Textbook of Criminal Law

Third Edition

Textbook of Criminal Law

Third Edition

Dennis J. Baker M.Phil., Ph.D. Jesus College, Cambridge
Lecturer in Law, King's College London

SWEET & MAXWELL

THOMSON REUTERS

Third Edition   2012   by Dennis J. Baker
Second Edition   1983   by Professor Glanville Williams
First Edition   1978   by Professor Glanville Williams

Published in 2012 by Sweet & Maxwell, 100 Avenue Road, London NW3 3PF part of
Thomson Reuters (Professional) UK Limited (Registered in England & Wales, Company No
1679046.
Registered Office and address for service: Aldgate House, 33 Aldgate High Street, London
EC3N 1DL)

For further information on our products and services, visit *www.sweetandmaxwell.co.uk*

Typeset by Letterpart Ltd, Reigate, Surrey

Printed and bound in Great Britain by CPI Group (UK) Ltd, Croydon, CR0 4YY.

No natural forests were destroyed to make this product; only farmed timber was used and
re-planted.

A CIP catalogue record of this book is available for the British Library.

ISBN: 978-041-404613-9

ACKNOWLEDGEMENTS

Grateful acknowledgement is made for permission to reproduce from the undermentioned works:

J.L. Mackie, *Ethics: Inventing Right and Wrong* (1977) at p.109. Reprinted with the permission of Penguin Books.

Jeffrie G. Murphy and Jules L. Coleman, *Philosophy of Law: An Introduction to Jurisprudence* (1989) at p.128. Reprinted with the permission of Westview Press.

Glanville Williams, *"Rape is Rape"* 142 NLJ 6534, p.11. Reprinted with the permission of the New Law Journal.

While every care has been taken to establish and acknowledge copyright, and contact the copyright owners, the publishers tender their apologies for any accidental infringement. They would be pleased to come to a suitable arrangement with the rightful owners in each case.

PREFACE

In the Preface of *Criminal Law: The General Part,* (1953), Professor Williams wrote: "Although this work is complete in itself, it is hoped to follow it later with a companion volume on specific crimes". The companion volume was his *Textbook of Criminal Law,* (1978). The second edition of the *Textbook* was published in 1983. I am pleased that I have been able to complete the third edition in 2011, as this year marks the 100th anniversary of the birth of Glanville Williams. Given that the *Textbook* has not been updated for nearly 3 decades, the changes in the law are too numerous to list in detail. A few of the main legislative changes include the *Fraud Act 2006*; the *Serious Crimes Act 2007*; the *Sexual Offences Act 2003*; *Immigration and Criminal Justice Act 2008*; *Protection from Protection from Harassment Act 1997*; *Police Act 1996*; *Police and Criminal Evidence Act 1984*; *Corporate Manslaughter and Corporate Homicide Act 2007*; *Coroners and Justice Act 2009*; and the list goes on and on. More than half this volume is new text.

A key feature of the earlier editions was the Socratic method that was used to get the reader to stop and think. The questions posed by the interlocutor throughout this treatise are not difficult, nor are they meant to be. They are easily answered. The aim is simply to get the reader to think as she reads. The interlocutor explains or asks the obvious at times, but as we will see, the obvious is not always that obvious, not even to some eminent judges.

I would like to acknowledge my criminal law colleagues: Professor Alan Norrie and Dr. John Stanton-Ife. I would like to especially thank Ms Anastasia Gorshkova for proof-reading the entire manuscript during her summer vacation; and Mr. Edward Warren for proof-reading several chapters. I would also like to thank the editorial team at Sweets including Nicola Thurlow, Laura Wood and David Lloyd. Coupled with this, I am immensely grateful to King's College London for its research support. I also acknowledge Dr. Lucy Zhao, Jianhua Li, Chengsheng Zhao, Gwen Mann, Laurie Baker, Jason Baker, Tina Baker, Shirley Meredith, Tanya Cherry, Graham Kenny and Dr. Martin Wood.

Dennis J. Baker
London
2011

TABLE OF CONTENTS

Part Two
The Protection of the Person

Part Three
Involvement in Crime

Part Four
Defences

Part Five
The Protection of Property

TABLE OF CASES

TABLE OF STATUTES

TABLE OF STATUTORY INSTRUMENTS

TABLE OF INTERNATIONAL LEGISLATION

PART ONE

GENERAL CONSIDERATIONS

CHAPTER 1

CRIME AND THE CRIMINAL LAW

"We come now to the principal object of law—the care of security. That inestimable good, the distinctive index of civilisation, is entirely the work of law. Without law there is no security; and, consequently, no abundance, and not even a certainty of subsistence; and the only equality which can exist in such a state of things is an equality of misery."

Jeremy Bentham[1]

"Whatever views one holds about the penal law, no one will question its importance to society. This is the law on which men place their ultimate reliance for protection against all the deepest injuries that human conduct can inflict on individuals and institutions. By the same token, penal law governs the strongest force that we permit official agencies to bring to bear on individuals. Its promise as an instrument of safety is matched only by its power to destroy. Nowhere in the entire legal field is more at stake for the community or the individual."

Herbert Wechsler[2]

1.1 SCOPE OF THE STUDY

To begin with territory: the subject of our study is the criminal law in force in England and Wales, the Scots being a law unto themselves. Parliament legislates for the whole of the United Kingdom, but it frequently needs to distinguish between Scotland on the one hand and England and Wales on the other, since the legal systems are largely different.

1–001

We refer to "England and Wales,"[3] because they are felt as two countries (at any rate by many Welshmen), but what is called England applies equally to Wales. For practically all legal purposes the territory is a single unit. It would be wrong to speak of "English and Welsh judges," because although we have both English and Welsh High Court and circuit judges they were not appointed on that basis. "English and Welsh law" would be even worse, since there are not two systems. One is compelled to say, therefore, that the Welsh are governed by English law, just as Americans and Australians have to express themselves in English language. Occasionally, for convenience, I even use the word "England"

---

[1] John Bowring (ed.), *The Works of Jeremy Bentham*, (Edinburgh: William Tait, 1838) at 307.
[2] "The Challenge of a Model Penal Code," (1952) 65 *Harv. L. Rev.* 1097 at 1089.
[3] Section 25 of the *Interpretation Act 1978* and Sch. 3 repeals the *Wales and Berwick Act 1746* under which the word "England" included Wales.

to stand for the orthodox and diplomatic expression "England and Wales," simply because the latter expression is too cumbrous.

The law of Northern Ireland, and indeed of the Republic of Ireland, is basically much the same as in England, though there are various statutory divergences. Also, many of the underlying concepts of criminal law are still recognized in other countries that started from English common law, such as the United States, Canada, Australia and New Zealand, and African states too numerous to mention. Overseas decisions based on the common law have persuasive authority in our courts and are referred to frequently in this book.

1.2   THE PROSECUTION OF OFFENCES

1–002 The police are charged with enforcing the criminal law in respect of the major crimes against the person, property and public order, and in respect of driving offences and miscellaneous minor offences. Prosecutions may also be instituted by the Director of Public Prosecutions (D.P.P.), particularly in the more serious or difficult cases. The Serious Fraud Office has special powers which enable it to investigate complex fraud and corruption cases. It is able to obtain and assess evidence for prosecuting fraudsters and can also freeze their assets.

Revenue offences are prosecuted by officers of the Revenue and Customs Prosecution Office. The Revenue and Customs Prosecution Office may also work with the Police and the Crown Prosecution Service when initiating a prosecution.[4] Other administrative or public welfare offences are prosecuted by inspectors and other officers of the Department concerned, for example, the Department of Trade (in respect of parts of the law within its purview, such as company law), health and safety inspectors of the Health and Safety Executive, and trading standards officers of the local authorities may prosecute matters such as public nuisance and offences against planning regulations and bylaws; some charges can be brought only by local authorities. Then there can be private prosecutions. Any queries so far?

1–003 **Do the police bring a charge whenever they have enough evidence?** They will nearly always bring proceedings for a major crime, provided that there is a reasonable prospect of conviction; but they exercise discretion in lesser cases, and in offences by youngsters.[5] They may content themselves with warning or cautioning the offender, even when they have evidence sufficient for a conviction. The same policy is followed by Government inspectors. It is not always wise, or even just, to let the heavy hand fall, and anyway the volume of offences is so large that charges have to be selective. To prosecute too often would soon lead to a collapse of the edifice of justice. But the consequence of the present policy of selective crackdown is that many regulations, even safety regulations, are inadequately enforced. Moreover, it is not entirely to be commended that enforcement policies should differ markedly between one Chief Constable and another, as they sometimes do.

---

[4] C.P.S., *Relations with other prosecuting agencies, http://www.cps.gov.uk/legal/p_to_r/prosecuting_ agencies_relations_with_other_agencies/#a20.*
[5] *R. v. Coxhead* [1986] R.T.R. 411.

When can a private prosecution be brought? In general, anyone can prosecute:[6] the greatest fetter is that legal aid is not available. Traders sometimes prosecute for theft, and members of pressure groups and vigilante groups occasionally prosecute for such offences as obscenity and cruelty to children. Private persons can prosecute even for murder and other serious offences against the person or property, and very occasionally do so when they can afford the expense. Exceptionally, the consent of some central officer such as the D.P.P. or Attorney-General is sometimes required. There will be cases where it is appropriate for the Crown Prosecution Service to take over the prosecution either to continue it or to discontinue it. If the offence is serious and there is a *prima facie* case, the Crown Prosecution Service will usually take over the prosecution.[7] It may also take it over to stop it, if the private prosecution interferes with the investigation of another criminal offence or if the prosecution is vexatious within the meaning of section 42 of the *Senior Courts Act 1981*, as amended by section 24 of the *Prosecution of Offences Act 1985*.[8]

1–004

Why need the private prosecutors seek permission? The requirement is put in as a safeguard against over-enthusiastic prosecutions. The Government Department or other body that devised the legislation may have been afraid that it had cast too wide a net, and may have relied on the discretion of the specified officer to confine charges to clear and flagrant cases. Or the legislation may be controversial, so that the requirement of an officer's consent is a compromise between the opinions of those who would have an unfettered offence and those who would support only a greatly restricted offence or none at all. It is even possible that the legislation is passed merely to satisfy those who wish Parliament to state what they consider to be a moral principle, without wanting to see many prosecutions brought under it. In other words, the law's bark is to be worse than its bite. Such considerations explain why, for example, the consent of the D.P.P. is required for a charge of abetting suicide.[9]

1–005

But if the D.P.P. can fix criteria to govern the giving of his consent, the same rules could have been incorporated in the offence. It is hard to deny that leaving the decision wholly to the D.P.P. is to delegate an essentially legislative decision to an executive officer.[10] The matter would stand differently if the D.P.P.'s consent were required merely to protect the individual against flimsy charges.

1–006

---

[6] Section 6 of the *Prosecution of Offences Act 1985*.

[7] *R. v. Tower Bridge Metropolitan Stipendiary Magistrate, Ex parte Chaudhry* [1994] Q.B. 340; *R. (on the application of Charlson) v. Guildford Magistrates Court* [2007] 3 All E.R. 163.

[8] It will also step in if a deal has been done whereby the defendant has been granted immunity from prosecution: *Jones v. Whalley* [2007] 1 A.C. 63; *Turner v. D.P.P.* (1979) 68 Cr. App. R. 70; *Raymond v. Attorney-General* [1982] Q.B. 839.

[9] See section 2 of the *Suicide Act 1961*. See also *Dunbar v. Plant* [1997] 3 W.L.R. 1261; *R. (on the application of Purdy) v. D.P.P.* [2010] 1 A.C. 345. See also Jaap Roording, "The Punishment of Tax Fraud," [1996] Crim. L.R. 240.

[10] D. A. Thomas, "Form and Function in Criminal Law," in P. R. Glazebrook, *Reshaping the Criminal Law: Essays in Honour of Glanville Williams*, (London: Stevens & Sons, 1978) at 30-31.

1–007   **What if the defendant admits guilt; must there be a full trial?** On a plea of guilty there is no trial, only sentence (or other disposal).

1–008   **Can a prosecutor drop the charge on condition of the defendant's paying a fine?** Generally not. Fines must be imposed by the court. But there are exceptional provisions whereby various officials may accept payment of a penalty in minor cases without court appearance. The Inland Revenue operates a system of "civil penalties" for breaches of the tax code; these can be collected, by agreement, without legal proceedings. The obdurate non-payer must be proceeded against before the General Commission or the High Court, but the proceedings for a civil penalty is civil, not criminal.[11]

Customs and Excise officers[12] and local vehicle licensing officers can also allow an offender to buy himself out of the court process. There are "fixed penalty" offences relating to vehicles (including parking, speeding, various vehicle defect offences and failing to comply with traffic directions) which retain their criminal character even though they need not come before the court; the payment of the penalty stated on the ticket saves a court hearing. A ticket-tearer can be prosecuted for the offence for which he was given the ticket. The spot fine system is still fragmentary, but these time-saving devices are likely to be extended in the future.

1–009   **Aren't spot fine provisions objectionable as reducing the awesome system of justice to a commercial transaction?** This criticism has, of course, been made. Lady Wootton said such provisions are "frank and final confessions that we have abandoned all hopes of enforcing the law, and that it is open to anyone with sufficient means to buy a right to lawbreaking in the same way as he might purchase a pound of cheese."[13] The criticism overlooks the fact that even where spot fines are not operated, magistrates' courts operate a tariff of fines that in effect enables the rich to buy "impunity" cheaply. Moreover, it is because ticket penalties are almost commercial transactions, so that the conduct in question is in effect decriminalized, that some people (like the owners of vehicles) can be made to pay penalties for the misbehaviour of others. They are induced to help in bringing pressure to bear on the real offenders to behave, and the efficacy of the law is increased without a strong sense of injustice building up. Looked at in aggregate, lawbreaking can be prevented far better by streamlining enforcement procedures for minor infractions than by trying to give such consideration to the individual case that the whole machinery fouls up.

---

[11] Section 100 of the *Taxes Management Act 1970*. *Flaxmode Ltd. v. Revenue and Customs Commissioners* [2010] S.F.T.D. 498.

[12] Section 152 of the *Customs and Excise Management Act 1979*. *Patel v. Spencer* [1976] 1 W.L.R. 1268.

[13] Barbara Wootton, *In a World I Never Made*, (London: Harper Collins, 1967) at 235.

1.3 WIDE AND NARROW OFFENCES

I should like you to imagine for a moment that you are engaged on a legislative exercise. Suppose that you are parliamentary counsel compiling a criminal code for a newly settled country (perhaps one day you will find yourself actually drawing one up for England and Wales, since we have none at present). You will obviously wish to include a provision punishing rape. Would you define the offence as one of rape, or would you leave rape as one example of the wider law of assault? Or would you have, perhaps, an even wider offence of "public mischief," covering not only assault but an indefinite number of other forms of misbehaviour? Either of the two latter solutions (assault or public mischief) would make a special law of rape unnecessary. What considerations would move you to define the offence one way or the other?

1–010

Calling it "public mischief" would be too wide. Rape is a public mischief, but no one could tell what else a judge might regard as public mischief. That is an important consideration. The law should tell us with reasonable clarity what it expects of us. Complete precision cannot be achieved, but very nebulous prescriptions should be avoided, because they give insufficient guidance to the citizen and correspondingly too wide a discretion to law enforcement agencies. The practical way in which law is administered would depend too much on the decisions of the police and other prosecutors, taken in private and without effective control.

1–011

There used to be a common law (*i.e.* judge-made)[14] offence of causing a public mischief, which allowed the courts to punish any conduct of which they disapproved. It was strongly criticized by commentators, and in practice prosecutors did not make much use of it; eventually the House of Lords overturned the previous learning on the subject and declared that the offence did not exist.[15] The notion of an offence of public mischief infringed the principle of legality—the proposition that there should be no criminal offence except one specified by pre-existing law (*nulla poena sine lege*, or *nullum crimen sine lege*).

Some statutory offences are open to the same objection of vagueness, though when they are only lightly punishable the objection has less force than for the common law offences just mentioned. An example is the offence of selling an article of food not of the nature, substance or quality demanded by the purchaser.[16] Under the predecessor of this provision the courts had to decide in every particular case whether a thing sold as a sausage was in truth a "sausage" or virtually a packet of breadcrumbs. Now, however, regulations require a pork sausage to contain at least 42 *per cent.* meat, and a beef sausage at least 32 *per cent.*[17] Obviously a strong case can be made for settling such a point uniformly by legislation, after consultation with manufactures and with consumer

---

[14] Some of the most serious offences found in English law such as murder and manslaughter are judge-made. As are many of the core defences including necessity, duress, automatism, mistake, intoxication and insanity.

[15] *D.P.P. v. Withers* [1975] A.C. 842. The courts neither have the power to invent nor abrogate offences. See *R. v. Rimmington* [2006] 1 A.C. 459.

[16] Section 14 of the *Food Safety Act 1990*.

[17] Sch. 2 of the *Meat Products (England) Regulations 2003/2075*.

organizations. To leave the question: What is a sausage? to the impressionistic decision by different magistrates when prosecutions are brought is inefficient, as well as unfair to manufacturers and traders who want to keep within the law if they can find out what the law is. Yet there are many articles of food (*e.g.*, minced meat)[18] where magistrates still have to find whether they are of proper quality without receiving any help from the law.

So, coming back to the question, the law should be reasonably precise. Opinions may differ about what is reasonably precise, but we can rule out having an offence of public mischief. Then what is the case for having an offence of rape? I think you will agree that your code must have an offence of assault (in the sense of a physical attack upon another person). So would you include an offence of rape as well?

1–012   **Rape is much more serious than ordinary assault, and needs a more severe punishment. So it must be a special offence.**   Your reasoning expresses the present legal position. Rape can be treated as a kind of indecent assault, but the maximum for an indecent assault (sexual assault) on a woman is ten years.[19] Rape is therefore made an offence on its own, punishable with life imprisonment.[20] (Of course, this does not mean that every rapist gets "life." The specification of a punishment in a statute is a maximum, so a rapist may be imprisoned for a fixed period of years or—theoretically—simply fined. In practice he is likely to get perhaps three or five years depending on the circumstances. The life sentence is reserved for a few people who are regarded as very dangerous—and does not usually last for life.)

We have here an illustration of the fact that the same conduct sometimes amounts to two or more offences of a different gravity. The graver offence (rape) carries a relatively maximum punishment. If for some reason the defendant cannot be convicted of that, he may be convicted of the lesser offence (sexual assault) carrying a lower maximum, this lesser offence being defined more broadly than the graver offence.

Other examples of such two-tier offences are murder and manslaughter; wounding with intent and unlawful wounding; robbery and theft and so on. The more serious offence includes some circumstance of aggravation that is not necessary for the less serious offence: perhaps a special mental element; or higher degree of damage, injury or alarm caused or likely to be caused by the offence.

1–013   It can be argued that the two-tier (or multiple-tier) arrangement is not strictly necessary. We could continue to use the name of the low-grade offence while attaching to it the maximum punishment of the more serious offence. So it would be theoretically possible to provide a maximum punishment of the more serious offence of life imprisonment for any sexual assault, which would mean that the special offence of rape could be abolished; and this has been seriously suggested. The court would be left to work out the right punishment in each case, with the safeguard of an appeal.

---

[18] See *Goldup v. John Manson Ltd.* [1982] Q.B. 161; *McDonald's Hamburgers Ltd. v. Windle* (1987) 151 J.P. 333.

[19] Section 3 of the *Sexual Offences Act 2003*.

[20] Section 1 of the *Sexual Offences Act 2003*.

This could be regarded as not involving a radical change, since the courts already operate a customary "tariff" of punishment which is generally well below the maximum allowed by Parliament for the offence. If the two-tier system were abolished, the law would be simplified. Some very serious cases of sexual assault, such as using threats to compel a woman to submit to providing "oral sex,"[21] could be punished as severely as rape.

We have already had some law reform along these lines. The *Criminal Damage Act 1971* abolished many offences of damage carrying different maxima and substituted broadly defined offences with a scale of maximum punishments that do not (in general) depend on the gravity of the harm done. The *Theft Act 1968* abolished a number of specific offences of theft carrying special penalties, leaving basically a single offence punishable with a maximum of seven years' imprisonment. Theft covers everything from treating the boss's tools as a kind of a "perk" to a highly organized raid upon a mail train; from the employee who cannot bring himself to disclose that there is too much in his pay packet to the bank clerk who embezzles tens of thousands of pounds to make good his betting losses. In practice thieves rarely get as much as seven years, and the great majority are not imprisoned at all. When the courts are given a wide discretion in sentencing they can take account of many circumstances of aggravation and mitigation. It is generally best this way. Singling out some circumstances of aggravation and putting them into special offences not only complicates the law but often makes it look arbitrary. The worst instances of the lesser, general, offence are often more anti-social and reprehensible than the most excusable instances of the serious offence. Moreover, complicated provisions increase the possibility of morally guilty people escaping on technicalities.

I am beginning to see the possibility of dispensing with the offence of rape. If   1–014
we can cover criminal damage and theft by wide offences without
subdivision, we might as well rest content with a wide offence of sexual
assault.   I have given you only one side of the argument. There are two persuasive reasons for not relying too much on "broad band" offences:

> The first reason is historical and psychological. Crimes like rape and murder are established in the public mind as special offences. There would be serious misunderstanding if a proposal were made to abolish them. The public would regard the effectiveness of the criminal law as being lessened, even though rape and murder might in fact continue to be punished in the same way under more general names. Words like "rape" and "murder" incorporate immemorial taboos, and if these words were not attached to the offence the force of the prohibition might be weakened.
> Widening the scope of serious offences reduces the function of the jury in the trial and may deny them the opportunity to decide the most important issue. To continue the previous example, whether the defendant raped the complainant or did not go beyond sexually assaulting her would be of great importance for sentence under any system of rules. If the question does not

---

[21] If D's oral sex involves him *penetrating* V with any part of his body other than his penis then section 2 of the *Sexual Offences Act 2003* would apply. That offence carries a life sentence.

enter into the definition of the crime the judge will have to decide it on his or her own. To some extent the judge is bound to decide questions of fact for the purpose of sentence; but very important questions, if they are capable of succinct and rational formulation in the definitions of offences, should be decided by the jury.[22]

1–015   So, as always, there is a golden mean. The law is a pragmatic compromise between opposing considerations. Strong arguments can be found for not simplifying its structure too radically. The grading of offences both limits and assists the judge; it also settles the function of the jury, helps to control the forum, and assists plea-bargaining. These points may be expanded:

- *Limiting the judge.* Although the courts do not generally use to the full the Draconian powers that Parliament may give them, it is accepted that judges ought not to be set completely free from statutory fetters. Imprisonment for "life," *i.e.* for an indeterminate period, is acceptable as a possible sentence for multiple rapists, but it would not be acceptable as a possible sentence for sexual assault (which such comparatively minor—though strongly resented—interferences as touching the breasts of a woman in a crowd).

  …The judge is limited not only by the legal maximum set by parliament but by the generally lower scales known as the "tariff" devised by appellate courts. (The courts are guided by the Sentencing Guidelines Council's guidelines. Section 125 of the *Coroners and Justice Act 2009* requires judges sentencing an offender for an offence committed on or after 6 April 2010, to follow any relevant sentencing guidelines, unless it is contrary to the interests of justice to do so.)[23] The theory is that the maximum sentence was intended only for the worst offence of its kind, and the judge must award less than that for other cases.[24]

- *Assisting the judge.* In the ordinary trial in the Crown Court, the evidence is listened to by the jury, for the purpose of deciding whether to convict, and by the judge, for the purpose of deciding what the sentence is to be in the event of conviction. It is the judge who decides whether there are aggravating or mitigating circumstances affecting the question of punishment.[25] But where there are two or more charges, and the jury acquit on the graver charge while convicting on the lesser charge, the rule is that the judge in sentencing for the lesser offence must pay due respect to the acquittal; hence he must assume (whatever his own opinion may be, and

---

[22] Thomas, *op. cit. supra*, note 10 at 21.

[23] To see the relevant guidelines, *http://www.sentencingcouncil.org.uk/guidelines/guidelines-to-download.htm*.

[24] *R. v. Mills* (1982) 146 J.N.P. 266. See generally, D. A. Thomas (ed.), *Current Sentencing Practice*, (London: Sweet & Maxwell, 2010). For a convenient and compendious discussion of the core issues, see Andrew Ashworth, *Sentencing and Criminal Justice*, (Cambridge: Cambridge University Press, 2010).

[25] The Court of Appeal generally discourages trial judges from questioning the jury as to matters not necessarily covered by the verdict. One reason is that the jury may not have reached agreement on such other matters. See the note to *R. v. Stosiek* [1982] Crim. L.R. 615. See also *R. v. Bertram* [2004] 1 Cr. App. R. (S.) 27.

however clear the evidence) that the circumstances of aggravation necessary for conviction of the graver charge were not proved.[26]

Many cases do not reach the jury. The defendant pleads (*i.e.* pleads guilty), and there is no trial. In legal parlance he is convicted on this plea, not by verdict. ("Plea" for lawyers always means a plea of guilty; when we refer to a lesser charge, and if the plea is accepted by the prosecution the judge will (after considering matters relevant to sentence) proceed to sentence; but he must honour the implied bargain and not sentence on the basis of any circumstances of aggravation that would have to be established for the graver charge.[27]) So far as the principle carried that even when only one offence is charged, if any aggravated form of the offence could have been charged the judge must not sentence on the basis that the offender committed the aggravated form.[28] It will be seen that having different grades of offences assists the judge because it helps to reduce the scope of his or her problem in choosing the proper sentence. This is not a very strong point, because even if two offences are charged and the defendant is convicted only of the lesser offence, this may still leave the judge with a wide range of discretion. Also, there are extreme cases, where the offender is looked upon as dangerous, that force the court to disregard the fact that a more serious charge has failed.[29]

- *Giving power to the jury.* The jury cannot take any part in sentencing as such, and this imposes a considerable strain upon their consciences. Are they to convict this nice-looking young fellow on a serious charge, if it means that that unending character on the Bench will send him to prison for many years? Giving the jury the opportunity to convict of a lesser offence means that they fetter the judge in his sentencing power. More important is the fact that by convicting of the lesser offence the jury send up a smoke signal that they want the offender to be treated fairly leniently. Indirectly, therefore, the jury are given a small measure of control over sentence, which may make the fact that they cannot directly control sentence more palatable to them. It is generally more in the public interest that the defendant should be convicted of the lesser offence than that he should, when guilty, escape with an outright acquittal.[30]

---

[26] See the commentary to *R. v. Davies* [1982] Crim. L.R. 243, deploring an isolated departure from the rule.

[27] An example is *R. v. Twomey* [[1964] Crim. L.R. 419: the prosecution accepted a plea of not guilty to robbery with violence that had caused the victim's injuries, and the appellate court reduced the sentence accordingly. Cf. *R. v. Denniston* (1977) 64 Cr. App. R. 119; *R. v. Fisher* (1981) 3 Cr. App. R. (S.) 313 (attempt). See also *R. v. Clark* [1996] 2 Cr. App. R. (S.) 351; *R. v. VV* [2004] EWCA Crim. 355.

[28] *R. v. Foo* [1976] Crim. L.R. 45. The rule is clear where the two offences are part of the same hierarchy, the prosecution charging the lesser offence and not the aggravated from. Where this is not strictly true, the application of the rule is more complicated. See *R. v. Rubinstein* (1982) 4 Cr. App. R. (S.) 202.

[29] *R. v. McCauliffe* (1982) 4 Cr. App. R. (S.) 13. See sections 224-239 of the *Criminal Justice Act 2003*.

[30] For a criticism of some modern legislation on the ground that it unduly reduces the function of the jury see D. A. Thomas, *op. cit. supra*, note 10 at 23-34.

- *Controlling the forum.* Another result of the grading of offences is that it helps to govern the selection of the court of trial. Graver offences are triable in the Crown Court, perhaps only there; lesser offences are triable in magistrates' courts, perhaps only there.
- *Assisting plea-bargaining.* The defendant through his advocate may offer to plead guilty to the lesser charge if the prosecution will withdraw the graver charge.[31] For example, the Crown sometimes charge the serious offence of "wounding with intent" when the facts only doubtfully warrant it. In that case, defending counsel may ask his opponent informally whether he will accept a plea (that is, a plea of guilty) to the lesser charge of unlawful wounding.[32] If the two sides reach an agreement, counsel for the Crown will explain the facts to the judge, and state why he would find difficulty in proving the more serious charge. The judge, if he approves the arrangement, will give leave to withdraw the count in respect of the graver charge, and will take the plea of guilty to the lesser. This saves the time of the court, the time of the witnesses and the strain upon them of giving evidence, and avoids the possibility that the defendant may succeed in getting off altogether. The defendant benefits on sentence.

1–016   It may be a matter of considerable difficulty for defending counsel to decide whether to advise his client to offer a plea. If he thinks he has a sporting chance of getting him off altogether, as on a defence of accident or self-defence, he may fight the case. If the defendant has a bad record, or the facts are black against him, counsel may think it wiser to attempt the compromise, for this will protect his client from the possibility of a conviction by the jury of the more serious charge, which may in turn lead to a stern sentence by the judge; and, quite apart from this, it is the custom to allow a "discount" for the mere plea of guilty, which saves the time of the court.

There is a darker side to plea bargaining. It is generally the police who first make the charge, when the defendant is before the magistrates, and although the charge may be varied later they retain considerable control over it. The police often overcharge, perhaps because they are not sure of the facts and wish to preserve all their options. So they may charge attempted murder, or wounding with intent, when it later transpires that the case amounts only to unlawful wounding. The fact that a very serious charge is included in the indictment is a source of great anxiety to the defendant, and a powerful inducement to him to try to settle the case by pleading to a lesser charge. If the lesser charge alone had been included, he might have been encouraged to adduce his evidence and perhaps win an acquittal. Sometimes the result is injustice.[33]

---

[31] For an historical overview of plea-bargaining see Mike McConville and Chester L. Mirsky, *Jury Trials and Plea Bargaining: A True History*, (Oxford: Hart Publishing, 2005).

[32] The defendant is allowed to plead guilty to an included offence: section 6(1)(b) of the *Criminal Law Act 1967*. For a discussion on included offences see Glanville Williams, "Alternative Elements and Included Offences," (1984) 43 *Cambridge L.J.* 290.

[33] John Baldwin and Mike McConville, *Negotiated Justice: Pressures on Defendants to Plead Guilty*, (London: Martin Robertson, 1979); Erica Hashimoto, "Toward Ethical Plea Bargaining," (2009) 30 *Cardozo L. Rev.* 949. For a recent example see Duncan Watson, "The Attorney General's Guidelines on Plea Bargaining in Serious Fraud: Obtaining Guilty Pleas Fairly," (2010) 74 *J. Crim. L.* 77.

1.4   THE JUDICIAL DEVELOPMENT OF THE LAW

The criminal law, like all our law, rests for the most part on statutes, but also, to a considerable extent, on decisions of the courts.

1–017

Hold on a moment. When you speak of a decision, who decides the case, judge or jury?   At a trial in the Crown Court, the judge instructs the jury on the law, and the jury then pronounce a verdict on the case as a whole. But when we speak of decided cases as one basis of the law we are generally referring to the decisions of the appellate courts, where there is no jury. (The direction to the jury given by the trial judge may be cited as an authority, but it is low in the hierarchy. What the jury decide, whichever way it is, is of no importance as a legal precedent.)

1–018

The non-lawyer who turns his attention to the law naturally begins by supposing that the law is a body of rules laid down in advance to govern people's conduct, and that these rules also govern the courts in deciding whether a breach has occurred. The reality is somewhat different. Many decisions as to what the law is are in reality only statements of what the law is going on after the decision. "That's not a regular rule," said Alice to the Queen; "You've just made it up." Not only is there inevitable uncertainty in applying the abstract rules to concrete facts, but even when the law is clear and capable of precise application the judges are smitten from time to time with the desire to change it in the act of adjudicating it.

Most decisions are, of course, routine. The judge functions in the way that is expected of him, ascertaining what the law is and applying it. Nevertheless, the judge has a measure of freedom to make law under the guise of exposition. He will often not be completely bound by a precedent. He may be able to overrule it or refuse to follow it, according to the rank of the court that decided it; and even if he is supposed to be bound by it, he may "distinguish" it by finding some real or quibbling point on which the precedent differs from the case before him. Lawmaking is, therefore, as we shall have much opportunity to observe in this book, part of the art and craft of deciding cases.

It is somewhat the same with statutory interpretation. The courts cannot manufacture statutes as they can precedents, but they can "interpret" them.[34] They can cut them down, or expand them. Courts still pay lip-service to the ancient principle that in case of doubt a criminal statute is to be "strictly construed" in favour of the defendant; but the principle is rarely applied in practice, if there are social reasons for convicting. Indeed, we may make bold to say that the looser the defendant's conduct, the more loosely the judges construe the statute designed to control him. When the defendant has acted immorally, nothing short of the most powerful reasoning based on the wording of the statute

1–019

---

[34] See Andrew Ashworth, "Interpreting Criminal Statutes: A Crisis of Legality?" (1991) 107 *L.Q.R.* 419; Timothy Endicott, "Law is Necessarily Vague," (2001) 7 *Leg. Theory* 379.

is likely to dissuade the judges from holding that the statute applies to him.[35] "Alas for law reform! Parliament proposes, but the Appellate Committee disposes."[36]

The law of prostitution supplies examples of both the legitimate and illegitimate interpretation of criminal statutes to cover peripheral cases. It has been held that the word "prostitute" includes a "masseuse" who, for hire, gives men manual stimulation.[37] This is not the usual idea of prostitution, and the court certainly did not apply a "strict construction" to the penal statutes in which the word occurred. The court proceeded entirely upon a purported interpretation of the word, and did not express any reasons of policy. However, such reasons could well be found. The ostensible "massage parlour" is open to some of the objections to a regular brothel, besides tempting some women into full prostitution. The police could not well control prostitution if they had to prove exactly what sexual practices went on in private. And although the decision stretches the meaning of the word "prostitution," it does not do so to breaking-point. For this reason I do not criticize the decision, but merely give it as an example of the court preferring the wider to the more usual narrower meaning of a word used in penal legislation when the meaning was in doubt.

The other decision passes from reasonable though wide interpretation to what is in reality covert legislation. It is not a representative specimen of the interpretation of statutes; on the other hand; it is not unique.

1–020 A statue makes it an offence for a person to solicit "in a street."[38] The courts hold that if a prostitute solicits by gestures when standing at the window of a room fronting the street, her gestures being directed at men in the street, she solicits in the street.[39]

Most people would, I think, be surprised at this interpretation. It rests on the following reasoning (which the court did not spell out as clearly as I am about to do):

1. The statute forbids a prostitute or other person to solicit in a street.
2. "Soliciting" refers to soliciting a man (and now a woman).[40]
3. Therefore the statute forbids a prostitute to solicit a person in a street.
4. Here the prostitute solicited a person in a street.

Therefore, she solicited in a street.

The fallacy should be obvious. The last premise 4. has implied hyphens in it: the prostitute solicited a-man-in-a-street. It does not follow from this that her

---

[35] Consider the massive argument that had to be mounted in the House of Lords in *R. v. Bloxham* [1983] 1 A.C. 109 to persuade it to reverse the plainly erroneous decision of the Court of Appeal, and the equally powerful argument that failed to persuade the House to uphold the plainly correct judgment of the Court of Appeal in *R. v. Lambie* [1982] A.C. 449. For a more recent example, see *R. v. Hinks* [2001] 2 A.C. 241.

[36] Glanville Williams, "The Lords and Impossible Attempts, or *Quis Custodiet Ipsos Custodes,*" (1986) 45 *Cambridge L.J.* 33 at 38.

[37] *R. v. Webb* [1964] 1 Q.B. 357, following earlier authority.

[38] Section 1 of the *Street Offences Act 1959* (as amended).

[39] *Smith v. Hughes* [1960] 1 W.L.R. 830. See also *Eastbourne BC v. Stirling* [2001] R.T.R. 7.

[40] See Sch. 1 of the *Sexual Offences Act 2003* and section 16 of the *Policing and Crime Act 2009.*

solicitation was in a street. (If a woman sang in her room for the benefit of someone in the street, we would hardly say that she sang in the street.) There are, in fact, indications in the statute that Parliament did not intend the *Act* to apply as the court said. In particular, the statute expressly defines "street" to include doorways, which shows that it was not intended to include rooms fronting the street.

Although the Court of Appeal has said that its own precedent is not binding on it when the precedent is "against the liberty of the subject," this rule is hardly ever applied in practice. Almost all errors of understanding or reasoning on the part of the judges, however flagrant, are healed by the miraculous powers of the doctrine of precedent. So every judicial extension of the law forms a firm base from which further sallies may be mounted. When the courts had decided that a prostitute in a room can solicit in a street, they proceeded to hold that she "solicits" if she displays herself passively at her window (scantily clad, however, and bathed in red light).[41] It is true that the prostitute's object in exhibiting herself was to attract custom. But in its ordinary meaning the word "solicits" implies an act of soliciting, not a mere appearance in a place. A provocatively dressed prostitute in a bar who hoped for custom but made no sexual approach to any person by word or gesture would not be said to solicit.

The decisions I have just mentioned are supported by general public opinion, and save us from sources of offence.[42] The doubt is not whether the rules they establish are good in their effect but whether the last two decisions I have mentioned are justifiable exercises of the judicial function.

So the judges concoct the law as they go along? That is an exaggeration, even   **1–021**
though it has a considerable measure of truth. It is an exaggeration because judges tend to be conservative and traditional. They like to think of themselves as administering a system of law, not merely "cadi justice," justice under a palm tree.

It is true because the common law is made, and statutes are interpreted, and therefore moulded, by the judiciary. Parliament is a legislature that intervenes only occasionally, and only in matters that it (or, more usually, some Minister) regards as of pressing importance. The day-to-day task of adjusting the law to present needs falls on the courts. In doing this they are strongly influenced by their own ideas of what conduct should be allowed. The tendency of the courts to create new criminal law is so pronounced that it is generally almost impossible to say with assurance what anti-social conduct (or conduct that the judges will regard as anti-social) is not criminal: only what is.

In some ways the continuous creation of law by the courts is a tremendous advantage for the legal system. It is particularly welcome when the judges create a new defence required by justice or social policy, as they very occasionally do (witness the celebrated direction to the jury by Macnaghten J. in *The King v.*

---

[41] *Behrendt v. Burridge* [1977] 1 W.L.R. 29.

[42] As we will see in Chapter 3, the case for criminalizing such conduct is negligible. Dennis J. Baker, *The Right Not to be Criminalized: Demarcating Criminal Law's Authority*, (Farnham: Ashgate Publishing, 2011) at Chap. 6; Joel Feinberg, *The Moral Limits of the Criminal Law: Offense to Others*, (New York: Oxford University Press, Vol. II, 1985).

Bourne.[43] But judges rarely invent restrictions on the criminal law. Their creative capacity goes in extending it. And the image of the judge as clandestine lawgiver, achieving this result by the cunning manipulation of words, rules and precedents, consorts ill with the image of the judge as an impartial adjudicator between State and subject.

We must keep a sense of proportion. Most judicial hawkishness is directed against people who would be accounted pests in any society. It is far removed from the tyranny of totalitarian regimes. Nevertheless, it constitutes a departure from the ideal of law as a pre-established and knowable body of rules of behaviour. Villains, and others who threaten the social order, and some people who are merely nonconformist, sexually or otherwise, can rarely be sure that the law will not be interpreted against them.[44]

1–022 **I should have thought that the law would quite clearly provide for the conviction of villains, at least.** The only way of making sure that the courts can convict all evilly disposed persons would be to have offences without firm limits. But, as was said before, a vague penal law is an evil for citizens who want to know how they stand. It may catch people who were not meant to be caught. So the modern tendency is to have laws defined with relative precision. Nevertheless, the more precise the law, the easier it is for evil-doers to skate around it. Some people commit "the oldest sins the newest kinds of ways," and judges want to deal with them, which they can do by reinterpreting the law. So the administering of criminal justice is the result of opposite pressures: the pressure to make the penal law certain, and the pressure to make it adaptable.

The argument for the second view is encapsulated in Shakespeare's vivid metaphor.

> "We must not make a scarecrow of the law,
> Setting it up to fear the birds of prey,
> And let it keep one shape, till custom make it
> Their perch and not their terror."

The argument for adaptability—that is, for judicial expansion of the law, where this is thought to be necessary—has been powerfully supported by judges in the past, and still has adherents; but to most commentators the contrary position now seems the more persuasive. The law ought not to be open-ended, and the judges should not break through its boundaries. The classical expression of this opinion was by Francis Bacon (Lord Chancellor Bacon):

> "Judges ought to remember that their office is *Ius dicere*, and not *Ius dare*; to interpret law, and not to make or give law."[45]

1–023 Notable support was given to the Baconian principle by Stephen J.—the revered Sir James Fitzjames Stephen, greatest criminal lawyer of his age, author of *A*

---

[43] [1939] 1 K.B. 687.

[44] *R. v. Gibson* [1990] 2 Q.B. 619. See further Dennis J. Baker "The Impossibility of a Critically Objective Criminal Law," (2011) 56(2) *McGill L. J.* 349.

[45] Francis Bacon, *Essays, Moral, Economical, and Political,* (London: printed by T. Bensley, 1798) at 198.

History of Criminal Law and the *Digest of Criminal Law*; principal author of the *Draft Code of 1879*, by means of which Britain presented a criminal code to various other parts of the world while rejecting it herself:

> "A considerable part of the law of England consists of judicial decisions, and in the very nature of things this must be so. Every decision upon a debated point adds a little to the law by making that point certain for the future. Indeed, whichever way this case may be decided, it will settle the law upon the precise point involved, and it is this which gives to judicial decisions their great importance.
>
> It seems to me, however, that in exercising the narrowly qualified power of quasi legislation which the very nature of our position confers upon us, we ought to confine ourselves as far as possible (there may be cases where such a course is not possible) to applying well-known principles and analogies to new combinations of facts, and to supplying to general definitions, and maxims, or to general statutory expressions qualifications, which though not expressed, are, in our opinion, implied. ... [I]f we go further and extend the law upon considerations of general expediency, we are, I think, invading the province of the legislature."[46]

In this passage Stephen J. did not draw certain distinctions that he might well have drawn. The objections to judicial legislation are much less (and therefore are much more easily counterbalanced) in the civil law than in criminal. The civil law does not generally lock people up or otherwise punish them.[47] Even in the criminal law, there is no reason why the judges should not expand justifications and excuses for crimes, for reasons of justice, or alter technical rules of procedure and evidence established at common law, when they impede the quest for truth. These are not matters on which people try to understand the law for the purpose of conforming their conduct to it. The issue concerns the expansion of the range of the substantive law of crime—the extension of criminal prohibitions. Here the Baconian principle has much stronger claim to recognition.

I think that your argument against the judges expanding crimes is too much   **1–024**
a counsel of perfection. When judges make the law more efficient they have general public support. No one wants to be governed by antiquated law. People generally don't know the law, but they do know when they are being knaves or brutes; so there is no harm in the judges manipulating the law to catch them. Brutes do not take legal advice in advance; knaves may, but the lawyer in advising will take the attitude of the judges into account when predicting their action. There is much force in what you say. But prediction is not so easy as you imply. Because judges vary in outlook, it is often hard to know in advance whether they will change the law or not. In the case of the prostitute at the window, if she had sought my advice beforehand I would have given my opinion that what she proposed to do did not fall within the statute, since all the legal arguments went that way, though I would have warned her of the possibility that the judges might take a different view. People do sometimes act upon an interpretation of what appears to be the present law, only to be confounded by a judicial decision that not only changes it but changes it retrospectively to their disadvantage.

Whatever the arguments, judicial legislation continues. Some common law crimes are so vaguely defined that it is easy to extend them when purporting to

---

[46] *R. v. Coney* 8 Q.B.D. 534 at 550-551.

[47] The most the civil law does allow for is punitive damages.

apply them. This is particularly true of public nuisance, a heterogeneous group of offences bearing a single name, which gives some signs of taking the place in the judicial armoury formerly occupied by public mischief.[48] The administration of justice, also, is protected by the amorphous crimes of interfering with justice, obstructing the police and contempt of court. Almost any misbehaviour in relation to the prosecution of offences can be punished under one or the other of these open-ended headings, without its being always clear in advance what the judges will regard as misbehaviour.

An example of how the law of contempt can involve controversial applications at the discretion of the judges is *Home Office v. Harman*,[49] where the House of Lords held (against the notable dissents of Lords Simon and Scarman) that it was a civil contempt of court for a solicitor to supply to a journalist copies of documents that had been disclosed for legal proceedings, even after they had been read out in open court during the trial.

1–025   Generally, the expansion of the law is unavowed, and takes place by small steps, the judges keeping up the pretence that they are mere mouthpieces of the law, *judex est lex loquens*. A judgment will marshal the authorities in a manner suggesting, to the uninitiated, that the court is ineluctably bound to reach the conclusion it does reach, when to the discerning eye it is often no more than what is popularly called "special pleading"—that is, rationalization accompanied by misdirection and legerdemain. The legal pros and cons are not fairly stated. (They cannot be, if the authorities are against the decision and if the court is not prepared to admit that it is changing the law.) The court selects the arguments and authorities leading to the conclusion it desires and minimizes or ignores the weight of authority or force of argument going the other way. Ordinary lawyerly reasoning, as generally employed in civil cases, may be rejected in favour of fallacious and shallow arguments. The unavowed premise is that those who break fresh ground in the annals of crime cannot rely upon any previously established rule of law being maintained in their favour. If the law were so-and-so, the court says, it would be absurd, and would fail to give sufficient protection to the public interest; therefore (the conclusion immediately follows) the law is *not* so-and-so.[50]

It would be wrong to give the impression that courts always construe the law against the defendant. We enjoy a blessed degree of political liberty, and part of the credit for this is due to the judges. From time to time some doubtful matters are resolved in favour of the defendant, even though he is a scamp. In matters of procedure and evidence the courts generally apply technical rules of common law with great rigidity in favour of defendants, guilty or innocent, although these rules are of far more assistance to the guilty than to the innocent.

Of course, judges differ in temperament. A few will, when stirred to action, play fast and loose with the authorities. Most, however, will genuinely try to

---

[48] *R. v. Norbury* [1978] Crim. L.R. 435; cf. *D.P.P. v. Fearon* [2010] 2 Cr. App. R. 22; *R. v. Rimmington* [2006] 1 A.C. 459.

[49] [1983] 1 A.C. 280.

[50] An example is *R. v. Instan* [1893] 1 Q.B. 450 at 454, where Lord Coleridge said that the failure to punish a niece who was living with her aunt and who let her aunt die "would be a slur upon and a discredit to the administration of justice in this country;" *therefore* the failure must be manslaughter.

follow authorities except in an extremely provoking case. So whether the defendant is acquitted or convicted may depend on whether he is tried before a judge of orthodox or adventurous views.

These facts are well known to lawyers, though they do not often find expression in forensic discussion. A rare example of judicial frankness is an utterance of Bridge L.J. (as he then was) speaking for the Court of Appeal:

> "[I]t is right, we think, to shun the temptation, which sometimes presses on the mind of the judiciary, to suppose that because a particular course of conduct, as was this course of conduct, was anti-social and undesirable, it can necessarily be fitted into some convenient criminal pigeon-hole."[51]

Accordingly, the court quashed the conviction. But mark the sequel. On further appeal the House of Lords succumbed to temptation and restored the conviction.[52]

You wouldn't argue, would you, that in case of doubt the law should always   1–026
be construed in favour of the rogue? Notwithstanding all the arguments against judicial legislation, it must be tolerated to some extent. The social interest in having an effective criminal law is great enough to justify some extensive interpretations of it. If the argument for conviction is supported by legal reasoning and authority (even though not so weighty a body of authority as the argument against), and if, in addition, it accords with clear social policy, and is not contrary to authority binding on the court, the court may properly decide in favour of conviction.

I would add this qualification: when the decision rests largely on considerations of policy, and particularly when a precedent in the defendant's favour is overruled, or distinguished virtually out of existence, the judges should, in honesty, admit that they are newly extending the law. The consequence that would inevitably follow from such candour would be that they would not be able, as now, to impose punishment on the person who occasions the extension of the law, and on others who offended before the new departure took place. They would have to give such persons at least an absolute or conditional discharge; and preferably they should acquit. Where the extension relates solely to the grade of the offence, or where the defendant intended to break the law, different considerations may apply.

As has already been intimated, the major cause of the trouble is that we have suffered centuries of neglect of the criminal law by the legislature. Parliament has been industrious in multiplying offences, very inarticulately drawn, but it is slow to remedy clear absurdities and deficiencies in the law as they come to light, and it has not bothered itself much in providing necessary defences. Under the present arrangements, both Government and Parliament are inadequate to meet all the demands made upon them.

Many Commonwealth countries have a code superseding the ramshackle creations of history; but proposals to this end have always been resisted in England. Two great efforts to produce a criminal code were made in the 19th

---

[51] *R. v. Charles* [1976] 1 W.L.R. 248 at 256C.
[52] *R. v. Charles* [1977] A.C. 177.

century, one from 1833 onwards on the initiative of Lord Brougham and another from 1878 by Stephen;[53] the reason for their failure was largely the opposition of the judges themselves, who wished to retain their discretionary powers.

1–027   **But isn't a statute a kind of code? You say that most criminal law is in statutes.**   A statute generally does not embody the common law, where much of the uncertainty in the criminal law occurs. Statutes, which are generally drafted by Government officials, often neglect juristic principles and often fail to define fundamental concepts. A well-drafted code should be the product of open government using the best brains of the legal profession. Not the least of its advantages for everybody except the lawyers would be that, by settling foreseeable difficulties in the law, it would save the taxpayer large sums spent on legal aid in appealing technical points. Moreover, a code would enable the whole body of law to be regularly checked by a supervisory commission.

New machinery for reform was introduced with the setting up of the Criminal Law Revision Committee ("C.L.R.C.") in 1959 and the Law Commission in 1965. While the former confined itself to proposing changes in the rules that have been found to be unsatisfactory, and steadfastly refused to codify even the branches of law on which it worked, the latter continues to make an effort to draft a code;[54] but the prospects of it being enacted are doubtful. The Commission has drafted a proposed code; it is valuable in itself and is suitable for adoption by Parliament (even though in some respect it could be improved upon); but it has not met with reasoned consideration and consensual amendment but with ministerial and bureaucratic indifference, passive resistance, and outright opposition. The same fate has befallen important legislative proposals of other Government committees, like those of the Butler Committee pertaining to criminal responsibility. The community at large is uninterested, and even within the legal profession as a whole there is no burning passion for rationalizing the criminal law.

1.5   THE CLASSIFICATION OF OFFENCES

1–028   The word "offence" is another name for a crime. Crimes in the broad sense include not only the major crimes (indictable offences) but summary offences. The latter regulate many trades and special activities (the so-called "regulatory offences"), as well as the conduct of ordinary people in their daily life.

In practice, a summary offence would not usually be referred to as a crime, which is felt to be too strong a description of it. To the extent that summary offences can result in six months' imprisonment, they are crimes.[55] However, we have become a bit squeamish about the word "crime." Just as we are now chary of blaming people for saying that they have done wrong (which may have been

---

[53] Also, an excellent code was produced by R. S. Wright in 1874; this failed because of Stephen's ungenerous opposition. See M. L. Friedland, "R. S. Wright's Model Criminal Code: A Forgotten Chapter in the History of the Criminal Law," (1981) 1 *Oxford J. Legal Stud.* 307.

[54] Law Commission, *A Criminal Code for England and Wales: Report and Draft Criminal Code Bill*, Law Com No 177 (London: H.M.S.O., 1989).

[55] Dennis J. Baker, "Constitutionalizing the Harm Principle," (2008) 27 *Crim. Just. Ethics* 3.

one of the reasons for the increase of criminality), so we do not seem to like saying that they have committed crimes. Even vile crimes like murder and rape are now termed "offences" in the statute-book. But it is not technically incorrect to call them crimes as well. Certainly we have no substitute for the expression "criminal law" (except "penal law," which is not much used); and the word "offence" happens not to yield a suitable adjective. In this book "crime" will continue to bear a generic meaning.

Summary offences are legion. If you are not an air pilot you may fondly believe that it is permissible to fly a kite 30 metres above ground level within the aerodrome traffic zone or 60 metres above ground anywhere else.[56] It is a summary offence to passively ask (beg) another for money in a public street;[57] to charge for supplying addresses of houses to let;[58] to collect from house to house for charity without a licence,[59] and selling fruit by the pound rather than by the kilogram could result in jail time.[60]

We must not make fun of the law. One or two of these offences may look like over-ebullience on the part of Parliament and the Government, but most have good reasons, or some sort of reason, when you come to think about them. Most summary offences are the result of prosaic efforts to improve standards, or to prevent petty fraud or oppression. Many occupations are regulated by statute, and it is generally made an offence to carry them on unless one is licensed, registered or otherwise qualified. Which occupations are thus favoured (or aimed at) often depends upon the accidents of political pressure. We went until 1975 (long after the age of the horse traffic was over) before it was thought necessary to enact that only qualified blacksmiths can shoe horses;[61] but at the time there was no law to stop anyone claiming to be a chiropodist and treating the feet of human beings.[62]

1–029

Most licensing provisions are a response to proved needs, particularly on grounds of public health and safety and the prevention of fraud. They can be of value in ensuring that standards are laid down and generally maintained, particularly where work is supervised by inspectors reporting to a supervising body. The licensing authority is frequently empowered to impose conditions and to withdraw the licence for misbehaviour; or a court on convicting of an offence may be authorized to order the revocation or suspension of a licence or registration—the best known example being disqualification from driving. (Even when an activity does not need a licence, the court on convicting of certain offences is sometimes empowered to make a disqualification order in respect of it. For example, convicted persons may be disqualified from managing companies for up to 15 years.)[63]

---

[56] Art. 164 of the *Air Navigation Order 2009*.
[57] Section 4 of the *Vagrancy Act 1824*.
[58] Section 1(1)(b) of the *Accommodation Agencies Act 1953*.
[59] *House to House Collections Act 1939*; see *Hankinson v. Dowland* [1974] 1 W.L.R. 1327.
[60] See *Weights and Measures Act 1985*.
[61] Section 16 of the *Farriers (Registration) Act 1975*.
[62] Chiropodists must now be registered with the Health Professions Council. Those who are unable to register because they do not have a diploma called themselves "Foot Health Practitioner," as there is no law requiring them to be registered to use such a title.
[63] See section 2 of the *Company Directors Disqualification Act 1986*.

What I have been saying about summary offences represents the lower reaches of the criminal law. You may at this point suppose that as this book proceeds it will give you further information on what people may and may not lawfully do. In fact, like every other discursive work on the criminal law, it will say little on this score that you do not know already. "Be honest and refrain from violence (including destructive acts against property)": these two commandments are almost the sum of it. Detailed and systematic information about the mass of regulatory offences is outside my purview. But dishonesty and violence and the legal structure erected to deal with them are sufficiently large topics for one book: too large to be dealt with except selectively. In addition, we shall be concerned with the general principles governing liability for crimes whether serious or trivial.

1–030   **What exactly is a summary offence?**   An offence triable only[64] in magistrates courts, which sit without a jury. In the clipped language of lawyers, a person charged with a summary offence has no "right" to trial," *i.e.* by a jury. His trial, if he contests the case, is by magistrates.

In contrast to summary offences, indictable offences committed by adult offenders are in principle triable in the Crown Court by jury. (The explanation of "in principle" will be given presently.) Cases tried in the Crown Court are said to be tried on indictment, the indictment being the formal document of accusation on which the trial by jury is based. The important characteristics of a trial on indictment are that it is always by jury and always in the Crown Court.

The term "summary offence" is now established, and is used in legislation; but it is somewhat inappropriate, since what is summary is not the offence itself but the mode of procedure. Even as applied to the procedure, "summary" is an infelicitous adjective, because the procedure of magistrates' courts is supposed to be as careful and formal as trial by jury. The chief differences between so-called summary trial and trial on indictment of an offence that is triable either way are that the latter is preceded by "committal proceedings" (the magistrates committing the defendant for trial in the Crown Court), and, of course, that there is no jury on summary trial. Committal proceedings do not apply in cases where the offence is *indictable only*. Section 51 of the *Crime and Disorder Act 1998* requires "indictable only" offences to be transferred directly to the Crown Court. Furthermore, any related either way offences will be transferred at the same time.[65] Committal proceedings are required to "commit" either way cases to the Crown Court, if there is no indictable only offence to which they are related.[66]

Indictable offences used to be divided into felonies (the graver class) and misdemeanours (graver than summary offences but not so grave as felonies). The distinction, at first of great importance, became eroded by various reforms, and the law was updated in 1967 by the simple expedient of applying the law for

---

[64] Section 5 and Sch. 1 of the *Interpretation Act 1978*.
[65] See also the proposed provisions in Sch. 3 of the *Criminal Justice Act 2003*. Cases can also be transferred to the Crown Court under section 4 of the *Criminal Justice Act 1987* (complex fraud cases); section 53 of the *Criminal Justice Act 1991* (certain child abuse cases); and under section 2(2) (b) of the *Administration of Justice (Miscellaneous Provisions) Act 1933*.
[66] See section 6 of the *Magistrates' Courts Act 1980*.

misdemeanours to felonies as well.[67] In consequence, we need no longer use either word. Not "felonies," because they no longer have distinctive features, and not "misdemeanours," because the whole point of that expression was to make a distinction from felonies. Besides, to designate murder as a misdemeanour would make it sound like a peccadillo.

How does one know whether an offence is indictable or summary? Summary offences are entirely the creatures of statutes. If Parliament has intended to make an offence punishable summarily, it should have made this clear in the statute. If Parliament prohibits an act without saying how a violation is to be tried, it becomes an indictable offence.[68]

    Some indictable offences exist at common law. But the great majority now rest on statute, even though some were originally judge-made.

So the beaks try summary offences, while the Crown Court tries indictable offences? Yes as regards the first part of your proposition, but the second part is over-simplified. Magistrates' courts can try some indictable offences, in addition to summary offences.

    To explain: practically every criminal case starts in the magistrates' court. The first step when proceedings are contemplated is to bring the suspect before the magistrates, either by arresting him or by serving him with a summons to attend.

    If the charge is of a summary offence the magistrates will normally try it themselves ("summary trial"). If the charge is of an indictable offence the magistrates may nevertheless have power to try it summarily. An indictable offence that can be tried summarily is said to be "triable either way." For such an offence, the magistrates first decide whether the case is suitable for summary trial. If it is, they proceed to act as "examining magistrates" conducting "committal proceedings." Their duty is to consider whether a *prima facie* case has been established. If they find in the affirmative (as they almost always do), they send ("commit") the defendant for trial before a jury ("trial on indictment").[69] There is a modern form of commitment on written statements, in which the magistrates need not consider the evidence if the defendant does not ask them to.[70] Committal proceedings can be held by one magistrate. If the magistrates decide that they can suitably deal with the case themselves, they can do so, subject to a qualification (as to the defendant's consent) to be mentioned

1–031

1–032

---

[67] Section 1 of the *Criminal Law Act 1967.*
[68] But where a statute imposes a "penalty" for an offence, the court may find an implication that the penalty is to be recoverable only in a magistrates' court: see *Johnson v. Colam* (1875) 10 Q.B. 544.
[69] The proceedings were formerly called the "preliminary examination" (or "enquiry"). "Commitment" or "committal" in its original meaning refers to imprisonment by order of the court; the word is generally confined to (1) imprisonment pending trial (as here), and (2) imprisonment for contempt of court. By an extension, we now speak of commitment on bail (which means freedom) as an alternative to commitment in custody.
[70] Section 6(2) of the *Magistrates Court Act 1980.*

presently.[71] (As said before, indictable only, and related triable either way offences, are transferred directly to the Crown Court and therefore are not preceded by a committal hearing).

1–033 **You say that some but only some indictable offences are triable either way. Which are they?** I will tell you how to find out. "Either way" offences are (a) those expressly stated to be triable either way in the legislation creating them, plus (b) the offences listed in the *Magistrates' Court Act* Schedule 1. There would be little point in reproducing the list here. All other offences are only summary or triable only on indictment. Let us call the latter "purely indictable" offences; they include all offences punishable with life imprisonment.

1–034 **Who decides how an offence either way is in fact tried? Is it for the prosecutor?** Neither the police nor private prosecutors can insist upon one form of trial rather than the other. The case will be tried on indictment if:

1. the magistrates consider the case more suitable for this form of trial, or
2. (although the magistrates consider it more suitable for summary trial) the defendant elects to "go for trial."

Otherwise the case will be tried summarily. It will be seen that ordinary charges of "either way" offences (those brought by the police or private prosecutors) are tried on indictment unless both the magistrates and the defendant are agreeable to summary trial.[72] This means that the defendant has an overriding right to be tried by jury. There is an elaborate—indeed, over-elaborate— procedure for informing him of his rights in this manner. Magistrates for their part will generally be prepared to try the case if the defendant will let them and if it is not too serious.

1–035 **Don't the magistrates listen to what the police have to say on this point?** The police may be happy to have the case tried summarily; it will save them time. If they want the defendant to be sent down for a good stretch they may try to persuade the magistrates that the offence is too grave for summary trial. (The police are dissatisfied by the excessive leniency of magistrates in some cases, particularly those involving violence against themselves.) But the only way in which the police can be sure of getting the case to the Crown Court is by charging a purely indictable offence. This is when the police are prosecuting on their own: the defendant's right to go for trial of an either way offence is excluded if the prosecution is brought by a Law Officer of the Crown (the Attorney-General or Solicitor-General) or (as much more commonly happens) the Director of Public Prosecutions.

---

[71] Section 41 of the *Criminal Justice Act 1988* provides: "Where a magistrates' court commits a person to the Crown Court for trial on indictment for an offence triable either way or a number of such offences, it may also commit him for trial for any summary offence with which he is charged ...".
[72] For more details see sections 17-27A of the *Magistrates Court Act 1980*.

The effect, then, is that on any serious "either way" charge a defendant who wants trial by jury will normally get it? Yes, and also on some charges that are not serious. Take petty theft as an example.[73] The defendant can insist on trial in the Crown Court, even though it is only a charge of theft of a Cohiba cigar worth £40 and the case is going to saddle the public with a bill of £10,000 in costs. If he is eventually convicted he may be ordered to pay the costs, but of course he may not have the means to do so.

1–036

Couldn't the law be rationalized? The law, like life in general, is a compromise. A section of opinion would strongly disapprove if people were deprived of their right of trial for theft, conviction of which is regarded as stigmatic. On the other hand, a number of very stigmatic offences are triable only summarily.

1–037

Generally the defendant will accept summary trial if offered, because he thinks the case will be heard more quickly by magistrates (though this is not always so). Also, magistrates' courts are less terrifying. On summary conviction the maximum punishment is generally six months' imprisonment and/or a pecuniary fine, and even within that limit offenders are likely to be treated more leniently by magistrates than if they had elected for trial in the Crown Court. (Judges and recorders regularly impose punishment on a scale that most magistrates would regard as monstrous. And conversely, changing the adjective to "derisory.") Occasionally the defendant will opt for the panoply (and expense) of the Crown Court because he wishes to air his defence before a jury (and more would do so if they were better advised).

Apart from the question of jurisdiction, are there any differences in law between indictable and summary offences? A few, but only one is important for substantive criminal law. An attempt to commit an indictable offence is itself an indictable offence, but an attempt to commit a summary offence is not punishable in the absence of an express statute. This difference is not accidental: summary offences are not sufficiently grave to make prosecutions for a mere attempt worthwhile.[74]

1–038

1.6 CRIMINAL AND CIVIL LAW

The layman tends to think of the law primarily as the criminal law; but most of it is civil, not criminal. In principle there are two sets of courts: criminal and civil (though the same court often has both kinds of jurisdiction). Similarly there are two kinds of legal procedure: civil and criminal. There criminal law is administered by criminal courts following criminal procedure, and similarly with civil law. An act can be a civil wrong (wrongful by the civil law) or a crime; or it

1–039

---

[73] Section 22 of the *Magistrates' Courts Act 1980* requires some offences involving loss of less than £5,000 to be tried summarily such as criminal damage and aggravated vehicle taking.

[74] A further procedural difference may be mentioned. Indictable offences can generally be prosecuted after any length of time, but summary offences cannot generally be charged after the lapse of six months. See section 127 of the *Magistrates' Court Act 1980*.

can be both. The part of the civil law bearing the strongest resemblance to the criminal law is the law of tort. Its effect is primarily to give an action for damages (compensation).

1–040　**Why are there two sorts of law?**　The criminal law is concerned primarily with the question of whether wrongdoers are to be punished (or compulsorily treated). The civil law is concerned with private rights: for example, enabling the owner of an article to get it back from someone who has gone off with it, or alternatively to get damages for its decision.

1–041　**Is libel a crime or a tort?**　Theoretically it is both; but it is now rarely prosecuted.[75]

1–042　**But surely people who libel others do find themselves in the dock from time to time?**　Not commonly in the dock, as the dock is a feature peculiar to the criminal courts. A libeller can be sued for damages in tort, and the damages are likely to be heavy. He may find himself in the witness box, giving evidence as a defendant in a civil action, but he is most unlikely to be in the dock.

1–043　**What if the libeller can't pay the damages; does he go to prison?**　No, he will go to the bankruptcy court. There is a big difference between civil damages and the criminal fine: a fine defaulter can in certain circumstances be sent to prison.[76]

1–044　**Can a criminal always be prosecuted for damages?**　Hold on: your terminology is mixed. Actions (not prosecutions) for damages are a matter of civil law. One sues (brings an action for) the civil wrong, prosecutes for the crime. No, every crime is not a civil wrong. Numerous offences under statutory regulations are not the subject of an action for damages.

1–045　**If I am injured in an accident with a drunken driver, can I sue him for damages for the offence of drunken driving?**　Not for the offence as such; you sue for damages for negligence, which is the tort.

1–046　**But his drinking was wilful. It is not a case of negligence.**　He drank intentionally (wilfully), but he did not injure you intentionally. Anyway, negligence covers cases of intention. In law we always speak of the minimum degree of fault necessary for liability, so a man who injures another intentionally is *a fortiori*[77] accounted negligent.

1–047　**Can anyone be prosecuted for breaking a contract?**　A few dangerous breaches of contract are criminally punishable,[78] and a few types of debt-frauds

---

[75] J. R. Spencer, "Criminal Libel: A Skeleton in the Cupboard," [1977] Crim. L.R. 383 at 465. See also *Gleaves v. Insall* [1999] 2 Cr. App. R. 466 at 478 *per* Kennedy L.J.

[76] Section 76 of the *Magistrates' Courts Act 1980*.

[77] With strong reason (generally anglicized in pronunciation as "ay forsheeohry").

[78] See G. H. Treitel, "Contract and Crime," in Colin Tapper (ed.), *Crime Proof and Punishment, Essays in Memory of Sir Rupert Cross*, (London: Butterworth, 1981) at 83. The criminal law also imposes various obligations on certain parties to contracts or proposed contracts: *id*. at 85-86.

are crimes,[79] but on the whole the law in this area is weak and under-enforced. For the most part a breach of contract is not a crime. Incurring a contractual debt by fraud could be criminal, but getting a contractual benefit and then dishonestly avoiding to pay for it is generally not. The remedy of the aggrieved party is to bring a civil action for debt, damages, specific performance or injunction. (A contracting party who fails to comply with the court's order of specific performance or injunction may be sent to prison for contempt of court, but the commitment is regarded as "civil" rather than "criminal").

But dishonesty in not paying contractual debts is rife. Many people nowadays delay payment of debts in order to profit by interest on the money retained, while others do their best to avoid paying at all. Why doesn't the criminal law reach such people? The chief reason is the fear that the law might be used to re-introduce what would be in effect imprisonment for debt, as we had in Dickensian times. Nevertheless, if it could be proved that the person had no intention of paying when he entered the contract; that person would be morally no different to a thief. He uses fraud to make off with the other person's goods or services. For example, the person who tricks a builder into installing a new kitchen in his house—that is, a kitchen he has no intention of paying for—could be brought within the purview of the *Fraud Act 2006*.[80]

1–048

When an act is both criminally and civilly wrong, is the wrongdoer punished twice? The damages in the civil action are regarded as compensation for the victim, not as punishment for the wrongdoer. Punitive damages are only awarded in exceptional cases, but are still a form of compensation.

1–049

If the same act can be both a crime and a tort, what is the difference between a crime and a tort? To say that an act is a tort or other civil wrong means that it can be followed by a civil action for damages, or other civil redress. To say that it is a crime means that it can be followed by a criminal prosecution. Not only the procedure and evidence but the outcomes differ.

1–050

The usual outcome for civil proceedings is:

- a judgment for debt; or
- damages; or
- compensation; or
- restitution; or

---

[79] See for example, section 40 of the *Administration of Justice Act 1970*. The *Fraud Act 2006* would also catch both the debtor and the payee, if fraudulent representations were made to intimidate the debtor into paying. Coupled with that, the debtor himself would be caught by the *Fraud Act 2006* if he were to make false representations to avoid paying his debt.

[80] This has caused issues in recent times, as solo tradesmen have complained that it is too expensive for them to launch civil proceedings to enforce debts. (It may also be remarkably time consuming). It does seem odd that a corporate giant such as John Lewis is able to have the state protect its property from shoplifters, but the humble plumber has to either forgo a debt or try to take civil action on his own account to recover his property and the money he is owed for his services. The core difference with the thief is that his culpability is much easier to infer where he has surreptitiously taken goods. *Per contra*, many debtors may have had the best intentions when they entered the contract, but foolishly lived beyond their means.

- an order for specific performance of contract; or
- an injunction to prevent the commission of a wrong, or its commission, or
- a declaration of rights.

There are also civil and equitable remedies in relation to the dissolution of marriage, care proceedings in respect of juveniles, other proceedings for transferring parental rights, and the application of judicial review. The latter asks the High Court to grant relief against improper conduct by public authorities and inferior tribunals; the relief may take the form of a declaration, injunction, damages, or one of the prerogative orders (*mandamus*, prohibition, *certiorari*), or the prerogative writ of *habeas corpus*. All these are distinctively civil orders.

1.7 THE DEFINITION OF A CRIME

1–051   We are now in a position to define a crime. A crime (or offence) is a legal wrong that can be followed by criminal proceedings which may result in punishment.

1–052   **Have you not produced a circular definition? We don't know whether an act is a crime unless it can be followed by criminal proceedings; and we don't know whether the appropriate proceedings are criminal unless we know that the act is a crime?** The question is a thoughtful one and deserves an answer. The answer is no. My definition is not circular, even though it may appear to be so. Criminal proceedings, that is to say a prosecution, can be described in great detail without ever using the word "crime," or at any rate without requiring the word "crime" to be defined for the purpose of understanding what is said.

Let me essay an outline of criminal proceedings. A person who is suspected of one of certain types of legal wrong (that is to say a crime, but, knowing that you are ready to pounce, I am avoiding the word) may be brought before the magistrates in custody, as a result of having been arrested without warrant or arrested on warrant. Alternatively he may come to court as a result of information leading to a summons directing him to appear.[81] Subsequent proceedings will depend upon whether the matter charged against him is indictable or summary. You will observe that so far I have not obliged to use the word "crime" or "criminal." And so I could go on with a complete description of criminal procedure and evidence, which differ in many ways (though not in all) from civil procedure and evidence. The fact that the wrong can be followed by this type of proceeding shows that it is a crime.[82]

To give a few examples in the High Court of the procedural differences between crimes and civil wrongs:

- A civil proceeding in the High Court is generally commenced by writ, whereas the document commencing a criminal trial in the Crown Court is

---

[81] Even when a person has been arrested the police have certain powers to release him on bail, or he may be given bail by the magistrates or by a High Court judge.

[82] Glanville L. Williams, "The Definition of a Crime," (1955) 8 *Current Legal Problems* 107 at 130. See also the penetrating discussion in Andrew Ashworth, "Is the Criminal Law a Lost Cause?" (2000) 116 *L.Q.R.* 225.

an indictment. At magistrates' court level, a document commencing a civil proceeding is called a complaint, whereas a document in a prosecution is, as we have seen, called an information.[83]

- Civil proceedings are, in general, brought by the person directly affected. Prosecutions can, in general, be brought by anyone, whether he is affected by the offence or not, subject to the restrictions that have already been noticed.

- The plaintiff in a civil action can abort the proceedings at any time, whereas they cannot be stopped by a Government officer. In contrast, no prosecutor except the Attorney-General and D.P.P. can be sure of being able to stifle a prosecution once started. If the prosecutor changes his mind about the case he may withdraw with the leave of the court; but if he does so without that leave a police officer or anyone else may continue proceedings on behalf of the public. The D.P.P. may take over the proceedings even without the prosecutor's consent, either in order to conduct the case more efficiently or even to discontinue it[84]—though he will intervene only in the most exceptional circumstances, as where the trial is improper for technical reasons, or the Government desires to protect a criminal who has "grassed" on his former companions.[85] The Attorney-General may stop any prosecution in the Crown Court by entering a *nolle proséqui*, though here again he rarely intervenes except when the trial is improper for technical reasons.[86]

Can I come again? Your description does not explain what a crime really is. It only states the consequences of crime.   The objection mistakes the purpose of definition. The object of a definition is to explain how words are used. Suppose that a Minister announces to Parliament that the Government intends to introduce legislation to make it a crime (or an offence) to join in unofficial strike. This means that a person who goes on unofficial strike will be subject to criminal proceedings (and we know what they are), the possible outcome being punishment (and we know what that is). So we know the meaning of saying that unofficial striking is to be a crime.

    I think you might want to know what ought to be a crime, rather than what *is* a crime—because what *is* a crime is anything the Government has chosen to criminalize. And it does this by making it an offence rather than a civil wrong. We will return to the question of what ought to be a crime soon.

1–053

---

[83] For an example of a complaint on a public matter see *Hereford and Worcester C.C. v. Newman* [1975] 1 W.L.R. 901.

[84] *Raymond v. Attorney-General* [1982] Q.B. 839; *R. v. D.P.P. Ex p. Hussein* [1990] C.O.D. 88; *R. v. D.P.P. Ex p. Chaudhary* [1995] 1 Cr. App. R. 136.

[85] Cf. *R. (on the application of Corner House Research) v. Director of the Serious Fraud Office* [2009] 1 A.C. 756.

[86] The Attorney-General cannot stop a summary prosecution, but, as was said above, the D.P.P. can take over any private prosecution in order to end it. See generally, J. Ll. J. Edwards, *The Law Officers of the Crown*, (London: Sweet & Maxwell, 1964) at Chap. 12.

1–054 **Can one say that the court order in civil proceedings is sought by and made for the benefit of the private individual, while the order of a criminal court is to protect society as a whole?** Alas, no, for an order mandamus[87] (which is civil, or at any rate non-criminal) requires the defendant to perform his public duty, and it is not intended to benefit one particular individual; while a criminal court can make an order for compensation which is intended to benefit an individual. There are two particular ways in which the line between civil and criminal law is blurred.

1. The practice of binding over straddles civil and criminal procedure. As an example of its criminal use, suppose that a private citizen charges another before the magistrates for assaulting him, and the defendant says that the prosecutor provoked him. The magistrates may metaphorically knock their heads together by requiring both to enter into recognisances, with or without sureties, to keep the peace. The recognisance (whether of the person bound over or of his surety) requires the payment of a sum of money in the event of breach. Refusal by the person bound over to enter into the recognisance or failure to find the required sureties can result in an immediate sentence of imprisonment (even when the person in question has broken no law). Breach of the recognisance when entered into can be punished by forfeiture of the whole part of the sums promised to be paid. The bind-over can also be used even when no criminal proceedings are in progress. If it is feared that a person will breach the peace he may be brought before a magistrates' court in civil proceedings (*i.e.* by complaint) and bound over to keep the peace. The recognisance may in appropriate cases be for a large sum. This procedure is sometimes used where a person has regularly flouted the law because the statutory fines are low; by binding him over the magistrates can mulct him in a heavier penalty next time.[88]

2. The civil courts can sometimes grant an injunction or declaration to prevent criminal offences. This can be done under the express or implied authority of a statute.[89] Also, the Attorney-General may sue at common law for an injunction to prevent a public nuisance or other breach of public duty; and a private person may, with the Attorney-General's consent, sue for the injunction in his name. This last is known as a relator action,[90] because the Attorney acts on the relation (*ex relatione*) of the citizen who is the real plaintiff and who has to foot the bill of the costs.

---

[87] "We command."

[88] See *Justices of the Peace Act 1361*; *R. v. Lincoln Crown Court Ex p. Jude* [1998] 1 W.L.R. 1403. For a fuller discussion see Glanville Williams, *Criminal Law: The General Part*, (London: Stevens & Sons, 2nd edn. 1961) at Chap. 16.

[89] In *Pharmaceutical Society of Great Britain v. Boots Cash Chemists (Southern) Ltd.* [1953] 1 Q.B. 401, the plaintiff society was required by statute to take steps to secure compliance with the statutory provisions (see now section 9(1) of the *Poisons Act 1972*), and instead of prosecuting for a summary offence under the Act it brought a civil action, apparently for an injunction or declaration. However, the House of Lords has now adopted a restrictive attitude in these actions: *RCA Corp. v. Pollard* [1982] 3 W.L.R. 1007.

[90] Accent on the second syllable.

Is the relation action civil or criminal, and is it brought for a crime or for a   1–055
civil wrong?   It is a civil action, but is brought on account of a crime or other
breach of public duty.

That seems a rare muddle. I thought you were saying that crimes are matters   1–056
for the criminal courts. But now you tell me that the civil courts can
interfere.   Yes in respect of apprehended crime. The action for an injunction (or,
as an alternative, for a declaration) is brought in the High Court, which has both
criminal and civil jurisdiction; the proceeding is governed by the rules of a civil
action and is not thought of as criminal because no question of punishment is
involved.

What is the point of bringing a relator action? Why not just prosecute for   1–057
the crime?   The crime may be threatened but not yet committed, and the
injunction may prevent it from being committed. Or the criminal penalty may be
only a modest fine, which is not enough to stop criminal activity from continuing,
whereas disobedience to an injunction can land the offender in jail.[91]

Why must the action be brought in the name of the Attorney-General when   1–058
the real plaintiff is a private person?   Relator actions are brought when the
defendant is in breach of his public duty, or threatens such breach. A barrow-boy
obstructs the street with his barrow; or buses park in the road in which you live
and cause congestion. No one has his individual rights infringed: the obstruction
of the highway is an infringement of the right of the public to pass without
hindrance, and is normally prosecuted as a summary offence. But the courts
allowed the Attorney-General to sue in the interest of the public, and the Attorney
in turn decided to allow his name to be used by members of the public. Since he
only consents to a single action being brought, this saves the vexation and waste
of money that would be involved if many people sued the same defendant.

What if the Attorney-General doesn't want the law to be enforced, and   1–059
refuses his consent?   The courts accord him an absolute discretion, and will not
interfere. The Attorney may refuse his consent, for example, if he thinks it unwise
to antagonize a powerful trade union. Whatever his reasons, good or bad, he need
not express them.[92] The only important exception to the Attorney's absolute
control over the action to protect public rights is that, by statute, a local authority
may sue to protect the interests of the local inhabitants.[93]

In short, the line between criminal and civil law is somewhat arbitrary. The
broad point remains that all crimes can legally be followed by punishment, and
that criminal courts generally punish (or sentence the defendant in a way that puts

---

[91] Cf. section 1 of the *Crime and Disorder Act 1998*, which is still in force at the time of writing. The coalition government has said it intends to repeal the provision.

[92] *Gouriet v. Union of Post Office Workers* [1978] A.C. 435; *Ashby v. Ebdon* [1985] Ch. 394.

[93] Section 222 of the *Local Government Act 1972*; *Kent CC v. Batchelor (No.2)* [1979] 1 W.L.R. 213; cf. *Birmingham City Council v. Shafi* [2009] 1 W.L.R. 1961, where it was held that the local authority should seek an ASBO (Anti-Social Behaviour Order) under the *Crime and Disorder Act 1998* and only use section 222 as a last resort. Obviously this situation will change if the Coalition Government fulfils its promise to abrogate the ASBO provisions.

him under a special risk of being punished, as in the case of probation or suspended sentence), while civil courts are not oriented to punishment in the same way. I have to say it is the broad point, because sometimes a civil court punishes, as when it orders a penalty to be paid.

1–060 **Why do we have *criminal* laws?** I can only give you an epigrammatic explanation of why we have law and enforcement institutions.[94] The object and function of law generally is not too different to that of conventional morality. The great Australian philosopher, J. L. Mackie, provides a superlative *précis* of the function of morality and its relation with law.

> "Protagoras, Hobbes, Hume, and Warnock are all at least broadly in agreement about the problem that morality [and ultimately law] is needed to solve: limited resources and limited sympathies together generate both competition leading to conflict and an absence of what would be mutually beneficial cooperation.[95]
>
> ....
>
> The essential device is a form of agreement which provides for its own enforcement. Each of the parties has a motive for supporting the authority who will himself have the job of punishing [or awarding private law remedies such as damages, injunctions and so forth] breaches of the agreement (and will himself have a motive for doing so). Consequently each party will have double reason for fulfilling his side of the bargain: the fear of punishment [or having to pay damages *etc.*] for breaking it, and the expectation of benefits from keeping it, because the fulfilment by the [majority] of other parties of their sides of the bargain is fairly well assured by the same motives."[96]

Whether we are talking about law by agreement[97] or the social contract[98] more generally, there is ample empirical evidence to support the claim that society is formed by some kind of agreement;[99] and also that some individuals are not going to keep their side of the bargain in such a big web of complex agreements and inter-agreements.[100] Consequently, informal moral commands are codified into law so that violations will be deterred with punishment or private law remedies. Mackie[101] cites game theory in his discussion of the evolution of morality, but is careful to note that even the most advanced theory could not explain how moral principles have evolved or why the majority conform. We benefit from the laws that are designed to preserve our individual financial and physical security. Health and safety standards and regulations against fraud and

---

[94] For a fuller discussion see Baker, *op. cit. supra*, note 42 at Chaps. 2 & 6.

[95] J. L. Mackie, *Ethics: Inventing Right and Wrong*, (New York: Penguin Books, 1977) at 111.

[96] *Id.* at 109. See also Nicola Lacey, "Social Policy, Civil Society and the Institutions of Criminal Justice," (2001) 26 *Austl. J. Leg. Phil.* 7; Stanley I. Benn and R. S. Peters, *Social Principles and the Democratic State*, (London: Harper Collins Publishers, 1971). See also John Gardner, "Ethics and Law," in John Skorupski (ed.), *The Routledge Companion to Ethics*, (London: Routledge, 2010).

[97] David Gauthier, *Morals By Agreement*, (New York: Oxford University Press, 1999).

[98] Thomas M. Scanlon, *What We Owe To Each Other*, (Cambridge MA: Harvard University Press, 2000).

[99] See generally F. J. M. Feldbrugge, *The Law's Beginnings*, (Leiden: Brill Academic Publishing, 2003); A. S. Diamond, *Primitive Law: Past and Present*, (London: Methuen & Co. Ltd., 1971).

[100] The hard empirical evidence is documented in the national crime statistics and in the tens of thousands of judgments flowing out of the courts each year concerning private disputes.

[101] Mackie, *op. cit. supra*, note 95 at 115 *et seq.*

deceptive practices serve such an end. Furthermore, each individual has an interest in maintaining the State and its institutions, because each member of society benefits from civilization.[102]

Professor Raz[103] notes that law serves a number of social functions including the prevention of undesirable behavior (this is mainly achieved by enacting criminal and tort laws); the provision of facilities and mechanisms to allow private arrangements to be regulated and protected between individuals; the provision of services and the redistribution of goods; and the provision of facilities for solving unregulated disputes. Society is necessary for the advancement and well-being of humanity and it is maintained and promoted directly and indirectly by law. Laws cover many areas because of the complexity of modern living. We have criminal law, contract law, family law, trusts law, consumer protection law, tort law, environmental laws, tax laws, *etc*. Tax laws have both an indirect and direct impact, as they force individuals to handover a portion of their income, but that income is spent on communal infrastructure, *etc*. Tax law allows revenues to be collected in a transparent way so that the public might benefit indirectly from the provision of universities, schools, roads, courts, police, welfare for the poor and so on. Welfare might also have an effect on crime rates, as it provides for those who lack the ability to provide for themselves.[104]

Principled criminal laws should comply with our basic principles of justice such as the harm principle,[105] the autonomy principle,[106] the culpability principle,[107] and the equality principle.[108] These are cardinal moral principles that have been developed and constructed by humans, and have improved as humans have gained better insights. Of course accounts of harm will vary given the limits of epistemological inquiry and of human rationality. Human agents invent crimes to manage conventional conflicts that arise from communal living. Criminal law is a system of social control[109] that allows a given community to manage itself. It is used to manage genuine conflicts, but unfortunately also to criminalize harmless wrongs; and to control the disadvantaged.[110]   **1–061**

Criminal laws that do not proscribe wrongs that are harmful, or otherwise violative of autonomy, are unprincipled. For example, the acts referred by Lord Devlin[111] (consensual prostitution and homosexuality) are not harmful or violative of the autonomy of others, because even conventional accounts of harm

---

[102] Alasdair MacIntyre, *After Virtue: A Study in Moral Theory*, (Notre Dame, IN: University of Notre Dame Press, 1984). S. Shapin, *A Social History of Truth: Civility and Science in Seventeenth-Century England*, (Chicago, IL: University of Chicago Press, 1994).

[103] Raz, *The Authority of Law*, (Oxford: Oxford University Press, 2009) at 168-179.

[104] Dennis J. Baker, "A Critical Evaluation of the Historical and Contemporary Justifications for Criminalizing Begging," (2009) 73(3) *J. Crim. L.* 212.

[105] Baker, *op. cit. supra*, note 42, Chaps. 2 & 6.

[106] J. B. Schneewind, *The Invention of Autonomy*, (Cambridge: Cambridge University Press, 1998).

[107] Rollin M. Perkins, "A Rationale of Mens Rea," (1939) 52 *Harvard Law Review* 905.

[108] W. T. Blackstone, "On The Meaning and Justification of The Equality Principle," (1967) 77(4) *Ethics* 239.

[109] Donald Black, *The Behaviour of Law* (New York: Academic Press, 1968), at 2.

[110] Richard Quinney, *The Critique of Legal Order*, (Boston: Little Brown, 1974), at 16; William Chambliss and Robert Seidmann, *Law, Order, and Power*, (Reading, MA: Addison-Wesley, 1982); Reiman, *The Rich Get Richer and the Poor Get Prison*, (Boston: Allyn & Bacon, 4th edn. 1995), at 7.

[111] Patrick Devlin, *The Enforcement of Morals*, (Oxford: Oxford University Press, 1965).

and wrong cannot explain how consenting adults engaging in homosexuality and prostitution harm or violate the autonomy of others. Devlin does not run into error by suggesting that without criminalization society would disintegrate, but rather he runs into error by postulating that certain harmless violations of conventional norms would cause social disintegration and thus should be criminalized. There is no empirical support for his claim that activities such as homosexuality and prostitution would cause the same type of social disintegration that would transpire if wrongful harms such as murder, rape, theft, robbery, *etc.* were not criminalized.

Rational lawmakers should draw on the best social information available including deep conventional understandings of justice, harm, privacy, autonomy and so on, when making criminalization determinations. Criminal law's evolution has often been shaped by unjust considerations, because lawmakers were not sufficiently enlightened and rational at various stages in our history to understand the injustice of some of their decisions.[112] In the 16th century the masses lacked the capacity to understand that humans could not really be witches and therefore many women were criminalized for allegedly engaging in witchcraft.[113] We no longer criminalize witchcraft as we have sufficient empirical information to be able to rationally understand that humans cannot have supernatural powers.[114] In summation: the criminal law aims to deter culpable harm-doing.

1–062   **Are there any criteria for determining whether to label a harmful wrong as a crime as opposed to labelling it as a civil wrong?** Professor Kleinig[115] notes that harm *per se* does not really explain why some forms of harm-doing are

---

[112] Sayre notes that: "primitive English law started from a basis bordering on absolute liability." Francis Bowes Sayre, "Mens Rea," (1932) 45 *Harvard Law Review* 974 at 977. See also the idiosyncratic prejudice that Stephen, like Devlin, tried to dress up as morality. James Fitzjames Stephen, *Liberty, Equality, Fraternity,* (Indianapolis: Liberty Fund, 1993).

[113] It has been noted that: "[e]ven if an illness was explicable by medical theory, it might still be seen as originating in the evil will of another person. A distinction was made between a cause in the mechanic sense—*how* a certain person was injured—and cause in the purposive sense—*why* this person not another was injured. When people blamed witches they did it not out of mere ignorance, but because it explained why a certain misfortune had happened to them, despite all their precautions; why for example, their butter did not 'come'." A. A. D. J. MacFarlane, "Witchcraft in Tudor and Stuart Essex," in J. S. Cockburn (eds.), *Crime in England 1550-1800,* (Cambridge: Methuen & Co., 1977) at 83.

[114] The badness and wrongness of many acts is conventionally contingent, but others acts are accepted as wrong and bad in nearly all jurisdictions. However, universal agreement very rarely extends far beyond a core set of primitive harms—harms that are biological and scientifically identifiable as bad and which impact all humans more or less in the same way. If you amputate a person's legs, she will be crippled regardless of whether she lives in Brazil or New York. In some sub-contexts, such harms may be welcomed (*i.e.* by sadomasochists—but I can think of no modern state where such a harm would be generally welcomed by the masses).

[115] John Kleinig, "Criminally Harming Others," (1986) 5 *Crim. Just. Ethics* 3. See also Benjamin C. Zipursky, "Two Dimensions of Responsibility in Crime, Tort, and Moral Luck," (2008) 9 *Theoretical Inq. L.* 97; Kenneth W. Simons, "Crime/Tort Distinction: Legal Doctrine and Normative Perspectives," (2008) 17 *Widener L.J.* 719; John C. Coffee, "Does Unlawful Mean Criminal: Reflections on the Disappearing Tort/Crime Distinction in American Law," (1991) 71 *B.U. L. Rev.* 193; Robert W. Drane and David J. Neal, "On Moral Justifications for the Tort/Crime Distinction," (1980) 68 *Cal. L. Rev.* 398; and also the collection of symposium papers on this topic in volume 76 of the *Boston University Law Review*.

criminalized while others are not. He suggests that moral culpability could play an important role in drawing a distinction between criminalizable wrongs and other wrongs, but notes that intentional harm doing (such as intentional breaches of contracts) is often regulated by the civil law.[116] There are various moral overlaps between crimes and torts.[117] It is not the degree of harm (or, other bad (but harmless) consequence such as the psychological distress suffered by V when she learns D has been covertly filming up her skirt)[118] alone that determines whether conduct should be criminalized. Some torts involve greater harm than criminal conduct. The negligent train driver is likely to cause greater harm than someone who deliberately drives her car over a single pedestrian. Similarly, the negligent banker[119] might cause more harm than a 1,000 pickpockets.[120] The lawmaker has to consider the degree of moral blameworthiness involved to determine whether the activities are sufficiently serious to warrant penal condemnation or a private law response.

There will always be some overlap. The private law also aims to prevent certain unwanted (usually harmful) bad consequences but compensates the wronged party.[121] Although a perfect line cannot be drawn, civil wrongs are distinguishable from crimes primarily because of the degree of culpability involved. Hampton,[122] like von Hirsch,[123] and Ashworth,[124] argues that the degree of culpability accompanying the harm doing is important for drawing a distinction between torts and crimes. Torts usually involve negligent harm doing, whereas crimes involve intentional, reckless or grossly negligent harm doing. Nevertheless, the degree of harm and culpability involved in some private wrongs could be sufficient to ground a case for criminalization (intentional defamation, intentional breaches of contracts without excuse or justification, and so forth), but wrongful harm does not necessarily have to be criminalized. It is important to note that wrongful harm provides a necessary condition for criminalization, but

---

[116] *Id.* at 6.

[117] To some extent this is attributable to the way in which the criminal and civil law evolved out of a single body of law. For a convenient and compendious overview of the criminal law's historical development and its relation to tort law, see Carleton Kemp Allen, *Legal Duties* (Oxford: Clarendon Press, 1931) at 221-52; J. A. Jolowicz, *Lectures on Jurisprudence*, (London: Athlone Press, 1963) at 344-58.

[118] *R. v. Hamilton* [2008] Q.B. 224.

[119] For example, James Gobert and Maurice Punch note that: "Before its collapse, Barings Bank was sending sums of money to Nick Leeson in Singapore for amounts that in some instances exceeded both the bank's assets as well as the limits set by the bank of England." James Gobert and Maurice Punch, *Rethinking Corporate Crime*, (London: Butterworths LexisNexis, 2003) at 19.

[120] Allen, *op. cit. supra*, note 117 at 255.

[121] Kleinig, *op. cit. supra*, note 115.

[122] Jean E. Hampton, "Liberalism, Retribution and Criminality," in *In Harms Way: Essays in Honour of Joel Feinberg*, ed. Jules L. Coleman and Allen Buchanan (Cambridge: Cambridge University Press, 1994) at 176 *et seq*. Cf. John Braithwaite and Philip Pettit, *Not Just Deserts: Republican Theory of Criminal Justice*, (Oxford: Clarendon Press, 1990).

[123] See Andrew von Hirsch, *Censure and Sanctions*, (Oxford: Clarendon Press, 1993) at 10.

[124] "'Result-crimes,' and many other crimes, impose liability on the basis of conduct which is preliminary to the infliction of harm, merely because of the intention with which the person acted." Andrew Ashworth, "Taking the Consequences," in *Action and Value in Criminal Law*, ed. Stephen Shute, John Gardner and Jeremy Horder (Oxford: Clarendon Press, 1993) at 116.

the state is not compelled to criminalize every form of wrongful harm-doing.[125] The fact that some harmful intentional wrongs are dealt with through the civil law helps to reduce the extent of criminalization. Ensuring that criminalization decisions meet the requirements of fairness is not about telling the lawmakers what they should criminalize, but what they may criminalize.[126] The criminal law should be used only as a last resort to prevent reasonably grave wrongs.

If lawmakers want to use the criminal law rather than a civil law response, then they have to show why the conduct is worthy of criminal condemnation. Having said that, it is important to note that in some cases, the case for criminalization will be so compelling that the state will be morally obliged to invoke the criminal law to protect the legitimate interests of its citizens. For example, in the 1990s lawmakers were compelled to criminalize marital rape.[127] It is the gravity and character of harm involved in culpable marital rape that makes it a moral issue that cannot be left to the parties concerned to resolve, especially in a humane society that cares for its members.[128] Furthermore, this type of wrong warrants a criminal law response rather than a private law response because "it would not be reasonable to expect one person to take proceedings on [her] own responsibility to put a stop to it, but . . . it should be taken on as the responsibility of the community at large."[129] Historically, publicness and the idea of the community being harmed has been used for identifying crimes. This approach is not valid for distinguishing crimes from torts, because it is clear that many private wrongs also harm the community.[130] The focus should be on whether the state has an obligation to use the criminal law, because of the gravity and character of the harm involved, and the degree of culpability involved. In less serious cases, wrongful harm is only a sufficient condition for criminalization.

1–063 The damage caused by a negligent train driver is every bit as grave as the harm caused by a single rape, but unless the harm has been caused by at least gross

---

[125] "It is important to point out that these proposed coercion-legitimizing principles do not even purport to state necessary and sufficient conditions for justified state coercion. A liberty-limiting principle does not state a *sufficient condition* because in a given case its purportedly relevant reason might not weigh heavily enough on the scales to outbalance the standing presumption in favour of liberty. That presumption is not only supported by moral and utilitarian considerations of a general kind; it is also likely to be buttressed in particular cases by appeal to the practical costs." Joel Feinberg, *The Moral Limits of the Criminal Law: Harm to Others*, (New York: Oxford University Press, 1984) at 10, 187-190.

[126] *Id*. at 4, 10.

[127] Marital rape was criminalized in some jurisdictions only in the 1990s. See *R. v. R.* [1991] 4 All E.R. 481.

[128] "It makes a great difference to the victim whether the community takes his wrong seriously, or passes it off as of no consequence. If he sees the man who cared nothing for him go scot-free, he is given to understand that society cares nothing for him either. But if the wrongdoer is made to see the error of his ways, the man to whom the wrong was done sees his rights vindicated, and is assured that society cares for him, even if one of its members does not, and will uphold his rights in face of assault and injury." J. R. Lucas, *Responsibility*, (Oxford: Clarendon Press, 1993) at 104.

[129] This is Lord Denning's test for ascertaining public nuisances. See his judgment in *Attorney-General v. PYA Quarries* [1957] 2 Q.B. 169.

[130] The current credit crunch exemplifies the public damage that can flow from private wrongs. The taxpayers arepaying for bailouts for corporations that have been mismanaged for decades. Clearly, the "negligent mismanagement of a company's affairs brings about a widespread and severe calamity." See Peter Brett, *An Inquiry Into Criminal Guilt*, (London: Sweet & Maxwell Ltd., 1963) at 6-7.

negligence, its gravity alone will not be sufficient to justify a criminal law response. Furthermore, the harmfulness of the consequences that flow from intentional defamation or from breaches of contractual duties means that such wrongs could be criminalized, but the nature of the harm is not sufficient to compel the state to criminalize these types of wrongs. It would not be fair to ask a person to commence proceedings on her own account to seek retribution for being raped (not only because it affects us all indirectly), but also because of the unequal bargaining position between the rapist and the victim. However, it would be reasonable to ask a person to commence proceedings on her own account to seek compensation for losses flowing from a breach of contract. In the end, only a crude line can be drawn.

Marshall and Duff[131] discuss the overlap between harm to individuals and harm to the community. They suggest that punishment should be considered in the context of the wrongdoer's relationship with the wider community as well as with the individual victim. By making the wrong done to a "rape victim 'ours,' rather than merely 'hers;' in thus understanding it as an attack on 'our' good, not merely on her individual good: we do not turn our attention *away* from the wrong that she has suffered, towards some distinct 'public' good. Rather, we share in the very wrong that she has suffered: it is not 'our' wrong instead of hers; it is 'our' wrong because it is a wrong done to her, as one of us—as a fellow member of our community whose identity and whose good is found within that community."[132] Likewise, C. K. Allen[133] is essentially correct in holding that: "Crime is crime because it consists in wrongdoing which directly and in serious degree threatens the security or well-being of society, and because it is not safe to leave it redressable only by compensation of the party injured." Wrongful harm criteria only provides a sufficient condition for criminalization, but in some cases the legislature will be compelled to act because of the serious nature of the harm involved.

Distinguishing wrongs that ought to be criminalized from those that may be criminalized is a matter of drawing a line somewhere along the continuum of culpability and the continuum of the nature and seriousness of the harm. There is also a continuum of fairness of enforcement, because in some cases as a matter of justice it would be unfair to ask individuals to take action to police harm that affects our collective interests more than it does our personal interests. The practicality constraint is especially relevant in the case of collective harms, such as littering. Littering may not be harmful in isolation, but in aggregate widespread littering would cause more harm to a city the size of London than a few incidences of other serious individualized harms such as homicide.[134] Because littering impacts our collective interests it would not be reasonable to expect one person to commence proceedings on her own initiative to put a stop to it. Instead, the community at large (by means of public institutions, such as the police, courts, government—and public mechanisms, such as criminal law and

---

[131] S. E. Marshall and R. A. Duff, "Criminalization and Sharing Wrongs," (1998) 11 *Can J. L. and Jurisprudence* 7 at 20-21.

[132] *Id.*

[133] Allen, *op. cit. supra*, fn. 117 at 233-35.

[134] Dennis J. Baker, "Collective Criminalization and the Constitutional Right to Endanger Others," (2009) 28 *Crim. Just. Ethics* 168.

punishment) is collectively responsible for protecting our collective interests (preventing littering, tax evasion, and so forth).

1–064 The fairness of enforcement justification for criminalization also applies in other areas. For example, *Ferguson v. British Gas Trading Ltd.* [2010] 1 W.L.R. 785 at 799, Sedley L.J. said:

> "Parliament's intention in passing the *Protection from Harassment Act 1997* was to criminalize the kind of serious and persistent unwarranted threat which is alleged here, giving a right of civil action as a fallback. In this situation it ought not to be left to hardy individuals to put their savings and homes at risk by suing. The primary responsibility should rest upon local public authorities which possess the means and the statutory powers to bring alleged harassers, however impersonal and powerful, before the local justices."

Civil law shares with the criminal law the aim of deterring people from harming others. This is one of the objects of the action for damages, and the action for injunction. The injunction orders the defendant not (for example) to continue a harmful nuisance, or not to publish, or continue publishing, a harmful[135] libel; and if he disobeys he can be committed (sent to prison) for contempt of court.[136] At its periphery, the civil law even allows people to be sent to prison for contempt of court. This offence is anomalous because there are both civil and criminal varieties. Civil contempt is committed chiefly where a person flouts an order of the court. Criminal contempt covers a miscellany of acts interfering with the work of the courts, ranging from contumely in court to the improper publication of matter that may influence the outcome of legal proceedings.[137] If a person is imprisoned for disobedience of a court order the court may order his discharge when he obeys.[138]

Other people who can be jailed on civil process are those who are in default of payment of income tax, rates, and similar public dues[139] (but not council house rents), and men who default on payment of maintenance for a wife or children (including illegitimate children). However, the defendant goes to prison not as a criminal but as a civil offender, and he receives certain concessions in prison that are not extended to criminals.

In conclusion, it appears that the general policy is not to use the criminal law if the civil law is sufficient to keep the conduct in check. Generally the criminal law has to be used to protect the public interest because there is no one who can be relied upon to take civil proceedings on behalf of the public. Also, the civil law has few terrors for the thoroughly impecunious.

---

[135] A libel could be offensive if it merely caused disgust, but could be harmful if the loss of reputation affects the victim's livelihood.

[136] Injunctions are not normally granted against apprehended personal injury. It is possible for certain potential victims to seek an injunction under Part IV of the *Family Law Act 1996*. Section 42 of the *1996 Act* allows V to apply for a non-molestation order. (It is an offence to breach it, section 42A).

[137] See David Eady and A. T. H. Smith, *Arlidge, Eady & Smith on Contempt*, (London: Sweet & Maxwell, 2009).

[138] By the *Contempt of Court Act 1981* committal is for a maximum of two years. The offender may also be fined.

[139] Including the payment of social security contributions.

1.8   THE JUSTIFICATION OF PUNISHMENT

As the last of these preliminaries, let us consider the proper basis of punishment.[140] This has greatly exercised the minds of both jurists and philosophers. Why are people punished, do you think?

1–065

I can answer promptly. Because they have done wrong and ought to be punished.   You have stated the theory of ethical (moral) retribution (otherwise called retributive justice, or desert), which holds that wrongdoers are punished in accordance with a moral law that requires this, or at any rate permits it. There is supposed to be some necessary moral connection between wrongdoing and punishment.

1–066

But moral blame and legal punishment are social reactions to what may broadly be called aggression—*i.e.* defiance of social standards of the moral code. Retributive justice can be explained as a refinement of the primitive urge to take revenge for injury, which has a biological explanation. A judicious measure of retaliation in addition to self-defence is, in the long run, beneficial to the defender by dissuading or disabling the attacker from repeating his aggression. So retaliation, and not merely defence, has survived value. Both fear and anger are defence mechanisms. Human beings still have these emotions, but we have sublimated our anger into moral disapproval and the legal system.

Philosophers have analysed the notion of retributive justice into two propositions, negative, and positive. The negative side of the proposition is that people ought not to be punished unless they have done wrong (which must mean moral wrong). We have a strong feeling (which we tend to regard as intuitive, though it is largely cultural) that punishment should not be given to anyone who is not guilty. Many utilitarians would support this negative proposition, because it is peculiarly offensive to our moral feelings if an innocent person is punished.

But we never would punish the innocent, except by mistake.   That is not entirely true. We often quite deliberately punish people who have not been at fault. This is called "strict liability," and some think it unjust. It is largely, though not entirely, confined to minor offences, generally summary offences.

1–067

Anyway, a person wouldn't be sent to prison unless he has been in some way at fault.   Probably never nowadays, though the courts have not always kept to this principle in the past. It is now generally agreed that a person should at least not be seriously punished unless he is at fault in breaking the law, and he should not be even mildly punished (as by fine) unless he is at fault or unless the offence

1–068

---

[140] On which see generally Andrew von Hirsch and Andrew Ashworth, *Proportionate Sentencing: Exploring the Principles*, (Oxford: Oxford University Press, 2005); Andrew von Hirsch, *Past or Future Crimes: Deservedness and Dangerousness in the Sentencing of Criminals*, (New Brunswick: Rutgers University Press, 1985); Jeffrie G. Murphy, *Retribution Reconsidered*, (Dordrecht: Kluwer, 1992); Joel Feinberg, *Doing and Deserving: Essays in the Theory of Responsibility* (Princeton: Princeton University Press, 1971); Stanley I. Benn, "An Approach To The Problems Of Punishment," (1958) 33 *Philosophy* 325.

is a minor one not involving much stigma. Qualified in this way, the negative side of the theory of justice can be regarded as agreed; and some would agree it without qualification.

1–069   **What is the positive side of the theory of justice?**   The one you stated at the beginning. Wrongdoers ought to be punished. No wrongdoer should escape, if we can help it, because haphazard punishment would be unjust.

I hope you will not be offended if I say that lawyers and philosophers are now practically unanimous in rejecting this proposition. Even philosophers who support retribution no longer argue that wrongdoing is a sufficient condition of punishment (they do not argue that all wrongdoers must be punished); they say only that it is a necessary condition (no one can properly be punished who is not a wrongdoer). Perhaps it is always just to punish the guilty, because that is the meaning of "just" in this context. But whether or not this is so, we no longer think that it is always justifiable to punish the guilty. Since this opinion is generally accepted, we allow the police and other prosecutors a discretion whether to prosecute at all. Also, in practically all crimes except murder we give sentencing judges a discretion whether to punish the convicted person. He may, for example, be put on probation (which is designed to help him not offend again), or be given an absolute discharge. In short, the theory of ethical retribution is now generally rejected by people who think about the subject, except as a limitation upon punishment.[141] The "just deserts" or "retribution" constraint is important as it ensures that the wrongdoer is punished in proportion with his past wrongdoing. That is, according to the culpableness and harmfulness of his past offending. We do not punish people for what they might do.[142]

1–070   **If we reject the demand for just punishment, on what basis do we punish?**   The only possible answer is the utilitarian opinion that punishment is preventive. Utilitarians (who take the view that the whole of morality is concerned with maximizing human happiness, or welfare) naturally conclude that offenders are punished for social reasons, looking to the future, not for metaphysical reasons, looking to the past. Bentham, the father of utilitarianism, wrote:

> "All punishment is mischief. All punishment in itself is evil. It ought only to be admitted in as far as it promises to exclude some greater evil."[143]

Punishment appears to look to the past, but for the utilitarian its real justification looks to the future. "Men are not hanged for stealing horses, but that horses may not be stolen."[144] There is no point doing the necessary maintenance on a

---

[141] Denis Galligan, "The Return to Retribution in Penal Theory," in Colin Tapper (ed.), *Crime Proof and Punishment, Essays in Memory of Sir Rupert Cross*, (London: Butterworth, 1981). H. L. A. Hart, *Punishment and Responsibility*, (Oxford: Oxford University Press, 1968).

[142] Dennis J. Baker, "Punishment without a Crime: Is Preventive Detention Reconcilable with Justice," (2009) 34 *Austl. J. Leg. Phil.* 120.

[143] Jeremy Bentham, *An Introduction to the Principles of Morals and Legislation*, (London: T. Payne, 1789), Chap. 15, § 1.

[144] George Savile (Marquis of Halifax), *Character of King Charles the Second: Political, Moral and Miscellaneous Thoughts and Reflections*, (London: J. & R. Tonson, 1750) at 114.

passenger ferry after it has sunk. Most of us support the idea of having criminal law and punishment as we want to avoid harm, not seek revenge. Most of us hope we will never be in a position where we will be seeking retribution, as we want to avoid ever being a victim. In other words, the utilitarian reason for punishment is either its effect upon the person punished (particular deterrence) or by serving as a warning to others (general deterrence). In addition, the penal process can have a certain educational effect. Punishment can bring an offender to a realization of the badness of his conduct.[145] The utilitarian goal provides a justification for having criminal law, punishment, a police force, a legal system and so on. It also is true that punishment deters the criminal and others like him, but that deterrence has to be achieved by punishing the individual offender in proportion with the harm he has caused.

Suppose a person does something wicked but it is quite certain that he will never repeat it. For example, a man murders his terribly spiteful and nagging wife, and it is inconceivable that he will be such an idiot as to marry another such. Would he be punished, on utilitarian theory? Obviously yes, for reasons of general deterrence. Similarly the spy in the Defence Establishment whose cover is blown is jailed in the hope of encouraging others in or under the Defence Ministry to resist any similar inclinations. If a prison officer helps a prisoner to escape by giving him an impression of the cell key for him to copy, the officer if discovered is dismissed, and will never be a prison officer again; but he is sent to prison all the same. Nevertheless, this can be achieved by punishing them proportionately for their past harm-doing.
1–071

What you say sounds all cut and dried, but punishment doesn't work very well, does it? No, but consider how much worse off we should be if we had no social provision for punishing evildoers.
1–072

To say that the rational justification of punishment is the prevention of crime is not to say that punishment always has this effect, or that it is wisely and moderately used. We have discovered comparatively mild punishments often have the same effect as comparatively severe ones, and that non-punitive disposals of the offender are often better at preventing a recurrence, or not worse, than a punitive sentence.

Which theory do the courts act on in sentencing: the retributive or the utilitarian? The courts accept the negative side of retributive theory as asserting the general principle that offenders should not be punished more severely than is proportionate to their guilt and the harmfulness of what they did. Every citizen has a basic right not to be unfairly criminalized. As we will see in Chapter 3, the main causes of unfair criminalization are: 1. unfair labelling (as far as criminalization is concerned, this occurs when innocuous conduct such as passive begging is labelled as criminal conduct); and 2. disproportionate punishment (this occurs when a person is unfairly punished—for example, it would be grossly unfair to send a person to prison for life for stealing video tapes,
1–073

---

[145] Nigel Walker, *Why Punish?*, (Oxford: Oxford University Press, 1990); D. M. Farrell, "Deterrence and the Just Distribution of Harm," (1995) 12 *Social Philosophy and Policy* 220.

but this has happened in advanced democracies).[146] The only way to reduce victimization numbers is to deter the victimizers by punishing them. The utilitarian aims of the criminal law would achieve more efficiency if we were to lock all offenders up for life, but such a system would be totally unjust. The burden of achieving harm prevention has to be distributed proportionately to those who have chosen to break the law. If you break the law many times, you will be punished many times. If you break it in a serious way, you will be punished more seriously.[147]

1–074 Parliament has recognized the importance of punishing people in proportion with their past wrongdoing. Section 143 of the *Criminal Justice Act 2003* provides:[148]

> "(1) In considering the seriousness of any offence, the court must consider the offender's *culpability* in committing the offence and any *harm* which the offence *caused*, was *intended* to cause or might forseeably have caused.
>
> (2) In considering the seriousness of an offence ("the current offence) committed by an offender who has one or more previous convictions, the court must treat each previous conviction as an aggravating factor if (in the case of that conviction) the court considers that it can reasonably be so treated having regard, in particular, to—(a) the nature of the offence to which the conviction relates and its relevance to the current offence, and (b) the time that has elapsed since the conviction."

To determine the length of a sentence the sentencing judge would consider the harmfulness of the conduct and the degree of culpability that the offender manifested in bringing the harm about. A crude formula might be: culpability × bad consequence, that is, $C \times BC$[149] (or in the case of *jail* sentences C × Harm (H) = sentence length).[150] Culpability would have three values: (1) gross negligence; (2) subjective recklessness (those who choose to take a risk); and (3) full intention (purpose). In this reverse order, as full intention would have the higher wrongfulness value of 3, with objective reckless having the lower value of 1.

Unlike culpability, harm cannot be divided into three broad categories because it varies significantly in degree and character. For instance, is physical assault worse than causing a person economic harm? What if the physical harm is minor and the economic harm is great? Harm impacts different people in different ways. Some people might prefer a black eye to having their new uninsured Bentley car destroyed by vandals. The best we can do is to make some basic generalizations about standard cases.[151] Harm could be divided into crude categories with murder having a value of 10 and littering at the other end of the scale having a value of 1.

---

[146] Baker, *op. cit. supra*, note 42 at Chaps. 2.

[147] For a profound and compendious discussion of how punishment should be distributed, see Paul H. Robinson, *Distributive Principles of Criminal Law: Who Should be Punished How Much?* (New York: Oxford University Press, 2008).

[148] Section 142 of the *2003 Act* makes it clear that the purpose of punishment is utilitarian—general harm prevention.

[149] Bad consequences (or risked bad consequences in the case of inchoate offending) might not always be harmful. The disgust caused by public nudity, hate speech, filming up skirts, and so on his harmless, but is a bad consequence which may require some form of regulation in extreme cases. But since these types of bad consequences are harmless, they should never be punished with jail terms.

[150] Nozick also suggests something along these lines. See Robert Nozick, *Philosophical Explanations*, (Oxford: Clarendon Press, 1981) at 363-97.

[151] See Minnesota Sentencing Grid. See also Richard S. Frase, "State Sentencing Guidelines Still Going Strong," (1995) 78 *Judicature* 173.

Deciding which of the ten categories to slot a given harm into would not be easy, but it certainly would not be impossible. I use categories rather than fixed rungs on a ladder because, like culpability, the harmfulness of a given bad consequence will be a matter of degree. It may very well fall between two rungs on the ladder. But there are many variables that need to be considered to determine how to categorize a particular harm. Economic harm could be measured to some extent by the value of the loss suffered by the victim in monetary terms, but we would also have to factor in other variables such as physical violence and intimidation if the economic harm was brought about in violent circumstances, as is the case with armed robbery. Furthermore, physical violence against others can be measured to some degree, by the extent of the physical injuries involved, though again we would have to consider other variables such as the psychological consequences that flow from certain physical attacks such as those that normally flow from rape.[152]

Another important variable is inchoateness, as is the case with attempts where the core moral justification for punishment and criminalization is moral culpability and bad action as opposed to actual consequences. Actual harm is not needed for the purpose of justifying penal detention in this context. Inchoate offences are designed to criminalize and punish conduct "in so far as it has an appropriate causal relationship to a primary harm, as making the occurrence of harm more likely; and the culpability of someone committing an inchoate offence, in so far as it involves more than the wilful performance of conduct defined by law as criminal, will consist essentially in her awareness of that relationship—in the fact that she knowingly, and avoidably, does what makes the occurrence of a primary harm more likely.[153]

1–075

The subjectivist argument for criminalizing attempts is that those who attempt to commit a criminal harm are morally no less culpable than those who succeed in doing so. For instance, if X shoots at N with the intention of killing N, but misses, she is no less culpable than if she had succeeded in killing N. There is no doubt that deliberately creating this type of danger should be criminalized and punished with a jail term. Coupled with this, the moral culpability element is sufficient to warrant a jail sentence when the harm aimed for is very serious. The wrongfulness element is present, but the bad consequence element is not satisfied. The bad acts/actions are sufficient to justify criminalization regardless of whether the consequences transpire. The controversy is in deciding if and to what extent any sentence should be discounted in cases in which the culpable offender has not caused any harm. Should moral luck play a role in grading and labelling offences? Clearly, in those cases in which the attempted harm was of a trivial nature, moral culpability alone would not be sufficient to justify jail sentences. It also seems fair to give a discount in serious cases, as the victim is not entitled to full retribution as she has not been fully harmed, endangerment is not as harmful as actually being killed. If it is fair to use constructive liability and

---

[152] There are many kinds of violence which impact different needs and interests. See for example, the discussion in Johan Galtung, "Cultural Violence," (1990) 27(3) *Journal of Peace Research* 291 at 292.
[153] R. A. Duff, *Criminal Attempts*, (Oxford: Clarendon Press, 1996) at 132-33.

moral bad luck to justify unlawful act manslaughter, then it must be fair to use moral good luck as a justification for less punishment for failed attempts.[154]

In summary, judges (including magistrates) generally sentence serious offenders on the basis of a rough assessment of what the offence is "worth." There is a customary tariff, the details of which are constantly being refined by the Court of Appeal; it is a mysterious mix of notions of ethical retribution, deterrence, reassuring the public, publicly repudiating the offence, and disabling the offender for a time. The tariff, it must be understood, is not a formal document, but has to be gathered from the appellate decisions. As said before, section 125 of the *Corners and Justice Act 2009* requires judges sentencing an offender to follow any relevant sentencing guidelines, unless it is contrary to the interests of justice to do so.

1–076   The tariff states not a definite sentence for a particular offence but the range of sentencing appropriate to ordinary circumstances, or to such special circumstances as may be specified in the tariff. The point at which the court fixes the sentence within the range depends in part upon the presence or absence of mitigating or aggravating circumstances. A bad criminal record, for example, is an aggravating circumstance, in the sense that it may dispose the court to sentence at the top of the scale—though the theory is that the court should never sentence *above* the tariff range on account of previous convictions, or for the purpose of general deterrence.

---

[154] *Contra*, Joel Feinberg, "Equal Punishment for Failed Attempts: Some Bad but Instructive Arguments Against It," (1995) 37 *Ariz. L. Rev.* 117.

CHAPTER 2

JUDGE AND JURY

"So prove it,
That the probation bear no hinge nor loop
To hang a doubt on."

Othello v. iii.

Before passing to the substantive law, we must consider part of the law of **2–001**
procedure and evidence that is intimately related to the substantive criminal law.
This concerns the burden of proof on the issues before the court and the
distribution of functions between judge and jury.

2.1. THE INCIDENCE AND QUANTUM OF THE BURDEN OF PROOF

An indictment (or information before magistrates) gives what are called **2–002**
particulars of the offence charged. For example, on a charge of theft in the Crown
Court, the particulars will say that AB, on the blank day, stole a wallet belonging
to CD. This does not expressly state all the elements of theft. In particular, it
leaves the mental element to implication, because the mental element is taken to
be comprised in the word "stole." Nor does it state where the alleged offence took
place, or the time of day. But the defendant is given formal notice, however
briefly, of the charge against him.

Suppose the jury or magistrate cannot make up their minds on whether the **2–003**
defendant is guilty or innocent?   Then they must find him not guilty.

So an acquittal is not a certificate that the defendant is innocent?   The jury **2–004**
or magistrates must acquit even though they believe the defendant to be guilty, if
the evidence leaves them with any reasonable doubt as to his guilt. The acquittal
does not mean that the defendant leaves the court without a stain on his character.
Whether it does will depend on the circumstances.[1]

The best-known statement of the burden of proof is in the celebrated case of
Woolmington v. D.P.P.[2] The old writers, notably Foster,[3] had declared that every
killing was presumed to be murder until the contrary was shown; and the

---

[1] An acquittal is generally taken as conclusive in the criminal law, but not for the purpose of later
civil proceedings. See Peter Mirfield, "Shedding a Tear for Issue Estoppel," [1980] Crim. L.R. 336 at
343 n. 33; see also *R. v. Mahalingan* [2008] 3 S.C.R. 316 at para. 123.
[2] [1935] A.C. 462; cf. *R. v. Hunt* [1987] A.C. 352.

statement was repeated in Archbold.[4] It was decisively rejected by the House of Lords, who asserted the fundamental presumption of innocence in criminal cases. When a defence to a charge of murder is accident or "loss of control," the onus rests on the prosecution to satisfy the jury that the killing was intentional and not provoked. Viscount Sankey L.C. said: "If the jury are left in reasonable doubt whether the act was unintentional or provoked, the prisoner[5] is entitled to be acquitted," that is, of murder. (There can still sometimes be a conviction of manslaughter.) The Lord Chancellor also put the point more generally in words that have run down the years: "Throughout the web of English criminal law one golden thread is always to be seen, that it is the duty of the prosecution to prove the prisoner's guilt, subject to the defence of insanity and subject also to any statutory exception."[6]

The burden of proof so placed upon the prosecution remains with them throughout the trial. Obviously it does not "shift" to the defendant merely because the prosecution make a *prima facie* case.[7] The criminal burden is contrasted with the civil one. In civil cases the burden of proof generally rests on the plaintiff, but he need only prove the case on the balance of probabilities.[8] The criminal law burden is supposed to be heavier.

2–005   **What is meant by reasonable doubt?**   The phrase is virtually indefinable. It can be said to mean not a mere fanciful doubt but one to which reasonable people would give weight—but how does that help? The best course for the judge is to state the rule without comment. Judges have tried to explain the phrase to juries, but often wrongly and convictions have sometimes been quashed in consequence. In 1952 the Court of Criminal Appeal suggested that it would be better to ask the jury whether they were "satisfied so that they can feel sure," or some similar phrase.[9] The change did not work well, and in 1979 the Judicial Committee of the Privy Council recommended a return to the time-honoured formula:

---

[3] Sir Michael Foster, *A Report of Some Proceedings on the Commission of Oyer and Terminer and Goal Delivery for the trial of the Rebels in the year 1746 in the county of Surry, and of other Crown Cases*, (Oxford: Clarendon Press, 1762) at 255.

[4] Robert E. Ross and T. R. F. Butler (eds.), *Archbold's Criminal Pleading and Evidence*, (London: Sweet & Maxwell, 29th edn. 1934) at 873.

[5] Formerly the judges spoke of the defendant on a felony charge as "the prisoner," but this fell into disuse with the abolition of the special incidents of felony; it was in any case pejorative for a person who had not been convicted. Both judges and statutes generally refer to the defendant as "the accused." But it is again an emotionally loaded word: if you were on trial for a crime, would you rather be called "the accused" or "the defendant"? It seems that the latter expression is preferable, as the more neutral.

[6] The splendour of this passage was marred by an examination candidate who reproduced the word "web" as "cobweb."

[7] *R. v. Stoddart* (1909) 2 Cr. App. R. 217 at 241-242.

[8] In some civil cases the criminal standard (or at any rate something higher than the usual civil standard) is applied.

[9] *R. v. Summers* [1952] 36 Cr. App. R. 14.

"Attempts to substitute other expressions have never prospered. It is generally sufficient and safe to direct a jury that they must be satisfied beyond reasonable doubt so that they feel sure of the defendant's guilt. Nevertheless, other words will suffice, so long as the message is clear."[10]

It is sometimes suggested that the degree of proof required varies directly with the seriousness of the charge;[11] but this is a suspect doctrine and it is virtually never invoked in practice. Occasionally the Court of Appeal has also laid down that it is not enough for the judge to say that the jury be sure of the defendant's guilt beyond reasonable doubt (the quantum of proof), without adding that the burden of proof is on the prosecution (the incidence of proof). This view is hard to follow, because the second proposition is contained in the first. There is no point in telling the jury what is inevitably implied. At any rate, the position now is that if a judge directs the jury merely in terms of quantum of proof, although the Court of Appeal may frown upon the direction as being unduly lax, an appeal may nevertheless be dismissed on the ground that it was not sufficient to make the conviction unsafe.[12] The appellate court now has less discretion for dismissing appeals on account of technical inadequacies in directions on the burden of proof than it used to have.[13] Even positive misdirections have been overlooked if no reasonable jury could have failed to convict on a proper direction.[14]

Can Parliament reverse the onus of proof?   Constitutionally the onus is on the State to prove its case beyond reasonable doubt; but the cardinal right to be presumed innocent until proved guilty is not always adhered to by Parliament.[15] Article 6 of the *European Convention for the Protection of Human Rights and Fundamental Freedoms*[16] provides, *inter alia*, "Everyone charged with a criminal offence shall be presumed innocent until proved guilty according to law." Hence, if the defendant is charged with any serious criminal offence (*i.e.* any summary or indictable offence which carries a jail term—even one day in prison is a serious violation of the defendant's liberty), then the prosecution has the onus of proving the defendant's guilt. The State has the persuasive burden in all but exceptional

2–006

---

[10] *Ferguson v. The Queen* [1979] 1 W.L.R. 94 at 99A. The Supreme Court of Canada recently expounded: "it is not essential to instruct jurors that a reasonable doubt is a doubt for which a reason can be supplied, and that it will suffice to instruct the jury that a reasonable doubt is a doubt based on reason and common sense." *R. v. Griffin* [2009] 2 S.C.R. 42 *per* Charron J. (Binnie, Deschamps, Abella, Rothstein JJ. concurring).

[11] Cf. *Bater v. Bater* [1951] P. 35; *Re H (Minors) (Sexual Abuse: Standard of Proof)* [1996] A.C. 563.

[12] *R. v. Mullen* [2000] Q.B. 520 at 536-537. Cf. *R. v. Friend* (1962) 46 Cr. App. R. 288; *R. v. Donoghue* (1988) 86 Cr. App. R. 267.

[13] Since the proviso was abrogated by section 1(2) of the *Criminal Appeal Act 1995*, the validity of the conviction will depend on its safeness. See the discussion *infra*.

[14] See *R. v. Stephens* [2002] EWCA Crim. 1529, where it was held that: "It was not helpful to the jury to seek to draw a distinction between being sure of guilt and being certain of guilt. However, that did not make S's conviction unsafe." See also *R. v. Majid* [2009] EWCA Crim. 2563; *Kwan Ping Bong v. The Queen* [1979] A.C. 609; *R. v. Folley* [1978] Crim. L.R. 556; *R. v. Hughes* [1963] Crim. L.R. 294.

[15] Andrew Ashworth, "The Presumption of Innocence in English Criminal Law," [1996] Crim. L.R. 307.

[16] 4 November 1950, 213 U.N.T.S. 222 (entered into force generally on 3 September 1953).

cases.[17] The post-*Human Rights Act* jurisprudence shows that the higher courts will rule enactments that reverse the onus of proof incompatible with Article 6(2), unless there are exceptional grounds for allowing the reversal. Such grounds will very rarely exist.[18] In *Sheldrake v. D.P.P.* Lord Bingham said:[19]

> "The overriding concern is that a trial should be fair, and the presumption of innocence is a fundamental right directed to that end. The Convention does not outlaw presumptions of fact or law but requires that these should be kept within reasonable limits and should not be arbitrary. It is open to states to define the constituent elements of a criminal offence, excluding the requirement of *mens rea*. But the substance and effect of any presumption adverse to a defendant must be examined, and must be reasonable. Relevant to any judgement on reasonableness or proportionality will be the opportunity given to the defendant to rebut the presumption, maintenance of the rights of the defence, flexibility in application of the presumption, retention by the court of a power to assess the evidence, the importance of what is at stake and the difficulty which a prosecutor may face in the absence of a presumption. Security concerns do not absolve member states from their duty to observe basic standards of fairness. The justifiability of any infringement of the presumption of innocence cannot be resolved by any rule of thumb, but on examination of all the facts and circumstances of the particular provision as applied in the particular case."

2.2. THE SUBMISSION OF "NO CASE"

2–007   The direction on the burden is not the only control over the jury. At the close of the case for the prosecution, you may hear counsel for the defence submitting to the judge that there is no case to answer. This is sometimes called an application for a directed verdict. If the judge (after hearing anything prosecuting counsel has to say) rules in favour of the submission, he will not leave the case to the jury's decision but will direct the jury to acquit.[20]

The submission is normally made after the jury have heard the prosecution evidence. There would be a danger of prejudice if they heard the submission being made, because if the judge rules that there is a case to answer the jurors may say to themselves: "The police think he did it, and now the judge thinks he did it as well." Accordingly, the accepted practice is that if the submission is made on the ground that the evidence for the Crown is insufficient to be left to the jury (as opposed, perhaps, to a submission that there is a purely technical defect in the prosecution case), the submission should be made and argued in the absence of the jury.[21]

---

[17] In *R. v. Webster* [2010] EWCA Crim. 2819 it was held that a national emergency such as the First World War would provide a sufficient justification for reversing the burden. This suggests that the courts will only override the defendant's right to be presumed innocent in extreme cases to prevent harm of an extraordinarily kind.

[18] The courts seem to be lifting the threshold for overriding the right. See *R. v. Webster* [2010] EWCA Crim. 2819; *Salabiaku v. France* (1991) 13 E.H.R.R. 379; *R. v. Lambert* [2002] 2 A.C. 545. See also *In re Winship*, 397 U.S. 358 (1970). For a penetrating discussion of the issue see Andrew Ashworth, "Four Threats to the Presumption of Innocence," (2006) 10 *International Journal of Evidence & Proof* 241.

[19] [2005] 1 A.C. 264 at 297; *R. v. Webster* [2010] EWCA Crim. 2819.

[20] See *R. v. Kahn* [2010] 1 Cr. App. R. 4. See also Glanville Williams, "Application for a Directed Verdict," [1965] Crim. L.R. 343, 410.

[21] *R. v. Falconer-Atlee* (1974) 58 Cr. App. R. 348 at 354; *Crosdale v. R.* [1995] 1 W.L.R. 864.

Why does the judge have to say that there isn't enough evidence? If the prosecution case is as pathetic as all that, the jurors wouldn't take long in coming to the answer themselves.   The rule is a safeguard for the defendant. He may want to cut short the proceedings by convincing the judge that the prosecution is mistaken in its view of the law. He may want to win an acquittal because of the weakness of the prosecution's case, without revealing the weakness of his own defence. Or he may want to avoid the risk of a perverse jury deciding against him without any real evidence at all. True, a perverse verdict might be set aside on appeal. But this procedure avoids the necessity for an appeal.

In other words, a submission of no case means "The prosecution have messed it up, hasn't it?"   Yes, but another translation of the submission is: "My client hasn't a dog's chance if you force him into the witness box, so I hope you'll find that the prosecution case has collapsed before it is his turn to speak." Putting this in formal language, the submission, if successful, protects the defendant from having to give evidence, when he may be forced under cross-examination to admit facts that prove the charge. Although the law does not compel him to give evidence, he may in practice be unable to avoid doing so if the submission is rejected, because of the bad impression that his silence may make on the jury.

These two reasons for the submission of no case may be viewed with mixed feelings. The first reason, the desirability of putting an end to a mistaken prosecution (both to save public money and to save the defendant from needless worry and the risk of a perverse verdict) is wholly in favour of allowing the submission to be made. The second reason will not be looked kindly upon by those who do not favour the defendant's so-called constitutional "right to silence."[22] It is a right that many offenders have had occasion to bless, since it has saved them from the practical necessity of having to own up; but that is not a reason why law-abiding citizens should look kindly upon it.

Can't the prosecution call the defendant as one of their own witnesses?   Dear me, no. It is the right of silence again. The defendant gives evidence only if he wants to, along with (almost always before) the other defence witnesses.

Why doesn't the judge stop the case on his own initiative? Is it that the defence prompt the judge in order to wake him up?   The judge does not regard it as his duty to attend to the sufficiency of the evidence at that stage, if counsel for the defence does not make a submission. He may let the case run, even if he detects deficiencies in the evidence for the Crown, if he thinks that the deficiencies may be made good by admissions extracted from the defence witnesses. However, if the defendant is unrepresented it seems to be the judge's duty to consider the point on his behalf.[23]

2–008

2–009

2–010

2–011

---

[22] *Murray v. U.K. (Right to Silence)* (1996) 22 E.H.R.R. 29.
[23] See [1981] Crim. L.R. 276.

2–012   **If the defendant submits no case and the prosecution realise at once that it has omitted to adduce evidence on something vital, can it make good the deficiency at that stage?**   Yes if the court (*i.e.* the judge or the magistrate) so allows; as in a proper case it can.[24] If the defect is purely formal or technical the court generally must allow the additional evidence, granting an adjournment if necessary.[25]

2–013   **Suppose the judge directs the jury to acquit but they are stiff-necked and want to make the true deliverance on their own whatever the judge thinks.**   If the foreman refuses to comply, the judge may tell him to stand down and may ask another juror to comply with his direction. If they persist in refusing he can empanel a more complaisant jury.[26] These are ridiculous subterfuges: we need a statute saying that the judge can enter an acquittal without having to overbear the jury.

2–014   **What if the judge fails to accede to a submission of no case when he ought to?**   If defence counsel has the courage to call no evidence, the Court of Appeal will quash a conviction if the judge ought to have accepted the submission. If, however, counsel continues with the case, practice has not been uniform. The Court of Appeal has on occasion looked at all the evidence to decide whether the verdict is "unsafe." On other occasions, however, the appellate court has taken the view that if the judge improperly rejected a submission on the evidence as it then stood, the impropriety is not cured by evidence given after the submission.[27]

The submission of no case and the possibility of an appeal mean that, in Lord Devlin's phrase, the jury are "limited at both ends"[28]—before they deliberate, and afterwards. Broadly speaking, they should not be allowed to decide a very shaky case (or rather a very shaky case of a certain type), and if they are allowed to decide it, and convict, the conviction may be quashed.

However, the test of shakiness differs at two stages. At the first stage it is a broad test. The Court of Appeal is directed by statute to quash a conviction if it is "unsafe."[29] A few years back there was authority for saying that the trial judge should apply the same test: would a conviction on this prosecution evidence be unsafe? But the Court of Appeal has now rejected this, and gone back to the traditional narrower rule, which is that on a trial by jury the judge is required to accept a submission of no case only if he decides that there is no evidence of guilt, or if the evidence is tenuous and the judge concludes that taken at its highest it is such that a properly directed jury could not properly convict on it.[30]

---

[24] *R. v. Doran* (1972) 56 Cr. App. R. 429; *Matthews v. Morris* [1981] Crim. L.R. 495; *R. v. Francis* [1990] 1 W.L.R. 1264; *Malcolm v. D.P.P.* [2007] 1 W.L.R. 1230.

[25] The permission may be granted even after the defendant has called evidence: *R. v. Doran* (1972) 56 Cr. App. R. 429. But if the submission of no case is overruled, and the defendant advocate announces that he will call no evidence and closes his case, the court cannot then allow the prosecution to call further evidence: *Saunders v. Johns* [1965] Crim. L.R. 49.

[26] 139 J.P.N. 159.

[27] *R. v. Juett* [1981] Crim. L.R. 113; cf. *R. v. Brown* [1998] Crim. L.R. 196.

[28] Patrick Devlin, *Trial by Jury*, (London, Stevens & Sons Ltd., 1956) at 65.

[29] Section 2 of the *Criminal Appeal Act 1968*.

[30] *R. v. Galbraith* [1981] 1 W.L.R. 1039; *R. v. Begum* [2010] EWCA Crim. 2647.

The professed reason for wording the rule in this severely limited way is that the judge must not usurp the function of the jury. The credibility of witnesses is supposed to be a matter for the jury alone. Therefore, the judge in ruling on a submission must pretend to himself that he believes evidence that in fact he regards as a pack of lies, or evidence that contradicts itself and is contradicted by overwhelming evidence to the contrary.[31] The judge must also, it seems, assume that there will be no evidence to displace inferences that might reasonably be drawn from the evidence in the absence of explanation.

2–015

This professed reason offered by the Court of Appeal is wholly unconvincing. We are told[32] that the jury should be allowed to decide the case because they have heard and seen the witnesses. But that is equally true of the trial judge. Moreover, the Court of Appeal, which has not heard and seen the witnesses, is allowed by statute to set aside a conviction on the general ground that it is unsafe; and it may therefore seem on the face of things to be remarkable that the trial judge, who *has* heard and seen the witnesses, is not required to intervene at an earlier stage when he could save the vexation, risk and waste of public money involved in a mistaken or ill-advised prosecution. While it is good to have the Court of Appeal as one safeguard against an unsound conviction, it would be better still to have two safeguards. The danger to justice is heightened by the fact that even the Court of Appeal refuses to consider questions of credibility of evidence.

But in human affairs arguments are rarely all one way, and things are not always what they seem. There is one strong reason for the present view of the Court of Appeal, which the court may have had in mind but was too discreet to parade in public. The submission of no case, as already explained, gives a powerful backing to the "right to silence," which is strongly supported by one body of opinion but at the same time causes failures of justice. If the judge is compelled to stop the trial on a submission of no case, the "right to silence" is fully protected. If he is allowed to reject the submission, the defendant may feel obliged to give evidence, and may be compelled in cross-examination to make admissions that defeat him. So those who think our criminal process is too indulgent are not keen on the submission of no case, except where the prosecution case is visibly misconceived. The difficulty hardly arises at that stage of appeal, because then all the evidence is generally in and the court can review it as a whole.

Some years ago the Criminal Law Revision Committee, in its Report on the Law of Evidence, proposed that the right to silence should be moderately curtailed by allowing the jury to take account of the defendant's failure to explain his conduct; but the proposal met with such outcry from eminent persons and bodies (including the Magistrates' Association) that not only was it dropped but the whole Evidence Report was jettisoned.[33] Yet no one notices when the judges

---

[31] There is authority for allowing the judge to stop the case if the prosecution evidence is inherently incredible: see Rosemary Pattenden, "The Submission of No Case—Some Recent Developments," [1982] *Crim. L.R.* 558 at 562-63. This does not apply merely because the prosecution evidence is contradicted by weightier evidence.

[32] *R. v. Galbraith* [1981] 1 W.L.R. 1039.

[33] Nevertheless, the court can draw adverse inferences from the defendant's silence in certain circumstances. See sections 35 to 37 of the *Criminal Justice and Public Order Act 1994*. Certain steps should be followed before adverse inferences are drawn from silence. "(1) The judge will have told

chip away at the right to silence by restricting the submission of no case. The more the submission is restricted, the more the defendant is put under pressure to enter the witness box to testify.

2–016   **Suppose that there is no successful submission of no case and the trial runs on. Can the judge afterwards stop the case on his own initiative when he finds that the prosecution case has really broken down?**   He has a discretion to so do at any time after the close of the prosecution case—even after all the evidence is in.[34] This in an important point, which is frequently overlooked. It means that the restrictive rules relating to a submission of no case apply only to the judge's duty to accept the submission, not to his power to do so if he pleases. There is no point in prolonging a trial at public expense if the trial judge, after hearing evidence from the prosecution (and also, perhaps, from the defendant, if he elects to give evidence), thinks there is no good reason for continuing.[35] The exercise of this discretion in suitable cases is the best way of solving the problem on the half-baked prosecution.

2–017   **Can a submission of no case be made in a magistrates' court?**   Certainly. The magistrates are judges and jury, but they rule on the submission by pretending that they are merely the judge, considering whether there is sufficient evidence of whether they should withhold the case from an imaginary jury.

The following peculiar situation can therefore arise: the defence advocate submits on case; the magistrates rule that there is a case to answer; the defence advocate then announces that he will call no evidence; the magistrates retire and decide to dismiss the charge! It may look like two inconsistent decisions, but the magistrates have acted properly in law. The first decision expressed not their opinion on the proper outcome of the case but a legal judgment.

---

the jury that the burden of proof remains upon the prosecution throughout and what the required standard is. (2) It is necessary for the judge to make clear to the jury that the defendant is entitled to remain silent. That is his right and his choice. ... (3) An inference from failure [to give evidence/to mention a fact] cannot on its own prove guilt. That is expressly stated in section 38(3) of the *1994 Act*. (4) Therefore, the jury must be satisfied that the prosecution have established a case to answer before drawing any inferences from silence ... (5) If, despite any evidence relied upon to explain his silence or in the absence of any such evidence, the jury conclude the silence can only sensibly be attributed to the defendant's having no answer or none that would stand up to [cross-examination/scrutiny], they may draw an adverse inference." In *R. v. Petkar* [2004] 1 Cr. App. R. 270 at 283 citing *R. v. Cowan* [1996] Q.B. 373 at 383 *per* Lord Taylor C.J. See also the six conditions laid down by Lord Bingham C.J. in *R. v. Argent* [1997] 2 Cr. App. R. 27.

[34] *R. v. Young* [1964] 1 W.L.R. 717 at 720. Cf. *R. v. Brown* [2002] 1 Cr. App. R. 5.

[35] Pattenden, *op. cit. supra*, note 32 at 565, says of this discretion that: "the Court of Appeal has criticised its exercise on so many occasions ... that it is difficult to envisage a case in which a trial judge would be justified in exercising the discretion." But she also gives as the reason for the objection a statement by Roskill L.J. that "it is not proper for a judge to invite a jury to stop a case. If a judge has doubts whether the evidence is sufficiently strong to justify a verdict of guilty then it is his duty to stop the case. It is not his duty to shift that responsibility to the jury." This does not say what Pattenden appears to understand by it; it says the opposite. See *R. v. C* (2007) 151 S.J.L.B. 572; *R. v. Speechley* [2005] 2 Cr. App. R. (S.) 15, where it was held that if the judge thinks the evidence is farcical, then he ought to take the responsibility upon himself to stop the case. Cf. *R. v. Brown* [2002] 1 Cr. App. R. 5.

There is, however, an important distinction between the powers of magistrates and those of the trial judge in the Crown Court. By a Practice Direction of 1962,[36] a submission in a magistrates' court that there is no case to answer may properly be upheld: (a) when there has been no evidence to prove an essential element in the alleged offence, or (b) when the evidence adduced by the prosecution has been discredited as a result of cross-examination or is so manifestly unreliable that no reasonable tribunal could safely act on it. Apart from these two situations "the decision should depend on whether the evidence is such that a reasonable tribunal might convict." This last is the same test as the Divisional Court uses on appeal from magistrates, so here the first—and second-stage controls coalesce, as they do not in jury trials. No satisfactory explanation has been given of the reason for the discrepancy,[37] but it probably is that at the time of the Practice Direction the law of jury trials was thought to be otherwise than it is now settled to be.

So what it comes to is that on a trial on indictment the prosecution must give enough evidence to take the case to the jury, and also give the possibly greater amount of evidence necessary to convince the jury? Quite. These two burdens are now frequently called the evidential and persuasive burdens respectively, or the burden of production and the burden of persuasion.   2–018

The distinction has only gradually made its way into legal thinking, and various expressions are used to denote it. English judges sometimes speak of the persuasive burden as the "ultimate" burden or "legal" burden or burden "at the end of the day," while the evidential burden is also called the "provisional" burden or "tactical" burden (both bad names)[38] or the "initial hurdle." However, the name "evidential burden" now has wide acceptance.[39]

Is there an evidential burden in respect of a question of law? Burdens are in respect of facts; questions of law are decided by the judge, without any question of burden. But some questions, such as the question of reasonableness, are in an intermediate position. They are value-judgments marking the boundary between criminal and non-criminal conduct, and therefore are really decisions of law; yet they are made by the jury, except that there must be evidence that, in the view of the trial judge, would justify the jury in finding that there has been reasonableness or unreasonableness or whatever.[40] For example, an allegation of negligence is not left to the jury unless there is evidence of negligence sufficient to support a conviction.   2–019

---

[36] *Practice Direction (Submission of No Case)* [1962] 1 W.L.R. 227; *D.P.P. v. SJ (A Juvenile)* [2002] EWHC 291. Cf. *R. v. Young* [1964] 1 W.L.R. 717.

[37] Archbold, 41ˢᵗ edn.

[38] "Provisional" is uninformative, and "tactical" misleading. Evidential burdens are imposed by law, not mere matters of tactics.

[39] The first acceptance of the term appears to have been in *R. v. Gill* [1963] 1 W.L.R. 841. Judges have sometimes made strange blunders in stating the theory of persuasive and evidential burdens.

[40] In *AK v. Western Australia* (2008) 232 C.L.R. 438 at 472-473.

2.3. RULES ASSISTING THE PROSECUTION

2–020   The prosecution's evidential burden is alleviated in two ways. First, the judge can draw common-sense inferences from evidence; and some of these have hardened into propositions of law. An illustration is the presumption arising when a person is found in possession of goods that have recently been stolen. He may be indicted for theft, for handling stolen goods, or for both; and on proof that the goods had recently been stolen and that the defendant was found in possession of them, the prosecution are entitled to have the case left to the jury.[41]

Although this presumption assists the prosecution to have the case left to the jury, satisfying their evidential burden, it does not shift the persuasive burden, the burden of proof. The jury must still be told that the burden of proving the case so that they feel sure of guilt is on the prosecution. Therefore, if the defendant gives any explanation of his possession consistent with his honesty so that the jury are left in doubt, he is entitled to an acquittal.[42]

This is traditionally expressed by saying that the presumption is only a presumption of fact; it would be better to be called an evidential presumption, discharging the evidential burden. It is a rule for the judge, instructing him to leave the case to the jury, not a rule for the jurors, directing them to find the defendant guilty. There is no occasion for the judge in directing the jury to refer to a "presumption" under that name, and it would be well for him not to do so, since an impromptu explanation of the meaning of a presumption is likely to muddle the jury on the persuasive burden. The jury can be adequately instructed on common-sense inferences without referring to presumptions. Where the defendant has been found in possession of goods recently stolen, and gives a somewhat lame explanation ("I bought them from a man who said they fell off the back of a lorry"), the jury can be told that the burden of proof beyond reasonable doubt rests on the Crown; that they can use their common sense in drawing inferences from the whole of the evidence given, and can convict on the evidence of possession if no explanation is given; but must give the defendant the benefit of any reasonable doubt. Such a formula avoids the language of presumption, which would almost certainly conflict in the minds of the jury with what they have been told on the burden of proof.

2–021   Again, on a charge of assault the burden is on the prosecution to adduce evidence that the complainant did not consent to the act.[43] But if the prosecution show that violence was used, this would be strong presumptive evidence of a lack of consent, and the judge would certainly leave the issue of consent to the jury. On the assault charge he may say that the man was a masochist and liked to be physically abused or that it was a friendly fight with mutual consent; the jury may or may not give sufficient credence to these defences to feel a doubt about the charge, but the question will be for them. Compare this to a charge of rape; if it is

---

[41] Hence, the celebrated marginal note to the report of *Clement's Case* (1830) 168 E.R. 980: "Possession in Scotland is evidence of stealing in England."

[42] *R. v. Schama* (1916) 11 Cr. App. R. 45; *The People v. Oglesby* [1966] I.R. 162; *R. v. Aves* (1950) 34 Cr. App. R. 159; *R. v. Moulding* [1996] Crim. L.R. 440; *R. v. Hepworth* [1955] 2 Q.B. 600. Cf. Sections 75-76 of the *Sexual Offences Act 2003*.

[43] *R. v. Donovan* [1934] 2 K.B. 498; *R. v. Meachen* [2006] EWCA Crim. 2414; *R. v. Brown* [1994] 1 A.C. 212.

proved that D had sexual intercourse with V, and at the time of having the intercourse "or immediately before it began," he used violence against V or caused V "to fear that immediate violence would be used against her"; and knew he had done so, "the complainant is to be taken not to have consented to the [sexual intercourse] unless sufficient evidence is adduced to raise an issue as to whether she consented, and the defendant is to be taken not to have reasonably believed that the complainant consented unless sufficient evidence is adduced to raise an issue as to whether he reasonably believed it."[44] The defendant is presumed to have had non-consensual sexual intercourse with the victim, because it is presumed that the violence negated the victim's consent. This presumption can be rebutted,[45] if the defendant is able to adduce appropriate evidence. For instance, he might produce evidence to show that he and the victim were sadomasochists who regularly attended sex parties. If there were credible evidence that the defendant and the victim were regular lovers who engaged in sadomasochism, then the judge might conclude that consent is a real issue that needs to be put to the jury. Section 75 does not shift the legal burden to the defendant; the defence team need only adduce sufficient evidence to raise an issue as to whether the victim consented. Once the defence has adduced an evidential case that raised an issue as to whether there was consent, the burden is on the prosecution to prove to the criminal standard that there was no consent.

These are ways in which the prosecution's evidential burden can be discharged. But, secondly, there are certain respects in which the prosecution are wholly relieved of the evidential burden, which is imposed instead on the defendant. This raises the question of defences, a subject to which we now turn.

2.4. DEFENCES

That a person does a forbidden act, even intentionally, does not mean that he is necessarily guilty of an offence. Various defences are recognized, quite apart from the defence of absence of the requisite mental element or degree of fault. Among the circumstances of justification or excuse are self-defence, public authority, and duress.   **2–022**

And alibi? Yes and no. The word "defence" is used in two different senses, broad and narrow. For the layman, in relation to argument, it means, broadly, anything that a person may urge to rebut a charge. Lawyers use the word in this way too. Yes, they speak of a defence of alibi; but an alibi is only a particular way of denying that the defendant did the act (he could not have done it, because he was elsewhere at the time). The defendant does not justify or excuse the alleged act, but denies that he did it.[46] Similarly a defence of accident, mistake or   **2–023**

---

[44] See section 75(1),(a),(b),(c) and 75(2),(a) of the *Sexual Offences Act 2003*. Violence is not the only factor that is presumed to negate consent, see subsections 75(2)(b)-(f).

[45] Section 76 of the *Sexual Offences Act 2003* contains a non-rebuttable presumption for cases involving consent obtained by deception or fraud.

[46] The defendant does not bear any burden of proving an alibi: *R. v. Denney* [1963] Crim. L.R. 191.

automatism usually denies that the defendant was at fault. Generally speaking, these defences do not introduce any further issue; they merely combat the allegations of the prosecution.

In the narrow (or, if you like, proper) sense a defence means a justification or excuse or one of certain technical points alleged by the defendant in order to avoid liability. It introduces a new issue into the trial.[47]

2–024   **You spoke of accident and mistake. What exactly is the difference?**   An accident is an unintended or unforeseen consequence of conduct. Mistake means a false understanding. Although in itself it is a mental fact, it may have physical consequences, and may therefore cause an accident; such as where a learner-driver by mistake presses the accelerator instead of the clutch.

2–025   **And what is the difference between a justification and an excuse?**   They are both defences in the full sense,[48] leading to an acquittal. However, when the act is not justified but only excused it is still regarded as being in some tenuous way wrong, for certain collateral purposes. Normally the justified actor can be said to have done the right thing all things considered. For example, if D tries to kill V, V would do the right thing if he were to act in self-defence to thwart D's unjustified attack. Meanwhile, the excused actor can usually be said to have done the wrong thing through no fault of his own. When a schizophrenic randomly stabs a passer-by to death because he has no idea what he is doing, he does not do the right thing. His insanity means that he does not act culpably, but there is no justification for his attack.[49] His attack was not intended to thwart some greater evil or to defend himself against an unwarranted attack.

A little bit of history: the term "justification" was formerly used for cases where the aim of law was not frustrated, while "excuse" was used for cases where it was not thought proper to punish. Killing a dangerous criminal who tried to avoid arrest was justified, since the law (if one may personify) wished this to happen, whereas killing in self-defence was merely *excused*. The distinction was important because justification was a defence to the criminal charge while excuse was not, being merely occasion for a royal pardon.[50] By the end of the Middle Ages (it is difficult to assign a fixed date) even excuses were recognised by the courts. After that it was frequently supposed that no occasion arose to distinguish between justification and excuse, but that is not entirely true. More of this anon.

---

[47] For the proposition that the word "defence" should be taken to refer only to mattes of procedure and evidence see Glanville Williams, "Offences and Defences," (1982) 2 *Legal Stud.* 233.

[48] However, there may be cases where D is partially excused because of diminished responsibility and so on.

[49] For a fuller discussion see Suzanne Uniacke, *Permissible Killing: The Self-Defence Justification of Homicide*, (Cambridge: Cambridge University Press, 1994).

[50] Anglo-Saxon law did not clearly exempt those who inflicted harm by accident or in self-defence, or when of unsound mind, though these facts went in mitigation of the penalty, or, after the Conquest, were grounds for the exercise of the prerogative of mercy. Later, courts took it upon themselves to accord a defence in these cases. Sporadic instances of acquittal for insanity in medieval times are recorded by N. D. Hunard, *The King's Pardon for Homicide before AD 1307*, (Oxford, Clarendon Press, 1969) at 166. The modern practice of acquitting on this account appears to date from 1505: Nigel Walker, *Crime and Insanity in England*, (Edinburgh: Edinburgh University Press, 1968) at 25-26.

On the rare occasions when the point matters the courts would nowadays regard self-defence as a justification not a mere excuse.

I suppose that the defendant bears the burden of proving defences in the proper sense?   Yes for some, but not all. He does not carry any burden of proof in respect of most of the common law defences, such as self-defence and duress. *Woolmington v. D.P.P.*[51] and the cases following it show that the burden rests on the prosecution to negative these defences, not upon the defendant to prove them.[52] In common law matters the courts laudably adopt the attitude that although the defence has come from the defendant, what has to be decided is the single issue of guilt, the burden of proving which rests on the prosecution. Moreover, when such a defence is in issue, it is not enough for the judge to direct the jury in general terms that the charge must be proved so that they feel sure of guilt. "Where the issue of self-defence is raised, a specific direction should be given on the law of self-defence and on the burden of proof on the prosecution."[53]

2–026

How does the defendant raise a defence?   He is not required to put it in a formal written pleading. Even if the matter is a defence in the strict (narrow) sense of that word, he puts it in issue merely by adducing evidence upon it.[54]

2–027

The evidential burden in respect of defences (in the strict sense) rests on the defendant. For example, it is not enough for defence counsel to argue that the defendant may have been acting in self-defence, or under a "loss of control," if he has not adduced some minimum of evidence to support the argument. The judge is not required to direct the jury on such a defence unless there is *"prima facie"* or a "proper foundation in the evidence" for it.[55] In such cases:[56]

> "Though questions as to whether evidence should or should not be accepted or as to the weight to be attached to it are for the determination of the jury, it is a province of the judge to rule whether a theory or a submission has the support of evidence so that it can properly be passed to the jury for their consideration. [I]t is not every facile mouthing of some easy phrase of excuse that can amount to an explanation. It is for a judge to decide whether there is evidence fit to be left to a jury which could be the basis for some suggested verdict."

Some judges have lately fallen into the habit of declaring that when a defence (such as self-defence or the prevention of crime) involves the question of whether the defendant acted reasonably, "what is reasonable in the circumstances is always a question for the jury, never a point of law of the trial judge."[57] In terms

---

[51] [1935] A.C. 462.

[52] For self-defence see *R. v. Julien* [1969] 1 W.L.R. 839.

[53] *R. v. Owen* [1964] Crim. L.R. 831; *R. v. Folley* [1978] Crim. L.R. 556; *R. v. Abraham* [1973] 1 W.L.R. 1270; *R. v. Cameron* [1973] Crim. L.R. 520.

[54] Therefore one should not, strictly, speak of a defendant to a criminal charge "pleading" insanity, self-defence *etc.*, though this loose language is often used for convenience, even by judges. The strictly correct phrase is that the defendant "adduced evidence of" the facts constituting the defence, or "raised" the defence.

[55] *Bratty v. Attorney-General of Northern Ireland* [1963] A.C. 386; *Hill v. Baxter* [1958] 1 Q.B. 277 at 284.

[56] *Bratty v. Attorney-General of Northern Ireland* [1963] A.C. 386 at 416–417 *per* Lord Morris.

[57] *Re Attorney-General of Northern Ireland's Reference (No.1 of 1975)* [1977] A.C. 105 at 137E *per* Lord Diplock; *R. v. Cousins* [1982] Q.B. 526 at 530C; *R. v. Fisher* [1987] Crim. L.R. 334.

of the traditional understanding of the law this is a misleading hyperbolic way of expressing the position. It is true that the question of reasonableness is for the jury, but it is not entirely one for the jury. For defences the rule is subject to the important proviso that the judge is entitled to decide whether there is any evidence of reasonable conduct for the jury's consideration. Could any reasonable jury find in favour of the defendant on the evidence?[58]

2–028 **How can one tell which evidential burdens lie on the prosecution and which on the defence?** Basically (and with exceptions) the distinction is between elements relating to the core of the offence and elements relating to an exception from liability or other defence. We may call these the prosecution (or definitional) elements and the defence elements respectively. There are difficulties in the distinction, but some distinction has to be made in distributing evidential burdens between the prosecution and defence.

2–029 **In assault, for example, the basis of the offence is that the defendant went up to the victim and punched him on the nose?** Yes; the charge of assault implies an intentional or reckless attack, and both the evidential and the persuasive burden of this is on the prosecution. Distinguish the defence of self-defence, where the evidential burden rests on the defendant.

2–030 **Well then, the defendant bears the burden of proof of defences.** Not necessarily. He generally bears the evidential burden, that is all.

2–031 **What is the difference between evidence and proof? Surely evidence is proof.** Evidence becomes proof only when the jury accept it as being sufficient for proof. When the defendant bears an evidential burden of a defence, he must adduce (or anyway there must be) enough evidence in favour of the defence to persuade the judge to leave it to the jury; but the judge must still direct the jury to acquit unless they are sure that the defence is not established.[59] (See 2.5 as to persuasive burdens on the defence).

2–032 **What's the point of putting an evidential burden on the defendant?** Whether the defendant bears an evidential burden or not, he is obviously going to adduce all the evidence he can on the issue. For this reason, the question whether he bears an evidential burden does not often arise. The point is that the judge may withdraw a merely fanciful defence from the jury, thus simplifying their task, and preventing the jury from accepting a defence where the defendant has made no sufficient efforts to back it up.[60] But even if the judge can withdraw

---

[58] For example, section 54(6) of the *Coroners and Justice Act 2009* provides: "For the purposes of subsection (5), sufficient evidence is adduced to raise an issue with respect to the defence [of loss of control] if evidence is adduced on which, in the opinion of the trial judge, a jury, properly directed, could reasonably conclude that the defence might apply."

[59] Do not speak of an "evidential burden of proof" resting on the defendant. An evidential burden is not a burden of proof. See *Jayasena v. The Queen* [1970] A.C. 618.

[60] *R. v. Critchley* [1982] Crim. L.R. 524.

the defence from the jury, it is rare in practice for him to do so, because he is not sure himself and is aware of the risk that if the Court of Appeal thinks he was wrong a conviction will be quashed.

The more important result of placing an evidential burden on the defence is to prevent the defendant submitting no case if the prosecution have led no evidence on that issue. The task of the prosecution is therefore simplified. (The same result, is as we have seen, sometimes achieved by creating a presumption, without imposing an evidential burden on the defendant.)

Let us revert to an example where the prosecution on a charge of assault give evidence that the defendant hit the victim. Suppose that at the close of the prosecution case the defending advocate rises and addresses the court thus: "An assault in law is not committed by a blow struck in lawful self-defence. The prosecution have given no evidence to negative the possibility that this blow was struck in self-defence. For all we know it was; therefore they have not given evidence of an assault in law, and there is no case for the defendant to answer." The judge (or magistrate) will override this submission, because although the premises are correct the submission overlooks the rule that the evidential burden of self-defence is on the defendant. If the defendant is going to raise a particular defence seriously he must have some evidence of it, and that evidence should be given. It is not enough for his counsel to make up a tale.

But can't the defendant tell the tale instead of his counsel?   The defendant   2–033
can give evidence to support his defence in the witness box. The point is that what his counsel says in argument is not evidence.

And counsel can't say: "My client says so-and-so"?   Certainly not. The   2–034
evidence must be given on oath (or affirmation), by the defendant or other witness.

Do the jury have to believe the defendant merely because he says   2–035
something?   They are not bound to believe him. But if the defendant testifies, that is evidence on which the jury should act if they think it sufficient to raise a reasonable doubt in his favour.

And when the defendant gives evidence he can be cross-examined and   2–036
perhaps tripped up?   Yes.

Aren't you forcing the defendant to convict himself? The poor chap is caught   2–037
either way. If he gives no evidence his defence won't be left to the jury; if he
does he can be shown up as a liar.   Putting the evidential burden on the defence does not necessarily mean that the defendant must give evidence. He may *adduce* evidence, by calling other witnesses to give evidence on his behalf. Or he may get the evidence before the court by extracting admissions from the prosecution witnesses under cross-examination.[61]

---

[61] It is sometimes said that when the prosecution witnesses supply evidence relating to a matter of defence, such as self-defence, no evidential burden in that respect rests on the defendant. Whether one puts it this way or says that there is an evidential burden that is discharged is purely verbal.

[59]

2–038   **But if the prosecution witnesses deny it flatly, and the defendant has no other witnesses, he will have to give evidence.**   In effect yes, but I think you are pushing your sympathy for the defendant to an extreme. If he cannot produce any evidence to support his defence, not even his own word, it is too bad for him. But if his tale is a plausible one and he stands up to cross-examination the jury are likely to give him the benefit of the doubt. I do not share the anxiety felt by some to protect a defendant from having to give evidence.

The test whether the evidence is sufficient is similar to that already stated in respect of prosecution evidence: is there before the court evidence that, if believed, and on the most favourable view,[62] could be taken by a reasonable jury to support the defence of loss of control,[63] self-defence,[64] duress,[65] "reasonable excuse" under statute,[66] "or whatever it may be"? The duty of the judge is to assume that the defendant's evidence, in so far as it can be reconciled with the unchallenged evidence in the case, is substantially true, and to ask himself whether it discloses some material suggesting a valid defence.

There is, however, this important difference between the position of the prosecution and that of the defence, namely that the persuasive burden generally rests on the prosecution. All that the defendant has to do is to bring before the court that small modicum of evidence that might be taken by a reasonable jury to raise doubt as to his guilt. In practice, the judge will never withdraw a defence from the jury if the defendant has himself given evidence in support of it, however unconvincing his evidence may appear.[67] It would almost seem as though the unavowed purpose of the law when it casts an evidential burden on the defendant is to put pressure on him to enter the witness box and submit himself to cross-examination. The only occasion on which the trial judge is likely to require more than the defendant's own evidence is when a medical question is involved, as when the defendant sets up a defence of automatism. Here, he must generally call medical witnesses.

2–039   If the defendant fails to support his defence to the extent just indicated, the judge may omit to mention the issue in his summing-up to the jury;[68] indeed, he may

---

[62] The expression used by Viscount Simon in *Holmes v. D.P.P.* [1946] A.C. 588. Cf. *Lee Chun Chuen v. The Queen* [1963] A.C. 220.

[63] See section 54(6) of the *Coroners and Justice Act 2009.* Cf. *Mancini v. D.P.P.* [1942] A.C. 1; *R. v. Hodges* [1962] Crim. L.R. 385.

[64] *R. v. Lobell* [1957] 1 Q.B. 547; *R. v. Abraham* [1973] 1 W.L.R. 1270; *D.P.P. v. Walker* [1974] 1 W.L.R. 1090; (the judge need not leave self-defence to the jury if the only evidence shows that it was unnecessary for the defendant to act in self-defence); *R. v. Bonnick* (1977) 66 Cr. App. R. 266; *R. v. Critchley* [1982] Crim. L.R. 524.

[65] *R. v. Gill* [1963] 1 W.L.R. 841; *R. v. Radford* [2004] EWCA Crim. 2878.

[66] See *R. v. John* [1974] 1 W.L.R. 624, where, under cover of the rule, the Court of Appeal limited the kinds of justifications that could be taken to be reasonable (religious belief is not a reasonable justification for failing to provide a specimen under the blood-alcohol legislation). Cf. Glanville Williams, "Law and Fact," [1976] Crim. L.R. 482, 539. Normally a judge must hear the evidence of the defence before ruling on a defence. (*R. v. Brown* [1974] R.T.R. 377), but perhaps that is not so where the defence of reasonable excuse raised by cross-examining the prosecution witnesses is incapable of being regarded as reasonable. See also *R. v. Leer* [1982] Crim. L.R. 310.

[67] This applies to questions of fact in the narrow sense, but not to matters of value-judgment like the issue of "reasonable excuse," where the courts exercise a considerable measure of control.

[68] *Mancini v. D.P.P.* [1942] A.C. 1; *D.P.P. v. Walker* [1974] 1 W.L.R. 1090.

positively direct the jury that there is no evidence on the issue for consideration.[69] Contrariwise, if the defence is clearly proved the judge can (and should) withdraw the case from the jury.[70]

In short, the rule imposing an evidential burden is applied by the judge, in deciding whether to leave an issue (the general issue or some specific question) to the jury. The rule imposing the persuasive burden is for application by the jury. Putting this in another way, the evidential burden governs what the judge does, in leaving the question to the jury or withdrawing it from them; the persuasive burden governs what he *says*, in directing the jury how they are to reach their verdict.

Suppose the defendant does not argue a particular defence, or mention it by name (*e.g.*, self-defence), but there is evidence before the court?   If there is evidence to support the defence the judge should leave it to the jury even though the defendant has not argued it. Lord Morris:[71]

2–040

> "It is always the duty of a judge to leave to the jury any issue (whether raised by the defence or not) which on the evidence in the case is an issue fit to be left to them."

The rule is particularly important where the defendant cannot raise the defence because it would be inconsistent with another defence (such as alibi).

2.5.   BURDENS OF PROOF ON THE DEFENCE

Harking back again to *Woolmington v. D.P.P.*, it will be remembered that Viscount Sankey said that: "it is the duty of the prosecution to prove the prisoner's guilt, subject to the defence of insanity also to any statutory exception." This remark, which has been judicially approved on a number of occasions, makes no exception for presumptions. In civil matters there are certain rebuttable presumptions of law which place the persuasive burden on the other side, but it seems that in criminal cases they do not operate in favour of the prosecution, but merely discharge the prosecution's evidential burden. "The accused does not need to establish, in the generality of cases, any defence or fact in order to secure an acquittal."[72]

2–041

The defence of insanity requires the defendant to prove his insanity on the balance of probabilities.[73] This will be dealt with in the Chapter on insanity. Many statutes shift the persuasive burden. As we have seen, it has become almost a matter of routine for Parliament, in respect of the most trivial offences as well

---

[69] *R. v. Bonnick* (1978) 66 Cr. App. R. 266; *R. v. Radford* [2004] EWCA Crim. 2878.

[70] *R. v. Ball* (1967) 131 J.P.N. 723.

[71] *Palmer v. The Queen* [1971] A.C. 814 at 823; *von Starck v. The Queen* [2000] 1 W.L.R. 1270. Cf. *R. v. Harvey* [2009] EWCA Crim. 469; *R. v. Keane* [2010] EWCA Crim. 2514; *D.P.P. v. Walker* [1974] 1 W.L.R. 1090.

[72] *R. v. Friend* (1962) 46 Cr. App. R. 288 at 289.

[73] The same applies where the defendant raises the partial defence of diminished responsibility to a murder charge. "On a charge of murder, it shall be for the defence to prove that the person charged is by virtue of this section not liable to be convicted of murder": section 2(2) of the *Homicide Act 1957* as amended by section 52 of the *Coroners and Justice Act 2009*. See generally, Timothy H. Jones, "Insanity, Automatism, and the Burden of Proof on the Accused," (1995) 111(3) *L.Q.R.* 475.

some serious ones, to enact that the onus of proving a particular fact shall rest on the defendant, so that he can be convicted "unless he proves" it.[74] This type of provision is used particularly in respect of circumstances of excuse, such as the possession of a licence, and of mental states such as the absence of knowledge.

An example is provided by section 2 of the *Prevention of Corruption Act 1916*[75]:

> "Where ... it is proved[76] that any money, gift, or other consideration has been paid or given to or received by a person in the employment of His Majesty ... by or from a person, or agent of a person, holding or seeking to obtain a contract from His Majesty ... the ... consideration shall be deemed to have been paid or given and received corruptly as such inducement or reward as is mentioned in such *Act* unless the contrary is proved."

Suppose that the director of a company that has a contract to supply red tape to a Government Department is friendly with a civil servant and pays him a sum of money. He is prosecuted for corruption, and gives evidence that he paid the money in discharge of a debt, thereby leading the jury to doubt whether the payment had been made "corruptly." If the burden of proving this lay on the prosecution, as in the absence of express statutory provision it would, the jury should acquit. But since it is here for the defendant to prove that the payment was *not* made corruptly, the judge must direct the jury to convict if the evidence leaves them in doubt on the point.[77]

2–042 **When a statute shifts the burden of proof, must the defendant prove the issue beyond reasonable doubt?** No: the courts alleviate his position by holding that he need only discharge the civil burden, establishing his case on a balance of probability.[78]

2–043 **Do you mean possibility?** If you like, but the meaning would be the same either way.

---

[74] Another formula is: "it shall be a defence to prove. ..." *Thurrock DC v. Pinch (LA&A)* [1974] R.T.R. 269.

[75] In *R. v. Webster* [2010] EWCA Crim. 2819, it was said: "We conclude that the imposition of the reverse burden was a necessary, reasonable and proportionate response to the circumstances in which it was introduced, that is, to counter a serious and growing problem involving the suspected corruption of public servants in a time of national emergency [the First World War]." *Id.* at para. 22. The court goes on to note: "In our judgment, by the time of the appellant's trial the imposition upon him of the legal burden of disproving guilt was no longer necessary and the means of imposition was unreasonable and disproportionate in that the presumption applied with full rigour to all gifts made by a person having or seeking a contract with a public body whatever the other circumstances may have been. In our view section 2 of the *Prevention of Corruption Act 1916*, as applied to section 1(2) *Public Bodies Corrupt Practices Act 1889* unjustifiably interferes with the Article 6.2 presumption of innocence." *Id.* at para. 27.

[76] These words are inept. If the defendant submits no case, on the ground that the consideration has not been proved to have been given corruptly, the judge is evidently intended to apply the section; yet before verdict nothing has been "proved"—only evidence has been given.

[77] *R. v. Evans-Jones* (1924) 17 Cr. App. R. 121.

[78] *R. v. Carr-Briant* [1943] K.B. 607; *Morton v. Confer* [1963] 1 W.L.R. 763.

The defendant has only to show that it could have been so?   No: that it was   **2–044**
so on a balance of probability, or "on the preponderance of evidence"—that is,
that the odds in his favour are better than evens.[79]

How do you work out the odds?   These things cannot be estimated with any   **2–045**
nicety. All that one can do is to give the general instruction to the jury: is it more
likely than not that the defence is true?

Why do statutes shift the burden of proof?   The answer, in part, is that it is   **2–046**
the result of confused thinking in relation to the common law. During the 19th
century, and for a good time afterwards, the distinction between the persuasive
and evidential burdens was not perceived; so it came to be held, as a rule of the
common law, that when a matter was particularly within the knowledge of the
defendant, the "burden of proof" was on him. This would have been a reasonable
proposition if it had referred only to the evidential burden; but why, because the
matter was particularly within the knowledge of the defendant, should he be
deprived of the benefit of the doubt?

A contributory factor in forming the law was that many judges came to
criminal courts with their minds influenced by the civil law, which they assumed
applied equally to criminal cases. They therefore held that the burden of proving
any exception from liability fell on the defendant (which was the civil rule).
These judges did not appreciate that the important difference between the
criminal and civil law is that the civil law does not set out to punish, as the
criminal law basically does.[80]

Anyway, this attitude of the judges influenced the legislature, and it is
reflected particularly in legislation now represented by section 101 of the
Magistrate's Court Act 1980, which places on the defendant in a magistrates'
court the burden of proving all matter of exception, excuse or qualification.[81] On
its face this would put the burden on the defendant in respect of common law
defences like self-defence, but magistrates' courts assume that it applies only to
exceptions to statutory offences and not to the traditional defences in criminal
law.

Woolmington v. D.P.P. was a recognition of the principle that a criminal   **2–047**
defendant should receive the benefit of the "presumption of innocence." As we
have seen, the courts accept the logical consequence that in common law matters
this applies to the whole issue of guilt. Unfortunately, our legislative masters
(meaning, in reality, parliamentary counsel and the bureaucrats in Government
Departments) continue in their bad old way, probably because they are not
satisfied that merely placing an evidential burden on the defence will prevent the
jury, or even magistrates, from swallowing a meretricious and meritless defence
too easily. But surely it is unjust for the judge to have to say in effect to the jury:
"You have heard evidence on this from both sides, and if in the end you are left in

---

[79] *Public Prosecutor v. Yuvaroj* [1970] A.C. 913.

[80] George P. Fletcher, *Rethinking Criminal Law*, (Boston: Little, Brown, 1978) at 524-532.

[81] Williams, *op. cit. supra*, note 47 at 236-238. See *R. (on the application of Grundy & Co Excavations Ltd.) v. Halton Division Magistrates Court* (2003) 167 J.P. 387.

a fog and don't know what to think you must convict the defendant, because English law presumes him to be guilty in respect of this issue unless he shows himself to be innocent."

The older attitude has also been preserved by some judges, who, blindly devoted to precedent, have continued to hold that the defendant, even in the Crown Court, must prove that he falls within any exception from the statutory offence on which he relies, even though the statute is silent on the burden of proof. For example, on a charge of selling liquor without a licence it is for the defendant to prove that he had a licence.[82] This rule, said the Court of Appeal in the leading case, *R. v. Edwards*:[83]

> "is limited to offences arising under enactments which prohibit the doing of an act save in specified circumstances or by persons of specified classes or with specified qualifications or with the licence or permission of specified authorities."[84]

The "limitation" is so broadly worded that it may seem at first sight to be no limitation at all. But it means, for example, that where a statute penalizes the doing of something without reasonable excuse, or lawful excuse, the burden of disproving the excuse rests on the prosecution, since the case does not fall within any excepted categories.[85] Also, the rule in *R. v. Edwards* does not apply to offences created by judges. Whether there is any rhyme or reason in these complexities is another question.

2–048 **So in effect the courts have added a third exception at common law to the two exceptions stated in *Woolmington v. D.P.P.*?** Yes.[86] That there were only two exceptions had been taken for granted in a number of cases since *Woolmington's* case, for example in *Mancini v. D.P.P.* where Viscount Simon said:[87]

> "The rule [in *Woolmington's case*] is of general application. . . . The only exceptions arise, as explained in *Woolmington's* case, in the defence of insanity and in offences where onus of proof is specially dealt with by statute."

It cannot plausibly be said that the onus of proof is "specifically dealt with by statute" where a statute merely enacts a licensing provision. Moreover, *R. v. Edwards* is inconsistent with authority in respect of acts prohibited "save in specified circumstances," for common assault is prohibited save in the "specified circumstances" of the victim's consent,[88] yet the burden of disproving these circumstances rests on the prosecution.

---

[82] *R. v. Edwards* [1975] Q.B. 27; *R. (on the application of Grundy & Co Excavations Ltd.) v. Halton Division Magistrates Court* (2003) 167 J.P. 387; cf. *R. v. Charles* [2010] 1 W.L.R. 644.

[83] [1975] Q.B. 27 at 40.

[84] This formula does not include the fault element required for the crime, and the burden of proving the issue clearly rests on the prosecution.

[85] Only an evidential burden rests on the defendant: *R. v. Cousins* [1982] Q.B. 526.

[86] And they have since added a fourth: the burden of proving a defence of previous acquittal or conviction rests on the defendant: *R. v. Coughlan* (1976) 63 Cr. App. R. 33; *Iremonger v. Vissenga* [1976] Crim. L.R. 524.

[87] [1942] A.C. 1 at 11.

[88] *Christopherson v. Bare* (1848) 116 E.R. 554. Cf. *R. v. Wilson* [1997] Q.B. 47.

An argument against shifting the burden of proof deserving more attention than it has received relates to the simplicity of the trial. If the evidential burden is placed on the defendant, the judge need not (and should not) direct the jury upon it; he himself decides whether the evidence is sufficient to take the defence to the jury, and if it is he merely directs the jury in the ordinary way that the burden of proof rests on the prosecution. But when the persuasive burden is on the defendant, the judge has to direct the jury that on certain issues the prosecution must prove the case beyond reasonable doubt, while on one particular issue the defendant must prove his defence on a balance of probability. This is a difficult intellectual task for the ordinary jury.

The Criminal Law Revision Committee in its Evidence Report[89] proposed that a statute should be passed putting the persuasive burden on the prosecution on all issues, except where subsequent legislation makes it clear that a persuasive burden is to rest on the defendant, and except also in cases where a statutory defence depends upon the defendant successfully throwing the blame on a third person. The Committee said:

2–049

> "We are strongly of the opinion that, both on principle and for the sake of clarity and convenience in practice, burdens on the defence should be evidential only."

In recent times the courts have tended to hold that statutory provisions expressly reversing the onus of proof are incompatible with Article 6 of the *European Convention for the Protection of Human Rights and Fundamental Freedoms*.[90] Given the requirements of Article 6, such provisions are likely to disappear from the legal landscape.

2.6. LAW AND FACT

The basic rule is that in the Crown Court the jury are the "tribunal of fact." It is for the judge to direct the jury on the relevant law,[91] always remembering the principle stated by Diplock L.J. (as he then was):

2–050

---

[89] (London: H.M.S.O., Cmnd. 4991, 1972) at paras. 137-142.

[90] *R. v. Lambert* [2002] 2 A.C. 545; *Sheldrake v. D.P.P.* [2005] 1 A.C. 264 at 297; *R. v. Webster* [2010] EWCA Crim. 2819; *D.P.P. v. Wright* [2010] Q.B. 224. See also *R. v. Charles* [2010] 1 W.L.R. 644, where it was held: "The effect of section 1(10) of the *Crime and Disorder Act 1998* in the instant case was to make criminal actions that would not otherwise be criminal. Therefore, it could not have been intended by Parliament to place any burden of proof on C under s.1(10) which criminalised conduct that Parliament itself had not criminalised and had not prescribed the terms in which that could be done." This decision is welcome. Cf. *R. v. Clarke* [2008] EWCA Crim. 893. See also, Ian Dennis, "Reverse Onuses and the Presumption of Innocence: in Search of Principle," [2005] Crim. L.R. 901.

[91] The judge may, even in advance of the trial, decide (on a motion to quash the indictment) whether the alleged offence exists in law, and for this purpose decide any relevant facts: *R. v. Goldstein* [1982] 1 W.L.R. 804.

> "The function of a summing-up is not to give the jury a general dissertation upon some aspect of the criminal law, but to tell them what the issues of fact on which they must make up their mind in order to determine whether the accused is guilty of a particular offence."[92]

The jury find the facts and apply the law to the facts by returning a verdict of guilty or not guilty; so they decide the case as a whole. The judge may review the facts and even suggest how the jury may find or regard them, so long as he says that the decision on the facts is for them.

2–051 **So it is for the judge to interpret the legislation and explain it to the jury?** The judge applies the principles of interpretation to the legislation in question, advises the jury which meaning is to be adopted in the case of ambiguity, and advises them also as to the meaning of technical legal words. For example, if the judge thinks that the statute impliedly requires *mens rea* he tells the jury that they cannot convict unless *mens rea* was present. (Not that he is likely to use the Latin phrase.)

2–052 **How do we know that the jury understand the judge's instructions on the law?** We don't. Authority has sternly set its face against any attempt, in Britain, to investigate how well the jury perform their allotted task. (To try to do so can even be a criminal contempt of court).[93] It seems reasonable to assume that the jury make many mistakes. A law student is selected for above-average intelligence, and spends considerable time studying the basic concepts of the criminal law under the guidance of a scholar with expertise in the subject area. A judge is expected to convey the same information to a randomly selected jury, who, if they are to do their work properly, must not only understand the concepts but apply them to an intricate web of evidence.

This suggests that the criminal law should be made as simple as possible. But it is better to have good rules, even though they are rather difficult for the jury to understand, than to have rules that have no other merit than simplicity of statement. There is at least the hope that the good rules will, for the most part, be properly applied.

2–053 **Where the facts are quite clear, can't the judge tell the jury so?** He may make the jury aware what his opinion is. In *D.P.P. v. Smith*,[94] a policeman clung to the defendant's car, trying to stop him, but the defendant drove on and the policeman fell off and was killed. The defendant said in evidence that he did not know the policeman was on the bonnet, and the trial judge directed the jury as follows:

---

[92] *R. v. Mowatt* [1968] 1 Q.B. 421. The judge need not explain the whole of a section, for instance, if only part is relevant: *Alford v. Magee* (1952) 85 C.L.R. 437 at 466. It is not customary to give the jury copies of the statute, because they should accept its meaning as explained by the judge. Cf. *R. v. Tennant* (1975) 23 CCC (ed) 82 (Ont.).

[93] Section 8 of the *Contempt of Court Act 1981*. See *Attorney-General v. Associated Newspapers Ltd. (1992)* [1993] 3 W.L.R. 74; cf. *R. v. Mirza* [2004] 1 A.C. 1118.

[94] [1961] A.C. 290 at 324. Cf. Lord Devlin in *Chandler v. D.P.P.* [1964] A.C. 763 at 803-804.

> "There is a limit, is there not, members of the jury, to human credulity, and you may think that the accused man's unsupported assertion on this part of the case goes well past it, that the evidence is overwhelming, and he knew his car was carrying the officer up the road? The matter is one for you, but if you arrive at the conclusion that, of course, he knew, it is one which I would regard as abundantly right. Indeed, on the evidence I do not see how you could properly arrive at any other conclusion. If that be so the defence of pure accident goes."

When the case came before the House of Lords Viscount Kilmuir L.C. commented that the judge's remarks were fully justified. Normally, the judge would not direct the jury so strongly as this, and, except where the facts are not in dispute,[95] he must never direct the jury to convict.[96]

Can the judge say to the jury: I direct you that the law is such and such, so if you find the facts to be such and such, then you must convict? Certainly, if the judge is merely telling the jury that they must take the law from him.

Apart from the judge's power to withdraw and issue from the jury, the only questions of fact decided by him in criminal cases are:

2–054

- Questions of fact relating to the admissibility of evidence (*e.g.*, whether a witness qualifies as an expert; and whether a confession was induced by promises, threats or oppression, in which case the jury are generally not allowed to hear evidence of it.
- Questions of fact in relation to sentence. While the jury are listening to the evidence for the purpose of convicting or acquitting, the judge is listening to it for the purpose of sentence in the event of conviction, and he may hear further evidence for this purpose after conviction. In sentencing, the judge acts on his own view of the facts.[97] If he wishes, he may ask the foreperson of the jury whether the verdict was based on one view of the facts or another; and if the judge does this he must accept the opinion expressed by the jury.

What is the line between fact and law? If the law refers to a "building," who decides whether a caravan is a building, judge or jury? You may be surprised to know that the general answer is: the jury.[98] Lawyers inveterately assume that questions of fact (and only questions of fact) are for the jury, but this involves giving a wide meaning to the phrase "questions of fact." Four types may be distinguished, and it is convenient to give them names[99]:

2–055

1. *Questions of primary fact.* Primary facts depend chiefly on whether a witness is to be believed in reporting what he did or perceived or mentally experienced (did he see black marks on the road?).

---

[95] *R. v. Goldstein* [1982] 1 W.L.R. 804.

[96] *R. v. Wang* [2005] 1 W.L.R. 661.

[97] *R. v. Whittle* [1974] Crim. L.R. 487. This is subject to the important qualification that the judge must not assume the defendant's guilt of an offence for which he has not been convicted, and in particular must honour an acquittal on another count.

[98] Cf. *R. v. Dhindsa* [2005] EWCA Crim. 1198, where it was held that it was a matter for the jury to decide whether the gold ring was an offensive weapon (a knuckleduster).

[99] See Williams, *op. cit. supra*, note 66 at 472, 532.

2. *Questions of inferential fact.* These concern the proper factual (non-verbal) inference to be drawn from the primary facts (were the marks caused by the defendant braking hard?).

3. *Questions of evaluative fact.* These principally concern the legal assessment of the fact as reasonable or negligent (if the defendant had to brake hard, does that mean he was driving too fast, and therefore negligently?).[100] All value-judgments relating to matters of reasonableness, such as "reasonable excuse" under statute, or whether a person who made an arrest had "reasonable cause to suspect an offence," are left to the jury, provided that there is sufficient evidence to support a positive finding. They are not really questions of fact, but the equation of jury questions and questions of fact means that they have to be pushed into this category.[101]

4. *Questions of denotative*[102] *fact.* These concern the application of ordinary (non-legal) words used in legal rules—subject to the observations that follow. To take your example, is a caravan a building?

2–056   In general, all four questions of fact (primary, inferential, evaluative and denotative fact) are for the jury. But:

1. The judge need not leave to the jury a question of fact that is not in dispute[103] (though he will generally do so, for safety's sake). This proposition does not apply where, although the brute facts are agreed, it is disputed whether they fall within a particular legal classification which has to be adjudicated by the jury.
   The fact that both sides agree that they are talking about a caravan and not a summer-house still leaves the jury to decide whether a caravan is a building. Another example is where it is disputed whether admitted facts

---

[100] See *AK v. Western Australia* (2008) 232 C.L.R. 438 at 472-473, the Australian High Court noted: "Lord Devlin considered that trial by jury had a 'unique merit' in 'that it allows a decision near to the *aequum et bonum* to be given without injuring the fabric of the law, for the verdict of a jury can make no impact on the law.' Thus Lord Devlin saw the jury as being for some purposes 'the best judicial instrument' (citing Lord Devlin, *Trial by Jury* (London: Stevens & Sons Ltd., 1966) at 158). A clear illustration of this role of the jury is seen when the jury decides whether the facts it finds answer certain *legal criteria.* That phenomenon is recognised by section 118(6) of the *Criminal Procedure Act* (Cth.), for the court may refuse to order trial by judge alone 'if it considers the trial will involve a factual issue that requires the application of objective community standards such as an issue of reasonableness, negligence, indecency, obscenity or dangerousness.' Other examples of factual issues requiring the application of 'objective community standards' include whether behaviour was 'threatening, abusive or insulting'; whether conduct was 'dishonest,' a matter to be decided by the jury 'according to the ordinary standards of reasonable and honest people'; whether an assault is 'indecent;' and whether an accused person had a particular intention." This process should be contradistinguished from the process of deciphering the meaning of words used within statutes. (Citations omitted.) It might pay to let you know that "unjust enrichment" is the label now given to the old doctrine of *aequum et bonum.*

[101] §6.10.

[102] In formal logic, denotation refers to the aggregate of objects of which a word maybe predicted, while connotation means the qualities that define the word.

[103] *R. v. Goldstein* [1982] 1 W.L.R. 804. "Where facts are proved and accepted, then whether those facts amount to a crime or not must be a question of law, not of fact:" *R. v. Larkin* [1943] 1 All E.R. 217 at 219. But even if the evidence is all one way, a fact will be regarded as disputed if the defendant or his counsel has invited the jury to disbelieve the evidence. *R. v. Leer* [1982] Crim. L.R. 310.

went far beyond mere preparation for the commission of the crime as to amount to criminal attempt,[104] or whether admitted harm amounts to grievous bodily harm. Here the issue must be left to the jury.

2. The judge may withdraw an issue from the jury if there is no sufficient evidence to support a finding on it, as already explained. A conspicuous example is the defence of "reasonable excuse" under statute, which judges are disposed to control quite tightly.[105]

3. An appellate court may quash a conviction if the verdict is unsafe, whatever type of question of fact is involved.

I still don't really see how you distinguish questions of law from questions of fact. Take the question whether D committed a burglary. That can involve both law and fact.   Whether D surreptitiously entered, say, a caravan while its normal inhabitants were away and stole something in it is a question of fact. Whether one can commit burglary in a caravan is a question of law, and the law answers it in the affirmative, provided that the caravan is inhabited. (Burglary can be committed in "an inhabited vehicle or vessel.")[106]

Although this distinction is clear, trouble can arise in applying words of the law to the facts. All words are to some extent imprecise, in the sense that difficulties can arise in applying them, and some words are very imprecise. A typical example is the question whether a particular injury amounts to "grievous bodily harm." Although this is a somewhat antiquated legal phrase, it merely means serious (or, some say, really serious) injury. Apart from that it has no specifically legal meaning. It involves a question of degree, and its application is chiefly one for the tribunal of fact. Similarly, the question whether a person is "driving" a car, within the meaning of a statute, is left to the jury. It is what we are calling a denotative fact. Philosophically speaking, of course, word-meanings are distinguished from questions of fact.

The jury wouldn't be allowed to find that a scratch was grievous bodily harm?   If that were the only evidence, the judge would not leave the case to the jury.

I can see that the jury must be left, within broad limits, to decide whether an injury is grievous bodily harm, because otherwise there would be nothing for them to decide. It is a question of degree, to be settled by a gut reaction. But whether a person can be said to be driving a car is different. It can depend on the shade of meaning you give to the word. Are you driving if you are being towed?   And is a passenger driving if he grabs the wheel in an emergency, when the driver has passed out? Or is a person driving if he releases the brake and lets the car coast downhill? Or if someone else is pushing the car and he walks beside it, controlling the steering through the open window? These questions are left to the jury, though the judge may advise the jury of what he thinks.

2–057

2–058

2–059

---

[104] *D.P.P. v. Stonehouse* [1978] A.C. 55.
[105] *R. v. John* [1974] 1 W.L.R. 624; *R. v. Brown* [1974] R.T.R. 377; *R. v. Leer* [1982] Crim. L.R. 310.
[106] Section 9(3) of the *Theft Act 1968*.

2–060 **But surely the judge ought not to leave the meaning of the words of the law to be decided by vox pop? One jury may jump one way, another a different way.** For hundreds of years judges took the view that it was part of their function to define words in statutes for the benefit of juries, thus creating a "judicial dictionary" of words commonly used for legal purposes. Then, suddenly, the House of Lords announced a new rule: the meaning of "ordinary" words is a question of fact for the jury. Although the judge may instruct the jury on the meaning of terms of legal art,[107] he is not supposed to lay down the law on the meaning of ordinary words: *Cozens v. Brutus*.[108] (This was an appeal from magistrates on a case stated, but the decision was intended to apply equally to findings by juries.)

The decision concerned the meaning of the word "insulting" in a statute making it a summary offence to use threatening, abusive or insulting words or language in a public place whereby a breach of the peace is likely. Brutus was one of some demonstrators who invaded a tennis court when a match was in progress, by way of protest against the presence of a South African player. The magistrates held that his act was not insulting; the Divisional Court reversed, offering an obviously wrong definition of the word; then the House of Lords, disagreeing with the Divisional Court's definition, restored the decision of the magistrates—not because all of their Lordships necessarily thought that the act was not insulting (though they probably thought it was not), but because they thought the question was for the magistrates. The opinions of the House make it plain that the same rule would apply where the application of the statute has to be made by a jury.

2–061 **So the jury look the word up in a dictionary?** They have no dictionary. They can use only the information they get in open court or what they have in their own heads.

2–062 **Can't they ask the judge for a dictionary?** They are unlikely to be given one. Dictionaries cannot define the word in its particular context, or pay attention to the questions of policy involved. The jury may go back into court, and the foreperson may ask for further guidance on the meaning of the word, and then perhaps the judge may read out the relevant entry in the dictionary to them, with an appropriate explanation. Or the judge may just tell the jury to go back and use their common sense.

---

[107] For example, the word "with" is not a term of art. See *R. v. DeBattista* [1986] 2 W.W.R. 722.

[108] [1973] A.C. 854; *R. v. Evans* [2005] 1 W.L.R. 1435 at 1441. But see Rupert Cross, *Statutory Interpretation*, (London: Butterworths, 1976) at 53-55, pointing out that the ordinary meaning of a word is not a question of fact in the usual sense, because evidence cannot be given upon it. The statute may contain a definition of a word it uses, in which case the judge must explain the statutory definition to the jury, who are then to apply it. In *R. v. Wheatley* [1979] 1 W.L.R. 144, the judge was held to be entitled, in view of the statutory definition, to direct the jury in effect that the defendant had no defence. Presumably this was because the application of the statutory definition to the facts was not in dispute. *R. v. Wheatley* also illustrates the point that the definition need not be in the statute creating the offence; it may be in another statute dealing with the same general subject matter (*in pari materia*), where the two statutes can be regarded as part of a legislative scheme. Further, Lord Reid in *Cozens v. Brutus* (at 861C) said that "if the context shows that a word is used in an unusual sense the court will determine in other words what the usual [unusual?] sense is."

Lord Reid, who gave the fullest reasons for the decision in *Cozens v. Brutus*, said that a dictionary would define "insulting" by giving synonyms; but, he said, "few words have exact synonyms." The alternative would be for the court to frame a definition, "but the purpose of a definition is not to limit or modify the ordinary meaning of a word and the court is not entitled to do that."

This remark does carry conviction. The object of the court's definition may be not to modify the ordinary meaning but to state it. As a definition of "insulting" in ordinary speech, I offer the following: language or conduct is not said to be insulting unless it is intended to show contempt or disesteem, or is understood by the hearer or observer to show this attitude. This was probably the meaning of the word that the magistrates had in mind, and they were right in holding that the defendant did not intend to insult the spectators or the game, even though his conduct was no doubt offensive to them. (Neither the magistrates nor the Law Lords seem to have considered the possibility that the demo was insulting to the South African player.)

The scope of the decision of the House of Lords is not entirely clear. Lord Reid said that if the context of the statute shows that the words are used in an unusual sense, the court will determine in other words what that unusual sense is. (He did not explain why the court could determine the unusual sense of words in a statute but not the usual sense.)[109] Conceivably a judge might say that the usual sense of driving a car is driving it under its own power, but that the policy of, say, the drink-drive offence is to forbid people who are under the influence of alcohol to have control of a vehicle while it is in motion, so that for this purpose the word has a wider meaning; and the judge might then, on Lord Reid's principle, instruct the jury in this wider meaning. But this still would not allow the judge to instruct the jury dogmatically on the ordinary meaning of an ordinary word like "insulting."

Suppose that this offence of insulting words were triable by jury, and the jury decided that a demo on a tennis court was insulting although the evidence was clear that it was not intended to express and was not understood to express any disrespect for anyone present, but was merely an offensive way of publicizing political opinions. Would the conviction be set aside on appeal? It might be.[110] Lord Reid said that "the question would normally be whether the decision was unreasonable in the sense that no tribunal

2–063

---

[109] "The judgment of Kitto J. in *N.S.W. Associated Blue-Metal Quarries Ltd. v. Federal Commissioner of Taxation* (1956) 94 C.L.R. 309 is illuminating. Kitto J. observed that the question whether certain operations answered the description "mining operations upon a mining property" within the meaning of section 122 of the *Income Tax Assessment Act 1936*, as amended, was a mixed question of law and fact. He went on to explain why this was so: "First it is necessary to decide as a matter of law whether the *Act* uses the expressions 'mining operations' and 'mining property' in any other sense than that which they have in ordinary speech." Having answered this question in the negative, he noted that the "common understanding of the words has … to be determined" as "a question of fact." *Hope v. Bathurst City Council* (1980) 144 C.L.R. 1 at 8 *per* Mason J. Recent decisions from the Australian High Court have applied this decision, see *Vetter v. Lake Macquarie CC* (2001) 202 C.L.R. 439 at 451; *Collector of Customs v. Agfa-Gevaert Ltd.* (1996) 186 C.L.R. 389 at 397. Cf. *Wyre Forest District Council Respondents v. Secretary of State for the Environment* [1990] 2 A.C. 357, where the meaning of the word was provided in the statute.
[110] *Edwards v. Bairstow* [1956] A.C. 14.

acquainted with the ordinary use of language could reasonably reach that decision." He was here presumably speaking of an appeal of law from magistrates. The formula he used does not apply to appeals from juries, where the question is whether the verdict is unsafe—though that probably gives the appellate court more control than the other.

2–064 **I have been saving up a supplementary for you. If the verdict would be upset as being unsafe, wouldn't it be more sensible for the trial judge to warn the jury how they are to interpret the word, so as to save all the trouble of a wrong conviction and an appeal?** That seems common sense. But it is uncertain how far the Lords would go in saying that the question is wholly for the jury and is not subject to appellate control.

The main objection to the rule in *Cozens v. Brutus* is that an appeal to common sense and to the jury's knowledge of the English language is an over-estimation of the jury's abilities, and also shows a misunderstanding of the function of language and a lack of appreciation of the peculiar difficulty of interpreting the law. As to the first point, there is no educational qualification for jurors; disgracefully, people are allowed to act on them without enquiry on whether they can read. No one even gives them a test to see whether they can understand spoken English.

It is true that anyone who knows English knows how to use common words. Whether words are used "properly" or not does not matter so long as information is conveyed. But to ask the jury to decide whether the words of a statute apply to a given situation is to set them a task to which they are wholly unaccustomed. Success in it depends not merely upon an ability to use words correctly but upon a consideration of the context in which the particular words appear, the general policy of the statute, and the practical result of giving the words one meaning or the other.

2–065 **What is the distinction between ordinary words and technical legal words?** The House of Lords gave no examples to help us. With rare exceptions, all words used in statutes are probably comprehensible in ordinary usage to every sixth-former, and the great majority of such words would be at least roughly understood by GCSE-level pupils. (Not that it can be assumed that jurors fell into either category at any time in their lives.) Statutes use "ordinary" words (that is, words found in compact dictionaries and used from time to time in general contexts) to express specialized legal concepts; we do not generally use outlandish words for legal purposes. Literally applied, therefore, the rule in *Cozens v. Brutus* would leave almost every statute to be interpreted by the jury. Yet the fact that the ordinary person can understand a word in ordinary use does not mean that he can understand it properly when it is used in a particular context in an Act of Parliament.

The Courts of first instance and intermediate appellate courts (Court of Appeal and Divisional Court) have on occasions shown a certain amount of healthy insubordination in respect of *Cozens v. Brutus*. (Even the House of Lords forgot it, or closed its eyes to it, on one occasion.)[111] The tendency is to hold that key

---

[111] *R. v. Caldwell* [1982] A.C. 341.

words in statutes, the words on which legal issues often hang, are not "ordinary," although the uninstructed observer might think they are. At any rate, the law reports contain a number of examples of judges very sensibly asserting as a matter of law what such words mean.[112]

Judges have ruled upon the meaning of the words "assist,"[113] "produce,"[114] "reckless,"[115] and "retention,"[116] in particular statutory offences. These are certainly important words in criminal matters, but they are not exclusively legal words. If they are ordinary words, and if *Cozens v. Brutus* is followed,[117] any conviction resulting from a positive direction by the judge on the meaning of a word should theoretically be open to attack on appeal; but often that is only theory, since the appellate court may be ready to dismiss an appeal. The more cautious judge will leave the meaning of the word to the jury while giving them a strong intimation of his own opinion.[118] Some judges, with regrettable reticence, offer the jury no help.[119] If, as a result, the jury convict, having attached a wholly unreasonable meaning to the word, the conviction can presumably be quashed on appeal as being unsafe, as already said. But since the prosecution cannot appeal, this control over the jury works only one way: if the jury attach a foolishly benevolent meaning to the word and acquit, the law provides no remedy.

---

[112] See the cases cited in *Coleman v. Power* (2004) 220 C.L.R. 1 at 38-42 concerning the word "insulting."

[113] *R. v. Vickers* [1975] 1 W.L.R. 811. (In ordinary English one who assists knows what he is doing and the purpose with which it is done).

[114] *D.P.P. v. Nock* [1978] A.C. 979 at 984E.

[115] Recklessness was defined by the Court of Appeal in *R. v. Briggs* [1977] 1 W.L.R. 605. The particular definition there favoured was disapproved in *R. v. Caldwell* [1982] A.C. 341, where Lord Diplock announced (on behalf of the majority) that recklessness is not a term of art but bears the meaning it has in ordinary speech; having said that, he laid down in express terms the definition of recklessness on which the jury were to be instructed. The two pronouncements cannot stand together. Either, "recklessness" is not an "ordinary word" bearing the meaning that it bears in ordinary speech or its meaning is a question for the jury—unless (happy thought) their Lordships are now prepared to repudiate *Cozens v. Brutus*. In *R. v. G* [2004] 1 A.C. 1034 it was held: "the majority's misinterpretation of 'recklessly' in section 1 of the *Criminal Damage Act* was offensive to principle and apt to cause injustice. Accordingly, the need to correct that misinterpretation was compelling." It seems fairly clear that whether "reckless" in a statute means subjective or objective recklessness is a question of law, and the question as to whether a particular act is of such a nature or kind as to fall within the legal definition of recklessness is a question of fact.

[116] *R. v. Pitchley* (1973) 57 Cr. App. R. 30 at 37; the Court of Appeal stated the meaning of "retention" even while saying that it was an "ordinary English word."

[117] It has been endorsed by the House of Lords in *Moyna v. Secretary of State for Work and Pensions* [2003] 1 W.L.R. 1929.

[118] In *Attorney-General's Reference (No.1 of 1976)* [1977] 1 W.L.R. 646 the Court of Appeal said that, on an issue as to the meaning of statutory words, it is proper that the judge should indicate to the jury his view that the case is all one way.

[119] Examples of the words that have been left unglossed for the jury to interpret are "appropriates" (*R. v. Hale* (1979) 68 Cr. App. R. 415); "obtains" (*R. v. Hayat* (1976) 63 Cr. App. R. 181); "dishonesty" (*R. v. Feely* [1973] Q.B. 530; *R. v. Ghosh* [1982] Q.B. 1053); "abusive action" (*R. v. Evans* [2005] 1 Cr. App. R. 32); "significant risk" (*R. v. Stephens* [2007] 2 Cr. App. R. 26); "premises" (*R. (on the application of Thames Water Utilities Ltd.) v. Water Services Regulation Authority* [2010] EWHC 3331); "persecution" (*Kagema v. Secretary of State for the Home Department* [1997] Imm. A.R. 137).

A striking example of the freedom that now may be left to the jury relates to the now repealed section 32 of the *Sexual Offences Act 1956*,[120] whereby it was an offence for a man to persistently solicit in a street for immoral purposes. The prudish wording, which studiously obscured the conduct that Parliament meant to prohibit, inevitably created problems. "Immoral purposes" was clearly intended to cover (and be confined to) sexual purposes, but what sexual purposes were to be regarded as immoral was left to the guesswork of those administering the law. After some vacillation the courts have now decided the point by not deciding it; they hold that the jury should be left to determine in each case whether or not the law covers a homosexual purpose! So under the old law, homosexuals seeking non-prostitute partners risked being treated as though they were soliciting prostitutes, since their conviction depended on the moral views of the particular jury, on a question that was plainly to be resolved as one of fixed law.[121]

2–066 **What about magistrates? Are they in the same position as juries?** One is tempted to say that *Cozens v. Brutus* has been a *brutum fulmen* in relation to magistrates, even though it was decided on an appeal from magistrates. Although the Divisional Court is supposed to hear appeals only on questions of law, it exercises tight control over magistrates' courts (and over the Crown Court on appeal from magistrates). It is strange that a random collection of jurors, who have perhaps never been in a court before, should be given a free hand, while magistrates, who are carefully selected and given some training, and generally have considerable experience, are kept on a close rein; but that is how it is. The Divisional Court will readily say that a summary conviction is perverse and also (since even the prosecution can appeal) that a summary acquittal is perverse. It will say this even where the task of the magistrates was to interpret an ordinary word in a statute.[122] But there is a certain area in between where the Divisional Court does not take a strong view and allows the court below to have its own way.

While the practice of the Divisional Court is socially beneficial (even if legally very questionable in view of the decision of the Lords), the contrast is strange with jury trial. The difference of treatment is practically anomalous in the case of either way offences. The appeal court may tell magistrates (carefully selected, experienced in administering the law) in no uncertain terms whether a particular person was "driving" a vehicle or not; yet when the identical question arises before a jury (unqualified, inexperienced) the judge is supposed to leave the matter to their unfettered discretion.

---

[120] The new law gets to the point. Section 51A(1) of the *Sexual Offences Act 2003* provides: "It is an offence for a person in a street or public place to solicit another (B) for the purpose of obtaining B's sexual services as a prostitute."

[121] *R. v. Gray* (1982) 74 Cr. App. R. 324. The Court of Appeal, in holding that the judge was wrong not to leave the question to the jury, nevertheless applied the proviso and affirmed the conviction on the ground that the jury, if properly directed, would inevitably have convicted. Cf. *R. v. Goddard* (1991) 92 Cr. App. R. 185.

[122] *Behrendt v. Burridge* [1977] 1 W.L.R. 29; *Chief Constable of the West Midlands v. Billingham* [1979] 1 W.L.R. 747; *Seamark v. Prouse* [1980] 1 W.L.R. 698; *Jones v. Pratt* [1983] R.T.R. 54.

2.7. APPELLATE CONTROL OVER JURIES

Although the Court of Appeal (like its predecessor the Court of Criminal Appeal)   **2–067**
has always had the power to quash erroneous convictions, it has been remarkably
disinclined to exercise the power where the rules of procedure and evidence have
been complied with. One reason is the strong feeling of English lawyers that the
responsibility for convicting rests with the jury.

As a general rule, only the defence can appeal to the Court of Appeal.[123]
However, appeals are also available in the lower courts. A person convicted in a
magistrates' court can appeal to the Crown Court. Furthermore, both the defence
and prosecution can appeal a point of law or an issue of excess jurisdiction by
"way of case stated" to the High Court. Our focus will primarily be on defence
appeals against conviction[124] to the Court of Appeal.

But doesn't the Court of Appeal fall down on its job if it allows an obviously   **2–068**
erroneous conviction to stand—or even one that is reasonably likely to be
erroneous?   I share your view. So did Parliament, when it passed section 2 of
the *Criminal Appeal Act 1968* (as amended by section 1(2) of the *Criminal
Appeal Act 1995*), requiring the Court of Appeal to allow an appeal if the
conviction is unsafe. But even this enactment has not produced a revolution in
judicial practice.

Before the 1995 amendment there were two bases for allowing an appeal,
namely that the court thinks that the conviction is "unsafe" or "unsatisfactory."
The pre-1995 law meant that the appellate court could apply what was called "the
proviso"—the concluding words of the former subsection, which allowed an
appeal to be dismissed although there had been a technical irregularity if no
miscarriage of justice had occurred.[125] The only basis for allowing appeal
nowadays is that the court regards the conviction to be "unsafe."[126]

Suppose that the appeal court takes the view that there was insufficient   **2–069**
evidence on a count on which the defendant was convicted, but that he was
undoubtedly guilty of some other offence. Can the court substitute a
conviction of that other offence?   Yes if it was one which the jury could have
convicted, on the indictment as it stood. But if the proper charge was not
expressly or impliedly included in the indictment, or if the jury have acquitted on

---

[123] Part 9 of the *Criminal Justice Act 2003* allows the prosecution to make interlocutory appeals to the
Court of Appeal in limited circumstances. Furthermore, section 36 of the *Criminal Justice Act 1988*
allows the Attorney-General to apply to the Court of Appeal to have a sentence reviewed. Section 36
of the *Criminal Justice Act 1972* allows the Attorney-General to refer a point of law to the Court of
Appeal. The prosecution is also able to appeal from the Court of Appeal to the Supreme Court.

[124] The defendant can also appeal against a sentence on the grounds that it is excessive.

[125] For example, in a number of cases the particulars specified in the indictment could not support a
conviction for the offences that had been charged, but the "proviso" was invoked to uphold the
convictions. (see *R. v. McHugh* (1977) 64 Cr. App. R. 92; *R. v. Molyneux* (1981) 72 Cr. App. R. 111;
R. v. Ayres (1984) 78 Cr. App. R. 232, [1984] A.C. 447; *R. v. Pickford* [1995] 1 Cr. App. R. 420).
Under the *post*-1995 law, such an irregularity would make the cases sufficiently unsafe to justify
allowing an appeal: *R. v. Graham* [1997] 1 Cr. App. R. 302 at 308-309.

[126] *R. v. Graham* [1997] 1 Cr. App. R. 302.

the proper charge, the court is helpless. Before the Court of Appeal can substitute a conviction for an alternative offence the prosecution has to establish:

> "(a)   that the jury could on the indictment have found the appellant guilty of some other offence, the allegation of which was expressly or impliedly included in the allegation in the particular count in the indictment, and
> (b)   that the jury must have been satisfied of facts which proved the appellant to be guilty of that other offence."[127]

2–070   **What if the conviction, though technically irregular, was substantially right? Can the Court of Appeal overlook the defect?**   It can if the defect is utterly trivial. Formerly, the practice was to uphold the conviction if there was almost any procedural irregularity at the trial, but the court has less discretion under the *1995 Act*. Lord Bingham C.J. (as he then was), discussing the 1995 amendment, said:[128]

> "[N]ow there is no proviso. Our sole obligation is to consider whether a conviction is unsafe. We would deprecate resort to undue technicality. A conviction will not be regarded as unsafe because it is possible to point to some drafting or clerical error, or omission, or discrepancy, or departure from good or prescribed practice. We would, for example, expect *R. v. McVitie* [1960] 2 Q.B. 483 to be decided under the new law in the same way as under the old. But if it is clear as a matter of law that the particulars of offence specified in the indictment cannot, even if established, support a conviction of the offence of which the defendant is accused, a conviction of such offence must in our opinion be considered unsafe. If a defendant could not in law be guilty of the offence charged on the facts relied on no conviction of that offence could be other than unsafe."

The way in which this power is exercised depends to some extent upon the facts. If there has been a breach of proper procedure (for example, where the defendant is clearly guilty, but of a crime different from the one charged against him) the Court of Appeal will generally quash his conviction, notwithstanding the words of the *Act*, since it regards the trial as being vitiated. In practice the defendant is not put on trial a second time, even though he generally could be.[129] So, obviously guilty people escape.[130] Although it has often been suggested that the Court of Appeal should have power in such circumstances to order a new trial, in order that the substantial question of guilt can be tried properly for the first time, the "sporting theory of justice" has hitherto prevailed, and the proposal has not been accepted.

---

[127] *R. v. Graham* [1997] 1 Cr. App. R. 302. Cf. *R. v. K* [2008] 1 Cr. App. R. 1.

[128] *R. v. Graham* [1997] 1 Cr. App. R. 302 at 309.

[129] And there are other restrictions as well: *e.g.*, the Court of Appeal cannot convict on a count that the trial judge has erroneously quashed. Nor under the old law could the court apply the proviso, because that only allowed an appeal to be dismissed when the jury could have convicted. See J. R. Spencer, "Criminal Law and Criminal Appeals—the Tail that Wags the Dog," [1982] Crim. L.R. 260 at 272-275. *Contra*, Andrew Ashworth, *Principles of Criminal Law*, (Oxford: Oxford University Press, 2009) at 360.

[130] The Court of Appeal cannot alter the *charge* and it can only substitute a *conviction* for an alternative offence if certain conditions are met. Consequently, the appeal courts have, on occasion, stretched the substantive criminal law beyond its limits to plug the lacuna. See *D.P.P. v. Gomez* [1993] AC 442; *R. v. Hinks* [2001] 2 A.C. 241.

The appellate court now allows appeals in a wider range of cases than it did before the enactment of section 1(2) of the *Criminal Appeal Act 1995*.[131] The legal principle is supposed to be that the appeal should be allowed if the conviction is unsafe, even if a reasonable jury, after being properly directed, on the evidence properly admissible, would have convicted. If there is any hint of the verdict being unsafe, the court is likely to allow the appeal. So, a conviction may be quashed as being unsafe even where the defendant has had a fair trial and there were no grounds for doubting his guilt.[132]

If the judge has usurped the function of the jury, *e.g.*, by wrongly telling them that the particular fact has been proved, then if the question is of primary or inferential[133] fact the appeal will most likely be allowed, and the conviction will be quashed. However clear the evidence may be against the defendant, the jury have a sacred right to be perverse if they want to. The appeal might also be allowed because the judge failed to sum up the defence.[134] Furthermore, appeals are usually allowed in relation to inadmissible[135] or fresh evidence.[136]

2–071

The Criminal Cases Review Commission can also refer cases to the Court of Appeal. Section 9 of the *Criminal Appeal Act 1995* provides:

"(1)   Where a person has been convicted of an offence on indictment[137] in England and Wales, the Commission—
    (a)   may at any time refer the conviction to the Court of Appeal, and
    (b)   (whether or not they refer the conviction) may at any time refer to the Court of Appeal any sentence (not being a sentence fixed by law) imposed on, or in subsequent proceedings relating to, the conviction.
(2)   A reference under subsection (1) of a person's conviction shall be treated for all purposes as an appeal by the person under section 1 of the *1968 Act* against the conviction.
(3)   A reference under subsection (1) of a sentence imposed on, or in subsequent proceedings relating to, a person's conviction on an indictment shall be treated for all purposes as an appeal by the person under section 9 of the *1968 Act* against—
    (a)   the sentence, and
    (b)   any other sentence (not being a sentence fixed by law) imposed on, or in subsequent proceedings relating to, the conviction or any other conviction on the indictment.

---

[131] In *R. v. Mullen* [2000] Q.B. 520 at 536-537, it was held "In arriving at this conclusion we strongly emphasise that nothing in this judgment should be taken to suggest that there may not be cases, such as *R. v. Latif* [1996] 1 W.L.R. 104 , in which the seriousness of the crime is so great relative to the nature of the abuse of process that it would be a proper exercise of judicial discretion to permit a prosecution to proceed or to allow a conviction to stand notwithstanding an abuse of process in relation to the defendant's presence within the jurisdiction. In each case it is a matter of discretionary balance, to be approached with regard to the particular conduct complained of and the particular offence charged." See also *R. v. Davis* [2001] 1 Cr. App. R. 8; *R. v. Smallman* [2010] EWCA Crim. 548; *R. v. Brady* [2004] 1 W.L.R. 3240; *R. v. Thomas* [2000] 1 Cr. App. R. 447.
[132] *R. v. Togher* [2001] 1 Cr. App. R. 33; *R. v. Early* [2003] 1 Cr. App. R. 19. See generally, J. R. Spencer, "Does Our Present Criminal Appeal System Make Sense?" [2006] Crim. L.R. 677; J. R. Spencer, "Quashing Convictions for Procedural Irregularities," (2008) 67(2) *Cambridge L.J.* 227.
[133] For example, intent in carrying a weapon that is offensive in law only if carried with offensive intent. See the strong decision in *R. v. Leer* [1982] Crim. L.R. 310. Cf. *R. v. Ptohopoulos* (1968) 52 Cr. App. R. 47.
[134] *R. v. Badjan* (1966) 50 Cr. App. R. 141.
[135] *R. v. Tricoglus* (1977) 65 Cr. App. R. 16.
[136] *R. v. Pendleton* [2002] 1 W.L.R. 72.
[137] As for summary offences, see section 11.

(4) On a reference under subsection (1) of a person's conviction on an indictment the Commission may give notice to the Court of Appeal that any other conviction on the indictment which is specified in the notice is to be treated as referred to the Court of Appeal under subsection (1).

(5) Where a verdict of not guilty by reason of insanity has been returned in England and Wales in the case of a person, the Commission may at any time refer the verdict to the Court of Appeal; and a reference under this subsection shall be treated for all purposes as an appeal by the person under section 12 of the *1968 Act* against the verdict."

Meanwhile, section 42 of the *Criminal Justice and Immigration Act 2008* provides:

"(1) This section applies where there is an appeal under this Part following a reference by the Criminal Cases Review Commission under section 9(1)(a), (5) or (6) of the *Criminal Appeal Act 1995* or section 1(1) of the *Criminal Cases Review (Insanity) Act 1999.*

(2) Notwithstanding anything in section 2, 13 or 16 of this Act, the Court of Appeal may dismiss the appeal if—
(a) the only ground for allowing it would be that there has been a development in the law since the date of the conviction, verdict or finding that is the subject of the appeal, and (b) the condition in subsection (3) is met.

(3) The condition in this subsection is that if—
(a) the reference had not been made, but
(b) the appellant had made (and had been entitled to make) an application for an extension of time within which to seek leave to appeal on the ground of the development in the law, the Court would not think it appropriate to grant the application by exercising the power conferred by section 18(3)."

CHAPTER 3

THE MORAL AND CONSTITUTIONAL LIMITS OF THE CRIMINAL LAW

"Liberty consists in the freedom to do everything which injures no one else; hence the existence of the natural rights of each man has no limits except those which assure to the other members of the society the enjoyment of the same rights. These limits can only be determined by law."[1]

"Law can only prohibit such actions as are hurtful to society. Nothing may be prevented which is not forbidden by law, and no one may be forced to do anything not provided by law."[2]

3.1. Constraints on the Substantive Criminal Law

An obvious moral basis can be found for criminalizing serious harms such as theft, fraud, rape, murder, assault, criminal damage, terrorism and so on. A more complex moral analysis is required for ascertaining the fairness of criminalizing borderline wrongdoing such as exhibitionism,[3] offensive speech, fox-hunting,[4] and so on. It is not clear why the crime label has been applied to a range of apparently innocuous activities such as passive begging,[5] feeding the homeless,[6] fornication,[7] possessing sex toys,[8] homosexuality,[9] possessing marijuana for personal use,[10] and attending live strip shows.[11] The majority in some societies

3–001

---

[1] Article IV of the *French Declaration of the Rights of Man and of the Citizen 1789*.

[2] Article V of the *French Declaration of the Rights of Man and of the Citizen 1789*.

[3] See section 5 of the *Public Order Act 1986*; and section 66 of the *Sexual Offences Act 2003*. Due to the wording of the *Sexual Offences Act* it's almost physically impossible for a woman to commit the offence unless she's doing cartwheels down the street. A woman could go topless without being punished, because a man can go topless in public places. Equality means both must be treated equally under the criminal law. See *People v. Santorelli*, 80 N.Y.2d 875 (1992).

[4] *Hunting Act 2004* (U.K.).

[5] It is worth noting the 800-year-old prohibition against begging of any kind is still in force and has been used to crackdown on passive begging. Section 3 of the *Vagrancy Act 1824* is the most recent of a long line of enactments *in pari materia*. See Dennis J. Baker, "A Critical Evaluation of the Historical and Contemporary Justifications for Criminalising Begging," (2009) 73 *J. Crim. L.* 212.

[6] Randal C. Archibold, "Las Vegas Makes It Illegal to Feed Homeless in Parks," (New York: *N. Y. Times*, 28 July 2006).

[7] See for example, *Lawrence v. Texas*, 539 U.S. 558 at 586; 592-594 (2003) *per* Scalia J.

[8] *Williams v. Pryor*, 240 F. 3d 944 at 949 (2001).

[9] *Lawrence v. Texas*, 539 U.S. 558 (2003).

[10] *Malmo-Levine* [2003] S.C.C. 74.

[11] *Barnes v. Glen Theatre, Inc.*, 501 U. S. 560, 574-575 (1991).

may not approve of homosexuality, prostitution, marijuana use or homelessness, but majority *mores* do not tell us why it is fair to criminalize such conduct. Why are those who engage in such activities deserving of criminal censure?

3–002 **Is there a specific constitutional right[12] not to be unfairly criminalized?** No. The British constitution does not expressly state that one has a right not to be unfairly criminalized.

3–003 **So no such right exists?** Not so. It does exist, but it cannot be found in a specific provision. There is no single right that expressly and specifically states: "No person shall be unfairly criminalised." Rather, this right can only be enforced by invoking other rights that achieve this effect. For example, the free speech right has been used to decriminalize begging in the United States.[13]

3–004 **But surely people do not have a right to go unpunished when they harm others?** Correct. No one has a right to "unjustifiably" or "inexcusably" harm another. But everyone has a right not to be criminalized when they do not unjustifiably or inexcusably harm others.[14] The right not to be criminalized is a basic human right that aims to protect individuals from unwarranted state interference of a penal nature. The right is not only a basic moral right,[15] but it is also a fundamental legal right.[16]

3–005 **You mentioned that the freedom of expression (or free speech right as it is called in the U.S.) right has been used to decriminalize passive begging? What other constitutional rights can be used to protect people from unfair criminalization?** A number of specific protections as well as the more general protections found in rights such as the right not to be unfairly deprived of your liberty, or the right not to be subjected to unusual and cruel (disproportionate) punishment, the right to control your private life and so on (see Articles 3, 5 and 8 of the *European Convention*),[17] can be used to ensure that people are not

---

[12] For present purposes, I treat European Conventional rights (see *European Convention for the Protection of Human Rights and Fundamental Freedoms*, 4 November 1950, 213 U.N.T.S. 222, (entered into force generally on 3 September 1953)) as though they are constitutional rights, even though they are not. They are not constitutional rights because they cannot be used to strike down unjust criminal laws. Rather they can only be used to highlight a particular substantive law's incompatibility with a given convention right. Nevertheless they are good as constitutional rights: the British government almost always repeals laws that are found to be incompatible with the European Convention, even though it is not legally required to do so.

[13] See *Benefit v. Cambridge*, 424 Mass. 918 (1997). Cf. *Loper v. New York City Police Dept.*, 802 F. Supp. 1029, 1042 (S.D.N.Y. 1992).

[14] Dennis J. Baker, *The Right Not to be Criminalized: Demarcating Criminal Law's Authority*, (Farnham: Ashgate Publishing, 2011). See also Douglas N. Husak, *Overcriminalisation: The Limits of the Criminal Law*, (Oxford: Oxford University Press, 2008).

[15] Human rights preserve human dignity and well-being and thus allow people to flourish in civilized states. See James Griffin, *On Human Rights*, (Oxford: Oxford University Press, 2008); Richard Kraut, *What is Good and Why: The Ethics of Well-Being*, (Cambridge MA: Harvard University Press, 2007).

[16] Baker, *op. cit. supra*, note 14.

[17] The right is better developed in the U.S. constitutional jurisprudence. In particular, the Fifth and Eighth Amendments of the *Constitution of the United States* 1787 have been read as incorporating a general liberty right. See also Part 1, section 2(b), *Constitution Act 1982* (Canada); and Articles 7, 9,

unfairly criminalized. The core rights that have been codified in various domestic constitutions and international conventions have a similar purpose and scope, even though their exact compass will vary slightly depending on the textual nature of the relevant provision. Various courts around the world use different standards of interpretation, but the differences are more formal than substantive. A careful analysis (that is, an examination that avoids dispensing with an analysis of the prudential and historical factors that typically inform judicial determinations of the rights individuals have in a given jurisdiction) of the right to private life and the unusual and cruel punishment type provisions found in the various constitutions and international conventions demonstrate that these types of rights, however differently worded and however differently interpreted in the past, contain a general right not to be criminalized.

The "evolutive interpretation" method used to determine rights in Europe allows the courts there to acknowledge that concepts can change over time and requires the courts to consider the E.C.H.R. in light of social and economic changes.[18] The "margin of appreciation" doctrine allows courts to take into account that the E.C.H.R. will be interpreted differently in different countries, but it should not permit the Strasbourg Court to endorse interpretations that would result in human rights abuses, such as allowing a person to be criminalized and jailed for engaging in innocuous conduct or allowing a person to be sent to prison for 40 years for shoplifting and so forth. Allowing someone to be jailed for 40 years for shoplifting contravenes our deeply held conventional standards of justice.

Specific rights such as the right to freedom of expression can be distinguished from the general right not to be criminalized. The European Convention does not contain a general right analogous to the one found in Articles IV and V of the *French Declaration of the Rights of Man and of the Citizen 1789*. But a similar result might be achieved by invoking specific rights such as the right to be free to make private decisions concerning personal matters that do not affect others; and the right not to be subjected to disproportionate punishment.[19] An express right not to be criminalized is urgently needed, but until such a right is incorporated into a British Bill of Rights, we will have to make do with the specific rights that are available.

Specific rights such as the freedom of expression right have been used to strike down a wide range of unjust criminal laws in the United States and Canada. When specific rights are involved the criminal law must violate an exercise of that specific right or the courts are unable to step in. For example, passive begging was not decriminalized in the United States[20] and Canada[21] because it

3–006

---

and 12 of the *Canadian Charter of Rights and Freedoms*. And also the corresponding rights in Articles 1, 3, 4, 5, 9, and 12 of *Universal Declaration of Human Rights*, GA Res. 217 A (III), U.N. Doc. A/810 (1948).

[18] See Eva Brems, *Human Rights: Universality and Diversity*, (The Hague: Martinus Nijhoff Publishers, 2001) at 396. Cf. Howard Charles Yourow, *The Margin of Appreciation Doctrine in the Dynamics of European Human Rights Jurisprudence*, (The Hague: Martinus Nijhoff Publishers, 1995) Cf. *Lawrence v. Texas*, 539 U.S. 558 (2003).

[19] Baker, *op. cit. supra*, note 14, Chap. 1.

[20] *Loper v. New York City Police Dept.*, 802 F. Supp. 1029, 1042 (S.D.N.Y. 1992); *Benefit v. Cambridge*, 424 Mass. 918 (1997).

contravened the beggar's general right not to be unfairly criminalized, but because it contravened his specific right to freedom of expression. Nevertheless, freedom of expression was not the real issue in those cases; the real issue was that the beggars were being unfairly criminalized. The effect of the decisions was to strike down the laws that were unfairly criminalizing the beggars.

The right not to be punished disproportionately has a much wider reach. On this point, the Eighth Amendment of the U.S. Constitution jurisprudence is instructive. It provides some ideas as to how Article 3 of *European Convention* could be interpreted to enforce the general right not to be criminalized. The Eighth Amendment is used to strike down crimes that carry disproportionate penal penalties. But how do we know when the punishment is disproportionate? Objective harm is an appropriate measuring stick for determining the proportionality of jail sentences, because jail harms the prisoner. Proportionality requires any jail term to be proportionate with the offender's culpability and the harmfulness of his wrongdoing.[22]

The harm and culpability criteria are the most appropriate criteria for determining the proportionality of criminalization, because criminalization harms the offender. "Even one day in prison would be a cruel and unusual punishment for the 'crime' of having a common cold."[23] Alas, in the United States the proportionate punishment constraint has been interpreted almost out of existence. This was not always the case, however. For instance, in *Solem v. Helm*,[24] the respondent was convicted for uttering a dud cheque for $100. The usual maximum punishment for that crime would have been five years imprisonment and a $5,000 fine. But the respondent was sentenced to life imprisonment without the option of parole under South Dakota's recidivist statute, because he had a number of prior convictions. The Supreme Court held that the "Eighth Amendment's proscription of cruel and unusual punishments prohibits not only barbaric punishments, but also sentences that are disproportionate to the crime committed."[25] *Per contra*, in *Harmelin v. Michigan*,[26] the Supreme Court held that the Eighth Amendment allowed a state to impose a life sentence without the possibility of parole for a drug possession offence.

3–007   The Eighth Amendment cases demonstrate that Western courts are willing to allow gross human rights abuses to go unchecked. What is clear is that Western states often pay no attention to fair labelling and proportionate punishment.[27] Britain only pays lip-service to the idea of proportionate punishment. In *Weeks v. United Kingdom*,[28] a 17-year-old man was given a life sentence for robbing a store with a starter pistol. The robbery merely involved a sum of 35 pence, which was eventually found on the shop floor. The defendant went to a pet shop with a starting pistol loaded with blank cartridges, pointed it at the owner and demanded

---

[21] *Federated Anti-Poverty Groups of British Columbia v. Vancouver (City)* [2002] B.C.S.C. 105.

[22] Baker, *op. cit. supra,* note 14, Chap. 2.

[23] *Robinson v. California*, 360 U.S. 660, 667 (1962).

[24] 463 U.S. 277 (1983).

[25] *Solem v. Helm*, 463 U.S. 277, 284-290 (1983).

[26] 501 U.S. 957 (1991).

[27] See Dennis J. Baker & Lucy X. Zhao, "Responsibility Links, Fair Labelling and Proportionality in China: A Comparative Analysis," (2009) 14(2) *UCLA J. Int'l L. & Foreign Aff.* 274.

[28] (1988) 10 E.H.R.R. 293.

the contents of the till. After committing the robbery he telephoned the police station and confessed and gave himself up. It emerged that he carried out the robbery because he wanted to pay back £3, which he owed his mother. Earlier that day his mother had threatened to evict him. Nevertheless, the court held that the life sentence was not contrary to Article 3 of the *European Convention*. In a line of other cases, the European Commission of Human Rights has erroneously held that the Convention does not contain a "general right to call into question the length of a sentence imposed by a competent court."[29]

The second fairly general right is the personal autonomy type right (right to private life), which derives either from the deprivation of liberty right or from the privacy right; and sometimes from a reading of both depending on the jurisdiction.[30] In this sense proportionality is about considering the seriousness, badness and intolerableness of the unwanted acts/consequences and their implications for society and its individual members. According to this standard it would be unfair to impede a person's freedom to do act *X*, unless act *X* results in (or risks) bad consequences that warrant a criminal law response. (I use the concept of "bad" rather than "harm," because some consequences may be criminalizable even though they are not harmful, such as public exhibitionism. If conduct is not criminalized because of its harmfulness, then it must be criminalized because it produces some other kind of bad consequences such as disgust,[31] if that is sufficiently bad to warrant a criminal law response. After all, we do not criminalize consequences or acts that are "perceived" to be good.)[32]

In *R. v. Malmo-Levine*,[33] Justices LeBel and Deschamps considered the general proportionality of criminalizing a person for possessing marijuana for

---

[29] See Michael Tonry and Richard S. Frase, *Sentencing and Sanctions in Western Countries*, (Oxford: Oxford University Press, 2001), at 363.

[30] In Canada these rights can also be read in conjunction with the disproportionate punishment provision to produce a rather wide personal autonomy protection. For instance, in *R. v. Malmo-Levine* [2003] S.C.C. 74 at para. 169, the Supreme Court of Canada held that the proportionality at issue was wider than mere disproportionality of penalty. It held that: "interaction by an accused with the criminal justice system brings with it a number of consequences, not least among them the possibility of a criminal record. We agree that the proportionality principle of fundamental justice … is not exhausted by its manifestation in s. 12."

[31] Joel Feinberg, *Offence to Others: The Moral Limits of the Criminal Law*, (New York: Oxford University Press, 1985). See *R. v. F* (2010) 174 J.P. 582, where D was engaging in self-abuse in his car in a public place. Section 66 of the *Sexual Offences Act 2003* makes it an offence to appear in public in a state of undress. Public nudity has been criminalized for hundreds of years in England (see *Le Roy v. Sr. Charles Sidley* (1662) 1 Siderfin 168, where D stood nude on a balcony in Covent Garden), but nudity *per se* most likely will not be criminalized 50 years from now.

[32] Nevertheless, lawmakers sometimes criminalize good acts because they mistake them for bad acts. For example, as noted above, in Las Vegas an ordinance makes it an offence to feed homeless people. Surely, running a mobile soup kitchen is a good act, not a bad one? See also Hamish Stewart, "Legality and Morality in H.L.A. Hart's Theory of Criminal Law," (1999) 52 *S.M.U. L. Rev.* 201.

[33] [2003] S.C.C. 74 at para. 280. Their Honours went on to note: "For the state to be able to justify limiting an individual's liberty, the legislation upon which it bases its actions must not be arbitrary. In this case, the legislation is arbitrary. First, it seems doubtful that it is appropriate to classify marijuana consumption as conduct giving rise to a legitimate use of the criminal law in light of the Charter, since, apart from the risks related to the operation of vehicles and the impact on public health care and social assistance systems, the moderate use of marihuana is on the whole harmless. Second, in view of the availability of more tailored methods, the choice of the criminal law for controlling conduct that causes little harm to moderate users or to control high risk groups for whom the effectiveness of deterrence or correction is highly dubious, is out of keeping with Canadian society's standards of

private use under section 7 of the *Canada Charter* (which protects life, liberty and security of the person).[34] The learned judges said:

> "[T]he harm that marihuana consumption for personal use may cause seems rather mild on the evidence we have. In contrast, the harm and the problems connected with the form of criminalization chosen by Parliament seem plain and important.... Jailing people for the offence of simple possession seems consistent with the perception that the law, as it stands, amounts to some sort of legislative overreach to the apprehended problems associated with marihuana consumption... Moreover, besides the availability of jail as a punishment, the enforcement of the law has tarred hundreds of thousands of Canadians with the stigma of a criminal record. The fundamental liberty interest has thus been infringed by the adoption and implementation of a legislative response which is disproportionate to the societal problems at issue and therefore arbitrary, and in breach of s. 7 of the *Charter.*"

3–008   In Canada and Europe[35] the privacy right, the right not to be arbitrarily detained, and the right not to be disproportionately punished, could be read conjunctively as providing a general right to do whatever you like so long as you do not wrong[36] others. Coupled with this, the other specific rights such as the right to freedom of speech and freedom of conscience could be read in sum where necessary to constrain unjust criminalization. If lawmakers want to criminalize conduct then they have to produce empirical evidence to explain not only how it wrongs, harms or disgusts others, but also to explain why criminalization is a proportionate state response. To satisfy the proportionality constraint when criminalizing harmless conduct such as exhibitionism, the courts might point to the need to strike a fair balance between the competing interest groups that use public spaces to justify using penal fines to restrict it to certain beaches and parks. The proportionality constraint means that the legislative responses must be proportionate for dealing with the social problem in question. In the United States the privacy right as delineated in *Griswold v. Connecticut*[37] was not an enumerated right; rather, it was constructed from the privacy interests that are implicit in the First, Third, Fourth, Fifth and Ninth Amendments. In *Roe v. Wade*,[38] the court said that the "right of privacy, whether it be founded in the Fourteenth Amendment's concept of personal liberty and restrictions upon state action, as we feel it is, or, as the District Court determined, in the Ninth Amendment's reservation of rights to the people, is broad enough to encompass a woman's decision whether or not to terminate her pregnancy." In the United

---

justice. Third, the harm caused by prohibiting marihuana is fundamentally disproportionate to the problems that the state seeks to suppress. This harm far outweighs the benefits that the prohibition can bring."

[34] Notably the European Human Rights Convention deals with this type of activity under Article 8 which deals with privacy, but also protects personal autonomy more generally. *Dudgeon v. United Kingdom*, (1981) 4 E.H.R.P. 149.

[35] The Canadian courts have tended to read section 7 of the Charter as containing a personal autonomy right. In Europe Articles 5 and 8 of the European Convention could be read together as providing a wide autonomy right.

[36] I use the concept of "wrong" here, even though it is too wide, because some consequences that might require a criminal law response are not harmful. For an account of wrongs that require a criminal law response, see Baker, *op. cit. supra,* note 14.

[37] 381 U.S. 479, 484 (1965).

[38] 410 U.S. 113, 153 (1973).

States, the privacy constraint has been used to protect personal decisions relating to marriage,[39] child rearing and education,[40] contraception,[41] and so forth.

The U.S. courts have often referred to criteria such as harm when interpreting the fairness of decisions that have overridden the right not to be criminalized in the privacy/personal autonomy context.[42] The privacy right in the U.S. has been given a fairly broad interpretation to allow a person the freedom to make personal choices in many areas. It has been used to decriminalize a range of conduct including homosexuality,[43] private marijuana use,[44] abortions, and so forth. For instance, in *Ravin v. State*[45] a law against private marijuana use was struck down for breaching the petitioner's privacy rights (privacy in this sense refers to personal autonomy more generally, as the only thing that is private about the personal choice to use marijuana is that it does not produce harmful consequences for others—it merely involves a personal lifestyle choice—a choice that does not impact on the lives of others). The court held that the privacy protection is absolute only "when private activity will not endanger or harm the general public."[46] Other courts have noted that the right to privacy derives primarily from "the long-standing importance in our Anglo-American legal tradition of personal autonomy and the right of self-determination."[47]

The majority in *Wisconsin v. Yoder* held that there is no longer an assumption "that today's majority is 'right' and the Amish and others like them are 'wrong.'" A way of life that is odd or even erratic but interferes with no rights or interests of others is not to be condemned because it is different.[48] In *Commonwealth v. Bonadio*[49] a state court invoked the personal autonomy and absence of harm to others justifications to strike down a law criminalizing homosexuals. The court quoting J. S. Mill said:[50]

3–009

> "'[T]he harm principle requires liberty of tastes and pursuits; of framing the plan of our life to suit our own character; of doing as we like, subject to such consequences as may follow:

---

[39] *Loving v. Virginia*, 388 U.S. 1 (1967).

[40] *Prince v. Massachusetts*, 321 U.S. 158 (1944); *Pierce v. Society of Sisters*, 268 U.S. 510 (1925).

[41] *Griswold v. Connecticut*, 381 U.S. 479 (1965); *Eisenstadt v. Baird*, 405 U.S. 438 (1972).

[42] See *Armstrong v. State*, 989 P. 2d 364, 372-74 (1999), (in which it was noted that: "John Stuart Mill recognized this fundamental right of self-determination and personal autonomy as both a limitation on the power of the government and as principle of preeminent deference to the individual. He stated: '[T]he only purpose for which power can be rightfully exercised over any member of a civilized community, against his will, is to prevent harm to others.'" See also *The Matter of Conservatorship of Groves*, 109 S.W. 3d 317, 328 (2003); and *Richards v. State*, 743 S.W. 2d 747, 751 (1987), (in which Levy, J. dissenting, quoted Mill before concluding that: "if we uphold the authority of the state to punish one's failure to use a seat-belt, we are one more step on our way to an Orwellian society in which the State can punish merely for smoking cigarettes, for not brushing one's teeth, or for being foolish."

[43] *Lawrence v. Texas*, 539 U.S. 558 (2003).

[44] *Ravin v. State*, 537 2d 494 (Alaska 1975).

[45] 537 P. 2d 494 (Alaska 1975).

[46] *Ravin v. State*, 537 2d 494 (Alaska 1975). See also *Cruzan v. Harmon*, 760 S.W. 2d 408, 417 (1988).

[47] *Thor v. Superior Court*, 855 P. 2d 375, 380 (1993); *Commonwealth v. Bonadio* 415 A. 2d 47, 96-98 (1980).

[48] 406 U.S. 205, 224 (1972).

[49] 415 A. 2d 47, 96-98 (1980).

[50] 415 A. 2d 47, 50-51(1980).

without impediment from our fellow creatures, so long as what we do does not harm them, even though they should think our conduct foolish, perverse, or wrong. [F]rom this liberty of each individual, follows the liberty, within the same limits of combination among individuals; freedom to unite, for any purpose not involving harm to others.

. . . .

'With respect to regulation of morals, the police power should properly be exercised to protect each individual's right to be free from interference in defining and pursuing his own morality but not to enforce a majority morality on persons whose conduct does not harm others. No harm to the secular interests of the community is involved in atypical sex practice in private between consenting adult partners. This philosophy, as applied to the issue of regulation of sexual morality presently before the court, or employed to delimit the police power generally, properly circumscribes state power over the individual.''[51]

In *Lawrence v. Texas*,[52] the United States Supreme Court interpreted the privacy right as protecting atypical sex practices in private between consenting adult partners. In that case, the majority overruled *Bowers v. Hardwick*[53] and held that: "It is a promise of the Constitution that there is a realm of personal liberty, which the government may not enter."[54] The majority held that the consensual conduct at issue (atypical sexual relations) was covered by that liberty. "[T]he Texas statute furthers no legitimate state interest which can justify its intrusion into the personal and private life of the individual."[55] A governing majority's belief that sexual immorality is unacceptable is not sufficient to override a person's right not to be criminalized. It is not good enough merely to claim something is harmful, it must be demonstrated that it is in fact harmful.

The right not to be criminalized cannot be enforced efficiently until the courts recognize that there is such a right. This right is found in the personal autonomy and proportionate punishment provisions in a number of international human rights documents. It also permeates nearly every other constitutionalized human right. It is a fundamental right and it is time for the courts to take it seriously. Once the courts recognize the right, it will then be necessary to undertake the task of determining when that right should be overridden.

3–010   **Would it not be better to have an express right similar to the one found in the Articles IV and V of the *French Declaration of the Rights of Man and of the Citizen 1789*?**   Yes. It is amazing that we lecture the world on the importance of human rights, but have never taken the step of incorporating an express right not to be unfairly criminalized into a modern Bill of Rights in our own jurisdiction. If such a step were taken, the courts would no doubt invoke the right more often than they currently do. The problem with relying on other rights such as the specific rights that exist is that the courts do not get the bigger picture: that is, that they are effectively enforcing the right not to be criminalized. This lack of vision means that the right's development has been hamstrung!

---

[51]   415 A. 2d 47, 49-50 (1980).

[52]   539 U.S. 558 (2003). While the judges in these cases do not always turn their minds to the distinction between objective and positive morality, they do seem to be engaging in a deliberative process that in many cases has allowed them to reach a conclusion that is reconcilable with fairness and justice.

[53]   478 U.S. 186 (1986).

[54]   *Lawrence v. Texas*, 539 U.S. 558, 578 (2003).

[55]   *Lawrence v. Texas*, 539 U.S. 558, 578 (2003).

When should the right be overridden?   A person's right not to be criminalized   **3–011**
can be overridden when he chooses to (unjustifiably and inexcusably) wrong
others. But, even if the conduct is worthy of the crime label, jail sentences should
not be used to deter the conduct unless it is conduct that is likely to cause "harm
to others."[56] It is one thing to be made to pay a fine for committing an offence,
but another to be sent to prison.

What counts as harm?   At the centre of the harm dartboard there is greater   **3–012**
agreement about what is objectively harmful, because of the primitive nature of
core harms such as those involving physiological pain and physical damage as is
the case with murder, starvation, limb amputation, torture and so on. These harms
impact humans more or less in the same way regardless of their culture or
context. But once we move concentrically away from the primitive-type harms to
more conventionally contingent harms, the case for punishment and criminalization is more difficult to identify.[57]

Does the exhibitionist harm others by cycling naked through the streets of   **3–013**
London?   No. He may cause offence to some sheltered folks, but he does not
cause his victims any economic or physical harm. The harmfulness of many acts
is dependent on convention and socialization. If *X* were to paint a bright yellow
stripe across the Mona Lisa his conduct would be classified as criminal damage,[58]
but unless we consider the underlying social norms it is not possible to
comprehend the wrongness, badness or harmfulness[59] of intentionally painting a
bright yellow stripe on an old painting. (If X were the owner of the Mona Lisa,
people would still object to him destroying it, even though he would only be
destroying his own property). Some might argue that the additional stripe is art in
itself and thus adds to the aesthetics of the original painting, if they have not been
socialized into perceiving it as a cultural artefact. Painting a stripe on it would not
diminish anyone's essential or primitive-type survival resources in the way that
destroying a remote tribe's only source of water and food would. There is
something much more universal about the latter harm, because suffering severe
dehydration and starvation would impact all humans in the same way.

---

[56] Dennis J. Baker, "Constitutionalizing the Harm Principle," (2008) 27 *Crim. Just. Ethics* 3. On the
harm criterion see Joel Feinberg, *Harm to Others: The Moral Limits of the Criminal Law*, (New York:
Oxford University Press, 1984).
[57] For a fuller picture see Dennis J. Baker "The Impossibility of a Critically Objective Criminal
Law," (2011) 56(2) *McGill L. J.* 349.
[58] This would be an offence under the *Criminal Damage Act 1971* (U.K.).
[59] Husak argues that the Harm Principle even belongs to the General Part of the Criminal Law.
Douglas N. Husak, "Limitations on Criminalization," in Stephen Shute and Andrew P. Simester (ed.),
Criminal Law Theory: Doctrines of the General Part, (Oxford: Oxford University Press, 2002) at
13-46.

3–014   **Surely conventional wrongs can cause great distress. If I am socialized to value privacy and my ex-lover uploads my nude photographs onto the Internet, this would cause me major distress. Would it not be fair to give him a short jail sentence even though he has not caused me any physical or economic harm? Surely psychological harm counts.**   If the conduct is merely offensive, jail sentences should not be used as a form of punishment. Disgusting others should only be criminalized in very extreme cases; and *a fortiori* should only be deterred with the threat of a prison sentence in the most extreme cases. But the type of conduct you refer to involves gross psychological distress[60] and thus could warrant a jail term.[61]

3.2.   NON-RETROACTIVITY

3–015   A person should only be made criminally liable for an act if the act was criminal at the time when it was done. It is not a crime to drink champagne in public places in England and Wales, but Parliament could change the law to make it a crime to drink alcoholic beverages in any public place. If Parliament were to change the law with the new law taking effect immediately, it would not be fair to charge those who were drinking in a public park a year ago with the new offence. It would be unjust if the police could sift through old CCTV footage to identify who was drinking in the park in the past and then charge them with the new offence. If it was not an offence to drink in public when the drinking took place, then no crime was committed. Such an offence would infringe the principle of legality—the proposition that there should be no criminal offence except one specified by pre-existing law (*nulla poena sine lege*, or *nullum crimen sine lege*).[62]

Article 7 of the European Convention provides:

> "No one shall be held guilty of any criminal offence on account of any act or omission which did not constitute a criminal offence under national or international law at the time when it was committed. Nor shall a heavier penalty be imposed than the one that was applicable at the time the criminal offence was committed.
> This article shall not prejudice the trial and punishment of any person for any act or omission which, at the time when it was committed, was criminal according the general principles of law recognized by civilized nations."

---

[60] In English law, psychological distress is only recognized as a harm when it causes the victim to suffer a recognized psychiatric illness. See Chap. 9.

[61] Cf. *R. v. Hamilton* [2008] Q.B. 224 (where a man went around filming up the skirts of ladies and was convicted of outraging public decency). Section 67 of the *Sexual Offences Act 2003* makes it an offence to engage in voyeurism.

[62] *R. v. Rimmington* [2006] 1 A.C. 459 at 483; *R. v. Secretary of State for The Home Department* [2004] 1 W.L.R. 2278 at 2289. See generally, Glanville Williams, *Criminal Law: The General Part*, (London: Stevens & Sons, 2nd edn. 1961) at 579-580; Jerome Hall, *General Principles of Criminal Law*, (Indianapolis: Bobbs-Merrill Co., 2nd edn., 1960) at 27-68; Francis A. Allen, "Crisis of Legality in the Criminal Law—Reflections on the Rule of Law," (1991) 42 *Mercer L. Rev.* 811; Paul H. Robinson, "Legality and Discretion in the Distribution of Criminal Sanctions," (1988) 25 *Harv. J. on Legis.* 393.

In *R. v. R*,[63] the House of Lords decided to create a new offence of marital rape by judicial fiat; or at least it abrogated the immunity for husband-rape. Until the decision in *R. v. R*, it was thought that a man could not be convicted of raping his wife. Commenting on *R. v. R*, Professor Glanville Williams said:

> "Dicey told us that in Britain the 'rule of law was supreme'. More than two centuries before Dicey, Hobbes had proclaimed that 'No law, made after a fact done, can make it a crime ... For before the law, there is no transgression of the law'. ... [The decision in *R. v. R*] was high-handed judicial action taken for a praiseworthy purpose, and differences of opinion have been expressed on whether the praiseworthiness redeemed the high-handedness... To abolish the rape exemption would in itself be a praiseworthy extension of human rights, but to abolish it retrospectively is another matter. If Parliament had passed a statute retrospectively abolishing the marital exemption there would be a distinct possibility of its being held to offend against Art. 7 of the *Convention on Human Rights*, in which case the Government would have to set aside all convictions and pay compensation to those convicted and punished... If, as seems likely, Art. 7 (2) does not validate retrospective penal legislation, how can it validate retrospective judicial action having the like effect?"[64]

These comments were made before the enactment of the *Human Rights Act 1998*. **3–016** Nevertheless, the *Human Rights Act 1998* has not changed the position. In *R. v. C*,[65] it was held that it was not an abuse of process for a defendant to be prosecuted for raping his wife in 2002, even though the alleged rape took place in 1970 when marital rape was not recognized as a crime. Apparently, this retrospective application of the new offence of marital rape (an offence that seems to have been created by judicial fiat in 1992),[66] did not breach a defendant's rights under the *European Convention*. In the Court of Appeal, Judge L.J. said:[67]

> "[In 1970, a solicitor would have explained the law of rape to his client] by pointing out to his client that to rape his wife would be barbaric, and that he would not condone it. He would then have told his client that the courts had developed and could be expected to continue to develop exceptions to the supposed rule of irrevocable consent, and that if ever the issue were considered in this court, the supposed immunity of a husband from a successful prosecution for rape of his wife might be recognized for what it was, a legal fiction."

This reasoning is not very convincing. The Court of Appeal suggests that a solicitor in 1970 would have told his client that marital rape is not a crime, but that the courts could make it one at anytime. But if it was not a crime in 1970, how could C commit the offence in 1970? Merely stating that the courts could have recognized the defence as a legal fiction at anytime will not do.[68] If it had not been recognized as a legal fiction in 1970, then it was not a legal fiction in

---

[63] [1992] 1 A.C. 599.

[64] Glanville Williams, "Rape is Rape," (1992) 142 *N.L.J.* 11.

[65] [2004] 1 W.L.R. 2098.

[66] *R. v. R* [1992] 1 A.C. 599.

[67] *R. v. C* [2004] 1 W.L.R. 2098 at 2103.

[68] The rule was not a mere legal fiction, it was accepted by authority not only in England, but throughout the common law world. It is still in force in some states in the United States. See *State v. Bell*, 90 N.M. 134 (1977); *People v. Brown*, 632 P.2d 1025 (1981); *Adams v. Com.*, 219 Ky. 711 (1927). According to Professor LaFave, "as recently as 1985 it could still be said that the exemption existed in about thirty states." See Wayne R. LaFave, *Substantive Criminal Law*, (West Publishing, Vol. II., 2003) at 653. In Australia the immunity was abolished by statute, but as a window-dressing exercise the High Court also held the immunity no longer existed at common law, but the rule was

1970. Coupled with this, the fact that the solicitor would have told his client that it is morally wrong to commit marital rape adds little, unless it is accepted that it was not "clear" that the act was not a criminal act when it was done.[69] Once again, principle has been abandoned because the wrong involved was particularly vile. Rape is a crime that stirs public sentiment. Very few of us have any sympathy for the defendants in the above cases, but we must remember that the cases will not always be concerned with vile behaviour.[70] It would be better to let a single cretin evade justice than to weaken the cardinal rights that we all rely on.

3.3. RES JUDICATA

3–017   This is a book on substantive criminal law, but it is worth making reference to couple of important procedural protections. The subject of multiple charges leads naturally to the subject of successive charges. Suppose that a transgressor is tried, even if he is let off very lightly, he cannot be tried a second time, even though on the second occasion the prosecution would be able to avoid the technicality and have better evidence. The defendant has what is termed, in legal Frenglish, the defence of autrefois acquit.

Similarly, if the defendant is convicted, even if he is let off very lightly, he cannot afterwards be charged on fresh evidence, because he will have the defence of autrefois convict.[71] These inelegant phrases have never been superseded, though they might well be called defence of "previous acquittal" and "previous conviction;" and *res judicata* (matter that has been decided) is a general name for both.

In 2005, sections 75 to 79 of the *Criminal Justice Act 2003* came into force. These provisions allow an acquittal to be quashed and the defendant to be retried for certain offences, but only if there is new and compelling evidence in relation to the offence and it is in the interests of justice to order a retrial.[72]

---

never applied retrospectively in that country. See *R. v. L* (1991) 174 C.L.R 379. But as Williams points out in the passage quoted in the text above, it is one thing to abrogate a law, it is another to apply the changed law retrospectively!

[69] Although, it might be said that he was skating on thin ice. The gist of the thin ice principle is "that citizens who know that their conduct is on the borderline of illegality take the risk that their behaviour will be held to be criminal." Andrew Ashworth, *Principles of Criminal Law*, (Oxford: Oxford University Press, 2009) at 63 citing *Knuller (Publishing, Printing and Promotions) Ltd. v. D.P.P.* [1973] A.C. 435 at 463 where Lord Morris said: "In many cases there can be no certainty as to what the decision will be. But none of this is a reflection upon the law. Nor do I know of any procedure under which someone could be told with precision just how far he may go before he may incur some civil or some criminal liability. Those who skate on thin ice can hardly expect to find a sign which will denote the precise spot where they may fall in."

[70] Cf. *Shaw v. D.P.P.* [1962] A.C. 220.

[71] Pronounced "ohterfoyz," with "acquit" and "convict" pronounced in English.

[72] *R. v. Dunlop* [2007] 1 W.L.R. 1657.

Suppose a person is acquitted of murder and afterwards writes an article for a newspaper describing how he committed it. Would he be safe from being charged again? He might be charged again if the court considers his confession to be "new and compelling evidence."[73] Furthermore, if he had given evidence falsely he could be prosecuted for perjury.

3–018

Does the new exception only apply to murder? No. It applies to a range of offences.[74]

3–019

If the offence is not one of those listed in Schedule 5 of the *Criminal Justice Act 2003*, autrefois acquit or autrefois convict can be invoked. However, the criminal law knows no doctrine of "issue estoppel." After an acquittal, the Crown cannot charge the defendant with the same offence, but it is not estopped (prevented) from saying *that* he was guilty of that offence if it brings proceedings for a *different* offence. Neither the Crown nor the defendant in the later proceedings is estopped from disputing the decision in the earlier proceedings on a particular issue. This is an example of the court making a law that is satisfactory on the facts before the court, but may be unsatisfactory in others. Where the allegation is one of perjury in the earlier proceedings, as was the case in *D.P.P. v. Humphrys*,[75] the rule laid down in that case is common sense, but in other situations the absence of a doctrine of issue estoppel in our law may work hardship, and also may produce inconsistent decisions as to bring the law into some measure of disrepute. It is hard on the defendant if, after he has at great cost in money and anxiety secured a favourable verdict from a jury on a particular issue, he must fight the battle over again when he is charged with a technically different offence arising out of the same facts. However, it is now recognized that the court has a discretion to stay the second proceedings as being vexatious or oppressive, and the use of this power can bypass the decision in *D.P.P. v. Humphrys*[76] and achieve the same effect as if there was an estoppel.[77]

Suppose a person is charged with driving a motorcycle with excess alcohol in his blood and also with riding a cycle (that is to say, the same motorcycle) without due care and attention, the two charges relating to the same incident. He elects to go to trial on the first charge, and is acquitted by the jury on his evidence that he was not in fact driving the vehicle. The police now restore to the list the summons for the offence of careless driving. If the case is heard, the police will be allowed to call evidence to the effect that the defendant was riding the cycle, notwithstanding his acquittal by the jury on this issue.[78] On one occasion the defendant in such circumstances obtained a High Court order of prohibition directed to the justices, on the ground that it would be oppressive and unfair to

---

[73] On similar facts in *R. v. Dunlop* [2007] 1 W.L.R. 1657 the acquittal was quashed and a new trial ordered.

[74] See the list of qualifying offences in Schedule 5 of the *Criminal Justice Act 2003*.

[75] [1977] A.C. 1.

[76] [1977] A.C. 1.

[77] *Dewhurst v. Foster* [1982] Crim. L.R. 582.

[78] *R. v. Z* [2000] 2 A.C. 483.

restore the charge to the list. However, the High Court said that it made the order only because there was another outstanding charge against the defendant in the Crown Court.[79]

It is not at all clear, therefore, that the discretion of the High Court to stay proceedings will be used in such a way as to prevent the criminal process being used vexatiously.[80] Although the House of Lords has now closed the door on issue estoppel in our law, there is much to be said for such a doctrine in circumstances like these.

3–020 **Suppose a prosecution is started but the authorities make some awful technical mistake. Can they abandon the proceeding half way and start again properly?** Yes. The defence of *res judicata* arises only when there has been a conviction or acquittal. Some writers use the expression "double jeopardy"[81] as another name for the *res judicata* doctrine, but it is misleading for English law. The defence is not given to a person merely because he was previously at risk of being convicted. The earlier proceedings must have gone to their conclusion.[82]

3.4. THE RIGHT TO A FAIR TRIAL

3–021 One of the most important procedural requirements is that the defendant be given a fair trial. This right is enshrined in Article 6 of the *European Convention for the Protection of Human Rights and Fundamental Freedoms*:[83]

> "In the determination of his civil rights and obligations or of any criminal charge against him, everyone is entitled to a fair and public hearing within a reasonable time by an independent and impartial tribunal established by law. Judgement shall be pronounced publicly by the press and public may be excluded from all or part of the trial in the interest of morals, public order or national security in a democratic society, where the interests of juveniles or the protection of the private life of the parties so require, or the extent strictly necessary in the opinion of the court in special circumstances where publicity would prejudice the interests of justice.
>
> Everyone charged with a criminal offence shall be presumed innocent until proved guilty according to law.
>
> Everyone charged with a criminal offence has the following minimum rights:
>
> (a)   to be informed promptly, in a language which he understands and in detail, of the nature and cause of the accusation against him;
>
> (b)   to have adequate time and the facilities for the preparation of his defence;
>
> (c)   to defend himself in person or through legal assistance of his own choosing or, if he has not sufficient means to pay for legal assistance, to be given it free when the interests of justice so require;
>
> (d)   to examine or have examined witnesses against him and to obtain the attendance and examination of witnesses on his behalf under the same conditions as witnesses against him;
>
> (e)   to have the free assistance of an interpreter if he cannot understand or speak the language used in court."

---

[79] *R. v. Cwmbran JJ., Ex parte Pope* (1979) unreported; see 143 J.P.N. 415, 568.

[80] Cf. the decision of the High Court of Australia in *R. v. Carroll* (2002) 194 A.L.R. 1.

[81] *Saeed v. Greater London Council* [1985] I.C.R. 637.

[82] *D.P.P. v. Nasrulla* [1967] 2 A.C. 238.

[83] See for example, *R. (on the application of Williamson) v. Secretary of State for Education and Employment* [2005] 2 A.C. 246.

Space prevents us from examining the compass of this right. There is an entire body of law on evidence[84] and procedure[85] that ensure that certain procedures are followed during the trial. Most of the challenges under Article 6 relate to the presumption of innocence, because Parliament has on numerous occasions attempted to reverse the onus of proof.[86] There are also rules that regulate police practices with respect to interviewing suspects; and also with respect to collecting evidence and so on.

---

[84] See Ian Dennis, *The Law of Evidence*, (London: Sweet & Maxwell, 2010).
[85] See Archbold, *Criminal Pleading: Evidence & Practice*, (London: Sweet & Maxell, 2012).
[86] 2.1.

CHAPTER 4

INTENTION

"Desire and force between them are responsible for all our actions; desire causes our voluntary acts, force our involuntary."

Blaise Pascal, *Pensées*[1]

4.1. ACTUS REUS AND MENS REA

The mere commission of a criminal act (or bringing about the state of affairs that the law provides against) is not enough to constitute a crime, at any rate in the case of the more serious crimes. These generally require, in addition, some element of wrongful intent or other fault. Increasing insistence upon this fault element was the mark of advancing civilization. In early law the distinction between what we now call crimes and civil wrongs was blurred, and liability in both was very strict.[2] Little or no mental element was requisite: the law hardly distinguished between intentional and unintentional acts. In the animistic period of legal thinking "punishment" was inflicted even upon animals and inanimate objects.[3]

4–001

The law followed a development that can still be seen among our own young. Small children think of wrongness as any disobedience to rules, irrespective of intention. Later they learn the relevance of wrongful intent,[4] and defend themselves by saying "I didn't mean to do it." Similarly, judges came to accept

---

[1] Translated into English by Joseph Walker, (London: Printed for Jacob Tonson *et al*, 1688).

[2] Francis Bowes Sayre, "Mens Rea," (1932) 45(6) *Harv. L. Rev.* 974 at 977. It was once normal for people to be prosecuted for any harm caused by their "slaves, animals, other members of their household, and even by inanimate things which belonged to" them. See Albert Levitt, "The Origin of the Doctrine of Mens Rea," (1923) 17 *Ill. L. Rev.* 117 at 120; Frederick Pollock and Frederick William Maitland, *The History of English Law Before the Time of Edward I*, (Cambridge: Cambridge University Press, Vol. II, 1923) at 470-480. See also Paul H. Robinson, "A Brief History of Distinctions in Criminal Culpability," (1980) 31 *Hastings L.J.* 815; Stephen J. Morse, "Inevitable Mens Rea," (2004) 27 *Harv. J.L. & Pub. Pol'y* 51.

[3] Payson Evans, *The Criminal Prosecution and Capital Punishment of Animals*, (London: Faber and Faber, 1987) at 184.

[4] Through the legal mechanism of a "bill of attainder," the legislature could declare a person or group of persons guilty of some serious crime without a trial. The bill of attainder was used to strip people of their property and to sentence them to death without the benefit of a trial. See Michael P. Lehmann, "The Bill of Attainder Doctrine: A Survey of the Decisional Law," (1978) 5 *Hastings Const. L. Q.* 767-1012 (1978). In ancient China family members were often held collectively responsible for the crimes of their relatives. See Dennis J. Baker & Lucy X. Zhao, "Responsibility Links, Fair Labelling and Proportionality in China: A Comparative Analysis," (2009) 14(2) *UCLA J. Int'l L. & Foreign Aff.* 274.

the maxim *Actus non facit reum nisi mens sit rea*[5] as a general principle (though one subject to exceptions) governing serious crimes. For example, assault involves an intentional or reckless interference with another. The requirement of a wrongful mental state is found not only in most common law crimes but also in nearly all statutory crimes if they are of any seriousness.[6] Thus criminal damage, a statutory crime, requires intention or recklessness. (Certain difficulties in the notion of recklessness will be discussed later).

If a penal statute does not include a mental element expressly, the courts will usually, sporadically and without much discernable principle, imply the requirement, on the assumption that Parliament intended the offence to be read in light of a general *mens rea* requirement.[7] The assumption ought to be made more regularly than it is. The operation of the criminal law in respect of offences traditionally regarded as serious ordinarily involves so drastic an interference with the liberty of the subject that it is not generally appropriate to those who are not deliberate offenders.[8]

4–002 **Do you mean that Oedipus did not commit incest, merely because he did not know Jocasta was his mother? What he knew made no difference to what he did. Surely he committed incest in fact.** The union was incestuous (it was subject to the genetic risks attaching to incest), but Oedipus did not commit incest morally or (under English law) legally. The crime of incest,[9] like nearly all serious crimes, has a mental component. If a driver accidentally kills a pedestrian, would you say that he commits murder "in fact"? He commits an act that would be murder if he had the necessary intent, which is however lacking. In lawyer's language, Oedipus and the driver commit the *actus reus* of the crime, without committing the crime.[10] This bit of legal jargon comes from the Latin maxim quoted above, which also gives us the corresponding term *mens rea*.

4–003 **I have a brilliant idea. Why not omit fault from the definition of crimes, and leave the judge to mitigate or remit punishment where fault is absent?** The idea is not so brilliant, though you are not the first to think it is. The scheme

---

[5] "An act does not make a man a criminal unless the mind be guilty": it may be anglicized in pronunciation as "actus non fasit reeum nysy mens sit reeah" (though nisi should properly be "nissy"). The brocade is of canonical origin; it is first found in the *Leges Henrici*, but goes back in one form to St. Augustine. It was not true for the run of crimes in Henry I's day. See L. J Downer, *Leges Henrici Primi* (Oxford: Clarendon Press, 1972).

[6] However, a "strict liability" "constituent" has crept into many crimes that are triable in the Crown Court. See Andrew Ashworth and Meredith Blake, "The Presumption of Innocence in English Criminal Law," [1996] Crim. L.R. 306. Furthermore, in *R. v. G* [2006] 1 W.L.R. 2052 it was held that strict liability for statutory rape did not contravene Art. 6(2) of the *European Convention for the Protection of Human Rights and Fundamental Freedoms*. See also *R. v. Deyemi* [2008] 1 Cr. App. R. 25.

[7] *Crown Prosecution Service v. M.* [2009] EWCA Crim. 2615.

[8] *B. (A Minor) v. D.P.P.* [2000] 2 A.C. 428.

[9] Section 65 of the *Sexual Offences Act 2003*.

[10] The criminal law does not accept the notion of what may be called *de facto* crime (crime in fact though not in law) for penal purposes, except for a limited purpose in relation to excuses. However, a non-penal statute referring, say, to incest may for some purposes be construed to mean incestuous acts objectively regarded, rather than the commission of crime. Cf. *Secretary of State for the Home Dept., Ex p. Khan* [1977] 1 W.L.R. 1466.

would remove the question of fault from the consideration of the jury, thus simplifying their task. But would you, if you have unluckily killed a pedestrian by pure accident when driving, appreciate being convicted of (or declared to have committed) unlawful killing? Would you be wholly comforted by the fact that the judge subsequently decides to remit punishment? Conviction without fault—that is, strict liability—gives no guidance to the police and others as to when they may properly prosecute, and imposes no limits upon the judge and magistrates as to whom they may punish. Also, our trial processes are not well suited to make full enquiry into matters of mitigation.[11]

I still do not know precisely what *mens rea* means. In Latin it means guilty   **4–004**
mind, but in legal use it denotes the mental state (subjective element) required for the particular crime in question. Or it can refer to the mental states commonly required for serious crimes (and a number of lesser offences). *Actus reus* denotes the external situation forbidden by law—the external elements of the offence.

Normally, the required mental element is either:

- an intention to do the forbidden act, or otherwise to bring about the external elements of the offence (whether you know of the legal prohibition or not), or
- (in most crimes) *recklessness* as to such elements.

Intention includes knowledge.

By "external elements" do you mean the parts of the offence that are not in   **4–005**
the mind?   Those that are not in the defendant's mind. Rape, for example, is (1) sexual penetration by a man of woman without her consent, (2) the man knowing that she does not consent or being negligent whether she consents or not. The elements that I have put (1) are the external elements, and they include lack of consent by the woman. The external elements are all the elements of the offence other than the *defendant's* mental element. They generally include some conduct by the defendant, and sometimes require a specified result to follow from his conduct.

You don't approve of my good ideas, but why not say that *mens rea* means   **4–006**
wickedness or moral guilt?   My dear imaginary interlocutor, do not be offended if I put down your ideas. After all, it is I who have put into your mouth some of the not-so-good ideas that have occurred to brilliant minds in the past! The answer to your present suggestion is that *mens rea* is merely convenient shorthand for the mental elements that are legally required for the crime. To say that a person did the *actus reus* with *mens rea* does not mean that he acted immorally. One who breaks the law with a good motive, or for conscientious

---

[11] See Sanford H. Kadish, "The Decline of Innocence," (1968) 26 *Cambridge L.J.* 273; Richard A. Wasserstrom, "H. L. A. Hart and the Doctrines of Mens Rea and Criminal Responsibility," (1968) 35 *U. Chi. L. Rev.* 92.

reasons, or from religious belief, still commits a crime. So also (in many cases) does a person who breaks the law in justifiable ignorance of its existence, or who misunderstands it.

R. v. Heron[12] may stand as an example. By statute, "every person who falsely makes or counterfeits any coin resembling any current coin" commits an offence. (The particular statute is now replaced by another statute in slightly different words.[13]) Heron[14] made coins resembling half-sovereigns, and when prosecuted submitted, through his counsel, that the Crown had to prove a dishonest intention—an intent to pass the counterfeit coins off as genuine. The House of Lords upheld the trial judge in holding that such proof was not required. Parliament wished to prevent counterfeit coins being made, because of the obvious danger that they might get into circulation. The only intent necessary was what Lord Simon called "basic intent" of doing the act, without regard to its purpose.

Their Lordships recognized that some crimes require more than a "basic" intent; they are crimes of "specific" (or, better, "ulterior") intent. The offence specifically requires some intent beyond the basic intent, or else it impliedly requires such an ulterior intent. (It is because the further requirement may be implied that the word "ulterior" is better than "specific".) A crime of basic intent, in contrast, merely requires that the physical act be done knowingly or (sometimes) recklessly.

4–007 An example of an ulterior intent expressly (specifically) required is the offence of delivering to another anything which is, and which the deliverer knows (the deliveree) shall pass to tender it as genuine.[15] Here the offender must have intentionally delivered the coin or note (basic intent) and must have had the further intent specified in the subsection as to what was to happen afterwards. The requirement of ulterior intent may also be indicated by the words "with intent to" or "dishonestly" or "fraudulent" in the definition of the offence.[16]

The requirement of an ulterior intent may be implied if the court thinks that that was the intention of the legislature. The section under which Heron was charged included the word "falsely," and this might in a different context have implied a requirement of dishonest intent—an intent to defraud.[17] The books contain many examples of the courts implying such a requirement of intent to

---

[12] [1982] 1 W.L.R. 451.

[13] Section 14(2) of the *Forgery and Counterfeiting Act 1981*. Lord Scarman said in *R. v. Heron* (at 458) that the decision had no bearing on this new provision, but the view may nevertheless be confidently held that the law is the same.

[14] In legal arguments and judgments the practice is to refer to the defendant by that title, or as the accused, and not by his proper name unless it is necessary to distinguish between joint defendants. In an appeal he is referred to as the appellant (accent on second syllable), except where the prosecution have been able to appeal in which case the defendant will become the respondent. But in my encapsulations of cases I customarily use proper names in the hope that repetition will assist the reader to remember the name of the case. Remembering the names of cases is not of great value in itself, but it is of some small utility in discussion.

[15] Section 15(1)(b) of the *Forgery and Counterfeiting Act 1981*.

[16] *Attorney-General's Reference (No. 1 of 1981)* [1982] 2 W.L.R. 875.

[17] See *Welham v. D.P.P.* [1961] A.C. 103; *Scott v. Commissioner of Police of the Metropolis* [1975] A.C. 819. Cf. *R. v. Terry* [1984] A.C. 374; *R. v. Macrae* [1994] Crim. L.R. 363; *Kensington International Ltd. v. Congo* [2008] 1 W.L.R. 1144.

defraud, or of an absence of a claim of right, in statutory offences.[18] Section 18 of the *Offences against the Person Act 1861* provides a further example. Under that section D would not be liable for intentionally wounding another unless his ulterior intent was to cause grievous bodily harm. An ear piercer would not be caught by section 18, even though he intentionally wounds his customer, because he pierces his customer's ear to achieve the ulterior end of providing a service for reward. He does not intentionally wound his customer with the ulterior aim of causing grievous bodily harm.

Part of the discussion of the mental element in crime concerns the meaning of the relevant terms. What precisely is to be understood by the words intention, recklessness and knowledge? We need to have reasonably precise definitions, not too far removed from the ordinary meanings of these words, so that the legislature can use them in defining offences and so that a trial judge can explain them confidently to a jury.

The other part concerns the issue of policy. How far is it proper to make a mental element an essential ingredient of an offence? Ought a particular offence require intention, or should it be capable of being committed by recklessness, or just negligence, or even strict liability, with virtually no element of fault? Primarily these questions are for the legislature to answer when it creates the offence.[19] But some offences rest on the common law, and even statutes are often silent or ambiguous on the mental element. Here the views of the judges on the social policy are important. **4–008**

Although the mental elements are basically simple, the courts have developed them in considerable confusion, partly because they feel a continual need to expand criminal liability on social or moral grounds. The easiest way to do this is to stretch the meaning of words used to define the liability. As a result of this, doubts still remain about the legal meaning of the *mens rea* words. It is lamentable that, after more than a thousand years of continuous legal development, English law should still lack clear and consistent definitions of words expressing basic concepts.

Doing the best we can to produce an intelligible scheme; we may say that legal fault[20] can be classified into mental elements (awareness, *mens rea*) and negligence. Negligence is legal fault although it is not (or is not necessarily) a mental element. The mental elements can be subdivided into intention and recklessness.[21]

This is a classification of positive mental states; but exceptionally a crime may require the *absence* of a particular kind of intention, knowledge or belief. This is **4–009**

---

[18] See *R. v. Allday* (1837) 8 Car. & P. 136; *R. v. Kemp* [1964] 2 Q.B. 341; *Moore v. Branton* [1974] Crim. L.R. 439. Cf. *Barrass v. Reeve* [1981] 1 W.L.R. 408; *R. v. Sood* [1998] 2 Cr. App. R. 355. See also Glanville Williams, *Criminal Law: The General Part*, (London: Stevens & Sons, 2nd edn. 1961) at 219 and 305-341. However, offences of forgery and such like do not require selfishness: a person may forge a will from motives of altruism. *R. v. Draper* [1962] Crim. L.R. 107.

[19] Subject of course to the constitutional constraints that apply to substantive criminal laws.

[20] "Fault" is a convenient generic term for *mens rea* and negligence, and it must be understood in this technical meaning. A person may break the law laudably or excusably and still be at fault in this sense.

[21] In *R. v. G* [2004] 1 A.C. 1034 the House of Lords overruled *Commissioner of Police of the Metropolis v. Caldwell* [1982] A.C. 341, so negligence applies in very few serious offences. Cf. *R. v. Adomako* [1994] Q.B. 302; *R. v. Morgan* [2007] EWCA Crim. 3313.

so, for example, with crimes of dishonesty, like theft and fraud. The crimes require an absence of honest intent. A person who has intentionally taken money from another may defend himself against a charge of theft by saying that he took it in order to recoup a debt owed to him. His intention to obtain payment of the debt can be regarded as an honest intention which removes the criminality of his intentional taking of the money.

The mental states may be required by implication. For example, as we have seen, statutes creating an offence of false statement are sometimes held to impliedly require an intent to deceive or defraud, even though there are no words to that effect; but on other occasions (as in *R. v. Heron*) it is held that the offence is committed merely by knowingly doing something that in fact violates the words of the statute. Sometimes, as we shall see in the Chapter on strict liability, offences of false statement are held to be matters of strict liability. It is hard to see a consistent pattern.

4.2. THE BASIC MEANING OF INTENTION

4–010   The general legal opinion is that "intention" cannot be satisfactorily defined and does not need a definition, since everyone knows what it means. This is largely true. Trouble has been caused in the past because when judges have provided the jury with definitions or tests of intention, they have used wide language going beyond the ordinary meaning of the word. The present practice is to leave the word without explanation, which in every case except one (to be discussed below) is perfectly acceptable. As a philosophical matter, however, intention is readily definable. With the one exception already mentioned, a consequence is said to be intended when the actor desires that it shall follow from his conduct.

I have many desires. Some I recognize to be visionary; some I lack the energy to implement. But if I decide to try to achieve my desire and start to act to that end, the desire becomes the intention with which I act.

The end aimed at may be a desire only in the sense that it is the lesser of two evils. When I am sitting in the dentist's chair, the last thing I "really" want to do is to open my mouth to have my tooth filled, yet I "really" want to do so, because I wish to avoid a toothache in the future. The desire need not be an end in itself (certainly having a tooth filled is not that) but may be a medial desire—a step on the way to something else (freedom from future toothache). The desire may be conceived on the instant, not premeditated. It need not be formulated in "interior language." Judges sometimes reject a definition of intention in terms of desire, but one reason may be that they overlook these explanations of the meaning of "desire." It is true, however, that in one respect the definition in terms of desire is too narrow: see 4.3. The idea of intention is expressed in law not only by the words "intention" or "with intent to" but also by other words, such as "with the purpose of" or "wilfully." (But the latter word often includes recklessness).

4–011   **Isn't the desire of a consequence the motive for acting, rather than intention?**   It can be regarded as either. In ordinary speech, "intention" and "motive" are often convertible terms. For the lawyer, the word "motive" generally refers to some further intent which forms no part of the legal rule.

If we say a man shot and killed his aunt with the motive of benefiting under her will, the immediate intent, which makes the act murder, is the intention or desire to kill, while the further intent or motive, which forms part of the definition of the crime of murder, is the intention or desire to benefit under the will. Other motives are the desire to obtain the satisfaction of revenge, or to get rid of a rival, or to promote a political object. (Such motives may also be expressed in abstract terms: "he killed her from a motive of greed/revenge/jealousy.") Motive in this sense is irrelevant to responsibility (guilt or innocence), though it may be relevant to proof, or to the quantum of punishment. The prosecution may prove a motive for the crime if it helps them to establish their case, as a matter of circumstantial evidence; but they are not legally bound to prove motive, because "motiveless" crime is still crime. Conversely, the defendant may adduce evidence of his good motive in order to reduce his punishment, perhaps to vanishing-point.

Exceptionally, the term "motive" is used in a sense of responsibility in the crime of libel.[22] Also, crimes of ulterior intent require two intents, one lying behind the other, and the second may be called motive. The crime of burglary is committed where a person enters a building or part of a building by way of trespass with intent to commit one of certain crimes therein. There is an intentional entry, with the ulterior intent of committing a crime in the house such as to steal or inflict on any person therein grievous bodily harm; this ulterior intent is the motive of the entry, and is sometimes referred to as such, yet here it forms part of the legal definition.

It is sometimes hard to determine from legislation what is to be regarded as an unlawful intention and what merely as irrelevant motive. In *Chandler v. D.P.P.*[23] a prosecution was brought against several persons who had organized a ban-the-bomb demonstration at the Royal Air Force station with the object of grounding aircraft. They were convicted of conspiring to commit a breach of section 1 of the *Official Secrets Act 1911*, namely, to enter the airfield "'for a purpose'" prejudicial to the safety or interest of the State. The trial judge had directed the jury to convict if they were satisfied that the defendants' immediate purpose was the obstruction of aircraft, and the conviction was upheld by the House of Lords. Their Lordships rejected the argument that the defendants' object was to get rid of nuclear weapons and thereby, in their view, to promote the safety and interests of the State. **4–012**

The various Lords gave somewhat discordant reasons, but perhaps the clearest way of expressing the decision would be to say that the defendants had two purposes: an immediate one, which in itself was illegal, and an ultimate one, which, although thoroughly well-intentioned, did not justify or excuse the illegality of the immediate purpose. Similarly, in *R. v. Jones*[24] the defendants were charged for criminally damaging a military airbase. "By way of defence they asserted that the United Kingdom's actions in preparing for, declaring and waging war in Iraq were unlawful acts [in international law] which they were justified in attempting to prevent by the use of reasonable force under section 3 of

---

[22] Cf. *R. v. Lemon* [1979] A.C. 617.

[23] [1964] A.C. 763.

[24] [2007] 1 A.C. 136.

the *Criminal Law Act 1967*." On this point, Lord Hoffman said,[25] "[b]ut if they are allowed to use force against military installations simply to give effect to their own honestly held view of the legality of what the armed forces of the Crown are doing, the *Statute of Treason* would become a dead letter."

4–013 **Why not allow good "motivations" (justificatory reasons for acting) to be used as defences?** Parliament does, but it narrowly defines the motives (justifications) that count so as to prevent abuse. A motive only counts if it is recognized as a legal justification for committing what is *prima facie* a criminal act. For instance, self-defence's *raison d'être* as a legal defence is that Parliament recognizes that it provides a legitimate "justification" for harming others. If D kills or injuries another in self-defence he acts to preserve his own physical integrity and any resulting harm is inflicted to achieve that end.[26] If a person kills because he was motivated by self-defence, then it is right to allow him to invoke the defence of self-defence.[27] *Per contra*, if a doctor decides to overdose his patient to kill him because the patient only has weeks to live and is in immense pain, he has no defence since Parliament has not recognized mercy killing as a defence. Since "mercy" is not recognized as lawful justification for killing, it is irrelevant that the doctor acted with mercy in mind. It is for Parliament to decide whether to enact a defence to cover doctors who aim to assist a consenting patient to end his life in such circumstances.

On rare occasions courts have recognized a good justification as a defence without referring to any legally recognized defence. Some judges have simply declared that a defendant lacked *mens rea* on the basis that they agree with the defendant's justifications or motivations for acting criminally.[28] Courts should always try to fit the conduct within one of the recognized justificatory defences, since a system of judge-made defences would be too unpredictable.[29] The potential unpredictability of such a system of defences is exemplified by some of

---

[25] *R. v. Jones* [2007] 1 A.C. 136 at 177 *per* Lord Hoffman.

[26] It is intended, as it is a necessary *means* for achieving the *end* of self-defence.

[27] Provided certain conditions are met see Chapter 21. For a discussion of the distinction between justificatory and excusatory defences, see George P. Fletcher, "Domination in the Theory of Justification and Excuse" (1996) 57 *U. Pitt. L. Rev.* 553; Kent Greenawalt, "The Perplexing Borders of Justification and Excuse," (1984) 84 *Colum. L. Rev.* 1897.

[28] See *R. v. Steane* [1947] K.B. 997, where the Court of Appeal basically held (although not explicitly) that the defendant's motivation to save his family was a defence which justified his intentional wrongdoing and thus negated his *mens rea*. But this finding is wrong in law, since his justification or motivation was underwritten by a legal defence. He intended to commit the crime; his *mens rea* was not negated, so the court should have invoked the defence of duress. See also *The King v. Ahlers* [1915] 1 K.B. 616. Some commentators argue that judges should consider motive (the morality of the reasons for committing the bad act more generally). See Douglas N. Husak, "Motive and Criminal Liability," (1989) 8 *Crim. Just. Ethics* 3; Alan Norrie, "Simulacra of Morality? Beyond the Ideal/Actual Antinomies of Criminal Justice," in R. A. Duff (ed.) *Philosophy and the Criminal Law*, (Cambridge: Cambridge University Press, 1998) at 101 *et seq.*; Martin R. Gardner, "The Mens Rea Enigma: Observations on the Role of Motive in the Criminal Law Past and Present," (1993) 1993 *Utah L. Rev.* 635.

[29] Whitley R. P. Kaufman, "Motive, Intention, and Morality in the Criminal Law," (2003) 28 *Crim. Just. Rev.* 317; Jeremy Horder, "On the Irrelevance of Motive in the Criminal Law," in Jeremy Horder (ed), *Oxford Essays in Jurisprudence*, (Oxford: Oxford University Press, 4th Series 2000). See also Nicola Lacey, "A Clear Concept of Intention: Elusive or Illusory?" (1993) 56 *Mod. L. Rev.* 621.

the medical cases.[30] In *Gillick v. West Norfolk and Wisbech AHA*[31] the House of Lords held that when a doctor commits a criminal offence for some good reason such as to further the "the physical, mental and emotional health of his patient," that "good reason" would be sufficient to exculpate him. Consequently, a doctor who gave a child contraceptive drugs, knowing that it would facilitate the child's endeavour to have sexual relations, was able to raise his good "motivation" to exculpate himself. Would the Lords have reached the same conclusion if the child had been 14 and the doctor knew she was having an affair with a 60-year-old? (Such a child might need prophylactics to avoid contracting H.I.V. rather than to avoid pregnancy). In other cases where doctors have arguably acted in the best interests of their patients, the courts have not been willing to recognize the "the best interests of the patient" motive as a defence.[32] The courts have also refused to accept the "motivation" of law enforcement as a worthy defence for officers who break the criminal law to entrap criminals.[33]

It is submitted that the courts should not create new defences by considering every possible good justification a given defendant might have had for offending. Instead, the courts should try to bring worthy conduct within one of the existing defences. In *Re A (Children) (Conjoined Twins: Surgical Separation)*,[34] conjoined twin girls were joined at the pelvis, with both having their own brains, hearts, lungs and other vital organs and own limbs. The medical evidence demonstrated that the stronger twin sustained the life of the weaker twin by circulating oxygenated blood through a common artery. The medical evidence also showed that the weaker twin's heart and lungs were too deficient to oxygenate and pump blood through her own body.

If the twins had not been separated the stronger twin's heart would have eventually failed and both twins would have died within a few months. The doctors argued that separating the twins would allow the stronger twin to survive and ultimately live a worthwhile life, but acknowledged that the weaker twin would die within minutes of the separation. The court upheld the defence of necessity and granted the doctors permission to operate. The stronger twin survived and has since lived a normal life. The doctors were exempted from any criminal liability. This is the right decision, because if the surgeons had not operated the result would have been far worse. The surgeons did not want to kill the weaker twin; her death was merely the inevitable side-effect of saving the stronger twin. As far as penal desert is concerned the evidence demonstrated that the surgeons acted for the good motive of saving the stronger twin and merely

---

[30] If a special defence is required for medics who are motivated to act in the best medical interests of their patients, then it should be done by Parliament. Cf. Andrew Ashworth, "Criminal Liability in a Medical Context: the Treatment of Good Intentions," in A.P. Simester and A.T.H. Smith (ed.) *Harm and Culpability*, (Oxford: Clarendon Press, 1996) at 173 *et seq.*

[31] [1986] A.C. 112.

[32] *R. v. Cox* (1992) 12 B.M.L.R. 38. Cf. *R. v. Adams* [1957] Crim. L.R. 365.

[33] *Yip Chiu-Cheung v. The Queen* [1995] 1 A.C. 111; *R. v. Smith* [1960] 2 W.L.R. 164.

[34] [2001] Fam. 147, 148.

accelerated[35] the inevitable death of the weaker twin.[36] The Civil Division of the Court of Appeal declared that the surgeon's intended actions would fit within the criminal defence of "necessity."[37]

4–014 **You have defined intention in relation to consequences. Don't we speak of an act itself as being intentional?** Yes. We may quite properly say, for example, that D intentionally trespassed on V's land,[38] or that D intentionally went through a bigamous ceremony of marriage—without referring to, or implying, any consequence. We say that bodily movement (like speaking, writing, gesturing, walking) is intentional if it is conscious or heedful, meaning that the actor in a sense knows what he is doing when he does it. He need not consciously attend to his movements, but they are purposive and are under his control.[39]

4–015 **How is the line drawn between an act and its consequence? If D shoots and kills V, is the killing D's act or its consequence?** As you like to regard it. Ordinarily language tends to blur the distinction between bodily movement and its consequences, since a statement that a person has acted in a particular way sometimes implies a consequence of acting. A statement that D has killed V implies that D has caused V's death. From one point of view the death is a consequence; from another point of view it can be regarded as part of D's movement.

If I perform the act of *crooking* my forefinger; since my finger is around the trigger of a loaded gun (a circumstance of my act of crooking my finger) I perform at the same time the act of firing the gun; since I have pointed the gun at a victim I also wound him; since he dies I also kill him; since his wife subsequently dies of a broken heart I *cause her death*. In all these examples, except the first and the last, a consequence can be spoken of as part of the act, because we happen to be provided with verbs (fire, wound, kill) that bring in the consequence. The last example must be excluded from the list of acts, because as soon as the word "cause" has to be used we do not regard the result as part of the act. But it is an accident that our language enables us to say "I killed him" rather than compelling us to say "I caused his death;" and similarly with all the other examples except the first and last. Only what I voluntarily do with my own body

---

[35] "[I]f the harm the defendant caused was about to be caused anyway by some natural occurrence, then the defendant may have a consequentialist, balance of evils defence, for his behaviour that would otherwise be unavailable." Michael S. Moore, *Counterfactual Dependence as an Independent, Non-Causal Desert-Determiner*, (2009) 34 *Austl. J. Leg. Phil.* 1 at 5. Such a case can be distinguished from cases where both lives have an equal chance of survival, as "counterfactual dependence" could not be invoked to provide guidance about which life should be sacrificed when all have an equal chance of survival.

[36] When such conundrums arise, philosophers use the doctrine of double-effect to explain the permissibility of harm-doing that has as a side-effect (or double-effect) of promoting some good end. See generally, Thomas A. Cavanaugh, *Double-Effect Reasoning: Doing Good and Avoiding Evil*, (Oxford: Clarendon Press, 2006); Thomas M. Scanlon, *Moral Dimensions: Permissibility, Meaning, Blame*, (Cambridge MA: Harvard University Press, 2008); Warren Quinn, "Actions, Intentions, and Consequences: The Doctrine of Double Effect," (1989) 18(4) *Philosophy and Public Affairs* 334.

[37] [2001] Fam. 147.

[38] In the discussions in this book, D of course stands for defendant, V for victim or alleged victim of an illegal act.

[39] Another element in the notion of intentional conduct will be considered in 6.2.

can indubitably be said to be an act and not the consequence of an act. Anything else *can* be called a consequence, though language may enable us to avoid calling it a consequence.

The way in which the accidents of language influence common notions of an act and its consequences may be further illustrated by considering wounding with a knife:

1. D, holding a knife, plunges it into V's body. Here we naturally say that D has stabbed V. We think of the wounding as practically a part of D's bodily movement; we speak of him as inflicting the wound rather than causing it.
2. D throws a knife at V and so causes a wound. Here we would probably not say that D has stabbed V, but rather that he has caused the wound. The wound is a consequence of his act of throwing the knife.

For legal purposes the situation is the same in both cases. In both, D has, in law, both wounded and caused a wound, and a wound is a consequence of D's bodily movement. There is no point in making a distinction, saying that the wound is a consequence of what D has done in the second case and part of what he has done in the first. The only qualification of the above remarks is that a lawyer's use of language may be controlled by the definitions of particular words. An example is the word "kill," which is used in the definition of murder and manslaughter; this is given a wider meaning by the law than it perhaps bears in ordinary speech, because, as we shall see, it covers the causing of death by some omissions and by some indirect means.

4–016

Another ambiguity may be noticed. If D murders V by shooting him, we say that D "intended to do it," or "meant to do it." Do what? D might have intended to shoot V in a non-vital part merely as a warning for the future. It would be wrong to say that because he intended to shoot, therefore he intended to kill. If we are speaking precisely we ought to speak about intending the consequence (if the consequence is important) rather than about intending the act. Clearly, the act must be intentional as to the relevant fact, whether bodily movement or consequence as the case may be:

> "Suppose that Winkle is out shooting partridges when his shot accidentally hits Tupman. We can say that Winkle intentionally fired the gun, and that he hit Tupman, but not that he intentionally shot Tupman. It would be an unscrupulous use of language to argue that Winkle committed an "intentional act and therefore an intentional crime. Yet sometimes, as we shall see, even the most eminent judges have made a mistake of this kind."[40]

The distinction between acts and their consequences has caused some judges (following a suggestion by Professor J. C. Smith) to classify crimes into two sorts: conduct crimes and result crimes. For the reasons already given the distinction, although sometimes useful, cannot be made perfectly precise.

Conduct crimes (such as assault) are those that are completed by the bodily movement (or other conduct) itself, with any requisite intent. Conduct crimes may be subdivided into the two sorts that we know already. Their common characteristic is that no result is required. (1) Some are crimes of basic (or

4–017

---

[40] See Lord Salmon's comments upon *R. v. Lamb* in *D.P.P. v. Newbury* [1977] A.C. 500 at 507–509.

general) intent, in the sense that the only mental element required is an intention to go through the bodily movements, coupled (generally) with one of various kinds of mental elements as to the relevant circumstances. Examples of such conduct crimes of basic intent are perjury, blackmail, and bigamy. (2) Other conduct crimes, while not requiring the achievement of a forbidden result, require an intention to achieve such a result, and therefore are crimes of ulterior intent. The definition of the crime contains two requirements: some specified criminal conduct, and an intention to produce a result. Examples are: theft (which involves dishonestly appropriating the property of another with intent to deprive him permanently of it), and burglary (which involves trespassory entry upon property with one of certain forbidden intents).[41]

Result crimes (such as murder) are those requiring some consequence to follow. Some require the result to be intended; these are crimes of ulterior intent in which the intent must be accomplished. Others are satisfied with recklessness or negligence as to the result, or even require no fault at all.

The distinction between conduct crimes and result crimes is unscientific because of the ambiguity discussed. Murder is a result crime if you think of it as causing death, but a conduct crime if you think of it as the act of killing. Unlawful wounding is a result crime if you think of it as causing a wound, but a conduct crime if you think of it as the act of wounding.

A third class of crimes does not fit neatly under either heading. They are what may be called crimes of pure intention (the "inchoate" crimes like attempt and conspiracy). They are not conduct crimes in the same sense as other conduct crimes, because no particular conduct is interdicted; and they are not result crimes, because the desired result need not be achieved. They are committed by doing any act that (within certain rules) manifests a sufficiently firm intention to bring about another crime.

It may be hard to determine whether Parliament meant to create a conduct crime or a result crime. In an offence allowing or permitting someone to do something, is the offence committed by giving the permission, or only when the permission is acted upon? The courts say the latter.[42]

4.3.   INDIRECT INTENTION: THE KNOWN SIDE-EFFECT

4-018   Even though a person's knowledge that a particular consequence will probably result from his act is an insufficient basis for saying that he intends it, there are strong reasons for holding that as a legal matter he can be held to intend something that he knows for sure he is doing. This is sometimes called "oblique" intent—not the result that is in the straight line of the defendant's purpose, but a side-effect that he accepts as inevitable.[43] Conceptually, indirect intention is not intention at all, but rather is a genus of "extreme subjective recklessness."[44] The

---

[41] See also Jeremy Horder, "Crimes of Ulterior Intent," in A.P. Simester and A.T.H. Smith (ed.) *Harm and Culpability*, (Oxford: Clarendon Press, 1996) at 153-172.

[42] *R. v. Diggin* [1981] 72 Cr. App. R. 204.

[43] Glanville Williams, "Oblique Intention," (1987) 46 *Cambridge L.J.* 417.

[44] Professor Duff also takes this view. See R. A. Duff, "Criminalizing Endangerment," in R. A. Duff and Stuart P. Green, *Defining Crimes*, (Oxford: Oxford University Press, 2005) at 52.

defendant intends to do *x* but does not intend it to result in *y*,[45] but *knows* that if he does *x* it will be *virtually impossible* for *y* not to occur. Since his state of mind is such that he as good as intended to bring about *y*, he is deemed to have intended *y*.

Clearly, a person can be "taken" to intend a consequence that follows under his nose from what he continues to do,[46] and the law should be the same where he is aware that the consequence in the future is the certain or practically certain result of what he does. As Lord Hailsham said in *Hyam v. D.P.P.*,[47] "intention" includes "the means as well as the end and the inseparable consequences of the end as well as the means." (What he meant was the consequences known to the defendant to be inseparable.) It is arguable that everyone would understand "intention" in this *extended* meaning; at any rate, the extension is not sufficiently great to depart seriously from ordinary ideas, while not to allow it would in some contexts make the concept of intention notably defective for practical purposes.[48]

Is this a case of intending a double-effect from one act?[49]   No. Cases   **4–019** involving oblique intention are not cases of double-effect as such, because the defendant's ulterior intent was not to bring about the harm which he is now being held responsible for. In *R. v. Woollin*,[50] the defendant lost his temper with his three-month-old baby because the baby was choking on his food and making a mess. To vent his anger, Woollin threw the baby as hard as he could and the impact caused the baby to die. Woollin's act of throwing the baby was intentional, but he did not intend the (double-effect) consequence. His ulterior intent was to let out his anger or perhaps to take some kind of sick revenge on the innocent baby, but it was not to kill the baby.

In *Hyam v. D.P.P.*[51] the defendant had had a relationship with a man who became engaged to another woman, V. The defendant went to V's house and

---

[45] Cf. John Finnis, "Intention and Side-Effects," in R.G. Frey & Christopher W. Morris (eds.), *Liability and Responsibility: Essays in Law and Morals*, (Cambridge: Cambridge University Press, 1991), at 32 *et seq.* See also Kimberly K. Ferzan, "Beyond Intention," (2008) 29 *Cardozo L. Rev.* 1147.

[46] Mere knowledge is not, of course, enough for constructing intention if there is nothing the defendant can do about it. This proposition is particularly important in relation to situational offences. If a patient in a hospital gets to know that his child at home is being neglected, he does not at that moment himself intentionally or wilfully neglect the child, if he cannot do anything to prevent the neglect continuing. See P. R. Glazebrook, "Situational Liability," in P. R. Glazebrook (ed.) *Reshaping the Criminal Law: Essays in Honour of Glanville Williams*, (London: Steven & Sons, 1978) at 117-18.

[47] [1974] A.C. 55 at 74.

[48] Kaveny notes that advocates of this approach "may argue that either in general or in the special case of homicide, it makes *practical* sense to expand the definition of intention to include consequences foreseen as virtually certain. Glanville Williams captures this pragmatic approach when he observes that 'to reject the doctrine of oblique intent would involve the law in fine distinctions, and would make it unduly lenient.' Williams' observation suggests that the pragmatic justification for [the constructed (extended) intent doctrine] has two components, one arguing for moral equivalence, and the other arguing for epistemological equivalence." M. Cathleen Kaveny, "Inferring Intention From Foresight," (2004) 120 *L.Q.R.* 81 at 85. Kaveny asserts that the "oblique intention" doctrine is not well suited for achieving moral equivalence. See also Alan Norrie, "After Woollin," [1999] Crim. L.R. 532. (I respectfully disagree with their views on this point).

[49] See the works cited *supra* note 36.

[50] *R. v. Woollin* [1999] 1 A.C. 82.

[51] [1974] A.C. 55.

poured petrol through her letterbox and ignited it. V escaped the ensuring blaze but her two daughters were killed by the fumes of the fire. Hyam's defence was that she had set fire to the house only in order to frighten V, as she wanted V to leave town. Hyam's act of lighting the fire was intentional, but her ulterior intent was not to kill V or V's daughters—it was merely to frighten V. *Per contra*, in the case of self-defence[52] the victim intends to harm the aggressor to achieve the ulterior end (the double-effect) of self-preservation. If the self-defender fires a bullet into an aggressor to thwart an unjustifiable attack and the aggressor dies instantly, the first effect of the self-defender's act is the aggressor's death; the second effect is the thwarting of the aggressor's attack. (The self-defender intends to use the means of "killing the aggressor" to achieve the ulterior end of self-preservation). Self-preservation is the desired end. In the case of oblique intention the defendant directly intends to do the harmful act (*i.e.* the act of throwing the baby, *etc.*), but does not do it with the aim of bringing about the side-effect—the baby's death, *etc.* D can only be said to have indirectly intended to bring about the undesired end—the baby's death, *etc.*

4–020　**Is this not merely a case of imputing intent to those who are "extremely (subjective) reckless"?**　The oblique intent is a different form of intent. Oblique intention is an independent form of *mens rea* which is treated as being equal to direct intention as far as punishment and labelling is concerned. The doctrine, however, will only apply in the most exceptional cases. To take a hypothetical case: suppose that a villain of the deepest dye sends an insured parcel on an aircraft, and includes in it a time-bomb by which he intends to bring down the plane and consequently to destroy the parcel. His immediate intention is merely to collect on the insurance. He does not care whether the people on board live or die, but he knows that success in his scheme will inevitably involve their deaths as a side-effect. On the theoretical point, common sense suggests that the notion of intention should be extended to this situation; it should not merely be regarded as a case of recklessness.[53] A consequence should normally be taken as intended although it was not desired, if it was foreseen by the actor as the virtually certain accompaniment of what he intended. This is not the same as saying that any consequence foreseen as probable is intended.

4–021　**Are you telling me there are two forms of intention to be found in the substantive criminal law?**　Yes. There is the standard form of intention which comes into play when the defendant intends to bring about the particular consequence. For example, D shoots V with the aim of killing him. The second substantive doctrine of intent is oblique intention. This catches D when he chooses to do *y* knowing it is virtually certain to result in *x*. If you know that *x* (the baby will suffer serious harm) is virtually certain to occur if you do *y* (throw the baby from the third floor of a house), then you should not do *y*. If you choose

---

[52] The same might be said of those who act out of necessity. Cf. *The Queen v. Dudley and Stephens* (1884-85) L.R. 14 Q.B.D. 273.

[53] Recklessness in the "normal" subjective rather than "extreme" subjective sense would only allow the defendant to be convicted of manslaughter, and yet, his extreme culpability makes it impossible to distinguish him from a murder—he did an act which he knew was certain to result in death for another.

to throw the baby when you know that it is virtually certain that he will suffer severe injuries, then in law you obliquely intend to injure the baby. In *R. v. Woollin*,[54] the House of Lords accepted the "oblique intention" doctrine as law by approving *R. v. Nedrick*.[55] Lord Steyn cited the following passages from Lord Lane C.J.'s judgment in *R. v. Nedrick*:

"(1)   Where the charge is murder and in the rare cases where the simple direction is not enough, the jury should be directed that they are not entitled to infer the necessary intention, unless they feel sure that death or serious bodily harm was a virtual certainty (barring some unforeseen intervention) as a result of the defendant's actions and that the defendant appreciated that such was the case.

(2)   Where a man realises that it is for all practical purposes inevitable that his actions will result in death or serious harm, the inference may be irresistible that he intended that result, however little he may have desired or wished it to happen. The decision is one for the jury to be reached upon a consideration of all the evidence."[56]

In *R. v. Woollin*, Lord Steyn also concluded: "[t]he use of the words 'to infer' in (1) may detract from the clarity of the model direction. I would substitute the words 'to find.'" In addition, "[t]he first sentence of (2) does not form part of the model direction. But it would always be right for the judge to say, as Lord Lane C.J. put it, that the decision is for the jury upon a consideration of all the evidence in the case."[57] If the jury find on the evidence that D knew that if he did *x*, the virtually certain consequence would be *y*, then it must find that he obliquely (indirectly) intended *y*.

Professor Glanville Williams expounds:[58]

"The proper view is that intention in its wider sense includes not only desire of consequence (purpose) but also foresight of the certainty of the consequence, as a matter of legal definition. What the jury infer from the facts is the defendant's direct intention or foresight of a consequence as certain; there is no additional element to be 'inferred.'"

A finding of oblique intention is not merely evidence from which the jury *might* infer that the defendant acted with direct intention. Once oblique intention is established, the jury ought to return a guilty verdict. If it were merely a rule of evidence the jury would be free to return a verdict of not guilty. Oblique intention is an alternative substantive form of intention. If the jury have found that the defendant foresaw the consequence was a virtual certainty, it would be nonsensical to treat their finding of indirect intention as mere evidence from which they could (at their own discretion) infer direct intention.[59] They should convict where oblique intention is established. If the jury is certain the defendant only obliquely intended to kill, it would be hard for it to infer that he directly intended to kill. The latter inference runs counter to its factual finding. However,

4–022

---

[54] *R. v. Woollin* [1999] 1 A.C. 82 at 96-97.

[55] [1986] 1 W.L.R. 1025. See also *R. v. Hancock* [1986] A.C. 455; *R. v. Moloney* [1985] A.C. 905. Cf. *Hyam v. D.P.P.* [1975] A.C. 55.

[56] *R. v. Woollin* [1999] 1 A.C. 82 at 96-97.

[57] *R. v. Woollin* [1999] 1 A.C. 82 at 96-97.

[58] Glanville Williams, "The Mens Rea for Murder: Leave it Alone," (1989) 105 *L.Q.R.* 387-388.

[59] Cf. *R. v. Matthews* [2003] 2 Cr. App. R. 30, where it was said, "If what was required was an appreciation of virtual certainty of death, and not some lesser foresight of merely probable consequences, there was very little to choose between a rule of evidence and one of substantive law."

a finding of oblique intention will allow the jury to infer that the defendant directly intended to kill, when it is fairly sure he is lying about not having a direct intent to kill.

Normally, intention means purpose, and it will be sufficient to tell the jury that, or indeed leave the word without explanation.[60] The oblique intention instruction need be given only when there was no desire to bring the particular event about.[61] So, if D puts a bomb in a carriage on the London tube during peak hour only intending to kill V1, a rival terrorist, his culpability comes within the normal doctrine of intention since his direct aim is to kill V1. Suppose his bomb goes off and not only kills V1, but 50 other innocent passengers. If D asserts that it was not his desire to kill anyone other than V1, and the evidence shows that he foresaw the death of all the passengers as a virtual certainty, then the instruction about oblique intention will need to be given.

This kind of intention should be sufficient to support a conviction of criminal attempt.[62] Suppose that in the example of the bomb on the aircraft, that the villain were arrested as he was about to put the bomb on the plane. To account him guilty only of recklessness (which is not sufficient for an attempt)[63] would make the notion of intention pedantically narrow. Whereas homicide can be committed in some cases by recklessness, attempted murder requires an intent to kill and is not committed by recklessness as to death. Here the villain would properly be held to have intended to kill.

4–023   **But is there a satisfactory line between foreseen certainty, which you say can be intention, and foreseen probability, which you deny is intention? The bomb might have gone off but the pilot might miraculously have brought the stricken plane to safely land.**   One specific argument in favour of recognizing oblique intention is that sometimes it is only a verbal question whether one regards the intention as direct or oblique. D helps a friend to evade justice because the friend offers him payment. One can say that D intends to help his friend to escape (direct intention), his motive being to earn money (the motive being legally immaterial), or one can say that D intends to earn money, knowing that in doing so he is helping his friend to evade justice (oblique intention). The facts are the same either way, and how one verbalizes them should make no difference. Similarly, if a porter at a ladies college, (perhaps Newnham College, Cambridge) smashes the glass dial on the fire alarm (without justification) because he wants to see how many men he can flush out of the ladies' rooms in the middle of the night, he could not argue that he did not intend to break the glass. His illegitimate motive for criminally damaging the College's property is

---

[60] *R. v. Moloney* [1985] A.C. 905 at 926. *R. v. Belfon* [1976] 1 W.L.R. 741.

[61] The circumstances in which a *Nedrick* direction will be required will be very rare. *R. v. McNamara* [2009] EWCA Crim. 2530; *R. v. Allen* [2005] EWCA Crim. 1344.

[62] Cf. *R. v. Hales* [2005] EWCA Crim. 1118. See also *R. v. Woollin* [1999] 1 A.C. 82 at 95.

[63] *R. v. Mohan* [1976] Q.B. 1.

legally immaterial.[64] He does not want to destroy the glass dial, but knows that he has to destroy it in order to achieve his end of setting the alarm off.[65]

These cases could be said to involve what might be described as absolute certainties, but one cannot confine the notion of foresight of certainty to certainty in the most absolute sense. It is a question of human certainty, or virtual certainty, or practical certainty. This is still not the same as speaking in terms of probability. The virtual certainty test will not catch many nasty types, but the line has to be drawn somewhere. Take the often cited example of the terrorist who places a bomb in a public place and then tips off the police. Suppose he does not intend to kill anyone but merely aims to attract publicity for his cause. Suppose also that he thinks no one will be hurt because his bomb is one that can easily be defused by a bomb disposal expert. However, on this occasion the bomb disposal expert is killed while he is trying to defuse it.[66] Is the terrorist guilty of manslaughter or murder? Lord Steyn answers this in the following passage:[67]

> "It is true that [the oblique intention doctrine] may exclude a conviction of murder in the often cited terrorist example where a member of the bomb disposal team is killed. In such a case it may realistically be said that the terrorist did not foresee the killing of a member of the bomb disposal team as a virtual certainty. That may be a consequence of not framing the principle in terms of *risk-taking*. Such cases ought to cause no substantial difficulty since immediately below murder there is available a verdict of manslaughter which may attract in the discretion of the court a life sentence. In any event,... to frame a principle for particular difficulties regarding terrorism 'would produce corresponding injustices which would be very hard to eradicate. I am satisfied that the *R. v. Nedrick* test, which was squarely based on the decision of the House in *R. v. Moloney*, is pitched at the right level of foresight."

So we are left with three rough distinctions: 1. those absolute certainties which are covered by the normal doctrine of intention, because the consequence is intended even though D has some other motive in mind (*e.g.*, D commits criminal damage by smashing glass to get the sound effect of broken glass for a short film he is producing); 2. foresight of inseparable or virtually certain consequences (*e.g.*, D throws a baby hard down a flight of steps foreseeing that the baby will be seriously injured); and 3. risk-taking involving probabilities (*e.g.*, D puts a bomb in a public place foreseeing that it is highly probable or at least probable that the bomb-disposal expert might not be able to safely defuse his bomb). Whether a

---

[64] Of course, it would be relevant if he has smashed the dial for a legitimate purpose such as warning the occupants about a raging fire.

[65] Professor Hart wrote, "For outside the law a merely foreseen, though unwanted, outcome is not usually considered as intended. ... The exceptions to this usage of 'intentionality' are cases where a foreseen outcome is so immediately and invariably connected with the action done that the suggestion that the action might not have that outcome would by ordinary standards be regarded as absurd, or such as only a mentally abnormal person would seriously entertain. ... Thus if a man struck a glass violently with a hammer, knowing that the blow would break it, he would be said to have broken the glass intentionally (though not, perhaps, to have intentionally broken the glass), even if he merely wanted the noise of the hammer making contact with the glass to attract attention." H. L. A. Hart, *Punishment and Responsibility: Essays in the Philosophy of Law*, (Oxford: Clarendon Press, 1968) at 120.

[66] *R. v. Moloney* [1985] A.C. 905.

[67] *R. v. Woollin* [1999] 1 A.C. 82 at 94-95.

case is one or the other will depend on the facts of the case, but it is clear only extreme cases will be caught by the oblique intention doctrine.[68]

4–024 **Does oblique intention apply to murder only?** That depends. What is the rationale of the doctrine? Its rationale in the homicide context is to ensure those who have the requisite culpability for murder are not labelled and punished as manslaughters. Therefore, it should only be invoked in cases where a lack of direct intent would see an equally culpable defendant being charged with an offence that does not reflect the culpableness and harmfulness of his offending. For instance, section 18 of the *Offences against the Person Act 1861* carries a life sentence, while section 20 of that *Act* does not. There is no reason why the oblique intention doctrine could not be invoked in exceptional circumstances to obtain a conviction under section 18, if it is clear that a section 20 conviction would be too lenient.

Per contra, it might be argued that murder is a special case because of the irreparable and grave harm involved and that the doctrine should not be used in other offences. It is also arguable that the doctrine does not apply to statutory offences that have been enacted in the 21st century. The "oblique intention" doctrine was developed by the courts towards the end of the 20th century. If Parliament had intended such a doctrine to apply in 21st century offences, then it would have expressly said so. For example, section 44(2) of the *Serious Crime Act 2007* provides "But he is not to be taken to have intended to encourage or assist the commission of an offence merely because such encouragement or assistance was a foreseeable consequence of his act." When the relevant Bill was introduced, the Parliamentary Under-Secretary of State for Justice said:[69]

> "The notion of intention is given a particular meaning by subsection (2) … I hope that it assists the Hon. Member for Hornchurch if I say that what we are trying to get at is that intention should be interpreted in a narrow way, and should exclude the concept of *virtual certainty*. It is equivalent to meaning that D's purpose must be to assist or encourage the offence."

4.4. THE PROOF OF INTENTION

4–025 As we saw in Chapter 2, the burden of proving a necessary mental element rests upon the prosecution. No presumption shifts the burden to the defendant. A defence that the defendant did not intend a consequence to follow from his act is frequently called a defence of accident, but this is merely a denial of intention and recklessness; and the burden of proving intention or recklessness rests on the Crown. In the same way, the prosecution must prove dishonesty and fraud, where these are required elements.[70] It makes no difference that the mental element is a matter lying peculiarly within the knowledge of the defendant.[71]

---

[68] Hyam was caught because subjective recklessness was sufficient *mens rea* for murder in those days. *Hyam v. D.P.P.* [1975] A.C. 55. It still is in many Australian jurisdictions. Cf. *Murray v. The Queen* (2002) 211 C.L.R.193; *Charlie v. The Queen* (1999) 199 C.L.R. 387. The Scots use a doctrine of "wicked recklessness": *Petto v. HM Advocate* (2009) S.L.T. 509.

[69] Hansard, HC Public Bill Committee, 6th Sitting, 3 July 2007, col.211.

[70] See *Ng v. The Queen* [1958] A.C. 173; *R. v. Lusty* [1964] 1 W.L.R. 606.

[71] *R. v. Spurge* [1961] 2 Q.B. 205.

I do not understand how intention is proved. Suppose the evidence is that   4–026
when V was ill D gave him a dose of arsenic. D says it was by mistake for a
sleeping powder; at least, that is what he told the police, but he does not give
evidence in court. Do you mean that the prosecution have the burden of
proving that D did not make a mistake and intended to kill V? How can they
do so if D does not give evidence and so lay himself open to cross-
examination? What D said to the police is not evidence in his favour. As the
case stands, therefore, the evidence is only that D gave V arsenic. The courts do
not generally impose an evidential burden on the defendant on the issue of *mens
rea* (as perhaps they should), but the facts you put would certainly be held
sufficient to discharge the prosecution's evidential burden. The jury must be
directed that the burden of proving the intention to kill (where the charge is of
murder) rests on the prosecution, and that such intention must be proved beyond
reasonable doubt; but they may also be told that they are entitled to infer an
intention from the evidence. In practice D may be bound to offer evidence of the
alleged mistake if he wants it to be considered;[72] but any evidence, however thin,
must be left to the jury.

But aren't there many cases where a court of law could not possibly   4–027
distinguish between "accidental" and "accidental on purpose"? Maybe; but
certain modes of proof are accepted as sufficient to distinguish between the
genuine and the feigned defence.

Facts are proved by direct evidence (the evidence of witnesses—including the
defendant himself—who perceived or experienced them) or by circumstantial
(indirect) evidence (the evidence of witnesses as to other facts, from which the
facts in issue are inferred). This is as true of the proof of intention as of the proof
of other facts.

(1)   Intention may be directly proved from what the defendant says. Evidence
      may be given of what he said contemporaneously with the act (by way of
      application of the so-called *res gestae* rule),[73] or of his prior or subsequent
      admission of what he intended to do. Such evidence is, of course, not
      conclusive in itself; it may be overborne by stronger evidence the other
      way; but usually it will be sufficient for a finding of intention. A subsequent
      admission of guilt is called a confession, whether it is made before or at the
      trial.

(2)   If the defendant does not give the court this assistance, the jury (or
      magistrates) will have no direct access to his mind.[74] Therefore, unless the

---

[72] Occasionally a mere statement of counsel as to the defendant's intention has been left to the jury as
though it were evidence; but it should not be.

[73] *Ratten v. The Queen* [1972] A.C. 378; *R. v. Andrews* [1987] A.C. 281.

[74] There is a machine known as the lie-detector or polygraph which is supposed to indicate whether a
lie is being told, by means of physiological changes resulting from the subject's emotional reactions;
but this device is not used in courts, partly because its scientific accuracy is disputed and partly
because the tradition is that defendants to a criminal charge are not subject to compulsory
interrogation. For a survey of opinion on the machine, see Julius Denenberg, "The Polygraph: Modern
Wizardry Unmasked," (1988) 55 *Def. Counsel J.* 278; David A. Weintraub, "Polygraph
Examination—A Valuable Arbitration Tool," (2009) 83(6) *Fla. B.J.* 97. Psychiatric evidence is not
admissible from either side on the issue of intention or other metal state except on the issue of

defendant confesses, the state of his mind at the time in question must be judged from his outward acts, whether they are contemporaneous or not:

- It may be gathered from previous or subsequent conduct on his part. There may be evidence of previous planning, or a subsequent flight from justice. An important part of the law of evidence relates to evidence of other offences. Normally, English law does not allow a charge of crime to be made out by showing that the defendant has committed other crimes; but if the various crimes exhibit striking similarities, so that it is impossible or difficult to imagine that they could all have been the result of coincidence, the other crimes (whether previous or even subsequent[75]) may be given in evidence in order to show that the defendant had a "system" of committing such crimes. This evidence may convince the jury not only that he did the act charged against him but that he did it with the requisite intent. Evidence of possible motive (*e.g.*, an expectation under a will) will be of some weight in supporting evidence.

- More frequently, the defendant's intention will have to be collected from the evidence of what he did on the occasion in question. If one man loads a revolver, points it at another, aims it carefully at the victim's heart and pulls the trigger, the jury will find that he intended to kill, because that is the only reasonable hypothesis to explain his conduct. They are not obliged to swallow a denial that is common-sense unswallowable.

4–028 **Doesn't it boil down simply to the probability of the consequence occurring?** Not quite. Probability is a guide, but it is not conclusive. This matter has a history. For many years the courts fudged the notion of intention. When a crime required intention and the judges thought this too narrow, they extended the law by the doctrine that a person was "deemed to intend the natural and probable consequences of his act." The principle reason was the desire of judges to procure and uphold the conviction of people who were public dangers or public nuisances. A contributory factor was that lawyers spent no time reflecting on their fundamental concepts. They were too slow in developing the concept of recklessness. When the only mental element they could think of was intention (or knowledge), they found that they needed to give it a wide definition which in effect covered recklessness. Unfortunately it then covered negligence as well.

But the maxim about intending probable consequences was always objectionable. It created a fictitious or "constructive" intention.[76] (A person who asserted that he knew that the driver who had had a nasty accident intended to cause it, when he knew full well that the driver had only taken a risk, would be regarded by everyone, except possibly a lawyer, as having told a lie.) It applied to some

---

insanity, diminished capacity, or automatism. See *R. v. Chard* (1972) 56 Cr. App. R. 268; *R. v. Henry* [2006] 1 Cr. App. R. 6. Cf. *R. v. Toner* (1991) 93 Cr. App. R. 382.

[75] *D.P.P. v. P* [1991] 2 A.C. 447; *R. v. Foster* [2006] EWCA Crim. 1275; *R. v. Hurren* (1962) 46 Cr. App. R. 323.

[76] A word is used in a constructive sense when the ordinary meaning is replaced by an artificial, technical meaning as a method of extending rules beyond their plain scope.

crimes but not to all, and when it did apply it turned negligence into intention. The maxim gained some plausibility from the fact it superficially resembled a common-sense rule of evidence. Often one can judge whether a man intended a consequence only by asking whether anyone in his shoes would have realized that the consequence was likely and whether there is any reasonable interpretation of his actions other than the hypothesis that he intended the consequence. The maxim was erroneous because it omitted the emphasized words.

Change in the law came at last as a reaction to the decision of the House of Lords in *Director of Public Prosecutions v. Smith*,[77] one of the most criticized judgments ever to be delivered by an English court. The Lords there applied the probable consequence maxim even to the crime of murder. They held that not merely could intent be inferred from the probability of the consequence but that the presumption of intent in such circumstances was irrebuttable. In other words, the judge could say to the jury:

> "Members of the jury, in deciding whether the defendant intended this consequence you merely have to consider whether a reasonable person would have foreseen it as probable. Do not enquire whether the defendant foresaw it, or whether he intended it. You can find that he intended it although you are sure he did not."

This preposterous rule was overthrown by section 8 of the *Criminal Justice Act 1967*, but the change of law has been blatantly disregarded by the courts in many cases. Section 8 provides: **4–029**

> "A court or jury, in determining whether a person has committed an offence,—
>
> (a)   shall not be bound in law to infer that he intended or foresaw a result of his actions by reasons only of its being a natural and probable consequence of those actions; but
>
> (b)   shall decide whether he did intend or foresee that result by reference to all the evidence, drawing such inferences from the evidence as appear proper in the circumstances."

Section 8 has no bearing on the substantive criminal law of intention. The section merely relates to the mode of proving any necessary intention or recklessness, and does not control the legal requirements of a particular offence.

Since *R. v. Woollin* has put an end to the mendacious definition of intention in terms of probability, what role does probability play under section 8? Section 8 merely holds that D's foresight of the probable consequences of doing x is evidence of an intent to bring about those consequences—nothing more. But this factor must be considered in light of all the other evidence in the case. The rule, however, suggests that establishing intention is to be ascertained by a "subjective" investigation—an investigation into the mind of the defendant— even though one can generally make this investigation only by studying his outward acts. The substantive law is now settled and it is clear that recklessness is distinct from intention, and that foresight of probability or likelihood is not part of intention, although it might be used to infer intention.

Section 8 establishes that intention and foresight are to be ascertained by a "subjective" investigation; but the judge may tell the jury that they may infer

---

[77] [1961] A.C. 290.

these mental states from what the defendant did, provided that they look at the whole of the evidence. If the jury after considering all the evidence conclude that the defendant realized for all practical purposes that it was inevitable that his actions would result in death or serious harm; this in itself is a finding that the defendant obliquely intended the consequences of his actions. If the jury have made such a finding there is no need for them to artificially use a finding of oblique intention to infer direct intention. If oblique intention is established then the jury should return a guilty verdict. Likewise, if direct intention is established the jury should return a guilty verdict.

4–030   **Suppose the defendant says that he was in a blind rage, or in the grip of fear, and did not know what he was doing. Might that get him off, if the offence charged requires intention or knowledge?**   Since the enactment of section 8 the defence would have to be left to the jury. But the judge would doubtless tell the jury that they are entitled to find that acts done in rage or fear can be found to be purposive, the emotional state overcoming the defendant's inhibitions rather than his awareness.[78]

4–031   **Does section 8 get rid of strict liability?**   The section applies only when the crime is one of requiring *mens rea*. It tells you that if a crime requires a mental element, that mental element must be genuinely ascertained, so far as this can possibly be done; and if it cannot be done, then the prosecution, who have the burden of proving the mental element, must fail. The section is inapplicable if the crime does not require a mental element.

4.5. GENERAL AND TRANSFERRED INTENTION

4–032   If the defendant did not aim at anyone in particular, he is still liable on the basis of what is sometimes called "general malice"—better, "general intention." The most obvious example is the terrorist "bomber." An intention to hit anyone within range is always, in logic and law, an intention to hit the particular person who is hit.

Another possibility is that D aims at V1 but accidentally hits V2. This is an instance of what is traditionally called "transferred malice"—more precisely, transferred intention. Although D aimed to hit V1, since his blow took effect on V2 it is deemed at common law to be an intentional attack upon V2. The rule is that D is guilty to the same extent as if he had intended to injure the person whom he actually did injure. The intention in respect of one victim is transferred by a legal fiction to another.

The doctrine is a general one, and applies whenever a wrongful intention is formed in respect of a person or thing but it takes immediate physical effect[79]

---

[78] Fear is likely to be regarded more indulgently than anger, see *Att-Gen. for Northern Ireland's Reference* [1977] A.C. 105, discussed in Glanville Williams, *Textbook of Criminal Law*, (London: Stevens & Sons, 1st edn. 1978) at 63. Cf. *R. v. Baker* [1997] Crim. L.R. 497.

[79] In justice, the doctrine should not be applied where the immediate injury to V2 is non-physical, even though an injury intended for V1 causes fright and consequent injury to V2, as in *R. v. Towers* (1874) 12 Cox C.C. 530. D's liability in respect of V2 should be adjudged without reference to his

upon another person or thing, where the intended and the actual "victim" (person or thing) fall within the definition of the offence.[80] Returning to the specific case of an assault, the argument is that D had the requisite *mens rea* for assault in hitting V2; therefore he has both the *mens rea* and *actus reus* for an assault on V2. The argument is of course fallacious, if D did not have *mens rea* in respect of V2. Still, many will think that the doctrine of transferred intention does practical justice in this application. It is closely similar to the case of mistaken victim, even though it is analytically distinct from it.

Suppose an attacker aims at a dog and hits a person, or *vice versa*? He cannot be charged either with an offence against the person or with an offence against property. There is no *actus reus* in respect of the dog and no intention in respect to person.

4–033

The fuller reason is that there is no statute under which he can be charged with a consummated intentional offence. No law makes it an offence to injure an "animal" in a sense of including both people and dogs. If there were such a law a charge would be available, the difference between the "animal" aimed at and the "animal" injured being immaterial. But under our law, dogs fall within the *Criminal Damage Act 1971* and the *Animal Welfare Act 2006* while human beings fall within the *Offences against the Person Act 1861*. On a charge of intentionally or recklessly damaging a dog under the *Criminal Damage Act*, *mens rea* would not be established by showing an intent to injure a person, because that would not be the *mens rea* required by the *Act*.[81] Similarly in the converse case. (But the attacker would be responsible if he were reckless in respect of the actual victim. And he can also be convicted of attempting to commit the offence that he tried to commit.)

The rule emerging from the above is that intention can be transferred only within the same crime, because the defendant must have the *mens rea* and commit the *actus reus* appropriate to the crime with which he is charged, even though they may exist in respect of different persons or objects.[82] Combining the elements of two different offences is not allowed.[83]

One other point; defences are transferred with the intention. So if D was acting in self-defence against V1, he will be deemed to have been acting in self-defence against V2.

---

intent against V1. The consequence of adopting the opposite rule was seen in the American case of *Ex parte Heigho* (1910) 18 Idaho 566, where D assaulted V1 and an onlooker, V2 died of fright; D was convicted of the manslaughter of V2!

[80] See Glanville Williams, *Criminal Law: The General Part*, (London: Stevens & Sons, 2nd edn. 1961), Chap. 4.

[81] This is the only logical interpretation of the decision in *R. v. Pembliton* (1872-75) L.R. 2 C.C.R. 119, even though the rule does not clearly appear from the judgments in that case.

[82] See the discussion in Chapter 13 regarding the problem that arises when D intends to kill V but kills a non-human foetus. An intent to kill a person is not an intent to kill a non-person, so D cannot be liable if he kills an unborn foetus—or a foetus that is born dead. See more generally, Jeremy Horder, "Transferred Malice and the Remoteness of Unexpected Outcomes From Intentions," [2006] Crim. L.R. 383; Michael Bohlander, "Transferred Malice and Transferred Defences: A Critique of the Traditional Doctrine and Arguments for a Change in Paradigm," (2010) 13 *New Crim. L. Rev.* 555.

[83] Exceptionally, and quite logically, intention may be transferred between two offences differently only in that one has elements of strict liability.

CHAPTER 5

RECKLESSNESS AND NEGLIGENCE

"'It's a poor sort of memory that only works backwards,' the Queen remarked."

The White Queen to Alice.[1]

5.1. RECKLESSNESS IN THE CRIMINAL LAW

We learn as a result of experience and instruction, and our learning brings awareness of the dangers of life. We can guess at the probable present even when we cannot directly perceive it, and can project ourselves into the future by foreseeing the probable consequences of our acts. Our memories work forwards.

5–001

This is the foundation of the notion of recklessness. "Reckless" is a word of condemnation. It normally involves conscious and unreasonable risk-taking, either as to the possibility that a particular undesirable circumstance exists or as to the possibility that some evil will come to pass. The reckless person deliberately "takes a chance." Other things being equal, this is evidently a less culpable mental state than intention, though worse than inadvertent negligence. Recklessness, like negligence, is unjustifiable risk-taking. It differs from simple negligence (or, if you like, objective recklessness) in that the risk is known. The culpability or recklessness depends on a number of factors, including the degree of known risk.

Some crimes can be committed only intentionally. But nearly all crimes requiring *mens rea* (which are, broadly speaking, the more serious crimes) now recognize recklessness as an alternative to intention. This proposition holds for most common law crimes;[2] and more recently parliamentary draftsman have begun to include it in their formulations of offences, as by making it an offence to do something "knowingly or recklessly." The courts were slow to develop the concept of recklessness of conduct; they tended to think only in terms of intention, negligence and strict liability. Recklessness was accommodated within intention by two lines of reasoning, one now discredited and the other, though still occasionally found in judicial rhetoric, highly suspect:

---

[1] Lewis Carroll, *Through the Looking Glass*, (London: Macmillan and Co. & 1872) at 36.

[2] Even where the common law crime has been traditionally stated in terms of intention, the courts may redefine it in terms of intention or recklessness, as they did, with regard to rape, in *D.P.P. v. Morgan* [1976] A.C. 182 at 230, 209, 225.

- The presumption about intending probable consequences was used to make the notion of intention cover what we now term recklessness (and it covered negligence as well).[3]
- The other technique was to speak of "intentionally creating (or taking) a risk,"[4] or "intending to do something whether or not something else happened or was present." The effect was again to lump recklessness with intention.

In *R. v. G*,[5] the House of Lords clearly differentiated the two ideas. Lord Bingham expounded the following standard:

> "A person acts recklessly... with respect to (i) a circumstance when he is aware of a risk that it exists or will exist; and (ii) a result when he is aware of a risk that it will occur; and it is, in the circumstances known to him, unreasonable to take the risk."[6]

5–002   **Isn't recklessness just extreme negligence? Why not use only the general category of negligence?**   The main answer is that even when inadvertent negligence is punishable the law often treats it as a less serious offence than offences of recklessness, because of the lower level of culpability. Moreover, whereas recklessness is recognized as a mode of committing most crimes, many cases of inadvertent negligence are left outside the criminal law as a matter of policy. So we need to have suitable terms to distinguish between (1) recklessness and (2) negligence not necessarily amounting to recklessness.

Although we have general offences of recklessness causing injury to the person or damage to property, we have no general offences of negligence (apart from driving offences[7] and homicide). The Law Commission decided against having an offence of negligent damage to property when it drafted what is now the *Criminal Damage Act 1971*, and Parliament accepted the decision. The Criminal Law Revision Committee decided against proposing an offence of negligent injury to the person when it considered the law of offences against the person.[8] Some Continental jurisdictions have general penal liability of this kind; but we have not hitherto found it to be necessary. Accepting negligence as a general mode of offending would either strain the overworked resources of the

---

[3] See for example, *The Queen v. Pembliton* (1872-75) L.R. 2 C.C.R. 119, particularly the judgment of Blackburn J.

[4] This was used by Lord Hailsham in *D.P.P. v. Morgan* [1976] A.C. 182. The technique does not work well. If "intentionally creating a risk" of a result is equivalent to intending the result, then the doer will be guilty even though the risk was justifiable. So a surgeon who operates with a slim hope in a desperate case, and who, therefore, "intentionally runs a risk," would be guilty in the same way as if he had intended the patient's death if that occurs. If he intended the death when doing what he did, the patient's desperate condition would be no defence. In order to avoid this conclusion Lord Hailsham spoke of "exposing the patient to the risk without lawful excuse." There can indeed be a lawful excuse for exposing the patient to a justifiable risk, but not for intentionally killing him. This shows that the rules of law for risking a result and intending a result are not the same. In fact two of the Lords in Morgan (Hailsham, in one place, and Edmund-Davies) spoke in terms of recklessness, which is obviously the proper word in relation to conscious risk-taking. See further, *R. v. G* [2004] 1 A.C. 1034.

[5] [2004] 1 A.C. 1034.

[6] *R. v. G* [2004] 1 A.C. 1034.

[7] *R. v. Reid* [1992] 1 W.L.R. 793.

[8] Working Paper on *Offences Against the Person* (London: H.M.S.O., 1976) para. 90.

penal system or bring about highly selective and indeed capricious enforcement. In general, negligence causing injury or loss is best left to the civil law; if it is to be dealt with penally, this should be done by specific provisions dealing with common categories of negligence.

5.2. SUBJECTIVE RECKLESSNESS

The subjective-objective controversy was put to rest by the House of Lords in *R. v. G.*[9] Before that case, the courts had hovered between the idea of recklessness as gross negligence (the "objective" definition) and the idea of recklessness as advertent recklessness:

5–003

1. The idea of recklessness as gross negligence proposes that recklessness is an extreme departure from the standard of conduct of the prudent person. Often the defendant will have adverted to the risk, but he may not have; and he can (on this view) be accounted grossly negligent whether he adverted to it or not. The tribunal of fact (jury or magistrates) does not attempt to look into his mind, but simply measures the degree of his departure from the proper standard.
2. The subjective definition, on the other hand, attempts to look into the defendant's mind. It asks whether he realized that there was a risk but carried on regardless.

The subjective definition is now fully accepted.

It's perfectly true that we sometimes consciously run a risk. But how can it be proved? When the affair is over, whatever realisation the defendant had at the time leaves no trace. If he says he didn't think, who can contradict him? One must admit that the subjective theory is an ideal imperfectly achievable. Even though it has been accepted in law, we have to use something suspiciously like an objective test. The jury may be instructed that if anyone would have realized the risk involved in the particular conduct, they may infer that the defendant did so. But:

5–004

*   There is a difference of degree between saying that the risk was so obvious that the defendant must have appreciated it (subjective recklessness), and saying that a reasonable person would have appreciated it but all the same quite a number of people might not have (when, in the absence of additional evidence, subjective recklessness cannot be inferred, though the defendant will be liable if there is a relevant offence of negligence).
*   If the jury are applying the doctrine of subjective recklessness they should regard themselves as trying to assess what the defendant must have foreseen (that is to say, did foresee); and if there is something in the particular facts indicating that he may not have appreciated the risk, that will be overriding. If the facts show that the defendant was or may have

---

[9] [2004] 1 A.C. 1034.

been momentarily careless, not appreciating the risk in what he did, he should be acquitted on the subjective theory.

5–005   **When the subjective definition refers to the defendant realizing that there was a risk, what degree of risk are we speaking of?**   Under the subjective definition of recklessness, the tribunal of fact would in theory enquire first what degree of risk the defendant foresaw, and would then determine whether that risk was a reasonable/justifiable one for the defendant to run. In practice the enquiry cannot be so fine-tuned. But the tribunal may ask itself whether there was any social justification for the defendant causing more than the usual accepted risks of life. If there was not, then if the tribunal believes that the defendant must at least have foreseen some small risk beyond these accepted risks in what he did, then he can be accounted reckless. In special cases the circumstances may be held to have justified him in running an appreciable degree of risk.[10]

5–006   **Is a person reckless if he intended the result?**   Certainly, *a fortiori*. And a person can be convicted of an offence of negligence if he was reckless or acted intentionally. The wider fault element includes the narrower one.

5–007   **Nevertheless I can't help feeling that subjective recklessness is a very narrow concept. A person may properly be punishable although he cannot be proved to have been subjectively reckless.**   The concept is narrow, but it is meant to be narrow. If the legislature wishes to create an offence wider in range, it can use the concept of negligence. The fear you have expressed is the main reason why the subjective definition met with resistance in the past.[11] The objective definition, in contrast, enables the jury to express its indignation at the defendant's conduct without bothering about what went on in his mind. But against this it may be said that to ask the jury whether the defendant departed grossly from the reasonable standard leaves them to make a value-judgment with very little assistance.

    Part of the trouble arises from the origin of the word "reckless." Etymologically, "recklessness" and "carelessness" mean the same; they refer to the state of mind of not caring, or "recking". In two cases, *Commissioner of Police of the Metropolis v. Caldwell*[12] and *R. v. Lawrence*,[13] Lord Diplock assumed that this meaning still held. Speaking of recklessness, he said: "The popular or dictionary meaning is: careless, regardless, or heedless, of the possible harmful consequences of one's acts;"[14] and assumed that this was also the legal meaning. Lord Diplock's words were unexceptionable if he was using "careless" as well as "reckless" in its literal or etymological sense. The reckless person pursues an object without caring, or without caring very much, whether he is creating danger or not. But it has already been observed that the word "careless" does not now mean this, either in its legal sense or in general use; nor did Lord Diplock suppose that it did. A careless person is one who does not take care, not

---

[10] For a fuller discussion see Glanville Williams, *Textbook of Criminal Law*, (London: Stevens & Sons, 1978) at 72-77.

[11] See *Commissioner of Police of the Metropolis v. Caldwell* [1982] A.C. 341.

[12] [1982] A.C. 341.

[13] [1982] A.C. 510.

[14] *Commissioner of Police of the Metropolis v. Caldwell* [1982] A.C. 341 at 351.

one who does not care. The careless driver certainly cares about having an accident, but for temperamental or other reasons is unable to drive in such a way as to avoid it. Lord Hailsham in *Lawrence*[15] remarked on this change in the meaning of carelessness and the consequent fallacy of identifying it with recklessness. He said: "Reckless has ... almost always ... applied to a person or conduct evincing a state of mind stopping short of deliberate intention, and going beyond mere inadvertence, or in its modern, though not its etymological and original sense, mere carelessness." He went on to say that the word retains its dictionary sense (the sense he had just explained) in legal contexts; but he also approved the "lucid legal interpretation" given to it by Lord Diplock—failing to perceive that Lord Diplock had accepted the possibility of finding recklessness without any state of mind. In the drowsy atmosphere of the committee room, the other Lords agreed both with Lord Diplock, that recklessness means carelessness, and with Lord Hailsham, that it does not.

5.3.   THE DEFINITION OF NEGLIGENCE

"Taint what men don't know that makes trouble in the world; it's what they know for certain that ain't so."

Josh Billings[16]

Intention is clearly a mental state, and a type of legal fault. Another type of legal fault, not necessarily involving a mental state, is negligence. Some accidents (or other events) are so unexpected that when they happen we can only say that they were unavoidable—in legal language, "inevitable." We cannot think of anything that a careful person would have done to avoid the evil result, if he had been in the shoes of the defendant. Other accidents happen because of the neglect of some precaution that a reasonable person would have used. (The reasonable person is sometimes, and better, called a prudent person.) Such accidents are the products of what we call negligence, or carelessness. Negligence, then, is failure to conform to the standard of care to which it is the defendant's duty to conform. It is failure to behave like a reasonable prudent person, in the circumstances where the law requires such reasonable behaviour. An employer may for example be negligent as to whether safety precautions are being used by his workpeople.

5–008

You mean the defendant was thoughtless?   Yes, or incompetent in a job (such as driving a car) in which he should have been competent. Or, worse still, he may actually have seen the danger and "chanced his arm." In the later cases he is advertently negligent, or in other words reckless. If he did not advert to the danger, or in other words realize there was a risk, when he ought to have, he is inadvertently negligent. Negligence means forbidden conduct where the defendant's liability depends on the fact that he failed to realize (foresee/know) what he ought to have realized, and failed to conform his conduct accordingly, or, *a fortiori*, that he did realize it and yet failed to conform his conduct as he should.

5–009

---

[15] [1982] A.C. 510 at 520.

[16] Josh Billings, *Everybody's Friend, or; Josh Billing's Encyclopedia and Proverbial Philosophy of Wit and Humor*, (Hartford, CT: American Publishing Company, 1874.) at 82.

The test of negligence in terms of the prudent person is called an "objective" standard, because it does not depend upon a finding of what passed in the defendant's mind.

5–010   **Why do you bring in the prudent person in defining negligence? Is it because otherwise the standard would vary for everyone?** There would be no standard at all. Every judgment of a person's conduct implies judgment measured against a standard external to him.

5–011   **Who is this "prudent person"? Is he the person in the street?** The person in the street, that legendary combination of sage and ignoramus, does not quite represent the idea. The "prudent person" or "reasonable person" of the lawyer's imagining is the exemplary person: the cautious, circumspect, anxiously calculating paragon who is held up by the judges as the model of behaviour. Sometimes, it is true, he is described as the ordinary person, or average person. But little effort is made at trials to find how ordinary people behave; and it would not be a cast-iron defence to a charge of negligence to show that other people are prone to do exactly as the defendant did. (At least, that is the position of the law of tort.) *Homo juridicus* is the ideal person, the moral person, the conscientious person—not setting the standard so high that life becomes impossible in ordinary terms, but nevertheless requiring the most careful consideration to be given, so that harm is avoided and the law is obeyed.

5–012   **Why not eliminate talk of a reasonable person by asking simply whether the harm was probable?** Probability is a matter of varying degree. Negligence consists in taking a risk of harm with such a degree of probability as to be socially unacceptable. This depends on what it is that is at stake. A surgeon may, if there is no other way of alleviating his patient's suffering or prolonging his life, perform an operation that carries a very high risk of killing his patient, without being adjudged negligent. An employer who, in order to increase production and profits, takes what is, statistically, a much smaller risk with the lives of his workpeople may well be held to be so.

5–013   **What should a prosecutor do to prove negligence?** In an action in tort for negligence the plaintiff must give particulars of the alleged negligence in his statement of claim. For example, in a running down case he will say that the defendant drove too fast, on the wrong side of the road, without keeping a proper look-out, and so on. There are no similar pleadings in criminal cases, but the prosecutor who alleges negligence must be prepared to say what the defendant could and should have done (or refrained from doing) in order to avoid the accident or other occurrence.

The evidence given on the negligence issue is almost exclusively evidence of what the defendant did (or failed to do).[17] After that, it is for the jury (or magistrates) to say whether the defendant's behaviour showed a lack of due caution. But occasionally experts called on behalf of the prosecution or defence, are allowed to say that a mistake made by the defendant in a technical matter was

---

[17] *R. v. Trafalgar Leisure Ltd.* [2009] Env. L.R. 29.

an understandable one,[18] or that the defendant behaved as people do in the particular occupation.[19] As said before, it is not necessarily a defence to show that the defendant complied with the average standard of conduct, because the tribunal may still say that this average standard was negligent; but the evidence may help the defence all the same.

A person who, otherwise than in an emergency, undertakes a task that can be safely performed only if he has special skill will be negligent if he does not possess that skill.[20] A person can be "careless" even where he cares deeply. A man may take all the care of which he is capable, and yet be accounted "careless" or negligent for failing to reach the objective standard. He may honestly (or, to use another expression, in good faith, *bona fide*[21]) believe that the facts are such that he is not imperilling anyone; but he may be held to have been negligent in arriving at that belief. An incompetent driver may be convicted of driving "without due care and attention" even though he was doing his level best. The careless person is the person who does not *take* the care he ought to take: never mind whether he *felt* careful. He can be held to be negligent in making a perfectly honest mistake.

Almost the only crime at common law carrying responsibility for negligence, certainly the only one of importance, is manslaughter; and here the courts have developed the restriction that the negligence must be "gross" in order to found criminal responsibility.[22] This means that a small lapse from reasonable conduct does not make a person punishable. Several other offences of negligence have been created by statute.[23] The legislature seems to prefer to speak of a failure to use care (as in the offence of careless driving) or of a requirement of due diligence[24] or reasonable conduct; but these are only different ways of referring to the concept of negligence. Statutes creating offences of omission often involve responsibility for negligence, because the purpose of such statutes is that the defendant should move himself to take positive steps to bring about the situations desired by the legislature.

5–014

---

[18] *R. v. Lamb* [1967] 2 Q.B. 981.

[19] The expert evidence given in *R. v. Adomako* [1995] 1 A.C. 171 overwhelmingly suggested that D had not behaved as a reasonable anaesthetist would.

[20] An everyday skill is not a specialist skill merely because it is used by someone in their profession. In *R. v. Bannister* [2010] 1 W.L.R. 870, a police officer argued "that his special training had provided him with the skill to drive safely at high speeds and in adverse conditions and that that was relevant to the question whether he had been driving dangerously." The Court of Appeal held: "that taking into account the driving skills of a *particular driver* in assessing whether his driving had been dangerous was inconsistent with the objective standard of what could be expected of the competent and careful driver set out in s. 2A(1)(3) of the *Road Traffic Act 1988*."

[21] Generally, pronounced "bohna fydee." Note that this means "in good faith," if you wish to speak Latin, it is *bona fides* (generally pronounced "bohna fydeez").

[22] *R. v. Adomako* [1995] 1 A.C. 171; *R. v. Morgan* [2007] EWCA Crim. 3313; *R. v. Evans* [2009] 1 W.L.R. 1999. See also Jeremy Horder, "Gross Negligence and Criminal Culpability," (1997) 47 *U. Toronto L.J.* 495.

[23] Some of these are rather serious indeed. Section 5 of the *Domestic Violence, Crime and Victims Act 2004* criminalizes those who recklessly or negligently cause or allow the death of a child; and can result in a maximum prison term of 14 years.

[24] Colin Manchester, "Knowledge, Due Diligence and Strict Liability in Regulatory Offences," [2006] Crim. L.R. 213.

When statutes create new offences of negligence, they do not specify the degree of negligence requisite for penal responsibility; and it might perhaps have been thought that, by analogy with the rule developed in manslaughter, the judges would have required all criminal negligence to be "gross." The rule is proposed in the American Law Institute's Model Penal Code.[25] English judges have not taken this line, so that, with us, statutory criminal negligence generally means any departure, however small, from the standard of the reasonable person. If some courts act more leniently, that is not reflected in the theory of the law.

5–015 **Do I gather that when considering negligence you entirely ignore the defendant's state of mind?** That would be going too far. One can imagine circumstances where an ordinary driver would not be careless in running a blind person down, if he did not know[26] he was blind and had no reason to suppose he would proceed as he did. But a driver who knew that the man was blind might on such facts be guilty of one of the negligent driving offences.[27]

5–016 **Is negligence a form of *mens rea*?** Some judges assume this, but there are substantial arguments the other way:

- Negligence is not necessarily a state of mind, so it is not properly called *mens rea*.
- The most serious and severely punishable crimes are defined to require intention or recklessness. If it were allowed that negligence is *mens rea*, the judges might extend the concept of recklessness to cover negligence (which some of them have done in the past),[28] and which would result in a great increase in severity of punishment).[29] The argument does *not* involve saying that negligence should not be punished: only that it should not generally be punished on a par with crimes requiring a mental element.[30]

Philosophers have tried all sorts of tricks to present criminal negligence as a form of subjective culpability, but have not managed to succeed.[31] It is said that some people have an "I could not care less" attitude, but an attitude cannot make a person subjectively culpable for risks he did not foresee. Many nasty people might not care less about others, but might be fortunate enough never to have an accident. Meanwhile, many people of exemplary character might be unfortunate enough to make grave slips. It is not clear how the attitude of the anaesthetist in

---

[25] See section 202(2)(*d*).

[26] "[R]egard shall be had not only to the circumstances of which he could be expected to be aware but also to any circumstances shown to have been within the knowledge of the accused." Section 30 (3ZA)(3) of the *Road Safety Act 2006*.

[27] See the offences found in section 2A(3) of the *Road Traffic Act 1988*; section 1 of the *Road Traffic Act 1991*; and section 20(1) of the *Road Safety Act 2006*.

[28] *Commissioner of Police of the Metropolis v. Caldwell* [1982] A.C. 341.

[29] See *Elliott v. C (A Minor)* [1983] 1 W.L.R. 939.

[30] Cf. George P. Fletcher, *Basic Concepts of Criminal Law*, (New York: Oxford University Press, 1998) at 117; George P. Fletcher, "Theory of Criminal Negligence: A Comparative Analysis," (1970) 119 *U. Pa. L. Rev.* 401.

[31] Cf. Victor Tadros, *Criminal Responsibility*, (Oxford: Oxford University Press, 2005) chap. 9; Michael D. Bayles, "Character, Purpose and Criminal Responsibility," (1982) 1 *Law and Phil.* 5 at 10.

R. v. Adomako was one of "I could not care less."[32] Nevertheless, he deserved to be punished. Adomako might have been very caring, but he got it wrong. A ruthless self-absorbed anaesthetist who attends operations while suffering from hangovers and sleep deprivation might never make a mistake. Some commentators refer to the idea of "culpable indifference," namely Duff and Simons. But to the extent "culpable" (subjective choice) "indifference"[33] means D chose "not to care," it is covered by the doctrine of subjective recklessness. If these theorists just mean "indifference,"[34] then that is negligence *a fortiori*. Attempts to extend subjective recklessness to cover objective recklessness can only go so far, because there is a conceptual divide that cannot be fused.

5.4. THE JUSTIFICATION OF PUNISHMENT FOR NEGLIGENCE

The reason for punishing negligence is the utilitarian one that we hope thereby to improve people's standards of behaviour.   **5–017**

Isn't the question one of moral wrong? It is wrong not to exercise   **5–018**
consideration for others. If inadvertent negligence results from not caring about other people, it is a defect of character and may be regarded as morally wrong. But what lawyers call inadvertent negligence is not always this kind. Negligence may be just a slip by a well-disposed person, and whether that should be accounted as morally wrong is open to debate.

Even though the offender did not realize the danger on the occasion in   **5–019**
question, he would have realized it if he had taken due precautions. So he
was morally to blame. I do not dissent; but we should keep our eyes open to the facts. Apply what you say to the particular case of the forgetful person. A person with a bad memory can often take steps to remedy his deficiency—by keeping a diary of his engagements and consulting frequently, and so on. But his memory may be so bad that one day he forgets to look in his diary, or forgets an item recorded in it. Perhaps, to overcome this risk, he takes additional steps, such as asking his wife to remind him of a particular engagement. But one day he forgets to ask his wife. Is he to think of another device to remind him to look at his diary or to ask his wife to remind him? What if he causes a fire by forgetting to turn off the oven or iron? Is it moral fault not to do so? What we are faced with is the plain fact that on the particular occasion the thought to take a particular

---

[32] [1995] 1 A.C. 171. See also *R. v. Misra* [2005] 1 Cr. App. R. 21.

[33] See for example, Kenneth W. Simons, "Does Punishment for Culpable Indifference Simply Punish for Bad Character," (2002-03) 6 *Buff. Crim. L. Rev.* 219; R. A. Duff, *Intention, Agency and Criminal Liability*, (Oxford: Basil Blackwell, 1990) at 160 *et seq.* See Stephen P. Garvey, "What's Wrong with Involuntary Manslaughter," (2007) 85 *Tex. L. Rev.* 333. Likewise, Garvey's "culpable failure to exercise doxastic self-control over one's beliefs" cannot be used to show that a defendant like Adomako subjectively risked the harm he brought about.

[34] That is to say, could not have modified if he had a normal make-up. As Moore notes, "What makes the intentional or reckless wrongdoer so culpable is not unexercised capacity—although that is necessary—but the way such capacity to avoid evil goes unexercised; such wrongdoer are not even trying to get it right. Their capacity goes unexercised because that is what they choose. Choice is essential to their culpability, not one way among others that they could have been seriously culpable." See Michal S. Moore, *Placing Blame*, (Oxford: Clarendon Press, 1997) at 590.

precaution never comes into his mind. That is a deficiency in his mental make-up which he cannot help. To search back into his past for the purpose of finding some defect in the arrangements made to remedy his failing, and blaming him on that account, often wears the appearance of being an unrewarding exercise in moralism.

It is not only a question of memory. Many studies have been made of accident proneness; and it has been found that large categories of people are more accident-prone than others. Old people are worse than younger people and children worse than adults and so on.[35] But some individuals are particularly accident prone. They are born with conditions that make them particularly inept,[36] or become so through their experiences. A person has an innate temperament, which may in the course of time be modified by many circumstances over which he has no control. The result may be that he is impulsive, unable to stop and consider the consequences of what he is doing, or too dull in mind to imagine them; that he is clumsy, unable to control his own movements (or those of a machine he is using) with due precision, or with a slow reaction-time in case of an emergency.

5–020   **If, as you say, the individual is unable to help these aspects of his mind or body, how can he be said to deserve punishment?**   This objection to imposing liability for negligence appeals particularly to those who take the "determinist" position, according to which all events (including human acts) are governed by pre-existing events which are their causes.[37] Everything we do is the product of our genetic constitution and personal history.

We need not go into voluminous arguments for and against determinism. It is sufficient to say that the determinist philosophy, even if true, is of little interest either to the lawyer or the moralist. The question in law and morals is whether the offender could have acted otherwise if he had willed. If he could, he is morally and legally responsible.[38] The further question "Was he able to will?" may be speculated on by philosophers, but is eschewed in law and morals for pragmatic reason. The object of the law and of the moral system is to influence our wills in a socially desirable direction. Once this simple point is grasped, the apparent difficulty of reconciling the utilitarian justification for punishment is slightly ameliorated. However, malfunctioning of the will is given moral and legal significance when it is associated with childhood or is regarded as a symptom of mental disorder.

---

[35] Knud Knudsen "Accident Risk in Middle Age Years and in Old Age," (1975) 18 *Acta Sociologica* 62. Cf. Liisa Hakamies-Blomqvist *et al.*, "Driver Ageing does not Cause Higher Accident Rates per km," (2002) 5(4) *Transportation Research: Traffic Psychology and Behaviour* 271. See also Frank P. Mckenna, "Accident proneness: A conceptual analysis," (1983) 15(1) *Accident Analysis & Prevention* 65.

[36] For example, those born with Attention Deficit Hyperactivity Disorder tend to be more accident-prone.

[37] See M. J. Julian, "A Determinist's Perspective of Criminal Responsibility," (1970) 8 *Alta. L. Rev.* 376; Joshua Dressler, "Professor Delgado's Brainwashing Defense: Courting a Determinist Legal System," (1979) 63 *Minn. L. Rev.* 335.

[38] Therefore, Professor Fletcher's criticism that an objective standard of negligence implies that negligence is not blameworthy, has to be rejected. See George P. Fletcher, *Rethinking Criminal Law*, (Boston: Little, Brown, 1978), 504-505.

Whether fault "exists" or not, the plain person thinks that it does exist. He is prepared to acknowledge that punishment for fault is just, when punishment without fault would be unjust. Therefore, we secure the best acceptance for the operation of the criminal law if we limit it to cases perceived as ones of fault—that is, cases where most people, *properly* conditioned, would have acted otherwise. Again punishment for what is seen as fault can affect future conduct and the conduct of others in a way that punishment without fault cannot.[39] Punishment for fault assumes that the offender could have prevented the occurrence—or, at least, that there were no circumstances outside the defendant's mental and bodily constitution that he could not have modified to prevent the occurrence; and we may entertain a hope that such punishment may cause him to act better afterwards. The application of punishment is a way of conditioning the offender for the future. But the real value in punishing such conduct is that it sends the "take care" message to the world at large. (Particularly, those who choose to engage in risky activities.)

The position is different if punishment is administered for inevitable accidents, **5–021** when it is admitted that no ordinary person doing what the offender was doing would have been able to avoid a recurrence of that situation, otherwise than by ceasing altogether from the class of activity in question—an activity which may be socially desirable. Here the offender is made to accept the risk of punishment as an unavoidable incident of the activity. This is the position with crimes of strict responsibility,[40] but from the moral point of view strict liability is highly suspect.

Liability for negligence is a way of sanctioning (punishing) common sense rules that in themselves have no legal force. There are well-known rules of prudence relating to the management of firearms, that one should never leave them loaded, or point them at anyone even though believed to be unloaded and so on. Again, it is only a rule of prudence, not explicitly one of law, that one should not pass on a blind corner (except that there is a law on the subject on the crossing of double white lines). Failure to observe these rules (which will

---

[39] Dennis J. Baker, "Punishment without a Crime: Is Preventive Detention Reconcilable with Justice," (2009) 34 *Austl. J. Leg. Phil.* 120; Peter Arenella "Convicting the Morally Blameless: Reassessing the Relationship between Legal and Moral Accountability," (1992) 39 *UCLA L. Rev.* 1511.

[40] Murphy and Coleman note: "Widespread strict liability would destroy meaningful lives because it would force us to be overly cautious in areas (*e.g.*, travel, pursuing ordinary activities, *etc.*) where we should not be overly cautious. But this is not true for all areas of social activity. Thus in order to prevent great harm, what is ultimately the matter with society saying this: 'Certain areas of activity (food processing, banking, sexual experimentation with children) have great potential for harm. Since individuals do not have fundamental rights to do those things and since there is no social value in having people casually experiment in these areas (indeed much potential for harm), then what is wrong with making the price for entry into these selected areas a willingness to risk strict liability prosecution. ...Even if one function of the criminal law is to express society's moral condemnation for certain acts and thereby stigmatise the criminal, a person who lacks the wisdom to heed the warning that he stay out of a dangerous area of conduct for which he is unsuited may not be an unfitting object for such ostracism.'" Jeffrie G. Murphy and Jules L. Coleman, *Philosophy of Law*, (Westview Press, 1990) at 128.

generally be an intentional or reckless failure) will readily be held to be negligence, and depending on the consequence could result in a conviction for a very serious offence.[41]

5–022 **The reason why drivers do not pass on blind corners is because they apprehend a consequence much more immediate and terrifying than what may afterwards happen in a court of law.** That is true, but the law of reckless and careless driving can add to the pressure to make bad drivers change their habits and in the last resort to give up driving. Carelessness with firearms is in a different legal position from careless driving. Such carelessness is not an offence in itself, and it is not an offence even if it causes severe injury, the reason evidently being that accidents with firearms are too uncommon to attract particular attention from the law. However, if the victim dies, a charge of manslaughter may be brought.

Paradoxically, the justification for punishing negligence is stronger in minor offences involving neither imprisonment nor odium than in major offences. "Regulatory offences" generally relate to the conduct of a business or other undertaking where the situation is a recurring one. Fines, and if necessary repeated fines, prod people into taking care.[42] On the other hand, a substantial sentence of imprisonment would make little sense, since it would be disproportionate to the occasion. As regards the offender himself it would be more likely to destroy his occupation than to improve his standards. Such a sentence, passed for reasons of general deterrence, is unlikely to make ordinary people attend more anxiously to the consequences of their conduct, except perhaps in the cases already mentioned where compliance may be demanded with some identifiable rule of prudence. Furthermore, even when the harm done is great, if the situation is one where it is not possible to link the harm to those who are most responsible for it, there may be little social advantage in inflicting heavy punishment on their agents simply because they were the immediate cause of the harm.[43]

In short, although there is little objection to fining the inadvertent offender, for reasons of general as well as particular deterrence, it seems right if possible to do so in summary proceedings for a breach of some specific regulation rather than by making negligence a serious and stigmatic offence. Lord Radcliffe observed that "there is a certain virile attraction in the idea of making a man answer for the foreseeable consequences of what he has done without troubling to search his

---

[41] See the offences found in section 2A(3) of the *Road Traffic Act 1988*; section 1 of the *Road Traffic Act 1991*; and section 20 of the *Road Safety Act 2006*.

[42] It would be harsh to jail a person for negligently failing to secure his rubbish cans, but a decent fine would be appropriate. Similarly, a business that is a repeat offender could have its trading licence revoked. Environmental vandalism will not always be a trivial matter. In some cases it will merely involve standard waste (litter, bottles and cans, *etc.*): *Milton Keynes Council v. Leisure Connection Ltd.* [2010] Env. L.R. 4; in other cases, it will involve toxic waste: *Transco Plc. v. HM Advocate (No.1)* [2005] B.C.C. 296.

[43] This has been a problem in the corporate manslaughter cases, as the immediate negligence is usually the product of a junior employee. See *Attorney-General's Reference (No. 2 of 1999)* [2000] Q.B. 796; *R. v. P&O European Ferries (Dover) Ltd.* (1991) 93 Cr. App. R. 72.

mind for motives or purposes: but it does not go well with the dock or the prison gate."[44] Responsibility for negligence is therefore exceptional for the more serious crimes.

There would be much to be said for enacting that no one should be sent to prison on account of negligence,[45] but there are rare cases where jail time is an appropriate state response. The deterrence justification is simply that the gravity of the harm involved in some negligent acts is much greater than it is in many intentional acts, so the criminal law should be used to get people to take care if they are engaging in risky activities such as driving cars, driving trains, flying planes, carrying our medical operations, labelling foods and medicines, handling firearms and so on. The harm that results when a person negligently fails to extinguish a campfire[46] may be much greater than the harm caused by someone who intentionally smashes a telephone receiver.[47]

5–023

5.5. THE DISABLED DEFENDANT

When comparing the physically and mentally disabled (blind, maimed, intellectually disabled, *etc.*) with the reasonable person, we suppose that the reasonable person suffers from the same disability. The defendant need only do his best with the body he has.[48] But it would generally be negligent for a disabled person to undertake something that could be done only safely by an ordinary person, if he has the opportunity not to do it.

5–024

What if the defendant is substandard in his abilities? The reasonable person is not imagined to be substandard in intelligence or foresight.[49] Some commentators argue that certain inabilities of the defendant should be considered when measuring whether his conduct fell below the standard expected of a reasonable person. Some call this subjectivizing the objective test. It is a matter of taking incapacitating traits of the defendant into account when considering whether he ought to have behaved better than he did. The question is not only whether he ought to have taken better care, but also whether he could have taken

5–025

---

[44] Lord Radcliffe, *Censors* (Cambridge: Cambridge University Press, The Rede Lecture, 1961) at 20.

[45] Jerome Hall, "Negligent Behavior Should be Excluded from Penal Liability," (1963) 63 *Colum. L. Rev.* 632. Cf. James B. Brady, "Punishment for Negligence: A Reply to Professor Hall," (1972-73) 22 *Buff. L. Rev.* 107.

[46] But even causing £1 million worth of damage has been held not sufficient to justify negligence lialbity. See *R. v G* [2004] 1 A.C. 1034.

[47] Criminal damage is a serious offence, so D must either intent to damage the property or foresee his behaviour will result in such damage. Cf. *R. v. Parker* [1977] 1 W.L.R. 600.

[48] See generally, Mayo Moran, *Rethinking the Reasonable Person*, (Oxford: Oxford University Press, 2003); Caroline Forell, "Essentialism, Empathy, and the Reasonable Woman," (1994) 1994 *U. Ill. L. Rev.* 769. See also Tatjana Hornle, "Social Expectation in the Criminal Law: The Reasonable Person in a Comparative Perspective," (2008) 11 *New Crim. L. Rev.* 1.

[49] See *R. v. C* [2001] 3 F.C.R. 409, where it was held that a defendant suffering from schizophrenia should be judged by the standards of the hypothetical reasonable person. The court was persuaded, it seems, by the fact that section 1(2) of the *Protection from Harassment Act 1997* was enacted to deal with stalkers and other who might have some kind of mild mental disorder. See also *R. v. Coles* [1995] 1 Cr. App. R. 157.

better care given his mental and physical disabilities. This type of individualiz-ing[50] of the prudent person test allows certain serious physical and mental disabilities to be considered.[51] (Of course, in some cases a person's physical disability will mean he should not have been doing what he was doing).

Decades ago Kitto J. expounded:[52]

> "The principle is of course applicable to a child. The standard of care being objective, it is no answer for him, any more than it is for an adult, to say that the harm he caused was due to his being abnormally slow-witted, quick-tempered, absent-minded or inexperienced. But it does not follow that he cannot rely in his defence upon a limitation upon the capacity for foresight or prudence, not as being personal to himself, but as being characteristic of humanity at his stage of development and in that sense normal. By doing so he appeals to a standard of ordinariness, to an objective and not a subjective standard. In regard to the things which pertain to foresight and prudence—experience, understanding of causes and effects, balance of judgement, thoughtfulness—it is absurd, indeed it is a misuse of language, to speak of normality in relation to persons of all ages taken together. In those things normality is, for children, something different from what normality is for adults; the very concept of normality is a concept of rising levels until 'years of discretion are attained'. …. [I]t seems to me that it would be contrary to the fundamental principle that a person is liable for harm that he causes by falling short of an objective criterion of 'propriety in his conduct'—propriety, that is to say, as determined by a comparison with the standard of care reasonably to be expected in the circumstances from the normal person—to hold that where a child's liability is in question the normal person to be considered is someone other than a child of corresponding age."

Certain limitations prevent certain people (in this case, very young children) from meeting the standards of the prudent adult. The entire rationale for punishing negligence is that a reasonable person would have acted differently. The message the law sends to the negligent wrongdoer is that he ought to have acted differently. If a reasonable child or disabled person could not have acted differently, it would be nonsensical to say: "we are punishing you because you ought to have acted differently." The general deterrence justification for punishment is baseless in such cases, because such people are incapable of acting differently to how they did. A child might commit some negligent act that even the most hopeless adult would not be silly enough to commit.

Likewise, it is necessary to individualize the prudent person when he is acting in a professional capacity. If a nurse and neurosurgeon are in the operating theatre, then we expect different things from each of them. Similarly, we would not expect a nurse to identify problems during an operation which are within someone else's skill range such as an anaesthetist's. Hence, the standard is what the reasonable person ought to have done in the circumstances. A child is not expected to act as a competent adult; a nurse ought not to be expected to have foreseen a risk which would have only been obvious to an anaesthetist and so on.

---

[50] Professor Weston prefers the term "individualizing": Peter Weston, "Individualizing the Reasonable Person in Criminal Law," (2008) 2(2) *Crim. L. & Phil.* 137 at 140.

[51] "It is not the handicap *per se* which bears on the excuse of mistake. It is the fact that the handicap results in the accused having to form his belief on a more limited set of information that is relevant, just as other external circumstances affecting the accused's opportunity to develop and test his perception are relevant." *R. v. Mrzljak* [2005] 152 A. Crim. R. 315 at 334 *per* Holmes J.

[52] *McHale v. Watson* (1966) 115 C.L.R. 199 at 213-214.

So have the courts been willing to consider the limitations of sub-groups of **5–026**
reasonable persons? Yes, but only in a limited way. In particular, they have
been willing to consider age. This is a modification of the usual rule requiring the
mental characteristics of the defendant to be ignored.[53] The courts should only
take traits into consideration that make it impossible for the defendant to act
reasonably. It would be unworkable to take gender into consideration, because it
is not a disability. Furthermore, one reasonable person of *x* gender might comply
and the next might not; this is different to saying that D could not comply because
he was in a wheelchair or suffered some mental impairment. Only serious and
clearly defined limitations should be considered, otherwise the objective standard
will spiral into free-for-all defence.

But wouldn't it be more just to have different standards of care for experts **5–027**
at one end of the scale and people of poor intelligence at the other? We were
all born green. Some people remain that colour, but even dullards are not immune
from the conditioning processes of life, including the law. The jury or magistrates
apply the negligence test, roughly speaking, by asking themselves: "Was the
defendant a bigger fool than I like to think I should have been in the same
circumstances?" That is a workable test, even though not very precise. But it
would be impossible and impolitic to have an array of standards varying with
position on an I.Q. scale. For example, an old man who has a driving accident
may decide to give up driving as a result of having to answer a charge of a
driving offence, quite apart from any disqualification that the court may impose
upon him. It would be absurd to say: the older or more stupid the driver, the lower
is the degree of care we expect from him.[54]

Moreover, if the law's reasonable person is to be invested with the defendant's
I.Q., there seems to be no reason why he should not be invested with the
defendant's emotional stability, and indeed with his whole character as resulting
from his genes and environment. But if the reasonable person is given all the
characteristics of the defendant, the standard of judgment wholly disappears, for
we can then compare the defendant's conduct only with the (presumably
identical) conduct of the fictitious construct who is like the defendant in every
conceivable way. However, where a person is mentally impaired (a technical
term), this can introduce the question of mental responsibility. (See Chapter 27).

If the defendant was drunk, do you suppose that a reasonable person was **5–028**
likewise? Obviously, the "reasonable drunken person" would be an unworkable
concept. The reasonable person is as sober as the proverbial judge. So on a charge
involving negligence no allowance is made for hallucinatory or disabling effects
of alcohol or other drugs when taken voluntarily. The rule is justified on social
grounds, since the criminal courts need the power to control those who are given
to drinking and who when in drink are dangerous. We will discuss this further in
later chapters.

---

[53] *Royal Society for the Protection of Animals v. C* (2006) 170 J.P. 463; *R. v. G.* [2004] 1 A.C. 1034 at
1037. Cf. *D.P.P. v. TY (No 2)* (2006) 14 V.R. 430. See also the civil law cases *Orchard v. Lee* [2009]
EWCA Civ. 295; *Blake v. Galloway* [2004] 1 W.L.R. 2844; *Mullin v. Richards* [1998] 1 W.L.R. 1304.
See *Attorney-General for Jersey v. Holley* [2005] 2 A.C. 580; *D.P.P. v. Camplin* [1978] 2 W.L.R. 679.
[54] *R. v. Bannister* [2010] 1 W.L.R. 870.

CHAPTER 6

FAULT AS TO CIRCUMSTANCES

"Doubtless it is the judicial unwillingness to make any case law at all which accounts for the sloppiness with which it is made, when it is. Discussion of general principle is not encouraged. Cases relating to *mens rea* as an element in crime live in a shambles from which academic writers try to rescue them."

Lord Devlin[1]

6.1. THE CIRCUMSTANCES OF AN ACT

Hitherto we have been primarily concerned with fault as to consequences, but similar problems can arise in relation to circumstances.   **6–001**

Could you give me a capsule definition of a circumstance? If a man seduces a French girl, is the fact that she is French one of the circumstances?   The circumstances are not all the facts surrounding the crime but the relevant circumstances—the facts existing at the time when the defendant acts, being facts specified in law as conditions of the offence. About the only offence that might be committed in the case you put is one of having sexual intercourse with a girl under 16.[2] The facts (1) that it is a girl; and (2) that she is under 16 are circumstances of the offence, being specified in the law; but her Frenchness is irrelevant. No consequence is required for this "conduct crime", only the act and the circumstances.   **6–002**

As another example, bigamy is committed where a man goes through a ceremony of marriage with a woman when he is already married to another (or similarly for a woman).[3] The offence is committed by the act of saying "I will" in the marriage ceremony. The fact that the defendant is already married is a circumstance of the offence. It is something specified in the statute that is not a consequence.

But isn't the consequence the fact that you become married?   The bigamous ceremony is null and void, and does not marry anybody. It has no operation in the civil law, even though it is a crime. But in any case, when one is analyzing the elements of a crime and speaks of the consequences, one means the physical consequences, not legal consequences. Bigamy is historically made an offence   **6–003**

---

[1] Baron Patrick Devlin, *The Judge* (Oxford: Oxford University Press, 1979).
[2] Section 9 of the *Sexual Offences Act 2003*.
[3] Section 57 of the *Offences against the Person Act 1861*.

[135]

because it is "the profanation of a solemn ceremony." Nowadays it is comparatively rarely prosecuted, and comparatively leniently treated, the main objection now seen to it being the opportunity that it gives to deceive the second "spouse," or perhaps third persons.

If the law were clear and rational, fault in relation to circumstances could be fairly easily stated. It would be this:

- An act is intentional as to circumstances if the actor knows that the circumstance is present.
- An act is reckless as to circumstances if the actor knows that the circumstance may be present and takes an unreasonable risk as to its presence.
- An act is negligent as to a circumstance if the circumstance, though perhaps not known, could have been discovered by reasonable enquiry.

We shall see that the courts have introduced doubts and difficulties into the first two of these propositions.

6–004   **I don't understand about being reckless as to a circumstance. A circumstance is a present fact. You can be reckless as to something happening in the future, but not, surely as to what has already happened.** The recklessness relates to the question whether or not the fact exists. You may throw a letter on the fire being reckless as to whether it contains cash. Part of the following discussion will be concerned with the effect of mistake, and it may be mentioned here that there are three kinds of mistake, only two of which concern us as affecting liability:

1.   Mistake as to a definitional fact (part of the definition of the offence). This is our concern at the moment, and the argument will be that such mistake is a defence if it negatives a required mental element forming part of the definition.
2.   Mistake as to the matter of defence (*e.g.*, mistaken belief in the necessity for self-defence).
3.   Mistake as to a jurisdictional or procedural fact, which does not affect culpability and so is no excuse (*e.g.*, a belief that you were acting in Scotland, when in fact you were acting in England, or a mistaken belief that you have diplomatic immunity). Of this kind of mistake we shall have no more to say.

6.2.   INTENTION AS TO CIRCUMSTANCES

6–005   Intention was previously defined in (4.2.) as relating to the result of an act, but we also speak of the act itself as being intentional. "The act itself" may mean *either* the bodily movement *or* the bodily movement plus the circumstances in which it was done. As applied to bodily movement the notion means that the movement was willed or volitional or purposive or done in a state of normal consciousness. (A sleepwalker does not intentionally walk, for legal purposes, because he is not in a state of normal consciousness.) As applied to the circumstances of the act, the notion of intention, according to the usual understanding, means that these circumstances were known to the actor. If for example we say that D intentionally trespassed on an airfield, we mean more than that D went for a walk. We mean that he knew he was on an airfield, and knew he had no right to be there.

Suppose he didn't know that where he was was part of the airfield but suspected it might be, and took his walk regardless?   The proper language then, surely, would be to say that D recklessly trespassed on an airfield, if such it was. Or, more fully, that he took a walk, being reckless as to whether he was on an airfield. There is surprisingly little authority on the legal point, because most *mens rea* offences can be committed intentionally or recklessly, in which case all the prosecution has to prove is recklessness. But the law should accept the ordinary use of language, so that an offence of intention (in the fullest sense of the word) should require knowledge of the circumstances, not just recklessness as to the circumstances. At the very least it should require one or the other.

6–006

Take the example of the person who held the arms of the police officer in order to persuade him that the person he was about to arrest was innocent.[4] He was convicted of wilfully obstructing the constable because he knowingly obstructed the constable, even though only for a moment. He knew that he was, for that moment, hindering the officer. If you know what you are doing, you do it intentionally. (The word "wilfully"[5] is sometimes construed to include reckless-ness, and a person might perhaps be convicted if he parked his car in a way that he knew might obstruct the police, and if in consequence he did obstruct them; but it would push the offence very far.)

Take rape as an example. This was defined at common law as sexual intercourse with a woman without her consent.[6] It has always been assumed that a mental element is required, but what mental element? Bridge J. (as he then was) declared in the Court of Appeal in *D.P.P. v. Morgan*[7] that the intention required for rape was simply to have sexual intercourse with a woman.[8] "Without her consent," he thought was not a part of the crime requiring a mental element. This strange idea was knocked on the head on appeal to the House of Lords,[9] which affirmed that rape does require a mental element, and not one that is merely confined to the act of sex.[10]

The loose thinking of some judges on the subject of rape was not due to judicial bashfulness as to making law, as Lord Devlin suggests in the passage at the head of this chapter. The courts, in my diagnosis, are far from unwilling to make law, if

6–007

---

[4] See *Hills v. Ellis* [1983] Q.B. 680.

[5] This word "wilfully" is also used in section 89 of the *Police Act 1996*. Section 89 replaced the old offence of obstructing found in section 51(3) of the *Police Act 1964*.

[6] The current statutory offence can only be committed by a man since the intentional penetration can only be done with a penis. See section 1 of the *Sexual Offences Act 2003*.

[7] [1975] 1 All E.R. 8.

[8] See the criticism by Lord Fraser in the House of Lords: *D.P.P. v. Morgan* [1976] A.C. 182 at 236-237. Yet Lord Fraser perpetrated the same error in regard to bigamy: *id* at 238.

[9] *D.P.P. v. Morgan* [1976] A.C. 182.

[10] Negligence as to whether the woman was consenting is now sufficient to ground a rape conviction: section 1(2) of the *Sexual Offences Act 2003*.

it is law extending offences and restricting defences. The reason why *mens rea* lives in a shambles—why judges incorrigibly defy the conventions of language and ordinary ideas of logic and justice, although their errors are continually being pointed out—is because they wish from time to time to exclude or restrict the *mens rea* doctrine.

D.P.P. v. Morgan concerned a crime the definition of which (at the time the case was decided) rested on the common law (it has since been put in statutory form).[11] Many other crimes are defined in statutes which do not expressly require a mental element. The traditional rule of the common law is that the requirement is nevertheless to be implied, but the courts frequently evade it.[12] One technique is to say (as the Court of Appeal did in *D.P.P. v. Morgan*) that although the offence impliedly requires an intent, that intent need relate only to the doing of the forbidden act, omitting any reference to the circumstances of the act. This merely pays lip-service to the requirement of intent.

The drastic effect that such language can have on the *mens rea* principle may be illustrated by bigamy. Bigamy is defined by statute as marrying again during the life of one's spouse. That is about all that the statute says on the basic requirements of the offence. The courts hold that the only mental element to be implied into the statute is an intent to do the forbidden act: in other words an intention to go through a marriage ceremony.[13] So everyone who gets married has the *mens rea* of bigamy! He is guilty of bigamy if, being already married, he is negligent as to the subsistence of the first marriage.

6–008 However, this severely restrictive attitude towards the mental element is generally found not in relation to technically serious crimes like bigamy but in relation to minor statutory offences, which are by this stratagem turned into offences of strict liability.

When a statute expressly requires a mental element, it seems that the courts will require the mental element to exist not merely as to the doing of the basic act but also to the circumstances of the offence. A mistake as to these circumstances can negative both intention and recklessness.[14] In other words, if the actor believed that the required circumstances, the definitional facts, were not present, then his act was neither intentional nor reckless to them. This proposition, which is the merest common sense, has been established for crimes of wilfulness by

---

[11] Section 1 of the *Sexual Offences Act 2003*.

[12] *R. v. Deyemi* [2008] 1 Cr. App. R. 25. Cf. *R. v. G* [2006] 1 W.L.R. 2052, which seems right doctrinally, since Parliament clearly intended section 5 of the *Sexual Offences Act* to operate as an offence of strict liability. However, it does suggest the constitutional principle of *mens rea* as stated in *B. (A Minor) v. D.P.P.* [2000] 2 A.C. 428 actually needs to be constitutionalized. This would allow the Supreme Court to strike down such offences. It is unjust to allow people to be jailed for years on the basis of strict liability. Sir Rupert Cross was essentially right in interpreting it as a constitutional principle, but it would have more bite if the legislature were to incorporate it in a codified Bill of Rights.

[13] See the *dictum* of Lord Fraser in *D.P.P. v. Morgan* [1976] A.C. 182 at 236-237.

[14] In *B. (A Minor) v. D.P.P.* [2000] 2 A.C. 428 at 462, it was noted: "The reasonableness or unreasonableness of the defendant's belief is material to the question of whether the belief was held by the defendant at all. If the belief was in fact held, its unreasonableness, so far as guilt or innocence is concerned, is neither here nor there. It is irrelevant. Were it otherwise, the defendant *would be convicted because he was negligent in failing to recognize that the victim was not consenting* . . . and so on." *Per* Lord Nicholls citing Lord Lane C.J. in *R. v. Williams* [1987] 3 All E.R. 411 at 415.

several decisions.[15] Nowadays the word "wilfully" is generally replaced in statutes by a requirement of intention or recklessness; and the same rule applies, as is shown by *R. v. Smith*.[16]

Section 1(1) of the *Criminal Damage Act 1971* provides "[a] person who without lawful excuse destroys or damages any property belonging to another intending to destroy or damage any such property or being reckless as to whether any such property would be destroyed or damaged shall be guilty of an offence." Smith was the tenant of a flat who made some additions to it with the consent of his landlady. These additions, being "affixed to the soil," became the property of the landlady; but believing them to be his own property he superficially damaged them in order to remove certain wiring. A totally unmeritorious prosecution was brought against him for criminal damage, on the extraordinary argument that he had intentionally damaged property that in fact (though he did not know it) belonged to another; therefore he had intentionally damaged property of another. This argument, believe it or not, was accepted by the trial judge, and Smith was convicted. James L.J., delivering the judgment of the Court of Appeal quashing the conviction, said that in construing section 1(1):[17]

> "[W]e have no doubt that the *actus reus* is 'destroying or damaging any property belonging to another'. It is not possible to exclude the words 'belonging to another' which describes the 'property'. Applying the ordinary principles of *mens rea*, the intention and recklessness and the absence of lawful excuse required to constitute the offence have reference to property belonging to another. It follows that in our judgment no offence is committed under this section if a person destroys or causes damage to property belonging to another if he does so in the honest though mistaken belief that the property is his own, and provided that the belief is honestly held it is irrelevant to consider whether or not it is a justifiable belief."

The judge says: "if the belief is honestly held." How could it be dishonestly held?   It could not be, of course. Judges in speaking of belief frequently say that it must be a genuine belief, an honest belief, a *bona fide* belief, a true belief, a belief held in good faith. But such qualifiers are unnecessary, because one cannot believe un-genuinely or dishonestly or in bad faith.[18] They seem to use the word "honestly" when they mean "actually." The decision in *R. v. Smith* illustrates two important propositions:

6–009

1.   Where a statute uses a *mens rea* word, this word should be taken to control the whole provision unless the contrary is clearly stated.[19] "Intending to damage any property belonging to another" does not mean "intending to

---

[15] *Moore v. Green* [1983] 1 All E.R. 663; *Ostler v. Elliott* [1980] Crim. L.R. 584; *Willmott v. Atack* [1977] Q.B. 498; *Eaton v. Cobb* [1950] 1 All E.R. 1016; *Wilson v. Inyang* [1951] 2 K.B. 799; *Bullock v. Turnbull* [1952] 2 Lloyd's Rep. 303.

[16] [1974] Q.B. 354.

[17] *R. v. Smith* [1974] Q.B. 354 at 360.

[18] If you dishonestly pretend that you believed *x* when you really believed *y*, then you never really believed *x*. So, the question is simply: Did you in fact believe *x*? If not, your dishonesty relates to your present lie in court, not your past belief because it was whatever it was.

[19] See *Cotterill v. Penn* [1936] 1 K.B. 53 (statute now repealed); *R. v. McPherson* [1980] Crim. L.R. 654.

damage any property, such property in fact belonging to another." It means "intending to destroy any-property-belonging-to-another." The *mens rea* word governs the whole.

Unhappily there have been occasions when judges have acted like the trial judge in *R. v. Smith*, defeating the plain intention of Parliament by construing an expressed mental element as applying only to part of the offence. Even where the statute included a word like "wilfully," the word was sometimes not construed to require knowledge of the circumstances required for the offence.[20] A considerable weight of authority, exemplified by *B. (A Minor) v. D.P.P.*,[21] now rejects this type of reasoning where the statute expressly requires *mens rea*. The defective authorities to the contrary relate to statutes now repealed, or are merely decisions by circuit judges, or have been reversed on appeal or overruled, or are either *obiter dicta*; so there is nothing in them to bind even the humblest court at the present day.

2.   As a corollary of the first proposition, intention in relation to circumstances requires knowledge, and negligence in not acquiring knowledge is insufficient.[22] You can neither intend to damage property belonging to another nor be subjectively reckless as to damaging such property if you believe that the property does not belong to another.

Here again *R. v. Smith* supplies a valuable corrective to some earlier pronouncements. There has been a tendency to say that the meaning of the word "intention" and its grammatical variants (intent, intended, *etc.*) is exhausted by requiring an act to be willed and a consequence to be intended or partly intended, so that no *mens rea* is required in respect of some of the circumstances or some of the required aspects of the consequences of the act. We may now assume that these remarks are wrong.

Another fallacy that is still distressingly embraced on occasion is that a person can be guilty of acting intentionally with respect to a particular fact even if he believes that the fact does not exist, if his belief is unreasonable.[23] This remarkable opinion arises because of the tendency of judges, on both sides of the Atlantic and indeed throughout the common law world, to suppose that the word "belief" can never be allowed to stand nude. Sometimes, as we have seen, the judges think they have decently covered it by speaking of an honest belief. That adjective is harmless, if useless. More often they qualify the noun by the word "reasonable." But to hold that an unreasonable belief that a fact is not present can make a person punishable for a crime of intention in relation to that fact means that negligence, which often means stupidity, can be punished as a serious crime.[24]

---

[20] See for example, *Cotterill v. Penn* [1936] 1 K.B. 53 (statute now repealed); *R. v. McPherson* [1980] Crim. L.R. 654.

[21] [2000] 2 A.C. 428. See also *R. v. K* [2002] 1 A.C. 462; *Crown Prosecution Service v. M* [2009] EWCA Crim. 2615.

[22] Cf. *R. v. G.* [2010] 1 A.C. 43.

[23] See *R. v. Z* [2005] 2 A.C. 467, affirming the rule that the defence of duress is only available to those who "reasonably" believed they were under threat. Cf. *R. v. Martin* [2000] 2 Cr. App. R. 42.

[24] That "unreasonable" means "negligent" is fairly clear. Reasonableness introduces an objective test.

Here is a particularly fine example of the self-contradictory nature of some assertions about reasonable belief:

6–010

> "Where the definition of the crime includes no specific mental element beyond the 'intention to do the prohibited act, the accused may show though he did the prohibited act intentionally he lacked *mens rea* because he mistakenly, but honestly and reasonably, believed facts which, if true, would have made his act innocent."[25]

If the defendant made such a mistake, it would be untrue to say that he did the prohibited act intentionally, because "the prohibited act" must be taken to include the relevant circumstances. A mistake as to the required circumstances negatives the intention.[26] Judges who regularly speak in terms of reasonable belief rarely explain why they think that a belief in a fact (or in the non-existence of a fact) must be reasonable if it is to exclude liability. However, two judges of eminence have risked an explanation. Lord Simon in his dissenting speech in *D.P.P. v. Morgan* (a case considered later), quoted with approval the reason offered by Bridge J. in the Court of Appeal:

> "A bald assertion of belief for which the accused can induce no reasonable ground is evidence of insufficient substance to raise any issue requiring the jury's consideration."[27]

This explanation fails for three reasons. First, it confuses the question whether there is evidence for the alleged belief with the question whether the belief was negligently arrived at. The genuineness of an unreasonable belief may be abundantly proved. An example is a decision on bigamy[28] where the defendant, who was seeking a divorce, received a letter from his solicitor saying: "We have your telegram and hope to send you papers for signature in the course of a day or two." The defendant, a man of little education, jumped to a hasty and mistaken conclusion: he clapped his hands and said, "Thank God my divorce has gone through," and immediately remarried. He was convicted (though sentenced only to a nominal one day's imprisonment); and an appeal was dismissed, the appeal court saying that there was no evidence that he had *bona fide* and on reasonable grounds believed that he was liberated by divorce from his lawful marriage. Obviously there was evidence that he believed it, so the negative pregnant must have meant that the belief, if entertained, was unreasonable. Lawyers readily suppose that all mistakes as to the law and legal status made by laymen

---

[25] *D.P.P. v. Morgan* [1975] 2 W.L.R. 913 at 921.

[26] A point recently highlighted by Lord Nicholls: "By definition the mental element in a crime is concerned with a subjective state of mind, such as intent or belief. To the extent that an overriding objective limit ('on reasonable grounds') is introduced, the subjective element is displaced. To that extent a person who lacks the necessary intent or belief may nevertheless commit the offence. When that occurs the defendant's 'fault' lies exclusively in falling short of an objective standard. His crime lies in his negligence. A statute may so provide expressly or by necessary implication. But this can have no place in a common law principle, of general application, which is concerned with the need for a mental element as an essential ingredient of a criminal offence." *B. (A Minor) v. D.P.P.* [2000] 2 A.C. 428 at 462. An example of a provision that expressly includes a negligence standard can be found in section 1 of the *Sexual Offences Act 2003*.

[27] *D.P.P. v. Morgan* [1976] A.C. 182 at 220.

[28] *The King v. Wheat* [1921] 2 K.B. 119.

(including people who are illiterate or totally unversed in business matters) are unreasonable, but it is strange that the jury in this case took the same view.

6–011   The second objection to the reasoning of the two judges is that it conveys a *suggestio falsi* as to the evidential burden. It implies that the rule about unreasonable belief in some way saves the jury time and trouble. This might be true if the evidential burden rested on the defendant, but it does not. In respect of the issues of intention and knowledge the evidential burden almost always[29] rests on the Crown, so these two issues are necessarily before the jury, whether the defendant gave evidence on them or not. The failure of the defendant to give convincing evidence (and the fact that his denial of the mental element involves setting up a mistaken belief) does not entitle the judges to withdraw the issue of *mens rea* from the jury merely because the judge believes the evidence is all one way. What the judge does is direct the jury that if they find the mistake unreasonable (a question primarily for them), then, however satisfied they may be that the mistake was made, they must regard it as being no defence. The appropriate direction for offences requiring proof of *mens rea* is a simple direction for the jury to consider whether the defendant had the belief in question. "While a defendant's belief need not be reasonable provided it is honest and genuine, the reasonableness or unreasonableness of the belief is by no means irrelevant. The more unreasonable the belief, the less likely it is to be accepted as genuine."[30]

A third error made by the two judges is the logical fallacy already mentioned, of supposing that a person can be convicted of an offence of intention or recklessness when he has made an unreasonable mistake as to the circumstances required for the offence. Even if the doctrine of unreasonable mistake has some social advantage, the judges have no right to superimpose it on a statute requiring proof of *mens rea*.[31] The logical point had been expounded by academic writers for many years before it found crucial acceptance in *D.P.P. v. Morgan*[32] by Lords Hailsham, Cross and Fraser.

Lord Hailsham's words in *D.P.P. v. Morgan* were as follows:

> "I cannot myself reconcile it with my conscience to sanction as part of the English law what I regard as a logical impossibility. ... Once one has accepted ... that the prohibited act in rape is non-consensual sexual intercourse, and that the guilty state of mind is an intention to commit it, it seems to me to follow as a matter of *inexorable logic* that there is no room either for a 'defence of honest belief or mistake', or of a defence of honest and reasonable belief or mistake. Either the prosecution proves that the accused had the requisite intent, or it does not. In the former case it succeeds, and in the latter it fails. ... Any other view, as for insertion of the word 'reasonable' can only have the effect of saying that a man intends something which he does not."

---

[29] One exception is in respect of the defence of automatism.

[30] *R. v. K* [2002] 1 A.C. 462 at 474 *per* Lord Bingham. See also *R v. Williams* [1987] 3 All E.R. 411 at 415; section 76 of the *Criminal Justice and Immigration Act 2008*.

[31] *B. (A Minor) v. D.P.P.* [2000] 2 A.C. 428.

[32] [1976] A.C. 182. And more recently in *B. (A Minor) v. D.P.P.* [2000] 2 A.C. 428; *R. v. K* [2002] 1 A.C. 462; *Crown Prosecution Service v. M* [2009] EWCA Crim. 2615.

Hence, a statute requiring intention means what it says, and must not be read as imposing liability for negligence. We are now in a position to state the complete definition of intention. For legal purposes it means, or should mean:

1. (if we are speaking of consequences of conduct) the desire that the consequence shall follow from a bodily movement (or omission to move), or realization that the consequence is virtually certain, or
2. (if we are speaking simply of the act itself) conscious movement (or conscious inactivity) with knowledge of the circumstances.

If a crime is declared in general terms to require intention, that should relate to all three elements—the act, the circumstances and the consequences.

Other aspects of the defence of mistake are considered in the rest of this chapter; and the subject of mistake as to the victim or kind of harm is considered in 6.9.

6.3. REQUIREMENTS OF KNOWLEDGE

As has been seen, a statute may require knowledge by requiring intention, but it may also require knowledge by using that word, or one of its grammatical variants. An example of an express requirement of knowledge is the offence of knowingly possessing explosives.[33] In legislation of this kind the requirement of knowledge is generally interpreted as applying to all the circumstances of the offence, unless the statute makes the contrary meaning plain. This is the same rule of knowledge as *R. v. Smith*[34] illustrates for offences of intention.

For example, an Act penalized any person who "knowingly makes any record without the consent in writing of performers." The court regarded the word "knowingly" as qualifying not only the making but the absence of consent.[35] The *mens rea* word applies to all the elements of the offence. Unfortunately, as we have seen and shall see further, the courts do not always interpret statutes as this principle would require.

Although the word knowingly is generally used in relation to circumstances, it is not incapable of applying to consequences. So, a person who arranges for goods to be sent from Kenya to the United Kingdom can be convicted of being "knowingly concerned in the fraudulent evasion of a prohibition applicable to those goods" when they arrive in the United Kingdom.[36]

What if a person knows something but then forgets? If he has truly forgotten, so that it is incapable of recall, he presumably no longer knows it. But if he can immediately recall it he knows it. However, courts have held that if a

6–012

6–013

6–014

---

[33] Section 4 of the *Explosive Substances Act 1883*. See *R. v. Berry (No. 3)* [1995] 1 W.L.R. 7, where it was held: "The Crown had to show that the person knew that what he was making or had in his possession or control was an explosive substance; that accordingly the trial judge ought to have identified *mens rea* as a specific ingredient of the offence under section 4...".

[34] [1974] Q.B. 354 at 360. See *R. v. Taaffe* [1984] A.C. 539; *R. v. Forbes* [2002] 2 A.C. 512.

[35] *Gaumont British Distributors Ltd. v. Henry* [1939] 2 K.B. 711.

[36] *R. v. Smith* [1973] Q.B. 924. The relevant provisions are now sections 68(2) and 170(1) of the *Customs and Excise Management Act 1979*.

defendant knew that he was in possession of drugs he remains in possession even if he forgets about the drugs—in other words he is deemed to know what he once knew and has now forgotten.[37]

6–015 **How can knowledge be proved?** The prosecution of course bear the persuasive burden,[38] and they may have problems. The mere fact that the defendant ought to have known, *i.e.* that he was negligent in not finding out, is insufficient. But although the jury may swallow an incredible tale, on account of the defendant's frank blue eyes, they are not bound to do so. In the first place if any ordinary person would have known a fact, the jury may infer that the defendant knew it, simply because they cannot believe that he did not, in the circumstances, know it.[39]

6–016 **Yet you say that it is not enough that the defendant was negligent in not finding out. I think the distinction is humbug. Whether the jury say that the defendant knew it because an ordinary person would have known it, or that he ought to have known it because a reasonable person would have known it, is merely a matter of words.** Very often there is no practical difference. But the point is legally important because it governs what the judge has to tell the jury. Besides, there are exceptional cases where the verdict can be influenced by evidence of: the sort of person the defendant is; his motives or lack of them in relation to the facts charged; his conduct before, at and after the time of the alleged offence; and so on. And even where particular evidence of this kind is lacking, the jury must be left free to decide how much weight to assign to the defendant's protestations of innocence. In short, the jury must be directed to consider all the evidence before drawing an inference of knowledge, as of any other mental state.

An important limitation on the evidence that can be adduced by the prosecution is the rule that, in general,[40] no testimony can be called as to the previous convictions of (or other similar conduct by) the defendant.

Suppose that D is charged with knowingly possessing explosives. It is proved that he was found in possession of a bag containing explosives. D's defence is that the bag was left in his custody by a friend from Italy, and he did not know what was in it. A hard-faced jury may refuse to credit this tale, and would undoubtedly be upheld in their refusal. But some juries may feel D should be

---

[37] *R. v. Jolie* [2004] 1 Cr. App. R. 3; *R. v. Martindale* [1986] 1 W.L.R. 1042; *R. v. McCalla* (1988) 87 Cr. App. R. 372; Cf. *R. v. Bello* (1978) 67 Cr. App. R. 288.

[38] *R v. K* [2002] 1 A.C. 462; *R. v. Curgerwen* (1865-72) L.R. 1 C.C.R. 1; *R. v. Cugullere* [1961] 1 W.L.R. 858.

[39] Cf. *Wilson v. Bird* [1963] Crim. L.R. 57.

[40] A core exception is found in the *Criminal Justice Act 2003*. In *R. v. Hanson* [2005] 1 W.L.R. 3169 it was held: "(1) under the *Criminal Justice Act 2003 s.103(2)* a defendant's propensity to commit offences of the kind with which he was charged could be established by evidence of conviction of an offence of the same description or category as the one with which he was charged, but by the *Criminal Justice Act 2003* s.103(3) that did not apply if the court was satisfied that that would be unjust by reason of the length of time since the conviction or for any other reason." Cf. section 78 of the *Police and Criminal Evidence Act 1984.*

given the benefit of the doubt, and acquit him. They would not do this if they knew that D had a previous conviction for possessing explosives, but they generally are not allowed to know it.

In the second place (to revert to what I was saying), the strict requirement of knowledge is qualified by the doctrine of wilful blindness.[41] This is meant to deal with those whose philosophy is: "Where ignorance is bliss, 'tis folly to be wise."[42] To argue away inconvenient truths is a human failing. If a person deliberately "shuts his eyes" to the obvious, because he "doesn't want to know," he is taken to know. While all the cases agree on this, they are sixes and sevens on what wilful blindness means. The best view is that it applies only when a person is virtually certain that the facts exist. The Law Commission, in the report now gathering dust on a bureaucratic shelf, proposed the following formula:[43]

6–017

> "The standard test of knowledge is—Did the person whose conduct is in issue either know of the relevant circumstances or have no substantial doubt of their existence?"

This very limited doctrine can reasonably be said to be an explanation of what is meant by knowledge as a matter of common sense, rather than a legitimate extension of the meaning of the term. If it does not give a sufficient extension to some particular offence, that is a matter for the legislature to consider when it is deciding between using the word "knows" and the words "knows or ought to know."

An example of wilful blindness in the proper sense is where an employer knew that his business was being run in an illegal way, and absented himself without having altered the arrangements; he was held to "know" that the law was being broken in his absence even though he had no direct information about what was happening then.[44]

Although courts have sometimes seemed to use the doctrine of wilful blindness to embrace "recklessness," they have also corrected the error. In a case of handling stolen goods knowing them or believing them to be stolen, the Court of Appeal said that "to direct the jury that the offence is committed if the defendant, suspecting that the goods were stolen, deliberately shut his eyes to the circumstances as an alternative to [directing them in terms of] knowing or believing the goods were stolen is a misdirection"; but "to direct the jury that, in common sense and in law, they may find that the defendant knew or believed the goods to be stolen because he deliberately closed his eyes to the circumstances is a perfectly proper direction."[45]

---

[41] See generally, Ira P. Robbins, "The Ostrich Instruction: Deliberate Ignorance as a Criminal *Mens Rea*," (1991) 81 *J. Crim. L. & Criminology* 191; Larry C. Wilson, "The Doctrine of Wilful Blindness," (1979) 28 *U.N.B.L.J.* 175; Douglas N. Husak, "Wilful Ignorance, Knowledge, and the Equal Culpability Thesis: A Study of the Deeper Significance of the Principle of Legality," (1994) 1994 *Wis. L. Rev.* 29; David Luban, "Contrived Ignorance," (1999) 87 *Geo. L.J.* 957.

[42] *The Zamora* [1921] 1 A.C. 801 at 812.

[43] Law Commission for England and Wales, *Report on Mental Element in Crime*, Law Com. No. 89 (London: H.M.S.O., 1978) at 58.

[44] *Ross v. Moss* [1965] 2 Q.B. 396.

[45] *R. v. Griffiths* (1974) 60 Cr. App. R. 14 at 18. This direction was cited with approval in *R. v. Saik* [2007] 1 A.C. 18 at 46.

6–018   **Can "belief" translate into knowledge?**   No. Belief can be used to construct knowledge, but not to demonstrate actual knowledge. X can say "I know that I am a woman," because she has firsthand access to information which allows her to know this. She also knows whether she has ever had a sex change. But X cannot say "I know Mona Lisa was a woman," because she does not have firsthand access to the relevant information. She has no way of knowing for sure. All she can do is form a belief by considering the available historical evidence. She might believe that it is highly probable that Mona Lisa was a woman, but this does not translate into actual knowledge. Since the subject of the Mona Lisa painting died in the 16th century, it is logically impossible for those living in the 21st century to know as a matter of fact that she was a woman. X might also believe that Edward de Vere, 17th Earl of Oxford, was the author of the plays and poems that have been attributed to William Shakespeare, but she could not claim to know this as a fact.[46] If you see a thief stealing goods which you know for a fact belong to your employer, your firsthand access to the relevant information (*i.e.* seeing the act of theft in motion) means you are in a position to know for a fact that the goods are stolen. If you do not witness the theft, but have access to other information such as the fact that the goods are very cheap, the seller has a reputation for dealing in stolen goods, the seller has asked to meet you in a dark lane at night to do the deal and so on, then, you could use this information to form a belief about whether or not the goods are stolen.[47] (But your belief could turn out to be incorrect!)

In *R. v. Saik*[48] Lord Nicholls said, "Knowledge means *true* belief." What he seems to be saying is that knowledge means that your belief turned out to be correct.[49] Firstly, qualifiers such as "true" are unnecessary when we are talking about "belief," because one cannot believe *untruly* or non-genuinely. You either have a belief or you do not. Lord Nicholls's statement could mean three things: 1. D truly held (did in fact hold the belief) the belief that the property was the proceeds of crime;[50] 2. D believed fact *X* did in fact (truly) exist and from the *ex post* perspective his belief was found to be correct; or 3. D in fact knew *X* to be true.

Lord Nicholls clearly had the third option in mind. Lord Nicholls said: "[a true belief] means that, in the case of identified property, a conspirator must be aware that the property was in fact the proceeds of crime. The prosecution must prove that the conspirator knew that the property was the proceeds of criminal conduct."[51] The options in 1 and 2 can only refer to constructive knowledge. If D

---

[46] A number of current and former Associate Justices of the United States Supreme Court including Blackmun, Scalia and Stephens J.J., have been or are "believers" of the Oxfordian theory of Shakespeare authorship. They might believe but they do not know!

[47] See the discussion in *R. v. Hall* (1985) 81 Cr. App. R. 260. For a convenient and compendious discussion of the belief/knowledge distinction, see Stephen Shute, "Knowledge and Belief in the Criminal Law," at 171 *et seq.*; and G. R. Sullivan, "Knowledge, Belief, and Culpability," at 207 *et seq.* in Stephen Shute and A. P. Simester (ed.), *Criminal Law Theory: Doctrines of the General Part*, (Oxford: Oxford University Press, 2001).

[48] [2007] 1 A.C. 18 at 36.

[49] Cf. *R. v. Zundel* [1992] 2 S.C.R. 731; *R. v. Stevens* (1995) 96 C.C.C. (3d) 238.

[50] This also means, D's actually held belief was that fact *X truly* existed (did in fact exist).

[51] *R. v. Saik* [2007] 1 A.C. 18 at 36. In that case, the Lords held that knowledge under the relevant provision, "meant awareness that the property *was in fact* the proceeds of crime or *intention that it*

believed facts existed which, if true, would have made his act criminal, then he would at best have constructive knowledge. A belief that the property is truly the proceeds of crime does not constitute actual awareness, once D becomes aware of the fact that the property is truly the proceeds of crime he then knows this for a fact. He no longer believes, because he knows. The words "truly knows" (does in fact know) should be used instead of the words "truly believes." So, if you see D taking a laptop from the Apple Store, which you mistakenly believe D has not paid for, you could not be said to truly know that it is stolen, even though you think you have seen the theft with your own eyes. True knowledge is knowledge that turns out to be correct when examined from the *ex post* perspective.

"Belief" is an important concept because it is sufficient for satisfying the **6–019** "knowledge" requirement when constructive knowledge is sufficient. For example, section 22 of the *Theft Act* provides, "A person handles stolen goods if … knowing or believing them to be stolen goods he dishonestly receives the goods…". Constructive knowledge is established by showing that even though D could not know for sure that the goods were stolen, he is liable because he believed as a matter of virtual certainty that they were stolen.[52] The culpability of a person who does *X* knowing fact *Y* exists is no different from a person who does *X* believing as a matter of certainty that fact *Y* exits. D might not know for sure whether it will rain in England within the next year, but unless he is deranged he will believe it is virtually certain that it will. If D is certain that goods are stolen should he be able to rely on the remote chance that what he believes to be true might be false to evade justice? I would think not! When D takes possession of goods which he believes as a matter of virtual certainty to be stolen, he effectively intends to receive stolen goods. His culpability is not materially different from that of the person who intends to receive stolen goods which he knows for certain are stolen. A person may believe something to be a possibility, a probability or a virtual certainty. Thus, when the word "believing" is used in a provision, it should be sufficient for the courts tell the jury that they may take a person to know a fact if they are satisfied that the defendant was virtually certain that the fact existed, or (in other words) that he had no substantial doubt that it existed.[53]

---

should be." This was a conspiracy case so an *intending that it would be* was sufficient, but it would only be an attempt in the case of stolen goods, if it turned out that the goods were not in fact stolen.

[52] This is the approach the courts have taken in the stolen goods cases. In numerous cases the courts have held that it is not enough to show that D was merely suspicious that the goods might be stolen: *R. v. Adinga* [2003] EWCA Crim. 3201; *R. v. Forsyth* [1997] 2 Cr. App. R. 299; *R. v. Toor* (1987) 85 Cr. App. R. 116; *R. v. Smith* (1977) 64 Cr. App. R. 217; *R. v. Ismail* [1977] Crim. L.R. 557; *R. v. Moys* (1984) 79 Cr. App. R. 72; *R. v. Reader* (1978) 66 Cr. App. R. 33; *Atwal v. Massey* (1972) 56 Cr. App. R. 6; *R. v. Grainge* [1974] 1 W.L.R. 619. See also *R. v. Havard* (1916) 11 Cr. App. R. 2; *R. v. Dykyj* (1993) 66 A. Crim. R. 567; *R. v. Fallon* (1981) 28 S.A.S.R. 394.

[53] The doctrine laid down in *R. v. Saik* [2007] 1 A.C. 18 seems too narrow in this sense, because one may be virtually certain that the property is the proceeds of crime, but might not know for sure. However, the Lords in that case said that if D intends the property to be the proceeds of crime then that will be sufficient—this was a conspiracy case. More generally, if D believes for certain that the property is the proceeds of crime, then this should satisfy the actual knowledge requirement.

6–020 **Why shouldn't one say that wilful blindness means recklessness? You agree that *mens rea* normally means intention or recklessness. Why not apply that principle here?** The courts sometimes do equate wilful blindness with recklessness, but they ought not to do so. If knowledge is judicially made to include wilful blindness, and if wilful blindness is judicially deemed to equal recklessness, the result is that a person who has no knowledge is judicially deemed to have knowledge if he is found to have been reckless—which is not what the statute says. The word "knowing" in a statute is very strong. To know that a fact exists is not the same as taking a chance whether it exists or not. The courts ought not to extend a *mens rea* word by forced construction. If, when Parliament says "knowing" or "knowingly," it does not mean actual knowledge, it should be left to say as much by amending the statute. Parliament can quite easily say: "knowing that the fact exists or being reckless whether it exists."[54]

The argument for giving the notion of knowledge a restricted meaning has particular point in relation to the offence of handling stolen goods. A trader may receive an offer of goods at a low price from someone who says that it is bankrupt stock. The trader realizes that the person may be a rogue, but he is by no means certain. The offer is a tempting one, and the trader has no time or inclination to investigate in depth; he must either accept or reject it. So he accepts it. The law is that the trader is not guilty of knowingly handling stolen goods if the goods turn out to be stolen. It would be vexatious to honest traders if the law were otherwise. In one application, however, the notion of knowledge may justifiably be held to include recklessness. This is in relation to the consequences of conduct. Take again a statutory offence that has already been mentioned, of being knowingly concerned in the fraudulent evasion of a prohibition of the importation of goods.[55] In *R. v. Smith*,[56] the defendant with others sent cannabis by air from Kenya addressed to Bermuda. He knew that the most likely route to Bermuda was via London. On the arrival of the packet at London airport it was held that Smith could be convicted of being "knowingly concerned" in the offence.

The court made no reference to the doctrine of wilful blindness, which is normally used in relation to circumstances and is inapposite to consequences. It seems reasonable to say that, in relation to consequences, the notion of knowledge is capable of comprising recklessness, in the sense of knowledge of the risk. In relation to the future we never know for sure, as we often can do for the present; so "knowledge" in relation to the future must embrace knowledge of probability.

---

[54] Cf. section 2 of the *Fraud Act 2006*.
[55] Sections 68(2) and 170(1) of the *Customs and Excise Management Act 1979*. See *R. v. Taaffe* [1984] A.C. 539; *R. v. Forbes* [2002] 2 A.C. 512.
[56] [1973] Q.B. 924.

6.4. OFFENCES OF PERMITTING

Minor offences are generally held to be of strict liability; but some statutory words are construed as impliedly requiring knowledge, even when they occur in minor offences. When a statue makes it an offence to "permit"[57] something to be done, or to "allow" or "suffer" it to be done, many authorities require that the defendant should (basically) have known the conduct or event[58] in question, since a person cannot be said to permit what he does not know about.[59] This is one of the few *mens rea* rules on which the courts have used almost every variety of language. Sometimes they have required knowledge, sometimes knowledge or "wilful blindness" (expressing this doctrine in a considerable range of ways), sometimes knowledge or recklessness, sometimes even negligence.

6–021

It can now be said that negligence is rejected, subject to the aberrant decision that is always possible. Whereas the civil law of property has a doctrine of constructive knowledge (meaning knowledge that a person could have had if he had taken reasonable steps), no such doctrine is recognized in the criminal law. The classic statement is by Devlin J. (as he then was):

> "The case of shutting the eyes to actual knowledge in the eyes of the law; the case of merely neglecting to make inquiries is not knowledge at all—it comes within the legal conception of constructive knowledge, a conception which, generally speaking, has no place in the criminal law."[60]

In *Westminster City Council v. Croyalgrange Ltd.*, Lord Bridge said:[61]

> "But it is perhaps worth remarking, in the hope that it may further allay the anxiety of the council about the enforcement of licensing control of sex establishments, that it is always open to the tribunal of fact, when knowledge on the part of a defendant is required to be proved, to base a finding of knowledge on evidence that the defendant had deliberately shut his eyes to the obvious or refrained from inquiry because he suspected the truth but did not want to have his suspicion confirmed."

The best view seems to be that offences of permitting can be committed either knowingly or recklessly,[62] and in no other way. The basis of this interpretation of the word "permits" is that person cannot permit what he does not know; he does not permit the use of a car in contravention of regulations if, although he permits the use of the car, he does not know that it is being used in contravention. But if he realizes that the car may be used in contravention and yet fails to take reasonable steps to prevent this, he may well be said to permit the improper use.[63]

6–022

---

[57] See for example, sections 35 and 36 of the *Sexual Offences Act 1956*; section 8 of the *Misuse of Drugs Act 1971*; section 136 of the *Licensing Act 2003*.

[58] The rule applies both where the defendant is charged with having permitted a person to do something and where the charge is of having permitted a state of affairs to occur.

[59] *R. v. Souter* [1971] 1 W.L.R. 1187; *R. v. Thomas* (1976) 63 Cr. App. R. 65; *Gray's Haulage Co Ltd. v. Arnold* [1966] 1 W.L.R. 534; *Latif v. Middlesbrough B.C.* [1997] C.O.D. 486.

[60] *Taylor's Central Garages v. Roper* [1951] 2 T.L.R. 284.

[61] [1986] 1 W.L.R. 674 at 684.

[62] *R. v. Brock* [2001] 1 W.L.R. 1159; *R. v. Auguste* [2004] 1 W.L.R. 917; *R. v. Brett* [1999] 1 W.L.R. 2109.

[63] In *Sweet v. Parsley* [1970] A.C. 132 at 162 Lord Diplock said that: "'permit' connotes at least knowledge or reasonable grounds for suspicion on the part of the permittor that the thing will be done

Although the law on this subject appears in general to be sweetly reasonable, the courts have not been able to save themselves from creating an anomalous exception on one point, namely in respect of offences of permitting the uninsured use of a motor vehicle. A person who permits the use of his vehicle is held to be strictly liable if the user happens to be uninsured.[64] So if you lend your car to a friend who says she has a driving licence when she has not, you will be criminally liable even though you were not at fault.[65] Where a statute makes it an offence to "cause" something to be done, this word is now often construed in the same way as "permit," to require knowledge (or, presumably, recklessness).[66]

6.5.   RECKLESSNESS AS TO CIRCUMSTANCES

6–023   An extract from the opinions in *D.P.P. v. Morgan*[67] has already been given; we may now add a statement of the facts. It concerned a prosecution for rape at common law. Morgan, an R.A.F. sergeant, invited three other men belonging to the R.A.F. to have intercourse with his wife. The three companions asserted (but Morgan denied) that Morgan told them that they must not be surprised if his wife struggled a bit since she was a bit kinky and that in reality she would welcome intercourse. The men had intercourse with the wife by force, and immediately afterwards Mrs. Morgan drove to a hospital and complained that she had been raped. The three men were charged with rape, and Morgan was also charged as a party to the rape ("aiding and abetting" it) because he incited it. The three men advanced a defence that Mrs. Morgan consented. (The *actus reus* in rape is sexual intercourse without the woman's consent, and her non-consent may be called a negative circumstance of the act.)

The trial judge directed the jury that if Mrs. Morgan did not consent, the fact that the defendants believed she consented (if they did so) would be no defence unless the belief was reasonable; and the jury convicted. Notwithstanding that the conduct of the men was abominable, the House of Lords by a majority of three to two disapproved the judge's direction. He should have asked the jury to decide whether the belief was actually held. An actual belief in the woman's consent

---

and an unwillingness to use means available to him to prevent it..." At 165 he repeated this but transposed "reasonable" to "grounds for reasonable suspicion." But the word "reasonable" appears to be superfluous; if it could be proved that the defendant suspected, even though on "unreasonable" grounds, and was nevertheless unwilling to prevent the act, Lord Diplock would probably find that he permitted the act, while if the defendant did not suspect, although he had reasonable grounds for suspecting, it could hardly be found that he was "unwilling" to prevent the act.

[64] *Sedgefield B.C. v. Crowe* [2009] R.T.R. 10; *Lloyd-Wolper v. Moore* [2004] 1 W.L.R. 2350; *Ferrymasters Ltd. v. Adams* [1980] R.T.R. 139. See also section 143(1)(b) of the *Road Traffic Act 1988*.

[65] See section 143(1)(b) of the *Road Traffic Act 1988*; *Baugh v. Crago* [1975] R.T.R. 453. But the courts draw a distinction: if you lend the car on condition that your friend obtains a licence, and if he does not, there is an exception to the exception; it is counted as a conditional permitting which (the condition being unfulfilled) is not a permitting, and you are not liable! See *Newbury v. Davis* [1974] R.T.R. 367; *Lloyd-Wolper v. Moore* [2004] 1 W.L.R. 2350.

[66] *R. v. G* [2004] 1 A.C. 1034 at 1057. An offence may be so worded as to require "objective recklessness," but the law should expressly state this. Cf. the express provision to the contrary in section 5 of the *Domestic Violence, Crime and Victims Act 2004*.

[67] [1976] A.C. 182.

would negative both the intention to rape and recklessness as to the lack of consent. However, the House felt able to uphold the conviction by applying the proviso.[68]

The case appears on its face to lay down two propositions:

1. A crime requires a mental element.
2. The requisite mental element as to the circumstances is knowledge of or subjective recklessness as to the circumstances. If the defendant lacked this mental element he is not rendered guilty of the offence by gross negligence in not ascertaining the facts.

With the decision in *D.P.P. v. Morgan* the *mens rea* doctrine irrupted into the popular consciousness, and great was the consternation. Women demonstrated in the streets of Dublin and Canberra. Letters were written to newspapers complaining that no man could now be successfully prosecuted for rape; all he had to do was to "persuade himself" that he believed the women consented. On the other hand, the decision on the point of law was greeted with approval by those lawyers who took a subjectivist position on the major crimes. The subjectivist theory requires fault: the constituents of a crime are harm (bad act or consequence) plus culpability. A crime requires wrongdoing—if a person is struck down by lightening she is harmed, but she is not wronged. A strike of lightening is an accident of nature, not a culpable choice by a human agent to harm another.[69] Common law jurisdictions have worked hard to develop principles of justice such as the culpability principle, so any departure from the subjectivist position would be a retrograde move.[70] The public tend to think it is fair to have negligence liability for some serious crimes but not for others. This is especially so when the crime evokes public sentiment as seems to be the case with terrorism, paedophilia and rape. But it makes no sense to require intention or subjective recklessness for some serious crimes and not for others simply because they evoke greater public sentiment.

6–024

I rather sympathize with the women's lib. A chap who forcibly rapes a woman ought not to be allowed to set up a cock-and-bull story about believing that she consented. Granting your opinion for the moment, perhaps you will agree that the question should be one for Parliament—one that it has since answered.[71] The courts should not turn serious crimes into offences of negligence on their own. Some commentators agree with you on the policy.[72] But

6–025

---

[68] As for the proviso, cf. *Criminal Appeal Act 1995*.

[69] Dennis J. Baker "The Impossibility of a Critically Objective Criminal Law," (2011) 56(2) *McGill L. J.* 349.

[70] Dennis J. Baker & Lucy X. Zhao, "Responsibility Links, Fair Labelling and Proportionality in China: Comparing China's Criminal Law Theory and Doctrine," (2009) 14(2) 14 *UCLA J. Int'l L. Foreign Aff.* 274.

[71] See section 1 of the *Sexual Offences Act 2003*.

[72] R. A. Duff, "Recklessness and Rape," (1981) 3 *Liverpool Law Review* 49; Toni Pickard, "Culpable Mistakes and Rape: Relating Mens Rea to the Crime," (1980) 30 *U. Toronto L.J.* 75; Celia Wells, "Swatting the Subjectivist Bug," [1982] Crim. L.R. 209. *Contra*, Rosanna Cavallaro, "A Big Mistake: Eroding the Defence of Mistake of Fact about Consent in Rape," (1997) 86 *J. Crim. L. & Criminology* 815.

if you were persuaded on the truth of the defence—that the defendant believed the woman was play-acting in putting up a resistance, and was enjoying the affair immensely—would you really want to punish him as a rapist? Of course, you would be extremely unlikely to believe the defence, or even to think it might be true, but that is a different matter.

Perhaps you fear that the jury will be taken in. However, we have little evidence that juries are hard to convince that a man is guilty of rape where he has used force. Most judges and practitioners believe that acquittals of rape are almost invariably justifiable or understandable on the facts given in the evidence.[73] Remember that a judge is perfectly entitled to tell the jury that the unreasonableness of an alleged belief is *evidence* that it was not held—they may refuse to credit that anyone could have held the absurd belief that the defendant puts forward. The jury in *D.P.P. v. Morgan* were clearly of this opinion.[74] In *B. (A Minor) v. D.P.P.*, Lord Nicholls said:[75]

> "[I cannot] attach much weight to a fear that it may be difficult sometimes for the prosecution to prove that the defendant knew the child was under 14 … A well known passage from a judgment of that great Australian jurist, Sir Owen Dixon, in *Thomas v. The King* (1937) 59 C.L.R. 279, 309, bears repetition: 'The truth appears to be that a reluctance on the part of courts has repeatedly appeared to allow a prisoner to avail himself of a defence depending simply on his own state of knowledge and belief. The reluctance is due in great measure, if not entirely, to a mistrust of the tribunal of fact—the jury. Through a feeling that, if the law allows such a defence to be submitted to the jury, prisoners may too readily escape by deposing to conditions of mind and describing sources of information, matters upon which their evidence cannot be adequately tested and contradicted, judges have been misled into a failure steadily to adhere to principle. It is not difficult to understand such tendencies, but a lack of confidence in the ability of a tribunal correctly to estimate evidence of states of mind and the like can never be sufficient ground for excluding from inquiry the most fundamental element in a rational and humane criminal code.'"

As for the defendants in *D.P.P. v. Morgan*, the jury did not buy their story; nor did the Lords who upheld the convictions on the grounds that the unreasonable belief in consent was not in fact held. The defendants were convicted because they were subjectively guilty and the evidence supported such a finding. So what is the problem?

6–026   **May an offence be so worded as to require intention as to consequences to be satisfied with subjective recklessness as to circumstances?**   Yes, of course, if the law expressly says so. If the defendant realized that the circumstance might have existed and took no steps to find out, he could be liable if the legislation merely requires recklessness as to circumstances or consequences. A problem arises only if the law requires intention as to the offence and does not provide for subjective recklessness as to circumstances. The law now holds that in such a

---

[73] Possibly, the women's lib was also concerned, in 1976, with the issue of the complainant's sexual history being generally admissible. But nowadays it can only be introduced in exceptional circumstances. See *R. v. Y* [2002] 1 A.C. 45.

[74] In *R. v. Cogan* [1976] Q.B. 217, where a man terrorized his wife into submitting to sexual intercourse with the defendant, the jury found that the defendant believed that the woman was consenting but had no reasonable grounds for his belief. Details of the evidence have not been published.

[75] [2000] 2 A.C. 428 at 465.

case knowledge (or belief in)[76] circumstances is required, not merely recklessness. An offence covering subjective recklessness as to circumstances is naturally thought of as an offence of recklessness, or an offence with a mixed mental element, rather than as a merely an offence of intention.

To take a hypothetical example, if at statute makes it an offence to harbour an escaped prisoner intentionally, the offence should not be committed if the defendant gave shelter to a person whom he suspected to be an escaped prisoner but without anything like certain knowledge. If the defendant has committed an offence on these facts it is more naturally described as one of recklessly harbouring a convict than as intentionally harbouring a convict.

However, the courts nearly always choose to give the wider rather than the narrower meaning to penal legislation if this is at all possible, but there is now high authority which should limit their ability to do so.[77] Many cases as to recklessness to circumstances can be made to appear as offences of intention by the "whether or not approach," which was used by Lord Cross and Lord Hailsham in *D.P.P. v. Morgan*. These two Lords sometimes spoke in terms of a rapist intending to have sexual intercourse and being reckless as to the woman's consent, and sometimes spoke of him as "intending to have intercourse whether or not the woman consents."[78] The latter formula makes the offence appear entirely one of intention, not as an offence of mixed intention and recklessness. Going back to the hypothetical of the escaped convict, it can be said, according to this line of reasoning, that the person who gives him shelter without knowing for certain that his guest is a convict intentionally harbours a convict, because he intends to harbour him whether or not he is a convict. He thus offends against the statute, and it is unnecessary to consider whether the statute covers recklessness. The practical effect is achieved without talking of recklessness.

Attractive as this argument may appear at first sight, it is open to objection. It conceals the concept of recklessness beneath the concept of intention. Where the two differ, it puts cases into the wrong category. Whether the theoretical point will persuade a court not to extend the offence to a case that it considers should be covered as a matter of policy is another matter.

6.6. NEGLIGENCE AS TO CIRCUMSTANCES

One can, of course, be negligent not only as to a consequence but as to a circumstance of one's act. In crimes requiring negligence, mistake of fact as to an element of the offence is no defence unless it is reasonable (*i.e.* non-negligent). Manslaughter, for example, can be a crime of gross negligence, from which it follows that a grossly unreasonable mistake is no defence. An illustration would be where a man shoots at another where it would be grossly unreasonable to believe that the other person is out of range.

6–027

---

[76] *B. (A Minor) v. D.P.P.* [2000] 2 A.C. 428; *R. v. K* [2002] 1 A.C. 462.

[77] *B. (A Minor) v. D.P.P.* [2000] 2 A.C. 428; *R. v. K* [2002] 1 A.C. 462.

[78] *D.P.P. v. Morgan* [1976] A.C. 182 at 203, 209.

As was mentioned before, the House of Lords accepted that *D.P.P. v. Morgan* is not merely a decision on the law of rape but is of more general application.[79] However, at least as far as rape is concerned, the decision of *D.P.P. v. Morgan* has been altered by legislation.[80] Section 1 of the *Sexual Offences Act 2003* provides:

> "(1)   A person (A) commits an offence if– (a) he intentionally penetrates the vagina, anus or mouth of another person (B) with his penis, (b) B does not consent to the penetration, and (c) A does not reasonably believe that B consents.
>
> (2)   Whether a belief is reasonable is to be determined having regard to all the circumstances, including any steps A has taken to ascertain whether B consents."

Hence, if D intends to have sexual intercourse and is negligent as to whether the victim consents, he will be caught by the new provision.

It remains to be noted that the language of reasonable belief and reasonable mistake has on various occasions been adopted by Parliament. When a statute expressly allows a defence of belief of mistake, the defence is generally qualified by inserting the word "reasonable."[81] This means that the crime is turned into one of negligence in respect of the ingredient in question, while the crime may require *mens rea* in other respects. It is now common form in statutes making an offence dependant on the age of another person to provide that the defendant can defend himself by proving that he believed the other person to be over the age in question and had reasonable grounds for that belief.[82]

6.7.   MISTAKES OF FACT UNDER STATUTES NOT EXPRESSING A MENTAL ELEMENT

6–028   We decided above that, notwithstanding some discordant authorities, an unreasonable mistake of fact (or other failure to know) can *negative* intention. An unreasonable mistake can negative knowledge, and an unreasonable mistake can negative recklessness. What if the statute does not use words expressly or impliedly requiring intention, knowledge or recklessness? The House of Lords has now more or less accepted that the same legal considerations apply as discussed above. Many judicial pronouncements can be cited for the view that even without apt words the graver statutory crimes imply the requirement of a mental element, which we now recognize as intention, knowledge or recklessness according to the context of the particular statute.[83] As has been shown, these requirements imply a mistaken belief inconsistent with the required mental element excuses from liability; indeed, this proposition being a tautology should

---

[79] *B. (A Minor) v. D.P.P.* [2000] 2 A.C. 428; *R. v. K* [2002] 1 A.C. 462. See also *Crown Prosecution Service v. M* [2009] EWCA Crim. 2615.

[80] See for example, *R. v. Doyle* [2010] EWCA Crim. 119. This issue is examined in detail in the chapter on sexual offences.

[81] For example, see section 28 of the *Misuse of Drugs Act 1971*.

[82] See section 24 of the *Firearms Act 1968*. Cf. sections 63(1) and 65(2)(b) of the *Criminal Justice and Immigration Act 2008*; section 58(1)(b) of the *Terrorism Act 2000*. See also *R. v. Cheung* [2009] EWCA Crim. 2963 and *R. v. G* [2010] 1 A.C. 43 respectively.

[83] *B. (A Minor) v. D.P.P.* [2000] 2 A.C. 428; *R. v. K* [2002] 1 A.C. 462. See also *Crown Prosecution Service v. M* [2009] EWCA Crim. 2615.

not need saying. The cases stem from *The Queen v. Tolson*,[84] where the court made contradictory pronouncements of the kind that will now be familiar to the reader, both requiring a mental element and saying that for a mistake to be a defence it must be "reasonable." *The Queen v. Tolson* has long been a celebrated affirmation of the general need for *mens rea* in crime, or at any rate for proof of fault. The prosecution was for bigamy, an ancient offence reproduced in section 57 of the *Offences against the Person Act 1861* (which is still in force). The gist of the section has already been given, but it may be set out virtually in full:

> "Whosoever, being married, shall marry any other person during the life of the former husband or wife, whether the second marriage shall have taken place in England or Ireland or elsewhere, shall be guilty of felony, and being convicted thereof shall be liable to be kept in penal servitude for any term not exceeding seven years. Provided, that nothing in this section contained shall extend to any second marriage contracted elsewhere than in England and Ireland by any other than a subject of Her Majesty, or to any person marrying a second time whose husband or wife shall have been continually absent from such person for the space of seven years then last past, and shall not have been known by such person to be living within that time, or shall extend to any person who, at the time of such second marriage, shall have been divorced from the bond of the first marriage, or to any person whose former marriage shall have been declared void by the sentence of any court of competent jurisdiction."

The facts before the court were as follows: Mrs. Tolson was deserted by her husband, and as a result of enquiries she was led to believe that shortly after leaving he had been drowned at sea. She waited six years without having word from him, after which time she married again. Thereupon her husband reappeared; and some stupid person prosecuted Mrs. Tolson for bigamy. Literally she had violated the words of the statute. The case was tried by Stephen J., and in order to raise an issue of appeal, to settle the law, he directed the jury that the belief in good faith and on reasonable grounds in the death of the other party to a marriage was no defence to the charge of bigamy. On this direction (which Stephen J. himself did not believe represented the law!) the jury convicted, and the judge passed a nominal sentence,[85] reserving for the Court of Crown Cases Reserved[86] the question whether his direction was right or wrong. He similarly reserved the case of another who was convicted before him on closely similar facts. The appellate court held that the directions were wrong, and the convictions were quashed.

But the woman did commit bigamy. They committed the outward fact of bigamy, the *actus reus*; and the second "marriage" was a nullity because of the subsistence of the earlier marriage; but these facts were held insufficient to constitute a crime.

6–029

---

[84] (1889) L.R. 23 Q.B.D. 168.

[85] Of one day's imprisonment, which meant the defendant's immediate discharge.

[86] This was a somewhat makeshift court of appeal in criminal cases. It was replaced in 1907 by a proper appellate court, the Court of Criminal Appeal, which in turn was superseded in 1966 by the Court of Appeal (Criminal Division). The position in 1889 was that the trial judge when convicting could take initiative in reserving a point of law for the consideration of a large number of his fellow judges, constituting the Court of Crown Cases Reserved, which could quash the conviction. Since it was not technically an appeal, the trial judge could himself take part in the deliberations of the court.

6–030   **Why not say that the woman was guilty, and simply take the facts as a reason for not punishing her?**   For a person who intended no harm it is terrible to be arrested, to face trial on a serious charge, and to be convicted, even though the conviction is not followed by punishment. The decision that the woman was not guilty meant that if such facts recurred, and the prosecuting authorities were satisfied of the genuineness of the defence, there would be no prosecution. The most admired of the judgments in the case is that of Stephen J. himself. The learned judge commenced with some remarks upon the meaning of *mens rea*, he then went on to state the view of the court that the bigamy section implied a requirement of fault even though none was expressed.

6–031   **But is it right that the courts should add words to a statute that are not there? Shouldn't they regard themselves as bound to enforce the statute as it stands?**   When a statute creates an offence, it does not recapitulate all the defences traditionally allowed by the criminal law; yet it must have been the intention of Parliament that these defences should apply. Similarly, since the requirement of *mens rea* is a cardinal principle of law, for serious crimes, it is reasonable to suppose that Parliament meant it to govern the statute.

Stephen J. stated this argument in a much-quoted passage.[87] It is too long to reproduce, but may be summarized. The judge begins by saying that "the full definition of every crime contains a proposition as to the state of mind." Then he spells out again by saying that if the mental element is absent there is no crime; and he clearly means this proposition to apply to crimes created by statute as well as by common law, so that all alike require a mental element. There follows a series of instances showing that where a person does not know[88] a fact required for the crime he lacks the mental element and so cannot be guilty. Finally, however, the judge confines his proposition to cases where the defendant's belief that the facts were innocent was not merely in good faith but was based on reasonable grounds. This implies that if the defendant genuinely but unreasonably believed in the existence of justifying facts he has no defence, even though in that case he lacked the mental element that is supposed to be required. The reference to reasonable grounds departs from the purely subjective element that the judge has hitherto been propounding, and introduces an objective test. There is, therefore, a basic contradiction in the judgment.

6–032   **Allowing a defence of belief in some circumstances of justification, based on reasonable grounds, still allows for a mental element. Belief is a mental element. So I don't see how the judgment contains a contradiction.**   You are going to see it. Stephen J. is assuming that the mental element required for a crime is knowledge of a particular fact, which we may call A (*e.g.*, "I am still married"). The defendant's defence is that he believes that the fact present was not-A ("I am not now married"). A defence of belief in not-A is of course the same thing as denying knowledge of A. But Stephen J. says that belief in not-A is no defence unless it is reasonable. If it is unreasonable, the defendant is convicted although he believed not-A, *i.e.* although he did not know A. So he contradicts

---

[87] (1889) L.R. 23 Q.B.D. 168 at 185 *et seq.*

[88] At present day we would generally want to add: "and is not reckless as to."

himself: *quod erat demonstrandum*. His judgment would make a person guilty of bigamy although the only mental element was that of intending to enter into a valid marriage—a state of mind that almost all of us possess at some time in our lives. Although the question of reasonable belief was not before the court in *The Queen v. Tolson*, and although Stephen J. and some other members of the court were clearly guilty of self-contradiction, the idea started in *The Queen v. Tolson* was perpetuated in later bigamy cases. Time and time again the judges have said that a mistake of fact, to be a defence to a charge of bigamy, must be reasonable.[89]

The Lords in *D.P.P. v. Morgan* were split on the question whether the general principle was represented by *Tolson* or that which was announced in *Morgan* for the common law offence of rape. They all made it plain that they did not intend to make a clean sweep of the cases stemming from *Tolson*, but they differed as to the weight that they would continue to allow to the principle in those cases. Of the three majority Lords, Lord Hailsham went no further than to say that he was inclined to view *Tolson* as a narrow decision based on the construction of a statute,[90] an opinion that would not attach to it any significance outside the law of bigamy. Lord Fraser's opinion may possibly be interpreted in the same way, but it was not clearly expressed. He distinguished *Tolson* from rape on the ground that "bigamy does not involve any intention except the intention to go through a marriage ceremony,"[91] but he did not explain why the *mens rea* should be so restrictively interpreted. He pointed out Lord Reid's error in a previous case in supposing that the *Tolson* rule (that a mistaken belief as to the required element be reasonable to be a defence) could co-exist with the proposition that the *mens rea* required for crime involves a subjective test;[92] yet he did not criticize the judgment in *Tolson* for making the same mistake!

The most uncompromisingly pro-*Tolson* member of the majority was Lord Cross, who confined his opinion to the law of rape and was prepared to give wide effect to the *Tolson* rule by applying it to all statutory offences that are "absolute" on their face—*i.e.* not expressly or by clear implication requiring a mental element. (He found that the statute on rape impliedly requires a mental element because that was the rule at common law for rape.[93] Similarly, a statutory offence of assault impliedly incorporates the mental element required at common law for that offence).[94] The argument is that when a statute makes no mention of a mental

---

[89] *R. v. Gould* [1968] 2 Q.B. 65. But see *Beaver v. R.* [1957] S.C.R. 531, where Cartwright J., speaking for the Supreme Court of Canada, commented that the requirement in *Tolson* that the mistake should be reasonable must now be read in light of *Wilson v. Inyang* [1951] 2 K.B. 799. This case, said Cartwright J., "rightly decides that the essential question is whether the belief entertained by the accused is an honest one and that the existence or non-existence of reasonable grounds for such a belief is merely relevant evidence to be weighted by the tribunal of fact in determining that essential question." And more recently another court in that jurisdiction noted: "It must be kept in mind that the honesty of the accused's belief, evaluated in light of the surrounding circumstances, is what is determinative. The reasonableness of the belief, however, is a factor to be weighed in the assessment of its honesty." See *R. v. Latouche* [2000] 147 C.C.C. (3d) 420 at para. 37.

[90] *D.P.P. v. Morgan* [1976] A.C. 182 at 215.

[91] *D.P.P. v. Morgan* [1976] A.C. 182 at 238.

[92] *D.P.P. v. Morgan* [1976] A.C. 182 at 238-239.

[93] *D.P.P. v. Morgan* [1976] A.C. 182 at 219-221, 234-235.

[94] *R. v. Kimber* [1983] 1 W.L.R. 1118.

element, directly or indirectly, and the requirement is merely implied by judges, why then can the judges "imply" it in such truncated form as they please; and what pleases them is to have a general rule requiring mistakes to be reasonable. The logicians are fended off by interpreting the crime not to contain a general requirement of intention or recklessness. The fact that *Tolson* itself requires the graver crimes to incorporate a mental element, and that the *Tolson* rule contradicts that requirement, was of no moment.

6–033 *Tolson* has no general application, because it cannot be reconciled with the general principle laid down in *B v. D.P.P.*[95] In that case, Lord Nicholls said:[96]

> "The 'reasonable belief' school of thought held unchallenged sway for many years. But over the last quarter of a century there have been several important cases where a defence of honest but mistaken belief was raised. In deciding these cases the courts have placed new, or renewed, emphasis on the subjective nature of the mental element in criminal offences. The courts have rejected the reasonable belief approach and preferred the honest belief approach. When *mens rea* is ousted by a mistaken belief, it is as well ousted by an unreasonable belief as by a reasonable belief.... Considered as a matter of principle, the honest belief approach must be preferable."
>
> ....
>
> "In principle, an age-related ingredient of a statutory offence stands on no different footing from any other ingredient. If a man genuinely believes that the girl with whom he is committing a grossly indecent act is over 14, he is not intending to commit such an act with a girl under 14."[97]

In *B (A Minor) v. D.P.P.*[98] the House of Lords held that the presumption of *mens rea*[99] operates "[a]s a constitutional principle which is not easily displaced by a statutory text."[100] Thus, beyond those regulatory type crimes mentioned above (*i.e.* regulatory offences concerning "permitting" and so on), the constitutional presumption of *mens rea* applies to the acts and attendant

---

[95] [2000] 2 A.C. 428.

[96] *B. (A Minor) v. D.P.P.* [2000] 2 A.C. 428 at 461-62 citing *R. v. Kimber* [1983] 1 W.L.R. 1118 at 1122; *R. v. Williams* [1987] 78 Cr. App. R. 276; these authorities concerned a range of offences. Lord Nicholls goes not to note: "By definition the mental element in a crime is concerned with a subjective state of mind, such as intent or belief. To the extent that an overriding objective limit ('on reasonable grounds') is introduced, the subjective element is displaced. To that extent a person who lacks the necessary intent or belief may nevertheless commit the offence. When that occurs the defendant's 'fault' lies exclusively in falling short of an objective standard. His crime lies in his negligence. A statute may so provide expressly or by necessary implication. But this can have no place in a common law principle, of general application, which is concerned with the need for a mental element as an essential ingredient of a criminal offence." *Id.* at 463.

[97] *B. (A Minor) v. D.P.P.* [2000] 2 A.C. 428 at 463.

[98] [2000] 2 A.C. 428. See also *R. v. K* [2002] 1 A.C. 462.

[99] In *Sweet v. Parsley* [1970] A.C. 132 at 148-149 Lord Reid said: "In such cases there has for centuries been a presumption that Parliament did not intend to make criminals of persons who were in no way blameworthy in what they did. That means that whenever a section is silent as to *mens rea* there is a presumption that, in order to give effect to the will of Parliament, we must read in words appropriate to require *mens rea* ... it is firmly established by a host of authorities that *mens rea* is an essential ingredient of every offence unless some reason can be found for holding that that is not necessary."

[100] *B. (A Minor) v. D.P.P.* [2000] 2 A.C. 428 at 470 *per* Lord Steyn. The basis of its constitutionality is not explained. It perhaps can be unwritten by the right not to be criminalized without fault: see generally, Dennis J. Baker, *The Right Not to be Criminalized: Demarcating Criminal Law's Authority*, (Farnham: Ashgate Publishing, 2011).

circumstances of serious criminal offences. Consequently, whenever a section is silent as to *mens rea* the prosecution will have to prove that the defendant intended to do the act and knew that the definitional circumstance was present.

6.8.   MISTAKEN BELIEFS OF FACT AND DEFENCES

During the 19th century there appears to have been no theory that an unreasonable belief as to a matter of defence could not justification or excuse. Even the mistaken belief of a drunkard as to the necessity for private defence (self-defence *etc.*) could putatively justify his attack on another person.[101] Later, however, the idea arose that belief had to be reasonable, and this view has continued for many mistakes as to the elements of defences.[102] The House of Lords in *D.P.P. v. Morgan* did not state that its decision would cover all mistakes of fact; the speeches were devoted to showing that the defendant's alleged mistake related to a definitional fact that was crucial to establishing that the defendant intended to commit the "offence" of rape.

6–034

If D accidentally takes the wrong umbrella when he is leaving the club, he does not intend to steal—he merely intends to take what he believes to be his own. However, if he takes the umbrella because he believes it is one which was stolen from him the week before, he intends to steal back what he believes is his own umbrella. If he is wrong and is charged with theft he may argue that he believed he had a claim of right. His mistake now relates to his claim of right. If D fires a bullet into the woods thinking he is killing a rabbit, but hits a human, he has committed the *actus reus* of murder. This is a mistake as to a definitional fact (since the offences against the person are confined to action against a human being), and he could not have been convicted of any offence, even if gross negligence had been established. D does not commit murder because he never forms the requisite *mens rea*. He does not intend to kill a human being.

What if D mistakenly believes he is about to be attacked and retaliates by wounding his putative aggressor?   In the case of self-defence the defendant clearly intends to assault (or otherwise harm his aggressor) and knows it is a crime to wound another human. Such a person intends to bring about the *actus reus* of an offence, but is legally justified in doing so. If the defender can show that he committed the *actus reus* of the given offence to achieve a lawfully justified goal such as self-defence, he will be excused. The self-defender lacks culpability in the wider legal sense, because he has a legally recognized motivation (or justification) for wounding the supposed aggressor.

6–035

One of the definitional requirements of the defence of self-defence is to show that the defendant believed that it was necessary to use force.[103] In *R. v. Williams*,[104] Lord Lane C.J. said: "[The self-defender] must then be judged

---

[101] *Marshall's Case* (1830) 168 E.R. 965; *R. v. Gamlen* (1858) 1 F. & F. 90. Cf. *R. v. Wardrope* [1960] Crim. L.R. 770; *R. v. O'Grady* [1987] Q.B. 995; *R. v. Hatton* [2006] 1 Cr. App. R. 16.

[102] *R. v. Howe* [1987] A.C. 417 at 459; *R. v. Z* [2005] 2 A.C. 467.

[103] *R. v. Williams* (1984) 78 Cr. App. R. 276 at 281-282; *R. v. Beckford* [1988] A.C. 130; *Blackburn v. Bowering* [1994] 1 W.L.R. 1324.

[104] (1984) 78 Cr. App. R. 276 at 281-282.

against the mistaken facts as he believes them to be. If judged against those facts or circumstances the prosecution fail to establish his guilt then he is entitled to be acquitted ....The reasonableness or unreasonableness of the defendant's belief is material to the question of whether the belief was held by the defendant at all." This has not always been the case (see Chapter 21). In *Albert v. Lavin*[105] the court overwhelmed by a mass of high-level *dicta* referring to reasonable belief, held that a mistaken belief in the necessity for private defence cannot justify unless it was reasonable. The law has changed for private and public defence, but not for the defence of duress.

6–036 **Anyway, you can't say that there is any logical fallacy in that, can you? One who wounds another in the mistaken belief that he has to act in self-defence has inflicted the wound intentionally. The question whether he was acting in self-defence or not does not bear on the question whether he was acting intentionally. So there is nothing illogical in saying that the wounding must be intentional but that an unreasonable belief as to self-defence is no justification.** I hope to convince you that it is illogical. Your argument assumes that no reference to defences is included in the definition of assault, but I would put it to you that the assumption is untrue. Wounding another is not an assault in itself, or any kind of wrongful act. Surgeons do it all the time. The wrong is in wounding another unlawfully, which implies an absence of a legal justification. Many definitions of assault (a common law offence) found in the books specify that an assault is an unlawful application of force, and this must be right. Now if the wounder believed that facts existed, and if, assuming those facts, then he would have been lawfully justified in causing the wound, he did not intend to cause the wound unlawfully.

Some commentators have argued that only reasonable mistakes of fact should count. Arguments against this are:

- Murder requires an intent to kill (or to inflict grievous bodily harm); so it is not murder to shoot and kill another by negligence, however gross. But if a person kills another in the convinced but mistaken belief that he himself is about to be killed by the other, he is theoretically guilty of murder, even though on the facts as he believed them to be he would not have been guilty of any crime. He believed the law allowed him to act as he did—he did not intend to break the law. Would it not be harsh to criminalize those who do not intend to act unlawfully? And (if it adds anything to the criticism) is it not illogical as well? Why should negligence be relevant in the one case but not in the other?
- Is public security appreciably improved by punishing the rare person who foolishly acts under supposed duress? Take the person who is sitting in his car in a car park when he is approached by two elderly ladies. Let us assume that he believes the ladies have been sent to kill him so he speeds off and in doing so crashes into another vehicle. Can he rely on "duress of

---

[105] *Albert v. Lavin* (1981) 72 Cr. App. R. 178.

circumstances" as a defence? Not if his mistake is found to be unreasonable.[106] Is it sensible to treat putative duress of circumstances differently to putative self-defence?

- It is fair to apply criteria of criminal negligence to a fearful situation? A person who acts under duress of circumstances may have to act in an instant, if he is to escape from the threat successfully; there may be virtually nothing he can do to test the validity of his fear before acting; yet he may be punished for an unreasonable mistake.[107] In contrast, a man who has intercourse with a woman without her consent has plenty of time to satisfy himself as to her consent if he is in any doubt on the matter; yet according to *D.P.P. v. Morgan* his unreasonable belief in her consent can excuse him. The courts proceed not upon an analysis of the various situations in terms of common sense or justice but by a mechanical application of an illusory distinction between offences and defences.
- No other rule of the substantive criminal law distinguishes between the definitional and the defence elements of a crime, and it is a distinction that is more useful to theorists than to judges and practitioners.[108] A rule creating a defence merely supplies additional details of the scope of the offence. To regard the offence as subsisting independently of its limitations and qualifications is unrealistic.[109] In terms of culpability the lawful justification and lawful excuse add an extra layer, but the effect is the same—they negate culpability. Neither justification or excuse have any bearing on the *actus reus* as that cannot be reversed or annulled, it is a past event. (A justification or excuse cannot un-kill someone). A mistake of fact might mean that the defendant never had any *mens rea* to begin with—*i.e.* he accidentally took an umbrella which he believed belonged to him. Or, a mistake of fact might mean that the defendant did not act culpably because he (*un*reasonably) believed he was lawfully justified in acting as he did. In the case of duress, the defendant's will is overborne whether or not his mistake is reasonable, if he in fact made the mistake. In both cases there is a lack of culpability.
- If it is generally accepted "as a matter of general principle that mistake, whether reasonable or not, is a defence where it prevents the defendant from having the *mens rea* which the law requires for the crime with which he is charged,"[110] why not allow it to cover supposed duress?

6.9.   MISTAKE AS TO VICTIM OR KIND OF HARM

A mistake as to the victim or as to the property concerned is legally immaterial if **6–037** it does not affect the category of the offence. So if a person makes a mistake as to the person he is assaulting, or the house he is burgling, the mistake does not let

[106] *R. v. Graham* (1982) 74 Cr. App. R. 235; *R. v. Howe* [1987] A.C. 417 at 459. Cf. *R. v. Safi* [2004] 1 Cr. App. R. 14.

[107] Cf. *R. v. Martin* [2000] 2 Cr. App. R. 42.

[108] Glanville Williams, "Offences and Defences," (1982) 2 *Leg. Stud.* 233.

[109] *R. v. Graham* (1982) 74 Cr. App. R. 235; *R. v. Howe* [1987] A.C. 417 at 459. Cf. *R. v. Safi* [2004] 1 Cr. App. R. 14.

[110] *B. (A Minor) v. D.P.P.* [2000] 2 A.C. 428 at 478 *per* Lord Steyn.

him out of liability. Even if the facts had been as he supposed, he would still have been guilty of an offence against the same legal provision.[111] Of course, if the mistake is relevant to guilt it is capable of negating *mens rea*, as where a householder uses force against an innocent person thinking he is a burglar. The fact that a mistake is immaterial as regards conviction does not mean that it is immaterial as regards sentence. For example, since the offence of criminal damage requires intention or subjective recklessness, a person who mischievously sets out to damage property that he thinks has small value should not have his sentence increased by the fact that the property was much more valuable than he thought.

It goes without saying that the position is different if the mistake is material. Where a person commits the external elements of a *mens rea* crime, thinking that he is committing a different one, he generally cannot be convicted of either. He may, however, be convicted of an attempt to commit the crime that he thought he was committing. He may, for example, think he is looking after a box of cocaine for a friend, and it turns out to be a gun. He cannot be convicted of unlawfully possessing cocaine, because he did not do it; and probably he cannot be convicted of unlawfully possessing a firearm,[112] because he did not know he had it.[113] The solution would be to convict him of attempting to possess cocaine.[114] As regards drug offences, when for example a person thinks he has cannabis when actually it is morphine, special provision is made for what may be called an interchangeable *mens rea*. Section 28 of the *Misuse of Drugs Act 1971* divides drugs of abuse ("controlled drugs"), in descending order of dangerousness, into "Class A drugs," "Class B drugs" and "Class C drugs," as defined in Schedule 2. Section 28(3) of the *Act* gives a person charged under the *Act* a limited defence of no *mens rea*, but not in such a way as to enable him to set up a mistake between the classes of drugs.

---

[111] In *R. v. McCullum* (1973) 57 Cr. App. R. 645 a woman was convicted of assisting in the handling of stolen guns and ammunition, even though it was not proved that she knew what the property was; she would have been convicted in the same way even though she thought the articles that were stolen were spades, though her moral offence would have been much less.

[112] *R. v. Taaffe* [1984] A.C. 539.

[113] "We are therefore satisfied that the Crown must prove that the defendant was aware of the kind of information which was in the document or record which he possessed. ... This does not mean, of course, that the Crown has to show that the defendant knew everything that was in the document or record. It is enough if he knew the nature of the material which it contains. That may often be apparent from the title of the document or from even a cursory glance at its contents. Nor can a defendant keep a document in his possession and claim ignorance of its contents by deliberately choosing not to inquire into them. If the document is hidden in some way, this will often be a basis on which the jury can be asked to infer that the defendant was aware of the nature of its contents." *R. v. G* [2010] 1 A.C. 43 at 77-78, referring to information kept for terrorism contrary to the *Terrorism Act 2000*.

[114] *R. v. Leeson* [2000] 1 Cr. App. R. 233; *R. v. McNamara* (1988) 87 Cr. App. R. 246.

Suppose a person is ignorant of the facts that make his act criminal (an *actus*   **6–038**
***reus*), but all the same knows that he is doing something morally wrong. You**
said that *mens rea* does not refer to knowledge of moral wrong, so I suppose
he won't be convicted?   On principle you are clearly right. In the well-known
case of *R. v. Prince*[115] a minority of judges held that a person who knew he was
committing a moral wrong could not set up the defence of mistake of fact, even
though on the facts as he believed them to be his act would not have been a crime
(but only a moral wrong). The idea resurfaces from time to time in the minds of
judges,[116] but that it is a confusion of thought can be proved by a multitude of
examples. To give only one: nearly everyone would call deer-stealing immoral,
but if a person believes he is unlawfully shooting at a deer when actually he is
shooting at a person, he could not possibly be convicted of murder.[117]

6.10. MENS REA, VALUE-JUDGEMENTS AND STRICT LIABILITY

Where a rule of law involves the making of a value-judgment, the doctrine of   **6–039**
mens rea doe not generally apply in respect of the value-judgment. On an issue of
negligence, for example, the question whether what the defendant did was
"negligent" on the one hand or "reasonable" on the other involves a judgment of
value made by the jury (or, of course, by magistrates), and the question whether
the defendant knew that he was being negligent is not controlling. Similarly a
defence of self-defence is excluded if the jury think he considered that it was
unnecessary (see Chapter 21); and a defence of necessity is excluded if the jury
think that what the defendant had in mind to do was not socially justified, even
though he thought it was. However, where the judge is of the opinion that no
reasonable jury would convict he should direct an acquittal. The instances just
given are all value-judgments, which are intermediate between questions of fact
and questions of law. As with questions of law, the defendant's failure to foresee
the decision of the court does not excuse him.

The *mens rea* doctrine is equally excluded in cases of strict liability, even
though a question of pure fact is involved. Here it is sufficient for the prosecution
to prove the doing of the prohibited act, the existence of the circumstance or the
happening of the consequence as the case may be.[118] In other words, a defence of
ignorance, mistake or reasonable care is excluded unless the law allows it to some
limited extent.[119] The reason offered by some judges for construing an offence as

---

[115] (1872-75) L.R. 2 C.C.R. 154. In *B. (A Minor) v. D.P.P.* [2000] 2 A.C. 428 at 466 Lord Nicholls
rejected Bramwell B.'s assertion in *Prince* that: "[t]he common law presumption was ousted because
the act forbidden was 'wrong in itself.'"

[116] A circuit judge in *R. v. McPherson* [1980] Crim. L.R. 654, used the moral wrong doctrine as one
of the grounds of his decision, which was clearly erroneous.

[117] See section 1 of the *Homicide Act 1957*.

[118] It is preferable not to say that an offence requiring the prosecution to prove negligence is one of
strict liability. Lord Diplock on one occasion said that careless driving is an offence of strict liability
(*Commissioner of Police of the Metropolis v. Caldwell* [1982] A.C. 341), but this would be
inconvenient usage. For other aberrational uses of the term, which sometimes result in faulty
conclusions see Glanville Williams "'Absolute liability,' in Traffic Offences," [1967] Crim. L.R. 142
at 143-145.

[119] Statutory rape (that is intercourse with a child under the age of 13) is a strict liability offence, so
raising a mistake of fact about the victim's age would be a futile exercise.

one of strict liability is that the statute is silent on the question of *mens rea*; but the law is that the requirement of *mens rea* is to be implied if the *Act* does not express the requirement, not *vice versa*.[120]

Strict liability is sometimes called "absolute liability," but this, although accepted usage, is a misnomer, because all the usual defences are available except the defences of lack of intention, recklessness or negligence. For example, a defendant can set up a defence of duress,[121] automatism,[122] and perhaps impossibility in some circumstances. An offence may be of strict liability in one respect but require a fault element in another. Driving while disqualified is an offence of strict liability in respect of the disqualification (the driver is guilty although he firmly, but mistakenly, believed that he was not then disqualified), but it requires an intentional act of driving. We call it an offence of strict liability because that is its predominant feature.

6–040   When it is held that an element of a serious crime is a matter of strict liability, this is probably because the courts fear that the prosecution would find it too difficult to establish *mens rea* in respect of that element. Serious problems arise when the element in question is highly speculative.

An example is the crime of blasphemous libel, commonly called blasphemy. This is a common law offence involving the publishing of matter that is "calculated to shock or outrage public feelings of Christians;" and here, as elsewhere, the courts distort the word "calculated" to make it mean something that is not calculated at all, but merely likely in the minds of the jury. The defendant must know that he is publishing something, and presumably he must know the meaning of the words he uses (lack of acquaintance with the English language could be a defence); but the question whether the words are calculated to shock involves only an objective question for the jury.[123] Likelihood of shock is a matter of strict liability or of negligence—the classification makes no difference.

The jury are allowed to find of their own knowledge that the publication would be likely to shock. Although the rule is worded in terms conveying the impression that the jury are to decide a question of fact, they are probably in reality deciding the evaluative question whether the publication is so scurrilous that its publication ought not to be allowed. (Nevertheless, it would be a misdirection to tell them this.) Obviously, the issue in blasphemy is extremely debatable in the modern world. Christians differ in the details and strength of their religious belief, and in their degrees of tolerance of dissenting opinion. If

---

[120] *B. (A Minor) v. D.P.P.* [2000] 2 A.C. 428; *Sweet v. Parsley* [1970] A.C. 132; *B. (A Child) v. DPP* [2000] 2 A.C. 428; *Crown Prosecution Service v. M* [2010] 2 Cr. App. R. 33; *R. v. Tolson* (1889) 23 Q.B.D. 168. For an overview of the older authorities see G. L., Peiris, "Strict Liability in Commonwealth Criminal Law," (1983) 3 *Legal Stud.* 117.

[121] *O'Sullivan v. Fisher* [1954] S.A.S.R. 33 at 37.

[122] See *R. v. Metro News Ltd.* (1986) 56 O.R. (2d) 321 (Can.) and *R.v. Stokes* (2009) O.N.C.J 8 at paragraph 10 citing Glanville Williams, *Textbook of Criminal Law*, (London: Stevens & Sons, 1978). In *R. v. Charlson* (1955) 1 W.L.R. 317 at 319; *State v. Kremer*, 262 Minn. 190 (1962); *Cordwell v. Carley* (1985) 31 A. Crim. R. 291; *State v. Campbell*, 117 Ohio App. 3d 762 (1997); *R. v. Hudson* [1971] 2 Q.B. 202.

[123] *R. v. Lemon* [1979] A.C. 617; *R. (on the application of Green) v. City of Westminster Magistrates' Court* [2008] E.M.L.R. 15.

questioned, some may profess shock about a particular publication (in the sense of strong disapproval), without being distressed otherwise than momentarily. The jury (who need not be Christians) are left to speculate, and the defendant is required, at the time of acting, to make an accurate forecast of the way in which they will decide.

Similar problems beset the crime of obscenity (the publishing of an obscene article, or having an obscene article for publication for gain), under the *Obscene Publications Act 1959* as amended by *Obscene Publications Act 1964*. The test of whether an article is obscene under section 1(1) of the *1959 Act*, as at common law, is whether: **6–041**

> "if its effect ... is, if taken as a whole, such as to tend to deprave and corrupt persons who are likely, having regard to all relevant circumstances, to read, see or hear the matter contained or embodied in it."

Here again the jury make the decision on the supposed question of fact without regard to what the defendant thought, and however reasonably he may have believed that the article would not deprave and corrupt.[124] The nebulous nature of the question gives the jury an extraordinary roving commission. As the courts have interpreted the legislation, the jury may find that the article tends to deprave if it encourages private sexual fantasies even without overt sexual activity[125] and the depravity need not relate to sex, since articles encouraging violence[126] or drug abuse[127] can be found to be obscene within the statutory definition. In short, it seems that the jury can condemn any publication tending to encourage a great departure from "current standards of ordinary decent people."[128] Given that these activities do not cause tangible harm to others, they should be decriminalized.[129] For that reason, we will not focus further on this area of the law in this book.

The laxity of craftsmanship of the obscenity offence has been strongly and justifiably criticized:

> "Extensive jury discretion of the kind that is created by the use of a vague statutory formula requiring the jury to determine for itself what the relevant standard should be is discretion in the most objectionable form, because the chances of structuring the exercise of that discretion by other means, whether administrative guidelines or information processes of discussion and consultation, are non-existent ... if the legislator wishes to use criminal sanctions to control behaviour of this kind he must accept the responsibility of defining the proscribed conduct

---

[124] Except that the defendant may prove that he had not examined the article and had no reasonable cause to suspect its nature: section 2(5) of the *1959 Act*. There is also a defence of public good under section 4 of the *1959 Act*, as amended by the *Criminal Law Act 1977*.

[125] *D.P.P. v. Whyte* [1972] A.C. 849; *R. v. Carleton* [1996] 1 Cr. App. R. 432.

[126] *R. v. Calder & Boyars Ltd.* [1969] 1 Q.B. 151 at 172.

[127] *John Calder (Publications) Ltd. v. Powell* [1965] 1 Q.B. 509.

[128] *Knuller (Publishing, Printing and Promotions) Ltd. v. D.P.P.* [1973] A.C. 435.

[129] For a general discussion of the case for decriminalization see Dennis J. Baker, "The Sense and Nonsense of Criminalising Transfers of Obscene Material," (2008) 26 *Sing. L. Rev.* 126; Dennis J. Baker, "Constitutionalizing the Harm Principle," (2008) 27 *Crim. Just. Ethics* 3. However, an exception needs to be made for child pornography, which clearly has to be criminalized because it is directly harmful to the children who are used to make it. See Dennis J. Baker, "The Moral Limits of Criminalizing Remote Harms," (2007) *New Crim. L. Rev.* 371 at 386-87.

more precisely, even if the resulting legislation makes distasteful reading, so that the jury is not required to go beyond the limits of its proper function."[130]

6–042   It is not a mere case of the jury having the discretion to determine whether a given act of "negligence" makes D responsible for a "particular harm;" rather it is also deciding what "harms" count.[131] If D negligently causes V's death, the jury do not decide whether that harm ("death of the victim") is criminalizable—because legislature has expressly stated the *actus reus* for homicide offences requires that particular result. In the case of obscenity the jury determines whether a particular act is harmful—it might decide that a particular publication is not harmful and that the next one is and so on.

To wind up this discussion on *mens rea*, it was the judges who invented the doctrine, but we have seen (and shall see at greater length as the book proceeds) that some have fought a long rearguard action against it. The mental element is being virtually eliminated from many serious offences, while it has been watered down in others. There are distressing examples of a crime that expressly requires *mens rea* being held to only require what may be called half *mens rea*—*mens rea* as to some elements of the offence but not to others. Sometimes the mental element has been qualified by insisting that lack of it (in cases of mistake) must be reasonable, which turns the offence into one of negligence. Even when intention was supposed to be required, there was for a long time a tendency (which some judges still cling to) to construe it "objectively," but there have also been great leaps forward. Recklessness is now a subjective standard for all offences, unless the legislature expressly states otherwise.

But the law of *mens rea* illustrates the eternal tension in the position of the judge. He is supposed to be an impartial adjudicator, applying the existing law and protecting the rights and liberties of the subject; but he is also a State instrumentality—in the wider sense, an organ of government. In general it is the second concept of the judge's role that shapes judicial attitudes on the issue of fault in the criminal law.

---

[130] D. A. Thomas, "Form and Function in Criminal Law," in P.R. Glazebrook (ed.), *Reshaping the Criminal Law: Essays in Honour of Glanville Williams*, (London: Steven & Sons, 1978), at 32.

[131] Cf. section 63 of the *Criminal Justice and Immigration Act 2008* which criminalizes the possession of extreme pornographic images. Section 63 clearly sets out what an extreme image must contain. In *R. v. Cheung* [2009] EWCA Crim. 2965 the Court of Appeal said that it was not enough for the prosecution to demonstrate that D was in physical possession of the offending article "as a matter of fact in the sense of it actually being within his custody or control." The prosecution must also establish to the criminal standard of proof that D "knew" of the existence of the article that was in his custody or control. Section 65(2)(b) of the *2008 Act* contains a statutory defence. The statutory defence allows the defendant to raise evidence to demonstrate that although he knew he was physically in possession of the object he was ignorant of the fact that it was of a kind which he should not have possessed. "If the jury are sure that the defendant was knowingly in possession of [the prohibited image] ... then the burden shifts to the defendant to establish on the balance of probabilities that the matters making up the statutory defence — in this case that he had not seen the image concerned and did not know nor had any cause to suspect it to be an extreme pornographic image." The section basically contains a no subjective recklessness defence—if D knows he has the image and suspects it is extreme, then it is reckless for him to keep it. Cf. section 58 of the *Terrorism Act 2000* where D must know that he possesses an incriminating item (material that can be used to support terrorism), but is exculpated if he can show an objectively reasonable excuse for his action or possession. See *R. v. G* [2010] 1 A.C. 43. See the discussion concerning possession of articles for use in fraud at 36.6.

CHAPTER 7

THE EXTERNAL ELEMENTS OF AN OFFENCE

"He dreamed that he stood in a shadowy Court,

Where the snark, with a glass in its eye,

Dressed in gown, bands and wig, was defending a pig

On the charge of dressing its sty. ...

The fact of Desertion I will not dispute:

But its guilt, as I trust, is removed

(So far as relates to the costs of the suit)

By the Alibi which has been proved."

Lewis Carroll, The Hunting of the Snark[1]

7.1. THE EXTENDED MEANING OF *ACTUS REUS*

Although lawyers find the expression *actus reus* convenient, it is misleading in one respect. It means not just the criminal act but all the external elements of an offence.

7–001

Ordinarily, there is a criminal act, which is what makes the term *actus reus* generally acceptable. But there are crimes without an act, and therefore without an *actus reus* in the obvious meaning of that term. The expression "conduct" is more satisfactory, because wider; it covers not only an act but an omission, and (by a stretch) a bodily position.[2] The conduct must sometimes take place in legally relevant circumstances. The relevant circumstances might include consent in the case of rape. The act of sexual intercourse becomes a wrongful act only if it is committed in circumstances where V does not consent. Other crimes require the act to produce a legally forbidden consequence. Such crimes are called result crimes. Unlike result crimes, conduct crimes do not require the act to cause a particular consequence. For example, crimes of endangerment do not require any particular harmful result, and therefore are conduct crimes. If X speeds through a school zone in a car at 125 m.p.h. without harming any pedestrians, X might be charged with dangerous driving. X's conduct (speeding through the school zone) endangers others even if it does not result in a harmful consequence. But if X kills a child on the crossing as X speeds through the school zone, X could be convicted of causing death by dangerous driving. The latter offence requires a

---

[1] Lewis Carroll, *The Hunting of the Snark*, (Macmillan and Co., London, 1876) at 53.

[2] *R. v. Larsonneur* 1933) 24 Cr. App. R. 74; *Winzar v. Chief Constable of Kent*, (*The Times*, May 1983).

particular consequence—the dangerous driving must cause a death. If no one is killed, the appropriate charge would be dangerous driving which is a conduct crime rather than a result crime. As a final complication, some crimes can be committed without any conduct by the defendant.

All that can truly be said, without exception, is that a crime requires some external state of affairs that can be categorized as criminal. What goes on inside a person's head is never enough in itself to constitute a crime, even though it might be proved by a confession that is fully believed to be genuine. English law has no instance of Orwell's "thought-crime," no equivalent of the adultery "in his heart" of the New Testament. Sir Edward Coke:[3]

> "No man ... shall be examined upon secret thoughts of his heart, or of his secret opinion: but something ought to be objected against him what he hath spoken or done."

7–002   The crime of attempt, for example, requires some kind of act directed towards the commission of the crime, going beyond mere preparation. It would be a great over-extension of the law to punish mere criminal fantasies which the defendant may lack the resolution to put into effect.

The proposition that there should be no criminal censure for thoughts will appeal to the civil libertarians, but it is itself a rather hollow liberty, since a private resolve without external expression cannot be satisfactorily proved, and its external expression can be a crime. If you think it is a good idea that the prime minister's house should be burgled, it is just as well not to express the thought to a cracksman, for you might in certain circumstances be liable for encouragement or conspiracy or as an accessory to the burglary if it is committed. What is important to the libertarian is the fact that our law does not generally penalize the expression of political opinion.

The necessity for both criminal conduct and co-existing *mens rea* in the more serious crimes may be shown by two instances.

1.   D, intending to steal V's umbrella, by mistake takes his own.
2.   D, intending to take his own umbrella, but by mistake takes V's.

In (1), D is not guilty of theft because, although he has the criminal state of mind, there is lacking the wrongful conduct required for this crime. Theft involves the dishonest appropriation of the property of another, and D has not done this.[4] In (2) he is not guilty of theft because, although he has thought about the situation against which the law provides, he lacks the criminal state of mind.

7–003   Older expressions having the same meaning as *actus reus* are *corpus delicti*[5] and "overt act." The latter means an act that is open to the world in the sense that it can be perceived by anyone placed to do so.

---

[3] (1607) 12 Coke Reports 26.

[4] See *R. v. Deller* (1952) 36 Cr. App. R. 184.

[5] There are two separate issues that the Crown must prove in every prosecution. Firstly, it must prove the *corpus delicti* (the body of the offence: the body of the offence is formed by the criminal harm or endangerment and the attendant circumstances); and it must be proved that the particular offender is causally responsible for the harm.

The *Treason Act 1351*[6] (which despite major amendments, is still in force) declares one form of treason to be "compassing or imagining" the death of the King, the Queen or their eldest son. "It is really too hard upon human nature," wrote George Eliot, "that it should be held a criminal offence to imagine the death of even the king when he is turned eighty-three."[7] But that is not what the statute is understood to mean; the judges require proof of an "overt act" evidencing an intention to kill the sovereign. However, an act done in secrecy is an overt act or *actus reus* if later it can be proved against the defendant (as if he confesses to it).

Although the term *actus reus* is convenient, it is in one respect misleading. The adjective *reus* does not imply that the act or other conduct must be obviously wicked or harmful in itself, apart from the intent that accompanies it. There may be an *actus reus* without any external consequence harmful to society. In the crime of conspiracy the fact of agreement is not in itself, and without more, harmful to society. Harm occurs only if the agreement is punishable because of its tendency to result in harm. The same applies to the act necessary for attempt, and to the persuasion necessary for the crime of incitement.

Another point on the term *actus reus* is that when a crime requires a *mens rea*, an *actus* cannot be legally *reus* (in the sense of involving criminal responsibility) unless there is *mens rea*. Therefore, it may appear self-contradictory to say: "There is an *actus reus*, but no *mens rea*." The solution of this difficulty is to define *actus reus* in a technical sense as meaning conduct that would be criminal provided that any necessary *mens rea* or other fault element was present. In other words, *actus reus* is the conduct that is forbidden by the rule of the criminal law, on the assumption that any necessary fault is found to exist. If we ever get a criminal code it may be expected to refer to the external elements of the offence rather than to the *actus reus*; but *actus reus* is a conveniently concise expression when discussing legal problems.

7.2. ACTS

Considerable confusion reigns in ordinary and legal speech, on what is meant by an act or a voluntary act. The most acceptable language is to say that an act means willed bodily movement, so that if A pushes B against C and thus causes C to fall over, we attribute the pushing of C to A, not to B. However, in a situation like this there is really no need to go into the meaning of an act. If B were charged with assaulting C, or with murdering C in the event of C's death, the obvious defence would be lack of mental element, and there would be no occasion to discuss whether B had "acted."

Lawyers sometimes speak of a voluntary act, meaning only that it was willed. Since every act is by definition willed, there is no need to call it voluntary.

7–004

---

[6] 25 Edw. III St. 5 c. 2.

[7] George Eliot, *Adam Bede*, (New York: Harper & Brothers, Publishers, 1859), 324. In *Powell v. State of Tex.*, 392 U.S. 514 at 543 (1968), the Supreme Court of the United States said: "As Glanville Williams puts it, '(t)hat crime requires an act is invariably true if the proposition be read as meaning that a private thought is not sufficient to found responsibility.'" Glanville Williams, *Criminal Law—The General Part*, (London: Stevens & Sons, 1961).

The element of volition in an act has greatly exercised the philosophers. Two of them, Ryle and Melden,[8] have attempted to argue away the notion of will. They build their case upon the difficulty of identifying conscious volitions accompanying bodily movement. Certainly it would be false to assume that every act is the result of deliberation: I may scratch my nose while thinking without knowing I am doing it or recollecting I have done it. Even when the act is conscious, introspection does not show a conscious exercise of will preceding conduct. When I move my arms, say in writing a letter, I do not consciously decide to move them before moving them. It is true that electrical impulses run from the motor nerve fibres to the muscles; and these muscles are under the control of the brain. But the mental functioning that controls movement is not conscious determination, and it takes place at practically the same time as the movement. Will is the mental activity accompanying the type of bodily movement that we call an act. It is, of course, possible to will the absence of an act, as when we sit still.

7–005 A bodily movement is said to be willed, generally speaking, when the person in question could have refrained from it if he had so willed: that is, he could have acted otherwise or kept still. Movements that are the result of epilepsy, for example, are involuntary or unwilled because the person concerned cannot by any mental effort avoid them. Whatever the difficulties in explaining what we mean by volition, everyone realizes the important difference between doing something and having something happen to one; and this distinction is a basic postulate of a moral view of human behaviour.

Crimes are not generally defined by reference to the doing of an act[9] in the abstract. A crime is committed in certain circumstances by appropriating property, or damaging property, or driving a vehicle, or killing someone. We can of course perceive a common element of an act in all these situations, but sometimes one has to look hard to find the *voluntary* conduct. There are many levels of involuntariness,[10] but our concern in this chapter is with physical involuntariness—that is, where an actor is physically/mechanically capable of acting but has no control over his mechanical actions. Most cases of automatism involve those who are not able to control their bodily movements because they are suffering from an impaired consciousness. Such people operate like a robot in automatic mode. In other cases, the actor is not able to control some external forces of which he has played some causative role in setting in motion. For example, where D drives through a red light because his brakes failed, he is controlled by the circumstances—the car is beyond his control even though he can control his action of pumping the brakes.

---

[8] Gilbert Ryle, *The Concept of Mind*, (London: Hutcheson, 1949); A. I. Melden, *Free Action*, (London: Routledge and Kegan Paul, 1961). See also Daniel M. Wegner, *The Illusion of Conscious Will*, (Cambridge MA: MIT Press, 2003). See more generally, George P. Fletcher, "On the Moral Irrelevance of Bodily Movements," (1994) 142 *U. Penn. L. Rev.* 1443.

[9] For a discussion of action see Donald Davidson, *Essays on Actions and Events*, (New York: Oxford University Press, 1980); Michael S. Moore, *Act and Crime: A Theory of Action and Its Implications for Criminal Law*, (Oxford: Clarendon, 1993); C. Arnold, "Conceptions of Action," (1977) 8 *Sydney L. Rev.* 86.

[10] For a deeper discussion of the various shades of voluntariness, see Joel Feinberg, *The Moral Limits of the Criminal Law: Harm to Self*, (New York: Oxford University Press, 1986) at 98-171.

Physical involuntariness is also different to moral involuntariness. The latter normally involves cases where people are compelled to act because of duress, necessity or duress of circumstances. A person does not act voluntarily if someone has a gun to his head, but he still has control over his willed voluntary actions. In the latter situation, D would commit the crime because he is being compelled to choose between doing the crime and forfeiting his life. A person who robs a store because someone has a gun at her back could choose to do otherwise, but she would also be choosing to sacrifice her own life. A person might be blackmailed or bullied into acting, but such a person still makes a conscious choice. When a person is coerced, he does not act as an automaton, but he does not have a wide range of choices and acts because of the pressure being asserted by the coercer.[11] This type of involuntariness will be discussed in the chapter on "Duress as a Defence".

7.3. OMISSIONS

A crime can be committed by omission,[12] but there can be no omission in law in the absence of a duty to act. The reason is obvious. If there is an act, someone acts; but if there is an omission, everyone (in a sense) omits. We omit to do everything in the world that is not done. Only those of us omit in law who are under a duty to act.[13]   **7–006**

When a statute expressly or impliedly creates an offence of omission, it points out the person under the duty by the wording of the offence. This is true, for example, of the offences of not stopping after a traffic accident,[14] of failing to fence dangerous machinery in a factory[15] and of failing to notify a change of

---

[11] For a good judicial discussion of moral involuntariness see *R. v. Ruzic* [2001] S.C.C. 24 (Can.) *per* LeBel J. Duress is available as a defence for non-homicide offences if the defendant can show that he acted because he was threatened and that the type of threats were "such that a sober person of reasonable firmness would not have resisted them." The defence would not be available if a reasonable person in the position of the defendant would have taken other measures to avoid the threatened harm such as calling the police. *R. v. Hudson* [1971] 2 Q.B. 202, 207. See also, Joshua Dressler, "Exegesis on the Law of Duress: Justifying the Excuse and Searching for Its Proper Limits," (1989) 62 *Cal. L. Rev.* 1331. Duress has both excusatory and justificatory aspects, as one might act as a matter of necessity to save one's family as the lesser of two evils, but does so with the further defensible element of excuse based on the fact that his freedom is not unfettered—he is forced to make a choice and is only given very limited options. See the facts in *R. v. Steane* [1947] K.B. 997.

[12] "To omit to perform an act is simply to fail to do it under circumstances in which one could have done it." Michael Gorr, "Actus Reus Requirement: A Qualified Defence," (1991) *Crim. Just. Ethics* 11 at 13.

[13] In *Mitchell v. Glasgow City Council* [2009] 2 W.L.R. 481 at 487 (civil case) Lord Scott noted: "A legal duty to take positive steps to prevent harm or injury to another requires the presence of some feature, additional to reasonable foreseeability that a failure to do so is likely to result in the person in question suffering harm or injury." That additional feature might arise because the "defendant has played some causative part in the train of events that have led to the risk of injury" or has a special relationship with the victim or has voluntarily assumed a duty of care and so on.

[14] Section 170 of the *Road Traffic Offenders Act 1988*. See also section 172 of the *Road Traffic 1988 Act*, which criminalizes failures to report road accidences and related offences.

[15] See for example, *R. v. EGS Ltd.* [2009] EWCA Crim. 1942 and the legislation cited therein.

circumstances regarding one's income.[16] Similarly, contractual relationships also create a legal duty to act in certain situations.[17] If an ambulance officer arrives at the scene of a car accident to discover his arch enemy in need of urgent medical assistance and refuses to assist, he would be criminally liable for his omission, because his employment contract requires him to render aid in such circumstances. The various offences of "permitting" something to be done can be committed not only by giving words of authorization but by failing to prevent conduct when one is in control of the situation, and here again the person who must not permit is specified.[18] Offences of possessing or retaining forbidden objects imply a duty to get rid of the object as soon as its nature is discovered. No general problem arises, except in deciding whether the offence was intended to be of strict liability or to require proof of negligence.

The law does not cast on us a general duty to play the Good Samaritan. The difficulty arises where the offence is worded in terms primarily suggesting active conduct, yet considerations of policy seem to suggest the desirability of extending the offence to omissions. In such circumstances, omitting to prevent a result will sometimes be regarded by the courts as equivalent to activity bringing it about.

7–007   Murder and manslaughter are the most prominent examples. These are common law crimes traditionally defined in terms of "killing" someone. The judges reason thus:

"Killing" means causing death. Agreed?

Well, then, you can cause death by omitting to save a person, as much as by stabbing him. Therefore you can be guilty of murder or manslaughter by omission.[19]

But that is conjuring with words: producing a rabbit from a hat that did not hold it. If I fail to warn a blind person that he is approaching a cliff, I may be morally guilty of "causing his death," or at any rate of letting him die, if he falls over, but I cannot in ordinary language be said to "kill" him. Besides, what if a whole crowd of people saw him walk to his death without intervening? Would they all "kill" him? The answer to your question, which I have not yet given, is no. You and the rest of the callous crowd in your hypothetical would not in law kill the unfortunate person, because you are not under a duty of care towards him.

---

[16] See *R. v. Tilley* [2009] 2 Cr. App. R. 31. Section 111A (1B) of the *Social Security Administration Act 1992* (as inserted by *Social Security Administration (Fraud) Act 1997* (c. 47), section 13 and the *Social Security Fraud Act 2001* (c. 11), section 16.

[17] *R. v. Pittwood* (1902) 19 T.L.R. 37; *R. v. Smith* (1869) 11 Cox C.C. 210; *R. v. Marriott* (1838) 173 E.R. 559; *R. v. Friend* (1802) Russ & Ry 20.

[18] A person would not be criminally liable for *failing* to police the omissions of others. A person cannot be liable for permitting or allowing another person to *deliberately* fail to report a change in her income to the Department for Work and Pensions (DWP), but he could be liable if he is married to the defendant and she needs the details of his income so that she can provide accurate details of their joint income to DWP and he omits to provide such information thereby causing her to (inadvertently) fail to provide details of her change of income. See *R. v. Tilley* [2009] 2 Cr. App. R. 31, where the husband was cleared, because he had provided his new wife with details of his income and it was her duty alone to pass this information on to the DWP, but she omitted to do so in order to keep her full social security income.

[19] *R. v. Evans* [2009] 1 W. L.R. 1999; *R. v. Stone and Dobinson* [1977] Q.B. 354. See also *Rex v. Smith* (1826) 172 E.R. 203.

Let me ask a counter-question. If parents deliberately starve their child to death, would not you say they have killed him?   That is an extreme case, and even there it might be truer to call it a bad case of child neglect rather than one of killing. Suppose parents fail to call a doctor to their sick child when they should, and the child dies in consequence. It is harsh to say that the parents have killed their child. The disease killed; the parents culpably let the child die. They should be guilty of child neglect, not of killing. Well put. The parents who bring about their child's death through want of medical treatment are regarded in law as killing the child, but it is stretching things.[20]

7–008

Since the judges formerly assumed that they had the power to invent new crimes whenever they felt the need,[21] it would have been better if they had invented a special offence of neglecting a duty to the helpless. But they prefer if possible to inflate crimes rather than create them; and extending the criminal law by attaching "constructive" meanings to words is one of the traditional weapons in the judges' armoury. So they made the word "kill," which primarily means killing by positive act, cover the causing of death by omissions. The lawyer takes straight the injunction in *The New Decalogue* which Clough meant as irony.[22]

> "Thou shalt not kill; but need'st not strive
> Officiously to keep alive:"

One such exception is the common law[23] duty of parents to look after their children, which can produce results in the law of murder and manslaughter. Parents (and others who have the charge of children) commit an offence if they wilfully neglect a child.[24] In many legal problems one finds oneself on a slippery slope, which it is all too easy to slither down. In this case, the judges extend the concept of killing by omission beyond parents who starve their children (where it might be regarded as common sense), and say that one who is in charge of any helpless person is under a duty, or can in certain circumstances be found by the jury to be under a duty,[25] to take reasonable steps to preserve his life (for example, by summoning medical assistance when needed), and "kills" him if he dies through neglect of the duty. To assert that if you fail to call a doctor to your

---

[20] *R. v. Lowe* [1973] Q.B. 702; *R. v. Sheppard* (1980) 70 Cr. App. R 210; *R. v. Gibbons and Proctor* (1918) 13 Cr. App. R. 134, *The Queen v. Senior* (1899) 1 Q.B. 283; *R. v. Conde* (1867) 10 Cox C.C. 547; *R. v. Russell* [1933] V.L.R. 59.

[21] As noted in Chapter 1, the courts have taken the view that they are not empowered to use stretched interpretations of vague provisions to created new offences. See *R. v. Jones*, [2007] 1 A.C. 136. Cf. *R. v. Manley* [1933] 1 K.B. 529 where a common law offence of "public mischief" was created to criminalize a woman who falsely claimed she had been robbed, because there was no existing offence for making false complaints to police.

[22] Shirley Chew, *Arthur Hugh Clough: Selected Poems*, (New York: Routledge, 2003) at 51.

[23] *R. v. Downes* (1875) 13 Cox C. C. 111; *R. v. Gibbons and Proctor* (1918) 13 Cr. App. R. 134, *The Queen v. Senior* (1899) 1 Q.B. 283; *R. v. Conde* (1867) 10 Cox C.C. 547; *R. v. Russell* [1933] V.L.R. 59.

[24] *R. v. Lowe* [1973] Q.B. 702; *R. v. Sheppard* (1980) 70 Cr. App. R 210.

[25] Whether there is a duty is a question of law, whether it is breached is a question of fact for the jury. See *R. v. Evans* [2009] 1 W. L.R. 1999; *R. v. Stone and Dobinson* [1977] Q.B. 354. For older cases giving rise to a legal duty, see *R. v. Instan* [1893] 1 Q.B. 450; *R. v. Nichols* (1874) 13 Cox C.C. 75.

sick lodger, and the lodger dies in consequence, you kill him is a colourful rather than a precise use of language; but it is the language that judges use in order to make the law of homicide apply.

7–009 **Suppose a squatter smokes a cigarette whilst in bed and as a result accidentally causes a small fire in the bed. He does not bother to put it out, so the fire spreads and destroys the house. Can he be convicted of arson?** By a brilliant exercise of imagination you have hit upon the very facts of the leading case of *R. v. Miller*.[26] The House of Lords affirmed the squatter's conviction for arson, because he had created the danger by his own act and had then intentionally or recklessly failed to avert it.

The facts were intermediate between an act and an omission. There was an act on the part of the defendant: Miller dropped the lighted cigarette that started the fire. He burnt the house down: there is no fiction, no contortion of language, involved in saying that. So he certainly committed the act necessary for arson.

There was an element of omission in the case, but it was not one of mere omission. In a case of mere omission the brute facts do not point the finger of blame at one omitter rather than another (even though we may conventionally regard some people as under positive duties and not others), while here they did.[27] Lord Diplock, delivering the opinion of the House, said that the defendant would not have been liable if his role was at no time more than that of a passive bystander. The defendant's earlier negligent acting set the harm in motion; therefore he had a duty to counteract the harm that he put in motion. Failing to act to counteract the harm would be to recklessly underwrite the earlier acting that set the harm in motion.

7–010 Of course, it is not enough to say that Miller burnt the house: arson also requires that the defendant should have intended or been reckless as to the burning. Here, Miller was at least reckless, in any meaning of the word, in letting the place burn down before his eyes. (To ground a manslaughter conviction by gross negligence, it would have to be demonstrated that the defendant was grossly negligent rather than merely inadvertent). It would not be difficult to demonstrate that Miller ought to have been aware of the risk he was running by not summoning the fire brigade or other assistance to remedy the fire he had started and of which was burning inside a building. So there would be both *actus reus* and *mens rea*.

The principle is that where a person accidentally creates a danger he can be liable for letting the danger eventuate. More technically, the rule is that where the law forbids a particular result (whether we call the crime a result crime or not), then *mens rea* conceived after the act and before the result occurs (but at the time when the defendant could still have prevented the result) can (as the law is now established by *Miller*) lead to liability, provided that the defendant's conduct falls within the terms of the offence. In *Miller* the House of Lords stated the rule only for criminal damage, but it could be applied more widely.

---

[26] [1983] 2 W.L.R. 539. In *R. v. Evans* [2009] 1 W. L.R. 1999, the *Miller* doctrine was invoked to ground a conviction for gross negligence manslaughter.

[27] This approach was first expounded in the United States in *Commonwealth v. Cali*, 247 Mass. 20 (1923).

What if the fire had not only destroyed the house, but had also killed an   7–011
occupant? Could Miller be convicted of gross negligence manslaughter? The
short answer is yes. In *R. v. Evans*,[28] Gemma Evans, a 24-year-old woman,
purchased heroin and supplied her 16-year-old sister, Carly. Carly self-injected in
a house in which she resided with Evans (the defendant) and her mother. After
injecting the drug she developed and complained of symptoms consistent with an
overdose. Evans appreciated that Carly's condition was very serious and
indicative of an overdose and, together with her mother, Andrea Townsend, who
was also convicted of manslaughter, believed that she was responsible for Carly's
care. "The appellant described in a later interview with the police that she had
seen that Carly's lips had turned blue, that she was 'in a mess', and was incapable
of responding to attempts to speak to her. The appellant and her mother decided
not to seek medical assistance because they feared that they themselves and
possibly Carly would get into trouble."[29] Instead, they put Carly in bed with the
hope that she would make a miraculous recovery. The defendant and her mother
checked on Carly occasionally and slept in the same room, but tragically, Carly
died during the night. The medical evidence demonstrated that the cause of death
was heroin poisoning. Evans and Townsend were charged with manslaughter.
Evans and her mother were also heroin addicts and knew the signs of an overdose
and were fully aware of the dangers involved, and merely needed to pick up the
phone and call an ambulance.

Evans appealed her conviction for gross negligence manslaughter. It was
argued by the defence team that the case should have been withdrawn from the
jury because the Crown failed to establish that Evans owed the victim a duty of
care. The Court of Appeal held that Evans' omission to summon medical help
after assisting her sister to create a dangerous situation for herself created a duty
of care.[30] The mother was convicted on the basis of her "familial duty or
responsibility which marked her relationship with the deceased" and which
required her to take reasonable steps to summon assistance for her young
daughter once she realized that she was critically ill and in need of urgent medical
attention.[31] Since Evans was an older half-sister, the court decided that she did
not come within the purview of the familial duty doctrine. Instead, Evans was
convicted on the grounds that but for her act of supply, her sister would not have
been able to create a dangerous situation for herself and thus would not have
overdosed. Since Evans assisted her sister's overdose by supplying the drug she
had a duty to summon help once she realized her sister was in peril: she had a
duty to take reasonable steps to counteract her sister's self-harming.

---

[28] [2009] 1 W. L.R. 1999.

[29] *R. v. Evans* [2009] 1 W. L.R. 1999 at 2002.

[30] This doctrine is not new. See variants in *Green v. Cross* (1910) 103 L.T. 279; *Commonwealth v. Cali*, 247 Mass. 20.

[31] The mother did not appeal and there is no discussion of the basis of her conviction in the *Evans* appeal, beyond a passing reference of her duty based on her familial relationship with the deceased, who was a minor. See *R. v. Evans* [2009] 1 W. L.R. 1999 at 2005.

7–013   **As the law stands, it means that if D "indirectly" helps another to harm herself, D can be held criminally responsible for a homicide offence? Evans's sister made an intervening choice to self-inject and it was her independent self-injection that was the direct cause of the dangerous situation.**   Evans's duty to act was grounded on the fact that she indirectly caused her sister to be put in peril. Her beach of the duty to act resulted from her failure to summon help when she became aware of the danger she had helped to create. She did not create the dangerous situation, but she did make an indirect causative contribution to the dangerous situation. If she had merely supplied the drugs and had left the scene,[32] and thus remained ignorant of the fact that her act of supply had facilitated the creation of a dangerous situation, her act of supply per se would not have been sufficient for a conviction of gross negligence manslaughter.[33] The Court of Appeal held:[34]

> "The duty necessary to found gross negligence manslaughter is plainly not confined to cases of a familial or professional relationship between the defendant and the deceased. In our judgment, consistently with *Adomako* and the link between civil and criminal liability for negligence, for the purposes of gross negligence manslaughter, when a person has created or contributed to the creation of a state of affairs which he knows, or ought reasonably to know, has become life threatening, a consequent duty on him to act by taking reasonable steps to save the other's life will normally arise."

R. v. Evans holds that if a person supplies dangerous drugs and becomes aware of the fact that her particular act of supply has put a given victim in peril, she will have a duty to take reasonable steps to counteract that danger. Reasonable steps would not require much more than calling an ambulance within an appropriate timeframe. American courts have imposed liability in situations similar to *R. v. Evans*.[35] The label of manslaughter, however, seems to be totally inappropriate given the level of culpability involved and the indirectness of Evans's contribution to the dangerous situation.

Mere supply does not amount to gross negligence manslaughter. If one sells a motorbike, sky-diving tickets, a light aircraft, a gun, or most commonly alcohol to another, knowing that the customer is making a fully informed choice to risk his life, one does not become that customer's guardian. It seems unfair that foolish individuals such as Evans are convicted of a homicide offence, because hardened drug dealers are able to escape liability for manslaughter because they are usually not present when their victims come to grief.[36]

---

[32] Cf. *R. v. Khan* [1998] Crim. L.R. 830.

[33] *R. v. Evans* [2009] 1 W. L.R. 1999 at 2003.

[34] In *Evans*, the Court cited a number of cases involving gross negligence manslaughter including *R. v. Willoughby* [2005] 1 Cr. App. R. 29; *R. v. Wacker* [2003] 1 Cr. App. R. 22; *R. v. Sinclair, Johnson and Smith* [1998] EWCA Crim 2590, and concluded: "These authorities are consistent with our analysis. None involved what could sensibly be described as manslaughter by *mere omission* and in each it was an essential requirement of any potential basis for conviction that the defendant should have *failed to act* when he was under a *duty to do so*." See *R. v. Evans* [2009] 1 W. L.R. 1999 at 2007.

[35] See *State v. Wassil*, 658 A.2d 548 (1995) (U.S.). In that case, the defendant created a dangerous situation by supplying drugs to the victim and omitted to seek assistance in a timely manner. He did eventually summon an ambulance, but the victim, while still alive, was too far gone to save.

[36] Cf. *R. v. Khan* [1998] Crim. L.R. 830.

Per contra, when a person supplies an "illegal" and dangerous drug to another and is present to see that its potential harmfulness is no longer a mere possibility but an actuality, it is not too much to demand that they take the simple step of calling an ambulance. Thus, some form of criminalization would not be too severe.[37] Similarly, the drug dealer knows that he is facilitating others who make the fully informed and independent choice to risk their lives and should be punished and labelled as a criminal at this remote level.[38] Deliberately supplying illegal and dangerous substances knowing that it will assist others to risk their lives is not the same as failing to summon help when the supplier has firsthand knowledge that a given act of supply has put his customer/sister/friend in peril. Professional dealers should be criminalized for "dealing," not for homicide.

Would Evans have been liable if her sister had died instantly upon injecting herself?   No. *R. v Kennedy (No. 2)*[39] makes it clear that dangerous supply alone is not sufficient to incur liability for manslaughter. And *R. v. Evans* only creates a duty to act to prevent the harm that V has caused for herself from materializing. Consequently, it must be shown that if D had acted it could have made some difference to the outcome that was already being caused by another or some other event. If a competent adult injects himself with a lethal overdose of heroin he causes his own death; and the supplier is only held liable if she fails to try to un-cause what she has facilitated.   **7–014**

If Evans's sister had died instantly, Evans's failure to summon help would not have breached her duty to un-cause what was already in motion, as any effort on her part would have made no difference.[40] (Similarly, if Evans had been in a remote part of Scotland, and were able to demonstrate that her sister would have died before help would have arrived, she would not have been able to reverse the harm that was already causing her sister's death.) All Evans had to do was summon an ambulance in a timely manner. If the medical team were not able to save her sister, Evans would have been exempt from any criminal liability, because she would have been able to demonstrate that she took reasonable steps to seek medical help as soon as she became aware of the dangerousness of the situation she had facilitated.

---

[37] The crime should be labelled and punished as a lesser serious offence of failing to summon help in circumstances where one had an indirect or direct link with the victim, rather than as a homicide offence. Cf. *R. v. Finlay* [1996] 17 O.T.C. 237.

[38] It is arguable, given the dangerousness of heroin and similar drugs, that supply should be labelled and punished as a serious offence *per se*.

[39] [2008] 1 A.C. 269. Evans did not deliberately or directly put her sister in danger. Cf. *R. v. Taber* [2002] 136 A. Crim. R. 478, where a robber tied up his victim and failed to adequately inform anyone of her whereabouts or of the danger he had put her in. Ultimately, she died from dehydration.

[40] Cf. *R. v. Pace* (2008) 187 A. Crim. R. 205; *R. v. Cato* [1976] 1 W.L.R. 110. See also *R. v. Cheshire* [1991] 1 W.L.R. 844; *R. v. Dalloway* (1847) 2 Cox C.C. 273.

7–015 **Does that mean that Evans would not have been under any duty to summon help, if she had not supplied the dangerous drugs? That would depend on whether Evans had voluntarily assumed a duty of care on some other basis, such as under the *R. v Stone and Dobinson*[41] doctrine.** In *R. v. Stone and Dobinson*, an intellectually disabled couple took in an eccentric 61-year-old relative who was suffering from anorexia nervosa. The relative became bedridden due to her ailing health and developed bed-sores, and other serious infections, and was clearly in need of medical attention. Stone and his mistress, Dobinson, failed to summon help and eventually the relative died. The defendants were convicted of negligent manslaughter on the basis that they voluntarily assumed a duty of care for the victim by taking her into their home and by providing for her in a minimal sense. Stone and Dobinson did not create any danger for the relative, rather the danger was a natural consequence of the relative's refusal to eat properly for years, which left her bedridden and in need of care from trained nursing staff. Dobinson's duty arose merely because she had washed the victim a few times and lived in the same house.

The *Stone and Dobinson* doctrine does not extend to cases such as *R. v. Evans*, because Evans's ineffectual acts of care were over hours not years. The *Stone and Dobinson* doctrine seems to apply to a narrow set of cases where substantial care has been provided for a considerable period of time; and where the defendants ought to have known that the victim was deteriorating and was in need of urgent medical assistance. If Evans had not supplied her sister with the dangerous drugs, but rather came home to find her sister self-injecting drugs which she had acquired by herself, then merely checking on her unconscious sister a couple of times in the hours before her death would not have been sufficient for holding that she has assumed a duty to try to "un-cause" or undo the harm her sister's self-injection was "causing."

Evans's sister was perfectly healthy when she decided to self-inject. Evans was not the victim's guardian[42] and it would be a very wide doctrine of liability, if the duty merely arose from blood ties between emancipated adults or from "a desultory attempt to be of assistance."[43] In *R. v. Sinclair, Johnson and Smith*, Johnson's conviction was quashed because his acts of assistance were not sufficient to constitute a voluntary assumption of a legal duty. Sinclair was found to owe a duty because there was evidence that he was a good friend of the adult victim, knew the victim was not an addict, and stayed with him throughout the period of his unconsciousness and waited 12 hours before calling an ambulance. More importantly, Sinclair supplied the victim with the lethal methadone.

7–016 Sinclair's friendship with the victim does not seem sufficient for imposing a duty of care for the purposes of establishing gross negligence manslaughter. Furthermore, it would be stretching it to argue that his presence and desultory attempts of assistance would be sufficient to ground a duty of care. Facilitating

---

[41] [1977] Q.B. 354. See also *R. v. Hood* [2004] 1 Cr. App. R. 73; *R. v. Nichols* (1874) 13 Cox C.C. 75. Cf. *R. v. Instan* [1893] 1 Q.B. 450.

[42] It was recognized long ago that a person does not have a legal duty to rescue or summon help for his sibling, see *R. v. Smith* (1826) 172 E.R. 203.

[43] *R. v. Evans* [2009] 1 W. L.R. 1999 at 2007 citing *R. v. Sinclair, Johnson and Smith* (1998) 148 N.L.J. 1353.

another's risk-taking does not seem enough for a homicide conviction even if that person foolishly fails to summon help after learning what she has facilitated has gone wrong. Criminalization would not be totally unfair, but a manslaughter conviction seems wrong given that the injector makes an independent choice to risk his or her own life.

Liability seems to hinge on the finest distinctions, because if the victim in *R. v. Evans* had obtained her own drugs her sister would have had no duty to summon help. Hence, she would have been able to sit by and watch her die without incurring liability. It seems that the act of supply is doing all the work: not the failure to summon help. Yet, she seems no less deserving of some form of criminalization and punishment in the latter situation. Likewise, if the victim had been 18 years old and had been living in her own flat, and if her mother had just happened to visit her at the point in time when she overdosed, the mother's familial relationship would be insufficient to establish a duty of care, because a parent has no duty to rescue emancipated offspring.[44]

In some jurisdictions the courts have taken a more expansive view. In *R. v. Finlay*,[45] a Canadian case, a man returned to his room in an intoxicated state and found his roommate suffering from severe injuries. The roommate had extensive bleeding. The defendant ignored the condition of his roommate and went to bed. The next morning he continued to ignore the condition of his roommate and went out for breakfast. The defendant was convicted of "criminal negligence causing bodily harm" and sentenced to nine months under house arrest followed by a two-year probation period with conditions. This approach is reconcilable with the requirements of proportionate punishment and fair labelling because the omission was not labelled as a form of homicide. Furthermore, the defendant was punished proportionately given that he did not inflict the injuries on his roommate, but merely failed to summon help after discovering his roommate's condition.

Defendants such as Stone, Dobinson, Evans, Findlay and Hood[46] are stupid rather **7–017** than dangerous and using "homicide" offences such as gross negligence manslaughter to criminalize them serves no retributive goal. If criminalization is appropriate in such cases, then proportionate punishment and fair labelling would require it not to be a form of homicide.[47] In *R. v. Hood*[48] the husband of the

---

[44] There is no duty to an emancipated off-spring, *R. v. Shephard* (1862) 9 Cox C.C. 123; *R. v. Kennedy (No. 2)* [2008] 1 A.C. 269. This is also the approach that has been adopted in some jurisdictions in the United States, see *People v. Beardsley*, 150 Mich. 206 (1907). However, many states do impose duties on those who are married to take reasonable steps to rescue their *dependent* adult spouses. This would be limited to those who are actually cohabiting together. However, in many of these marital cases, the facts have been such that the duty could just as easily be explained as a creation of danger case based on the creation of danger doctrine. For an overview of the U.S. position, see Jennifer M. Collins *et al.*, "Punishing Family Status," (2008) 88 *B.U.L. Rev.* 1327.

[45] [1996] 17 O.T.C. 237.

[46] *R. v. Hood* [2004] 1 Cr. App. R. 73.

[47] Professor Williams notes: "A purely moralistic approach, attempting to calibrate the degree of moral turpitude in omitting with the tragedy of the fatal result, as though the defendant had recklessly acted to cause the result instead of merely failing to prevent it, leads to the kind of judicial cruelty practised upon Mr. Stone. So my support would be given only on condition that the maximum penalty is a fine and/or community service, the preferred outcome being either a discharge with a warning or an order for some kind of education or training." Glanville Williams, "Criminal Omissions—The Conventional View," (1991) 107 *L. Q. R.* 86 at 90.

victim was jailed for 30 months notwithstanding that his wife refused to go to hospital. Coupled with this, his negligence was not the cause (rather he failed to un-cause what was already being caused by other events) of his wife's death. (He did eventually summon help, but not in time to save his wife.) It would be fairer to convict this type of defendant of some lesser negligence offence. Likewise, Evans did not directly create a situation of danger for her sister. Her contribution to the danger was indirect and remote. Her sister directly endangered her own life by making the independent choice to inject the heroin into her own arm. Direct endangerment only materialized when she self-injected the heroin. Evans's indirect contribution was merely a but for causative contribution and would be better labelled as something less serious than manslaughter.

A special offence of neglecting a duty to summon help when one has a duty to do so might provide an alternative. (It would not be harsh to extend such a duty to anyone who has a *link* to the victim such as a relative, a friend, or a stranger who has started to render assistance, *etc.*) In all the aforementioned cases it was reasonable to hold that the defendants had a duty to act, but the breach should have been labelled as "causing bodily harm by neglecting a duty to summon help" rather than as homicide. *Per contra*, Miller was the direct cause of the danger that caused the building to burn down. Miller directly created the danger and if lives had been lost, the appropriate label would have been gross negligence manslaughter.[49]

7–018 **Should a person have a general duty to summon help for strangers in need?** If adult D is on a footpath near a very busy road and she sees a two-year-old child running towards the road as a lorry is about to pass, it is not too much to ask D to reach out and grab the child.[50] Does a ship's captain have a duty to rescue a passenger who falls overboard because of his own recklessness?[51] Should a person have a duty to report a neighbour who is physically abusing his children?[52]

A general duty of easy rescue does not seem too unreasonable,[53] if it merely requires a rescue in narrowly defined circumstances. In jurisdictions where such laws exist, the general duty usually only requires the rescuer to assist a person who is in great peril and only when the rescuer can assist without endangering

---

[48] [2004] 1 Cr. App. R. 73.

[49] Cf. *R. v. Johnson* (2009) 2 Cr. App. R. 28, where a builder received a two-year sentence for negligently blocking a chimney thereby causing the occupant to die from carbon monoxide poisoning.

[50] See generally, Glanville Williams, "What Should the Code Do about Omissions," (1987) 7 *Legal Stud.* 92. For an overview of Good Samaritan laws in the United States, see Joshua Dressler, "Some Brief Thoughts (Mostly Negative) About 'Bad Samaritan' Laws," (2000) 40 *Santa Clara L. Rev.* 971; Alison McIntyre, "Guilty Bystanders? On the Legitimacy of Duty to Rescue Statutes," (1994) 23 *Phil. & Pub. Aff.* 157. Daniel B. Yeager, "A Radical Community of Aid: A Rejoinder to Opponents of Affirmative Duties to Help Strangers," (1993) 71 *Wash. U.L.Q.* 1. For a deeper philosophical discussion, see Stephen Mathis, "A Plea for Omissions," (2003) 22 *Crim. Just. Ethics* 15.

[51] There is no tort duty to act. See *Wright v. Dunlop Rubber Co. Ltd.* (1971) 11 K.I.R. 311. See also *Vanvalkenberg v. N. Navigation Co.* [1913] 30 O.L.R. 142.

[52] In California, the *Sherrice Inversion Good Samaritan Law* criminalizes those who witness an assault of a minor under the age of 14 without notifying the police.

[53] See generally Andrew Ashworth, "The Scope of Criminal Liability for Omissions," (1989) 105 *L.Q.R.* 424.

himself.[54] Furthermore, if such a law merely labelled the failure to act as an independent less serious form of petty offending, then it might not be too burdensome. It might, however, be difficult to enforce such a law in practice. If there are many potential rescuers should they all be held liable? Obviously, if someone is already providing assistance, then the need for others to get involved dissipates. A strong argument for resisting criminalization for failure to rescue might be that it would serve little purpose in practice. It is arguable that most people would try to provide basic assistance or at least summon help in an emergency. Given the cardinal value of personal autonomy, any enactments in this area should be narrowly tailored to deal with extreme cases.

Should there be a duty to report or prevent serious crimes? Unlike the easy **7–019** rescue cases, there may be crimes committed in gang type situations where the bystanders are quasi-complicit in the primary criminality, but not sufficiently so to be caught by the law of complicity. Given the propinquity of such offenders with the substantive offending, it might be possible to identify them for the purposes of enforcing omissions liability. If a person is in a public bar and witnesses a woman being raped on the counter, is it too much to ask that person to call the police? Compounding the crimes of others might provide a rationale for criminalization in some cases, as the bystander benefits from the crime that she is witnessing.

Compounding or extraction-complicity liability arises when people benefit from the criminality of another, but have not directly encouraged or assisted[55] the perpetrator's substantive offending.[56] Examples of crimes enacted to criminalize those who benefit from the criminality of others include crimes that prohibit people purchasing or possessing child pornography or elephant ivory. The primary harm is carried out by the person who produces the child pornography or the poacher who hunts the endangered elephants. Such purchases are outlawed because the suppliers have criminally harmed children and endangered species to produce the end product. A more familiar example is the prohibition against purchasing stolen goods. The purchaser of the stolen goods is not a thief, but he benefits from the thief's thieving, because it allows him to purchase cheap goods. If a person makes a big saving by purchasing stolen goods from a thief, he compounds the thief's original theft. The traditional common law offence "of compounding a felony" covered situations where a person took money or some other benefit to conceal another's crime.[57]

There is no reason why compounding liability cannot be extended to those who obtain minor benefits from the serious crimes of others. In a recent tragedy

---

[54] Thomas Lateano *et al.*, "Does the Law Encourage or Hinder Bystander Intervention? An Analysis of Good Samaritan Laws," (2009) 44(5) *Crim. L. Bulletin* ART 4.

[55] If they encouraged or assisted the perpetrator, then they would be caught by sections 44-46 of the *Serious Crime Act 2007.*

[56] Dennis J. Baker, "Collective Criminalization and the Constitutional Right to Endanger Others," (2009) 28(2) *Crim. Just. Ethics* 168; Dennis J. Baker, "The Moral Limits of Criminalizing Remote Harms," (2007) 10(3) *New Crim. L. Rev.* 370.

[57] Section 5(5) of the *Criminal Law Act 1967* replaces the common law offence of "compounding a felony". For an application of section 5(5) see *R. v. Panyiotou* [1973] 1 W.L.R. 1032. For an application of the old "compounding a felony" offence see *The Queen v. Burgess* (1885-86) 16 Q.B.D. 141.

in California, a 15-year-old school girl was raped for two hours by up to ten youths while 20 onlookers either cheered or did nothing.[58] The girl was found with a badly swollen face because she had been violently beaten during the public rape. None of the bystanders attempted to help the young woman, nor did any of them attempt to call the police. It was only reported to the police sometime later when a member of the public discovered the naked victim lying under a park bench with severe injuries. The benefit for the majority of the passive bystanders was the perverted thrill they got by staying on for two hours to see the innocent girl being publicly brutalized and raped. It is debatable as to what kind of benefit this is, as normal people would not want to see such a thing, but many of the bystanders filmed the rape with their mobile phones for their own perverted purposes. One argument for criminalizing the bystanders is that they benefited from the crime by obtaining "footage of a rape" and by watching it for so long.

7–020   This rape involved high school students at a high school dance, and no doubt the gang mentality[59] involved was part of the reason for the spectators filming it. The proximate spectators compounded the rapists' criminality. A general offence requiring people to report a serious crime could be enacted to catch this type of wrongdoing. It should be enforced with two layers of wrongdoing in mind. First, those who merely fail to report a crime because they do not want to get involved should be subject to pecuniary fines.[60] Second, those who benefit from the criminality or standby for a lengthy period of time should be taken as compounding the criminality and should be subject to a more severe sentence including jail terms were appropriate.

Complicity liability would not be wide enough to catch passive witnesses of such crimes.[61] If the bystanders thoroughly enjoyed seeing the rape and took delight in the victim's misery, they would not be complicit in the rape unless they encouraged it or assisted it in some way. Arguably, filming it might be a form of encouragement—but it might also be a form of discouragement depending on the reasons that the filming party has for filming it. The person filming it might film it intending to provide the footage to the police. Those cheering it would be caught by the law of complicity, because that is a form of encouragement.

A general duty to report violent crime in circumstances where the immediacy of the violent attack means that the spectator's action could prevent a rape or further violence does not seem to be too burdensome. But the failure to do so would not make the spectator a rapist; rather he should be criminalized independently of the rapist for failing to report a violent crime which he

---

[58] Michelle Quinn, "Richmond Gang Rape: Coping With the Shock," (New York: *New York Times*, 5 November 2009).

[59] Paul O'Connell *et al.*, "Peer Involvement in Bullying: Insights and Challenges for Intervention," (1999) 22(4) *Journal of Adolescence* 437.

[60] Interestingly, Californian law makes it a crime not to report a crime against a child under 14 (see the *Sherrice Inversion Good Samaritan Law*), but this girl was 15 so the offenders did not come within the law's purview. In the United States the misprision of felony offence has been interpreted as requiring affirmative acts of concealment, a mere failure to report a crime is not enough to ground liability. See *U.S. v. Davila*, 698 F. 2d 715 (1983); *United States v. Johnson*, 546 F. 2d 1225 (5ᵗʰ Cir. 1977). Cf. *State v. Hann*, 40 N.J.L. 228 (1878).

[61] *R. v. Clarkson* (1971) 55 Cr. App. R. 445, where it was held that being present at the crime scene without something more would not be enough to constitute complicit encouragement.

witnessed firsthand. Proportionate punishment would require such an offender to be punished and criminalized independently as a person who has compounded the criminality of another or as a person who has failed in his duty to report a serious crime that was taking place in his presence, when it was reasonable for him to do so. It is important not to extend this to all serious crimes such as fraud, theft, and so on.

As noted above, there used to be a common law offence of "misprision of felony,"[62] which required people to report felonies. But it would be too great an extension of criminal responsibility and too great a restriction on the potential defendant's freedom to require him to report serious crimes in general. If there is no immediacy, and no violence involved, then it is for the police to seek out the defendants. As Professor Williams warns:[63]

7–021

> "[M]isprision of felony ... was an offence abolished in 1967 because it was found to be productive of such severe problems as to be unusable. It would have required people to report on their companions and acquaintances, including their best friends and near members of their family, whatever might be the degree of seriousness of the particular felony in question. This would be an appalling way of extending the circle of criminality beyond the immediate doers and omitters and their accomplices."

An offence criminalizing failures to report *violent* crimes would not require the live witness to intervene. All the witness would be required to do is call the police. When there are many bystanders responsibility becomes more diffuse or collective and individual bystanders are more reluctant to take action.[64] In gang situations some of the members may also be reluctant to act because of a fear of reprisals. Nonetheless, there is no reason why all those present in such cases could not be charged if there is sufficient evidence to demonstrate that they were in a position to call the police. Enforcement might not always be easy, but such a law would act as a deterrent in situations involving publicly committed crimes. CCTV and other forms of recording also mean that it might be possible to identify onlookers when these crimes are committed in public places. The gang rape mentioned above took place at a school dance, so it would be possible to narrow down those who were present. Such a duty should perhaps be limited to reporting sexual offences, offences against the person, homicide offences and misprision of treason and other acts of terrorism.[65]

---

[62] The misprision of felony offence was an "[i]ndictable misdemeanour at common law, and a person was guilty of the crime if knowing that a felony had been committed he failed to disclose his knowledge to those responsible for the preservation of the peace, be they constables or justices, within a reasonable time and having a reasonable opportunity for doing so". *Sykes v. Director of Public Prosecutions* [1963] A.C. 528. See also *R. v. Lucraft* (1966) 50 Cr. App. R. 296; *R. v. King* [1965] 1 W.L.R. 706. The offence was abolished when the *Criminal Law Act 1967* was enacted.

[63] William, *loc. cit. supra*, note 46.

[64] Gregory K. Gruder *et al.*, "Group Cohesiveness, Social Norms, and Bystander Intervention," (1983) 44(3) *J. Personality & Soc. Psych.* 545; Bibb Latané and John M. Darley, "Group Inhibition of Bystander Intervention in Emergencies," (1968) 10 *J. Personality & Soc. Psych.* 215.

[65] Section 19 of the *Terrorism Act 2000* retains the latter offence.

7.4. POSSESSION

7–022   The judges ultimately refused to recognize any offences of illicit possession as a matter of common law, saying that possession was not an act;[66] and such offences of the kind as we have are statutory.

The acquisition of possession usually involves an act (an act of grasping an object, for example), in which case there is no difficulty. Even where a person delivers goods to my premises without my touching them, I shall usually have ordered him to do so. However, one can instance cases where there is no relevant act. Take the statutory offence of "knowingly possessing explosives."[67] A man is in possession of a package which, when he first received it, he did not realize contained explosives, but he has later come to know it does. There is no "act" on his part after he acquires the knowledge. The courts hold that he commits an offence if he retains the explosives, unless he retains it for some lawful purpose[68] such as to inform the police.[69] In this respect, therefore, the offence is one of omission in breach of duty. The person who is under the duty to act is clearly pointed out by the statute, as being the person in possession of the property.[70]

It is sometimes hard to tell whether, when a person is in possession of contraband (an expression used in this book to denote any forbidden object), his possession will be treated in law as shared by another. The answer many sometimes depend on the particular offence charged, but the general principle is that a person may possess through another (particularly an agent or accomplice) if, though not in physical possession of the thing, he intends to exercise prior joint or sole control over it.[71]

7–023   The courts are generally reluctant to hold that an employee possesses his employer's goods of which he is left in charge, for the purpose of convicting the employee of an offence of unlawful possession. The possession is generally regarded as being solely in the employer. This is so, for example, with regard to possessing unfit food for sale. But the attitude of the court will naturally depend upon the offence charged, upon the degree of control exercised by the employer over the article, and upon the discretion given to the employee. The manager of a shop would readily be convicted of possessing contraband stock when he is

---

[66] *Dugdale v. The Queen* (1853) 118 E.R. 717; P. R. Glazebrook, "Criminal Omissions: the Duty Requirement in Offences against the Person," (1960) 76 *L.Q.R.* 386.

[67] Section 4(1) of the *Explosive Substances Act 1883.*

[68] *R. v. Riding* [2009] EWCA Crim. 892.

[69] Similarly with the offences of handling stolen goods by retention: *R. v. Brown* [1970] 1 Q.B. 105; *R. v. Pitchley* (1972) 57 Cr. App. R. 30. As to the qualification see *R. v. Wuyts* [1969] 2 Q.B. 474: here the statute defined the offence as being committed only when the possession was "without lawful authority or excuse," but these words would anyway be implied. See *R. v. Selby* [1972] A.C. 515 (possession of counterfeit coins).

[70] Whereas a person who consciously keeps a contraband object in order to inform police is not liable, one who holds it not knowing its nature can, paradoxically, be liable for an offence of strict liability. Cf. *R. v. Deyemi* (2008) 1 Cr. App. R. 25.

[71] In *R. v. Stong* [1989] 86 10 L.S.G. 41 it was held that joint possession could be imputed to co-defendants so long as "each had a right to say what should be done with the contents." Knowledge *per se* does not amount to control. *R. v. Searle* [1971] Crim. L.R. 592; *R. v. Bland* [1988] Crim. L.R. 41.

effectively in sole charge of the business; and even more low-level employees may sometimes be held to have been placed in possession.[72]

The *actus reus* might involve the positive act to obtain contraband or an omission to rid oneself of contraband after realizing that one is in control or possession of it. The mental element permeates the *actus reus* requirement, because a possessor's duty to dispossess himself of contraband depends not only on his control or physical possession of the contraband, but also on his awareness of that control or possession and knowledge of the potential nature of the substance that is controlled or possessed.[73] Section 5(3) of the *Misuse of Drugs Act 1971* makes it an offence to be found in possession of drugs such as heroin. Section 28 of the *Misuse of Drugs Act 1971* allows the possessor to avoid criminal liability, if he can establish that he was not suspicious or aware of the fact that he was in possession of an illegal substance.

In *Warner v. Metropolitan Police Commissioner*[74] it was held that if a possessor fails to check the nature of contraband in his possession when he has an opportunity to do so, knowledge of its nature will be imputed to him. If D slips a packet of heroin into V's pocket without V's knowledge, V will be in physical control of the heroin but the offence is not made out because V did not know or have reason to believe that he was in control of the drug. If V discovers the package and has reason to suspect that it is a prohibited drug, then V has a legal duty to get rid of the package. There would be no liability if V did not have sufficient time or opportunity to dispossess himself of the drugs. It is the omission to take positive steps to hand over the contraband to the police upon learning of its potentially illegal nature that forms the actus reus in such cases. Similarly, section 58 of the *Terrorism Act 2000* makes it an offence to possess information for a terrorist purpose. It must not only be shown that the defendant possessed such information, but that he also possessed it for terrorist purposes. The defendant has to know that he is in control of the information that is likely to be useful for terrorism; and also know the nature of the information.[75] Once the defendant realizes that he has such material he has a duty to dispossess himself of such material.

7.5. THE CONCURRENCE OF ACT AND INTENT

Normally, *actus reus* and *mens rea* must concur in point of time. If a person innocently acquires goods, he does not become guilty of receiving stolen goods by reason of subsequently finding out that they are stolen. Nor does a person who has been given stolen goods become guilty of theft in acquiring them by reason of the fact that he subsequently finds that he has not obtained a good title to them. But the rule is not so simple as it may at first seem. In the second hypothetical, the donee of the goods can become guilty of theft by dishonestly keeping them

7–024

---

[72] *D.D.P. v. Brooks* [1974] A.C. 862 shows that an employee (in that case a van driver) can be guilty of an offence of possessing a controlled drug even though he possesses only for his employer.

[73] If the possessor thought she was in possession of drugs, then it does not matter if the drug is not the exact drug she suspected it might be. *R. v. Leeson* (2000) 1 Cr. App. R. 233; *R. v. Lambert* [2002] Q.B. 1112; *R. v. Choudhury* [2008] EWCA Crim. 3179.

[74] [1969] 2 A.C. 256. Cf. *R. v. Lewis* (1988) 87 Cr. App. R. 270.

[75] *R. v. G* [2010] 1 A.C. 43. See the fuller discussion in Chapter 36.

after he comes to know that they do not belong to him. The theft is not the original acquisition but the subsequent guilty retention, and this retention is an *actus reus* concurrent with the *mens rea*.

Moreover, some criminal acts are regarded as continuing over a period of time. If the act is continuing, a guilty intent formed towards the end of this period can still make the actor guilty of the crime. A good example is false imprisonment (*i.e.* unlawful detention), which is committed for as long as the imprisonment lasts. If a library assistant locks me in the library by mistake, he does not at that moment commit false imprisonment. But if he subsequently sees me through the window trying to get out, and decides to leave me in overnight to teach me to be more careful next time, he commits false imprisonment.[76] The same would apply if a person was engaged in consensual sexual intercourse, but was asked not to continue. At the point in time when consent is withdrawn, the intercourse becomes rape unless the defendant desists.

This point was involved, but not clearly perceived, in *Fagan v. Metropolitan Police Commissioner*,[77] the case of "parking on a police officer's foot." Fagan, having accidentally brought his car to rest on the foot of a police officer, refused to remove it when asked to do so. After a short time he relented and moved the car. He could have been prosecuted for false imprisonment, but that is purely indictable, so he was brought before the justices on a charge of assaulting a constable in the execution of his duty. The difficulty was that an assault cannot be committed by omission, and when Fagan drew up on the officer's foot he lacked *mens rea* for an assault. However, he was convicted.

7–025 On appeal the Divisional Court was quite clear that it wished to affirm the conviction, but took no pains to find a convincing reason. The court said that Fagan committed an *act* in keeping his car where it was, because he (1) remained in the car and (2) switched off the ignition. But was remaining in the car an act? And would the court have quashed the conviction if Fagan had left the engine running and got out of the car? If not, the reason offered was not a convincing reason. And, of course, the policeman's complaint was not that Fagan remained in the car and switched off the engine; his complaint was that Fagan did not move the car, which in itself looks like an omission.

The proper decision would have been that the offence of assault continued for as long as force was being applied to the policeman as a direct result of Fagan's act. That force was the force of gravity. The point is supported by civil cases.[78] On this view, Fagan's intent and unlawful act concurred in point of time. The

---

[76] It is assumed in the hypothetical that the librarian believes that the "reader" is not a trespasser. False imprisonment is a common law offence. See *R. v. Rashman* (1985) 81 Cr. App. R. 349.

[77] [1969] 1 Q.B. 439.

[78] The crime of assault stems from the old writ of tress pass, which also gave us the tort of trespass to land. It is clear law that a person who places trespassory articles on the land of another is guilty of a continuing trespass as long as they continue there. There is no reason why the same principle should not apply where trespassory pressure is exercised upon the body of another.

alternative approach is to apply *R. v. Miller*.[79] Fagan may have accidentally created a situation of danger, but once he realized the danger he had a duty to counteract it.[80]

If D kills someone by committing a sequence of interconnected acts, need his   7–026
***mens rea* concur with the actual act that causes V's death?**   No. If the acts are temporally connected and relate to a single criminal "event" the courts will most likely apply the doctrine of extended concurrence.

In *Meli v. The Queen*[81] four men were convicted of murder. They had allegedly taken the victim to a hut and plied him with beer before striking him on the head with an instrument. Believing they had killed him, they took his body outside and dumped it. The medical evidence showed that the victim's death was not caused by the blows in the hut, but from exposure. It was contended on behalf of the defendants that two separate acts were involved. First, there was the attack in the hut; and, second, there was the dumping of the body outside afterwards. It was asserted that the defendants' lacked *mens rea* for murder, because they did not intend to kill the victim when they did the second act. The Privy Council upheld a conviction for murder on the ground that the defendants had set out to do all the acts (including the disposal of the body) as part of a plan; and it did not matter that they thought that their purpose had been achieved (that the victim had been killed) earlier than it had been. An English case followed this and took the same position.[82]

The courts have reached their decisions by enquiring whether there was a preconceived plan covering what was done, or whether there was a continuing series of acts; but these enquires are unsatisfactory substitutes for a basic decision of policy. The proper view is that this is a situation where the act and intent need not concur. In this case, the initial assault was accompanied by the requisite intention, and the subsequent act was temporally and culpably connected with the preceding act. The "disposal of the body" did not relate to a different crime at a different point in time, but to the very crime which they had just committed.

But suppose that the defendant says that when he killed the victim he had no plan   7–027
to dispose of the body, and only decided to do that when he had the "body" on his hands? The point arose in the Supreme Court of South Africa (Appellate

---

[79] [1983] 2 A.C. 161.
[80] Cf. *R. v. Taber* [2002] 136 A. Crim. R. 478, where D's deliberate failure to summon help continued for days and this caused V to die from dehydration. In that case, D, a robber, tied his victim up and left her in her home. D tried to alert the authorities of her whereabouts and of the dangerous situation he had created for her, but the emergency services thought it was a prank call so did not respond.
[81] [1954] 1 W.L.R. 228; *sub. nom.*
[82] *R. v. Moore* [1975] Crim. L.R. 229. *R. v. Church* [1966] 1 Q.B. 59 may seem on its face to be to the same effect, but the Court of Appeal somewhat fudged the rule. Purporting to follow *Meli v. The Queen*, the court said, *obiter*: "The jury should have been told that it was still open to them to convict of murder, notwithstanding that the appellant may have thought his blows and attempt at strangulation had actually produced death when he threw the body into the river, if the appellant's behaviour from the moment he first struck her to the movement when he threw her into the river was a series of acts designed to cause death or grievous bodily harm." The obvious difficulty is that the disposal of the "body" was not one of "a series of acts designed to cause death *etc.*" It lay outside any such series, because when it was done the defendant thought the victim was dead. For this reason, a direction in the terms suggested would be self-contradictory.

Division), and it was held that the killer could be convicted of murder even though the disposal of the supposed corpse was not part of a plan conceived before the murderous attack.[83]

The decision in *Meli v. The Queen* seems right in principle, because the defendants intended to kill V and managed to achieve this end by committing a number of acts which were temporally and culpably intertwined. Likewise, in *R. v. Church*, D had attempted to kill the deceased prior to inadvertently causing her death. The victim had been brutally beaten and strangulated to the point of unconsciousness before Church threw her into the river. It was his act of covering up the horrific crime he had just committed that caused her death. In these cases, the defendants had the requisite intent when they initially embarked on the course of conduct which caused the victim's death. The actual acts that caused the victims' death were so interconnected with the initial acts that it would be pure fiction to isolate them.

7–028   **Does it make a difference if by his first act D did not intend to kill?** No. "If a killing by the first act would have been manslaughter, a later destruction of the supposed corpse should also be manslaughter."[84] In *R. v. Le Brun*,[85] D accidentally killed his wife when he was attempting to cover up the fact that he had unlawfully assaulted her. Le Brun did not intend to do her serious injury, nor did he intend to kill her. He had an argument with his wife in a public street and knocked her semi-conscious. The wife was lying on the footpath and was unable to get up. Le Brun tried to pick her up and attempted to drag her to their home which was nearby, as he wanted to cover up what he had done. In doing the latter, he accidentally dropped her, fractured her skull, and thus killed her.

Lord Lane C.J. said:[86]

> "The guilty intent accompanying that blow was sufficient to have rendered the appellant guilty of manslaughter, but not murder, had it caused death. But it did not cause death. What caused death was the later impact when the wife's head hit the pavement. At the moment of impact the appellant's intention was to remove her, probably unconscious, body to avoid detection. To that extent the impact may have been accidental. May the earlier guilty intent be joined with the later non-guilty blow which caused death to produce in the conglomerate a proper verdict of manslaughter?
>
> ....
>
> It seems to us that where the unlawful application of force and the eventual act causing death are parts of the same sequence of events, the same transaction, the fact that there is an appreciable interval of time between the two does not serve to exonerate the defendant from liability. That is certainly so where the appellant's subsequent actions which caused death, after the initial unlawful blow, are designed to conceal his commission of the original unlawful assault."[87]

---

[83] *State. v. Masilela* (1968) 2 S.A. 558. See also the decision of the South Australian Supreme Court in *R. v. Hallett* [1969] S.A.S.R. 141. In *R. v. Ramsay* [1967] N.Z.L.R. 1005 the New Zealand Court of Appeal held that the supposed corpse doctrine in murder applied only where there was an intention to kill, not where the murderous malice involved an intention to injure or risk causing injury; but that limitation is unlikely to be accepted in England and Wales. See *R. v. Moore* [1975] Crim. L.R. 229.

[84] Glanville Williams, *Criminal Law: The General Part*, (London: Stevens & Sons, 2nd edn. 1961) at 174 cited with approval in *R. v. Le Brun* [1992] Q.B. 61 at 68 *per* Lane C.J.

[85] [1992] Q.B. 61.

[86] *R. v. Le Brun* [1992] Q.B. 61 at 66.

[87] *R. v. Le Brun* [1992] Q.B. 61 at 68.

Lord Lane C.J. also held that if the defendant had been trying to rescue his wife, instead of concealing his initial unlawful act, he would not have been liable.[88] This, perhaps, is because his culpability for the initial wrongdoing would have entirely ceased. There is nothing culpable about trying to pick someone up to race them to hospital, *etc.* Such a person acts to remedy his initial unlawful harm-doing, so he cannot be said to be culpably taking a risk to make it worse. Nor could it be said, that such a defendant was aiming to further a criminal goal.

7.6. OFFENCES WITHOUT RELEVANT CONDUCT

Parliament sometimes makes a person guilty by reason of his bodily position, voluntarily assumed, as in the offence of being found on certain private premises for an unlawful purpose. Some conduct can be seen, but the offence consists in the bodily position resulting from conduct rather than in the conduct itself.   **7–029**

On at least one occasion (which we have noticed before) the courts created such an offence by "interpretation." A statute makes it an offence for a prostitute to solicit in any street. A prostitute showed herself provocatively in a window fronting the street, without making a sign or other movement, but intending by her self-display to attract customers. It was held that she was guilty of soliciting in a street.[89] She had, of course, moved herself into the offending position, but it was her position and its accompaniments that were held to fall within the notion of soliciting.

What if there is no conduct at all—not even the conduct of taking up a position?   Remarkable as it may at first appear, Parliament not infrequently imposes (or is interpreted as having imposed) penal liability upon people who have not in any sense done anything, and who may not be at fault. To give this a distinguishing name, the term "situational liability" has been suggested.[90] Situational offences are committed by those who find themselves in a specified situation not involving any relevant conduct on their part. The most important illustrations turn on the attributed (vicarious) liability. Situational liability does not offend our sense of justice in the "ticket" cases, when the penalty is light and imposed without court proceedings, or when it requires fault by the defendant, but grave doubts arise when the liability is both situational and strict. Offences of this kind strike one as being particularly tyrannical. The British used collective responsibility for serious offences including capital offences until 1798.[91] Through the legal mechanism of bill of attainder, the legislature could declare a   **7–030**

---

[88] "The judge was drawing a sharp distinction between actions by the appellant which were designed to help his wife and actions which were not so designed: on the one hand that would be a way in which the prosecution could establish the connection if he was not trying to assist his wife; on the other hand if he was trying to assist his wife, the chain of causation would have been broken and the nexus between the two halves of the prosecution case would not exist." *R. v. Le Brun* [1992] Q.B. 61 at 71.

[89] *Behrendt v. Burridge* [1977] 1 W.L.R. 29.

[90] P. R. Glazebrook, "Situational Liability," in P. R. Glazebrook (ed.), *Reshaping The Criminal Law*, (London: Steven & Sons, 1978).

[91] Michael P. Lehmann, *The Bill of Attainder Doctrine: A Survey of the Decisional Law*, (1978) 5 *Hastings Const. L. Q.* 767-1012.

person or group of persons guilty of some serious crime without a trial. The bill of attainder was used to strip people of their property and to sentence them to death without the benefit of a trial.[92] The criminal code of Stalin's Russia provided a scandalous example in the offence of being a "relative of an enemy of the people." In our law these offences arise partly because of the wording of some legislation and partly because of the failure of the courts to develop a liberal principle of interpretation.

A case that is generally regarded as marking the extreme of severity in this country is *R. v. Larsonneur*,[93] where a Frenchwoman who went from England to Ireland was arrested by the Irish police and delivered by them in custody back to the Welsh police at Holyhead. The police charged her with the offence under the *Aliens Order* of being an alien who was "found" in the United Kingdom without permission; they had, of course, "found" her in their own custody when they received delivery of her protesting body from the Irish police. The London Sessions sentenced her to imprisonment of three days with a recommendation for deportation, and the conviction and sentence was upheld by the Court of Criminal Appeal. The peculiar oppression of this decision did not lie in the mere fact that it imposed liability without any act or culpable omission. There are many offences of strict and attributed liability, to be studied in the last part of this book, which can also result in unjust condemnations; but they generally concern business matters, and result merely in a fine, so that, although they may be regarded as unjust, the injustice is perhaps not felt strongly. In *R. v. Larsonneur*, on the other hand, the events concerned the defendant's private life, and the sentence was one of imprisonment, even though for only a short time.

It is difficult to understand why the unfortunate woman was prosecuted, since she could simply have been send back to her native country without prosecution. Nor was there any exegetical necessity for the court to read the *Aliens Order* as creating an offence in the absence of a culpable act or omission: the word "found" might well have been interpreted as meaning "found at liberty"—not "found" in police custody. Alternatively, the court might have extended the defence of duress to include compulsion by law, or compulsion of circumstances.

7–031   Although the decision in *R. v. Larsonneur* has been condemned by most commentators, a similar attitude was adopted by a court in a case of 1983.[94] The defendant was brought to hospital on a stretcher; the doctor discovered that he was merely drunk, so the police were called. They removed the defendant to their car on the roadway, and then charged him with being found drunk in a highway. His conviction was affirmed by a Divisional Court.

The proper mode of construing such legislation was exemplified by the Supreme Court of Alabama[95] in a case where the police came to the defendant when he was sitting drunk in his house, carried him out on the street, and then arrested him for being drunk and disorderly in a public place. The statute under

---

[92] *Ibid.*

[93] (1933) 24 Cr. App. R. 74. Cf. *Chia Gee v. Martin* (1906) 3 C.L.R. 649. The decision of the Privy Council in *Lim Chin Aik v. R.* [1963] A.C. 160 may be quoted *contra*.

[94] *Winzar v. Chief Constable of Kent, The Times*, (May 1983). *Contra*, *McKenzie v. Police* [1956] N.Z.L.R. 1013. See also *Lehr v. City of Sacramento*, 624 F.Supp.2d 1218 (2009); *Finger v. State*, 117 Nev. 548 (2001).

[95] *Martin v. State*, 31 Ala. App. 344 (1944).

which the defendant was charged referred to "any person who, while intoxicated or drunk, appears in any public place ... and manifests a drunken condition by boisterous or indecent conduct," *etc.* Literally the defendant had "appeared" on the street, but the court declared that "under the plain terms of this statute a voluntary appearance is presupposed."

It was remarked just now that there is no objection on principle to convicting a person of a situational offence if he was culpable in bringing about the situation. So a person who creeps into someone's house, drinks himself silly, is found by the owner and is ejected on to the street, could properly be convicted of being drunk in a public place because he might reasonably have foreseen that he would end up drunk in a public place. *R. v. Larsonneur*, likewise, has been supported on the ground that she had been ordered to leave the United Kingdom and did so by going to the Irish Free State; she should have foreseen that she might be expelled from Ireland back to the United Kingdom.[96]

In some cases a defendant's prior blameworthy acts make it fair to impute blame to him, even though he was not acting voluntarily when the final harm or wrong eventuated. In the 21st century most people know that they need a visa to enter other countries and would also realize that travelling to a country without a visa would be risky, as it is likely to result in deportation, and not necessarily to their home country. But this would be expecting prescience of Larsonneur in 1933. It was surely quite reasonable for her to think that even if she should prove to be unwelcome to the Irish as she was to the English, she would be allowed to make her own way back from Ireland to France. Although situational offences may be unobjectionable if some kind of culpability is required, it would be strained to find any culpability in *Larsonneur*, and no such finding was in fact made.

7.7.   THE MISSING ELEMENT

Suppose a person thinks he is committing a crime, but a bit of the *actus reus* is missing. It goes without saying that the offence is not committed. For example, a person who believes he has brought off a successful fraud resulting in a profit cannot be convicted of fraud by false representation if it turns out that what he said happened to be true.[97] And if a man who has been estranged from his wife thinks that he is marrying another woman bigamously, but it transpires that his wife died just before the ceremony, he is not guilty of bigamy. The marriage that he thinks is bigamous is perfectly valid.

However, the would-be cheat could be convicted of trying to obtain property by making a false representation (an inchoate offence under section 2 of the *Fraud Act 2006*), and the would-be bigamist could be convicted of an attempt to commit bigamy—just as a person who shoots a tree stump believing it to be a human being can be convicted of attempted murder. In practice the question of attempt would be unlikely to arise, because the police would probably be satisfied with charging a firearms offence, or having the offender bound over, or perhaps just cautioning him. But it might arise if there was a prosecution for the

7–032

---

[96] D. J. Lanham, "Larsonneur Revisted," [1976] *Crim. L.R.* 276.
[97] *R. v. Deller* (1952) 36 Cr. App. R. 184.

completed crime and it was only discovered during the trial that the completed crime could not be established. In that case the prosecution might press the charge of attempt.

7–033 **But your would-be fraudster is only committing fraud in his heart, and the would-be bigamist is only committing bigamy in his heart. What he does is perfectly legal, so how can it be a crime? You said, didn't you, that our law does not go in for thought-crime.** It is not merely punishing for thoughts. These people have gone beyond thinking. They have taken steps. Yes, what they did was perfectly legal, apart from the law of attempt!

The act of attempt need not be illegal apart from its being the crime of attempt. If a person puts her own rat poison into her own bowl of soup and offers it to her husband with intent to murder him, she is guilty of an attempt even though, apart from the law of attempt, everything she has done is legal. It is not merely a thought-crime: she has actually offered her husband what she believes to be deadly poison.

7–034 **I still don't see why you should say that the intended bigamist commits an attempt. He has gone through what he imagined was a bigamous ceremony, and it was not. Why should he be guilty of attempted bigamy? And so forth for the fraudster. They have done everything they intended to do, and it was not a crime. The question of attempt does not come into it.** Your difficulty is one that eminent judges have shared. As a result, the courts used to limit attempt at common law to cases where all the required circumstances for the complete offence were present, or the forbidden consequences might happen. One could not "attempt the impossible." But the rule worked badly; it meant, for example, that the "dip" who tried to steal from an empty pocket could not be convicted of attempted theft, since one of the requirements of theft (property belonging to another as the subject of theft) was missing. Because of these and other problems the "impossibility rule" in the law of attempt was abolished by the *Criminal Attempts Act 1981.*

To return to where we started, whether a person is guilty of completed crime when he mistakenly believes that a fact is present depends, of course, on what facts are needed for the crime. Difficulties can arise if a penal statute does not explain whether it is speaking of a mental state or an external element. The point is illustrated by section 22(1) of the *Theft Act 1968,* which provides:

> "A person handles stolen goods if (otherwise than in the course of stealing) knowing or believing them to be stolen goods he dishonestly receives the goods…"

Here "believing them to be stolen" means "being almost sure that they are stolen, and being right, because they are stolen." So the subsection requires the goods to be stolen. This point may not be immediately obvious. In some contexts the words "believing them to be stolen" could mean "correctly or mistakenly believing them to be stolen." The word "know" refers exclusively to true knowledge; we are not said to "know" something that is not so. Belief, on the other hand, can include a mistaken belief, a subjective conviction whether right or wrong. But this is not the only meaning; "belief" can refer to the degree of belief ("I do not know it is so; I am not 100 *per cent.* sure; but I believe it is so—with something less than complete certainty"). This must be the meaning in the subsection, because it opens with the words "a person handles stolen goods." It takes for granted as the *actus reus* the fact that the goods are stolen and handled, and concerns itself only with the *mens rea*. If the goods turn out not to be stolen, the would-be handler is guilty of an attempt.[98]

Does the rule for offences apply similarly to defences? I readily see that a person cannot be convicted of an offence merely because he believed he was committing it. Can he be convicted of an offence notwithstanding that on the facts he would have had a defence, if he did not know the facts gave him a defence? Defences may be classified as excuses and justifications. In the former, the social mischief has happened but the defendant is allowed a defence on personal grounds. Examples of excuses are duress and (in murder) diminished responsibility. The essence of such a defence is that some pressure acted on the defendant's mind at the time. He must have been affected by the duress, or the "loss of control", and therefore must have known of it or believed it existed. Justifications are allowed by law where it is thought that, on the facts, the defendant was perfectly right in acting as he did. In principle, such defences should operate even if the defendant only believed the facts creating the justification existed.[99]

7–035

---

[98] *R. v. Shivpuri* [1987] A.C. 1 at 2.
[99] See *The Queen v. Dadson*, 169 E.R. 407 (1850).

CHAPTER 8

CAUSATION

"I only assisted natur', ma'am, as the doctor said to the boy's mother, arter he'd bled him to death."[1]

8.1. KILLING IN HOMICIDE

Causation is a central issue in result crimes, because causation is used to link the defendant with the result (harm). It is not about imputing blame to the defendant, but rather about demonstrating that his conduct was an imputable (sufficiently proximate) cause of the harm. The question of fault only arises after causation has been established. The defendant must take responsibility for any harm he has caused where he acted with the requisite fault. Causation is rarely an issue in non-homicide cases, and is not an issue at all in conduct crimes. Homicide provides the best exemplar for examining the dimensions of causation, so my discussion on causation will predominantly be centred on homicide cases. The common law definition of murder, and similarly that of manslaughter, required that the defendant should have "killed" his victim, and that the death should follow within a year and a day. The year-and-a-day rule has now been abolished by the *Law Reform (Year and a Day Rule) Act 1996*. If "the injury alleged to have caused the death was sustained more than three years before the death occurred" proceedings for murder or manslaughter can be commenced only if the Attorney-General grants permission. Since medicine and science has improved dramatically in recent years, it is possible to trace causation over a number of years without causing any grave injustice.[2]

A killing can take place by any means. There need be no direct physical act. If the victim asks his way on a dark night, and the defendant, intending to cause his death, directs him to a path that he knows will bring him to a cliff edge, and the victim suffers a fatal fall, this is clearly murder, though the defendant has done nothing more than utter words. So we may say that "killing" means conduct causing death in any way that the law regards as sufficient.[3] What these ways are has to be considered.

8-001

---

[1] Charles Dickens, *The Posthumous Papers: the Pickwick Club*, (New York: J. Van Amringe, 4th edn.1840) at 505.

[2] See generally, Donald E. Walther, "Taming a Phoenix: The Year-and-a-Day Rule in Federal Prosecutions for Murder," (1992) 59 *U. Chi. L. Rev.* 1337.

[3] It can be unlawful homicide to cause a person to catch a disease of which he dies: *Castell v. Bambridge* (1729) 93 E.R. 894. The case might be reasonably straightforward where a person is imprisoned with a carrier of smallpox and dies reasonably soon after contracting the disease.

8–002 **What of accelerating the victim's death?** This is a "killing" in law. Since we are fated to die at some time, every instance of killing is an instance of accelerating death; and even if death is hastened by as little as five minutes it is still a criminal homicide. So it is no defence to a person who stabs another to death to show that the victim was already dangerously ill.[4] All the same, as we shall see, there are some cases where the courts will ignore minimal causation.

8–003 **Why require that the death must follow within three years?** In origin the year-and-a-day rule was perhaps dictated by the desire to limit difficult problems of causation.[5] Some time limitation seems reasonable on the ground that it would be wrong for a person to remain at risk of a charge of homicide for a long time. A person may have been convicted and sentenced for a serious injury; if the victim then dies from the injury, it would be undesirable to have a fresh trial for murder. The year-and-a-day rule is a relic from a time when medicine was not sufficiently developed to allow medical scientists to identify the exact cause of a death after a year or so had passed. Similarly, it dates from a time when people could not be kept alive on life support for years after being stabbed, shot, and so on. Given the advances in medicine and science, it seems perfectly reasonable to extend the timeframe to three years.[6]

8–004 **Do problems of causation arise only for homicide cases?** These are the most important in practice, but a causal question is capable of arising in other offences, particularly those against the person or property. For example, the offence under section 18 of the *Offences against the Person Act 1861* is of causing grievous bodily harm. The wording of sections 20 and 47 is different: the one speaks of inflicting grievous bodily harm and the other of occasioning actual bodily harm, but these verbs also imply a requirement of causation. Similarly, the offences under the *Criminal Damage Act 1971* imply that the act of the defendant has caused the damage. The notion of causation may also appear in general penal legislation, where the context may give the word a special meaning. "Causing" something to be done sometimes bears the narrow meaning of giving an order or direction to do it.[7]

8.2. BUT-FOR CAUSATION

8–005 An important distinction must be taken. The question of causation, as it is generally used in the law, involves both a problem of causation *sine qua non*, and a problem of imputability. A convenient English equivalent of the term causation

---

However, in the H.I.V. transmission cases, it can take decades for the victim to die. See Dennis J. Baker, "The Moral Limits of Consent as a Defence in the Criminal Law," (2009) 12(1) *New Crim. L. Rev.* 93. Cf. *State v. Govan*, 744 P.2d 712 (1987), where the chain of causation was traced back to an event five years earlier in order to uphold a manslaughter conviction.

[4] *R. v. Dyson* [1908] 2 K.B. 454; *R. v. Pankotai* [1961] Crim. L.R. 546.

[5] *R. v. Dyson* [1908] 2 K.B. 454.

[6] Professor LaFave is critical of the rule for this reason. He notes: "Now that doctors know infinitely more, it seems strange that the year-and-a-day rule" survives in some U.S. jurisdictions. Wayne R. LaFave, *Substantive Criminal Law*, (Minnesota: West Group, Vol. 1, 2003) at 500.

[7] *Shave v. Rosner* [1954] 2 Q.B. 113 (on the *Construction and Use Regulations*).

sine qua non is but-for causation (properly speaking, but-for ... not causation). For a factor to be a but-for cause, one must be able to say that but for the occurrence of the antecedent factor the event would not have happened.

Surely the notion of but-for causation is ridiculously wide, because it would take us back to Adam and Eve. The criminal's mother is a but-for cause of his crimes, and so is his grandmother, and all his ancestors to infinity. That is perfectly true, but two factors limit judicial enquiry. First, one starts with the defendant who is charged; his mother does not come into it, much less Adam and Eve. Secondly, but-for causation is only half the story; the defendant who was a but-for cause of the harm is not responsible unless his conduct was also the imputable cause. We still have to deal with imputable causation.[8]

8–006

Is the notion of but-for a useful one? Where the cause is a positive act, isn't it too obvious to be worth stating? If D shoots V and V drops down dead, surely you don't have to prove that the bullet entering V's heart caused him to die? When but-for causation is obvious (as it usually is), it is not discussed. Certainly the answer to your last question is in the negative. But occasionally an issue of this kind may require expert assistance. D may administer poison to V, who may die shortly afterwards, yet an autopsy may reveal that V died not of the poison but of heart disease. There will then be medical evidence at D's trial to the effect that the poison did not cause the death, meaning that V would in any case have died at the time and in the way he did, and that the poison did not play any contributory part. If the jury believe this evidence, or, rather, if they are not sure that it is untrue, they must acquit of murder—though D may, of course, be convicted of the attempt.[9]

8–007

We may summarize, then, by saying that but-for causation is of legal interest only in the comparatively rare cases where, notwithstanding appearances, it is absent; that when it is alleged to be absent, this raises a question of fact for the jury, who may decide by ordinary experience but may have to be assisted by expert evidence; and the burden is on the Crown to prove beyond reasonable doubt that the defendant's act (or omission) was a but-for cause.[10]

The last point occasions some difficulty in respect of expert evidence, because an expert may not be willing to commit himself to more than the statement that the result would "probably" not have happened as it did apart from the defendant's act or omission. Notwithstanding that the expert will not commit himself to more, the jury (somewhat strangely) are entitled to draw a sure inference of causation from the evidence.[11] Nonetheless, they should be reminded

---

[8] The maxim *in jure non remota causa sed proxima spectatur* (only proximate causes are considered in law) is not too helpful as many indirect and remote causes can be fairly imputed to individuals.

[9] *The King v. White* [1910] 2 K.B. 124. For a good discussion of the general concepts in causation theory see Richard W. Wright, "Causation Responsibility, Risk, Probability, Naked Statistics, and Proof: Pruning the Bramble Bush by Clarifying the Concepts," (1988) 73 *Iowa L. Rev.* 1001.

[10] *R. v. Dyos* [1979] Crim. L.R. 660.

[11] *R. v. Cato* [1976] 1 W.L.R. 110; *R. v. Stone and Dobinson* [1977] 2 W.L.R.169 at 173.

that they themselves must be sure; and the hesitation or reserve of the expert should surely be a factor leading the appeal court to scrutinize a conviction with care.[12]

8–008   **The courts assume in manslaughter cases like *R. v. Stone and Dobinson* that an omission can be a cause. But surely a non-event cannot be a but-for cause of an event.** Whatever the philosophical view[13] may be, the courts certainly assume, and must assume, that an omission can be a cause (just as a lack of oxygen or food is commonly regarded as a cause of death). If D leaves the manhole uncovered and V falls 100 metres to her death, D's omission has indirectly, but substantially, contributed (causally) to her death. If D had not been reckless, the manhole would have been covered and V would not have fallen to her death. D's omission is an indirect cause of V's fall; the direct cause is her inability to see the uncovered manhole and her physical steps into it. However, a court can, and should, say that a reference to causation in a statute does not cover omissions, in the absence of express words or necessary implication.[14] That is not a rule of causation but a question of legal import of words. The application of the usual burden of proof to the issue of causation is of considerable importance in cases of omission, and sometimes gives the court the opportunity of arriving at a merciful conclusion.[15] On any charge involving causation by omission it behoves the defence to go into the evidence of causation most carefully.

8–009   **What about two but-for causes contributed by different defendants? Doesn't your definition imply the paradox that if two persons independently cause an event, neither causes it?** To provide for this, an exception for cases of multiple-causation has to be inserted into the definition. It is possible for two sufficient causes, C1 and C2, to be present together, so that E follows both, when usually it follows only one or the other. Both C1 and C2 are causes, even though in the particular situation one or the other (as the case may be) was not necessary to be present. An example is where two fatal wounds are given independently at the same time. On the other hand, suppose that D1's shot entered the lung and would have caused the victim's death in an hour, but D2's entered the heart and killed him instantaneously? Then of course, only D2 has killed him. D1 is guilty of an attempt. The but-for cause is sometimes referred to as the factual cause, or the *de facto* cause, or scientific cause. The important thing is to distinguish it from cause in another sense, the "imputable" (or "legal" or "effective" or "direct" or "proximate") cause, to which we now turn.

---

[12] See *R. v. Clark* [2003] EWCA Crim. 1020; and *R. v. George* [2007] EWCA Crim. 2722, where inferences drawn from uncertain expert evidence led to miscarriages of justice. See also Law Commission, *The Admissibility of Expert Evidence in Criminal Proceedings in England and Wales*, Consultation Paper, No 190 (London: 2009).

[13] See Judith Jarvis Thomson, "Causation: Omissions," (2003) 66(1) *Philosophy and Phenomenological Research* 81; Sarah McGrath, "Causation by Omission: A Dilemma," (2005) 123 *Philosophical Studies* 125; Arthur Leavens, "A Causation Approach to Criminal Omissions," (1988) 76 *Cal. L. Rev.* 547.

[14] In *R. v. Tilley* [2009] 2 Cr. App. R. 31 the Court of Appeal, correctly, refused to read a statute so as to impose omissions liability on a third party for another's omissions.

[15] *The Queen v. Morby* (1882) 8 Q.B.D. 571. Graham Hughes, "Criminal Omissions," (1958) 67 *Yale L.J.* 590.

8.3. IMPUTABLE CAUSATION

When causation is in issue, the defendant's act (or omission) must be shown to be **8–010** not only a but-for cause but also an imputable or legal cause of the consequence. Imputable causes are some of the but-for causes. In other words, the defendant's acts, being a but-for cause, must be sufficiently closely connected with the consequence to involve him in responsibility. The lawyer is interested in the causal authorship of events, not in their causal ancestry. The United States Model Penal Code expresses the principle by stating that a person is not criminally responsible for a result if it is "too remote and accidental in its occurrence to have a just bearing on the actor's liability or on the gravity of his offence."[16]

Several attempts have been made to find a suitable name for this second notion of cause. To call it the "direct" or "proximate" cause (as is often done) is misleading, because several stages may intervene between the so-called direct cause and the effect. D may send poisoned chocolates to V, who lives at the other side of the world; if V eats the chocolates and dies, the law will certainly regard D as responsible for the death, though his act was far removed in space and considerably moved in time from its effect. To call D's act the "effective" cause is unhelpful, because every cause must by definition be effective—if an act is not effective to produce a given result, it is not a cause of it.

Sometimes (looking at the situation backwards instead of forwards) imputable causation is stated in terms of "remoteness of consequence." To say that a particular consequence is "too remote" is only another way of saying that the defendant's act (or omission) is not an imputable cause.

Going back to the formulation in the Model Penal Code, the use of the word "just" indicates the true nature of the problem. When one has settled the question of but-for causation, the further test to be applied to the but-for cause in order to qualify it for legal recognition is not a test of causation but *a moral reaction*. The question is whether the result can fairly be said to be imputable to the defendant. Sometimes the question of fairness is settled by rules of law, sometimes it is left for impressionistic decision in the individual case. If the term "cause" must be used, it can be distinguished in this meaning as the "imputable" or "responsible" or "blameable" cause, to indicate the value-judgment involved. The word "imputable" is here chosen as best representing the idea. Whereas the but-for cause can generally be demonstrated scientifically,[17] no experiment can be devised to show that one of a number of concurring but-for outcomes is more substantial or important that another, or that one person who is involved in the causal chain is more blameworthy than another.[18]

What are the principles governing imputable causation? Hitherto the judges **8–011** have made little progress in establishing such principles. Generally, of course, no problem arises. Where causation is obvious, the judge may give no direction upon it, even in a homicide case, and even though the burden of proof of causation is

---

[16] American Law Institute's Model Penal Code (1985), §2.03(b), (3)(b).

[17] But only when the relevant features of the situation can be reported as an experiment, so that the effect of removing the alleged but-for cause is revealed.

[18] Unless of course, the experiment merely seeks to summarize people's opinion as to what act is blameworthy.

supposed to rest on the prosecution. "In homicide cases," said Goff L.J., "it is rarely necessary to give the jury any direction on causation as such."[19] Even when a direction is given, it is usually in very general terms, without so much as distinguishing between factual and legal causation. The judge will use one of the adjectives already mentioned, telling the jury that the defendant's act must have been the "sufficient" or "direct" or "proximate" or "substantial" cause of the result, or something beyond a trivial cause, or that the result must not have been too "remote." Or he may tell them that in law the defendant's act need not be the sole cause, of even the main cause, of the result, it being enough that the act contributed "significantly" to that result.[20]

This is good enough if the defendant's act was clearly an imputable cause, and it may be good enough in cases where no precise rule can be formulated. It is unsatisfactory in some of the cases to be discussed in this chapter, where the proper result may seem doubtful to the layperson and a vague direction may produce discordant verdicts which could have been avoided if more specific guidance had been given. The direction to the jury should distinguish, where necessary, between the two kinds of causation, and the jury should be informed with some precision of any rules of law that are involved. If the issue is one of but-for causation, it should be enough to ask the jury whether the defendant's act (or omission) was a cause of what happened in any case. There is no need to talk about "substantiality."[21] But if the issue is whether the alleged cause was an imputable cause, and if the proper view is that for some reason the alleged cause was not or may not have been an imputable cause in law, it should be a misdirection to instruct the jury no more fully than this.[22]

The harm must be imputable to the person whom is being held responsible for it. In the more complex cases involving intervening acts, something more than a but-for cause analysis is needed. It must be shown that the harm was caused by the defendant rather than by some other coincidental or intervening event. In most cases, the application of the common-sense test of causation is enough to determine whether the defendant's act is sufficiently significant to make him causally liable for the end harm. But establishing legal causation by referring to a simple common-sense standard is more problematic when the harm would not have resulted but-for some intervening act or omission (failure to accept lifesaving medical treatment) of the victim or some other party.

8–012   The courts have outlined a number of legal tests for guiding such decisions including:

---

[19] *R. v. Pagett* (1983) 76 Cr. App. R. 279 at 288 *per* Goff L.J.

[20] *R. v. Pagett* (1983) 76 Cr. App. R. 279.

[21] *R. v. Cato* [1976] 1 W.L.R. 110, where the issue was one of but-for causation, the court said that the act had to be the substantial cause of death, or at any rate something more than "the mere *de minimis* contribution." Even indirect contributions, as seen in *Pagett,* are substantial, because the event would not have happened but-for him forcing the policeman's hand as so to speak. What makes the harm imputable to Pagett is his indirect causal contribution and the foreseeable result of making this kind of indirect contribution. In terms of culpability, he also had a culpability link with the end harm.

[22] In *R. v. Cato* [1976] 1 W.L.R. 110, a conviction was upheld although the judge had merely asked the jury whether the defendant's act caused, contributed to or accelerated the death, the court saying that "the jury knew perfectly well that he [the judge] was talking about something more than a mere *de minimis* contribution." If there had been any issue on imputable causation the direction should have been regarded as inadequate.

- the operating and substantial cause test;
- the natural consequence test;
- the reasonable foresight of the intervention and its consequences test; and
- the *novus actus interveniens* test, which is used sometimes in conjunction with and sometimes independently of other tests.

The theoretical problem as far as causation directions for the jury are concerned, may be clarified if we distinguish between cases where there is and is not a relevant rule of law on the subject of imputable causation. If no satisfactory rule can be formulated, and it is a matter of "gut reaction,"[23] the proper verdict on the point being subject to legitimate doubt, the jury can be told that they must decide whether in fairness the result should be attributed to the defendant. The direction is unnecessary if the harm obviously is imputable to the defendant. If a rule can be formulated, which ought to govern similar situations (which was the case in Pagett), the judge should be entitled to announce it firmly to the jury, and where necessary to exclude irrelevant evidence.

The last proposition is supported by *R. v. Malcherek*,[24] where control of the trial judge was emphasized. Malcherek stabbed his wife in the abdomen; her heart stopped in hospital and she was put on a ventilator, but, her brain being irretrievably damaged, she was taken off the ventilator. On a charge of murder the trial judge refused to leave the issue of causation to the jury, and D was convicted. On appeal the defence sought to introduce evidence to suggest that the doctor had switched the machine off prematurely, but the court refused to hear the evidence. In such circumstances, the court declared, where a doctor decides "that the patient is for practical purposes dead," and switches off the ventilator, this does not in law prevent the assailant from being held responsible.

Granted, then, that rules of imputable causation are rules of law, we must consider what these rules are. Subject to what is to be said as to new intervening acts, no problem generally arises when the defendant has intentionally produced the consequence.[25] The chief difficulties relate to unintended consequences.

It may be suggested that five rules are supported either by authority or common sense:

- the rule that negligence must be relevant;
- the minimal causation principle;
- the ordinary hazard principle;
- the reasonable foresight principle;
- the principle of the new intervening act.

8–013

---

[23] As the Australian High Court puts it: "It is enough if juries are told that the question of cause for them to decide is not a philosophical or a scientific question, but a question to be determined by applying their common sense to the facts as they find them, they appreciating that the purpose of the inquiry is to attribute responsibility in a criminal manner." *Royall v. The Queen* (1991) 172 C.L.R. 378, 379 (Aust.) *per* Mason C.J., Brennan, Dawson, and McHugh J.J.

[24] [1981] 1 W.L.R. 690. Cf. the *obiter dictum* in *R. v. Blaue* (1975) 61 Cr. App. R. 271.

[25] Cf. *R. v. Lewis* (1922) unreported, where the intended consequence was held not to be caused in law.

8.4. CAUSATION AND NEGLIGENCE

8–014   Where negligence (or recklessness) is in issue, a limiting rule straddles the divide between but-for and imputable causation. The rule is that the negligence proved against the defendant must be negligence in a relevant respect. The case must be such that the accident would not have happened if he had not been negligent. In other words, the defendant is not liable for an event that is not causally connected with the feature of his conduct that was negligent. The rule has some application to manslaughter and causing death by dangerous driving.

An illustration in the reports is *R. v. Dalloway*.[26] The driver of a horse and cart let the reins lie loose on the horses back. This was of course a negligent way of driving. A child ran across the road, and was knocked down and killed. Erle J. directed the jury that if the driver by using the reins could have saved the child he was guilty of manslaughter, but that if they thought he could not have saved the child by pulling the reins they must acquit him. In other words, the question was this. Assuming that the defendant had been driving carefully, holding the reins, would the death have occurred? A defendant is not guilty of causing a death by negligence if the victim ran out at a moment when no one—not even a person who had been behaving carefully throughout—could have pulled up.

In *Dalloway* there was an element of but-for causation connecting the defendant's driving with the death of the child. Had Dalloway not been travelling in his vehicle at that time and that spot, his vehicle would not have hit the child. Moreover, he was negligent, perhaps grossly negligent. But it was also necessary to show (on a charge of manslaughter) that the death was causally connected with the negligent failure to hold the reins. If a person was charged with causing death by dangerous driving, it would be necessary to demonstrate that the death would not have occurred but-for the negligence. If it would have occurred regardless of the driver's negligence, then the *Dalloway* doctrine could be invoked.

8.5. THE DEFENCE OF MINIMAL CAUSATION

8–015   Of the assorted adjectives mentioned above, "significant" currently finds the greatest favour; and if this word is used in instructing the jury a conviction is pretty safe from being upset on appeal. However, the Court of Appeal regards it as being too favourable to the defendant.[27] The preferred direction is to tell the jury that they can convict the defendant if his conduct (for example, dangerous driving) was "a cause" of the death, being something more than a negligible cause (a *de minimis* contribution, as it is ungrammatically termed). The reference to "a cause" is presumably a but-for causation, while the reference to minimal contribution seems to express the idea that imputable causation is lacking. The direction at least gives the jury some pointer to the fact that they are entitled to use common sense (moral instinct) on questions of causation. In *R. v. Cheshire* as much was recognized:[28]

---

[26] (1847) 2 Cox C.C. 273. See also *R. v. Lowe* (1850) 175 E.R. 152; *R. v. Haines* (1847) 2 C. & K. 368.

[27] The preferred word adopted in *R. v. Hennigan* [1971] 3 All E.R. 133 was "substantial".

[28] *R. v. Cheshire* [1991] 1 W.L.R. 844 at 851–852.

"In a case in which the jury have to consider whether negligence in the treatment of injuries inflicted by the defendant was the cause of death we think it is sufficient for the judge to tell the jury that they must be satisfied that the Crown have proved that the acts of the defendant caused the death of the deceased adding that the defendant's acts need not be the sole cause or even the main cause of death it being sufficient that his acts contributed significantly to that result. Even though negligence in the treatment of the victim was the immediate cause of his death, the jury should not regard it as excluding the responsibility of the defendant unless the negligent treatment was so independent of his acts, and in itself so potent in causing death, that they regard the contribution made by his acts as insignificant. .... It is not the function of the jury to evaluate competing causes or to choose which is dominant provided they are satisfied that the defendant's acts can fairly be said to have made a significant contribution to the victim's death. We think the word 'significant conveys the necessary substance of a contribution made to the death which is more than negligible."

It may have been a notion of minimal causation that was in the mind of Devlin J. in *R. v. Bodkin Adams*.[29] The acceleration of death is supposed to be enough for criminal liability, so that the defendant is not normally allowed to say that the victim would have died before long. But in *R. v. Adams* Devlin J. directed the jury that when health cannot be restored, a doctor "is still entitled to do all that is proper and necessary to relieve pain and suffering even if measures he takes may incidentally shorten life." The passage as a whole seems to imply the view that what the doctor does by way of approved medical practice is not a cause in law. It plays such a minor part in causing the death that it can be excluded from consideration.

A more satisfactory reason would be the doctrine of necessity, at which Devlin J. perhaps glanced in his use of the word "necessity."[30] Arguably accelerating a harmful result as a *matter of necessity* for a legitimate purpose in cases where the harm is virtually certain to transpire within a short timeframe, ought to be grounds for extending the necessity defence (depending on the facts) to cover doctors and stranded sailors and the like, because such people are not motivated by evil. They act knowing that the end harm is about to transpire anyway and that by accelerating it some greater harm might be avoided.[31] A doctor who genuinely tries to relieve his patient's pain knowing that it might accelerate her death is motivated by the necessity to act in her best interests. Therefore, his conduct should be treated as being lawfully justified. However, as noted in Chapter 4, good motives only count when they are underwritten by a valid legal defence. (The courts seem to take the view if the pain relief is absolutely necessary and is administered according to standard medical practice that the doctor is exempt from liability even though he foresaw that the side-effect of the treatment would be the acceleration of his patient's death.)[32]

---

[29] [1957] Crim. L.R. 365. See also Glanville Williams, *The Sanctity of Life and the Criminal Law*, (London: Faber, 1958) at 289.

[30] Other interpretations have been offered. H. L. A. Hart and A. M. Honoré, *Causation in the Law*, (Oxford: Clarendon, 1959) at 308-309, suggest that Devlin J. might have rested his opinion on "absence of intent when the effect of the drug is not known," but that would not let the doctor out if the side-effect was known, and the judge gave no indication that he regarded this as the decisive point.

[31] See Michael S. Moore, "Counterfactual Dependence as an Independent, Non-Causal Desert-Determiner," (2009) 34 *Austl. J. Leg. Phil.* 1 at 5. Cf. *Re A (Conjoined Twins Surgical Separation)* [2000] 4 All E.R. 961.

[32] *Airedale N.H.S. Trust v. Bland* [1993] A.C. 789.

Alternatively, if a doctor euthanizes his patient and foresees that the side-effect of doing so will be that she will no longer be in pain, he clearly has no defence. In *R. v. Cox*[33] the patient was dying and was in serious pain. She lost her sight just days before dying and expressed a wish to die. The consultant rheumatologist treating her administered two ampoules of potassium chloride, but evidence showed that the doctor's aim was to relieve her pain by ending her life. The medication was injected in a manner and quantity that served no therapeutic purpose for the patient while she was living. The patient died within minutes of receiving the injection. It was held that Dr. Cox could only escape liability if his primary *purpose* was to alleviate pain and suffering, rather than to bring the life of the patient to an end. His motive may have been reasonable but it provides no defence under the current law. Dr. Cox was convicted of attempted murder, even though he committed murder.

8.6. THE UNEXPECTED TWIST

8–016   Most problems of causation[34] relate to what may be called the unexpected twist, which is to occupy the rest of this chapter. Subject to what is to be said later, an unexpected twist in the outcome of conduct does not necessarily put the end result outside the mental element, or mean that the conduct is not the punishable cause of the result. For example, D attacks V intending to stab him in the arm, but V jumps back, falls and cracks his head. Assuming that both the harm intended and suffered was grievous bodily harm, there is no difficulty from the point of view either of *mens rea* or of causation in convicting D of causing grievous bodily harm with intent. Under section 18 of the *Offences against the Person Act 1861* the legal category is "grievous bodily harm," and it does not matter that the defendant intended one form and did another.[35]

Such facts are very similar to transferred intention, except that here the intention takes effect upon the person intended, and the only variation is in respect of the way in which it takes effect or in respect of the precise description of the injury. The unexpected twist principle does not supplant the primary requirement of a mental element for the particular crime. In a crime of intention, the ultimate result must be as intended by the defendant;[36] but the *mode* by which the intended result occurred need not have been intended.[37]

Where, as in the case of criminal damage, the offence is defined in broad terms so that it covers a great variety of causal nexus, the unexpected twist principle can have unwelcome results, particularly in making the defendant subject to conviction for doing much greater damage than he expected. The solution here would be to sentence on the basis of what was within the range of what the defendant would have foreseen. A problem of justice can also arise where the

---

[33] (1992)12 B.M.L.R. 38.

[34] Cf. Michael S. Moore, "Foreseeing Harm Opaquely," in Stephen Shute *et al.*, (eds.) *Action and Value in Criminal Law*, (Oxford: Clarendon Press, 1993) at 125 *et seq.*

[35] A neat illustration from Papua and New Guinea is *R. v. Kilpali-Ikarum* [1967-68] P. & N.G.L.R. 119. It would probably be necessary that what happened should be reasonably foreseeable, as explained below; but this could easily be established on the facts given.

[36] Subject to the law of transferred intention.

[37] Another good example of the unexpected twist principle is *R. v. Michael* (1840) 173 E.R. 867.

defendant is still at an early stage in his effort to commit a crime when events are, so to speak, taken out of his hands. Professor Smith suggests that the defendant can be liable for the result if he had reached the stage of attempt, but otherwise not.[38] He provides two hypothetical examples.

D prepares a poisoned drink with the intention of giving it to his wife, V, to eat **8–017** tomorrow. V finds the poisoned apple today, eats it and dies. Alternatively, D is cleaning his gun with the intention of shooting V tomorrow. The gun goes off accidentally and kills V.

It would obviously be too harsh to convict D of murder in the second case; his liability, if any, would be for manslaughter. As to the first case, the answer may depend on the more detailed facts. If D put the poison by his wife's bedside, intending to administer it to her when she woke up, the jury should be allowed to find that he has launched himself sufficiently far on his ghastly plan to be guilty of an attempt, and therefore (according to Smith's suggestion) to be guilty of murder if the wife unexpectedly wakes up and drinks the poison herself.[39] If on the other hand the poisoned drink is still in the kitchen, the result should probably be different.

Whatever the theory may be, the law is not always applied with full rigour. On a charge of murder the trial judge may permit or encourage the jury to return a verdict of manslaughter. Or he may accept a plea to manslaughter, even when in strict law it is murder. The unexpected twist principle would probably meet with general acceptance in obvious cases.[40] But the criminal law should, so far as possible, avoid saddling people with liability for results markedly different from what was intended or foreseen. So it is important not merely that the law should be applied with discretion but that we should find rules that satisfactorily state what twists in the outcome are to be regarded as beyond the range of responsibility ascribed to the defendant.

8.7. THE ORDINARY HAZARD PRINCIPLE: COINCIDENCE IS NOT CAUSATION

In many situations giving rise to criminal liability, the death or harm is not **8–018** directly caused by the defendant's wrongdoing. Instead, it results from intervening forces or events such as lightning strikes, tsunamis, escape attempts, negligent medical treatment, and the negligent and intentional acts of the victim and third parties. The ordinary hazard principle deals with those situations where natural or coincidental events have the effect of cutting off the causal chain between the defendant's actions and the end harm. D attacks V intending to stab him to death; V runs away, and in his flight is struck by lightning and dies. The

---

[38] J. C. Smith, "Commentary," [1983] Crim. L.R. 105.

[39] In *Cassell v. Commonwealth*, 248 Ky. 579 (1933) (U.S.), it was held that the defendant was criminally liable for his wife's death whether he administered the poison himself or whether he put the poison in her way to take innocently.

[40] If the defendant is violently assaulting the victim in an apartment six floors up, and the victim unexpectedly jumps to her death believing it is her only way of escaping a murderous attack, then "it is no defence to murder that it *caused death* at a time and in a way that was to some extent unexpected." *Royall v. The Queen* (1991) 172 C.L.R. 378, at 379 *per* Mason C.J., Brennan, Deane, Dawson and McHugh J.J.

lightning was the *coup de grace*. One would say that D is not guilty of murder, though he is guilty of attempted murder. D's actions did not cause V's death, but rather it was caused by the coincidental lightning strike? In the response cases the result would be different. If V, in response, had jumped over a cliff or into a river in an effort to escape, or to commit suicide in despair,[41] or had accidentally fallen over the cliff or into the river in his flight, D would have been accountable for the death, and we should not have said that it was not D who killed V but the water or the hard ground. Similarly, the terrorists who flew planes into the World Trade Center in New York in 2001 caused those who were trapped in the burning floors above to jump to their deaths—they had the choice of staying and being burnt to death or chancing an 80-floor jump.

If D beats V unconscious and leaves V on the high ground well away from the waterline[42] and V is killed by a tsunami, the death results from the coincidence of the tsunami. D will not be guilty of murder, but he would be if the normal tide took V out to sea, as that would be a foreseeable consequence of D's criminal conduct, and therefore the law considers the legal chain of causation to be unbroken. The rationale for the principle is that people should not be held responsible for pure coincidences. If D left V unconscious in the snow, then the foreseeable consequence is death. If D left V unconscious in Hyde Park on a summer's night, and a gang came along and burnt unconscious V to death, the chain of causation would be broken because the original injuries were not life-threatening and were not a concurrent cause of death.

When a person is struck by lightning while running away from an attacker, the attack is not a concurrent cause of that person's death. He may have been struck by lightning just by being in that area at that time. The attacker has not significantly increased the victim's risk of being the victim of a lightning strike. Another example of the ordinary hazard principle is where the victim of an attack dies in a traffic accident when he is being conveyed by ambulance to hospital, or dies as a result of a fever which sweeps through the hospital. Assuming that his death was not contributed to by his weak condition, the attacker is not guilty of it, because the effect of the attack was merely to place the victim in a geographical position where another actor or event was able to cause his death. The attack did not significantly increase the risk or the fatal result, because anyone may die in a traffic accident or epidemic.[43] Of course, a reasonable person mulling over all the

---

[41] *R. v. Mackie* (1973) 57 Cr. App. R. 453. See also *Royall v. The Queen* (1991) 172 C.L.R. 378; *R. v. Demirian* [1989] V.R. 97 at 113; *Commonwealth v. Rementer*, 598 A.2d 1300 (1991).

[42] In *R. v. Hallett* [1969] S.A.S.R. 141 at 149 the court applied the "substantial, operating cause doctrine of causation" in a case where the deceased drowned after being left unconscious on a beach. The Court expounded: "The death of the deceased is the material event. The question to be asked is whether an act or series of acts (in exceptional cases an omission or series of omissions) consciously performed by the accused is or are so connected with the event that it or they must be regarded as having a sufficiently substantial causal effect which subsisted up to the happening of the event, without being spent or without being in the eyes of the law sufficiently interrupted by some other act or event."

[43] Cf. *Bush v. Commonwealth*, 78 Ky. 268 (1880), where the defendant was acquitted of unlawful homicide even though the disease was communicated to the victim by a surgeon operating on a bullet wound inflicted by the defendant.

possible consequences of an attack might think of these possibilities; but they would not be possibilities rendered any more likely by the fact of the attack.[44]

What if V catches a fatal disease while in hospital? Even if it could be shown that there was slightly more risk of dying of fever in hospital than elsewhere (perhaps because of the presence in hospital of resistant bacteria), this would probably be accounted too insignificant to impact the decision. Contrast the case where the victim died of hospital fever, but a contributory factor was the weakness caused by his injuries, so that he would not have died if it had not been for his weakness. Probably the attacker would then be guilty of criminal homicide (murder or manslaughter), for on these facts there is a medical (and not *merely fortuitous*) connection between the wound and the death. It is like the case of the wound turning gangrenous and causing death, where the wounding is clearly the cause of death. The ordinary hazard principle in most, but not all applications, can be regarded as a particular application of a test of reasonable foresight, on which decided cases can be found.

8–019

8.8. THE REASONABLE FORESIGHT PRINCIPLE

Normally a person is guilty for the harm that he directly causes, but under the foresight principle a person will be criminally liable when his acts indirectly cause harm and it was foreseeable that the harm would be caused by his remote acts. There is no need for a direct application of force. To say that a consequence, to be imputed to the defendant, must be within the risk that would be apprehended by a reasonable person is much wider than the ordinary hazard principle. The "reasonable foreseeability" of risk standard has been discussed by writers on the tort of negligence, and has also been developed incrementally in numerous criminal cases.[45]

8–020

The principle was expounded rather adequately in *R. v. Roberts.*[46] Roberts was driving a girl from a party, and according to the view of the facts that (in the opinion of the Court of Appeal) the jury must have taken, he pestered her with advances, held her coat and told her that he had beaten girls who had refused him. She jumped out of the moving car and suffered injury. The chairman of Sessions directed the jury that on these facts Roberts would be guilty of an assault

---

[44] See *R. v. Carey* [2006] EWCA Crim. 17, where a 15-year-old girl died after running from an affray. She had a serious heart condition. The victim and her parents did not know about the heart condition. The Court of Appeal held that the manslaughter count should not have been put to the jury, because the bullying resulted only in slight injuries, and none of the defendants intended to cause really serious harm; nor did they intend to kill the victim. Some harm was foreseeable, but not death as the heart attack was a mere coincidence.

[45] In particular, *R. v. Pitts* (1842) Car. & M. 284; *R. v. Curley* (1909) 2 Cr. App. R. 96; *R. v. Beech* (1912) 7 Cr. App. R. 197; *R. v. Mackie* (1973) 57 Cr. App. R. 453; *Director of Public Prosecutions v. Daley* [1980] A.C. 237; *R. v. Corbett* [1996] Crim. L.R. 594; *D.P.P. v. Santa-Bermudez* [2004] Crim. L.R. 471.

[46] (1971) 56 Cr. App. R. 95. In *Sanders v. Commonwealth*, 244 Ky. 77 (1932), a conviction was upheld when a woman jumped from a travelling car because her husband threatened her with a deadly weapon. Cf. *People v. Beard*, 74 A.D. 2d 926 (1980) (U.S.), where there were no threats, but there was other extenuating circumstances that made it reasonably foreseeable that the passenger might jump from the moving car.

occasioning actual bodily harm under section 47 of the *Offences against the Person Act 1861*. Roberts was convicted, and the conviction was affirmed on appeal, the court said: "The test is: Was it [the injury] the natural result of what the alleged assailant said and did, in the sense that it was something that could reasonably have been foreseen as the consequence of what he was saying or doing?"

In previous cases of similar type, the test laid down had generally been whether the victim acted reasonably in his endeavour to escape. *Roberts* widens the area of liability, but is best read as requiring the victim's response to be proportionate (not to be a "draft"[47] response). Whether it is prudent for a woman to jump from a rapidly moving car to avoid rape is a question on which opinions may differ, but at any rate it is fully understandable, and the possibility of it could well have been foreseen by the attacker. The reasonable foresight principle gives the jury the opportunity of exempting the defendant where what happened is particularly unusual and it would be unfair to hold the wrongdoer liable. But the intentional wrongdoer will rarely be advantaged by it. Although he has a theoretical opportunity of escaping a consequence brought about by the victim's unforeseeable reaction, a jury would probably be loath to describe an act done to escape as not reasonably foreseeable. Anyone who makes a serious or distressing attack on another should realize that the victim may try to escape, and in panic may try to escape in a very dangerous way. It is not a case of asking whether the defendant was negligent or otherwise at fault; it is about asking whether he caused the victim to bring the end harm on herself. The reasonable foreseeability test merely allows the jury to infer that the defendant caused the victim to act as she did. If the victim acted as any reasonable person might have acted, then it is fair to infer that the defendant caused her to so act.

8–021　**Does this mean that D can be held criminally responsible for murder/ manslaughter even though he only intended g.b.h. and did not expect the death to be caused the way it was?**　The short answer is yes.[48] The *mens rea* question is not to be conflated with the causation question. In murder cases, the defendant's mental state is determined independently by examining whether he intended to cause g.b.h. or death.[49] The reasonable foreseeability negligence standard is used to limit the defendant's liability in causal terms. When we ask

---

[47] *R. v. Roberts* (1971) 56 Cr. App. R. 95 at 102. See also *R. v. Lewis* [2010] EWCA Crim. 151 ("The nature of the flight or escape had to be a foreseeable consequence of the unlawful act, and not such an unreasonable response as to break the chain of causation."); *R. v. Williams* [1992] 1 W.L.R. 380. Cf. *R. v. Girdler* [2010] R.T.R. 307 at 321, where the car D was driving collided with a taxi. The taxi lost control and collided with another car. This resulted in the deaths of both the taxi driver and the driver of the other car. In the Court of Appeal Hooper L.J. said: "We suggest that a jury could be told, in circumstances like the present where the immediate cause of death is a second collision, that if they were sure that the defendant drove dangerously and were sure that his dangerous driving was more than a slight or trifling link to the death(s) then: 'The defendant will have caused the death(s) only if you are sure that it could sensibly have been anticipated that a fatal collision might occur in the circumstances in which the second collision did occur.'"

[48] *R. v. Demirian* [1989] V.R. 97 at 113.

[49] If the victim does not die, D will only be liable for attempted murder if he intended to kill. See *R. v. Donovan* (1850) 4 Cox C.C. 401, where it was held that if a woman jumps out of a window for the purpose of avoiding the violence of her husband, and sustains dangerous bodily injury, her husband cannot be convicted of "an attempt to murder, unless he intended by his conduct to make her jump out

was the intervention by the victim or some other party reasonably foreseeable, we are merely eliminating coincidental causes. It is a case of the jury using its common sense to ascertain whether a particular intervention was too fanciful to be regarded as having any causal bearing. It is well established that a harmful result can be imputed to a defendant even if his actions were not the direct cause of it, such as where the victim directly brings about the final harm because defendant has induced her to do so. The *novus actus* principle does not apply if it can be shown that the victim acted: "[i]n an attempt to preserve himself or herself from physical harm which unlawful conduct on the part of the accused has induced the victim to fear, and the victim's attempt at self-preservation was reasonable having regard to the nature of the accused's conduct and the fear it was likely to have induced (or, as I would prefer, provided the attempt is proportionate to that conduct and the fear it was likely to have induced)."[50]

In *Royall v. The Queen*,[51] the defendant was charged with the murder of a woman who jumped or was pushed from the bathroom window of a sixth-floor flat. The defendant admitted that prior to the victim's fatal fall he had backhanded her, had punched her twice in the nose, and had grabbed her by the hair and shook her. Photographs showed that the deceased had sustained significant facial injuries and that she had bruises around her throat and a dislocated nose. She had also suffered considerable bleeding. There had clearly been considerable violence. The victim's blood was found throughout the flat including in the bathroom where the victim was eventually cornered; and from where she was forced to jump because of duress of circumstances.

The deceased locked herself in the bathroom but the defendant broke in and started to pound into her with a heavy glass ashtray. There was ample evidence to demonstrate that the victim had been brutally beaten before she jumped from the sixth-floor window of the flat to her death. It was held that even if the victim made the independent choice to jump, that it was a reasonable and proportionate response given the threat she was attempting to avoid. She did not do so freely even if voluntarily, as she did not have an unfettered freedom. The chain of causation between the defendant's intentional violence and the end result was not broken. The question of whether the intervening acts of the victim were reasonably foreseeable involves the jury examining the facts to determine whether the victim over-reacted or acted proportionately given the nature of the threat.

The jury have to ascertain whether the end result can be linked to the defendant's **8–022** bad acting. In this case, his gross acts of violence. This issue is independent to the *mens rea* question. If the jury decides that the defendant's intended g.b.h. or death, then it needs to examine whether his intentional bad acting also caused the victim's death. Royall clearly had the requisite *mens rea* for murder as he had already intentionally inflicted g.b.h. upon his victim. Nevertheless, if lightning

---

of the window." An intention to inflict g.b.h. is sufficient *mens rea* for a murder conviction if V dies. See *R. v. Cunningham* [1982] A.C. 566; *R. v. Rahman* [2009] 1 A.C. 129 at 145.

[50] *Royall v. The Queen* (1991) 172 C.L.R. 378 at 398 *per* Brennan J. in the High Court of Australia citing the following English precedents as authority for this statement of the law: *R. v. Pitts* (1842) Car. & M. 284; *R. v. Curley* (1909) 2 Cr. App. R. 109; *Director of Public Prosecutions v. Daley* [1980] A.C. 237.

[51] (1991) 172 C.L.R. 378.

had struck her though the bathroom window before she had a chance to jump, his criminal liability would have only been for aggravated assault and possibly attempted murder. A lightning strike is an act of nature and it is not reasonably foreseeable that if a person beats another that it will result in lightning striking her though an open window. It is foreseeable that a person who is being bashed in the head with a heavy glass ashtray whilst she is trapped in a small room may jump to escape from the attack.

Only the harm caused by reasonably foreseeable intervening acts can be imputed to the defendant. This prevents every possible remote cause being imputed to the defendant. Since Royall gave his victim a serious reason (inducement—indirect causation) to take equally serious action, the harm was causally linked to his wrongdoing. Royall intended to kill or at least cause g.b.h. to his ex-girlfriend and it was reasonably foreseeable that V would jump in such circumstances. Therefore, it was irrelevant that he did not intend to harm her by using the mode of forcing her to jump.

On the other hand, if N tells her boyfriend F that she will leave him for another man if he does not jump from the 50th floor of their apartment block, it would be unreasonable for him to jump. It would be an unforeseeable and disproportionate response,[52] given the nature of the threat. N could not be said to have caused him to take such drastic action, as her actions would not be sufficient to induce a rational and autonomous adult to commit suicide. D is not causally responsible.[53] When harm is intended, but results from an unexpected mode; and the victim has over-reacted, it is most likely that the jury will conclude that the defendant did not cause the victim to act as he did. In other words, such a response would be regarded as too coincidental or independently unnecessary to count.

8–023   Does this mean a victim's independent and unreasonable (disproportionate) response will break the chain of causation?   Not quite! In *R. v. Blaue*[54] the victim's unreasonable failure to accept lifesaving medical treatment did not operate as a *novus actus interveniens*.

In *R. v. Blaue* the victim refused a blood transfusion because it was against her religious beliefs to have a blood transfusion. The case is commonly cited as providing an example of the "thin skull rule," but the victim did not exactly have a thin skull. She was perfectly normal in physical terms. The victim was not old, disabled, or frail; she merely had strong personal beliefs about blood transfusions

---

[52] For a case involving an unnecessary and foolish act, which broke the chain of causation see *State v. Preslar*, 48 N.C. 421 (1856).

[53] Cf. *Commonwealth v. Bianco*, 388 Mass. 358 (1984) (U.S.). In that case the victims jumped into their car as it was rolling towards a lake to avoid mere assault and ended up drowning. It was held that the threat of assault was not sufficient justification for the victim's actions. This case was borderline, as it was recognized by the dissenting judges that the jury could reasonably infer that the victims were escaping further harm.

[54] [1975] 1 W.L.R. 1411. See also *People v. Goodman*, 182 Misc. 585 (1943); *People v. Webb*, 415 N.W. 2d 9 (1987) where the victim initially refused help from the paramedics which resulted in his death. Cf. *People v. Velez*, 602 N.Y.S. 2d 798 (1993); *State v. Pelham*, 746 A.2d 557 (1998) where the victims had their life support removed, but because their quality of life had been reduced significantly by the physical injuries that D had inflicted. The victims were bedridden.

being wrong and refused to have one. If a person has a personal conviction[55] about medicine being bad or about not wanting a doctor of a particular race treating him, and refuses necessary treatment at the cost of dying, the chain of causation will not be broken. This is so even if beliefs are unreasonable and irrational when judged objectively. An *obiter dictum* in *R. v. Blaue* noted that under the special sensitivity rule, that "those who use violence on other people must take their victims as they find them." The court said: "This in our judgement means the whole man, not just the physical man. It does not lie in the mouth of the assailant to say that his victim's religious belief's which inhibited him from accepting certain kinds of treatment were unreasonable."

Probably the *obiter dictum* was meant only to explain the actual decision; if it applied more widely it would have sweeping results. D assaults V, cutting his finger in a remote village; V could seek medical treatment, but the only available doctor in the village is black. Because V is racist[56] V prefers to bleed to death rather than seek treatment from a black doctor. Are racist convictions, neurosis or vengefulness or stupidity to be reckoned as part of the victim that D must "take"? Yes, since the victim is not on trial—it is D's wrong that counts. If the bigot is to be ridiculed for his views then so be it, but V's independent wrongdoing does not negate D's harm-doing or culpability—nor does it break the chain of causation. The defendant cannot evade justice because he picks a victim who has terrible or unorthodox religious views, *etc.*

The rule excluding from consideration the contributory negligence of the victim **8–024** to his first injury does not necessarily entail the conclusion that the attacker is liable for an aggravation of the injury brought about by the victim. This is a separate question. As a matter of justice, it might be thought that the attacker ought not generally to be liable for the result of the aggravation; but the cases go the other way. First, it is clear that if D inflicts a serious injury on V, and V refuses, however unreasonably, to receive medical treatment and so dies from the

---

[55] Generally, there is a right to freedom of *conscience* which allows people to have particular beliefs and to live particular lifestyles, regardless of whether that lifestyle is associated with their religious belief or their secular convictions. The freedom of a person to wear a bangle as a part of the cultural norms that are associated with his religious lifestyle would not violate a school's no-jewellery policy providing it did not harm or interfere with the rights of others—but nor would the secular decision of a youth who decides to wear jewellery and purple hair as an exercise of his freedom of conscience and expression. Freedom of religion is too narrow in that it protects only the harmless cultural practices that can be linked to religious ideology. The focus should be on the more general conscience right, which could be invoked to protect non-religious people who refuse medical treatment because of their deep personal convictions. However, freedom of religion and freedom of conscience does not give one *carte blanche* to do whatever one likes in the name of conscience or religious conviction. If a person were to import endangered monkeys because eating monkey meat is a part of the social norms associated with his religious belief, the harm principle could be invoked to justify criminalization. A person can have beliefs without slaughtering endangered species. See *U.S. v. Manneh*, 645 F.Supp.2d 98 (2008). On objectivity, cultural practices and criminal responsibility, see Dennis J. Baker & Lucy X. Zhao, "Responsibility Links, Fair Labeling and Proportionality in China: Comparing China's Criminal Law Theory and Doctrine," (2009) 14 *UCLA J. Int'l L. For. Aff.* 274.

[56] Some of these examples are not as fanciful as they may sound. See Andrew Levy, "Mother Facing Prosecution 'For Asking Ethic Hospital Staff to be Removed from Birthing Room," (London: *Daily Mail*, 29 October 2009).

injury, D is responsible for the death. In *R. v. Blaue*[57] the defendant stabbed the victim, penetrating her lung. She was taken to hospital, but, being a Jehovah's Witness, refused to have a blood transfusion, and died. The transfusion would probably have saved her. The judge directed the jury that they would get some help from the cases to which counsel had referred in their speeches, and said that they might think they had little option but to reach the conclusion that the stab wound was a cause of death—or a substantial cause of death. The jury convicted of manslaughter by reason of diminished responsibility (the diminished responsibility, of course, having nothing to do with the question of causation), and the conviction was affirmed on appeal.

We have seen that the courts have held that where the victim sustains injury in an attempt to escape,[58] the test of imputable causation is one of reasonable foresight. This is a useful test and it seems appropriate to invoke it in cases where the victim does some positive act which might otherwise be said to break the chain of causation. In *R. v. Blaue* the court thought that on the undisputed evidence the stab wound inflicted by Blaue caused the death, and that the judge could have told the jury so. Of course it was a cause of death, but V's refusal of treatment was an additional but-for cause. The court described the defendant's act as "the physical cause of death," and regarded that as conclusive. The best reason for the decision, though not one in the judgment, is that Blaue would have been guilty of unlawful homicide if the victim had no chance of obtaining medical assistance, and therefore (it may be said) should be equally liable if the victim chose not to avail herself of such assistance. Still, there is a difference. But it seems reasonable to hold Blaue responsible for the victim's failure to try to reverse his harm-doing, because unlike the positive response cases it was his act which caused the harm. In the positive response cases, the actual cause of harm is dependent on the victim's positive act (the act of jumping from the window, *etc.*), so if the victim puts herself in peril by jumping from a window, it seems fair to ask whether it was reasonable for her to take such action before holding another responsible for it.

In *R. v. Blaue* the victim refused to take action which might have stopped the stabbing which was already "causing" her death from succeeding. In *Royall v. The Queen* the victim's act caused her own death, but the defendant caused her to do the act which caused her death. Justice McHugh notes:[59] "But in each case, the death occurs only because of conduct on the part of the victim which is unreasonable by objective standards. It is not easy to see any distinction in principle between the two cases. It is even more difficult to see why the conduct of the victim should absolve the accused in one case and not the other." The foreseeability test is used to demonstrate a reasonable link between the

---

[57] (1975) 61 Cr. App. R. 271. Carlson argues that a reasonable Jehovah's Witness would accept a blood transfusion. B. L. Carlson, "Blood and Judgment: Inconsistencies Between Criminal and Civil Courts When Victims Refuse Blood Transfusions," (2004) 33 *Stetson L. Rev.* 1067 at 1078-79.

[58] *R. v. Pitts* (1842) Car. & M. 284; *R. v. Curley* (1909) 2 Cr. App. R. 96; *R. v. Beech* (1912) 7 Cr. App. R. 197; *R. v. Mackie* (1973) 57 Cr. App. R. 453; *Director of Public Prosecutions v. Daley* [1980] A.C. 237; *R. v. Corbett* [1996] Crim. L.R. 594; *DPP v. Santa-Bermudez* [2004] Crim. L.R. 471.

[59] *Royall v. The Queen* (1991) 172 C.L.R. 378 at 450.

defendant's choices and the victim's choices—a person cannot be held responsible for harm that was not intended and of which no reasonable person could have foreseen.

There is a crucial difference between unreasonably refusing treatment to reverse what a defendant is already causing (or has set in motion), and unnecessarily harming yourself by taking disproportionate positive steps and then expecting someone else to be held responsible for your self-harming choice. Blaue committed horrific acts of violence and it was only by pure chance (moral luck)[60] that a chance arose for third parties (the medical team) and the victim to undo what he had set in motion. The victim's acceptance of treatment could have helped prevent or reverse the harm that the defendant's stabbing was already causing, but Blaue was morally unlucky as the victim was not willing to take reasonable steps to reverse or stem the damage that he had put in motion. The rationale for punishment is that the wound would have been fatal without the treatment. Not only was the end harm foreseeable, but it was also reasonably foreseeable that such wounds might not be curable, and that it is only a matter of luck whether the doctors will be successful or whether a chance will even arise for medical intervention.

8–025

A problem for justice arises when the defendant kills a haemophilic by merely pin-picking her as a joke, if the defendant did not know of her sensitivity.[61] In such cases, the defendant will normally avoid conviction as he will not have the requisite fault for manslaughter or assault.

What if the victim is guilty of a positive act of foolishness aggravating his injury? In general the aggravation will again be placed at the door of the defendant, at any rate if the victim's act was within the range of reasonable foresight. In *R. v. Dear*[62] the defendant slashed the victim repeatedly with a Stanley knife because he was of the belief that the victim had sexually interfered with his 12-year-old daughter. The victim refused medical treatment and died two days later from bleeding. The defendant argued that the chain of causation was broken because the defendant failed to seek treatment that would have prevented his death. There was also evidence to suggest that the victim had reopened the wounds as a way of committing suicide, as he was found with a suicide note. The court said: "It would not be helpful to juries if the law required them to decide causation in a case such as the present by embarking on an analysis of whether a victim had treated himself with mere negligence or gross neglect, the latter breaking but the former not breaking the chain of causation…"[63] It was noted that the cause of the victim's death was the bleeding that resulted from the original wounds inflicted by the defendant. And that it did not matter whether or not the resumption or continuation of the bleeding was deliberately caused by the victim.

8–026

---

[60] Where the defendant is morally unlucky, the wrongness of his actions is no different. The moral bad luck merely gives society a chance to learn about the character of the individual. See Anders Schinkel, "The Problem of Moral Luck: An Argument Against its Epistemic Reduction," (2009) 12 *Ethic. Theory Moral Prac.* 267.

[61] *State v. Frazer*, 98 S.W.2d 707 (1936).

[62] [1996] Crim. L.R. 595.

[63] *R. v. Dear* [1996] Crim. L.R. 595 at 596. Cf. *R. v. Wall* (1802) 28 State Tr. 51; *R. v. Flynn* (1867) 16 W.R. 319 (Ir.). See also *R. v. Mubila* (1956) (1) S.A. 31.

8–027 **If the victim commits positive acts which are designed to worsen his condition, or open wounds that have healed, this surely should break the chain of causation. Would it be reasonably foreseeable that a person would reopen his wounds and refuse medical treatment?** If the victim has healed and is out of danger, then the defendant's original acts would no longer be a (concurrent) cause of the end harm. In *R. v. Dear*, the defendant was found with a suicide note and there was some evidence that suggested that he wanted to die rather than face the shame of being found out as a child molester. The evidence was not conclusive on this point and the judgment does not give a clear account of what really happened. Unreasonable positive acts should be distinguished from unreasonable omissions to reverse harm that is already being caused by the defendant's past acts. In *R. v. Dear* it appears the court took the view that there was insufficient evidence to show that the victim had taken steps to reopen the wounds. An as there was no duty for the victim to try to reverse Dear's harm, the chain of causation was not broken.

The cases that are more problematic are those where there is no temporal or direct causal connection between a given bad act and the end harm. A defendant's many acts of domestic violence might have the cumulative effect of causing a victim to suffer psychological injury, and that harm might cause the victim to harm herself by committing suicide. But can the collateral harm (the suicide) be causally linked to the defendant's many acts of violence over many years? The courts have suggested that it can.[64] It will be difficult to prove that there was a strong causal link in most cases, because it will not only be necessary to prove that the defendant caused the victim's psychological injury, but also that the injury prevented the victim from making a fully informed and voluntary decision as far as the suicide is concerned. If D knocks V semi-conscious and V walks into the path of a train and is killed because of her state of semi-consciousness, then D has caused her death. Here, V's death is temporally connected to D's original harm-doing. D caused her to be in a state of semi-consciousness and thus caused her to walk "blindly" into the path of the train.

In the suicide cases there is no temporal link between a given act of domestic violence and the victim's psychological injury. Consequently, given that suicide itself is a somewhat irrational and unreasonable response,[65] it will be very

---

[64] *R. v. Dhaliwal* [2006] 2 Cr. App. R. 348. Horder and McGowan see domestic violence as a form of gross negligence which might cause psychological injury, which in turn might cause the psychologically injured party to eventually harm herself. Jeremy Horder and Laura McGowan, "Manslaughter by Causing Another's Suicide," [2006] Crim. L.R. 1035. Alas, in practice it would be nearly impossible to prove a strong connection. It might be better do more to target the domestic violence directly, as prevention is better the cure when the harm is irreversible as it was in *R. v. Dhaliwal*. Domestic violence is difficult to counter at the best of times, but the problem is acerbated in certain communities where the victims are blamed for being a victim. Cf. *Corr v. I.B.C. Vehicles Ltd.* [2008] 1 A.C. 884, a civil negligence case.

[65] Cf. *People v. Lewis*, 124 Cal. 551 (1899) (U.S.). In that case, there was a temporal link between the victim's suicide and the defendant's wrongdoing. The defendant mortally wounded the victim by shooting him. The victim was dying and was in pain so he acted by cutting his own throat to accelerate his death. He made a rational choice to accelerate his inevitable death as a temporal or *chronological* response to the mortal wounding. See also *People v. Duffy*, 79 N.Y.2d 611 (1992), where "[D's] conduct was a sufficiently direct cause of the death of a suicide victim to support D's conviction of ... manslaughter for engaging in reckless conduct which resulted in another person committing suicide ... D gave the suicide victim a rifle and a number of rounds of ammunition

difficult to prove not only that there was a chain of causation, but also that it was not severed by the suicide. Unlike the victims in *Royall v. The Queen* and *R. v. Roberts*, the victim *R. v. Dhaliwal* was not compelled to take drastic steps as a matter of urgency to avoid an immediate threat. Mrs. Dhaliwal had other options such as leaving her husband, calling the police when he started assaulting her many years before, and so on. It will be necessary to show that her suicide was involuntary. Again, it may end up being a question of whether this was the only escape route given the threat of future violence.

Doesn't the risk principle, as applied to crimes requiring intention, contradict that requirement? The objection overlooks the fact that the rule of causation cannot make the defendant guilty of a crime of intention unless he intended the event specified in the law (such as the death of a human being). All that the rules do is settle the question of liability where the event occurs in an unexpected way. The foreseeability rule is a limitation upon the general principle relating to the unexpected twist. 8–028

How does the rule in manslaughter excluding the victim's special sensitivity from consideration square with the risk principle? These special grounds start from the observation that the risk principle does not operate to negative liability if the event happened precisely as the defendant intended. Suppose that he aimed at the victim with a rifle and all the experts would have said that the victim was out of range; but he hoped to hit the victim and by some freak did so. The defendant is clearly responsible for hitting the victim. Questions of foreseeable risk arise only when there is some slight shift from the events that the defendant intended. 8–029

All the authorities on the special sensitivity rule seem to relate to manslaughter, where there was no intention to kill; but it can hardly be doubted that the same rule applies to murder. If the defendant intended to cause death and actually did so, it is irrelevant that the injury that he inflicted would not have caused a normal person to die. This is somewhat similar to the case just put of the victim being out of normal range of the weapon. However, it is not quite so straightforward. The defendant may have aimed to stab the victim through the heart, but only succeeded in cutting him slightly, but the victim was a haemophiliac and bled to death.[66] There is here a shift in the intended chain of causation, though (perhaps it may be said) only a slight shift. At any rate, it is intelligible that a court should refuse to pay attention to the victim's parlous state of health, if the defendant has substantially achieved his purpose.

The special sensitivity rule does not or should not qualify a requirement of *mens rea* or fault for the particular offence. An attacker whose *mens rea* is limited

---

knowing full well that V had been drinking heavily and was in an extremely depressed and suicidal state; D taunted V to 'put the gun in his mouth and blow his head off.' V's act of loading the rifle and using it to kill himself did not constitute an intervening cause which—as a matter of law—relieved D of criminal responsibility. The jury could rationally have concluded that the risk of V taking these actions was something which D should have, under the circumstances, plainly foreseen." In England and Wales, it is a statutory offence to assist suicide. See section 2 of the *Suicide Act 1961* as amended by section 59 of the *Coroners and Justice Act 2009*.
[66] *State v. Frazer*, 98 S.W.2d 707 (1936).

to the infliction of slight injury cannot become guilty of murder if, owing to the victim's sensitivity, the slight injury becomes serious and leads to death. A person who is negligent as to causing slight injury should not be guilty of manslaughter if, owing to the special sensitivity of the victim, the slight injury proves to be fatal. Manslaughter should require gross negligence as to death, or at any rate as to grievous bodily harm.

The law of constructive manslaughter is anomalous, because if strictly applied it turns a minor assault into criminal homicide if the victim dies because of his peculiar physical condition. The interpretation of section 47 of the *Offences against the Person Act 1861* as creating an offence of half *mens rea*[67] can also have the same effect that a person may be convicted of aggravated assault although he neither intended to inflict bodily harm nor was reckless or even negligent as to it, if bodily harm follows because of the victim's special sensitivity. But if the bodily harm follows only because of the victim's efforts to escape, it is clear from the above discussion that the attacker is not liable under this section unless what the victim did was reasonably foreseeable.

8–030   **Does the risk principle apply to the doctrine of transferred intention?** Apparently not. No case decides that it does, and one suggests that it does not.[68] It may be thought that in *R. v. Gore*[69] the defendant could not reasonably have foreseen that the apothecary would be poisoned, yet her intention was transferred. In *Philips v. Commonwealth*,[70] the Supreme Court of Kentucky developed a doctrine of "transferred wantonness". In other words, it used a theory of transferred recklessness to convict a defendant for the wanton murder of a victim who was shot, as she sat next to the defendant in the front seat of a car during an exchange of gunfire between defendant and a co-defendant. The defendant, Philips, was verbally abused by the co-defendant, Johnson, and a gun exchange resulted. Johnson shot at Philips and killed the woman sitting next to Philips. The defendant was held criminally liable because his act provoked another to inadvertently kill an innocent third party. The court held that even though the co-defendant was the one who shot the victim, the defendant was acting with aggravated wantonness with respect to co-defendant, and the victim was resultantly killed for this reason. The defendant was in a rough area doing a drug deal, went armed, and should have known that shooting at someone in that area would result in return fire, but choose to shoot at Johnson even though he had a young woman sitting next to him. As far as psychological causation (moral involuntariness) is concerned, D caused (induced) the gunman to return fire. Johnson and Philips were strangers, so accessorial liability was not available. (Self-defence is not an issue where gangsters engage in a mutual gunfight, because they deliberately risk being shot at by seeking out their fellow gangster.

---

[67] See the discussion *infra*.

[68] *R. v. Latimer* (1886) 17 Q.B.D. 359.

[69] (1611) 9 Co. Rep. 81a.

[70] 17 S.W.3d 870 (2000). The court noted that the state code "creates the concept of transferred wantonness, a theory of criminal liability unfamiliar to our common law. Under (3)(a), a defendant is guilty of wanton murder if, under circumstances manifesting extreme indifference to human life, he wantonly engages in conduct which creates a grave risk of death to one person (V-1) and thereby causes the death of another (V-2)." Cf. *R. v. Pagett* (1983) 76 Cr. App. R. 279.

One can hardly go looking for trouble and then raise self-defence when he finds it—there is no necessity for self-defence in such circumstances. The need to act in self-defence can be avoided by staying away from the rival gangster.)

8.9. REMOTE HARMS AND NEW INTERVENING ACT

An extreme view of criminal responsibility might be that a person is under a duty **8–031** to act in such a way that others are not led to cause harm, so that in some circumstances he could be responsible for harm that is directly caused by others, even though without his authorization or encouragement. In *R. v. Tilley*,[71] the defendant was prosecuted for failing to police his wife's criminal omissions. The defendant was charged with offences contrary to section 111A(1B) of the *Social Security Administration Act 1992* on the basis that he "dishonestly caused or allowed his wife [the co-defendant] to fail to give a prompt notification of a change of circumstance which he knew would affect her entitlement to benefit". Nicola Tilley married D who was earning considerable income from his employment. The marriage meant that her financial circumstances changed. Nicola Tilley failed to notify the relevant authority of the change in her financial circumstances. It was held that under the legislation the primary obligation to notify a change of circumstance was on the person whose entitlement to benefit was liable to be reduced. In this case, the husband was not receiving any benefits and therefore had only a secondary obligation, which was owed not to the authority but to the recipient of the benefit, his wife. He committed an offence only if he caused or allowed her to be in a position where she was unable to give the appropriate notification to the authorities about her financial situation.

Lord Justice Scott Baker, correctly, interpreted the legislation as requiring the husband only to inform his wife of any changes in his income, rather than as requiring him to police her criminal omissions by reporting her for failing to pass on information that he had made available to her. The Court of Appeal summed up by noting: "We think the critical question is whether there was evidence of anything the defendant could have done that would have prevented Nicola Tilley's failure to give notice, bearing in mind that the obligation to give prompt notification was hers not his."[72] The husband and wife had a joint bank account, so the wife had full knowledge of her husband's income. Therefore, the husband had done all he needed to do. There was nothing further he could do to enable her to provide the details of their joint income to the relevant authority. In *R. v. Tilley* the Court of Appeal implicitly recognized the cardinal principle that a person is primarily responsible only for what he himself does or incites. The fact that his own conduct provided the background[73] for some consequential wrong act by another, and that he should have foreseen this act, does not make him responsible for it.

---

[71] (2009) 173 J.P. 393.

[72] *R. v. Tilley* (2009) 173 J.P. 393.

[73] I have examined this issue at length elsewhere, see Dennis J. Baker, "The Moral Limits of Criminalizing Remote Harms," (2007) 10(3) *New Crim. L. Rev.* 370; Dennis J. Baker, "Collective Criminalization and the Constitutional Right to Endanger Others," (2009) 28(2) *Crim. Just. Ethics* 168.

Putting the rule in terms of causation, the new intervening act (*novus actus interveniens*) of a responsible actor, who has full knowledge of what he is doing, and is not subject to mistake or pressure, will normally operate to relieve the defendant of liability for a further consequence, because it makes the consequence "too remote." Underlying this rule there is, undoubtedly, a philosophical attitude. Moralists and lawyers regard the individual's will as the autonomous prime cause of his behaviour. What a person does (if he has reached adult years, is of sound mind and is not acting under mistake, intimidation or other similar pressure) is his own responsibility, and is not regarded as having been caused by other people. An intervening act of this kind, therefore, breaks the causal connection that would otherwise have been perceived between previous acts and the forbidden consequence. (An intervening wrongful omission does not break it.)

8–032
The rule can be rationalized in psychological terms by saying that the intervention of the responsible actor diverts our retributive wrath from the defendant, the previous actor, who may appear to be so much less culpable than the later actor, and this switching of retributive feeling is expressed in causal language. Sometimes, too, we may feel that making people responsible for the subsequent behaviour of others, merely because they foresaw or could have foreseen that behaviour, would be too great a restriction upon liberty. Yet another way of explaining the rule would be to say that part of the object of the criminal trial is to dramatize society's rejection of the deed, and this is adequately done by prosecuting the immediate author. There is no pressing necessity to regard more remote authors as responsible for the harm itself, though they may well be prosecuted for other offences, such as attempt, or in appropriate circumstances as accessories. It is important that the law should not saddle a person with liability for consequences where not only he but also the general public would blame someone else.

To take a fanciful case, suppose that D1 prepares a poisoned drink, intending to offer it to D2, who has his own score to settle with V, and who has observed D1's preparations, offers the drink to V, who takes it and dies. D2 was not acting in collaboration with D1. D2 is guilty of murder and D1 is not. If the poison which D1 left for V to drink had been administered to V by someone who did not know it was poisoned, D1 would have been guilty of murder. As it is, D2's criminal intent insulates D1 from liability.[74]

Another example of the rule, a person who provokes another to kill without encouraging him to do so does not become guilty of murder or manslaughter, even though he realized or should have realized what the effect of his conduct would be.[75] Similarly, unintentionally provoking another person to break the peace[76] or to drive recklessly[77] does not make the provoker criminally

---

[74] Cf. *People v. Elder*, 100 Mich. 515 (1894). For a less obvious illustration see *R. v. Hilton* (1838) 2 Lewin 214. The doctrine of remoteness has been used to mitigate some extreme applications of the law of constructive manslaughter: *R. v. Bennett* (1858) 169 E.R. 1143.

[75] Cf. *R. v. Dubois* (1959) 32 C.R. 187 (Quebec).

[76] *Beatty v. Gillbanks* (1882) 9 Q.B.D. 308; *Redmond-Bate v. D.P.P.* (1999) 163 J.P. 789. For an extensive discussion of this issue see Baker, *supra* note 73. See also the discussion in *Mitchell v. Glasgow City Council* [2009] 2 W.L.R. 481 at 487, where it was held that the law "does not impose a duty to prevent a person from being harmed by the criminal act of a third party based simply upon

responsible. Generally, the courts have refused to allow people to be held liable for being a mere but-for cause (an enabling factor) of someone else's criminal harm-doing. Let us take the example of X, the owner of a corner store. X sells an ice cream to customer Y, and Y subsequently walks out of X's shop and throws the ice cream's packaging on the ground. Should X be held responsible for Y's littering? The harm is contingent on Y making an intervening choice to throw the packet on the ground, but it would not have come about but-for X selling the ice cream to Y. Nevertheless, it is clear why X is not morally blameworthy (criminally condemnable) for this kind of remote harm. The appropriate measure is to punish those who actually throw papers on the street.[78]

The *novus actus* rule is of fundamental importance at common law, because it underlies the doctrine of accessoryship. If D2 incites D1 to kill V, and D1 complies, D2 has prompted (in ordinary speech, indirectly made a causal contribution) D1 to perpetrate the crime, and is himself an accessory to the crime, but he has not directly caused V's death. Professor Fletcher states the principle as follows. "Aiding the crime of a responsible, self-acting perpetrator does not 'cause,' 'control' or 'determine' the latter's conduct. The accessory contributes to the crime, but the execution is not his doing."[79] There are certain important differences between the liability of the accessory and that of the perpetrator. If it were not for the *novus actus* rule the successful encourager would be liable as perpetrator, which would require the law of complicity to be rewritten.[80] The point just made also shows that the *novus actus* principle is distinct from the requirement of reasonable foreseeability. If D2 pays an assassin D1 to kill V, of course he foresees that D1 will do the killing, so that the requirement of foreseeability is satisfied; but still D2 is not a perpetrator of the crime.

8–033

The *novus actus* rule does not prevent liability for joint negligence in concerted action, even though it is the act of only one of the parties that produces the evil result.[81] The law of complicity creates liability where the normal rule for causation would not.[82] Although a *novus actus* rule is recognized in the law of

---

foreseeability." In *R. (on the application of Laporte) v. Chief Constable of Gloucestershire* [2007] 2 A.C. 105 at 155, Lord Brown said: "Take Mr. Beatty, the Salvation Army captain, or Ms Redmond-Bate, the Wakefield preacher. The Divisional Court was in each case clearly right to have set aside their respective convictions. I repeat, the police's first duty is to protect the rights of the innocent rather than to compel the innocent to cease exercising them." See also *Austin v. Commissioner of Police of the Metropolis* [2008] Q.B. 660 at 680-681.

[77] *R. v. Mastin* (1834) 172 E.R. 1292.

[78] *Schneider v. New Jersey*, 308 U.S. 147 (1939). Lawmakers have also relied on remote harm arguments to justify *ex ante* criminalization. See Dennis J. Baker, "A Critical Evaluation of the Historical and Contemporary Justifications for Criminalising Begging," (2009) 73(3) *J. Crim. L.* 212.

[79] George P. Fletcher, *Rethinking the Criminal Law*, (Boston: Little, Brown, 1978) at 582. Cf. John Gardner, "Complicity and Causality," (2007) 1 *Crim. L. & Phil.* 127. This issue is discussed fully in the chapter on complicity *infra*.

[80] The *novus actus* rule is also capable of explaining the doctrine of innocent agency, for the act of an innocent agent is not a *novus actus*.

[81] As in *R. v. Salmon* (1880) 6 Q.B.D. 79 and *R. v. Reid* (1975) 62 Cr. App. R. 109.

[82] Where, however, there is no concerted action but only concurrent acts of negligence, the one party is not liable for the results of the negligence of the other, even though his own negligence is equal to that of the other and he might have foreseen the evil result of the affair in which both were engaged. The point emerges sharply by comparing *R. v. Swindall* (1846) 175 E.R. 95 with *R. v. Mastin* (1834) 172 E.R. 1292.

tort, it differs from the criminal rule in that if A instigates B to commit a tort, both A and B are regarded as causing the result as joint tortfeasors. The law of tort does not distinguish between degrees of complicity as the criminal law does.

The *novus actus* is so potent that it has even rescued a defendant from strict liability. In *Impress (Worcester) Ltd. v. Rees*[83] the appellant company's fuel store leaked oil into the Severn River, after an unknown person had tampered with the valve. Normally (it was assumed) the leak would have been an offence of strict liability, but the Divisional Court held that the company was not liable, because the intervening act of the stranger was an "intervening cause of so powerful nature that the conduct of the appellants was not a cause at all but was merely part of the surrounding circumstances."[84] The pollution of the river was, of course, factually caused in part by the circumstance in that the company had accumulated fuel near the river. But this was merely the background of the matter; in law the only operative cause was the act of the mischief-maker. The distinction is between something operating only indirectly through the wrongful intervener.

Nevertheless, the House of Lords did not adopt this line of reasoning in *Environmental Agency v. Empress Car Co. (Abertillery) Ltd.*[85] The facts of that case were almost identical. An unknown third party opened a tap allowing a significant amount of the defendant's diesel to flow into a storm drain and from there into a nearby river. Empress Car Co. was negligent in that it stored large quantities of diesel on its premises, left the controlling tap unlocked, stored the diesel in an area that was accessible to the public and failed to implement procedures for controlling any overflows.[86] At best these factors only contribute indirectly by making it easier for a wrongdoer to commit his independent criminality. Such an argument is no different to asserting that a person is responsible for the theft of her laptop because it was stolen in circumstances where she failed to lock her window properly.[87] But this would merely be the background of the matter.

8–034   **Does this mean that indirect but-for contributions are sufficient for holding a drug dealer criminally liable for manslaughter when his client over-doses?** *Empress* was a case dealing with a regulatory offence and in circumstances where strict liability would not have been patently unfair. Any unfairness in such cases could be counteracted by providing a "due diligence"

---

[83] [1971] 2 All E.R. 357.

[84] [1971] 2 All E.R. 357 at 359.

[85] [1998] 1 All E.R. 481.

[86] Arguably it would be fair to impose strict liability for this type of regulatory offence, but fair warning would require the Parliament to do this at the *ex ante* legislative stage.

[87] The core difference, however, might be that the firm was storing a dangerous polluting substance in large quantities and therefore had a special duty to ensure it was kept reasonably secure. It arguably failed to take sufficient steps to prevent strangers from releasing the oil. Cf. Vera Bergelson, "Conditional Rights and Comparative Wrongs: More on the Theory and Application of Comparative Criminal Liability," (2005) 8(2) *Buff. Crim. L. Rev.* 567; Heidi M. Hurd, "Blaming the Victim: A Response to the Proposal That Criminal Law Recognise a General Defence of Contributory Responsibility," (2005) 8(2) *Buff. Crim. L. Rev.* 503.

defence.[88] But it would be grossly unfair to use this type of vicarious and strict liability in cases concerning serious *malum in se* criminality, because the penal consequences are much greater. The House of Lords recognized as much in *R v. Kennedy (No. 2).*[89] In that case, the defendant prepared a syringe of heroin and gave it to B. B immediately injected himself. B died within an hour of injecting the drugs into himself. The defendant was charged with manslaughter, even though he merely prepared and supplied the drug. The critical question was whether mere supply was an act causative of B's death given that B injected himself. The House of Lords held that the ultimate harm could not be imputed to the defendant as B's autonomous fully informed choice broke the chain of causation.

It is important to understand the limits of indirect but-for causation. Conceptually, indirect but-for facilitation (supplying a deadly drug) cannot factually cause another to make the independent criminal choice to use that assistance. The House of Lords recognized the limits of indirect causation in the following passage:[90]

> "...the doctrine of secondary liability was developed precisely because an informed voluntary choice was ordinarily regarded as a *novus actus interveniens* breaking the chain of causation: 'Principals cause, accomplices encourage (or otherwise influence) or help. If the instigator were regarded as causing the result he would be a principal, and the conceptual division between principals ... and accessories would vanish. Indeed, it was because the instigator was not regarded as causing the crime that the notion of accessories had to be developed. This is the irrefragable argument for recognising the *novus actus* principle as one of the bases of our criminal law. The final act is done by the perpetrator, and his guilt pushes the accessories, conceptually speaking, into the background."

When a person is given no choice and is used as a mere instrument then the party using her as an instrument is the direct factual cause of that person's wrongdoing. Pimp X might factually cause trafficked woman Y to be raped if X imprisons Y and forces Y to have non-consensual sexual intercourse with X's unsuspecting clients, but in these circumstances X is the perpetrator—there is no secondary party. There is a distinction between mere but-for facilitation and overbearing coercion. Likewise, when a woman is abducted and forced to prostitute herself, her unsuspecting customer could be said to have made a causal contribution to her rape, but he does not make a (culpable) contribution to her rape: the innocent agent, prostitute-user, is a mere non-culpable instrument who

---

[88] It is a cost of doing business that hazardous materials should be properly stored. For an example of a "due diligence" defence, see section 39(1) of the *Consumer Protection Act 1987*, which allows the defendant to demonstrate he took all reasonable steps and exercised all due diligence to avoid the criminal harm that transpired. In *Empress* this could have been achieved by implementing procedures and building facilities for dealing with spills, and also by ensuring that the fuel was secured.

[89] [2008] 1 A.C. 269.

[90] *R. v. Kennedy (No. 2)* [2007] UKHL 38 at para. 17 citing Professor Glanville Williams, "Finis for Novus Actus?" (1989) 48 *Cambridge L.J.* 391 at 398. The Law Lords also cited the following passage from page 392 of Professor Williams' article: "I may suggest reasons to you for doing something; I may urge you to do it, tell you it will pay you to do it, tell you it is your duty to do it. My efforts may perhaps make it very much more likely that you will do it. But they do not cause you to do it, in the sense in which one causes a kettle of water to boil by putting it on the stove. Your volitional act is regarded (within the doctrine of responsibility) as setting a new 'chain of causation' going, irrespective of what has happened before."

is used by the pimp to rape the trafficked women for money-making purposes. The direct legal cause of the rape is the pimp's culpable decision to factually force a non-consenting woman to have sex.

Kennedy's act of supplying the drug was a mere indirect but-for cause. He did not put a gun to B's head and demand B to inject himself. He was not an innocent agent as he knew well that he was injecting himself with a life-threatening drug. Kennedy's indirect assistance might be sufficient to ground derivative liability in the right circumstances (*i.e.* where it is culpably designed to facilitate some primary criminality of a principal), but B was not a principal committing self-manslaughter—there is no such offence. Nor was he attempting suicide; his death was accidental. The only act he committed was self-injection, which is not a crime. Adults with full capacity are able to make their own decisions when it comes to risking *self*-harm. When a person makes a voluntary and informed decision to engage in self-harm it seems pointless to punish their addict associates, who on a different occasion would have been the recipient of the supply.

8–035   **You told me in the last chapter that D can be liable for manslaughter if she supplies drugs to another and that person kills herself by self-injecting.** As noted in the last chapter, in the recent case of *R. v. Evans*,[91] the *Miller*[92] doctrine was wrongly invoked to sustain a conviction of gross negligence manslaughter. It does not mean that supply in itself is sufficient to constitute gross negligence manslaughter. The supplier will only be held criminally liable for gross negligence manslaughter if she indirectly assists another to create a dangerous situation for herself and becomes aware of the danger she has helped to create, and fails to take reasonable steps to counteract that danger when it was possible for her to do so. Hence, if the victim's deliberate self-injection is causing her death, the defendant (supplier) has a duty to try to un-cause what the victim's self-injection is causing, because she has facilitated the victim's risk-taking and is aware of the fact the victim has put herself in peril by using the drugs.

The defendant is held liable for failing to take reasonable steps to counteract the danger that she helped create. In most cases, the supplier is somewhat removed from the drug-user, and thus will not come within the purview of the *R. v. Evans* doctrine. The supplier would have to be present when it became apparent that the victim has overdosed and is in peril.[93]

---

[91] *R. v. Evans* [2009] 1 W.L.R. 1999. Some courts in the U.S. have also adopted this approach. See *State v. Wassil*, 658 A.2d 548 (1995) (U.S.). Cf. *R. v. Creighton* [1993] 3 S.C.R. 3, where D was directly responsible for creating the dangerous situation as he injected the drugs into V. See also Dennis J. Baker, "Omissions Liability for Homicide Offences: Reconciling *R v Kennedy* with *R v Evans*," (2010) 74 *J. Crim. L.* 310. It is also open to the objection that the courts cannot create further situations where a duty will be imposed breach of which will amount to manslaughter. See *R. v. Rimmington* [2006] 1 A.C. 459. Hence, the categories should be regarded as closed. Therefore, since the case is not covered by the *R. v. Stone* [1977] Q.B. 354 category, the court should have held that there was no duty of care.

[92] [1983] 2 W.L.R. 539. Followed also by the court in *DPP v. Santa-Bermudez* [2004] Crim. L.R. 471.

[93] Cf. *R. v. Khan* [1998] Crim. L.R. 830.

But surely the act of supply was merely the background of the matter; the 8–036
only operative cause was the act of the self-injector. Is the Court of Appeal
suggesting that if Miller had given X a lighted cigar and had been present to
see X accidentally cause a fire with it, that Miller would have been liable
too? Yes. But the court is clearly wrong on this point. Merely facilitating
another's accidental harm-doing should not be sufficient for holding that the
facilitator has a duty to act to try to undo or un-cause what that other person's act
is accidentally causing—a building to burn, an addict to die, *etc.*

You told me before, that since the stab wounds Blaue[94] inflicted on his V was 8–037
"causing" her to die when she failed to accept a blood transfusion (a
transfusion which might have reversed or stemmed the harm that Blaue's
past wrongdoing was already causing) that V's omission did not break the
chain of causation. V's omission was not a further cause of her death, but an
omission to attempt to try to stop the stab wounds from causing her to die.
Since Blaue's victim had no duty to act, her omission did not break the chain
of causation. Could not one argue that Evans's sister's self-injection was
causing her death when Evans failed to summon help, so her omission to summon
help was merely a failure to stem or reverse what her sister's past acting was
already causing? Such an argument is perfectly plausible, because Evans's
omission did not cause her sister's death. Her omission was a mere failure to
reverse or stop what her sister had caused for herself. *Per contra*, if Evans had
injected the drug into her sister's arm she would have set the harm in motion, and
thus would have had a duty to act to try to stop the harm from materializing.

But, if the Court of Appeal was right to hold that merely supplying the drug 8–038
created a duty to act, then there is no need to show that the defendant caused
the victim's death. After all, was not Stone's sister's choice not to eat and not
to seek medical attention for herself the direct cause of her death?[95] If there
is a legitimate duty to act, then omissions liability does not hinge on the
prosecution demonstrating that the defendant caused the victim's death. Instead,
it hinges on showing that the defendant failed to take an opportunity to un-cause
or undo harm that was being caused by another or some other event, when he had
a duty and a reasonable opportunity to do so. If a strong wind is about to blow
your child off a cliff and you can easily reach the child and pull him back, then
you are liable for failing to prevent the wind from "causing" your child's death.
This is so, since a parent has a duty to protect his child, when it is reasonable to
do so. (The same can be said if the child is drowning in a puddle.) The duty to act
which was imposed on Evans was not recognized in the authorities; basically the
Court of Appeal extended the *R. v. Miller* doctrine by judicial fiat.

---

[94] The defendant in *R. v. Blaue* [1975] 1 W.L.R. 1411.

[95] The same argument seems to catch *R. v. Stone* [1977] Q.B. 354, as well; unless we accept that one
can cause by omission. But clearly one cannot cause by omitting to do something (see the penetrating
discussion in Michael S. Moore, *Act and Crime: A Theory of Action and Its Implications for Criminal
Law*, (Oxford: Clarendon, 1993) at 267 *et seq.*) So the courts hinge liability on those who have a duty
to stop what someone else or some other natural force is causing.

8–039   **What if Evans had died instantly upon injecting?**   I will answer this for you too: if Evans's sister had died instantly, Evans's *failure* to try to undo the harm that her sister's self-injection had caused (*no longer causing*) would not have made her liable.[96] (Similarly, if Evans had been in a remote part of the Lake District, and were able to demonstrate that her sister would have died before help could have arrived). *R. v. Evans* only creates a duty to act to try to un-cause something that is still operating as a cause. If the end consequence is caused instantly, then one does not have an opportunity to try to un-cause it. Consequently, it must be shown that if D had acted, it could have made some difference to the outcome that was being caused by V or some other event.[97] So even though, in omission cases, it need not be shown that D's omission caused the harm, it must be shown that but-for the omission the harm might have been un-caused.

8–040   **Does *Kennedy (No. 2)* mean that when a police officer makes an independent choice to shoot at D who is holding an innocent human shield, and accidentally kills the human shield, that the officer's independent decision to shoot will relieve D of criminal liability?**   Not unless that choice is fully unfettered. In *R. v. Pagett*[98] it was held that the police officer's act of killing an innocent human shield did not break the chain of causation. In that case the defendant was armed with a shotgun and shot at police officers who were attempting to arrest for other serious offences. There was a 16-year-old girl in the flat with the defendant, and when he made his escape he fired at the police, and against the girl's will he used her body to shield himself from any retaliation by the officers. The officers in fact returned the appellant's fire and as a result the girl was killed. The facts showed as far as causation was concerned, the defendant had fired first at the officers and thus induced (caused) them to respond in self-defence with the result that the girl was killed. The court held that the independent actions of the officers were not a *novus actus*, because "the police acted reasonably[99] either by way of self-defence or in the performance of their duties as police officers."

Pagett was not the direct cause of the victim's death, but his indirect inducement was a more than negligible cause in that it pressured the police to respond in the way they did. The police were acting under pressure caused by the defendant, and so were not exercising the unfettered volition presupposed by the *novus actus* rule. However, what was equally important was the court's view that the police were not independently culpable. The direct cause of death was the shot fired by the officer; but it was the defendant's indirect causal contribution that provided the stimulus for the direct reaction of the officer. The defendant had a direct culpability link with the end result and an indirect but significant causal link. Therefore, it was appropriate to impute the ultimate harm to him. The

---

[96] Cf. *R. v. Cato* [1976] 1 W.L.R. 110. See also *R. v. Cheshire* [1991] 1 WLR 844; *R. v. Dalloway* (1847) 2 Cox C.C. 273.

[97] *R. v. Morby* (1882) 15 Cox C.C. 35; *R. v. Pace* (2008) 187 A. Crim. R. 205.

[98] [1983] 76 Cr. App. R. 279.

[99] When we discuss defences below we will see that self-defence can be based on an unreasonable but honest mistake about the need to act in defence. But any forced used must be reasonable and proportionate to the value being defended—for example, a person's life is worth more than property.

indirect contribution made by the defendant caused the intervening non-culpable agent to kill. Similarly, if an insane person calls for a gun so that he can kill, and you provide it, you will be guilty as an accessory even though the direct cause of harm results from the non-responsible (insane) agent's act.

The chain of causation was not broken in *Pagett*, because there was not any free, deliberate and unfettered intervening acting. If the police had acted recklessly, then the chain of causation would have been broken. For example, if the defendant had been armed only with a knife and was threatening to use it to kill the hostage, the police would act unreasonably and disproportionately if they were to fire and kill the hostage. In these circumstances, the police are not compelled to use lethal force in self-defence and there is an innocent life at stake. Police have specialist training and it would be wrong for them to use other culpable wrongdoers to disguise their own acts of recklessness—they too should be accountable in such circumstances.

If the police had been reckless, would not the consequences of Pagett's actions have been a concurrent cause? Concurrent causation occurs where the actions of two independent wrongdoers make equal causal contributions at the same time.[100] An example is where D1 fires at D2 and D2 grabs innocent third party V1 and uses her as a shield. But-for D1 attempting to kill D2, V1 would not have been killed. Furthermore, but-for D2 pulling V1 into the firing line so as to use her as a shield, V1 would not have been shot; instead D2 would have been shot. D1 would be caught by the transferred malice doctrine and thus is liable for murder. Furthermore, since V1 was an innocent bystander D2 will not be able to raise self-defence against her, and as we will see later in this book, necessity (assuming using the bystander was the only means of survival) is not a defence to murder. The actions of both parties are concurrent causes of the innocent bystander's death and the *novus actus* doctrine does not apply, because there is no intervening act—they both acted independently and at the same time.

8–041

Let us consider a further example, suppose that D1 and D2 successively and independently wound V with murderous intent, and V dies from the loss of blood alone. Beginning with D2, the later assailant, he is guilty of murder, since he must take his victim as he finds him—in this case, weakened and bleeding from the first wound. As regards liability of D1, the question is moot. On the one hand it may be argued that he is not guilty of murder if the wound he inflicted would not have caused the death, because he is not responsible for the subsequent act of a fresh agent. The argument the other way is that both causes are physically operating to bring about death. The *novus actus* doctrine does not insulate D1 from liability in respect of the death when his harm-doing is a concurrent and more than negligible cause of the victim's death.

---

[100] See *Attorney-General's Reference (No. 4 of 1980)* [1981] 1 W.L.R. 705.

8.10.   THE NON-RESPONSIBLE INTERVENER

8–042   If D causes an innocent agent to commit a criminal act, and the innocent agent does so, D is regarded as perpetrating the crime. Put in terms of causation, the rule is that if D has done the last act that he intended to do (instructing the innocent agent), he causes the result notwithstanding that the immediate cause was the act of another (the innocent agent), if there was no subsequent criminal volition of another. This principle is wider than the simple doctrine of innocent agency, as *R. v. Michael*[101] shows. Michael, a single woman, had an illegitimate baby boy a few months old whom she boarded out with a foster-mother. Intending to murder the infant she bought a bottle of laudanum, told the foster-mother that it was medicine, and directed her to give the infant a teaspoonful every night. The woman gave none, but put the bottle on the mantelpiece, where a few days later her own small boy, aged about five, being left alone with the infant, took the bottle down and administered half its contents to the infant, who died. Michael was convicted of murder, and the conviction affirmed by the Court of Crown Cases Reserved.

No clear reason was given by the court for holding Michael responsible, but we may rationalize as follows. Michael intended to poison her baby with laudanum administered by the hand of another, and this very thing happened. The fact that she intended the killing process to be spun out was immaterial. The trial judge in directing the jury assumed that it was necessary for the prosecution to show that a single teaspoonful of the liquid—the dose directed by Michael—was enough to kill the baby; but nowadays this would be regarded as too lenient a direction. Even if the dose of a teaspoonful each night would have killed only by reason of having a cumulative effect, the variation whereby half the bottle was administered at once would have been immaterial.

The more striking deviation from Michael's plan was the intervention of a different, and unforeseen, actor. The small boy was innocent, being under the age of criminal responsibility, and Michael was responsible for the result that he helped to bring about, even though he was not Michael's intended tool. Michael had done the last act that she intended to do, and there was no affront to the sense of justice in saying that the variation in the chain of causation was immaterial.

The negative rules we are now studying are cumulative in effect. It is not enough to show that there was no new intervening act of a responsible actor; it must also be shown that what happened was reasonably foreseeable. There was ample evidence in Michael that the latter rule was satisfied. The defendant had placed the poison in the room where the baby was, and had described it as medicine for the baby. It seems likely that the boy of five who had administered it to the baby had been told or otherwise had come to believe that it was the baby's medicine, though the jury were not asked to consider this point. The fact that some other member of the foster-mother's family might do the actual administrating of the medicine was clearly within the risk she created, though of course the question was one for the jury. Where the third party acts with full

---

[101] (1840) 173 E.R. 867.

knowledge, but not in concert with the defendant, his conduct will be caught by the general principle of causation that free, deliberate and informed intervention breaks the chain of causation.[102]

8.11. CONTRIBUTORY NEGLIGENCE OF THE VICTIM

The principle is that the victim's contributory negligence is no answer to a charge **8–043** or crime.[103] In other words, it is generally no defence that the victim laid himself open to the act, or was himself guilty of negligence in bringing it about. This rule can have strange results. Suppose there are two burglars engaged together in blowing a safe in a grossly negligent way. If one is killed the other is presumably guilty of manslaughter, even though the victim participated throughout in the act of negligence.[104] It can be argued that there should be a defence of negligent joint enterprise, but the courts have not hitherto recognized it. In *R. v. Willoughby* the evidence showed that a fire recklessly set by the defendant and his accomplice had resulted in the accomplice's death. The fact that an accomplice may have been negligent with respect to his own safety does not relieve a defendant of criminal liability. It is not treated any different than if the accomplice had been an innocent victim who made a negligent contribution.[105]

Occasionally the contributory fault of the victim may be so great that the defendant's act is held not to be the imputable cause of the harm. And illustration is the "exhaustion of danger" principle, where the risk created by the defendant is at an end before the victim commits the careless act. In *R. v. Waters*[106] the defendant Waters, being on board a ship, and V, who was in a boat alongside, disputed about payment for some goods, both being intoxicated. There was a conflict of evidence as to what subsequently happened, but according to one witness Waters, to get rid of V, pushed away the boat with his foot; V, reaching out to lay hold of a barge, to prevent his boat from drifting away, overbalanced, fell into the water, and was drowned. Park J. ruled that even if this evidence were accepted it was not a case of manslaughter. No reason was given for the ruling, but a reason can easily be framed. If V had fallen into the water immediately upon his boat being pushed, it might perhaps have amounted to manslaughter, supposing that Waters knew that V was unsteady on his feet and probably too drunk to swim. But this is not what happened. V remained safe in his boat, and the only effect of the push was to cause him the inconvenience, in having the boat drift from the place where he wanted it to be. At that point the risk caused by Waters' act was exhausted.

---

[102] *R. v. Latif* (1996) 2 Cr. App. R. 92.
[103] The rule is well settled; a modern instance is *R. v. Hennigan* [1971] 3 All E.R. 133.
[104] Cf. *R. v. Willoughby* [2005] 1 W.L.R. 1880; *State v. Pellegrino*, 480 A.2d 537 (1984).
[105] See, *mutatis mutandis*, *R. v. Evans* [2009] 1 W.L.R. 1999.
[106] (1834) 6 Car. & P. 328.

8.12.   DEATH THROUGH FRIGHT OF SHOCK

8–044   Where a person is attacked he does not commonly die of fright or shock, but if he does, his death may perhaps be attributed to the attacker on the special sensitivity principle.[107] A person cannot reasonably foresee that another will die of fright when the other is not himself in danger. The law of constructive manslaughter and transferred intention should not be pushed so far as to say that if D assaults V1 he becomes guilty of the manslaughter of V2, a mere spectator, who, remarkably, dies of fright or shock in witnessing what happens to V1.[108] However, if D threatens and frightens V in circumstances where he foresees that V might suffer a heart attack he will be held liable for the resulting harm or death. In *R. v. Dawson*[109] some men tried to rob a petrol station that was being manned by a 60-year-old attendant. After the robbers fled the attendant suffered a heart attack and died. The Court of Appeal quashed their convictions for manslaughter because the defendants did not foresee that the emotional disturbance they caused by committing the robbery would cause the victim to have a heart attack. The robbers had no knowledge of the victim's heart condition. (Even though the robbery did *in fact* cause the victim's heart attack, the defendants were not liable for constructive manslaughter because the act was not objectively dangerous.)

In *R. v. Watson*[110] an 87-year-old man died of a heart attack 90 minutes after he was burgled. The Court of Appeal held that a person can be liable for constructive manslaughter when he frightens a very old and frail victim, if he foresees that the victim might suffer a heart attack.[111] In *R. v. Watson* the defendants were not aware of the victim's frailty when they commenced the burglary, but they abused the elderly man and remained in his house and continued their threats after learning of his age and frailty. The defendants were able to evade justice, because the victim suffered the heart attack 90 minutes after the burglary. The Court of Appeal held that the time delay meant that it was not clear that the burglary had "caused" the heart attack, as it may have been caused by the additional disturbance that resulted when the police and the window repairman arrived at

---

[107] See *R. v. Towers* (1874) 12 Cox C.C. 530; *R. v. Dugal* (1874) 4 Que. L.R. 350 (Can.).

[108] In the American case of *Re Heigho*, 18 Idaho 566 (1910) the defendant was convicted of manslaughter, though the only person killed was an onlooker. The onlooker who died was the mother-in-law of the person assaulted—she died of fright. The medical opinion is that an ordinary person is not likely to suffer any permanent effects from shock unless he is himself involved: John Havard, "Reasonable Foresight of Nervous Shock," (1956) 19 *Mod. L. Rev.* 478. Technically, no doubt a combination of the law of constructive manslaughter and transferred intention would support *Re Heigho*; but it would be open to a court to refuse to combine the two doctrines. In *R. v. Towers* (1874) 12 Cox C.C. 530 the evidence showed that the attacker was negligent and even reckless towards the baby (since the girl when attacked might have dropped it), and the way in which the baby actually died could perhaps be regarded as a mere difference of mode; even so, the decision was severe.

[109] (1985) 81 Cr. App. R. 150. See also *R. v. Carey* [2006] EWCA Crim. 17; *R. v. Lewis* [2010] EWCA Crim. 151; *Todd v. State*, (1992) 594 So.2d 802.

[110] [1989] 1 W.L.R. 684. In *People v. Aponte*, 369 N.Y.2d 342 (1975) the 49-year-old victim was punched by the defendant following a traffic altercation. When the defendant challenged the victim to a fight the victim made it clear he was a "very sick man" and could not fight. The defendant landed a punch and the victim died from heart failure after being knocked unconscious. The conviction was upheld because the defendant was given notice of the victim's condition.

[111] *R. v. Watson* [1989] 1 W.L.R. 684 at 686. Cf. *R. v. Carey* [2006] EWCA Crim. 17; *R. v. Hayward* (1908) 21 Cox C.C 692.

the old man's house. The evidence was not sufficient for the jury to infer that the burglary was *in fact* the cause of the heart attack.

The American courts have not been so generous. In *Matter of Anthony M*[112] a conviction was upheld where an 83-year-old woman died from a heart attack ten days after being mugged. In that case, the defendant deliberately targeted the victim because of her age and thus had the requisite *mens rea* for constructive manslaughter. Furthermore, a reasonable jury could infer that such an attack was the cause of the elderly victim's (reasonably proximate) heart failure.

Fright is more likely to result in death when it causes/induces the victim to make an effort to escape (as by jumping out the window). We have seen that the attacker can be convicted of murder or manslaughter if the victim's response was reasonably foreseeable, provided that there is the mental state or other fault on part of the attacker necessary for the type of homicide or other crime with which he is charged. The interpretation of section 47 of the *Offences against the Person Act 1861* as an offence of half *mens rea* means that, provided that the flight reaction and consequent injury were foreseeable by a reasonable person, they need not have been foreseen by the defendant.[113] Here, the reasonable foreseeability test is being used to establish causation, not fault. Similarly, he can be convicted of constructive manslaughter if death results.[114] **8–045**

Authority from the Victorian era declares that a person who treats another unkindly is not liable if the other dies of grief.[115] Generally, there is insufficient science to support the empirical claim that grief can lead to death, and furthermore, in many cases the grief will not connect with any fault on the part of the person who has caused the grief. An adulterer might cause grief, but surely would not be criminally responsible for any harm stemming from the grief. An American court has held that if D tortures V and causes V to commit suicide as the only means of escape, D will be guilty at least of manslaughter.[116] In England too, D may be criminally liable when he assaults his wife repeatedly for years and this causes her to suffer a mental disorder, which in turn causes her to commit suicide.[117] (The causal connection in the latter case is not only indirect, but is weakened almost to vanishing point, since V harms herself in circumstances

---

[112] 63 N.Y.2d 270. See also *Schlossman v. State*, 105 Md. App. 277 (1995), where non-life-threatening conduct such as kicking dirt and poking a homeless person with a stick was held to have a causal connection with the V's heart attack. See also *Baraka v. Com.*, 194 S.W.3d 313 at 317 (2006) and the many cases cited therein; *Terry v. Associated Stone Co.*, 334 S.W.2d 926, 928 (1960); *State v. Shaw*, 260 Kan. 396 (1996) where an 86-year-old man suffered a heart attack after being left tied up by a burglar; *State v. Washington*, 581 A.2d 1031 (1990), where a 73-year-old rape victim suffered a heart attack while being raped. In all these cases, V's death or injury was unintended but was a "foreseeable" and "factual" result of D's conduct; the law considers the chain of legal causation unbroken in such cases. See the discussion in *State v. Spates*, 176 Conn. 227 at 235 (1978).

[113] See D. W. Elliot, "Frightening a Person into Injuring Himself," [1974] Crim. L.R. 15.

[114] *Director of Public Prosecutions v. Daley* [1980] A.C. 237.

[115] *R. v. Murton* (1862) 3 F. & F. 492. In that case, the husband had used violence against his wife ten days before her dead, but there was no evidence to demonstrate that the physical attack caused her death. Instead, it was accepted that she died of grief because the husband had brought a couple of ladies of the town home and kicked her out of the matrimonial home at the request of the ladies.

[116] As in *Stephenson v. State*, (1932) 124 Cal. 551, where a rape victim poisoned herself while being held captive.

[117] *R. v. Dhaliwal* [2006] 2 Cr. App. R. 348.

where she is not forced to do so by the urgency of the situation, and her response is a sudden response to a stimulus which has been unleashed cumulatively over many years.)

In most cases the *novus actus* principle will relieve the wrongdoer of criminal liability, if the victim acts independently and unnecessarily takes his own life, even if the defendant's behaviour was atrocious.[118] If the suicide was a necessary, immediate and proportionate response to the defendant's violence, then the chain of causation will not be broken. In *People v. Lewis*[119] the victim had been shot and would have died in an hour or so, but accelerated his own death by cutting his own throat. The court said it would not be homicide by D, if the wounded condition of the victim was "merely the occasion upon which another cause intervened, not produced by the first wound, or related to it in other than a causal way" (as if the deceased had been run over on the way to hospital). It was also said that the case would have stood otherwise if the wound, though painful, had not been dangerous, and V had known it was not dangerous but had taken his life to escape pain. If D's wounding was no longer causing V's death, then the subsequent suicide would have broken the chain of causation. Hence, if V had cut his own throat ten weeks later, and after he had basically recovered, the chain of causation would have been broken.

8.13. IMPROPER MEDICAL TREATMENT

8–046 As a general rule, if the defendant's wrongdoing is a more than insignificant (concurrent) cause of the end harm, the chain of causation will not be broken even if there are multiple sufficient causes. When a person has injured another, who dies, the courts are very chary of allowing the assailant to adduce evidence suggesting that the doctors were in some way at fault in their treatment of the victim, in order to escape liability for causing death. The doctors are not on trial, and are not represented; and even if it is alleged that the medical treatment fell short of perfection, whether by act or omission, the court will now generally exclude evidence on the subject, on the ground that it could make no difference to the outcome. We have already seen one example of this in *R. v. Malcherek and Steel*.[120]

In *R. v. Malcherek and Steel*[121] the facts clearly showed that the brain deaths of the victims were a direct consequence of the defendants' violence. Mrs. Malcherek's original injury caused her to gain a clot which caused her heart to stop and it was 30 minutes before the doctors could remove the clot and restart her heart. This resulted in severe brain damage and she was being kept alive on a life-support machine. Likewise, Ms Wilkinson was left brain-dead because Steel had bashed her head in with a rock. The medical team in both cases did a number of tests and decided there was no point in continuing life support. The defendants argued that turning off the life support was an intervening act breaking the chain causation. The Court of Appeal dismissed these arguments, because the evidence

---

[118] *R. v. Sawyer* (1887) 106 Sess. Pap. 301.
[119] (1899) 124 Cal. 551.
[120] [1981] 1 W.L.R. 690.
[121] [1981] 1 W.L.R. 690 at 692.

showed that the victims were left brain dead as a direct result of the original injuries. There was no evidence of gross negligence to put to the jury. In such a clear-cut case there is no need for the jury to consider causation.[122] Clearly, a doctor who tries his "[c]onscientious best to save the life of a patient brought to hospital in extremis, skilfully using sophisticated methods, drugs and machinery to do so, but fails in his attempt and therefore discontinues treatment, cannot be said have caused death of the patient."[123]

The courts may perhaps be persuaded to admit evidence of gross negligence if the injury inflicted by the defendant was demonstrably not serious or had almost healed. A line of precedents suggest that negligent medical treatment will only break the chain of causation if it is the sole cause of V's death or other injury. The more general rule is that the intervening medical negligence would break the chain of causation if the defendant's wrongdoing was no more than a *de minimis* concurrent cause.[124] If the defendant's contribution remains a more than negligible cause, then it does not matter that the medical negligence was a greater concurrent cause. In *R. v. Jordon*[125] the medical negligence was sufficient to break the chain of causation, because it was the sole cause of the victim's death. The defendant's contribution had become nothing greater than coincidental in that it merely caused the victim to be in the wrong place at the wrong time. If the victim had not been in hospital (the wrong place) at the wrong time, the gross negligence may not have affected him as opposed to someone else. Even if the defendant's contribution concurrently remained a cause, it was nothing more than a *de minimis* cause, because the wounds had "mainly heeled at the time of death" and were no longer life threatening.[126] The direct and immediate cause of death was not the almost heeled wounds, but rather it was the antibiotic (terramycin) which was administered negligently by the treating doctors on several occasions after they had already discovered that the victim was allergic to that particular drug.

In *R. v. Smith*[127] the intervening negligent acts of third parties including the treating doctors did not break the chain of causation, because the original wound remained a more than negligible (concurrent) cause of the victim's death. In that case, the court took the view that any kind of foreseeable wrongdoing or negligence by a third party would not break the chain of causation. If the original cause is no longer a factual cause, foreseeability is irrelevant. *R. v. Smith* is best described as a case where the wounds would likely have been fatal without treatment and therefore the bad medical treatment was not sufficient to break the chain of causation. It was held that the chain of causation will not be broken if at the "time of death the original wound is still an operating cause and a substantial

---

[122] "The issue of the cause of death in a trial for either murder or manslaughter is one of fact for the jury to decide. But if, as in this case, there is no conflict of evidence and all the jury has to do is apply the law to the admitted facts, the judge is entitled to tell the jury what the result of that application will be. In this case the judge would have been entitled to have told the jury that the defendant's stab wound was an operative cause of death". *R. v. Malcherek and Steel* [1981] 1 W.L.R. 690 at 696.

[123] *R. v. Malcherek and Steel* [1981] 1 W.L.R. 690 at 697.

[124] *R. v. Cheshire* [1991] 1 W.L.R. 844 at 850.

[125] (1956) 40 Cr. App. R. 152.

[126] (1956) 40 Cr. App. R. 152 at 157.

[127] [1959] 2 Q.B. 35.

cause." The adjective "operative" is superfluous, as it is merely asking whether the act remained a cause at the time of death—if it remains a cause then it is a cause. The word "substantial" is now interpreted as requiring a not insignificant or more than negligible cause. Similarly, in *R. v. Cheshire*[128] the Court of Appeal said that even gross medical negligence will not break the chain of causation where D's act remains one of the causes of V's injury. The original act does not have to be the sole cause or even the greater (main) cause, but it has to remain as something more than an insignificant cause.

---

[128] [1991] 1 W.L.R. 844 at 850.

PART TWO

THE PROTECTION OF THE PERSON

CHAPTER 9

NON-FATAL OFFENCES AGAINST THE PERSON

"A man's body and his mind, with the utmost reverence to both I speak it, are exactly like a jerkin and a jerkin's lining: rumple the one, you rumple the other."

Laurence Sterne[1]

9.1. THE TWO KINDS OF ASSAULT

This chapter and the next chapter are concerned with what may be called the right to bodily integrity: non-fatal injuries to the person (or other threats of injury), brought about with an element of intention or recklessness.[2] This chapter focuses on offences of a non-sexual nature (or not necessarily of a sexual nature). How much intention or recklessness, we are to consider. The basic offences are assault and battery, but they have been fortified by a number of statutory offences.

9–001

Assault and battery are now statutory offences.[3] Section 39 of the *Criminal Justice Act 1988* provides:

> "Common assault and battery shall be summary offences and a person guilty of either of them shall be liable to a fine not exceeding level 5 on the standard scale, to imprisonment for a term not exceeding six months, or to both."

Since the *Criminal Justice Act* makes them summary offences, they cannot be attempted. The notion of assault enters into various crimes. In its simple form, known as common assault (the subject of this section), it is punishable summarily. The definition of assault and its sister offence battery are the same in crime or tort, except that consent as a defence in tort is probably wider than it is in crime.[4] The required mental element is intention or subjective recklessness.[5]

---

[1] *The Life and Opinions of Tristram Shandy, Gentleman*, (London: James Cochrane & Co. 1832) at 146.
[2] As we will see in the next chapter, negligence as to circumstances is enough for some sexual offences such as rape.
[3] *D.P.P. v. Taylor* [1992] Q.B. 645.
[4] In criminal law, consent is sometimes disregarded on grounds of policy (see *R. v. Brown* [1994] 1 A.C. 212), but this is probably not so for civil law. Formerly, a tortious battery (unlike a criminal one) could be committed negligently. But the courts now treat a negligent battery as being an instance of the tort of negligence, not of battery, though the point has no practical importance since anyway the defendant is liable in damages for negligence. See *Gorely v. Codd* [1967] 1 W.L.R. 19 at 25.
[5] *R. v. Savage* [1992] 1 A.C. 699.

An example of recklessness is where a person, lying on the ground, kicks out at random towards other people around him.[6] He may not have hoped to hurt someone, but anyway is reckless.[7]

9–002 Mere negligence is not sufficient *mens rea* for assault. Only in modern times was the idea of reckless assault accepted by the courts, and it was certainly not thought of as applying to cases of negligence.[8] If a person light-heartedly swings his umbrella without thinking that someone may be behind him, his liability if any for hitting the other person should be for negligence, not recklessness; and it is a civil liability, not a criminal one.

Certain defences such as consent,[9] self-defence, public authority, necessity and duress are of general importance in crime, and are therefore dealt with not here but in later chapters.

Ordinary usage creates certain difficulty in pinning down the meaning of "assault." Etymologically, the word is compounded of the Latin *ad-saltare*, to jump at. In popular language, it has always connoted a physical attack. When we say that D assaulted V, we have a mental picture of D attacking V, by striking or pushing or stabbing him.

In the middle ages, however, the terms "assault" and "battery" were given technical meanings which they have retained ever since. It became settled that though an assault could be committed by physical contact, it did not require this, since a show of force raising an apprehension in the mind of the victim was sufficient. Also, a "battery" did not require an actual beating; the use of any degree of force against the body would suffice. The acts of spitting[10] on a person and kissing[11] without consent are both batteries.[12]

9–003 **So an assault is a threatened battery?** An assault can consist of a threatened battery. But, unfortunately, lawyers have continued to use the word "assault" also in the sense of a battery.

Both in the interpretation of statutes and in ordinary legal discussions "assault" is regularly used to include or mean a battery—for example, in the statutory expressions "assault occasioning actual bodily harm" and "sexual assault."[13] Also, the word "battery" is now almost out of use, except when the

---

[6] *D v. D.P.P.* [2005] EWHC 967.

[7] *R. v. Venna* [1976] Q.B. 421. That negligence is not enough was decided in *Ackroyd v. Barett* (1894) 11 T.L.R. 115; indeed, the court there said that it was insufficient that the defendant acted "recklessly," but the word was evidently intended to mean "with gross negligence."

[8] *R. v. Venna* [1976] Q.B. 421; *R. v. Spratt* [1990] 1 W.L.R. 1073; *R. v. Savage* [1992] 1 A.C. 699; *R. v. Ireland* [1997] Q.B. 114; *D.P.P. v. DA (A Child)* [2001] Crim. L.R. 140.

[9] See generally, Dennis J. Baker, "Moral Limits of Consent as a Defence in the Criminal Law," (2009) 12 *New Crim. L. Rev.* 93.

[10] *R. v. Cotesworth* (1704) 87 E.R. 928; *R. v. Smith* (1866) 176 E.R. 910; *Ray v. U.S.*, 575 A.2d 1196 (1990). Similarly, if D squirts baby oil and throws water on V he commits a battery. See *State v. Padilla*, 123 N.M. 216 (1997); *Pursell v. Horn* (1838) 112 E.R. 966. Blowing cigar smoke into another's face has also been held to constitute a battery: *Leichtman v. WLW Jacor Communications, Inc.*, 634 N.E.2d 697 (1994).

[11] *R. v. Dungey* (1864) 176 E.R. 485.

[12] In *Fagan v. Commissioner of Police of the Metropolis* [1969] 1 Q.B. 439 at 444F it was said that "assault may be committed by the laying of a hand upon a person."

[13] See for example, section 3 of the *Sexual Offences Act 2003*.

speaker tries to make his meaning abundantly clear by using the phrase "assault and battery." One could not talk of a "battery" without being thought to use the word oddly. The noun "battery" has never given an acceptable verb for expressing the range of the offence; we say that D assaulted V, but it would sound archaic and misleading to describe D's act in shooting and stabbing V in words "D battered V," or "D beat V."

For these reasons, the word "assault" has to be recognized as covering not only an assault in the sense of an act causing apprehension but also what was formerly called a battery. Speaking of the former statutory offence of "indecent assault," Lord Goddard C.J. said:

> "An assault can be committed without touching a person. One always thinks of an assault as giving a blow to somebody, but that is not necessary. An assault may be constituted by a threat or a hostile act committed towards a person."[14]

The last sentence gives examples of assaults, but it should be noticed that a non-hostile but unwelcome application of "force" can also be an assault.[15]

The double meaning of "assault" creates a somewhat awkward linguistic **9–004** situation. Assault in the wide sense means (1) a battery or (2) a threatened battery, according to context or circumstance. Kissing the Sleeping Beauty is an assault in the sense of battery, while it is not an assault in the sense of apprehension. If a threatened battery is an assault, and a battery is assault, it follows that a threatened assault is an assault!

The most convenient solution would be to recognize "assault" as the generic expression, consisting in certain kinds of unlawful interference with another. This interference may be either (1) a physical assault, an unlawful bodily contact, that is to say a battery, or (2) a psychic assault, an assault in the sense of a threatened battery. If this terminology is accepted, we can talk sense instead of paradox; we can say that a psychic assault is a threatened physical assault. Since physical assault is by far the commonest form of assault to come before the courts, it is usually referred to as "assault" simply.

Although this suggested language may assist clarity of thought, it does not mean that assault in the generic sense is a single offence. The only offences are psychic assault and physical assault, and they are different offences.[16] There may be one without the other. An example of a psychic assault without a physical assault is a threatened blow. An example without a psychic assault is giving a

---

[14] *R. v. Rolfe* (1952) 36 Cr. App. R. 4 at 6.
[15] *In re: F (Mental Patient: Sterilisation)* [1990] 2 A.C. 1 at 73 *per* Lord Goff. Cf. *R. v. Brown* [1994] 1 A.C. 212 where the Lords suggested "hostility" is required. The facts in that case showed that the sadomasochists did not act with hostility: harm-doing does not always involve hostility. If a doctor botches a medical procedure thereby leaving his patient permanently scarred, we cannot say he was hostile in negligently causing such harm to his patient.
[16] Notwithstanding that they have been put in statutory form. *R. v. Beasley* (1981) 73 Cr. App. R. 44 illustrates the anomaly of having two offences going by the same name. They should have different names, such as "assault" and "threatened assault."

blow from behind, or giving a blow (or, as said before, a kiss) to a sleeping person, where there is no previous apprehension.[17]

The general impression that there can be a conviction of "assault and battery" is therefore, strictly speaking, erroneous, for there cannot be a single conviction of two crimes. But a conviction in these traditional terms should be upheld as meaning a conviction of battery only.[18] In the consolidated appeals in *D.P.P. v. Taylor, Little*,[19] it was held that "assault" and "battery" remain independent offences. Therefore, the information should charge one or the other. (It would be pointless to charge them in the alternative, as a conviction of either one would achieve the same end.) Even where alternative counts are appropriate, the defendant cannot be convicted of both. "That principle applies not only where the alternatives are mutually exclusive but also where the more serious offence necessarily includes the lesser alternative."[20]

9–005 **Is any threat a psychic assault?** A psychic assault is a threat creating an apprehension of immediate force, made intentionally or recklessly. The threat may be by conduct, or by spoken[21] or written[22] words; this will be discussed later. The force apprehended must be unlawful force to the body of the victim, and the victim must believe that the force is about to be applied to him.

It will be seen that there are two separate states of mind to be considered: that of the victim, and that of the actor:[23]

---

[17] Hawkins says that: "every battery includes an assault," *i.e.* a psychic assault, but this is evidently a mistake. William Hawkins, *A Treatise of the Pleas of the Crown*, (London: His Majesty's Law Printers, 6th edn. 1777) at 586. Cf. J. W. C. Turner, *Russell On Crime*, (London: Steven & Sons, 12th edn. 1964) at 655.

[18] In drawing an indictment or information the word "assault," if standing alone, will be taken to refer to a psychic assault or physical assault or both. So the charge will be valid whichever the evidence establishes. But if the draftsman contrasts "assault" and "battery," by charging that the defendant "did unlawfully assault or beat" the victim, the word "assault" will be read as meaning a psychic assault and the charge will then, be bad for duplicity: *Jones v. Sherwood* [1942] 1 K.B. 127. In *D.P.P. v. Taylor* [1992] Q.B. 645 at 653 Mann L.J. held: "[A] charge of common assault should be formulated so as to avoid duplicity where the case is one of actual as well as apprehended unlawful force. The form which is hallowed by long use is 'did assault *and* beat' the victim … this form has been described as 'lazy "conventional" language.' A proper language would be 'assault by beating' where force had been used and 'assault by threatening' where it had not. … [U]ndeniably a more accurate form would avoid a *conjunction* and use a *preposition*. Thus 'assault by beating' would be *immune* from argument. … I think that in the future prosecutors should avoid conjunctive forms."

[19] [1992] Q.B. 645.

[20] *R. v. S* [2007] EWCA Crim. 2247 at para. 12 *per* Toulson L.J.

[21] *R. v. Ireland* [1998] A.C. 147 at 166H *per* Lord Hope. Cf. *Chappell v. D.P.P.* (1989) 89 Cr. App. R. 82 with respect to section 5 of the *Public Order Act 1986*.

[22] *R. v. Constanza* [1997] 2 Cr. App. R. 492.

[23] The term "actor" (or "doer") is a convenient general expression for the person doing the act in question. Usually it will be the defendant to a criminal charge, though occasionally it may be the prosecutor or some other person. For example, where the defendant claims that he acted in self-defence because the prosecutor had first assaulted him, if the issue is as to the alleged assault by the prosecutor, the prosecutor will be the "actor" within the rule stated in the text.

1.   The victim must expect that force is about to be applied to him.[24] He need not experience fear, provided that he has the expectation.[25] (Aiming a gun at a sleeping person would not constitute assault, because the victim does not expect that force is about to be applied to him. He expects nothing as he is not aware of the potential attack.)[26]

2.   The actor must intend to create the expectation or be reckless as to it. In other words, it is sufficient that he knows he is doing something from which the belief is likely to arise.

No blow need be struck; the actor need only do something inducing the victim to believe that he will instantly receive a blow (or other application of force) unless he does something to avoid it, as by striking in self-defence or retreating. It is immaterial that the actor is not at that moment within striking distance,[27] but he must, normally, be sufficiently near to apply the force *then and there*, and he must do some act (such as the act of making a silent phone call[28]—or uttering some words) inducing the victim's apprehension.

A case going to the limit of the law was one where the defendant entered a garden of a house and looked through a window of a woman's bedsitting room, intending to frighten her. When she screamed he went away. It was held that he was guilty of assault (and in consequence, was guilty of being found on enclosed premises for an unlawful purpose). Yet the only movement he made was in going to the spot, and he could not have harmed the victim except by somehow getting into the house.[29] More recently, the House of Lords have relaxed the "immediacy" requirement further. It appears that a psychic assault is now a threat creating an apprehension of "imminent" force, made intentionally or recklessly. In *R. v. Burstow*,[30] the defendant had been in a relationship with the victim, but she ended it. He could not accept her decision, so he began a campaign of harassment. The harassment involved, among other things,[31] him making

---

[24] It was once held that a mother's abandonment of her baby in a ditch was not assault upon it, because the baby did not know what was happening: *R. v. Renshaw* (1847) 3 Cox C.C. 285. At present day the charge of assault on such facts could be read as a charge of battery; but even then the charge ought to be dismissed as merely a legal ploy to treat what is really an omission to look after a child as a positive act. The proper charge is one of child neglect. See section 1 of the *Children and Young Persons Act 1933*.

[25] *State v. McMahon*, 81 P.3d 508 (2003); *State v. LaMere*, 621 P.2d 462 (1980). Cf. *R. v. Lamb* [1967] 2 Q.B. 981, where the victim of a shooting was not put in fear, as the gun fired accidentally as his mate played with it.

[26] *State v. Barry*, 124 P. 775 (1912); cf. *R. v. St. George* (1840) 173 E.R. 921.

[27] *Mortin v. Shoppee* (1828) 172 E.R. 462; *Stephens v. Myers* (1830) 172 E.R. 735.

[28] The conduct might involve making repeated silent phone calls of a harassing nature. In *R. v. Ireland* [1998] A.C. 147 at 166H, Lord Hope said: "In my opinion silent telephone calls of this nature are just as capable as words or gestures, said or made in the presence of the victim, of causing an apprehension of immediate and unlawful violence."

[29] *Smith v. Superintendent of Working Police Station* [1983] Crim. L.R. 323. A psychic assault can be committed on the other side of a locked door, if the victim believes that the attacker is about to break it down. See *R. v. Mostyn* (2004) 145 A. Crim. R. 304. Cf. *R. v. Beach* (1912) 7 Cr. App. R. 197. Query, *Smith v. Newsam* (1673) 84 E.R. 728.

[30] [1998] A.C. 147 at 162.

[31] Some of his calls were not silent. He also distributed offensive cards in the street where she lived. He frequently turned up at her place of employment and surreptitiously took photographs of the victim and her family. In addition, he sent her menacing letters.

numerous silent telephone calls to her. It was found that his repeated silent phone calls caused the victim to develop a recognized psychiatric illness.

9–006 The House of Lords had to decide whether the making of silent telephone calls causing psychiatric injury was capable of constituting an assault. Lord Steyn said:

> "That brings me to the critical question whether a silent caller may be guilty of an assault. The answer to this question seems to me to be 'Yes, depending on the facts'. It involves questions of fact within the province of the jury. After all, there is no reason why a telephone caller who says to a woman in a menacing way 'I will be at your door in a minute or two' may not be guilty of an assault if he causes his victim to apprehend immediate personal violence. Take now the case of the silent caller. He intends by his silence to cause fear and he is so understood. The victim is assailed by uncertainty about his intentions. Fear may dominate her emotions, and it may be the fear that the caller's arrival at her door may be imminent. She may fear the possibility of immediate personal violence. As a matter of law the caller may be guilty of an assault: whether he is or not will depend on the circumstance and in particular on the impact of the caller's potentially menacing call or calls on the victim."

According to Lord Steyn, if the jury find that V feared that D might strike (apply unlawful force) within minutes of her receiving his silent call, then assault could be made out.

But, if a person merely fears that a battery is likely in the near future, she does not fear that it will take place immediately. "Imminent" means liable to happen in the near future—not the immediate future. In some contexts an event will be imminent if it is due to take place in a few days. In other contexts, "imminence" will be measured in minutes or hours. An event that is likely to happen in the future is not likely to happen here and now—in the instant. Lord Steyn suggested that the concept of "immediate" could be stretched to cover events that are likely to take place in the imminent future. This line of reasoning is conceptually problematic. A threat to inflict violence in 30 minutes time is not a threat to inflict it here and now.[32] This judicial extension of the law should be interpreted as requiring the victim to fear that the force will be applied within a minute or two (at the most) of her receiving the silent call.[33] Mobile phones may not have been in common use in the 1990s (when Ireland and Burstow were playing havoc with their victims), but they are now omnipresent. Consequently, it would not be too fanciful to argue that a silent telephone call (text message, e-mail and so on) could cause a victim to fear that the caller could strike within a minute. After all, the caller could already be on your doorstep! The implicit threat of physical violence made by making a silent telephone call could constitute an assault, provided it causes the victim to apprehend "immediate" or "almost immediate" physical violence.

---

[32] *R. v. Knight* (1988) 35 A. Crim. R. 314.

[33] "[I]f the fear so intentionally created is of harm in the future, not being the immediate future, then whilst the fear may be equally harmful and distressing to the victim, it would not fulfil the requirement of immediacy or imminence that is an element of an assault not involving a battery." *R. v. Gabriel* (2004) 182 F.L.R. 102 at 114 *per* Higgins C.J. Chief Justice Higgins also said: "The ordinary meaning of the term 'immediate' is that the consequence follows 'at once, without delay' (*The Concise Oxford Dictionary* 5th edn.). The term 'imminent' means 'impending, soon to happen.' I do not consider that a consequence which is not to follow *without delay* but which *may or may not happen in the more distant future* satisfies this requirement. ... Of course, the apparent time between the threat and its execution must involve some lapse of time. A fist formed and shaken may indicate an impending blow. That blow, if struck, may take a few seconds to follow." (Emphasis added.)

When a person receives a silent call, it is not possible for her to ascertain whether the caller is within immediate striking distance or not. In many cases the victim will only believe that it is possible that violence will be inflicted within a minute or two. The Lords held that a belief in the possibility of violence is sufficient. The victim has no way of knowing whether the silent caller is on her doorstep with his mobile telephone, or whether he is around the corner in the red telephone kiosk. Nor is it possible for the victim to ascertain which call might result in the defendant subjecting her to unlawful force. The victim would not be able to distinguish one implied threat of immediate violence from the next. Every silent call might be perceived as an implied threat of immediate violence. If the silent caller gives his victim the impression that he is at her door and will be in her house striking her within a minute, this will be sufficient for grounding an assault conviction.

9–007

However, if the victim knows that the defendant is calling from overseas or from a reasonable distance, she would not apprehend an immediate infliction of unlawful force.[34] She might fear a future attack, but that is not the same as fearing an immediate attack. If it is clear that the attack is likely to occur in the more distant future (after some delay), then it is neither imminent[35] nor immediate.[36] So, if X telephones Y at 11:00 *a.m.* and says: "When I get out of prison this afternoon at 2:00 *p.m.* I am going to find you and give you a beating," he does not commit assault. (This is assuming that Y knows for a fact that X is still in prison and that he is yet to be released.)

Some of the old books define a psychic assault as an attempted impact,[37] but they are wrong. Psychic assault and attempted physical assault were two distinct offences. If D clenches his fist and threatens V, intending only to create apprehension, he is guilty of psychic assault even though (since he does not intend to strike) he is not guilty of an attempted physical assault. Conversely, if D *tries* to strike V from behind, he is guilty of an attempted physical assault even though (since V does not know of his danger) there is no psychic assault.[38] As said before, common assault can no longer be attempted, since it is now a summary offence.

The confusion between psychic assault and attempted physical assault is responsible for the notion in some of the old cases that it is no assault to point an unloaded gun at another, even though the actor knows that the other thinks the gun is loaded.[39] Although the older authorities are in conflict,[40] it is now settled

9–008

---

[34] *R. v. Knight* (1988) 35 A. Crim. R. 314.

[35] As far as the law of assault is concerned, "imminent" should be given a restrictive interpretation: it should be regarded as meaning "almost immediately."

[36] *R. v. Gabriel* (2004) 182 F.L.R. 102 at 117; *Slaveski v. State of Victoria & Ors* [2010] V.S.C. 441 at para. 238.

[37] Hawkins, *op. cit. supra*, note 17 at 585; Edward H. East, *A Treatise of the Pleas of the Crown*, (London: printed by A. Strahan, Vol. I, 1803) at 406.

[38] Cf. *State v. Wilson*, 218 Or. 575 (1959); *State v. Garcias*, 679 P.2d 1354 (1984); cf. *People v. Jones*, 443 Mich. 88 (1993). See also *R. v. Doiron* (1960) 34 C.R. 188 (Brit. Col.).

[39] Cf. *R. v. Everingham* (1949) 66 W.N. (N.S.W.) 122, where this was held to be an assault. See also *Commonwealth v. Howard* 386 Mass 607 (1982); *R. v. Standley* (1996) 90 A. Crim. R. 67.

[40] See Glanville Williams, *Textbook of Criminal Law*, (London: Stevens & Sons, 1978) at 138 n. 16.

that such an act is an assault.[41] The reason is that the culprit has deliberately raised apprehension in the mind of the victim, which is precisely what a psychic assault is. The actor's belief that he can put the threat into execution was necessary for an attempted battery, but not for a psychic assault.

As will be shown in the next section, a conditional threat can be an assault.

9.2. ASSAULT BY WORDS

9–009   To constitute a psychic assault the victim must apprehend immediate force. It is not an assault if the defendant shows clearly in words that no immediate attack is intended, even if he makes a show of aggression. In the antique case of *Tuberville v. Savage*:[42]

> "Tuberville and Savage exchanged quarrelsome words; Tuberville laid his hand on his sword and said to Savage: 'If it were not assize-time, I would not take such language from you.' These words showed that Tuberville's menacing gesture was pure bravado; so far from being a threat, the words were a reassurance. But Savage thrust at Tuberville and put out his eye. Tuberville sued for damages for assault; Savage pleaded self-defence because he feared an attack. It was held that Tuberville had not opened the hostilities, because his words showed no present intention to do violence. Consequently, Savage was not entitled to claim that he acted in self-defence."

It will be seen that this case did not raise the neat question whether the plaintiff, Tuberville, committed assault. Quite possibly he did commit an assault when he made the menacing gesture of laying his hand upon his sword, if he did not utter his emollient words quickly enough to destroy the defendant's momentary apprehension. But, whether this was so or not, his words showed that he had no present intention of being an aggressor. Once he had uttered them, the defendant could not claim that his retaliatory act was in self-defence.

The problem of conditional threat arose again in *R. v. Light*.[43] Light held a shovel over his wife's head and said: "If it were not for the policeman outside I would split your head open." The judges differed on the question whether this was a criminal assault, and the two reports of the case are not completely in accord on what the judges said. But it seems a fair inference from the various opinions expressed that the test is this: did Light's words so neutralize the menacing character of his acts as to prevent a reasonable person from feeling apprehension?

It seems right to say that where the act is of a very menacing character, as it was in *R. v. Light*, the mere fact that words are spoken indicating no present intention to assault does not necessarily negative an assault in law. If a man raises a shovel to a position where he can bring it down on his wife's head, she will in all probability feel fear, and her fear will prevent her from listening carefully to what he says and coming to the calm conclusion that no assault is intended. Even if the reassuring words are heard and attended to, they may be wholly outweighed

---

[41] *Logdon v. D.P.P.* [1976] Crim. L.R. 121.

[42] (1669) 86 E.R. 684.

[43] (1857) 169 E.R. 1029.

by the menace of the act. The victim may well fear that the aggressor will suddenly change his mind and attack notwithstanding the fact that the condition he has stated is not fulfilled.

Then what if one says to another: "Be quiet or I will blow your brains out," **9–010** **pointing a gun at him a moment afterwards? Is this an assault?** Such a situation is clearly distinguishable from that in *Tuberville v. Savage*, for there the words referred to an extraneous condition ("If it were not assize-time") which the victim knew was not fulfilled. There was, therefore, no present threat. But if the words fetter the victim's present freedom, an assault is committed.[44]

In these cases the requirement that the threat be to inflict harm immediately is qualified: it need only be a threat of force to follow immediately upon disobedience, provided that the obedience is required then and there. Were it otherwise, the highwayman who says "Stand and deliver," at the same time pointing a gun, would not be guilty of an assault—a conclusion that it is impossible to accept. The victim of the threat realizes that he has to regulate his movements carefully if he is to avoid being shot. Even if he decides to comply with the demand, the fear of being shot, perhaps as a result of misunderstanding by the aggressor, is not absent from his mind. Quite apart from this argument, it is a salutary rule that persons should not be allowed to constrain the conduct of others by threats of immediate physical force, and will be held guilty of assault if they attempt to do so.

Suppose you don't point a gun; can there be an assault by words alone? It **9–011** is said in most of the standard authorities on criminal law and the law of tort that words cannot constitute an assault, in the absence of accompanying gestures;[45] but the judicial authority for this supposed limitation is of the slightest. Ordinarily, perhaps, a spoken threat would not arouse an apprehension that violence is imminent, but some threats obviously may. There is no good reason for requiring a menacing gesture, if the words themselves are such as to arouse immediate apprehension.

Take again the case of the highwayman. Suppose that the highwayman is well known for his evil deeds, and that he stands in the road before a coach of people, saying laconically "Your money or your life," but not troubling to pull out one of the weapons with which he bristles, because he is confident that his threat will exact compliance. There is no solid reason for doubting that this is a psychic

---

[44] *Read v. Coker* (1853) 138 E.R. 1437; (threat, accompanied by conduct, to break the other's neck if he did not leave the premises); *Logdon v. D.P.P.* [1976] Crim. L.R. 121; *Rozsa v. Samuels* [1969] S.A.S.R. 205. Cf. *Genner v. Sparkes* (1704) 91 E.R. 74. V came lawfully to arrest D; D kept him off by holding up a farm fork and retreating. The court said, *obiter*, that D's act was an assault. V had a right to advance, and D prevented him from doing so. The act of holding up the fork was in effect a conditional threat. See also Glanville Williams, "Assault and Words," [1957] Crim. L.R. 216 at 222-223; *Police v. Greaves* [1964] N.Z.L.R. 295. *Contra, Blake v. Barnard* (1840) 173 E.R. 985, where a quite inadequate direction to the jury is attributed to Lord Abinger by notoriously unreliable reporters.

[45] The court inclined to this view (without deciding it) in *R. v. Springfield* (1969) 53 Cr. App. R. 608 at 612.

assault, and the conclusion is supported by medieval and later authorities.[46] (In any case, the highwayman could be guilty of a false imprisonment, an attempted robbery, and blackmail.)

Another line of argument leads to the same conclusion, in the civil case of *Read v. Coker*,[47] D collected some men who mustered around V, tucking up their sleeves and threatening to "break his neck" if he did not leave the premises. V left, and successfully sued D for assault. In essence the assault was by words. There was, in a sense, some conduct in addition on the part of D and his men, for they tucked up their sleeves. But when a number of men propose to eject a single person from premises, it is not at all necessary that they should first tuck up their sleeves. This is merely a conventional way of conveying a threat, an alternative to words as a mode of expressing an intention. Symbolical gestures of this kind are logically the same as the utterance of words, for words are symbols. There would be no sense in attaching legal significance to the one that is not attached to the other.

It is now beyond dispute that mere words are sufficient. If implying a threat by making a silent telephone call is sufficient, then *a fortiori* threats expressed in words are sufficient. In *R. v. Constanza*,[48] one of the submissions was that an assault could not be committed by words alone. The Court of Appeal said:

> "We reject that submission. What is important for the prosecution to prove is that the fear was there in the complainant's mind. How it got there, whether by seeing an action or hearing a threat and whether that threat was conveyed verbally through words spoken either directly in the presence of the complainant or over the telephone or whether the fear was aroused through something written whether it be a letter or a fax seems to us wholly irrelevant."

9–012   **What of a threat by e-mail sent from a smartphone?** This would normally lack the immediacy necessary for an assault. Besides, the assaults punished in the past have always involved personal presence; they have been what Roman lawyers called *corpore corpori* (by body to a body). It is inconceivable that an isolated threat by letter, for instance, could be an assault; and the same should apply to a threat by e-mail. But an e-mail sent from an i-Phone normally informs the receiver that it has been sent from an i-Phone, so the receiver might believe that the sender is at his front door and is ready to strike. As we have seen, cases may arise in which the courts may be willing to find an assault. But the prosecution would have to demonstrate that the victim feared the unlawful force would be applied in the immediate future. If D e-mails/texts/telephones V and says threateningly: "Get out of your house this moment: a bomb is due to go off in 30 minutes," the threat might have the same psychological effect as if made by one who is present. All the same, it should not be regarded as an assault, because that would be getting too far away from the common understanding of the word. Conduct of this kind should be punished as a threat to kill or as a misuse of telecommunications.[49]

---

[46] Cf. *R. v. Wilson* [1955] 1 W.L.R. 493 at 494.

[47] (1853) 138 E.R. 1437.

[48] [1997] 2 Cr. App. R. 492 at 495 *per* Schiemann L.J. See also *R. v. Ireland* [1998] A.C. 147 at 166H.

[49] See section 16 of the *Offences against the Person Act 1861*; section 127 of the *Communications Act 2003*. If the threat results from a course of conduct, it would be caught by section 4 of the *Protection from Harassment Act 1997*.

9.3. THE REQUIREMENT OF FORCE

It was said at the beginning that a physical assault requires some degree of **9–013** "force" applied against the body of the victim. So poisoning a man's coffee, whereby he becomes ill, is not a physical assault (battery).[50] It is, as we shall see, a statutory crime.[51] Again, merely pulling away from one who seeks to arrest you is not a physical assault—even though the arrest is lawful.[52] It is the distinct offence of escape, assuming of course that the arrest has been properly effected and is lawful.[53] Pulling an article from another's grasp is not an assault, even though it is with intent to steal.[54] But to push or strike the victim would be; and it seems clear that even a pulling of an article would be an assault if this is known to involve injury or pain to the victim, as where an ear-ring is ripped from the lobe of the ear.[55]

As said before, the "force" used in a physical assault may be very slight. Unlawful touching is enough. According to an ancient maxim, the law does not take trifles (*de minimis non curat lex*), but this is a very misleading generalization. If the physical assault is trivial the court may grant an absolute discharge,[56] but, even so, the fact that an assault has been committed can have importance. It gives the person assaulted the right to act in reasonable self-defence, and where the assault is by a policeman it means that defensive force used to repeal the assault is not an assault upon the officer in the execution of his duty—either because the defensive force is reasonable and lawful, or, in any case, because the officer is not acting in the execution of his duty when the force is used.

"Ordinary social contact" (tapping a person on the shoulder to attract his attention) is not an assault.[57] The rule may be based on the necessities of social intercourse. The exemption applies only to non-hostile acts, for, in the words of Holt C.J., "the least touching of another in anger is a battery."[58]

---

[50] *R. v. Hanson* (1849) 175 E.R. 383; *R. v. Walkden* (1845) 1 Cox C.C. 282.

[51] See sections 23 and 24 of the *Offences against the Person Act 1861*.

[52] *R. v. Sherriff* [1969] Crim. L.R. 260.

[53] *R. v. Iqbal* [2011] 1 Cr. App. R. 317, where it was held: "The common law offence of escape from custody did not cover those who escaped from police restraint or control before they had been arrested and the ambit of this criminal offence could not be widened by making it apply to those whose arrest had been deliberately postponed."

[54] *Ansell v. Thomas* [1974] Crim. L.R. 31.

[55] *R. v. Lapier* (1784) 168 E.R. 263. Some U.S. courts have been less indulgent. In *State v. Ortega*, 113 N.M. 437 (1992), it was held that the act of knocking a torch from a policeman's hand constituted a battery. See also *Watson v. U.S.*, 979 A.2d 1254 (2009), where D snatched a mobile telephone from V. If the snatching is done in a threatening manner, it could also involve a psychic assault.

[56] Section 44 of the *Offences against the Person Act 1861* gives magistrates the power to draw up a certificate of dismissal if the assault was so trifling as not to merit punishment. This power can now be regarded as an instance of the general power to grant a discharge, except that it has the peculiar property of barring a civil action.

[57] *Coward v. Baddeley* (1859) 157 E.R. 927; *Collins v. Wilcock* [1984] 1 W.L.R. 1172.

[58] *Cole v. Turner* (1704) 90 E.R. 958. The *dictum* does not mean that anger is required. See also *Wilson v. Pringle* [1987] Q.B. 237.

9–014 **Is it a physical assault if a policeman puts his hand on my arm and says he wants to speak to me?** On principle, yes. The police have no general power to detain people for questioning, even those who are strongly suspected of crime. The police may of course ask people questions, just as you or I can, but they cannot require them to stop to be questioned.[59] If the person accosted is willing to answer questions, he can be spoken to without the necessity to lay hands upon him. If he is unwilling, the officer's laying a hand upon him in order to make him stop and listen should be accounted an assault.

However, there are indications that the courts are in the process of changing the rule to a rule more favourable to the police.[60] Undoubtedly the police still lack power to detain anyone for questioning (apart from the law of arrest and certain powers of search);[61] yet it has been held that a police officer commits no assault if he taps a pedestrian repeatedly on the shoulder after the person so accosted has expressed an objection to speaking to the officer.[62] The point is important if the person accosted strikes the officer in order to prevent him continuing his unwelcome attentions. In the case just referred to the person accosted was held to have no right of self-defence, because in law he had not been accosted.

The court did not make it clear why the officer was not regarded as committing an assault. It did not use the phrase "social contact," but something like that concept would seem to have been the officer's only defence.[63] Nevertheless, it is extremely dubious whether an officious tapping on the shoulder by a person invested with the authority of a police officer can properly be so characterized. Perhaps a better way of deciding the case would have been to say that the officer was behaving (or proposing to behave) unlawfully, but that the use of anything but the gentlest force by way of defence was unreasonable when the apprehended assault was so trivial. Even so, a trivial bodily interference constantly repeated can be very irritating. If the citizen is not allowed to reply to it with some force, and if in addition he is held not even to have been assaulted

---

[59] *Rice v. Connolly* [1966] 2 Q.B. 414; *Kenlin v. Gardiner* [1967] 2 Q.B. 510; *Ansell v. Swift* [1987] Crim. L.R. 194; *Collins v. Wilcock* [1984] 1 W.L.R. 1172; *Cumberbatch v. Crown Prosecution Service* (2010) 174 J.P. 149.

[60] Cf. *McMillan v. Crown Prosecution Service* (2008) 172 J.P. 485; *Weight v. Long* [1986] Crim. L.R. 746.

[61] *R. v. Faraj* [2007] 2 Cr. App. R. 25. See also *Gillan v. United Kingdom* (2010) 28 B.H.R.C. 420. The powers in section 60 of the *Criminal Justice and Public Order Act 1994* and section 1 of the *Police and Criminal Evidence Act 1984* are not general powers.

[62] *Donnelly v. Jackman* [1970] 1 W.L.R. 562; cf. *Ludlow v. Burgess* (1982) 75 Cr. App. R. 227; *Wood v. D.P.P.* [2008] EWHC 1056.

[63] In *McMillan v. Crown Prosecution Service* (2008) 172 J.P. 485 a police officer took intoxicated M by the arm and led her from her daughter's garden without arresting her. The Divisional Court held that this did not go "beyond the generally acceptable conduct of touching a person to engage their attention." The special facts of the case seemed to sway the court: McMillan was intoxicated and on *steep steps* and could have fallen. However, this surely did not give the officer the right to lead her any further than the foot of the steps. If the police officer had grabbed intoxicated McMillan to stop her from walking into the path of a car, then clearly his doing the right thing (acting as a matter of necessity to save her from certain harm) would not have made him liable for assault. See *Coward v. Baddeley* (1859) 157 E.R. 927. See also *Semple v. D.P.P.* [2010] 2 All E.R. 353, where the police were acting within the terms of section 143(4) of the *Licensing Act 2003*, when they used reasonable force to remove an intoxicated person from licensed premises.

(so as to have a remedy in the courts on that account), his right to freedom from physical interference by the police will lack effective sanction.

Must the attack be on the body? What about an attack on the clothes a person is wearing?   An attack upon clothes is certainly an assault if it causes the victim to feel pain, or apprehension in respect of his own safety.[64] The better view is that it is an assault in any event, since clothes are so intimately connected with the wearer that offensive conduct against them is likely to be taken as an affront to the wearer.[65] The basis of the crime of assault is the desire of the law to preserve the peace.

9–015

Must the force be applied directly? What of the practical joker who balances a pail of water on a half-opened door? Or the reckless driver who strikes his passenger with a parked car?   The old law was that the force had to be applied "directly" (without intervening causation), and this is still so as far as autonomous intervening agents are concerned. More generally, the courts have accepted that people can use many means to directly harm others.

9–016

The offence of assault at common law derived from the old writ of trespass, which has also given us the tort of assault. In general, an injury had to be direct and forcible before it (or the threat of it) came within the writ of trespass. Some slight degree of delayed or indirect action is tolerated. A physical assault is held to be committed if the defendant sets a dog on a person,[66] or strikes a horse to make it throw its rider,[67] or throws over a chair in which another person is sitting.[68] But, according to the old authorities, it is not a trespass, and so not an assault, to erect an obstruction that causes another person to fall, since here the injury is too "indirect" to come within the crime.[69] The standard illustration was as follows: if a person throws a log of wood out of his window, and hits a passer-by, this is a trespass, and an assault; but if the log falls on the highway and a passer-by trips over it, it is not.[70] It made no difference that throwing the log on to the highway involved the use of force; the force was not direct. In general this is still true, unless the facts are such that the defendant intended or was reckless as to whether it would physically strike his victim. But, if a person merely stands stock still, being "entirely passive like a door or a wall" as it was put in one case, it is not an assault, however inconvenient his presence at the particular spot may have been;[71] but it is a false imprisonment if the victim does not know that another exit exists.

The old law held that it cannot be an assault to engineer a downfall of another by making use of his momentum. When a person trips over a log of wood on the

[64] *The Queen v. Day* (1845) 1 Cox. C.C. 207; *R. v. Thomas* (1985) 81 Cr. App. R. 331; *R. v. H* [2005] 1 W.L.R. 2005.
[65] It has been held that a tightly held purse was an object that had such an intimate connection with the person as to be regarded as a part or extension of the person. *Nash v. State*, 766 So. 2d 310 (2000).
[66] *Murgatroyd v. Chief Constable of West Yorkshire Police* [2000] All E.R. (D) 1742; *J. A. T. v. State*, 133 Ga.App. 922 (1975). Cf. *R. v. Dixon* [1993] Crim. L.R. 579.
[67] *Dodwell v. Burford* (1670) 86 E.R. 703.
[68] *Hopper v. Reeve* (1817) 129 E.R. 278 *per* Gibbs C.J.
[69] *Innes v. Wylie* (1844) 174 E.R. 800.
[70] *Scott v. Shepherd* (1773) 96 E.R. 525.
[71] *Innes v. Wylie* (1844) 174 E.R. 800 at 803 *per* Denman C.J.

highway, his momentum causes him to fall, yet it is not an assault—not even if the injury was intended. Logically, therefore, it could not be an assault to cause injury by breaking ice just in front of a skater,[72] or by stretching a wire to bring off a motor-cyclist, or by taking up the rails before an approaching train;[73] still less in your hypothetical of driving into a parked car. When the victim sees the danger ahead he may be very frightened, but is not psychically assaulted; and when the danger materializes he is not, on historical principles, physically assaulted.

9–017   Some of these acts amount to other offences such as wilful obstruction of the highway,[74] a railway offence,[75] or careless driving.[76] If grievous bodily harm is caused it is an offence under section 18 of the *Offences against the Person Act 1861*. But the sousing of the skater is no offence if it is held not to be a battery and if the harm suffered is not serious. If the skater case comes before the courts the judge will undoubtedly be strongly inclined to extend the law of assault. Judges do not like letting mischief-makers go scot free.

The weight of authority now holds that indirect causation is sufficient for grounding a conviction for physical assault. Two members of the court in *R. v. Clarence*[77] thought that a physical assault would be committed by a "man who digs a pit for another to fall into, whereby that other is injured," and one of these two thought that there was also an assault on the facts of *R. v. Martin*,[78] to be considered presently.[79] Moreover, it seems that under the present law an assault can be committed by applying light, heat, electricity, gas, or odour to the victim, in uncomfortable quantities.[80] The force might also be applied directly by using an innocent agent. If D grabs V1's fist and rams it into V2's face, he should be liable for battery against both V1 and V2.[81]

In your hypothetical booby-trap involving the bucket of water on the door, the traditionalists would see the victim's act in opening the door as a direct cause of his wetting, not the setting of the trap by the practical joker; but since the victim acted without knowing the circumstances and without foreseeing the consequence, the person who set the trap should be regarded as having applied the

---

[72] *Contra*, J. W. C. Turner, *Kenny's Outlines of Criminal Law*, (Cambridge: Cambridge University Press, 18th edn. 1926) at 209.

[73] *Contra*, *R. v. Jolly* [1923] A.D. 176 (South Africa).

[74] Section 137 of the *Highways Act 1980*. See also section 21 of the *Town Police Clauses Act 1847*.

[75] Section 32 of the *Offences against the Person Act 1861*.

[76] See section 3 of the *Road Traffic Act 1988*.

[77] (1888) 22 Q.B.D. 23 at 36, 45 (Wills and Stephen J.J.).

[78] (1881-82) 8 Q. B. D. 54.

[79] In *Fagan v Commissioner of Police of the Metropolis* [1969] 1 Q.B. 439 at 444D a [psychic] assault was defined as "any act which intentionally—or possibly recklessly—causes another to apprehend immediate and unlawful personal violence." Perhaps the concept "immediate" was meant to carry the sense of "directness;" in any case the violence before the court in *Fagan* was direct.

[80] See J. W. C. Turner, *Russell on Crime*, (London: Stevens & Sons, 12th edn. 1964) at 652–653.

[81] See *Short v. Lovejoy* (1752) Bull. N.P. 16 *coram* Lee C.J., where D pushed an intoxicated man (an innocent agent) against V. See further Isaac 'Espinasse, *A Digest of the Law of Actions and Trials at Nisi Prius*, (Dublin: printed for E. Lynch *et al.*, 2nd edn. 1794) at 313.

force directly. The booby trap is the "means" used to directly inflict the injury. Such an approach was adopted by a Divisional Court in *D.P.P. v. K.*[82]

In that case, D, a schoolboy aged 15, stole some concentrated sulphuric acid from his school's chemistry laboratory during a lesson. It was contained in a test tube. He took the tube of acid to the lavatory and was messing about with it when he heard footsteps. He panicked and poured the acid into the upturned nozzle of an air hand-*face* drying machine. When the footsteps receded, he returned to his class. He disposed of the test tube on his way back to his lesson. It was argued on his behalf that he intended to return to the lavatory to clean the acid out of the hand-face dryer. However, before he cleaned the dyer another pupil went to the lavatory to wash his hands. When the pupil turned on the dryer acid was sprayed into his face, leaving a permanent scar. The defendant was charged with assault occasioning actual bodily harm contrary to section 47 of the *Offences against the Persons Act 1861*.

9–018

The Divisional Court held that: "it was clear that D knew full well that he had created a dangerous situation and the inescapable inference was that he decided to take the risk of someone using the machine before he could get back and render it harmless or gave no thought to that risk."[83]

Parker L.J. concluded:[84]

> "A defendant, who pours a dangerous substance into a machine, just as truly assaults the next user of the machine as if he had himself switched the machine on. So, too, in my judgment would he be guilty of an assault if he was guilty of relevant recklessness."

Does that mean that a person who accidentally creates a booby trap has a duty to warn others of its potential dangerousness? He does if it poses a present threat to another person and he is capable of providing a warning. An omission to take reasonable steps to prevent the booby trap from harming another could constitute a physical assault. If a person inadvertently creates a booby trap or some other dangerous situation, he has a duty to take reasonable steps to ensure that others are not harmed by it.[85]

9–019

In *D.P.P. v. Santa-Bermudez*, V and other police officers had been called to Stockwell Underground Station where ticket touts were operating. The victim was in full uniform when she saw D by the ticket machines and apparently acting as a tout. V approached D and asked him to accompany her to the station

---

[82] [1990] 1 W.L.R. 1067. See also *R. v. Roberts* (1972) 56 Cr. App. R. 95; *R. v. Halliday* (1889) 54 J.P. 312; *Haystead v. Chief Constable of Derbyshire* [2000] 2 Cr. App. R. 339; *Scott v. Shepherd* (1773) 96 E.R. 525; *Com. v. Parker*, 522 N.E.2d 2 (1988); *Com. v. Bianco*, 388 Mass. 358 (1983); *Clark v. State*, 783 So. 2d 967 (2001). The same might be held for the case of the *crashing driver*. Here, D imparts momentum to V's body without an assault, and then suddenly and purposely causes P to collide with something, or to fear he will do so. An example would be where V is D's passenger in a car, and D deliberately collides with a building, or causes V to fear that a collision is imminent. See *People v. Moore*, 3 N.Y.S. 159 (1888).

[83] *D.P.P. v. K* [1990] 1 W.L.R. 1067 at 1071.

[84] *D.P.P. v. K* [1990] 1 W.L.R. 1067 at 1071 quoting *R. v. Clarence* (1888) 22 Q.B.D. 23 at 45, where Stephen J. held: "If a man laid a trap for another into which he fell after an interval the man who laid it would during the interval be guilty of an attempt to assault and of an actual assault as soon as the man fell in."

[85] See *D.P.P. v. Santa-Bermudez* (2004) 168 J.P. 373.

supervisor's office. V informed D that she intended to carry out a full body search.[86] V asked D to turn out all his pockets and to place the contents on a table. D emptied all his pockets with the exception of two small breast pockets at the top of his jacket. The linings of these pockets could not be pulled out. D was asked whether there were any sharp items in these pockets. He replied: "No". The officer searched the pockets by running her fingers through them. When she withdrew her fingers from the pocket she saw that her middle finger had been pierced by a hypodermic needle which was still inserted in her fingertip.

The Divisional Court held him liable, because he failed to disclose the details of the danger that lurked in his pocket. He may have accidentally created the dangerous situation, but he knew full well that it existed. Consequently, he could have discharged his duty by removing the needles himself or by warning the officer. If a police officer pricks herself on a needle while searching an unconscious person's pocket to ascertain his identity, the unconscious person is not liable for assault since he is not capable of taking reasonable steps to disclose the danger. If the dangerous situation causes V to suffer a.b.h. or g.b.h., then D may be liable under section 20 or 47 of the *Offences against the Person Act 1861.*[87]

9–020   You will recall Mr. Miller.[88] He accidentally started a fire and was liable because he failed to summon help after he became aware that he had set harm in motion. He had a duty to summon help to try to counter the harm his accident was causing. Miller was charged with arson, contrary to section 1(1) and (3) of the *Criminal Damage Act 1971*, since his omission did not kill or harm any *person*. Nevertheless, if Miller had seen a fellow homeless person sleeping soundly in the next room of the burning house, he would have had a duty to wake him and warn him that he was in danger of being burnt. Similarly, if Miller had seen a person trapped within the burning building he would have a duty to try to either rescue that person himself (if physically possible) or to summon help in a timely manner. In such a situation, the author of the dangerous situation has a duty to act. That duty might be fulfilled by summoning help or by warning others about the danger. It does not matter that he did not intend to create a dangerous situation (booby trap and so on). If Miller had failed to warn a sleeping person about the ensuring fire (assuming he had a fair opportunity to do so), he could have been liable for any harm caused by that omission. If his omission had resulted in the sleeping person being killed, then he could have been held liable for manslaughter.[89] If his omission had caused the sleeping person to suffer actual

---

[86] In accordance with section 1 of the *Police and Criminal Evidence Act 1984*.

[87] Santa-Bermudez's blood, when tested, proved positive for HIV and Hepatitis C. If he had caused the officer to be infected with these diseases, then he would have been responsible for causing her to suffer grievous bodily harm. See *R. v. Dica* [2005] EWCA Crim. 2304; *R. v. Konzani* [2005] 2 Cr. App. R. 141; *R. v. B* [2007] 1 W.L.R. 1567. See also *Houghton v. Western Australia* [2006] 163 A. Crim. R. 226; *R. v. Mwai* [1995] 3 N.Z.L.R. 149; *State v. Gonzalez*, 796 N.E.2d 12 (2003); *State v. Elliott*, 663 N.E.2d 412 (1995).

[88] *R. v. Miller* [1983] 2 A.C. 161.

[89] *R. v. Evans* [2010] 1 All E.R. 13. However, in *R. v. Evans* the Court of Appeal went too far in holding that a person can be liable for merely "facilitating" another to create a dangerous situation for herself. For a critique, see Dennis J. Baker, "Omissions Liability for Homicide Offences: Reconciling *R. v. Kennedy* with *R. v. Evans*," (2010) 74 *J. Crim. L.* 310 (2010).

bodily harm (perhaps mild burns or mild smoke inhalation)[90] or grievous bodily harm (severe burns of a permanent nature), then he could have been convicted of an offence contrary to either section 47 or 20 of the *Offences against the Person Act 1861*. These offences will be discussed shortly.

9.4.   THE PLACE OF ASSAULT IN THE LAW

Psychic assault is the only crime in which the evil of the act consists merely in creating fear or apprehension in the mind of the victim. Historically speaking, the object of the law, in giving a remedy for this wrong, is to offer the victim some means of vindicating his own dignity and security without recourse to fighting. But nowadays the police rarely prosecute for psychic assault, or even for physical assault if no great harm is done. They take assaults as being of everyday occurrence, and cannot be bothered with them.

9–021

The police are most likely to make a charge for assaults occurring in a public place, but even then the charge is generally for insulting behaviour rather than for assault.[91] The victim may bring a private prosecution, but probably the assaulter will only be bound over to keep the peace; and if the victim contributed in any way to the affair (as he often has) he will be lucky not to be bound over too. However, the law retains some importance because the notion of assault enters into the law of tort and also into some of the more serious criminal offences.

The dismissive attitude of the police towards complaints of assault results in part from the dismissive attitudes of magistrates. A charge of assault can only be tried summarily,[92] and many courts are pretty lenient. An unprovoked attack with heavy blows to the face, perhaps breaking the victim's nose, is frequently followed by a fine—not a high price to pay for the satisfaction of giving vent to aggressive feelings. Another common outcome is an order binding the defendant over. Regarding small cases as a waste of time, the chairman or clerk to the magistrates may warn both parties of such a possible outcome in order to promote the withdrawal of the proceedings. When the assault is by a person of substance the aggrieved party may be better advised to sue in a civil court and obtain damages, which may well be considerable, and will have the added attraction of going into his own pocket.[93]

---

[90] It has been held (in a civil case in the U.S.) that blowing cigar smoke into another's face constitutes a battery. *Leichtman v. WLW Jacor Communications, Inc.*, 634 N.E.2d 697 (1994). Severe smoke inhalation would result in at least actual bodily harm if not grievous bodily harm.

[91] Sections 4–5 of the *Public Order Act 1986*.

[92] Section 39 of the *Criminal Justice Act 1988*. But aggravated forms of assault can be tried on indictment in the Crown Court.

[93] In *Reynolds v. Comr. of Police*, (*The Times*, 21 May 1982), where the plaintiff was unlawfully arrested and detained at a police station for one day, the jury were upheld in awarding £12,000 damages for false imprisonment.

9–022   Before we consider the individual offences, it is worth considering the overall scheme that is provided by sections 18, 20 and 47 of the *Offences against the Person Act 1861*. Those offences focus on the harm caused rather than on the way it was caused. The offences grade harm according to its gravity and type. The two grades of harm are grievous bodily harm (the most serious form of harm) and actual bodily harm. Harm that is below actual bodily harm will be caught by the offence of common assault. As for the type of harm, sections 18 and 20 single out "wounding" as a special type of harm that warrants criminalization. Nevertheless, it would be better just to focus on the gravity of the harm rather than on the type of injury it has caused. Any reform in this area should merely refer to harm according to its gravity. The law has evolved in this area so as not to try to list all the ways in which harm can be caused or inflicted. It would be pointless to list every possibility such as D caused g.b.h. by throwing a beer bottle at V's head, *etc.*[94] Wounding itself could constitute grievous bodily harm, but it may also constitute something less. The wrongness of harms against the persons can be measured by positioning two ladders side by side. The ladders are the "harm ladder" and the "culpability ladder."[95] A serious wrong will involve harm and culpability that will sit at the top of the "crime seriousness ladder."

CRIME SERIOUSNESS LADDER

HARM	*CULPABILITY*
1. Grievous Bodily Harm (serious harm) • (Covered by 18 and 20)	1. Intention (Section 18)
2. Actual bodily harm (not as serious harm) • (Covered by section 47)	2. Intention and Recklessness (Section 20)
3. Minor harm (not serious) • (Section 39 of the *Criminal Justice Act 1988*)	3. Intentionally or recklessly committing common assault is sufficient *mens rea* for section 47

A given harm may very well fall between two rungs on the metaphoric ladder. There are many variables that need to be considered to determine how to categorize a particular harm.[96] As we will see, grading harm is not an exact science. If an offence clearly states that the offender is liable if he intends to bring about a particular level of harm, then he should not be held liable for accidentally bringing about greater harm than he intended. Similarly, if the offence clearly

---

[94] Cf. the *1997 Criminal Code of the People's Republic of China.*

[95] For a good discussion of some of the problems in lining up the ladders, see Sir Anthony Bottoms, "Five Puzzles in von Hirsch's Theory of Punishment," in Andrew Ashworth and Martin Wasik (ed.), *Fundamentals of Sentencing Theory: Essays in Honour of Andrew von Hirsch*, (Oxford: Clarendon Press, 1998) at 53 *et seq.*

[96] Elsewhere, I argue that there are about ten core grades of harm. See Dennis J. Baker, "Constitutionalizing the Harm Principle," (2008) 27 *Crim. Just. Ethics* 3 at 17. See also Glanville Williams, "Force, Injury and Serious Injury," (1990) 140 *N.L.J.* 1227.

states that the offender should be reckless as to a particular level of harm, he should not be held liable if he was merely reckless as to some lesser harm. His culpability should correspond with the relevant harm on the seriousness ladder, unless the wording of the offence makes it clear that something less will do. As we will see, constructive liability means that the offender's culpability need not relate to the harm that he is held responsible for causing. Constructive liability distorts the seriousness ladder, as it allows the courts to focus purely on the "harm ladder." When the courts hold a person constructively liable, they ignore the culpability ladder. This basically involves the courts holding the offender strictly liable for any harm that he has caused, regardless of whether he intended to cause that level of harm or foresaw that it would result.

The crimes that we are to consider in the following sections are the major offences under section 18 of the *Offences against the Person Act 1861* and the medium offences under sections 20 and 47, together with some miscellaneous offences against the person.

A rational legal system probably grades attacks upon the person (not resulting in **9–023** death) in three categories. At the low order of gravity there would be assaults in which bodily harm is not an element; these were considered in the last section. At the other extreme there would be the crime of intentionally (or recklessly) causing serious injury. In between there would be attacks of medium gravity, where bodily harm (not necessarily serious) is caused intentionally or recklessly.

The *Act of 1861* establishes something like the last two classes, but the crimes of medium gravity are expressed in language of unnecessary complexity. The luxuriant growth of decided cases on the *Act* makes it impossible to state the law in a clear and satisfactory way. Simplification has been recommended by the Criminal Law Revision Committee,[97] but at the time of writing there is no sign of legislation.

Section 18, as amended,[98] runs essentially as follows:

> "Whosoever shall unlawfully and maliciously by any means whatsoever wound or cause[99] any grievous bodily harm to any person, with intent, to do some grievous bodily harm to any person, or with intent to resist or prevent the lawful apprehension or detainer of any person, shall be ... liable to be kept in penal servitude for life".

This section has two conduct elements, either of which can be committed with **9–024** any of three intents. Separating them out, they may be as follows:

1.   Unlawfully and maliciously wounding any person:
       i.   with an ulterior intent to do g.b.h. to any person, or
      ii.   with an ulterior intent to resist the lawful[100] apprehension of any person, or

---

[97] Criminal Law Revision Committee, *Offences Against the Person*, Fourteenth Report, (London: H.M.S.O., Cmnd. 7844, 1980) at paras. 149–157.

[98] By the *Criminal Law Act 1967*, Sched. 3 Pt. III.

[99] The word "cause" probably does not cover causing by omission. *R. v. Brown* [1970] 1 Q.B. 105. On causing otherwise than by assault see *R. v. Clarence* (1888) 22 Q.B.D. 23 at 36.

[100] In order for the defendant to be guilty of an intent to resist or prevent lawful apprehension the arrest must be authorized by law. If it is illegal, the defendant is not guilty under section 18 merely

    iii.   with an ulterior intent to prevent the lawful apprehension of any person.

2.   Unlawfully and maliciously causing any g.b.h. to any person:

    i.   with intent to cause it to any person, or

    ii.   with an ulterior intent to resist the lawful apprehension of any person, or

    iii.   with an ulterior intent to prevent the lawful apprehension of any person.

The section is compendiously referred to in legal discussions as creating the crime of "wounding with intent," but this is only half of it, since causing grievous bodily harm with intent is an alternative. The abbreviation "g.b.h." is frequently used in conversation, though not in court.

9–025   **What is a "wounding"?** For a "wounding" the skin must be broken (the dermis as well as the epidermis),[101] and this need not amount to a grievous bodily harm. A scratch is not a wound;[102] nor is an internal rupture. Generally, grievous bodily harm involves a wound, but it need not always do so—for example, where the skin is extensively bruised or burned, or a bone is broken.

9–026   **Is not a wounding merely a type of grievous bodily harm?** Not always. The wounding might be too minor to even count as actual bodily harm.

9–027   **Well answer me this, does that mean that section 18 applies only to a wounding that is so serious that it *per se* constitutes grievous bodily harm?** My dear imaginary interlocutor, you are making too much sense. A wound is a wound regardless of its gravity. However, in practice the prosecutor is not likely to charge a defendant under section 18 unless the wound constitutes grievous bodily harm. So the prosecutor has all the say once again.

9–028   **Has "grievous bodily harm" a fixed meaning?** The phrase means "really serious harm"[103]—a matter for the jury to decide.[104] The equiparation was established in the House of Lords in *D.P.P. v. Smith*,[105] the well-known case on

---

because of his intent to frustrate the arrest. (He will, however, be guilty under this section if his intent was to do grievous bodily harm.) Whether the arrest is illegal or not will depend upon the common law or statutory powers of arrest.

[101] *JJC (a Minor) v. Eisenhower* [1984] Q.B. 331. See also *R. v. M'Loughlin* (1838) 8 C. & P. 635; *R. v. Waltham* (1849) 13 J.P. 183.

[102] *R. v. Morris* [2005] EWCA Crim. 609.

[103] In *R. v. Saunders* [1985] Crim. L.R. 230, it was held that a jury direction omitting the "word 'really' before 'serious injury' made no difference at all in this case, since a broken nose on any view was really serious bodily harm." See also *R. v. Janjua* [1999] 1 Cr. App. R. 91.

[104] The jury determine the conduct's harmfulness by judging it "objectively according to ordinary standards of usage and experience and on all the evidence, not subjectively from the standpoint of the victim." *R. v. Brown* [1998] Crim. L.R. 485 at 486.

[105] [1961] A.C. 290 at 333–335.

murder, and has been followed for the offence under section 18.[106] The lack of any clear definition leads to the possibility that different juries may apply different tests.

Bodily, used singly, means pertaining to the body; but does the body include the mind? In *R. v. Chan-Fook*[107] Hobhouse L.J. said: "The body of the victim includes all parts of his body, including his organs, his nervous system and his brain. Bodily injury therefore may include injury to any of those parts of his body responsible for his mental and other faculties." This line of reasoning is perfectly reasonable. A person might be harmed less by having to have an orthopaedic cast put on her arm, than if she were to be hospitalized for mental illness. A loss of normal mental functioning might incapacitate the victim in a serious way. A psychological injury that does not involve a "recognized psychiatric illness" will not be treated as grievous bodily harm.[108] The mental illness must also be serious if it is to be treated as grievous bodily harm. It should be regarded as serious if the victim requires prolonged psychiatric treatment or loses the capacity to live a normal life for any length of time. If the victim is hospitalized for a month because of mental illness, then clearly she loses her capacity to live a normal life for a month. Let us assume that the victim is a law student. Would her life be set back more by having two legs in orthopaedic casts for three months or by being mentally incapacitated for three months? The broken legs would not stop her from getting on with her studies and social life, but a serious psychiatric injury could.

Harm has many forms—it can be economic, psychological or physical. Destroying another's property might cause him economic harm, but it will not necessarily cause him bodily harm. Although burning a person alive in his own home would have the effect of achieving both. In the context of offences against the person, we are focusing on damage or harm to the body of a human being. A person might not only suffer harm from having her leg blown off, but also from being terrorized in the middle of the night by silent telephone calls. Regardless of whether the harm caused is psychological or physical, it must be serious if it is to fall within the concept of grievous bodily harm.

How do we measure its seriousness?   The best we can do is to provide some   **9–029**
rough criteria. For example, R.C. § 2901.01(5) of the *Ohio Penal Code* defines serious harm as follows:[109]

> "Serious physical harm to persons means any of the following:
> (a)   Any mental illness or condition of such gravity as would normally require hospitalization or prolonged psychiatric treatment;
> (b)   Any physical harm that carries a substantial risk of death;
> (c)   Any physical harm that involves some permanent incapacity, whether partial or total, or that involves some temporary, substantial incapacity;

---

[106] *R. v. Metharam* (1961) 45 Cr. App. R. 304.

[107] [1994] 1 W.L.R. 689 at 695. Approved by *R. v. Ireland* [1998] A.C. 147. See also, *McLoughlin v. O'Brian* [1983] 1 A.C. 410 at 418.

[108] Nor will it constitute actual bodily harm. *R. v. Dhaliwal* [2006] 2 Cr. App. R. 348. Cf. *R. v. Miller* [1954] 2 Q.B. 282.

[109] See *Baldwin's Ohio Revised Code Annotated*, Title XXIX. Crimes—Procedure: Chapter 2901.

(d)   Any physical harm that involves some permanent disfigurement or that involves some
        temporary, serious disfigurement;

(e)   Any physical harm that involves acute pain of such duration as to result in substantial
        suffering or that involves any degree of prolonged or intractable pain."

The definition is helpful for distinguishing non-serious mental illness from a serious mental illness. Even if a psychiatrist is able to cure the victim in weeks, her mental illness should still be classified as grievous bodily harm if it has caused her to lose the capacity to live a normal life during that time. (As would be the case if she had been forced to live in a mental hospital.)

It seems perfectly fair to look at the aggregate and long-term accumulative effect of the harm as well. If a number of injuries aggregate to leave a victim in a serious condition, then courts will most likely treat it as g.b.h.[110] Where D has caused V to suffer a long-term illness, the seriousness of V's injury should be assessed by considering the accumulative impact of that illness. If D has infected V with a debilitating disease that requires long-term treatment, it is neither here nor there that it does not cause V substantial suffering in the short-term. The courts have held that infecting a person with H.I.V. causes her grievous bodily harm.[111] A serious temporary incapacity could cover situations where the victim has been left with broken legs or arms, or it might even cover cases where the victim's mental illness is so bad that she requires hospitalization. Broken-bones or severe burns would also be caught, as they would cause substantial suffering. (However, at the lower end of the scale burns and broken bones might be treated as actual bodily harm.) The test of permanent disfigurement is rather wide, as any little wound could leave a permanent scar. It is submitted that the permanent disfigurement should be sufficiently prominent to cause the victim substantial stress. Obviously, if the disfigurement is serious as would be the case where the victim has obvious scars, it should be treated as g.b.h.

9–030   Inflicting a deep wound in the head or trunk is indubitably grievous bodily harm because of the evident danger to life, unless the wound is in some non-vital part such as the ear or shoulder. But the test of danger to life, though a clear positive test of grievous bodily harm, is not a reliable negative one, since (as was held in *D.P.P. v. Smith*) harm can be grievous although it really is not dangerous to life. For example, blinding a person or shooting him in the leg would be really serious harm, though there is no risk of death.

The Crown Prosecution Service provides the following guidance:

"[I]t is for the jury to decide whether the harm is serious. However, examples of what would
usually amount to serious harm include:[112]
•   injury resulting in permanent disability or permanent loss of sensory function;
•   injury which results in more than minor permanent, visible disfigurement;
•   broken or displaced limbs or bones, including fractured skull;

---

[110] *R. v. Bollom* [2004] 2 Cr. App. R. 6; *R. v. Birmingham* [2002] EWCA Crim. 2608 at para. 11; *R. v. Grundy* [1989] Crim. L.R. 502. (The harm should also be measured against the victim's vulnerability. The impact of the harm might be much greater for an infant, disabled victim, or an elderly victim.) Cf. *R. v. Brown* [2005] EWCA Crim. 359, where the harm was delivered over several days.

[111] *R. v. Dica* [2005] EWCA Crim. 2304; *R. v. Konzani* [2005] 2 Cr. App. R. 14; *R. v. B* [2007] 1 W.L.R. 1567.

[112] C.P.S. Charging Standard—Offences Against The Person: *http://www.cps.gov.uk/legal/l_to_o/ offences_against_the_person/#P48_1458.*

- compound fractures, broken cheek bone, jaw, ribs, *etc.*;
- injuries which cause substantial loss of blood, usually necessitating a transfusion;
- injuries resulting in lengthy treatment or incapacity; psychiatric injury.
- As with assault occasioning actual bodily harm, appropriate expert evidence is essential to prove the injury."

The suggestion has been made that juries can utilize the uncertainty of the meaning of "grievous" to regard the harm as grievous or not according to other circumstances, *e.g.*, the degree of provocation if any. They are very likely to do this, and the judge need not stop them by telling them not to. But he is not supposed to encourage them.[113] Provocation (loss of control) is not in theory allowed to be taken into consideration by the jury, because it is feared that this would unduly lengthen trials.

What mental element is required under section 18? A charge of wounding or **9–031**
causing grievous bodily harm with intent to cause g.b.h. clearly requires an actual intention, and not mere knowledge of the possibility of g.b.h.[114] Of course, intent may be inferred from conduct as a matter of fact. The courts are also likely to hold that the doctrine of "oblique intention" applies. If a person realizes that it is for all practical purposes inevitable that his actions will result in grievous bodily harm, then he should be held liable under section 18. If D foresees that it is inevitable (virtually certain) that he will cause his baby grievous bodily harm if he throws it down a flight of stairs, then what is wrong with holding him liable under section 18?[115] Why not charge him with attempted murder? It was argued in (4.3), that oblique intention should be sufficient to support a conviction of criminal attempt, but such a proposition is yet to be tested in the courts. Consequently, the "baby thrower" might be able to evade a conviction for attempted murder by arguing that he was not (directly) intending to kill his baby. He might argue that he was just letting off steam and had no intention whatsoever of killing his child.

This will pose no significant problem for justice if oblique intention is invoked to ground a section 18 conviction, as it carries a life sentence. Of course, section 20 would catch his conduct, but it only carries a 5-year sentence. Such a sentence might not be sufficient, if D has caused grave harm of an irreversible kind. Would five years be enough if the baby has been left a quadriplegic? I would think not. The proposition that oblique intention applies to section 18 seems unassailable, but the question of whether it applies to criminal attempts awaits judicial pronouncement.

It was said before, that a recognized mental illness of a serious nature constitutes grievous bodily harm. This may be true, but in practice it will be difficult to prove, if not impossible, that the defendant intended to send his victim mad. In most cases he will not have such an aim: his aim will be merely to terrorize his victim. It might also be impossible to prove that he obliquely intended to send his victim mad. Therefore, a section 18 conviction is likely to be rare when the grievous bodily harm is mental illness.

---

[113] *R. v. Hamilton* [1980] Crim. L.R. 441.
[114] *R. v. Belfon* [1976] 1 W.L.R. 741.
[115] See the facts in *R. v. Woollin* [1999] 1 A.C. 82.

It is well settled that "malice" in statutes means intention or subjective recklessness.[116] In relation to the intent to do grievous bodily harm the word "recklessness" is surplusage, since the requirement of intent means that recklessness is not enough. But in relation to the intent to resist or prevent apprehension the word has certain effect. Suppose that D, endeavouring to avoid being lawfully arrested by V, knowingly subjects V to a risk of serious injury, and V is in fact wounded or seriously injured.[117] D did not intend V to be injured, but he is guilty under the section because he was malicious (subjectively reckless) as to the injury and he intended to resist a lawful arrest.[118] (He would be guilty under the section even if the arrest that he was trying to prevent was the arrest of someone else.)[119]

9–032　**Need D foresee that his intentional act of preventing or resisting the lawful apprehension of any person *will* result in g.b.h.? Or will foresight of any minor harm do?**　It is submitted that he should be reckless as to g.b.h. It would be wrong for the courts to use both elements of constructive liability and recklessness to ground a conviction for an offence that *prima facie* requires intention.[120] Furthermore, the offence carries a life sentence.

9–033　**Can intention be transferred under the section?**　The wording is clearly designed to allow this. The doctrine of transferred intention applies to crimes at common law, such as murder; but the courts have found difficulty in applying it to the construction of statutes unless the statute is aptly framed. Section 18 is an example of suitable wording. It repeats the phrase "any person" ("whosoever shall … wound or cause any grievous bodily harm to any person, with intent to do some grievous bodily harm to *any* person"—not "*such* person"). The object is to indicate that the intention can be transferred from the intended victim to the actual victim.[121]

---

[116] *R. v. Cunningham* [1957] 2 Q.B. 396; *R. v. G* [2004] 1 A.C. 1034; *R. v. Savage* [1992] 1 A.C. 699. See also *B (A Child) v. DPP* [2000] 2 A.C. 428.

[117] If, however, D intends to inflict g.b.h. with the ulterior intent of preventing the lawful apprehension of any person, his indictment need only refer to his intent to cause g.b.h. See *R. v. Gillow* (1825) 168 E.R. 1195.

[118] *R. v. Morrison* (1989) 89 Cr. App. R. 17; *R. v. Farrell* [1989] Crim. L.R. 376.

[119] If V goes to arrest D1, and D1 and D2 use force to thwart the arrest, it seems that D1 "resists" the arrest and D2 "prevents" it. D1 can also "prevent" his own arrest, it would seem, by rigging up a trap to incapacitate V.

[120] Cf. *R. v. Mowatt* [1968] 1 Q.B. 421.

[121] But it was ruled in *R. v. Monger* [1973] Crim. L.R. 301 that the indictment must be worded appropriately to cover the case. See also *R. v. Hewlett* (1858) 175 E.R. 640; *R. v. Ryan* (1839) 174 E.R. 266. It must charge an intention against V1 and wounding, *etc.*, of V2; see Andrew Ashworth, "Transferred Malice and Punishment for Unforeseen Consequences," in P. R. Glazebrook, *Reshaping the Criminal Law: Essays in Honour of Glanville Williams*, (London: Stevens & Sons, 1978) at 84–85. The doctrine of transferred intent also applies to the offence of battery. Cf. *Mordica v. State*, 618 So. 2d 301 (1993); *People v. Eyman*, 222 Ill. App. 3d 1097 (1991); *Wieland v. State*, 643 A.2d 446 (1994).

9.6. *OFFENCES AGAINST THE PERSON ACT* SECTION 20

The statutory crimes of medium gravity are generally known as "unlawful wounding" and "assault occasioning actual bodily harm." They are created by sections 20 and 47 respectively. The penalty for each is the same—five years' imprisonment.[122]

9–034

Section 20 has two alternative conduct elements: "unlawfully and maliciously *wound[ing] or inflict[ing] any grievous harm upon* any other person." Section 47 penalizes "any assault occasioning actual bodily harm."

The two sections are very similar, and the more one studies them the more similar they seem to become. The most obvious difference is in respect of the outcome of the attack. Section 20 requires a wound or *grievous* bodily harm. Section 47 requires only *actual* bodily harm. Every wound (or almost every wound) must be actual bodily harm, and of course grievous bodily harm is an aggravated form of actual bodily harm. So section 47 is from this point of view the wider section.

What mental element is required under section 20? "Maliciously" in section 20 means, as we already know, that the act must be done intentionally[123] or recklessly, that is to say with foresight of the likelihood or possibility[124] of the consequence; it does not include inadvertent negligence in respect of the consequence. This appears plainly from *R. v. Cunningham*,[125] a case on poisoning, where the Court of Criminal Appeal held that the word "malice" in a penal statute is a term of art meaning:

9–035

> "either (1) An actual intention to do the particular kind of harm that in fact was done; or (2) recklessness as to whether such harm should occur or not (*i.e.* the accused has foreseen that the particular kind of harm might be done and yet has gone on to take the risk of it)."

Incidentally, this much-quoted passage shows that the judges recognize the difference of meaning between "actual intention" and "recklessness," even though the use of the adjective "actual" improperly suggests the possibility of some kind of legal intention that is not actual intention. The definition is also significant in clearly recognizing the subjective meaning of recklessness. The

---

[122] The length of the term is stated in section 1 of the *Penal Servitude Act 1891*. By section 17(2) of the *Firearms Act 1968*, it is an offence punishable with 7 years' imprisonment to be in possession of a firearm or imitation firearm at the time of committing or being arrested for a number of specified offences, including under sections 20 and 47 of the *Offences against the Person Act 1861*. Whereas a charge under section 18 cannot be tried by magistrates, a charge under the other two sections can both be. These two crimes are treated in practice as founding alternative charges, so that if there are counts for both, and the jury convict on one, they should be discharged from giving a verdict on the other: *R. v. Cowdell* [1962] Crim. L.R. 262. (The jury are not directed to *acquit* on the other two counts; it is left alive, so to speak, so that if, on appeal, the verdict on the one count is set aside, the appellate court can substitute a conviction on the other.)

[123] But the implied inclusion of intention in the section adds nothing to it, because of the practice of the courts in the sentencing.

[124] It is enough that D foresaw that the harm *might* result; there is no need to show that he believed it *would* result. *R. v. Rushworth* (1992) 95 Cr. App. R. 252. This is unobjectionable, since the section merely requires subjective risk taking. It does not require oblique intention.

[125] [1957] 2 Q.B. 396 at 399. See also *R. v. Brady* [2006] EWCA Crim. 2413.

House of Lords[126] have confirmed that section 20 requires subjective recklessness. Alas, the Lords also held that constructive fault is sufficient for grounding a section 20 conviction. Hence, to establish an offence under section 20 the prosecution only need prove that "D intended or that he actually foresaw that his act would cause physical harm to some person, albeit that it was harm only of a minor character."[127]

9–036 **So, according to *R. v. Savage*, if a person intends to inflict actual harm and causes grievous harm, when his act was neither intentional nor reckless in respect of grievous harm, he can be convicted under section 20?** That would be the logical consequence of the decision. The courts tend to punish more severely under section 20 for grievous harm than under section 47 for lesser harm, and the logic of the *mens rea* requirement implies that it should govern the *extent* as well as the *existence* of criminal responsibility. A conviction under section 20 would not be possible if the rule in *R. v. Cunningham* were applied, in the absence of intention or recklessness as to grievous bodily harm; and that would be the proper rule.

However, the courts have now veered away from *R. v. Cunningham* on this point. *R. v. Savage*[128] decides that a person may be convicted of maliciously wounding or inflicting grievous bodily harm although he did not intend to inflict such harm and was not reckless as to it—notwithstanding that "maliciously" is supposed to mean "intentionally or recklessly." According to *R. v. Savage*,[129] foresight of some minor physical harm is sufficient. The effect of this decision is to confirm that something less than full *mens rea* is sufficient under section 20. Although the defendant can be punished on the basis of having caused grievous bodily harm, his *mens rea* need only be as to a lesser degree of bodily harm. From this point of view, the offence is what might be categorized as one of incomplete *mens rea*. The Lords admitted that the section requires intention or subjective recklessness as to harm, in accordance with *R. v. Cunningham*, but announced that under section 20 "the particular kind of harm" means any physical harm, not necessarily grievous. So although the *actus reus* involves grievous bodily harm, the *mens rea* may be as to something less: the required *mens rea* does not correspond to the required *actus reus*. The section requires the infliction of the grievous bodily harm, accompanied by intention or subjective recklessness, which according to *R. v. Cunningham* means as to the "particular kind of harm." The particular degree of harm in this context, should surely mean the grievous bodily harm that is mentioned in the section.

In *R. v. Savage* the Lords approved of *R. v. Mowatt*,[130] notwithstanding that the latter decision had been subjected to reasoned criticism by leading commentators.[131] The interpretation is open to the objection that it is contrary to the rule

---

[126] *R. v. Savage* [1992] 1 A.C. 699 at 751 *per* Lord Ackner; Lords Kinkel, Brandon and Lowry concurring.

[127] [1992] 1 A.C. 699 at 729 *et passim*.

[128] [1992] 1 A.C. 699 approving *R. v. Mowatt* [1968] 1 Q.B. 421.

[129] [1992] 1 A.C. 699 at 752.

[130] [1968] 1 Q.B. 421.

[131] For a penetrating critique, see Glanville Williams, *Textbook of Criminal Law*, (London: Stevens & Sons, 1978) at 189–190.

(accepted both in the American Model Penal Code and by the House of Lords)[132] that a requirement of *mens rea* is to be read as applying to all the external elements of the offence. Moreover, the interpretation as applied to section 20 has to meet a special difficulty. Section 20 creates two offences, unlawfully and maliciously wounding, and unlawfully and maliciously inflicting grievous bodily harm. Mowatt was convicted of unlawfully and maliciously wounding. This particular offence makes no reference to bodily harm in general or to grievous bodily harm in particular, but only to *wounding*. It is impossible to see what warrant there is for deciding the mental element by reference to foreseen bodily harm. The foresight must be of wounding, and nothing else.

In *R. v. K*[133] Lord Steyn said: "It is well established that there is a constitutional **9–037** principle of general application that 'whenever a section is silent as to *mens rea* there is a presumption that, in order to give effect to the will of Parliament, we must read in words appropriate to require *mens rea*.'" If one accepts the principle that every (major) crime implies a state of mind, this offence would require a mental element as to the degree of harm mentioned in the section. The courts should not interpret section 20 as an offence of half *mens rea* and of half strict liability. Strict liability should not be used to construct a higher degree of subjective fault. We can presume that Parliament did not intend to hold people strictly liable for unforeseen g.b.h. under section 20, because otherwise it would have said so.[134] The correspondence principle is subsumed in the presumption of *mens rea*, since the presumption means that the defendant should not be liable under section 20, unless he intends to cause g.b.h. (wounding) or foresees it as a possibility.

Per contra, Gardner[135] asserts: "Fortunately, this correspondence principle is not and never has been a principle of English law." According to Gardner, once a person engages in crime (changes his normative position) he ought to be held strictly liable for any consequences that follow.[136] Such a theory would allow a person to be held liable for consequences that even a reasonable person would not have foreseen. Gardner[137] incorrectly asserts that Glanville Williams was wrong

---

[132] *D.P.P. v. Morgan* [1976] A.C. 182.

[133] [2002] 1 A.C. 462 at 477. See also *R. v. Tolson* (1889) 23 Q.B.D. 168.

[134] One of the core reasons Lord Ackner gave for reading section 20 as an offence of "constructive liability" was that constructive liability is sufficient for some common law offences such as constructive manslaughter and murder. (See *R. v. Savage* [1992] 1 A.C. 699 at 752). However, section 20 is a statutory offence created by Parliament.

[135] John Gardner, *Offences and Defences*, (Oxford: Oxford University Press, 2007) at 41–42. Gardner misses the point made by Glanville Williams, which is simply that the correspondence principle is effectively enforceable to the extent that it is subsumed in other doctrines such as the presumption of *mens rea*.

[136] Cf. Andrew Ashworth, "A Change of Normative Position: Determining the Contours of Culpability in Criminal Law," (2008) 11 *New Crim. L. Rev.* 232.

[137] Gardner, *op. cit. supra*, note 135 at 41 n. 19. Gardner does not explain what is wrong with requiring Parliament to state in advance that the offence is one of constructive liability. Williams simply argued that one effect of constructive liability is that it imposes strict liability for any unintended consequences. This element of strict liability is only permissible if the statute expressly provides for it. See the discussion in *State v. Brown*, 140 Wash.2d 456 at 473–474 (2000). In *R. v. Tolson* 23 Q.B.D. 168 at 170 Stephen, J. held: "Section 57 of the *Offences against the Person Act 1861* should be construed in accordance with the well-known principle of English criminal law that in order to constitute crime there must be a *mens rea*, or guilty intention: *non est reus, nisi mens sit rea*.

to argue that the presumption of *mens rea* militates against a constructive interpretation of sections 20 and 47 of the *1861 Act*.[138]

Professor Williams does not misinterpret either the presumption of *mens rea* or the authorities that underwrite it. Furthermore, he states the implications that the presumption of *mens rea* has for the correspondence principle with precision. Williams rightly asserted that certain violations of the correspondence principle contravene the presumption of *mens rea*. Since *R. v. Mowatt* does not require the defendant's *mens rea* to correspond with the harm he causes, it is open to the objection that it imports a considerable measure of strict liability into a crime purportedly dependent on proof of subjective fault. Once *mens rea* is introduced into a statutory offence it governs the whole in absence of an expressed intention to the contrary.[139] According to the majority of their Lordships in *D.P.P. v. Morgan*,[140] where an offence imports *mens rea* there must be *mens rea* even as to the circumstances of the offence. *A fortiori*, then, there must be *mens rea* as to a specified consequence of the act required for the commission of the offence. The whole does not merely refer to all external elements and relevant circumstances, but also to the proscribed harm that is mentioned in the offence. Anything less would allow a person to be held strictly liable for unforeseen consequences, and this would contravene the presumption of *mens rea*. If Parliament wants to make a person strictly liable for serious harm merely because he foresaw that some minor harm might result were he to do so X (change his normative position), then it should express such an intention in the given statute.

9–038 Section 20 would satisfy the presumption of *mens rea*, if it were reworded to provide: "Whosoever shall unlawfully and maliciously wound or inflict any grievous bodily harm upon any other person ... shall be liable," *regardless of whether he intended to do so, if he foresaw that he might cause some physical harm to any other person*. However, such an enactment would be unconstitutional.

A further argument against constructive liability is that it ultimately results in disproportionate punishment and unfair labelling. Lord Steyn assumed that it is well established that the presumption of *mens rea* is a constitutional principle. Such an assessment is perfectly plausible, if the principle can be underwritten or linked to a more substantive constitutional right.[141] As a matter of constitutional

---

It is true that the legislature may for its own reasons dispense in any given case with the necessity for a *mens rea*, and may constitute certain acts crimes in themselves; but this it generally does in very clear language."

[138] See Glanville Williams, *Textbook of Criminal Law*, (London: Steven & Sons, 2nd edn. 1983) at 189–192 (and also at page 930, where Professor Williams makes explicit reference to strict liability in relation to half *mens rea*—lack of correspondence). Professor Williams argued that the presumption of *mens rea* militates against both a constructive interpretation of section 47 and also of section 20. See also Glanville Williams, *Textbook of Criminal Law*, (London: Steven & Sons, 1st edn. 1978) at 157–159; 160-161.

[139] *State v. Brown*, 140 Wash.2d 456 at 473–474 (2000); *Sweet v. Parsley* [1970] A.C. 132; *B (A Child) v. DPP* [2000] 2 A.C. 428; *Crown Prosecution Service v. M* [2010] 2 Cr. App. R. 33.

[140] [1976] A.C. 182; *R. v. K* [2002] 1 A.C. 462.

[141] *R. v. Secretary of State for the Home Department Ex p. Simms* [2000] 2 A.C. 115 at 131, Lord Hoffmann said: "Fundamental rights cannot be overridden by general or ambiguous words. This is because there is too great a risk that the full implications of their unqualified meaning may have passed unnoticed in the democratic process. In the absence of express language or necessary

justice all serious crimes (that is, crimes carrying prison sentences) require a mental element that corresponds[142] with the proscribed harm, since anything less would violate the offender's constitutional right not be unfairly criminalized.[143]

Is *R. v. Savage* affected by section 8 of the *Criminal Justice Act* 9–039 1967? Logically it should be. Malice meaning intention or recklessness: section 8 states in effect that the intention or recklessness must be genuinely ascertained. This seems to be inconsistent with inferring the required mental state from a different and lower mental state.

But there is a loophole in the section, by which courts are enabled to evade it. The section merely relates to the mode of proving any necessary intention or recklessness, and does not control the legal requirements of a particular offence. So all the judges have to do, to evade the operation of the section, is to abrogate the *mens rea* requirement, either in whole or part. This has happened in the present instance. It may be concluded, therefore, that the rule in *R. v. Savage* will be regarded as unaffected by section 8.

The Criminal Law Revision Committee[144] long ago proposed the statutory reversal of *R. v. Mowatt*, but nothing has happened. That decision was not necessary for the protection of the public against evildoers, because section 47 allows for a conviction of an assault occasioning actual bodily harm without the harm being grievous, and the section therefore imposes a lighter burden of proof on the prosecution than section 20. All that is required, to obtain a conviction without any legal problems, is to charge the offence under section 47. When prosecutors do not do this, the courts rescue them by distorting the accepted meaning of statutory malice.

---

implication to the contrary, the courts therefore presume that even the most general words were intended to be subject to the *basic rights of the individual*."

[142] Jeremy Horder rightly asserts that the correspondence principle "ought to be styled the 'proximity' principle, since there are so many instances where it would be wrong to require an exact match between *actus reus* and *mens rea*, rather than simply a close approximation." See Jeremy Horder, "A Critique of the Correspondence Principle in Criminal Law," [1995] Crim. L.R. 759. Only obvious and gross departures from the correspondence principle would result in unfair criminalization. (See for example, the severe decisions in *R. v. Mallett* [1972] Crim. L.R. 260; *R. v. Mitchell* [1983] 2 W.L.R. 938.)

[143] Proportionate punishment is about holding D responsible according to the culpableness and harmfulness of his acting. Fair labelling means he should not be criminalized merely in accordance with the harm he has caused, but also in accordance with his culpable link to that harm. The formula for fair criminalization is: *harmfulness x culpableness* = sentence length/crime label. See Dennis J. Baker, *The Right Not to be Criminalized: Demarcating Criminal Law's Authority*, (Farnham: Ashgate Publishing, 2011) at Chap. 2. See Articles 3, 5 and 8 of the *European Convention for the Protection of Human Rights and Fundamental Freedoms*, 4 November 1950, 213 U.N.T.S. 222 (entered into force generally on 3 September 1953). However, the courts have not taken this right seriously. It has only been acknowledged when the disproportionality has been very gross. (And even then, there is no guarantee that the court will uphold the right.) Cf. *United Kingdom v. Weeks* (1988) 10 E.H.R.R. 293; *R. v. Lichniakde* [2003] 1 A.C. 903; *Boucherville v. Mauritius* [2008] 25 B.H.R.C. 433. See also Alan Brudner, "Imprisonment and Strict Liability," (1990) 40 *U. Toronto L.J.* 738.

[144] Criminal Law Revision Committee, *Offences Against the Person*, Fourteenth Report, (London: H.M.S.O., Cmnd. 7844, 1980) at para. 6.

9–040 **Push it a stage further. The defendant did not intend to cause g.b.h., but he intended to give the other a severe fright, and did so in a way that created a risk of injury and actually caused serious injury. Couldn't the frightener be made liable under section 20?** The frightener may be liable under section 47, and he will be liable under section 20 if he was reckless as to causing harm (*R. v. Savage*). But, correcting some earlier pronouncements, the courts now hold, in accordance with principle, that an intention to frighten is not sufficient to create liability under section 20, in the absence of recklessness as to causing harm.

So where a gamekeeper fired a shot towards a bush, thinking that a poacher might be there and wishing to "startle" him into coming out of hiding, but not believing that anyone was within range and not foreseeing the possibility of causing direct physical injury, but in fact caused g.b.h. to a man who was hiding in the bush, the gamekeeper's appeal against conviction under section 20 was allowed.[145]

9–041 **But surely the gamekeeper was reckless. Would he have shot towards the bush if he had known his wife or daughter was in it?** That would be a good question to ask him in cross-examination. If the magistrates had found that the gamekeeper foresaw even a very small possibility of hitting someone, he would have been reckless as to causing harm, because no foreseen risk would have been justifiable in the circumstances. But the appeal court was bound by the magistrates finding of fact.

Before this case the judges had created a further form of constructive intention, holding that the intent to frighten made the defendant automatically liable for harm resulting from the fright, even though the harm was not only unintentional but even unforeseen. The Criminal Law Revision Committee recommended that this rule should be reversed by statute; and although no statute has yet appeared, the courts by remoulding the common law (for once in the direction of restricting liability) have made the change themselves. It represents a minor success for the subjectivist approach to criminal liability.

One application of the old rule needs special mention. It was formerly held that if a person did an act with intent to frighten, and the victim injured himself in trying to escape, the intention to frighten was sufficient for conviction under sections 20 or 47, so that the doer could be punished for causing the injury even though he did not intend to cause injury and was not reckless as to it.[146] We can assume that these decisions are no longer law in respect of section 20. The frightener is liable under section 20 only for intention or recklessness as to injury.

9–042 **You are not telling me that if D scares the daylight out of V, who injures herself trying to escape, that D should not be accountable?** The frightener will generally be guilty of a (psychic) assault, and/or of a crime of uttering threats.[147] Often the tribunal of fact will be able to infer recklessness as to causing injury, which would be sufficient under section 20. According to the authorities

---

[145] *Flack v. Hunt* (1979) 70 Cr. App. R. 51, cf. *W (A Minor) v. Dolbey* (1989) 88 Cr. App. R. 1.

[146] See particularly, *R. v. Halliday* (1890) 54 J.P. 312. This was followed by a number of cases. See *R. v. Beech* (1912) 7 Cr. App. R. 197; *R. v. Lewis* [1970] Crim. L.R. 647; *Cartledge v. Allen* [1973] Crim. L.R. 530.

[147] See section 4 of the *Public Order Act 1986*.

the frightener can in any case be made liable under section 47.[148] But the law now is that an intention to frighten is not in itself *mens rea* as to bring about a wound or cause grievous bodily harm, which is the charge under section 20. Nor should it be so regarded. The Criminal Law Revision Committee, agreeing with this opinion has recommended that the frightener should never be liable for an aggravated assault merely because he intended to frighten.[149]

Can intention be transferred under section 20?   Yes. There is nothing in the wording of the section to prevent such transfer.[150]   **9–043**

One thing puzzles me. If recklessness as to mental harm is sufficient for grounding a conviction under section 20, am I liable if I dump my girlfriend knowing this will cause her to suffer a mental breakdown?   Clearly not! But what if the mental breakdown causes her serious psychiatric injury? This is not a case of "take victim as you find her." The prosecution would have to prove that you caused her breakdown. This is an objective question which must be assessed by considering the relevant expert evidence. Even though you foresaw that she might suffer a serious psychiatric injury, you did not cause it. A normal person would not be seriously injured in a psychiatric sense from being told that a relationship is over. You did not intend to cause such an injury but merely foresaw it as a side-effect of you exercising your lawful right to live your own life as you please. Forcing X to stay in a relationship with Y might have the effect of preventing Y from suffering a mental breakdown or from committing suicide, but the criminal law cannot be used to force a person to stay in a relationship that is not working. Since the expert evidence is likely to demonstrate that the actual cause of her injury was her underlying mental condition, you should not be liable. It would be almost impossible to prove that your isolated one-off act of ending the relationship caused her mental breakdown.[151]   **9–044**

Hence, in cases like your hypothetical there would usually be no *mens rea*, because the mental breakdown would not be foreseeable. Even where D foresees the harm (for instance, where he knows his girlfriend has psychological problems); he surely could end his relationship with her as a matter of necessity. He could end the relationship as it would be necessary to do so if he were to preserve his own freedom and autonomy. The same would apply if a professor was forced to fail a Ph.D. candidate, or refuse to promote an employee.

9.7.   *OFFENCES AGAINST THE PERSON ACT* SECTION 47

The uncertainty about grievous bodily harm affects the notion of "actual bodily harm" in section 47 ("a.b.h." in police jargon). This is a silly expression—as though there were some kind of contrasting bodily harm that was not "actual"! Presumably it means "more than trifling." Transitory pain is obviously not   **9–045**

---

[148] *R. v. Roberts* (1972) 56 Cr. App. R. 95.

[149] *Offences Against the Person*, Fourteenth Report, (London: H.M.S.O., Cmnd. 7844, 1980) at para. 6.

[150] *R. v. Latimer* (1886) 17 Q.B.D. 359.

[151] However, compare the civil negligence case: *Corr v. I.B.C. Vehicles Ltd.* [2008] 1 A.C. 884.

enough, but a bruise is.[152] But it need not involve pain at all, if there is actual physical damage. A miscreant who wrongfully cuts off a damsel's tresses could be convicted under section 47.[153] It is not necessary to demonstrate that the defendant physically injured the victim. The physical harm requirement should be satisfied if the defendant subjects the victim to pain, even if he does not cause any injury. If D repeatedly zaps V with an electric prodder,[154] V would find it painful but would not be physically injured. He would not be injured in the sense of suffering physical damage, but he would be harmed since this type of conduct would interfere with his health and comfort.[155] There is no doubt that this type of conduct is harmful, even if it does not physically injure or damage the victim. A momentary loss of consciousness has been held to constitute bodily harm, even though it caused no physical damage.[156]

Per contra, we have seen that psychological harm only counts if it in fact injures the victim. The defendant must in fact cause the victim to suffer a recognized psychological injury. "Actual" does not mean physical as opposed to mental, because the phrase has been ruled to include psychiatric injuries. In *R. v. Chan-Fook*[157] Hobhouse L.J. said:[158]

> "Accordingly the phrase 'actual bodily harm' is capable of including psychiatric injury. But it does not include mere emotions such as fear or distress nor panic nor does it include, as such, states of mind that are not themselves evidence of some identifiable clinical condition. The phrase 'state of mind' is not a scientific one and should be avoided in considering whether or not a psychiatric injury has been caused; its use is likely to create in the minds of the jury the impression that something which is not more than a strong emotion, such as extreme fear or panic, can amount to actual bodily harm. It cannot. Similarly juries should not be directed that an assault which causes a hysterical and nervous condition is an assault occasioning actual bodily harm. Where there is evidence that the assault has caused some psychiatric injury, the jury should be directed that that injury is capable of amounting to actual bodily harm; otherwise there should be no reference to the mental state of the victim following the assault unless it be relevant to some other aspect of the case, as it was in *R. v. Roberts*, (1971) 56 Cr. App. R. 95. It is also relevant to have in mind the relationship between the offence of aggravated assault comprised in section 47 and simple assault. The latter can include conduct which causes the victim to apprehend immediate and unlawful violence ... To treat the victim's fear of such unlawful violence, without more, as amounting to actual bodily harm would be to risk rendering the definition of the aggravated offence academic in many cases."

---

[152] In *Taylor v. Granville* [1978] Crim. L.R. 482 magistrates were held to be entitled to infer that "bodily harm, however slight," must have resulted from a blow to the face. But query whether the extension of a.b.h. to include very slight harm gives proper weight to the meaning of the word "actual" in the context. In *R. v. Christopher* [1981] Crim. L.R. 119 the court said that to describe minor abrasions and a bruise on the face as a.b.h. "went to the very margin of what was meant by that term," and that to impose a term of imprisonment was incorrect.

[153] *D.P.P. v. Smith* [2006] 1 W.L.R. 1571.

[154] An electric prodder is device that is designed to get cattle to move about when being yarded. If D were to use something more powerful such as a taser gun, then one zap would be sufficient. (One zap from a taser might also cause g.b.h.)

[155] *R. v. Donovan* [1934] 2 K.B. 498; *R. v. Miller* [1954] 2 Q.B. 282 at 292; *R. v. Brown* [1994] 1 A.C. 212.

[156] *T v. D.P.P.* [2003] Crim. L.R. 622.

[157] [1994] 1 W.L.R. 689 at 696. Approved by *R. v. Ireland* [1998] A.C. 147. See also *McLoughlin v. O'Brian* [1983] 1 A.C. 410 at 418.

[158] [1998] A.C. 147. *R. v. Miller* [1954] 2 Q.B. 282 is no longer good law. In that case, a trial judge ruled that where D physically assaulted V, who was in consequence put into "a hysterical and nervous condition," the latter was actual bodily harm and D was liable for it under section 47.

This ruling obviously presents some danger of an over-extension of the offence, but Hobhouse L.J. was careful not to extend actual bodily harm to cover *any* mental hurt. Mental harm is only covered if it constitutes a "recognized psychiatric illness." That a recognizable mental illness should be actual bodily harm is beyond doubt.[159] It is not necessary to show that the victim suffered some recognizable mental illness, if the mental harm is connected with some physical harm. Concussion, for example, is obviously bodily harm even where the injury to the skull is minimal. In such a case there is an injury to the brain, even though it is temporary.[160] But the phrase "actual bodily harm" should surely connote something more than a trivial injury. Minor physical harm should not be regarded as sufficient unless there is psychiatric evidence of a recognized mental disorder. The above passage suggests that the courts will recognize this limitation.[161]

The prosecution charging guidelines suggest that the following injuries should be prosecuted under section 47: "loss or breaking of tooth or teeth; temporary loss of sensory functions, which may include loss of consciousness; extensive or multiple bruising; a displaced broken nose; minor fractures; minor, but not merely superficial, cuts of a sort probably requiring medical treatment (*e.g.*, stitches); psychiatric injury that is more than mere emotions such as fear, distress or panic."[162]

What mental element is required under section 47?   Section 47 does not   **9–046**
expressly state the mental element required, but it postulates an assault, and we have also seen that an assault requires intention or recklessness. We have seen that recklessness for this purpose should be taken as being subjective recklessness.

The Court of Appeal has held that an intention to frighten is sufficient. A person who assaults another physically or psychically, with the result that the other tries to escape and suffers actual bodily harm, is guilty under the section without proof that the assaulter foresaw the harm, at least if the harm was reasonably foreseeable.[163] Of course, *mens rea* is present as to the assault, but there need be none as to the harm. The crime is one of negligence as to the circumstance of aggravation, the occasioning of bodily harm. In *R. v. Savage* Lord Ackner said:[164]

---

[159] *R. v. Dhaliwal* [2006] 2 Cr. App. R. 24.

[160] *T v. D.P.P.* [2003] Crim. L.R. 622.

[161] There is no technical reason why the victim's mental suffering should not inflate the sentence if the actual bodily harm has been occasioned. In *R. v. Maguire* (1982) 146 J.N.P. 314 the defendant was convicted under section 47 where he had inflicted only slight bodily harm by sexual assault (some grazing and bruising, but where he caused severe shock). A sentence of two years' imprisonment was upheld, the Court of Appeal assuming without firm evidence that the victim might suffer lasting psychological damage. Yet apart from the assumed psychological damage the evidence of the bodily harm seems to have gone to "the very margin of what was meant by that term".

[162] http://www.cps.gov.uk/legal/l_to_o/offences_against_the_person/#P48_1458.

[163] *R. v. Roberts* (1972) 56 Cr. App. R. 95.

[164] *R. v. Savage* [1992] 1 A.C. 699 at 742, Lords Keith, Brandon and Lowry concurring.

"[T]he decision in *R. v. Roberts*[165] was correct. The verdict of assault occasioning actual bodily harm may be returned upon proof of an assault together with proof of the fact that actual bodily harm was occasioned by the assault. The prosecution are not obliged to prove that the defendant intended to cause some actual bodily harm or was *reckless* as to whether such harm would be caused."

9–047 **The law is in a shambles, admittedly, but I don't think you sufficiently acknowledge the difference between the two sections. Section 20 has an express mental element, section 47 hasn't. Parliament may well have intended that section 47 was to be an offence of strict liability in respect of the consequence. Section 47 implies a mental element as to assault, but no more.** Let me explain why I do not agree with that view. Suppose that the statute had simply made it an offence to occasion actual bodily harm. If one accepts the constitutional presumption of *mens rea*, then this offence like the offence found in section 20, requires a mental element as to the harm. Now suppose that, as is the case with section 47, the statute specifies that the harm must be caused by an assault. This cuts down the ways in which the harm is caused, but why should it eliminate the mental element as to the harm?

Even if the authorities are wrong, so that section 47 carries a full *mens rea* requirement, it seems likely as a matter of general principle that when an attacker is reckless as to causing a particular type of bodily harm, he is liable under section 47 even though he caused some other type of bodily harm as to which he was not reckless. It would be pushing insistence on the mental element too far to require it to be as to the specific type of harm described in the section—actual bodily harm. Consequently, since mental harm can be bodily harm, if the defendant caused mental harm resulting in a recognized psychiatric illness, the jury may convict whether he intended or was reckless as to either bodily or mental harm of that degree.

9.8. THE REQUIREMENT OF ASSAULT

9–048 There is a difference between the two sections in that section 47 on its face requires an assault while section 20 does not. Section 20 merely requires harm to be "inflicted." In the ordinary use of language harm may be inflicted without an assault (for example, by poisoning). But the courts have not found the question simple.

For more than a century before 1983[166] it had been supposed that section 20, too, requires an assault. The leading authority was the decision of the Court of Crown Cases Reserved in *R. v. Clarence*.[167]

Clarence, who had communicated venereal disease to his wife, was indicted under section 20. It was held that he was not guilty because an "infliction" under the section could only be by way of assault. "The words appear to me" said Stephen J. (with whom three other judges concurred) "to mean the direct causing of some grievous bodily injury to the body itself. ... I think the words imply an assault and battery of which a wound or grievous bodily harm is the manifest

---

[165] (1972) 56 Cr. App. R. 95.
[166] *R. v. Wilson* [1983] 1 W.L.R. 356.
[167] (1888) 22 Q.B.D. 23.

immediate and obvious result." Here there was no assault, because an assault presupposes a lack of consent, and the wife had consented to the contact.

Obviously Clarence did not assault his wife. Her ignorance or mistake was as to the consequence of the act, not as to the act itself. The gravamen of the charge against Clarence was that he had communicated a disease. Can one communicate a disease to another person without touching him or her?[168] We shall return to the disease point when we come to the law on administrating noxious things.

Why did the court in *Clarence* require an assault? It seems to me that 9–049
Clarence did inflict a.b.h. on his wife. What did it matter whether it was by
an assault or not? It is difficult to say why. The court in *R. v. Clarence* was partly following precedent, and partly, perhaps, giving effect to the notion of policy.

We do not know who decided to charge Clarence with a crime, but the charge was unprecedented. Millions of men and women must have infected their consorts with VD without being prosecuted. Perhaps the court in *R. v. Clarence* merely disliked the idea of bringing the marital bed into the criminal law. However, the situation is different where a person deliberately passes on a lethal disease.[169] It is one thing to pass on a minor disease, but another to deliberately pass on a lethal disease. The carriers of H.I.V. should take the simple precaution of using a prophylactic when they engage in sexual relations. The H.I.V. carrier should tell his partner of his condition so that she can decide whether to risk her life by having sexual relations with him. Even if the victim consents to contracting a lethal disease, her consent is unlikely to be sufficient to provide the defendant with a defence.[170]

If *R. v. Clarence* was right (and until 1983 it was always accepted as representing the law) both sections would require an assault, the one section expressly and the other impliedly by using the word "inflict." A consequence of the decision was that (as had, indeed, been held before *R. v. Clarence*) both assault and the offence under section 47 were wholly charged when section 20 was charged.[171] However, in *R. v. Wilson*,[172] by an astonishing reversal of view, the Court of Appeal held that this is too narrow an interpretation of section 20. Although a section 20 offence can be committed by an assault, it can, in the alternative, be committed "by doing something intentionally, which, though it is not itself a direct application of force to the body of the victim, so that he suffers grievous bodily harm."

---

[168] Biological weapons do not require any touching: it would be enough to circulate the disease via an office building's air-conditioning system.

[169] Or at least (recklessly) caused their lovers g.b.h., by concealing their own infection. *R. v. Konzani* [2005] 2 Cr. App. R. 14; *R. v. Dica* [2005] EWCA Crim. 2304.

[170] *R. v. Konzani* [2005] 2 Cr. App. R. 14 suggests that V's consenting to contract H.I.V. would provide D with a defence even though this involves D causing grievously bodily harm to V. It is submitted this cannot be correct, since in *R. v. Brown* [1994] 1 A.C. 212 the House of Lords held that a person cannot consent to actual bodily harm or greater harm. See Dennis J. Baker, "The Moral Limits of Consent as a Defence in the Criminal Law," (2009) 12 *New Crim. L. Rev.* 93.

[171] *R. v. Taylor* (1869) 1 C. C. R. 194; *R. v. Snewing* [1972] Crim. L.R. 267.

[172] [1983] 1 W.L.R. 356.

9–050 The decision in *R. v. Wilson*[173] had a long-term advantage in that it gives legitimacy to the old case of *R. v. Martin*,[174] which had previously been in doubt. Martin was one of the unfunny jokers who appear from time to time in the law reports. According to the special verdict of the jury he extinguished the light in a theatre "with the intention of causing terror and alarm," and placed a bar across the door "with the intention of wilfully obstructing the means of exit." Persons were injured in the ensuring pandemonium, and the Court for Crown Cases Reserved held that Martin could be convicted of maliciously inflicting grievous bodily harm under section 20.

The court proceeded on the assumption that "maliciously" in the statute covered an act done with intent to frighten, and in that respect the case is no longer law. The more recent cases discussed above show that an intention to frighten is not sufficient under section 20. The jury should therefore have been directed to consider whether they were satisfied beyond reasonable doubt that Martin either intended to cause the bodily harm or was reckless as to it. If he foresaw even the slightest risk of causing harm (as he must have done), that would make him reckless. The lack of a direction along these lines was a flaw in the conviction, according to present ideas, but, applying the subsequent decision in *R. v. Clarence*, there was another much more serious defect. As we have seen, section 20 was construed in *R. v. Clarence* to require an assault, and on traditional principles there was no assault in *R. v. Martin*. Assuming Martin realized the danger he was creating, all he did was to set up a situation that he knew would cause panic, and then leave the members of the audience to injure each other. It cannot be said (if the decencies of language are observed) that he directly inflicted force upon the injured persons, so as to make him guilty of an assault. So he should not have been liable under either section.

The court in *R. v. Martin* did not decide that Martin had committed an assault. It just did not consider that an assault might be necessary under the section. In *R. v. Clarence*, Wills J. expressed the opinion that in *R. v. Martin* there was a direct infliction of force, and therefore an assault.[175] But the other members of the court in *R. v. Clarence* did not deal with the matter, and Wills J.'s opinion stretches the notion of an assault, and of the direct infliction of force, well beyond its common legal understanding. If Martin was guilty of a physical assault when the members of the audience injured each other, he was guilty of a psychic assault when a member of the audience was frightened on seeing the crowd surging towards him, but it is impossible to believe that such fright could properly been held to make Martin guilty of a psychic assault.

On appeal, in *R. v. Wilson*,[176] Lord Roskill said:[177]

> "I am content to accept … that there can be an infliction of grievous bodily harm contrary to section 20 without an assault being committed."

---

[173] [1984] A.C. 242.
[174] (1881) 8 Q.B.D. 54.
[175] 22 Q.B.D. 23 at 36.
[176] [1984] A.C. 242.
[177] *R. v. Wilson* [1984] A.C. 242 at 260–261.

Does "inflict" simply mean "cause"?[178] That is the way the cases are unfolding. Lord Steyn has observed:[179] "[It is] clear that in the context of the *Act of 1861* there is no radical divergence between the meaning of the two words." Lord Hope said: "for all practical purposes there is, in my opinion, no difference between these two words. ... But I would add that there is this difference, that the word 'inflict' implies that the consequence of the act is something which the victim is likely to find unpleasant or harmful. The relationship between cause and effect, when the word 'cause' is used, is neutral. It may embrace pleasure as well as pain. The relationship when the word 'inflict' is used is more precise, because it invariably implies detriment to the victim of some kind."[180] "Inflict" naturally refers to cases where the defendant deliberately or recklessly causes harm to the victim. "Cause" in the wider sense would cover cases where he innocently causes harm to the victim.

9–051

Consensual sexual intercourse does not involve an assault or a battery. Similarly, consent makes a battery lawful if it does not cause actual bodily harm. Consent coverts what would otherwise be unlawful and unwanted assault and battery into something that is a lawful activity. Non-consensual sexual intercourse is violent rape, whereas consensual intercourse is lovemaking.[181] A person like Clarence would be convicted (even though no non-consensual force was involved in communicating VD), and a person like Martin would be convicted (because he caused members of the audience to inflict force on each other). However, in the ordinary case under section 20 the "force" would be inflicted by way of assault.

9.9. ASSAULTING PARTICULAR CLASSES OF VICTIMS

Laws have been enacted to increase the sentence of those who make offensive comments about a victim's ethnicity, religion and/or sexual orientation during the course of an assault. We need to tread carefully when we dish out higher sentences for conduct that causes public outrage, because public outrage can result in disproportionate and unprincipled criminalization. Terrorists,[182] paedophiles,[183] racists, homophobes,[184] and religious haters evoke strong public sentiment. Laws have been enacted to target those who are motivated to assault others because of their sexual orientation, race and/or religion, but there are

9–052

---

[178] [1998] A.C. 147 at 160. See also *D.P.P. v. K* [1990] 1 W.L.R. 1067; *D.P.P. v. Santa-Bermudez* (2004) 168 J.P. 373.

[179] "It would ... introduce extreme and undesirable artificiality into what should be a very practical area of the law if we were to hold that, although grievous bodily harm includes psychiatric injury, no offence against section 20 is committed unless such psychiatric injury is the result of physical violence applied directly or indirectly to the body of the victim." *R. v. Ireland* [1998] A.C. 147 at 155 *per* Lord Steyn quoting Lord Bingham C.J. in the court below.

[180] *R. v. Ireland* [1998] A.C. 147 at 160, 164.

[181] *R. v. B* [2007] 1 Cr. App. R. 29.

[182] Provisions were enacted to allow terrorist suspects to be detained without a trial. See *A v. United Kingdom* (2009) 49 E.H.R.R. 29.

[183] Dennis J. Baker, "Punishment without a Crime: Is Preventive Detention Reconcilable with Justice," (2009) 34 *Austl. J. Leg. Phil.* 120.

[184] See for example, "Former public schoolgirl Ruby Thomas grinned as she kicked gay man to death," (London: *The Mirror*, 17 December 2010).

dozens of motivations that are as evil as these. Why single out these motivations? Sir John Smith, referring to section 29 of the *Crime and Disorder Act 1998*, said:

"It is deplorable that the Government is able to find time for ill-considered, 'politically correct,' legislation of this kind when the very fully considered proposals for the much-needed reform of the law of non-fatal offences against the person gather still more dust. ... All that has happened is that the law which was acknowledged to be 'archaic and unclear and ... now in urgent need of reform' has been further complicated by the new racially aggravated versions of that archaic legislation."[185]

Sir John Smith was not one for mincing words. Is there any merit in Professor Smith's provocative claim? The laws are well intended, but such evils should not be criminalized as a form of bodily harm. Is the actual bodily harm increased when the harmer has a particular evil motive? It appears not. The motivation for causing harm does not make the defendant's actions less or more harmful. Nor does an offender's motivation necessarily make him any less or more dangerous in terms of statistical risk. (Statistically, intoxicated offenders commit the majority of assaults. If the statistical risk posed by the particular class of offender is the rationale for the greater sentence, intoxicated offenders should be punished very severely.)

Generally, those who wantonly injure other human beings are motivated by a hatred and disrespect for humanity *simpliciter*. Those who make hateful or offensive comments during the course of an attack commit an independent wrong, but the motivation for making such comments normally has nothing to do with the motivation for physically injuring the victim. Many bigots make hateful comments without physically attacking anyone. Only haters who also have no respect for the humanity of their victims take the further step of physically attacking the victim. There are two wrongs here and they should be criminalized as independent offences. It is one thing to verbally attack another and something quite different to physically attack him. The *Offences against the Person Act 1861* should not be used to tackle hate speech. The courts have held that psychological distress *per se* does not constitute harm for the purposes of the *Act of 1861*. Even though the offensive speech is not likely to result in g.b.h. or a.b.h.,[186] it has been used to justify increasing, the sentence of hate motivated assaults. The sentence is nearly doubled for aggravated assault[187] and quadrupled for common assault. (We all detest such offenders, but we must keep a level head when formulating criminal law.)

9–053   Section 29 of the *Crime and Disorder Act 1998* provides:

"(1)   A person is guilty of an offence under this section if he commits—(a) an offence under section 20 of the *Offences against the Person Act 1861* (malicious wounding or

---

[185] J.C. Smith, Commentary on *D.P.P. v. Pal* [2000] Crim. L.R. 756 at 757.

[186] At least not harm as recognized in English law; because short-lived psychological annoyance does not count. See *R. v. Dhaliwal* [2006] 2 Cr. App. R. 348.

[187] In practice, the courts might not increase the sentence by more than 20 *per cent.* (*R. v. O'Callaghan* [2005] 2 Cr. App. R. (S.) 83). But that is still a big increase for offensive speech that does not result in a.b.h. or g.b.h. This will teach the wrongdoer a well-deserved lesson, but will do little to offer all *victims* equal protection under the criminal law regardless of their individual characteristics.

grievous bodily harm); (b) an offence under section 47 of that Act (actual bodily harm); or (c) common assault, which is racially or religiously aggravated[188] for the purposes of this section.

(2) A person guilty of an offence falling within subsection (1)(a) or (b) above shall be liable—(a) on summary conviction, to imprisonment for a term not exceeding six months or to a fine not exceeding the statutory maximum, or to both; (b) on conviction on indictment, to imprisonment for a term not exceeding seven years or to a fine, or to both.

(3) A person guilty of an offence falling within subsection (1)(c) above shall be liable—(a) on summary conviction, to imprisonment for a term not exceeding six months or to a fine not exceeding the statutory maximum, or to both; (b) on conviction on indictment, to imprisonment for a term not exceeding two years or to a fine, or to both."

Section 28(1) provides:

"An offence is racially or religiously aggravated for the purposes of sections 29 to 32 below if—(a) at the time of committing the offence, or immediately before or after doing so, the offender demonstrates towards the victim of the offence hostility based on the victim's membership (or presumed membership) of a racial or religious group; or (b) the offence is motivated (wholly or partly) by hostility towards members of a racial or religious group."

Where the offender commits certain offences against the person and utters xenophobic or anti-religious comments, he may get a sentence that is four times longer than if he had kept his offensive thoughts to himself. (In practice, the penalty is not likely be increased that much, however.) If D were to punch a person whom he believes to be Jewish and gestures a Nazi salute "immediately before or after doing so," his hostility towards the victim could be held to be based "on the victim's membership (or presumed membership) of a racial or religious" group. But does the grossly offensive but otherwise harmless gesture make his assault four times worse than if he had just walked off? The maximum sentence for common assault is six months imprisonment, but it is two years when it involves hostility that can be linked to race or religion. In the case of the offences found under sections 20 and 47, the sentence can be extended from five years to seven years. Hence, the maximum sentence is nearly half as long again, because of the hate[189] speech/expression component.

---

[188] Meanwhile, section 146 of the *Criminal Justice Act 2003* provides: "(1) This section applies where the court is considering the seriousness of an offence committed in any of the circumstances mentioned in subsection (2). (2) Those circumstances are—(a) that, at the time of committing the offence, or immediately before or after doing so, the offender demonstrated towards the victim of the offence hostility based on—(i) the sexual orientation (or presumed sexual orientation) of the victim, or (ii) a disability (or presumed disability) of the victim, or (b) that the offence is motivated (wholly or partly)—(i) by hostility towards persons who are of a particular sexual orientation, or (ii) by hostility towards persons who have a disability or a particular disability." See also sections 39–41 of the *Anti-terrorism, Crime and Security Act 2001*.

[189] In many cases the offensive comments will not be motivated by a hatred of people with the particular characteristic. For example, X punches Y because Y has taken the car space which X was about to use to park his car. Let us assume that Y is enormously fat, and as X punches him he shouts: "That will teach you, you fat fool." X's fattist comments do not mean he was motivated by a hatred of fat people. He was motivated by the fact he felt cheated, and his response manifests a general hatred and lack of respect for the humanity of others.

9–054　　**What if the defendant is of the same race as the victim?**　In *D.P.P. v. Pal*[190] one man assaulted another man from his own ethnic background and called him: "a white man's a … licker" and a "brown Englishman." The Divisional Court held that this type of name calling did not manifest racial hostility. It is difficult to see why not. The court held that D's hostility stemmed purely from his hatred of V, rather than a hatred of V's race.[191] This suggests that the extra punishment is designed to punish the wrongdoer for having a bad *motivation*, rather than for causing deep offence.[192] But surely, any unlawful and unworthy motivation for wantonly assaulting a human being is equally deserving of punishment.

9–055　　**What if the defendant is not motivated by racial or religious hatred, but makes racists comments to irritate V?**　In *D.P.P. v. Wood*,[193] it was held that there was no need to show that the offender was "motivated solely, or even mainly, by racial malevolence." The offence covers "cases which may have a racially neutral gravamen but in the course of which there is demonstrated towards the victim hostility based on the victim's membership of a racial group."[194] Section 28(a) "is concerned with the objective view of whether racial hostility had been demonstrated, in part because of its effect upon the victim, rather than being concerned with a subjective motivation of the defendant." Meanwhile section 28(b) allows for a consideration of D's subjective motivation. If he can show that he was not motivated by racial hatred but by a desire to incense V, then he will not be liable.[195]

---

[190] [2000] Crim. L.R. 756.

[191] In *D.P.P. v. Pal* [2000] Crim. L.R. 756 the Divisional Court also held: "an offence of racially aggravated common assault might be made out if, for example, one white man were to assault another white man and to make a grossly offensive remark, such as 'nigger lover' to that man upon seeing his victim rejoin a group of black friends." This cannot be right as D's hostility has nothing to do with the victim's membership of a religion or ethnic group. The victim does not become a member of another racial group merely because he is friends with members of it. Cf. *R. v. White* [2001] 1 W.L.R. 1352.

[192] The courts have been able to stretch the law to criminalize offensive speech. In *Kendall v. South East Magistrates' Court* [2008] EWHC 1848; *Norwood v. D.P.P.* [2003] Crim. L.R. 888. (It would have been better to have charged Kendall and Nowood under section 1 of the *Indecent Displays (Control) Act 1981*, because this offence targets the specific *wrong* involved.) In other cases, the courts recognized the cardinal value of freedom of expression: *Percy v. D.P.P.* [2002] A.C.D. 24. Unless hate expression causes a.b.h. or g.b.h., it should be tolerated as the dangers of criminalizing it are much greater than debating it. See Joel Feinberg, *The Moral Limits of the Criminal Law: Offense to Others*, (New York: Oxford University Press, Vol. II, 1985); Eric Heinze, "Viewpoint Absolutism and Hate Speech," (2006) 69 *Mod. L. Rev.* 543; Simon W. Thomas, "Fighting Racism: Hate Speech Detours," (1993) 26 *Ind. L. Rev.* 411. One important advance in modern society is that debate and publicity has the effect of treating the bigot as less than a full member of society. The person making the offensive comment is confronted and is made to feel ashamed—that is, made to feel less than a full member of society. Many people in public life have been forced to apologize for making silly comments which were not intended to be racist. See Amelia Hilland Lee Glendinning, "Politicians condemn Prince Harry over 'racist' remark," (London: *The Guardian*, Sunday, 11 January 2009). A non-penal option would be to order those who make offensive comments to seek counselling to confront their phobia.

[193] [2002] EWHC 85 at para. 12; *D.P.P. v. M* [2004] 1 W.L.R. 2758; *D.P.P. v. Green* [2004] EWHC 1225.

[194] *Jones v. D.P.P.* [2010] 3 All E.R. 1057.

[195] *D.P.P. v. Pal* [2000] Crim. L.R. 756.

Is a mere reference to V's nationality sufficient? What if I call an Anglo-Australian a "foreigner" and tell him to go back to Australia? It is neither here nor there that your Australian victim is an Anglo-Saxon.[196] You need only refer to the victim's ethnicity,[197] nationality,[198] immigration status[199] or religious status. It must be demonstrated that you manifested a hostility towards the victim because of his religion, nationality, immigration status or ethnicity. Your words need not be offensive *per se*. Most people would not be offended if someone were to refer to their ethnicity or nationality, but some people might be deeply offended if they were denigrated because of their ethnicity or nationality.

9–056

Is there not a danger that the law will only protect people who follow traditional religions? The follower of a religion lives his life in accordance with its prescribed social practices. The freedom of religion right basically protects cultural practices,[200] as it allows people to follow certain social norms in accordance with the ideology of that culture. A follower of a certain religion might be required to wear religious habits, crosses, bracelets, turbans, burqas, and so on. Generally, the freedom of religion right has the effect of protecting the religious person's right to carry out certain social rituals that are associated with her religion.[201] It is the rituals and social practices that are protected in practice,

9–057

---

[196] See *Johnson v. D.P.P.* (2008) 105(10) L.S.G. 27, where a black man told two white parking officers to get back to their white neighbourhood. Cf. *D.P.P. v. Balham* [2004] EWHC 2990, where it was held: "'foreigner' was capable of being construed as expressing hostility by reference to race since it arguably included all those whose family origins were not in this country."

[197] Such as calling an African person an African, or a Scottish man a Scotsman, or a Frenchman a Frenchman and so on. See *R. v. White* [2001] 1 W.L.R. 1352. See also *Mandla v. Lee* [1983] 2 A.C. 548.

[198] *R. v. Rogers* [2007] 2 A.C. 62. In *D.P.P. v. M* [2004] 1 W.L.R. 2758, the victims were resident in the U.K., so the term "foreigner" was taken to refer to their ethnicity. Cf. *R. (on the application of Taffurelli) v. D.P.P.* [2004] EWHC 2791, where D threatened violence and called his neighbours "lesbian bull dykes". Interestingly, the court did not treat the homophobic comments as an aggravating feature as it could have done pursuant to section 146 of the *Criminal Justice Act 2003*.

[199] *Re Attorney-General's Reference (No.4 of 2004)* [2005] 1 W.L.R. 2810.

[200] For example, a Sikh teenager who was excluded from school for refusing to remove a religious bracelet at school was held to have the right to do so, even though not being able to wear it could not really stop her from believing her ideology. Denying her the right not to wear it merely denied her the right to follow the social practices and rituals associated with her religion. *R. (on the application of Watkins-Singh) v. Aberdare Girls' High School Governors* [2008] 3 F.C.R. 203. It might also be the social practice of a young atheist girl living in modern Britain to wear jewellery, but she would not be able to invoke the freedom of religion right to gain the freedom to wear it in school, because her social practice cannot be linked to a particular ideology. In both cases, the girls should be allowed to wear their jewellery, because they do not *harm* others by doing so.

[201] This is because it is impossible to stop people from believing what they choose to believe. If a state tried to brainwash its members then it would violate their freedom of conscience right. If a state tried to curb a group's ability to present its ideology to the public or to discuss it publicly, it would violate the group's freedom of expression right. However, a person can believe in an ideology without carrying out all of its rituals; and the believer should not be allowed to carry out harmful rituals in the name of religion. In a United States case, D smuggled smoked bushmeat (known colloquially as monkey meat) into the U.S. in violation of a number of domestic laws and international treaties designed to protect endangered species. The judge held that it was not necessary for her to eat endangered monkeys in order to maintain her religious beliefs. *U.S. v. Manneh*, 645 F.Supp.2d 98 (2008). (The focus should be on "conscience" not "religion," as that would allow all cultural groups to practice their way of life when doing so does not *harm others*.)

because a person's religious beliefs are hidden until expressed. If they are expressed, then they will be protected by the right of freedom of expression.

9–058   **Does that mean that a "nudist" might be covered by section 29 if she is attacked for believing in nudism or for appearing on a nude beach wearing only sunscreen lotion?**   If a religious group is merely a cultural group,[202] then technically nudists fall within the definition of a religious group. The nudist might have no problem demonstrating that the hostility was based on her membership of her group, but she might struggle to get the courts to recognize nudism as a religion. It is doubtful that the nudist would be protected. Consequently, if D vehemently hates V because she is a member of a nudist group or some other peripheral cultural group, his sentence for assaulting her will not be increased under section 29. The courts will probably construe the provision so that it will only cover conventional religions. Some religions are clearly linked to philosophers (*e.g.*, Confucianism) rather than a divine rule, but would surely count for the purpose of section 29. (These are controversial issues, which cannot be fully addressed in this work on criminal law.)

9–059   **Does that mean that if the victim is from a certain religious/racial background, she will automatically get the extra protection provided by section 29?**   No. The attacker will only be liable under section 29, if it can be proved that he demonstrated hostility based on the victim's membership of a racial or religious group. If the defendant keeps his motivation secret, then V will get no greater protection than the next person. If the attacker is a recidivist he will probably be too cunning to make his motivation known.

9–060   **What if the defendant makes his racist comments 20 minutes after he physically attacks V?**   He will not be liable, because his offensive comments are not immediately connected with the assault.[203] D must make the comment during the attack or immediately before or after. Immediately after would catch those who make such comments as they are leaving the scene of the crime. If D has completed his attack and has left the scene, his comments will not be immediate. However, the courts are likely to be stricter in cases where the comments are made in the lead up to the attack, as the racist or anti-religious sentiment could be playing on D's mind in the lead up to the attack.[204]

9–061   **Need the racist comments be hostile? Suppose a white man approaches a black woman in a club and says: "Miss, I want to kiss a black woman; I want to see what it is like to kiss a black woman."**   If the facts are such that he commits a psychic assault,[205] he could get a maximum prison sentence of two years rather than one of six months. However, it appears that the offender in your

---

[202] See Ian Hacking, *The Social Construction of What?* (Cambridge Mass: Harvard University Press, 1999).

[203] *Parry v. D.P.P.* [2005] A.C.D. 64.

[204] *R. v. Babbs* [2007] EWCA Crim. 2737.

[205] In *Lynch v. Com.*, 131 Va. 762 (1921), D said these exact words to V and put his hand on V's arm. It was held he had committed an assault. If there is a battery of a sexual nature, then it could be caught by section 3 of the *Sexual Offences Act 2003*.

hypothetical did not demonstrate towards the victim hostility based on her membership (or presumed membership) of a racial group. There is no doubt that his encounter was racially motivated, but it would be difficult to show that he was hostile towards the victim because of her race.

From the victims' perspective, section 29 of the *Crime and Disorder Act 1998* 9–062
seems to contravene the equality[206] and proportionate punishment princi-
ples.[207] Should not all victims be entitled to equal protection and equal
retribution under the criminal law?   As far as proportionality in punishment is concerned, the hate expression component does not seem sufficient for justifying four times the sentence for common assault and nearly half the sentence again for the section 20 and 47 offences. It treats the physical harm as less worthy of deterrence than the offensive speech. (The offensive speech only counts as harm if it causes its victim to suffer from a recognized mental illness, which will hardly ever be the case.) As far as the principle of equal protection under the criminal law is concerned, some victims are deemed to be worthy of less protection because they do not belong to a particular social group. Regardless of the background of the victim, the defendant should be punished equally where the harm is equal.

Another objection is that this provision punishes conduct that is not otherwise criminalized. It is not generally a crime to call European ladies "bloody foreigners."[208] If this conduct is not criminalized *per se*, how can it be used to justify a double or quadruple sentence? If D uttered the words "foreigners" in a rude way without committing an assault, he would not commit a crime. If such comments or motivations are to be criminalized, then the appropriate way to do it would be to criminalize the offensive expression itself. This would allow the lawmaker to impose an appropriate sentence, which would normally be a fine. It would also give the wrongdoer fair warning as to what he should not be doing. Hate speech should only be punished with jail terms if it incites harm to others.

The higher sentences are designed to offer greater protection to certain humans on the basis of their sexual orientation, race, and so on. In the case of disabled people, it is arguable that a higher sentence is justifiable because of the special vulnerability of the victim. A disabled person has less means of escape, and it seems fair to punish those who take advantage of vulnerable people more severely. As for other characteristics such as sexual orientation, race and religion, a higher sentence cannot be reconciled with the fundamental principle that all humans are equal and are entitled to equal protection under the law. Why is the victim of an honour killing worthy of greater protection from her potential killer

---

[206] W. T. Blackstone, "On The Meaning and Justification of The Equality Principle," (1967) 77(4) *Ethics* 239; John Stanton-Ife, "Should Equality be a Constitutional Principle?" 11 *K.C.L.J.* 133 (2000). In *Hunt v. Cromartie*, 526 U.S. 541 (1999), the United States Supreme Court held that: "All laws that classify citizens on the basis of race … are constitutionally suspect and must be strictly scrutinized under the Equal Protection Clause of the Fourteenth Amendment" of the *United States Constitution*. (It is the victim that is treated unequally, but procedurally a bigot who suffers xenophobia might argue that his punishment for causing g.b.h. should be the same as it is for the non-xenophobic who causes g.b.h.)

[207] For a good account of the theory of proportionate punishment, see Andrew von Hirsch, *Censure and Sanctions*, (Oxford: Clarendon Press, 1993).

[208] See *R. v. Rogers* [2007] 2 A.C. 62.

than any other member of society is from her potential killer? Those who physically harm others are motivated by all sorts of equally vile considerations. The attacker might be motivated by a hatred of disabled people, women,[209] rich people,[210] fat people, gay and lesbian people, old people,[211] and so on.

9–063 Let us assume that D throws acid into X's eyes because she is fat. Suppose also that D does the same thing to Y because Y is Spanish. Let us also assume that X and Y are both blinded for life by D's attack. Why is the fat victim worthy of less protection than the Spanish victim? The evilness of D's motivation does not change the harmfulness of what he did to Y—nor does it mean that people belonging to Y's group are worthy of greater protection than people belonging to X's group. Furthermore, both victims are entitled to the same level of retribution:

> "It makes a great difference to the victim whether the community takes his wrong seriously, or passes it off as of no consequence. If he sees the man who cared nothing for him go scot-free, he is given to understand that society cares nothing for him either. But if the wrongdoer is made to see the error of his ways, the man to whom the wrong was done sees his rights vindicated, and is assured that society cares for him, even if one of its members does not, and will uphold his rights in face of assault and injury."[212]

It must make a great difference to X whether the community takes her blindness as seriously as it does Y's blindness. The same would apply if X had not been fat. If a person is harmed simply because the attacker has no respect for her as a human being, he disrespects her dignity and human worth no less than if he had been motivated to attack her because of her lesbianism and so on.

9–064 **Surely if D1 is motivated to attack V1 because of her sexual orientation, race or religion he is more evil than D2 who is motivated to attack V2 merely because of his hatred of her as a human being?** I cannot see how. Both seem to disrespect the dignity of their victims equally. It is oxymoronic to argue that if D intentionally blinds X (a lesbian) and also blinds Y (a Spanish lady), that he respected X's humanity and dignity more because he did not mention her sexual orientation as he blinded her. Similarly, the disrespect he has for Y is equal regardless of whether he mentions her ethnicity. Anyone who is willing to blind another human being has no respect for that person's dignity or humanity.[213] Is the animal activist worthy of less punishment than the terrorist if he causes as much injury to his victims as the terrorist did to his? Does it matter that the terrorist was motivated by religious hatred, while the animal activist was motivated by a desire to spare animals from being used in experiments? It is hard

---

[209] Ironically, some criminal laws criminalize women because of their status. A man can go topless in a public park, but a woman is liable to be arrested for a public order offence. However, women surely have an equal right to go topless on a summer's day. See *People v. Santorelli*, 80 N.Y.2d 875 (1992).
[210] Or could the poor be a special class worthy of special protection, even though they are the majority of the populace. See the interesting discussion in Henry Rose, "The Poor as a Suspect Class under the Equal Protection Clause: An Open Constitutional Question," (2009) 34 *Nova L. Rev.* 407.
[211] Sixth Report—*Shipman Inquiry*, (London: H.M.S.O., 2005).
[212] J. R. Lucas, *Responsibility*, (Oxford: Clarendon Press, 1993) at 104. See also Stephen P. Garvey, "Self-Defence and the Mistaken Racist," (2008) 11 *New Crim. L. Rev.* 119.
[213] Dennis J. Baker, "The Harm Principle vs Kantian Criteria for Ensuring Fair, Principled and Just Criminalisation," (2008) 33 *Austl. J. Leg. Phil.* 66.

to see why one is deserving of more punishment than the other, if they have both managed to inflict an equal amount of harm on the same number of victims.

Whatever the motivation of the defendant we are surely entitled to equal protection under the criminal law and to equal retribution. The majority of assaults are not motivated by homophobia and xenophobia; rather the cause is often excessive alcohol consumption. Consequently, if "specific" deterrence is the aim of such laws, then they should also penalize alcohol related violence.[214] Intoxicated offenders as a class pose the greatest statistical risk.[215] Similarly, the homophobe or xenophobe is normally motivated by a hatred of humanity *simpliciter*. Besides that, offending rates do not provide a rational basis for formulating penal policy. Proportional punishment and fair labelling is about punishing people for their individual wrongdoing.[216]

Welcoming these offences is tempting if we just consider the offender's evil character, as it is difficult to have sympathy for such offenders. As a society we have an obligation to do all we can to counter these forms of hatred, but the criminal law should only be used to achieve such a objective in extreme cases. Soft-power is likely to be more effective. Attempting to force tolerance by criminalizing the intolerant is not likely to work. Jail time is not likely to make the hater love what he hated when he is released from prison. Debate and education is a better way to deal with such people. (There may be a strong case for enacting independent hate speech offences, but J. C. Smith is probably right to suggest that it should not be done by tagging them on to the end of an antiquated set of offences that target physical harm.)

From the victim's perspective the offences are unjust and unconstitutional. The proponents of "unequal protection" need a theory that can explain to the victims why they are not entitled to equal protection under the criminal law for equal harm. It is easy to see how grossly offensive comments can arouse public sentiment, but a person who attacks another because he hates humanity is no less deserving of punishment than one who provides the victim with an explanation of why he hates humanity "at the time of committing the offence, or immediately before or after doing so." The gravamen of offences against the person is disrespect for the victim as a person. A person's characteristics are subsumed by her personhood—they are a part of her. The gravamen of offensive expression is that it causes profound disgust, but the disgust does not cause the type of harm that the *Act of 1861* criminalizes. The latter requires the psychological distress to cause the victim to suffer from a recognized mental illness, anything less is not regarded as a.b.h. or g.b.h.[217]

---

[214] Similarly, it would be wrong to punish an offender less or more merely because they belong to a class of people who statistically commit more crimes. Cf. William J. Stuntz, "Unequal Justice," (2008) 121 *Harv. L. Rev.* 1669.

[215] Even though there has been an increase in racist and anti-religious assaults, such assaults only make up a small share of the total. See Fowles and Wilson, "Racist and Religious Crime Data," (2004) 43 *Howard J. Crim. Just.* 441.

[216] Dennis J. Baker, "Collective Criminalization and the Constitutional Right to Endanger Others," 28 *Crim. Just. Ethics* 168.

[217] Repeated abuse could culminate in harm. Alternatively, it could be tackled by invoking the *Protection from Protection from Harassment Act 1997.*

If the hate speech does not cause physical or psychological harm, then the defendant should be prosecuted under section 5 of the *Public Order Act 1986*. That offence is designed to criminalise offensive and hatred words; a separate charge under this Act would allow the judge to impose a separate sentence for the psychological distress component of the wrong.[218] It would be appropriate to also charge the offender with an offence under the *Act of 1861* for any physical harm that he may have caused. Extreme hate speech inciting actual violence is harmful and thus is clearly worthy of criminalization.

9.10. PERMISSIBLE ALTERNATIVE VERDICTS

9–065 The effect of the decision in *R. v. Wilson*[219] in the Court of Appeal was that assault and the offence under section 47 were no longer included offences on a charge under section 20. The facts were that Wilson was driving a car when he had a "misunderstanding" with a pedestrian. The misunderstanding was unfortunate for the pedestrian, because the result of it was that Wilson punched him to the extent of seriously injuring him. Wilson was charged on an indictment containing a single count under section 20. The judge directed the jury that if they were satisfied that actual bodily harm was inflicted but no more, they might convict under section 47 as an included offence; and this they accordingly did. In giving his instruction the judge was faithfully following precedents dating from 1869 which were binding on him. On appeal, the Court of Appeal quashed the conviction. The judge had conducted the trial properly; the conviction was fair, and was in accordance with the law when it was rendered; but the judge, not being a clairvoyant, had failed to take account of the rule (stated above) that the Court of Appeal had invented for the first time.

But the jury found that Wilson committed an assault which occasioned actual bodily harm. Surely, therefore, they found all the essential elements necessary for a conviction under section 47. The question is not what the jury find but what has been expressly or impliedly charged. The relation of an included offence to the express charge may be visualized as a step (the included offence) leading to a platform (the offence charged), where the step must be mounted in order to reach the platform. If you can reach the platform by a straight jump, then the step is not an included offence. Since the Court of Appeal held that the offence charged under section 20 could be proved without mounting the step (proof of assault), it was thought that the offence under section 47 was not an included offence.

In the House of Lords, Lord Roskill said:[220]

> "The allegations in a section 20 charge 'include either expressly or by implication' allegations of assault occasioning actual bodily harm. If 'inflicting' can, as the cases show, include 'inflicting by assault', then even though such a charge may not necessarily do so, I do not for

---

[218] *Offence to others* should be punished with fines. *Offence to others* that causes or incites harm-doing should be punished with proportionate jail terms. See Dennis J. Baker, "Constitutionalizing the Harm Principle," 27 *Crim. Just. Ethics* 3.

[219] [1983] 1 W.L.R. 356.

[220] *R. v. Wilson* [1984] A.C. 242 at 260–261.

myself see why on a fair reading of section 6(3) of the *Criminal Law Act 1967*[221] these allegations do not at least impliedly include 'inflicting by assault'. That is sufficient for present purposes though I also regard it as also a possible view that those former allegations expressly include the other allegations. … [I]t follows that both the learned judge and learned recorder were correct in leaving the possibility of conviction of the section 47 offences to the jury in these cases."

Section 6(3) of the *Criminal Law Act 1967* means it is open to the jury to convict a defendant of an offence under section 20 of the *Offences against the Person Act 1861* as an alternative to a charge under section 18 of that *Act*.[222] And as we have just seen, section 6(3) of the *Criminal Law Act 1967* means it is open to the jury to convict a defendant of an offence under section 47 as an alternative to a charge under section 20.[223] In a trial on indictment any obvious and viable alternative verdict should be left to the jury if there is clear evidence to support it. The fact that the parties might not want the verdict left to the jury is of no consequence.[224]

9.11. PROTECTION FROM HARASSMENT

We have a number of offences of harassment. It is provided by statute that a landlord commits an offence if he harasses a "residential occupier" with intent to cause him to give up occupation, or with intent to make him refrain from exercising a right that he has as a tenant.[225] This covers not only physical "winking" by locking the tenant out, but threatening him and his family with violence, or withdrawing services.[226]

9–066

---

[221] The latter constitutes "another offence" within the ambit of section 6(3) of the *Criminal Law Act 1967*. It provides: "Where, on a person's trial on indictment for any offence except treason or murder, the jury find him not guilty of the offence specifically charged in the indictment, but the allegations in the indictment amount to *or* include (expressly or by implication) an allegation of another offence … the jury may find him guilty of that other offence or of an offence of which he could be found guilty on an indictment specifically charging that other offence." Glanville Williams has observed: "Section 6(3) was obviously intended to restate the long-standing rule at common law that an offence is not included in another unless all its ingredients are so included in the other that they can be regarded as implicitly alleged in an allegation of the other." Glanville Williams, "Alternative Elements and Included Offences," (1984) 43 *Cambridge L.J.* 290 at 299.

[222] *R. v. Mandair* [1995] 1 A.C. 208.

[223] *R. v. Wilson* [1984] A.C. 242.

[224] *R. v. Coutts* [2006] 1 W.L.R. 2154. See also *R. v. Griffiths* [2005] EWCA Crim. 237; *R. v. Swift* [1992] Crim. L.R. 48; *R. v. Savage* [1992] 1 A.C. 699.

[225] Section 1 of the *Protection from Eviction Act 1977*. See *R. v. Phekoo* [1981] 1 W.L.R. 1117; *West Wiltshire DC v. Snelgrove* (1998) 30 H.L.R. 57. The offence is triable either way, so if the landlord has used violence in order to enter it may be preferable (in order to stop him claiming jury trial) to charge the purely summary offence of violent entry under section 6(1) of the *Criminal Law Act 1977*. Cf. section 3 of the *Caravan Sites Act 1968*.

[226] The landlord's success in *Westminster City Council v. Peart* (1968) 19 P. & C.R. 736 was apparently due to a mistake made by the court as to the law of pleading: see *R. v. Abrol* [1972] Crim. L.R. 318. The Committee on the *Rent Acts* received "horrifying stories" of harassment by landlords by tenants to prevent them from pursuing their remedies ("Report of the Committee on the Rents Act," (1971) 34 *Mod. L. Rev.* 427 at 431) but no offence of this character was created.

Harassment of contractual debtors is also an offence.[227] It can be committed by over-frequent demands for payment, if they are calculated to subject the debtor or members of his family or household to alarm, distress or humiliation. Widely as the statute is drawn, the courts administer it with due restraint, though the use of a van marked "Debt Collection" in visiting the debtor would undoubtedly call forth a penalty.

In 1997 three further harassment offences were enacted to tackle certain forms of personal harassment.[228] The offences were designed to address the shortfalls of the law of assault. It was said before, that assault does not criminalize threats of future violence. The problem with the law of assault is that it only deals with threats against the *person*, and only threats of immediate violence.[229] Consequently, those who threaten property are not covered. Nor does the law of assault cover other forms of harassing conduct such as where D installs C.C.T.V. cameras to keep his neighbour under constant surveillance. If X films Y while he is in his own backyard he would violate his privacy. Since this could have the effect of causing the householder or members of his family alarm, distress or humiliation, the courts are likely to hold that it is a form of harassment. The conduct need not be related to threats of physical violence. It need only be harassing. If D tells his former girlfriend he is going to post her nude photographs/videos on Facebook (where they may have many common friends),[230] he does not threaten immediate violence, so is not caught by the law of assault. But he does threaten to totally humiliate his victim. A series of threats (that is, two or more threats) of this nature would constitute harassment, even though it would not be caught by the law of assault. Similarly, if D sends his former lover dozens of begging letters to try to rekindle their relationship; his letters might not be directly threatening (they may say the nicest things, or merely beg for forgiveness), but repeatedly sending letters to a person that does not want to receive them could have the effect making that person feel threatened or harassed.[231]

9-067   Section 1 of the *Protection from Harassment Act 1997* provides:

---

[227] Section 40 of the *Administration of Justice Act 1970*. In addition, subs. 1(*b*) makes it an offence to falsely represent that criminal proceedings lie for failure to pay a debt; (*c*) penalizes a false representation that one is authorized in some official capacity to claim payment; and (*d*) penalizes false representations that a document has some official character. Unfair debt-collecting methods may be reported to the local trading standards officer, and the Office of Fair Trading may then put the debt collector out of business by revoking his licence under the *Consumer Credit Act 1974*.

[228] For a discussion of the "stalking" phenomenon see L. F. Lowenstein, "Stalking Phenomenon," (2000) 73 *Police J.* 153; Kenneth Campbell, "Stalking around the Main Issue," (1998) 8 *K.C.L.J.* 128; Ursula Smart, "The Stalking Phenomenon: Trends in European and International Stalking and Harassment Legislation," (2001) 9 *Eur. J. Crime Crim. L. & Crim Just.* 209.

[229] See for example, *R. v. Medley* [2009] EWCA Crim. 1604, where D telephoned his ex-girlfriend and said: "'Are you ready to drop the charges?' ... At 8 o'clock, later that morning, she received a further telephone call and the defendant on this occasion said: 'I'm getting closer to doing some serious damage, you little bitch.'" Assault is not made out on these facts, as there was no threat of immediate violence.

[230] *King v. D.P.P.* [2001] A.C.D. 7; *R. v. Stender* [2004] 188 C.C.C. (3d) 514. For examples of very intimate material being posted on the Internet, see Dennis J. Baker, "The Sense and Nonsense of Criminalising Transfers of Obscene Material," (2008) 26 *Sing. L. Rev.* 126.

[231] Cf. *Crawford v. CPS* [2008] EWHC 148, where a barrister was held liable for harassing his solicitor wife.

"(1)   A person must not pursue a course of conduct—(a) which amounts to harassment of another, and (b) which he knows or ought to know amounts to harassment of the other.

(1A)   A person must not pursue a course of conduct—(a) which involves harassment of two or more persons, and (b) which he knows or ought to know involves harassment of those persons, and (c) by which he intends to persuade any person (whether or not one of those mentioned above)—(i) not to do something that he is entitled or required to do, or (ii) to do something that he is not under any obligation to do.

(2)   For the purposes of this section, the person whose course of conduct is in question ought to know that it amounts to or involves harassment of another if a reasonable person in possession of the same information would think the course of conduct amounted to or involved harassment of the other."

Section 2 provides:

"(1)   A person who pursues a course of conduct in breach of section 1(1) or (1A) is guilty of an offence."

The offence is a summary offence. The legislation targets two forms of harm: 1) the direct harm that is caused by the harassment itself (that is, the intimidation and annoyance that results from D repeatedly interfering in V's life); and 2) the greater harm that is likely to result in cases where the harasser becomes obsessive. An obsessive stalker might end up raping or murdering his victim. So long as a crime lies in the mind it is not punishable, because criminal thoughts often occur to people without any serious intention of putting them into execution. The position is different when some step is taken to put the desire into effect. The harassment offences allow a person who starts harassing another to be checked before his harassment leads to something more serious. The harassment laws not only criminalize a consummated harm (intimidation and personal annoyance), but also allow the police to step in before some greater harm is done.

If the threat is a direct threat to kill the victim, then it would come within the purview of section 16 of the *Offences against the Person Act 1861*. If the threat is made on more than one occasion then it could also be charged under section 4 of the *Protection from Harassment Act 1997*. The threats may be serious or trivial. Obviously, if the threat is of a serious nature then a single threat in itself would be harassing. But a single threat is not caught by the *1997 Act*. The threat (or, other harassing act) has to be repeated at least once for it to constitute a course of conduct.

9–068

The *Act* criminalizes any trivial annoyance so long as it is repeated at least once. Obviously, if the conduct is very trivial it will have to be repeated many times to pass the "unreasonableness" requirement.[232] Other innocuous interferences will also come within the purview of the *Act*, if they are repeated more than once. For instance, X does not harm Y by sending her red roses. The act of sending red roses is hardly threatening, but it might be oppressive and intimidating where the woman has rejected the advances of the sender many times before. If the roses are sent repeatedly after the receiver has made it clear that she is not interested, then the receiver might start to fear for her safety.[233] The

---

[232] For example, making 90 or more telephone calls within an hour would be unreasonable and harassing. See *D.P.P. v. Hardy* (2009) 173 J.P. 10.

[233] Cf. *King v. D.P.P.* [2001] A.C.D. 7. In such a case, it would be difficult for D to argue this conduct was reasonable.

sender's obsessive behaviour implies that he might not be mentally stable, as he is unable to respond to normal social cues. The degree of alarm and distress would vary depending on the context and on V's past experiences with the stalker and so on. It is for this reason that the *1997 Act* criminalizes a course of conduct. The *Act* aims to criminalize acts that are harmful in aggregate.

9–069   **Cannot a single act be calculated to subject the victim to alarm, distress or humiliation?**   The Court of Appeal has tried to explain the concept of harassment in the following passage:[234]

> "To harass ... is to 'torment by subjecting to constant interference or intimidation'. The conduct must be unacceptable to a degree which would sustain criminal liability and also must be oppressive. Section 7 of the *1997 Act* does not purport to provide a comprehensive definition of harassment. There are many actions that foreseeably alarm or cause a person distress that could not possibly be described as harassment. It seems to me that section 7 is dealing with that element of the offence which is constituted by the effect of the conduct rather than with the types of conduct that produce that effect. ... The *Act* does not attempt to define the type of conduct that is capable of constituting harassment. 'Harassment' is, however, a word which has a meaning which is generally understood. It describes conduct targeted at an individual which is calculated to produce the consequences described in section 7 and which is oppressive and unreasonable. The practice of stalking is a prime example of such conduct."

If X telephones Y and says, "I am going to rape you when I get out of jail next month," he would not have to repeat the threat for it to cause the victim great angst. If a rapist telephones the person he raped before being sent to prison to tell her that he intends to rape her again when he is released, this clearly could have the effect of making the victim constantly fear his release. Even though this is a very serious threat which may have grave consequences for the victim, it will not be caught by either the law of assault or the law of harassment. As we will see, a one off threat does not constitute a course of conduct.

9–070   **The definition provided by the Court of Appeal sounds rather circular to me; it appears that the magistrates get to decide whether or not the harassment is criminal conduct.**   The way the courts have conceptualized harassment may not be perfect, but it is the conduct that varies not the concept. It is true, that like the concept of negligence and reasonableness, to a large degree, harassment is a factual issue that requires the application of objective community standards.[235] Nevertheless, it is possible to draw some fairly clear legal lines. The "intimidation" criterion is not controversial. Repeatedly intimidating another is harassment and should be criminalized. The definition is also fairly clear as far as repeated interference is concerned. A person should not have to put up with repeated interferences, even if they are trivial.[236]

---

[234] *R. v. Curtis* [2010] 1 W.L.R. 2770 at 2777 citing Lord Phillips of Worth Matravers M.R., with whom Jonathan Parker L.J. and Lord Mustill agreed, in *Thomas v. News Group Newspapers Ltd.* [2002] E.M.L.R.78, paras. 29, 30.

[235] See 2.3. n. 40.

[236] "[T]he frequency of acts, may well throw light on whether [the conduct] amounts to harassment." *R. v. Curtis* [2010] 1 W.L.R. 2770 at 2778. See also *Pratt v. D.P.P.* [2001] EWHC 483 at para. 10.

The interference need not be serious and need not be aimed at any particular victim. In *R. v. Lindsky*,[237] D repeatedly annoyed his neighbours by going naked in his own backyard. It was the repetitious nature of his conduct that made his conduct a criminal matter: one neighbour was too scared to host a birthday party for her young child because she feared D would appear in his backyard in the nude. She cancelled the party because she did not want to risk having the children see him. The focus here is on the unjustified "interference" in the lives of others. Notwithstanding that the sight of a naked person is not threatening in itself, a person should have the freedom to be spared such information when she is in her own backyard. The homeowner has the right to be spared from receiving D's very intimate information when she is trying to enjoy her own home; and she should have the right to decide whether she wants her small children to see a naked man. The act might not be threatening or harmful *per se*, but it interferes with the neighbour's right to be let alone in her own backyard, and since it is repeated over and over it seems to warrant a criminal law response.[238]

What is less clear is what is meant by the "to a degree that would sustain criminal liability" standard. It would make sense to hold that many repeated trivial interferences warrant a criminal law response, such as dozens of phone calls, or harassing letters from a firm demanding payment of a debt that is not due and so on.[239] But the *Act* only requires the interference to be repeated once. And as we will see, the *Act* has been used to criminalize trivial interferences that do not warrant a criminal law response. At the other end of the scale no such problem arises. It is fairly clear that serious interferences that are designed to intimidate, humiliate and terrorize the victim warrant a criminal law response. Obviously, repetition is not a major issue when the interference is serious. It seems fair to criminalize these types of interferences if they occur on more than one occasion. Take for example the conduct in *R. v. Lewis*.[240] In that case, D conducted a campaign of harassment against V, a lady who lived next door to him. His acts of interference included sending her an obscene and aggressive Valentine's card; sending controversial letters to the local press in her name; arranging for suitors in a lonely hearts column to contact her; displaying in a local bus shelter a poster of a woman offering sexual services giving her name and address; and forging a cheque purporting to come from her and using it to place an order in her name for sex aids. No one should have to endure this type of repeated harassment. These types of interferences are clearly designed to cause the victim serious humiliation and distress and thus are the business of the criminal law.

The core problem with the summary offences of harassment is that they cast the net too wide. They have the potential to catch many offenders for merely annoying the victim. In particular, it could be used to sort out neighbourly disputes that should not be the business of the criminal law. If an uneducated

9–071

---

[237] [2009] EWCA Crim. 2721. Cf. the offence in section 42A of the *Criminal Justice and Police Act 2001* vis-à-vis dwellings.

[238] Dennis J. Baker "The Impossibility of a Critically Objective Criminal Law," (2011) 56(2) *McGill L. J.* 349.

[239] *Ferguson v. British Gas Trading Ltd.* [2010] 1 W.L.R. 785.

[240] *R. v. Lewis* [2003] EWCA Crim. 395.

person is extremely rude and uses foul language to try to vent his grievances with social services on more than one occasion he could be liable for harassment, even when it is clear that he poses no danger to anyone. In *James v D.P.P.*[241] a conviction for harassment was upheld because the disabled defendant verbally abused the victim who had telephoned him. He was trying to complain about the poor quality of care he had been provided, but was extremely rude in doing so.[242] Surely, the appropriate response would have been for the social worker to hang the telephone up. It seems a great waste of taxpayers' money to prosecute an uneducated person who is too inarticulate to complain in strong but non-abusive terms. The offences should target conduct that is repeated many more times than twice, if it is to be used to criminalize the types of everyday disputes that arise in workplaces and neighbourhoods.[243] In life people have to tolerate a certain amount of annoyance. The criminal law[244] should only be invoked to tackle sufficiently grave forms of harassment.

Another case that should never have made it to the courts is *R. (on the application of Jones) v. Bedfordshire and Mid Bedfordshire Magistrates Court.*[245] In that case D was convicted of harassment, because she engaged in petty name-calling and made a threat to paint her own garage door an ugly colour. Surely this type of wrongdoing is too trivial to be the business of the criminal law. The law of harassment is being used to solve silly neighbourhood disputes that do not involve harm to others. Criminalizing offensive speech of a non-threatening kind between neighbours is too great an extension of the criminal law and too great a restriction of liberty. People have to tolerate some name-calling and trivial abuses in the real world. This type of criminalization could have the effect of disproportionately catching those who are too inarticulate to disguise their verbal abuse. A sophisticated verbal-abuser is more likely to act in a passive aggressive way. Furthermore, the law could be used as a weapon of revenge by a party to a neighbourhood dispute, even when he does not have clean hands himself. The law should only provide the victim with a shield, not with a shield and a sword!

---

[241] [2009] EWHC 2925, where it was also said in the head-note: "The fact that D had not made the telephone calls himself was irrelevant. D had known that V was obliged, as manager of the adult care team, to return his calls. In any event, even if the calls had not been directly initiated by D, if an individual was continually abusive to someone who came within his vicinity, that would still amount to a course of conduct, even if the victim chose to come within his vicinity." The "reasonableness" defence could apply here if D could show that the person had been asked to stay away from him, but repeatedly approached him when there was no cause for doing so.

[242] "He apparently said that he could not promise that he would allow Mrs. Thomas [the social worker] to leave his house without an axe in her head." This was said over the telephone, and Mrs. Thomas had no obligation to visit him so how serious one would take the threat is not clear. But that aside, this type of threat is not mere abuse, it is intimidation of the worst kind, and it is little wonder the court was swayed to uphold his conviction. *James v D.P.P.* [2009] EWHC 2925 at para. 4.

[243] Cf. *Kellett v. D.P.P.* [2001] EWHC Admin. 107.

[244] See *Ferguson v. British Gas Trading Ltd.* [2010] 1 W.L.R. 785, where it was held even the civil law should only be invoked to tackle harassment that is reasonably grave.

[245] [2010] 3 All E.R. 1057. In a U.S. case a court applied the *de minimis* infraction defence (see 24.11. *infra*) to dismiss charges of harassment where the harassment was trivial: *State of N.J. v. Bazin*, 912 F. Supp. 106 (1995).

What is meant by two or more persons?   This provision is designed to cover   9–072
groups of people who may be harassed for belonging to a particular collective.
The collective might be as small as a family. Suppose that D says to his
neighbour X, "I am fed up with your barking dog, if I hear it again I will kill it."
Suppose a week later D sees X's wife and repeats his threat. Here D has
threatened two members of the same household and the threats have been made
more than once, *caeteris paribus*,[246] he could be liable for harassment. The "two
or more persons" protection aims to cover members of collectives such as
employees of a scientific laboratory that uses animals for research or the
employees of a farm that breeds guinea pigs for research.[247]

Animal activists have targeted people to try to get them to stop doing what
they have a lawful right to do. In one case, militant animal activists carried out a
vicious campaign of harassment to persuade a guinea pig farmer from farming
guinea pigs (*i.e.* to persuade him "not to do something that he is entitled or
required to do"). The campaign was not only aimed at the farmer but also his
employees and anyone associated with the farm. The militant activists removed
the remains of his family member from a grave, started a smear campaign
alleging that he was a paedophile, cut the electricity supply to his farm and
committed various other acts of criminal damage.[248] Alas, the activists got their
way, because the harassment was sufficient to persuade the family to close its
farm. To the extent that these activists try to persuade employees from working
for such an organization, it is enough that they target one employee today and a
different one tomorrow. After all, their aim is to persuade two people from the
same collective of individuals from doing something they are entitled to do. The
complainants should be members of a close-knit, definable group and the conduct
should be "clearly aimed at all of them on each occasion, although only one had
been present."[249]

What is meant by a course of conduct?   The defendant engages in a course of   9–073
conduct by committing a series of harassing acts. One harassing act in isolation is
not a course of acts. It is about doing two or more acts which objectively judged
have one end: the harassment of the victim.

What if activist X helps activist Y to make a threat to V on Monday, and X   9–074
repeats the threat himself on Friday?   This will constitute a course of
conduct. X will be liable pursuant to section 7(3A) of the *1997 Act* as inserted by
section 44 of the *Criminal Justice and Police Act 2001*.

---

[246] D might be able to show he acted reasonably if there is strong evidence that the dog kept the
neighbourhood awake at night by barking, and that repeated polite requests to the owners to do
something about it were to no avail. (Of course, the most reasonable response would be to report the
dog to the relevant authorities.)

[247] Often the organization will seek a civil injunction to prevent the harassment. See *EDO MBM
Technology Ltd. v. Campaign to Smash EDO* [2005] EWHC 837; *Hall v. Save Newchurch Guinea
Pigs (Campaign)* (2005) 102(21) L.S.G. 33.

[248] "Hundreds of people were terrorized by the protesters. Threats had been made against anyone who
was associated with the family who own the farm, who were themselves the subject of paedophilia
smears." Jonathan Brown and Robert Dex, "Animal rights activists condemned as guinea pig farm
gives up fight," (London: *The Independent*, Wednesday, 24 August 2005).

[249] *D.D.P. v. Dunn* [2001] 1 Cr. App. R. 22. Cf. *D.P.P. v. Dziurzynski* [2002] A.C.D. 88.

9–075 **What if a bitter union boss sends Baroness Thatcher a nasty letter each year on the anniversary of her reforming the mining industry? Does a one year gap between the acts of harassment prevent them from forming an interconnected series of harassing acts?** No. But such cases are likely to be rare.[250] The stalker is normally more persistent than this. In most cases a one year gap will prevent the sequence of acts from forming a course of conduct. Acts that are remotely connected in time will not normally be sufficient to constitute a course of conduct. The word "course" refers to a continuous pattern of conduct. There should be a series of acts that have some temporal and purposeful connection with each other. Since the acts in your hypothetical are sequential and singularly purposeful, they would form a course of conduct.

At the other end of the spectrum, the acts may be so close in time as to constitute a single act. In *Kelly v. D.P.P.*,[251] D made three telephone calls within five minutes to his former partner. The Divisional Court held that that these independent calls constituted a course of conduct. It might be argued that acts this close in time should be treated as one bout of harassment. But technically the series of calls are not a continuous act. One sensible reason for treating each call as a separate incident is that the defendant could repeat the calls at a minute interval *ad infinitum*.

9–076 **Need the acts be identical?** No. But they must be of a similar nature (*i.e.* of a harassing nature). They must also relate to a particular course of harassment. It is not enough that D stalked V 20 years ago and has started to do so again.

Suppose D telephones V to tell her that he is going to destroy her car, because it was parked a bit close to his driveway thereby making it a little difficult for him to access his driveway. Suppose also that he telephones her the next day to apologize and to withdraw his threat. When he telephones the second time he says, "I am very sorry for complaining about your car being parked too close to my driveway yesterday and for threatening to damage it, I was slightly inebriated and I am deeply sorry for making such a silly threat." The acts are interconnected and sequential, but they are not both of a "harassing" nature. The second act negates the threat made in the first act, and is intended to put the victim's mind at ease.

Take a further example. Suppose D verbally abuses V (a 50-year-old lesbian), because V has been seeing his 20-year-old daughter without his permission. D says, "I do not want my daughter seeing a lesbian 'bull dyke,' she was an innocent girl before you got your hands on her." By pure chance, a month later V accidentally bumps into D's car at the local shopping mall car park. As a consequence, D flies into a rage and once again abuses V. This time he says, "I

---

[250] See *Pratt v. D.P.P.* [2001] EWHC 483 at para. 10 *per* Latham L.J. See also *Lau v. D.P.P.* [2000] 1 F.L.R. 799 at 801. In the latter case it was held: "the fewer the number of incidents and the wider the time lapse, the less likely such a finding would be justified." Furthermore, the statutory limitation for summary offences is six months. It has been held that the last act in the series of acts has to have been committed in the six months prior to D being prosecuted. *D.P.P. v. Baker* (2005) 169 J.P.N. 78. But if the first act was three years before, this type of continuous act theory seems rather strained indeed!

[251] [2003] A.C.D. 4.

would not expect a stupid lesbian 'bull dyke' to know how to drive, you filthy lesbian." Is this a course of conduct? No, because the acts are isolated and "random."[252]

Would a tough boss be liable for harassment merely for criticizing the poor performance of his staff? What if he gives lots of orders? If the orders and criticisms relate to the employee's employment duties then the boss should not be liable.[253] If, however, the oppressive and critical comments are of a personal nature and have nothing to do with giving orders in the line of duty as so to speak, then he may be liable. We are already over-criminalized, so the law of harassment should only be used as a last resort to sort out office politics amongst adults.

9–077

Would the offence catch the paparazzi? Parliament has not yet found itself able to make harassment by journalists an offence, but extreme cases could be brought within the purview of the *Act*. However given the value of free speech, the content of media reports should not be censored by judges sitting in criminal courts. Such matters should be left to the civil law.

9–078

What mental element is required? The defendant need not intend to harass the victim. It is only necessary to show that a reasonable person in his position (*i.e.* armed with the information he had) would have realized that his course of conduct would have the effect of harassing the victim. Would a reasonable person who has been rejected many times by V realize that continuing to send her roses could amount to harassment? I would think so. If so, it does not matter the defendant did not realize as much. The test is purely objective. Consequently, mental illness and other characteristics of the defendant will not be taken into consideration. If a schizophrenic harasses V, it is no defence for him to argue that his illness prevented him from understanding that his conduct amounted to harassment. Since a reasonable person without his mental illness would understand that continuing to send roses to a woman who has repeatedly asked to be let alone would amount to harassment, he will be liable.[254]

9–079

Is it a defence for D to show that he negligently performed the acts of harassment? No. In *Ferguson v. British Gas Trading Ltd.*[255] the claimant commenced proceedings in the civil courts for the tort of harassment, pursuant to sections 1 and 3 of the *Protection from Harassment Act 1997*. British Gas had been Ms. Ferguson's gas supplier prior to her transferring to another provider. For a period of about five months after the claimant had transferred to another gas supplier she received a series of computer-generated bills and letters claiming sums which she did not owe. The letters also threatened to commence legal

9–080

---

[252] Furthermore, acts that are incidental in that they are part of a two-way and ongoing domestic dispute will not necessarily be acts that form a course of conduct. See *R. v. Curtis* [2010] 1 W.L.R. 2770 at 2778; *R. v. Hills* [2001] 1 F.L.R. 580. Cf. the offence in section 42A of the *Criminal Justice and Police Act 2001*, which covers a resident in the victim's home.

[253] Cf. *Dowson v. Chief Constable of Northumbria* [2010] EWHC 2612; *Lipscombe v. Forestry Commission* [2008] EWHC 3342.

[254] *R. v. C* (2001) 165 J.P.N. 1019; *R. v. Pelham* [2007] EWCA Crim. 1321.

[255] [2010] 1 W.L.R. 785.

proceedings and to report her to credit rating agencies. The claimant wrote to British Gas and made numerous telephone calls to inform it of its error, but this was to no avail. The Civil Division of the Court of Appeal held: "it was, at the very least, strongly arguable that British Gas's conduct in repeatedly sending a former customer unjustified bills and threatening letters was of sufficient gravity to constitute harassment in breach of the *Protection from Harassment Act 1997*."

The court also said the case was an appropriate one for criminal prosecution. Jacob L.J. said:[256] "I would think it entirely proper for a prosecutor, such as a trading standards officer, to bring criminal proceedings in respect of a case where there has been such a period of persistent conduct and such threats as are pleaded here." It was also held that there was no reason why a large corporation should evade liability for engaging in this type of harassment. The corporation attempted to argue that it did not intentionally send out the harassing letters, as they were generated automatically by its staff and computer system. The defendant said its acts of harassment were accidental, because it did not know its computer was sending the threats. The Court of Appeal said, "It was notable that the *1997 Act* did not provide any defence for 'accidental'[257] harassment."[258] Surely it meant negligence harassment.

9–081   **What is the purpose of the section 4 offence?**   Section 4 creates an offence which is triable either way.[259] It carries a maximum sentence of five years imprisonment, and specifically targets conduct that causes the victim to fear violence. Section 4 provides:

> "(1)   A person whose course of conduct causes another to fear, on at least two occasions, that violence will be used against him is guilty of an offence if he knows or ought to know that his course of conduct will cause the other so to fear on each of those occasions.
>
> (2)   For the purposes of this section, the person whose course of conduct is in question ought to know that it will cause another to fear that violence will be used against him on any occasion if a reasonable person in possession of the same information would think the course of conduct would cause the other so to fear on that occasion.
>
> (3)   It is a defence for a person charged with an offence under this section to show that—(a) his course of conduct was pursued for the purpose of preventing or detecting crime, (b) his course of conduct was pursued under any enactment or rule of law or to comply with any condition or requirement imposed by any person under any enactment, or (c) the pursuit of his course of conduct was reasonable for the protection of himself or another or for the protection of his or another's property."

This provision only covers harassment which results in the particular victim fearing that he will be subjected to violence. Again, the course of conduct element must be satisfied. D must cause V to fear violence on at least two occasions. It is not enough to show that members of V's family feared violence.

---

[256] *Ferguson v. British Gas Trading Ltd.* [2010] 1 W.L.R. 785 at 791.

[257] Perhaps, it should have said, "grossly negligent" harassment, since the customer repeatedly told the staff working for British Gas of the error.

[258] *Ferguson v. British Gas Trading Ltd.* [2010] 1 W.L.R. 785 at 795. It is arguable that the corporation and its employees were grossly negligent if not reckless in sending out the threats, since the claimant (and no doubt thousands of others like her) told them repeatedly of their mistakes.

[259] On a trial on indictment, the jury may find a defendant guilty of an offence under section 2, as an alternative to convicting on a charge under section 4. *R. v. Curtis* [2010] 1 W.L.R. 2770 at 2775.

The victim must himself fear the violence.[260] As was said before, there is no need to show that V feared that the violence would be inflicted in the immediate future. Since an unjustified threat of violence is by its very nature a form of harassment, the offence is not as vague as the offence found in section 2.

A shortfall of the offence is that the victim must actually fear that the violence "will" be inflicted. If the victim only fears that D might subject her to violence, the offence will not be made out.[261] Therefore, the likes of Ireland and Burstow[262] might not be caught by the section 4 offence, even though they would be caught by the section 2 offence.

What mental element is required under section 4? The defendant need not intend to cause the victim to fear that violence will be used against him. Nor need he recklessly cause the victim to fear that violence will be used against him. It is only necessary to prove that he ought to have known that his conduct would have the effect of causing the victim to fear that violence would be used against him. If a reasonable person would have realized that the conduct would have such an effect, the defendant will be liable.[263] In other words, mere negligence is sufficient for grounding a conviction under section 4. This is objectionable, since the offence carries a sentence of up to five years' imprisonment.

9–082

Are there any defences? Yes. It is a defence under sections 1(1), 1(2), and 4 to show that the conduct was reasonable,[264] or was lawful, or was aimed at preventing or detecting crime. So, the police officer who has been staking out a house for two weeks could argue that he was not aiming to harass the victim, but was merely trying to prevent a crime from being committed. He might be able to show that V was a notorious drug dealer and that he had strong grounds for having him under surveillance. It would be necessary to show that the surveillance was aimed at preventing or detecting crime, rather than solving a past crime.

9–083

More generally, it is a defence to show that the conduct was reasonable. If the media run a campaign against a suspected criminal, it should be able to argue that it was exercising its right to freedom of expression.[265] The public, after all, have

---

[260] *Caurti v. D.P.P.* [2001] EWHC Admin. 867.

[261] *R. v. Henley* [2000] Crim. L.R. 582.

[262] *R. v. Ireland* [1998] A.C. 147.

[263] The fact that D lacked the capacity to understand what a reasonable person ought to have understood is irrelevant. *R. v. C* (2001) 165 J.P.N. 1019; *R. v. Pelham* [2007] EWCA Crim. 1321.

[264] But conduct will only be reasonable under section 4(C) if it was reasonable for the protection of D or another, or for the protection of D's or another's property. There is no similar restriction in subsection 3(c) apropos sections 1 and 1A.

[265] Cf. *Thomas v. News Group Newspapers Ltd.* [2002] E.M.L.R.78, where it was held that *The Daily Sun* newspaper harassed a woman by unnecessarily mentioning that she had made trouble for a colleague who had verbally abused her at work thereby causing members of the public to harass her. (But it is those members of the public that should have been held liable for harassment, not the newspaper since it did not intend to encourage the public to harass the victim by sending her hate mail, see Dennis J. Baker, "The Moral Limits of Criminalizing Remote Harms," (2007) 10 *New Crim. L. Rev.* 370.) The newspaper was using gutter press tactics; it reported that the woman had caused someone to be demoted by complaining of his offensive jokes. But the court understated the importance of free speech. It overlooked the fact that the article also had the effect of sending a warning to many others: "Do not make grossly offensive jokes in the workplace." Furthermore the

an interest in knowing what is going on in the world. However, in some cases, it might be possible to show that the story was of no great public value and that the coverage was excessive, since the victim was merely a suspect—not a convicted offender.[266]

Protestors not only have a right to freedom of expression under Article 10 of the *European Convention for the Protection of Human Rights and Fundamental Freedoms*, but also have a right to freedom of movement (Protocol 4), and freedom of association and assembly under Article 11. These are cardinal rights that should only be overridden in extreme cases. The courts will balance the reasonableness of the conduct against the defendants' basic human rights.[267] A protestor cannot dig up a person's remains or commit criminal damage and then dress these horrific acts as an exercise of his fundamental rights. A person can express his opposition to animal testing without interfering with the corpse of an innocent person who had no connection with animal testing; and without criminally damaging the property of those who are engaging in lawful activity—farming, scientific research and so on. Nor is it necessary for such groups to continuously make bomb threats to a leading research university. Peaceful protest might also cause harassment, for example, if the protestors stand outside a scientific laboratory or farm day after day with their placards, but if it is peaceful the courts will most likely hold that it is reasonable. Peaceful speech that does not encourage violence should generally not be criminalised in a democratic state.

There is also an aggravated form of the offence, which targets racially and religiously motivated harassment. Given the dangers of sexually motivated stalking, it is odd that there is no an aggravated offence to deter sexually motivated harassment.

---

decision means a serious criminal (or, suspect) could use the law of harassment to prevent the media from reporting his wrongdoing, if it has the effect of making the public harass him by sending him hate mail.

[266] There has to be some limits. An example of *direct* media harassment is the media crusade that followed the high profile murder of Joanna Yeates. This murder happened just before Christmas 2010, so it attracted mass media coverage. That coverage involved the media putting a key suspect's house under surveillance 24/7 for many weeks. The media also revealed the most personal details of the suspect's life. The suspect, Christopher Jefferies, a retired teacher who had taught English at an elite school, has since been released, and the real killer (Vincent Tabak) has been convicted of murder. One would have thought that the harassing coverage Jefferies received would have been reserved for a convicted offender rather than for a mere suspect. For more details of the case, see Caroline Gammell, "Joanna Yeates: police arrest architect's landlord on suspicion of murder," (London: *The Telegraph*: 11:55am GMT 30 December 2010).

[267] Cf. the civil case, *Howlett v. Holding* (2006) 150 S.J.L.B. 161. (But conduct will not be reasonable if it involves a deliberate violation of an injunction). *D.P.P. v. Moseley* (*The Times*, 23 June 1999).

9.12. Offences of Poisoning

The poisoner usually works in the traditional Borgia fashion,[268] poisoning the chalice which the victim then unsuspectingly puts to his own lips. This does not involve an assault,[269] but it is one of the two statutory crimes of poisoning under the *Offences against the Person Act 1861*. Both specify an *act* of maliciously administrating to any person (or causing to be taken by any person) any poison or other noxious thing.

9–084

What if the victim knows that the chalice contains poison, but puts it to his own lips anyway? If V makes an autonomous and fully informed decision to consume the poison, D will not be liable under section 23 or 24 of the *Offences against the Person Act 1861*.[270] If V intended to kill himself, D may be liable for a statutory offence.[271]

9–085

The expressions "administrating" and "causing to be taken" both mean that the poison must actually enter the victim's system: it is not enough that his food is poisoned, if he does not eat it.[272] There is an "administrating" even though the poison is unknowingly taken by the victim.[273] Generally, therefore, "administrating" and "causing to be taken" are convertible expressions. But a possible small difference is that poison is administered if it is brought into injurious contact with the victim's skin,[274] although this is perhaps not causing it to be "taken."

What is a "poison or other noxious thing"? Before answering this question we need to consider the more specific features of the two offences. Maliciously administrating a noxious thing to any person:

9–086

1. so as thereby to endanger the life of such person or to inflict[275] upon him grievous bodily harm is punishable with imprisonment for 10 years[276] (section 23);

---

[268] Legend has it that Lucrezia Borgia wore a hollow ring so she could store poison. Lucrezia furtively dispersed the poison into the wine chalices of her enemies. See William Le Queux, *The Closed Book: Concerning the Secret of the Borgias*, (London: The Smart Set Pub. Co., 1904).

[269] *R. v. Hanson* (1849) 175 E.R. 383; *R. v. Walkden* (1845) 1 Cox C.C. 282.

[270] See *R. v. Kennedy (No.2)* [2008] 1 A.C. 269, cf. *R. v. Harley* (1830) 172 E.R. 744 where V drank her coffee without realizing it has been poisoned.

[271] Section 2 of the *Suicide Act 1961* as amended by section 59 of the *Coroners and Justice Act 2009*.

[272] *R. v. Walford* (1899) 34 L. Jo. 116; *R. v. Cadman* (1825) 168 E.R. 1206; *R. v. Gillard* (1988) 87 Cr. App. R. 189.

[273] *R. v. Harley* (1830) 172 E.R. 744.

[274] In any case it is an offence under section 23 to sue a corrosive or destructive substance with intent to burn or cause g.b.h. to any person. This provision was used in an unreported case of 1973 when a thwarted lover sprayed paint stripper on the crotch of his beloved's underclothes. See also *R. v. Dones* [1987] Crim. L.R. 682; *R. v. Gillard* (1988) 87 Cr. App. R. 189.

[275] Notice that the word "inflict" is here used in the *Act* to cover cases where there is clearly no battery. Cf. *R. v. Dica* [2005] EWCA Crim. 2304; *R. v. Konzani* [2005] 2 Cr. App. R. 14; *R. v. B* [2007] 1 W.L.R. 1567.

[276] If poison is administered (or even it if is merely mixed with food or drink that another is expected to consume), with intent to murder, this is an attempt to murder. Also, if the intent is to cause grievous bodily harm short of death, and the poison has this effect, the administration is punishable with imprisonment for life under section 18 of the *Offences against the Person Act 1861*.

2.   with intent to injure, aggrieve or annoy such person is punishable with imprisonment for five years (section 24).[277]

The broad difference is that it is the graver offence when g.b.h. is actually inflicted, and the lesser offence when it amounts merely to an attempt to do harm (though with the actual administration of the poison). The lesser offence does not require that harm be actually done. Also, the lesser offence is committed where the intent is merely to annoy.[278]

To return to your question of what is noxious: if the drug has endangered life or inflicted g.b.h. under section 23 there can be no question but that it is noxious. The interpretation of the word is more difficult if the drug has merely been administered with intent to annoy contrary to section 24.[279] The rule as now settled in *R. v. Marcus*[280] gives the word a wide meaning. Until this case it had not been definitely settled that "noxious" covered ordinary sleeping tablets, administered for the purpose of making the victim fall into an unwanted sleep. In *R. v. Marcus* the Court of Appeal announced that a substance is noxious under section 24 even if it is merely "obnoxious, *i.e.* objectionable or unwelcome." (The word "obnoxious" as an equivalent for "noxious" appeared in a dictionary.) Consequently it was held that sleeping tablets administered in a normal dose are noxious; and the court said that even causing an unsuspecting victim to take a bottle of ginger beer with a snail in the bottom would constitute the offence, because of the revulsion that would be caused to the drinker on discovering the snail after drinking the ginger beer.

9–087   **Can I first pounce on the snail? Thank you. Noxious doesn't mean obnoxious, whatever the dictionary says. A nice lamb chop would be obnoxious to a vegetarian, but it would do him a power of good if someone got him to eat it by pretending that it was a clever concoction of soya. And an innocuous snail isn't noxious.**   The last remark of the court, anent the snail in the bottle, certainly goes beyond anything that had been decided or even suggested before. Whether or not "noxious" sometimes means "obnoxious," it should be elementary that a dictionary only gives approximate synonyms for words, with perhaps an indication of the shades of meaning that they may possess in different contexts. If the court had paid attention to the present context it would have found that the statute not only makes "noxious" an alternative to "poisonous" (a strong word) but makes it alternative to "destructive" (also a strong word). One would have thought that in the context of the section

---

[277] The punishment under section 24 now depends upon the *Penal Servitude Act 1891*. To administer or attempt to administer chloroform or other stupefying drugs in furtherance of any indictable offence, even though no harm results, is punishable with imprisonment for life: section 22 of the *1861 Act*. The narrower offence under section 61 of the *Sexual Offences Act 2003* with a maximum sentence of 10 years, seems unnecessary as section 22 carries a life sentence.

[278] Although section 24 is in effect an attempt provision, there is no reason why a person should not be charged with an attempt to commit the offence where the poison is not in fact administered.

[279] *R. v. Hill* (1986) 83 Cr. App. R. 386; *R. v. Gantz* [2005] 1 Cr. App. R. (S.) 104.

[280] [1981] 1 W.L.R. 774.

"noxious" carries at least a whiff of the meaning of "poisonous" and "destructive." If this is so, a solution of the decomposed snail doing no harm is not noxious.

Nevertheless, it was not an intolerable extension of the meaning of the word to make it cover sleeping tablets, which can induce an unwanted unconsciousness and therefore affect bodily (including mental) function. The idea that a harmless solution of snail is noxious merely because it is repugnant to the drinker goes too far, and the point was not before the court in *R. v. Marcus*. A thing should not be held to be noxious unless it either is harmful or interferes with bodily function (even though only slightly and temporarily).

What about lacing a teetotaller's lemonade with a couple measures of gin?   It may be argued that the social acceptance of alcohol prevents it from being accounted noxious in law. But it interferes with bodily function, and here is known to be unwelcome to the recipient. Presumably, the question would be left to the free discretion of the jury, turning them into *ad hoc* lawmakers.   **9–088**

Couldn't the joker say that in his opinion gin is a blessing to mankind and not noxious?   The court would undoubtedly hold that if the defendant knows what he is (or may be) administering, and knows that it has (or may have) the effect that makes the jury find it to be noxious, then he cannot say that in his opinion the effect is not noxious. Any mistake is one of law.   **9–089**

"It is usually said that a poison in a small dose is a medicine, while a medicine in a large dose is a poison."[281] But it has sometimes been thought that a recognized poison is noxious even though administered in a harmless quantity.[282] This opinion always had its difficulties, and it seems now to be disapproved by a *dictum* in *R. v. Marcus* that the quantity of the drug must be considered.[283] Some recognized poisons are harmless (and even beneficial) when taken in very small doses. *Botulinum toxin* (known colloquially as Botox) is one of the most powerful neurotoxins known. It is a deadly poison,[284] but it is harmless when injected in small doses. I have not heard of any aging celebrity dying from his or her Botox injections. To administer a harmlessly small dose of a recognized poison is equivalent (for the purpose of section 24) to administering water, and it should

---

[281] Alfred Swaine Taylor, *On Poisons, In relation to Medical Jurisprudence and Medicine*, (London: Churchill, 1848) at 2.

[282] There is a somewhat ambiguous *dictum* of Lord Cockburn C.J. in *R. v. Hennah* (1877) 13 Cox C.C. 547 which may be read as meaning this; however, he also said that "unless the thing is noxious in the quantity administered, it seems exceedingly difficult to say that logically there has been a noxious thing administered." Cf. Field J. in *R. v. Cramp* (1880) 5 Q.B.D. 307 (a decision on the g.b.h. under section 23 that there can be no question but that it is noxious).

[283] Cf. *R. v. Cato* [1976] 1 W.L.R. 110, where Lord Widgery C.J. said that: "an article is not to be described as noxious merely because it has a potentiality for harm if taken in overdose." "Overdose" tends to beg the question, so perhaps the statement can be amended to read: "if taken in a larger quantity than that administrated."

[284] It is one of the most acutely toxic substances known. Depending on the method used to administer it, a mere 90–270 nanograms of botulinum toxin could be enough to kill an average 90 k.g. person. See Stephen S. Arnon *et al.*, "Botulinum Toxin as a Biological Weapon: Medical and Public Health Management," (2001) 285(8) *Journal of the American Medical Association* 1059.

not be an offence under the section. If the person who administers such a dose believes it to be harmful he would be guilty of attempting to administer a poison.

9–090 **But he wasn't attempting to administer a poison, because it wasn't poison.** It was a poison in his own mind. The type of argument you have advanced was successful when the "impossibility" rule held sway, before the enactment of the *Criminal Attempts Act 1981*. The intention of the *Act* was to get rid of this rule.

A difficult intermediate case is where the would-be poisoner administers a first harmless dose of a poison that has a cumulative effect, his intention being to follow this up with further doses in order to harm the victim. If the first dose is harmless it would seem that the poisoner's only guilt is for an attempt.[285]

It need hardly be said that the noxious thing need not be in solid or liquid form. Coal gas[286] and electricity[287] are noxious things within the sections.

9–091 **It appears that a drug may be noxious in law although it is not likely to cause death or g.b.h. So suppose that D has administered something that he knew to be noxious, because of its soporific effect. He did not know that it was likely to cause death or g.b.h., but he unknowingly gave an overdose and so caused g.b.h. Would he be liable under section 23?** The difficulty is the familiar one of determining the elements of the offence to which a requirement of *mens rea* applies. It is possible to read section 23 as dividing into two distinct parts:

> "(1)   Whosoever shall unlawfully and maliciously administer to or cause to be administered to or taken by any other person any poison or other destructive or noxious thing,
>
> (2)   so as thereby to endanger the life of such person, or so as thereby to inflict upon such person any grievous bodily harm..."

On this reading, the equipment of malice applies only to the elements in (1), and the elements in (2) can be interpreted as being of strict liability.[288] But the principle of construction contended for in previous chapters is that a serious crime should impliedly require *mens rea* as to all the external elements, in the absence of an expression of the contrary intention, and that *a fortiori* a statutory requirement of *mens rea* should apply to all the other elements of the offence, again in the absence of a contrary intent (which is not expressed in the present section). It is not permissible to split a statutory offence in two and apply a requirement of a mental element only to the half in which the requirement happens to be expressed. Authorities for this proposition are *R. v. Smith*[289] and some of the cases on offences of knowledge (6.3.). Unfortunately, the authorities on section 23 are in a difficult state.

---

[285] *R. v. White* [1910] 2 K.B. 124.

[286] *R. v. Cunningham* [1957] 2 Q.B. 396; *R. v. Gillard* (1988) 87 Cr. App. R. 189.

[287] *R. v. Donald* (1955) *The Times* (9 May 1955).

[288] The higher courts insist on fault unless the statute states otherwise, see *R. v. K* [2002] 1 A.C. 462; *B (A Child) v. D.P.P.* [2000] 2 A.C. 428; *Crown Prosecution Service v. M* [2010] 2 Cr. App. R. 33. *A fortiori* this must mean *full* fault as to the prohibited harm unless the statute states otherwise.

[289] [1974] Q.B. 354. For a particularly powerful argument to this effect, see the opinion of Madsen J. in *State v. Brown*, 140 Wash.2d 456 at 473–474 (2000).

The case of *R. v. Cunningham*,[290] was at first thought to settle all these problems in relation to statutory offences of malice.

Roy Cunningham wrenched away a gas coin meter to steal the contents, and left coal gas escaping from the pipe, which partially asphyxiated a woman who was asleep next door. The Court of Criminal Appeal held that, notwithstanding that Cunningham was engaged on a criminal enterprise, he was not guilty of maliciously causing a noxious thing to be taken, under section 23, in the absence of foresight that it would or might be taken. The court required proof that "the accused has foreseen that the particular kind of harm might be done and yet has gone on to take the risk of it. ... the word 'maliciously' in a statutory crime postulates foresight of consequence."

This *dictum* is not as specific upon the mental element under section 23 as may appear at first sight. "The particular kind of harm" and the "consequence" referred to by the court may conceivably mean merely the harm and consequence of taking a noxious thing into the body. On this reading the court was considering only the defendant's foresight that the coal gas (which of course he knew to be noxious) might be inhaled by someone, and did not require foresight that the noxious thing would endanger life or might inflict g.b.h. But the more natural reading is that the court was referring to both elements: not merely to the noxious nature of the substance and its inhalation but to the harm and consequence specified in the section as a result of taking the substance, namely the danger to life or g.b.h.

9–092

If this is the correct interpretation of *R. v. Cunningham*, its effect, unfortunately, has been reduced by the later case of *R. v. Cato*.[291]

V produced heroin and syringes and invited Cato to have a "fix" with him. Each took a syringe, filled it to his own taste with a mixture of heroin and water, and was injected by the other. They did this several times during the night, and in the morning V died, there being evidence from which the jury could (and did) infer that the death was a consequence of the administration of the drug. Cato's conviction under section 23, and also of manslaughter, was upheld on appeal.

This was the first time that section 23 was held to apply to the administration of a drug with consent. The decision rests upon the principle that it is not competent for a person to consent to suffer death or grievous bodily harm.

There are considerable difficulties with it. All the previous cases under the section had concerned the administration without the recipient's consent. Clearly, consent is not a defence to murder, nor does it provide a defence where the defendant causes the consenter to suffer actual bodily harm.[292] However, the drug cases can be contradistinguished from cases where the harm-doer intentionally inflicts a.b.h. or g.b.h. on the consenter. In those cases, the harm-inflictor aims to harm the victim. In the drug cases, the harm-inflictor does not aim to inflict harm, he aims to assist his fellow addict to enjoy his "fix." The death is a mere side-effect of what he intends to do. Arguably, those involved with heroin must at least foresee a user's death as a remote possibility. (The risk might be sufficiently

9–093

---

[290] [1957] 2 Q.B. 396.
[291] [1976] 1 W.L.R. 110.
[292] *R. v. Brown* [1994] 1 A.C. 212.

high to justify invoking the criminal law to prevent the accidental harm-inflictor from taking the risk. It might not be too much to require the accidental harm-inflictor to say to the consenter, "Inject yourself, I do not want to risk killing you.")

Even if the principle is accepted that the consensual administration of a drug can be an offence under section 23,[293] the question remains whether heroin presents the degree of danger specified in section 23. Heroin addiction involves serious physical and mental consequences,[294] but there appears to have been no evidence offered in *R. v. Cato* that a single dose, or a short series of doses, was necessarily dangerous, apart from the long-term danger of creating or increasing addiction. The injections did in fact endanger (and more than endanger) the friend's life; but the point as to the mental element remains. Should not a conviction under section 23 require proof of a mental element beyond the mere intention to administer heroin?

The trial judge in this case had partly applied *R. v. Cunningham*, because he had required the jury to find whether the defendant knew that heroin was likely to do some harm. (This was not fully applying *R. v. Cunningham*, if we are right in our interpretation of that case, since *R. v. Cunningham* spoke of "the particular kind of harm," and, as already said, the particular kind of harm in section 23 may be thought to be the endangering of life or causing g.b.h.). The jury found that Cato had such knowledge (though on what evidence does not appear). On appeal the Court of Appeal not only affirmed the conviction but held that no direction as to foresight of harm was necessary.

9–094 The court distinguished *R. v. Cunningham*, not (be it noted) as a case where the defendant may not have realized that the stuff would be "administered," but as a case where the injury to the victim was done "indirectly," the gas having escaped into an adjoining house or part of the house.

> "We think in this case where the act was entirely a direct one that the requirement of malice is satisfied if the syringe was deliberately inserted into the body of [V], as it undoubtedly was, and if the appellant at a time when he so inserted the syringe knew that the syringe contained a noxious substance."[295]

This is the worst kind of restrictive distinguishing, where an accidental factor present in the earlier case is regarded as part of the *ratio decidendi* merely for the purpose of disregarding the earlier case, although the factor has no logical relevance and the earlier court attached no significance to it. As the Law Commission has pointed out, criticizing *R. v. Cato*, the distinction means that Cato would not have been regarded as "malicious" if he had offered his friend a

---

[293] This is highly unlikely, cf. *R. v. Evans* [2009] 1 W.L.R. 1999; *R. v. Andrews* [2002] EWCA Crim. 3021.

[294] See generally, David Nutt *et al.*, "Drug Harms in the UK: A Multicriteria Decision Analysis," (2010) 376 *The Lancet* 1558; Robin Room, "The Dangerousness of Drugs," (2006) 101 *Addiction* 166; J. Neeleman & M. Farrell, "Fatal methadone and heroin overdoses: time trends in England and Wales," (1997) 51 *J. Epidemiol. Community Health* 435.

[295] *R. v. Cato* [1976] 1 W.L.R. 110 at 120.

glass containing the drug,[296] but was "malicious" because he injected it.[297] There is no rhyme or reason in such a rule. Its sole merit, if the word is appropriate, was that it served to uphold the conviction.

Apart from the common sense of the matter, there were authorities against the distinction. Section 23, in encompassing both administering and causing to be taken, shows that it is meant to cover both direct and indirect causation without discriminating between them. Further, the court took no account of *R. v. Mowatt*.[298] In this case (which, it will be remembered, arose under section 20) the Court of Appeal held that, even in the case of a direct attack on the victim, statutory malice required an awareness of the possibility of causing some harm. It is true that in *R. v. Mowatt* the court watered down *R. v. Cunningham* to the extent necessary to affirm Mowatt's conviction, but it did not go so far as to exclude the question of foresight altogether, even though the harm inflicted was direct. *R. v. Cato* waters down not only *R. v. Cunningham* but also *R. v. Mowatt*, and the reason the court gave for distinguishing *R. v. Cunningham* did not distinguish *R. v. Mowatt*. Both *R. v. Mowatt* and *R. v. Cato* are open to the objection that they import a considerable measure of strict liability into a crime purportedly dependent on proof of "malice," as well as introducing complexity and artificiality into the law.

We are left in a state of some doubt as to the present law. The court in *R. v. Cato* might have decided that section 23 creates an offence of strict liability in respect of the danger involved, but it did not do this. It seemed content to accept that where the noxious thing is indirectly administered *R. v. Cunningham* requires that the defendant should have foreseen the danger specified in the last part of section 23. But when the noxious thing is directly administered, such foresight is not required. In view of the weakness of the reasoning in *R. v. Cato*, it may perhaps be reconsidered if the point arises again.

Consider the owner of the factory who knows that it is belching out noxious fumes in a populous area. Could he be convicted under section 23 if people suffer grievous bodily harm?   No reason why not. He recklessly causes the noxious thing to be taken. No such prosecution has yet been brought, but conservationists might like to take one.[299]   **9–095**

Could it be an offence under section 23 to communicate a disease?   It was said in *R. v. Clarence*[300] that "infection is a kind of poisoning. It is the application   **9–096**

---

[296] It is for this reason that secret poisoning is not an assault. *R. v. Hanson* (1849) 175 E.R. 383.

[297] The Law Commission of England and Wales, *Report on the Mental Element in Crime*, Law Commission Report No. 89, (London: H.M.S.O., 1978) at 15.

[298] [1968] 1 Q.B. 421. However, V's self-administration would break the chain of causation. If V (an autonomous adult) took a glass and poured its contents down his own throat with knowledge of its dangerous contents, the chain of causation would be broken: *R. v. Kennedy (No 2)* [2008] A.C. 269. Cf. *R. v. Evans* [2009] 1 W.L.R. 1999 where it was held that mere supply would be enough to ground a conviction for gross negligence manslaughter, if the supplier saw the consequence of her supply and failed to summon help when doing so would have made a *causal* difference.

[299] However, if life is not endangered and serious injury is not caused no prosecution would lie under section 23; and none would lie under section 24, which requires intention (being in the nature of an attempt) and cannot be committed recklessly.

[300] (1888) 22 Q.B.D. 23.

of an animal poison" (Stephen J.). Yet it may seem rather forced to say that the communication of microscopic bacteria or viruses is the administration of a "noxious thing." If this extensive interpretation of "noxious thing" is accepted, it means that Clarence could have been successfully indicted under section 23, assuming that he was reckless as to the communication of venereal disease to his wife. But, as was remarked before, it is not the practice to prosecute in respect of this type of *minor* disease.[301]

9–097 **Can intention be transferred under the sections?** Yes under section 23, but not under section 24. The curious point may be elaborated as follows. Suppose that D puts a noxious thing into V1's lemonade, intending to injure him, and the liquid is actually consumed by V2, who suffers grievous bodily harm. D is guilty under section 23, which does not require the person injured to be the person aimed at. The section applies whenever one person maliciously administers a noxious thing to "any other person" (V2) so as thereby to endanger the life of "such person" (V2) or to inflict upon "such person" (V) grievous bodily harm. This formula fits the above facts. The mental element is supplied by the word "maliciously", but this word is to be interpreted in accordance with the general common law principle permitting transferred intention, where this is not inconsistent with the wording of the statute. Therefore, it does not matter under section 23 that the intent was in respect of V1.

Contrast the position under section 24. Suppose in the case put that although V2 suffered harm, it was not grievous. Section 23 does not apply because the effects specified therein do not occur, and section 24 does not apply because it requires a malicious administration to "any other person" (V2) with intent to injure "such person" (V2), and here there is no intent to injure V2. The doctrine of transferred malice cannot be applied when this would be inconsistent with the words of the statute.[302]

9–098 **Does the mental element in section 24 raise similar issues as section 23?** No. Section 24 applies where the defendant has unlawfully and maliciously administered "[o]r caused to be administered or to be taken by any other person any poison or other destructive or noxious thing," if he acted with the ulterior *intent* of injuring, aggrieving or annoying that person.

9–099 **Suppose I put some hot chillies in a soup I intend to serve to guests at a dinner party. Suppose also that I put the chillies in the soup because I know that my sister will be bringing her boyfriend and he does not like hot food. I also know that all my other guests love chillies and will enjoy the soup immensely. Can I be liable under section 24 for annoying him?** The fact you intended to annoy one of the guests will not be enough. Nor does it matter

---

[301] Cases involving serious diseases are likely to be prosecuted under section 18 or 20. See *R. v. Konzani* [2005] 2 Cr. App. R. 14, where the disease caused g.b.h.

[302] If the point were free from authority it might be held that D's intent in respect of V1 was in law an intent in respect of V2. But the cases seem to be against this view. See Ashworth, *op. cit. supra*, note 121 at 85; *R. v. Monger* [1973] Crim. L.R. 301. The opinion in the text is supported by the contrast wording of sections 18 and 24.

whether you in fact annoy him. The House of Lords has held that:[303] "the test to be applied is whether a defendant intended to cause harm to the health of the victim." Chillies can be lethal, and certainly can cause harm if delivered in a large dose.[304] However, the question is whether your small dose was intended to cause harm or injury to your guests. If you were merely intending to annoy a particular guest with a perfectly safe concoction of chilli soup, then you will not be liable under section 24.

In *R. v. Hill*[305] a paedophile fed slimming tablets to two little boys aged 11 and 13. He told the boys that the tablets would make them happy. The boys were harmed by the slimming tablets, as they caused the boys to vomit and suffer diarrhoea. Lord Griffiths said:[306]

> "The summing up read as a whole, as a summing up should always be read, made it clear beyond peradventure that the jury should only convict if they were sure that the respondent intended to injure the boys in the sense of causing them physical harm by the administration of the drugs. This was a correct direction. The respondent did, in fact, cause some physical harm and there was overwhelming evidence that this was his intention. I would accordingly allow this appeal and restore the convictions."

9.13.   OTHER ASSAULTS AND THREATS

Various other elements may affect the maximum punishment for assault and other similar crimes. An assault made with intent to rob is an indictable offence carrying a possible life sentence.[307] Assaults may be charged under other names. There are statutory offences of attempting to choke. *etc.* a person or to chloroform, *etc.* him, with intent to commit an indictable offence.[308] Assaults committed by the driving of vehicles are generally charged as driving offences. Cruelty to children may be prosecuted as an ordinary offence against the person, such as assault or manslaughter or murder. But it is also covered by a special provision, section 1 of the *Children and Young Persons Act 1933* (as amended), creating offences of cruelty and wilful neglect.[309] The social and medical aspects of cruelty to children are of great importance, but limitations of space prevent them from being considered here. Mention may also be made of an offence of ill-treating a patient in a psychiatric hospital.[310]

9–100

Lesser charges may be brought for other offences arising out of public disorder. Particular mention may be made of section 1(1) of the *Prevention of Crime Act 1953*, which makes it an either way offence where:

---

[303] *R. v. Hill* (1986) 83 Cr. App. R. 386.

[304] Steve Bird, "Keen cook died after eating red-hot chilli sauce as a dare," (London: *The Times*, 29 September 2008).

[305] (1986) 83 Cr. App. R. 386.

[306] *R. v. Hill* (1986) 83 Cr. App. R. 386 at 390.

[307] Section 8(2) of the *Theft Act 1968*. Other aggravated assaults, rarely charged, are in sections 36–37 of the *Offences against the Person Act 1861*.

[308] Sections 21–22 of the *Offences against the Person Act 1861*.

[309] On the offence of wilful neglect, *R. v. Sheppard* [1981] A.C. 394, overruling previous cases, attached a fairly reasonable meaning to "wilfully." See also *R. v. D* [2008] EWCA Crim. 2360; Glanville Williams, "Recklessness Redefined," (1981) 40 *Cambridge L.J.* 252 at 257–258, 266.

[310] Section 127 of the *Mental Health Act 1983*. A single assault can constitute ill-treatment. *R. v. Holmes* [1979] Crim. L.R. 52.

"Any person who without lawful authority or reasonable excuse, the proof whereof shall lie on him, has with him in any public place any offensive weapon shall be guilty of an offence."

The terms used in this definition are themselves defined, both by the *Act* itself and by a considerable body of case-law.[311] The firearms legislation controls possession of firearms and creates a number of serious offences in relation to their improper use.[312] A string of offences concern the use of explosives for criminal ends.[313] Section 85 of the *Postal Services Act 2000* has a provision about dangerous things sent by post. There are various offences of endangering passengers by rail;[314] and it is an offence maliciously to impede escape from wrecks or to impede one who is endeavouring to save the life of a person escaping from a wreck.[315]

Outside the law of assault, our law of threats is a thing of shreds and patches. It is an offence, punishable with ten years' imprisonment, to threaten to kill the person to whom the threat is made or anyone else, without lawful excuse;[316] but this does not touch threats to torture or maim,[317] which, if made merely by word of mouth or in writing, are generally no offence at all (except for it could involve a psychic assault). Menaces made through public electronic communications are an offence under section 127 of the *Communications Act 2003*. Bomb hoaxes constitute an offence under section 51 of the *Criminal Law Act 1977*. Not to the mention the spate of enactments which aim to prevent terrorists from committing mass murder.[318] The *Public Order Act 1986* also has a number of statutory offences that tackle various forms of public violence such as riot (section 1), violent disorder (section 2), affray (section 3), causing fear or provocation of violence (section 4) and causing harassment, alarm or distress (section 5).

9.14. FALSE IMPRISONMENT

9–101   It is convenient to include this here, although false imprisonment need not involve injury in the narrow sense of the expression. False imprisonment is the third traditional species of criminal trespass to the person, the other two being assault and battery (psychic and physical assault). It is a common law offence; but it differs from some common law offences in that no statute provides a ceiling

---

[311] *C (A Juvenile) v. D.P.P.* [2001] EWHC Admin. 1093; *Bates v. Bulman* [1979] 1 W.L.R. 1190; *Bradley v. Moss* [1974] Crim. L.R. 430; *Copus v. D.P.P.* [1989] C.O.D. 428; *D.P.P. v. Gregson* (1993) 96 Cr. App. R. 240; *D.P.P. v. Hynde* [1998] 1 W.L.R. 1222; *D.P.P. v. Patterson* [2004] EWHC 2744; *R. v. Archbold* [2007] EWCA Crim. 2137; *R. v. Formosa* [1991] 2 Q.B. 1. See *I v. D.P.P.* [2002] 1 A.C. 285.

[312] *Firearms Act 1968.*

[313] Sections 22–30, 64 of the *Offences against the Person Act 1861*; sections 2–3 of the *Explosive Substances Act 1883* (as amended).

[314] Sections 32–34 of the *Offences against the Person Act 1861* (as amended); section 36 of the *Malicious Damage Act 1861* (as amended) (see *R. v. Jones* [2006] EWCA Crim. 2942).

[315] Section 17 of the *Offences against the Person Act 1861.*

[316] Section 16 of the *Offences against the Person Act 1861*. See *R. v. Cousins* [1982] Q.B. 526.

[317] It is an offence to commit torture, however. See section 134 of the *Criminal Justice Act 1988.*

[318] *Terrorism Act 2000*; *Terrorism Act 2006*. See also *Anti-terrorism, Crime and Security Act 2001*; *Counter-Terrorism Act 2008*; *Prevention of Terrorism Act 2005.*

to the possible punishment.[319] It is, therefore, punishable with imprisonment and fine at discretion. Proceedings for the offence are not brought lightly, because it is punishable only on indictment.

What is false "imprisonment"? This is an archaic name for the unlawful   **9–102** detention of a person. It usually involves an application of force to the body, when it amounts also to a physical assault. But false imprisonment is committed by a person who unlawfully turns the key on someone who is already in the room; and here there is no assault.[320] Logically, such an act should not have been regarded as falling within the notion of trespass of the person, but it was made to do so.

Does false imprisonment require physical detention? False imprisonment is   **9–103** a total restraint of liberty, but it may be committed without physical detention—for example, by compelling the victim to go to a particular place.

Whenever a police officer (or other person) purports to make an arrest, even though it is only by using words of arrest, and the person so addressed submits to the arrest, this is an imprisonment in law; and if the arrest is not legally justified it is a false imprisonment. The reason is that an arrester impliedly threatens the use of force if his demand for submission is not complied with.[321] Similarly, if a police officer announces that he will arrest a person unless he gives up a certain thing, and the other complies, this seems to be a sufficient constraint upon the person to amount to imprisonment.[322] The reason again is that the officer who makes such a threat is implicitly saying that the other must not go out of his presence until he complies with the condition. The threat becomes an imprisonment if the other party submits and remains with the officer while he complies with the officer's demand. Or perhaps the making of the demand, with the implied threat of force, is an assault in the absence of justification or excuse.[323]

The police evade restrictions on their powers of arrest by inviting suspects (or telling them) to accompany them to the police station, where they are questioned. The judges have remained quiescent on this practice. What is supposed to keep it legal is the free consent of the suspect to go to the police station and remain there. But the ordinary person is likely to interpret the request made by a police officer

---

[319] *R. v. Rahman* (1985) 81 Cr. App. R. 349.

[320] *R. v. Linsberg* (1905) 69 J.P. 107; *Hunter v. Johnson* (1884) 13 Q.B.D. 225.

[321] Glanville Williams, "Requisites of a Valid Arrest," [1954] Crim. L.R. 6 at 11–12.

[322] *Grainger v. Hill* (1838) 132 E.R. 769 at 772–773. In a U.S. case it was held: "[T]he defendant need not use physical violence or lay hands on the plaintiff to be liable for false imprisonment. *People v. Scalisi*, 154 N.E. 715, 722 (1926). It is sufficient to show that at any time or place the defendant in any manner restrained the plaintiff of her liberty without sufficient legal authority. *Lindquist v. Friedman's, Inc.*, 8 N.E.2d 625, 627 (1937). Unlawful restraint may be effected by words alone, by acts alone or both. *Lopez v. Winchell's Donut House*, 466 N.E.2d 1309, 1312 (1984). It is essential, however, that the confinement be against the plaintiff's will. If a person voluntarily consents to the confinement, there can be no false imprisonment." *Campbell v. AT&T Communications, Inc.* (1994) WL 380620.

[323] There are also limited statutory offences of detaining adults: section 11 of the *Habeas Corpus Act 1679* (sending a prisoner out of England). For a further discussion of false imprisonment see works on tort.

in uniform, even if worded politely, as a command backed by the implied threat of force. It could well be argued that if the police use ambiguous language ("I want you to come with me to the police station") this is a deprivation of the suspect's liberty which can be justified only under the law of arrest. Either the police should arrest the offender, complying with the legal requirements of arrest, or they should make it plain that the suspect is not legally bound to accompany them.

9–104   There is authority for saying that it is a false imprisonment (or, at least a kidnapping[324]) to cause a person by deception to remain in a place or go to a place.[325] However, a person who is deceived may be caused to behave in a certain way but might not necessarily be deprived of his liberty.[326] There are precedents for saying that an offence of doing something "against the will" of someone covers the getting of consent by fraud,[327] but fraud would also have to result in the victim being deprived of her liberty if the charge were to be false imprisonment.

Prosecutions for false imprisonment are uncommon because the damages obtainable in a civil action are likely to be far higher than the criminal penalty.[328] Another effective civil remedy is an application for writ of *habeas corpus*, and anyone who impedes the process on *habeas corpus* can be committed to prison for contempt of court.

9–105   **What is the difference between "false imprisonment" and "kidnapping"?**   There is a common law offence going by the name "kidnapping,"[329] which is committed by carrying a person away without his consent. In *R. v. D*[330] the House of Lords held that the offence of kidnapping contains four ingredients: (i) the taking or carrying away of one person by another; (ii) by force or fraud; (iii) without the consent of the person so taken or carried away; and (iv) without lawful excuse. It is supposed to be a particularly serious form of false imprisonment, but over the years the courts have, in familiar fashion, attenuated the circumstances of aggravation, so that now the only distinguishing feature is that the imprisonment, to amount to an aggravation, must involve either the secreting of the victim or carrying him away from a place where he wishes to be.[331] It may be either by force or by threat of force. (As was said before, the courts have extended it to taking by deception.)

---

[324] *R. v. Cort* [2004] 1 Cr. App. R. 18; *R. v. D.* [1984] A.C. 778.

[325] *R. v. Hendy-Freegard* [2008] Q.B. 57 at 67.

[326] Lord Phillips quoted this assessment as originally stated in the second edition of this book with approval in *R. v. Hendy-Freegard* [2008] Q.B. 57 at 66.

[327] *R. v. Wellard* [1978] 1 W.L.R. 921; *R. v. Hopkins* (1842) 174 E.R. 495. Cf. *R. v. Linekar* [1995] Q.B. 250.

[328] A customer who was mistakenly arrested on a charge of theft in a supermarket was awarded £6,000 damages by a jury way back in 1978. (*The Times*, 20 January 1978).

[329] *R. v. Reid* [1973] Q.B. 299. There is a statutory form of the offence under the *Taking of Hostages Act 1982*, which is punishable wherever committed. On false imprisonment and kidnapping in general see B. W. Napier, "Detention Offences at Common Law," in P. R. Glazebrook (ed.), *Reshaping the Criminal Law: Essays in Honour of Glanville Williams*, (London: Steven & Sons, 1978) at 190 *et seq.*

[330] [1984] A.C. 778 at 801.

[331] *R. v. Wellard* [1978] 1 W.L.R. 921, shows that carrying away for 100 yards is enough. Lawson L.J. seems to have regarded it as for the jury to decide whether the transporting of the victim went

Although the maximum punishment is the same as for false imprisonment, sentences for kidnapping are generally more severe; "life" imprisonment is possible.

Does there have to be a total restraint on liberty? Suppose there is an escape route, but a very awkward one? A man offers his dancing partner to drive her home, but deceitfully drives her to his own house. Thereafter, he refuses to drive her home. She stays the night because it would be a long and possibly dangerous walk home. Is that imprisonment? Deceitfully taking a woman to the wrong place might be held to be false imprisonment or kidnapping. A court would certainly say that a dangerous escape route is no escape route. We do not know whether the judge would direct a jury to take extreme inconvenience or hardship in making an escape into account. Very likely he would. The courts might convict him of kidnapping his dance partner because he "carried her away without her consent," as her consent was vitiated by fraud.[332] But unless the carrying away is contemporaneously connected to the deprivation of liberty, the charge will have to one of false imprisonment.[333]

There is a case for having a statutory offence of fraud to cover a "marooning" of this kind. Since your dancer intends to detain his dance partner until he is ready to drive her home he should be liable for kidnapping. He used fraud to carry her away and it appears that he had no intention of taking her home until he was ready. If you take a woman to your desert island on your boat and refuse to return her to the mainland when she asks to return, you clearly deprive her of her liberty.

Kidnapping is a serious offence, so it should not be extended to catch those who merely inconvenience others by forcing them to find an alternative form of transport to get home. Marooning someone at Heathrow Airport would not deprive her of her liberty, because there are plenty of convenient ways to get out of such a location. Nevertheless, where D has used fraud to strand V, he should be held liable if he refuses to take her back to where he took her from—or to some other location where she will be able to use reasonably convenient means to make her own way back.

The carrying away must be connected to a deprivation of liberty. In *R. v. Cort*[334] **9–107** D stopped his car at a bus stop and falsely told those present that the bus had broken down. He then offered a lift to a single woman standing in the queue. He did this on numerous occasions. Normally his offer was rejected, but two ladies were foolish enough to accept a ride. The first changed her mind as soon as she

9–106

---

sufficiently far to be accounted a carrying away. But surely there must be some rule of law on the subject. In the old law of larceny, the least movement of an article constituted a carrying away, but that can hardly apply to kidnapping.

[332] *R. v. Cort* [2004] 1 Cr. App. R. 18.

[333] The act of carrying the victim away would have to be contemporaneous with the deprivation of liberty. If D were to use fraud to get V to travel to London with him for some innocent purpose but thereafter decided to lock her up in his apartment, he would not commit kidnapping. He would have to form the intent to deprive her of her liberty before he carried her away or while he was in the act of carrying her away. If he forms it at some later stage, the carrying away will have no temporal connection with the deprivation of liberty.

[334] [2004] Q.B. 388.

entered the car and asked to be let out of the car. D willingly let her out of the car. The second was taken by him to her destination. Buxton L.J.[335] held that he had kidnapped the women, because his fraud enabled him to carry them away. In other words, he carried them away without their consent. It is true that they would not have entered his car but for his lie about the bus being broken down. It is also true that the second lady was actually carried away. However, it is not clear that they were deprived of their liberty. He did not prevent them from leaving the car and in the case of the second lady he drove her to where she wanted to go. (There is no doubt he was up to something sinister, but he had not got to the stage of actually depriving the ladies of their liberty.)

In *R. v. Hendy-Freegard*,[336] Lord Phillips said:

> "We cannot see that there was justification for extending the offence of kidnapping to cover the situation in which the driver of the car has no intention of detaining his passenger against her will nor of doing other than taking her to the destination to which she wishes to go, simply because in some such circumstances the driver may have an objectionable ulterior motive. The consequence of the decision in *R. v. Cort* would seem to be that the minicab driver, who obtains a fare by falsely pretending to be an authorised taxi, will be guilty of kidnapping."

9–108 **If "deprivation of liberty" is the gravamen of the offence, why require it to involve (or be preceded by) a "physical carrying away"?** In many cases the "carrying away" will be merely incidental to the actual deprivation of liberty. In other cases, the carrying away will be incidental to some crime that has nothing to do with kidnapping or false imprisonment.[337] Consequently, this requirement seems to unnecessarily limit the scope of the offence. Suppose a man enters a woman's flat and holds her at gun point. Is he liable for "kidnapping" or the lesser offence of "false imprisonment"? The answer, of course, is false imprisonment as he does not carry his victim away.

It means that the offence will only catch those who were present. In *R. v. Hendy-Freegard*,[338] the defendant (a notorious fraudster) told numerous lies to convince his victims to take a road trip. Hendy-Freegard was meant to go on the road trip with his victims, but for various reasons did not go with them. He used lies to send his victims on a wild goose chase, but did not personally carry them anywhere. Nor did he force them to go anywhere. It was the Crown's case that: "the element of 'taking and carrying away' can be achieved by causing the victim to move from one place to another, even where the victim is unaccompanied." It

---

[335] *R. v. Cort* [2004] Q.B. 388 at 390.

[336] [2008] Q.B. 57 at 71. His Lordship also notes: "One thing is quite plain and that is that in *R. v. Wellard* [1978] 1 W.L.R. 921 deprivation of liberty was treated as an essential ingredient of the offence of kidnapping" [2008] Q.B. 57 at 69.

[337] If D forcefully carries V for a few metres this will constitute a carrying away, but it also constitutes a complete deprivation of liberty, even though it is only ephemeral loss of liberty. See *R. v. Dzokamshure* [2009] 1 Cr. App. R. (S.) 112; *R. v. Wellard* [1978] 1 W.L.R. 92. Hence, if D breaks into V's house and carries her from her living room to her bedroom to rape her, technically he could be liable for both kidnapping and rape. But it would not be appropriate to charge both when the "carrying away" was "concomitant" with the rape. If D had detained V independently of raping her, then he should be charged with both rape and kidnapping (that is, where he detains her before or after the rape). Cf. *People v. Dugger*, 5 Cal.2d 337 (1936); *People v. Rangel*, (unreported, 2010 WestLaw 5124954; Cal.App. 3 Dist. 16 December 2010); *People v. Martinez*, 20 Cal.4th 225, at 232 (1999).

[338] [2008] Q.B. 57 at 63.

was held that causing a person by fraud to go from one place to another unaccompanied cannot amount to kidnapping. On the facts of the case, this was the correct result as the defendant did not kidnap his victims.

Would the result be different if Hendy-Freegard had used *threats* rather than *fraud* to get his victims to drive to a particular location?   No. If he had said to his victims: "Drive to X and wait there for 12-hours or I will kill your mother," he would not be liable for kidnapping, since he does not physically carry them away. This type of "duress"[339] could compel a victim to drive himself to a particular location and wait there, but causing someone to "carry herself away" is not the same as "carrying her away."[340]

    9–109

This seems to leave a lacuna in the law. Take the example of a woman who has been forced into prostitution. In many cases the pimp is able to force young women to stay in a brothel at night time and return to it each night by making threats against her life and the life of her family. The sexual offences apart,[341] surely there is also a false imprisonment here. Similarly, if a morbidly jealous boyfriend tells his girlfriend not to leave the house while he is at work, he falsely imprisons her. It is not difficult to imagine cases where the victim will be too terrified to disobey the person making the threats. Nevertheless, a villain is only liable for kidnapping if he personally carries his victim away.

I recall you telling me before that the offence of "false imprisonment" does not require the defendant to "physically" restrain the victim. Does this mean that those who make threats that have the effect of causing the victim to imprison herself could be charged with false imprisonment rather than kidnapping?   Yes. Furthermore, the threat need not be made against the actual person imprisoned. It would be enough if D said to V: "Do not leave this flat today or I will kill your mother." A threat used to get the victim to stay in a particular location may "extend to a threat against the welfare or safety of another person."[342]

    9–110

In *R. v. Garrett*,[343] von Doussa J. said:

> "As a proposition of law, I do not think there is any arbitrary rule that the threat which causes the person to submit to confinement against his will must be a threat of physical force to [the actual victim]. The will of a person may be at least as effectively overborne by threats of physical force to other people, or even by threats of damage to valuable personal property. In my view, it is sufficient that the defendant restrains the liberty of a person against his will by threats of immediate physical force to the safety of another person or by other immediate

---

[339] *R. v. Ruzic* [2001] S.C.C. 24 (Can.) *per* LeBel J.

[340] The "taking away" requirement imposes an unnecessary limitation in this respect. The focus should be on the deprivation of liberty, not on the physical "carrying away" element.

[341] In many of these cases there will be actual trafficking involved, which will involve a "carrying away." The pimp will usually be an accessory. There are also special statutory provisions which target this type of conduct.

[342] See the decision of the Supreme Court of South Australia in *R. v. Garrett* (1988) 50 S.A.S.R.392 *per* King C.J., Jacobs and von Doussa JJ. Cf. *R. v. Linsberg* (1905) 69 J.P. 107.

[343] (1988) 50 S.A.S.R.392 at 405. A headmaster could order a student to stay in class after school hours to write lines without needing to use physical force—he need not even be present as the student might be too scared to leave if he has been ordered to stay. This would be a false imprisonment: *Hunter v. Johnson* (1884) 13 Q.B.D. 225.

intimidating conduct intended to bring about that result. [But] there can be no false imprisonment if the alleged victim agrees to go or to remain in a particular area nominated by the defendant of his own free will and not out of submission to a threat."

Many states in the United States have criminal coercion offences. For example, §9A.36.070 of the *Revised Code of Washington* provides:

"(1) A person is guilty of coercion if by use of a threat he compels or induces a person to engage in conduct which the latter has a legal right to abstain from, or to abstain from conduct which he has a legal right to engage in.

(2) 'Threat' as used in this section means: (a) To communicate, directly or indirectly, the intent immediately to use force against any person who is present at the time; or (b) Threats as defined in RCW 9A.04.110 (25)(a), (b), or (c).

(3) Coercion is a gross misdemeanour."[344]

Given that the offence of blackmail is a property offence, and considering that many forms of coercion will not involve false imprisonment, a general coercion offence might not be unwelcome in England and Wales.

9.15. ABDUCTION OFFENCES CONCERNING CHILDREN

9–111 Some of the statutory offences of abduction are designed to safeguard the right of custody possessed by a parent or guardian. The *Child Abduction Act 1984* specifically targets interferences with custody. Nevertheless, mass immigration has made this an international issue in the 21st century.[345] In many cases, fathers have abducted their children and taken them to their country of origin.

Section 1 of the *Child Abduction Act 1984* criminalizes child abductions by parents and guardians:

"(1) Subject to subsections (5) and (8) below, a person connected with a child under the age of sixteen commits an offence if he takes or sends the child out of the United Kingdom without the appropriate consent.

(2) A person is connected with a child for the purposes of this section if—
 (a) he is a parent of the child; or
 (b) in the case of a child whose parents were not married to each other at the time of his birth, there are reasonable grounds for believing that he is the father of the child; or (c) he is a guardian of the child; or (ca) he is a special guardian of the child; or 2(d) he is a person in whose favour a residence order is in force with respect to the child; or (e) he has custody of the child.

(3) In this section 'the appropriate consent', in relation to a child, means —(a) the consent of each of the following—(i) the child's mother; (ii) the child's father, if he has parental responsibility for him; (iii) any guardian of the child; (iiia) any special guardian of the child; 3(iv) any person in whose favour a residence order is in force

---

[344] See also New York Penal Law 135.60.

[345] Wibo van Rossum, "The Clash of Legal Cultures over the Best Interests of the Child Principle in Cases of International Parental Child Abduction," (2010) 6 *Utrecht L. Rev.* 33; Michael R. Walsh and Susan W. Savard, "International Child Abduction and the Hague Convention," (2006) 6 *Barry L. Rev.* 29 (2006); Peter McEleavy, "The New Child Abduction Regime in the European Union: Symbiotic Relationship or Forced Partnership," (2005) 1 *J. Priv. Int'l L.* 5; Mónica Herranz Ballesteros, "International Child Abduction in the European Union: The Solutions Incorporated by the Council Regulation," (2004) 34 *Rev. Gen.* 343. See also *Convention on the Civil Aspects of International Child Abduction* (Hague, 25 October 1980; T.S. 66 (1986); Cm. 33); the *Child Abduction and Custody Act 1985*.

with respect to the child; (v) any person who has custody of the child; or (b) the leave of the court granted under or by virtue of any provision of Part II of the *Children Act 1989*; or (c) if any person has custody of the child, the leave of the court which awarded custody to him."

The offence of taking is not considered to be as serious as kidnapping a stranger.[346] This is perhaps because it can only be committed by a person who has some connection with the child. In most cases, the offence will be committed by a parent taking his or her own child; and since the offence of kidnapping is a very serious offence, it should only be used as a last resort in serious cases where the child is endangered.[347] The offence only applies to children under the age of 16. A connected person includes a legally recognized parent or guardian; or a man who has reasonable grounds for believing that he is the biological father of the victim. This also covers those who have a current residence or contact order for the child.[348]

What does the taker need to do to obtain consent to take the child? He   9–112
needs to seek permission from those listed in section 1(3).

Section 2 of the *Child Abduction Act 1984* criminalizes child abductions by other persons:

"(1)   Subject to subsection (3) below, a person, other than one mentioned in subsection (2) below, commits an offence if, without lawful authority or reasonable excuse, he takes or detains a child under the age of sixteen— (a) so as to remove him from the lawful control of any person having lawful control of the child; or (b) so as to keep him out of the lawful control of any person entitled to lawful control of the child.

(2)   The persons are—(a) where the father and mother of the child in question were married to each other at the time of his birth, the child's father and mother; (b) where the father and mother of the child in question were not married to each other at the time of his birth, the child's mother; and (c) any other person mentioned in section 1(2)(c) to (e) above.

(3)   In proceedings against any person for an offence under this section, it shall be a defence for that person to prove—(a) where the father and mother of the child in question were not married to each other at the time of his birth—(i) that he is the child's father; or (ii) that, at the time of the alleged offence, he believed, on reasonable grounds, that he was the child's father; or (b) that, at the time of the alleged offence, he believed that the child had attained the age of sixteen."

This section catches abductors other than the parents/guardians of the victim.

If an adult takes away a juvenile with his consent but without the consent of   9–113
his parents, is this the more serious offence of "kidnapping"?   Not according
to the ruling of House of Lords in *R. v. D.*[349] But it may constitute child abduction

---

[346] Section 5 of the *Child Abduction Act 1984* provides: "Except by or with the consent of the Director of Public Prosecutions no prosecution shall be instituted for an offence of kidnapping if it was committed—(a) against a child under the age of sixteen; and (b) by a *person connected with the child*, within the meaning of section 1 above."

[347] *R. v. C* [1991] 2 F.L.R. 252.

[348] See section 8(1) of the *Children Act 1989*.

[349] [1984] A.C. 778 at 809, where Lord Brandon said: "That third ingredient, as I formulated it earlier, consists of the absence of consent on the part of the person taken or carried away. I see no good reason why, in relation to the kidnapping of a child, it should not in all cases be the absence of the child's consent which is material, whatever its age may be. In the case of a very young child, it

contrary to sections 1 and 2 of the *Child Abduction Act 1984*. This section only applies if the child is under the age of 16. Section 1 expressly states that any consent must come from the parent or guardian. Section 2 does not expressly state who can give consent, but the section is designed to prevent a child from being taken out of the control of "any person having lawful control of the child." It goes without saying, that a child's consent is irrelevant as far as this section is concerned. The focus is on whether any person having lawful control has consented to the child being taken out of his control. This is also supported by the fact that subsection 2(3), is silent as to whether a child's consent could provide a lawful excuse.

In many of these cases it is doubtful whether there will be genuine consent. In *R. v. Leather*,[350] a paedophile stopped a number of children on different occasions in the street and told them that his bike had been stolen. On each occasion he managed to get the children to go with him to try to find his bike. All the children consented, but that consent was surely vitiated by D's fraud. If the D had told the truth the children would not have agreed to accompany him. The children would not have accompanied him if he had said, "I am a dangerous paedophile, will you accompany me to the woods?" rather than, "Can you help me find my stolen bike?"[351] There was no carrying away in these cases, so kidnapping would not be available. Furthermore, the undisputed facts were that:

> "Throughout the three incidents the appellant made no attempt at any time to touch any one of the children. All the children said that the appellant did not try to stop them from leaving. They all felt that they could have left at any point if they had wanted to. No doubt they could have left, and certainly the case seems to have proceeded on that basis."[352]

Consequently, it would be difficult to charge false imprisonment. There seems to be no evidence of a deprivation of liberty or of a false imprisonment, it did not get to that stage. Nevertheless, a charge is available under section 2 of the *Child Abduction Act 1984* where a child has been taken "from the lawful control of the person having lawful control." A person having lawful control might be a school teacher, a nurse, a nanny, a parent, grandparent, and so on. "Taking" does not have to constitute a "detaining."

9–114 The subsection refers to "takes" and "detains" as alternative ways of committing the offence. Of course, the act of taking might also involve an act of detaining. Furthermore, there is no need for an act of detaining to be preceded by an act of

---

would not have the understanding or the intelligence to give its consent, so that absence of consent would be a necessary inference from its age. In the case of an older child, however, it must, I think be a question of fact for a jury whether the child concerned has sufficient understanding and intelligence to give its consent; if, but only if, the jury considers that a child has these qualities, it must then go on to consider whether it has been proved that the child did not give its consent. While the matter will always be for the jury alone to decide, I should not expect a jury to find at all frequently that a child under 14 had sufficient understanding and intelligence to give its consent. ... [T]he absence of the consent of the person having custody or care and control of a child is not material, [but] the giving of consent by such a person may be very relevant to ... a defence of lawful excuse." See also *R. v. Hale* [1974] Q.B. 819, following *People of Ireland v. Edge* [1943] I.R. 115.

[350] (1994) 98 Cr. App. R. 179.

[351] *R. v. Leather* (1994) 98 Cr. App. R. 179.

[352] *R. v. Leather* (1994) 98 Cr. App. R. 179 at 182.

taking. If a parent leaves a child at another's house, that person may have permission to control the child for the time being, but once the parent/guardian revokes his permission the child must be let return to his parent or guardian. If D were to keep a child in his house after a parent has asked for him to be released, he would come within the purview of section 2.[353] This would also constitute false imprisonment.

In the case of "taking" a child out of the control of those who have lawful control, it only need be shown that the defendant caused the child not to be in the control of his lawful controller—this might occur if D convinces V to follow him to a location. Since he "takes" the child to that location by "leading" him to it, he "removes" him from the control of his parents. If the parents were still in control, they would be ordering their child not to wander into the forest with a stranger who has paedophilic predilections. The courts have held that a "taking out of control" does not refer to physical, spatial or geographical control as such.[354] This is the right conclusion. If a man is found within five metres of a school leading children in the direction of a nearby forest, it should be no defence that he only got five metres away from the school before being caught. Once he causes the child to start following him to an isolated location, he has taken the child out of the control of the school teachers (other persons having lawful control) and ultimately out of the control of their parents. It is exactly this type of activity that Parliament was intending to target when it enacted section 2 of the *1984 Act*.

The Court of Appeal has said the question is simply:[355]

> "Was the child concerned, without any lawful authority or reasonable excuse, deflected by some action of the accused from that which with the consent of his parents, or other person at the time having lawful control, he would otherwise have been doing into some activity induced by the accused? If, as must have been the case, the answer to that question was 'yes', then it was open to the jury to say that the offence was made out."

This is a little wide as it would also catch online activities[356] that deflect the child from doing as his parents wish, but obviously the latter would not be charged as abduction. A firmer test might be to ask: Was the child effectively under the unjustifiable and inexcusable control of the abductor?[357] The control should relate to the concept of "abduction," not to some remote controlling or manipulating of the child's actions. Obviously, if the child has been convinced to accompany D, he is effectively under D's control.[358] The parents and other persons having lawful control have lost control, because if they were present they would say, "Do not go with that strange man."

---

[353] *R. v. Norman* [2009] 1 Cr. App. R. 192.

[354] *R. v. Leather* (1994) 98 Cr. App. R. 179 at 184.

[355] *R. v. Leather* (1994) 98 Cr. App. R. 179 at 184.

[356] The paedophile might use an online chat-room to groom a child, and thereby deflect the child from using her computer to do her homework as her parents have asked her to do. But the gravamen of this wrong is not even remotely connected to the concept of abduction.

[357] Cf. *R. v. Norman* [2009] 1 Cr. App. R. 192 at 199.

[358] There is no need to show that D had an absolute control over the children as he would if he had physically detained them. It is only necessary to show that he had "effective" control.

9–115   **What mental element is required under section 2?** Firstly, the defendant must in fact do something to remove the child from the control of those who have lawful control. His actions must have the effect or objective consequence of removing the child from the control of those who have lawful control. This might result because he has detained the child without permission, or because he has caused the child to accompany him without the permission of the child's parents and so on. As for the mental element, it must be shown that the defendant either intentionally or recklessly brought about that objective consequence. In *Foster v. D.P.P.*, Pitchford J. said:[359] "For my part, I would conclude that the *mens rea* of the offence of abduction under section 2 is an intentional or reckless taking or detention of a child under the age of 16, the effect or objective consequence of which is to remove or to keep that child within the meaning of section 2(1)(a) or (b)."

9–116   **What if a 17-year-old man convinces a 15-year-old girl to go to the cafe with him for a milkshake?** He may have a defence if at the time of taking her to the cafe he genuinely believed that the child had attained the age of 16.[360]

There is one further defence mentioned in subsection 2(3) above. This only applies if the abductor can prove that he is the child's father or has reasonable grounds for believing he is; and where it can be proved that "the father and mother of the child in question were not married to each other at the time of his birth."

9.16. LAWFUL DETENTION AND ARREST

9–117   If a person has been lawfully arrested then the police may detain him. The police may also stop and search people in specified circumstances.[361] Apart from this, and from powers of arrest, the common law recognizes no power to detain except in certain situations of extreme necessity.[362] The procedure laid down by statutes and by the judges for the exercise of the power of arrest would be set at naught if the police could achieve the same purpose by purporting to detain without arresting.[363] In particular, the police have no general power to detain suspects for

---

[359] [2005] 1 W.L.R.1400 at 1407.

[360] See *Foster v. D.P.P.* [2005] 1 W.L.R.1400 at 1402.

[361] Section 60 of the *Criminal Justice and Public Order Act 1994*. See also sections 1 and 2 of the *Police and Criminal Evidence Act 1984*, section 2 sets out the steps that must be followed before a search is conducted. If these steps are not followed, the search will be unlawful: *Bonner v. D.P.P.* [2005] A.C.D. 56.

[362] *Austin v. Commissioner of Police of the Metropolis* [2009] 1 A.C. 564; *R. (on the application of Laporte) v. Chief Constable of Gloucestershire* [2007] 2 A.C. 105; *O'Kelly v. Harvey* (1883) L.R. 14 Ir. 105; cf. *R. v. Faraj* [2007] 2 Cr. App. R. 25.

[363] *Rice v. Connolly* [1966] 2 Q.B. 414. In *Gillan v. United Kingdom* (2010) 50 E.H.R.R. 45 it was held that the stop and search powers found in section 44 of the *Terrorism Act 2000* violated the appellants' right to respect for their private life under Article 8 of the *European Convention for the Protection of Human Rights and Fundamental Freedoms*, 4 November 1950, 213 U.N.T.S. 222 (entered into force generally on 3 September 1953). It contravened that right, because "the officer's decision to stop and search would be based exclusively on his professional intuition. Not only was it unnecessary for him to demonstrate the existence of any reasonable suspicion, he was not required even subjectively to suspect anything about the person stopped and searched."

questioning without arresting them (and even upon arrest their powers of interrogation are supposed to be limited).

Illegal detention is a false imprisonment,[364] and in practice would generally involve an assault; and the suspect's refusal to stay or to answer questions is not an obstruction of the police in the execution of their duty.[365] An imprisonment will be unlawful if it results from an unlawful arrest. The law of arrest was for centuries an Augean stable, but the stable has now been cleared.[366] An arrest may be on warrant or without a warrant. The police have a general power to arrest on warrant. Warrants of arrest are obtained from magistrates, and there are certain rules limiting their issue.[367] In practice the police generally try to get along without warrants. Section 24 of the *Police and Criminal Evidence Act 1984* provides:

"(1)   A constable may arrest without a warrant—(a) anyone who is about to commit an offence; (b) anyone who is in the act of committing an offence; (c) anyone whom he has reasonable grounds for suspecting to be about to commit an offence; (d) anyone whom he has reasonable grounds for suspecting to be committing an offence.

(2)   If a constable has reasonable grounds for suspecting that an offence has been committed, he may arrest without a warrant anyone whom he has reasonable grounds to suspect of being guilty of it.

(3)   If an offence has been committed, a constable may arrest without a warrant—(a) anyone who is guilty of the offence; (b) anyone whom he has reasonable grounds for suspecting to be guilty of it.

(4)   But the power of summary arrest conferred by subsection (1), (2) or (3) is exercisable only if the constable has reasonable grounds for believing that for any of the reasons mentioned in subsection (5) it is necessary to arrest the person in question.

(5)   The reasons are—(a) to enable the name of the person in question to be ascertained (in the case where the constable does not know, and cannot readily ascertain, the person's name, or has reasonable grounds for doubting whether a name given by the person as his name is his real name); (b) correspondingly as regards the person's address; (c) to prevent the person in question—(i) causing physical injury to himself or any other person; (ii) suffering physical injury; (iii) causing loss of or damage to property; (iv) committing an offence against public decency (subject to subsection (6)); or (v) causing an unlawful obstruction of the highway; (d) to protect a child or other vulnerable person from the person in question; (e) to allow the prompt and effective investigation of the offence or of the conduct of the person in question; (f) to prevent any prosecution for the offence from being hindered by the disappearance of the person in question.

(6)   Subsection (5)(c)(iv) applies only where members of the public going about their normal business cannot reasonably be expected to avoid the person in question."

When will a constable have reasonable grounds for suspecting that a person should be arrested?   The adjective reasonable is meant to give reassurance to the public that arrests will be made only on solid grounds, but in practice it is rare for either magistrates or the higher courts to find that a suspicion felt by the police was unreasonable. Claims that an arrest was made for a reasonably

9–118

---

[364] *R. v. Governor of Brockhill Prison Ex p. Evans (No 2)* [2001] A.C. 19.

[365] *Bentley v. Brudzinski* (1982) 75 Cr. App. R. 217; *Cumberbatch v. Crown Prosecution Service* (2010) 174 J.P. 149.

[366] Section 26 of the *Police and Criminal Evidence Act 1984* repealed a plethora of earlier statutory provisions.

[367] Section 1 of the *Magistrates Court Act 1980*. Cf. section 6 of the *Constables Protection Act 1750*; *Bell v. Chief Constable of Greater Manchester* [2005] EWCA Civ. 902.

apprehended breach of the peace are allowed by the courts so routinely that the inclusion of the word "reasonably" is generally functionless.

It seems, though the matter is not that clear, that:

- Wording in terms of "reasonable grounds for suspecting" does not require the arrester to believe with the certainty required for a conviction.[368]
- A person who arrests on "reasonable suspicion" need not positively believe that the arrestee has committed an offence;[369] it is enough that he reasonably believes that grounds exist for bringing him before the magistrates.[370]
- The question of whether the arresting officer had reasonable grounds for his suspicion is an objective question based on matters known to him at the time.[371] It is a case of asking would a reasonable person in the same circumstances as the officer have thought that it was necessary to make the arrest.

A person is empowered to arrest when he reasonably suspects an offence is about to be committed, but there should be evidence that there were reasonable grounds for suspecting; he should give evidence that he himself suspected.[372] The arrester should say in court (the validity of the arrest being under enquiry) that he suspected that an offence was about to be committed.[373]

9–119 **Arrest on a correct "hunch."** It may be strongly argued that if the statute allows an arrest where an offence is being committed, then if the offence was in fact committed the arrest is lawful even though the arrester's suspicion was unreasonable. But that is not the law. It may be difficult for an arrester to forecast whether a court will subsequently regard his suspicion as reasonable; but the question will be raised. If there are no reasonable grounds for believing that it is necessary to make an arrest, the arrest will be unlawful. The criticism of this approach is that the law in giving a power of arrest does so in order that offenders may, where necessary, be brought to justice. If this end has been secured, the

---

[368] *Buckley v. Chief Officer of Thames Valley* [2009] EWCA Civ. 356.

[369] *O'Hara v. Chief Constable of The Royal Ulster Constabulary* [1997] A.C. 286 at 293 said: "(1) In order to have a reasonable suspicion the constable need not have evidence amounting to a *prima facie* case. *Ex hypothesi* one is considering a preliminary stage of the investigation and information from an informer or a tip-off from a member of the public may be enough. (2) Hearsay information may therefore afford a constable reasonable grounds to arrest. Such information may come from other officers. (3) The information which causes the constable to be suspicious of the individual must be in existence to the knowledge of the [arresting police officer], as Lord Diplock described it in *Mohammed-Holgate v. Duke* [1984] A.C. 437 at 446, vests in the constable, who is engaged on the decision to arrest or not, and not in his superior officers."

[370] *Al-Fayed v. Commissioner of Police of the Metropolis (No.3)* (2004) 148 S.J.L.B. 1405; *Ricketts v. Cox* (1982) 74 Cr. App. R. 298.

[371] *Alford v. Chief Constable of Cambridgeshire* [2009] EWCA Civ. 100; *Raissi v. Commissioner of Police of the Metropolis* [2009] Q.B. 564.

[372] *Siddiqui v. Swain* [1979] R.T.R. 454; *Chapman v. D.P.P.* (1989) 89 Cr. App. R .190, 196–197; *Paul v. Chief Constable of Humberside* [2004] Po. L.R. 179 at para. 34–35.

[373] *Siddiqui v. Swain* [1979] R.T.R. 454.

arrester ought to be given qualified praise, and ought not to be penalized merely because he did not accurately know or believe the facts. What he did was objectively lawful.[374]

Duty to release when innocence is established.   Where an arrest is allowed on reasonable suspicion, the arrester must, of course, release the suspect as soon as he realizes that his suspicion is unfounded.[375]   **9–120**

Arrest where no offence has been committed.   When the police exercise this power it is not clear what they arrest for. Of course, if the suspect has reached the stage of attempt the police can arrest him for that. The question whether he has reached that stage need not be considered until the question of charging arises.[376] Even if the suspect has not yet committed an attempt, the police may after arresting him find evidence that he was committing or had committed some offence, such as "going equipped."[377] They can charge such other offence, or simply warn the suspect and release him. The only other possibility is to bring the suspect before magistrates and have him bound over. The suspect cannot be bound over unless he agrees; but if he does not agree he can be immediately sent to prison.[378]   **9–121**

Are there any other conditions for a valid arrest?   A constable or other person who proposes to make an arrest may not merely announce the arrest to the suspect. He must use clear words: a polite request to the suspect to accompany him to the police station is insufficient. He must ensure that the arrestee understands that he is no longer a free man.[379]   **9–122**

If the suspect submits, he is taken to be under arrest. If he does not submit, there is no arrest until the arrester touches the suspect, telling him that he is under arrest. Thus if a suspect, on being told that he is under arrest, runs away, the policeman must pursue him and touch him before he is legally arrested.[380] If he cannot touch him, then words should be sufficient to make the arrest lawful.[381] The suspect's running away before arrest is not an offence itself.[382] But if he runs while the officer is trying to arrest him, then he could be liable for "resisting"

---

[374] However, this exception should not be used to allow the police to injure an offender when they do not have a reasonable belief that it is right or necessary to do so. Allowing the officer to risk making a wrongful arrest is tolerable because the consequences for the victim are not too serious, but allowing an officer to risk injuring a suspect in a serious way would not be tolerable. See *The Queen v. Dadson* (1850) 169 E.R. 407.

[375] *Wiltshire v. Barrett* [1966] 1 Q.B. 312.

[376] Charging means the making of the formal charge in the police station; it is a matter of police practice and has no legal effect as a matter of substantive law.

[377] Section 25 of the *Theft Act 1968*.

[378] *Everett v. Ribbands* [1952] 2 Q.B. 198; Glanville Williams, "Preventive Justice and the Rule of Law," (1953) 16 *Mod. L. Rev.* 417 at 425.

[379] *R. v. Inwood* [1973] 1 W.L.R. 647.

[380] *R. v. Brosch* [1988] Crim.L.R. 743.

[381] *Alderson v. Booth* [1969] 2 Q.B. 216.

[382] The courts now treat this as an "obstruction of a constable in the execution of his duty" contrary to section 89(2) of the *Police Act 1996*, even if the constable makes no attempt to arrest the suspect and has no intention of arresting him: *Sekfali v. D.P.P* (2006) 170 J.P. 393. See the discussion in the following sections of this Chapter.

arrest (see the discussion below). If he runs away after he has been arrested he is guilty of an escape, and anyone who assists him are guilty of rescue.[383] If, after being arrested, he simply refuses to accompany the officer, he is doubtless guilty of obstructing the officer in the execution of his duty.[384]

Where immediate action is required the arrester may, it seems, use immediate force to detain the suspect; the force is legally justified,[385] but it would seem that the arrest is not complete until the arrester has made proper communication to the person arrested. The suspect must be informed at the time of arrest what essentially is alleged against him. This rule was established as common law in the celebrated case of *Christie v. Leachinsky*.[386] It requires the arrester to tell the suspect briefly the act for which the arrest is made (you killed X; you stole a jacket from the Next store), unless in the circumstances this is obvious to the suspect[387] or communicating with him is impracticable, as where the suspect fights[388] or runs away.

9–123   Where the arrest is on warrant common sense suggests that the arrester should, in addition, state this fact. A statute requires that the warrant should, on the demand of the arrestee, be shown to him as soon as practicable;[389] and obviously the suspect can ask to see the warrant if he has not been told that it exists. In one case the court, in an *obiter dictum*, said that a person is not entitled to know whether his arrest is on warrant or not, so long as he is told the act for which he is arrested;[390] but this cannot be right.

An arrest that is initially invalid can be subsequently (though not retrospectively) legalized—for example, by telling the arrestee the ground of the arrest when he arrives at the police station. The suspect is then lawfully arrested from that moment, but can still complain of his former illegal detention.[391]

Various other problems relating to arrest have been omitted from this discussion, such as those relating to the right of entry upon premises to make an arrest (although this is mentioned in passing in the following sections), the duty to bring the suspect before magistrates, interrogation, search, fingerprinting,

---

[383] *R. v. Dhillon* [2006] 1 W.L.R. 1535; *R. v. Montgomery* [2008] 1 W.L.R. 636 (escaping). *The King v. Burridge* (1734) 93 E.R. 202; *Bensted's Case* (1640) 79 E.R. 1101 (rescuing).

[384] *Sekfali v. D.P.P* (2006) 170 J.P. 393.

[385] Section 117 of the *Police and Criminal Evidence Act 1984*.

[386] [1947] A.C. 573 applied by the Court of Appeal in *Taylor v. Chief Constable of Thames Valley* [2004] 1 W.L.R. 3155 with reference to section 28(3) of *Police and Criminal Evidence Act 1984*. In that case it was held that the arrestee should be "told, in simple non-technical language that he can understand, the legal and factual grounds for his arrest," so that he will have an opportunity to provide an explanation for his alleged conduct such as point out that he is being mistaken for someone else. See also *Fox v. U.K.* (1991) 13 E.H.R.R. 157.

[387] Cf. *Waters v. Bigmore* [1981] R.T.R. 356.

[388] "Where it was not practicable for an officer to inform a detainee of the reason for his arrest, the arrest should be maintained until it was possible to inform him of the reason. But any delay in informing B of the reason for his arrest for the assault could not retrospectively render unlawful his correct and lawful arrest by the officer for breach of the peace." *Blench v. D.P.P.* [2004] EWHC 2717; *D.P.P. v. Hawkins* (1989) 88 Cr. App. R. 166.

[389] Section 96(4) of the *Access to Justice Act 1999*. See also section 125 of the *Magistrates' Court Act 1980*.

[390] *R. v. Kulynycz* [1971] 1 Q.B. 367 at 372.

[391] *Lewis v. Chief Constable of South Wales* [1991] 1 All E.R. 206; *Dawes v. D.P.P.* [1995] 1 Cr. App. R. 65; *R. v. Kulynycz* [1971] 1 Q.B. 367.

medical examination and identification procedures. These matters fall outside the scope of this work. The aim in this section has been to provide essential details about lawful detention because of its relevance to false imprisonment. (However, this brief overview of the law of arrest also sets the scene for the discussion below concerning the offence of obstructing a constable in the execution of his duty.) Before we move on, we need to briefly consider a couple of other forms of lawful detention.

Can a person be lawfully detained without being arrested?   Yes. The term **9–124** "arrest" is generally used in connection with arrest for offences. In addition, the law gives certain powers to detain apart from offences or the suspicion of offences. For example, some mentally disordered persons may be removed to hospital;[392] and an officer who has required a driver to supply a specimen under the excess alcohol provisions may detain him temporarily after he has provided the specimen;[393] and the police may detain people temporarily to search them for firearms[394] or illicit drugs.[395] Section 105 of the *Merchant Shipping Act 1995* provides: "The master of any United Kingdom ship may cause any person on board the ship to be put under restraint if and for so long as it appears to him necessary or expedient in the interest of safety or for the preservation of good order or discipline on board the ship."

Are there any private defences?   A person is entitled to use reasonable force to **9–125** defend his property and that force might involve detaining a person who he (unreasonably) believes to be a burglar. The force used must not be excessive, but the defendant can make an unreasonable mistake as to whether the person he detains is a burglar.[396] If he honestly believes that the person he has detained is a burglar, then detaining such a person might not necessarily involve an unreasonable use of force. Whether or not the force is unreasonable depends on the facts. It would be unreasonable to use gross force to prevent a suspected burglar from escaping, such as blowing his legs off with a shotgun. The value of property is not sufficiently important to justify this type of gross violation of another human's dignity.

Compare this with the case where X (a non-police officer) arrests V mistakenly believing V was the person he saw smashing the local bus shelter two weeks earlier. Here, X would not be acting to protect property as the criminal damage was committed two weeks earlier. Since X is making an arrest under section 24A of the *Police and Criminal Evidence Act 1984*, he must have reasonable grounds for detaining the suspect. X might argue that he detained V and arrested him because he believed that V committed an indictable offence. But he would have to have reasonable grounds for suspecting V of being guilty of criminally damaging the bus shelter (section 24A(2)(b)). Furthermore, he would

---

[392] Particularly under sections 135 and 136 of the *Mental Health Act 1983*.

[393] Section 7 of the *Road Traffic Act 1988*. The driver would obstruct the officer in the execution of his duty if he were to drive off before the officer could assess his level of intoxication. See *D.P.P. v. Carey* [1970] A.C. 1072; *Scheiner v. D.P.P.* [2006] EWHC 1516.

[394] Section 47 of the *Firearms Act 1968*.

[395] Section 23(2)(a) of the *Misuse of Drugs Act 1971*.

[396] *R. v. Faraj* [2007] 2 Cr.App.R. 25.

have to satisfy the requirements of section 24A(4). He might do this by arguing that he believed that V would make off before a constable could "assume responsibility for him" (section 24A(4)(d)). Again, he must have reasonable grounds for believing that V would make off before a constable could assume responsibility for him, and so on. If the evidence shows that his mistaken belief that it was V who damaged the bus shelter was totally unreasonable, his arrest and detention will be unlawful.

9.17. ASSAULTING AND WILFULLY OBSTRUCTING THE POLICE

9–126 Section 89 of the *Police Act 1996* creates two core offences:

> "(1) Any person who assaults a constable in the execution of his duty, or a person assisting a constable in the execution of his duty, shall be guilty of an offence and liable on summary conviction …
>
> (2) Any person who resists or wilfully obstructs a constable in the execution of his duty, or a person assisting a constable in the execution of his duty, shall be guilty of an offence and liable on summary conviction …"

To come within the purview of section 89(1) the defendant must "assault" a constable in the execution of his duty, or a person assisting a constable in the execution of his duty. The section 89(2) offence targets those who do anything to "resist" or "obstruct" a constable in the execution of his duty.

In addition, it is an offence contrary to section 38 of the *Offences against the Person Act 1861* to assault "any person with intent to resist or prevent the lawful apprehension or detainer of himself or of any other person for any offence."[397] The latter offence is made out if the defendant commits an assault or battery with the ulterior intent of preventing his own or someone else's lawful apprehension.[398] A peculiarity of the section 38 offence is that it does not apply if the offender is resisting arrest for a non-criminal wrong such as a breach of the peace.[399] The fact the defendant is mistaken about the lawfulness of his arrest is no defence, if the arrest is in fact lawful.[400] Hereinafter our focus will be on the section 89 offences.

---

[397] Section 38 of the *Offences against the Person Act 1861*.

[398] *R. v. Lee* [2001] 1 Cr. App. R. 19.

[399] *Davies v. Griffiths* [1937] 2 All E.R. 67; *R. v. County of London Quarter Sessions Appeals Committee, Ex. p Metropolitan Police Comr.* [1948] 1 K.B. 670; *Williamson v. Chief Constable of the West Midlands Police* [2004] 1 W.L.R. 14. Cf. *Hewitt v. D.P.P.* [2002] EWHC 2801 where D was charged under section 4 of the *Public Order Act 1986*. (Conceptually, a breach of the peace is a crime, since it can result in an indefinite prison sentence where the offender is a serial breacher: see Heidi Blake, "Naked Rambler Faces Life in Prison", (London: *The Telegraph*, 13 January 2010.)

[400] *R. v. Fennell* [1971] 1 Q.B. 428.

Would it be a good riposte to the charge of assaulting a constable that the defendant did not know that the person he was hitting was a constable? No. The defendant is allowed to say that he was not guilty of assault—for example, because he honestly[401] believed that he had to act in self-defence.[402] But, given the assault, he is not allowed to say that he did not know the person he hit was a police officer;[403] so the offence is one of half *mens rea*.[404] If, for example, the defendant assaulted a person who unbeknown to him was a plain clothes detective, he can be convicted of the offence under the *Police Act 1996* even though he had no means of knowing the status of the person he was assaulting.[405]

9–127

Isn't that unjust? If a detective in plain clothes wishes to receive the special protection given by the law to police officers, surely he should show his warrant card. If he chooses to remain incognito, there is no reason why the defendant should be convicted of the special offence. The rule is remnant of the principle, formerly advocated but now generally abandoned, that an intent to commit a moral wrong, or a lesser crime, is sufficient *mens rea* to convict of a crime.[406] The rule in respect of assaulting a constable is anomalous, and its abolition has been recommended by the Criminal Law Revision Committee.[407]

9–128

What is meant by "in the execution of his duty"? Does it mean that the police officer must be on duty? The question is whether he is doing what he may lawfully do in his capacity of a police officer. He may be on duty and yet not be acting in the execution of his duty, because he may be acting unlawfully.

9–129

---

[401] If D is unreasonably mistaken about the need to defend himself, his unreasonable belief must be honestly held. *R. v. Williams* (1984) 78 Cr. App. R. 276; *R. v. Beckford* [1988] A.C. 130; *R. v. Kimber* [1983] 1 W.L.R. 1118. See also *Ashley v. Chief Constable of Sussex* [2008] 1 A.C. 962 at 972. Cf. *R. v. Mark* [1961] Crim. L.R. 173.

[402] *Ansell v. Swift* [1987] Crim. L.R. 194; *Kenlin v. Gardiner* [1967] 2 Q.B. 510; *Blackburn v. Bowering* [1994] 1 W.L.R. 1324; *R. v. Fennell* [1971] 1 Q.B. 428.

[403] *R. v. Forbes* (1865) 10 Cox C.C. 362; *R. v. Maxwell* (1909) 2 Cr. App. R. 26. Furthermore, there is no need to show that D knew or believed that the constable was acting in the execution of his duty. The half *mens rea* provision violates the presumption of *mens rea* (*R. v. K* [2002] 1 A.C. 462), but the courts will most likely hold Parliament intended section 89(1) to incorporate an element of strict liability, since section 89(2) makes an express reference to wilfully. It is worth noting that in most states in the United States, the defendant's knowledge of the victim's status is expressly required by statute. See the statutes cited in *State v. Brown*, 140 Wash.2d 456 at 472 (2000).

[404] "Strict criminal liability is strongly disfavoured in the law. ... While RCW 9A.36.031 is not a pure strict liability statute—the mental element for the *actus reus* of assault contemplates knowing or purposeful conduct ... it nevertheless, under the majority's interpretation, contains a strict liability element [a person is strictly liable for the more serious offence of assaulting a law enforcement officer even if he had no way of knowing that his victim was a law enforcement officer]. Given the "nature of the crime ... and the harshness of the potential punishment, legislative intent to dispense with a mental element should be clear before the court concludes the statute defines a strict liability crime." *State v. Brown*, 140 Wash.2d 456 at 473–474 (2000) *per* Madsen J.

[405] *Lavin v. Albert* [1982] A.C. 546.

[406] The rule was stated by Bramwell B., delivering the minority judgment in *R. v. Prince* (1875) 2 C.C.R. 154.

[407] Criminal Law Revision Committee, *Offences Against the Person*, Fourteenth Report, (London: H.M.S.O., Cmnd. 7844, 1980) at para. 256.

9–130   **If the court holds that the officer was acting outside his duty, because he was acting illegally, I suppose the defendant can still be convicted of a common assault on him if hitting the officer was unjustified?**   Yes.

9–131   **Doesn't the reference to the policeman's duty mean what the policeman is bound to do, rather than merely what it is proper for him to do?**   The courts give it the latter, and wider, meaning. The phrase is interpreted to refer to the functions of the police in arresting, searching, asking questions, setting traps, seizing evidence, maintaining the peace, protecting people and their property, preventing and detecting crime,[408] directing traffic,[409] and so on—anything lawful that the police choose to do as police officers. The slightest act of interference with the police in these circumstances is likely to be held to be an obstruction.

An arrest need not result in a conviction, but it must be lawful.[410] If the officer's actions are unlawful he will not be acting in the execution of his duty. He must not, for instance, be trespassing[411] or committing an assault.[412] A constable would act unlawfully if he were to physically escort or restrain a person who has not been arrested.[413] An officer must follow the correct procedures when he his arresting a suspect or is carrying out a search of the suspect's premises.[414] If an officer enters a property as a trespasser he will cease to be a trespasser if some overriding factor gives him a right to remain. For instance, if he remains on the premise or enters other parts of the premises purely for the purpose of preventing an imminent breach of the peace.[415]

---

[408] *Coffin v. Smith* (1980) 71 Cr. App. R. 221; *Ludlow v. Burgess* [1971] Crim. L.R. 238; *Waterford v. Lynn* [1964] 1 Q.B. 164.

[409] *Johnson v. Phillips* [1976] 1 W.L.R. 65.

[410] In *Burrell v. Crown Prosecution Service* [2005] EWHC 786, D was lawfully arrested, but the grounds for arresting him were weak.

[411] *Syed v. D.P.P.* [2010] 1 Cr. App. R. 34; *Baker v. Crown Prosecution Service* (2009) 173 J.P. 215; *Robson v. Hallett* [1967] 2 Q.B. 939. If the constable has permission (either express or implied) to enter D's premises, he must be given a reasonable opportunity to leave if that permission is revoked. "The question has arisen whether the revocation of a licence depends on the understanding of the owner of the premises, or of the person who has come on to the premises, or whether the test is an objective one, that is whether an *objective bystander would conclude that permission to be on the premises had been withdrawn.*" See *R. (on the application of Fullard) v. Woking Magistrates Court* [2005] EWHC 2922 at para. 19. The court held that it is an objective test. Certain provisions provide the police with a statutory right of entry: *e.g.*, section 180 of the *Licensing Act 2003*; section 143 of that *Act* allows an officer to use reasonable force to remove an intoxicated patron from licensed premises. See *Semple v. D.P.P.* [2010] 2 All E.R. 353.

[412] *Cumberbatch v. Crown Prosecution Service* (2010) 174 J.P. 149.

[413] *C v. D.P.P.* [2003] EWHC 2780; *Wood v. D.P.P.* [2008] EWHC 1056; cf. *McMillan v. Crown Prosecution Service* (2008) 172 J.P. 485.

[414] *Saliu v. D.P.P.* [2005] EWHC 2689; *McBean v. Parker* [1983] Crim. L.R. 399. See also *McLorie v. Oxford* [1982] Q.B. 1290. A constable may use reasonable force to enter a property, but "unless it was impossible, impracticable or undesirable to do so" he should "give the occupant of the property reasons for his seeking to gain" entry: *O'Loughlin v. Chief Constable of Essex* [1998] 1 W.L.R. 374. See also *Mullady v. D.P.P.* [1997] C.O.D. 422; *Edwards v. D.P.P.* (1993) 97 Cr. App. R. 30.

[415] *Lamb v. D.P.P.* (1990) 154 J.P.N. 172. A breach of the peace can take place on private premises: *McConnell v. Chief Constable of Greater Manchester* [1990] 1 W.L.R. 364; *Friswell v. Chief Constable of Essex* [2004] EWHC 3009; *McQuade v. Chief Constable of Humberside* [2002] 1 W.L.R. 1347.

Suppose the defendant admits that he knew he was belabouring a police officer, but says that he did not know the officer was acting in the execution of his duty?   What the execution of duty by the police is, in the abstract, is a question of law. It is taken to be part of the criminal law, and the citizen could not defend himself by saying that he did not know this part of the law.[416]

9–132

The rule about ignorance of the criminal law operates with great rigour in this application, because the legal powers of the police (in entering premises, seizing goods, interfering with the person) are in doubt on many particulars—the courts themselves are uncertain about them. In effect the position is that no one can safely use force against the police, because he cannot—or can rarely—be certain that the police have no right to detain him, enter his premises, or seize his goods, as they claim to do—or will not be given the right *ex post facto* by the judiciary. Even if the defendant sets up a mistake of fact, such that if the facts had been as he believed the officer would have been acting outside his duty;[417] still if the defendant is guilty of assaulting the officer he is, almost certainly, guilty also of assaulting him in the execution of this duty, this being as much a matter of strict liability as the fact that he is assaulting an officer. It is generally regarded as oppressive to charge this offence of assaulting the police if the assault is technical or trivial.

What if the constable mistakenly believes he is acting lawfully?   The question of whether a constable is acting in the execution of his duty is objective. If the constable's actions are in fact unlawful, then his mistaken belief cannot make them objectively lawful. A constable who restrains or forcibly escorts a person because he mistakenly believes that she has been arrested by another officer will not be acting in the execution of his duty.[418]

9–133

What mental element is required under section 89(1)?   The defendant must be shown to have had the requisite *mens rea* for assault/battery. If the offender assaults the constable because he honestly believes he is being attacked by a thug, he will lack the *mens rea* for assault. The offender lacks the requisite *mens rea* because he does not intend to apply unlawful force to the constable. Nor does he intend to make the constable apprehend unlawful violence. The offender merely intends to defend himself from what he genuinely believes is an unlawful attack. Furthermore, he does not act recklessly because he honestly believes that the constable is an unlawful attacker. But he must not use unreasonable force.

9–134

When will a person be liable for resisting or obstructing a constable contrary to section 89(2)?   Section 89(2) has two alternative conduct elements "resisting"[419] and "obstructing" a constable in the execution of his duty. The

9–135

---

[416] *R. v. Bentley* (1850) 4 Cox C.C. 406; *Agnew v. Johnson* (1877) 13 Cox C.C. 625; *Gelberg v. Miller* [1961] 1 W.L.R. 153. Cf. *McGrath v. Vipas* [1984] R.T.R. 58.

[417] Similarly, a mistaken belief that excessive force was being used in the course of an arrest by a police officer is no defence to a charge of assault. *R. v. Fennell* [1971] 1 Q.B. 428. See also *R. v. Ball* (1990) 90 Cr. App. R. 378.

[418] *Kerr v. D.P.P.* (1994) 158 J.P. 1048; see also *Cumberbatch v. Crown Prosecution Service* (2010) 174 J.P. 149; *Bentley v. Brudzinski* (1982) 75 Cr. App. R. 217.

[419] This might be satisfied if D pulls away from an officer. See *R. v. Sherriff* [1969] Crim. L.R. 260.

offender must in fact obstruct or resist the constable, as an attempt to obstruct or resist the constable will not be enough.[420] This offence and the offence of "assaulting" a constable in the execution of his duty have been developed by the courts into a barbed-wire entanglement protecting the operations of the police and the courts from all manner of interferences.

9–136   **Suppose that the police want to interview me about a crime, either because I am a witness or because I am possibly the culprit, and I refuse to talk to them. Am I guilty of obstructing them in their constabulary duty?**   No. Apart from certain powers of arrest and detention, the police cannot force themselves upon people in order to interview them, and they have no power to compel answers to be given to their questions.

9–137   **But part of the duty of the police is to investigate crime. How is it that I do not commit obstruction if I refuse to help them in their investigation?**   The answer I would like to give to you is: because an obstruction of the police means an active obstruction, not a failure to help them. Regrettably, the courts have developed a doctrine of obstruction by non-cooperation, so this is not the right legal answer.

It is clear that when the offence of wilfully obstructing a constable first appeared on the statute-book it was intended to deal only with physical obstructions, which is how the Scottish judges still interpret it.[421] But the English judges conceived the idea that an obstruction can be non-physical, which means that they have been able to bring extensive new areas of conduct under control. For example, it has been held that a person can frustrate the police by warning offenders of their presence.[422] So the question was raised whether an obstruction can be brought about by an omission.

At first the courts held not, and this is shown by the much misunderstood case of *Rice v. Connolly*.[423] A Divisional Court there reached an impeccable conclusion for a reason that was slightly flawed but substantially sound. The impeccable conclusion was that a citizen who refused to answer questions of the police is not guilty of wilfully obstructing them in the execution of their duty.[424] The slightly peccable reason, contained in the leading judgment of Lord Parker C.J., was that the offence requires wilfulness, which implies an absence of lawful excuse; and the citizen has a lawful excuse for not answering questions, presumably because of his "right to silence."[425] The objections to this line of argument are; first, that questions of excuse have nothing to do with the mental state of wilfulness. Secondly, the logical and proper reason why a failure to

---

[420] As section 89(2) is a summary offence it cannot be attempted. See *Bennett v. Bale* [1986] Crim. L.R. 404; *D.P.P. v. Glendinning* [2006] A.C.D. 21.

[421] *Curlett v. M'Kechnie* (1939) S.L.T. 11; *Carmichael v. Brannan* (1985) J.C. 82.

[422] But there can be no obstruction of a constable in the exercise of his duty unless Ds were committing or were likely to commit the crime. *D.P.P. v. Glendinning* [2006] A.C.D. 21; *Betts v. Stevens* [1910] 1 K.B. 1; *Green v. Moore* [1982] Q.B. 1044. These decisions make it clear that *Bastable v. Little* [1907] 1 K.B. 59 is unlikely to be followed.

[423] [1966] 2 Q.B. 414.

[424] Cf. *Dibble v. Ingleton* [1972] 1 Q.B. 480 at 488, where it was said that obstruction cannot be committed by a failure to act.

[425] *Murray v. U.K. (Right to Silence)* (1996) 22 E.H.R.R. 29.

answer the question of the police is not an obstruction is not because of any specific right the citizen has but simply because an "obstruction" must be taken to mean an *active* obstruction, not a mere failure to co-operate. If we are to be put under a legal duty to help the police, it must be by an *Act* of Parliament; and Parliament should say in what respects we are required to help the police on their request, and it should provide proper exemptions, and name the appropriate penalty for refusal. The job ought not to be done by judicial "interpretation" of the obstruction offence, which was obviously designed to do nothing more than prevent active obstructions.

To be fair to Lord Parker, although he started on the wrong foot he arrived at the right conclusion, because he said: "Though every citizen has a moral duty ... to assist the police, he has no legal duty to that effect." Since the notion of an omission makes no sense in the absence of a legal duty to act, one might have supposed that it was for Parliament to provide a list of these legal duties imposed upon people, not for the judges to make up the duties as the cases come before them. Parliament has, in fact, provided some specific offences of failing to comply with the orders of the police,[426] which seems to indicate an opinion that specific legislation is necessary. This opinion is supported by the fact that the giving of powers to the police involves sensitive issues of civil liberty. The courts recognize this in generally continuing to affirm that although it is an important function of the police to obtain evidence of offences, a person commits no offence in refusing to answer questions.[427]

    So far, all that is fairly clear. Unfortunately, the courts in their anxiety to uphold the actions of the police are now using *Rice v. Connelly* to reach a result that is the reverse of Lord Parker's conclusion. They do this by taking a single sentence out of context, and not even reading it properly. Lord Parker said: "to 'obstruct' is to do any act which makes it more difficult for the police to carry out their duty." This does not mean, as is sometimes supposed, that everything making it more difficult, *etc.* is an obstruction. For one thing, Lord Parker said "any *act*." For another, he was obviously speaking only of the lawful activities of the police. But the courts nowadays seem almost to say that because the police are doing something or other, they must be doing it lawfully.

    The following cases show that the police can require the active co-operation of the citizen in two important spheres of action: in preventing offences, and in protecting life and property, so that a refusal of the citizen to help them in these two matters is an obstruction.

9–138

When a person obstructs the highway by congregating with others in a demonstration, and fails to go away when told by the police to move on, he may

9–139

---

[426] See for example section 163 of the *Road Traffic Act 1988* (failure to give a constable an address on demand); and section 167 (driver failing to stop when so required by a constable in uniform).

[427] *Rice v. Connolly* [1966] 2 Q.B. 414. On the question of whether telling lies to the police in answer to questions is an obstruction: see Glanville Williams, "Evading Justice," [1975] Crim. L.R. 479 at 481 *et seq. R. v. George* [1981] Crim. L.R. 185. It is an obstruction to hinder the police in their questioning of a third party, *e.g.*, by telling the third party not to answer questions: *Green v. D.P.P.* (1991) 155 J.P. 816. But it would be an obstruction to step between the police and the person they sought to arrest: *Hills v. Ellis* [1983] Q.B. 680.

be charged with obstructing the highway⁴²⁸ or, alternatively, with obstructing the police, since it is the duty of the police to remove obstructions to the highway.⁴²⁹ And when a person has the keys of a car that is obstructing the highway, and refuses to surrender them to the police who wish to move the car, he obstructs the police by refusing to give the keys up.⁴³⁰ Similarly, a driver can be ordered to pull over so that he can be breathalysed.⁴³¹

Quite apart from their power to prevent offences, the police are invested by the courts with a general power to protect life or property; and in the exercise of this power they may even direct the citizen to commit what would normally be a minor offence, and prosecute him for obstruction if he refuses.⁴³² Since the police have a duty to prevent offences, and particularly breaches of the peace, an officer may lawfully require a person to desist from provocative (though lawful) behaviour, if this reasonably seems to be the only way of preventing a breach of the peace by others; and if the person so addressed refuses to desist he is guilty of obstruction.⁴³³Although it may seem right in the abstract that the police should have this power, they have sometimes been allowed to claim a fear of breach of the peace on indefensibly tenuous grounds, merely because the defendant was addressing a meeting or distributing pamphlets.⁴³⁴

The police can take action to prevent an imminent breach of the peace, but only if it is clear that a breach is almost certain to take place in the immediate future. In *R. (on the application of Laporte) v. Chief Constable of Gloucestershire*⁴³⁵ the claimant was a passenger on a coach travelling from London to a protest demonstration at an air base in Gloucestershire. The police stopped the coach she was travelling on and escorted it back to London. The coach was one of three containing 120 protesters. There was no evidence that the majority of the protesters intended to do anything other than protest in a peaceful manner. Lord Bingham said:⁴³⁶

> "It is not enough to justify action that a breach of the peace is anticipated to be a real possibility, and neither constables nor private citizens are empowered or bound to take such steps as on the evidence before them they think proper."

Thereafter Lord Brown said:

> "[N]o power (or duty) arises to take any preventive action whatever unless and until the constable (or citizen) reasonably apprehends that an actual breach of the peace is imminent (about to happen)."⁴³⁷

---

⁴²⁸ Section 137 of the *Highways Act 1980*.
⁴²⁹ *Parkhurst v. Jarvis* (1910) 101 L.T. 946.
⁴³⁰ *Stunt v. Bolton* [1972] R.T.R. 435; *Liepens v. Spearman* [1986] R.T.R. 24.
⁴³¹ Section 7 of the *Road Traffic Act 1988*.
⁴³² *Johnson v. Phillips* [1976] 1 W.L.R. 65; *Stunt v. Bolton* [1972] R.T.R. 435; *Broome v. D.P.P.* [1974] A.C. 58; *Re Kavanagh* [1974] Q.B. 600; *Tynan v. Balmer* [1967] 1 Q.B. 91.
⁴³³ *Humphries v. Connor* (1864) 17 I.C.L.R. 1.
⁴³⁴ *Duncan v. Jones* [1936] 1 K.B. 218.
⁴³⁵ [2007] 2 A.C. 105. Cf. *R. (on the application of Hawkes) v. D.P.P.* [2005] EWHC 3046.
⁴³⁶ *R. (on the application of Laporte) v. Chief Constable of Gloucestershire* [2007] 2 A.C. 105 at 131.
⁴³⁷ Quoting Profesor Glanville Williams in his 1954 article "Arrest for Breach of the Peace," [1954] Crim L.R. 578, where he said an imminent breach would involve "a sufficiently real and present threat." Lord Brown said that the lower courts went wrong, because under "their approach the police

Since the enactment of the *Human Rights Act 1998*, the courts have held that the police will be able to curtail the lawful activities of innocent bystanders only to prevent a breach of the peace, if it is absolutely necessary to do so.[438] In *Austin v. Commissioner of Police of the Metropolis* Clarke M.R. (as he then was) said:[439] **9–140**

> "(i) where a breach of the peace is taking place, or is reasonably thought to be imminent, before the police can take any steps which interfere with or curtail in any way the lawful exercise of rights by innocent third parties they must ensure that they have taken all other possible steps to ensure that the breach, or imminent breach, is obviated and that the rights of innocent third parties are protected; (ii) the taking of all other possible steps includes (where practicable), but is not limited to, ensuring that proper and advance preparations have been made to deal with such a breach, since failure to take such steps will render interference with the rights of innocent third parties unjustified or unjustifiable; but (iii) where (and only where) there is a reasonable belief that there are no other means whatsoever whereby a breach or imminent breach of the peace can be obviated, the lawful exercise by third parties of their rights may be curtailed by the police; (iv) this is a test of necessity which it is to be expected can only be justified in truly extreme and exceptional circumstances; and (v) the action taken must be both reasonably necessary and proportionate."

Nevertheless, the courts have been less indulgent in other areas. Take the case where two police officers attempted to question two men on the street. One of the two men became abusive and tried to walk away. He was convicted of obstructing the officers in the execution of their duty, and the conviction was upheld on appeal.[440] No satisfactory reasons were given. If a person is not obliged to stay while he is being questioned by the police (which is undoubted law),[441] it is impossible to see why his refusal to stay, accompanying a refusal by abuse and threats, makes him guilty of obstruction. Whatever the defendant threatened, the police could not have reasonably believed that they were in danger of being assaulted, because they knew that all they had to do in order to close the incident was to cease pestering him with unwelcome questions. The decision seems to be the result of confused ideas that because the police are acting in the pursuance of their general duty to enforce the law, therefore they have the right to interfere with the liberty of the citizen, as by compelling him to stop to answer questions. In fact the general "duty" of the police to enforce the law operates only within the legal powers and liberties allowed to them.

---

are under a duty to take reasonable steps to prevent a breach of the peace *from becoming imminent* (rather than which is *imminent*). The duty they postulate would allow for reduced imminence for lesser restraint (*i.e.* for preventive action short of arrest) on some sort of sliding scale." *R. (on the application of Laporte) v. Chief Constable of Gloucestershire* [2007] 2 A.C. 105 at 151–152.

[438] See *Beatty v. Gillbanks* (1882) 9 Q.B.D. 308 (where appellants assembled with others for a lawful purpose, and with no intention of carrying it out unlawfully, but with the knowledge that their assembly would be opposed by the Skeleton Army); and *Redmond-Bate v. D.P.P.* (1999) 163 J.P. 789 (where a woman was arrested for breach of the peace when she had refused to stop preaching to a hostile audience from the steps of Wakefield Cathedral.) In *R. (on the application of Laporte) v. Chief Constable of Gloucestershire* [2007] 2 A.C. 105 at 155, Lord Brown said: "Take Mr. Beatty, the Salvation Army captain, or Ms Redmond-Bate, the Wakefield preacher. The Divisional Court was in each case clearly right to have set aside their respective convictions. I repeat, the police's first duty is to protect the rights of the innocent rather than to compel the innocent to cease exercising them."

[439] [2008] Q.B. 660 at 680–681.

[440] *Ricketts v. Cox* (1982) 74 Cr. App. R. 298. See also *Donnelly v. Jackman* [1970] 1 W.L.R. 562; *Ledger v. D.P.P.* [1991] Crim. L.R. 439.

[441] *Rice v. Connolly* [1966] 2 Q.B. 414; *Bentley v. Brudzinski* (1982) 75 Cr. App. R. 217.

In *Sekfali v. D.P.P.*[442] three defendants were seen acting suspiciously in a clothing store in London. Members of staff from the store called the police. Plainclothes detectives spotted the suspects in a nearby street not long after they had left the store. The detectives approached the suspects and identified themselves as police officers. When they showed their warrant cards the three suspects ran in different directions. All three were apprehended. One was found to be carrying a stolen jacket, which had allegedly been taken from the store. The suspects were charged with wilful obstruction of the police contrary to section 89(2) of the *Police Act 1996*. It was argued on their behalf that they had no duty to remain or to answer questions, because they had not been arrested. The court held that they had a duty to remain even though they had no duty to answer questions or to do anything else to assist the police:

> "The appellants would have been entitled to remain silent and not answer any questions put to them. They could have refused, if they had not been arrested, to accompany the police to any particular place to which they might have been requested by the police to go. They could have said that they had no intention of answering questions and they could, no doubt, have said that as a result they were intent on going on their way and have done so without giving rise to a case which would entitle the court to conclude that in departing they were intending to impede the police officers and obstruct the police officers in the execution of their duty. Had they responded in that way, then it would have been for the police to have decided whether to arrest them; but they ran off, as the magistrates found to avoid apprehension. That being a wilful act, taken so as to obstruct the police, was an act capable of constituting an offence contrary to section 89(2)."[443]

This means that even though the police cannot detain a suspect without arresting him,[444] the suspect is required to stay put until the police have had a reasonable opportunity to determine whether to arrest him. The law would be pushed to the limit if the police were allowed to require a person to remain for more than ten minutes or so.[445] If the police do not intend to arrest the suspect, then they should not detain him more than momentarily. Walking away from an officer as he is asking questions cannot amount to an obstruction, because the officer is not entitled to receive answers. If the police want the walker to stop walking then they should arrest him, if they have grounds for making an arrest. The rule in *Sekfali v. D.P.P.* should only apply in cases where the police intend to make an arrest and where there is clear evidence that the offender is running because he suspects he is about to be arrested.

---

[442] (2006) 170 J.P. 393.

[443] *Sekfali v. D.P.P* (2006) 170 J.P. 393 at para. 10.

[444] *R. v. Inwood* [1973] 1 W.L.R. 647; *Pedro v. Diss* (1981) 72 Cr. App. R. 193.

[445] Cf. *Lodwick v. Saunders* [1985] 1 W.L.R. 382, where it was held a constable who suspected that the vehicle was stolen was entitled to take reasonable steps to detain the vehicle for a reasonable time to effect an arrest. See also *Leach v. D.P.P.* [1993] R.T.R. 161. In *D.P.P. v. Hawkins* [1988] 1 W.L.R. 1166 it was held that, although under section 28(3) of the *Police and Criminal Evidence Act 1984* an arresting officer is required to state the ground for the arrest as soon as possible he was entitled to "*maintain* the arrest until it was practicable to inform the arrested person of that ground." In that case, the police officer omitted to provide reasons when it was practicable to do so, but this was not enough to retroactively nullify the arrest.

If the police can rope people in to prevent obstruction of the highway, could   **9–141**
they organize a press-gang of passers-by to clear rubble from the street,
prosecuting any recalcitrant person for obstructing them in the execution of
their duty? The decisions have concerned only people who were personally
obstructing the highway or who (by possessing the keys of an obstructing car)
were in a special position to prevent its continuance. Obviously the answer to
your question is no. In general, the right of the police to require co-operation to
prevent crime has been recognized only against those who were in some way
involved in the crime as fomenters or otherwise.[446] But it is not at all clear how
far the court's line of reasoning will be pushed; a new departure may be made at
any time. The traditional rule, supported by many decisions, is that to justify
interference with individuals the police must adduce specific legal authority. It is
not enough for them to show that they were performing their general functions.

A special problem concerns trespass to land and buildings. It has always been
assumed that although the police have the right to enter premises to prevent a
breach of the peace or serious offence,[447] they generally have no such right
merely for the purpose of obtaining evidence of past offences; and the correctness
of this opinion was confirmed by a decision that it is not an obstruction to deny a
police officer entry to premises to search for incriminating evidence when he has
no warrant permitting him to do so.[448] Similarly, it has been supposed that a
police officer cannot call upon people to help him make an arrest (unless a breach
of the peace has been committed in his presence by two or more persons);[449] and
the correctness of this was confirmed by a case of 1861, where it was held that an
occupier of premises is not guilty of obstruction if he refuses to help the police to
find a criminal who is hiding on his premises. It this still the law? Yes. And does
a landlord commit obstruction in refusing to allow the police to search his
lodger's belongings for evidence to incriminate the lodger? It seems that in fact
the offence of obstruction has never been extended to a person's failure to help
the police make an arrest or collect evidence of crime.

Even *R. v. Brown*[450] is not likely to be followed in the 21st century. It would be
too much to allow a police officer to call on innocent bystanders to help them
make an arrest to prevent a breach of the peace which has been committed in his
presence by two or more persons. Given that the modern police force has
immense resources, it would be inappropriate to criminalize untrained members

---

[446] In *Sekfali v. D.P.P* (2006) 170 J.P. 393 at para. 10 it was observed: "The position is that a citizen
has no legal duty to assist the police. As it happens, probably most people would accept that they have
a moral and social duty to do so; but it is clear that no legal duty to assist exists."

[447] *Handcock v. Baker* (1800) 126 E.R. 1270; *Thomas v. Sawkins* [1935] 2 K.B. 249; *McGowan v.
Chief Constable of Kingston-upon-Hull* [1967] Crim. L.R. 34.

[448] *Syce v. Harrison* [1980] Crim. L.R. 649; cf. *Chapman v. D.P.P.* (1989) 89 Cr. App. R. 190. In *R.
(on the application of Rottman) v. Commissioner of Police of the Metropolis* [2002] 2 A.C. 692, it was
held that an arresting officer has the power to search the room in which a person has been arrested.
See also *Bhatti v. Croydon Magistrates' Court* [2010] 3 All E.R. 671; *R. v. Commissioner of the City
of London Police* [2009] 1 W.L.R. 2091.

[449] It is an offence at common law for a person to refuse without lawful excuse to help a constable to
quell a riot when he has seen a breach of the peace committed by two or more persons and there is a
reasonable necessity for calling on help (this only applies if defendant, without any physical
impossibility or lawful excuse refuses to assist): *R. v. Brown* (1841) 174 E.R. 522. Presumably the
refusal could now be punished instead as an obstruction.

[450] (1841) 174 E.R. 522. See also *R. v. Atkinson* (1869) 11 Cox C.C. 330.

of the public for refusing to get involved in dangerous police work. It would also seem unnecessary to involve the public.[451] *Per contra*, where a person is able to assist without unwarranted restriction of his own liberty, such as where a landlord can use his key to open a door to help the police rescue people from a burning building, he should be liable if he fails to assist.[452] He might also be summarily liable for the statutory offence of obstructing an emergency worker,[453] if he were to refuse to assist the worker by using his key to open the door. So the courts have apparently, in an inarticulate and unsystematic way, arrived at a rough division of the functions of the police for the purpose of deciding what co-operation can be exacted from the public.[454]

9–142   **Does the mental element for section 89(1) differ from that for section 89(2)?** You will recall the subsection provides: "Any person who resists or wilfully obstructs a constable in the execution of his duty." The word "wilfully" only applies to obstructing. Perhaps this means that a person can be liable for recklessly resisting[455] a constable in the execution of his duty. Nevertheless, the wilfulness requirement makes it explicitly clear that the defendant will only be liable for obstruction, if he intended to obstruct the officer in the execution of his duty. There is no need to show that the defendant was acting hostilely, as the defendant's motivation is irrelevant.[456] He may have been acting with the best of intentions, but if he knew that his conduct would hinder the police, he may be liable. It is no defence to say, "I knew I was obstructing or hindering the officer from carrying out his duties, but I had a good reason for hindering him."

The wilfulness requirement provides the defendant with one further advantage. The requirement of wilfulness for the offence of obstructing the police means that mistake of fact by the defendant as to the official status of the person he is obstructing can be a defence;[457] but once again a mistake of law (*e.g.*, as to what is the officer's duty) is not a defence.

9.18.   Negligent Injuries to the Person

9–143   There is no general offence of negligently causing injury to the person. At common law, almost the only offence of this kind is manslaughter, which requires death to occur (by gross negligence or in certain other ways). Similarly, there is no general statutory offence of injury by negligence. But provisions aimed

---

[451] Since *R. v. Brown* (1841) 174 E.R. 522 requires innocent bystanders to take positive action, it would surely be subject to the necessity conditions laid down in *R. (on the application of Laporte) v. Chief Constable of Gloucestershire* [2007] 2 A.C. 105 (Lord Rodger quotes the case at 132, but skirts the issue); and *Austin v. Commissioner of Police of the Metropolis* [2008] Q.B. 660 at 680–681.

[452] Cf. *Lunt v. D.P.P.* [1993] C.O.D. 430.

[453] See sections 1 and 2 of the *Emergency Workers (Obstruction) Act 2006*.

[454] *R. v. Green* (1861) 8 Cox C.C. 441.

[455] Perhaps, the courts will hold that recklessness is sufficient. Suppose D unintentionally resists a police officer in the execution of his duties, because he is too intoxicated to know what he is doing. He would not be liable if the section requires a specific intent to resist, but he would be if recklessness were sufficient *mens rea*. The courts are likely hold that it is a crime of basic intent.

[456] *Hills v. Ellis* [1983] Q.B. 680; *Lewis v. Cox* [1985] Q.B. 509; *Smith v. Reynolds* [1986] Crim. L.R. 559; *Mauritius v. Hurnam* [2007] 1 W.L.R. 1582.

[457] *Ostler v. Elliott* [1980] Crim. L.R. 584.

against those who negligently create the risk of injury in particular circumstances have been seeping into the statute-book. The best-known is the offence of careless driving, but we now have in addition wide offences under the *Health and Safety at Work etc. Act 1974.*

Section 2(1) provides:

> "It shall be the duty of every employer to ensure, so far as is reasonably practicable, the health, safety and welfare at work of all his employees."

Section 3(1):

> "It shall be the duty of every employer to conduct his undertaking in such a way as to ensure, so far as is reasonably practicable, that persons not in his employment who may be affected thereby are not thereby exposed to risks to their health or safety."

This provision travels far outside the short title of the *Act*, and could be used if noxious factory chimneys injure the health of the surrounding population. Section 4 imposes similar wide duties on persons concerned with work premises (including employees who have duties in relation to the premises), to ensure that the premises (and any plant or substance in the premises) are safe and without risks to health. Section 6 imposes a duty on any person who designs, manufactures, imports or supplies any article for use at work to ensure, so far as it is reasonably practicable, that the article is designed and constructed as to be safe and without risks to health when properly used; and there are subsidiary provisions requiring testing and research, and similar provisions relating to the supply of substances for use at work.

Section 7 shows an unusual lack of bias in this type of legislation by extending a **9–144** general duty to employees. It is:

> "the duty of every employee while at work—
> (a)   to take reasonable care for the health and safety of himself and, of other persons who may be affected by his acts or omissions at work; and
> (b)   as regards any duty or requirement imposed on his employer or any other person by or under any of the relevant statutory provisions, to co-operate with him so far as is necessary to enable that duty or requirement to be performed or complied with."

Meanwhile section 8 provides:

> "No person shall intentionally or recklessly interfere with or misuse anything provided in the interests of health, safety or welfare in pursuance of any of the relevant statutory provisions."

Penalties are provided by section 33 (as amended), which makes it an offence to fail to discharge any of these duties (or contravene section 8). The offence is triable either way.[458]

These provisions are the most general of a mass of safety provisions in industrial legislation, failure to comply with which is an offence. In addition there is a considerable body of law for the protection of consumers and the environment, which cannot even be touched upon here. When an activity

---

[458] The last phrase is widely defined in section 53(1).

involves risk, it is frequently confined to qualified persons—either those professionally qualified, or those with licences from the public authorities; and it is made an offence for unqualified persons to act. For example, sections 78 and 84 of the *Medicines Act 1968* create an offence of pretending to be a chemist; but the punishment is a fine only, even if many people have been negligently poisoned.

9–145   **Why not have a general offence instead of all these detailed offences? If there is an offence of manslaughter by gross negligence, I don't see why there shouldn't be a general serious offence of causing injury by gross negligence, or indeed an offence of being grossly negligent. Liability should not depend on the accident of the outcome.** Some take this view, on logical grounds which I do not find persuasive. The offence of manslaughter by gross negligence has not worked satisfactorily, as we shall see. And even if it is thought worth preserving, we have got on well enough without a general offence of negligence not resulting in death. We have an embarrassing number of wicked people in prison and do not need to add incautious ones to them. If we are to have any offences of negligence they had better be summary, finable ones; and that is how nearly all the statutory offences just mentioned work in practice, even if most of them could as a matter of law be tried on indictment.

CHAPTER 10

SEXUAL AGGRESSION

"We do not discount the seriousness of rape as a crime. It is highly reprehensible, both in a moral sense and in its almost total contempt for the personal integrity and autonomy of the female victim and for the latter's privilege of choosing those with whom intimate relationships are to be established. Short of homicide, it is the 'ultimate violation of self.'"[1]

10.1.   THE CLASSIFICATION OF SEXUAL OFFENCES

To speak of sexual offences as a class is somewhat misleading, since there are important differences of types. The two main groups are sexual aggression and breaches of sexual taboo. In this book we are almost exclusively concerned with the first.   **10–001**

Those in the first group consist of injuries to a non-consenting victim, while in the second group the conduct is illegal whether or not the victim consents. The distinction is not precise, because of ambiguity of the concept of "consent." Misbehaviour by an adult with a consenting severely impaired person is normally assigned to either group, the consent of the protected person being disregarded for the purpose of certain offences.[2] If the defendant is in a position of trust and his victim is aged 16 or 17, the law deems that the victim's consent is negated even if it was otherwise valid.[3] In the case of a very young victim it is in any case unrealistic to speak in terms of consent.

The present chapter is concerned with those offences where the predominant motive of the law is to protect an innocent person against an aggressor. The *Sexual Offences Act 2003* decriminalized many of the more controversial offences that fell in the second category, namely homosexual offences[4] (buggery, and gross indecency between men).[5] Others offences seem to straddle both categories such as indecent exposure.[6] Public nudity might not flout our social

---

[1] *Coker v. Georgia*, 433 U.S. 584 at 597 (1977).

[2] Sections 38–41 of the *Sexual Offences Act 2003*.

[3] Sections 16–19 of the *Sexual Offences Act 2003*.

[4] The word comes not from the Latin *homo*, man, but from the Greek *homos*, the same, and refers to an attraction to the same sex, whether male or female. There has never been a specific offence of female homosexual behaviour.

[5] See the now repealed sections 12 and 13 of the *Sexual Offences Act 1957*.

[6] Section 66 of the *Sexual Offences Act 2003*. The police do not seem to prosecute nude protestors and the like these days, but would certainly prosecute a flasher. Similarly, it is not likely that the

norms if it takes place on a clothes optional beach, but would be a form of sexual aggression if it involved a flasher exposing himself to a young lady for his own sexual gratification.

10–002 Even the general class of sexual offences is not clearly demarcated, because almost any crime can be committed from a sexual motive. Murder may have an overt or hidden sexual motive, ranging from the common case of jealousy or the desire to be rid of a sexual partner to the uncommon case of the necrophiliac.[7] Sadism, another perversion of the sex instinct, may result in an offence of causing actual bodily harm.[8] Sexual acts between consenting adults in public places such as public lavatories are criminalized,[9] because it is necessary to ensure public spaces are available for all to use.[10] No one is going to want to use a public amenity, if there are sexual encounters taking place in it. Bestiality is not harmful to humans, but there is no reason why harm to animals should not be criminalized.[11] Incest is criminalized, not only because it flouts social conventions, but because there is a danger that it might produce a disabled child.[12] A fetishist may steal a sexual object (such as underclothes from a clothes line). The nuisance committed opportunistically by a Peeping Tom (one type of voyeur) is in general so slight that it is not worth specifically dealing with by law, but it is now criminalized.[13] The gravamen of voyeurism from the victim's perspective is a loss of privacy, rather than a sexual violation as such.[14]

The *Sexual Offences Act 2003* recast the law, largely as a result of the recommendations made by the Home Office.[15] (All references in this chapter are to this *Act*, unless the contrary is expressed or clearly implied.) The *Act of 2003*

---

police would charge a person for changing a baby's nappy in a public place in the 21st century. Cf. *R. v. Clark* (1883) 15 Cox C.C. 171, where D was convicted of an offence for having a naked newborn baby in a public place.

[7] Necrophilia is now caught by section 70 of the *Sexual Offences Act 2003*. It is not harmful to the living, but it could cause serious distress to the victim's living relatives, if he/she has any. People with such propensities could be dangerous in other ways. See *R. v. Coutts* [2007] 1 Cr. App. R. 60 at 78.

[8] *R. v. Brown* [1994] 1 A.C. 212.

[9] See section 71 of the *Sexual Offences Act 2003*.

[10] See Dennis J. Baker "The Impossibility of a Critically Objective Criminal Law," (2011) 56(2) *McGill L. J.* 349; Joseph Raz, *Ethics in the Public Domain* (Oxford: Clarendon Press, 1995) at 162 *et seq.*

[11] See section 69 of the *Sexual Offences Act 2003*. For a fuller discussion of the moral rationale of criminalizing harm to animals, see Dennis J. Baker, *The Right Not to be Criminalized: Demarcating Criminal Law's Authority*, (Farnham: Ashgate Publishing, 2011) at 82–83; 158.

[12] Sections 64 and 65 of the *Sexual Offences Act 2003* do not catch cousins. Therefore, it is not clear that the "disabled off-spring" argument had much influence on Parliament. Professor Baroness Deech claims that many people from certain ethnic groups are married to their first cousins and that this has resulted in a third of the children born to such parents having recessive genetic disorders. See Frances Gibb, "Rise in marriages between cousins 'is putting children's health at risk'", (London: *The Sunday Times*, 10 March 2010). Professor Deech said one ethnic group represented 3 *per cent.* "of all births in Britain but one third of children with recessive disorders." The child that is born is harmed directly because it is born disabled. It also results in a remote harm, because taxpayers have to fund the National Health Service.

[13] Section 67 of the *Sexual Offences Act 2003*.

[14] See *R. v. Hamilton* [2008] Q.B. 224. See generally, Dennis J. Baker, "The Sense and Nonsense of Criminalising Transfers of Obscene Material," (2008) 26 *Sing. L. Rev.* 126.

[15] Home Office, *Setting the Boundaries: Reforming the Law on Sex Offences*, (London: Home Office Communication Directorate, 2000).

created more than 70 new offences, but space prevents us from examining them all in detail in this treatise. In this chapter we will examine the core offences involving aggression. There is a great deal of overlap between the adult offences, child offences and the mentally disordered offences. In this chapter, the core principles will be set out with reference to the adult offences. However, where the child offences and mentally disordered offences incorporate a distinct concept such as "incitement," that concept will be discussed in detail with reference to the given offence.

The core offences include rape (section 1), assault by penetration (section 2), sexual assault (section 3), and causing another to engage in sexual activity (section 4). We will also examine the child version of these offences; and the specific offences that aim to protect the mentally disordered. A concept that lies at the heart of sexual offences is "consent." Consent will not be discussed in detail here, because it is covered in great detail in Chapter 23. Many of the non-core offences such as indecent exposure, sex in a public lavatory, voyeurism, incest, and so on, will not be discussed further.

10.2. Rape

Rape is punishable with imprisonment for life.[16] The offence was not given statutory definition until 1976, when the *Sexual Offences (Amendment) Act 1976* put the decision in *D.P.P. v. Morgan*[17] on a statutory footing. The latest formulation of the offence appears in section 1 of the *Sexual Offences Act 2003*. **10–003**

Section 1 provides:

"(1) A person (A) commits an offence if–
(a) he intentionally penetrates the vagina, anus or mouth of another person (B) with his penis,
(b) B does not consent to the penetration, and
(c) A does not reasonably believe that B consents.
(2) Whether a belief is reasonable is to be determined having regard to all the circumstances, including any steps A has taken to ascertain whether B consents."

The offence can only be perpetrated by a male, since only a male has a penis. A person is not convictable of rape where he uses an innocent agent to perpetrate rape,[18] because the wording of the section seems to preclude such an application. Parliament intended such cases to be prosecuted under section 4. Section 4 creates a new offence of causing a person to engage in sexual activity. A woman could be convicted of rape if she assists or encourages another to perpetrate a rape.[19] The male appendage need not be an original. If the defendant has had a sex change his new part will be regarded as a penis as far as the law of rape is concerned. Similarly, if the victim was formerly a man and has been converted

---

[16] Section 1(4) of the *Sexual Offences Act 2003*.
[17] [1976] A.C. 182.
[18] See *R. v. Cogan* [1976] Q.B. 217.
[19] *R. v. Ram* (1893) 17 Cox C.C. 609; *Lord Baltimore* (1768) 98 E.R. 136; *D.P.P. v. K* [1997] 1 Cr. App. R. 36; cf. *R. v. Eldershaw* (1828) 172 E.R. 472. Such a woman could be convicted of rape by means of section 8 of the *Accessories and Abettors Act 1861*, but she might instead be convicted of an independent inchoate offence under section 44 or 45 of the *Serious Crime Act 2007*.

into a woman, her surgically constructed vagina will be treated as a vagina under the subsection.[20] The victim can be male or female, since all humans have an anus and a mouth.

10–004 There were two classes of person who were exempt from the law of rape. Formerly husbands were a class of person who could not commit rape, but this is no longer the case.[21] The reason traditionally given for the general rule was the totally unconvincing one that the wife's consent is given on marriage, and she cannot revoke it.[22] This antediluvian view of the rights of the husband was not in keeping with modern standards of equality. Nonetheless, husbands should not be prosecuted for old rapes that took place before the law was reformed.[23]

The other person who could not be convicted of rape under the previous law was a boy under 14, the reason advanced being that he was irrebuttably presumed not to have reached the age of puberty.[24] The presumption was abrogated by section 1 of the *Sexual Offences Act 1993*. Therefore, the only persons that remain exempt from the law of rape are children under the age of 10 (28.2).

The penetration requirement is satisfied by the least degree of penetration.[25] The carnal act will normally be *per vaginam*; but penetrating the mouth or anus of the victim with a penis is also rape. The inclusion of the mouth is a major extension to the law of rape. Penetrating the victim's mouth is not as harmful as penetrating her vagina or anus, because penetrating the former is less likely to result in physical damage or transmit a dangerous disease. Nevertheless, it does not seem unjust to label this type of sexual violation as rape, even though most lay people would not think of it as an act of rape.[26] The jury can convict the defendant even if it is not clear which cavity he penetrated, but it must be proved that he penetrated one or the other.[27] The act of penetration is a continuing act. If D's initial penetration is consensual he will only commit rape if he continues to penetrate the victim after consent has been withdrawn. As soon as consent is withdrawn he must withdraw or he will face a rape charge.[28]

It must be proved that the act of penetration was non-consensual. The absence of consent from the complainant converts what would otherwise be lovemaking

---

[20] Section 79(3) of the *Sexual Offences Act 2003*.

[21] *R. v. R.* [1992] A.C. 599.

[22] *R. v. Clarence* (1889) 22 Q.B.D. 23 at 51 *per* Hawkins J.

[23] In *R. v. C* [2004] 1 W.L.R. 2098 a husband was convicted of rape for raping his wife in 1970, but the marital rape exemption was abrogated 22 years after that rape took place. This decision was contrary to the rule of law. No one would deny that it was a good thing to change the law so that a husband can be convicted for raping his wife (a heinous crime, indeed), but allowing judges to act as legislatures, and to apply such a change retroactively, is contrary to the rule of law. See Glanville Williams, "Rape is Rape," (1992) 142 *N.L.J.* 11.

[24] *The King v. Groombridge* (1836) 173 E.R. 256.

[25] The *Act* says "penetration," but it is declaratory of the common law which declared that the least degree of penetration was sufficient. Emission is unnecessary. See *R. v. Dermody* [1956] I.R. 32; *R. v. Lines* (1844) 174 E.R. 861; *R. v. Hughes* (1841) 173 E.R. 1038; *R. v. Gammon* (1832) 172 E.R. 994.

[26] It will be more difficult to collect DNA samples from the mouth of the victim, because she will no doubt rinse her mouth at the first opportunity.

[27] *R. v. K* [2009] 1 Cr. App. R. 24.

[28] See section 79(2) of the *2003 Act*. See also *Kaitamaki v. The Queen* [1985] A.C. 147; *R. v. Schaub* (1994) 138 S.J.L.B. 11. Cf. *State v. Baby,* 946 A.2d 463 (2008); *People v. Dancy*, 124 Cal. Rptr. 2d 898 (2002); *State v. Bunyard*, 133 P.3d 14 (2006).

into a serious and violent wrong. The requirements of consent are discussed in Chapter 23. (The section 75 and 76 presumptions apply to the offence of rape.)

What is the mental element for rape?   The defendant must intentionally   **10–005**
penetrate the victim in circumstances where the victim is not consenting. There is no need to show that the defendant intended to have sexual intercourse in circumstances where the victim was not consenting, it is only necessary to show that the act of penetration was intentional and that he was negligent as to whether or not the victim was consenting. If the penetration is involuntary such as where the defendant acts as an automaton, the defendant cannot be said to have intentionally penetrate the victim.[29] Similarly, if a couple are rolling around naked in circumstances where the woman has made it clear that she does not mind a naked cuddle and kiss, but does not want to have sexual intercourse, D will not be liable if his excited penis accidentally rubs into V's vagina and thus penetrates her slightly. (This is a most fanciful example, but it makes a conceptual point.) In this type of improbable scenario, D recklessly penetrates V. He is not reckless (or negligent) as to whether she is consenting as he knows she is not consenting to penetration and he does not intend to penetrate her.

Are you telling me that the defendant can be liable even if he did not realize   **10–006**
that the victim was not consenting?   Yes. It is only necessary to show that the defendant did not have reasonable grounds for believing that the victim was consenting. This requires a consideration of whether the defendant had reasonable grounds for believing that the victim was consenting, not a consideration of what a reasonable person would have believed. It is a question of whether the given defendant had reasonable grounds for *his* belief.

In the majority of cases it will be obvious that the victim is not consenting. But in the absence of protest from the victim, it may not be obvious that the victim is incapable of consenting. In *R. v. Cooper*[30] the victim fellated the defendant without objection, because her mental disorder caused her to mistakenly believe that she would be harmed if she did not comply with his request to be fellated. In that case the defendant did not threaten the victim, he merely asked her to fellate him. However, the defendant had just met the victim at a psychiatric clinic, had been told by her that she had mental health problems, and had been told by her that she believed that she had to leave the area because people were trying to kill her. The facts were such that defendant could not argue that he had reasonable grounds for believing that the victim was consenting. The defendant offered to help her escape from what *he* believed to be imaginary enemies. He took her to his friend's house where he encouraged her to consume crack cocaine. After he got her to take several doses of the crack cocaine he cornered her in a bathroom and asked her to fellate him. Given the information that was available to him he could have easily formed the opinion that the victim was in no position to give true consent (23.7).

---

[29] See *R. v. Luedecke* [2008] 236 C.C.C. 3d 317, where a man in a sleepwalking trance raped a woman.
[30] [2009] 1 W.L.R. 1786.

10–007	**What if a man picks up a mentally impaired woman and has sexual relations with her without realizing that she lacks the capacity to consent?** No ordinary man, who does not know what diagnosis has been made, is likely to be able to tell the difference between an impaired and a severely impaired women, at any rate in quite a broad band of marginal cases—even if he knew the legal definition of the degree of mental impairment required. To look for *mens rea* or an unreasonable failure to spot the girl's mental incapacity when a man in a cinema finds a complaisant girl next to him and has intercourse with her, she being in fact severely impaired, is a controversial undertaking.

The offences make special provision for the defendant's mistake. The defendant must have reasonable grounds for believing that the victim is not impaired and thus is giving true consent. He will not have reasonable grounds for his belief, if the victim's impairment was apparent in her appearance, demeanour, speech and or general pattern of behaviour. The impairment would have to be obvious from the perspective of the reasonable bystander. If his mistake is reasonable, he will not be liable.

10–008	**What if the defendant's own mental impairment causes him to make a mistake that a reasonable person would not have made?** The offences in sections 1–4 of the *Act of 2003* adopt the following test:

> "Whether a belief is reasonable is to be determined having regard to all the circumstances, including any steps A has taken to ascertain whether B consents."

Suppose the defendant is mentally impaired, but understands that it is wrong to have sexual intercourse with a mentally impaired person who is not capable of giving genuine consent. Let us assume he meets a young woman in the park and forms a relationship with her. After a few weeks he and the young lady engage in sexual intercourse. Unbeknown to him, she lacks the mental capacity to provide true consent because she is severely impaired. A reasonable person would have detected her impairment, but the defendant was unable to because of his own mental impairment.

On similar facts in *R. v. Mrzljak*,[31] the Supreme Court of Queensland accepted that the defendant's mental impairment was "the primary reason why he could not evaluate whether, what appeared to him in the absence of protest to be the complainant's consent, was given with cognitive capacity. Had someone taken the appellant aside and explained that she was intellectually handicapped he would not have had sex with her." The defendant was unable to pick up the social cues that would have allowed him to make a rational judgment as to whether the victim had sufficient capacity to be able to consent, not only because of his own impairment, but also because he was a migrant with poor English skills. His mental impairment and poor English prevented him from accessing and assessing the available information in the same way that a reasonable person would have accessed and assessed it. A reasonable person armed with the same limited information would have made the same mistake. "A jury might be prepared to

---

[31] [2005] 152 A. Crim. R. 315.

accept that a belief which would not be reasonable if held by a native English speaker of normal IQ, was honestly held by the appellant on reasonable grounds."

In *R. v. Mrzljak*, Holmes J. said:[32]   **10–009**

> "It is not the handicap *per se* which bears on the excuse of mistake. It is the fact that the handicap results in the accused having to form his belief on a more limited set of information that is relevant, just as other external circumstances affecting the accused's opportunity to develop and test his perception are relevant. A jury cannot assess the rationality of a belief in isolation from the circumstances in which, and the information on which, it is formed."

His mistake was one that a reasonable person would have made in the same circumstances. The words "having regard to all the circumstances" mean that the courts will be required to consider whether the given defendant had reasonable grounds for the belief. Therefore, the question of whether the given defendant reasonably believed that the victim was consenting may depend not only on his mental capacity, but also on certain other characteristics such as deafness and blindness. The fact that the defendant did not speak the same language as the victim might also be considered, because a reasonable person speaking the same language as the victim would act in circumstances where he would have a fair opportunity to assess the victim's mental capacity by having a conversation with her.[33] This approach seems fair, because a person can only be expected to act as a reasonable person armed with the same information would have acted in the circumstances.[34] A person will act in different ways depending on the circumstantial information that is available to him.

Parliament had this type of approach in mind when it enacted the *Act of 2003*. In the Standing Committee on the Bill for this *Act* in the House of Commons the Minister said:

> "[W]e accept that in some circumstances it is fair for the jury to take relevant characteristics of the defendant into account when considering whether he reasonably believed that the complainant consented. That is why the reasonableness test does not rule out that possibility. In appropriate cases, if a defendant is very young or has a mental disorder, the jury will take that into account when considering whether his belief in consent was reasonable."[35]

---

[32] *R. v. Mrzljak* [2005] 152 A. Crim. R. 315 at 334. See also *Daniels v. The Queen* (1989) 1 W.A.R. 435 at 445, where it was held that the reasonableness of the mistake would depend "on whether an ordinary and reasonable man would have made it in the circumstances which the jury found to have existed that night." See also *Aubertin v. Western Australia* (2006) 167 A. Crim. R. 1 at para. 29, where it was said: "The reasonableness of the accused's belief is an objective factor to be judged by the standard of a reasonable person of the same age, background and level of intellectual functioning as the accused, and familiar with all the circumstances that were known to the accused at the relevant time."

[33] See *TS v. R.* [2008] EWCA Crim. 6. For a discussion of the unfairness of imposing the strict liability standard on mentally impaired defendants, see Elizabeth Nevins-Saunders, "Incomprehensible Crimes: Defendants with Mental Retardation Charged with Statutory Rape," (2010) 85 *N.Y.U. L. Rev.* 1067.

[34] Because the negligence requirement is contrary to the requirement that liability for serious offences should be based on subjective fault, the "in all the circumstances" element is needed to strike a fair balance.

[35] Hansard, H.C. Standing Committee B, 1st Sitting, 9 September 2003, col.18.

10–010 **Are you telling me that the offender is only required to act as reasonably as any other person who is afflicted by his mental imperfections? Does the law allow the courts to invest the reasonable person with all the defendant's characteristics?** No. A person's gender would not be relevant nor would age unless the defendant is so immature that he is unable to access and assess the circumstantial information that a reasonable person would be able to access and evaluate. A reasonable person who is blindfolded or made to wear earplugs is likely to make mistakes he would not otherwise make. Similarly, a reasonable person who is severely impaired because he is concussed or has been drugged will make mistakes that he would not otherwise make. The circumstances are that he is concussed or drugged.

10–011 **What about if the defendant has full capacity but arrogantly believes that a woman is consenting when she is not?** He will be liable for rape. His subjective evaluation of the reasonableness of his conduct is irrelevant. Strong medical or other evidence would have to be produced to explain why he could not access and evaluate information that any reasonable person would have been able to access and evaluate in the given circumstances. A person of normal capacity with no disability would not convince a jury that his belief was reasonable, because he is expected to discover facts that any reasonable person would discover.

10–012 **What about self-induced impairment. Suppose a man mistakenly ends up in the wrong bed because he has had too much to drink and as a consequence starts to penetrate the wrong woman. Is he liable for rape?** Yes. Rape is a basic intent crime as far as fault relates to the circumstances such as whether or not the woman is consenting. Consequently, mistakes that result from voluntary intoxication are not excused.[36]

10.3. ASSAULT BY PENETRATION

10–013 Assault by penetration is punishable with imprisonment for life.[37] The offence of assault by penetration was enacted to cover non-penile penetration. Section 2 provides:

> "(1) A person (A) commits an offence if–
>   (a) he intentionally penetrates the vagina or anus of another person (B) with a part of his body or anything else,
>   (b) the penetration is sexual,
>   (c) B does not consent to the penetration, and
>   (d) A does not reasonably believe that B consents.
> (2) Whether a belief is reasonable is to be determined having regard to all the circumstances, including any steps A has taken to ascertain whether B consents."

---

[36] *R. v. Fotheringham* (1989) 88 Cr. App. R. 206; *R. v. Woods* (1982) 74 Cr. App. R. 312; *R. v. Heard* [2008] Q.B. 43. Cf. *Attorney-General's Reference No. 79 of 2006* [2007] 1 Cr. App. R. (S.) 752, where intoxication was not raised.

[37] Section 2(4) of the *Sexual Offences Act 2003*.

The offence can be perpetrated by a man or a woman, since the penetration may be done with any body part or with an instrument. It would also cover cases where a man has penetrated a woman with his penis when it cannot be proved that he used his penis as opposed to some other body part or object. If the evidence shows he penetrated the victim with his penis, he should be charged with rape. Rape is a more serious offence, because penile penetration exposes the victim to other risks such as H.I.V. infection. A person could be liable as an accessory if he assists or encourages another to penetrate the victim. If the victim was formerly a man and has been converted into a woman, her surgically constructed vagina will be treated as a vagina under the subsection.[38] The victim can be male or female, since all humans have an anus.

The penetration requirement is satisfied by the least degree of penetration.[39] The section does not criminalize non-penile penetration of a person's mouth. So if D were to stick his fingers in V's mouth, he would have to be charged with sexual assault. If his act of sticking his fingers in the victim's mouth was not sexual, he could be charged with simple assault. The act of penetration is a continuing act. If D's initial penetration is consensual he will commit assault by penetration if he continues to penetrate the victim after consent has been withdrawn.[40]

Consent will be withdrawn where it is vitiated by fraud. Suppose a radiographer inserts an ultrasound transducer into the vagina of V purely for diagnostic purposes. If after he inserts the instrument he keeps it in there for longer than necessary to seek sexual gratification, his continuing penetration would be without the victim's consent. As soon as his purpose changes the victim's consent is vitiated. The victim only consents to the instrument being inserted for medical purposes, so if the defendant acts in part to seek sexual gratification he could be liable for assault by penetration.[41]   **10–014**

It must be proved that the act of penetration was non-consensual. The requirements of consent are discussed in Chapter 23. (23.1–23.9 should be read in conjunction with this section.)

What is the mental element for assault by penetration?   The defendant must   **10–015** intentionally penetrate the victim in circumstances where the victim is not consenting. There is no need to show that the defendant intended to penetrate the victim in circumstances where the victim was not consenting, it is only necessary to show that the act of penetration was intentional and that he was negligent as to whether or not the victim was consenting. If the penetration is involuntary such as where the defendant acts as an automaton, the defendant cannot be said to have intentionally penetrated the victim.[42]

---

[38] Section 79(3) of the *Sexual Offences Act 2003*.

[39] *R. v. Dermody* [1956] I.R. 32.

[40] See section 79(2) of the *2003 Act*.

[41] In *R. v. Mobilio* [1991] 1 V.R. 339; D was convicted of rape under the Victorian law of rape. On acting for dual purposes, one legitimate and the other illegitimate, see *R. v. Kumar* (2006) 150 S.J.L.B. 1053.

[42] See *R. v. Luedecke* [2008] 236 C.C.C. 3d 317, where a man in a sleepwalking trance had sexual intercourse with a woman.

As for when the defendant will be held to have reasonably believed the victim was consenting, the test is the same as it is for rape. (The requirements of consent are discussed in Chapter 23.) (The section 75 and 76 presumptions apply to the offence of assault by penetration.)

10.4. SEXUAL ASSAULT

10–016 The old offence of indecent assault supposed that there was an assault in the generic sense, accompanied by a circumstance of a sexual nature. Since the word "assault" in statutory language means either a psychic or a physical assault, an indecent assault could be of the same two varieties. You will recall the double meaning of "assault" creates a somewhat awkward linguistic situation. Assault in the wide sense means (1) a battery or (2) a threatened battery, according to context or circumstance. Kissing the Sleeping Beauty is an assault in the sense of battery, while it is not an assault in the sense of apprehension.[43] In *R. v. Rolfe*[44] Lord Goddard C.J., delivering the judgment of the court, said: "An assault can be committed without touching a person. One always thinks of an assault as the giving of a blow to somebody, but that is not necessary. An assault may be constituted by a threat or a hostile act committed towards a person." It was therefore held that a man who indecently exposed himself and walked towards a woman with his person exposed, making an indecent suggestion to her, could be convicted of indecent assault. It may be questioned, however, whether the court paid sufficient attention to the requirement that the victim of a psychic assault must apprehend a physical assault.[45] If, in the case before the court, the woman was merely disgusted and disturbed by the behaviour, and did not apprehend that she would be touched, the case should not, on principle, have been regarded as an indecent assault, though it could now be treated as an offence of exposure.[46]

The new offence of sexual assault requires more than a psychic assault; there must be an actual physical touching.

Section 3 of the *Sexual Offences Act 2003* provides:

"(1)   A person (A) commits an offence if–
    (a)   he intentionally touches another person (B),
    (b)   the touching is sexual,
    (c)   B does not consent to the touching, and
    (d)   A does not reasonably believe that B consents.
(2)   Whether a belief is reasonable is to be determined having regard to all the circumstances, including any steps A has taken to ascertain whether B consents."

The notion of assault does not require any knowledge on the part of the victim as to what is happening. A wrongful interference with a sleeping person or an infant would clearly be an assault. Such an assault, if sexual in nature, will be a sexual assault.

---

[43] In many of the sexual assault cases the victim will also apprehend physical violence. See *R. v. Beaney* [2010] EWCA Crim. 2551.

[44] (1952) 36 Cr. App. R. 4 at 5.

[45] See *R. v. Hudson* [1966] 1 Q.B. 448, where the court gave an indulgent interpretation to "had reason to suspect."

[46] See section 66 of the *Sexual Offences Act 2003*.

Are you telling me that sexual assault only covers what might be thought of as a sexual battery?   Yes. It targets those who "touch" others in a sexual way.   **10–017**

What do you mean by "sexual"?   The touching must be "overtly sexual." Two propositions may be advanced: **10–018**

1.   An assault is not sexual if it is neither intended by the defendant nor interpreted by the other party as having a sexual purpose. A doctor who makes an intimate examination of a woman for medical reasons is not guilty of sexual assault, because he acts from a non-sexual motive, though if it were a sexual assault the consent of the girl would be no defence because she only consents to a medical touching—not a sexual touching (23.5).
2.   The mental states of the defendant and of his victim are not the only elements in a sexual assault. There must, it seems, be a situation that would appear to the ordinary observer as sexual.

Section 78 provides:

> "Penetration, touching or any other activity is sexual if a reasonable person would consider that–
> (a)   whatever its circumstances or any person's purpose in relation to it, it is because of its nature sexual, or
> (b)   because of its nature it may be sexual and because of its circumstances or the purpose of any person in relation to it (or both) it is sexual."

Section 78(a) will not apply in many cases, because there are very few acts that could be regarded as being inherently sexual—or purely sexual. The obvious type of non-penetrative touching that could be regarded as sexual by its very nature is oral sex. Oral sex is not likely to serve any purpose other than to provide sexual stimulation. Consequently, section 78(b) will do most of the work. Most acts will have to be assessed under the latter subsection, because most acts could be performed for more than one purpose.

A person might even kiss another's penis for a non-sexual purpose.[47] Think of all   **10–019**
the reasons why a man might fondle a woman's breasts: 1) for sexual gratification; 2) to carry out a legitimate medical examination; 3) to apply makeup to them for a nude photo shoot; 4) to tattoo the breast and so on. It is only the first purpose that is caught by section 78(b), and only if, the fondling is done without the woman's consent. Many of these acts will be completely innocuous accept for where they are done for a sexual purpose, and without the consent of the victim.

---

[47]   See *State v. Kargar*, 679 A.2d 81 (1996), where D's conviction for gross sexual assault was vacated under a *de minimis* statute. The Supreme Judicial Court of Maine said: "Although D's kissing his infant son's penis fell within the literal definition of the offense of gross sexual assault, the legislature had not envisioned the extenuating circumstances of the case, in that D's conduct was accepted practice in his culture as a sign only of love and affection for the child, there was nothing sexual about D's conduct, and the child was not harmed, and thus the *de minimis* statute required vacation of convictions to avoid injustice." (This seems a strange cultural practice, but the court accepted that is all it was.) Cf. *R. v. Davies* [2005] EWCA Crim. 3690.

In a case at Lincoln Assizes,[48] the defendant was a shoe fetishist who attempted to remove the shoe from a girl's foot, the act giving him a perverted sexual gratification. It was ruled that this was not an indecent assault, because there were no circumstances of indecency towards the girl. This was an indulgent decision that is not likely to be followed. Under the *Act of 2003*, if it is proved that defendant removed a shoe for the purpose of seeking sexual gratification, he would be liable.[49] His purpose would have to be established, because the act of removing a shoe is not inherently sexual.

Unless the defendant confesses that he acted for a sexual purpose,[50] prosecutors will have great difficulty in establishing that the defendant acted for such a purpose. In *R. v. Court*[51] the defendant repeatedly struck a 12-year-old girl on the outside of her shorts on her buttocks. When the police asked the defendant why he had struck the girl's backside he said, "I don't know—buttock fetish." The defendant tried to have the evidence of his confession excluded but failed. This type of evidence would be relevant under section 78(b), because it is evidence of "the purpose of any person in relation to" the sexual assault.

10–020   The reasonable person standard governs both subsection 78(a) and (b).[52] Therefore, if a reasonable person would have been aware of the fact that the touching was sexual because of its nature or of its circumstances, it will be deemed to have been sexual regardless of the defendant's purpose. "Purpose" is referred to in subsection (b), but this does not mean that the defendant can assert that his purpose was not sexual. It is for the defendant to state what his purpose was for touching V and for the jury to decide whether a reasonable person would consider the stated purpose to be a sexual purpose. This part of the offence is satisfied as long as the defendant was negligent.

Where the objective evidence is strong the jury will be able to infer that the defendant was acting for a sexual purpose. In *State v. Chabot*[53] the defendant was meant to be alone with a female patient for the purpose of giving her a bath. The curtains around the bed were drawn when another nurse entered the room in search of the defendant and found him standing over the patient with his trousers unzipped and his testicles and erect penis exposed. The patient, who suffered from an organic brain disease, was lying in a V position with her buttocks exposed. This type of objective evidence would allow a reasonable jury to infer that the defendant was sexually excited and was about to sexually assault or rape the patient. Nevertheless, in many cases this type of objective evidence will not be available. The aforementioned nurse may have fantasized about many other patients while bathing them. A reasonable person would not consider the act of bathing a patient as sexual. If there were no overt signs of his sexual purpose, then he cannot be prosecuted for doing the job he was paid to do. The problem is that people like this may use a legitimate purpose to disguise a sexual purpose. His purpose for bathing the patients might be as much about doing his job as it is

---

[48] *R. v. George* [1956] Crim. L.R. 52. Cf. *R. v. Kumar* (2006) 150 S.J.L.B. 1053.

[49] *R. v. H* [2005] 1 W.L.R. 2005 at 2008.

[50] In *R. v. Court* [1989] A.C. 28; the defendant admitted that he touched the girl to gain sexual gratification.

[51] [1989] A.C. 28.

[52] *R. v. Grout* [2011] 1 Cr. App. R. 472 at 480; *R. v. H* [2005] 1 W.L.R. 2005 at 2008.

[53] 478 A2d 1136 (1984).

about him seeking sexual gratification. It will be difficult to prosecute this type of defendant where his impure thoughts stay in his mind. It will only be possible to convict this type of cretin where the evidence allows the jury to establish that he was acting not only to do his job, but also to seek sexual gratification.[54]

In *R. v. Kumar*,[55] a medical doctor carried out an examination of a young woman's breasts. The examination was needed and was conducted for medical purposes. However, the doctor fondled the patient's breasts excessively and pressed his head hard against the patient for 5 minutes. It was clear by the way that he had carried out the examination that he was seeking some kind of sexual gratification. If he had carried out the procedure according to standard practice, it would have been impossible to detect his sexual purpose. In many cases the defendant's sexual purpose will be adequately disguised by his legitimate purpose.

What if the side-effect of the doctor doing the breast examination is that he becomes sexually excited? If the only reason he has for examining the patient's breasts is that it is required to provide a medical diagnosis, he should not be liable for sexual assault. This is assuming that his sexual excitement is a side-effect of him doing what he is medically required to do. It would have to be shown that he had no sexual motivation for carrying out the procedure. But if the doctor is half way through a breast examination when he becomes sexually excited and continues the examination in part to seek sexual gratification, he will be liable for sexual assault. The patient's consent is vitiated as soon as the doctor starts to act for a sexual purpose, because the patient has not consented to a sexual touching. The prosecution will have to prove that he continued the procedure not only to provide a medical service, but also to seek sexual gratification. The problem is that the doctor may continue a legitimate medical examination while he is sexually excited without anyone being the wiser.[56] Alas, in many of these cases the sexual assaults will be disguised as legitimate medical procedures and thus will not be detected. **10–021**

Does this mean that indecent acts that are not sexual will not come within the purview of section 3? Yes. Disgusting acts are not always sexual acts. If a person vomits and forces another to eat his vomit he behaves indecently, but he does not come within the purview of section 3. His act is not sexual and no stretch of the imagination can make it sexual. This type of disgusting behaviour would have to be punished as a non-sexual assault. There will be borderline cases where a bully will try to humiliate a person by forcing him to kiss a private part such as his backside and so on. These cases should be put to the jury as sexual assaults, because a reasonable jury is likely hold that the forcing a person to kiss a backside is sexual. **10–022**

---

[54] *R. v. Kumar* (2006) 150 S.J.L.B. 1053.

[55] (2006) 150 S.J.L.B. 1053.

[56] Cf. *R. v. Kumar* (2006) 150 S.J.L.B. 1053; similarly in *Bhatt v. General Medical Council* [2011] EWHC 783 (Admin).

10–023 **Is it a sexual assault if the defendant does not actually touch the victim?** Yes. If the defendant touches the victim's clothes, this will be considered to be a touching for the purposes of section 3.[57] It is also enough to show that the defendant used some instrument or other thing to touch the victim.

Suppose a group of university students are having a summer picnic when D notices that V is not wearing anything under her T-shirt. D decides to throw a bucket of water on her to make her top transparent. He does this to seek sexual gratification.

D will be liable for sexual assault even though there was no direct connection between him and the victim. It does not matter that the water left the bucket and moved in midair before landing on the victim's blouse,[58] because the direct and immediate consequence of his action was that the water touched the victim.[59]

10–024 **What is the mental element for the section 3 offence?** The defendant must intentionally touch the victim in a sexual way and in circumstances where the victim is not consenting. There is no need to show that the defendant intended to touch the victim in circumstances where the victim was not consenting, it is only necessary to show that the act of touching was intentional and that he did not have reasonable grounds for believing that the victim was consenting. If the defendant touches someone in an inherently sexual way while acting as an automaton, he will not be liable under section 3.[60] Suppose D is packed like a sardine in the London tube between two pretty ladies. He may find this sexually gratifying, but he does not commit an offence because the touching is unintentional. (Accidental touching does not count.) Suppose D and V are playing beach volleyball and D trips and lands on V; suppose he displays signs of sexual arousal before he has a chance to climb off V. This type of unintentional touching is not sufficient to make him liable for sexual assault. (If he intentionally took longer than necessary to climb off her, then that would be another matter).[61]

There are some *obiter* statements that suggest that the "touching" element only requires basic intent.[62] Clearly, this is not the law and it is doubtful future courts will hold otherwise. These statements are fallacious, because the touching element of the offence requires specific intent. In *R. v. Heard*[63] police officers took an injured man to hospital so that he could have a cut treated. The man had been drinking heavily and was utterly inebriated. The officers were waiting with

---

[57] *R. v. H* [2005] 1 W.L.R. 2005.

[58] Cf. *R. v. Cotesworth* (1704) 87 E.R. 928; *R. v. Smith* (1866) 176 E.R. 910; *Ray v. U.S.*, 575 A.2d 1196 (1990). Similarly, if D squirts baby oil and throws water on V he commits a battery. See *State v. Padilla*, 123 N.M. 216 (1997); *Pursell v. Horn* (1838) 112 E.R. 966. Blowing cigar smoke into another's face has also been held to constitute a battery: *Leichtman v. WLW Jacor Communications, Inc.*, 634 N.E.2d 697 (1994).

[59] Section 79(8) provides: "Touching includes touching—(a) with any part of the body, (b) with anything else, (c) through anything, and in particular includes touching amounting to penetration."

[60] *R. v. Heard* [2008] Q.B. 43. Cf. *R. v. Luedecke* [2008] 236 C.C.C. 3d 317. This is assuming that section 3 is in part a specific intent crime. See 19.4.

[61] The Court of Appeal has made it clear that accidents not involving any hint of reckless are exempt; see *R. v. Heard* [2008] Q.B. 43 at 51.

[62] *R. v. Heard* [2008] Q.B. 43 at 55 *et passim*.

[63] [2008] Q.B. 43.

him when he put his hand on his groin and started to dance suggestively. Thereafter, he punched one of the officers and undid his trousers, took his penis in his hand and rubbed it up and down the officer's thigh. He was arrested and when he was being questioned at the police station, said: "The only way I can make money is by moving my hips in a sexual way in Soho and I thought I would get away with doing it to you but I obviously didn't."

The question of whether the touching element only requires a basic intent was not really in issue in *R. v. Heard*, because Heard had deliberately pulled his part from his pants and put it on the officer's leg. His act of touching was not reckless, accidental or unintentional. He was found guilty because a drunken intent is still an intent.[64] Furthermore, a reasonable jury could infer that his act of rubbing his penis on the thigh was sexual in the circumstances.

Since it is enough to show that a reasonable person would have known that the officer was not consenting to the penis rubbing, intoxication is irrelevant as far as this element is concerned.[65] It is enough that a reasonable person would have realized that it was sexual, as he would have, if he had been sober (see Chapter 19). As for when the sober defendant will be held to have reasonably believed the victim was consenting, the law is the same as it is for rape. The requirements of consent are discussed in Chapter 23. (The section 75 and 76 presumptions apply to the offence of sexual assault.)

10.5. CAUSING A PERSON TO ENGAGE IN SEXUAL ACTIVITY

This offence seems to be aimed at those cases where people use duress to force others to engage in sexual activity. It also covers the situation where an innocent agent is used as an instrument to rape or otherwise violate others in a sexual way. **10–025**
  Section 4 provides:

"(1) A person (A) commits an offence if—(a) he intentionally causes another person (B) to engage in an activity, (b) the activity is sexual, (c) B does not consent to engaging in the activity, and (d) A does not reasonably believe that B consents.

(2) Whether a belief is reasonable is to be determined having regard to all the circumstances, including any steps A has taken to ascertain whether B consents.

(3) Sections 75 and 76 apply to an offence under this section.

(4) A person guilty of an offence under this section, if the activity caused involved—(a) penetration of B's anus or vagina, (b) penetration of B's mouth with a person's penis, (c) penetration of a person's anus or vagina with a part of B's body or by B with anything else, or (d) penetration of a person's mouth with B's penis, is liable, on conviction on indictment, to imprisonment for life.

(5) Unless subsection (4) applies, a person guilty of an offence under this section is liable—(a) on summary conviction, to imprisonment for a term not exceeding 6 months or to a fine not exceeding the statutory maximum or both; (b) on conviction on indictment, to imprisonment for a term not exceeding 10 years."

---

[64] This is a basic intent element: see Chap. 19. *R. v. Heard* [2008] Q.B. 43 at 49; *R. v. Kingston* [1995] 2 A.C. 355.

[65] *R. v. Fotheringham* (1989) 88 Cr. App. R. 206; *R. v. Woods* (1982) 74 Cr. App. R. 312; *R. v. Heard* [2008] Q.B. 43.

10–026   **Does a punter "cause" a prostitute to engage in sexual activity with him by falsely promising to pay her for her services? Can he be liable under section 4 for failing to pay her?**   My dear interlocutory friend, if that is all that were required by the causation requirement, the offence would be completely boundless. The punter is not liable because the prostitute consents to the sexual intercourse.[66] The only thing she does not consent to is the non-payment (see 23.5).

10–027   **How can a person cause another to do something that she does not want to do? Would not the victim's independent action break the chain of causation?**   Nothing short of duress would be sufficient to cause someone to do something he does not want to do. The issue of consent overlaps with the issue of causation in cases where this provision applies. If D overbears V's will by forcing her to engage in sexual activity, he "causes" her to engage in sexual activity. What is more, there will be no consent.

Causation as required by the subsection means that D would have to do something to override V's will. When D offers V money in return for V working in her brothel she provides V with an incentive for engaging in sexual activity, but she does not cause her to engage in such activity. *Per contra*, when D smuggles women into England and forces them into prostitution, he causes them to engage in sexual activity.[67] People traffickers[68] and pimps smuggle women into this country and force them to work as prostitutes.[69] They are used as sex slaves and the customers often have no idea that they are having sexual intercourse with a non-consenting woman. The customers are basically used as instruments of rape so that the brothel owner can make money. The women are often told that their family members in their home countries will be harmed, if they do not work in the brothel.

In *R. v. Tang*[70] the High Court of Australia upheld a slavery conviction where a brothel owner had forced women to work in her brothel. In that case a brothel owner obtained illegal visas for five women from Thailand and made them work in her Australian brothel. They became "contract workers" at the brothel. The victims had been charged between $42,000AUD and $45,000AUD each for the fake visas that Tang had acquired for them. They were forced to repay the debt by working six days a week at the brothel servicing up to 900 customers per week. The customers were charged $110 for the complainants' services, all of which was retained by Tang. For each customer serviced, the "debt" owed by each

---

[66] *R. v. Linekar* [1995] Q.B. 250; *R. v. Jheeta* [2008] 1 W.L.R. 2582 at 2590. Cf. *Michael v. Western Australia* [2008] 183 A. Crim. R. 348.

[67] Some of these operators also commit slavery offences, see sections 2, 10, 11 of the *Slave Trade Act 1824*. Slavery is contrary to the rights guaranteed by Art.4 of the European Convention, *Siliadin v. France* (2006) 43 E.H.R.R. 16.

[68] Section 57 of the *Sexual Offences Act 2003* makes it an offence to traffic people into Britain for sexual exploitation. See also section 58, which makes it an offence to traffic within Britain for sexual exploitation; and section 59, which makes it an offence to traffic people out of the Britain for sexual exploitation. See also *R. v. M(L)* [2011] 1 Cr. App. R. 135.

[69] For a fuller account of this disturbing trade, see Michelle M. Dempsey, "Sex Trafficking and Criminalization in Defence of Feminist Abolitionism," (2010) 158 *U. Pa. L. Rev.* 1729 at 1758 *et passim*.

[70] (2008) 237 C.L.R. 1. (This case includes an excellent judicial discussion of the concept of slavery.)

complainant was reduced by $50. Tang also confiscated the complainants' passports and prevented them from leaving her premises until the debt was paid in full.

This type of conduct would be caught by section 4. There was clearly no real consent in this case. A person does not consent to have sexual intercourse in circumstances where she has had her passport taken, has been locked up, and is ordered to handover 100 *per cent.* of her income. The brothel owner basically caused these women to engage in sexual activity of the most serious kind; repeated sexual intercourse with thousands of strangers for no reward beyond paying an illegal and unjust debt. The victims had no reasonable means of escape.

10–028

There is a cardinal difference between providing a person with an incentive to do something and forcing or causing him to do it. In the thoroughly nasty case of *R. v. Bourne*,[71] the defendant compelled his wife to commit bestiality with a dog. Bestiality was an offence, but at that time it was not an offence to cause another to engage in bestiality.[72] The wife had the defence of duress, and she was not charged. In *State v. B.H.*[73] an extremely violent man forced his wife to engage in sexual activity with their 7-year-old son. The woman was suffering from battered woman's syndrome and knew the type of violence the defendant was capable of inflicting. The defendant had his hands around her neck and was threatening violence when he demanded that she engage in the sexual activity with the young boy. Clearly, section 4 covers these types of cases as there is no real consent, and the defendant does not merely provide the victim with an incentive for engaging in the sexual activity. The victim is not given any real choice. In *R. v. Ayeva*,[74] D grabbed V from behind and bent her arm behind her back, forced her to take hold of his erect penis and to masturbate him. This is an example of a victim being "physically" caused to engage in sexual activity. Her hand was used as an instrument—there was no voluntary action on her part.

The causation requirement will not be satisfied unless the victim's will is overborne or she is physically forced to take part in the sexual activity. It should be shown the victim had no reasonable alternative but to engage in the sexual activity. Otherwise any incentive will count. A person does not cause a hit-man to do an assassination by offering him a million pound payment, he merely provides him with an incentive to do it. The assassin can only cause himself to do it, his will is not overborne and he has other options. Most law abiding citizens would not choose to do an assassination, not even for a million pounds. (They might decide otherwise where there is a gun pointed at their heads.) The hit-man has the freedom to make his own choice unless he acts under duress.

---

[71] (1952) 36 Cr. App. R. 125. See also *R. v. H* [2008] EWCA Crim. 1202, where V forced D to take a dog's erect penis into his mouth; and also forced it in V's anus.

[72] See the repealed Section 12(1) of the *Sexual Offences Act 1956*. Cf. section 69(2) of the *Sexual Offences Act 2003*, which makes it an offence to "cause" another to commit bestiality: "A person (A) commits an offence if—(a) A intentionally *causes,* or *allows*, A's vagina or anus to be penetrated, (b) the penetration is by the penis of a living animal, and (c) A knows that, or is reckless as to whether, that is what A is being penetrated by."

[73] 834 A.2d 1063 (2003). See also *R. v. Basherdost* [2009] EWCA Crim. 2883, where a man used violence and threats of violence to compel a couple to engage in sexual activity in his presence.

[74] [2010] 2 Cr. App. R. (S.) 22. See also *R. v. C* [2006] EWCA Crim. 3428, where D took V's hand and put it down his trousers onto his penis.

10–029   In *R. v. Devonald*[75] the Court of Appeal implied causation where there was none and thus wrongly held there was an absence of consent. In that case D provided V with an incentive for engaging in self-abuse in front of a web camera. D was able to incentivize V to self-abuse (masturbate) himself in front of the web camera by pretending to be a 20-year-old female called "Cassey." Cassey was invented by D, because he wanted to humiliate V. (D was seeking revenge because V had jilted his daughter.) Since Cassey did not exist outside of cyberspace, V's consent was not vitiated on the grounds that D had impersonated someone personally "known" to V.[76] Nevertheless, the Court of Appeal erroneously held that V did not understand the nature and purpose of the act and therefore his consent was vitiated. This finding is wrong, because V understood that he was engaging in sexual activity for another human being. The only thing he did not know was D's ulterior motive for encouraging him to engage in the conduct. D's ulterior motive was non-sexual. It was merely to get revenge for his daughter.

The consent issue need not concern us further here as it is discussed in Chapter 23.[77] As for the causation issue, it was clear that V caused *himself* to engage in the sexual activity in front of the webcam. D provided V with an incentive; the incentive was simply the sexual gratification that might be gained by engaging in sexual activity for the curiosity of a young woman. V self-abused himself because he wanted the thrill of showing off sexually in front of a young lady. It is true that he only acted as he did because he believed he was putting on a sexual show for a young lady, but he was not forced or compelled ("caused") to act as he did. His decision to act as he did was a calculated risk: he chose to risk putting on a show for a stranger who could have been of any age or sex. He took no steps to confirm the identity of the person at the other end of the line. For all he knew it could have been a 12-year-old girl[78] or an 80-year-old woman.

If a young lady goes to the beach in a string bikini she does not cause a pervert to masturbate in the nearby sand dunes. She might inadvertently provide the pervert with an incentive for engaging in sexual activity, but she does not cause him to engage in such activity. Even if the young lady takes her bikini top off intending to provoke a man at the beach to act in a sexual way, she could not be said to have caused him to so act. He is responsible for his own independent choices. Likewise, Devonald did not cause V to abuse himself, he merely provided him with an incentive.

It is patently clear that Parliament did not intend to criminalize mere "encouragement" or "incentivizing," because it enacted special incitement provisions. The incitement provisions cover vulnerable victims, because mere encouragement could be enough to cause such victims to engage in sexual activity.[79] Children should not be encouraged to engage in sexual activities period, because they are children. There is nothing wrong with encouraging/inciting a competent adult to engage in sexual activity, since such a person is able to consent.

---

[75] [2008] EWCA Crim. 527.

[76] Se section 76(2)(b) of the *Sexual Offences Act 2003*.

[77] See 23.6.

[78] If it had been a 12-year-old girl, V himself would have been liable for an offence under section 12.

[79] See for example, sections 8, 10, 17, 26, 31, 39, and 48 of the *Act of 2003*.

May I bring you back to the case of forced prostitution? I am wondering if the men who copulate with these ladies can be convicted of the offences found in sections 1–4. Not unless they had reasonable grounds for believing that the women were not consenting. If the punter arrives at the brothel and sees a woman being pushed into the bedroom at gunpoint, he might have reasonable grounds for believing that the woman will not be consenting to have sexual intercourse with him. If in those circumstances he copulates with her, he could be liable for rape.

10–030

But the story does not end there. A draconian provision has been enacted which goes even further than this. Section 53A of the *Sexual Offences Act 2003* provides:

> "(1) A person (A) commits an offence if—(a) A makes or promises payment for the sexual services of a prostitute (B), (b) a third person (C) has engaged in exploitative conduct of a kind likely to induce or encourage B to provide the sexual services for which A has made or promised payment, and (c) C engaged in that conduct for or in the expectation of gain for C or another person (apart from A or B).
>
> (2) The following are *ir*relevant—(a) where in the world the sexual services are to be provided and whether those services are provided, (b) whether A is, or ought to be, aware that C has engaged in exploitative conduct.
>
> (3) C engages in exploitative conduct if—(a) C uses force, threats (whether or not relating to violence) or any other form of coercion, or (b) C practises any form of deception."

This is a strict liability offence, because the defendant need not have any knowledge of the fact that the prostitute has been forced into prostitution. This offence seems to be a move towards having an absolute prohibition against all forms of prostitution.[80] As we saw in Chapter 3, adults have a constitutional right to engage in consensual conduct that does not harm others. An absolute prohibition could not be justified, since many forms of prostitution involve consenting adults who do no harm others.

What is the mental element for the section 4 offence? The defendant must intentionally cause the victim to engage in sexual activity in circumstances where the victim is not consenting. It is not enough to show that he recklessly caused the person to engage in sexual activity. It must be shown that when the defendant intentionally caused the victim to engage in the sexual activity he had no reasonable grounds for believing that she was consenting. As for whether the defendant will be held to have reasonably believed the victim was consenting, the test is the same as it is for rape. See the discussion above. The requirements of consent are discussed in Chapter 23. (The section 75 and 76 presumptions apply to the offence of causing another to engage in sexual activity.)

10–031

---

[80] This type of criminalization contravenes the principle that a person should only be held responsible for his own culpable harm-doing. See Dennis J. Baker, "The Moral Limits of Criminalizing Remote Harms," (2007) 10(3) *New Crim. L. Rev.* 370; Dennis J. Baker, "Collective Criminalization and the Constitutional Right to Endanger Others," (2009) 28(2) *Crim. Just. Ethics* 168.

10.6. Sexual Offences against Children under 13

10–032 All the aforementioned offences are restated as specific offences that can be committed against children under the age of 13. Section 5 makes it an offence to rape a child under 13; section 6 makes it an offence to assault a child under 13 by penetration; section 7 makes it an offence to sexually assault a child under 13; and section 8 makes it an offence to cause or *incite* a child under 13 to engage in sexual activity.

The *actus reus* for child rape is the same as it is for adult rape, except for the fact that the victim must be under 13. Similarly, the *actus reus* for the assault by penetration and sexual assault of a child under 13 are the same as for the adult offences. The core difference is that these offences deem that children under the age of 13 are absolutely incapable of consenting. This is because very young children lack the capacity to understand the harmful implications (that simple fact that they are not physically developed for such activity) of engaging in sexual activity, and thus cannot give true consent. Parliament also deems that no person could ever have reasonable grounds for believing that a child aged under 13 could be older. Therefore, any person who engages in sexual activity with a child who is in fact under 13 is deemed to have known that the child was under 13, even if he had reasonable grounds for believing that the child was older. Hence, D will be liable for committing these offences regardless of whether the victim consented or whether he had reasonable grounds for believing that the victim was consenting, and regardless of whether he had good reason for believing that the victim was over 13.

10–033 **Does strict liability as to the victim's age bar the defence of automatism? Or are these offences what might be termed as offences of partial strict liability?** If the offender has intercourse with the underage victim while in a state of automatism, he will have a full defence, because his actions are involuntary. The offence requires voluntary and intentional action. Strict liability only covers the circumstance element.

10–034 **Most of us have little sympathy for those who engage in sexual experimentation with young children. But would not strict liability be harsh where the offender is also a child of a similar age and the sexual activity is consensual?** It is difficult to believe that a 60-year-old man could reasonably believe that a girl of 12 is over 13, but a boy of 12 might reasonably believe that she is. If underage sexual intercourse is an inherent harm in accordance with the harm principle,[81] then there is nothing wrong with treating an underage offender as an adult offender.[82] An act of penetration perpetrated by an underage offender is no different than one perpetrated by an adult offender: physically it is identical. If a healthy 12-year-old girl asked her 13-year-old boyfriend to chop her finger

---

[81] Baroness Hale asserts that underage sexual intercourse involves inherent dangers: *R. v. G.* [2009] 1 A.C. 92 at 110.

[82] Cf. Siji A. Moore, "Out of the Fire and Into the Frying Pan: Georgia Legislature's Attempt to Regulate Teen Sex Through the Criminal Justice System," (2009) 52 *Howard L.J.* 197; see also J. R. Spencer, "The *Sexual Offences Act 2003*: (2) Child and Family Offences," [2004] Crim. L.R. 347 at 355.

off, we would not say his act was harmless merely because he was around the same age as the consenting victim. If consensual sexual activity involving a person under the age of 13 is objectively harmful, then the defendant's age cannot make it objectively harmless.[83] A justificatory defence could not be developed for young offenders, because the act is objectively harmful regardless of the age of the offender.[84] However we might "excuse" a boy of a similar age, because his innocence, immaturity and hormones might compel him to engage in sexual activity with someone of his own age.

A further problem in cases involving consensual underage sexual activity is that in some cases it will be impossible to identify the instigator. In many cases both parties will be treated as perpetrators of one or more of the available offences. If a 12-year-old boy and a 12-year-old girl have sexual intercourse, the boy will be liable for perpetrating rape under section 5; and they will both be liable under section 7 for sexually assaulting a child under 13. In addition, they both engage in sexual activity with a child under 13 contrary to section 9 of the *Act of 2003*. The instigator would also be liable under section 8 for causing or inciting a child under 13 to engage in sexual activity.

If a 12-year-old girl fellates her sleeping 12-year-old boyfriend and he awakes and fails to tell her to stop, he does not commit rape because he does not intentionally penetrate the vagina, anus or mouth of another person with his penis; nor does he incite or cause her to engage in sexual activity. His mere omission does not make him liable for conduct that requires intentional action on his part. The 12-year-old girlfriend would be liable for committing the offences found in sections 7 and 8.

Obviously, the Crown Prosecution Service will have to use a lot of common sense when charging these offences. Its guidelines suggest it will,[85] but guidelines are not law—they do not provide legal immunity for young people.[86] Clearly, the criminal justice system should not be used to regulate the sexual development of the rebellious youth. The rationale for such legislation is to protect children from older youths; and also adult paedophiles and pederasts; and yet, it catches naive youngsters who are doing little more than learning the facts of life.

I notice that the section 8 offence differs to the section 4 offence in that it includes an offence of incitement. Does this mean that the section 8 offence includes two independent offences? Yes.[87] It enacts a substantive offence which criminalizes those who cause children under 13 to engage in sexual activity. The elements of this offence are identical to those found in section 4. The

10–035

---

[83] See Dennis J. Baker, *The Right Not to be Criminalized: Demarcating Criminal Law's Authority*, (Farnham: Ashgate Publishing, 2011) at Chap. 6.

[84] Baroness Hale seems to accept such an argument: "In view of all the dangers resulting from under-age sexual activity, it cannot be wrong for the law to apply that label even if it cannot be proved that the child was in fact unwilling. The fact that the defendant was under 16 is obviously relevant to his relative blameworthiness and has been reflected in the second most lenient disposal available to a criminal court. But it does not alter the fact of what he did or the fact that he should not have done it."*R. v. G.* [2009] 1 A.C. 92 at 110.

[85] http://www.cps.gov.uk/legal/s_to_u/sexual_offences_unlawful_sexual_intercourse/#Code_for_Crown_Prosecutors.

[86] Prosecutorial discretion is not likely to be exercised in rape cases. See *R. v. G.* [2009] 1 A.C. 92.

[87] *R. v. Grout* [2011] 1 Cr. App. R. 472 at 479-480; *R. v. Walker* [2006] EWCA Crim. 1907.

only difference is that the offence imposes strict liability as far as consent and the age of the victim is concerned. The causing[88] must be intentional; "recklessness or less will not do."[89]

Section 8 also enacts an inchoate offence of incitement. The incitement offence is wider than the causing offence, because it is inchoate. The inchoate offence is committed as soon as D incites the victim to engage in sexual activity. D will be liable whether the child engages in the sexual activity or not. D must intend[90] to incite a child under 13 to engage in sexual activity; it need not be a particular child. Furthermore, the victim need not in fact be under 13.[91]

10–036 **Does that mean that where the putative 12-year-old is an adult police officer D is still liable?** The defendant will be liable if he was trying to incite a person whom he believed to be under the age of 13 to engage in sexual activity. If he had no belief about the age of the potential victim and it turns out the victim is over 16, he will not be liable for the section 8 offence. However, he may be liable under section 10 if he intended to incite an under 16 to engage in sexual activity. If, on the other hand, the victim is in fact under 16, he may be liable for the section 10 offence where it can be shown that he did "not reasonably believe that" V was 16 or over. If the adult police officer turns out to be a 12-year-old girl, he is strictly liable as to age.

10–037 **Does strict liability as to age mean that he is strictly liable if he recklessly causes a child under 13 to engage in sexual activity?** No. He is only strictly liable as far as age and consent are concerned. As far as the act of incitement is concerned, he must intend to incite a child under the age of 13 to engage in sexual activity. It is not enough that he writes graffiti on a wall where youths hang out urging everyone to participate in London's naked bike ride.[92] The situation would be different where his message urges under 13s to contact him for sexual relations.[93]

If a person writes a message on the back of a door in a public lavatory asking children under 13 to contact him for the purpose of having sexual intercourse, he has performed the *actus reus* of the offence. A suggestion may, of course, be incitement in itself, particularly for those who, as Shakespeare put it, "take suggestion as a cat laps milk." The act of incitement is complete as soon as he writes the message on the wall.[94] Section 8 does not require either the victim or the defendant to have engaged in sexual activity; it merely requires the defendant to intentionally incite a child to do so. It is the intentional act of incitement that is

---

[88] It was noted above, "causation" requires more than mere encouragement/incitement. However, in the case of very young children mere incitement or encouragement might be enough to also cause them to do something, because they are very impressionable. Their youth and inexperience means that they could be caused to do something without any trickery or great pressure being applied.

[89] *R. v. Grout* [2011] 1 Cr. App. R. 472 at 479–480.

[90] *R. v. Grout* [2011] 1 Cr. App. R. 472 at 479–480.

[91] *R. v. Jones* [2008] Q.B. 460.

[92] Notably, some would argue that the basic act of getting undressed for a nude protest is not of a sexual nature and thus does not involve sexual activity.

[93] *R. v. Jones* [2008] Q.B. 460; cf. *Baney v. State*, 42 So.3d 170 (2009).

[94] See 17.2. See also *Invicta Plastics Ltd. v. Clare* [1976] R.T.R. 251; *R. v. Goldman* [2001] EWCA Crim. 1684; *R. v. Marlow* [1998] 1 Cr. App. R. (S.) 273.

criminalized, not the actual sexual activity. If the defendant does in fact engage in sexual activity with the child, he will be charged with one of the offences that cover consummated offending.

In *R. v. Jones*,[95] a disturbed paedophile wrote graffiti on the back of the doors in public lavatories seeking girls aged 8 to 13 for sex in return for payment. His messages requested that they contact him on a given mobile telephone number. The facts were as follows:

> "A journalist, Ms Ruth Lumley, when travelling on a train to Brighton, saw graffiti of this type on the toilet door. The message was in capital letters in black marker pen and as she could best recall stated: 'Wanted for sex girls from 8–13. Text only [mobile number].' Ms Lumley telephoned the number twice. (a) It was not answered, but within 30 minutes she received a text from the number she had rung: 'U male or female How old whr u c my number? Txt bk only.' (b) She sent a text message back: 'Female on train, 11'. (c) Within minutes she received the reply, 'U up 4 it r u a virgin or not wht skol u go 2 whr u live tx bk. My name Dave. What urs what time train u c number? Tx bk.'"

The messages were reported to the police and an undercover operation was **10–038** commenced. The police used an officer who pretended to be a 12-year-old girl called Amy. Amy (the adult police officer) responded to the defendant's advertisement by sending a text in which she introduced herself as Amy. She also texted that she had seen his message on a train and that she was on holiday. Furthermore, she expressly asked if he would really pay. He texted back within 90 minutes to ask her how old she was and where she was holidaying. The exchange of texts went as follows:

> "Amy. 'Hi am12. Am near Brighton how old r u'.
> The defendant. 'I am 35 how long are u on hol 4. R u a virgin. Tx bk'.
> Amy. 'Cpl of weeks staying with Nan yes I am. Why?'
> The defendant. 'Can you be on Brighton pier Saturday at about 5.30 and can you wear a nice short skirt. You ever sucked a cock or wanked 1'."

The language is rather shocking (and not only grammatically), but I have left it in to highlight that this individual had only one thing in mind. It is very clear that this type of explicit and direct request for a child under the age of 13 to engage in sexual activity is caught by section 8. D is guilty at the moment of incitement. The section 8 offence of incitement is committed when one person incites a child under the age of 13 to engage in sexual activity, whether or not that child does what she was urged to do. (If she does the defendant will be liable for consummating one of the other offences such as child rape, penetration of a child under 13, sexual assault of a child under 13 and so on.)

Since the police officer was not really a 12-year-old girl, the defendant argued that it was not possible for him to commit the offence:

- Firstly, if the defendant had sent the abovementioned messages to a 12-year-old girl the issue of attempt would not have arisen. His text messages were intended to persuade the putative 12-year-old girl to engage in sexual activity and if he had in fact managed to send them to a

---

[95] [2008] Q.B. 460.

12-year-old girl (instead of to an adult police officer) the incitement offence would have been consummated upon her receiving them.

- Secondly, it is possible to be guilty of attempting to incite.[96] For instance, if the defendant's text messages had failed to send for some technical reason, we could then say he only attempted to incite a child under the age of 13 to engage in sexual activity. The same applies if he posts a letter which never reaches the child because her mother finds it and hands it to the police. If the words of incitement never reach its intended audience, D could only be prosecuted for attempting the incitement offence. A further example of an attempted incitement is where D tries to send text messages to a child under 13 but mistakenly sends them to an adult police officer. D in fact incites an adult,[97] but he is attempting to incite a child under the age of 13 to engage in sexual activity with him.

- Thirdly, it is no defence to assert that you attempted the factually impossible.[98]

10–039   An impossible attempt is not made out unless the defendant "intends" to do the impossible. Jones attempted to do the impossible because he intended to incite a girl under the age of 13 to engage in sexual activity. This is what Jones believed he was doing, and it is what he intended to do. His conviction was rightly upheld. Section 8(2) provides: "A person guilty of an offence under this section, if the activity caused or incited involved—(a) penetration of B's anus or vagina, (b) penetration of B's mouth with a person's penis, (c) penetration of a person's anus or vagina with a part of B's body or by B with anything else, or (d) penetration of a person's mouth with B's penis, is liable, on conviction on indictment, to imprisonment for life." Where these physical elements remain inchoate the sentence will be lighter.

If Jones had not targeted a particular age group and had merely intended to incite adult swingers and doggers to meet him for a sexual encounter, he would not have been liable for the section 8 offence. It is not enough to show that he negligently exposed a child to his words of incitement.

10.7.   SEXUAL OFFENCES AGAINST CHILDREN UNDER 16

10–040   There are a number of offences that target consensual sexual activity between children under the age of 16 and adults. Since a child under the age of 16 cannot consent to sexual activity, consent is no defence. Parliament has deemed that

---

[96] *R. v. Chelmsford Justices Ex p. Amos (JJ)* [1973] Crim. L.R. 437. Cf. section 1(4) of the *Criminal Attempts Act 1981*. This excludes "aiding, abetting, counselling, procuring or suborning the commission of an offence" from the class of accountable crimes. However, it seems to have been intended to exclude only acts of attempted accessoryship, *i.e.* acts charged as an attempt to become an accessory to a crime. It does not, apparently, exclude a charge of attempting to commit the inchoate crime of incitement. When Parliament wishes to refer to incitement as an inchoate crime it uses that word, not language of "aiding, abetting, counselling and procuring."

[97] It is not an offence to incite a competent adult to engage in sexual activity.

[98] *R. v. Shivpuri* [1987] A.C. 1; *R. v. Jones* [2008] Q.B. 460 at 473–474. See also Glanville Williams, "The Lords and Impossible Attempts, or *Quis Custodiet Ipsos Custodes,*" (1986) 45 *Cambridge L.J.* 33.

children under 16 are incapable of consenting. However, the under 16 offences do allow for reasonable mistakes as to age. The core offences overlap with the abovementioned offences concerning children under the age of 13. Section 9 makes it an offence to engage in sexual activity with a child under 16. Meanwhile, section 10 makes it an offence to cause or incite a child under 16 to engage in sexual activity.[99] The *actus reus* for these offences is the same as for the under 13 offences.[100]

There are also a number of grooming offences. Section 12 makes it an offence to cause a child to watch a sexual act. Section 14 makes it an offence to arrange or facilitate the commission of a child sex offence; and section 15 makes it an offence to meet a child that has been groomed.[101]

The mental element is different for the under 16 offences, because reasonable mistakes as to age can be used to negate *mens rea*. If the child is over 13 and under 16, the defendant will not be found guilty unless the prosecution prove that the defendant did not reasonably believe the child was over 16. This applies to all the offences found in sections 9–12; and 15. As far as the offences in sections 9–12 are concerned, if the defendant is under 18 he will get a lighter sentence.[102]

10.8. VICTIMS WHO ARE DEEMED INCAPABLE OF CONSENTING

Certain offences deem that youths aged 16–17 are irrebuttably presumed not to have consented where D has influence over them because of a position of trust he occupies. A person who is in a position of trust commits an offence if he engages in sexual activity with a person who is over 16 but under 18 (section 16); or if he causes or incites such a victim to engage in sexual activity (section 17); or if he engages in sexual activity in the presence of such a victim (section 18); or if he causes such a victim to watch a sexual act (section 19).

10–041

There is no need for there to be an actual abuse of trust, it is only necessary to show that the defendant was in a position of trust. If the defendant is in a position of trust he will be deemed to have abused it if he engages in sexual activity with a consenting youth within the relevant age bracket. For example, a school teacher is in a position of trust[103] and thus would commit an offence if he were to kiss

---

[99] Section 9(2) and 10(1) include the following provision: "A person guilty of an offence under this section, if the touching involved—(a) penetration of B's anus or vagina with a part of A's body or anything else, (b) penetration of B's mouth with A's penis, (c) penetration of A's anus or vagina with a part of B's body, or (d) penetration of A's mouth with B's penis, is liable, on conviction on indictment, to imprisonment for a term not exceeding 14 years."

[100] These offences also make reference to under 13s.

[101] For a discussion of grooming see Suzanne Ost, *Child Pornography and Sexual Grooming*, (Cambridge: Cambridge University Press, 2009).

[102] Section 13 of the *Act of 2003* provides: "(1) A person under 18 commits an offence if he does anything which would be an offence under any of sections 9 to 12 if he were aged 18. (2) A person guilty of an offence under this section is liable—(a) on summary conviction, to imprisonment for a term not exceeding 6 months or a fine not exceeding the statutory maximum or both; (b) on conviction on indictment, to imprisonment for a term not exceeding 5 years."

[103] For a list of the people who are deemed to be in a position of trust see sections 21–22 of the *Act of 2003*.

one of his 17-year-old students.[104] This extension of the law seems to rest on the idea that the victim cannot give true consent because she will be spell bound by her carer/supervisor/teacher. It is irrebuttably presumed that the complainant did not consent.

Elsewhere, the law provides that it is not harmful for those who are aged 16 and over to engage in sexual activity. If it is not harmful for them to engage in consensual sexual activity, then the above offences must presume there is no consent. As should be apparent, it is total fiction to presume that the relationship of trust negates consent in all cases. The law deems that even though the consent may be valid it is to be taken to be invalid. It is presumed that any consent that may be given will only be given because there was undue influence. The reality is that in many of these cases the consent will be genuine. Given the coverage of the *Act of 2003*, these offences seem unnecessary. It would be better to ascertain whether the victim did in fact consent, because where there is genuine consent the criminal law has no role to play. The fact that there was a relationship of trust between the defendant and the victim adds nothing where the sexual actively is in fact consensual. A 16-year-old can refuse lifesaving treatment, can consent to have an abortion and so on (see 23.10), so it is a little incongruous that she is barred from consenting to sexual activity with an adult in certain contexts. It seems that it would be enough to fire the teacher if he has an affair with a student who is aged under 18.

If the defendant reasonably believes the victim is 18 or over, the mental element will not be made out. Similarly, the defendant might argue that he did not know or could not reasonably have been "expected to know of the circumstances by virtue of which he was in a position of trust in relation to" the victim, but in many cases this will not be an issue. In the school teacher cases quoted in the preceding footnotes, the defendant knew for a fact that he was in a position of trust and that the victim was under 18.

10–042   **Will D, a school teacher, be liable for one of the aforementioned offences if he has sexual intercourse with his 17-year-old neighbour?**   Not unless she is also one of his students. If she is not enrolled in his school he will not be liable for any offence, because there will be no relationship of trust. Furthermore, if the teacher manages to elope with one of his students he will have a defence. Section 23 provides:

> "(1)   Conduct by a person (A) which would otherwise be an offence under any of sections 16 to 19 against another person (B) is not an offence under that section if at the time–
>   (a)   B is 16 or over, and
>   (b)   A and B are lawfully married or civil partners of each other.
> (2)   In proceedings for such an offence it is for the defendant to prove that A and B were at the time lawfully married or civil partners of each other".

---

[104] *R. v. Lamb* [2007] EWCA Crim. 1766; *R. v. Lister* [2006] 1 Cr. App. R. (S.) 69; *R. v. Healy* [2010] 1 Cr. App. R. (S.) 105; in *R. v. Wilson* [2008] 1 Cr. App. R. (S.) 90, a trainee teacher had a consensual affair with a 17-year-old girl and was jailed. The sentencing judge noted: "A very considerable penalty had been paid by Wilson for his behaviour. His career in teaching was over and he would remain on the sexual offenders register for years to come and would never work with children again."

If a teacher and a student strike up a friendship, the teacher will not be liable for any of the abovementioned offences as long as he does not allow the relationship to get physical before he marries the student. It is not clear why Parliament presumes such a person is able to consent to marital sexual intercourse with someone whom she has met through a relationship of trust, but is not capable of otherwise consenting to have sexual intercourse with such a defendant.

The familial child sex offences found in sections 25–26 of the *Act of 2003* also aim to protect children who are vulnerable because of their relationship to the defendant. Coupled with this, sexual relations between blood relatives flout deeply held conventional norms against incest.[105]

10.9. DEFENCES FOR SECONDARY PARTIES

Section 73 of the *Act of 2003* provides: **10–043**

"(1) A person is not guilty of aiding, abetting or counselling the commission against a child of an offence to which this section applies if he acts for the purpose of—
  (a) protecting the child from sexually transmitted infection,
  (b) protecting the physical safety of the child,
  (c) preventing the child from becoming pregnant, or
  (d) promoting the child's emotional well-being by the giving of advice, and not for the purpose of obtaining sexual gratification or for the purpose of causing or encouraging the activity constituting the offence or the child's participation in it.
(2) This section applies to—
  (a) an offence under any of sections 5 to 7 (offences against children under 13);
  (b) an offence under section 9 (sexual activity with a child);
  (c) an offence under section 13 which would be an offence under section 9 if the offender were aged 18;
  (d) an offence under any of sections 16, 25, 30, 34 and 38 (sexual activity) against a person under 16.
(3) This section does not affect any other enactment or any rule of law restricting the circumstances in which a person is guilty of aiding, abetting or counselling an offence under this Part."

This provision is fairly self-explanatory. It designed to protect doctors and other professionals who provide advice which is designed to protect a child. For instance, a health worker might advise a child to use a prophylactic to ensure that she does not contract H.I.V. This is in line with the decision of the House of Lords in *Gillick v. West Norfolk and Wisbech AHA*.[106]

10.10. MENTALLY DISORDERED VICTIMS

There are a number of offences that specifically target those who have sexual **10–044** relations with anyone who is suffering from a mental disorder. For example, section 30 of the *Act of 2003* provides:

---

[105] For a discussion of the problem of criminalizing incest between consenting adults behind closed doors: see Dennis J. Baker, "Constitutionalizing the Harm Principle," (2008) 27 *Crim. Just. Ethics* 3 at 14–15.
[106] [1986] A.C. 112.

"(1)   A person (A) commits an offence if—
    (a)   he intentionally touches another person (B),
    (b)   the touching is sexual,
    (c)   B is unable to refuse because of or for a reason related to a mental disorder, and
    (d)   A knows or could reasonably be expected to know that B has a mental disorder and that because of it or for a reason related to it B is likely to be unable to refuse.

(2)   B is unable to refuse if—
    (a)   he lacks the capacity to choose whether to agree to the touching (whether because he lacks sufficient understanding of the nature or reasonably foreseeable consequences of what is being done, or for any other reason), or
    (b)   he is unable to communicate such a choice to A.

(3)   A person guilty of an offence under this section, if the touching involved—
    (a)   penetration of B's anus or vagina with a part of A's body or anything else,
    (b)   penetration of B's mouth with A's penis,
    (c)   penetration of A's anus or vagina with a part of B's body, or
    (d)   penetration of A's mouth with B's penis, is liable, on conviction on indictment, to imprisonment for life.

(4)   Unless subsection (3) applies, a person guilty of an offence under this section is liable—(a) on summary conviction, to imprisonment for a term not exceeding 6 months or to a fine not exceeding the statutory maximum or both; (b) on conviction on indictment, to imprisonment for a term not exceeding 14 years."

Section 30(3) mirrors the under 13 offence found in section 8 in that it carries a life sentence if the sexual activity involves any of the conduct mentioned in the subsection. Like subsections 8(2), 9(2) and 10(2), subsection 30(3) does not mention penile penetration of the vagina. Technically, subsection 30(3)(a) covers penile penetration because it refers to "penetration of B's anus or vagina with a part of A's body." A penis is the part of A's body if A is a man. Nevertheless, cases involving penile penetration should be charged as rape under section 1. Once we take rape out of the equation it emerges that section 30 overlaps with sections 2–3 of the *Act of 2003*. Section 31 makes it an offence to cause or incite a person with a mental disorder to engage in sexual activity. Section 31 not only overlaps with section 4 (causing a person to engage in sexual activity without consent), but also creates an inchoate offence of incitement similar to the one found in the child offences.[107]

10–045   **If this conduct (with the exception of incitement) is covered elsewhere in the *Act*, why create special offences for mentally disordered people? Surely, they should not be treated any differently to any other adult citizen living in the community. If they have consented then they have consented.**   There is no doubt that people suffering mental disorder may be more vulnerable than the average person, but in our haste to protect them we must be careful not to jump onto the paternalism treadmill.[108] The law should do all it can to allow such people as much sexual freedom as possible. If a mentally disordered person is merely responding to "animal instincts" and there is no exploitation,[109] there is no case for invoking the criminal law.[110]

---

[107] See also section 32 (engaging in sexual activity in the presence of a person with a mental disorder); and section 33 (causing a person with a mental disorder to watch a sexual act).

[108] The offences in sections 38–41 seem somewhat paternalistic.

[109] In *R. v. Mrzljak* [2005] 152 A. Crim. R. 315 V and D seem to have been driven by their animal instincts. As we saw above, both parties were mentally impaired and there was no evidence that the

Is the mental element the same as it is for the offences found in sections   **10–046**
1–4?   It is as far as the section requires any sexual activity to be intentional. If D
is acting as an automaton he will not be liable because his touching will not be
volitional. The sexual activity must involve intentional touching (subsection
30(1)(a)). Subsection 30(1)(a) governs the conduct referred to in subsections
30(3)(a)–(d).

The mental element for this offence differs as far as mistakes as to whether the
mentally disordered person is consenting are concerned. As you will have
noticed, subsection 30(1)(d) provides:

> "A knows or could reasonably be expected to know that B has a mental disorder and that
> because of it or for a reason related to it B is likely to be unable to refuse."

You will recall that the offences found in sections 1–4 used a slightly different
test. The test in those sections goes as follows:

> "•   A does not reasonably believe that B consents.
> •   Whether a belief is reasonable is to be determined having regard to all the
>   circumstances, including any steps A has taken to ascertain whether B consents." [111]

In either case the defendant will be liable if he is negligent as to whether the   **10–047**
victim is consenting. However, the latter provision makes reference to "all the
circumstances." As we have seen, if the defendant makes a mistake as to whether
the victim is consenting because he too is mentally disordered, the court can
consider this as one of the circumstances. In other words, it will be able to
enquire as to whether a reasonable person armed with the same information as the
mentally disordered defendant would have made the same mistake. Alas, the
offences found in sections 30–33 make no such concession. It seems odd not to
have expressly included this concession in these offences, because in certain
institutional contexts mentally disordered persons are more likely to meet up with
other mentally disordered persons, and thus the mistaken consent rates could be
higher in such contexts. (For a fuller discussion of when a mentally disordered
person's consent is vitiated, see 23.7).

If you are not fed up with the repetition and the utter unnecessary overlap in
the provisions of the *Act*, let me give you a bit more repetition. Sections 34–37
create a further set of offences. These offences target those who use "inducement,
threat or deception" to procure sexual activity[112] with a person with a mental
disorder. We need consider only the wording of section 34 to get an idea of how
these offences operate. Section 34 provides:

---

man exploited the girl. D was 50 and V was only 18, but such an age difference alone should not be
deemed as evidence of exploitation. Courts are likely to draw the wrong conclusion when there is this
type of age difference, but age might not make any difference where the parties are driven by their
basic "animal instincts;" and both are mentally impaired.
[110] *R. v. Morgan* [1970] V.R. 337; *In Re F. (Mental Patient: Sterilisation)* [1990] 2 A.C. 1.
[111] See subsections 1(1)(c) and 1(2); 2(1)(d) and 2(2); 3(1)(d) and 3(2); and 4(1)(d) and 4(2).
[112] Section 35 targets those who use inducement, threat or deception to cause a person with a mental
disorder to engage in or agree to engage in sexual activity; section 36 targets those who engage in
sexual activity in the presence, procured by inducement, threat or deception, of a person with a mental
disorder; and section 37 targets those who cause a person with a mental disorder to watch a sexual act
by inducement, threat or deception.

"(1)   A person (A) commits an offence if—
    (a)   with the agreement of another person (B) he intentionally touches that person,
    (b)   the touching is sexual,
    (c)   A obtains B's agreement by means of an inducement offered or given, a threat made or a deception practised by A for that purpose,
    (d)   B has a mental disorder, and
    (e)   A knows or could reasonably be expected to know that B has a mental disorder.
(2)   A person guilty of an offence under this section, if the touching involved—
    (a)   penetration of B's anus or vagina with a part of A's body or anything else,
    (b)   penetration of B's mouth with A's penis,
    (c)   penetration of A's anus or vagina with a part of B's body, or
    (d)   penetration of A's mouth with B's penis, is liable, on conviction on indictment, to imprisonment for life."

These provisions do not require the defendant to know that the victim cannot refuse consent because of her mental disorder. The defendant need only have reasonable grounds for believing that the victim was suffering from a mental disorder. If a reasonable person would have known that the victim was mentally disordered, this element will be satisfied. It does not matter that a reasonable person would have believed that V's mental disorder was not preventing her from giving true consent as long as there was some kind of threat, deception, or inducement. It is not clear what this type of provision adds. If the threat, inducement or deception negates consent, then why not charge the defendant with one of the offences under sections 1–4? Or is this another case of Parliament deeming there was no consent even if there was? If the treat, deception or inducement does not negate consent, then the criminal law should not be invoked. The fact that there was a threat or deception could be sufficient to negate V's consent, but that will depend on the type of threat or deception involved (see Chapter 23). As for inducement, it seems this has been included because mere inducement may be enough to cause mentally disordered people to engage in sexual activity, when it would not be enough to cause a normal person to do so. But this question is best dealt with under the general head of consent.

There is a final set of offences that are worth mentioning. The offences in sections 38–41 criminalize consensual sexual relations between care workers and adults who suffer some kind of mental disorder regardless of whether their disorder renders them incapable of giving a valid consent. Given that mental disorder is widespread in modern society, the focus should be on whether there was in fact genuine "consent," not on the relationship of trust. If a psychiatrist has a sexual affair with his beautiful patient,[113] he should only face a jail term when it is established that his patient was not in fact consenting. The fact that he is technically a care worker should not make him liable for a serious offence where there is genuine consent.[114] These provisions seem to go too far. All adult citizens are entitled to equal sexual freedom regardless of their disabilities. These provisions seem to deem that mentally disordered people who are under the care

---

[113] The great Vivian Leigh had bipolar disorder. Recently, Catherine Zeta Jones checked into a hospital to seek treatment for manic depression. See Alex Spillius, "Catherine Zeta Jones 'received treatment for manic depression'," (London: *The Telegraph*, 13 April 2011). These high profile cases demonstrate that autonomous adults of all walks of life might have their sexual liberty restricted by such laws.

[114] Section 42 of the *Act of 2003* sets out the hospitals and care homes that are covered by the offences found in section 38–41. It appears that a psychiatrist working in an independent hospital

of others are not fully autonomous. The focus should be on the quality of the consent, not on the nature of the relationship between the victim and the defendant. (Adults should not be criminalized for engaging in sexual relations with each other.) It is too much to deem there is no consent merely because the victim has a sexual relationship with a person who has been entrusted to care for her. It treats mentally disordered patients as less than full members of the community. Mental disorder can effect the quality of a person's consent to many degrees, but it might not affect it at all in many cases. These provisions are meant to protect vulnerable people, but they seem to also limit their sexual freedom.

---

would be caught. No doubt these types of hospitals house people from all walks of life (sick actors, doctors, lawyers, bankers and so on). At the other end of the scale, there are care homes which house very vulnerable people.

CHAPTER 11

MURDER

"There's scarlet thread of murder running through the colourless skein of life, and our duty is to unravel it, and isolate it, and expose every inch of it."

Sir Arthur Conan Doyle[1]

11.1. THE PUNISHMENT OF MURDER

Killing a person, whether lawfully or unlawfully, is called "homicide," but this is only a literary expression. There is no crime of "homicide." Unlawful homicide at common law comprises the two crimes of murder and manslaughter. Other forms of unlawful homicide have been created by statute: certain forms of manslaughter (homicide with diminished responsibility, loss of control,[2] and suicide pacts), infanticide, and causing death by dangerous driving.

11–001

The classic definition of murder is that of Sir Edward (Chief Justice) Coke,[3] though its antiqued wording requires careful glossing:

> "Murder is when a man ... unlawfully killeth ... any reasonable creature in *rerum natura* under the king's peace, with malice forethought, either expressed by the party, or implied by law, so as the party wounded, or hurt, *etc.* die of the wound, or hurt, *etc.* within a year and a day after the same."[4]

"Any reasonable creature" means any human being (a demented person being protected), and "*in rerum natura*" (in being) excludes the unborn child. But as we will see in Chapter 13, a foetus may be covered if it is born alive. "Under the King's peace" covers everyone except the enemy killed in operations of war.[5]

The *actus reus* is simply the unlawful killing of another human being. As we will see in the next Chapter, a person may be classified as dead once he is "brain dead."[6] If the brain dead victim is on life support, the *actus reus* of murder or

---

[1] *A Study of Scarlet*, (London: Ward, Lock & Co., 1888) at 65.

[2] Sections 52–54 of the *Coroners and Justice Act 2009*.

[3] Pronounced "Cook."

[4] Sir Edward Coke, *Institutes of the Laws of England*, (London: Printed for E. and R. Brooke , Pt III, 1797), Chap. 7, at 47.

[5] *Maria v. Hall* (1807) 1 Taunt 33; *Wells v. Williams* (1697) 91 E.R. 45; *R. v. Page* [1954] 1 Q.B. 170. See also Michael Hirst, "Murder under the Queen's Peace," [2008] Crim. L.R. 541.

[6] "Physicians, health care workers, members of the clergy, and laypeople throughout the world have accepted fully that a person is dead when his or her brain is dead." Eelco F.M. Wijdicks, "The Diagnosis of Brain Death," (2001) 344 *N. Engl. J. Med.* 1215. See also *Airedale NHS Trust v. Bland* [1993] A.C. 789, *per* Lords Keith, Goff, and Browne-Wilkinson, *obiter dicta*; *Re A* (1992) 3 *Med. L. Rev.* 303.

manslaughter will normally be complete once the doctors switch it off.[7] (It is noted in the next Chapter, that a doctor's act of removing a patient from life support will not normally sever the chain of causation between the defendant's act or omission and the patient's death.) Causation has been discussed at length in Chapter 8, so we need not revisit that issue. But it is worth recapping one point. You will recall that the year-and-a-day rule has been abolished.[8] Therefore, if D causes V's brain death and V is kept on a ventilator for more than three years, proceedings for murder or manslaughter can be commenced only if Attorney-General grants permission. (When life begins and ends and the matter of prolongation of life is dealt with at length in the next two chapters.)

11–002   **What if a doctor accelerates V's death by providing standard pain relief?**   The acceleration of death is supposed to be enough for criminal liability, so the defendant is not normally allowed to say that the victim would have died before long. But in *R. v. Bodkin Adams*[9] Devlin J. directed the jury that when health cannot be restored a doctor "is still entitled to do all that is proper and necessary to relieve pain and suffering even if measures he takes may incidentally shorten life." The passage as a whole seems to imply the view that what the doctor does by way of approved medical practice is not a cause in law. It plays such a minor part in causing the death that it can be excluded from consideration. But clearly it is a cause.

A more satisfactory reason would be the doctrine of necessity, at which Devlin J. perhaps glanced in his use of the word "necessity." Arguably accelerating a harmful result as a matter of necessity for a legitimate purpose in cases where the harm is certain to transpire (within a reasonable timeframe),[10] ought to be grounds for extending the necessity defence (depending on the facts) to cover doctors,[11] because such people are not motivated by a desire to kill for the sake of killing.[12] They are accelerating death by a very short period of time and in exceptional circumstances. A doctor who genuinely tries to relieve his patient's pain knowing that it might accelerate her death is motivated by the necessity to relieve her immense pain. Therefore, his conduct should be treated as being lawfully justified. However, as noted in Chapter 4, good motives only count when they are underwritten by a valid legal defence. Since necessity is not generally a defence to murder, being motivated by necessity might not provide a defence.[13]

The courts seem to take the view if the pain relief is absolutely necessary and is administered according to standard medical practice that it is irrelevant that the doctor foresaw that the side-effect of the treatment would be the acceleration of

---

[7] *R. v. Malcherek* [1981] 1 W.L.R. 690 at 694.

[8] Section 3(2) of the *Law Reform (Year and a Day Rule) Act 1996*.

[9] [1957] Crim. L.R. 365. See also Glanville Williams, *The Sanctity of Life and the Criminal Law*, (London: Faber, 1958), 289.

[10] See Michael S. Moore, "Counterfactual Dependence as an Independent, Non-Causal Desert-Determiner," (2009) 34 *Austl. J. Leg. Phil.* 1 at 5; *Re A (Conjoined Twins Surgical Separation)*, [2000] 4 All E.R. 961.

[11] See generally, Andrew Ashworth, "Criminal Liability in a Medical Context: The Treatment of Good Intentions," in A. P. Simester and A. T. H. Smith, *Harm and Culpability*, (Oxford: Clarendon Press, 1996).

[12] Cf. *R. v. Cox* (1992)12 B.M.L.R. 38.

[13] Cf. *Re A (Conjoined Twins Surgical Separation)*, [2000] 4 All E.R. 961.

his patient's death.[14] Alternatively, if a doctor euthanizes his patient and foresees that the side-effect of doing so will be that she will no longer be in pain, he clearly has no defence.[15]

How are murder and manslaughter distinguished?   The requirements for **11–003** both are the same except in respect of the fault element and mitigating circumstances. Murder requires, positively, the mental element traditionally known as "malice aforethought," and, negatively, the absence of certain mitigating circumstances (such as "loss of control" or "diminished responsibility") that would turn the case into one of manslaughter.

During the formative period of the common law the distinction between murder and manslaughter was of great moment for the defendant, because murder was punished by death, unless the Crown respited the sentence, whereas a person convicted of manslaughter generally escaped that penalty owing to the indulgence known as benefit of clergy; when benefit of clergy was abolished the sentence was changed to a maximum of imprisonment for life. The death penalty for murder continued until 1965, when it was replaced by a mandatory[16] sentence of imprisonment for life.[17]

You referred to a mandatory life sentence. Do you mean that the offender **11–004** **must be sentenced for life imprisonment whatever the circumstances of the** **murder?**   Yes if he is convicted of murder. However, "loss of control,"[18] and "diminished responsibility,"[19] for instance, are partial defences to murder, reducing the charge to manslaughter.

But isn't that manslaughter. It's murder.   Killing by "loss of self control" is **11–005** in fact mitigated murder, but in law it is called manslaughter. The purpose of calling it manslaughter was in the old days to escape capital punishment, and is now to give the judge a discretion as to sentence.

What term do murderers in fact serve?   There is an eradicable idea in the **11–006** minds of the public that the term is for life, but most offenders serve no more than 15 years.[20] All offenders must serve a minimum term before they can apply for parole. At the end of the minimum term the offender will remain in prison until he is granted parole. After the offender is released on parole he will be supervised

---

[14] See Lord Goff's judgment in *Airedale N.H.S. Trust v. Bland* [1993] A.C. 789. However, as noted in the next chapter, withdrawing treatment or life support is not sufficient to break the chain of causation.
[15] *R. v. Cox* (1992)12 B.M.L.R. 38.
[16] A command to the court, leaving it no discretion. Accent on the first syllable.
[17] *Murder (Abolition of Death) Act 1965* (subsequently made perpetual by resolutions in Parliament). A person under 18 at the time of the crime is sentenced to be detained in accordance with *Powers of Criminal Courts (Sentencing) Act 2000*. The death penalty, though abolished, remained on the statute book for some offences until 1998. In 1998 section 36 of the *Crime and Disorder Act 1998* abolished it for treason and piracy.
[18] Sections 54 and 55 of the *Coroners and Justice Act 2009*.
[19] See also section 52 of the *Coroners and Justice Act 2009*.
[20] The starting tariff may be much less, however. It could start at 8 years, but now days would not normally be much less than 13 years. See *R. v. Oyediran* [2010] EWCA Crim. 2431.

for the rest of his life by the Probation Service. He may be recalled to prison to continue serving his life sentence, if there is evidence that it is in the public interest to recall him.

The minimum term will depend on the nature of the murder, but will normally be:

- a whole life term, or
- 30 years, or
- 15 years.

Section 269 of the *Criminal Justice Act 2003* requires the sentencing judge to consider the guidelines found in Schedule 21 of that *Act*, when determining the minimum sentence that an offender should serve before being considered for parole. The judge may decide not to follow the guidelines, but if he does not follow them he is required to provide reasons to explain why he departed from them. The guidelines recommended that the starting point is life where the offender has committed multiple murders (the murder of two or more people) involving "substantial premeditation, the abduction of the victim, sexual or sadistic conduct, the murder of a child if involving the abduction of the child or sexual or sadistic motivation, a murder done for the purpose of advancing political, religious, racial or ideological causes (terrorism), or the offender has previously been convicted of murder."

Where the offender has committed multiple murders (of in some cases a single murder of a particular nature) the starting point for his minimum term should be 30 years, if the murder(s) involved any of the following factors:

"(a) the murder of a police officer or prison officer in the course of his duty,
(b) a murder involving the use of a firearm or explosive,
(c) a murder done for gain (such as a murder done in the course or furtherance of robbery or burglary, done for payment or done in the expectation of gain as a result of the death),
(d) a murder intended to obstruct or interfere with the course of justice,
(e) a murder involving sexual or sadistic conduct,
(f) the murder of two or more persons,
(g) a murder that is racially or religiously aggravated or aggravated by sexual orientation."[21]

Most other offenders should be subject to a minimum term of 15-years.

11–007 **What about the barmy ones? Must they too be sentenced for life?**   Yes, if they are convicted of murder; but they will not be. A mentally disordered defendant (note the proper expression) can in appropriate circumstances set up either an insanity defence, resulting in a special verdict, or a defence of diminished responsibility, resulting in a conviction of manslaughter.

11–008 **Why was the life sentence made mandatory? Why wasn't the judge given a discretion?**   Several answers may be given. The most obvious is that murder was thought to be a bad crime that had to have a terrible punishment. The

---

[21] Schedule 21 of the *Criminal Justice Act 2003*.

punishment for murder in the old days was a mandatory death sentence; now, by a quirk of language, it was to be a mandatory "life" sentence.

More realistically, the mandatory sentence was a political compromise arrived at in order to get capital punishment abolished.[22] A subsidiary (but thoroughly unconvincing) reason for denying the discretion to the judge was that it was desired to keep murder separate from manslaughter. For manslaughter the judge has a discretion. He may sentence the offender to imprisonment for any term up to (and of course including) life; but on the other hand he may save the defendant from a prison sentence: for example, by merely fining him or putting him on probation or (conceivably) granting a discharge. To make a distinction from manslaughter, the mandatory life sentence for murder was an obvious, if unsatisfactory, expedient. (In fact the two offences could have been retained without making any distinction in respect of sentencing powers.)

Yet another reason was that it was thought unsafe for the judge to be allowed to sentence a murderer to anything less than "life"—the judge may underestimate the danger he presented to society. (This is made nonsense of by the fact that if the killer is suffering from mental disorder and gets a verdict of diminished responsibility, the judge has a complete discretion as to sentence. Mentally disordered killers are in general more dangerous and unpredictable than other killers.)[23]

11.2. INTENT TO KILL

The mental element in murder is "malice aforethought," but this is a term of art, if not a term of deception. Murder does not require either spite or premeditation. Mercy-killing can be murder, and so can a killing where the intent is conceived on the instant. Malice aforethought is present in contemplation of law whenever there is: **11–009**

- an intent to unlawfully[24] kill,[25] or
- an intent to inflict grievous bodily harm,[26] or
- an oblique intent to unlawfully kill or inflict grievous bodily harm.[27]

This treatise will simply refer to "intention" and "oblique intention" as opposed to "malice aforethought." Let us start by examining intention. Since the enactment of section 8 of the *Criminal Justice Act 1967* the courts have dropped

---

[22] D. A. Thomas, "Form and Function in the Criminal Law," in P. R. Glazebrook (ed.) *Reshaping the Criminal Law: Essays in Honour of Glanville Williams,* (London: Stevens & Sons, 1978) at 25–29.

[23] See Dennis J. Baker, "Punishment Without a Crime: Is Preventive Detention Reconcilable with Justice," (2009) 34 *Austl. J. Leg. Phil.* 120.

[24] The killing will be unlawful if the defendant killed without a legal justification (*e.g.*, in self-defence) or without legal excuse (*e.g.*, the defendant was insane).

[25] Traditionally, an "intention to kill" was referred to as "express malice." See *R. v. Vickers* [1957] 2 Q.B. 664.

[26] Traditionally, an "intention to cause g.b.h." was referred to as "implied malice." See *R. v Cunningham* [1982] A.C. 566.

[27] It was noted in Chap. 4 that "oblique intention" in the pure sense is not intention at all, but a form of extreme subjective recklessness. It is about choosing a virtually certainty. See *R. v. Woollin* [1999] 1 A.C. 82.

the notion of an entirely "objective" intention that was expressed in *D.P.P. v. Smith*.[28] As we have seen, the better view, and the predominant judicial view, is that intention now bears its natural meaning. As a general rule, its natural meaning need not be explained to the jury:

> "The golden rule should be that, when directing a jury on the mental element necessary in a crime of specific intent, the judge should avoid any elaboration or paraphrase of what is meant by intent, and leave it to the jury's good sense to decide whether the accused acted with the necessary intent, unless the judge is convinced that, on the facts and having regard to the way the case has been presented to the jury in evidence and argument, some further explanation or elaboration is strictly necessary to avoid misunderstanding."[29]

11.3.   INTENT TO INFLICT GRIEVOUS BODILY HARM

11–010   Murder requires a killing, so the normal principle should be that the *mental element* in murder should refer to *death*, not to harm short of death. But the law holds otherwise. The mental element for murder can be made out even where the defendant does not intend to kill the victim as long as he intended to inflict grievous bodily harm.[30]

A charge of attempted murder requires an intention to kill, and cannot be established by proof of intent to do grievous bodily harm.[31] It may seem remarkable that a person cannot be convicted of attempt to murder when he deliberately inflicts g.b.h. upon another, and yet can be convicted of murder, if, as a result of the injury, the victim dies. On a charge of attempted murder the jury must distinguish between an intent to kill and an intent to injure, the latter not being sufficient for the charge of attempt. A charge of attempt always requires proof of an intention to achieve the forbidden result; here the forbidden result is the death of another, and there must be intention as to that.

11–011   **Why is an intention to cause grievous bodily harm sufficient *mens rea* for murder?**   This form of constructive intent is the "residue" of a much greater doctrine of constructive intention. A historical note on constructive intention may assist understanding. We have always had a law of murder, but only the name has remained unchanged. Formerly, there was the doctrine of "constructive malice" in murder which greatly extended the scope of the crime. The word "constructive" is used by lawyers to mean "fictitious" or "non-actual"; it signifies that a word is being stretched beyond its natural meaning.[32] Constructive malice was found whenever a killing occurred (however accidentally) in the course of an

---

[28] [1961] A.C. 290.

[29] *R. v. Moloney* [1985] A.C. 905 at 926 *per* Lord Bridge.

[30] So long as the g.b.h. causes the victim's death. On causation, see Chap. 8 of this book.

[31] The rule goes back to *R. v. Donovan* (1850) Cox. C.C. 399; cf. *R. v. Grimwood* [1962] 2 Q.B. 621. The defendant can, of course, be convicted of intentionally causing g.b.h., or of an attempt to do so, which are punishable as severely as attempted murder.

[32] "To constitute a constructive offence, the words of the original offence are made to signify that which in their natural and ordinary sense they do not signify": Criminal Law Commission, Sixth Report, *Parl. Papers* x 16, (London: 1841). For the complicated origin of murder and manslaughter, see J. M. Kaye, "Early History of Murder and Manslaughter," (1967) 83 *L.Q.R.* 365 at 383 *et seq*. See also Jeremy Horder, "Two Histories and Four Hidden Principles of *Mens Rea*," (1997) 113 *L.Q.R.* 95.

unlawful act. Coke, writing in the reign of James I, and regarded as an authority of the law of his own day, gave a strong example:

> "As if A, meaning to steale a deere in the park of B, shooteth at the deer, and by a glance of the arrow killeth a boy that is hidden in a bush: this is murder, for that act was unlawful, although A had no intent to hurt the boy, nor knew not of him."[33]

The defendant was "constructively" deemed to have intended the consequence of death, because he caused it while committing some other crime. This rule, typical of the pedantry and barbarity of the ancient common law, could not endure. It became confined by judicial decision to killing in the course of serious "felonies" (such as robbery, rape and arson), or killing in the course of resisting arrest or escaping from custody. But even in this attenuated form the doctrine of constructive malice was unacceptable to the rational mind, and it was eventually abolished by section 1 of the *Homicide Act 1957*:

> "(1)   Where a person kills another in the course or furtherance of some other offence, the killing shall not amount to murder unless done with the same malice aforethought (express or implied) as is required for a killing to amount to murder when not done in the course or furtherance of another offence.
>
> (2)   For the purposes of the foregoing subsection, a killing done in the course or for the purpose of resisting an officer of justice, or of resisting or avoiding or preventing a lawful arrest, or of effecting or assisting an escape or rescue from legal custody, shall be treated as a killing in the course or furtherance of an offence."

Now there was another form of malice aforethought at common law: the one we are concerned with—killing as a result of an intention to inflict grievous bodily harm.[34] The legal question is whether this form of intention (malice) was abolished by section 1 of the *1957 Act*. In *R. v. Vickers*[35] the Court of Appeal held that it was not; causing grievous bodily harm was not "some other offence" within section 1. It might be thought that this decision flies in the face of section 1, and in *Hyam v. D.P.P.*[36] discordant opinions were expressed about it. Lords Hailsham and Dilhorne held that *R. v. Vickers* was rightly decided. Lords Diplock and Kilbrandon thought it was wrong: an intention to cause grievous bodily harm is not sufficient *mens rea* for murder unless the defendant realized that his act was likely to endanger life. The fifth judge was Lord Cross, and he confessed that he had grave difficulty in understanding the doctrine because as a Chancery lawyer he had never before "had to grapple with this obscure and highly technical branch of the law."[37] He therefore took the extraordinary course of assuming, without deciding, that *R. v. Vickers* was right; so in the result he joined Lords Hailsham and Dilhorne.

This creates a puzzling question on the doctrine of precedent: is it competent for a judge to assume that the law is so-and-so as the basis of his judgment without deciding it? Whatever the theoretical answer may be, it is clear that a

---

[33] Coke, *op. cit. supra*, note 4 at 57.
[34] It has long been held that an intent to inflict serious injury is sufficient *mens rea* for murder. See *Errington's Case* (1838) 2 Lewin 217; *Halloway's Case* (1628) 79 E.R. 715.
[35] [1957] 2 Q.B. 664.
[36] [1975] A.C. 55.
[37] *Hyam v. D.P.P.* [1975] A.C. 55 at 96.

"residual" form of "constructive intent" still applies as far as the offence of murder is concerned. Its continued existence in modern law was reaffirmed by the House of Lords in *R. v. Cunningham*[38] and more recently in *R. v. Rahman*.[39] Lord Edmund-Davies in *R. v. Cunningham* pointed to another disquieting aspect of the rule in that it accounts a person guilty of murder although the harm he intended to inflict was unlikely to kill:

> "I find it passing strange that a person can be convicted of murder if death results from, say, his intentional breaking of another's arm, an action which, while undoubtedly involving the infliction of 'really serious harm' and, as such, calling for severe punishment, would in most cases be unlikely to kill."[40]

11–012   **So the defendant need not intend to inflict harm that he believes is likely to kill, because any "serious harm" will do.**   That is correct. The courts attach the same meaning to "grievous bodily harm" as in the context of aggravated assaults; it means "really serious harm, whether or not it is likely to kill." The rule was reaffirmed in *R. v. Cunningham*.[41] What is a really serious bodily harm is a question for the jury. In practice, deaths caused with this form of *mens rea* are generally treated as manslaughter, unless the defendant was engaged in a villainous enterprise.

11–013   **Will D be guilty of murder, if he intentionally pinpricks V without realizing that V is a haemophiliac and this causes V to bleed to death?**   He will not be liable for murder unless he intended to inflict grievous bodily harm. He could not have intended to inflict g.b.h., if he was unaware of his victim's special sensitivity. If he knew that his victim was a haemophiliac and believed a pinprick would cause him serious injury by causing major bleeding, then he could be liable for murder if the victim bleeds to death. In the latter situation, he intends to inflict g.b.h. This is no different than if he had intended to slash open a major artery on a person of normal sensitivity to cause major bleeding. The focus has to be on the intended harm, not the means used to achieve it. The means might not seem too evil where the defendant deliberately and intentionally takes advantage of the victim's special sensitivity, but the intended harm may be.

11–014   **Doesn't this residual form of constructive intent leave the prosecution too much discretion?**   An even more serious objection to the rule is that it leaves so much to prosecutorial discretion.[42] In practice deaths caused with this form of *mens rea* are generally treated as manslaughter, unless the defendant was engaged in a villainous enterprise. A parent who inflicts grievous bodily harm on his child,

---

[38] [1982] A.C. 566; *R. v. Rahman* [2009] 1 A.C. 129 at 145.

[39] [2009] 1 A.C. 129 at 144 *per* Lord Bingham; at 156 *per* Lord Roger; and at 160 *per* Lord Brown.

[40] [1982] A.C. 566 at 582–583.

[41] [1982] A.C. 566. The words "serious" and "injury" are to be given their ordinary meaning. *R. v. Bollom* [2004] 2 Cr. App. R. 6; *R. v. Janjua* [1999] 1 Cr. App. R. 91.

[42] The substantive provisions found in some U.S. jurisdictions allow for even greater prosecutorial flexibility. See generally, Carolyn B. Ramsey, "Homicide on Holiday, Prosecutorial Discretion, Popular Culture, and the Boundaries of the Criminal Law," (2003) 54 *Hastings L.J.* 1641.

so causing its death, is often charged with manslaughter only,[43] and if the conviction is for murder the sentencing judge is likely to set a fairly low minimum term.[44] Or the judge may refrain from leaving the question of murder to the jury. If the defendant is convicted under section 5 of the *Domestic Violence, Crime and Victims Act 2004*, for allowing or causing the death of her child she might receive a prison term of less than six years.[45] So the rule in *R. v. Cunningham* is merely a rule that a person may be convicted of murder if he both falls within the rule and is unlucky in his choice of prosecutor, judge and jury.

Notwithstanding these objections, the rule was approved by the Criminal Law Revision Committee, though with the important qualification that it should be confined to cases where the act was known to the defendant to involve a risk of causing death.[46] The argument for the rule is that when a person shoots or stabs another, his act is sufficiently grave to justify a conviction of murder if death results, even though his intention was only to disable a person from whom he wished to steal, or to stop a pursuer when he was running away after a robbery, or to mutilate someone by way of revenge, or to stop a person giving an alarm. The human body is fragile, and a person who shows himself willing to inflict serious injury to another, thus causing his death, is so little less blameable than the intentional killer that the law is right in not making a distinction.[47] (This argument would be stronger, if serious bodily injury referred to acts intended to bring the victim close to death.)

There is also the argument that if the law were otherwise a truly intentional killer would be encouraged to run a false defence in the hope of bamboozling the jury. But this is unconvincing, because on a charge of attempted murder the jury must distinguish between false and true defences of lack of intent to kill.

The core objection, however, remains. It is unacceptable to invoke the doctrine of constructive intention given that the penalty is a mandatory life sentence. Recently, the Law Commission recommended that murder be split into two categories:[48]

11–015

---

[43] Cf. *R. v. Henderson* [2010] 2 Cr. App. R. 24; *R. v. Ikram* [2009] 1 W.L.R. 1419. In the United States, the conviction can be for second degree murder. See *Fisher v. State*, 128 Md.App. 79 (1999); *Simpkins v. State*, 596 A.2d 655 (1991) (where the parents let their two-year-old daughter die of starvation); *Duley v. State*, 467 A.2d 776 (1983); *Moore v. State*, 291 A.2d 73 (1972).

[44] The minimum term served in prison would normally be approximately 13 years in such cases, but could be much lower. See *R. v. Oyediran* [2010] EWCA Crim. 2431. In *R. v. Essilfie* [2009] 2 Cr. App. R. (S.) 11, it was held "A life sentence with a specified minimum term of 13 years was appropriate in the case of a father who had murdered his six-month-old child during a violent incident when he had lost his temper in the heat of the moment."

[45] See *R. v. V* [2010] 2 Cr. App. R. (S.) 108, where D caused the death of a child by giving it adult drugs to keep it calm.

[46] Criminal Law Revision Committee, *Offences Against the Person*, Fourteenth Report, (London: H.M.S.O., Cmnd. 7844, 1980) at para. 31.

[47] In *R. v. Rahman* [2009] 1 A.C. 129 at 153, Lord Bingham expounded: "The rationale of that principle plainly is that if a person unlawfully assaults another with intent to cause him really serious injury, and death results, he should be held criminally responsible for that fatality, even though he did not intend it. If he had not embarked on a course of deliberate violence, the fatality would not have occurred. This rationale may lack logical purity, but it is underpinned by a quality of earthy realism."

[48] Law Commission, *Murder, Manslaughter and Infanticide*, Report 304, (London: H.M.S.O., 2006) at paras. 9.5 and 9.6.

1.   First degree murder should encompass:

> "(1)   intentional killings, and
> (2)   killings with the intent to cause serious injury where the killer was *aware* that his or her conduct involved a serious risk of causing death."

2.   Second degree murder should encompass:

> "(1)   killings intended to cause serious injury; or
> (2)   killings intended to cause injury or fear or risk of injury where the killer was aware that his or her conduct involved a serious risk of causing death; or
> (3)   killings intended to kill or to cause serious injury where the killer was aware that his or her conduct involved a serious risk of causing death but successfully pleads [loss of control], diminished responsibility or that he or she killed pursuant to a suicide pact."

The Law Commission recommended the mandatory life penalty be maintained for first degree murder and that a discretionary penalty with a maximum of life be introduced for second degree murder. This would take the constructive sting out of cases leading to a mandatory life sentence. Nevertheless, the Government's response was merely to reform the partial defences of provocation and diminished responsibility. Given that there has since been a change of government, and that reforming homicide laws is a political minefield, it is unlikely that we will see further reforms in the immediate future.

11.4.   OBLIQUE INTENTION

11–016   Whether some degree of risk-taking suffices for murder was formerly in some doubt; all that we know for certain is that cases on the subject were meagre. However, an affirmative answer was given by the House of Lords in *R. v. Woollin*.[49] The Lords have made it clear that nothing less than oblique intention will do. The earlier cases held that mere recklessness was sufficient. Firstly in *D.P.P. v. Smith*[50] and then again in *Hyam v. D.P.P.*;[51] neither case is any longer binding as far as this point is concerned.

Mrs. Hyam, being animated by malice against Mrs. B, poured half a gallon of petrol through Mrs. B's letter box in the small hours of the morning and set it alight. Mrs. B's two daughters died in the fire. Hyam was charged with murder. Her defence was that she had started the fire only to frighten Mrs. B into leaving the neighbourhood. The judge directed as follows: "The prosecution must prove, beyond all reasonable doubt, that the accused intended to kill or do serious bodily harm to Mrs. B the mother of the deceased girls. If you are satisfied that when the accused set fire to the house she knew that it was highly probable that this would cause death or serious bodily harm then the prosecution will have established the necessary intent. It matters not if her motive was, as she says, to frighten Mrs. B."

It will be seen that this direction starts by requiring intention to bring about the specified consequence, but then says that Hyam's knowledge that the consequence was highly probable would in law be an intention to bring it about.

---

[49] *R. v. Woollin* [1999] 1 A.C. 82 at 96–97.
[50] [1961] A.C. 290.
[51] [1975] A.C. 55.

There was no need for the judge to use language in this way. He could have said that Hyam was guilty of murder if she either intended to cause death or serious bodily harm or knew that such a consequence was highly probable. In the House of Lords, Hyam's conviction of murder was affirmed by three out of the five lords, and all five agreed that a person could be guilty of murder if he caused death as a result of consciously taking a specified degree of risk as to causing death. Differing views were expressed as to the precise rule of law.

I thought that people who killed as a result of deliberately taking a risk were guilty of manslaughter. If they are guilty of murder, how do you distinguish the two crimes? Taking that as a rhetorical question, it is the most important argument against the wider view of murder. Everyone assumes that the reckless person who takes a chance and causes a fatal accident is guilty of manslaughter, not murder. If recklessness were sufficient for murder such a person would be guilty of murder. Since the conclusion is absurd the premise must be wrong, so that recklessness cannot rationally be regarded as sufficient for murder. Murder by risk-taking is in fact an example of Orwellian "doublethink"; it is a principle applied against those who are thought to deserve it, but is never contemplated in relation to those who do not. Killing by taking risks is clearly the province of the law of manslaughter, not of murder.

11–017

Killing the children was not a part of Mrs. Hyam's direct intention, nor is it reasonable to say that it was part of her intention in a wider sense. She did not believe that their deaths would be an inseparable consequence of what she intended. If Mrs. Hyam had encircled the house with jet fuel and had barricaded all the windows and doors before setting it alight, then the jury might have been able to find that she must had foreseen that it was virtually certain that the occupants would be killed.

Only oblique intention (or *extreme* subjective recklessness, if that helps you understand the conceptual nature of oblique intention) is an alternative *mens rea* for murder.[52]

As mentioned in Chapter 4,[53] there are two substantive doctrines of intention:

(1) There is the intention in the pure sense, which comes into play when the defendant *intends* to kill the victim. This is satisfied when the evidence shows that the defendant's purpose or aim was to kill the victim.

(2) There is oblique intention. Oblique intention comes in to play when the defendant foresees V's death as a virtually certain consequence of his offending.

In *R. v. Woollin*,[54] House of Lords adopted Lord Lane C.J.'s[55] formulation of the oblique doctrine:[56]

11–018

---

[52] *R. v. Woollin* [1999] 1 A.C. 82.

[53] See the discussion in Chap. 4 of this book.

[54] *R. v. Woollin* [1999] 1 A.C. 82 at 96–97.

[55] *R. v. Nedrick* [1986] 1 W.L.R. 1025. See also *R. v. Hancock* [1986] A.C. 455; *R. v. Moloney* [1985] A.C. 905. Cf. *Hyam v. D.P.P.* [1975] A.C. 55.

[56] [1986] 1 W.L.R. 1025. See also *R. v. Hancock* [1986] A.C. 455; *R. v. Moloney* [1985] A.C. 905. Cf. *Hyam v. D.P.P.* [1975] A.C. 55.

"(1) Where the charge is murder and in the rare cases where the simple direction is not enough, the jury should be directed that they are not entitled to infer the necessary intention, unless they feel sure that death or serious bodily harm was a virtual certainty (barring some unforeseen intervention) as a result of the defendant's actions and that the defendant appreciated that such was the case."[57]

Lord Steyn qualified Lord Lane C.J.'s statement of the doctrine by holding that: "[t]he use of the words 'to infer' in (1) may detract from the clarity of the model direction. I would substitute the words 'to find.'"[58]

Oblique intention is an independent form of *mens rea* that can be used to satisfy the fault requirement for murder. It is not a mere rule of evidence.[59] The oblique intention doctrine catches a person who chooses to do *y* believing it is virtually certain that *y* will cause *x's* death.

11–019   **Is it enough that D only obliquely intended to inflict "grievous bodily harm"?**   Yes. If you know that *x* (the baby will suffer serious injury) is virtually certain to occur if you do *y* (throw the baby from the window), then you will be liable for murder if the baby dies as a result of you throwing it from the third floor. If you choose to throw the baby when you know that it is virtually certain that he will suffer severe injuries, then in law you indirectly intend to injure the baby. Once again, constructive liability "rears her hideous head." Obliquely intending to inflict g.b.h. without lawful excuse is sufficient *mens rea* for murder, if the victim dies as a result of his injuries.

If the jury find on the evidence that D believed that if he threw the baby across the room, that it was virtually certain that it would suffer grievous bodily harm, the jury must "find" that D indirectly intended to kill the baby. The rationale for the doctrine is that the defendant's foresight of such a virtually certain consequence (g.b.h.) means that he as good as intended to kill the victim. Combining constructive intention with oblique intention seems to go too far. But that is the law. Perhaps, as far as murder involving a mandatory life sentence is concerned, oblique intention should be limited to cases involving foresight of death. The Law Commission has made such a proposal.[60]

11–020   **Is not oblique intention merely extreme subjective recklessness?**[61]   One specific argument in favour of recognizing oblique intention is that sometimes it is only a verbal question whether one regards the intention as direct or oblique. D helps a friend to evade justice because the friend offers him payment. One can say that D intends to help his friend to escape (direct intention), his motive being to earn money (the motive being legally immaterial), or one can say that D intends to earn money, knowing that in doing so he is helping his friend to evade

---

[57] *R. v. Woollin* [1999] 1 A.C. 82 at 96-97.

[58] See also the discussion in Chap. 4 of this book.

[59] Glanville Williams, "The Mens Rea for Murder: Leave it Alone," (1989) 105 *L.Q.R.* 387–388.

[60] Law Commission, *Murder, Manslaughter and Infanticide*, Report 304, (London: H.M.S.O., 2006) at para. 9.5.

[61] See John Finnis, "Intention and Side-Effects," in R.G. Frey & Christopher W. Morris (eds.) *Liability and Responsibility: Essays in Law and Morals*, (Cambridge: Cambridge University Press, 1991), at 32 *et seq*. See also Kimberly K. Ferzan, "Beyond Intention," (2008) 29 *Cardozo L. Rev.* 1147.

justice (oblique intention). The facts are the same either way, and how one verbalizes them should make no difference. Similarly, if D smashes the glass table belonging to another (without lawful excuse) to get the sound effect of glass breaking for a short film he is making, he could not argue that he did not intend to break the glass. His motive for criminally damaging the property is legally immaterial. He does not want to destroy the glass table, but knows that he has to destroy it in order to achieve his end of getting the sound of broken glass.[62]

These cases could be said to involve what might be described as absolute certainties, but one cannot confine the notion of foresight of certainty to certainty in the most absolute sense. It is a question of human certainty, or virtual certainty, or practical certainty. This is still not the same as speaking in terms of probability. The virtual certainty test will not catch some nasty types, but the line has to be drawn somewhere. That there is a difference in formulations may be illustrated by considering a case where a person places a bomb in a store and gives the people inside two or three minutes to get out before the bomb explodes. Suppose that, for some reason, one of these people fails to escape and is killed. (A deaf and arthritic person, who did not notice what was happening until too late.) The oblique intention doctrine would only make the bomber guilty of murder if he believed that someone was virtually certain to be killed, which would not be easy for the jury to find in these circumstances.

The *Hyam v. D.P.P.*[63] requirement of knowledge of high probability might be easier for the jury to find, if the bomber gave the public a "fair" chance to escape. Such a finding would mean that the bomber would only be guilty of manslaughter. The high probability might be difficult to satisfy as well, if high probability means *much more* likely than not. A similar problem would arise if the bomber's bomb had killed a bomb disposal expert.

We need not enter further into the difficulties of quantifying risk-taking for the purpose of murder. We are left with three rough distinctions: **11–021**

- Absolute certainties which are covered by the normal doctrine of intention, because one effect is intended to achieve the other effect (*X kills D in self-defence*). Such cases are best conceptualized as cases of "double-effect." D is motivated by self-defence, but intends to kill. He also intends the double-effect of avoiding being killed. (Both effects are aimed for.)
- Foresight of virtually certain consequences (*D throws a baby across the room to let off steam, but foresees its death as a virtual certainty*). This is not a case of "double-effect" as the baby's death is not aimed for to achieve the end of anger release. Instead, the act of throwing *per se* is meant to allow D to vent his anger. The baby's death is an unwanted (but foreseen as a virtually certain) side-effect of the act of anger release: "the throwing." *Per contra*, when one kills in self-defence it would be odd to say that she

---

[62] "Thus if a man struck a glass violently with a hammer, knowing that the blow would break it, he would be said to have broken the glass intentionally (though not, perhaps, to have intentionally broken the glass), even if he merely wanted the noise of the hammer making contact with the glass to attract attention." H.L.A. Hart, *Punishment and Responsibility: Essays in the Philosophy of Law*, (Oxford: Clarendon Press, 1968) at 120.

[63] [1975] A.C. 55.

does not want to kill, because she does. The difference is that she does it for a lawful reason. The fact that she would not kill if she had other options does not mean that she does not intend to kill.

- Risk-taking involving probabilities (*D puts a bomb in a public place foreseeing that it is (highly) probable that the bomb disposal expert might not be able to safely defuse his bomb*). In statistics, probability means the whole range of possibility between impossibility and certainty (in mathematical terms, between nought and one). "Chance" is a non-technical synonym for probability, as also is "risk" (the chance of an untoward fact or event). The degree of probability is expressed either as a vulgar fraction or as a decimal fraction. So one can speak of a probability of 1/100 or .01, meaning that it is a chance of one in a hundred, or that the odds are 99 to one against. "Probability" means a substantial chance, but no one knows whether this means a probability of at least .34, .51, (more likely than not), .67, .80 or what. It could mean something less than those figures. Probability, however, has no memory.

How do we distinguish Mrs. Hyam from Mr. Woollin? The core difference is that one is less culpable than the other. The oblique intender does not merely run a risk. Rather, he chooses to do an act believing that the unwanted consequence is virtually certain to follow. Chance is not the issue, as the oblique intender's moral culpability is based on what he believed would happen if he acted as he did. The oblique intention doctrine poses no problems to the extent that it is used to impute intention to those who believe that it is virtually certain that they will kill if they do X. If D obliquely intends to kill V by pushing him over a cliff, then what is wrong with holding him liable for attempted murder, if by pure chance his victim survives the fall? Hence, D's moral culpability does not depend on V being killed or on the likelihood of V being killed, but rather it hinges on his belief that it is virtually certain that the victim will be killed. In most cases what the defendant believes will happen, will in fact happen, but it does not follow that he is less culpable if by pure chance it does not happen.

The defendant might believe that if he pushes a person from the tenth floor of a building that he will die. If an experimenter were to drop 10,000 people from the same floor he would probably find that all of them would be killed. The oblique intender's culpability does not depend on factual or empirical certainties. The jury should merely decide whether the defendant was culpable: that is, acted with oblique intention. The issue is whether the consequence was *in fact* virtually certain to follow the particular act. All the jury have to do is determine whether the defendant believed it was a virtual certainty. If D believes that he can kill his mistress by pushing her off the roof of his single story garage, and he kills her by doing so, it should not matter that many others would not die from such a short fall, or that many others would have believed it impossible to kill someone by pushing them from a single story garage. The defendant was culpable and thus should be liable for his culpable act of killing.

The problem with the current law is that the prosecution has to prove that the consequence was a virtual certainty as a matter of fact. In addition, it has to prove that the defendant believed or foresaw that such a consequence was a virtual certainty. But as we have just seen, whether or not the consequence was in fact a virtual certainty seems to have little to no bearing on the defendant's culpability. The focus should be on the defendant's subjective belief.[64] This would save the jury estimating the factual certainty of consequence X following act Y.

Is a finding of oblique intention enough to ground a conviction? You will recall, that it was explained in Chapter 4 that the oblique intention doctrine is a substantive criminal law doctrine. Hence, a finding of oblique intention means the jury must return a guilty verdict.

11–022

If the jury find that D foresaw the consequence was a virtual certainty, it would be nonsensical to treat their finding of indirect intention as something from which they could (at their own discretion) infer direct intention.[65] How can the jury infer that the defendant directly intended to kill, if they have concluded that he only indirectly intended to kill? If the oblique intention doctrine is treated as a mere rule of evidence, then it is adds nothing. The jury can already infer that the defendant intended something even though he claims he did not intend it. The jury need not believe the defendant's tales. In *R. v. Woollin* the evidence clearly suggested that Woollin did not intend to kill the baby. Therefore, a finding that he did because he indirectly (or obliquely intended to kill the baby) would be absurd. The jury are not required to infer the required mental state from a different and lower mental state. Rather, they are to ask whether on the evidence the lower mental state is available because the higher one is not. If the higher one is made out on the facts, then there is no need to look any further. Of course, a finding of oblique intention might allow the jury to infer that D is lying when he claims he did not directly intend to kill.

If the doctrine were merely one of evidence, a sympathetic jury could let certain offenders walk free, even though they obliquely intended to kill. The better view is that the oblique intention doctrine is a substantive criminal law doctrine.[66] And since it is a substantive criminal law doctrine a finding of oblique intention means that the jury *must* return a guilty verdict. On an ordinary charge of murder where there is clear evidence of intention to cause death or grievous bodily harm, the trial judge is well advised not to direct the jury on oblique intention, since this would complicate the issues unnecessarily.

---

[64] See Law Commission, *Murder, Manslaughter and Infanticide*, Report 304, (London: H.M.S.O., 2006) at para. 3.27, where it is recommended that such a formulation be put into statutory form.

[65] Cf. *R. v. Matthews* [2003] 2 Cr. App. R. 30, where it was said, "If what was required was an appreciation of virtual certainty of death, and not some lesser foresight of merely probable consequences, there was very little to choose between a rule of evidence and one of substantive law."

[66] It has been treated as such in other jurisdictions. See *Mata-Medina v. People*, 71 P.3d 973 at 978 (2008), where it was held that: "to constitute murder in the second degree the actor must 'knowingly cause the death of a person.' (Colorado Penal Code, § 18-3-103(1)). A person acts knowingly when 'he is *aware* that his conduct is *practically certain* to cause the result.' (Colorado Penal Code § 18-1-501(6)). Thus there are two elements of second-degree murder, '[f]irst, the death must have been more than merely a probable result of the defendant's actions. Second, the defendant must have been aware of the circumstances that made death practically certain.' ... The first element is objective; the second is subjective." As noted above, the objective or empirical estimate of whether or not the consequence was a certainty seems irrelevant if D believed it was a certainty, and if it in fact has resulted in a death. It would be better to have a one prong subjective test, as this would keep the focus on the defendant's culpability.

11.5. TRANSFERRED INTENTION

11–023 The doctrine of transferred intention applies in murder, an early example being *Agnes Gore's Case*.[67] Agnes Gore was a murderess, but not in the way that you might think. She mixed ratsbane with her husband's medicine. He took it, and, his condition suddenly worsening, the medicine was suspected. The apothecary who had compounded it, to prove there was nothing wrong with it, swallowed some himself and soon after died. Agnes was convicted of the murder of the apothecary, because "the law conjoins the murderous intention with the event which thence ensured."

A slightly different form of transferred intention occurred in the case of *Sanders and Archer*,[68] dramatically reported by Foster as follows:

> "Saunders with intention to destroy his wife, by the advice of one Archer mixed poison in a roasted apple, and gave it to her to eat. She having eaten a small part of it gave the remainder to their child. Saunders at this dreadful moment made a faint attempt to save the child; but conscious of the horrid purpose of his own heart, and unwilling to make his wife a witness of it, desisted; and stood by and saw the infant he dearly loved eat the poison, of which it soon afterwards died. It was ruled without much difficulty that Saunders was guilty of murder of the child."

Saunders would have been just as guilty if his wife had passed the poisoned apple to the child in Saunders' absence and without his knowledge. But if the wife had come to know that the apple was poisoned, and had passed it to the child in his absence with the object of causing Saunders to feel remorse for the child's death, Saunders would not have been guilty of murder of the child, because the effective cause of the child's death would then have been the conscious act of the wife. (Saunders would, however, have remained guilty of attempting to murder his wife.) The responsibility of Archer on the above facts will be discussed when we come to the subject of complicity.[69]

11–024 **If D shoots to kill V's dog but hits V instead, is he liable for murder?** No, because he does not intend to kill a person.

11–025 **Does this mean that if D stabs pregnant V with an intent to kill her, that he does not commit murder if he destroys her unborn foetus?** The short answer is yes.[70] The transferred intention doctrine cannot be invoked, because that applies only when the defendant intends a particular crime, and commits the *actus reus* of that crime (though with a different victim). If the defendant intends to kill the mother and as a consequence brings about an abortion by killing her unborn foetus, he does not murder the foetus because it cannot be a victim of murder. In law a foetus is not regarded as a person.

---

[67] (1611) 9 Co. Rep. 81.

[68] Sir Michael Foster, *Crown Law*, (London: Printed by W. Strahan and M. Woodfall, 1776) at 371.

[69] Archer was acquitted because Saunders, when he knowingly allowed the plan to miscarry, put the result outside the common purpose. This did not affect Saunders's liability as perpetrator on the basis of transferred intention.

[70] *Attorney-General's Reference (No. 3 of 1994)* [1998] A.C. 245.

Once a foetus is "born alive," however, it becomes a person. One view is that the *unborn foetus* and the corresponding *born alive infant* are the same person.[71] If the "born alive" rule means that the foetus can be deemed to have been a person from the time it was stabbed, on the basis that it is a person (born alive) when the stabbing causes its death, then it is only necessary to transfer D's intent to kill the pregnant mother to the born alive infant. That is, from one person to another person. If we accept this view D could be liable for murder if he stabs V and this causes her "born alive" infant to die.[72] (For a fuller discussion of this theory, see Chapter 13.) Nevertheless, the Lords have held that it cannot be murder,[73] because that would involve transferring D's intent to kill the pregnant mother to the foetus and then from the foetus to the born alive infant. This would involve a transfer from a person (the pregnant mother), to a non-person (the foetus) and then back to a person (the born alive infant). As we just saw, this would not be the case if the corresponding foetus and born alive infant were deemed to be one continuous person, which is what the "born alive" rule seems to provide for.

If he intended merely to destroy the foetus he could be charged with some other offence such as abortion,[74] but in abortion there is no offence against the person.[75]

11.6. KILLING A SUPPOSED CORPSE

Murder is committed by an act (or omission) causing death, and the question arises whether the mental element must exist at the time of the act of causing death. **11–026**

Suppose that D inflicts a series of knife wounds on V, intending to kill him. The medical evidence is that the last stab killed V, but at that time D was pretty sure that V was already dead, and delivered this last stab just to make sure. Clearly, he is guilty of murder, because when he delivered the last blow he had a conditional intention to kill—an intention to kill if the victim should still be alive.

Yes, but suppose that, at the time of the act that killed, D fully believed V to be dead. D stabbed V intending to kill him. Believing him to be dead, D threw him over the cliff, or into a river, in order to conceal his crime; and the medical evidence is that V died from the fall or from drowning. Is this murder? Although the authorities are not as precise as might have been wished, it can be said with some assurance that D's conduct will be viewed as a whole, and he will be guilty of murder. **11–027**

---

[71] The Supreme Court of Conneticut has held that the "born alive" rule can be applied in tandem with the "transferred malice" doctrine to ground a murder conviction. See *State v. Courchesne*, 296 Conn. 622 at 678–679 (2010). The Court's judgment runs for nearly 200 pages and thoroughly examines the common law position.

[72] *Trespasse and Assault v. Sims* (1600) 75 E.R. 1075; *R. v. West* (1848) 2 Car. & K. 784 at 786, 788; *R. v. Kwok Chak Ming* [1963] H.K.L.R. 226; *State v. Courchesne*, 296 Conn. 622 at 678–679 (2010).

[73] *Attorney-General's Reference (No. 3 of 1994)* [1998] A.C. 245.

[74] See section 58 of the *Offences against the Person Act 1861* (abortion); and section 1 of the *Infant Life (Preservation) Act 1929* (child destruction).

[75] At least to the extent it concerns the unborn foetus.

The abstract principle is cumbersome to formulate, but it would run something like this. A person may commit two acts against another. (1) An unlawful act reducing him to a state in which the actor mistakenly believes him to be dead; this is such that, if the victim had died as an immediate result, it would have been murder. (2) An act of disposal of the victim's body, which brings about the victim's death; this act is such that, if the actor had known that the victim was alive when he did it, the actor would have been guilty of murder. When these conditions are fulfilled, the actor is guilty of murder.[76]

11–028 **Isn't there a problem? Normally, the defendant's act and his *mens rea* co-exist in point of time. In the present situation, D had the *mens rea* before he committed the act that immediately caused the death (throwing the body over the cliff); but when he committed this act he had no *mens rea* in respect of killing. In the ordinary case a person who thinks he is dealing with a corpse and who destroys it would not be guilty of murder even though the supposed corpse was alive, because there would be no intent to kill. Why should his prior and abortive intent to kill make any difference?** The courts have rejected such an argument. The justification for not insisting on concurrence in these types of special cases is based in policy. In many of these cases, D had an intent to kill, caused the condition which put V in an unconscious and helpless state and thought he had killed. Consequently, the temporally intertwined act of disposal is not sufficiently removed to warrant a strict application of the concurrence principle. When D causes the condition which leaves V unconscious and helpless, he causes V to be in a position where she could not respond or act to save herself. Her death eventually results from his act of finishing off or concealing his putative murder.[77]

---

[76] Or manslaughter, depending on the facts, *R. v. Le Brun* [1992] Q.B. 61 at 66. A similar principle would apply where (1) above is an unlawful omission.

[77] *R. v. Church* [1966] 1 Q.B. 59; see also, *R. v. Moore* [1975] Crim. L.R. 229; *R v Hallett* [1969] S.A.S.R. 141.

CHAPTER 12

INVOLUNTARY MANSLAUGHTER

"Crime is regarded as somewhat down-market by civil lawyers. Bankers and property developers are thought to be more desirable customers than indecent assaulters or petty thieves, or at least create a better impression when they are sitting around in the waiting-room. And yet, while civil law is nearly always about money, criminal law is concerned with more vital matters, such as life, love and liberty of the subject."

John Mortimer[1]

12.1.　THE KINDS OF MANSLAUGHTER

Death is not always the worst evil that can befall us, but we mostly regard it as so. **12–001** For this reason, various kinds of unlawful killing short of murder are grouped under what is the serious crime of manslaughter.

The ingredients of manslaughter are supposed to be the same as that of murder, except that the requirements of oblique intention or actual intention as to killing are omitted. In fact the two crimes differ in a further respect, that certain exceptions from murder (loss of self control,[2] diminished responsibility,[3] suicide pacts[4]), not stated in the traditional definition, reduce the offence to manslaughter. Manslaughter falls into two categories:

1.　Voluntary manslaughter occurs when:
　　i.　D with the requisite fault for murder kills V, but successfully raises the partial defence of "loss of control."[5]
　　ii.　D with the requisite fault for murder kills V, but successfully raises the partial defence of "diminished responsibility."[6]
　　iii.　Where V1 and V2 agree to take their lives as a part of a suicide pact, section 4 of the *Homicide Act 1957* provides: "(1) It shall be manslaughter, and shall not be murder, for a person acting in pursuance of a suicide pact between him and another to kill the other or be a party to the other being killed by a third person."

---

[1] *Clinging to the Wreckage: A Part of Life*, (London: Weidenfeld & Nicolson, 1982).
[2] See Chap. 22 *infra*.
[3] See Chap. 28 *infra*.
[4] See 23.13.
[5] Sections 54 and 55 of the *Coroners and Justice Act 2009*.
[6] See section 52 of the *Coroners and Justice Act 2009*.

"Loss of control," "diminished responsibility," and "suicide pact" are legal defences that can be a raised against a murder charge, but do not necessarily allow the defendant to go free. If the jury accept one or more of the defences they are directed to return a verdict of manslaughter (which, as usual, is regarded as an included offence on a charge of murder). This is the form known as voluntary manslaughter, because the defendant intended to kill or otherwise had the mental element for murder. The judge has the usual wide discretion in sentencing for manslaughter. Since voluntary manslaughter depends on the defendant successfully raising a defence, it will not be the subject of this chapter. The partial defences of loss of control and diminished responsibility are discussed in Part IV of this book.

2. Involuntary manslaughter covers:
   i. Gross negligence manslaughter;
   ii. Constructive manslaughter;
   iii. Subjective recklessness manslaughter; and
   iv. Corporate manslaughter.[7]

Our focus in this chapter will be on gross negligence manslaughter and constructive manslaughter. Corporate manslaughter is discussed independently, as it involves the issue of collective responsibility. The theory of collective responsibility is set out in the final chapter of this book, as is the issue of collective (or corporate/entity) liability for manslaughter.

12–002 Manslaughter is a built-in alternative to a charge of murder. All its essentials are supposed to be comprised in the charge of murder, so the jury may on the indictment for murder convict of manslaughter as an included offence. The theory is false, since it is not enough to convict of manslaughter merely to show that all the essentials of murder other than an intention to kill are present; but the result of the false theory is convenient, and it is confirmed by statute.[8]

If the jury return the lenient verdict, the judge in sentencing is bound to give effect to the view of the facts implicit in it. He must assume that the facts were not such as to justify a verdict of murder, even though in his opinion they were. In the ordinary course of events this means that the judge must give a significantly reduced sentence. However, in the specific case of diminished responsibility a sentence of life imprisonment may be justified. The judge may sentence the defendant to life imprisonment for manslaughter (which would be the same as the sentence for murder) on the ground of the defendant's mental instability. The latter sentence cannot be justified by pointing to purely punitive or deterrent considerations.[9]

---

[7] See Chap. 38 *infra*.

[8] See also section 6(2) of the *Criminal Law Act 1967*. The judge was said in *D.P.P. v. Daley* [1980] A.C. 237 to be under a duty to direct the jury on manslaughter (so as to leave them with the choice) if there is evidence to make the propriety of a murder conviction at all doubtful. Previously the judge had an option except in cases of provocation, and the Privy Council does not seem to have been aware that it was requiring a change of practice; but the change is beneficial.

[9] Dennis J. Baker, "Punishment without a Crime: Is Preventive Detention Reconcilable with Justice," (2009) 34 *Austl. J. Leg. Phil.* 120.

Must the judge tell the jury about the merciful option open to them? He 12–003
need not; and he may even direct the jury positively that it is a case of murder or
nothing at all, by way of trying to stop them from returning a lenient compromise
verdict.[10] In the grim old phrase, he may make it "neck or nothing." But a judge
who acts in this way must be very sure that there are no facts that might justify
the jury returning a verdict of manslaughter.[11] In particular, where evidence
indicates a possible case of "loss of control," or "diminished responsibility" the
judge must direct the jury on the possibility of a manslaughter verdict even when
the defence has not been set up.[12] In *R. v. Coutts*,[13] the House of Lords held:
"[T]he jury should be directed on manslaughter whenever ... it arises as a viable
issue on a reasonable view of the evidence, a failure by the judge to give the
direction will amount to a material misdirection in law."

Assuming that the case is not one of murder, what precisely must be proved 12–004
to make the killing amount to manslaughter? The law-books recognize two
forms of manslaughter, voluntary and involuntary, though the verdict of the jury
does not distinguish between them.

Voluntary manslaughter means an act of murder reduced to manslaughter on
account of the mitigating circumstances already mentioned (loss of control;
diminished responsibility; suicide pact).

Involuntary manslaughter, the subject of this chapter, means the form in which
there is (or need be) no intention (*voluntas*)[14] to kill or do grievous bodily harm (a
strange meaning of "involuntary"). There are two subspecies, both of them, as
will be painfully seen in this chapter, exhibiting the common law at its worst. We
can give them uncontroversial names, since the courts have settled clearly what
fault element is involved; in this book the first will be called "gross negligence
manslaughter," though the concept of "gross negligence" will give us trouble.
The other subspecies is constructive manslaughter.

12.2. GROSS NEGLIGENCE MANSLAUGHTER: POSITIVE ACTS

This form of manslaughter requires the prosecution to prove that the defendant 12–005
caused the death in question by an act or omission, amounting in either case to
what is called objective recklessness (in a special sense) in breach of a duty of
care.

---

[10] *Contra, R. v. Nuttall* [1968] Crim. L.R. 173, which is out of line with other authorities.

[11] *Mensah v. The King* [1946] A.C. 83; *Rumping v. D.P.P.* [1964] A.C. 814 at 820–822; *R. v. Singh* [1962] A.C. 188 at 195. And if the jury indicate that *they* see facts (or fail to see facts) so that manslaughter becomes a live issue, the judge must at that stage give a direction upon it. See *R. v. Weston* [1966] Crim. L.R. 512. It was said by the High Court of Australia in *Beavan v. The Queen* (1954) 92 C.L.R. 660 at 662 that if the jury specifically ask whether they may bring in a manslaughter conviction, the judge must tell them that they can, but he may add an expression of his own opinion that on no view of the evidence that the jury may reasonably take can it be manslaughter. However, the tendency of the English cases is that the judge may tell the jury that they cannot bring in manslaughter.

[12] Cf. *R. v. Greenwood* (1857) 7 Cox C.C. 404; *R. v. Taylor* (1857) 169 E.R. 1011.

[13] [2006] 1 W.L.R. 2154 at 2189.

[14] That is, wish, intend.

One is always under a duty of care not to cause the death of another by positive acts of negligence, so that nothing turns in practice on the requirement of duty in cases of this sort.[15] A criminal even has a duty not to risk the life of his fellow criminal(s) while carrying out a dangerous criminal enterprise with him.[16] The maxim *ex turpi causa non oritur actio*[17] means that the "civil law" of negligence does not normally recognize the "relationship between those involved in a criminal enterprise as giving rise to a duty of care owed by one participant to another." It is true that the general "principles of the law of negligence apply to ascertain whether or not the defendant has been in breach of a duty of care towards the victim who has died,"[18] but that does not mean that technical rules from the civil law can be used to usurp the criminal law. If there is any conflict, the criminal law takes precedence. Thus, a person has a duty not to negligently cause the death to his accomplice(s) during the course of a joint criminal enterprise:

"Why is there, therefore, this distinction between the approach of the civil law and the criminal law? The answer is that the very same public policy that causes the civil courts to refuse the claim points in a quite different direction in considering a criminal offence. The criminal law has as its function the protection of citizens and gives effect to the state's duty to try those who have deprived citizens of their rights of life, limb or property. It may very well step in at the precise moment when civil courts withdraw because of this very different function. The withdrawal of a civil remedy has nothing to do with whether as a matter of public policy the criminal law applies. The criminal law should not be disapplied just because the civil law is disapplied. It has its own public policy aim which may require a different approach to the involvement of the law."[19]

The duty of care does, however, call for consideration in connection with manslaughter by omission. The problem of causation has been discussed in Chapter 8. This leaves us at this place to discuss the fault element.

During the second half of the 19th century it came to be limited to gross negligence. The classic definition is in *R. v. Bateman*,[20] where the Court of Criminal Appeal said:

"The foregoing observations deal with civil liability. To support an indictment for manslaughter the prosecution must prove ... that the negligence or incompetence of the accused went beyond a mere matter of compensation and showed such disregard for the life and safety of others as to amount to a crime against the State and conduct deserving punishment."

12–006 **Isn't that a circular definition?** It is true that the definition serves to tell us little more than that the negligence necessary for the crime of manslaughter must be criminal—a fact that we knew to start with. It fails to express whether the defendant must have appreciated the risk, though perhaps this requirement is to be understood from the reference to a "disregard for the life and safety of others;" one cannot disregard a risk of which one is unaware. A minor objection is that the

---

[15] *R. v. Doherty* (1887) 16 Cox C.C. 306; *R. v. Willoughby* [2005] 1 W.L.R. 1880; *R. v. Litchfield* [1998] Crim. L.R. 507.

[16] *R. v. Willoughby* [2005] 1 W.L.R. 1880.

[17] From a dishonourable cause an action does not arise.

[18] *R. v. Adomako* [1995] 1 A.C. 171 at 187 *per* Lord MacKay.

[19] *R. v. Wacker* [2003] Q.B. 1207 at 1216–1217.

[20] (1927) 19 Cr. App. R. 8 at 13.

concluding words mistakenly suggest that it is for the jury to consider whether punishment is to be awarded. That is not their function. A conviction for manslaughter may be legally justified even though the judge afterwards grants a discharge.[21]

Whatever may be thought of the definition in *R. v. Bateman*, it has been frequently approved since. Not all judges have followed it exactly. Some have merely told the jury that the negligence must be of a high degree, or must be "gross negligence" or "criminal negligence." Others have expressly required what they refer to as recklessness (without explaining it), or some kind of mental element. During the 1930s the view emerged that "recklessness" was a good word to use in explaining the fault required, but the cases favouring this word were most unsatisfactory. Sometimes the jury were instructed in terms of recklessness but were left to make what they could of it. ("After all," said Lord Widgery C.J., "recklessness is a perfectly simple English word. Its meaning is well known and it is in common use.")[22] Sometimes they were specifically told that they must find a mental element of recklessness, inadvertence not being enough. Sometimes the fault element was described in words so chosen that the reader or hearer was left in doubt whether it was objective or subjective, part of the judge's description fitting the one view, part the other—the judge apparently being unconscious that he was floundering between alternatives.[23]

The decision of *R. v. Lamb*,[24] the revolver case, may be offered as a further example of the imprecision of the judges' language in the earlier cases. Much of the discussion on appeal in this case concerned the law of constructive manslaughter, which will be considered presently, but some remarks were made on manslaughter by negligence. The court laid it down generally that *mens rea* is now an essential ingredient in manslaughter, and proceeded:

> "When the gravamen of a charge is criminal negligence—often referred to as recklessness—of an accused, the jury have to consider among other matters the state of his mind, and that includes the question of whether or not he thought that that which he was doing was safe. In the present case it would, of course, have been fully open to a jury, if properly directed, to find the defendant guilty because they considered his view as to there being no danger was formed in a criminally negligent way. But he was entitled to a direction that the jury should take into account the fact that he had undisputedly formed that view and that there was expert evidence as to this being an understandable view." (The direction being at fault, the conviction was quashed.)

What is one to make of this? The initial reference to *mens rea* and to the consideration of what the defendant thought suggests that the court had a subjective test in mind. Then this seems to be rejected, because we are told that the defendant can be guilty of negligent manslaughter although he thought that what he was doing was safe. So why were the jury bidden to enquire into the latter question? Well, the direction proceeds, they should take it into account.

12–007

---

[21] To avoid the second objection, it was proposed by the Criminal Court of Appeal in *Andrews v. D.P.P.* [1937] A.C. 576 that the concluding words should be altered to: "and to call for a conviction."

[22] *R. v. Cato* [1976] 1 W.L.R. 110 at 119C.

[23] The cases are collected in Glanville Williams, *Textbook of Criminal Law*, (London: Stevens & Sons, 1st edn. 1978) at 225 *et seq.*, and the speech of Lord Atkin in *Andrews v. D.P.P.* [1937] A.C. 576 at 583.

[24] [1967] 2 Q.B. 981 at 990.

They take it into account, but it does not countervail evidence of negligence. So for what purpose is it to be taken into account? Some other decisions are more indulgent, at least in words.

Consider *R. v. Cato*,[25] where a drug addict died as a result of an injection of heroin given to him by the defendant. The judge directed the jury that it was manslaughter to cause death by an act that was "grossly negligent or, in other words, reckless"[26]—on its face, a similar equation to that propounded in *R. v. Lamb*. A conviction of manslaughter was upheld on appeal. One might have thought that the judge meant to convey to the jury that gross negligence was sufficient. But the Court of Appeal seemed to understand the direction as meaning the opposite: that the gross negligence required had to involve subjective recklessness, so that it had to be shown that the defendant knew that injecting heroin could give rise to death or grievous bodily harm. The defendant in giving evidence had said that he had no idea that the injection could cause death or serious bodily harm, and on this the court commented that "of course in deciding whether the appellant had himself acted recklessly one would have to have regard to the fact, if it was accepted, that he did not know about the potentiality of the drug." Apparently the view of the court was that the jury had had their minds directed to the issue, and were free to find, notwithstanding the defendant's denial, that he was aware of the danger specified.

This is a very casual treatment of the matter. The heroin had been produced by the deceased himself, who had made up the syringe, and in these circumstances it is difficult to see how the defendant was reckless as to any special danger (unless a reasonable person[27] would have foreseen an overdose as a real possibility), other than the danger of producing addiction. It is little use having a rule of law requiring a mental state if the jury are allowed to convict without any evidence of that state.

12–008 The theoretical law is one thing, practical realities another. Generally, a person who makes an honest mistake, who has not clouded his own judgment by taking drugs, and who has not undertaken an obviously risky course of conduct, is pretty safe from a conviction of manslaughter: and it is not normally the practice even to bring a charge in these circumstances. But if the defendant has taken drugs (including alcohol) and has killed, he is likely to be charged and convicted, and may be severely punished. (See further the Chapter on intoxication.)

Previous practice has now been clarified by the decision in *R. v. Adomako*.[28] In that case the House of Lords made it clear that the fault required for gross negligence manslaughter is gross negligence. The negligence required has to involve gross negligence, so that it has to be shown that risk of death (the focus

---

[25] [1976] 1 W.L.R. 110.

[26] [1976] 1 W.L.R. 110 at 114, 115.

[27] As we are about to see, the test is now one of gross objective recklessness. *R. v. Adomako* [1995] 1 A.C. 171; *R. v. Morgan* [2007] EWCA Crim. 3313.

[28] [1995] 1 A.C. 171 *per* Lord Mackay at 187. Cf. the aberrant decision in *R. v. Seymour* [1983] 2 A.C. 493 where the Lords endorsed *R. v. Caldwell* [1982] A.C. 341 objective recklessness as the standard. For a fuller critique of *R. v. Seymour* see Glanville Williams, *Textbook of Criminal Law*, (London: Stevens & Sons, 1983) at 261. See also Glanville Williams, "Misadventures of Manslaughter," (1993) 143 *N.L.J.* 1413.

on negligence as to the consequence of death led to a narrowing in the law) would have been blatantly obvious to a reasonable person in the offender's position.

In *R. v. Adomako*, D, an anaesthetist, was responsible for doing the anaesthesia for an eye operation. Adomako was in charge of the patient during the latter part of the operation. The patient had been paralysed by the injection of the drug and an endotracheal tube had been inserted to enable the patient to breathe by mechanical means. During the course of the operation the endotracheal tube disconnected. Consequently, the supply of oxygen to the patient ceased and this caused the patient to die from cardiac arrest. The defendant failed to notice or remedy the disconnection. He was aware that something was wrong as an alarm sounded on the Dinamap machine, which was being used to monitor the patient's blood pressure. The expert witness attested that such an alarm would normally sound 4 minutes after a tube disconnection. When the alarm sounded D responded by checking the equipment and by administering atropine to raise the patient's pulse, but he failed to check the tube connection. The evidence showed that the tube had been disconnected for some 11 minutes. The defendant was convicted of gross negligence manslaughter, because he failed to fulfil his duty to take adequate steps to try to preserve the life of the patient. It was found that he had been grossly negligent in failing to preserve the patient's life, because a reasonable anaesthetist would have realized that the patient's life was in grave danger and would have checked the endotracheal tube connection immediately.

The House of Lords said gross negligence manslaughter is made out when the following conditions are satisfied:[29]

1. The defendant owed the victim a duty of care.
   a. Whether the defendant had a duty to try to prevent V's death is a question of law, therefore, it is question for the judge to determine.[30]
2. The defendant breached the duty he owed the victim.
   a. "Ordinary principles of the law of negligence apply to ascertain whether or not the defendant has been in breach of a duty of care towards the victim who has died."[31]
3. The breach of duty caused the death of the victim.
   a. In the case of "omissions" the death will be caused by external factors or by another's actions, but the defendant is held liable for failing to act to prevent those independent events or persons from causing V's death.[32]

---

[29] *R. v. Adomako* [1995] 1 A.C. 171 at 187 *per* Lord MacKay.

[30] "[T]he criminal trial decisions of fact are the exclusive responsibility of the jury and questions of law are for the judge. In principle therefore the existence, or otherwise, of a duty of care or, we would add, a duty to act, is a stark question of law: the question whether the facts establish the existence of the duty is for the jury." *R. v. Evans* [2009] 1 W.L.R. 1999 at 2009–2011. Cf. *R. v. Willoughby* [2005] 1 W.L.R. 1880. See also Jonathan Herring and Elaine Palser, "The Duty of Care in Gross Negligence Manslaughter" [2007] Crim. L.R. 24.

[31] *R. v. Adomako* [1995] 1 A.C. 171 at 187 *per* Lord MacKay.

[32] It was noted in Chap. 7 above, that an omission does not cause a result: instead liability hinges on D failing to take steps to try to un-cause what is already causing V's death. If V is dying from a heroin overdose, it is the drug overdose that is causing her to die. If D fails to call an ambulance, she fails to try to reverse what is already causing V to die. And if the court decides she had a duty to try to reverse

4.   If the duty has been breached and the breach has caused the victim's death (or the defendant breached his duty by unreasonably failing to take positive steps to un-cause or prevent certain events or persons from causing the victim's death), "the jury must go on to consider whether that breach of duty should be characterized as gross negligence ..."[33]

12–009   **Are you telling me that the jury decides whether negligently performing an operation should be a crime?**   No. There are several ways to restrict the jury's discretion.

Firstly, the *actus reus* of gross negligence manslaughter is an act or omission which causes[34] a particular result—that is, the *death* of a human being.[35] The corollary of this is that the gross negligence is required to be as to death. This is because the fault element in a crime should relate to the prohibited outcome, which in this case is death. In *R. v. Misra*[36] the Court of Appeal said:

> "In our judgment, where the issue of risk is engaged, *R. v. Adomako* demonstrates, and it is now clearly established, that it relates to the risk of death, and is not sufficiently satisfied by the risk of bodily injury or injury to health. In short, the offence requires gross negligence in circumstances where what is at risk is the life of an individual to whom the defendant owes a duty of care. As such it serves to protect his or her right to life."

The jury do not decide whether the *actus reus* of gross negligence manslaughter is an act or omission of causing the death of a human being, because this is the law. The jury merely decide whether the act or omission did in fact cause the victim's death. In the case of omissions, the jury has to decide that the defendant did in fact fail to prevent other events (or persons) from causing the victim's death when he had a duty to prevent them from doing so.

12–010   Secondly, the question of whether or not the defendant had a duty to preserve the victim's life is a question of law.

Thirdly, the fault element is gross negligence. Again, this is the law. The jury do not decide whether the offence requires subjective recklessness or objective recklessness, or whether it should be gross negligence or mere negligence. The law is clear: it requires gross negligence. "On proper analysis, therefore, the jury is not deciding whether the particular defendant ought to be convicted on some unprincipled basis. The question for the jury is not whether the defendant's negligence was gross, and whether, additionally, it was a crime, but whether his behaviour was grossly negligent and consequently criminal. This is not a question of law, but one of fact, for decision in the individual case."[37]

---

or "un-cause" what was already being caused by some external event (*i.e.* V's independent act of self-injection, V's refusal to eat, and so on), D will be liable. See for example, *R. v. Evans* [2009] 1 W.L.R. 1999.

[33] *R. v. Adomako* [1995] 1 A.C. 171 at 187 *per* Lord MacKay.

[34] Legal causation covers omissions, even though theoretically the omission does not directly cause the death. The law merely requires the prosecution to prove that if D had acted he *could* have made a difference.

[35] *R. v. Misra* [2005] 1 Cr. App. R. 328.

[36] [2005] 1 Cr. App. R. 328 at 344.

[37] *R. v. Misra* [2005] 1 Cr. App. R. 328 at 348.

If the expert or other evidence clearly demonstrates that the particular defendant acted in a way that no reasonable person with his skill and training would have acted, the jury will normally accept that the facts demonstrate that he was grossly negligent rather than merely negligent. The fault element does allow for some jury discretion, because the jury has to decide whether the facts were such that D objectively risked causing the death of V. The jury merely decide, given the facts, whether the risk of death would have been patently obvious to a reasonable person with D's skill and training.

It is true that the jury is left to make their own value-judgment based on the expert or other evidence. Where the rule of law involves the making of a value-judgment, the doctrine of *mens rea* does not generally apply in respect of the value-judgment. On an issue of negligence, for example, the question whether what the defendant did was "negligent" on the one hand or "reasonable" on the other involves a judgment of value made by the jury (or, of course, by magistrates), and the question of whether the defendant knew that he was being negligent is not controlling. Similarly a defence of self-defence is excluded if the jury think that the defendant reacted disproportionately, even though he considered that it was proportionate; and a defence of necessity is excluded if the jury think that what the defendant had in mind to do was not justified, even though he thought it was. However, where the judge is of the opinion that no reasonable jury would convict he should direct an acquittal. The instances just given are all value-judgements, which are intermediate between questions of fact and questions of law. As with questions of law, the defendant's failure to foresee the decision of the court does not excuse him.

Was Adomako grossly negligent in failing to notice the disconnection of the endotracheal tube? Would not a reasonable anaesthetist have realized that the patient's life was in grave danger? Yes. (And there was no doubt that a reasonable anaesthetist would have realized that the tube had detached, because an alarm sounded.) Well, then, would a reasonable anaesthetist have immediately checked the endotracheal tube connection? The expert evidence clearly suggested that a reasonable anaesthetist would have, because that is what anaesthetists are trained to do. The jury do not decide whether his conduct was criminal, but whether the evidence demonstrates that he in fact had the requisite fault for gross negligence manslaughter.   **12–011**

Would a reasonable person check for passers-by before firing a high powered rifle in Kensington Gardens?[38] Of course he would. A reasonable hunter/shooter would not even shoot in such a location; nor would a reasonable person. In other areas, the reasonableness (or grossness) of the defendant's failure to realize the risk to the victim's life will be determined by asking whether a reasonable professional with his training would have noticed that he was risking another's life. Would a reasonable air hostess or host check her or his aircraft's fuel supplies before takeoff? No, but a reasonable airline pilot would because his

---

[38] *R. v. Salmon* (1880–81) L.R. 6 Q.B.D. 79.

training requires him to check the fuel gauges before takeoff. Would a reasonable doctor check the dosage of the drug that he is about to inject into his patient?[39] He most certainly would.[40]

According to the theory of "gross negligence," a high degree of negligence—that is to say, a gross departure from the standard of care of the reasonable person—is required for a conviction of manslaughter, even though the defendant did not consciously take any abnormal risk. As a matter of law, a person only commits gross negligence manslaughter if a reasonable person would have foreseen that by acting as the defendant did, that it was highly probably that the victim would be killed.

12.3. HOMICIDE BY OMISSION: THE DUTY

12–012   Omissions resulting in death can be regarded as either murder[41] or manslaughter according to the fault element. In practice charges are rarely brought, and even if a charge of murder might technically succeed the indictment is almost invariably for manslaughter.

If we had a statutory duty to render assistance to specified classes of persons in immediate danger, as there is in many mainland European countries, it is to be expected that the penalty would be relatively light, reflecting the moral difference between killing and letting die. The prohibition of killing is the most urgent requirement of any society, whereas the intervention of the criminal law to promote the giving of assistance to those in distress is little needed for the general safety. Apart from the upbringing of children, it is only rarely that sick people are left without necessary assistance by their relatives and acquaintances, at least to the extent of informing the social service authorities of their plight.

Moreover, while those who deliberately kill commit an offence that is regarded as very wrong because of the offender's culpableness and the harmfulness of his actions, a person may neglect a child or invalid from his own inadequacy or selfishness rather than malevolence.[42] The harm is not less, but his moral culpableness is less. When a lodger (for example) falls ill, his landlord does not initiate his distress, but may merely fail to cope. Yet the courts, by extending the law of homicide to these omissions, have at the same time caused such offences to be treated with something of the same severity as other cases of homicide; and the severity evokes no protest from a legal profession that has become habituated to the rule.

---

[39] Cf. *R. v. Taylor* (1983) 9 A. Crim. R. 358; *R. v. Pace* (2008) 187 A. Crim. R. 205.

[40] Medical doctors are normal people with a vocation like any other. Medics do noble work, but are not above the criminal law. We would not excuse a flight engineer for failing to properly maintain a passenger airliner. Cf. *R. v. Johnson* [2009] 2 Cr. App. R. 28; *R. v. Yaqoob* [2005] EWCA Crim. 2169 and *R. v. Misra* [2005] 1 Cr. App. R. 21. *Contra*, Oliver Quick, "Medical Killing: Need for a Special Offence," in C. M.V. Clarkson and Sally Cunningham, (eds.) *Criminal Liability for Non-Aggressive Death*, (London: Ashgate Publishing, 2008).

[41] *R. v. Gibbins* (1919) 13 Cr. App. R. 134.

[42] See *R. v. Johnston* (2007) 173 A. Crim. R. 540.

The courts first perceived the duty to act for the helpless as arising from status. Where a person was under a duty imposed by the Poor Law[43] to maintain another, who was unable to look after himself, the neglect of that duty, where the other died in consequence, was manslaughter. The rule applied to husbands in respect of wives, and parents in respect of un-emancipated children.[44]

Did the poor law make it manslaughter to neglect wives and children? No. **12–013** It merely established financial responsibility for them. What the judges were really doing, of course, was to turn morality (or perhaps retributive instinct) into law;[45] but they were chary about admitting this, and preferred to find some kind of legal basis for the conclusion even though it was not logically compulsive.

Once the concept of a duty to save life became established as the basis of a conviction of manslaughter, it was possible to expand the list of duties. Thus a duty was also imposed as a result of contract, where an employer received an employee or apprentice into his house.[46] The employer was regarded as impliedly undertaking to provide the necessities of life if the other became incapacitated or was unable to withdraw from his control. In the second half of the 19th century the duty was extended to voluntary undertakings, as where the defendant had received a young child or a lunatic into his house.[47] The undertaking was expressly or impliedly given to a relative or the previous custodian of the person received.[48]

The next step was to extend the duty to cases where there was no promise to care for the person received. At this point we must notice an ambiguity in the word "undertaking." It may mean either a promise to do something or actually doing it. If the defendant has received a foundling (like Tom Jones in Fielding's novel)[49] there may be nobody to whom he makes a promise, yet he may still be said to have "undertaken" the child's care in the sense that he has actually taken its care upon himself. Such ambiguity can be used as a cover for an extension of the law, as may be seen in *R. v. Stone*.[50]

The two defendants were Stone, a man of 67, of "low average" intelligence, **12–014** partly deaf and almost blind, and his mistress Mrs. Dobinson, aged 43, who was ineffectual and somewhat inadequate. Stone's sister Fanny came to live with the couple as a lodger; she developed *anorexia nervosa* (a pathological condition

---

[43] For the history of the poor laws, see Dennis J. Baker, "Critical Evaluation of the Historical and Contemporary Justifications for Criminalising Begging," (2009) 73(3) *J. Crim. L.* 212 (and the works cited therein); Jacobus TenBroek, "California's Dual System of Family Law: Its Origin, Development, and Present Status," (1964) 16 *Stan. L. Rev.* 257.

[44] *R. v. Shephard* (1862) 9 Cox C.C. 123; *R. v. Russell* [1933] V.L.R. 59; *R. v. Bubb* (1859) 4 Cox C.C. 455.

[45] *R. v. O'Connor* [1908] 2 K.B. 26; *R. v. Senior* (1899) 1 Q.B. 283.

[46] See *R. v. Smith* (1837) 8 Car. & P. 153; *R. v. Smith* (1826) 172 E.R. 203; *R. v. Lowe* (1850) 3 Car. & K. 123. Cf. the more recent cases, *R. v. D.P.P. Ex p. Jones* [2000] I.R.L.R. 373; *R. v. Clothier* [2004] EWCA Crim. 2629.

[47] *R. v. Instan* [1893] 1 Q.B. 450. See also, *R. v. Bonnyman* (1943) 28 Cr. App. R. 131.

[48] On the history generally, see P. R. Glazebrook, "Criminal Omissions: The Duty Requirement in Offences against the Person," (1960) 76 *L.Q.R.* 386; George P. Fletcher, *Rethinking Criminal Law*, (Boston: Little, Brown, 1978) at 611–634.

[49] Henry Fielding, *The History of Tom Jones, a Foundling*, (London: Andrew Millar, 1749).

[50] [1977] Q.B. 354.

involving an extreme disinclination to eat), became very weak, and refused to reveal the name of her doctor (because she was afraid of being "put away"). The defendants tried without success to find her doctor, walking a very considerable distance to do so (they were unable to use a telephone). They also tried unsuccessfully to find another doctor, but took no other steps, not even mentioning the problem to a social worker who used to visit Stone's mentally retarded son at his house. Meanwhile Fanny had taken permanently to her bed, eating only "biscuits and pop." When she died, in dreadful degradation because of a lack of nursing care, the two defendants were convicted of manslaughter, and their conviction was affirmed on appeal. The old man received an exceedingly unkind prison sentence of 12 months, "if for nothing at least to mark public disapproval of such behaviour." Mrs. Dobinson received only a suspended sentence.

The Court of Appeal's idea of the function of a prison sentence is highly questionable, and in point of justice it insufficiently takes account of Stone's poor intelligence and his evident sense of hopelessness in the face of his sister's refusal to accept treatment. The fact is that the problem was too big for him. Important as it is to maintain the principle that helpless invalids must be cared for, no great public harm would follow if indulgence were shown to inadequate people and those who do not wish to force ministrations upon others; and Stone fell into both categories.[51] But what concerns us here is not the courts lack of human understanding but the principle upon which it found a duty of care to have been established. It was expressed in the following words:

> "[W]hether Fanny was a lodger or not she was a blood relation of the appellant Stone; she was occupying a room in his house; Mrs. Dobinson had undertaken the duty of trying to wash her, of taking such food to her as she required. ...[52] All these were matters which the jury were entitled to take into account when considering whether the necessary assumption of a duty to care for Fanny had been proved."[53]

The observation that Fanny was a blood relative of Stone was surely irrelevant. Stone would *not* have been under a duty towards his adult sister if she had not been under his roof, and, contrariwise, we may be sure that he *would* have been regarded as under a duty to Fanny, a person under his roof, even if she had not been his sister.[54]

12–015   **I still don't understand in what way the defendants assumed a duty to Fanny.**   The court found the language of assumption of duty in the precedents, so it sought somehow to apply it to the facts, but unconvincingly. If the idea that when you allow your sister (or, surely, anybody else) to come to live with you, you impliedly promise to give her necessary aid if she falls ill, that is merely a "construction of law," and the court might as well state the reality of the rule,

---

[51] Generally they were right not to do so.

[52] The words omitted from the quotation related to the defendants' knowledge of Fanny's condition and their failure to provide effective help. These matters are generally thought of as relating to the questions of breach of duty rather than to its existence. It is strange that the court thought that such facts could serve to prove an assumption of duty by the defendants.

[53] *R. v. Stone* [1977] Q.B. 354 at 361.

[54] See *R. v. Sinclair* (1998) 148 *N.L.J.* 1353. Cf. *R. v. Khan* [1998] Crim. L.R. 830.

which is that the occupier of the house must take reasonable steps in these circumstances. The rule, as a rule, would be a reasonable one.[55] (On that view of the law, however, it is strange that the judge should have left it to the jury to decide the question of whether Stone was under a duty. If the matter was settled by law, as a conclusion from the mere fact that Fanny was incapacitated in Stone's house, the jury could and should have been explicitly directed on the point.)

All right: a person must look after someone who falls ill in his house. But what about Mrs. Dobinson? It wasn't her house. She had "undertaken the duty" of trying to wash Fanny, in one meaning of the phrase, by reason of the fact that she did try to wash Fanny. But she undertook the duty only in the sense that she tried to perform a self-imposed duty, not in the sense that she promised Fanny or anyone else to perform it. Suppose that Mrs. Dobinson did nothing for Fanny after Fanny took to her bed; would she have been acquitted? The judgment of the Court of Appeal on this point leaves the law quite obscure. The court is evidently seeking some fact that can plausibly be pointed to as an "assumption of a duty to care for Fanny." As you imply, to find such an assumption in the fact that Mrs. Dobinson tried to wash her and took her food implies that if Mrs. Dobinson had made no such efforts she would not have assumed the duty. But it is contrary to common sense to say that a person who voluntarily begins to help another is by reason of that fact subjected to a duty to continue to help, even though by giving the help he did (to say the least) no damage to the other, in comparison with his position if no help had been provided. It looks very much as though the court has hit upon an equivocal phrase and is proceeding to draw inadmissible conclusions from it.

12–016

The only reasonable ground for holding that Mrs. Dobinson (who was not related to Fanny) owed a duty to her would have been to say that she was an adult member of a household in which Fanny became ill, and as such was under the same duty (whatever it might be) as the occupier, Stone. That would be an acceptable rule[56] (except that it is harsh to regard the breach of the duty as so

---

[55] It is a reasonable one to the extent that those who have a more than temporary relationship with the victim, should have a duty to summon help. Not to rescue but merely to summon help. However, any criminal liability for breaching such a duty should not result in a manslaughter conviction. Instead, a new offence of "criminal negligence" is required to criminalize those who fail to summon help when the victim is well known to them and has lived with them for more than mere weeks. Punishment should be limited to fines and very short jail terms, as there is no direct harm-doing. See Dennis J. Baker, *The Right Not to be Criminalized: Demarcating Criminal Law's Authority*, (Farnham: Ashgate Publishing, 2011) at Chap. 2.

[56] Extraordinary as it may seem, section 5(1)(d)(ii) of the *Domestic Violence, Crime and Victims Act 2004*, works in this way. See *R. v Owen* [2009] EWCA Crim. 2259 at para. 8 where it is noted that the offence covers a wide range of conduct and that: "At the lower end, where it is allowing rather than causing the death, it may be little more than the *lack of will* in a dominated weak person who *fails* to stand out for the sake of the child against what he or she knows is going on. What is certainly clear is that the essence of this offence in many cases will be a *culpable failure to protect the child from others* rather than the use of physical violence oneself. That failure may be more or less culpable according to the circumstances of the principal perpetrator and of the second defendant." See also *R. v. Ikram* [2009] 1 W.L.R. 1419; *R. v. Khan* [2009] 1 W.L.R. 2036. (However, the provision only requires the fellow resident of the household to report (or otherwise try to prevent), "unlawful acts" not "unlawful omissions," that pose a risk to the vulnerable victim.)

grave a crime as manslaughter).[57] There is no reason why the duty should be confined to the occupier. If a landlord suddenly falls ill in his house, why should not a duty be imposed on the lodger on his behalf, just as it is presumably imposed on the landlord on behalf of the lodger? But if Stone and Mrs. Dobinson were legally on a par, as being members of the household, it is difficult to justify the distinction made between them in the matter of punishment. Mrs. Dobinson would seem from the facts stated to have been the more competent of the two, and therefore more responsible.

Nevertheless, the decision in *R. v. Sinclair*[58] makes it clear that an occupier has no duty to summon help for a person who ends up in peril in his house.[59] *R. v. Stone* can be distinguished from *R. v. Sinclair*, because the victim was resident in Stone's house for a lengthy period of time. The victim in *R. v. Sinclair* was a casual visitor who had only spent a day in the occupier's house. In that case, Sinclair (a drug addict) and his friend Coleman went to Johnson's and Smith's flat at about 3:00 p.m. to buy methadone from Smith. Johnson and Smith were also drug addicts. Sinclair and Coleman each injected themselves at Johnson's flat with the methadone they had obtained. Within ten minutes of injecting Coleman became unconscious. He never regained consciousness and died the following morning. Not long after Coleman overdosed, Johnson prepared a saline solution and injected him in the hope of bringing him around. After Johnson did this the deceased coughed and spluttered but remained comatose. Johnson and Smith then left the flat to go to London to buy more drugs and did not return until about 5 hours later. During their absence, Sinclair remained in the flat with Coleman, but many others also visited the flat. The Court of Appeal said:

> "The evidence was that [Sinclair] was a close friend of the deceased for many years and the two had lived together *almost* as brothers. It was Sinclair who paid for and supplied the deceased with the first dose of methadone and helped him to obtain the second dose. He knew that the deceased was not an addict.[60] He remained with the deceased throughout the period of his unconsciousness and, for a substantial period, was the only person with him. In the light of this evidence, there was in our judgment material on which the jury properly directed, could have found that Sinclair owed the deceased a legal duty of care. The judge was therefore correct to leave Sinclair's case to the jury on this aspect."

12–017 Sinclair could not be said to have assumed a duty merely because he was Coleman's friend. Nor could the duty be based on the fact that Sinclair and Coleman had been housemates for 18 months; otherwise every undergraduate

---

[57] Dennis J. Baker, "Omissions Liability for Homicide Offenses: Reconciling *R. v. Kennedy* with *R. v. Evans*," (2010) 74 *J. Crim. L.* 310. See also *R. v. Finlay* [1996] 17 O.T.C. 237.

[58] (1998) 148 *N.L.J.* 1353.

[59] *R. v. Sinclair* (1998) 148 *N.L.J.* 1353, it was held that the occupier of premises where V overdosed on drugs owed no duty to summon help, even though he had attempted to resuscitate V. The courts said as far as Johnson (the occupier of the premises) "is concerned, there is no English authority in which a duty of care has been held to arise, over a period of hours, on the part of a medically unqualified stranger. ... But Johnson did not know the deceased. His only connection with him was that he had come to his house and there taken methadone and remained until he died. ... The fact that Johnson had prepared and administered to the deceased saline solutions does not, as it seems to us, demonstrate on his part a voluntary assumption of a legal duty of care rather than a desultory attempt to be of assistance."

[60] It is not clear how this makes a difference. If he had been an addict would that provide a defence? The evidence also showed that even though he was not an addict, he had used methadone before.

would have such a duty in relation to their housemates. Even if they were brothers, a person is not assumed to owe a duty of care to emancipated adults merely because they are related to them. The "time" argument is also very unconvincing: it is true that Sinclair was present for a few more hours than Johnson and Smith, but the latter were present at all material times. Coleman was clearly in peril before Johnson and Smith went to collect more methadone. Coupled with this, Johnson tried to resuscitate Coleman—Johnson prepared and administered a saline solution in an attempt to save him. To hold that Johnson did not voluntarily assume a duty of care merely because he was present and offered assistance over a six hour period as opposed to a twelve hour period is nonsensical. Sinclair might have been a housemate with Coleman for 18 months, but he had not cared for him for 18 months. In fact he had never cared for him before the night in question. Sinclair might have known Coleman for years, but he had not cared for him for years. He had not been caring for him before the overdose. Coleman was a perfectly healthy (autonomous) adult before his overdose. Sinclair's care lasted for hours, not days, weeks, months or years. The only thing Sinclair did that Johnson did not, was *pay* for drugs.

The decision in *R. v. Sinclair* is totally unsound. More recently, the Court of Appeal has steered clear of *R. v. Sinclair*. In *R. v. Evans*[61] the Court of Appeal tried a new approach. *R. v. Evans* was a case with similar facts. The core difference being that Evans supplied her sister with drugs. (Sinclair did not supply Coleman with the drugs; he merely paid for the drugs that Smith had supplied to Coleman.) In *R. v. Evans*, the Court of Appeal decided not to apply the "voluntarily assumption of a duty" doctrine. Instead, the court extended the doctrine laid down in *R. v. Miller*.[62]

The *R. v. Miller* doctrine (as far as manslaughter is concerned) is:

- D has a duty to take steps to try to preserve the life of V if D has directly created a situation that has put V's life at risk.

The *R. v. Evans* extension of the doctrine (as far as manslaughter is concerned) is:

- D has a duty to take steps to try to preserve V's life where V herself has done something to put her own life at risk, if D facilitated[63] V's self-harming actions.

---

[61] [2009] 1 W.L.R. 1999.

[62] [1983] 2 A.C. 161.

[63] Basically she is complicit in her sister's act of self-harming, but that act was not a criminal act. She cannot be held liable for complicity in manslaughter as there is no such thing as *self*-gross-negligence manslaughter. A further incongruity relates to the severe sentence in which she received. If Evans had deliberately assisted her sister to *kill herself* (that is, help her sister in circumstances where she knew her sister was intending to use the help to kill herself), she would get a lighter sentence under section 2 of the *Suicide Act 1961* as amended by section 59 of the *Coroners and Justice Act 2009*, than she would for gross negligence manslaughter. She would be more culpable if she had intentionally facilitated a deliberate act of suicide, than for accidentally assisting an act of unintended self-killing, but would most likely get a higher sentence for the latter.

12–018   The Court of Appeal's decision in *R. v. Evans* is not supported by the authorities, but it will be binding unless the Supreme Court decides otherwise. What concerns us here is the principle upon which the court in *R. v. Evans* found a duty of care to have been established. You will recall that Miller accidentally started a fire by dropping his lit cigarette. The court held that since his act of dropping the cigarette was the direct cause of the damage to the building, he had a duty to summon help. If Miller had provided X with a lighted cigarette, and X had accidentally started a fire with it, surely Miller would not have been liable for manslaughter if he stood by and watched the building burn. X would have the duty since X directly started the fire. Similarly, Evans merely supplied her sister. It was her sister who created the dangerous situation by *directly* injecting the drugs into her own arm. *R. v. Evans* is untenable: it is too much to hold someone liable for manslaughter for merely facilitating the victim's autonomous self-harming risk-taking. If Evans had directly injected the drugs into the victim, then that would be a different matter. There is no doubt that if a person supplies drugs to another and hangs around to watch her die that she should be punished, but not for manslaughter.

The legal development sketched in these pages leaves us with a tentative list of duties towards helpless persons based upon:

- The defendant's status (marriage[64] and parenthood[65]).
- The defendant voluntarily assuming a duty to care.[66]
- The defendant indirectly assisting V to create a dangerous situation for herself.[67]
- The defendant directly creating a dangerous situation for V.[68]

There are two bases for determining whether the defendant owed the victim a duty of care.

1)   The duty can be based on the defendant's *relationship* with the victim (*i.e.* parent/child; doctor/patient, and so on).

2)   The defendant's *conduct* prior to his omission may give rise to a duty (*i.e.* D took care of the victim over a period of months and thus voluntarily assumed a duty of care; or D accidently created a dangerous situation and thus now has a duty to take reasonable steps to try to prevent that danger from causing criminal harm).

In addition, the law still recognizes duties owed to others (not necessarily helpless persons) arising from contractual duties or in some cases from having given an undertaking to take safety precautions (a level-crossing gatekeeper);[69] but the authorities are not wholly consistent, and anyway prosecutions on this

---

[64] *R. v. Hood* [2004] 1 Cr. App. R. 73.
[65] Those *in loco parentis. R. v. Sheppard* [1981] A.C. 394.
[66] *R. v. Stone* [1977] Q.B. 354; *R. v. Sinclair* (1998) 148 *N.L.J.* 1353.
[67] *R. v. Evans* [2009] 1 W.L.R. 1999.
[68] *R. v. Miller* [1983] 2 A.C. 161.
[69] *R. v. Pittwood* (1902) 19 T.L.R. 37.

ground, for pure omission,[70] seem to be brought rarely, though one is always possible where gross negligence is involved. There may be duties of positive action outside these categories, but in view of the cautious attitude of prosecutors the question seems theoretical.

The law of manslaughter by omission remains one of the chief areas in which **12–019** English law rejects the principle *Nulla poena sine lege*.[71] Yet when the Criminal Law Revision Committee discussed the subject of offences against the person the majority were against having any statutory formulation of the duty to act, for the purpose of the law of murder and manslaughter, preferring to leave it to the courts to decide in each case whether there is a legal duty.[72] "The main reason for this view," said the Committee "is that the boundaries of the common law are not clearly marked and there would be difficulty in setting them out in statutory form." If the top lawyers in a Government committee find the law hard to state clearly, what hope have the Stones and Dobinsons of this world of ascertaining their legal position, in advance of prosecution, when they find themselves landed with a hunger-striking relative? Would the advice to Mrs. Dobinson be: on no account do anything for the invalid? The Committee not only expressed satisfaction with the present law of homicide but even recommended that the courts should be entrusted with a similar roving commission to create positive duties in respect of certain other offences falling short of homicide.

More recently, the Law Commission recommended that gross negligence manslaughter be defined as:[73]

"(1)   a person by his or her conduct causes the death of another;

(2)   a risk that his or her conduct will cause death ... would be obvious to a reasonable person in his or her position;

(3)   he or she is capable of appreciating that risk at the material time;[74] and

(4)   ... his or her conduct falls far below what can reasonably be expected of him or her in the circumstances ..."

---

[70] See *R. v. Johnson* [2009] 2 Cr. App. R. 28, where "a builder repairing a chimney caused the chimney to become blocked, with the result that the householder died from carbon monoxide poisoning." The case involves positive acts which endangered V; and omissions to correct the danger that V had been exposed.

[71] It is also open to the objection that the courts cannot create further situations (or declare further relationships such as roommate/roommate) where a duty will be imposed the breach of which will amount to manslaughter. See *R. v. Rimmington* [2006] 1 A.C. 459. Hence, the categories should be regarded as closed. Since the case is not covered by the *R. v. Stone* [1977] Q.B. 354 category, the court should have held that there was no duty of care. There is nothing wrong with applying *R. v. Miller* [1983] 2 A.C. 161 to a manslaughter case; but the court extended the *Miller* doctrine to cover mere facilitation, and then applied that new doctrine to manslaughter and in doing so created a new basis for a duty of care for manslaughter. Its creation of the new duty contravenes the ruling in *R. v. Rimmington* [2006] 1 A.C. 459, which holds that judges cannot extend common law offences to cover new forms of conduct. It is one thing to apply an existing doctrine to new facts, and another to apply it to conceptually different conduct.

[72] Criminal Law Revision Committee, *Offences Against the Person*, Fourteenth Report, (London: H.M.S.O., Cmnd. 7844, 1980) at para. 256.

[73] Law Commission, *Murder, Manslaughter and Infanticide*, Report 304, (London: H.M.S.O., 2006) at para. 3.60.

[74] Such a formulation seems better suited for dealing with cases such as *R. v. Stone* [1977] Q.B. 354.

12.4. CAUSATION IN OMISSIONS

12–020   **One other question seems to need answering. Suppose that Stone had called a doctor to Fanny. What could the doctor have done, if Fanny had still refused food and treatment? Could she have been forcibly fed?** It is pointed out later that a sane adult cannot be subjected to compulsory medical treatment when he is ill.[75] To interfere with a person by force without his consent and without the authority of law is an assault; and there is no authority for allowing paternal interference except in limited circumstances that ought not to be taken as being present in cases such as *R. v. Stone*. This freedom from a duty to submit to compulsory treatment is what is sometimes called a citizen's right of self-determination. If there is such a right, it should follow that the spouse or other person who refrains from obtaining medical treatment for the sufferer when he does not want it cannot be guilty of manslaughter if the sufferer dies, because the law does not impose a duty to commit an illegality.

There is one complicating factor. Statutory powers exist to remove to hospital or some other place people who are suspected of mental disorder or who are unable to cope.[76] If Fanny wanted to die at home in filth, and if the defendants were prepared to let her, their failure to put compulsory powers in motion should not have counted against them. Besides, even if Fanny had been institutionalized, that would not have given the institution the right to force feed her. So there is no assurance that the move would have saved her life. (Which is another argument against conviction: a person cannot be convicted of manslaughter by omission unless it can be proved beyond reasonable doubt that action by him could have saved the life of the supposed victim.) In other words, it has to be shown that the defendant not only had a duty to act, but that his failure to do so could have made a difference. There would have to be evidence to support such a claim. Perhaps, evidence showing that Fanny had been offered medical assistance on other occasions, but had always refused to accept it. Such evidence would show that continued attempts to seek help would have made no difference.[77]

Similarly, if the sister in *R. v. Evans* had died within minutes (or instantly) of overdosing, Evans would not have been liable since her failure to act would have made no difference. You cannot save someone who is already dead. In *R. v. Evans*, the victim caused her own death by self-injecting, but Evans was liable because she failed to take steps to "un-cause" what the victim's self-injection was already causing. Evans's sister was dying—but Evans had a chance to stop her from dying. All she had to do was summon help in a timely manner. If she had done so, she would not have been liable even if the help had failed to save her

---

[75] *Secretary of State for the Home Department v. Robb* [1995] 2 W.L.R. 722 (where it was held that a sane prisoner on a hunger strike could not be force fed). But it may be permissible to force feed a person who is mentally ill: *Re JR18's Application for Judicial Review* [2008] M.H.L.R. 50. See also *Re C (Adult: Refusal of Medical Treatment)* [1994] 1 W.L.R. 290; *R. (on the application of Burke) v. General Medical Council* [2006] Q.B. 273; *St George's Healthcare NHS Trust v. S* [1999] Fam. 26.

[76] See for example, section 3 of the *Mental Health Act 1983*. See also *Mental Health Act 2007*. For an overview, see Neil Allen, "The Bournewood Gap (as amended?)," (2010) *Med. L. Rev.* 78. See also *J v. Foundation Trust* [2010] Fam. 70.

[77] *R. v. Dalloway* (1847) 2 Cox C.C. 273. See also *Com. v. Williams*, 1 A.2d 812 (1938); *King v. Commonwealth*, 6 Va. App. 351 (1988); *People v. Mulcahy*, 318 Ill. 332 (1925). Cf. *R. v. Williams* [2011] 1 W.L.R. 588.

sister. If the evidence had showed that Evans's sister died instantly or would have died before an ambulance could have reached her, Evans could have rebutted a showing of causation by demonstrating that the harm would have occurred regardless of her omission.

We do not know whether Evans's sister was beyond saving, but the evidence showed that she died over hours not minutes. Therefore, there was a substantial chance that she could have been saved. In some omissions cases, it will be possible to hold that "but for" the defendant's omission the result would have almost certainly been different. In *R. v. Adomako*, it was fairly clear that if the anaesthetist had reattached the endotracheal tube, the patient would have lived. Adomako did nothing to cause the patient's death. He did not even insert the endotracheal tube into the patient, as he was present only for the second part of the operation. The tube had been inserted earlier by another anaesthetist. Nor did he pull the tube out. The patient's death was caused by the disconnection of the tube, not by Adomako's omission. However, if Adomako had not failed to detect the disconnection the patient would almost certainly have lived. He failed to act to take adequate steps to try to un-cause what was being caused by some other event. Adomako had a duty to try to stop the tube disconnection from causing the patient's death and it was his failure to do so that made him causally responsible.

Nevertheless, the omission will not always involve the defendant failing to un-cause what is being caused by some other event. In some cases, the defendant's omission will be the cause of the death. For example, if a station-master forgets to flick a switch and this causes a train to derail, his omission is a cause of the derailment.[78] The same can be said if the station-master forgets to shut the boom-gate thereby allowing a car to collide with an oncoming train.[79] The omission is a cause of the harm; if he had fulfilled his duty the harm causing condition (the open boom-gate) would not have existed. Counterfactually, the collision would not have transpired but for him leaving the gate open. The open gate and the moving car and train are necessary causal conditions of the collision. These cases do not involve the defendant having a duty to reverse some harm that is already in motion, but a duty to take precautions to prevent harm from occurring. And this is sufficient for a manslaughter conviction.

12.5. CONSTRUCTIVE MANSLAUGHTER: DANGEROUSNESS

We face more technicalities, but first a historical note by way of explanation. At one time it was held that a killing, though unintentional, was murder if it occurred in the course of any unlawful act; so an accidental killing while trying to steal a fowl was murder.[80] This doctrine of constructive murder was limited in the course of time by judicial decision and statute; and the area progressively freed from the law of murder was simultaneously and automatically occupied by the doctrine of

12–021

12–022

---

[78] *State v. O'Brien*, 3 Vroom 169 (1867).
[79] *R. v. Pittwood* (1902) 19 T.L.R. 37; *R. v. Smith* (1869) 11 Cox C.C. 210; *R. v. Benge* (1865) 176 E.R. 665.
[80] Sir William Oldnall Russell, *A Treatise on Crimes and Indictable Misdemeanours*, (Philadelphia: P. H. Nicklin and T. Johnson, Vol. I, 1831) at 59. Cf. Sir James Fitzjames Stephen, *A History of the Criminal Law of England*, (Macmillan & Co, Vol. III, 1883) at 57 *et seq*.

constructive manslaughter.[81] What had been murder became manslaughter. Hence, for several centuries, it was axiomatic that a killing in the course of an unlawful act was at least manslaughter by construction of law.

Just as the judges steadily diminished the law of constructive murder, so they came to whittle down the law of constructive manslaughter.[82] The present law contains some firm rules and some outstanding doubts. It may be summarized as follows. For the doctrine to operate:

- there must be an act (an omission is insufficient)
- which is unlawful, within certain rules, and also
- dangerous.
- The death must be a direct consequence of the unlawful act.

Two illustrations may be given of the working of the law.

In *D.P.P. v. Newbury*[83] two 15-year-old boys pushed a piece of paving stone[84] from a railway bridge into the path of an oncoming train. The case for the defence was that they intended only to cause it to hit the roof of the driving cab or a coach, where it might have done some damage but not injured anybody (no reference to this defence is made in the report). Unfortunately the stone went through the window of the driving cab and killed the guard who was inside. The trial judge instructed the jury in terms of constructive manslaughter; the jury convicted, and the conviction was affirmed by the House of Lords.

12–023 The decision was followed by the Privy Council in a case where the defendants threw stones at V who ran away from them. As he ran he tripped and was later found dead, it being possible that the death was caused by the fall rather than by hits with the stones. The judge in summing up said that "where one person causes in the mind of another by violence or the threat of violence a well-founded sense of danger to life or limb as to cause him to suffer or [and?] to try to escape and in the endeavour to escape he is killed, the person creating the state of mind is guilty at least of manslaughter." The jury convicted of manslaughter, and the conviction was upheld on appeal.[85]

In both cases the law of constructive manslaughter offered a short cut to conviction, but in neither was it socially necessary. In *D.P.P. v. Newbury* the lads were guilty of a statutory offence (of negligence or strict liability) in "endangering the safety of any person upon a railway."[86] Apart from that, the jury would very probably have convicted of gross negligence manslaughter on a

---

[81] This pejorative but convenient expression assumes that manslaughter is first defined to require criminal negligence as to death or g.b.h., and is then extended by an irrebuttable presumption of criminal negligence in the case of an unlawful act causing death. The conviction for "manslaughter" only; a separate crime of constructive manslaughter is not known to the law.

[82] For an account of the development see Glanville Williams, "Constructive Manslaughter," [1957] Crim. L.R. 293; W. T. Westling, "Manslaughter by Unlawful Act: The Constructive Crime Which Serves No Constructive Purpose," (1973–76) 7 *Sydney L. Rev.* 211.

[83] [1977] A.C. 500.

[84] So the report states, but counsel for the defence said that it was in fact about a quarter of a paving stone.

[85] *D.P.P. v. Daley* [1980] A.C. 237.

[86] Section 34 of the *Offences against the Person Act 1861*.

decision couched in terms of gross negligence. The lads could even have been found subjectively reckless if they must have foreseen at least a slight possibility of the stone causing serious injury to someone. Conviction would have been even more likely if the prosecution had refrained from charging manslaughter and instead charged criminal damage to property intending to endanger life or being reckless as to such danger.[87] But not all cases of constructive manslaughter are as serious as the two just instanced.

We will commence to sort out the law by considering the definition of a dangerous act. A few decades ago the law of constructive manslaughter operated with great severity. People were convicted notwithstanding that death would not have occurred but for some abnormal sensitivity of the victim which the attacker had no reason to know.[88] A trivial physical assault or even a mere psychic assault resulting in death could amount to manslaughter, although the intention of the defendant was only to frighten or to perpetrate a stupid joke involving minor physical contact. The assault might be against a third party.

Nowadays the courts generally maintain that there must, at least, be subjective fault as to the risk of causing some harm. The modern rule stems from *R. v. Church*,[89] where the Court of Appeal said:

> "[A]n unlawful act causing the death of another cannot, simply because it is an unlawful act, render a manslaughter verdict inevitable. For such a verdict inexorably to follow, the unlawful act must be such as all sober and reasonable people would inevitably recognize must subject the other person to, at least, the risk of some harm resulting therefrom, albeit not serious harm."

12–024

The correctness of this statement was recognized by the House of Lords in *D.P.P. v. Newbury*. Their Lordships added the observation that the defendant need not know that this act was dangerous. Although this must be accepted, the point remains that there must be an unlawful act, which may involve a mental element. The requirement was unfortunately misunderstood and obscured by Lord Salmon, as we shall see in the next section.

The statement refers to "some harm." Presumably what is intended is the "actual bodily harm" of section 47 of the *Offences against the Person Act 1861*.

But that may be a very small amount of harm: for instance a mere bruise.[90] So, is the law much improved from the bad old days of which you spoke before? Not much. But the whole point of constructive manslaughter is that it can arise from an unlawful act that was only likely to do minor injury. If the act was likely to kill or do g.b.h. the doer would invariably be guilty of reckless manslaughter,[91] so in that case there is no need for a doctrine of constructive manslaughter.

12–025

---

[87] Section 1 of the *Criminal Damage Act 1971*.

[88] *R. v. Mawgridge* (1706) Kel. 119; *R. v. Martin* (1832) 5 Car. & P. 128; *R. v. Plumer* (1844) 1 Car. & K. 600; *R. v. Murton* (1862) 3 F. & F. 492; *R. v. Hayward* (1908) 21 Cox C.C. 692.

[89] [1966] 1 Q.B. 59 at 70. See also *R. v. Carey* [2006] EWCA Crim. 17.

[90] *R. v. Jones* [1981] Crim. L.R. 119; *Taylor v. Granville* [1978] Crim. L.R. 482.

[91] For instance, since Mrs. Hyam (*Hyam v. D.P.P.* [1975] A.C. 55.) foresaw g.b.h. as highly probably she would now be liable for reckless manslaughter rather than murder: *R. v. Woollin* [1999] 1 A.C. 82.

An example of the potential severity of the law is the old case of *R. v. Towers*,[92] where the defendant assaulted a girl who was nursing an infant. The girl screamed, and this so frightened the infant that he became black in the face; later he had a convulsion, and died. Towers was convicted of manslaughter of the infant.[93]

Presumably all sober and reasonable people would inevitably recognize that assaulting a girl with an infant in her arms might lead her to drop and injure the infant; and if so a man like Towers could still be convicted of manslaughter, even though the particular mode of the infant's death was not reasonably foreseeable. No judge has explained on what ground of justice or policy a person who has made a minor assault should be rendered guilty of manslaughter by reason of an unknown weakness of the victim. All that can be said is that, the judges having invented the idea of constructive manslaughter it is now a part of the order of the universe and the judges are powerless to change it. (The courts often seem to treat the criminal law as a militaristic State treats its territory: something that can always be extended but must never be given back again.)

12–026 **"All sober and reasonable people would inevitably recognize." Is that a gross negligence test?** One would have thought so, but the language of gross negligence is not used in relation to constructive manslaughter. Presumably the phrase means: consider the responsible and careful people you know. Do you thing they would all say that this act carried a foreseeable danger of causing some injury? If you think they might be divided in opinion, constructive manslaughter is not made out. (But, of course, you do not sound the opinions of any actual people. And there is a whiff of begging the question about the test, because if a minority of the friends who you imagine you are consulting report, in your imagination, that they do not think the act is dangerous, you may rule them out of consideration as not being sober and reasonable people after all!)

12–027 **Does grave harm (such as death) count if a reasonable person would not have foreseen it as a possibility? Take for example the case where a person is frightened to death in circumstances where a reasonable person would not have foreseen this as possible.** In such cases, the victim's death may perhaps be attributed to the attacker on the thin skull rule.[94] However, the law of constructive manslaughter and transferred intention should not be pushed so far as to say that if D assaults V1 he becomes guilty of the manslaughter of V2, a mere spectator, who, remarkably, dies of fright or shock in witnessing what

---

[92] (1874) 12 Cox C.C. 530.

[93] There was probably an assault upon the child who died, because the defendant could have been found to have been reckless as to the child; but no point was made as to this, and the judge took the case merely on the assault of the girl. Cf. *R. v. Bruce* (1847) 2 Cox C.C. 262; *Re Heigho*, 18 Idaho 566 (1910); *R. v. Mitchell* [1983] 2 W.L.R. 938, where, however, the question of foreseeability was not made an issue.

[94] See *R. v. Towers* (1874) 12 Cox C.C. 530; *R. v. Dugal* (1874) 4 Que. L.R. 350 (Can.).

happens to V1.[95] If D threatens and frightens V in circumstances where he foresees that his threat might cause V to suffer a heart attack, then he will be held liable for the resulting harm or death.

In *R. v. Dawson*,[96] some men tried to rob a petrol station that was being manned by a 60-year-old attendant. After the robbers fled the attendant suffered a heart attack and died. The Court of Appeal quashed their convictions for manslaughter, because the defendants lacked the requisite *mens rea* for manslaughter. The robbers did not envisage that *any* harm would result from their threats. Even though they in fact cased the victim's heart attack, they did not intend to, nor did they foresee it as a possibility of frightening him.[97]

In *R. v. Watson*[98] an 87-year-old man died of a heart attack 90 minutes after he was burgled. The Court of Appeal held that when a person creates an emotional disturbance and continues to do so after learning that the victim that he is terrorizing is very old and frail, it would be reasonably foreseeable that the victim might suffer a heart attack.[99] In *R. v. Watson* the defendants were not aware of the victim's frailty when they commenced the burglary, but they abused the elderly man and remained in his house and continued their threats after learning of his age and frailty. The defendants were able to evade justice, because the victim suffered the heart attack 90 minutes after the burglary. The Court of Appeal held that the time delay meant that it was not clear that the burglary had caused the heart attack, as it may have been caused by the additional disturbance that resulted when the police and the window repairman arrived at the old man's house. The defendants in that case had the requisite *mens rea* for constructive manslaughter as they could see that by remaining they might cause the old man to suffer a heart attack, but causation was not made out. The evidence was not sufficient, according to the court, to demonstrate that the burglary was in fact the cause of the heart attack. The defendants were let off the hook because causation was not established.[100]

---

[95] In the American case of *Re Heigho*, 18 Idaho 566 (1910) the defendant was convicted of manslaughter, though the only person killed was an onlooker. The onlooker who died was the mother-in-law of the person assaulted—she died of fright. Technically no doubt, a combination of the law of constructive manslaughter and transferred intention would support *Re Heigho*; but it would be open to a court to refuse to combine the two doctrines.

[96] (1985) 81 Cr. App. R. 150. In *Todd v. State* (1992) 594 So.2d 802, V got in his car and went after a petty thief and suffered a heart attack while in pursuit. Cf. *People v. Hiraldo*, 676 N.Y.S.2d 775 (1998).

[97] As for the limitations of claiming that psychic harm was foreseeable: *R. v. Ireland* [1998] A.C. 147.

[98] [1989] 1 W.L.R. 684. In *People v. Aponte*, 369 N.Y.2d 342 (1975) the 49-year-old victim was punched by the defendant following a traffic altercation. When the defendant challenged the victim to a fight the victim made it clear he was a "very sick man" and could not fight. The defendant landed a punch and the victim died from heart failure after being knocked unconscious. The conviction was upheld because the defendant was given notice of the victim's condition.

[99] *R. v. Watson* [1989] 1 W.L.R. 684 at 686. Cf. *R. v. Carey* [2006] EWCA Crim. 17; *R. v. Hayward* (1908) 21 Cox C.C. 692.

[100] Cf. *In Matter of Anthony M*, 63 N.Y.2d 270 (1984). See also *Schlossman v. State*, 105 Md. App. 277 (1995), where non-life threatening conduct such as kicking dirt and poking a homeless person with a stick was held to have a causal connection with V's heart attack. See also *Baraka v. Com.*, 194 S.W.3d 313 at 317 (2006) and the many cases cited therein; *Terry v. Associated Stone Co.*, 334 S.W.2d 926, 928 (1960). See *State v. Shaw*, 260 Kan. 396 (1996) where an 86-year-old man suffered a heart attack after being left tied up by a burglar; and *State v. Washington*, 581 A.2d 1031 (1990), where a 73-year-old rape victim suffered a heart attack while being raped. In all these cases, V's death or

12–028 **Would X be liable for manslaughter if she scratches Y who unbeknown to her is a haemophiliac and as a result he bleeds to death?** She would be if she knew he was a haemophiliac. But if she had no way of knowing about his special sensitivity (his so-called thin skull),[101] then she would only be liable for constructive manslaughter if some harm was foreseeable.[102] The test of dangerousness is an objective one. Would a reasonable person have foreseen that Y would die from a scratch if she had not known of his special sensitivity? The answer is, of course, no. Nevertheless, a reasonable person most likely would foresee that "scratching" another is an act that is likely to result in some harm even if not serious harm.[103] Consequently, X may be liable for manslaughter.[104] The act of scratching is unlawful battery.

In Australia the defendant is only liable if a reasonable person would have foreseen that the unlawful act could result in serious injury.[105] The Law Commission has recommended that manslaughter should encompass:[106]

> "(1) killing another person through gross negligence ('gross negligence manslaughter'); or
> (2) killing another person:
>   (a) through the commission of a criminal act intended by the defendant to cause injury, or
>   (b) through the commission of a criminal act that the defendant was aware involved a serious risk of causing some injury ('criminal act manslaughter')."

According to this proposal, subjective foresight of any injury will do. Suppose D punches X whom he believed has slandered him and X falls awkwardly and dies.[107] Suppose also that D foresaw that it was virtually certain that if he punched X that he would cause some injury. Under the proposals put forward by the Law Commission, D would be no better off than he would be under the current law.

---

injury was unintended but it was foreseeable that the victims would suffer some harm. Furthermore, D's conduct was in fact the cause of their deaths. See also the discussion in *State v. Spates*, 176 Conn. 227 at 235 (1978).

[101] *R. v. Blaue* [1975] 1 W.L.R. 1411.

[102] *R. v. Dawson* (1985) 81 Cr. App. R. 150.

[103] In *R. v. Mallett* [1972] Crim. L.R. 260, D punched V whom he believed had slandered him. D fell awkwardly suffered brain injuries and died. Mallett did not foresee that he would kill V, but a reasonable person would have foreseen that a punch could be dangerous.

[104] Cf. *State v. Frazier*, 339 Mo. 966 (1936), where D was convicted of manslaughter because he punched a haemophiliac, which caused him to bleed to death.

[105] This is the approach taken in Australia. See *Wilson v. The Queen* (1992) 174 C.L.R. 313; *D.P.P. v. Singleton* (2010) V.S.C. 428.

[106] Law Commission, *Murder, Manslaughter and Infanticide*, Report 304, (London: H.M.S.O., 2006) at para. 9.9.

[107] Arguably, Mallett intended to cause some injury to his neighbour when he punched him, otherwise he would not have bothered to do so. Furthermore, he must have foreseen that it was highly probably (if not virtually certain) that his punch would cause some injury. See *R. v. Mallett* [1972] Crim. L.R. 260.

12.6. THE UNLAWFUL ACT

The other main limit upon the doctrine of constructive manslaughter is that it **12–029** applies only when the defendant committed an unlawful act, not including a merely negligent act. Negligence is not an unlawful act for the purpose of constructive manslaughter even when it constitutes a specific statutory offence. This was settled by the House of Lords in *Andrews v. D.P.P.*[108]

It was held that the mere fact that a person committed the offence of dangerous driving, and killed in consequence, did not make him guilty of manslaughter. Dangerous driving, though a statutory offence of negligence created for the protection of life, did not necessarily connote the same degree of negligence as that required for negligent manslaughter; and the commission of the statutory offence was not to be used to lay a foundation for a charge of constructive manslaughter.

The general proposition that negligence is insufficient for constructive manslaughter is also illustrated by *R. v. Lamb*,[109] a case that we have come across before. Since Lamb knew that his friend regarded the affair as a joke, he was not guilty of an assault on the friend, and committed no unlawful act, when he pointed the gun and pulled the trigger. The act was negligent; but negligent acts are not unlawful at the moment when they are done, even though they create liability in tort if they cause damage. This point was accepted in the Court of Appeal as a conclusive reason why Lamb was not guilty of constructive manslaughter. The court said:[110]

> "[Counsel for the Crown] rightly conceded that there was no evidence to go to the jury of any assault of any kind. Nor did he feel able to submit that the acts of the defendant were on any other ground unlawful in the criminal sense of that word. Indeed no such submission could in law be made: if, for instance, the pulling of the trigger had had no effect because the striking mechanism or the ammunition had been defective no offence would have been committed by the defendant. … Unfortunately [the trial judge] fell into error as to the meaning of the word 'unlawful' in that passage [in *R. v. Church*,[111]]. … The trial judge took the view that the pointing of the revolver and the pulling of the trigger was something which could of itself be unlawful even if there was no attempt to alarm or intent to injure."

And the trial judge was wrong in doing so. The simple point was gravely **12–030** misunderstood by Lord Salmon, stating the opinion of the House of Lords in *D.P.P. v. Newbury*:[112]

> "[I]n manslaughter there must always be a guilty mind. This is true of every crime except those of absolute liability.[113] The guilty mind usually depends on the intention of the accused. Some crimes require what is sometimes called a specific intention. … Other crimes need only what is called a basic intention, which is an intention to do the acts which constitute the crime. Manslaughter is such a crime. … *R. v. Lamb* is certainly no authority to the contrary. … The

---

[108] [1937] A.C. 576 at 585.
[109] [1967] 2 Q.B. 981.
[110] *R. v. Lamb* [1967] 2 Q.B. 981 at 985 *per* Sachs L.J.
[111] [1966] 1 Q.B. 59 at 70.
[112] [1977] A.C. 500 at 509B.
[113] Lord Salmon evidently took crimes of negligence to involve a guilty mind—a deplorable use of language to say the least. Cf. §2.02 of the American Law Institute's Model Penal Code.

defendant was convicted but his conviction was quashed on appeal because, luckily for him, there had been a series of serious misdirections by the learned trial judge."

If this means that Lamb could have been convicted of gross negligence manslaughter on a proper direction, it may be true but irrelevant. Perhaps he could have been, though improperly in my view. Lamb was not guilty of gross negligence, notwithstanding the disastrous results. (On every charge of manslaughter the defendant has produced disastrous results, because he has caused death; that mere fact cannot turn tort negligence into gross negligence.) However, Lord Salmon was speaking primarily in the context of constructive manslaughter, and he was clearly in error in suggesting that on a proper direction Lamb's conviction would have been upheld on the basis that he had committed an unlawful act. Lord Salmon and the other lords who concurred with him were perhaps going upon a faded memory of the case; they could have corrected their mistake if they had re-read the head-note. (It correctly summaries the decision in these words: "manslaughter could not be established in relation to the first ground [the doing of an unlawful act] without proving the element of intent without which there could be no assault.") Besides, one does not need authority for saying that negligence is not an unlawful act for constructive manslaughter. If it were, constructive manslaughter would virtually[114] swallow up gross negligence manslaughter, whereas everyone agrees that they are separate concepts.

Lord Salmon's use of the notion of crimes of basic intention is also a most regrettable muddle. The misleading nature of the phrase "intention to do the acts which constitute the crime" may be shown by an example. When a driver "intentionally" drives in a certain way which the court regards as dangerous, he has, in a sense, an "intention to do the acts which constitute the crime," but this does not make him guilty of constructive manslaughter if his dangerous driving causes a death. It would be quite untrue in the ordinary understanding of words to say that the driver has intentionally committed an unlawful act. His offence is one of negligence, not intention.[115] It follows that what can be said (in a strained and misleading sense) to be an intention to do the acts which constitute the crime is not necessarily sufficient for constructive manslaughter.

12–031   Lord Salmon was derailed by the language of "crimes of basic intention," which he found in cases of voluntary intoxication.[116] It was there invented as what can only be called a piece of legal hocus-pocus in order to convict drunkards and evade section 8 of the *Criminal Justice Act 1967*. For this purpose, the courts say that assault is a crime of basic intent, in which all that is required for the drunkard to be convicted is an intent to do the acts constituting the crime. The falsity of the proposition that this is the only *mens rea* in assault which can be seen from *R. v. Lamb*. Suppose for a moment that Lamb had wanted to frighten his friend, and had done so by pointing the loaded gun. Let us imagine (contrary to the facts of the case) that his friend became frightened that Lamb was about to shoot him,

---

[114] The only negligent manslaughter that would be left outside constructive manslaughter would be one in which there is no "act," as where a woman carrying a baby negligently trips and drops the baby. But in such circumstances it would be rare for the negligence to be accounted sufficiently gross for negligent manslaughter.

[115] *Attorney-General's Reference (No. 4 of 2000)* [2001] 2 Cr. App. R. 22.

[116] See Chap. 19 *infra*.

though Lamb neither intended to do so nor realized that his friend would suppose the affair to be anything but fun. On such facts, he would not have committed an assault, and would not have committed an unlawful act, because he lacked the intent. Intending to do the acts which constitute the offence is *not* sufficient for the crime of assault. What is required is a further intent, to frighten or cause contact with the victim.

The point that emerges is that an act is not unlawful for constructive manslaughter unless it satisfies all the requirements of unlawfulness. It is not unlawful as a lesser crime unless the defendant has the requisite fault required for that lesser crime. Their Lordships announced in *D.P.P. v. Newbury*[117] that the defendant need not have known that his act was unlawful; and the statement was given added weight by being repeated by the Privy Council on a subsequent occasion.[118] But why their Lordships troubled to say it is a mystery. With rare exceptions the prosecution need never show that the defendant knew the law, and there was no occasion to state this elementary rule in the two cases in question. The statement in *D.P.P. v. Newbury* cannot be understood to mean that a mistake of fact is excluded. Lamb was not guilty of assault, and consequently was not guilty of constructive manslaughter, because, although he shot his friend, he believed that his revolver would not fire. For constructive manslaughter you need not know that your act is unlawful, but it must *be* unlawful; and when a mistake of fact negatives the required intention it also negatives constructive manslaughter.

The next qualification upon the "unlawful act" rule is that a tort (a civil wrong) is not an unlawful act for the purpose of constructive manslaughter. The law of constructive manslaughter can operate to turn a minor crime into manslaughter if death follows, but it does not turn a tort into manslaughter. There is an old case which is directly on point: *R. v. Franklin*.[119] Although only a ruling by a puisne judge, it has been widely approved.

Franklin took up a good-sized box from a refreshment stall on a pier and **12–032** wantonly threw it into the sea; the box struck a swimmer underneath and caused his death. The prosecution urged that, death having been caused by an unlawful act, Franklin was guilty of manslaughter irrespective of negligence. Field J. said: "The mere fact of a civil wrong committed by one person against another ought not to be used as an incident which is a necessary step in a criminal case. ... I have a great abhorrence of constructive crime." He therefore left the case to the jury only on the basis of negligence. (Field J. did not expressly notice that Franklin was also, presumably, guilty of theft of the box; but doubtless regarded the offence against property as equally irrelevant.)

R. v. Franklin was approved in *R. v. Lamb*, where the Court of Appeal was laudably careful to speak not of an unlawful act simply but of an act that is "unlawful in a criminal sense of the word." "When using the phrase 'in the criminal sense of the word' the court has in mind it is long settled that it is not in point to consider whether an act is unlawful merely from the angle of civil

---

[117] [1977] A.C. 500 at 507A.
[118] *D.P.P. v. Daley* [1980] A.C. 237.
[119] (1883) 15 Cox C.C. 163. See also *R. v. Criminal Injuries Compensation Board, Ex parte Webb* [1986] Q.B. 184 at 188.

liabilities."[120] Grateful as we may be for the clear lucid reasoning in *R. v. Lamb*, it is a pity that the court chose the circumlocution instead of dropping the talk of an "unlawful act" and speaking instead of "a crime."

12–033   **Then where was the unlawful act, or crime, in *D.P.P. v. Newbury*? The boys' act was not unlawful merely because it was negligent, and it was not unlawful merely because it involved the tort of damage to the train (or, we suppose, criminal damage to the train).** Remarkably, the Lords did not endeavour to pinpoint the unlawful act committed by the boys. Lord Salmon merely said: "[Counsel for the defendant] did not and indeed could not contend that the appellant's act was lawful."[121] Of course it was not lawful (if that was the only question); the act damaged the train. But we cannot suppose that their Lordships meant to overrule *R. v. Franklin* and to disregard the settled opinion. Similarly, we cannot suppose that they intended to depart silently from their own previous decision in *Andrews v. D.P.P.* (it was referred to in argument, but not in Lord Salmon's speech).

There is, however, one possible explanation of the decision in *D.P.P. v. Newbury*. The boys intended to frighten the crew and passengers in the train, or were reckless as to frightening or hurting them; and the jury could clearly have decided that they were guilty of assault on this basis. Since the direction to the jury is not reported, we do not know whether they were directed in these terms. Obviously, a jury should not be left to find that the defendant's act was unlawful without being told the law.

One other case may be mentioned as an example of judicial laxity in finding an unlawful act. This is *R. v. Cato*,[122] the facts which will now be familiar. D injected V with heroin. V died from an overdose and D was convicted of manslaughter and of administering a noxious thing, contrary to section 23 of the *Offences against the Person Act 1861*. The judge left the manslaughter charge to the jury on two alternative grounds: (1) that the death was caused by Cato's "recklessness or gross negligence"; and (2) that it was caused by the injection of heroin which, as Cato knew, was likely to do harm to the person injected. On appeal from conviction, it was argued that the injection of heroin is not an unlawful act for the purpose of constructive manslaughter. Possessing or supplying heroin is a statutory offence, but Cato did not supply it to the deceased, because he had received it from the deceased for the express purpose of administering it to him.[123] The prosecution had to show that the administration of heroin is an offence. The court held that it is, being an offence of administrating a noxious thing so as to endanger life under section 23 of the *Offences against the Person Act 1861*, the consent of the person injected being no defence. The court

---

[120] *R. v. Lamb* [1967] 2 Q.B. 981 at 988D.

[121] *D.P.P. v. Newbury* [1977] A.C. 500 at 507A.

[122] [1976] 1 W.L.R. 110.

[123] *R. v. Harris* [1968] 1 W.L.R. 769, where it was held "a person who injects another with that other's heroin does not 'supply' a dangerous drug ..." Cf. *R. v. Maginnis* [1987] A.C. 303, where it was held: "that 'supply' did not necessarily involve supplying from the suppliers own resources, and if the drugs were to be returned with the intention that the friend use them for his own purposes, that constituted 'intention to supply' [contrary to sections 4(1)(b), 5(3) of the *Misuse of Drugs Act 1971*]."

added that anyway there was an unlawful act of "injecting [V] with heroin which the accused had unlawfully taken into possession."

Whether it was good law to hold that V's consent was no defence under section 23 will be discussed in the Chapter on Consent and Entrapment below.[124] The serious difficulty presented by the decision for the modern law of constructive manslaughter relates to the court's second ground (which in view of the first ground, relating to section 23 of the *Offences against the Person Act 1861*,[125] was unnecessary for the decision). The court acknowledged that there was no statutory offence of administering heroin. Even if Cato's momentary possession were regarded as sufficient for the statutory offence of possession, it was not his possession that killed. The illegality found by the court in the injection of heroin could therefore only be at common law.[126] This case is controversial, as it was, as it is not a crime to administer heroin. The victim was technically nothing more than a self-harmer; he would have injected himself if it had not been easier to have the defendant administer the injection containing the (dangerous) recreational drug.

Can a criminal omission be an "unlawful act"?   The answer, on authority, is no.[127] The answer is given in *R. v. Lowe*,[128] where the Court of Appeal held, refusing to follow *R. v. Senior*,[129] that the mere fact that a parent is guilty of the statutory offence of wilful neglect of a child, whereby the child dies, does not make the parent automatically guilty of manslaughter. This seems reasonable to the extent that such a person is merely negligent in omitting to fulfil his duty, since the law may impose low duties obliging to positive conduct (with a penalty of say, a fine), and these ought not automatically be translated into the far more serious duties implied by the law of manslaughter. (What's more, gross negligence manslaughter now requires gross negligence as to the consequence of death. It would apply if a reasonable person would have foreseen that the omission might cause the victim's death.)   **12–034**

However, it is difficult to make a distinction in cases where the defendant deliberately fails to act when he has a duty to act. If a person deliberately omits to take positive steps to counteract or prevent the victim from dying, and has a duty

---

[124] See also, Dennis J. Baker, "Moral Limits of Consent as a Defence in the Criminal Law," (2009) 12 *New Crim. L. Rev.* 93.

[125] See *R. v. Andrews* [2002] EWCA Crim. 3021, where D was found guilty of committing the statutory offence of "administering a prescription only medicine when not qualified to do so in contravention" of sections 58(2)(b) and 67 of the *Medicines Act 1968*. It was also held that consent provided no defence as far as the statutory offence was concerned.

[126] See *R. v. Kennedy (No. 2)* [2008] 1 A.C. 269 at 274 *per* Lord Bingham. (V instructs D to inject him, as drug addicts seem to encourage other-injecting—perhaps it is difficult for them to self-inject, but in following V's instructions, D is a direct cause of the administration of the substance.) In *R. v. Dias* [2002] 2 Cr. App. R. 96 at 99, it was held that self-injection is not an unlawful act, therefore, those who assist another to self-inject cannot be an accessory to a crime, as there is no crime to aid or abet. The section 23 of the *Offences against the Person Act 1861* was not available in that case, as V administered drugs to himself.

[127] Cf. *R. v. Khan* [1998] Crim. L.R. 830, where it was asserted that omissions should be brought within the purview of gross negligence manslaughter.

[128] [1973] Q.B. 702.

[129] [1899] 1 Q.B. 283. For a discussion of the case, see Glanville Williams, *Textbook of Criminal Law*, (London: Stevens & Sons, 1978) at 88.

to take such steps, then he technically performs an unlawful and dangerous omission (act), and thus seems to fall within the purview of the unlawful dangerous act doctrine.[130] In cases where the omission is deliberate and the defendant intends to produce a particular consequence by omitting to fulfil his duty, such as where a parent sits by and watches his child drown in a puddle of water because he wants the child to die, the unlawful dangerous act doctrine is not needed, because a charge of murder would be available.[131]

12–035 **What if D punches V in self-defence and accidently kills him?** If he satisfies the conditions of self-defence, then his conduct will be lawful.

12.7. THE UNLAWFUL ACT AND CAUSATION

12–036 The unlawful dangerous act must cause the victim's death.[132] In *R. v. Watson*,[133] the defendants escaped a manslaughter conviction because it could not be proved that their unlawful act (the burglary) caused the victim's heart attack.

Suppose X is driving in an absolutely safe and careful manner when a child jumps in front of his car. Unfortunately, the child is killed. Suppose X has been driving for 20 years' and has never had an accident, but when the police arrive they discover that X's licence has just expired.[134]

X should not be liable for unlawful act manslaughter (intentionally driving without a licence or insurance is not a case of negligence), because the unlawfulness of his act was not the cause of the victim's death.[135] The fact that his licence had expired did not cause the child to jump in front of his car. But surely if he waited to renew his licence he would not have been driving on the day in question and therefore would not have hit the child? A person who commits some unlawful act is not absolutely liable for the accidental death of another person, if the death was a mere coincidence and not a consequence of the unlawful act. It is true that D would not have been driving at that place or at that time "but for" the fact that he chose to drove without a licence, but the unlawfulness of his otherwise faultless driving did not cause V's death.[136] However, he may be convicted of a statutory offence contrary to section 3ZB of

---

[130] Cf. *R. v. Sheppard* [1981] A.C. 394.

[131] *R. v. Gibbons* (1919) 13 Cr. App. R. 134.

[132] *R. v. Watson* [1989] 1 W.L.R. 684.

[133] [1989] 1 W.L.R. 684.

[134] On similar facts in *Com. v. Williams*, 1 A.2d 812 (1938), a U.S. court acquitted the defendant because the unlawfulness of his driving (driving without a current licence) did not cause him to crash and thereby kill his passenger. He crashed his car because another car forced him to swerve and this resulted in him hitting the telephone pole.

[135] *R. v. Dalloway* (1847) 2 Cox C.C. 273.

[136] In *People v. Mulcahy*, 318 Ill. 332 (1925) it was held that: to "convict one of manslaughter for killing a person while in the commission of an unlawful act, the state must show more than a mere coincidence of time and place between the wrongful act and the death." Similarly, in *King v. Commonwealth*, 6 Va. App. 351 (1988) it was held: "Criminal liability for felony-murder requires more than a finding that 'but for' the felony the parties would not have been present at the time and location of the accidental death." See also *Davis v. Commonwealth*, 404 S.E.2d 377 (1991).

the *Road Traffic Act 1988*.[137] Unintentional killings resulting from driving offences are covered by special statutory provisions.[138] If, however, D uses his car to intentionally kill a pedestrian, he will be liable for murder.

In *R. v Carey*[139] a group of girls attacked and chased another group of girls. One of the girls in the victim group suffered a heart attack as she tried to run from her attackers. Her heart attack was a mere coincidence and not a consequence of the unlawful affray. She was only 15 years old, but was suffering from a rare heart condition. The evidence suggested that her rare heart condition was the cause of the heart attack. It is irrelevant that a reasonable person would have foreseen that the unlawful assault could result in some harm, because the actual harm inflicted did not in fact cause her to have a heart attack. It was coincidental. If the victim had run into the path of a car and had been killed while trying to escape the unlawful attack, causation might have been established.[140]

12–037

In *R. v. Kennedy (No. 2)* the House of Lords said:[141]

> "To establish the crime of unlawful act manslaughter it must be shown, among other things not relevant to this appeal: (1) that the defendant committed an unlawful act; (2) that such unlawful act was a crime; ... and (3) that the defendant's unlawful act was a significant cause of the death of the deceased. ... There is now, as already noted, no doubt but that the appellant committed an unlawful (and criminal) act by supplying the heroin to the deceased. But the act of supplying, without more, could not harm the deceased in any physical way, let alone cause his death. ... '[T]he supply of drugs would itself have caused no harm unless the deceased had subsequently used the drugs in a form and quantity which was dangerous'. So, as the parties agree, the charge of unlawful act manslaughter cannot be founded on the act of supplying the heroin alone."

R. v. Kennedy (No. 2) does not affect the established rule that a person who secretly administers a dangerous drug to another and unintentionally kills him can be convicted of constructive manslaughter, because here the victim takes the drug unwittingly. The distinction between these cases and *R. v. Cato*, apparently is that Cato himself injected his friend, whereas as Kennedy left the friend to inject himself.

The rule does not require the defendant to directly aim for the victim. The defendant may cause the victim's death by trying to injure a third party or while trying to commit criminal damage.[142] In *R. v. Mitchell*,[143] D's unlawful act was not directly aimed at the victim, but it was the direct cause of her death. In that

12–038

---

[137] In *R. v. Williams* [2011] 1 W.L.R. 588 it was said: "sometimes *non-dangerous driving* will be a sufficient cause [to convict a person of *causing* death by dangerous driving], the simple question for the court is whether the death was caused by driving without insurance or without a driving licence."

[138] See the *Road Traffic Act 1988*.

[139] [2006] EWCA Crim. 17. See also *R. v. DJ* [2007] EWCA Crim. 3133; *R. v. Williams* [1992] 1 W.L.R. 380; *Royall v. The Queen* (1991) 172 C.L.R. 378.

[140] *R. v. Lewis* [2010] EWCA Crim. 151.

[141] *R. v. Kennedy (No. 2)* [2008] 1 A.C. 269 at 274 *per* Bingham L.J. His Lordship, citing Glanville Williams, "Finis for Novus Actus?", 48 *Cambridge L.J.* 391 at 392, went on to hold that: "D is not to be treated as causing V to act in a certain way if V makes a voluntary and informed decision to act in that way rather than another."

[142] *Attorney-General's Reference (No. 3 of 1994)* [1998] A.C. 245; *R. v. Pagett* (1983) 76 Cr. App. R. 279.

[143] [1983] Q.B. 741. See also *R. v. Ball* [1989] Crim. L.R. 730.

case, D tried to force himself into a queue in a busy post office. V1 remonstrated D, so D punched V1 thereby causing V1 to fall against V2, an 89-year-old woman. V2 suffered a broken femur as a result of which she underwent an operation. She was making a good recovery when she died suddenly as a result of a pulmonary embolism caused by thrombosis of the left leg veins, which in turn was caused by the fracture of the femur. The defendant was convicted of manslaughter of V2 and of assault occasioning actual bodily harm to V1. Even though D's unlawful act was aimed at V1 it directly caused V2's death.

Similarly, in *R. v. Goodfellow*,[144] D set fire to his council house because he wanted to be relocated to a different house. He thought that if he made it look as though his house had been firebombed he would be relocated. Unfortunately, the fire got out of control and killed not only his wife and their son, but also his new girlfriend. D's unlawful act was aimed at the building not his family, but it was the direct cause of their deaths. He was rightly convicted of manslaughter. This decision may be taken to reinforce the opinion that a tort in respect of property is not unlawful act manslaughter. The aggravated form of criminal damage (damage intending, *etc.* to endanger life)[145] is clearly a sufficient unlawful act, but this crime requires proof of an intention or recklessness as to the endangering of life; and proof of this mental element should be necessary, as requisite to the proof of the unlawful act, notwithstanding what was said in the Lords about the defendant not having to know that his act was dangerous.

12–039 **Is it constructive manslaughter if an illegal abortionist accidentally kills his patient?** If the abortionist has supplied the woman with an abortifacient drug,[146] which kills her, he may be able to defend himself against a charge of manslaughter by virtue of the rule in *R. v. Kennedy (No. 2)*. But in the more usual case, where the abortionist has used an instrument on the woman and kills her, he is, anomalously, guilty of manslaughter.

At one time abortion was a felony, so if it resulted in the patient dying it was automatically treated as murder. The Parliament mercifully removed that possibility.[147] But even a conviction of manslaughter is against principle, since the abortionist commits no crime against the woman.[148] Abortion (in effect feticide) is not homicide, because in law *foetus* is not homo. It is somewhat artificial to hold that an intention to abort a foetus becomes manslaughter of the woman if she accidentally dies.

---

[144] (1986) 83 Cr. App. R. 23.

[145] See section 1 of the *Criminal Damage Act 1971*.

[146] Cf. *R. v. Gaylor* (1857) Dears. & B. 288. See also section 58 of the *Offences against the Person Act 1861*. Of course, if D kills during the course of doing an illegal abortion he is liable, since he commits a potentially harmful crime. *R. v. Creamer* [1966] 1 Q.B. 72; *R. v. Buck* (1960) 44 Cr. App. R. 213. Cf. *R. (on the application of Smeaton) v. Secretary of State for Health* [2002] 2 F.L.R. 146.

[147] Section 1(1) of the *Homicide Act 1957*.

[148] This is if we accept consent as a defence. It seems plausible given that abortion is legal if two doctors approve. However, to the extent that it results in actual bodily harm, consent is no defence. See *R. v. Brown* [1994] 1 A.C. 212.

Some people would say that there is no moral difference between killing a mature foetus and killing a baby.   I am not debating the moral issue, but only the legal one. Ever since the time of Coke it has been accepted that unlawful homicide (murder or manslaughter) is the killing of "a reasonable creature who is in being," and "in being 'means' fully born alive."[149] Many authorities demonstrate this limitation to murder and manslaughter. So, in abortion, there is certainly no intention to commit an offence against the person.[150]

12–040

The doctrine of transferred intention cannot be invoked, because that applies only when the defendant intends a particular crime, and commits the *actus reus* of that crime (though with a different victim). Here the defendant intends an abortion; what he does is, in addition,[151] to kill the woman; but the killing of the woman is a different crime—murder or manslaughter in some circumstances, but not abortion.

The judges have tried to explain the law by saying that abortion always involves considerable risk to the person, however carefully performed;[152] but this is probably false. Abortion is dangerous in unskilled hands, but as safe as any other operation in skilled hands; and the law of constructive manslaughter is occasionally used even against skilled surgeons if they operate illegally and are unlucky enough to cause death. If the abortionist kills by gross negligence he is guilty of manslaughter for that reason. Otherwise, the law of abortion is sufficiently severe in itself. In the 21st century abortions are common place, and widely available through officially sanctioned clinics, so in practice, a prosecution under the old abortion laws is likely to be rare.

Is there anything to be said for constructive manslaughter, ever? Why should punishment be increased simply because there is a corpse?   Some kind of answer can be made. Killings attract public attention, and condign punishment may affect general deterrence, enabling other offenders who happen not to kill to be let off more lightly. But the counter-argument is the stronger: that the penal system should not be administered as a lottery.

12–041

Judges who compiled a memorandum on punishment as long ago as 1901 agreed that in manslaughter cases where death results from an assault the punishment should pay regard only to the injury that might reasonably be expected from the assault.[153] The logical conclusion is that there is no point in charging constructive manslaughter: the prosecution might just as well charge gross negligence manslaughter, or assault or some other lesser crime. Some decisions on manslaughter seem to accept the principle stated in 1901; but in

---

[149] *C v. S* [1988] Q.B. 135.

[150] Although abortion appears in the *Offences against the Person Act 1861*, the name of the *Act* cannot be relied upon as a reason for departing from the established rule that a foetus is not a person. The *1861 Act* also has a section on bigamy, which is clearly not an offence against the person in any reasonable meaning of those words.

[151] Generally in addition; but the abortion offence is worded as using "means" to procure a miscarriage, and it is committed even though the woman happens not to be pregnant. *R. v. Gaylor* (1857) Dears. & B. 288.

[152] *R. v. Buck* (1960) 44 Cr. App. R. 213.

[153] Richard M. Jackson, *Enforcing the Law*, (London: Macmillan, 1967) at 5.

other cases, even a near-accident, the punishment is occasionally severe, apparently because different judges hold different opinions on sentencing and policy.[154]

It seems that we will have to put up with this tedious, unnecessary and unjust part of the law for much longer. The Criminal Law Revision Committee long ago recommended the abolition of constructive manslaughter, on the ground that "the offender's fault falls too far short of the unlucky result."[155] As noted above, more recently the Law Commission has proposed something in between, but the Government response to the Law Commission's recommendations concerning homicide was merely to reform the partial defences of provocation and diminished responsibility.

12.8.   KILLING A SUPPOSED CORPSE

12–042   The problem involved where a person has killed another by getting rid of his supposed corpse has already been discussed in connection with murder. The problem arises again for manslaughter. Although the killer will almost certainly not get off a charge of manslaughter by the "supposed corpse" argument, divergent legal theories have been invoked to justify this result.

The first is that the killer's attack of his victim and his subsequent disposal of the supposed corpse are a "series of acts" which the jury can regard as a single act. This principle was applied in *R. v. Church*[156] in relation to both murder and manslaughter. We have seen that the formulation of the rule, at least in relation to murder, was illogical because it was self-contradictory. However, in relation to manslaughter the court also quoted with approval the opinion that "if killing by the first act would have been manslaughter, a later destruction of the supposed corpse should also be manslaughter."[157] This is the right rule, and the one required by policy. Contrary to the apparent opinion of the court, it does not involve any necessity to ask the jury to decide the metaphysical question whether there was a "series of acts."

The second line of approach was utilized in *Attorney-General's Reference (No.4 of 1980)*.[158] This was a case in which the prosecution were under the embarrassment of not being able to prove whether the death was occasioned by the attack or by the act of "disposal." The Court of Appeal held that the jury should be asked two questions. (1) Was the deceased's injury caused by an intentional act by the defendant which was unlawful and dangerous? (2) Was the defendant's treatment of the supposed corpse an act of gross criminal negligence? If the answer to both questions is in the affirmative, the defendant must be guilty

---

[154] See generally, Andrew Ashworth, *Sentencing and Criminal Justice*, (Cambridge: Cambridge University Press, 2010).

[155] Criminal Law Revision Committee, *Offences Against the Person*, Fourteenth Report, (London: H.M.S.O., Cmnd. 7844, 1980) at para. 120.

[156] [1966] 1 Q.B. 59; *R. v. Le Brun* [1992] Q.B. 61.

[157] [1966] 1 Q.B. 59 at 71 quoting Glanville Williams, *Criminal Law: The General Part*, (London: Stevens & Sons, 2nd edn. 1961) at 174.

[158] [1981] 1 W.L.R. 705.

of manslaughter, since he is guilty of that crime whether the death resulted directly from the attack in (1) or from the act in (2).[159]

It seems to follow the decision on (2)[160] that what the court thought of as negligent manslaughter can be committed in respect of a supposed corpse even when the defendant was not guilty of any act causing the victim's unconsciousness. The decision is also supported by the fact that negligent manslaughter does not require subjective recklessness. The decision in *Attorney-General's Reference (No.4 of 1980)* is slightly more indulgent to the defendant than the principle stated at the beginning which was approved in *R. v. Church*, because, unlike *R. v. Church*, it requires the jury to find that the defendant's dealing with the body was grossly negligent. Conceivably the jury may refuse to make this finding, in which case the rule would acquit the defendant of manslaughter—a result of which few would approve. Was Le Brun grossly negligent in trying to drag his unconscious wife into their house?[161] *R. v. Church* is a more clear-cut case, as most reasonable persons would think it grossly negligent to throw an unconscious body into a river, if one were not medically qualified to establish whether that person was still alive.

Another difficulty with the principle stated in *Attorney-General's Reference (No.4 of 1980)* is that it cannot be successfully adapted where the facts leave the cause of death in doubt and the defendant had a murderous intent. D attacks V with a murderous intent. Believing him to be dead, he throws the supposed corpse into the river. It cannot be established which act caused the death. On a charge of murder, the "either way" approach does not work, because a person who throws a supposed corpse into a river cannot by reason of that act alone be guilty of murder. If he is to be convicted of murder it must be because of his bad intent. The only practicable rule for murder is to say that in these circumstances the act and mental state need not concur; and if that is the rule for murder there is no reason why it should not also be the rule for manslaughter. It may be noticed that the court did not deny that the rule might be stated in these terms, but simply held that the case before it could be decided without going into the question. In doing so it put the law into unnecessary doubt.

12.9. KILLING AND THE PROLONGING OF LIFE

Exceptions apart, no one can treat a patient without his consent; so if a dying patient requests that no steps should be taken to prolong his life,[162] we are bound to comply with his request, and therefore cannot be under a legal duty to not ignore it.[163]

12–043

12–044

---

[159] "Where two possible means of a killing are completely different acts, happening at different times, the jury ought to be unanimous on which act has lead them to a decision to convict." *R. v. Boreman* [2000] 2 Cr. App. R. 17.

[160] This point was also an alternative ground of the decision in *R. v. Church*.

[161] *R. v. Le Brun* [1992] Q.B. 61.

[162] *Re B (Consent to Treatment: Capacity)* [2002] Fam. Law 423.

[163] *R. (on the application of Burke) v. General Medical Council* [2006] Q.B. 273; *St George's Healthcare NHS Trust v. S* [1999] Fam. 26; *Bolton Hospitals NHS Trust v. O* [2003] 1 F.L.R. 824; *Winnipeg Child and Family Services (Northwest Area) v. G* [1997] 3 B.H.R.C. 611 (Can. Sup. Ct.).

12–045 **Suppose that the dying patient is unconscious and cannot express a wish?** On principle, the attending physician is entitled to give up treatment when he thinks that it is of no practical value and is in the best interests of the patient to do so. More fully stated, the point is that a doctor must never do anything actively to kill his patient.[164] But he is not bound to fight for the patient's life forever.[165] His duty in this respect is to make reasonable efforts, having regard to the customary practice and expectations, and in particular having regard to the benefit to the patient to be expected from further exertions. He need not and should not crassly fix his attention upon mere (artificially ventilated) heart-beats. Hence the legal importance in this situation, of the distinction between an act and omission, between killing and letting die.

Suppose that a patient with brain damage is on a ventilator (a respirator); he is unconscious, but the machine keeps his heart and lungs going mechanically. A number of independent doctors decide that there is no chance of recovery, so the doctor directly in charge of the patient "pulls the plug." There is general agreement that he is entitled to do so in exceptional circumstances where there is no doubt that that patient is brain dead.[166] This is not a case where, by continuing to treat the patient, the doctor has put him in some peril to which he would not otherwise have been subject.

Justifications may be available for allowing a medical team to withdraw life support, in exceptional circumstances (that is, where many years, or at least months, have passed[167] and the medical evidence suggests that no advances in either the patient's condition or in medical practices are likely to change the result in the foreseeable future) where it is clear that the patient's brain death cannot be reversed. The core justification is that the patient is already dead: on this view, turning off the ventilation does not kill him.

12–046 The problem of the time of death is important in various contexts:

1. *Property rights.* A corpse cannot have property or succeed to property. Suppose that X is an old man who has left Y a large sum in his will. Y is himself in a coma with a flat EEG (electroencephalograph) reading, but his relatives see that he is kept "alive" on a ventilator because they want X's money. As soon as X dies the ventilator is switched off and Y is buried. Will the dodge be successful, Y being regarded as still alive when X dies, so that his family become entitled to the property through him when the machine is switched off? Or is the patient with a flat EEG already dead, so that he cannot be entitled to property?

---

[164] Cf. *A (Children) (Conjoined Twins: Medical Treatment) (No.1)* [2001] 2 W.L.R. 480. This case is discussed *infra* in Chap. 24.

[165] *Airedale NHS Trust v. Bland* [1993] A.C. 789; *Re OT* [2009] EWHC 633 (Fam.).

[166] *Airedale NHS Trust v. Bland* [1993] A.C. 789; *Re B (Consent to Treatment: Capacity)* [2002] Fam. Law 423.

[167] There is a danger that neurosurgeons could push families into agreeing to end life support as soon as possible once they have determined that a particular patient is "brain dead," but such an approach should be resisted. Patients in highly advanced nations where there are adequate health care resources should be kept on life-support for a reasonable period of time, because medical science does not always provide accurate answers.

2. *Taking transplants.* Transplants organs are best used when fresh: is it permissible to take them from a decerebrate "donor" before the life-support system is removed?[168] Transplants cannot lawfully be taken from a living patient (if he cannot live without the part taken), but (subject to conditions)[169] can be taken from a dead one; so is the patient alive or dead?

3. *The responsibility of the doctor for* switching *off the machine.* He can be saved from responsibility if life is regarded as already extinct, for a corpse cannot be killed.

4. *The responsibility of an assailant for bringing the patient to such a pass.* Is the assailant guilty of murder or manslaughter in having caused the death when the ventilator is switched off, or is the cause of the death taking the patient off the ventilator? The question would arise in another form if the assailant kept his victim "alive" on a ventilator in order to avoid a conviction of murder or manslaughter. Could there nevertheless be a conviction, when the victim's heart is still beating?

Formerly, the legal attitude was that death was something that could be left to the doctors to certify, but with the advance of science complications and doubts have set in. It used to be thought that death occurred when the heart stopped, but the French noticed that when an aristocrat or criminal was guillotined his heart continued to function for some seconds after his head was off. Was he still alive? The definition of death in terms of heart death was obviously suspect.

The doubts increased with the increase of medical skill. In open-heart surgery the patient's heart is temporarily stopped, but he is not regarded as dying. Conversely, when a hopelessly comatose patient is kept going on a ventilator, can he be regarded as dead? It has come to be realized that a person's passing, like his creation, is a continuous process, and that there is no scientifically ascertainable moment of death. Different parts of the body die at different times (the skin remains alive for some time after cessation of heart and brain activity, and hair goes on growing for another two days). So in attempting to pinpoint the death of the human person we are engaged in an evaluative exercise, a question of naming, and not primarily a scientific one.

Who is to do the naming? Not necessarily doctors. It was always a mistake to **12–047** regard life and death as exclusively medical questions.[170] Of course, in defining death judges will pay great attention to the state of medical science and the opinions of doctors, as well as to the practical consequences of choosing one definition rather than another. Moreover, it is the doctor who has to apply the legal definition by giving expert evidence. But the fact remains that although the diagnosis of death is medical, the definition must be legal. The law protects the living and ceases to protect the dead (at any rate, in the same way); and the line between the two has to be drawn by the law.

---

[168] Kenneth E. Wood *et al.*, "Care of the Potential Organ Donor," (2004) 351 *N. Engl. J. Med.* 2730, cf. Markus Weber *et al.*, "Kidney Transplantation from Donors without a Heartbeat," (2002) 347 *N. Engl. J. Med.* 248.

[169] Section 33 of the *Human Tissue Act 2004*.

[170] Sometimes, it will be a purely legal question. The law regards a person as dead if she has not been heard of for at least seven years: *Chard v. Chard* [1955] 3 W.L.R. 954. See also section 184 of the *Law of Property Act 1925*.

The doctors have now made up their minds in favour of brain death instead of heart death. The Conference of Medical Royal Colleges and their Faculties of the United Kingdom have resolved that when irreversible brain damage is diagnosed, and it is established by tests that none of the vital centres in the brain stem is still functioning, the patient is to be accounted dead, though the decision to cease artificial support should be taken by two doctors.[171] This has now become accepted by the courts.[172]

The pronouncement is important in relation to transplants. It will encourage doctors to remove kidneys while the patient is still on the respirator, thus increasing the likelihood that the organ will be an effective transplant. A surgeon who did this would be guilty of assault if the patient were not dead. The law never fixed on the heart death as the sole relevant point of time, because formerly it was not possible to distinguish for practical purposes between heart death and brain death. Now that the question has become a practical one, the courts have adopted the definition of death in terms of brain death.[173]

12–048   **Are you telling me that a doctor would not be liable if he withdrew life support from a brain dead patient since the patient is already dead?** The doctor who switches off the machine does not cause the patient to die, because he died when D caused his brain death.

This line of argument would not help as regards property rights and the taking of transplants, but is a way of protecting the doctor from responsibility for stopping the ventilator. It is supported by the ruling in *R. v. Malcherek*,[174] where the trial judge refused to ask the jury to decide whether the fact that the doctors took the patient off the ventilator affected the defendant's liability for murder. On appeal the Court of Appeal similarly declined to hear the alleged evidence that the doctors had not acted in accordance with approved medical practice.

There is no reason why the law should not adopt such an argument in order to promote a beneficial outcome. Brain-death, when it can be established, could well be taken as death for legal purposes. No one could then gain a legal advantage by ventilating what is to all intents and purposes a corpse. Even when brain death cannot be established, but all efforts to restore consciousness have failed, the doctors may be entitled in exceptional circumstances to turn off the respirator when this is a reasonable course of action; and they should not be saddled with liability merely because they were unable to reverse what the defendant caused. The brain death theory involves the application of scientific

---

[171] Conference of Medical Royal Colleges and their Faculties in the United Kingdom, "Diagnosis of Brain Death," (1976) 2 B.M.J. 1187 (1976). Recent science supports this conclusion. Academy of Medical Royal Colleges, *A Code of Practice for the Diagnosis and Confirmation of Death*, (London: 2008); Conference of Medical Royal Colleges and their Faculties in the United Kingdom, "The Permanent Vegetative State," (1996) 30 *Journal of the Royal College of Physicians* 119; *Airedale NHS Trust v. Bland* [1993] A.C. 789, *per* Lords Keith, Goff, and Browne-Wilkinson, *obiter dicta*.
[172] *Airedale NHS Trust v. Bland* [1993] A.C. 789.
[173] *R. v. Malcherek* [1981] 1 W.L.R. 690 at 694; *Airedale NHS Trust v. Bland* [1993] A.C. 789; *Re A* (1992) 3 *Med. L. Rev.* 303.
[174] [1981] 1 W.L.R. 690 at 694.

criteria in virtually an automatic way. But in other cases, it would be up to the doctors (or the patient if she is conscious)[175] to decide whether the victim's life will have any value.

Are you telling me that if a patient is "brain dead" that the doctor is not   **12–049**
deciding that she should die when he turns off the ventilator?   Yes. But, what if the patient is merely in a "persistent vegetative state"? A patient who has not yet suffered death of the brain-stem may be in a deep coma with irreversible brain damage, which means that he is in a persistent vegetative state. If he is not being artificially supported, doctors might do nothing, but simply refrain from giving him medical treatment or food intravenously. If he is on a ventilator they will eventually switch it off. The general view is that this cannot be justified by saying that the patient is dead, though some would extend the notion of death to all irreversibly comatose individuals.[176]

If the patient is in a persistent vegetative state, he is not only legally alive but also medically alive. This is an area where medics, judges and lawyers should tread with caution. Utilitarian considerations (such as making hospital beds available) should never count when determining what constitutes death, because such arguments could allow the status of "dead" to be bestowed upon those are not brain dead. In a rich nation where taxes are high and healthcare resources plentiful, the utilitarian gain of ending the life of a few hundred people each year to free up their intensive care places would not be measurable. The right to life should not be trumped merely to free up hospital beds.[177]

---

[175] *Brightwater Care Group (Inc.) v. Rossiter* [2009] W.A.S.C. 229.
[176] P. D. G. Skegg, "Irreversibly Comatose Individuals: Alive or Dead," (1974) 33 *Cambridge L.J.* 130. See also Peter Singer, *Rethinking Life and Death: The Collapse of Our Traditional Ethics*, (Oxford: Oxford University Press, 1995). A different and even more puzzling problem of definition arises when a patient whose heart beat has stopped is afterwards resuscitated. If the doctor were to say that the patient was dead but has been restored to life the court would not accept his language, because the legal consequences would be too upsetting. On the death of his patient his estate would pass irrevocably to his executors and any life interest that he held in property would come to an end; so that if it were held that he was later restored to life, he would come back into the world a pauper. The law must say that the patient never died. This implies that the cessation of the heart beat, respiration and even brain activity need not signify death if the patient is afterwards resuscitated. The problem is whether the possibility of resuscitation (when the patient is not in fact resuscitated) is to be taken as postponing the legal time of death. For example, the patient's legatee, to make sure that he is not resuscitated, plunges a dagger into his heart. Has an unlawful homicide been committed? The answer would seem to be that the legal moment of death is not to be postponed by reference to a possible resuscitation that does not take place, because the contrary view would create formidable difficulties.
[177] If, however, after many years on life-support, perhaps 5 years depending on the wishes of the family, it becomes patently obvious that given all the advances in science that there is no hope of the patient recovering or any hope of advances in medicine coming up with some miracle cure in the foreseeable future, then it may be in the patient's best interest to end life-support and let nature takes its course.

In recent years the courts[178] have been willing to grant doctors permission to end the life of people in a persistent vegetative state.[179] The usual justification is that it is in the patient's best interests,[180] but this is a broad and contested justification, since it is difficult to see how it is in a person's interest to have all hope taken from him.[181] It may also be in the patient's interests to wait to see if a cure is around the corner. These are thorny ethical issue which we cannot address here.[182] Generally, a doctor should not be allowed to end the life of a person who is not brain dead. In exceptional cases a civil court might grant a doctor permission to withdraw life support. Nevertheless, the civil courts should not permit the withdrawal of life support from a person in a persistent vegetative state, if his family insists that it should not be withdrawn. If the patient is still alive (not brain dead), then he or his family should have the right to demand that treatment continue. If there is no hope and the person is permanently unconscious, then the family might decide, after seeking appropriate medical advice, that it is no longer in his best interests to be kept on life support. In such cases, the hospital should seek a declaration from the courts before it withdraws that patient's life support.

12–050   Obviously, if the patient is brain dead, then the withdrawal of treatment changes nothing: it merely ends a phantasmagorical display of life. That is, it ends the artificial breathing which allows the other parts of the body to display the normal signs of life. Of course, there is a fine line here, but a line has to be drawn somewhere. If a person is brain dead then he is in no better position than a person who has been killed instantly. The defendant has effectively killed him, because he has deprived him of his brain.

However, the situation is not so clear-cut when the victim has been left in a persistent vegetative state. In the latter situation the victim is still alive. He is badly damaged but alive. It is clear that if the doctors withdraw life support from a brain dead person, that the defendant will be liable for either manslaughter or murder depending on his culpability.[183] It is also arguable that if the doctors are forced to take a patient who is in a persistent vegetative state off life support,

---

[178] *A Hospital v. W* [2007] EWHC 425 (Fam.), (however, "W's husband and immediate family supported H's application for the declaration."); *Trust A v. M* [2005] EWHC 807 (Fam.). It is hoped, that the courts will never allow the family's wishes to be overridden, when the patient is still alive, as is the case with those in "a persistent vegetative state."

[179] Such people are clearly not dead. There is a difference between being in "a persistent vegetative state" and being "brain dead." Eelco F.M. Wijdicks, "The Diagnosis of Brain Death," (2001) 344 *N. Engl. J. Med.* 1215.

[180] *Airedale NHS Trust v. Bland* [1993] A.C. 789. The counter argument is the doctor has no duty to treat such patients: given that doctors are paid a fortune and choose to work in such an industry one wonders why!

[181] Keown asserts: "the question is always whether the treatment would be worthwhile, not whether the patient's life would be worthwhile. Were one to engage in judgments of the latter sort, and to conclude that certain lives were not worth living, one would forfeit any principled basis for objecting to intentional killing." John Keown, "Restoring Moral and Intellectual Shape to the Law after Bland," (1997) 113 *L.Q.R.* 481. Quoted with approval by Ward J. in *In Re A (Children) (Conjoined Twins: Surgical Separation)* [2001] Fam. 147 at 187.

[182] Glanville Williams, *The Sanctity of Life and the Criminal Law*, (London: Faber, 1958); Ronald Dworkin, *Life's Dominion: An Argument About Abortion and Euthanasia*, (London: Harper Collins, 1993).

[183] *R. v. Malcherek* [1981] 1 W.L.R. 690 at 694.

because he has been on life support for a lengthy period of time and has not regained consciousness, that the defendant should be convicted of murder or manslaughter depending on his culpability.

What if a fully "conscious" patient demands to be taken off life support? [184] **Would not the victim's fully informed choice to have his treatment withdrawn break the chain of causation?**   No.[185] The removal of life support from a conscious victim who is not brain dead is not a sufficient intervening cause to relieve the defendant from criminal liability.   **12–051**

A person relying on life support to survive is dying "but for" the life support, so if he refuses further treatment the defendant has to take the consequences of what he has set in motion. The chain of causation will not be broken because the victim's failure to accept further treatment is not what is causing him to die. The victim is dying because the defendant has shot him, stabbed him, run him down with a car, *etc*. The victim's refusal (omission) to accept further treatment is merely a failure to take a further chance of trying to prevent the injuries that D has inflicted from killing him. The defendant is responsible for those injuries not the patient. And it is those injuries that are causing the victim to die. The victim is not responsible merely because he has decided that it is no longer worth trying to un-cause or undo what the defendant's act is causing. Unlike the harm inflicted on the victim in *R. v. Blaue*,[186] usually the harm caused to those who have been left on life support for a very lengthy period of time is irreversible. If Blaue's victim had accepted a blood transfusion, it is highly probable that it would have stopped the injuries that Blaue had inflicted from causing her death. Where the victim is in a position to refuse further treatment, the decision will not be one for the doctors.[187]

Couldn't you avoid the niceties of charnel knowledge by saying simply that the doctor who switches off the machine when the patient is in an irreversible coma is not guilty of murder because he does not perform an act of killing, but merely decides not to fight any more to try to revive the patient.   This is a possible solution of the problem mentioned at the outset. It is capable of providing a defence to the doctor even where the patient has not suffered death of the brain stem but is irreversibly comatose all the same. The argument is that stopping the ventilator is in substance not an act but an omission to struggle. And the omission is not a breach of duty by the doctor, because he is not obliged to continue in a hopeless case.   **12–052**

The better view seems to be to accept that turning off the machine is a positive act, but not one that causes the patient's brain death. The latter has already been caused. Switching of the machine is merely an act of stopping it from ventilating a corpse. It has the effect of shutting down the rest of the body, which has only

---

[184] *Re B (Consent to Treatment: Capacity)* [2002] Fam. Law 423.
[185] *R. v. Blaue* [1975] 1 W.L.R. 1411. Cf. *People v. Velez*, 602 N.Y.S. 2d 798 (1993); *State v. Pelham*, 746 A.2d 557 (1998) where the victims had their life support removed, but because their quality of life had been reduced significantly by the physical injuries that D had inflicted. The victims were bedridden.
[186] [1975] 1 W.L.R. 1411.
[187] *R. v. Blaue* [1975] 1 W.L.R. 1411; *Re B (Consent to Treatment: Capacity)* [2002] Fam. Law 423.

been operating in a mechanical sense. The great difficulty of course involves those cases where the patient is permanently unconscious, but is not brain dead. In such a case, the civil courts are only likely to grant a doctor permission to withdraw life support in exceptional cases. Clearly, if the civil courts have granted the hospital permission, then the defendant should take the consequences of what he has caused. As far as causation is concerned, the doctors are in a similar position to the victim in *R. v. Blaue*, except they have done all they could to try to stop the defendant's harm-doing from causing the victim's death.

CHAPTER 13

THE FOETUS AND THE NEW-BORN CHILD

"For Man to tell how human Life began
It is hard: for who himself beginning knew?"

John Milton[1]

13.1.   HOMICIDE AND THE NEW-BORN

The law protecting neonates and the unborn is not ordinarily met with in legal   **13–001**
practice; but it is of importance for obstetric surgeons and is a matter of
philosophical and human interest. It is also the subject of strongly-felt differences
of moral opinion.

The definition of homicide requires the victim to be in *rerum natura* or "in
being," which means that he must be "completely born alive."[2] Although injuries
to a foetus[3] causing death do not generally amount to homicide, there is a curious
rule by which they can do so. If a foetus is injured in the womb and is
subsequently born alive[4] but dies as a result of the prenatal injury, this is murder[5]
or manslaughter according to the mental element.[6]

When exactly does life begin?   The two requirements, birth and live birth, must   **13–002**
be taken separately. The rule for birth is simple: the child must have been wholly

---

[1] John Milton, *Paradise Lost*, (London: Peter Parker, 1667), Book 3.

[2] *C v. S* [1988] Q.B. 135.

[3] Often spelt "fetus," as the American spelling is preferred in medical writing. The *e* is long.

[4] For a lengthy judicial discussion of the "born alive" rule, see *State v. Courchesne*, 296 Conn. 622 at 678–679 (2010), where the Supreme Court of Connecticut, in a 170 page opinion, examined the doctrine's common law roots. See also Clarke D. Forsythe, "Homicide of the Unborn Child: The Born Alive Rule and Other Legal Anachronisms," (1987) 21 *Val. U. L. Rev.* 563.

[5] *Trespasse and Assault v. Sims* (1600) 75 E.R. 1075, cf. *Attorney-General's Reference (No. 3 of 1994)* [1998] A.C. 245. Coke said: "if the childe be born alive, and dieth of the potion, battery, or other cause, this is murder: for in law it is accounted a reasonable creature, *in rerum natura*, when it is born alive." Edward Coke, *Institutes of the Laws of England*, (London: Printed by M. Flesher, for W. Lee, and D. Pakeman, Pt. III, 1648) at 48. It has been consistently accepted that: "The killing of an infant in its mother's womb is confessedly not murder; but on the authority of *R. v. Senior* (1832) 1 Mood. 346, it appears to be laid down by the text-writers as the better opinion, that if an injury be received by the child in the womb, *and the child afterwards, born alive, dies of that injury*, it is murder or manslaughter, according to the circumstances of the case." *R. v. West* (1848) 2 Car. & K. 784 at 786, 788; *R. v. Kwok Chak Ming* [1963] H.K.L.R. 226. It is premised on the infant being born alive, so a threat to kill would not be sufficient for a conviction under section 16 of the *Offences against the Person Act 1861*: *R v Tait* [1990] 1 Q.B. 290.

[6] *Attorney-General's Reference (No. 3 of 1994)* [1998] A.C. 245.

extruded from the body of the mother. No part of the child must remain within the parts of the mother if it is to be regarded as born. Even if the child is deliberately throttled when only its head is protruding this is not murder.[7] An infant is born alive "if, after birth, it exists as a live child, that is to say, breathing and living by reason of its breathing through its own lungs alone, without deriving any of its living or power of living by or through any connection with its mother."[8]

The question of birth has given rise to confusion in the past, because of arguments on the question of "independent existence." Subject to what is to be said later, the law as now settled is that a child is regarded as born alive whenever it is fully born (as above defined) and is alive, the test of the latter being the functioning of the heart.[9] It does not matter that the umbilical cord, whereby the child is connected to the mother, had not been severed at the time when the defendant killed the child.[10] Nor need the child have taken its first gasp,[11] since this may not occur for some little time after birth. Some authorities lay it down that the child must have had a circulation independent of the mother, but this proposition is based on a biological misconception, since the "independent circulation" exists before birth. For several months the foetus has had a circulation independent of the mother in the sense that the embryonic heart maintains a foetal blood-stream, which does not directly communicate with the maternal blood. The two blood-streams are separated by a thin membrane, through which oxygen and nutrients pass to the foetus, and waste products back to the mother. When the child is born, if it does not breathe, its existence is dependent on the umbilical cord, through which its blood-stream is passing in both directions, and so long as the umbilical cord is pulsating in this way the child is dependent on its mother for life.[12]

13–003 **Are you telling me that D could be liable for double homicide if he shoots a pregnant woman in the back of the head and this causes her baby to be born dead?** No. The infant must be born alive, but D will be liable if it subsequently dies from injuries that D inflicted on it while it was a foetus.[13] If D causes the infant to be *born dead*, he cannot be liable for homicide. Is an infant born alive if it is born "brain dead"? An anomaly would be created if a person could be

---

[7] *R. v. Enoch* (1833) 5 Car. & P. 539.

[8] *Rance v. Mid-Downs Health Authority* [1991] 1 Q.B. 587 at 621 *per* Brooke J.; *R v Handley* (1874) 13 Cox C.C. 79.

[9] Suppose that a doctor, having fertilized an ovum in a test tube (in vitro in medical parlance), in order to produce a "test-tube baby," finds that it will no longer be required, and throws it/him/her away. Is this murder? The embryo has not been "born," but it has an existence independent of the mother; biologically it is alive, but is not legally alive if the law makes heart-beat the test! The sensible solution is to say that the embryo has not reached a sufficient stage of development to be "a reasonable creature" within the law of homicide.

[10] *R. v. Reeves* (1839) 173 E.R. 724; *R. v. Poulton* (1832) 172 E.R. 997.

[11] *R. v. Brain* (1834) 172 E.R. 1272.

[12] On the whole subject see Glanville Williams, *The Sanctity of Life and the Criminal Law*, (London: Faber, 1958) at 19–23.

[13] The Lords applied the "born alive" rule in *Attorney-General's Reference (No. 3 of 1994)* [1998] A.C. 245 at 263. See *State v. Courchesne*, 296 Conn. 622 at 678–679 (2010), where a retrial was ordered because the prosecution had failed to prove that the baby which had been kept alive for 40 days on life support was born alive.

convicted of murder or manslaughter when he causes "brain death" in a victim,[14] but is unable to avoid a murder or manslaughter conviction when he causes an infant to be born "brain dead." The "born alive" rule is of ancient origins and the authorities demonstrate that if the infant is born with an independent heartbeat, no matter how momentarily,[15] it is born alive.[16] Nevertheless, if an infant is born brain dead (*i.e.* an electroencephalography (EEG) shows that there is no brain activity), the court is likely to hold that he was born dead.[17]

A flat EEG might not be conclusive as far as the born alive rule is concerned. (An EEG is not likely to be carried out before the infant is fully delivered, and it could lose what life it has before the EEG is conducted.[18]) In *R. v. Iby*[19] the expert witness said: "EEG does not measure subcortical structures underneath the cortex or in the brain stem. Dr. Stack expressed the opinion, albeit in a tentative manner, that the presence of a heartbeat and of blood circulation indicated that some part of the brain stem was functioning. There was also evidence that 22 *per cent.* of children survived after an EEG that indicated a flat line." If it is determined that V was born "brain dead" because he exhibited no brain activity, then it is not likely that there will be any other signs of life. If the infant is born dead and is kept alive on a ventilator, D will not be held liable unless it can be shown that the infant was independently alive before he was put on life support.

Suppose D shoots (with a high powered gun) his pregnant girlfriend six times   **13–004**
in the abdomen with an intent to kill her. Suppose he succeeds and her baby
is born alive, but dies within 3 days. Is he liable for double murder?   He could be liable for double murder, but that would depend on your interpretation of the born alive rule. As far as the Lords are concerned the born alive rule does not make the foetus a person retroactively, so such a case is likely to be treated as murder and manslaughter, not as murder and murder.[20]

On similar facts,[21] the Lords have held it is not possible to transfer D's intent to kill pregnant X to foetus Y and then to born alive infant Y-y. The older authorities make it clear that it was possible to do this, but the Lords thought that the "felony-murder" rule did most of the work in the older cases. Under the abrogated felony murder rule, a person was liable for murder if he killed another

---

[14] In *R. v. Malcherek* [1981] 1 W.L.R. 690 at 694 it is asserted: "There is, it seems, a body of opinion in the medical profession that there is only one true test of death and that is the irreversible death of the brain stem, which controls the basic functions of the body such as breathing. When that occurs it is said the body has died, even though by mechanical means the lungs are being caused to operate and some circulation of blood is taking place."

[15] *Brock v. Kellock* (1861) 66 E.R. 322; *State v. Courchesne*, 296 Conn. 622 (2010).

[16] See the survey of the older English cases in *R. v. Iby* (2005) 154 A. Crim. R. 55.

[17] "Physicians, health care workers, members of the clergy, and laypeople throughout the world have accepted fully that a person is dead when his or her brain is dead." Eelco F.M. Wijdicks, "The Diagnosis of Brain Death," (2001) 344 *N. Engl. J. Med.* 1215. Academy of Medical Royal Colleges, *A Code of Practice for the Diagnosis and Confirmation of Death*, (London: 2008); Conference of Medical Royal Colleges and their Faculties in the United Kingdom, "The Permanent Vegetative State," (1996) 30 *Journal of the Royal College of Physicians* 119; *Airedale NHS Trust v. Bland* [1993] A.C. 789 *per* Lords Keith, Goff, and Browne-Wilkinson, *obiter dicta*.

[18] See *People v. Hall*, 557 NYS (2d) 879 (1990).

[19] (2005) 154 A. Crim. R. 55. Cf. *State v. Cornelius*, 448 N.W.2d 434 (1989).

[20] *Attorney-General's Reference (No. 3 of 1994)* [1998] A.C. 245.

[21] *Attorney-General's Reference (No. 3 of 1994)* [1998] A.C. 245.

while committing a felony. Russell sums the rule up by referring to Coke's classic example: "Whenever an unlawful act, an act *malum in se*, is done in prosecution of a felonious intention, and death ensures, it will be murder: as if A shoots at the poultry of B intending to steal the poultry, and by accident kill a man, this will be murder by reason of the felonious intention of stealing."[22] Therefore, if D unlawfully stabbed V in the abdomen and thereby caused the death of born alive V2, he committed murder.

Under the felony-murder rule it was not necessary to show that D intended to kill anyone, therefore, a conviction could be upheld without transferring D's intent to kill V1 (the pregnant mother) to V2 (a foetus) and then to V3 (born alive infant). All the prosecution had to do was demonstrate that D's unlawful act caused a person's death. Since the infant was born alive and thus was a person when D's unlawful (felonious) act caused his death, D could be held liable for murder. D had the requisite intent when he caused the injuries to the foetus because he had a felonious intent and since there was a sufficient causal link between his unlawful (felonious) act and the born alive infant's death, he could be held liable for murder. The prenatal injuries were the direct cause of the born alive infant's death—the latter being a person.

In *Attorney-General's Reference (No. 3 of 1994)*[23] the Lords invoked the constructive manslaughter doctrine, because the felony murder form of constructive liability[24] is no longer sufficient *mens rea* for *murder*. The *actus reus* for unlawful act manslaughter is complete once D's unlawful act causes the death of another person. The born alive infant is a person so if D causes his death the *actus reus* is complete. The question then is whether D had the requisite *mens rea* for manslaughter. In *Attorney-General's Reference (No. 3 of 1994)* D stabbed his girlfriend thereby causing her born alive infant to die, so he clearly had the requisite *mens rea* for unlawful act manslaughter. Furthermore, his unlawful act was a substantial and operating cause of the born alive infant's death. Lord Mustill said:[25]

> "[A]ctus reus and *mens rea* must coincide. A continuous act or continuous chain of causes leading to death is treated by the law as if it happened when first initiated. The development of this ... rule, which links an act and intent before birth with a death happening after a live delivery, causes a little more strain, given the incapacity of the foetus to be the object of homicide. If, however, it is possible to interpret the situation as one where the mental element is directed, not to the foetus but to the human being when and if it comes into existence,[26] no fiction is required.
> ...
> "In a case such as the present, therefore, responsibility for manslaughter would automatically be established, once causation has been shown, simply by proving a violent attack even if (which cannot have been the case here) the attacker had no idea that the woman was pregnant.

---

[22] Sir William Oldnall Russell, *A Treatise on Crimes and Indictable Misdemeanours*, (Philadelphia: P. H. Nicklin and T. Johnson, Vol. I, 1831) at 59. Cf. Sir James Fitzjames Stephen, *A History of the Criminal Law of England*, (Macmillan & Co, Vol. III, 1883) at 57 *et seq.*

[23] [1998] A.C. 245 at 261.

[24] Constructive intention is no longer sufficient for grounding a murder conviction: section 1 of the *Homicide Act 1957.*

[25] *Attorney-General's Reference (No. 3 of 1994)* [1998] A.C. 245 at 261.

[26] His Lordship seems to be suggesting that if D intends (or obliquely intends to kill or cause g.b.h to the foetus) then he is basically intending or obliquely intending the same against the born alive infant, and therefore, could be liable for murder.

On a broader canvas, the proposition involves that manslaughter can be established against someone who does any wrongful act leading to death, in circumstances where it was foreseeable that it might hurt anyone at all; and that this is so even if the victim does not fall into any category of persons whom a reasonable person in the position of the defendant might have envisaged as being within the area of potential risk. This is strong doctrine, the more so since it might be said with some force that it recognises a concept of general malice (that those who do wrong must suffer the consequences of a resulting death, whether or not the death was intended or could have been foreseen) …"[27]

The House of Lords thought that the involuntary manslaughter route was more feasible as it does not require the prosecution to prove that D intended to kill V (the born alive infant). Rather, it is only necessary to demonstrate that D caused V's death as a result of his unlawful acting.

13–005

As Lord Hope puts it:

"As D intended to commit [an unlawful dangerous act], all the ingredients necessary for *mens rea* in regard to the crime of manslaughter were established, irrespective of who was the ultimate victim whom of it. The fact that the child whom the mother was carrying at the time was born alive and then died as a result of the stabbing is all that was needed for the offence of manslaughter when *actus reus* for that crime was completed by the child's death. The question, once all the other elements are satisfied, is simply one of causation."

Could D be convicted of murder where he intends to kill the foetus?[28]

13–006

That might depend on whether the foetus and the born alive infant are regarded as the same person. Technically, D only intends to commit feticide or abortion. In *Attorney-General's Reference (No. 3 of 1994)*,[29] Lord Mustill seems to have accepted that if D intends to kill the foetus rather than the mother, D will be liable for murder where the foetus is born alive. (The *actus reus* and *mens rea* would coincide, because the foetus and the born alive infant are deemed to be the same person.)

In your hypothetical, D did not intend to injure the foetus with an ulterior aim of causing it to be born alive so that it could then die! Feticide is not homicide! (Intent for one type of crime cannot be transferred to a different type of crime).[30] A foetus *per se* is not a person, so unless the born alive infant is deemed to be the same person (foetus) that was attacked, D cannot be held liable for murder. It is not murder to kill a foetus in itself, but a born alive foetus can be deemed to have been a person from the moment it was attacked in the womb on the basis that it has been born alive. In the United States a number of courts have held that the born alive rule makes it possible to deem that born alive foetuses were persons at the point in time when they were attacked in the womb. Technically, the victim might not have been a person before he was born, but he is when he dies. And because the foetus and born alive infant is the same victim, it is feasible to deem them to be one and the same. (If this approach is adopted, the issue of double transferred intention does not arise: D's intent to kill pregnant X is transferred directly to V, the foetus/born alive infant—who was "a continuing person.")

---

[27] [1998] A.C. 245 at 263–64.

[28] In *R. v. Virgo* (1988) 10 Cr. App. R. 427, D intended to kill the foetus, but managed to kill it before it could be born alive, so could not be convicted a homicide offence.

[29] [1998] A.C. 245 at 261.

[30] *The Queen v. Pembliton* (1872–75) L.R. 2 C.C.R. 119.

13–007 **It is feasible to transfer intent from one "person" to another "person", but is it feasible to deem that the foetus and the born alive infant was a single person under the born alive rule?** The Lords[31] held that D's intent to kill the mother could not be transferred directly to the born alive infant, because this would involve transferring D's intent to kill a pregnant woman to a non-person (a foetus: and an intent to commit feticide is a different crime, which could constitute a criminal act of abortion or child destruction but is not a intent to kill a human) to the born alive infant (a person). If the foetus and born alive infant is treated as one continuing human life, then the double transfer problem does not arise.

In the United States a number of jurisdictions have upheld murder convictions in cases where defendants have caused the deaths of born alive infants. And courts have achieved this in a number of jurisdictions without invoking the felony-murder rule. Instead of invoking the felony-murder rule, the courts have simply held that the "born alive rule" means that born alive infants are "persons" from the moment when they were injured in the womb. The transferred intent doctrine can be applied in such cases as the intent is simply being transferred from one person (the pregnant mother) to another person (the born alive infant). Hence, if the foetus and the born alive infant constitute the same person, then it is possible to transfer D's intent to kill X (the mother) to Y (the born alive infant). There is no need to transfer D's intent to kill pregnant X to foetus Y and then to born alive infant Y-y, as Y and Y-y are one and the same.[32] Thus, if D intends to kill X and in doing so kills Y-y (her born alive infant), he is liable for murdering the infant because he intended to kill a "person" and in fact killed a person (the born alive infant). If he kills both the mother and the born alive infant, he could be liable for double murder.

Since the Lords did not treat the unborn infant and the born infant as "one in the same"[33] under the "born alive" rule, they were unable to invoke the transferred intention doctrine.[34] But if the unborn infant and the born alive infant are "deemed" to be one person under the born alive rule, the transferred intention doctrine allows those who aim to kill a pregnant woman to be convicted of murdering her infant, *if it manages to be born alive*. If it is not born alive, then a homicide conviction is not possible since a foetus is not a person.

---

[31] *Attorney-General's Reference (No. 3 of 1994)* [1998] A.C. 245.

[32] *State v. Courchesne*, 296 Conn. 622 (2010). See also *U.S. v. Spencer*, 839 F.2d 1341 (2008); *Ranger v. State*, 249 Ga. 315 (1982); *People v. Bolar*, 109 Ill.App.3d 384 (1982); *Jones v. Commonwealth*, 830 S.W.2d 877, 880 (1992); *Williams v. State*, 316 Md. 677 (1989); *State v. Anderson*, 135 N.J.Super. 423 (1975); *People v. Hall*, 557 N.Y.S.2d 879 (1990); *Cuellar v. State*, 957 S.W.2d 134 (1997); *State v. Cornelius*, 152 Wis.2d 272 (1989); *State v. Cotton*, 197 Ariz. 584 (2000).

[33] Although, Lord Mustill struggled to maintain such a distinction: "If, however, it is possible to interpret the situation as one where the mental element is directed, not to the foetus but to the human being when and if it comes into existence, no fiction is required." *Attorney-General's Reference (No. 3 of 1994)* [1998] A.C. 245 at 261.

[34] *Attorney-General's Reference (No. 3 of 1994)* [1998] A.C. 245.

The Supreme Court of Connecticut thoroughly examined the issue in a judgment that runs for almost 200 pages and concluded:[35] **13–008**

> "[T]he born alive rule operates to render the foetus a person for purposes of murder or manslaughter if that foetus, having been injured *in utero*, nevertheless is born alive and then dies of the injuries sustained *in utero*. Put differently, in that particular factual scenario, the foetus is treated like any other person. ... In other words, because a foetus that is born alive is a person for purposes of homicide, the transferred intent provisions are equally applicable to a foetus that is born alive as they are to any other person."

The Lords were right not to transfer D's intent from the mother to the foetus (a non-person) to the born alive infant (a person). But if the U.S. interpretation of the common law born alive rule is adopted, there is no need to transfer intent from a person to a thing to a person, since a *born alive* infant is the exact same person throughout—it is not two persons—nor is it a *thing* and a *person*. It is one person as deemed by the born alive rule.

If D intends to kill a pregnant woman and obliquely intends to kill her foetus, then what is wrong with constructively deeming the foetus was born alive when he tried to kill it, if it is subsequently born alive? The culpability involved in repeatedly firing bullets through a pregnant woman with an intent to kill her and also obliquely intending to destroy her foetus, is no different than repeatedly firing bullets through a woman who has a one-year-old child strapped to her back. Intending to kill a woman and obliquely intending to kill the child on her back is not too different from intending to kill her and obliquely intending to destroy her foetus. This is assuming the facts support a claim of oblique intention as far as the foetus/infant is concerned. (If D had no way of knowing that the woman was pregnant or that she had a child strapped to her back, then constructive manslaughter would be back in play.) The constructive manslaughter doctrine holds D liable for manslaughter when he unintentionally causes the death of another. Often there is no comparison between the death D caused and the consequences he actually intended.[36] *Per contra*, those who stab and shoot woman who are visibly[37] pregnant are held liable for the type of consequences they intended or obliquely intended—their convictions are barely tinted with constructiveness.

If D fires twenty bullets into pregnant X's abdomen, could it not be argued that he obliquely intended to kill both X and her born alive infant? **13–009** Your argument would only be plausible if it could be shown that D foresaw the born alive infant's death as a virtually certain consequence, barring some unforeseen intervention, of his act of firing twenty bullets into his girlfriend's womb area.

---

[35] *State v. Courchesne*, 296 Conn. 622 at 720 (2010). The Supreme Court of Connecticut applied the common-law "born alive" rule and the "transferred malice" doctrine rather than the felony/murder rule, to allow for a murder conviction. Cf. *Attorney-General's Reference (No. 3 of 1994)* [1998] A.C. 245 at 265 *per* Lord Mustill.

[36] *R. v. Mitchell* [1983] 2 W.L.R. 938.

[37] Or women (girlfriends, wives, *etc.*, who they know to be pregnant as a matter of fact).

The jury would have to find that the defendant "had appreciated that such was the case; the decision being one for them to be reached on a consideration of all the evidence."[38]

13–010   **The problem with your argument is this: if D fires twenty bullets into V's lower abdomen, it is virtually certain that the foetus will be killed there and then. If D thinks it is virtually certain that the foetus will be killed *in utero*, he cannot also believe that it is virtually certain it will be born alive and then die. Therefore, he obliquely intends to kill the foetus, not a born alive infant?**   It is worth noting that a similar finding would not be available regarding the pregnant mother. If D had shot the womb area repeatedly with an intent to kill the foetus[39] and it had been born alive and subsequently died, he would be liable for causing its death.[40] Furthermore, if he appreciated that the bullet wounds were such that his girlfriend's death was a virtual certainty, barring some unforeseen intervention, he would be liable for murdering her as well. Clearly, the latter is foreseeable as a virtual certainty.

13–011   **Could a person who causes a born alive infant to die be convicted of procuring an abortion?**   Apparently not: abortion is only committed when the foetus is killed in the womb or caused to be prematurely born. Abortion is inapplicable to an act done when the child has left the womb during birth. We shall see that the crime committed is child destruction. A foetus (or unborn child) is not a legal person, and so cannot (for example) own property; but its existence is recognized by law in some ways. The foetus becomes a legal person when it is born alive.

13–012   **The "born alive" rule seems too narrow: D could fire a bullet through the womb of V, who just happens to be 8½ months pregnant thereby killing her foetus and evade liability for murder or manslaughter, simply because he killed the foetus in the womb. Whereas the next person might be unlucky in that his victim is born alive?**   Abortion is applicable to an act done when the child is in the womb. It seems incongruous to label those who deliberately stab or shoot a woman as mere abortionists. Furthermore, it is not clear that they will always have sufficient *mens rea* to come within the purview of section 58 of the *Offences against the Person Act*.[41] If it could be shown that D obliquely intended (a jury is likely to find that D foresaw a miscarriage as a virtually certain consequence of stabbing a woman several times in the abdomen—or of shooting her in the back of the head)[42] to procure V's miscarriage, D could be caught by

---

[38] *R. v. Woollin* [1999] 1 A.C. 82.

[39] Cf. the facts in *R. v. Virgo* (1988) 10 Cr. App. R. 427.

[40] See Lord Mustill's comments in *Attorney-General's Reference (No. 3 of 1994)* [1998] A.C. 245 at 261.

[41] In some cases it will be difficult to establish that D intended to procure an abortion if he merely sees it as a side-effect of attacking the pregnant victim. In other cases, D might try to encourage a third party to do the abortion. See *R. v. A* [2010] EWCA Crim. 1949, this again, makes it difficult to apply section 58.

[42] See *State v. Latour*, 886 A.2d 404 (2005); *State v. Cotton*, 197 Ariz. at 584 (2000).

section 58.[43] It is worth noting that section 58 carries a life sentence. Arguably, if D uses a gun or knife to seriously injure or kill an obviously pregnant woman, he must obliquely intend to use such means to procure her miscarriage.

But Parliament would have to enact a new offence if it were to treat feticide and child destruction as homicide. It could enact a special provision to make it clear that viable foetuses and born alive infants are persons for the purposes of murder and manslaughter. The born alive rule was designed to guard "against the danger of erroneous accusation, therefore the law [presumed] that every newborn child had been born dead, until the contrary appeared from medical or other evidence."[44] In earlier times stillbirths were common and since no one knew for sure whether a foetus was alive in the womb or whether it had any chance of being born alive, it was not homicide to kill a foetus in the womb. "Recent advances in medical science have prompted a number of state courts [in the U.S.] to depart from the born alive rule in favour of a rule of viability, under which 'a viable[45] foetus can be the victim of homicide,' regardless of whether it is born alive." It is for this reason that thirty-eight jurisdictions in the United States have enacted foetal homicide laws. The foetal homicide laws in most states deem that viable foetuses are human beings and thus are capable of being the victims of homicide.[46] Several states treat the killing of a foetus as a form of aggravated assault rather than as homicide.[47] In other states, even non-viable foetuses are protected.[48] (However, as far as the offences of murder and manslaughter are concerned, personhood should not be extended to cover non-viable foetuses.)

13.2. CHILD DESTRUCTION

If a child is purposely killed in the process of being born, this should rationally be the offence of abortion. But it was thought that this offence did not apply to an act done during birth. Accordingly, the *Infant Life (Preservation) Act 1929* created an additional offence of child destruction, punishable (like abortion) with imprisonment for life. The only situation for which the *Act* was required was where a baby was killed after being partly extruded; but it was given wider ambit, overlapping the crime of abortion. The offence is committed by:[49]

13–013

> "any person who, with intent to destroy the life of a child capable of being born alive, by any wilful act causes a child to die before it has an existence independent of its mother."

---

[43] Cf. *R. v. Bond* [1906] 2 K.B. 389.

[44] Alfred S. Taylor, *Medical Jurisprudence*, (Philadelphia: Blanchard & Lea, 7th edn. 1861) at 411.

[45] The word "viable" is derived from the French word "vie," meaning "capable of living."

[46] "[T]he rationale for the 'born alive' rule no longer exists because medical science has now advanced to a stage that the viability, health, and cause of a foetus's death can be determined." See *State v. Courchesne*, 296 Conn. 622 at 688–689 (2010). See also *McCarty v. State*, 41 P.3d 981 (2002), where it was held that if the foetus has reached 24 weeks gestation and medical testimony shows the unborn child is viable, killing the foetus would constitute first-degree murder. Not all states have such provisions. See *Meadows v. State*, (1987) 722 SW2d 584 (1987); *State v. Beale*, 376 SE2d 1 (1989); *Hollis v. Commonwealth*, 652 SW2d 61 (1983), where D was not liable for killing another *person* when he forcefully aborted his girlfriend's pregnancy.

[47] *State v. Courchesne*, 296 Conn. 622 at 690 (2010) and statutes cited therein.

[48] *State v. Courchesne*, 296 Conn. 622 at 690 (2010) and statutes cited therein.

[49] Section 1 of the *1929 Act*.

This legislation is supposed to cover the last part of the period of gestation, namely, when the child is capable of being born alive—commonly, though perhaps misleadingly, called the time of viability.[50] In order to determine the period more precisely, the *Act* provides a presumption that the child is capable of being born alive after the 28th week of pregnancy, *i.e.* the seventh lunar month. The statute expressly provides that no person shall be found guilty unless it is proved that the act was not done in good faith for the purpose only of preserving the life of the mother. This legalizes an operation like craniotomy, designed to reduce the bulk of mature foetus, which intentionally sacrifices the foetus in order to save the life of the mother. The mother's interests take precedence.[51]

13–014 **Suppose a newly born baby is found dead. May not the prosecution find it hard to prove whether the baby was killed or not, and if so whether it was killed before birth or after?** The *Act of 1929* does not help on this. It does not save the jury from the difficulty of making up their minds whether the child was fully born alive at the time when the criminal act was committed, because when the child is fully born alive (having an existence independent of its mother) the crime of child destruction becomes inapplicable and the crime of murder takes over. However, the indictment, and the jury will be left to choose between them.

13–015 **If the child destruction statute does not help with problems of proof, I don't really see why it was passed.** Because it was thought that abortion could not be committed during the birth. This was purely a technical difficulty: it would have been simpler to enact that abortion can be committed up to the moment when the child is born.

13.3. CONCEALMENT OF BIRTH

13–016 The difficulty of proof of the unlawful homicide of new-born infants has lead to an intervention by the legislature. It is an offence, punishable with two years' imprisonment, by any secret disposition of the dead body of a child to endeavour to conceal its birth.[52] The statute is of doubtful justice, because a woman who has

---

[50] "In giving the judgment of the Court of Appeal [in *C. v. S.* [1988] Q.B. 135], Sir John Donaldson M.R., rejected the proposition that a foetus between 18 and 21 weeks of age was, or might be, a child 'capable of being born alive,' in these words, at 151: 'the foetus, even if then delivered by hysterectomy, would be incapable ever of breathing either naturally or with the aid of a ventilator. It is not a case of the foetus requiring a stimulus or assistance. It cannot and will never be able to breathe . . . If [this foetus] has reached the normal stage of development and so is incapable ever of breathing, it is not in our judgment "a child capable of being born alive" within the meaning of the *Act [of 1929]* . . .'" *Rance v. Mid-Downs Health Authority* [1991] 1 Q.B. 587 at 621 *per* Brooke J. (Civil Division).

[51] Cf. *St George's Healthcare NHS Trust v. S* [1999] Fam. 26; *Vo v. France* (2005) 40 E.H.R.R. 12.

[52] Section 60 of the *Offences against the Person Act 1861*; *R. v. Kersey* (1909) 1 Cr. App. R. 260. See also D. Seaborne Davies, "Child-Killing in English Law—Part I," (1937) 1 *Mod. L. Rev.* 203; Stanley B. Atkinson, "Life Birth and Live-Birth," (1901) 20 *L. Q. Rev.* 134; P. H. Winfield, "The Unborn Child," (1944) 8 *Cambridge L.J.* 76. The present tendency is to construe the statute restrictively: it does not apply to concealment of a nonviable foetus: *R. v. Holt* (1937) 2 *J. Crim. L.* 69. Where there is no suspicion of foul play or negligence the outcome of the proceeding is usually indulgent. *R. v. Mortimer* (1938) 3 *J. Crim. L.* 39; *R. v. English* (1968) 52 Cr. App. R. 119.

given birth to an illegitimate child, which dies soon after, may wish to conceal its birth for reasons that do not indicate her responsibility for its death. For instance, she might be a member of an extremely conservative and culturally segmented part of our society. The statute is not required in order to secure the public notification of births, because this is provided for in other legislation.

Nevertheless, the offence does have some merit:

"Withholding a child's dead body from the state's regulatory and investigatory regimes effectively frustrates the ability to determine whether criminal liability exists for the commission of other crimes relating to a child ... whether committed before or after the dead child's birth. The absence of the body of a deceased infant, or access to decayed remains only long after birth, effectively counteracts the government's ability, on behalf of society as a whole, to determine whether the child was still-born or born alive and the cause of death. Motives other than foul play have of course always existed for a person disposing of the body of a child with intent to conceal that the birth occurred, including panic or ignorance of what to do, shame or embarrassment, inability to finance a funeral, *etc.* .... Timely post-mortem examination of a baby may reveal that an infant died a non-accidental death not from natural causes. Where circumstances point toward the deceased's mother as the party responsible for the death, and death is pinpointed to be soon after birth, infanticide may be the appropriate charge not murder or manslaughter. In these cases, because of the mother's mental disturbance and profile of being in denial about killing her child, often there is difficulty ensuring that the appropriate defence is advanced. It is not in the public interest to have such accused charged with and convicted of a more serious crime properly reserved for deliberate killing motivated by stress or simply a disinclination to care for an unwanted baby."[53]

13.4. ABORTION

Abortion (or miscarriage) may occur spontaneously, in which case it is of no interest to the criminal law; or it may be deliberately induced, when it is a serious crime.[54] For legal purposes, abortion means feticide: the intentional destruction of the foetus in the womb, or any untimely delivery brought about with intent to cause the death of the foetus. It is not criminal for a doctor to induce premature birth, when he has no intention to cause the death of the child; and he does not become criminally responsible even if he accidentally causes death.

13–017

Why do you keep referring to the foetus? Would it not be better to admit that we are talking about killing an unborn child?   There is a linguistic point, and a philosophical point. Ordinary language is uncertain: people used to speak of a pregnant woman as being "great with child," but on the other hand the woman might say that she has no child yet. She is "in the family way" rather than having a family. It is quite natural to speak of a mature foetus as an "unborn child," but it would be odd to refer to a microscopic fertilized ovum in that way.

The philosophical debate is whether there is a difference in moral status between the foetus and the born child. Only by stages do women come to regard

13–018

---

[53] *R. v. Levkovic* [2008] 235 C.C.C. (3d) 417 at paras.143–144. For a good historical overview of the offence see, Mark Jackson (ed.) *Infanticide: Historical Perspectives on Child Murder and Concealment, 1550–2000*, (London: Ashgate Publishing, 2002).

[54] Although "abortion" and "miscarriage" are now used by doctors as synonyms, the word "miscarriage" in medical usage formerly referred only to the miscarriage of a foetus of an appreciable degree of development, which is an argument for saying this is its meaning in section 58 of the *Offences against the Person Act 1861*.

the embryo as a separate entity from themselves. Most people agree that at some point of development a foetus has or should have rights, but not the full rights of a born child.[55] We cannot go into the problem further, and it is enough to say that the word "foetus" is here used to cover the product of conception before birth. A foetus is not a legal person, and so cannot (for example) own property; but its existence is recognized in law in some ways.

The early Church accepted, and transmitted to the Middle Ages, the generally held belief of antiquity that the soul entered the human foetus at some time after conception; this was called the theory of mediate animation, since "animation" was supposed to occur at some medial time in pregnancy. The common law absorbed this theory, and fixed the time of animation at the time of quickening, when the foetus moved in the womb, and even that usually occurs about half-way through the pregnancy (the 20th week), though at no fixed point. Abortion before quickening was not a crime punished at common law (though there are records of its being punished by ecclesiastical courts);[56] even abortion after quickening was not murder, because no "reasonable creature" was involved but it was a common misdemeanour, being the killing of a human being or potential human being presumably already possessed of a soul. Thus the common law distinguished between the moral status of the foetus and that of the child, according a lower protection to the former.

13–019 People's thinking on the subject was confused, partly because the term "animation" might refer either to the entry of life (*animus*) or to the early soul (*anima*). No one can prove when—or if—a "soul" enters; but to say that the foetus becomes alive only when it moves is a palpable error. The Roman Church had never regarded the time of quickening as decisive on the entry of the soul, and during the 19th century most Catholic theologians came to support the theory of immediate animation—that is, that the human soul enters at the time of conception. Protestant theology paid virtually no attention to the question,[57] but the claims of logic or supposed logic were sufficiently strong to procure a stiffening of the common law. By a statute of 1803, attempting to procure a miscarriage even before quickening became a crime triable before ordinary courts.[58]

---

[55] See Allen W. Wood "Kant on Duties Regarding Nonrational Nature," (1998) 72 *Proceedings of the Aristotelian Society* 189; Onora O'Neill, "Kant on Duties Regarding Nonrational Nature," (1998) 72 *Proceedings of the Aristotelian Society* 211; Glanville Williams, "Fetus and the Right to Life," (1994) 53 *Cambridge L.J.* 71; Elizabeth Harman, "Creation Ethics: the Moral Status of Early Foetuses and the Ethics of Abortion," (1999) 28 *Philosophy and Public Affairs* 310; Robert J. Araujo, "Abortion, Ethics, and the Common Good: Who Are We—What Do We Want—How Do We Get There," (1993) 76 *Marq. L. Rev.* 701; John Keown, "Back to the Future of Abortion Law: Roe's Rejection of America's History and Traditions," (2007) 22 *Issues L. & Med.* 3; Bonnie Steinbock, *Life Before Birth: The Moral and Legal Status of Embryos and Foetuses*, (New York: Oxford University Press, 1992).

[56] Williams, *op. cit. supra*, note 12 at 139 *et seq.*; Anthony N. Cabot, "History of Abortion Law," (1980) 1980 *Ariz. St. L.J.* 73 at 85 *et seq.*

[57] *Human Reproduction*, (London: British Council of Churches, 1962) at 44.

[58] Though a distinction was still made in respect of punishment, abortion after quickening being capital. For fuller discussion of the post 1803 law, see John Keown, *Abortion, Doctors and the Law: Some Aspects of the Legal Regulation of Abortion in England from 1803 to 1982*, (Cambridge: Cambridge University Press, 1988).

Strangely, the law does not make the abortion itself a crime; the crime consists of an act done with intent to procure (cause) an abortion. It now rests on section 58 of the *Offences against the Person Act 1861*:

> "Every woman, being with child, who, with intent to procure her own miscarriage, shall unlawfully administer to herself any poison or other noxious thing, or shall unlawfully use any instrument or other means whatsoever with the like intent, and whosoever, with intent to procure the miscarriage of any woman, whether she be or be not with child, shall unlawfully administer to her or cause to be taken by her any poison or other noxious thing, or shall unlawfully use any instrument or other means whatsoever with the like intent, shall be guilty of felony, and being convicted thereof shall be liable to be kept in penal servitude for life".

It will be seen that the *Act* covers two cases. First, it covers a pregnant woman who uses any means with intent to procure her own miscarriage. Although these words still stand in the statute book, women are not prosecuted for procuring abortion themselves, perhaps because of the difficulty of getting a jury to convict a woman for an act committed in extreme distress, and the unlikelihood that if convicted she will receive anything more than a nominal sentence. A further good reason for not prosecuting (whether or not it weighs with the police) is that a woman who has operated on herself, or taken drugs, will frequently have caused herself such injury as to necessitate medical attention; and it would be most undesirable that she should be deterred from seeking this attention through the threat of punishment.[59]

Secondly, where anyone else unlawfully uses means with such intent, whether the woman is pregnant or not. A woman who goes to an illegal abortionist becomes an accessory, but in practice she is not charged. Legally, using means with intent is the full offence under the section. Presumably the *Act* was drafted like this in order to save the prosecution from having to prove that an abortion was caused.

13–020

Instances of means in the statute are "poison or other noxious thing"[60] and "any instrument." The statute is not confined to these two instances, and it has been held to apply to an abortion attempted by manipulation with the hand.[61] Where a drug is administered, the judges insist that it must be noxious in itself to be a "noxious thing" within the statute: a harmless dose does not become noxious because the drug in question would be noxious if taken in excess.

Where exactly is the line drawn between contraception and abortion?[62]   Formerly it was thought that the vital point of time was fertilization, the fusion of spermatozoon and ovum, but it is now realized that this position is not maintainable, and that conception for legal purposes must be dated at earliest from implantation. The legislation is unspecific. The abortion section does not expressly refer to conception; it speaks merely of a "miscarriage." There is, therefore, nothing to prevent the courts interpreting the word "miscarriage" in a way that takes account of customary and approved birth control practices.

13–021

---

[59] In 1977 a girl of 13 who was convicted of trying to give herself a miscarriage received a free pardon and apology.

[60] *R. v. Spicer* (1955) 39 Cr. App. R. 189.

[61] *R. v. Hollis* (1873) 28 L.T. 455.

[62] See *R. (on the application of Smeaton) v. Secretary of State for Health* [2002] A.C.D. 70.

After fertilization the human egg stays in the uterine tube for three days, then descends to the uterus and on about the 10th day after fertilization attaches itself to the uterine wall ("implantation" or "nidation"). The widely-used "emergency contraceptive", in common parlance as a morning-after pill, works by destroying the blastocyst (the developing egg) or preventing it from implanting itself in the wall of the womb. If, therefore, conception refers to fertilization, the morning-after pill should be named post-conceptive rather than contraceptive. So-called oral contraceptives may also act in this way, for as well as suppressing ovulation there is evidence that they can prevent the fertilized ovum implanting or for long remaining implanted. That is certainly the mechanism of post-coital oestrogen and progesteron administration, these substances (the so-called morning-after pill) being effective if used within 72-hours of coitus.[63]

If these methods of birth control are abortifacient they are illegal, unless administered by a doctor with the specified opinions of two doctors and in a hospital or registered nursing home under the *Abortion Act 1967*. But no one who uses the morning-after pill supposes that it is illegal or governed by the *Abortion Act 1967*. The only way to uphold the legality of present medical practice, to make the morning-after pill contraceptives and not abortifacients, is to say for legal purposes conception is not complete until implantation. The line of argument is that such pills are designed to inhibit implantation and therefore are not abortifacient. The legal argument is that the word "miscarriage" in the abortion section means the miscarriage of an implanted blastocyst.[64]

13–022   This line of argument would uphold the legality of a universal medical practice, and would therefore provide a partial solution to immediate problems. But our birth control methods have a devastating effect upon the anti-abortion argument that there is something magical or divine about the moment of fertilization which brings about a new "human person" who must be fully protected by law. If all abortion is a kind of murder, it must be recognized, in the words of anti-abortionists, that uncounted thousands of human beings are slaughtered each day by widely accepted birth control devices, as well as by the pill. (It is not clear where all these people are going to fit or how they are all going to be fed: India provides a stark example of the dangers of gross over-population.[65]) Those who are unwilling to denounce these forms of birth control cannot consistently argue for the prohibition of abortion from the moment of fertilization.

Even dating the prohibition of abortion from implantation does establish the legality of the gel and prostaglandin preparations, now being developed, which expel the foetus at an earlier stage after implantation. There is an argument for interpreting the word "miscarriage" to allow still a little more leeway on this question. "Miscarriage" may be interpreted to mean the miscarriage of a foetus

---

[63] *R. (on the application of Smeaton) v. Secretary of State for Health* [2002] A.C.D. 70.

[64] *R. (on the application of Smeaton) v. Secretary of State for Health* [2002] A.C.D. 70.

[65] See Thomas R. Malthus, *An Essay on the Principle of Population*, (London: J. Johnson, 1807). Frank W. Elwell, *A Commentary on Malthus's 1798 Essay on Population as Social Theory*, (Lewiston, NY: Edwin Mellen Press, 2001); L. T. Evans, *Feeding the Ten Billion—Plants and Population Growth*, (Cambridge, UK: Cambridge University Press, 1998); and Antony Trewavas, "Malthus Foiled Again and Again," *Nature* 418 (2002): 668; Lester R. Brown, *Outgrowing the Earth: The Food Security Challenge in an Age of Falling Water Tables and Rising Temperatures*, (New York: W. W. Norton, 2005); John J. Ray, *Conservatism as Heresy*, (Sydney: A.N.Z. Book Co., 1974).

when it has achieved a certain degree of recognizable human organization. In particular, those whose objection to abortion depends upon belief in the soul may be impressed by the fact that until two weeks after conception it remains uncertain whether the egg will become twins (or quins) instead of a single person. Since theology has never contemplated the division of the soul, this implies that the soul cannot enter the body for at least a fortnight after conception. So this argument takes us back to "mediate animation."

The issue was decided upon recently, when the Queen's Bench Division was asked to decide whether the morning-after pill was an abortifacient. In *R. (on the application of Smeaton) v. Secretary of State for Health*[66] the claimant sought a declaration that:

"(i)   a person who administers Levonelle [a brand-name for the morning-after pill] to a woman with the intention of causing any embryo which exists to be expelled commits an offence under section 58 of the of the *Offences against the Person Act 1861*;

(ii)   a person who supplies Levonelle intending that the patient use it for a like purpose commits an offence under section 59 of the *1861 Act*."

The issue was whether the morning-after pill operates in such a way as to cause a "miscarriage" within the meaning of sections 58 and 59 of the *1861 Act*. The claimant sought to argue that Levonelle is not a contraceptive but an abortifacient—and therefore should only be made available in accordance with the procedures laid down in the *Abortion Act 1967*. The *Abortion Act* requires two medical practitioners acting in good faith to certify that the conditions set out in the *Act* are satisfied. If an "abortifacient" is not prescribed in accordance with the conditions laid down in the *Abortion Act 1967*, it is a criminal offence to supply it "knowing that the same is intended to be … used … with intent to procure the miscarriage of any woman."[67] In addition, it may also be an offence to administer the abortifacient, if it the administration is intended to procure a "miscarriage."[68] If the morning-after pill is an abortifacient rather a contraceptive, it would be a crime for pharmacists to dispense it. Permitting a pharmacist to dispense such drugs without requiring a prescription, allows women to access such contraceptives more readily on weekends, public holidays and more generally. Are there not "overwhelmingly strong reasons why it is better to provide emergency contraception than to put more women in the position where they may need to seek an abortion"?[69]

After examining the issues in a very lengthy judgment, Munby J. concluded:[70]

13–023

"[P]rofessor Williams … in the second edition of his *Textbook of Criminal Law* (1983) … states that there is no reason why [the word 'miscarriage' should not be construed to allow a little more leeway]; that is plainly right. …. I have come to the conclusion that I should adopt the narrower interpretation of this part of section 58, and hold that the word 'miscarriage' in this context relates to the spontaneous expulsion of the products of pregnancy. I further hold,

---

[66] [2002] A.C.D. 70.

[67] Section 59 of the *Offences against the Person Act 1861*.

[68] Section 58 of the *Offences against the Person Act 1861*.

[69] *R. (on the application of Smeaton) v. Secretary of State for Health* [2002] A.C.D. 70 at paras. 71, 136.

[70] *R. (on the application of Smeaton) v. Secretary of State for Health* [2002] A.C.D. 70 at paras. 249–250.

in accordance with the uncontroverted evidence that I have heard, that a pregnancy cannot come into existence until the fertilized ovum has become implanted in the womb, and that that stage is not reached until, at the earliest, the 20th day of a normal 28-day cycle, and, in all probability, until the next period is missed.

...

"The word 'miscarriage' as a matter of language presupposes some prior carriage. There can be no miscarriage (or what is by common consent its synonym, abortion) in the absence of true carriage. Prior to implantation there is no true carriage. It may be theoretically possible to argue that carriage can occur when the embryo is free floating in the fallopian tube or in the uterus. However, the much more natural meaning involves not merely presence in the woman's body and interaction with it, but attachment to it in a real sense such as occurs only with implantation."[71]

Since the court declared the morning-after pill (and similar products) as contraceptive rather than abortive, it is not an offence to supply such products. It appears any product preventing implantation within the first 20-days is covered.

13–024 **Do abortionists ever get as much as life?** The maximum sentence is never awarded. In practice, 6 years is the utmost, even for the professional abortionist. Many receive much shorter sentences, and some are merely fined. The ready availability of legal abortions in the 21st century means that prosecutions are rare.

13–025 **When did abortion come to be recognized as proper on medical grounds?** In 1929 Parliament perceived the need to qualify the child destruction statute by a provision for preserving the life of the mother, but crassly failed to add a similar exception to the abortion section. In 1861 (when the *Offences against the Person Act* was passed as a consolidating measure) medical science was not sufficiently advanced to make it safe to terminate pregnancy, so this *Act* makes no exception for therapeutic (health) abortions.

With increasing skill it became medical practice to perform the operation on urgent medical grounds, and the legality of this was established in dramatic circumstances in *R. v. Bourne*.[72]

An eminent gynaecologist aborted a girl of 14 who was pregnant as the result of multiple rapes. He justified his action on health grounds, and was acquitted after a favourable direction by Macnaghten J. The judge rested his direction on the presence in the statute of the word "unlawfully," which he took to signify that some terminations of pregnancy were lawful. In itself this was not a strong ground, but he also referred to the choice of values or choice of evils that is generally known as the doctrine of necessity. He said: "The unborn child in the womb must not be destroyed unless the destruction of that child is for the purpose of preserving the yet more precious life of the mother."[73]

13–026 To expand this point: the woman is a developed human being, sensitive to pain and anxiety. She is established in the affections of her family, and upon her the welfare of other children and of a husband may depend. It is far more important

---

[71] *R. (on the application of Smeaton) v. Secretary of State for Health* [2002] A.C.D. 70 at para. 353.
[72] [1939] 1 K.B. 687. The judge's direction to the jury is reported presumably verbatim as delivered in [1938] 3 All E.R. 615. The variations between this report and that in the Law Reports are so great that the judge must have almost re-written his direction for the Law Reports version.
[73] From the report in [1938] 3 All E.R. 615 at 620. For some reason Macnaghten J. excised the sentence from the Law Reports version.

to consider her life and health than that of an early foetus, representing only a child-to-be, which has not yet been fully formed, cannot feel pain, cannot live outside the womb, and has not entered the human community.

Bourne's acquittal did not at once produce a large increase in medical abortions. The attitude of the medical profession in general was hostile, and tragic cases continued to occur. A girl of 12, pregnant by her father, was refused an abortion.[74] Special boarding schools were opened for expectant mothers aged from 12 upwards, in order that they might continue their lessons while looking after their babies. Women who had been raped, women deserted by their lovers or husbands, and overburdened mothers living in poverty with large families, also failed to get a medical abortion. One "liberal" hospital in London and one in Newcastle performed the operation comparatively freely, and abortions could be readily bought in Harley Street; but in general the mass of women could only go to a "back-street abortionist," wielding a knitting needle, syringe or stick of slippery elm, or to a skilled operator acting illegally for large fees. Some unwilling mothers-to-be used dangerous methods on themselves,[75] or occasionally committed suicide. Although illegal abortions ran into thousands each year, convictions were comparatively few (less than a hundred a year), largely because women who had sought the help of an abortionist were unwilling to give him away, but partly because the police themselves tended not to look upon abortion as a real crime.[76]

The only people who were effectively deterred by the law were the doctors, who alone could operate safely. The problem was common to all Christian countries that started with an unqualified prohibition on abortion. At the same time these evils were beginning to be acknowledged, the opinion arose that a woman had the right to control her own fertility. But against the pro-abortionists was arrayed a powerful religious lobby basing itself upon the "sanctity of life." The *Abortion Act 1967* was a compromise measure which did not concede all the demands of the libertarians and feminists but substantially liberalized the law. In England and Scotland it supersedes the case-law, including *R. v. Bourne*.

Section 1 of the *Act of 1967* provides:

> "(1)   Subject to the provisions of this section, a person shall not be guilty of an offence under the law relating to abortion when a pregnancy is terminated[77] by a registered medical practitioner[78] if two registered medical practitioners are of the opinion, formed

---

[74] *Per contra*, more recently the courts have held that an abortion is in the child's best interests, because of her extreme youth. *B (Wardship: Abortion)* [1991] 2 F.L.R. 426.

[75] On one occasion a teenage girl who took quinine to produce a miscarriage became blind. Other women became paralysed for life or gravely impaired in health. See Glanville Williams, *Textbook of Criminal Law*, (London: Stevens & Sons, 1983) at 296.

[76] Ben Whitaker, *The Police*, (London: Penguin Books, 1964) at 36–37.

[77] Or, surely, attempted to be terminated. An attempt to terminate within the *Abortion Act* is not an attempt to commit a crime. This opinion was expressed by Lord Edmund-Davies and apparently also by Lord Diplock in *Royal College of Nursing v. DHSS* [1981] A.C. 800, but Lord Wilberforce differed. The Law Officers expressed the opinion in 1979 that a doctor who performs "menstrual aspiration" at a time when it is not known whether the woman is pregnant or not is protected by the *Abortion Act* if one of the grounds of termination specified in the *Act* is present.

[78] It is sufficient if the doctor makes the medical decision and performs such parts of the treatment as necessitate his particular skill, other parts being performed by nurses, even though in his absence. *Royal College of Nursing v. DHSS* [1981] A.C. 800.

in good faith—(a) that the pregnancy has not exceeded its twenty-fourth week and that the continuance of the pregnancy would involve risk, greater than if the pregnancy were terminated, of injury to the physical or mental health of the pregnant woman or any existing children of her family; or (b) that the termination is necessary to prevent grave permanent injury to the physical or mental health of the pregnant woman; or (c) that the continuance of the pregnancy would involve risk to the life of the pregnant woman, greater than if the pregnancy were terminated; or (d) that there is a substantial risk that if the child were born it would suffer from such physical or mental abnormalities as to be seriously handicapped.

(2)   In determining whether the continuance of a pregnancy would involve such risk of injury to health as is mentioned in paragraph (a) or (b) of subsection (1) of this section, account may be taken of the pregnant woman's actual or reasonably foreseeable environment.

(3)   Except as provided by subsection (4) of this section, any treatment for the termination of pregnancy must be carried out in a hospital vested in the Secretary of State for the purposes of his functions under the *National Health Service Act 2006* or the *National Health Service (Scotland) Act 1978* or in a hospital vested in a Primary Care Trust or a National Health Service trust or an NHS foundation trust or in a place approved for the purposes of this section by the Secretary of State.

(4)   Subsection (3) of this section, and so much of subsection (1) as relates to the opinion of two registered medical practitioners, shall not apply to the termination of a pregnancy by a registered medical practitioner in a case where he is of the opinion, formed in good faith, that the termination is immediately necessary to save the life or to prevent grave permanent injury to the physical or mental health of the pregnant woman."

13.5. THE FOETAL GROUND

13–027   The foetal ground (section 1(1)(b)) does not need extensive consideration. It is sometimes justified for eugenic reasons,[79] but in fact the contribution that abortion is likely to make to the betterment of man's genetic inheritance is slight. No: the argument for abortion on the foetal indication relates to the welfare of parents, whose lives may well be blighted by having to rear a grossly defective child, and perhaps secondarily by consideration for the public purse.[80] That this is the philosophy of the *Act* is borne out by the fact that it allows termination only where the child if born would be seriously handicapped, not where it is merely carrying undesirable genes.

Whereas the health grounds recognized in the *Act* merely enlarge on the attitude of the judge in *R. v. Bourne*, that the health of full human beings is to be preferred to that interest of the foetus in being born alive where the two interests conflict, the foetal ground marks a new departure. The foetus is destroyed not necessarily in its own interest (the physician need make no judgment that life be a burden for it), but in the interest either of the parents or of society at large, though of course only upon the request of the mother.

Even though the argument whether abortion should be permitted merely as a matter of convenience to the woman continues, in practice the issue is settled as abortions are readily available under the mental health prong (*i.e.* to prevent injury to the mental health of the pregnant woman)—which seems to permit

---

[79] Cf. *Jepson v. Chief Constable of West Mercia* [2003] EWHC 3318.

[80] Professor Baroness Deech claims that people are married to their first cousins and that this has resulted in a third of the children born to such parents having recessive genetic disorders. See Martin Beckford, "Baroness Deech: risks of cousin marriage not discussed for fear of offending muslims," (London: *The Telegraph*, 23 March 2010). This could have long term fiscal implications for the N.H.S. and social costs for the community involved.

abortions that are primarily needed as a matter of convenience.[81] That aside, the foetal ground is almost universally accepted. But it is of some interest to note that anyone who does accept the foetal ground for abortion commits himself to the view that the moral status of the foetus is not the same as that of a child. After all, we do not permit children to be killed because they are seriously handicapped.

13.6. THE HEALTH GROUNDS

The health grounds subdivide in relation to the health of the woman and the health of the existing children in her family.   **13–028**

Where pregnancy is terminated on the ground of risk of injury to health,   **13–029**
how great must the risk be to justify the termination? There is no need to
show that the mother was exposed to a physical risk, because the risk of mental
injury is sufficient. When the Abortion Bill came before the House of Lords,
much attention was given to this question. The adjectives "serious," "grave" and
"substantial" were considered, but their Lordships finally adopted Lord Parker
C.J.'s suggestion (moved in absence by Lord Dilhorne, a strong opponent of
relaxing the law), which now appears in the *Act*. The injury feared from allowing
pregnancy to continue must be "greater than if the pregnancy were terminated."
Lord Parker C.J. said of his amendment that the doctor's decision was to be
arrived by comparing one risk with another, and only if the risk in continuation
were greater than the risk in termination would a defence be created under the
Act. If that was the test, he said, it would be unnecessary and wrong to talk about
risk as being "serious" or "substantial."

In making this move some of the opponents of freer abortion were perhaps
misled by the propaganda emanating from their own side. It had been widely
argued, against the practice of abortion, that it was a dangerous operation, and on
this supposition the formula was a restrictive one. Even so, the formula was a
doubtful advantage for the restrictionists, because no one knew how long it might
be before the danger of the operation was reduced, thus extending its legality. But
in any case the assumption that the operation was particularly dangerous was
wrong even in 1967, at least in cases where the termination was performed early
enough. Figures from Eastern Europe indicated that the operation, properly
performed within the first trimester[82] (the first three months of pregnancy), was
much safer (at least from the point of view of morality) than normal childbirth.

The wording of the *Act*, then, suggests the argument that first-trimester
abortions are now left to medical discretion in the sense that if the doctor comes
to the conclusion that, as the figures firmly show,[83] the general mortality risk of a

---

[81] In 2008 there were 195,296 legal abortions in England and Wales. See Abortion Statistics, England and Wales: 2008 (*Statistical Bulletin*: Department of Health, 2009). Most of these were funded by the N.H.S.

[82] Accent on middle syllable.

[83] See Abortion Statistics, England and Wales: 2008 (*Statistical Bulletin*: Department of Health, 2009).

first-trimester abortion is less than maternal mortality, and if he further believes[84] that the morbidity risk does not affect the general conclusion that abortion is safer,[85] and that there is nothing in his patient's condition to affect the application of the statistical argument to her case, he is entitled to terminate an early pregnancy without finding a more specific ground for termination. Although this argument has not been ventilated in court, and would doubtless be regarded with extreme reserve by the judges, there is no logical answer to it. The risks associated with normal maternity must be among the risks resulting from a decision not to terminate, so that they can enter into a calculation of the risks that are "greater than if the pregnancy were terminated;" and if these risks by themselves are greater than the risks of termination; no other question need logically be asked.[86]

13–030   **But that would mean that we have abortion on demand, which Parliament never intended. So the *Act* ought not to be interpreted in that way.**   Some would say so. The opposing view is that Parliament consciously settled for a certain test for the legality of abortion; that test is acceptable to very many people, and the courts should apply it according to its wording. It is not for the courts to speculate whether Parliament made some mistake of fact, and how it would have worded the *Act* if it had not made that mistake.

Most doctors accept the above argument and assume that the *Act* enables them to terminate on the ground of hardship and distress, provided that they act early enough. There have been nearly 1,000,000 abortions performed in England and Wales in the last five years.[87] A minority of doctors, however, disapprove of abortion, and therefore construe the *Act* restrictively; so that some variation still exists between different parts of the country.

13–031   **Can the doctor act at a very early stage, before it has been established whether the woman is pregnant?**   No reason why not: the doctor may act on the ground that *if* the woman is pregnant it will be bad for the pregnancy to continue. This point is important because the practice of menstrual aspiration at an early date when the diagnosis of pregnancy may be uncertain. It may of course be argued, against the legality of operating, that the *Abortion Act* validates the proceeding only if the woman is in fact pregnant, because it supposes that "a pregnancy is terminated." But this would overlook the question of the *mens rea*

---

[84] It seems that on the wording of the *Act* a doctor who terminates where there is a proper ground under the *Act* is technically guilty if he does not have it in mind to terminate on that ground. But this is against principle: Glanville Williams, "Offences and Defences," (1982) 2 *Legal Stud.* 233.

[85] The conflicting evidence on morbidity associated with abortion is largely explicable by the fact that the research is coloured by moral views. See Betty Sarvis and Hyman Rodman, *The Abortion Controversy*, (New York: Columbia University Press, 1973). It is hard to measure the long-term psychological effects of forcing the mother to have the child, as many may, after experiencing motherhood, end up being pleased that they did not abort—or *vice versa*.

[86] A doctor would, however, not be protected if he has not examined the patient. See *R. v. Smith* [1973] 1 W.L.R. 1510, where a doctor was convicted partly because of this fact.

[87] See the Abortion Statistics, England and Wales: 2005, 2006, 2007, 2008, and 2009 (*Statistical Bulletins*: Department of Health).

required for the offence under section 58 of the *1861 Act*. Because of this consideration, the Law Officers of the Crown expressed the opinion in 1979 that menstrual aspiration is lawful.

Although the section makes it an offence to use means to procure the miscarriage of a woman who is not in fact with child, it obviously supposes that the defendant believed that the woman was or might be with child. Now the attitude of the doctor in the case we are considering is this. If the woman is with child, then what he does will result in an abortion, and it will be lawful under the *Abortion Act*. If the woman is not with child, then there will be no abortion. Either there will be no abortion, or it will be a lawful abortion. The doctor's intention being not to procure any abortion except a lawful abortion, it cannot reasonably be argued that an offence is committed.

What is meant by "the mental health of the pregnant woman"? Narrowly 13–032 interpreted, it may require the doctor to fear that the patient will suffer from what is commonly called a mental illness, whether a psychosis or severe neurosis. This may include a depressive psychosis; the British Medical Association has long recognized that termination may properly be advised on account of a "reactive depression," that is, the state of hopeless despair in which the patient finds herself.[88] If the question is one of mental illness, the natural course would be to call a psychiatrist, a specialist in mental disorder.

But "mental health" is susceptible of a wider meaning. The definition of health advanced by the World Health Organization is that it is "state of complete physical, mental and social well-being and not merely the absence of disease or infirmity." Gynaecologists who take this broad view do not insist upon a psychiatric opinion, but are ready to act on their own opinion of the case, backed by the family doctor.

Can the doctor take account of the fact that the woman is a suicide risk? A 13–033 serious threat of suicide can clearly be taken into account, because it indicates the depth of the woman's depression.

Can the doctor take account of a risk to the health of the woman arising not 13–034 during the pregnancy but as a consequence of her having to rear the child if it is born? The words of the *Act* suggest answers both ways. The *Act* refers to "risk of injury to the health of the pregnant woman," and one may argue that when the child has been born the woman is no longer pregnant. Moreover, it must be "continuance of pregnancy" that produces this risk, and it is perhaps slightly strange, though not impossible, to say that the burden on the mother of having to rear the child was a result of "continuance of the pregnancy."

On the other hand there are two clues in the *Act* making it reasonably clear that the wider meaning was intended by Parliament.

The words just quoted are used with regard to both the health of the woman and the health of existing children of her family. If one pays regard to the health of existing children, as the *Act* allows, it would be illogical to do this only during the time of gestation of the new addition to the family. What was evidently

---

[88] [1968] 1 *B.M.J.* 171.

intended was that existing children might be adversely affected by the extra child being born and having to be brought up by an already overburdened mother.

Subsection (1)(2)(1) provides that "account may be taken of the pregnant woman's actual or reasonably foreseeable environment." This is not, as has sometimes been thought, a purely "social" ground for termination, since it is related to the question of health. It does not allow the operation merely because the patient will otherwise lose her job or her husband. Still, the statutory words make it clear that the question of health is to be considered broadly. There is not much point in directing the doctor to look ahead to the woman's future environment if he is to consider only the time of pregnancy. So it is really quite clear that the *Act* is intended to provide for the case of the overburdened mother.

13–035 **The *Act* allows termination out of consideration for existing children of the family. How can the health of existing children be affected by their mother having another child?** Sometimes it may be reasonable to make this judgment. Consider the mother of a "problem family." She is living in poverty, with a large brood of children. Her *de facto* lover has been in prison and has now been arrested again. Her existing children are badly cared for and play truant. Now she is pregnant once more. It may confidently be predicted that if the pregnancy is allowed to go to term, matters will be worsened for the existing children to the extent that their health may be affected. In practice, doctors who terminate on this ground generally tick it as an extra to the health of the woman.

13–036 **Can the doctor take the poverty of the family into account?** Not directly, but he can if the woman's poverty, aggravated by the addition to her family, is likely to affect her health or that of her other children.

13.7. LIMITATIONS OF THE ABORTION ACT

13–037 The *Act* does not provide for termination on the ground that the pregnancy was the result of rape. In human terms there is a strong argument for this, but the proposal was successfully resisted in Parliament. The position generally taken was that the abortion was immoral except when performed on health or eugenic grounds. Also, many doctors objected that they could not decide whether a rape had been committed. (This was really no argument against allowing the doctor to act where he thought the facts were clear—*i.e.* where charges have been laid against an identified rapist.) All agreed, however, that the fact of rape could influence the decision of the doctor in invoking the health ground. In effect, doctors were encouraged to stretch their professional consciences, in order to enable the supposed moral principle to be preserved.

13–038 **What if the woman is under the age of consent to sexual intercourse?** The position is much the same as for rape. There is no specific statutory provision. But the doctor can take youth into account in judging the probable effect of a continuation of the pregnancy on her mental health. Here again the *Act* probably invites a degree of benevolent hypocrisy on the part of doctors, since the real argument for terminating in these cases may be social rather than medical.

The *Act* does not allow termination on the ground that the child would be unwanted, the woman having used a method of contraception that failed on the particular occasion. Again, it is no ground for termination that the mother has been convicted of baby-battering. The fact that the child when born is likely to be cruelly neglected or ill-treated is not considered. The only ground relating to the foetus is that of serious handicap.

Does the *Act* cut down the defence under *R. v. Bourne*? It imposes two   **13–039** procedural restrictions, which did not exist for the common law defence:

1. The treatment must be given in an N.H.S. hospital or other approved clinic/hospital. Such institutions are inspected and tightly controlled.
2. Two registered medical practitioners[89] must have found the opinion in good faith that the case falls within section 1.

The reasonableness of the opinion is not in issue, though, of course, an alleged opinion that is grossly unreasonable may be held not to have been formed in good faith. The doctor giving the treatment need not be one of those who gave the required opinion, though he may be. Nor is it required that both or either of the doctors be a consultant, and gynaecologists commonly rely to a considerable extent on the opinion of the woman's general practitioner as to her mental condition in relation to the pregnancy. It seems that in a suitable case one doctor would be justified in relying implicitly on the judgment of another; what he himself contributes to the case is his knowledge of the experience of his colleague. Owing to a defect in the wording of the *Act*, both doctors must act in good faith before either falls within the protection given by its wording. But if a case arose in which one of two doctors alone acted in good faith, it could be argued in his defence that the general principles of *mens rea* save him from conviction. Believing that his companion acted in good faith, he would not have the necessary intent to commit an offence.

The two procedural safeguards do not apply in serious emergencies, as specified in section 1(4) (though even in an emergency the termination must be by a doctor).

The draftsman evidently thought that by providing for an emergency he had   **13–040** rendered the common law wholly unnecessary, and section 5(2) accordingly provides that "for the purpose of the law relating to abortion, anything done with intent to procure the miscarriage of a woman is unlawfully done unless authorised by section 1 of this *Act*." This strikes down one of the reasons for the decision in *R. v. Bourne*, and was certainly intended to get rid of that decision in order to prevent the procedural safeguards from being circumvented. However, the total elimination of the defence of necessity, if that is what the subsection does, was of doubtful wisdom.

Another procedural provision in the *Act* relates to notification (section 2). Non-compliance with this is a summary offence. Compliance is not a condition of the defence given by the *Act* to a charge of abortion.

---

[89] For qualifications in respect of visiting forces, *etc.*, see section 3 of the *Act of 1967*.

13–041   **Can an abortion be lawfully performed under the *Abortion Act* at any stage in the pregnancy?**   Section 5(1) of the *Abortion Act* provides:

> "(1)   No offence under the *Infant Life (Preservation) Act 1929* shall be committed by a registered medical practitioner who terminates a pregnancy in accordance with the provisions of this *Act*."

Formerly, the *Act* criminalized the destruction of a child capable of being born alive except to preserve the patient's life, and the *Act* created a presumption that a foetus of 28 weeks' gestation could be born alive. Since the enactment of the *Human Fertilisation and Embryology Act 1990*, this limitation has been removed. A doctor no longer commits an offence for the purpose of the *1929 Act*, if he aborts a foetus capable of being born alive, if he complies with the conditions laid down in the *Abortion Act*.

13.8.   THE SUPPLY OF THINGS FOR ABORTION

13–042   Partly to put down abortions, and partly in order to prevent women who desire abortions from endangering themselves, it is made an offence unlawfully to supply or procure any noxious thing, instrument, "or thing," with knowledge that it is intended to be used to procure a miscarriage, whether the woman be or be not with child.[90] However, procuring a thing for use in abortion is not the same as procuring an abortion, the former is caught by section 59, and the latter by section 58.[91] A thing does not include an "act of abortion"—one does not supply or procure a thing for use in abortion by procuring a medical doctor to do the abortion.

In *R. v. A*,[92] a young woman from Pakistan entered an arranged marriage with a man double her age. When she fell pregnant he attempted to trick her into having an abortion by taking her to a clinic for an allegedly routine operation. She could not speak English so the husband acted as an interpreter and convinced the staff that she wanted an abortion. Before the abortion went ahead, the general manager of the clinic asked an Urdu speaking nurse to speak to the complainant. When the complainant learnt she had been brought in for an abortion she became very upset. She claimed that she believed she was having a minor operation to cure something that was wrong with her blood. She refused to have the abortion and fled to Bristol where she had relatives. Subsequently, she gave birth to the child and applied for leave to remain in the United Kingdom.

The case against the defendant was that he had unlawfully procured a "thing," namely a surgical procedure at the clinic "knowing that this procedure was intended to be used unlawfully to procure the complainant's miscarriage." It was

---

[90] Section 59 of the *Offences against the Person Act 1861. R. v. Titley* (1880) 14 Cox C.C. 502. It has been held that the supplier or procurer may be convicted under this section though he is the only person who has the criminal intent: *R. v. Hillman* (1863) Le. & Ca. 343, *sed quaere. R. v. Mills* [1963] 1 Q.B. 522, gives a very limited meaning to the word "procure." A person may be convicted of an attempt at common law to commit an offence under section 59. If the noxious thing is taken by the woman, the supplier will generally be guilty under section 58, not merely section 59. *R. v. Turner* (1910) 4 Cr. App. R. 203. See also *R. v. Marlow* (1965) 49 Cr. App. R. 49.
[91] *R. v. A* [2010] EWCA Crim. 1949.
[92] [2010] EWCA Crim. 1949.

asserted in the alternative, that "if the word 'thing' is apt only to describe an object or article, rather than a procedure, then D must have procured the surgical instruments that must have been available to carry out the procedure had it gone ahead."

The Court of Appeal said:[93]   **13–043**

> "[S]ection 59 is concerned in short with the procuring or supply of something intended for use in procuring an unlawful miscarriage. ... Even if the indictment had been correctly drawn, it is our view that no offence contrary to section 59 would have been made out on the facts of this case. The appellant clearly did not supply or procure any poison, any other noxious thing or any instrument. Recognising that, the respondent is impelled to argue that the appellant supplied or procured a 'thing' within the meaning of that word where it appears for the second time in section 59, the 'thing' being the anticipated medical or surgical procedure. In our judgment, however, the juxtaposition of the word 'thing' with the word 'instrument' which almost immediately precedes it, indicates that the 'thing' must be some sort of article or object rather than something such as a medical procedure which has no physical existence. We are fortified in this conclusion by comparing section 59 with section 58 of the *1861 Act*. The latter section makes it an offence, amongst other things, for any person with intent to procure a miscarriage of a woman unlawfully to 'use any instrument or other means whatsoever'. The use of the word 'means' almost immediately after the word 'instrument' in section 58 is to be compared and contrasted with the use of the word 'thing' almost immediately after the word 'instrument' in section 59. The word 'means may well have been apt to encompass a surgical procedure or efforts made to procure one, though it does not follow that section 58 would have been apt to meet the circumstances of this particular case."

D could not be charged under section 58 as he had not carried out the abortion and nor had the doctors. Could he have been charged for attempting to carry out the abortion? No, because he only attempted to encourage the doctors to do so. Nor is he an accessory under the *Accessories and Abettors Act 1861*, because the doctors did not go through with the abortion.[94] Furthermore, if the doctors had acted lawfully and in good faith there would be no crime for him to procure or encourage. (But the clinic might have been sued for negligently failing to ascertain the patient's fully informed consent.) Nevertheless, D could be convicted of an inchoate offence contrary to sections 44 and 47(5)(iii) of the *Serious Crime Act 2007*. He encourages the doctors to perform an abortion on a non-consenting woman. The doctors are innocent agents, as they are acting in good faith. D, however, has the requisite fault for the offence found in section 58. Furthermore, the new inchoate offences apply regardless of whether the doctors perform or attempt to perform the abortion.

---

[93] *R. v. A.* [2010] EWCA Crim. 1949 at paras. 10–14.Cf. *R. v. Magira* [2009] 1 Cr. App. R. (S.) 390.
[94] Cf. *R. v. Sockett* (1908) 1 Cr. App. R. 101. Nor was there a conspiracy between D and the doctors. Cf. *R. v. Whitchurch* (1890) 24 Q.B.D. 420.

PART THREE

INVOLVEMENT IN CRIME

CHAPTER 14

COMPLICITY

"For the sin ye do by two and two
ye must pay for by one!"

Joseph Rudyard Kipling, *Tomlinson*

14.1.   THE DEGREES OF COMPLICITY: PERPETRATORS

Complicity in crime extends beyond the perpetrator to accessories.[1] Both the perpetrator and the accessories are regarded by law as participants in the crime, and are called accomplices. The perpetrator is an accomplice of the accessories, and they are accomplices of the perpetrator and of each other.[2] An accessory (sometimes called a secondary party) may be either an encourager or an assister. He is one who encourages or assists the commission of an offence by the perpetrator. There is a small problem of terminology. At common law the person here called the perpetrator was called the principal in the first degree. Those who assisted at the time of the crime ("aided and abetted") were termed principals in the second degree. Those who successfully encouraged ("counselled or procured") the crime, were termed accessories (before the fact) in felonies, principals in misdemeanours and summary offences.

14–001

The *Criminal Law Act 1967* abolished the distinction between felonies and misdemeanours, applying the misdemeanour rules to all indictable offences. The effect is to abolish accessories and make everyone a principal—if the old terminology is kept. But there is no point in continuing to speak of a principal if he is not contrasted with a non-principal. Evidently, new language is needed. The Law Commission Working Party proposed to speak of the doer as the principal and all other accomplices as accessories.[3] Accessories, therefore, are both the former accessories in felony and the former principals in the second degree. While this extended notion of "accessories" is acceptable, there is one serious objection to the continued use of the term "principal" to denote the perpetrator. In the civil law (the law of contract and tort), where A directs B to do something on his behalf, A, the commander, is called the principal and B, the doer, his agent. It

---

[1] See further, Glanville Williams, *Criminal Law: The General Part*, (London: Stevens & Sons, 2nd edn., 1961), Chap. 9.

[2] The word "accomplice" is used chiefly in relation to the rule of evidence that the judge must warn the jury of the danger of convicting on the uncorroborated evidence of an accomplice.

[3] Law Com., *General Principles, Parties, Complicity and Liability for the Acts of Another*, Working Paper 43 (London: H.M.S.O. 1972).

seems unfortunate to call B the principal in criminal law, when he is the agent in civil law.[4] Let it be known, therefore, that the name "perpetrator" is adopted in the present book.[5]

The "perpetrator" (or, if you will, the principal) means, and means exclusively the person who in law performs the offence. More precisely, the perpetrator is the person who, being directly struck at by the criminal prohibition, offends against it with the necessary *mens rea* or negligence (if either is required). He is normally indicated by the wording of the legal rule. In murder, he is the person who kills; in burglary, the person who trespasses with the requisite intent; in forgery, the person who makes or uses the forged document.

14–002   The perpetrator may do the deed by his own hand, or he may procure an innocent agent (or set up an instrumentality) to do it. In other words he may use a cat's paw to pull his chestnuts from the fire. He may, for example, get another to make false representations on his behalf by concealing facts from him, or he may (keeping more closely to the fable) train a dog to steal meat. Also, an employer who is attributively responsible (that is, responsible for his employee) is a perpetrator if the act amounts to an offence, because he is regarded as doing the act through his employee. So the full definition offered by the Law Commission Working Party on Codification is as follows. I quote it with an addition of my own in square brackets:

"(1)   A principal in an offence is one who, with any necessary fault element, [and possessing any qualification required for the offence,] does the acts constituting the external elements of the offence.

(2)   A person does such an act not only when he does it himself but also when he—

(a)   acts through an innocent agent; or

(b)   is otherwise responsible for the act of another which constitutes an external element of an offence."[6]

Innocent agency and attributed responsibility will be studied later. At present we are concerned only with the sub-rule (1). The sub-rule as worded by the Working Party did not say, as properly it should have, that a person cannot be a perpetrator unless he possesses a qualification required for the offence. Bigamy, for example, can be perpetrated only by a married person ("Whosoever, being married, shall marry ..."),[7] so if a married man goes through a bigamous ceremony of marriage with a spinster, the spinster cannot be guilty of bigamy as perpetrator, even if she knows of the bigamous character of the ceremony. (In the latter event she is guilty as accessory.)

---

[4] A further reason for abandoning the word "principal" in the criminal law is that it is liable to mislead when the older authorities are read. Before 1967 an abettor was a principal in felonies and all parties were principals in misdemeanours; since the misdemeanour rules have been generalized, all parties to all crimes are principals on the old terminology, but they were and are not all principals in the first degree (which is what we are now talking about). To abbreviate to "principals," simply, is capable of producing false reasoning.

[5] An incidental advantage of the word "perpetrator" is that it gives the verb "perpetrate"; the word "principal" yields no verb.

[6] *Working Paper 43, supra,* note 3.

[7] Section 57 of the *Offences against the Person Act 1861.*

Two persons may be guilty as joint perpetrators;[8] and part of a crime may be committed by one perpetrator, another by another. Thus, in robbery, which involves the two elements of theft and threat, one person may steal while his companion makes the threat of force, and the two are co-perpetrators. The most common form of co-perpetration is where two join in committing an offence so that their respective contributions are indistinguishable. If two ruffians belabour a man about the head and he dies as a result of the combined blows, both are perpetrators of murder.

Suppose Dirk stabs a man while his companion Dastard pinions the man's arms so as to prevent him from defending himself. Are they joint perpetrators of the stabbing? A perpetrator must himself do the criminal act, apart from the exceptional cases in sub-rule (2) above. In your hypothetical the criminal act, the act of killing, is the stabbing. Dastard is an accessory.[9] As another example, if D gives V a lethal pill to help V kill himself, V on taking the pill and dying commits suicide, but D is not guilty as perpetrator of a murder, because he did not do the act of killing. He is an accessory to the self-killing (suicide) by V, and commits a special statutory offence.[10] If on the other hand D stabs V at V's request, and so kills him, he is guilty of murder, as consent is not a defence to murder.[11]

14–003

---

[8] *R. v. Bingley* (1821) 168 E.R. 890; *R. v. Kirkwood* (1831) 168 E.R. 1281; *Tyler v. Whatmore* [1976] R.T.R. 83.

[9] A tendency to inflate the category of perpetrators, perhaps because of confusion arising from the old law, is visible in some judicial *dicta*, and is encouraged by Fletcher, who argues that all conspirators become co-perpetrators when the crime is committed. George P. Fletcher, *Rethinking Criminal Law*, (Boston: Little, Brown, 1978) at 634 *et seq*. For a refutation see David Lanham, "Complicity, Concert and Conspiracy," [1980] 4 *Crim. L.J.* 276 at 286–288.

[10] See section 2 of the *Suicide Act 1961* as amended by section 59 of the *Coroners and Justice Act 2009*. See also *R. (on the application of Purdy) v. D.P.P.* [2010] 1 A.C. 345 at 352, where it was argued that the provision violated a terminally ill person's right to have herself euthanized, because "first, section 2(4) (taken together with the general *Code for Crown Prosecutors*) does not enable a person affected by the prohibition in section 2(1) to know in advance the factors relevant to whether a person who assists her suicide will or will not be prosecuted for an offence under section 2(1) so as to enable her or him to regulate her or his conduct accordingly". On this point, the Lords concluded, "In most cases its application will ensure predictability and consistency of decision-taking, and people will know where they stand. But that cannot be said of cases where the offence in contemplation is aiding or abetting the suicide of a person who is terminally ill or severely and incurably disabled, who wishes to be helped to travel to a country where assisted suicide is lawful and who, having the capacity to take such a decision, does so freely and with a full understanding of the consequences. There is already an obvious gulf between what section 2(1) says and the way that the subsection is being applied in practice in compassionate cases of that kind." *Id.* at 395. (The prosecution service will no doubt amend its guidelines to make it clear that any assistance that is jurisdictionally relevant will be caught by section 2(1)(4)). *Per contra*, physician assisted euthanasia has been decriminalized in some U.S. states, see *Baxter v. State*, 224 P.3d 1211 (2009); cf. *People v. Minor*, 898 N.Y.S.2d 440 (2010), where D was convicted of murder because he "actively participated in an act causing the victim's death by allegedly holding the butt of a knife against a steering wheel while the victim repeatedly lunged himself forward onto the knife".

[11] See Dennis J. Baker, "The Moral Limits of Consent as a Defence in the Criminal Law", 12 *New Crim. L. Rev.* 93. Nor is it a defence for D to assist the consenter (V) to euthanize herself: *Pretty v. U.K.* (2002) 35 E.H.R.R. 1.

14.2. ACCESSORIES

14-004 The courts made accessories liable as a matter of common law, and this was put on a statutory footing by section 8 of the *Accessories and Abettors Act 1861*:

> "Whosoever shall aid, abet, counsel, or procure the commission of any indictable offence, whether the same be an offence at common law or by virtue of any *Act* passed or to be passed, shall be liable to be tried, indicted, and punished as a principal offender."

The four verbs used at the beginning of this section are the traditional way of expressing acts of accessoryship, and are still used in indictments (though there is no law compelling them to be used). Any one of the four verbs may be charged,[12] or all four may be charged together (with the conjunctive "and") in the same count. Charging all four is the safest thing to do, because the shades of difference between them are far from clear.[13]

14-005 **Suppose you counsel someone to commit a crime, and he does not do it?** I should not be an accessory, because that supposes that the crime has been committed. I should be guilty of an inchoate crime for trying to encourage another to commit a crime.[14]

14-006 **Can the accessory be tried by himself?** Yes. As a practical matter, it is highly desirable that all the alleged parties to a crime should be indicted and tried together; as they can be. When they are jointly charged, a court is rarely well advised to consent to an application for separate trials. Still, if it is only possible to charge the accessory (*e.g.,* because the perpetrator has escaped), there is no legal objection to it. Of course, the prosecution must establish the commission of the crime just as if the perpetrator were before the court.

Let us consider a few details of evidence. Suppose the perpetrator has already been convicted. The conviction is not evidence against the alleged accessory to show that the offence was committed. It is *res inter alias acta.*[15]

Suppose the alleged perpetrator has already been acquitted. The acquittal will probably not bar the subsequent trial of the accessory, if the prosecution's acquittal was merely the result of a lack of evidence against the perpetrator, or some other special ground which does not apply when the accessory comes to be charged.[16]

---

[12] Each word was said in *Attorney-General's Reference (No.1 of 1975)* [1975] Q.B. 773 at 779 to have a different meaning. In *D.P.P. for Northern Ireland v. Lynch* [1975] A.C. 653 at 678 "aid" and "abet" were said to be synonymous; but see *id.* at 698.

[13] J.C. Smith, "Aid, Abet, Counsel or Procure", in P.R. Glazebrook (ed.), *Reshaping the Criminal Law: Essays in Honour of Glanville Williams*, (London: Stevens, 1978) at 120 *et seq.*

[14] See sections 44–46 of the *Serious Crime Act 2007.*

[15] See *Hui Chi-Ming v. R.* [1992] 1 A.C. 34; *R. v. Hassan* [1970] 1 Q.B. 423 at 426. The Latin expression means "a thing done between others".

[16] *R. v. Humphreys* (1966) 130 J.P. 45; *R. v. Davis* [1977] Crim.L.R. 542, see also *Remillard v. R.* (1921) 62 S.C.R. 21; *Warren v. The Queen* [1987] W.A.R. 314.

Suppose that D2 counsels D1 to commit a crime, and D1 complies. D2   **14–007**
confesses but D1 does not.   D2's confession is admissible in evidence against
him but not against D1; consequently, the case against D1 may break down for
lack of evidence, but that is no reason why D2 should not be convicted on his
confession.[17] Similarly, if D1 is acquitted on some procedural ground, it is still
possible to convict D2.[18]

The distinction between perpetrator and accessories does not, in law, control
the punishment. Accessories are subject to the same maximum as that laid down
by law for the perpetrator. On conviction of murder they are subject to the
mandatory life sentence.[19] Except in murder, the court may of course differentiate
between the accomplices in sentencing.[20] The accessory may get more
punishment than the perpetrator, as when he is the master-mind behind the crime;
or he may get less, as when a stupid youth plays a subordinate part in a scheme
initiated by another. That is a matter for the judge or magistrates. But the
sentencing judges will be constrained by the tariffs for the given offence,
remember if you assist a robbery, you will be convicted and sentenced as a
robber, so a judge's sentencing discretion does not allow him to label the offence
as something it is not, or impose a sentence which is below the absolute
minimum for robbery and so on.[21] (One of the objections to the fixed penalty for
murder is that the judge is not allowed to differentiate the sentence in this case.)

What about disqualification? Dan has had a number of stiff whiskies and his   **14–008**
blood-alcohol content is obviously above the norm. Dare encourages him to
drive, but does not drive himself, though he happens to possess a licence. If
Dan is disqualified from driving by the court, can Dare be disqualified as
well?   Yes. In the case of the perpetrator, disqualification is certain for this
offence in the absence of special reasons.[22] If there were no statute in point the
court might say that the disqualification applies only to the driver; but under the
Road Traffic Act 1988 there is a discretionary disqualification for the accessory.[23]
So it is for the court to decide whether to disqualify Dare.

---

[17] Cf. *R. v. Fuller* [1998] Crim. L.R. 61.

[18] This is borne out by certain old authorities and now seems clear since the decision of the House of
Lords in the conspiracy case of *D.P.P. v. Shannon* [1975] A.C. 717. See also *R. v. Zaman* [2010] 1
W.L.R. 1304; *R. v. Burke* [2006] EWCA Crim. 3122. As we shall see below, it has even been held in
some cases that a person can be convicted as accessory although the alleged perpetrator is shown to
have a personal defence.

[19] The sentencing judge would have some discretion if the accessory were charged with one of the
new inchoate offences of "encouraging" and "assisting" found in sections 44–46 of the *Serious Crime
Act 2007*, but not if the prosecution uses its discretion to charge under *Accessories and Abettors Act
1861*. See Dennis J. Baker, "Complicity, Proportionality and the Serious Crime Act", (2011) 14(3)
New Crim. L. Rev. 403.

[20] *R. v. Height* [2009] 1 Cr. App. R. (S.) 117.

[21] After all, section 8 of the *Act of 1861* provides that the assister/encourager is "liable to be …
punished as a principal offender". The sentence for robbery may vary depending on the facts, but it
does have a minimum threshold. See *R. v. Roe* [2010] All E.R. (D) 228.

[22] See sections 4(2) and 5(2) of the *Road Traffic Act 1988*.

[23] See also *Ullah v. Luckhurst* [1977] R.T.R. 401; *Makeham v. Donaldson* [1981] R.T.R. 511.

14-009 **What if the prosecutor cannot be certain before the trial, or the jury cannot be certain at the trial, which of several people who were in cahoots with one another was the perpetrator and which were the accessories?** If the Crown is only able to demonstrate that either D1 or D2 committed the offence, then both have to be acquitted.[24] In this situation, the Crown is unable to prove that D was actually assisted or encouraged. But, if it can be proved that one of them had to be the perpetrator and the other the accessory, and *vice versa*, then they will both be liable.[25] In contemplation of law, both the perpetrator and the accessories "commit" the offence, and there are procedural provisions whereby accessories can be charged and convicted as perpetrators and *vice versa*.

An indictment may allege that the defendant D2 on the blank day of blank *murdered* V, instead of alleging (as the fact is) that he counselled and procured D1 to murder V, or aided and abetted D1 to murder V. This saves the prosecution and the jury from embarrassment if it is not clear who perpetrated the offence and who incited or helped.

14-010 **In other words, the legal distinctions between perpetrator and accessories have been wiped out?** That is a tempting view, but it is not quite right. One can "commit" an offence as a perpetrator or "commit" it as an accessory, but the two forms of legal commission remain distinct.

- The chief distinction is that, as will be shown, the mental element for the accessory is not necessarily the same as for the perpetrator.
- Someone must be proved to have been the perpetrator; there cannot be an accessory without a perpetrator. This rule seems to have been qualified (14.18), but it has not been entirely abolished.
- The distinction is also relevant to the problem on self-manslaughter discussed in 23.13.

14-011 **You said that a husband can be an accessory to a rape on his wife.[26] Can a woman commit rape, as accessory to rape by a man?** Certainly.[27] A person can be guilty as accessory although he could not commit the crime as perpetrator. Similarly, if a particular offence can be committed only by a person holding a licence to sell liquor, another person (such as a barman) can nevertheless be convicted of abetting him.

---

[24] *King v. The Queen* [1962] A.C. 199; *R. v. Abbott* [1955] 3 W.L.R. 369; *R. v. Richardson* (1785) 168 E.R. 296. So, if it is only known that one or other of two people perpetrated the offence, and is not clear that the other (whichever it was) helped him, neither can be convicted. But *Marsh v. Hodgson* [1974] Crim. L.R. 35 holds that in some cases an evidential burden lies on each person present to negative complicity (husband and wife jointly in charge of a child who was intentionally injured by one or the other of them). Cf. section 5 of the *Domestic Violence, Crime and Victims Act 2004*. See also *R. v. Lane* (1986) 82 Cr. App. R. 5; *R. v. Ikram* [2009] 1 W.L.R. 1419; *Collins v. Chief Constable of Merseyside* [1988] Crim. L.R. 247.
[25] *R. v. Giannetto* [1997] 1 Cr. App. R. 1; *Smith v. Mellors* (1987) 84 Cr. App. R. 279; *R. v. Swindall* (1864) 175 E.R. 95; see also Glanville Williams, "Which of You Did It," (1989) 52 *Mod. L. Rev.* 179.
[26] *R. v. Lord Audley* (1631) 3 St. Tr. 401.
[27] *R. v. Ram* (1893) 17 Cox C.C. 609; *Lord Baltimore* (1768) 98 E.R. 136; *D.P.P. v. K* [1997] 1 Cr. App. R. 36; cf. *R. v. Eldershaw* (1828) 172 E.R. 472.

Reverting to the procedural point, although the wording of the charge generally does not matter, it is customary and wise for the prosecution to charge the perpetrator and accessories in appropriate terms where the evidence is clear.[28] The statement of the offence will give the name of the crime, but the particulars of the offence should, when possible, state that the defendant is charged with having aided, abetted, counselled or procured the crime, if such be the fact. In bigamy, for example, where a married man has married a spinster who knows the bigamous nature of the ceremony, the spinster is an accessory and can be convicted of "bigamy," but it would be absurd for the particulars of the offence to charge her of that, being married, she has married again. In a case like this the accessory should be charged in express terms as accessory.[29]

Although the four traditional verbs are still used, the language is antiquated. This might be simplified into two words. "Aiding and abetting" could be interpreted as "assisting", and "counselling and procuring" could be interpreted as "encouraging".[30] This simplified language will be used in the present book. However, the concept of "procure" has been given an extended meaning; it has been used to hold a person responsible for causing another to commit the *actus reus* of an offence. In cases requiring fault, the "procurer" has been held to be the "perpetrator".[31]

Does the rule that ignorance of the criminal law is no defence apply to accessories? Yes.[32] In this application the rule is very severe. The perpetrator of one of the innumerable offences in relation to business or some other specialized activity such as driving can reasonably be expected to acquaint himself with the law relating to it. But he may use the services of many other people: suppliers, repairers, carriers, consultants, accountants, and so on. It is remarkable that they, too, are expected to learn the specialized law of all their customers and clients.

14–012

14.3. ENCOURAGEMENT

The word "encouragement" generally speaks for itself, but includes advice, incitement and authorization,[33] as well as persuasion by threats. (The phrase used in the old books was "counsel, procure or command".) Encouragement may be

14–013

---

[28] The high desirability of this was emphasized in *D.P.P. of Northern Ireland v. Maxwell* [1978] 1 W.L.R. 1350.

[29] But even if the indictment was glaringly at fault a conviction may be upheld on appeal. See *R. v. Cogan* [1976] Q.B. 217 at 224.

[30] This book has used the categories of "incitement" (encouragement) and "helping" (assistance) since 1978. See Glanville Williams, *Textbook of Criminal Law*, (London: Stevens & Sons, 1978). See also Law Commission, *Inchoate Liability for Assisting and Encouraging Crime*, Report 300 (London: H.M.S.O., 2006). Sections 44–46 of the *Serious Crime Act 2007* use the words: "encouraging or assisting".

[31] *R. v. Millward* (1994) 158 J.P. 1091. Cf. the position when the offence is a no fault (strict liability) offence. *Attorney-General's Reference (No.1 of 1975)* [1975] Q.B. 773.

[32] *Johnson v. Youden* [1950] 1 K.B. 544. See also *R. v. Sterecki* [2002] EWCA Crim. 1662.

[33] For authorization see *Derrick v. Cornhill* [1970] R.T.R. 341.

given expressly or may be implied from conduct.[34] So if a gang of rowdies proceed along a street, some members of it damaging property as they go, the others will very likely be found to have encouraged them by remaining part of the mob and moving with it. They will therefore be accessories, and all the mob can be charged with the offence without the prosecution being under the necessity of identifying the perpetrators.[35]

14–014   **Suppose D3 encourages D2 to procure D1 to commit a crime, and all works out according to plan. Is D3 a party to the crime?**   Certainly. He has encouraged at one remove.[36]

14–015   **Can a person encourage an indefinite series of crimes?**   A person who exhorts another to commit a series of crimes will become an accessory to all of them when they are committed; but common sense is needed in applying this rule. If D2 persuades D1 to commit a series of murders for a political object, D2 will be inculpated in each of them. However, the position is surely different if D2 merely encourages D1 in his general criminal tendencies,[37] or even in the commission of crimes of a particular kind—as if he advises D1 that burglary affords a good opening. It would be too severe to say that such general encouragement makes D2 a participant in every crime that is thereafter committed by D1 within the terms of the encouraging words. There must be an element of particularity in the crime that is counselled in order to make the counsellor a party.

14–016   **Need there be an element of particularity in the people who are encouraged? What about an appeal to the general public to murder all members of the Cabinet?**   Presumably the accessory must have communicated with an individual (or group of nameable individuals). He will not be an accessory to crimes committed by random members of the public. A person who incites the public generally to commit a particular crime is guilty of encouragement of murder as an inchoate crime,[38] but no case decides that he becomes an accessory to all the murders that are carried out in consequence of his encouragement. In common sense, there is a difference between "encouragement" as an inchoate crime (which is fully committed as soon as the encouragement is uttered) and encouragement as making a person accessory to crime when it is committed.

14–017   **Will you be an accessory if you do something that you know will encourage a crime, but without intent to encourage?**   It depends on the circumstances. If I act in co-operation with someone, and my doing so encourages him in illegality, I shall not be heard to say that I did not intend to encourage. But if there is no

---

[34] An example of implied encouragement was suggested in *Drake v. Morgan* [1978] I.C.R. 56 (agreeing to indemnify against a fine for a future offence).

[35] Cf. *Macklin and Murphy's Case* (1838) 168 E.R. 1136.

[36] *The King v. Macdaniel* (1755) 168 E.R. 60 at 62.

[37] *R. v. Bainbridge* [1960] 1 Q.B. 129.

[38] See generally, sections 44–46 of the *Serious Crime Act 2007*.

co-operation between us I shall not be liable.[39] There must be an intention to encourage. Even recklessness as to encouraging is not enough.

The manager of a shop owned by a company sets out his wares on the pavement, where they may be picked up by a passer-by. He knows that some people will be tempted to steal articles from time to time. So he knows that he is (in a sense) encouraging people to steal (and also that he is making it easy for them to steal, and to that extent assisting them to do so). But obviously when a theft takes place he is not an accessory to the theft from his employer, which he certainly does not want to encourage or promote.

There is authority for saying that every conspirator becomes a procurer in law when the crime is committed, and therefore becomes a party to the crime.[40] But this opinion should be rejected, because it inflates the notion of complicity beyond reason. However difficult it may be to formulate the rule, liability for complicity in crime should be confined to those who are in some appreciable way involved in the crime itself, either by encouraging the actual participants in some fairly proximate way or otherwise. It is noticeable, for example, that members of the Provisional I.R.A. have not been charged with murder merely on the basis of their membership, though the conspiracy theory would suggest liability. The murderers are those who take part in the actual murder or who encourage the murderers with some realistic degree of proximity.[41]

14.4. ASSISTANCE

The accessory's assistance may be given before or during the crime. Examples of **14–018** assistance given before the crime are supplying tools or materials of crime, imparting the "know-how", and opening a bank account in a false name in expectation that a forger will pay into it the proceeds of forged cheques.[42]

In *R. v. Bainbridge*[43] a thief broke into a bank with oxygen cutting equipment supplied by Bainbridge. It was held that Bainbridge was liable as accessory if he knew that a crime of breaking and entering premises (the former name used to describe offences like burglary) and stealing property therein was intended. It was not necessary that he should know when and where the offence was to be committed. As we shall see, a person like Bainbridge would now be liable even if he knew only that burglary was one of the crimes within the contemplation of the person he helped.

As another example, in a New Zealand case, where D2 wrote a letter to D1 at his request describing how to break open a safe with explosives, knowing that a crime was afoot, he was held to be a party to the crime committed by D1 in attempting to break open a safe with the information provided.[44]

---

[39] *R. v. Swindall* (1846) 175 E.R. 95; *R. v. Mastin* (1834) 172 E.R. 1292.

[40] *R. v. Croft* [1944] K.B. 295.

[41] Williams, *op. cit. supra*, note 1 at 363.

[42] On the bank account see *Thambiah v. The Queen* [1966] A.C. 37. Contrast, *R. v. Scott* (1979) 68 Cr. App. R. 164; *R. v. Farr* [1982] Crim. L.R. 745, on supplying premises for producing drugs, is not in accord with principle. See also *R. v. Brown* [2001] EWCA Crim. 1771.

[43] [1960] 1 Q.B. 129.

[44] *The King v. Baker* (1909) 28 N.Z.L.R. 536.

14–019   Assistance also includes co-operation. So, as was said before, the other party to a bigamous ceremony is an accessory. If a statute forbids the selling of something, a person who buys the thing can be liable as accessory, since there can be no seller without a buyer.[45] The Law Commission Working Party[46] proposed a partial definition in order to extend "assisting" to cases that clearly need to be covered. (The primary purpose of the Working Party's propositions was to form the foundation of a code, but the propositions are sufficiently close to the present law to make them a useful basis of discussion.) The partial definition is as follows:

Assists includes—

(a)   "Assistance given which the principal was unaware;[47] and
(b)   conduct of a person which leads the principal to believe when committing the offence that he is being helped or will be helped if necessary, by that person in its commission."

Paragraph (b) (to start with that) is declaratory of the present law. Examples are:

- Acting as a look-out. The look-out person is an accessory even though the gang are not in fact disturbed; he is ready to give a warning if necessary, and his presence is a comfort to them.[48]
- Manning a get-away car. Here again the driver gives encouragement and psychological assistance even though all the accomplices are arrested before the car can be used.

14–020   **Couldn't all these assisters be regarded as encouragers, and therefore as inciters, so that the category of assisters is not needed?**   Many assisters can be regarded as encouragers as well, but some cannot be.

If D1 goes to D2 and asks for the loan of D2's gun for a robbery, and D2 complies, it is unrealistic to say that D2 has incited or encouraged D1. D2 said nothing by way of incitement or encouragement, but he assisted, and he is an accessory.

Again, one who, knowing that a person is going to be murdered, off his own bat lulls the victim's suspicions and directs him to the spot planned for the murder is an accomplice although he did not communicate with the actual murderer. He has purposely assisted.

---

[45] *Sayce v. Coupe* [1953] 1 Q.B. 1 at 7–8.

[46] *Working Paper 43, supra*, note 3. See also, Law Com., *Assisting and Encouraging Crime,* Consultation Paper No. 131 (London: H.M.S.O., 1993).

[47] And, it may be added, assistance given to a person of whose identity the assister is unaware. On the question whether D2 is an accessory by reason of assistance intended to be given to X but actually used by D1, see J. C. Smith, "Secondary Participation and Inchoate Offences", in C. Tapper (ed.) *Crime, Proof and Punishment*, (London: Butterworths, 1981). See also *State v. Tally*, 15 So. 722 (1894).

[48] *S v. D.P.P.* [2003] EWHC 2717.

Another illustration of the same point is *Attorney-General's Reference (No.1 of 1975).*[49] A driver was convicted of having an excess of alcohol in his blood, and in order to persuade the court that there were "special reasons" for not disqualifying him from driving he offered evidence that his drink had been surreptitiously "laced" with spirits by a friend. Probably (although the report does not say so) the story was corroborated by his friend; at any rate the friend was then indicted for aiding and abetting the offence, on the basis that he knew that the driver would shortly be driving the car home. (One does not need to be told that the object of the prosecution was to reduce the popularity of the "spiked drink" excuse.) The judge ruled that there was no case to answer, and the Attorney-General referred the question to the Court of Appeal under section 36 of the *Criminal Justice Act 1972.* (Although the prosecution cannot appeal from an acquittal on indictment, this procedure allows them to obtain a decision of the Court of Appeal that the acquittal was wrong in law, so that the error is not perpetuated in future cases.) It was held that the ruling was wrong, the friend being an accessory because, in the words of the indictment, he "procured" the offence by reason of having caused it.[50]

On its face the decision implies that a person can procure an offence by another when the other is unaware of the procurement; but this may be questioned. "Counsel or procure" in the *Accessories and Abettors Act 1861* and in the indictment should be taken to mean what is here called encouragement or incitement, and should presuppose that the counselling or procuring comes to the knowledge of the perpetrator. The indictment in this case had charged the friend in the usual blunderbuss language with aiding and abetting, counselling and procuring the offence, and the proper basis of the decision was surely that the friend had aided and abetted it, not that he had procured it. Lord Widgery C.J. said:[51] **14–021**

> "It may very well be… difficult to think of a case of aiding, abetting or counselling when the parties have not met and have not discussed in some respects the terms of the offence which they have in mind."

That is partly true for counselling (though an actual meeting is not necessary); but is it at all true for aiding and abetting? D1 and V are fighting; D2, without prior agreement, holds V for D1 to punch or kick him. Is this not a clear case of aiding? And did not the defendant before the court also aid the offence by supplying the "material" by which it came to be committed? The offence was one of strict liability for the driver, but alcohol was necessary for its commission and the friend supplied the alcohol. It is settled law that a person who supplies the tools or materials of crime can be a party to it.

On the other hand, incitement or encouragement means words or conduct operating on the mind of another person and intended to persuade him to adopt a line of conduct. There can be no encouragement that does not come to the knowledge of the person encouraged. The same should be true of "procuring" at

---

[49] [1975] Q.B. 773.
[50] Cf. *R. v. Millward* (1994) 158 J.P. 1091.
[51] *Attorney-General's Reference (No.1 of 1975)* [1975] Q.B. 773 at 779.

any rate where the procuring takes the form of encouraging. If one calls every assisting a "procuring", then it need not come to the perpetrator's knowledge, but such a use of language is not very apt.

In *Attorney-General's Reference (No.1 of 1975)* the defendant gave assistance and so caused the offence to be committed. (The only special feature of the case was that the "assistance" caused the person "assisted" to commit an offence of strict liability of which he was unaware.) But no authority holds that the law of complicity extends to a person who causes an offence without encouraging it or assisting in its commission. The mere fact that a person is pursuing his lawful occasions,[52] not designing to bring about a crime or assisting another to commit a crime in any way, does not make him party to a crime committed by that other, even though the first knows that what he is doing will be made occasion of crime by the other.

14–022   The leading authority for this proposition is *Beatty v. Gillbanks*.[53] The Salvation Army was accustomed to hold Sunday meetings in Weston-super-Mare, and a hostile organization, called the Skeleton Army, was formed to break it up. A Divisional Court held, on a case stated, that the leaders of the Salvation Army could not be convicted of a breach of the peace merely because of what the Skeleton Army might do. Field J. said that there was no authority for the proposition that a man may be convicted for doing a lawful act if he knows that his doing it may cause another to do an unlawful act.

In so far as *Attorney-General's Reference (No.1 of 1975)* purports to decide that merely causing an offence can be said to be a procuring of it, it should be regarded as too incautious a generalization. The decision is supportable, and supportable only, on the ground that the materials of the offence had been provided, so that its commission had been assisted.

14–023   **But the spiker did not merely provide the materials of the offence. He concealed the fact that what he did caused the offence. If he had not concealed it, he would not have been liable. If I throw a party with plenty of liquid refreshment, I am not my guest's keeper. All I do is to give a party. I am not responsible if my bibulous friends choose to drive home.** That is a reasonable view, but it is hard to see how you can avoid responsibility under the law as it stands. Your guests commit an offence in driving home, and you have supplied the materials for it, and you knew they were going to commit it.

In *Attorney-General's Reference (No.1 of 1975)* the Court of Appeal struggled with this question because it sensed the danger of extending the law too widely. Reasons were offered why the ordinary host could not be convicted, but they were somewhat obscure and unconvincing. It was suggested that where the host does not act surreptitiously he may properly leave the guest to make his own

---

[52] Or even unlawful occasions. The mere fact that A commits a crime parallel with the crime of B, and so causes B to commit his crime, does not make A an accomplice in B's crime. See *R. v. Mastin* (1834) 172 E.R. 1292.

[53] (1881–82) 9 Q.B.D. 308. See Dennis J. Baker, "The Moral Limits of Criminalizing Remote Harms", (2007) 10 *New Crim. L. Rev.* 370; Audrey Rogers, "Accomplice Liability for Unintentional Crimes: Remaining within the Constraints of Intent", (1998) 31 *Loy. L. A. L. Rev.* 1351.

decision. But what if the host knows for a fact that the guest is becoming "tiddley" and yet does not withdraw the bottles, as he could legally do?

Granted that mere causation is not enough to make a person an accessory, would it be true to say that a person cannot be an accessory unless he caused the perpetrator to do as he did?   No. Encouragement must come to the knowledge of the person encouraged, but the prosecution need not prove that it decisively affected his mind. Similarly the prosecution need not prove that the perpetrator would not have committed the crime if it had not been for the assistance given by the defendant.[54] Such a requirement would present the prosecution with an impossible task.

14–024

A different problem: one who supplies a tool for crime, such as a burglar's jemmy, may know that it will be used for a large number of crimes. The same can be said with respect to know-how. Does he become implicated in every one of the crimes in which the tool or information is used?   This is another form of the problem discussed in the last section, concerning complicity in an indefinite series of crimes. It may be suggested that the rule is that the assister is not an accessory unless at the time of the assistance (1) the perpetrator had a particular crime in mind (or one of a number of possibilities) and (2) the assister knew this. The assister will become party only to this one crime (or a crime of the group).[55] However, it is not clear that the courts will restrict the law in this way.

14–025

But if my burglar friend writes to me asking me for information on how to open safes, and I reply, I may not have the slightest idea whether he has a particular job in mind or simply wants to improve his own criminal education. Does my liability depend on the jury deciding whether I thought it was one or the other?   It can only be said that the law on this question is obscure.[56]

14–026

Need the assister have the mental state required for the perpetrator?   No. It is enough that he knows the perpetrator's intention (within limits to be discussed).

14–027

---

[54] *R. v. Luffman* [2008] EWCA Crim. 1739; *R. v. Calhaem* [1985] Q.B. 808.

[55] The matter was touched upon by Lowry C.J. delivering the judgment of the Court of Appeal of Northern Ireland in *D.P.P. of Northern Ireland v. Maxwell* [1978] 1 W.L.R. 1363 at 1375 "Such questions must we think, be solved by asking whether the crime actually committed is fairly described as the crime or one of a number of crimes within the contemplation of the accomplice."

[56] The voluntary Euthanasia Society published a booklet for its members describing methods of committing suicide. It is an offence to aid suicide so the Attorney-General sought a declaration that the supply of the booklet was unlawful: *Attorney-General v. Able* [1984] Q.B. 795. Woolf J. refused that declaration but also refused to declare that the supply was lawful. In his opinion a supplier could be guilty of the statutory offence if he intended to assist someone to commit suicide by means of the booklet and the person in question was assisted or encouraged to try to do so. It did not matter that the supplier did not know the state of mind of the recipient. A similar (but morally different) problem arises with regard to terrorist manuals describing methods of blowing up bridges, *etc.* No prosecutions have been brought for these matters.

For example, if D2 hands a knife to D1 knowing that he is going to use it for a section 18[57] offence, D1 must intend to do g.b.h., but provided that D1 has that intent, D2 need not share it. He can be an accessory even though he has no interest in the question whether g.b.h. is inflicted or not.

That is a somewhat unlikely hypothetical, but less dramatic illustrations of the principle can be found in the reports. Where D2 lent a car to D1 knowing that the latter intended to use it to "break and enter", he was held to be a party to D1's offence;[58] and where D2 lent a car to D1 to drive, knowing that D1 was disqualified from driving, he became a party to D1's offence.[59] In neither of these cases did D2 have a personal interest in the offence.

14–028 **You say that the accessory by assisting must know the perpetrator's intention. Must not he also himself intend to assist?** In no realistic sense was there an intent to assist in *Attorney-General's Reference (No.1 of 1975)*.[60] Such an intent, although sometimes postulated by the judges, is not necessary as a general rule. The accessory must know he is "assisting"; he need not intend to assist in the sense that he wishes to encourage the crime. See the next section. But there is one type of case where the absence of an intent to assist will negate liability, namely where a crime is facilitated without communication with the suspect and with intent to obtain evidence against him. The manager of a shop, suspecting an employee of theft, puts marked money in a cash box, leaves the box unlocked, and lies in wait. The suspect enters and steals from the box. Obviously, the manager is not an accessory to theft from his employers; yet he assisted the theft in fact.

14.5. ORDINARY BUSINESS SUPPLY

14–029 The law of complicity constantly threatens to expand beyond reasonable bounds. One reason for this is the tendency of the courts to apply the rules mechanically, without considering the need to resolve the conflict between the necessary protection of society and the freedom of ordinary people to live their lives without harassment from the criminal law. This happened in *National Coal Board v. Gamble*.[61] The decision, shortly stated, was that when the seller of goods knew that the goods would overload a lorry in which the buyer intended to drive them away, the seller became a party to the buyer's offence of driving an overloaded lorry.

Presumably this means that a filling attendant who fills up a car that he sees has worn tyres or is otherwise unfit for the road becomes a party to the offence of using an unfit car when the customer drives off. If he knows that the driver has no licence or insurance, he is a party to the offence of driving without a licence or insurance. If you help to pull a friend's car out of a ditch so as to put it on the road again, after noticing that it is decrepit to the point of illegality, you too will

---

[57] *Offences against the Person Act 1861.*
[58] *R. v. Bullock* [1955] 1 W.L.R. 1.
[59] *Pope v. Minton* [1954] Crim. L.R. 711.
[60] [1975] Q.B. 773.
[61] [1959] 1 Q.B. 11.

become a criminal by reason of your friendly act. A barman who supplies a customer till he is "over the limit", knowing that he intends to drive home, becomes an accessory to driving with excess alcohol. (We have already noticed this problem in the last section, in connection with a host at a party.) But is this all really so? Will not, should not, a point be reached at which assistance is too minor, or too much a matter of ordinary business or social practice, to be counted?[62]

The fuller facts of the case just mentioned were as follows. The National Coal Board sold a bulk quantity of coal. A carrier's lorry was sent to fetch part of it; the lorry was loaded with a quantity of coal, and the N.C.B.'s weighbridge clerk (whose task was simply to find how much coal had been loaded in order to charge for it) then discovered that the load was in excess of what was allowed to be carried in the lorry on the highway. At that point he could have insisted that the lorry be relieved of sufficient coal to make it law-abiding. But all he did was to call the attention of the driver to the overload. The driver said he would risk it, and the clerk handed him the weighbridge ticket (this act passing the ownership of the coal to the buyer), and allowed him to drive away with his load. It was held that the weighbridge operator, and through him the National Coal Board as his employer, became a party to the offence of driving the lorry when overweight.

The decision proceeded solely on the fact that the clerk knew of the intended offence and could have prevented it. The court did not consider the wider implications relating to the proper scope of the law of complicity. The Board did not contest that they were liable if the clerk was liable, and that decision proceeded solely on the law of complicity. It has since become clear that the conviction of the Board was wrong, because it did not know of the offence.[63] This does not affect the decision on the question of the clerk's liability.

14–030

The argument in favour of the decision is that the clerk knowingly assisted in the commission of the offence. The offence could not have been committed without an excessive load, and the clerk knowingly allowed that excessive load to be carried. He contributed *more* to the offence than a person who lends a gun for a robbery, because a robbery can be committed without a gun, but a lorry cannot be driven overweight without an excessive load.

But the clerk's job was to weigh the coal for his employer's purposes, and he simply did this job. He did nothing exceptional or unusual to assist the offence. He was under no duty to investigate what load the lorry was permitted to carry. It was pure accident, presumably, that he happened to know what this weight was. He called the driver's attention to the overloading as a good citizen, leaving the decision whether to commit an offence to him. It seems a strong thing to hold that a person who is simply pursuing his ordinary and lawful vocation, and takes no

---

[62] These minor reckless (non-purposive) contributions to the crimes of others should be dealt with, if at all, under sections 44–46 of the *Serious Crime Act 2007*. This would allow for fair labelling and proportionate punishment. Baker, *op. cit. supra*, note 19. Surely, if conduct such as kerb-crawling and prostitution is sufficiently harmful to warrant criminalization, which is doubtful, there is no need to also criminalize the car hire firm for letting the kerb-crawler hire a car for such a purpose; or those who dry clean the prostitute's dress. These activities are so trivial that there is no need for secondary liability. Cf. *R. v. Shaw* [1962] A.C. 220; *Bowry v. Bennet* (1808) 170 E.R. 981; *Lloyd v. Johnson* (1798) 126 E.R. 939.

[63] *Henshall (Quarries) v. Harvey* [1965] 2 Q.B. 233.

special steps to assist illegalities, becomes involved as a party to a crime committed by the customer merely because he realizes that his customer will be enabled by what he himself does to commit such a crime.

14–031 The decision was a turning-point in the law of complicity. The dissenting judgment of Slade J. shows that it was still possible at that date to hold the opinion that the prosecution had to prove that the abettor intended to aid the offence. Slade J. read this as meaning that the abettor must act "with the motive of endorsing the commission of the offence". Lord Goddard C.J. took the opposite view, quoting authority for holding that "if he knew all the circumstances constituted the offence ... that was enough to convict him of being an aider an abettor". The third member of the court, Devlin J. (as he then was), held the balance between these two opposites with a judgment of unwonted indecision. He sided with Slade J. in requiring not merely knowledge on the part of the abettor but an intent to aid, and said expressly that "proof that the article was knowingly supplied is not conclusive evidence of intent to aid". But then he turned over to the side of the Chief Justice by invoking the tired maxim that "*prima facie* a man is presumed to intend the natural and probable consequences of his acts". Since the consequence of supplying essential material was that assistance was given to the criminal, and the clerk had not given evidence of his real intention, he thought that the presumption stood and was enough to justify the verdict. We are left in the dark about what the outcome would have been if the clerk had given evidence. Devlin J. did not suggest what the clerk could have said about his "real intention" that would have rebutted the supposed presumption. The only hint we have is Devlin J.'s statement that if it had been shown that the clerk was confused about the legal position and thought he was not entitled to withhold the weight ticket, he would not have been liable, since he would then have no intention to aid. In effect this allows a defence of claim of right or mistake as to the civil law. Apart from this point, *National Coal Board v. Gamble* is theoretically inconclusive; but it is generally taken to settle that mere knowledge of facts is enough to make aiding a crime itself criminal; and this is also borne out by other decisions.[64]

Somewhat similar to the decision in *National Coal Board v. Gamble* is the holding in another case that a criminal offence of offering contraband for sale is abetted by the publisher who publishes an advertisement of the offer for sale.[65] The publisher has no interest in the commission of the crime, and merely accepts the advertisement as one of thousands of others that he publishes. But he knowingly assists in the offer for sale, and his assistance is much more positive than that given by the clerk in *National Coal Board v. Gamble*, which amounted to little more than a failure to prevent the lorry from being driven away with its excess load.

In these cases it can at least be said that the defendant was directly implicated in the offence. In *National Coal Board v. Gamble* the offending load was to be driven directly away from the defendant's premises. But suppose a person supplies goods or services in the ordinary course of business, knowing that after they are supplied they will assist the customer in some illegal activity, but the

---

[64] *R. v. Bryce* [2004] 2 Cr. App. R. 592 at 604; *D.P.P. v. Anderson* [1990] R.T.R. 269.
[65] *R. v. De Marny* [1907] 1 K.B. 388; *Poultry World v. Conder* [1957] Crim. L.R. 803.

supplier does not adjust them to any special criminal requirements or charge an additional price to compensate for the legal risks. The supplier knows that if he refuses to make the supply it will be obtained by some competitor (who may not know the facts as he does). There is no English authority for exempting the supplier, but well-known American cases do so. One case, for example, concerned a sugar retailer who made a normal sale to persons who he knew would use it for the illegal distillation of spirits. These cases exculpate the supplier from liability for both conspiracy and complicity.[66]

The difficulty is to formulate a satisfactory rule of exemption. One writer **14–032** suggests that the defendant, to be liable, "must in some sense promote the venture himself, make it his own, have a stake in the outcome".[67] (As applied to English law the last phrase is inconsistent with the advertisement cases.) The supplier must, in a different phrase, "intend to further the illegal activity", but this is too stringent a test for English law as it would have allowed some to evade justice where some form of criminalization seems appropriate. The supplier of a murder weapon may not care whether it is used for murder or not, but he would certainly be implicated if he knew the purpose. The other suggested phrases do not sufficiently identify the activity that is to be regarded as criminal.

The difficulty of the problem would be reduced if the grip of the criminal law were relaxed in respect of summary offences.[68] Parliament decided in 1981 to keep summary offences out of the law of criminal attempts,[69] and there are equally strong arguments for removing them from the law of complicity. As for those selling everyday items which they know D intends to use to cause grave harm, such as fertilizer to build a bomb to blow a nightclub to smithereens, there would be no great injustice in holding such a seller equally liable for this type of conduct, but only if he knew that it was virtually certain that D would use the fertilizer for such a purpose. As we will see shortly, the current law only requires the fertilizer seller to believe that there is a "substantial" or "real" possibility that it will be used for such a purpose. In the latter case, the appropriate charge would be one under section 45 of the *Serious Crime Act 2007*; not only because it gives the sentencing judge greater discretion, but also because it saves the careless shopkeeper from being labelled a terrorist.

---

[66] *U.S. v. Falcone*, 109 F.2d 579 (1940); *Snell v. State*, 13 Ga. App. 158 (1913); *United States v. Gallishaw*, 428 F.2d 760 (2d Cir.1970). Cf. *State v. Maldonado*, 137 N.M. 699 (2005); *People v. Harsit*, 193 Misc.2d 680 (2002).

[67] Fletcher, *op. cit. supra*, note 9 at 675.

[68] See also, Joshua Dressler, "Reforming Complicity Law: Trivial Assistance as a Lesser Offense", (2008) 5 *Ohio St. J. Crim. L.* 427; Robert Weisberg, "Reappraising Complicity", (2001) 4 *Buff. Crim. L. Rev.* 217.

[69] Section 1 of the *Criminal Attempts Act 1981*.

14.6. ACTS DONE UNDER LEGAL DUTY

14–033   It should need no demonstration that an act done in fulfilment of legal duty cannot be a crime. But this is an unreliable defence for a person charged as accessory, because the court can so easily nullify it by holding that there is no legal duty to participate in a crime. We are faced with two opposing arguments, each of them circular.

The law compels the performance of this duty; therefore doing it cannot be a crime. To do this would be a crime; therefore doing it cannot be a legal duty.

The question has arisen when a person returns an article that he has been keeping for the owner, knowing that the owner means to commit a crime with it. It can also arise in other cases, as when a person who has sold a thing comes to realize after the sale and before delivery that the buyer has a criminal purpose. The cases are in a difficult state, but it may be said with some assurance that a person will not be an accomplice if he acts in the belief (correctly or otherwise) that he is bound by law to deliver the article, or if he is uncertain as to the legal position. If he believes that he is not bound to deliver that article, or has no opinion one way or the other, but nevertheless delivers it, he will very likely be made liable by a court of first instance, though the matter requires further consideration at a higher level.

14–034   The first case of importance on the subject is the jemmy case, *R. v. Lomas*.[70]

Lomas had borrowed a jemmy from a burglar. He returned it to the burglar on request, thus restoring the *status quo ante*. He was held not to be implicated in a burglary subsequently committed with it.

There have been doubts as to the basis of the decision. Devlin J. approved it in *National Coal Board v. Gamble*[71] on the ground that (i) the owner had the right to demand his article back and (ii) Lomas in giving it back was not doing anything positive; he was simply refraining from using force to keep the article, which was only a "negative act", *i.e.* an omission. This was a broad-minded construction of the facts, since the verdict stated that Lomas handed the jemmy back to its owner—he did not merely permit the owner to retake it. As for the owner's right to demand his article back, Devlin J. recognized that Lomas would have the right to detain the article forcibly "in the case of felony", apparently without noticing that burglary, the crime in question, was a felony. Although the special rules for felonies are now abolished, section 3(1) of the *Criminal Law Act 1967* allows the use of force in the prevention of crime (see Chapter 21), which would presumably cover Lomas.[72] It is not clear from the judgment whether Devlin J. put the main weight of his approval of the decision on the supposed fact that Lomas was bound to give the jemmy back (which the judge's own remarks contradicted) or on the fact that giving it back was regarded as being in substance a mere omission.

Whatever the civil law may say on the duty or otherwise to give back property intended to be used for crime, Devlin J.'s instinct was surely right in approving

---

[70] (1914) 9 Cr. App. R. 220. *R. v. Salford H.A. Ex p. Janaway* [1989] A.C. 537.

[71] [1959] 1 Q.B. 11 at 20 (where the words "former" and "latter" are inadvertently transposed).

[72] Section 3 in terms merely allows the use of force, and there is no indication that Lomas needed to use force; perhaps the lender did not know where his jemmy was. But presumably the right to detain a criminal article peaceably follows *a fortiori* from the right to use force to retain it.

the outcome in *R. v. Lomas*. It would be too severe to treat as an accessory a person who has done nothing to encourage the crime and whose only act of assisting is to return property to its owner. *R. v. Lomas* concerned a planned burglary, a serious crime. Even if the decision had been the other way, on the ground that Lomas had a right to detain a burglarious tool and should have exercised that right, it may be doubted whether one has a duty to exercise the right to detain an article from its owner in order to prevent him from committing a minor offence (withholding the key of his car because he is proposing to commit a parking offence, or because it is known that he always exceeds the speed limits).[73]

Unfortunately, the law was thrown into doubt by the decision in *Garrett v. Arthur Churchill (Glass) Ltd*.[74] It was held there that when an agent who had bought a goblet for his principal handed it to his principal, the owner, at the latter's request on the termination of his agency, knowing that the owner intended to export it illegally, the (former) agent was not bound to hand it over for the illegal purpose, and was therefore himself guilty of being "knowingly concerned in the exportation of goods" with intent to evade a prohibition (a statutory offence) if by returning it he "lent himself to the idea of exporting it without the necessary documents". This was not a case of accessoryship, but the principle involved would appear to have been the same. *R. v. Lomas* was not considered.

The meaning of the figurative phrase about "lending himself to the idea" was not analysed, and may involve the court in a delicate enquiry as to the defendant's motives. It seems that when the owner demanded the transfer of his goblet he had not at that time committed any offence. If the agent is entitled to detain the owner's property because he knows (or thinks he knows) that the owner intends to commit an illegality with it, for how long is he entitled to do so? If the owner assures him that he has now changed his mind, can he safely accept the assurance? Who pays for the insurance of the article while it is detained? What steps can the agent take to protect himself from an action in tort by the owner?[75] To none of these questions did the court address itself in the goblet case.

---

[73] "Force may be used in such a case because there is a common law authority in any person to take reasonable steps to restrain a breach of the peace which he reasonably apprehends is about to be committed in his presence (*Albert v. Lavin* [1982] A.C. 546 at 565), and the person who exercises that authority is not exposed to a civil liability in trespass or detinue because he takes possession of the weapon being used in breaching the peace." *Gollan v. Nugent* (1988) 166 C.L.R. 18 at 32-33 *per* Brennan J. It might be fair to provide a defence for those who use force to prevent a breach of the peace, but a person surely has no duty to do so if another is demanding their property back and they are physically much stronger than the detainer.

[74] [1970] 1 Q.B. 92. Cited in *Webb v. Chief Constable of Merseyside Police* [2000] Q.B. 427 at 431, in support of the principle that: "Compliance by the police [or anyone else] with a civil law obligation would be no defence to a criminal charge."

[75] "There are other instances where an intention to use a thing in the commission of crime may affect the extent of the liability of one who takes or keeps the thing. Thus, if one person who is drunk goes to drive his car and a second person takes the key out of the ignition, the second person incurs no liability in trespass for damages for depriving the driver temporarily of the key. Nor is he liable in detinue for damages for refusing the driver's immediate demand to return the key, but he would be liable in detinue if he did not return the key when the driver had sobered up or directed delivery of the key to a third person. These are cases where the act on which the plaintiff founds his claim for relief

A point made at the beginning of this discussion was that a person is not an accomplice if he believes that he is legally bound to do what he does. As was observed in the last section, this opinion was held by Devlin J. in *National Coal Board v. Gamble*.[76] Indeed, the judge's words may be taken to mean that the clerk's doubt as to the legal position would have been sufficient to justify him in refraining from taking strong action, and this would be common sense. Much the same point appears from *Garrett v. Arthur Churchill (Glass) Ltd.*, where the justices were asked to decide the question of intent in the following terms. "Did he then only hand over because he felt that he had to as his agency was terminated, or did he at that stage lend himself to the idea of exporting this without the necessary documents?" The formula perhaps suggests that the defendant would be deemed to "lend himself to the idea" of illegality unless he believed that it was his duty to return the goblet.

14–035 Most people are hazy as to the law. (The courts themselves are hazy as to this point of law.) Suppose the buying agent says, when charged: "I had no idea as to the law, but I handed over the goblet because that was my business obligation" (or, "my moral obligation"). Should not that also be a defence? Or suppose he says: "I thought that perhaps I could have handed it to the police, or just detained it; but I don't agree with all these export restrictions." If the one defence is good and the other bad, does not this involve the criminal court going into the difficult question of the defendant's motive?

14–036 **Suppose you are a Licensee and one of your patrons has put his motorbike under your control by giving you its keys for safekeeping. If the patron becomes totally intoxicated do you have a duty to keep his keys so that he cannot use the motorbike whilst intoxicated?** In *CAL No. 14 Pty. Ltd. v. Motor Accidents Insurance Board*,[77] the High Court of Australia took the view that the licensee of the hotel did not have a right to prevent an intoxicated patron from using his property to commit a crime—that is, to use his motorbike whilst in a state of intoxication. The court noted that the licensee had no criminal or civil law duty to stop the patron from using his own property in such circumstances. (Of course, there would be a moral obligation to try and stop him and also to inform the police of his dangerous plans.[78]) But everyday citizens cannot be expected to police the world at large. In a joint judgment three of the judges said:

> "The Licensee had a statutory duty to refuse Mr. Scott service and not to supply him with liquor if he appeared to be drunk, to require him to leave the Hotel, and to take reasonable steps to prevent the commission of an offence–but only on licensed premises. A police officer had power to arrest Mr. Scott if that officer had reasonable grounds to suspect that Mr. Scott

---

is an offence or an intended offence and the general principle precludes the grant of relief in respect of the criminal use or proposed use of the thing possessed." *Gollan v. Nugent* (1988) 166 C.L.R. 18 at 32–33 *per* Brennan J.

[76] [1959] 1 Q.B. 11 at 25. See further, on mistake of the civil law, 18.4.

[77] (2009) 239 C.L.R. 390. (In this case (a civil negligence case), V "demanded that he be given the motorcycle on which he was riding. He had previously agreed that the motorcycle should be locked in a storeroom at the hotel when it was rumoured that the police were operating a breathalyser or speed camera in the vicinity of his home.")

[78] Section 3(1) of the *Criminal Law Act 1967* would give the licensee a right to take reasonable steps to prevent the crime. But he would have no duty to do so if he did not want to intervene.

had committed an offence by driving a vehicle under the influence of liquor to the extent that he was incapable of having proper control of a vehicle. A police officer had power to forbid Mr. Scott to drive the motorcycle if that officer was of the opinion that he was incapable of having proper control of it, to direct him to deliver up the keys of the motorcycle, and to take such steps as may have been necessary to render the motorcycle immobile or to remove it to a place of safety. As Crawford C.J. pointed out [in the court below], the legislation did not give power of this kind to citizens who were not police officers. ... These provisions leave no room for the suggestion that the law relating to the tort of negligence gave the Licensee, without regard to the careful statutory safeguards against abuse of police power, a power to arrest Mr. Scott or control his freedom to use property—the motorcycle and its keys—to which he had a right of possession."[79]

In short, the sensible rule would be that when a person acts in pursuance of either a legal duty (or what would be a legal duty if it were not for the law of complicity) or of a moral or business obligation, he should not be accounted an accomplice.[80] If any exceptions are to be made from this principle for serious crimes they should be made by express legislation.

14.7. WHEN AN OMISSION CAN BE ASSISTANCE

The weighbridge clerk in *National Coal Board v. Gamble* did a positive act: he handed over the ticket, which (the court held) gave the lorry driver a clearance. It seems plain from the judgments that if the clerk had done nothing at all, he would not have been liable. A person does not become an accessory merely by failing to prevent an offence; I am not my brother's keeper. This is so however morally culpable the defendant was. "It is not a criminal offence to stand by, a mere passive spectator of a crime, even of murder."[81] **14–037**

If a particular provision criminalizes a person's failure to act, what role does the law of complicity play?[82] An omission will not always be a crime in itself. For example, a librarian who deliberately omits to close a window in the rare books room in the library so that her cousin can burglarize the library does not necessarily commit an offence. After all, there is no offence "of deliberately leaving a window open." But she does assist her cousin to burglarize the library and should be liable as an accessory to burglary.[83] **14–038**

---

[79] (2009) 239 C.L.R. 390 at 407–409 *per* Gummow, Heydon and Crennan J.J. See also, Hilary R. Weinert, "Social Hosts and Drunken Drivers: A Duty to Intervene" (1985) 133 *U. Pa. L. Rev.* 867. Cf. *State v. Scott*, 285 Kan. 366 (2007) *vis-à-vis* alcohol service and causation.

[80] Glanville Williams, "Obedience to Law as a Crime", (1990) 53 *Mod. L. Rev.* 445.

[81] *R. v. Coney* (1881–82) 8 Q.B.D. 534 at 557–558 *per* Hawkins J. In *R. v. Allan* [1965] 1 Q.B. 130 it was held that an onlooker's intention to join in an affray if his help were needed did not make him a party to the affray. Cf. *Smith v. Baker* [1971] R.T.R. 350.

[82] For example, it is an offence in itself for a person not to give society security officials information regarding any change in his financial circumstances. See *R. v. Tilley* [2009] 2 Cr. App. R. 31. Furthermore, parents who fail to protect their children are liable for their omission: *R. v. Lowe* [1973] Q.B. 702; *R. v. Sheppard* (1980) 70 Cr. App. R. 210; *R. v. Gibbons and Proctor* (1918) 13 Cr. App. R. 134; *The Queen v. Senior* (1899) 1 Q.B. 283; *R. v. Conde* (1867) 10 Cox C.C. 547; *R. v. Russell* [1933] V.L.R. 59. Similarly, those who fail to summon help after creating a dangerous situation are criminalized for the omission itself. *R. v. Evans* [2009] 1 W. L.R. 1999; *R. v. Stone and Dobinson* [1977] Q.B. 354.

[83] Cf. *R. v. Johnson* (1841) Car. & M. 218; *R. v. Egginton* (1801) 2 Bos. & Pul. 508 at 513.

14–039   **But may not a person's presence at the scene of the crime sometimes amount to an encouragement of the crime?**   If a person, knowing that an offence is going to be committed, arranges with the intending perpetrator to be present, this will almost inevitably be construed as an encouragement. The question for the jury presumably is whether, by agreeing to be present, the defendant encouraged the perpetrator in the act and knew that he was giving his encouragement.[84] Where there is no arrangement, presence should not generally be enough, even though the defendant went to the scene of the offence out of curiosity or otherwise—for he does not intend to encourage the offence, and generally has no reason to suppose that his mere presence encourages.

In *R. v. Clarkson*[85] two men were charged as accessories to rape. They heard indications that a woman was being raped in another room, and they entered it and remained while the offence was committed. It was held by the Courts-Martial Appeal Court that the defendant could not be convicted if they had merely entered the room as voyeurs. To be guilty, they must have intended to encourage the act of rape, and have given actual encouragement. Since the direction was unsatisfactory on this, the conviction was quashed. So far the decision is to be welcomed; but at the end of its judgment the court said: "While we have no doubt that those inferences [as to encouragement] could properly have been drawn in respect of each defendant, so that verdicts of guilty could not have been returned, we cannot say that the courts-martial, properly directed, would necessarily have drawn those inferences." On the facts reported it is difficult to see what evidence there was before the court on which an inference of encouragement could properly have been found.[86]

14–040   **But if a person deliberately goes to watch a crime being committed, isn't that evidence of encouragement?**   It is easy to slip from the proposition that A is evidence of B to the proposition that you only have to prove A to prove B. That merely creates a legal fiction that A = B. To constitute encouragement in these circumstances, for the purpose of complicity, the court should be satisfied both that the defendant intended to encourage the crime and that the perpetrator realized he had an approving audience. In any case, it may be doubted whether liability for a crime should be extended to mere spectators, whether they express approval of it or not (cf. 7.3).

---

[84] *C v. Hume* [1979] Crim. L.R. 328 is an indulgent decision, in respect of the charge of taking the vehicle. Had the defendant been older the conviction would surely have been upheld.

[85] [1971] 1 W.L.R. 1402. Cf. *Smith v. Reynolds* [1986] Crim. L.R. 559, where it was held that the defendants gave encouragement to the driver of a van who was disobeying police instructions, by merely remaining in the van with him. See also *R. v. Ellis* [2008] EWCA Crim. 886.

[86] "The fact that a person was voluntarily and purposely present witnessing the commission of a crime and offered no opposition, though he might reasonably be expected to prevent it and had the power to do so, or at least express his dissent, may in some circumstances afford cogent evidence upon which a jury would be justified in finding that he wilfully encouraged the person committing the crime. It is a question of fact for the jury..." *R. v. McCarry* [2009] EWCA Crim. 1718 at para. 21. Nevertheless in that case, D2 provided substantial assistance and encouragement to D1. Cf. *R. v. Atkinson* (1869) 11 Cox C.C. 330.

What if a person who is supposed to be in control of a situation neglects to prevent an offence by someone under his authority? Does the controller become an accomplice? Yes, at least sometimes. This rule is particularly applied against the owner of a car who allows himself to be driven in an illegal manner, whether by his employee or by someone else: ownership is assumed to give sufficient control to entail responsibility. In *Du Cros v. Lambourne*,[87] the owner of a car who sat beside the driver was convicted of abetting him in driving at a dangerous speed, although there was no evidence of positive encouragement. Again, the supervisor of the learner-driver is assumed by reason of his position to have authority to control the learner, and can be convicted as accessory to the learner's traffic offences if he knowingly fails to take steps to do so.[88]

14–041

So if the car you drive happens to be in the name of your rich mother-in-law who is sitting in the back seat and cannot drive, she becomes responsible to try to control your driving? In *Du Cros v. Lambourne* the owner was sitting in the front, but the question is not where the owner is sitting but whether he or she knows that facts constituting offences are occurring or are about to occur.

14–042

It looks as though that is encouraging "back-seat driving". Passengers in a car, even owner passengers, are normally justified in leaving the driver to make decisions. The proposition seems to be that if the dangerous driving or other breach of law comes to the knowledge of the owner-passenger he must protest.

14–043

What about a passenger who is not the owner? If he is a possessor of the car (*e.g.*, a hirer) he is in the same position as the owner. If he is a mere passenger he has no right to control the driver and would not be liable. The responsibility for driving rests on the driver and no social purpose is served by punishing the passengers. (It may be said that the argument based on social purpose applies equally where the passenger happens to be the owner.[89]) However, the passenger may be convicted where it can be inferred that he and the driver had set out with an intention of proceeding in a dangerous manner, or otherwise illegally.[90]

14–044

Suppose you find that you are being driven by someone who is the worse for drink? The same principles apply. In certain circumstances you might evade liability,[91] but you would normally be liable if you were the owner of the car, or if you had been drinking with the driver and so encouraging him to drink

14–045

---

[87] [1907] 1 K.B. 40. See also *R. v. Webster* [2006] 2 Cr. App. R. 6.
[88] *R. v. Harris* [1964] Crim. L.R. 54; *D.P.P. v. Anderson* [1990] R.T.R. 269; *Carter v. Richardson* [1974] R.T.R. 314.
[89] See the comments made upon *Du Cros v. Lambourne* in *Dennis v. Plight* (1968) 11 F.L.R. 458.
[90] Cf. *R. v. Baldessare* (1931) 22 Cr. App. R. 70: two took a car unlawfully for "joy-riding," and a death was caused; both the driver and passenger were convicted of manslaughter. But the fact that the car was taken unlawfully should not have been regarded as relevant. For evidence of association between driver and passengers in taking a car unlawfully, see *Ross v. Rivenall* [1959] 1 W.L.R. 713.
[91] Cf. *Smith v. Baker* [1971] R.T.R. 350; *D (an infant) v. Parsons* [1960] 1 W.L.R. 797.

excessively before driving.[92] If you permit an intoxicated person to drive your car then you act negligently if not recklessly.[93]

In *R. v. Webster*[94] D2 gave D1 and a number of others a lift. At some point during the journey D2 permitted D1 to drive. D1 drove erratically and at excessive speed and eventually lost control of the vehicle. As a result, one of the passengers was killed. The evidence showed that D1 lost control of the vehicle because he was intoxicated. D1 pleaded guilty to an offence of causing death by dangerous driving and D2 was charged with aiding and abetting that offence. D2 was alleged to have assisted D1 by (1) permitting him to drive to start with; and (2) by failing to take steps to stop him from continuing to drive when it became apparent that he was driving in a dangerous manner.

The Court of Appeal held that in order to prove that D2 was guilty of aiding and abetting D1 to drive dangerously, it was necessary to prove that at the time D2 permitted D1 to drive he foresaw that D1 was likely to drive in a dangerous manner. If you know someone is in a state of intoxication and you let him have your vehicle, then there is no injustice in holding you equally responsible for his harmful actions.[95] In *R. v. Webster* D2 failed to intervene even though he knew that D1 was driving dangerously and he had a reasonable opportunity to intervene. "[I]t was Webster's failure to take that opportunity and exercise his right as owner of the vehicle that [allowed the] inference [to be drawn] that he was associating himself with the dangerous driving."

If D2 allows a drunkard to drive his car, he clearly assists the drunkard's illegal driving. But if D2 lets a sober person drive his car and that person only starts driving dangerously after they are on the road, D2 does not assist D1's dangerous driving. A person cannot be said to have assisted dangerous driving, if at the time of handing his car keys over he had no idea that the driver would drive dangerously. But if D1 starts driving dangerously after they are on the road, D2 has a duty to try and stop the driver. If D2 fails to try to stop the dangerous driver, the courts are likely to hold that he *encouraged* it, even though he did nothing to encourage it. All he did was *fail* to *discourage* it.

14–046   The common law rarely pursues an undeviating course, and the stringent rule applied in the foregoing cases may be qualified by the decision in *Cassady v. Morris (Reg) (Transport) Ltd.*;[96] where it was held that an employer's failure to forbid an employee was evidence, but only evidence, of encouragement by the employer. Consequently, if on a summary charge the justices find that there was no encouragement or assistance the employer must be acquitted; and the rule was applied notwithstanding that the principal offence was one of omission. This is

---

[92] Where two intoxicated persons set out in a car, each driving at different times, and killed a man, it was held in *Manitoba* that both could be convicted of criminal negligence causing the death, whichever of them was driving at the time of the accident. *R. v. Lachance* [1962] 132 C.C.C. 202. See also *Smith v. Mellors* (1987) 84 Cr. App. R. 279.

[93] *R. v. Cramp* (1999) 110 A. Crim R. 198.

[94] [2006] 2 Cr. App. R. 6.

[95] In *R. v. Webster* [2006] 2 Cr. App. R. 6 it was held: "The condition of the driver, in this case attributable to drink, was relevant and admissible but it did not determine whether the way in which the driver drove was dangerous. To establish secondary liability against the appellant the question was whether he foresaw the likelihood that the driver would drive in a dangerous manner."

[96] [1975] R.T.R. 470. See also *R. v. J.F. Alford Transport Ltd.* [1997] 2 Cr. App. R. 326.

certainly the right rule, but the appellate courts have failed to give any clear guidance on what is required, beyond the non-control, to constitute encouragement. *Cassady v. Morris (Reg) (Transport) Ltd.* did not involve dangerous conduct.

The driving cases do not suggest that the owner's liability depends upon anything more than the fictitious encouragement held to result from non-control. At all events, it can be assumed that the person who has the right of control need do no more than is reasonable. The owner-passenger in a car must protest against the illegality in driving, but is presumably not expected to require the car to be stopped so that he can get out and walk, if it would be unreasonable to expect this of him (as it would be where the offending is trivial such as where the driver is not wearing a seatbelt). It would be reasonable to make a special exception to the rule that there must be some encouragement or assistance, in the driving cases, because a motorcar is an inherently dangerous piece of equipment when it is in the hands of an intoxicated driver. The general public are endangered by such a driver. In *R. v. Webster* there was factual assistance as it appears that the owner knew that the driver was intoxicated when he first permitted him to drive. The general "power to control" rule should only apply in exceptional cases.

The rule that a person who had some special legal duty to stop an offence is an accessory on the ground of real or fictitious encouragement if he does not take reasonable steps to stop it is applied against a publican who fails to eject a customer at closing time. Owing to a quirk of legislative drafting, it is only the dilatory customer who perpetrates the offence of late drinking, but the courts use the law of complicity to bring in the publican as an accessory, since the pub is his (or he is in control of it).[97] So, would a landowner be accessory to murder if he fails to try to eject a would-be murderer as a trespasser? Could Clarkson have been convicted of rape if he had owned the premises in which the rape was committed?[98] If you find that your guest is in possession of cannabis, do you become an accessory to his possession if you do not endeavour to persuade him to flush it down the lavatory? (An occupier is guilty of a statutory offence if he allows his premises to be used for smoking cannabis,[99] but that is a special offence and does not make him an accomplice in the illegality.)[100]

The decision in *Cassady v. Morris (Reg) (Transport) Ltd.* puts the law on a better footing than previously, but it is doubted whether it can be reconciled with the other cases, and to what extent it will be followed. At the same time, the decision is to be welcomed in point of policy. The Law Commission Working Party thought that it ought to be put on a statutory footing in the following words: **14–047**

---

[97] *Tuck v. Robson* [1970] 1 W.L.R. 741; *Duxley v. Gilmore* [1959] Crim. L.R. 454.

[98] Cf. *R. v. McCarry* [2009] EWCA Crim. 1718 where D2 allowed D1 to rape and kill in his presence in his motorcar.

[99] Section 8 of the *Misuse of Drugs Act 1971*. Curiously, the section does not extend to occupiers who permit their premises to be used for the injection of heroin, or for any other consumption of a controlled drug except the smoking of cannabis, cannabis resin or prepared opium.

[100] In *R. v. Bland* [1988] Crim. L.R. 41, a drug possession case, it was held that: "The fact that B lived together with R in the same room was insufficient evidence from which an inference of assistance could be drawn. Assistance required more than mere knowledge that R was drug-dealing." See also *R. v. Searle* (1971) 115 S.J. 739; *R. v. Kousar* [2009] 2 Cr. App. R. 5.

"A person who is in a position to prevent an offence, because he is in control of property or for some other reason, it is not to be taken to be an accessory merely because he fails to prevent an offence."[101]

If that were the law, Parliament would have to make special provision whenever it wished to make a person liable for not preventing an offence.

And would that not be a desirable state of affairs? In fact, Parliament already takes this responsibility in respect to certain offences, by creating the offences of "permitting" or "suffering" or "allowing" other offences, which we have already studied (6.4). A person convicted of permitting, *etc.*, does not become a party to the offence permitted: his liability is a distinct one.

The courts have left open the question whether the inclusion in legislation of an offence of permitting impliedly excludes the law as to accessoryship in relation to the permitter.[102] In other words, is the only possible charge one of permitting, or can the permitter in a suitable case be charged also as accessory? The reasonable answer is that the permitting offences merely extend liability to people who are inactive, and do not exclude the application of the ordinary law of complicity to those who are active.

14.8. PERFORMANCES WITH SPECTATORS

14–048 Few performances with spectators are illegal. The most likely instance of illegality is an obscene performance, which is primarily the responsibility of the producer and performers. The question arises whether members of the audience are liable as accessories if they knew the nature of the performance beforehand. This is not a case of mere omission, since the spectators would have knowingly come. Nor is it a case where the illegality would take place independently of the audience. There would be no spectacle if there were no spectators (whether the spectators pay for admission or not). It may therefore seem logical to hold that the spectators are accomplices, just as one who knowingly buys from an illegal seller is an accomplice in the sale.[103] Evidence of acts of encouragement during the performance would not, on this view, be necessary for liability, since in the nature of the case the mere presence of the audience is not only an encouragement but a determining factor.

But this conclusion involves absurdities. A law that seems to require or at any rate to allow the police to charge hundreds or even thousands of people as spectators of an event, or as an audience at a seditious lecture, would be unworkable. Moreover, each individual member of the audience may quite reasonably feel that the show does not depend on him; if he does not attend, many others will, and it will still take place. Some members of the audience may attend disapprovingly, to satisfy themselves of the full heinousness of what is being done, or perhaps to get evidence for a prosecution. If attendance at a seditious lecture (*e.g.*, a lecture inciting terrorism and intolerance) involves the audience, then buying a seditious publication would involve the purchaser. The conclusion

---

[101] *Working Paper No. 43, op. cit. supra*, note 3.
[102] *Carmichael & Sons Ltd. v. Cottle* [1971] R.T.R. 11; *Crawford v. Haughton* [1972] 1 W.L.R. 572.
[103] *Sayce v. Coupe* [1953] 1 Q.B. 1 at 7–8.

is intolerable. So the only wise course for the courts is to rule that, as a matter of law, members of the audience are not accomplices by reason of being there, and that neither payment nor applause by them makes them accomplices.

The courts have not gone as far as this, but the law is not altogether clear. The position is said to be that a spectator does not become an accessory merely by being present with knowledge of what is proceeding;[104] but, as already noticed, the clarity of this rule is marred by judicial expressions of willingness to accept presence as "evidence" of encouragement.[105] In one case it was suggested that spectators of an illegal prize fight would become implicated if they applauded.[106] In *R. v. Giannetto*[107] the Court of Appeal said: "Any involvement from mere encouragement upwards would suffice." Nevertheless, it may be strongly doubted whether either applause or laughter by a *spectator* ought to be taken as extending liability beyond those who put on the performances, however disgusting the affair may be to the right-minded citizen.

This is another example of a point that has already been emerging in this chapter; that the logic of accessoryship can be pressed too far. It is not a head of liability that should be applied blindly. Some curtailment is necessary if the law is to be kept within reasonable limits.[108]

14.9. THE MODES OF PARTICIPATION

In the standard case of accessorial liability D2 purposely assists or encourages D1 **14–049** to commit a crime. If a person supplies a gun for a murder or advises another to commit murder, then he makes a contribution to that person's criminality. But a person does not have to make a direct contribution to be ditto as an accomplice. There are three basic forms of participation.

1. Intentional participation: In the pure case of participation D2 not only intentionally assists or encourages D1, but also intends that the perpetrator succeed in committing the particular offence.[109] Under this doctrine it is not enough to show that D2 sold D1 a gun believing D1 would use it to commit

---

[104] *R. v. Coney* (1881–82) 8 Q.B.D. 534; *R. v. Clarkson* [1971] 1 W.L.R. 1402; *R. v. Tait* [1993] Crim. L.R. 538.

[105] In *Wilcox v. Jeffery* [1951] 1 All E.R. 464, there was evidence beyond that of mere attendance. See Williams, *op. cit. supra*, note 1 at 359.

[106] *R. v. Coney* (1881–82) 8 Q.B.D. 534 at 557 ("actions intended to signify approval").

[107] [1997] 1 Cr. App. R. 1 at 13. The Court of Appeal referred to the following hypothetical: "Supposing somebody came up to D and said, 'I am going to kill your wife', if he played any part, either in encouragement, as little as patting him on the back, nodding, saying, 'Oh goody', that would be sufficient to involve him in the murder, to make him guilty, because he is encouraging the murder."

[108] A technical reason for exempting spectators may sometimes be found by attaching a particular construction to the statute under which they are charged. Cf. *Jenks v. Turpin* (1884) 13 Q.B.D. 505. But the question should also be dealt with by a suitable refinement of the law of complicity.

[109] In the pure case an accomplice is only inculpated if he: "[i]n some sort associates himself with the venture, that he participate in it as in something that he wishes to bring about, that he seek by his action to make it succeed. All the words used—even the most colourless, 'abet'—carry an implication of purposive attitude towards it.' The majority of states in the U.S. have adopted this purpose-based standard:" *Wilson-Bey v. U.S.*, 903 A. 2d 818 at 831–32 (2006) citing Judge Learned Hand in *United States v. Peoni*, 100 F.2d 401 (2d Cir.1938).

murder. It must also be shown that D2 shared that aim—i.e. wanted the murder to take place. Similarly, if D1 and D2 agree to rob a bank so that they can share the proceeds, it is irrelevant that D2 might have only supplied the gun, because it is clear that D2 intended to assist D1 and also intended that D1 succeed in committing the robbery.[110] (Australia[111] and almost half the states in the U.S.[112] adopt this approach). If D1 and D2 commit the actus reus of an offence simultaneously, then obviously they are joint perpetrators. For example, if D1 grabs V's feet and D2 grabs his hands so that they can jointly and simultaneously cause his death by throwing him over a cliff, they are joint perpetrators of the murder.

2. Active participation: The "active participation" mode of participation requires much less. D2 must intentionally "assist", "encourage" or "procure" D1's offending (for example, D2 might intentionally sell D1 a gun—the act of selling the gun is an intentional act),[113] but need not be shown to have intended that the perpetrator succeed in committing a robbery with the gun and so on. It is sufficient to show that D2 intentionally sold the gun (the intentional act of handing it over the counter and taking cash for it and so on) and was subjectively reckless as to whether his intentional sale would assist D1 to commit a crime with the gun. D2 need only foresee D1's use of the gun to commit a particular crime as a "real possibility".[114] This type of participation involves D2 making a direct factual contribution to D1's offending.

3. Passive participation or common purpose participation: Theoretically speaking this is an independent head of complicity. It does not require D2 to "actively" assist or encourage D1's "collateral" offending. It only applies, however, if D2 and D1 are jointly involved in some "underlying" offence. For example, if D2 and D1 jointly rob a bank (the underlying offence) and D1 panics and kills the security guard (the collateral offence), both may be held liable for the collateral offence even though D1 committed it and D2 did nothing to directly assist or encourage the collateral offending. D2 is held liable if he foresaw the collateral offending as an incident of committing the robbery, because it is presumed that the

---

[110] As Sir Robin Cooke puts it: "a person acting in concert with the primary offender may become a party to the crime, whether or not present at the time of its commission, by activities variously described as aiding, abetting, counselling, inciting or procuring it. In the *typical case* in that class, the same or the same type of offence is actually intended by all the parties acting in concert." *Chan Wing-Siu v. The Queen* [1985] A.C. 168 at 175.

[111] "For the purposes of many offences it may be true to say that if an act is done with foresight of its probable consequences, there is sufficient intent in law even if such intent may more properly be described as a form of recklessness. There are, however, offences in which it is not possible to speak of recklessness as constituting a sufficient intent. [These include] aiding and abetting and counselling and procuring. [D's] participation must be intentionally aimed at the commission of the acts which constitute it." *Giorgianni v. The Queen* (1985) 156 C.L.R. 473 at 506. But the Australian courts have developed a subjective foresight standard in the "common purpose" cases. *Chan Wing-Siu v. The Queen* [1985] A.C.168 followed the Australian cases, see in particular *Johns v. The Queen* (1980) 143 C.L.R. 108; and the English "common purpose" cases have been heavily influenced by the more recent decision of the Australian High Court in *McAuliffe v. The Queen* (1995) 69 A.L.J.R. 621 at 624.

[112] Wayne R. LaFave, *Substantive Criminal Law*, (West Publishing, Vol. II, 2003) at 345 *et seq.*

[113] Or lends a knife, see *R. v. Reardon* [1999] Crim. L.R. 392.

[114] *R. v. Bryce* [2004] 2 Cr. App. R. 592.

robbery had the indirect effect of making the collateral offending more likely. D2's liability will depend on whether he contemplated that D1 would commit the conduct element of the collateral offence. If D2 knows that D1 is a violent person who is carrying a gun, then the jury is likely to infer that he subjectively foresaw the collateral offence as a possibility. D2 does not make a direct contribution to D1's collateral offending, rather he indirectly underwrites it.

14.10. THE MENTAL ELEMENT FOR ACTIVE PARTICIPATION

Both "common purpose" participation (passive participation) and active participation require some *prima facie* intentional act from the secondary party. In the case of common purpose participation, D2's *prima facie* intentional acting takes place when he jointly commits the underlying offence. For example, where D2 joins with D1 to rob a bank he intentionally robs the bank, even though he does not intentionally encourage D1 to kill the security guard (commit the collateral offence). In the case of active participation, the defendant intentionally does the act that provides assistance or encouragement such as selling a gun, even though he might not intend it to be used by his customer to kill another.

14–050

Hence, in the case of common purpose participation D2 *intentionally* co-perpetrates the *underlying crime* "believing" that it might lead to *collateral offending* by D1. In the case of active participation the defendant does not necessarily commit a crime (unless he sells a stolen gun and so on), but believes that his intentional act might assist or encourage another to commit a crime. Nevertheless, once we get past the *way* in which the accomplice became involved in the perpetrator's crime, the focus moves to "subjective recklessness," unless it is a pure case where the accomplice shares the perpetrator's criminal purpose. The touchstone for imputing fault in both active and passive involvement cases is one of "foresight".[115]

The *actus reus* requirements vary depending on the mode of participation. But both modes of participation have two basic fault elements (1) intention; and (2) foresight. The defendant must always start by intentionally doing some act, because without a culpable act there would be no foreseen consequences of any relevance to the defendant. If D has not intentionally engaged in a joint enterprise; or intentionally assisted, encouraged or procured a crime, the issue of foresight does not arise.

We will start by considering the fault element for "active participation" and thereafter we will consider "common purpose" participation. As said before, the decision in *National Coal Board v. Gamble*[116] was a turning-point in the law of complicity. The dissenting judgment of Slade J. shows that it was still possible at that date to hold the opinion that the prosecution had to prove that the abettor intended to aid the offence. Slade J. read this as meaning that the abettor must act

14–051

---

[115] *R. v. Rahman* [2009] 1 A.C. 129 at 146 *per* Lord Bingham. See also *R. v. Mendez* [2011] 1 Cr. App. R. 109.
[116] [1959] 1 Q.B. 11. See also *Johnson v. Youden* [1950] 1 K.B. 544 at 546; *D.P.P. of Northern Ireland v. Maxwell* [1978] 1 W.L.R. 1350. Cf. *R. v. Antonelli* (1905) 70 J.P. 4.

"with the motive of endorsing the commission of the offence". The courts have followed this approach ever since.[117] Professor Williams rightly observes:[118]

> "Before *Maxwell*, in nearly all the decisions on the subject the accessory by helping knew the facts, not merely the possibility of the facts, and many *dicta* assumed that this positive knowledge was necessary. ... Heavy artillery is needed on this, since some judges and writers have expressed a contrary opinion. ... It would be unacceptable to hold that a man who lets a car on hire to another becomes a party to the latter's drink-driving, or to arson committed with the aid of the car (neither act being any part of his own purpose), if he is merely aware of the possibility (including probability, but not virtual certainty) of the car being used in this way by the borrower ..."

An accessory should *only* be held liable if he does act A, believing that it is *certain* or *virtually certain* that in doing act A the perpetrator will (or will be assisted to) do act B, which is an illegal act.[119] Alas, that is not the law.

14–052   **In the case of active participation the encourager/assister will be liable for what he intends to do (*i.e.* where he "intends" to sell a gun to D) and for what he "knows" might happen in the particular circumstances (*i.e.* where he believes D might use the gun to kill).** The accomplice need only appreciate that there is a "real" or "substantial" possibility that the perpetrator will use his assistance to commit a crime or that his actions will encourage the perpetrator to commit a particular crime.[120] The standard is not one of knowledge, so D need not have foreseen the perpetrator's offending as a virtual certainty.[121] In *R. v. Bryce*[122] the Court of Appeal held that in the case of active participation that prosecution must prove:

> "1. an act done by D which in fact assisted the later commission of the offence,
> 2. that D did the act intentionally realizing that it was capable of assisting the offence, and
> 3. that D at the time of doing the act contemplated the commission of the offence by A, *i.e.* he foresaw it as a 'real or substantial risk' or 'real possibility'."

The assistance must be used. The accomplice must in fact assist or encourage the perpetrator—if D2 sells D1 a gun and D1 uses a knife to kill his victim, D2 is not liable as an accessory to murder because he did not in fact assist D1's offending. Similarly, the encouragement need not provide the sole impetus for D's offending, but it must be part of the reason for it.[123] A person is not held

---

[117] See for example, *R. v. Bryce* [2004] 2 Cr. App. R. 592. Cf. section 45 of the *Serious Crime Act 2007*.

[118] Glanville Williams, "Complicity, Purpose and the Draft Code: Part 2," [1990] Crim. L.R. 98 at 100–101.

[119] The exception being: in crimes of *mens rea* where recklessness is sufficient for the perpetrator it is also sufficient for the accessory.

[120] This should not be conflated with requiring actual knowledge. See *Giorgianni v. The Queen* (1985) 156 C.L.R. 473.

[121] As noted in Chapter 6, "actual knowledge" is present knowledge of a risk that is virtually certain to materialize. A person cannot know the future, but if he believes that X is almost certain to transpire, then that constitutes "actual knowledge" for legal purposes.

[122] [2004] 2 Cr. App. R. 592 at 611.

[123] "The prosecution do not have to satisfy a 'but for' test, *i.e.* that P's act would not have happened but for D's assistance or encouragement: *Attorney-General v Able* (1984) 78 Cr. App. R. 197 at 208; [1984] Q.B. 795 at 812 and *R. v. Calhaem* (1985) 81 Cr. App. R. 131. To require the prosecution to

liable as an accomplice for attempting to assist or encourage, even though he might be liable for an inchoate offence.[124]

Suppose V, D2 and D1 are playing a game of cards; and that D2 discovers that V has been cheating. D2 knowing that D1 is a former boxer encourages him to inflict g.b.h. on V. D1 refuses to do so because he thinks the card game is no big deal. Coincidentally, D1 receives a telephone call just as he is about to leave the card game. The telephone call is to inform him that V has been having an affair his wife. On learning this, D1 flies into a rage and inflicts g.b.h. on V. Clearly, D2 is not liable because he only attempted to encourage D1 to inflict g.b.h.—D2's encouragement did not in fact encourage D1.[125]

The accomplice's act of assistance or encouragement must be intentional. Although a person may be held liable for *intentionally* assisting or encouraging crimes of recklessness or negligence,[126] he cannot be held liable for recklessly or negligently assisting the intentional crimes of others. If D carelessly leaves his car unlocked with the key in the ignition while he quickly goes into a store to get a newspaper, and a robber steals it to make a getaway, D could not be said to have intentionally provided his car to assist the robber. His reckless or negligent act does in fact assist the robber, but this is not sufficient for holding him liable as an accessory.[127] **14–053**

If the defendant has factually[128] assisted or encouraged the perpetrator, the focus then turns to whether he realized that his act of assistance was capable of assisting the offender. Suppose D1 purchases a standard physics textbook and says to the cashier, "I am going to use this book to work out how to build a bomb to blow up the underground". Is the cashier liable if D1 succeeds in his endeavour? D2 might argue that he did not think the textbook was enough to equip D1 for building bombs. If the book's usefulness for making bombs is

---

satisfy a 'but for' test would be to place an impossible burden on them in many cases and would be liable to produce perverse and unprincipled results. Where a victim (V) is attacked by a group, it may well be the case that if any one of the group had not taken part in the attack the outcome would have been the same. If the prosecution had to satisfy a 'but for' test in relation to each defendant, the result would be that no defendant had committed the offence, whereas it is proper to regard each as having contributed to it. So it is no defence for D to say that without his assistance or encouragement the offence would still have occurred. However, in both *Attorney-General v Able* and *Calhaem* the court recognized that there must be a connecting link between D's assistance or encouragement and P's act, without attempting a precise definition of the connection, other than to say (in *Calhaem*) that P's act must be done within the scope of D's authority or advice. As an example, the court postulated a case where D encouraged P to kill V, and soon afterwards P became involved in a football riot in which he used a weapon and killed V, without realising that the person he attacked was the same person as D had encouraged him to kill. Although P had done what D encouraged him to do, there would have been no link between D's encouragement and P's act. For D to be found guilty jointly with P, D's conduct must (objectively) have constituted assistance or encouragement at the time of P's act, even if P (subjectively) did not need assistance or encouragement." *R. v. Mendez* [2011] 1 Cr. App. R. 109 at 117 *per* Toulson L.J. It is not really a question of causation: it is a question of whether D's encouragement was the reason (or a significant reason) why the perpetrator perpetrated. The encouragement must be shown to have in fact provided the perpetrator with a reason for acting.

[124] Sections 44–46 of the *Serious Crime Act 2007*.

[125] Cf. *The Queen v. Most* (1881) 7 Q.B.D. 244.

[126] *R. v. Webster* [2006] 2 Cr. App. R. 6; *R. v. Cramp* (1999) 110 A. Crim R. 198.

[127] *R. v. Webster* [2006] 2 Cr. App. R. 6.

[128] See *R. v. Mendez* [2011] 1 Cr. App. R. 109 at 117–118.

minimal, the jury might infer that D2 did not contemplate that there was a "real possibility" that D1 would be able to use the book to commit an act of terrorism.

14–054 **Might not the salesperson be held liable if D1 "attempts" to make the bomb?** It would depend whether D1 gets past the more than merely preparatory stage. The law of complicity criminalizes those who assist both consummated and non-consummated criminality,[129] but assisting anything less than an attempt is not criminalized. (And remember, assisting an attempt is different to attempting to assist a consummated crime, or attempting to assist an attempt.) Again, the jury is likely to accept that D2 did not believe that there was a substantial possibility that D1 would be able to use the book to commit terrorism. The standard is one of foresight: did D foresee that there was "real or substantial risk" or "real possibility" that the perpetrator would in fact be equipped to build a bomb? D2 would hardly believe this if he genuinely believed the textbook would be useless for such a purpose.

The facts of *R. v. Bryce* were that D1 was a runner for a drug dealer who ordered him to kill *X*. D2 assisted D1 by transporting him and the gun (the murder weapon) to a caravan near *X's* home so that D1 could wait for an opportunity to carry out the killing. D2 also organized a "safe house" (a caravan) within the vicinity of where the victim lived so that D1 would be able to hide out while waiting to strike. Bryce was convicted of murder since the evidence was sufficient for the jury to infer that he intentionally assisted D1 "[k]nowing or contemplating as a real possibility that the perpetrator, with the help he supplied would or might kill the victim deliberately and unlawfully, intending to do so, or at least would or might have intentionally done some serious harm to the victim."[130] Bryce was not a passive participant; he *actively* provided assistance by arranging a hideout, by transporting the killer and so on. The act of driving the perpetrator to the crime scene was an intentional act and Bryce had full knowledge of the essential matters. Bryce knew that the perpetrator had been sent to kill and knew that there was a real or substantial risk that the crime would be committed. He intended to assist, even though he might not have desired the end result.

14–055 **Are assisters and encouragers caught by the same rule?** If D2 encourages D1 to buy a device the only *raison d'être* of which is an illegal use, knowing that there is a real or substantial possibility[131] that D1 will put it to such use, but (shall we say) not being interested in whether he uses it or not, this is sufficient encouragement for legal purposes.[132]

14–056 **Does the accomplice have to foresee the exact crime that his "active" assistance or encouragement will facilitate?** Where a person assists (or encourages) another in a crime, it is enough that he knows that the crime in

---

[129] *R. v. Dunnington* [1984] 1 Q.B. 472.
[130] [2004] 2 Cr. App. R. 592 at 619. See also *R. v. Luffman* [2008] EWCA Crim. 1739.
[131] *R. v. Webster* [2006] 2 Cr. App. R. 6.
[132] *Invicta Plastics Ltd. v. Clare* [1976] R.T.R. 251.

contemplation would be one of a certain range.[133] He is then an accessory to whichever crime within the range was actually in the perpetrator's mind. This was established by the House of Lords in *D.P.P. of Northern Ireland v. Maxwell*.[134] Maxwell was told to drive a car to an inn. He was a member of a terrorist organization and knew that he was to act as a guide to others who would follow him in another car and who would attack either the inn or the people inside or would make some other terrorist attack in the vicinity; and he knew that the car following his car would contain weapons. Apparently he did not know whether the attack would be by means of guns or by planting a bomb in the inn. The House of Lords held that Maxwell was rightly convicted as accessory to an offence under the *Explosive Substances Act 1883* of doing an act with intent to cause an explosion likely to endanger life or cause serious injury to property (section 3(a)), and to an offence of being in possession of a bomb with the same intent (section 3(b)).

It could hardly be said that Maxwell intended to cause an explosion, because he did not know for sure that that was the plan of the people he was assisting. For all he knew, the plan might have been to start a fire with a few cans of petrol. But it was enough, to convict him as accessory, that he knew that causing an explosion ranked among the possible plans of his confederates. Knowledge of what the perpetrator might do is sufficient, without having the intent yourself. Similarly, on the charge of being an accessory to possession, knowledge of the possibility of the perpetrator's possession is sufficient. The conviction seemed anomalous on its face because the prosecution had charged Maxwell as perpetrator, and their Lordships pointed out the undesirability of doing this when the defendant was clearly an accessory.

If D2 lends cutting equipment to D1, and under cross-examination admits that he knew it was intended to be used for some dishonest acquisition of property, it is open to the jury to find that the range of acquisitive offences (theft, robbery, burglary, handling) came within his contemplation, even though he did not sit down and work them all out.[135] If the foregoing reasoning is correct, it is a mistake to suppose that *Maxwell* extends liability to the accessory only when the accessory contemplated that a crime of some definite "type" would be committed. The majority opinions in the Lords are not limited in this way. All that they require is that the crime should be one of those in the defendant's contemplation. Of course, when the defendant does not know the precise crime it is likely that he will expect it to belong to some particular genus, *e.g.*, "terrorist crime" or "profitable fraud". But not necessarily so: the range of crimes in his mind as possibilities may include an assortment resulting from his past experience of what the perpetrator is accustomed to do.

---

[133] *R. v. Rahman* [2009] 1 A.C. 129.

[134] [1978] 1 W.L.R. 1350.

[135] *D.P.P. of Northern Ireland v. Maxwell* [1978] 1 W.L.R. 1350 overrules *R. v. Bainbridge* [1960] 1 Q.B. 129 on this point.

14–057 **In these cases the accessory doesn't write a completely blank cheque. The crimes in his contemplation are supposed to be limited in some way. What if all that the alleged accessory knew was that shady work was afoot?** The answer is unclear. In *R. v. Scott*[136] the defendant opened a bank account in a bogus name on behalf of two men. She knew that something illegal was going on. In fact the men were illegally importing cannabis. It was held that the defendant was not a party to import cannabis.

Presumably the court would have held that she was not an accomplice either; but the decision looks indulgent. Suppose that under cross-examination the defendant admitted that "something illegal" included the importation of drugs, as a purpose within the range of what her associates might do. It is difficult to see why she should not be inculpated.[137] If so, the defendant should be liable as accessory without express admission if the jury can conclude from the evidence that the offence was one of the types of illegality that may fairly be taken as having been within the defendant's contemplation. If the associates had been planning to murder and rob, this might well be outside the range of illegality in the defendant's contemplation.

14–058 **Couldn't accessorial liability be extended also to a case where the offence committed is very similar to that contemplated? D2 supplies D1 with cutting tools thinking D1 means to use them to cut into a safe that has already been stolen by someone else. In fact they are used for another burglary. The two crimes are similar in that both involve dishonesty in relation to property. Shouldn't D2 be regarded as an accomplice?** If liability is extended by consideration of whether crime A is like crime B, we lack any firm limit to the rule. Polonius readily gave his assent to several successive propositions: that the same cloud was very like a camel, a weasel and a whale. Similarity is in the eye of the beholder.

The opinions delivered by three of the five Lords in *Maxwell* (Edmund-Davies, Fraser, and Scarman) are perfectly clear on this. All three agree that the question, and the only question, is the range of the defendant's contemplation. All three referred with approval to the judgment of Lowry C.J. in the court below, where he said:

> "The situation has something in common with that of two persons who agree to rob a bank on the understanding, either express or implied from conduct (such as the carrying of a loaded gun by one person with the knowledge of the other), that violence may be resorted to. The accomplice knows, not that the principal will shoot the cashier, but that he may do so, and if the principal does shoot him, the accomplice will be guilty of murder. A different case is where the accomplice has only offence A in contemplation and the principal commits offence B. Here the accomplice … is not guilty of aiding and abetting offence B. …. The relevant crime must

---

[136] (1979) 68 Cr. App. R. 164. *Per contra, Thambiah v. The Queen* [1966] A.C. 37, where it was assumed that the defendant knew that "some profitable fraud" was projected, and this made her an accessory to forgery. She might have been held, more broadly, to have contemplated that some profitable non-violent illegality was in the air (*e.g.*, smuggling cannabis); indeed, any profitable illegality might have been furthered by the help she gave.

[137] In *Tek v. The Queen* [1990] 2 A.C. 333 the wife of a corrupt official deposited large sums in a bank account for him. The Privy Council held: "if there is evidence as to her state of mind while associated with him showing that she knew the money came from a corrupt source she will be guilty of aiding and abetting him."

be within the contemplation of the accomplice and only exceptionally would evidence be found to support the allegation that the accomplice had given the principal a completely blank cheque."[138]

Similarly, Lord Fraser said of the defendant in the particular case:[139]

"The possible extent of his guilt was limited to the range of crimes any of which he must have known were to be expected that night. Doing acts with explosives, and possessing explosives were within that range and when they turned out to be crimes committed on that night he was therefore guilty of them. If another member of the gang had committed some crime that the appellant had no reason to expect, such as perhaps throwing poison gas into the inn, the appellant would not have been guilty of using poison gas."

By "had no reason to expect" his Lordship evidently meant "cannot be inferred to have been expected."[140] Maxwell knew that some crime was going to be committed, and was merely uncertain which it would be. The same principle, must, however, apply where the defendant is uncertain whether the other person intends to commit a particular crime or intends a lawful act such as giving someone a warning. A historical note will assist understanding of the previous case law. The requirement of knowledge by the accessory was developed by the courts principally in the "common purpose" rule, it being said that the accessory is not responsible for an act going beyond the "common purpose". This way of putting the matter is doubly misleading: **14–059**

1. It suggests that the accessory is liable for an act within the common purpose. This is correct if the act is fully within the common purpose, but the accessory is not liable for the use of un-agreed means towards the common purpose, which means themselves amount to the charged crime. Two robbers agree that they will use slight force but will not use a weapon. If one of them uses a weapon in committing the robbery, both are liable for the robbery, but the one who did not use the weapon is not liable for inflicting injury even though, as it turned out, the infliction of the injury was the only way of successfully carrying out the robbery. A person is not liable as accessory merely because the crime serves the general aim.

2. It suggests that there must be a common purpose. In the typical case of two or more persons going out to rob there may be said to be a common purpose to rob. But when a rogue lends another a gun for the commission of a robbery, the lender is not intending to take any other part or to share the proceeds, talk of common purpose is hardly apt. The lender may be

---

[138] *D.P.P. of Northern Ireland v. Maxwell* [1978] 1 W.L.R. 1363 at 1374–75.

[139] *D.P.P. of Northern Ireland v. Maxwell* [1978] 1 W.L.R. 1350 at 1361.

[140] It may be suggested that in the case of encouragement, where the perpetrator's departure from the plan is merely in the manner of execution, the encourager may be liable if the perpetrator thought that he was carrying out the encourager's purpose. See later. This rider is inapplicable to the accessoryship by assisting if, as in *Maxwell*, the perpetrator is the dominating criminal and has no intention of trying to act within the alleged accessory's purpose. Even so, Lord Fraser's example of an act outside the purpose is unconvincing. Terrorism involves the commission of dreadful crimes, chosen for their dreadfulness, and murder by poison gas, although not usually undertaken by terrorists, is not outside their general purpose.

indifferent to the question whether robbery is committed or not, or devoutly hope that it will not be, but he knows of the plan and that makes him an accessory.[141]

14.11. COMMON PURPOSE PARTICIPATION

14–060   Common purpose complicity is a mode of complicity that has deep roots.[142] In some U.S. states it hinges on what a reasonable person would have contemplated to be the "natural-and-probable-consequences"[143] of engaging in crime X with D1. Common purpose participation has emerged as a doctrinally distinct mode of complicity.[144] Its conduct element is indisputably distinct, because there is no direct assistance or encouragement of the collateral offending. The active participation cases require the accomplice to make a contribution in circumstances where he foresees D's offending as a "real" or "substantial" possibility. It has been suggested that the common purpose doctrine requires a lower level of foresight (subjective fault),[145] but if this was once the case,[146] it no longer is.[147] In both cases, knowledge or wilful blindness will do.[148] Consequently, the rules for imputing fault for the two forms of complicity are not too different, even though the modes of participation are different.

---

[141] *R. v. Bryce* [2004] 2 Cr. App. R. 592 at 619; *R. v. Luffman* [2008] EWCA Crim. 1739.

[142] *Three Soldiers' Case* (1697) Fost. 353.

[143] For a convenient and compendious overview of the U.S. doctrine, see John F. Decker, "The Mental State Requirement for Accomplice Liability in American Criminal Law", (2009) 60 *S. C. L. Rev.* 237. The penal code in Israel also makes special provision for this mode of complicity. See, Daniel Ohana, "The Natural and Probable Consequence Rule in Complicity: Section 34A of the Israeli Penal La –Part I", (2000) 34 *Isr. L. Rev.* 321.

[144] See *Chan Wing-Su v. The Queen* [1985] A.C. 168. See also *R. v. Stewart* [1995] 1 Cr. App. R. 441. Cf. John C. Smith, "Criminal Liability of Accessories: Law and Law Reform", (1997) 113 *L.Q.R.* 453 at 461-462. For an overview of the Law Commission's proposal to enact such a separate "common purpose" offence, see Law Commission, *Inchoate Liability for Assisting and Encouraging Crime*, No. 300 (London: Cm. 6878, 2006) at 19.

[145] See generally, Andrew Simester, "The Mental Element in Complicity", (2006) 122 *L.Q.R.* 578.

[146] The difference in degree of recklessness probably derives from the probable consequence doctrine. In England, "The Draft Code of 1879 stated the rule, which was thought to represent the common law, that a secondary party was responsible for a consequence that he knew or *ought* to have known to be likely or probable, and this was adopted in the codes of Canada and Australia. ... It is submitted that the rule is inconsistent with the general principle that the secondary party must know the facts." Williams, *op. cit. supra*, note 1 at 402 n. 1. Australian courts use the "natural-probable-consequence" doctrine in common purposes cases, but require subjective foresight as to those consequences: *Johns v. The Queen* (1980) 143 C.L.R. 108; *Brennan v. The King* (1936) 55 C.L.R. 253. This doctrine has a long history in one shade or another; Forster said: "So where the principal goeth beyond the terms of the solicitation, *if in the event the felony committed was a probable consequence of what was ordered or advised*, the person giving such order or advice will be an accessory to that felony. *A.*, upon some affront given by *B.*, ordereth his servant doth so, and *B.* dieth of this beating. *A.* is accessory to this murder." Sir Michael Foster, *Crown Cases*, (Oxford: Clarendon Press, 1762) at 370. See also Sir Matthew Hale, *Historia Placitorum Coronae*, (London: printed by E. and R. Nutt *et al.*, 1736) at 617.

[147] *R. v. Bryce* [2004] 2 Cr. App. R. 592 at 619; *R. v. Luffman* [2008] EWCA Crim. 1739; cf. *R. v. Rahman* [2009] 1 A.C. 129.

[148] *R. v. Antonelli* (1905) 70 J.P. 4; *R. v. J.F. Alford Transport Ltd.* [1997] 2 Cr. App. R. 326; *Blakely v. D.P.P.* [1991] R.T.R. 405; *Carter v. Richardson* [1974] R.T.R. 314; *Poultry World v. Conder* [1957] Crim. L.R. 803; *R. v. Webster* [2006] 2 Cr. App. R. 103 at 111; *R. v. Hyde* [1991] 1 Q.B. 134.

How is the mode different?   In the case of active participation, the accessory   **14–061**
must provide factual assistance or encouragement in circumstances where he
believes it will facilitate another person's offending. In such cases, that
accomplice makes a direct contribution to the perpetrator's crime by providing
factual assistance or encouragement. In the active participation cases there is a
direct nexus between D2's encouragement or assistance and D1's offending. In
the case of common purpose participation, the accessory does not actively
participate in the collateral crime. His liability hinges on his active involvement
in the underlying crime and on his foresight of the joint enterprise resulting in
collateral offending by his associate(s).[149] There is only an indirect nexus
between his active involvement in the underlying offence and the perpetrator's
collateral offending. The accomplice does not directly assist or encourage D, but
rather he indirectly encourages D's collateral offending by being a party to the
joint enterprise.

Let us take an obvious example. D2 and D1 agree to rob X bank. D2 knows
D1 always carries a high powered pistol. D2 also knows that D1 is
quick-tempered and capable of becoming very violent. On the way to the bank
D1 says to D2, "The bank's security guard is always armed, but I will shoot him
if it comes to a showdown." In response D2 says, "Please do not shoot him, it
would be better to leave empty handed." D2 does not want to see the security
guard come to grief, but participates in the robbery anyway. D2 and D1 get to the
bank and demand cash, but as they are leaving the security guard fires a bullet at
them and D1 shoots back and kills the guard. D2 did not assist or encourage D1
to commit the collateral offence—he was totally inactive. But he did play an
active role in bringing about the underlying offence (the bank robbery); and did
so with a subjective awareness of the fact that D1 was armed, quick-tempered,
and willing to shoot it out if confronted. He subjectively risked D1's collateral
offending by actively participating in the underlying offence.

The defendants had a common purpose as far as the robbery and its associated
risks were concerned. At different levels they both risked D1's collateral
offending. The accessory made a deliberate and informed choice to *risk* the
perpetrator's collateral offending, because he *foresaw* that there was a possibility
that D1 would kill during the course of the robbery. *D.P.P. of Northern Ireland v.
Maxwell* demonstrates that the so-called "common purpose" rule is not to be read
narrowly. Maxwell was a very subordinate member of the gang and left it to his
companions to decide which crime was to be committed. It is now clear that if D1
and D2 set out to rob and D2 knows that D1 may be carrying a gun and *may* use
it, D2 will be an accomplice in an offence committed by D1 with the gun, if it is
in the course of the robbery or of escaping afterwards.[150]

The rationale for criminalizing D2's indirect participation in the collateral crime   **14–062**
is that he indirectly supports it. His indirect support stems from his participation
in the joint enterprise. It is the joint enterprise that put D1 in a "position" to

---

[149] It might be argued that by merely engaging in the underlying crime D2 encourages D1 to do any
closely related collateral crime, but this would surely be stretching the concept of encouragement
beyond its limits.
[150] Cf. *R. v. Short* (1932) 23 Cr. App. R. 170, where D was not held responsible because he did not
anticipate the use of a gun during their escape.

endanger others: a position from where he was much more likely to commit the collateral offence. If D2 had not supported and encouraged D1 to engage in the joint enterprise, then D1 might not have been in that particular "dangerous position". D1 may have done the robbery on his own if D2 had not agreed to help, but that is irrelevant. In many of these cases the support of a gang or other participants emboldens the author of the collateral offence and puts him in a position where he is more likely to offend—a position he might not have chosen to be in if he had acted alone. If D2 had said to D1, "I will not rob a bank with you", D1 might not have proceeded with his plan. More directly, D2 is criminalized for personally choosing to engage in dangerous conduct—the joint enterprise (robbery, gang violence, and so on) is dangerous because of the collateral risks that are likely to transpire. Since D2 is criminalized for his subjective risk taking, it is important to demonstrate that he foresaw the collateral offending as a *possibility*.

14–063 **What if a random passerby discovers D1 robbing a jewellery store and decides to grab a few jewels for himself as he passes the store?** Randomly taking advantage of a robbery would not be sufficient to make the passerby a joint participant in the robbery. And if he is not a joint participant in the robbery he cannot be held liable for any collateral offending that stems from the robbery. There must be a joint enterprise. If the passerby merely snatched a few loose items without making any threats he is likely to be charged with theft, but nothing more.

However, there is no need to show that the passerby had agreed in advance to be a participant.[151] If the passerby were to tacitly or expressly indicate to the robber that he is willing to help him complete the robbery, then he joins the robber's enterprise. He would have to do something to make this patently clear. In *R. v. Petters*[152] two individuals arrived in a park independently of each other and started kicking and punching X. One of the blows killed X. The Court of Appeal said: "[w]hat needed to be said to the jury was that the common purpose or intention had to be more than merely them both separately intending to do some harm to X. They had to share a common purpose to harm X, and make it clear by their actions to the other that that was their common intention."

14–064 **Suppose D2 arms himself with a pistol and goes to confront a rival gangster, D1. Suppose also that when D2 arrives at D1's house to settle their dispute, D1 comes out on to the public footpath and starts firing bullets at D2. D2 shoots back and the ensuing gun battle results in an innocent passerby being shot dead. And it is D1's bullet that kills the passerby. Is D2 equally liable for murder?** By a brilliant exercise of imagination you have hit upon the very facts of the case of *R. v. Gnango*.[153] First, the transferred malice doctrine means that D1 is liable for murder. Is D2 liable for murder as an accessory? If D2 had been

---

[151] *R. v. Mohan v. The Queen* [1967] 2 A.C. 187; *R. v. Gnango* [2011] 1 All E.R. 153.

[152] *R. v. Petters* [1995] Crim. L.R. 501. See also *R. v. Uddin* [1999] Q.B. 431.

[153] [2011] 1 All E.R. 153. Cf. the recent German case, BGHSt 11, 268 (2010), where D1 accidentally shot D2 when they were escaping from a bank robbery, because D1 mistook D2 as a security guard, who he thought was chasing him to apprehend him. The German court held them both liable for attempted murder, because they had agreed in advance that they would use lethal force against anyone

encouraging D1 to shoot at him, the transferred malice doctrine would also catch him. Nevertheless, it would not be plausible to argue that the D2 was intentionally "encouraging" D1 to kill him, or *vice versa*. Nor would it be plausible to argue that that was their common purpose.[154] Neither party wanted to encourage the other to kill him.

As it was not possible to argue that D2 was encouraging D1 to kill him, the prosecution tried to identify an underlying crime so that it could invoke the common purpose doctrine to catch the murder as a collateral offence. The prosecution argued that even though it was not their common purpose to kill each other, they had jointly committed affray contrary to section 3 of the *Public Order Act 1986*. The prosecution thought that if it could show that the defendants had jointly committed affray (an underlying crime), it could argue that D2 foresaw that there was a possibility that the joint affray would result in someone being killed or seriously injured (the collateral offending). This argument would have been perfectly plausible, if the facts had shown that an agreement had been formed *vis-à-vis* the affray. The Court of Appeal said: "An agreement to commit an offence might arise on the spur of the moment. Nothing need be said at all. It could be made with a nod or a wink or just a knowing look or by taking the first step in committing an offence in which the other then joined, so that the agreement could be inferred from their behaviour."[155] Nevertheless, the facts showed that D1's and D2's breaches of the peace were wholly independent of each other. Since D2 was not involved in a joint enterprise, he could not be held responsible for D1's collateral offending.

Could the gangster be convicted of "obliquely" intending to encourage the other gangster to endanger the lives of passersby?   There is no such offence. **14–065** Furthermore, Gnango's bullet did not cause V's death. Thus, he did not commit manslaughter or murder. Since D1 was charged with murder, D2 could not be held liable for "encouraging" manslaughter.[156] Gnango might not have intended to encourage D1 to shoot him, but he obliquely intended D1 to endanger

---

who tried to apprehend them during or after the robbery, and it was only an accident that D1 shot D2 rather than a genuine apprehender. In effect, D2 was held liable for abetting his own attempted murder.

[154] In *R. v. Gnango* [2011] 1 All E.R. 153 at para. 58 the court: "Two people who voluntarily engage in fighting each other might, exceptionally, be acting together or in concert, but ordinarily they are not. It is not realistic to say that they acted in concert to cause fear; they acted independently and antagonistically in a manner which did so. Absent a shared purpose to shoot and be shot at, the submission made by the appellant was correct that there was no room on the *facts for any other common purpose*." Cf. the old duelling cases, *R. v. Taverner* (1619) 1 Ro. R. 360; *R. v. Rice* (1803) 3 East. 581; *R. v. Young* (1838) 8 C. & P. 644; *R. v. Cuddy* (1843) 1 C. & K. 210.

[155] *R. v. Gnango* [2011] 1 All E.R. 153 at para.19.

[156] Cf. *R. v. English* [1999] A.C. 1 at 30 *per* Lord Hutton; *Attorney-General's Reference No. 3 of 2004* [2005] EWCA Crim.1882 at paras. 44–47. Since Gnango was not involved in a joint enterprise, whether he foresaw the relevant harm to V was not an issue. If Gnango and the other gangster had been engaged in a joint enterprise, the foreseen bullet wound (g.b.h.) would have been sufficient to convict Gnango of murder: *R. v. Lovesey* [1970] 1 Q.B. 352.

others.[157] Parliament should enact a special endangerment offence to deal with those who engage in gun fights and other dangerous gang fights in public places. Such offenders do not intend to encourage their rivals to harm them, but they obliquely intend to encourage their rivals to endanger innocent passersby.[158]

14–066 **The "foresight" doctrine seems to be very sweeping, because a nervous criminal is likely to think of many possibilities before participating in a robbery or a violent gang fight. Does he need to foresee the future with exactitude or will any small variation exempt him from being held responsible for another's collateral offending?** D2 will not be held liable for the D1's collateral offending, if D1's collateral offending is fundamentally different from anything D2 contemplated as a possible incident of the joint enterprise. Again, let us start with an obvious example.

Suppose D2 agrees to rob a jewellery store with D1 and it all goes well. Let us assume that the pretty saleslady hands over all the diamonds without any resistance, but when the defendants are leaving D1 decides to sexually grope and kiss the saleslady. Both D2 and D1 are convicted of robbery and sexual assault.[159] In this case, D2 might argue that he did not foresee that D1 would sexually assault the saleslady. Sexual assault is hardly something that is likely to transpire during the course of a normal robbery. Unless D2 had some information that made him subjectively aware of the risk that D1 would sexually assault the saleslady, the jury are likely to infer that he did not foresee sexual assault as an associated risk of committing the robbery.

Compare this with the situation where D2 participates in the robbery knowing that his accomplice has a gun and is willing to use it. If D1 uses the gun to kill the saleslady, then D2 may be liable for murder. Similarly, if D2 knows that D1 is bad tempered and likes smashing things, and thus foresees that D1 might smash

---

[157] Cf. *R. v. Swindall* (1846) 2 Car. & K. 230, where the defendants' intentionally encouraged each other to engage in dangerous conduct—cart racing. Cf. *R. v. Turner* [1991] Crim. L.R. 57, where the defendants negligently (if not, recklessly) encouraged each other to engage in the dangerous conduct—cart racing.

[158] In some U.S. states, the law is more amenable when it comes to inculpating the likes of Gnango. See *State v. Spates*, 779 N.W.2d 770 at 775 (2010), where the court referred to the following direction: "If you find that either of the defendants, or any person or persons that either of the defendants was acting together with, were voluntarily engaged in *mutual* combat by shooting guns at each other and that, by exchanging gunfire, *they jointly* created a zone of danger likely to result in the death or injury of innocent bystanders, then you may also find that each of the combatants, including the defendant, aided and abetted each of the other combatants and it makes no difference which of the combatants fired the first shot or which of the combatants fired the shot which struck and killed [the victim]." Gnango might not have intended to encourage D1 to shoot him, but by voluntarily engaging in gunfire a public place he knew that it was virtually certain that bullets would fly—by voluntarily engaging in gunfire in a public place he procured (or caused) D1 to endanger innocent others. See also *People v. Ross*, 66 Cal. Rptr. 3d 438 (2007); *Sanders v. State*, 659 S.E.2d 376 (2008); *Hudson v. State*, 280 Ga. 123, 623 S.E.2d 497 (2005). "Other jurisdictions have extended proximate cause liability to participants in gun battles, finding that an individual's participation in such a battle represents a *depraved indifference to human life* such that he or she meets the *mens rea* for second-degree depraved heart murder. Further, courts have determined that the combined hail of bullets that result from such a battle are jointly responsible for the fatal injury, such that a determination of which defendant's bullet 'actually' caused the death is unnecessary." See *Roy v. U.S.*, 871 A.2d 498 at 507 (2005).

[159] See section 3 of the *Sexual Offences Act 2003*.

the glass displays containing the jewellery rather than wait for the saleslady to hand over the jewels, he could be liable for criminal damage as well. In fact, he could be liable for a chain of collateral offences, so long as he foresees that it is possible that D1 will commit those offences.

As far as the sexual assault in your hypothetical is concerned, the jury is likely to hold that D2 did not contemplate that D1 would sexually grope the saleslady. D2 should be able to establish that the sexual assault was fundamentally different to any crime he envisaged D1 committing during the course of the robbery.   **14–067**

An accessory is only held responsible for the risks that he chose to run by engaging in the joint enterprise. When a person chooses to engage in a dangerous joint enterprise he risks the foreseeable consequences. But if the particular risk did not occur to the defendant then he will not be liable. In this country, the question is not: "Would a reasonable person have foreseen the collateral offending as the natural-probable-consequences of engaging in the particular joint enterprise?" Rather, it is: "Did the defendant foresee the collateral offending as a possible incident of the joint enterprise?"

You told me earlier that a person can be held constructively liable for murder,[160] because the *mens rea* for murder is satisfied if D either intended to kill or intended to cause really serious injury. Does that mean that if D2 and D1 jointly inflict g.b.h. on V, that D2 will be liable for murder if D1 kills V?   Yes. D2 and D1 are equally liable for the unforeseen consequences of their joint conduct. It need only be shown that the "[k]illing stroke was an act within the scope of the joint enterprise on which the parties had embarked".[161] As Lord Lane C.J. said in *R. v. Hyde*:[162]   **14–068**

> "If B realises (without agreeing to such conduct being used) that A may kill or intentionally inflict serious injury, but nevertheless continues to participate with A in the venture, that will amount to a sufficient mental element for B to be guilty of murder if A, with the requisite intent, kills in the course of the venture."

Suppose D2 and D1 agree to inflict g.b.h. on V by beating him with steel poles. Suppose also that D1 secretly intends to kill V by hitting him as hard as he can on the nose. Will D2 be liable as an accessory to murder if D1 succeeds in killing V?   Yes. In *R. v. Rahman*[163] the House of Lords held that an accomplice can be liable for murder if he participates in a joint enterprise with an associate whom he knows intends to inflict g.b.h., if that g.b.h. causes the victim's death. As long as the accomplice believes that the perpetrator intends to inflict g.b.h., there is no need to show that he also believed that the perpetrator intended to kill the victim.   **14–069**

In *R. v. Rahman*, Lord Bingham said:[164]

---

[160] *R. v. Cunningham* [1982] A.C. 566.
[161] *R. v. Rahman* [2009] 1 A.C. 129 at 155.
[162] [1991] 1 Q.B. 134 at 139.
[163] [2009] 1 A.C. 129.
[164] [2009] 1 A.C. 129 at 153.

"In the prosecution of a principal offender for murder, it is not necessary for the prosecution to prove or the jury to consider whether the defendant intended on the one hand to kill or on the other to cause really serious injury. That is legally irrelevant to guilt. The rationale of that principle plainly is that if a person unlawfully assaults another with intent to cause him really serious injury, and death results, he should be held criminally responsible for that fatality, even though he did not intend it. ... To rule that an undisclosed and unforeseen intention to kill on the part of the primary offender may take a killing outside the scope of a common purpose to cause really serious injury, calling for a distinction irrelevant in the case of the primary offender, is in my view to subvert the rationale which underlies our law of murder."

14–070   **Would not this be a fundamentally different act to that which caused the death?**   Yes. A person cannot be held liable for murder if his act did not cause V's death. Nor can he be held liable for another's murderous act (the cause of the death) if he did not subjectively risk it—that is, contemplate it as a possible incident of their joint enterprise. This is starkly illustrated in *R. v. Gamble*.[165] In that case, four men (Gamble, Boyd, Douglas and McKee) agreed to inflict serious harm on V, but did not agree to kill him. Nor did they agree to inflict life threatening injuries (that is, if we accept that "kneecapping" is not life threatening). The victim was shot twice in the head and these wounds would have been fatal but for the fact his throat was cut, which killed him instantly. Gamble and Boyd deliberately and forcefully killed the victim by cutting his throat.[166] Douglas and McKee foresaw and intended that V should be "kneecapped" (that is, have his kneecaps blown off with a gun) and beaten, but did not contemplate that their associates would "deliberately" kill the victim by cutting his throat. They argued that they should not be held liable for their associates' murderous act, because they did not foresee it as a possible incident of their joint enterprise.

Since the kneecapping did not in fact cause V's death, it would not have been right to hold Douglas and McKee constructively liable for murder on the basis that they intended (or foresaw) that particular act of g.b.h. They intended to inflict g.b.h. or at least foresaw that Gamble and Boyd would inflict g.b.h., but the act that they intended and/or foresaw as a possible incident of the joint enterprise did not cause V's death. (This would not have been a barrier to conviction, except that the wounds that were inflicted resulted from an act that was fundamentally different from anything Douglas and McKee had envisaged.)

The serious injury that caused V's death was the cut to his throat. If we want to hold Douglas and McKee criminally responsible for that act, then we need link them to it. Were they culpably linked to that act? There is no need to demonstrate a causal nexus between Douglas's and McKee's participation in the joint enterprise and V's death, but it is necessary to demonstrate that there was a causal

---

[165] [1989] N.I. 268. See also *R. v. Rafferty* [2007] EWCA Crim. 1846. Cf. *R. v. Rahman* [2009] 1 A.C. 129 at 160 where a gang of men jointly attacked another man. The gang members had various weapons at their disposal including metal poles, blocks of wood and so on. The actual joint attack was the direct cause of the victim's death, and where all the participants were found to have contemplated that one of their fellow attackers might be carrying a knife, among other weapons, and might misuse it in the heat of the moment. As Lord Rodger said: "In joining in the attack, the appellants [must chose to take] the risk of anything that any of their number might do with the weapon at his disposal in the heat of the moment. In these circumstances any decision to kill did not 'relegate into history' the events in which the appellants were involved. Rather, the killing *flowed directly* from the *joint attack* in which the appellants had decided to participate."

[166] Gamble had not foreseen killing with a knife or firing bullets into the head, but had contemplated the kneecapping.

connection between Gamble's and Boyd's act and V's death. Once that is established, it is necessary to demonstrate that Douglas and McKee were culpably involved in that act, because it is that act which caused V's death. They would have been culpably involved if they had made a choice to normatively underwrite the throat cutting, and that would have been the case if they had contemplated it (or something similar) as a possible incident of the original joint enterprise. If V had died from being kneecapped then all of the defendants would have been guilty of murder.

Constructive liability for murder can only apply to secondary parties if they choose to risk the acts which cause the victim's death. In *R. v. Gamble*, Douglas and McKee risked the kneecapping but did not choose to risk their associates' fully independent and unforeseeable criminal choice to cut V's throat. Therefore, the court was right to let them go. Anything less would cause the "common purpose" rule to collapse into the old "felony murder" rule. Where an associate makes a fully autonomous choice to kill, the public can be protected adequately if he alone is punished for it.

I appreciate that D must foresee the particular type of acts which caused V's death as a possible incident of the joint enterprise, but surely similar acts can be substituted for each other?   14–071 The act that causes the death must not be fundamentally different to anything the defendant had in mind. Many of these cases are determined by drawing very fine distinctions. In *R. v. Rahman*[167] at least two of the Lords suggested that if the victim in *R. v. Gamble* had died from being shot in the head, all the defendants would have been liable for murder. Lord Neuberger took the view that deliberately shooting the victim in the head would not have been fundamentally different from deliberately shooting him in the kneecaps. After all, both involve using a lethal weapon against the person of a human being. And in both cases, the dangerousness of doing so would be perfectly foreseeable:

> "Where B joins with A in what he intends to be a kneecapping of V, he foresees, indeed intends, that V should be seriously injured with a gun. The 'departure' he relies on is A's intention to kill with the gun combined with the fact that A aims at V's head rather than at his knees. On the face of it, that appears to be no more than a specific example of the type of case summarised in para. 76. ... To my mind, the conclusion that B is guilty of murder on facts such as those in this case and on facts such as those in *R. v. Gamble* (on the assumption that V was killed by shooting him in the head) can be justified on the basis of policy and principle.[168] As to the principle, I have already dealt with it: given that intention to cause serious injury is sufficient *mens rea* for murder, if B foresaw that serious injury will be caused to V by A using

---

[167] [2009] 1 A.C. 129. In particular, see Lord Neuberger's comments at 170–172. See also the judgment of Lord Rodger.

[168] I think his Lordship's analysis is erroneous. There is a fundamental difference between foreseeing g.b.h. that might result in death, and foreseeing a deliberate and unplanned act of killing. The act of cutting V's throat was designed to kill him instantly, whereas the kneecapping was not intended to result in his death, although that would not have mattered if the kneecapping had been the cause of death. We do not know whether it would have caused V's death, since the act of cutting his throat broke the chain of causation and ended his life almost instantly. Similarly, if D had deliberately shot V in the head to kill him instantly that would clearly be fundamentally different from kneecapping which might not be designed to kill instantly.

a particular weapon, he should not escape a murder conviction merely because A intended (or may have intended) to kill V when he attacked him with that very weapon."[169]

This overlooks the fact that kneecapping is widely used by gangsters as a form of punishment and is not usually lethal. *Per contra*, firing a bullet into a person's head is a particularly lethal act, as is the act of cutting a person's throat. Clearly, the latter acts are fundamentally different to kneecapping.[170]

14–072   **Does the type of weapon tell us much about the nature of the act? Gamble and Boyd ended up killing their victim with a knife and a knife is not as lethal as a gun.**   Clearly the type of weapon can change the nature of the act. It is one thing to strike someone over the head with a fly swat and another to do the same with a cricket bat. The type of weapon is something to be considered along with the context and all the other evidence. If the defendant did not know that his associate was carrying a gun or a knife, this along with all the other evidence, will allow the jury to draw appropriate inferences as to what the accessory foresaw. Possession of a gun or a knife is not of itself conclusive, it is merely evidence from which the jury can infer D foresaw that his associate might do the particular dangerous act.[171] As *R. v. Gamble*[172] shows, it might also be necessary to demonstrate that D foresaw that the gun would be *used* in a particular way, because the *use* of a gun might not be life threatening if it were merely used to knock V unconscious or to frighten V. It is necessary to consider the overall dangerousness of the contemplated act.[173]

In *R. v. Rahman*[174] V was attacked by a group of persons who were armed with various blunt weapons. The mob used metal poles, chair legs and a miscellany of objects to beat V to a pulp. During the course of the attack one of the gang members fatally wounded V by stabbing him with a knife. Each defendant had realized that one or more of the attackers might produce and use a knife to inflict really serious injury on the victim. There was no evidence that the defendant was the one who used the knife. Nevertheless, the defendant was convicted for his part in the joint enterprise. The jury were able to infer that Rahman foresaw that a stabbing was a possibility. Since Rahman foresaw that one of his fellow attackers might use a knife during the course of the joint-attack, he risked such a weapon being used.

Rahman was found guilty of the murder as an accessory because the jury was able to infer from the evidence that he foresaw a stabbing or an equally grave act

---

[169] The case given at paragraph 76 of the judgment was: "The fundamental issue raised on this appeal can be reduced to the following facts. A and B jointly attack V. B intends to cause V serious injury, but not to kill him. B believes that A has the same intention. In the course of the attack A kills V, intending to kill him. Can B avoid conviction for murder by saying that he should not be criminally liable for V being killed as a result of A intending to kill him, rather than as a result of A intending seriously to injure him?" See *R. v. Rahman* [2009] 1 A.C. 129 at 167.

[170] *Attorney-General's Reference (No.3 of 2004)* [2005] EWCA Crim. 1882 at para. 43.

[171] *R. v. Rahman* [2009] 1 A.C. 129 at 147 *per* Lord Bingham.

[172] [1989] N.I. 268.

[173] *R. v. Uddin* [1999] Q.B. 431 at 441.

[174] [2009] 1 A.C. 129.

(smashing someone's head in with a metal pole does not seem any less grave than stabbing him) as a possible incident of the joint enterprise. The attack was particularly ferocious.[175]

In *R. v. Rahman* Lord Bingham said:[176]

14–073

> "[I]f parties embark on a punishment exercise that carries with it the foreseeable possibility of death of the victim, the instruments used for that purpose seem to me of much less importance than the purpose itself. ...This constitutes, in my opinion, a far more satisfactory means of dealing with those whose liability for the unlawful killing is secondary than a rule which would exonerate them from criminal liability on the ground that they did not know or suspect that the primary party was carrying the particular weapon that delivered the fatal blow."

In cases of violence, the focus will usually be on dangerousness or lethalness of the collateral offending (for example, it is much more dangerous to shoot someone at point blank in the head than to use the gun to kneecap him).[177] In other cases dangerousness will offer little guidance (for example, where the collateral offending is a property offence). A person charged as accessory is responsible only for crimes committed within his own purpose, or within the purpose of the other perpetrator of which he has knowledge, and a question on this should always (in case of doubt) be left to the jury,[178] whether the defendant has raised the point or not.[179] Granted that as a general rule the defendant that is charged as accessory must have known what the crook was crooking, so to speak, the facts of the case may show that he had only a misty idea of what was in the perpetrator's mind. To what extent does this afford him a defence?

The practical problems that arise relate to evidence. Wrongdoers are not likely to admit what their contemplation was; and indeed they may not have clearly envisaged what might be done. In practice, the tribunal of fact (whether jury or magistrates) is forced to draw common-sense inferences from the events proved. If two criminals both use force in committing a crime, the jury will readily infer, and be allowed to infer, that both had agreed to use force, so that each will be

---

[175] Compare this to *R. v. English* [1999] 1 A.C. 1, where D2 and D1 gave a police officer a beating with a couple of wooden pegs. During the course of the attack D1 stabbed the officer and killed him. The attack only involved two people and the weapons were not inherently lethal. Thus, it was accepted that D1's act was fundamentally different to anything D2 had envisaged. (It hardly needs saying, but if English had participated in the attack after learning of the knife, he would have been liable. Once D learns of a weapon, he has the choice of immediately withdrawing from the enterprise or of taking the consequences of remaining as a participant.) Cf. *R. v. Yemoh* [2009] EWCA Crim. 930.

[176] [2009] 1 A.C. 129 at 155.

[177] It is also fundamentally more dangerous to deliberately drown someone than merely to give him a beating with your fists. See *R. v. Rafferty* [2007] EWCA Crim. 1846.

[178] As for jury directions, in *R. v. Rahman* [2009] 1 A.C. 129 at 153 Lord Bingham said: "The Court of Appeal ... dismissed the appellants' appeals for reasons with which I agree. In para. 69 of their judgment they tentatively suggested a series of questions which a trial judge might invite a jury to consider in a case such as this. There is, and can be, *no prescriptive formula for directing juries*. Having made clear the governing principle, it is for trial judges to choose the terms most apt to enable juries to reach a just decision in the particular case. I would for my part, however, prefer the judge's four questions (amended to remove the overly favourable direction in question 3) to the questions proposed in para. 69." His Lordship was referring to the trial judge's questions as cited by the Court of Appeal in *R. v. Rahman* [2007] 1 W.L.R. 2191 at 2196.

[179] *R. v. Lovesey* [1970] 1 Q.B. 352 at 356; *R. v. Dunbar* [1970] 1 Q.B. 352.

responsible for the force used by the other. The same will apply if they both use force trying to escape after the crime. But this is so only if the acts of force are roughly commensurate. If D2 uses mild force, and his companion D1 unexpectedly uses greater force (as, by using a gun which D2 did not know him to be carrying), D1's conduct may be regarded as going beyond the common purpose.[180]

14–074   If the evidence shows that D2 knew that D1 was carrying the weapon,[181] the inference will be almost irresistible that the use of the weapon was contemplated by D2.[182] However, it is not a fixed rule of law that D2 must be convicted in these circumstances. If D2 can convince the jury (or convince them of the reasonable possibility) that, although he knew that D1 was carrying a gun, he thought that this was merely a matter of habit, or underworld prestige, or of defence against a rival gang, and did not know of D1's intention to use it on this occasion against this victim, he will not be a party to such a use.[183] There is merely a common sense inference that criminals who carry weapons do so for a purpose. The inference should not be drawn if the evidence excludes it.

The upshot seems to be, in this type of case, that D2 is liable for the force used by D1 if D2 intended such force to be used or knew that D1 might use such force in the pursuance of this known purpose or would use it if the circumstances seemed to him to require it. D2 is not liable if he believed that D1 would not use such force or if the use of such force was specifically excluded by agreement between them, but not if in the latter case, D2 realized that D1, being an unreliable person, might possibly use it.

14–075   **It is common practice for only one of a gang of robbers to carry a gun, the others being armed with coshes, pick-handles or ammonia. Suppose that the gun-carrier uses the weapon to kill or inflict harm. The others say that they thought that the gun would be used only to frighten. Assuming that the jury credit the defence, what is the position?** If the gunman used the gun intentionally, that would obviously be outside his purpose as known to his companions (the "common purpose" as it is usually known). The others would be guilty neither of murder nor of manslaughter.[184] If the gunman accidentally shot and killed, when intending only to frighten, he would be liable for manslaughter, both negligent and constructive—the latter because using a loaded gun to frighten was an unlawful act (assault), and everyone would realize the risk of some harm resulting. The law of constructive manslaughter applies to accessories as much as it does to the perpetrator, so if they knew that the gun was or might be loaded they will be accessories to manslaughter.[185]

---

[180] *R. v. English* [1999] 1 A.C. 1; *R. v. Rahman* [2009] 1 A.C. 129; *R. v. Miah* [2009] EWCA Crim. 2368.

[181] *R. v. Powell* [1999] 1 A.C. 1; *R. v. Mendez* [2011] 1 Cr. App. R. 109.

[182] *R. v. Smith* [1963] 1 W.L.R. 1200; *R. v. Matthew* [2010] EWCA Crim. 1859.

[183] *R. v. Betty* (1964) 48 Cr. App. R. 6; *R. v. Stewart* [1995] 1 Cr. App. R. 441; *Three Soldiers' Case* (1697) Fost. 353.

[184] *Attorney-General's Reference (No.3 of 2004)* [2005] EWCA Crim. 1882.

[185] Cf. *R. v. Perman* [1996] 1 Cr. App. R. 24 at 36. See also *Attorney-General's Reference (No.3 of 2004)* [2005] EWCA Crim. 1882 at paras. 65–70; *R. v. Mahmood* [1995] R.T.R. 48.

If D1 and D2 jointly rob a store and D2 foresees that D1 will punch V, but believes the punch will only cause V to suffer actual bodily harm, D2 might be liable for manslaughter if the punch kills V.[186] But if D1 intends to kill V when he delivers the punch and succeeds because the punch is enough to cause V to lose balance and hit his head on the kerb, D1 would be liable for murder.[187] In these circumstances, D2 would not be liable for murder but should be liable for manslaughter, because D1's concealed intent to kill does not change the nature of the act that caused V's death; and D2 foresaw this particular act as an incident of their unlawful dangerous enterprise.[188]

If the gunman, intending to frighten, accidentally caused injury, he is liable under section 47 of the *Offences against the Person Act 1861*, apparently, since the section creates a degree of strict liability but not under section 20 of the *1861 Act* which requires *mens rea* as to causing injury. The same propositions apply to the other members of the gang. If the use of the gun to frighten was within the contemplated purpose, they are liable (presumably)[189] under section 47 but not section 20.

What if Donald tells Ronald to assault someone and Ronald goes beyond his instructions and assaults the victim so seriously as to kill him. Ronald is convicted of murder. Donald is not an accessory to murder, but can he be convicted as accessory to assault or manslaughter? Yes as to assault. The fact that Ronald has not been convicted of assault is immaterial.[190] The killing being outside Ronald's known purpose, Donald would not be guilty of manslaughter in respect of it. He has authorized only a non-lethal assault.[191] Whether or not this rule is strictly logical, it is merciful.

14–076

To recap very briefly, I understand that a person is liable as accessory for acts that are within the perpetrator's known purpose, and also for consequences of acts within the known purpose that are a matter of strict liability. Suppose the perpetrator commits the intended crime in a different way from that intended? The general answer is undoubtedly that the alleged accessory it not responsible for a deliberate change of plan by the perpetrator, but is for his accident or mistake in carrying out the plan.

14–077

---

[186] *R. v. Yemoh* [2009] EWCA Crim. 930; *R. v. Parsons* [2009] EWCA Crim. 64.

[187] *R. v. Yemoh* [2009] EWCA Crim. 930; *R. v. Parsons* [2009] EWCA Crim. 64.

[188] The jury could convict D2 of manslaughter if they find that D1 formed the intention to kill or cause g.b.h. to V only after the commencement of the assault and that D2 had never intended to cause death or g.b.h. to V. If D1 does not form an intention to kill or to inflict g.b.h., both D1 and D2 would be guilty of manslaughter only. *R. v. Reid* (1976) 62 Cr. App. R. 109 at 112; *R. v. Roberts* [2001] EWCA Crim. 1594. See also *R. v. Stewart* [1995] 1 Cr. App. R. 441; *R. v. Perman* [1996] 1 Cr. App. R. 24 at 36-37; *R. v. Barlow* (1997) 188 C.L.R. 1; *R. v. Jackson* [1993] 4 S.C.R. 573 at 585.

[189] This is on the assumption that the principle of *R. v. Creamer* [1966] 1 Q.B. 72 extends to other unintended consequences for which there is strict liability.

[190] *Trial of Lord Mohun* (1692) Holt, K.B. 479.

[191] *R. v. Lovesey* [1970] 1 Q.B. 352 at 356. The head-note to *R. v. Betty* (1964) 48 Cr. App. R. 6, is misleading, since the killing was not there held to be within the common purpose. The killer's accomplice can be implicated in an accidental killing.

14–078   **I don't see why a deliberate change of plan should let the accessory out, if it is still the same crime as he encouraged or assisted. Iago said: "Do it not with poison; strangle her in bed," and Othello complied. Had Othello, ignoring Iago's advice, used poison to kill Desdemona, that would surely not have exempted Iago form liability as an accessory.**   The theory of the common law is that the alleged accessory is entitled to delimit the scope of his participation in the intended crime. This is the basis of the "contemplated purpose" rule. If the encourager or assister says: "You may overpower the night watchman and tie him up, but you must not use a weapon or do him serious injury", this means that he is not a party to anything intentionally done against his instructions. Similarly, to take a more horrific example, if the satanic inciter says: "I have insured my wife against a traffic accident, and I want to see that she falls under a lorry this afternoon", he is on principle not guilty of murder if the assassin then uses a knife. But in your variant of the Othello story the jury would undoubtedly be encouraged to find that the purpose contemplated by Iago (or the purpose understood by Othello to be contemplated by Iago) was merely the killing of Desdemona, and that Iago's remark about the method was merely a matter of tactics which did not delimit the purpose.[192]

It may be suggested, then, that the rule is that the encourager or assister is liable if (1) the crime committed was within his contemplation (putting aside the merely tactical details, as already noticed), or (2) the crime committed was of the same abstract kind as the one contemplated, and the perpetrator tried to carry out what he understood to be the alleged accessory's intention.

The second part of the rule may be illustrated as follows. Suppose that in the previous example the instigator did not make it clear that it was important for him that his wife should be killed in a particular way. The perpetrator therefore thought that the instigator merely wanted the victim killed, and thought that the mention of a faked traffic accident was only a suggestion as to the best means. In that case the instigator would presumably remain a party to a murder of the wife committed by some other method.

14–079   On the question of mistakes in carrying out the plan, the Law Commission Working Party expresses the rule as follows:

> "The accessory is liable notwithstanding that the principal makes a mistake as to the identity of the victim or of the property affected by the offence, or a mistake as to the victim or property intended by the accessory to be affected."[193]

This is right on principle, because the perpetrator is trying to carry out the offence that was within the accessory's contemplation. But, it may be suggested,

---

[192] "To this extent there must clearly be, first, contact between the parties, and, secondly, a connection between the counselling and the murder. Equally, the act done must, we think, be done within the scope of the authority or advice, and not, for example, accidentally when the mind of the final murderer did not go with his actions. For example, if the principal offender happened to be involved in a football riot in the course of which he laid about him with a weapon of some sort and killed someone who, unknown to him, was the person whom he had been counselled to kill, he would not, in our view, have been acting within the scope of his authority." *R. v. Calhaem* [1985] Q.B. 808 at 813; *R. v. Mendez* [2011] 1 Cr. App. R. 109 at 117.

[193] *Working Paper 43, supra* note 3.

the inciter will not be responsible if the perpetrator misunderstands his instructions to the extent of committing a different crime, such as murder instead of burglary.[194]

What about a case of transferred intention?   The Law Commission Working Party proposes a principle similar to that already stated for mistake:

> "The accessory is liable to the same extent where the intended offence takes effect on an unintended victim or property, unless the principal consciously allows the plan to miscarry,"

The last words mean that if the perpetrator deliberately changes the victim, and so acts outside the inciter's contemplation, the inciter is not a party to that crime. So if the inciter gives the perpetrator a gun and tells him to murder the Prime Minister, and the perpetrator shoots his wife's lover instead, the inciter is not a party to this murder.[195]

Why not? The encourager incited a murder, and a murder was committed with the weapon that he supplied.   The fact that you supply an accomplice with a gun with murderous intent does not involve you in every murder that the accomplice chooses to commit with the weapon. The inciter does not become involved in a murder merely because he encouraged murder in the abstract. He must have encouraged the particular murder, the factual situation—though he will be responsible for an accidental miscarriage of the plan, and probably for some degree of misunderstanding of the perpetrator, as before explained.

Does this mean that if you encourage a burglary, you can get off by saying that they deliberately burgled some house other than the one you instructed?   In acquisitive crimes the judge might encourage the jury to find that the defendant was principally concerned to get money dishonestly, and that some change of plan to suit the circumstances or the opportunity was within his contemplation. Whether this inference can be drawn as a matter of common sense depends upon the facts. Alternatively, it may be suggested, the defendant is liable if the crime committed is the same in the abstract as the one contemplated, and the perpetrator believed that he was acting within the encourager's intention.[196]

What if the perpetrator lets the plan miscarry without having intended that things should take the course they do?   That is a borderline case. There are two extreme situations. On the one hand, the perpetrator may deliberately change

14–080

14–081

14–082

14–083

---

[194] For another treatment, see David Lanham, "Accomplicies and Transferred Malice," (1980) 96 L.Q.R. 110 at 117-119.

[195] R. v. Leahy [1985] Crim. L.R. 99.

[196] The general question is discussed by Lanham, op. cit. supra, note 193 at 123-124. He puts the case of D2 ordering D1 to steal an ox (as a draught animal); D1 cannot find an ox, so he steals a horse. Lanham says that D2 "ought to be liable even though he did not authorise or command the theft of the horse". I would suggest that D2 is liable only if it is found as a fact that the theft of the horse, as a draught animal, was in the circumstances within the terms of his command, or was believed by D1 to be within those terms. No doubt this question will usually give the same result as Lanham's more simple-seeming (but analytically more dubious) question: was the crime the direct consequence of what was commanded etc.?

the plan, when the inciter (as already said) is not inculpated in the unauthorized crime. On the other hand, the perpetrator may muff it, when the inciter is liable as an accessory. The intermediate situation is where the perpetrator sees that the plan is miscarrying and allows it to do so. This is illustrated by the case of our old acquaintances, Saunders and Archer.[197]

Archer, you remember, counselled Saunders to murder Mrs. Saunders by giving her a poisoned apple, and Saunders allowed the apple to be eaten by his child instead. He did not have the courage to confess that he had planned to kill his wife, or the wit to make some excuse for taking the apple from the child. It was held on these facts that Archer was not guilty as an accessory to the murder of the child. He had counselled the murder of the wife, whereas Saunders had with full knowledge brought about the death of his child.

In order to understand the extent of the decision, let us imagine some slight changes of fact. (*a*) Suppose that Archer had counselled Saunders to murder his wife by shooting her, and that in attempting to carry out this proposal Saunders had accidentally shot his child instead. On these facts Archer would clearly have been guilty. The intention would have been transferred in law for both Saunders and Archer. (*b*) Now suppose the actual facts of the case except that Saunders was not present when his wife passed on the apple to the child. Here again, it seems, Archer would have been guilty. The apple would be like a bullet that by accident found its mark in the wrong person.

The point of difficulty about the actual facts of the case was that Saunders realized what was happening and consciously, deliberately, allowed his child to become the victim rather than his wife. This was taken to be the same as if Saunders had purposely changed his mind and decided to kill his child rather than his wife. It was a change of plan which meant that Saunders was no longer carrying out Archer's plan at all. Put in this way, the decision sounds reasonable, though it is near the line. The court might have held that the miscarriage of the plan was involuntary rather than intentional, since Saunders was trapped in a situation resulting from his criminal purpose. He could not (or thought he could not) save the child except by avowing his own guilt. Still, the point is sufficiently doubtful to justify leniency.[198]

---

[197] *R. v. Saunders and Archer* (1577) 2 Plow. 473.

[198] For a survey of the conflicting theories and conflicting overseas decisions on transferred intention see Lanham, *op. cit. supra*, note 193 at 110-117, 119-121. His discussion seems to confirm the wisdom of the rule suggested by the Law Commission Working Party. At p. 121 he puts a case where D2, a terrorist leader, sends D1 to murder X, a public figure; X is not available so D1 murders Y, a colleague of X's. Lanham suggests that D2 is liable for this because the killing of Y is a direct result of his orders. It seems to me that this is too broad a test. The killing is not the direct result of D2's orders if D1 deliberately changed the plan. D2 may be held to be an accessory only if killing Y was (or was thought by D1 to be) within D2's plan (D2's principal object being to procure the murder of a public figure, and the particular victim not being material). Lanham then expresses the opinion that *Saunders and Archer* is on all fours with his hypothetical, but it is not. In the absence of evidence as to Archer's intention, there is no warrant for supposing that he would have regarded the change of victim as being within the advice he gave. *R. v. Saunders and Archer* (1577) 2 Plow. 473 was decided in 1575, when the inchoate offence of incitement had not been developed. At present day, a person like Archer could be convicted of an offence under section 44 of the *Serious Crime Act 2007*. (Notice that when the alleged perpetrator and accessory are indicted together, the perpetrator's name stands first.)

14.12. RECKLESSNESS AS TO CIRCUMSTANCES

Normally the accessory by encouragement intends the offence to be committed, either in all events or if the circumstances so require. But it seems reasonable to say that he (and also the assister) can be implicated by subjective recklessness, provided that the offence can be perpetrated recklessly and that the perpetrator acts within the contemplated purpose. Take the following example. **14–084**

D2 encourages D1 to hit a night watchman over the head in order to render him unconscious. D1 does so and thereby inflicts grievous bodily harm on the watchman. D1 is liable for recklessly inflicting the harm, and D2 doubtless is too.

D2 encourages D1 to send a begging letter making a representation of fact, as D2 knows, might be false. If it is false, both D1 and D2 are guilty of fraud by false representation contrary section 2 of the *Fraud Act 2006.*

These examples show that when the courts say, as they frequently do, that a person charged as accessory must know the facts, this is too narrow a statement of law. In crimes of *mens rea* where recklessness is sufficient for the perpetrator it is also sufficient for the accessory.

In the forgoing examples the encourager desires the perpetrator to perform the reckless act that constitutes the crime. But is it enough that the encourager knows that by doing act A, that it is certain or virtually certain that D2 will also do act B, which is an illegal act? The encourager is liable for what he intends and for what he knows the perpetrator will do in the particular circumstances.[199]

The following decision bears out this view of the law. **14–085**

In *Carter v. Richardson,*[200] the supervising driver of a learner-driver whose blood-alcohol was above the limit (this being an offence of strict liability for the learner-driver) was held to have aided and abetted the offence because the supervisor "was aware that the principal consumed an excessive amount of alcohol or was reckless as to whether he had done so". The supervisor had not actively contributed to the offence, but in continuing to sit with the driver and thus legalizing the act of driving he had implicated himself in it. (The supervisor had brought himself to the unfavourable attention of the police by claiming at first to have been the actual driver, in order to protect the learner-driver, and confessed the truth only after it was established that he himself was above the blood-alcohol limit. Would he have been charged if it had not been for this?)

Since the particular offence was one of strict liability for the perpetrator, it could *a fortiori* be committed recklessly by him. It is true that numerous authorities say that a person is not an accessory to an offence of strict liability unless he actually knows the facts; but recklessness as to circumstances must be accommodated within the rule.

---

[199] Cf. *R. v. Turner* [1991] Crim. L.R. 57. Arguably, Turner obliquely intended to encourage D to speed, and knew that he was encouraging D to commit the conduct element of the offence in question—dangerous driving.
[200] [1974] R.T.R. 314.

14.13. WHERE THE PERPETRATOR IS LIABLE FOR NEGLIGENCE

14–086   In offences of negligence, like manslaughter (on one view) and dangerous driving, a person will be liable as accessory if what the perpetrator did was within his contemplation and if he knew (or was reckless as to) the facts that made the conduct negligent. In *R. v. Salmon*,[201] several people went together to practise with a rifle which could be deadly at a mile. They fired at a target 100 yards away in a field; one of the shots killed a boy in a garden 400 yards away. It was held by the Court of Crown Cases Reserved that they all could be convicted of manslaughter by negligence,[202] though it could not be proved who fired the fatal shot.

It appears that not one of the defendants realized the danger or knew of the presence of the boy within range; yet this possibility did not prevent the conviction of accessories. Presumably the explanation is that each defendant, regarded as an accessory, knew the facts that made the conduct negligent on the part of whoever was the perpetrator. They all knew that the shooting was taking place with a rifle and that people might be within range.

The same rule is applied to negligent races on the highway.

Two persons agreed expressly or by mutual understanding to race their horses and carts on the highway. Both drove with gross negligence, and a pedestrian was killed by one of them (it was not known which). Both were held guilty of manslaughter, since each had encouraged the other and it did not matter who was the perpetrator.[203]

The point seems to have been that as regards each driver, looked upon as an accessory, what mattered was not his own negligence but the fact that he knew that his friend (regarded as the perpetrator) was driving as he was and knew all the circumstances that made the driving negligent. In addition to having this knowledge, each driver intentionally encouraged the other in the dangerous course of conduct, for the sake of having a race. Similarly, if D1 (a 56 year old man) asks an intoxicated teenage girl (D2) to drive his car after plying D2 with drinks; and then urges D2 to speed thereby causing the death of a pedestrian, D1 could be held liable as an accessory.[204]

14–087   Can a person be held liable for "negligently" encouraging reckless or negligent wrongdoing?   It should not be.[205]

---

[201] (1880-81) L.R. 6 Q.B.D. 79.

[202] The question was left open in *R. v. Cramp* (1999) 110 A. Crim R. 198, but clearly the same would apply.

[203] *R. v. Swindall* (1846) 2 C. & K. 230; cf. *R. v. Baldessare* (1931) 22 Cr. App. R. 70; *R. v. Cramp* (1999) 110 A. Crim R. 198.

[204] In some of these negligence and recklessness cases accomplice liability is not always needed, as the accomplice's own negligence is enough to make him liable for the consequences of it. See *R. v. Cramp* (1999) 110 A. Crim R. 198; *State v. Anthony*, 151 N.H. 492 (2004); *Freeman v. State*, 211 Tenn. 27 (1962). Cf. *R. v. Loukes* [1996] 1 Cr. App. R. 444.

[205] *R. v. Roberts* [1997] R.T.R. 462; and *Blakely v. D.P.P.* [1991] R.T.R. 405 as to recklessness *vis-à-vis* the conduct element.

Cf. *State v. McVay*, 132 A. 436 (1926); *State v. Anthony*, 151 N.H. 492 (2004).

Suppose D1, driving a car, passes D2. D2 angered by this, accelerates to pass D1; and so a kind of competition develops between the two drivers, and each driver at a negligent speed. A pedestrian is killed by one of the drivers, it is not known which.

The driver who killed the pedestrian should be guilty of causing death by dangerous driving;[206] and if his identity cannot be established, neither driver can be convicted of this crime. Here neither driver wished the other to drive at speed or intended to give him encouragement in the affair.[207] The best that could be said is that they recklessly encouraged each other to speed. If D1 had only attempted to pass D2 once and D2 sped up thereby causing D1 to have a head on collision, it would be difficult to demonstrate that D1 knew that his single act of overtaking was virtually certain to encourage D2 to speed up. It is one thing to intend to encourage D to act[208] negligently or recklessly, but something rather different to negligently encourage D to act negligently or recklessly.[209]

In many of the racing cases D1 will be subjectively aware of the fact that his racing is likely to encourage D2 to also race—and therefore he risks encouraging D2 to engage in dangerous conduct.[210]

14.14. WHERE THE PERPETRATOR IS STRICTLY LIABLE

Where the offence is one of strict liability for the perpetrator, this kind of liability does not extend to the accessory. The accessory is not liable without *mens rea*—a principle testified by an almost unbroken line of authority since *Callow v. Tillstone*.[211] This was what is sometimes known as a "strong" decision, meaning one of doubtful justice. **14–088**

Callow, a veterinary surgeon, gave a farmer a certificate that his meat was fit for human consumption. The farmer knew that the meat was unfit because the animal, a heifer, had died from eating yew. Callow knew that two other cattle that had been feeding with this heifer died from eating yew, and the examination he made of the dead heifer was utterly perfunctory. The farmer sold the meat to a butcher, who exposed it for sale; the meat was then condemned as unfit. It was held that although the butcher was strictly liable for exposing unfit meat for sale, Callow could not be convicted as accessory since all that was found against him was negligence.

This means that in regulatory offences the doctrine of strict responsibility in respect of circumstances of an offence applies only to the perpetrator.

---

[206] Section 1 of the *Road Traffic Act 1988*.

[207] Cf. *R. v. Gnango* [2011] 1 All E.R. 153.

[208] See *R. v. Turner* [1991] Crim. L.R. 57 (perhaps, explainable as a case where D1 obliquely intends to encourage D2); cf. *R. v. Gnango* [2011] 1 All E.R. 153.

[209] *R. v. Mastin* (1834) 6 Car. & P. 396; *R. v. Roberts* [1997] R.T.R. 462; *R. v. Lee* [2006] EWCA Crim 240.

[210] See further, Sanford H. Kadish, "Reckless Complicity", (1997) 87 *J. Crim. L. & Criminology* 369; Glanville Williams, "Complicity, Purpose and the Draft Dode: Part 2", [1990] Crim. L.R. 98.

[211] (1900) 64 J.P. 823. Cf. *Bowker v. Woodroffe* [1928] 1 K.B. 217; *Dial Contracts v. Vickers* [1971] R.T.R. 386; *Ferguson v. Weaving* [1951] 1 K.B. 814; *R. v. Tinsley* [1963] Crim. L.R. 520; *D Stanton & Son Ltd. v. Webber* [1973] R.T.R. 86; *D.P.P. v. Anderson* (1991) 155 J.P. 157.

Accomplices require *mens rea*.[212] The remarkable result in *Callow v. Tillstone* was that the shopkeeper, who was utterly without fault, could be convicted, while the negligent author of the offence could not be. However, it would seem that Callow could now be convicted on the basis of recklessness if the court were satisfied that he had no belief that the meat was fit.

14–089   **The law seems to me to be illogical. If an offence of recklessness is equally an offence of recklessness for the accessory, and an offence of negligence is equally ditto for the accessory, I don't see why an offence of strict liability should not be at least an offence of negligence for the accessory. In fact, I don't see why it shouldn't be an offence of strict liability for him.**   I should be reluctant to see strict liability extended, but there would be much to be said for the rule that in offences of strict liability the accessory is liable for negligence. That however, is not the law as it stands. One of the few cases holding that strict liability extends to accessories is *R. v. Creamer*.[213] The Court of Criminal Appeal there held that the only mental element necessary for constructive manslaughter is intending to commit a dangerous unlawful act. Then, if death follows, it is manslaughter. The court held that a person could be convicted as accessory to the manslaughter if he knew of the dangerous and unlawful act (meaning, the facts making it dangerous and unlawful); it was not required that he, any more than the perpetrator, should foresee the death.

Reverting to *Callow v. Tillstone*, although the decision looks unjust on the particular facts, the principle can be defended in most cases on the ground that accessories generally have less control over and knowledge of the situation than the perpetrator. In particular, it is generally the perpetrator (the factory owner or seller or other person carrying on a business directly affected by law) who is expected to know what he may and may not do, and to take anxious precautions to comply.

The rationale would suggest that ignorance of the specialized law should be a defence to a person charged as accessory; yet it is not. One would have thought that the same reasoning gave the alleged accomplice a defence of ignorance of fact would have given him a defence of ignorance of law where the relevant law is highly specialized. Anyway, in *Callow v. Tillstone* the vet must have known the law, and was being paid in order to make sure it was complied with; yet he was allowed the defence of ignorance of fact; so the legal position is indefensible on any view. Perhaps a reasonable rule would be to say that where the alleged accomplice himself carries on the specialized business or profession, or is so closely associated with it that he ought to know the relevant law, he is strictly liable in the same way as the perpetrator, but otherwise can set up a defence of ignorance of fact or law. Alternatively, the question could be left to be settled by the legislation in question.

Parliament has in fact accepted the responsibility in some instances, though it has not allowed a defence of ignorance of law nor distinguished between those

---

[212] If this approach is followed in serious offences, D2 might not be liable for statutory rape if he lets D1 use his apartment so that D1 can seduce V, if he has no idea that V is under 13.

[213] [1966] 1 Q.B. 72 at 82. The High Court of Australia examines this issue in *R. v. Chai* (2002) 128 A. Crim. R. 101. See also *R. v. Trinneer* [1970] S.C.R. 638; *R. v. Jackson* [1993] 4 S.C.R. 573.

who are and are not involved in the specialized activity. Modern statutes often include a provision extending strict liability to accessories, and do it in a wholesale way because they bring in everyone who contributes to bring about the offence, whether he is carrying on a related business or profession or not. Such a provision would not operate if the facts of *Callow v. Tillstone* occurred again.

Suppose that the defendant is a company, as in *National Coal Board v.*   **14–090 *Gamble*. How can you speak of knowledge or recklessness in relation to a company?**   A company is affected by the knowledge of its governing director or manager, but not by the knowledge of a subordinate employee (see Chapter 38). It follows that a company can be accessory to an offence only if one of its directing officers has the requisite mental state.[214] That is why the conviction of the National Coal Board was wrong, whether the weighbridge clerk could rightly have been convicted or not.

14.15. Police Informers

Consider the case where a police informer pretends to help but really intends to   **14–091** frustrate the crime. He should not, in common sense, be an accessory, even though he gives what is technically an act of help, and even though in the event he fails to frustrate the crime. The Law Commission expressed this by proposing a defence for a person who acted with the purpose of preventing the commission of an offence:

> "We recommend that it should be a defence to liability for an offence as a secondary party if D proves that:
> (1)   he or she acted for the purpose of:
>   (a)   preventing the commission of either the offence that he or she was encouraging or assisting or another offence; or
>   (b)   to prevent or limit the occurrence of harm; and
> (2)   it was reasonable to act as D did in the circumstances."[215]

Obviously, you might prevent an assault by assisting it and then having the assaulter arrested. When drinking after hours has taken place, the "effects" are not nullified by arresting the drinker. For the most part, therefore, the police and their informers would not be able to argue that it was reasonable to drink in such circumstances. However, common sense suggests that the occurrence of harm that transpires from theft may be reduced or prevented by allowing it to occur but having the guilty parties arrested immediately after so that the property is restored unharmed to its owner. In such circumstances the informer does not intend that the owner shall be permanently deprived of his property, which is what the law of theft aims against.[216] The same would not apply to offences of violence. Such offences involve irreversible harm and should be thwarted before

---

[214] *Henshall (John) (Quarries) v. Harvey* [1965] 2 Q.B. 233.

[215] Law Commission, *Participating in Crime*, No. 305 (London: Cm. 7084, 2007) at para. 5.23.

[216] *The Case of Macdaniel* (1748) Fost. 121, it was held that D was guilty as accessory to robbery when he arranged that the robber should be stimulated to commit robbery, his object being to claim that reward for apprehending a highway robber. There was no evidence that D's object was to see that the property was returned to the victim. Even so, the apprehensions of the robber would have meant

they are consummated. However, the defence (which the courts could implement as a matter of common law, if they wished) could allow police informers to abet (but not perpetrate) any acquisitive offence if they intended to see that the criminals were frustrated after committing the offence.

14.16. WITHDRAWAL

14–092 A person who has incited a crime can still (in general) escape complicity in it if he expressly and clearly countermands the crime or withdraws his assent in due time before it is committed[217] (*i.e.* in time to enable the perpetrator to prevent its commission); but he will remain liable for any previous encouragement or conspiracy, as an inchoate offence.[218] There need not even be an express withdrawal of advice and consent, if the encourager has made his change of heart clear by conduct, as by quitting the gang.[219] He must, however, make it clear he is no longer in the game and wants no part of it. Probably he can also avoid complicity by going to the police, or by giving a timely warning to the intended victim. If he informed D of his intention to inform the police or the victim, this would be strong evidence that he does not want D to use the advice, encouragement or information which he provided at some earlier point in time.[220] Similarly, if he phones or e-mails D over and over to tell him he does not want D to go through with the crime or use the information or advice he provided, then this should also be sufficient.[221]

The above rule applies only when the defendant has done no more than encourage or otherwise incite the commission of the crime, as by agreeing to take part in it. If he has acted positively to assist the crime, he must, it seems, do his best to prevent its commission, by warning the victim or by other means, short perhaps of going to the police.[222] Nevertheless, reporting the crime to the police would provide fairly powerful evidence of his withdrawal from the criminal venture. D need not succeed in preventing the crime, but he should show that his

---

that there was a good chance of the victim getting his property back, and it would seem that in such circumstances there was no theftous intent on D's part. The point was not argued.

[217] *R. v. Croft* [1944] K.B. 295; *R. v. Barnard* (1980) 70 Cr. App. R. 28; *R. v. Baker* [1994] Crim. L.R. 444; *R. v. Rook* [1993] 1 W.L.R. 1005; *R. v. Whitefield* (1984) 79 Cr. App. R. 36.

[218] Cf. *R. v. Mitchell* (1998) 163 J.P. 75. He could also be caught by one of the inchoate offences found in sections 44–46 of the *Serious Crime Act 2007*.

[219] Foster, *op. cit. supra*, note 142 at 354. In the case of spontaneous violence, it has been held that dropping one's weapons and walking off is sufficient to isolate one's early participation from acts which may transpire post withdrawal: *R. v. Mitchell* (1998) 163 J.P. 75; *R. v. O'Flaherty* [2004] 2 Cr. App. R. 20. See also *R. v. Mendez* [2011] 1 Cr. App. R. 109.

[220] *R. v. Grundy* [1977] Crim. L.R. 543.

[221] *R. v. Grundy* [1977] Crim. L.R. 543.

[222] David Lanham, "Accomplices and Withdrawal", (1981) 97 *L.Q.R.* 575 at 579–585. Some American decisions suggest that a person who has given help must either withdraw the help or, if he cannot do that, must go to the police. But the American Law Institute's Modal Penal Code s.206(6) requires only that the defendant "gives timely warning to law enforcement authorities or otherwise makes proper effort to prevent the commission of the offence". Going to the police was not made a requirement in *R. v. Grundy* [1977] Crim. L.R. 543. Likewise, in *R. v. O'Flaherty* [2004] 2 Cr. App. R. 20 at paras 61–62, it was said that: "There is no to a requirement that reasonable steps must have been taken to prevent the crime."

attempt to prevent it was genuine and serious.[223] D must do something to neutralize his assistance. If D has supplied the perpetrator with a gun, then he should take reasonable steps to recover it, or to make sure that it will not be used to commit a crime, and so on.[224]

Where a person who, having given information enabling a burglary to be committed, repented and tried to stop his companion going on with the project for two weeks before the companion committed the crime, this was held to be sufficient to let him out of liability for the crime[225] (though he would remain liable for conspiracy). But where one burglar gave a knife to his companion to use against anyone who might interrupt them, but on someone approaching, said: "Come on, let's go", suiting the action to the word, this was held to be insufficient to exempt him from complicity in a stabbing that his companion proceeded to inflict with the knife; and the Court of Appeal seemed to indicate that the defendant could on the facts have dissociated himself from the crime only by physically intervening to prevent the use of the knife.[226]

This restriction upon the right of withdrawal is an exception to the usual requirement that *mens rea* and *actus reus* must be contemporaneous. In effect the defendant is made liable for negligence in failing to prevent the crime.

If one of a band of criminals is arrested, does this prevent him from being responsible for what his companions afterwards do in pursuance of the common purpose? He remains responsible if his arrest is unknown to the others.   14–093

In *R. v. Johnson*[227] D1 and D2 entered a house with intent to steal; D2 was apprehended, without D1 becoming aware of the fact, and D1 afterwards stole an article in the house. The trial judge, Maule J., ruled that D2 could be convicted as accessory.

If the arrest is known to the others, it would seem that the arrest should be accounted an involuntary withdrawal from the plan, so that the party arrested is liable only to the extent that he would be liable on a voluntary withdrawal. If for example, a number of criminals make forcible resistance to arrest, and one of them is arrested, and ceases resistance and encouragement to his companions, it seems that he will not ordinarily be implicated in an act of force subsequently committed by another of the gang.[228] The reason is that when he is seen to be arrested the encouragement he has given his companions by joining their forcible resistance comes to an end. But if he has supplied a companion with a weapon to be used in resisting, the arrest will not end his liability for the use of the weapon, any more than in the case of voluntary withdrawal, unless perhaps he offers to try to persuade his companion not to use the weapon.

In a pre-planned joint enterprise D may communicate his withdrawal simply by telling his co-perpetrators that he has no intention of continuing with the plan, and that they too should abandon it. Merely not showing up on the day will not be

---

[223] *R. v. O'Flaherty* [2004] 2 Cr. App. R. 20.
[224] *R. v. Becerra* (1976) 62 Cr. App. R. 212.
[225] *R. v. Grundy* [1977] Crim. L.R. 543.
[226] *R. v. Becerra* (1976) 62 Cr. App. R. 212.
[227] (1841) Car. & M. 218.
[228] *R. v. Jackson* (1673) 1 Hale P.C. 464.

sufficient: he must communicate his withdrawal in unequivocal terms and before the criminality is underway. In the case of spontaneous gang violence, a participant might not think to categorically state that he or she is no longer willing to participate and thus is withdrawing. Often the withdrawal in such cases will involve nothing more than the accomplice running off before the fatal blow is delivered to the victim.

14–094 **If the joint enterprise is still underway, how do we decide whether D is still in it or whether he has withdrawn?** If a person puts a boulder in motion and it rolls down the hill and kills a child, it will not be easy for him to distance himself from it. Similarly, if a person participates in savage gang violence, it will not be easy for him to distance himself from what he has helped to put in motion. But human beings are not boulders, they are autonomous rational creatures and thus if a participant takes reasonable steps to either dissuade his fellow gang members from proceeding with their attack, or to show that he no longer supports it, and thinks it should stop immediately, he may be able to convince the jury that he withdrew from the enterprise.

D will need to communicate his change of heart to his fellow gang members. If he is the ring leader, or a major player, the others might also desist if he does. It will be extremely difficult for D to establish that he made an effective withdrawal when he has willingly participated in spontaneous gang violence. However, if he were to drop his weapon[229] and yell: "I am out: this has to stop it has gone too far", he might have a chance. Of course, if he took extra steps such as trying to protect the victim, or to disarm his former accomplices, he might be able to convince a jury that he effectively withdrew from the joint enterprise. Merely running away because it looks as though it is getting too risky would not be enough.[230]

14–095 **If there is a lull in violence during a vicious gang attack upon V, is D liable for harm caused after the lull if he does not join the attack after the lull?** Perhaps! It will depend on whether the violence was fundamentally different to anything D had anticipated,[231] or whether he effectively withdrew before the second round of violence kicked off:

> "If a group of men, in a spontaneous joint enterprise of violence are chasing another man armed with weapons, bottles and sticks through the streets of a town, and at a point when the man being chased and the remaining chasers turn a corner out of the sight of one of the attackers, and that one attacker then stops, puts down his weapon and walks back the way he had come, and does not go round the corner, he does not participate any further in the attack which culminates two streets later with the death of the man being chased. In such a case, a

---

[229] *R. v. Mitchell* (1998) 163 J.P. 75.

[230] *R. v. Perman* [1996] 1 Cr. App. R. 24 at 34.

[231] These are two different ways of exculpating D and should not be conflated: 1. The fundamentally different act rule applies even if D does not withdraw, but did not foresee the fatal blow, *etc.* as a possible incident of the joint enterprise. 2. The withdrawal rule applies even if the act was not fundamentally different, so long as D has effectively withdrawn. Cf. *R. v. Rafferty* [2007] EWCA Crim. 1846.

jury may well conclude that that one man, by stopping and acting as he did, had withdrawn from the joint enterprise of which he was at one stage a willing member. It is a question of fact and degree in every case."[232]

In *R. v. Mitchell*,[233] Mitchell and her co-defendants jointly attacked three victims in a car park following a dispute over a taxi. During the attack there was a lull in the violence, because some of the co-defendants went to a nearby house to fetch weapons. Mitchell remained in the car park and claimed she only remained as she was searching for her shoes, which she had lost during the initial part of the attack. When the violence resumed one of the co-defendants stamped so hard on the head of one of the victims that it killed him. Mitchell and her co-defendants were charged with murder. Mitchell claimed that there was more than one joint enterprise, because there was a lull in the violence and that she did not participate in the violence after the lull. The Court of Appeal rejected this submission, because Mitchell played a leading role in instigating the violence and had foreseen "within the scope of the enterprise that one of the others might kill with the intention of killing or causing really serious bodily injury and that the actions of, the killer, were not outside that scope." Furthermore, Mitchell was still in it. She had not effectively withdrawn before the fatal blow was delivered; she was present when the blow was delivered. The court held that the evidence was sufficient for the jury to infer that the lull in violence did not end the original joint enterprise—it continued and Mitchell stayed in the game. As she remained present before and after the lull in violence she clearly had not withdrawn from it.[234]

This is clearly the right decision. A lull in violence should not be used to split what is in effect a continuing act of violence. Only in exceptional circumstances would a lull in violence be sufficient to sever proximate and sequential acts of violence. That aside, if D is present when the fatal blow is delivered and is a member of the gang that delivers it, she can hardly claim that she was not involved. She would only evade liability if she could show that the fatal blow was an act fundamentally different to anything she had envisaged; or where she could show she withdrew.[235]

14.17. LEGISLATIVE EXCLUSION

The law of complicity is very wide, but it is well known, and normally the legislature may fairly be presumed to intend it to apply to its new edicts. **14–096**

Occasionally, however, the court may feel able to collect from the statute a legislative policy exempting the unnamed party from responsibility. An example is where legislation is designed for the protection of a certain class of persons, who are not directly struck at by it, and who by reason of nonage, poverty, social isolation or the like are deemed by the courts to be unable to protect themselves

---

[232] *R. v. Mitchell* [2009] 1 Cr. App. R. 438 at 448. See also *R. v. O'Flaherty* [2004] 2 Cr. App. R. 20. Cf. *R. v. Rafferty* [2007] EWCA Crim. 1846.

[233] [2009] 1 Cr. App. R. 438.

[234] *R. v. Mitchell* [2009] 1 Cr. App. R. 438 at 452.

[235] *R. v. O'Flaherty* [2004] 2 Cr. App. R. 20.

fully against exploitation.[236] Such persons do not become accessories to an offence committed in respect of them by giving their consent to it.[237]

The only clear instance in the reports is in respect of the crime of unlawful sexual intercourse with a girl under 16.[238] The statute is intended to protect young girls even against themselves. Therefore, the girl who consents to or instigates her own seduction is not an accessory to an offence committed by the man.[239]

14–097 The "victim" rule, as it may be called, applies only where the person who is in the vulnerable position is excluded from the class of perpetrators. If a person can be called a perpetrator, then *a fortiori* he can be an accessory. The unresolved issue is what to do with two 15-year-old lovers. Since under the *Sexual Offences Act 2003*, both can be perpetrators and both can be victims! For example, even a youth under 16 can perpetrate a consensual sexual assault upon a girl under 16. He will therefore be an accessory if he encourages such a female to commit a sexual assault upon him, and *vice versa*. A youth under 16 can perpetrate sexual assault upon another; he can therefore abet acts of these kinds committed upon him. Even girls under 16 can be convicted of sexual assault upon boys under 16; they can be convicted as perpetrators, and therefore can be convicted as accessories. There was no legislative intent to exempt consenting youngsters from the operation of the *Sexual Offences Act 2003*.[240] If 15-year-old D1 goes all the way with his 15-year-old girlfriend both are criminals—one as an accessory and the other as perpetrator.

It appears, however, the normal rule could apply if an adult took advantage of a consenting underage victim, since the law clearly aims to protect underage consenters from being sexually exploited by adults. A minor does not have the capacity to consent to sexual relations, they are assumed to be victims even though they consent.[241] The absurdity caused by allowing one to be an accessory when she consents to have sexual intercourse with someone her own age is not really caused by the "victim" rule, but rather by the fact that consensual underage sex is criminalized by the *Sexual Offences Act 2003*. (Clearly, the criminal law is not the way to protect underage people from the dangers of engaging in "consensual" sexual activity when they are "very" close in age—and are both underage.)

Per contra, if a father has an incestuous relationship with his daughter under 16, the daughter does not commit incest: not as perpetrator, because the statute expressly excludes girls under 16, and not as accessory, because the exclusion of

---

[236] See for example, section 50 of the *Serious Crime Act 2007*.

[237] See Glanville Williams, "Victims as Parties to Crime—A Further Comment", [1964] Crim. L.R. 686.

[238] *R. v. Tyrrell* [1894] 1 Q.B. 710.

[239] The provisions in the *Sexual Offences Act 2003* are also designed to protect underage boys, so the rule would also apply to a boy under 16. The victim rule has been recognized in connection with conspiracy: *R. v. Whitehouse* [1977] Q.B. 868. For another possible instance of the rule see *Grace Rymer Investments Ltd. v. Waite* [1958] Ch. 831 at 845–846. See also *R. v. Morris* [1923] 1 K.B. 166 at 169, 171-172.

[240] *R. v. G.* [2006] 1 W.L.R. 2052. One U.S. case has held, that a minor could not be an accessory *State v. Hayes*, 351 N.W.2d 654 (1984).

[241] For a fuller discussion of the limits of consent as a defence, see Dennis J. Baker, "The Moral Limits of Consent as a Defence in the Criminal Law", (2009) 12 *New Crim. L. Rev.* 93. See also Glanville Williams, "Victims and Other Exempt Parties in Crime", (1990) 10 *Legal Stud.* 245.

such girls as perpetrators implies their exclusion as accessories. The point arose in *R. v. Whitehouse*,[242] where the court reached the right result but gave the wrong reason. It was held that the girl could not be an accessory because she was the "victim" of the offence. This is wrong because incest is not an offence against the person. Its basis is either "moral" (incest is widely thought to be wrong in itself) or eugenic, not a matter of protecting the young, as is shown by the fact that it applies to intercourse between fathers and adult daughters and between adult brothers and sisters. The decision cannot be grounded on the "victim" rule as a matter of law. The offence found in the former section 11 of the *Sexual Offences Act 1956* was not aimed at protecting a special category of victim. Since incest is considered to be a victimless crime, at least, if it merely involves consenting adults, V could only be regarded as falling into a special victim category if a different offence had been charged.

It is true that a girl under 16 was omitted from the former offence of incest (and is also omitted from the replacement offences found in sections 64 and 65 of the *Sexual Offences Act 2003*), whether committed with her father, brother, or any other male or female within the forbidden degrees; but this is probably because it was thought when the legislation was passed that most of the girls under 16 who participate in incest will have been sexually imposed upon, and therefore it would not be right to include any young girls in the law. Of course, nowadays the father would be charged with rape of a child or with engaging in sexual activity with a child family member.[243]   **14–098**

So the proper reason for holding in *R. v. Whitehouse* that the girl was not within the law of incest was simply that it was the intention of the statute to exclude her.[244] If a 14-year-old girl seduces her 15-year-old brother; she could hardly be said to be the victim. The offences aimed at protecting children found in the *Sexual Offences Act 2003* treat all underage persons as victims, whether the perpetrator is an adult or not. Not only do children lack the capacity to give fully informed consent, they are in a vulnerable position where they could be easily coerced. We might call this type of victim an "assumed" victim. Accessorial liability is excluded when the offence is specifically designed for the protection of such persons, because even though they may be willing participants, they are

---

[242] [1977] Q.B. 868.

[243] This conduct is caught by sections 25 and 26 (and also 63 and 64 for adults) of the *Sexual Offences Act 2003*.

[244] For a similar reason, *R. v. Sockett* (1909) 1 Cr. App. R. 101 appears to be wrongly decided. It was held in that case that a non-pregnant woman could be convicted as accessory to a man's attempt to abort her, although, because of the wording of the statute, she could not have been convicted of an attempt to abort herself. Why Parliament exempted non-pregnant women from liability for attempting to abort themselves is a matter of speculation, but it may have been because many women who mistakenly believed themselves to be pregnant attempted abortion, and no good reason was seen for rendering them liable to prosecution. On the other hand the Parliament that passed the *Offences against the Person Act 1861* evidently saw good reason for punishing the pregnant woman who operated on herself and also the professional abortionist who operated on any woman, pregnant or not. That was all that the Parliament expressly said. It probably forgot about the law of complicity; but the rational view is that since Parliament exempted the non-pregnant woman who acted for herself it would surely have intended to exempt her from complicity in an abortion if the matter had been brought to its attention.

assumed to be unwilling.[245] If the incest involves consenting adults, then they will both be criminalized because they are assumed not to be victims but willing perpetrators. (In reality, the child participant is a victim of a sexual violation, rather than incest *per se*.)

14–099   **Does not the law also assume that consenting adults can also be victims? If adult V encourages adult D to nail his hand to a plank, will V be held criminally liable as an accessory?**   The harm-doer could be charged with an offence under *Offences against the Person Act 1861*,[246] but should the *consenter* be charged as an accessory given the law is designed to protect him? As a matter of principle he should not be charged as an accessory. He should be exempt if his encouragement only leads to harm against himself. In an Australian case, a woman was convicted of assisting her estranged domestic partner to breach a restraining order, because she asked him to visit her home to take care of their infant child.[247] One wonders what the social benefit is in convicting such persons. Similarly, if a person goes to a euthanasia clinic and the physician is arrested just before he delivers the fatal dose, it would be absurd to hold the consenting V liable as an accessory to her own attempted murder.

14–100   **Can it not be said that every case where Parliament penalizes one party to a bilateral transaction, it must have intended to leave the other party free from liability? Yet you said earlier that the law is otherwise. For example, where a statute makes it an offence to sell something, the buyer is counted as an accessory. If Parliament meant that, it would surely have brought both of them within the prohibition.**   This is quite an important point, on which the American[248] and English courts have diverged. When a statute makes it an offence for one party to enter into a transaction, the English courts automatically

---

[245] As a U.S. court recently put it, children cannot consent to sexual molestation because they do not have the capacity to do so. See *Bazin v. State*, 683 S.E.2d 917 (2009). See also *People v. Burnham*, 222 Cal. Rptr. 630 (1986).

[246] *R. v. Brown* [1994] 1 A.C. 212. Cf. *R. v. Wright* (1603) Co.Lit. f. 127 a-b.; (1613) 1 East P.C. 396.

[247] *Keane v. Police* (1997) 69 S.A.S.R. 481. (In this case, the mother put the children at risk by allowing him to visit, but if she were merely to risk harm to herself, it would be wrong to criminalize her). Cf. *State v. Dejarlais*, 944 P.2d 1110 (1997). See Joel Feinberg, *Harm to Self: The Moral Limits of the Criminal Law*, (New York: Oxford University Press, 1986).

[248] Courts in the United States have rejected such an approach. In *Robinson v. State*, 815 S.W.2d 361, at 363-364 (1991), the Court of Appeals of Texas said: "Numerous jurisdictions [in the U.S.] have addressed the question presented here, and all have reached the same result. See *Thompson v. State*, 1386 (Ala.Crim.App.1977); *Sweatt v. State*, 473 S.W.2d 913, 914-15 (1971); *People v. Lamb*, 285 P.2d 941, 942-43 (1955); *State v. Hayes*, 351 N.W.2d 654, 657 (1984); *Tellis v. State*, 445 P.2d 938, 940 (1968); *People v. Tune*, 479 N.Y.S.2d 832, 834 (1984); *State v. Nasholm*, 467 P.2d 647, 648 (1970); *State v. Fox*, 313 N.W.2d 38, 40 (S.D.1981); *Brown v. State*, 557 S.W.2d 926 (1977); *State v. Berg*, 613 P.2d 1125, 1126 (1980); *State v. Warnock*, 501 P.2d 625, 625-26 (1972); *Wheeler v. State*, 691 P.2d 599, 602 (1984). The opinion of the Supreme Court of Wyoming in Wheeler provides a good example of the reasoning employed in these decisions: There is a definite distinction between a seller and a buyer. Their separate acts may result in a single transaction, but the buyer is not aiding the 'selling act' of the seller and the seller is not aiding the 'buying act' of the buyer. The buyer and seller act from different poles. They are not in association or confederacy. An accomplice is one who participates in the same criminal conduct as the defendant, not one whose conduct is the antithesis of the defendant, albeit the conduct of both is involved in a single transaction."

convict the other party as accessory if he knew the facts.[249] In the example you give, although the buyer is not within the definition of the offence as a perpetrator, there is no indication that buyers are in any sense a protected class (unless, of course, the legislation is clearly intended for the protection of buyers).[250] In the English opinion, therefore, such a statute does not show an intention to exclude buyers in the same way as some sexual offences exclude girls under 16. The American courts hold the opposite, and have the better reason.[251] When the legislature has referred to bilateral transaction and made it an offence in one party only, it is improper to extend the law to catch the other party under the doctrine of accessoryship, because the legislature, when it applied the offence to sellers, must have considered whether to bring buyers within the prohibition also, and its silence on this point is an indication of an intention not to bring the buyer in.

In consequence of the English rule, it has been held that a thief who disposes of goods to a handler (receiver) can be convicted as accessory to the handling.[252] Normally, of course, a thief will be charged with theft; but if he is charged with handling, the prosecutor believing that he was himself the thief who sold to a handler, he can frequently be convicted under the indictment for handling.

The decision looks wrong. Handlers are subject to a higher maximum punishment than thieves. Since the legislature has distinguished between thieves and handlers, it is unsound to hold that a thief can be a handler by reason of accessoryship. In *Mallan v. Lee*,[253] Dixon J. said: "the application of sections dealing with aiding and abetting, may be excluded by the nature of the substantive offence or the general tenor or policy of the provisions by which it is created." In *Keane v. Police*, King C.J. said:[254]

---

[249] *Sayce v. Coupe* [1953] 1 Q.B. 1; *R. v. Potts* (1818) Russ. & Ry. 353.

[250] An example might be the person who buys drugs for his own consumption from a trafficker. Although drug addicts can commit an offence of illegal possession, there would be no good reason for bringing them into the more serious offence of trafficking (section 3 of the *Misuse of Drugs Act 1971*) as accessory, since the statute against trafficking was obviously made for their protection. A similar provision was considered by the High Court of Australia. Justice Kirby, in dissent, said: "In textual terms, the appellant cannot be deemed 'to have taken part in committing the offence' and to be 'guilty of the offence' because an essential element of 'the offence' is that the offender must be the supplier and not the recipient of the dangerous drug. By the terms of the offence, the offender cannot be placed on both sides of the equation. In accordance with the *Act*, he cannot at once be the person who 'supplies' and 'the person to whom the thing is supplied' within the institution. No general aiding and abetting provision can change this fundamental character and expression of the offence." *Maroney v. The Queen* (2003) 216 C.L.R. 31 at 46. As a general rule this is correct. But the majority upheld the conviction because the receiver was a prisoner who had taken deliberate steps to organize his "own supply". Cf. *R. v. Latif* [1996] 1 W.L.R. 104.

[251] See for example, *State v. Utterback*, 240 Neb. 981 (1991); *United States v. Farrar*, 281 U.S. 624 (1930); *In re Cooper*, 121 P. 318 (1912); *Commonwealth v. Boynton*, 116 Mass. 343 (1875).

[252] *Carter Patersons & Pickfords Carriers Limited v. Wessel* [1947] K.B. 849.

[253] (1949) 80 C.L.R. 198.

[254] (1997) 69 S.A.S.R. 481 cited with approval by Kirby J. in *Maroney v. The Queen* (2003) 216 C.L.R. 31 at 44.

"It may, therefore, be inapplicable to a person of a class whom the substantive offence is designed to protect ...; or in respect of whose participation some lesser punishment is imposed...[255] It may also be inapplicable where the substantive offence itself involves some element of secondary participation..."[256]

14–101   The furthest the English courts have gone is to hold that complicity is to some extent excluded where the offence is defined in terms too narrow to involve some of those who (in a sense) take part in its commission. A statute makes it an offence to keep (meaning to manage) a betting house or brothel, or to carry on a prohibited business. For example, players at an unlawful game do not aid the occupier in using the premises for unlawful gaming, because "using" is held not to mean "managing".[257] The Law Commission Working Party has proposed that the American rule should be adopted in the projected code:

"A person does not become an accessory to an offence if the offence is so defined that his conduct in it is inevitably incidental to its commission and such conduct is not expressly penalised."[258]

It seems right in such a case that the legislature should be required to state fully the persons who are to be liable.

14.18. COMPLICITY AND LIMITATIONS ON THE CRIMINAL LAW

14–102   Traditionally, the liability of the alleged accessory depends on that of the perpetrator. The basis of the common law is that the accessory's liability is derivative from that of the perpetrator. The rule may seem like the most obvious common sense, for unless there is a perpetrator there cannot have been a crime, and "there will be no foundation on which accessory crime can rest" (Lord Denman C.J.).[259] (Lord Denman did not speak with complete precision, because at common law there is no "accessory crime"; there is a single crime with several parties.) The general rule is not merely a piece of pedantry. The law of complicity cannot turn non-crimes into crimes. It is not a crime for a man to desert his wife, so, obviously, it ought not to be a crime for another person to help him desert his wife.

14–103   **Yes, but that is a case where the act is not prohibited. Suppose that a person commits what may be called a criminal act but is not responsible. Why should not an accessory be made liable?** Here courts are generally able to surmount the difficulty by a technique already mentioned: the physical actor is treated as a puppet, so that the guilty actor who activates him to do the mischief becomes responsible not as accessory but as a perpetrator acting through an innocent agent. The Law Commission Working Party formulated the following definition of an innocent agent:

---

[255] Citing *Ellis v. Guerin* [1925] S.A.S.R. 282.

[256] Cf. *Jenks v. Turpin* (1884) 13 Q.B.D. 505 at 526; *Carmichael & Sons (Worcester) Ltd. v. Cottle* [1971] R.T.R. 11 at 14.

[257] *Jenks v. Turpin* (1884) 13 Q.B.D. 505.

[258] *Working Paper 43, supra*, note 3 at 8–12.

[259] *R. v. Tyler* (1838) 8 Car. & P. 616 at 618.

"A person acts through an innocent agent when he intentionally causes the external elements of the offence to be committed by (or partly by) a person who is himself innocent of the offence charged by reason of lack of a required fault element, or lack of capacity."

For instance, one can murder or wound through an innocent agent, such as a person who is irresponsibly insane. Not only common law but statutory offences can be committed by proxy, as the example just given of wounding shows. When Fagin sends Twist (aged under 10)[260] to steal handkerchiefs, Fagin "appropriates" a handkerchief, within the meaning of the *Theft Act 1968*, at the moment when Twist takes it. Fagin is the perpetrator, although absent, since a child under 10 cannot commit a crime.[261] If Dodge gets Dupe to write a false document (or "instrument" as the law of forgery calls it), so that it would be forgery if he wrote it himself, then if Dupe does not know of the falsity Dodge can be held responsible for "making" a forgery by the hand of Dupe.

It does not matter that it was the "innocent agent" who started the affair.[262] The innocent agent need not be instructed to commit the criminal act; it is enough that he is caused to commit it (as where he is told that he may, thus leading him to believe that the act is lawful).[263] Where a person manipulates an innocent agent in these ways it is the same as if he acted through a robot or an animal: in law the act is his.

We saw above that the perpetrator will often remain guilty of the crime even though his purpose takes effect by accident upon a different victim, or upon a mistaken victim, or in an unintended mode. This rule applies equally to acts through innocent agents.[264]

So the doctrine of innocent agency avoids any failure of justice that might   **14–104**
otherwise occur as a result of the rule that there cannot be an accessory without a perpetrator? It does so largely,[265] but not entirely:

- The doctrine of innocent agency applies only when the perpetrator intended the offence be committed, not when he was merely negligent as to whether it would be committed.[266]
- There is the further limitation that the doctrine can be used only when it is plausible to say that the defendant did the forbidden act in the forbidden circumstances. The Law Commission Working Party puts it thus:

---

[260] If the child is 10 or over he may on the facts not be an innocent agent: *D.P.P. v. K* [1997] 1 Cr. App. R. 36.

[261] *R. v. J.T.B.* [2009] 1 A.C. 1310; *Walters v. Lunt* (1951) 35 Cr. App. R. 94.

[262] *R. v. Tyler* (1838) 8 Car. & P. 616.

[263] *R. v. Walkley* (1833) 6 Car. & P. 175.

[264] Illustrations are *R. v. Saunders and Archer* (1577) 2 Plow. 473, and *R. v. Michael* (1840) 9 Car. & P. 356. Michael intended to act through the nurse as innocent agent; in fact the nurse's child took over, but Michael was still responsible for the act of the child, since substantially her criminal purpose was carried out. (Incidentally, this again illustrates the point that an "innocent agent" need not be an agent in the sense of one having authority to act.) Saunders did not intend to act through an innocent agent, but his wife became one when she passed on the poisoned apple to the child. Saunders's intention was transferred as a matter of law from her to the child, for it was upon the child that his evil took effect.

[265] Glanville Williams, "Innocent Agency and Causation", (1992) 3(2) *Crim. L.F.* 289.

[266] Cf. *R. v. Loukes* [1996] 1 Cr. App. R. 444.

"A person is not guilty of committing an offence through an innocent agent when the law provides or implies that the offence can be committed only by one who complies with a particular description which does not apply to that person, or specifies the offence in terms implying personal conduct on the part of the offender."[267]

An example of the first of these limitations (where the law specifies a particular description) is as follows.

It was an offence under section 2 of the now repealed *Licensing Act 1872* for the holder of a justices' licence to sell liquor to a police officer if he knew he was on duty.[268] A person who ordered a drink for such an officer, could not be convicted for falsely telling the publican that the officer was not on duty. He himself was not the holder of a justices' licence, and did not sell the drink; so he could not qualify to be a perpetrator.[269] The publican did not perpetrate the offence either, because he did not know the officer was on duty. So there was no offence to which the liar could be an accessory, at any rate if the traditional principles are applied.

14–105   An example of the second limitation (where the law implies personal conduct) is *Thornton v. Mitchell*.[270]

A bus was being reversed, and the conductor in accordance with the usual custom assisted the driver by signalling that all was clear at the back. On this occasion the conductor negligently gave the all-clear signal when there was a pedestrian behind the bus; the driver backed and the pedestrian was injured. The driver was charged with driving without due care and attention, and the conductor was charged as abettor. The charge against the driver was dismissed, because he had *reasonably relied* on the signal given by the conductor, and so had not acted negligently. This meant that the conductor had to be acquitted also, because there could be no abettor to an offence that had not been committed.

14–106   **Could the conductor have been convicted of negligently conducting?**   There is no such offence. Most people who act negligently are safe from the criminal law. As we have seen, it is only in exceptional cases, as with the offence of dangerous driving, that negligence is punished. There is a general tort of negligence, but not a general crime of negligence.

14–107   **Could the conductor have been convicted of driving carelessly through the innocent agency of the actual driver?**   This argument was not considered by the court, but on principle it should fail. First, the conductor did not intend to commit an offence; and the recent practice of applying the doctrine of innocent agency to those who have negligently caused (or if you like, procured) an innocent agent to carry out the conduct element of an offence,[271] is doctrinally and conceptually flawed. The notion of driving in the *Road Traffic Act 1988*,

---

[267] *Working paper 43, supra,* note 3. See also Law Commission, *Participating in Crime,* No. 305 (London: Cm 7084, 2007) at 99–106.

[268] Cf. *Sherras v. De Rutzen* [1895] 1 Q.B. 918.

[269] That only the holder of the licence could be convicted as perpetrator in such cases is the foundation of the law of "delegation". See 40.3.

[270] [1940] 1 All E.R. 339.

[271] Cf. *R. v. Loukes* [1996] 1 Cr. App. R. 444; *R. v. Millward* (1994) 158 J.P. 1091.

cannot be extended to cover people who do not actually drive, because it would lead to absurdities. The driver of a vehicle must pass the driving test and have a driving licence. If the conductor of a bus, or a passenger in a car, were deemed to drive whenever he gave instructions to the driver, it would follow that such a conductor or passenger would be required himself to take the test and hold a licence. This would be unreasonable. The word "drive" must be taken to have such a strong bodily connotation that only the actual driver can be the perpetrator of a driving offence.

The decision in *Thornton v. Mitchell* does not mark the end of the story. Two sex cases arose, in which the courts were determined to uphold a conviction; and to do this they invented new and remarkable doctrines. First there was the thoroughly nasty case of *R. v. Bourne*.[272]

Bourne compelled his wife to commit bestiality with a dog. (Bestiality was an offence at the time, but it is now an offence to cause another to engage in bestiality.)[273] The wife had the defence of duress, and she was not charged. Bourne was tried on his own for abetting her, and was convicted. On appeal the obvious objection was raised that Bourne could not abet an offence that was not committed—a point which one could have thought that the authorities were completely solid. The Court of Appeal, driven to desperation, invented a concept of *de facto* crime for the purpose of upholding the conviction. The court held that the wife committed the offence in contemplation of law even though she could not be punished for it.

It does not seem to have been contemplated that Bourne could be convicted as perpetrator of bestiality. There was an obvious reason. The definitions of sex crimes refer strongly to personal bodily behaviour. Only by a violent wrench of the English language could it be said that Bourne himself committed the act of bestiality.   **14–108**

Instead, it was assumed that there was an offence to which he could be an accessory. The wife's defence of duress, said Lord Goddard C.J., was simply a "prayer by her to be excused from punishment", so that she was not guilty of the offence. This does not truly represent the effect of duress, which is not a mere matter of mitigation: success in the defence results in a verdict of not guilty, which would mean that the wife did not commit an offence on traditional principles. It is conceptually improper, according to the theory of the common law, to imagine some ghostly offence committed by the wife for the purpose of convicting the husband as accessory.[274]

---

[272] (1952) 36 Cr. App. R. 125.

[273] See the repealed section 12(1) of the *Sexual Offences Act 1956*. Cf. section 69(2) of the *Sexual Offences Act 2003*, which makes it an offence to "cause" another to commit bestiality: "A person (A) commits an offence if– (a) A intentionally *causes,* or *allows*, A's vagina or anus to be penetrated, (b) the penetration is by the penis of a living animal, and (c) A knows that, or is reckless as to whether, that is what A is being penetrated by."

[274] See the criticism of the decision by Lord Edmund Davies in *D.P.P. v. Lynch* [1975] A.C. 653 at 710 citing Williams, *op. cit. supra*, note 1 at 710. And, in the same case in the court below by Lowry L.C.J. However, there are circumstances were it is impossible to avoid the concept of an excused defence, as in the offence of an attack by a lunatic.

In the second case, *R. v. Cogan*,[275] the Court of Appeal took the step of applying the doctrine of innocent agency to an act of sexual intercourse.

14–109   A husband compelled his wife to have sexual intercourse with Cogan, who believed that the wife was consenting. Cogan having had his conviction of rape quashed on appeal, the question arose whether a conviction of the husband as aider and abettor could stand. The Court of Appeal held that it could, since the defendant was liable as perpetrator and the form of the conviction did not matter.

The decision saved the law from much public odium, but its legal basis is demonstrably unsound. Lawton L.J., delivering the judgment of the court, advanced two reasons. The first and chief one was that the husband could have been indicted as principal and "convictions should not be upset because of mere technicalities of pleading". To the argument that the husband could not rape his own wife the court replied that the reason for that rule was that the law presumes consent from the marriage ceremony,[276] and that there was no such presumption on the facts of the present case.

Although this may sound like robust common sense, the fact remains that it was the first occasion on which a person was convicted of a crime as perpetrator for doing something through an innocent agent when he could not have been convicted had he done it himself. Moreover, the court directed itself exclusively to the difficulty that the defendant was the husband, and did not consider the wholly distinct difficulty arising from the bodily connotation of rape.

14–110   The decision was rendered possible by the fact that the defendant happened to be a man. Rape can be perpetrated only by a man; the statute says so. If Parliament had entertained the extraordinary notion of raping by means of the genitals of another, it would not have limited the offence to males.[277] As it is, the position is that if duress is applied by a woman it would need an even greater degree of hawkishness than that displayed by the court in *R. v. Cogan* to call her a constructive man. Yet it is highly illogical that a man can commit rape through an innocent agent when a woman cannot, because if the notion of innocent agency is held to be applicable, so that the bodily acts of the innocent agent are attributed to the instigator, the sex of the instigator (the fact that the instigator lacks the sex organ of the innocent agent) becomes irrelevant.

The second ground taken by the court, though apparently only by way of *obiter dictum* and not as a final opinion, was that the husband was rightly convicted of procuring the offence (that is, as accessory) because the woman had been raped: "No one outside a court of law would say that she had not been." Speaking, as always, with every respect to the Queen's justice, this will not do at all. It uses popular or sociological language, on the question whether the fact of "rape" has occurred, instead of legal language, on the question whether the crime of rape has been committed. It is in effect the same doctrine as that in *R. v. Bourne*, that an offence that is excused for the "perpetrator" is still an offence in law, to which there can be an accessory.

---

[275] [1976] Q.B. 217.

[276] This is no longer the case, see *R. v. R* [1992] 1 A.C. 599, where it was held that a husband could rape his wife.

[277] Parliament has since entertained the extraordinary notion, see section 2 and 4 of the *Sexual Offences Act 2003*; section 47(6) of the *Serious Crime Act 2007*.

Can one recklessly cause an innocent agent to commit the conduct element of an offence? If this is the law, it is law newly minted by the courts. In *R. v Millward*,[278] D2 instructed D1 (his employee) to take a tractor and trailer onto a public road, even though he knew the hitch attaching the trailer was faulty. The pin broke and the runaway trailer struck a car and killed the driver. Both D1 and D2 were charged with the former offence of causing death by reckless driving. Since D1 was not aware of the faulty tow hitch and thus lacked *mens rea* he was not liable. D2 could not be charged as an accessory, as there was no offence for his liability to derive from. To solve this problem the court invoked the innocent agency doctrine which allowed Millward to be convicted on the basis that he had caused D1 to commit the *actus reus* of the offence. Millward did not cause his employer to kill, but rather caused him to drive "recklessly" which in turn caused a death. If Millward had driven the tractor himself, he would have been held liable for the consequence, so it is neither here nor there that he did not intend D1 to cause death. The act of driving an unsafe vehicle (or speeding) is criminalized not because that particular act is harmful *per se*, but because it risks harm. If that harm transpires, then the offending will come within the purview of a more serious criminal label.[279] If a person chooses to do a dangerous act and is subjectively aware of the dangerousness of what he is doing, then he chooses to risk the harmful consequences of doing that act.

In *R. v. Millward* the act of driving the unfit vehicle on the road was objectively dangerous. The dangerous act resulted in actual harm—it caused a person to be killed. But it is not clear that Millward intended to cause his employee to do the reckless act. Millward certainly intended to encourage his employee to take the vehicle onto the public road, but did he intend him to take a dangerous vehicle onto the road? Given that Millward knew the vehicle was in a dangerous state, he must have obliquely intended his employee to perform the conduct element of the offence. The reckless driving (the endangerment that resulted as soon as the innocent agent took the vehicle onto the road) was an inseparable consequence (state of affairs)[280] of the vehicle being driven on a public road. Millward knew the "endangerment" was a virtually certain and inseparable consequence (state of affairs) of causing the vehicle to be taken on the road, even though he did not foresee as a matter of virtual certainty that the "endangerment" would result in the consequence of V being killed.[281]

---

[278] (1994) 158 J.P.N. 715.

[279] For example, "dangerous driving causing death" is labelled and punished as a more serious offence than dangerous driving without such a result. Section 1 of the *Road Traffic Act 1988* as amended by the *Road Traffic Act 1991*.

[280] Endangerment is arguably a consequence, because the consequence is that V was in fact endangered: this is a real consequence for V.

[281] *Attorney-General's Reference (No.1 of 1975)* [1975] Q.B. 773 at 779 seems to require something stronger: "To procure means to produce by endeavour. You procure a thing by setting out to see that it happens and taking the appropriate steps to produce that happening."

14–112   **What if Millward had not known of the vehicle's unsafe condition? Does the procurement doctrine apply when one negligently causes another to commit a (*blameless*) act of dangerous driving?**   The courts have held that negligence is not sufficient.[282] In *R. v. Loukes*,[283] D2, a partner in a haulage firm, was responsible for overseeing the maintenance of the firm's fleet of vehicles. D2 sent his employee (D1) onto the motorway in a truck that was in a dangerous state. A large part fell off the truck and struck and killed a passing motorist. Since D1 had no knowledge of the vehicle's dangerous state his act of dangerous driving was an innocent act. Nevertheless, D2 was convicted of aiding, abetting, counselling or procuring the offence of causing of death by dangerous driving contrary to section 1 of the *Road Traffic Act 1988*. He appealed and his conviction was quashed. The Court of Appeal said:[284]

> "That Mr. Loukes could not procure an offence, the *actus reus* of which—all of the offence in this case—has not been committed. ... If we are correct in our interpretation of the new provisions, a person who, knowing of the dangerous state of a vehicle, procures another innocent of that dangerous state to drive it, and where there is no evidence that that state would have been obvious to a competent and careful driver will escape conviction."

It was also said:

> "Accordingly, we are of the view that the *Millward* principle does not enable conviction of an alleged procurer of causing death by dangerous driving where the dangerous driving as defined in section 2A(2) has not been established. In our view, this case is governed by *Thornton v. Mitchell*. A man cannot be convicted of procuring an offence where the *actus reus* is not established."[285]

14–113   **Are you telling me that there is no liability for negligently causing an innocent agent to perform the act of dangerous driving?**   Yes, but not for the reason given by the court in *R. v. Loukes*. In *R. v. Loukes* the Court of Appeal suggested that D1 did not in fact commit the *actus reus* of the offence, but this analysis seems wrong. D1 clearly (even if innocently) committed the *actus reus* in full. He did this by driving (an intentional act) a vehicle that was in a dangerous state (the relevant circumstances) onto a public highway. The offence can be committed in two ways. First, it can be committed if a person drives in a careful manner, but drives a vehicle that is in a dangerous state. Secondly, it can be committed when D drives in a dangerous manner—for example, if D drives through a school zone in a perfectly safe car, but at 100 m.p.h. The jury determine whether the "manner" of the driving is dangerous by asking whether it met the standard that would be expected of a competent and careful driver. Similarly, it determines whether D drove a car that was in a dangerous state by asking whether its dangerousness would have been "obvious to a competent and careful driver".

Cases where an innocent agent drives a vehicle that is in a dangerous state are likely to be more common. In these types of cases the *actus reus* is committed by the driver even though he was not negligent. In *R. v. Loukes* the innocent agent committed the *actus reus* because he drove the vehicle on a highway (an

---

[282] *R. v. Roberts* [1997] R.T.R. 462; *R. v. J.F. Alford Transport Ltd.* [1997] 2 Cr. App. R. 326.
[283] [1996] 1 Cr. App. R. 444.
[284] *R. v. Loukes* [1996] 1 Cr. App. R. 444 at 453.
[285] *R. v. Loukes* [1996] 1 Cr. App. R. 444 at 450.

intentional act) and it was in an unsafe condition (the relevant circumstances).[286] D1's lack of knowledge of the vehicle's dangerous state cannot change the objective dangerousness of his innocent acting. He did not act as an automaton; rather he acted non-culpably since he was not negligent in not discovering the vehicle's dangerousness.

An innocent agent will not normally drive in a dangerous "manner". A bank robber might jump into a stranger's car and force the driver at gun point to drive at dangerous speeds to help him escape from a robbery, but the driver is not a mere instrument, he knows that he is committing a criminal offence.[287] His dangerous driving may be excused as he was acting under duress, but that is a different matter. *Thornton v. Mitchell* can be distinguished. In *R. v. Loukes* the truck was a time bomb waiting to explode and the act of driving it did in fact endanger others. Existentially, there was an act and it endangered others, as evidenced by the fact that it led to a death. If a person drives a truck with faulty brakes he drives dangerously, even though he was not negligent in not discovering the truck's dangerousness.

It is difficult to imagine a situation where a person could procure an act of careless driving.[288] How do you cause someone not to pay attention? Distractions can be provided, but surely the onus is on the driver to pay attention. Nevertheless, a person can drive carefully and still kill a pedestrian. Take the example of the cautious driver who hits and kills a drunk who has foolishly jumped in the path of his moving car. In this case it is the pedestrian who is not careful, so there is no *act* of careless driving. There is an act of "careless pedestrianism". This is why there was no conviction in *Thornton v. Mitchell*. In that case the only person who acted carelessly was the conductor. It was his careless conducting that caused the injuries and his act of carelessness in no way changed the manner or nature of the driver's driving. If a person carelessly falls on a train track, it would be absurd to suggest his carelessness meant that the careful and cautious train-driver acted carelessly. In *Thornton v. Mitchell*, the conductor was negligent in not spotting the pedestrian, but that was a wholly independent act of carelessness. The fact the conductor was negligent in not spotting the pedestrian did not change the nature of the driver's careful driving. (And presumably it did not change the nature of the pedestrians' careful pedestrianism.) The driver was paying attention, but unfortunately he paid careful attention to the conductor's careless instructions. The pedestrians perhaps were also a bit careless.

14–114

---

[286] Cf. *R. v. Marchant* [2004] 1 W.L.R. 442.

[287] (Similarly, if a nine-year-old child knows that it is wrong to steal and understands that it is against the criminal law to do so, he is not used as a mere instrument if his father asks him to steal. But nor is he liable, since he is exempt from prosecution: but an exempt (or excused) agent is conceptually distinct from an "innocent" one. An innocent agent is a mere "instrument".) Of course, if you encourage a friend to drive at dangerous speeds and she willingly does so, you would be an accomplice in the traditional sense. See *R. v. Webster* [2006] 2 Cr. App. R. 6; *R. v. Cramp* (1999) 110 A. Crim R. 198.

[288] Section 20(1)(2B) of the *Road Safety Act 2006* provides: "A person who causes the death of another person by driving a mechanically propelled vehicle on a road or other public place without due care and attention, or without reasonable consideration for other persons using the road or place, is guilty of an offence."

Therefore, the better reason for acquitting Loukes is that he lacked *mens rea*. Loukes intentionally procured the act of driving, but he did not intentionally procure an act of dangerous driving. Nor did he recklessly procure an act of dangerous driving, because he was not reckless in not discovering that the truck was in a dangerous condition. That is different to holding that the act of driving never took place, or that the truck's faults did not in fact exist at the time it was driven, because clearly they did exist. Objectively judged there was a dangerous (non-culpable) act of driving. The truck was in fact in a dangerous state.

To put it another way, he would not have been negligent if he had driven the truck himself because the vehicle's dangerous state was not "obvious to a competent and careful" driver, so he did not culpably use an innocent instrument to commit the offence. In *R. v. Roberts*[289] it was held that it must be "made clear that D2 must have known that it was or should have been obvious to a competent and careful driver having D1's knowledge that driving the lorry in its current state would be dangerous." If D2 intentionally causes D1 to drive a vehicle[290] which he knows to be in a dangerous state, he will be liable for procuring an act of dangerous driving.[291] But it should be proved that he either knew the vehicle was in a dangerous state or believed that it was.[292]

14–115   **So that unsettles that. How does one state the present law?**   Whatever the technical deficiencies of *R. v. Bourne*; *R. v. Cogan* and *R. v. Millward*, these decisions undoubtedly reached a desirable result. The best way to put the new rule is to say that when a person commits what may be called a criminal act, for which he is not responsible because he lacks *mens rea* or other requisite fault element or has some other excuse, another person can be convicted as perpetrator if he is in fact responsible for the act (that is to say, would be legally responsible if he had satisfied the requisite fault element and lacked any excuse).[293] The difficulty with the rule is that the conviction registers a falsehood and wrongly labels the "perpetrator". For example, Millward is convicted of aiding and abetting reckless driving by the driver, when he did not drive recklessly. The only completely satisfactory solution to these problems is by legislation.

---

[289] *R. v. Roberts* [1997] R.T.R. 462 at 473.

[290] It would not be enough to show that D2's recklessness or negligence led to D1 accessing and driving a vehicle that was in a dangerous state. Suppose D2 knows that one of his trucks is in a dangerous state because the brakes are faulty. Suppose also that D2 puts it aside so that it might be repaired but is reckless or negligent in that he leaves the keys in the ignition and fails to put a notice on it to warn his drivers not to use the vehicle as it is out of service. If one of D2's drivers use the vehicle, D2 will not be liable for recklessly causing D1 to drive the vehicle.

[291] *R. v. Millward* (1994) 158 J.P. 1091.

[292] Cf. *R. v. Webster* [2006] 2 Cr. App. R. 103 at 111; *R. v. J.F. Alford Transport Ltd.* [1997] 2 Cr. App. R. 326; *Blakely v. D.P.P.* [1991] R.T.R. 405; *Carter v. Richardson* [1974] R.T.R. 314; *Poultry World v. Conder* [1957] Crim. L.R. 803.

[293] Although the courts may now apply such a rule, it considerably alters the previous understandings of the law. For example, it would have secured a different outcome in *R. v. Kemp* [1964] 2 Q.B. 341: the alleged perpetrator having been held on appeal to be not guilty for lack of *mens rea*, the conviction of an alleged accessory (who possessed the *mens rea* and had engineered the whole affair) was quashed. The point was not argued, because it was thought too clear for argument. The rule assumed to be the law in *R. v. Kemp* is the foundation of the law of innocent agency (which was invented to get round it), and also of liability of publicans for the acts of their delegates (a matter to be considered in 36.3).

The objection to this extension of the law of complicity is that it is a gross distortion to use the innocent agency doctrine to criminalize this kind of direct recklessness.[294] We need more offences which are specially devised to deal with the difficulty revealed by these cases. In recent times there has been a move towards enacting offences to deal with those who cause innocent agents[295] to perform the *actus reus* of certain offences. Organized prostitution involves the use of many women who are nothing short of sex slaves.[296] Since these women are forced to have sexual contact with non-suspecting customers they are effectively raped by innocent agents—the customers. The pimps and people traffickers cause them to be raped by the innocent and non-suspecting customers.[297] Parliament has enacted an offence which catches men or women who sexually penetrate another person; and a further offence which catches those who cause[298] a person to engage in sexual activity without consent.[299] These narrowly tailored offences are preferable to stretching doctrine and language beyond judicious limits.

In addition, the general reforms proposed by the Law Commission seem to cut through some of the fiction and thus could result in clarity. In particular, it has recommended:

1. replacing the common law doctrine of innocent agency with a statutory version of the doctrine; and
2. that a new offence be enacted to directly criminalize those who cause "a person to commit a no-fault offence".[300]

The Law Commissions recommendations in full: **14–116**

> "(1)   if D uses an innocent agent (P) to commit an offence ("the principal offence"), D is guilty of the principal offence.
>
> (2)   P is an innocent agent if: (a) he or she commits the conduct element of the principal offence; and (b) he or she does not commit the principal offence itself solely because:

---

[294] Cf. *Giorgianni v. The Queen* (1985) 156 C.L.R. 473.

[295] Some offences even impose strict liability on the innocent agent: see section 53A of the *Sexual Offences Act 2003*.

[296] For a good judicial discussion of sex slavery, see the decision of the High Court of Australia in *R. v. Tang* (2008) 237 C.L.R. 1. See also Michelle M. Dempsey, "Sex Trafficking and Criminalization in Defence of Feminist Abolitionism", (2010) 158 *U. Pa. L. Rev.* 1729 at 1758 *et passim*.

[297] Section 53A of the *Sexual Offences Act 2003* also criminalizes the innocent agent, even though he lacks any fault. It is sufficient that the innocent agent "ought" to have known the prostitute was being forced into prostitution by a third party. These new offences cannot be reconciled with the constitutional principles of justice including the presumption of *mens rea*. See Dennis J. Baker, "Collective Criminalization and the Constitutional Right to Endanger Others", (2009) 28 *Crim. Just. Ethics* 168 at 189-190.

[298] For a penetrating discussion of the dimensions of causation in complicity, see Sanford H. Kadish, *Blame and Punishment*, (New York: Macmillan Publishing Co., 1987) at 135 *et seq.*; Michael S. Moore, "Causing, Aiding, and the Superfluity of Accomplice Liability", (2008) 156 *U. Pa. L. Rev.* 395.

[299] See sections 2 and 4 of the *Sexual Offences Act 2003*. However, the "causing" only has a maximum sentence of 10 years, whereas the section 2 offence carries a maximum penalty of life.

[300] Law Commission, *Participating in Crime*, Report 305 (London: H.M.S.O., 2007) paras.427 and 4.37.

(i) he or she is under the age of 10;[301] (ii) he or she has a defence of insanity;[302] or (iii) he or she acts without the fault required for conviction of the principal offence.

(3) D uses P to commit the principal offence if: (a) D intends to cause a person (whether or not P) to commit the conduct element of the principal offence; (b) D causes P to commit the conduct element of the principal offence; and (c) D is at fault in relation to the principal offence.

(4) D is at fault in relation to the principal offence if: (a) where conviction of the principal offence requires proof of fault, D's state of mind is such that, were he or she to commit the conduct element of the principal offence, he or she would do it with the state of mind necessary to be convicted of the offence; or (b) where conviction of the principal offence does not require proof of fault, D knows or believes that were a person to commit the conduct element of the principal offence, that person would do so: (i) in the circumstances (if any); and (ii) with the consequences (if any) proof of which is required for conviction of the principal offence.

(5) D may be guilty of the principal offence through using P to commit the offence: (a) even though the principal offence is one that may be committed only by a person who meets a particular description; and (b) D does not meet that description."

Causing a person to commit a no fault offence:

"(1) there should be an offence of causing the commission of a no-fault offence which D would commit if he or she caused another person to commit a no-fault offence and (a) it was D's intention that a person should commit the offence; or (b) D knew or believed that his or her behaviour would cause a person to commit it;

(2) a person convicted of the offence should be liable to any penalty for which he or she would be liable if convicted of the no-fault offence concerned."

14.19. UNDERCOVER PERSONS AS INNOCENT AGENTS

14–117   One other exception to the doctrine of innocent agency is based upon the notion of justice, and is similar to the rule already stated for accessories. The Law Commission Working Party again speaks:

> "A person is not guilty of committing an offence through an innocent agent when the innocent agent acts with the purpose of preventing the commission of the offence or of nullifying its effects.[303]"

If D asks X to help him in committing a crime, and X assents purely for the purpose of procuring D's conviction, and obtains the consent of the intended victim, what X does is not attributed to D. Anything that D does will, of course, inculpate him; and he will be guilty of an inchoate offence of encouragement (dealt with in Chapter 17); but it would be unjust to allow X in these circumstances to manufacture a consummated crime on the part of D by conduct of his own.[304] The point is carried by the old case of *R. v. Egginton*.[305] Egginton

---

[301] It is worth noting that the Law Commission could not have meant that all persons under the age of 10 are innocent agents. It appears the Law Commission is stating that they should be "deemed" innocent agents, even though a nine-year-old who knows that it is a criminal offence to steal does not act innocently if he is encouraged to steal. Instead, he is an exempt agent—because the law holds that nine-year-olds do not know right from wrong, legal from illegal and so on.

[302] An agent who is innocent because he is excused.

[303] *Working Paper 43, supra*, note 3 at 8–12.

[304] Cf. *Pinkstone v. The Queen* (2004) 219 C.L.R. 444.

[305] (1801) 2 Bos. & P. 508. Cf. George P. Fletcher, "The Metamorphosis of Larceny", (1976) 89 *Harv. L. Rev.* 469 at 496.

tried to persuade the watchman of a building to help him to steal from it. The watchman informed his employer, who told him to pretend to co-operate. He opened the yard door for Egginton, and they went together through an open door into the building (the latter door had also, apparently, been opened by the watchman). It was held that Egginton could not be convicted of burglary because at common law (which required a "breaking" in a technical sense) there was no "breaking" of the building by Egginton. There would have been a "breaking" if Egginton had opened the door; but he could not be made responsible for the "breaking" by the watchman, when the watchman was intending only to incriminate him.

In *Pinkstone v. The Queen*[306] D sent a package containing drugs from Sydney airport to Perth in Western Australia. When the box arrived in Perth airport undercover police officers intercepted it and delivered it to the intended recipient. D was found guilty of supply of a prohibited drug contrary to section 6(1)(c) of the *Misuse of Drugs Act (W.A.)*. D appealed on the basis that he had not consummated the act of supply, because the police did this by intervening and thereafter delivering drugs to the intended recipient. The issue was whether the prosecution had proved that D had "supplied;" or whether the act of "supply" was performed by the police officer. The High Court of Australia held that an act of supply is consummated as soon as D "knowingly places the drug in a mail delivery system with the intention that it be received by the other person at a particular place, regardless whether the drug ultimately reaches the intended recipient".

The majority reasoning is less than convincing.[307] This is nothing more than an attempt to supply.[308] The act of "supply" was near completion, but was never completed because the police intervened. D was not trying to supply the airport, nor was he trying to supply the police. Rather, he was trying to supply a particular drug dealer and he failed to *supply* him, because the police intercepted the package in transit. If the police had allowed the airline to complete its delivery at the other end, then the supply would have been completed as the recipient would have been supplied. If D had been caught with the package as he was driving to the airport in Sydney, would that have constituted a supply too? If we accept the majority's analysis, D would attempt to supply by driving to the airport or the post office with such a package; and would consummate that attempt by leaving that package with the airline or postal service for transportation.

14–118

The interesting point for present purposes is what was said with respect to innocent agency and entrapment.[309] The innocent agent in this case was the airline, because it was ignorant of the fact that the box contained a prohibited

[306] (2004) 219 C.L.R. 444.

[307] *Pinkstone v. The Queen* (2004) 219 C.L.R. 444 *per* Gleeson C.J., McHugh, Gummow and Heydon J.J.

[308] See *R. v. Robinson* [1915] 2 K.B. 342; *R. v. Gullefer* [1990] 1 W.L.R. 1063; *Comer v. Bloomfield* (1971) 55 Cr. App. R. 305; *R. v. Murray* [1982] 1 W.L.R. 475; *Kyprianou v. Reynolds* (1990) 91 Cr. App. R. 356; *R. v. Widdowson* (1986) 82 Cr. App. R. 314; *R. v. Ilyas* (1984) 78 Cr. App. R. 17.

[309] The dissenting judgment of Kirby J. is to be preferred. *Pinkstone v. The Queen* (2004) 219 C.L.R. 444 at 477 *et seq*. See also *R. v. Maginnis* [1987] A.C. 303.

drug.[310] Clearly, the police were not innocent agents, since they did not lack responsibility. The police officers were not innocent agents, because "[t]hey were not 'supplying' the drug to [D's intended recipient] for D but solely for the purposes of the pre-arranged police plan to complete the offence and, if the cargo contained a prohibited drug (as the police believed) to secure the conviction of the appellant." So, if the police had intercepted D on his way to the airport in Sydney, and had thereafter organized for the package to be shipped to Perth, the majority would have been willing to accept that the police rather than D had consummated the act of supply. But if the police had caught him at Sydney airport just after he had signed the parcel in with the airline, and had thereafter organized for it to be shipped to Perth, they would not have consummated D's act of supply, because the parcel was already in the mail system when the police took control of it. This finding seems to have turned on the special words of the provision.[311] In this country "supply"[312] has been given a more restricted meaning, so the *R. v. Egginton* doctrine would apply.[313]

14.20. THE SEMI-INNOCENT AGENT

14–119   There may be different degrees of *mens rea* between the instigator and the actor, and it is possible for the instigator to have the higher degree, or of course the lower degree.[314]

D1 incites D2 to assault V, knowing that V has a weak heart and hoping he will die. D2 assaults V thinking that no more is intended, and V dies. Assuming that

---

[310] "However it is well settled at common law that a person who commits a crime by the use of an innocent agent is himself liable as a principal offender. That is so not only where the agent lacks criminal responsibility, as, for example, when he is insane or too young to know what he is doing, but also where the agent, although of sound mind and full understanding, is ignorant of the true facts and believes that what he is doing is lawful." *White v. Ridley* (1978) 140 C.L.R. 342 at 346 *per* Gibbs C.J.

[311] The Western Australian provision uses a number of substitute words to cover "supply" including "dispense", "deliver", "distribute", "furnish". All of these imply that the "supply" must be effective—that is, the recipient must actually be *supplied*. To put it another way, the intended recipient must in fact receive the supplied article otherwise he has not been supplied. Notwithstanding that this is clearly the aim of the provision, the drafters threw in the word "forward" for good measure; and it was the distinct concept of "forward" that allowed the majority to collapse attempted supply into supply. A person cannot supply, dispense, deliver, or furnish thin air, but he can "forward" something on a plane bound for nowhere! "Forward" is conceptually very distinct to supply, deliver, dispense, distribute. The word "forward", technically, would allow for inchoate liability, but it is doubtful that is what the Western Australian Parliament had in mind when it enacted the provision.

[312] "The word 'supply', in its ordinary natural meaning, conveys the idea of furnishing or providing to another something. The additional concept is that of enabling the recipient to apply the thing handed over to purposes for which he desires or has a duty to apply it." *R. v. Maginnis* [1987] A.C. 303 at 309 *per* Lord Kinkel.

[313] In *R. v. Latif* [1996] 1 W.L.R. 104 the Lords held that offences "could be committed through an innocent agent, [but in the case at hand] the conduct of the customs officers, who had acted in full knowledge of the content of the packages and not in concert with S., but deliberately for their own purposes, fell within the general principle of causation that the free, deliberate and informed intervention of a second person, intending to exploit a situation created by the first but not acting in concert with him, relieved the first of criminal responsibility."

[314] Williams, *op. cit. supra*, note 1 at 390 n. 1. Where a perpetrator goes *outside* the contemplated purpose and commits a murder, his companion is not guilty of manslaughter. See *R. v. Lovesey* [1970] 1 Q.B. 352 at 356.

D2 is not guilty of murder, the question is whether D1 can nevertheless be convicted of committing murder through an innocent agent. In fact D2 is a semi-innocent agent.

It is now clear that an instigator can be guilty of a crime of greater enormity than that intended by the person who physically did it.[315] This rule is stated by the institutional writers,[316] and it follows logically from the doctrine of innocent agency. It means, for example, that while a person who kills under a "loss of control"[317] is guilty only of manslaughter, another who assists the killing and who is not affected by a "loss of control" can, on principle be convicted of murder.

However, a complication was introduced into the law in *R. v. Richards*.[318] In that case the defendant, Mrs. Richards, told two accomplices to beat up her husband badly enough to put him in hospital for a month. She held a light at the window to indicate when her husband left the house, and the accomplices then attacked him, but only so as to inflict a comparatively slight injury. The accomplices were convicted of unlawful wounding contrary to section 20 of the *Offences against the Person Act 1861*, but Richards was convicted of wounding with intent to cause him grievous bodily harm contrary to section 18. On appeal Richards's conviction was reduced to unlawful wounding, on the ground that Richards, not being present, and could not by reason of incitement be convicted of a crime of higher degree than the persons who actually did it. **14–120**

The decision introduced a needless technicality into the law and it is little wonder that the Lords have since overruled it.[319] There is no reason for distinguishing between an accessory who is present and the accessory who is absent. A core criticism is that there is no mention in the judgment of the doctrine of innocent agency, which applied to felonies in the old law as much as to misdemeanours. If a person can act through a completely innocent agent, there is no reason why he should not act through a semi-innocent agent. It would be wholly unreasonable that the partial guilt of the agent should operate as a defence to the instigator.

14.21. STATUTORY OFFENCES BY COMPANY OFFICERS

For company officers, the common law of accessoryship is supplemented by statutory provisions. Many statutes creating particular offences, especially those relating to trade, provide that a director or other officer of an incorporated **14–121**

---

[315] *R. v. Howe* [1987] A.C. 417. Cf. *R. v. Selvaratnam* [2006] EWCA Crim. 1321.

[316] Particularly, E. H. East, *A Treatise of the Pleas of the Crown*, (London: J. Butterworth, 1801), i 350. See also *Salisbury Case* (1553) 1 Plow. 97.

[317] See section 54 of the *Coroners and Justice Act 2009*. Cf. *Osland v. The Queen* (1998) 197 C.L.R. 316.

[318] [1974] Q.B. 776 overruled by *R. v. Howe* [1987] A.C. 417. See also *Hui Chi-ming v. The Queen* [1992] 1 AC 34 at 41–45.

[319] "[I] would affirm [Lord Lane C.J.'s] view that where a person has been killed and that result is the result intended by another participant, the mere fact that the actual killer may be convicted only of the reduced charge of manslaughter for some reason special to himself does not, in my opinion in any way, result in a compulsory reduction for the other participant." *R. v. Howe* [1987] A.C. 417 at 456 *per* Lord Mackay. For further critical analysis, see the discussion in the second edition of this book at 374.

company that is guilty of an offence under the *Act* shall be implicated in the offence if it was committed by his consent or connivance, or even merely facilitated by his negligence. Some of the older statutes go further and shift the burden of proof: they require the officer to prove that he did not know of the offence or connive in it, but this is no longer the practice in drafting.[320]

14.22. ASSISTANCE AFTER THE CRIME

14–122   The law of complicity is, with one exception, confined to acts done before or at the time of the crime in question. A person who assists a criminal after he has committed the crime to avoid apprehension or conviction does not become a party to the crime, though he may himself commit various offences in doing so. The one exception relates to treason.[321] Formerly, persons who helped felons to escape were "accessories after the fact". The law is now gone, but those who help traitors to escape are still "principals after the fact" to treason, since the reform of this antiquated branch of the law has not hitherto seemed sufficiently pressing to justify parliamentary time being spent on it. We will not spend our time on it either.

A person who tries to assist his friend to evade justice may be guilty of perjury (if he lies under oath), or of contempt of court, or of an offence under section 4 of the *Criminal Law 1967*[322] of impeding the apprehension or prosecution of a person who has committed a "relevant offence".[323] But the most general offences, which can be committed both before and after the crime in question, are those of obstructing the police and obstructing justice. Merely associating with another directly after he has committed a crime cannot be said to be an active

---

[320] See for example, section 50(2) of the *Children and Families (Wales) Measure 2010*; section 61 of the *Data Protection Act 1998*; section 65 of the *Charities Act 2006*; section 87 of the *Childcare Act 2006*; section 143 of the *Adoption and Children Act 2002*; section 39 of the *Bank of England Act 1998*; section 7 of the *City of Westminster Act 1996*; section 4(6) of the *Children and Young Persons (Protection from Tobacco) Act 1991*; section 52 of the *Clean Air Act 1993*; section 50 of the *Aviation and Maritime Security Act 1990*; section 195 of the *Broadcasting Act 1990*; section 78 of the *Airports Act 1986*; section 11(9) of the *Anatomy Act 1984*; section 11 of the *Animal Health and Welfare Act 1984*; section 14 of the *Atomic Energy Act 1946*; section 99 of the *Civil Aviation Act 1982*; section 2 of the *Agricultural Land (Removal of Surface Soil) Act 1953*; section 110 of the *Agriculture Act 1970*; section 19 of the *Agriculture and Horticulture Act 1964*; section 9(5) of the *Building Control Act 1964*; section 55 of the *Cable and Broadcasting Act 1984*; section 64 of the *Coal Industry Act 1994*; section 10 of the *Coinage Act 1971*; section 40(2) of the *Consumer Protection Act 1987*; section 87 of the *Control of Pollution Act 1974*; section 14 of the *Deer Act 1991*; section 108 of the *Electricity Act 1989*; section 45 of the *Gas Act 1986*; section 314 of the *Highways Act 1980*; section 432(2) of the *Insolvency Act 1986*; section 48 of the *London Local Authorities Act 1995*; sections 10(4) and 41(3) of the *Petroleum Act 1998*; section 36 of the *Plant Varieties Act 1997*; section 36 of the *Radioactive Substances Act 1993*; section 147 of the *Railways Act 1993*; section 177 of the *Water Act 1989*; section 210 of the *Water Industry Act 1991*; section 82 of the *Weights and Measures Act 1985*; reg. 23 of the *Merchant Shipping and Fishing Vessels (Health and Safety at Work) (Biological Agents) Regulations 2010*; reg. 15 of the *Wine Regulations 2009*; section 14 of the *Bribery Act 2010*, among others. See also Williams, *op. cit. supra*, note 1 at §284.

[321] See section 5(5) of the *Criminal Law Act 1967*. See also *R. v. Rafique* [1993] Q.B. 843 at 851; *R. v. Panayiotou* [1973] 1 W.L.R. 1032 at 1037.

[322] *R. v. Spinks* [1982] 1 All E.R. 587.

[323] The words "arrestable offence" were removed by *Serious Organised Crime and Police Act 2005* c.15 Sch.7(3) para.40(2)(a)(ii).

encouragement, because his offending is in the past.[324] Even if D1 associates with D2 within seconds of D2 having committed a crime, he will not become an accessory since the offending is over and done.[325]

---

[324] In *R. v. Rose* [2004] EWCA Crim. 764 at para. 18, it was said: "there was no evidence of any involvement or encouragement at the scene by Madden, after the altercation between Rose and Cagney, Rose then joined Madden within 30 seconds of the altercation ending and the two of them went off together. In our view, there was no evidence fit for the jury's consideration that Madden was involved in encouraging Rose to assault Cagney."

[325] *Michaels v. Highbury Corner Magistrates Court* [2010] Crim. L.R. 506; *R. v. Brown* [2004] EWCA Crim. 744; *R. v. Rowell* [1978] 1 All E.R. 665; *R. v. Machin* (1980) 71 Cr. App. Rep. 166; *R. v. Selvage* [1982] Q.B. 372; *R. v. Ali* [1993] 2 All E.R. 409; *R. v. Stally* [1960] 1 W.L.R. 79; *R. v. Vreones* [1891] 1 Q.B. 360. See also Glanville Williams, "Evading Justice", [1975] Crim. L.R. 430.

CHAPTER 15

ATTEMPT

"The attempt and not the deed confounds us."

Macbeth II ii.

15.1. INCHOATE OFFENCES

So long as a crime lies in the mind it is not punishable, because criminal thoughts often occur to people without any serious intention of putting them into execution: **15–001**

> "Others, I am not the first,
> Have willed more mischief than they durst."[1]

The position is different when some step is taken to put the desire into effect. A man who starts on a criminal path but who is checked before he can accomplish his purpose may commit what is in itself an offence—conveniently called an inchoate offence. This may be defined as an offence committed by doing an act with the purpose of effecting some other offence (called the "substantive offence" or "consummated offence" or "completed offence").

Anciently the law was otherwise, no penalty being provided for those who did not accomplish their criminal object. At that time, the criminal law was not clearly separated from the law of tort, which provided compensation only when some injury had actually been inflicted. "The idea of punishment is but slowly severed from that of reparation, and where no harm is done there is none to be repaired."[2] The change in the law was largely the work of the King's courts. From the latter part of the 17th century onwards, they developed the three inchoate crimes of attempt, conspiracy and incitement.[3]

---

[1] A. E. Housman, *A Shropshire Lad*, (London: Richards, 1896).
[2] S. F. C. Milsom, *Historical Foundations of the Common Law*, (London: Butterworths, 1969), at 373 finds traces of an earlier development in the local courts. Credit for the development has also been given to the Star Chamber (see Thomas G. Barnes "Star Chamber and the Sophistication of the Criminal Law," [1977] Crim. L.R. 316 at 325-326), but the evidence is thin.
[3] Barnes, *ibid*. The common law offence of incitement has been replaced with a statutory offence of encouraging. See sections 44-46 of the *Serious Crimes Act 2007*, discussed in the next chapter.

15.2. THE RANGE OF THE LAW OF ATTEMPT

15–002 The offence of attempt at common law was put into statutory form, with some amendments, by the *Criminal Attempts Act 1981*. References in this chapter are to this *Act*, unless otherwise stated. Examples of punishable attempts are:

- attempting to steal a wallet from an empty pocket;
- attempted arson by soaking a building with petrol in order to set it on fire; and
- attempted murder by trying to draw a pistol upon the victim.

Sometimes an attempt to commit one crime is at the same time another completed crime. Apart from a few statutory exceptions, of small importance,[4] an attempt may be to commit "any offence which, if it were completed, would be triable in England and Wales as an indictable offence."[5] This means for example, that even offences of unlawful possession can be attempted,[6] and so can offences that may be regarded from one point of view as being themselves "inchoate" (*e.g.*, psychic assault). The question of attempt to commit offences of omission will be briefly considered later. The most important restriction is that an attempt to commit a summary offence is not criminal unless some special statute so provides.

15–003 **What about offences triable either way?** An attempt to commit such an offence is similarly triable either way.[7] One difference between trial on indictment and summary trial may be noted. On a trial on indictment, if the jury acquit of the substantive offence they may, by statute, convict of an attempt to commit it, without any necessity for an express count for attempt in the indictment.[8] Unfortunately this is not possible in the magistrates' courts, where for some unfathomable reason, express charges are required.[9]

The inconvenience of this can be avoided if the informations are laid both for the consummated offence and for the attempt, the two charges being tied together.[10] If the prosecution have forgotten to lay an information for the attempt, they may, on an acquittal of the completed offence, immediately lay an information for an attempt; but the witnesses must then be heard over again!

---

[4] Section 1(4)(c) excludes conspiracy and offences under the *Criminal Law Act 1967* sections 4 (assisting offenders) and 5(1) (agreeing for a consideration not to disclose an arrestable offence).

[5] Section 1(1) of the *Criminal Attempts Act 1981*.

[6] Such prosecutions are not infrequent, and have not been challenged on the point of law. See *R. v. Foo* [1976] Crim. L.R. 456.

[7] *Magistrates Court Act 1980* Sched. 1 para. 4.

[8] Section 6(4) of the *Criminal Law Act 1967*.

[9] *Pender v. Smith* [1959] 2 Q.B. 84; *Re Crown Court at Manchester, ex p Hill* (1985) 149 J.P.N. 29.

[10] Section 4(2); the rule has now been generalized by judicial decision: *D.P.P. v. Humphrys* [1977] A.C. 1. The difficulty can also be got over by charging an attempt whenever the position is doubtful. If it turns out that the defendant completed the offence he can still be convicted of the attempt. Cf. for the Crown Court section 6(4) of the *Criminal Law Act 1967*; *Webley v. Buxton* [1977] Q.B. 481.

What if the court is sure that the defendant was up to no good, and in fact attempting to commit some crime, but is not sure which?   He cannot be convicted of an attempt, because the prosecution can only charge an attempt to commit a particular crime. In practice, obvious suspects can often be convicted of some offence. Burglary, for example, can be committed with one of a number of intents, and the prosecution need not prove which the defendant had.[11] Again, the defendant may be convicted of a possession offence like possessing a firearm or other offensive weapon, or of "going equipped,"[12] or interfering with a vehicle.[13] These offences either do not require proof of intent to commit some other crime or allow conviction where the defendant evidently had one of the specified range of intents but it may not be certain which.

15–004

Are attempts often prosecuted?   Notwithstanding the range of the offence, the police and other prosecuting authorities do not generally wish to add to their load by prosecuting attempts. The required intention is frequently hard to prove, and anyway the police may think that a warning is sufficient. If they make a charge, they may well prefer a charge of a specific offence like carrying a firearm. Nevertheless, attempts to commit serious crimes are prosecuted; and the law of attempt frequently supplies a justification for arresting a would-be offender.

15–005

15.3. THE PUNISHMENT OF ATTEMPT

On conviction of attempt the court may (with a few exceptions) impose any penalty that would be within its power for the completed offence.[14] In practice, the punishment for an attempt will generally be less than for a consummated crime. If a person shoots at another, intending to kill him, and succeeds, he is sentenced for "life." If he misses, although he could receive a life sentence, in practice he will be treated much more leniently.[15] Often the attempter receives a discount of 50 *per cent.* or more.

15–006

Why should the law punish a mere attempt? The attempter thinks he will succeed. If all those who succeed are punished, then people will be sufficiently deterred even from making a bid. So couldn't the mere attempter be let off?   An attractive argument if it is not your head that the bullet has just missed. To start with the criminal law not only targets harm; but the risk of harm. Criminalization is a mechanism for censuring and punishing a person for his culpable act when it harms others or subjects them to the risk of harm. Otherwise, we would not bother to have an offence of dangerous driving. It would not be enough to only punish the dangerous driver when his driving results

15–007

---

[11] Section 9 of the *Theft Act 1968*.

[12] Section 25(1) of the *Theft Act 1968*; see also, section 6 of the *Fraud Act 2006*.

[13] Section 9 of the *Criminal Attempts Act 1981*.

[14] Section 4 of the *Criminal Attempts Act 1981*.

[15] In the particular example the use of the firearm could still result in a substantial sentence. But in some other cases great indulgence is shown. In *Roy Jones, The Times,* 3 March 1976, a father who attempted to murder his two daughters after his wife had left him, by giving them drugged ice-cream, was given a jail sentence of two years, suspended. Examples of the more usual outcome are *R. v. Taylor* [1978] Crim. L.R. 236 and *R. v. Townsend* (1980) 144 J.P.N. 12.

in harm. Suppose X fires a rifle at Y but misses him. Since X misses his target, Y, he only endangers Y. If Y was not aware of the attempt, then he could not be said to have been harmed either physically or psychologically. But Y has been endangered regardless of whether he was aware of the fact that a sniper took a shot at him.[16] If he had been aware of the attempt he might have also suffered psychological harm. "Creation of risk of harm is not necessarily a harm in itself. But acts which create only a risk of harm may in fact cause harm. Swinging a fist at a person may not injure him as intended, but it may cause apprehension of injury that is itself a harm."[17] The harm principle is satisfied since the lawmaker can demonstrate that the proscribed activity risks harm to others. It is also worth keeping in mind that the attempter is just as culpable as the succeeder.

Clearly, the police who find a person attempting a crime must be given power to foil him. Often they can do this only by detaining him, and detention normally presupposes the making of a charge. It therefore presupposes an offence. This is by no means a strong reason in itself, but it is supported by others. We may feel it necessary to punish the unsuccessful attempter by way of particular deterrence. Otherwise, he might merely resolve to be more careful in future. To some extent, letting off the attempter would also weaken general deterrence, which depends upon society's success in making things unpleasant for malefactors. Furthermore, since the attempter exposes his victim to a risk of harm, his victim is entitled to some retribution. The victim has been wronged and exposed to a risk of harm, even if he has not been harmed in the fuller sense.

These arguments are, I think, persuasive where the crime attempted is one of those distinctly betokening a criminal mentality. They are not so persuasive in respect of minor offences—which is one reason why summary offences are not made the subject of criminal attempt.

15–008   **Then let me change my previous stance, because I am also vexed with the opposite doubt. If you punish attempts at all, surely leniency is irrational. Why not punish them like consummated crimes? Attempters are just as wicked, and often just as dangerous, as those who complete the crime—if the attempter doesn't repent and is just dished. The difference between murder and attempted murder may be due not to the skill or lack of it shown by the attacker in carrying out his purpose but to the skill or lack of it shown by a doctor treating the victim, or the speed with which the victim is transported to hospital.** The subjectivist justification for punishing attempts is that those who have completed their attempt[18] are morally no less culpable than if they had succeeded and therefore should be punished as though they had succeeded. Subjectivists argue that moral luck does not justify a sentence discount for complete attempts. Feinberg asserts: "The principle of proportionality, after all, does not decree that the severity of the punishment be proportionate to the

---

[16] Dennis J. Baker, "Collective Criminalization and the Constitutional Right to Endanger Others," (2009) 28 *Crim. Just. Ethics* 168; Jerome Hall, "Science and Reform in Criminal Law," (1952) 100 *U. Pa. L. Rev.* 787 at 801.

[17] Robinson, "A Theory of Justification: Societal Harm as a Prerequisite for Criminal Liability," (1975) *UCLA L. Rev.* 266 at 268.

[18] Andrew Ashworth, "Criminal Attempts and the Role of Resulting Harm under the Code, and in the Common Law," (1988) 19 *Rutgers L.J.* 725 at 739–744.

offender's good or bad luck, but rather to his good or bad deserts, or blameworthiness."[19] But, if "bad luck" makes a difference to the way a crime is labelled and punished, why shouldn't "good luck" make a difference?[20] Moral bad luck is sufficient to ground constructive liability for murder, manslaughter[21] and so on. As far as just deserts (proportionate punishment) is concerned, a discount does seem appropriate for attempts. General deterrence is achieved by making the individual offender pay for his particular offending. A person should only be punished for his own wrongdoing and only in proportion to the culpableness and the harmfulness of his actions.[22] The basic formula for proportionate punishment is: Harm x Culpability = Punishment.[23] Since attempts risk harm they should not be regarded as purely harmless, but as less harmful.

The absence of consummated harm should not be completely ignored when determining the gravity of attempts. Retribution is about inflicting hard treatment on those who have wronged others. Proportionality means that both harm and culpability need to be considered by those who grade offences and set sentences. A proportionate and fair sentence should reflect the gravity of the harm to the victim. Non-consummated harm (risk) is not as *bad* as consummated harm; therefore, an appropriate discount should be provided to reflect the lower level of harm. In addition, it would provide D with an incentive for desisting before the harm is actually consummated. It seems clear that the victim is not entitled to as much retribution when she has only been exposed to a risk of harm, because endangerment is not as bad as actual harm. If we accept that retribution is not merely about seeking revenge, but is a form of psychological reparation for the victim (or when the victim has been killed—for the victim's family, friends, community and society more generally) then "results" matter.

This type of retributive psychological security and satisfaction[24] cannot be substituted with pecuniary compensation, although the latter too could offer further comfort to the victims of crime. It also matters to the rest of the

---

[19] Joel Feinberg, "Criminal Attempts: Equal Punishment for Failed Attempts," in J. Feinberg, *Problems at the Roots of Law*, (New York: Oxford University Press, 2003) at 100. Cf. Lawrence Crocker, "Justice in Criminal Liability: Decriminalizing Harmless Attempts," (1992) 53 *Ohio St. L.J.* 1057. For a most interesting account of the wrongness of attempts see Stephen P. Garvey, "Are Attempts Like Treason," (2011) 14 *New Crim. L. Rev.* 173.

[20] It plays a role in other areas: for instance, dangerous driving is not punished equally with dangerous driving causing death. The unlucky dangerous driver who causes death is no less culpable than the lucky one who does not, but is punished and labelled differently.

[21] For a stark example of bad (moral) luck resulting in a manslaughter conviction, see *R. v. Mitchell* [1983] Q.B. 741.

[22] Andrew von Hirsch, *Censure and Sanctions*, (Oxford: Clarendon Press, 1993).

[23] The formula is not Culpability x Purely Potential Harm. See Dennis J. Baker, "Constitutionalizing the Harm Principle," (2008) 27 *Crim. Just. Ethics* 3.

[24] As J. R. Lucas notes: "It makes a great difference to the victim whether the community takes his wrong seriously, or passes it off as of no consequence. If he sees the man who cared nothing for him go scot-free, he is given to understand that society cares nothing for him either. But if the wrongdoer is made to see the error of his ways, the man to whom the wrong was done sees his rights vindicated, and is assured that society cares for him, even if one of its members does not, and will uphold his rights in face of assault and injury." J. R. Lucas, *Responsibility*, (Oxford: Clarendon, 1993), 104. See also Theodore Y. Blumoff, "A Jurisprudence for Punishing Attempts Asymmetrically," (2003) 6 *Buff. Crim. L. Rev.* 951; Michael Davis, "Why Attempts Deserve Less Punishment than Complete Crimes," (1986) *Law and Phil.* 1; Nils Jareborg, "Criminal Attempts and Moral Luck," (1993) 27 *Isr. L. Rev.* 213.

community, as we all have a stake in seeing that those who try to commit gross harms are proportionately incapacitated, deterred[25] and punished for their past wrongs. While the absence of consummated harm in inchoate criminality does not reduce the wrongdoer's culpability, it does give the victim (if alive) less to be distressed about. If a failed attempt means the victim has escaped theft or injury, she is going to feel much happier (and her life will be less affected) than a victim who has lost property or has suffered injury. At this level results matter and thus provide a justification for granting a lighter sentence. In cases where the harm would have been "irreparable" if it had been consummated (as would be the case with attempted murder) the attempter should not get much of a sentence discount.

15–009   Failing to consider the overall normative impact of the wrongdoing for the victim would allow the victim to benefit from moral luck (escape harm) and receive full retribution as if she had been harmed. This type of distortion would not only prevent the offender from benefiting from moral luck, but also force her to suffer retribution for consequences that did not eventuate.

Judges never say why the sentence should be reduced for failure. Probably the reason is that they think in retributive terms. We do not feel so angry with people who fail, and who in fact do no harm, as with people who succeed in their mischief. But if one thinks in terms not of simple vengeance but of moral culpability, it seems hard at first sight to resist the argument that the attempter is morally just as guilty as the succeeder.

However, there are also solid utilitarian reasons for comparative leniency in the case of attempters. Two may be mentioned in particular:

- The institution of punishment works best when the punishment is felt by those who receive it to be deserved. A person who actually does harm frequently feels the sense of guilt, and accepts punishment as being just. If no harm occurs he is unlikely to feel guilty, or at any rate as much guilt. It might be counterproductive to treat the attempter the same as a succeeder if our conventional understandings of just deserts suggests that lighter punishment is sufficient.[26]

- Even the utilitarian, who himself rejects retribution as a basis of punishment, may take it into account in the way just suggested and also as a statement of the attitude of the general public. In a democracy, the administration of law must to some extent take note of public opinion. Where the act does not evoke alarm, punishment can be lenient without producing a general feeling that the courts are becoming soft; and severe punishment might be thought unjust. Now as to attempts, since many people take the crude retributive position, requiring punishment to balance the harm actually inflicted, a law that punished attempts as severely as

---

[25] The utilitarian effect is to send a message to potential wrongdoers that wrongdoing results in proportionate hard treatment from the state.

[26] See generally, Paul H. Robinson and John M. Darley, "Objectivist Versus Subjectivist Views of Criminality: A Study in the Role of Social Science in Criminal Law Theory," (1998) 18 *Oxford J. Legal Stud.* 409; Paul H. Robinson, *Distributive Principles of Criminal Law: Who Should be Punished How Much?* (New York: Oxford University Press, 2008) at 175 *et seq.* See also Sanford Kadish, "The Criminal Law and the Luck of the Draw," (1994) 84 *J. Crim. L. & Criminology* 679 at 689.

consummated crimes would give the appearance of harshness; and the law would tend to lose public support. Utility is also severed if D is left with some incentive to desist before the crime is consummated.

- As far as utility is concerned, it is important to note the distinction between complete and incomplete attempts, since if the attempt is complete then desistance ceases to be possible. A complete attempt takes place when D does all that is needed to attempt the crime. For example, if D fires a bullet at V but misses because he is a bad shot, he has completed his attempt. If, however, D is arrested by the police just as he is taking aim; or at some earlier point in time, his attempt remains incomplete, because he never fires the gun. Depending how close he got to completing his attempt, there may have still been ample opportunity for him to desist.[27]

The comparatively mild attitude of the courts towards attempts shows the practical importance of the doctrine of transferred intention. If D shoots at V1 and hits V2, he can be convicted of attempting to wound V1 or actually wounding V2; but the punishment on the latter charge is likely to be considerably more severe than on the former. The lenient treatment of attempts depends upon the fact that the evil result has not occurred. Where evil has transpired, even though to a person or property that was not intended; general opinion would probably regard the law as inadequate if the case were treated as mere attempt.[28]

15.4. THE MENTAL ELEMENT

Section 1(1) of the *Criminal Attempts Act 1981* defines a criminal attempt:

15–010

> "If, with intent to commit an offence to which this section applies, a person does an act which is more than merely preparatory to the commission of the offence, he is guilty of attempting to commit the offence."

Attempt normally requires an intention to commit the crime in question. The requirement of intent (at least as to consequences) restates the common law. Its effect is powerfully shown by the rule for attempted murder.[29] Murder can be

---

[27] See Ashworth, *op. cit. supra*, note 18 at 739-744.

[28] Professor Ashworth is unimpressed by arguments like the above. He would punish cases of transferred intention as attempts, but would punish attempts as consummated crimes. So in relation to transferred intention his two proposals cancel out. See Andrew Ashworth, "The Elasticity of Mens Rea," in C. Tapper (e.d.), *Crime Proof and Punishment: Essays in Memory of Sir Rupert Cross*, (London: Butterworths, 1981); Andrew Ashworth, "Transferred Malice and Punishment for Unforeseen Consequences," in P. R. Glazebrook (ed.), *Reshaping Criminal Law: Essays in Honour of Glanville Williams*, (London: Sweet & Maxwell, 1978). See also Andrew Ashworth, "Taking the Consequences," in S. Shute *et al* (ed.), *Action and Value in Criminal Law*, (Oxford: Clarendon Press, 1993).

[29] See generally, Michael T. Cahill, "Attempt, Reckless Homicide, and The Design of Criminal Law," (2007) 78 *U. Colo. L. Rev.* 879; Arnold N. Enker, "*Mens Rea* and Criminal Attempt," (1977) 1977 *Am. B. Found. Res. J.* 845.

committed by a person who intends only to do grievous bodily harm; but for attempted murder the prosecution must prove an attempt to kill; an intent to do grievous bodily harm is not enough.[30]

15–011 **If a terrorist places a bomb by the front door of a cabinet minister, which does damage but fortunately does not kill anyone, could this be an attempt to murder?** If there were evidence that the terrorist hoped to kill, it would be. But if there were no evidence on the intent, and the inference from the evidence could be no more than that the terrorist was completely reckless as to killing, his particular object being to explode a bomb to create a sense of insecurity and to draw attention to his cause, then it would not be an attempt to murder. The terrorist could be dealt with for an offence in relation to explosives, under the *Explosives Act 1883*.[31]

15–012 **Isn't it rather narrow to insist upon intention? Can't one ever attempt recklessly?** Recklessness as to consequence is certainly not enough. It was held by the Court of Appeal in *R. v. Mohan*[32] that attempt at common law required intention in the true sense, and mere knowledge of the probability or high probability or likelihood of the consequence was not enough. The offence requires "proof of specific intent, a decision to bring about, in so far as it lies within the accused's power, the commission of the offence which it is alleged that the accused attempted to commit."

15–013 **Does that mean that if a terrorist kills half the passengers in a fully occupied carriage on the London underground by detonating a bomb, that he will not be liable for attempting to murder the survivors if he was merely "intending" to attract attention to his cause?** No. The terrorist would be caught by the "oblique intention" doctrine. If a terrorist bombs a train foreseeing the death of the passengers as a virtually certain consequence of bombing it, he would be liable for murdering those who die and for attempting to murder those who survive.[33] There is no reason for limiting the "oblique intention" doctrine to consummated offending. Clearly, the terrorist obliquely intended to kill the injured survivors as much as he obliquely intended to kill those whom he in fact killed with his bomb.

The requirement of intention results in part from the ordinary meaning of the word "attempt." One would not be said to attempt a wicked result if one went some part of the way towards it by accident. Suppose that D is throwing stones in the hope of breaking a window. He knows perfectly well that people are standing

---

[30] *R. v. Walker* (1990) 90 Cr. App. R. 226; *R. v. Grimwood* [1962] 2 Q.B. 621; *R. v. Whybrow* (1951) 35 Cr. App. R. 141; *R. v. Donovan* (1850) 4 Cox C.C. 401.

[31] He would also be liable for criminal damage contrary to section 1(1) of the *Criminal Damage Act 1971*. There are also terrorism offences which apply to acts associated with terrorism. See the examples in *R. v. G.* [2010] 1 A.C. 43 at 48, 64.

[32] [1976] QB 1 at 10-11. See also *R. v. Pearman* (1984) 80 Cr. App. R. 259; *R. v. Saik* [2007] 1 A.C. 18 at 24.

[33] *R. v. Walker* (1990) 90 Cr. App. R. 226; *R. v. Pearman* (1984) 80 Cr. App. R. 259. See also *R. v. MD* [2004] EWCA Crim. 1391; *R. v. Woollin* [1999] 1 A.C. 82. Cf. *Commonwealth v. Maloney*, 399 Mass 785 (1987), where D set fire to a house while the occupants slept and then denied that he intended to kill them; the jury was able to infer from the evidence that he did intend to kill.

near and that he is in danger of hitting one of them instead. He is, therefore, reckless as to hitting a person; but we would not say that he is attempting to hit a person. His object is to break the widow. Attempts go with objects, aims and purposes, not with collateral risks. The law reflects common speech on this matter, or tries to do so. However, there is no reason why "oblique intention" should not be sufficient.[34]

So "recklessness" as to the "consequence elements" of an offence is not **15–014** **sufficient for an attempt conviction.** Correct, but one decision suggests otherwise. In *Attorney-General's Reference (No. 3 of 1992)*,[35] the Court of Appeal erroneously treated the "consequence of endangerment" as though it was a "circumstance." In that case the defendants were in a moving vehicle from which a petrol bomb was thrown at an occupied car. The bomb missed the car and hit a garden wall, but did not cause any damage. The defendants were charged with attempted aggravated arson, contrary to section 1(2) of the *Criminal Damage Act 1971*, which provides:

> "A person who without lawful excuse destroys or damages any property, whether belonging to himself or another—
>
> (a)   intending to destroy or damage any property or being reckless as to whether any property would be destroyed or damaged; and
>
> (b)   intending by the destruction or damage to endanger the life of another or being reckless as to whether the life of another would be thereby endangered;…"

The offence is similar to the simple offence of criminal damage found in section 1(1) of the *Criminal Damage Act 1971*, except that it applies where a person damages his own property, as well as where he damages the property of another. It is confined to cases where life is intentionally or recklessly endangered. This element is thought to justify the increase in the maximum punishment to imprisonment for life. It should be noted that the offence can be committed although no one was in fact endangered (as where no one was in fact in the building). The consummated offence is made out so long as D intentionally or recklessly brings about the proscribed consequences (that is, the consequence of damage to property, and the collateral consequence of endangerment). If D intentionally or recklessly destroys property and this results in someone being endangered, the consummated offence is made out. Alternatively, if D destroys property with an intent to endanger others, the consummated offence is made out even if no one is endangered (as where no one was in fact in the building).[36]

---

[34] It may be said that oblique intention is included in the formula in *R. v. Mohan* [1976] QB 1; the defendant who foresees a consequence as a certainty resulting from his act has taken a "decision" to bring it about.

[35] [1994] 1 W.L.R. 409.

[36] D putatively endangers life. For example, D might destroy a building believing that it is occupied, but it turns out that he was wrong. Even though he has not in fact endangered life, he was reckless in taking the risk. In the case of conspiracy or attempt he would have to be more than reckless, he would have to intend to endanger life. If D blows up what he believes to be an occupied building it is irrelevant that it is impossible for him to endanger anyone because the building is really empty, because if the facts had been as he believed it would have been possible for him to endanger the occupants.

Endangerment is a consequence: if D fires a bullet at V and it misses V by an inch, the consequence is that V has been endangered, even if he has not been harmed.[37]

Therefore, a person could only attempt to commit this offence if he intended both to damage property and also to endanger others.[38] If a person intends to cause only criminal damage, he does not intend to endanger others. Why should he be held liable for attempting the "aggravated" form of the criminal damage offence, if he does not intend to endanger others? D could only attempt this offence if he intended to bring about the consequence of property damage as well as the collateral consequence of endangerment. In *Attorney-General's Reference (No. 3 of 1992)* the trial judge correctly held that "recklessness as to the (collateral) consequences of such damage for the lives of others was not enough to secure a conviction for attempt," although it was sufficient for the completed offence. The trial judge held that before a defendant could be convicted of attempting to commit the offence it had to be shown that he "intended that the lives of others should be endangered by the damage which he intended."[39] The Court of Appeal rejected such an argument:

> "[I]n addition to establishing a specific intent to cause damage by fire to the first named property, it is sufficient to prove that the defendant was reckless as to whether any second named property was damaged and reckless as to whether the life of another would be endangered by the damage to the second named property."[40]

15–015 Endangerment cannot be attempted if it is not aimed for. The collateral consequence of "endangerment" is used to justify grading this offence as a more serious offence than simple criminal damage, so it would be wrong not to require D to also attempt the collateral consequence of endangerment. In effect, the Court of Appeal has held that it is enough to attempt simple criminal damage so long as it results in endangerment! The distortion is twofold: 1) D did not attempt to endanger others because he in fact consummated that physical element of the offence. Hence, D cannot attempt to endanger if he has in fact endangered. 2) D did not intend to bring about the collateral consequence of endangerment so he could not be said to have been attempting to bring it about. One does not attempt accidentally. D did intend to cause damage to property, but failed to do so. Clearly, he could have been convicted of attempting criminal damage *simpliciter*, since he intended to cause damage to property. He could not have been convicted of consummating the aggravated form of the offence, because he only consummated the endangerment element. And it is not a crime in itself to

---

[37] The "result" of throwing a petrol bomb is that it is "thrown," the consequence might be property damage, but the double-effect of the act of throwing it could be the further consequence of endangerment. Throwing a petrol bomb near or past people would produce a state of affairs in which they could be said to have been endangered. For a more penetrating discussion, see Georg Henrik von Wright, *The Varieties of Goodness*, (London: Routledge & Kegan Paul, 1963) at 116 *et seq.*

[38] See Glanville Williams, "Intents in the Alternative," (1991) 50 *Cambridge L.J.* 120; R. A. Duff, *Criminal Attempts*, (Oxford: Clarendon Press, 1996) at 10 *et passim*; Jeremy Horder, "Varieties of Intention, Criminal Attempts and Endangerment," (1994) 14 *Legal Stud.* 335. Cf. John E. Stannard, "Making Up for the Missing Element – A Sideways Look at Attempts," (1987) 7 *Legal Stud.* 194 at 199.

[39] *Attorney-General's Reference (No. 3 of 1992)* [1994] 1 W.L.R. 409 at 418.

[40] *Attorney-General's Reference (No. 3 of 1992)* [1994] 1 W.L.R. 409 at 420.

endanger others.[41] This might explain why the court was keen to stretch the doctrine of attempt beyond judicious limits to uphold his conviction.

Schiemann J. thought that since D consummated the endangerment element that the *mens rea* for the consummated form of the offence would be sufficient for that element. The consummated form of the offence only requires the defendant to be reckless as to endangerment. In addition, Schiemann J. thought because the defendant intended to bring about the "the non-consummated element" (the "missing element"—the damage to property), that could be combined with the consummated element to ground a conviction for attempted aggravated criminal damage.[42]

So what should constitute attempted "aggravated" criminal damage? Suppose D attempts to blow up the underground, but fails because his bomb was too weak. If he bombed the train with an intent not only to destroy it, but also to kill the passengers, he attempts the aggravated from of criminal damage.[43] If he does not intend to destroy property with the ulterior intent of endangering others (or does not foresee endangerment as a virtually certain consequence of damaging the target property), he does not attempt the aggravated form of the offence. *Attorney-General's Reference (No. 3 of 1992)* cannot be reconciled with requirement of intent as to proscribed consequences as set down in *R. v. Mohan*,[44] and therefore, it is hoped that the higher courts will correct it rather than follow it.[45]

15–016

Can't one attempt an offence of strict liability? Yes if it is indictable, but the attempt requires intention, even though the offence attempted does not. *Gardner v. Akeroyd* [46] concerned wartime regulations under which it was an offence to sell meat at above fixed prices, or to attempt to do so or to do acts preparatory to doing so. An inspector found parcels of meat in Akeroyd's butcher shop bearing the names of purchasers and marked with prices exceeding the maximum. The tickets had been prepared and fixed by Akeroyd's assistant, during Akeroyd's

15–017

---

[41] D.W. Elliott, "Endangering Life by Damaging Property," [1997] Crim. LR 382 at 393-394.

[42] *Attorney-General's Reference (No. 3 of 1992)* [1994] 1 W.L.R. 409 at 417. A wholly unsatisfactory aspect of the decision is the tendency of the court to cite *R. v. Khan* [1990] 1 W.L.R. 813, as if consequences and circumstances were one in the same. This decision did not cause any injustice, but the reasoning is utterly unconvincing. D clearly did not attempt the aggravated form of the offence and the decision would also allow negligence to be used so long as it related to the consummated element, when clearly one cannot negligently intend! Parliament should, however, plug the lacuna by enacting a general endangerment offence.

[43] Cf. *R. v. Dudley* [1989] Crim. L.R. 57; *R. v. Webster* [1995] 1 Cr. App. R. 492; *R. v. Millard* [1987] Crim. L.R. 393.

[44] [1976] QB 1 at 10-11. (An intention to bring about the proscribed consequence(s) is a necessary element of an attempt to bring them about). This cardinal rule is adopted throughout the common law world. See *R. v. Ancio* [1984] 1 S.C.R. 225; *Braxton v. U.S.*, 500 U.S. 344 at 350-351 (1991); *Alister v. The Queen* (1984) 154 C.L.R. 404 at 422; *R. v. LK* (2010) 4 A.L.J.R. 395.

[45] Cf. Lord Nicholls in *R. v. Saik* [2007] 1 A.C. 18 at 31.

[46] [1952] 2 Q.B. 743. Some jurisdictions have expressly excluded the requirement of intention for attempts involving strict liability offences. Cf. *R. v. Lau Sai-wai* [1985] H.K.L.R. 423; *HKSAR v. Kan Chung Hung* [2001] 3 H.K.L.R.D. 834; *HKSAR v. Kwok Chu Ho* [2007] H.K.E.C. 178. The criminalization of conduct involving "no fault" and "no harm" is a gross violation of the constitutional right not to be criminalized. See the discussion in Chapter 3.

absence and without his knowledge. Had the meat been sold, the full offence would have been committed by Akeroyd, for he would have been vicariously responsible for the act of his assistant, and the regulations did not require *mens rea*. Since the meat had not been sold, Akeroyd was charged with doing an act preparatory to the commission of the offence. It was held that knowledge of the facts was necessary for an attempt, and was also necessary for the statutory offence of doing an act preparatory; consequently, Akeroyd was not responsible.

Although the observations of the court on the law of attempt may strictly be said to have been *obiter*, they were the foundation of the decision, for the opinion was that what was true for attempt must *a fortiori* be true for the statutory offence of preparation. The opinion of the court on the law of attempt was, therefore, a step in the reasoning leading to the determination of the case.

15–018   **It isn't very sensible to settle the limits of a crime by reference to the popular meaning of the word by which the crime happens to be called. What reason of substance is there why a crime of strict liability cannot be attempted without a mental element? Or a crime of recklessness or negligence? Some people can be dangerous although they do not consummate any crime and are not intending to do so. Workmen in demolishing a building may do so recklessly or carelessly, with the result that other people narrowly escape with their lives. It is not manslaughter if no one is killed; but why shouldn't it be inchoate manslaughter?**   I can only answer by saying that it would be going too far to hold that an attempt can be committed negligently. If a person has not actually brought about the legally proscribed state of affairs, there seems to be no sufficient ground for using the criminal law to punish incipient negligence (in the absence of specific statutory provision),[47] still less for punishing those who are wholly without fault. Most people would think it over-severe to use the criminal law in these cases. There may, of course, be specific statutory offences (such as dangerous driving) that do not require a harmful outcome.[48]

Even recklessness should generally be regarded as insufficient. For one thing, it would sound odd to speak of someone unintentionally but recklessly attempting. More important than the linguistic point is the question of policy. The law of attempt is a very large extension of legal liability. It is tolerable when confined to intention; but the jury or magistrates should not have general permission to convict on the basis of recklessness where nothing untoward happened. If inchoate offences of recklessness are to be created it should be done by special statute—and only if the lawmaker can provide a compelling case for enacting such offences.

One exception may be made to the requirement of intention for an attempt. It seems acceptable to say that although attempt requires intention as to consequences, recklessness can be sufficient as to circumstances.

---

[47] See for example, *R. v. Lau Sai-wai* [1985] H.K.L.R. 423.
[48] Causing death by dangerous driving is an independent head of liability.

If you attach importance to the ordinary meaning of "attempt," then surely   **15–019**
recklessness as to circumstances (as distinct from consequences) should be
enough. If a man tries to have sexual intercourse without knowing or caring
whether the woman is consenting, and in fact she does not consent, everyone
would say that he has attempted to rape her. It was, indeed, held in *R. v.*
Pigg,[49] just before the *Criminal Attempts Act* came into force, that the man in
such circumstances was guilty of an attempt at common law. In other words, one
could attempt at common law if one was reckless as to the circumstances,
provided that such recklessness was sufficient for the consummated offence, and
that one intended any necessary consequence or conduct. It has also been
confirmed that this is still the position under the *Act*.[50] Technically, D only
attempts to rape when he knows for a fact that V is not consenting but attempts to
have intercourse with her. But where D attempts to have intercourse with a
woman who he believes might not be consenting, he is at least attempting to risk
raping her.

The courts have regarded the *Criminal Attempts Act's* requirement of intention
for attempts as merely reaffirming the common law as stated in *R. v. Mohan*,[51]
and the courts did not regard the rule in *R. v. Mohan* as excluding liability for
attempts that were reckless as to circumstances. The same rule applies to the
construction of the *Act*, and it is in the public interest that it should. Therefore,
recklessness as to circumstances is sufficient under the *Act*, if the consummated
offence only requires recklessness as to circumstances. There is no inconsistency
between requiring intention for the crime in general (as *R. v. Mohan* did at
common law), that is to say intention as to the physical act and its required
consequence, if any, and being satisfied with recklessness as to circumstances. If
that is so, it must be the same where the requirement of intention is laid down by
statute.

If you say that recklessness as to circumstances is sufficient for an attempt   **15–020**
where such recklessness is sufficient for the consummated crime, then why
not say that negligence as to circumstances is sufficient where negligence is
sufficient for the consummated crime? After all, the current law of rape only
requires "negligence" as to circumstances.[52] One would prefer the courts not
to take the law of attempt beyond subjective recklessness, but *R. v. Mohan* does
not exclude liability for attempts that were negligent as to circumstances if that is
all that is required for the consummated offence. The Law Commission takes the
view that attempt liability should not be grounded on anything less than
subjective recklessness as to circumstances.[53] What if a man unreasonably thinks
that a woman he has known for years is consenting and he gets as far as stripping
her naked? Should he evade justice completely merely because he has not
consummated the rape and was only negligent as to whether she was

---

[49] [1982] 1 W.L.R. 762.
[50] *R. v. Khan* [1990] 1 W.L.R. 813; *Attorney-General's Reference (No.3 of 1992)* [1994] 1 W.L.R. 409.
[51] *R. v. Pearman* (1984) 80 Cr. App. R. 259.
[52] Section 1(2) of the *Sexual Offences Act 2003*.
[53] Law Commission, *Conspiracy and Attempts*, L.C.C.P.183 (London: H.M.S.O., 2007) at 194-97.

consenting?[54] Would not that allow the likes of Morgan and his confederates (see *D.P.P. v. Morgan*[55]) to try, unreasonably, to rape a woman and escape any liability for trying merely because they were negligent as to whether she was consenting? Perhaps not, because in such cases the jury is likely to infer that the defendants were subjectively reckless as to the circumstances. The courts are likely to hold that negligence as to circumstances is not sufficient for attempt liability, because those who are negligent merely attempt to commit the innocuous act of love-making, *etc.* They are not subjectively aware of the fact that they are attempting an offence, because they are not aware of the fact that the circumstances may not be as they believe.

15–021 **Does strict liability as to circumstances apply to attempts?** In *R. v. Collier*,[56] D was charged with attempting to have intercourse with a girl under 16. Being under the age of 24 he sought to raise the statutory defence of reasonable belief that the girl was over 16.[57] The trial judge ruled that it was available to him. This implied that, apart from the defence, the attempt was an offence of strict liability. The learned judge did not notice that on a charge of attempt *mens rea* should have been required, even though the consummated offence was in general one of strict liability.

The preferable *mens rea* would be either knowledge of the circumstances or recklessness as to them. The courts are likely to hold that strict liability as to circumstances is not sufficient for attempt liability, even where strict liability is sufficient for the consummated crime. Thus, if a person tries to sexually fondle a girl under the age of 13, he will most likely not be held liable for attempting to sexually assault a child under the age of 13.[58] The fact that he may have believed the girl was over the age of 16 does not provide a defence for the consummated crime, but may do for the attempt.[59] The American Law Institute's Model Penal Code provides that negligence (and even strict liability) as to circumstances is sufficient for attempt liability, if that is all that is required for the consummated

---

[54] Of course, he would not evade justice completely if he got as far as stripping her naked, as that in itself would involve a sexual assault. Cf. *Attorney-General's Reference (No. 1 of 1992)* [1993] 1 W.L.R. 274.

[55] [1976] A.C. 182.

[56] [1960] Crim. L.R. 204. Strict liability as to circumstances would be inconsistent with the reasoning in *Gardner v. Akeroyd* [1952] 2 Q.B. 743. Cf. *R. v. Lau Sai-wai* [1985] H.K.L.R. 423; *HKSAR v. Kan Chung Hung* [2001] 3 H.K.L.R.D. 834; *HKSAR v. Kwok Chu Ho* [2007] H.K.E.C. 178.

[57] See the now repealed section 6(3) of the *Sexual Offences Act 1956*.

[58] Section 7 of the *Sexual Offences Act 2003*.

[59] Most U.S. states allow strict liability as to circumstances where that is all that is required for the consummated crime. See *e.g.*, *Maxwell v. State*, 168 Md. App. 1 (2006); *State v. Chhom*, 128 Wash.2d 739 (1996); *Matter of Brion H*, 555 N.Y.S.2d 881 (1990). Cf. Law Commission, *Conspiracy and Attempts*, L.C.C.P.183 (London: 2007) at 196, where it is asserted: "to be found guilty of an attempt to rape a child under 13, it [should] have to be proved that D called on V (with a view to having sexual intercourse with her) *realising* that there was a risk that she might be under 13." See also Audrey Rogers, "New Technology, Old Defences: Internet Sting Operations and Attempt Liability," (2004) 38 *U. Rich. L. Rev.* 477.

crime.[60] But as said before, the Law Commission has suggested that subjective recklessness should be required as a bare minimal.

Is it possible to attempt a "conduct" crime?   Yes, but the violation would   15–022
have to be intentional. A person can intend to engage in conduct which has been criminalized because of its dangerousness, even though he does not intend it to result in specific harm. If D intends to drive a car which he knows has faulty brakes and attempts to do so, he attempts to endanger others even though he does not intend to harm anyone.[61] If he is caught trying to start a vehicle that has faulty brakes, he might be convicted of attempting to drive dangerously. As far as attempt liability is concerned,[62] it would not be enough to show that he ought to have known the vehicle was in a dangerous state, rather it would be necessary to show that he knew for a fact (or believed correctly and for certain) that it was in such a state, and that he made a deliberate choice to drive it in that state. There is no need for the prosecution to prove that D intended to endanger others, but it must prove that he was intending to engage in the criminal "conduct"— dangerous driving. If D intends to commit a "conduct" crime, then his attempt to do so should be punished. Similarly, if a person intends to drive a car even though he knows he is totally intoxicated, he intends to engage in criminal conduct even though he does not intend to harm anyone. Thus, if a policeman catches a drunk trying to start his car, he could charge him with attempting to drive whilst under the influence of alcohol.[63]

Does that mean a person can attempt to cause "death" by dangerous   15–023
driving?[64]   No. A person might attempt to engage in dangerous "conduct," drive dangerously, but he cannot attempt to bring about an unintended "consequence." An unintended consequence cannot be intended! Just as there can be no conviction of attempted involuntary manslaughter based on the defendant's negligent or reckless behaviour, there cannot be a conviction of attempting to cause "death" by dangerous driving unless D intended to bring about the prohibited result, "death." If D accidentally hits a child as he speeds through a school zone, he causes a consequence that he did not intend. D intended his conduct (speeding), but did not intend the consequence which resulted from his speeding (injury to a child). It would be absurd to argue that he attempted to kill the child, as that was not his intention—he merely intended to engage in the

---

[60] See Larry Alexander and Kimberly D. Kessler, "Mens Rea and Inchoate Crimes," (1997) 87 *J. Crim. L. & Criminology* 1138 at 1159-63; Paul H. Robinson and Jane A. Grall, "Element Analysis in Defining Criminal Liability: The Model Penal Code and Beyond," (1983) 35 *Stan. L. Rev.* 681 at 740-743).

[61] Glanville Williams, *Criminal Law: The General Part*, (London: Stevens & Sons, 1961) at 619.

[62] The substantive offence is made out if D was negligent as to the vehicle's dangerous state: but obviously one cannot attempt negligence, because one cannot *negligently intend*. Thus, if the police caught D trying to start a car with faulty brakes, D would not be liable for attempting to drive dangerously unless he knew for a fact that the brakes were faulty.

[63] See section 5 of the *Road Traffic Act 1988*; *Mason v. D.P.P.* [2010] R.T.R. 11. Mason was able to avoid a conviction because he had not tried to start his vehicle and thus had not gone past the more than mere preparation stage. Meanwhile, intoxicated Moore attempted to drive onto a public highway: *Moore v. D.P.P.* [2010] EWHC 1822.

[64] See section 2 and 2A of the *Road Traffic Act 1988*.

criminal "conduct" of speeding. Otherwise, we could argue that he attempted to kill everyone within the school zone. If he intends to run down and kill a pedestrian, then he attempts murder. So if D uses his car to *try* to run down and kill a rival, not only would his dangerous driving be intentional, but so would his attempt to kill his rival.[65] A person can be held liable for intentionally attempting to bring about results that are proscribed by law or for intentionally attempting to engage in "conduct" that is proscribed by law.

15.5. THE ACT OF ATTEMPT

15–024   Section 1(1) of the *Criminal Attempts Act 1981* defines an attempt as the doing of an act, and there should be no question, therefore, that an omission cannot be an attempt (whether to commit a crime of positive action or of omission).[66] If the rule of law is not to be reduced to something like a game of croquet in *Alice in Wonderland*, where the mallets were flamingos which wandered about during the game, a measure of fixity must be given to the basic legal terms, and for this reason the word "act" in a statute should not include an omission, in default of clear language on the subject.[67] Unfortunately, it is never certain that the courts will adopt this interpretation in a given case.[68]

Once an intending criminal goes as far as to perform an act of attempt, his liability for that offence becomes fixed, whatever happens afterwards:

- It does not matter that the attempter subsequently gives up the attempt—for example, because he finds that someone is watching him,[69] or because he

---

[65] Cf. *State v. Frohlich*, 729 N.W.2d 148 (N.D. 2007), where D attempted to kill his girlfriend by deliberately speeding through a red light.

[66] That does not mean it would be unjust to amend the law to cover attempts by omission which may warrant criminalization. The Law Commission recently proposed that attempt by omission should be criminalized. See Law Commission, *Conspiracy and Attempts*, Report 318 (London: H.M.S.O., 2009) at 151. The Law Commission provides examples of parents starving their children: it is assumed that the Law Commission is not referring to cases such as *R. v. Stone and Dobinson* [1977] Q.B. 354, but rather cases where the omission is *intended* to bring about the criminally proscribed *consequence*, death, *etc.* You can attempt to bring about a consequence by omission if you intend to do so. (However, the starvation cases normally involve recklessness or negligence as to consequence). Nevertheless, if a father sits by while his child nearly drowns in a puddle because he wants the child to die, but it is saved by a stranger—he clearly attempts to murder his child by omission. Cahill also argues that certain cases involving "zero action" and "zero harm" are worthy of criminalization. See the examples and discussion in Michael T. Cahill, "Attempt by Omission," (2009) 94 *Iowa L. Rev.* 1207.

[67] Cf. *R. v. Ahmad* (1987) 84 Cr. App. R. 64.

[68] It was the intention of the Government that crimes of omission should be attemptable, but this was not written into the *Act*. See generally, Ian Dennis "The Criminal Attempts Act 1981," [1982] Crim. L.R. 5. In *R. v. Arthur*, (*The Times*, November 5, 1981), which arose before the *Act*, the judge allowed a charge of attempted murder by omission to go to the jury. Dr. Arthur committed an "act" in proscribing nursing care only, meaning that for the time being the child was not to be fed. But if non-feeding is an omission, an order not to feed should surely be held to be an omission not an act.

[69] *R. v. Taylor* (1859) 1 F. & F. 511.

has a change of mind. (But if he changes his mind the court may possibly find that this indicates he never had a firm purpose.)[70]

- Nor does it matter that he goes on and completes the crime: his attempt does not "merge" in the crime.[71] Of course, if the police have evidence of a completed crime they will charge that. But if they charge attempt, the defendant's impudent defence that he succeeded will not avail him. The same is true of conspiracy.

What does section 1(1) mean by saying that the act must be "more than merely preparatory to the commission of the offence"? If I lift my arm in order to strike someone on the head, I am preparing to strike him, but am also attempting to strike him, because when I bring my arm down I have struck him. It seems to me that every act done in order to commit the crime is preparation for committing it. That is literally true. But the "more than merely preparatory" rule has a special meaning for lawyers. It implies that one has to draw the line. At common law the courts distinguished between acts that were merely preparatory to the offence, which could not be an attempt, and proximate acts, which could.[72] In some degree the decision depended on what is politely called a visceral reaction. Judges frequently construe the notion of a "more than merely preparatory" act so narrowly that obvious rascals who have gone very far towards committing the intended offence are acquitted. This is perhaps because the judges are inclined to think that no act could be "more than merely preparatory" to the offence unless it actually involves the defendant "trying" to do the offence in question;[73] or at least something very near indeed[74] (which is indeed, the classical meaning of the word). The *Criminal Attempts Act 1981* therefore discards the language of proximity while leaving the other half of the rule, or the other side of the coin (that the act must go beyond mere preparation), untouched.

The change has one obvious effect: it deprives us of convenient language. We no longer have a word for the act that goes beyond mere preparation, but must use the whole of that cumbrous phrase. As we will see, the phrase has had little effect upon the post-*Act* decisions.

15–025

---

[70] See Stuart, "*Actus Reus* in Attempts," [1970] Crim. L.R. 505 at 519-541. Some foreign codes provide no punishment if the defendant desists; and the Model Penal Code allows a defence of repentance, under careful conditions.

[71] Section 6(4) of the *Criminal Law Act 1967*; *Webley v. Buxton* [1977] Q.B. 481.

[72] The law of attempt was developed by the courts in the late 1600s, at which time the rule was that any act manifesting a felonious intent was a misdemeanour. The law was not limited by any notion derived from the word "attempt." In time the law was both extended and restricted: it was extended to cases where the intent was to commit a misdemeanour, and it was restricted (by the decision in *R. v. Eagleton* (1855) Dears. 376) to cases where there was a proximate act of attempt—which gives us the present law. See P. R. Glazebrook, "Should we have a Law of Attempted Crime?" (1969) 85 *L.Q.R.* 28 at 29-35, esp. at 33 n. 26. Having introduced the proximity test, the courts quite possibly became influenced by the language of attempt; but it would have been better if they had said that the limits of the law were to be settled by considerations of policy, not by pseudo-logical derivations from the notion of attempt.

[73] See *e.g.*, *R. v. Geddes* [1996] Crim. L.R. 894 at 895 *per* Lord Bingham L.C.J.

[74] See *e.g.*, *R. v. Tosti* [1997] Crim. L.R. 746.

15–026   **Surely there was some principle upon which the courts would generally hold that an act went beyond mere preparation?**   Various ideas were mooted, by judges and commentators, but none of them gave much assistance, and one or two were positively misleading.[75]

15–027   **Why bother drawing a line between perpetration and preparation?**   The "more than mere preparation" rule may be regarded as deriving from the motto that one must draw the line somewhere. It also rests, in part, upon the fact that the offence happens to be called an "attempt." We would not say that a person is attempting to counterfeit bank notes if he has only got to the stage of sitting in the British Library studying works on engraving. The mere preparation rule is designed to distinguish relatively innocuous activities of the mere preparer from those of the fully prepared *trier*.[76] If the defendant is still at the stage of remote preparation, we are not sure that he would have the ability or constancy of purpose to go on with his plan. A person who takes only the first step in preparation, as when he studies a book on engraving with a view to becoming a forger, may be barely distinguishable from a person who merely has criminal fantasies.[77] Since most of us have inhibitions against criminality, there is no telling that such a person will get further, though the further he proceeds the less likely it becomes that he will repent. It is not reasonable to punish a person for an attempt until he has gone far enough to show that he has broken through the psychological barrier to crime.

15–028   **Can one explain the more than merely preparatory rule by saying that a person should not be convicted of an attempt if his conduct is at all ambiguous?**   Some courts have toyed with this idea in the past,[78] but it has been abandoned. And for good reason too. The idea is that the defendant's acts should be regarded as more than merely preparatory if and only if they are unequivocally indicative of the criminal intention. But this test is too circumscribed to offer any guidance. True, a very commonplace act, such as carrying a box of matches, may be held not to be an attempt, on the ground that it does not take the defendant sufficiently far beyond mere mental resolution, which the law does not punish.

---

[75] On two of these see Glanville Williams, *Textbook of Criminal Law*, (London: Stevens & Sons, 1978) at 379-382. For some other examples, see Hamish Stewart, "The Centrality of the Act Requirement for Criminal Attempts," (2001) 51 *U. Toronto L.J.* 399; Barbara Baum Levenbook, "Prohibiting Attempts and Preparations," (1981) 49 *UMKC L. Rev.* 41.

[76] The Court of Appeal has held that an attempt requires the defendant to actually try to commit the offence in question. See *R. v. Geddes* [1996] Crim. L.R. 894 at 895.

[77] Some statutory provisions make mere preparation a substantive offence; therefore, attempting such an offence can be caught by the *Criminal Attempts Act 1981* even if D has not got past the mere preparation stage. See *R. v. R.* [2009] 1 W.L.R. 713.

[78] The test seemed to be approved by the Divisional Court in *Davey v. Lee* [1968] 1 Q.B. 366, but a retreat was made from this position in *Jones v. Brookes* (1968) 52 Cr. App. R. 614. The equivocality test was at one time applied by the New Zealand courts, but it was found to work badly and has now been abolished by statute. Section 72(3) of the *Crimes Act 1961* (N.Z.). It has also surfaced in some U.S. jurisdictions. See Wayne R. LaFave, *Substantive Criminal Law*, (West Publishing, Vol. II, 2003) at 225 n. 58.

But it would be too narrow a rule to say that any reasonable ambiguity in what the defendant has done involves a consequence that his act is mere preparation and not an attempt.

To put the objection of the suggested rule in a nutshell, it confuses proof of intent with proximity of the act of attempt. One may concede that ambiguity in the defendant's conduct may make it impossible to conclude from this evidence alone that he had a criminal intent. But a criminal intent may be proved otherwise than by evidence of the defendant's conduct at the time: it may, as we have seen, be proved by his subsequent confession. Once the jury are satisfied that the defendant had a criminal intent, the fact that his conduct was objectively capable of an innocent interpretation is not decisive to the question of whether he was at the merely preparatory stage.

An example may highlight the incoherency of the "ambiguity" or "unequivocal act" rule. Suppose that a number of haystacks have been set on fire in a particular locality. One night the defendant enters a farmer's field, goes to a haystack, puts a cigarette in his mouth and lights a match. The police emerge from the depths of the stack, where they have been concealed, and arrest him. If the defendant is charged with attempted damage, and these are the only facts given in evidence, the case is likely to break down for lack of satisfactory proof of criminal intent. On the other hand, he might have been about to set fire to the stack before lighting the cigarette; but he might merely have intended to light the cigarette. The difficulty relates to proof of *mens rea*, not to whether he had got past the mere preparatory stage. Suppose after being arrested, this defendant confesses that his intention was to burn the stack. If his confession is believed, his criminal intention is proved; and there can be no doubt that he had reached the stage of attempt, because in lighting the match he commenced the act of trying to burn it.

What about if the defendant has done the "last act" required to effect his   **15–029**
attempt? The courts at one time used the "last act" principle to determine whether D had done acts that were more than merely preparatory, but this principle was of very limited use. If the defendant has done the last act that was needed for him to perpetrate the crime, he has inevitably passed beyond mere preparation.[79] If therefore, D encourages X as an innocent agent to commit a crime, expecting that he will then commit it without further instruction, D can, on principle, be found guilty of an attempt to commit it (and will be the perpetrator if X does commit it).[80] If on the other hand D encourages a guilty agent to commit a crime, D, although he is guilty of the special crime of encouragement,[81] and although he will become an accessory if the perpetrator commits the crime, he is not guilty of an attempt by reason of his encouragement. Otherwise every encouragement would be an attempt. The rule is confirmed by an express

---

[79] *D.P.P. v. Stonehouse* [1978] A.C. 55; *R. v. Eagleton* (1855) Dears. C.C. 515.
[80] Cf. *R. v. R.* [2009] 1 W.L.R. 713.
[81] See section 44 of the *Serious Crime Act 2007*.

provision in the *Criminal Attempts Act*.[82] In short, the law of attempt applies only to would-be perpetrators, not to would-be accessories. We shall return to this point later.

What is "the last act" that is needful for him to perpetrate the crime depends in part on the law of causation, which may in turn depend in part on the law of attempt. The case has already been put of a person preparing poison to give to his wife, when the wife unexpectedly drinks it without assistance, and dies. It may be said that the man can be found guilty of murder on the "unexpected twist" principle, so that if he had been arrested immediately after preparing the poison he would have been guilty of an attempt on the last act principle. But against this it may be said that his act had not gone beyond mere preparation, so that he had not reached the stage of attempt, and from this it may be concluded that the man is not guilty of murder if the wife unexpectedly drinks the poison. It was suggested before that the solution should depend upon how close the man got towards administrating the poison.

The more than mere preparation standard is evidently wider than the "last act" standard. An attempt can be committed where other acts remain to be done.

15–030 A man draws a revolver from his pocket, intending to kill another, but his arm is seized before he can take aim. Clearly he is guilty of attempted murder; yet he has not reached the last act of pulling the trigger.[83]

Similarly, it was held before the *Act* that when a person got into the driving seat of another's car he was guilty of an attempt to steal even though he had not yet started the engine or put the car in gear.[84]

It was even held that the first of a series of similar acts intended to result cumulatively in the crime could be a sufficient attempt.[85] The principal case concerned a deep-dyed villain going incongruously by the name of White.[86] White put two grains of cyanide of potassium in his mother's nectar, intending to kill her. The dose was insufficient to kill, and the mother did not even drink the nectar, but, by coincidence, she died from natural causes a short time after. It was held that White was guilty of attempt to murder, whether he thought that the dose was sufficient to kill in itself, or whether he intended to kill by giving a series of

---

[82] Section 1(4) of the *Act* "applies to any offence which … other than—(a) conspiracy … (b) aiding, abetting, counselling, procuring or suborning the commission of an offence…".

[83] *R. v. Linneker* [1906] 2 K.B. 99; *R. v. Jones* [1990] 1 W.L.R. 1057.

[84] *R. v. Cook* (1964) 48 Cr. App. R. 98. (Under the *Theft Act 1968* it is quite possible that the full offence of theft is committed when the thief touches the car, or at any rate when he opens the car door. If so, the attempt comes at a still earlier time.) Opening a van door was held to be an attempt to steal an article inside: *R. v. Hussein* [1967] Crim. L. R. 219. And a man who pushed his motor cycle towards the entrance of a public road, with intent to ride it, was held to attempt to ride it on the road: *Shaw v. Knill* [1974] R.T.R. 142. Cf. *D.P.P. v. Mason* [2010] R.T.R. 11, where it was held that opening the door of a car with an intent to drive was not an attempt to drive whilst intoxicated!

[85] The act might also be a continuing act. For example, if intoxicated D drives around a private field and all of a sudden forms the intent to drive on a public highway, and tries to do so, he would be liable for attempting to drive under the influence on a public highway. If he formed the intent to drive onto the highway when he first started the car then his putting the key in the ignition would be an attempt to drive on the highway while intoxicated. If, instead, he formed the intent to drive on the public highway after commencing to drive around the field, he would have attempted from that point in time onwards. Cf. *Moore v. D.P.P.* [2010] EWHC 1822.

[86] [1910] 2 K.B. 124.

doses having cumulative effect; and in the latter event it made no difference that in fact cyanide of potassium has no cumulative effect. Clearly, White was trying to kill; he had commenced his acts of *trying* to kill.

So these old tests are of no use. What test is in vogue? Does the offender   **15–031**
actually have to "*try* to consummate" his crime or will it be enough to show
that he was on the "*brink* of consummating" it?   The weight of authority suggests that the offender will have to *try* to consummate his crime. In *R. v. Jones*,[87] the defendant had done acts which were more than preparatory to the offence of murder, because he got into the victim's car and pointed a loaded gun at him with the intention of killing him. He did not get a chance to actually try to do the act that was necessary to kill the victim, that is, pull the trigger. He did not get a chance to complete his attempt before he was disarmed by the victim. The victim disarmed the defendant before he could remove the safety catch and try to press the trigger, but he was clearly on the brink of pulling the trigger.

Nevertheless, a line of cases have generally held that being on the brink of committing the crime is not enough. But some decisions have gone the other way.[88] A farcical example of the restrictive approach to the law of attempts was *R. v. Geddes*.[89] It seems to show that to be guilty of an attempt the defendant must actually be "in the act" of attempting, or to put it another way, must actually commence his attempt (that is, try to consummate the crime in question). This is generally referred to as a question of "whether the defendant has embarked on the crime proper; but it is not necessary that he should have reached a 'point of no return' in respect of the full offence."[90]

In *R. v. Geddes* D was charged with attempted false imprisonment. Geddes was spotted trespassing in the boys' lavatory block at a school. A police officer was visiting the school at the time, but was unable to prevent him from escaping. D's rucksack was found nearby. The rucksack contained a large kitchen knife, some lengths of rope and a roll of masking tape. The prosecution argued that D was equipped to catch and restrain any boy who ventured into the lavatory. The defendant was merely waiting for a boy to enter so that he could pounce. Notwithstanding that the defendant was a trespasser, was temporally positioned to pounce, was fully prepared and on the brink of attempting to grab a boy, the Court of Appeal held that he had not attempted to falsely imprison any boys. The Court of Appeal held:[91]

> "There was no rule of thumb test, and there must always be an exercise of judgment based on the particular facts of the case. It was an accurate paraphrase of the statutory test to ask whether the available evidence, if accepted, could show that a defendant had done an act showed that he had actually tried to commit the offence in question, or whether he had only got ready or put himself in a position or equipped himself to do so. ... It was true that he had entered the school, but he had never had any contact or communication with, nor had

---

[87] [1990] 1 W.L.R. 1057. See also *Attorney-General's Reference (No.1 of 1992)* [1993] 1 W.L.R. 274, where D was clearly in the process of attempting to rape his victim: he had removed her underwear and was holding her down.
[88] Cf. *R. v. Tosti* [1997] Crim. L.R. 746.
[89] *R. v. Geddes* [1996] Crim. L.R. 894 at 895.
[90] *R. v. G* [2010] 1 A.C. 43 at 48 citing *R. v. Gullefer* [1990] 1 W.L.R. 1063 at 1066.
[91] *R. v. Geddes* [1996] Crim. L.R. 894 at 895 *per* Lord Bingham L.C.J.

confronted, any pupil at the school. The whole story was one which filled the court with the gravest unease, but on the facts of the case the court felt bound to conclude that the evidence was not sufficient in law to support a finding that the appellant had done an act which was more than merely preparatory to wrongfully imprisoning a person unknown."

Basically, Geddes would only have been guilty if he had tried to grab a boy;[92] or perhaps, if he had at least tried to communicate with one of the boys. As he did not actually try to pounce, (*i.e.* grab a boy—or try to persuade a boy to go with him), he did not attempt to falsely imprison a boy.

15–032   The restrictive approach to the law of attempts is reinforced by *R. v. Campbell*.[93] Campbell was convicted of attempted robbery. The police had a tipoff that a robbery was going to go down at a particular post office, so they put it under surveillance. Campbell was seen to be loitering in the vicinity of the post office. Campbell was searched and was found to be carrying sunglasses, a gun[94] and a demand note. He admitted that he intended to rob the post office, but asserted that he had changed his mind and was not going to go through with it. Watkins L.J. said:[95]

> "If a person, in circumstances such as this, has not even gained [access to] the place where he could be in a position to carry out the offence, it is extremely unlikely that it could ever be said that he had performed an act which could be properly said to be an attempt."

If Campbell had entered the post office, would that have been enough? In *R. v. Geddes* it was held that Geddes's presence in the lavatory was not enough. But what if a boy had entered the lavatory while Geddes was present? That logically should not make any difference if the restrictive approach is followed. If a boy had entered the lavatory Geddes would have perhaps pounced, but the boy's action of entering the lavatory cannot change the nature of the defendant's actions. (What if he had run off upon seeing a boy enter?)

If Campbell had decided to abandon his robbery after entering the post office and seeing an armed guard, would his temporary presence in the post office have made any difference? The courts continue to prefer the restrictive approach. In *Mason v. D.P.P.*[96] it was held that a drunk had not attempted to drive his car merely by opening the door to get into the driver's seat. Mason admitted that he intended to drive it and that his attempt was only frustrated because he was robbed of his car as he opened its door. It appears that he would only have been liable if he had got in the driver's seat and had attempted to start the engine; but

---

[92] Cf. *R. v. Dagnall* (2003) 147 S.J.L.B. 995, where D grabbed a girl and told her he was going to rape her.

[93] (1991) 93 Cr. App. R. 350.

[94] The gun was an imitation, but that is irrelevant.

[95] *R. v. Campbell* (1991) 93 Cr. App. R. 350 at 355.

[96] [2010] R.T.R. 11. Cf. *Moore v. D.P.P.* [2010] EWHC 1822. Under section 5(1)(b)(2) of the *Road Traffic Act 1988*: "It is a defence for a person charged with an offence under subsection (1)(b) above to prove that at the time he is alleged to have committed the offence the circumstances were such that there was no likelihood of his driving the vehicle whilst the proportion of alcohol in his breath, blood or urine remained likely to exceed the prescribed limit." See *Drake v. D.P.P.* [1994] R.T.R. 411, where it was factually impossible for D to drive his vehicle because it was wheel-clamped. And he had full knowledge of the impossibility. Cf. *D.P.P. v. Watkins* [1989] Q.B. 821.

surely if the engine had fired he would have consummated the offence. If he had been caught inserting the key into the ignition, that should have been sufficient.

The courts also adopted a similarly restrictive approach to the law of attempts in **15–033** a number of pre-*Act* decisions, but the earlier cases were less borderline than the three just mentioned. For example, in *R. v. Robinson*[97] an impecunious jeweller attempted to swindle his insurers. When the curtain rises, Robinson is discovered inside his shop with his legs and one hand tied. He is shouting "I am bound and gagged: open the door." A passing policeman hears the cries and blows his whistle. (How Robinson manages not merely to articulate but to make his words heard in the street outside when he is gagged we do not know, but I tell the tale as it is told in the Law Reports.) Reinforcements arrive; the officers burst into the shop and release Robinson, who explains that he has been robbed of jewellery in his safe. The police with their quick thinking look behind the safe, where they find the jewellery, which Robinson has of course insured against theft.

On the facts Robinson was convicted by a jury of attempting to obtain money from the insurers by false pretences (an offence now replaced by that of fraud). But the conviction was quashed by the Court of Criminal Appeal, which held that the police had moved too fast. They should have waited for Robinson to write to the company to claim the money. As it was, Robinson had merely prepared the background for the fraud, and was not guilty of attempt.

But Robinson's intention in staging his tableau was clear. An act does not **15–034** become an attempt merely because the *mens rea* is obvious. Although the decision has been criticized,[98] it is by no means obviously wrong in terms of the traditional law of attempt. If Robinson bought a rope with which to truss himself up for the purpose of his intended fraud that would obviously be merely preparatory. The court was not demonstrably in error in holding that staging the robbery was merely a preparatory act to making a claim on the insurers. Robinson's fraudulent behaviour did, however, go further along the path of criminality than merely buying a rope.

The courts have taken the same view in the post-*Act* cases. For example, in *R. v. Gullefer*,[99] the defendant backed a greyhound to win a race, but after the race commenced it became clear that he had backed a loser. The defendant ran on to the track to distract the dogs, because he wanted the race to be declared a "no

---

[97] [1915] 2 K.B. 342. Cf. *Comer v. Bloomfield* (1971) 55 Cr. App. R. 305, where the fraudster actually wrote to the insurers asking whether he could make a claim; again it was held not to be an attempt. Contrast *R. v. Murray* [1982] 1 W.L.R. 475, where the false information in fact reached the knowledge of some of the persons intended to be deceived.

[98] See in particular the reservation repressed by Lord Edmund-Davies in *D.P.P. v. Stonehouse* [1978] A.C. 55 at 75.

[99] (1990) 91 Cr. App. R. 356. See *R. v. Widdowson* (1986) 82 Cr. App. R. 314, where D put his neighbour's details on a form so that he would pass a credit check which would have allowed him then to gain a hire purchase contract. In *R. v. Ilyas* (1984) 78 Cr. App. R. 17, D falsely reported to the police and his insurance company that his car had been stolen, and obtained, but did not complete, a claim form from the insurance company. It was held that D "had plainly not done every act which was necessary for him to do to achieve the result he intended; *i.e.* all he had done was to obtain a claim form, that act and all the other acts which preceded it in point of time, were merely preparatory and remote from the contemplated offence of dishonestly attempting to obtain money from the insurance company…".

race" as he hoped this would mean that the bookmakers would have to return all stakes. He was charged with attempting to steal his stake. The Court of Appeal held that his actions were not enough to constitute an attempt. According to the court, he would only have attempted to steal his stake if he were to present his ticket to his bookmaker. In other words, use his preparation to try to seek his stake.

Whatever the theoretical argument may be, the decision in a case like *R. v. Robinson* puts the police "on the spot." As soon as Robinson realized that he was found out he desisted from the enterprise: there was no longer any point in claiming from the insurance company. But if the police had refrained from searching until after the fundamental letter was written and posted, they might not have found the jewellery, because by that time Robinson might have hidden it better. Good police practice demands prompt action, but the law of attempt stultifies it. (A latter-day Robinson could, however, be convicted of the summary offence of making a false report and wasting the time of the police.)[100]

15–035   Another merry anecdote, equally infuriating for the police, is *Kyprianou v. Reynolds*.[101] Kyprianou approached drug pedlars and said, or perhaps hissed: "What you got tonight boys—hash or heroin? I got money upstairs." At this point Kyprianou observed for the first time that police officers were listening. It was held that he was not guilty of attempting to obtain cannabis or heroin, because he had, in the phrase used in the law of contract, merely issued an "invitation to treat." Presumably an offer to buy would have been an attempt.

15–036   **What other acts have been held not to be attempts?**   Reconnoitring, or looking for an opportunity to commit a crime, was never held to be anymore than mere preparation. The following illustrations have not been the subject of decisions, but pretty clearly would be mere reconnoitring, not going beyond preparation.[102]

A person is seen going along a row of terraced houses, pausing at each and appearing to examine them to see if they are secure; whenever anyone passes he conceals himself. He has convictions for burglary.

In a busy market a youth successfully follows a number of women whose purses can be seen at the top of their shopping bag or pram; he runs off when spoken to.

A person drifts along a road and knocks on houses to see if anyone is at home. When challenged he fails to give a convincing explanation of his behaviour.

If two men behaved like this together they could, theoretically, be convicted of conspiracy to steal. But a conspiracy charge is not of much use to the police in small cases, because it is purely indictable. Before the *Act* the police could charge a summary offence of "being a suspected person loitering with intent to commit

---

[100] Section 5 of the *Criminal Law Act 1967*.

[101] (1969) 113 S.J. 563. The *Fraud Act 2006* targets inchoate conduct, and would catch any false representation that is made for the purpose of making a gain or causing a loss. Under that *Fraud Act 2006* there is no need to show that D actually made a gain or caused a loss, it is sufficient that he made the false representation with an intent to gain or cause a loss or expose another to a risk of loss. But the representation must in fact be made.

[102] They were given in a police memorandum to the House of Commons Committee on the Criminal Attempts Bill, 10 February 1981, paras. 147-148, 163.

an arrestable offence;" but this "sus" law came under attack because it was alleged to be used oppressively against the ethnic population. So the offence was abolished by the *Act*. This piece of history makes it even less likely that the law of attempt will be extended to reconnoitring cases.

Another type of conduct that may safely be said not to amount to an attempt is the **15–037** acquisition of information or materials for a proposed crime. Before the *Act* there was some authority for saying that acquiring materials for certain crimes was either an attempt or a special common law offence; but the *Act* (section 6(1)) expressly abolishes these special offences. Clearly the intention is that they shall not be punishable except under express statutory provisions.[103]

Even lengthy pursuit of an unsuspecting victim was ruled in one case not to amount to an attempt. The case was *R. v. Komaroni*[104] where the two defendants admitted that they had driven after a lorry at night with the intention of stealing from it when the driver should leave it unattended to get a meal. During the journey, when the lorry got stuck on an ice-bound hill, the defendants, abhorring violence, helped the driver to start it moving again. The driver, suspicious of his escort, drove through the night without stopping. It was ruled by Streatfeild J. that the defendants' conduct amounted to mere preparation.

Here the plotters were not merely looking for their victim; they had actually found him. What if the defendants were armed and intended to murder the driver when he stopped? Would it still have been held that they were not guilty of attempt until the moment when they had him in their gunsights? If so, the law of attempt is allowed very little operation. The two defendants did not go without punishment, because they pleaded guilty to conspiracy; but the question of attempt retains practical importance in a case of this kind where there is only one attempter.

Somewhat inconsistently, there were cases holding that it could be an attempt to commit a consensual sexual offence (such as unlawful sexual intercourse with a young girl) if the defendant enticed the other party to go to the place contemplated for the commission of the offence, provided that the defendant made known to such party what was intended. The logical relevance of the qualification is obscure, but appears to no longer apply.[105]

Could anything be done to improve the law?   A Working Party appointed by **15–038** the Law Commission proposed that these problems should be resolved by enacting that an attempt is committed by taking a "substantial step"[106] towards committing the crime. Both Geddes and Campbell (and also Mason) clearly took a substantial step. Instead of beginning with the crime, and looking backwards to see what was proximate, one would begin with the defendant's intention and look forward to see what was a substantial step in pursuance of it. This would give the law of attempt a wider scope. The Working Party also proposed that the statute

---

[103] See for example, section 6 of the *Fraud Act 2006*, and also section 25 of the *Theft Act 1968*.
[104] (1953) 103 L. Jo. 97.
[105] See *R. v. Nash* [1999] Crim. L.R. 308. Thus, even a solicitation by letter can be an attempt. (Or even by words to a third party: *R. v. R.* [2009] 1 W.L.R. 713). See also *R. v. Gammon* (1959) 43 Cr. App. R. 155; *R. v. Cope* (1922) 16 Cr. App. R. 77. See further, Glanville Williams, *Criminal Law: The General Part*, (London: Stevens & Sons, 2nd edn. 1961) at 628 n. 26.
[106] Law Commission, *Published Working Paper* No. 50.

should contain illustrative examples, so that the legislature could make its own "case-law" on what is essentially the political matter of deciding when the law of attempt should begin to operate; these examples could show both what is an attempt and what is not. That is the rule proposed in §5.01(c) of the American Law Institute's *Model Penal Code*.

15–039   **But even with a "substantial step" test, we should still have a somewhat untidy mass of cases going one way or the other, and the decision would often be unpredictable, just as it is now.**   True. But the only alternative would be to enact that any step, even a preparatory act, should be a sufficient act of attempt if accompanied by the requite intent.[107] What's more, a substantial step will often be nothing more than mere preparation. And that is politically "not on."[108] Members of Parliament would point out that such a law would enable suspicious magistrates to convict an unemployed person of attempted theft if he merely set foot in a car park—indeed, theoretically he could be convicted of attempted theft the moment he set foot outside his own door, if the police gave evidence that upon being interrogated he admitted to a criminal intent. Additionally, it is not clear how an elaborate set of examples would guide courts better than the plethora of examples found in the precedents.

15–040   **Would it not be better to have a standard which covers those who are on the *brink* of "actually trying to commit" the offence in question?**   Such a test would have to focus on the temporal and spatial aspects of the defendant's attempt. In *R. v. Tosti*[109] a conviction was upheld even though the defendant had not "[d]one an act that showed that he had actually tried to commit the offence in question."[110] In that case the defendant was convicted of attempted burglary. The defendant was seen with an accomplice just before midnight examining the padlock on a barn door. Once they realized they were being watched they took off. Oxyacetylene equipment was found hidden in a hedge near the barn. The Court of Appeal applied the *R. v. Geddes* standard and held that "the facts proved in evidence were sufficient for the judge to leave to the jury the question of whether 'defendant had done an act which showed that he had actually tried to commit the offence.'"

The court got the right result, but for the wrong reason. The defendants did not "actually try" to commit the offence. They were fully prepared and were positioned to strike, but they were yet to strike. In other words, they were on the "brink" of trying to commit the offence. If a person is fully prepared and is in a position to strike as so to speak, then clearly he is no longer merely preparing to strike. The Court of Appeal wrongly suggested that he had actually tried to burgle the building: he did not try to enter, he did not try to cut the lock, he did not even get the oxyacetylene equipment within reach of the door—it was still in the nearby hedge. But he was no longer "merely" preparing either. He was prepared

---

[107] The Law Commission now proposes exactly this: it wants to criminalize mere preparation as a separate offence.

[108] Unless, of course, the offence is one which causes public outrage. Cf. section 14 of the *Sexual Offences Act 2003* as discussed in *R. v. R.* [2009] 1 W.L.R. 713.

[109] [1997] Crim. L.R. 746.

[110] To borrow the standard proposed in *R. v. Geddes* [1996] Crim. L.R. 894 at 895.

and on the brink of trying to bring about the burglary. The latter is more than enough to ground an attempt conviction. *R. v. Tosti* needs to be explained properly so that the courts might distil a principle to guide future cases. The decision is best explained as a case where the defendant was no longer merely preparing even though he had not commenced trying either. He was equipped and positioned to consummate the crime within minutes.

The courts should focus on whether the defendant is fully prepared and is on the brink of using that preparation to strike. Geddes and Campbell were no longer preparing, they were both on the brink of striking and should have been convicted. The restrictive approach adopted in those cases is unacceptable, because the subsection does not require the defendant to actually try. It requires only that the defendant advance past the merely preparatory stage, as Geddes, Campbell and Tosti had. Nevertheless, evidence of whether D was fully prepared and in a position to consummate his planned crime is something to be considered along with the context and all the other evidence. Mason[111] was equipped to drive whilst under the influence of alcohol (he was intoxicated, had his keys, and was trying to open the door to his car), but he may have only been attempting to sleep in his car, rather than drive it.

If the evidence shows that D was fully prepared and on the brink of consummating the crime, the inference will be almost irresistible that he was attempting to commit the crime. However, it is not a fixed rule of law that D must be convicted in these circumstances. If D can convince the jury (or convince them of the reasonable possibility) that, although he was fully prepared and positioned to consummate the particular crime, that there was a reasonable alternative explanation for his preparation and position, then he may be let off the hook. Clearly, Geddes, Campbell and Tosti would struggle to convince a jury that they were attempting to do something legitimate; and since they had crossed the threshold of merely preparing for their crime they should have been convicted.

Well, suppose the judge now wishes to give the jury a genuine instruction on the current law, and not merely to lead them by the noses, what is he to say? The judge should not refer to any formal tests—especially the pre-*Act* tests. The best he can generally do is to tell the jury that: "before you, the jury, can convict the defendant you must be satisfied so as to feel sure of two things: first, that he intended to commit [the offence]; and, secondly, that with that intent he did an act which was more than an act of preparation to commit that offence. It is for you to decide whether the act relied upon by the prosecution was more than merely preparatory."[112] It is a question of fact to be decided in each case.

15–041

In a jury trial, who decides whether the act goes beyond mere preparation: judge or jury? Section 4(3) of the *Criminal Attempts Act* enacts:

15–042

"Where, in proceedings against a person for an offence under section 1 above, there is evidence sufficient in law to support a finding that he did an act falling within subsection (1) of that section, the question whether or not his act fell within that subsection is a question of fact."

---

[111] *Mason v. D.P.P.* [2010] R.T.R. 11.

[112] *R. v. Campbell* [1991] 93 Cr. App. R. 350 at 354.

This puts the common law, as declared (or rather changed) by the House of Lords in *D.P.P. v. Stonehouse*,[113] into statutory form. The effect is that:

1.   The trial judge can rule as a matter of law whether the evidence is sufficient to support a finding that the act did go beyond mere preparation; if he concludes that there is insufficient evidence in law to support such a finding he can withdraw the case from the jury.
2.   If the judge thinks that the act can reasonably be regarded as having gone beyond mere preparation he should leave the question to the jury; but he may sum up, it was judicially said, "in such a way as to make it plain that he considers that the accused is guilty and should be convicted."[114] He may not rule as a matter of law that the act went beyond mere preparation,[115] even though it plainly did. He must, in theory, leave the jury to ponder the question, telling them that the matter is for them.[116]

The rule is really rather silly. It means that the jury, who may be thoroughly mystified by the judge's direction, must be given the opportunity to return a perverse or stupid verdict of acquittal even though an attempt was quite clearly committed on the undisputed facts. Before the decision in *D.P.P. v. Stonehouse* the courts treated the question of proximity in attempt, quite rightly, as one of law—which was why the appellate court felt able to quash convictions. Since *D.P.P. v. Stonehouse* and section 4(3) of the *Act*, previous decisions such as *R. v. Robinson* can be given legal force only by "reinterpreting" them, so that instead of being decisions that as a matter of law an attempt was not committed, they become decisions that as a matter of law there was no evidence for the jury that an attempt was committed. On its face the *Act* seems to leave a large scope to the jury to make their own decision; but it does not absolutely oblige the courts to change their former practice in ruling against liability.[117]

15.6.   IMPOSSIBILITY

15–043   The *Act* abolishes the former rule that one cannot attempt the impossible. The *Act* deals with the matter in the following two subsections of section 1 of the *Criminal Attempts Act 1981*:

> "(2)   A person may be guilty of attempting to commit an offence to which this section applies even though the facts are such that the commission of the offence is impossible.
> (3)   In any case where—
>   (a)   apart from this subsection a person's intention would not be regarded as having amounted to an intent to commit an offence; but

---

[113] [1978] A.C. 55. In Canada the Criminal Code expressly states that this is a question of law. *United States v. Dynar* [1997] 2 S.C.R. 462 at para. 17.

[114] *D.P.P. v. Stonehouse* [1978] A.C. 55 at 80 *per* Lord Salmon.

[115] *R. v. Griffin* [1993] Crim. L.R. 515. Questions of fact are for the jury alone: *R. v. Wang* [2005] 1 W.L.R. 661.

[116] If the judge fails to do so an appeal can no longer be dismissed under the proviso, as it no longer exists: *Criminal Appeal Act 1995*. An unsafe conviction would be quashed.

[117] See further Glanville Williams, *Textbook of Criminal Law*, (London: Stevens & Sons, 2nd edn. 1983) at 416-417.

(b)   if the facts of the case had been as he believed them to be, his intention would
        be so regarded,

then, for the purposes of subsection (1) above, he shall be regarded as having had an
intent to commit that offence."

This rather cumbrous provision boils down to the rule that in an attempt you take the facts as the defendant believed them to be. If, on the supposed facts, he would have been guilty of an attempt, then he is guilty of it. Impossibility falls into three categories:

1.   Legal impossibility (D attempted to do a legal act rather than an illegal one).
2.   Factual impossibility. A crime might been factually impossible to consummate because the "means" used were insufficient (the gun could not shoot the distance aimed for, *etc.*); or because the facts or circumstances were not as D believed, such as the goods were not stolen, there was no wallet in the pocket he tried to pickpocket, the person he stabbed was a pillow, the drugs he imported was talcum powder, the intended rape victim was consenting and so on.
3.   A further category of factual impossibility concerns "inherent factual impossibility." The latter usually concerns cases where it was absolutely impossible for D to commit his intended crime because of the insufficiency of the means he used. For example, D attempts to shoot down a passenger jet (criminal end) by using a water pistol (inherently insufficient means).

Legal and "inherent" factual impossibility will normally exempt the defendant from liability, but "standard" factual impossibility will not.

Suppose a person thinks he is smuggling sugar into the country. There is a sugar shortage, and he thinks, mistakenly, that it is an offence to import sugar. Is that an attempt?   No, because the "offence" that he has in mind to commit does not exist as an offence. Legal impossibility in the pure sense will exempt D from prosecution, because there is no offence to prosecute. He is attempting an imaginary crime, so there is no crime to attempt. In considering impossible attempts we are speaking only of mistakes of fact, not mistakes of law. A seven-year-old boy could not be convicted of attempted theft, since it is legally impossible for him to commit theft.[118]

15–044

The rule about intention works both ways. It makes a person guilty of an attempt according to his intention, and it prevents him from being guilty of an attempt if he did not intend to commit an offence (that is to say, to commit the acts amounting to an offence—he need not know the law.)[119]

---

[118] A child under the age of ten cannot be held criminally responsible for theft because it is presumed that he is *doli incapax*—incapable of fully comprehending the wrongness of criminal acts. *R. v. J.T.B.* [2009] 1 A.C. 1310; *Walters v. Lunt* (1951) 35 Cr. App. R. 94.

[119] If you think you are committing a crime when you are not, your moral culpability for that act cannot be transferred to some other *actus reus* which you might have inadvertently committed. If a man intends to import currency and it is not a crime to do so, he cannot be convicted of importing cannabis merely because he was sent cannabis instead of currency, if he never intended to import cannabis. *R. v. Taaffe* [1984] A.C. 539. (A person cannot attempt what he does not intend—and it will

15–045 **Suppose a person thinks he is smuggling cocaine into the country. He thinks, mistakenly, that it is cocaine but it is sugar. Does the fact that it is factually impossible for him to import cocaine on this occasion provide him with a defence?** No.[120] The defence of "factual impossibility" advanced in *Haughton v. Smith*[121] was abrogated by the *Criminal Attempts Act 1981*.[122] If factual impossibility were a defence, the morally culpable defendant would evade justice. If you attempt to import drugs, why should you have a complete defence just because your supplier has tricked you? It is by pure chance that D has imported sugar rather than cocaine. If the facts had been as D believed, he would have imported cocaine. He was morally unlucky in not getting his drugs, but morally lucky in not importing drugs; but neither reduce his culpability. The rationale for criminalizing such an offender is that he was fully culpable and he completed his attempt to import what he assumed to be drugs. His criminal end would have been achievable if the facts had been as he believed them to be. D is rightly censurable for his wrongdoing, even though on this occasion it was impossible for him to consummate his intended crime.

15–046 **Suppose it isn't a question of impossibility but of lack of an ingredient of the crime? A man receives goods mistakenly believing that they are stolen. Can he be convicted of attempting to receive stolen goods? One of the conditions required by law for the full crime is missing,[123] namely stolen goods.** Apply the plain words of subsection (3): if the goods were stolen, as the defendant believed them to be, he "shall be regarded as having had an intent to commit that offence." (The reason for the wording is that before the *Act* the judges had convinced themselves, by obviously fallacious reasoning, that the defendant did not intend to commit the offence.)[124] Clearly, if D believes the goods are stolen as

---

not do to substitute the intent of some imaginary crime for a real crime where the *actus reus* of the real crime was committed without fault). If, a man tries to fondle a woman's breasts thinking that is rape, he cannot be charged with attempted rape if all he intended was to grope her breasts. However, he might be charged with a sexual assault as he has consummated that offence and seems to have intended to sexually touch the woman.

[120] *R. v. Shivpuri* [1987] A.C. 1 at 22-23 *per* Lord Bridge. The Australian courts also prefer this approach. See *Onuorah v. The Queen* (2009) 234 F.L.R. 377 and the precedents cited therein.

[121] [1975] A.C. 476.

[122] *R. v. Shivpuri* [1987] A.C. 1. Cf. *Anderton v. Ryan* [1985] A.C. 560.

[123] The Americans refer to this as "Hybrid Legal Impossibility," but in effect, it is really nothing more than factual impossibility. Dressler notes that the doctrine caused so much confusion in the U.S. that most states abolished it. See Joshua Dressler, *Understanding Criminal Law*, (Neward, N.J.: LexisNexis, 2006) at 437. Therefore, those jurisdictions now treat hybrid legal impossibility as a factual impossibility. And rightly so—anything else would rob the law of attempt of much of its usefulness!

[124] For a penetrating discussion of the fallacious reasoning in *Anderton v. Ryan* [1985] A.C. 560, see Glanville Williams, "The Lords and Impossible Attempts, or *Quis Custodiet Ipsos Custodes*," (1986) 45 *Cambridge L.J.* 33. This article was influential in having the law changed. As Lord Bridge noted: "I cannot conclude this opinion without disclosing that I have had the advantage, since the conclusion of the argument in this appeal, of reading an article by Professor Glanville Williams entitled 'The Lords and Impossible Attempts, or *Quis Custodiet Ipsos Custodes*?' ... The language in which he criticises the decision in *Anderton v. Ryan* is not conspicuous for its moderation, but it would be foolish, on that account, not to recognise the force of the criticism and churlish not to acknowledge the assistance I have derived from it." *R. v. Shivpuri* [1987] A.C. 1 at 23. See also H.L.A. Hart, *Essays in Jurisprudence and Philosophy*, (Oxford: Clarendon Press, 1983) at 367-391.

a matter of certainty, then he must intend to receive stolen goods. Since the goods turn out not to be stolen, D would be convicted of attempting to receive stolen goods rather than with receiving stolen goods. If he had actually received stolen goods, then his offence would have been consummated. The rationale for attempts is to criminalize those who try to succeed at bringing about some criminal end: if they succeed then they will be charged with the consummated form of the offence.

This type of case involves a mistake of fact not one of law; D is mistaken about whether or not the goods are stolen, not about whether or not it is a crime to receive stolen goods. The crime exists—it is not an imaginary crime and D tries to succeed at it. The Lords once thought that when an essential ingredient of the full crime was missing that the crime became a legal impossibility. But as Professor Williams perspicaciously remarks:[125]

> "To accept the argument that:
> Some part of the full crime is missing;
> Therefore the act is lawful;
> Therefore it is not an attempt would abolish the law of attempt."

There is no analytical difference between your "question of impossibility" and your "lack of an ingredient of the crime." In the case of the supposed corpse, or an attempted theft from an empty pocket, which everyone will agree are cases of impossibility, one of the ingredients or conditions of the full crime is missing (a live human being who can be killed; property belonging to another), but obviously the intention of the *Act* is that an attempt can be committed. The same can be said of your case of receiving stolen goods.

No problem arises in drafting a charge of attempting to receive stolen goods, because the charge may follow the words of the offence and say: "attempted to receive stolen goods, *believing* them to be stolen." It is true that this would involve a play upon words. In relation to charges of completed offences, "believing" refers to near-certain and correct knowledge (6.3). But in relation to a charge of attempting to handle stolen goods that are in fact not stolen, we wish to make it bear the different meaning of positive but mistaken belief. The courts will probably refuse to attach any significance to this subtle change of meaning. It is simply a fortunate accident that the offence of handling is drafted in terms that prevent difficulty on a charge of attempting the impossible.

15–047

There may be a slight hitch with a charge of, say, attempting to possess articles in the mistaken belief that they were explosives, where the substantive charge is of knowingly possessing explosives (the substantive charge in this case not allowing the alternative of belief). If the charge of attempt said: "attempted to possess articles knowing them to be explosives," the charge would not be made out, on a strict interpretation, because you cannot know what is not so. If it said: "attempted to possess articles believing them to be explosives," the objection might be advanced that since there is no offence of possessing articles believing them to be explosives (as opposed to knowing them to be explosives) the charge would not state an attempt to commit an offence known to law. It should be held,

---

[125] *Id.* at 60.

however, that in the case of an attempt the word "knowing" can properly be transposed into "believing," since it is a convention of our language that the word "know" cannot be applied to a mistaken belief.

15–048 **Could a man be convicted of attempted rape for trying to have sexual intercourse with a woman who he mistakenly believed was not consenting?** Yes, if it his purpose to have intercourse without her consent.[126] That seems odd since he would not commit rape if he had actually had intercourse. You are right, but that is why he is charged with attempted rape. Since it is his purpose to rape a woman, it is neither here nor there that on this occasion rape was impossible because consent would have been given. If he in fact had consensual intercourse under the belief that he was having non-consensual intercourse, the same would apply. It is not the attempt that was impossible, but the completed offence. It was impossible for him to consummate his criminality on this occasion because the victim was consenting; but rape is an offence that he could have committed if the facts had been as he believed.

15–049 **So Bluebeard would be guilty of an attempt to murder if he gave his helpmate a glass of water to drink, believing it to be a lethal dose of poison?** Yes. It is possible to commit the crime of murder by giving another a sufficient dose of the right poison. If the facts had been as Bluebeard believed, he would have consummated his murderous act. His mistake of fact meant that it was only possible for him to attempt murder.[127]

15–050 **Suppose D thinks he has actually committed a crime? He stabs a corpse thinking it is still alive, and thinks he has killed it.** He is still guilty of an attempt. Again, if the facts had been as D believed, it would have been *possible* for D to consummate his intended crime, murder.

15–051 **Is there a difference between attempting the possible and the "inherently" impossible?** A careful distinction needs to be made between the "possible" (that is, would have been possible if the facts had been as D believed) and the "inherently impossible." It is possible to steal from a pocket if it contains money; it is possible to kill a person if he is alive; it is possible to import drugs if what is imported is drugs. These crimes are not inherently impossible to commit in the sense that they can never be committed by anyone in any circumstances—they are only impossible in certain circumstances. *Per contra*, if "inherently insufficient means" are used to commit a given crime; it will be impossible for D or anyone else to consummate that crime with those means regardless of the circumstances.

Suppose D wants to take revenge on an airline because it lost his luggage. In order to do this, he attempts to shoot down one of its jumbo jets with the aim of destroying the plane and killing all those on board. Does he attempt to commit murder and criminal damage? Let us assume that he uses an air rifle to shoot down the aircraft which is 35,000 feet above. It is inherently impossible for D to

---

[126] Cf. *Police Service for Northern Ireland v. MacRitchie* [2009] N.I. 84.
[127] Cf. *R. v. White* [1910] 2 K.B. 124.

achieve his criminal aim with his chosen method. An air rifle cannot hit a target 35,000 feet away, and even it if could, its projectile would not have sufficient velocity to bring down a jumbo jet. (If you want and even more unassailable example, assume he uses the same method in an attempt to bring down the International Space Station, with an intent to kill its visiting expedition crew).[128]

Take another example. D is a disgruntled voter who is fed up with the Labour party, because it left Britain in financial ruin and sold its gold reserves. Consequently, he tries to assassinate all its members by using a voodoo doll. V believes that if he puts a pin in the heart of the voodoo doll that this will cause all the members of the party to suffer heart failure. Again, the method used is futile. It is inherently impossible to kill another human being by merely pinning a voodoo doll.[129]

The crimes attempted in the above hypotheticals do exist and it would be possible to consummate those crimes (murder, criminal damage and so on), if the right means were used. It is possible to commit murder and criminal damage, but not by using the means used by D. D's criminal ends are inherently unachievable, since he cannot succeed by using "the acts" that he has used (that is, the firing of the air rifle and the pinning of the voodoo doll).

Are you telling me that if D uses a gun which only has a range of one mile to kill a person who is two miles away he will be exempt from liability? No, because his goal is remotely achievable. The "inherent impossibility" defence should only apply in exceptional circumstances. Inherent impossibility refers to absolute impossibility. If the means used make the end remotely achievable, then D should be held liable for an attempt. Anything less might allow culpable and dangerous offenders to evade justice. Your gunman might only have a one-in-a-thousand chance of killing his target (if his gun only has a range of one mile), but his chosen means do not make his criminal end inherently unachievable. **15–052**

So when will my witch be liable for trying to cast a death spell? Assuming your witch is not insane,[130] she is probably exempt from liability simply because her actions do not get far past the "thought crime" stage, because her act (casting a spell) is not even mere preparation. Her actions have no relevance to the crime she is trying to achieve; she might as well go and boil her kettle to make a cup of tea as that would be just as effective for achieving her end—that is, totally ineffective! Similarly, if your witch believes that she can bring down the International Space Station with a water pistol, she does not do acts that go **15–053**

---

[128] It would be inherently impossible for him to shoot down the space station; he would not be able to see it with his naked eye, nor could a pellet from an air rifle reach it let alone bring it down.

[129] It has never happened, and it would be extremely unlikely, but D might use a voodoo doll to cause a superstitious person to die of fright (see 8.12). D would have to target a particular victim, and the victim would have to be aware of the curse if a causal connexion were to be established. In primitive societies where beliefs in magic might be the norm cursing could have a powerful psychological impact. See Glanville Williams, *Criminal Law: The General Part*, (London: Stevens & Sons, 1953) at 502.

[130] A person might believe in these methods because she is suffering from mental illness, but in some cases the user of such methods will be sane and thus will not be able to invoke the insanity defence.

beyond the mere thought crime or preparation stage. (Such acts are not even preparation, as they do not do anything to prepare her for achieving her criminal end.)

The courts recognized this long ago. In *Attorney-General v. Sillem*, Pollock C.B.[131] said, *obiter*:

> "If a statute simply made it a felony to attempt to kill any human being, or to conspire to do so, an attempt by means of witchcraft, or a conspiracy to kill by means of charms and incantations, would not be an offence within such a statute. The poverty of language compels one to say 'an attempt to kill by means of witchcraft, but such an attempt is really no attempt at all to kill. It is true the sin or wickedness may be as great as an attempt or conspiracy by competent means; but human laws are made, not to punish sin, but to prevent crime and mischief."

Inherent impossibility provides a defence—or it at least negatives the *actus reus* requirement, since attempts require acts that are more than mere preparation. If a robber standing outside the front of a post office waiting to enter is "not on the job proper,"[132] then, the person who uses a water pistol to try to bring down the International Space Station certainly isn't.

15–054   Nevertheless, when a person tries to steal from an empty pocket his act of dipping his hand in the pocket is more than mere preparation given the putative facts: it is a complete attempt. Similarly, if a man rapes a corpse mistakenly thinking it is a living woman he completes his attempt, he does acts which are more than mere preparation. His acts would have been enough to consummate the crime if the facts had been as he believed.[133] (D is liable because he got beyond the mere preparation stage, and since it would have been "possible" for him to consummate his crime if the facts had been as he believed.) *Per contra*, in the inherent impossibility scenario, D believes the impossible, *not the putatively possible*. No reasonable person would believe his chosen means were useful for achieving his chosen crime.[134] There is a difference between attempting what would have been possible if the facts had been as D had believed, and attempting what is impossible regardless of belief. In the inherent impossibility case, D believes in something that can never happen in the way he thinks it can.

There is also the issue of whether it is appropriate to punish these types of innocuous attempts. Plenty of ink has been spilt on this issue.[135] Commentators

---

[131]   (1863) 159 E.R. 178 at 222.

[132]   Cf. *R. v. Campbell* (1991) 93 Cr. App. R. 350; *Mason v. D.P.P.* [2010] R.T.R. 11.

[133]   Cf. the shocking facts in *United States v. Thomas*, 32 C.M.R. 278 (1962), where a corpse was raped.

[134]   The defence of inherent impossibility is recognized in the U.S. Professor Hall suggests that the question is: "What seems defensible is not the 'reasonable man's expectation in particular cases, but the 'reasonable man's' expectation (informed by expert opinion in certain cases) in all cases of that type." Jerome Hall, *General Principles of Criminal Law*, (Indianapolis: Bobbs-Merrill, 2nd edn. 1960) at 598. So if a reasonable person concluded that the chosen means meant that it was absolutely impossible for D to achieve his criminal end, he should have a defence.

[135]   For a detailed discussion of the pros and cons of criminalizing inherently impossible attempts, see Peter Westen, "Impossibility Attempts: A Speculative Thesis," (2008) 5 *Ohio St. J. Crim. L.* 523 at 544; Kevin Cole, "The Voodoo We Do: Harm, Impossibility, and the Reductionist Impulse," (1994) 5 *J. Contemp. Legal Issues* 31; John Hasnas, "Once More unto the Breach: The Inherent Liberalism of the Criminal Law and Liability for Attempting the Impossible," (2003) 54 *Hastings L.J.* 1; Kenneth

have debated whether punishment can deter[136] the sane who use such fanciful methods. Obviously, if the sane sorcière believes she is committing a crime by using a voodoo doll, then she could be deterred with the threat of punishment as much as the next criminal. Retributively speaking, nothing would be gained by punishing those who try to use inherently non-dangerous and ineffective methods. The law might as well be used to criminalize thought crimes, if it is going to be extended to such remote and fanciful attempts. Some commentators have argued that if we do not deter these types of fanciful attempts, that the attempter might try more effective means next time, such as poison, a gun, or a high powered missile rather than a voodoo doll or a water pistol.[137] Nevertheless, the better argument is that if a person's actual wrongdoing (pinning the voodoo doll) is innocuous *per se*, then there is nothing to be gained by punishing her for what she might do in the future.[138] If she decides to attempt murder with a gun next time, then punish her for that independent act of wrongdoing when she does it!

15.7.   ATTEMPTS AND ACCESSORIES

A person may be an accessory to an attempt.[139]   **15–055**
Take for example the case where D encourages X to commit a crime:

- D is guilty, at the moment of encouragement.[140] (And if, as would be usual, D and X act by arrangement together, both are guilty of conspiracy to commit the crime.)
- When X attempts to commit the crime, D becomes an accessory to the attempt.
- When the attempt succeeds, D becomes accessory to the crime.

D's liability as accessory at the second stage presupposes three things:

1.   That an act of attempt was committed.
2.   That the attempt was encouraged (or assisted) by D.

W. Simons, "Mistake and Impossibility, Law and Fact, and Culpability: A Speculative Essay," (1991) 81 *J. Crim. L. & Criminology* 447 (1991); Bebhinn Donnelly, "Possibility, Impossibility and Extraordinariness in Attempts," (2010) 23 *Can. J. L. & Jurisprudence* 47.

[136] Steven Shavell, "Deterrence and the Punishment of Attempts," (1990) 19 *J. Legal Stud.* 435; cf. David D Friedman, "Impossibility, Subjective Probability, and Punishment for Attempts," (1991) 20 *J. Legal Stud.* 179. (Friedman is right, if these folks are rational they can be deterred, but that does not explain why it is fair in retributive terms to punish them.) Shavell, to some extent, presents a fairly convincing case apropos the disutility of punishing such conduct.

[137] *Ibid.*

[138] On the inappropriateness of punishing people for what they might do next time, see Dennis J. Baker, "Punishment Without a Crime: Is Preventive Detention Reconcilable with Justice?" (2009) 34 *Austl. J. Leg. Phil.* 120.

[139] *R. v. Dunnington* [1984] 1 Q.B. 472. See more generally, John C. Smith, "Secondary Participation and Inchoate Offences," in C. Tapper (ed.) *Crime, Proof and Punishment*, (London: Butterworths, 1981); J.C. Smith, "Criminal Liability of Accessories: Law and Law Reform" (1997) 113 *L.Q.R.* 453.

[140] Section 44 of the *Serious Crime Act 2007*.

3.   That D intended the crime be committed, or at any rate knew that its commission was a "real possibility."[141]

As to (1), if X has not reached the stage of attempt, D's encouragement or effort to assist does not make him a party to an attempt, because there is no attempt by the contemplated perpetrator yet.[142]

To put the matter in a nutshell, the law under section 8 of the *Accessories and Abettors Act 1861* is that one can be accessory to an attempt when there is an attempt, but one cannot attempt to commit a crime as accessory—one cannot attempt to abet. To attempt means to attempt to perpetrate a crime, not to attempt to abet it. If somebody does attempt to perpetrate the crime, then others can be guilty of abetting the attempt, but that is a different matter. However, one can be charged with an "independent offence" under sections 44-46 of the *Serious Crime Act 2007*, because those sections criminalize attempts to assist and encourage as well as actual assistance and encouragement.

15–056   **If a person can conspire to commit an offence as accessory, I don't see why he can't attempt it as accessory.**   The reason is that conspiracy as a crime is not limited by the beyond-preparation doctrine, as attempt is. It would be strange if a person could be guilty of attempting a crime as accessory when the intended perpetrator has not reached the stage of attempt. Suppose that X asks D for the loan of a knife, saying that he wants to kill V. D lends him the knife, but X does not use it or try to use it. X has not attempted to commit murder, and the same principle that exempts X from liability for attempt (namely, that the stage of attempt has not been reached) protects D also.

Reverting to rule 3 above, this is important in respect of police informers. If such an informer has infiltrated a gang and assisted them in attempting a crime, intending that they shall be frustrated by the arrival of the police, the informer is not an accessory to attempt, any more than he will be accessory to the full offence if (contrary to his plan) it is carried out. Just as the perpetrator of an attempt must intend to bring about the crime in view, and not merely go through the motions of an attempt, so must his assister.

It logically follows that if D2 hands D1 some liquid which he falsely says is poison, and encourages him to put it into V's coffee for the purpose (in D1's mind) of killing V, and D1 does so, D1 is guilty as perpetrator of an attempt to murder, but D2 is not an accessory. The intention to murder was that of D1 alone. If D2 were accessory to the attempt, the police informer discussed in the previous paragraph would also be an accessory, which would be absurd. The difference between the police informer and the practical joker is that the informer is acting in the public interest while the joker is a mischief-maker, but this is only a difference in their motivation, not in their intention.

---

[141] *R. v. Bryce* [2004] 2 Cr. App. R. 35.

[142] He could be liable for an offence of assisting or encouraging contrary to sections 44-46 of the *Serious Crime Act 2007*. See generally Dennis J. Baker, "Complicity, Proportionality and the Serious Crime Act," (2011) 14(3) *New Crim. L. Rev.* 403.

CHAPTER 16

CONSPIRACY

"Open-ey'd Conspiracy
His time doth take."

The Tempest II. i.

16.1. CONSPIRACY AND ITS OBJECTS

Conspiracy, the most complex of the inchoate offences at common law, may seem **16–001** somewhat arbitrary. Conspiracy allows the police to intervene before the conspirators manage to consummate their planned crime, but it also allows the police to pounce before the conspirators take any physical steps towards putting their criminal plans into action. If the mere intention of one person to commit a crime is not criminal, why should the agreement of two people to do it make it criminal? The only possible reply is that the law (or, if you prefer, the establishment) is fearful of numbers, and that the act of agreeing to offend is regarded as such a decisive step as to justify its own criminal sanction.[1]

It is true that certain crimes are more likely to succeed if more than one person is involved. For instance, a group of robbers might take different roles (that is, one might take on the role of gunman, another might act as getaway driver, another might act as lookout and so on) to increase their chance of succeeding. The lone robber's robbery has less chance of succeeding not only because he does not have the moral support of a group,[2] but because he does not have a lookout, a getaway driver and so on. Obviously, organized crime relies on many players working in different capacities to achieve some criminal goal. It would be difficult if not impossible for a lone operator to effectively carry out a large scale terrorist attack, grand fraud, money laundering, tax evasion, narcotics trade and

---

[1] Here, as generally in law, "sanction" means punishment. See further on the history and justification of (or reasons against) the law of conspiracy Francis B. Sayre, "Criminal Conspiracy," (1922) 35 *Harv. L. Rev.* 393; Percy Winfield, "Early History of Criminal Conspiracy," (1920) 36 *L.Q. Rev.* 240; Benjamin F. Pollack, "Common Law Conspiracy," (1947) 35 *Geo. L. J.* 328; Robert S. Wright, *The Law of Criminal Conspiracies and Agreements*, (London: Butterworths, 1873); James W. Bryan, *The Development of the English Law of Conspiracy*, (Baltimore: The Johns Hopkins Press, 1909); Ian H. Dennis, "The Rationale of Criminal Conspiracy," (1977) 93 *L.Q.R.* 39.

[2] The U.S. Supreme Court uses the "group offending" concept to support a "*doubly* remote harm" justification for criminalizing conspiracy. It argues that conspiratorial offending has a tendency to lead to other offending that is unrelated to the original plan. See *U.S. v. Jimenez Recio*, 537 U.S. 270 (2003). But this rationale for criminalizing conspiracy has to be rejected, because it would punish people *not* for what they have agreed to do, but for what they might (agree) do. See generally, Dennis J. Baker, "The Moral Limits of Criminalizing Remote Harms," (2007) 10 *New Crim. L. Rev.* 370.

so on. Is there any great benefit in punishing group "agreement" *per se*?[3] As for the "danger in numbers" argument, an alternative to conspiracy would be to punish those who offend collectively more severely when they consummate their planned crime. A person who consummates a robbery as a part of a group effort might be deterred from doing so, if the sentence were (proportionately)[4] greater for those who act collectively.

16–002   At common law there could be a criminal conspiracy to commit various non-criminal acts, such as a tort, and even acts that were not legally wrong at all but were thought by judges to be sufficiently improper to be repressed by the law of conspiracy. So, even where it was not legally wrong for one person to do the act, it could be a crime for two persons to agree to do it. After prolonged argument this doctrine was expunged from the law by the *Criminal Law Act 1977*; apart from two partial survivals which were intended to be temporary, but are still with us:

1.   Conspiracy to defraud at common law is preserved. It was meant to be abrogated with the enactment of the *Fraud Act 2006*, but it remains in force. (Conspiracy to defraud *infra*, see 34.9).

2.   There are vague common law offences of conduct tending to corrupt public morals or outrage public decency. Such acts are probably punishable even when committed by individuals,[5] in which case a conspiracy to do them is now a statutory conspiracy. To the extent that they are only punishable as conspiracies, they are excluded from the *Act*, so that such conspiracies remain governed by the common law; but again it is proposed to supersede these common law offences in due course by more specific statutory offences. (Perhaps, the most needed offence is one that criminalizes gross privacy violations, since the digital age has made it particularly easy for rogues to covertly record people in locker rooms and so on.)[6] Whether they

---

[3] Johnson provides some fairly powerful arguments for decriminalizing conspiracy. See Phillip E. Johnson, "The Unnecessary Crime of Conspiracy," (1973) 61 *Cal. L. Rev.* 1137. See also Abraham S. Goldstein, "Conspiracy to Defraud the United States," (1959) 68 *Yale L.J.* 405.

[4] The "danger in numbers" rationale for greater punishment would have to be supported with empirical evidence. But if it could be shown the threat of harm was greater, then a slightly higher sentence for the individual players would be justified.

[5] Outraging public decency has been recognized as an offence *per se*. See *R. v. Gibson* [1990] 2 Q.B. 619; *R. v. Hamilton* [2008] Q.B. 224; *HKSAR v. Chan Sek Ming* [2006] H.K.E.C. 1769. Cf. *Knuller (Publishing, Printing and Promotions) Ltd. v. D.P.P.* [1973] A.C. 435. Those who argue that such conduct should be criminalized should demonstrate that the given instance of "corruption" of public morality is objectively harmful. Long ago Bray C.J. said: "I cannot accept the argument that Parliament by the *Police Offences Act 1953* (S.A.) meant to stereotype for all time the standard of sexual morality at that prevalent in 1953. I think, on the contrary, that what is set is a standard intended to vary with the manners and customs of the age and that, just as conduct which might have been held not to be negligent in 1873 may well be held to be negligent in 1973, so what would have been regarded as having a tendency to deprave or corrupt in 1873, or even in 1953, need not necessarily be so regarded in 1973." *Popow v. Samuels* (1973) 4 S.A.S.R. 594 at 609. See further Dennis J. Baker "The Impossibility of a Critically Objective Criminal Law," (2011) 56(2) *McGill L. J.* 349.

[6] See generally, Dennis J. Baker, "The Sense and Nonsense of Criminalising Transfers of Obscene Material," (2008) 26 *Sing. L. Rev.* 126. The *Sexual Offences Act 2003* does criminalize some types of voyeurism. Even though the motivation of some offenders will be commercial (they aim to cash in on

will be superseded in this way, having regard to the limited powers of the Law Commission and the inanition that generally attends efforts at law reform, remains to be seen. In any case these matters lie outside the scope of the present work.

16.2. THE DEFINITION OF STATUTORY

Except as just stated, the common law of conspiracy has been superseded by the **16–003** *Criminal Law Act 1977*. The rest of this chapter is concerned with conspiracies under the *Act*. For reasons of space, it does not, in general, deal with the common law, except where this is the same as statutory conspiracy.

Section 1(1) of the *Criminal Law Act 1977*[7] provides the central definition of the statutory offence:

> "(1) If a person agrees with any other person or persons that a course of conduct shall be pursued which, if the agreement is carried out in accordance with their intentions, either—
>   (a) will necessarily amount to or involve the commission of any offence[8] or offences by one or more of the parties to the agreement, or
>   (b) would do so but for the existence of facts which render the commission of the offence or any of the offences impossible, he is guilty of conspiracy to commit the offence or offences in question."

This definition substantially repeats the common law, except that:

- It is more restricted than the common law in requiring the object of the conspiracy to be criminal.
- It is wider than the common law in not requiring the object of the conspiracy to be possible.
- It creates doubts as to the mental element which did not exist at common law.

The conspiracy may be to commit a mere summary offence, though in that case a prosecution requires the consent of the Director of Public Prosecutions.[9] Trial must be by jury, since the conspiracy charge is thought to raise too many difficulties of substance and procedure for magistrates to try. (A more solid reason is that conspiracy may lie so much in the mind and so little in the outward manifestation of illegality that the safeguard of the jury trial is thought essential.)

---

the black market in pornography rather than to seek sexual gratification), they would be caught by section 67(3) of the *Sexual Offences Act 2003*, since they produce the material for a third party's sexual gratification. But, if a computer repairman finds nude images of his client on his client's computer and uploads them on the World Wide Web, he would not be caught by the *Sexual Offences Act 2003*. Furthermore, it is also difficult to see how he would outrage public decency or corrupt morality, if such images are widely available on the Web! Cf. *R. v. Hamilton* [2008] Q.B. 224.

[7] *Criminal Law Act 1977* as substituted by the *Criminal Attempts Act 1981*.

[8] An offence triable in England and Wales: section 1(4).

[9] Section 4(1) of the *Criminal Law Act 1977*. If the summary offence can be prosecuted only with the consent of the Attorney-General, a conspiracy charge requires his consent in place of the D.P.P.: section 4(2).

16.3. THE AGREEMENT

16–004   There must be a common agreement to which all of the alleged conspirators are privy. Any agreement to commit the crime, communicated to the other party or parties,[10] constitutes a conspiracy.[11] The essence of criminal conspiracy is the agreement.[12] The focus has to be on the agreement, not merely on the fact that there was more than one offender. The fact that there were two or more offenders is totally irrelevant, unless those offenders shared a criminal goal which they mutually intended to bring about.

Agreement requires more than mere knowledge of another's criminal plan. Suppose X is in his gun shop when two potential customers (D1 and D2) walk in and ask for a large hunting gun. Suppose also that X asks, "Are you going to do a spot of hunting?" and is told, "No, we are going to rob Y-bank." If X sells the gun believing that D1 and D2 might rob Y-bank he may become an accessory to the robbery if the robbery is consummated or attempted, or may be charged with an offence under sections 44 or 45 of the *Serious Crime Act 2007* if it is not, but the fact that he knows about D1's and D2's criminal plans does not mean he intends to join their conspiracy. He would only become a conspirator if he decided to join their conspiracy by agreeing with them that the robbery should be brought about. He would have to share D1's and D2's criminal goal and also intend that it be carried out. Since he is an uninterested third party, he could hardly be said to be a part of the conspiracy. X does not work in unison with the robbers. D1's and D2's mutual goal is to rob Y-bank and they both intend to carry out the robbery, whereas X's only goal is to make a profit by selling a gun.

Similarly, a person does not become a party to a conspiracy merely by associating with the wrong people, there has to be a meeting of the minds. If X is out on the town with his fellow gang members who (unbeknown to X) have agreed in advance that they will rob a convenience store, X does not become a party to that conspiracy merely because he is a gang member who is present when the store is robbed. He would have to agree to the plan and intend that the robbery be carried out.

16–005   **Isn't there a danger that the law of conspiracy may be used to punish some nebulous agreement that the schemers might never have had the courage or ability to carry out?**   Some prosecutorial discretion may be exercised in respect of vague conspiracies. But the only limitation upon the law is that there must be a

---

[10] *R. v. Scott* (1979) 68 Cr. App. R. 164.

[11] It might possibly be held, notwithstanding the statutory definition, that a conspirator must either encourage (or otherwise incite) the others or undertake (expressly or impliedly) to assist. If A and B tell C that they have decided to commit a crime, and C indicates general approval without having any task assigned to him or inciting them, he could hardly be said to be a party to an agreement that the crime shall be committed. Of course, if C is to receive part of the proceeds that would be authorization, and therefore incitement.

[12] *D.P.P. v. Nock* [1978] 3 W.L.R. 57 at 66.

concluded agreement to commit the wrong, not just the negotiation for such an agreement.[13] An agreement to commit the wrong on a condition, namely, if the opportunity shall arise, is sufficient.[14]

What if A thinks he is agreeing to do crime Y with B, but B thinks he is agreeing to do crime X with A?   In *R. v. Barnard*[15] A and B agreed to carry out a property offence, but A thought he was agreeing to commit robbery, while B thought he was agreeing to commit theft. Normally this will mean that there was no agreement.[16] However, in cases where a lesser offence is clearly included in a greater the courts are likely to hold there was an agreement to carry out the lesser. In *R. v. Barnard* the defendant only agreed to commit theft, so he could not be held liable for agreeing to commit the more serious offence of robbery. If he had agreed to commit robbery he could have been held liable for conspiracy to commit theft, even if the other parties only had robbery in mind. This would not create any injustice, as one cannot agree to commit robbery without agreeing to commit theft. Since robbery is theft with the additional ingredient of the use or threat of force, a "person convicted of robbery must, by statutory definition, also be guilty of theft."[17] The greater covers the lesser, if all the parties intend to carry out the lesser offence.[18] The lesser cannot cover the greater. A person cannot be held strictly liable for conspiring to commit a greater offence than he agreed to commit, merely because his co-conspirators had it in mind. Robbery is not theft, so it would have to be shown that the defendant, like is co-conspirators, intended to carry out a robbery.

16–006

Conspiracies are hatched in private. How can they be proved?   It is true that only rarely it is possible to establish a conspiracy by direct evidence. Usually, both the fact of the conspiracy and its objects have to be inferred from conduct.

16–007

A conspiracy charge can be embarrassing to the defence because of its vagueness, but this can be avoided if the prosecutor includes in the indictment particulars of the acts ("overt acts") alleged against each defendant sufficient to

---

[13] *R. v. Walker* [1962] Crim. L.R. 458; *R. v Mills* [1963] 1 Q.B. 522; *R. v. O'Brien* (1974) 59 Cr. App. R. 222; *R. v. El-Ghazal* [1986] Crim. L.R. 52.

[14] *R. v. King* [1966] Crim. L.R. 280.

[15] (1980) 70 Cr. App. R. 28.

[16] *R. v. Siracusa* (1990) 90 Cr. App. R. 340, where it was held that "a conspiracy to import heroin could not be proved by an agreement to import cannabis.")

[17] *R. v. Guy* (1990) 93 Cr. App. R. 108.

[18] There will not be many offences where a lesser offence is clearly included in some greater offence. But at a stretch the doctrine could be applied to other offence such as drug offences. Drug offences are graded in seriousness according to the Class (dangerousness) of the drug that is being imported or possessed and so on. Therefore, no great injustice is caused when D1 is convicted of conspiring to important a Class C drug (a less dangerous drug—and less serious offence) if he thought he was agreeing to import a Class A drug (a more dangerous drug—and more serious offence). See *R. v. Taylor* [2001] EWCA Crim. 1044 (where D agreed to import Class B drugs, but not Class A drugs; he was only convicted of conspiracy to import Class B drugs). See also *R. v. Broad* [1997] Crim. L.R. 666 (where D1 and D2 both agreed to import a Class A drug, but where one thought it was heroin and the other cocaine—clearly nothing turns on this since they both intended to commit the crime that they did in fact commit).

enable him to know as precisely as possible what is being alleged against him.[19] Particulars are important when the conspiracy is inferred from conduct. If the conspiracy charge is left vague, as unhappily it may be, each defendant will have to pick out the material allegations against him from the statements taken for the purposes of trial, which may be voluminous.

The overt acts in a conspiracy charge may be acts signifying agreement, acts preparatory to offences, or the offences themselves. Such acts are, of course, only evidence of the agreement. So if three people conspire to steal, one, A, agreeing only to a non-violent theft while B and C secretly agree between themselves to use force, and in fact commit robbery with violence, the commission of this robbery by B and C does not make A guilty of conspiracy to rob.[20]

16–008   **If a band of crooks have committed offences, can they be charged in the same indictment both with the offences and with conspiracy?**   Yes.

16–009   **And the jury can convict both of the main offences and of the conspiracy?**   Yes. Conspiracy does not merge in the consummated crime.[21]

16–010   **How do you settle the limits of a conspiracy? If terrorists foregather and plan to cause explosions in general, following this with more detailed plans to cause particular explosions, are these charged as one conspiracy or as many conspiracies?**   The prosecution are not allowed to charge two conspiracies in one count. But they may charge a general conspiracy, and in support of that charge may adduce evidence of specific offences, such as (in the case instanced) an explosion in Manchester and one in London. These could have been charged as separate conspiracies,[22] but that does not affect the validity of the general count.[23]

However, if all that the prosecution can prove is that the defendants D1 and D2 conspired in respect of the Manchester bomb, and that D3 and D4 conspired in respect of the London bomb, all four defendants cannot be convicted on the one count for the two conspiracies. A single count can charge only one offence, though the count may be against two defendants. The best that the prosecution can do *if* they have included only the general count is to ask for a conviction of, say, D3 and D4 on the general count, while accepting an acquittal of D1 and D2.

---

[19] *R. v. Hancock* [1996] 2 Cr. App. R. 554; *R. v. Cushnie* [2005] EWCA Crim. 962; *R. v. Landy* [1981] 1 W.L.R. 355.

[20] See [1980] Crim. L.R. 236, commenting on *R. v. Barnard* (1980) 70 Cr. App. R. 28, where there are misleading *dicta* on this point. The decision in *R. v. Barnard* is to be explained by the fact that A either had never conspired or had withdrawn from the conspiracy before it was carried out. Cf. *R. v. Crothers* [2001] N.I. 55.

[21] In the event of such double conviction, there should be no more than a nominal sentence on the conspiracy count. *D.P.P. v. Stewart* [1983] 2 A.C. 91.

[22] *R. v. Coughlan* (1976) 63 Cr. App. R. 33; *R. v. Cooke* [1986] A.C. 909 at 931; *R. v. Hobbs* [2002] 2 Cr. App. R. 324 at 330-331.

[23] *R. v. Greenfield* [1973] 1 W.L.R. 1151; *R. v. Mintern* (2004) 148 S.J.L.B. 146; *R. v. Mirza* [2007] EWCA Crim 1125; cf. *R. v. Marchese* [2009] 1 W.L.R. 992.

Or conversely. This is a strange result, because it allows the prosecution in effect to choose which of the defendants are to be convicted, even though all have been shown to be guilty.[24]

Can conspirators adhere to the pact at different times? Certainly. Any **16–011** number of people may join a conspiracy, and may join at different times.[25] The conspirators can be convicted even though the wrong plotted was to be committed only in the distant future, and though the plot immediately started to fall apart at the seams.[26] The act of conspiracy is itself regarded as a sufficient step in fulfilling the plan to be punishable.[27] Conspirators may, for example, be enrolled in a chain—A enrolling B, B enrolling C, and so on; and all will be members of a single conspiracy if they so intend, even though each member knows only the person who enrolled him and the person who he enrols. Similarly, there may be a kind of umbrella-stroke enrolment,[28] a single person at the centre doing the enrolling and all the other members being unknown to each other by name, though they know that there are to be other members.

Provided that the mutual intent is present, therefore, persons may be members of a single conspiracy even though each is ignorant of the identity of many others. But if A intends to conspire solely with B, and C intends to conspire solely with B, there can be no common conspiracy involving A and C, since neither intends to conspire with anyone but B. The chain is broken. The two conspiracies involving different people cannot be charged in the same indictment.

Furthermore, the fact that the two conspiracies have a common member, B, does not make them one conspiracy.

As an example, suppose that an accountant proposes to each of a number of **16–012** clients a particular means of defrauding the Revenue, and each client accepts the proposal. There is then a conspiracy between the accountant and each client separately, but not between the clients; and it makes no difference that the fraud is similar in all cases. Even if the clients know that others are committing the same fraud, that does not make them conspirators with each other. The purpose of the various parties must be not merely *similar* but *agreed*.[29]

There would only be a common intent in such cases if each member shared the end of seeing each other succeed in the fraud. This was clearly not the case in *R. v. Griffiths*, since the individual members only intended to defraud the Revenue

---

[24] A general count for conspiracy will be struck out if the court itself and the statements show that there was no single conspiracy between the defendants but only a number of separate conspiracies: *per curiam* in *R. v. Greenfield* [1973] 1 W.L.R. 1151 at 1156.

[25] *R. v. Murphy* (1837) 173 E.R. 502; *R. v. Sweetland* (1958) 42 Cr. App. R. 62 at 67; cf. *D.P.P. v. Doot* [1973] A.C. 807.

[26] And though the defendant immediately afterwards withdrew from the conspiracy. See Martin Wasik, "Abandoning Criminal Intent," [1980] Crim. L.R. 785 at 788 n. 21.

[27] *R. v. Hobbs* [2002] 2 Cr. App. R. 22; *R. v. Bolton* (1992) 94 Cr. App. R. 74.

[28] Usually called a "cartwheel" conspiracy. Some commentators refer to the "rim" of the wheel being formed as a way of illustrating a common intent and design between the individual spokes (members). It is a way of saying that the individual spoke members are not only in agreement with the hub, but are all in agreement with each other and share a common goal. See *R. v. Ardalan* [1972] 1 W.L.R. 463 at 470.

[29] *R. v. Griffiths* [1966] 1 Q.B. 589. See also *R. v. Barnes* [2003] EWCA Crim. 2138; *R. v. Barratt* [1996] Crim. L.R. 495. Cf. *R. v. Meyrick* (1930) 21 Cr. App. R. 94.

for their own benefit and could not care less whether others succeeded in doing the same. The individual fraudsters did not share a single objective; rather they had their own individual objectives. Each person may have had the same type of objective when viewed individually, but there was no community of interest between those individuals. There individual agreements were independently formed.

16–013   **What if a plain-clothes police officer or his undercover agent, coming to know that some nefarious scheme is afoot, pretends to join it, in order to secure the conviction of the other parties? Is he guilty himself?**   Not if his intention is to frustrate the conspiracy. In the discussion of complicity it was suggested that a person should not be an accessory if he took part only with the purpose of preventing the commission of the offence. No such limitation is incorporated into the rules for conspiracy in the *Criminal Law Act 1977*. But if the police informant never intended the object of the conspiracy to be carried out, he cannot be a party to a conspiracy.[30] If the police informant is the only other party to the conspiracy, then no conspiracy is formed as there is no common intention (between him and the other party) that the object of the conspiracy be carried out. The same does not apply if the police informant intends the object of the conspiracy be carried out, as he might do if he is trying to entrap potential offenders. If he intends the object of the conspiracy be carried out he will be held to be one of the conspirators,[31] unless the courts let him out by holding that his mental reservation meant that he did not "really" agree. In *Chiu-Cheung v. The Queen*, Lord Griffiths said:[32]

> "In these circumstances it was argued that it would be wrong to treat the agent as having any criminal intent, and reliance was placed upon a passage in the speech of Lord Bridge in *R. v. Anderson* [1986] A.C. 27, 38-39.... There may be many cases in which undercover police officers or other law enforcement agents pretend to join a conspiracy in order to gain information about the plans of the criminals, with no intention of taking any part in the planned crime but rather with the intention of providing information that will frustrate it. It was to this situation that Lord Bridge was referring in *R. v. Anderson*. The crime of conspiracy requires an agreement between two or more persons to commit an unlawful act with the intention of carrying it out. It is the intention to carry out the crime that constitutes the necessary *mens rea* for the offence. As Lord Bridge pointed out, an undercover agent who has no intention of committing the crime lacks the necessary *mens rea* to be a conspirator."

It is expected that the Crown Prosecution Service will use its discretion appropriately when deciding whether to prosecute such offenders. The Law Commission has recommended that "the defence of acting reasonably provided for by section 50 of the *Serious Crime Act 2007* should be applied in its entirety to the offence of conspiracy."[33] It was thought important to have a wider defence

---

[30] *R. v. Anderson* [1986] A.C. 27, 38-39. See also *United States v. Dynar* [1997] 2 S.C.R. 462 at paras. 86-88.

[31] *Chiu-Cheung v. The Queen* [1995] 1 A.C. 111.

[32] [1995] 1 A.C. 111 at 117-119. Cf. *R. v. Edwards* [1991] Crim. L.R. 45.

[33] Law Commission, *Conspiracy and Attempts*, Report 318 (London: H.M.S.O., 2009) at 93-104. Cf. the discussion in *R. v. McPhillips* [1989] N.I. 360. In the United States, government agents participating in "sting" operations have long been exempt from conspiracy liability. See *U.S. v. Strickland*, 245 F.3d 368 (2001); *U.S. v. Hayes*, 775 F.2d 1279, 1283 (1985).

that would not only cover the police but also ordinary citizens who act to thwart crime. Such a reform would be welcome.

16.4. CONSPIRACY IN RELATION TO OTHER INCHOATE CRIMES

By statute, a person cannot be convicted of attempting to conspire (whether to commit a statutory conspiracy or to defraud).[34] The reason given is that it would push liability too far back, to a stage where there is no agreement to commit the offence. The reason is highly questionable, and it would seem that all or almost all cases of encouragement (or attempts to conspire) could be charged as encouragement to commit the crime under sections 44-46 of the *Serious Crime Act 2007*. The latter no doubt would catch most attempts to conspire. If D tries to encourage an undercover police officer to join with him in selling drugs he attempts to conspire, but also tries to encourage another to commit a crime contrary to section 44 of the *Serious Crime Act*.[35]

16–014

Intending accessories may be parties to a conspiracy, if they have a mutual intent that the object of the conspiracy be carried out. If D1, D2 and D3 conspire that D2 and D3 are to place a ladder against a building, so that D1 shall subsequently use the ladder to enter the building and steal, all three are guilty of conspiring to burgle (*i.e.* conspiring that a burglary shall be perpetrated by D1). The position is different if they merely conspire to be accessories.

Suppose D1 and D2 are in the pub when they overhear D3 saying that he is going to burgle house X. Let us assume house X belongs to D1's and D2's arch rival, Y. Even though they do not know D3 and do not communicate with him, they decide that it would be a good idea to make it easy for D3 to burgle Y's house, so they leave a ladder by the front of house X. When D3 gets to the house he loses confidence and decides not to do the burglary. Since D1 and D2 had no agreement with D3 they were not conspiring to commit burglary. At most they were conspiring to assist D3's crime. But since encouragement and assistance *per se* is not a crime[36] (at least not under the *Accessories and Abettors Act 1861*), they do not conspire to commit a crime and thus do not commit a statutory conspiracy. Complicity liability (under 8 of the *Accessories and Abettors Act 1861*) is derivative in that it only derives when the substantive offence is attempted[37] or consummated.

Obviously, however, a conspiracy to encourage or assist a person to commit a crime contrary to section 44 of the *Serious Crime Act 2007* would constitute a statutory conspiracy. Encouragement being itself a crime,[38] the conspiracy is to commit a crime. So if D1 and D2 agree to encourage assassin X to kill D1's arch rival, they conspire to commit an offence contrary to section 44 of the *Serious Crime Act 2007*. A conspiracy to encourage a person to commit a crime, either as

---

[34] Section 1(4) of the *Criminal Attempts Act 1981*.

[35] For some justifications for "double inchoate" criminalization, see generally, Ira P. Robbins, "Double Inchoate Crimes," (1989) 26 *Harv. J. on Legis.* 1. In England, however, the gaps have been adequately plugged by the *Serious Crime Act 2007*.

[36] *R. v. Kenning* [2009] Q.B. 221. But if Kenning had been charged under section 44 of the *Serious Crime Act 2007*, the position would have been different.

[37] *R. v. Dunnington* [1984] Q.B. 472.

[38] Section 44 of the *Serious Crime Act 2007*.

perpetrator or as accessory, is criminal. This offence is not "derivative" and thus is a crime regardless of whether the encouragement fails to influence the assassin to commit the assassination.

16.5. PROS AND CONS OF THE CONSPIRACY COUNT

16–015   Conspiracy charges used to be the bogey of the political left, because of their use against people who take part in industrial and political disorder.[39] But considerable changes have been made in the law, and at the present day the charges are neither so oppressive as their critics fear nor so efficacious as prosecutors seem to believe. The question mark that hangs over them is, in fact, whether they are worthwhile, having regard to the complexity they tend to add to the trial.

Although conspiracy is generally considered, and treated in the books, as an inchoate crime, in practice it is rarely prosecuted at the purely inchoate stage. Almost always some substantive crime has been committed in pursuance of it, for which all or most of the conspirators could be prosecuted as accomplices. As an inchoate crime, therefore, the law of conspiracy serves little social purpose.

16–016   **If a charge of conspiracy as an inchoate crime is of small use, isn't the same even more true of a charge of conspiracy when the crime has been committed? Why not charge the crime?**   As was mentioned before, the prosecution can charge both. They gain two minor advantages in adding a conspiracy count to a charge for consummated crime:

1.   In theory, and to some small extent in practice, adding the conspiracy count guards against the risk that the prosecution may fail to prove the consummated crime, while being able to prove the conspiracy. Difficulty might be caused if there were not a conspiracy count. It would add to the costs, and might look like harassment, to indict members of a gang for conspiracy after they have been acquitted of the substantive crime. But in fact the problem rarely arises: that a crime was committed is generally quite clear, and the only question is whether the defendant was a party to an agreement to commit it. Alternatively, if the substantive crime cannot be proved (as in a fraud case), the conspiracy charge generally falls also.

2.   At common law, conspiracy, like all other common law misdemeanours, was not subject to any maximum punishment. This rule was a target for the reformers, who argued that there was no reason why two people who committed a crime together should, by the addition of a conspiracy count, become liable to a higher sentence than the person who gave a solo performance. The *Criminal Law Act 1977* acknowledges the justice of the criticism to some extent, since it provides that conspiracy is subject to the

---

[39] See the radical, jaundiced, and somewhat flawed but interesting polemic by Robert Spicer, *Conspiracy: Law, Class and Society*, (London: Lawrence and Wishart, 1981). See also, Wes Wilson, "Political Use of Criminal Conspiracy," (1984) 42 *U. Toronto Fac. L. Rev.* 60; Jeffrey S. Kahana, "*Imperium in Imperio* and the Political Origins of the American Labour Conspiracy Doctrine," (2008) 30 *Law & Pol'y* 364.

same maximum term of imprisonment as the completed offence.[40] But the old anomaly is allowed to remain in one respect: a conspiracy to commit a summary offence is punishable (on indictment, of course) by an unlimited fine, whereas if the summary offence were actually committed the fine that could be imposed by a magistrates' court would be limited by statute.

At common law, charges of conspiracy provided the prosecution with an unfair trump, since by charging it the prosecution freed itself from the time-limit on prosecution[41] or the necessity for the consent of the Director of Public Prosecutions or other person. For statutory conspiracy, these rules are now altered by the *Criminal Law Act 1977*,[42] so that in these respects the advantages of adding a conspiracy charge disappear. Conspiracy counts are sometimes said to help the jury to understand the "overall criminality" of what the defendants have done;[43] but it may be doubted whether they can do any more in this respect than could be done by the specific counts, including, if necessary, representative counts. Conspiracy charges are sometimes thought to allow the Crown to adduce evidence that would otherwise be inadmissible, but again this may be strongly doubted.[44]

Counterbalancing the two advantages for the prosecution in including a conspiracy count are two disadvantages: **16–017**

1. If the evidence is that the offences were committed in concert and the jury convict of the offences but acquit of conspiracy, or *vice versa*, the conviction may be quashed for inconsistency with the acquittal.[45]
2. The addition of an unnecessary count increases the possibility of a mistake being made at the trial.

Quite apart from the above matters, there has long been an impression that the addition of a conspiracy count where the crimes in view are alleged to have been consummated is procedurally unfair to the defendants. Accordingly, the judge is required (by a practice direction[46]) to call upon the prosecution to justify the joinder, and if they fail to do so they will have to elect whether to proceed upon

---

[40] Section 3. On conviction of conspiracy to murder, the judge has a discretion as to sentence. Where several crimes are committed, the sentence for these crimes (if they are not part of the single transaction) can be cumulative, but on a charge of conspiracy to commit them the maximum imprisonment is for the longest term applicable to any of the crimes contemplated, for a cumulative term.

[41] *R. v. Simmonds* [1969] 1 Q.B. 685.

[42] Section 4(3), (4). The officer's consent must be specifically to a charge of conspiracy: *R. v. Pearce* (1981) 72 Cr. App. R. 295; *R. v. Keyes* [2000] 2 Cr. App. R. 181. But one anomaly remains: since time runs from the commission of the offence, a conspiracy charge is not subject to a time limit attaching to the offence where the offence is not committed. And conviction of conspiracy does not enable the court to make a forfeiture order as for the completed crime: *R. v. Cuthbertson* [1981] A.C. 470.

[43] *Per* James L.J. in *R. v. Jones* (1974) 59 Cr. App. R. 120 at 124.

[44] Glanville Williams, *Criminal Law: The General Part*, (London: Stevens & Sons, 2nd edn. 1961) at §218.

[45] *R. v. Sweetland* (1958) 42 Cr. App. R. 62.

[46] *Practice Direction (Crime: Conspiracy)* [1977] 1 W.L.R. 537; *R. v. Watts* (1995), *The Times*, (April 14).

the substantive or the conspiracy counts. In any case, now that the conspiracy count no longer enables the prescribed maximum term of imprisonment to be disregarded, the attractiveness of the count to the prosecution largely disappears.

Whether there is any real unfairness in a conspiracy count, as such, that could not be rectified by the sensible conduct of the trial, may be questioned.[47] Obviously it is desirable to confine trials to a relatively small number of defendants (the chief offenders), and to a reasonably narrow class of acts, whether a conspiracy count is added or not; otherwise the jury may become confused.

A defect in the present procedure is that when the jury return a verdict of guilty they are not asked whether they find all the defendants to have participated in all the overt acts alleged against them. Judges appear to assume that the verdict means this, but obviously it may not do so, so that considerable injustice is possible. It may be that there is only one really serious overt act alleged (planting a bomb in a crowded store, which failed to go off), and if the jury are not satisfied that a particular defendant agreed to that the finding ought to be known.

16.6. THE CRIMINAL PURPOSE

16–018 It will be remembered that section 1(1) of the *Criminal Law Act 1977* speaks of the purpose of the conspiracy as being to pursue "a course of conduct which, if the agreement is carried out in accordance with their intentions, either (*a*) will necessarily amount to or involve the commission of any offence or offences by one or more of the parties to the agreement ..." or (*b*) would do so but for impossibility.

The meaning of "necessarily" has been the subject of speculation. The word is unfortunate, because it gives the impression, wrongly, that the only plans that can amount to a statutory conspiracy are those that are either absolutely infallible or absolutely impossible. In reality, many gradations can be found between these extremes, where "the best laid schemes o' mice and men gang a-ley"[48] and yet are punishable in appropriate circumstances as conspiracies. The following hypothetical will illustrate the point.

D1 and D2 agree to snipe at V from the roof of a building, hoping to kill him. They think that he is or may be within range, but in fact he is out of range of the gun that they use. They are guilty of conspiracy to murder, it being immaterial that there are "facts [the positive fact that V is out of range, or negative fact that V is not within range—it does not matter how one words it] which render the commission of the offence impossible." (The singular in statutes includes the plural, and the plural the singular, unless the contrary intention appears.)[49]

16–019 Although these facts are clearly covered under (*b*), they might be slightly different. It might be uncertain whether V was out of range or not, in which case it may be moot whether a conspiracy can be found under (*a*). Even if V was within range, it would not be certain that the assassins would hit him. They might

---

[47] 128 N.L.J. 24.
[48] Robert Burns, *To A Mouse.*
[49] Section 6(c) of the *Interpretation Act 1978.*

shoot at him and miss. So (it may be argued) they will not "necessarily" kill him; so it is not a conspiracy within the section.

The argument has some attraction but of course the result would be absurd. The answer to it is that the "course of conduct" envisaged by the agreement means not only the physical acts of the conspirators but the intended result. In our hypothetical the intended "course of conduct" is not only shooting at V but killing him. When this "course of conduct" is "carried out in accordance with their intentions," it will necessarily be murder. (It is a mark of the defective wording of the *Act*, as it emerged from the parliamentary process, that such lengthy reasoning has to be set out in order to arrive at the common-sense conclusion. The defects in the wording were immediately pointed out by the commentators,[50] yet no relevant changes were made—except on the impossibility issue—when the subsection, originally in the *Criminal Law Act 1977*, was replaced by a new version in the *Criminal Attempts Act 1981*.)

Doesn't your argument mean that the word "necessarily" is otiose? Not necessarily! Donaldson L.J. (as he then was) gave the following illustration of how it is capable of having a practical effect:[51]   16–020

> "A and B agree to drive from London to Edinburgh in a time which can be achieved without exceeding the speed limits, but only if the traffic which they encounter is exceptionally light. Their agreement will not necessarily involve the commission of any offence, even if it is carried out in accordance with their intentions. ... Accordingly the agreement does not constitute the offence of the statutory conspiracy."

Well, suppose that A and B agree to export aluminium. There is emergency legislation in force making such export an offence, but it is quite possible that the legislation will be repealed by the time the export is to take place. Would Donaldson L.J. say that that is not a conspiracy? The courts would probably distinguish a case where the parties gamble on a change in the law, as in your instance. And the courts would probably require a substantial possibility that the agreement may be carried out lawfully.[52]   16–021

Then suppose that A and B agree to make a trespassory entry into a building in order to photocopy secret documents, and to shoot anyone who attempts to impede them. They expect to be able to do the job without interference, but there is a substantial possibility that they will have to shoot. Isn't that a conspiracy to wound? It appears so.[53] But it is difficult to distinguish your hypothetical from that put by Lord Justice Donaldson. Perhaps one can say that   16–022

---

[50] See Glanville Williams, *Textbook of Criminal Law*, (London: Stevens & Sons, 1st edn. 1978) at 355-356.

[51] *R. v. Reed* [1982] Crim. L.R. 819.

[52] *R. v. Buckingham* (1976) 63 Cr. App. R. 159; *Attorney-General's Reference (Nos.1 and 2 of 1979)* [1980] Q.B. 180. *R. v. Saik* [2007] 1 A.C. 18 at 32.

[53] In *R. v. Saik* [2007] 1 A.C. 18 at 61-62 Lord Brown said: "If two men agree to burgle a house but only if it is unoccupied or not alarmed they are clearly guilty of conspiracy to burgle notwithstanding that their intention may be thwarted. And if they take a weapon albeit to be used only if strictly necessary they are, the better view suggests, guilty also of conspiracy to wound. Consistently with this approach convictions were upheld (a) of conspiracy to aid and abet suicide where it was agreed that the accused would visit individuals contemplating suicide and either seek to discourage them or

the offence of wounding will be committed in certain foreseen circumstances if the agreement is carried out in accordance with their intentions. They have an intent (often referred to as a conditional intent) to shoot if they are interfered with.

16–023   **Is there such a thing as a conditional intent?**   The whole idea of a conditional intent seems oxymoronic, either you intend or you do not. In these cases, it is perfectly plausible to assert that the intent has been formed and the agreement concluded. They have already agreed to do a criminal act; whether they act or not does not depend on their intentions, but on circumstances and future conditions that are beyond their control. Their level of culpability is not reduced merely because the circumstances that eventuate may be such that they may not want to risk committing the crime. Once they have formed an intent to commit a crime, it is a matter of pure luck whether or not they will feel that it is safe for them to carry it out, or whether they need to carry out some collateral or alternative criminal plan. Their intent is only conditional in the sense that the planned criminality is contingent on the circumstances as they may arise. The intent is firm, but the agreement's actuation depends on the circumstances that may arise.

If D1 and D2 agree to drive from Cambridge to London within an hour, and agree that they will not stop for pedestrians on zebra crossings as this will slow them down, it is irrelevant that by pure chance there were no pedestrians on any of the crossings when they happened to chance their way through.

The concept of "circumstance contingent" offending must not be applied so widely as to efface the distinction between intention and recklessness, but there is no reason why it should not be used to extend the *mens rea* for conspiracy to cases where the criminal intends to do something if necessary to effect his unscrupulous purpose.[54] If the offenders agree to speed through a school zone if necessary to get to a destination on time, then they conspire to commit dangerous driving. But they cannot be held liable for conspiring to commit murder, because they have not agreed to kill if necessary.

16–024   **But then, A and B in Donaldson L.J.'s example had an "intent" to exceed speed limits—an intent to exceed them if the traffic should be heavy.**   Yes, and the Lord Justice said that it is a conspiracy to agree to rob a bank "if when they arrive at the bank it seems safe to so do." That must be the law, since every conspiracy is dependent on its seeming to be safe to act at the time. The actual decision in the case before Donaldson L.J. in the Court of Appeal was that it is a conspiracy to aid and abet suicide for the parties to agree to assist a person to commit suicide if upon investigation this seems the best course in the

---

actively help them commit suicide depending on his assessment of the appropriate course of action (*R. v. Reed* [1982] Crim L.R. 819); (b) of conspiracy to pervert the course of public justice where three men agreed that a fourth man, under trial for burglary, should be shot in the leg so as to provide him with mitigation in the event he were convicted (*R. v. Jackson* [1985] Crim. L.R. 442) and (c) of conspiracy to cause explosions where members of the IRA during the IRA cease-fire agreed to make bombs for use only if the cease-fire came to an end: *R. v. O'Hadhmaill* [1996] Crim. L.R. 509." Cf. for a decision on a different part of the law, *R. v. Buckingham* (1976) 63 Cr. App. R. 159.

[54] Lord Nicholls held: "Fanciful cases apart, the conditional nature of [an] agreement is insufficient to take [a] conspiracy outside section 1(1)." *R. v. Saik* [2007] 1 A.C. 18 at 32.

circumstances. If the parties had not agreed to speed, they would not be liable for conspiring to commit an lawful act simply because it might be hypothetically impossible to achieve their goal without breaking the law. They would have to agree to break the law to achieve their otherwise lawful goal, should it be necessary for them to do so to achieve that end.

If the conspirators agree to commit theft if condition A is present, and as an alternative, burglary if condition B is present, and as a further alternative, robbery if condition C is present, are they liable for conspiring to commit the crimes of theft, burglary and robbery? Or are they only liable for the crime they go on to commit? It need only be shown that the defendants agreed not only to commit theft, but also burglary or robbery if necessary.[55] Conspiracy is forward looking, so the conspirators are liable for what they agree to do in the future, not for what they have done in the past. They are liable as soon as the agreement is made. The evidence might be sufficient to show that the defendants agreed to commit a range of alternative offences, if so, they will be liable for conspiring to commit all the offences they agreed and intended to carry out in alternative of each other.[56] D1 and D2 might agree to steal a rare painting and agree to commit burglary or robbery rather than theft if the need arises. It would be absurd to hold that they were not agreeing to commit any property offence, simply because did they did not know which offence they might have to commit to get the property. They were willing to do all three. The three could be charged as a single conspiracy. In certain circumstances it will be appropriate to charge the defendants for committing multiple conspiracies.[57]

16–025

As for included offences, in *R. v. Roberts*[58] Phillips L.J. said:

> "If a single count charges a conspiracy in relation to the commission of more than one offence, each offence probably constitutes an essential element of the conspiracy so that, unless the Crown proves that the conspiracy extended to all the offences alleged, the charge will not be made out. We think that it is quite plain that, as the maximum sentence is governed by that which attaches to the ulterior offence that carries the longest term of imprisonment, the jury must be satisfied that the conspiracy embraced at least that offence."

---

[55] In *Attorney-General's Reference (No 4 of 2003)* [2005] 1 W.L.R. 1574 at 1579 the court referred to this example and said: "The fact that the agreement to burgle or rob is contingent on the particular circumstances, does not affect the nature of the conspiracy." …. "Thus an agreement to commit a number of different offences remains an offence under section 1 of the *1977 Act* even if only one, or even none, of those offences is in fact committed. It is the agreement which constitutes the offence. Equally, if the agreement is to commit either of two offences, that is also an indictable conspiracy." See also *R. v. El-Kurd* [2001] Crim. L.R. 234.

[56] *R. v. Hussain* [2002] 2 Cr. App. R. 363 at 372.

[57] Cf. *R. v. Lavercombe* [1988] Crim. L.R. 435, where A and B were caught in Thailand with drugs which they intended to bring back to England where they plead guilty to keeping possession of the cannabis for sale. When they returned to England they were charged with conspiracy to import the cannabis. The Court of Appeal said: "that possession which was necessary under the foreign charge was not necessary under the English charge, there was no charge of exporting in Thailand, and there were two distinct conspiracies, one to violate Thai law, one to violate English law."

[58] [1998] 1 Cr. App. R. 441 at 449. See also *D.P.P. v. Stewart* [1983] 2 A.C. 91.

16.7. THE MENTAL ELEMENT

16–026 The statutory conspiracy needs a common intention that the crime shall be committed, using the word "intention," as always, to include knowledge of circumstances. It was noted above, that in *Chiu-Cheung v. The Queen*, Lord Griffiths said:[59] "The crime of conspiracy requires an agreement between two or more persons to commit an unlawful act with the intention of carrying it out. It is the intention to carry out the crime that constitutes the necessary *mens rea* for the offence."

Therefore, the defendant must:

1. intend to enter into the agreement;[60]
2. intend that the object of the agreement will be carried out;[61] and
3. intend or know the relevant circumstances.[62]

The first requirement normally does not raise any issues. If the conspirator is a fully autonomous adult (that is, mentally sound and sober), then it should not be too difficult to determine whether he entered into the agreement willingly. The second requirement is that the parties intend that the object of the conspiracy be carried out. Only those who intend that the agreed crime be carried out become parties to the conspiracy.

In *R. v. Saik*, Lord Nicholls said:

> "Thus under this subsection the mental element of the offence, apart from the mental element involved in making an agreement, comprises the intention to pursue a course of conduct which will necessarily involve commission of the crime in question by one or more of the conspirators. The conspirators must intend to do the act prohibited by the substantive offence."[63]

---

[59] [1995] 1 A.C. 111 at 117-119.

[60] *Churchill v. Walton* [1967] 2 A.C. 224.

[61] The decision of Lord Bridge (Lords Scarman, Diplock, Kinkel and Brightman concurring) in *R. v. Anderson* [1986] A.C. 27 at 39E holds otherwise. Lord Bridge took the view that the conspirators would have to intend to play a part in bringing about the offending conduct, but would not need to intend that the planned crime be carried out. The lower courts have been unable to follow this statement of the law because it makes no sense. It is logically impossible to agree to "commit" a crime if you do not intend that it be "committed." Furthermore, it seems erroneous to suggest that a conspirator such as a gang leader, who agrees with gang members that a rival gangster should be assassinated, is liable for conspiracy to murder only if he intended to play a part in carrying out the killing. Does this mean that if the agreement was that the junior members of the gang would carry out the killing, the gang leader is exempt from liability? The better argument is that the gang leader is liable for conspiracy to murder because he agrees that the rival gangster should be killed and intends it to be carried out by his fellow conspirators. It is irrelevant that he does not intend to play an active role in carrying out the killing. See *R. v. Siracusa* (1990) 90 Cr. App. R. 340; *R. v. Harvey* [1999] Crim. L.R. 70; *R. v. Ashton* [1992] Crim. L.R. 667; *R. v. Edwards* [1991] Crim. L.R. 45; *R. v. McPhillips* [1989] N.I. 360; *R. v. Crothers* [2001] N.I. 55. See also *U.S. v. Lopez*, 443 F.3d 1026 (2006), where it was held: "a defendant may be convicted for even a minor role in a conspiracy, so long as the government proves beyond a reasonable doubt that he or she was a member of the conspiracy."

[62] *R. v. Saik* [2007] 1 A.C. 18.

[63] [2007] 1 A.C. 18 at 31.

(1) No liability where consequence unintended and not foreseen as certain. On a **16–027** superficial reading, section 1(1) of the *Act* may seem to impose liability for conspiracy on a person who did not intend the criminal consequence that he is charged as conspiring to bring about. It may seem to imply that if D1 and D2 agree on a course of conduct, D1 having a criminal intent and D2 not, both parties will be guilty of a criminal conspiracy if the agreement when carried out will involve D1 in liability for an offence—in other words, D1's guilt will bring in D2. An effort must obviously be made to avoid this result. Consider the following hypothetical.

D1 falsely tells D2 that V has asked D1 to burn down an old shed for him. D2 agrees to help, and together they take petrol to the site, where they are apprehended. D1 and D2 are charged with conspiring to commit arson.

Here it is true to say, in some sense, that D2 has agreed that a course of conduct shall be pursued which, when carried out, will amount to the commission of the offence of arson (by D1); and from this the conclusion may perhaps be drawn that both parties are guilty of conspiracy to commit the offence. But this would be a misreading of the subsection, for two reasons. First, arson involves burning a building without lawful excuse. D2 thought he had a lawful excuse. Therefore he has not agreed to a course of conduct involving an offence; he has agreed to a course of conduct, and the course of conduct will amount to an offence, but he has not agreed to one of the elements of the conduct that amount to the offence, because he did not know of this particular element among the other facts of the case.

Secondly, the carrying out of the agreement "in accordance with their intentions" will not involve the commission of an offence, since D2's intention extended only to the burning of the shed with lawful excuse. What brings about the offence is not the mere burning of the shed but its burning without lawful excuse; D2 did not know of the absence of lawful excuse, and it was not part of his intention. In short, the word "intentions" in the subsection must be construed to refer to the common intention of the parties, and to include only items of unlawfulness known to both of them.[64]

What if two terrorists agree to bomb a fully occupied passenger aeroplane **16–028** **merely to attract attention to their cause? Could they argue that they did not** **intend to kill the passengers and therefore are not liable for conspiracy to** **murder?** No. The terrorists should be caught by the "oblique intention" doctrine. If the terrorists agree to blow up a passenger jet and intend to carry out the bombing foreseeing the death of the passengers as a virtually certain consequence of doing so, they should be liable for conspiring to murder the passengers.[65] There is no reason for limiting the "oblique intention" doctrine to

---

[64] *R. v. Saik* [2007] 1 A.C. 18. In *United States v. Dynar* [1997] 2 S.C.R. 462 at paras. 86-88, the Supreme Court of Canada said: "Where one member of a so-called conspiracy is a police informant who never intends to *carry out the common design*, there can be no conspiracy involving that person…. A common design necessarily involves an intention. Both are synonymous. *The intention cannot be anything else but the will to attain the [criminal] object of the agreement.*"

[65] Cf. *R. v. Walker* (1990) 90 Cr. App. R. 226; *R. v. Pearman* (1984) 80 Cr. App. R. 259. See also *R. v. MD* [2004] EWCA Crim. 1391; *R. v. Woollin* [1999] 1 A.C. 82. Cf. *Commonwealth v. Maloney*, 399

consummated offending. Clearly, the terrorists intended to carry out the bombing and obliquely intended to kill the passengers.

(1) Recklessness as to consequence is insufficient. The wording of section 1 is evidently intended to exclude this form of *mens rea* from statutory conspiracy, since a requirement of intention or knowledge is inconsistent with mere recklessness.[66]

The only qualification is that, if "intention" is understood to include realization of the virtual certainty of the consequence, this realization will be sufficient for conspiracy under section 1(1). But the plain meaning of section 1(1) of the *1977 Act* makes it clear that subjective recklessness or less is not sufficient. This makes a point of difference between conspiracy (and other inchoate offences as well) and accessoryship. We saw above that a person can be an accessory to an offence of *mens rea* or negligence if, in general, he has the same fault element in relation to the consequence as is required for the perpetrator. Conspiracy is different: recklessness or negligence as to the consequences is not enough, even though they are enough for the perpetrator.

16–029   Consider again the facts of *R. v. Salmon*.[67] If D2 encourages D1 to fire a gun negligently, and D1 kills someone, D2 is accessory to manslaughter. But if D1 did not kill anyone, he and D2 could not be convicted of conspiring to commit manslaughter.

The reason for the distinction is that where the crime is completed the courts wish to avoid the difficulties of proof that would result from distinguishing too finely between the perpetrator and the accessories, so they hold that it is possible to encourage manslaughter by negligence; whereas if the crime remains inchoate the element of intention assumes prominence.[68]

In *R. v. Saik*,[69] Lord Nicholls said:

Mass 785 (1987), where D set fire to a house while the occupants slept and then denied that he intended to kill them; the jury was able to infer from the evidence that he did intend to kill.

[66] Professor Smith takes a wider view of the offence (J.C. Smith, "Conspiracy under the *Criminal Law Act*," [1977] Crim. L.R. 638-639). He seems to hold that if the consummated offence can be committed recklessly, then recklessness in relation to the consequence is sufficient *mens rea*, provided that the consequence would necessarily follow, granted the circumstances "intended or known" to the defendants. So if two parties agree to take a risk of inflicting serious injury on another, such that if death occurs they will be guilty of manslaughter, and if in the circumstances "intended or known" to them death was necessarily involved, then this would be conspiracy to commit murder, even though the parties did not know that death was necessarily involved. A practical case raising this problem is difficult to imagine, but the theoretical answer is surely that section 1(1) on is proper interpretation requires that the defendant must have *known* that the course of conduct agreed would necessarily (that is, inevitably, or at least practically inevitably) involve the commission of the consummated offence. Liability for conspiracy is fixed at the time when the conspiracy is entered into, and does not depend upon what happened afterwards; so "necessarily" in the subsection must mean "necessarily" in the expectation of someone; and that someone, surely, is the defendant. The overriding purpose of section 1(1) is to make a person liable for conspiracy on the basis of his intention. In any case, the parties would on the facts supposed be saved from liability for conspiracy by subsection 2.

[67] (1880-81) L.R. 6 Q.B.D. 79.

[68] For an extended discussion see G. Orchard, "Agreement in Conspiracy," [1974] Crim. L.R. 297 at 335.

[69] [2007] 1 A.C. 18 at 31.

> "The conspirators state of mind must also satisfy the mental ingredients of the substantive offence. If one of the ingredients of the substantive offence is that the act is done with a specific intent, the conspirators must intend to do the prohibited act and must intend to do the prohibited act with the prescribed intent. A conspiracy to wound with intent to do grievous bodily harm contrary to section 18 of the *Offences against the Person Act 1861* requires proof of an intention to wound with the intent of doing grievous bodily harm. The position is the same if the prescribed state of mind regarding the consequence of the prohibited act is recklessness. Damaging property, being reckless as to whether life is endangered thereby, is a criminal offence: *Criminal Damage Act 1971*, section 1(2). Conspiracy to commit this offence requires proof of an intention to damage property, and to do so recklessly indifferent to whether this would endanger life."

Lord Nicholls first example seems to run counter to his second.[70] Surely, one cannot conspire to commit aggravated criminal damage if one only intends to damage property and is recklessly indifferent as to whether that damage will result in endangerment to others.[71] Endangerment to life is a consequence not a circumstance, so it is not sufficient merely to show that the conspirators knew that the circumstances would be such that if they were to commit criminal damage they would endanger life. Rather, it should be shown that they intended to destroy the property with an ulterior intent to endanger life. If D1 and D2 agree to blow an "occupied" building to smithereens, the fact that the building will be occupied is a circumstance, whereas the fact that the bombing will endanger the occupants is a consequence. It is something that will happen to the occupants. From the *ex post* perspective the occupants have been endangered, if not harmed. This is a consequence of the bombing. A person cannot conspire to endanger the life of others unless he intends (or obliquely intends) to endanger those lives.

Nor does it matter that Ds could have consummated the aggravated form of **16–030** criminal damage without in fact endangering anyone. They would be liable for the substantive offence as long as they putatively endangered life. For example, Ds might destroy a building believing that it is occupied, but it turns out that they were wrong. Even though they have not in fact endangered life, they were reckless in taking the risk. In the case of conspiracy or attempt they would have to be more than reckless, they would have to intend to endanger life. If D2 and D1 agree to destroy a building believing that it "will" be occupied when they destroy it, they will be liable for conspiracy to commit aggravated criminal damage even if unbeknown to them the building is no longer occupied because it is being renovated. It may be impossible for them to endanger anyone because the building will in fact be empty when they carry out their bombing, but they will be liable because if the facts had been as they believed it would have been possible

---

[70] As far as the aggravated form of criminal damages is concerned, perhaps Lord Nicholls had the "missing element" theory in mind (see *Attorney-General's Reference (No. 3 of 1992)* [1994] 1 W.L.R. 409), but such talk is unhelpful given that conspiracy is forward looking. When we consider the *mens rea* for inchoate offences we must assume they have not been consummated in full or part. (Furthermore, even if we accept the missing element theory, it would only apply if one of the physical elements had been consummated).

[71] *R. v. Roberts* [1998] 1 Cr. App. R. 441. See *State v. Beccia*, 505 A.2d 683 (1986) where it was held that: "A conspiracy to commit arson was not a cognizable offense because 'conspirators cannot agree to accomplish a result recklessly when that result is an essential element of the crime' . . . . There is just no such crime as would require proof that one intended a result that accidentally occurred."

for them to endanger the occupants. (It might also be put this way, they intend the circumstance of occupation to exist at the time when they plan to destroy the building.)

In *R. v. Saik*[72] Lord Hope said:

> "Section 1(2) ... was designed to make it clear that, while ignorance of the law was no excuse, full knowledge of the consequences of the agreement was required. It was designed also to exclude recklessness as to the consequences."

Since the aggravated form of the offence of criminal damage is labelled as a more serious offence than criminal damage *simpliciter*,[73] it is important to ensure that the conspirators intend that that form of criminal damage be carried out. Those conspiring to commit criminal damage could only be held liable for conspiring to commit the aggravated form of the offence if they intend: (1) to damage property; and (2) intend (or obliquely intend) to endanger lives in the process. Recklessness as to consequences may suffice for D's culpability for the consummated crime, but it cannot be used to convict the conspirators because they do not agree nor intend to bring about the unintended result—endangerment.[74]

16–031 **You have already mentioned that recklessness as to "circumstances" is *not* sufficient for grounding a conspiracy conviction. I recall you telling me that recklessness as to circumstances is sufficient for "attempts,"[75] so why is not sufficient for "conspiracy"?** The *Criminal Law Act 1977* is again badly drafted as far as this point is concerned. It makes one undesirable change in the law and, for the rest, succeeds only in making obscure what was almost entirely plain before.[76]

There is no reason why the mental element for a conspiracy should differ from that for attempt, and probably it does not, except in respect of the one change in the law already mentioned. In other words, the mental element should basically be intention, with question marks added in respect of two possible extensions: foresight of certainty (oblique intention) and recklessness as to circumstance. The *Act* removes the question mark as to recklessness by giving the wrong answer. Recklessness as to circumstances is now not enough for a conspiracy, since the plain words of the *Act* exclude it.[77] This is because of section 1(2). The subsection is mind-twisting:

> "(2)   Where liability for any offence may be incurred without knowledge on the part of the
> person committing it of any particular fact or circumstance necessary for the

---

[72] [2007] 1 A.C. 18 at 44.

[73] See *R. v. Roberts* [1998] 1 Cr. App. R. 441 at 448.

[74] *R. v. Siracusa* (1990) 90 Cr. App. R. 340. See further, *Com. v. Weimer*, 977 A.2d 1103 (2009); *State v. Almeda*, 189 Conn. 303 (1983); *Conley v. State*, 247 S.E.2d 562, 565 (1978). *State v. Wilson*, 43 P.3d 851 (2002).

[75] *R. v. Khan* [1990] 1 W.L.R. 813; *Attorney-General's Reference (No.3 of 1992)* [1994] 1 W.L.R. 409.

[76] See *Churchill v. Walton* [1967] 2 A.C. 224 at 237 *per* Viscount Dilhorne. Cf. Glanville Williams, "The New Statutory Offence of Conspiracy-I" (1977) 127 *New L. J.* 1164.

[77] *R. v. Saik* [2007] 1 A.C. 18. Cf. *R. v. Mawbey* (1796) 6 Term Rep. 619. See also Glanville Williams, *Textbook of Criminal Law*, (London: Stevens & Sons, 1st edn 1978) at 359.

commission of the offence, a person shall nevertheless not be guilty of conspiracy to commit that offence by virtue of subsection (1) above unless he and at least one other party to the agreement intend or know that that fact or circumstance shall or will exist at the time when the conduct constituting the offence is to take place."

In other words, where an offence can be committed without the perpetrator knowing of a required circumstance (*e.g.*, where he is liable for recklessness or negligence as to the circumstances), there can be no conspiracy except between those who intend that the circumstance shall exist at the time of the offence or know that it will. In *R. v. Saik*[78] Lord Nicholls said: "Section 1(2) qualifies the scope of the offence created by section 1(1). This subsection is more difficult. Its essential purpose is to ensure that strict liability and recklessness have no place in the offence of conspiracy."

So if the operator of a bureau de change agrees to convert banknotes which he **16–032** strongly suspects will be the proceeds of crime, and at that time does not know for certain that the notes will be the proceeds of crime, he might be guilty of a substantive offence if recklessness as to circumstances is sufficient for that offence,[79] but he will not be guilty of conspiracy contrary to section 1(1) of the *Criminal Law Act 1977*.

Section 1(2) was probably not drafted for the purpose of reaching this result, but it is the consequence of the wording. If you are still with me you will be asking what the position is if the offence requires knowledge on the part of the perpetrator.[80] Take for example the offence of knowingly possessing explosives. D1 and D2 agree to receive a bag from X and to keep it for him. D1 knows that the bag will contain explosives. D2 knows that it may but is not by any means sure. Again D2 is not guilty of conspiracy. A person cannot attempt to conspire by recklessness to commit a crime requiring knowledge, because what he does in consequence of the attempt or conspiracy will not be the completed crime in question. This being so, D1 is probably not guilty of conspiracy either.[81]

Reverting to the hypothetical about the money laundering, if the defendant is found to have been "wilfully blind" to the possibility that the banknotes were the proceeds of crime, he may be held to have known that the they were the proceeds of crime, but the doctrine of wilful blindness should not be used to extend a requirement of knowledge to cases of mere recklessness (6.3).[82]

---

[78] [2007] 1 A.C. 18 at 32.

[79] See for example the fault requirement for the substantive offence in section 327 of the *Proceeds of Crime Act 2002*. "In this respect the mental element of conspiracy is distinct from and supersedes the mental element in the substantive offence. When this is so, the lesser mental element in the substantive offence becomes otiose on a charge of conspiracy. It is an immaterial averment. To include it in the particulars of the offence of conspiracy is potentially confusing and should be avoided." *R. v. Saik* [2007] 1 A.C. 18 at 32. See also *R. v. LK* (2010) 84 A.L.J.R. 395 at para. 77 *per* French C.J.

[80] "[T]he assumption underlying section 1(2) is that, where knowledge of a material fact is an ingredient of a substantive offence, knowledge of that fact is also an ingredient of the crime of conspiring to commit the substantive offence. ... In my view, therefore, the preferable interpretation of section 1(2) is that the subsection applies to all offences. It applies whenever an ingredient of an offence is the existence of a particular fact or circumstance. The subsection applies to that ingredient." *R. v. Saik* [2007] 1 A.C. 18 at 33-34 *per* Lord Nicholls.

[81] Cf. the example given by Lord Hope in *R. v. Saik* [2007] 1 A.C. 18 at 51.

[82] *R. v. Saik* [2007] 1 A.C. 18.

16–033 This leaves a lacuna in the law, since a person can agree to do something which he suspects is criminal (have sexual intercourse with a girl he suspects to be aged 15), but can evade justice if he does not know for sure that she is or will be that age at the time when he plans to have intercourse with her. The Law Commission has recommended that the law be amended to remedy this situation:[83]

> "[W]here the substantive offence requires no proof of fault in relation to a circumstance element, or proof only of negligence (or an equivalent, objectively determined, state of mind, such as an unreasonable belief), the prosecution should be required to show that an alleged conspirator was reckless concerning the possible presence or absence of the circumstance element at the relevant time."[84]

The proposed amendment would mean that those who conspire to rape a woman would have to be subjectively reckless as to whether or not she was consenting (a circumstance), even though negligence would be sufficient for the substantive offence. If D1 and D2 independently have sexual intercourse with a woman and are independently negligent as to whether she is consenting they would be independently liable for rape. But if they agree with each other that one of them (or both of them) will have sexual intercourse with the woman, then the prosecution would have to show that they were "aware" of the fact that she might not consent. Similarly, if D1 decides to have sexual intercourse with a child under the age of 13 he commits statutory rape, even though he might have genuinely believed that the child was 16. If, however, D1 agrees with D2 that they should have sexual intercourse with a person who just happens to under the age of 13, they would not be liable unless they were "aware" that the child might be under 13. Under the current law, they would not be liable even if they were subjectively reckless as to the relevant circumstances.[85] Consequently, the Law Commission proposals would expand the law, but not so far as to require the same fault as is required for the substantive offence.

Why require subjective recklessness as to the relevant circumstances if negligence or strict liability is sufficient for the consummated offence? The justification for requiring subjective fault as to the relevant circumstances in conspiracy cases seems to hinge on the fact that the offender's culpable agreement is only remotely connected to its potential harm. When an offence is consummated the harm is not a remote probability, rather it is a past fact. Conspiracy is highly inchoate, because unlike attempts it does not require any

---

[83] See clause 1(3) of the *Conspiracy and Attempts Draft Bill* as outlined in Law Commission, *Conspiracy and Attempts*, Report 318 (London: H.M.S.O., 2009) at 10.

[84] Such an approach has been adopted by some federal courts in the U.S. including the Supreme Court. *U.S. v. Feola*, 420 U.S. 671 (1975); *U.S. v. Rosa*, 17 F.3d 1531 (1994). Even strict liability as to circumstances has been held to be sufficient for some conspirators. See *U.S. v. Mack*, 112 F.2d 290 (1940). See *also* Herbert Wechsler *et al.*, "The Treatment of Inchoate Crimes in the Model Penal Code of the American Law Institute: Attempt, Solicitation, and Conspiracy," (1961) 61 *Colum. L. Rev.* 957 at 941 citing *Wilkerson v. United States*, 41 F.2d 654 (1930).

[85] Requiring intention as to "circumstances" is surely too restrictive: D1 and D2 could agree to have sexual intercourse with V even though they suspect she is underage, or will not consent. If they think V might be underage or might not consent, then they are aware of the possibilities that make their agreement wrong. They are agreeing to do an act which they are aware might cause grave harm to V. It seems absurd that they cannot be criminalized for *agreeing to take a risk* which they are aware could result in serious harm for V.

kind of overt act[86]—there is no need to show that the defendant started to act. Conspiracy can be used to criminalize attempts to commit substantive crimes before those attempts reach the stage of attempt in law,[87] so long as there is an agreement to commit those crimes.[88] The agreement itself is sufficient for grounding a conviction. The remoteness of the potential harm involved in conspiracy is one justification for maintaining the current "actual knowledge" standard.[89] Given the highly inchoate nature of conspiracy and the procedural and evidential advantages that a conspiracy charge provides for the prosecution, it seems reasonable to require nothing less than recklessness as to circumstances.

(1) *A person is not liable for conspiracy if he believed that the required circumstances would not exist at the time of the intended conduct.* This conclusion follows *a fortiori* from our previous conclusion as to recklessness in relation to circumstances. If a person is not guilty of conspiracy on account of recklessness as to circumstances, it follows that he is not liable if he believed that the required circumstances would not exist. But the subsection is not necessary to reach this conclusion in the case of crimes of intention. Section 1(1) is not drafted to deal with the question of knowledge of circumstances, but the right result can be achieved if the reference as to the "intentions" of the parties is held to exclude liability where the party believed the circumstances necessary to make the act a crime were not present. Subsection (2) makes it plain that a similar rule applies even though what is plotted will be an offence of recklessness, negligence or strict liability. Hence it is a defence to a charge of statutory conspiracy to show that the defendant was under a misapprehension, such that if the facts had been as he supposed his conduct would not have been criminal.

16–034

Is oblique intention as to circumstances sufficient? The Lords have not provided a clear answer on this point.[90] It was said that the conspirators must know or intend the circumstances. If D1 and D2 agree that they will have sexual intercourse with a girl that they know for a fact has just turned 12, they will be liable for conspiring to commit the substantive offence of child rape. If a person knows that a child has just turned 12, then he must know this circumstance will exist if he has intercourse with her in the imminent future. But if they do not know her age for sure, they will only be caught if it can be shown they intend to have sexual intercourse with a girl aged 12.

16–035

---

[86] Some Australian and U.S. states require an "overt act." See for example, section 11 of the *Criminal Code* (Cth.). For a survey of the U.S. statutes requiring an overt act, see Wayne R. LaFave, *Substantive Criminal Law*, (West Publishing, Vol. II, 2nd edn. 2003) at 271 *et seq.*

[87] You will recall that attempts require acts that are more than merely preparatory to the commission of the substantive offence.

[88] *Board of Trade v. Owen* [1957] A.C. 602 at 626 *per* Lord Tucker.

[89] The Law Commission notes in its report that: "The Criminal Bar Association, Professor Spencer Q.C., Mr. Krolick Q.C., and Mrs. Padfield all considered that there is no need to change the present (more stringent) requirement of knowledge as to circumstances." See also Law Commission, *Report on Conspiracy and Criminal Law Reform*, (London: H.M.S.O. Law Com. No. 76, 1976), para. 1.41; Criminal Law Officers Committee of the Standing Committee of Attorney-Generals, Model Criminal Code, Chapter 2: *General Principles of Criminal Responsibility*, Final Report, (December 1992) at 99-101. *Per contra*, as far as the English law is concerned, Lord Nicholls said the current law is "not altogether satisfactory in terms of blameworthiness." *R. v. Saik* [2007] 1 A.C. 18 at 37.

[90] *R. v. Saik* [2007] 1 A.C. 18.

Arguably, it is enough to show that the conspirators obliquely intend the circumstance to exist at the time when they carry out the substantive offence. If this is not enough, then conspirators who believe that a circumstance is virtually certain to exist when they carry out their planned crime will walk free. For instance, if D1 and D2 agree to have sexual intercourse with any woman they meet in a nightclub, they might not be liable since they might argue that there was a remote chance that she would consent. Nevertheless, if the evidence is particularly strong the jury should be allowed to infer that the defendants intended the circumstance (absence of consent) to exist. If D1 and D2 believe that it is virtually certain that a woman will not consent to having sexual intercourse with them, then they must intend to have sexual intercourse in circumstances where the woman will not be consenting.

In *R. v. Saik*[91] Lord Hope said: "It may be open to the Crown to prove that D knew very well that the purpose of the agreement was to [launder money]. It might be going too far to say that he knew that the cash would be [the proceeds of crime] when he came to deal with it. But it could be inferred that he intended that the cash would be [the proceeds of crime], because he knew that that was the only purpose of the transaction." In other words, if there is objective evidence showing that D had agreed to deal with the proceeds of crime, such as phone records, or C.C.T.V. footage of D being told that the money would be the proceeds of crime, then that would be sufficient to show that he intended the future circumstance. He need not know for sure that the given bundle of cash will be the proceeds of crime, because he intends to deal with what he believes will, ("at the time when the conduct constituting the offence is to take place,") be the proceeds of crime.

16–036 **How can one intend circumstances? I intend to go to the beach tomorrow to do a bit of sunbathing, but only if it is a sunny day. A sunny day is a circumstance of which I cannot intend, even though I might desire or hope it will exist.** There is some merit in what you say. The word "intend" is not the most apt word for describing a person's state of mind with respect to future facts, because it refers to what one has in mind as one's purpose. It cannot be your aim or purpose to make the sun come out, since you have no control over such matters. Of course, a person can have limited control over some circumstances. Take the situation where D lures V to an isolated location so that he can kill him. Let us assume that D telephones V and convinces him that they need to meet in the isolated place for some legitimate purpose. Suppose V swallows D's incredible story and goes to meet him. D through his deliberate actions has managed to bring about a circumstance of which he intended to bring about (that is, V's presence at a particular place at a particular point in time). Nevertheless, in most cases the defendant will not be in a position to bring about a desired circumstance, even though he might be able to plan things so that he might take advantage of existing circumstances.

Take the terrorist who wants to blow up a tube carriage on the London underground. If the carriage is full of passengers, we might say the fact that it is fully occupied is a present fact. The terrorist might plan his attack for rush hour so that it will take place in circumstances where the tube carriage is fully

---

[91] [2007] 1 A.C. 18 at 51.

occupied, but the fact that passengers just happened to be travelling at that point in time on the day in question is a circumstance that he had no control over. He may have hoped for it or believed as a matter of certainty that it would exist, but he did not intentionally bring it about. The terrorist merely intends to take advantage of a circumstance that he believes is virtually certain to exist at the time when he plans to commit his attack.

Can a rapist intentionally bring about a circumstance such as a woman's lack of consent? Can a paedophile intentionally bring about a child's age? How can a rapist intend a woman's lack of consent? He does not intentionally bring her lack of consent about, rather he chooses to have sexual intercourse in circumstances where V is not consenting. Likewise, a paedophile might intend to sexually assault children, but he cannot bring about their age? A child's age exists regardless of what the paedophile intends. He can, however, intend to molest a child whom he knows (or believes) is under the age of 13. He intends to take advantage of a circumstance that already exists. He intends to sexually assault a child (the conduct) and intends the child to be under the age of 13. He can intend to target underage children and thus intend to take advantage of certain circumstances, but technically he does not intend the circumstance itself. Similarly, if two men conspire to rape a woman, and have it has their common purpose only to have non-consensual intercourse. Hence they can only intend a circumstance in the sense that it is their purpose to take advantage of what they believe will be an existing circumstance at the time when they commit their offence.

Does a person become a conspirator by agreeing to help in an illegal plan of which he knows no details?   It has already been mentioned that a negative answer was given in *R. v. Scott*,[92] but that case is perhaps not the last word on the subject.   16–037

As with accessories, a person charged with conspiracy need not know that what is agreed upon is a breach of the law, where ignorance of the law would be no excuse in respect of the consummated offence.[93]

Does a person become a conspirator by knowingly supplying an article? A gang plan to commit a robbery. Needing a gun, they approach D, who, knowing of their purpose, supplies them with a weapon for a suitable consideration. The police have been on their tracks, and intervene before the robbery is committed. Is D guilty of conspiracy?   The answer is clearly no. If D initiated the plan, or if he shared the other gang members' intent that the crime be committed, he could be found to be a conspirator. If he merely agreed to provide a service for a fixed reward at the time of the crime, such as by driving the robbers to the bank, it would be reasonable to regard him as one of the plotters. But it would be going too far to say that a person has agreed that a crime shall be committed if he merely supplies the instrument of crime and realizes that   16–038

---

[92] (1979) 68 Cr. App. R. 164 . Cf. *R. v. Brown* [2001] EWCA Crim. 1771.

[93] This is clear from the wording of section 1 of the *Criminal Law Act 1977*, following the common law.

it might be used to commit a crime. Knowledge of the conspiracy is not sufficient to link him to it if he does not intend to be a part of it, nor intend that it be carried out.

The evidence would have to show that D was not merely intending to assist the planned criminality, but also shared the conspirators' intent that the crime be committed. Suppose D1 and D2 agree to break someone out of prison, but that D1 only agrees to supply cutting equipment because he wants to make some money. D1 would be liable for conspiracy if he shared D2's intent that the crime be carried out. The fact that he only supplied cutting wire is neither here nor there, if he agreed to do the prison break and intended it to be carried out. But if he were merely agreeing to supply cutting wire without a care about whether it would be used to break someone out of prison, and with no intention of being involved in the overall scheme, he would not be a conspirator. He may be charged as an accessory if the object of the conspiracy is attempted or consummated. If it is not attempted or consummated, he could be convicted of assisting the substantive offence under sections 44 or 45 of the *Serious Crime Act 2007*.

16–039   **Now if all the above made sense to you, you had better brace yourself for some *non*sense.** The natural mental element required for conspiracy is basically one of intention, but an abominable decision from the Lords has distorted this requirement. Notwithstanding that the wording of section 1 of the *Criminal Law Act 1977* makes it clear that the accused must intend the object of the conspiracy and its consequences, the Lords have held that the accused need not intend the crime be committed.[94]

In *R. v. Anderson*[95] D1 and D2 were on remand in prison and spent one night in the same cell. Before D1 was released on bail he agreed with D2 to participate in a scheme to effect X's escape from prison. There were to be two other participants in the scheme. D1 was to be paid £20,000 to acquire diamond wire that could be used to cut through metal bars, which he was to give it to one of the other participants. He was subsequently paid £2,000, but was injured before he could supply the wire and took no further part in the scheme. He was charged with conspiracy to effect the escape of a prisoner. D1 asserted that he lacked *mens rea*, because he had never intended the escape plan to be carried into effect and did not believe it could possibly succeed.

It was argued on his behalf that the subsection "requires that the party charged should not only have agreed that a course of conduct shall be pursued which will necessarily amount to or involve the commission of that offence by himself or one or more other parties to the agreement, but must also be proved himself to have intended that that offence should be committed." Lord Bridge rejected this argument:[96]

> "Parliament cannot have intended that such parties should escape conviction of conspiracy on the basis that it cannot be proved against them that they intended that the relevant offence or offences should be committed."

---

[94] *R. v. Anderson* [1986] A.C. 27. Cf. *R. v. McPhillips* [1989] N.I. 360.
[95] [1986] A.C. 27.
[96] [1986] A.C. 27 at 38.

Are you telling me that the accused must intend or know the relevant circumstances, but need not intend the crime to be committed? That is what 16–040
Lord Bridge seems to be suggesting. Not only is the decision irreconcilable with the pre-*Act* position,[97] but it is at odds with the law in every major common law jurisdiction.[98] The decision is binding on the lower courts, but has not been followed.[99] Nor is it likely to be followed, since it is too vacuous to apply in practice. If the gravamen of the offence of conspiracy is the common intent to commit a crime, then all the conspirators would have to share that intent. Those who do not share that intent cannot be a part of the conspiracy. A statutory conspiracy can only be formed if all the conspirators share the intent that the object of the conspiracy be carried out. Those who do not share such an intent do not become a member of the conspiracy, because it is that intent that brings them in. The common intention of the conspirators cannot be anything other than the intention to attain the object of the agreement. The word "conspire" comes from two Latin words, "con" and "spirare," which translate to breathe together.[100] If one of the conspirators does not breathe with the others, or to put it another way, does not share their aim of seeing the target crime carried out, then he cannot be a party to the conspiracy.

Is it possible to make any sense of Lord Bridge's judgment? No! He surely 16–041
did not mean to suggest that a conspiracy can be formed if none of the conspirators intend to commit a crime. It appears that he was suggesting that if at least two conspirators intend that the crime be committed, that a conspiracy is formed and therefore others can be linked to it so long as they have knowledge of it and intend to facilitate it. (Lord Bridge stretches the law of conspiracy to cover an accessory, because accessorial liability is only an option when the substantive offence is attempted[101] or consummated.)[102] But in doing this, he suggests that conspiracy has different *mens rea* requirements for different people, when that clearly cannot be the case. The crime of conspiracy has a set mental element that must apply to all offenders in the same way. So, either no party is required to intend that the object of the conspiracy be carried out, or all are required to intend that it be carried out. The weight of recent authority makes it pertinently clear that all the parties to a conspiracy must intend that the object of the conspiracy be

---

[97] *R. v. Thomson* (1966) 50 Cr. App. R. 1; *Mulcahy v. R.* (1868) L.R. 3 H.L. 306 at 317 where it was said: "A conspiracy consists not merely in the intention of two or more, but in the agreement of two or more to do an unlawful act, or to do a lawful act by unlawful means. So long as such a design rests in intention only, it is not indictable. When two agree to *carry it into effect*, the very plot is an act in itself, and the act of each of the parties, promise against promise, *actus contra actum*, capable of being enforced, if lawful, punishable if for a criminal object or for the use of criminal means."

[98] See *Chiu-Cheung v. The Queen* [1995] 1 A.C. 111 at 117-119; *People v. Cortez*, 960 P.2d 537 (1998); *United States v. Dynar* [1997] 2 S.C.R. 462; *Gerakiteys v. The Queen* (1984) 153 C.L.R. 317.

[99] *R. v. Siracusa* (1990) 90 Cr. App. R. 340; *R. v. Harvey* [1999] Crim. L.R. 70; *R. v. Ashton* [1992] Crim. L.R. 667; *R. v. Edwards* [1991] Crim. L.R. 45; *R. v. McPhillips* [1989] N.I. 360; *R. v. Crothers* [2001] N.I. 55.

[100] *R. v. Cotroni* [1979] 2 S.C.R. 256 at 276 *per* Dickson J.

[101] (An attempt requires the perpetrators to get past the mere preparation stage.) *R. v. Dunnington* [1984] Q.B. 472.

[102] This is no longer a problem since the *Serious Crime Act 2007* catches those who attempt to assist and encourage others to commit crimes.

carried out.[103] Therefore, if the matter comes before the Supreme Court, it is likely to hold that D must (1) intend to enter the agreement; (2) share the intent of the other conspirators that the object of the conspiracy be carried out; and (3) intend or know the relevant circumstances.

16.8.   THE NECESSITY FOR TWO CONSPIRATORS

16–042   The rule that there must be at least two conspirators[104] has been used to reach the conclusion that husband and wife cannot conspire together, where there is no third party, because they are one person in law.[105] The reason is false, and the rule is of doubtful policy; but it is expressly preserved by the *Criminal Law Act* (section 2(2)(a)). The provision in the *Act* emanated from the Law Commission Working Party, a majority of which defended the rule on the ground that it prevents the police from bringing improper pressure to bear on criminals. A man may be made to confess by threatening him that otherwise his wife will be charged with conspiracy with him. A weakness of this argument is that no steps have been taken to negate other ways in which the wife may become liable in crime. A wife may certainly be convicted as accessory to her husband's crime,[106] or presumably of encouraging her husband to crime.[107] And there may be a conviction of conspiracy between a husband, wife and a third person.[108] No sufficient reason can be found for singling out conspiracy as the one crime that husband and wife cannot commit together.[109]

16–043   **It may be known that the defendant has conspired with someone else, a shadowy figure whom the police never lay their hands on. Can the defendant nevertheless be convicted?**   He may be indicted for conspiracy with a person unknown.[110] Obviously, the evidence would have to be strong. If D1 and D2 were caught on C.C.T.V. agreeing to do some abominable crime, then it should not matter that D2 disappears like a Chinese wish lantern into the night sky.

16–044   **D1 weaves a plot with D2. They are found out, but D2 escapes. D1 is tried and convicted of conspiracy. Then D2 is caught and put on trial. Is the conviction of D1 admissible in evidence against him?**   This is now governed by sections 74, and 78 of the *Police and Criminal Evidence Act 1984*. Technically

---

[103] *R. v. Siracusa* (1990) 90 Cr. App. R. 340; *R. v. Harvey* [1999] Crim. L.R. 70; *R. v. Ashton* [1992] Crim. L.R. 667; *R. v. Edwards* [1991] Crim. L.R. 45; *R. v. McPhillips* [1989] N.I. 360.

[104] Cf. *R. v. McDonnell* [1966] 1 Q.B. 233; *Stone & Rolls Ltd. (In Liquidation) v. Moore Stephens* [2009] 1 A.C. 1391 at 1491.

[105] See generally the scholarly judgment of Oliver J. in *Midland Bank Trust Co. Ltd. v. Green (No.3)* [1979] Ch. 496 at 510 *et seq.*, affd. *Midland Bank Trust Co. Ltd. v. Green (No.3)* [1982] 2 W.L.R. 1. See further Glanville Williams, "The Legal Unity of Husband and Wife," (1947) 10 *Mod. L. Rev.* 16.

[106] *R. v. Manning* (1849) 2 Car. & K. 887 at 904; *Browning v. Floyd* [1946] K.B. 597; See also Williams, *op. cit. supra*, note 44 at §123 n. 14.

[107] See sections 44-45 of the *Serious Crime Act 2007*.

[108] *R. v. Lovick* [1993] Crim. L.R. 890; *R. v. Chrastny* [1991] 1 W.L.R. 1381.

[109] The Law Commission has recommended that the exemption be abrogated. Law Commission, *Conspiracy and Attempts*, Report 318 (London: H.M.S.O. 2009) at para. 5.16.

[110] *R. v. Niccolls* (1944) 93 E.R. 1148; *R. v. Kenrick* (1843) 5 Q.B. 49; *The King v. Plummer* [1902] 2 K.B. 339; *R. v. Phillips* (1988) 86 Cr. App. R. 18.

the conviction would be admissible, but D2 is entitled to fight the issue of his own innocence, without being prejudiced by the conviction of D1.[111]

What if D1 and D2 are tried together for conspiring together (without any other parties being named)? Can the jury convict D1 and acquit D2? The common law was in a muddle on this, but the position is now clarified by the *Criminal Law Act 1977*.[112] The answer is that in a suitable case they can. For example, D1 may have confessed, and his confession is admissible against him but not against D2. However, if the evidence against the two defendants is substantially the same the judge should direct the jury that it would not be right for them to convict one of conspiracy and acquit the other. If there is any doubt as to the case against one, they should acquit both.[113]

16–045

I don't understand why D1's confession that he conspired with D2 is not evidence against D2. It is if the confession is made in the witness box at the joint trial. But if it was made to the police it is hearsay evidence in respect of D2, though it is admissible against D1 as a confession. Even if D1 pleads guilty, this is not evidence against D2, because it is not a statement made on oath but only a statement of intention not to contest the charge.[114]

16–046

But if D1 pleads guilty, so that there is no trial of the case against him, and then D2 gets off, D1 will have a sense of grievance. If D1 is acquitted the judge may allow D1 to withdraw his plea and be tried, when it seems on the evidence that there might otherwise be a miscarriage of justice.[115] But when the evidence explains the situation, D1's conviction will doubtless be allowed to stand. The rules and evidence do not affect the proposition that on a charge of conspiracy against a particular person it must be proved that he and another person took part with the required guilty state of mind.

16–047

16.9. LIABILITY OF AN EXEMPT PARTY

The next question is whether a person can be liable for conspiracy to commit a crime that he cannot commit himself. He ought not be, and generally he is not, but there are anomalous exceptions.[116] First as to the general rule: where a person would not be liable for the consummated crime because he lacks the mental

16–048

---

[111] In *R. v. Robertson* [1987] Q.B. 920 it was held: "Section 74 should be sparingly used. Occasionally evidence may be technically admissible but its effect is likely to be so slight that it will be wiser not to adduce it, particularly where there is any danger of contravening section 78. Where the evidence is admitted, the judge should be careful to explain to the jury the effect of the evidence and its limitations."

[112] Sections 5(8) and (9). When the two are tried together the judge must decide on the evidence whether: "the two cases are different to a substantial degree; but that is a matter for his assessment and not for the jury's." *R. v. Testouri* [2004] 2 Cr. App. R. 26 at 29.

[113] *R. v. Longman* (1981) 72 Cr. App. R. 121; *R. v. Holmes* [1980] 1 W.L.R. 1055; *R. v. Roberts* (1984) 78 Cr. App. R. 41; *R. v. Testouri* [2004] 2 Cr. App. R. 26.

[114] The conditions for admitting hearsay evidence are set out in section 114 of the *Criminal Justice Act 2003*.

[115] Cf. *R. v. Drew* [1985] 1 W.L.R. 914.

[116] *R. v. Duguid* (1906) 70 J.P. 294.

element, then he is also free from liability for conspiracy. (Even if the consummated crime does not require a mental element, a person cannot be liable for conspiracy unless he knows the facts: see in particular section 1(2) of the *Act*, already discussed).

Where a person cannot by law perpetrate a crime, owing to some special exemption, he can still, obviously, be guilty of conspiring to commit the crime if he can be an accessory to it. So if a woman, D1, who cannot generally perpetrate a rape upon another woman,[117] agrees with her friend to help the friend (a man) to rape V, D1 and D2 can be guilty of conspiring together. This was so at common law,[118] and remains so under the wide words of section 1(1).

The anomalous cases are those arising from the wording of section 1(1), which makes D1 guilty of conspiracy if he agrees that D2 shall do what will for D2 be a crime, notwithstanding that D1 could not himself commit the crime, even as accessory. Provided that D1 has the requisite mental element, he becomes a conspirator.

16–049 Let us take a common law example. At common law a parent or guardian of a child (*e.g.*, the mother) could not be guilty of the offence of taking the child from its parent or guardian (*e.g.*, the father);[119] and it may well be (though the point has not been decided) that the mother in the example is not guilty of abetting a third party (such as her brother) to abduct the child. But in such circumstances the mother, though not guilty of the substantive offence, appears to be made guilty of conspiracy by the *Act*. Her brother will commit the offence of child abduction (assuming that he knew that the mother had been deprived of her right to custody of the child, so that he has no claim of right). Therefore, the case falls within section 1(1):[120] the mother and her brother have agreed that something shall be done that will be an offence for her brother. The mother is not the victim of the offence; so she is guilty of conspiracy.[121]

There seems to be no great injustice in roping in such people, but Parliament doubtless did not intend this result to apply across the board. Special provision is made by the *Act* on one point. Suppose that a girl under 16, who cannot be party to her own seduction, is charged with conspiring with her seducer. In this

---

[117] *D.P.P. v. K & B* [1997] 1 Cr. App. R. 36.

[118] In *R. v. Whitchurch* (1890) 24 Q.B.D. 420 a woman who (not being pregnant) could not have been convicted of perpetrating an abortion on herself was convicted of conspiring with another that that other should perpetrate the abortion on her. This can be explained by reference to the later case of *R. v. Sockett* (1909) 1 Cr. App. R. 101, where it was held that such a woman could be accessory to her own abortion. Clearly, a person can conspire to commit an offence where he would be accessory to the offence. It may be doubted, however, whether *R. v. Sockett* was correctly decided. The court might well have discovered a legislative intention to exempt the non-pregnant woman. Even so, she may now be convicted of conspiracy by reason of the unhappy wording of the *Criminal Law Act 1977*.

[119] This example is based on the old case of *R. v. Duguid* (1906) 70 J.P. 294. Such an exemption no longer applies, see section 1 of the *Child Abduction Act 1984*; *R. v. Taylor* [1997] 1 Cr. App. R. 329 (where a mother was convicted of abducting her child).

[120] *R. v. Sherry* [1993] Crim. L.R. 536.

[121] To add another anomaly, if the brother had a claim of right because he did not know that the mother had been deprived of the legal custody of the child, the mother would not be guilty of conspiracy because section 1 of the *Criminal Law Act 1977*, while not requiring double liability for the consummated offence, requires double knowledge of the facts.

particular case she is exempted by reason of the fact that she is the victim of the intended offence. Section 2(1) of the *Act* provides:

"(1)   A person shall not by virtue of section 1 above be guilty of conspiracy to commit any offence if he is an intended victim of that offence."

Although this provision meets the particular point, it is clumsy draftsmanship, because it is capable of being construed too widely, and yet, in one respect, it is too narrow. However, problems are not likely to occur frequently. The provision is wider in that it could be construed to apply to anyone who is regarded as adversely affected by the offence. The word "victim" has been traditionally construed to mean a person who cannot *perpetrate the offence*, and who cannot be convicted as accessory to it because, being the victim of the offence, he is assumed to fall outside its scope.[122]

Contrast the masochist who conspires to have a sadist inflict actual bodily harm on him, not being exempted from the offence found in section 47 of the *Offences against the Person Act 1861*,[123] he cannot be regarded as the "victim" of that offence as a matter of law if the *Tyrrell*[124] doctrine is invoked, even though he may be regarded as the victim from the moral point of view. Since he can be convicted as perpetrator, it follows that he can be convicted as accessory; and therefore he should be liable for conspiring, and there is no reason why section 2(1) should apply.[125]   **16–050**

It was said above, that "the application of sections dealing with aiding and abetting may be excluded by the nature of the substantive offence or the general tenor or policy of the provisions by which it is created."[126] The general tenor of sections 18, 20 and 47 of the *Offences against the Person Act 1861* is to protect people from being subjected to physical violence. These offences aim to stop people from inflicting violence on others. The *Act of 1861* does not aim to criminalize what is effectively self-harm, even though the victim could also be a perpetrator on a different day.[127] The wording of section 2 of the *Criminal Law Act 1977* is such that the courts could apply it to victims more generally. There would be nothing to prevent the courts extending it to cases involving masochists so long as the masochists have not "agreed" to "reciprocate" the harm they have conspired to have inflicted upon themselves.[128] If they intend to reciprocate the harm by giving their harmer a thrashing and *vice versa*, then they intend to act as perpetrators as well as victims and would not be protected by section 2 of the *Criminal Law Act*.

If two people agree to duel each other they would intend to harm each other and thus intend to perpetrate crimes, even though they risk being a victim. But the

---

[122] *The Queen v. Tyrrell* [1894] 1 Q.B. 710; *R. v. Whitehouse* [1977] Q.B. 868.
[123] *R. v. Brown* [1994] 1 A.C. 212.
[124] *The Queen v. Tyrrell* [1894] 1 Q.B. 710.
[125] *R. v. Wright* (1603) Co.Lit. f. 127 a-b.; (1613) 1 East P.C. 396.
[126] *Mallan v. Lee* (1949) 80 C.L.R. 198 *per* Sir Owen Dixon J.
[127] Only the person inflicting the harm should be criminalized rather than the consenting victim and this is so even if the victim has encouraged the offending: see Dennis J. Baker, "The Moral Limits of Consent as a Defence in the Criminal Law," 12 *New Crim. L. Rev.* 93.
[128] Of course, such a victim would be caught by section 44 of the *Serious Crime Act 2007*.

situation would be different if V went to a euthanasia clinic. Here the victim has no intention of harming the physician: she merely intends that she be harmed. She should not be charged with conspiring to have herself murdered. (Compare section 2 of the *Suicide Act 1961*.)

16–051 **Can D rely on the "victim" exemption if he has conspired to have drugs supplied to himself?** No. He receives an illegal benefit, as does the lady who seeks an abortion.[129] If the illegal drug use goes wrong, then he will be a victim of his own stupidity,[130] but the mere receipt of the drug from his supplier does not mean that the supplier has victimized him.[131]

16–052 **But is it going too far to criminalize agreements by two persons where they are merely the supply and demand sides (as so to speak) of one criminal transaction?** In some U.S. states the courts invoke what has become known as the "Wharton Rule"[132] Wharton's Rule has been applied restrictively, however:[133]

> "Historically, Wharton's Rule was only a narrow common law exception that provided that a defendant cannot be punished for conspiracy and a substantive offense if the substantive offense itself requires the participation of two persons. 'The basic idea of Wharton's Rule is that where a [substantive] crime requires a plurality of agents for its commission, a charge of conspiracy cannot be used to impose a heavier penalty. ... Wharton's Rule reflects an era where conspiracy law was still developing, and it traditionally applied to offenses such as adultery, incest, bigamy, and duelling that were 'characterized by the general congruence of the agreement and the completed substantive offence ....'"

The Wharton Rule does not exempt bilateral transactions from criminalization, it merely aims to prevent the parties to such a transaction from being disproportionately punished.[134] There is nothing to be gained from exempting those who conspire to get others to supply drugs to them, or conspire to have a duel or gang battle in a London street.[135] Why wait for the duellers or gangsters to fight it out thereby allowing them either to kill each other or an innocent

---

[129] Cf. *R. v. Whitchurch* (1890) 24 Q.B.D. 420.

[130] *R. v. Kennedy (No 2)* [2008] 1 A.C. 269.

[131] *R. v. Drew* [2000] 1 Cr. App. R. 91; *R. v. Jackson* [2000] 1 Cr. App. R. 97. See also *Maroney v. The Queen* (2003) 216 C.L.R. 31.

[132] Named after its author, Professor Francis Wharton. Francis Wharton, *Criminal Law*, (Rochester, New York: Lawyers Co-operative Publishing Co., Vol. II, 12ᵗʰ edn. 1932) at 1862.

[133] *U.S. v. McNair*, 605 F.3d 1152 at 1215 (2010). In *McNair* the United States Court of Appeals (11ᵗʰ Circuit) refused to apply the Wharton Rule to conspiracy to commit bribery, since "'the consequences of bribery not only affect the parties to the crime but have a negative effect on society at large,' ... the agreement connected with the substantive offence of bribery ... poses 'the distinct kinds of threats to society that the law of conspiracy seeks to avert.'"

[134] A Federal Court in the U.S. recently held: "'Wharton's Rule is, to some extent a relic of the discredited merger doctrine and should be interpreted narrowly' and explaining 'the Rule does not forbid charging both a conspiracy and the substantive offense, even when it applies' as it 'merely forbids sentencing on both counts.')" *U.S. v. McNair*, 605 F.3d 1152 at 1215 (2010). And it has also concluded that it should only apply when the legislature has expressed intent that crimes should not merge. *Iannelli v. U. S.*, 420 U.S. 770 (1975).

[135] *R. v. Drew* [2000] 1 Cr. App. R. 91; *R. v. Jackson* [2000] 1 Cr. App. R. 97. See also *Sayce v. Coupe* [1953] 1 Q.B. 1 at 7-8. If two gang members agree to meet in a London street for a shootout, then they should be held liable for conspiring to murder each other. It is best that the law steps in before the situation ends up as it did in *R. v. Gnango* [2011] 1 All E.R. 153.

passerby? Conspiracy aims to nip such offending in the bud before it is consummated or even attempted. Most of these cases would now be caught by the offences found in sections 44-46 of the *Serious Crime Act 2007*. The victim rule does not exempt those who engage in bilateral offending. A dueller is not merely a victim since he is both a potential victim and a potential perpetrator. Consequently, the dueller is not protected by the victim exemption. Those who try to bribe government officials are not victims, nor are those who seek the illicit benefits of drug use, so they too would not be protected by the victim exemption.

A person who conspires to have herself euthanatized should be exempt from conspiring to have herself murdered. Similarly, there is little to be gained from criminalizing the masochist who seeks to have only himself harmed; and who has no intention of reciprocating that harm. He could not be punished for the substantive offence contrary to section 47 of the *Offences against the Person Act 1861*, because he would not satisfy the *mens rea* and *actus reus* requirements of that offence, if he were simply allowing himself to take a whipping. Society is sufficiently protected if the person inflicting the harm is criminalized. There is little to be gained from criminalizing the receiver of the harm, when the receiver has no intention of reciprocating the harm or engaging in any other form of substantive criminality. However, such offenders could come within the purview of the offences found in sections 44-45 of the *Serious Crime Act 2007*, as it only exempts victims in the narrower sense.[136] In practice, the prosecution does not normally charge such victims.

In another respect the provision in the *Criminal Law Act 1977* is too narrow as far **16–053** as victims are concerned. The rule that an intended victim of an offence is not an accessory to it is merely one instance of what should be regarded as a wider proposition, that a person is not an accessory to a statutory offence if it was evidently the intention of the legislature to exempt him. The *Act* fails to provide exemption from conspiracy on this wider, ground, so the possibility arises of a person who cannot be convicted as accessory to an offence when it is committed being liable for conspiracy to commit it.

The case of *R. v. Whitehouse*[137] has already been party considered. The court held that if a person defiles his daughter aged under 16, she cannot be convicted of incest[138]—not as perpetrator, because the statute leaves her out of the wording of the offence, confining the offence to adults, and not as accessory, because she was the victim of the offence. No doubt a future court will accept this reason and hold, in consequence, that the girl is the "victim" of the offence within section 2(1) above, and so cannot be guilty of conspiring to commit it. But it has already been suggested that the court was wrong in applying the "victim" rule in *R. v. Whitehouse*, and should have put the exemption on the wider ground that the legislature showed an intention not to include the daughter in the offence. If the exemption is placed on this wider ground, and not on the "victim" rule, section 2(1) would not apply. Section 1(1) would make her liable, since she is party to an

---

[136] Section 51 of the *Serious Crime Act 2007* makes it clear that the exemption applies only if the offence "exists (wholly or in part) for the protection of a particular *category* of person…".

[137] [1977] Q.B. 868.

[138] This conduct is caught by sections 25 and 26 (and also sections 63 and 64 for adults) of the *Sexual Offences Act 2003*.

agreement for an offence to be committed by her father. There would be a considerable anomaly if the daughter were to be held not guilty as accessory to incest when it is committed, because of the obvious intention of the statute, and yet be guilty of conspiracy to commit it because of the inept wording of the *Criminal Law Act 1977*.

Although the problem can be avoided for incest (as it is now likely to be charged merely as a sexual offence against a minor) if the court uncritically accepts the *ratio decidendi* of *R. v. Whitehouse*, there are other possible situations that cannot be dealt with in this way. The victim rule is only one example of the proposition that the courts may find that a person is excluded by implication from liability as accessory to a statutory offence. Others may be suggested. There is a long and well understood tradition in our law that prostitution is not an offence in itself. But the prostitute is hedged about by restrictions, so that it is quite difficult for her to continue her way of life within the law, and the law also directs itself against those who help her in her trade. For example, it is a statutory offence for the occupier of premises to permit them to be used for habitual prostitution.[139] Suppose a man who has a woman lodger permits her to use her room for habitual prostitution. The man commits an offence under the statute, but it would be wrong to convict the woman as accessory to the offence, because that would run counter to the policy that can be seen to underlie all the legislation, of leaving untouched the prostitute who carries out her occupation in accordance with the rules restricting the ways in which she can do so.[140]

16.10.   AGREEMENT WITH AN EXEMPT PARTY

16–054 The previous discussion concerned the liability for conspiracy of an exempt party, where he entered into an agreement with one whom we may call a liable party. We must now consider the liability for conspiracy in these circumstances of the liable party. Granted that he will be liable for the consummated offence when it is committed, is he liable for conspiracy if his agreement to commit the crime is with an exempt party and no one else?

The Law Commission reached a clear and satisfactory decision on this question. In their view, the liable party should never in these circumstances be liable for conspiracy. His liability should be left to the law of incitement, attempt and complicity.[141] The Bill proposed by the Commission would have given effect to this proposal, but it was amended in the House of Lords in a way that makes it

---

[139] Section 36 of the *Sexual Offences Act 1956*.

[140] The point has not arisen above magisterial level. In *R. v. King* (1914) 10 Cr. App. R. 117 the Court of Criminal Appeal held that a prostitute who gave her immoral earnings to a man was not an accessory to his offence of living on her immoral earnings, for the purpose of the "accomplice warning" in the law of evidence; but no reason was offered. In *R. v. Pickford* (1914) 10 Cr. App. R. 269, the rule was approved and the reason given was that the woman might have acted under compulsion. The reason is clearly mistaken: an accessory need not have the qualification required for a perpetrator. The best justification for the rule in *R. v. King* is that the statute is intended, at least in part, to protect the prostitute from exploitation. But this is not the only reason for the statute: another is to prevent men from building up illicit fortunes by organizing prostitution. This would suggest that the woman should be regarded as an accomplice.

[141] Law Commission, *Report on Conspiracy and Criminal Law Reform*, (London: H.M.S.O. Law Com. No. 76, 1976), paras. 1.50-1.58.

somewhat obscure. If you would like to have a summary of the resulting provision in tabloid form, it is that (1) the liable party is not liable for conspiracy if the other party (or all the other parties) lacked *mens rea*, but (2) is liable if the other party is exempted by reason of some special rule of law, except in two cases: where the other party is either a small child or the victim:

(1) We will begin with cases where the other party is exempt because he lacked *mens rea*. It has already been argued that section 1 requires all parties to a criminal conspiracy to know the facts (note the words "their intentions" in section 1(1), and the additional provision in section 1(2)). If the other parties are not guilty of conspiracy because they did not know the facts, then the defendant is not guilty of conspiracy either.

An illustration would be where D1 engages D2, an innocent agent, to handle stolen goods. D2 is not guilty of conspiring to handle stolen goods, because he lacks the intention, so D1 is not guilty either, because section 1(1) requires a joint intention. This construction of the *Act* is in accordance with the common law.[142]

A problem arises for the police and their informers. Suppose that D1, wishing to steal V's furniture, is looking for an assistant. He ropes in D2, who unfortunately for him is a policeman. D2 pretends to agree, in order to frustrate the plan. Is D1 guilty of conspiracy?

It has already been suggested that D2 may perhaps be held not guilty of conspiracy because he does not really agree to the commission of the offence, but only pretends to agree. If that is so, D1 is not guilty either. Section 1(1) does not apply, for the same reason as before: it requires two or more "intentions," and here there is only one. The fact that D2 thinks that D1 is agreeing with him does not matter. There is no conspiracy within the subsection. The exemption of D1 may not be sound policy on common sense, but the *Act* does not embrace him. If, however, D2 is held guilty, then of course D1 can be convicted of conspiracy with him.[143]

(2) Next, the fiddling rules for cases where the exempt party is exempt by reason of some special rule of law. The effect of the *Act*, reversing the proposal of the Law Commission, is presently to be noted. The *Act* therefore preserves the effect of *R. v. Duguid*,[144] a case on abducting children.   **16–055**

It was held Duguid could be convicted at common law of conspiring with a mother to abduct her child from its guardian; yet the mother herself could seemingly not have been convicted of conspiracy, since she was not within the scope of the consummated crime.[145]

We have already seen that owing to the incompetent wording of the *Act* the mother herself would now be liable for conspiracy, there being nothing in the *Act* to exempt her, notwithstanding that it was the intention of the section 56 of the

---

[142] *R. v. Curr* [1968] 2 Q.B. 944.

[143] If policeman intends that the object of the conspiracy be carried out so that he might entrap D (rather than frustrate the object of the conspiracy), then D will be liable, as might the policeman. *Chiu-Cheung v. The Queen* [1995] 1 A.C. 111.

[144] (1906) 70 J.P. 294.

[145] The last point was left open in *R. v. Duguid* (1906) 70 J.P. 294.

Offences against the Person Act 1861 to exempt her from liability for the consummated offence. So the problem under discussion would no longer present any difficulty in this particular case.

The *Act* establishes certain exceptions to the general principle. Section 2(2):

> "A person shall not by virtue of section 1 above be guilty of conspiracy to commit any offence or offences if the only other person or persons with whom he agrees are (both initially and at all times during the currency of the agreement) persons of any one or more of the following descriptions, that is to say—
> (a)   his spouse [or civil partner];
> (b)   a person under the age of criminal responsibility; and
> (c)   an intended victim of that offence or of each of those offences."

16–056   Paragraph (*a*) has already been dealt with. Paragraph (*b*) means that an agreement between an adult and a child under 10 cannot be a conspiracy. This is important chiefly for sexual offences. The child may encourage an adult to commit the offence, and the adult may agree; if matters remain at that stage, it would be harsh to hold the adult guilty. If on the other hand the adult encourages the child, this could be held to be an attempt on this part to commit the offence.[146] So there is no need to treat the case as one of conspiracy, and solid argument against doing so.

Paragraph (*c*) has the same effect where a man agrees with a girl under 16 that they shall have sexual intercourse together. The girl will be in law regarded as the victim of the offence, even if she instigated it, and the man will escape a conspiracy charge.

16.11. IMPOSSIBILITY

16–057   We have already considered impossibility in the context of attempts. It was noted that there are three forms of impossibility: (1) legal impossibility; (2) factual impossibility; and (3) inherent factual impossibility. It was also noted, that only legal impossibility and inherent factual impossibility provide defences. Is the situation the same in the context of conspiracy? Section 1(1) of the *Criminal Law Act 1977* catches agreements even if the facts "render the commission of the offence or any of the offences impossible."

If the agreement constitutes a statutory conspiracy, factual impossibility will not provide a defence. However, factual impossibility does provide a defence where the conspiracy is a "common law" conspiracy.[147] Common law conspiracies are likely to be far and few between if the Crown Prosecution Service clutch the *Fraud Act 2006* with alacrity. Of course, legal impossibility exempts the would-be conspirators from being convicted of statutory conspiracy, as the agreement must be to commit a crime.

Suppose two foreign tourists agree to go swimming at a public beach wearing nothing but a bikini bottom. They believe that it is a criminal offence to wear so little on a public beach in England and Wales, but agree to do it anyway.

---

[146] The *Sexual Offences Act 2003* contains a range of incitement offences which specifically aim to protect children.
[147] *D.P.P. v. Nock* [1978] A.C. 979.

Is this an insufficiency of means case or legal impossibility? If they really intend to commit indecent exposure then it would be a case of insufficient means—in that they have not taken enough off.[148] But if they merely think that it is criminal to wear a bikini on the beach, then they conspire to do a lawful act. If they believe that it is criminally indecent to wear red lipstick they would not commit statutory conspiracy, because again they conspire to do an innocuous and lawful act. The same applies if D1 and D2 agree to take a bottle of whisky with them for their picnic in Hyde Park thinking that it is an offence to drink alcohol in the park. Since it is not an offence to do so, they do not conspire to commit a criminal offence. 16–058

Nevertheless, a conviction for statutory conspiracy will stick regardless of whether it was factually impossible for the conspirators to achieve their aim. After all, their aim would have been achievable if the facts had been as they believed (*i.e.* if the pocket they conspired to pickpocket had a wallet in it, theft would have been achievable.)

What if D1 and D2 conspire to murder X, but agree to use (inherently insufficient) means that would make such a crime unattainable? Suppose they intend to commit the murder by merely sticking a pin in a voodoo doll. It was noted above, that in the context of attempts that this could not really be regarded as an act that has gone beyond the mere preparation stage, since objectively judged it is no different to someone learning how to use a gun in the months before he uses it to commit murder. Each time he practices using the gun he might envisage his intended victim as the target, but he is merely running through the motions—he is not on the job. He is not aiming at the actual target. Those who pin voodoo dolls are in the same position—they run through the motions but they are not on the job proper. The latter does not pass the evil thoughts stage! However, in the case of conspiracy this should not be a bar to conviction. 16–059

The conspirators in your hypothetical have agreed to commit the criminal offence of murder. This alone should be sufficient for grounding liability. They are not criminalized on the basis of whether or not they agree to use effective means, but on the basis that they agree to do a criminal act. They should be liable as they have agreed to kill another human being: it is irrelevant that the act would not even constitute mere preparation in the law of attempts, because the law of conspiracy reaches back further. As Lord Tucker put it long ago: "[I]t seems to me that the whole object of making such agreements punishable is to prevent the commission of the substantive offence before it has even reached the stage of an attempt, and that it is all part and parcel of the preservation of the Queen's peace within the realm."[149]

---

[148] The wording of section 66 of the *Sexual Offences Act 2003* means it would be almost physically impossible for a woman to commit the offence unless she does cartwheels down the street. It is not an offence to go topless on a public beach *per se*; nor are the police likely to treat it as a public order offence if the conduct takes place on a beach. See section 5 of the *Public Order Act 1986*. Equality means both men and women must be treated equally under the criminal law, so women should be allowed to take their tops off on the beach or in the park. See *People v. Santorelli*, 80 N.Y.2d 875 (1992).

[149] *Board of Trade v. Owen* [1957] A.C. 602 at 626 *per* Lord Tucker.

Thus, inherent factual impossibility is likely to be excluded as a defence to statutory conspiracy. The courts might distinguish inherent factual impossibility by holding that pinning a voodoo doll is not a "course of conduct" that would "necessarily amount to or involve the commission of any offence," since its impossibility does not depend on the "existence of facts which render the commission of the offence or any of the offences impossible." It is inherently impossible: it is not the facts on the day in question that make it impossible, but it is impossible at all times for all people to achieve. Nevertheless for the reasons already given, the courts are not likely to make any distinction between factual and inherent factual impossibility.[150]

---

[150] *D.P.P. v. Nock* [1978] A.C. 979 itself could be explained as an inherent factual impossibility case, as the defendants might as well have conspired to extract drugs from lemonade. And it is doubtful any court would let their like evade a statutory conspiracy conviction merely because what they conspired to do was inherently unachievable given the means they adopted.

CHAPTER 17

OTHER INCHOATE OFFENCES

"When you have said a thing, that fixes it, and you must take the consequences."[1]

The Red Queen to Alice.

17.1. INCITEMENT

At common law the offence of incitement (or solicitation) was committed when a person "counselled, procured or commanded" another to commit a crime, whether as perpetrator or as accessory, and whether or not the person incited did what he was urged to do. If he did, the inciter would of course have been an accomplice and would normally have been charged as such; but on a charge of incitement it was no defence to show that the crime was actually committed. Incitement only covered acts of persuasion or encouragement, so it did not cover attempts to assist another to commit a crime.

17–001

The assister of crime did not commit an offence at common law if the crime was not committed. After supplying assistance an accomplice can make quite strenuous attempts to prevent it being *used* and thus might evade liability, but under the *Serious Crime Act 2007* he will be liable even if he prevents his assistance from being used. (All references in this chapter are to this *Act*, unless the contrary is expressed or clearly implied.) It was this small gap in the law, among other things,[2] that provided the impetus for the enactment of the offences found in sections 44-46 of the *Serious Crime Act 2007*. The *2007 Act* criminalizes those who "encourage" or "assist" others to commit substantive offences regardless of whether those others actually attempt to commit the anticipated offence.[3]

The fact that the common law did not cover attempts to assist meant that there was a gap in the law. The Law Commission took the view that the gap was a serious one:

---

[1] We might add, or "When you have done a thing."

[2] The common law offence of incitement also warranted a tidy up. One issue that has not been addressed in the *Act of 2007* is the defence of impossibility, which applied to the common law offence of incitement. The new *Act* makes no mention of it.

[3] I use the label "anticipated offence" (as used in the *2007 Act*) as the inchoate offences are substantive offences too.

> "Parliament has enacted a considerable number of statutory offences that criminalise particular instances of inchoate assistance.[4] However, there are no statutory inchoate offences of *assisting* some of the most serious, including murder, robbery, blackmail or burglary. … We agree with Professor Spencer that there 'is a general problem, and it needs a general solution."[5]

17–002   The Law Commission's recommendations led to major reform. The straightforward offence of incitement was abrogated and replaced with three rather cumbersome offences:

1.   Intentionally encouraging or assisting an offence.
2.   Encouraging or assisting an offence believing it will be committed.
3.   Encouraging or assisting offences believing one or more will be committed.

As originally conceived by the Law Commission, these offences were to replace complicity. Unfortunately, the Government when enacting these new offences decided not to reform[6] complicity. So they live side by side but they are separate. This allows the prosecutor to cherry-pick, if the encouraged or assisted perpetrator actually attempts or consummates the anticipated substantive crime, the prosecutor will be able to charge under the *Accessories and Abettors Act 1861*, which in effect allows the defendant to be convicted and sentenced as a perpetrator. If the perpetrator does not commit (or attempt) the anticipated substantive crime, the prosecutor can go for one of the inchoate offences found in sections 44-46 of the *Serious Crime Act 2007*.

17–003   **Is the assister/encourager labelled as a perpetrator of the anticipated substantive offence?**   No. If D attempts to assist a murder, he will not be labelled as a perpetrator of murder. The encourager/assister is not punished or convicted for anything other than an inchoate offence.

17–004   **Is the encourager/assister subject to the same punishment as is available for the anticipated offence?**   Section 58(1) provides:

(1)   Subsections (2) and (3) apply if–
    (a)   a person is convicted of an offence under section 44 or 45; or
    (b)   a person is convicted of an offence under section 46 by reference to only one offence ("the reference offence").
(2)   If the anticipated or reference offence is murder, he is liable to imprisonment for life.

---

[4] Citing the *Treason Act 1351*; section 39 of the *Prison Act 1952*; section 17(1) of the *Forgery and Counterfeiting Act 1981*; section 2(1)(b) of the *Computer Misuse Act 1990*; sections 12(2) and 17 of the *Terrorism Act 2000*; section 4(2) of the *Asylum and Immigration (Treatment of Claimants) Act 2004*.

[5] Law Commission, *Inchoate Liability for Assisting and Encouraging Crime*, Report 300, (London: H.M.S.O., 2006) at para. 3.7.

[6] The Law Commission later realized this would be a mistake, so proposed that complicity should be reformed so that it would only apply to those who intentionally encourage or assist the attempted or consummated offending of others. See Law Commission, *Participating in Crime*, Report 305, (London. H.M.S.O., 2007).

(3)   In any other case he is liable to any penalty for which he would be liable on conviction of the anticipated or reference offence.

(4)   Subsections (5) to (7) apply if a person is convicted of an offence under section 46 by reference to more than one offence ("the reference offences").

(5)   If one of the reference offences is murder, he is liable to imprisonment for life.

(6)   If none of the reference offences is murder but one or more of them is punishable with imprisonment, he is liable–(a) to imprisonment for a term not exceeding the maximum term provided for any one of those offences (taking the longer or the longest term as the limit for the purposes of this paragraph where the terms provided differ); or (b) to a fine.

(7)   In any other case he is liable to a fine.

Section 58 allows for punishment equal to that available for the reference offence, but that does not mean the court has to impose the maximum penalty. The assister/encourager may receive the maximum sentence for the crime encouraged or assisted under the *Serious Crime Act 2007*, but that is within the discretion of the court. So in a case where the crime assisted or encouraged is murder, the defendant may receive a life sentence alongside the perpetrator, the murderer, if, say, his potential assistance would have been substantial and he shared a common purpose with the perpetrator. Nevertheless, the defendant may receive a much lesser sentence if his assistance was not substantial and he did not share a common purpose with the perpetrator. Contrast if the defendant was charged as an accomplice to the perpetrator's murder under the *Accessories Abettors Act 1861*. Here, he would be labelled and punished as a perpetrator of murder.

Under the law of complicity, reckless[7] and insubstantial assistance is enough to allow the defendant to be labelled and sentenced as a perpetrator. As an accomplice to murder, a defendant would be guilty of murder and subject to the mandatory life sentence. Consequently, if a defendant sells a gun believing that it might be used to kill, he is treated no different to the defendant who supplies a gun "intending" it will be used to kill. The new offences have the advantage of providing an opportunity for the sentencing judge to consider D's level of culpability and the magnitude of his acts of encouragement and assistance.

Are the offences triable either way?   Section 55(1) provides "An offence under section 44 or 45 is triable in the same way as the anticipated offence." And section 55(2) "An offence under section 46 is triable on indictment."   **17–005**

17.2.   INTENTIONAL ENCOURAGEMENT AND ASSISTANCE

Section 44 of the *Serious Crime Act 2007* criminalizes those who intentionally encourage or assist another to commit an offence. The crime is made out regardless of whether the anticipated crime is attempted or committed. Section 44 provides: **17–006**

---

[7] See *R. v. Bryce* [2004] 2 Cr. App. R. 592.

"(1)   A person commits an offence if–
    (a)   he does an act capable of encouraging or assisting the commission of an offence; and
    (b)   he intends to encourage or assist its commission.
(2)   But he is not to be taken to have intended to encourage or assist the commission of an offence merely because such encouragement or assistance was a foreseeable consequence of his act."

The section 44 offence replaces the common law offence of incitement. The common law offence of incitement (or solicitation) was committed when one person "counselled, procured or commanded" another to commit a crime, whether as perpetrator or as accessory, and whether or not the person incited did what he was urged to do. The section 44 offence works in the same way, since the encouragement need not actually encourage the potential perpetrator to act. But it is more expansive in that it also covers attempted assistance—or to put it another way assistance that is provided but is not used. Any persuasion or encouragement (including a threat)[8] is sufficient for the purposes of section 44.

17–007   When is an act "capable" of encouraging or assisting?   The defendant must do some act which is "capable" of assisting or encouraging the perpetrator to commit a crime. The *Act* probably does not catch acts (incomplete attempts to assist or encourage) that are putatively capable of assisting or encouraging the defendant to commit a crime. If D1 mails a gun to D2 so that D2 might use it to kill a rival, D1 should not be liable if the gun gets lost in the post. D1's act is not *in fact* capable of assisting D2, because the gun never arrives. D2 cannot kill or attempt to kill his rival with a gun he does not have. Compare this to the situation where the gun does arrive, but D2 decides not to use it. In the latter situation, D1's act is in fact capable of assisting D2 to kill.

Section 44 also has to be read in conjunction with subsection 47(8) of the *Act*, which provides: "Reference in this section to the doing of an act includes reference to–(a) a failure to act; and (b) the continuation of an act that has already begun…". Consequently, encouraging or assisting someone who is in the middle of raping a woman would be caught, since the sexual intercourse is a continuing act.[9] Furthermore, an omission that is capable of assisting or encouraging another to commit a crime comes within the purview of the offences.

17–008   If a disgruntled jewellery shop employee deliberately leaves his employer's shop window open believing it will facilitate a burglary, is he liable?   Section 65(2)(b) provides: "A reference in this Part to a person's doing an act that is capable of encouraging or assisting the commission of an offence includes a reference to his doing so" by "failing to take reasonable steps to discharge a duty." In your hypothetical the disgruntled employer not only failed to take reasonable steps to discharge his duty, but deliberately left the window open intending to assist burglars. If he had merely forgotten to close the window, he would not be caught by the subsection.

---

[8] Section 65 of the *Serious Crime Act 2007*.
[9] *Kaitamaki v. The Queen* [1985] A.C. 147; *R. v. Schaub* [1994] Crim. L.R. 531. D would not be liable for merely standing by and watching a continuing act of rape, unless he had a duty to take reasonable steps to prevent it. Cf. *R. v. Clarkson* [1971] 1 W.L.R. 1402.

What constitutes an act of encouragement? Is a cool suggestion, without attempt to persuade, the suggester having no interest in the matter one way or the other, sufficient? A suggestion may, of course, be encouragement in itself, particularly for those who, as Shakespeare put it, "take suggestion that as a cat laps milk." The section 44 offence (leaving the assistance side of the equation aside for the moment) applies only to intentional persuasions or encouragements to crime.

17–009

Let us take an obvious example. In the old incitement case, *R. v. Fitzmaurice*,[10] the defendant approached X and informed him of a proposed robbery, inviting his cooperation, for which he promised reward. Fitzmaurice's conviction of incitement was upheld on appeal, the court saying that the trial judge had "rightly focused the attention of the jury on the element of persuasion which it was necessary for the prosecution to prove." As an example of a case where this element would be lacking, the Court of Appeal instanced the case of a person whose role is "limited to informing certain named individuals that the planner of the enterprise would like to see them." He would not be guilty in the latter situation.

It is presumed that section 44 will require this type of purposeful encouragement—purposeful in that it is a straightforward request that X commit a particular offence. If X has not been asked to commit an offence, then the act of "inviting him" to meet with a gang leader who may thereafter encourage him to commit an offence is not in itself capable of encouraging him to commit an offence—as there is no mention of crime. But by taking X to meet the gang leader, D assists the gang leader to commit the section 44 offence. The gang leader commits the section 44 offence by asking D to bring X (and also by encouraging X to commit the crime he has in mind) to him so that he can encourage X to commit an offence, so D will liable under section 44 himself, because he assists the gang leader to commit the section 44 offence.

What if instead of inviting X to meet the gang leader, D had merely passed on a message of encouragement from the gang leader? "If a person (D1) arranges for a person (D2) to do an act that is capable of encouraging or assisting the commission of an offence, and D2 does the act, D1 is also to be treated for the purposes of this Part as having done it."[11] For example, if D1 and D2 pay D3 £1,000 to arrange for V to be beaten, all three will be liable for encouraging the attack. As another example, D1 might encourage D2 to encourage "a person or persons unknown, to murder X."[12] An example involving assistance might be where D3 encourages D2 to assist D1 in the commission of crime to be perpetrated by D1. Let us assume that D3 asks D2 to supply D1 with a gun so that D1 can kill V. D3 is regarded as having supplied the gun himself. The act of supplying a gun is an act which is capable of assisting D1 to commit murder. Another example might be where D1 writes a letter to X encouraging him to

17–010

---

[10] [1983] 2 W.L.R. 227.

[11] Section 66 of the *Serious Crime Act 2007*. For some pre-*Act* examples, of incitement to incite, see *R. v. Bodin* [1979] Crim. L.R. 176; *R. v. Sirat* (1986) 83 Cr. App. R. 41.

[12] In *R. v. Evans* [1986] Crim. L.R. 470, Evans "offered B £1,000 to see someone who could 'put a contract out' on X, saying she wanted X dead."

commit a crime and D2 knowingly delivers the missive for him. At common law, D2 could have been treated as an accessory of D1's incitement.

17–011   **Suppose a person facilitates a crime by supplying tools, materials or information, so that if the crime is committed he would be an accessory.[13] If it is not committed or attempted, is he an encourager/assister under section 44?**   Yes, it does not matter that his attempt to encourage or assist the commission of the crime was not successful.[14] He could also be charged under section 44, if the crime is consummated. It is not an offence that targets purely inchoate conduct.

17–012   **Where a statute makes it an offence to sell something, is the buyer counted as an assister/encourager?**   Can it not be said that every case where Parliament penalizes one party to a bilateral transaction, it must have intended to leave the other party free from liability? In relation to complicity, it was said above that this is quite an important point, on which the American[15] and English courts have diverged. When a statute makes it an offence for one party to enter into a transaction, the English courts sometimes convict the other party as accessory if he knew the facts.[16] A single bilateral transaction could involve independent acts of encouragement and assistance. Therefore, a single transaction could result in more than one party committing an inchoate offence.

The *Act* clearly catches straightforward bilateral transactions. For example, in *R. v. Goldman*,[17] Goldman was convicted of attempting to incite his potential supplier to distribute photographs of children under the age of 16.[18] Goldman had responded to an advertisement placed by X (the potential supplier) by requesting pornographic video tapes of girls aged 7 to 13. Goldman sent X payment for the video tapes, but X did not supply them. Goldman was convicted because he had tried to encourage X to "distribute" the illegal videos.

Nevertheless, it would be wrong to leave X out of the equation, as he was the original instigator. Arguably, X was trying to encourage Goldman and his ilk to possess child pornography.[19] X might not have encouraged Goldman to distribute

---

[13] You will recall that a person is only an accessory under the *Accessories and Abettors Act 1861*, if the offence that he has encouraged or assisted is attempted or consummated. His liability derives from the perpetrator's (principal's) attempt or successful commission of the substantive offence.

[14] See section 49 of the *Serious Crime Act 2007*. Cf. the common law offence of incitement: Glanville Williams, *Textbook of Criminal Law*, (London: Stevens & Sons, 1983) at 439.

[15] Courts in the United States have rejected such an approach. In *Robinson v. State*, 815 S.W.2d 361, at 363-364 (1991), the Court of Appeals of Texas said: "Numerous jurisdictions [in the U.S.] have addressed the question presented here, and all have reached the same result. ... There is a definite distinction between a seller and a buyer. Their separate acts may result in a single transaction, but the buyer is not aiding the 'selling act' of the seller and the seller is not aiding the 'buying act' of the buyer. The buyer and seller act from different poles. They are not in association or confederacy. An accomplice is one who participates in the same criminal conduct as the defendant, not one whose conduct is the antithesis of the defendant, albeit the conduct of both is involved in a single transaction."

[16] *Sayce v. Coupe* [1953] 1 Q.B. 1; *R. v. Potts* (1818) Russ. & Ry. 353.

[17] *R. v. Goldman* [2001] EWCA Crim. 1684.

[18] Goldman attempted to commit a substantive offence. The substantive offence of which he attempted to incite another to commit is set out in section 1 of the *Protection of Children Act 1978*.

[19] There were jurisdictional issues involved, however.

the videos, but his advertisement surely encouraged him to possess them.[20] X must have believed that by encouraging people to purchase child pornography those same people "would" commit the offence of possessing it. If the supplier is the person who initiated the idea, then he has obviously encouraged the crime. But, if the would-be perpetrator goes to the supplier and asks for the supply, the fact of supply in itself should not be regarded as an encouragement, any more than it should be regarded as conspiracy.

The fact that a shop sells knives does not mean it encourages the world at large to use them to kill others. (Everyday articles can, however, be distinguished from articles that can be used for no other purpose but to commit crime, such as radar detectors and so on.) Nor is the supplier guilty of attempting to abet the crime, for the reason given before: the law does not know the doctrine of attempted abetment.[21]

Since possessing child pornography is an offence in itself, X could have been convicted of encouraging Goldman to commit an offence contrary to section 160(1) of the *Criminal Justice Act 1988*?   It appears that he would be caught by one of the offences found in sections 44 and 45 of the *Serious Crime Act 2007*. It is an offence in itself to possess such images. Therefore, X would be liable for encouraging D to commit the possession offence[22]—and *vice versa*. (Goldman would be liable for encouraging X to commit the "distribution" offence). And since the offences are inchoate, it does not matter that Goldman did not in fact obtain possession of the videos nor does it matter that X did not in fact supply them.   **17–013**

Is the act of placing an advertisement "capable" of encouraging a person to possess child pornography? Do cretins with such predilections need any encouragement?[23]   In one of the old incitement cases, *Invicta Plastics Ltd. v. Clare*,[24] a company advertised in a periodical a device that when installed in a car warned the driver that a police radar trap was operating. The company was convicted of inciting readers of the publication to use the unlicensed apparatus for wireless telegraphy in contravention of the *Wireless Telegraphy Act 1949*. This form of encouragement might also be caught by section 44 of the *Serious Crime Act*.   **17–014**

---

[20] Section 1(c) of the *Protection of Children Act 1978* criminalizes only those who possess the images for the purpose of distribution or for the purpose of showing others them. If the paedophile intends only to look at them himself, then he is not caught by that provision. For a discussion of the moral justification for criminalizing mere "possession," see Dennis J. Baker, "The Moral Limits of Criminalizing Remote Harms," (2007) 10(3) *New Crim. L. Rev.* 370.

[21] A person can be held liable as an "accessory" if he assists an "attempt" by the perpetrator (principal), but could not be held liable (under the *Accessories and Abettors Act 1861*) for attempting to assist. *R. v. Dunnington* [1984] Q.B. 472.

[22] See also section 63 of *Criminal Justice and Immigration Act 2008*, which criminalizes those who possess "extreme" images. See further *R. v. Chen* [2009] EWCA Crim. 2965; *Attorney-General's Reference (No.55 of 2008)* [2009] 1 W.L.R. 2158; *Crown Prosecution Service v. LR* [2010] 2 Cr. App. R. 9; *R. v. Hancock* [2010] EWCA Crim. 390.

[23] Arguably not! See Dennis J. Baker, "Punishment Without a Crime: Is Preventive Detention Reconcilable with Justice?" (2009) 34 *Austl. J. Leg. Phil.* 120; Suzanne Ost, *Child Pornography and Sexual Grooming*, (Cambridge: Cambridge University Press, 2009) at 108-134.

[24] [1976] R.T.R. 251.

Nevertheless, there is a fine distinction between this type of case and those cases where possession *per se* is criminalized. It is a crime to possess child pornography, articles for use in fraud,[25] certain types of illicit drugs,[26] and so on. Those who advertise such goods directly encourage others to commit "possession" crimes. In *Invicta Plastics Ltd. v. Clare*,[27] the drivers would have been convicted of an offence only if they had used the radar detection devices. It was not an offence merely to possess such a device. It appears the court was of the view that since the devices could serve no purpose other than a criminal one, that encouraging people to possess such devices was a way of encouraging them to use them. It was an offence to use such devices rather than to possess them. (Those who actually sell such a device at least attempt to "assist" the purchaser to speed and thus should come within the purview of the *Act of 2007*. They have done and act capable of assisting speeding.)

Similarly, it is not an offence to possess information about cultivating cannabis, even though it may be an offence to possess cannabis. Thus, if D provides information in a gardening book about growing cannabis, does he really encourage others to grow it? The courts think so.[28] Surely the autonomous agent is not so easily encouraged.[29] All D does is "assist" those who are already minded to engage in such conduct. It is his attempt to assist that is wrong. It would be possible to convict him under section 45 of the *2007 Act* if he intends or believes that one of his customers "will" be assisted. The encouragement may be directed to persons generally, as it was in *Invicta Plastics Ltd. v. Clare*,[30] and it may encourage a general course of crime.[31] If the person encouraged gives ear and assents to the plan proposed, he and the encourager become conspirators.

17–015 **But surely D would not encourage X to distribute child pornography if he took advantage of a self-service setup?** You are right—he should not be liable. If D serves himself, then he is the one who distributes the pornography. It would be too great an extension of criminal liability to classify self-serving as an act "capable" of encouraging other-serving. Self-service or self-distribution is not capable of encouraging others to distribute, as it does not require the distributor to do anything. D should only be brought within the purview of the *Act* if he makes a specific request and conveys, or attempts to convey, that request to the potential distributor. If D fills in an electronic form requesting pornographic videos which

---

[25] Section 6 of the *Fraud Act 2006*.

[26] Sections 5 and 28 of the *Misuse of Drugs Act 1971*.

[27] [1976] R.T.R. 251.

[28] *R. v. Marlow* [1998] 1 Cr. App. R. (S.) 273.

[29] On at least one occasion, the court has held that selling articles that could only be used to commit fraud to a middle man who would then encourage others to use them was not sufficient for establishing incitement at common law. As the defendants had not encouraged the middle man personally to use the articles, they were able to evade justice. See *R. v. James* (1986) 82 Cr. App. R. 226. However, they would now be caught by section 66 of the *Serious Crime Act 2007* which criminalizes indirect encouragement. In addition, such defendants directly encourage the middle man to possess an article for use in fraud, and thus encourage him to commit an offence contrary to section 6 of the *Fraud Act 2006*. The *Fraud Act* does not require the middle man to use the articles himself; it merely requires him to possess them intending that they be used in fraud.

[30] [1976] R.T.R. 251. See also *R. v. Jones* [2008] Q.B. 460; cf. *Baney v. State*, 42 So.3d 170 (2009).

[31] Section 67 of the *Serious Crime Act 2007*.

have to be physically sent to him, he would encourage X to send the videos. Similarly, he might convey his request by sending an e-mail or by posting a letter. So long as the encouragement is capable of encouraging an act of distribution on the distributor's part, D should be liable. D would be liable, for instance, if he encouraged X to e-mail images to him. But if the entire distribution is automated, in that D downloads a picture from a website and automatically transfers money to X's account, D's acts would not be capable of encouraging X to distribute.

When many paedophiles purchase child pornography they create the demand for the market in child pornography. But this type of remote encouragement is not caught by the *2007 Act*. The *Act* does not criminalize paedophiles at large merely because they collectively encourage others to go into the business of supplying child pornography. Rather, there has to be an individualized act of encouragement. The *2007 Act* deals with individual requests (acts of encouragement) for such material when those requests are conveyed (or there is an attempt to convey such requests) to a particular supplier. It is true that paedophiles create the demand for self-service websites containing these ghastly materials, but if they serve themselves they have not encouraged another to serve them. A supplier is encouraged to stay in business as the funds accumulate automatically into his account, but he is not encouraged to distribute to a particular individual. If a person leaves a pile of melons and pumpkins on an old table on the side of a highway, and leaves an honesty box on the table, he encourages the world at large to purchase his goods, but he himself is not encouraged by any particular individual to supply that individual. In the criminal law, responsibility is individual not collective; the criminal law targets individuals not collectives.[32]

Need the potential perpetrator be aware of the encouragement? Must it be communicated? It appears not.[33] It is only necessary to show that the "words," "acts," "actions," and so on were capable of encouraging the potential perpetrator, not that they did, or that they were communicated. Unused assistance is enough. If D sends X a letter to encourage him to suicide bomb the London underground, D will be liable so long as the words in his letter would have been capable of encouraging X and his ilk to commit such an atrocity. (It does not matter that the letter lies unopened on X's desk, as its delivery is the completion or consequence of an act that is *capable* of encouraging X to commit a crime).
    17–016

What mental element is required under section 44? D1 is liable under section 44 if he intends to encourage or assist D2 to commit an offence. Intention does not include oblique intention. It is not enough that D1 foresees that his act will almost certainly assist or encourage D2 to commit an offence. D is clearly caught by section 44 if he shares the perpetrator's purpose that the "anticipated or reference" offence be committed. The defendant must by his assistance or
    17–017

---

[32] Dennis J. Baker, "Collective Criminalization and the Constitutional Right to Endanger Others," (2009) 28(2) *Crim. Just. Ethics* 168.

[33] *Per contra*, the common law offence of incitement required actual "communication." *R. v. Banks* (1873) 12 Cox C.C. 393. The *Act of 2007* regards attempted assistance and encouragement as being no different than actual assistance or encouragement.

encouragement seek to bring about the perpetrator's offending.[34] A clear example is where D1 gives D2 his gun to commit murder, because he hates the person that he knows D2 intends to kill. Since D1 provides the gun and hopes D2 will succeed in killing the intended victim, he is caught by section 44.

D1 does an act which is capable of assisting the commission of the anticipated substantive offence and he intends to do this act (supply a gun) and intends to assist the perpetrator to commit murder. Furthermore, he also intends the potential consequences—he intends to assist for the purpose of ensuring that the perpetrator succeeds in killing V. This is a most straightforward case.

17–018   **Suppose D sells a gun in the ordinary course of business as a gunsmith. Is he liable if he believes his customer "might" use it to kill?**   If he merely believed his assistance (supply of a gun) might be used by D2 to commit an offence, he will not come within the purview of section 44.

17–019   **What if he believes that his customer is virtually certain to use the gun to kill?**   Again he should not come within the purview of the subsection. Section 44(2) expressly provides that D "is not to be taken to have intended to encourage or assist the commission of an offence merely because such encouragement or assistance was a *foreseeable consequence* of his act." Parliament intended to exclude "oblique intention" from section 44.[35] Thus, it is not enough for D to obliquely intend to assist or encourage an "act." The defendant must intend to assist or encourage the actual "act"—the shooting, the beating, the stabbing, *etc.* A person does not intend to assist or encourage a shooting merely because he sees it as a virtually certain consequence of selling a gun.

Nevertheless, section 47(2) provides: "If it is alleged under section 44(1)(b) that a person (D) intended to encourage or assist the commission of an offence, it is sufficient to prove that he intended to encourage or assist the doing of an *act* which would amount to the commission of that offence."[36]

Suppose D1 gives D2 a baseball bat intending to assist D2 to inflict grievous bodily harm upon V. D1 would be liable under section 44, because he intended to assist an act (the infliction of grievous bodily harm) which would amount to an offence under section 18 of the *Offences against the Person Act 1861*.

---

[34] The test would be akin to that expounded by Judge Learned Hand in *United States v. Peoni*, 100 F.2d 401 at 402 (2d Cir.1938), where he said: "[I]t [is] ... nothing whatever to do with the probability that the forbidden result would follow upon the [assister's/encourager's] conduct,... he must in some sort associate himself with the venture, in that he participates in it as in something that he wishes to bring about, that he seek by his action to make it succeed."

[35] When the relevant Bill was introduced, the Parliamentary Under-Secretary of State for Justice said: "The notion of intention is given a particular meaning by subsection (2) ... I hope that it assists the hon. Member for Hornchurch if I say that what we are trying to get at is that intention should be interpreted in a narrow way, and should exclude the concept of *virtual certainty*. It is equivalent to meaning that D's *purpose must be to assist or encourage the offence.*" (Hansard, HC Public Bill Committee, 6th Sitting, 3 July 2007, col.211.) *Pepper v. Hart* [1993] A.C. 593 means that courts should look at Parliamentary proceedings in Hansard "for the purpose of resolving ambiguity in the construction of statutes."

[36] *Serious Crime Act 2007.*

If D2 accidentally kills V, he is liable for murder. Is D1 liable for assisting murder or the section 18 offence?   Either way D1 is liable under section 44. However, when the case involves unintended consequences we need to look a little further. After all, it would make a difference as to the relevant sentence, since a non-mandatory life sentence is available when the reference offence is murder.

17–020

To ascertain whether D1 is liable for assisting or encouraging murder, we will need to examine the rules set out in sections 47(5), (6) and (7) of the *Serious Crime Act 2007*. If you enjoy verbal puzzles, the subsections may amuse you. If, on the other hand, you believe that the object of penal legislation is to give clear guidance to the citizen, judges and magistrates' clerks, advocates and legal advisors, its wilful opacity will lower your spirits. The subsection provides:

> "In proving for the purposes of this section whether an act is one which, if done, would amount to the commission of an offence–
>
> (a)   if the offence is one requiring proof of fault, it must be proved that–
>> (i)   D believed that, were the act to be done, it would be done with that fault;
>> (ii)   D was reckless as to whether or not it would be done with that fault; or
>> (iii)   D's state of mind was such that, were he to do it, it would be done with that fault; and
>
> (b)   if the offence is one requiring proof of particular circumstances or consequences (or both), it must be proved that–
>> (i)   D believed that, were the act to be done, it would be done in those circumstances or with those consequences; or
>> (ii)   D was reckless as to whether or not it would be done in those circumstances or with those consequences."

Unriddle me that.   Section 44 has to be read in conjunction with these cumbersome subsections. It is gobbledygook,[37] but careful thought will extract some sense from it. Subsections 47(5)(a)(i) and (ii) simply means that if the anticipated offence requires proof of fault:

17–021

1.   The encourager/assister must "believe" or "suspect" that the perpetrator will commit the *actus reus* with any fault required for it.
2.   If the anticipated offence requires proof of fault as to circumstances or consequences, then the encourager/assister must believe or suspect:
   a.   that if he assists or encourages the perpetrator to commit the *actus reus* of the anticipated offence that those consequences will result;
   b.   that if he assists or encourages the perpetrator to commit the *actus reus* of the anticipated offence that it will be committed in circumstances that make it criminal (*i.e.* that the perpetrator's act of sexual intercourse with V will be done in circumstances where she is not consenting).

---

[37] "The desideratum of clarity represents one of the most important ingredients of legality." Lon L. Fuller, *The Morality of Law*, (New Haven: Yale University Press, 1969), at 63, aptly cited by Professor Ibbetson as his opening line in David Ibbetson, "Encouraging or Assisting an Attempt," (2009) *Arch. News* 8. The practitioner is bound to find the provisions flummoxing; not to mention the undergraduate!

The overriding factor relates to the defendant's intention as far as the act or offence is concerned. If the defendant does not intend to assist or encourage the perpetrator to inflict grievous bodily harm there is no need to consider section 47, because section 44 has not been satisfied.

In your hypothetical D2 accidentally killed V, but D1 clearly intended to assist D2 to inflict grievous bodily harm. Since the *mens rea* for murder merely requires the perpetrator to intentionally inflict g.b.h., D1 must have also believed that D2 would act with the requisite fault for murder.

17–022 **But did X foresee the consequences?** Subsections 47(5)(b)(i) and (ii) mean that D1 will be liable so long as he believed or suspected that D2 might kill V or cause him g.b.h. Murder is an offence which requires proof as to consequences, so it must be shown that D1 believed or suspected that D2 would kill V.

Suppose D2, an 80-year-old man, asks D1 to drive him to V's house (V is a 25-year-old champion boxer) so that he can give V a clip under the ear for getting his 20-year-old granddaughter pregnant. D1 believes or suspects that D2 intends to cause V actual bodily harm and believes that the old man will act with the requisite fault for the offence found in section 47 of the *Offences against the Person Act 1861*. (Let us assume D1 intends to assist D2 to cause V to suffer a.b.h., because he wants to see an 80-year-old take on a young boxer). Unfortunately, when D2 pokes V with his walking stick V looses balance and hits his head on the corner of a table and dies. Is D1 liable for assisting manslaughter?

He will not be liable because he did not believe or suspect that V would be killed or would be caused g.b.h. (These are different consequences, but either consequence will do for the purposes of convicting him under the *Act of* 2007, as it is an independent offence. He is not charged with murder or an offence under the *Offences against the Person Act 1861*, but with an offence under the *Act of 2007*.) The subsection requires nothing less than subjective recklessness as to consequences.

17–023 **Are there cases where D believing or suspecting that a perpetrator will act with the requisite *mens rea* for the anticipated offence means that D must *a fortiori* believe or suspect that that particular consequence will transpire?** Perhaps there are.

Suppose D2, a drug dealer, wants to punish a customer who owes him money by throwing him from the sixth floor of an apartment building. D2 does not intend to kill the customer but merely wants him to suffer grievous bodily harm. Suppose also that D2 lives on the ground floor of his apartment building, so asks his friend, D1, who lives on the sixth floor, for permission to use his apartment to throw the customer out the window. D1 lets D2 use his apartment intending to assist his act of defenestration, because he owes D2 a favour.

A jury could infer "that death or serious bodily harm had been a virtual certainty (barring some unforeseen intervention) as a result of the defendant's actions and that the defendant had appreciated that such was the case."[38] Now, if D1 suspected or believed that D2 was obliquely intending to kill the customer,

---

[38] Arguably, on these facts a jury would hold that D2 foresaw the consequence of death as a virtual certainty. *R. v Woollin* [1999] 1 A.C. 82.

then D1 must have at least obliquely intended the consequences of the defenestration. Even if D1 did not envisage such a consequence as a virtual certainty, since the section only requires D1 to be reckless as to consequences he will be liable. In many of these cases the nature of the assisted or encouraged act will make it difficult for the assister/encourager to deny that he did not obliquely intend the consequences.[39]

If the drug dealer's customer dies, D1 would also be an accessory to murder. If the customer survives D2 might be liable for attempted murder and D1 as an accessory. What does section 44 add? Well, it could cut in if the attempt has not got past the more than merely preparatory stage. If D1 had given his apartment keys to D2 and said, "Use the apartment whenever you want to throw V out the window," D1's receipt of the keys would only be a preparatory act as far as his substantive offending is concerned. But D1's act of providing D2 with the keys to his high-rise apartment would be an act capable of assisting D2 in his quest to throw V from the window of a high-rise. In the latter situation, D1 would be liable under section 44, but D2 would not be liable for anything because the act of receiving the key would not be more than mere preparation.

What if D1 had only suspected that D2 might use his apartment for such a purpose?   He would not be liable because section 44 would not be satisfied. He would have to intend to assist the very act which caused the death: that is, the act of defenestration. Before recklessness or belief as to consequences becomes an issue, the assister/encourager must intentionally assist or encourage the perpetrator to do the criminal act that causes the consequences. Section 44 does not apply to situations where the assister/encourager recklessly assists or encouragers the perpetrator to commit the *actus reus* of the anticipated offence.   17–024

Suppose D2 has lost his house because of a bank foreclosure. D2 jokingly says to D1, "I should rob a bank, those rotten banks have taken it all from me." Suppose three days later D2 asks D1 if he can use D1's gun for a hunting trip. D1 is suspicious because the hunting season has not started. Furthermore, D2 has been acting a little odd and seems depressed. Nevertheless, D1 gives D2 "the benefit of the doubt" and thus lets him borrow the gun. The next night D2 commits armed robbery and kills a security guard during the robbery.

D1 is not liable for encouraging and assisting D2's act of robbery, as he did not intend to assist or encourage D2 to commit robbery. He merely intended to assist his hunting. He may have been reckless as to whether D2 was really going to use the gun for hunting, but this is not sufficient for grounding a conviction under section 44. Nor would it be enough to ground a conviction under sections 45 or 46 for assisting the robbery or murder, because D1 did not "believe" or "suspect" that D2 would use the gun to rob and kill. A reasonable person might have foreseen that D2 would do something bad, but the test is subjective not objective—and as we will see, sections 45-46 require a high degree of

---

[39] Section 47(7) provides: "In the case of an offence under section 44–(a) subsection (5)(b)(i) is to be read as if the reference to 'D believed' were a reference to 'D intended or believed;' but (b) D is not to be taken to have intended that an act would be done in particular circumstances or with particular consequences merely because its being done in those circumstances or with those consequences was a foreseeable consequence of his act of encouragement or assistance." This provision seems to add little, since mere recklessness is an alternative to intention as to consequences and circumstances.

recklessness. D2 could have committed suicide or done a number of bad things with the gun; D1's conjecturing about the possibilities does not make him liable.

17–025 **Is recklessness as to circumstances sufficient where it is for the anticipated reference offence?** Yes. Technically, it should not be enough for section 44, because that offence requires actual intention. Nevertheless, as we have seen the provisions in section 47 dispenses with that requirement in a number of ways.

Suppose Y had met and befriended V at a pub where they were both drinking heavily. Y arranges to meet X, who drives them all to a remote area. Y then has non-consensual sexual intercourse with V. Let us assume that X knew that Y intended to have sexual intercourse with V, and that he intended to assist Y to have sexual intercourse.[40]

Technically, if section 44 requires actual intention X should only be liable if he knew for a fact that the woman would not be consenting and that Y intended to have sexual intercourse in circumstances where she would not be consenting. If this were the case, X could be shown to have intended to assist an act of rape.

17–026 But there are two other possibilities:

1. X merely suspected that Y might have non-consensual intercourse with V;
2. X was negligent as to whether Y would have non-consensual sexual intercourse with V.

Since it is sufficient to prove that X "intended to encourage or assist the doing of an act which would amount to the commission of that offence,"[41] he will be caught by section 44. It is a criminal offence to have sexual intercourse with a woman in circumstances where a reasonable person would realize that she was not consenting,[42] so *a fortiori* it is a criminal offence for a person to have sexual intercourse in circumstances where he believes or suspects the victim might not be consenting. Since the act of non-consensual sexual intercourse would amount to a criminal offence, X will be liable, if it can be shown that he intended to assist Y to have sexual intercourse and believed or suspected that the victim would not be consenting. It must also be shown that he believed or suspected that Y had the requisite fault for the substantive offence.

17–027 **Is negligence as to circumstances sufficient where it is for the anticipated reference offence?** No. The defendant must believe or suspect the relevant circumstances will exist. It is not enough to show that the defendant negligently assisted the doing of an *act* which would amount to the commission of that offence. Nor is it enough to show that he was negligent as to whether the defendant would commit the crime with the requisite fault, or that he was negligent as the relevant circumstances.

---

[40] Cf. *R. v. McCarry* [2009] EWCA Crim. 1718.

[41] Section 47(2) of the *Serious Crime Act 2007*.

[42] The requisite fault for rape is intentional intercourse and negligence as to whether V is consenting. See section 1 of the *Sexual Offences Act 2003*.

Being reckless as to whether the defendant would commit the substantive **17–028**
offence in certain circumstances is one thing if the substantive offence only
requires the perpetrator to be negligent as to those circumstances, but
another if it requires the perpetrator to almost obliquely intend those
circumstances, is it not? You raise an important point. Suppose D2 tells D1
that he needs to pick up a shipment of cheap iPhones. D2 asks D1 to assist him by
driving him to pick them up. D2 will only be liable for the substantive offence of
receiving stolen goods if he knows or believes the goods are stolen. D1 could be
liable for assisting him, so long as he suspects the goods are stolen. Nevertheless,
all D1 intends to do is to assist D2 to risk handling stolen goods. He knows he is
assisting D2 to do an act that might (not "will") amount to the commission of an
offence. He could only intend to assist D2 to receive stolen goods, if he knew for
a fact that the goods that he was assisting D2 to collect were stolen. One cannot
intend chances.

Reverting to section 47(2); you will recall that subsection merely provides: "If
it is alleged under section 44(1)(b) that a person (D) intended to encourage or
assist the commission of an offence, it is sufficient to prove that he intended to
encourage or assist the doing of an *act* which would amount to the commission of
that offence."[43] It does not say that the defendant must know that the act would
amount to the commission of an offence. The act of picking up a shipment of
goods does not amount to an offence in itself. It would only amount to an offence
if the goods were stolen. Similarly, the act of having sexual intercourse does not
amount to the commission of an offence in itself. It would amount to the
commission of an offence if the woman was not consenting. Section 47(2) merely
requires the act to be of a kind that would amount to the commission of the
offence that the defendant was potentially assisting or encouraging. If the
defendant has been charged with assisting or encouraging the perpetrator to
receive or handle stolen goods, it need only be shown that the act of receiving the
stolen goods or handling them would amount to the commission of that offence.
The only foresight the defendant need have as to the potential criminality of the
innocuous act of collecting the goods is that stated in section 47(5). All that is
required is that it be demonstrated that he believed or suspected that the
circumstances were such that the goods might be stolen.

Again, section 47 seems to be in conflict with the strict intention requirement
found in section 44. This is particularly problematic in cases where it is the
circumstances that determine whether or not the act that was assisted would have
been an offence. The way the law stands, the defendant could commit the section
44 offence if he intentionally assists/encourages another to risk receiving stolen
goods, even if the goods turn out not to be stolen. All that needs to be shown is
that he believed or suspected that they were stolen, intended to assist the
perpetrator to receive and handle them, and believed or suspected that the
perpetrator knew or believed[44] the goods were stolen. (However, if he suspects
that latter, he perhaps also knows or believes the goods are stolen).

---

[43] *Serious Crime Act 2007.*
[44] See section 22 of the *Theft Act 1968*. To commit the substantive offence the perpetrator would have
to know for a fact that the goods are stolen or believe that they are. Mere suspicion is not enough. *R.
v. Adinga* [2003] EWCA Crim. 3201; *R. v. Moys* (1984) 79 Cr. App. R. 72.

Contrast the stolen goods case with the example given above, where the defendant intended to inflict grievous bodily harm on V, but in doing so caused his death. Assault is a crime in itself, so it is enough to show that the defendant intended to assist or encourage that crime, and believed or suspected it would have certain consequences.

17.3. ENCOURAGING AND ASSISTING A NON-CRIMINAL

17–029   This requires a discussion of the rationale for the alternative mental element found in section 47(5)(a)(iii). That subsection holds that D will be liable for trying to encourage or assist the criminality of another if: "D's state of mind was such that, were he to do it, it would be done with that fault." The subsection has to be read in conjunction with section 47(6) which provides: "For the purposes of subsection (5)(a)(iii), D is to be assumed to be able to do the act in question."

Under the *2007 Act* it is irrelevant that the encouraged party lacks *mens rea* or is exempt from liability for some other reason. If D encourages an exempt party (a child under 10) to steal a watch from a store, he is caught by section 47(5)(a)(iii) because he intends the store to be permanently deprived of its property. He encourages the child to steal knowing that the child cannot be convicted of theft because he is exempt from criminal liability. He uses an innocent (sometimes the agent is not innocent but is still exempt from liability as is the case with minors—*some* minors will know full well that they are committing a criminal wrong) agent to bring about the *actus reus* of the offence. D intends to encourage the child to commit the act of theft. D's state of mind is such that, if he were to steal the watch, he would intend to permanently deprive the store of it. D can be guilty of intentionally encouraging or assisting an offence because he intended the *actus reus* of the substantive offence to be committed and he had the requisite *mens rea* for that offence. It is irrelevant that he knew that the party he was encouraging or assisting could not in law commit the offence.

Section 47(5)(a)(iii) not only catches cases involving encouraged parties who are "exempt"[45] from criminal liability, but also "innocence agents" in the pure sense. In *R. v. A*,[46] the defendant took his non-English speaking wife to an abortion clinic and asked the medical team to perform an abortion on her. D acted as her interpreter and falsely told the medical team that his wife wanted an abortion, when he knew she did not. He told his wife that she was having a minor operation to cure her blood.[47] His false representations were discovered before the abortion took place. If the abortion had been performed the doctors would not have been liable as they were acting lawfully.[48] D was effectively using the doctors as innocent agents. The doctors were being conned into performing an

---

[45] Some exempt parties, of course, may also be innocent agents in that they do not understand that they are being used to commit a crime. A 15-year-old girl is not likely to be an innocent agent in this sense, if she realizes that her father is committing a crime by trying to sleep with her. Similarly, some children under the age of 10, exempt from liability, will understand that they are being used to commit a crime.

[46] [2010] EWCA Crim. 1949.

[47] The wife was a young woman who was brought from Pakistan as a part of an arranged marriage, and the husband was 20 years her senior.

[48] It is assumed they were acting within the terms of the *Abortion Act 1967*.

(illegal) abortion, as the pregnant patient was not consenting. If D had performed the abortion himself, he would have committed an offence contrary to section 58 of the *Offences against the Person Act 1861*. Additionally, D's state of mind was such that, were he to do the abortion himself, it would have been done with the fault required by section 58 of the *1861 Act*.

You will recall that in *R. v. Cogan*,[49] the Court of Appeal took the step of applying the doctrine of innocent agency to an act of sexual intercourse.   **17–030**

A husband compelled his wife to have sexual intercourse with Cogan, who believed that the wife was consenting. Cogan having had his conviction of rape quashed on appeal, the question arose whether a conviction of the husband as aider and abettor could stand. The Court of Appeal held that it could, since the defendant was liable as perpetrator and the form of the conviction did not matter.

The decision was rendered possible by the fact that the defendant happened to be a man. Rape can be perpetrated only by a man; the statute says so. Parliament has now embraced the extraordinary notion of raping by means of the genitals of another, and thus has taken steps to make sure that those who cause another to be sexually violated come within the ambit of the criminal law.

Take bordello madam X, who uses trafficked ladies from the third-world in her London brothel. Let us assume she takes their passports, locks them up, and forces them to have sexual intercourse with non-suspecting customers. Suppose she encourages the customers to use the ladies by advertising her services on a website. The advertisements include rates and photos of scantily-clad ladies. If the customers are innocent agents (mere instruments), because they have no idea that the women are not consenting, then they are used by X to rape Vs. Organized prostitution involves the use of many women who are nothing short of sex slaves.[50] Since these women are forced to have sexual intercourse with non-suspecting customers they are effectively raped by innocent agents—the customers. The pimps and people traffickers cause them to be raped by the innocent and non-suspecting customers.[51]   **17–031**

X knows the customers will not have the requisite *mens rea* for rape, so she does not come within the purview of section 47(5)(a)(i), and (ii), or (b)(i) and (ii). But, she would be caught by section 47(5)(a)(iii). While your bordello madam cannot commit rape herself, she "is to be assumed to be able to do the act in question." In addition, she has the requisite *mens rea* for rape. She intends to encourage the customers to have sexual intercourse with the victims and is at least negligent as to whether they are consenting. The shady underworld figures who force women to prostitute themselves are usually more than negligent as to whether their victims are consenting; in most cases they are fully aware that they

---

[49] [1976] Q.B. 217.

[50] Michelle M. Dempsey, "Sex Trafficking and Criminalization in Defence of Feminist Abolitionism," (2010) 158 *U. Pa. L. Rev.* 1729 at 1758 *et passim*.

[51] Section 53A of the *Sexual Offences Act 2003* also criminalizes the innocent agent, even though he lacks any fault. It is sufficient that the innocent agent "ought" to have known that the prostitute was being forced into prostitution by a third party. These new offences cannot be reconciled with the constitutional principles of justice including the presumption of *mens rea*. See Dennis J. Baker, "Collective Criminalization and the Constitutional Right to Endanger Others," (2009) 28 *Crim. Just. Ethics* 168 at 189-190.

are not. Consequently, their "state of mind" is normally such that were they to have sexual intercourse with their victims, it would be done with the requisite fault for rape.

D's encouragement of an innocent agent was not incitement at common law, since incitement presupposed a guilty incitee. Suppose that D has been "working on" the innocent agent, trying to get him to agree to do the act, and much remains to be done by D by way of preparation if the agent does agree to do it. The encouragement may not be sufficiently proximate to be an attempt. The problem at common law was that it did not constitute incitement either. It had been held that one could only commit incitement of a guilty agent, so to speak, not to an innocent one. If, for instance, a person tried to encourage another to commit the *actus reus* of a crime requiring *mens rea*, concealing from him the facts that made the act criminal, he would not have been guilty of incitement.[52] Moreover, by concealing his defence from the prosecution until the trial was half way through he might have avoided having a count for attempt added to the indictment.

17–032   **What if D1 encourages an exempt party to commit a crime that would not be a crime were D1 to commit it himself?**   Suppose D1, an adult, encourages a 14-year-old boy, D2, to sodomize him. Since, it would not be an offence for D1 to sodomize another adult he does not seem liable for any offence. He is encouraging the boy to do an act which he could legally do himself, that is, sodomize an adult. It would be different if D1 encouraged the boy to sodomize another underage boy, as he would commit a crime himself if he were to do the act of sodomizing an underage boy.

A historical note will help you understand the problem at hand. The rule attracted public attention by reason of the decision in *R. v. Whitehouse*,[53] the facts of which were partly given before.[54] Whitehouse was charged not only with conspiring with his daughter to commit incest but with inciting her to commit incest with him (it was not shown that incest was actually committed), and the Court of Appeal held that he was not liable on either count. Since the girl was exempt from committing incest, her father could not be guilty of inciting her to commit it, for "the crime of incitement consists of inciting another person to commit a crime."

Although this premise may sound common sense, it is in fact ambiguous. Why should not the crime of encouragement include incitement of an exempt agent to commit what will be a crime for the encourager? The point would not be of great importance if the act of encouragement of an exempt party were held to amount to an attempt, and on principle it always should be, yet this possibility was apparently ruled out by the prosecuting authorities in *R. v. Whitehouse*.

17–033   The *Criminal Law Act* met the specific situation in *R. v. Whitehouse* by creating a new offence for the case where a man incited his granddaughter, daughter or

---

[52] *R. v. Curr* [1968] 2 Q.B. 944. *Contra, D.P.P. v. Armstrong* [2000] Crim. L.R. 379; *R. v. C* [2006] 1 Cr. App. R. 20. Latter courts have held that the knowledge of *mens rea* of the incitee was irrelevant. Section 47(5)(iii) and 47(6) of the *Serious Crime the 2007* also make it clear that the incitee's state of mind is irrelevant.
[53] [1977] Q.B. 868. See also *R. v Pickford* [1995] Q.B. 203; *R. v. Claydon* [2006] 1 Cr. App. R. 20.
[54] 14.17.

sister, being under 16.[55] This was botching legislation of an objectionable kind. If *R. v. Whitehouse* was regarded as unfortunately decided, the proper course was to reverse it in principle, not merely in the instance. The argument for punishing Whitehouse is no stronger than the argument for punishing a man who incites a child under 14 to do an act of gross indecency with him; yet the latter remained un-punishable for the incitement until the *Sexual Offences Act 2003* was enacted.[56]

On this front, it is not clear that the *Serious Crime Act 2007* has fully rectified the problem. But in practice there are not likely to be many cases where the encourager could not be held liable if he were to do what he has encouraged the exempt party to do. Many of the areas where it might have been possible for the encourager to encourage another to do what would have been a non-criminal act for both the encourager and encouraged involved sexual offences with minors, but it appears the enactment of the *Sexual Offence Act*[57] has plugged the worse gaps.

17.4. RECKLESS ENCOURAGEMENT AND ASSISTANCE (PARTICULAR CRIMES)

Section 45 of the *Serious Crime Act 2007* criminalizes those who encourage or assist another to commit a crime "believing" it will be committed. Section 45 provides:

17–034

> "A person commits an offence if–
> (a) he does an act capable of encouraging or assisting the commission of an offence; and
> (b) he believes– (i) that the offence will be committed; and (ii) that his act will encourage or assist its commission."

The *actus reus* for this offence is the same as for the section 44 offence. The defendant must do some act which is capable of encouraging or assisting another to commit an offence. The core difference between the section 44 and 45 offences relates to the mental element.

What mental element is required under section 45?   Under section 45 the defendant need not intend to assist or encourage the perpetrator's offending. It is enough that he "believes" his encouragement or assistance "will" assist or encourage the perpetrator and that the perpetrator "will" commit the anticipated offence. The section does not require oblique intention,[58] but it clearly requires a very high level of subjective recklessness. It requires the defendant to "believe" not only that the perpetrator will commit the anticipated offence, but also that his assistance/encouragement "will" assist or encourage the perpetrator to do so. The fact that the defendant must "believe" that the perpetrator "will" rather than "might" commit the anticipated offence means that it will not be enough to show

17–035

---

[55] This conduct is now covered by the *Sexual Offences Act 2003*.

[56] *R. v. Claydon* [2006] 1 Cr. App. R. 20.

[57] See sections 10, 17, 26, 31, 39 and 48 of the *Sexual Offences Act 2003*.

[58] Professor Ashworth suggests that the level of recklessness required is so high that it is virtually indistinguishable from oblique intention. See Andrew Ashworth, *Principles of Criminal Law*, (Oxford: Oxford University Press, 2009) at 460.

that the defendant foresaw the perpetrator's offending as a real possibility.[59] It will be necessary to show that the defendant had no substantial doubt that the offence would be committed with his assistance or encouragement. This may allow some to escape, but given the inchoateness of the offences found in the *Serious Crime Act 2007*, this will not cause any injustice. Of course, if the anticipated offence is attempted or consummated, the encourager/assister will be an accessory.

17–036   **Suppose D sells a gun to X suspecting that X "might" use it to kill. Even though D is suspicious he makes the sale as he needs the money to make the payments on his gunsmith. Is he liable?**   No. Section 45 requires more than mere recklessness. It requires D to hand over the gun believing that X "will" use the gun to kill. D must also believe that his assistance or encouragement "will" assist or encourage X to commit the anticipated offence.[60] In your hypothetical, D only suspects that the perpetrator "might" commit the offence. It is not enough to show that the defendant believed that the perpetrator "might" have gone on to commit the anticipated offence. A strong suspicion would not be enough, because the defendant must form a firm belief that the anticipated offence will be committed.[61] If D has no substantial doubt that his assistance or encouragement will facilitate D2's offending, then he could be said to have believed it would.[62]

Section 47(5) discussed above, applies as far as circumstances and consequences are concerned. Consequently, if D1 gives a cricket bat to D2 believing the D2 will use it to inflict grievous bodily harm on V, D1 could be liable for assisting and encouraging murder if D2 kills V. But it would be necessary to prove that D1 believed or at the very least suspected, that D2's assault could kill V.

Hence, the encourager/assister will be liable where he:

1.   recklessly assists or encourages the perpetrator's (potential) offending;
2.   believing or suspecting that the perpetrator would commit the anticipated offence with the requisite fault for that offence; and
3.   "if the offence is one requiring proof of particular circumstances or consequences (or both);" believing or suspecting that the perpetrator would commit the anticipated offence "in those circumstances or with those consequences."

---

[59] Dennis J. Baker, "Complicity, Proportionality and the Serious Crime Act," (2011) 14 *New Crim. L. Rev.* 403. Cf. *R. v. Bryce* [2004] 2 Cr. App. R. 592.

[60] An analogous standard of "belief" can be found in the stolen goods jurisprudence: *R. v. Adinga* [2003] EWCA Crim. 3201; *R. v. Toor* (1987) 85 Cr. App. R. 116; *R. v. Smith* (1977) 64 Cr. App. R. 217; *R. v. Ismail* [1977] Crim. L.R. 557; *R. v. Moys* (1984) 79 Cr. App. R. 72; *R. v. Reader* (1978) 66 Cr. App. R. 33; *Atwal v. Massey* (1972) 56 Cr. App. R. 6; *R. v. Grainge* [1974] 1 W.L.R. 619.

[61] See Glanville Williams, *Criminal Law: The General Part*, (London: Stevens & Sons, 2nd edn. 1961) at 159.

[62] Law Commission, *Report on Mental Element in Crime*, Law Com. No. 89 (London: H.M.S.O., 1978) at 58 proposed the following test: "The standard test of knowledge is—Did the person whose conduct is in issue either know of the relevant circumstances or have no substantial doubt of their existence?"

As far as the offence of receiving stolen goods is concerned, the same issues arise as were discussed above with reference to section 44. (The assister/ encourager need only suspect that the goods are stolen, whereas the perpetrator must believe they are stolen.)

If I do some "lawful act" which I believe will "encourage" X to commit a 17–037 **crime, am I liable simply because I also believe X will commit the anticipated substantive offence?** That will depend on the facts. You should be able to invoke the reasonableness defence,[63] if you were exercising your lawful rights.[64]

Media coverage of violent street protests could influence some quasi-political groups to organize such protests so as to attract publicity for their grievances. Likewise, media coverage of prison riots could encourage further rioting. When a television station broadcasts prisoners on the rampage on a prison roof, destroying property and displaying banners, it could encourage the prisoners to continue rioting so as to attract further publicity for their grievances.[65] In *Beatty v. Gillbanks*[66] it was held that the Salvation Army had acted lawfully in congregating in Weston-super-Mare even though its officers knew from past experience that this would cause an opposing organization, the Skeleton Army, to attack them. The Salvation Army believed it would be attacked by the Skeleton Army if it exercised its lawful right to have a public meeting, but it was not its purpose to encourage this unlawful behaviour. Its purpose was merely to congregate to conduct its own business.

Should a journalist be held liable simply because he believed that covering a 17–038 **riot would encourage the rioters to continue rioting?** Clearly, it was not the journalist's purpose to encourage the criminal activities of the rioters and protestors. But since the subsection does not require actual purpose, the journalist will have to invoke the reasonableness defence, if he is to avoid being held liable under section 45. It is important not to allow people's rights to be curtailed by the fear that others will engage in criminal conduct. It is "the unlawful that must yield to the lawful, and not *vice versa*." [67]

It is arguable that in the context of encouraging, it would have been better if the new offences had limited liability to cases where it was the encourager's purpose to encourage the anticipated offence. It seems wrong that a person has to

---

[63] See section 50 of the *Serious Crime Act 2007*.

[64] In *R. (on the application of Laporte) v. Chief Constable of Gloucestershire* [2007] 2 A.C. 105 at 155, Lord Brown said: "Take Mr. Beatty, the Salvation Army captain, or Ms Redmond-Bate, the Wakefield preacher. The Divisional Court was in each case clearly right to have set aside their respective convictions. I repeat, the police's first duty is to protect the rights of the innocent rather than to compel the innocent to cease exercising them." See *Redmond-Bate v. D.P.P.* [2000] H.R.L.R. 249.

[65] Glanville Williams, "Complicity, Purpose and the Draft Code: Part 1," [1990] Crim. L.R. 4 at 9; Dennis J. Baker, "The Moral Limits of Criminalizing Remote Harms," (2007) 10 *New Crim. L. Rev.* 370 at 384-385.

[66] (1892) 9 Q.B.D. 308.

[67] *Beatty v. Gillbanks* [1882] 9 Q.B.D. 308; *Howard E Perry & Co. Ltd. v. British Railways Board* [1980] 1 W.L.R. 1375.

go to court to defend lawful conduct. Professor Glanville Williams, discussing encouragement in the law of complicity, said:[68]

> "It will be suggested that what is primarily needed in stating the mental element for complicity is a distinction between complicity by encouraging or influencing the perpetrator of crime, on the one hand, and complicity by helping him in its commission, on the other. The latter requires only knowledge, while the former requires some tinge of purpose. This I believe to be broadly the result of the present authorities... Another difference in the facts is that influencing a person towards the commission of a crime is (generally) more remotely connected with the crime than helping him in its commission. Most important of all, whereas knowing assistance in crime is reprehensible, knowingly influencing another in crime is not necessarily so, if the influencer did not directly intend (had no purpose) to influence."

If the subsection required actual purpose in cases involving encouragement, the prosecution would have the burden of proving beyond reasonable doubt that the defendant had such a purpose. But as the law stands, the burden is on the defendant to prove that he acted reasonably.[69] It seems morally objectionable to require the encourager to prove his innocence merely because he foresaw the perpetrator's offending as a definite side-effect of his lawful conduct. It is true that assistance raises similar issues: why should the gunsmith forgo a gun sale if it will pay his bills just because some cretin intends to misuse it? The right to sell a gun is not of the magnitude of the right of freedom of expression or freedom of movement, so restricting a sale where it is clear that it will be misused does not seem unreasonable. In this respect, the reasonableness defence does allow for a more flexible balancing approach. (See the discussion below.)

17.5. RECKLESSLY ENCOURAGING AND ASSISTING A CRIME WITHIN A PARTICULAR RANGE

17–039 Section 46 of the *Serious Crime Act 2007* provides:

> "(1)   A person commits an offence if– (a) he does an act capable of encouraging or assisting the commission of one or more of a number of offences; and (b) he believes–
>
> (i)   that one or more of those offences will be committed (but has no belief as to which); and
>
> (ii)   that his act will encourage or assist the commission of one or more of them.
>
> (2)   It is immaterial for the purposes of subsection (1)(b)(ii) whether the person has any belief as to which offence will be encouraged or assisted.
>
> (3)   If a person is charged with an offence under subsection (1)– (a) the indictment must specify the offences alleged to be the "number of offences mentioned in paragraph (a) of that subsection; but (b) nothing in paragraph (a) requires all the offences potentially comprised in that number to be specified."

The *actus reus* for this offence is the same as for the sections 44 and 45. The defendant must do some act which is capable of encouraging or assisting another to commit one or more offence within a certain range. For example, if D1 gives D2 a gun, he does an act that is capable of assisting a number of offences. D2 might use it to commit murder, or to commit robbery, to commit rape, to abduct a

---

[68] Glanville Williams, "Complicity, Purpose and the Draft Code: Part 1," [1990] Crim. L.R. 4 at 9.

[69] The reasonableness defence found in section 50 of the *Serious Crime Act 2007*, in this respect, does not respect the defendant's right to be presumed innocent until proven guilty.

child, to commit criminal damage, and so on. The core difference between the section 44 offence and the section 46 offence relates to the mental element.

What mental element is required under section 46?   Under section 46 the **17–040** defendant need not intend to assist or encourage the perpetrator's offending. It is enough that he believes his encouragement or assistance will assist or encourage the perpetrator to commit one or more offences within a certain range, and that the perpetrator will commit one or more of the anticipated offences. Section 46 requires the defendant to "believe" not only that the perpetrator "will" commit one of the anticipated offences, but also that his assistance/encouragement "will" assist or encourage the perpetrator to do so.[70] The section requires a very high degree of subjective recklessness as far as these elements are concerned.

This offence is designed to deal with two situations:

1. Cases where the defendant believes he is assisting or encouraging the defendant to commit more than one offence. D1 might give D2 a jemmy bar so that he can burglarize houses X, Y, and Z. If D1 believes that D2 will burglarize those houses, and that the jemmy bar will assist D2 to do so, then he is liable. But if D2 used the jemmy bar to burglarize a fourth house, he should not be liable, unless he believed D2 would also burglarize that house.

2. The assistance or encouragement might also be designed to facilitate alternative offences, that is, offences that will be committed in alternative to each other depending on the circumstances. For instance, D1 might give D2 a gun believing he will use it to commit a robbery and that it will assist him to do so, but also believing that if the robbery goes wrong and D2 is cornered by the police or security guards, that he will use it to kill.[71] Or he may supply the perpetrator with oxyacetylene cutting equipment, which he suspects will be used to commit some kind of property offence, such as melting down stolen goods, or burglary and so on.[72]

The latter scenario is where the section is most likely to be applied. You will recall the facts of *D.P.P. of Northern Ireland v. Maxwell*,[73] where Maxwell was a member of a terrorist organization that used firearms and bombs to carry out attacks against Roman Catholics and their property. Maxwell was told by a member of the organization to act as an escort for another car containing a number of men. Maxwell was asked to lead them to a particular inn. After Maxwell reached the inn he drove off. But one of the men he had led to the inn

---

[70] Dennis J. Baker, "Complicity, Proportionality and the *Serious Crime Act*," (2011) 14 *New Crim. L. Rev.* 403.

[71] D need only encourage or assist acts which would amount to offences. "If it is alleged under section 46(1)(b) that a person (D) believed that one or more of a number of offences would be committed and that his act would encourage or assist the commission of one or more of them, it is sufficient to prove that he believed–(a) that one or more of a number of *acts* would be done which would amount to the commission of one or more of those offences; and (b) that his act would encourage or assist the doing of one or more of those acts": section 47(4) of the *Serious Crime Act 2007*.

[72] Cf. *R. v. Bainbridge* [1960] 1 Q.B. 129.

[73] [1978] 1 W.L.R. 1350.

attempted to bomb it. Maxwell was charged and convicted of unlawfully and maliciously doing an act with intent to cause an explosion likely to endanger life, contrary to section 3(a) of the *Explosive Substances Act 1883* and possession of the bomb, contrary to section 3(b) of the *Act*. Maxwell's defence was that he did not know which crime would be committed out of the range of crimes that he believed the terrorists could commit.

17–041 What if Maxwell believed that the possible offences included murder, criminal damage, terrorist offences, and so on? Under the law of complicity, he would only be liable for the offences which were actually attempted or consummated. Under section 46, it would be necessary to demonstrate that he believed the perpetrator would commit anyone of those offences. It is not necessary to demonstrate that he believed that a particular alternative was more likely than the others, but it must be proved he believed that one of those offences would be committed. It is not enough to show that D believed crime X *would* be committed and that crimes Y and Z *might* be committed. It has to be shown that D believed X, Y, and Z would be committed; or that D believed X would be committed, or alternatively Y would be committed, or alternatively Z would be committed; or that D believed that X and Y or Z would be committed and so on. He is only liable for encouraging the offences he believed would be committed. The question will always be: did the defendant believe that the perpetrator would commit the particular offence(s) which he is now being held liable for encouraging and assisting?

Like sections 44 and 45, if the anticipated offence is one requiring proof of fault, the offence is governed by section 47(5)(a)(i) and (ii). Therefore, D1 will only be liable if he believed or suspected the perpetrator had the requisite fault for the anticipated offence. If not, it will be sufficient to show that if D were to do the offence himself that he would have the requisite fault for the anticipated offence: section 47(5)(a)(iii). Like sections 44 and 45, if the anticipated offence is one requiring proof of particular circumstances or consequences (or both), it is governed by section 47(5)(b)(i) and (ii). It must be shown that D1 believed that the perpetrator would commit one of the anticipated offences, and also believed or suspected that "it would be done in those circumstances or with those consequences."

17.6. ENCOURAGEMENT, ASSISTANCE AND OTHER INCHOATE CRIMES

17–042 Section 44 has to be read in conjunction with subsection 47(8)(c) of the *Act*, which provides: "Reference in this section to the doing of an act includes ... (c) an attempt to do an act (except an act amounting to the commission of the offence of attempting to commit another offence)."[74] It is worth noting, that a person who encourages another to attempt a crime necessarily encourages him to commit it.

---

[74] The befuddling subsection left two Cambridge professors in a state of utter bewilderment! See John Spencer and Graham Virgo, "Encouraging and Assisting Crime: Legislate in Haste, Repent at Leisure," (2008) *Arch. News*, 7-9. The learned scholars concluded: "Can any reader of this paper make sense of the wording of subsection 47(8)(c)? The authors of this article cannot—and think that if anybody can, they deserve to win a prize."

The focus is on the act that the encourager/assister does. The subsection seems to hold that even if D's attempt to assist or encourage the perpetrator is capable of doing so, it will not count if the act *per se* is an attempt to commit some other substantive crime. Instead, D should be charged with attempting that crime. If D meets X to go for a walk with him, intending to encourage X to commit an offence of indecency with him, and having arranged the walk for that purpose, this could be an attempt to encourage X to do the act of indecency; yet it is not an attempt to perpetrate the act of indecency, as the walking alone may not be sufficiently proximate to the perpetration of the crime ultimately in view.[75] If D (the encourager) removes his shirt and is about to remove his pants in an attempt to encourage X to make love to him in a public park, he would then be attempting to commit an act of indecent exposure. (This might also be an act capable of encouraging a like-minded person to do the same).[76] If the police arrest him before he is able to consummate the act of indecent exposure, then he should be charged with attempting to commit the indecent exposure offence contrary to section 66 of the *Sexual Offences Act 2003*.[77] Subsection 47(8)(c) suggests that he should not also be charged with the inchoate offence of attempting to encourage X to commit indecent exposure, because he did an "act amounting to the commission of the offence of attempting to commit another offence."[78]

Incomplete attempts to assist or encourage are probably not enough to satisfy sections 44-46 of the *Act*, unless the incomplete attempt itself was sufficient to constitute an act "capable" of encouraging or assisting the commission of an offence. If D attempts to purchase explosives from an undercover police officer so that he can resell them to X who intends to use them to commit an act of terrorism, D attempts to assist X but does not succeed as his act is not an act capable of assisting X. Nor has he got to the stage of attempting to assist. His attempt to purchase the explosives is an "act amounting to the commission of the offence of attempting to commit another offence." His failed attempt to obtain the explosives is not an attempt to assist X, since he has not attempted to supply X. He was merely equipping himself so that he would be in a position to attempt to assist or actually assist X by selling him the explosives.

---

[75] *R. v. Miskell* [1954] 1 W.L.R. 438. This type of activity might now be caught by sections 66 or 71 of the *Sexual Offences Act 2003*, depending on the nature of the acts and the context. It might also be caught by section 5 of the *Public Order Act 1986*.

[76] This phenomenon is known as "dogging." It involves couples meeting in public locations of ill repute to have sexual intercourse in front of other like-minded individuals. See Richard Savill, "PC Sacked for Joining in with 'Dogging' Couple," (London: *The Telegraph*, 15 Sep 2006).

[77] An alternative example might be where D2 assists D1 in attempting to kill V by keeping lookout as D1 shoots, but misses. This is a case in which D2's acts are in fact those amounting to an attempt (via complicity) to commit murder.

[78] Section 66 of the *Sexual Offences Act 2003* would have to be charged on indictment, since summary offences cannot be attempted. It might be argued that he was attempting to "outrage public decency," but attempt normally requires an intention to commit the crime in question. Therefore, it would have to be shown that D was intending to "outrage public decency" rather than seek a quick thrill. On the common law offence of "outraging public decency," see *R. v. Hamilton* [2008] Q.B. 224; *R. v. Gibson* [1990] 2 Q.B. 619.

17–043 **What if D1 encourages D2 to commit an "attempt" which is a crime in itself?** Suppose D1 sends a letter to D2 to encourage him to attempt to strangle V to frighten her into having non-consensual sexual intercourse with D1. Here, D1 has attempted to encourage D2 to attempt to strangle V. An attempt to strangle or choke another "to enable … any other person to commit, or … assist any other person in committing, any indictable offence,"[79] is a substantive offence in itself.[80] Here, D1 encourages D2 to commit the offence found in section 21 of the *Offences against the Person Act 1861*, since this is a substantive offence *per se* subsection 47(8)(c) is not relevant.

17–044 **Can one inchoately commit an inchoate offence?** There is no reason why not, although there are some limits.[81] The Law Commission recognized as much when it proposed the new statutory offences:

> "[W]e are recommending that it should be an offence to do an act, with the requisite fault element, capable of encouraging or assisting another person to commit an offence. Accordingly if P asks D to supply him or her with an article [*e.g.*, a gun] so that P can commit an offence [*e.g.*, commit murder], P is doing an act capable of encouraging D to do an act capable of assisting P to commit an offence [*i.e.* he encourages D to assist a murder and it is an offence to assist another to commit murder]. In other words, if D supplies the article to P, not only is D committing an offence contrary section 45 of the *2007 Act* but, by encouraging D to commit that offence, P is committing an offence contrary to section 44."[82]

The section 44 offence applies to all offences including itself, other inchoate offences, and also other types of statutory incitements.[83] Consequently, it is possible to commit the section 44 offence by intentionally encouraging and assisting another person to commit the section 44 offence. If D3 intentionally encourages D2 to intentionally encourage D1 to kill V, then he commits the section 44 offence.[84] But if D3 sells a gun to D2 "believing" that D2 "will" give it to D1 and that D1 will use it to kill or to rob, D3 is not liable for committing either a section 45 or 46 offence. D3 is liable only if he intends D2 to assist or encourage D1. And since it was not his intention that D2 should give D1 the gun or that D1 should use it to kill, he is not liable under section 44.

These provisions seem spectacularly wide. Nevertheless, they do have the potential to rope in the likes of Anderson. You will recall Anderson[85] attempted to

---

[79] Rape is an indictable offence. See section 1 *Sexual Offences Act 2003*.

[80] Section 21 of the *Offences against the Person Act 1861*.

[81] A person cannot be liable under sections 45 or 46 for encouraging and assisting a section 44, a 45 or a 46 offence. Sections 49(3) and (4) of the *Serious Crime Act 2007* provide: "(3) A person may, in relation to the same act, commit an offence under more than one provision of this Part. (4) In reckoning whether– (a) for the purposes of section 45, an act is capable of encouraging or assisting the commission of an offence; or (b) for the purposes of section 46, an act is capable of encouraging or assisting the commission of one or more of a number of offences; offences under this Part and listed offences are to be disregarded." The listed offences mainly cover statutory incitements, see list of offences in Schedule 3 of the *Act*. Corporate manslaughter is also excluded.

[82] Law Commission, *Inchoate Liability for Assisting and Encouraging Crime*, Report 300, (London: H.M.S.O., 2006) at para. 4.26.

[83] For a list of the statutory incitements of which D could intentionally assist or encourage contrary to section 44, see Schedule 3 of the *Serious Crime Act 2007*.

[84] See section 66 of the *Serious Crime Act 2007*.

[85] *R. v. Anderson* [1986] A.C. 27.

assist a prison escape. Anderson agreed to supply cutting wire to assist a couple of conspirators who were planning to help a hoodlum to escape from prison. If we accept Anderson's story that he did not share the conspirator's purpose, then he was not a conspirator. And since the conspirators did not even attempt their daring plan, Anderson could not be held liable as an accessory either.[86] But a person could be held liable under sections 44-46, if he assisted or encouraged a conspiracy regardless of whether the conspirators manage to consummate or attempt the planned substantive offence. Notwithstanding this, Anderson would not be caught by the new provisions, because he was hurt in a car accident before he got a chance to do an act which would have been capable of assisting the conspirators to attempt or consummate the anticipated offence.

At common law conspiracy, also, could be compounded with other inchoate **17–045** offences, so there could be an incitement or attempt to conspire. These possibilities are abolished by section 5(1)(7) of the *Criminal Law Act 1977*, in order to preclude the argument that a mere negotiation for an illegal agreement, though not itself a conspiracy is an attempted conspiracy or incitement to conspire. Incitement to conspire was abolished on the proposal of the Law Commission, which though that this form of incitement put liability too far back; once it is realized that the incitement to conspire is in fact, in virtually every case, an incitement to either perpetrate or to abet, the fallacy of the Law Commission's reasoning becomes apparent.

Once again, the position has been reversed, so it is now possible to encourage and assist a conspiracy.[87] (1.) If D3 encourages D2 to perpetrate a crime, D3 is guilty of encouragement. (2.) Equally, where he encourages D1 and D2 to perpetrate the crime jointly, even though this involves encouraging them to conspire. (3.) Equally where he encourages D1 to commit it with the aid of D2, even though this involves the creation of a conspiracy. (4.) And equally, surely, where he encourages D2 to assist D1 (by arrangement) to commit the crime. Obviously, however, a conspiracy to encourage or assist a person to commit a crime contrary to section 44 of the *Serious Crime Act 2007* would constitute a statutory conspiracy. Encouragement being itself a crime,[88] the conspiracy is to commit a crime. So if D1 and D2 agree to encourage assassin X to kill D1's arch rival, they conspire to commit the section 44 offence.

Of course, it has always been possible to convict those who assist and encourage "attempts" as the attempter's accessory, so the new provisions do not expand the law as far as attempts are concerned.[89] A person, however, cannot be liable for encouraging or assisting attempts or a conspiracy under sections 45 and 46.[90]

These crimes can be applied to achieve double inchoate criminalization: so there can be a conviction of encouragement to encourage, or attempt to encourage. The justice and need to allow the law to reach such remote wrongs is

---

[86] *R. v. Kenning* [2009] Q.B. 221.
[87] See the former section 5(1)(7) of the *Criminal Law Act 1977*, repealed by *Serious Crime Act 2007*.
[88] Section 44 of the *Serious Crime Act 2007*.
[89] *R. v. Dunnington* [1984] Q.B. 472.
[90] Schedule 3 of the *Serious Crime Act 2007*.

questionable.[91] The operation of the law is pushed back in the realm of what (from the point of view of the ultimate criminal intent) is not much more than an overt manifestation of a "thought crime"!

17.7. DEFENCES

17–046 Section 50 of the *Serious Crime Act 2007* provides a defence for those who acted reasonably:

> "(1)   A person is not guilty of an offence under this Part if he proves–(a) that he knew certain circumstances existed; and (b) that it was reasonable for him to act as he did in those circumstances.
>
> (2)   A person is not guilty of an offence under this Part if he proves– (a) that he believed certain circumstances to exist; (b) that his belief was reasonable; and (c) that it was reasonable for him to act as he did in the circumstances as he believed them to be.
>
> (3)   Factors to be considered in determining whether it was reasonable for a person to act as he did include–(a) the seriousness of the anticipated offence (or, in the case of an offence under section 46, the offences specified in the indictment); (b) any purpose for which he claims to have been acting; (c) any authority by which he claims to have been acting."

We have already seen one area where the defence might apply. If a political group is set upon for exercising their freedom of expression rights, it would be too much to hold them responsible for an inchoate offence merely because they believed they would encourage others to attack them if they exercised their lawful rights.[92] The executives at the B.B.C. believed that their decision to allow the British National Party leader to participate in one of their live broadcasts would encourage others to riot,[93] but they were merely exercising their right of freedom of expression, which in a democracy, allows all sides to express their political views regardless of whether some of those views are detestable. It was mentioned before, that in *Beatty v. Gillbanks*[94] the Salvation Army had acted lawfully in congregating in Weston-super-Mare even though its officers knew from past experience that this would cause an opposing organization, the Skeleton Army, to attack them. The Salvation Army believed it would be attacked by the Skeleton Army if it exercised its lawful right to have a public meeting, but it was not its purpose to encourage this unlawful behaviour. Its purpose was merely to congregate to conduct its own business.

The reasonableness defence requires the court to weigh the harmfulness of D's act of assistance or encouragement against the social value of his conduct (free speech, entrapment, *etc.*) and the extent of intrusion upon his choices that

---

[91] For a discussion of the reasonable limits of "inchoate" criminalization, see Douglas N. Husak, "The Nature and Justifiability of Non-consummate Offences," (1995) 37 *Ariz. L. Rev.* 151; Ira P. Robbins, "Double Inchoate Crimes," (1989) 26 *Harv. J. on Legis.* 1.

[92] *Beatty v. Gillbanks* (1892) 9 Q.B.D. 308.

[93] John Bingham, "BBC facing protests over BNP invitation to Question Time," (London: *The Telegraph*, 6 September 2009).

[94] (1892) 9 Q.B.D. 308.

criminalization would involve.[95] Since free speech is a cardinal value it should never be criminalized merely because it is offensive. Given that freedom of expression and freedom of movement are cardinal rights, they should only be overridden when D's conduct directly encourages people to attack others. To put it another way, when it directly and purposely encouragers third parties to harm others. Hate speech is detestable, but in itself should not be criminalized merely because it is grossly offensive,[96] as this approach pushes the haters underground,[97] and could allow the majority to determine what is grossly offensive according to their own inter-subjective whims.[98] (The defence may lead to courts making some controversial decisions about what is reasonable, but most cases will probably involve nothing more controversial than issues of entrapment.)

The standard cases are more likely to involve those who encourage or assist **17–047** another's offending with the aim of entrapping him. If X encourages D to commit a crime, and X does so purely for the purpose of procuring D's conviction, X, of course, inculpates himself; and he will be guilty of an inchoate offence of encouragement, unless the reasonableness defence applies. Again, the court will consider the seriousness of the crime which X encouraged or assisted, the purpose for which he claims to have encouraged or assisted it, and any authority he claims to have been acting with.

If the crime is serious and the police have no intention of allowing it to be consummated, then the court is likely to allow the defence. If, however, the police intend to consummate the crime,[99] or assist or encourage the perpetrator to consummate the crime,[100] it will have to demonstrate it had the authority to do so, that the crime's seriousness warranted the entrapping action, and that real victims were not put in danger. If the police were to assist a thief so as to crack a crime syndicate, this would perhaps be tolerable as the crime is serious but its harmfulness is reversible (or compensable) and the social value of busting a large crime syndicate would be rather high.[101] The same could not be said if the police were to assist an assassin to consummate an assassination, or a rapist a rape, and so on.

---

[95] The court would need to invoke something akin to Professor von Hirsch's "Standard Harms Analysis." See Andrew von Hirsch, "Extending the Harm Principle: 'Remote' Harms and Fair Imputation," in Andrew P. Simester and A.T.H. Smith (eds.), *Harm and Culpability*, (Oxford: Clarendon Press, 1996) at 261 *et seq.*

[96] Joel Feinberg, *Offense to Others: The Moral Limits of the Criminal Law*, (New York: Oxford University Press, 1985).

[97] Frederick M. Lawrence, "Resolving the Hate Crimes/Hate Speech Paradox; Punishing Bias Crimes and Protecting Racist Speech," (1993) 68 *Notre Dame L. Rev.* 673; Arnold H. Loewy, "A Dialogue on Hate Speech," (2009) 36 *Fla. St. U. L. Rev.* 67; Richard Delgado and Jean Stefancic, "Four Observations about Hate Speech," (2009) 44 *Wake Forest L. Rev.* 353.

[98] See Scalia J.'s opinion in *Lawrence v. Texas*, 539 U.S. 558 (2003).

[99] *R. v. Latif* [1996] 1 W.L.R. 104; *Pinkstone v. The Queen* (2004) 219 C.L.R. 444.

[100] Obviously, if the police officer pretends to be the putative victim, he does not intend to allow the defendant to consummate the crime. A police officer pretending to be a child in response to encouragement from a paedophile who is attempting to incite a child to engage in sexual activity, is not an act of encouragement or assistance as far as the police officer is concerned. *R. v. Jones* [2008] Q.B. 460. Nor would impossibility be a defence. *D.P.P. v. Armstrong* [2000] Crim. L.R. 379.

[101] Cf. *Chiu-Cheung v. The Queen* [1995] 1 A.C. 111 at 117-119; Cf. *R. v. Edwards* [1991] Crim. L.R. 45.

If a manager of a large retail outlet were to encourage employees to steal from his employer in order to test the firm's security systems, he would be less likely to satisfy the reasonableness defence. He might be able to rely on the defence if he could show that he was acting with his employer's authority, but he would still have to explain why it was justifiable for him to encourage otherwise lawful citizens to commit crimes which they might not have otherwise committed.[102]

The defence is more likely to be successful in cases involving police and other state agents, who take steps to entrap drug smugglers and the like, but only where they follow careful procedures to ensure that if any crime is consummated, that it will result in less overall harm than if they had not allowed it to be consummated. The issue of whether the defence involves a question of law, or should be left purely to the discretion of the jury as a question of fact, is more controversial. It seems wrong to allow the jury to have *carte blanche* to decide what is reasonable (not criminal) and what is unreasonable (criminal).

17.8.   THE VICTIM EXEMPTION

17–048   **Can a person encourage the commission of a crime upon himself?**   Not if his consent negatives the crime.[103] He cannot be criminally liable for encouraging someone to burgle his house, for instance. Yes, generally, in other cases (such as inciting another to kill him). However, the rule that the protected victim of crime cannot be a party to it applies to the offences found in the *2007 Act*.

Section 51 of the *Serious Crime Act 2007* exempts victims who encourage another to victimize them, but only if they fit within a very narrow class. It is to be regretted that the Law Commission did not consider this issue in more depth:

> "(1)   In the case of protective offences, a person does not commit an offence under this Part by reference to such an offence if–
> (a)   he falls within the protected category; and
> (b)   he is the person in respect of whom the protective offence was committed or would have been if it had been committed.
> (2)   Protective offence means an offence that exists (wholly or in part) for the protection of a particular category of persons ('the protected category')."

The victim exemption only applies to protected victims in the narrow sense. The "victim" rule, as it may be called, applies only where the person who is in the vulnerable position is expressly excluded from the *class of perpetrators*. Such a person cannot be convicted of encouraging the commission of a crime upon himself. If a person can be called a perpetrator, then *a fortiori* he can be an assister or encourager. The legislative policy is evidently the same, whether or not the offence is encouraged or committed.

17–049   The same issue was discussed in the previous chapter concerning the victim rule. Does it cover the masochist who does not reciprocate the harm he encourages others to inflict on him? There is no reason why not, as the *Offences against the*

---

[102] Cf. *R. v. Shaw* [1994] Crim. L.R. 365.
[103] *R. v. Brown* [1994] 1 A.C. 212. See the fuller discussion in the preceding chapters. See also Dennis J. Baker, "The Moral Limits of Consent as a Defence in the Criminal Law," 12 *New Crim. L. Rev.* 93.

Person Act 1861 views such a person as a victim—not as a perpetrator. Similarly, is the 14-year-old boy who encourages another 14-year-old to sodomize a fellow 14-year-old boy exempt? He apparently is not exempt. The problem is more acute when it involves consensual lovemaking between two 15-year-olds. Is the 15-year-old who suggests the lovemaking session liable, while her consenting partner is not? Clearly, an express provision is needed to exempt children over the age of 13 and under age of 16 who engage in consensual sexual activity, so long as both parties are within that age range. There should be no exemption, if either party is under the age of 13.

Meanwhile, section 51A of the *Serious Crime Act 2007* holds that the section 44 offence does not apply to those who commit an offence contrary to section 2(1) of the *Suicide Act 1961* as amended by the *Coroners and Justice Act 2009*.

17.9. IMPOSSIBILITY

Can one encourage or assist an impossible crime, if one believes it to be possible? Not at common law, but the position under the *Act* is yet to be determined. At common law one could not attempt to conspire or do the impossible, unless the impossibility related solely to means and not to the end in view.[104] The rule was changed by statute for attempt and conspiracy,[105] but nothing was enacted for incitement, and it was held in *R. v. Fitzmaurice*[106] that the impossibility rule governed the common law offence of incitement.   **17–050**

Many decades ago, the Law Commission[107] in recommending the change for attempt and conspiracy, refrained from making any recommendation for incitement, chiefly because the Commission expressed the opinion that the courts might be able to declare that the law of incitement is in line with the law for the other offences, without statutory help. The suggestion was received with some scepticism, and has now been falsified by the decision in *R. v. Fitzmaurice*. However, the court made it clear that nothing but the most complete impossibility would exclude liability. If the projected crime, though impossible at the time, might become possible before it was expected to be committed, the incitement would be an offence.[108]

When the Law Commission[109] revisited the issue in 2006, it thought that it was unnecessary "for the Bill to include a clause expressly addressing the issue of [impossibility]." The reason being, that the inchoate nature of the offences, mean that they would catch the standard cases of factual impossibility—attempts to steal from an empty pocket, attempts to kill a person who is already dead, attempts to import drugs and so on. If D encourages X to steal from V's pocket he is liable as soon as he utters his encouragement, it does not matter whether the

---

[104] On the difficulty of the means-end distinction see *R. v. Harris* (1979) 69 Cr. App. R. 122.

[105] Section 1(2) and section 5 (1) of the *Criminal Attempts Act 1981*.

[106] [1983] 2 W.L.R. 227. See also Glanville Williams, *Criminal Law: The General Part*, (London: Stevens & Sons, 2nd edn. 1961) at para. 194.

[107] Law Commission, *Criminal Law: Attempt and Impossibility in Relation to Attempt, Conspiracy and Incitement*, Report 102, (London: H.M.S.O., 1980), Part IV.

[108] See *R. v. Shepherd* [1919] 2 K.B. 125.

[109] Law Commission, *Inchoate Liability for Assisting and Encouraging Crime*, Report 300, (London: H.M.S.O., 2006) at para. 6.62.

pocket contains a wallet. Similarly, if D pays X to kill V, it is neither here nor there that V is killed in a car accident before X gets the chance to carry out the assassination.[110] X's liability depends on whether his act was capable of encouraging X to kill and on his culpability for the inchoate offence.

Nevertheless, given that this gap in the law was seen as one of the core problems with the common law offence of incitement, it is difficult to understand why the Government in enacting the *Serious Crime Act 2007* made no attempt to expressly state that impossibility is no defence. Even though the *Act* makes no reference to impossibility, standard factual impossibility clearly will not provide a defence, because the inchoate nature of the offending means that it does not matter whether the perpetrator could have consummated the anticipated offence if the facts had been as he believed. Since the *Act* makes no reference to impossibility, a defendant could argue that Parliament did not intend to abolish the impossibility defence as far as *inherent* factual impossibility is concerned. Thus, if X sells a voodoo doll believing that D will use it to try to kill V, he might point to the fact that he was merely assisting an innocuous activity, as he wanted to make the sale and so on. He might also point to the reasonableness defence.[111] The core problem with the defence is that it is subject to the whims of the jury, and the burden is on the defendant.

17.10. OTHER INCHOATE OFFENCES

17–051   The inchoate offences we have been considering are sweeping, but there are some other statutory specimens. Statutory offences relating to selling goods are now generally worded so as to include not only attempting to sell but also displaying for sale. Statutes create various offences of possessing prohibited articles, the object of which is frequently to prevent the articles from being used for criminal purposes. Examples are statutory offences of possessing explosives[112] or firearms,[113] and possessing implements for certain forgeries and counterfeiting,[114] articles for use in fraud,[115] and possessing anything with intent to commit an indictable offence against the person[116] or any damage to property.[117] See also the long list of statutory incitements as listed in Schedule 3 of the *Serious Crime Act 2007*.

As noted above, these incitements cannot be encouraged or assisted contrary to sections 45 and 46 of the *Act of 2007*, but they can be contrary to section 44 of the *Act*. Some of these other statutory offences may themselves be the subject of a common law attempt, so that the operation of the law is pushed still further back in the realm of what (from the point of view of the ultimate criminal intent)

---

[110] Cf. *D.P.P. v. Armstrong* [2000] Crim. L.R. 379.

[111] See the discussion in the preceding chapters concerning inherent factual impossibility.

[112] Section 4(1) of the *Explosive Substances Act 1883*.

[113] Section 16 of the *Firearms Act 1968*.

[114] Section 17 of the *Forgery and Counterfeiting Act 1981*.

[115] Section 6 of the *Fraud Act 2006*. See also section 25(1) of the *Theft Act 1968*.

[116] Section 64 of the *Offences against the Persons Act 1861* as amended by the *Criminal Law Act 1967*.

[117] A conditional intent, namely to use the article if necessary, is sufficient, *R. v. Buckingham* (1976) 63 Cr. App. R. 159.

is mere preparation. For example, it is a statutory crime to supply or produce a thing for the purpose of abortion[118] and there may be an attempt at common law to commit the statutory offence of procuring.[119]

As was remarked before, the line between inchoate and substantive offences is not firm, for a number of crimes are defined in such a way as to include what the person in the street might regard as an attempt. This is so with assault, abortion, and blackmail. The full crime of burglary is committed as soon as the premises are trespassed upon with the requisite intent.[120]

---

[118] Section 59 of the *Offences against the Person Act 1861*.

[119] *People v. Thornton* [1952] I.R. 91. It was also noted above that one can be liable for encouraging another to commit the substantive attempt found in section 21 of the *Offences against the Person Act 1861*.

[120] See Chapter 32.

PART FOUR

DEFENCES

We have seen that the dividing line between the constituent elements of an offence and defences is largely arbitrary, though it has some importance in relation to the drafting of charges, burdens of proof, evidential burdens, and (in respect of unreasonable mistakes.) The title of this Part must be taken merely as a convenient rubric gathering together certain restrictions upon liability, common to more than one offence, that are suitable to be dealt with at this point. The restrictions may pertain either to what may be thought of as the definition of defences or to what may be thought of as defences.

CHAPTER 18

IGNORANCE OF LAW

"God forbid that it should be imagined that an attorney or a counsel or even a judge is bound to know all the law."[1]

18.1.   THE GENERAL RULE

Almost the only knowledge of law possessed by many is that ignorance of it is no excuse (*ignorantia juris non excusat*). This maxim was originally formulated at a time when the list of crimes, broadly speaking, represented current morality (*mala in se*), but we now have many other crimes that are the result of administrative or social regulation (*mala prohibita*), which are equally governed by the maxim.   **18–001**

The rule is, then, that whereas ignorance of fact can excuse, to the extent that it negatives any necessary *mens rea* or fault, even reasonable ignorance of the law generally does not.

What is the distinction between fact and law? Is a matter one of fact because it is left to the jury?   The distinction now under discussion does not fully correspond to that drawn in relation to the functions of judge and jury. The judge will often leave the jury to decide the application of ordinary words in statutes (2.6). In that context, the meaning of statutory words may be said to be one of fact, in the sense that it is a jury question. But in the present context it is one of law. The citizen must accurately forecast not only the way in which the judge will interpret a statute, so far as he regards it as his function to do so, but also the way in which the jury will, so far as the question is left to them. (We have already noticed the rule in connection with value-judgments required to be made by the law: 6.10).   **18–002**

So, not only is the citizen expected to know the existence and precise terms of all penal legislation pertaining to him, however obscure its wording or chaotic its arrangement, but he is required at his peril to make a correct forecast of the way in which the court will resolve any ambiguity. A barrister may, after research in a law library, write an opinion saying that the provision cannot be interpreted with any certainty; yet every member of the public is required to have precognition of the way in which the court will apply it.

To add to the anomaly, a judge in interpreting a statute may use a vast range of materials outside the statute or statutory instrument itself. He may refer to

---

[1] *Montriou, Gent v. Jefferys* (1825) 172 E.R. 51 at 54 *per* Abbott C.J.

decided cases on the same and other statutes; and an *Act* may be interpreted in light of other *Acts*—even repealed *Acts*. So it is not enough for the anxious layperson to consult the legislation currently in force; he needs a law library of a size that can be found in very few towns, and to which, when it exists, he may have no right of access. He also needs a legal training to understand the material when he has found it.

18–003 **What is the reason for the rule? How can Joe Bloggs be expected to know the law, particularly if he has no money to pay a lawyer?** An excellent question, which is not at all easy to answer. A critic might say that it is because lawyers are insensitive to the plain man's difficulties; and there would be a lot in that. But the orthodox answers are two:

1. The difficulty of proving that the defendant knew the law.
2. The risk that such a defence would make it advantageous for people to refrain deliberately from acquiring knowledge of their legal duties.

The reasons may look persuasive at first sight, but they have not prevented certain other systems of law allowing a limited defence.[2] In particular, the German Supreme Court has, off its own bat, decided to allow a defence of unavoidable ignorance of law. The German citizen is, of course, expected to find out what his legal obligations are, and the fact that he disagrees with the legal norm is no defence; but even with these limitations the rule is a significant concession. Professor Fletcher comments:

> "In its scope and sophistication, in the self-confidence of the judicial role conveyed, this opinion by the German Supreme Court has no equal in Anglo-American precedents on substantive criminal law."[3]

The general refusal of the English courts to allow a defence of reasonable mistake of law is one instance of their disinclination to all new defences. In *Abbott v. The Queen*,[4] for example, Lord Salmon, delivering the opinion of the Judicial Committee, declared that their Lordships had no power to invent a new defence for murder even if they approved of it (although what was in issue was actually not the creation of an entirely novel defence but only the question of its limits).

18–004 Why do the courts limit themselves in this way? Utilitarian theory and ordinary notions of justice would suggest that there should be nothing to prevent the courts inventing new defences where this is desirable, because it does not violate the

---

[2] Cf. for Scandinavian law, J. Andenaes "*Ignorantia Juris* in Scandinavian Law," in Gerhard O.W. Mueller (ed.), *Essays in Criminal Science*, (London: Sweet & Maxwell, 1961). More generally, see Dan M. Kaham, "Ignorance of Law in an Excuse—But Only for the Virtuous," (1998) 96 *Mich. L. Rev.* 127; George Rutherglen, "Dilemmas and Disclosures: A Comment on Client Perjury," (1992) 19 *Am. J. Crim. L.* 278.

[3] George P. Fletcher, *Rethinking Criminal Law*, (Boston: Little, Brown, 1978) at 736-758. See also Douglas Husak and Andrew von Hirsch, "Culpability and Mistake of Law," in Stephen Shute *et al.*, (eds.) *Action and Value in Criminal Law*, (Oxford: Clarendon Press, 1993) at 160 *et seq.*; George P. Fletcher, *Basic Concepts of Criminal Law*, (New York: Oxford University Press, 1998) at 148 *et seq.*

[4] [1977] A.C. at 755 at 767.

maxim *Nulla poena sine lege*,[5] as extending the ambit of crimes does.[6] The argument for allowing reasonable mistake of law as a defence is particularly strong where the law is unclear even to the lawyer, and even stronger where it appears to be clear but is retrospectively changed by the courts.[7] Neither of the two objections (stated above) to allowing a defence of mistake of law justifies the courts in extending the penal law under the pretence of applying it, and then punishing the person who is the occasion of the extension. The justification for judicial activism is twofold: that the courts must, as part of their function of applying the law, clear up its obscurities; and the failure of Parliament to keep the law up to date means that this task must in large degree be performed by the courts. The argument would be more acceptable if the courts gave the protagonist in the leading case an absolute discharge.

Take the facts of *Shaw v. D.P.P.*[8] Shaw published a booklet called *The Ladies' Directory*, being a directory of prostitutes, with photographs of some of them in the nude, and indications in code of their sexual practices. Before publishing it, being disposed to keep within the law, he consulted the police to find out whether it would be legal, and they refused to advise him. Apparently he did not go to the length of consulting a lawyer. Had he done so, he might well have been advised that there was no direct precedent for saying that the publication was unlawful; that, having regard to the advice of the Wolfenden Committee on Homosexuality and Prostitution[9] that prostitution should continue to be regarded as a permitted occupation, though subject to severe restrictions, a liberal-minded judge might well rule that the publication was lawful; but that a judge who looked at it in a moral light might equally well extend some offence or other to embrace it. In the result, Shaw was convicted of no fewer than three offences; publishing an obscene book (though it appears that the book was not sexually titillating as hardcore pornography is); being a male living on the earnings of prostitutes (an offence designed to catch pimps; Shaw merely supplied the prostitutes with a commercial service on a contractual basis, and could not have been convicted of this offence if he had been a woman);[10] and a vague common law offence of conduct intended to corrupt public morals. On this basis, Shaw was sentenced to nine months' imprisonment.

A further point arises out of this one: the citizen generally has no real means of obtaining an authoritative ruling from a governmental agency on the meaning of penal legislation which may affect him. He may have in mind some costly

---

[5] "No penalty without a law."

[6] See Glanville Williams, "Necessity," [1978] Crim. L.R. 128. A reason sometimes advanced for not extending defences is the fear that people who had been convicted under the previous law would then be queuing up at the Home Office for pardons and compensation. This is bureaucratic rather than judicial reasoning, and the objection could be met by the court assuming power to declare that its decision in any particular case is not retrospective in respect of penalties already imposed.

[7] Before *R. v. Hinks* [2001] 2 A.C. 241, most people would not have thought it would be theft to ask (or even to pressure, within in reason) a friend for a gift.

[8] [1962] A.C. 220.

[9] *Report of the Committee on Homosexual Offenses and Prostitution*, (London: Home Office, Cmd. 247, 1957) at paragraphs 13 and 61.

[10] See *Bowry v. Bennet* (1808) 170 E.R. 981; *Lloyd v. Johnson* (1798) 126 E.R. 939. If this type of remote harm argument is accepted, it would support the absurd proposition that those who dry clean a prostitute's garments and so on must also live on the earnings of prostitutes.

enterprise, with no certain inexpensive way of knowing whether it will be stopped. Why should not a Department entrusted with the administration of the particular branch of law be empowered to give a decision on its meaning which, if in favour of the subject, and until successfully challenged in the courts, would protect him against criminal proceedings?[11]

18–005 Some slight movement can be detected on this matter. The civil courts will now hear an action for a declaration brought against the Attorney-General or a Government Department, the most important condition being that criminal proceedings must not already have been started.[12] The court has a discretion whether to hear the case, and it is unknown whether an action by someone whom the judges regard as unsavoury (such as a prostitute) would be allowed. If the outcome of the action is favourable to the citizen, this may persuade the authorities not to prosecute him; but, astonishingly, some judges have said that the favourable outcome will be no defence to him if he is charged.[13]

There are exceptions to the rule that ignorance of the law is no defence, the following being the most important.

18.2. MAKING THE LAW ACCESSIBLE

18–006 Although a statute takes effect without promulgation, there is authority for saying that it will not operate upon a continuous proceeding (such as making a voyage) until a reasonable time has been allowed for discontinuance; and unavoidable ignorance of the statute will be relevant in enquiring what is a reasonable time.[14]

Further rules apply to subordinate legislation. The more important legislative products of Government Departments (Government orders) are "statutory instruments," and in proceedings for an offence under a statutory instrument it is a statutory defence to prove that the instrument had not been issued by Her Majesty's Stationery Office, unless reasonable steps had been taken to bring its purport to the notice of those affected.[15]

This provision does not apply to sub-delegated legislation or to local authorities' bylaws, or even (presumably) to statutory instruments that are allowed to go out of print after being issued, though in these cases the common

---

[11] Legislation confers jurisdiction upon a Government agency to determine certain points, and the giving of an informal assurance to the citizen is a determination.

[12] See particularly Woolf J. in *Royal College of Nursing of the United Kingdom v. Department of Health and Social Security* [1981] 1 All E.R. 545. The case, which went to the House of Lords on the point of substance, shows the danger to the citizen that he will incur great costs if he seeks clarification of the law in this way, even if he is ultimately successful.

[13] See Lords Denning and Roskill in *Royal College of Nursing of the United Kingdom v. Department of Health and Social Security* [1981] 1 All E.R. 545. Brightman L.J. in the Court of Appeal, while giving an opinion on the specific question put to him, refused to provide detailed guidance on what precisely was required to make a medical abortion lawful, saying: "It is not the function of the court to decide how close to dangerous waters it is possible to sail without actually being shipwrecked." ([1981] 2 W.L.R.279 at 288C). The effect is that citizens must refrain from doing not only what the statute clearly forbids but also what tight-lipped judges or future juries may conceivably hold that it forbids, a view that hardly seems consistent with ordinary notions of the rule of law. Cf. *Re A (Children) (Conjoined Twins: Medical Treatment) (No.1)* [2001] Fam. 147.

[14] *Burns v. Nowell* (1880) 5 Q.B.D. 444 at 454.

[15] Section 3(2) of the *Statutory Instruments Act 1946*.

law may have something to say. Bailhache J. held that no delegated legislation comes into force until it is published, so that ignorance due to non-publication is a defence.[16] Also, the Judicial Committee of the Privy Council has held that when a Government order is made in respect of a particular person, and no provision is made for acquainting him of it, he cannot be convicted of an offence under it committed at a time when he did not know that it had been made.[17] The opinion gives no indication that it is intended to apply where the order is in respect of a class of person, or the public at large. But the courts may come to the view that any failure by the authorities to enable people to discover the relevant law can found a defence to a criminal charge, for example where a statute or statutory order is allowed to go out of print.[18]

These rules merely require the legislation to be made available to the diligent **18–007** enquirer. Government orders affecting a particular trade will generally reach those affected by being noticed in trade journals; and there will often have been prior consultation between the Government Department and representatives of the trade. But departmental draftspersons who are responsible for this legislation, with little effective control from Parliament, are not always alive to the importance of confining the duty to the smallest possible class of people and to those who are likely to come to know it. Parliament itself is a sinner in this respect. When it was decided to impose an official specification for motorcycle helmets, and to make noncompliance with regulations an offence, Parliament chose to word the offence as one committed by anyone who sells an infringing helmet—instead of confining the duty to the comparatively small number who manufacture or import such helmets.[19]

Government departments sometimes bring new legislation to the public notice by advertisements. One of the most ambitious efforts to alleviate our ignorance is the Highway Code; but even this is silent on many topics of road traffic law, and when a subject is touched upon the details are omitted.

The general rule is that *mens rea* may be present notwithstanding ignorance of law. If a defendant who knew the criminal law would have had *mens rea*, then one who does not know the law has *mens rea* also. Exceptionally, ignorance of the law is sometimes allowed to produce an absence of some particular form of *mens rea*. The insane are excused from liability where their insanity prevented them from comprehending the criminal nature of their actions; and children under the age of ten are exempt from liability even if they understood they were committing a crime, because it is presumed that children under the age of ten are unable to understand what is and is not a crime (Chapter 28). Further exceptions or possible exceptions relate to superior orders, ignorance of the civil law, and the effect of particular statutory expressions.

---

[16] *Johnson v. Sargant & Sons* [1918] 1 K.B. 101; *Bugg v. D.P.P.* [1993] Q.B. 473 at 478.

[17] *Lim Chin Aik v. R.* [1963] A.C. 160.

[18] Andrew Ashworth, "Excusing Mistake of Law," [1974] Crim. L.R. 652 at 654.

[19] See the now repealed section 32(2) of the *Road Traffic Act 1972*.

18.3.   OFFICIAL ORDERS AND ADVICE

18–008   Superior orders are not generally a defence to a charge of crime, but it has been suggested that a limited exception should be recognized for members of armed forces. A soldier, sailor or airman is bound by military law to obey lawful commands without question; but he may not find it easy to decide on the spur of the moment whether a particular command is lawful or not. The *Manual of Military Law* adopts the harsh view that, whatever the dilemma, the serviceperson has no defence to a criminal charge if the order is in fact unlawful.[20]

The authorities are sparse and in conflict. In the old case of *R. v. Thomas*[21] a naval sentinel who, being ordered to keep off all boats, fired at a boat and killed a man in it, was convicted of murder, notwithstanding that the jury found that he fired under a mistaken impression that it was his duty. Thus, the current position is that no such defence exists in English law.[22]

In *R. v. Smith*,[23] a soldier (during the Boer war) was ordered to shoot at Boer civilian if he did not fetch a bridle, and obeyed the command by killing the Boer. He was acquitted of murder although the command was unlawful. Solomon J. said: "If a soldier honestly believes he is doing his duty in obeying the commands of his superior, and if the orders are not so manifestly illegal that he must or ought to have known that they are unlawful, the private soldier would be protected by the orders of his superior officer." In *U.S. v. Pacheco*[24] it was held "a subordinate must obey all orders except those that are 'palpably' illegal."

18–009   The enlightened Model Penal Code of the American Law Institute allows a defence of unlawful military orders if the defendant did not know the order to be unlawful.[25] In *U.S. v. Smith*,[26] Baker J. said: "'Obedience to lawful orders' is an affirmative defence on which the military judge has a *sua sponte* duty to instruct if the defence is reasonably raised. ... Specifically, [i]t is a defence to any offense that the accused was acting pursuant to orders unless the accused knew the orders to be unlawful or a person of ordinary sense and understanding would have known the orders to be unlawful."

A serviceman may say that he obeys orders because they are orders; he does not enquire whether they are lawful or not. It would be proper, however, for a

---

[20] Great Britain. Ministry of Defence, *Manual of Military Law*, (London: H.M.S.O., 1972) at Pt 1, Ch.VI, para.24. This has long been the law: For a fuller discussion see Ian D. Brownlee, "Superior Orders—Time For a New Realism?" [1989] Crim. L.R. 396.

[21] (1815) 105 E.R. 897.

[22] *Axtell's Case* (1660) 1 East P.C. 7; see also the *obiter* statements in *R. v. Clegg* [1995] 1 A.C. 482 at 498; *Chiu-Cheung v. The Queen* [1995] 1 A.C. 111 at 118. This also remains the position in Australia. See *White v. Director of Military Prosecutions* (2007) 231 C.L.R. 570 at 592 *per* Gummow, Hayne and Crennan J.J.

[23] (1900) 17 Cape of Good Hope SC Reports 561.

[24] (2001) 56 M.J. 1 at 7.

[25] Model Penal Code, §2.10.

[26] (2010) 68 M.J. 316 at 319. Baker J. also said: "The essential attributes of a lawful order include: (1) issuance by competent authority—a person authorized by applicable law to give such an order; (2) communication of words that express a specific mandate to do or not do a specific act; and (3) relationship of the mandate to a military duty." (Erdmann, Stucky, and Ryan, J.J., concurring. Effron, C.J., filed a separate opinion concurring in part and in the result.) The case was heard in U.S. Court of Appeals for the Armed Forces.

court to enquire whether it was reasonable for the defendant to obey the order, having regard to its gravity and apparent necessity, and to the consequences of disobedience to the defendant. In particular, the defence may be withheld where the act is a violation of the laws of war or would be regarded as an atrocity. There is a strong reason for viewing servicemen sympathetically, because they are liable to severe punishment for disobeying orders. There is also an argument, though not so strong, for granting exemption to civilians on the ground of apparently reasonable civilian orders, as in the case of the police. Hitherto the argument has not met with a favourable response from the courts.[27]

A related question concerns persons who follow official advice. Some authorities from the United States hold that a person is protected from prosecution if he makes a mistake of law resulting from an "official statement of the law;"[28] it does not include unofficial advice from the police[29] (except where the police officer asks for help in making an arrest, and thus impliedly represents that he is acting lawfully.) In some jurisdictions it is a defence to culpability, but it is not an affirmative defence.[30] There is much to be said in favour of the American rule, but it has been steadfastly rejected in the birthplace of common law.[31] (A Delaware court has even held it to be a defence that the defendant used diligence to obtain professional legal advice and acted upon it,[32] but this opinion is exceptional in the United States;[33] it carries obvious dangers, and has failed to find favour in England.)[34] English courts convict even when the defendant has been misled by official action into supposing that his conduct was lawful.[35] There is nothing in the books to suggest that a defence is allowed in such circumstances, so, of course, it cannot be allowed.[36] Although the Supreme Court theoretically can still take a more enlightened view in respect of official advice or misdirection, their Lordships have never hinted that they will do so.

---

[27] Lord Goddard C.J. said in *Brannan v. Peek* [1948] 1 K.B. 68 at 72 that the police have no right to commit offences to detect crime. That is undoubted, and indeed tautologous; but it does not preclude the possibility of allowing an excuse of reasonable reliance on superior orders. Nor does it necessarily deny that the intention of the police officer may negative a crime on his part.

[28] *Walker v. Com.*, 127 S.W.3d 596 (2004); *State v. Norton*, 67 P.3d 1050 (2003); *People v. Studifin*, 504 N.Y.S. 2d 608 (1986); *Kratz v. Kratz*, 477 F Supp. 463 (1979); *State v. Leavitt*, 107 Wash. App. 361(2001).

[29] The defence is unavailable where a person (even if reasonably) relies on a police officer's or other subordinate's mistaken statement or interpretation of the law: *Stevens v. State*, 135 P.3d 688 (2006). The statement of the law must have an authoritative source. *People v. Aresen*, 91 Cal.App.2d 26 (1949).

[30] See for example, *State v. Cote*, 286 Conn. 603 (2008).

[31] See for example, *Brook v. Ashton* (1973) 231 E.G. 615; *Surrey CC v. Battersby* [1965] 2 Q.B. 194; *R. v. Arrowsmith* [1975] Q.B. 678; *Cooper v. Hall* [1968] 1 W.L.R. 360; *George Cohen 600 Group Ltd. v. Hird* [1970] 1 W.L.R. 1226; *R. v. Bowsher* [1973] R.T.R. 202; *R. v. Jacey* [1975] Crim. L.R. 373.

[32] *Long v. State*, 65 A.2d 489 (1949); see also *Kipp v. State*, 704 A.2d 839 (1998); *Bryson v. State*, 840 A.2d 631 (2002).

[33] See *People v. Carmichael*, 164 Cal.Rptr. 872 (1980) where it was held that advice from a private lawyer is not sufficient.

[34] *Cooper v. Simmons* (1862) 158 E.R. 654.

[35] See for example, *Burgess v. West* [1982] R.T.R. 269 (misleading speed-limit signs).

[36] Cf. *Postermobile Plc. v. Brent L.B.C.* (*The Times*, December 1997), where D appealed by way of case stated against convictions of displaying advertisements without the appropriate planning consent. The Court of Appeal held that: "it was an abuse of process for the prosecutions to proceed, as it would

Sometimes express rules of law confer immunity for an apparently lawful act. In particular, a jailer or other officer who carries out an irregular sentence or order of the court is protected if the court has jurisdiction, and perhaps even if it had not.[37] Section 3(4)(a)(i) of the *Control of Pollution Act 1974* marks a welcome departure in regulatory legislation in allowing a defence of misleading information "from persons who were in a position to provide the information," and also a defence of apparently lawful order from an employer.

18.4. IGNORANCE OF THE CIVIL LAW

18–010 By far the most important limitation of the *ignorantia juris* rule is that it applies only to ignorance of the criminal law. Ignorance of the civil law can be a defence in offences requiring *mens rea*, because it can negative the *mens rea*. In relation to offences against property, this proposition used to be expressed by saying that the offence was committed only by a person who acted "without a claim of right." Sometimes the defence of claim of right was rested on the fact that the statute had used the word "maliciously" or "unlawfully," which was thought to be of special significance;[38] but in fact these two words were not essential. At the present day a claim of right, in the sense of a mistaken belief that the civil law confers a legal right to do the act charged, may be said to be a defence to a charge of damaging property even when the statute has made no kind of reference to it.[39] In other words, in charges of crimes against property a mistake as to property rights is regarded as pertaining to civil law. There is a limit to the amount of law that the citizen can be expected to know, and the law of property falls beyond that limit. As we shall see in 35.6, this rule is applied under the *Criminal Damage Act 1971*. In relation to theft, since the *Theft Act 1968* the language of "claim of right" has been abandoned and we speak instead of the offence being committed "dishonestly." A defence of honesty or claim of right is equally effective whether it rests on a mistake of fact (the defendant thought that the owner in handing over the thing had intended to give it to him), or a mistake of the civil law (the defendant thought that he could seize possession as executor, but the will under which he acted was invalid).

Nor is this type of defence limited to offences against property. On a charge of bigamy, the defendant will not be heard to say that he did not know that bigamy was a crime, but it will be a defence that he (mistakenly but reasonably) thought that his first marriage was dissolved by divorce at the time of the bigamous ceremony, when as a matter of civil law the supposed divorce was invalid

---

be unfair for D to be tried. BLBC's officers had clearly represented that D did not require planning consent and D had been entitled to rely on their advice." See also *R. v. Croydon Justices, Ex parte Dean* [1993] Q.B. 769.

[37] *Williams v. Williams* (1937) 2 All E.R. 559; *Mackalley's Case* (1611) 77 E.R. 828; *R. v. Drury* (1848); *Howard v. Gossett* (1845) 10 Q.B. 411 at 453-4 (confining the rule to orders of the superior courts); *Raja v. Van Hoogstraten (No 9)* [2009] 1 W.L.R. 1143 at 1148.

[38] Glanville Williams, "Offences and Defences," (1982) 2 *Legal Stud.* 233; Glanville Williams, *Criminal Law: The General Part*, (London: Steven & Sons, 2nd edn., 1962) at §§108-109.

[39] *R. v. Smith* [1974] Q.B. 354. For the old authorities see Williams, *The General Part*, at §§107.

because it was pronounced by a court not having jurisdiction.[40] The law of divorce is not part of the criminal law, so a mistake as to it can be a defence.

In one respect the law of bigamy is anomalous. Ordinarily, when ignorance of the civil law negatives *mens rea*, it does not matter whether the ignorance is reasonable or not. But, owing to the peculiar development of the law of bigamy, the defence of mistake in that crime requires that the mistake should have been reasonable; and the same may be true of other statutory offences not incorporating an express requirement of *mens rea* (6.7).

As another example of the width of the principle under discussion, it seems to be the general rule that a person does not become an accessory to an offence if he does only what he believes to be required by the civil law (14.6).

What precisely is the difference between mistake of the criminal law and of the civil law? The word "precisely" asks for more than can be given. Obviously a mistake as to the law of tort, contract, trusts, property or family law relates to the civil law. On the other hand, offences against the person do not easily let in the defence, because they are regarded as being (for the most part) completely or exclusively defined by the criminal law itself. The law of private defence and arrest, for example, are exceptions from the criminal prohibition that are taken to be part of the criminal law.[41] The citizen is expected to know not only the law relating to the essentials of criminality but also the law relating to the main defences. They would appear in a well drafted criminal code. (Perhaps a more persuasive reason is the importance of protecting the body from harm; yet it may be gravely doubted whether a restriction of defences has any substantial effect in promoting bodily security.) Exceptionally a mistake as to the law of property can be a defence even to a charge of crime against the person. If a person mistakenly believes he is the owner of an article, and uses moderate force to obtain possession of it, he is entitled to be judged as if he were in truth the owner.

18–011

Where the crime is one of strict liability, there will be no scope for a defence of claim of right. Since, for instance, a motorist is liable for driving without insurance even if he believed that he was insured, it is irrelevant whether his mistake was as to a pure matter of fact (the date when the policy expired) or as to the validity of the policy on some abstruse point of insurance law.[42]

---

[40] Cf. *R. v. Gould* [1968] 2 Q.B. 65. In that case the mistake was one of pure fact, but it seems clear that the decision would have been the same if it had related to the law of divorce.

[41] *R. v. Bentley* (1850) Cox C.C. 406; *Agnew v. Jobson* (1877) 13 Cox C.C. 625; *The Queen v. Tolson* (1889) 23 Q.B.D. 168 at 188; *Gelberg v. Miller* [1961] 1 W.L.R. 153; cf. *R. v. Reid* [1973] 1 W.L.R. 1283 at 1289; *D.P.P. v. Fountain* [1988] R.T.R. 385; *R. v. Barrett* (1981) 72 Cr. App. R. 212 (mistake as to the validity of court process); *Hills v Ellis* [1983] Q.B. 680.

[42] Cf. section 143(3)(a)(b)(c) of the *Road Traffic Act 1988*. See also *R. v. Williams* [2011] 1 W.L.R. 588.

18.5. THE EFFECT OF PARTICULAR STATUTORY EXPRESSIONS

18–012 In general, *mens rea* words do not let in a defence of ignorance of the criminal law. To take an obvious example, the offence of knowingly possessing explosives does not require knowledge of the statutory offence.[43] Some statutes creating offences stipulate that the act must be "without lawful excuse."[44] The phrase may be a useful reminder of the existence of general justifications and excuses, to those who are apt to forget them; but logically it should be unnecessary.[45] It is not read as exempting people from the duty to know and interpret all the relevant provisions, however, obscure or complicated, of the statute under which they are charged.[46]

Ignorance of the law is not in general a "reasonable excuse" within a statutory exemption. For instance: a statute empowered the police to require a driver to take a breath test in certain circumstances if he was driving or attempting to drive. The defendant, a driver, got out of his car and a policeman then required him to take a breath test. The defendant was word-perfect on the legislation, and declined to take the test on the ground that he was at that moment neither driving nor attempting to drive—which was, in the ordinary meaning of the words, the fact. He did not know that the courts had interpreted the statute in a common sense way to include a driver who had only momentarily interrupted his driving. He was convicted of the offence of failing without lawful excuse to take the breath test, the trial judge having refused to leave the question of reasonable excuse to the jury; and the conviction was upheld on appeal.[47]

It is understandable that the courts should say that an unlawful refusal to comply with the directions of the police, on a layman's view of the law, when the law (to a lawyer) is quite clear, cannot constitute a reasonable excuse. One may hope, however, that decisions like this will not be taken as finally settling that no wrong opinion as to the law (including a wrong guess as to how the courts will decide a disputed point) can be reasonable.[48] A person who has mistakenly relied upon an official statement of the law should certainly be allowed a defence of reasonable excuse. Further, a misunderstanding of the law should be a reasonable excuse if the law is obscure even to a lawyer who applies himself diligently to its interpretation. As Maule J. put it, in his inimitable way:

> "[T]here may be such thing as a doubtful point of law. If there were not, there would be no need of courts of appeal, the existence of which shews that judges may be ignorant of law."[49]

The word "wilfully" generates some problems. It has been mentioned that the courts construe it to mean "acting intentionally or recklessly without lawful

---

[43] Section 4 of the *Explosive Substance Act 1883*.

[44] For example, threatening to kill (section 16 of the *Offences against the Person Act 1861*) and threatening to commit criminal damage (section 2 of the *Criminal Damage Act 1971*).

[45] *R. v. G* [2004] 1 A.C. 1034.

[46] *Cambridgeshire and Isle of Ely CC v. Rust* [1972] 2 Q.B. 426.

[47] *R. v. Reid* [1973] 1 W.L.R. 1283. (The new legislation covers those who have been driving). See also *McGrath v. Vipas* [1984] R.T.R. 58.

[48] See Ashworth, *op. cit. supra* note 18.

[49] *Martindale v. Falkner* (1846) 135 E.R. 1124 at 1130.

excuse;"[50] and the same meaning is read into statutory malice.[51] Nevertheless, for the reasons already given, ignorance of law should not in general be read as a lawful excuse.

Cases on the statutory offence of wilfully obstructing the highway illustrate the point. Certain justifications for obstruction are recognized,[52] such as reasonable temporary obstruction in the exercise of rights, and temporary obstruction under licence given under the authority of statute; but on a proper analysis the cases may merely illustrate the meaning of "obstruction," and do not turn on the notion of wilfulness. Several cases show that a person's belief that the statutory offence contains an exception that it does not contain is no defence. If the defendant mistakenly believes, for example, that he has a right to hold a public meeting on the highway,[53] or to erect a bollard on the highway in order to protect his premises,[54] he will be convicted even of the offence of wilfulness, since these are mistakes as to the scope of the offence. However, the cases on the word "wilfully" are not entirely uniform, and there are instances of a person who has committed a public nuisance under a claim of right being acquitted.[55] **18–013**

Some particular *mens rea* requirements in a statutory offence may indicate that the offence does not apply to those who mistake the law—even the law of which the statutory offence forms part. The courts have reached this conclusion in cases turning on the words "properly" and "qualified," both of which impliedly refer to the law.

In the first case, a statute (now repealed) made it an offence for any person to obtain a family allowance "knowing that it was not properly receivable by him." It was held that a woman who received a family allowance on behalf of another person, in breach of the regulations but not knowing that she was doing anything wrong, had a defence. The offence was not committed unless the woman knew that her receipt of the money was improper under the regulations.[56]

The statute (now repealed) in the second case made it an offence for a person to act as an auditor of a company at a time when he knows he is disqualified for appointment to that office. Another statutory provision stated that an officer of a company is not qualified for appointment as an auditor of that company. The defendant was a director (and therefore an officer) of a company, and acted as an auditor for it, but he did not know the law and did not know that he was disqualified. A Divisional Court held that he was not guilty of the offence. Courts so often quibble by saying that regulatory offences are "not truly criminal" that it is refreshing to find the court on this occasion asserting roundly that it was a criminal offence, so that the word "knows" in the statute had to be read as **18–014**

---

[50] J. A. Andrews, "Wilfulness, a Lesson in Ambiguity," (1981) 1 *Legal Stud.* 303.

[51] *R. v. Cunningham* [1957] 2 Q.B. 396.

[52] *Herrick v. Kidner* [2010] P.T.S.R. 1804 at 1814; *Torbay Borough Council v. Cross* (1995) 159 J.P. 682.

[53] *Arrowsmith v. Jenkins* [1963] 2 Q.B. 561; *Birch v. D.P.P.* [2000] Crim. L.R. 301; *Kent CC v. Upchurch River Valley Golf Course Ltd.* (1998) 75 P. & C.R. D37. Cf. *D.P.P. v. Jones* [1999] 2 A.C. 240.

[54] *Dixon v. Atfield* [1975] 1 W.L.R. 1171.

[55] See Williams, *op. cit. supra*, note 39 at §109.

[56] *R. v. Curr* [1968] 2 Q.B. 944.

meaning "knows."[57] (Apparently the word "knows" in the statute had to be read as meaning "knows" in a non-criminal statute!) It is to be noticed that the notion of disqualification is itself entirely a matter of law; consequently, a contrary decision would have deprived the requirement of knowledge of almost all meaning.

18.6. FALSE REPRESENTATIONS AND FRAUD

18–015 The word "false" in a penal statute is *prima facie* an *actus reus* word. When a statute prohibits the making of a false representation, the adjective is needed to express the fact that the making of a true representation is not forbidden. When the offence is of a serious kind the courts may treat the adjective as carrying also a *mens rea* implication, so that a person does not offend unless he knows or believes his representation to be false;[58] but in minor offences the presence of the word "false" need not prevent the statute from being construed as imposing strict liability.[59]

Assuming that "false" is read as a *mens rea* word, or that there are other indications in the statute that *mens rea* is required, will a person be liable if his representation is false because of his mistake of law? Many of our utterances that we may think of as simple representations of fact contain elements of law. For example, "I am the son of X (by adoption); I am married to Y; I have bought furniture; I have passed a driving test and have a driving licence." None of these statements would involve me in liability for a wilfully false statement if, unknown to me, they were false by reason of my mistake of law. This is obviously so if, as in these examples, the mistake relates to civil law. Thus it has been held that a person who makes a representation in good faith but who misunderstands the civil law is not guilty of perjury,[60] or of a statutory offence of making a false statement,[61] or of forgery.[62] But where *mens rea* is required the judges occasionally go further than this, and, allow a defence of mistake relating to a statutory scheme of which the penal clause forms part. The principle is, or should be, that where a statute penalizes the making of a false representation, and

---

[57] *Secretary of State for Trade and Industry v. Hart* [1982] 1 W.L.R. 481. Cf. *Attorney-General's Reference (No.1 of 1995)* [1996] 1 W.L.R. 970 at 980, where the Court of Appeal, considering a different statute, said: "A [company] director who knows that acts which can only be performed by the company if it is licensed by the bank are being performed when in fact no licence exists and who consents to that performance is guilty of the offence charged. The fact that he does not know it is an offence to perform them without a licence, *i.e.*, ignorance of the law, is no defence."

[58] Or that it might be false, see section 2 of the *Fraud Act 2006*.

[59] *Laird v. Dobell* [1906] 1 K.B. 131; cf. *Consumer Protection from Unfair Trading Regulations 2008*. Regulation 17 contains a "due diligence" defence which provides: "17(1) In any proceedings against a person for an offence under regulation 9, 10, 11 or 12 it is a defence for that person to prove—(a) that the commission of the offence was due to— (i) a mistake; (ii) reliance on information supplied to him by another person; (iii) the act or default of another person; (iv) an accident; or (v) another *cause beyond his control*; and (b) that he took all reasonable precautions and exercised all due diligence to avoid the commission of such an offence by himself or any person under his control."

[60] *R. v. Crespigny* (1795) 170 E.R. 357.

[61] *R. v. Dodsworth* (1837) 173 E.R. 467.

[62] *Ocean Accident & Guarantee Corp Ltd. v. Cole* [1932] 2 K.B. 100.

expressly or impliedly confines the offence to representations that are wilfully or knowingly false, a mistake of law affecting the truth of the statement can be a defence.

An important example is *Wilson v. Inyang*.[63] This turned on a section in the *Medical Act 1858* (now repealed). To explain it, something should be known of the law relating to professional practice.

A few professions are protected by statutes which make it an offence for an unqualified person to engage in the profession. A prominent example is the profession of solicitor; another is the profession of veterinary surgeon. Only a vet can operate on animals, and only a qualified doctor or dentist can practice dentistry.[64] With doctors who treat humans the position is different. The establishment by statute of the profession of registered medical practitioners did not put an end to osteopaths (bone-setters), chiropodists, naturopaths, herbalists faith-healers and others, who may be unlikely to be described as "quacks" (though they often perform useful services and are sometimes called in aid by doctors themselves). Such persons were allowed to practice without any kind of qualification,[65] the only penal rule being that they might not call themselves doctors or anything like it.

18–016

The rule against unqualified persons calling themselves doctors in the *Medical Act 1858* is now found in sections 49 and 49A of the *Medical Act 1983*, which replaces the earlier legislation in the same terms. This makes it a summary offence wilfully and falsely to take one of a number of medical titles, including that of physician, doctor of medicine, and surgeon. The settled interpretation of the section is that a person who is not registered under the *Act* must not appropriate one of the taboo words even though he adds some qualifying adjective. Thus in a case where the unqualified defendant argued that his use of the word "manipulative" before "surgeon" made his use of the term "surgeon" lawful because it told the public that he was not registered, the court drily remarked: "If the respondent is, as we must take him to be, sincere, there are many ways open to him of telling the public that he is not a surgeon other than the way of telling them that he is a surgeon."[66]

What, then, is the effect of the words "wilfully and falsely" in the section? In *Wilson v. Inyang*,[67] Inyang was an African who had lived in England for two years and who had taken a correspondence course in "drugless therapy." He set up in practice and called himself a "naturopath physician, N.D., M.R.D.P." On a prosecution under the *Act of 1858* the magistrate took the view, in accordance with the authorities, that Inyang's use of the word "physician" (even though qualified by "naturopath") was not allowed under the section, but he held that Inyang could not be convicted because, on the facts, he honestly believed that he was entitled to use that expression. On appeal the Divisional Court (speaking

---

[63] [1951] 2 K.B. 799.

[64] Section 49 of the *Medical Act 1983* provides: "Any person who wilfully and falsely pretends to be or takes or uses the name or title of physician, doctor of medicine... shall be liable on summary conviction to a fine..." See also section 38 of the *Dentists Act 1984*.

[65] Some of these occupations are now regulated.

[66] *Jutson v. Barrow* [1936] 1 K.B. 236 at 245.

[67] [1951] 2 K.B. 799.

through Lord Goddard C.J.) affirmed the acquittal, saying that the question was not whether Inyang acted reasonably but whether he acted in good faith.

18–017 In a case decided under the same section two years before, Lord Goddard had said that a mistake, to be a defence, must be based on reasonable grounds. But he now recanted and said that reasonableness was simply evidence of honesty, and not essential evidence. "A man may honestly believe that which no other man of common sense would believe. If he has acted without any reasonable ground, and has refrained from making any proper enquiry, that is generally good evidence that he is not acting honestly. But it is only evidence. ... In this case the magistrate ... saw the defendant, heard his evidence, and formed an opinion as to his credibility and honesty. In view of his findings I do not think that the court can interfere."

The decision is an early example of a shift of judicial opinion from an objective to a subjective test of criminal responsibility. It is useful authority for the proposition that a requirement of wilfulness lets in a defence of mistake. However, the court did not avert to the problem of ignorance of law. Lord Goddard spoke as though the fact that *mens rea* was in issue automatically brought knowledge of law in issue, which is not always so. Inyang did not make any relevant mistake of fact. Even if he thought that the title he assumed was not misleading to the public, the offence did not require that the title should be misleading. If he had put up a brass plate saying "A B Inyang, physician and surgeon (not a registered medical practitioner)," this would hardly have been misleading but would pretty clearly have been unlawful, since the courts do not allow the use of taboo words even with explanation and qualification. Consequently, Inyang's mistake was purely as to the penal statute and its judicial interpretation.

Nevertheless, it is acceptable to say (and there were precedents for saying)[68] that the statutory offence in terms of "wilfully and falsely" taking a medical title was not committed, owing to the defendant's ignorance of law, even though the ignorance related to the very section under which the charge was made. A persuasive reason in support of the decision is that if it had been otherwise the statutory requirement of wilfulness would have had practically no effect. A person can hardly use the title of "physician" or "surgeon" without knowing that he is using it, and he can hardly make any mistake on the question of whether he is registered under the *Medical Act* or not. However, *Wilson v. Inyang* should be regarded as resting on the word "falsely" (read as a *mens rea* word) and not on the word "wilfully" taken by itself.

18–018 Contrast the decision in *Roberts v. Duce*.[69] Roberts was granted legal aid on the basis of his declaration as to his "disposable income." He later received an educational grant (to buy books, *etc.*), and, naturally thinking that this was not "disposable income," did not notify the legal aid authority. It was held that the grant was disposable income within the *Legal Aid and Advice Act 1949*, and Roberts was accordingly guilty of "wilfully" failing to notify it.

---

[68] Particularly *Hunter v. Clare* [1899] 1 Q.B. 635 and *Younghusband v. Luftig* [1949] 2 K.B. 354.
[69] [1974] Crim. L.R. 107.

This accords with a number of cases on statutory wilfulness, but overlooks the fact that those cases were concerned with physical acts, not the utterance of words. It seems reasonable to say that any *mens rea* offence of false representation lets in the defence of mistake as to the law affecting the truth of the statement, even where the defendant has used an expression having a legal meaning without knowing the meaning, and the same should apply to the offence of failing to make a true statement.[70] On this view, *Roberts v. Duce* was wrongly decided.

The rule just suggested for the offences involving knowledge or wilfulness in relation to false representations or statements is confined to the question of truth of the representation. A person can be convicted of an offence of wilfully or knowingly making a false representation if he says what he knows is false, even though he wrongly believes that the falsity is on a matter with which the statutory requirement of truth is not concerned.

D claimed sickness benefit and made a knowingly false statement that he had not **18–019** worked during a certain period. However, he did not think that the false statement would affect the amount of benefit, and told the lie only because he did not want his employer to know that he had worked elsewhere. He was convicted of knowingly making a false statement for the purpose of claiming benefit.[71]

For reasons similar to those for making false statements, offences of fraud are regularly held to admit a defence of mistake of law. Whether these offences admit of a general defence of honesty or good faith need not be considered here.

---

[70] On failing to make a disclosure, see for example, *R. v .Tilley* [2010] 1 W.L.R. 605.
[71] *Barrass v. Reeve* [1981] 1 W.L.R. 408; see also *Harrison v. Department of Social Security* [1997] C.O.D. 220; *R. (on the application of Hastings BC) v. Jones* [2004] R.V.R. 270.

CHAPTER 19

INTOXICATION

"Oh God; That men should put an enemy in their mouths, to steal away their brains."

Othello II. iii

19.1. THE EFFECT OF INTOXICANTS

The effect of alcohol on the brain is depressant from the beginning. Its apparently **19–001** stimulating effect is due solely to the fact that it deadens the higher control centres (and progressively the other centres as well), so weakening or removing the inhibitions that normally keep us within the bounds of civilized behaviour. It also impairs perception, reasoning, and the ability to foresee consequences.[1]

Alcohol is quite strongly associated with crimes of violence, but this does not necessarily mean that it is a causal factor.[2] We all know many people who drink a social glass; most perhaps become inebriated, without being violent. However, case histories show that a few people, who are generally peaceable, for some idiosyncratic reason become highly violent and dangerous in their coupes of Dom Perignon.[3]

Alcohol is generally distinguished from drugs as a matter of speech, though scientifically speaking it is a drug. As regards the effect on *mens rea*, nearly all cases concern alcohol, but other psychedelic drugs have come to present similar legal problems which are answered on the same principles as those established for alcohol.[4] Cocaine, which is frequently injected with heroin, is an intense stimulant which in large doses causes acute paranoia. Stimulants (such as amphetamines) and tranquillizers and other sedatives (such as barbiturates) do not generally produce criminal behaviour (although theft and forgery are

[1] Jennifer R. Redman *et al*., "Intoxication and Criminal Behaviour," (2000) 7 *Psychiatry Psychol. & L.* 59; Michael G. Weil and Winifred Rosen, *From Chocolate to Morphine: Everything You Need to Know About Mind-altering Drugs*, (New York: Houghton Mifflin Co., 2004).
[2] Research shows that there is a correlation between binge drinking and crime. See Anna Richardson and Tracey Budd, "Young Adults, Alcohol, Crime and Disorder," (2003) 13(1) *Criminal Behaviour and Mental Health* 5; Susan E. Martin, "The Links Between Alcohol, Crime and the Criminal Justice System: Explanations, Evidence and Interventions," (2001) 10(1) *American Journal on Addictions* 136; Gavin Dingwall, *Alcohol and Crime*, (Portland: Willan Publishing, 2006). The Law Commission observes that "there were 1,087,000 violent incidents in 2006/2007 where the victim believed the offender … was under the influence of alcohol." Law Commission, *Intoxication and Criminal Liability*, Law Com. No. 314, (London: H.M.S.O. Cm. 7526, 2009) at para. 1.1.
[3] Jeffrey Fagan, "Intoxication and Aggression," (1990) 13 *Crime & Just.* 241.
[4] *R. v. Lipman* [1970] 1 Q.B. 152 at 156A.

[657]

committed in order to obtain them).[5] However, large overdoses can result in violence, sometimes apparently, as the result of producing psychosis (insanity).

In the vast controversy surrounding cannabis (marijuana, hashish, pot and so forth—to use colloquial terms), the evidence of any connection with criminality is almost entirely negative. Only occasionally, it seems, does its use precipitate a psychotic state. The hallucinogens, including LSD, produce hallucinations, as their name implies; under their influence repressions and learned patterns of behaviour are dissolved away. But again the connection with criminal behaviour is very slight.

19.2. INTOXICATION AND RESPONSIBILITY

19–002 In times gone by voluntary intoxication was treated as an aggravating feature of a crime, but now it is seen as a potential excuse. In *R. v. Fogossa*, it was said:[6]

> "As if a person that is drunk kills another, this shall be felony, and he shall be hanged for it, and yet he did it through ignorance, for when he was drunk he had no understanding nor memory; but inasmuch as that ignorance was occasioned by his own act and folly, and he might have avoided it, he shall not be privileged thereby. And Aristotle says, that such a man deserves double punishment, because he has doubly offended, viz. in being drunk to the evil example of others, and in committing the crime of homicide. And this act is said to be done *ignoranter*, for that he is the cause of his own ignorance: and so the diversity appears between a thing done *ex ignorantia*, and *ignoranter*."

Nowadays intoxication itself is not treated as an aggravating feature. Instead, in certain cases the defendant is permitted to raise evidence of his intoxication to demonstrate that he was too intoxicated to form the specific intention[7] required for the offence he committed. (As we will soon see, the defendant will usually be convicted of some lesser crime where recklessness or negligence is sufficient to satisfy the mental element.) Intoxication *per se* is only criminalized in certain circumstances.[8] The most important are:

- being found drunk in a public place;[9]
- being drunk and disorderly in a public place;[10]

---

[5] Sam Wright and Hilary Klee, "Violent Crime, Aggression and Amphetamine: What Are the Implications for Drug Treatment Services? (2001) 8(1) *Drugs: Education, Prevention, and Policy* 83.
[6] [1550] 75 E.R. 1 at 32. See also Sir Matthew Hale, *Historia Placitorum Coronae: The History of the Pleas of the Crow*, (London: Printed for E. and R. Nutt, Vol. I, 1736) at 32-33.
[7] Specific intent refers to direct intention in its pure form: that is where D has it as his purpose to do a certain action to bring about a certain result.
[8] Certain forms of drunkenness have been criminalized in one form or another for centuries. See for example, 4 Jac. 1, c. 5 (1606). See also Glanville Williams, *Criminal Law: The General Part*, (London: Steven & Sons, 1953) at 373; James Fitzjames Stephen, *History of the Criminal Law of England*, (London: Macmillan, Vol. II, 1883) at 410; William Hawkins, *A Treatise of the Pleas of the Crown*, (London: printed by Eliz. Nutt, 1716) at 8.
[9] Section 12 of the *Licensing Act 1872*. Notwithstanding widespread public drunkenness in the 21st century, this offence is still charged. See also *R. v. McGrath* [2005] 2 Cr. App. R. (S.) 85; *R. v. Liverpool City Justices* (1983) 76 Cr. App. R. 170; *Lewis v. Dodd* [1919] 1 K.B. 1.
[10] *Carroll v. D.P.P.* (2009) 173 J.P. 285; *Neale v. RMJE (A Minor)* (1985) 80 Cr. App. R. 20.

- being drunk on an aircraft;[11]
- being drunk in a public place in possession of a loaded firearm;[12]
- being found drunk in a place in charge of a child under seven;[13]
- driving a motor vehicle, or being in charge of a motor vehicle, when under the influence of drink or drugs;[14]
- driving a motor vehicle or being in charge of a motor vehicle with alcohol concentration above the prescribed limit;[15] and
- a drunk or disorderly person commits an offence if, without reasonable excuse—(a) he fails to leave relevant licensed premises when requested to do so.[16]

Intoxication is an element of these crimes; therefore, the issue of whether evidence of intoxication can be raised to negate *mens rea* does not arise. Legislation also strikes at the possession of what are compendiously described as "controlled drugs."[17] In this Chapter, we will focus on intoxication as a potential excuse.

Intoxication presents problems in the theory of responsibility. One who does a criminal deed when intoxicated may previously have led a blameless life. Drink (or a drug) perhaps had an unexpected effect on him, and the act may not reflect his real character. So it may look harsh to convict him of a crime, particularly of a very serious crime like murder. Moreover, the evidence of intoxication may satisfy the jury that he lacked the intention or other mental element normally required for the crime.

    19–003

    On the other hand, many offenders have imbibed before committing the criminal act, and this cannot be allowed as a general defence. By becoming intoxicated a person voluntarily impairs his own self-control and good judgment. He must be subjected to social control if there is a possibility that his mischievous conduct will be repeated.

Why not treat the drunkard as insane? The poisoning of the brain with alcohol or other drugs is a self-induced condition and thus is not an uncontrollable condition. Volition enters into it in a way that it does not into insanity. The threat of punishment may cause a person to moderate his intake of intoxicants, and it may cause even the intoxicated person to control himself. Some may be inclined to dispute this assumption; but obviously it would be inimical to the safety of all of us if the judges announced that anyone could be excused from criminal liability by getting drunk.[18]

    19–004

---

[11] See *Air Navigation (No.2) Order 1995* Art.57 and section 61 of the *Civil Aviation Act 1982; R. v. Tagg* [2002] 1 Cr. App. R. 22.

[12] See section 12 of the *Licensing Act 1872*. See also *Seamark v. Prouse* (1980) 70 Cr. App. R. 236.

[13] See sections 1 and 2 of the *Licensing Act 1902*. See *Alabusheva v. D.P.P.* [2007] EWHC 264 (Admin).

[14] Section 4 of the *Road Traffic Act 1988*.

[15] Section 5 of the *Road Traffic Act 1988*.

[16] Section 143 of the *Licensing Act 2003*.

[17] *Misuse of Drugs Act 1971* and Regulations thereunder.

[18] In United States Supreme Court in *Montana v. Egelhoff*, 518 U.S. 37 at 50 (1996), Scalia J. said: "The rule … serves as a specific deterrent, ensuring that those who prove incapable of controlling

19–005   **Is it not possible to be both drunk and insane?** The distinction between intoxication and insanity is not entirely realistic: an addict is as much in the grip of his own failing as a psychotic. Alcoholic addiction may culminate in serious brain damage. Drunkenness is not itself insanity, but drinking may result in what is thought of as insanity (for example, *delirium tremens*), or it may be symptomatic of insanity, or bring out latent insanity. The same is true for other drugs. Here the ordinary defence of insanity is open, within the rules to be discussed in Chapter 27. If it succeeds there must be a special verdict, and the defendant may go to hospital.

If the cause of the defendant's insanity is his chronic alcoholism, he should be able to raise the defence of insanity. In a United States case, *West v. State*,[19] it was said: "Temporary insanity arising from *present* voluntary intoxication is no defence to criminal charge, but if the accused is suffering from settled or fixed insanity caused by long continued alcoholic indulgence, the rule is the same as in case of insanity arising from any other cause." Here, the defendant raises the defence of insanity, not the issue of intoxication. His chronic alcohol abuse causes his insanity and it is his insanity that prevents him from knowing he is committing a crime. Hence, the insanity must operate on its own: it has to be shown that the source of the insanity is some underlying disease or defect of the mind rather than the ephemeral effects of the alcohol itself.[20] Once it is established that a person is legally insane he will be able to raise the defence of insanity, even if he was intoxicated when he committed the offence. It does not matter that he was intoxicated when he committed the crime, as long as his underlying insanity prevents him from knowing right from wrong.[21] Nor will it matter that he caused his own insanity by consuming alcohol and (other) drugs over many years. Furthermore, a partial defence of diminished responsibility might be based on "alcohol dependency syndrome,"[22] but, "*voluntary* consumption of alcohol, however excessive, does not constitute an abnormality of the mind."[23]

So the insane drunk walks free. The courts do not draw the line as sharply as may appear. On the one hand, a person who successfully sets up a defence of insanity is not necessarily released: if his crime is serious he is likely to go to a

---

violent impulses while voluntarily intoxicated go to prison." *Per contra*, in *R. v. Connor* (1980) 146 C.L.R. 64 at 79, Barwick C.J., in the High Court of Australia, said: "whatever the risks in a trial by jury, they do not justify, in my opinion, such a departure from fundamental principles of criminal responsibility as to my mind is involved in the decision of *Majewski's Case*. It is clear, I think, that no common law offence is made out by proof of the *actus reus* alone. In the case of all such crimes, at least an actual intent to do the physical act involved in the crime charged must be established."

[19] 511 So.2d 258 (1987); see also *R. v. Davis* (1881) 14 Cox C.C. 563; *R. v. Burns* (1974) 58 Cr. App. R. 364; *State v. Hartfield*, 388 S.E.2d 802 (1990); *State v. Salmon*, 226 NE 2d 784 (1967); Meloy J. Reid, "Voluntary Intoxication and the Insanity Defence," (1992) 20 *J. Psychiatry & L.* 439; Stanley Yeo, "Intoxication and Mental Disorder Defences," (2004) 16 *S. Ac. L.J.* 488 (2004). Cf. *Villarreal v. State*, 661 S.W.2d 329 (1983); *Carter v. State*, 248 Ga.App. 139 (2001); *Hewitt v. State*, 575 So.2d 273 (1991).

[20] *Attorney-General of Northern Ireland v. Gallagher* [1963] A.C. 349 at 382.

[21] The *M'Naghten* rules would have to be satisfied. *R. v. M'Naghten* (1843) 10 Cl. & Fin. 200 at 211. See also *R. v. Kingston* [1995] 2 A.C. 355 at 369, *per* Lord Mustill.

[22] Cf. *R. v. Tandy* [1989] 1 W.L.R. 350; *R. v. Stewart* [2009] 1 W.L.R. 2507; *R. v. Stewart* [2010] EWCA Crim. 2159. Cf. *State v. LaCroix*, 911 A.2d 674 (2006); *R. v. Elias* [2010] Y.J. No. 174.

[23] *R. v. Wood* [2009] 1 W.L.R. 496.

psychiatric hospital for as long as he is thought to be a public danger. On the other hand, an alcoholic or drug addict who is convicted of crime need not be punished: the court may put him on probation for treatment, if considerations of deterrence are not paramount and if treatment is available. Most drunkards who commit serious crimes are sent to prison (and on conviction of murder the court has no option); whereas an irresponsibly insane person who sets up his insanity as a defence may have a "special verdict" (of insanity), in which case he will at least be safe from prison. If an insane person does not specifically set up an insanity defence even he may go to prison, as we shall see, though this outcome is now unlikely.

From the social point of view confinement in a special hospital may not be the preferred outcome. A supervision order would be better,[24] since it is unlikely that either a special hospital or an NHS hospital would willingly accept an alcoholic as an inpatient for any length of time, if at all. Such methods of treatment as exist require the active desire of the patient for treatment, and the problem is one of motivation. The desirable solution is some legal mechanism by which the alcoholic or drug-addict can be held to be legally responsible, and therefore punishable—not by way of retribution, but in order to induce him to accept treatment or otherwise to discontinue the habit, or in the last resort to confine him for the protection of the public. What we have to consider is how legal responsibility can be secured. **19–006**

19.3.   INTOXICATION AND INTENTION

The House of Lords in *Commissioner of Police of the Metropolis v. Caldwell*[25] solved the problem of the intoxicated offender by creating a kind of constructive recklessness. If the courts had begun with this solution it is unlikely that they would have felt the need for any other. An explanation must start in the 1920s, when it was thought that the ordinary *mens rea* principles applied to the ascertainment of intention even when the defendant was drunk.[26] **19–007**

So drunks were let off these charges?   Not necessarily. The law was, and is, that evidence of intoxication is not a passport to an acquittal. The mere fact that a person was drunk when he committed a criminal act is not an excuse. Drink may have loosened his inhibitions, made him more irascible, caused him to do terrible **19–008**

---

[24]   Schedule 1A to the *Domestic Violence, Crime and Victims Act 2004* provides: "(1) In this Schedule 'supervision order' means an order which requires the person in respect of whom it is made ('the supervised person') to be under the supervision of a social worker or an officer of a local probation board ('the supervising officer') for a period specified in the order of not more than two years. (2) A supervision order may, in accordance with paragraph 4 or 5 below, require the supervised person to submit, during the whole of that period or such part of it as may be specified in the order, to treatment by or under the direction of a registered medical practitioner."

[25]   [1982] A.C. 341.

[26]   *D.P.P. v. Beard* [1920] A.C. 479.

things that he would not have otherwise done when sober; but on none of these accounts would he be entitled to an acquittal. An intoxicated intent is still an intent.[27]

19–009   **Can the drunk get off on a charge of murder in this way?**   Yes, if his state of intoxication was sufficient to prevent him from forming a specific intent to commit murder.[28] If he did not form the intent, he cannot be convicted of murder.

19–010   **But if the evidence of intoxication gets him off, then intoxication is a passport to an acquittal.**   Whether the evidence leads to an acquittal depends on the circumstances and on the view taken by the jury. An intoxicated person can decide to kill somebody. If he rushes at the victim and stabs him, the jury may come to the conclusion that he intended to kill.[29] Suppose a man, having taken drink, in a fit of temper pushes his wife under a bus. The jury may be satisfied that he intended to kill her, and convict him of murder. Indeed, the fact that the man was intoxicated may make them more convinced that he lost his temper to such a fearful extent. But if the evidence seems to show that he only stumbled against his wife, the fact that he was intoxicated may fortify any doubt the jury may have had about his intention, and lead them to acquit him of murder (and also of wounding with intent).[30]

19–011   **So the question is whether the evidence of intoxication negatives the capacity to form the required intent?**   If you summed up to the jury in that way a conviction would be quashed on appeal; but you would not be the first judge to step on that particular banana-skin. Such a direction puts the matter too favourably to the defendant. Of course, if he couldn't form the intent, he didn't; but the converse is not true. As I said, a person who is under the influence may have been quite capable of deciding to kill someone, but the evidence may indicate that he did not so decide. The simple question for the jury is: Are you sure that the defendant had the requisite state of mind? For this purpose it is irrelevant to consider the fact of intoxication.[31]

19–012   **I do not want to come another tumble, but how sloshed must a person be before he gets off a charge of murder by giving evidence of intoxication?**   Once more: it is not the simple fact of intoxication that puts the defendant in the clear, so we do not need a rule about the degree of intoxication that has to be regarded. A person who is charged with theft of an umbrella may give evidence that he is an absent-minded professor and did not think what he was doing, or that he was drunk; the evidence may help him to an acquittal, but what

---

[27] See *R. v. Kingston* [1995] 2 A.C. 355, where a pederast was not able to avoid conviction, because the drugs only had the effect of reducing his inhibitions—he still intended to violate the boy.

[28] *R. v. Sheehan* [1975] 1 W.L.R. 739; *D.P.P. v. Beard* [1920] A.C. 479.

[29] *R. v. Kingston* [1995] 2 A.C. 355.

[30] In which case the prosecution bear the usual burden of proof of intent: *R. v. Sheehan* [1975] 1 W.L.R. 739.

[31] *R. v. Sheehan* [1975] 1 W.L.R. 739; *R. v. Pordage* [1975] Crim. L.R. 575; *R. v. Hayes* [2002] EWCA Crim. 1945.

gets him off is not the fact that he is a professor, or was drunk, or both, but that the jury or magistrates are not sure that he intended to steal.

What if a person deliberately gets drunk for the sake of "Dutch courage" to commit murder or some other serious crime?   That is a special case. He can probably be convicted even though he was an "automaton" at the moment of acting.

19–013

A person decides to commit murder, and gets drunk in order to nerve himself to carry it out; in fact he gets so drunk that the jury feel unable to say that when he did the deed he had any idea what he was doing. To acquit him would obviously be too lenient. Indeed, the probability is that even in his drunken state he remembered the intent that he formed when sober—because otherwise it would be difficult to explain his actions. However that may be, it is an intelligible rule that the defendant is to be held guilty of a crime of intention in such circumstances because his conduct must be regarded as a whole; and Lord Denning on one occasion expressed an opinion to this effect.[32] Suppose, to take an analogy, that a man sets a time-bomb to kill people, and is asleep when it goes off; obviously he is guilty of murder. Similarly, if he fuddles himself with drink in order to commit murder, he turns himself into a kind of human time-bomb.[33]

During the 1920s it was thought that this was the whole of the law on the subject of intoxication in relation to the mental element. But some judges were apprehensive that we were being too lenient to drunkards, and so they set about to change the law by introducing a distinction between what they called crimes of specific intent and crimes of basic intent. The old law continues to apply to crimes of specific intent, but in crimes of basic (or general) intent the jury will be instructed not to take evidence of voluntary intoxication into account in deciding the issue of intention. The seal of approval was placed on this development by the House of Lords in *D.P.P. v. Majewski*.[34]

I gather from what you have said before that murder[35] is a crime of specific intent, where the old law still applies. What others are there?   The principal are wounding with intent,[36] criminal damage with intent to endanger life,[37] theft,[38] robbery, burglary, handling stolen goods,[39] and an attempt to commit any offence.[40]

19–014

---

[32] *Attorney-General of Northern Ireland v. Gallagher* [1963] A.C. 349 at 382. The majority did not express concurrence in Lord Denning's view, because they decided the case on a different point. It had been argued that the defendant was irresponsibly insane, and the majority held that the question of insanity was to be judged by reference to the time of the act, not some earlier time when he took alcohol (because at that earlier time he might not have been insane, yet he might have been insane at the time of the act). Lord Denning's opinion, on the other hand, supposed that insanity was out of the case; on that assumption it was surely right.

[33] The *mens rea* antedates the *actus reus*.

[34] [1977] A.C. 443. The name is anglicized in pronunciation as spelt.

[35] *D.P.P. v. Beard* [1920] A.C. 479.

[36] *R. v. Pordage* [1975] Crim. L.R. 575.

[37] *R. v. Durante* [1972] 1 W.L.R. 1612.

[38] *Ruse v. Read* [1949] 1 K.B. 377; *R. v. Foote* [1964] Crim. L.R. 405; *R. v. Kindon* (1957) 41 Cr. App. R. 208. Nor would the drunken taker be convicted on the basis of recklessness, since theft cannot be committed recklessly. Offences involving an intent to deceive or defraud are also taken to be of specific intent: *R. v. Durante* [1972] 1 W.L.R. 1612. For example, under section 2 of the *Fraud*

Although the defendant is acquitted of one of these serious crimes by reason of evidence of intoxication, there will generally be a fall-back offence of which, under the dispensation established in *D.P.P. v. Majewski*, the prosecution can get him convicted, because it is an offence of basic intent which is not disproved by evidence of intoxication. For example, the drunken killer may be acquitted of murder because he did not intend to kill; but he will be convicted of manslaughter (as he always could be). So broad is the law of manslaughter that it applies even when a person has killed another when in a state of minimal consciousness.

In *R. v. Lipman*,[41] the defendant killed his lover when he was under the influence of LSD (hallucinating that he was fighting snakes at the centre of the earth). He was convicted of constructive manslaughter because he had committed an unlawful act, and sentenced to six years' imprisonment. The decision caused discomfort to commentators, but the House of Lords regarded it as authoritative in *D.P.P. v. Majewski*. It is clear from the latter case that Lipman's "unlawful act" was in attacking his female companion. This attack was an assault, his state of confused consciousness being the result of voluntary intoxication.

19–015 Similarly, the drunkard (I call him a drunkard, but he may be equally incapacitated by (other) drugs, which are legally regarded in the same way as alcohol) may be acquitted of wounding with intent, but may be convicted of various lesser crimes because they are regarded as crimes of basic intent: assault, unlawful wounding, *etc.*[42] He may be acquitted of criminal damage with intent to endanger life, but on certain lesser charges evidence of intoxication will generally be of no help to him: criminal damage being reckless whether life will be endangered, or criminal damage simply, whether of the intentional or reckless variety.[43] These are crimes of basic intent.

The drunkard may be acquitted of theft, which involves an intent to deprive the owner permanently of the thing. So if he comes out of a pub after a merry evening and rides off on someone else's bicycle by mistake, the evidence of intoxication will help to get him off the charge of theft. Also of burglary when that involves an intent to steal. But he may (it is held) be convicted of taking a conveyance without the owner's consent (sometimes called the joyriding offence). This is supposed to be a crime of basic intent to which evidence of intoxication is irrelevant.[44] (But the opinion has to be qualified, as we shall see (19.6).)

Act 2006 a person commits an offence if he "dishonestly makes a false representation, and (b) *intends*, by making the representation– (i) to make a gain for himself or another."

[39] *Commissioner of Police of the Metropolis v. Caldwell* [1982] A.C. 341.

[40] *Per* Lord Salmon in *D.P.P. v. Majewski* [1977] A.C. 443 at 483D; see also *R. v. Mohan* [1976] Q.B. 1.

[41] [1970] 1 Q.B. 152. The basis of the decision has been debated (see Glanville Williams, *Textbook of Criminal Law*, (London: Stevens & Sons, 1978) at 435-436), but it is now in line with *Commissioner of Police of the Metropolis v. Caldwell* [1982] A.C. 341.

[42] Also assault occasioning actual bodily harm, or assault on a constable in the execution of his duty.

[43] For the proposition that intentional damage under section 1(1) of the *Criminal Damage Act 1971* is an offence of basic intent see *Jaggard v. Dickinson* [1981] Q.B. 527; *Commissioner of Police of the Metropolis v. Caldwell* [1982] A.C. 341.

[44] *R. v. MacPherson* [1973] R.T.R. 157; *D.P.P. v. Majewski* [1977] A.C. 443 at 477D; *R. v. Gannon* (1988) 87 Cr. App. R. 254.

Suppose the thing the drunkard takes is not a vehicle but something else,   19–016
such as a watch. In that event there is generally no lesser charge that can be
used against him. However, even if the evidence of intoxication saves him from
being convicted in respect of the original taking of the watch, he can be convicted
of theft if he decided to keep it after he had sobered up.

If theft of the watch is a crime of specific intent, what is the corresponding   19–017
crime of basic intent? There is no crime of basic intent applicable in this case.
A crime of specific intent means an act intentionally done with a certain specific
intent. Consequently, one cannot always find a crime of basic intent underlying a
crime of specific intent. When a conveyance is taken, we happen to have the
joyriding offence[45] (basic intent) underpinning the crime of theft (specific intent)
but no lesser offence of basic intent generally applies to the taking of other
objects. As another example of this, attempt is classified as a crime of specific
intent,[46] but the act of attempt need not be an offence apart from attempt. (This
means, for instance, that intoxication must be taken into account on a charge of
attempted rape,[47] though it is not on a charge of rape itself!)[48] If the drunkard gets
off the charge of attempt he will generally be safe from any other charge in
respect of that incident.

Why ever do we have these terms "specific intent" and "basic intent"? I   19–018
don't really see that the law makes sense. The way in which we came to have
these expressions, as a historical matter, is perfectly clear. They result from the
desire on the part of the judges to change the law. I will tell you the story; it is of
interest as a case-study in the way the judges see their own role, and the kind of
manipulation of the law that they consider proper; but otherwise it is purely
historical.

Before *D.P.P. v. Majewski* the leading case on the subject of intoxication was
D.P.P. v. Beard.[49] Lord Birkenhead, delivering in effect the judgment of the
House of Lords, stated that evidence of intoxication could be taken into
consideration in deciding whether the defendant had a "specific intent essential to
constitute the crime." He did not explain what he meant by "specific," but we can
say with some confidence that his judgment indicates that he had nothing very
much in mind, and it is a great pity that he did not cross the word out of his

---

[45] Section 12 of the *Theft Act 1968*.

[46] *D.P.P. v. Majewski* [1977] A.C. 443 at 477D at 483D.

[47] A man cannot attempt to rape a woman if he has no awareness of her non-consent. (In *R. v. Khan*
[1990] 1 W.L.R. 813, it was held that a man could attempt rape if he attempted to have intercourse
knowing there was a risk that V was not consenting, but such a rapist might be too intoxicated to even
be aware that there is a "risk" that his victim is not consenting.) Even though the offence of rape under
section 1 of the *Sexual Offences Act 2003* only requires negligence as to circumstances, conceptually
a man cannot attempt to rape as opposed to attempt to love make, if he does not know that his victim
is not consenting. *Contra*, *United States v. Short*, 16 C.M.R. 11 (1954). Cf. *U.S. v. Langley*, 33 M.J.
278 (1991), where D committed the ulterior intent crime of assault with intent to rape.

[48] There may be rare rape cases where intoxication will be relevant, because the defendant's act of
intercourse is not purposive or intentional. But it is difficult to imagine a person having sexual
intercourse as a drunken automaton. Nonetheless, an automaton might be capable of having sexual
intercourse. See *R. v. Luedecke* [2008] 236 C.C.C. 3d 317.

[49] [1920] A.C. 479.

speech before delivering it.[50] That he attached no significance to the word is shown in the fact that immediately after the sentence in question he repeated it in essence but modified it by omitting the word "specific" and substituting the phrase "the intent necessary to constitute the crime."[51] Moreover, at the end of his speech he stated expressly that his remarks were meant to apply not only to crimes requiring a "specific intent" but also to crimes not requiring a "specific intent," "for," he said, "speaking generally (and apart from certain special offences), a person cannot be convicted of crime unless the *mens rea* was *rea*."[52] He could hardly have made it clearer that, whatever distinction he had in mind between specific intents and other intents, he (and therefore the House of Lords for whom he was speaking) meant his remarks to apply to all intents. That, indeed, was how his opinion was understood for many years.

But judges then conceived the fear that gullible juries would turn dangerous drunks loose upon the community (there is little or no evidence that they have done so.)[53] Since so many crimes were worded to require a mental element, and since nothing was to be expected from the Government and Parliament, which do not think it an important part of their function to settle legal difficulties, the judges silently came to the conclusion that the only remedy was the accustomed one of do-it-yourself. The technique was to take Lord Birkenhead's phrase "specific intent" and to assert that what he said applied *only* to crimes having that requirement (whatever meaning might be found for it, Lord Birkenhead having assigned none). In *D.P.P. v. Majewski* the Law Lords were pressed with the argument that Lord Birkenhead did not mean what he was now supposed to have meant, but they brushed aside the argument with the assertion that he could not have meant what he said.

We must now study the highly obscure distinction between specific and basic intent in greater depth.

19.4.   SPECIFIC AND BASIC INTENT

19–019   The rule in *D.P.P. v. Majewski* depends upon the assumption that an intelligible distinction can be made between specific and basic intent. But the higher courts in that and other cases, while unanimous that there is such a distinction, and while agreeing on some of its applications, have failed to agree on a definition of the two intents. What can be said is that the definition is the one we had before for what we then preferred to call "direct intent" or "purpose."[54] (But this definition does not necessarily fit well with all the decisions, or with the definition representing the dominant judicial opinion.) In *D.P.P. v. Majewski*, Lord Elwyn-Jones L.C. said that specific intent refers to an "ulterior intent."[55] If this

---

[50] Some of the old cases used the term merely to note that the defendant should have the specific harm in mind that he is being held liable for. *R. v. Cruse* (1838) 173 E.R. 610.

[51] [1920] A.C. 479 at 501-502.

[52] [1920] A.C. 479 at 504.

[53] See for example, Victorian Law Reform Commission, *Criminal Responsibility: Intention Gross Intoxication*, (Melbourne: V.L.R.C., 1986) at 19. In that part of Australia, the *D.P.P. v. Majewski* rule is not recognized by the courts.

[54] 4.1-4.2. See *R. v. Heard* [2008] Q.B. 43.

[55] [1977] A.C. 443 at 470.

were right, only crimes of ulterior intent require a specific intent. We know this cannot be right, because the specific intent doctrine has been applied in numerous cases where the offender has not committed an ulterior intent crime.

However, the ulterior intent idea is conceptually a form of direct or purposive intent. A specific intent is an intent going beyond the intent to do the act in question.[56] The body movement is willed or intentional, and it is done with some further intent specified in the offence.[57] In murder (the judges appear to suppose), specific intent where an act is done with intent to cause death (if a doctor wounds a patient as a part of an operation, he does not wound him for the purpose of killing him). Similarly, if a person takes a wallet from a pocket for a joke, he does not take the wallet for the purpose of permanently depriving the owner of it, so he does not commit theft. If a doctor intentionally fondles a woman's breasts for the purpose of carrying out a medical examination, his purpose is not to seek sexual gratification. Originally, it was said that the ulterior intent crimes provided the best example of crimes requiring a specific intent, because such crimes usually require the defendant to do some act for some ulterior purpose. For example, in burglary, trespass with certain unlawful intents, and so on. It is clear, however, that the "ulterior intent" conceptualization of specific intent is too simplistic— after all, the most serious specific intent crime is murder and it is not an ulterior intent crime.

Why is murder a crime of specific intent? Surely the intent is "basic," as you   19–020
defined this word. The murderer intends to kill; he need have no intent
beyond that. A motiveless murder is still murder. Similarly with the
wounder.   I am glad that you have clutched the gist of the above argument with alacrity. It followed that given by the courts, but in common sense, as you say, murder and wounding with intent (or, at least, the commonest forms of the latter crimes) are not ulterior intent crimes. In neither murder nor causing g.b.h. with intent to cause g.b.h. does the law specify any result that must be intended to follow the attack.

The courts have not stated how they conceive the intent as specific. Perhaps in the case of causing g.b.h. they do not realize that the words "with intent" are used in a usual sense, or it does not suit their purpose to advert to this. The phrase "with intent" in the definition of a crime normally refers to an ulterior intent (*e.g.*, in the crime of assault with intent to rob, or wounding with intent to resist arrest),

---

[56] *Jaggard v. Dickinson* [1981] Q.B. 527 at 532H, *per* Donaldson L.J. "The distinction between a general or basic intent and a specific intent is that whereas the former extends only to the *actus reus*, a specific intent extends beyond it." By *actus reus* he evidently intended the physical act, regarding a specified consequence as not part of the act (though in another use of language it could be so regarded). For discordant views in the House of Lords see Williams, *op. cit. supra*, note 45 at 429-430.

[57] Cf. *Parker v. The Queen* [1964] A.C. 1369 at 1391; *Maddy's case* (1671) 86 E.R. 108, referring to premeditation. Russell also said: "Where upon, a charge of murder, the material question, is, whether the act was premeditated or done only with sudden heat and impulse, the fact of the party being intoxicated has been holden to be a circumstance proper to be taken into consideration." William Oldnall Russell, *A Treatise on Crimes and Indictable Misdemeanours*, (Boston: Lilly and Watt, Vol. I, 1831) at 8.

but in the crime of causing g.b.h. with intent to cause g.b.h. no such ulterior intent is required. Causing g.b.h. with intent to cause it merely means intentionally causing g.b.h.

A better explanation depends on the facts pointed out before,[58] that while some verbs have consequences wrapped into them, some have not. When we talk of killing (or wounding) a person, we may conceptualize or verbalize the event in either of two ways. We may take killing (or wounding) to mean doing an act (striking *etc.*) that causes death (or a wound), where the act and its consequences are treated as two separate events; or we may have a composite notion of "doing an act of killing" (or "an act of wounding"), where the result is included in the notion of the act. The choice is only a question of words, but it is a choice with legal implications under the *D.P.P. v. Majewski* rule. Traditionally, murder is thought of as a "killing," and that is how it is legally described. But, the judges scheme being to have a rule that will let the drunkard off the graver charge only, they decide to think of murder for this particular purpose as "an act done with intent to cause death (and succeeding in that purpose)" rather than as a self-contained act of "intentional killing." Similarly, they regard an intentional wounding as "doing an act with intent to cause a wound" rather than an act of "intentional wounding."

19–021   It is not even true that murder is necessarily an intentional killing. Intentionally causing grievous bodily harm without intent to kill is murder if death results. (This anomaly is not caused by the concept of direct intention, but by the fiction created by constructive liability.)[59] But, if one can turn a crime into one of specific intent by saying that achieving a result by doing an act with intent to achieve it involves a specific intent, then I commit a crime of specific intent when I move my fist with intent to bring it into painful contact with your nose, and succeed in doing so, or when I put your car in motion as a result of having done something (started the engine, *etc.*) with that purpose; yet neither of these crimes (assault, and taking a conveyance) involves a specific intent in law. That may be so, but that does not mean that you cannot commit such crimes with a specific intent! So in legal terms, it appears that a person has a specific intent when it is his purpose to perform the *actus reus* of an offence in circumstances where he should not do so. He has sexual intercourse for the purpose of raping his victim, when he knows for fact that the circumstances are that she is not consenting. Negligence as to circumstances is a basic intent element, but it does not mean that the defendant cannot form a specific intent to have sexual intercourse in such circumstances. Or he stabs a person for the purpose of killing him. He intends to stab—and he intends to kill; his intentional act of stabbing is done for the purpose of killing.

---

[58]   4.2.

[59]   Murder is made out if D's direct intent is either to kill or cause g.b.h. Nonetheless, D must still have a specific intent to cause the g.b.h.; and the latter may be negated if he is severely intoxicated. (Technically, the constructive liability that is used to make him responsible for murder rather than for the offence found in section 18 of the *Offences against the Person Act 1861*, is a form of basic intent. That is, the constructive gap rests on a basic intent notion: D intends to cause g.b.h. and is reckless as to whether this might kill V, and thus is forced to take the consequences of intending g.b.h. He is held constructively liable even if he did not envisage death as a potential consequence of inflicting g.b.h. upon his victim.)

This might make things clearer in conceptual terms, but anomalies arise because crimes have been enacted for centuries with sober offenders in mind—not intoxicated ones. For example, there is no social difference between stealing someone else's watch and deliberately smashing someone else's watch, but the first (theft) is regarded as a crime of specific intent while the second (criminal damage) is a crime of basic intent.

Another anomaly emerges when one compares criminal damage with wounding with intent. "Wounding with intent" under section 18 of the *Offences against the Person Act 1861* in most cases means intentionally wounding, and it is precisely analogous to intentionally damaging property. Now if a drunkard on the rampage swings an iron bar at a window and smashes it, the jury (or magistrate) can convict him under the rule in *D.P.P. v. Majewski* of culpably damaging the window, the jury being instructed to disregard his intoxication when the offence is one of basic intent, as this offence is. But if he had wounded a man by doing essentially the same thing, his intoxication would have been taken into account on a charge under section 18 of the *Act of 1861* to help show that he did not intend to wound anyone, the crime under section 18 being one of specific intent. There is no relevant difference between the two cases on the facts. The defendant broke the window, or he caused the window to be broken; he wounded the victim, or he caused the victim to be wounded. (Nonetheless, section 18 is underwritten by section 20, a basic intent crime.)

Further anomalies can be attributed to the fact that many offences have both **19–022** specific intent (purposive/direct intent) elements and basic intent (recklessness/ negligence) elements. Take the intoxicated man who intentionally has sexual intercourse with a woman who he mistakenly believes is consenting. The act of intercourse must be intentional,[60] if the defendant's intoxication means that he is an automaton, he will not form the specific intent required for this element of the offence of rape. This means he cannot be convicted of rape.[61] Clearly, if intoxication negates D's specific intent for a given element of the offence, he will not have the requisite *mens rea* for that element. Unless the specific intent element (*i.e.* a requirement that the sexual intercourse be intentional) is underwritten by a basic intent element (*i.e.* a requirement that the sexual intercourse be either intentional or reckless), D does not commit rape. The offence is not one of negligently doing the act of intercourse; it is one of intentionally[62] doing the act of intercourse. (Negligence only goes to the circumstance of consent.) This seems extreme, but thankfully such a case will

---

[60] This was overlooked in the past because the English courts focused on ulterior intent crimes without realizing that conceptually rape and murder fit within the specific intent framework. The pre-*2003* offence of rape did not expressly require the act of intercourse to be intentional, but that did not mean that there was no implied requirement that it be intentional. The only reason the offence of rape was treated as entirely one of basic intent, is that in all the cases where intoxication was an issue, it related to the basic intent element.

[61] Professor LaFave (very correctly, in my view) asserts that: "[R]ape requires an intent to do the physical act of accomplishing sexual intercourse with the victim." Wayne R. LaFave, *Substantive Criminal Law*, (West Group Publishing, Vol. II, 2003) at 45 n.20. LaFave also notes that if the specific intent element is blotted out, then rape is not made out: *id.* at 45-46. He is critical of a number of U.S. decisions that have overlooked this distinction.

[62] Cf. *R. v. G* [2009] 1 A.C. 92.

hardly ever arise. The action of sexual intercourse will nearly always be intentional, because a drunken intent is still an intent.[63]

There would have to be compelling evidence to convince the jury that the act of intercourse was unintentional. A person might suffer an illness that may cause him to rape whilst in a trance, but such cases are exceptional.[64] Nor is it likely that someone would subjectively be reckless as to whether he is engaging in sexual intercourse as opposed to dancing or some other activity. It is difficult to imagine a situation where a person might believe his act of sexual intercourse is not sexual intercourse, but that there is a risk that it could be. Even the most naive person would know that sexual intercourse is not a form of dancing, or is not the act of riding an exercise bike. (Suppose X is having sexual intercourse with Y but believes he is merely dancing with Y; but in the back of his mind he believes that there is a chance that he engaging in sexual intercourse—not dancing. Here, we might say that he is reckless as to whether he is engaging in the act of sexual intercourse. If he does not think of the risk that it might be sexual intercourse rather than dancing, he is not subjectively aware of the risk that it might be sexual intercourse.) As you can see, this is different to knowing for a fact that you are engaging in sexual intercourse, but being negligent as to whether the other party is consenting.

Since the idea of sexual intercourse being unintentional or reckless is extremely fanciful, it is little wonder that Parliament required the act of intercourse to be intentional. Once it is established that the sexual intercourse was intentional (which will normally be the case), the focus will be on the basic intent element. That is, whether a reasonable person[65] *would* have believed that the victim was not consenting had the hypothetical reasonable person not been intoxicated.

19–023 In *R. v. Heard*,[66] the Court of Appeal embarked on an ill-considered legislative venture. The court decided to consider whether the offence of sexual assault found in section 3 of the *Sexual Offences Act 2003* is a basic intent crime. Speaking through Hughes L.J., the court proposed (*obiter*) a new rule, one of policy but conjured out of the authorities by carrying selection to extreme lengths. The court's own reasoning is contradictory and fallacious. Hughes L.J. said:

---

[63] *R. v. Heard* [2008] Q.B. 43 at 49-51; *R. v. Kingston* [1995] 2 A.C. 355.

[64] I searched for cases in every common law jurisdiction and could only find one case of rape by an automaton in the last 800 years; and his automatism was not the result of voluntary intoxication. See *R. v. Luedecke* [2008] 236 C.C.C. 3d 317.

[65] Since rape only requires negligence as to the circumstance of whether or not the victim was consenting, a reasonable person standard is applicable. (The question need not be framed in this way for cases involving negligence, because a reasonable person is axiomatically a sober person.) Where the basic intent element requires subjective recklessness, the question will be whether the *defendant* would have realized his mistake had *he* been sober.

[66] [2008] Q.B. 43 at 50-51.

"We are in the present case concerned with element (a),[67] the touching. The *2003 Act* says that it must be intentional. We regard it as clear that a reckless touching will not do. The *Act* plainly proceeds upon the basis that there is a difference between intentionally and recklessly. Where it wishes to speak in terms of recklessness, the *2003 Act* does so: see for example sections 63(1), 69(1)(c)(2)(c) and 70(1)(c)."

Remarkably, Hughes L.J. goes on to conclude the opposite:[68]

"Element (a) (the touching) in sexual assault contrary to section 3 of the *Act of 2003* is an element requiring no more than *basic intent*. It follows that voluntary intoxication cannot be relied upon to negate that intent."

One would have thought that the Court of Appeal was interpreting the pre-*2003* law. The new offence found in section 3, like many of the new sexual offences, clearly has a specific intent element. The touching must be intentional in that the defendant must intend to touch another human being. It must be his purpose to touch a human being rather than a chair, or a kettle and so on. This is not merely a volitional requirement, as suggested by the court. If it is a specific intent element, the defendant cannot be liable unless his touching is intentional. It was held in *R. v. Bailey*[69] that the fact that automatism was self-induced could not make a defendant guilty of a crime of specific intent. A person who brings about the *actus reus* of an offence while in a state of self-induced automatism, can only be convicted of a basic intent crime.

The problem is that sexual assault is not a purely basic intent crime. It is patently **19–024** clear that the touching must be purposive (blameworthy),[70] that is, intentional. In *R. v. G*[71] the House of Lords said the offence of raping a child under 13 was not entirely an offence of strict liability, because "the penetration had to be intentional." This is clearly correct. To suggest, as Hughes L.J. does, that the Parliament merely used the word "intentional" in a range of sexual offences to mean "non-intentional" but "volitional," is nonsensical. Serious offences such as those found in the *Sexual Offences Act 2003*, require fault beyond mere negligence or strict liability as to circumstances.[72]

---

[67] You will recall, section 3 provides: "(1) A person (A) commits an offence if–(a) he intentionally touches another person (B), (b) the touching is sexual, (c) B does not consent to the touching."

[68] [2008] Q.B. 43 at 55. Cf. *People in the Interest of J.A.*, 733 P.2d 1197 (1987), where a U.S. court interprets a similar provision as creating a specific intent requirement. See also *State v. Bicknese*, 285 N.W.2d 684 (Minn.1979).

[69] [1983] 1 W.L.R. 760.

[70] The Court of Appeal contradicts itself further by asserting that subjective recklessness (clearly a form of fault) would not be enough, but that nothing else is needed.

[71] [2009] 1 A.C. 92 at 96H. Lord Hoffman said: "The mental element of the offence under section 5, as the language and structure of the section makes clear, is that penetration must be intentional but there is no requirement that the accused must have known that the other person was under 13." Lord Hope (at 100H) said: "The offence ... is one of strict liability in the sense that proof of the intentional penetration of a child under 13 is all that is needed for a conviction." And Baroness Hale (at 108C) said: "Thus there is no strict liability in relation to the conduct involved. The perpetrator has to intend to penetrate. Every male has a choice about where he puts his penis. ... There is nothing unjust or irrational about a law which says that if he chooses to put his penis inside a child who turns out to be under 13 he has committed an offence." At 101C, Lord Hope said that sexual touching must also be intentional.

[72] *R. v. G* [2009] 1 A.C. 92.

As said before, the "intentional" requirement in offences such as rape and sexual assault will hardly ever be an issue. In most cases, the defendant will be asserting that his intoxication affected the element of the offence that merely requires recklessness or negligence. For example, he might assert that he was not aware that his intentional touching was sexual or that he was not aware of the fact that the victim was not consenting to have sexual intercourse with him. Here evidence of his intoxication will not help him, because the latter are basic intent elements. If a drunkard gropes a woman's breasts, his act of groping is likely to be held to be intentional and purposive, unless he was an automaton.[73] Therefore, his intoxication will not get him off the hook.

The basic intent element in the offence of sexual assault is superlatively exemplified in section 78 of the *2003 Act*. That section provides:

> "For the purposes of this Part ... penetration, touching or any other activity is sexual if a reasonable person would consider that–
> (a)   whatever its circumstances or any person's purpose in relation to it, it is because of its nature sexual, or
> (b)   because of its nature it may be sexual and because of its circumstances or the purpose of any person in relation to it (or both) it is sexual."

19–025   The reasonable person standard governs both subsection (a) and (b), so if a reasonable person would have been aware of the fact that the touching was sexual because of its nature or of its circumstances, then it will be deemed to have been sexual regardless of the defendant's purpose. "Purpose" is referred to in subsection (b), but this does not mean that the defendant can assert that his purpose was not sexual. It is for the defendant to state what his purpose was for touching the V and for the jury to decide whether a reasonable person would consider the stated purpose to be a sexual purpose. This part of the offence is satisfied as long as the defendant was negligent.

It has to be remembered that most offenders will be sober; therefore the intention requirement should not be removed from the statute by unelected judges. It would cause too many distortions in everyday cases where intoxication is not an issue. Parliament could have covered the risk of someone recklessly touching another in a sexual way, but it seems to have taken the view that unintentional touching is not likely to be sexual. This means that a voluntarily

---

[73] If Lipman had sexually molested his victim while he was in his drug induced trance, he could not have been said to have intentionally touched her. Therefore, Lipman and his ilk would not be liable under section 3 of the *Sexual Offences Act 2003*; or for rape (*R. v. Luedecke* [2008] 236 C.C.C. 3d 317, Luedecke's automatism was not self-induced, however.) Cf. *R. v. Lipman* [1970] 1 Q.B. 152 (where Lipman, acting as no more than an automaton, killed his girlfriend because his intoxication caused him to see her as a snake at the centre of the earth). However, an automaton would have been liable under the old law, since a reckless battery would have been sufficient to satisfy the "assault" element in the old "indecent assault" offence. See *R. v. Rolfe* (1952) 36 Cr. App. R. 4; *R. v. Burns* (1974) 58 Cr. App. R. 364. The *Act of 2003* requires the battery (or touching) to be intentional. Compare the completely different wording of the old rape offence under section 1 of the *Sexual Offences (Amendment) Act 1976*, where a man committed "rape if—(a) he has unlawful sexual intercourse with a woman who at the time of the intercourse does not consent to it..." Under this wording it was presumed that the offence of rape was entirely one of basic intent: see *R. v. Woods* (1982) 74 Cr. App. R. 312; *R. v. Fotheringham* (1989) 88 Cr. App. R. 206. See also *U.S. v. Zachary*, 61 M.J. 813 at 820 (2005), where the wording of the statute did not include a specific intent requirement—but one should have been read in.

intoxicated automaton will be able to evade justice where his touching is unintentional. Such a case is not likely to arise in practice, because drunkards usually act with a drunken intent.

The *obiter* statements in *R. v. Heard* effectively hold that a person is deemed to have had the specific intent required for any elements of an offence requiring specific intent, so long as the offence has a basic intent element—even if that basic intent element is not a substitute for the specific intent element. The court achieved this result by simply stating that the only fault element in the offence is the one concerning negligence as to the sexual nature of the touching. But the basic intent element concerning the "nature" of the touching is not a substitute for the specific intent required concerning the "physical action" that brings the touching about.[74]

Can I switch to ask about crimes of basic intent? When a crime of this kind is charged, do the courts refuse to allow the defendant to adduce evidence of intoxication? They allow evidence to be given by either side.[75] The prosecution may give it to show the background of the case, and even to support the contention that the defendant intentionally did the dreadful thing charged against him, because the drug had weakened his inhibitions. The defendant is free to give it in the hope of persuading the jury that he was fuddled with drink and had no illegal intention. But the judge, applying *D.P.P. v. Majewski*, will direct the jury that the evidence cannot negative the "basic intent" required for the crime.

19–026

The appellant judgments are vague about the practical implications of the rule, but what it means, almost certainly, is no more than that the jury must disregard the evidence of intoxication in determining the defendant's intention. They can and should have regard to any other evidence on the subject. Therefore, the jury must decide how they would have viewed the case if the defendant had not been intoxicated.[76]

If a drunkard makes a fire on the floorboards or hits someone very hard over the head, and afterwards says that he intended no damage or injury, the tribunal of fact should have no difficulty in saying that if he had been sober he would have foreseen that by doing so he might cause damage or injury, if only because he would have realized that damage or injury was inevitable; so they could dismiss the argument that the drunkard was not reckless.[77] But if, in the case of a sober defendant, the evidence would be consistent with his not intending the result, then the tribunal should not find an intoxicated person was reckless (unless, conceivably, the fact of intoxication itself tips the balance and persuades the tribunal that the intoxicant had reduced the defendant's inhibitions).[78] If the

---

[74] Basic intent only works as a substitute where the offence provides that the *actus reus* may be brought about either intentionally or recklessly. See for example, *Commissioner of Police of the Metropolis v. Caldwell* [1982] A.C. 341.

[75] "It is a common misapprehension that voluntary intoxication in the case of a crime of basic intent precludes any defence of lack of *mens rea*. In truth there is no rule that evidence of intoxication at the time of a criminal act turns the crime into one of strict liability and must inevitably lead to a conviction." Glanville Williams, "Two Nocturnal Blunders," (1990) 140 *N.L.J.* 1564.

[76] *R. v. Richardson* [1999] 1 Cr. App. R. 392; *R. v. Aitken* [1992] 1 W.L.R. 1006.

[77] *R. v. Richardson* [1999] 1 Cr. App. R. 392; *R. v. Aitken* [1992] 1 W.L.R. 1006.

[78] *R. v. Kingston* [1995] 2 A.C. 355.

drunkard is not to be treated more leniently than the sober-sides in the findings of fact, he is not to be treated more severely either.

19–027 **This is expecting the jury to perform awful mental gymnastics.** It is, but there seems to be no other practical interpretation of the law, so long as the rule in *D.P.P. v. Majewski* prevails.

The alternative that comes to mind is for the trial judge to instruct the jury that, the defendant having given evidence of voluntary intoxication, they need not consider the question of intention, the crime now having become one of strict liability. The trouble is that this would raise the question as to the degree of intoxication required to bring the rule into operation. The law can hardly be that the evidence (perhaps introduced by prosecution witnesses, or elicited from the defendant in cross-examination) that the defendant had consumed a couple of pints of beer turns what would otherwise be an offence requiring *mens rea* into an offence of strict liability. It is only intoxication of a certain degree that could possibly do this. But how can one define the degree? This difficulty is so serious that we can safely take the view previously stated as being the correct one. Nevertheless, there are indications that the rule in *D.P.P. v. Majewski* is misunderstood by some judges and magistrates, who assume that when evidence of intoxication is given there is nothing to be decided on the issue of intention.

The type of problem that can arise may be illustrated by a hypothetical based on an incident that occurred in New Zealand. At a midnight party at which liquor has flowed, a number of young men are capering about dressing in grass haka skirts. They are in high spirits, and one of them, merely to add to the merriment, takes a flaring torch and sets his friend's skirt alight. The friend is seriously burnt. When charged with inflicting g.b.h. under section 20 of the *Offences against the Person Act*, the doer of the stupid act gives evidence that although he was rather tipsy he certainly thought that the fire would be immediately and easily put out, so that there was no risk; otherwise he would never have done such a thing.

19–028 Recall that the mental element under section 20 is intention or recklessness. On the argument previously advanced, if the prosecution rest their case on intention the jury are not absolved from deciding that issue because evidence of intoxication has been given. They must decide whether the evidence, putting aside the evidence of intoxication, shows that the defendant intended to do g.b.h.,[79] or leaves them in doubt on the subject; and in the above hypothetical they will probably have no difficulty in finding at least a doubt, so that they acquit on that charge.[80]

If, as is likely, there is an alternative charge alleging recklessness, the jury must then decide whether the doer was reckless as to causing the harm. The defendant will still get off if the court thinks that a sober person might have made the same mistake. We have seen that the general rule for recklessness (apart from intoxication) rests on a concept of subjective recklessness, and thus only applies where the defendant thought that what he was doing was unsafe.[81] Hence, the

---

[79] The evidence of intoxication may be such that it shows that D acted with a drunken intent. *R. v. Kingston* [1995] 2 A.C. 355.

[80] *R. v. Aitken* [1992] 1 W.L.R. 1006.

[81] *R. v. G* [2004] 1 A.C. 1034; see also *R. v. Brady* [2006] EWCA Crim. 2413.

general rule is that the court will be required to determine whether the defendant (rather than a reasonable person) *would* have been aware of the risk had he been sober.[82]

Is oblique intention (legally) a form of specific intent? Yes. The law treats it as a form of specific intent, even though conceptually it a form of basic intent.[83] The oblique intention doctrine has been applied in murder cases since the 1990s,[84] but there has been no move to treat murder as a basic intent crime. It is surely right (at least for legal purposes) to treat oblique intention as a form of specific intent, not only because it prevents a mass of further legal anomalies from arising, but because it is a substitute for specific intention—not a substitute for basic intention. It is a substitute for the highest level of culpability. The type of recklessness involved in becoming intoxicated has little moral equivalence with subjective recklessness, let alone oblique intention, so it is best to regard mental elements that can be satisfied by either oblique intention or direct intention as specific intent elements.

19–029

Can we now draw a sensible line between specific and basic intent crimes? I think we can. First, it has to be acknowledged that some crimes may have both specific intent and basic intent mental elements. Such crimes are neither basic intent nor specific intent crimes. Rather, evidence of intoxication can be raised where the defendant is charged with such a crime to negate any specific intent elements, but not to negate any basic intent elements:

19–030

- Specific intent refers to purposive behaviour. The only exception is that made for crimes that use oblique intention as a substitute for direct intention. These crimes are treated as specific intent crimes (for example, murder).
  - o A person specifically intends to bring about a consequence, if it is his purpose to bring it about. (Or, if he foresees it as a virtually certain consequence of his action).
  - o A person specifically intends to engage in conduct if it is his purpose to do so. If D intends to speed in a car at 100 m.p.h., but does not intent to kill a child on a zebra crossing—he specifically intends to engage in the conduct of speeding, but does not specifically intend to kill a child.

---

[82] *R. v. Richardson* [1999] 1 Cr. App. R. 392; *R. v. Aitken* [1992] 1 W.L.R. 1006. See also section 6(5) of the *Public Order Act 1986* which expressly states: "For the purposes of this section a person whose awareness is impaired by intoxication shall be taken to be aware of that of which he would be aware if not intoxicated, unless he shows either that his intoxication was not self-induced or that it was caused solely by the taking or administration of a substance in the course of medical treatment."

[83] See John Finnis, "Intention and Side-Effects," in R.G. Frey & Christopher W. Morris (eds.) *Liability and Responsibility: Essays in Law and Morals* (Cambridge: Cambridge University Press, 1991) at 32 *et seq.*

[84] *R. v. Woollin* [1999] 1 A.C. 82.

    o   A person specifically intends a circumstance, if he knows or believes that it exists or will exist. If D knows for a fact that the woman he is having sexual intercourse with is not consenting, he must intend to rape her.

- Basic intent crimes are those where negligence or recklessness is available as an alternative form of fault for all the elements of the offence. Most elements of most offences can be satisfied where the defendant acts either intentionally or recklessly (for example, assault and battery can be committed intentionally or recklessly).

19–031   **You said above that on a charge involving specific intent, such as murder or wounding (or causing g.b.h.) with intent, the defendant would be acquitted if the evidence was that owing to intoxication he accidentally lurched against someone, who fell under a bus. Do I gather that he could be convicted on those same facts of unlawful wounding or assault? He did not attack anybody.** The only member of the House of Lords to deal with this problem in *D.P.P. v. Majewski* was Lord Salmon, and he appears to have contemplated that the drunkard would not be liable for a "pure accident."[85] This seems reasonable at first sight. *D.P.P. v. Majewski* may be said to apply only to what may be called acts of aggression, where the defendant tried, in however confused a way, to interfere with the person or property of another. For (the argument may run) the rationale of the intoxication rule does not apply to acts of intoxicated clumsiness. In *R. v. Heard*,[86] Hughes L.J. said: "A judge might well find it useful to add to the previously-mentioned direction that 'a drunken intent is still an intent,' the corollary that 'a drunken accident is still an accident.'"

    The solution lies in the argument previously advanced, that even on a charge of basic intent the jury must have regard to all the evidence except the evidence of intoxication in determining the defendant's intention. If the evidence is that the defendant stumbled against someone who then fell under a bus, the defendant's explanation that he fell, from whatever cause, would readily be accepted as negativing intention in the absence of evidence of malign motive.[87]

---

[85] Lord Salmon (at 481-482) said: "[A]n assault committed accidentally [*sic*] is not a criminal offence. A man may, *e.g.*, thoughtlessly throw out his hand to stop a taxi, or open the door of his car and accidentally hit a passer-by and perhaps unhappily cause him quite serious bodily harm. In such circumstances, the man who caused the injury would be liable civilly for damages but clearly he would have committed no crime.... A man who by voluntarily taking drink and drugs gets himself into an aggressive state in which he does not know what he is doing and then makes a vicious assault can hardly say with any plausibility that what he did was a pure accident which should render him immune from any criminal liability." This implies that if the case is not one of assault (or, presumably, of intentional attack upon property) but of "pure accident" even an intoxicated person can escape liability.

[86] [2008] Q.B. 43 at 51.

[87] *R. v. Brady* [2006] EWCA Crim. 2413.

19.5. THE CONSTRUCTIVE RECKLESSNESS JUSTIFICATION

It has long been held that voluntary intoxication (alternatively called "self-induced" intoxication") presents a problem for the subjectivists. A person may severely wound another, or set fire to a building, and when charged may say that he was so drunk (or so much under the influence of other drugs) that he did not know what he was doing.

19–032

So, when he was consuming such a quantity of drink he must have known that he was impairing his self-control, and was therefore reckless. I am not speaking of self-control. Failure of self-control through intoxication is clearly no defence. The problem arises when the intoxication brings about a failure to perceive risk.

19–033

In getting drunk a person knew there was a risk that he might injure someone, so he was reckless. Your theory of recklessness in imbibing has been twice accepted by the House of Lords,[88] but it involves problems. Whether a person knew he was creating a risk by getting drunk is a question of fact in each case. Perhaps he has got very drunk many times before, and on all previous occasions has fallen peacefully asleep. Britain has a binge drinking culture, but many very intoxicated individuals make their way home nightly without harming others. Drinking could only be described as a remote form of recklessness (prior fault) where the defendant knows or firmly believes that there is a good chance that he will go berserk and harm others if he drinks. If a person knows that he cannot handle drink and that he misbehaves when he drinks, he risks behaving criminally simply by drinking.

19–034

But should he not be held responsible even if he has no idea that he might commit a crime if he drinks too much? "Regarding" or "deeming" someone to be something when you do not know he is, or know he is not, is to create a legal fiction, and a fiction does not explain anything—it is merely a disguised restatement of the rule. It is a fiction because the drunkard is held liable on the basis that he would have foreseen the danger if he had not made the choice to drink. All the court asks is: Would you have foreseen the danger involved in doing X if you had been sober? If so, you must take the consequences of your mindless actions. The actions are mindless, because the defendant did not know what he was doing. If he did, fault could be proved in the normal way.

19–035

What is clear is that such a person does not fall within the definition of subjective recklessness as it relates to the elements of the relevant offence. Nor does he come within the concept of prior fault, unless he realized there was a risk that he might offend while intoxicated. But intoxication is so common an accompaniment of violent and destructive behaviour that it ought not to be allowed as a let-out from criminal responsibility. Two reasons may be assigned

---

[88] See Lord Elwyn-Jones *D.P.P. v. Majewski* [1977] A.C. 443 at 474-475, cited with approval by Lord Diplock in *Commissioner of Police of the Metropolis v. Caldwell* [1982] A.C. 341. Neither Lord recognized that the proposition could not be supported as an unqualified statement of fact, and that as a statement of legal fiction it could not afford a rational justification for any rule.

for taking this line. First, although it may be unlikely that an intoxicated person is unable to realize what he is doing, the jury (or magistrates) may have difficulty in deciding such an issue. Secondly, drink and (other) drugs being frequently matters of habit or addiction, there is a substantial possibility that the harmful conduct will be repeated if the offender is not made to alter his ways. If one could be sure both that the defendant did not realize the danger on the present occasion and that he would not inactivate his reasoning powers again, there would be no case for punishing him. But one generally cannot be sure, and anyway the question is best left to the judge in sentencing. By holding the defendant liable, the court is able to consider whether to apply pressure to him to make him avoid becoming intoxicated in the future, the pressure taking the form either of punishment for what he has just done or of some form of imposed treatment for addiction.

19–036   **Instead of departing from subjectivism in the major offences, why not provide for the dangerous drunk by a new offence of strict liability?**   This has been suggested, but the objections to it have been thought to be too great. The proposal was rejected by the Criminal Law Revision Committee partly because it was thought too difficult to draft satisfactorily. It would complicate the trial by giving the jury another offence to consider. It might encourage lenient juries to go for the new offence instead of for the serious offence that has in fact been committed. And to deal with the very dangerous offender the maximum for the new offence would have to be high. For these reasons the Criminal Law Revision Committee, in its report on offences against the person, followed the ALI Model Penal Code in recommending legislation to make an exception from the ordinary subjective definition of recklessness. The Committee thought it should be provided that:[89]

> "in offences in which recklessness constitutes an element of the offence, if the defendant owing to voluntary intoxication had no appreciation of a risk which he would have appreciated had he been sober, such lack of appreciation is immaterial."

We have seen that the courts have adopted this approach. The Law Commission thinks it is the right approach too. It has recommended that it be codified as follows:[90]

> "There should be a general rule that:
> (1)   if D is charged with having committed an offence as a perpetrator;
> (2)   the fault element of the offence is not an integral fault element (for example, because it merely requires proof of recklessness); and
> (3)   D was voluntarily intoxicated at the material time; then, in determining whether or not D is liable for the offence, D should be treated as having been aware at the material time of anything which D would then have been aware of but for the intoxication."

This rule is generally acceptable in point of policy, though (as a matter of present law) it cannot be reconciled with section 8 of the *Criminal Justice Act*

---

[89] Criminal Law Revision Committee, *Offences Against the Person*, Fourteenth Report, (London: H.M.S.O., Cmnd. 7844, 1980).
[90] Law Commission, *Intoxication and Criminal Liability*, Law Com. No. 314, (London: H.M.S.O. Cm. 7526, 2009) at para. 3.35.

1967. If it should happen that a person intoxicates himself to escape temporarily from the stress of life, and under the influence of the drug commits some mindless and dreadful act, of which he had no expectation or premonition (prior *fault* as such),[91] there is no evidence upon which he may be said to have been in fact reckless as to the result. So the rule is not an application of the notion of recklessness to cases of voluntary intoxication. It merely makes a pretence of finding recklessness, for reasons of policy. All that is done is to deem recklessness to be present, and judges, of course, can deem anything, since there is no one to say to them nay.

How do the courts get round section 8 of the *Criminal Justice Act*? Some of the Lords who took part in the decision in *D.P.P. v. Majewski* resolved that problem by disregarding it. Lord Elwyn-Jones L.C. (with whom several other Lords concurred) confronted the statute and attempted the perilous task of offering a reason for not applying it. His words were as follows: **19–037**

> "In referring to 'all the evidence [the section] meant all the *relevant* evidence. But if there is a substantive rule of law that in crimes of basic intent, the factor of intoxication is irrelevant (and such I hold to be the substantive law), evidence with regard to it is quite irrelevant."[92]

It is true, too, that if the courts treat a particular crime as being of strict liability, intent is not in issue and evidence on that question would be logically irrelevant to the matters to be decided. But crimes of basic intent are not of strict liability. As their description indicates, they are crimes of subjective fault.[93] The interpretation reduces section 8 to impotence. It means that anything that would have been withheld from the jury's consideration before the section was passed can still be withheld from them because the judges declare it to be irrelevant. The only basis for it is that the evidence of intoxication, if accepted by the jury would negate the basic intent element, and since as a matter of policy the voluntarily intoxicated defendant is deemed to have had a basic intent by virtue of the fact that he has committed a crime whilst intoxicated, it seems pointless to consider his recklessness in the normal way with reference to evidence of intoxication. After all, he most likely will have already used that evidence to negate any specific intent elements and thus have already shown that he was mindless when he committed the offence.

You approve of the intoxication rule as a matter of policy, but is it not very harsh to say not merely that the drunkard is guilty of an offence, but is guilty of even the gravest offences on the basis of fictitious recklessness? Lord Edmund-Davies thought so, in his dissenting opinion in *Commissioner of Police of the Metropolis v. Caldwell*.[94] Everything depends on the circumstances, and on   **19–038**

---

[91] *R. v. Lipman* [1970] 1 Q.B. 152.
[92] [1977] A.C. 443 at 476A.
[93] For example, the Court of Appeal said in *R. v. Mowatt* [1968] 1 Q.B. 421 that under section 20 of the *Offences against the Person Act 1861* the defendant must have "an awareness that his act may have the consequence of causing some physical harm to some other persons." (see 9.6.) Yet according to *D.P.P. v. Majewski* the jury are not allowed to consider evidence of voluntary intoxication as negativing this awareness.
[94] [1982] A.C. 341.

the humanity of the courts in sentencing. If they sentence as the judges did in *R. v. Lipman*, it would indeed be harsh. Even murder may be caught by the rule.[95]

19.6. INTOXICATION AND MISTAKE

19–039 The drunkard (or, of course, drug-taker) who does what may be called a criminal act (the *actus reus* of a crime) owing to a mistake of fact is the target of three rules. It seems the legal problem in this area can best be solved by asking three questions; and they must be asked in the following order.

19–040 **First question: does the offence include a requirement of knowledge or belief that facts exists?** If the offence requires proof of knowledge of a fact, evidence of intoxication can help to negative that knowledge. For example, take the offence of handling stolen goods knowing them to be stolen. A person may buy goods at a low price from a suspicious looking character in a public house, and when charged with handling stolen goods he may support his defence of innocence by saying that he was a bit light-headed and did not notice circumstances that otherwise he would have noticed. It has been judicially assumed that the defence is allowable.[96] Handling is a crime with a specific requirement of knowledge; and the courts, very properly, do not feel able to exclude evidence of intoxication in adjudicating whether the statutory requirement of knowledge was present.

Awkwardly, the law is different if it refers not to knowledge but to intent (even though intention includes knowledge). Suppose, to take a hypothetical based on an actual incident, a man charged with assaulting a policeman gives evidence in his defence that after taking a drug he hallucinated and thought he was about to be attacked by a great black bear. The "bear" was a policeman. All the offences against the person presuppose action directed against a human being, and if the drug-taker's hallucination were treated the same way as a sober mistake it would give immunity from conviction of a crime of intent. Now the law according to *D.P.P. v. Majewski* states that assault is a crime of basic intent and that evidence of voluntary intoxication cannot negative the intent. So our drug abuser would be convicted of assault.[97]

19–041 **I don't see why there should be this distinction between the issue of knowledge (on which you say that evidence of intoxication can afford a defence, even in crimes of basic intent) and the issue of intention (where, on a charge of a crime of basic intent, such evidence is unlikely to exclude liability).** The distinction is illogical, but it does not seem to work too badly in the present instance. The decision in *D.P.P. v. Majewski* is motivated chiefly by a desire to secure the conviction of drunkards who act aggressively, and the main crimes of aggression are defined in terms of intention or recklessness, not knowledge.

---

[95] *R. v. Hatton* [2006] 1 Cr. App. R. 247. Cf. *R. v. Conlon* (1993) 69 A. Crim. R. 92.

[96] *R. v. Durante* [1972] 1 W.L.R. 1612.

[97] If the assault resulted in the policeman's death, the drug abuser would be liable for manslaughter. See *R. v. Lipman* [1970] 1 Q.B. 152.

Some offences do not expressly require the prosecution to prove the defendant's knowledge that a fact was present but allow a defence of belief that the fact was absent, which (apart from the burden of proof) comes to very much the same thing. The effect of such a provision was before the court in *Jaggard v. Dickinson*,[98] a prosecution under section 1(1) of the *Criminal Damage Act 1971*.

Ms Jaggard after a convivial evening in a tavern bethought herself of sleep. She seems to have been on very good terms with the owner of a certain house, because he (if it was a "he") had given her permission to use it as if it were her own. History does not record whether she was living in it, but we are told that was the house to which she chose to repair for a slumber. All the doors of the house she tried were locked, so she had to break a window to get in. As you may have guessed, from the lady's appearance in the law reports and this textbook, she had selected the wrong house.

She was charged with criminal damage under section 1(1); evidence was given of **19–042** her intoxication and consequent mistake; but the justices nevertheless convicted. They reasoned that this was a crime of basic intent (as it was), Jaggard's intoxication was voluntary (it was), and so *D.P.P. v. Majewski* told them to ignore evidence of intoxication on the issue of intent (it did). Full marks for the justices? No. Marvellous to relate, the conviction was reversed by the Divisional Court.

Under the definition of the offence in section 1(1),[99] if it had stood alone, Jaggard's conviction would quite possibly have stood. The evidence of intoxication would have had to be ignored on the question of intention (the crime being one of basic intent), and by closing their eyes to such evidence the justices might have been justified in finding that the defendant damaged the property of another without lawful excuse. But the *Act* contained a further provision. Although the wording of the offence does not say in express terms that the owner must not have consented to the act, or that the offender must have known that he had no right to damage the property, section 5(2)(a) covers a good deal of the ground by allowing a defence of belief in the existence of certain exempting facts. This provision, like the rest of the *Act*, was the work of the Law Commission, who were thorough-going subjectivists and wished to make sure that the issue of belief in right would be judged according to the defendant's real state of mind.

The subsection accordingly provides in effect that the defendant has a defence if he believed that the owner (i) had consented or (ii) would have consented if he had known the circumstances. Jaggard's belief was that she was acting with the owner's consent (as she would have been, if it had been the right house). Section 5(3) provides, to make assurance doubly sure, that "for the purposes of this section it is immaterial whether a belief is justified or not if it is honestly held." The Divisional Court applied the section and allowed a defence according to its terms. In adjudicating whether Jaggard had the requisite belief one had to look at all the facts, including the evidence of intoxication.

---

[98] [1981] Q.B. 527.

[99] Section 1(1) provides: "A person who without lawful excuse destroys or damages any property belonging to another intending to destroy or damage any such property or being reckless as to whether any such property would be destroyed or damaged shall be guilty of an offence."

19–043   It is difficult to fit this decision in with some other cases dealing with the same point. The decision in *Jaggard v. Dickinson* can be technically, very technically, distinguished from *D.P.P. v. Majewski* by saying that the latter case applies only to statutory requirements of intention, whereas *Jaggard v. Dickinson* involves an issue of knowledge. The *Criminal Damage Act 1971* is not merely worded in terms of intention or recklessness; it also contains the specifically subjective provision in section 5(2). Donaldson L.J. said that section 5(2) and (3) had to be applied so as to give a defence even to drunkards, because it was illegitimate to read the section as though it contained an exception for voluntary intoxication.

What, then, if the facts were slightly varied so as to fall outside section 5 altogether? Suppose Jaggard had besottedly believed that the house was her own. She would then not have had any belief that the owner "consented." (You can hardly talk of your own consent to what you do yourself.) So section 5(2) would not have applied according to its words; and probably the court would not have stretched the words to cover the case—even though in common sense the case would be on all fours with the situations mentioned in section 5, or, indeed, *a fortiori*. The court would probably decide to leave the case to fall under Question 3. This does not mean that the defendant would be convicted. On principle, she should still be acquitted, as long as she would have made the same mistake had she not been intoxicated. And that is common sense, for if a drunkard is acquitted when he thinks he is breaking into a friend's house with his permission, it would be strange indeed if he were convicted when his belief was that he was breaking into his own house.

The earlier decision of *R. v. McPherson*,[100] which at first sight looks very similar in point of principle, was not cited in *Jaggard v. Dickinson*. *R. v. McPherson* held that the offence of taking a conveyance, being one of basic intent, did not permit evidence of intoxication to show that the defendant did not form the relevant *mens rea*. The section of the *Theft Act 1968* creating this offence contains a provision (section 12(6) virtually identical with that in section 5(2)(*a*) of the *Criminal Damage Act 1971*) saying that no offence is committed if a conveyance is taken in the belief that he would have the owner's consent if the owner knew of the circumstances, but counsel for McPherson did not rely on this provision.

19–044   The two cases differ in one relevant respect. McPherson's defence was not one of belief in the owner's consent; it was one of complete absence of any mental state, and so did not fall within section 12(6) which requires the defendant's positive belief. So the case is properly distinguishable from *Jaggard v. Dickinson*. Evidently, if Jaggard's defence had been that she was too drunk to know what she was doing, she would have been convicted.

These subtleties are highly unsatisfactory, particularly because the outcome of the case may depend on the wording of legislation that was drafted without the problem of intoxication in mind.

---

[100] [1973] R.T.R. 157; cf. *R. v. Gannon* (1988) 87 Cr. App. R. 254.

Second question: does the issue relate to a definitional element or to a matter   **19–045**
of defence?   I revert to the supposition that you have some problem case on intoxication, and I know that your case does not concern a requirement of knowledge or belief. You are therefore driven to consider the difficult and obscure distinction between the definition of an offence and matters of defence. If the mistaken belief relates to the definition of the offence (such as a man's belief that the woman with whom he is performing the act of sex has consented; this belief was held in *D.P.P. v. Morgan*[101] to relate to a definitional element), then you pass to Question 3.[102]

If the mistake relates to a matter of defence, then evidence of intoxication will not negate the mistake. In the 19th century, in the happy days before the invention of basic intent and the rule against intoxicated mistaken defence, the drunkard who attacked in imaginary defence was let off a charge of assault and everything else except manslaughter and the special intoxication offences such as being drunk and disorderly.[103] Now, in our more enlightened and tolerant age, he can be guilty even of a crime of specific intent.[104]

In *R. v. O'Grady*,[105] Lord Lane C.J. said:

> "How should the jury be invited to approach the problem? One starts with the decision of this court in *R. v. Williams* (1983) 78 Cr. App. R. 276, namely, that where the defendant might have been labouring under a mistake as to the facts he must be judged according to that mistaken view, whether the mistake was reasonable or not. It is then for the jury to decide whether the defendant's reaction to the threat, real or imaginary, was a reasonable one. The court was not in that case considering what the situation might be where the mistake was due to voluntary intoxication by alcohol or some other drug.
>
> We have come to the conclusion that where the jury are satisfied that the defendant was mistaken in his belief that any force or the force which he in fact used was necessary to defend himself and are further satisfied that the mistake was caused by voluntarily induced intoxication, the defence must fail. We do not consider that any distinction should be drawn on this aspect of the matter between offences involving what is called specific intent, such as murder,[106] and offences of so called basic intent, such as manslaughter. Quite apart from the problem of directing a jury in a case such as the present where manslaughter is an alternative verdict to murder, the question of mistake can and ought to be considered separately from the question of intent."

Since the decision of the Court of Appeal in *R. v. Hatton*,[107] this is now the law in   **19–046**
England and Wales. If for example, a person kills another in the firm but drunken and mistaken belief that he has to act immediately in self defence, he can

---

[101] [1976] A.C. 182.
[102] In the "black bear" hallucination discussed previously, the mistake should be regarded as definitional, notwithstanding that it also relates to the necessity for self-defence.
[103] Drunken mistake as to the necessity for self-defence had been accepted in *Marshall's Case* (1830) 168 E.R. 965; *R. v. Gamlen* (1858) 175 E.R. 639.
[104] *R. v. Hatton* [2006] 1 Cr. App. R. 247; *R. v. O'Grady* [1987] Q.B. 995.
[105] [1987] Q.B. 995 at 999.
[106] Since the appellant was only appealing against a manslaughter conviction, the point was only *obiter* as far as murder was concerned.
[107] [2006] 1 Cr. App. R. 247; see also *R. v. O'Connor* [1991] Crim. L.R. 135.

(astonishingly as it may appear) be convicted of murder.[108] (Not that he is likely to be; a verdict of manslaughter would be wangled somehow.)[109]

The Law Commission thinks this is the correct approach for a number of reasons:[110]

1. "Our first reason for rejecting the critics' argument is that it fails to address the important fact that self-defence is a *general* defence and that, accordingly, it is a defence which should in principle be available on the same basis in relation to all crimes, regardless of the nature of the fault alleged."

2. "The question of mistake can and ought to be considered separately from the question of intent .... because [where] D is aware that he or she is inflicting harm against a person [rather than a snake or a bear] his or her conduct requires a truly compelling justification or excuse."

3. "Allowing a distinction to be drawn between the situation where the prosecution alleges an integral fault element and the situation where no such element is alleged would be difficult to apply and extremely confusing for the jury."

As for the first point, the focus should be on how the mistake affected the defendant's specific intent. The focus has to be on the intoxicated mistake and its impact on the quality of the defendant's intent. The mistake changes the nature of the defendant's intention, because it means he has a putative legal justification for killing. His justification for killing is lawful self-defence: if the motive is to do a supposed lawful act, it can be material.[111] The quality of his "specific intent" is altered by his lawful motive which hinges on his mistaken belief that it is necessary for him to defend himself. It is not clear why an "unreasonable mistake" about the need to act in self-defence is not a "truly compelling justification"[112] for an intoxicated person, if it is for a sober person.[113] Especially, if the mistaken party would have made the same mistake if he had been sober. Nor does it seem right to assert that this type of offender is more culpable because he aims to kill a human being rather than a snake or a black bear. There is no moral difference whatsoever, because the absence of subjective fault is equal in both cases. (The self-defender is no less convinced that he needs to act to defend himself, than the snake killer is convinced that his victim is a snake rather than a human.) I think this answers the Law Commission's first and second points of contention.

19–047 If his mistake is totally unreasonable and is one that the defendant would not have made if he had been sober, he should not walk free. In such cases he should be

---

[108] *R. v. Hatton* [2006] 1 Cr. App. R. 247; see also section 76(5) of the *Criminal Justice and Immigration Act 2008*.

[109] *R. v. O'Connor* [1991] Crim. L.R. 135.

[110] Law Commission, *Intoxication and Criminal Liability*, Law Com. No. 314, (London: H.M.S.O. Cm. 7526, 2009) at paras. 3.53-3.63.

[111] In this sense, intent cannot be considered independently of the relevant mistake.

[112] In the words of the Law Commission.

[113] It will provide a defence for a sober person as long as the jury can be convinced it was in fact held, if any force used is reasonable.

convicted of a crime of basic intent, if there is one available. The Law Commission was right to recommend that: "D's mistaken belief should be taken into account *only* if D would have held the same belief if D had not been intoxicated."[114]

As for the Law Commission's third point, I am not convinced that the jury could not be carefully directed on the aforementioned issues. There is no reason why the jury could not be asked to determine whether the defendant's intoxicated mistake was genuine. If so, it could be held that his purpose was not to kill for the sake of it, but rather was to lawfully defend himself. This should be enough to hold that he did not form the specific intent that is normally required for murder.[115] The defendant would still have to answer a manslaughter (or other basic intent) charge.

Third question: is the offence one of specific or basic intent? If no statute   **19–048**
introduces the issue of knowledge or belief, and if the defendant sets up a mistaken belief as to a definitional element and not as to a matter of defence, you come to the *D.P.P. v. Majewski* question. Is the offence one of specific or basic intent?

The reasoning then bifurcates.

- If the offence you are considering is of specific intent, the evidence of intoxication will be taken into account on the issue of intention or knowledge.
- If it is an offence of basic intent *D.P.P. v. Majewski* will apply, and will render evidence of intoxication legally irrelevant on the issue of intent.

Go back to the hypothetical of the woman like Jaggard breaking into someone else's house when drunk, except that in this hypothetical her drunken belief is that it is her own house. She is not protected by section 5, so you passed to Question 2. Here you would have found that her mistake relates to a definitional fact ("whether she is damaging property belonging to another," as section 1(1) of the *Criminal Damage Act* specifies). This means that you did not consider it as a defence element in Question 2, but went on to the present Question. *R. v. Smith*[116] shows that the mistake would be a complete defence for a sober person, on general *mens rea* principles. But it is an offence of basic intent; so a mistake due to intoxication is affected by *D.P.P. v. Majewski* (as regards intention) as well as recklessness.

We may consider more closely the question for the jury (or, of course, for magistrates) in the above hypothetical. It seems that the question for the jury on intention would be: Notwithstanding the evidence on intoxication you have heard, would you, with that evidence, have found that beyond any reasonable doubt the defendant intended to damage the property of another, *i.e.* that he knew

---

[114] *Id.* at para. 3.53.

[115] An intent/motivation to kill in self-defence would not be sufficient for convicting a sober person of murder, as long as any force used was not disproportionate.

[116] [1974] Q.B. 354.

that this property belonged to another, and is not telling the truth when he now says that he believed it was his own? A drunken intent is still intent.[117]

19–049 On the issue of recklessness, the question for the jury is: Are you sure that if the defendant (not some hypothetical reasonable person)[118] had been sober he would not have made a mistake? If you are sure, find him reckless; if not, acquit.

There is no inevitability of a conviction on the issue. The defendant may give evidence that he mistook the house; the two houses (his own; and the one he broke into) may be close together and look much alike; the visibility may have been bad; the defendant has never been convicted of an offence of dishonesty or damage; he did not steal anything, and had no ascertainable motive for breaking into the neighbour's house, and so on. So the jury may acquit the defendant, even though he was intoxicated. They would believe the defendant when he said he mistook the house, even leaving aside the evidence of intoxication; or at least they would not disbelieve him.[119]

These points were not taken up in *Jaggard v. Dickinson*, but they may be thought to show that the magistrates would have been wrong in convicting even if section 5 had not been included in the *Act*. The magistrates laboured under what seems to be a common misapprehension, that voluntary intoxication in the case of a crime of basic intent precludes any defence of lack of *mens rea*.[120]

Apply the same two questions to a charge of rape where the defendant sets up a defence of belief in consent resulting from his intoxication. The jury would probably find it easy to reach the conclusions (i) that (on the issue of intention or knowledge) if they had not heard evidence of intoxication they would have found that the defendant knew that the woman was not consenting, and (ii) that (on the issue of recklessness/negligence) if he had been sober he would have known the risk (or of the fact) that she was not consenting. So the man would probably go down on both counts, of intention and negligence.

19–050 **What if liability depends on nothing more than negligence?** Offences of negligence require, at most, a basic intent, but some of them do not require that. The principle clearly is that the intoxicated defendant must comply with the same standard of care as the sober one.[121]

19.7. INVOLUNTARY INTOXICATION

19–051 We have been speaking of "voluntary" ("self-induced") intoxication. The qualifiers must be read in a technical sense; neither is completely satisfactory. Intoxication may be the result of the defendant's own act and yet not be thought of as self-induced—namely, where the defendant did not know he was taking an intoxicant. Intoxication is voluntary for the present purpose even though the defendant did not mean to become intoxicated, if he knew he was taking an

---

[117] *R. v. Kingston* [1995] 2 A.C. 355.
[118] See *R. v. Richardson* [1999] 1 Cr. App. R. 392.
[119] See Glanville Williams, "Two Nocturnal Blunders," (1990) 140 *N.L.J.* 1564.
[120] *R. v. Richardson* [1999] 1 Cr. App. R. 392.
[121] *R. v. Lipman* [1970] 1 Q.B. 152, where, however, the decision was put on constructive manslaughter.

intoxicant. The law is different for involuntary intoxication, as where I think I am partaking of some innocent libation when in fact my companion has laced it with gin;[122] or where I become unwittingly affected by medicine, not having been warned by my doctor.[123] The intoxication might be involuntary because of fraud (drink spiking), accident (an overdose of medicine), a reasonable mistake (misunderstanding your doctor's directions), duress, and so on.

In crimes of specific intent the only question is one of *mens rea*. In crimes of basic intent, the House of Lords recognized in *D.P.P. v. Majewski* that involuntary intoxication negativing *mens rea* would be a defence, even though voluntary intoxication would not. The distinction between voluntary and involuntary intoxication depends upon whether the defendant knowingly took an intoxicating substance otherwise than under medical advice.[124]

The level of involuntary intoxication must in fact negate the defendant's *mens rea*. In *R. v. Kingston*,[125] a pederast with a penchant for young boys was drugged and thereafter lost his inhibitions and violated a boy. Kingston's coffee had been laced with a powerful drug. Even though he had a penchant for young boys, he normally controlled his criminal desires. Even though his intoxication was involuntary, he was unable to evade justice because it merely reduced his inhibitions. He knew what he was doing and thus was found guilty, because a drunken intent is still an intent.

Isn't the distinction whether the defendant was at fault?   No: whether he   **19–052**
knowingly took a drug that in sufficient quantity would be intoxicating. It seems that intoxication would be regarded as voluntary if the defendant knowingly took an intoxicating substance, even though it had an unexpectedly great effect upon him.[126] He need not, apparently, have set out to become intoxicated.

What if a person fails to take a standard medicine on doctor's orders   **19–053**
knowing that it might cause him to misbehave?   In *R. v. Bailey*[127] the
defendant was charged with wounding with intent to cause grievous bodily harm contrary to section 18 of the *Offences against the Person Act 1861* and, in the alternative, with unlawful wounding contrary to section 20 of that *Act*. Bailey was a diabetic whose defence was that he had acted in a state of automatism caused by hypoglaecemia, because he failed to take food after a dose of insulin. It was held, first, that the fact that the automatism was self-induced could not make the defendant guilty of a crime of specific intent; so such evidence could not support a conviction under section 18.

Secondly, the court pointed out that even for crimes of basic intent the rule relating to self-induced incapacity applies only in respect of intoxication. It does not apply, for instance, to a diabetic who fails to take food after insulin. The rule

---

[122] *R. v. Kingston* [1995] 2 A.C. 355.
[123] For an example of a drug taken under medical advice see *R. v. Quick* [1973] Q.B. 910. The intoxication of an addict is not thought of as involuntary.
[124] *R. v. Hardie* [1985] 1 W.L.R. 64; *R. v. Bailey* [1983] 1 W.L.R. 760.
[125] [1995] 2 A.C. 355.
[126] *R. v. Allen* [1988] Crim. L.R. 698.
[127] [1983] 1 W.L.R. 760.

in *D.P.P. v. Majewski* was invented with the sole reference to the problem of voluntary intoxication, and the decision in *R. v. Bailey* fortunately excludes this possibility.

The decision in *R. v. Bailey* is supported by the earlier decision of *R. v. Stripp*,[128] where the Court of Appeal expressed the opinion that automatism can be a defence if:

- it was caused by concussion, even though it might have been caused by an accident that was due to the taking of alcohol; and it can also be a defence if:
- it was caused partly by the concussion aforesaid and partly by the continuing effect of alcoholic intake. "If it was a question of two causes operating, we venture to think that the prosecution would not be able to discharge the burden of proof," *i.e.* of the mental element.

19–054   If concussion caused by voluntary intoxication can found a defence of automatism, it follows that, in general, all other fault-factors can found the defence. Recklessness apart, the single exception is voluntary intoxication directly operating in isolation from other factors to negative a basic intent or the *actus reus*.

The court in *R. v. Bailey* did not altogether rule out criminal liability for injuries inflicted in a confusional state resulting from hypoglycaemia. A person can, it was held, be liable for recklessness causing the commission of a crime of basic intent if he knew what would happen if he did not take food after his insulin and if there were no circumstances excusing his failure to take food. This is another instance of the mental element antedating and not being concurrent with the physical act causing the injury. The court made it clear that it was not speaking of the fictitious recklessness attributed to drunkards in *D.P.P. v. Majewski*, but meant real recklessness: knowledge by the defendant that in failing to take precautions against a loss of consciousness he was endangering others.

In *R. v. Hardie*,[129] the defendant accidentally induced his own state of intoxication by taking a soporific or sedative drug (valium) and it was held that he had a defence to an offence of basic intent. Hardie was upset after the breakdown of his relationship with a woman. He took valium (a sedative drug) without knowledge of the possible effects. As a result he started a fire in his ex-girlfriend's flat and was charged in one count with "intent to endanger life and being reckless" as to the same. The Court of Appeal held that in the case of standard medicines such as soporific or sedative drugs, the jury should consider whether the taking of the drug was itself reckless.

In crimes of negligence, an exemption for involuntary intoxication (or, rather, non-negligent intoxication) is obviously required by both logic and justice. Where a hopelessly drunk person does some fuddled act that is legally characterized as negligent, his real negligence consists in having incapacitated himself by drink. So if he was not negligent in getting drunk, he should be excused.

---

[128] (1979) 69 Cr. App. R. 318.
[129] [1985] 1 W.L.R. 64.

CHAPTER 20

DISCIPLINE AND AUTHORITY

"Make your educational laws strict and your criminal ones can be gentle; but if you leave youth its liberty you will have to dig dungeons for ages."

Michel Eyquem de Montaigne[1]

20.1. DISCIPLINE

Parents have a right to use reasonable disciplinary measures against their children, but what is reasonable will vary according to the spirit of the time.[2] The right lasts up to the age that it is not altogether clear but is perhaps 16 and certainly no higher than 18.[3] Section 58 of the *Children Act 2004* provides:

20–001

"(1)   In relation to any offence specified in subsection (2), battery of a child cannot be justified on the ground that it constituted reasonable punishment.

(2)   The offences referred to in subsection (1) are–
    (a)   an offence under section 18 or 20 of the *Offences against the Person Act 1861* (c. 100) (wounding and causing grievous bodily harm);
    (b)   an offence under section 47 of that *Act* (assault occasioning actual bodily harm);
    (c)   an offence under section 1 of the *Children and Young Persons Act 1933* (c. 12) (cruelty to persons under 16).

(3)   Battery of a child causing actual bodily harm to the child cannot be justified in any civil proceedings on the ground that it constituted reasonable punishment.

(4)   For the purposes of subsection (3) "actual bodily harm" has the same meaning as it has for the purposes of section 47 of the *Offences against the Person Act 1861*."

Furthermore, section 93 of the *Education and Inspections Act 2006* provides:

"(1)   A person to whom this section applies may use such force as is reasonable in the circumstances for the purpose of preventing a pupil from doing (or continuing to do) any of the following, namely–
    (a)   committing any offence,
    (b)   causing personal injury to, or damage to the property of, any person (including the pupil himself), or
    (c)   prejudicing the maintenance of good order and discipline at the school or among any pupils receiving education at the school, whether during a teaching session or otherwise.

---

[1] Quoted in John Ruskin, *Munera pulveris: Six Essays on the Elements of Political Economy*, (London: Printed by Smith, Elder, 1872).

[2] *R. v. Smith* [1985] Crim. L.R. 42.

[3] It hardly need be said that husbands have no right to chastise or imprison their wives: *R. v. Reid* [1973] Q.B. 299.

(2) This section applies to a person who is, in relation to a pupil, a member of the staff of any school at which education is provided for the pupil.

(3) The power conferred by subsection (1) may be exercised only where–
  (a) the member of the staff and the pupil are on the premises of the school in question, or
  (b) they are elsewhere and the member of the staff has lawful control or charge of the pupil concerned.

(4) Subsection (1) does not authorise anything to be done in relation to a pupil which constitutes the giving of corporal punishment within the meaning of section 548 of *Education Act 1996*.

(5) The powers conferred by subsection (1) are in addition to any powers exercisable apart from this section and are not to be construed as restricting what may lawfully be done apart from this section.

(6) In this section, "offence" includes anything that would be an offence but for the operation of any presumption that a person under a particular age is incapable of committing an offence."

Discipline includes the use of force to restrain the juvenile from misbehaving. At common law it includes corporal punishment. Such punishment can now, according to the circumstances, be regarded as a breach of the *European Convention for the Protection of Human Rights and Fundamental Freedoms*.[4]

20–002 School-teachers are no longer permitted to administer discipline in respect of matters pertaining to the school. They once had a right to use reasonable discipline; the right rested on the notion that parents impliedly delegated the right to discipline to them.

Section 548 of the *Education Act 1996* provides:

"(1) Corporal punishment given by, or on the authority of, a member of staff to a child (a) for whom education is provided at any school, or (b) for whom education is provided, otherwise than at school, under any arrangements made by a local authority, or (c) for whom specified nursery education is provided otherwise than at school, cannot be justified in any proceedings on the ground that it was given in pursuance of a right exercisable by the member of staff by virtue of his position as such.

(2) Subsection (1) applies to corporal punishment so given to a child at any time, whether at the school or other place at which education is provided for the child, or elsewhere.

(3) The following provisions have effect for the purposes of this section.

(4) Any reference to giving corporal punishment to a child is to doing anything for the purpose of punishing that child (whether or not there are other reasons for doing it) which, apart from any justification, would constitute battery.

(5) However, corporal punishment shall not be taken to be given to a child by virtue of anything done for reasons that include averting—(a) an immediate danger of personal injury to, or (b) an immediate danger to the property of, any person (including the child himself).

(6) 'Member of staff', in relation to the child concerned, means — (a) any person who works as a teacher at the school or other place at which education is provided for the child, or (b) any other person who (whether in connection with the provision of education for the child or otherwise)— (i) works at that school or place, or—(ii) otherwise provides his services there (whether or not for payment), and has lawful control or charge of the child.

(7) 'Child' (except in subsection (8)) means a person under the age of 18."

---

[4] 4 November 1950, 213 U.N.T.S. 222 (entered into force generally on 3 September 1953). See *A v. United Kingdom* (1999) 27 E.H.R.R. 611; *R. (on the application of Williamson) v. Secretary of State for Education and Employment* [2005] 2 A.C. 246.

In *R. (on the application of Williamson) v. Secretary of State for Education and Employment*,[5] the claimants were at independent private schools which had been founded to provide Christian education. The joint claimants were the parents of the students who attended those schools. The teachers at those schools, with the full support and consent of the parents, wanted to maintain the right to administer corporal punishment. It was contended on behalf of the claimants that they had a fundamental right to use corporal punishment because it was part of their fundamental Christian beliefs that such discipline should be administered. It was also asserted that such discipline was efficacious. Some of the teachers in some of the schools had administered corporal punishment, but in other schools the parents had administered it. All the claimants asserted that the teachers had the right to use corporal punishment. As we have seen section 548 of the *Education Act 1996* has taken this right away from teachers. The claimants contended that section 548 interfered with their freedom of religion contrary to article 9(1) of the *Convention for the Protection of Human Rights and Fundamental Freedoms*, as scheduled to the *Human Rights Act 1998*, and with their right to educate their children in conformity with their religious convictions, contrary to article 2 of the *First Protocol to the Convention*, as well as their right to respect for their family life, contrary to article 8 of the Convention.

20–003

The House of Lords dismissed the appeal. Lord Bingham said:

> "I am in no doubt this interference is, within the meaning of article 9, 'necessary in a democratic society ... for the protection of the rights and freedoms of others'. The statutory ban pursues a legitimate aim: children are vulnerable, and the aim of the legislation is to protect them and promote their wellbeing. Corporal punishment involves deliberately inflicting physical violence. The legislation is intended to protect children against the distress, pain and other harmful effects this infliction of physical violence may cause. That corporal punishment may have these harmful effects is self-evident. .... Further, the means chosen to achieve this aim are appropriate and not disproportionate in their adverse impact on parents who believe that carefully-controlled administration of corporal punishment to a mild degree can be beneficial, for this reason: the legislature was entitled to take the view that, overall and balancing the conflicting considerations, all corporal punishment of children at school is undesirable and unnecessary and that other, non-violent means of discipline are available and preferable."[6]

The general subject of parental and school discipline is treated in works on the law of tort and will not be further considered here.

Some disciplinary powers are given by legislation. This is so for discipline in prisons and armed forces (though corporal punishment has been abolished). At common law the master even of a merchant vessel may take all reasonable means to preserve discipline by crew and passengers,[7] and the authority is now supplemented by statute for ships,[8] and aircraft.

20–004

For example, section 94 of the *Civil Aviation Act 1982* provides:

---

[5] [2005] 2 A.C. 246.

[6] *R. (on the application of Williamson) v. Secretary of State for Education and Employment* [2005] 2 A.C. 246.

[7] *The Lima* (1837) 166 E.R. 434; *Hook v. Cunard Steamship Co.* [1953] 1 W.L.R. 682.

[8] Section 105 of the *Merchant Shipping Act 1995*.

"(1) The provisions of subsections (2) to (5) below shall have effect for the purposes of any proceedings before any court in the United Kingdom.

(2) If the commander of an aircraft in flight, wherever that aircraft may be, has reasonable grounds to believe in respect of any person on board the aircraft—

 (a) that the person in question has done or is about to do any act on the aircraft while it is in flight which jeopardises or may jeopardise—(i) the safety of the aircraft or of persons or property on board the aircraft, or (ii) good order and discipline on board the aircraft, or

 (b) that the person in question has done on the aircraft while in flight any act which in the opinion of the commander is a serious offence under any law in force in the country in which the aircraft is registered, not being a law of a political nature or based on racial or religious discrimination, then, subject to subsection (4) below, the commander may take with respect to that person such reasonable measures, including restraint of his person, as may be necessary—(i) to protect the safety of the aircraft or of persons or property on board the aircraft; or (ii) to maintain good order and discipline on board the aircraft; or (iii) to enable the commander to disembark or deliver that person in accordance with subsection (5) below, and for the purposes of paragraph (b) of this subsection any British-controlled aircraft shall be deemed to be registered in the United Kingdom whether or not it is in fact so registered and whether or not it is in fact registered in some other country.

(3) Any member of the crew of an aircraft and any other person on board the aircraft may, at the request or with the authority of the commander of the aircraft, and any such member shall if so required by that commander, render assistance in restraining any person whom the commander is entitled under subsection (2) above to restrain; and at any time when the aircraft is in flight any such member or other person may, without obtaining the authority of the commander, take with respect to any person on board the aircraft any measures such as are mentioned in that subsection which he has reasonable grounds to believe are immediately necessary to protect the safety of the aircraft or of persons or property on board the aircraft.

(4) Any restraint imposed on any person on board an aircraft under the powers conferred by the preceding provisions of this section shall not be continued after the time when the aircraft first thereafter ceases to be in flight unless before or as soon as is reasonably practicable after that time the commander of the aircraft causes notification of the fact that a person on board the aircraft is under restraint and of the reasons therefor to be sent to an appropriate authority of the country in which the aircraft so ceases to be in flight."

Of course, the commander's discipline does not mean lashing or putting the offender in irons; it involves no more than restraining passengers or crew who are endangering the aircraft/vessel or those aboard, or who are seriously disrupting life aboard.

CHAPTER 21

PRIVATE AND PUBLIC DEFENCE

"Self-defence is the clearest of all laws: and for this reason—the lawyers didn't make it."

Douglas Jerrold[1]

21.1.   THE SCOPE OF PRIVATE DEFENCE

Jerrold was not a lawyer, or he would have known that lawyers did create the right of self-defence, or at least restored it after taking it away. In early times, a homicide in self-defence or by misadventure "deserved but needed a pardon."[2] In the reign of Henry VIII such "excusable" homicides came to result in an acquittal. The limits of the right of self-defence are very much a matter of law, and, perhaps because lawyers did make it, the right has been fraught with difficulty and doubt. We may start with the generalization that self-defence is, within limits, a justification for any crime against the person or property.   **21–001**

May one defend a stranger?   Some old books merely state a right to use force necessary to protect oneself and one's family, as though it does not extend to protecting strangers. Morally and rationally it ought to allow the defence to anybody. But the authorities, ancient and modern, take the sensible view that the right to defend others is not limited by a family relationship.[3] In our own times judges have evaded the issue by saying that, whether or not one can defend a stranger, one can prevent the commission of a crime against a stranger—which comes to much the same thing.[4]   **21–002**

Because defence is not limited to self-defence, it is convenient to use "private defence" as a more general expression. Another useful term for force used in private defence is "protective force" (adopted in the ALI's Model Penal Code). Protective force can be used to ward off unlawful force, to prevent unlawful force, to avoid unlawful detention and to escape from such detention.

---

[1] *The Catspaw: A Comedy*, (London: Bradbury & Evans, 1850) at 22.
[2] Frederick Pollock and Frederic William Maitland, *The History of English Law before the time of Edward I*, (Cambridge: Cambridge University Press, 1895) at 477 *et seq.* 574.
[3] *Walter v. Jones* (1634) Rolle's Abridgement 526 (C) 3. *R. v. Tooley* (1709) 88 E.R. 1015 at 1020; *R. v. Prince* (1875) 2 C.C.R. 154 at 178.
[4] *R. v. Duffy* [1967] 1 Q.B. 63. In *Devlin v. Armstrong* [1971] N.I. 13 at 35-36 it was specifically denied that the right of self-defence applied in respect of strangers; but that was the last of seven reasons for dismissing a hopeless appeal.

21–003 **In the event of aggression, may one use protective force against someone who is not the aggressor? For example, could one take a hostage from the aggressor's family?** No. But self-defence may be exercised against one who may be called an innocent aggressor, such as where an absent minded insane person, or a small child, starts firing a gun at the defender. In other words, protective force may be used only, against one who himself uses or is about to use (or is honestly believed to be using or to be about to use) force that is unjustifiable in law, or who is (or is honestly believed to be) guilty of false imprisonment. If any wider defence is allowed by law, it can only be under the doctrine of necessity.

21–004 **But if a raving lunatic attacks you and he doesn't know what he is doing he doesn't commit a crime; so how come you can defend yourself against him? Surely you can't defend yourself against a lawful act.** The lunatic has an excuse, on the ground of lack of *mens rea*; but his act of aggression is not authorized by law. It is not *justified*. This is one of the differences in law between a justification and an excuse.[5]

21–005 **If two men fight, and one says he was acting in self-defence, isn't there a formidable problem of proof?** Yes, and, in particular, a person who kills in what he conceives to be self-defence is subject to the serious risk that the emergency will not appear to the jury in the same light that it appeared to him.

When looking back at the incident, the fact likely to make the strongest impression is that a person has been killed; the transitory fear felt by the person prosecuted has left no memorial to compare with the tragic reality of the corpse. If there is a survivor of the incident on the other side, his account of what happened is likely to differ essentially from that of the defendant before the court. Even impartial spectators are unreliable witnesses to a sudden affray that is over in a few minutes or seconds. When the issue is one of self-defence, everything depends on which side the aggressor was on, and the temporal order of events is therefore of high importance. But experiments indicate that this is difficult to establish by oral evidence. In particular, witnesses have been shown to have been unable to recall events with accuracy.[6] Hence arise two dangers in the administration of the law: unjust conviction; and unmerited acquittal after a concocted defence. Of the two risks, the former has to be taken more seriously, and for this reason the law casts the burden of negativing the defence of

---

[5] For a general insight into the widely discussed justification/excuse distinction, see George P. Fletcher, "Domination in the Theory of Justification and Excuse" (1996) 57 *U. Pitt. L. Rev.* 553; Gauthier David "Self-Defence and the Requirement of Imminence: Comments on George Fletcher's Domination in the Theory of Justification and Excuse," 57 *U. Pitt. L. Rev.* 615; Larry Alexander, "Self-defence, Justification, and Excuse," (1993) 22 *Philosophy and Public Affairs* 53; Kent Greenawalt, "The Perplexing Borders of Justification and Excuse," (1984) 84 *Colum. L. Rev.* 1897; Heidi M. Hurd, "Justification and Excuse, Wrongdoing and Culpability," (1999) 74 *Notre Dame L. Rev.* 1551; Mitchell N. Berman, "Justification and Excuse, Law and Morality," (2004) 53 *Duke L.J.* 1.
[6] Glanville Williams, *Proof of Guilt: Study of the English Criminal Trial (Hamlyn Lecture)*, (London: Stevens & Sons, 3rd edn., 1963), Chap. 5; David F. Ross *et al.*, *Adult Eyewitness Testimony: Current Trends and Developments*, (Cambridge: Cambridge University Press, 1994); Bob Uttl *et al.*, (eds.) *Memory and Emotion: Interdisciplinary Perspectives*, (Oxford: Wiley-Blackwell, 2006).

self-defence upon the prosecution, only the evidential burden rests on the defendant.[7] If the case is clearly one of self-defence the judge will not even allow the case to go to the jury.[8]

The position is easier if there is a past history that helps to establish who was at fault or what a party may be expected to have believed. Evidence is admissible as to previous friction or threats to show which was the aggressor,[9] or what the actor feared from his assailant.[10] It seems that the evidence may even include the character habits of the assailant.[11] Evidence may also be given of previous crimes in the neighbourhood, to help support the actor's belief that another attack was imminent.[12]

21.2.   THE NECESSITY FOR DEFENCE

The defence of private defence resembles that of preventing crime in the twin requirements that the act must be immediately necessary (there must be no milder way of achieving the end) and proportional to the harm feared. In the past both questions, the factual and the evaluative, have frequently been left to the jury as a single, unanalysed, question of reasonableness. This saved the trouble of sorting them out, but led to regrettable confusion. **21–006**

Necessity: A behaves aggressively towards B; B squares up to him and A makes to retreat, showing clearly that he has thought better of attacking. A blow given to him by B cannot be justified, because the necessity for the defence has passed.[13]

Proportionality: A is about to slap B's face; B is a weakling who can avoid the slap only by using a gun. B is not justified in shooting, but must submit to being slapped.

Private defence is construed in a subjective sense, as far as the necessity for the intervention prong is concerned, but not as far as the question of proportionality is concerned.

On the necessity question, is a pre-emptive strike allowed?   It is sometimes thought that the defence is allowed only against immediately threatened **21–007**

---

[7] For a direction to the jury see *R. v. Abraham* [1973] 1 W.L.R. 1270. It is not clear whether the judge must leave private defence to the jury if the evidence clearly indicates that the defendant went beyond the necessity of the defence. Generally, the judge should only leave the issue to the jury when the evidence makes it clear that it is appropriate to leave it to them: *D.P.P. v. Walker* [1974] 1 W.L.R. 1090; *R. v. Bonnick* (1978) 66 Cr. App. R. 266. See also *Palmer v. R.* [1971] A.C. 814; *R. v. Williams* (1994) 99 Cr. App. R. 163.

[8] In *R. v. Ball* (1967) 131 J.P. 723 an angry crowd besieged Ball's house, threw bricks through his windows and shouted threats. Ball appeared at his window and, after shouting due warning, fired a shotgun, wounding one of the rioters. Roskill J. not only directed Ball's acquittal on a charge of wounding but bound over six prosecution witnesses to keep the peace. Cf. *R. v. Franklin* (1972) *The Times*, May 11.

[9] *R. v. Humphreys* (1920) 14 Cr. App. R. 85.

[10] *R. v. Gunn* (1943) 7 *J. Crim. L.* 28.

[11] *R. v. Griffin* (1871) 10 SRNSW 91.

[12] *Viliborghi v. State*, 45 Ariz. 275 (1935).

[13] *Priestnall v. Cornish* [1979] Crim. L.R. 310; *R. v. Martin* [2003] Q.B. 1.

violence.[14] Clearly, force may not be used to meet a threat of violence in the future,[15] when there is still time for the person threatened to seek police protection. If he acts prematurely the judge may perhaps withdraw the defence from the jury, on the ground that there was no evidence of necessity when the defendant acted. But, as was said before in connection with the prevention of crime, there is a distinction between the immediacy of the necessity for acting and the immediacy of the threatened violence. The use of force may be immediately necessary to prevent an attack in the future. If, for example, there is a present hostile demonstration indicating that violence is about to be used, the defender[16] need not wait until his assailant comes within striking distance, or gets his finger on the trigger.[17] Moreover, force may lawfully be threatened in advance of the immediate necessity for using it.[18] For these reasons it is best to regard the question of immediacy as something that enters into the calculation of necessity, rather than as an independent rule.

21–008   **To what extent can one carry weapons by way of defence? Could I carry a hefty spanner to use if I am attacked on the street at night?**   Not legally. It is, you will remember, an either way offence under section 1 of the *Prevention of Crime Act 1953*[19] for a person to have "with him" an offensive weapon in a public place without "reasonable excuse". Offensive weapons are (1) those that are offensive *per se*,[20] and (2) those that are capable of an innocent use (your spanner) but are carried for the purpose of causing injury to the person. It does not matter that the injury contemplated will be defensive.

21–009   **But you said that reasonable excuse is a defence. Why isn't self-defence a reasonable excuse?**   We are not allowed to make a habit of carrying a weapon for defence, because every weapon could be used by thugs as well as by honest

---

[14] In *Devlin v. Armstrong* [1971] N.I. 13, Lord MacDermott L.C.J. said that where the defence is against an expected attack, "the anticipated attack must be imminent," quoting *R. v. Chisam* (1963) 47 Cr. App. R. 130 at 134.

[15] *R. v. Meade* (1823) 168 E.R. 1006; *R. v. Rashford* [2005] All E.R. (D) 192. Cf. *R. v. Shannon* (1980) 71 Cr. App. R. 192.

[16] The "defender" need not be the defendant; the question of the lawfulness of force in self-defence may arise if such force was used by the victim of the force used by the defendant; as on an issue of provocation. But I shall in general use "defendant" to mean defender, because that is the more convenient word to use for the typical case where the defender is being prosecuted.

[17] See *Beckford v. The Queen* [1988] A.C. 130 at 144, where it was said: "a man about to be attacked does not have to wait for his assailant to strike the first blow or fire the first shot; circumstances may justify a pre-emptive strike." In *Attorney-General of Northern Ireland's Reference (No. 1 of 1975)* [1977] A.C. 105 at 136D, Lord Diplock said: "The facts ... are not capable in law of giving rise to a possible defence of 'self-defence.' The deceased was in fact, and appeared to the accused to be, unarmed. He was not attacking the accused: he was running away." But later he said (at 138B): "There is material upon which a jury might take the view that the accused had reasonable grounds for apprehension of imminent danger to himself and other members of the patrol if the deceased were allowed to get away and join armed fellow-members of the Provisional I.R.A. who might be lurking in the neighbourhood;" so he held that the defence of preventing crime could avail. Cf. Joseph H. Beale, "Homicide in Self-Defence," (1903) 3 *Colum. L. Rev.* 526 at 529.

[18] *R. v. Cousins* [1982] Q.B. 526.

[19] See also section 139(4) of the *Criminal Justice Act 1988*.

[20] "In themselves." Examples are flick knives (*Gibson v. Wales* [1983] Crim. L.R. 113) and coshes (*Grieve v. Macleaod* [1967] Crim. L.R. 424).

people. The defence of reasonable excuse is available, but it is given a restricted interpretation; it might justify a person in carrying a weapon after being attacked within the last day or two,[21] or perhaps a little longer; but even the fact that he has been mugged does not give him an indefinite licence to carry a weapon. There must be "an imminent particular threat affecting the particular circumstances in which it was carried."[22]

In *Attorney-General's Reference (No. 2 of 1983)*,[23] D, whose property was attacked and damaged by rioters, feared that there would be further attacks. Consequently, he made some petrol bombs, which he intended to use for the purpose of keeping the rioters at bay. He was tried for having made an "explosive substance in such circumstances as to give rise to a reasonable suspicion that he had not made it for a lawful object," contrary to section 4(1) of the *Explosive Substances Act 1883*. The court held that his possession of the petrol bombs was lawful because his aim was to protect his family and their property. In this type of case the court considers the lawfulness of the "precautions" taken by the defendant. The defendant was merely equipping himself so that he would be able to defend his property if the need arose in the immediate future. The court had to consider whether it was reasonable for the defendant to take such precautions. It was held that he could take such precautions, because further attacks seemed imminent. In coming to this conclusion, the Court of Appeal had to accept that if the petrol bombs had been used to thwart the rioters, this would have been a necessary and proportionate response.[24]

By the way, if you carried the spanner without any intention to strike anyone with it, but only to frighten off an attack, it would not be an "offensive weapon," not being offensive *per se* and not being carried for the purpose of causing injury.[25] And if you did not intend to strike anyone with the spanner when you carried it, but used it on the spur of the moment when attacked, it would still not be an "offensive weapon" so you would still not be guilty of having it with you for an offensive purpose.[26]

Again, you would not commit an offence under the *Act of 1953* if you used a spanner that you snatched from an assailant in order to strike him, or one that you happened to see when you were being attacked, for the same reason as before—it would not be an "offensive weapon" and you would not "have it with you."[27] These two escape-routes from the *Act of 1953* (depending on the understanding of what is an offensive weapon and when the user had it "with him") are quite distinct from the question of what is a reasonable excuse. The question of

---

[21] *R. v. McAuley* [2010] 1 Cr. App. R. 148. (This was the real issue in, *Attorney-General's Reference (No. 2 of 1983)* [1984] Q.B. 456, but that case is often cited as authority for the proposition that one can pre-emptively defend himself even where there is no imminent threat of harm.)

[22] *Evans v. Hughes* 1972] 1 W.L.R. 1452 at 1455G; *R. v. Archbold* (2007) 171 J.P. 664. Cf. *Malnik v. D.P.P.* [1989] Crim. L.R. 451; *R. v. Salih* [2008] 1 W.L.R. 2627.

[23] [1984] Q.B. 456.

[24] The decision seems somewhat indulgent; but not if one considers the special facts of the case. The evidence suggested that the police were not on top of the riots and that D was resorting to self-help as a matter of necessity.

[25] *R. v. Rapier* (1980) 70 Cr. App. R. 17; *R. v. Snooks* [1997] Crim. L.R. 230.

[26] *R. v. Humphreys* [1977] Crim. L.R. 225.

[27] *Bates v. Bulman* [1979] 1 W.L.R. 1190.

reasonable excuse is one for the jury or magistrates, but the magistrates, at least, will be expected to guide themselves by the above principle stated by the higher courts.

21–010   **Are guns in the same position?**   Most guns are offensive weapons within the *Prevention of Crime Act 1953*, and in addition, the private possession of firearms is strictly controlled under the *Firearms Act 1968* and other *Acts*. Even if you have a licence from the police to possess a firearm, carrying a weapon is an offence under section 19 of that *Act*, except that the courts will allow the statutory defence of "reasonable excuse," which is construed in the same way as in the *Prevention of Crime Act 1953*. The fact that you were acting under this general permission does not allow you to shoot. When you can do so, depends on the law of private defence.[28]

21–011   **If I were carrying a gun or spanner illegally I might be punished for it, but all the same I would use the weapon if I were being murderously attacked.**   On principle you would be within your rights in doing so. The fact that your possession of the weapon is punishable under statute is no more relevant to a charge of assault or manslaughter than would be the fact that you have stolen it. Such is the logic of the matter. When the defendant has armed himself against attack, and particularly when he has armed himself illegally, this is quite likely to be a circumstance of prejudice against him; he will not be looked upon so benignly as the defendant who possessed himself of a weapon in the stress of the moment.

21–012   **If a person is set upon, is he obliged to try to run away, if he can, instead of acting in self-defence?**   The law now is that he is not under a duty to retreat as such, but he must take any opportunity of disengaging himself. The Court of Appeal formulated the rule in the following terms:

> "It is not, as we understand it, the law that a person threatened must take to his heels and run in the dramatic way suggested by counsel for the appellant; but what is necessary is that he should demonstrate by his actions that he does not want to fight. He must demonstrate that he is prepared to temporise and disengage and perhaps to make some physical withdrawal; and that that is necessary as a feature of the justification of self-defence is true, in our opinion, whether the charge is a homicide charge or something less serious."[29]

The defender must, therefore, whenever possible, make a kind of symbolic retreat, or use words having a similar effect, in order to demonstrate that he is not the aggressor. If he makes a lusty defence, the aggressor may suddenly find that he himself has to act in defence; and there is an obvious danger that both parties may then conceive themselves as defenders. To avoid this, each party is required to make his stance clear to the other, whatever the origin of the affair may have been.

---

[28] See *R. v. Martin* [2003] Q.B. 1.

[29] *R. v. Julien* [1969] 1 W.L.R. 839 at 843. Cf. *R. v. McInnes* [1971] 1 W.L.R. 1600. But a "failure to demonstrate unwillingness to fight [is] not fatal to a plea of self-defence." See *R. v. Bird* [1985] 1 W.L.R. 816.

The importance of this rule becomes apparent when one considers the ordinary brawl. Group fights in public houses and elsewhere tend to escalate as friends of the original antagonists decide to join in. Gang members take very seriously the need to show loyalty to their friends who become involved in fights.[30] Those who go immediately to the assistance of a defender are acting lawfully, so long as they keep to the limits of defence; but as more join in on each side it becomes more difficult, as a practical matter, to maintain a distinction between attack and defence, especially when the legal question is not how the fracas started but what each new entrant believes. The fact that the defendant must do what he can to indicate to his adversary that he is willing to discontinue the fight is sufficient to show that the rules of private defence and the prevention of crime[31] are different.

There may be no duty to retreat as such, but the "necessity" requirement means that in cases where the defender can retreat without his liberty being unduly restricted, he will be required to retreat. If the defendant can easily avoid the need to act in self-defence, then he should do so. For example, if the defendant is in his car and a thug is approaching with a baseball bat, he should drive off. If he decides to stay to fight it might be difficult for him to argue that he had no choice but to defend himself. Requiring a defender to retreat on a single occasion (as long as he is not being forced to retreat from his dwelling) would not unduly burden his liberty. *Per contra*, it would be too much to require a defender to take onerous precautions to avoid a conflict such as requiring him to flee from his own home.[32] A defender does not have to forego the right to visit a village or use certain public streets (his right to freedom of movement), even though such action might allow him to avoid a conflict.[33]

Can the victim act to save his own life from a defender who is using excessive force in response to the victim's original attack?　The traditional view is that the defence is not allowed in such circumstances.[34] However, the better view is that where a combatant attempts to disengage himself, but is compelled to go on fighting in self-defence, his acts should on principle be lawful, even though he was originally the aggressor. So if he is at that stage compelled to kill in defence, he should not be guilty of murder or manslaughter. His liability should be for what he did originally.[35] The Court of Appeal has held: "self-defence may arise in

21–013

---

[30] Martin Bouchard and Andrea Spindler, "Groups, Gangs, and Delinquency: Does Organization Matter?" (2010) 38(5) *Journal of Criminal Justice* 921; Scott H. Decker and G. David Curry, "Gangs, Gang Homicides, and Gang Loyalty: Organized Crimes or Disorganized Criminals," (2002) 30(4) *Journal of Criminal Justice* 343.

[31] See section 3 of the *Criminal Law Act 1967*.

[32] "It is the unlawful that must yield to the lawful, and not *vice versa*." *Howard E. Perry & Co. Ltd. v. British Railways Board* [1980] 1 W.L.R. 1375 at 1385, *per* Sir Robert Megarry V.C. See also *R. (on the application of Laporte) v. Chief Constable of Gloucestershire* [2007] 2 A.C. 105 at 155-156.

[33] *R. v. Field* [1972] Crim. L.R. 435. Cf. *U.S. v. Moore*, 35 C.M.R. 159 (1964).

[34] See *R. v Browne* [1973] N.I. 96 at 107, where Lowry L.C.J. said: "The need to act must not have been created by conduct of the accused in the immediate context of the incident which was likely or was intended to give rise to that need." See also *Richard Mason's Case* (1748) 168 E.R. 66.

[35] For considerations of policy in not removing a justification on account of prior misconduct, see Paul H. Robinson, "Criminal Law Defences: A Systematic Analysis," (1982) 82 *Colum. L. Rev.* 199; Andrew J. Ashworth, "Self-Defence and the Right to Life," (1975) 34 *Cambridge L.J.* 282.

the case of an original aggressor but only where the violence offered by the victim was so out of proportion to what the original aggressor did that in effect the roles were reversed."[36]

21.3.   THE PROPORTIONALITY RULE

21–014   Consider again the example where: A is about to slap B's face; B is a weakling who can avoid the slap only by using a gun. In this example the use of the gun may be "necessary" to avoid the apprehended evil of being slapped, but its use would be a disproportionate way to avoid that evil, and therefore unlawful. "For every assault it is not reasonable a man should be banged with a cudgel" (Holt C.J.).[37] The proportionality rule is based on the view that there are some insults and hurts that one must suffer rather than use extreme force, if the choice is between suffering hurt and using extreme force.

The previous examples of the proportionality rule are too trivial to be helpful. The real-life problem arises where a person is fiercely attacked by a bully whom he can resist only by the use of a lethal weapon. It is now so common for brutal men to kick their opponents about the head after he has been felled to the ground that anyone who is attacked may reasonably dread the possibility of being left with permanent brain damage or worse. Their right to avoid the harmful results of this type of beating has to be balanced against the attacker's right not to be harmed. When the harms are equal proportionality will not be an issue, because the aggressor is in the wrong. It is not only a case of balancing the relative harms, but also of considering whether the defender acted to avoid harm that he should not have been forced to endure. It is one thing to require a person to take a slap across the face if he can only avoid it by killing the aggressor, but another thing to require him to endure a violent beating including kicks to the head. A person should not have to lie on the ground and risk serious brain injury or worse, even if doing so would save him from taking the life of his aggressor. In such a situation the aggressor chooses to risk[38] forfeiting his right to life and therefore is not wronged.[39] In most situations the aggressor's right to life will outweigh the defender's right not to be assaulted or unlawfully detained.[40] However, if the aggressor is trying to inflict grievous bodily harm upon the defender, and the defender has no way of knowing whether the attack will cost him his own life, he should be able to use extreme force including lethal force in response.

---

[36] *R. v. Keane* [2010] EWCA Crim. 2514 at para. 17; see also *R. v. Harvey* [2009] EWCA Crim. 469; *R. v. Rashford* [2005] All E.R. (D) 19.

[37] *Cockcroft v. Smith* (1705) 91 E.R. 541.

[38] An analogy can be drawn with the soldier who chooses to go to war to fight for his country: the soldier chooses to risk his life for his country. Likewise, the wrongful aggressor chooses to risk his life when he decides to inflict serious injuries upon another, because he knows that lethal force might be used in response.

[39] The right to life is not inalienable; it may be forfeited. See Joel Feinberg, "Voluntary Euthanasia and the Inalienable Right to Life," (1978) 7(2) *Philosophy and Public Affairs* 93. See also Suzanne Uniacke, *Permissible Killing: the Self-defence Justification of Homicide*, (Cambridge: Cambridge University Press, 1994).

[40] Killing results in irreparable harm of an extraordinary grave kind. Therefore, the threatened harm would have to be of comparable weight to counterbalance it.

The older authorities try to clarify the law of private defence by declaring that extreme force (otherwise called "deadly force," that is, force involving the intentional or reckless infliction of death or serious injury) may be used to avoid extreme harm, but not otherwise. "Extreme harm" includes death or serious injury but might also include other serious harms such as rape.[41] The modern authorities, however, leave the rule of "reasonable relationship" at large, at least in the case of defence of the person.

The abandonment of the relative precision of the old law seems unfortunate. **21–015** Would it not be desirable, for the sake of protecting defendants from the vagaries not only of juries (one must add) of judges, and from gusts of public opinion, that certain fixed rules should be laid down beforehand as to the occasions on which extreme force can be used for self-preservation? The list need not be exhaustive, for the rule could be that extreme but necessary force can be used in specified cases (*a*), (*b*), *etc.*, "and in all other cases where such force would not be regarded by any reasonable person as disproportionate to the threat."

In order to give proper width to the right of self-defence an Australian court stated the law negatively: "Would a reasonable person in the defendant's situation have regarded what he did as out of all proportion to the danger to be guarded against?"[42]

Section 76 of the *Criminal Justice and Immigration Act 2008* provides:[43]

"(1)   This section applies where in proceedings for an offence—(a) an issue arises as to whether a person charged with the offence ('D') is entitled to rely on a defence within subsection (2), and (b) the question arises whether the degree of force used by D against a person ('V') was reasonable in the circumstances.

(2)   The defences are—(a) the common law defence of self-defence; and (b) the defences provided by section 3(1) of the *Criminal Law Act 1967* … (use of force in prevention of crime or making arrest).

(6)   The degree of force used by D is not to be regarded as having been reasonable in the circumstances as D believed them to be if it was disproportionate in those circumstances."

The rule involves a community standard of reasonableness,[44] and is left to the consideration of the jury.[45] It can bear hardly on the defender, but much depends on the way in which judges and juries administer it; and that, again, may depend on whether they happen to empathize with the frightened defender or with his injured (or dead) assailant. If the defendant's reaction was disproportionate, the attack he feared or was resisting will go only in mitigation.

In *R. v. Shannon*[46] the deceased, a heavily built man who had convictions for **21–016** violence, had been making threats against Shannon for having (as he believed) "grassed" him. Shannon, who had no history of violence or aggression, must have

---

[41] A. V. Dicey, *Introduction to the Study of the Law of the Constitution*, (London: Macmillan, 8th reprint edn., 1924).

[42] *R. v. Rainey* [1970] V.R. 650.

[43] Section 76 is not substantive law; rather it "is intended to clarify the operation of the existing defences mentioned in subsection (2)."

[44] *R. v. Owino* [1996] 2 Cr. App. R. 128; *R. v. Rashford* [2005] EWCA Crim. 3377.

[45] Subject to the usual rule that there must be evidence for the jury.

[46] (1980) 71 Cr. App. R. 192.

been living in fear of attack for some time. When the attack came he fought back, the fight (though evidently largely one-sided) being described by a bystander as "pretty frightening." Shannon's evidence was that he was being held very tightly by the neck and was being dragged down and "kneed;" he feared that if he fell while in the grip of his attacker he would have "got beat up by his feet." He lashed out with a pair of scissors and inflicted a fatal blow. On the issue of self-defence the judge left the case to the jury with the bald question: Did the defendant use more force than was necessary in the circumstances? On this the jury, surprisingly, returned a conviction of manslaughter. The conviction was quashed, for inadequate direction to the jury; but the Court of Appeal expressed no other criticism of the verdict. Shannon was not mistaken about the need for action and seems to have used reasonable force given the nature of the attack, but we are left with the impression that if in a similar case the judge reads out the wording of section 76(7) of the *Criminal Justice and Immigration Act 2008*[47] to the jury, who nevertheless convict, the conviction will stand.

21–017 **Suppose Shannon had used his scissors upon a mugger; would the view of the court have been the same?** If the thief were trying to drag his bag from him, and the victim of the robbery stabbed the thief only to avoid losing his property, this will be regarded as a disproportionate response. All that one can clearly do by way of defence against robbery is to give the robber blows and threaten him with a weapon.[48] For some reason that is not clear, the courts occasionally seem to regard the scandal of the killing of a robber (or of a person who is feared to be a robber) as of greater moment than the safety of the robber's victim in respect of his person and property.[49]

21.4. MISTAKEN BELIEF

21–018 It is enough that the defendant was under the belief[50] that the force was necessary, even though he made a mistake—subject to an argument on whether the belief must be reasonable. Nearly all the earlier authorities required the belief to be reasonable.[51] They took the "objective" view that the defendant's honest belief is no defence to the charge if it was unreasonably arrived at. The argument in favour of the objective view is that it may be difficult to decide whether an alleged belief was actually held or not (see 6.8.). Since the burden is on the Crown to negative

---

[47] The wording of this provision is taken from Lord Morris's *dictum* in *Palmer v. The Queen* [1971] A.C. 814 at 831, where he said: "If there has been attack so that defence is reasonably necessary it will be recognised that a person defending himself cannot weigh to a nicety the exact measure of his necessary defensive action. If a jury thought that in a moment of unexpected anguish a person attacked had only done what he honestly and instinctively thought was necessary that would be most potent evidence that only reasonable defensive action had been taken."

[48] *R. v. Cousins* [1982] Q.B. 526.

[49] In *R. v. O'shea* (1978) 142 J.P.N. 472 a man who feared he was about to be set upon by a gang of youths was sent to prison for four years for accidentally killing one of them in the course of defensive action.

[50] The word "belief" is sometimes qualified by adjectives like "honest" or "genuine" or "*bona fide*," which (as has been pointed out before) are strictly tautologous.

[51] For example, *R. v. Hassin* [1963] Crim. L.R. 852. Cf. A. Zuckerman, "Assault or Not Assault," (1972) 88 *L. Q. Rev.* 246 at 260 *et seq.*

self-defence, if that issue is raised by evidence given on behalf of the defendant, the Crown may be unable to prove beyond reasonable doubt that the defendant did not act under the particular belief that he alleges. It is said that the objective view enables the jury under the direction of the judge, or the magistrates, to do substantial justice in the circumstances of the particular case. The defendant's belief will be a factor in deciding whether what he did was justified or not, but will not be conclusive under the objective standard. The objective standard is still applied to the question of whether or not the force used was proportionate. However, the objective standard no longer holds sway as far as the mistaken "necessity" element is concerned.

Are you telling me that a police officer can kill X if he mistakenly believes X **21–019** **is a suicide bomber who is about to blow up a train carriage full of people, even if no reasonable person would have made the same mistake?** Yes, if the jury accept that he in fact held such a belief. His belief that it was necessary to act might have been totally unreasonable,[52] but the degree of forced used was proportionate (it seems "reasonable" to use lethal force to prevent a putative terrorist from killing many innocent people), so he should be able to raise the section 3 of the *1967 Act* defence.

Is it really fair to maintain the subjective standard in such cases? You will **21–020** recall that *D.P.P. v. Morgan*[53] decided that when the offence charged requires a mental element at common law or expressly by a statute or by implication from a statute, the defendant's mistake of fact can be a defence even though it was unreasonable. The question is whether we have to distinguish between the *mens rea* required for the basic elements of the offence (the definitional elements); and that required for defence. It may be said that the offence of assault or murder requires an attack upon a person (definitional element); the question whether the attack had to be made by the defendant in self-defence is a defence element; not a definitional element, and the question of fault may not be the same.

In answer to this argument, and in favour of the subjective view, it is said that if the defendant, believing that he has to act urgently in self-defence, kills or wounds a person who is completely innocent, this must be accounted a tragic accident, and it is pointless to punish for it. The following additional arguments are advanced for the subjective position:

- It accords with the general principle that serious crimes, and particularly offences against the person, require a mental element. This mental element should be required for all the circumstances of the case, and is lacking if the defendant believes that a situation calling for self-defence has arisen. For example, on a charge of wounding with intent, where the defendant has in fact inflicted a wound, it is not sufficient for conviction to show that, without intending to wound, he unreasonably failed to realize the danger in what he was doing. So why should it be sufficient that he unreasonably believed that he was being attacked and thus responded in self-defence? If

---

[52] We would need more facts than we have here to decide one way or the other.
[53] [1976] A.C. 182.

it were the case that an unreasonable belief in the need for self-defence was no justification, the defendant would be liable to be convicted of a crime of unlawful intention, when in fact his only fault would be one of negligence. Such a defendant does not intend to break the law. Rather, he intends to rely on the law so that he can defend himself against what he in fact believes to be an attack. Justificatory defences allow certain motivations to be considered. A person who kills in self-defence is motivated by a desire to preserve his own life. Because self-defence is recognized as a legal justification for killing, those who are motivated by self-defence lack culpability in the wider sense. If the motive is to do a lawful act, it can be material (cf. 4.2.).

- When the law requires beliefs to be "reasonable," it generally does so in order to compel people to take steps to verify their beliefs before acting. Alternatively, the object is to compel compliance with well-know rules of prudence. But in a situation where a person believes that he must act in self-defence, he must act on the instant. Suppose that the defendant suddenly saw a figure looming before him in the dark, and, seized with an unreasonable panic, he took a heavy stick and inflicted serious injury on the other. He believed for the moment that he was about to be gravely attacked, but can now offer no grounds for his belief. If we disallow the defence of self-defence because the defendant's fear was unreasonable, and therefore punish him for the attack, are we not inflicting an injustice on him without retributive or utilitarian purpose? No rule of prudence decides the question whether another person is about to launch a fierce attack on you. Generally there will be no way in which the defender can check the validity of his belief; and such a situation is so unlikely to be repeated that he will probably not benefit from experience. Also, a defender is subject to the strong emotion of fear, which may well warp his judgment. If the law is to allow self-defence at all, it has to allow it on the facts as they appear to the defendant.[54]

- When the charge is manslaughter, gross negligence is in issue, and some cases in which the court required the defendant's belief to be reasonable may perhaps be explained on the ground that this was the charge being considered.[55] Even so, it would be wrong, for the reasons given, to apply principles of negligence to this situation. At the least, a person should not be convicted of manslaughter unless he were guilty of gross negligence. It should therefore be a misdirection, even in cases of manslaughter, to ask the jury whether the defendant's belief in the necessity for protective force was reasonable; if such an instruction is given at all, the question should be

---

[54] *R. v. Williams* (1984) 78 Cr. App. R. 276 at 281-282, *per* Lord Lane C.J.

[55] *R. v. Wardrope* (1959) 24 *J. Crim. L.* 178; *R. v. Chisam* (1963) 47 Cr. App. R. 130. Other possible misunderstandings that may underlie the objective view are a condition between the required mental state and evidence of it, and a confusion between the necessity rule and the proportionality rule.

whether his belief was grossly unreasonable.[56] A mistake as to the necessity for self-defence made in the heat of the moment would rarely if ever amount to gross negligence.

- The objective test is inadequately justified by referring to the prosecution's difficulty of proof. For the objective test was stated a rule of substantive law,[57] which meant that even if the tribunal had been fully satisfied that the defendant believed that he had to act in self-defence, it was still required to convict if that belief was adjudged unreasonable.

   In so far as the subjective test causes difficulty for the prosecution in proving its case, this is so for all issues as to the mental element in crime. However, the difficulty is not so great as may at first appear, because it is for the defendant to satisfy the "evidential burden," or jump the "initial hurdle," of offering enough evidence of his belief to raise the issue. Almost inevitably this means that he must give evidence, and he may then be cross-examined as to the grounds of his belief. Moreover, the unreasonableness of the defendant's belief is evidence that he did not in fact hold it. To quote the words of Lord Parker C.J. in a different context, the proper direction to the jury is in terms of the defendant's genuine belief, "subject to this, that it would be right to tell the jury that they can use as a test, though not a conclusive test, whether there were any reasonable grounds for that belief."[58] All the same, where a person has to respond to a crisis a court should be slow to reject a defence of self-defence unless there is positive evidence that the act was done in anger or revenge rather than in fear. For example, if the defendant followed his retreating adversary and killed him in flight, the issue would be whether the defendant believed that it was necessary to kill in order to prevent an immediate renewal of the attack. Evidence that the attacker had been put to flight may negative a belief, beyond all reasonable doubt.[59] It would not be enough for the defendant to say, what might well be believed, that he feared that if he did not kill on this occasion his opponent would take a later opportunity to kill him when he was defenceless. The same analysis holds where the defendant has knifed his opponent lying helpless on the ground. In all such cases a defence of belief in necessity to use force is almost as likely to fail as the defence of reasonable belief.

The subjective view was recognized in *R. v. Williams*,[60] where Lord Lane C.J. said: **21–021**

---

[56] Cf. Herbert Wechsler and Jerome Michael, "Rationale of the Law of Homicide," (1937) 37 *Colum. L. Rev.* 701 at 726: "It is difficult to see why negligence in judging the existence of grounds for justification should be treated more severely than negligence in judging the character of one's own acts."

[57] See *R. v. Hassin* [1963] Crim. L.R. 852.

[58] *R. v. Waterfall* [1970] 1 Q.B. 148 at 151.

[59] *R. v. Martin* [2003] Q.B. 1.

[60] (1984) 78 Cr. App. R. 276 at 281-282. See also *Beckford v. The Queen* [1988] A.C. 130; *R. v. Wilson* [2006] EWCA Crim. 1880.

"What then is the situation if the defendant is labouring under a mistake of fact as to the circumstances? What if he believes, but believes mistakenly, that the victim is consenting or that it is necessary to defend himself, or that a crime is being committed which he intends to prevent? He must then be judged against the mistaken facts as he believes them to be. If judged against those facts or circumstances the prosecution fail to establish his guilt then he is entitled to be acquitted ....

The reasonableness or unreasonableness of the defendant's belief is material to the question of whether the belief was held by the defendant at all. If the belief was in fact held, its unreasonableness, so far as guilt or innocence is concerned is neither here nor there. It is irrelevant."

21–022   **Should the subjective test be applied not only to the existence of the danger but also to its magnitude?**   The defendant's belief that danger is imminent may have been well founded, but he may have over-estimated its seriousness. He may, for example, have used a knife in self-defence, believing that his life was in danger, when in fact his antagonist intended only a common assault. The law must be prepared, so far as it can do so, to look into the mind of the defendant and give him the benefit of the facts as they appear to him.

Section 76 of the *Criminal Justice and Immigration Act 2008* covers this type of mistake:

"(3)   The question whether the degree of force used by D was reasonable in the circumstances is to be decided by reference to the circumstances as D believed them to be, and subsections (4) to (8) also apply in connection with deciding that question.

(4)   If D claims to have held a particular belief as regards the existence of any circumstances—(a) the reasonableness or otherwise of that belief is relevant to the question whether D genuinely held it; but (b) if it is determined that D did genuinely hold it, D is entitled to rely on it for the purposes of subsection (3), whether or not—(i) it was mistaken, or (ii) (if it was mistaken) the mistake was a reasonable one to have made.

(7)   In deciding the question mentioned in subsection (3) the following considerations are to be taken into account (so far as relevant in the circumstances of the case)—(a) that a person acting for a legitimate purpose may not be able to weigh to a nicety the exact *measure* of any necessary action; and (b) that evidence of a person's having only done what the person honestly and instinctively thought was necessary for a legitimate purpose constitutes strong evidence that only reasonable action was taken by that person for that purpose."

21–023   **On subsection 76(7), it is not easy to see how "what the defendant thought" could be evidence of what it was reasonable for him to do. The usual opinion is that the question what is reasonable, in the multifarious applications of that word, is for the unaided vote of the jury, and is not a matter for "evidence" in the ordinary way. It looks very much as though the subsection is a way of escaping from the test of reasonableness without acknowledging the fact.** Reasonableness in the subsection merely relates to the level of harm that the defendant thought it was necessary for him to use. So, if Y kills innocent X because he unreasonably believes X is a suicide bomber, Y's unreasonable mistake will be regarded as reasonable as long as he did in fact believe X was a terrorist. He will be judged on the facts as he believed them to be. Once the jury accept that Y did in fact believe that X was a terrorist, it will then apply the objective standard to determine whether lethal force was a reasonable response for stopping a supposed terrorist from killing a train full of people. (Obviously the latter will be held to be a proportionate response.)

In *R. v. Martin*,[61] the Court of Appeal overlooked this important requirement. If a person unreasonably believes that X is a suicide bomber, he is allowed to use whatever force would be reasonable to stop him. His unreasonable mistake is not about the extent of the threat, but merely about whether the threat is in fact real. The force used to prevent the supposed offending need only be proportionate to the supposed extent of the threat—it does not have to be proportionate with the actual threat. When such mistakes are made, the defender only discovers that the supposed threat did not in fact exist *ex post facto*.

Compare this with the situation where the defender not only mistakenly believes that V is going to slap him across the face, but also mistakenly believes that it is reasonable for him to kill V to avoid being slapped. Here the defender's response will be judged according to the threat that he mistakenly believed existed. Since the only threat he believed existed was a slap in the face, his response will be judged by the jury to be disproportionate. A reasonable jury would not hold that it is reasonable to kill another human being to avoid being slapped in the face. Hence, the reasonableness of the force used will depend on what degree of harm the defender "thought" was being threatened.

What if the defender's voluntary intoxication led him to mistakenly believe that it was "necessary" for him to defend himself? Since *D.P.P. v. Majewski*[62] a drunken (and therefore unreasonable) mistake as to the necessity for self-defence is no answer to a charge of assault, this being held not to be a crime of "specific intent." This involves a reversal of the previous law.[63] The adoption of the objective test is a good illustration of the contradiction implicit in the prevailing view of the law. Murder being a crime of "specific intent," evidence of intoxication is allowed on the issue of intention to kill;[64] yet the same evidence is, it is said, no defence when the defendant says that he believed that he was being attacked and had to act in self-defence, if a sober person would not have been under the same belief.[65] Why should not the mental element necessary for the definitional elements of the offence apply also to the defence elements? Therefore, if the voluntarily intoxicated defender kills a person he mistakenly thought was trying to kill him, he will be liable for murder if his intoxication does not prevent him from forming the "specific intent" required for that offence. It was said before that the motive for doing the act can be material. When an intoxicated person kills in mistaken defence, he believes he is lawfully justified even though he is not. Since his voluntary intoxication causes him to mistakenly believe he has a right to kill, he should be charged with a basic intent crime.

21–024

---

[61] [2003] Q.B. 1.

[62] [1977] A.C. 443. Section 76(5) of the *Criminal Justice and Immigration Act 2008* affirms this rule: "Subsection (4)(b) does not enable D to rely on any mistaken belief attributable to intoxication that was voluntarily induced."

[63] Drunken mistake as to the necessity for self-defence had been accepted in *Marshall's Case* (1830) 168 E.R. 965; *R. v. Gamlen* (1858) 175 E.R. 639; *R. v. Wardrope* [1960] Crim. L.R. 770.

[64] *R. v. Lipman* [1970] 1 Q.B. 152.

[65] *R. v. Hatton* [2006] 1 Cr. App. R. 247; *R. v. O'Connor* [1991] Crim. L.R. 135; *R. v. O'Grady* [1987] Q.B. 995. The Law Commission support the approach adopted in *R. v. Hatton*. See Law Commission, *Intoxication and Criminal Liability*, Law Com. No. 314, (London: H.M.S.O. Cm. 7526, 2009) at para. 3.53.

The nonsensicality of distinguishing between definitional and defence elements is exemplified by *R. v. Lipman*.[66] Lipman killed his girlfriend because he mistakenly believed that she was a serpent. Lipman was in an intoxicated trance, but he did form the specific intent to kill. However, he only intended to kill a serpent, not a human being. He was able to evade a murder conviction because he did not form a specific intent to kill a human being. If he had mistakenly killed his girlfriend on the belief that she was a large man attacking him, he would have been convictable of murder because he intended to kill another human being.[67] People like Lipman are no less blameworthy than the likes of Hatton and O'Grady, but because their mistakes relate to a definitional element they will be convicted only of a basic intent crime and thus will be punished much less.

21–025 **What if the defender's mental disorder led him to mistakenly believe that it was "necessary" for him to defend himself?** Since the test is subjective, he will be judged according to the circumstances as believed them to be.

21–026 **What if a person's mental disorder prevents him from judging the appropriate level of force that is required to thwart an attack?** It has been noted that any force used must be reasonable. Would a reasonable person with the same information as the defender has (a belief that V will assault him), use lethal force to thwart a common assault? One would think not! The mentally disordered offender is required to act as a reasonable person would have acted, even though it may be impossible for him to act in this way.[68] The reason a reasonable person is judged against the standard of his peers is that on reflection he can be expected to understand that standard, but a mentally disordered person might be unable to comprehend such a standard under any circumstances. In borderline cases, a person's mental impairment might cause him to make a mistake that is not terribly unreasonable, so a purely objective test seems severe. Nevertheless, in extreme cases it will be perfectly clear that no reasonable person would have made the same mistake. Mental disorder should be taken into account, but where the mistake is blatantly unreasonable the defendant should be subject to a special verdict of insanity. A fair balance has to be struck, if a person is so deranged that he makes mistakes that no reasonable person would make, and those mistakes cost other people their lives, psychiatric incarceration is appropriate.

21.5.   THE UNKNOWN NECESSITY

21–027 It was just said that there is a requirement of necessity or of belief in necessity, but the question whether the first of these alternatives really needs to be inserted requires further consideration. Can one act in self-defence by accident, so to speak? D fires at V, intending to murder him. Unknown to D, V was at that moment about to kill him, and D's act, objectively regarded, was necessary in

---

[66] [1970] 1 Q.B. 152.
[67] *R. v. Hatton* [2006] 1 Cr. App. R. 247.
[68] *R. v. Martin* [2003] Q.B. 1.

self-defence, although he did not know it. The question is whether D's act in shooting V (and thereafter in saving his own life) was lawful.

Put in more general form, the question is whether, to justify a conviction, all the external elements of the defence must be absent, just as all the external elements of the definition must be present. The question is of theoretical interest, even though it rarely arises.[69] Clearly, the defender cannot rely on self-defence if he killed or injured the victim for some other reason.[70] Justificatory defences simply recognize that the defendant was legally motivated. The courts recognize self-defence as a lawful justification[71] for committing the *actus reus* of certain crimes. If a person kills in self-defence he lacks *mens rea* because he is acting lawfully. If a person kills for revenge he is culpable, because revenge is not recognized as a lawful justification for killing (cf. 4.2).

21.6. FORCE TO PREVENT CRIME AND ARREST CRIMINALS

Force used in arrest and for the prevention of crime is legalized by section 3 of the *Criminal Law Act 1967*, and this is almost the sole authority to be considered for the modern law: **21–028**

> "(1) A person may use such force as is reasonable in the circumstances in the prevention of crime, or in effecting or assisting in the lawful arrest of offenders or suspected offenders or of persons unlawfully at large.
>
> (2) Subsection (1) above shall replace the rules of the common law on the question when force used for a purpose mentioned in the subsection is justified by that purpose."

Before the *Act of 1967* it was doubtful how far the police or private persons could use force to prevent minor offences.[72] The police have unlimited powers under the section, subject to the requirement of reasonableness.[73]

In theory the section applies equally to private persons, but the ordinary citizen would be unwise to use force to prevent a motor cyclist from riding without protective headgear, for instance. He would run the risk of finding that no force could "reasonably" be used to prevent such an offence. The section does not say that moderate (non-extreme) force can always be used when necessary to prevent crime, so the citizen has to decide two questions: whether it is necessary to use any force, and if so what force is reasonable.[74]

It is sometimes suggested that section 3 of the *Criminal Law Act 1967* has swallowed up the law of private defence, or else that its limitations have

---

[69] For an example where it did arise see *R. v. Dadson* (1850) 175 E.R. 499. Cf. *United States v. Dynar* [1997] 2 S.C.R. 462 at para. 175.

[70] Cf. Paul H. Robinson, *Structure and Function in Criminal Law*, (Oxford: Clarendon Press, 1997) at 100 *et seq.*

[71] One only acts lawfully, if one's motivation for committing the offence is recognized as a lawful justification. See *Beckford v. The Queen* 1988] A.C. 130 at 144, *per* Lord Griffiths.

[72] The case law showed that the police could use force to prevent unlawful intimation (*Tynan v. Balmer* [1965] 3 All E.R. 99), the obstruction of the highway (*Despard v. Wilcox* (1910) 22 Cox C.C. 258); and sedition (*Timothy v. Simpson* (1835) 149 E.R. 1284).

[73] *Kelly v. United Kingdom* (1993) 16 E.H.R.R. CD20.

[74] Criminal Law Revision Committee, 7th *Report*, (London: H.M.S.O., Cmnd. 2659, 1965) at para. 23, states: "In the case of very trivial offences it would very likely be held that it would not be reasonable to use even the slightest force to prevent them."

somehow superimposed themselves upon the defence;[75] but there is no reason why this should be so. When a person has two defences (private defence and public authority; private defence and loss of control, *etc.*), he is allowed the benefit of whichever is the most favourable to him on the facts. It is true that section 3(2) states that section 3(1) replaces the previous rules of the common law in relation to the purpose of preventing crime and arresting offenders, but the "purpose" of private defence is different, and is not affected.

21–029 Section 3 of the *Act of 1967* was passed to deal with the prevention of crime and the arrest of offenders, not with private defence. Where the defendant acted under section 3 to prevent a crime, it would seem, according to the words of the section, that there must have been a crime in contemplation or thought to be in contemplation. What if the defendant knew that the person against whom he acted would have a defence to a charge of crime, for example on the ground of insanity or duress? Assuming that section 3 does not apply to these circumstances, private defence can do so: it can be exercised (as was said before) against a lunatic or a small child who has armed himself with his father's revolver. Again, the ejection of trespassers is private defence but not the prevention of crime. Even when exercised against offenders, the right of private defence may sometimes be wider than the right to prevent crime and arrest offenders; in particular, private defence seems to be wider in respect of the protection of the dwelling (see the discussion below). Of course, a defendant may be able to rely on both section 3 and on private defence, so he may argue both or may choose the more favourable defence in the circumstances.

21–030 **Need it be apprehended that the crime will be committed immediately?** No.[76] But the force must be immediately necessary. You may have to use force if it is immediately necessary to disarm a person who is running off to commit a crime elsewhere.[77]

21–031 **Isn't this talk about reasonable force merely a disguise for the fact that there is no rule? Suppose someone is making off with my valuables, and I happen to have my shotgun handy. I want to know whether I can shoot. If the law simply tells me that I can do what is reasonable, that is pure waffle.** Your impeachment cannot be altogether contradicted. Section 3 gives no real guidance on the question when extreme force (involving the infliction of death or serious injury) may be used for the prevention of crime. Before the *Act* there was authority for saying that anyone might kill to prevent a robbery,[78] "manifest theft,"[79] burglary,[80] arson,[81] rape,[82] or, in general, any atrocious[83] crime (whatever that meant). It would have been politically impossible in 1967 to get

---

[75] J. C. Smith and Brian Hogan, *Criminal Law*, (London: Butterworths, 4th edn., 1978) at 325.

[76] *R. v. Cousins* [1982] Q.B. 526.

[77] *Farrell v. Secretary of State for Defence* [1980] 1 W.L.R. 172 at 179C-E.

[78] Sir Matthew Hale, *Historia Placitorum Coronae: The History of the Pleas of the Crow*, (London: Printed for E. and R. Nutt, Vol. I, 1736) at 481.

[79] George P. Fletcher, *Rethinking Criminal Law*, (Boston, Little, Brown, 1978) at 860-861.

[80] Hale, *op. cit. supra*, note 78 at 42; *R. v. Dennis* (1905) 68 J.P. 256.

[81] *Id.*, at 488.

[82] *Id.*, at 486.

any such rules through Parliament; the best that could be done was to ask Parliament to approve a rule so vague that it is hardly a rule at all. So we are given only the test of reasonableness; and the old law is expressly abolished. On a charge of murder or manslaughter (to take examples), the jury are left to decide whether it was lawful to kill.

Like private defence, reasonableness in public defence only concerns the reasonableness of the force used. The defence raises the same two questions:

1. Was the force used *necessary*, or in fact believed to be necessary to prevent the offences? If force had to be used—did the defender in fact believe a smaller degree of force would have been sufficient?) This is a question of fact.
2. Was the force *proportionate* to the evil to be avoided? This is a question of evaluation or social judgment.

We may call these factual and evaluative questions respectively. They are the same as the principles applied in relation to private defence.

On the factual question, suppose that the force used was not necessary in fact   **21–032**
but the defendant mistakenly thought it was. Do you mean that if his belief
in necessity was unreasonable he has a defence under the section? Yes. The
courts have been disposed to hold that the question of reasonableness is to be
judged on the facts as the defendant believed them to be—in other words that his
belief that it was necessary to use force need not be held on reasonable grounds.[84]
On this construction, the question is whether the force would be reasonable on the
assumption that the defendant in fact believed it was necessary to use force. The
defendant's conduct will be held to be reasonable even if he mistakenly kills an
innocent person, if he in fact believed it was necessary to kill, and if killing that
person would have been a reasonable response to prevent the victim from
committing the crime he mistakenly believed he was going to commit.

In *Attorney-General of Northern Ireland's Reference (No. 1 of 1975)*,[85] a
soldier in Northern Ireland shot and killed a suspected terrorist who had started to
run away when challenged. The man turned out not to be a terrorist. The judge in
Northern Ireland, sitting without a jury, acquitted the soldier of murder, one of the
reasons given being the somewhat surprising one that he had not intended to kill
or seriously injure the deceased. On a reference to the House of Lords, their
Lordships, while expressing no disapproval of the judge's finding of fact, also
discussed the legality of the shooting in terms of the legislative provision in
Northern Ireland in terms with section 3 of the *Act of 1967*. Lord Diplock said:

> "Are we satisfied that no reasonable man (a) with knowledge of such facts as were known to
> the accused or ... believed[86] by him to exist (b) in the circumstances and time available to him

---

[83] Sir William Blackstone, *Commentaries on the laws of England*, (Oxford: Clarendon Press, 6th edn., Vol. IV, 1778) at 180.

[84] See section 76(6), (7) of the *Criminal Justice and Immigration Act 2008*.

[85] [1977] A.C. 105.

[86] Lord Diplock thought both the belief in the necessity for acting, and the amount of force required, had to be reasonable. This is clearly no longer the law.

for reflection (c) could be of opinion that the prevention of the risk of harm to which others might be exposed if the suspect were allowed to escape justified exposing the suspect to the risk of harm to him that might result from the kind of force that the accused contemplated using?"[87]

With the alleviations accepted by Lord Diplock there is probably little difference in practice, so far as the police and armed forces are concerned, between a defence of reasonable belief and a defence of belief, since an allegation of a wholly unreasonable belief would in any case be unlikely to be credited.[88]

21–033 However, a woolly word like "reasonable" is quite capable of a surreptitiously differential application, being adjudged indulgently for the forces of law and strictly for the private citizen.[89] There seems to be nothing reasonable about shooting a person dead merely because he appears to be a terrorist who may escape and commit acts of terrorism. The appropriate response would be to let him go and use intelligence to track him down. We cannot licence the police to kill anyone who flees upon being questioned, simply because that person fits the profile of the standard terrorist.[90] However, the case might be different if the police in fact believe that it is necessary to shoot a person whom they believe is a suicide bomber who is about to detonate a bomb on the crowded London underground. If the police believe a person is armed with a bomb and is about to detonate it in a crowded train carriage, it seems that they would have a defence, even if it was totally unreasonable for them to believe that the particular person was a terrorist; or that he had a bomb, because the force used would be reasonable. It would be reasonable to kill a suicide bomber to save the lives of many innocent people. As long as the jury accept that they in fact held the unreasonable belief that the victim was a terrorist who was about to kill many, the defence should be available where the force used is proportionate to the putative threat. The unreasonable mistake about whether or not the victim is a suicide bomber does not mean the force used was unreasonable—the force used to prevent the supposed offending need only be proportionate to the supposed threat—it does not have to be proportionate with the actual threat. When such mistakes are made, the defender only discovers that the supposed threat did not in fact exist *ex post facto*. (Alas, unreasonable mistakes can have tragic consequences.)[91]

Another example, of the evaluation question, somewhat more clear-cut than that presented in the Northern Ireland case, may be helpful. A group of strikers are trying to prevent me from driving along a stretch of highway leading to a factory. Assume that they are not exercising their statutory right of peaceful picketing. They form a line across the road. I am no match for them in a fight, but I can break the blockade by driving at them, with the risk of killing one of them. I do this, and run one of them down. Suppose that I am charged with

---

[87] *Attorney-General of Northern Ireland's Reference (No. 1 of 1975)* [1977] A.C. 105.

[88] See sections 76(3), (4) of the *Criminal Justice and Immigration Act 2008*.

[89] *Kelly v. United Kingdom* (1993) 16 E.H.R.R. CD20.

[90] See *Juozaitiene v. Lithuania* (2008) 47 E.H.R.R. 55; *McCann v. United Kingdom* (1996) 21 E.H.R.R. 97.

[91] James Burleigh and Ben Fenton "Bomb suspect gunned down on Tube after frantic chase with armed police," (London: *The Telegraph*, 23 Jul 2005).

manslaughter and set up a defence under section 3. On the question of fact, whether there was any other way in which I could enforce my right of passage, it may be argued that I should have driven slowly forward to give the strikers the chance to move away; but then they might have clambered on the car, obstructed my vision and prevented me from proceeding. However, this factual question is answered, the legal position obviously is that my right of passage along the highway is not sufficiently important to justify me in deliberately killing an obstructer or inflicting serious injury upon him. The legal point is so clear that the judge could probably direct the jury as a matter of law that they need not consider the defence under section 3.[92] The governing consideration is not the factual question but the evaluative one.

As the *Report of the Criminal Code Bill of 1879* put it:

> "We take one great principle of the common law to be, that though it sanctions the defence of a man's person, liberty and property against illegal violence, and permits the use of force to prevent crimes, to preserve the public peace, and to bring offenders to justice, yet all this is subject to the restriction that the forced used is necessary; that is, that the mischief sought to be prevented could not be prevented by less violent means; and that the mischief done by, or which might reasonably be anticipated from the force used, is not disproportionate to the injury or mischief which it is intended to prevent."[93]

Apart from such generalities, little guidance is to be obtained from the authorities on what is reasonable to prevent crime. The only safe course for the citizen is not to use more than mild force. He may threaten more force than he may lawfully use.[94] He is not well advised to kill or inflict serious injury in defence of property or economic interests; the spirit of the time is against it. Don't "have a go;" let the criminal get on with it. This course may be pusillanimous, but the law has to strike a fair balance between the rights of the defender and the rights of the offender. The offender does not choose to risk forfeiting (or alienating)[95] his right to life or his right not to be seriously injured merely by choosing to commit minor property offences. You might restrain someone who is shoplifting in your store, but you could not shoot him in the back if he were to escape your grip and run. Nor should you give him a brutal beating. Your right to keep your goods does not compete with his right to life and limb.[96] If the thief is an armed robber, lethal or extreme force might be a proportionate response. It would depend on what the robber was armed with and on the type of threats he made. If he is armed with a shotgun and is threatening to kill a bank teller, then lethal force would be a proportionate response.

Difficulty might arise in cases where unarmed thieves are escaping with very valuable property. Such cases are likely to be rare, because those who commit

21–034

---

[92] *Attorney-General of Northern Ireland's Reference (No. 1 of 1975)* [1977] A.C. 105.

[93] C. 2345 at 11.

[94] *R. v. Cousins* [1982] Q.B. 526.

[95] A person chooses to risk forfeiting his right to life when he starts firing bullets at other innocent people, because he knows that the result will be return (defensive) fire. He only "risks" forfeiting his life, because he does not know for sure that he will be killed, but must know that there is a risk that he will be killed. See the facts of *R. v. Pagett* (1983) 76 Cr. App. R. 279, Pagett chose to risk his own life (as well as that of the innocent girl who he used as a human shield) by deliberately firing bullets at the police.

[96] *R. v. Martin* [2003] Q.B. 1.

large scale thefts very rarely go unarmed and are usually willing to use whatever arms they have to escape. In practice, the courts are likely to hold that it would be reasonable for the police to use lethal force to stop a gang escaping with national treasures of immense value. This would, however, mean giving property a higher value than human life. (Many jurors might be willing to do so in exceptional cases.)

21–035 **Does the section allow the use of force against third parties?** One can imagine a case where the use of mild force against an innocent third party would be adjudged reasonable and lawful. But injuring or endangering third parties would be unlikely to be held reasonable unless it were to avoid even greater danger to life, when the question in effect becomes one of necessity (24.6).

21–036 **Is it justifiable to commit a minor offence in order to frustrate a serious offender?** Section 3 will apply if the minor offence is one of using force. The section does not expressly authorize mild non-forcible measures to prevent crime.[97]

21–037 **Could the police be justified in using force to enter and remain on property in order to prevent crime?** Yes according to the general formula of the section, but difficulties loom up. In the pre-*Act* case of *Thomas v. Sawkins*[98] the police entered a public meeting on private premises, believing that if they were not present seditious speeches would be made, and incitements to violence would occur. They were requested to leave, but used mild force in order to remain, and this was held to be justified as an exercise of the power of the police to prevent crime at common law.

One reason given for the decision was that the police had a right to be at the meeting because it was advertised as a public meeting and the police were members of the public; but this was obviously fallacious. Ordinary members of the public could have been requested to leave. Another reason was that since the police could use force to prevent crime, they could, *a fortiori*, enter premises to prevent crime. The decision was, of course, unpalatable to civil libertarians, and its authority remained doubtful before the *Criminal Law Act 1967*; but the *Act* now seems to allow the use of force without restriction (save as to reasonableness), and therefore seems to allow force to be used to enter and remain on private property—whether a public meeting is taking place or not.

The *a fortiori* argument would suggest that if the police can fight their way in to private premises, then they can enter surreptitiously without force, if this is necessary to prevent crime; and that having entered they can, subject to the same restriction, blow open safes and copy private documents! But, as Pollock C.B. once said, "an argument can be pressed to an absurdity, as a bubble may be blown until it bursts."[99] It seems very unlikely that when Parliament passed the *Act* of 1967 it intended to allow the police to do a kind of "Watergate" for law-promoting reasons; or to sit in on a private meeting of an extreme political

---

[97] See *Blake v. D.P.P.* [1993] Crim. L.R. 586.
[98] [1935] 2 K.B. 249.
[99] *White v. Bluett* (1853) 23 L.J. Ex. 36.

group, merely because the police reasonably feared that seditious statements would be made. Hence, the better argument is that section 3 would not allow the police to remain on premises to prevent a crime, because passively entering and remaining on premises does not involve an exercise of force.[100] Nevertheless, the police might be able to remain in certain restricted circumstances to prevent an imminent breach of the peace.[101]

Suppose that an offence has been committed. What guidance does section 3 give in respect of the amount of force that can be used in making a "lawful arrest" for the crime that is not of great gravity?   When force is used to arrest, a distinction must be drawn between the resisting and the fleeing suspect—fleeing, that is, without violent resistance. Where the suspect flees, the officer's justification for the use of force rests exclusively on section 3(1). Hale lays it down as clear law that the officer may in the "last resort" use fatal force, irrespective of the crime for which he is arresting.[102] The legal result is that an officer endeavouring to effect an arrest is not obliged to back off, but may press forward against resistance, meeting the resistance with self-defence according to the usual rules, except that he is clearly under no duty to retreat. As the struggle gains in ferocity, and the officer is obliged to use more and more extreme measures against the offender if he is to avoid being disabled, the point is reached at which the officer comes to fear that he will himself suffer death or grave harm unless he retreats or uses extreme violence, and in such circumstances he may use that violence. The fact that section 3 and the right of defence act together in this way shows that the right of defence remains separate from section 3.

21–038

The abstract principles are the same as those already considered, and, once more, they give little help. Before the *Act* there was authority for saying that even a sneak thief (if a felon) could be shot in order to prevent the theft or prevent his escape.[103] But this was never beyond doubt; and anyway section 3 abolishes the common law. Nowadays the citizen would be ill advised to use a gun against a fleeing thief, at any rate if the theft is a minor one.

In a case before magistrates, the defendant fired at a man who, being surprised when attempting to break into his house, was running away; the intruder fell, and was discovered to be a notorious burglar whom the police had been seeking for ten years, and was rewarded by being fined for unlawful wounding.[104] The doubt concerning the law affects the police and the armed forces. The subsection requires the force used to be reasonable, which seems to mean that the harassed officer has to decide not only whether he has power to act and whether the force

---

[100] Cf. *Blake v. D.P.P.* [1993] Crim. L.R. 586, where it was held that writing protest messages on a wall did not involve force. In *Hutchinson v. D.P.P.* (*The Independent*, November 20, 2000), it was held cutting though a fence did not involve the use of force.

[101] *McLeod v. Commissioner of Police of the Metropolis* [1994] 4 All E.R. 553; *Addison v. Chief Constable of the West Midlands* [2004] 1 W.L.R. 29; *R. (on the application of Laporte) v. Chief Constable of Gloucestershire* [2007] 2 A.C. 105.

[102] Hale, *op. cit. supra* note at 78 at 117-118. Cf. Blackstone, *op. cit. supra*, note 83 at 179; Sir Michael Foster, *Crown Law*, (London: Printed by W. Strahan and M. Woodfall, 1776) at 270-271; James Fitzjames Stephen, *A History of The Criminal Law of England*, (London: MacMillan and Co., Vol. I, 1883) at 193. *Mackalley's Case* (1611) 77 E.R. 824 at 828; *R v. Simmonds* (1965) 9 W.I.R. 95.

[103] *R. v. Dadson* (1850) 175 E.R. 499. *Contra, R. v. Murphy* (1839) 1 Craw. & Dix. 20.

[104] 133 J.P.N. 337, 547.

he uses is necessary to stop the suspect in his tracks but in addition, and on the spur of the moment, a question of social values. In the past the police have been saved the difficulty of decision by the fact that they were unarmed; but nowadays if they are after armed people they are likely themselves to be armed.

21–039   The power to arrest is now found in section 24 of *Police and Criminal Evidence Act 1984*. Section 24 is governed by section 117 of the same *Act*, which provides:

> "Where any provision of this *Act*—(a) confers a power on a constable; and (b) does not provide that the power may only be exercised with the consent of some person, other than a police officer, the officer may use reasonable force, if necessary, in the exercise of the power."

Lethal force would have to be absolutely necessary[105] for it to be regarded as a "last resort" response.[106] The use of lethal force has to be balanced against the victim's right to life.[107] In *McCann v. United Kingdom*[108] it was held that the deprivation of a suspect's life would not be regarded as inflicted in contravention of Article 2 of the *European Convention for the Protection of Human Rights and Fundamental Freedoms*:[109]

> "[W]hen it results from the use of force which is no more than absolutely necessary:
> a.   in defence of any person from unlawful violence;
> b.   in order to effect a lawful arrest or to prevent the escape of a person lawfully detained;
> c.   in action lawfully taken for the purpose of quelling a riot or insurrection.
> The use of force which has resulted in a deprivation of life must be shown to have been 'absolutely necessary' for one of the purposes set out in the second paragraph. In the context of the other provisions of the Convention, the test of necessity includes an assessment as to whether the interference with the Convention right in question was proportionate to the legitimate aim pursued. In the context of Article 2 and the use of lethal force, the qualification of the word 'necessary' by the adverb 'absolutely' indicates that a stricter and more compelling test of necessity must be applied."

Where the offender is armed with a lethal weapon, the fatal point in the struggle may be reached quickly, the legal analysis of the situation being in no way affected. Nor is the legal position any different in theory where both parties are armed with firearms. In such circumstances the officer must, for his own protection, shoot first if the other shows any sign of reaching for his gun. If the suspect is being besieged and is armed, the police are frank that when they decide to shoot, they shoot to kill.[110] The law allows this, even though the result is that

---

[105] "In truth, if any officer reasonably decides that he must use lethal force, it will inevitably be because it is absolutely necessary to do so. To kill when it is not absolutely necessary to do so is surely to act unreasonably. Thus, the reasonableness test does not in truth differ from the Article 2 test as applied in *McCann v. United Kingdom* (1996) 21 E.H.R.R. 97:" *Bennett v. United Kingdom* (2011) 52 E.H.R.R. 101 at 106; the court went on to note at 117: "[T]he High Court and Court of Appeal were correct in stating that the domestic 'reasonableness' test effectively incorporated 'absolute necessity' standards". And at 118: there is "no sufficiently great difference between the English definition of self-defence and the 'absolute necessity' test for which art.2 provides."

[106] *Stewart v. United Kingdom* (1985) 7 E.H.R.R. CD453.

[107] *R. (on the application of Bennett) v. HM Coroner for Inner South London* [2006] H.R.L.R. 22; *McCann v. United Kingdom* (1996) 21 E.H.R.R. 97.

[108] (1996) 21 E.H.R.R. 97.

[109] 4 November 1950, 213 U.N.T.S. 222 (entered into force generally on 3 September 1953).

[110] Peter Kennison and Amanda Loumansky, "Shoot to Kill–Understanding Police use of Force in Combating Suicide Terrorism," (2007) 47(3) *Crime, Law and Social Change* 151.

the police bring back not the suspect but a corpse.[111] The duty is not merely to arrest but, if they cannot arrest a dangerous offender, to prevent him from continuing at liberty. Lethal force could only be used in the most exceptional cases.[112] It has to be remembered that a suspect is a suspect, not a convicted offender. In cases where the suspect poses a clear and immediate threat to others such as in a hostage or suicide bomber situation, lethal force would be permissible. Lethal force is used in these situations as a last resort to save innocent lives. The police have to recognize public opinion is sensitive on the use of guns by the police.[113]

These rules apply whether the suspect is presenting his face to the officer engaged in a "running fight," firing perhaps from the rear of a car.[114] Since the right to kill a resisting criminal depends upon the law of self-defence[115] combined with the officer's right to make a lawful arrest, it applies to all manner of lawful arrests and not merely to arrest for serious crimes. If a desperado, wanted on any ground, barricades himself with arms in a house he may be deliberately shot if that is the only way to quell his dangerous resistance.[116] Under section 18 of the *Offences against the Person Act 1861* it is a crime to wound to resist arrest, and, where this crime is committed or attempted, an additional ground is furnished for using force against the resisting criminal, even when his original crime was not of a character to justify the use of fatal force in arrest apart from resistance. The arrester, as soon as the weapon is used against him, may ignore the original charge and proceed to use force on the basis that he is arresting for the crime of attempting to wound to resist arrest. Always bearing in mind that the lethal force should only be used as a last resort, and only, where it is absolutely necessary.

The officer can reckon to be safe in shooting an escaping murderer or escaping terrorist or other violent offender if he fears immediate danger from him to himself or others.[117] But the law seems otherwise if he only fears possible danger in the future, or if he merely seeks to arrest for a past murder without fearing any danger from this offender for the future. It also seems clear that it would not be reasonable for an officer (when he cannot otherwise effect an arrest) to shoot or otherwise use deadly force against someone who has not used or threatened force but is going off with the proceeds of a burglary, or a Rolls Royce; or against one of the innumerable petty offenders that he has to deal with. The rule seems to be that the police are legally entitled to use fatal force to arrest terrorists, murders and others who pose an immediate threat of danger to the wider community. In

21–040

---

[111] *R. (on the application of Bennett) v. HM Coroner for Inner South London* [2006] H.R.L.R. 22.

[112] *McCann v. United Kingdom* (1996) 21 E.H.R.R. 97.

[113] See Rhona Smith, "Police, the Public, 'Less Lethal Force' and Suspects: Deconstructing the Human Rights Arguments," (2009) 82(3) *Police Journal* 194, noting "that mid-range 'less-lethal' weapons such as TASER stun guns and other electronic control devices (ECD)" could be used in many cases instead of lethal force to "incapacitate the suspect temporarily" thereby neutralizing the threat that he poses to the public.

[114] But the police could not lawfully shoot the passengers in a fleeing car where the occupants are unarmed and pose no danger other than that they will evade arrest for a driving offence. *Juozaitiene v. Lithuania* (2008) 47 E.H.R.R. 55.

[115] *R. (on the application of Bennett) v. HM Coroner for Inner South London* [2006] H.R.L.R. 22.

[116] *Bubbins v. United* Kingdom (2005) 41 E.H.R.R. 24.

[117] See Lord Diplock's restricted statement in *Attorney-General of Northern Ireland's Reference (No.1 of 1975)* [1977] A.C. 105 at 136D.

other cases, the police would be allowed to use necessary force short of the infliction of death or grievous bodily harm.

21.7.   DEFENCE AGAINST THE POLICE

21–041   The right of self-defence avails against the police, so the citizen is permitted (in theory) to use reasonable force against an officer to avoid being illegally arrested. He is not guilty of assaulting the officer in the execution of his duty for two separate reasons: the officer is not acting in the execution of his duty, and there is no assault.

The French have a doctrine of *rebellion*, according to which it is unlawful to resist a police officer even though he is acting illegally: the citizen must submit, and seek his remedy afterwards in the courts. But in Britain the normal right of self-defence exists, even where the only purpose of the defendant is to avoid being arrested[118] or detained,[119] and even where the police believe themselves to be acting in the execution of their duty (see 9.17), if in fact they are acting illegally.[120] Whether our rule is politic, or fair to the police, may be questioned;[121] but in practice, because the law relating to police power is so obscure, it gives people very little freedom to defy the police with safety.

21–042   **Can you use force against police officers after being arrested, to prevent them from taking liberties with you that they ought not take?**   Yes. Persons in custody have been upheld by the courts in forcibly resisting the taking of fingerprints outside statutory powers,[122] and the removal of a woman's brassiere without adequate cause.[123]

21–043   **How much force may you use against the police?**   The practical answer, as regards the attitude of some courts, is: "only force that is so mild as to be ineffective."

In the bra case, the defendant, resisting having the garment taken, scratched the policewoman's hand and kicked her knee. The Divisional Court, while allowing her appeal against a conviction of assaulting the officer in the execution

---

[118] *R. v. Mabel* (1840) 173 E.R. 918; *Kenlin v. Gardiner* [1967] 2 Q.B. 510; *Wood v. D.P.P.* [2008] EWHC 1056; cf. *Semple v. D.P.P.* [2011] P.T.S.R. 111.

[119] *R. v. Iqbal* [2011] 1 Cr. App. R. 317.

[120] Glanville Williams, "Requisites for a Valid Arrest," [1954] Crim. L.R. 6 at 8-11; *Townley v. Rushworth* (1963) 107 S.J. 1004. "If in fact acting illegally" includes cases where the courts invent a new rule *ex post facto*, making the conduct of the police illegal when there was no direct authority for saying so before. Conversely, if the courts suddenly invent new powers for the police, making resistance to them illegal when there was no previous authority in point.

[121] The ALI's Model Penal Code, POD section 3.04(2)(a), provides that "the use of force is not justifiable under this section to resist arrest which the actor knows is being made by a peace officer, although the arrest is unlawful." The Comment to the Tentative Draft says: "There ought not to be a privilege to employ force against a public officer who, to the actor's knowledge, is attempting only to arrest him and subject him to the process of law."

[122] *R. v. Jones* (1978) 67 Cr. App. R. 166.

[123] *Lindley v. Rutter* [1981] Q.B. 128; *Brazil v. Chief Constable of Surrey* [1983] 1 W.L.R. 1155; *Oscar v. Chief Constable of the Royal Ulster Constabulary* [1992] N.I. 290; see also *Secretary of State for the Home Department v. GG* [2010] Q.B. 585.

of her duty, said, *obiter*, that she was guilty of common assault on the officer because she (the defendant) had used more force than was necessary. This opinion was particularly strange because in fact the force used had been unavailing: the bra had been removed. Apparently the only lawful force, in the view of the court, was something less than that required to make the police desist from what they unlawfully wanted to do. (If a male officer removes a defendant's clothes and attempts to rape her, surely the defendant would be entitled to use whatever force is necessary to thwart the officer's unlawful attack.) Similarly, if an officer is brutally beating an innocent person who is caught up in a public protest, surely that person is entitled to respond with proportionate violence.

Such pronouncements on the question of necessity and reasonableness of force stultify the right of self-defence, and so are too absurd to be accepted with patience; but the issue of proportionality is difficult. A strongly-built man who tries to resist an illegal arrest by a single officer will very likely not succeed unless he inflicts some injury on the officer; and if he does, a judge might suggest to the jury that the infliction of injury on one who is known to be a police officer would be disproportionate to the evil involved in an illegal but temporary deprivation of liberty. Possibly the judge might even withdraw the defence from the jury, for reasons similar to those already discussed in relation to the prevention of crime. An attempt by the police merely to take an impression of fingerprints or to remove a bra might be regarded as justifying an even smaller degree of force in resisting. There is, therefore, a head-on clash between the idea that the citizen can use force to prevent illegal action against him by the police and the proportionality rule. In view of the obscurity of the law and the fact that courts are understandably reluctant to allow people to fight the police, the practical advice to everyone is not to do so unless the circumstances are exceptional such as where the police use excessive force.[124] The resister or passive passerby is likely to get the worse of it, one way or the other.[125]

Can you resist arrest on the ground that you are innocent, if you are innocent?   Not necessarily. Most powers of arrest are worded or interpreted in terms of reasonable suspicion (9.16). If the officer has reasonable grounds for suspecting that someone has committed a crime, the arrest is not made invalid by the suspect's innocence.   21–044

What if you resist arrest, believing the arrest to be unlawful when in fact it is lawful?   Ignorance of the criminal law is no excuse, and for this purpose the law of arrest (as well as the law of self-defence) is regarded as part of the criminal   21–045

---

[124] See Murray Wardrop and Richard Edwards, "G20 protests death: Ian Tomlinson shoved to ground by police officer, video shows," (London: *The Telegraph*, 07 Apr 2009), where it is reported: "Ian Tomlinson, the man who died during the G20 protests in London, was charged from behind and shoved to the ground by a police officer wielding a baton, damning video footage has shown." Mr. Tomlinson was not a protestor, but a humble labourer making his way home from work. Such victims, if not killed outright by the police, should be able to use necessary and proportionate force to stop this kind of police brutality.

[125] *Id.*

law,[126] for obvious reasons of policy. Hence a person who violently resists a lawful arrest believing it to be unlawful but not mistaking any fact can be convicted—even of the serious offence under section 18 of the *Offences against the Person Act 1861*.

This rule, which is inevitable, makes nonsense of the supposition that the right to resist an illegal arrest by the police is a valuable safeguard of liberty. So great is the complexity of the law that no wise person would resist arrest, even if he suspects it to be illegal, because he cannot be sufficiently sure of his opinion. The safest ground for resistance is that the officer has not stated the reason for the arrest.

21–046   **But you may use force against a person if you reasonably think he is a thug, although in fact he is a police officer who is properly trying to arrest you under a statutory power?**   Yes. Even if the plain-clothes officer tries to establish his status, the suspect may lawfully defend himself by force if he believes that the officer's claim to official status is a pretence.[127] On such facts, each party is lawfully permitted to use force against the other. This means that, as said before,[128] the offence of assault upon a constable in the exercise of his duty is one of full *mens rea* in respect of the assault element.[129] To this extent the defendant's ignorance of the officer's status can avail him.

21–047   **Suppose the arrest is lawful but the police officer uses unreasonable force. May the arrestee defend himself against the unreasonable force?**   In theory yes, to avoid being hurt. I say "in theory" because where there is a conflict in the evidence between a police officer and a citizen the officer tends to be believed. If therefore the defendant says that he was submitting to arrest but the officer aimed a blow at him, and that he only hit the officer to avoid being hit himself, while the officer denies the blow and says that the defendant was resisting arrest, the officer is likely to be believed in a magistrates' court, which does not wish to brand him a liar. There is more chance of an acquittal on a trial by jury. (The case would be different if there were plenty of eyewitness, or CCTV footage available.)

21–048   **If your friend has been arrested, may you wade in to rescue him provided you believe that the arrest is unlawful?**   Consider this chain of reasoning:

1.   Protective force may be used both against unlawful injury and against unlawful detention.
2.   It may be used on the facts as they appear to be.
3.   It may be used to protect third persons, at any rate one's child.
4.   It may be used against the police.

---

[126] *R. v. Bentley* (1850) Cox C.C. 406; *Agnew v. Jobson* (1877) 13 Cox C.C. 625; *The Queen v. Tolson* (1889) 23 Q.B.D. 168 at 188; *Gelberg v. Miller* [1961] 1 W.L.R. 153; cf. *R. v. Reid* [1973] 1 W.L.R. 1283 at 1289; *D.P.P. v. Fountain* [1988] R.T.R. 385; *R. v. Barrett* (1981) 72 Cr. App. R. 212 (mistake as to the validity of court process); *Hills v Ellis* [1983] Q.B. 680.
[127] *Kenlin v. Gardiner* [1967] 2 Q.B. 510; *R. v. Williams* (1984) 78 Cr. App. R. 276.
[128] 9.17.
[129] Cf. section 89 of the *Police Act 1996*.

Therefore protective force may be used by a person, if on the facts as he believes them to be this is necessary to prevent the unlawful detention of his child by the police.

All the premises in this argument are amply supported by authority, and the conclusion follows inexorably from them. But the Court of Appeal in *R. v. Fennell*[130] fractured two of the links leading to the conclusion, and so enabled itself to dodge the conclusion. The case is probably of small importance, and its chief interest is in showing how some judges will go to considerable lengths to evade the operation of settled legal principles for pragmatic reasons.

Fennell's son had been arrested for taking part at 11:15 p.m. in a street fight which took the police some time to stop. Fennell, protesting a belief in his son's innocence, told one of the officers that he would hit him unless his son was released. As the officer did not respond Fennell hit him on the jaw. Fennell was prosecuted for assault on the police constable, and it was argued in his defence that if he genuinely believed on reasonable grounds that the restraint of his son was unlawful he was justified in using reasonable force to free him. The proposition of law was rejected by the trial judge and on appeal; and Fennell was convicted.

Understandably, the judges did not relish the idea that a father could rescue his son from the police, but the problem was to escape from the precedents. The Court of Appeal improvised a solution by drawing a distinction within proposition 1, between injury and detention, for which there was no previous authority, and by curtailing proposition 2 so as to make the offence of assaulting a constable one of strict liability in respect for which there was again no previous authority. Widgery L.J.:[131]

21–049

> "It was accepted in the court below that if the arrest had been, in fact, unlawful the appellant would have been justified in using reasonable force to secure the release of his son. This proposition has not been argued before us and we will assume, without deciding it, that it is correct.... Where a person honestly and reasonably believes that he or his child is in imminent danger of injury it would be unjust if he were deprived of the right to use reasonable force by way of defence merely because he had made some genuine mistake of fact. On the other hand if the child is in police custody and not in imminent danger of injury there is no urgency of the kind which requires an immediate decision and a father who forcibly releases the child does so at his peril."

Therefore, since the detention of the son was lawful, the defendant's belief (even if reasonable) that the facts of the case made it unlawful was no defence.

As was said before, the earlier authorities held that the offence of assaulting a constable was not entirely of strict liability, but required *mens rea* in respect of the requirement of an assault. We now are told that it is of strict liability even in respect of the assault, if the defendant was acting against the police to free another person. But the court would apparently still allow a person to use force against the police to secure his own freedom from illegal detention,[132] and it would certainly allow a father to use force against the police to prevent them

---

[130] [1971] 1 Q.B. 428.
[131] *R. v. Fennell* [1971] 1 Q.B. 428 at 431.
[132] *R. v. Iqbal* [2011] 1 Cr. App. R. 317.

from illegally injuring his child.[133] In short, the exception made by this decision from the previous rules is directed exclusively to the facts of the particular case.

21–050 The problem that vexed the court could have been settled, without departing from the authorities, by a different line of reasoning. The argument that Fennell honestly and reasonably believed that the arrest was unlawful and therefore was justified in using force contained an ambiguity:

- If it meant that Fennell did not know the law of arrest, that was his look-out. We are supposed to know the law of arrest, or at least cannot take any advantage from not knowing it.
- If it meant that Fennell believed in facts that made the arrest unlawful, we must consider what those facts were. The police had a right to arrest on various grounds:
  o   at common law for breach of the peace committed in their presence;
  o   for assault occasioning actual bodily harm (if the police suspected him of that); this was punishable with five years' imprisonment and therefore was an arrestable offence.

These grounds of arrest certainly cover cases of reasonable even if mistaken suspicion. From this conclusion follows that to justify the attempted rescue it was necessary that Fennell should have believed either that the officer did not have reasonable grounds for suspecting that his son had committed these offences or that there were no facts that could give the officer reasonable grounds for suspicion. For Fennell to say: "I know my son was innocent" would, even if correct in fact, not exclude the possibility that the arrest was lawful. Now it is virtually impossible to credit a defence that the defendant knew or believed that the officer did not know or believe any fact that would create a reasonable suspicion against his son. The evidence in the case fell far short of establishing such a remarkable frame of mind on the part of Fennell. The appeal could have been dismissed on that ground.

It might be good policy to enact that no one is entitled to use force for the purpose of rescuing another from the custody of the police who act in the belief that they are within the law. But at present we have no such legislation, and on principle there is a right to rescue if the arrest is in fact unlawful or the police seem to be using excessive force. It is anomalous, therefore, to deny that operation of the usual *mens rea* principle in these circumstances. Nor is there any need to deny it, because it cannot advantage a would-be rescuer like Fennell.

---

[133] *R. v. Williams* (1984) 78 Cr. App. R. 276. Again, if the father mistakenly believed the police were using excessive force to arrest his son, he would be strictly liable for assault if he intervened. See *R. v. Ball* (1990) 90 Cr. App. R. 378. Ignorance of how much force the police are legally allowed to use would be no defence.

21.8.   DEFENCE OF LAND AGAINST TRESPASSERS

A person is entitled to use necessary and reasonable force in defence of **21–051** property.[134] He may use such force to prevent trespass or to eject trespassers, to re-enter upon land (subject to what is to be said in 21.10), and to defend and recapture chattels (21.11). For all these purposes the force must not only be the minimum necessary and reasonable to achieve the object but also (according to the older authorities) be moderate—that is, must fall short of the intentional or reckless infliction of death or grievous bodily harm.[135] There is an authority that holds that death may be inflicted in defence of a dwelling house (21.9), but this authority is probably no longer binding given the recent focus on reasonableness. (The defendant would have difficulty in showing that it was reasonable for him to kill in order to protect his dwelling *per se*.)

In *D.P.P. v. Bayer*[136] Brooke L.J. said:

> "[T]he statutory defence contained in section 5(2)(b) of the *Criminal Damage Act 1971* [provides a] person who commits what would otherwise be regarded as criminal damage [with] a statutory defence of 'lawful excuse': 'if he damaged ... the property in question ... in order to protect property belonging to ... another ... and at the time of the ... acts alleged to constitute the offence he believed—(i) that the property ... was in immediate need of protection; and (ii) that the means of protection adopted ... were ... reasonable having regard to all the circumstances.' ... The common law defence of defence of property has different ingredients. ... If the common law defence is raised ... a court should first ask itself: are the defendants contending that they used reasonable force in order to defend property from actual or imminent damage[137] which constituted or would constitute an unlawful[138] or criminal act? If the answer to this question is 'No', as in the present case, the defence is not available. If the answer is 'Yes', then the court must go on to consider the facts as the defendants honestly believed them to be, and should then determine objectively whether the force they used was no more than was reasonable in all the circumstances, given their beliefs."

It appears that the old restriction that the force be moderate no longer survives. The rule now appears to be simply that any force used in defence of property be reasonable, which means the jury are left to decide generally whether the force was necessary and reasonable, *i.e.* proportionate. But, on principle, the judge retains the power to withdraw the defence from the jury if it is not supported by evidence on which a reasonable jury could act.

---

[134] Including trespassers on a vehicle, like a ship: *Canadian Pacific Railway v. Gaud* [1949] 2 K.B. 239; a person may also inflict actual bodily harm upon a trespasser to eject her from a motorcar if he has not promised that she can remain for a certain purpose: *R. v. Burns* [2010] 1 W.L.R. 2694.

[135] The well known case on the limitation is *R. v. Moir* (1828) Roscoe, Cr. Ev. (16th edn.) cited in J. W. C. Turner, *Russell On Crime*, (London: Steven & Sons, 12th edn., 1964) at 441. See also *Wild's Case* (1837) 168 E.R. 1132; *Taylor v. Mucklow* (1973) 117 S.J. 792.

[136] [2004] 1 W.L.R. 2856 at 2864.

[137] There is no requirement that there be a threat of damage—a trespasser does not necessarily damage property by trespassing. Nor does he necessarily damage chattels by unlawfully holding them for ransom.

[138] "Unlawful" means that civil wrongs such as trespass are covered. See *R. v. Pratt* (1855) 119 E.R. 319; *Taylor v. Jackson* (1898) 78 L.T. 555; *Harrison v. Duke of Rutland* [1893] 1 Q.B. 142; *R. v. Jones and Smith* [1976] 1 W.L.R. 672. In some jurisdictions, trespass is a criminal offence *per se*. See *Giddings v. Director of Public Prosecutions (N.S.W.)* (2008) 181 A. Crim. R. 536, where there was no criminal trespass, so the defence was not available.

21–052 **Must the owner ask the trespasser to leave before forcibly ushering him out?** The requirement that any force be necessary and reasonable means that the trespasser must be asked to leave (or to desist from an attempted entry), and a reasonable time allowed for compliance, before force is used against him, for otherwise it is not clear that force is necessary. That the occupier must first require the trespasser to leave or desist is not an inflexible rule of law (though it is often said to be):[139] if the trespasser is evidently determined to use force to enter, reasonable force may be used to expel him without any words being uttered.

21–053 **What if the trespasser fights back?** The occupier (or person acting under his authority) may go on using necessary and reasonable force. It seems clear that it would not be reasonable or necessary for the defendant to escalate to extreme force for his own safety, if he can avoid the necessity by allowing the trespasser to remain.[140]

21–054 **What if the person was not a trespasser but the occupier thought he was?** The law of trespass and title to land is regarded as belonging to the civil law, not the criminal law, and a mistake as to it can be a defence. So, if the occupier believes that the person ejected is a trespasser, he commits no offence. In *R. v. Burns*,[141] the defendant's mistake of civil law was overlooked. D thought he had a right to eject a prostitute from his motorcar. The Court of Appeal held that he had no right to eject the prostitute from his car in the middle of nowhere, because he had promised to return her to the place where he had picked her up. Lord Judge C.J. said:[142]

> "(1) Recognising that to be lawful the use of force must always be reasonable in the circumstances, we accept that it might be open to the owner of a vehicle, in the last resort and when all reasonably practicable alternatives have failed, forcibly to remove an individual who has entered into his vehicle without permission and refuses to leave it. However, where that individual entered the car as a passenger, in effect at the invitation of the car owner, on the basis that they mutually understood that when their dealings were completed she would be driven back in the car from whence she had come, the use of force to remove her at the appellant's unilateral whim, was unlawful.
> (2) In any event, the resort to self-help was not justified in the circumstances of this case because the appellant could readily have regained exclusive possession to his vehicle by means not involving the use of force, that is, by simply driving the complainant back to the starting point."

The reference to unlawful in the first point refers to civil unlawfulness. If the Court of Appeal was right in holding that Burns had no civil law right to eject the prostitute,[143] Burns mistaken belief that he did was a mistake of civil law. On the

---

[139] David Lanham, "Defence of Property in Criminal Law," [1966] Crim. L.R. 368 at 372.
[140] Cf. *R. v. Faraj* [2007] 2 Cr. App. R. 322.
[141] [2010] 1 W.L.R. 2694.
[142] [2010] 1 W.L.R. 2694 at 2698.
[143] It is not clear that civil law requires a person to return a prostitute to the exact location from where he took her from, even if he has promised to do so. Some of the old licensee cases suggest that a person need not leave premises until he has started to misbehave: *Howell v. Jackson* (1834) 172 E.R. 1435; *Constantine v. Imperial London Hotels* [1944] K.B. 693; *Sealey v. Tandy* [1902] 1 K.B. 296. But a licence to enter premises (including a motor vehicle) based in contract (if the contract between

other hand if the occupier mistakenly believes that he is entitled to shoot the trespasser he does commit an offence in shooting, because the limits of the power to eject trespassers are part of the criminal law. These limits are stated in the rule that any force must be necessary and reasonable.

On the second point concerning necessity, Lord Judge C.J. was right to hold that the force was not necessary, because Burns could have got the prostitute out of his car by returning her to where he found her, as he promised to do. The latter was not such a burdensome step that it made the ejection necessary.

Can the occupier of property who is pestered by a trespasser ask a police officer to help him? Traditionally, the police do not generally assist in the eviction of trespassers, because they see this as a civil matter. Sometimes, however, they do so: they may eject trouble-makers from a football ground, acting on behalf of management. Section 143 of the *Licensing Act 2003* makes it a criminal offence not to leave licensed premises when "drunk or disorderly and requested to leave by the licence holder, specified members of staff, or a police constable."[144] This saves them time: if they arrested offenders, they would have to go to the station with them. **21–055**

Could a student evict a trespasser from his college room, or from his room in lodgings? Primarily, the right of defence of property is given to the occupier (possessor). It seems, however, that even a licensee of land (like the student in your question) can eject trespassing strangers,[145] though he cannot eject the occupier or someone permitted to be there by the occupier.[146] **21–056**

Where actual damage to property is apprehended, it is possible that even a stranger might defend it on the owner's behalf against a wrong-doer. As we shall see,[147] the *Criminal Damage Act 1971* allows anyone to damage property in defence of the property of another (killing a marauding dog in defence of a neighbour's sheep),[148] and there is no good reason why the use of force against a human being should not be allowable on the same ground. A dog might also be shot dead in defence of a human, if it is attacking a person.[149]

Since we are in the area of judge-made law, the judges can go on making up new rules. It has been held that where a statutory body has the legal right to enter

---

the prostitute and the punter is not void for illegality), would allow the occupier to eject anyone at anytime without giving any reasons: see *Cowell v. Rosehill Racecourse Co. Ltd.* (1937) 56 C.L.R. 605; *Heatley v. Tasmanian Racing and Gaming Commission* (1977) 137 C.L.R. 487 at 506. I am not convinced that the punter was lawfully required to return the prostitute to the location from where he took her. He certainly had a moral obligation to return her, but that was all. If he had left her completely stranded, perhaps he could have been convicted of false imprisonment. The latter would not be easy to establish, however (see 9.14).

[144] *Semple v. D.P.P.* [2011] P.T.S.R. 111. See also *Porter v. The Commissioner of Police for the Metropolis* (1999) 1999 WL 852129 (unreported).

[145] *Hall v. Davis* (1825) 172 E.R. 16; cf. *R. v. Tao* [1977] Q.B. 141.

[146] *Dean v. Hogg* (1824) 131 E.R. 937. One joint occupier cannot eject another, even if he is making a nuisance of himself; but see the *dictum* in *Holmes v. Bagge* (1853) 118 E.R. 629.

[147] 35.6.

[148] It must be shown that it was necessary to kill the dog. If the dog has fled this will not be the case. See *Wright v. Ramscot* (1666) 85 E.R. 93; *Cresswell v. Sirl* [1948] 1 K.B. 241. See also section 9(1)(a) of *The Animals Act 1971* (a tort statute).

[149] *Morris v. Nugent* (1836) 173 E.R. 252.

land for a specified purpose, it can use the force reasonably necessary to remove demonstrators who try to obstruct its operations.[150]

21–057 **Can a trespasser be detained until he gives his name and address?** The answer to your question is in the negative. Trespass is not generally a crime, and the landowner's remedy is supposed to be to sue for damages in tort; but the law does not enable him to find out who the trespasser is. This proposition was overlooked in *R. v. Bow*.[151] A gamekeeper found Bow and other men on a private estate in the early hours armed with air rifles. Reasonably suspecting them of poaching, he blocked their escape with his Land Rover, driving it across the lane. (The report does not specify, but presumably this lane was a private road on the estate.) Bow got into the Land Rover, released the hand-brake and cruised down the lane to a spot where he could pull off the lane. He and his companions then made off in their own car. Bow was convicted of taking a conveyance under section 12(1) of the *Theft Act 1968*, and the conviction was affirmed on appeal, the court holding that it was immaterial that Bow's purpose was to remove an obstruction to his own exit.

This is a disappointingly simple-minded manner of interpreting penal legislation, which one would have hoped the courts had outgrown. The statute was not passed to prevent people removing cars that were obstructing, and it was a sharp interpretation to say that Bow had committed a "taking" in this case. Moreover, there was the question of implied exceptions from the offence. All such legislation should be read, *prima facie*, as subject to the general law allowing excuses or justifications, and it is not good enough to affirm a conviction merely by saying, as the court did, that "motive is immaterial." If the motive is to do a lawful act, it can be material. The gamekeeper might have arrested the men under section 31 of the *Game Act 1831*,[152] and his obstruction of the lane would then have been lawful as part of the arrest; but he did not say that he was making an arrest. That being so, one would have thought that he had no right in law to prevent them from making an exit by driving out. Perhaps Bow should have asked the gamekeeper to move the Land Rover before doing so himself, but since the gamekeeper was evidently determined not to do so, Bow's failure to make the request should not have been sufficient to convict him of the offence. His moving the vehicle should have been justified by necessity. Putting aside mere matters of prejudice, the case was a simple one in which A drives his car to a spot and leaves it there for the sole purpose of blocking B's exit. To hold that B commits an offence in moving it in order to get out is astonishing. Even if the court failed to find any justification for Bow's act, there was the question of excuse: the statute explicitly makes belief in lawful authority a defence.

21–058 **Can one set up static deterrents such as man-traps?** The former practice of setting spring guns or man-traps to injure trespassers is specifically prohibited by

---

[150] *R. v. Chief Constable of Devon and Cornwall Ex p. Central Electricity Generating Board* [1981] 3 W.L.R. 967 at 975E, 977F, 982G.

[151] [1977] R.T.R. 6.

[152] Provided that they had refused to give their name and address.

statute, unless they are set in a dwelling house between sunset and sunrise.[153] The general answer, therefore, is that man-traps are unlawful. Even traps not mentioned in the statute are unlawful. If, for example, a shopkeeper rigs up a device to electrocute intruders, and someone is killed by it, this is manslaughter.[154]

But what about the exception? Is it lawful to set a man-trap in a dwelling house at night?   The section does not positively authorize the setting of infernal machines in a dwelling house at night, but merely says that nothing in the section shall make such an act unlawful. It is still possibly open to argument that one who sets such a machine in a dwelling house at night, with the result that an intruder is killed, is guilty of manslaughter, or, if the intruder is grievously injured, is guilty of the crime of wounding with intent under section 18 of the *Offences against the Person Act 1861*. Similarly, such a person might be convicted of malicious wounding under section 20, or of an assault occasioning actual bodily harm under section 47.[155] Unlawfully giving someone an electric shock is the offence of administering a noxious thing,[156] so an electrocution device could result in liability on this score.

21–059

This is an area where the law is quite capable of clashing with public opinion. There would be little public sympathy for the landowner who is punished when he sets horrible traps for small-time poachers. But what if a person who has been plagued by repeated burglaries booby-traps his premises with an explosive device and gives full notice of it? (In France, where one thief was killed and his companion lost an eye as a result of such a device, set in such circumstances, a petition bearing thousands of signatures was organized to protest against the property-owner being prosecuted.)[157]

What about revolving spikes and guard dogs?   The rule at common law can probably be said to be that things like spikes or broken glass on walls are lawful as devices to deter trespasses if they are not likely to cause serious injury and if the device is stationary and visible in ordinary daylight and its use is otherwise reasonable in the circumstances.[158] Revolving spikes might quite possibly be held to be unreasonable; they may perhaps be held to be reasonable to prevent burglaries but perhaps not simple trespass. Keeping a dog for defence of property

21–060

---

[153] Section 31 of the *Offences against the Person Act 1861*. The law relating to the duty to give a name and address is in a highly defective condition. See Glanville Williams, "Demanding Name and Address," (1950) 66 *L.Q.R.* 465.

[154] In *R. v. Pratt* (*The Times*, 9 October 1976), the defendant pleaded guilty to manslaughter on such facts and received a suspended sentence.

[155] *R. v. Cockburn* [2008] Q.B. 882.

[156] *R. v. Donald* (*The Times*, 1955).

[157] *The Times*, 27 April 1978. Public attitudes do not seem to have changed much in the last few decades. More recently, there was a public outcry when a farmer was convicted for shooting a burglar in the back. See generally, Michael Jefferson, "House-holders and the Use of Force against Intruders," (2005) 69 *J. Crim. L.* 405 at 407.

[158] *R. v. Cockburn* [2008] Q.B. 882.

is time-hallowed,[159] but it would not be lawful to train a dog to be unreasonably solicitous of your interests (gripping an intruder by the throat). The owner of the dog would become guilty of one of the usual crimes (such as manslaughter) on principles relevant to them. In addition, there are special statutory provisions for keeping guard dogs under full control.[160] (Guard dogs in private homes or on agricultural land are exempt.)

21.9. DEFENCE OF THE DWELLING

21–061   The law has always looked with special indulgence on a man who is defending his dwelling against those who would unlawfully evict him. When necessary, he may even go as far as to take a life, for "the house of everyone is to him as his castle and fortress."[161] This ancient rule was reaffirmed by the Court of Appeal in *R. v. Hussey*,[162] when, remarkably, it was assumed to give a tenant the right to shoot a lessor (his landlady) who had given him notice to quit that happened to be invalid.[163] The landlady evidently thought that the notice was valid, and so (as the tenant must have known) thought she had a legal right to enter the premises to evict the tenant. Hussey did not fear death or injury; he simply faced eviction. It seems extraordinary that the right to shoot should have been extended to these circumstances. The decision in *R. v. Hussey* has been criticized, but if the doctrine of precedent retains any force it represents the law. It appears it will not be followed, because the courts now require defensive force in the dwelling context to be reasonable. "The householder must honestly believe that he needs to [use force] and must do so in a way which is reasonable." [164]

The condition is important: we have observed several instances of modern courts rewriting the law to suit their own opinions, and no one would be well

---

[159] See section 5(3)(b) of the *Animals Act 1971*; this is a tort statute recognizing the right to keep a dog in reasonable circumstances for protection against trespassers. See *Cummings v. Grainger* [1976] Q.B. 397.

[160] Section 1 of the *Guard Dogs Act 1975*. Cf. *Hobson v. Gledhill* [1978] 1 W.L.R. 215; *Kelly v. D.P.P.* [2008] EWHC 597 (Admin).

[161] This proverbial remark is in *Semayne's Case* (1604) 77 E.R. 194 at 195. The rule as stated in the text above is not laid down in that case, but it goes back to Bracton. See Henry Bracton, *On the Laws and Customs of England*, (Cambridge MA: Belknap Press of Harvard University Press, translated by Samuel E. Thorne, 1968) at 372. The rule is supported by the older authorities: *Cooper's Case* (1639) 79 E.R. 1069 (holding: "A master, lodger, or sojourner in a house, who kills a person breaking into it with intent to commit burglary or homicide, are exempt from guilt by 24 Hen. 8. c. 5."); *Cook's Case* (1639) 79 E.R. 1063 (holding: "To kill a sheriff's officer voluntarily while he is attempting to break into a house for the purpose of executing civil process, is man-slaughter, and not murder; for it is not lawful to break open doors for such purpose, and every man has a right to defend his own house."). See also Michael Foster, *Crown Law*, (London: Printed by W. Strahan and M. Woodfall, 1776) at 298. Many U.S. states have put the castle doctrine into statutory form. See Catherine L. Carpenter, "Of the Enemy within, the Castle Doctrine, and Self-Defence," (2003) 86 *Marq. L. Rev.* 653; Christine Catalfamo, "Stand Your Ground: Florida's Castle Doctrine for the Twenty-First Century," (2007) 4 *Rutgers J. L. & Pub. Pol'y* 504. Some of the U.S. statutes effectively give the householder a licence to kill.

[162] (1925) 18 Cr. App. R. 160.

[163] It is doubtful that the defence would apply if the defendant knew that the landlady was lawfully evicting him. See *Williams v. State*, 41 So. 992 (1906).

[164] *R. v. Faraj* [2007] 2 Cr. App. R. 322 at 328.

advised to act on the assumption that *R. v. Hussey* would now be followed. Further support for not following the ancient law can be found in the right to life jurisprudence.[165] Lethal force would only be necessary and reasonable if it were used to prevent an intruder from seriously injuring the occupants. "The theory of using deadly force to protect one's dwelling is not for the protection of the physical dwelling itself; rather, it is for the protection of the individuals therein."[166]

In the Irish Court of Criminal Appeal decision in *D.P.P. v. Barnes*,[167] Hardman J. said:

> "This court wishes to make it clear, in the absence of other express Irish authority to this effect, that to the extent that the common law permitted the killing of a burglar by a householder simply for being a burglar, and no matter what the other circumstances, it no longer does so in this jurisdiction. It has not done so for at least 70 years. Many social and historical reasons could be cited to support this conclusion but in reality it is unnecessary to cite more than one: the Constitution of Ireland. This provides at Article 40.3.1: 'The State guarantees in its laws to respect, and, as far as practicable, by its laws to defend and vindicate the personal rights of the citizen.' ... It seems an elementary proposition, in the light of such provisions, that a person cannot lawfully lose his life simply because he trespasses in the dwelling-house of another with intent to steal. In as much as the State itself will not exact the forfeiture of his life for doing so, it is ridiculous to suggest that a private citizen, however outraged, may deliberately kill him simply for being a burglar."

Nowadays it is virtually unknown for anyone to be evicted from a dwelling house except by someone who thinks he has some sort of right to do so, and public policy pretty clearly indicates that the occupier should have no right to use extreme force against such an evictor even though the eviction is illegal. However, it is not uncommon in modern times for burglars to be caught in the act by residents. Abolition of the right to shoot to kill burglars would not affect the right to shoot by an occupier who fears that the burglar is intent on killing him or causing him serious injury. However, such an occupier would have no right to shoot a fleeing burglar in the back.[168] Nor could he shoot a burglar without trying to defuse the situation by threatening the burglar and demanding that he get out of the premises. If the burglar becomes violent, then the normal rules of self-defence would be activated.

21–062

The courts are likely to hold that lethal or extreme force is only justified where the defendant acts to defend himself or his family from personal injury. The normal private and public defence rules are likely to be applied. The courts will

---

[165] *Bennett v. United Kingdom* (2011) 52 E.H.R.R. 101.

[166] *People v. Morris*, 516 N.E.2d 412 (1987). In most U.S. states a person is allowed to use extreme force including fatal force to prevent someone from entering his home, if he believes that the trespasser is trying to gain entry to kill or seriously injure the occupants: *People v. Eckert*, 919 P.2d 962 (1996); *Falco v. State*, 407 So. 2d 203 (1981); *People v. McNeese*, 892 P.2d 304 (1995); *Crawford v. State*, 190 A.2d 538 (1963); *Lester v. State*, 862 So. 2d 582 (2004); *State v. Lyons*, 459 S.E.2d 770 (1995); *State v. Pellegrino*, 577 N.W.2d 590 (1998); *People v. Sizemore*, 69 Mich. App. 672 (1976). If the trespasser gains entry, as a general rule the normal rules of private defence apply. *State v. Marshall*, 414 S.E.2d 95 (1992). Even though the normal rules of self-defence apply once the intruder has gained entry, there is "no duty of retreat cast upon one attacked in his own home." *State v. Brookshire*, 353 S.W.2d 681 (1962); *State v. Ivicsics*, 604 S.W.2d 773 (1980); *State v. Bottenfield*, 692 S.W.2d 447 (1985).

[167] [2007] 3 I.R. 130 at 146-147.

[168] See *R. v. Martin* [2003] Q.B. 1; *People v. Torres*, 645 N.E.2d 1018 (1995).

require any force used to defend a dwelling to be necessary and proportionate. But the courts will probably hold that those confronted in their own dwelling have a right to stand their ground even when they could easily flee. To ask a person to flee his own home would place undue burden on his liberty. Therefore, if a person stands his ground and uses proportionate force to thwart an attack from an intruder, he should be able to rely on private defence or the section 3 defence. It is irrelevant that force was not "necessary" in the sense that he could have easily fled from his own home and thereby avoided the conflict.

21–063 **Suppose the defender sees an armed burglar approaching his house. Suppose also that the defender could easily escape from a back window and call the police on his mobile telephone, but decides to stay to defend his property. If the defender ends up in a struggle with the intruder and kills him to save his own life, will the defence of self-defence be available?** Your defender's lethal force seems to have been necessary and proportionate. It was only "unnecessary" in the sense that he could have escaped from his dwelling and thereby avoided the need to defend himself.[169] But he stood his ground as he was entitled to do and therefore found it necessary to act to save his own life. A man, said Cardozo J., "is under no duty to take to the fields and the highways, a fugitive from his own home."[170] The proposition that a person who is attacked in his own home is not bound to run away is a qualification upon the general rule that the defence is limited to acts of necessity. Another qualification is that a person is entitled to reject an unlawful demand. If V says to D: "If you don't do as I tell you I will kill you," D is clearly entitled to refuse to obey the order and to resist any consequent attack upon him by V, even though he could have avoided the necessity of self-defence by complying with the order.

Where an occupier is faced (especially at night) with an unknown intruder who may inflict serious injury on himself or his family, he will readily be understood to have feared injury, and will be likely to be thought justified in resisting with any necessary and proportionate force, even to the extent of using a lethal weapon. However, no more than reasonable force may be used against a gate-crasher at a party, say. The mere fact that the trespasser is in a dwelling-house does not justify the infliction of excessive injury.

---

[169] *R. v. Frankum* (*The Times*, 11 May 1972) where Cusack J. directed the acquittal of a householder who fatally stabbed a drunkard who was endeavouring to break in at night. See also *R. v. Faraj* [2007] 2 Cr. App. R. 322, where it was held that one could imprison a suspected burglar to ascertain his identity.

[170] *People v. Tomlins*, 213 N.Y. 240 (1914). See also *People v. Jones*, 788 N.Y.S.2d 651 (2004), where the defender killed his much smaller girlfriend in their shared apartment. It was held that the "Statutory exception to duty to retreat before responding to deadly force in kind, where one is attacked at home, applies when the assailant and the defender share same dwelling." (A battered woman would have no duty to retreat from her own home, but she should have to prove that her force was necessary to prevent imminent harm.) In *D.P.P. v. Barnes* [2007] 3 I.R. 130 at 150 it was said: "It is, in our view, quite inconsistent with the constitutional doctrine of the inviolability of a dwelling-house that a householder or other lawful occupant could ever be under a legal obligation to flee the dwelling-house or, as it might be put in more contemporary language, to retreat from it. It follows from this, in turn, that such a person can never be in a worse position in point of law because he has decided to stand his ground in his house."

21.10.   RE-ENTRY UPON LAND

The general principle at common law is that a person may use moderate force **21–064**
when exercising a right of re-entry on land (including buildings). This principle,
however, is qualified by section 6(2) of the *Criminal Law Act 1977*, which
extends the offence of violence for securing entry to cover even those who have a
right to possession of the premises. The owner of a factory is therefore forbidden
to use violence to eject workers who are engaged in a sit-in. The offence does not
extend to those who have a right of entry not based on an interest or right to
possession or occupation of the premises (so it does not affect rights of entry
possessed by the police), nor to the displaced residential occupier of the
premises.[171] This means that a person who has been wrongfully evicted from his
dwelling (that is, from any house, flat, room, caravan, *etc.* in which he was living)
can still exercise his right of re-entry to the same extent as at common law; but a
landlord cannot use violence to expel his tenant at the end of the tenancy, unless
the landlord wishes to live in the house himself.[172]

The upshot is that the displaced residential occupier[173] and those acting on his
behalf can use necessary and reasonable force to effect a re-entry.[174] The right
probably exists even though the wrongful possessor is known to be acting under a
claim of right.[175] But he in turn is probably entitled to defend the possession
which he believes himself entitled;[176] so blows may be exchanged without either
party being criminally liable for them.

21.11.   THE PROTECTION OF MOVABLES

Necessary and reasonable force may be used to prevent unlawful damage to **21–065**
movables (chattels), or to prevent their dispossession.[177] The requirement of
moderation would certainly be stressed if the attacker is known to be acting

---

[171] See sections 6(1A) and 12(3) of the *Criminal Act 1977*.

[172] See section 12A of the *Criminal Law Act 1977*. The use of force by a landlord without a court order is also an offence under section 1 of the *Protection from Eviction Act 1977*. Cf. *R. v. Davidson-Acres* [1980] Crim. L.R. 50; *Haniff v. Robinson* [1993] Q.B. 419. It seems that an owner who forcibly enters property in breach of the *Criminal Law Act 1977* or the *Rent Act 1977* could be charged with an offence against the person instead of an offence under those *Acts*. The *Acts* have not, however, abrogated the common law right of forcible entry. In *Secretary of State for the Environment, Food and Rural Affairs v. Meier* [2009] 1 W.L.R. 2780 at 2788-2789, Baroness Hale said: "In considering the nature and scope of any judicial remedy, the parallel existence of a right of self-help against trespassers must not be forgotten, because the rights protected by self-help should mirror the rights that can be protected by judicial order, even if the scope of self-help has been curtailed by statute. No civil wrong is done by turning out a trespasser using no more force than is reasonably necessary: see *Hemmings v Stoke Poges Golf Club Ltd.* [1920] 1 K.B. 720."

[173] Section 6 of the *Criminal Law Act 1977* provides an exception for a "displaced residential occupier" or "protected intending occupier": section 6(1A) as inserted by section 72(2) of the *Criminal Justice and Public Order Act 1994*.

[174] *McPhail v. Persons, Names Unknown* [1973] Ch. 447 at 456.

[175] On the analogy of *Blades v. Higgs* (1865) 144 E.R. 1087; *R. v. Hussey* (1925) 18 Cr. App. R. 160.

[176] Glanville Williams, *Criminal Law: The General Part*, (London: Stevens & Sons, 2nd edn., 1961) at §115 at note 20.

[177] *Green v. Goddard* (1704) 91 E.R. 540; *Russell v. State*, 219 Ala. 567 (1929).

honestly (under a claim of right). If the attacker is a would-be robber, extreme force may be used under section 3 of the *Criminal Law Act 1967* if it is reasonable in the circumstances.

In *Blades v. Higgs*,[178] the House of Lords accepted the unseemly proposition that an owner of goods may use force to recover them from a wrongful possessor, even though that possessor was a shopkeeper who had paid for the goods. The Supreme Court of New South Wales adopts a more civilized principle that force in recaption may be used only against one who took by way of trespass;[179] the *bona fide* purchaser (or *mala fide donee*, for that matter) must be sued if he is to be made to give up the goods.[180]

21.12.   ABATEMENT OF NUISANCE

21–066   Another form of self-help is abatement of nuisance, as where a member of the public removes an obstruction from the highway. The right extends even to a private nuisance, where there is an obstruction to a private right of way.[181] Presumably there is a right to use reasonable force to get past a person who is deliberately obstructing a highway or other way.[182] Lord Denning M.R. put the law even more widely:

> "Every person who is prevented from carrying out his lawful pursuits is entitled to use self-help, so as to prevent any unlawful obstruction."[183]

This proposition goes beyond the decisions, but it is a useful principle that might well be developed. In any case the law of abatement of nuisance can perhaps be supplemented by the defence of necessity.

---

[178] (1865) 144 E.R. 1087. See also *R. v. Milton* (1827) 173 E.R. 1097; *Abbott v. New South Wales Mont de Piete Company* (1904) 4 SR (NSW) 336; *Janson v. Brown* (1807) 170 E.R. 869.

[179] Cf. *Toyota Finance Australia Ltd. v. Dennis* [2002] N.S.W.C.A. 369, where Sheller J.A., Meagher J.A. (in the Court of Appeal of the Supreme Court of New South Wales, providing a detailed analysis of the issue in a 55 page judgment) held that: "where the chattel was taken by a trespass 'there is clear authority that the owner is entitled to use such force as is reasonably necessary to wrest control of the chattel from the trespasser...' The right of seizure of chattels using reasonable force is limited to situations of wrongful appropriation." See also *R. v. Mitchell* [2004] R.T.R. 14.

[180] An approach long adopted in Canada. See *Devoe v. Long* [1951] 1 D.L.R. 203; *J.J. Riverside Manufacturing Ltd. v. E.J.W. Development Co.* [1981] 5 W.W.R. 607.

[181] A public nuisance is a crime as well as (in some cases) a tort, whereas a private nuisance is only a tort except where it is made a specific statutory offence. *R. v. Rimmington* [2006] 1 A.C. 459.

[182] *Beatty v. Gillbanks* (1881-82) 9 Q.B.D. 308.

[183] *R. v. Chief Constable of Devon and Cornwall Ex p. Central Electricity Generating Board* [1982] Q.B. 458 at 470.

CHAPTER 22

LOSS OF CONTROL

"Reason only controls individuals after emotion and impulse have lost their impetus."

Carlton Simon

22.1.   THE SCOPE OF THE DEFENCE

The old partial defence of "provocation"[1] has been replaced with a new defence   **22–001**
of "loss of control."[2] Section 56(7) of the *Coroners and Justice Act 2009* holds
that: "A person who, but for [the partial defence of loss of control], would be
liable to be convicted of murder is liable instead to be convicted of
manslaughter." The *Coroners and Justice Act 2009* recast the law, largely as a
result of recommendations made by the Law Commission.[3] (All references in this
chapter are to this *Act*, unless the contrary is expressed or clearly implied.) If the
defence is made out, the killing will be treated as a case of voluntary
manslaughter. It is *voluntary* manslaughter because the killer intends to kill. His
act of killing is voluntary and intentional. All the elements of the offence of
murder will be made out.

Many intentional killings of adult males are in rage or quarrel, in jealously and
revenge. The two emotions involved are anger and fear. Anger clearly comes
within the domain of the law of "loss of control," but fear seems to fall in the
domain of the law of private defence. Nevertheless, there may be rare cases
where fear could cause a person to lose control. For example, a women suffering
from battered woman's syndrome might kill her abuser because she is terrified
about the prospect of facing a further beating. The new partial defence pays more
attention to fear than the old defence of provocation did. A loss of control that
results from "anger" provides the defendant with a partial excuse, because he
would not have acted as he did if the anger had not prevented him from
controlling his behaviour. A loss of control that results from "fear" might also
provide the defendant with an excuse for the same reason, but also seems to

---

[1] For a detailed study of the former partial defence of provocation see Jeremy Horder, *Provocation and Responsibility*, (Oxford: Clarendon Press, 1992); for a discussion of the defence's rationale, see Mitchell N. Berman and Ian P. Farrell, "Provocation Manslaughter as a Partial Justification and Partial Excuse," (2011) 52 *Wm. & Mary L. Rev.* 1027.

[2] Section 56 of the *Coroners and Justice Act 2009*.

[3] Law Commission, *Partial Defences to Murder*, (London: H.M.S.O, Law Com. No.290 (2004); Law Commission, *Murder, Manslaughter and Infanticide*, (London: H.M.S.O., Law Com. No.304, 2006).

provide a justification. It is justificatory to the extent that it is necessary for the battered woman to kill to prevent herself from being killed or seriously injured.

It is worth asserting at the outset that this defence should have been abrogated.[4] It is extraordinary that this defence survives in the 21st century. Most criminality could be said to be linked to a loss of control. The kleptomaniac cannot control himself, nor can the greedy thief who is not a kleptomaniac. The majority of violent offending results from a loss of control: how many criminals regret their criminal violence with the benefit of hindsight? Many I suspect. Coupled with this, the great majority of people are able to control themselves even when they are enraged. Many victims of adultery, theft, criminal vandalism, slander, violence and so on fly into a rage when they discover they have been wronged, but manage to control their anger. The criminal law should not offer a concession to those who are unable to control their actions, because they pose a great threat to others.

22–002   The defence would have been abrogated in its entirety, if academics had not drawn attention to the plight of battered women who kill out of desperation. It was argued that a partial defence was needed to cover battered women who may lose control slowly rather than suddenly. This argument gained traction because society has failed to find a way to protect such women. The reality is that the criminal law is unable to protect a small minority of battered women who are effectively left with no option but to kill their abuser. This is an important consideration, but I am not convinced that the new defence provides an apt solution. Battered women kill to avoid further violence, not because they have lost control. "Fear" is more likely to result in controlled defensive action rather than uncontrolled violence. The reality is that killing by battered women is the product of desperation in intolerable circumstances—not the product of a loss of control! It would have been better to reform the defence of self-defence to allow such women a full defence, where appropriate, because the loss of control defence does not provide an apt solution.[5]

Parliament and the Law Commission tried to tackle this problem by removing the "sudden loss of control" requirement from the new defence,[6] but it is doubtful that the new defence provides such women with much protection. It is difficult to imagine cases where the so-called "slow burning" idea of "loss of control" will be present. A person either looses self-control in an ephemeral sense, or he does

---

[4] Three Australian states have abolished the partial defence. The state of Tasmania has abolished it completely, while the states of Victoria and Western Australia have replaced it with new offences of "unreasonable self-protective killings." For a detailed discussion of those reforms see Carolyn B. Ramsey, "Provoking Change: Comparative Insights on Feminist Homicide Law Reform Criminal Law," (2010) 100 *J. Crim. L. & Criminology* 33 at 57 *et seq.*

[5] Cf. section 9AD of the *Crimes (Homicide) Act of 2005* (Vic.). See also Joshua Dressler, "Battered Women Who Kill their Sleeping Tormenters: Reflections on Maintaining Respect for Human Life while Killing Moral Monsters," in Stephen Shute and A. P. Simester, *Criminal Law Theory: Doctrines of the General Part*, (Oxford: Oxford University Press, 2002) at 258. See also Patricia J. Falk, "Novel Theories of Criminal Defence Based Upon the Toxicity of the Social Environment: Urban Psychosis, Television Intoxication and Black Rage," (1996) 74 *N.C. L. Rev.* 731. Falk is critical of the growing number of new defences; people are relying on everything from battered women's syndrome to social deprivation to excuse their appalling criminal behaviour.

[6] See Alan Norrie, "The Coroners and Justice Act 2009—Partial Defences to Murder (1) Loss of Control," [2010] Crim. L.R. 275.

not. It is difficult to conceptualize the idea of a person losing control over a period of days or months—even though anger might build over days or months. Similarly, the effect of fear may have some kind of cumulative effect, but the ultimate loss of control will be ephemeral. Even though the law no longer requires a sudden loss of control, the defence is more likely to be successful in cases where the loss of control was sudden. The excusatory rationale for the defence is that D has lost the mental capacity to control his behaviour in way that he would have, if he had not been enraged or overwhelmed with fear. It is difficult to see this state of mind lasting for days or months, unless the defendant is suffering some kind of mental illness. If the latter is the case, then the partial defence of diminished responsibility or defence of insanity may be more appropriate. Any advantage gained by removing the "sudden" loss of control requirement from the new defence is undercut by the fact that there must in fact be a "loss of control."

How does loss of control affect crimes other than murder?   For crimes in general, loss of control is a matter of mitigation, to be considered by the judge in his discretion after conviction.[7] There are no limiting rules. (Even a person who takes umbrage and assaults someone when under the influence of alcohol may receive some consideration on account of loss of control). 22–003

Murder is an exception. Loss of control is a legal defence, but not one that necessarily allows the defendant to go free. If the jury accept the defence they are directed to return a verdict of manslaughter (which, as usual, is regarded as an included offence on a charge of murder). This is the form known as voluntary manslaughter, because the defendant intended to kill or otherwise had the mental element for murder. The judge has the usual wide range of discretion for manslaughter.

The life sentence is never given for a killing that results from the defendant losing control, even though it is theoretically possible. The courts take the view that if the jury have accepted the defence of loss of control, or if the defendant to a murder charge has been allowed to plead guilty to manslaughter, the judge must accept the view of the facts implicit in the conviction, notwithstanding that he himself thinks there was no sufficient loss of control. He must give a discount—generally a substantial discount—on what would have been the term served for murder. With rare exceptions the sentence is now likely to be between four and nine years.[8]

Is loss of control a defence when the defendant actually intended to kill?   It has sometimes been thought not. But the law is now clear that the answer is yes.[9] 22–004

---

[7] See for example, *Attorney-General's Reference (No. 95 of 2009)* [2010] 2 Cr. App. R. (S.) 83, where it was held that: "A suspended sentence of two years' imprisonment imposed on an offender for wounding with intent was not unduly lenient where the offender, who had been attacked in his home by the victim with an axe, stabbed the victim once under serious provocation." However, the sentence in that case was unlawful for other reasons.

[8] *R. v. Daley* [2008] 2 Cr. App. R. (S.) 534; see also the *Sentencing Guidelines Council: Manslaughter by Reason of Provocation Guideline*, (London: Sentencing Council, 2005).

[9] *R. v. Martindale* [1966] 1 W.L.R. 1564.

22–005   **If the defendant was obviously provoked, and severely provoked at that, will the prosecution even reduce the charge to manslaughter off their own bat?**   The prosecution do not indict for voluntary manslaughter. The indictment is for murder, the jury being left to convict of manslaughter if they think fit. Under the old law of provocation, occasionally, however, magistrates took the merciful course of committing for trial on the manslaughter charge only.[10] The defendant when charged with murder may offer a plea of guilty to manslaughter, and if this is accepted there will of course be no trial. The Crown often accepts a plea to voluntary manslaughter when the case does not fall within the rules for "loss of control" to be studied in the following pages.

22–006   **Why do we need this law of loss of control in murder? If we allowed the judge to have discretion in sentencing for murders, would there then be any point in having a defence of loss of control?**   It is sometimes said that even then the judge would derive help from the verdict of the jury. In other crimes loss of control can reduce punishment, but only in murder does it regularly have a dramatic effect. So the jury relieve the judge of some responsibility.

22–007   **Yes, but you say that on a verdict of voluntary manslaughter the judge may in practice give anything from nine years to a full discharge. So the verdict of the jury does not really afford him much assistance. The punishment he actually metes out must depend on his own view of the facts as given in the evidence. So I still don't see the point of taking the verdict of the jury. Why not let the judge decide on loss of control himself?**   I have given you the orthodox answers. My own answer would be twofold. First, the conviction of manslaughter instead of murder explains to the public the leniency of the sentence. It avoids the headline: "Murderer gets suspended sentence."

Secondly, the defence of loss of control resulting in a conviction of manslaughter serves the same function as other "included offences": it allows the jury to participate to a limited extent in sentencing. For most crimes they are expected to trust the judge to give the right sentence, but for a crime as serious as intentional homicide, where there are circumstances that appeal strongly to the sense of sympathy, it would impose a strain on the jury if they were not allowed to express a finding of mitigation.

22–008   **But loss of control is not the only point that may appeal strongly to the sense of sympathy. If it is a question of sympathy, why not allow a defence in all cases of murder (reducing it to manslaughter) where the jury think there are strong grounds of mitigation?**   A partial answer is that the law does allow the defence of diminished responsibility in murder, which has the same effect as the defence of loss of control. Diminished responsibility is supposed to be confined

---

[10] A rare example is *R. v. Symondson* (1896) 60 J.P. 645.

to circumstances of mental malfunctioning,[11] but in practice it has been stretched to cover some other circumstances calling strongly for compassion, such as killing by a battered woman.[12]

It is true, however, that we have no general defence of mitigating circumstances in murder. There would be much to be said for allowing the jury a general discretion to return a verdict of murder with mitigating circumstances, if it were not for the fact that this would enable terrorists when put on trial to protract the proceedings with evidence of their supposed grievances. Mitigating circumstances can of course be taken into account by the parole board in deciding when to recommend parole.

You say that loss of control is a defence to murder. In that case, isn't it also a defence to attempted murder?   The short answer to your question is that it has not yet called for consideration by the Court of Appeal. The long answer is that the point is puzzling because logic gives conflicting answers. The logic of legal rules is this: if the crime intended had been committed it would not have been murder, so failure cannot amount to attempted murder. A person can attempt a crime only if he would be guilty of the crime if he succeeded. Logically, the case should be one of attempted manslaughter, and there is no reason why there should not be a conviction of this, though the point has never been brought before the courts.   **22–009**

Ah, but there is an opposing logic. This rests not on the legal rules but on the reasons for them. Loss of control is allowed as a defence in murder (it is said) only because murder carries a fixed sentence.[13] Attempted murder does not carry a fixed sentence, so that the loss of control may be allowed for in the punishment. There is no more reason for having the defence of loss of control to attempted murder than to any other crime not carrying a fixed sentence. Therefore, the killer in the case under discussion is guilty of attempted murder.

A possible answer to the latter argument is that not only murder but also attempted murder is so serious a crime that it is right that the existence of the loss of control should be registered in the verdict, reducing the crime to attempted manslaughter. (Or, of course, if the defendant wounded the other party he could be convicted of wounding).

Formerly, the law was clear that the case was not one of attempted murder,[14] but in recent years trial judges have assumed the contrary, the older authorities not having been brought to their attention.[15] As said before, the question has not

---

[11] The defence of diminished responsibility is only available if D's abnormality of mental functioning arose from a recognized medical condition: section 52(1)(a) of the *Coroners and Justice Act 2009*.

[12] Cf. *R. v. Ahluwalia* (1993) 96 Cr. App. R. 133; *R. v. Thornton (No. 2)* [1996] 1 W.L.R. 1174.

[13] This is the general opinion: *sed quaere*.

[14] *R. v. Thompson* (1825) 168 E.R. 1193; *R. v. Bourne* (1831); *R. v. Beeson* (1835) 173 E.R. 63; *R. v. Thomas* (1837) 7 C. & P. 817; *R. v. Hagan* (1837) 173 E.R. 445. The cases were decided on the special offence of wounding with intent to murder, which is now merged in the general crime of attempt to murder (section 15 of the *Offences against the Person Act 1861* having been repealed by the Schedule 3 of the *Criminal Law Act 1967*).

[15] *R. v. Bruzas* [1972] Crim. L.R. 367. In *R. v. Peck* (*The Times*, 5 December 1975), a man who stabbed his wife after he had caught her in her nightdress with his friend was convicted of attempted murder and sentenced to 12 years' imprisonment. It is very doubtful, on the authorities, whether the conviction was right, the question of provocation presumably not having been left to the jury. In any

been decided at the appellate level; but the Criminal Law Revision Committee has recommended the legislative reinstatement of the old rule.[16] However, Parliament overlooked this matter when it replaced the law of provocation.

22–010 **Is the defence automatically available to joint-perpetrators and accomplices?** No. Section 54(8) of the of the *Act of 2009* provides: "The fact that one party to a killing is by virtue of this section not liable to be convicted of murder does not affect the question whether the killing amounted to murder in the case of any other party to it." Consequently, the accomplice or joint perpetrator will have to show that he also lost control at the same time. (There may be cases where two people lose control at the same time and thus jointly perpetrate murder. Such cases are likely to be extremely rare, but might include a mother and daughter who act together to kill a violent husband/father.)

22.2. LOSS OF CONTROL

22–011 Loss of control as a defence to murder, unlike loss of control as mitigation in other offences, had attained a degree of legal definition before the enactment of section 54 of the *Act of 2009*.[17] Section 54 of the *Coroners and Justice Act 2009* provides:

> "(1) Where a person ('D') kills or is a party to the killing of another ('V'), D is not to be convicted of murder if—
>   (a) D's acts and omissions in doing or being a party to the killing resulted from D's loss of self-control,
>   (b) the loss of self-control had a qualifying trigger, and
>   (c) a person of D's sex and age, with a normal degree of tolerance and self restraint and in the circumstances of D, might have reacted in the same or in a similar way to D.
> (2) For the purposes of subsection (1)(a), it does not matter whether or not the loss of control was sudden."

The factual question is sometimes expressed in purportedly psychological terms. Did the circumstances take the defendant over his threshold of tolerance? Could he prevent himself from acting as he did? Or—the favourite—did he lose his self-control?

These seem to be useless or misleading formulations. By hypothesis the defendant passed his limit of tolerance, because he killed. To ask whether a person could prevent himself from doing something conjures up the absurd notion that he is two people, one trying to act and the other trying to stop him. Talk about losing self-control is acceptable as a way of speaking of an act done in the heat of anger or fear, but it means no more than that. The angry or fearful

---

case, 12 years would be out of line with normal sentencing practice on a conviction of manslaughter by reason of loss of control due to provocation. It is anomalous if the judges regard killing more indulgently than an attempt to kill. Cf. *D.P.P. (Vic.) v. McAllister* (2007) 177 A. Crim. R. 467; *R. v. Pepper* (2007) 177 A. Crim. R. 456.

[16] Criminal Law Revision Committee, *Offences Against the Person (Report 14)* (London: H.M.S.O., Cmnd. 7844, 1980).

[17] For a detailed discussion of the old law see Glanville Williams, *Textbook of Criminal Law*, (London: Stevens & Sons, 1983) at Chap. 24.

person who kills in the heat of anger or fear has presumably lost his self-control; the angry or fearful person who does not kill (when he would rather like to) has to that extent kept his self-control; what does the test of self-control add to the test of killing in anger or fear? And what is the point of saying that killing in the heat of anger or fear involves a loss of control? One who kills in a rage does what he wants to do in those circumstances (as does one who kills out of fear), just as much as the calculating robber does. There is a difference in his emotional state, in motivation, and in the degree of reflection, but that is not well expressed by speaking of self-control. (Indeed, the killer may have evinced ample retention of self-control and yet have the defence of loss of control: he may have killed with one calculated thrust of a knife, when if he had gone completely berserk he might have delivered 20 wounds[18]).

When a person acts deliberately to seek revenge he may be in full control of his actions. He may not want to suffer the consequences of killing in revenge (a conviction for murder), but might balance the pros and cons and choose to take the consequences. He might prefer to go to jail rather than forego the chance to seek vengeance. Compare this to the case where the defendant is so enraged or fearful that he has been dethroned of his reason. The law of loss of control presumes it is possible for fear or anger to rob a person of his full mental powers of control.[19] It is this partial loss of capacity that provides the rationale for the partial excuse. (The law seems to be based on the notion that such a defendant suffers a partial loss of his mental ability to control his actions—a loss akin to a temporary bout of partial insanity.) But at the same time the law recognizes that the defendant has significant control over his actions, because it allows for a manslaughter conviction. The manslaughter conviction is allowed because the defendant's partially uncontrolled behaviour incorporated the controlled choice to intentionally kill another human being: he was not acting as an uncontrolled automaton.

22–012

This leaves us with two propositions. (1) The defendant must have killed because he was provoked by one of the qualifying triggers (that is, he must have been provoked by fear of violence or a "thing or things done or said (or both) which—(a) constituted circumstances of an extremely grave character, and (b) caused D to have a justifiable sense of being seriously wronged"), not merely because the qualifying trigger (provocation) existed.[20] There must be a causal relationship between the loss of control and the killing. So if the defendant sought the provocation in order to kill his opponent the killing will not be mitigated.[21] Except in such circumstances the requirement of causal relationship hardly limits

---

[18] This was also a problem for the old defence of provocation: Andrew Ashworth, "Doctrine of Provocation," (1976) 35 *Cambridge L.J.* 292 at 306.

[19] I am not convinced that anger or fear robs a person of his powers of control and therefore take the view that the defence should be completely abrogated. *Per contra*, others take the view that a person can lose the ability to control his actions: see Richard Holton and Stephen Shute, "Self-control in the Modern Provocation Defence," (2007) 27(1) *Oxford J. Legal Stud.* 49.

[20] *R. v. Tran* [2010] 3 S.C.R. 350 at para. 37 quoting Glanville Williams, *Textbook of Criminal Law*, (London: Stevens & Sons, 1978) at 480.

[21] See section 55(6)(b) of the *Coroners and Justice Act 2009*. This was also the case under the old law. See *Richard Mason's Case* (1748) Fost. 132; *R. v. Mawgridge* (1706) 84 E.R. 1107; *R. v. Lynch*

the defence, because where there is provocation followed by a killing (especially if immediately) the causal relationship will be readily inferred unless there is evidence of premeditation.

22–013 **Such as evidence that he was carrying the weapon about with him?** A person who carries a weapon with which he kills will be in danger of failing in the defence of loss of control if the jury think that the loss of control was a mere pretext for the use of the weapon. But there is no rule excluding the defence merely because the defendant had the weapon on him. Even though he was carrying the lethal weapon, the defence of loss of control is capable of succeeding if he had no intention of using the weapon before the provocation was offered.[22]

(2) The law attempts to distinguish between killing in cold anger, when there is a deliberate decision to kill after weighing up the pros and cons, and an impulsive killing in hot blood where there is no weighing up at all. In the past the distinction generally depended upon the immediacy of the defendant's response to the provoking event. Even though the sudden loss of control requirement has been removed from the new defence, the defence is more likely to succeed where the loss of control was sudden. If the provoking event is very recent this may be strong evidence of the defendant being passionately affected by it at the moment of killing.

Where provocation has been given and cooling time has elapsed, smaller incidents may reopen the provocation than would be sufficient to constitute a trigger if there had been no previous incident.[23] A number of triggering events (for example, frequent beatings by a violent husband) might culminate in immense fear; therefore, the person who kills when smarting under a fresh attack will be entitled to be judged on the whole background of her act.

22–014 The immediacy (or sudden loss of control) requirement that existed in the old law was considered to be too restrictive. It meant that the defence was excluded when the killer killed in response to affronts over a long period of time; affronts that may have induced her to take defensive action. The new defence aims to recognize the effect of cumulative provocation. In cases where a woman has been battered over a long period (*i.e.* where she has been subject to continuing provocation and emotional distress), it is no longer necessary to find something that can be called provocation immediately before the killing. But it must be shown that she had in fact lost control.

The defendant bears the evidential burden in respect of loss of control. Section 54(6) provides: "For the purposes of subsection (5), sufficient evidence is adduced to raise an issue with respect to the defence if evidence is adduced on which, in the opinion of the trial judge, a jury, properly directed, could reasonably conclude that the defence might apply." Therefore the judge can withdraw the

---

(1832) 172 E.R. 995; *R. v. Selten* (1871) 11 Cox C.C. 674; *R. v. Kirkham* (1837) 173 E.R. 422, *per* Coleridge J. Cf. *R. v. Johnson* [1989] 1 W.L.R. 740; it appears that *R. v. Johnson* would no longer hold sway.

[22] This was also the case under the old law: see *R. v. Fantle* [1959] Crim. L.R. 584.

[23] See *R. v. McCarthy* [1954] 2 Q.B. 105.

defence if the evidence is not sufficient to demonstrate a factual loss of control.[24] Nevertheless, judges rarely withdraw the issue from the jury on the factual question, though the judge has sometimes told the jury that the evidence of loss of control is extremely thin, or even that he himself cannot seen any such evidence.

22.3.   THE QUALIFYING TRIGGERS

Loss of control refers to action in the heat of the moment, or action that is the product of desperation in intolerable circumstances. Section 55 of the *Act of 2009* provides:

22–015

"(1)   This section applies for the purposes of section 54.

(2)   A loss of self-control had a qualifying trigger if subsection (3), (4) or (5) applies.

(3)   This subsection applies if D's loss of self-control was attributable to D's fear of serious violence from V against D or another identified person.

(4)   This subsection applies if D's loss of self-control was attributable to a thing or things done or said (or both) which—

(a)   constituted circumstances of an extremely grave character, and

(b)   caused D to have a justifiable sense of being seriously wronged.

(5)   This subsection applies if D's loss of self-control was attributable to a combination of the matters mentioned in subsections (3) and (4).

(6)   In determining whether a loss of self-control had a qualifying trigger—

(a)   D's fear of serious violence is to be disregarded to the extent that it was caused by a thing which D incited to be done or said for the purpose of providing an excuse to use violence;

(b)   a sense of being seriously wronged by a thing done or said is not justifiable if D incited the thing to be done or said for the purpose of providing an excuse to use violence;

(c)   the fact that a thing done or said constituted sexual infidelity is to be disregarded."

Section 55 almost abrogates the defence of loss of control, because provocation will only count if it is extremely grave and unjustifiably wrongful according to contemporary social standards.[25] Coupled with this, infidelity, one of the most common triggers, no longer counts as a trigger. Section 55(6)(c) of the *Act of 2009* provides "the fact that a thing done or said [*sic*][26] constituted sexual infidelity is to be disregarded." In *Mawgridge's Case* it was said:[27] "Where a man is taken in adultery with another man's wife, if the husband shall stab the adulterer, or knock out his brains, this is bare manslaughter; for adultery is the highest invasion of property, and there cannot be a greater provocation: and jealousy is the rage of a man." Infidelity may be no less provocative for some in the 21st century, but people are now expected to control their rage when they learn of their lover's infidelity. A person is not wronged if his lover decides to

---

[24] As we will see, the judge might also withdraw the defence from the jury if there is no evidence to support the other elements of the defence.

[25] Cf. *R. v. Tran* [2010] 3 S.C.R. 350 at para. 19.

[26] It is not clear that mere talk can constitute infidelity: the provision seems to have been poorly drafted on this point. A person might be said to commit infidelity by calling a telephone sex line to talk sex, but this does not encapsulate the popular meaning of infidelity. It appears that Parliament was aiming to exclude verbal taunts as triggers (*i.e.* taunts from a lover about his infidelity.)

[27] (1706) Holt K.B. 484.

leave him to start a new life with another man, even if he might be morally wronged when his lover cheats on him while he is still in a committed relationship with her. In the latter situation, the character of the wrongful provocation is not extremely grave, so even if it were not expressly excluded from the new defence, it would not come within its purview. Some people will in fact lose control upon learning of their lover's infidelity, but they will not be able to rely on that loss of control as an excuse. (Nor will it make any difference that the defendant learnt of the infidelity from a third party, because the policy for excluding it as a general trigger is clear.)

Where the trigger qualifies, it will not matter that a third party relays a provocative message. Suppose X and her husband go to pick up their child from the local kindergarten. The husband waits in their motorcar in front of the kindergarten while his wife goes in to pick up their young child. When X gets into the building she discovers a paedophile teacher molesting her child. X telephones her husband on her mobile telephone and tells him what is happening and he runs in and kills the teacher. The husband was provoked by the news of his child being molested, but the source of the provocation was the teacher's act of molesting his child. Since the latter would constitute a qualifying trigger, it does not matter that it was relayed to the defendant by a third party.

22–016 **Is it not illogical to only allow the defence if the loss of control results from certain types of provocative acts? If a person has lost control then he has lost control.** Yes, but Parliament was aiming to abrogate the defence. Instead of abrogating it outright, it decided to retain a truncated form of the defence. The new defence will only be available in extreme cases. Besides, there is no longer any reason why the defence should be available to the jilted lover who kills the object of his affection or her lover.[28]

The second qualifying trigger will also have the effect of precluding the defence from being considered in many cases where it may have once been considered, such as where a man kills his daughter for choosing her own boyfriend,[29] or the parent who kills a constantly crying baby.[30]

---

[28] In the recent case of *R. v. Tran* [2010] 3 S.C.R. 350, D had clearly lost control when he found his estranged wife in bed with her new boyfriend, because he went berserk and stabbed her boyfriend 17 times. In the Supreme Court of Canada, Charron J. (Binnie, Deschamps, Fish, Abella, Rothstein, Cromwell J.J. concurring) said: "the appellant's view of his estranged wife's sexual involvement with another man after the couple had separated—found at trial to be the 'insult'—cannot in law be sufficient to excuse 'a loss of control in the form of a homicidal rage' and constitute 'an excuse for the ordinary person of whatever personal circumstances or background.'" Later in the opinion, Charron J. (at para. 19) said: "By incorporating [an] objective element, the defence of provocation is necessarily informed by contemporary social norms and values. These include society's changed views regarding the nature of marital relationships and the present reality that a high percentage of them end in separation."

[29] *R. v. Mohammed* [2005] EWCA Crim. 1880. Or where a parent engages in vigilantism. *R. v. Baillie* [1995] 2 Cr. App. R. 31.

[30] *R. v. Doughty* (1986) 83 Cr. App. R. 319.

Could not a father who commits an "honour killing" argue that finding his 18-year-old daughter in bed with a man constituted circumstances of an extremely grave character, and that this caused him to have a justifiable sense of being seriously wronged? I would think not. His subjective view of right and wrong does not count. The question is whether a person of normal restraint and control would have felt wronged, or would have found the circumstances to be of an extremely grave character. A properly directed jury is not likely to accept that a father finding his adult daughter having sexual intercourse with her boyfriend to be circumstances of an extremely grave character, or that the father was unjustifiably wronged in a serious way.

22–017

What if the jury accepted honour killing as a qualifying trigger? The law allows the jury to consider whether, on the facts as they appeared to the defendant, the provocation can reasonably be regarded as a sufficient (justifiable) ground for loss of self-control leading that defendant to react against the victim with murderous intent. But the jury does not have *carte blanche* to decide whether the defence is available on the facts, because the judge has the power to remove cases that are not supported with sound evidence from the jury's consideration.[31] The judge looks at the evidence and asks himself could a reasonable jury reach such a conclusion on this evidence. A jury should not be allowed to consider whether an honour killing is a qualifying trigger within subsections 55(4)(a) and (b), because a reasonable jury could not find that defence was made out in such circumstances.

22–018

This assumes that the jury is made up of fair minded people who support British values. What if the defendant is from a different cultural background? This is an irrelevant consideration. The criminal law judges a person by the norms and standards of the society in which it operates. If a person chooses to live in China, then he must comply with the criminal law in that country; likewise if he chooses to sets up camp in Britain. "Nay, I hope, as I have temperance to forbear drink, so have I patience to endure drink: Ile do as company dooth; for when a man doth to Rome come, he must do as there is done."[32] Besides, murder is a very serious offence in nearly every modern society that exists in the world today. Coupled with this, there is no society where the criminal law provides a legal defence of honour killing. The honour killer may have in fact lost self-control, and may have felt that he had been unjustifiably wronged to a great degree; but a person of normal control and restraint would not kill his adult daughter for having consensual sexual intercourse with a man of her own choosing. Moreover, it may be said that making any concession on the ground of culture may be socially divisive, and may, in addition, land the courts in having to view sympathetically some ferocious "subculture" to which the defendant belongs.[33]

22–019

---

[31] Section 54(6) of the *Act of 2009*.

[32] Henry Porter, *The Pleasant History of the two angry women of Abington*, (London: Imprinted for Ioseph Hunt and William Ferbrand, 1599).

[33] See further, on variant cultures and provocation, Glanville Williams, *Textbook of Criminal Law*, (London: Stevens & Sons, 1978) at 490-493.

22–020   **Can a jury take account of the defendant's culture as making him more susceptible to a particular kind of affront, if it is not directed against his culture as such? Suppose that in a particular culture it is a point of deeply-ingrained honour to react strongly against a particular type of insult.**   On one occasion, an Italian in England who was provoked to homicidal frenzy by a remark directed against his lady friend was judged by English standards, neglecting the fact that this type of insult is regarded far more seriously in Mediterranean countries than in Britain.[34] The Italian (like those who are taunted about their culture, race, religion, sexual orientation),[35] may receive favourable consideration not because, as an Italian, he is particularly excitable, but because some insults are more grievous to him than they would be to an English person. It must be confessed, however, that the distinction is fine. The other limits found in the new defence means that a verbal insult is not likely to qualify as a trigger. The circumstances of such a provocation are not extremely grave when measured against the conventional standards of the reasonable jury.

The juror will probably always have one question in the back of his mind: You killed someone for this? From this premise, the reasonable juror will require the circumstances to be extremely grave. If a man found his 12-year-old daughter being raped by a school teacher, the jury would most likely accept that the provocation occurred in circumstances of an extremely grave character; and that the rape of a child would cause a parent to have a justifiable sense of being seriously wronged. The jury would then consider whether "a person of D's sex and age, with a normal degree of tolerance and self-restraint and in the circumstances of D, might have reacted in the same or in a similar way to D." (See the discussion in the next section).

22–021   **What if a heterosexual loses control and kills a homosexual who has propositioned him?**   It is doubtful that any court would consider such circumstances to be of an extremely grave character. Nor would a court accept that the defendant was caused to have a justifiable sense of being seriously wronged.[36] Women are propositioned by unattractive men in bars all the time, but they do not respond by killing. One can easily walk away from this type of encounter; and a person of normal restraint and control would not kill in such circumstances. If a lesbian woman is propositioned by a man she is not likely to pull out a gun and kill him. "It must not be light provocation, it must be grave provocation."[37]

If the gay man tried to sexually assault (penetrate, *etc.*) the defendant, then the defence could be put to the jury.[38] There is a great difference between being propositioned and being sexually assaulted, regardless of the sexual orientation of the attacker. In the latter situation, a reasonable person would find the

---

[34] *R. v. Semini* [1949] 1 K.B. 405.

[35] "To taunt a person because of his race, his physical infirmities or some shameful incident in his past may well be considered by the jury to be more [provocative] to the person addressed, however equable his temperament, if the facts on which the taunt is founded are true than it would be if they were not." *R. v. Camplin* [1978] A.C. 705 at 717, *per* Lord Diplock.

[36] Cynthia Lee, "The Gay Panic Defence," (2008) 42 *U.C. Davis L. Rev.* 471.

[37] To use the words of Hannen J. in *R. v. Selten* (1871) 11 Cox C.C. 674.

[38] Cf. *R. v. Martin* [2011] V.S.C. 217; *R. v. Hansford* [1987] 33 C.C.C. (3d) 74.

circumstances to be of an extremely grave character and would no doubt hold that a reasonable person would have a sense of being seriously wronged in such circumstances.

So if the Minister for Universities and Science addresses a students' meeting, and a student, taking umbrage because the Minister says that he has to raise tuition fees, shoots him dead, this would not come within the loss of control defence.   Under the old law of provocation this would have been left to the jury to decide, though I hasten to add that the jury would have been unlikely to have allowed it to be the act of a reasonable person. Under the new law a judge would remove such a case from the jury's consideration. Some jurors might consider that an announcement of a steep rise in tuition fees could have caused D to have a justifiable sense of being seriously wronged, but a judge is no longer required to leave the defence to the jury where the provocation is not grave; or where there is no evidence that "a person of D's sex and age, with a normal degree of tolerance and self-restraint and in the circumstances of D, might have reacted in the same or in a similar way to D."

22–022

And if a bank clerk refuses to hand the keys of the strong room to a robber, and the robber shoots him, this would not come within the loss of control defence?   The judge would remove the evaluative question from the jury. He might also withdraw the defence on the factual question, because the evidence that the robber carried a gun showed premeditation. The court would most likely hold that such circumstances are outside the notion of loss of control. The qualifying trigger requires a wrongful act, even though the notion of wrongfulness is extended to include moral wrongs.

22–023

Where D's loss of self-control was attributable to D's fear of serious violence from V, the defence may be available because this is a qualifying trigger. But would not the defence of self-defence provide a more appropriate defence?   It may if the conditions of that defence are made out. In *R. v. Ahluwalia* the defendant, after enduring many years of violence and humiliation from her husband, threw petrol in his bedroom and set it alight and thus killed him.[39] A woman who kills her sleeping husband cannot be said to have been acting in self-defence. Even though the "sudden" loss of control requirement has been removed from the law of loss of control, it may be difficult for a battered woman to demonstrate that her fear was such that she had in fact lost control. She may strike pre-emptively because she fears that she is about to encounter another beating, but the deliberation and planning involved in pre-emptive strikes mean that it will be difficult for her to show that it resulted from a loss of control. Nevertheless, she might show that she was in a constant state of panic and fear and thus ultimately snapped. (But again, the idea of someone "snapping" conjures up an image of a sudden rather than a slow-burning loss of control.)

22–024

Isn't loss of control in such circumstances just a form of revenge?   Killing in loss of control is indeed a kind of killing in revenge, but we refrain from calling

22–025

---

[39] (1993) 96 Cr. App. R. 133; *R. v. Thornton (No. 2)* [1996] 1 W.L.R. 1174.

it that. The term "revenge" is used for retaliatory action that is planned and cold-blooded. Section 54(4) of *Act of 2009* provides: "Subsection (1) does not apply if, in doing or being a party to the killing, D acted in a considered desire for revenge." Parliament took this precaution, because it was concerned that abolishing the immediacy requirement would extend the defence to cover revenge-killing.

The no revenge requirement is likely to pose another barrier for the battered woman. An example may be given. In one case, two sisters, together with their mother, had to deal with a brutal and drunken father. When he was in one of his violent rages they floored him over the head, and the sisters resolved that if he was again violent towards them after coming round they would kill him. He attacked them again, and one of them stabbed him to death. In strict law this could have been murder, because of the deliberate planning; but the jury returned a verdict of manslaughter. The older sister, aged 21, was sent to prison for three years, upheld upon appeal.[40] Under the new law, the defence of loss of control will not be available unless it can be proved that the revenge was merely a background factor and that the killing was in fact the result of a loss of control.

22.4. THE EVALUATIVE QUESTION

22–026 The evaluative question refers to the supposed conduct of the ordinary person, meaning a reasonable person of the defendant's age and gender. We have already seen, the question of whether the qualifying trigger found in section 55(4)(a) and (b) is established, involves an evaluative question. While gender is not likely to have any bearing on normalness, Parliament threw it in for good measure. The governing provisions are subsections 54(1)(c) and (3) of the *Act of 2009*:

> "D is not to be convicted of murder if—'a person of D's sex and age', with a normal degree of tolerance and self-restraint and in the circumstances of D, might have reacted in the same or in a similar way to D....
> In subsection (1)(c) the reference to 'the circumstances of D' is a reference to all of D's circumstances other than those whose only relevance to D's conduct is that they bear on D's general capacity for tolerance or self-restraint."

The jury decide whether a normal person[41] of D's age and gender would have acted as the defendant did; and they decide it according to their opinion. As a corollary of the first point, the subsections prevent the judge from telling the jury as a matter of law how an ordinary person of that age and gender would behave. He cannot direct the jury as a matter of law that an ordinary person of that age and gender would not have behaved like that, for it would be stultifying to leave the defence to the jury and at the same time direct them that they cannot entertain it. That would amount in effect to not leaving the defence to them. There would be no harm in suggesting how a reasonable person might be expected to act, but

---

[40] *R. v. Maw* (1980); see 130 N.L.J. 1163.
[41] "Normal person" hereinafter refers to a person who has "a normal degree of tolerance and self-restraint." In *R. v. Tran* [2010] 3 S.C.R. 350 at para. 30 it was said: "The use of the term 'ordinary person' therefore reflects the normative dimensions of the defence; that is, behaviour which comports with contemporary society's norms and values will attract the law's compassion. Meeting the standard, however, will only provide a partial defence."

certainly the judge could not lay it down to the jury. However, if there is an insufficient evidential basis for any element of the defence, the judge should not allow the defence to be put to the jury. The evidence must be "reasonably capable of supporting the inferences necessary to make out the defence."[42]

The *Act of 2009* continues the objective test, yet it seems strange to suppose that a reasonable person would ever kill as the result of a merely verbal insult. Did we not as children incant the lines: "Sticks and stones may break my bones but words will never hurt me"? Although it will hardly even be open to the jury to consider a defence based on insults, the question may be left to them if section 55(4) is satisfied.

The use of the person of a normal degree of tolerance and self-restraint in the law **22–027** of loss of control is problematic. Elsewhere the "reasonable person" test is used to indicate a standard of care required by law. The normal person (or reasonable person) is careful, moral, prudent, calculating and law-abiding. How absurd, then, to imagine that he is capable of losing all control of himself and thereby commits a crime punishable with imprisonment for life! To say that a "normal" person would commit this crime in the same circumstances is hardly less inapt. The reason why provoked homicide is punished is to deter people from committing the offence, and it is a curious (and erroneous) forecast of failure for the law to assume that, notwithstanding the possibility of heavy punishment, any normal person will commit it.[43]

Killing upon provocation is very unusual. This is particularly true of killing in jealously which is a long established instance of provocation.[44] Infidelity affects tens of thousands of people every year, but, the instances of murder accompanying infidelity is insignificant.[45]

Perhaps the loss of control must be great enough to make the normal person **22–028** **wobble.** This will be a hard test to pass. We might be more realistic if instead of speaking of all normal people we spoke of a normal person. But the provision seems to require the judge to ask the jury to consider what the normal person *may* do, rather than what the (or a) normal person *would* do. Not all normal people kill their husbands because they have suffered long-term abuse at his hands, but one normal person in a few million may do so. It is nevertheless an odd conception of the normal person. Besides, since no one supposes that the law's normal person exists, there is no sense in a statistical probability of his occurrence.

---

[42] To use the apt words of Charron J. in *R. v. Tran* [2010] 3 S.C.R. 350 at para. 41.

[43] Section 54(6) of the *Act of 2009*.

[44] Pieternel Dijkstra *et al.*, "An Inventory and Update of Jealousy-evoking Partner Behaviours in Modern Society," (2010) 17(4) *Clinical Psychology & Psychotherapy* 329.

[45] Adrian J. Blow and Kelley Hartnett, "Infidelity in Committed Relationships II: A Substantive Review," (2005) 31(2) *Journal of Marital and Family Therapy* 217; Bruce Elmslie1 and Edinaldo Tebaldi, "So, What Did You Do Last Night? The Economics of Infidelity," (2008) 61(3) *Kyklos* 391. The media give the impression that infidelity is almost a norm these days. See Polly Vernon, "Is anyone faithful anymore? Infidelity in the 21st century," (London: *The Observer*, Sunday 7 March 2010).

22–029 **So we just shunt the question off to the jury. What on earth are the poor things going to go on?** Perhaps they do not trouble with it, and simply ask themselves whether the defendant was gravely provoked or unjustifiably wronged. Or perhaps they try to imagine whether they would have done it themselves. Gross variation of judgment is possible, because people's capacity for sympathetic self-identification with others (empathy) varies.

Take the question of the honour killing. Many jurors will say to themselves with complete truth and conviction that they would never kill their daughter for dating a chap from a different religious or racial background; but under the old law of provocation they were allowed by legal tradition to say that the normal person would, or at least may. To empathize successfully they have to imagine not merely that they have been disobeyed by their daughter but that they were as distraught as the defendant was. Whether they find loss of control may depend on their success in making the effort of imagination. Again, how successful is the average juror likely to be in imagining his own behaviour if he were not from the same cultural background as the defendant.

22–030 **You said before that the person of normal control and restraint is supposed to be afflicted by the defendant's physical imperfections if the question is how he is to be imagined reacting to an insult. Does the law always allow the jury to invest the normal person with the defendant's characteristics?** A historical note will help your understanding here. In *R. v. Camplin*,[46] Lord Diplock, speaking with the concurrence of the other Lords on this particular point, explained it in the following terms:

> "In my opinion a proper direction to a jury on the question left to their exclusive determination by section 3 of the *Act of 1957* would be on the following lines. The judge should state what the question is using the very terms of the section. He should then explain to them that the reasonable man referred to in the question is a person having the power of self-control to be expected of an ordinary person of the sex and age of the accused, but in other respects sharing such of the accused's characteristics as they think would affect the gravity of the provocation to him; and that the question is not merely whether such a person would in like circumstances be provoked to lose his self-control but also whether he would react to the provocation as the accused did."

As we have seen, the *Act of 2009* refers to "a person of D's sex and age, with a normal degree of tolerance and self-restraint."[47] Elsewhere in his opinion Lord Diplock made it clear that the "ordinary person" into who the reasonable person is thus turned is not to be discovered by observation. He is "possessed of such powers of control as everyone is entitled to expect that his fellow-citizens will exercise in society as it is today."[48] A value-judgment is involved, and it is made by the jury. No evidence is allowed to be given on how reasonable people behave, or even on "how a pregnant woman or a 15-year-old boy or a hunchback would, exercising reasonable self-control, react in the circumstances."[49]

---

[46] [1978] A.C. 705 at 718E.

[47] See also the pre-*Act* decisions in *Attorney-General for Jersey v. Holley* [2005] 2 A.C. 580; *R. v. Smith* [2001] 1 A.C. 146.

[48] *R. v. Camplin* [1978] A.C. 705 at 717A. Lord Morris regarded the reasonable person as a "mythical person:" (at 719H), evidently meaning an imaginary person.

[49] *R. v. Camplin* [1978] A.C. 705 at 716E, 727F.

That factual evidence is impossible on how reasonable people behave is obvious, since such evidence would be question-begging. (The scientific witness cannot select his exemplars of behaviour without first having decided that they are reasonable persons.) That passage, as worded, does not conclude the question whether evidence is admissible to show how pregnant women, *etc.* do behave, but Lord Diplock probably meant to say that it is not admissible; and the *Act of 2009* suggests the same conclusion.

I think I am now quite lost. To start with, I don't understand why "age and   22–031
sex" should come into it. We are talking about a standard, aren't we? Surely
we expect youths and women to restrain themselves from killing just as
much as adult males. In fact the female of the species is less dangerous than
the male, but the point should have no legal relevance. Your words come
like a breath of fresh air. The legal relevance of age was first decided in *R. v.
Camplin*, and the decision perhaps resulted in part from analogy of the law of
negligence. Negligence is considerably concerned with questions of judgment
and experience, which depend on age; whereas loss of control is concerned with
self-control, which, in the basic matter of not killing, should be acquired
contemporaneously with the acquisition of physical power to kill. However, it is
human to say that the jury can take youth into account; whether it is logical or
not, the rule works in the direction of leniency.

It is difficult to see why Parliament included sex in the *Act of 2009*. Sex should
be completely irrelevant. Lord Diplock spoke as if there were or might be some
sex difference in respect of the power of self-control in the abstract. That
proposition, if seriously advanced, would operate to the disadvantage of the
gentle sex. It must be so much easier to restrain oneself from violence if one has
oestrogen in one's blood instead of androgen; so a woman who gives way to an
impulse to violence must be more blameworthy than a man! This would be a
paradoxical result of introducing a reference to sex here. In fact no one would
want to pursue such a line of reasoning.

Lord Diplock's reference to pregnant women did not imply that any special
legal considerations were involved in pregnancy; in fact he said the opposite. It
has not been suggested that the pregnant woman as a class are unduly prone to
violence. Under the *Act of 2009*, pregnancy is simply one of the facts of existence
that may sometimes lead to tragedy. A woman may be depressed by her
pregnancy, and may perhaps kill her former lover who rejects her; but that is
merely an instance of the circumstances that drive people to great anger. The jury
may have to consider any one of the infinite number of such circumstances. (That
a male juror may have to imagine himself as a pregnant woman may sound
strange, but it is no harder for him to imagine himself as a pregnant woman who
has been jilted than it is for a female juror to imagine herself as a youth who has
been taunted for impotence by a prostitute.)[50]

---

[50] See the facts in *Bedder v. D.P.P.* [1954] 1 W.L.R. 1119.

22–032	**Well, then, with age and sex cleared out of the way as being very largely red herrings (though I appreciate that they must now be mentioned to the jury—as though jurors hadn't got enough to bother them already), what about other "circumstances"? Is the *Act of 2009* merely referring to circumstances that may give sting to a jibe?** To some extent that is what Parliament had in mind. It is not only a question of jibes. In one case the court accepted that knocking away a man's crutch could be provocation, taking account of the fact that the man was one-legged.[51] His disability was his very sore spot. All the pain and inconvenience suffered from it in the past were concentrated into rage when an attack was directed against the thing that did something to alleviate the disability and was at the same time its symbol. Sex may itself be a circumstance from this point of view, as where (to take an illustration given by Lord Simon in *R. v. Camplin*) a woman is taunted as a whore.[52]

The *Act of 2009* expressly answers the question whether "circumstances" can be matters that bear on the particular qualifying trigger; circumstances may be considered to the extent that they affect the gravity of the provocation. However, the defendant's general capacity to control his reaction to the provocation is to be regarded as independent of his "personal characteristics." Although the defendant has only one leg, he can (or should be able to) control his temper as well as the next person; but his handicap may determine the circumstances that infuriate him. This leads to the conclusion that the circumstances, other than age and sex, will only be considered to the extent that they relate to the gravity of the provocation. Under the *Act of 2009*, the defendant who fails to show normal self-control is not entitled to a manslaughter verdict merely because he had an artificial leg, was impotent, had a low IQ or was suffering from Post Traumatic Stress Disorder (P.T.S.D.).[53] Similarly, evidence that a woman was suffering from battered woman's syndrome may show that the threat of a further beating was a particularly provocative threat for her, but its effect on her general capacity for self-control cannot be considered. Hence, such factors may be raised only to the extent that they show that the trigger was particularly provocative for the given defendant. Once it is established that the provocation was particularly grave for the defendant because he only had one leg and so on, the jury will determine whether a normal person would have responded to that degree of provocation in the same way as the defendant did.

A case such as *R. v. Raven*[54] would be decided differently under the *Act of 2009*. In that case, a Recorder of London, purporting to apply *R. v. Camplin*, ruled that a man whose physical age was 22 but whose mental age was only nine years was to be judged by reference to "a reasonable person who has lived the same type of life as the defendant for 22 years but who has the mental age of the defendant." This would mean that a reasonable person in these circumstances must be assumed to be mentally deficient! The rule may be perhaps justified as an extension to "mental age" of the *Camplin* rule for ordinary age. At the same time, it must be said that the concept of "mental age" is only a convenient expression

---

[51] *R. v. Raney* (1944) 29 Cr. App. R. 14.
[52] [1978] A.C. 705 at 724E. Cf. Lord Morris at 721E.
[53] See Heathcote W. Wales, "Causation in Medicine and Law: The Plight of the Iraq Veterans," (2009) 35 *New Eng. J. Crim. & Civ. Confinement* 373 at 392.
[54] [1982] Crim. L.R. 51.

for performance of an intelligence test, and is not normally regarded either in law or in psychology as a substitute for actual age. The ruling was a merciful concession to people who are very mentally retarded; that is all.

In *R. v. Reynolds*[55] the defendant was able to invoke the partial defence of diminished responsibility, because she was suffering from premenstrual syndrome and postnatal depression.[56] A woman might lose control in circumstances where she is menstruating, but to the extent that circumstance affects her general capacity for tolerance or self-restraint, it cannot be considered under the *Act of 2009*. In *R. v. Camplin*[57] Lord Simon, seeking some reason for introducing a reference to the reasonable woman, suggested that it would "presumably" be relevant to provocation that a female defendant was menstruating or was menopausal when provoked. The fact that the woman is menstruating or about to do so does not relate to a particular qualifying trigger (or is most unlikely to do so). It may affect her general capacity for self-control and restraint, because it makes her irritable; but that is generally regarded as being governed by the objective test, which does not vary as between women who are menstruating and those who are not; and the same applies to menopause (which of course may affect men as well). To hold that evidence may be given to show that the defendant was in some way particularly liable to be provoked because of his own make-up and not for any reason connected with the particular provocation is not permissible, for the rule is that the peculiar irritability or sensitivity or excitability of the defendant does not affect the evaluative test; and this, indeed is expressly stated in the new statute. It is the whole purpose of the evaluative question: "We boil at different degrees," said Emerson;[58] but the law has a notion of normal boiling point. For these reasons the *dicta* about menstruation and the menopause must be regarded as irreconcilable with the new statute.

22–033

Suppose that the defendant believed that something provoking had happened, when it had not.[59] Does the reasonable person test mean that the defendant has no defence of loss of control unless his mistake was reasonable? The person of normal restraint and control test does not necessitate saying that the defendant's mistake must be reasonable. It would be perfectly possible to apply the test to the facts as the defendant believed them to be (reasonably or not).[60] What the evaluative test is concerned to exclude is unusual deficiency of self-control, not the making of an error of observation, or of inference on a point of fact. The present determination of the courts to recognize mistakes relating to defences, if they are reasonable, means this is probably now the law.

22–034

---

[55] [1988] Crim. L.R. 679.

[56] See Bernadette McSherry, "The Return of the Raging Hormones Theory: Premenstrual Syndrome, Postpartum Disorders and Criminal Responsibility," (1993) 15 *Sydney L. Rev.* 292.

[57] [1978] A.C. 705.

[58] Ralph Waldo Emerson, *Complete Works of Ralph Waldo Emerson*, (Cambridge: Riverside Press, 1903) at 222.

[59] See for example, *R. v. Ghazlan* [2011] V.S.C. 178.

[60] In *R. v. Manchuk* [1938] S.C.R. 18, a mistaken belief was allowed as creating a case of provocation although it seems to have been wholly unreasonable.

The point has chief practical importance in connection with intoxication, for a person under the influence of drink or drugs is practically prone to mistake the intention of another.[61] The courts have in the past been ready to allow the drunkard a defence of provocation, with no restriction on reasonableness.[62] They have recently become more severe on intoxicated mistakes;[63] but it may still be argued that since it is only a question of palliating the offence, intoxication can be given in evidence on the question of putative loss of control, even though alcoholism is not a characteristic that can be considered as far as the general capacity for self-control is concerned.

22.5. NON-IMMINENT THREATS AND EXCESSIVE DEFENCE

22–035   A person in a panic may go far beyond what is necessary for his own safety. Suppose a person over-reacts to an attack by killing his adversary when this is not justified by the law of self-defence. On principle he is still entitled to the loss of control defence, reducing his guilt to manslaughter. A person who reacts to a blow often does so in mixed fear and anger, and it is now clear that the loss of control defence is not strictly confined to action in anger. Both fear and anger release hormones that prepare the body for violent action, and both tend to result in violence:

> "There's no philosophy but sees
> That rage and fear and one disease;
> Though that may burn, and this may freeze,
> Theyre both alike in ague."[64]

That excessive action in self-defence can reduce murder to manslaughter has been recognized by overseas courts, and in *R. v. McInnes*[65] Edmund Davies L.J. conceded, what was obvious, that "the facts upon which the plea of self-defence is unsuccessfully sought to be based may nevertheless ... go to show that [the defendant] acted under provocation." Long before the *Coroners and Justice Act 2009* it had been established that an apprehended attack can constitute provocation, even though the defendant has not sustained a blow.[66] From this it seems to follow that in every case in which the defendant believes that he has to defend himself against the threat of serious violence,[67] but for some reason oversteps the limits of self-defence (because the attack he fears is not sufficiently

---

[61] An extraordinary instance is that of Booth the actor (brother of Lincoln's assassin), who on one occasion, when he was playing Macbeth under the influence of liquor, refused to be killed, and chased Macduff murderously through the stalls.

[62] *R. v. Letenock* (1917) 12 Cr. App. R. 221; *R. v. Raney* (1944) 29 Cr. App. R. 14; *R. v. Wardrope* [1960] Crim. L.R. 770.

[63] *R. v. Hatton* [2006] 1 Cr. App. R. 247; *R. v. O'Connor* [1991] Crim. L.R. 135; *R. v. O'Grady* [1987] Q.B. 995.

[64] Samuel Taylor Coleridge, *Biographia Literaria*, (London: Rest Fenner, 1817) at Chap. 2.

[65] [1971] 1 W.L.R. 1600 at 1608.

[66] *R. v. Kessal* (1824) 171 E.R. 1263; *R. v. Greening* (1914) 9 Cr. App. R. 105; *R. v. Letenock* (1917) 12 Cr. App. R. 221; *R. v. Semini* [1949] 1 K.B. 405 at 409; *R. v. Cornyn* [1964] Crim. L.R. 484. Evidence may be given of past attacks by the deceased to show the nature of the attack that is feared: *R. v. Hopkins* (1866) 31 J.P. 105; *R. v. Ahluwalia* (1993) 96 Cr. App. R. 133.

[67] Section 55(3) of the *Act of 2009*.

imminent or serious enough to justify killing in self-defence), the circumstances can still amount to loss of control. The loss of control defence will be available, not only where the defendant makes a genuine mistake about the need to kill, but also where she mistakenly believes that killing is not an excessive (disproportionate) response.[68]

The fear of violence trigger was included in the new defence to provide battered women and the like with a partial defence where self-defence cannot be made out. Professor Norrie notes: "Where an abused woman kills her partner out of fear of violence, such conduct often does not bring the defendant within self-defence, either because she reacted disproportionately or because it would be hard to claim that she acted in response to a fear of imminent violence."[69] As we have seen, the new defence does not provide an adequate solution, because where the defendant does not in fact lose control the defence is not available. In many of the battered women cases the defendant will not have in fact lost control. Coupled with this, there will be battered women who have acted disproportionately, but may be deserving of a full defence rather than a mere partial defence. The legal reforms in some Australian states deal with this problem squarely. Ramsey summaries the gist of the Australian reforms in the following passages:[70]

> "The Victorian Law Reform Commission report recommended two steps—reforming self-defence law to make it more inclusive of women's experiences and adopting a partial defence of excessive self-defence to provide mitigation for defendants who honestly but unreasonably believed in the necessity of lethal action. In either case, the defendant's conduct would likely be fear based, though the existence of anger would not negate the claim unless it constituted a 'premeditated desire for revenge'. ... Perhaps the most significant feature of this self-defence proposal was its assertion that '[t]here may be circumstances in which the D's belief in the need to take action is reasonably held where the danger is not immediate, but is inevitable'. ... Another notable aspect of the V.L.R.C. proposal involved proportionality, which the pre-reform law in Victoria did not expressly require. The V.L.R.C. declined to impose a strict proportionality element due to common size-and-strength disparities between aggressors and those who attack and the fact that women may use a weapon or choose a non-confrontational moment to strike their abusers in compensation for such disparities.
> In short, the V.L.R.C. recommendations essentially proposed codifying pre-emptive strikes as potentially reasonable, depending on the circumstances, in cases where the deceased posed an ongoing, unlawful threat of death or serious injury to the accused. This recommendation proved influential. The self-defence provision enacted statutorily in Victoria in 2005 tracked the V.L.R.C. proposal by omitting any requirements of proportionality or imminence, and the 2008 homicide amendments in Western Australia expressly allowed self-defence acquittals of defendants who used deadly force to defend themselves or another person 'from a harmful act, including a harmful act that is not imminent."[71]

---

[68] Proportionality in self-defence should not be confused with the abrogated "reasonable relationship" rule. Under the old defence of provocation the reasonable person test applied not only to the fact of killing but also to the mode of killing. For a discussion of the abrogated "reasonable relationship" rule see Glanville Williams, *Textbook of Criminal Law*, (London: Stevens and Sons, 1983) at 543. Nor does the loss of control defence under the *Act of 2009* require the killing to be proportionate with the level of provocation received, because killing could never be proportionate in this sense. Cf. the pre-*Act* decision in *R. v. Van Dongen* [2005] 2 Cr. App. R. 38.

[69] Norrie, *op. cit. supra*, note 6 at 285.

[70] Ramsey, *op. cit. supra*, note 4 at 73-74. See also Victorian Law Reform Commission, *Defences to Homicide: Final Report*, (Melbourne: Victorian Government Printer, 2004); New Zealand Law Commission, *The Partial Defence of Provocation, Report 98*, (Wellington: Law Com., 2007).

[71] Section 9AD of the *Crimes Act 1958* (Vic.) provides: "A person who, by his or her conduct, kills another person in circumstances that, but for section 9AC, would constitute murder, is guilty of an

22–036   There is much to be said for the automatic rule recognized in varying degrees in other jurisdictions (and hinted at in some of the older authorities in England)[72] that whenever the defendant directs himself to using force in private defence but exceeds the limits allowed for private defence he is entitled to a verdict of manslaughter rather than murder.[73] This rule, however, only applies where the imminence requirement is satisfied.

The rule is supported by certain passages in the old books,[74] and was accepted by Macaulay and the other Commissioners for the Indian Penal Code,[75] and by the Criminal Law Commissioners of 1833.[76] In consequence, it passed in a number of overseas codes.[77] It has been accepted in the Republic of Ireland[78] and by the High Court of Australia[79] as a statement of the common law; and in Victoria a killing is also held to be mitigated if it is the result of excessive force used in arresting a criminal, or even in defending property.[80] "If the occasion warrants action in self-defence or for the prevention of felony or the apprehension of the felon but the person taking action acts beyond necessity of the occasion and kills the offender the crime is manslaughter—not murder" (Lowe J.). As Macaulay and the other Commissioners of the India Code pointed out, when the use of moderate force is completely lawful, it is too extreme to regard the actor as a murderer on account of excess of force. It may be said that he is less culpable than the killer who acts on provocation in anger, because the defender has the right to use some force and it may be hard for him to form a cool judgment as to when to stop. The principle should apply equally to killing in cases of attempts to prevent crime[81] or of necessity or duress, where the fatal force is not totally excused in the circumstances but should nevertheless be mitigated. However, our courts have been extraordinarily resistant to attempts to procure the recognition of the rule in modern English law, and the House of Lords

---

indictable offence (defensive homicide)." The "offence" of defensive homicide replaces the partial "defence" of provocation. See also section 9AH; and *D.P.P. v. Edwards* [2009] VSCA 232; *R. v. Creamer* [2011] V.S.C. 196.

[72] Peter Smith, "Excessive Defence—A Rejection of Australian Imitative," [1972] Crim. L.R. 525; Sean Doran, "The Doctrine of Excessive Defence: Developments Past, Present and Potential," (1985) 36 *N. Ir. Legal Q.* 314.

[73] In England and Wales the House of Lords has held that: "where a person used a greater degree of force in self-defence than was necessary in the circumstances he was guilty of murder." See *R. v. Clegg* [1995] 1 A.C. 482.

[74] Michael Foster, *Crown Law*, (London: Printed by W. Strahan and M. Woodfall, 1776) at 277; Edward Hyde East, *A Treatise of the Pleas of the Crown*, (London: Printed by A. Strahan, for J. Butterworth, 1803) at 243.

[75] Hannah More Trevelyan (ed.), *The Works of Lord Macaulay*, (London: Longman's, Green & Co., Vol. VII, 1866) at 505.

[76] *Fourth Report of Her Majesty's Commissioners on Criminal Law*, (London: H.M.S.O., 1839) 271 art. 40.

[77] See the Penal Codes quoted in *R. v. Rolle* [1965] 1 W.L.R. 1341.

[78] *People v. Dwyer* [1972] I.R. 416.

[79] *The Queen v. Howe* (1958) 100 C.L.R. 448; see also *R. v. Walden* (1986) 19 A. Crim. R. 444. It has also been put into statutory form in the *Criminal Code* of Western Australia.

[80] *R. v. McKay* [1957] V.R. 560.

[81] In *R. v. Clegg* [1995] 1 A.C. 482 the House of Lords held that where a person uses excessive force in self-defence he will be guilty of murder. It was also said: "that there was no distinction to be drawn between the use of excessive force in self-defence and the use of excessive force in the prevention of crime or in arresting an offender."

has expressly rejected it.[82] The latter approach will be of little assistance to battered women, unless they have killed in response to an imminent threat. Therefore, if the battered woman has not in fact lost control, she will receive a mandatory life sentence for murder.

As the law now stands, therefore, defence counsel who set up self-defence in answer to a murder charge should always consider carefully whether to rest his defence on the alternative of loss of control.

Need the judge direct the jury on loss of control if the defendant has not raised the defence?   Defending counsel are well aware of the truth of Aldous Huxley's adage that several excuses are always less convincing than one. If the defendant says that he did not strike a blow, it would be fatal to the credibility of the defence if it were to be said, in the alternative, that if the defendant struck a blow it was provoked. So the general principle is that on the charge of murder, if the evidence suggests that a jury, properly directed, could reasonably conclude that the defence might apply, the judge should instruct the jury on that issue. If the judge fails to do so and the jury convict of murder, the conviction cannot be upheld if there is sufficient evidence which a verdict of manslaughter could have been given.[83] In such circumstances the Court of Appeal will substitute a conviction of manslaughter.[84]

22–037

22.6.   LOSS OF CONTROL AND MENTAL DISORDER

Loss of control is traditionally a defence for "normal" people. Abnormal people can shelter under it, but only on the same conditions as apply to normal ones.[85] If they want their abnormality to be taken into account they must raise a defence appropriate to them—insanity or diminished responsibility.

22–038

The latter defence now found in section 2 of the *Homicide Act 1957* (as amended by section 52 of the *Coroners and Justice Act 2009*)[86] has greatly alleviated the responsibility for murder of those who have some degree of mental disorder. The defence can include even a difficulty with controlling one's actions, provided that it is due to an abnormality of mental functioning,[87] "which arose from a recognised medical condition."[88]

The courts allow the defendant to raise the defences of loss of control and diminished responsibility together, and either of them, if successful, will result in

---

[82] *R. v. Clegg* [1995] 1 A.C. 482 following *Palmer v. The Queen* [1971] A.C. 814.

[83] The evidence would have to be such that "a jury, properly directed, could reasonably conclude that the defence might apply." See section 54(6) of the *Coroners and Justice Act 2009*.

[84] Cf. *R. v. Cambridge* [1994] 1 W.L.R. 971; *Mancini v. D.P.P.* [1942] A.C. 1; *R. v. Porritt* [1961] 1 W.L.R. 1372; *Lee Chun Chuen v. The Queen* [1963] A.C. 220; *R. v. Robinson* [1965] Crim. L.R. 491; *Rolle v. The Queen* [1965] 1 W.L.R. 1341; cf. *R. v. Bonnick* (1978) 66 Cr. App. R. 266.

[85] Cf. *R. v. Smith* [2001] 1 A.C. 146 where it was held that the "jury was entitled to take into account the effect of the defendant's depression in relation to the question whether he had measured up to the standard reasonably required of him." *Contra, Attorney-General for Jersey v. Holley* [2005] 2 A.C. 580. Section 54(3) of the *Coroners and Justice Act 2009* makes it clear that mental disorder is not to be considered.

[86] See Chapter 27.

[87] *R. v. Bryce* [1960] 2 Q.B. 396.

[88] See section 2(1)(a) of the *Homicide Act 1957*.

a manslaughter verdict.[89] The judge may ask the jury, for the purpose of sentence, whether they put their verdict on one ground or the other,[90] but the jury may put it on both grounds.[91]

Strictly, the defence of loss of control ought not to succeed in such circumstances unless the jury think that, notwithstanding the evidence of diminished responsibility, an ordinary person would have done as the defendant did. In other words, the evidence of diminished responsibility will not in law assist the verdict of loss of control. No doubt in practice it may. Success in the combined defence of loss of control and diminished responsibility has an advantage for the defendant in respect of sentence: it may well result in a more lenient outcome than a defence of loss of control alone.[92]

---

[89] *R. v. Campbell* [1997] 1 Cr. App. R. 199; *Luc Thiet Thuan Appellant v. The Queen* [1997] A.C. 131; *R. v. Taylor* [2003] EWCA Crim. 2447; *R. v. Walker* [2009] EWCA Crim. 1829; *R. v. Gilliatt* [2007] 1 Cr. App. R. (S.) 78. Often the evidence of diminished responsibility is raised after a plea of loss of control has failed: see *R. v. Andrews* [2003] EWCA Crim. 2750. See also *R. v. Ellis* [2003] EWCA Crim. 3930, where the diminished responsibility defence was applied 50 years after the murder took place.

[90] *R. v. McPherson* (*The Times*, 18 June 1963).

[91] In *R. v. Wright* [1995] 16 Cr. App. R. (S.) 877 it was held that: "there was a strong possibility that if the jury had considered the issue of diminished responsibility; they would have found the appellant guilty of manslaughter on that basis. The appellant should have been sentenced on the basis that he was both provoked and suffering from diminished responsibility. The sentence would be reduced to four years' imprisonment." *R. v. Holford* (*The Times*, 29, 30 March 1963); the case did not go on appeal. In *R. v. McPherson* (*The Times*, 18 June 1963), the C.C.A. held that the jury have put their verdict on both grounds. Cf. *R. v. Ahluwalia* (1993) 96 Cr. App. R. 133, where the evidence of diminished responsibility was only raised at the appeal level. The appeal was allowed and the conviction of murder quashed and a re-trial ordered. See also *R. v. Evans* [2009] EWCA Crim. 2243, where the defendant tried to raise both defences.

[92] *R. v. Wright* [1995] 16 Cr. App. R. (S.) 877.

CHAPTER 23

CONSENT AND ENTRAPMENT

"For when success a lover's toil attends
For ask if force or fraud attained his ends."

Alexander Pope *The Rape of the Lock*[1]

Few, perhaps, but among them are likely to be police, prosecution, judges and juries.

23.1.   THE IMPORTANCE OF CONSENT

To begin at the beginning: the notion of consent enters into a discussion of offences both on the negative and on the positive side:

23–001

1.   Negatively: things may not be done to a person without his consent, merely on the ground that they are done for his benefit. This protects us from busybodies who think they know what is good for us better than we do ourselves. The exceptions to the principle (in relation to sane adults) are narrow, and the most important of them will be indicated in the next chapter.

2.   Positively: anything may be done to a person[2] (within certain legal limits)[3] if he consents to it, whether it is for his benefit or not. Just as we can decide what we do not want done to us, so we can decide what we do. Again the principle is not without exceptions.

Examples of the second (positive) principle: a person impliedly consents to being tackled when he plays rugby, to being punched when he boxes, and to having his tooth extracted when he visits the dentist. These consents prevent the act from being an assault. Similarly, a passenger's consent to travel in an aircraft means that there is no false imprisonment; and a human "guinea pig" who voluntarily takes a noxious drug for the purpose of medical research is not the victim of a crime of poisoning.

---

[1] *The Works of Mr. Pope*, (London: W. Bowyer, Vol. I, 1717) at 125.

[2] Or in respect of his property. The present chapter is chiefly concerned with consent to what would otherwise be an offence against the person. Consent in relation to property is more specifically considered in the chapter on property offences. The owner of a listed house or other real estate cannot consent to having such property destroyed without falling afoul of the law. Similarly, there are various laws regulating those who own cultural artefacts and noted works of art.

[3] *R. v. Brown* [1994] 1 A.C. 212.

The details of the defence are judge made. As we have seen (2.4), the burden of negativing consent rests on the prosecution. The defendant probably does not carry even an evidential burden,[4] though the evidence of assault, or rape, or other offence against the person, given by the prosecution will normally be sufficient to discharge their evidential burden of non-consent and to take the case to the jury. Evidence of the use of force, or the threat of force, or the use of certain serious frauds upon him, to prevent him from making opposition, is sufficient to negative consent without asking the complainant in the witness box whether he consented.

23–002 **Can consent be retrospective? What if the victim of a crime, not having consented beforehand, now wishes to hush the matter up?** The law does not allow him to do so. If the police think that the victim has been intimidated they may bring the offender to court. On the other hand, if they think that no good purpose would now be served by prosecuting they may hold their hand.

23.2. THE MANIFESTATION AND VITIATION OF CONSENT

23–003 Consent is hard to define. To consent to do something, and to wish or want to do it, are not the same. Suppose my classmate asks me to join her in serving soup to the homeless on Christmas morning. I may consent to assist, when I decidedly "do not want" to go. I do it because my classmate asks me to volunteer with her. I go because I do not want to offend her, since I have a faint hope of dating her. But I would much rather be at home opening my gifts and enjoying a feast. As I keep telling you, I do not want to go, but I consent to go. Everyone who goes, consents to go, unless he is shanghaied or goes at pistol point or is tricked by being told that he is going somewhere else. I think that every reader will recognize this as a statement of the way in which we use the word "consent;" yet I have not succeeded in giving a positive content to the word.

Since offences against the person and property generally require *mens rea*, the prosecution must show not merely that the complainant did not consent but that the defendant *knew* that the complainant was not consenting or might not be consenting. ("Might not be" to provide for "recklessness.") In the case of rape and certain other serious sexual offences, the defendant need only be "negligent" as to whether the complainant was consenting.[5]

Problems rarely arise if consent is expressly given. As to implied consent, the defendant is entitled to infer the complainant's consent if all the following circumstances are present:

1. The complainant knows that the act is being or is proposed to be done in respect of his body (or property) by the defendant who is present before him. The requirement of knowledge on the part of the complainant follows

---

[4] If the sexual intercourse took place in particular circumstances such as those mentioned in section 75(2)(a)-(f) of the *Sexual Offences Act 2003*, the defendant will have to raise evidence to rebut the presumption that the victim did not consent. See also the conclusive presumptions set out in section 76 of the *2003 Act*.

[5] The offences found in sections 1-4 of the *Sexual Offences Act 2003* only require the prosecution to prove that the defendant did not "reasonably" believe the victim was consenting. Cf. *D.P.P. v. Morgan* [1976] A.C. 182.

from the very meaning of "consent." "Consent" means consent *to* something. One cannot consent *in vacuo*. But whether the details of what is done must be known—ah! that is a question. We shall revert to that question below.

2. The complainant has the ability to signify refusal of consent. This condition and the previous one mean that an unconscious person cannot consent[6] (unless a question arises as to his previous consent continuing to be valid after he fell unconscious).[7] The present condition means in addition that a person who, though aware of what is happening, is paralysed or overpowered does not consent.

3. The complainant fails to signify his refusal. Refusal of consent may be signified either symbolically (by words or gestures) or by physical resistance. Words withholding consent (or even token resistance to a sexual overture) may be belied by absence of strong resistance where such resistance is possible and is to be expected if consent is withheld.

As an illustration: if a patient in hospital is told by a doctor he is to have a certain   **23–004**
operation, and does not signify dissent but allows himself to be wheeled to the operating theatre, he would normally be taken to consent; and the fact that he is very doubtful in his mind about agreeing to the operation is irrelevant.[8] Similarly, a woman who submits to sexual intercourse that she finds disagreeable, when she could decline it, consents to it; how little she likes it is of no legal interest. It does not matter in these cases whether we say that the complainant actually consented as a matter of law or that the defendant was entitled to suppose that he or she was consenting.

There are these classes of case in which though consent may appear to have been given it will be deprived of its legal effect:

1. Where certain circumstances detract from the effectiveness of choice. Rules of law decree that an apparent consent is "vitiated" if it is produced by mistake or fear of certain kinds. (The two forms of vitiation reflected in rules 1 and 2 above. Mistake can prevent such consent as was given from being relevant to what was actually done, and coercion producing fear prevents the victim from signifying refusal.)

2. Where the complainant is one of certain classes of person who are deprived by law of the "capacity" (ability) to consent, because of the likelihood that

---

[6] Nor can a person who is semi-conscious, if this prevents her from comprehending to what she is consenting. See *R. v. Stein* (2007) 179 A. Crim. R. 360, where V was unable to withdraw consent because he was gagged. See also *The Queen v. J.A.* [2011] S.C.C. 28 (in particular, the dissenting judgments of Binnie and LeBel J.J.); *R. v. Bree* [2008] Q.B. 131; *R. v. Camplin* (1878) 1 Cox C.C. 220; *R. v. Lang* (1976) 62 Cr. App. R. 50; *R. v. Malone* [1998] 2 Cr. App. R. 447; *R. v. Francis* [1993] 2 Qd. R. 300; *R. v. Blayney* (2003) 87 S.A.S.R. 354.

[7] See *R. v. Pike* [1961] Crim. L.R. 114, 547, where the defendant procured his mistress to be anaesthetized, with her consent, his object being to gratify his sexual perversion of copulating with an unconscious woman. See also *R. v. Meachen* [2006] EWCA Crim. 2414.

[8] Cf. *O'Brien v. Cunard SS Co.* (1891) 154 Mass. 272.

such persons by reason of disability cannot choose in the normal way. The people so disabled are certain juveniles and certain mentally disordered persons.[9]

3. Where rules of public policy deprive us all of the legal ability to consent to certain acts that are regarded as immoral or socially injurious.[10]

Although the name "public policy" is given only to the third situation, an element of public policy enters into the first two. All three bristle with philosophical as well as legal problems. A discussion of them will occupy the rest of the chapter. We begin with the rules (so far as they can be stated) on the vitiation of consent, starting with fear. They are so uncertain in many respects that they afford much opportunity to the activist judge to extend the empire of the penal law.

23.3. THE VITIATION OF CONSENT BY LACK OF FREEDOM

23–005   Section 74 of the *Sexual Offences Act 2003* expressly provides: "For the purposes of this Part, a person consents if he agrees by choice, and has the freedom and capacity to make that choice." Capacity is an issue we can leave a side for the moment. Let us consider the concept of "freedom." Does the threat have to be such that it completely overbears the victim's will or is it enough that it substantially overbears her will? If a woman is physically pinned to the ground and is raped, she has no freedom whatsoever to resist the threat. She is physically constrained and her decision to refuse to have sexual intercourse with the defendant has been overridden by him. Here there is not only physical involuntariness, but also moral involuntariness. If she is not physically restrained, but is told that if she does not comply she will be seriously injured or killed, her freedom to say no is almost non-existent.[11] However, there are many other cases where it might be said that the victim did not have a fully unfettered freedom to say no, but where her freedom was not fettered significantly. In fact, in some cases the threatened harm may be so minor that the victim's freedom might be said not be to be fettered in any real sense.

Speaking of interferences with the person generally, and not merely rape, pressure to consent may take the form of various persuasions—the appeal to the conscience of the complainant to permit medical experimentation upon him, the invocation by the experimenter of his scientific authority, the threat by a man to give up his association with a woman if she does not consent to sexual intercourse, the offer of a bribe. Inducements of these kinds may sometimes be regarded as morally improper, or as fit for prosecution as a statutory offence of threats,[12] without reaching the conclusion that they are such as to negative

---

[9] *R. v. Cooper* [2009] 1 W.L.R. 1786.

[10] See *R. v. Brown* [1994] 1 A.C. 212.

[11] In the duress jurisprudence this is referred to as "moral involuntariness." "In using the expression 'moral involuntariness,' we mean that [V] had no 'real' choice but to [yield to the threat]. This recognizes that there was indeed an alternative to [yielding to the threat], although in the case of duress that choice may be even more unpalatable — to be killed or physically harmed." *R. v. Ruzic* (2001) 153 C.C.C. (3d) 1 at para. 39, *per* Lebel J.

[12] See the repealed section 2(1) of the *Sexual Offences Act 1956*.

consent in law. Employers, for example, have no power to search employees on suspicion of theft without their consent, but they may search an employee with his consent, but the employee realizing that if he refuses consent the employer is likely to call the police. It would be absurd to regard the consent as thereby vitiated.

Many decisions that we take in life are the result of choosing between evils. We opt for one course, which we dislike, because the alternative is more objectionable still. This unpleasantness of choice does not, in ordinary language, destroy the reality of the choice or the existence of consent.

However, there are extreme cases where fear resulting from threats will nullify consent in law. It would not commend itself to public opinion to say that a man who has obtained sexual intercourse by threatening a woman with a knife is not a rapist. The line between using force to overcome a woman and using a serious threat to prevent her from offering resistance is too fine to be the basis of a legal definition. It is a purely verbal question whether the second case should be regarded as one in which the woman consents under compulsion or as one in which she does not truly *consent* but simply gives *submission, acquiescence* or *complaisance*. However one expresses it, there is no effective consent in law.

23–006

The threat need not be of extreme violence. Common sense suggests that a person who submits to an act only because he believes that otherwise he will be overpowered and have it done to him anyway does not consent in law, even though the force necessary to overpower him will be small and non-injurious.[13]

Suppose that the police illegally require a suspect to make an impression of his finger-prints.[14] If an officer presses the suspect's finger on the scanner, the suspect co-operating by placing his fingers in the place on the scanner, this can be regarded as an assault, because the suspect believes that if he resists force will be used. The doctrine of vitiation of consent enables the law to be invoked against the officer.

Probably the threat need not be of force to the complainant: a threat in respect of, say, the complainant's children is sufficient.[15] It may be implied from conduct: an intruder in a house who orders the female occupier to submit to sexual intercourse would not need to back his command with an express threat. It may be implied from past conduct: the woman may know from unhappy experience that it is useless to resist.[16] It may be implied from numbers, as in a "gang

23–007

---

[13] *R. v. Hallett* (1841) 173 E.R. 1036; *R. v. Day* (1841) 173 E.R. 1026.

[14] It is unlawful to obtain fingerprints from suspects unless certain conditions are met: see section 61 of the *Police and Criminal Evidence Act 1984*.

[15] Cf. *R. v. Garrett* (1988) 50 S.A.S.R. 392.

[16] *R. v. Jones* (1861) 4 L.T. 154. See *State v. B.H.*, 834 A.2d 1063 (2003), where a husband threatened to give his wife a serious beating if she did not engage in sexual activity with their seven-year-old son. The woman was suffering battered woman's syndrome because of the husband's past violence. If the case had been tried in this country under the post-2003 law, the husband would be guilty of causing a person to engage in sexual activity without consent contrary to section 4 of the *Sexual Offences Act 2003*. See also *R. v. Bourne* (1952) 36 Cr. App. R. 125, where Bourne compelled his wife to commit bestiality with a dog. Bourne could now be charged under section 69(2) of the *Sexual Offences Act 2003*, so long as he causes his wife to be penetrated by the sex organ of the animal. Again, the threat of violence in that case was such that the wife could not be said to have been consenting.

rape."[17] And if a man takes advantage of a state of fear induced in the victim by another, it will be the same as if he had induced it himself.

In the last of these situations the requirement of the threat by the defendant vanishes, and the truth is that no threat is necessary. What matters is not the threat but the woman's belief as to what will happen if she does not acquiesce. If she submits to sexual intercourse from fear of force, and the man knows (or ought to know) this, her consent is vitiated and the man has the requisite *mens rea* for rape, even though he did nothing to cause the fear. Where the threat does not relate to the use of force, the traditional and proper view is that the obtaining of sexual intercourse by means of the threat is not rape.

23–008 **Isn't that too narrow a view of the law? Oughtn't the rule be that a woman's mere submission to sexual intercourse is not enough to establish her consent if there was some constraint operating on her mind?** One reason for having a narrow rule is that threats vary greatly in their weightiness, the least serious amounting to little more than the offer of an improper bargain. Rape is such a serious crime, and regularly attracts such severe sentences, that it is important that it should apply only to the gravest cases.

The opinion I have just offered as to the proper rule is supported in all the authorities except the case of *R. v. Olugboja,*[18] which goes much further. In this case your "constraint" idea was accepted by the trial judge, and not emphatically rejected by the Court of Appeal. Olugboja's conduct was so unscrupulous and overbearing that if we had a crime of obtaining sexual intercourse by gross sexual imposition (otherwise than by rape) he would rank as a prime candidate for conviction. He might even have been convicted of rape, without any commentator voicing criticism, if the female complainant had given evidence that she feared the use of force and if the direction to the jury had been in conventional terms. But apparently the female complainant was not asked the vital question: Why did you take off your trousers? And the conviction for rape was procured and justified on grounds so woolly that we now seem no longer to have any firm bounds to the crime. (Alas, section 74 of the *2003 Act* does not specify how unfettered V's freedom need be, before her consent will be vitiated.)

The facts of *R. v. Olugboja* cannot be shortly summarized without the risk of creating an unfair impression. The complainant was a girl of 16; the parties had started together on a social basis; and the sexual intercourse was admitted. The evidence creating difficulty for the prosecution in obtaining a conviction of rape on normal principles was that the complainant removed her own trousers on being directed by Olugboja to do so; that Olugboja uttered no threat of violence, and the complainant apparently did not say at the trial that she feared the use of force; that she did not resist the sexual penetration, though she struggled when she thought that after penetration Olugboja was going to ejaculate inside her, and

---

[17] *R. v. Hallett* (1841) 173 E.R. 1036; cf. *R. v. Hodgon* [1962] Crim. L.R. 563; *Whittaker v. Campbell* [1984] Q.B. 318 (taking conveyance).

[18] [1982] Q.B. 320. Cf. *R. v. Aiken* (2005) 157 A. Crim. R. 515. See also *R. v. Sutton* (2008) 187 A. Crim. R. 231, where the complainant acknowledged that there was nothing to prevent him from leaving the bed, getting dressed and going home. He also acknowledged that he had been *in no way threatened by the appellant.* He said, however, that "he felt intimidated by the appellant's relatively greater physical size." See also *Holman v. The Queen* [1970] W.A.R. 2 at 6.

he accordingly withdrew; and that after Olugboja had taken her home she complained to her mother, the police and a doctor about the conduct of Olugboja's companion (who had raped her shortly before), but not about Olugboja (who, she even said, had not touched her, though that was evidently false).

The trial judge introduced an innovation in the direction to the jury by making "constraint" a ground for vitiating consent. "You will ... decide whether or not there were any constraints operating on her will, so that you are satisfied that in taking her trousers down and letting him have sexual intercourse with her, she was not, in fact, consenting to it." Apparently the judge did not spell out to the jury what "constraints" he had in mind, but presumably they were that the complainant and her girlfriend had been tricked by the two defendants into allowing themselves to be driven to the bungalow where the events occurred; that she was dependent on the defendant or his companion to drive her home again; that she had reason to believe that she was not going to be driven home immediately; and that she had just seen Olugboja's companion dragging her friend into a bedroom to rape her.

23–009

Dunn L.J., delivering the judgment of the Court of Appeal said:[19]

> "We do not think that the issue of consent should be left to a jury without some further direction. ... They should be directed that consent, or the absence of it, is to be given its ordinary meaning and if need be, by way of example, that there is a difference between consent and submission; every consent involves a submission, but it by no means follows that a mere submission involves consent.[20] ... In the less common type of case where intercourse takes place after threats not involving violence or the fear of it, ... [the jury] should be directed to concentrate on the state of mind of the victim immediately before the act of sexual intercourse, having regard to all the relevant circumstances; and in particular, the events leading up to the act and her reaction to them showing their impact on her mind. ... [T]he dividing line in such circumstances between real consent on the one hand and mere submission on the other may not be easy to draw. Where it is to be drawn in a given case is for the jury to decide. ...Looked at in this way we find no misdirection by the judge in this case. We think it would have been better not to use the word 'constraint' in explaining the offence, but whenever he used it the judge linked it with the word 'fear',[21] so that in the context the word seems to us to be unexceptional [sic]."

These remarks are disturbing, because they suggest that the judge can direct the jury with great laxity, uttering a series of platitudes without giving them any

---

[19] *R. v. Olugboja* [1982] Q.B. 320 at 332.

[20] Both parts of this statement are wrong. A consent eagerly given between equal partners does not involve a submission (which implies giving in to a dominant will), and a mere submission does involve consent if there are no vitiating factors. Many a wife (or cohabite) has submitted to the attentions of a man with whom she is bored, because for one reason or another she does not care to reject them; and in so doing she consents to the contact. The court quoted one of a series of cases in the earlier 19th century holding that a youngster who is sexually interfered with by an adult (particularly by one who is in some authority over him) does not "consent" but only "submits," this mode of reasoning became unnecessary when legislation created sexual offences by adults that did not require proof of non-consent; and the special doctrine of submission was not extended to complaisances by adults. This reasoning was applied in *R. v. Ramsay* (1999) S.K.Q.B. 173, where a 14-year-old girl was blackmailed into having sexual intercourse with an adult man who was a police officer in uniform.

[21] He did not. Even when the judge added a reference to fear, he stated this as an alternative to constraint; and he does not seem to have suggested what the complainant's fear might have been.

real guidance. The court assumes that fear can vitiate consent in rape even though it is not fear of violence (or, presumably, of force short of violence); and yet the court makes no effort to specify the sort of fear or threat that has this effect. A threat in the wide sense is simply a statement by X that he will act in some way that Y will not like if Y acts in some other specified way; and the jury are apparently left as a kind of sovereign legislature to decide what statements of this kind in a sexual case will make X a rapist. Moreover, the court seems to think that consent is a state of mind which the jury can distinguish factually from "submission" without any criteria enabling a line to be drawn. The judgment astonishingly misunderstands the authorities it cites on this question.[22]

If the complainant did not fear force, there was apparently no direct evidence before the court as to what she did fear. If she submitted herself to the defendant because she thought it would be the quickest way of getting home, was he properly convicted of rape?

23–010 **But the statutory definition of rape is that it is unlawful sexual intercourse without consent. Surely the question must be left to the jury in general to decide whether the threat, of whatever kind it was, was such as to negative any real consent.**   That was the reasoning on which the court proceeded, but it overlooks the history of the law on this subject, as well as the philosophical difficulty in defining consent.

The old writers defined rape as involving an act against the woman's will by force, fear or fraud,[23] but in fact the cases went no further than to allow the "will" or consent to be vitiated by one kind of fear (namely, of force) and one kind of fraud (namely, as to the nature of the act). The change from "will" to "consent" took place in the 19th century, so that the *Sexual Offences (Amendment) Act 1976* was purely declaratory. The change was made simply to make it plain that sexual intercourse with an unconscious woman (where she had no "will" *either way*) could be rape. It was certainly not the intention to set the jury free to decide in general whether or not there was "real" consent.

23–011 **The point remains that consent must be voluntarily given. So it must be a question of fact in each case whether it was.**   Yes, in a sense; but everything depends on what you are looking for to establish or negative voluntariness of consent, only a negative test. Consent is voluntary when it is not given as a result of certain pressures. Questions of policy are involved in deciding what pressures are sufficient to nullify consent, and guidance must be given by the rules of law.

The paradox of the voluntary–involuntary distinction is that it is the positive-looking member of the pair (voluntary) that carries the negative meaning (here, no relevant threat or fear), and the negative-looking word (involuntary) that has positive force. We shall see that the same is true in the law of duress (where the distinction is equally useless as a guide to reasoning); and the words play the same trick in the law of evidence, where they are used in connection with

---

[22] The court quoted the (Report of the *Advisory Group on the Law of Rape* (1975) (Cmnd. 6352)) and the C.L.R.C., for the proposition that consent may be vitiated by intimidation other than threats of force; but in fact the two reports did not say or intend anything of the kind.

[23] *R. v. Lang* (1976) 62 Cr. App. R. 50.

confessions. A confession is "voluntary," and therefore admissible in evidence, if it is not "involuntary," the latter signifying "the result of promises, threats or oppression by a person in authority." In all three contexts "voluntary" has no meaning except as to the negation of the certain factors.

Among the threats other than of force that may possibly vitiate consent, the strongest candidates are threats of imprisonment or of prosecution (whether on good grounds or maliciously).

In a South African case[24] a threat of malicious prosecution for an imprisonable **23–012** offence by a policeman was held to vitiate a woman's consent to sexual intercourse, so that the officer could be guilty of rape. But in England a judge directed the acquittal of a policeman on a charge of rape founded on an allegation of such a threat.[25] The point is important as far as the offence of sexual assault is concerned. On one occasion a probationary officer who found a youth committing some misdemeanour gave him the option of going to court or taking a flogging; the youth chose the flogging and was hit on the bare buttocks. As a result, the constable was charged in the Crown Court with this and other sexual assaults. The age of the youth is not stated in the brief report, and in any case the matter was not argued because the constable pleaded guilty on all counts.[26]

Reverting to the vitiation of consent in rape, if a threat of imprisonment is to be accepted as sufficient it must, surely, be a threat of something more than temporary restraint. A temporary restraint would be sufficient where the defendant threatens to lock a person whom he knows suffers from claustrophobia in a small space, because such a threat might be sufficient to overbear the will of such a victim. Even if in *R. v. Olugboja* there was an implied threat to keep the complainant in the bungalow for the night if she did not yield herself, that should not have been accounted a sufficiently serious threat to make the threatener guilty of so serious a crime as rape. Even on that view of the facts, the case should not have been treated as anything more than the statutory offence of threats, which was still in force when that case was decided.[27]

Before the upheaval in the law created by the decision in *R. v. Olugboja* one could at least have been reasonably certain that economic pressure was insufficient. "My poverty, but not my will, consents" is a distinction hitherto unknown to law. (Were it is recognized, anyone without an independent income who took a job on the factory floor or at a desk would be able to bring proceedings for false imprisonment; for in performing his job he is psychologically chained to one place.) Again, what courts of equity call undue influence has always been thought to be insufficient; and a man who compels a woman to submit to his unwelcome attention by threats of exposing her past life has never been imagined to be guilty of sexual assault or rape. If a person reluctantly agrees to have sexual intercourse with the defendant to avoid him revealing her past cannabis use to her parents, she seems to make a free choice to have sexual intercourse. It seems to be a question of whether the pressure applied to get the victim to yield to the threat was equal to or greater than the pressure to resist. If a

---

[24] *State v. Volschenk* (1968) (2) P.H. H 283 (D).
[25] *R. v. Kirby*, (1961) *The Times* (December 19).
[26] 136 J.N.P. 264.
[27] See section 2(1) of the *Sexual Offences Act 1956*.

person is adamant that she does not want to have sexual intercourse with the defendant under any circumstances, the threat would have to be fairly serious to pressure her into agreeing. If the threat is trivial, then it might be held that the victim's will was not completely overborne. Given the gravity of rape, those who consent because someone has threatened to reveal a bit of past gossip seem to freely choose to consent to the sexual intercourse. A reluctant consent is still consent.[28]

23–013 In the civil case of *Latter v. Braddell*,[29] it was held that no assault was committed when a mistress required her maid to be medically examined to see if she were pregnant. The maid submitted to the examination, under tearful protest, and her action against the mistress for assault failed. Perhaps there was economic coercion and perhaps there was undue influence, but neither vitiates consent in the law of tort. It must be said, however, that even *Latter v. Braddell* was one of the cases lumped together by the court in *R. v. Oblugboja* as those where a criminal jury could find lack of consent on an "appropriate direction." This contemplates that a jury in a criminal case can ignore general principles established in the civil law, even in relation to so serious a crime as rape.

In the first edition of this book the decision of the Rhodesian case of *R. v. McCoy*[30] was characterized as wrong, but no firm opinion on any of these topics can now be entertained. It was an extreme case of what is now known as sexual harassment, the abuse of economic power in the work-place.

An airhostess broke a regulation of the company, and McCoy, the manager, offered her a caning as an alternative to being disciplined by being grounded, which would have meant loss of pay. She accepted, and the caning was administered in humiliating circumstances. There is certainly a case for saying this conduct should be reached by the criminal law. One way of looking at it would be to say that McCoy was in breach of his duty to his employer, the company, in turning to his own advantage the authority given to him. A way of dealing with the malpractice would be a statute forbidding employers and their agents to abuse their economic power by imposing certain socially undesirable penalties or substitutes for penalties (particularly sexual submissions) upon employees. Since we lack any specific statute on the subject,[31] if a case of gross abuse of power by an employer or his manager comes before the court the judges are very likely to express their disapproval by manipulating the doctrine of consent. But, reverting to the case of *R. v. McCoy*, if one looks at the matter from the point of view of the particular woman employee involved in the case, it may be said that she exercised the choice that McCoy gave her in the way that suited her own interest. Assuming that in the regular course McCoy would have ordered the woman to be grounded, and that this would have been the proper action on his part, what happened was that he offered to be bribed by her, in a non-pecuniary way, not to do his duty. She herself thought the humiliation and pain of the caning preferable to the official penalty, and she was benefited by being given the option.

---

[28] *Holman v. The Queen* [1970] W.A.R. 2 at 6. Cf. *Michael v. Western Australia* [2008] 183 A. Crim. R. 348.
[29] (1881) 50 L.J.Q.B. 116, 448.
[30] [1953] 2 S.A. 4.
[31] Cf. section 15 of the *Employment Rights Act 1996*.

McCoy's real offence was one of abusing his position to obtain sexual favours; behaviour like his needs to be punished on public grounds, but would best be dealt with by having a special provision.[32]

The decision cannot be reconciled with the principles of the crime of assault, because, in the first place, the harm done appears to have been insufficient to negative consent on account of the seriousness of the injury,[33] and, in the second place, economic pressure should be regarded as insufficient to negative consent. The court said that "the complainant's consent was not real in that she did not give it freely and voluntarily," but this is the fallacy already considered, of supposing that one can make deductions from the notion of voluntariness without considering its technical legal meaning.

23–014

Suppose that the manager had offered the woman sexual intercourse as an alternative to being grounded, and that she had accepted. If her consent were regarded as being nullified, the manager would be guilty of rape, which would be absurd. If she had said "no" he would not have dared take her by force, since he would not have wanted to commit a serious criminal offence or rape a woman. He was trying to commit some lesser wrong: that is, he was seeking a particular kind of bribe. (After all, he makes the offer because he wants to obtain consensual sexual intercourse/activity—not because he wants non-consensual intercourse.) To carry the point further: suppose it was the woman who took the initiative in offering to participate in a sexual act, in return for the manager's changing his intention to ground her. Here the initiative in that act of bribery would come from the woman, but her state of mind would be exactly the same as before: one of accepting the sexual act in order to buy off the discipline that could lawfully be imposed. Could it possibly be said that her consent was not "real" and should be ignored?[34]

---

[32] The provision might target those who make threats or intimidate a person to get her to take part in any act of a sexual nature. Otherwise, the courts will be forced to water down the consent requirement. There is a moral difference between the character who takes advantage of a reluctant consent and the one who acts without consent.

[33] Technically, a caning could constitute actual bodily harm, which means consent would not provide a defence: *R. v. Brown* [1994] 1 A.C. 212. But the better view is that a person can consent to being exposed to this type of trivial and transient from of harm; and the decision in *The King v. Donovan* [1934] 2 K.B. 498 is open to objection to the extent it holds otherwise. Cf. *R. v. Wilson* [1997] Q.B. 47.

[34] If economic pressure were accepted as negativing consent, the question would arise whether the degree of pressure must be balanced against the degree of harm to which consent is obtained. It may be argued that a threat to dismiss a woman employee vitiates her consent to being beaten but not to sexual intercourse, on the assumption that her reluctance to be beaten is stronger than her reluctance to submit to intercourse. But of course this assumption would only be true for some women, and might depend on such factors as the degree of pain expected in the proposed beating. A rule of this kind would be unworkable. By hypothesis the woman has submitted to the unwelcome act, and by hypothesis has done so under the threat in question; so she has indicated her own view that the threat implied an evil worse than the submission. It seems, then, that the only practicable rule is in terms of the kind of threat made, irrespective of the magnitude of the evil to which the complainant is caused to submit. (Whether a person is able in law to give consent to certain serious harm is an independent question to be discussed later.)

We come back, then, to the proposition that the best policy is to limit rape to acts done by force or under the threat of force (which is its ordinary meaning).[35] This might also be extended to cover cases where the threat is not of force, but where the threatened harm is greater or equal to the sexual violation that the victim will experience if she does not comply, because in such cases it might be said that the victim could not reasonably be expected to resist the threat. For example, D might threaten to report V for committing £500,000 fraud; V, a lawyer realizes she could be sent to jail for many years. She also believes that if she is prosecuted she will be totally humiliated and struck of the roll for life. Coupled with this, she may fear that in prison she will be strip-searched, raped repeatedly by the guards, assaulted by hardened criminals, and be denied regular access to her children. It is arguable that the magnitude of what is threatened is sufficient to vitiate her consent: her consent is vitiated because from her perspective the gravity of the harm threatened is equal or greater than that what is likely to result from engaging in the unwanted sexual intercourse.

23–015 In *R. v. Aiken*[36] a man offered not to report a lady's shoplifting on the condition that she provide him with sexual favours. The great majority of people would probably prefer to be charged with shoplifting, rather than engage in unwanted sexual intercourse with a stranger. In cases like *McCoy* and *Aiken* it is possible to say that the alternatives available to the victims were better than rape or sexual assault. They freely consented to the sexual intercourse/assault "as a result of a non-violent threat and could ... in the circumstances be reasonably expected to resist the threat."[37]

A more borderline case is where D threatens to upload his ex-girlfriend's sex videos on Facebook.[38] Some people would resist such a threat, since they might be exhibitionists. But many would find such a threat difficult to resist; the humiliation and gross loss of privacy might be too shocking for some to bear. There are no privacy or blackmail offences that would protect such a victim. It is one thing to threaten to reveal a person's past, but another to threaten to upload very intimate images onto the Internet.

The now repealed section 2(1) of the *Sexual Offences Act 1956* provided:[39]

---

[35] Cf. *R. v. Shaw* [1996] 1 Qd. R. 641, where D put a knife to V's throat; clearly if one is only able to choose between having her throat cut or submitting to sexual intercourse, she is given no choice but to submit.

[36] (2005) 157 A. Crim. R. 515 at 521.

[37] See the repealed section 65A of the *Crimes Act 1989* NSW. "(1) In this section: 'non-violent threat' means intimidatory or coercive conduct, or other threat, which does not involve a threat of physical force. (2) Any person who has sexual intercourse with another person shall, if the other person submits to the sexual intercourse as a result of a non-violent threat and could not in the circumstances be reasonably expected to resist the threat, be liable to imprisonment for 6 years."

[38] Cf. *R. v. Davis* [1998] N.J. No. 16, where D tried to obtain sexual favours by threatening to release compromising photographs of the victim. The court held that this type of blackmail would vitiate consent, but this is surely questionable. In *R. v. Stender* [2004] 188 C.C.C. (3d) 514, another Canadian court also held that such consent is not voluntary and therefore is no consent at all. But §135 of the *Criminal Code of Canada* expressly states: "a male ... commits rape when he has sexual intercourse with a female ... without her consent; or with her consent if the consent is extorted by threats or fear of bodily harm..."

[39] This offence provided a useful supplement to the law of rape, but no similar statutory provision supplemented the offence of "sexual assault." So even under the old law, threatening to cause a

"It is an offence for a person to procure a woman, by threats or intimidation, to have unlawful sexual intercourse in any part of the world."

This offence was not replaced when the *Sexual Offences Act 2003* was enacted. **23–016** This has left a lacuna in the law. The provision should have been replaced, because in many cases the coercion will not have the effect of annulling the victim's consent. Under the current law such a person will not be liable for any crime, unless the court holds that a reluctant consent is no consent at all. But a reluctant consent is still consent. Those who take advantage of a reluctant consent are not as morally reprehensible as those who intend to operate without any consent. Consequently, they should not be treated as rapists. In the United States, most states have tackled such conduct by enacting criminal coercion type offences.[40] This is preferable to treating such conduct as rape. Rape and assault by penetration are very serious offences and they should not be charged in cases where the victim has chosen to consent for her own benefit, even though she reluctantly consented.

The important difference between the offence under section 2(1) of the *1956 Act* and the offences found in sections 1-4 of the *Sexual Offences Act 2003*, among others, is in respect of the threats. "Threats or intimidation" were not defined, and they were taken to include more than the threats that traditionally vitiate consent at common law. "Intimidation" presumably covered implied threats. But even non-violent threats have to have some limits, and it would seem reasonable to say that, if the threat is not of a kind to vitiate consent, it must be a threat of such a nature as is likely to overcome resistance by an ordinary woman, and must not be merely a threat to withhold a benefit from her. The magnitude of the threatened harm (for example, the potential distress and actual fear of seeing her sex movies uploaded onto the Internet, *etc.*) would have to be balanced against the harmfulness of having to have sexual intercourse with the coercer.

It cannot be imagined that an offence is committed if a man, faced with a rebellious mistress (or a woman faced with a rebellious toy-boy), tells her that unless cohabitation is resumed she shall not have a mink coat, or will be turned out of her Kensington flat. A proposal to withhold a benefit that the defendant is not bound to give cannot reasonably be described as a threat sufficient for negating consent. The question is not, or should not be, how important it is for the woman to receive the benefit. The mistress's flat may be her only home, but that is not a reason for saying that the man's threat to evict her is a threat within the meaning of the offences found in sections 1-3 of the *Sexual Offences Act 2003*.[41]

---

woman economic loss or social injury if she did not submit to having her breasts fondled was no offence, unless the court regarded her consent as vitiated. Similarly, section 57(1) of the *Crimes Act 1958* (Victoria) provides: "A person must not by threats or intimidation procure a person to take part in an act of sexual penetration."

[40] See law as surveyed in Michal Buchhandler-Raphael, "Criminalizing Coerced Submission in the Workplace and in the Academy," (2010) 19 *Colum. J. Gender & L.* 409 at 439 *et passim*; and Patricia J. Falk, "Rape by Fraud and Rape by Coercion," (1998) 64 *Brook. L. Rev.* 39 at 89 *et seq.* See also Stuart P. Green, "Theft by Coercion: Extortion, Blackmail, and Hard Bargaining," (2005) 44 *Washburn L.J.* 553 at 558 *et seq.* As to the case for criminalizing such conduct, see Joel Fienberg, "Victims' Excuses: The Case of Fraudulently Procured Consent," (1986) 96 *Ethics* 330.

[41] Nor would such a threat have been caught by the offence of obtaining coition by threats. See the now repealed section 2(1) of the *Sexual offences Act 1956*.

The man is entitled to leave the woman, to whom he is not married, and it would be wrong and impolitic to say that if he expostulates with her, pointing out that the inevitable consequence of her present conduct will be the rupture of their relations, the result, if he succeeds in changing her attitude and sexual intercourse is resumed, is that he commits an offence. Even a threat to deprive the woman of something she is entitled to expect should not necessarily be sufficient (a threat by her debtor not to pay £1,000 he owes her).[42]

23–017 But the court in *R. v. Olugboja* thought that all such cases could be left to the jury with what it vaguely called "an appropriate direction." This is one more manifestation of the deplorable tendency of the criminal courts to leave important questions of legal policy to the jury.

A person who uses non-violent coercion to obtain sexual intercourse deserves criminal censure, but not for rape. Those who use large bribes or mediocre threats to obtain a woman's "consent" to have sexual intercourse differ from the rapist in the pure sense. This type of character is despicable, but he is not a rapist. He merely makes an offer which the offeree can reasonably resist if she chooses to do so. He uses unscrupulous threats/offers to obtain the victim's consent to have sexual intercourse, but only uses threats that can be resisted. He is trying to induce the victim to have consensual sexual intercourse with him, but would not dare to take the victim by force. Rather, he uses unscrupulous means to try to persuade the victim to have consensual sexual intercourse with him, because he does not want "non-consensual" intercourse. He leaves enough latitude so that the victim might resist his offer. Autonomous adults have to take some responsibility for their own well-being. If a person offers not to report another's petty theft if she provides him with sexual favours, then it is up to her to say, "No thank you, report it but I will not sleep with you." Hence, the victim is still able to say, "No." That choice has not been taken from her. Unscrupulous persuasion does not constitute a criminal offence.[43]

---

[42] Cf. *Michael v. Western Australia* [2008] 183 A. Crim. R. 348 (Steytler P., Miller J.A. with EM Heenan A.J.A. dissenting), where it was held that a prostitute's consent was vitiated because she only consented to have sexual intercourse with D for a discounted rate (and on other occasions for free) because he pretended to be a police officer and told her he could arrest her for engaging in illegal prostitution. Clearly, in this case there was genuine consent even if it was given reluctantly. Such a case could not be treated as rape in England and Wales, because the prostitute agrees by choice, and has the freedom and capacity to make that choice. *Per contra*, section 319(2)(a) of the *Criminal Code* (Western Australia) is a sweeping provision that deems that consent is vitiated (even if it is not in fact vitiated), if it "is obtained by *force, threat, intimidation*, deceit, or any fraudulent means…"

[43] In *R. v. Aiken* (2005) 157 A. Crim. R. 515 at 521, Studdert J. said: "However, must there be a threat of physical violence as opposed to some lesser threat? It cannot be that any type of threat necessarily [will do]. For instance, it does not seem to me that a despicable threat by an employer that he would block an employee's prospects of promotion at work unless she had intercourse with him would suffice, without more to vitiate consent." Studdert J. also noted under the N.S.W. law as it stood at the time: "A further matter of significance in section 65A of the *Crimes Act 1900* N.S.W. is that to prove an offence under that section the Crown must prove not only submission to intercourse as a result of a non violent threat, but also that the victim could not in the circumstances be reasonably expected to resist the threat offered." The latter is a very sensible limitation! Such an approach allows rape in the pure sense to be distinguished from cases where V chooses to have sexual intercourse to avoid a lesser harm such as topless photos being revealed, her past cannabis use being revealed and so on.

23.4.   THE VITIATION OF CONSENT BY MISTAKE

It is often said that consent is vitiated by fraud, but the point is not limited to fraud. Fraud can induce the complainant to make some mistake of fact, but it is also possible for the complainant to make a spontaneous mistake, which raises the same legal problem. To what extent does the complainant's mistake as to what is happening nullify or preclude his consent?

23–018

Consider the case where a man makes a false statement to a woman in order to obtain her consent to sexual intercourse. If he represents himself as being rich when he in fact is poor, few would argue that her consent is "vitiated," so that the man is guilty of rape or assault. The traditional view for both these offences is that they are acts done with consent. When, if ever, is fraud so serious that it can be said to destroy any "real" consent?

The answer is given by the previous observation that consent always means to something. If you consent to A, you do not for that reason consent to B. The converse is true too. If you do not consent to B, you do not for that reason not consent to A. If V permits D to have sexual intercourse with her (A), she does not automatically consent to D exposing her to H.I.V. (B). But, the latter is an independent wrong. If D had told his lover of his H.I.V. status, she may very well have permitted him to have sexual intercourse with a prophylactic: it is not the intercourse that concerns her as D is her lover—rather it is the H.I.V.[44] It may be said that in rape, the issue is the woman's consent to sexual intercourse with this man. If she does not know that the act is one of sexual intercourse, or if she is mistaken as to the identity of the man, then she does not consent, but otherwise she does. One must have regard to the decencies of language, and it cannot properly be asserted that the woman does not consent where she merely mistakes some attribute of the man (that he has career prospects, that he has been vasectomized, that he intends to marry her, that he is free from venereal disease). If a side-effect of the consensual sexual intercourse is that the victim is harmed in some other way, and she has not consented to that harm, the defendant should be criminalized for causing that harm.[45] There is, therefore, no need to inflate the grave offence of rape to make it cover deceits in general.

The law was settled in this sense in *R. v. Clarence*,[46] which has already been discussed in connection with section 20 of the *Offences against the Person Act 1861*. It will be remembered that the facts were that Clarence, knowing that he was suffering from venereal disease, had intercourse with his wife, and thus communicated the disease to her. In holding that Clarence was not guilty under section 20, because there was no assault, the Court of Crown Reserved took the view that the wife's consent to the contact was not vitiated by Clarence's

23–019

---

[44] In *R. v. B* [2007] 1 W.L.R. 1567 at 1571, Latham L.J. said: "Where one party to sexual activity has a sexually transmissible disease which is not disclosed to the other party any consent that may have been given to that activity by the other party is not thereby vitiated. The act remains a consensual act. However, the party suffering from the sexually transmissible disease will not have any defence to any charge which may result from harm created by that sexual activity, merely by virtue of that consent, because such consent did not include consent to infection by the disease."

[45] For example, V does not consent to being infected with H.I.V. if D does not tell her that is what she is risking by having unprotected sexual intercourse with him.

[46] (1889) 22 Q.B.D. 23.

nondisclosure of his condition; and Stephen J. expressly held that the rules for both rape and assault were the same. He stated the law thus: "The only sorts of fraud which so far destroy the effect of a woman's consent as to convert a connection consented to in fact into rape are frauds as to the nature of the act itself, or as to the identity of the person who does the act.[47] I should myself prefer to say that consent in such cases does not exist at all, because the act consented to is not the act done."

It would be ludicrous to classify the act as rape merely because the man did not tell the woman that he was diseased. The same moral offence would be committed by a woman who knowingly transmits disease to a man;[48] but a woman cannot rape. Many high powered bankers, barristers, and celebrities use high class escorts,[49] presumably they are willing to sleep with the escorts regardless of whether they have H.I.V. so long as a prophylactic is used. It is not a case of them not being willing to have sexual intercourse with a potentially H.I.V. positive escort, since many punters would be. It is a case of them not consenting to being deliberately and unnecessarily exposed to H.I.V.

Suppose a male gigolo supplies his own prophylactics, but is fed up with sleeping with elderly ladies for money so decides to insert pinholes through the prophylactics before using them. His aim is to infect the ladies with H.I.V. to teach them a lesson for cheating on their husbands. He does not aim to sexually violate them. Instead, he aims to please them sexually so that he can achieve his ulterior end of causing them to become infected with H.I.V. Let us assume that he is successful in achieving his evil end. It would be nonsensical to say that his customer did not want to have sexual intercourse; given that she paid him a large sum for that exact service. She also consents to the risk of H.I.V., since anyone with enough money to pay for a high class gigolo must have some awareness of H.I.V.; and must realize that gigolos and prostitutes are in a high risk group as far as H.I.V. infection is concerned.[50] Such a person would also know that prophylactics do not guarantee absolute protection. The defendant's criminal wrong is that he deliberately causes the victim to suffer grievous bodily harm. In such a case the defendant does not rape the victim, because the sexual aspects of the transaction were welcomed by her. It is true that if he had said to his customer, "I have punched small holes into the prophylactics so that I might infect you with H.I.V.;" she would not have consented to the sexual intercourse. But it is only the risk of infection that she is refusing to take, she wants the sexual intercourse but wants any risks to be minimized.

---

[47] This has been put into statutory form in section 76 of the *Sexual Offences Act 2003*. The latter sets out substantive principles, even though the section gives the impression that it only lays down evidential rules.

[48] In one case, a female singer infected a string of men with H.I.V. Allan Hall, "German Singer Admits not Telling Sexual Partners she was HIV Positive," (London: *The Telegraph*, 16 August 2010).

[49] A recent high profile case of such *use* was that involving Eliot Spitzer, the former governor of New York. Spitzer paid $U.S.5,000 for a night in the arms of a high class prostitute. He was not alone; see Russ Buettner and Ray Rivera, "Behind the Emperor's Club Escort Service," (New York: *New York Times*, 7 April 2008).

[50] Cf. *R. v. Lee* (1991), 3 O.R. (3d) 726, where V knew D was homosexual and was an intravenous drug user who shared needles.

The victim is not harmed in a sexual way, because she wants the sexual **23–020** intercourse. She is harmed in a non-sexual sense. The sexual intercourse is merely the means used by the defendant to cause the victim to suffer grievous bodily harm. The victim consents to the sexual intercourse, but does not consent to the harm that is incidental to it. It is best to criminalize this type of harm-doing as a non-sexual offence against the person. The focus should not be on the innocuous *means* used to achieve such an end. If a person poisons a delicious chocolate bar to kill V, he will be liable for murder. It does not matter that he did not use force to kill V, or that V consented to eating the chocolate. The harm is the actual killing and it is that which is criminalized, not the act of giving another a chocolate. Similarly, if X, a heroin addict, shares needles with heroin addict Y, without disclosing his H.I.V. status and thus infects Y he could be liable for an offence under sections 18 or 20 of the *Offences against the Person Act 1861*. But the act of sharing needles (means used) is not harmful *per se*. Clearly, the rape charge would merely be a device for punishing a totally different type of harm. Again, the legal question of transmitting disease can arise if disease is transmitted otherwise than by consensual intercourse. It would be most unsatisfactory to make the issue of criminal liability turn on the question whether the communication happened to be by physical contact that was otherwise unobjectionable.[51]

In *R. v. Cuerrier*,[52] the Supreme Court of Canada held: "The dishonest act must relate to obtaining consent to engage in sexual intercourse, and consists of either deliberate deceit respecting H.I.V. status or non-disclosure of that status. Without disclosure of H.I.V. status there can be no true consent. The consent cannot be simply to have sexual intercourse. Rather, it must be to have intercourse with a partner who is H.I.V.-positive." As we have just seen, this line of reasoning is fallacious. The Canadian courts have also held that "consent is vitiated only when there is a substantial risk of serious bodily harm."[53] Clarence would not be convicted of rape under the latter doctrine, because exposing V to the risk of contracting "V.D." would not expose her to a substantial risk of serious bodily harm. *Per contra*, Dica would be liable for rape, because H.I.V. infection is a serious injury.[54] In that jurisdiction, whether or not the non-disclosure of the sexually transmittable disease will vitiate consent depends on its harmfulness and on the gravity of the risk of transmission.[55] Alas, this approach fails to distinguish sexual harm from normal harm.

---

[51] It was suggested in *R. v. Clarence* that the defendant might have been liable for administering a noxious thing, on the assumption that disease germs were noxious things. If this application of the poisoning offence is justified, consent would clearly be no defence, because the victim did not consent to being given the disease. However, the poisoning offence has not in fact been charged in the case of communicating disease. Section 23 of the *Offences against the Person Act 1861* has the advantage of carrying a 10 year sentence; section 20 only carries a 5 year sentence.

[52] [1998] 2 S.C.R. 371.

[53] See *R. v. Mabior* [2010] M.J. No. 308.

[54] *R. v. Dica* [2004] Q.B. 1257.

[55] *R. v. T.* (J.A.) (2010) B.C.S.C. 766. Cf. Jonathan Herring, "Mistaken Sex," [2005] Crim. L.R. 511 at 517, where he asserts that if: "A does not disclose his criminal past to his sexual partner, B, where B would not have consented to the activity had she known of it, B should be taken to have not consented." Under this test, if a man secretly films his consensual lovemaking with V, he is liable for

Stephen J.'s rule does something to nail down the doctrine of vitiation of consent. If it be granted, it must necessarily govern spontaneous mistake as well as mistake produced by fraud; indeed, there was no fraud in *R. v. Clarence.* The point was made by the High Court of Australia:

"In considering whether an apparent consent is unreal it is the mistake of misapprehension that makes it so. It is not fraud producing the mistake which is material so much as the mistake itself."[56]

We now consider in more detail the two kinds of fundamental mistake identified long ago by Stephen J., since these have since been put into statutory form.[57]

23.5. MISTAKE AS TO THE NATURE OF THE ACT

23–021   An example of a mistake as the nature of the act is the unlikely case of *R. v. Flattery.*[58] Flattery induced a woman to submit to intercourse by pretending to perform a surgical operation. Although the report is not altogether clear, it may be taken that the woman did not know the physical nature of the act. Flattery was convicted of rape.

Here the woman submitted to the act and made no protest. She did not scream and shout for help, but accepted what was happening, and perhaps found the supposed surgery unexpectedly pleasant. There is a great factual difference between the violently resisting or terrified woman in the ordinary case of rape and the woman who happily submits because she has been deceived. In the latter case any mental discomfort she feels is only in retrospect when she discovers the truth,[59] though of course she may suffer the physical consequence of being pregnant or infected with a disease. Still, it is not unreasonable to say, where the error is as fundamental as this, that one of the essential elements of consent is lacking.

On the other hand, the decision of the Court of Criminal Appeal in *R. v. Williams*[60] is clearly wrong. Williams was a singing master who persuaded a female pupil to submit to intercourse under the pretence that it was treatment for breathing. His conviction of rape was affirmed. The conviction accorded with principle if the woman knew nothing about sex and thought that what her instructor was doing was merely an exercise to improve her lungs. If on the other hand she knew the facts of life and was willing to be persuaded that one of the

---

rape if she would not have had sex with him if she had known he was filming it. (But, surely the gravamen of the latter offence has to be the privacy and trust violation: as there was no sexual violation).

[56] *Papadimitropoulos v. The Queen* (1957) 98 C.L.R. 249 at 260, *per* Dixon C.J., McTiernan, Webb, Kitto and Taylor J.J.

[57] Section 76 of the *Sexual Offences Act 2003.*

[58] (1876-77) 2 Q.B.D. 410. The defendant's conduct in this case also amounted to sexual assault. *R. v. Case* (1850) 169 E.R. 381.

[59] For a fuller discussion of the wrongness and harmfulness of sexual violations that are discovered *ex post facto*, see Dennis J. Baker, "The Harm Principle vs. Kantian Criteria for Ensuring Fair, Principled and Just Criminalisation," (2008) 33 *Austl. J. Leg. Phil.* 66 at 78 *et seq.*

[60] [1923] 1 K.B. 340.

benefits of the act of sex was an improvement in breathing, then she did not mistake the nature of the act, even though in her innocence she may not have realized that the man's motives had nothing to do with singing.[61] Since the court did not enquire into the question, the decision must be regarded as unsound. This is borne out by the judgment of the High Court of Australia already referred to, given after a full review of the authorities:

> "[R]ape is carnal knowledge of a woman without her consent: carnal knowledge is the physical fact of penetration; it is the consent to that which is in question; such a consent demands a perception as to what is about to take place, as to the identity of the man and the character of what he is doing. But once the consent is comprehending and actual the inducing causes cannot destroy its reality and leave the man guilty of rape."[62]

Would a radiographer be liable for rape for inserting an ultrasound transducer into the vagina of V solely for his sexual gratification, if V consented to the insertion of the instrument only for medical diagnostic purposes?[63]　No, because he does not use his penis. But he would be liable for assault by penetration contrary to section 2 of the *Sexual Offences Act 2003*. 　23–022

What if the radiographer was merely doing his job, but gets a sexual thrill "after" he has inserted the ultrasound transducer?　If the only reason he has for inserting the instrument is that it is required to provide a medical diagnosis, he should not be liable for assault by penetration. This is assuming that his sexual excitement is a side-effect of him doing what he is medically required to do. Hence, it would have to be shown that his purpose for carrying out the procedure was not sexual. He might not have carried out the procedure for the purpose of seeking sexual excitement, but if he gets sexually excited from carrying out routine medical procedures there is always the danger that he might perform unnecessary procedures for his own sexual gratification. But we cannot punish him for what he might do.[64] 　23–023

If he carries out a legitimate medical examination and performs it with the dual aim of seeking sexual gratification he will be criminally liable for committing assault by penetration and perhaps sexual assault, depending on the facts.[65] It is important to focus on his purpose for inserting the instrument;[66] not

---

[61] See *R. v. Mobilio* [1991] 1 V.R. 339.

[62] *Papadimitropoulos v. The Queen* (1957) 98 C.L.R. 249 at 261. Cf. *R. v. Devonald* [2008] EWCA Crim. 527, where the Court of Appeal failed to identify this very obvious line of reasoning.

[63] On similar facts in the Australian case of *R. v. Mobilio* [1991] 1 V.R. 339, D was charged with rape. See also *R. v. Green* [2002] EWCA Crim. 1501; *R. v. BAS* [2005] Q.C.A. 97; *R. v. Chen* [2003] B.C.S.C. 1363.

[64] Dennis J. Baker, "Punishment Without a Crime: Is Preventive Detention Reconcilable with Justice," (2009) 34 *Austl. J. Leg. Phil.* 120.

[65] *R. v. Kumar* (2006) 150 S.J.L.B. 1053. There would need to be some objective evidence for the jury to be able to infer that the defendant was acting for a sexual rather than medical or other purpose. The evidence might involve a nurse reporting that she noticed that he was in a visible state of lust on many occasions while performing the procedure. Often this will be impossible to prove, since his lust may be hidden beneath his white overcoat; or might not go beyond him fantasizing. Cf. *State v. Chabot*, 478 A.2d 1136 (1984), where D, a male nurse, was found standing over an unconscious patient with his male part exposed and erect—he was meant to be giving the patient a sponge bath.

[66] It is also important to consider whether the victim was misled about the purpose. *R. v. Green* [2002] EWCA Crim. 1501.

on his afterthoughts. However, if it can be proved that he continued the procedure partly for a sexual purpose he should be liable for continuing the penetration with a sexual purpose in mind.[67] The patient's consent is vitiated from the moment in time when the defendant becomes sexually motivated to continue the procedure. The defendant should not continue with a medical procedure if part of his reason for continuing it is to seek sexual gratification. Instead, he should stop the procedure and ask another doctor to takeover. It is no defence for him to argue that when he started the procedure he did not act for a sexual purpose, if he continues the procedure in part to seek sexual gratification. The patient's consent relates to the entire penetration; and if that consent is only to the medical procedure, it is vitiated when the doctor starts acting for a non-medical purpose. Unfortunately, most of these kinds of sexual assaults will be cloaked as legitimate medical procedures.

In *R. v. Rosinski*,[68] Rosinski for his own lewd purposes undressed a woman and rubbed her with some liquid, causing her to believe that this was necessary for therapy. It is not clear from the reports whether he also pretended to have a medical qualification, but when the case was decided many unqualified persons purported to perform cures. Rosinski was convicted of assault, and the conviction was upheld by the C.C.C.R.

23–024   The rule for the vitiation of consent applies as much to sexual assault[69] as to rape. For sexual assault, as for rape, the fraud must be as to the nature of the act or the identity of the actor. By a stretch, the woman's mistake induced by Rosinski may be said to have related to the nature of the act. She thought it was a medical treatment, whereas Rosinski's purpose was carnal. On the other hand, her mistake did not relate to any of the objective facts, but only to what was in the defendant's mind.[70]

The foundation of the doctrine of mistake in relation to consent is the truism that a person who consents to A does not thereby consent to B. A man who consents to having his appendix out does not consent to having his *vas deferens* cut when he is unconscious (and even if he were conscious he would not know what the surgeon was doing). Stephen J. therefore explained the doctrine of vitiation of consent by saying that "the act consented to is not the act done."[71] But the complainant in *R. v. Rosinski* knew exactly what act was done. She knew that Rosinski was rubbing a liquid on her body. To say that she did not consent, if that denial is rested on "the nature of the act," is to make that notion distinctly metaphysical. When the true objection to what the defendant has done is that he

---

[67] See section 79(2) of the *2003 Act*. See also *Kaitamaki v. The Queen* [1985] A.C. 147; *R. v. Schaub* (1994) 138 S.J.L.B. 11. Cf. *State v. Baby*, 946 A.2d 463 (2008); *People v. Dancy*, 124 Cal. Rptr. 2d 898 (2002); *State v. Bunyard*, 133 P.3d 14 (2006).

[68] (1824) 168 E.R. 941.

[69] See section 3 of the *Sexual Offences Act 2003*.

[70] If the defendant acted from a mixed motive, partly proper and partly improper, the complainant's consent will be vitiated. But if V consents to the *core* act involved, the fact that she did not consent to some incidental act or event will not vitiate her consent as far as the core act is concerned. In *Bolduc v. R.* (1967) 63 D.L.R. 2d 82, the Supreme Court of Canada held that consent to a genuine medical examination was not vitiated by the fact that, unknown to the patient, a man accompanying the doctor was not medically qualified. See also *R. v. Richardson* [1999] Q.B. 444.

[71] *R. v. Clarence* (1889) 22 Q.B.D. 23 at 44.

was fraudulent and has invaded the victim's privacy, his conduct is turned into an assault by the pretence that consent is lacking.

Are you telling me that if the victim understands the basic physical "nature of the act" (for example, that her vagina is being penetrated with an ultrasound transducer), she consents to being assaulted by penetration? That is the logical conclusion. But as far as the core offences found in Part 1 of the *Sexual Offences Act 2003* are concerned, section 76(2) provides a solution. Under the subsection it is irrebuttably presumed that the "complainant did not consent to the relevant act… if the defendant intentionally deceived the complainant as to the nature or purpose of the relevant act." "Purpose" in the subsection refers to the defendant's purpose for doing the act. It is no defence for the defendant to assert that the victim understood the basic physical aspects of the act—the physical nature of oil being rubbed on her back, or the physical nature of her breasts being fondled,[72] or the physical nature of an ultrasound transducer being inserted into her private, if she does not understand his purpose for doing such acts. The victim would have to have full knowledge of the fact that the defendant his seeking sexual gratification.

23–025

Suppose D asks several women to take part in a breast cancer survey to enable him to prepare a computer software package for sale to medical doctors. Let us assume that he fondles their breasts only for this purpose. Is he liable for sexually assaulting the woman contrary to section 3 of the *Sexual Offences Act 2003*, if he intentionally deceives the victims as to the extent of his medical qualifications, rather than as to his purpose for acting? It appears that he has not committed a sexual assault.[73] His act is intended to be medical not sexual. His victims have not been deceived "as to the [medical] nature or purpose of the relevant act."

23–026

However, the courts have held that non-consensual contact with another's body is indecent assault, if the contact is with a body part that could serve some sexual purpose. A woman's breasts are commonly known to have two core functions: (1) they can be used for breast feeding a baby; and (2) they function to attract men. They are regarded as a private part of the woman and are not normally put on public display. Nor are they normally available for strangers and acquaintances to touch, as a "hand" might be. Handshaking between strangers is common in our society, but breast touching is not. A medically qualified person might touch a woman's breast if it is for the legitimate purpose of providing her with treatment. In *R. v. Tabassum*[74] the Court of Appeal held that it was "indecent"[75] assault where a woman consented to the touching of her breasts in the mistaken belief that D was medically qualified. In that case the defendant had asked several women to take part in a breast cancer survey so that he could prepare a computer software package for doctors. The defendant told the victims

---

[72] If a man cons a girl into taking fake first aid lessons so that he can fondle her breasts and kiss her lips, his deception will vitiate the girl's consent. See *H.K.S.A.R. v. Chan Wai Hung* [2000] H.K.E.C. 504.

[73] *R. v. Richardson* [1999] Q.B. 444.

[74] [2000] 2 Cr. App. R. 328.

[75] Now labelled as sexual assault.

that he had appropriate medical qualifications, but his medical knowledge was limited. Notwithstanding this, it appears that the defendant was not sexually motivated. It seems he was trying to develop the software to make money and to increase his chances of being accepted into a medical school.[76]

The Court of Appeal said:[77]

> "The nature and quality of the defendant's acts in touching the breasts of women to whom, in sexual terms he was a stranger, was unlawful and an indecent assault unless the complainants consented to that touching. ... On the evidence, if the jury accepted it, consent was given because they mistakenly believed that the defendant was medically qualified ... trained at Christie's and that, in consequence, the touching was for a medical purpose. As this was not so, there was no true consent. They were consenting to touching for medical purposes not to indecent behaviour, that is, there was consent to the nature of the act but not its quality. ... The touching was *prima facie* indecent, as we have said. Whether the defendant had any sexual motive or intent was irrelevant."

23–027   The conclusion is not supported by the facts of the case, because breast touching is not inherently indecent. Furthermore, there was no evidence to support the claim that Tabassum had committed sexual assault rather than assault pure and simple. The evidence suggested that he was genuinely attempting to construct a scientific database. Under the *Sexual Offences Act 2003* he could not be said to have "intentionally deceived the complainant as to the nature or purpose of the relevant act," merely because he deceived them of his medical qualifications. The decision would be on solid ground if the evidence had shown that Tabassum acted partly or solely for his own sexual gratification.[78] But the findings of fact showed otherwise. Nor can the decision be reconciled with *R. v. Richardson*,[79] where it was held that a dentist had not assaulted his patients merely because he treated them while he had been suspended from practice. Richardson's lies about his qualifications did not go to the nature or purpose of the act.

In *R. v. Tabassum* the court misconceptualizes the concept of "indecent." It is not true that every fraudulent touching of a body part that has a sexual function is inherently indecent. There is nothing "sexual" about a deregistered medical doctor examining breasts, penes and vaginas for medical purposes, if he acts merely to obtain money and intends to supply a proper medical service. If such a doctor pretends to be registered so that he can continue to practice because he has a large mortgage and needs the money, his fraud does not go to the nature and purpose of the act. Nor is it indecent (or sexual) for a makeup artist to apply body makeup to the naked body of a model, or for a tattoo artist to tattoo breasts and buttocks, or for a body-piercer to pierce a breast nipple or other private parts, if he merely does this as a part of his job to earn a living.

---

[76] It was suggested in evidence that he was obsessed with becoming a medical doctor.

[77] *R. v. Tabassum* [2000] 2 Cr. App. R. 328 at 336-337.

[78] By "quality" the court seemed to mean "purpose." It was held that: "There was consent to the *nature* of the act but not its *quality*." *R. v. Tabassum* [2000] 2 Cr. App. R. 328 at 337. In other words, the women knew that the nature of the act was that their breasts were being touched, but did not know exactly what they were being touched for. They were being touched for a non-legitimate medical purpose.

[79] [1999] Q.B. 444.

What if Tabassum has said he was testing the safety of a therapeutic ointment, when he was really testing the safety of a cosmetic? Does the fact that he rubbed it on a body part that has more than one function including a sexual function make his experimenting a sexual act? Clearly not. It should be fairly obvious by now, that *R. v. Tabassum* does not make a distinction between medical and sexual acts. The women who Tabassum deceived understood the nature of the breast examinations. Tabassum's lies about his qualifications did not go to the nature or purpose of the act. Fraud as to having a medical qualification is fraud as to a personal attribute, not as to the nature or purpose of what the person without those attributes did.[80]

23–028

Do you mean to say that a gentleman from the Subcontinent with a bogus medical degree who undertakes a serious surgical operation and makes a hash of it is not guilty of an aggravated assault? He ought to be guilty of an offence in a rational system of law.[81] It is arguable that when a person is inadequately qualified to perform a particular medical procedure, that his concealment of his inadequacies goes to the nature and purpose of the act that he performs. An operation carried out by a skilled surgeon is fundamentally different to one carried out by a person who is not qualified to perform such an operation. (One is therapeutic the other is butchery.) If the person is qualified but is not registered, or is only marginally unqualified, then the nature and the purpose of his act is not kept from the victim.[82]

23–029

Where the defendant is substantially under-qualified, and as a result recklessly causes grievous bodily or actual bodily harm to his deceived victim, he should be liable for aggravated assault. He should not be able to rely on the patient's apparent consent as a defence, because the nature and the purpose of his attempted treatment is fundamentally different from what the patient thought she was consenting to have done to her. She thought she was consenting to standard or close to standard medical treatment; not to having her life and health put in jeopardy by a non-medical person. (Sexual assault is not an issue, because shoddy surgery in itself is not of a sexual nature.)

What if a punter runs off without paying for the services of a lady of the night? He does not commit rape, because V is not deceived as to the nature and purpose of the act.[83] The prostitute knows that she is being asked to engage in

23–030

---

[80] Cf. *R. v. Wellard* [1978] 1 W.L.R. 921, where the defendant, pretending to be a police officer, required a girl to accompany him. The jury found that the girl felt compelled to do so, and convicted the defendant of kidnapping, the verdict being upheld. There was no discussion of vitiation of consent. It may be tempting to suppose that the girl's consent was vitiated by fraud. But, for reasons stated above, it causes fewer problems to regard her consent as vitiated by duress, the threat of force being applied.

[81] Section 49 of the *Medical Act 1983* makes it an offence for any unqualified person to falsely pretend to be medical doctor. See *R. v. Grimshaw* (1984) unreported. See also section 38 of the *Dentists Act 1984*.

[82] *R. v. Richardson* [1999] Q.B. 444.

[83] *R. v. Linekar* [1995] Q.B. 250; *R. v. Jheeta* [2008] 1 W.L.R. 2582 at 2590. Cf. *Michael v. Western Australia* [2008] 183 A. Crim. R. 348, where the Supreme Court of Western Australia examines this issue at length in a 114 page judgment. (That case, however, is best explained as one where V's consent was vitiated by non-violent threats, which are provided for in the law of that jurisdiction.)

sexual intercourse and agrees to have sexual intercourse—there is consensus *quoad hoc*. She also consents to act A (sexual intercourse), even though she does not consent to B (not being paid). Nor is the punter's identity an issue, so there is consensus *quoad hanc personam*.[84]

If this type of fraud is to be criminalized, then it should be done by enacting a special provision.[85] It does not involve a sexual violation as grave as rape in the *pure* sense. It appears the gravamen of the wrong has more to do with fraud than it does with a sexual violation,[86] because the woman was going to have intercourse with the punter anyway. There was nothing about the punter that was preventing her from consenting—she was more than willing to lie down with him. The prostitute would not have provided the service if the punter had said in advance: "I am not going to pay you." But her loss is pecuniary. It is not a case where she would not have slept with the punter under any circumstances. She was entirely willing to provide the service, but expected payment. It was the non-payment that she was not willing to accept—not the sexual intercourse.

23.6.   MISTAKE AS TO THE IDENTITY OF THE ACTOR

23–031   At common law false impersonation did not turn an act of sexual intercourse into rape, though it was an assault (an odd distinction). A woman who yielded believing that the man was her husband gave consent to the act and so was not regarded as being raped.[87] The rule was reaffirmed by the Court Crown Cases Reserved in 1868.[88] It was strictly logical. If a man slips into bed with a woman pretending to be her husband, and has intercourse with her, the woman happily accepts the intercourse as she would if it were in fact her husband. It does not look at all like rape, which was originally based upon the notion of force and still normally involves force. However, the lack of legal provision for such an escape was naturally liable to cause public outcry. The law of obtaining sex by fraud could not be used against the man where, as in the case just mentioned, he did not make any representation as to his identity but merely relied on a spontaneous mistake by the woman. Parliament therefore intervened by including a provision in an *Act of 1885*, now represented by section 76 of the *Sexual Offences Act 2003*:

---

[84] *R. v. Linekar* [1995] Q.B. 250 at 257.

[85] In at least one Australian state this type of conduct is covered by a special provision, see section 57(2) of the *Crimes Act 1958* (Vic.) which provides: "A person must not by any fraudulent means procure a person to take part in an act of sexual penetration." In *R. v. Rajakaruna* (2004) 8 V.R. 340, D repeatedly used prostitutes without paying for their services. He was convicted of (among other things) procuring sexual penetration by fraudulent means.

[86] In England and Wales it is probably covered by section 2 of the *Fraud Act 2006* as a property offence.

[87] See *R. v. Saunders* (1838) 173 E.R. 488; *R. v. Jackson* (1822) 168 E.R. 911; *R. v. Clarke* (1854) Dears C.C. 397; *R. v. Dee* (1884) 15 Cox C.C. 57; *R. v. Williams* (1838) 173 E.R. 497. This despite the traditional definition of rape, stemming from the institutional writers, that the offence can be committed "by force, fear or fraud." The decisions rejecting false impersonation (and therefore, *a fortiori*, all other kinds of fraud, except fraud as to the nature of the act, as founding a charge of rape) refute the last item in the definition.

[88] *R. v. Barrow* (1868) L.R. 1 C.C.R. 156.

"(1) If in proceedings for an offence to which this section applies it is proved that the defendant did the relevant act and that any of the circumstances specified in subsection (2) existed, it is to be conclusively presumed—(a) that the complainant did not consent to the relevant act, and (b) that the defendant did not believe that the complainant consented to the relevant act.

(2) The circumstances are that– (a) the defendant intentionally deceived the complainant as to the nature or purpose of the relevant act; (b) the defendant intentionally induced the complainant to consent to the relevant act by impersonating a person known personally to the complainant."

If it is proved that D did the relevant act and that he intentionally deceived V as to the nature or purpose of the act, or intentionally induced V to consent to the act by impersonating a person known personally to her, it is to be irrebuttably presumed that V did not consent to the act and that D did not believe that V consented to it. This is in effect a substantive doctrine of criminal law, because section 76 prevents D from claiming that he had reasonable grounds for believing that V would consent regardless of his deceit.

It is difficult to fathom a case where D could have reasonable grounds for believing that V is consenting even though he is impersonating another person known to the victim. Suppose D is lost at sea and end ups stranded on a desert island for a year. Eventually he is discovered and is brought back to England, only to discover his fiancée is dating someone else. He does not want to ruin her new life, but is desperate to see her again so sneaks into her bedroom at night and pretends to be her current boyfriend. This leads to sexual intercourse. Could he argue that he had reasonable grounds for believing that she would consent either to him or her current boyfriend making love to her?

He might, but because he has impersonated a person known to V, the irrebuttable presumption of no consent applies. It is presumed that there was no consent and that he knew that there was no consent, regardless of whether he had reasonable grounds for believing otherwise. He "impersonates" a person known to the complainant by acting like that person in a situation where he knows that the woman is mistaken. The *Sexual Offences Act 2003* unlike the *1885* and *1956 Acts*, applies to the impersonation of a woman's lover. Presumably the Parliament of 1885 thought that women who took lovers were not worthy of any special protection against imposters; and the *Act of 1956* was merely consolidating.

23–032

The same irrebuttable presumption of no consent applies when the victim has been deceived as to the nature and purpose of the act. If a doctor inserts an ultrasound transducer into the vagina of V for his own sexual gratification, it is irrebuttably presumed that V did not consent. Likewise, if the Crown shows that he examined a patient's breasts to seek sexual gratification, the irrebuttable presumption of no consent applies. The issue of whether he had reasonable grounds for believing that the victim was consenting will not be considered, since it is presumed there was no consent. All the prosecution has to do is show that the victim was in fact deceived as to the nature and purpose of the act.

23–033 In Guy de Maupassant's *Boule de Suife*[89] there is a saucy tale of a man who masquerades as a woman and acts as a lady maid, bathing his mistress. Is he guilty of sexual assault if the bathing involved touching his mistress sexually? On principle no. The mistress's mistake as to the gender of her "maid" is a mistake as to attribute, not as to identity, and so does not vitiate her consent even if a mistake as to identity does so. In a modern context, this might occur if a man dresses as a woman to lure other men in a public bar—as unbelievable as it sounds, some men have actually been taken in by such persons. The victim might discover his mistake if the encounter advances to a more intimate encounter in a hotel room, but by then he would have already been sexually molested by a man whom he believed to be a woman.

23–034 **I should have thought that the gender of the person is so important that it should go to identity.** My own view is that the law would become undesirably imprecise if a mistake as to some characteristic of a person, even so important a characteristic as gender, were regarded as a mistake of identity. Where would it end? Would it catch a 30-year-old woman who pretends to be 22 years of age? In the real world characteristics such as gender are patently obvious to most people.

The distinction between identity and attributes is drawn by the civil courts. A mistake of identity occurs only where the person under the mistake confuses two real people, X and Y, by supposing X is Y. It is not a mistake of identity when you think that a man is a woman, unless you think that he is some specific woman; or that you believe an unqualified person to be a qualified doctor, unless you believe him to be some other real person who is a doctor. That, at any rate, is the meaning of mistake of identity in the law of contract,[90] and there is no reason why this concept should be any different in the criminal law.

23–035 **Then what offence has the man committed?** None. We have no crime of procuring submission to a bodily interference by fraud. We should have, but we have not. If D's gender does not affect his identity, it must affect the nature and the purpose of sexual act, must it not? A sexual act is a sexual act; such an act does not become sexual just because the fondler happens to be a man rather than a woman.

Nevertheless, there is an aberrant authority which suggests otherwise. In *R. v. Devonald*,[91] D incentivized V (an adult male) to engage in self-abuse in front of a web camera. D was able to encourage V to self-abuse himself (masturbate) in front of the web camera by pretending to be a 20-year-old female called "Cassey." Cassey was invented by D, because he wanted to humiliate V. (D was seeking revenge because V had jilted his daughter.) Since Cassey only existed in cyberspace, V's consent was not vitiated on the grounds that D had impersonated someone personally "known" to V. Section 76(2)(b) of the *Sexual Offences Act 2003* only applies if the defendant impersonates someone whom the victim in fact knows. V did not know Cassey, because she only existed in cyberspace.

---

[89] Published in Paul Alexis *et al.*, *Les soirées de Médan: nouvelles*, (Paris: Charpentier, 1880).

[90] Glanville Williams, "Mistake as to Party in Law of Contract," (1945) 23 *Can. B. Rev.* 271; 380.

[91] [2008] EWCA Crim. 527.

The case should never have made it to court. The victim was not totally innocent. People have to take some responsibility for their own actions. The person on the other end of the Internet cable could have been a 12-year-old girl. Thus, V should not have been exposing himself to the world at large; especially as he did not know who was at the other end of the line. That aside, D's behaviour was reprehensible, so the Court of Appeal in typical fashion decided to do a bit of inventing of its own. It held that it was open to the jury to conclude that V had been deceived as to the purpose of the masturbation. In particular, it held that V "had been deceived into believing that he was indulging in sexual acts with, and for the sexual gratification of, a young woman with whom he was having an online relationship." The court held that V had been deceived as to the purpose of the act, because he believed that he was acting to provide a 20-year-old woman with sexual gratification, not to provide a man with revengeful gratification.

The court's analysis is erroneous, because the purpose and nature of the act are **23–036** inseparable in this context. They are one in the same. The purpose of the act was sexual: D wanted V to engage in sexual activity. D's ulterior intent was to seek to revenge, but his primary purpose was to have V engage in sexual activity. D's ulterior aim did not change the purpose or nature of the acts he asked V to perform. His purpose was to have V perform sexual acts. More importantly, the victim knew that he was being asked to perform a sexual act, he knew that the nature and purpose of what he was doing was sexual.[92] The victim intended to do a sexual act and knew the exact nature of what he was doing. The ulterior motive of the viewer did not change the nature or purpose of the act. D's ulterior motive was not sexual—he was merely seeking revenge.

Furthermore, D's gender cannot be said to have made any difference. Would it have made any difference if D had sought revenge by asking a 20-year-old female to trick D into performing sexually in front of the webcam? What if the woman gained some pleasure out of seeing V engaging in self-abuse? Would it matter that her ulterior aim was to seek revenge for her friend, and so on? Does the pathetic individual who pays for telephone sex have a case if a 65-year-old lady tells him she is a 21-year-old aerobics instructor? I would think not. People have to take some responsibility for their own stupidity. If a person is willing to perform lewd acts online, then he must expect that his performance might be recorded and uploaded onto the Internet for the world at large to view, or that anyone could be at the other end of the line. Such a person should also know that the person at the other end could have many ulterior aims! (Hence, Devonald knew he was doing a sexual act; he just did not know *why* he had been asked to do it.)

---

[92] Section 76 of the *2003 Act* is only concerned with the "relevant act;" it does not criminalize bad motives if the nature and purpose of what V consented to was clearly sexual. "In our judgment the ambit of section 76 is limited to the 'act' to which it is said to apply. In rape cases the 'act' is vaginal, anal or oral intercourse. Provided this consideration is constantly borne in mind, it will be seen that section 76(2)(a) is relevant only to the comparatively rare cases where the defendant deliberately deceives the complainant about the nature or purpose of one or other form of intercourse. No conclusive presumptions arise merely because the complainant was deceived in some way or other by disingenuous blandishments or common garden lies by the defendant. These may well be deceptive and persuasive, but they will rarely go to the nature or purpose of intercourse." See *R. v. Jheeta* [2008] 1 W.L.R. 2582 at 2590.

23.7. INCAPACITY, MENTAL DISORDER AND CONSENT

23–037 As far as sexual offences are concerned, the victim's consent will only be valid where she has sufficient capacity to be able to make an informed choice.[93] A person many not be able to consent because she is physically incapacitated such as where she is unconscious or semi-paralysed. There may be an implied consent even though a person is not physically able to communicate her assent. Take the woman who has been put in a medically induced comma to help her recover from a medical operation. If her husband visits her in hospital while she is comatose and holds her hand and kisses her on the forehead, he should not be liable for sexual assault. Clearly, the husband has reasonable grounds for believing that his wife would welcome his affection and comforting support during her recovery. However, cases where a defendant can be said to have reasonable grounds for believing that a physically incapacitated person (that is, a person who is physically unable to communicate her wishes one way or the other) was consenting will be rare.

Our focus in the rest of this section will be on mental incapacity. A person may be mentally incapacitated because of intoxication or simply because she suffers some kind of mental disorder or mental impairment. A person may be so subnormal in intelligence, or so mentally ill, that she cannot consent to sexual intercourse, but the Supreme Court of Victoria rightly allowed this possibility very limited scope.[94] That a mentally retarded person readily gives way to "animal instincts" is not to the purpose.[95] The Australian court said that for a woman to lack capacity to consent to intercourse:

> "it must be proved that she has not sufficient knowledge or understanding to comprehend
> (a)   that what is proposed to be done is the physical fact of penetration of her body by the male organ or, if that is not proved,
> (b)   that the act of penetration proposed is one of sexual connection as distinct from an act of a totally different character."[96]

In *D Borough Council v. AB*,[97] Mostyn J. said that the victim should have an

> "understanding and awareness of:
> • the mechanics of the act;
> • that there are health risks involved, particularly the acquisition of sexually transmitted and sexually transmissible infections; and
> • that sex between a man and a woman may result in the woman becoming pregnant."

---

[93] See section 74 of the *Sexual Offences Act 2003*.

[94] *R. v. Morgan* [1970] V.R. 337. The rule would be more clearly expressed in positive terms: the woman must both know the physical facts and know that the connection is sexual; failing either knowledge, she does not consent in law. This formulation is greatly superior to the English pronouncement of the 19th century. See *R. v. Barratt* (1873) L.R. 2 C.C.R. 81.

[95] *R. v. Barratt* (1866) L.R. 1 C.C.R. 39; cf. *R. v. Fletcher* (1859) 169 E.R. 1168 at 1172.

[96] *R. v. Morgan* (1970) V.R. 337.

[97] (2011) 161 N.L.J. 254 at para.42.

This goes too far. A mentally disabled person should be able to maintain a sexual relationship without fully understanding all the implications of pregnancy.[98] If the alleged victim gives what consent she can, then it should count for something. Furthermore, many sexual acts will not involve intercourse and thus the risk of pregnancy or of being infected with a sexually transmitted disease will not be an issue. For example, a man might fondle a mentally impaired woman's bosom and so on. In such cases, it will be essential to prove that the victim understood the fondling, *etc.* was done for a sexual purpose and that she welcomed it for that reason.

The requirement has to be lower than Mostyn J. suggests. There are two reasons **23–038** for making the requirement low. First, this is necessary to prevent men who have intercourse with willing but sexually innocent girls from being convicted of rape. Secondly, it is necessary in order not to forbid sexual expression to women and men of low intelligence.[99] Every offence has the effect of diminishing the liberty of the defendant, but when a person is convicted on account of a consensual activity the practical result is to restrict not only his liberty but that of the person with whom he acts. Great care must be taken to allow mentally handicapped individuals to have some sexual freedom.

Section 2 of the *Mental Capacity Act 2005* provides: "a person lacks capacity in relation to a matter if at the material time he is unable to make a decision for himself in relation to the matter because of an impairment of, or a disturbance in the functioning of, the mind or brain." Likewise, the definition of mental disorder is very wide.[100] If a person's incapacity relates to a recognized mental disorder he will be covered by the specific offences found in sections 30-37 of the *Sexual Offences Act 2003*.

These offences cover those whose "mental disorder" impedes their capacity to make an informed choice about whether to consent to the sexual activity.

For example, section 30(1) of the *Sexual Offences Act 2003* provides:

"(A)   commits an offence if–
    (a)   he intentionally touches another person (B),
    (b)   the touching is sexual,
    (c)   B is unable to refuse because of or for a reason related to a mental disorder, and
    (d)   A knows or could reasonably be expected to know that B has a mental disorder and that because of it or for a reason related to it B is likely to be unable to refuse.
(2)   B is unable to refuse if–
    (a)   he lacks the capacity to choose whether to agree to the touching (whether because he lacks sufficient understanding of the nature or reasonably foreseeable consequences of what is being done, or for any other reason), or
    (b)   he is unable to communicate such a choice to A."

---

[98] *In Re F. (Mental Patient: Sterilisation)* [1990] 2 A.C. 1.

[99] *In Re F. (Mental Patient: Sterilisation)* [1990] 2 A.C. 1, a 36-year-old woman with the mind of a small child desired sexual relations because of her innate instincts and was sterilized as a matter of necessity so that she could enjoy what limited sexual freedom she had. She did not fully understand the consequences of having sexual intercourse, but the court thought that she should be allowed to have some sexual freedom.

[100] Mental disorder means "any disorder or disability of the mind." See section 1 of the *Mental Health Act 1983* (as amended by section 1 of the *Mental Health Act 2007*).

23–039 The victim's inability to understand the nature of the sexual act may not be the only reason for her not being able to make an informed choice about whether she wants to engage in the sexual activity. The victim may have a full comprehension of the nature of the proposed sexual activity, but may lack the capacity to understand that she can assent or dissent.[101] The victim may understand that what is proposed is sexual intercourse that could result in pregnancy or in her contracting a sexually transmitted disease, but might consent to the intercourse because she mistakenly believes that she will be harmed if she does not. If it was her mental disorder that caused her to make such a mistake, she will be covered by the specific provisions found in sections 30–37 of the *Act of 2003*. Consent generally is about choice. Did the victim have the capacity to balance the relevant information to make an informed choice about whether to consent?[102] A person's consent will only be valid if she is capable of understanding the act and its consequences and is sufficiently able to understand that she can chose either to assent or dissent.

In *R. v. Cooper*[103] the victim had a history of mental illness. The victim visited a community mental health team resource centre and was seen by a consultant forensic psychiatrist. The psychiatrist formed the view that she was in such a state that it would be best to have her compulsorily admitted to hospital. The victim walked out of the session with the psychiatrist. After she left the centre she met the defendant (who was also a user of the resource centre) in the centre car park. The victim told the defendant that she had been in and out of psychiatric hospitals for many years. She also told him that she wanted to leave the area (Croydon), because she believed that people were after her and were going to harm her. The defendant told her that he could help her. The defendant sold the victim's mobile telephone and bicycle and thereafter took her to his friend's house where he repeatedly encouraged her to consume crack cocaine. While at the house the victim went into the bathroom. She was in the bathroom when the defendant cornered her and asked her to fellate him. The victim was in an irrational state and this caused her to mistakenly believe that if she did not comply with the defendant's request for oral sex, she would not be able to get out of the situation she was in without being harmed. She would not have complied but for this irrational belief; and the belief was caused by her mental disorder. In other words, she lacked the mental capacity to ascertain whether or not she would be forced to do the act if she did not comply:

> "She had an irrational fear that she needed to get out of Croydon because her life was under threat. In these circumstances, having thrown herself upon the mercy of the appellant in order to escape from Croydon, she found herself confined with him, unable by reason of irrational fear either to refuse sexual activity, or to communicate her refusal."[104]

---

[101] *R. v. Cooper* [2009] 1 W.L.R. 1786.

[102] Section 3 of the *Mental Capacity Act 2005* provides some guidance: "a person is unable to make a decision for himself if he is unable–(a) to understand the information relevant to the decision, (b) to retain that information, (c) to use or weigh that information as part of the process of making the decision, or (d) to communicate his decision (whether by talking, using sign language or any other means)."

[103] [2009] 1 W.L.R. 1786.

[104] *R. v. Cooper* [2009] 1 Cr. App. R. 211 at 225.

In the House of Lords Baroness Hale said:[105]

> "the case law on capacity has for some time recognised that, to be able to make a decision, the person concerned must not only be able to understand the information relevant to making it but also be able to 'weigh [that information] in the balance to arrive at [a] choice'. ... [A] person's delusions that she was being commanded by God to have sexual intercourse, an act which she was perfectly capable of understanding, might make her incapable of exercising an autonomous choice in the matter."

In this case the victim's irrational belief caused her to comply with the defendant's request for oral sex. She did not want to have oral sex with him, but formed the irrational belief that it was the only way for her to get herself out of the situation in which she found herself. Baroness Hale said: "The words 'for any other reason'[106] are clearly capable of encompassing a wide range of circumstances in which a person's mental disorder may rob them of the ability to make an autonomous choice, even though they may have sufficient understanding of the information relevant to making it." The victim was robbed of the ability to make an autonomous choice because of her schizophrenia. If she had not been in an irrational state she would have been able to assess the nature of any threat posed by the defendant (and would have realized that those others who she thought were out to kill her were just a figment of her own imagination) and thus would have had sufficient understanding of the circumstantial facts to be in a position to make a genuine choice about whether to comply with his request for oral sex.

23–040

Baroness Hale went on to say:[107]

> "It is, perhaps, easier to understand how the test of capacity might be 'act-specific' but not 'person-specific' or 'situation-specific' if intellectual understanding were all that was required. The complainant here did know what a 'blow job' [oral sex] was. ... Once it is accepted that choice is an exercise of free will, and that mental disorder may rob a person of free will in a number of different ways and in a number of different situations, then a mentally disordered person may be quite capable of exercising choice in one situation but not in another. The complainant here, even in her agitated and aroused state, might have been quite capable of deciding whether or not to have sexual intercourse with a person who had not put her in the vulnerable and terrifying situation in which she found herself on 27 June 2007. The question is whether, in the state that she was in that day, she was capable of choosing whether to agree to the touching demanded of her by the defendant."

The talk of "situation-specific" adds little. Take the situation in *R. v. Cooper*. If a reasonable person would not have responded to Cooper's request for oral sex by providing it, then the fact that there was an element of duress involved (if approaching someone in a bathroom and asking for oral sex *per se* constitutes an implied threat),[108] does not tell us why the victim did not have the capacity to refuse. If anyone else would have refused in that situation, then the only

---

[105] *R. v. Cooper* [2009] 1 W.L.R. 1786 at 1793 quoting *In re C (Adult: Refusal of Treatment)* [1994] 1 W.L.R. 290 at 295; *In re MB (Medical Treatment)* [1997] 2 F.L.R. 426 at 433.

[106] See section 30(2)(a) of the *Sexual Offences Act 2003*.

[107] *R. v. Cooper* [2009] 1 W.L.R. 1786 at 1794.

[108] We have to remember he had also sold her bicycle and mobile telephone; had stripped naked in another room in front of her and had encouraged her to do the same; had told her he was going to get her pregnant; and had repeatedly pushed her to consume crack cocaine. It would appear to any reasonable bystander that he only had one reason for giving her his crack cocaine!

explanation for the victim not refusing is that she was mentally impaired. This is just a way of saying this victim complied with his request for oral sex even though a reasonable person in the same situation would not have complied, because her mental disorder prevented her from making a proper assessment of the situation she found herself in.

23.8.   INTOXICATION AND CONSENT

23–041   There is no special rule on the subject of drink, (other) drugs, and consent. A surgical consent form signed when the patient is under such heavy sedation that he is unable to understand the form would obviously be worthless. If a man, in order to cause a woman to succumb to his wishes, stupefies her by drugs so that she does not know what is happening or is physically unable to make resistance, then of course she does not consent, so he may be guilty of an offence under the *Sexual Offences Act 2003*. There is also a statutory offence covering preparatory acts. Section 61 of the *Sexual Offences Act 2003* targets those who drug others so that they or someone else might engage in sexual activity with V. If X drugs Y so that either he or T can sexually fondle her breasts, or rape her, X will be liable regardless of whether any sexual activity takes place.[109] Suppose X has drugged Y and is about to rape her when the police discover him. Since Y has already been drugged, X will be liable under section 61 even though he did not get a chance to rape her.[110]

23–042   **Alcohol is a kind of drug. What about the man who makes an attempt on a lady's virtue by plying her with unsuitable liquors?**   If the effect is to overcome the woman, in the way just stated, the man will if successful in his endeavour be guilty of rape. But the usual effect of alcohol is merely to reduce self-control, so that a woman who would not normally submit to sexual intercourse may offer no resistance to it. She may know what is happening, and be physically able to express dissent, but have her normal inhibitions removed by alcohol.[111] In such circumstances there is consent to the sexual act, since a

---

[109] If a woman goes with a man and pretends that she is going to have sexual intercourse with him, but drugs him and steals his wallet, she would not be caught by this section because she does not drug him for the purposes of engaging in sexual activity. See *R. v. Hakki* [2006] 1 Cr. App. R. (S.) 46.

[110] Inchoate liability can also be extended further back. Falk notes that in many U.S. jurisdictions it is a crime to possess or distribute common rape drugs such as gamma hydroxy butyrate (GHB), flunitrazepam (Rohypnol) and ketamine. See Patricia J. Falk, "Rape by Drugs: A Statutory Overview and Proposals for Reform," (2002) 44 *Ariz. L. Rev.* 131.

[111] *R. v. Bree* [2008] Q.B. 131. For a deeper discussion of the issue, see Peter Westen, *The Logic of Consent*, (Burlington VT: Ashgate Publishing, 2004); Alan Wertheimer, *Consent to Sexual Relations*, (New York: Cambridge University Press, 2003) at 232 *et passim*; Sharon Cowan, "The Trouble with Drink: Intoxication, (In)Capacity, and the Evaporation of Consent to Sex," (2008) 41 *Akron L. Rev.* 899. Goodman argues the more intoxicated the victim, the more explicit her consent should be. (Presumably, this only applies where the higher level of intoxication is patently obvious to the defendant. If a totally intoxicated victim seems only mildly intoxicated, then the standard adds nothing.) Christine C. Goodman, "Protecting the Party Girl: A New Approach for Evaluating Intoxicated Consent," (2009) 2009 *BYU L. Rev.* 57. This approach also seems to overlook the fact that a drunken intent is still an intent.

drunken consent is still consent.[112] But if the victim's intoxication causes her to temporarily lose her capacity to choose whether or not to have intercourse, she will not be consenting, "and subject to questions about the defendant's state of mind, if intercourse takes place, this would be rape."[113]

In *R. v. Bree*, the Court of Appeal said:[114]

> "[W]here the complainant has voluntarily consumed even substantial quantities of alcohol, but nevertheless remains capable of choosing whether or not to have intercourse, and in drink agrees to do so, this would not be rape. We should perhaps underline that, as a matter of practical reality, capacity to consent may evaporate well before a complainant becomes unconscious. Whether this is so or not, however, is fact-specific, or more accurately, depends on the actual state of mind of the individuals involved on the particular occasion."

It will be important for the court to establish whether the victim's mental incapacity was such that it made the intercourse non-consensual. The defendant must have reasonable grounds for believing that the intoxicated victim is consenting. The victim may be fully conscious and realize what is happening, but may be too intoxicated to resist or communicate her resistance.[115] If the victim is fully aware of what is happening and is not consenting in her mind, but is too intoxicated to resist or to convey her absence of consent, she does not in fact consent. The defendant will be liable unless he can convince the jury he reasonably believed she was consenting.[116] The victim should be sufficiently coherent to understand that she is being asked to have sexual intercourse. If she fully understands the nature of what she is being asked to do and agrees to do it then she consents. If she understands what she is agreeing to do and decides to do it, she cannot later say, "I really regret making that decision, I would not have 'agreed' but for the fact that I was drunk."

What has just been said is subject, as always, to judicial vagaries. In a New Zealand case, a driver was suspected by the police of being under the influence of drink. He stoutly maintained that he was sober, and, to prove it, rolled up his sleeve for the doctor to take a blood sample. The test revealed a blood alcohol level of 170 mg. per 100 ml., and the man then succeeded in obtaining damages against the doctor on the argument that he was too drunk to be capable of consenting to the assault.

---

[112] *R. v. Bree* [2008] Q.B. 131.

[113] *R. v. Bree* [2008] Q.B. 131 at 140.

[114] [2008] Q.B. 131 at 140.

[115] See *R. v. Blayney* [2003] 140 A. Crim. R. 249, where the victim was so intoxicated that she could not move or say anything. She drifted in and out of consciousness and could not remember any act of sexual intercourse.

[116] *R. v. Wright* [2007] EWCA Crim. 3473. In *R. v. Francis* [1993] 2 Qd. R. 300 at 305 it was said: "The critical question [is] whether the complainant had, by reason of sleep or a drunken stupor, been rendered incapable of deciding whether to consent or not." In *C v. T* (1995) 58 F.C.R. 1 at 18, the court (quoting Cussen J., in *R. v. Lambert* [1919] V.L.R. 205 at 213) said: "rape was 'committed by violating a woman when she is in a state of insensibility and has no power over her will ... [and where] the accused [ought to have known] at the time that she [was] in that state.'" Cf. *R. v. Cooper* [2009] 1 W.L.R. 1786.

23–043 **What if the complainant cannot remember whether she consented or not?** The case should still be put to the jury, because there may be other evidence that shows that she did not consent. In *R. v. H*[117] a 16-year-old girl, who was inebriated after drinking a litre of vodka with friends during New Year celebrations, became separated from her friends and was picked up by a group of three men whom she had never met before. She got into the backseat of their car and was raped by one of the men. She was unable to remember what she had said to the man, but remembered that she did not want to have sexual intercourse with him. The trial judge accepted the defence's submission of no case to answer on the basis that V could not remember whether she had consented. The trial judge also held that there was insufficient evidence of her incapacity. On appeal the Court of Appeal held: "There was sufficient evidence of rape to be left to the jury. V had insisted during re-examination that she did not want to have sex when she got into the car and had told the man to get off during the course of intercourse."

The prosecution is not required to prove that the victim communicated her dissension to the defendant. Furthermore the prosecution does not have to prove that the victim was incapable of saying no. "In order to obtain a conviction there will no doubt have to be some evidence of lack of consent to go before the jury. That evidence will depend on the particular circumstances of the case."[118] In *R. v. H* there was ample evidence to go before the jury. The circumstances were that the victim was a 16-year-old girl who had never met the defendant before and who had told him that she did not want to have sexual intercourse, and also had asked him to get off her during the intercourse. If a person can give evidence that she did not consent while she was mentally coherent, then it can hardly be said that she consented when she was mentally incoherent or unconscious.[119]

23.9. SEXUAL OFFENCES AND THE REBUTTABLE PRESUMPTIONS

23–044 In the foregoing sections consent has been discussed predominantly with reference to sexual offences. In the following sections the discussion will focus more on bodily harm of a non-sexual nature. Before we proceed to that discussion, it is necessary to consider the above heads of vitiation as far as they are covered by the rebuttable presumptions found in section 75 of the *Sexual Offences Act 2003*. (As we have already seen, the presumptions found in section 76 are conclusive and thus cannot be rebutted).

Section 75 of the *Act of 2003* provides:

> "(1) If in proceedings for an offence to which this section applies it is proved–(a) that the defendant did the relevant act, (b) that any of the circumstances specified in subsection (2) existed, and (c) that the defendant *knew* that those circumstances existed, the complainant is to be taken not to have consented to the relevant act unless sufficient evidence is adduced to raise an issue as to whether he consented, and the defendant is to be taken not to have reasonably believed that the complainant consented unless sufficient evidence is adduced to raise an issue as to whether he reasonably believed it.
>
> (2) The circumstances are that–

---

[117] [2007] EWCA Crim. 2056.

[118] *R. v. Malone* [1998] 2 Cr. App. R. 447; *R. v. H* [2007] EWCA Crim. 2056.

[119] See *R. v. Blayney* [2003] 140 A. Crim. R. 249.

(a)   any person was, at the time of the relevant act or immediately before it began, using violence against the complainant or causing the complainant to fear that immediate violence would be used against him;[120]

(b)   any person was, at the time of the relevant act or immediately before it began, causing the complainant to fear that violence was being used, or that immediate violence would be used, against another person;

(c)   the complainant was, and the defendant was not, unlawfully detained at the time of the relevant act;

(d)   the complainant was asleep or otherwise unconscious at the time of the relevant act;[121]

(e)   because of the complainant's physical disability, the complainant would not have been able at the time of the relevant act to communicate to the defendant whether the complainant consented;

(f)   any person had administered to or caused to be taken by the complainant, without the complainant's consent, a substance which, having regard to when it was administered or taken, was capable of causing or enabling the complainant to be stupefied or overpowered at the time of the relevant act."

On a charge of rape, must the prosecution prove an absence of the woman's consent, or is it for the defence to prove consent?   The burden rests on the prosecution, just as it does in cases of assault by penetration and sexual assault. (As it does for the other offences found in the *Act of 2003*.)   **23–045**

Once the prosecution have established that the sexual activity in fact took place in circumstances where the victim was unlawfully detained, or was unconscious, or was physically unable to communicate her consent one way or the other, or was under the influence of stupefying drugs, or had been subjected to violence immediately prior to the sexual activity, the victim is presumed not to have consented. (In many cases, more than one of these circumstances will exist when the offending takes place.) The prosecution must also demonstrate that the defendant *knew* that the sexual activity was taking place in such circumstances. The persuasive burden is not put on the defendant, but he will be required to produce evidence to rebut the presumption of no consent. The evidence will have to be sufficiently cogent to make consent an issue. Even if the defendant is able to produce sufficient evidence to rebut the presumption of no consent, the prosecution will still have the option of proving the absence of consent in the normal way under section 74.

It is not a matter of the defendant producing evidence to show there was no violence or that the victim was not unconscious and so on, because the prosecution will have already proved the contrary. If the prosecution has not proved that the given circumstance existed, then the presumption will not arise. The defendant is merely required to produce evidence to show that the victim consented notwithstanding the violence, unconsciousness and so on.

Violence: The defendant might be able to rebut the presumption that the victim did not consent by raising evidence to show that any violence that immediately   **23–046**

---

[120] The violence might be consensual and thus punishable as an assault, as consent is no defence. *R. v. Brown* [1994] 1 A.C. 212. If the violence kills the consenter, the charge may be for murder or manslaughter, depending on the facts. See *R. v. McIntosh* [1999] V.S.C. 358; *R. v. Stein* (2007) 179 A. Crim. R. 360.

[121] See *R. v. Pike* [1961] Crim. L.R. 114, 547, where the defendant procured his mistress to be anaesthetized, with her consent, his object being to gratify his sexual perversion of copulating with an unconscious woman. The consenter was accidentally killed.

preceded the sexual activity was consensual. For instance, the defendant might be able to produce compelling evidence to demonstrate that he and the victim often engaged in consensual sadomasochism or bondage sessions. If the violence was not inflicted immediately before the sexual activity took place, then the presumption does not arise. This is presumably because the threat of imminent harm would override the victim's will. In such circumstances it is reasonable to presume that the victim did not consent.[122] If the threat is of future violence the matter is less clear and is best tested in the normal way under section 74. It is perhaps for this reason that threats to property are not sufficient to raise the presumption of no consent. The presumption will arise in any case where the defendant has used some violence. All too often cretins grab lone girls in public places and rape them. The physical clutching of the girl would be sufficient violence to raise the presumption of no consent.[123]

Unlawful detention: It is of little surprise that Parliament decided to include unlawful detention within its list of rebuttable presumptions. Many offenders find it necessary to unlawfully detain their victims for the purpose of sexually violating them.[124] Such defendants hold their victims captive because it makes it easier for them to rape their victims. A common scenario is where men in motorcars pick up young intoxicated women, who have become separated from their friends during an evening of drinking, and rape them. (Another common scenario is where a man holds his estranged wife/girlfriend captive for the purpose of raping her.)

It is difficult to imagine a hypothetical where the defendant might be able to produce evidence to suggest that the unlawful detention did not vitiate the victim's consent. A fanciful example might be where the defendant has locked up his self-harming girlfriend because she has threatened to commit suicide. The defendant might raise evidence of her mental instability to convince the court that he had a good reason for detaining her. If his evidence is accepted, she will not be presumed to have not consented to the relevant sexual activity. However, it would be still open to the prosecution to prove that she did not consent pursuant to section 74 of the *Act of 2003*.

---

[122] A reasonably short gap between the violence and the sexual violation would not prevent the presumption from arising. For example, if D hits V in his car and within an hour has sexual intercourse with her in her apartment against her will, the presumption should be satisfied. See the facts in *R. v. C* [2003] Q.C.A. 561.

[123] For example, pulling the victim's hair in order to restrain her to rape her would be enough. See *R. v. Dagnall* (2003) 147 S.J.L.B. 995.

[124] *Attorney-General's Reference (Nos. 7, 8 and 9 of 2009)* [2010] 1 Cr. App. R. (S.) 67 (where a gang of youths unlawfully detained a young girl and made her provide oral sex to 12 of them); *R. v. CV* [2010] EWCA Crim. 695 (where a gang of drug dealers kidnapped a woman who owed them money for drugs and held her against her will in a flat where one of the gang raped her); *R. v. Brand* [2009] EWCA Crim. 2878 (where there was both an unlawful detention and violence; the intoxicated victim was picked up from the roadside and held in a car against her will by a group of men she did not know, and was driven to an isolated spot where the men dragged her with force from the car and raped her). *Attorney-General's Reference (No. 73 of 2008)* [2009] EWCA Crim. 913 (where a man was kidnapped and made to fellate a homosexual defendant); *R. v. Harris* [2007] EWCA Crim. 3472 (where a taxi-driver took a young female passenger to an isolated location and forced her to engage in sexual activity with him); see also *R. v. Keown* [2010] EWCA Crim. 2385.

Unconsciousness: Women are often raped while they are asleep or unconscious **23–047** from drink.[125] Presumably the victim would have to remain unconscious until the sexual touching or penetration commences.[126] This was clearly the case in *Attorney-General's Reference No. 104 of 2004*[127] where the victim woke up to find a man digitally penetrating her. It is difficult to imagine a case where the defendant will be able to produce cogent evidence to rebut the presumption that the victim was not consenting to any sexual activity that took place while she was unconscious. In *R. v. Pike*[128] the defendant anaesthetized his mistress with her consent. His object was to gratify his sexual perversion of copulating with an unconscious woman. In this type of case the evidential burden rests with the defendant. The defence would have to produce evidence to rebut the presumption that V was not consenting. If a person has not consented while conscious, then she can hardly consent while unconscious.[129]

Physical disability: If a person is so inebriated that she is physically unable to move or "communicate" her assent or dissent, it will be presumed that she did not consent to engage in sexual activity with the defendant. It is not enough to show that the victim was physically unable to move or resist the defendant's advances. It must be shown that she was physically unable to communicate. Thus, if she is bedridden but can speak and think and is able to communicate the presumption of no consent will not arise. The defendant might be able to rebut this presumption by showing that the intercourse was with his own girlfriend/wife and that they regularly engaged in sex where she was paralysed from the effects of booze and drugs. If the encounter is with a stranger, the defendant will have great difficulty in rebutting the presumption of no consent.

Stupefying drugs: In *R. v. Meachen*[130] there was evidence that both parties agreed to take a stupefying drug before they engaged in sexual relations. Under this subsection the victim is only presumed to have not consented where the drugs were plied without her consent. This provision is aimed to counter the recent phenomena of drug assisted rape. Cretins sometimes use drugs such as Rohypnol to stupefy their victims so that they can engage in non-consensual sexual activity with them.[131] The victim might also be fooled into self-administering the drug to herself. The presumption might also apply where a person deliberately spikes another's drinks with alcohol to stupefy her.

---

[125] Cf. *R. v. Blacklock* [2006] EWCA Crim. 1740; *R. v. Johnston* [2003] All E.R. (D) 266; *R. v. Larter* [1995] Crim. L.R. 75; *R. v. Mayers* (1872) 12 Cox C.C. 311; *R. v. Young* (1878) 14 Cox C.C. 114. See also *Banditt v. The Queen* (2005) 224 C.L.R. 262.

[126] The slightest degree of penetration will do. *R. v. Lines* (1844) 174 E.R. 861; *R. v. Hughes* (1841) 173 E.R. 1038.

[127] [2005] 1 Cr. App. R. (S.) 117.

[128] [1961] Crim. L.R. 114, 547. Cf. *R. v. Evans* [2009] 1 W.L.R. 1999, where it was held that if D assists V to engage in risky conduct, D can be liable for gross negligence manslaughter if the risk-taker dies. However, D is only liable if it became obvious that the risk-taker was in peril (for example, dying from a drug overdose), and if, armed with that knowledge, D failed to summon help.

[129] See *R. v. Blayney* [2003] 140 A. Crim. R. 249.

[130] [2006] EWCA Crim. 2414.

[131] See *R. v. Wright* [2007] 1 Cr. App. R. (S.) 661. However, alcohol is the drug used most often in drug-assisted rapes. See Miranda Horvath and Jennifer Brown, "Alcohol as Drug of Choice; is Drug-assisted Rape a Misnomer?" (2007) 13(5) *P.C. & L.* 417.

23.10. MINORS

23–048 The law relating to consent by and on behalf of minors is not altogether clear, but a measure of certainty is given by the section 8 of the *Family Law Reform Act 1969*:

> "(1) The consent of a minor who has attained the age of sixteen years to any surgical, medical or dental treatment which, in the absence of consent, would constitute a trespass to his person, shall be as effective as it would be if he were of full age; and where a minor has by virtue of this section given an effective consent to any treatment it shall not be necessary to obtain any consent for it from his parent or guardian.
>
> (2) In this section 'surgical, medical or dental treatment' includes any procedure undertaken for the purposes of diagnosis, and this section applies to any procedure (including, in particular, the administration of an anaesthetic) which is ancillary to any treatment as it applies to that treatment.
>
> (3) Nothing in this section shall be construed as making ineffective any consent which would have been effective if this section had not been enacted."

The particular purpose of the section is to clarify the law for the reassurance of doctors. It is limited to "treatment," which would cover not only (as it says) diagnostic but also preventive procedures. Independently of the section, a youngster over 16 can presumably give consent to a blood donation, organ transplant, plastic surgery, or medical experiment, even if they are not "treatment" (which may perhaps be regarded as an open question). In any case he can do so at 18, which is the age of majority.[132]

23–049 **Suppose an adolescent over 16 refuses consent to an operation: can his parent nevertheless give it?** The section is silent, but the reasonable implication is that when the youngster has attained 16 only he can consent to medical treatment.

23–050 **Can an under-16 consent?** A child may be so young as to make it unreal to say that he understands what is proposed and can consent. The determining age is sometimes referred to as "the age of discretion."

In general, persons under 16 can consent to bodily contacts, and therefore (according to the better view) can consent to therapy. Furthermore, a girl of (say) 15 who knows the facts of life can give consent to a doctor giving her contraceptives[133] or to receiving a blood transfusion.[134] The House of Lords has held that minors can consent on their own behalf to certain medical procedures, so long as they fully understand what they are authorizing.[135] This suggests that a girl under 16 can consent to an abortion without the concurrence of her parents. Nevertheless, if the child lacks the capacity to understand what she is authorizing,

---

[132] Section 1 of the *Family Law Reform Act 1969*.

[133] *Gillick v. West Norfolk and Wisbech AHA* [1986] A.C. 112; *R. (on the application of Axon) v. Secretary of State for Health* [2006] Q.B. 539.

[134] *E (A Minor) (Wardship: Medical Treatment)* [1993] 1 F.L.R. 386.

[135] *Gillick v. West Norfolk and Wisbech AHA* [1986] A.C. 112.

her parents have an almost absolute right to decide for her. This right will only be overridden in exceptional circumstances.[136]

A particularly thorny problem is presented by the search for a kidney from the family of a patient needing a transplant. The survival rate is greatest from donors who are close blood relatives, particularly identical twins. But much unhappiness may be caused within the family when the question of offering a transplant arises, and most surgeons will perform transplants from living donors only if persuaded that the donor will feel deprived if he is not allowed to help his elderly dearly beloved relative. On the other hand, the giving of a successful transplant is often a cause of great satisfaction to the donor, while failure to offer it may bring about self reproach. The problem should be regarded as one of medical ethics, not a matter for legal control, provided that the youngster has reached the age of discretion and consents. His consent to surrender an organ should be valid.

If an under-16 consents, can a parent veto it?   Where a child under 16 gives   **23–051**
what from his point of view is a valid consent to some interference with his body, it would seem on principle that the fact that the parent forbids the interference does not make it illegal.

Obviously, a father who forbade his young daughter to engage in sexual intercourse would not thereby make the intercourse rape on the part of the boyfriend,[137] for rape requires non-consent by the sexual partner; non-consent of parents is irrelevant. For the same reason it would seem that there can be no assault on a child when the child gives a valid consent so far as he is concerned. This means that a parent could not forbid a doctor to perform an abortion[138] on his daughter with her consent. It is also clear that a parent cannot forbid lifesaving treatment.[139] Whether a child is capable of giving the necessary consent would depend on the child's maturity and understanding and the nature of what the consent is required for.

If an under-16 can consent at common law when of the age of discretion,   **23–052**
what is the point of the provision in the *Family Law Reform Act* for the
over-16s?   It seems that the section does nothing that would not be so without it, but it gives a measure of reassurance to doctors.

Can a parent give consent on behalf of his child under 16?   Parents certainly   **23–053**
have some authority to give consent for under-16s, but the limits are doubtful. If the child lacks the capacity to consent for himself, then his parents have the right to consent on his behalf. They also have the right *not* to consent on his behalf, if he lacks capacity to withhold consent.

---

[136] See *MAK v. United Kingdom* [2010] 2 F.L.R. 451 at 466; *O and J (Children) (Blood Tests: Constraint)* [2000] 2 W.L.R. 1284.

[137] However, if the child is over 13 but under 16 and D does not reasonably believe that she is 16 or over, he could be liable for a number of offences under the *Sexual Offences Act 2003*. This is so even if V is 15, has reached the age of discretion, and consents to have sexual intercourse with another 15-year-old. V cannot consent to sexual intercourse if she is under 16.

[138] *Gillick v. West Norfolk and Wisbech AHA* [1986] A.C. 112; *R. (on the application of Axon) v. Secretary of State for Health* [2006] Q.B. 539.

[139] *E (A Minor) (Wardship: Medical Treatment)* [1993] 1 F.L.R. 386.

In *MAK v. United Kingdom*[140] a girl aged nine years was taken out of the custody of her parents and placed in hospital, because her local doctor suspected that she had been the victim of child abuse. However, it emerged that the child had been suffering from a rare blood condition, which had caused bruise marks on her skin. Before this was discovered, the medical team at the hospital took blood samples from the girl and also took intimate photographs of her.

The European Court of Human Rights said:[141]

> "In the present case the patient was 9 years old. It has not been suggested that she had the capacity to consent to any medical intervention. The consent of either the first applicant or his wife was, therefore, required before any medical intervention could take place. On leaving the hospital … the … applicant informed the medical staff that no further tests should be carried out until his wife arrived in approximately one hour's time. These instructions were confirmed by his wife in a telephone call to the hospital.
>
> ....
>
> In view of her parent's express instructions, the only possible justification for the decision to proceed with the blood test and photographs was that they were required as a matter of urgency. In this regard, the court does not accept the Government's submission that there was a pressing social need to treat the child's symptoms. There is no evidence to suggest that the child's condition was critical, or that her situation was either deteriorating or was likely to deteriorate before her mother arrived. Moreover, it has not been suggested that she was in any pain or discomfort. Finally, there was no reason to believe that her mother would withhold consent, and even if she had, the hospital could have applied to the court for an order requiring the tests to be conducted. In the circumstances, the court can find no justification for the decision to take a blood test and intimate photographs of a nine-year-old girl, against the express wishes of both her parents, while she was alone in the hospital."

As for therapeutic procedures; it is accepted that a parent can consent on the child's behalf when the child is too young to consent, being too young to understand what is proposed to be done. When the child is above the ill-defined "age of discretion," the ideal is to have the concurrent consent of the parent and child. The position is also clear if the child, being old enough to consent, withholds consent: in such a case a doctor's hands would most likely be tied by the law.[142] However, if the child is under 16 and the parents insist on him having life saving treatment, the courts will most likely hold that the child has not reached the "age of discretion" (even if he has), and allow the parent's consent to override the child's non-consent.

23–054 **Can an under-16's parents refuse to allow him to have lifesaving treatment?** No. If a child below the age of discretion requires life saving treatment his doctors will most likely seek a declaration from the courts if his parents refuse to allow them to treat him.

In *E (A Minor) (Wardship: Medical Treatment)*,[143] a boy, aged nearly 16, and his family were Jehovah's Witnesses. The boy required a life-saving blood transfusion because he was suffering from leukaemia. Alas, the boy refused to have the blood transfusion for religious reasons. His parents shared his religious

---

[140] [2010] 2 F.L.R. 451 at 466.

[141] *MAK v. United Kingdom* [2010] 2 F.L.R. 451 at 466.

[142] Cf. *E (A Minor) (Wardship: Medical Treatment)* [1993] 1 F.L.R. 386, where the child lacked the capacity to understand the nature of what he was refusing to consent to have done.

[143] [1993] 1 F.L.R. 386. See also *L (Medical Treatment: Gillick Competence)* [1998] 2 F.L.R. 810; cf. *Queensland v. B* [2008] 2 Qd. R. 562.

convictions and therefore they too refused to authorize the use of blood transfusions. The boy was in a critical condition and required medical treatment as a matter of necessity. The court took the view that the boy did not understand the implications of his decision and therefore held his refusal to consent was irrelevant.[144] Would an ordinary parent regard it to be in his child's best interest to deny him life saving treatment?[145] If not, it does not matter that a "Jehovah's Witness" parent would deny his child such treatment? The court said the child's welfare "demanded that the hospital should be at liberty to give treatment, including the use of blood transfusions."

What if a 15-year-old girl wants to have her breasts enlarged because she falsely believes that without the augmentation she will not be successful in life?[146] The child's parents would be the best judges of whether she should be allowed to have unnecessary cosmetic surgery. The courts should be careful not to allow medical doctors to dress up unnecessary medical treatment as necessary treatment. A doctor might have a basic undergraduate degree in medicine, but this does not mean he is in a better position than a parent to assess the appropriateness of unnecessary cosmetic treatment. There is all too much evidence that such procedures can go horribly wrong. Since the doctor makes a financial gain from carrying out such surgery, it should only be permitted if the patient has been assessed by at least two child psychologists, and only if she has reached the age of 16.

23–055

If the evidence shows that the child is suffering acute anxiety because of her insecurities about her image, then surely the appropriate treatment would be counselling. This seems a case for a child psychologist, not one for a cosmetic surgeon. Besides that, the child's parents cannot be forced to pay for unnecessary plastic surgery, and since it is unnecessary it should not be billed to the taxpayers either. (If the parents consent and are willing to pay, and the child fully understands the implications of her decision, then it appears that the doctor will be able to perform the operation.)

Obviously a parent should not authorize non-therapeutic intervention where it is clear that it may adversely affect her child, but there may be differences of opinion on what will adversely affect the child. In *Re: Jamie (Special medical procedure)*,[147] Dessau J. in the Family Court of Australia granted the parents of a 10-year-old boy permission to consent on his behalf to him having hormone replacement treatment to become a girl. This decision goes too far, a single judge should not be allowed to authorize such a life a changing procedure for such a

---

[144] The same would apply if he had been brought in to the hospital unconscious and thus were physically unable to consent.

[145] "The welfare of the child was to be determined by an objective standard of the ordinary parent." *E (A Minor) (Wardship: Medical Treatment)* [1993] 1 F.L.R. 386.

[146] See Helen Carter, "Parents defend breast implants for girl, 15," (London: *The Guardian*, Jan. 5, 2001), where it is noted that a girl of 15 had breast implants inserted, because she believed she would not be able to succeed in life without them. (She had held this absurd belief from the age of 12.) We need not produce empirical evidence to highlight the patent falseness of this belief. It is doubtful that such a young person would understand the "potential complications and the downside of the operation." It is arguable that there should be tighter regulatory controls over the cosmetic surgery industry, since this type of surgery should not be carried out on under-16s.

[147] [2011] Fam. C.A. 248.

young child. Many children who suffer gender identity dysphoria grow out of it, so it would be better to wait until the child is at least 15 or 16 to see if he is going to grow out of it. A child could still have the treatment when he turns 15 or 16,[148] so there is no need to allow a 10-year-old to have such treatment.

When it is desired to have a judicial ruling on a particular proposal, this can be done by having the child made ward of court.[149] Many circuit judges are empowered to act in wardship proceedings, and a decision can generally be obtained in urgent cases almost immediately. Any person having a proper interest in the child can apply, as may the child himself by his next friend. The court acts in what it judges to be the best interests of the child. This procedure is preferable to having a care order made by magistrates in favour of the local authority, for the purpose of overruling the parents.[150]

23–056 **Can a mother cause her child grievous or actual bodily harm, and rely on her own consent as a defence?** No, the mother cannot consent on the child's behalf. Nor can the child consent on his own behalf, since the harm is too great.

In 1975 a Nigerian woman who incised the cheeks of her two sons, aged 9 and 14, with their consent and approval at a family ceremony, found herself in the Central Criminal Court and was convicted under section 47 of the *Offences against the Person Act 1861*. She was given an absolute discharge, but the judge uttered a warning against any repetition of the offence by those from Nigeria "or any other part of Africa."[151] As we will see below, the House of Lords has since held that even a fully competent adult cannot consent to actual bodily harm.[152] If a person cannot consent to receiving actual bodily harm on his own behalf,[153] then *a fortiori* a parent should not be able to consent to such harm on his behalf.

Notwithstanding the many doubts that have been expressed, the reasonable view is that a parent can authorize anything to be done to the child that is (or the parent believes to be) not against his interest, and even something against his interest if it is compensated by sufficient advantage to others and is not seriously detrimental to the child—though probably not, in either case, if the child is old enough to understand what is involved and is either left uninformed or withholds assent, and certainly not if the operation involves the unjustifiable infliction of grievous bodily harm (and graver forms of actual bodily harm—whatever that may be held to be) without compensating advantage to the child.

---

[148] *Re: O (Special medical procedure)* [2010] Fam. C.A. 1153.

[149] See *In Re A (Children) (Conjoined Twins: Surgical Separation)* [2001] Fam. 147 at 179-180. See also the restrictions on use of wardship jurisdiction as set out in section 100 of the *Children Act 1989*. The High Court can invoke its inherent jurisdiction. See *A Local Authority v. DL* [2011] Fam. Law 26; *In Re F (Adult: Court's Jurisdiction)* [2001] Fam. 38 at 43.

[150] See section 31 of the *Children Act 1989* as applied in *A and D (Non Accidental Injury: Subdural Haematomas)* [2002] 1 F.L.R. 337.

[151] *R. v. Adesanya (The Times*, 16, 17 July 1974).

[152] *R. v. Brown* [1994] 1 A.C. 212.

[153] *R. v. Brown* [1994] 1 A.C. 212.

23.11.   "INFORMED CONSENT" AND OPERATIONS

The limits of the legal notion of consent are of great importance to doctors as a matter of civil law, but a criminal prosecution of a doctor, on the ground that he has not fully informed his patient of the nature or effects of an operation, is unlikely.

23–057

Suppose that a patient assents to an operation, but does not realize that it will render him impotent. Does he "consent?" Even if he is held not to, the surgeon will not be liable for a criminal assault if he believed that the patient consented. But sometimes the surgeon may be constrained to admit that he knew that his patient did not realize the possibility of a certain side-effect of the operation. There would obviously be great danger for surgeons if patients could prosecute or sue in respect of all side-effects that were unknown to them.

American courts have developed a doctrine of "informed consent": a consent not based upon proper understanding of the relevant facts is no consent.[154] Although the proposition may be accepted to a certain extent, great caution is needed in its application.

It may be that as a matter of civil law a surgeon is under a duty of care and a contractual duty to give the patient reasonable information about a proposed operation.[155] Whether that is so or not, it ought not to be accepted as representing the criminal law. There is nothing to prevent a patient putting himself generally into the hands of the surgeon, without enquiring too specifically what is to be done; in other words, he can consent generally to such surgery as is thought necessary.[156] Even if his consent is to a particular operation, the operation does not become a criminal assault just because the surgeon omits to give him information as to its effects.

23–058

Supposing (against the above argument) that some disclosure were required from the surgeon, it would be wrong to expect him to catalogue the possible adverse effects and to give his patient a full balance-sheet of the pros and cons of the operation. A patient who asks for medical advice inevitably puts himself in the hands of his doctor. The patient is often in a highly emotional state and may be frightened out of his wits if the surgeon offers him a recital of past medical disasters.[157] It is the doctor who has to take the difficult medical decision, not the patient. A doctor should not be criminally liable even if he unduly minimizes the risks of therapeutic procedure.

---

[154] See generally, Jaime S. King and Benjamin W. Moulton, "Rethinking Informed Consent: The Case for Shared Medical Decision-Making," (2006) 32 *Am. J.L. & Med.* 429; Peter J. Buenger and Brittany H. Southerland, "Health—Consent for Surgical or Medical Treatment," (2008) 24 *Ga. St. U. L. Rev.* 161.

[155] It would not be unfair to allow a person to sue his surgeon where the surgeon has failed to advise of a risk which he ought to have made known to his patient. See for example, *Chappel v. Hart* (1998) 195 C.L.R. 232; and *Rogers v. Whitaker* (1992) 175 C.L.R. 479.

[156] See generally, P. D. G. Skegg, "English Medical Law and Informed Consent: An Antipodean Assessment and Alternative," (1999) 7 *Med. L. Rev.* 135; Sirko Harder, "Medical Non-Disclosure and Hypothetical Consent," (2009) 20 *K.C.L.J.* 435.

[157] Anyone doubting this should read the amusing piece by William P. Irvin reprinted in Jay Katz, Joseph Goldstein and Alan M. Dershowitz (eds.), *Psychoanalysis, Psychiatry and Law*, (New York: Free Press, 1967) at 716.

A doctor who engages in medical experiments with human beings may have his conduct more severely scrutinized than one who acts for the purpose of therapy. There is here no obvious need for not alarming the patient.[158] As a matter of good practice, the doctor should make the fullest disclosure. At the same time, it would seem to be wrong to use the criminal law to control the amount of disclosure required. Such legal control as is needed can, surely, be provided by the civil law.

23–059 While our courts are likely to treat doctors with great consideration, and while on principle there is no difference between the doctrine of consent in relation to doctors and to unqualified practitioners, human justice does not always follow the rules of logic. Judges are likely to react against unqualified people who indulge in doubtful practices against the bodies of others, and the doctrine of consent is sufficiently malleable to enable convictions to be upheld.

In *Burrell v. Harmer*[159] a tattooist tattooed two boys aged 12 and 13, causing their arms to become inflamed and painful. The magistrates convicted him of an assault occasioning actual bodily harm, rejecting his defence that the boys consented, on the ground that they did not understand the nature of the act; and the conviction was upheld on appeal.

These boys did not expect the painful result. But it is difficult to see how the doctrine of consent can rationally distinguish between a surgeon and a tattooist, and equally hard to imagine that the courts attitude would have been the same if a surgeon and orthodox surgery had been involved. The judges were, of course, actuated by a desire to protect boys from tattooists, and to do that they were prepared to bend the notion of consent. It would have been better to leave the problem to Parliament; and in fact Parliament acted two years later by making the tattooing of minors (persons under 18) a specific offence.[160] As we shall see, later developments in the doctrine of consent may have made tattooing illegal even for adults.

23.12. CONSENT AND PUBLIC POLICY

23–060 The relation between criminal law and morality has been much discussed. It usually comes down to the question of whether society, through the law, has any right to interfere with solitary conduct, or conduct between consenting adults, that does not affect any third person.[161] The rest of this chapter will consider the question in some limited contexts. We shall be concerned not with problems of law and law reform in relation to specifically crimes that cause disgust and

---

[158] Bernard M. Dickson, "Information for Consent in Human Experimentation," (1974) 24 *U. Toronto L.J.* 381; Maxwell J. Mehlman and Jessica W. Berg, "Human Subjects Protections in Biomedical Enhancement Research: Assessing Risk and Benefit and Obtaining Informed Consent," (2008) 36 *J.L. Med. & Ethics* 546.

[159] [1967] Crim. L.R. 169.

[160] Section 1 of the *Tattooing of Minors Act 1969*, applied in *Harvie v. Stewart* (2010) G.W.D. 27-533. On the rationale, see Brian Hogan, "Modernising the Law of Sexual Offences," in P. R. Glazebrook (ed.) *Reshaping the Criminal Law: Essays in Honour of Glanville Williams*, (London: Steven & Sons, 1978) at 180.

[161] See Dennis J. Baker, *The Right Not to be Criminalized: Demarcating Criminal Law's Authority*, (Farnham: Ashgate Publishing, 2011) at Chap. 5 & 6.

offence, such as exhibitionism,[162] still less with questions of public policy relating to the control of drugs, gambling, and suchlike, but only with the extent to which consent is vitiated on grounds of public policy in crimes like murder, manslaughter and assault.

The two sides that line up on the issue are one aspect of the same schism between the philosophy of libertarianism and that of authoritarianism.

Libertarians support the individual's claim to autonomy.[163] Everyone prizes the right to live his own life, not to be made to conform to important decisions made on his behalf by others. This principle yields the two postulates stated in 23.1—that, in general, (1) nothing must be done to a person without his consent and (2) anything can be done to him with his consent. (In this section we are chiefly concerned with the second of these postulates.) Our own courts have not formulated the principle categorically, but it was neatly expressed by an American judge. "Anglo-American law," declared Schroeder J. "starts with the premise of thorough going self-determination."[164]

For English law this is a large overstatement. Cases like *R. v. Brown*[165] and *R. v. Stone*[166] show that our courts are unstable in their allegiance to the principle, and often seem to be more interested in inventing exceptions to it than in giving effect to it. In other words they frequently prefer the opposing philosophy, that of authoritarianism (legal moralism) or paternalism,[167] which again has two postulates. The one relevant to this chapter is that nothing must be done to a person, even with his consent, if it is to his disadvantage or is otherwise regarded as anti-social. (The other, to be considered in the next chapter, is that anything can be done to a person, even without his consent, if this is necessary for his own or the public good, as seen by the legislature or the courts.)

23–061

The leading philosophical exponents of the libertarian view were the individualists of the 19th century, led by J.S. Mill, who contended[168] that the law could properly be used against the individual only to prevent him from harming others. Its most celebrated affirmation in the 20th century was by the Wolfenden Committee on Homosexuality and Prostitution,[169] though neither they nor Mill considered the principle in the context of the consensual infliction of harm.[170]

---

[162] See further Dennis J. Baker "The Impossibility of a Critically Objective Criminal Law," (2011) 56(2) *McGill L. J.* 349.

[163] See the essays collected in Jules L. Coleman and Allen Buchanan (ed.), *In Harm's Way: Essays in Honour of Joel Feinberg*, (Cambridge: Cambridge University Press, 1994).

[164] *Natanson v. Kline*, 350 P.2d 1093 at 1104 (1960).

[165] [1994] 1 A.C. 212.

[166] [1977] 2 W.L.R. 169.

[167] For a thorough discussion on the inappropriateness of invoking paternalism as a justification for criminalization, see Joel Feinberg, *The Moral Limits of the Criminal Law: Harm to Self*, (New York: Oxford University Press, Vol. III, 1986); John Kleinig, *Paternalism*, (Manchester: Manchester University Press, 1983).

[168] J. S. Mill, *On Liberty*, (London: John W. Parker & Son, 1859).

[169] *Report of the Committee on Homosexual Offenses and Prostitution*, (London: Home Office, Cmd. 247, 1957) at paras. 13 and 61.

[170] Cf. the magisterial work of Joel Feinberg, *The Moral Limits of the Criminal Law: Harmless Wrongdoing*, (New York: Oxford University Press, Vol. IV, 1988) at 165 *et seq.*; Feinberg Vol. III, *op. cit. supra*, note 167 at 175-305.

Legal moralists are concerned with what they see as social or conventional harms as well as the more obvious and indisputable harms perceived by the libertarians. The best-known statement of legal moralism in the present context is that by Lord Devlin. In his view, the consent of a person against whom force is used is no excuse to the person who uses the force, if the basic common morality of society is infringed.[171]

It is true that consent is sometimes regarded as nullified on grounds of public policy. But it is going too far to say that the mere infringement of "basic common morality" nullifies consent.[172] If that were so, fornication would involve an assault (at least by the man), or would have done so when it was more discountenanced by opinion than it is now. So would mutual masturbation by males. The extent of the doctrine of public policy requires careful consideration, which we must now give it. We commence with the most extreme alteration of the personal condition known to mankind: death.

23.13.   ABETTING SUICIDE

23–062 The response of the Christian religion and consequently the common law to the human tragedy of suicide was to condemn it. Suicide was regarded as a crime, and this had a number of consequences.

The superstitious horror of suicide in European culture has partly pagan origins. The notion of suicide as a sin is not biblical; it was invented by St. Augustine of Hippo, and he intimates pretty clearly what his reason was. Some Christians were choosing to end their lives immediately after baptism, in the belief that this was the only sure way of avoiding sin and proceeding to heaven. To prevent this decimation of believers, Augustine taught that suicide was itself a sin greater than any that was likely to be committed by remaining alive. So English law stigmatized suicide as a felony; the *felo de se's* property was forfeited, leaving his family impoverished; and his body was denied Christian burial. Even when these unfeeling practices were given up, suicide remained legally equivalent to self-murder for a number of purposes, including, to some extent, the law of attempt.[173]

The law was changed by section 1 of the *Suicide Act 1961*, which enacts that "the rule of law whereby it is a crime for a person to commit suicide is hereby abrogated." One result is that it is no longer a crime to attempt suicide; also, there is now no question of transferred intention in these cases. If D shoots at his own head with intent to commit suicide, but misses and kills V, this is not now murder of V as it used to be, though D is likely to be convicted of manslaughter on the ground of gross negligence.

---

[171] Patrick Devlin, *The Enforcement of Morals*, (Oxford: Oxford University Press, 1965) at Chap. 1.

[172] See Dennis J. Baker, "Moral Limits of Consent as a Defence in the Criminal Law," (2009) 12 *New Crim. L. Rev.* 93; see also Hamish Stewart, "The Limits of Consent and the Law of Assault," (2011) 24 *Can. J.L. & Juris.* 205.

[173] See Glanville Williams, *The Sanctity of Life and the Criminal Law*, (New York: Alfred Knopf, 1957) at Chap. 7; Norman St John-Stevens, *Life, Death and the Law*, (London: Eyre and Spottiswoode, 1961) at Chap. 6; Maximilian Koessler, "Comparative Aspects of the English *Homicide Act of 1957*," (1960) 25 *Mo. L. Rev.* 107 at 143. Legal rules have never prevented a high rate of suicide.

The *Suicide Act 1961* (as amended)[174] does not altogether efface the religious prohibition of suicide from the law, because it expressly continues to impose a considerable measure of responsibility upon persons other than the suicide or would be-suicide. At common law, one who incited or assisted another to do away with himself was guilty of inciting and abetting a crime, as a deduction from the supposed guilt of the deceased. This way of looking at the matter is no longer possible, but the *Suicide Act* in effect continues the old law by making it a statutory crime to encourage or assist the suicide or attempted suicide of another person. We may call it "abetting suicide" for short. The offence carries a very severe penalty of 14 years' imprisonment, to provide for those who induce the suicide of others for some nefarious purpose of their own; but the wording is not limited to cases of bad intention. The offence can be committed "whether or not a suicide, or an attempt at suicide, occurs."[175]

23–063

Do you abet someone's suicide by deciding not to prevent it?   No, since a bare omission is not included in abetment as a form of complicity in crime. A person who fails to prevent a voluntary death by starvation or by the rejection of medical assistance may be in peril of being convicted of manslaughter, but he can only be convicted by the disregard of an important legal duty.

23–064

Furthermore, the offence expressly requires the defendant to do some positive act. The defendant must do some act that is "capable[176] of encouraging or assisting the suicide or attempted suicide of another person."[177] The defendant must by his act intend to encourage or assist suicide or an attempt at suicide.

Suppose V asks D if she can borrow his gun for a spot of hunting. Suppose also that D knows that V has lost her job and husband, and also has massive debts. D is a little suspicious because he cannot recall V ever hunting before, but gives her the benefit of the doubt. V uses the gun to commit suicide.

Is D liable? No, because he was only reckless. D did not intend to assist V to commit suicide. He was merely reckless as to whether she might use the gun for such a purpose.

The question of principle is: if one can lawfully commit suicide, why should it be an offence for another to help him?   Can I offer an explanation? It is because we still think suicide immoral. We no longer punish attempted suicide, because punishment is not likely to deter, and because it can only aggravate the depression of the person who has attempted suicide, and make it more likely that he will repeat the attempt. These reasons do not prevent helpers from being punished.

23–065

---

[174] Section 59 of the *Corners and Justice Act 2009* amended section 2 of the *1961 Act* to create a single offence of encouraging or assisting the suicide or attempted suicide of another person. Section 59 of the *2009 Act* replaced the former offences under section 2(1) of *1961 Act* and section 1 of the *Criminal Attempts Act 1981* with a single offence.

[175] See section 1(1B) of the *Suicide Act 1961*.

[176] Section 2A(2) of the *Suicide Act 1961* deals with "impossibility": "(2) Where the facts are such that an act is not capable of encouraging or assisting suicide or attempted suicide, for the purposes of this *Act* it is to be treated as so capable if the act would have been so capable had the facts been as D believed them to be at the time of the act or had subsequent events happened in the manner D believed they would happen (or both)."

[177] Section 2(1)(a) of the *Suicide Act 1961*.

23–066   **Yes, but why should the law deny the terminally ill patient the right to obtain help from others to control the time and manner of his dying?**   There is a case for punishing those who assist suicide by young people (who may go through a temporarily difficult phase, and whose suicide is a cruel blow to parents), or who *persuade* others to commit suicide, or use fraud, or assist the act for selfish reasons. But it is sensible and humane that doctors, (or, in extreme cases, even relatives), should be inhibited from providing a person who is dying in immense pain with the passport to oblivion that he seeks.

There may be a case for exempting people from liability where they merely *assist*[178] another to commit suicide as a last resort. This exemption should only apply where the person committing suicide is forced to do so as a last resort. If the victim is healthy (or has many years of life left) then the exemption should not apply.[179] A healthy disabled person (even if severely disabled) should not be treated any differently to any other healthy person who has a long life ahead of him. The important consideration is the concept of "acceleration." If D merely assists V to accelerate her imminent death (there should be compelling medical evidence to show that V only has weeks or a month or two at the most to live), because V is in immense pain, then what she does is not morally reprehensible. We should not continue to criminalize those who merely assist others to bring their death forward by a very short period of time, when they act solely because the assisted parties are being tortured by the pain of their illness, are bedridden and have no quality of life left. Basically, such people are only being kept alive so that they can endure the torture of their illness for a few more weeks or a couple of months. This would only be so in the most extreme cases, since modern painkillers would relive the bulk of the pain in many cases.

As far as the harm principle is concerned, V is not harmed if her suicide is designed to avoid the greater harm of being tortured by immense pain for a few more weeks. The immense pain serves no purpose, since she is going to die anyway in the very near future. If the pain was a part of longer term rehabilitation, then her suicide would not be permissible. Using the criminal law to make it impossible for V to commit suicide without the assistance of another, could force her to commit suicide earlier when she is able to do so without assistance. V might kill herself even though she still has some quality of life, if

---

[178] It should always be a crime to *encourage* another to commit suicide, since V's decision to take such drastic action should be entirely her own.

[179] A cure could be around the corner, and it is wrong to allow people to assist severely disabled people to end their lives if they are not in pain where they have a long life ahead of them. Cf. *Brightwater Care Group (Inc.) v. Rossiter* [2009] W.A.S.C. 229, where the Supreme Court of Western Australia declared that a healthy quadriplegic (Mr. Rossiter was not terminally ill, nor was he dying) had the right to starve himself to death. It said that his carers could not force feed him or force him to receive medical treatment that would prolong his life, if he did not want that treatment. It seems grossly inhumane to allow a person to starve to death merely because of his status as a quadriplegic: it also has the effect of undervaluing the lives of many other healthy quadriplegics who wish to live. Nonetheless, this case did not involve active assistance; it was merely a case of the victim exercising his right not to be force fed or forced to receive medication that he did not wish to receive. The result would have been different, if he had asked his carers to take positive steps to kill him, such as by lethal injection. (A further danger is the healthy quadriplegic has healthy organs which may be in high demand, whereas the organs of those who are terminally ill may not be of much use.)

she knows that she may get to a point where she will be forced to exist in immense pain for weeks on end and where she will not be able to seek assistance to die.

The exemption should apply only where the abettor has merely assisted V to kill herself (for example, where D merely drives V to the euthanasia clinic and so on). If D kills V to put her out of her misery, he should be liable for murder. We do not want individuals going around killing others, because this could affect their mental well-being. It could also have a dangerous desensitizing effect. We do not want people becoming desensitized to killing.[180] (If there is to be any active killing, it should be done in a specialized euthanasia clinic by a medically qualified person.) It should not be done in a normal hospital or by everyday doctors, since they work in an environment where the professional culture has to be one of saving life, not life ending. We do not want to socialize lifesavers into being live-enders.[181] (Anyway, as the law stands those who assist could spend up to 14 years in jail.)

23.14. CONSENT-KILLING AND DEATH PACTS

A person cannot consent to his own death. The rule is not based upon utilitarian considerations even though these may sometimes buttress it.[182] It is a theocratic survival in our predominantly secular law; and religious ("transcendental") arguments are still its main support.

23–067

What is the difference between killing a person with his consent and assisting his suicide? The first is generally, murder, while the second is still the statutory offence just considered. The distinction between them is the distinction between

23–068

---

[180] A similar argument is often raised for not having the death penalty: What does it do to us as individuals to use killing as a way of solving our problems?

[181] Assistance is a better way to handle the problem, as it is the victim who does the killing. If we were to ask a doctor to deliver a lethal injection we would be asking him to become an executioner (regardless of the good motive); the effect is that this person would be asked to kill day in and day out in his clinic. Does this mean that this doctor will eventually suffer posttraumatic stress disorder in the long-term in the way that soldiers do after returning from war? (See Thomas L. Hafemeister and Nicole A.Stockey, "Last Stand—The Criminal Responsibility of War Veterans Returning from Iraq and Afghanistan with Posttraumatic Stress Disorder," (2010) 85 *Ind. L.J.* 87. If so, does it mean he may eventually become a danger to society? Routine killing is different to routine lifesaving. Could this lead to a situation where doctors start killing consenting patients who have healthy organs to get them for transplant patients? These are ethical dilemmas that run beyond the scope of this book. See the interesting report by David Wilson, "From cure to kill," (London: *The Guardian*, Monday 8 February 2010); where Wilson boldly observes: "The medical profession has regularly been mired in ignominy as far as serial killers are concerned –whether we are discussing GPs from our own time such as Harold Shipman (who murdered at least 215 of his elderly and mostly female patients), nurses like Beverly Allitt or Colin Norris (who also murdered elderly women), or from earlier in our history, Dr Thomas Neill Cream, who liked to poison the prostitutes that he had engaged (and who was once believed to have been Jack the Ripper) or Dr John Bodkin Adams who was suspected of having murdered over 100 of his elderly, female patients in the decade after the second world war." Cf. Penney Lewis, "The Empirical Slippery Slope from Voluntary to Non-Voluntary Euthanasia," (2007) 35 *J.L. Med. & Ethics* 197.

[182] It might be difficult to determine whether a dead person really consented, since it is not possible to cross-examine a corpse. See further, Terrance C. McConnell, *Inalienable Rights: The Limits of Consent in Medicine and the Law*, (Oxford: Oxford University Press, 2000) at 44 *et seq.*

perpetrators and accessories. If a doctor, to speed his dying patient's passing, injects poison with the patient's consent, this will be murder;[183] but if the doctor places the poison by the patient's side, and the patient takes it, this will be suicide and the doctor's guilt will be of the abetment offence under the *Suicide Act 1961* (not abetment in murder). Although this is the theoretical distinction, a case of consent-killing is occasionally reduced to one of assisting suicide.[184]

The distinction may be thought to have no moral relevance, since the doctor assists the patient's death in both cases. But one or two points may be made. If V asks D to help him to die, D may reasonably say: "I do not approve of what you propose, and will not do the job for you. But you are entitled to act on your own responsibility; and since you are ill and cannot obtain the means of suicide yourself, I do not mind supplying them to you." Besides this, the fact that the patient takes the poison with his own hand helps to allay fears that perhaps he did not really consent. Suicide is more clearly an act of self-determination than consent to be killed, and requires greater strength of purpose.[185]

The question may again be asked whether there is any social value in denying the doctor's right to help his patient in this way in terminal cases. Several unsuccessful attempts have been made to change the law, but they have foundered because of the united opposition of the churches and the medical profession itself. Doctors fear that if they were given the legal power to terminate their patient's lives, although with consent, they would lose the confidence of their patients.[186]

23–069 The only alleviation of the traditional attitude is that according to a ruling of Devlin J.,[187]a doctor is entitled to administer drugs in order to relieve pain even if the side-effect is to shorten the patient's life. Devlin J. based his conclusion on the doctrine of causation, which is unconvincing because it obscures the value-judgment involved. However, the practical effect of the judge's direction is welcome. It could well be supported on other grounds by saying the administration of pain-killing drugs in these circumstances is justified by necessity. It is necessary to relieve the pain, and it should not matter that the doctor foresees death as a probable or even virtually certain side-effect of relieving this type of pain where the patient is near death. When, in the last stages of illness, a certain amount of drug is administered in order to deaden pain, it may lawfully be administered even though the physician knows that it will also accelerate the patient's death.[188] But he may not deliberately choose an amount of

---

[183] *R. v. Cox* (1992)12 B.M.L.R. 38.

[184] *R. v. Robey* (1979) 1 Cr. App. R. (S.) 127.

[185] On the ethics of the matter see Feinberg Vol. III, *op. cit. supra*, note 167 at 344 *et seq.*

[186] Euthanasia has been legalized in some jurisdictions, see Penney Lewis, "Euthanasia in Belgium Five Years after Legislation," (2009) 16 *Eur. J. Health L.* 125; Raphel Cohen-Almagor, "Euthanasia Policy and Practice in Belgium: Critical Observations and Suggestions for Improvement," (2009) 24 *Issues L. & Med.* 187. The literature on this issue is too vast to cite. But, for a good comparative study see Penney Lewis, *Assisted Dying and Legal Change*, (Oxford: Oxford University Press, 2007).

[187] *R. v. Bodkin Adams* [1957] Crim. L.R. 365.

[188] For ecclesiastic opinions in support see the Bishop of Exeter's sermon printed in [1960] *B.M.J.* 128, and Pope Pius XII's remarks reported in *The Times*, 18 September 1958. Dr. Coggan (the Archbishop of Canterbury at the time), in his Stevens Memorial Lecture, approved the following statement of Chancellor E. Garth Moore: "It would seem reasonably certain that the giving of a pain-killing drug to a patient in extremis can be justified, not only by the theologian's law of double

the drug that is not necessary to relieve pain and that is designed solely to kill.[189] (The latest research suggests that drugs used to provide pain relief cannot accelerate a terminally ill patient's death, if administered properly.)[190]

Humanitarian feeling is allowed to prevail in respect of the duty to make positive exertions to prolong life in terminal illnesses. A doctor could not successfully be charged with murder, manslaughter or abetting suicide merely because, in the terminal stages of disease, he does not take exceptional measures to prolong a doomed existence, whether at the patient's request or not.[191] This could be put on the ground that he has not actively shortened life, and that his decision not to intervene is justifiable in the circumstances.[192] It would also seem that no question of assisted suicide is involved in a patient's decision not to struggle further for existence.[193]

What if the position if two lovers make a suicide pact with each other, and one survives?   Two forms of death pact (suicide pact) must be distinguished: the killing-suicide pact and the double-suicide pact.

23–070

The killing-suicide pact is an agreement between A and B that A shall first kill B and then commit suicide. If A performs the first part and then fails to complete the bargain, his responsibility is reduced from murder (as at common law) to manslaughter by the *Homicide Act 1957*.[194]

The double-suicide pact, where each party agrees to kill himself, is in legal analysis a case of mutual abetment of suicide. The responsibility of the survivor therefore rests on the *Suicide Act 1961* (for abetting suicide), not on the *Homicide Act* (for killing).

How exactly is the line drawn between the two kinds of death pact?   The answer is again given by a simple application of the law of complicity. It depends on who does the act of killing. If a husband and wife agree to commit suicide, and together they seal their garage and sit inside, one of them starting the car engine, then if, say, the husband survives and the wife dies, the husband's guilt will depend on who started the car. If he did, he will be guilty at common law of

23–071

---

effect, but also by the Common Law doctrine of necessity, even where one of the effects of the drug is the probable shortening of the patient's life. This is because the evil averted, namely the agony of the patient, is greater than the evil performed, namely an act leading to the probable shortening of his life . . ." See H. D. Coggan, "On Dying and Dying Well: Moral and Spiritual Aspects," (1977) *Proc. R. Soc. Med.* 75 at 76.

[189] *R. v. Cox* (1992)12 B.M.L.R. 38. However, Dr. Cox was treated leniently in that he was only convicted of attempted murder, even though the evidence showed that he had consummated the killing. See section 6(4) of the *Criminal Law Act 1967*.

[190] Susan A. Fohr, "The Double Effect of Pain Medication: Separating Myth from Reality," (1998) 1 *Journal of Palliative Medicine* 315.

[191] Cf. *Brightwater Care Group (Inc.) v. Rossiter* [2009] W.A.S.C. 229.

[192] Cf. *Airedale NHS Trust v. Bland* [1993] A.C. 789. On passive and active euthanasia, see Gwen M. Sayers, "Non-Voluntary Passive Euthanasia: The Social Consequences of Euphemisms," (2007) 14 *Eur. J. Health L.* 221.

[193] *Brightwater Care Group (Inc.) v. Rossiter* [2009] W.A.S.C. 229.

[194] Section 4. The burden of proving the existence of the pact is placed upon the defendant, and it must be shown that he himself had a settled intention of dying at the time when he killed his companion in pursuance of the pact. Although the statute does not expressly make a suicide pact a defence to a charge of attempted murder, it should logically be a defence.

murdering his wife, though since it was a suicide pact his guilt will be reduced to manslaughter under section 4 of the *Homicide Act 1957*. If the wife started the car it will be suicide by her, and the husband will be guilty under the *Suicide Act 1961* of abetting suicide.

23–072   **But it may be a pure accident which of them started the car and which of them survived.**   No doubt, but the distinction between the perpetrator and the accessory necessitates the enquiry.

There is little practical difference between the two statutes, but the proper statute must be referred to in the indictment.[195] It hardly needs to be said that a suicide pact requires an agreement. If, for example, a husband tells his wife that he is going to commit suicide by taking tablets, and his wife says that in that case she is going to join him, then if both take tablets (neither assisting or encouraging the other) and one survives the survivor cannot, on those facts alone, be convicted. It is merely a case of two concurrent decisions to commit suicide, each of which is lawful.

23.15.   CONSENT AND BODILY HARM: FIGHTS

23–073   Killing in a duel is murder, consent not being recognized as a defence to this charge.[196] The judges have set their faces even against fisticuffs (whether as public spectacles, or in anger, or as a way of settling a dispute), and hold that consent of the combatants is again, in general, no defence. The present law rests on *Attorney-General's Reference (No. 6 of 1980)*,[197] where it was held that the combatants were guilty of assault (or an aggravated assault) if they intended to inflict actual bodily harm or were reckless as to it.

Although most fights have always been discountenanced, the scope of the prohibition has been variously stated, and the objection to consensual fights has been put on different grounds at different times. Sometimes it was the likelihood of serious injury to the combatants, sometimes the fact that public fights encouraged idleness and indulgence in betting. The Court of Appeal has not put the law on a definite and comprehensive footing. The court held that a fight is unlawful even though it takes place in private, with fists only; even though there is no question of any wider breach of the peace; even though there is no question of grievous bodily harm; and even though it is a consensual fight engaged in as a means of settling a quarrel—if, in any of these cases, actual bodily harm is intended or caused;[198] and the court clearly contemplated that a bleeding nose and

---

[195] The difference of penalty—life against 14 years—is only theoretical. In particular the charge under the *Homicide Act 1957* arises only on the prosecution for murder, which will be undertaken by the Director of Public Prosecutions. The consent of the D.P.P. is expressly required under section 2(4) of the *Suicide Act 1961*. This should be a safeguard against callous prosecution, but instances of these have occurred.

[196] *R. v. Rice* (1803) 102 E.R. 719; *R. v. Cuddy* (1843) 174 E.R. 779; *R. v. Gnango* [2011] 1 All E.R. 153.

[197] [1981] Q.B. 715 applied by the House of Lords in *R. v. Brown* [1994] 1 A.C. 212.

[198] The court said "intended and/or caused," presumably meaning that the parties must either intend such harm or be "reckless" as to it.

bruises to the face would be "actual bodily harm." In such circumstances each party is guilty of assault upon the other, the consent to fight being rendered ineffective in law as a matter of policy.

This wide doctrine of vitiation of consent on grounds of policy is a judicial invention for putting the law of assault to a purpose for which it was not intended. It turns an offence designed for the prevention of aggression into one that gives a judge and jury discretion to punish people for what they deem to be improper. Since this was an Attorney-General's reference and no defendant was before the court, the court did not find it necessary to pretend that it was merely stating the existing law. The precedents directly in point were of low order of authority, while other cases indicated that the law was narrower. The only relevant English case cited in the judgment was a 19th century decision on prize fights; such fights involved a considerable risk of death or grievous bodily harm and presented a much more serious social problem than a fist fight between two disputing teenagers (which was the occasion of the particular reference).

The attitude of the court was that it could nullify a person's consent in any case where the public interest did not require that consent should be a defence, and, in the opinion of the court, it "is not in the public interest that people should try to cause, or should cause, each other actual bodily harm for no good reason." **23–074**

These are wide words, but if the decision is read as being confined to the subject of unregulated fights the policy is understandable. Such fights involve the appreciable possibility of causing more injury than the combatants intend or contemplate such as severe brain damage. They tend to occasion apprehension among members of the public and can spread into wider disorder; and the police in putting them down may themselves be injured. Moreover, when the giving and accepting of challenges to fight are socially allowable, the acceptance of a challenge is apt to be forced on a person as a matter of "honour." It is true that the courts had, by receiving the law of public disorder, provided themselves with a powerful weapon for dealing with major public disorder; but by now extending the law of assault they enabled magistrates' courts to be used to suppress minor fights.

Then what about boxing and other bouts by way of sport? Lord Lane C.J., after the sentence just quoted, added: **23–075**

> "Nothing which we have said is intended to cast doubt upon the accepted legality of properly conducted games and sports, lawful chastisement or correction, reasonable surgical interference, dangerous exhibitions, *etc.* These apparent exceptions can be justified as involving the exercise of a legal right, in the case of chastisement or correction, or as needed in the public interest, in the other cases."[199]

Apart from chastisement or correction, the legality of the items in this list will normally depend on consent, which is allowed to operate in these cases.[200] Although the list is presented as a statement of matters to which the court's outlawing of bodily injury will not extend, there is the disturbing thought that in fact the list may operate to extend that pronouncement. Were it not for the list of

---

[199] *Attorney-General's Reference (No. 6 of 1980)* [1981] Q.B. 715 at 719.
[200] *R. v. Billinghurst* [1978] Crim. L.R. 553.

"apparent exceptions" the decision might have been regarded as confined to injuries inflicted in fights. But the "apparent exceptions" seem to imply that the judges have empowered themselves to declare that the occasioning of any injury, even by consent, is unlawful except to the extent that they are prepared to accept "apparent exceptions" in the public interest; and "in the public interest" simply means that the judges approve of the activity. Traditionally they approve of boxing; presumably this is "needed in the public interest."

23–076 **Why is boxing needed? Is it not the point rather that there is no public interest against it?—though serious doubts are now felt on the subject of head injuries in this sport.** It needs some knowledge of social history to understand and evaluate the old authorities. The medieval joust involved great risks for the combatants and on that ground come to be regarded as illegal, unless it took place by the King's command.[201] A lesser degree of danger in friendly combat was tolerated. Cudgelling and wrestling, said Foster,[202] are lawful. "Here is indeed the appearance of a combat it is in reality no more than a friendly exertion of strength and dexterity. ... They are manly diversion, they tend to give strength, skill and activity, and make fit people for defence." East[203] commented that: "if the possibility of danger were the criterion by which lawfulness of sports and recreations were to be decided, many exercises must be proscribed which are in common use, and were never heretofore deemed unlawful." Everything depended, therefore, on whether the court, adjudicating *ex post facto* a charge of manslaughter, regarded the weapon used as lawful or unlawful, this depending on the degree of apparent danger. A man could not consent to the risk of being killed by a dangerous weapon, even in a friendly combat.[204]

Views expressed upon these matters often exhibited confusion between the question of physical risk, and objections to a large assembly of spectators, at a time when the constabulary was weak. East, for example, says, of medieval jousts: "They drew together a great concourse of unruly spirits, not always consistent with public tranquillity, and seldom ending without bloodshed."[205]

Most of the discussion came to centre on what were called prize-fights. Basing himself upon the literature of the period, Pollock expressed the opinion that the prize-fight of the Restoration and the early 18th century was a fight with swords, the weapon being the single-edged cutting "backsword," not the small-sword carried by gentlemen.[206] By the later part of the 18th century the contest was pugilistic, no gloves being worn. Even so, death and injury in the ring were common, since the rules were few and ineffective, and fights reached almost the limits of brutality. Strangely, the objection first voiced against these fights were only that they attracted the masses from work. Foster, after the passage previously quoted, added: "I would not be understood to speak of prize-fighting and public boxing-matches, or any other exertions ... of the like kind which are

---

[201] Sir Michael Foster, *Crown Law*, (London: Printed by W. Strahan and M. Woodfall, 1776) at 260.
[202] *Id.* at 260.
[203] Sir Edward Hyde East, *A Treatise of the Pleas of the Crown*, (London: Printed by A. Strahan, for J. Butterworth, 1803) at 268.
[204] See the discussion of *Sir John Chichester's Case* (1646) 82 E.R. 888, in East, *ibid.*
[205] *Id.* at 270.
[206] *Notes*, (1912) 28 *L. Q. Rev.* 125.

exhibited for lucre and can serve no valuable purpose, but on the contrary encourage a spirit of idleness and debauchery." His objection was to fighting matches as what we now call a spectator sport, particularly because they encourage betting. This was in accordance with the spirit of the age. In the same vein, an *Act of 1739*[207] was passed to "restrain and prevent the excessive increase of horse races." It recited that "the great number of horse races for small plates, prizes and sums of money, have contributed very much to the encouragement of idleness, to the impoverishment of many of the meaner sort of the subjects of the kingdom." Borrough J. a notable opponent of prize-fights, added another reason for objecting to them:

> "It cannot be disputed that all these fights are illegal, and no consent can make them legal, and all the country being present would not make them less an offence. They are unlawful assemblies.... The inconvenience in the country is not so great, but nearer London the quantity of crime that these fights lead to, is immense."[208]

Notwithstanding the hostility of the law and sporadic prosecutions, fisticuffs by professionals remained enormously popular among all classes. Magistrates might intervene personally to ban a fight, but in other areas they attended as appreciative spectators. Fights were sponsored by the nobility and by businessmen, and were witnessed by many thousands.[209] Although the crowds were occasionally riotous, they often were at the races and cricket matches too. The occasion of the riot was that the onlookers, to save their bets, might cut the ropes and forcibly put an end to the fight. But this was by no means an invariable occurrence.

23–077

While the origin of the objection to prize-fights was the desire to keep the lower classes in their place, in time, with a certain softening of manners, the high rate of death and injury among the pugilists became a matter of additional concern. For these reasons, the judges came to say that a knuckle-fight was indictable not only as an unlawful assembly, and in case of death as manslaughter, but as mutual assaults, even though there was no death and no rioting.[210] Although assault was still said to presuppose an absence of consent by the victim, the consent of combatants was no defence. The rule was applied even though the fight was not for reward, if it was before a crowd of spectators.[211]

We may safely say that this special rule for prize-fights, so-called, is obsolete with the passing of forms of the public behaviour that gave rise to it. Certainly the fact that a fight is for money would no longer be sufficient to make it illegal: professional boxing and wrestling are for money. In any case, the view that charges of assault could be brought against the combatants merely because the spectators might be unruly was illogical, just as much as if it were now held that violence by fans at football matches makes the players liable for mutual

---

[207] 13 Geo. 2 c. 19.

[208] *R. v. Billingham* (1825) 172 E.R. 106. Borrough J. seems to be suggesting that those who follow such sports engage in other crime, if this is so, then criminalize the offenders when they commit those other independent crimes.

[209] John Ford, *Prizefighting: The Age of Regency Boximania*, (London: Newton Abbot, 1971).

[210] *R. v. Perkins* (1831) 172 E.R. 814; *R. v. Lewis* (1844) 174 E.R. 874; *R. v. Hunt* (1845) 1 Cox C.C. 177.

[211] *R. v. Coney* (1881-82) 8 Q.B.D. 534.

assaults.[212] Such violence, when it occurs, is merely a reason for treating those responsible as guilty of public order offences.

23–078   There remains one ground upon which a fight can be unlawful. (1) The relatively clear ground is where the circumstances make it likely that injury, or (at least) actual bodily harm[213] or greater will be caused. This was one of the reasons, and the only good reason, given for saying that prize-fighting involved mutual assaults.[214] "The fists of trained pugilists are dangerous weapons which they are not at liberty to use against each other."[215] The courts here take a paternalist view, repudiating the right of self-determination.

In order to preserve pugilism as an activity and as a spectacle, the Queensbury rules were framed with the object of making boxing sufficiently safe to be accounted legal. This was in 1890, the rules being an improvement on rules for boxing contests that had already been drawn up in 1865. Even the earlier rules had an immediate reflection in legal pronouncements. In 1866,[216] and again in 1878,[217] juries were directed that an encounter was lawful if it were a mere exhibition of skill in sparring; but the judges continued to insist that if the combatants intended to fight until one gave in from exhaustion it was a criminal offence.[218] Similarly, such sports as single-stick, wrestling and fencing remain lawful if reasonably conducted.

At present day, prosecutions for consensual combats are almost unknown, notwithstanding that fierce forms like all-in wrestling have been displayed in public. Jousting has been revived as a spectator sport without intervention by the law.

23–079   In recent years medical opinion has been hardening against the risks involved in boxing.[219] When compared with some other sports such as motor-racing and football,[220] boxing is not the most hazardous, but death and injuries are not uncommon; moreover the object of the boxer is to inflict at least temporary damage on his opponent's brain by the knock-out, whereas in the other sports mentioned no injury to the person of any kind is intended. Nevertheless, efforts to legislate against it have met with no success. Apologists for boxing argue that it encourages the manly art of self-defence, that it is an outlet for aggression or

---

[212] Such a justification for criminalization would contravene the "remote harm" constraint against criminalization. See Baker, *op. cit. supra*, note 162 at 101 *et seq.*

[213] Cf. *R. v. Jobidon* [1991] 2 S.C.R. 714; *R. v. Camelon* [2011] O.J. No. 1182, at para. 100, where it was held that consent is a defence to harm that is not serious.

[214] *R. v. Coney* (1881-82) 8 Q.B.D. 534, *per* Stephen, Hawkins, and Matthew J.J.

[215] *R. v. Coney* (1881-82) 8 Q.B.D. 534 at 547.

[216] *R. v. Young* (1866) 10 Cox C.C. 371.

[217] *R. v. Orton* (1878) 14 Cox C.C. 226. Cf. *Pallante v. Stadiums Pty. Ltd. [No 2]* [1976] V.R. 331; *R. v. Raabe* (1985) 14 A. Crim. R. 381.

[218] See J. W. Cecil Turner, *Russell on Crime*, (London: Steven & Sons, 12th edn., 1964) at 463-464.

[219] C. Constantoyannis and M. Partheni, "Fatal Head Injury from Boxing: A Case Report from Greece," (2004) 38 *British Journal of Sports Medicine* 78; C. D. Herrera, "The Search for Meaningful Comparisons in Boxing and Medical Ethics," (2004) 30 *J. Med. Ethics* 514; Mario F. Mendez, "The Neuropsychiatric Aspects of Boxing," (1995) 25 *The International Journal of Psychiatry in Medicine* 249.

[220] Steven T. DeKosky *et al.*, "Traumatic Brain Injury — Football, Warfare, and Long-Term Effects," (2010) 363 *N. Engl. J. Med.* 1293.

frustration, and that the public appreciate it as a spectacle. These arguments have not been ventilated in court because prosecutors no longer feel called upon to take an interest in the matter.

In *R. v. Brown*, Lord Mustill said:[221]

> "That the court is in such cases making a value-judgment, not dependent upon any general theory of consent is exposed by the failure of any attempt to deduce why professional boxing appears to be immune from prosecution. For money, not recreation or personal improvement, each boxer tries to hurt the opponent more than he is hurt himself, and aims to end the contest prematurely by inflicting a brain injury serious enough to make the opponent unconscious, or temporarily by impairing his central nervous system through a blow to the midriff, or cutting his skin to a degree which would ordinarily be well within the scope of section 20. The boxers display skill, strength and courage, but nobody pretends that they do good to themselves or others. The onlookers derive entertainment, but none of the physical and moral benefits which have been seen as the fruits of engagement in manly sports. … It is in my judgment best to regard this as another special situation which for the time being stands outside the ordinary law of violence because society chooses to tolerate it."

It is not clear that society is willing to tolerate it in the 21st century.[222] In *R. v. Brown*,[223] the House of Lords expressly reserved the right of judges (with the assistance, of course, of juries) to pronounce upon what consensual harm-doing (including grievous bodily harm-doing) should be exempt from criminalization. The courts recognized a number of exceptions including: (1) surgical operations; (2) adornment;[224] (3) properly conducted games; (4) dangerous feats and exhibitions; (5) horseplay;[225] and (6) that a person may risk grievous bodily harm by consenting to risk contracting H.I.V.[226]

Does this mean that the courts can extend the list in an *ad hoc*   23–080
fashion? There is some looseness in the drafting of the list given in *R. v. Brown*; but what seems to emerge is that in the matter of bodily injuries, widely interpreted, three Lords sitting in the House of Lords have now legislated judicial paternalism to the full extent. The Lords in the majority in *R. v. Brown*, accepted without scrutiny, Lord Lane C.J.'s statement of the law as laid down in *Attorney-General's Reference (No. 6 of 1980)*.[227] Although Lord Lane C.J. mentioned that he had heard "interesting legal and philosophical debate," no echo of any philosophy is heard in the judgment. The court did not utter a word in support of the idea that people have a right to do what they like with their own bodies, so long as they do not harm others.

---

[221] *R. v. Brown* [1994] 1 A.C. 212 at 263.
[222] British Medical Association, *The Boxing Debate*, (London: British Medical Association, 1993).
[223] [1994] 1 A.C. 212.
[224] *R. v. Wilson* [1997] Q.B. 47.
[225] *R. v. Jones* (1986) 83 Cr. App. R. 375.
[226] *R. v. Dica* [2004] Q.B. 1257; *R. v. Konzani* [2005] 2 Cr. App. R. 198.
[227] [1981] Q.B. 715.

23.16.   CONSENT AND DESIRED INJURIES

23–081   The courts punish a person who intentionally inflicts a certain (rather uncertain) degree of injury on another, even though not in a fight, any consent of the other notwithstanding. A good legal case can be made for this rule in relation to injuries that amount to grievous bodily harm or injuries that endanger life. But as we will see, slight harm will do.[228]

However, there is no direct authority for saying that a person commits a crime in injuring himself, even seriously. This cannot be an assault, which presupposes an offender and victim.[229] An ancient crime of maim still exists;[230] but there is no recorded instance of such a charge being brought for an injury inflicted by a person on himself, or to attempt to do so. It would be somewhat illogical to punish him for inflicting upon himself a lesser degree of injury, particularly if this is in the course of an attempt to destroy himself.[231]

As to what is maim, the ancient notion was that it was a permanent injury that rendered a man less able to fight in defence of himself or his country.[232] Since one basis of the law of maim was that the king had an interest in his subject's ability to fight, it is intelligible that on a charge of maim the victim's consent should not be a defence; and this is commonly assumed. However, the only reported decision capable of bearing on the point is the old case of *R. v. Wright*,[233] where the facts, as recorded by Coke, were as follows:

> "A young strong and lustie rogue, to make himself impotent, thereby to have more colour to begge or to be relieved without putting himself to any labour, caused his companion to strike off his left hand; and both of them were indicted, fined and ransomed therefore."

23–082   It will be noticed that both parties had entered into a conspiracy to defraud the public. Still, the companion would very likely have been convicted even if his act had not had this object.

Self-injury is not infrequent in the 21st century. Mentally disturbed people, particularly young people and particularly young girls,[234] practise various kinds of self-abuse and self-mutilation, from sticking pins in their own legs to arm-slashing.[235] Some are given to swallowing objects, so that they have to receive continual operative treatment. This type of self-harm differs to

---

[228] *R. v. Brown* [1994] 1 A.C. 212.

[229] There is a theoretical problem on section 18 of the *Offences against the Person Act 1861*, which unlike section 20 and the poisoning sections, does not say "any other person." But it is hard to imagine that self-injury would be held to be both unlawful and "malicious," and anyway no prosecutor has yet charged under section 18 for such an act.

[230] *R. v. Povey* [2009] 1 Cr. App. R. (S.) 42. Cf. *The King v. Lee* (1763) 168 E.R. 128; *The King v. Tickner* (1778) 168 E.R. 196; *R. v. Akenhead* (1816) 171 E.R. 308.

[231] See Feinberg, *loc. cit. supra*, note 170.

[232] Sir Edward Coke, *Institutes of the Laws of England*, (London: Printed for E. and R. Brooke, Pt I, 1794) at 288a; James Fitzjames Stephen, *Digest of Criminal Law*, (London: MacMillan, 1904) at 165.

[233] (1603) Co.Lit. f. 127 a-b.; (1613) 1 East P.C. 396.

[234] Keith Hawton and Athony James, "Suicide and Deliberate Self-harm in Young People," (2005) 330 *B.M.J.* 891.

[235] See Stacy S. Welch, "A Review of the Literature on the Epidemiology of Parasuicide in the General Population," (2001) 52 *Psychiatr. Serv.* 368; Armando Favazza, *Bodies Under Siege: Self-mutilation in Culture and Psychiatry*, (Baltimore: John Hopkins University Press, 1996).

parasuicide in that it does not necessarily result in the self-harmer attempting suicide.[236] Prosecutions are unknown.[237]

If it is accepted that self-mutilation is not a crime, the conclusion should follow that those who encourage[238] it or aid and abet[239] it are not guilty either, provided that they do not inflict the injury. The encourager should not be guilty of "causing" grievous bodily harm under section 18, because the subsequent voluntary act of the self-harmer severs the chain of imputable causation.[240] The encourager or assister is not guilty as accessory, because there is no crime, not even the ghostly crime involved in the doctrine of *R. v. Bourne.*[241] To argue otherwise involves asserting that section 2 of the *Suicide Act*, making it an offence to abet suicide, was unnecessary. There is no statutory provision for abetment of self-maim as there is with suicide. However, if the self-maim is an attempted suicide, abetting it comes within the *Suicide Act 1961.*

The position is different when the injury is inflicted by another. The weight of 19th century authority favoured the view that it was unlawful to inflict on another an injury amounting to a maim or endangering life.[242] (A maim probably always involved grievous bodily harm, since it had to render the victim less able to fight in defence of himself and country.) However, the courts since extended the rule so that it now covers actual bodily harm.   **23–083**

The decision in *R. v. Donovan*[243] loosened the law. *R. v. Donovan* concerned sadism (the association of the sexual impulse with cruelty). Donovan privately caned a girl of 17, for the purpose of gratifying his sexual tastes. On being charged with common assault and indecent (sexual) assault he offered evidence that the girl had consented. The evidence of consent seems, from the summary of it given in the judgment, to have been cogent; yet the jury convicted, perhaps because they disapproved of Donovan and his ways. They found in effect that the girl had not consented. The verdict was quashed on appeal for misdirection, but the Court of Criminal Appeal took occasion to go into the general question whether the girl's consent, if established, would be a defence in law. The view expressed was that "if the blows struck were likely or intended to do bodily harm to the prosecutrix," her consent would be no defence:

---

[236] E. David Klonsky, "Non-suicidal self-injury: An introduction," (2007) 63 *Journal of Clinical Psychology* 1039.

[237] One justification for criminalizing this type of self-harm is that the injured person is more likely to become a charge upon the taxpayer. But such an argument is nonsensical, since treatment would cost less than trying and jailing the self-harmer. Furthermore, if this type of remote harm justification were to be applied uniformly, it would be necessary to criminalize alcohol consumption, motorcar use and so on. See Dennis J. Baker, "The Moral Limits of Criminalizing Remote Harms," (2007) 10 *New Crim. L. Rev.* 370.

[238] See section 44-46 of the *Serious Crime Act 2007.*

[239] See section 8 of the *Accessories and Abettors Act 1861.*

[240] *R. v. Kennedy (No. 2)* [2008] 1 A.C. 269. Glanville Williams, "Finis for Novus Actus?" (1989) 48 *Cambridge L.J.* 391 at 398.

[241] (1952) 36 Cr. App. R. 125.

[242] See Glanville Williams, *Textbook of Criminal Law*, (London: Stephen & Sons, 1978) at 538 *et seq.*

[243] [1934] 2 K.B. 498.

"For this purpose we think that 'bodily harm has its ordinary meaning and includes any hurt or injury calculated to interfere with the health or comfort of the prosecutor. Such hurt or injury need not be permanent, but must, no doubt, be more than merely transient and trifling."[244]

In laying down this wide rule (which was entirely *obiter*) the court was perhaps influenced, like the jury, by its aversion to the defendant's conduct. It exercised the prerogative of discriminating between activities of which it approved and those of which it disapproved. Swift J. said:[245] "Nothing could be more absurd or more repellent to the ordinary intelligence than to regard his conduct as comparable with that of a participant in one of those 'manly diversions.'" Although the criminal law had directed itself against homosexual deviations, it had not specifically provided for heterosexual sadism. By ruling that the consent of the victim was no defence in respect of "bodily harm," including even an interference with comfort, the court in effect proposed to extend the operation of the law of assault to cover a sexual quirk.

23–084   The reasoning in the judgment commenced as follows:

"If an act is unlawful in the sense of being in itself a criminal act, it is plain that it cannot be rendered lawful because the person to whose detriment it is done consents to it. No person can license another to commit a crime. So far as the criminal law is concerned, therefore, where the act charged is in itself unlawful, it can never be necessary to prove absence of consent on the part of the person wronged in order to obtain the conviction of the wrongdoer. There are, however, many acts in themselves harmless and lawful which become unlawful only if they are done without the consent of the person affected."[246]

This passage is open to the obvious objection that it is a tautology. The first three sentences say merely that if an act is a crime irrespective of consent, then consent is no defence, while the last says that if the act is a crime only when done without consent, then consent is a defence. Such premises do not assist in the determination of the case.

The court proceeded to say that "as a general rule, although it is a rule to which there are well-established exceptions, it is an unlawful act to beat another person with such a degree of violence that the infliction of bodily harm is a probable consequence." For this proposition no authority was offered. If it is correct, the legality of professional boxing matches, where the object is to knock the opponent senseless, should also be treated as criminal acts. The proposition is true where the victim does not consent, and also for injury inflicted in unregulated fights, but whether it is true for a sexual beating with consent needed consideration. In any case, there is no reason to suppose from the facts stated that bodily harm in any realistic sense was likely.

23–085   The court in *Attorney-General's Reference (No. 6 of 1980)*,[247] accepted the criticism of *R. v. Donovan* that the reasoning was tautologous, but said nothing further in opposition to it. Moreover, the court's general statement of principle was evidently meant to approve the decision. The Court of Appeal, like the Court of Criminal Appeal in *R. v. Donovan*, started from the premise that all infliction

---

[244] *R. v. Donovan* [1934] 2 K.B. 498 at 509.

[245] *R. v. Donovan* [1934] 2 K.B. 498 at 509.

[246] *R. v. Donovan* [1934] 2 K.B. 498 at 506.

[247] [1981] Q.B. 715.

of bodily harm is unlawful unless it is for the public benefit; if this proposition is accepted, and since no one argues that the sadistic beating is for the public benefit, such a beating must be unlawful. But the proposition is open to the criticism that it attaches no value to the individual's autonomy. The proper question should be not whether consensual beating is required by the public interest but whether there is anything against it.

Legal intervention is most likely where, as in *R. v. Donovan* and more recently in *R. v. Brown*,[248] the conduct in question is regarded as *contra bonos mores et decorum*.[249] The decision of the House of Lords in *R. v. Brown* can be read as vitiating consent to any bodily injury, unless some excuse or justification can be raised, as may be the case where a surgeon performs a necessary operation.

In *R. v. Brown* a group of homosexual sadomasochists voluntarily and enthusiastically committed acts of violence against each other, because they achieved sexual gratification from being subjected to violence and pain. The appellants were arraigned on various counts under sections 20 and 47 of the *Offences against the Person Act 1861*, for inflicting wounds and actual bodily harm on the genital and other areas of the bodies of each other.

The trial judge stated that consent was not a viable defence to intentionally inflicting harm beyond a certain threshold (actual bodily harm or greater). The appellants appealed unsuccessfully to the House of Lords. It was held: **23–086**

> "although a prosecutor had to prove absence of consent in order to secure a conviction for mere assault it was not in the public interest that a person should wound or cause actual bodily harm to another for no good reason and, in the absence of such a reason, the victim's consent afforded no defence to a charge under section 20 or 47 of the *Act of 1861*."[250]

The House of Lords held that satisfying sadomasochistic desires did not provide the appellants with a good reason for inflicting actual bodily harm on each other. If the injuries had amounted to grievous bodily harm, it would have been reasonable for the Lords not to allow consent to operate as a defence in *R. v. Brown*.[251] This level of harm is where the line should have been drawn, not at the level of actual bodily harm. The appellants had committed violent acts against each other including nailing their prepuces and scrota to a board, inserting hot wax into their urethras, burning their penes with candles and incising their scrota with scalpels.[252] Clearly, the hot waxing would not amount to anything greater

---

[248] [1994] 1 A.C. 212, where the Lords applied *R. v. Donovan* [1934] 2 K.B. 498.

[249] This type of reasoning harks back to a time gone by. See *Jones v. Randall* (1774) 98 E.R. 954 at 956 where Lord Mansfield said: "The question then is, whether this wager is against principles? If it be contrary to any, it must be contrary either to principles of morality; for the law of England prohibits everything which is *contra bonos mores*." See also *Shaw v. D.P.P.* [1962] A.C. 220 at 268, where offences *contra bonos mores* were described as "those offences which are prejudicial to the public welfare."

[250] *R. v. Brown* [1994] 1 A.C. 212 at 233, *per* Lord Templeman; *per* Lord Jauncey (at 243); *per* Lord Lowry (at 253-254), all three quoting Lane C.J. in *Attorney-General's Reference (No. 6 of 1980)* [1981] Q.B. 715 at 719.

[251] The value we put on humanity means that we would not want to allow people to go around inflicting grievous bodily harm upon their fellow human beings. If consent were allowed to justify all types of gross harms the harmers would be desensitized as to the value of humanity. Baker, *op. cit. supra*, note 172.

[252] *R. v. Brown* [1994] 1 A.C. 212 at 246.

than actual bodily harm. The incising and nailing of the penes to the board clearly involved wounding, but probably fell short of being grievous bodily harm.

The Lords should have distinguished actual bodily harm from grievous bodily harm, because consent should provide a defence in the case of actual bodily harm. We would not want to allow the defence where the consenter consents to have her arms amputated, or her eyes poked out, because it would clearly be wrong for the person inflicting the harm to rely on another's consent to treat his fellow human so inhumanely. Of course, if he were to blind the consenter by poking her eyes out it would be him, not her, that we would criminalize. The consenter is not a harm-doer, so unless she reciprocates the harm, she will not be liable. The sadist is the harm-doer and the masochist is the harm receiver. Sadomasochists are both, because they reciprocate the harm that they receive.

23–087   As we have seen, actual bodily harm seems to cover everything from trivial discomfort right through to a broken tooth (9.7.). That aside, even the most serious form of actual bodily harm is not grave enough to deny the defence of consent. *R. v. Brown* means that consent is vitiated not only in respect to the more serious forms of actual bodily harm such as a broken tooth, but also in respect to slight harm. It would be better to draw the line at death or grievous bodily harm, since the higher threshold would provide firmer guidance. It would prevent the courts from holding that consent is vitiated even when the harm is slight.[253]

It may be strongly doubted whether the very rare show trial for consensual immoral acts serves any social purpose.[254] Moreover, a law is objectionable if, while general in its terms, it is used only against those who engage by mutual consent in deviant activity. The result is to give full rein to the prejudices of prosecutors, judges and juries. This was starkly illustrated by the Court of Appeal in *R. v. Wilson*.[255] In that case a man used a hot brand to burn his initials into the buttocks of his wife, with her consent. The court held that unlike sadomasochism, hot-branding did not involve aggression.[256] Would the court have come to such a conclusion if the branding had been non-consensual? The court took the view that the defendant was not inflicting the harm for the sake of causing harm, but to

---

[253] The Supreme Court of Canada has held consent is not a defence if the harm is reasonably serious. See *R. v. Jobidon* [1991] 2 S.C.R. 714; *R. v. Camelon* [2011] O.J. No. 1182, at para. 100. In *R. v. Brown* [1994] 1 A.C. 212 at 276, Lord Slynn (dissenting) said: "If a line has to be drawn, as I think it must, to be workable, it cannot be allowed to fluctuate within particular charges and in the interests of legal certainty it has to be accepted that consent can be given to acts which are said to constitute actual bodily harm and wounding. Grievous bodily harm I accept to be different by analogy with and as an extension of the old cases on maiming. Accordingly, I accept that other than for cases of grievous bodily harm or death, consent can be a defence."

[254] See Cheryl Hanna, "Rethinking Consent in a Big Love Way," (2010) 17 *Mich. J. Gender & L.* 111; Vera Bergelson, "Consent to Harm," (2008) 28 *Pace L. Rev.* 683; Kelly Egan, "Morality-Based Legislation Is Alive and Well: Why the Law Permits Consent to Body Modification but Not Sadomasohistic Sex," (2007) 70 *Alb. L. Rev.* 1615.

[255] [1997] Q.B. 47.

[256] "Mrs. Wilson not only consented to that which the appellant did, she instigated it. There was no aggressive intent on the part of the appellant." *R. v. Wilson* [1997] Q.B. 47 at 50, *per* Russell L.J. But the sadomasochists in *R. v. Brown* by consenting and by asking others to beat them, also instigated the assaults against themselves.

achieve the end of adornment. Normally good motives do not count, but they do if they can be linked to a recognized defence.[257]

Moreover, Russell L.J. said:[258]

> "[W]e are firmly of the opinion that it is not in the public interest that activities such as the appellant's in this appeal should amount to criminal behaviour. Consensual activity between husband and wife, in the privacy of the matrimonial home, is not, in our judgment, normally a proper matter for criminal investigation, let alone criminal prosecution. Accordingly we take the view that the judge failed to have full regard to the facts of this case and misdirected himself in saying that *R. v. Donovan* ... and *R. v. Brown* ... constrained him to rule that consent was no defence. .... In this field, in our judgment, the law should develop upon a case by case basis rather than upon general propositions to which, in the changing times in which we live, exceptions may arise from time to time not expressly covered by authority."

The court held that the defence was available because the defendant did not intend to harm his wife, but merely intended to adorn her. At this level it was thought that it was no different to tattooing. There is some merit in the argument that tattooing and cosmetic surgery might be treated differently to sadomasochism, because the former involves a one-off infliction of harm for a long-term benefit. *Per contra*, it is not enough for the sadist to harm the masochist only once; he has to inflict the same harm on the masochist every time the masochist wants a thrill. The initial harm provides no long-term benefit. Nevertheless, if the repeated harm does not involve anything more than actual bodily harm, consent should provide a defence. The repeated instances of injury and pain are probably less than that experienced by many Olympic athletes; and others who labour for a living. (See 23.18).

If a person consents to be injured, and if inflicting such injury is an assault (*e.g.*, because it amounts to a.b.h.), is he an accessory to the offence of inflicting the injury upon himself?   There is no authority.[259] If the view is accepted that a person ought not to be criminally liable for self-injury, it should follow that for the same reason he should not be liable as accessory if he consents to be injured. There is a certain justification for the law directing itself against the other person who inflicts the injury amounting to grievous bodily harm, but not against a person who is so abnormal that he seeks it.[260]

23–088

23.17.   RECKLESS HARM-DOING AND CONSENT

If the defendant is reckless in causing the victim to suffer actual bodily harm, it will be no defence for him to show that the victim consented to the risk.[261] Suppose V prepares herself a shot of heroin and asks D to inject it into her arm. If D foresees that the heroin might cause V actual bodily harm, he cannot raise her consent as a defence. If he was not reckless in injecting her, and merely thought

23–089

---

[257] See 4.2.

[258] *R. v. Wilson* [1997] Q.B. 47 at 50.

[259] The old case of *R. v. Wright* (1603) Co.Lit. f. 127 a-b.; (1613) 1 East P.C. 396, which is distinguishable, was discussed above.

[260] See Baker, *op. cit. supra*, note 172.

[261] *R. v. Barnes* [2005] 1 W.L.R. 910.

he was helping her for recreational purposes, then he will not be liable for any unforeseen harm arising from the battery/wounding.[262]

23–090 **Are you telling me that if D is not reckless, he will not be liable even if he causes really serious harm?** Correct. In *R. v. Meachen*,[263] a woman met a man in a public house and took him home for the night. During the course of the night the couple engaged in what can only be described as rather disturbing sexual activities. These activities involved the man inserting his fingers into the woman's rectum. After he inserted his fingers into her rectum, she apparently rode up and down on them.[264] This resulted in her being seriously injured; her injuries were so severe that she had to be fitted with a colostomy bag. Simple assault would have been made out had there not been consent, because Meachen had committed a battery by inserting his fingers into the woman's rectum. His battery was not unlawful, because her consent made it lawful.[265] Consent is not sufficient to make actual bodily harm lawful, but the defendant did not intend or foresee that the victim would suffer actual bodily harm. The Court of Appeal correctly held that it was "necessary for the prosecution to show that the offender intended to cause some bodily harm or caused such harm recklessly."[266]

23–091 **What about if D accidentally kills V while engaging in consensual activity?** In *R. v. McLeod*,[267] an old New Zealand case, an expert marksman who, in the course of a performance of his skill, invited a member of the audience to hold a cigarette in his mouth which was to act as a target. The invitation was accepted, and McLeod aimed at the cigarette ash with the object of knocking it away. No injury would have occurred but for the fact that the voluntary assistant moved his head just before the defendant fired, which caused the bullet to enter his cheek. It was held by the Court of Appeal, on the construction of the section of the New Zealand Code, that if the assistant had died it would have been manslaughter, since "a lethal weapon was used and in risky circumstances." It may be doubted whether the fact that a potentially lethal weapon was used was itself sufficient to carry the decision, for it was not used with the intention of causing injury. Moreover, if some element of risk in the performance was enough to make it illegal at common law, many other exhibitions and feats of endurance would come under the same condemnation.

Under the current law in England and Wales, if it can be shown that the defendant foresaw that it was highly probable that V would be killed or seriously

---

[262] *R. v. Meachen* [2006] EWCA Crim. 2414 at para. 39; *R. v. Slingsby* [1995] Crim. L.R. 570. (Any wounding that does not constitute actual bodily harm should be protected by the consent defence.) If it becomes obvious that V has overdosed, D has a duty to summon help; and if he fails to try to save V he may be liable for gross negligence manslaughter. See *R. v. Evans* [2009] 1 W.L.R. 1999; cf. *R. v. Kennedy (No.2)* [2008] 1 A.C. 269.

[263] *R. v. Meachen* [2006] EWCA Crim. 2414 at para. 39.

[264] At least this was what the defendant had alleged. V could not remember whether she had acted in this way.

[265] *R. v. Slingsby* [1995] Crim. L.R. 571.

[266] *R. v. Meachen* [2006] EWCA Crim. 2414 at para. 37.

[267] *R. v. McLeod* [1915] 34 N.Z.L.R. 430.

injured, he will be liable for "reckless manslaughter."[268] If the defendant foresees that the victim might suffer actual bodily harm, he would be liable for aggravated assault contrary to section 47 of the *Offences against the Person Act 1861*. The doctrine of constructive manslaughter would only apply if both the "unlawful act" and "dangerous act" requirements are met. Since the conduct in *R. v. McLeod* was only dangerous;[269] rather than unlawful *and* dangerous, he could not be convicted of "unlawful act" manslaughter. (Furthermore, his conduct comes within the "dangerous exhibition" exception; so consent could provide a full defence regardless of the level of harm inflicted.) If D does some unlawful dangerous act that exposes V the risk of suffering actual bodily harm, V's consent will be irrelevant.[270]

Is consent a defence to a charge of gross negligence manslaughter? The **23–092** courts most likely will not allow the defence to be raised in cases where the victim's implied consent arises in the context of a joint criminal enterprise.[271]

Consent will hardly ever be an issue in negligence cases, because it will not play on the defendant's mind. When a person commits simple battery against another person with his consent, the consent is a defence because it negates the defendant's *mens rea*. The defendant is able to say, "I did not 'unlawfully harm' V, because he agreed to the risk of being harmed." The defendant cannot assert that he did not "harm" V, because he has in fact harmed V. If V asks D to blind him with acid, D might not wrong V, but he certainly harms him.[272] V is permanently disabled and that is an objective fact. The defendant has committed the *actus reus* of a serious offence.[273] He does not wrong V, because V desired the injury. Nonetheless, the law *deems* that he has wronged V, because the law holds that consent does not provide a defence where the defendant deliberately or

---

[268] *R. v. Lidar* [2000] *Archbold News* 3, where the Court of Appeal held that a person could be liable for "reckless manslaughter" if he does some act foreseeing that it will kill V, or will at least cause him serious injury. The defendant must foresee that it is highly probable that if he does act X (for example, tries to shoot an ash of the end of a cigarette in V's mouth), that it might cause V serious injury. See also *Gray v. Barr* [1971] 2 Q.B. 554 at 557. If V had died in *R. v. Emmett* (*The Times*, 15 October 1999), D would have been liable for "reckless manslaughter," because he foresaw death or serious injure as a highly probable consequence of putting her head in a plastic bag as a part of the sex game. If reckless manslaughter is charged, there is no need to identify an unlawful act.

[269] See the discussion above (§12.6.) *vis-à-vis R. v. Lamb* [1967] 2 Q.B. 981.

[270] See *R. v. Stein* (2007) 179 A. Crim. R. 360, where D bound and gagged V as a part of a sex game. In that case, it appeared that V only consented to simple assault; and was deprived of the ability to withdraw his consent to greater harm because he was gagged. The act of gagging V was a dangerous and unlawful act, as it deprived him of the ability to warn that the sadomasochistic session was getting out of hand. See also *R. v. McIntosh* [1999] V.S.C .358, where a masochist consented to the risk of actual bodily harm. The Supreme Court of Canada has held that an unconscious person cannot consent to activities that take place after she is unconscious, because she is deprived of the opportunity to withdraw her consent: *The Queen v. J.A.* [2011] S.C.C. 28 (but see the dissenting judgments of Binnie and LeBel J.J.).

[271] In *R. v. Wacker* [2003] Q.B. 1207 at 1217. Kay L.J. said: "Further the criminal law will not hesitate to act to prevent serious injury or death even when the persons subjected to such injury or death may have consented to or willingly accepted the risk of actual injury or death." Quoted in *R. v. Willoughby* [2005] 1 W.L.R. 1880 at 1885.

[272] D could be convicted of an offence under section 29 of the *Offences against the Person Act 1861*, even if he did not intend to permanently disable V. See *R. v. James* (1980) 70 Cr. App. R. 215.

[273] See section 18 of the *Offences against the Person Act 1861*.

recklessly causes V actual bodily harm or greater harm. If the harm is less than actual bodily harm, D can raise the defence of consent to show that he acted for a lawful purpose, because the law deems that this is sufficient to negate any wrongful intent. In the case of sexual offences such as rape, consent negates the *actus reus*. Consent changes the nature of the act, because it converts what would be rape into the innocuous act of lovemaking. (In the latter case, D might also lack any wrongful intent. But this will not always be the case: D might intentionally have sexual intercourse with V hoping that she is not consenting when unbeknown to him she is consenting. D is culpable because he attempts to rape V; V's consent means it is impossible for D to consummate the *actus reus* of the offence.)

If the defendant does not foresee the harm as a possibility, how can he assert that he did not wrong V because he thought V was consenting? If consent did not enter his mind it cannot be used to justify his actions. In most cases where the defendant has not foreseen the risk of harm, the victim probably has not foreseen it either. The victim cannot be said to have consented to a risk that he did not believe existed. The victim does not impliedly consent to being exposed to the risk of being harmed merely because a reasonable person would have foreseen the risk of harm.[274] In *R. v. Wacker*[275] 58 illegal immigrants were asphyxiated in the shipping container in which they were being trafficked. It is doubtful that the victims impliedly consented to take the risk of being asphyxiated. Arguably, the only risk they had in mind was that they might get caught at the border into England. Nor did the defendant think of the risk or consider whether the victims' might have impliedly consented to take such a risk.[276]

23–093 **Are there any special exceptions where reckless harm-doing is exempt where intentional harm-doing is not?** As we have seen, it was decided by a majority in *R. v. Brown* that the infliction of actual bodily harm with consent is unlawful, unless it comes within one of the exceptions that the courts have created as matter of public policy. If the conduct comes within one of the established exceptions, the defendant will be able to raise consent as a defence even if he intentionally caused V to suffer actual bodily harm. This was starkly illustrated with reference to boxing.

It appears that dogging[277] and swinging[278] are exempt as a matter of public policy.[279] Perhaps casual sex is so common that it would be too great a restriction of personal liberty and too great of an extension of the criminal law to try to police those who frequently have one night stands and engage in other risky

---

[274] Consent to injury cannot arise where neither the harmer or consenter anticipated or considered it. See *R. v. Slingsby* [1995] Crim. L.R. 571.

[275] [2003] Q.B. 1207.

[276] Cf. *R. v. Sullivan* [2011] N.L.C.A. 6.

[277] "Dogging combines voyeurism, exhibitionism, public sex and partner-swapping or multi-partner sex, and predominantly takes place in secluded sites on the urban fringe, accessed by car." David Bell, "Bodies, Technologies, Spaces: On 'Dogging'," (2006) 9(4) *Sexualities* 387.

[278] Swingers are people who randomly have group sex with strangers. See generally, Meg Barker and Darren Langdridge, "Whatever happened to non-monogamies? Critical Reflections on Recent Research and Theory," (2010) 13(6) *Sexualities* 748.

[279] *R. v. Dica* [2004] Q.B. 1257; *R. v. Konzani* [2005] 2 Cr. App. R. 198. See also Margo Kaplan, "Rethinking HIV-Exposure Crimes," (2012) 87 *Ind. L. Rev.* (forthcoming).

sexual practices of a non-violent nature.[280] Many of these folks would foresee that there is a possibility that one of their sexual encounters might leave them with a nasty infection such as H.I.V. If a person has sexual relations with another believing that the other could have H.I.V., he impliedly consents to the risk of being infected. Those who engage in casual sexual relations cannot be criminalized for doing so. Such an exception is analogous to the exceptions for sport, horse-play and dangerous feats, in that the harm-doer is only exempt when he recklessly causes bodily harm. For example, if a bowler bowls a cricket ball and accidentally hits the batsperson in the eye thereby blinding him, the batsperson's consent (implied by the fact that he willingly plays cricket knowing that such an injury is a possibility), will provide the bowler with a defence. If the bowler deliberately bowls the ball at the batsman purely for the sake of causing him serious injury, consent will only provide a defence if the resulting harm is less than actual bodily harm.[281]

If the defendant intentionally causes the victim to be infected with H.I.V., the victim's consent will not provide him with a defence. Suppose V knows that D is a H.I.V. carrier. Suppose also that V asks D to draw some of his infected blood into a syringe and thereafter asks him to inject her with it. Because D deliberately aims to infect V with H.I.V. (cause her g.b.h.), he will not be able to rely on V's consent to justify his actions. Similarly, if a H.I.V. carrier has consensual sexual intercourse with the aim of infecting the other with H.I.V., the victim's consenting to be infected will be no defence.[282] The defendant is not liable when he recklessly risks infecting the victim, because both parties should be able to take such a risk. It would be too much to criminalize an infector where he did not even know he was a carrier, because those engaging in casual sex know the risks. People should be able to take such risks if they want.

23.18. CONSENT, SURGERY AND ADORNMENT

The previous discussion has shown that the validity of consent to harm is a grey area in the law. It is sufficiently uncertain to have given rise to the option that the judges have a commission to pronounce upon the legality of all forms of surgery; and certainly the pronouncement in *R. v. Brown*, conferring benediction of the Lords on "reasonable surgical interference," seems to confirm that opinion. In practice, of course, the courts would find in favour of such interferences if the question ever arose, almost as a matter of routine.

23–094

There have been doubts about unnecessary cosmetic surgery. However, many dangerous and unnecessary cosmetic procedures have come to be accepted as lawful. Many people have died from having liposuction,[283] yet it does not even

---

[280] See generally, Raymond Ku, "Swingers: Morality Legislation and the Limits of State Police Power," (1999) 12 *St. Thomas L. Rev.* 1.

[281] This is assuming that for some bizarre reason the batsman has asked the bowler to injure him.

[282] Those who infect others with diseases will be liable for aggravated assault contrary to sections 18 and 20 of the *Offences against the Person Act 1861. R. v. Konzani* [2005] 2 Cr. App. R. 198.

[283] Frederick Grazer, "Fatal Outcomes from Liposuction: Census Survey of Cosmetic Surgeons," (2000) 105 *Plastic & Reconstructive Surgery* 436; Susan F. Ely, *et al.*, "Deaths Related to Liposuction," (1999) 340 *N. Eng. J. Med.* 1471. Liposuction deaths are usually caused by the anaesthesia.

remove the most dangerous fat.[284] Numerous procedures have been recognized as lawful including sex-changes. A change from male to pseudo-female sex organs involves castration: the penis and testicles are removed and a pseudo-vagina constructed from the scrotum. Now castration was regarded as maim at common law, because it was thought to reduce the will to fight. Yet the male-"female" sex-change is performed openly by qualified surgeons. If the issue were raised, the operation could be supported as conducive to the patient's mental health; and Ormrod J. accepted its legality on this ground.[285] Again, no one has ever doubted the legality of the operation of prefrontal leucotomy, which, by severing the frontal lobes of the brain, changes the personality of the patient in certain cases of mental illness. (However, this would now be caught by *R. v. Brown*, as removing a person's mental capacity is clearly bodily harm.) Therapy also gives moral support to a wide range of cosmetic surgery, but not all. The justification for augmenting bosoms, chiselling noses, lifting faces and eyelids, and ear-pinning to name a few, is that the patient is pleased and may be socially advantaged, rather than that the operation is a psychiatric necessity.

The surgical removal of healthy limbs from physically healthy young adults has been justified as a psychiatric necessity.[286] Those who suffer Body Integrity Identity Disorder[287] desire that their healthy limbs be surgically removed. In a case in Scotland a surgeon amputated a healthy young man's foot, because the patient said he could not identify with it, and that it was causing him great annoyance and metal distress. The surgeon was not prosecuted, so we do not know whether consent would have been an effective defence.[288] Clearly, removing the limb from a non-consenting person would be a maiming at common law, and would also result in grievous bodily harm. If a person's feet or legs are removed, he is permanently disabled. *R. v. Brown* means consent would be no defence in such cases. In extreme cases the defence of medical necessity could be raised, but there are not likely to be many cases where the mental harm would outweigh the long-term physical disablement. (If the surgery involved removing a person's legs, it would also mean this person would then need carers to help him

---

[284] Liposuction removes only the surface fat that forms just below the skin; it does not remove the most dangerous kind of fat (*i.e.* visceral fat deposits, which are located inside the abdominal cavity). Samuel Klein *et al.*, "Absence of an Effect of Liposuction on Insulin Action and Risk Factors for Coronary Heart Disease," (2004) 350 *N. Engl. J. Med.* 2549.

[285] *Corbett v. Corbett* [1971] P. 83 at 99.

[286] Bayne and Levy argue that "if such patients are experiencing significant distress as a consequence of the rare psychological disorder named Body Integrity Identity Disorder (BIID), such operations might be permissible." Tim Bayne and Neil Levy, "Amputees By Choice: Body Integrity Identity Disorder and the Ethics of Amputation," (2005) 22(1) *Journal of Applied Philosophy* 75.

[287] There are three main disorders that cause young people to desire that their limbs be removed: (1) Body Integrity Identity Disorder involves the consenter not wanting his limbs because he has no awareness of them or believes that they belong to another person. (2) Body Dysmorphic Disorder is a "condition in which the individual believes, incorrectly, that a part of their body is diseased or exceedingly ugly;" and therefore should be removed. (3) Apotemphilia. "Apotemnophiles are sexually attracted to amputees, and sexually excited by the notion that they might become amputees themselves." *Id.* at 75-78.

[288] *Id.* at 75.

bathe, cook, clean and so on.)[289] A clear case of medical necessity is the taking of an organ for transplant, such as a kidney. No serious legal doubts have been expressed about such operations upon adult donors, where a paired organ is surrendered to save the life of another.

Given *R. v. Brown*, it may be questioned whether the criminal law has no acceptable place in controlling operations that result in the patient being permanently (and unnecessarily) disabled or disfigured. If the surgery permanently disfigures or disables the patient for no good reason, then the criminal law should come into play. It is difficult to reconcile the spanking in *R. v. Donovan* with some of the procedures that medically qualified people are allowed to perform for pecuniary reward. Can the cosmetic surgeon provide dangerous and unnecessary surgery, so long as the price is right?[290] It appears so. Controls exercised by the medical profession itself will be sufficient in most cases, but there may be extreme cases (such as where the patient is addicted to cosmetic surgery and the repeated procedures are likely to result in long-term health problems)[291] where the criminal law should be invoked. Medics should not be licensed to assist people to permanently disable or disfigure themselves. The surgeon does aim to leave her patient permanently disfigured or disabled, but if she foresees long-term disablement or disfigurement as a virtually certain consequence of performing the operation, she should not perform it. That is, unless it is a case of medical necessity. If a surgeon amputates a patient's legs to prevent gangrene spreading, he could be said to have provided life saving treatment as a matter of necessity. However, if he amputates his patient's legs merely because the patient does not want her legs anymore, he would have difficulty in satisfying necessity as a defence.[292]

23–095

---

[289] The remote harm involved is that society has to pay for the amputee's care. Remote harms are not usually the business of the criminal law, but they should be where the harm is great and where the harm is not self-inflicted. (Hence, the surgeon should be liable.)

[290] Many celebrities are disfigured not because they have one or two cosmetic procedures, but because they become addicted to surgery and insist on having many procedures. (We need only think of the late 20th century singer, Michael Jackson.) The grievous bodily harm might result from the person developing a recognized psychiatric illness. See the tragic cases reported in the media by John Naish, "When Looks Can Kill," (London: *The Daily Mail*, 25 January 2011).

[291] See for example, Virginia L. Blum, *Flesh Wounds: The Culture of Cosmetic Surgery*, (Los Angeles: University of California Press, 2003).

[292] Clearly if the patient has attempted to amputate his own foot, because the doctor has refused to operate, the defence of necessity might be raised: the lesser evil would be for the doctor to remove the foot in controlled conditions using proper medicine and science. See David Veale, "Outcome of Cosmetic Surgery and 'DIY' Surgery in Patients with Body Dysmorphic Disorder," (2000) *Psychiatric Bulletin* 218, where it is noted that some mentally disordered people have tried to perform their own cosmetic surgery.

23–096 **Wilson[293] was not a medical doctor, nor is hot-branding a normal form of an adornment in our society. You said above that his conduct might be distinguished from sadomasochism because he did not harm his wife merely for the sake of harming her. But could not the sadomasochist say the same? Why does motive matter?** The medical cases might be distinguished on two grounds. (1) Medical necessity. (2) The grievous bodily harm (or actual bodily harm) is merely a means for providing therapy.

The threshold for overriding consent has to be very high. The physical wounds involved in unnecessary plastic surgery could be worse than those witnessed in *R. v. Brown*. A person is able to consent to dangerous cosmetic surgery that is not necessary, such as repeated breast augmentation procedures; and repeated facelifts. The benefits of this sort of unnecessary cosmetic surgery are not as valuable as life-saving surgery or surgery that is needed to correct severe disfigurement. This kind of cosmetic surgery merely provides a psychological benefit to those who are narcissistic. What makes cosmetic surgery morally permissible? Surgery involves intentional violence that may cause serious bodily harm, but the purpose of the surgery is to advance the patient's long-term interests. Any short-term harm (wounding, pain, *etc.*) is a mere means to an end. The end is to give the patient a psychological boost.

23–097 **This all seems to be sitting on loose sand. Suppose Wilson had branded a big W on his wife's forehead. Would the court have held that type of adornment is in the public interest?** The decision would have almost certainly been different, if that had been the case. The adornment cases seem to be no different to cosmetic surgery, the wounding, burning, *etc.*, is a means to achieve the adornment. Once the wound or burn heals the consenter is able to enjoy the long-term benefit of having the adornment. The only difference is that adornments are normally done by people who are not medically qualified. However, the processes used to achieve adornment normally only cause the consenter to suffer superficial wounds. Even though cosmetic surgery is carried out in a controlled medical environment by medically qualified operators, it is inherently more dangerous.[294] Cosmetic surgery uses more extreme means (invasive surgery) to achieve the end of adornment. The adornment (larger breasts, a more youthful face, and so on) is a long-term benefit from the consenter's perspective. And society seems to accept that these extreme forms of adornment are beneficial for those who desire them. Of course, if it all goes horribly wrong it may result in permanent misery for the consenter.

23–098 **But the sadomasochists were not merely injuring each other for the sake of injuring each other; the injuring was a means for achieving sexual satisfaction, was it not?** That is what they argued. The sadomasochists might argue that the *telos* of the participants' activities in sadomasochism is merely to achieve sexual gratification. But every time they want to achieve the ulterior aim of sexual gratification, they need to harm each other. The harm has to be repeated

---

[293] *R. v. Wilson* [1997] Q.B. 47.

[294] Risks for any surgery include, bleeding, infection, risks of being killed by the anaesthesia, reactions to the drugs, respiratory problems, pneumonia and so on.

each time the recipient wants to receive sadomasochistic pleasure. The two are inseparable—the sexual gratification can only be achieved while the harm is being inflicted. *Per contra*, adornment procedures only involve a one-off wounding, burning, *etc.*, which results in a long-term benefit. There is nothing unreasonable about preventing people from repeatedly inflicting grievous bodily harm upon others, merely because they want to repeat the ephemeral sexual thrill it gives them. Nonetheless, it seems that this argument should not apply to actual bodily harm. Those who regularly inflict actual bodily harm on themselves by smoking and drinking excessively are not criminalized, nor are those who supply them with the instruments of harm. Similarly, professional athletes regularly subject their bodies to actual bodily harm, but recover.

It is submitted that if the sadomasochists are only inflicting actual bodily harm on each other, that the criminal law should not be invoked. It is a complete waste of taxpayer funds trying and jailing such people. The harm is ephemeral (Donovan's mistress's bottom no doubt was not permanently injured), trivial and not worthy of punishment. The ephemeral nature of the harm means that repeat performances, unlike repeat alcohol and nicotine consumption, would not culminate in harm any greater than actual bodily harm.

23.19. CONSENSUAL RISK-TAKING: DANGEROUS FEATS, SPORT AND HORSEPLAY

23–099 The foregoing discussion has concentrated on where hurt is intentionally inflicted. We now turn to those where the "victim" knowingly assumes the risk of being hurt (or killed). The only purpose of the defendant is to do something that, as he knows, involves the risk of hurt to another, the other consenting to run the risk.

According to the *dictum* in *Attorney-General's Reference (No. 6 of 1980)*,[295] the courts are even prepared to countenance "dangerous exhibitions." No qualification about reasonableness appears here, but it would be unwise to rely on the omission; a judge could always defeat the argument by pointing out that Lord Lane was merely endorsing the "accepted legality" of such exhibitions, and did not say how far the "accepted legality" went.

23–100 **But why are dangerous exhibitions needed in the public interest?**[296] The law relating to dangerous feats and performances, such as the climbing of vertical surfaces and brief defiances of the law of gravity on the flying trapeze or hang-glider, is obscure. Certainly no crime is committed if the whole affair is reasonable; but can one go further and say that the law does not interfere even if it is reckoned unreasonable? Granted the power of the courts to nullify consent to hurts intentionally inflicted, it does not follow that the general criminal law dictates what dangers may be lawfully encountered in behaviour that is not only unaggressive but not intended to harm.

---

[295] [1981] Q.B. 715.

[296] In a recent stunt gone wrong, a stuntman was killed when his safety net failed. See Mark Hughes, "Human Cannonball Killed After Missing Safety Net," (London: *The Telegraph*, 26 April 2011).

One way of settling many problems is by pointing out that there is not, and never has been, any crime of self-manslaughter. Suicide has always meant intentional suicide:[297] in effect (though not in legal theory) self-murder. For no purpose is it a crime for a person to kill himself negligently.[298] Anyone who incites or helps him cannot be guilty of manslaughter as a perpetrator, because he is not the perpetrator; and he cannot be guilty as accessory, because of the absence of the crime.

This point was overlooked in *R. v. Pike*.[299] Pike anaesthetized his mistress with her consent, or encouraged her to administer the anaesthetic to herself—the evidence did not make it clear which. His object was to gratify his sexual perversion of copulating with an unconscious woman. The anaesthetic was a wholly improper and dangerous one, and caused her death. The trial judge, Hilbery J., directed the jury that, given the requisite *mens rea*, the defendant could be convicted of manslaughter whether he administered the anaesthetic himself or provided it for the deceased woman to take.

23–101　The court did not focus on the self-manslaughter point, and the ruling is clearly contrary to principle. Since the case might have amounted to accidental killing, rather than to a killing by Pike, he should have been acquitted.

It is true, according to *R. v. Bourne*[300] and *R. v. Cogan*,[301] a person may be an accessory to a non-existent crime, or may commit the *actus reus* through an innocent agent. But even if these decisions are given their fullest width, they do not apply here. Suppose for the sake of argument that the two cases decide that where the alleged perpetrator has a personal defence, an alleged accessory not having that defence can be held liable. The difficulty is not that the mistress has a personal defence. There is no *actus reus*. Since the *Suicide Act 1961*, even intentional self-killing is a perfectly lawful activity; and negligent self-killing always was lawful. It took express provision in the *Suicide Act 1961* to make the abetment of suicide a crime, and there is no statute making the abetment of negligent self-killing a crime. The decisions in *R. v. Bourne* and *R. v. Cogan* should not be taken as making a person guilty as accessory in these circumstances.

Nor does the doctrine of innocent agency affect the question. It could not be argued that Pike killed his mistress with her own hand, because the doctrine of innocent agency has not been extended to negligent acts.[302] Besides, it is not proper to use the doctrine where the alleged agent is innocent because the act is

---

[297] *R. v. HM Coroner for the City of London Ex p. Barber* [1975] 1 W.L.R. 1310.

[298] Glanville Williams, *Criminal Law: The General Part*, (London: Stevens & Sons, 2nd edn. 1961) at 393-394.

[299] [1961] Crim. L.R. 114, 547. Cf. *R. v. Evans* [2009] 1 W.L.R. 1999, where it was held that if D assists V to engage in risky conduct, D can be liable for gross negligence manslaughter if the risk-taker dies. However, D is only liable if it became obvious that the risk-taker was in peril (for example, dying from a drug overdose), and if, armed with that knowledge, D failed to summon help.

[300] (1952) 36 Cr. App. R. 125.

[301] [1976] Q.B. 217.

[302] Cf. *R. v. Millward* (1994) 158 J.P.N. 715, where there D arguably obliquely intended the innocent agent to perform conduct element.

perfectly lawful. The doctrine applies only where the act would be unlawful for the agent, but for the lack of fault by the agent or some personal defence that he (or she) has.

Apart from these technical arguments, it would be unfortunate if the accessory to **23–102** *de facto* self-manslaughter could be convicted, because it would mean that people who help mountaineers, yachtspersons and others to fit out foolhardy expeditions might be convicted of manslaughter if a member of the party dies. There has never been any such prosecution, and it would be undesirable to have a rule of law making the prosecution possible.[303]

The foregoing reasoning helps the defendant only when he does not do the act that kills. If he does, he must find his defence along some other line.[304] One solution would be to seize upon the only fully liberal phrase in the judgment in *Attorney-General's Reference (No. 6 of 1980)*,[305] permitting "dangerous exhibitions." It has already been noticed that the liberality may be illusory, because of Lord Lane's reference to "accepted legality". But if dangerous exhibitions are truly allowed, then dangerous feats not intended as exhibitions must presumably be allowed as well. In other words, "assumption of risk" must be a defence to a manslaughter charge in these cases. Alternatively, it is always possible for the court to regard the value of the activity, taken in conjunction with the voluntariness of participation, as excluding a finding of negligence.

The proper rule would be that the common law has no application to feats of skill or endurance. There have always been people who have taken pleasure in such things; and few would count the preservation of life as the worthiest way of living. "Surely," said R. L. S., "the love of living is stronger in an Alpine climber roping over a peril, or a hunter riding merrily at a stiff fence, than in the creature that lives upon a diet and walks a measured distance in the interest of his constitution."[306] Activities like these are valued not only because they present difficulties to overcome but often, paradoxically, because of the danger. Motorcycle racing and bull-riding are conspicuous examples. These activities attract participants and spectators precisely because of the risks—even though the organizers take great pains to minimize them. The same is true of those who climb down dark holes, or who make free-fall parachute descents, or go white water rafting. The soundest policy for the criminal courts would be to dissociate themselves from these questions, by holding that consent of a person to run the risk of death, otherwise than in combats,[307] is a defence to a charge of manslaughter. Unless the law abrogates control over this area, the courts will be faced with the invidious task of deciding between risks that people may and may not legitimately run in respect of their own bodies.

---

[303] Cf. *R. v. Evans* [2009] 1 W.L.R. 1999, which comes very close to creating such a rule.

[304] If the act is an unlawful dangerous act *per se*, then consent will be no defence. *R. v. Stein* (2007) 179 A. Crim. R. 360.

[305] [1981] Q.B. 715.

[306] Robert Louis Stevenson, *Essays,* (New York: C. Scribner, 1906) at 49.

[307] Cf. *R. v. Gnango* [2011] 1 All E.R. 153.

23–103   The proposition should be accepted not only for open-air sports but for cinema "stuntmen" and circus entertainers. Risks are taken every day in these performances, and sometimes accidents happen, but the police rightly take no notice.

That dangerous performances should not be controlled by the operation of the common law of manslaughter seems to be supported by the fact that Parliament has itself made a notably limited entry into the field. Sections 23-24 of the *Children and Young Persons Act 1933* contains prohibitions in respect of dangerous performances by persons under the age of 16;[308] and the *Hypnotism Act 1952* allows the local authority, or other body that licenses places of public entertainment, to regulate exhibitions of hypnotism; section 3 of the latter *Act* provides that hypnotism must not be demonstrated on a person under 18.

We may end this discussion by observing that Parliament has not entirely excluded consensual and self-directed negligence from penal restraint. The *Health and Safety at Work etc. Act 1974* imposes a duty on employees to take care even for themselves. It has long been accepted that employees may properly be made liable, at least in theory, for not using safety precautions like goggles: factory workers are subject to a great temptation not to use them when they are uncomfortable or hinder earnings, so paternalistic considerations are allowed to prevail—even though prosecutions of employees may be very rare. Enforcement is by inspectors who primarily use persuasion. It is different when an effort is made to impose safety precautions on the general public, because here enforcement is necessarily by the police, who are not well utilized on matters not relating to public order. However, after heated debate Parliament made the wearing of crash helmets compulsory for motorcyclists, and the wearing of seatbelts compulsory in vehicles.[309] Strain upon the National Health Service is not in general a reason for proscribing dangerous activities, if it were, there would be a strong case for outlawing all alcohol consumption and also for outlawing private motorcar ownership in large cities, because the overall economic benefit would be enormous.[310] However, when the safety precaution is simple and causalities are high the medical argument can outweigh that based on personal liberty.

23–104   **Are not many sports a dangerous feat?**   Games like football, while very dissimilar from fights or bouts, have the common feature of involving the use of force between the players in accordance with the rules. The consent by the players to the use of moderate force is certainly valid. Whether the courts will, or should assert any control over games on account of danger to the participants has hitherto not been debated in this country. In the case of gridiron football there is a remote risk of serious harm transpiring, but the harm is a mere side-effect of playing a risky sport. The participants in a football match do not intentionally aim to harm their fellow players.

---

[308] The cut-off age in section 24 of the *1933 Act* is under 12. See also *Children (Protection at Work) Regulations 1998/276*.

[309] See sections 14-18 of the *Road Traffic Act 1988*.

[310] Dennis J. Baker, "Collective Criminalization and the Constitutional Right to Endanger Others," (2009) 28 *Crim. Just. Ethics* 168.

In practice the legal questions, when they arise, turn on the limits of the consent actually given.[311] It might seem that consent is given only to force that is within the rules of the game, and that force applied outside these rules, if it is deliberate and not an accident, is an assault.[312] A player may, however, be convicted of assault or manslaughter if he does an act with intent to harm outside the bounds of the sport.[313] The bounds of the game can only be established by looking at the rules, because it will be necessary to establish that the defendant's conduct was within or outside the consent or was reckless.[314]

There are no rules of the game in horseplay, so how will the limits of consent   **23–105**
be determined? Most youths know that one of the side-effects of engaging in rough horseplay is that someone might get hurt. Those who participate in horseplay impliedly consent to take the risk of being harmed when they willingly participate knowing that there is a risk that they might be injured.[315] If the harm is not a foreseeable consequence of the horseplay, the victim cannot be said to have risked it.

In *R. v. Jones*[316] a group of school boys grabbed two boys and tossed them high into the air. When the boys come down to ground they were seriously injured. The facts were that the victims were protesting and trying to get away. Clearly, if a person is saying do not throw me into the air and is trying to escape, he is not consenting to being tossed in the air. Nevertheless, it was held that the question of whether the boys genuinely believed the victims were consenting should have been left to the jury. In *R. v. Aitken*[317] three R.A.F. officers, after consuming a large quantity of alcohol, engaged in some horseplay at a party. The horseplay included them setting light to the fire resistant suits of two officers. Those two officers treated it as a joke. Later in the evening the defendants decided to set fire to another officer's fire resistant suit. The officer struggled, but was too intoxicated to defend himself. The flames flared up rapidly and he was severely burned. The court held that it was not a question of whether the victim was in fact consenting, but a question of whether the defendants in fact believed he was consenting. Since the officers believed (even if unreasonably) that the victim was consenting, the defence of consent was available.

If the victim is not willingly participating in the horseplay, then he cannot be said to be consenting to the foreseen risks of engaging in such horseplay. If he does not want to be a part of the horseplay, is trying to resist and so on, then there will be no implied consent. But the defence will be available where the defendant makes an unreasonable mistake as to whether the victim is consenting.[318]

---

[311] *R. v. Barnes* [2005] 1 W.L.R. 910. See also *R. v. Ciccarelli* (1989) 54 C.C.C. (3d) 121.

[312] *R. v. Barnes* [2005] 1 W.L.R. 910; see also *R. v. Anderson* [2000] 40 C.R. (5th) 329; *R. v. Krzysztofik* [1992] 79 Man. R. (2d) 234; *R. v. Brown* [1994] 1 A.C. 212 at 266.

[313] *R. v. T. (G.)* [1996] 18 O.T.C. 73.

[314] To the extent that *R. v. Moore* (1898) 14 T.L.R. 229, suggests that the rules of the game are not admissible evidence, it should not be followed.

[315] *R. v. Aitken* [1992] 1 W.L.R. 1006.

[316] (1986) 83 Cr. App. R. 375.

[317] [1992] 1 W.L.R. 1006.

[318] *R. v. Jones* (1986) 83 Cr. App. R. 375.

If the defendant's belief is totally unreasonable, the jury need not accept that he in fact held such a belief.[319] In *R. v. P*[320] the defendant appealed against his conviction of manslaughter. In that case, the defendant and another youth had pushed a school colleague from a bridge into a river. The victim could not swim and drowned. The defendant claimed that the victim was only thrown into the river as a prank and that he consented to being thrown in the river. The Court of Appeal rightly held that it had been open to the jury to conclude that there was no consent. The evidence showed that he was not consenting when he was thrown into the murky river and that the defendant did not in fact believe he was. Therefore, the horseplay exception was not relevant.

23.20.   ENTRAPMENT

23–106   The courts of the United States have created a defence of entrapment where a defence to which the actor was not "predisposed" has been actively instigated by the police or by an undercover agent on their behalf.[321] English courts reject the defence.[322] Whether this is the right attitude is a matter of opinion, but a workable rule would be somewhat difficult to draft and administer.

Of course, entrapment can be a matter of mitigation where the offender was not the prime mover in the scheme and might have refrained from committing any offence if he had not been tempted. Entrapment is not even mitigation if the undercover agents merely pretend that they are in the market to buy things like drugs or obscene publications, and do not use extraordinary persuasion in order to overcome reluctance.[323] The courts recognize that the consensual offences (such as in the realm of sex, drink, drugs, and gambling)[324] generally cannot be detected without some testing of the suspects, and criminal organizations frequently have to be infiltrated by police spies who must necessarily show enthusiasm for the undertaking.

Judges have sometimes spoken strongly against the police using *agents provocateurs*,[325] in the sense that people should not cause offences to be committed.[326] One principle that has been distinctly laid down is that where an informer has been employed in such a way as to affect "the quality of the offence," this fact must be disclosed at trial.[327] However, when a police officer

---

[319] Cf. *D.P.P. v. Morgan* [1976] A.C. 182.

[320] *R. v. P* [2005] EWCA Crim. 1960.

[321] *Soriano v. State*, 248 P.3d 381 (2011); *U.S. v. Theagene*, 565 F.3d 911 (2009); *Jacobson v. U.S.*, 503 U.S. 540 (1992). The basis of the defence is controversial. See George Fletcher, *Rethinking Criminal Law*, (Boston, Little, Brown, 1978), at 541-544. See also Dru Stevenson, "Entrapment and the Problem of Deterring Police Misconduct," (2004) 37 *Conn. L. Rev.* 67; Derrick A. Carter, "To Catch the Loin, Tether the Goat: Entrapment, Conspiracy and Sentencing Manipulation," (2009) 42 *Akron L. Rev.* 135.

[322] *R. v. Sang* [1980] A.C. 402; *R. v. Jones* [2010] 2 Cr. App. R. 69.

[323] *R. v. Thornton* [2003] EWCA Crim. 919 at paras. 23-26; *R. v. Mayeri* [1999] 1 Cr. App. R. (S.) 304.

[324] See for example, *R. v. Jones* [2008] Q.B. 460. Cf. *State v. Nero*, 1 A.3d 184 (2010).

[325] See the discussion in *Nottingham City Council v. Amin* [2000] 1 W.L.R. 1071.

[326] Responsive to this opinion, the Direct or Public Prosecutions may abandon charges that appear to have been induced by an *agent provocateur*.

[327] *R. v. Birtles* [1969] 1 W.L.R. 1047.

gives evidence that he acted "on information received," the defendant cannot cross-examine him to ascertain the identity of his informant; so if the defendant alleges that he was unfairly tricked and the police deny it, he may have considerable difficulty in proving his contention.

Can the court stay the proceedings for abuse of process?   The courts will   **23–107** only exclude evidence obtained by entrapment in exceptional cases. The courts have to balance the requirement that criminals should be caught and punished against the requirement that there should be no abuse of process. If an abuse of process is significant, it would bring the criminal justice system into disrepute.[328] The courts consider a number of factors to ensure that a fair balance is struck. In *Re Attorney-General's Reference (No.3 of 2000)*, Lord Nicholls said:[329]

> "On this a useful guide is to consider whether the police did no more than present the defendant with an unexceptional opportunity to commit a crime. I emphasize the word 'unexceptional'. The yardstick for the purpose of this test is, in general, whether the police conduct preceding the commission of the offence was no more than might have been expected from others in the circumstances."

The courts will balance a number of considerations to determine whether the police went too far including the nature of the offence (the police should show there was no reasonable alternative available for thwarting the given type of offence)[330] and whether the police were acting in good faith. Did they have reasonable grounds for targeting the defendant? Or were they acting merely to seek revenge and so on? However, the most important consideration concerns the nature of the police's participation in the crime.[331] What lengths did the police go to encourage the defendant to commit the crime?:

> "The greater the inducement held out by the police, and the more forceful or persistent the police overtures, the more readily may a court conclude that the police overstepped the boundary: their conduct might well have brought about commission of a crime by a person who would normally avoid crime of that kind. In assessing the weight to be attached to the police inducement, regard is to be had to the defendant's circumstances, including his vulnerability. This is a recognition that what may be a significant inducement to one person may not be so to another. For the police to behave as would an ordinary customer of a trade, whether lawful or unlawful, being carried on by the defendant will not normally be regarded as objectionable."[332]

A policeman cannot be said to have caused the commission of the offence, rather than have merely provided an opportunity for the defendant to commit it, if

---

[328] *R. v. Latif* [1996] 1 W.L.R. 104 at 112, *per* Lord Steyn.

[329] [2001] 1 W.L.R. 2060 at 2069 quoting McHugh J. in *Ridgeway v. The Queen* (1995) 184 C.L.R. 19 at 92 where he said: "once the state goes beyond the ordinary, it is likely to increase the incidence of crime by artificial means."

[330] *Re Attorney-General's Reference (No. 3 of 2000)* [2001] 1 W.L.R. 2060 at 2079, *per* Lord Hoffman.

[331] *Re Attorney-General's Reference (No. 3 of 2000)* [2001] 1 W.L.R. 2060 at 2075, *per* Lord Hoffman.

[332] *Re Attorney-General's Reference (No. 3 of 2000)* [2001] 1 W.L.R. 2060 at 2070, *per* Lord Nicholls.

he behaved as an ordinary member of the public would have behaved.[333] If the police officer merely asks to purchase cocaine from a suspected dealer, he cannot be said to have encouraged the defendant to commit a crime that he would not otherwise have committed. Such a defendant is willing to sell the drugs to anyone who presents himself as a willing customer. If the police offered a massive financial incentive to a suspected drug dealer to encourage him to *start* growing cannabis, they would cross the line. It would be necessary to show that the defendant committed the crime simply because he had been encouraged to do so by the enforcement officer.[334]

In *Re Attorney-General's Reference (No. 3 of 2000)*, Lord Hoffman said:

> "A good example of a straightforward application of the distinction between causing the commission of the offence and providing an opportunity for it to be committed is *Nottingham City Council v. Amin* …. Mr. Amin owned a taxi which was not licensed to ply for hire in Nottingham. Two plain clothes policemen who saw him driving down a street in Nottingham in the middle of the night flagged him down. He stopped and upon request agreed to take them to the destination which they named. When they arrived, the policemen paid the fare and then charged him with the offence of plying for hire without a licence. …. [T]he policemen behaved like ordinary members of the public in flagging the taxi down. They did not wave £50 notes or pretend to be in distress."[335]

23–108 **Can evidence obtained by entrapment be excluded?** Perhaps. Under section 78(1) of the *Police and Criminal Evidence Act 1984* a court may exclude evidence "if … having regard to … the circumstances in which the evidence was obtained, the admission of the evidence would have an adverse effect on the fairness of the proceedings." Section 78 would provide a remedy in cases where it would be unfair to allow the evidence to be admitted. If the defendant claims he was entrapped and that he would not have committed the crime but for the incentive and encouragement provided by the law enforcement officers, then the appropriate remedy is to have the proceedings stayed. Such a defendant is arguing that it is unfair to try him at all, not that the evidence of his wrongdoing would make his trial unfair. However, the effect might be the same.[336] Lord Hoffman and Lord Hutton said "where to exclude evidence under section 78 is, in substance, an application to stay on the ground of entrapment, a court should apply the principles applicable to the grant of a stay."[337]

---

[333] *Re Attorney-General's Reference (No. 3 of 2000)* [2001] 1 W.L.R. 2060 at 2075, *per* Lord Hoffman.

[334] *Nottingham City Council v. Amin* [2000] 1 W.L.R. 1071 at 1076–1077, *per* Lord Bingham.

[335] [2001] 1 W.L.R. 2060 at 2075-2076, *per* Lord Hoffman.

[336] Article 6(1) of the *European Convention for the Protection of Human Rights and Fundamental Freedoms* might be invoked in extreme cases, see *Ramanauskas v. Lithuania* (2010) 51 E.H.R.R. 11, where European Court of Human Rights held: "[T]he public interest could not justify the use of evidence obtained as a result of police incitement, since to do so would risk depriving the accused of a fair trial from the outset. Police incitement occurred where the officers involved did not confine themselves to investigating criminal activity in an essentially passive manner, but exerted such an influence on the subject as to incite the commission of an offence that would otherwise not have been committed, in order to make it possible to establish the offence. In order for a trial to be fair within the meaning of art. 6(1), all evidence obtained due to police incitement had to be excluded." Of course, the exclusion of this evidence might have the effect of staying the proceedings, since there might not be much left to base the case on.

[337] *Re Attorney-General's Reference (No. 3 of 2000)* [2001] 1 W.L.R. 2060 at 2075; 2092.

CHAPTER 24

NECESSITY

"In all human institutions, a smaller evil is allowed to procure a greater good."

Oliver Goldsmith[1]

The fact that the defendant broke the letter of the law in mitigating circumstances may be a ground for reducing or cancelling punishment, but it is not generally a defence in the sense that it prevents conviction. Although from the human point of view we may understand the strength of a temptation to which the defendant was subjected, still we say that he did wrong, and we express the opinion by registering a conviction, even though this is followed by giving the defendant an absolute discharge or other virtual let-off. But there are certain situations—necessity, duress and self-defence among them—where (at least in some circumstances) the defendant is entitled to be acquitted, and not merely to be treated leniently in the matter of punishment.

24–001

24.1. THE THEORY OF NECESSITY

The word "necessity," as we customarily use it, has a special meaning. A particular act is never necessary in the sense that there is literally no option. Some choice is always present, even though one of the alternatives is to meet one's own death. Necessity in legal contexts involves the judgment that the evil of obeying the letter of the law is socially greater in the particular circumstances than the evil of breaking it. In other words, the law has to be broken to achieve a greater good.

24–002

But good can never come out of evil.   If I give an instance where good comes out of what seems to have been evil, are you then going to say that the apparent evil was not really evil? For, if so, I can obviously never defeat your proposition; but the proposition will then be uninformative, because it is tautologous.

24–003

Certainly we should be very cautious about inflicting an admitted evil in the hope that good will come. Generally it would not be justifiable to do so. The doctrine of necessity concerns cases in which it is justified.

Surely necessity can never justify a breach of the law?   As we shall see, the defence of necessity is controversial. Judges are suspicious of it because they fear that it may be subversive. But if the validity of the defence is acknowledged, then

24–004

---

[1] *The Vicar of Wakefield*, (Edinburgh: Oliver & Boyd, 1823) at 175.

it is only the letter of the law, or the apparent law, that is broken under necessity. If necessity is a legal justification, the law itself is not truly broken.

24–005 **It is said that good motive is no defence. How does necessity differ from this?** One who acts from necessity acts from a kind of good motive. Good motive falling outside the doctrine of necessity is not a defence to a criminal charge,[2] though it may be a ground for reducing punishment.

24–006 **But does our law recognize the defence?**   There are two views:

1.   The first is that necessity is not a general defence, but is recognized within the definitions of some particular offences.[3] A few statutes painstakingly provide for the defence, at least in part, such as the *Control of Pollution Act 1974*,[4] which allows a defence that the acts were done "in an emergency in order to avoid danger to the public." But Parliament is not generally so imaginative. The more usual position in this country is that the statute is silent about emergencies, but may incorporate wide words that could give the courts an excuse for reading in the defence of necessity. For example, if negligence or unreasonableness or even recklessness is in issue, necessity can be taken into account. (A man charged with careless driving says that he had to cross over to the wrong side of the road to avoid a collision.) It seems even to be allowed that the fact that a person is driving in an emergency is a factor to be weighed in deciding whether his driving was without due care.[5] Criminal damage requires that the damage be caused without lawful excuse; so if there is a rail accident and a passenger breaks into an unoccupied house in order to telephone for help, it may be contended that his damage to the door is not an offence because he has a lawful excuse. Or if the aforesaid passenger seizes a motorcycle in order to go for help, his consumption of the petrol would be held not to be dishonest, and therefore not to be theft, dishonesty being part of the definition of theft. If a statute prohibits something being done "wilfully," the courts hold that this word implies that the conduct is unlawful only if done "without lawful excuse."[6] The weakness in arguments built upon this last phrase is that it is (very reasonably) held not to let in defences not otherwise recognized by law.[7] Conversely, it can be argued with much force that a word like "unlawfully" should not be required in order to ensure that ordinary legal justifications are implied in the definition of the offence.[8] A

---

[2] *Chandler v. D.P.P.* [1964] A.C. 763; *R. v. Jones* [2007] 1 A.C. 136.

[3] In support of this see P. R. Glazebrook, "The Necessity Plea in English Criminal Law," (1972) 30 *Cambridge L.J.* 87. In *D.P.P. for Northern Ireland v. Lynch* [1975] A.C. 653 at 691F Lord Simon declared that the defence of necessity "has been decisively rejected in the criminal law generally," but this was dissenting *obiter*, and in support he mentioned only *R. v. Dudley* (1884-85) 14 Q.B.D. 273 and theft by starving, and neither is conclusive, as will be shown.

[4] Section 3(4)(d). See also section 1(4)(a) of the *Control of Pollution (Amendment) Act 1989*; section 18 of the *Animal Welfare Act 2006*; and section 44 of the *Fire and Rescue Services Act 2004*.

[5] *Wood v. Richards* (1977) 65 Cr. App. R. 300.

[6] *Rice v. Connolly* [1966] 2 Q.B. 414.

[7] *R. v. Tegerdine* (1982) 75 Cr. App. R. 298.

[8] Cf. the discussion in *R. v. Quayle* [2005] 1 W.L.R. 3642 at 3673.

more generous phrase is "without reasonable justification or excuse," which plainly admits justifications not otherwise recognized by law.

2. The alternative view is that necessity or lesser evil is a general defence in the criminal law, like nonage, insanity, self-defence and duress. In English common law it has been recognized mainly in the medical necessity cases,[9] and has been supported by a number of writers including Sir James Fitzjames Stephen.[10] There is little logic in saying that necessity can justify where the offence happens to have the word "unlawfully" or some such expression in the definition but not where there are no words upon which the defence can be hung; for it must often be an accident of drafting whether a word like "unlawfully" is put in or not. Moreover, to say that necessity can come in as a "lawful excuse" under statute presupposes that it is recognized by law as a lawful justification.[11] If it is, there is no reason why its availability should depend upon the statutory phrase.

The old books contain a plethora of maxims justifying necessity as a defence.[12] **24–007** The specific instances commonly given were pulling down houses to prevent the spread of fire, and entering upon land to dig trenches and bulwarks against the enemy. It was also recognized that prisoners could lawfully leave a prison in the case of fire, even though prison-break was a crime under a statute that made no mention of the defence of necessity. The prisoner, as the judges forcibly expressed it, "is not to be hanged because he would stay burnt." In *Reniger v. Fogossa*[13] it was said:

> "As the breaking of prison is felony in the prisoner himself by the Statute 1 Ed. 2. *de Frangentibus Prisonam*: yet if the prison be on fire, and they who are in break the prison to save their lives, this shall be excused by the law of reason, and yet the words of the statute are against it. So the jurors who were sworn upon an issue for fear of a great tempest, departed thence and dispersed themselves, and it was there held that they should not be amerced, and that their verdict afterwards was good, and that they did not do ill; which was so held in regard of the necessity of the occasion, but otherwise they should have been grievously punished."

---

[9] See *Gillick v. West Norfolk and Wisbech AHA* [1986] A.C. 112; *In re: F (Mental Patient: Sterilisation)* [1990] 2 A.C. 1 at 73–77; *Re A (Children) (Conjoined Twins: Medical Treatment) (No.1)* [2001] Fam. 147.

[10] See James Fitzjames Stephen, *A Digest of Criminal Law*, (London: MacMillan & Co., 1904) at 24.

[11] Cf. *R. v. Quayle* [2005] 1 W.L.R. 3642 at 3673–3674. See also *R. v. Bourne* [1939] 1 K.B. 687. The rule that "without lawful excuse" does not let in a defence of ignorance of the criminal law, since the law does not recognize such a general defence. *Dixon v. Atfield* [1975] 1 W.L.R. 1171, indicates an exception that proves the rule: the law allows reasonable temporary obstructions to a highway, but not unauthorized permanent obstructions. The latter therefore, unlike the former, cannot come within the phrase "lawful authority or excuse" in section 148(c) of the *Highways Act 1980*: *Putnam v. Colvin* [1984] R.T.R. 150.

[12] See Glanville Williams, *Criminal Law: The General Part*, (London: Stevens & Sons, 2nd edn. 1961) at 724–725.

[13] (1551) 1 Plow. 1 at 22 argued before the Earl of Wilt, Sir John Baker, and all the Justices of England. Cf. *State v. Lovercamp*, 43 Cal App 3d 823 (1974) (justifiable to escape prison to avoid homosexual attacks); *United States v. Bailey* (1980) 444 US 394 (not justifiable to escape prison to avoid intolerable prison conditions).

Wills J. on one occasion said that "a municipal regulation may be broken to save life or put out a fire,"[14] and it may be supposed that his mention of municipal regulations and fires was by way of illustration only, to save going into details. In a storm at sea, the cargo may be jettisoned for the safety of the passengers.[15] There is a right to land on the shore (even where it would otherwise be a trespass) in cases of peril or necessity,[16] and travellers who find the highway (including a footpath) "foundrous" may proceed on the adjoining land. It has also been held justifiable to burn a strip of heather to prevent a fire from spreading.[17]

Of all the instances of necessity, the saving of life is of course the strongest. Devlin J. said, in a civil case:

> "The safety of human lives belongs to a different scale of values from the safety of property. The two are beyond comparison and the necessity for saving life has at all times been considered a proper ground for inflicting such damage as may be necessary upon another's property."[18]

There are authorities of more recent date supporting the defence.[19] We may notice here, as elsewhere, that the enthusiasm of the courts in developing criminal liability is but imperfectly matched by their readiness to recognize proper defences.

24–008 **Is a defence of necessity really required, when the court can in a proper case give an absolute discharge?** An absolute discharge vindicates the defendant to a considerable extent, and although it follows what is technically a conviction, the conviction is eliminated for most purposes. Still, this is not a completely satisfactory solution from the defendant's point of view:

- The court cannot give a discharge where the conviction is of murder. Here the only possibility is a pardon, and on this the remarks of Lord Morris in *D.P.P. for Northern Ireland v. Lynch*[20] are worth quoting:

  > "It is most undesirable that cases should arise in which a just conclusion will only be attained by the prerogative of pardon. I would regret it if on an application legal principles such as cases could arise. Such principles and such approach as will prevent them from arising would seem to be more soundly based."

- If the defendant is regarded as having acted rightly, even the technical conviction seems obnoxious.
- A professional person like a doctor wishes to comply with the law in his practice (partly, but not entirely, because of the fear of disciplinary proceedings). It is the conviction, not a fine, that he particularly wants to avoid. And many non-professional people feel the same way.

---

[14] *R. v. Tolson* (1889) 23 Q.B.D. 168 at 172.
[15] *Mouse's Case* (1608) 77 E.R. 1341.
[16] Cf. *Perka v. The Queen* [1984] 13 D.L.R. (4th) 1.
[17] *Cope v. Sharpe* [1912] 1 K.B. 496.
[18] *Esso Petroleum Co Ltd. v. Southport Corp.* [1956] A.C. 218 at 228.
[19] See *Re A (Children) (Conjoined Twins: Medical Treatment) (No.1)* [2001] Fam. 147. Cf. *R. v. Rodger* [1998] 1 Cr. App. R. 143.
[20] [1975] A.C. 653 at 672E.

- When the court gives an absolute discharge it cannot award costs against the prosecution, as it can in the case of acquittal. So the defendant may be badly out of pocket.
- The court has a discretion whether to give a discharge or not, and there may be no certainty that it will do this. Some judges are powerfully influenced by the fact that, in their view, the law has been broken. And the possibility of being punished may be a disincentive to act in a way that is socially desirable.

At this stage in the discussion it will have become obvious that the defence of necessity involves fundamental questions as to the morality of conduct. The notion of necessity easily earns a bad name because it is invoked equally by despots and by rebels:

"So spake the Fiend, and with necessity,
The tyrant's plea, excus'd his devilish deeds.[21]"

Little as we may relish abuses of the doctrine, from the autocrat's *raison d'État* to the Marxist-Leninist advocacy of violent revolution against democratic governments, necessity has been accepted by overseas courts as a justification for governmental action after the collapse of lawful authority. Still, in the ordinary working of the criminal law necessity cannot be allowed as a justification for the wholesale disregard for rules.[22] Rules are meant to supersede individual judgment, where individual judgment has been found by experience to be unreliable. Necessity can be recognized only where the application of the rules would be disastrous, and in a genuine emergency, so specific in character that the acceptance of the defence does not imperil the general rule. On multifarious occasions it would be highly convenient and quite safe to violate the traffic law, as by judicious excess of speed limits or careful crossing of the lights against the red. The private necessity of getting to an important appointment cannot be recognized, because to recognize it would destroy the rule and impair the important purposes that the rule subserves.

---

[21] John Milton, *Paradise Lost*, (London: Peter Parker, 1667), Book 4, 390.

[22] *Southwark L.B.C. v. Williams* [1971] Ch. 734; *R. v. Jones* [2007] 1 A.C. 136; *R. v. Burns* [2010] 1 W.L.R. 2694. See also *R. v. Quayle* [2005] 1 W.L.R. 3642; *R. v. Altham* [2006] 1 W.L.R. 3287, where the defendants tried to raise medical necessity as a justification for using marijuana for pain relief, even though there was little evidence that a lawful alternative was not available. Some U.S. states allow cannabis to be used for pain relief as a matter of necessity, but only if there is no better lawful alternative. See *State v. Otis*, 151 Wash. App. 572 (2009); *State v. Hastings*, 118 Idaho 854 (1990). See also the *Compassionate Use Act 1996* (CUA) as discussed in *People v. Windus*, 81 Cal. Rptr. 3d 227 (2008). See also *City of Garden Grove v. Superior Court*, 157 Cal. App. 4th 355 (2007). Cf. *State v. Poling*, 207 W. Va. 299, (2000) where the defence was unavailable in West Virginia, because the legislation treated it as a controlled substance and provided no express defence for medical use.

24.2.   THE DEFENCE OF NECESSITY

24-009   The defence of necessity in its pure sense has been developed in the medical necessity cases.[23] In *R. v. Shayler*, Lord Woolf C.J. said:"Apart from some of the medical cases the law has tended to treat duress of circumstances and necessity as one and the same." This is an oversimplification, because the defences are very distinct. The rationale for the defence of duress of circumstances is that the harm-doer's "will" is overborne. The defendant who raises that defence must show that he acted to avoid imminent harm that was otherwise unavoidable; and that he acted because the threat overbore his will.[24] For example, if D drives a getaway car for a bank robber, because the robber has a loaded gun pointed at D's head, he might argue that he only assisted the robber because he was forced to make such a choice.

The basis for the defence of duress of circumstances is "moral involuntariness,"[25] the defendant must commit the crime only because his will was overborne. It is true that in many necessity cases the actor's mind will also be irresistibly overcome by external pressures, but in many necessity cases that will not be so. For instance, in many of the medical necessity cases the surgeon does not act because his will is overborne. "The basis for the defence of necessity is that the conduct in question is not regarded as harmful because on a comparison of two evils the choice of avoiding the greater harm was justified."[26] Nevertheless, the duress of circumstance cases are important, since that defence and the defence of necessity have common elements.

The elements of the defence of necessity include:

(i)   the criminal act must in fact be necessary to avoid inevitable and irreparable evil;

(ii)   no more was done than was reasonably necessary for the purpose to be achieved;

(iii) the evil inflicted was not disproportionate to the evil avoided.[27]

The common elements of the two defences seem to include:

(i)   there was no legislative intent to exclude the defence;[28]

(ii)   the defendant acted on the facts as they reasonably appeared to him to be;[29] and

---

[23] *In Re F (Mental Patient: Sterilisation)* [1990] 2 A.C. 1.

[24] *R. v. Z* [2005] 2 A.C. 467.

[25] See the discussion in the next chapter.

[26] *Re A (Children) (Conjoined Twins: Medical Treatment) (No.1)* [2001] Fam. 147.

[27] *Re A (Children) (Conjoined Twins: Medical Treatment) (No.1)* [2001] Fam. 147 at 240 *per* Brooke L.J. quoting James Fitzjames Stephen, *A Digest of Criminal Law*, (London: Macmillan, 1887).

[28] *R. v. Quayle* [2005] 1 W.L.R. 3642.

[29] The word "reasonably" is inserted because the decision that putative defences require reasonableness. But this was not always so: in *R. v. Bourne* [1939] 1 K.B. 687, the doctor was said to be protected if he acted in good faith. See also *R. v. Z* [2005] 2 A.C. 467. Cf. *R. v. Williams* (1984) 78 Cr. App. R. 276; *Beckford v. The Queen* [1988] A.C. 130; *R. v. Wilson* [2006] EWCA Crim. 1880.

(iii)   the defendant was not responsible for the circumstances occasioning the necessity.[30]

The harm need not be imminent,[31] but there must be no other available legal alternative for avoiding it. The proportionality requirement means that the harm to be avoided must be greater than the harm that will be caused by the criminal act. The defendant should also have reasonable grounds for believing that his criminal act is necessary and would be successful in averting the greater harm.

24.3.   NECESSITY AS A REASON FOR KILLING

The doctrine of necessity is an expression of the philosophy of utilitarianism; but utilitarianism does not exercise undisputed sway over our minds. Many people give allegiance to a notion of human rights or fundamental values; and sometimes, at least, these interests do not merely enter into the utilitarian calculus but supersede it. As an example, a doctor could not take blood from an unwilling patient in order to save the life of another patient, even though the blood-group is a rare one and the blood can be obtained in no other way.[32] This particular conclusion can perhaps be reconciled with utilitarian theory by saying that if we are able to have a scheme of compulsory blood donation it must be done by proper statutory arrangement, not left to the arbitrary decision of individual doctors. It is also pointed out that the recognition of important values does not entirely exclude a defence of necessity, for, first, these values can be given special weight in estimating the balance of interests, and, secondly, their existence does not affect that determination of cases where they do not appear.[33] In any event, the theoretical difficulty is no greater than in the law of tort, where the defence of necessity is relatively well established. In order to make the position clear, it may be desirable for a penal code to make certain express provision of the supremacy of human rights, at least in relation to the individual right of self-determination (to be discussed below). The main problem presented by human rights is in respect to the right to life.

    Some of the instances of necessity given above may seem acceptable because they involve clear social preferences. In particular, everyone agrees nowadays that property rights are subject to the social interest; we no longer believe in the sacred right to property.[34] But many of us do believe in the sanctity of life—the "natural right" of every person to his own life—and consequently believe that

24–010

---

[30] *R. v. Shepherd* (1987) 86 Cr. App. R. 47; *R. v. Sharpe* [1987] Q.B. 853.

[31] "The existence of an emergency in the normal sense of the word is not an essential prerequisite for the application of the doctrine of necessity." *Re A (Children) (Conjoined Twins: Medical Treatment) (No.1)* [2001] Fam. 147 *per* Brooke L.J. at 239. The principle is one of necessity, not emergency. Cf. the defence of duress of circumstances which has an imminent harm requirement.

[32] This point is made by Glazebrook, *op. cit. supra*, note 3 at 99.

[33] Paul H. Robinson, "Criminal Law Defences: A Systematic Analysis," (1982) 82 *Colum. L. Rev.* 199.

[34] See generally, Jeremy Waldron, "Community and Property – For Those Who Have Neither," (2009) 10 *Theoretical Inq. L.* 161 and the works cited therein.

killing is absolutely wrong.[35] This is an area, therefore, in which the defence of necessity, if allowed at all, is given a very narrow scope.

24–011   **But one can kill in self-defence. Isn't that just an example of necessity?**   No. Private defence overlaps necessity, but the two are not the same:

- Unlike necessity, private defence involves no balancing of values. Not only can a person kill by way of self-defence, but he can kill any number of aggressors to protect himself alone.
- On the other hand, private defence operates only against aggressors (voluntary or involuntary). With rare exceptions the aggressors are wrongdoers, while the persons against whom action is taken by necessity may not be aggressors or wrongdoers.

As we have seen, the decision in *R. v. Bourne*[36] can be regarded as an example of the defence of necessity, though it was not a case of homicide but of feticide. The decision has perhaps ceased to be important in England in abortion cases, since they are now governed by the *Abortion Act 1967*[37] which seems to supersede the common law defence. At the same time, the decision remains an excellent example of the basis of the doctrine of necessity.

24–012   **Might the defence apply where a parent has killed his severely disabled infant?**   Doubtless not.[38] It may of course be argued that the value of such an infant's life, even to himself, is minimal or negative, and that if parents are obliged to rear him they may be disabled from having another (normal) child. But it is not a case for applying the doctrine of necessity as usually understood. The child when born, unlike the foetus, is regarded as having absolute rights.[39] Besides, there is no emergency. It is said that malformed neonates are from time to time discreetly disposed of in maternity hospitals; but we must wait for public opinion to crystallize before the law can provide for it.[40] (The question of letting a malformed infant die is of course different.)

The usual view is that necessity is no defence to a charge of murder.[41] This, if accepted, is a non-utilitarian doctrine; but in case of a serious emergency is it wholly acceptable? If you are roped to a climber who has fallen, and neither of you can rectify the situation, it may not be very glorious on your part to cut the

---

[35] Cf. Judith Jarvis Thomson, *Realm of Rights*, (Cambridge MA: Harvard University Press, 1990) at 176 *et seq.*

[36] [1939] 1 K.B. 687.

[37] Section 5(2) provides: "For the purposes of the law relating to abortion, anything done with intent to procure [a woman's miscarriage (or, in the case of a woman carrying more than one foetus, her miscarriage of any foetus)] is unlawfully done unless authorised by section 1."

[38] Cf. *R. v. Latimer* [2001] 1 S.C.R. 3.

[39] Ronald Dworkin, *Life's Dominion: Argument About Abortion and Euthanasia*, (New York: Knopf, 1993).

[40] On the moral and policy questions, see Marvin Kohl, *Infanticide and the Value of Life*, (New York: Prometheus Books, 1978).

[41] See generally, John A. Cohen, "Homicide by Necessity," (2006) 10 *Chap. L. Rev.* 119; Gary T. Trotter, "Necessity and Death: Lessons from Latimer and the Case of the Conjoined Twins," (2003) 40 *Alberta. L.R.* 817.

rope, but is it wrong? Is it not socially desirable that one life, at least, should be saved? Again, if you are flying an aircraft and the engine dies on you, it would not be wrong, but would be praiseworthy, to choose to come down in a street (where you can see you will kill or injure a few pedestrians) rather than in a crowded sports stadium.

But in the case of cutting the rope you are only freeing yourself from someone who is, however involuntarily, dragging you to your death. And in the case of the aircraft you do not want to kill anyone; you simply minimize the slaughter that you are bound to do one way or the other. The question is whether you could deliberately kill someone for calculating reasons. We do regard the right to life as almost a supreme value, and it is very unlikely that anyone would be held to be justified in killing for any purpose except the saving of other life, or perhaps the saving of great pain or distress. Our revulsion against a deliberate killing is so strong that we are loathe to consider utilitarian reasons for it. 24–013

But a compelling case of justification of this kind is the action of a ship's captain in a wreck. He can determine who are to enter the first lifeboat; he can forbid overcrowding; and it makes no difference that those who are not allowed to enter the lifeboat will inevitably perish with the ship. The captain, in choosing who are to live, is not guilty of killing those who remain. He would not be guilty even though he kept some of the passengers back from the boat at revolver-point, and he would not be guilty even though he had to fire the revolver.

Here the captain or commander is exercising authority, and in any event he is defending others from what is in fact dangerous aggression. That does not support a general defence of necessity. The fact that the case involves an exercise of authority does not mean that it cannot be regarded as an instance of necessity. Moreover, a case of necessity need not be a case of aggression in the ordinary sense. 24–014

Suppose that the boat was overcrowded from the start, so that some of those in it must be sacrificed if the boat is to be saved from capsizing. This situation arose in the American case of *United States v. Holmes*.[42]

Holmes was a member of the crew of a boat after a shipwreck who had, under the orders of the mate, thrown out 16 male passengers. The grand jury refused to indict him for murder, and instead he was charged with manslaughter.

The judge directed the jury that Holmes's act was illegal, but only for two specific reasons: (1) such sailors as were not necessary for navigation ought to have been sacrificed before the passengers, and (2) the choice of these sailors, and of any passengers who had to be thrown out with them, should have been determined by lot, there being plenty of time to do so. Holmes was convicted of manslaughter and sentenced to six months' imprisonment.

---

[42] (1842) 26 F.Cas. 360.

24–015   The first ruling now looks old in our less class-conscious society,[43] and even the second is open to doubt on the facts of the case. The drawing of lots may commend itself to the devout as an appeal to Providence. A secular justification would be that, if a dreadful choice of victim has to be made, and everyone realizes it has to be made, the drawing of lots is the fairest and most civilized method. But when it is a question of an overloaded boat, it may be sensible to decide that the weightiest members of the party shall go first—there would hardly be justification for throwing two thin members overboard to save one bulky member! The appeal of the lottery is that it prevents purely personal consideration entering into the choice; but there are other ways of excluding personal considerations.[44] If a sailor is detailed to lighten the boat by so many souls, and simply pitches out those who first come to hand, the selection of victims is just as haphazard as if determined by lot. This may be both a kinder and a more practicable way of performing the operation than by going through the agonizing process of drawing lots. However this may be, the decision in *United States v. Holmes* does recognize that, in extreme emergency, and subject to reasonable conditions, a deliberate killing can be justified by the necessity of saving lives. If the choice is between doing nothing, when the whole boat will founder, and throwing out half the people, with the chance of saving the rest, it is useless for the law to continue its usual prohibition of murder.

An early English decision concerning this issue is *R. v. Dudley and Stephens*.[45] The crew of the yacht Mignonette were cast away in a storm, and were compelled to get into an open boat: in this boat they had no water and little provisions. On the 20th day, having had nothing to eat for eight days, and being 1,000 miles from land, two of the crew (named Dudley and Stephens) agreed that the cabin-boy should be killed with a knife in order that they might feed upon his body; and one of them carried out the plan. On the fourth day after that they were rescued by a passing vessel, in the lowest state of prostration. The two men were charged with murder, but the jury refused to take the responsibility of convicting in such tragic circumstances. They found a special verdict in which they declared that:

> "if the men had not fed upon the body of the boy they would probably not have survived to be so picked up and rescued, but would within the four days have died of famine; that the boy, being in a much weaker condition, was likely to have died before them; that at the time of the act there was no sail in sight, nor any reasonable prospect of relief;… that assuming any necessity to kill any one, there was no greater necessity for killing the boy than any of the other three men; but whether, upon the whole matter, the prisoners were and are guilty of murder, the jury are ignorant, and refer to the Court."

The question was considered by the Divisional Court of five judges, who held that the act was murder.

---

[43] Sailors are regarded as owing a special duty to protect passengers, but that duty hardly means that a sailor is a special subject of sacrifice where no activities are called for on his part and he is adversely affecting the passenger merely by his existence.

[44] See Jeremy Waldron, "Majority in the Lifeboat," (2010) 90 *B.U. L. Rev.* 1043; cf. Ronald Dworkin, *Justice for Hedgehogs*, (Cambridge MA: Harvard University Press, 2011).

[45] (1884-85) 14 Q.B.D. 273.

So the men were supposed to lie down and die? Theoretically yes, but their **24–016** sentence of death for murder was commuted by the Crown to one of six months' imprisonment. So, one could say that they were allowed to survive at a bargain price.

Most of the judgment is unconvincing, but ultimately, perhaps, it depended on the view taken by the court of the particular facts.[46] The court might conceivably have allowed the defence if it had been persuaded that the act was really necessary at the time when it was done (though it may be added that the court's refusal to accept that this was the case was highly questionable). Even if the case decides that the justification of necessity can never apply to the taking of life, it is now clear that necessity is a defence for lesser departures from the ordinary law.

To bring out the stark question in *R. v. Dudley*, let us suppose that the boat was equipped with an experimental radio transmitter, although radio-telephony was not in general use. The crew were able to make contact with Whitehall, which arranged for a ship to go to the rescue, but it could not arrive in seven days. The boat was lying off the trade routes, so it was unlikely that any other vessel would effect a rescue. The crew had reached such a stage of exhaustion that very soon none of them would be able to wield a knife. In these circumstances they asked to speak to the Home Secretary. They put the question to him: should they all accept death, or may they draw lots, kill the one with the unlucky number, and live on his body? What would you reply, if you were the Home Secretary?

Although *R. v. Dudley* concerned the relative force of necessity and the right to life, the facts were very special. It was a case of a number of persons involved in a common disaster all of whom were likely to die in a matter of days and hours if no action were taken to save some of them. The victim was alive, but his prospect of remaining alive for more than a short time was minimal, so that his "right to life" was of very small value. These considerations suggest that the defence of necessity might have been accepted without imperilling the general supremacy of the right to life.

If it had been accepted that Dudley and Stephens had a right to kill the cabin **24–017** **boy, wouldn't it follow that the cabin boy had no right to act in self-defence?** Your suggested conclusion does not follow. It would be possible for the law to refrain from intervening either way. The killing of the cabin boy might be justified as a matter of necessity, while defensive action by the cabin boy might be justified as self-defence, or by reason of "duress of circumstances," an arguable defence to be noticed later.[47]

You say that necessity is a matter of the lesser evil. Assuming that it may **24–018** **justify killing one to save two or more, could it ever justify killing one to save** **one other?** Only where necessity overlaps self-defence, which is as much as to say no. A person can certainly be killed by a person who is threatened by an aggressor. If V is a culpable aggressor against D1, he can be killed by D1 in

---

[46] For a full examination see Glanville Williams, "A Commentary on *R. v. Dudley and Stephens*," (1977) 8 *Cambrian L. Rev.* 94.

[47] 25.4. A situation in which each of the two contending parties is justified or excused (for different reasons) in using force against the other is not unknown in the law.

self-defence, or by D2 in defence of D1. Even if V is a lunatic who is not criminally responsible, he can be killed in private defence.

Another example of a case that can be analysed as one of private defence is as follows. A shipwrecked person is clinging in the sea to a plank, but the person in possession beats the assailant off, and the latter is drowned. This may look like a situation of necessity, but the act can be adequately justified as one of private defence, the assailant's attack being technically wrongful.

24–019   **Suppose the assailant had shaken off the man who was first in possession of the plank, and that the latter had drowned?**   Lord Chancellor Bacon discussed this case[48] and thought that the assailant's act would be justified as necessity. This seems hard to support, on the doctrine of necessity as now understood, for that doctrine applies only where the value preserved is greater than the value destroyed in breaking the letter of the law. Where it is merely a case of life for life, the doctrine of necessity must generally be silent, because the two lives must be accounted equal in the eye of the law and there is nothing to choose between them. Necessity cannot justify here, but circumstances may go so strongly in alleviation that the defendant is pardoned or his sentence greatly shortened. (An alternative solution, for which indeed Bacon's hypothetical may be cited in support, would be to recognize an excuse of compulsion (duress) of circumstances, as before mentioned).[49]

24–020   **May not necessity sometimes justify action even if it is a case of one for one, where the two people you are weighing against each other are not really equal? Could not a doctor take an organ from a dying patient to transplant to a patient who can be saved?**   No: and although that answer is obvious, a thoroughgoing utilitarian who supported it would be hard pressed to justify his position. Few people are wholly inconsistent utilitarians, because, as was said before, our thinking is tinged with notions of human rights and moral absolutes. Transplants are taken from fresh cadavers, or (in the case of paired organs) from living volunteers, not from unwilling donors.[50]

---

[48] Sir Francis Bacon, *The elements of the common laws of England*, (London: Printed by the Assignes of I. More, Esq., 1630) at 32.

[49] Cf. section 25 of the *Criminal Code* of Western Australia, which provides: "Subject to the express provisions of this Code relating to acts done upon compulsion or provocation or in self-defence, a person is not criminally responsible for an act or omission done or made under such circumstances of sudden or extraordinary emergency that an ordinary person possessing ordinary power of self-control could not reasonably be expected to act otherwise." In *Johnson v. Western Australia* (2009) 194 A. Crim. R. 470 at 494 the Court of Appeal of the Supreme Court of Western Australia held that section 25 provided a defence to all offences including murder.

[50] Setting aside the special problem where a patient who has suffered "brain death" and is on a ventilator has his organ removed for transplantation while his heart is still beating under the action of the ventilator. This problem involves the problem of the time of "death." See 12.8.

What if the less equal person (the dying one) is also killing the more equal   **24–021**
person (the one with a chance of living a normal life-span)? Take the case of
the conjoined twins where the weaker twin is involuntarily killing the
stronger. It has been decided in a couple of cases that it is permissible to kill
the weaker twin in such circumstances.[51]

In the famous case of *Re A (Children) (Conjoined Twins: Surgical
Separation)*,[52] conjoined twin girls were joined at the pelvis with both having
their own brains, hearts, lungs and other vital organs and own limbs. The medical
evidence demonstrated that the stronger twin sustained the life of the weaker twin
by circulating oxygenated blood through a common artery. The medical evidence
also showed that the weaker twin's heart and lungs were too deficient to
oxygenate and pump blood through her own body. If the twins had not been
separated the stronger twin's heart would have eventually failed and both of them
would have died within a few months. The doctors argued that separating the
twins would allow the stronger twin to survive and ultimately live a worthwhile
life, but acknowledged that the weaker twin would die within minutes of the
separation. The surgeons did not want to kill the weaker twin; but knew her death
was an inevitable side-effect of saving the stronger twin.[53]

It was held that necessity provided a defence to murder in such circumstances,
but only if certain conditions were satisfied:[54]

"(1)   that it must be impossible to preserve the life of X without bringing about the death of Y;

(2)   that Y by his or her very continued existence will inevitably bring about the death of X within a short period of time; and

(3)   that X is capable of living an independent life but Y is incapable under any circumstances, including all forms of medical intervention, of viable independent existence."

The decision seems to rest on three justifications:

1.   The "lesser evil" principle;
2.   The "acceleration of inevitable and reasonably imminent harm" principle; and
3.   The "defence from an involuntary aggressor" principle.[55]

---

[51] *Re A (Children) (Conjoined Twins: Medical Treatment) (No.1)* [2001] Fam. 147; *Queensland v. Nolan* (2002) 122 A. Crim. R. 517.

[52] [2001] Fam. 147.

[53] Thus, the doctors acted with sufficient *mens rea* for murder. See *R. v. Woollin* [1999] 1 A.C. 82.

[54] *Re A (Children) (Conjoined Twins: Medical Treatment) (No.1)* [2001] Fam. 147 at 205 *per* Ward L.J.

[55] Walker L.J. said (*Re A (Children) (Conjoined Twins: Medical Treatment) (No.1)* [2001] Fam. 147 at 255): "There is on the facts of this case some element of protecting Jodie against the unnatural invasion of her body through the physical burden imposed by her conjoined twin. That element must not be overstated. It would be absurd to suggest that Mary, a pitiful and innocent baby, is an unjust aggressor. ... Nevertheless, the doctors' duty to protect and save Jodie's life if they can is of fundamental importance to the resolution of this appeal." Brooke L.J. cited Sir James Stephen's criteria for satisfying the necessity defence (at 240); but Stephen's criteria did not include the self-defence element. Nevertheless, there is no doubt that Brooke L.J. thought it a relevant consideration. At 227, Brooke L.J. (quoting with approval the reasoning of Glanville Williams, *Textbook of Criminal Law*, (London: Stevens & Sons, 1983) at 26.3), accepted that it might be

24–022   While the "lesser evil" argument was the predominant justification given by the Court of Appeal for its decision, it alone was not sufficient to justify the decision. If the twins had been born independent of each other and one had needed an organ from the other, the doctors would not have been permitted to kill one to save the other.

Suppose twins X and Y are born separate and each has a viable independent existence. Let us assume that the doctors discover that X has only one kidney, which is malfunctioning. Therefore, she needs a kidney transplant if she is to survive. Alas, her sister Y also has only one kidney, so Y will die if the doctors take her kidney for X. Let us assume that the incontrovertible medical evidence is that X will live if given Y's kidney and that Y will die within weeks (anyway) because she has an incurable heart condition.

24–023   **Can the doctors take Y's healthy kidney to save X simply because Y is going to die anyway?**   No. They could if the only consideration was "lesser evil," because it would be better to save one twin rather than let them both die. Similarly, the "acceleration of inevitable and reasonably imminent harm" principle would be satisfied, because Y's heart condition will cause her to die within weeks. (Thus, she will only use the organ for a few weeks and thereafter it will be wasted). The element that is not satisfied is the "defence from an involuntary aggressor" requirement. If the twins are born independently of each other and have a viable independent existence, it could not be said that the twin needing the kidney is being involuntarily killed by the one who has the healthy kidney. Consequently, killing Y by taking her kidney could not be justified on the ground that "Y by her very continued existence will inevitably bring about the death of X within a short period of time." Y's existence would not cause X's death anymore than any other potential kidney donor's failure to donate would.

If the twins had an equal chance of dying within a month, the doctors would not have operated at all—they would have let nature take its course. If they had had an equal chance of surviving the doctors would most likely have operated to try to save them both, but they would not have been liable for murder if one or both of the twins had died as a result of the operation, because the doctors would not have foreseen the death of either twin as a virtual certainty. All operations involve some risk; and foresight of some risk would not be enough to ground a murder conviction.

24–024   **Would the doctrine protect the likes of Dudley and Stephens?**   No. The doctrine as developed in *Re A (Children) (Conjoined Twins: Surgical Separation)* is very narrow. The lesser evil prong would be satisfied, because the cabin boy was sacrificed to save two. The "acceleration of inevitable and reasonably imminent harm" prong would be satisfied, as the evidence showed that the cabin boy was weaker than the others (did not have an equal chance of surviving) and would have died within a day or two. However, the "defence from an involuntary aggressor" prong would not be satisfied. The cabin boy was not involuntarily

---

permissible for a mountain climber to cut a rope that he shares with another climber if both are being dragged to their death, because do so would allow him to free himself "from someone who is, however involuntarily, dragging [him] to [his] death."

causing the deaths of the other sailors. However, the Supreme Court might decide that the latter prong is not essential in all cases, as it is not included in Sir James Stephen's general formulation. If so, the likes of Dudley and Stephens would come within the purview of the defence. It would be better to develop the defence of duress of circumstances to cover such cases (see 25.9), since this would allow the courts to limit the defence so that it only applies in cases where the circumstances are so extreme that the killer's "will is overborne." This would put a check on unbridled utilitarianism. After all, the doctor who takes organs from one patient to save the lives of many others would have difficulty in proving that his "will was overborne."

24.4. NECESSITY AND STARVATION

According to the institutional writers, the poor (even if starving) are not allowed to take the law into their own hands.[56] The law does not recognize a necessity to eat.[57] Although one may steal food in certain contexts, such as where he is lost in the mountains and discovers a cabin with supplies, since he would be able to demonstrate that he had no reasonable alternative except to steal the food. A face-saving reason formerly advanced for the rule was that sufficient provision was made for the poor in this country by charity and State aid. The reason has attained greater reality in modern times, though for one reason or another (usually drug addiction) people may still be utterly destitute. If someone steals as the only way to relieve hunger he will be convicted, but will certainly receive a discharge, with the assistance of the probation officer to obtain social security payments, and quite possibly a gift from the poor box to tide him over.

24–025

It was no doubt with this position in mind that Edmund-Davies L.J. (as he then was) said on one occasion[58] that although necessity "may in certain cases afford a defence ... [in] an urgent situation of imminent peril," it is not a defence to murder or theft. Both exceptions are too absolutely stated. There can be no reasonable doubt that necessity would be a defence where hunger arises in an extraordinary situation from physical and not economic causes, as where a group of miners are trapped underground and have to consume the rations of their comrades who have escaped or are dead. In any case, such conduct would not be theft because it would not be dishonest, as theft requires. The miners would be entitled to assume the consent of those who owned the food.

Another dire conflict between extreme need and the maintenance of public order arises in relation to housing. In the case just mentioned, the Court of Appeal

---

[56] Glazebrook, *op. cit. supra*, note 3 at 115-117.

[57] In *People v. Fontes*, 89 P.3d 484 at 486 (2003), the Colorado Court of Appeals said: "While we are not without sympathy for the downtrodden, the law is clear that economic necessity alone cannot support a choice of crime. Although economic necessity may be an important issue in sentencing, *People v. Turner*, 619 N.E.2d 781 (1993), a choice of evils defence cannot be based upon economic necessity. See *State v. Moe*, 174 Wash. 303, (1933) (unemployed workers who marched on a commissary and stole groceries could not raise the defence of economic necessity); see also *People v. McKnight*, 626 P.2d 678 (Colo.1981) (to rely on the choice of evils defence, the defendant must show that he or she had no reasonable alternative except to commit the crime charged)."

[58] *Southwark L.B.C. v. Williams* [1971] Ch. 734 at 745. Cf. Lord Denning at 743-744. See also *People v. Fontes*, 89 P.3d 484 (2003); *People v. Brante*, 232 P.3d 204 (2009).

held that necessity does not justify the homeless in "squatting" in unoccupied buildings. The court gave a certain support to the defence of necessity, while not applying it to the facts of the case.

24.5.   NECESSITY AND DRIVING OFFENCES

24–026   The law makes a certain provision for emergencies in driving. Firemen, the police and ambulances are expressly exempted from speed limits,[59] if observance "would be likely to hinder the use of the vehicle for the purpose for which it is being used on that occasion."

The question is how the court will allow drivers in general to disobey traffic rules under the doctrine of necessity. There is plenty of indication that they will.[60] At about the same time as the "squatting" case just mentioned, and before the aforesaid regulations had been made, a differently constituted Court of Appeal denied (*obiter*) that necessity could justify the driver of a fire-engine in crossing against the lights, even to save life.[61] This was understandable, since the question of a fire-engine crossing against the lights is not one of unforeseen emergency but of proper practice on the part of the fire service; if an exemption were thought proper, it was to be expected that the legislature would make it—as after it did.

In *D.P.P. v. Harris*,[62] Curtis J. said: "Necessity is, in my judgement, a defence both to reckless driving and careless driving in cases other than the present one. …. On the facts of this case, this defence was not open to this respondent because, looking at his driving from an objective standpoint, he cannot be said to have been acting reasonably and proportionately—on his own account—to avoid the threat of death or serious injury." In that case, the police officer endangered others by unnecessarily running the red in a dangerous manner.[63]

More questionable was a decision that where a man woke up intoxicated in a car, to find it coasting downhill, and steered it to a grass verge to avoid a possible collision, he was guilty of driving it while under the influence of drink.[64] Since the defence of necessity was, surprisingly, not raised, the case is no authority on the question; but in fact a clear occasion for recognition of the defence could hardly be imagined. A driver who has too much to drink and who goes to sleep in his car before driving off again can be convicted of being under the influence of drink when in charge of his car. But if (as in the case just mentioned) it is a passenger who is drunk and asleep in the car, and if he wakes up to find that the vehicle is running downhill, and all that he does is to bring it to a safe stop, what is wrong in his conduct?[65] What do we expect him to do: remain passive while a

---

[59] Section 87 of the *Road Traffic Regulation Act 1984*.

[60] *R. v. Conway* [1989] Q.B. 290 at 297; *R. v. Martin* (1989) 88 Cr. App. R. 343 ("duress of circumstances" was raised in those cases, so "lesser evil" was not a consideration).

[61] *Buckoke v. Greater London Council* [1971] Ch. 655 at 668.

[62] [1995] 1 Cr. App. R. 170 at 181. See also *R. v. Backshall* [1998] 1 W.L.R. 1506.

[63] A police officer will not be liable for running a red light unless he does so "in a manner or at a time likely to endanger any person." See Reg. 36 of the *Traffic Signs Regulations and General Directions* 2002 (S.I. 2002 No. 3113).

[64] *R. v. Kitson* (1955) 39 Cr. App. R. 66.

[65] Some U.S. courts have accepted that the defence of necessity should be available in such cases, see *Toops v. State*, 643 N.E.2d 387 (1994) (where an intoxicated passenger took control of a car when the

fatal accident takes place? The authorities suggest the defence would now be available in such a case, since such a driver could be said to be acting reasonably and proportionately in order to avoid the threat of serious injury. The threat of injury has to be imminent and continuing, if the "duress of circumstances" defence is to be invoked.[66] But the traditional defence of necessity would also be available, since the driver acts to prevent a greater harm (a potential collision) from eventuating.

24.6. THE ENFORCEMENT OF LAW AND RIGHTS

One of the most celebrated pronouncements in our law repudiates the doctrine of necessity as a means of enlarging the powers of the Executive:

24–027

> "And with respect to the argument of State necessity, or a distinction that has been aimed at between State offences and others, the common law does not understand that kind of reasoning, nor do our books take notice of any such distinctions."[67]

All that this means, however, is that the courts are not supposed to extend governmental powers merely by reference to the necessities of government. If the Government wants powers, it must obtain them from Parliament; and when it has obtained them, it must keep within them, not stretch them under the plea of necessity. The principle is not regarded as impeding the grant of powers at common law for certain recognized purposes, such as the preservation of the peace and the saving of life. In *Humphries v. Connor*,[68] for instance, it was held that a constable may commit what would otherwise be an assault upon an innocent person in order to remove a provocative emblem he is wearing if that is the only way of preserving the peace. At the present day action of this kind may be justified under section 3 of the *Criminal Law Act 1967*; but only if it complies with the victim's rights under the *European Convention for the Protection of Human Rights and Fundamental Freedoms*.[69]

---

driver abandoned it in motion because he panicked when he saw the police); *Bodner v. State*, 752 A.2d 1169 (2000) (where the driver abandoned the car on a rail-track when it stalled; and where the intoxicated passenger removed the car as a matter of necessity to prevent a potential collision with a train).

[66] If the threat of injury has disappeared, the defences of "necessity" and "duress of circumstances" will not be available. Cf. *D.P.P. v. Tomkinson* [2001] R.T.R. 38; *Crown Prosecution Service v. Brown* [2007] EWHC 3274; *D.P.P. v. Jones* [1990] R.T.R. 33; *D. v. Donnelly* (2009) S.L.T. 476.

[67] Lord Camden in *Entick v. Carrington* (1765) 19 St. Tr. 1029.

[68] (1864) 17 I.C.L.R. 1.

[69] 4 November 1950, 213 U.N.T.S. 222 (entered into force generally on 3 September 1953). See the discussion at 9.17. See also *Beatty v. Gillbanks* (1882) 9 Q.B.D. 308 (where appellants assembled with others for a lawful purpose, and with no intention of carrying it out unlawfully, but with the knowledge that their assembly would be opposed by the Skeleton Army); and *Redmond-Bate v. D.P.P.* (1999) 163 J.P. 789 (where a woman was arrested for breach of the peace when she had refused to stop preaching to a hostile audience from the steps of Wakefield Cathedral.) In *R. (on the application of Laporte) v. Chief Constable of Gloucestershire* [2007] 2 A.C. 105 at 155, Lord Brown said: "Take Mr. Beatty, the Salvation Army captain, or Ms Redmond-Bate, the Wakefield preacher. The Divisional Court was in each case clearly right to have set aside their respective convictions. I repeat, the police's first duty is to protect the rights of the innocent rather than to compel the innocent to cease exercising them."

Of course the officer or informer may escape conviction in particular circumstances for lack of *mens rea*: for example, for lack of intention in theft or burglary. He is not guilty of attempt or conspiracy or as accessory if he intended to frustrate the commission of the full offence.[70] His mere pretence at being a conspirator will probably not make him an accessory to the crime when it is committed, if his pretence was not causally connected with the crime. If, however, he went beyond mere concurrence and encouraged or assisted the commission of the crime, without intending to frustrate it, he would be in breach of the law, notwithstanding that his intention was only to expose others, and the doctrine of necessity would not be taken as a reason for the extension of police powers.

There is no indication in the authorities that private persons can break the letter of the law in order to prevent serious crimes. The provision in section 3 of the *Criminal Law Act 1967* probably does not justify the commission of offences in general, but in extreme circumstances the doctrine of necessity should do so. For example, to prevent a burglary (or to arrest the burglars) it might be necessary to drive an uninsured car to inform the police.

24–028   **If I find someone's car occupying my parking space, or if he has left his car blocking my exit from the car park, can I, by way of defence of my interests, break his window in order to move his car?**   As to the first part of your question, probably yes: you are ejecting a trespassing object.[71] As to the second part, a person who is unlawfully imprisoned can obviously break out, even though the property of innocent third parties is damaged in the process. But the courts have been unsympathetic to claims to preserve mobility where no false imprisonment was involved. Reference may again be made to *R. v. Bow*,[72] where the relevance of the defence of necessity was overlooked. Magistrates have convicted motorists who, when their exits were blocked on private premises, damaged other cars or jammed the exit barrier of a car park in order to get free. The value of personal mobility is recognized in law in the defence of abatement of public nuisance, which justifies the removal of an obstruction to the highway. There is no reason why the law should not equally allow the removal of unjustifiable obstructions to egress from private premises, where this is reasonable in the circumstances; and the German courts have in fact allowed it as an example of private defence.[73] (Wherever possible, of course, the help of the police should be invoked before taking drastic action, and an unreasonable failure to do this would bar the defence.)

---

[70]   14.13.

[71]   A Twickenham solicitor who did this had his conviction of criminal damage set aside by the Crown Court: Middlesex Chronicle, 20 August 1982.

[72]   (1977) 64 Cr. App. R. 54.

[73]   George P. Fletcher, *Rethinking Criminal Law*, (Boston: Little, Brown, 1978) at 864.

24.7. OPERATIONS UPON SANE ADULTS

Since necessity involves an evaluation, the right of self-determination is one of **24–029** the values taken into account. Accordingly, the general principle of law is that a person cannot be medically treated without his consent.[74] The point is more likely to concern legal practitioners in the civil courts than in the criminal, since it is highly improbable that a prosecution would be brought against a doctor who has transgressed in good faith in the interest of the patient. But to doctors themselves the matter appears in reverse: whereas a civil action can be settled out of court, and the doctor will be defended and the damages paid by his defence society, the remotest fear of a criminal prosecution is of grave concern to him. The criminal law, therefore, is almost entirely self-operative upon doctors, without any need for actual enforcement.

One who is suffering from an infectious disease may be quarantined in exceptional circumstances as a matter of necessity;[75] this is for the protection of the public, not particularly for his benefit, and it does not mean that anything may be done to him in hospital, beyond keeping him quarantined in the usual way.

There is an unqualified rule that if an adult patient of sound mind utters any words forbidding an operation the doctor's hands are tied. People are not bound to accept even the unanimous opinions of the doctors.[76] Partly this is because medicine is not an exact science. Notwithstanding every advance, cases still occur where operations are performed mistakenly and disastrously. (Surgeons are notoriously reluctant to submit to the scalpel themselves.) But the more important reason is the general agreement that this area of personal liberty must be preserved. There is no overwhelming public interest in compelling people to submit to the cure of non-infectious complaints. Members of the religious sect known as Jehovah's Witnesses think that blood transfusions are wrong, and will not accept them even when they know that they will otherwise die; and doctors respect their wishes, as they must.[77]

Any dying patient has the right to refuse further treatment even though his only object is to make an end of his own sufferings.[78] In practice, such requests

---

[74] *Secretary of State for the Home Department v. Robb* [1995] Fam. 127 (where it was held that a sane prisoner on a hunger strike could not be force-fed). But it may be permissible to force feed a person who is mentally ill: *Re JR18's Application for Judicial Review* [2008] M.H.L.R. 50. See also *Re C (Adult: Refusal of Medical Treatment)* [1994] 1 W.L.R. 290; *R. (on the application of Burke) v. General Medical Council* [2006] Q.B. 273.

[75] See for example, *Greater Glasgow Health Board v. W* (2006) S.C.L.R. 159; *Enhorn v. Sweden* (2005) 41 E.H.R.R. 30; cf. the repealed sections 37 and 38 of the *Public Health (Control of Disease) Act 1984*.

[76] *St George's Healthcare NHS Trust v. S* [1999] Fam. 26, where it was held that an "unborn child was not a separate person from its mother and its need for medical assistance did not prevail over her right not to be forced to submit to an invasion of her body against her will, whether her own life or that of her unborn child depended on it."

[77] *R. v. Blaue* [1975] 1 W.L.R. 1411.

[78] See *Brightwater Care Group (Inc.) v. Rossiter* [2009] W.A.S.C. 229, where the Supreme Court of Western Australia said that a healthy quadriplegic (Mr. Rossiter was not terminally ill, nor was he dying) had the right to starve himself to death. It said that his carers could not force feed him or force him to receive medical treatment that would prolong his life, if he did not want that treatment. See also *People v. Velez*, 602 N.Y.S. 2d 798 (1993); *State v. Pelham*, 746 A.2d 557 (1998) where the victims demanded to have their life support removed.

are from time to time ignored, for various reasons: the doctor's training biases him towards treatment, and imbues him with the idea that he knows what is best for the patient; he fears criticism if he allows the patient to die; and the dying patient is often in great pain or is otherwise seriously ill, so it is easy to subject the seriously ill patient to a kind of "Catch 22": either he is of sound mind, in which case he will obviously want to live, or he is not, in which case other people must take the decision for him. The defender of the patient's autonomy will of course dismiss such arguments. To disregard the expressed wish of the dying patient on the ground that he cannot really mean what he says is to substitute paternalism for self-determinism. It should be beyond doubt that a doctor who does anything to his patient without consent is guilty of assault. No question can arise of abetting suicide, first because it would seem that inaction by the patient cannot be a suicide in law, and secondly because, since the law gives the doctor no authority to act against his patient's wishes, his failure to do so is not the breach of any duty by him and cannot be abetment.

24–030   **What if the patient's consent cannot be asked for? A person is found injured and unconscious; he is rushed to hospital, where he is operated upon to save his life.**   The operation is clearly lawful.[79] The principle was stated by an eminent United States judge, Cardozo J.:

> "Every human being of adult years and sound mind has the right to determine what shall be done with his own body. ... this is true except in cases of emergency where the patient is unconscious and where it is necessary to operate before consent can be obtained."[80]

We have here a kind of hybrid between the defences of necessity and consent. It is not an ordinary case of consent, because consent is not in fact given; so from that point of view the justification must be one of necessity. On the other hand, the justification would clearly not avail if the surgeon ascertained, before the patient fell unconscious, that the patient withheld his consent. So it is not a case where social necessity overrides a refusal of consent. American writers have called the defence, with more punch than accuracy, "future consent."[81] The surgeon is entitled in the circumstances to suppose that what he does will be ratified by a grateful patient, having nothing to cause him to believe the contrary; and he will be protected in law even though the patient turns out to be ungrateful. His defence must, to repeat, be grounded on necessity; the only distinctive feature is that the defence is curtailed when it conflicts with the patient's exercise of his right to self-determination.

It would be an illegitimate application of the doctrine of future consent to subject a depressed and protesting patient to a brain operation on the ground that the operation will change the patient's personality and he will then be pleased he

---

[79] *In Re T (Adult: Refusal of Treatment)* [1992] 3 W.L.R. 782; *In re: F (Mental Patient: Sterilisation)* [1990] 2 A.C. 1 at 73-77; *Airedale N.H.S. Trust v. Bland* [1993] A.C. 789, 842, 864.

[80] *Schloendorff v. Society of New York Hospital* (1914) 105 N.E. 92; quoted with approval in *In re: F (Mental Patient: Sterilisation)* [1990] 2 A.C. 1 at 73; *Airedale N.H.S. Trust v. Bland* [1993] A.C. 789, 842, 864.

[81] David B. Wexler, "Therapeutic Justice," (1973) 57 *Minn. L. Rev.* 289 at 334.

had it. That is a bootstrap argument, and ought to be rejected. The general question of operations on the mentally disordered will be briefly considered in the next section.

Sometimes, in the course of an operation, a surgeon sees a need for some other operation. He is generally protected in performing this by the consent form signed by the patient, which authorizes such further or alternative operative measures as may be found to be necessary. But sometimes a consent form has not been offered to the patient, as when a maternity patient is under anaesthetic when it is discovered that delivery by caesarean section is necessary. In such circumstances the practice is to do what is required, the justification being implied consent or necessity. The surgeon would of course be ill-advised to perform an unexpected operation having serious consequences if there is no great urgency for it.[82]

24.8. PERSONS UNDER DISABILITY

Persons under disability lack the full right to self-determination, so that various things may be done to them without their consent, either under the authority of explicit rules of law or generally because of the necessity of the case.[83] For example, as we have seen, a parent may to some extent give consent on behalf of his young child. When he sends his child to hospital, he does not thereby surrender to the doctor in charge his parental right to decide what is good for the child; the doctor must, at least in the first place, seek the parent's consent for an operation to the same extent as he would seek the consent of an adult patient.[84]   **24–031**

But what if it is a question of saving the life of the child? Must the doctor watch the child's life ebb away if the child can't give consent and the doctor can't get the parent's consent to act?   If the parent cannot be consulted, the doctrine of future consent may be applied: the doctor is entitled to believe that what he does will be ratified by the parent.   **24–032**

The difficulty arises where the parent is consulted and wishes his child to be allowed to die. The problem has been encountered with Jehovah's Witnesses who refuse to let a child have a blood transfusion. Here it is generally agreed that the turning-point is reached: the doctor can refuse to allow the parent's wishes to prevail over the child's "right to life."[85] However, the theoretical basis on which the hospital doctor is allowed to act is in doubt. The clearest ground is the doctrine of necessity.[86] If the doctor wants specific legal protection he can have the child made a ward of the court and ask for the judge's authority to proceed.

---

[82] *Re F (Mental Patient: Sterilisation)* [1990] 2 A.C. 1 at 77-78.
[83] *Re F (Mental Patient: Sterilisation)* [1990] 2 A.C. 1; *R. v. Bournewood Community and Mental Health NHS Trust, Ex p. L* [1999] 1 A.C. 458.
[84] *MAK v. United Kingdom* [2010] 2 F.L.R. 451 at 466.
[85] *E (A Minor) (Wardship: Medical Treatment)* [1993] 1 F.L.R. 386; *L (Medical Treatment: Gillick Competence)* [1998] 2 F.L.R. 810; *E (A Minor) (Wardship: Medical Treatment)* [1993] 1 F.L.R. 386.
[86] *In Re F (Mental Patient: Sterilisation)* [1990] 2 A.C. 1 at 73-77 *per* Lord Goff.

24-033 **When can mentally disordered people be taken to hospital without their consent?** Those who come within a statutory definition may be taken to hospital on the certificate of two doctors (exceptionally, one doctor), either for their own protection or for that of the public.[87] This is commonly called "civil commitment" (as opposed to "criminal commitment" resulting from a prosecution, which is to be studied in Chap. 28). The technical name for it, however, is "admission" to hospital, not commitment, a word that is thought to be too stigmatic.

If a constable finds a person who appears to him to be mentally disordered in a public place, he may take him off for medical examination under section 136 of the *Mental Health Act 1983*. Or, if two doctors[88] come to the conclusion that a person is mentally disordered they may certify for his or her emergency admission to hospital for assessment under section 2. The *Act* does not empower the doctor to enter premises or to examine the patient by force, but once the certificate has been given and other procedures have been complied with the patient may be taken to hospital. There are also powers to remove people from their homes when they have reached the "last stage of all," or are otherwise unable to cope.

An old, mentally disordered person may be unable to look after himself properly in his house, and may be living in squalor. Wide powers are available to move him compulsorily to hospital. One is given by the *Mental Health Act 1983*. When a person is believed to be suffering from mental disorder and is being ill-treated or neglected, or, being unable to care for himself, is living alone, a magistrate may issue a warrant authorizing a constable to enter the premises and remove such a person to a "place of safety;" he may then be medically examined and, if thought fit, civilly committed.[89] Equally draconic powers are given by section 47 of the *National Assistance Act 1948* (as amended).

The uprooting of old people under these powers, though sometimes unavoidable, has often been resorted to readily. It has been called "slow euthanasia," because the old people when moved, though well looked after physically, generally suffer from apathy and dejection, often amounting to intense grief. A quarter of them die within three months of admission; yet some of these were physically healthy when admitted. For others, death is long drawn out and miserable.[90] Although in extreme cases an old bod's right of self-determination has to be overridden, it is far better to arrange for insanitary conditions to be cleaned up, and domiciliary and health services provided, and to put up with the mess, than to move anyone forcibly from his home if this can be avoided. Nowadays the Government tries to ensure that the elderly stay in their homes for

---

[87] Under the *Mental Health Act 1983* Pt. I.

[88] Section 2(3) of the *Mental Health Act 1983* provides: "An application for admission for assessment shall be founded on the written recommendations in the prescribed form of two registered medical practitioners, including in each case a statement that in the opinion of the practitioner the conditions set out in subsection (2) above are complied with." As for judicial review see *R. (on the application of H) v. Secretary of State for Health* [2006] 1 A.C. 441.

[89] Section 135 of the *Mental Health Act 1983*.

[90] A. A. Baker, "Slow euthanasia—or 'she will be better off in hospital'" [1976] 2 *B.M.J.* 571.

as long as possible; it is considered to be more beneficial for them and also more economical for the state to provide homecare rather than move such people to nursing homes.

When a person has been moved to hospital or an institution in this way, can he be compulsorily treated?   The powers just described to remove people from their homes do not carry powers of compulsory treatment. Nevertheless, Parts IV and IVA of the *Mental Health Act 1983* contain certain powers of compulsory medical treatment.[91]   **24–034**

Does the rule against interfering with people mean that a person can never be forcibly prevented from committing suicide?   It seems reasonable to say that if a person is found attempting to commit suicide and nothing is known about his state of mind, the attempt is evidence of mental disorder. Anyone is entitled at common law to apprehend a person who is mentally disordered and who is a danger to himself or others, the purpose of the apprehension, of course, being to get him to a doctor.   **24–035**

Unfortunately, a limitation on this rule is that the person so detained must actually be mentally disordered, so if a person attempting suicide turns out to be *compos mentis* it seems that the detention is unlawful, and constitutes at least the tort of assault and false imprisonment. Even so taking the instruments of suicide away from him might be justified under the doctrine of necessity, since this doctrine, unlike the law relating to arrest and detention, always allows a person to act on the facts as they reasonably appear to him to be.[92] The powers given by the *Mental Health Acts* may, of course, be invoked.[93]

While cases may occur in which hospitalization would clearly be justified, particularly in the case of young people, the fact remains that the law does not provide for anyone being kept alive without his consent. Formerly, suicide was a felony; so interfering with a would-be suicide could be justified as the prevention of felony; but now, by the *Suicide Act 1961* (as amended), suicide is legal. If a patient has a perfectly sound reason for desiring not to "keep right on to the end of the road" (as if he is suffering a fatal and painful disease), a doctor has no

---

[91] See generally, *R. (on the application of B) v. S (Responsible Medical Officer, Broadmoor Hospital)* [2006] 1 W.L.R. 810; *R. (on the application of B) v. Haddock (Responsible Medical Officer)* [2006] H.R.L.R. 40.

[92] The word "reasonably" is inserted because the decision that putative defences require reasonableness. But this was not always so: in *R. v. Bourne* [1939] 1 K.B. 687, the doctor was said to be protected if he acted in good faith. The rule is embodied in the *Abortion Act 1967*. Specifically on the subject of preventing suicide see *Meyer v. Supreme Lodge K. of P.*, 70 N.E. 111 (1904) (New York) (administering antidote to would-be suicide lawful). A Canadian court held that a would-be suicide who forcibly resists an attempt by a police officer to stop him can be convicted of assaulting the officer in the execution of his duty. *R. v. Dietrich* [1978] 39 C.C.C. (2d) 361.

[93] In *Savage v. South Essex Partnership NHS Foundation Trust* [2009] 1 A.C. 681, the Lords said: "a public authority's obligations under Article 2 of the *Convention for the Protection of Human Rights and Fundamental Freedoms* ... applied to a health authority's obligations to prevent patients detained in hospital under section 3 of the *Mental Health Act 1983* from committing suicide." It was held that Article 2 of the *Convention for the Protection of Human Rights and Fundamental Freedoms* required the authority to do all it could to prevent its patients from committing suicide.

warrant to interfere with him.[94] Some would say that even a mentally ill patient should be allowed to drink the hemlock; and that is a reasonable view if medication has failed to make the patient change his mind. Indeed, the Samaritans (who do noble work in trying to help people so that they do not commit suicide), if they are called to someone who has committed a suicidal act and who wishes to die, do not attempt to save his life, but simply hold his hand while he is dying, taking the view that they have no right of duty to interfere. But these considerations do not mean that people who have intervened in good faith in an emergency have much to fear from the law. Even if the law does not technically validate what they do, they would almost certainly, if prosecuted, be given an absolute discharge.

24–036 **If a person is not mentally ill within the meaning of the *Mental Health Act 1983*, can he be compulsorily treated?** Yes, but only if he is mentally incompetent.[95] In numerous cases over the last two decades the courts have invoked the doctrine of necessity ("by way of declarations") to allow doctors and others to act in the best interests of vulnerable adults who were not mentally ill within the *Mental Health Act 1983*.[96]

In *In Re F (Mental Patient: Sterilisation)*,[97] a 36-year-old woman with the mental age of a small child formed a sexual relationship with a male patient in the mental hospital where she resided. The hospital staff and her mother considered that she would not be able to cope with the effects of pregnancy and giving birth. It was also clear she would not be able to raise a child. It was determined that it would be necessary to sterilize her so that she would be able to enjoy her limited freedom to engage in sexual activity. It was necessary for her to have the medical procedure in the not too distant future, but the case was not one of emergency. Nevertheless, the necessity doctrine can be invoked in non-emergency situations. *In Re F (Mental Patient: Sterilisation)* Lord Goff said:

"Take the example of an elderly person who suffers a stroke which renders him incapable of speech or movement. I can see no good reason why the principle of necessity should not be applicable in his case .... [T]he permanent state of affairs calls for a wider range of care than may be requisite in an emergency which arises from accidental injury. When the state of affairs is permanent, or semi-permanent, action properly taken to preserve the life, health or well-being of the assisted person may well transcend such measures as surgical operation or

---

[94] See *Secretary of State for the Home Department v. Robb* [1995] Fam. 127; *Brightwater Care Group (Inc.) v. Rossiter* [2009] W.A.S.C. 229; *People v. Velez*, 602 N.Y.S. 2d 798 (1993); *State v. Pelham*, 746 A.2d 557 (1998).

[95] In special circumstances, a local authority might seek a declaration from the High Court so that it might act in the best interests of a "mentally competent" person: see *A Local Authority v. DL* [2011] Fam. Law 26. But it can never seek a declaration to compulsorily treat a mentally competent person.

[96] In *A Local Authority v. DL* [2011] Fam. Law 26 Wall J. said: "[I]t is ... well established that the inherent jurisdiction of the High Court exists to remedy *lacunae* left by the common law or Statute. There is no doubt also, I think, that in the years leading up to the passing of *Mental Capacity Act 2005* and the plugging of the Bournewood Gap [see *R. v. Bournewood Community and Mental Health NHS Trust Ex p. L* [1999] 1 A.C. 458] by means of the amendments to *Mental Capacity Act 2005* by the *Mental Health Act 2007*) there was a considerable development of the High Court's inherent jurisdiction over vulnerable adults who were not mentally ill within the *Mental Health Act 1983*, but who were in need of protection." See also *In Re F (Adult: Court's Jurisdiction)* [2001] Fam. 38 at 43.

[97] [1990] 2 A.C. 1.

substantial medical treatment and may extend to include such humdrum matters as routine medical or dental treatment, even simple care such as dressing and undressing and putting to bed."[98]

Can a hunger-striker prisoner be forcibly fed? No.[99] In *Secretary of State* **24–037** *for the Home Department v. Robb*,[100] it was held that a prisoner had the right to refuse to consume food or water, because he had the mental capacity to understand the consequences of his decision. Thorpe J. said:[101]

> "The first principle is that every person's body is inviolate and proof against any form of physical molestation.[102] ... Secondly, the principle of self-determination requires that respect must be given to the wishes of the patient. So that if an adult of sound mind refuses, however unreasonably, to consent to treatment or care by which his life would or might be prolonged the doctors responsible for his care must give effect to his wishes even though they do not consider it to be in his best interest to do so."[103]

24.9. JUDGE AND JURY

Where a statute allows "reasonable excuse" as a defence, the judges are disposed **24–038** to place strict limits upon it. Magistrates are virtually directed by the Divisional Court whether they can or cannot allow the excuse in the particular case. Judges are directed by the Court of Appeal not to leave the defence to the jury except in circumstances that seem right to the Court of Appeal. So "reasonable excuse," although it is a defence for breaking the letter of the law, is itself a matter of law.

The position should be the same for the defence of necessity. When a judge rules on particular facts that necessity is *not* a defence, he is deciding the question of values, namely that the importance of obeying the letter of the law is supreme on those facts. It may be thought that the positive decision, that necessity is an allowable defence in the particular case, should also belong to the judge, assuming that the jury find the facts necessary to support it. Necessity is essentially a normative doctrine, it curtails legal rules. The evaluation should be by the judge both because uniformity of decision is important and also because the judge is better qualified to pronounce on traditional values. In *R. v. Bourne*[104] it was clearly the judge who laid down the new rule for therapeutic abortions; all that he left the jury to decide was whether the doctor had acted in good faith for the purpose specified by the judge as constituting a valid defence.

If it is accepted that the evaluation of necessity is for the judge, this makes a point of difference from other doctrines such as dishonesty in theft, which, as said before, may operate very much like a defence of necessity. These matters are for the jury, subject however to a certain control by the judge.

---

[98] *In Re F (Mental Patient: Sterilisation)* [1990] 2 A.C. 1 at 77.

[99] *Secretary of State for the Home Department v. Robb* [1995] Fam. 127. Cf. *Leigh v. Gladstone* (1909) 26 T.L.R. 139.

[100] *Secretary of State for the Home Department v. Robb* [1995] Fam. 127.

[101] [1995] Fam. 127 at 130.

[102] *In Re F (Mental Patient: Sterilisation)* [1990] 2 A.C. 1.

[103] *In Re T (Adult: Refusal of Treatment)* [1993] Fam. 95; *Airedale N.H.S. Trust v. Bland* [1993] A.C. 789.

[104] [1939] 1 K.B. 687.

Some of the authorities supporting the defence show that although the evidential burden of raising it rests on the defendant, the persuasive burden of negativing it rests on the prosecution.[105]

24.10. IMPOSSIBILITY

24–039   Little discussion of a defence of impossibility is to be found in the books. In so far as the courts allow it, this is generally done under other rubrics, such as the mental element, negligence or duress. But in two types of case impossibility should be a defence independently of any other.

1.   In offences of omission, if the act to which the law obliges cannot be preformed, and the defendant was not at fault in bringing about the impossibility, he should not be held liable for the failure.[106] In other words, sheer impossibility should be an excuse for not performing a positive obligation. It is no use the law's butting its head against a brick wall. Sometimes, but by no means always, the courts accept this. An affirmative example is an old case holding that a person is not liable for not repairing a road if the road has been washed away by the sea.[107] But the more common case of impossibility by failure of subject-matter is that of failing to produce a piece of paper or article that one is expected to have; and here the courts have shown no indulgence. A person who has borrowed a car and who does not produce a test certificate to the police as required is not allowed the defence that no certificate exists, even though its non-existence was not his fault.[108] This is in accordance with the general practice of the courts for regulatory offences, where absence of fault does not excuse.[109] But it should not apply to offences carrying jail terms.[110] Of course, the difficulty of ensuring that one has a test certificate is not comparable with the difficulty of replacing a road over land eroded by the sea. The problem presented by offences of strict liability is to be discussed in Chapter 36.

2.   Certain cases of inconsistent duties can be regarded as impossibility of full performance, because both duties cannot be discharged. In the example of an air pilot whose engine fails, he is under a duty not to kill people on the street and also not to kill people in the sports stadium; and he best

---

[105] *R. v. Bourne* [1939] 1 K.B. 687; *R. v. Trim* [1943] V.L.R. 109. It seems right that the prosecution should bear the burden of negativing the defence. See *Johnson v. Western Australia* (2009) 194 A. Crim. R. 470; *Taiapa v. The Queen* (2009) 240 C.L.R. 95 at 106.

[106] Cf. *Oakley-Moore v. Robinson* [1982] R.T.R. 74.

[107] *R. v. Bamber* (1843) 114 E.R. 1254.

[108] *Sparks v. Worthington* [1986] R.T.R. 64; *Davey v. Towle* [1973] R.T.R. 328; *Stockdale v. Coulson* [1974] 1 W.L.R. 1192. Cf. *Pilgram v. Dean* [1974] 1 W.L.R. 601.

[109] *Strowger v. John* [1974] R.T.R. 124; *City of London Corp v. Eurostar (UK) Ltd.* (2005) 169 J.P. 263.

[110] *Barnfather v. Islington Education Authority* [2003] 1 W.L.R. 2318; *Hampshire CC v. E* [2008] E.L.R. 260.

reconciles the conflicting demands of the law by killing the smaller number of people in the street. It is impossible for him to fulfil both duties.[111]

24.11. MINIMAL VIOLATIONS

English law is popularly supposed not to concern itself with trifles (*De minimis non curat lex*).[112] A number of U.S. jurisdictions have put the *de minimis* defence into statutory form. In *State v. Sorge*, the Superior Court of New Jersey, referring to the codification of the defence in that state, said:[113]

24–040

> "In criminal law enforcement, many agencies exercise discretion as to the appropriateness of prosecution in a particular case. The police constantly must make decisions as to whether to arrest or, after arrest, whether to proceed with the case. Thereafter, both the prosecutor and the jury are charged with the obligation of determining both the sufficiency of the evidence to proceed and the appropriateness of doing so. Further, at least as to the Municipal Courts, experience has shown that judges will, on occasion, enter a finding of not guilty even in the face of proven guilt because, under the circumstances, a conviction is considered to be inappropriate. The drafters of the Model Penal Code summarize all of this as a 'kind of unarticulated authority to mitigate the general provisions of the criminal law to prevent absurd applications. In order to bring this exercise of discretion to the surface and to be sure that it is exercised uniformly throughout the judicial system, this [defence has been put in statutory form]."[114]

Those who believe their conduct will be exempt from punishment on the basis that it was only trivially criminal are likely to get a surprise in court. In England and Wales, if the words of a statute have clearly been offended against, an infraction will generally be found although the defendant meant no harm, or only minimal harm.[115] In particular, the courts will strictly enforce rules that are accurately quantified.

A driver who exceeds the speed limit by one mile an hour would be liable for conviction, but in practice the police do not prosecute for small excesses. The alcohol limits for drivers have been strictly applied, an excess of as little as one mg. in 100 ml. of urine leading to conviction, but in calculating the excess the justices are (very questionably) allowed to make a deduction to allow for a margin of error in the laboratory test.[116] The court in one case[117] expressed the view that the police should not prosecute when the excess of alcohol is truly minimal, but the indulgence would be against the public interest. There is a distinction from speeding offences: if a speed limit were enforced rigorously, no

---

[111] Cf. *Re A (Children) (Conjoined Twins: Medical Treatment) (No.1)* [2001] Fam. 147, where it was impossible for the doctors to fulfil their duties to both twins, since allowing the weaker twin to live would have meant allowing the stronger twin to forfeit a fairly normal life span.

[112] In *State v. Evans*, 774 A.2d 539 at 541 (2001), Petrella P.J.A.D. said: "The *de minimis* statute vests the assignment judge with discretion to dismiss certain charges to avoid an absurd application of the penal laws."

[113] 591 A.2d 1382 at 1384-1385 (1991).

[114] See *De minimis* infractions N.J.S.A. 2C:2–11.

[115] *Wells v. Hardy* [1964] 2 Q.B. 447.

[116] *Walker v. Hodgins* [1984] R.T.R. 34; cf. *Oswald v. D.P.P.* [1989] R.T.R. 360; *Stephenson v. Clift* [1988] R.T.R. 171; *Hussain v. D.P.P.* (2008) 172 J.P. 434. See also sections 7 and 11 of the *Road Traffic Act 1988*.

[117] *Delaroy-Hall v. Tadman* [1969] 2 Q.B. 208.

driver could safely drive at the limit (speedometers are imperfect, and anyway one cannot watch the dial the whole time), so that traffic in a 30 m.p.h. area would be slowed to a maximum of say 25 m.p.h., which is unlikely to be what Parliament intended. In contrast nothing but good would result if no one consumed alcohol before driving. The figure of 80 mg.[118] allowed is a concession to a pernicious practice, and the concession having been made ought not to be extended to police discretion, which is likely to continue ingrained social attitudes. Drivers under the influence of alcohol do not go by scientific measurements, and they presumably know that unless they keep well within the permitted maximum they are at risk.

24–041   When the offence is not numerically quantified, and the application of a word involves questions of the little less and the little more, the courts have more leeway to disregard trifles, but they generally do not choose to do so.[119] They rarely adopt the maxim *De minimis non curat lex* in words, and almost as rarely apply it in practice. A few examples of *de minimis* may be harvested. Where a driver unintentionally immobilized another car for a very short time, and the car was easily restarted, magistrates were held to be entitled to find that no "accident" had occurred.[120] And where a moneylender was under an obligation to make a memorandum of a loan, it was held that clerical errors would not necessarily invalidate it.[121] Any obstruction of a highway, even of the smallest degree, is said to be a public nuisance; but at the same time it is allowed that an obstruction may be so trifling (particularly, though not only, when it is temporary) that it does not "in law" amount to an obstruction.[122] In effect, though not avowedly, these cases accept the *de minimis* principle.

A physical assault is defined as the application of force, however slight, and this enables the courts to administer due punishment to the rascal who steals a

---

[118] See section 11(2)(b) of the *Road Traffic Act 1988*.

[119] See for example, *Davies v. Heatley* [1971] R.T.R. 145; *O'Halloran v. D.P.P.* [1990] R.T.R. 62; cf. *Herron v. Parking Adjudicator* [2010] A.C.D. 82. The usual, and proper rule applied by the courts is that if traffic signs *etc.* (see *Traffic Signs Regulations and General Directions 2002*; and section 85 of the *Road Traffic Regulation Act 1984*) do not conform strictly to the statutory conditions they are inoperative. It might be thought that what is law for the defendant is law for the prosecutor, but on more than one occasion this was not so. See *Briere v. Hailstone* [1969] Crim. L.R. 36; *Spittle v. Kent County Constabulary* [1986] R.T.R. 142; *Canadine v. D.P.P.* [2007] EWHC 383. Cf. *Jones v. D.P.P.* [2011] EWHC 50 (Admin) where it was held: "It was not only non-compliance with the *Traffic Signs Regulations and General Directions 2002* within the *de minimis* principle that could be disregarded in determining whether a person had protection from conviction. A purposive approach had to be taken to determining whether a motorist was entitled to protection from conviction under section 85(4) of the *Road Traffic Regulation Act 1984*. Where a local traffic authority had not strictly complied with its duties under section 85(2) of that *Act*, it was necessary to ask whether the driver had been given adequate guidance as to the speed limit to the extent that the signs on the relevant part of the road did comply with the *Traffic Signs Regulations and General Directions 2002*."

[120] *R. v. Morris* [1972] 1 W.L.R. 228 at 231; cf. *R. v. Currie* [2007] 2 Cr. App. R. 18; *Torbay Borough Council v. Cross* (1995) 159 J.P. 682, a small protrusion is too minor to count as an obstruction of the footpath/highway.

[121] *London and Harrogate Securities Ltd. v. Pitts* [1976] 1 W.L.R. 264; on appeal [1976] 1 W.L.R. 1063.

[122] *Scott v. Mid-South Essex Justices* [2004] EWHC 1001 (Admin); *D.P.P. v. Jones* [1999] 2 A.C. 240; *Almeroth v. Chivers & Sons* [1948] 1 All E.R. 53.

kiss from a sleeping beauty,[123] or where he squirts her with a water pistol.[124] There are obvious reasons for understanding the word "force" in this technical sense; normally, a slight touching would be dismissed from consideration as an ordinary social contract.[125]

The most striking rejection of the *de minimis* maxim is in relation to the unlawful possession of controlled drugs (drugs of abuse). The statute is held to apply to the smallest quantity of the drug. "If the scale do turn but in the estimate of a hair, thou diest." This was a decision of the House of Lords. Previously, the Court of Appeal had arrived at the sensible principle that there was no offence in possessing minute quantities of a forbidden drug, if they were too small to be usable. But the Lords took an about turn in *R. v. Boyesen*.[126] The possession of 5 mg. of cannabis resin (the normal range for a reefer cigarette being 50-100 mg.) was held to be a sufficient quantity to be unlawfully possessed. Lord Scarman, speaking for the House, said:

> "[T]he possession of any quantity, which is visible, tangible, measurable, and 'capable of manipulation', ... is a serious matter to be prohibited if the law is to be effective against trafficking in dangerous drugs and their misuse."[127]

Lord Scarman conceded that the quantity must be sufficient to amount, as a matter of common sense, to "something." Therefore, microscopic traces of a drug in the defendant's pockets, pipe or hypodermic syringe would not be sufficient.[128] He also recognized that quantity can be relevant to the issue of knowledge; if the amount is very small the prosecution may be unable to prove that the defendant knew he had anything.

24–042

The decisions assembled above are not entirely satisfactory. They fail to organize any coherent principle, and in the drugs case, *R. v. Boyesen*, the Lords

---

[123] Cf. the disturbing case of *State v. Kargar*, 679 A.2d 81 (1996), where D's conviction for gross sexual assault was vacated under a *de minimis* statute. The Supreme Judicial Court of Maine said: "In determining whether to dismiss the prosecution under the *de minimis* statute permitting dismissal when D's conduct could not reasonably be regarded as envisaged by the legislature in defining the crime, the focus is not on whether the conduct falls within the reach of statute criminalizing it, but on whether the possibility of the result of conviction in the particular case could not have been anticipated by the legislature when it defined the crime." It was also said: "Although D's kissing his infant son's penis fell within the literal definition of the offense of gross sexual assault, the legislature had not envisioned the extenuating circumstances of the case, in that D's conduct was accepted practice in his culture as a sign only of love and affection for the child, there was nothing sexual about D's conduct, and the child was not harmed, and thus the *de minimis* statute required vacation of convictions to avoid injustice." (Many Westerners will have great difficulty in fathoming this cultural practice.)

[124] See the facts in *R. v. Smith* (1866) 176 E.R. 910. In some U.S. jurisdictions the *de minimis* defence has provided an effective defence against assault charges. See for example, *State v. Cabana*, 716 A.2d 576 (1997); cf. *Watson v. U.S.*, 979 A.2d 1254 (2009).

[125] *McMillan v. Crown Prosecution Service* (2008) 172 J.P. 485. There is less justification for the decision that "actual bodily harm" means "bodily harm, however slight," since that repeals the word "actual."

[126] [1982] A.C. 768.

[127] *R. v. Boyesen* [1982] A.C. 768 at 777.

[128] Cf. *State v. Fukagawa*, 60 P.3d 899 (2002); *State v. Oughterson*, 54 P.3d 415 (2002). See also *State v. Rapozo*, 235 P.3d 325 (2010), where D's "possession of a live bullet for the asserted purpose of making it into a charm for a bracelet" was held to be sufficient to threaten "the harm or evil sought to be prevented by statute prohibiting possession of any firearm or ammunition by a convicted felon."

seem to have lost their usual sense of fairness. The argument they accepted, that the *Misuse of Drugs Act 1971* cannot be confined to the possession of drugs in "usable" quantities because that word does not appear in the *Misuse of Drugs Act*, is unconvincing. The words "capable of manipulation" do not either, though Lord Scarman was apparently prepared to accept them as a limitation of the offence. If their Lordships' decision appears reasonable, it is because a person who possesses residual traces of a drug has probably possessed a larger quantity in the past. But on that basis the proper course would be to convict the defendant of having possessed the drug in the past.[129] Such a conviction is all that is required for the proper enforcement of the law, and it is one to which no one could possibly object. In contrast, a person who is convicted of possessing drugs when he only has an unusably[130] small amount in his possession may understandably feel that he is the victim of legal pedantry or chicanery, since an unusable amount (if there is no question of the amount being saved up to be accumulated) is not within the mischief aimed against by the *Act*. At any rate, as a matter of general principle the rule stated in §2.12 of the American Law Institute's *Model Penal Code* is surely right, that an act that is so trivial as to be outside the harm or evil sought to be prevented and punished by the offences is outside its range.[131] However, the principle should not apply to rules stated in terms of numerical quantities.

---

[129] The possession of traces may be evidence of an offence of possession having been committed previously. It is sometimes objected that on such a charge the court would have to weigh the possibility that the defendant came into possession of the container when it was in its present condition, *i.e.* virtually empty; and also of the possibility that when the defendant came into possession of the full container he immediately emptied out the contents because he did not wish to have them. However, these would seem to be fanciful speculations in absence of evidence, and the tribunal of fact would normally be justified in inferring the prior possession of the larger quantity. *Contra, R. v. Carver* [1978] Q.B. 472 at 478B.

[130] In *State v. Fukagawa*, 60 P.3d 899 (2002), the *de minimis* defence did not apply, even though D only possessed .018 grams of the controlled drug. The evidence showed that .018 grams was a "usable" quantity in that it was sufficient to produce a pharmacological effect.

[131] In *People v. Curtis*, 784 N.Y.S.2d 922 (2003), the Criminal Court, City of New York held: "[D] did not cause significant harm by her actions. The court recognizes that there is harm created by shoplifting. Nonetheless, the *de minimis* value of the item taken, a $6.59 bottle of Advil pain medication, which occasioned a *de minimis* harm, allows the court to regard the character, history and personal circumstances of [the] defendant in order to fairly balance her interest against that of the community. ... The harm caused by defendant's act was *de minimis* and fundamental justice requires that this defendant be released from further prosecution due to her singular lapse in judgement and unique personal circumstances." *Contra, State v. Evans*, 774 A.2d 539 at 543 (2001) where it was noted: "Turning to the question of triviality, we note that attempts to define triviality by a monetary amount are fraught with potential dangers. The proposition, for example, that shoplifting items of a certain value or less, say $13 or less in this case, would send the wrong message."

CHAPTER 25

DURESS AND COERCION

"In the calm of the court room measures of fortitude or of heroic behaviour are surely not to be demanded when they could not in moments for decision reasonably have been expected even of the resolute and well disposed."

Lord Morris of Borth-y-Gest[1]

25.1. DURESS AS A DEFENCE

A person may be "compelled" by a threat to do something to which he is strongly adverse. Happily, the law on this subject is not shrouded in quite the same doubt as the defence of necessity. Subject to certain rules, a threat that is sufficiently grave to be accounted "duress"[2] can operate as a defence. This was established by the House of Lords in *D.P.P. for Northern Ireland v. Lynch*[3] following earlier authorities.[4] It is equally well settled that the burden of negativing the defence, once raised, rests on the Crown,[5] though an evidential burden rests on the defendant.[6]

Certain distinctions between the defences of duress, necessity and private defence are perhaps worth stating. Private defence does not excuse one for acting against an innocent third party, as duress does. And private defence can justify the defence of property, while duress in respect of property is not a defence. There is a closer kinship between duress and necessity.[7] Many cases of duress could be resolved as cases of necessity, by balancing of values. If a gunman threatens to

25–001

---

[1] *D.P.P. for Northern Ireland v. Lynch* [1975] A.C. 653 at 670.

[2] The term "duress" has different meanings in different branches of the law. The "duress" that makes a contract voidable may include threats of imprisonment by legal process; and the "duress" that enables a payment to be recovered back in quasi-contract may include the so-called "duress of goods." Duress as vitiating consent in an interference with the person was studied in Chap. 24.

[3] [1975] A.C. 653.

[4] See *R. v. Gotts* [1992] 2 A.C. 412 and the cases cited therein.

[5] See *R. v. Z* [2005] 2 A.C. 467 at 510-511; *R. v. Fitzpatrick* [1977] N.I. 20. For a discussion of the Law Commission's proposal to put the persuasive burden of proving duress, on the balance of probabilities, on the defence, see Jeremy Horder, "Occupying the Moral High Ground? The Law Commission on Duress," [1994] Crim. L.R. 334 at 341-342.

[6] If there is no evidence fit to go to the jury on the issue of duress or necessity, the trial judge should not allow it to go to the jury. The defence should only be put to the jury if the defendant has discharged the evidentiary onus in that respect. See *Taiapa v. The Queen* (2009) 240 C.L.R. 95 at 106 quoting Glanville Williams, *Textbook of Criminal Law*, (London: Stevens & Sons, 1983) at 49. See also *R. v. Rogers* (1996) 86 A. Crim. R. 542.

[7] See generally, Jeremy Horder, "Self-Defence, Necessity and Duress: Understanding the Relationship," (1998) 11 *Can J. L. and Jurisprudence.* 143; Michael Bayles, "Reconceptualising

shoot my wife immediately if I do not give him the keys of my employer's safe, and I yield to the threat, I could justify invoking the lesser evil defence; in any case I have the defence of duress.[8]

But, first, we have seen that doubts exist about the lesser evil doctrine, particularly in relation to murder, while the law of duress is much clearer. The courts have made it clear that duress is not a defence to murder in any circumstances.[9] Secondly, in necessity the balancing of evil against evil is left at large, and this often presents hard problems. It is both possible and desirable to achieve a greater precision with the defence of duress.

25–002 The defences of "duress" and "duress of circumstances" share some common elements with the defence of "necessity," but they are distinct defences with distinct requirements. In *R. v. Shayler*, Lord Woolf C.J. said:[10]

> "[T]he distinction between duress of circumstances and necessity has, correctly, been by and large ignored or blurred by the courts. Apart from some of the medical cases like *In re F (Mental Patient: Sterilisation)* [1990] 2 AC 1 the law has tended to treat duress of circumstances and necessity as one and the same."

Lord Woolf C.J. does not explain why the medical cases are treated differently, but I can give you a fairly good reason. The duress of circumstances defence cannot cover such cases, because the operating surgeon's "will" is not normally overborne, because the threatened harm is not usually "imminent." Of course, in some cases the surgeon will be compelled to perform an operation under emergency conditions to save the life of an accident victim and so on, but in many cases the surgeon will have weeks or even months to decide whether to perform the operation to prevent inevitable harm from transpiring. Hence, the defence of duress of circumstances differs from the defence of necessity, because the defence of necessity can be invoked even if the defendant's mind is not irresistibly overcome by external pressures. In *Re A (Children) (Conjoined Twins: Medical Treatment) (No.1)*,[11] the surgeon's "will" was not overborne. Nor was the threatened harm to the stronger twin imminent in that it was likely to transpire almost immediately. As we will see, the defences of duress and duress of circumstances have an "imminent harm" requirement. That means that the doctor would have to act to prevent harm that is likely to transpire almost immediately; not harm that could transpire in the future—even if that future is only days away.

The defence of duress only applies if the coercer threatens to kill or cause serious injury to the defendant, whereas the defence of necessity applies more generally. The defence of necessity might allow a person to take proportionate action to preserve his property or even his pet cat.

Necessity and Duress," (1987) 33 *Wayne L. Rev.* 1191; Winnie Chan and A. P. Simester, "Duress, Necessity: How Many Defences," (2005) 16 *K.C.L.J.* 121.

[8] For example, see *R. v. Pommell* [1995] 2 Cr. App. R. 607 at 615.

[9] *Contra*, "necessity" does provide a defence to murder in extreme circumstances. See the position with respect to necessity. *Re A (Children) (Conjoined Twins: Surgical Separation)* [2001] Fam. 147.

[10] [2001] 1 W.L.R. 2206 at 2226.

[11] [2001] Fam. 147.

Suppose D's cat has consumed a poisoned rat[12] and is dying as a result. Suppose **25–003** also that D lives in a remote village and the nearest vet is 30 minutes away. Let us assume D reasonably believes that the cat will die if he does not get it to the vet within 30 minutes. To save his cat, he decides to drive (all the way) at 5 miles over the speed limit. In such a case, D might be able to raise the defence of necessity. However, if he sped at 100 m.p.h. the courts would hold that the greater evil was his dangerous driving, because the risk to his cat's life cannot outweigh him risking human lives by driving dangerously. The latter is clearly a greater harm.

The idea of duress as involving a choice of evils has had some influence on legal thought. In particular, it underlies some (not all) of the remarks in *D.P.P. for Northern Ireland v. Lynch*.[13] But the argument the other way is now preferred, because duress can be invoked even if the evils are equal.[14] In *Re A (Children) (Conjoined Twins: Surgical Separation)*[15] Brooke L.J. said:

> "I have described how in modern times Parliament has sometimes provided 'necessity' defences in statutes and how the courts in developing the defence of duress of circumstances have sometimes equated it with the defence of necessity. They do not, however, cover exactly the same ground. In cases of pure necessity the actor's mind is not irresistibly overborne by external pressures. The claim is that his or her conduct was not harmful because on a choice of two evils the choice of avoiding the greater harm was justified."

The defence of duress (specifically defined) is not a justification of the crime (as necessity is) but an excuse.[16] The defence is allowed not because it achieves the greater good or lesser evil but because the defendant acts without a fully unfettered freedom.[17] It would be difficult to conceptualize D robbing an innocent third party as a justified robbery.[18] D might assert that he robbed V to

---

[12] That is a rat that the owner knows has died from eating rat poison.

[13] Glanville Williams, *Textbook of Criminal Law*, (London: Stevens & Sons, 1978) at 579-580. Cf. *R. v. Howe* [1987] A.C. 417 at 433, where Lord Hailsham said: "Other considerations necessarily arise where the choice is between the threat of death or *a fortiori* of serious injury and deliberately taking an innocent life. In such a case a reasonable man might reflect that one innocent human life is at least as valuable as his own or that of his loved one. In such a case a man cannot claim that he is choosing the lesser of two evils. Instead, he is embracing the cognate but morally disreputable principle that the end justifies the means." At 435 Lord Hailsham concludes: "Duress, as I have already pointed out, is a concession to human frailty in that it allows a reasonable man to make a conscious choice between the reality of the immediate threat and what he may reasonably regard as the lesser of two evils." See also *R. v. Shepherd* (1988) 86 Cr. App. R. 47 at 50 *per* Mustill L.J.

[14] In some cases the coerced party might even commit a greater evil (*i.e.*, he might cause serious injury to three people to protect two people from serious injury as might be the case where he acts to protect his wife and child).

[15] [2001] Fam. 147 at 236.

[16] *Per* Lord Bingham in *R. v. Z* [2005] 2 A.C. 489. Peter Westen and James Mangiafico, "The Criminal Defence of Duress: A Justification Not An Excuse—And Why It Matters," (2003) 6 *Buff. Crim. L. Rev.* 833 (2003); Kyron Huigens, "Duress Is Not a Justification," (2004) 2 *Ohio St. J. Crim. L.* 303 (2004); Joshua Dressler, "Exegesis on the Law of Duress: Justifying the Excuse and Searching for Its Proper Limits," (1989) 62 *Cal. L. Rev.* 1331.

[17] *Dixon v. U.S.*, 548 U.S. 1 at 6-7 (2006).

[18] "Moral involuntariness is also related to the notion that the defence of duress is an excuse. Dickson J. maintained in *Perka v. The Queen* [1984] 2 S.C.R. 232 that an excuse acknowledges the wrongfulness of the accused's conduct. Nevertheless, the law refuses to attach penal consequences to it because an 'excuse' has been made out. In using the expression 'moral involuntariness,' we mean

save his wife from being shot by D2, but he cannot assert that robbing an innocent third party is justified conduct. He can, however, assert that his decision to commit the robbery was not an entirely fully voluntary decision. The fact that D acted to prevent some greater evil is only a supplementary consideration, it might be considered when the court determines whether he acted "reasonably and proportionately in order to avoid a threat of death or serious injury."[19]

25–004 **So the idea is that duress makes the act involuntary?**   When Widgery L.J. spoke of the will being overborne, he used figurative language. A person who is acting under duress makes a decision to give way to duress.[20] The view taken by the majority of the House of Lords in *D.P.P. for Northern Ireland v. Lynch* was that duress is a defence on its own, and does not negative either the doing of the act charged or the *mens rea*.[21] This is plainly right. If D1 seizes D2's hand and by direct force makes D2 pull the trigger of a revolver which kills V, we would certainly say that the killing was done by D1 and not by D2. But if D2 is persuaded by threats to shoot V, it is proper to say that D2 has killed him, though perhaps under duress.

Aristotle suggested, as one reason for classifying such an act as voluntary, that "an individual may resist the threat and suffer the evil rather than do what he thinks to be wrong; he will then be praised, and his resistance will show that it was not inevitable that a person should submit to the threat."[22] Similarly, in *Benyon v. Evelyn* it was said:

> "If rebels come to men's houses, and *pro timore mortis* they give them victuals, and go along with them, *et quod recesserunt quam cito potuerint*, this was adjudged no treason in Sir John Oldcastle's case; yet to have refused to have given them victuals had been more heroical."[23]

---

that the accused had no 'real' choice but to commit the offence. This recognizes that there was indeed an alternative to breaking the law, although in the case of duress that choice may be even more unpalatable — to be killed or physically harmed." *R. v. Ruzic* (2001) 153 C.C.C. (3d) 1 at para. 39 *per* Lebel J. See also *Tofilau v. The Queen* (2007) 231 C.L.R. 396 at 516 *et seq.*

[19] *R. v. Martin* (1989) 88 Cr. App. R. 343.

[20] Duress has been conceptualized as "moral involuntariness." It is different from physical involuntariness, since the actor still has the capacity to choose to resist the threat. See *R. v. Ruzic* (2001) 153 C.C.C. (3d) 1 at para. 39.

[21] For this reason, it seems that *R. v. Steane* [1947] K.B. 997 should have been decided on duress, not on the absence of intent. See Glanville Williams, *Criminal Law: The General Part*, (London: Stevens & Sons, 2nd edn. 1961) at 18. See also *Dixon v. U.S.*, 548 U.S. 1 (2006); *R. v. Hibbert* [1995] 2 S.C.R. 973.

[22] *Nicomachean Ethics*, Book 3, Chap. 1. (For example, if D threatens to cause X to suffer grievously bodily harm unless he rapes V, X might say, "I can stand a beating, but I cannot rape anyone, so please beat me."). Cf. *R. v. Luedecke* [2008] 236 C.C.C. (3d) 317, where a man raped a woman while in a state of automatism and was able to raise the issue of automatism (physical involuntariness).

[23] (1664) 124 E.R. 614 at 633. Because a human life is regarded as having an absolute value, duress is no defence to murder. It is irrelevant that D only kills because his will is overborne, because the defence is excluded as a matter of policy. He is expected to sacrifice his own life rather than that of another human being. See *R. v. Howe* [1987] A.C. 417 at 432, where Lord Hailsham said: "I do not at all accept in relation to the defence of murder it is either good morals, good policy or good law to suggest, as did the majority in *Lynch* and the minority in *Abbott* that the ordinary man of reasonable fortitude is not to be supposed to be capable of heroism if he is asked to take an innocent life rather than sacrifice his own."

We may add that the notion that the act is involuntary would automatically make duress a defence to all charges of crime, whereas the courts treat the question whether exceptions should be made as one of policy.

What limitations are placed on the defence of duress? In *R. v. Z*[24] Lord **25–005**
Bingham said: "it seems to me important that the issues the House is asked to resolve should be approached with understanding of how the defence has developed, and to that end I shall briefly identify the most important limitations.":

"(1)   Duress does not afford a defence to charges of murder, attempted murder and, perhaps, some forms of treason.

(2)   To found a plea of duress the threat relied on must be to cause death or serious injury.

(3)   The threat must be directed against the defendant or his immediate family or someone close to him. [T]he threat must be directed, if not to the defendant or a member of his immediate family, to a person for whose safety the defendant would reasonably regard himself as responsible.

(4)   The relevant tests pertaining to duress have been largely stated objectively, with reference to the reasonableness of the defendant's perceptions and conduct and not, as is usual in many other areas of the criminal law, with primary reference to his subjective perceptions.

(5)   The defence of duress is available only where the criminal conduct which it is sought to excuse has been directly caused by the threats which are relied upon.

(6)   The defendant may excuse his criminal conduct on grounds of duress only if, placed as he was, there was no evasive action he could reasonably have been expected to take.

(7)   The defendant may not rely on duress to which he has voluntarily laid himself open."

25.2.   THREATS OF DEATH AND SERIOUS INJURY

For practical reasons duress is confined to threats of death or serious personal **25–006**
injury. Widgery L.J. expressed the law thus:

"[I]t is clearly established that duress provides a defence in all offences including perjury (except possibly treason or murder as a principal) if the will of the accused has been overborne by threats of death or serious personal injury so that the commission of the alleged offence was no longer the voluntary act of the accused.[25]"

Moreover, it is a question of policy what should be counted as duress. The Law Commission, in an important Report,[26] put forward two propositions:

1.   Certain very terrible threats should excuse all crimes.
2.   Less terrible threats should be a matter of mitigation only. If the crime is a minor one the mitigation may result in an absolute discharge, but that is in the discretion of the judge.

As to what threats should fall within proposition 1, the Law Commission adopted the rule stated by Widgery L.J., that duress must amount to a threat of

---

[24]   [2005] 2 A.C. 467 at 490–491.
[25]   *R. v. Hudson* [1971] 2 Q.B. 202 at 206.
[26]   Law Commission, *Criminal Law: Report on Defences of General Application*, (London: Law Com No. 83, 1977), at Pt. II.

death or serious injury, with the modification that the injury threatened may be physical or mental,[27] and may be to the defendant or to another; also, what matters is not what threat was intended but what threat the defendant believed to exist. The Commission slipped in the qualification that the threat must be such that in all the circumstances of the case the defendant could not reasonably have been expected to resist it.

25–007 **May there not be serious threats other than those mentioned by Widgery L.J. and the Law Commission? What about a threat to destroy a person's dwelling?[28] Or to cause him to lose his job? Or a blackmailing threat to his character?[29]** Many of us are subject to pressures, external and internal, to cause harm to others. The law is by definition a system of counter-pressure, its aim being to influence individuals to make acceptable social decisions. This counter-pressure cannot be lifted merely because the individual finds strong personal reasons for acting contrary to the law. Constraint is a defence only when it is so immediate and pressing in character that it seems futile or unconscionably harsh to maintain the prohibition. As a practical matter, the threats you mention must be left to general mitigation, though the threat to burn a person's dwelling could afford him a defence for some minor transgression under the doctrine of necessity. I think, however, that a threat to torture should be added to the Widgery list as a case of duress, since a person may find torture unendurable even though it does not involve physical injury.[30]

25–008 **You agree that if the threat is not of death or serious injury (or perhaps torture) the question has to be left to the judge as a matter of mitigation. Why not do so in all cases? Why let the judge come into the picture when the threat is of some particular kind?** Voices are still raised to say this. But the question whether a person ought to be punishable in such cases is one of general policy, resting upon an assessment of what the criminal law is capable of effecting and what it is right that it should try to do; and the matter ought not to be left to the shifting sands of discretion.

For good measure, three other reasons may be advanced for allowing duress as a defence, and not simply as a matter of mitigation:

---

[27] In *R. v. Baker* [1997] Crim. L.R. 497 it was held that "duress of circumstances could not be extended to circumstances where the defendant had feared serious psychological injury." This makes sense in that this type of injury cannot be inflicted in one blow. The harm would normally not be imminent, because it would be almost impossible to cause another to instantly suffer a recognized psychiatric illness. (See *R. v. Dhaliwal* [2006] 2 Cr. App. R. 348). The victim would normally have time to contact the police.

[28] See *Alexander M'Growther's Case* (1746) Fost. 13 at 14 (a treason case), where Lord Chief Justice Lee said: "that there is not, nor ever was, any tenure which obligeth tenants to follow their lords into rebellion. And as to the matter of force, he said, that the fear of having houses burnt or goods spoiled ... is no excuse in the eye of the law for joining and marching with rebels." See also *R. v. Crutchley* (1831) 172 E.R. 909; *D.P.P. v. Milcoy* [1993] C.O.D. 200, where it was held the defence is not available where the defendant merely threatens to harm the coerced party's dogs and ponies.

[29] *R. v. Singh* [1972] 1 W.L.R. 1600 at 1604.

[30] For example, sleep deprivation. However, most forms of torture will have the double-effect of causing serious injury.

1. Allowing a specific defence means that the evidence is brought out fully before the jury. It is a criticism of our trial system that where evidence is admissible only in mitigation, so that it is no concern of the jury, it is not considered and probed with the same thoroughness as evidence going to liability.[31]

2. There is a special argument for murder. If duress were not allowed as a defence (and it is not) the judge would have to pass a life sentence.

3. A last argument is perhaps the most decisive. In a case of overwhelming duress, no punishment can in justice be imposed on the unhappy victim of the duress. The moral rigorist may assert that there must nevertheless be a conviction, to maintain the supremacy of the higher morality. But, as Rupert Cross remarked, "an absolute discharge or an instant release under the prerogative mercy are strange methods of enforcing absolute moral prohibitions."[32]

25.3. CRIMES EXCEPTED FROM THE DEFENCE

It will be remembered that Widgery L.J. mooted two exceptions from the defence: treason and murder as principal. Prosecutions for treason are virtually confined to the circumstances of war.[33] Perhaps in war even the private citizen is expected to cast himself in a heroic mould. But remarks in *D.P.P. for Northern Ireland v. Lynch*,[34] as well as the weight of earlier authority, are in favour of allowing the defence of duress to a charge of treason.[35]

25–009

As for murder, the decision in *D.P.P. for Northern Ireland v. Lynch* was that duress can be a defence to a person charged as accessory to murder (even though he is what used to be called a principal in the second degree, assisting at the time of the crime). This decision is no longer the law. The House of Lords has since held that the defence of duress is not available to a person who is an accessory to murder.[36] Nor is the defence of duress available to a person who has attempted to commit murder. "Accordingly, duress is no defence to murder in whatever capacity the accused is charged with that crime."[37] It has never been suggested that the defence of duress is denied to the attempted perpetrator of murder. Yet the punishment of attempt is at the discretion of the court, while that of murder is fixed by law, so that, on grounds of justice, a defence to the charge of murder is much more important for the person accused of murder than for one accused of attempt to murder.

---

[31] Cf. Lord Edmund-Davies in *D.P.P. for Northern Ireland v. Lynch* [1975] A.C. 653 at 707E.

[32] Rupert Cross, "Murder under Duress," (1978) 28 *U. Toronto L.J.* 369 at 376.

[33] Cf. *Alexander M'Growther's Case* (1746) Fost. 13.

[34] [1975] A.C. 653 at 672E, 791E, 708C.

[35] See *Oldcastle's Case* (1414) 1 St. Tr. 225, (where the defendants merely provided food and provisions—assisted the act of treason). See also *R. v. Prudy* (1946) 10 *J. Crim. L.* 182; and the cases discussed in J. Ll. J. Edwards, "Compulsion, Coercion and Criminal Responsibility," (1951) 14 *Mod. L. Rev.* 297.

[36] *R. v. Howe* [1987] A.C. 417. If endangering the lives of hundreds of passengers by high-jacking a passenger jet can be excused (see *R. v. Safi* [2004] 1 Cr. App. R. 157), there is no reason why minor acts of treason might not be excused.

[37] *R. v. Gotts* [1992] 2 A.C. 412 at 424.

The defence could be invoked in cases where a person is forced to commit some act such as speeding in a motorcar and that act in turn causes the death of an innocent pedestrian. Suppose a fleeing bank robber randomly carjacks D's car and orders him at gunpoint to drive at great speeds to help him escape from the scene. If the dangerous driving (speeding) causes the death of a pedestrian, the defendant should be able to invoke the defence of duress.[38] Similarly, if a person is ordered at gunpoint to inflict actual bodily harm on V, he would be able to rely on the defence of duress if V slips and hits his head and dies. A person who inflicts grievous bodily harm on another can set up a defence of duress; but if the victim happens to die, and the charge is murder, the defence may be ousted. This seems absurd, but it is the law.

25–010   Additionally, duress would be a defence to the offences found in sections 44-45 of the *Serious Crime Act 2007*.

Suppose D1 sells D2 a pack of bullets for his gun believing he will use them to kill V. D1 only sells the ammunition to D2 because D2 puts a gun to D1's head.[39] D1 sells the bullets because he believes D2 will kill him if he does not supply him with them. Unfortunately, D2 uses the bullets to kill V.

Can D1 rely on the defence of duress? If the prosecution decide to charge D1 with an offence under sections 44 or 45 of the *Serious Crime Act 2007*, the defence of duress should be available to him. The *Serious Crime Act* offences are independent offences, so a person cannot be convicted of murder under those provisions. If he is charged as an accessory to murder under the *Accessories and Abettors Act 1861*, the defence of duress will not be available. Under the latter *Act* the defendant is convicted of murder, if that is the substantive offence that he assisted or encouraged. It seems unreasonable to exclude the defence of duress to an accessory on a charge of murder where the accessory has done something quite trivial, like handing over a pack of bullets because he had a gun at his head. There can be no advantage to a person in refusing to hand over a pack of bullets if he can be shot and the bullets taken from his dead body.

25–011   **That is a highly tendentious example. What the defendant did may not be trivial. Do you say that if a terrorist threatens Droop to injure him seriously if he does not make a telephone call that will lure an unsuspecting victim to his death, and Droop complies, Droop should not be guilty of murder?**   We would admire Droop if he rejected the proposal and accepted the injury. The doctrine of necessity would hardy justify such a deed as proposed to him, because the injury to Droop is not demonstrably a greater evil then the death of the victim.

---

[38] Cf. *R. v. B, JA* [2007] 99 S.A.S.R. 317, where the defence was not available in a dangerous driving case because the defendant did not honestly believe on reasonable grounds that he was placed in a position of imminent peril.

[39] See *R. v. Wilson* [2007] 2 Cr. App. R. 411 at 420-421, where Lord Phillips C.J. said: "There may be grounds for criticising a principle of law that does not afford a 13-year-old boy any defence to a charge of murder on the ground that he was complying with his father's instructions, which he was too frightened to refuse to disobey. But our criminal law holds that a 13-year-old boy is responsible for his actions and the rule that duress provides no defence to a charge of murder applies however susceptible the defendant may be to the duress, absent always any question of diminished responsibility, and applies whether the defendant is a principal in the first or the second degree." Cf. *Jupiter v. State*, 616 A.2d 412 (1992).

But if Droop lacks the moral fibre to resist the threat, it seems pointless to treat him as a murderer as well. (And if you still despise Droop, consider that the threat may not be to injure him but to torture him, and not only him but his wife and children).

What would you say if the defendant has helped to plant a bomb that kills   25–012
scores of people? Is he to be permitted to save his own skin in that way? In
the Nuremberg trials those who took part in the mass extermination of Jews
were not allowed to defend themselves by saying that they themselves feared
that they would be executed if they disobeyed orders.   The point you make about the Nuremberg trials is powerful, but the problem of atrocities committed by soldiers and others who are under orders has special features. If members of the armed forces are allowed defences of duress and superior orders, responsibility is confined to a very few people at the top. Perhaps, for overwhelming social reasons, these defences have to be withheld from members of the armed forces (or others subject to discipline) in respect of acts of killing or torturing that are clearly contrary to civilized standards of behaviour. In practice, because of the number of people involved, it would be only those with appreciable authority who would be prosecuted. But whatever solution is found need not govern ordinary cases involving civilians.

Your question about the bomb raises difficult issues of morality and social policy. There is an argument for saying that we should nourish the hope, however faint, that the threat of punishment may be enough to tip the balance of decision by those who have only doubtfully sufficient fortitude to undergo martyrdom for the sake of moral principle. But even though duress is not a defence in your hypothetical, the circumstances would go so strongly in mitigation of punishment that the defendant would probably serve only a proportionately just sentence, which in itself would probably (if he knew it beforehand) be insufficient to avail against the threat. There is also the question whether the conviction and punishment in what may be highly unusual circumstances are likely to be known later on to other people who are similarly placed. (Lawyers exaggerate the extent to which decisions of the courts are known to and remembered by the populace.)

But surely a distinction between the perpetrator and the accessory is   25–013
indefensible. There may be no moral difference between them.   That is true. Compare the person who is forced to drive a bomber to a crowded pub and someone who is forced to carry the bomb into the pub and leave it there. The former is an accessory, the latter the perpetrator; but on facts like these the legal distinction is too fine to be morally or psychologically relevant. For this and other reasons the Law Commission proposed that the defence of duress should be extended by statute to all crimes.[40]

In *D.P.P. for Northern Ireland v. Lynch*, Lord Morris suggested a reason for the distinction: under terrible threat, many temporize by assisting in the plan while hoping that something will intervene to save the victim, whereas a perpetrator knows that he is doing the immediate killing. But this distinction does not quite

---

[40] Law Commission, *Murder, Manslaughter and Infanticide*, (London: H.M.S.O. No. 304, 2006) at para. 612 *et passim*.

fit. A perpetrator who sets a bomb because he is under duress may hope that it will not go off, or that someone will find it in time, while an accessory who assists in the killing of a victim then and there has no hope that anyone will intervene.

Something depends on how the line between perpetrators and others is drawn. In *Abbott v. The Queen*, the defendant held the victim (a girl) while a hired assassin attempted to stab her to death; however, she was still alive when the defendant and others joined in burying her. The Judicial Committee of the Privy Council said: "The facts make it obvious that the appellant was a principal in the first degree in that he took an active and indeed a leading part in the killing."[41] But this has never been the test of a principal in the first degree. An accessory may take "a leading part in the killing" by devising the plan and supervising its execution; this does not make him a perpetrator.[42] On traditional principles, what made Abbott a perpetrator was not the fact that he held the victim while she was stabbed but only the fact that he took an immediate joint part in her final dispatch by burying her alive (even though at the time she was mortally wounded). Morally, the former conduct was worse than the latter, because the latter conduct, though very cruel, merely accelerated the girl's death by a short time.

25–014 The absurdity of the distinction was adverted to by the Court of Appeal in *R. v. Graham*,[43] a case of murder so cold-blooded and brutal that it makes the demand for the restoration of capital punishment understandable. Graham set about helping to throttle his wife by pulling the plug at one end of an electric flex, which was around her neck, while his companion in inequity pulled the other end. The wife was killed, but Graham said that in fact he did not take an effective part because the plug came off in his hand when he began to pull it. If that was so, his guilt was only that of an accessory (abettor) by being present and encouraging, not that of perpetrator. The court commented that the jury would be puzzled to be told that Graham's guilt depended on whether the plug did come off in his hand.

But the decision in that case presents its own problems. The trial judge left the defence of duress to the jury without asking them to find whether the defendant was the perpetrator of the murder. In effect he decided not to follow *Abbott v. The Queen* (as technically he was not obliged to do).[44] The objection to the judge's ruling is that there was no evidence of duress. The evidence was merely that Graham's companion was sometimes given to violence. The report gave no indication that a threat was made to Graham, and Graham took an active part in arranging that his wife should be murdered. Obviously it cannot found a defence of duress to show merely that the defendant voluntarily associated with a man of whom he was rather afraid, and took part with him in planning and executing the crime. A defence of duress requires a threat, express or implied, not merely general evidence of fear. Remarkably, counsel for the Crown conceded that it was open to the defendant to raise the defence; equally remarkably, the trial judge

---

[41] [1977] A.C. 755 at 762B.

[42] 15.1.

[43] [1982] 1 W.L.R. 294.

[44] Decisions of the Judicial Committee of the Privy Council are treated with great respect by the United Kingdom courts (as the House of Lords was, and the Supreme Court is), but are not binding upon them.

accepted this opinion without question, and left the defence to the jury; more remarkably still, the Court of Appeal did not voice even the mildest criticism of the judge's pusillanimity. The court did indeed "doubt" whether counsel for the Crown were right to concede that the question of duress arose; "the words and deeds of King relied on by the defence were far short of those needed to raise a threat of the requisite gravity." But the court went on to say that the Crown having made the concession, the judge was right to leave the question of duress to the jury in the way it did. The puzzle is why the Court of Appeal thought he was right to leave it to them at all. Judges are not bound to accept concessions made by counsel in a criminal case.

25.4. THE SUBJECTIVE AND OBJECTIVE PRONGS

The defence of duress applies where a person is able to demonstrate that another person made threats which persuaded him to commit a crime which he otherwise would not have committed. The threat "must involve a threat of such a degree of violence that 'a person of reasonable firmness' with the characteristics and in the situation of the defendant could not have been expected to resist."[45]   **25–015**

In *R. v. Graham*,[46] Lane C.J. laid down the following test for determining whether the defence applies in a given case:

> "(1) Was the defendant, or may he have been, impelled to act as he did because, as a result of what he reasonably believed [the coercer] had said or done, he had good cause to fear that if he did not so act [the coercer] would kill him or (if this is to be added) cause him serious physical injury?
>
> (2) If so, have the prosecution made the jury sure that a sober person of reasonable firmness, sharing the characteristics of the defendant, would not have responded to whatever he reasonably believed [the coercer] said or did by taking part in the killing? The fact that a defendant's will to resist has been eroded by the voluntary consumption of drink or drugs or both is not relevant to this test."

The first question is always a subjective one. It is the question of whether the defendant did in fact hold the belief that the threat would be carried out. It must also be shown that he in fact held the belief that it was necessary for him to commit the nominated crime to avoid the threat. If he did not in fact believe that the threat would be carried out and that it was necessary for him to commit the nominated crime to avoid the threat, he will not be able to show that his "will" was in fact overborne.

The second question is whether the defendant had reasonable grounds for believing that the threat would be carried out. The defendant must also have had reasonable grounds for believing that it was necessary for him to commit the crime to avoid the threat. This is an objective standard and it has two prongs: **25–016**

1. The defendant must have reasonable grounds for believing that the threats could be carried out.

---

[45] *R. v. Howe* [1987] A.C. 417 at 426.
[46] [1982] 1 W.L.R. 294 at 300. See also *R. v. Z* [2005] 2 A.C. 467.

2.   It must be shown that a person of reasonable firmness in the same circumstances would have committed the crime to avoid being killed or seriously injured. (The defendant must not yield to the threat, if a person of reasonable firmness sharing his characteristics would not yield to it.)

If it can be shown that he did not have reasonable grounds for believing the threat would be carried out, the second prong need not be considered.

25–017   **Would it not be fairer to allow the defence so long as the defendant honestly, even if unreasonably, believed that the threat would be carried out and that it was necessary to commit the crime to avoid the threat?**   If the defendant's belief that the threat would be carried out were tested subjectively, the defence of duress would be brought into line with public and private defence.[47] But the courts have not developed the defence of duress in the same way. Therefore, the defendant's beliefs are tested objectively.

25–018   **Are you telling me that the defence is not available for a person who unreasonably believes that he will be seriously injured?**   Correct, it does not matter that his fear may have been genuine and his belief very real for him. Let us take an extreme example to shed some light on the test.

Suppose a physically strong 21-year-old man is terrified of older men because he was abused as a child. Suppose also that an unarmed 80-year-old man orders him to steal some cigars from a shop. The old man threatens to break both his legs if he does not comply, so the young man yields to the threat.

A physically strong 21-year-old of reasonable firmness would not be terrified of having his legs broken by an 80-year-old, because he would believe that he could easily escape such an attack by running off. Most people of reasonable firmness would assume that an unarmed 80-year-old would not be able to carry out such a threat. The abuse he suffered as a child may have in fact caused him to genuinely believe that the old man could break his legs, but a reasonable person without his past would not have formed such an unreasonable belief.[48]

However, the cases will not always be this extreme. There may be borderline cases where the defendant will unreasonably believe that the threat will be carried out if he does not commit the nominated offence; and where he may unreasonably believe that it is necessary for him to commit the nominated crime to avoid being killed or seriously injured. A subjective standard would allow the jury to decide whether the defence is available by considering whether the defendant in fact held the belief that it was necessary for him to commit the

---

[47] When *R. v. Graham* [1982] 1 W.L.R. 294 was decided the defence of self-defence by and large incorporated an objective test. The courts have since held that an unreasonable belief is sufficient so long as it was in fact held. See *R. v. Williams* (1984) 78 Cr. App. R. 276; *Beckford v. The Queen* [1988] A.C. 130; *R. v. Wilson* [2006] EWCA Crim. 1880. Cf. *R. v. Martin* [2000] 2 Cr. App. R. 42, where the court invoked the subjective test in a duress case. (The latter is the preferable view, but it is not supported by the authorities.)

[48] *R. v. Hurst* [1995] 1 Cr. App. R. 82.

nominated crime to avoid being killed or injured almost immediately. If the belief is utterly fanciful,[49] the jury is likely to infer that the defendant did not in fact hold it.[50]

Suppose that the defendant was very cowardly. Someone with more backbone and intelligence might have seen that the threat was probably only a bluff, and might have called the bluff. Is the defendant still allowed the defence? The defence will be allowed only to those who showed reasonable firmness. The objective limitation upon the defence means that the threat must be such that the defendant could not reasonably be expected to resist.

25–019

Does it matter that there was in fact no threat, if the defendant reasonably believed that there was a threat and that it would be carried out? The defendant could raise the defence. It does not matter that there was in fact no threat, so long as a reasonable person would have believed that there was a threat.[51]

25–020

You told me that the second prong of the objective standard excuses the defendant for responding to the threat by committing a crime, only if a person of reasonable firmness would have believed he needed to commit the crime to avoid imminent harm. Is the defendant of reasonable firmness imbued with certain characteristics? Yes. In *R. v. Bowen*[52] Stuart-Smith L.J. said:

25–021

"(1)   The mere fact that the defendant is more pliable, vulnerable, timid or susceptible to threats than a normal person is not a characteristic with which it is legitimate to invest the reasonable/ordinary person for the purpose of considering the objective test.

(2)   The defendant may be in a category of persons whom the jury may think less able to resist pressure than people not within that category. Obvious examples are age, where a young person may well not be so robust as a mature one; possibly sex, though many women would doubtless consider they had as much moral courage to resist pressure as men; pregnancy, where there is added fear for the unborn child; serious physical disability, which may inhibit self protection; recognised mental illness or psychiatric condition, such as post-traumatic stress disorder leading to learnt helplessness.

(3)   Characteristics which may be relevant in considering provocation, because they relate to the nature of the provocation itself, will not necessarily be relevant in cases of duress. Thus homosexuality may be relevant to provocation if the provocative words or conduct are related to this characteristic; it cannot be relevant in duress, since there is no reason to think that homosexuals are less robust in resisting threats of the kind that are relevant in duress cases.

(4)   Characteristics due to self-induced abuse, such as alcohol, drugs or glue-sniffing, cannot be relevant.

(5)   Psychiatric evidence may be admissible to show that the defendant is suffering from some mental illness, mental impairment or recognised psychiatric condition provided

---

[49] If the claim is too fanciful and thus is not founded on evidence the judge should not let the jury consider it. The Canadian courts apply what they call the "air of reality" test. It is applied "to avoid having to consider defences which have been described as meritless, outlandish, fanciful, far-fetched, speculative and not founded on evidence." *R. v. Cinous* (2002) 162 C.C.C. (3d) 129. *R. v. Savoury* (2005), 201 O.A.C. 40.

[50] Cf. *D.P.P. v. Morgan* [1976] A.C. 182.

[51] *R. v. Cairns* [1999] 2 Cr. App. R. 137; *R. v. Conway* [1989] Q.B. 290; *R. v. Safi* [2004] 1 Cr. App. R. 157.

[52] [1997] 1 W.L.R. 372 at 379-380.

persons generally suffering from such condition may be more susceptible to pressure and threats and thus to assist the jury in deciding whether a reasonable person suffering from such a condition might have been impelled to act as the defendant did. It is not admissible simply to show that in the doctor's opinion a defendant, who is not suffering from such illness or condition, is especially timid, suggestible or vulnerable to pressure and threats. ..."

The decision in *R. v. Bowen* allows certain defendants to have the reasonableness of their beliefs tested against what people like them would regard as reasonable. The court made some suggestions about the types of characteristics that might be considered, including age, disability, gender, pregnancy and mental illness. The court seems to be suggesting that because these types of people might be more susceptible to pressure, the question is whether a reasonable person with their characteristics would have believed it was necessary to commit the nominated crime to avoid serious injury or death.

A pregnant woman or disabled person might give way to the threat simply because they believe they are physically less able to withstand or avoid the threat. A pregnant woman might also be concerned about the life and health of her unborn child. Her physical condition is akin to a contextual factor or circumstance, because it does not affect her ability to make a rational decision. Rather, it is a factor that will help her determine whether it is necessary for her to yield to the threat in the given context. If she were not pregnant she might just run or if she were not physically disabled she might have been able to stand up to the coercer. The standard is still objective in that the defendant will be judged against the standard expected of a similarly situated person with identical characteristics.

25–022 In the case of mental illness, the defendant might not be in a position to make a rational decision about whether or not it is necessary for him to yield to the threat.[53] If the mental illness caused a person to unreasonably yield to a threat, then unless a subjective standard is applied it is difficult to see how she could rely on the defence of duress. In extreme cases the defence of insanity may be available, but diminished responsibility only provides a partial defence to murder.[54] Similarly, battered women's syndrome would not be difficult to apply under a subjective standard, but may be difficult to consider under an objective standard. It seems to make a complete nonsense of the objective standard to allow the defence to be raised where a person has made an unreasonable mistake because of his mental illness. (In some cases, the belief that it is necessary to yield to the threat will clearly be reasonable even though the defendant had a diminished capacity. For instance, in most cases where a woman is suffering from battered woman's syndrome the threatened violence is usually serious enough to provide the defendant with reasonable grounds for believing it was necessary to

---

[53] See *R. v. Horne* [1994] Crim. L.R. 584; *R. v. Hegarty* [1994] Crim. L.R. 353; *R. v. Hurst* [1995] 1 Cr. App. R. 82.

[54] In some U.S. states the partial defence of diminished responsibility has been applied to a range of offences. (See for example, *State v. Jones,* 920 P2d 225 (1996); *U.S. v. Murphy*, 556 F. Supp. 2d 1232 (2008)). The problem is that where there is no lesser offence, diminished responsibility can only be considered as a mitigating factor by the sentencing judge. Some states allow it to be raised to negate the specific intent required for certain crimes, but convict the defendant of a basic intent crime where one is available. See *State v. Lowe*, 318 S.W.3d 812 (2010); *State v. Jimenez*, 880 A.2d 468 (2005).

commit the nominated offence.)[55] It is one thing to ask whether the defendant committed the nominated crime because his mind had been overborne by threats of death or serious bodily violence that would have induced an average person of ordinary firmness of mind, of a like age, gender, and physical ability, in like circumstances to act in the same way; but something entirely different to ask whether a person suffering from mental illness would have yielded to the threat.

There is no such thing as a person of ordinary mental disorder, if such a characteristic is to be considered then it would be better to have a subjective standard. A person suffering from a recognized mental illness might be more likely to make an unreasonable mistake as to whether the threat will be carried out. Furthermore, such a person is more likely to make an unreasonable mistake about whether it is necessary to commit the nominated crime to avoid the threat.

If the courts were to adopt a purely objective standard, even the age of the coerced party would be irrelevant. But a purely subjective standard might allow some fairly fanciful claims to be put to the jury, but only if the defendant has satisfied the evidential burden. If the defendant's failure to resist the threat is totally unreasonable, the jury could infer that he did not in fact believe that it was necessary for him to yield to the threat. The Law Commission has recommended that the objective standard be maintained. It has proposed:[56]

"(1)   In deciding whether a person of reasonable firmness might have acted as D did, the jury should be able to take into account all the circumstances of D, including his or her age, other than those that bear upon his or her capacity to withstand duress.

(2)   D's belief as to the existence of the threat and its being implemented must be not only honestly but also reasonably held."

The case for maintaining a purely objective standard is questionable, because the courts have decided that mental illness is a characteristic that should be considered. Applying the objective standard to such cases would be fraught with difficulty and will most likely produce absurd results. It would be better just to adopt a wholly subjective standard. The direction in *R. v. Graham* accepts the test of a person of reasonable firmness (qualifying this by postulating that he is a

25–023

---

[55] However, the courts have held that battered women's syndrome is a characteristic that can be considered when determining whether the defendant has reasonable grounds for yielding to the threat. In *State v. B.H.*, 834 A.2d 1063 (2003) is was said: "[W]e conclude that evidence that [the] defendant suffered from battered woman's syndrome as a result of [D's] prior abuse was relevant to the jury's determination whether she was coerced by fear of serious harm to herself or her daughter that was honestly held and reasonable 'in her situation.' That situation may include a history of battering and the condition known as battered woman's syndrome." See also *R. v. Runjanjic* (1991) 56 S.A.S.R. 114 at 120 *per* King C.J. If the offending has taken place on many occasions over a considerable period of time, it will be very difficult for the defendant to establish that she had no reasonable opportunity to escape the threatened harm. Cf. *R. v. Emery* (1993) 14 Cr. App. R. (S.) 394 at 398 (where D "was unable to resist or stand up to the father of her child, as a result of his treatment of her, and this resulted in the child's death." She was convicted on the basis that she had failed to protect the child.). See further *State v. Brennan*, 870 A.2d 292 (2005); *Re Glenn G.*, 587 N.Y.S.2d 464 (1992).
[56] Law Commission, *Murder, Manslaughter and Infanticide*, (London: H.M.S.O. No. 304, 2006) at para. 6.12. Professor Ashworth asserts: "The Commission's argument that the reasonableness requirement is right because the duressee usually has 'time to reflect' does not convince; and its claims about the relative difficulties of proving the qualifying conditions of duress are inadequately grounded." Andrew Ashworth, "Principles, Pragmatism and the Law Commission's Recommendations on Homicide Law Reform," [2007] Crim. L.R. 333 at 341.

person "sharing the characteristics of the defendant;" it is impossible to reconcile this wholesale importation of personal characteristics, especially characteristics such as mental disorder, into the supposedly objective test).[57] Whether an objective limitation upon the defence in these terms is necessary or desirable may be doubted. It spoils such precision as the rule for duress would otherwise have. Also, it puts great strain on the notion of reasonableness. Normally, in law, this word implies a value-judgment. The jury cannot be asked whether it was moral for the defendant to give way to the threat; that would be a hard question to answer, and to ask it would largely renounce the decision of the House of Lords in point of policy to allow duress as a defence. There would be the same objection if the jury were asked to consider whether it is politic to allow the defence in the circumstances—whether allowing the defence might lead to an increase in terrorism. Policy questions were decided in *D.P.P. for Northern Ireland v. Lynch*,[58] and there is nothing left under this head for the consideration of the jury.

The direction does not explicitly require a threat, but presumably the circumstances envisaged are those in which there would be at least an implied threat.[59] (In view of the absence of evidence of a threat in *R. v. Graham* it is surprising that the Court of Appeal did not require the jury to be expressly directed on the point). The requirement of reasonable firmness would usually mean that the person who thinks he is being threatened by implication must if possible put his fears to the test by trying to temporize, arguing with the person making the demand if this can be done with safety. He will then discover whether or not he is under threat.

25–024 **Does the seriousness of the offence committed tell us anything about the reasonableness of failing to resist the coercer's threat?** On one side of the scales there is the threat of serious injury or death for the defendant. On the other side of the scales there are offences ranging from innocuous conduct such as shoplifting right through to aircraft hijacking. (Of course, murder and some forms of treason are not put on the scales, as the defence does not cover them). Serious harm is serious harm regardless of who the victim is, but serious harm itself can gradate. It would be one thing to threaten to cut off the end of a person's finger and another to threaten to blind a person for life by throwing acid in her eyes.[60]

---

[57] The phrase is evidently an echo of Lord Diplock's opinion in *R. v. Camplin* [1978] A.C. 705, the provocation case. But Lord Diplock put in an objective criterion ("having the power of self-control to be expected of an ordinary person") of which there is no analogue in the model direction in *R. v. Graham* [1982] 1 W.L.R. 294.

[58] [1975] A.C. 653.

[59] Previous authorities assumed that there must be a threat, express or implied. No express threat was uttered in *D.P.P. for Northern Ireland v. Lynch*, but the person who gave the order was a ruthless gunman, and the manner of his instructions indicated that he would tolerate no disobedience. Cf. [1975] A.C. 653 at 679B, C. There was therefore evidence from which the threat could be implied; but this was a totally different case from *R. v. Graham*, where evidence of a threat or even an instruction appears to have been completely lacking.

[60] This example is not as fictitious as it may sound. See Myles Burke, "Acid attack model talks about recovery," (London: *The Telegraph*, 20 October 2009), where V was "left in a critical condition when her ex-boyfriend raped her and then arranged for another to throw sulphuric acid on her. The acid burned through four layers of skin and left her blinded in one eye."

Clearly, a person is likely to yield very quickly to avoid being permanently blinded. In other cases the serious harm will be more general such as broken bones resulting from an aggravated assault. In such cases the coerced party might withstand the assault, if it means avoiding committing a particularly gross offence such as raping his or her own child.

Should a person be required to withstand even the most serious injury to avoid committing a horrendous crime?   There is no such requirement because the defence is available if the defendant's will was overborne, unless he commits murder or treason.[61]   **25–025**

State v. B.H.[62] provides us with a disturbing and utterly shocking example. In that case a man forced his wife to have sexual intercourse with their seven-year-old son. He did not threaten to kill her, but he threatened to cause her serious injury. Arguably, a man of reasonable firmness and even some women of reasonable firmness would rather suffer serious injury than cause their child to suffer in this way. But the coerced party was not a woman of reasonable firmness, since she had battered woman's syndrome.

Many women might not yield to the threat, because they would perhaps not want to cause their child to endure such a horrendous experience. Forcing a mother to have sex with her own child would not only have long-term (damaging) psychological effects for her, but also long-term (damaging) psychological effects for the child. In *State v. B.H.*,[63] the husband had his hands around the coerced party's neck and was squeezing as he made his threat, and the coerced party had been physically and mentally abused by him for years, so a similarly situated woman sharing her characteristics would most likely have yielded to the threat.

What is clear is that when the offence is trivial it will be much easier for the defendant to raise the defence of duress, because on the other side of the scales the weights are always heavy. Those weights are serious injury and death. A person of reasonable firmness is likely to yield to the threat if he is being asked to commit some trivial crime, if it means avoiding death or serious injury. In some cases the courts have held that the crime committed must be proportionate to the threat.[64] But a proportionality analysis adds little, because the only crimes that are   **25–026**

---

[61] Cf. *Abbott v. The Queen* [1977] A.C. 755 at 773 where Lord Edmund-Davies said: "But the realistic view is that, the more dreadful the [crime], the heavier the evidential burden of an accused advancing such a plea, and the stronger and more irresistible the duress needed before it could be regarded as affording any defence." His Lordship is merely suggesting that the evidence will have to be strong in such cases, but it is not clear why, because surely the opposite would be the case. Surely, the fact that a mother rapes her own child suggests she must have been under enormous pressure!

[62] 834 A.2d 1063 (2003).

[63] 834 A.2d 1063 (2003).

[64] See *R. v. Martin* (1989) 88 Cr. App. R. 343. In *Bayley v. Police* (2007) 99 S.A.S.R. 413 at 427-428, Gray J. said: "Assuming there was an imminent peril, a defendant must have honestly believed on reasonable grounds that it was necessary for him to do the acts which are alleged to constitute the offence in order to avoid the threatened peril. That test will, as a matter of fact, not be met if it is proved that the conduct was disproportionate to the threat. A response is not proportionate to the threat if there are reasonable grounds for believing there were alternative courses of action available." See also *R. v. Ruzic* [2001] 1 S.C.R. 687.

considered to be a disproportionate response are murder and some forms of treason! Hence, any lesser crime is regarded as a proportionate way of avoiding the threat of death or serious injury.

Nonetheless, the proportionality principle might make a difference in special cases.[65] In *R. v. Abdul-Hussain*[66] the defendants hijacked a Sudanese Airbus on a flight from Khartoum to Amman and forced it to fly to England, because they thought that the Sudanese authorities would send them back to their own country, Iraq. They alleged that were they to be sent back to Iraq they would have been imprisoned and tortured. During the flight from Africa to England the hijackers seized an airhostess and threatened her with a knife and produced a grenade and threatened to blow up the aircraft. The hijackers also held a knife to the captain's back for most of the flight. Coupled with this, one of the hijackers told his accomplice to blow up the plane if anyone moved. The aircraft had to land at Larnaca in Cyprus to refuel. When it landed in Cyprus the cabin crew asked the hijackers to release the women and children, but the hijacker refused to release them. While some of the forgoing acts might have been necessary for the hijackers to achieve their aim of fleeing from Sudan, forcing the women and children to fly from Cyprus to Britain in terrifying conditions was clearly an unreasonable and disproportionate way for them to avoid the very remote threats that were allegedly being made by the Iraqi regime. Even if we accept that it was reasonable for them to fly from Cyprus to Britain to avoid imminent harm,[67] it was not reasonable for them to take the women and children on the second part of the flight given the terrifying conditions. A proportionate response would have been merely to take the flight crew and a few of the male passengers.

25.5. THE SUBJECT OF THE THREAT

25–027   It was noted above that Lord Bingham said the threat should be directed against the defendant, his immediate family, or "someone close to him." In *R. v. Shayler*[68] it was held that: "the evil must be directed towards the defendant or a person or persons for whom he has responsibility or, we would add, persons for whom the situation makes him responsible." This will not only cover immediate blood relatives, but also a *de facto* wife/husband and step-children.

---

[65] Of course, proportionality plays a greater role in the defence of necessity, because it involves a balancing of the harms.

[66] [1999] Crim. L.R. 570.

[67] Cyprus is clearly a safe country where the hijackers could have disembarked and claimed refugee status. There was no threat of imminent harm in Cyprus; and arguably none in Sudan. If the threat has dissipated, then the defence is not available. See *D.P.P. v. Tomkinson* [2001] R.T.R. 38; *Crown Prosecution Service v. Brown* [2007] EWHC 3274; *D.P.P. v. Jones* [1990] R.T.R. 33.

[68] [2001] 1 W.L.R. 2206 at 2226 *per* Lord Woolf C.J. Approved by Lord Bingham in *R. v. Z* [2005] 2 A.C. 467 at 490-491. See also the original statement by Rose L.J. in *R. v. Abdul-Hussain* [1999] Crim. L.R. 570.

Does "someone close to him" cover his best friend?   There is no reason why   **25–028**
it should not cover his best friend. Most people would feel compelled to act to
prevent a close friend from being seriously injured or killed.[69]

Is it enough that he yields to the threat to protect a stranger from being   **25–029**
killed or seriously injured?   There is no reason why not. Many people would
feel compelled to act to prevent a stranger from being seriously injured or
killed.[70] If the courts hold that duress only counts when the defendant yields to a
threat to protect a family member or a close friend, the law may produce absurd
results. There could be situations where a person commits a crime to protect
people he has never met before. Such a person should not be punished for acting
to prevent a stranger from being killed or seriously injured. Most jurisdictions in
the United States do not require the coerced party to be closely connected to the
person who is the target of the threat.[71]

In *U.S. v. Haney*,[72] the United States Court of Appeals (Tenth Circuit) said:

> "It is true that, as the government observes, most cases of third-party duress involve familial
> relationships between the defendant and the threatened individual; however, neither logic nor
> practicality supports such a 'family relationship' limitation. Returning to our basic illustration
> of the duress defence above, why should it matter whether C (who jaywalks in order to prevent
> A from shooting B) enjoys a family relationship with B; in either case, permitting C to jaywalk
> avoids the greater social harm."

The requirement that the threat be made against someone close to the
defendant or against someone for "whom he has responsibility or ... for whom
the situation makes him responsible," is unprincipled and unduly restrictive. The
test of whom the defendant "reasonably regards himself as responsible for" is too
vague. One professor might feel responsible for his adult students, and another
might not. Similarly, one adult student might regard himself as responsible for
protecting his professor, and countless others might not. One hairdresser might
feel responsible for a regular customer, but countless others might not. However,

---

[69] It has been held that a boyfriend or girlfriend counts, see *R. v. Wright* [2000] Crim. L.R. 510.
Obviously, people are closer to their girlfriend than they are to their best friends, but it seems
plausible to allow the defence in both cases. In *R. v. Conway* [1989] Q.B. 290, D acted to protect a
passenger in his car, and this was held to be sufficient.

[70] Lord Woolf C.J. rightly asserts that it should cover "the situation where the threat is made to set off
a bomb unless the defendant performs the unlawful act. The defendant may not have had any previous
connection with those who would be injured by the bomb but the threat itself creates the defendant's
responsibility for those who will be at risk if he does not give way to the threat." *R. v. Shayler* [2001]
1 W.L.R. 2206 at 2224.

[71] *U.S. v. Haney*, 287 F.3d 1266 at 1271-1272 (2002).

[72] 287 F.3d 1266 at 1271-1272 (2002). The court goes on to note: "Not only is the government's
'family members only' limitation unprincipled, it is unworkable. Under the government's proposed
limitation, the duress defence would presumably remain available where B and C enjoy a mother-son
or husband-wife relationship but not where B and C merely find themselves seated next to each other
on a public bus. A family relationship, however, is somewhat difficult to identify: what of a couple
engaged to be married, an aunt and nephew, in-laws, distant cousins who know each other well,
siblings who have never met, unmarried co-habitants, *etc.*? The government's failure to offer guidance
on these issues is surely a product of the unprincipled line drawn by the 'family relationship' test. ...
And, again, how are any of these relationships meaningfully distinct, for purposes of application of
the duress defence, from the relationship between two close friends, long-time roommates, work
colleagues, a teacher and student, *etc.*?"

the courts are not likely to reject the defence in genuine cases where people have been forced to act to save a stranger or acquaintance[73] from being seriously injured or killed.

25.6. THE IMMINENT PERIL REQUIREMENT

25–030 If a person when threatened is able make resistance or to flee from the wrongdoer, he must of course do so rather than give way to duress. The facts must be such that there was no way (known to the defendant) of avoiding the threat without committing the infraction or one of greater gravity. If on the uncontradicted evidence the defendant could have made his escape, then, on principle, there is no evidence of duress for the consideration of the jury—though the trial judge may think it safer to leave this question to the jury, while directing them upon it.

Before the surprisingly indulgent decision in *R. v. Hudson*[74] it was thought that the defence was not open if the defendant could seek police protection, whether or not the police were able to defend him effectively. Otherwise, a terrorist could confer standing immunity on any timorous citizen for doing terrible deeds.

In *R. v. Hudson*, two girls, aged 19 and 17, committed perjury when giving evidence at a criminal trial, because (they said) of threats of injury made before the trial and the presence in court during it of one of those who had uttered the threats. They were indicted for perjury. The trial judge declined to leave the defence of duress to the jury, on the ground that the girls were in a court of law when they committed the offence, and protection was readily available for them if they had asked for it. They were convicted. The Court of Appeal, however, took the view that the defence ought to have been left to the jury, and the conviction was quashed.[75]

25–031 The decision seems to have owed more to the judges' innate chivalry than to a steely-hearted consideration of what public policy required. The girls could have sought police protection immediately after giving evidence; and although they might have thought, with good reason, that the police would not be able to shield them indefinitely, yet that consideration should not be sufficient to support the defence. Notwithstanding *R. v. Hudson*,[76] in *R. v. Z*, Lord Bingham (with whom Lords Steyn, Rodger, and Brown concurred) said:[77]

---

[73] See for example, *R. v. Conway* [1989] Q.B. 290.

[74] [1971] 2 Q.B. 202.

[75] *Contra, R. v. Taonis* [1974] Crim. L.R. 331, where the Court of Appeal assumed that the traditional restriction was valid, though the appeal before them was only against sentence.

[76] In *R. v. Z* [2005] 2 A.C. 467 at 494-495, Lord Bingham said: "*R. v. Hudson* [1971] 2 Q.B. 202 ... was described by Professor Glanville Williams, *Textbook of Criminal Law*, (London: Stevens & Sons, 2nd edn. 1983), at 631, as 'an indulgent decision,' and it has in my opinion had the unfortunate effect of weakening the requirement that execution of a threat must be reasonably believed to be imminent and immediate if it is to support a plea of duress."

[77] [2005] 2 A.C. 467 at 494-495. See also *R. v. Cole* [1994] Crim. L.R. 582; *D.P.P. v. Mullally* [2006] EWHC 3448.

"It should ... be made clear to juries that if the retribution threatened against the defendant or his family or a person for whom he reasonably feels responsible is not such as he reasonably expects to follow immediately or almost immediately on his failure to comply with the threat, there may be little if any room for doubt that he could have taken evasive action, whether by going to the police or in some other way, to avoid committing the crime with which he is charged."

In *R. v. N*[78] the Court of Appeal said:

"[T]he defence of duress ... excuses an offender who genuinely and reasonably believes that he has no escape from death or grave injury at the hands of another unless he commits the crime in question. ... The judge's direction in the present case conforms with Lord Bingham's statement in *R. v. Z* [2005] 2 A.C. 467 at 494. *R. v. Abdul-Hussain*,[79] properly understood, is nothing to the contrary. *R. v. Hudson* was a case decided on its own facts. Any different understanding of *R. v. Abdul-Hussain* or *R. v. Hudson* would as we see it lead to a wholly unjustified extension of the special and particular defence of duress."

Duress should not be allowed as a defence if the defendant had an opportunity to seek official protection. If the threat no longer exists because the defendant has managed to put himself beyond the coercer's reach, the defence will not be available. Therefore, if an intoxicated person is being attacked and decides to speed off in her car, she should stop the car as soon as she is out of danger. If she is caught driving many miles away from where the alleged attack took place, the courts are likely to hold that she was no longer driving to avoid a threat of imminent harm.[80]

The defendant should desist from continuing his offending as soon as he **25–032** reasonably can. It does not matter that his continuation of the offence would not expose others to any danger. In *R. v. Pommell*[81] the defendant was found in his bed with a sub-machine gun. He was charged under section 5(1)(a) of the *Firearms Act 1968* for possessing a firearm without authority. He asserted that he took possession of a firearm during the night to prevent his acquaintance from using it to harm others. It was also contended on his behalf that he intended to give it to the police at daybreak. The Court of Appeal held that the defence of duress of circumstances was open to the defendant in respect of his acquisition of the gun. As to the continued possession of the gun, it was held that he should have desisted from possessing the gun as soon as he reasonably could. This

---

[78] *R. v. N* [2007] EWCA Crim. 3479 paras. 11 and 12.

[79] It is difficult to see where the threat of imminent harm was in *R. v. Abdul-Hussain* [1999] Crim. L.R. 570. As said before, even if the threat of imminent harm was present in Sudan, there was no such threat in Cyprus. The only threat they faced in Sudan was deportation and there was no evidence that deportation was imminent. If the deportation had been imminent, then they might have been able to argue that the only way they could avoid the threat of harm in Iraq was to avoid being deported from Sudan. Similarly, the decision in *R. v. Safi* [2004] 1 Cr. App. R. 157 seems indulgent. The hijackers could have taken refuge in either Kazakhstan or Russia when they landed in those places, but decided to make the additional trip to England. Clearly, the threat of harm ended once they landed in Moscow. It has been reported that individuals from Afghanistan constitute the largest number of successful asylum seekers in Russia. Thus, Russia was a safe country where Safi and is confederates could have sought asylum (see *http://www.unhcr.org/3eb13b4d4.html*).

[80] *D.P.P. v. Tomkinson* [2001] R.T.R. 38; *Crown Prosecution Service v. Brown* [2007] EWHC 3274; *D.P.P. v. Jones* [1990] R.T.R. 33; cf. *D.P.P. v. Bell* (1992) R.T.R. 335.

[81] [1995] 2 Cr. App. R. 607.

means that the defendant should have taken the gun to the police as soon as he took possession of it. Nevertheless, the court said:

> "We accept that in some cases a delay, especially if unexplained, may be such as to make it clear that any duress must have ceased to operate. ... There would then be no reason to leave the issue to the jury. However, the situation does not seem to us to have been sufficiently clear cut to make that an appropriate step in the present case. In the first place, the delay of a few hours overnight might not be regarded as being unduly long and, secondly, the defendant did offer an explanation for it, therefore, in our judgment, the proposed defence should have been left to the jury."[82]

A thornier question arises if a member of the defendant's family is kidnapped and if the defendant is threatened that the victim will be killed or seriously injured if he does not commit some criminal act.[83] The defendant goes to the police, but obviously the police cannot prevent the carrying out of the threat, so the defendant does as the thug tells him. The Law Commission proposed that the defence should be excluded, by means of a provision that:

> "the fact that any official protection which might have been available in the circumstances would or might not have been effective to prevent the harm threatened is immaterial."[84]

This is a severe rule, but it is required by public policy.[85] Otherwise the possibility arises of a person being free in society, programmed to commit a list of heinous crimes without legal sanction because a relative of his has been kidnapped. The recognition of such a rule might even increase kidnappings, and it would probably increase the readiness of the person threatened to comply with the demands.

25–033 Nevertheless, the defence might be allowed in extreme cases where there is clear evidence that it would be almost impossible for the police to intervene to protect the hostage. In *R. v. Ajami*, [86] Ms Ajami, a 24-year-old university graduate, and her family were Lebanese immigrants living in Canada. Ms Ajami was based in Canada but her close relatives, including her sister and her uncle, still resided in Lebanon. Ms Ajami fraudulently obtained a $45,000 automobile from a Mercedes-Benz dealership. The automobile was recovered from a shipping container at the port of Montreal before it could be shipped to Lebanon. She was charged with a fraud offence under the law of that province. She admitted committing the offence, but raised the defence of duress. In her evidence she asserted that she committed the offence "because members of her family in Lebanon were being held hostage and that their captors, Karim Ghandour and his son Kamal, threatened to kill them unless she committed this offence as well as other crimes...."[87]

---

[82] *R. v. Pommell* [1995] 2 Cr. App. R. 607 at 616.

[83] See for example, *R.I. Recreation Center v. Aetna Casualty & Surety Co.*, 177 F.2d 603 (1949); *U.S. v. Alicea*, 837 F.2d 103 (1988); *R. v. Hurley* [1967] V.R. 526.

[84] Law Commission, *Criminal Law: Report on Defences of General Application*, (London: H.M.S.O., No. 83, 1977) Pt.II.

[85] Cf. *R. v. Ajami* [2010] O.N.C.J. 284 at para. 38 *et passim*.

[86] [2010] O.N.C.J. 284.

[87] *R. v. Ajami* [2010] O.N.C.J. 284 at para. 4.

Kamal Ghandour turned up at Ms Ajami's family home in Canada without warning and was accompanied by Ajami's sister, Nicole, who had been living in Lebanon.[88] Ms Ajami's sister was apparently in a distressed and agitated state when they arrived. Ghandour told Ms Ajami that her uncle, Jean Ajami, was being held hostage in southern Lebanon by his confederates. He threatened that the uncle would be killed unless Ms Ajami and her family committed a number of property offences to raise ransom money. Ghandour told Ms Ajami that he was connected to Hezbollah[89] and that he had contacts within the Canadian police force. The defence team called Det. Kelly Labonte of the Ontario Provincial Police Anti-Terrorism Section, Intelligence Unit, who attested the Ghandours were known criminals who had connections to Hezbollah.

The court allowed the defence of duress. On the question of whether Ms Ajami had a safe means of escape, it was held that she did not. Even though she could have easily called the police from the car dealer's office or from her apartment, she feared if she did her uncle would be killed in Lebanon. It was held the defendant had reasonable grounds for believing that going to the police would not provide her with a means of escape. Schwarzl J. said:

"Her belief was later reinforced in Lebanon when she came to reasonably believe that the Ghandours had the Lebanese police in their pockets. … I find her subsequent knowledge and experience in Lebanon consistent with her concerns about Ghandour's ties to police in Canada. … Consequently, I am satisfied that Ms. Ajami honestly and reasonably felt that she had no safe means of escaping the clutches of the Ghandours and was compelled to participate in this crime against her will."[90]

Surely Ajami could have called the Ontario Provincial Police Anti-Terrorism Section, the Royal Canadian Mounted Police or the Canadian Security Intelligence Service, when the fraud was being committed.   The judge held 25–034 that the defendant had reasonable grounds for believing that these agencies were not fully independent of the police in Lebanon where Ghandour had contacts. The decision seems wrong on the facts, because a reasonable person would not believe that the likes of Ghandour would have contacts in all the police and intelligence agencies in Canada. It is also doubtful that Ajami had reasonable grounds for believing that the Canadian intelligence agencies would inform Ghandour or random offices in the Lebanon police force of her complaint. (A reasonable person would most likely believe that the Canadian agencies would work with Interpol to ensure that Ghandours' contacts in Lebanon would not get a tip off.)

How could a reasonable person believe that an agency such as the Ontario Provincial Police Anti-Terrorism Section would assist a terrorist such as Ghandour? A stronger argument would have been that the defendant had reasonable grounds for believing that the Canadian police would do their best to protect her uncle, but that that would not be enough to save him. She seems to have had reasonable grounds for believing that the Canadian police would not be

---

[88] It is worth noting that the defendant had never met Kamal Ghandour before he arrived at her family home; and that there was no evidence of her having any other association with the likes of Ghandour.
[89] "Hezbollah is a recognized, and highly entrenched, terrorist group which has full control in southern Lebanon." *R. v. Ajami* [2010] O.N.C.J. 284 at paras. 14-17.
[90] *R. v. Ajami* [2010] O.N.C.J. 284 at para. 39, 41.

able to do much to protect her uncle, because he was being held by terrorists in a foreign country. Not only was he being held in a foreign country, but he was being held in a country where Hezbollah had enormous influence and where Ghandour had contacts in the police force. *R. v. Ajami* is an extreme case, because it seemed that it would have been virtually impossible for the Canadian police to protect the hostage. Ajami had reasonable grounds for believing that reporting the matter to the Canadian police would not have prevented Ghandour carrying out his threats.[91] Ms Ajami seemed to have had reasonable grounds for believing that she could protect her uncle *only* by committing the fraud.

The English courts will most likely allow the defence in a "hostage" case, if it can be shown that the defendant had reasonable grounds for believing that reporting the matter to the police would not have been enough to stop the threat being carried out.[92]

25–035   **Is it not enough to show that the harm "could" have been inflicted immediately? Ghandour had the means to have her uncle killed instantly, because all Ghandour had to do was send a text message from a mobile telephone to his confederates in Lebanon.**   The threat must be to carry out the threat almost immediately. It is true that the threat could have been carried out almost immediately, but the threat was not to kill the uncle in the immediate future. Ghandour was threatening to have the uncle killed in the future, but only if Ajami failed to carry out the fraud in the future.

Suppose Ghandour had arrived at Ms Ajami's apartment and said: "You are going to accompany me to a car dealership where you are going to use fraud to obtain a car; if you do not, I will send a text message to my associates in Lebanon and your uncle will be killed instantly." The defence of duress would be available in these circumstances, because it would not be possible for Ms Ajami to call the police or to warn the car dealership in such circumstances. Since Ghandour would have her under guard she would not be able to call the police or warn the car dealer without risking him pushing the send button on his mobile telephone. One wrong move and Ghandour would send an SMS to his associates to have her uncle killed instantly. This is starkly different to the situation where the coerced party has ample opportunity to make a private call to the police.[93]

---

[91] Cf. *R. v. Hudson* [1971] 2 Q.B. 202, where it was not virtually impossible for the police to prevent the girls from being beaten; in that case there was only a remote risk that the coercer would have carried out his threats if the police had been informed of his plans. He was a local thug who could easily be monitored by a modern police force.

[92] The High Court of Australia has held that the defence should be allowed in such cases, if the defendant can satisfy the evidential burden. See *Taiapa v. The Queen* (2009) 240 C.L.R. 95 at 109.

[93] See *R.I. Recreation Center v. Aetna Casualty & Surety Co.*, 177 F.2d 603 (1949); *R. v. Le (No 3)* [2010] N.S.W.D.C. 37.

25.7. CAUSATION AND THE NOMINATED CRIME

The defence is available if the defendant would not have committed the nominated crime "but for" the threat.[94] Did the defendant commit the offence only because of the threats? It has been held that the threat of serious injury or death must provide the sole impetus for the defendant's offending.[95] In *R. v. Valderrama-Vega*,[96] the defendant imported controlled drugs because his wife and his family had been threatened by a Mafia-type organization with serious injury or death and he had been threatened with disclosure of his homosexuality. His poor financial position also incentivized him to commit the offence. His conviction was upheld because the threat against his family *per se* was not the only reason for his offending. The defence of duress requires the defendant's will to be overborne by threats of death or serious injury, not by a combination of factors.

25–036

This seems to be a severe rule, it might be better to have a rule that allows the defence where the defendant can show that he would not have committed the nominated crime "but for" the coercer's threat. If the threat of injury or death *per se* is sufficient to overbear the defendant's will, then it should not matter that he was also influenced by other factors. In *R. v. Valderrama-Vega*, the evidence suggested that all these factors influenced the defendant to commit the nominated crime. No doubt, a major consideration for Valderrama-Vega was his poor financial position. Therefore, the decision seems right in principle. Valderrama-Vega might have been willing to commit the nominated crime to solve his financial problems and to prevent his closet homosexuality from being disclosed. It was not clear that he would not have committed the nominated crime "but for" the fact that his wife and his family had been threatened by a Mafia-type organization with serious injury or death.

Need the villain have instructed the defendant to commit the offence? Suppose the defendant, in fear of the villain, simply committed the offence in his endeavour to get away? On principle, the offence must be one expressly or impliedly ordered by the villain, the order being backed up by his threat. (Or the defendant must have believed that.) Of course, in cases involving duress of circumstances, there will be no express or implied command for the defendant to commit a nominated crime. Rather, the defendant may commit a range of crimes (speeding, criminal damage and so on) to escape the threatened harm. In such cases the source of the threat may be manmade such as where a person fires a gun at the defendant and this causes him to speed off in a car or break into a building to seek shelter. As we will see, the threats may also arise because of a natural event, such as where the defendant takes another's motorcar without permission

25–037

---

[94] See *R. v. Valderrama-Vega* [1985] Crim. L.R. 220, where D had a number of reasons for acting including threats that his family would be seriously injured and that his homosexuality would be disclosed. He also was under enormous financial pressure. The evidence seemed to suggest that all these factors influenced the defendant to commit the nominated crime. (No doubt, a major consideration for the defendant was the fact that by importing the drugs he would be able to make some money to pay his bills).

[95] *R. v. Valderrama-Vega* [1985] Crim. L.R. 220; *The Queen v. Fisher* [2004] EWCA Crim. 1190.

[96] [1985] Crim. L.R. 220.

to escape from an emerging tsunami. (The latter might also be treated as a case of necessity, rather than one of duress of circumstances.)

An illustration of this limit upon the defence of duress in its pure form is the extraordinary case of *R. v. Jones*.[97] Two plain-clothes police officers went to investigate Jones, who was sitting in a parked car, at 1:20 a.m. Thinking that they were thugs Jones drove through the built-up area at up to 50 m.p.h., going through traffic lights on red, and ending up outside a police station where he dashed inside for "safety." He was convicted of dangerous driving and did not appeal. He did not have a defence of duress, because he had not been ordered to drive dangerously, and did not think he had been. He did not have the defence of self-defence, since the defence is presumably available only in respect of acts done against an aggressor, or one thought to be an aggressor. Dangerous driving affected the public at large.

25–038   **So why was it not a case of necessity or duress of circumstances?**   It would now be treated as a case of duress of circumstances. Unlike duress in its pure form, duress of circumstances would apply.[98] Nevertheless, the doctrine had not been developed in 1963.

25–039   **Are you telling me that if the case is not one of duress of circumstances cases, the defendant will only be able to rely on the defence of duress if he is ordered to commit a particular crime and it is that crime that he commits?** As a matter of justice the defence should only be available where the defendant commits a crime that he has been directly coerced to commit.[99] In *R. v. Cole*[100] the defendant robbed two building societies. His defence was that he was unable to repay moneylenders who had threatened him, his girlfriend and child. The trial judge ruled that duress was only available where the defendant commits the crime that he was ordered to commit. Cole was not ordered to rob a bank; he was merely told that he and his family would be seriously harmed if he did not come up with money.

The Court of Appeal said:[101]

> "Cole could not rely on duress by threats since the moneylenders had not stipulated that he commit robbery to meet their demands. Imminent peril, which was a necessary pre-condition to the defence of duress properly arising, was also lacking."

The court was influenced by the fact that the imminent harm requirement had not been met. Cole had ample opportunity to seek the assistance of the police. The rule does allow for some leeway, however. The courts are likely to hold that the defence is available if the defendant commits a crime within a range of crimes

---

[97] (1963) *The Times*, December 18.

[98] On analogous facts in *R. v. Conway* [1989] Q.B. 290 the defence of duress of circumstances was allowed.

[99] He might argue that he had to commit some crime as a matter of necessity to pay his drug debts, but such an argument should be rejected by the courts. Not only has he created the conditions of his own defence, but such a defence would open the floodgates for many unworthy defendants. Cf. *Southwark L.B.C. v. Williams* [1971] Ch. 734; *R. v. Ali* [1995] Crim. L.R. 303.

[100] [1994] Crim. L.R. 582.

[101] *R. v. Cole* [1994] Crim. L.R. 582.

that the defendant was ordered to commit in alternative of each other. Suppose D is ordered to get money within an hour or else his family will be killed. Suppose he is told that he should either rob someone or pickpocket him. If he commits either robbery or theft the defence should be available, because he commits one of the nominated crimes.[102] It will be necessary to show that the defendant only committed one of the nominated crimes. In most cases, it will not be necessary to show that the defendant targeted a nominated victim. For example, if he is ordered to rob a bank on the Strand, it should not matter which bank he robs.

Suppose gang members threaten to kill a passerby unless he helps them to commit a robbery. It would be incongruous to allow the defence if he avoids the threat by assisting the robbery and to disallow it if he were to escape the threat by stealing a car and speeding off, would it not?   Yes. But clearly the defence of duress of circumstances would protect his conduct in the latter situation. *R. v. Cole*[103] can be contradistinguished, since it was not a case of duress of circumstances. Cole had plenty of time to seek the protection of the police, and that is what he should have done.

25–040

25.8.   VOLUNTARY EXPOSURE TO THE THREAT OF COERCION

The defence will not be available if the defendant voluntarily put himself in a position where he knew or ought to have known that the coercer might force him to commit a crime by threatening to kill him or cause him serious injury.[104]

25–041

Consider the terrorist organization with a single boss and an iron discipline. Every member carries out orders, knowing that if he refuses he will be shot or kneecapped. If you allow duress as a defence, only the boss can be punished.   The defence is not open to people who voluntarily expose themselves to the risk of being coerced into committing an offence. A clear example is where a person voluntarily joins a criminal enterprise.[105] In *R. v. Sharpe*[106] the defendant voluntarily joined a gang of armed robbers and participated in a robbery which resulted in the gang leader killing a postmaster. The defendant was convicted of manslaughter and raised the defence of duress. Sharpe asserted that he wanted to pull out of the robbery, but continued to participate because the gang leader pointed a gun at him and threatened to blow

25–042

---

[102] Cf. *R. v. Ali* [1995] Crim. L.R. 303, where the defence was not available because he created the conditions of his own defence, he caused the coercer to coerce him by stealing the coercer's drugs and by refusing to repay him for the value of the drugs. He chose to associate with dangerous drug dealers and must have foreseen the consequences of stealing drugs from such persons.

[103] [1994] Crim. L.R. 582.

[104] *R. v. Z* [2005] 2 A.C. 467.

[105] *R. v. Shepherd* (1987) 86 Cr. App. R. 47; *R. v. Sharpe* [1987] Q.B. 853.

[106] [1987] Q.B. 853. For a wider discussion of defences that may be excluded where the defendant voluntarily brings about the conditions for invoking the defence, see Paul H. Robinson, "Causing the Conditions of One's Own Defence: A Study in the Limits of Theory in Criminal Law Doctrine," (1985) 71 *Va. L. Rev.* 1.

his head off. It was held that the defence of duress was not available, because the defendant had voluntarily joined the criminal gang knowing that its members could force him to commit an offence.

Similarly, if a defendant joins an organization[107] which he knows or ought to know engages in criminal activity, the defence will not be available to him if the members of that organization force him to commit an offence. The defendant has voluntarily exposed himself to the risk of being coerced into offending.[108] If the defendant chooses to associate with a motorcycle gang that he knows engages in criminal activity, he will not be able to raise the defence of duress if its members force him to commit a crime.[109] It does not matter that the gang's *raison d'être* is not solely to engage in criminal activity. It is enough that they from time to time engage in such conduct and that the defendant knew that or ought to have known that he might be forced to commit a criminal act of some kind.

25–043   **Must it be shown that the defendant ought to have foreseen that he would be forced to commit the crime which he in fact committed? Or is it enough to show that he ought to have foreseen he could be forced to commit a criminal act of some kind?**   It would be too much to allow the defence in any case where the defendant did not foresee the "type" of crime he would be asked to commit.[110] A fair balance could be struck by allowing the defence in cases where a reasonable person would not have foreseen that he would be coerced into committing a criminal act of some kind. Nevertheless, in *R. v. Z*, Lord Bingham said:[111]

> "There need not be foresight of coercion to commit crimes, although it is not easy to envisage circumstances in which a party might be coerced to act lawfully."

In *R. v. Ali*[112] the Court of Appeal said:

> "[T]he Judicial Studies Board specimen directions makes clear, the core question is whether the defendant voluntarily put himself in the position in which he foresaw or ought reasonably have foreseen the risk of being subjected to any compulsion by threats of violence. As a matter of fact, threats of violence will almost always be made by persons engaged in a criminal activity; but in our judgment it is the risk of being subjected to compulsion by threats of violence that must be foreseen or foreseeable that is relevant, rather than the nature of the activity in which the threatener is engaged."

---

[107] See *R. v. Fitzpatrick* [1977] N.I. 20.

[108] See also *R. v. Heath* [2000] Crim. L.R. 109; *R. v. Lewis* [1993] 96 Cr. App. R. 41; *R. v. Ali* [1995] Crim. L.R. 303; *R. v. Ali* [2008] EWCA Crim. 716 at para. 12.

[109] In *R. v. Sandham* (2009) 70 C.R. (6th) 203, members of Bandidos Motorcycle Club carried out a number of execution style killings. The killers relied on the assistance of several fellow gang members to carry out the executions. The defence of duress was not available to either the perpetrators or accessories. See also *R. v. Li* [2002] 162 C.C.C. (3d) 360.

[110] *R. v. Z* [2005] 2 A.C. 467 at para. 497-498, overruled *R. v. Baker (No.1)* [1999] 2 Cr. App. R. 335 at 344 where Roch L.J. said: "This again, in our view was a misdirection. What a defendant has to be aware of is the risk that the group might try to coerce him into committing criminal offences of the *type* for which he is being tried by the use of violence or threats of violence."

[111] *R. v. Z* [2005] 2 A.C. 467 at para. 498.

[112] [2008] EWCA Crim. 716 at para. 12.

Judicial Studies Board specimen directions provide guidance for trial judges, but they are not binding law.[113] If *R. v. Ali* were followed, a woman could be barred from raising the defence where her violent partner forces her to commit a crime on the basis that she ought to have foreseen that she might be "subjected to compulsion by threats of violence." *R. v. Ali* holds that if she continues to associate with her violent husband/partner she will be responsible for any crimes that he forces her to commit. You will recall *State v. B.H.*,[114] where B.H.'s husband forced her to engage in sexual activity with their seven-year-old son. B.H. was suffering from battered women's syndrome and thus was aware of the fact that she was associating with someone who might "subject her to compulsion by threats of violence."

Suppose over the years D's husband has forced (under the threat of serious violence) her to do many non-criminal acts such as serving him beer while he watches television. Suppose also that out of the blue he forces her to engage in sexual activity with their son. Is the defence of duress open to her? Not if we apply *R. v. Z* and *R. v. Ali*. Since she knew he had been coercing her by threats of violence to serve him beer (a non-criminal act from her perspective), *R. v. Z* and *R. v. Ali* mean she is liable for any crime that he might force her to commit. 25–044

This surely must be wrong. The better view is that the defence is only excluded where the defendant has recklessly or negligently exposed himself to the risk of being forced to engage in some kind of criminal activity.[115] In *R. v. Z*, Baroness Hale, also referring to the battered woman situation, said:[116]

> "The battered wife knows that she is exposing herself to a risk of unlawful violence if she stays, but she may have no reason to believe that her husband will eventually use her broken will to force her to commit crimes. For the same reason, I would say that it must be foreseeable that duress will be used to compel the person to commit crimes of some sort."

Baroness Hale's statement of the law is preferred. Lord Bingham was right to hold that the prosecution need not prove that the defendant foresaw the exact "type" of offence he might be forced to commit, but was wrong to suggest that the defendant (or a reasonable person) need not foresee that he might be forced to do a criminal act of some kind. It was also made clear in *R. v. Z*, that those who negligently (or recklessly) expose themselves to the risk of being coerced would be barred from raising the defence of duress.

---

[113] *R. v. Ramchurn* [2010] 2 Cr. App. R. 18.

[114] 834 A.2d 1063 (2003).

[115] Section 32 of the *Criminal Code of Western Australia* excludes the defence of duress if: "the threat is made by or on behalf of a person with whom the person under duress is voluntarily associating for the purpose of —(a) doing an act or making an omission of the *kind in fact done* or made by the person under duress; or (b) *prosecuting an unlawful purpose* in which it is reasonably foreseeable such a threat would be made." This is much more restrictive than the U.S. standard, which merely requires negligence as to the probability of being coerced into committing some kind of criminal act.

[116] *R. v. Z* [2005] 2 A.C. 467 at 512.

Given that mere negligence is enough to exclude the defence, the test should be whether the coerced party "[r]ecklessly or negligently placed himself in a situation in which it was probable that he would be forced to commit a criminal act."[117]

25–045   **If a battered woman hasn't the strength of will to leave her coercive husband, would it not be fair to say that her association with the coercer is involuntary. Does she not have a reasonable excuse for risking being coerced into offending?**   In the case of domestic relationships, the defendant should be able to raise the defence of duress. A court in the U.S. has held that such a defendant does not negligently or recklessly expose herself to the risk of being coerced and therefore should be able to raise the defence of duress.[118] A stronger argument would be that she does not voluntarily associate with someone whom she knows or ought to know might force her to commit a criminal act. The fact that she lacks the strength of will to leave her abuser should be enough to provide her with a reasonable excuse for associating with him.[119]

25–046   **Does it matter if the threat resonates from the subject himself?**   If the defendant is the source of the threat against himself then he will not be able to raise the defence of duress.[120] Take the example of the person who is suicidal because he does not like being in prison. In *R. v. Rodger*, the defendants were convicted of breaking prison. They were serving a lengthy sentence for murder and became depressed and suicidal in prison. It was argued on their behalf that they had escaped from prison because they would have committed suicide if they had remained in prison. The Court of Appeal held that the defence was not available unless the "causative feature of the commission of the offence was extraneous to the offender.":

> "These appeals it was solely the suicidal tendencies, the thought processes and the emotions of the offenders themselves which operated as duress. That factor introduced an entirely subjective element not present in the authorities."[121]

It might also be argued that they voluntarily exposed themselves to the risk of developing suicidal tendencies by committing murder, which they must have known would result in a lengthy sentence.

25–047   **Does that mean that if the causative feature of the commission of the offence is not extraneous to the offender the defence will not be available?**   Not necessarily. The court also suggested that if there is a strong objective element that the defence would apply. Therefore, if a person was suffering some immense pain (assuming that amounts to serious injury, if not he will have to raise the

---

[117] That is the standard applied in the U.S., see *U.S. v. Burnes*, 666 F. Supp. 2d 968 (2009); *U.S. v. Gamboa*, 439 F.3d 796 (2006); *U.S. v. Montes*, 602 F.3d 381 (2010).

[118] See *U.S. v. Ceballos*, 593 F.Supp.2d 1054 at 1063 (2009), where it was said: "the Court finds that Defendant has made a *prima facie* case that it was not negligent or reckless for her to be in an abusive relationship where the abuser would later try to force her to commit a crime."

[119] See Baroness Hale's observations in *R. v. Z* [2005] 2 A.C. 467 at 511.

[120] [1998] 1 Cr. App. R. 143.

[121] *R. v. Rodger* [1998] 1 Cr. App. R. 143 at 145.

defence of necessity) that only cannabis can relieve, he should be able to raise the defence unless the defence is excluded by legislation.[122] The objective element could be satisfied by producing compelling medical evidence to show that the person is suffering from a recognized medical condition that is extremely painful, and that cannabis is the *only* effective way to treat that pain.[123]

In the case of duress of circumstances, it would be necessary to satisfy all the other elements of the defence. As for possession of cannabis, the defence would clearly be available if a person was forced at gunpoint to take possession of it. Similarly, the defence might be raised where it can be shown there was no other reasonable alternative available.

Suppose a group of students go camping in the Lake District and one falls down a ravine. Let us assume that he is badly injured and is in immense pain. Suppose that the students have no painkillers and it is a three-hour walk back to their motor vehicle. It just happens that one of the students has some cannabis with him, which he offers to the injured party to help relieve his pain.

Would the injured party be able to argue the he was compelled to use the cannabis to relieve his immense pain? In these circumstances he should be able to raise the defence of duress as long as he can satisfy the "moral involuntariness" and "imminent harm" requirements, since there seems to be no lawful alternative available.[124] It is also worth noting that he was not blameworthy in bringing about the conditions that caused him to rely on the cannabis as a form of pain relief.

25.9. DURESS OF CIRCUMSTANCES

If the reason for allowing the defence of duress is the unlikelihood that the law's threats will be effective on a person who is wrongfully threatened with death or serious injury, the same reason should support a defence where the duress arises not from a direct human threat, but from pressure of circumstances. The circumstances may be an act of nature or may be manmade. If D starts shooting at V and as a result V commits criminal damage by breaking into a house to take refuge, the circumstances that force him to commit criminal damage are manmade. If D takes a motor vehicle without authority to escape from a village because he knows it will be engulfed by a tsunami within 20 minutes, the

25–048

---

[122] In *R. v. Quayle* [2005] 1 W.L.R. 3642 at 3675-3676, it was said: "The necessitous medical use on an individual basis which is at the root of the defences suggested by all the appellants … is in conflict with the purpose and effect of the legislative scheme. First, no such use is permitted under the present legislation, even on doctor's prescription, except in the context of the ongoing trials for medical research purposes. Secondly, the defences involve the proposition that it is lawful for unqualified individuals to prescribe cannabis to themselves as patients or to assume the role of unqualified doctors by obtaining it and prescribing and supplying it to other individual 'patients.'" See also *R. v. Altham* [2006] 1 W.L.R. 3287.

[123] Some U.S. states have accepted such a defence, see *State v. Otis*, 151 Wash. App. 572 (2009); *State v. Hastings*, 118 Idaho 854 (1990). See also the *Compassionate Use Act 1996* (CUA) as discussed in *People v. Windus*, 81 Cal. Rptr. 3d 227 (2008). See also *City of Garden Grove v. Superior Court*, 157 Cal. App. 4th 355 (2007). Cf. *State v. Poling*, 207 W. Va. 299, (2000) where the defence was unavailable in West Virginia, because the legislation treated it as a controlled substance and provided no express defence for medical use.

[124] See *R. v. Quayle* [2005] 1 W.L.R. 3642 at 3676.

circumstances that force him to take the vehicle are created by a natural event. Therefore, this is another way of looking at some (by no means all) cases of necessity, and it should be a valid argument even if the courts reject the defence of necessity. The defence has been called duress of circumstances.[125] It operates not theoretically as a justification (as necessity is) but as an excuse, similar to the excuse of duress in the pure sense.[126] This may be more palatable to some people on facts like those in *R. v. Dudley*,[127] where a moralist may be unwilling to accord a justification but will accord an excuse. (D's will is overborne).

The defence of duress of circumstances was first recognized in *R. v. Willer*.[128] It has since been developed in a number of decisions.[129] The requirements for the defence are the same as those that have been developed under the traditional doctrine of duress: (1) the circumstances must threaten death or serious injury; (2) the defendant must have reasonable grounds for believing that the circumstances are such that he could be killed or seriously injured and for believing it was necessary for him to commit a crime to avoid the threat; (3) the harm must be imminent; and (4) the offence must be committed *only* to avoid the threat.

The core difference between duress in the pure sense and duress of circumstances is that the threat need not have a human source. Where there is no human source, there is no need to show that the defendant was ordered to commit a particular crime. Similarly, if the threatening circumstances are created by a human source such as where a person starts firing a gun at the defendant, there is no need to show that the gunman also ordered the defendant to commit a nominated crime. If the defendant steals a motor vehicle to avoid being shot, it is enough to show that the defendant committed the crime to avoid the threatened harm. In *R. v. Conway*[130] the defendant was in the same state of fear as if he had been ordered by a thug at gunpoint to drive at that speed. So it was decided that the law should not distinguish between traditional cases of duress and such a case of compulsion of circumstances.

25–049 **Should the defence be extended to all crimes?** The defendant may commit any crime (apart from murder, attempted murder and some forms of treason), if he had reasonable grounds for believing that it was necessary for him to commit the crime to avoid the threatened harm. Such a defence is recognized in the statutory law of a number of countries.[131] The Commonwealth of Australia has

---

[125] *R. v. Shayler* [2001] 1 W.L.R. 2206 at 2224.

[126] Duress in the pure sense involves direct commands: D1 commands D2 to commit crime X, and threatens death or serious injury to get D2 to follow his command.

[127] (1884) 14 Q.B.D. 273.

[128] (1986) 83 Cr. App. R. 225.

[129] *R. v. Conway* [1989] Q.B. 290 at 297; *R. v. Martin* (1989) 88 Cr. App. R. 343; *R. v. Pommell* [1995] 2 Cr. App. R. 607; *R. v. Shayler* [2001] 1 W.L.R. 2206.

[130] [1989] Q.B. 290.

[131] Cf. section 25 of the *Criminal Code* of Western Australia, which provides: "Subject to the express provisions of this Code relating to acts done upon compulsion or provocation or in self-defence, a person is not criminally responsible for an act or omission done or made under such circumstances of sudden or extraordinary emergency that an ordinary person possessing ordinary power of self-control could not reasonably be expected to act otherwise." In *Johnson v. Western Australia* (2009) 194 A. Crim. R. 470 at 494 the Court of Appeal of the Supreme Court of Western Australia noted: "The

provided for a defence of sudden or extraordinary emergency in its Criminal Code.[132] In *Tran v. The Commonwealth*, Cowdroy J. said:[133]

> "There can be no doubt that the Criminal Code was intended to provide a principled and logical analytical regime for Commonwealth criminal law and thus substantially remove inconsistencies found in the common law. For example, the defence of necessity at common law did not apply to murder: see *R. v. Dudley and Stephens* (1884) 14 Q.B.D. 273. However, the defence of sudden or extraordinary emergency is not so limited in the Criminal Code and it applies to all Commonwealth offences."

Suppose that in the *Mignonette's* boat there was an armed man who threatened to shoot Dudley if he did not hold the cabin boy while his throat was cut. Dudley might have a defence in some jurisdictions if he complied with the demand.[134] The reason why he would be allowed the defence (if it applied to murder)[135] is that he cannot be expected to resist.

- Cases of involuntary "aggression" may be treated in the same way. The notion of an involuntary aggressor would include the mountaineer whose weight is dragging another to his death (where the rope may be cut), and other instances where it is the existence of the victim that is specifically creating the danger to the person who kills him. This might be extended to Bacon's suppositional case about the plank.[136]
- The same might possibly apply in a variant of the plank case, where a swimmer dislodges the swimmer who is in possession of the plank. It is not a case of necessity (since there is an equality of evil),[137] or of self-defence; but an excuse might be allowed, on the principle *sauve qui peut*,[138] because legal regulation seems hopeless.[139]

The examples are distinguishable from general cases of necessity in that they involve fear of death or serious injury, and do not necessarily involve a choice of

---

defence recognised in section 25 applies generally to offences against the criminal law of Western Australia. Section 25 is not confined to specific offences or categories of offences." The other code states in Australia also have a defence of "sudden or extraordinary emergency." See section 25 of the *Criminal Code* (Queensland); section 33 of the *Criminal Code* (Northern Territory); and Section 41 of the *Criminal Code* (A.C.T.). See also §35.05(2) of the *N.Y. Penal Law* (New York).

[132] Section 10.3(1) of the *Criminal Code Act 1995* (Cth.).

[133] [2009] F.C.A. 474.

[134] Cf. *Re A (Children) (Conjoined Twins: Surgical Separation)* [2001] Fam. 147, where the harm was not imminent; and where the operation was not carried out in emergency conditions. It was not a matter of someone being raced to a hospital unconscious and the doctor operating without consent as a matter of urgency.

[135] See *D.P.P. for Northern Ireland v. Lynch* [1975] A.C. 65; cf. *R. v. Howe* [1987] A.C. 417.

[136] Sir Francis Bacon, *The elements of the common laws of England*, (London: Printed by the Assignes of I. More, Esq., 1630) at 32.

[137] Cf. *Re A (Children) (Conjoined Twins: Surgical Separation)* [2001] Fam. 147, where there was not any equality of evil since one twin would have died within weeks for certain, whereas the other had a chance of not only surviving, but also of leading a normal life. The twin that survived has gone on to live a normal life.

[138] "Let him save (himself) who can."

[139] Rupert Cross, "1968 Turner Memorial Lecture—Necessity Knows No Law," (1968-1970) 3 *U. Tas. L. Rev.* 1 at 3.

the lesser evil from the public point of view. They are distinguished from duress in the pure sense in that the fear is not necessarily caused by a criminal threat.

25–050 The argument for recognizing an excuse as a defence to murder holds even where the defendant has chosen what is on utilitarian theory the greater evil. Consider the following hypotheticals.

D, driving along a narrow road with a sheer drop on one side, suddenly finds two drunkards fallen senseless in front of him. (1) By his side is a terrorist, fleeing from the police; he forces D at gunpoint to drive over the two drunks. D has the defence of duress, at any rate if he only injures the men. (2) But suppose there is no terrorist, and no duress, but D's brakes fail, and he is faced with the choice of either running down and killing the two drunks or himself plunging to this death over the cliff. D chooses to stay on the road.[140]

Necessity could not possibly justify in case (2), if utilitarian principles are applied, since it is a case of two-for-one. Nor is it a case of duress of circumstances, unless that defence is extended to cover murder.

25.10. OTHER FORMS OF COMPULSION

25–051 There is a defence of coercion, akin to but distinct from duress, which is open only to married women who act under coercion from their husbands and in the husband's presence; it does not extend to treason or murder.[141] Details have not been clarified by the courts because the defence is rarely raised; but a circuit judge left it to the jury in general terms, explaining that it included "moral coercion," the only condition being that the wife must prove that her "will was overborne" so that she was "forced unwilling to participate."[142] It was also held in *R. v. Shortland*[143] that the threat need not be one of force. So there is no need to show that the husband threatened to kill or seriously injure his wife, it might be enough to show that he threatened to commit adultery with her best friend or sister, or that he threatened to kidnap their children and so on. In *R. v. Shortland*[144] it was also held that it is not enough to show that the wife committed the offence out of loyalty to her husband. Rather, "to establish the defence of marital coercion under section 47 of the *Criminal Justice Act 1925* a jury had to be satisfied, on the balance of probabilities, that the will of the defendant wife

---

[140] This problem is posed by Sanford H. Kadish, Stephen J. Schulhofer and Monrad G. Paulsen, *Criminal Law and its Process: Cases and Materials*, (Boston: Little, Brown; 4th edn. 1983) at 798.

[141] Section 47 of the *Criminal Justice Act 1925*. See also Glanville Williams, *Criminal Law: The General Part*, (London: Stevens & Sons, 2nd edn. 1961) at 248; *D.P.P. for Northern Ireland v. Lynch* [1975] A.C. 653 at 694D, 713A.

[142] *R. v. Richman* [1982] Crim. L.R. 507. In *R. v. Ditta* [1988] Crim. L.R. 42 it was held that a woman cannot rely on the defence unless she is in fact a wife of the man who coerced her. The defence is not available even if the supposed wife believed, even on reasonable grounds, that the coercer was in fact her husband.

[143] [1996] 1 Cr. App. R. 116.

[144] [1996] 1 Cr. App. R. 116.

was so overborne by the wishes of her husband that she had been forced to participate unwillingly."[145] The Law Commission has recommended the abolition of the defence.[146]

---

[145] *R. v. Shortland* [1996] 1 Cr. App. R. 116.
[146] Law Commission, *Criminal Law: Report on Defences of General Application*, (London: Law Com No. 83, 1977).

CHAPTER 26

AUTOMATISM

"To define true madness,
What is't but to be nothing else but mad?"

Hamlet II. ii

26.1.   INVOLUNTARINESS: IMPAIRED CONSCIOUSNESS

The most prominent instances of mental disorder negativing criminality yet not   **26–001**
amounting to insanity are those that are sometimes called "involuntary acts" but
now more frequently go by the name of automatism, or, more fully, non-insane
automatism. A person should not be held responsible for events that are beyond
his physical control. An act is not voluntary or willed if a person is unable to
control it.[1] The defence of automatism is made out where the defendant can show
that he was unable to control his physical actions. The defendant may be unable
to control his physical actions where his consciousness is impaired or where he
suffers a muscle spasm. A muscle spasm is an involuntary and sudden contraction
of a muscle. The physical movements of a person's limbs might also be
involuntary where another person uses his fist as an instrument. For instance, if X
forces Y's fist into S's face, Y does not act—the movement of his fist is not
voluntary. Y has not acted at all; his fist was used as an instrument.

Insane automatism is regarded as a form of insanity although conceptually it is
different.[2] Insane automatism is established where the automatism is caused by
some internal condition that affects the defendant's ability to control his physical
actions such as where the defendant suffers epilepsy. Meanwhile, sane
automatism is established where the automatism is caused by some external
condition such as where the defendant suffers concussion after hitting his head on
a wooden beam. The defence of automatism is only available if there is a "total
loss of voluntary control."[3]

The "voluntary act" requirement is not to be confused with the intentional act
requirement. When a person acts as an automaton he lacks *mens rea*, but it is not
only *mens rea* that is negated by automatism. The voluntary act (volitional acting)

---

[1] H.L.A. Hart, *Punishment and Responsibility*, (Oxford: Clarendon Press, 1968) at 181.
[2] See the detailed discussion in Deborah W. Denno "Crime and Consciousness: Science and
Involuntary Acts," (2003) 87 *Minn. L. Rev.* 269 at 337-355. See also Robert F. Schopp, *Automatism,
Insanity, and the Psychology of Criminal Responsibility*, (Cambridge: Cambridge University Press,
1991); Michael Corrado, "Automatism and the Theory of Action," (1990) 39 *Emory L.J.* 1191.
[3] *Attorney-General's Reference (No. 2 of 1992)* [1993] 3 W.L.R. 982.

requirement is also negated. When Y rapes X while he is in an automatistic state medically characterized as sexsomnia,[4] he physically penetrates the victim, but his physical movements are involuntary; they are robotic and unwilled. Automatism is regarded as being incompatible not only with the mental element in crime but also with the notion of an act.[5] If it were a matter of pure theory this could be characterized as unnecessary refinement, but the "act" doctrine has the advantage of making automatism a defence to an offence of strict liability requiring an act.[6]

In automatism cases the defendant is only acting in a mechanical sense—he is the unwilling author of his body's mechanical actions. The brain will be sending sufficient messages for his limbs to operate and for those movements to harm others. It is illogical to argue that automatons[7] do not act at all in a physical sense,[8] but it is not illogical to argue that they did not act at all in a legal sense. The law does not target this type of acting. Automatons can be distinguished from those who are used by others as an instrument, because their brains are allowing them to make mechanical movements that harm others. Automatism is not about showing that there were no actions at all, but just that the actions were not voluntary. Bodily actions become uncontrollable when a person's consciousness is sufficient for his body to act as an automaton and inflict harm, but not sufficient for him to control those harmful actions when normally he would. The acting might not be totally non-volitional, but the wrongdoer does not have sufficient consciousness to control what he is doing.

26–002   **Does automatism mean that the behaviour is virtually mindless?**   Yes in medical usage, but the legal meaning has developed far beyond that. The term "automatism" is used medically in connection with epilepsy, and in its proper medical sense it is rare even in that disease. Although attacks of *grand mal* and even *petit mal* very occasionally result in violence, this is usually not because the sufferer is a complete automaton but because of confusion or delusion or a rage

---

[4] See *R. v. Luedecke* [2008] 236 C.C.C. 3d 317, where a sleepwalker was acquitted of rape. See also *R. v. Spence* (2008) 2008 O.N.C.J. 104; *R. v. Pond* (2007) Carswell Ont. 8055. In *R. v. S* [2009] EWCA Crim. 783, D's claim that his offending occurred because of sexsomnia was not supported with cogent evidence. See also *State v. Myers*, WL 4642928 (Utah App., 2008). Unconscious and subconscious acting can be coordinated and directive. See Peter B.C. Fenwick "Automatism," in Robert Bluglass and Paul Bowden (eds.), *Principles and Practice of Forensic Psychiatry*, (Edinburgh: Churchill Livingston, 1990) at 271-85.

[5] *R. v. Charlson* (1955) 1 W.L.R. 317 at 319, where it was held that the prosecution did not have to prove intent in relation to the third charge relating to the infliction of grievous bodily harm, but that it had to prove that the harm was caused by "a conscious act of the accused". See also *Bratty v. Attorney-General for Northern Ireland* [1963] A.C. 386 at 405 *per* Lord Denning. Cf. the opinions of Lord Kilmuir at 407 and Lord Morris at 415.

[6] See *State v. Kremer*, 262 Minn. 190 (1962); *Cordwell v. Carley* (1985) 31 A. Crim. R. 291; *Police v. Barber* [2010] S.A.S.C. 329 at para. 16, 31-33; *R. v. Connor* (1980) 146 C.L.R. 64. Strict liability for quasi-acting—that is, for an *actus reus* that is quasi because the volitional element incorporated in that notion is missing, would be contrary to the requirements of proportionate punishment. *State v. Campbell*, 117 Ohio App. 3d 762 (1997). See also *R. v. Metro News Ltd.* (1986) 56 O.R. (2d) 321 (Can.); and *R. v. Stokes* (2009) O.N.C.J 8 at para. 10 citing Glanville Williams, *Textbook of Criminal Law*, (London: Stevens & Sons, 1978).

[7] This term is convenient for referring to people who are in automatic mode.

[8] See Bernard Williams, "The Actus Reus of Dr. Caligari," (1994) 142 *U. Pa. L. Rev.* 1664 *et seq.*

response.[9] On the lips of lawyers, however, automatism has come to express any abnormal state of consciousness (whether confusion, delusion or dissociation) that is regarded as incompatible with the existence of *mens rea*, while not amounting to insanity.[10] It is sometimes called "altered" or "clouded" consciousness; perhaps "impaired consciousness" is the best name, but the orthodox one can be used if we bear in mind that it does not mean what it says.[11]

What do we mean by consciousness? A bee perceives the symbolic dances of other bees, and is genetically programmed to make the appropriate response by following the direction indicated; but we have no warrant to describe a bee as being "conscious" in any sense relevant to human activity. Consciousness, for humanity, means not simple perception, the awareness of the here-and-now, but the ability, at least in limited degree, to remember the past and foresee the future, so as to make informed choices.[12] On principle, therefore, a disease or other event seriously impairing consciousness in this sense exempts the affected party from liability. Putting aside two or three ill-considered decisions, the great weight of authority shows that a person whose consciousness is badly impaired can have the defence of automatism even though he is still able to co-ordinate his movements.[13]

In some situations, the actor's bodily movements will be voluntary, but they will have an inverse relation with the harm that he causes such as where he strikes pedestrians with his car because its brakes have failed. D may be voluntarily pumping the brake pedal to no avail. Such a driver is not blameworthy if he kills the pedestrians, because he was merely one of the "but for" causes of the uncontrollable concatenation of events. He might be liable if the prior fault doctrine is made out, such as where he made a conscious choice to drive a vehicle with faulty brakes.[14] Involuntariness in this context is not about involuntary acting, because the driver's actions are voluntary. External physical events cause the driver and his car to be dragged into the pedestrians against his will. The driver is conscious and in is full control of his own bodily actions, but is unable to control the events that he has, without any culpability, put in motion.[15] Another

---

[9] John Gunn and George Fenton, "Epilepsy, Automatism and Crime," (1971) 297 *The Lancet* 1173.

[10] Lord Kilmuir in *Bratty v. Attorney-General for Northern Ireland* [1963] A.C. 386 at 401 accepted the definition of automatism "as connoting the state of a person who, though capable of action, is not conscious of what he is doing. … It is a defence because the mind does not go with what is being done."

[11] Because automatism is a legal concept, a psychiatrist should be asked to testify to the mental condition as psychiatrically recognized, not to "automatism." It is for the judge to make the translation. In most of the conditions referred to legally as automatism the psychiatrist would speak of an altered state of consciousness.

[12] For a more detailed discussion of the intricacy of consciousness, see John R. Searle, *The Mystery of Consciousness*, (New York: NYREV., 1997); Daniel C. Dennett, *Consciousness Explained*, (New York: Back Bay, 1991); Thomas Nagel, "What Is It Like to be a Bat?" (1974) 483 *Phil. Rev.* 435.

[13] See for example, D's behaviour in *R. v. Burgess* [1991] 2 W.L.R. 1206.

[14] Under the *Road Traffic Act 1988* mere negligence as to the vehicle's dangerous state is sufficient for grounding a conviction. See *Attorney-General's Reference (No.4 of 2000)* [2001] 2 Cr. App. R. 22; *R. v. Loukes* [1996] 1 Cr. App. R. 444 at 453.

[15] *State v. Kremer*, 262 Minn. 190 (1962). A latent defect of which the driver is unaware can provide a defence: *Oakley-Moore v. Robinson* [1982] R.T.R. 74; *Burns v. Bidder* [1966] 3 W.L.R. 99. Cf. *Hughes v. Hall* [1960] 1 W.L.R. 733; *Neal v. Bedford* [1966] 1 Q.B. 505. This type of situation can be distinguished from those where a fully conscious person causes an accident and continues to drive not

example of involuntary acting that involves circumstantial events (rather than impaired consciousness), is where a swarm of bees attack a driver and thus cause him to crash into a crowd of people.[16]

26–003 A person's physical involuntariness might also result from a reflex reaction. In *Ryan v. The Queen*,[17] a young man tried to imitate a robbery that he had read about in a novel. He robbed a petrol station at gun point. Throughout the robbery his gun was loaded and cocked without the safety catch being applied and was pointed at the attendant. After the service station attendant gave the defendant the money, the defendant with the loaded gun in one hand tried to use his free hand to tie up the attendant. The attendant moved suddenly as the defendant attempted to tie him up and this caused the gun to discharge. The attendant was killed because the gun was pointed directly at the back of his head. The defendant said he did not pull the trigger. He argued that when the attendant moved suddenly, the gun discharged because he stepped back suddenly in surprise of the attendant's sudden movements. The police replicated the incident many times and in every re-enactment the gun discharged. Barwick C.J. outlined the explanations for the action as follows: "(1) The applicant's explanation could be disbelieved, and it could be concluded that he had fired the gun intentionally—that is to say, both as a voluntary act with the intention to do the deceased harm. (2) That he fired the gun voluntarily, not intending to do any harm to the deceased but merely to frighten him as a means of self-protection. (3) That being startled, he voluntarily but in a panic, pressed the trigger but with no specific intent either to do the deceased harm or to frighten him. (4) That being startled so as to move slightly off his balance, the trigger was pressed in a reflex or convulsive, unwilled movement of his hand or of his muscles."[18] The latter of course being involuntary.

26–004 **Which side bears the burden of proof?** Although the "black-out" defence is legally recognized, it is a defence too easily feigned to be accepted without severe scrutiny. So the courts have laid down that the evidential burden in respect of the issue of non-insane automatism rests upon the defendant,[19] and, moreover, that medical evidence must (where appropriate) be given in support before the judge is bound to leave this issue to the jury. There must be a proper foundation for the automatism which involves presenting not merely evidence that the defendant acted unconsciously or in a subconscious state, but that his mental state prevented him from controlling his actions.[20]

---

realizing he has done so. In such a case the driver acts consciously but lacks *mens rea*, because he was not aware that he had hit a pedestrian, *etc*. Cf. *R. v. Racimore* [1975] 25 C.C.C. (2d) 143. Likewise, if a driver hits the accelerator instead of the brakes by accident, he acts voluntarily. See *Attorney-General's Reference (No. 4 of 2000)* [2000] *Crim. L.R.* 578.

[16] See *Kay v. Butterworth* (1945) 61 T.L.R. 452.

[17] (1967) 121 C.L.R. 205.

[18] *Ryan v. The Queen* (1967) 121 C.L.R. 205 at 209.

[19] *Hill v. Baxter* [1958] 1 Q.B. 277; *Bratty v. Attorney-General (Northern Ireland)* [1963] A.C. 386 at 405.

[20] *Re Attorney-General's Reference (No. 2 of 1992)* [1994] Q.B. 91; *R. v. Burgess* [1991] 2 W.L.R. 1206.

26.2. INSANE AND NON-INSANE AUTOMATISM

It would be better to call insane automatism "treatable automatism" and non-insane automatism "general automatism". The traditional labels are insane and non-insane automatism, but as we will see, the label insane automatism is a misnomer, because it has been applied to automatism that has little to do with insanity.

26–005

What is insane automatism? Insane automatism is not about asking if the defendant understood what he was doing was wrong, as is the case with establishing insanity.[21] Insanity more broadly involves not only demonstrating that the defendant lacked volition because he suffered a disease of the mind, but also that the disease resulted in him having a lack of cognition—that is, an ability to know right and wrong or to understand the nature or quality of his act. In the case of insane automatism, it is only necessary to demonstrate that the defendant's condition ("disease of the mind") resulted in a lack of volition.

26–006

As things have developed, judges have been forced to attach their own meaning to "insanity," because this expression (or its equivalent "disease of the mind") denotes the distinction between the kind of acquittal called the special verdict, which can result in the defendant being consigned to a psychiatric hospital,[22] and the ordinary acquittal whereby he walks out of court a free person. For example, the law obviously distinguishes between a sane mistake (or ordinary forgetfulness) as to a relevant fact and an insane delusion. In neither case does the defendant "know the nature and quality of his act," while in the latter there must be a special verdict.

An illustration of the former is *R. v. Clarke*,[23] where a woman was charged with theft from a supermarket. Her defence was that she had taken the goods in a state of absent mindedness resulting from depression. She was convicted, but the conviction was quashed on appeal. Depression can amount to a psychosis, but a court would naturally be reluctant to say that simple forgetfulness, even if resulting from psychotic depression, manifests a "defect of reason of the mind" within the *McNaghten* Rules.[24]

The courts tend to examine the "cause" of the automatism to determine whether it is insane or non-insane automatism. If the automatism is caused by a condition that exists within the defendant such as epilepsy,[25] hyperglycaemia,[26] and perhaps sleepwalking,[27] it is labelled as insane automatism. The courts presume that internal disorders that cause a person to act as an automaton are likely to recur, but this is not necessarily true. These forms of automatism are labelled as insane automatism because they are caused by triggers that exist in the defendant. Epilepsy is a condition that exists within the physical being of the defendant—it

26–007

---

[21] Stanley Yeo, "Clarifying Automatism," (2002) 25 *Int'l J. L. & Psychiatry* 445.

[22] Section 2 of the *Trial of Lunatics Act 1883* (as amended).

[23] [1972] 1 All E.R. 219.

[24] *R. v. M'Naughten* (1843) 8 E.R. 718.

[25] *Bratty v. Attorney-General (Northern Ireland)* [1963] A.C. 386; *R. v. Sullivan* [1983] 3 W.L.R. 123.

[26] *R. v. Hennessy* [1989] 1 W.L.R. 287.

[27] *R. v. Burgess* [1991] 2 W.L.R. 1206. The Canadian Supreme Court held otherwise. See *R. v. Parks* [1992] 2 S.C.R. 871.

is not injected into him as drugs might be. It exists as a part of his biological makeup. If a person's automatism results from him having an epileptic or diabetic fit, he may be labelled as an insane person and therefore will not get an unqualified acquittal. The internal cause test is illogical, because it brings a range of defendants within the purview of the special verdict, who do not require ongoing treatment and would not benefit from a supervision or hospital order.[28] Under this test, diabetics and epileptics have been labelled as insane, even though they are not, and even though they do not require supervision or psychiatric treatment. In fact, a psychiatric hospital would not take such a person.

Epilepsy is certainly a disease of the brain, but it is not classified as a psychosis, and sufferers are rarely dangerous to others even during an attack. Epilepsy, hyperglycaemia and sleepwalking do not predispose to criminal conduct in the usual sense, but can result in harm on rare occasions if not controlled by treatment.[29] An actor will be incapacitated not only by a *grand mal* attack (the epileptic fit in the usual sense) but by *petit mal* epilepsy in which his mind simply fails to function for a few seconds. Also, the sufferer may in rare instances perform complicated acts in a somnambulist condition (the psychomotor attack), and these may unintentionally cause injury. Although most patients can be helped by drugs to lead a normal life, a few severely brain-damaged patients require long-term medical supervision.

Formerly, epilepsy was automatically treated as a kind of insanity, future danger or not. In one case a woman, having an epileptic seizure while filling a kettle to put on the fire, put the kettle in the oven and her child on the fire. This was a pure mishap, which might happen to any of the thousands of epileptics who lead an almost normal life in society; yet the unfortunate woman was immured in Broadmoor, away from her husband and friends—a tragic reproach to the law of mandatory commitment and the incompetence of the Home Office of the day.[30] More recently, the courts have accepted on a number of occasions that when the injury inflicted by the sufferer from an ordinary epileptic fit is the merest accident, and there is no reason to suppose that he presents a continuing source of danger, a verdict of automatism is appropriate. A psychiatric hospital would not accept such a patient under a hospital order, except perhaps briefly for assessment, since he would not be regarded as in need of in-patient treatment; and there would be no social purpose in an insanity verdict on such facts. In driving cases, particularly, epilepsy is now regularly regarded as being distinct from insanity. In *R. v. Quick*,[31] the Court of Appeal accepted overseas authorities to the effect that an epileptic seizure can be regarded as producing non-insane automatism. However, we also have powerful authority the other way.

In *Bratty v. Attorney-General (Northern Ireland)*,[32] the House of Lords held that the medical evidence in the case pointed to the defendant's alleged state of

---

[28] 27.7.

[29] See R. D. Mackay and Markus Reuber, "Epilepsy and the Defence of Insanity: Time for Change? [2007] *Crim. L.R.* 782; William Wilson *et al.*, "Violence, Sleepwalking and the Criminal Law: Part 2 The Legal Aspects," [2005] *Crim. L.R.* 614.

[30] W. C. Sullivan, *Crime and Insanity*, (London: Edward Arnold & Co., 1924), Chap. 9. Cf. *R. v. Perry* (1920) 14 Cr. App. R. 48 at 51.

[31] [1973] Q.B. 910 at 922.

[32] [1963] A.C. 386.

psychomotor epilepsy at the time when he killed a young girl as being a disease of the mind within the *M'Naghten* rules. There may appear at first sight to be a conflict between *Bratty* and the authorities previously quoted, but the reconciliation is that the statements holding that epileptic attacks did not amount to insanity were made in cases where the injury was accidental and unlikely to be repeated, whereas in *Bratty* the court thought that the defendant might present a continuing danger. A verdict of insane automatism is given in cases where the automatism has been found to have been caused by any mental disease or defect ("disease of the mind") of which the defendant suffered. Disease of the mind is a legal standard,[33] any condition internal to the accused counts.

What is sane automatism?   Like insane automatism, non-insane automatism is   **26–008**
made out where the defendant suffers an obscuration of his mental capacities, if this causes him to act involuntarily. The automatism will be deemed to be sane automatism if it has an external cause. It appears that the courts treat automatism that has an external cause as sane automatism because an external trigger is not a disease of the mind, and because a person is not likely to be hit by lightening twice. Hence, if a person suffers concussion after being hit over the head by a robber, there is little to suggest he will be hit over the head by another robber in the future; but if he has some internal condition such as diabetes, he may have future attacks.

If a person is held down and is injected with a powerful drug and as a result acts as an automaton, the external cause of his automatism is the drug,[34] even though the drug is also an internal cause of the automatism. The drugs are an internal cause as soon as they enter the body and start affecting its processes. But the drugs are regarded as an external cause of the automatism, because they do not exist in the defendant as a part of his biological makeup. Another simple example of an external cause is where a person has been hit over the head and is left concussed. Concussion can cause automatism. Obviously, concussion does not require ongoing medical monitoring.

Can you tell me which cases of automatism should be subject to the special   **26–009**
verdict?   We need to distinguish those who require supervisory treatment from those who do not. The best approach would be to focus on whether the defect that caused the automatism requires treatment of the kind that the special verdict allows for. As far as the diabetic or epileptic is concerned, there is no justification for subjecting him to the special verdict, because he does not require treatment in a psychiatric hospital, nor does he require treatment that requires supervision.

The Supreme Court of Canada has proposed some criteria for determining whether automatism should be categorized as sane or insane automatism. In *R. v. Stone*[35] the defendant claimed that he killed as an automaton in a state of

---

[33] On the problems of defining such diseases and conditions see Bernadette McSherry, "Defining What is a 'Disease of the Mind': The Untenability of Current Legal Interpretations," (1993) 1 *J. L. and Medicine* 76.

[34] *Broome v. Perkins* (1987) 85 Cr. App. R. 121; *R. v. Bailey* [1983] 1 W.L.R. 760; *Watmore v. Jenkins* [1962] 3 W.L.R. 463. *R. v. Quick* [1973] Q.B. 910.

[35] [1999] 2 S.C.R. 269.

"disassociation." The Supreme Court posed three questions for determining whether a defendant acted as a result of a disease of the mind:

1. Was the volitional incapacity caused by some internal condition peculiar to the defendant?
2. Was the condition one that posed continuing danger?
3. Are there any policy reasons for allowing the defendant to invoke the defence of non-insane automatism even though his wrongdoing resulted from some internal condition?

26–010 **I see the first consideration is whether the automatism is caused by some internal condition peculiar to the defendant, but you have already told me that the internal cause test should be abandoned.** The internal cause test is too wide as it brings too many defendants that are not likely to suffer a future attack of automatism. There is a difference between internal conditions that require ongoing psychiatric treatment[36] or supervision and those that merely require the defendant to take basic medication such as insulin. If a person's automatism was caused by sleep deprivation and it could be shown that he was not in need of psychiatric treatment[37] or other forms of rehabilitation, then his automatism should be labelled non-insane automatism.[38]

The illogicality of applying the internal/external cause test in isolation is best exemplified by referring to the hypoglycaemia (high blood sugar levels) and hyperglycaemia (low blood sugar levels) cases. Both conditions constitute diabetes, but when a person acts as an automaton because of high blood sugars, he is subject to a special verdict. In *R. v. Hennessy*[39] the defendant took a motor vehicle without consent and attempted to raise sane automatism as a defence by arguing that he was affected by stress, anxiety and depression. He also claimed that he was suffering hyperglycaemia because he had not taken his insulin for three days. The Court of Appeal held that the defence of sane automatism was not available unless it could be shown that the defendant's lack of capacity was due to some external factor and that stress, anxiety and depression were not separately or together external factors capable of causing sane automatism. It also concluded that hyperglycaemia is an inherent defect that is a disease of the mind and therefore comes within the purview of the *M'Naughten* rules as insane automatism.

Hypoglycaemia is a deficiency of blood sugar and it too can impair the consciousness and induce an aggressive outburst. It may come about as the result of fasting followed by the consumption of alcohol, or when a diabetic takes an overdose of insulin or subjects himself to unusual fatigue or lack of food. Hypoglycaemia has come before the courts in a number of cases and is clearly

---

[36] For a discussion of mental disorders requiring psychiatric treatment see Michael G. Gelder *et al.*, *New Oxford Textbook of Psychiatry*, (Oxford: Oxford University Press, 2009).

[37] See *State v. McClain*, 678 N.E. 2d 104 (1997).

[38] Cf. *J v. Foundation Trust* [2010] 3 W.L.R. 840, where J's mental illness prevented him for taking his insulin for diabetes and thus resulted in him having dangerous fits.

[39] [1989] 1 W.L.R. 287.

held to be capable of producing a state of non-insane automatism. In *R. v. Quick*[40] the defendant, charged with assault, was a diabetic who had taken insulin, as prescribed, on the morning of the assault, and had drunk a quantity of spirits and eaten little food thereafter. He contended that at the time of the assault he was in a state of automatism due to hypoglycaemia, but the trial judge intimated that this would be taken as an insanity defence, so Quick changed his plea to guilty. The conviction was reversed on the ground that if Quick's condition produced automatism it would not amount to insanity. Illogically, a diabetic whose automatism is caused by an overproduction of insulin in his body (an internal cause) is regarded as legally insane, but those whose automatism is caused by an insulin overdose (an external cause) are treated as sane and are entitled to a full acquittal with no strings attached. But both suffer the same disease—sugar diabetes—and neither the hypoglycaemic nor the hyperglycaemic pose a danger to the community. Similarly, most sleepwalkers are not dangerous, but it too has been labelled as insane automatism.[41]

So the internal test should be abandoned.   Yes. The focus should be on   **26–011** whether the defendant's condition is likely recur and thus cause him to reoffend. The special verdict aims to ensure that dangerous offenders receive appropriate treatment. In *R. v. Sullivan*[42] the appellant suffered from *petit mal* and attacked a friend by kicking him about the head and body. The House of Lords held that if the effect of a disease such as epilepsy prevents the defendant from knowing what he is doing, or if he did know, that he did not know it was wrong, it should be treated as insane automatism where there is evidence that further dangerous bouts were likely to recur.

The special verdict should only be invoked where there is strong evidence that the defendant is unlikely to accept treatment unless kept under supervision or hospitalized. Lord Denning expounded this test in the following terms:

> "It seems to me that any mental disorder which has manifested itself in violence and is prone to recur is a disease of the mind. At any rate it is the sort of disease for which a person should be detained in hospital rather than be given an unqualified acquittal."[43]

A criticism of this is that the statement is inadequate as a definition of "disease of the mind" unless it is accompanied by the converse proposition that for legal purposes a disease of the mind is an affliction that is likely to manifest itself again in a dangerous way. In other words: future danger, disease of the mind; no future danger, no disease of the mind.[44] This converse or negative side of Lord Denning's definition is necessary to prevent the special verdict having too wide an application. The dangerousness test should not be used to determine whether epilepsy, hypoglycaemia and sleepwalking are "diseases of the mind," but rather whether the given medical condition is worthy of a special verdict because the

---

[40] [1973] Q.B. 910. See also *R. v. Bailey* [1983] 1 W.L.R. 760; *Moses v. Winder* [1980] Crim. L.R. 232.

[41] *R. v. Burgess* [1991] 2 W.L.R. 1206. Cf. *R. v. Parks* [1992] 2 S.C.R. 871.

[42] [1984] A.C. 156.

[43] *Bratty v. Attorney-General for Northern Ireland* [1963] A.C. 386 at 412.

[44] The negative proposition was rejected by the Supreme Court of Canada in *R. v. Rabey* [1980] 2 S.C.R. 513. See also the comments of Lord Lane in *R. v. Burgess* [1991] 2 W.L.R. 1206 at 1212.

defendant requires treatment to prevent him from having another attack. As a matter of policy the aim should be to ensure that those who are likely to suffer automatism in the future are brought within the purview of the special verdict, if they are treatable and require supervision.[45] The defendant might not require psychiatric counselling, but may require supervision[46] because he has a tendency to forget to take his insulin and so on.[47]

26–012   Dangerousness should not be read as meaning violent outbursts: the kleptomaniac who repeatedly steals in a state of dissociation and refuses treatment[48] is only dangerous in the sense that he threatens the property interests of others, but there is no reason why he should not be made to accept treatment where he has a history of offending and it seems that treatment is necessary to prevent him from reoffending. (Mind you, most kleptomaniacs do not operate as automatons.)[49] The public have a right to be protected from property crimes.

There is no point in merely focusing on internal and external causes, because the automatism may result from a combination of both. For instance, the sleepwalker's automatism may be caused by a combination of internal factors such as the genetic makeup of the defendant and external factors such as sleep deprivation and alcohol consumption.[50] One sleepwalker may be willing to ensure that he gets adequate sleep and that he only drinks in moderation; meanwhile, another sleepwalker may have the opposite attitude. Their medical records might have to be considered to determine whether they pose a future threat to the community. The distinction between insane automatism and sane automatism can be maintained, but the emphasis should be on whether the defendant requires treatment to prevent him from threatening the interests of others.

26–013   **If the question is one of the defendant's future dangerousness, who decides it, judge or jury?**   *M'Naghten* seemed to suppose that the question of sanity or insanity was for the jury. This is certainly so on the question of whether the defendant knew what he was doing, *etc.*; but in *R. v. Kemp*[51] Devlin J. held that the question of whether evidence showed insanity as opposed to non-insane

---

[45] See also *Bratty v. Attorney-General (Northern Ireland)* [1963] A.C. 386 at 412 *per* Lord Denning.

[46] A supervision order is "an order which requires the person in respect of whom it is made ('the supervised person') to be under the supervision of a social worker or an officer of a local probation board ('the supervising officer') for a period specified in the order of not more than two years. (2) A supervision order may, in accordance with paragraph 4 or 5 below, require the supervised person to submit, during the whole of that period or such part of it as may be specified in the order, to treatment by or under the direction of a registered medical practitioner." See Schedule 1A of the *Domestic Violence, Crime and Victims Act 2004*.

[47] Cf. *J v. Foundation Trust* [2010] 3 W.L.R. 840, where J kept forgetting to take his insulin and as a result had dangerous fits.

[48] Cognitive-behavioural therapy is the standard treatment. See Aaron T. Beck, *Cognitive Therapy and the Emotional Disorders*, (New York: Penguin, 1993).

[49] It is doubtful the compulsion involved in kleptomania would be accepted as a defence of automatism, as it seems to fall short of non-volitional acting and is more akin to duress. See for example the comments in *Allstate Ins. Co. v. Jarvis*, 195 Ga. App. 335 (1990). Cf. *United States v. McGauley*, 279 F.3d 62 (2004); *United States v. Lake*, 910 F.2d 414 (1990).

[50] *R. v. Burgess* [1991] 2 W.L.R. 1206.

[51] [1957] 1 Q.B. 399. See also *R. v. Sullivan* [1983] 3 W.L.R. 123.

automatism was one of law for the judge, and Lord Denning approved his view. It has also been approved by the Supreme Court of Canada. Ritchie J. said:[52] "The general rule is that it is for the judge as a question of law to decide what constitutes a 'disease of the mind,' but that the question of whether or not the facts in a given case disclose the existence of such a disease is a question to be determined by the trier of fact."

26.3. DISSOCIATION AND AUTOMATISM

Dissociation is said to involve: **26–014**

> "'a disruption of the usually integrated functions of consciousness, memory, identity, or perception of the environment'. From a psychological perspective, the presence of dissociation is usually inferred from amnesia for events that have been externally verified as having happened (such as failed recollection of a traumatic experience like rape) and from subjective descriptions of the loss of volitional control of one's conduct (such as the commission of a violent act that was unintended and not controllable)."[53]

Dissociation is difficult to diagnose with certainty because the psychiatrist can only accept the patient's word, apart from considering what the patient now avers in relation to his general conduct at the time. Whether dissociation is accepted as negativing criminal liability depends upon the circumstances and the strength of the psychiatric evidence. The defence should produce convincing psychiatric evidence confirming the defendant's alleged involuntariness. A claim of dissociation automatism could be supported with evidence showing that the defendant had a "medical history" of suffering automatistic-like dissociative states.[54] It could also be supported with corroborating evidence from bystanders, evidence of "motive," and evidence that the "stimulus" for the dissociation was "extremely shocking."[55] Regardless of whether the automatism is labelled as insane or non-insane automatism, the evidence must show that the defendant acted involuntarily because of his impaired consciousness.

There is considerable danger of a miscarriage of justice if the sufferer is unaware of what happened because of his affliction. Therefore, a defence to a charge of shoplifting that "I had a blackout" or "something came over me" ought not to be scornfully rejected without a medical examination precluding the possibility of a brain abnormality, unless of course the evidence is convincing that the defendant was acting purposefully—and even this evidence may be misleading.

Should dissociation resulting from external causes such as "psychological   **26–015**
blows" be treated as sane automatism?   In England and Wales, the defence has been recognized by the lower courts. In *R. v. T*[56] the defendant stabbed a

---

[52] *R. v. Rabey* [1980] 2 S.C.R. 513.

[53] Hamish J. McLeod *et al.*, "Automatism and Dissociation: Disturbances of Consciousness and Volition from a Psychological Perspective," (2004) 27 *Int'l J. L. and Psychiatry* 471.

[54] *R. v. Stone* [1999] 2 S.C.R. 290 at 291-293. See also *R. v. Rabey* [1980] 2 S.C.R. 513. See also *R. v. Ansari* [2009] B.C.W.L.D. 719.

[55] *R. v. Stone* [1999] 2 S.C.R. 290 at 291-293.

[56] [1990] Crim. L.R. 256.

person in an armed robbery. It was argued on her behalf that she did not know what she was doing because she had been raped just days before carrying out the robbery. T was suffering from post-traumatic stress and was in a dissociative state when she carried out the robbery. There was medical evidence available to verify that she had been raped. The Crown Court held that rape could be a sufficient external factor to cause a malfunctioning of the mind. It was also held that this would not be a disease of the mind, therefore if the evidence was accepted the defendant would be entitled to rely on sane automatism. In Australia a general defence of dissociation has been recognized by the High Court of Australia. That court[57] has held that psychiatric evidence of dissociation is relevant for determining whether the defendant's wrongdoing occurred "independently of the exercise of" his will.

If a defendant asserts that he acted in a dissociative state because of some psychological blow, there should be evidence of "an extremely shocking" trigger if non-insane automatism is to be established.[58] The defendant who kills his wife in a stabbing frenzy, stabbing her 47 times merely because she was nagging him or verbally abusing him, does not act rationally given the triviality of the "psychological blow," and is likely to pose a continuing threat to society.[59] The Canadian Supreme Court has taken the view that where the "involuntariness was caused by mere stress it is presumed to be triggered by a factor internal to the accused, and as such gives rise to a defence of insane automatism only."[60] If there is no evidence to demonstrate that the trigger was an extreme psychological blow of a kind that would cause a normal person to dissociate, then only insane automatism should be put to the jury.[61] Dissociation will be interpreted as insane automatism where the defendant's reaction to the "psychological blow" was not a response that would be expected of a normal person and it appears it might be triggered again.[62]

In a joint judgment in *R. v. Falconer*,[63] Mason C.J., Brennan and McHugh J.J. said:

---

[57] *R. v. Falconer* (1990) 171 C.L.R. 30 at 31. "In practical terms a claim of involuntariness which is not based on mental illness is almost certain to be treated as frivolous unless supported by medical evidence that identifies a mental state in which acts can occur independently of the will, assigns a causative explanation for that state and postulates that the accused did or may have experienced that state." *Id*. at 83 *per* Gaudron J.

[58] *R. v. Stone* [1999] 2 S.C.R. 290 at 291-293.

[59] *R. v. Stone* [1999] 2 S.C.R. 290 at 291-293.

[60] *R. v. Stone* [1999] 2 S.C.R. 290.

[61] This approach was expounded by the Supreme Court of Canada. Given the potential dangerousness of those who commit gross criminal acts merely because of stress such an approach is very laudable and should be followed in Britain. *R. v. Stone* [1999] 2 S.C.R. 290.

[62] "[T]he law must postulate a standard of mental strength which, in the face of a given level of psychological trauma, is capable of protecting the mind from malfunction to the extent prescribed in the respective definitions of insanity. That standard must be the standard of the ordinary person: if the mind's strength is below that standard, the mind is infirm; if it is above that standard, the mind is sound or sane." *R. v. Falconer* (1990) 171 C.L.R. 30 at 55. If the mind is sane, then general automatism is available.

[63] (1990) 171 C.L.R. 30 at 55.

"In a given case, if the psychological trauma causes a sound mind, possessed of the requisite standard of strength, to malfunction only transiently so as to produce the effects mentioned in the *M'Naghten Rules*, the malfunction cannot be attributed to mental infirmity but to 'the nature of man: that is to say, a malfunction which is transient and not prone to recur and to which the mind of an ordinary person would be subject if exposed to the same psychological trauma is neither a mental disease nor a natural mental infirmity. It is not an instance of unsoundness of mind under the common law. Having regard to the reason for distinguishing between sane and insane mental irresponsibility in *Hill v. Baxter*, there is no reason to require such a malfunction of the mind to attract a qualified verdict of acquittal."

You have just told me that dissociation not involving a sufficient (shocking) psychological (external) blow would, if anything, only provide a defence of insane automatism. But what needs to be established?   It must be demonstrated that the condition of dissociation caused the defendant to act non-volitionally. The evidence would have to be compelling to convince a jury where there is no clear medical defect. In an earlier English case where a defendant, having caused a collision, drove dangerously in order to evade the police, making a clean get-away so that they were not able to arrest him until some time later, the trial judge took a strong line by withholding a defence of hysterical fugue from the jury. The Court of Appeal upheld the decision, notwithstanding psychiatric evidence that the defendant's subconscious mind took over so that he would not have appreciated what he was doing.[64] The case was unpropitious for the recognition of the defence. One finds it hard to believe that a man who was obviously trying to evade the police did not know what he was doing; in fact the psychiatrist called by the defence, who talked about the defendant's subconscious mind taking over, admitted his belief that the defendant knew he was driving away from the accident, and intended not to allow the police to stop him. So the psychiatrist's evidence was self-contradictory. Nevertheless, the court's judgment is itself unsatisfactory.

The court excluded the defence on the ground that the defendant's mind "was working to some extent." This remark is true, but, because it is unaccompanied by further explanation, it fails to carry complete conviction. In sleepwalking cases (which are often diagnosed as states of dissociation) the sleeper's mind is working "to some extent" (as a dreamer's is), and his acts may be purposive or directive.[65] An example is where he dives out of the bedroom window, evidently under the impression that he is diving into a pool. Because we all dream, and because the fact of sleepwalking is well authenticated, a defence of sleepwalking can be intrinsically probable, while the driver's defence of dissociation during his waking hours, when he has a strong motive for lying, is intrinsically improbable; but is not the question of probability for the jury? The difference is that for the window-diver there is no pool, whereas the driver in the present case was in fact successfully shaking off the police. The driver certainly seems to have had more control than the lorry driver did in *Attorney-General's Reference (No. 2 of 1992)*.[66] In that case, the driver was unable to raise the defence of automatism because he maintained some control.

26–016

---

[64] *R. v. Isitt* (1978) 67 Cr. App. R. 44.
[65] *R. v. Prescott* [2008] O.N.C.J 604.
[66] [1994] Q.B. 91 at 95-96.

26.4.   AUTOMATISM AND PRIOR FAULT

26–017   Self-induced automatism does not provide a defence. The issue of "prior fault" arises where the automated actor had prior warning of his potential dangerousness. The prior wrongdoing might involve unlawful acting such as dangerous driving. Prior fault does not refer to the fictitious recklessness attributed to intoxicated defendants under the *D.P.P. v. Majewski* doctrine.[67] It refers to real recklessness: knowledge by the defendant that in failing to take precautions against a loss of consciousness he was endangering others.[68] As we saw above, the defendant in *The Queen v. Ryan*[69] robbed a service station and accidentally killed the attendant when he was attempting to tie the attendant up. While the action that caused the gun to fire was involuntary, his prior actions were voluntary. The defendant was acting recklessly in the moments prior to the gun being discharged by his reflex action. "[A]lthough a voluntary act is an absolute requirement for criminal liability, you do not have to find that every single act in the circumstances presented to you was voluntary".[70] In situations where a defendant's prior recklessness is linked to the involuntary action, it is fair to impute any resulting harm to him. It is reckless to hold a loaded gun point-blank at the head of a fellow human being and it is reasonably foreseeable that a reflex (non-motivational/non-volitional) action could trigger it in such circumstances.

Similarly, there may be evidence of fault in cases where drivers cause the death or injury to others by falling asleep while driving. If a driver goes on driving knowing that he is tired and is about to fall asleep he can foresee the potential danger and his choice to continue driving is reckless. The driver is not guilty of dangerous or careless driving by reason of what he does when asleep; but all the same he can be convicted for dangerous driving if he falls asleep at the wheel, on the theory that he was guilty of the offence not at the moment when the crash occurred but at the prior moment when he should have realized that he was sleepy and should have stopped driving.[71] Similarly, a driver may be guilty of dangerous driving if he drives knowing that he is subject to an epileptic attack or a diabetic coma;[72] in theory the driver is guilty of careless or dangerous driving even when he is driving perfectly well and nothing untoward occurs.[73]

It is rare for a driver to fall fast asleep at the wheel, but a momentary loss of consciousness may occur, and is now a recognized phenomenon under the name

---

[67] [1977] A.C. 443.

[68] Cf. 19.5.

[69] (1967) 121 C.L.R. 205. See also *R. v. Jiminez* (1992) 173 C.L.R. 572; *R. v. Clarke* (2003) 87 S.A.S.R. 203.

[70] *State v. Burrell*, 609 A.2d. 751 at 753 (1992). Similarly in *Rogers v. State*, 105 S.W.3d. 630 at 638 (2003) it was held that the "voluntary act requirement does not necessarily go to the ultimate act (*e.g.*, pulling the trigger), but only that criminal responsibility for the harm must 'include an act' that is voluntary (*e.g.*, pulling the gun, pointing the gun, or cocking the hammer)."

[71] *Kay v. Butterworth* (1945) 173 L.T. 191; *Henderson v. Jones* (1955) 119 J.P. 305.

[72] In *Moses v. Winder* [1980] Crim. L.R. 232 a driver who fell into a diabetic coma was convicted of careless driving, but the reason given was that he had forewarning and did not take adequate steps. Presumably he would also have been convicted if he knew the coma would befall him without warning.

[73] *R. v. Spurge* [1961] 2 Q.B. 205 at 210.

of "microsleep."[74] A sleep-deprived person can lose consciousness for a few seconds, when the eyes remain open because the mechanisms that keep the body alert are momentarily switched off; and he will not afterwards know what happened. If he is driving he may be involved in a "mystery accident." A defence based on this hypothesis is unlikely to succeed, because in the evidence it would be accounted a "fanciful doubt" and dismissed from consideration.[75] Presumably the only concrete evidence that would be adduced (apart from expert evidence as to the possibility of the condition) would be evidence that the defendant was deprived of sleep; but then his driving in that condition would be found reckless for that reason.

What if a person who is at the wheel but is in a state of automatism fails to give way at a Give Way sign? It was held in *Hill v. Baxter*[76] that the former offence of reckless driving was an offence of strict liability,[77] but that automatism could exculpate. The defence failed on the facts because the defendant had not given sufficient evidence to raise it.

26–018

What if the driver was at fault in losing consciousness just before he came to the traffic sign? In *Hill v. Baxter*, Lord Goddard C.J. declared that the evidence was compatible with the driver having fallen asleep at the wheel, which could not be a defence. The last part of this statement may frequently be true for a charge of careless driving, when the carelessness can be backdated to the driving while awake. But as regards the failure to conform to the traffic sign, there is an obvious difficulty. When the defendant failed to conform to the sign, he was asleep and not "driving." At the earlier time when he was awake, he did not fail to conform to the sign in question because he had not then reached it. The problem is part of the general question of whether automatism induced by the defendant's own fault is a defence. In these cases, prior fault arises if the defendant was aware that he was becoming sleepy and made a choice to continue to drive anyway. The actual accident might not have resulted from a voluntary act because the driver was unconscious at the time of the impact, but his involuntary driving was caused by his prior choice to continue driving even though he knew he was sleepy. If the offence is one of negligence, he should still be liable because a reasonable person would not drive whilst drowsy:

26–019

> "Every act of falling asleep at the wheel is preceded by a period of driving while awake and therefore, assuming the absence of involuntariness arising from other causes, responsible for his actions. If a driver who knows or ought[78] to know that there is a significant risk of falling

---

[74] See further J. A. Horne and S. D. Baulk, "Awareness of Sleepiness When Driving," (2004) 41 *Psychophysiology* 161; K. Kaplan *et al.*, "Awareness of Sleepiness and Ability to Predict Sleep Onset: Can Drivers Avoid Falling Asleep at the Wheel?" (2008) 9 *Sleep Medicine* 71; A. Akerstedt *et al.*, "Impaired Alertness and Performance Driving Home from the Night Shift: A Driving Simulator Study," (2005) 14 *Journal of Sleep Research* 17.

[75] *Oakes v. Foster* [1961] Crim. L.R. 628; *Richards v. Gardner* [1974] Crim. L.R. 119.

[76] [1958] 1 Q.B. 277.

[77] In *R. v. Gosney* [1971] 3 W.L.R. 343 the Court of Appeal held that the former offence of reckless driving was not a strict liability offence and therefore the defendant was entitled to raise a defence of honest reasonable mistake.

[78] See *Attorney-General's Reference (No.4 of 2000)* [2001] 2 Cr. App. R. 22.

asleep at the wheel, and continues to drive the vehicle, he is plainly driving without due care and may be driving in a manner dangerous to the public. If the driver does fall asleep and death or bodily injury results, the driving prior to the falling asleep is sufficiently contemporaneous with the death or bodily injury to be regarded as the cause of death or bodily injury."[79]

A properly licensed driver in the 21st century ought to foresee the dangerousness of driving whilst in a sleepy state. The driver's decision (or negligence) to drive when he knows that he is not fit to do so is made immediately prior to falling asleep and therefore his prior fault is sufficiently contemporaneous with the involuntary harmful driving.

26–020 **How far gone must the driver be, not to be accounted "driving"?**   Of course this question cannot be answered in the abstract, but the weight of authority holds that if the defendant was driving in what is legally accepted as a state of severely impaired consciousness, then he is not "driving" in contemplation of the law. Severely impaired consciousness has been interpreted as excluding cases where the defendant maintains a fraction of control or awareness.[80] In *Re Attorney-General's Reference (No. 2 of 1992)*,[81] a heavy goods lorry was driving down the motorway when his lorry wandered into the hard shoulder (emergency lane) and continued driving down it until it collided with a parked vehicle. The impact of the collision killed two people. The driver admitted that he felt sleepy but the evidence showed that he had taken the necessary respite breaks as required by law. The defence of automatism was raised, based on expert evidence of a condition of "driving without awareness". According to the evidence, the driver had become unaware of what was in front of him because he was suffering a special kind of fatigue. The Court of Appeal held that the fatigue could only operate as a defence if it resulted in the driver suffering "a total loss of voluntary control, not just impaired or reduced control."[82] Since the driver was able to respond to strong stimuli such as flashing lights, it was held that he did not suffer a complete loss of control.

If a driver is aware that he is very fatigued, his decision to continue driving would come within the purview of the prior fault doctrine. Notwithstanding this, the decision in *Re Attorney-General's Reference (No. 2 of 1992)* is wholly unsatisfactory. There may be cases where a person without prior fault has not suffered a complete destruction of voluntary control, but has no real control. A significant loss of voluntary control (let us say, an 80 *per cent.* loss of control—if such a thing can be quantified) is the same as a total loss of voluntary control. If a person has only 20 *per cent.* control, he can hardly be said to be in control of his bodily movements. A person may maintain some control, but may be too far gone to regain sufficient control to make a difference. The lorry driver seems to have crossed the threshold of no return!

---

[79] *R. v. Jiminez* (1992) 173 C.L.R. 572 at 587 citing *R. v. Kroon* (1990) 52 A. Crim. R. 15; *McBride v. The Queen* (1966) 115 C.L.R. 44.
[80] *Re Attorney-General's Reference (No. 2 of 1992)* [1994] Q.B. 91; *Watmore v. Jenkins* [1962] 2 Q.B. 572.
[81] [1994] Q.B. 91 at 95-96.
[82] *Re Attorney-General's Reference (No. 2 of 1992)* [1994] Q.B. 91, at 95-96.

The previous discussion leads on to a wider question. How far is the automatism displaced by evidence that the condition was produced wholly or in part by the defendant's voluntary intoxication? Automatism resulting from voluntary intoxication will not provide the defendant with a defence.

26–021

Would a person foresee that by drinking all day he might become a robotic murderer? Voluntary intoxication involving alcohol does not necessarily involve prior fault, as consuming a legally acceptable social drug such as alcohol over many hours is different to driving whilst sleepy. Unlike the sleeping driver the drunkard might not foresee the potential harmfulness of him continuing to drink. If D has been at the cricket or horse races all day drinking, it can hardly be said that he foresaw that by drinking all day he would become intoxicated and kill someone later that night. In England and Wales many thousands of people drink themselves into oblivion on a daily basis without going on to engage in crime. The decision to drink alcohol cannot be linked to the end crime. Hence, the term prior fault is a misnomer to the extent that it is applied to alcohol related automatism, because drinking alcohol is criminally faultless prior conduct (or at least faultless to the extent that it is independently criminal conduct that has no relation to the offence being charged).[83]

26–022

Automatism induced by voluntary intoxication is punished for policy reasons. The voluntarily intoxicated automaton is held constructively liable for choosing to get intoxicated, because it is assumed that if he had not been intoxicated he would not have committed the offence. The general policy argument for dispensing with the fault requirement in such cases is that many crimes are committed by intoxicated defendants.[84] Lawmakers also find it difficult to believe that alcohol causes a complete loss of control in the majority of cases, so it is assumed that charging the defendant with a lesser basic intent offence strikes a fair balance.

The harshness of the liability without fault approach adopted in the voluntary intoxication cases is softened slightly by the application of the *R. v. Majewski* rule.[85] If the crime is of specific intent, automatism is a defence in the usual way. If it is of basic intent, voluntary intoxication producing the automatism is fatal to the defence (whether the automatism is regarded as negativing the intent or the act). Putting this another way, it may be said that in crimes of basic intent *D.P.P. v. Majewski* rides rough-shod over all doctrines of *mens rea* and *actus reus*. The evidence of voluntary intoxication and its consequential muddled state of mind are to be ignored in deciding whether the defendant intended the result in question. This interpretation of the law is essential, because the law would be even more confused than it now is if the courts distinguished between "ordinary"

---

[83] An intoxicated defendant might commit manslaughter in a public place and thus would not only be criminally liable for manslaughter but also the offence of being drunk and disorderly in a public place pursuant to section 91 of the *Criminal Justice Act 1967*. But the latter is a totally independent and unrelated form of criminality and it has no relation to the non-contemporaneous act of killing which occurs after the defendant has become an automaton. This involves criminal liability without *relevant* fault—not criminal liability without *contemporaneous* fault.

[84] Gavin Dingwall, *Alcohol and Crime*, (London: Willan Publishing, 2006).

[85] [1977] A.C. 443.

voluntary intoxication and such intoxication resulting in automatism. Intoxication resulting in a confusional state is both intoxication and automatism, and is governed by *D.P.P. v. Majewski*.[86]

26–023   Compare this with the diabetes type cases where the defendant has caused his own state of automatism by failing to follow medical advice in circumstances where the defendant knew of the potential harmfulness of not doing so. These types of cases fall within the purview of the prior fault doctrine because the defendant is aware of the danger posed by failing to take his insulin, but runs the risk.[87] The court in *R. v. Bailey*[88] did not altogether rule out criminal liability for injuries inflicted in a confusional state resulting from hypoglycaemia. A person can, it was held, be liable for recklessness causing the commission of a crime of basic intent if he knew what would happen if he did not take food after his insulin and if there were no circumstances excusing his failure to take food. This is another instance of the mental element antedating and not being concurrent with the physical act causing the injury. The court made it clear that it was not speaking of the fictitious recklessness that was attributed to the drunkards in *D.P.P. v. Majewski*, but meant real recklessness: knowledge by the defendant that in failing to take precautions against a loss of consciousness he was endangering others.

26–024   **What about when the automatism is produced by a combination of intoxication and another cause?**   Surprising as it may seem, it is now well settled that such circumstances are to be judged as cases of automatism without applying the rule in *D.P.P. v. Majewski*. In other words, the intoxication can be a defence even in crimes of basic intent. *D.P.P. v. Majewski* operates only where the confusional state is produced by voluntary intoxication alone. The intervention in substantial degree of any other causal factor means that the confusional state can be found to be inconsistent with, and therefore to negative, the required mental element.[89] The combination of factors just referred to may occur in different ways:

1.   Voluntary intoxication may bring about some factor or event that itself wholly produces the state of automatism. A drunkard staggers and falls, hitting his head; he then inflicts some injury without knowing what he is doing. The medical evidence is that the defendant was concussed, and that his confusional state was, medically speaking, due entirely to the concussion, the defendant's intoxication being merely a historical cause of the concussion. Here the usual defence of automatism will avail. The rule would be obvious if the concussion were not causally connected with the intoxication, but it is applied also where (as in this example) the concussion is produced as a result of the defendant's intoxicated state.

---

[86] See Chapter 19.

[87] *R. v. Bailey* [1983] 1 W.L.R. 760.

[88] [1983] 1 W.L.R. 760.

[89] *R. v. Roach* [2001] EWCA Crim. 2698; *R. v. Burns* (1973) 58 Cr. App. R. 49; *R. v. Budd* [1962] Crim. L.R. 49; *Police v. Barber* [2010] S.A.S.C. 329. Likewise, if a defence of insanity is available, then intoxication will not matter, see *D.P.P. v. Beard* [1920] A.C. 479; *R. v. Davis* (1881) 14 Cox C.C. 563. See also *R. v. McEachem* [2003] A.W.L.D 209.

2.   As in case 1, except that the medical evidence is that the defendant's confusional state was the result both of voluntary intoxication and (in substantial degree) of another cause. For example, the evidence may be that it was immediately caused by the combination of concussion and voluntary intoxication. Here again it has been held that automatism is a defence.[90] What will create a flutter of dovecotes will be a case in which evidence of alcoholic intake is combined with evidence from a friendly psychiatrist that when the defendant imbibed he was in a highly emotional state, the result being to produce dissociation which would not have occurred without the presence of both factors![91]

3.   As in case 2, but the second factor is the taking of a drug which potentiates the intoxicant and increases its effect. If the drug was taken for the purpose of increasing intoxication, the case is obviously governed by *D.P.P. v. Majewski* (indeed Majewski himself had produced his condition by taking drugs as well as drink). On the other hand, if the drug was taken for some other purpose, as for a stomach upset, the defendant not realizing the effect it would have, and if the intoxicant would not have produced the state of automatism by itself, the defence of automatism is available.[92] This is only another way of saying that the intoxication is not regarded as voluntary, and therefore is not covered by *D.P.P. v. Majewski*.

4.   As in case 2, except that the second factor is a "disease of the mind." A person who is prone to psychotic outbursts triggers such an outburst by drinking. As a matter of common sense it would seem that the verdict on such facts should be one of insanity.[93] One case holds that a verdict of non-insane automatism would be permissible.[94]

---

[90] *R. v. Stripp* (1978) 69 Cr. App. R. 318.

[91] Cf. *R. v. Prescott* [2008] O.N.C.J 604; *R. v. Talock* [2003] 238 Sask. R. 130.

[92] *R. v. Hardie* [1981] 1. W.L.R. 64.

[93] Lawrence P. Tiffany and Mary Tiffany, "Nosologic, Objections to the Criminal Defence of Pathological Intoxication: What do the Doubters Doubt?" (1990) 13 *Int'l J. L. & Psychiatry* 49; Lawrence P. Tiffany, "The Drunk, the Insane, and the Criminal Courts: Deciding What to Make of Self-Induced Insanity," (1991) 69 *Wash. U.L.Q.* 221.

[94] *R. v. Burns* (1973) 58 Cr. App. R. 49.

CHAPTER 27

CRIMINAL CAPACITY AND INSANITY

"The misery of the insane more thoroughly excites our pity than any other suffering to which humanity is subject; but it is necessary that the madness should be acknowledged to be madness before the pity can be felt."[1]

27.1. STATE IMMUNITIES

Who is answerable to the criminal law? Natural persons are answerable for violations of the criminal law unless they are able to show that they lacked the capacity to understand that what they were doing was wrong in the sense that it violated the criminal law.[2] Certain fictitious legal entities such as corporations are also answerable for various violations of the criminal law. It is the corporation itself (a legal creation) that is labelled a criminal, although the natural persons who control it can also be labelled as criminals. The corporation is treated as a natural person,[3] but a corporation cannot be jailed or experience the shame or stigmatizing effects of criminalization. Nor can it lose its mind. Certain persons are exempted from the operation of the criminal law, or from its effects, on the ground of official status: the sovereign,[4] foreign visiting sovereigns,[5] foreign diplomats,[6] and members of foreign armed forces.[7]

A rule of construction of statutes declares that they do not bind the Crown in the absence of express words or necessary implication, and this sometimes has the result of exempting officers of the Crown from the operation of penal statutes when such officers are acting on behalf of the Crown.[8] Apart from this rule, officers of the Crown are fully subject to the criminal law in their private

27–001

---

[1] Anthony Trollope, *He Knew He Was Right*, (London: Smith and French, Vol. II, 1869), 491.

[2] *R. v. Johnson* [2007] EWCA Crim. 1978.

[3] *DPP v. Kent and Sussex Contractors Ltd.* [1944] K.B. 146.

[4] *Cooke's Case* (1660) 5 How. St. Tr. 1077 at 1113; *Tobin v. R.* (1864) 33 L.J.C.P 199. Cf. *R. v. Mary, Queen of Scots* (1586) 1 St. Tr. 1161, where the immunity was not extended to the exiled Queen Mary of Scots; she was executed for treason for planning to have Elizabeth I assassinated.

[5] Section 20(1), (2) of the *State Immunity Act 1978.*

[6] *Diplomatic Privileges Act 1964*; *International Organisations Act 1968*. The protection is more limited for diplomatic agents who are citizens of the United Kingdom or of one of its colonies; or are permanently resident in the United Kingdom. *R. v. Bow Street Stipendiary Magistrate, Ex p. Pinochet Ugrate (No. 3)* [2000] 1 A.C. 147.

[7] Section 3 of the *Visiting Forces Act 1954.*

[8] The *Crown Proceedings Act 1947*. See also *Thomas v. Pritchard* [1903] 1 K.B. 209; *BBC v. Johns* [1964] 1 All E.R. 923.

capacity[9] (that is to say, they are liable to pay any fine themselves, unless the Crown does so *ex gratia*).[10] The Crown itself cannot be prosecuted, for that would be *Regina v. Reginam*, which is thought to be impossible (it is not, of course); and the same rule applies in favour of Government Departments and other Crown agencies.[11] On the other hand, some public bodies are not regarded as emanations of the Crown.

The immunity of the Crown is an indefensible exception from the rule of law. It means, for example, that Government Departments and certain other public bodies are generally not bound by public welfare legislation. Nevertheless, the *Corporate Manslaughter and Corporate Homicide Act 2007* largely removes Crown immunity as far as it applies to corporate manslaughter. Coupled with this, the *Food Safety Act 1990* does not allow prosecutions but it does allow the courts to declare certain acts of the Crown as unlawful.[12] These matters are discussed more fully in specialized works, including works on constitutional and international law, and need not concern us further.

27.2. CHILDHOOD

27–002   A child under the age of ten cannot be held criminally responsible for his harmful actions because it is presumed that he is *doli incapax*—incapable of fully comprehending the nature of criminal wrongs.[13]

27–003   **Why the magic of the age of 10? Why not 12, or 14, or 16?**   The age at common law was the age of seven. Section 50 of the *Children and Young Persons Act 1933* raised it to eight and section 16 of the *Children and Young Persons Act 1963* raised it to ten. Although children are now responsible from the age of ten onwards, at one time those under 14 received the benefit of a rule at common law that a child in this age-group could not be convicted, however uncontrollable he was, unless he knew that what he did was wrong—which seemed to have meant either legally wrong or morally wrong.[14] This rule was abolished by section 34 of the *Crime and Disorder Act 1998*.[15] This was confirmed in *R. v. JTB*[16] where the defendant was tried on indictment for causing or inciting another child to engage in sexual activity. The defendant was only 12-years-old when the alleged offending took place. It was argued on his behalf that he was incapable of

---

[9] See the discussion in *M. v. Home Office and Another* [1994] 1 A.C. 377.

[10] Cf. *Barnett v. French* [1981] 1 W.L.R. 848, where the nominated defendant's fines were covered by the Crown.

[11] Cf. section 1 of the *Corporate Manslaughter Act 2007*, which applies to corporations and government bodies and other bodies as listed in Sch. 1 (as amended).

[12] "Unlawfulness declarations" are also permitted by other enactments such as the *Environmental Protection Act 1990*; the *Environmental Act 1995*; *Transport Act 2000*; the *Chemical Weapons Act 1996*.

[13] See generally, Joseph B. Sanborn, "Juveniles' Competency to Stand Trial: Wading Through the Rhetoric and the Evidence," (2009) 99 *J. Crim. L. & Criminology* 135; Stephen Morse, "Immaturity and Irresponsibility," (1998) 88 *J. Crim. L. & Criminology* 15.

[14] *C (A Minor) v. D.P.P.* [1996] 3 A.C. 1 at 23; *R. v. JTB* [2009] 2 W.L.R. 1088 at 1092-96.

[15] For a critical evaluation of the pre-1998 presumption see the judgment of Laws J. in *C (A Minor) v. D.P.P.* [1994] 3 W.L.R. 888.

[16] [2009] 2 W.L.R. 1088.

committing the offences because he lacked the capacity to understand that what he did was wrong. The House of Lords held that section 34 of the *Crime and Disorder Act 1998* had abolished the rebuttable presumption that a child aged between 10 and 14 was *doli incapax*.

Of course any age must be arbitrary. The governing considerations are pragmatic. At what age does one wish to be able to administer legal punishment to a juvenile? Even if it is only to be a fine, if the outcome is punitive in intent this implies that the offender must be legally responsible. Precocious children get to know the age of criminal responsibility and are quite apt to say to a policeman: "You can't touch me. I'm under ten." Even if punitive sanctions are intended to be used only for particularly bad offenders, they still imply that criminal responsibility must be attributed to offenders of that age. (It is true that punishment could be meted out in nominally civil proceedings,[17] or by way of school discipline under legal auspices. But the abandonment of criminal procedure would carry some danger of either injustice or ineffectiveness or both).

You have just told me that defendants over the age of ten are treated as adults because (barring some other disability) they know right from wrong? Does that also mean that such defendants are presumed to have the mental capacity to participate effectively in complex criminal proceedings? Would it not be unfair to try a very young defendant of low intelligence? A low IQ or other types of mild mental impairments do not necessarily mean that a defendant will not be able to follow or understand his trial.[18] The issue is more complicated when the mildly impaired or not so bright defendant is also very young. There is no doubt that a normal 11-year-old would be sufficiently mature to understand that it is wrong to kill another.[19] But given the intricacy of a murder trial, he might struggle to fully understand all the complexities involved.[20] It cannot be forgotten that such defendants are still children. Defendants aged 13 or 14 would be in a better position in this respect. But there is no denying that some young offenders (even 11-year-olds) are repeat offenders who understand what they have done is very wrong.[21] The courts have held that trying those who are affected by a combination of youth and low intelligence does not lead to a breach of Article 6 of the *European Convention*.[22] In *R. (on the application of P) v. West London Youth Court*[23] the defendant had the intellect of an eight-year-old, but was fifteen years old. The defendant was facing charges of robbery and attempted

27–004

---

[17] In some cases it will be appropriate to apply for a supervision order under the *Children Act 1989*. See the discussion in *Crown Prosecution Service v. P* [2008] 1 W.L.R. 1005.

[18] *R. v. M and Another* [2006] All E.R. 43.

[19] James Bulger was killed by two 10-years-old boys. See *V v. United Kingdom* (2000) 30 E.H.R.R. 121.

[20] Andrew Ashworth, "Case Comment: Human Rights: Article 6(1)—Right to Fair Trial of Defendant Aged 11," [2005] Crim. L.R. 132.

[21] The young defendant in *SC v. United Kingdom* [2005] 1 F.C.R. 347 had a long history of offending and clearly knew he was acting wrongly when he robbed an 87-year-old woman. Despite his youth and low intelligence, the court was of the view that he had understood the trial process sufficiently, because he was no stranger to the legal system and had ample support.

[22] *European Convention for the Protection of Human Rights and Fundamental Freedoms*, 4 November 1950, 213 U.N.T.S. 222, (entered into force generally on 3 September 1953).

[23] [2006] 1 All E.R. 477.

robbery and it was argued on his behalf that he would not be able to understand a criminal trial and thus would not be able to participate effectively in the trial in accordance with the requirements of Article 6. The court held the defendant could be tried where:[24]

> "i.   [h]e had understood what he is said to have done wrong;
> ii.   the court was satisfied that the claimant when he had done wrong by act or omission had the means of knowing that was wrong;
> iii.   he understood what, if any, defences were available to him;
> iv.   he has a reasonable opportunity to make relevant representations if he wished;
> v.   he has the opportunity to consider what representations he wishes to make once he has understood the issues involved. He has to be able to give proper instructions and to participate by way of providing answers to questions and suggesting questions to his lawyers in the circumstances of the trial as they arise."

Youth and a limited intellectual capacity will not prevent a person from having a fair trial. The focus has to be on whether the particular defendant is able to participate effectively in the trial, not on his age and intelligence. Even a very young offender would be able to participate effectively in a trial if he has a history of offending and has been through the process several times before. Nevertheless for many very young offenders it will be their first time in court, so care will have to be taken to ensure that they get a fair trial. Very young defendants are usually tried summarily in the youth court, as its processes are better equipped for ensuing that they are able to participate in the trial. A specialist tribunal such as the youth court is especially designed to ensure children are given a fair trial. When a young defendant is being tried in the Crown Court, the court should:[25]

- "keep his level of cognitive function in mind;
- use concise and simple language;
- have regular breaks;
- take additional time to explain court proceedings;
- be proactive in ensuring the claimant has access to support;
- explain and ensure the claimant understands the ingredients of the charge;
- explain the possible outcomes and sentences; and
- ensure that cross-examination is carefully controlled so that questions are short and clear and frustration minimised."

This approach is better than not trying them at all,[26] because some young offenders repeatedly engage in violent crimes such as robbery and attempted murder[27] and understand that it is wrong to do so. Such offenders are dangerous and require detention and rehabilitation.

---

[24] *R. (on the application of P) v. West London Youth Court* [2006] 1 All E.R. 477 at 480.

[25] *R. (on the application of P) v. West London Youth Court* [2006] 1 All E.R. 477 at 486.

[26] *R (on application of C) v. Sevenoaks Youth Court* [2009] EWHC 3088, where it was held that a young defendant with a learning disability should have had an intermediary to explain the process to him. It was also held that the lawyer alone was not sufficient for this purpose.

[27] For example, see *R. v. W* [2009] 2 Cr. App. R. 94.

27.3. FITNESS TO PLEAD

Responsible is used in different meanings. An employer giving a reference to an employee may say that he is a "responsible person," meaning that he is of good character, efficient in work, and so on. Obviously that is not the meaning of "responsibility" in the criminal law. The worse a person's character is (that is to say, the more irresponsible he is), the more firmly he must be held "responsible" in the sense of "accountable."

27–005

We are speaking, therefore, of responsibility in the sense of moral or legal accountability. A person is morally responsible if he can justly be blamed and perhaps punished when he does wrong. We do not regard a dog as responsible, or a babe in arms, or a gibbering lunatic. On much the same principle they are not regarded as legally responsible, *i.e.* legally liable to punishment through the agency of the courts.

Society has two alternative ways of dealing with mischief-makers. Normally we regard them as responsible, which means that they can be left free in society, subject to punishment when they misbehave, the punishment being designed either to correct the offender for the future or to serve as a retributive warning to others, or both. But there are those such as young children and the severely mentally ill or mentally handicapped,[28] where we think it would be useless or wrong to invoke the criminal law. Although they are not responsible, the fact that they are not subject to punishment through the courts does not mean that they are left without social control. If a defendant is not fit to plead but facts show that he did the crime, he may, *inter alia*, be subject to detention in a mental hospital. If he is fit to plead, but was incapable of understanding the wrongness of his criminality at the time of offending, he may raise the substantive criminal law defence of insanity at his trial. However, successfully raising the defence might still result in the defendant being sent to a mental hospital.

Does this mean that the defendant has be to mentally fit to plead before the substantive defence of insanity can be considered?   Yes.

27–006

You told me earlier that low intelligence and immaturity will not necessarily mean that the defendant is unfit to plead. Why is this so?   It is all a matter of degree. "An accused is 'unfit to plead' if by reason of a disability, such as mental illness, he has—'insufficient intellect' to instruct his solicitors and counsel, to plead to the indictment, to challenge jurors, to understand the evidence, and to give evidence."[29] Low intelligence in itself does not prevent a person from understanding criminal proceedings. A first class honours law student obviously understands criminal law better than a student who has just passed the subject, but it could not be said that the latter does not understand criminal law. Similarly, an exceptionally bright youth might understand the trial process better than an adult who is intellectually challenged. "The whole purpose of sections 4 and 4A *Criminal Procedure (Insanity) Act 1964* is to protect a person who is unfit to

27–007

---

[28] This term is unfortunate, but it is not meant to be pejorative.
[29] *SC v. United Kingdom* [2005] 1 F.C.R. 347 at 357.

stand trial against the return of a verdict of guilty."[30] Therefore, justice requires that the defendant not be tried when he does not have a reasonable understanding of what is taking place. The interests of justice are served as long as the defendant has a very basic understanding of the process.

The question whether or not a defendant is fit to plead will be decided by a judge[31] after considering the written or oral evidence of at least two medical experts, one of whom should be recognized by the Home Secretary as a medical expert for this purpose. The issue of fitness to plead may be raised by the prosecution or the defence and if neither the prosecution nor defence team raise the issue the judge can where he thinks it is necessary to do so. Obviously, if the medical experts present evidence to show that the defendant has no sense of reality, the trial should not proceed.[32] The unfitness need not be related to mental illness as such. A person may be unfit to plead because he is a deaf mute and so on. The unfitness issue is normally determined at the arraignment before the trial commences, but the court may find that it is in the interests of the defendant to postpone the consideration of the question of fitness to be tried. It may postpone the question "until any time up to the opening of the case for the defence."[33]

Once it is determined that the defendant is not fit to plead, a jury will decide whether he did the act or made the omission.[34] If it is found that the defendant did the act or made the relevant omission, the judge may make a hospital order against the defendant. The purpose of subjecting those who are unfit to plead to a hospital order is to protect the public until they are fit to be tried. Obviously, in some cases detention will not be necessary, but monitoring may be.[35] Where it is found that the defendant did not do the act or make the omission, he will be entitled to an acquittal.

---

[30] *R. v. Antoine* [2001] 1 A.C. 340 at 351.

[31] Section 4(2) of the *Criminal Procedure (Insanity) Act 1964* (as amended).

[32] Under section 48 of the *Mental Health Act 1983*, the Secretary of State may use her discretion to order the defendant be sent to a mental hospital for treatment without trial. However, this only applies where "(a) that person is suffering from mental disorder of a nature or degree which makes it appropriate for him to be detained in a hospital for medical treatment; and (b) he is in urgent need of such treatment; and 1(c) appropriate medical treatment is available for him." The provision applies where the defendant is being held in a prison or remand centre. If the defendant no longer requires treatment he should be released or sent back to prison to await his trial.

[33] The judge may leave the issue of unfitness to plead until the prosecution has concluded its case, because it may emerge that there is no case to answer.

[34] Sections 4A of the *Criminal Procedure (Insanity) Act 1964* (as amended). The defendant can appeal against a finding that he was unfit to plead and that he did the act or made the omission: sections 15-16 of the *Criminal Appeal Act 1968*. However, the Court of Appeal cannot order a retrial: see *R. v. Norman* [2009] 1 Cr. App. R. 192 at 201-202.

[35] Section 5(2) of the *Criminal Procedure (Insanity) Act 1964* (as amended) provides: "The court shall make in respect of the accused–(a) a hospital order (with or without a restriction order); (b) a supervision order; or (c) an order for his absolute discharge."

Can the defendant raise a defence even though he has been found unfit to plead?   No, the trial should be postponed. Substantive defences and mistakes often amount to a denial of *mens rea* and thus should not be considered in a hearing where the defendant is unfit to plead.[36]

27–008

Are you telling me even if there is compelling evidence to show that the defendant acted in self-defence or made a mistake that he will have to wait until he is fit to plead to raise that defence?   Yes. Nevertheless, in *R. v. Antoine*,[37] Lord Hutton made some cursory comments towards the end of his judgment to the contrary.[38] Lord Hutton said:

27–009

> "If there is objective evidence which raises the issue of mistake or accident or self-defence, then the jury should not find that the defendant did the 'act unless it is satisfied beyond reasonable doubt on all the evidence that the prosecution has negatived that defence. For example, if the defendant had struck another person with his fist and the blow had caused death, it would be open to the jury under section 4A(4) to acquit the defendant charged with manslaughter if a witness gave evidence that the victim had attacked the defendant with a knife before the defendant struck him. Again, if a woman was charged with theft of a handbag and a witness gave evidence that on sitting down at a table in a restaurant the defendant had placed her own handbag on the floor and, on getting up to leave, picked up the handbag placed beside her by a woman at the next table, it would be open to the jury to acquit."

Self-defence is something that would have to be tested in a criminal trial, especially when it is raised against a charge as serious as murder. Even powerful (objective) evidence showing that the defendant was acting in self-defence such as C.C.T.V. footage, cannot tell us whether he believed it was necessary for him to act in self-defence, or whether he was acting in revenge and so on. Similarly, C.C.T.V. footage may suggest that the defendant mistakenly took the wrong handbag, but that does not mean she was honest. It is not possible to determine whether she acted honestly where she is not sufficiently alert to deny that she was intending to permanently deprive the owner of the handbag, or to assert that she thought she had a claim of right. Lord Hutton's suggestion that a witness statement would be sufficient to allow a court to acquit when the act has been done is not supported by the wording of sections 4 and 4A of *Criminal Procedure (Insanity) Act 1964*. If the evidence is exceptionally compelling, then it would be appropriate for the prosecution to drop the charges.

---

[36] As the court noted in *R. v. Grant* [2002] Q.B. 1030 at 1048: "it would be unrealistic and contradictory, in relation to a person unfit to tried, that a jury should have to consider what effect the conduct of the deceased [provocation] had on the mind of that person."

[37] *R. v. Antoine* [2001] 1 A.C. 340 at 376-377 *per* Lord Hutton. See also *R. v. Jagnieszho* [2008] EWCA Crim. 3065.

[38] *Criminal Procedure (Insanity) Act 1964*.

27.4.   WHEN MENTAL DISORDER IS A DEFENCE

27–010   "Mental disorder" is the widest possible expression for disorder of the mind: it is much too wide to be recognized as a complete defence to a charge of crime. The definition in section 1(2) of the *Mental Health Act 1983*[39] is as follows:

> "'Mental disorder' means any disorder or disability of the mind."

The definition is so wide that it would cover mere neurosis, such as claustrophobia (fear of confined spaces). If a claustrophobic on Dartmoor punches someone on the nose, his malady is not a reason for letting him off a charge.

27–011   **It would not be causally connected with the assault. But suppose the claustrophobic panicked when he was in a car, and struck out?**   Even then he would not have a defence, though the medical evidence would no doubt induce the court to treat him leniently.

27–012   **But surely insanity is a defence?**   The general principle of English law may sound strange: even those mentally disordered people who may be called insane can be held responsible. Insanity *per se* is not a defence.

27–013   **What if the person was completely off his head and did not know what he was doing?**   In that case he would lack the mental element necessary for the crime. The law still rests on the answers given by the House of Lords in *M'Naghten's* case (1843).[40] The facts that gave rise to this famous pronouncement are now only of historical interest, but may be mentioned briefly. One Daniel M'Naghten shot Sir Robert Peel's secretary, perhaps thinking that it was Peel himself. M'Naghten, who suffered from what today would be called paranoia, was actuated by the morbid delusion that he was being persecuted by the "Tories." He was acquitted on the ground of insanity, being committed to hospital in the usual way; but the supposed leniency of the verdict caused a public outcry. The law of insanity was debated in the House of Lords, and their Lordships decided to ask the judges to advise them on the relevant legal principles. Theoretically this type of advisory opinion is not binding as precedent. The joint answer given by fourteen judges as a result of the *M'Naghten* case has, however, been so frequently followed and approved that it must be taken as authoritative, at any rate for the most part.

---

[39] The former definition referred to "arrested or incomplete development of mind, psychopathic disorder and any other disorder or disability of mind." Presumably, the reference to "disability" in the new provision will cover those who are mentally impaired because they are mentally handicapped and so on.

[40] 10 Cl. & Fin. 200. For discussion of the history of the excuse of insanity see Cynthia G. Hawkins-León, "'Literature as Law': The History of the Insanity Plea and a Fictional Application Within the Law and Literature Canon," (1999) 72 *Temp. L. Rev.* 381; Anthony Michael Platt and Bernard L. Diamond, "The Origins and Development of the 'Wild Beast' Concept of Mental Illness and Its Relation to Theories of Criminal Responsibility," (1965) 1 *J. Hist. Behav. Sci.* 355. See also the dissenting judgment of McDevitt J. in *State v. Searcy*, 798 P.2d 914 at 928-931 (1990).

The answer reads, in its essential portion, as follows. (I have inserted the lettering and numbering.):

> "The jurors ought to be told in all cases that every man is to be presumed to be sane, and to possess a sufficient degree of reason to be responsible for his crimes, until the contrary be proved to their satisfaction; and that to establish a defence on the ground of insanity, it must be clearly proved that, (A) at the time of committing the act, the accused was labouring under such a defect of reason, from disease of the mind, (B) as not to know (1) the nature and quality of the act he was doing, or, if he did know it, (2) that he did not know he was doing what was wrong."

The judges added (3) that if the defendant "labours under [a] partial delusion only, and is not in other respect insane, we think he must be considered in the same situation of responsibility as if the facts with respect to which the delusion exists were real."

The judges' explanation was as follows: **27–014**

> "For example, if under the influence of his delusion he supposes another man to be in the act of attempting to take away his life, and he kills that man, as he supposes, in self-defence, he would be exempt from punishment. If his delusion was that the deceased had inflicted a serious injury to his character and fortune, and he killed him in revenge for such supposed injury, he would be liable to punishment."[41]

This answer lays down a double test for exemption. (A) The defendant must have been suffering from "a defect of reason, from disease of the mind." (B) If he was, there are two or perhaps three further questions for the jury:

1.   Is it the case that, in consequence of this defect of reason, the defendant did not know the nature and quality of his act?
2.   If he did, did he not know it was wrong?
3.   Was he under a delusion?—if that question can ever arise, having regard to question 1.

Although the *M'Naghten* rules save the defendant from criminal liability, they do not, of course, exempt him from the special verdict.

What is "a defect of reason, from disease of the mind"?   "Disease of the   **27–015**
mind" is no longer in medical use, though doctors (psychiatrists) are still prepared to humour lawyers by saying in court that a particular person suffers or does not suffer from it. The current medical phrases are mental illness and (a wider expression) mental disorder. But these do not precisely indicate the meaning of "disease of the mind." The judges in *M'Naghten* appear to have used the phrase convertibly with "insanity," but this is an equally baffling expression. Lawyers used to believe that insanity was a medical term, yet psychiatrists have long declared that they do not know what it means, and assert that it can only be

---

[41] *R. v. M'Naghten* (1843) 10 Cl. & Fin. 200 at 211. Daniel M'Naghten was acquitted by the jury before the formulation of the rules now associated with his name; but under those rules he should have been convicted because he formed the intent to kill a person.

a legal concept, which in fact it is. Insanity is a social judgment founded upon, but not precisely representing, a medical diagnosis.

A rough medical translation of "psychosis," means a condition involving a more serious kind of mental illness, generally involving hallucinations or delusions.[42] But as was noted above in the discussion on automatism,[43] there are many conditions that are internal to the defendant that can cause a loss of cognition/volition, that have little to do with psychosis. Almost any condition that arises internally in the defendant will amount to insanity at law when it causes a sufficient loss of cognition. The *M'Naghten* rules focus exclusively on cognitive impairments caused by diseases of the mind. Examples of conditions that are typically related to a person's internal biological makeup include schizophrenia, manic-depression and cerebral[44] arteriosclerosis.[45] Some internal conditions have external causes such as Post Traumatic Stress Disorder (P.T.S.D.), which a person might suffer after fighting in a war.[46] (The war is the external event that causes the internal condition to develop.)

Other impairments are directly related to the biological makeup of the defendant such as personality disorders,[47] epilepsy,[48] diabetes,[49] sleep disorders[50] and so on. Some mental conditions do not produce the degree of cognitive impairment required by the *M'Naghten* rules and thus do not come within the purview of the insanity defence. Examples might include battered women's syndrome,[51] premenstrual syndrome[52] or a homophobic panic attack.[53] The latter conditions do not normally prevent a person from knowing right from wrong or from understanding the nature or quality of his act.

27–016   **What must the defendant know to be wrong?**   The three *M'Naghten* questions are principally concerned with cognition and ultimately whether the

---

[42] An hallucination is a disturbed perception—the patient hears "voices" or sees apparitions. A delusion is a belief resulting from disturbed thinking, such as the paranoia suffered by M'Naghten.

[43] See Chapter 26.

[44] Pronounced "*ser*ebral."

[45] *R. v. Kemp* [1957] 1 Q.B. 399.

[46] See *United States v. Tracy*, 36 F. 3d 187 (1st Cir. 1994); Heathcote W. Wales, "Causation in Medicine and Law: The Plight of the Iraq Veterans," (2009) 35 *New Eng. J. Crim. & Civ. Confinement* 373 at 392.

[47] *United States v. Denny-Shaffer*, 2 F. 3d 999 (10th Cir. 1993). See the discussion of this case in J. C. Oleson, "Is Tyler Durden Insane?" (2007) 83 *N.D. L. Rev.* 579 at 615. See also Elyn R. Saks, "Multiple Personality Disorder and Criminal Responsibility," (2001) 10 *S. Cal. Interdisc. L.J.* 185.

[48] *R. v. Sullivan* [1983] 3 W.L.R. 123; *Bratty v. Attorney-General for Northern Ireland* [1963] A.C. 386.

[49] *R. v. Hennessy* [1989] 1 W.L.R. 287. Cf. *R. v. Bailey* [1983] 1 W.L.R. 760.

[50] *R. v. Burgess* [1991] 2 W.L.R. 1206.

[51] Although it has been sufficient to ground a defence of diminished responsibility, see *R. v. Ahluwalia* [1992] 4 All E.R. 899.

[52] See *R. v. Reynolds* [1988] Crim. L.R. 679 where the defendant was able to invoke the partial defence of diminished responsibility, because she was suffering from premenstrual syndrome and postnatal depression. See more generally, Bernadette McSherry, "The Return of the Raging Hormones Theory: Premenstrual Syndrome, Postpartum Disorders and Criminal Responsibility," (1993) 15 *Sydney L. Rev.* 292.

[53] Cynthia Lee, "The Gay Panic Defence," (2008) 42 *U.C. Davis L. Rev.* 471 at 491-94. Cf. Patricia J. Falk, "Novel Theories of Criminal Defence Based Upon the Toxicity of the Social Environment: Urban Psychosis, Television Intoxication and Black Rage," (1996) 74 *N.C. L. Rev.* 731.

defendant's cognitive incapacity meant that he did not form the *mens rea* for the offence. *M'Naghten* was decided at a time when the doctrine was still cloudy. Looking back, we can see that the judges' answers amount to little more than an assertion that the defendant cannot be convicted without the necessary mental element. Question 1: "Did he know the nature and quality of his act?" means "Did he know what he was doing?" (Did he know that he was killing someone; did he know that he was sticking a knife into someone; did he know he was burning someone's house down?) This is a *mens rea* question. If D squeezes her boyfriend's throat, believing that she is strangling a deadly snake, she is not aware of the nature of what she is doing and does not comprehend the physical and normative implications of her actions; therefore she does not form the *mens rea* for murder.[54] There is no *mens rea* because D does not intend to kill a human being.

Suppose that the defendant attacked someone in the insane belief that he was acting in self-defence. He knew he was hitting the victim on the head. Would he be said to have known the nature and quality of his act?   If an insanity defence is raised in such a case it may be held that since the defendant did not apprehend all the circumstances relevant to liability for the crime, he has the defence under question 1. But if the judge is in any doubt as to the law he can instruct the jury under question 3, the delusion question, and this clearly lets the defendant out. Had the facts been as he supposed, it would not have been a crime.[55] If D, a member of a university rowing team, travels from Oxford to Cambridge to kill the team's captain, because his delusions cause him to be believe that the captain is planning to kill him and that he has to strike first to save his life, the defence of insanity would not apply because the delusion has not lead him to believe that he was in imminent danger, which if true, would ground the defence of self-defence.[56]

27–017

But surely the same result could be obtained by considering the second question; the third does not seem to add much?   This is true. If a person's delusions cause him to believe that he is acting lawfully when in fact he is not, then the defence of insanity would be available either under question 2 or question 3. However, question 3 seems to cover only legal wrongness—not moral *and* legal wrongness. It seems to cover cases where the defendant understands the nature and quality of his act (that he is killing a human being) and understands that it is wrong to kill a human being (he might not only understand that it is

27–018

---

[54] *R. v. Codère* (1917) 12 Cr. App. R. 21; *R. v. Johnson* [2007] EWCA Crim. 1978.

[55] Cf. the Privy Council decision in *Moore v. Trinidad and Tobago* [2001] U.K.P.C. 4.

[56] See *Finger v. State*, 117 Nev. 548 at 576 (2001), where a United States court held: "So, if a jury believes he was suffering from a delusional state, and if the facts as he believed them to be in his delusional state would justify his actions, he is insane and entitled to acquittal. If, however, the delusional facts would not amount to a legal defence, then he is not insane. Persons suffering from a delusion that someone is shooting at them, so they shot back in self-defence are insane under *M'Naghten*. Persons who are paranoid and believe that the victim is going to get them some time in the future, so they hunt down the victim first, are not."

morally wrong, but also that it is also a serious crime), but where he believes his act of killing is lawfully justified. This is explained nicely in the following passage:

> "An individual who labours under the total delusion that he is a soldier in a war and is shooting at enemy soldiers is not capable of forming the intent to kill with malice aforethought. His delusional state prohibits him from forming the requisite *mens rea*, because he believes that his killing is authorized by law. He is legally insane under *M'Naghten*. Anytime a statute requires something more than the intent to commit a particular act, then legal insanity must be a viable defence to the crime and involves both tests under the *M'Naghten* rule."[57]

This analysis might also apply to the defence of duress of circumstances. For instance, an insane person might speed off in a motor vehicle because his delusions cause him to perceive an approaching police officer as an approaching assassin. As for the defence of self-defence, it does not seem to add much because that defence is available where a person genuinely believed it was necessary for him to act in self-defence.

27–019 **What is the difference between a delusion and a mistake?** The psychotic patient with a delusion persists in his false belief despite evidence to the contrary which an ordinary person would accept. It can be a difficult distinction. The psychiatrist may have to assess (for example) whether the defendant was labouring under an insane delusion that his brother was trying to kill him, or a stupid suspicion to the same affect. The answer may depend on the degree of absurdity of the belief, the tenacity with which it was held in the face of the evidence, *etc.*, in practice a delusion is not a single false belief, but spreads out into abnormal beliefs over a segment of life.

In summation, the *M'Naghten* rules can be interpreted as saying little more than that insanity may negative *mens rea*. However, they are not well framed to express this. In particular, question 3 (whether the defendant laboured under a partial delusion) is misleading. It suggests that although the defendant may not be liable in full degree he may be liable in some lesser degree. Normally, at least, this is not so. If his delusion was as to some ingredient legally necessary for the crime, he cannot be convicted.

The only one of the *M'Naghten* rules not going to *mens rea* as that is now interpreted[58] and understood is question 2, relating to knowledge of wrong. This is held to mean knowledge of legal wrong. Unless very benevolently interpreted it adds almost nothing to the other questions. The reason for saying this is that in practice insanity is never set up in the Crown Court except on charges of the gravest crimes; and a person would have to be very deranged not to know that killing or stabbing a person or burning a house is illegal; so deranged that the jury would probably refuse to find that he knew what he was doing. For instance, if D kills her five children because she believes God[59] has ordered her to kill them, she commits murder. She commits murder because she intends to kill human

---

[57] *Finger v. State*, 117 Nev. 548 at 574-575 (2001).

[58] *R. v. Windle* [1952] 2 Q.B. 826; *R. v. Johnson* [2007] EWCA Crim. 1978.

[59] Interestingly, if she believed God was telling her to kill, then she might have a special defence (the "deific decree defence") in some U.S. jurisdictions, even if she realized that the act was legally wrong. See *State v. Applin*, 116 Wash. App. 818 (2003).

beings. She will only be able to rely on the insanity defence when she does not realize that it is a crime to kill a human being. The wrongness question in the second prong of *M'Naghten*, unless interpreted as referring to moral wrongness, adds nothing to the other questions.

Are you telling me that insane defendants could be jailed even though they did not understand what they were doing as long as they realized that they were committing a criminal act?   Yes. Those who are very deranged but have sufficient cognitive awareness to realize the criminal nature of what they are doing, may not be able to raise the defence of insanity in England and Wales. Since these defendants have *mens rea* in a narrow legal sense, they will be held responsible for their insane acting. This is unjust in moral terms, because such defendants are not "morally culpable." They do not understand the moral wrongness of their actions. Since moral culpability in the wider sense underwrites the *mens rea* concept, insane defendants do not really act with legal *mens rea* either. The union of harm and culpability provides a sound basis for criminalization. A person should not be criminalized merely for knowing that something is legally wrong.[60] Where a person intends to commit a legal crime such as killing another person, because he believes it will prevent the world from being sucked into a black hole, he does not act with the type of moral culpability that the sane murderer acts with.[61] He is only culpable in a narrow legal sense. The defendant's insane delusions cause him to genuinely believe that he is morally justified in committing the particular criminal act.[62] This type of insane defendant may be blameworthy in a technical legal sense, but he is not morally culpable. It would be unjust to punish people when no retributive or deterrent objective is served.[63]

In *R. v. Johnson*,[64] the appellant (a paranoid schizophrenic) stabbed his neighbour because he believed that the victim had molested his sister.[65] The Court of Appeal held that the defendant was sufficiently cognitive to realize that his acts were legally wrong, and that it was therefore irrelevant that he was insane and could not comprehend the moral wrongness of what he had done. The Court of Appeal's analysis of the earlier law is not convincing. Hopefully, the Supreme

27–020

---

[60] Dennis J. Baker, "Constitutionalizing the Harm Principle," (2008) 27 *Crim. Just. Ethics* 3 at 7-9.

[61] Dennis J. Baker, *The Right Not to be Criminalized: Demarcating Criminal Law's Authority*, (Farnham: Ashgate Publishing, 2011) at Chap. 2.

[62] "Similarly, persons who thought they were soldiers in the middle of a battlefield, and that the individuals they were killing were enemy forces, would meet the second factor of *M'Naghten*. Such persons would know they were shooting and killing human beings, but would not understand that it was wrong because of their delusional belief they were in the middle of a war." *Finger v. State*, 117 Nev. 548 at 557 (2001).

[63] "This is because sane people are presumed to have the capacity to distinguish between right and wrong — if a sane person is of the opinion that murder is not wrong, his opinion makes him 'bad' (as opposed to sick) because he has the capacity to distinguish right from wrong." *R. v. Chaulk* [1990] 3 S.C.R. 1303 at para. 30 *per* Lamer J. This refers to "moral culpability", which clearly is necessary to demonstrate *mens rea* in the wider moral sense.

[64] [2007] EWCA Crim. 1978. However on the borderline facts in that case, the jury might have also concluded that his condition did not distort his perception of reality so severely that he could not understand the moral wrongness of his actions.

[65] His delusions caused him to falsely believe that many other people were also "noncing" (a colloquial term for "molesting") his sister.

Court will overturn *R. v. Johnson* when an opportunity arises. As long ago as 1933, the distinguished Australian jurist, Sir Owen Dixon, said:[66]

> "The other head is of quite a different character, namely, that his disease or disorder or disturbance of mind was of such a character that he was unable to appreciate that the act he was doing was wrong. It is supposed that he knew he was killing, knew how he was killing and knew why he was killing but that he was quite incapable of appreciating the wrongness of the act.... If through the disordered condition of the mind he could not reason about the matter with a moderate degree of sense and composure it may be said that he could not know what he was doing was wrong. What is meant by 'wrong'? What is meant by wrong is wrong having regard to the everyday standards of reasonable... people. [If it is found that] he was quite incapable of taking into account the considerations which go to make right or wrong, then you should find him not guilty ..."

Justice Dixon framed the following direction:

> "[the defendant] was disabled from knowing that it was a wrong act to commit in the sense that ordinary reasonable men understand right and wrong and that he was disabled from considering with some degree of composure and reason what he was doing and its wrongness."

27–021   His Honour affirmed this principle later as the Chief Justice of the Australian High Court in *Stapleton v. R.*[67] In *R. v. Chaulk*[68] the Supreme Court of Canada overruled its earlier ruling on this point and cited *Stapleton v. R.* as providing the correct interpretation of the law. It is also worth noting that more than half the states in the U.S. allow the defence for those who do not realize the moral wrongness of their actions.[69] In *R. v. Chaulk*[70] it was said:[71]

> "In my view, [this court's earlier ruling in *R. v. Schwartz*] had the effect of expanding the scope of criminal responsibility unacceptably to include persons who, by reason of disease of the mind, were incapable of knowing that an act was wrong according to the normal and reasonable standards of society even though they were aware that the act was formally a crime.
>
> ....
>
> "'The Nature of the Insanity Provisions', rests on the belief that persons suffering from insanity should not be subject to standard criminal culpability with its resulting punishment and stigmatization. This belief, in turn, flows from the principle that individuals are held responsible for the commission of criminal offences because they possess the capacity to distinguish between what is right and what is wrong."

The analysis in *R. v. Chaulk* is much more convincing than the terse analyses provided by the Court of Appeal in the English cases.[72] The core points in support of such interpretation can be summed up as:

---

[66] *The King v. Porter* (1933) 55 C.L.R. 182 at 189-190.

[67] (1952) 86 C.L.R. 358.

[68] [1990] 3 S.C.R. 1303 overruling *R. v. Schwartz* (1976) 29 C.C.C. (2d) 1.

[69] See Joshua Dressler, *Understanding Criminal Law*, (Newark N.J.: LexisNexis, 2006) at 376.

[70] [1990] 3 S.C.R. 1303. See also *R. v. Hussey* [2007] N.L.T.D. 4 at para. 38 (Can.).

[71] [1990] 3 S.C.R. 1303.

[72] *R. v. Codère* (1917) 12 Cr. App. R. 21; *R. v. Windle* [1952] 2 Q.B. 826; *R. v. Johnson* [2007] EWCA Crim. 1978.

- The second limb adds little to nothing if it means that the defendant can only rely on the insanity defence when he is so deranged that he does not realize he is committing a crime.[73]
- The authorities antedating *M'Naghten's* case[74] and earlier common law standards for determining the criminal responsibility of insane persons was "whether the particular accused had the capacity to distinguish between conduct that was good or evil, right or wrong." *M'Naghten* did not depart from or distinguish that standard.[75]
- *M'Naghten* drew a clear line between knowledge of illegality and knowledge of moral wrongness.[76]
- If wrong simply meant "illegal" the court would basically be prevented from considering the defendant's incapacity.[77] Such an approach would inject "a formalistic legalism into the insanity equation to the disregard of the psychological underpinnings of legal insanity."[78] A person suffering from extreme psychosis might be aware that the act is illegal but might lack the capacity to understand its wrongness and therefore face criminal censure.
- Finally, the contention that a moral standard would favour amoral offenders overlooks the fact that the loss of cognition has to be linked to disease of the mind.

If the insanity defence is primarily a negation of *mens rea*, does that mean it would not provide a defence where the offence carries strict or absolute liability?   There is no reason why the defence of insanity, to the extent that it relates to committing the *actus reus* of an offence, should not be available for   27–022

---

[73] A converse problem also arises: "One line of cases interpreting the *M'Naghten* test seems to require that defendant know that the act is wrong under societal standards of morality and is also illegal. ... This conjunctive test would appear to be unnecessarily rigid and would apparently exonerate a person by reason of insanity when the person knew that act was morally wrong but, as a result of a mental disease of defect, was not aware that it was contrary to law." *People v. Serravo*, 823 P. 2d 128 at 135 (1992).

[74] For an compendious and illuminating discussion of the moral right-wrong standard as developed in *M'Naghten,* see Antony Platt and Bernard L. Diamond, "The Origins of the 'Right and Wrong' Test of Criminal Responsibility and Its Subsequent Development in the United States: An Historical Survey," (1966) 54 *Cal. L. Rev.* 1227 at 1233-1237.

[75] *R. v. Chaulk* [1990] 3 S.C.R. 1303 at para. 100.

[76] *R. v. Chaulk* [1990] 3 S.C.R. 1303 at 100 where it is asserted that the distinction was "revealed in the following passage in *M'Naghten's Case* (at 723): If the accused was conscious that the act was one which he ought not to do, and if that act was at the same time contrary to the law of the land, he is punishable ...".

[77] "The object of [the second prong of *M'Naghten*] is to protect individuals who do not have the capacity to judge whether an act is wrong; the inquiry as to the capacity of an accused to reason must not end simply because it is determined that the accused knew that the act was a crime." *R. v. Chaulk* [1990] 3 S.C.R. 1303 at para. 101. In the U.S. in *People v. Serravo*, 823 P. 2d 128 at 135 (1992), it was said: "The *M'Naghten* judges expressly held that a defendant who knew nothing of the law would none the less be responsible if he knew that the act was wrong, by which, therefore, they must have meant, if he knew it was morally wrong. ... That must certainly have been the test under the older law when the capacity to distinguish between right and wrong imported a capacity to distinguish between good and evil as abstract qualities."

[78] *People v. Serravo*, 823 P. 2d 128 at 135 (1992).

absolute liability offences.[79] The Court of Appeal[80] has erroneously held that insanity only negates *mens rea* and therefore is not a defence for strict liability offending. The non-cognitive actor is in many senses a non-volitional actor. Automatism is available as a defence for non-voluntary acting, because the *actus reus* element of an offence has a volitional ingredient. Similarly, the insane person who harms others is not really in control of his bad actions (his cognitive disability prevents him from choosing not to act.)[81]

Insanity excuses a person from criminal responsibility when his mental condition deprives him of the capacity to avoid making choices that harm others. In *D.P.P. v. Harper*[82] the Court of Appeal were right to hold that *mens rea* is axiomatically satisfied when the offence is one of strict liability, but it erred when it failed to carry out an independent analysis of the insanity defence and its effect on the quality of the *actus reus*. It should have examined whether the *actus reus* was merely the product of non-cognitive acting. Generally, defences should be available in strict liability cases when the defence is unrelated to the issue of *mens rea*.[83] It would be contrary to justice to invoke criminal punishment in an attempt to deter non-cognitive harm-doing.

27–023 **One thing puzzles me. If the *M'Naghten* rules predominantly work as a denial of *mens rea*, why can't the defendant say: "I am not setting up a defence of insanity—I am denying *mens rea*, with the aid of medical evidence, and although I may be a bit wonky upstairs I want an ordinary acquittal, not your 'strings attached' insanity verdict"?** It depends upon what you mean by "wonky upstairs." If the mental disorder was a temporary affliction, you are right in suggesting that the defendant may sometimes get a clean acquittal as his *mens rea* is negated. But if the defendant was insane it is different. The law now accepted is that if the defending counsel adduces evidence that the defendant's mind was disordered at the time of the deed, for the purpose of negativing *mens rea*, counsel for the Crown may show that the particular abnormality from which the defendant was suffering amounted to insanity in law, in order to ensure that the defendant is subject to the special verdict. As noted above, if the condition is labelled as a "disease of the mind," even general automatism will be brought within the purview of the insanity defence.

---

[79] Insanity is a defence for strict liability offending in many U.S. states. See for example, *State v. Olmstead*, 310 Or. 455 (1990); *Tollefson v. State*, 525 So. 2d 957 (1988). It has also been recognized as a defence in all jurisdictions in Canada. See *R. v. Stokes* (2009) O.N.C.J 8 at para. 10; and *R. v. Metro News Ltd.* (1986) 56 O.R. (2d) 321 at para. 33 where the court (citing the first edition (at 906) and the second edition (at 142) of this book respectively) held that defences such as insanity, automatism or duress were available for absolute liability offences when the defence concerned the defendant's actions in committing the *actus reus* of the offence. The defence would also arise if the insanity caused a substantial lack of consciousness: *People v. Halvorsen*, 64 Cal. Rptr. 3d 721 (2007); *People v. Newton*, 8 Cal. App. 3d 359 (1970).

[80] *D.P.P. v. Harper* [1997] 1 W.L.R. 1406.

[81] In the U.S. insanity has also been recognized as a defence for strict liability involving non-automatistic (moral involuntariness) involuntary acting involving duress or compulsion. See *State v. Riedi*, 15 Kan. App. 2d 326 (1991); *State v. Rasmussen*, 524 N.W. 2d 843 (N.D. 1994). See also *R. v. Ruzic* [2001] S.C.C. 24 (Can.) *per* LeBel J.

[82] [1997] 1 W.L.R. 1406.

[83] *Tollefson v. State*, 525 So. 2d 957 at 961 (1988); *State v. Olmstead*, 800 P.2d 277 (1990).

It is worth observing that some U.S. states have abolished the insanity defence and have legislated to allow evidence of insanity to be used only to negate *mens rea*.[84] In the states where the insanity defence has been abolished defendants are only able to introduce evidence of mental illness to "show that the level of *mens rea* the state is required to prove as an element of a crime was not possessed by the defendant due to his mental condition."[85] These reforms have led to totally insane defendants being convicted because they were not able to negate the *mens rea* element.

Take the example of Mrs. Yates who killed her five children because she believed that God had ordered her to kill them. The *M'Naghten* rules (if the second prong requires an awareness of the moral wrongness of the particular acts of killing) would provide Mrs. Yates with an excusatory defence, because she did not know that what she did was wrong. Mrs. Yates believed that she was morally justified in drowning her children.[86] Merely producing evidence of mental illness would not be sufficient to negate *mens rea*, because Mrs. Yates acted intentionally (in the narrow legal sense) when she killed her five children. She also realized that it was a criminal offence to kill the children and that she was in fact killing children—she knew she was not merely drowning animals. Her mental illness did not negate her *mens rea*. The second prong of *M'Naghten* would, if it is read as requiring the defendant to understand the moral wrongness of her actions, as this would involve an evaluation of the defendant's moral culpability rather than her *mens rea* in the narrow legal sense.

27.5. M'NAGHTEN, NEGLIGENCE AND RECKLESSNESS

On its face, the first *M'Naghten* question is concerned with the defendant's knowledge (which means, also, his intention); but the topics of recklessness and negligence also need to be considered.   **27–024**

Whether *M'Naghten* applies to crimes of negligence remains uncertain; it has not been tested in the courts, because no lunatic having an adviser in his senses would set up an insanity defence to a charge of negligence.

A more substantial problem arises for recklessness, particularly because there may be the possibility of bypassing *M'Naghten* and obtaining an ordinary acquittal. Suppose a man is charged with arson, and says that he did not realize that the small fire he lawfully made would spread to other people's property, or that he did not realize that life would be endangered; and suppose that to support this defence he offers evidence that he has a low IQ. If the defence is credited (or not discredited), what should be the outcome?

Before *Commissioner of Police of the Metropolis v. Caldwell*[87] the courts on three occasions recognized that evidence of mental illness (schizophrenia) or

---

[84] See the discussion in Jean K. Gilles Phillips and Rebecca E. Woodman, "The Insanity of the *Mens Rea* Model: Due Process and the Abolition of the Insanity Defence," (2008) 28 *Pace L. Rev.* 455.

[85] Henry F. Fradella, "From Insanity to Beyond Diminished Capacity: Mental Illness and Criminal Excuse in the Post-Clark Era," (2007) 18 *U. Fla. J.L. & Pub. Pol'y* 7 at 35.

[86] See *Yates v. Texas*, 171 S.W.3d 215 (2005). The nortiorous serial killer, Peter Sutcliffe (now using the alias of Coonan) claimed that God told him to kill prostitutes: the facts are restated in his recent appeal: *R. v. Coonan* [2011] EWCA Crim. 5 at 12.

[87] [1982] A.C. 341.

mental "backwardness" or "limited intelligence" could be given to enable the defendant to win an outright acquittal on a charge involving recklessness. This was when the fully subjective theory of recklessness prevailed, and was a consequence of the Court of Appeal's loyal acceptance of section 8 of the *Criminal Justice Act 1967*.[88] Following the introduction of the objective theory of recklessness in *Caldwell*, the position was uncertain.[89]

27–025   **But surely a person who gives evidence that he is mentally disordered and therefore did not see a risk that anyone else would have seen in what he did; and that he did not know the nature and quality of his act, should get an insanity verdict?**   This point has not been argued, but since the subjective approach is now back in vogue (and is likely to stay with us),[90] it seems to be maintainable. It involves holding that the "nature and quality" of the act includes its foreseeable consequences, and that is not too broad an interpretation of the word "quality." This given, there would be no theoretical difficulty in bringing in schizophrenics who take insane risks, and the same rule should apply to the mentally impaired. If the defendant is so low in intelligence that it can seriously be argued that he set fire to a house, for instance, without realizing that this involved danger to those sleeping inside, and if evidence of the mental impairment is given, then on principle he should not be entitled to an ordinary acquittal but at best should have an insanity verdict. (And if he merely gives evidence that he did not realize the danger, the Crown should on principle be allowed to give evidence to show that his mental impairment amounts to insanity in order to ensure that he does obtain a complete acquittal). Although mental impairment is not insanity in the ordinary use of language, there is authority for saying that it can amount to insanity in law.

In M'Naghten's time even doctors spoke of "insanity" as including imbecility,[91] and there are later legal approvals of this usage,[92] though the matter has not been finally decided.[93] Sometimes, however, evidence has been given on behalf of the defendant that he was of inferior intelligence, for the purpose of showing that he did not intend or foresee a result of his conduct that the jury might otherwise have inferred that he intended or foresaw; and the evidence was not taken to require an insanity verdict as opposed to an ordinary acquittal. An impaired person may, because he is stupid, accidentally set fire to a house, but if it is an accident it is unlikely to be repeated and the defendant can safely be given an ordinary acquittal.

An impaired person might also take an unreasonable risk as to whether another is consenting to sexual intercourse, a risk that a person of ordinary cognition

---

[88] *R. v. Hudson* [1966] 1 Q.B. 448; *R. v. Wallett* [1968] 2 Q.B. 367; *R. v. Stephenson* [1979] Q.B. 695.

[89] See *Elliott v. C (A Minor)* [1983] 1 W.L.R. 939.

[90] *R. v. G* [2004] 1 A.C. 1034.

[91] This term is unfortunate, but it is not meant to be pejorative.

[92] See Nigel Walker, *Crime and Insanity in England*, (Edinburgh: Edinburgh University Press, 1968) at 116.

[93] The U.S. Supreme Court has rejected low intelligence even as a form of diminished responsibility. *Stewart v. United States*, 366 U.S. 1 at 9 (1961). See also the discussion in Charles M. Lamb, "Warren Burger and the Insanity Defence—Judicial Philosophy and Voting Behaviour on a U.S. Court of Appeals," (1975) 24 *Am. U.L. Rev.* 91 at 104.

would not take. In this context the impairment may be taken into consideration without any need to consider the issue of insanity. Take the example of rape where a negligent mistake as to whether a person is consenting to sexual intercourse is sufficient to ground a conviction. Under section 1 of the *Sexual Offences Act 2003* D is negligent as to whether V consents to the sexual intercourse if he "does not reasonably believe that V consents." Section 1(2) of the *Act of 2003* provides: "Whether a belief is reasonable is to be determined having regard to all the circumstances, including any steps A has taken to ascertain whether B consents."

In *R. v. Mrzljak*,[94] the Queensland Court of Appeal held that D's mental impairment was relevant to an assessment of the reasonableness of his belief that V was consenting.[95] It is not D's mental impairment "*per se* which bears on the excuse of mistake. It is the fact that the handicap results in the accused having to form his belief on a more limited set of information that is relevant, just as other external circumstances affecting the accused's opportunity to develop and test his perception are relevant. A jury cannot assess the rationality of a belief in isolation from the circumstances in which, and the information on which, it is formed."[96] In other words, it might be demonstrated that D's impairment prevented him from accessing the relevant information that an ordinary person would have accessed and thereby prevented him from understanding that he was committing a wrongful rape. The jury could find that the defendant was not guilty of rape without considering the insanity issue. Where a mentally impaired defendant has sexual intercourse with a women because his cognitive incapacity affected his ability perceive that the victim was not consenting, the big hurdle for the insanity defence will be in demonstrating that the "impairment" or "low intelligence" constituted a sufficient cognitive impairment to be brought within the purview of the *M'Naghten* rules. Nevertheless, for the same reason insanity should be a defence where an element of an offence merely requires negligence.[97]

27–026

In *R. v. Mrzljak*, the intercourse was consensual in that both parties were mentally impaired and seemed to be driven by their animal instincts, but if D had taken an innocent woman by force, a special verdict would have been appropriate. If a person's impairment prevents him from realizing that he must not rape women, then he is a danger to society and therefore a jail term or hospital order would be appropriate.

---

[94] [2005] 152 A. Crim. R. 315. See also *R. v. Hudson* [1966] 1 Q.B. 448; *R. v. Cooper* [2009] 1 W.L.R. 1786.

[95] See *R. v. Mrzljak* [2005] 152 A. Crim. R. 315. Section 27(1) of the Criminal Code (Qld.) is analogous to section 1 (C) of the *Sexual Offences Act 2003* (U.K.) in that it has an objective element: "A person who does or omits to do an act under an honest and *reasonable*, but mistaken, belief in the existence of any state of things is not criminally responsible for the act or omission to any greater extent than if the real state of things had been such as the person believed to exist."

[96] *R. v. Mrzljak* [2005] 152 A. Crim. R. 315 at 334.

[97] Cognitive acting that is voluntary could not provide a defence as far as a strict liability element of an offence is concerned. A person who is insane within the *M'Naghten* rules would be able to raise insanity as a defence to statutory rape, but a mentally impaired person would not be able to raise that defence, unless he also comes within the *M'Naghten* rules. (He might get in under the third question, if his impairment caused him to mistakenly believe he was acting lawfully.)

27.6. IRRESISTIBLE IMPULSES AND CRIMINALITY

27–027   **Suppose a person has some "disease of the mind" that results in an "irresistible impulse" for committing crime. Would the *M'Naghten* rules provide him with a defence?**   No. A person is not entitled to a defence when he knows that he is committing a crime and it is wrong do to so, just because he finds the temptation irresistible. The law still has the potential to deter this type of criminal, because he understands the nature of what he is doing.[98] If any protection is to be accorded, then it should be taken care of at the sentencing stage.

The humane use of hospital orders and other non-punitive disposals does not provide a complete answer to the demand that the test of mental incapacity to commit a crime should be modernized. At one time there was a movement to exempt people who suffered from "insane impulse" or "irresistible impulse." Although this has been incorporated in the statutes of several common law countries, the argument that it should excuse from responsibility has never been accepted in our law as a full defence,[99] largely because it is thought that an irresistible impulse is unprovable.[100] Professors Morse and Hoffman observe:[101] "The problem in cases of alleged lack of self-control is distinguishing the disordered person from any other agent who also wants to do something very badly that the agent should not do, such as the very greedy person tempted terribly to steal."

A criticism of the *M'Naghten* rules is that they only allow for an evaluation of the defendant's cognitive incapacity. *M'Naghten* does not allow for an evaluation of the defendant's volitional incapacity. We are not talking about automatistic acting or physical involuntariness, but a type of moral involuntariness. The narrowness of the *M'Naghten* rules led to reform in many U.S. jurisdictions. In the United States, the notion of irresistible impulse was espoused in the Model Penal Code, but with a certain change of language. To avoid giving the impression that the irresistible drive must be impulsive or of sudden occurrence, the Code speaks instead of "capacity to conform to the law." The ALI test as formulated in the Model Penal Code provides that "a person is not responsible for criminal conduct if, at the time of such conduct as a result of a mental disease or defect, [the defendant] lacks the substantial capacity to appreciate the criminality of his conduct or to conform his conduct to the requirements of law." Nevertheless, a majority of states in the U.S. reverted to the *M'Naghten* rules

---

[98] Christopher Slobogin, "The Integrationist Alternative to the Insanity Defence: Reflections on the Exculpatory Scope of Mental Illness in the Wake of the Andrea Yates Trial," (2003) 30 *Am. J. Crim. L.* 315.

[99] For example, an "irresistible impulse" might be sufficient to establish the partial defence of diminished responsibility. See *R. v. Khan* (2010) 1 Cr. App. R. 4; *R. v. Byrne* [1960] 2 Q.B. 396. Cf. section 52 of the *Corners and Justice Act 2009*.

[100] *R. v. Kopsch* (1927) 19 Cr. App. R. 50 at 51 it was famously stated that it is a "fantastic theory … which if it were to become apart of out criminal law, would be merely subversive." See also *Attorney-General of South Australia v. Brown* [1960] A.C. 432.

[101] Stephen J. Morse and Morris B. Hoffman, "The Uneasy Entente Between Legal Insanity and *Mens Rea*: Beyond *Clark v. Arizona*," (2007) 97 *J. Crim. L. & Criminology* 1071at 1095.

after John Hinckley used the ALI type defence[102] to get off the hook.[103] Hinckley attempted to kill the hugely popular President Reagan.[104] The attempted assignation was designed to impress Jodie Foster, a first-year student at Yale University and actress.[105] The irresistible impulse component of the ALI test was criticized as protecting impulses that should have and could have been resisted.[106]

A fatal objection to the practicality of the solution is the impossibility of drawing **27–028** a line between an impulse that is irresistible and one that is merely not resisted. Take two schizophrenics, A and B, whose clinical symptoms appear to be the same. Both are involved with their friends in arguments that cause them to go into towering rages, but whereas A stabs to death his opponent in the argument, B does not. If A is prosecuted for murder, a psychiatrist may be ready to testify that by reason of his disease he was deprived of capacity to conform to the law, as is indeed shown by the fact that he did not conform to it. B, not having stabbed, does not appear before the court, so we do not hear psychiatric evidence about him; but presumably our psychiatrist would say that he had the capacity to conform to the law, as is shown by the fact that he conformed. All that we ever observe is that individuals conform or fail to conform. For practical purposes, therefore, a judgment that the defendant by reason of mental disease lacked the capacity to conform to the law does not differ in any way from a judgment that he suffered from a mental disease and by reason of that disease did not conform to the law.

The usual question is whether the defendant would have committed the crime if the police were present. In most cases the defendant would probably control his actions if the police were present, so it is argued that the criminal law still has a deterrent role to play.[107] Generally, autonomous agents should be held responsible for their harmful choices. There is no doubt that some defendants such as paedophiles have psychological problems which make it difficult for them to resist harming children, but such people are dangerous and make the deliberate choice to harm their innocent victims.[108] Similarly, drug addicts might find it necessary to burgle others to fund their habit and their condition might make it very difficult for them to resist the temptation to burgle, but they make a

---

[102] "Hinckley asserted the insanity defence, alleging he was under an irresistible compulsion brought on by a mental disease or defect. Hinckley would not have been able to assert his defence under the *M'Naghten* rule, but was successful in convincing a jury that he was legally insane under the lesser standards embodied by *Durham v. United States*, 214 F.2d 862 (D.C.Cir.1954), that governed his trial. … While his thought process was clearly irrational, Hinckley knew that he was shooting at a human being and that such an action was illegal, indeed Hinckley intended to commit murder." See *Finger v. State*, 117 Nev. 548 at 560 (2001).

[103] Lisa A. Callahan *et al.*, "Insanity Defence Reform in the United States Post-Hinckley", (1987) 11 *Mental & Physical Disability L. Rep.* 54 at 54-59.

[104] Michael L. Perlin, "Unpacking the Myths: The Symbolism Mythology of Insanity Defence Jurisprudence", (1990) 40 *Case W. Res. L. Rev.* 599 at 637-638.

[105] *United States v. Hinckley*, 672 F.2d 115.

[106] Stephen J. Morse, "Culpability and Control", (1994) 142 *U. Pa. L. Rev.* 1587 at 1600-1601.

[107] There is evidence to suggest most of these criminal urges are no greater than normal urges: Paul S. Appelbaum *et al.*, "Violence and Delusions: Data from the MacArthur Violence Risk Study," (2000) 157 *Am. J. Psychiatry* 556.

[108] Dennis J. Baker, "Punishment Without a Crime: Is Preventive Detention Reconcilable with Justice?" (2009) 34 *Austl. J. Leg. Phil.* 120.

fully informed choice to harm others for their own benefit. The *M'Naghten* rules would not allow drug addicts and paedophiles to avoid penal censure for their autonomous criminal choices, and therefore is the preferred model.

Some medical condition might increase a person's desire or propensity for committing certain criminal acts, but such a person knows that he is doing the wrong thing. The appropriate solution is to consider his condition as a mitigating factor when determining his sentence. His diminished capacity or partial responsibility could be taken into consideration at the sentencing stage or it might provide a partial defence. In this country, diminished responsibility is only a partial defence to murder, but there is no reason why partial responsibility cannot be considered as a mitigating factor where there is compelling medical evidence which demonstrates that the defendant was not fully culpable. Such cases are likely to be very exceptional, as the medical evidence would have to demonstrate that the actor acted almost as an automaton.

27.7. THE SPECIAL VERDICT AND DISPOSAL

27–029 Where insanity negatives the mental element necessary for the crime, it might seem that the defendant would be entitled to an ordinary acquittal. Not so. The verdict returned by the jury is one of "not guilty by reason of insanity,"[109] known succinctly as the special verdict. It finds that the defendant did the act[110] (otherwise the verdict would be a plain not guilty),[111] but fell within the *M'Naghten* rules.

A general observation is that the question of responsibility can be dodged, or deprived of much of its significance, by blurring the responsible/non-responsible distinction. This is now what the law largely does. Offenders (*i.e.* legally responsible wrongdoers) can generally be treated by a court as if they were non-responsible: they can be sent to hospital, or simply discharged, instead of being punished. Conversely, people who could claim non-responsibility may be punished if (as may quite understandably happen) they do not choose to rely upon their immunity.

The subject of mental disorder as it appears to the lawyer is closely connected with admission to a mental hospital, the current euphemism for which is "psychiatric hospital." The police may decide not to charge a minor offender who is mentally disturbed, and may permit him to return to his relatives or to enter hospital voluntarily ("informally"). Or a person may in some cases (*e.g.*, if he is mentally ill) be compulsorily admitted to hospital on a medical certificate without

---

[109] Section 2 of the *Trial of Lunatics Act 1883* (as amended).

[110] This must be understood to mean "went through the motions alleged against him." In *R. v. Sullivan* [1983] 2 W.L.R. 123 at 396 it was expounded: "If a man does not know what he is doing, in no legal sense can the physical movements of the limbs which cause injury or damage to others be said to be his acts." Nonetheless, the court recognized that the insanity defence would be available and assume that there would be a special verdict—not noticing that the special verdict must find the relevant "act" was committed, The only possible explanation is that the *Act of 1964*, like the legislation it replaced, used the word "act" in a sense that was "no legal sense." Therefore, a non-volitional *act* is sufficient. This seems fair, because those who are unable to control the harmful physical movements of their limbs might require monitoring and supervision for medical purposes.

[111] *Attorney-General's Reference (No.3 of 1998)* [2000] Q.B. 401 at 409.

court proceedings (civil confinement), whether he has committed an offence or not.[112] The commitment (or, in legal terms, admission) to hospital may be "for assessment," under a comparatively simple procedure, or "for treatment." The latter requires two medical certificates, which (in the case of mentally ill patients) must certify that the admission is necessary for the health and safety of the patient for the protection of other persons.[113]

As we have seen, certain procedures apply specifically to persons suspected of criminal acts:

27–030

- If a person is charged with an offence and remanded in custody (*i.e.* to prison) before trial or sentence, he may be transferred to hospital by administrative direction.[114]
- If he is on trial he may be found by a judge to be unfit to stand trial[115] ("unfit to plead," "insane on arraignment"); he may be sent to a hospital. Alternatively, he may be made the subject of a supervision order; or an order for his absolute discharge.[116] (A deaf and mute person who cannot communicate can also be found to be unfit to stand trial.)
- If he is tried, he may succeed on an insanity defence, when again the court must make him the subject of the special verdict.
- If the defence is not set up, or it is rejected by the jury or magistrates, the defendant can still (in many cases) be sent to hospital by a judge or magistrates.
- Or, if sent to prison, he can be administratively transferred to hospital, but this will not in practice be done unless the mental disorder is "frank" and the defendant is obviously an unsuitable person to be kept in prison.

A verdict of not guilty by reason of insanity from 1800 until 1991[117] required the judge to order the defendant to be detained. This was known as mandatory commitment. Formerly he was detained at the "pleasure" of the Sovereign (acting on the advice of the Home Secretary); but later the discretion was given to the Home Secretary. The terms of the order under the pre-1991 law was that the defendant be admitted to a hospital specified by the Home Secretary. Where he remained until the Home Secretary otherwise directed. Fortunately, there are a now a number of disposal options available to the courts including hospital orders, an order of absolute discharge and supervision orders:

- Supervision orders mean "an order which requires the person in respect of whom it is made ('the supervised person') to be under the supervision of a social worker or an officer of a local probation board ('the supervising officer') for a period specified in the order of not more than two years. (2) A supervision order may, in accordance with paragraph 4 or 5 below,

---

[112] Part II of the *Mental Health Act 1983*.

[113] Section 3 of the *Mental Health Act 1983*.

[114] Section 48 of the *Mental Health Act 1983*.

[115] And it has also been found that he did the act or made the omission charged against him.

[116] Section 5 of the *Criminal Procedure (Insanity) Act 1964*.

[117] *Criminal Procedure (Insanity and Unfitness to Plead) Act 1991*.

require the supervised person to submit, during the whole of that period or such part of it as may be specified in the order, to treatment by or under the direction of a registered medical practitioner."[118]

- A hospital order means that "the court may by order authorize D's admission to and detention in such hospital as may be specified in the order or, as the case may be, place him under the guardianship of a local social services authority or of such other person approved by a local social services authority as may be so specified."[119]

- A restriction order is "Where a hospital order is made in respect of an offender by the Crown Court, and it appears to the court, having regard to the nature of the offence, the antecedents of the offender and the risk of his committing further offences if set at large, that it is necessary for the protection of the public from serious harm so to do, the court may … further order that the offender shall be subject to the special restrictions."[120] The restriction order will normally set the minimum of time for which the defendant must be detained.

27–031   A hospital order is not inevitable. If the defendant is seen to be pretty harmless (perhaps he is aged, or his disorder has been brought under control since the event charged, or his offence was not serious) he may simply be made the subject of a supervision order, (usually with a condition of mental treatment, whether as an out-patient, or less usually, as an in-patient), or even given an absolute discharge.

Since a homicidal manic cannot be automatically set at large, the law is that in murder cases the judge must make a hospital order with a restriction order.[121] Detention is frequently in a special hospital (Broadmoor, Ashworth and Rampton), but may be in a local psychiatric hospital. When a hospital order is made on the ground of mental illness, two doctors must certify that the offender is suffering from mental illness "of a nature or degree which makes it appropriate for him to be detained in a hospital for medical treatment."

27–032   **If the main question for the hospital order is whether the offender is treatable, the judge must have to decide whether the defendant was responsible for his actions?**   The abstract question of responsibility rarely enters in. Usually, if the court has medical evidence that the defendant is treatable and should go to hospital, and if a hospital is prepared to take him, the judge will be glad to make a hospital order instead of adding one more inmate to the prisons.

---

[118] Schedule 1A of the *Domestic Violence, Crime and Victims Act 2004*.

[119] Section 37 of the *Mental Health Act 1983*.

[120] Section 41 of the *Mental Health Act 1983*. See *R. v. Steward* [2008] M.H.L.R. 148; *R. (on the application of Jones) v. Isleworth Crown Court* [2005] M.H.L.R. 93.

[121] Section 5(3) of the *Criminal Procedure (Insanity) Act 1964* provides: "(a) the offence to which the special verdict or the findings relate is an offence the sentence for which is fixed by law, and (b) the court have power to make a hospital order, the court shall make a hospital order with a restriction order (whether or not they would have power to make a restriction order apart from this subsection)." See also section 37 of the *Mental Health Act 1983*.

But hospital orders are made because the chap is round the bend at the time 27–033
of sentence, where as *M'Naghten* relates to his condition at the time of the
act.   True. If the evidence is that the offender was disordered at the time of the
act but has recovered since, a hospital order cannot be made, but the judge may of
course release him under supervision or give him an absolute discharge.

Does the present law give the disturbed offender sufficient protection? I can 27–034
see that the judge will make a hospital order if he is of the opinion that this is
the most suitable method of disposing of the case. But the judge may think
that the most suitable method of disposing the case is to send the offender to
prison. So what protection has a mentally ill offender against a severe judge?
The defendant can only be sent to prison when he has been convicted of
committing a crime.[122] Doctors cannot retain patients in hospital merely by way
of preventive detention after treatment has failed, or if it is producing no further
results; yet a psychopath who is untreatable may still need detention in the public
interest.[123]

   If the convicted defendant is sent to prison even though he requires treatment,
he can appeal from a sentence of imprisonment and ask to have a hospital order
substituted.[124] In practice, if a hospital order can be made and seems necessary
the judge will almost always make it.

"Almost always?" If the offender is mentally ill, surely it should be "always." 27–035
A person ought not to be punished for being ill.   It does not follow that the
offence was the result of the illness.[125] And sometimes the necessity to keep the
offender from doing it again is an overriding consideration.[126]

   The choice between prison and hospital is often not straightforward, either
from the point of view of the community or even that of the offender. As regards
incapacitation, a mentally disordered person may be detained in a special hospital
in conditions that protect the public to the same extent as if he were in prison.
Since he may be kept in hospital for longer than he would have been kept in
prison on tariff principles,[127] the protection to the public may be even greater. But
there is great pressure on the special hospitals, which cannot always take patients
who are not in the highest degree dangerous. Moreover, the patient's disorder and
objectionable conduct may not be sufficiently serious to justify his prolonged

---

[122] In *R. v. Drew* [2003] 1 W.L.R. 1213, it was said: "as a matter of national law it could not be wrong
in principle to pass a sentence of imprisonment on a mentally disordered defendant who was
criminally responsible and fit to be tried."

[123] *R. v. Wood* [2010] 1 Cr. App. R. (S.) 6; *R. v. Welsh* (2011) 119 B.M.L.R. 21.

[124] See *R. v. Morris* [1961] 2 Q.B. 237; cf. *R. v. Wood* [2010] 1 Cr. App. R. (S.) 6; *R. v. Welsh* (2011)
119 B.M.L.R. 21; *R. v. Cox* [1968] 1 W.L.R. 308.

[125] *R. v. Dass* [2009] M.H.L.R. 288; *R. v. IA* [2006] 1 Cr. App. R. (S.) 91.

[126] *R. v. Wood* [2010] 1 Cr. App. R. (S.) 6; *R. v. Welsh* (2011) 119 B.M.L.R. 21.

[127] Cf. sections 222-229 of the *Criminal Justice Act 2003*. See generally, Dennis J. Baker,
"Punishment Without a Crime: Is Preventive Detention Reconcilable with Justice?" (2009) 34 *Austl.
J. Leg. Phil.* 120; Andrew von Hirsch and Andrew Ashworth, *Proportionate Sentencing: Exploring
the Principles*, (Oxford: Oxford University Press, 2005) at 50 *et seq.*; R. A. Duff, *Punishment,
Communication, and Community*, (Oxford: Oxford University Press, 2001), at 165 *et seq.*; Richard L.
Lippke, "No Easy Way Out: Dangerous Offenders and Preventive Detention," (2008) 27(2) *Law &
Phil.* 383.

detention on medical grounds. Doctors object to being "jailers in white coats," and N.H.S. hospitals in particular will let out patients as soon as they feel they can do nothing further for them. So the judge may feel obliged to send the offender to prison.

Then there is the question of deterrence. In some forms of mental illness the best hope of preventing a recurrence of the objectionable conduct will lie in treating the illness rather than punishing the offender. However, mental illness cannot always be cured even if it can be alleviated. Many people suffering from schizophrenia are at large in the community and manage to maintain themselves in employment. They may be helped by drugs but cannot be permanently cured. There is no point in keeping them in hospital unless their behaviour is too objectionable to allow them to continue at liberty. If such a person commits some minor offence (a petty theft for example), it may be better from every point of view to treat him as responsible and give him some minor punishment in the ordinary way, or put him under supervision, rather than subject him to the serious loss of liberty that may be involved in commitment to hospital. It is good social policy to try to convey even to mentally or socially handicapped people that good behaviour is expected of them, and that they are accountable for what they do—unless a therapeutic approach offers either a better promise of improving their conduct or a humane alternative to a severe and profitless prison sentence.

27–036   **Is there a form of the special verdict for magistrates' courts?**   No. A person who is tried summarily can set up mental disorder to negative *mens rea* and the court may give him an ordinary acquittal.[128] Alternatively, the magistrates may find that he did the act (or made the omission) and, without recording a conviction, make a hospital order.[129] This is a discretionary power, and one rarely used; the magistrates generally prefer to discharge the defendant, perhaps arranging for him to be examined with a view to being civilly committed to hospital.[130] Because of the wide discretion of magistrates as to disposal, in contrast to the rigorous rule that was available for those tried in the Crown Court prior to 1991 and 2004,[131] defences based on mental disorder were much more frequent on summary trial than on indictment. But the new disposal powers available in the Crown Court are encouraging more defendants to invoke the insanity defence.[132]

---

[128] *R. v. Horseferry Road Magistrates Court Ex p. K* [1997] Q.B. 23.

[129] Section 37(3) of the *Mental Health Act 1983*. The offence must be punishable by the magistrates with imprisonment. Justices may use this power where it is uncertain whether the defendant is fit to stand trial: *R. v. Lincoln Magistrates Court Ex p. O'Connor* [1983] 1 W.L.R. 335; *R. v. Stratford Magistrates' Court* [2007] 1 W.L.R. 3119. Of course, the magistrates' have no power to determine such issues where the offence is triable on indictment only: *R. v. Chippenham Magistrates Court Ex p. Thompson* (1996) 160 J.P. 207.

[130] A police officer may take him to hospital pursuant to section 136 of the *Mental Health Act 1983*.

[131] See *Criminal Procedure (Insanity and Unfitness to Plead) Act 1991* and section 24 of the *Domestic Violence, Crime and Victims Act 2004*.

[132] R. D. Mackay *et al.*, "Yet More Facts About the Insanity Defence," [2006] Crim. L.R. 399.

CHAPTER 28

DIMINISHED RESPONSIBILITY

"It is very difficult to put it in a phrase, but it has been put in this way: that there must be aberration or weakness of mind; that there must be some form of mental unsoundness; that there must be a state of mind which is bordering on, though not amounting to, insanity; that there must be a mind so affected that responsibility is diminished from full responsibility to partial responsibility—in other words, the prisoner in question must be only partially accountable for his actions."

Lord Justice Clerk[1]

28.1. DIMINISHED RESPONSIBILITY: THE NATURE OF THE DEFENCE

Except in cases of murder the judge has a discretion in sentencing that enables **28–001** him to deal sensibly with the mentally disordered. For murder, legislation is needed. The Government, having seen insuperable difficulties in a proposal by the Royal Commission on Capital Punishment to extend the defence of insanity exemption, decided instead to extend the discretion of the judge by allowing a defence of "diminished responsibility." Section 2 of the *Homicide Act 1957* (as amended)[2] reads as follows:

"(1) A person ('D') who kills or is a party to the killing of another is not to be convicted of murder if D was suffering from an abnormality of mental functioning which—
  (a) arose from a recognised medical condition,
  (b) substantially impaired D's ability to do one or more of the things mentioned in subsection (1A), and
  (c) provides an explanation for D's acts and omissions in doing or being a party to the killing.
(1A) Those things are—
  (a) to understand the nature of D's conduct;
  (b) to form a rational judgment;
  (c) to exercise self-control.
(2) On a charge of murder, it shall be for the defence to prove that the person charged is by virtue of this section not liable to be convicted of murder.
(3) A person who but for this section would be liable, whether as principal or as accessory, to be convicted of murder shall be liable instead to be convicted of manslaughter.
(4) The fact that one party to a killing is by virtue of this section not liable to be convicted of murder shall not affect the question whether the killing amounted to murder in the case of any other party to it."

---

[1] *H. M. Advocate v. Savage* (1923) J.C. 49 at 51.
[2] See section 52 of the *Coroners and Justice Act 2009*.

The general notion of diminished responsibility (as it is called in the margin of the section) was borrowed from Scotland,[3] where it had been developed as judge-made law; and section 2 of the *Homicide Act 1957* has in turn been adopted in some other parts of the common law world. If the defence is established (and the burden of proving it on a balance of probability rests on the defendant),[4] the jury convict of manslaughter, which means that the judge has the usual wide range of discretion as to disposal.

28–002   **Should not diminished responsibility be accounted automatism?**   Permit me to say that your question shows a certain confusion. If the defendant's mental disorder amounts to automatism, he receives a plain acquittal and there is no need for the defence of "diminished responsibility" (as it is sometimes abbreviated in informal speech). To amount to automatism, the disorder must cause the defendant to act involuntarily and must also negative *mens rea*. If the disorder does not negative *mens rea*, and if the charge is murder, the defendant (assuming that he has no other defence) must be convicted of something. The advantage of the defence of diminished responsibility is that it reduces the conviction from one of murder to one of manslaughter.

28–003   **Yes, but why shouldn't it be provided that diminished responsibility is a complete defence?**   That is out of the question. Diminished responsibility targets those who retain a degree of culpability. It does not aim merely to protect those who lacked any culpability. Where the defendant has committed the forbidden act with the forbidden state of mind, it would be against public policy to exempt him from responsibility and therefore from all forms of social control.

28–004   **Do the prosecution ever charge manslaughter by reason of diminished responsibility, or do they always charge murder?**   The latter. The issue arises only if the defendant introduces it or sets up a *M'Naghten* defence.[5]

In practice the defence of diminished responsibility cannot be set up, for obvious reasons, if the defendant denies that he committed the act. So if the denial is disbelieved, the conviction will be of murder, notwithstanding that evidence of diminished responsibility could have been given. This is an unhappy situation for the defendant, who can give no evidence in mitigation after a murder conviction.[6] It is another argument against the mandatory sentence in murder.

---

[3] See *H. M. Advocate v. Dingwall* (1867) Irvine 466.

[4] *R. v. Dunbar* [1981] 1 Q.B. 36. The persuasive burden resting on the defence implies an evidential burden as well, and the judge will not leave the defence to the jury in the absence of medical evidence: *R. v. Dix* (1981) 74 Cr. App. R. 306. See also *R. v. Lambert* [2002] Q.B. 1112.

[5] There is no good reason why the charge should always be one of murder. Generally, it is true, it must be of murder because medical evidence is not available when the defendant is arraigned; but if the necessary evidence becomes available in time the trial should be for manslaughter, except in the unlikely event of the defence resisting the evidence.

[6] If the defence is not advanced at the trial, the Court of Appeal may refuse to hear medical evidence on the subject, particularly if the medical reports do not clearly support the defence. See *R. v. Melville* [1976] 1 W.L.R. 181; *R. v. Straw* [1995] 1 All E.R. 187. Cf. *R. v. Erskine* [2010] 1 W.L.R. 183 at 193, where Lord Judge C.J. said: "Virtually by definition, the decision whether to admit fresh evidence is case—and fact-specific. The discretion to receive fresh evidence is a wide one focussing on the interests of justice. The considerations listed in subsection (2)(a) to (d) of the *Criminal Appeal Act*

When a person is charged with murder, can he plead guilty to manslaughter on the ground of diminished responsibility? He is allowed to do so, though the usual qualification applies that the defendant cannot insist upon pleading to the lesser offence. His plea needs to be accepted by the prosecution, who then ask for the leave of the court. The prosecution doctors almost always support the defence, and the plea is generally accepted.[7]

28–005

Does the defence apply to attempted murder? No.[8] Attempted murder does not carry a mandatory life sentence, so there is no point in invoking the defence of diminished responsibility in attempted murder cases. (See also the discussion at 22.1).

28–006

28.2. Scope of the Defence of "Diminished Responsibility"

The defence requires the defendant to have an abnormality of mental functioning arising from a recognized medical condition; and that it substantially impair the defendant's ability:

28–007

- to understand the nature of his conduct;
- to form a rational judgment;
- to exercise self-control.

What is abnormal mental functioning? It is mental functioning that is not normal according to the standards of society. Interpreting the old law, Lord Parker C.J. said: "'Abnormality of mind', which has to be contrasted with the time-honoured expression in the *M'Naughten* rules 'defect of reason', means a state of mind so different from that of ordinary human beings that the reasonable man would term it abnormal. It appears to us to be wide enough to cover the mind's activities in all its aspects, not only the perception of physical acts and matters, and the ability to form a rational judgment as to whether an act is right or wrong, but also the ability to exercise will power to control physical acts in

28–008

1968 are neither exhaustive nor conclusive, but they require specific attention. The fact that the issue to which the fresh evidence relates was not raised at trial does not automatically preclude its reception. However it is well understood that, save exceptionally, if the defendant is allowed to advance on appeal a defence and/or evidence which could and should have been but were not put before the jury, our trial process would be subverted. Therefore if they were not deployed when they were available to be deployed, or the issues could have been but were not raised at trial, it is clear from the statutory structure, as explained in the authorities, that unless a reasonable and persuasive explanation for one or other of these omissions is offered, it is highly unlikely that the 'interests of justice' test will be satisfied." As far as Erskine's appeal was concerned, Lord Judge C.J. (at 207-208) said: "It is overwhelmingly clear that at the time when the appellant appeared at trial, there was unequivocal contemporaneous evidence that his mental responsibility for his actions at the time of the killing was substantially impaired. In addition, there was contemporaneous evidence which suggested that as a result of reduced mental acuity, not amounting to unfitness to plead, but part and parcel of his illness, the decision not to advance the defence was irremediably flawed....The interests of justice require us to admit the fresh evidence.... We shall substitute convictions of manslaughter on the grounds of diminished responsibility."

[7] See Law Commission, *Partial Defences to Murder*, Report 290, (London: H.M.S.O., 2004) appendix B.

[8] *R. v. Campbell* [1997] Crim. L.R. 495.

accordance with that rational judgment."[9] Medical evidence will have to be presented to the jury before they will be able to determine whether the defendant's medical condition was one which could have caused abnormal mental functioning. If an expert attests that a diabetic fit could cause a person to go into a semi-conscious trance or that bipolar disorder could cause a person to suffer delusions, then the jury should not have any difficulty forming the view that a normal person does not go around in a semi-conscious trance, suffer delusions and so on. (Of course, there will be some guesswork at the edges, because some medical conditions such as "adjustment disorder" do not cause delusions or trances, but something much less measurable such as feelings of sadness and stress. The problem is that the latter states of mind are endured by ordinary people in the normal course of life.) Once the jury is convinced that the medical condition is one that could cause abnormal mental functioning, it will consider the facts to determine whether the particular medical condition impacted the defendant's mental functioning when he committed the offence.

28–009 **You have just told me that the abnormal mental functioning must substantially impair the defendant's ability (1) to understand the nature of his conduct; (2) to form a rational judgment; and (3) to exercise self-control. Why single out those effects?** Although the old section 2 may be said in a sense to have "worked" (indeed, it had highly beneficial results), it meant that psychiatrists were put under pressure to testify in terms that went beyond their professional competence. This did not cause them to express much open discontent. When their sympathies were engaged they adapted themselves to any legal formula.

The former section 2 of the *Homicide Act 1957*[10] did not refer to "mental functioning." The old law with its requirement that the defendant's abnormality of mind should have substantially impaired his "mental responsibility," was as embarrassing a formula for a scientifically-minded witness as could be devised.

- "Mental responsibility" was an ill-chosen expression, since responsibility is a legal or ethical notion, not in itself a clinical fact relating to the defendant. One can intelligently speak of "legal responsibility" (liability to conviction) or of "moral responsibility" (liability to moral censure). But the draftsperson avoided the words "moral responsibility," because he did not want to bring moral questions into the criminal law. And it would make no sense to talk about substantial impairment of legal responsibility, because legal responsibility in the sense of liability to conviction either exists or does not. (It is true that section 2, when it operates, downgrades the responsibility from murder to manslaughter. But this downgrading cannot be used as a criterion for operating the section: that would be begging the question.)

---

[9] *R. v. Byrne* [1960] 2 Q.B. 396 at 403 *per* Lord Parker C.J.

[10] Before section 52 of the *Coroners and Justice Act 2009* amended section 2 of the *Homicide Act 1957* it read as follows: "Where a person kills or is party to the killing of another he shall not be convicted of murder if he was suffering from a condition of arrested or retarded development of mind or any inherent causes or induced by disease or injury) as substantially impaired his mental responsibility for his acts and omissions in doing or being a party to the killing."

- The difficulty was compounded by the use of the word "substantial." Even if there were a scientific test of impairment, the question of substantial impairment is one of subjective estimation, not of medical science. The intention of the *Act* was that the jury should decide the substantiality of the impairment, but they are unfitted to do this without help, and doctors are prepared to testify on it.
- Section 52 of the *Coroners and Justice Act 2009* addresses this by requiring the impaired mental functioning to affect the defendant's ability to (1) understand the nature of his conduct; (2) to form a rational judgment; and (3) to exercise self-control.

If the defendant's abnormality of mental functioning meant that he did not understand the nature of his conduct, wouldn't it be better for him to invoke the full defence of insanity?   The requirement in section 2(1A)(a) of the *Act of 1957* bears a stark resemblance to the first limb of the *M'Naghten* rules. But as far as the defence of diminished responsibility is concerned, the defendant need only be shown to have had some understanding of the nature of his conduct. It is only necessary to show that he did not fully comprehend the nature of what he was doing because of his abnormal mental functioning. A person who relies on the partial defence of diminished responsibility is partially culpable, whereas a person who relies on the defence of insanity is not culpable at all.

28–010

Can the defence be set up in a case really falling within the insanity defence?   Yes. But, by statute, the prosecution can reply with evidence of insanity,[11] and if the jury accept that it is really a *M'Naghten* situation they will return a special verdict accordingly.[12]

28–011

Does the jury merely guess whether the defendant's mental impairment was substantial?   Medical evidence will be presented to the jury and it will determine whether the defendant's medical condition substantially reduced his ability to understand the nature of his conduct, to form a rational judgment, and to exercise self-control.[13] Basically, the jury determines whether the defendant's medical condition reduced his ability to comply with the criminal law. The notion that ability to conform to the law can be measured is particularly puzzling. The position seems to be that if the doctors say the defendant's ability to do the things mentioned in section 2(1A) of the *Homicide Act 1957* was substantially limited; the jury is likely to assume that this implies "substantial" impairment of his

28–012

---

[11] Section 6 of the *Criminal Procedure (Insanity) Act 1964*. It is also worth noting that where there is a defence of insanity, the prosecution can show that the case is in reality one of diminished responsibility.

[12] If the jury reject the defence and convict of murder, the Court of Appeal may take a different view and substitute a conviction of manslaughter: *R. v. Spratt* [1980] 1 W.L.R. 554.

[13] See *R. v. Khan* [2010] 1 Cr. App. R. 74. In *R. v. Walker* [2009] EWCA Crim. 1829 it was held that "the jury was not obliged to accept expert medical evidence of abnormality of mind put forward in a defence of diminished responsibility in relation to a murder charge merely because there is no contradictory medical evidence." The jury is not bound to accept the medical evidence, but if medical evidence is categorical the jury are bound to accept it otherwise the verdict will be set aside on appeal. See *R. v. Sanders* (1991) 93 Cr. App. R. 245.

ability to do those things.[14] In most cases, D will deny that he understood the nature of his conduct or that he was able to form a rational judgment, *etc.* The jury will determine whether he is to be believed by considering the medical evidence and the facts of the case.

Lord Parker C.J. recognized some of the problems:

> "'[T]he step between 'he did not resist his impulse' and 'he could not resist his impulse' is, as the evidence in this case shows, one which is incapable of scientific proof. *A fortiori* there is no scientific measurement of the degree of difficulty which an abnormal person finds in controlling his impulses. These problems which in the present state of medical knowledge are scientifically insoluble, the jury can only approach in a broad, common-sense way."[15]

Lady Wootton's comment on this was:

> "Apart from admiration of the optimism which expects common sense to make good the deficiencies of science, it is only necessary to add that the problem would seem to be insoluble, not merely in the present, but indeed in any, state of medical knowledge ... Neither medical nor any other science can even hope to prove whether a man who does not resist his impulses does not do so because he cannot or because he will not."[16]

28–013   **Isn't it possible that the killer suffered from abnormality of his mental functioning at the time of the killing, and so can plead diminished responsibility, and yet is not mentally ill, *etc.* (within the terms of the *Mental Health Act 1983*), so that a hospital order cannot be made?**   Certainly! A multitude of conditions are recognized by the scientific community as medical conditions.[17] While section 2(1)(a) of the *Act of 1957* requires the abnormality of mental functioning to result from a medical condition, it does not require the condition to be of a psychiatric kind. There are numerous conditions that may have some impact on a person's capacity for rational thought and self-control including post-traumatic-stress disorder,[18] gender identity disorder,[19] personality disorders,[20] paedophilia, paraphilia, psychosexual disorder,[21] epilepsy, diabetes,

---

[14] Cf. *R. v. Byrne* [1960] 2 Q.B. 396.

[15] *R. v. Byrne* [1960] 2 Q.B. 396 at 404; see also *R. v. Khan* [2010] 1 Cr. App. R. 74.

[16] Barbara Wootton, *Crime and the Criminal Law: Reflections of a Magistrate and Social Scientist,* (London: Stevens & Sons, 1981) at 77-78.

[17] See World Health Organisation, *International Classification of Diseases: ICD-10,* (Geneva: W.H.O., 2007).

[18] *American Psychiatric Association, Diagnostic and Statistical Manual of Mental Disorders,* (Washington, D.C.: American Psychiatric Association 4th edn. 2000) at 463.

[19] See also *Re: Jamie (Special medical procedure)* [2011] Fam. C.A. 248; *Brian L. v. Administration for Children's Services,* 51 A.D.3d 488 (2008).

[20] *State v. King,* 387 N.J.Super. 522 (2006).

[21] *Diagnostic and Statistical Manual of Mental Disorders, supra* note 18 at 571; *Kansas v. Hendricks,* 521 U.S. 346 (1997); *Erler v. State,* 921 N.E.2d 52 (2010). See also Michael B. First and Robert L. Halon, "Use of DSM Paraphilia Diagnoses in SVP Commitment Cases," (2008) 36(4) *J. Am. Acad. Psychiatry Law* 443; Cf. Richard Green, "Is Paedophilia a Mental Disorder? (2002) 31(6) *Achieves of Sexual Behaviour* 467.

sleep apnea, attention-deficit hyperactivity disorder,[22] autism, alcohol dependency syndrome,[23] and the list goes on *ad infinitum.*

If the medical condition is said to relate to a mental disorder, the court would do well to start by consulting the *American Psychiatric Association, Diagnostic and Statistical Manual of Mental Disorders* (2000). If the medical condition that causes the abnormal mental functioning is some common illness such as diabetes, the court could take "judicial notice" of the fact that it is a recognized medical condition. Of course, D's medical records would have to show that he had the particular medical condition. An idiosyncratic claim from an expert witness that a certain condition is a medical condition will not be sufficient to satisfy the requirements of the legislation. If the claim is supported by an emerging body of scientific research, the court might accept that it is a recognized medical condition even though it may not be listed in the standard works. It would have to be established that a large minority of the scientific community recognize the relevant condition as a medical one.

Mercy killers and battered women who kill will not be able to raise the defence of diminished responsibility merely by referring to their emotional state and the stress that they were under when they killed. Although stress does not constitute diminished responsibility in itself, it can trigger off "inherent causes." The cumulative effects of being battered for years could cause a person to develop a recognized medical condition such as post-traumatic-stress disorder. The latter would count as far as the defence of diminished responsibility is concerned, but it would have to be established that it was the post-traumatic-stress disorder that caused the defendant's abnormal mental functioning.[24] The medical condition must cause the defendant's abnormal mental functioning. It is not enough to show that it could have caused him to function abnormally, if it did not have that effect on him when he committed the crime. The "recognized medical condition" constraint precludes a defendant from using low intelligence and mental immaturity as a basis for the defence. If a person has the intelligence of a child aged ten or older, he is expected to comply with the criminal law. This makes perfect sense, since a 10-year-old is expected to comply with the criminal law.

Reverting to your question; the defence may successfully be raised on medical grounds that have little to do with mental illness and where there is clearly no reason for using a hospital order. The sentence may be anything from a life

---

[22] Tim Kendall *et al.*, "Diagnosis and Management of Attention-Deficit/Hyperactivity Disorder in Children, Young People, and Adults," (2008) 337 *B.M.J.* 1239; Marsha D. Rappley, "Attention Deficit–Hyperactivity Disorder," (2005) 352 *N. Engl. J. Med.* 165.

[23] *R. v. Stewart* [2009] 1 W.L.R. 2507 at 2510; *R. v. Wood* [2009] 1 W.L.R. 496; *State ex rel. Harper v. Zegeer*, 296 S.E.2d 873 at 875 (1982).

[24] In *State v. Townsend*, 186 N.J. 473 at 491-492 (2006), Wallace J. said: "It is beyond debate that battered women's syndrome has gained general acceptance as a scientific doctrine within the professional community. Recently, we noted that the syndrome has become widely accepted as admissible evidence in self-defence cases because it has been determined to be useful in explaining conduct exhibited by battered women toward their abusers." *State v. B.H.*, 183 N.J. 171, 183 (2005). We further explained that although battered woman's syndrome is not included as a psychological syndrome in the *Diagnostic and Statistical Manual of Mental Disorders*, battering is considered 'a potential triggering event for Post Traumatic Stress Disorder.'" Cf. *R. v. Dhaliwal* [2006] 2 Cr. App. R. 348.

sentence[25] in jail down to a virtual let-off,[26] depending on the circumstances and the judge. A defence of diminished responsibility, supported with sound medical evidence, is a safe course for a defendant if he is clearly not a public danger.

28–014 **Why limit the defence to those who have a recognized medical condition?** The object of this restriction was to exclude such emotions as rage, fear, jealousy and hate. It excludes vague diagnoses that are not based on science from being used to raise the defence. This prevents the courts from accepting medical evidence saying little more than that the defendant was severely affected by provocative or stressful events, in effect disregarding the requirement that the "abnormality of mental functioning" provide an explanation for the defendant's conduct, and making the defence overlap with (and, indeed, extend) that of "loss of control" when it has the blessing of a doctor.[27]

Commenting upon the artificiality of the defence in such cases, Lady Wootton wrote:

> "When homicide has resulted from such common human motives as sexual jealousy or the desire to escape from pecuniary embarrassment, it is hard not to believe that juries were moved more by the familiarity than by the abnormality of the offender's mental processes." [28]

A particular curiosity of some psychiatric diagnoses is that they seem to dress everyday "stress" up as some kind of "mental disorder."[29] There is of course a personal factor, but so there always is in human conduct, which is never completely uniform and predictable.

In short, under the old law the defence of diminished responsibility could be interpreted in accordance with the morality of the case rather than as a strict application of psychiatric and medical concepts. Where sympathy is evoked,[30] as Lady Wootton observed long ago, it "seems to be dissolving into what is virtually the equivalent of a mitigating circumstance."[31] But the complaisance of some doctor was still required to give legal admissibility to the defence.

28–015 One may question whether leniency went too far under the old law; but there can be no doubt that it had a beneficial effect in allowing a partial defence in the mercy-killing cases. In some of the cases under the old law, it had been invariably accepted by the jury on the flimsiest medical evidence, and was used by the judge as a reason for leniency. While the outcome of these cases may have been humane, it was achieved only because the courts were willing to rely "upon psychiatrists interpreting what [was], often, a rational act in terms of mental

---

[25] *R. v. Wood* [2010] 1 Cr. App. R. (S.) 6.

[26] *R. v. Webb* [2011] EWCA Crim. 152.

[27] As in *R. v. Coles* (1980) 144 J.P.N. 528. Coles had slept on his wrath before killing his wife, so that he was presumably outside the defence of loss of control. See also *R. v. Ahluwalia* (1993) 96 Cr. App. R. 133.

[28] Wootton, *op. cit. supra*, note 16 at 73.

[29] In *R. v. Webb* [2011] EWCA Crim. 152, the evidence merely suggested that D was under considerable stress, but a benevolent psychiatrist dressed this up as "adjustment disorder."

[30] See *R. v. Ahluwalia* (1993) 96 Cr. App. R. 133.

[31] Wootton, *op. cit. supra*, note 16 at 73.

abnormality, referring in justification to the stress, anxiety or even depression associated with the pain and helplessness of watching a relative die."[32]

In a 1965 case, a father who killed his Down's Syndrome infant successfully relied on the defence.[33] In 1971, a man who placed his severely handicapped son in the River Stour and watched him float away received the same clemency.[34] Evidence had been that the boy functioned at the level of a baby and had a short life expectancy. The judge told the defendant that he would be required to "undergo treatment as a doctor may prescribe for the next few weeks or so," and he added: "I hope that in the passage of time you will be able to forget about this matter."

In *R. v. Webb*,[35] V had been suicidal for many months and kept begging her husband to help her to kill herself. V believed that she was terminally ill, but she was not. Nevertheless, she was afflicted by a number of other non-life-threatening illnesses. One evening V took an overdose of Lorazepam tablets in an attempt to kill herself. V told her 73-year-old husband that if the tablets did not work that he should kill her. Her sleep became lighter and D began to fear that she would wake up. "As her sleep became lighter, he took a plastic bag and a towel and smothered her." This was not a case of assisted suicide, as the chain of causation was broken by D's deliberate intervention. D caused V's death by smothering her.[36] D raised the defence of diminished responsibility on the basis that he was suffering from "adjustment disorder," which was caused by the stress of caring for his mentally ill wife over a long period of time.

Lord Judge C.J. said: **28–016**

> "The evidence at trial included that of two distinguished psychiatrists. The jury concluded that the appellant had suffered from diminished responsibility at the time of the killing; in short that, as a matter of law, his mental responsibility for his actions at the time when he killed his wife was substantially impaired. It is clear from the evidence and from our summary of the facts that the mental turmoil engendered by the impossible situation in which he found himself must have been intolerable."[37]

The defence was supported by a benevolent psychiatrist who attested that:

> "... there is a significant body of research that demonstrates the negative psychological impact of being a full-time carer for another person who is suffering from both physical and psychiatric disorder. In my view, that psychological effect will have been compounded uniquely by the complex relationship that must have existed between Mr. Webb and his wife."[38]

---

[32] Robert Bluglass, *Psychiatry, the Law and the Offender: Present Dilemmas and Future Prospects*, (London, Institute for the Study and Treatment of Delinquency, 1980) at 10-11.

[33] *R. v. Gray* (1965) 129 J.P.N. 819.

[34] *R. v. Price (The Times*, 22 December 1971).

[35] [2011] EWCA Crim. 152. Cf. *R. v. Inglis* [2011] 1 W.L.R. 1110, where a mother was not able to raise the defence because she made a deliberate and calculated choice to kill her disabled son. The facts were that she had attempted to take his life on more than one occasion.

[36] *R. v. Webb* [2011] EWCA Crim. 152 at paras. 11 and 12.

[37] *R. v. Webb* [2011] EWCA Crim. 152 at para. 15.

[38] *R. v. Webb* [2011] EWCA Crim. 152 at para. 15.

According to the evidence, Webb's diminished capacity was caused by "adjustment disorder." Webb was successful in raising the defence of diminished responsibly and the Court of Appeal reduced his sentence of two years' imprisonment to a suspended sentence of twelve months. In doing this, Lord Judge C.J. remarked that the sentence would allow "this lonely old man [to] receive the help that he will need to come to terms with the disaster that has overtaken him."[39]

28–017   Loosely defined medical conditions such as "adjustment disorder"[40] will still give the benevolent psychiatrist some room to move, but cases like *R. v. Webb* would be decided differently under the current law. The new partial defence of diminished responsibility would not be available for someone like Mr. Webb. Under the new law Webb would get a mandatory life sentence, because his diminished capacity did not affect his ability to understand the nature of his conduct, to form a rational judgment or to exercise control. Webb's decision was calculated and rational. He was in full control[41] when he made the decision to assist his suicidal wife by killing her. He also understood that he was committing murder and that it was the wrong thing to do. It was noted in the judgment that:

> "The appellant's responsibility was diminished, not extinguished. He knew what he was doing and that what he did was unlawful; and the possible consequences of what he was doing when he was doing it. The judge was concerned that to pass a sentence short of immediate custody, even in the circumstances of this case, would give a wholly erroneous indication that such killings did not warrant punishment."[42]

The judges have tried to strike a balance on humane grounds in the mercy-killing cases, but the invocation of the psychiatrist could not have been regarded as necessary for any of the purposes for which those persons are normally used. It was merely an attempt by the judge to render workable a law that is grossly out of accord with present thought, and to maintain, as is required by his office, an appearance of official disapproval towards the act that most people nowadays would regard as a normal reaction to an impossible situation.

Clemency could not be so readily exercised if the offence were not characterized by the jury as murder. What is important about the doctrine of diminished responsibility is not only that it gives the judge a discretion in

---

[39] *R. v. Webb* [2011] EWCA Crim. 152 at para. 26.

[40] It is noted in one of the leading textbooks of psychiatry that: "The adjustment disorder construct is often criticized for a lack of scientific support, and there are few controlled studies of the adjustment disorders in the literature to date. ...The diagnosis of adjustment disorder strays from the general phenomenological approach of the fourth revised edition of the *Diagnostic and Statistical Manual of Mental Disorders* (DSM-IV-TR). The diagnosis provides little in the way of observable symptom criteria. Instead, it provides an etiological model linking a stressor to symptom formation. This model is unique to adjustment disorder..." See Benjamin J. Sadock *et al.*, *Kaplan and Sadock's Comprehensive Textbook of Psychiatry*, (Philadelphia: Wolters Kluwer Health/Lippincott Williams & Wilkins, 9th edn., 2009.) at Chap. 22.

[41] The fact that Webb's wife had been suicidal for a long period of time, and the fact that she had some non-life-threatening ailments might have provided him with a strong incentive for killing, but it is doubtful that this strong incentive combined with "adjustment disorder" substantially reduced his ability to control himself.

[42] *R. v. Webb* [2011] EWCA Crim. 152 at para. 17.

sentencing but that it enables him to exercise that discretion leniently, by removing the emotive reference to murder.

28.3. CAUSATION

Section 2(1)(c) of the *Act of 1957* requires the abnormality of mental functioning **28–018** to provide "an explanation for D's acts and omissions in doing or being a party to the killing." Meanwhile, section 2(1B) provides:

> "For the purposes of subsection (1)(c), an abnormality of mental functioning provides an explanation for D's conduct if it causes, or is a significant contributory factor in causing, D to carry out that conduct."

So there must be a nexus between D's abnormal mental functioning and his **28–019** **offending. Would the sexually motivated serial killer be able to raise the defence where he is able to show that his mental disorder prevented him from resisting the impulse to kill?[43]** Yes, but he may still get a life sentence, or if he is treatable, life in a mental hospital.[44] The provision requires the "abnormal mental functioning" to be a significant cause, which means it need not be the predominant cause.[45] It need not be the sole cause, but if the non-medical condition cause (*e.g.,* voluntary intoxication)[46] is the predominant cause this would suggest that the "abnormal mental functioning" that is linked to the defendant's recognized medical condition[47] is not a significant cause. To put it another way, if the evidence is that the defendant's abnormal mental functioning was such that his ability to understand the nature of his conduct, *etc.* would not have been substantially reduced had he been sober, he should not be able to raise the defence of diminished responsibility. It is not necessary to show that he would not have killed if he had been sober, it is only necessary to show that the medical condition was not a significant cause of the abnormal mental functioning that was present when the defendant killed.[48] The courts will probably hold that the intervention in substantial degree of any other causal factor means that the

---

[43] See *United States ex rel. Gacy v. Welborn*, 1992 WL 211018 (N.D.Ill. Aug. 26, 1992) (unpublished decision), where D, (who had been diagnosed as "borderline" with the psychosexual disorders of fetishism, homosexuality, sexual sadism, and necrophilia) killed 33 boys. See also *R. v. Byrne* [1960] Q.B. 396.

[44] *R. v. Wood* [2010] 1 Cr. App. R. (S.) 6. See also *Care and Treatment of Barlow v. State*, 250 S.W.3d 725 (2008).

[45] Cf. *R. v. Roach* [2001] EWCA Crim. 2698; *R. v. McEachem* [2003] A.W.L.D 209 (the latter is a decision of the Alberta Court of Queen's Bench).

[46] "On its own, voluntary intoxication falls outside the ambit of the defence. This is consistent with the general approach of the law that, save in the context of offences of specific intent and proof of that intent, criminal acts committed under the influence of self induced intoxication are not for that reason excused." *R. v. Wood* [2008] 2 Cr. App. R. 507 at 513-514.

[47] The state of being intoxicated causes an independent bout of abnormal mental functioning. Abnormal mental functioning resulting from intoxication is ephemeral.

[48] "[T]he subsection does not require the abnormality of mind to be the sole cause of the defendant's acts in doing the killing. In my opinion, even if the defendant would not have killed if he had not taken drink, the causative effect of the drink does not necessarily prevent an abnormality of mind suffered by the defendant from substantially impairing his mental responsibility for his fatal acts." *R. v. Dietschmann* [2003] 1 A.C. 1209 at 1217B *per* Lord Hutton discussing the former section 2.

abnormality of mental functioning that relates to the medical condition was not a significant cause of the defendant's impairment.

It would have been better if Parliament had made the test one of "predominance" rather than "significance," because a significant cause test could allow any cause that is not trivial to be considered. What will create a flutter of dovecotes will be a case in which evidence of alcoholic intake is combined with evidence from a friendly psychiatrist that when the defendant imbibed he had some kind of mild mental disorder, the result being that his ability to understand the nature of his conduct, *etc.* was diminished, which would not have occurred without the presence of both factors!

28–020   **Can D raise the defence even though he has induced his own abnormality of mental functioning?**   The medical condition that causes D's abnormal mental functioning may be a precursor to the abnormal mental functioning that actually causes D to be unable to fully understand the nature of his conduct, *etc.* when he kills. Take for example those who suffer from alcohol dependency syndrome; this medical condition *per se*[49] does not necessarily prevent the sufferer from fully understanding the nature of his conduct, *etc.*[50] It prevents the defendant from making a rational choice about avoiding alcohol. A person suffering alcohol dependency syndrome might kill whilst inebriated, but if he were sober he would have no problem in fully understanding that murder is wrong and that it is irrational to kill. Likewise, alcohol dependency syndrome does not cause a person to have an urge to kill.[51] The effect of alcohol dependency syndrome is simply that it results in the sufferer having an irresistible impulse for drinking alcohol. It affects his mental functioning to that extent only. Alcohol dependency syndrome, however, has a chain effect, because the sufferer becomes intoxicated as a matter of routine. The intoxication is an independent source of abnormal mental functioning. The question is whether abnormal mental functioning that is only indirectly caused by a recognized medical condition is sufficient for raising the defence of diminished responsibility.

If a person's medical condition causes him to drink large quantities of alcohol and his state of intoxication substantially reduces his ability to understand the nature of his conduct, to form a rational judgment and to exercise control, he may

---

[49] Long-term alcohol abuse can result in brain damage, but one can suffer alcohol dependency syndrome without also having brain damage.

[50] In *R. v. Wood* [2008] 2 Cr. App. R. 507, the defence of diminished responsibility did not rest on D having "brain damage," but merely on his "alcohol dependency syndrome"; a syndrome that in itself did not substantially reduce his ability to understand the nature of murder, to form a rational judgment about murder, or to resist the impulse to kill; the condition only reduced his ability to resist the impulse to drink.

[51] For a discussion of the medical conditions that might cause a person to have such an urge, see Zelda G. Knight, "Some Thoughts on the Psychological Roots of the Behaviour of Serial Killers as Narcissists: An Object Relations Perspective," (2006) 34(10) *Social Behaviour and Personality* 1189; William B. Arndt, Tammy Hietpas and Juhu Kim, "Critical Characteristics of Male Serial Murderers," (2004) 29(1) *American Journal of Criminal Justice* 117; J. M. W. Bradford, "The Paraphilias, Obsessive Compulsive Spectrum Disorder, and the Treatment of Sexually Deviant Behaviour," (1999) 70(3) *Psychiatric Quarterly* 209.

be able to raise the defence.[52] This is not a case of contributory causes working in tandem; it is a case of causes operating in a domino effect. The medical condition (alcohol dependency syndrome) causes D to drink excessively and this results in D becoming intoxicated, and the intoxication substantially diminishes D's ability to understand the nature of his conduct, to form a rational judgment, and to exercise control.

Technically, there is no direct causal link between his medical condition (alcohol dependency syndrome) and his act of killing, but there is an indirect causal link. It appears this will be enough to satisfy the requirements of the defence.[53] Support for the indirect causation approach can be found in *R. v. Wood*,[54] where Lord Judge C.J. said:

> "If the syndrome does not constitute such an abnormality of mind, diminished responsibility based on the consumption of alcohol will fail. If, on the other hand, it does, the jury must then be directed to address the question whether the defendant's mental responsibility for his actions at the time of the killing was substantially impaired as a result of the syndrome. In deciding that question the jury should focus exclusively on the effect of alcohol consumed by the defendant as a direct result of his illness or disease and ignore the effect of any alcohol consumed voluntarily. Assuming that the jury has decided that the syndrome constitutes an abnormality of mind induced by disease or illness, its possible impact and significance in the individual case must be addressed. The resolution of this issue embraces questions such as whether the defendant's craving for alcohol was or was not irresistible, and whether his consumption of alcohol in the period leading up to the killing was voluntary (and if so, to what extent) or was not voluntary, and leads to the ultimate decision, which is whether the defendant's mental responsibility for his actions when killing the deceased was substantially impaired as a result of the alcohol consumed under the baneful influence of the syndrome."

The amended section 2(1)(c) of the *Act of 1957* would also allow for such an interpretation, because it merely requires the abnormal mental functioning to provide "an explanation for D's acts and omissions in doing or being a party to the killing." The alcohol dependency syndrome is a significant contributory factor in causing the defendant's intoxication which in turn causes his abnormal mental functioning at the time when he kills. The "explanation" is that the defendant could not help drinking and as a result of his involuntary drinking he substantially reduced his capacity to understand the nature of his conduct, to form a rational judgment and to exercise control.[55]

28–021

---

[52] *R. v. Wood* [2008] 2 Cr. App. R. 507. Cf. *R. v. Tandy* [1989] 1 W.L.R. 350. See also Lawrence P. Tiffany and Mary Tiffany, "Noslogic, Objections to the Criminal Defence of Pathological Intoxication: What do the Doubters Doubt?" (1990) 13 *Int'l J. L. & Psychiatry 49*; Lawrence P. Tiffany, "The Drunk, the Insane, and the Criminal Courts: Deciding What to Make of Self-Induced Insanity," (1991) 69 *Wash. U.L.Q.* 221.

[53] *R. v. Wood* [2008] 2 Cr. App. R. 507 at 520. *R. v. Stewart* [2009] 1 W.L.R. 2507 at 2512H. Cf. *R. v. Inseal* [1992] Crim. L.R. 36; *R. v. Tandy* [1989] 1 W.L.R. 350; *R. v. Atkinson* [1985] Crim. L.R. 314; *R. v. Egan* (1992) 95 Cr. App. R. 278.

[54] *R. v. Wood* [2008] 2 Cr. App. R. 507 at 520.

[55] Manslaughter is a basic intent crime, so the result would be the same if his voluntary intoxication prevented him from forming the specific intent to kill a human being.

28.4. SENTENCING FOR DIMINISHED RESPONSIBILITY

28–022 The defence of "diminished responsibility" has the superficial attraction of offering an escape from the mad-bad dichotomy. It enables (so it may be thought) a transition to be made from complete responsibility to complete irresponsibility. Those who are completely normal are completely responsible; those who are so insane as to come within the *M'Naghten* rules are irresponsible; those who are on the borderline of such extreme insanity have diminished responsibility.

There is a danger in such reasoning. The law appears to imply that dangerous killers may be entitled, on account of their supposed mental disorder, to receive a comparatively light sentence, and thus may be turned loose on the community after a very few years in confinement.

This was in fact the line taken by some judges in the first case that arose under the *Act*. But the absurdity came to be recognized, and the general practice arose of sentencing dangerous offenders convicted under section 2 of the *Act of 1957* to imprisonment for life.[56] The paradoxical result was that a person who "won" a defence of "diminished responsibility" was often sentenced in the same way as if he had lost on that defence and had been convicted of murder.

When the *Mental Health Act 1959* came into force, it was realized that the new powers would be partially appropriate to cases under section 2 of the *Homicide Act 1957*. In *R. v. Morris*[57] the Court of Criminal Appeal laid down as a general principle that "in the ordinary case where punishment as such is not intended, and where the sole object of the sentence is that a man should receive mental treatment and be at large again as soon as he can safely be discharged, a proper exercise of the discretion [resulting from a finding of diminished responsibility] demands that steps should be taken to exercise the powers" of that *Act*, that is, to make a hospital order.

28–023 **Do the courts still send people to prison who have succeeded in the defence?** Imprisonment remains quite a common outcome, being imposed in the majority of cases of diminished responsibility.[58] Many offenders, however, receive hospital orders, and some are dealt with without the assistance of custody.

The rule in *R. v. Morris* was expressed only "in the ordinary case where punishment as such is not intended."[59] The court added, though without explanation, that even where there was substantial impairment of responsibility the offender might still "have some responsibility for the act he has done, for which he must be punished." This may suggest that the offender is, say, one-half

---

[56] See Law Commission, *Partial Defences to Murder*, Report 290, (London: H.M.S.O., 2004) appendix B at 14, where Professor MacKay writes, "It is interesting to note from ... the 126 diminished responsibility verdicts, 49.2% (n=62) resulted in a restriction order and six in a hospital order, while 46% (n=58) were punished in the normal way." It is also noted that around 40 *per cent.* received a life or discretionary life sentence.

[57] [1961] 2 Q.B. 237 at 243. See also *R. v. Bourne* (1995) 16 Cr. App. R. (S.) 237; *R. v. Chambers* (1983) 5 Cr. App. R. (S.) 190.

[58] Cf. *R. v. Wood* [2010] 1 Cr. App. R. (S.) 6; *R. v. Welsh* (2011) 119 B.M.L.R. 21; cf. *R. v. Drew* [2003] 1 W.L.R. 1213.

[59] Cf. *R. v. Wood* [2010] 1 Cr. App. R. (S.) 6.

responsible and so should receive half the normal sentence. But in fact the courts often sent these offenders to prison for life, if they are sent to prison at all.

The conditions upon which a judge may jail a dangerous offender to protect the public are found in section 225 of the *Criminal Justice Act 2003*. That provision provides:

"(1)   This section applies where—
    (a)   a person aged 18 or over is convicted of a serious offence committed after the commencement of this section, and
    (b)   the court is of the opinion that there is a significant risk to members of the public of serious harm occasioned by the commission by him of further specified offences.
(2)   If—
    (a)   the offence is one in respect of which the offender would apart from this section be liable to imprisonment for life, and
    (b)   the court considers that the seriousness of the offence, or of the offence and one or more offences associated with it, is such as to justify the imposition of a sentence of imprisonment for life, the court must impose a sentence of imprisonment for life or in the case of a person aged at least 18 but under 21, a sentence of custody for life."

Section 225 of the *Act of 2003* means that a life sentence is only likely to be given in cases where the defendant poses a significant threat to society and where he killed without a very substantial diminution of mental functioning.[60]

In *R. v. Wood*,[61] D was convicted of murder and sentenced to life imprisonment **28–024** with a minimum term of 18 years' imprisonment. The Court of Appeal quashed his conviction for murder and substituted a conviction for manslaughter on the ground of diminished responsibility. The murder involved Wood killing a homosexual. The attack involved extreme and repeated violence. The post-mortem examination of the deceased showed that he had been hit or stabbed some 53 times with a meat cleaver and a lump hammer. The defendant claimed he was visiting the victim when he made a homosexual advance to him, but the evidence revealed that the defendant had taken a meat cleaver to the deceased's home in a rucksack. Coupled with this, the defendant had an extensive criminal record which showed he had a history of violent offending. A psychiatric report indicated that he had the ability to cause serious harm in the context of interpersonal conflict, especially when he was under the influence of alcohol. This was an important consideration, because D's abnormality of mind arose from alcohol dependency syndrome.

Lord Judge C.J. said:[62]

"Although reference was made to a hospital order if recommended by a psychiatric report and justified, where the defendant constituted a danger to the public for an unpredictable time, the right sentence would probably be life imprisonment. However if the defendant's responsibility for his acts was so grossly impaired that his degree of responsibility was minimal, then a lenient course would be open, but the length of any determinate sentence depended on the judge's assessment of the degree of the defendant's responsibility and his assessment of the

---

[60] *R. v. Welsh* (2011) 119 B.M.L.R. 21. Cf. *R. v. Dighton* [2011] EWCA Crim. 1372, where D's sentence was reduced to 12 years, because there was substantial diminished responsibility.
[61] [2010] 1 Cr. App. R. (S.) 6.
[62] *R. v. Wood* [2010] 1 Cr. App. R. (S.) 6 at 12.

time for which the accused would continue to represent a danger to the public. At the time when *R. v. Chambers*[63] was decided imprisonment for public protection was not available. Nevertheless *R. v. Chambers* remains relevant to our decision. This is because the judge concluded that, notwithstanding the acceptance by the prosecution of manslaughter on the grounds of diminished responsibility, what the judge described as a 'very substantial amount of mental responsibility remained.'"

...

"The conclusion which follows from this observation is that the mere fact that the case is one of manslaughter on the grounds of diminished responsibility does not preclude a sentence of imprisonment for life. In reality this sentence will be rare in such cases, usually reserved for particularly grave cases, where the defendant's responsibility for his actions, although diminished, remains high."[64]

So the upshot of the tale, with our national genius for compromise, we have solved the problem of distinguishing legal irresponsibility from responsibility by making almost everyone responsible but entrusting the judge with a wide discretion which is generally exercised on pragmatic grounds.[65] If there are the requisite medical recommendations the judge will normally make a hospital order.[66] If, for one reason or another, the offender has to be sent to prison and is regarded as extremely dangerous, the sentence will normally (and should) be for "life."

28–025   The following are the chief reasons why the offender may go to prison:

- No hospital will take him, or the judge thinks the offender can only be entrusted to a special hospital and no special hospital will take him.
- The doctor cannot hold out any substantial hope of improving the offender's behaviour, and it is plain that if the proposed treatment proves to be ineffective the offender will soon be discharged from hospital and will be a menace or a serious threat to the community. As was pointed out in Chapter 27,[67] no hospital (not even a special hospital) can keep a patient under a hospital order merely because he is thought to be dangerous, if nothing further can be done for him. Even so, the judge will often chance a hospital order, on the argument that it offers a better hope of improving the offender's conduct than a prison sentence would do. But sometimes the judge may feel that, since medical science offers no assurance, he must pin his faith on old-fashioned incapacitation and deterrence.
- The defendant disputes the medical evidence and prefers prison.
- The defence of diminished responsibility was combined with one of loss of control, and was really a way of escaping from a limitation on the law of loss of control.

---

[63] (1983) 5 Cr. App. R. (S.) 190.
[64] *R. v. Wood* [2010] 1 Cr. App. R. (S.) 6 at 14.
[65] Cf. Lord Judge C.J.'s decision in *R. v. Webb* [2011] EWCA Crim. 152.
[66] *R. v. Welsh* (2011) 119 B.M.L.R. 21.
[67] 27.7.

Is not the problem that we lack any institution for people who are so   **28–026**
mentally affected that we feel it unjust to send them to an ordinary penal
institution as though they were normal, and yet who are not certainly
treatable and must be confined indefinitely in the public interest?   That
may be so. The special hospitals like Broadmoor formerly fulfilled this role, but
the hospital order no longer gives assurance that the offender will be kept under
control for as long as the public interest may demand.

Although we have swept the problem of responsibility under the carpet, its
continued existence is shown by the case of Sutcliffe, the multiple murderer (the
"Yorkshire Ripper") (1981).[68] All the doctors (including the prison medical
officers) concurred in the view that he suffered from paranoid schizophrenia and
would be properly convicted of manslaughter on the ground of diminished
responsibility.[69] The prosecution were therefore agreeable that he should plead to
manslaughter. The course, while making no difference to the sentence, would
have saved the expense of the trial and spared the feelings of the relatives who
would otherwise have to hear the horrible details of how their loved ones died.
But the judge rightly refused to accept the plea; Sutcliffe was tried for murder, the
psychiatrists were subjected to gruelling cross-examination, and the jury
convicted of murder. Leave to appeal was refused by the Court of Appeal.

The jury's verdict can technically be justified on the ground that although
Sutcliffe satisfied the medical criteria for the defence, his responsibility (having
regard, perhaps, to the gravity and persistence of his crimes, and his cunning in
avoiding detection—showing that he was not entirely beyond the restraint of the
law) was nevertheless not "substantially" diminished. But this is only a form of
words, which means little when we have no clear idea of the "responsibility" we
are talking about. The reality is that the jury thought Sutcliffe should go to prison
for an indeterminate time. Everyone would agree with that, however Sutcliffe's
mental state may be categorized, such a man must be detained for the indefinite
future. The only certain way of achieving this is a sentence of life
imprisonment.[70] (Sutcliffe began his sentence in prison, but was transferred to
Broadmoor in 1984 after being diagnosed as a schizophrenic. Section 47 of the
Mental Health Act 1983 allows for such a transfer to be made.)

It seems strange that the law of diminished responsibility adds yet another   **28–027**
form of manslaughter. Does it not make things difficult for the judge in
sentencing to have so many different variants of this crime? How does the
judge know which sort the jury have found?   You are right in suspecting the
existence of a problem. We have manslaughter by gross negligence, constructive
manslaughter, loss of control killing and diminished responsibility—all in theory
punishable with imprisonment for life. But loss of control killing by itself very

---

[68] For the case in the Court of Appeal, see *The Times*, 26 May 1982.
[69] Cf. *R. v. Coonan* [2011] EWCA Crim. 5. Sutcliffe now uses the alias Coonan.
[70] *R. v. Coonan* [2011] EWCA Crim. 5.

rarely attracts a life sentence, while killing with diminished responsibility may well do so. In practice, if there is evidence to support both defences, the judge will try not to give a life sentence.[71]

The general answer to your question is that the judge may question the foreperson as to the basis of the verdict, for the purpose of sentence.[72] He is not obliged to do so,[73] but if he does they must accept the opinion as to the facts reported by the foreperson.

28.5. INFANTICIDE

28–028   A forerunner of the general defence of diminished responsibility was the special rule for infanticide, which is still in force. At common law, infanticide by the mother was murder, but there were generally circumstances of mitigation which prompted a widespread desire for a change in the law. In the days of capital punishment it was highly distasteful to pass a death sentence that everyone in court—apart perhaps from the unfortunate woman herself—knew would not be carried out. Consequently, a special rule was passed.

The present law rests on section 1 of the *Infanticide Act 1938*.[74]

> "(1)   Where a woman by any wilful act or omission causes the death of her child being a child under the age of twelve months, but at the time of the act or omission the balance of her mind was disturbed by reason of her not having fully recovered from the effect of giving birth to the child or by reason of the effect of lactation consequent upon the birth of the child, then, [if] the circumstances were such that but for this *Act* the offence would have amounted to *murder* [or *manslaughter*], she shall be guilty of felony, to wit of infanticide, and may for such offence be dealt with and punished as if she had been guilty of the offence of *manslaughter* of the child.
>
> (2)   Where upon the trial of a woman for the murder of her child, being a child under the age of twelve months, the jury are of opinion that she by any wilful act or omission caused its death, but that at the time of the act or omission the balance of her mind was disturbed by reason of her not having fully recovered from the effect of giving birth to the child or by reason of the effect of lactation consequent upon the birth of the child, then the jury may, [if] the circumstances were such that but for the provisions of this *Act* they might have returned a verdict of *murder* [or *manslaughter*], return in lieu thereof a verdict of infanticide."

Infanticide is punishable like manslaughter, so the judge has a complete discretion as to sentence. In many cases, the outcome was always a hospital order or probation order; in more recent years the woman has simply been given a discharge.[75]

---

[71] *R. v. Wright* [1995] 16 Cr. App. R. (S.) 877. However, he may be compelled to impose a life sentence where the offender is extremely dangerous and thus poses a threat to society.

[72] *R. v. Matheson* [1958] 1 W.L.R. 474; *per* Diplock L.J. in *Warner v. Commissioner of Police of the Metropolis* [1967] 1 W.L.R. 1209 at 1213-1214; *R. v. Lamb* [1967] 2 Q.B. 981 at 984. The decision *contra* in *R. v. Larkin* [1943] K.B. 174 is now disregarded. A verdict is valid although the jury fail to pronounce upon a particular fact as the judge requests: *The Mayor and Burgesses of Devizes v. Clark* (1835) 111 E.R. 506.

[73] Subject to any guidance given by the verdict or plea, the judge sentences on his own view of the facts. For making a hospital order, all that he needs is the appropriate medical evidence.

[74] As amended by section 57 of the *Coroners and Justice Act 2009*.

[75] R. D. Mackay, "The Consequences of Killing Very Young Children," [1993] Crim. L.R. 21.

The prosecution normally charge infanticide and not murder if the evidence of mental unbalance is available to them; and the Director of Public Prosecutions will exert himself to obtain such evidence if it is obtainable. If murder or manslaughter[76] is charged, the woman may be allowed to plead infanticide (in which case there is no trial and no medical evidence), or if the case goes to the jury they may find her guilty only of infanticide. Infanticide can be raised as a defence to a charge of murder, but it is an independent criminal offence. If infanticide is raised as a defence, the prosecution have the burden of disproving the defendant's claim. And its burden is to disprove it "beyond reasonable doubt."

28–029

Although "puerperal psychosis"[77] appears in the books, and depression after childbirth is common,[78] women now rarely kill their babies for this reason. The reason is that at the first sign of mental trouble the baby is removed from its mother. Studies have shown that women who have killed their babies found no particular association with the period following childbirth.[79] As for a reference in the statute to lactation, the evidence that this is associated with mental disturbance is very weak indeed.[80] The association is a legal fiction, designed to extend the lesser offence to the full year of childbirth. In reality, the operative factors in child-killing are often the stress of having to care for the infant, who may be unwanted or difficult, and personality problems (in short, the "battered baby" syndrome); these stresses affect the father[81] as well as the mother, and are not confined to a year after birth.[82]

The advantage of including lactation is that the defendant only has to produce evidence to demonstrate that at the time of the killing the balance of her mind was disturbed by the birth or subsequent lactation. Whereas if she were to rely on insanity, the evidence would have to demonstrate that her mental disorder was such that she did not understand the nature and quality of her act of killing. Often the mother will not be legally insane, so the defence of insanity will not be

---

[76] See *R. v. Gore* [2007] EWCA Crim. 2789. However, section 1 of the *Infanticide Act 1938*, as amended by section 57(1) of the *Coroners and Justice Act 2009*, makes it clear it does not substitute other offences.

[77] Puerperal psychosis is a recognized mental illness so would also be caught by the partial defence of diminished responsibility, and perhaps in extreme cases the full defence of insanity. See Ian F. Brockington, *Motherhood and Mental Health*, (Oxford: Oxford University Press, 1996) at chapter 4.

[78] It has been noted that postpartum *depression* is the most common complication of childbearing. It affects 13 *per cent.* of women (one of every eight) after delivery. See Katherine L. Wisner *et al.* "Postpartum Depression," (2002) 347 *N. Engl. J. Med.* 194.

[79] D. J. West, *Murder Followed by Suicide*, (London: Heinemann, 1965) at 147; Ian D. Lambie "Mothers Who Kill: The Crime of Infanticide," (2001) 24(1) *International J. L. & Psychiatry* 71.

[80] Velma Dobson and Bruce Sales, "The Science of Infanticide and Mental Illness," (2000) 6(4) *Psychology, Public Policy, and Law* 1098. Cf. Maureen Marks, "Infanticide," (2009) 8(1) *Psychiatry* 10.

[81] Notably, fathers and other carers are not covered by the infanticide alternative. The ready acceptance of parliamentary diagnosis was travestied by an examination candidate who wrote: "The shock of childbirth may produce an effect that no man can tell, and may cause lactation."

[82] Michelle Oberman, "Mothers Who Kill: Coming to Terms with Modern American Infanticide," (2005) 8 *DePaul J. Health Care L.* 3; Karen Brennan, "Beyond the Medical Model: A Rationale for Infanticide Legislation," (2007) 58 *N. Ir. Legal Q.* 505; Bernadette McSherry, "The Return of the Raging Hormones Theory: Premenstrual Syndrome, Postpartum Disorders and Criminal Responsibility," (1993) 15 *Sydney L. Rev.* 292; Emma Cunliffe, "Infanticide: Legislative History and Current Questions," (2010) 55 *Crim. L.Q.* 94; Elizabeth Rapaport, "Mad Women and Desperate Girls: Infanticide and Child Murder in Law and Myth," (2006) 33 *Fordham Urb. L.J.* 527.

available, and the partial defence of diminished responsibility is only available if the mother was suffering from a recognized medical condition.[83] (If the defendant raises the partial defence of diminished responsibility, she will have the burden of proving it on the balance of probabilities.)

28–030 The *Infanticide Act* is the result of the sympathetic feelings of the judges and others, but it also reinforces them. When a woman does away with her infant everyone assumes, on slight evidence, that she was mentally unbalanced by reason of the consequences of childbirth. But if the woman botches the killing and merely injures the child, the Act does not apply; she will be charged with attempted murder or wounding with intent, and is quite likely to go to prison. Or if a mother kills her newborn baby and an older child, notwithstanding that any mental disturbance from which she suffered would have affected both killings. Of course, she can set up a defence of diminished responsibility in respect of the older child, but only if she was suffering from a "recognized medical condition." Furthermore, the latter only reduces murder to manslaughter. It does not apply to other offences against the person.

The Law Commission recently concluded: "We believe that although the *Infanticide Act 1938* has been subject to criticism, it is a practicable legal solution to a particular set of circumstances. Therefore, we will be recommending that the offence/defence of infanticide should be retained without amendment."[84] The Law Commission's conclusion seems balanced. Widening the offence/defence to cover those who killed because of the social pressures of parenting seems unnecessary.[85] Nor is there a strong case for including fathers. The defence/offence should really be kept in bounds: the father does not endure the hormonal and physical trauma of giving birth or of lactating. The physical trauma of giving birth and the changes it causes to a woman's body are bound to have psychological implications. If the "balance of her mind was disturbed by reason of her not having fully recovered from the effect of giving birth," then it seems appropriate to proportionately excuse her for her harm-doing. There is no doubt that social conditions can also play a role, but they should be considered as a mitigating factor by the sentencing judge. Social pressures of parenting *per se* do not excuse killing. Although, the "lactation" prong seems questionable, it does provide for an appropriate degree of leeway.

The Law Commission, however, recognized the need for procedural reform to protect mothers who are in a state of denial about what they did.[86] If the mother denies killing the infant because of her mental disturbance, "it is virtually

---

[83] See also April J. Walker, "Application of the Insanity Defense to Postpartum Disorder-Driven Infanticide in the United States: A Look Toward the Enactment of an Infanticide Act," (2006) 6 *U. Md. L.J. Race, Religion, Gender & Class* 197.

[84] Law Commission, *Murder, Manslaughter and Infanticide*, Report 304, (London: H.M.S.O., 2006) at para.8.3. Cf. Criminal Law Revision Committee, *Offences Against the Person*, Fourteenth Report, (London: H.M.S.O., Cmnd. 7844, 1980) at paras. 106-108.

[85] If a person chooses to have seven children and through her gross negligence causes the death of her latest infant; the fact that she has seven children, chooses to ignore medical advice, and so on does not do much to mitigate her culpableness. See *R. v. Johnston* (2007) 173 A. Crim. R. 540. Not every act of murder can be converted into one of infanticide merely because the victim is an infant—similar social conditions would not excuse those who cause the death of older children.

[86] See *R. v. Kai-Whitewind* [2005] 2 Cr. App. R. 31.

impossible under the adversarial system to obtain and present psychiatric evidence in order to found a plea or charge of infanticide. As a result, if the mother's denial is rejected by the jury such cases lead to a murder conviction with a mandatory life sentence." [87] The Law Commission proposed that:[88]

> "in circumstances where infanticide is not raised as an issue at trial and the defendant (biological mother of a child aged 12 months or less) is convicted by the jury of murder ..., the trial judge should have the power to order a medical examination of the defendant with a view to establishing whether or not there is evidence that at the time of the killing the requisite elements of a charge of infanticide were present. If such evidence is produced and the defendant wishes to appeal, the judge should be able to refer the application to the Court of Appeal and to postpone sentence pending the determination of the application."

---

[87] Law Com. *Murder, Manslaughter and Infanticide*, at para.8.44.
[88] *Id.* at para. 8.46; and para. 8.50 for the limitations of this solution.

PART FIVE

THE PROTECTION OF PROPERTY

CHAPTER 29

THEFT

"Property and the law are born and must die together."

Jeremy Bentham[1]

29.1. TYPES OF PROPERTY OFFENCES

Offences in respect of property may be divided in various ways. Most are **29–001** acquisitive offences (the main offence of dishonesty), but there are also offences of damage and destruction which are non-acquisitive. Offences of dishonesty do not necessarily relate to property (one may, for example, commit perjury in the hope of avoiding going to prison), but the great majority of them do. Some offences of dishonesty concentrate on the interest invaded, while others focus on the defendant's conduct. The present chapter will deal with theft. The following chapters will deal with the fraud, blackmail, burglary and handling stolen goods. It can be an offence:

- to appropriate a person's property dishonestly; or
- to make temporary use of his property.

29.2. THEFT: THE HISTORY

The common law got itself into a tangle over theft, or larceny as it was called.[2] **29–002** Basically, this crime was confirmed to be the taking of a thing from the possession of another without his consent. It did not cover misappropriation by a possessor of the thing (he could not take what he already possessed), and it did not (at least in its original form) cover the theft of a notional balance of account.

However, the proposition that possessors could not steal was eroded by subtle rules. For example, a servant (employee) was said not to possess his master's article, although he held it in his hands. He only had custody of it; his master retained possession; so a dishonest appropriation by the servant was a "taking" from his master's possession and therefore larceny. The artificiality of the rule was shown by the fact that if a wrong-doer stole the thing from the servant, the

---

[1] John Bowring (ed.), *The Works of Jeremy Bentham*, (Edinburgh: William Tait, 1838) at 307.
[2] The offence of larceny has survived in many U.S. jurisdictions. For an overview of the U.S. position see Wayne R. LaFave, *Substantive Criminal Law* (West Publishing, Vol. III 2003) at 55 *et seq*. It also survives in some Australia jurisdictions, but some states (most notably Victoria) adopted the U.K. *Theft Act* model in 1968. See also the *Theft Act 1969* for Northern Ireland.

servant was regarded as being in possession. The indictment could "lay the property" in the servant. So the servant was both in possession and not in possession: not in possession if the question were whether he stole from the master, and in possession if the question were whether a stranger stole from him. The object of these two contradictory rules was simply to procure the conviction of wrongdoers; but the practical necessity for the law to contort itself in this way showed that the premise from which it proceeded was socially inadequate.

Even heroic judicial action was found not to be enough to cure the defects of the common law. Sundry statutory offences had to be created—obtaining by false pretences, embezzlement, larceny by bailee, fraudulent conversion, obtaining credit by fraud, false accounting, and a number of summary offences.

29–003 The *Theft Act 1968* recast the law, largely as a result of recommendations made by the Criminal Law Revision Committee (C.L.R.C.).[3] (All references in this chapter are to this *Act*, unless the contrary is expressed or clearly implied.) The *Theft Act* abandons the Latinate term "larceny"[4] in favour of the Old English "theft" and it makes it clear that we can use "steal" as the verb. Theft is no longer confined to taking of specific corporeal things. The *Theft Act* sweeps away all the offences specifically mentioned in the last paragraph and replaces them by a series of simpler offences, chief among which is theft. Theft rolled up what was larceny, embezzlement and fraudulent conversion in the old law, while offences of deception replaced[5] obtaining by false pretences and obtaining credit by fraud.

One effect of the new definition of theft is to abolish the rule that possessors cannot steal. Therefore, there is little necessity nowadays to assert pedantically that an employee only has custody of his employer's goods and not possession. The object of this proposition in the old law was to enable the employee to be convicted. Since it is no longer needed for that purpose we might well admit that he has possession. But the old ways of speaking are likely to persist, and on occasions may still arise (though no longer in relation to theft) where the lawyer may think it important to assert that the employer who entrusts an article to an employee does not part with possession of it.

29.3. THE DEFINITION OF THEFT

29–004 The offence of theft created by the *Theft Act 1968* was intended to be as free from technicality as human ingenuity could devise. Things have not worked out like that. Troublesome questions of interpretation have arisen. Still, it is true that almost everyone[6] whom common sense would regard as a thief is now a thief in law, if the *Theft Act* departs from common sense, that is chiefly because it brings

---

[3] See the C.L.R.C., Eighth Report: *Theft and Related Offences*, (London: Cmnd. 2977, 1966).

[4] The word "larcenous" was formerly in use as the adjective from "larceny." There is no accepted adjective from "theft," but the word "theftous" will here be used.

[5] The *Fraud Act 2006* now covers deception.

[6] Even the facts of *R. v. Hinks* [2001] 2 A.C. 241 seem to fit. What does not fit, are the statements of the Lords suggesting that a valid gift can be the object of theft. On the facts, it appears that Mrs. Hinks's gift would have been invalid at civil law, as she used "undue influence" and no doubt fraudulent tactics to obtain it. It is argued below, some unlawfulness in civil law is required, but this is only a sufficient condition—civil law unlawfulness would need to do more than invalid the gift to warrant a criminal law response, rather than pure remedial response in equity.

within the notion of theft some forms of dishonesty that some people might prefer to call by other names (breach of trust, fraud or deception).[7] If the *Theft Act* is sometimes hard to apply, that is chiefly because it has to operate against the background of the law of property, which is itself complicated.

Theft is defined in section 1(1):

> "A person is guilty of theft if he dishonestly appropriates property belonging to another with the intention of permanently depriving the other of it; and 'thief' and 'steal' shall be construed accordingly."

Does that mean that you can't steal from a possessor who is not the owner, such as a hirer or a borrower? A thief can be charged with stealing either from the owner or from the possessor, as the prosecutor pleases. Ever since earliest times the law has to some extent muddled up the notions of possession and ownership, because it traditionally regards the possessor as being the owner, the proprietor, as against third parties, unless such third parties have a better right to possess than he has. In other words, the law protects the possessor against wrongdoers as though the possessor were the owner. This is expressed in section 5(1):

29–005

> "Property shall be regarded as belonging to any person having possession or control of it, or having in it any proprietary right or interest (not being an equitable interest arising only from an agreement to transfer or grant an interest)."

The effect of the subsection is that the prosecutor when drawing the indictment may "lay the property" either in the owner or in a bare possessor.

Can property be laid in an owner who has never been in possession? Yes. If A sells goods to B, so that the property (ownership, title) passes to B, and the goods are stolen before being delivered to B, the property may be laid either in A (who is now only the possessor) or in B (the owner who has not yet taken possession). It may be noticed here that the word "property" has two meanings. Sometimes it refers to physical property (furniture, *etc.*), while sometimes it means property rights—ownership, the right of property. If I say that "the property in this furniture is in me," I mean that the ownership is me—that I am the owner. (The double use of the term "property," as meaning both physical things and ownership, was the basis of a witticism of G. K. Chesterton's "Thieves respect property; they merely wish the property to become their property that they more perfectly respect it."[8] What thieves do not respect is the right of ownership.)

29–006

Suppose A lends £5 to B, and while B is walking away with it a bandit steals it from him. Is this a theft of the debt by the bandit? No, it is not, because the lender continues to be owed the money by the borrower. The thief has simply stolen money from the borrower. The thief has not stolen anything from the

29–007

---

[7] As we will see below, some deception cases have been charged as simple theft rather than as "obtaining by deception" under the repealed section 15 of the *Act*, which has resulted in the courts stretching the notion of "appropriation" beyond is conceptual limits.

[8] G. K. Chesterton, *The Man Who Was Thursday – A Nightmare*, (Bristol: Arrowsmith, 1908) at 32.

lender, because the money became the borrower's when it was "lent" to him. Legally there is a difference between the loan of a chattel and the loan of money. If I ask you for the "loan" of a bicycle, and you comply, you will remain the owner of the bicycle, and I shall obtain only possession; in law I shall be a bailee. But if I ask you for a "loan" of money, and you comply, I shall obtain ownership of the notes and coins that you hand to me. This is because you do not expect me to return the money *in specie* (as lawyers say); you merely have a right *in personam* against me for the repayment of an equivalent sum.[9]

29–008   **But surely a creditor can get a bank loan back from a debtor?**   He can bring an action and get judgment for payment of the money. But the creditor cannot just walk into the debtor's house and make off with money in the drawer, or with a television set, in repayment of the loan. The creditor does not own any property of the debtor's. If a judgment remains unsatisfied he can apply to have a bailiff of the court levy execution on the debtor's property, selling his furniture if necessary to satisfy the judgment. In the case of the loan of a bicycle, on the other hand, the lender still owns the bicycle.

29–009   **What was that bit in section 5(1) about an equitable interest?**   Do not trouble about the bracketed words in the subsection at the moment. Suffice it here to say that property ordinarily exists at law; that is, it was recognized by the old courts of common law. This is legal property, or property without complications. But property can also exist in equity behind a trust; this was the invention of the former Court of Chancery.[10] In other words, the legal title to property may be vested in trustees, who hold it on trust for a beneficiary; the beneficiary is the owner in equity, and may be said to have the equitable title. (The above is a simplified account of the position, but it is good enough for our purposes) either the trustee or the beneficiary may be named in the indictment as the person to whom the property "belongs;" no question will be raised.

29–010   **What if the indictment lays the property in the wrong person?**   Happily, the mistake is usually harmless. Provided that there has clearly been a theft from someone, it does not matter that the indictment names the wrong owner, unless the circumstances are very unusual and mentioning the wrong owner has misled the defendant in his defence. Normally the trial court can, upon application, give leave to amend the indictment or information, and even if no amendment is made

---

[9] Of course, if I "borrow" a £50 note for performing a party trick, I am a bailee of the note, because the specific note is supposed to be given back. Similarly, rare vintage coinage lent to a museum would not be fungible—as the specific coins would not necessarily be interchangeable for modern coins or even coins of the same age and kind—as the value of vintage coins would depend on their rareness and condition.

[10] For a detailed discussion of equitable and legal interests see R.P. Meagher *et al.*, *Meagher, Gummow and Lehane, Equity: Doctrines and Remedies*, (Sydney, LexisNexis, 2002).

a conviction to correct a mistake as to ownership will be upheld on appeal. The comforting rule for prosecutors is that the ownership of the property is an "immaterial averment."[11]

What is an appropriation?   This was chosen as a wider term than the "taking" previously required for theft. In order to make the meaning clearer, section 3(1) provides that "any assumption by a person of the rights of an owner amounts to an appropriation."

29–011

I am glad you think that makes it clearer. It's far from being clear to me. Does it mean that the thief assumes the owner has rights?   No. The thief assumes to himself, *i.e.* grabs for himself, so far as he can what would otherwise have been the rights of the owner.

29–012

But theft does not alter the ownership. The owner still has all his rights. So how can the thief have assumed them?   The section must refer to the thief taking for himself some of the advantages to which the owner is entitled, such as possession of the thing. In short, "appropriation" means the *usurpation* of rights. This does not have to result in acquisition of possession or ownership—it covers any interference that involves an owner's rights.

29–013

A word as to sentencing, the maximum sentence for theft is seven years' imprisonment,[12] but this is meant only for cases of the utmost seriousness, and the ordinary offender, particularly the first-time offender, can expect lenient treatment. Theft is triable either way, and the vast majority of charges are tried summarily.[13] In the following pages we shall frequently speak of the jury as the triers of fact, but wherever the context so admits this expression is intended to include magistrates on summary trial.

29.4.   THEFT: THE *ACTUS REUS*

The *actus reus* of theft may be discussed under five propositions:

29–014

1. There must be property.
2. The property must belong to another.
3. The thief must appropriate the property.
4. It is immaterial that the owner is induced by fraud, threats and undue influence to consent to parting with the title to the property;
5. but in other cases it is doubtful how far theft can be committed if the act of appropriation is lawful in civil law.

---

[11] *Pike v. Morrison* [1981] Crim. L.R. 492; *Etim v. Hatfield* [1975] Crim. L.R. 234; *R. v. Gregory* [1972] W.L.R. 991. If information arises which allows for an amendment then it is good practice to do so.

[12] Section 7 of the *Theft Act 1968* as amended by *Criminal Justice Act 1991*.

[13] So magistrates, rather than juries determine honesty in such cases.

29–015   That there must be property is an independent requirement of the law of theft. My small son "belongs" to me, and is in my possession or control; but he is not stealable under the law of theft because he is not property. An employee who spends hours on Facebook while at work may be said to be dishonest with his employer's time and equipment,[14] but he does not steal because time is not property (although he may be fired for ineptitude). It is impossible to filch from another his good name, except by poetic licence, because a good name is not property. The notion of property, therefore, is a key concept in the law of theft. It is a notion of the civil law, so the ambit of the law of theft depends directly upon the civil law.

The property alleged to have been stolen is stated in the indictment, but only in a general way. The following is an example:

Statement of Offence

Theft, contrary to section 1 of the *Theft Act 1968.*

Particulars of Offence

AB on the ____ day of ____ stole 400 shirts belonging to Shirt Inc.

Almost every prosecution for theft starts as an information before magistrates, which is somewhat similar to the indictment (except that there are no counts in an information, which must not charge more than one offence). Theft is triable either way, so if the defendant consents he can be tried summarily on the information instead of being "sent for trial."[15]

29–016   **In the above example, don't you need a count for each separate shirt?** Where many articles are stolen together, or even over a period of time in a continuous course of conduct, so that separate thefts cannot be identified, the theft of all may be charged in one count. If the separate thefts are identifiable the court might treat the individual takings as a "continuous theft."[16] If the thefts

---

[14] He might also be liable for dishonestly obtaining a service contrary to section 11 of the *Fraud Act 2006*. But unless his employer is in the business of providing such a service, it will be difficult to prove D had the requisite *mens rea*. If D works for an Internet café and decides to sit on Facebook all day, he might know that he is dishonestly acquiring a service that the café is in the business of providing for payment. Cf. *People v. Weg*, 450 N.Y.S. (2d) 957 (1982), where it was held that the defendant was not guilty of obtaining a service when he used the Education Board's computer for his own use, because the Board was not in the business of supplying such a (computer) service. Similarly, the U.S. courts have held that labour is not property, see *Chappell v. United States*, 270 F. 2d. 274 (9th Cir. 1959). In that case, an Air Marshal ordered junior officers, who were on duty, to paint three houses belonging to him. See also *U.S. v. Lewis*, 938 F. Supp. 683 (1996); See *U.S. v. Delano*, 55 F. 3d 720 (1995).

[15] This book covers substantive criminal law. Those who are looking for more detail on criminal law procedure will no doubt consult *Archbold: Criminal Pleading, Evidence & Practice* (London: Sweet & Maxwell, 2012).

[16] *Barton v. D.P.P.* (2001) 165 J.P.N. 887; *R. v. Jackson (No. 2)* (1991) reported in *Guardian*, Nov. 20 (1991).

occur in different places (even if only in different departments of a department store, on the same occasion) it is safer to charge them in separate counts.[17]

Suppose it can only be proved that 100 shirts were stolen? The defendant can be convicted under the indictment (or information) of stealing the part of the property charged that he is proved to have stolen. There is no need to amend the charge.

29–017

Suppose that the prosecution is against the manager of the shop who is 400 shirts down on his stock. He has given evasive explanations of the shortage and is obviously dishonest. Is he charged with stealing the shirts or the proceeds? It would be safest to charge him with stealing the money. In practice, the jury or magistrate would be strongly inclined to assume that the manager had sold the shirts in the shop, at the prices he was supposed to sell them at, and convict him of dipping into the till, since the great probability is that that is what he did.[18]

29–018

Couldn't one just charge the defendant with theft, without mentioning the property? The court upon the defendant's application would require such an indictment (or information) to be amended to state the property. It need not state the serial numbers of the currency notes or the brands of the shirts, but it must state in general what is alleged to have been stolen.

29–019

What is covered by the term "property"? Property is defined for the purpose of theft in section 4(1) of the *Theft Act 1968*:

29–020

> "'Property includes money and all other property, real or personal, including things in action and other intangible property."

What is the difference between real and personal property? "Real property" (otherwise called "reality") means freehold land. "Personal property called "personalty") means all other property, including leasehold land, movables ("chattels"), and money.

29–021

Can one steal a thing of no value? At common law the thing had to have some value, but the rule was so interpreted that it had practically no effect, except in wholly artificial applications. Anyway it is not repeated in the *Theft Act*. One may steal, for example, a commercially worthless piece of paper, because there are many pieces of paper that people want to keep, even though they have no market value. If a thing were derisively worthless, like a used matchstick, the prosecution could not establish dishonesty.

29–022

---

[17] *R. v. Wilson* (1979) 69 Cr. App. R. 83; *R. v. Fyffe* [1992] Crim. L.R. 442.

[18] Of course it is necessary to prove that the defendant took the particular property he has been accused of taking. See *Machent v. Quinn* [1970] All E.R. 255.

29–023 **Can one steal a corpse, or a bit of the human body such as hair?** The traditional rule is that there is no property in a corpse,[19] which was accordingly regarded as not larcenable (unless labour had been expended on it, as by reducing it to an anatomical skeleton).[20] The same rule applies to theft.[21] There are also a number of situations where the law allows for possession but not outright ownership, such as for post mortems[22] and burials.[23] Notwithstanding that a corpse cannot be stolen, there is a plethora of offences relating to corpses at common law and under statute such as using a corpse to create a nuisance,[24] preventing or leaving a corpse unburied,[25] wrongfully removing a corpse from a grave,[26] using it for sexual[27] and pornographic purposes[28] and so forth. For the purpose of this book it is enough to say that almost any wrongful disposal of or interference with human remains is an offence.[29]

A miscreant who wrongfully cuts off a damsel's tresses could be charged with an offence against the person.[30] If the miscreant dishonestly takes the tresses after someone else has cut them off for the victim's benefit,[31] he could be charged with theft,[32] since a person is regarded as owning parts of his body after they have been severed or otherwise discharged.[33]

In *R. v. Bentham*[34] the House of Lords held that:

> "An un-severed hand or finger is part of oneself. Therefore, one cannot possess it. ... What is possessed must under the definition be a thing. A person's hand or fingers are not a thing. If they were regarded as property for the purposes [of the *Act* in question] the court could, theoretically, make an order depriving the offender of his rights to them and they could be taken into the possession of the police."

---

[19] *Hanydyside's Case* (1749) 2 East. P.C. 652; *R. v. Sharpe* (1857) 169 E.R. 959 at 960 *per* Erle J; *The Queen v. Price* (1884) 12 Q.B.D. 247 at 253 *per* Stephen J; *Williams v. Williams* (1882) 20 Ch. D. 659 at 644; *Pierce v. Swan Point Cemetery*, 4 Am. Rep. 667 (1872).

[20] *Doodeward v. Spence* (1908) 6 C.L.R. 406. See also section 32(9)(c) of the *Human Tissue Act 2004*; and sections 5, 6 and 9 of the *Anatomy Act 1984*.

[21] *R. v. Kelly* [1999] Q.B. 621. See also *Dobson v. North Tyneside Health Authority* [1997] 1 W.L.R. 596.

[22] *A v. Leeds Teaching Hospitals NHS Trust* [2005] Q.B. 506.

[23] *Dobson v. North Tyneside Health Authority* [1997] 1 W.L.R. 596.

[24] *R. v. Clark* (1883) 15 Cox C.C. 171; *R. v. Price* (1884) 12 Q.B.D. 247.

[25] *R. v. Hunter* [1973] 3 W.L.R. 374; *R. v. Pedder* (2000) 2 Cr. App. R. 36; *R. v. Whiteley* [2000] All E.R. 1888. It is also an offence to refuse access to a corpse: *The King v. Soleguard* (1738) 95 E.R. 376.

[26] *R. v. Jacobson* (1880) 14 Cox C.C. 522. Generally, it is not a defence to demonstrate good motives: *R. v. Sharpe* (1857) 169 E.R. 959. However, the courts may permit the removal of a corpse from a grave if it is in the public interest: *Re St Mary, Sledmere* [2007] 2 All E.R. 75.

[27] Section 70 of the *Sexual Offence Act 2003*.

[28] Section 63(1),(7) of the *Criminal Justice and Immigration Act 2008*.

[29] *The King v. Cundick* (1822) 171 E.R. 900; *R. v. Stephenson* (1884) 13 Q.B.D. 331; *R. v. Le Grand, Townsend and Cooper* [1983] Crim. L.R. 626.

[30] *D.P.P. v. Smith* [2006] 1 W.L.R. 1571.

[31] The damsel might have asked a hairdresser to cut them off so that she could sell them to a wigmaker.

[32] *R. v. Rothery* (1976) Cr. App. R. 231; *R. v. Welsh* [1974] R.T.R. 478.

[33] In *Yearworth v. North Bristol NHS Trust* [2009] 3 W.L.R. 118, it was held that the appellants had ownership in their own sperm because they had generated it and dispensed it for their own benefit.

[34] [2005] 1 W.L.R. 1057 at 1060. "*Dominus membrorum suorum nemo videtur*: no one is to be regarded as the owner of his own limbs": *id.* at 1061.

Parts of a person's body that remain attached to a person do not constitute property under section 4 of the *Theft Act*, but the removal of tissue and other transplantable material from living human beings may be caught by more specific offences.[35] Given that a person is able to donate his body for medical research, and that medical research centres are able to possess and control corpses for research purposes, it seems appropriate to recognize a corpse as property. Might not the corpse of a person who was suffering some rare condition be extremely valuable to a scientific team?[36] Propertizing[37] and commercializing body parts and corpses raises profound ethical issues that cannot be explored in this treatise.[38] Criminalization is necessary in certain cases, but in many other cases private law regulation would be sufficient. For present purposes, we need merely bear in mind that certain discharged bodily fluids and severed body parts constitute property as far as section 4 of the *Theft Act 1968* is concerned.

29.6.   CORPOREAL PROPERTY

The title of this section is the general name for tangible property, whether land or chattels. The common law declared, with superficial logic, that there could be no larceny of land. That a person could not steal the sitfast acres was obvious, in days when stealing involved a taking and carrying away. But the courts (with a view, it is said, to restricting capital punishment) went further, and held that parts of the land (gravel, growing timber, buildings) could not be stolen even by being severed and carried off.   **29–024**

The basic rule that there can be no theft of land survives the sweep of the new broom. The Book of Deuteronomy pronounces a curse on the person who dishonestly "removeth his neighbour's landmark";[39] but the framers of the *Theft Act* decided not to take a cue from this, even though dishonest practices are not unknown when new housing estates are being laid out. The worst curse laid upon the boundary-mover by English law is to make him or her liable for civil trespass. After occupying his ill-gotten strip for 12 years he will get title to it as a "squatter."[40] (If you were to take Caravaggio's *Conversion of Saint Paul* from the

---

[35] See section 33 of the *Human Tissue Act 2004*. Sections 1–12, 14 and 57 of the *Human Tissue Act 2004* allows a person to consent to his body or any part of it being used for medical research.

[36] Charlotte H. Harrison, "Neither Moore Nor the Market: Alternative Models for Compensating Contributors of Human Tissue," (2002) 28 *Am. J. L. & Med.* 77.

[37] For a general discussion of the concept of property, see James E. Penner, *The Idea of Property in Law*, (Oxford: Clarendon Press, 1997).

[38] See generally, J. W. Harris, "Who Owns My Body?" (1996) *Oxford J. Legal Stud.* 55; Loane Skene, "Arguments Against People Legally 'Owning Their Own Bodies, Body Parts, and Tissue'", (2002) 2 *Macquarie L.J.* 165; Rosalind Atherton, "Claims on the Deceased: The Corpse as Property," (2000) 7 *J. L. & Med.* 361; Prue Vines, "The Sacred and the Profane: The Role of Property Concepts in Disputes about Post-Mortem Examination," (2007) *Sydney L. Rev.* 255; Michele Goodwin, "Empires of the Flesh: Tissue and Organ Taboos," (2009) *Ala. L. Rev.* 1219; Gloria J. Banks, "Legal and Ethical Safeguards: Protection of Society's Most Vulnerable Participants in a Commercialised Organ Transplantation System," (1995) 21 *Am. J. L. & Med.* 45.

[39] George Adam Smith, *The Book of Deuteronomy*, (Cambridge: University Press, revised edition, 1918) at 305.

[40] *JA Pye (Oxford) Ltd. v. Graham* [2003] 1 A.C. 419; *Ashe v. National Westminster Bank Plc.* [2008] 1 W.L.R. 710. See also, Michael J. Goodman, "Adverse Possession of Land—Morality and Motive,"

Chapel Santa Maria Del Popolo and care for it for 12 years you would not get title, so why should you get the title to another's reality?)

Generally, land theft will involve fraud, false representations,[41] forged conveyances and so on. Thus, it is better dealt with as a fraud offence. The law's benevolence to squatters is meant to assist in settling disputed claims, particularly in respect of boundaries, which are often hazy on the title deeds.[42] It makes for easy decision to say that the occupier who has mown or seeded the boundary strip for 12 years shall be entitled to it. Would it not be anomalous (the argument runs) if a squatter, notwithstanding that he has obtained title to land, could be charged with theft of it? But the argument is defective. There is no reason why the squatter should not be subject to the law of theft before he gets his title by lapse of time. When the squatter does get title, he would naturally be in a different position. In effect, there would be a 12-year time limit on prosecution. Given the munificent provision of public housing, housing benefit and welfare in England and Wales, it seems unreasonable to ask those who are paying taxes to fund such benefits to have their property rights subject to the insecurities of a system of winner takes title. Why should one compete civilly for title one has paid for?[43] It would be much easier to send the police to charge squatters with theft and likely to be a greater deterrent. This solution not having been adopted, the *Theft Act* has the unhappy result of perpetuating in the criminal law the archaic distinction between land and chattels. The squatter does not engage in fraud so he would not be caught by the *Fraud Act 2006*.

29–025   The restriction upon the scope of theft is effected by section 4(2) of the *Act*, but some important qualifications are imposed upon it. Omitting some of the rigmarole, it runs as follows:

> "A person cannot steal land, or things forming part of land and severed from it by him or by his directions, except in the following cases:
> (a)   when he is a trustee, and he appropriates the land by dealing with it in breach of the confidence reposed in him; or
> (b)   when he is not in possession of the land and appropriates anything forming part of the land by severing it; or

---

(1970) 33 *Mod. L. Rev.* 281. Cf. *Callan v. Superior Court in and For San Mateo County*, 204 Cal. App. 2d 652 (1962); American Law Institute: *Model Penal Code* (1985), §223.0(6).

[41] The former section 15 of the *Theft Act 1968* caught those who obtained title to land by deception. This would now be caught by the *Fraud Act 2006*. For an example of deceptive behaviour involving land: see *Sylvan Lake Golf & Tennis Club Ltd. v. Performance Industries Ltd.* (2002) S.C.C. 19, where the victim was tricked into selling more of his land than he had agreed to sell because he thought he was keeping a 110 *yard* wide strip, when in fact the conveyance misstated it as 110 *foot* wide strip of land.

[42] Land does not include incorporeal hereditaments such as easements, *profits á prendre*, rent-charges and so forth. Therefore, these rights can be the subject of theft. *Per contra*, the dishonest creation of a lease or easement cannot constitute theft from the owner of the land affected by the lease or easement—as the fraud creates something new. "A freeholder granting a lease could never own the leasehold estate as it would merge in the freehold interest." *Chan Wai Lam v. The Queen* [1981] Crim. L.R. 497.

[43] Taxpayers have funded civil proceedings to recover housing that was set aside for veterans. Helen Pidd, "Exodus across London as 120 evicted squatters move into homes for veterans," (London: *The Guardian*, Thursday 28 August 2008). These takeovers will not always involve a billionaire's 100th residence. See Jon Swaine, "Squatters move into £4.5m Hampstead Mansion," (London: *The Telegraph*, 10 April 2009).

(c)   when, being in possession under a tenancy, he appropriates any fixture."

A trustee would be guilty of theft if he sold real property that he was holding on trust for another. This is an exception to the rule that reality does not constitute property for purposes of the *Theft Act*. Similarly, if the trustee sells land for less than its market value (perhaps to a confederate or relative), he could be guilty of theft. Such a case is yet to come before the courts.

A squatter can be convicted of theft of chattels that he finds on the land, though not part of the land itself, or of buildings on it. To illustrate the refinements of the law, the following are chattels; a mobile caravan,[44] windfall apples,[45] and a heap of dung. All these are personal property, which the squatter (or anyone else) takes on peril of being convicted of theft. The following are "part of the reality"; a caravan on fixed brick piers, growing apples,[46] a farm gate,[47] and dung[48] spread on the land;[49] these things the trespasser can steal by severing them: but a squatter cannot steal them because he is in possession of the land. The squatter might dig up part of the land and take it, take a growing apple or chattels that have been affixed to the land such as a manmade hut. Nevertheless, it is arguable that a squatter is no more than a trespasser and only takes lawful possession (and title) after his 12 years of occupancy has passed. If so, he will be treated like any other trespasser and will be liable if he steals "realty" as so to speak.[50] Things that form a part of the land become a part of it and thus are real property.[51] All the same, taking away a building like a fixed caravan would be criminal because it would amount to criminal damage.

So what might a tenant *in possession* make off with?   A bucket of soil,[52] as it is not a fixture but forms part of the land. This exception seems to have been geared towards protecting tenants who carried out landscaping and other renovations. Technically, section 4(2)(c) only protects the holder of the tenancy, rather than his family and friends. If a tenant of a farm allowed his friend from the city to dig up some topsoil for his garden, his friend would be liable for theft. **29–026**

---

[44] Even a bolted down hut might pass. See *Billing v. Pill* [1954] 1 Q.B. 70. Cf. *Wessex Reserve Forces & Cadets Association v. White* [2005] 3 E.G.L.R. 127.

[45] *R. v. Friend* (1931) 22 Cr. App. R. 130.

[46] See *The Queen v. Foley* (1889) 17 Cox C.C. 142, where D was convicted for cutting grass "on the said lands with a scythe."

[47] *R. v. Skujins* [1956] Crim. L.R. 266.

[48] His Honour Sir Edward Abbott Parry in *My Own Way*, (London: Cassell and Company, 1932) at 250 relates an Irish case that furnishes an apt commentary upon these distinctions. The question was whether dung was real property. A lawyer made an admirable argument to show that it was. The farmer was called upon to reply and said: "I'm puzzled indeed by all these strange words. But the lawyer says, fair play to him, that cows are personal property, and the hay they eat is personal property, and I ask your Honour, as one man to another, how, baiting miracles, personal property can go on eating personal property and evacuating ['—he used a homelier verb']—real property—well, your Honour, it's beyond my understanding."

[49] *Carver v. Pierce* (1648) 82 E.R. 534.

[50] A trespasser might find herself guilty of theft if she decides to sublet such premises in which she is squatting: *R. v. Edwards* [1978] Crim. L.R. 49.

[51] Whether or not the thing has been annexed to the land is a question of degree. See *Elitestone v. Ltd. Morris* [1997] All E.R. 513; *Chelsea Yacht and Boat Club Ltd. v. Pope* [2001] 2 All E.R. 409.

[52] Cf. *R. v. Bleasdale* (1848) 175 E.R. 321, where D took coal from a mine.

The tenant might also be an accessory, depending on his culpability. If a tenant takes chattels that have not been affixed to the land then he would be guilty in the normal way. If a tenant takes chattels that have obviously been affixed to the land then he would be caught by section 4(2)(c) of the *Act*. The section makes a distinction between chattels that are affixed to the land and those that form a part of the land. Exactly when a fixture forms part of the land is a question of degree, but asking whether the item in question was affixed by human intervention would be a starting point. If the tenant were to remove doors from buildings, fences and so on section 4(2)(c) would catch him. The subsection does not catch squatters (or it appears licencees)[53] as they are not tenants, so if they are not *trespassers* (which is still unclear in the case of squatters) they have more rights to deal with property belonging to others than does a tenant or the casual passerby.

29–027   **What if the tenant tires to sell an antique doorknob, but does not attempt to sever it?**   He could still be liable as the subsection does not require severance.

29–028   **Is it theft to take wild flowers and plants?**   The answer is given by section 4(3). Picking wild mushrooms, flowers, fruit or foliage is theft only if the taking is for reward or for sale or other commercial purpose. Commercial purpose might include situations where a person sells wild mushrooms regularly at a weekend market stall. It ought not, however, catch the casual seller such as a little old lady who is paid for picking a few extra mushrooms for her neighbour. Notably, if a person is growing wild mushrooms or flowers as a part of a commercial venture, it would be theft to take flowers or mushrooms from his plot. The modern interest in conservation has resulted in a statute making it an offence, in general, to uproot any wild plant without reasonable excuse.[54] This does not apply to the mere picking of flowers, but some rare specimens that are threatened with extinction are forbidden to be picked. Beware, therefore, of plucking a posy consisting of any of the listed plants within the *Act*.[55] The taker might also be guilty of criminal damage if he visibly damages the rest of the plant (as if he clumsily tears off branches). Some bylaws in public parks and nature reserves make it an offence to pick anything.[56]

29–029   **What about poaching?**   For tens of thousands of years man was a hunter, and even after the rise of agriculture the chase remained a passion of the nobility, as poaching was of the peasantry. Notwithstanding the desire of the privileged classes to preserve their game, the law of larceny was not applied because wild animals were not regarded as property.[57]

The provision in the *Theft Act* starts with what appears to be a bold rejection of this rule, but speedily relapses into orthodoxy. Section 4(4):

---

[53] *Gray v. Taylor* [1998] 1 W.L.R. 1093; *Camden LBC v. Shortlife Community Housing Ltd.* (1993) 25 H.L.R. 330.

[54] See section 13 of the *Wildlife and Countryside Act 1981*.

[55] See Sch. 8 of the *Wildlife and Countryside Act 1981*.

[56] See in particular section 20 of the *National Parks and Access to Countryside Act 1949*.

[57] *R. v. Howlett* [1968] Crim. L.R. 222.

"Wild creatures, tamed or untamed, shall be regarded as property; but a person cannot steal a wild creature not tamed nor ordinarily kept in captivity, or the carcass of any such creature, unless either it has been reduced into possession by or on behalf of another person and possession of it has not since been lost or abandoned, or another person is in the course of reducing it into possession."

This means that the poacher does not steal, though he commits an offence under antiquated legislation known as the *Game Acts* and *Poaching Acts*.[58] While a wild animal remains alive there can be no absolute property in it. In broad terms it is a question of law whether an animal is wild (*ferae naturae*) or domesticated (*mansuetae naturae*).[59] In *Cresswell v. D.P.P.*[60] it was recognized that once a wild animal is killed it becomes the property of the owner of the land on which it is killed, unless hunting rights have been granted by the owner to another.[61] There is qualified property in living wild animals in three circumstances:[62]

Per industriam: "Wild animals become the property of a person who takes or tames or reclaims them until they regain their natural liberty and have not the intention to return."
Ratione impotentiae et loci: "The owner of land has a qualified right in the young animal born on the land until they can fly or run away."
Ratione soli and ratione privilegii: "An owner of land who has retained the exclusive right to hunt, take and kill wild animals on his land has a qualified property in them for the time being while they are there but if he grants to another the right to hunt, take or kill them then the grantee has a qualified property."

Although the judges held that animals were not property when in the wild state, they withheld the benefit of this rule from poachers who were so unsporting as to go off with a creature that someone else had shot. As soon as the animal falls dead it is regarded, by the occult operation of the law, as falling into the possession and ownership either of the shooter (if he has not abandoned the chase) or, failing him, of the landowner.[63] Poaching legislation is intended to protect the person having the sporting rights. Other legislation, having the different object of conserving endangered species of wild animal makes it an offence to kill, *etc.* certain protected species.[64] It is also an offence to possess such animals, live or dead, for sale.[65]

29–030

---

[58] *Night Poaching Act 1828*; *Game Act 1831* as amended by the *Game Laws (Amendment) Act 1960*; *Poaching Prevention Act 1862*; *Salmon and Freshwater Fisheries Act 1975*; *Deer Act 1991*.

[59] *Cresswell v. D.P.P.* [2006] EWHC 3379 (Admin).

[60] [2006] EWHC 3379 (Admin).

[61] *Cresswell v. D.P.P.* [2006] EWHC 3379 (Admin).

[62] *Cresswell v. D.P.P.* [2006] EWHC 3379 (Admin). Furthermore, certain wild animals are the property of the Queen by prerogative right, such as swans, whales and sturgeon. See *Case of Swans* (1592) 7 Co. Rep. 15 and section 1 of the *Wild Creatures and Forest Laws Act 1971*. (Fellows of St John's College, Cambridge are the only people outside the Royal Family granted the right to eat unmarked mute swans).

[63] *Blades v. Higgs* (1865) 11 H.L. Cas. 621. See also *Yanner v. Eaton* (1999) 201 C.L.R. 351.

[64] See generally the *Wildlife and Countryside Act 1981*. Cf. the *Hunting Act 2004*, which targets wanton use.

[65] See generally the *Wildlife and Countryside Act 1981*.

The taker or killer of wild animals will not be guilty of theft unless the animals have been reduced (or are being reduced[66]) into another's possession.[67] If possession of a wild animal is lost, then the former possessor will no longer have property in them, so theft will not be possible.[68] If a person kills a number of grouse only to discover that a stranger has been picking them up and loading them into his car, he would not only have a right to retrieve the birds,[69] but also to have the taker prosecuted for theft. Similarly, if D decides to take some emus from V's emu farm he will be liable for theft,[70] because the wild animals are being farmed as a part of a commercial enterprise. It is possible to steal wild animals that are a part of a zoo or farm[71] or have otherwise been reduced into possession (*e.g.*, bees that are being farmed, or identifiable homing pigeons that have been kept for racing and return home regularly,[72] a pet snake and so on).[73]

29–031 **Can you steal things that come out of tubes—such as gas and water or over wire—such as electricity?** Domestic gas is personal property,[74] so a householder who fraudulently by-passes the meter to burn gas for nothing commits theft of the gas. He is entitled to use the gas only if it goes through the meter in the proper way.

Electricity is not scientifically regarded as a physical thing, like gas, but is a form of energy. A cyclist who holds on to the back of a lorry appropriates energy but does not commit theft; so appropriating electricity is not regarded as theft either.[75] To solve the problem of classifying electricity, its dishonest use, waste or diversion achieves the dignity of a special offence, under section 13 of the *Theft Act*. (The name used in the marginal note is "abstracting of electricity"; this is not very apt, since unlawfully used electricity returns to the power station,[76] though at a reduced voltage; it is true, however, that power is abstracted.) Abstract in the real world refers to use, or consumption. The defendant would be liable under section 13 of the *Act* if he were to use electricity without paying for it regardless of whether he also tampered with the meter.[77] The defendant might obtain free electricity merely because his meter is faulty or he may be a squatter who decides to use the electricity in another person's vacant holiday cottage and has no intention of paying for it. A conviction under section 13 requires that the

---

[66] *Cresswell v. D.P.P.* [2006] EWHC 3379 (Admin). If V is in the course of reducing the animal into possession then an intervening taking would be theft. Cf. *The King v. Stride and Millard* [1908] 1 K.B. 617.

[67] *R. v. Howlett* [1968] Crim. L.R. 222.

[68] *Kearry v. Pattinson* [1939] 1 K.B. 471; *R. v. Petch* (1878) 14 Cox C.C. 116.

[69] *Blades v. Higgs* (1865) 11 H.L. Cas. 621.

[70] *R. v. Shears* (1980) 2 Cr. App. R. 223; *Hamps v. Darby* [1948] 2 All E.R. 474; *R. v. Cory* (1864) 10 Cox C.C. 23.

[71] *R. v. Shears* (1980) 2 Cr. App. R. 223.

[72] Farmed bees and homing pigeons have the intent to return to their owner: *animus revertendi*.

[73] *Blades v. Higgs* (1865) 11 H.L. Cas. 621.

[74] *R. v. White* (1853) 3 Car. & K. 363; *R. v. Firth* (1869) L.R. 1 C.C.R. 172.

[75] Hence an entry to make dishonest use of electricity is not burglary: *Low v. Blease* [1975] Crim. L.R. 513.

[76] Cf. *Clinton v. Cahill* [1998] N.I. 200.

[77] *R. v. McCreadie, Tune* (1993) 96 Cr. App. R. 143. See also *R. v. Harrison* [2001] All E.R. 42, where the defendant did not tamper with the meter but dishonestly took advantage of a faulty meter. See also section 31 of the *Electricity Act 1989* as amended by the *Utilities Act 2000*.

defendant was also dishonest.[78] An intent to pay is merely a factor that the jury would consider along with any other relevant factors in determining D's culpability.[79]

Could a thief be charged under the section (do you call it an electric charge?) 29–032
for pressing the starting-button of someone else's car? Most likely not, but it
is technically possible. Technically a person could be convicted under section
13 of the *Theft Act* for using up the battery in another's torch, electric car and so
on. Electric cars are becoming the norm and will no doubt be the predominant
type of car on our roads within a few years. The car thief might not only be liable
for theft of the car, but also for theft of the electricity stored in its massive
batteries. No doubt charging the batteries of this type of motorcar is likely to be
rather expensive. But the prosecutor is likely to be satisfied with charging the
defendant for the theft of the car *per se*. Some of the older cases treated the theft
of the car and the petrol in the tank as theft of two different things.[80]

Might it also be possible to convict someone of theft for consuming
(abstracting) electricity when he uses a landline to make an international
telephone call? A telephone would use little more than the most trivial amount of
electricity. Criminalizing this type of use seems to be overkill given that there are
other offences that are better suited for dealing with those who use another's
telephone unlawfully.[81] Similarly, if a person unlawfully extracts information (a
million pound trade secret) from a computer he can be charged with dishonestly
using electricity under section 13 unless he is authorized to use the computer. But
the victim is not going to be too worried about the trivial cost of the electricity
used; rather he is going to be concerned about his trade secret. The most serious
part of the wrong is the theft of the confidential information, so that theft should
be criminalized directly. Alternatively, the defendant could be charged under
section 2 of the *Computer Misuse Act 1990*,[82] which makes it an offence to access
a computer without authorization.

Water[83] in a pipe or other container is the subject of property, though a
prosecution for drawing water from a tap is highly unlikely. When water is
standing on land in a pond, lake or reservoir it is regarded as land, and is no more
the subject of theft than is land in general. Percolating water is ownerless, *res*

---

[78] *R. v. Ghosh* [1982] Q.B. 1053. Cf. *Boggeln v. Williams* (1978) 67 Cr. App. R. 50 at 54 (now
overruled by *Ghosh*).
[79] Cf. *Boggeln v. Williams* (1978) 67 Cr. App. R. 50 at 54.
[80] See for example, *R. v. Williams* [1962] 1 W.L.R. 1268.
[81] Section 125 of the *Communications Act 2003*. See *R. v. Nadig* (1993) 14 Cr. App. R. 49. Free calls
would not be covered as no payment is involved. Thus, if an airline has a free-call number and D uses
V's telephone to book his flights then the section would not apply. There are numerous other offences
covering the use of electronic equipment with the aim of dishonestly receiving some kind of service
such as broadcasts (section 297(1) of the *Copyright and Designs Act 1988* catches this), but the
telephone example is sufficient for making the point that trivial (inadvertent) electricity abstraction is
not what makes the defendant reprehensible in such cases. Instead, the defendant is reprehensible for
trying to obtain the broadcast, telephone call and so on without paying. The issue of electricity does
not even enter such a defendant's mind—he does not intend to avoid paying for the electricity but
rather for the telephone call *etc*. Cf. *R. v. Allen* [1985] 1 W.L.R. 50 *vis-à-vis* intent not to pay.
[82] Section 1 of the *Computer Misuse Act 1990*, is a summary offence which deals with less serious
cases.
[83] *Ferens v. O'Brien* (1883) 11 Q.B.D. 21.

nullius, so that (apart from statutory regulations about to be mentioned) any landowner may abstract as much as he pleases. When the water is flowing in a defined channel (as a stream or river) the rights of the riparian owner to abstract it are limited, but if he exceeds his rights section 4(2) probably saves him from a charge of theft, even though his appropriation is a tort to the lower riparian owners. Subject to certain exceptions, it is an offence to abstract water from any source in a river authority area without a licence from the authority.[84]

29.7.   INCORPOREAL PROPERTY

29–033   Section 4(1) of the *Theft Act* mentions "things in action and other intangible property" as the subject of theft. "Things in action" (also archaically called "choses[85] in action") are rights that can be enforced only by bringing an action and not by taking possession; they are "property rights" to the extent that they can be bought and sold.[86] The most obvious thing in action is the creditor's right to payment of a debt. Shares, patents, copyrights, and trade marks have also been called things in action, but Parliament has taken away that name from patents (which, however, remain intangible property, otherwise called incorporeal property.)[87]

29–034   **Should I entangle the police if I illegally download a movie from the Internet?**   Infringing a copyright or trade mark is not theft. However, pirating, or any other infringement of copyright[88] or of a trade mark,[89] is an offence. Copyright and patents in effect are used to criminalize the theft of "information" or at least the right to control certain (intangible property) information such as the design of a new plane, the contents of the latest blockbuster and so on. If none of these infringements is theft, why does the *Act* say that things in action are property for the purpose of theft? Theoretically there can be theft of these rights, but only when the whole copyright or trade mark is appropriated, as in the highly unlikely event of a trustee of a copyright wrongfully selling it for his own benefit. A "patent" is not a thing in action, but is intangible property.[90]

---

[84] See section 24 of the *Water Resources Act 1991*.

[85] Pronounced "shozes."

[86] Certain quota rights are also a form of intangible property which may be bought and sold. Selling another's quota rights for way less than they are worth could constitute an appropriation. See *Attorney-General of Hong Kong v. Chan Nai-Keung* [1987] 1 W.L.R. 1339.

[87] Section 30(1) of the *Patents Act 1977*.

[88] See sections 107-109, 198 of the *Copyright, Designs and Patents Act 1988*. See section 109 of the *Patents Act 1977* with respect to interferences with patent registration.

[89] See section 92 of the *Trade Marks Act 1994*. For a good discussion of these offences, see *R. v. Johnson* [2003] 3 All E.R. 884.

[90] See section 30 of the *Patents Act 1977*. Export quotas have also been held to be "intangible" property. See the discussion in *Chan Man-sin. v. The Queen* [1988] 1 W.L.R. 196.

Does this mean that I am free to steal your confidential informa- **29–035**
tion?[91]   Generally, confidential information has been held not to constitute
property for the purposes of section 4 of the *Theft Act*.[92] If you are able get your
hands on a valuable trade secret, or a university's examination paper, and
memorize the contents for your own benefit, you might walk free. The law of
theft would not get in your way. It is absurd and disgraceful that we should still
be making do without any legislation specifically designed to discourage this
modern form of commercial piracy. Abstracting or divulging an official secret is
an offence under section 1 of the *Official Secrets Act 1911*;[93] but Leviathan is not
much concerned to protect the secret and immensely valuable know-how of its
subjects.

The law of theft does not criminalize individuals[94] for copying or memorizing
confidential information, but such conduct may be caught by other specific
offences such as data protection laws, copyright offences, trade mark offences,
patents offences, fraud offences, and computer misuse offences. The Law
Commission[95] considered the situation in the context of trade secrets and
concluded that confidential information could not be brought within the purview
of the *Theft Act*, because "it is difficult to see how there is any question of
deprivation where someone has, in breach of confidence, forced the original
holder to share, but not forget, his secret."[96]

Are you telling me that if V accidentally leaves her digital camera **29–036**
(containing nude photographs of herself)[97] on the back seat of a taxi, that the
taxi driver does not commit theft if he downloads a copy of the photographs
onto his I-Phone?[98]   Yes, if *Oxford v. Moss*[99] is followed. The right to control
important confidential information (intangible property) is a property right
analogous to copyright, but it has not been recognized by the English courts. The
only authority in support of this narrow reading of section 4 of the *Theft Act* is

---

[91] There is some very limited protection of certain personal information pursuant to the *Data
Protection Act 1998*. It might also constitute an "article for use in frauds" pursuant to section 6 of the
Fraud Act 2006. See the discussion in the chapter on fraud.

[92] *Oxford v. Moss* (1979) 68 Cr. App. R. 183.

[93] See also the *Official Secrets Act 1989*.

[94] A conspiracy to defraud another of a trade secret would have to involve more than one party. See
Scott v. Commissioner of Police of the Metropolis [1975] A.C. 819.

[95] Law Commission, Consultation Paper 150, *Legislating the Criminal Code: Misuse of Trade
Secrets*, (London: H.M.S.O., 1997) at 7.

[96] *Ibid.* Compare the discussion below *vis-à-vis* section 6 of the *Theft Act 1968*.

[97] If the photos were downloaded from a very sophisticated mobile telephone such as an I-Phone,
then copying the information might be caught by the *Computer Misuse Act 1990*. But a standard
digital camera is not a computer.

[98] In a scandal in Hong Kong an actor's laptop was sent for repair and the repairman found many
nude images of the actor copulating with a number of starlets. The repairman copied the images and
uploaded them on the World Wide Web. If the information was taken from a laptop in this jurisdiction
such a defendant would be caught by the *Computer Misuse Act 1990* (U.K.). The computer repairman
might also be charged with public decency and invasion of privacy type offences for uploading the
material. See generally, Dennis J. Baker, "The Sense and Nonsense of Criminalizing Transfers of
Obscene Material," (2008) 26 *Sing. L. Rev.* 126. See also *State v. Nelson*, 842 A.2d (2004).

[99] (1979) 68 Cr. App. R. 183.

found in the divisional court judgment of *Oxford v. Moss*.[100] In *Oxford v. Moss* an engineering student from Liverpool University stole an examination script and photocopied it and then returned it. It was held that secret information is not property.

The finding in *Oxford v. Moss* is out of step with other major common law jurisdictions. Industrial and trade secrets are often immensely valuable, are legitimately bought and sold, and for some purposes regarded as property. In *Carpenter v. United States*[101] the U.S. Supreme Court correctly held that though the victim "did not suffer monetary loss; it was sufficient that it was deprived of its right to exclusive use of information, as exclusivity is an important aspect of business information." In *Carpenter* the victim did not lose a tangible thing; rather it lost its exclusive right to keep to itself its own commercial information. The defendant's use of its information deprived it of the ability to use its property as it pleased.

Civil courts will award an injunction or damages in respect of a breach of confidence or a breach of contract relating to confidential information of commercial value.[102] Furthermore, having the right to keep certain intimate information private is extremely important in Western society.[103]

29–037   Free speech has to be balanced against the right to privacy. The public have no right to access intimate personal information such as images of a person dressing in a locker room. We would not want to criminalize journalists for exposing secrets that the public have an interest in knowing about. Should a photographer be convicted of theft for taking photographs of a topless celebrity on a public beach? One would hope not. Obviously, that would raise free speech issues. More generally, however, the cases where the criminal law should be invoked are fairly obvious. If the theft involves a PIN code, door key, trade secret, sensitive or intimate information (photographs of the victim in the nude, or her medical records),[104] then the criminal law should offer an appropriate form of protection.

In most cases it will be patently clear that the information in question is worthy of protection. In *State v. Nelson*[105] a tradesman found nude photographs of his client on her bedroom floor. He secretly borrowed the photographs and scanned the images into his computer before returning them. The court held that he had deprived the owner of her right to "select who would have access to view" the photographs. When another assumes the right to control (even intangible property such as digital images) property that belongs to another he deprives the owner of her right to control and exclusively use that property. There is a general right to have one's property respected, and if confidential information is property,

---

[100] (1979) 68 Cr. App. R. 183.

[101] 484 U.S. 19, at 27 (1987).

[102] John T. Cross, "Protecting Confidential Information Under the Criminal Law of Theft and Fraud," (1991) 11 *Oxford J. Legal Stud.* 264. See also John C. Coffee, "Hush! The Criminal Status of Confidential Information After McNally and Carpenter and the Enduring Problem of Over-criminalisation," (1988) *Am. Crim. L. Rev.* 121.

[103] Dennis J. Baker, *The Right Not to be Criminalized: Demarcating Criminal Law's Authority*, (Farnham: Ashgate Publishing, 2011) at Chap. 6.

[104] Dennis J. Baker "The Impossibility of a Critically Objective Criminal Law," (2011) 56(2) *McGill L. J.* 349.

[105] 842 A. 2d 83 (2004).

then one has a right to keep it confidential. All its value is used up once it is made public.[106] But the gravamen of the defendant's wrongdoing in *State v. Nelson* was not the theft, because the victim was really trying to prevent an invasion of privacy. Therefore, a more specific privacy offence is required.[107]

In *Dreiman v. State*[108] the defendant entered his former girlfriend's residence and took her house and automobile keys and made copies of them before returning the originals to her dwelling. The defendant argued that he could not be guilty of burglary because he did not have the specific intent to commit theft by stealing keys because he returned those items after he copied them. The court held that:

> "[c]opying the key was equivalent to taking something from her and depriving her of her right to have exclusive access to her trailer house and automobile. Unauthorized copies of a person's keys diminish the value of the original keys—keeping unwanted persons out of the trailer. ... Thus, although the owner may retain possession of the original property, there has been nevertheless a deprivation of property when a copy is made and retained by another."

In *People v. Kwok*[109] the defendant befriended the victim and pretended that he **29–038** was fixing her door lock, but instead removed it and took it to a locksmith and had a key cut for it. He returned to her home nine days later, let himself in and assaulted her. He was charged with a number of offences including theft. The defendant argued that his temporary removal of the door lock was not theft because there was no evidence that he intended to deprive the victim permanently of any property. Even if the English courts do not recognize confidential information as property, as will be seen below, this type of conduct would be caught by section 6 of the *Theft Act 1968*, because the door lock has been returned in a valueless state. The defendant only borrowed the lock for a few hours to enable the locksmith to study its insides to gain the necessary information for making a template key. He in effect was stealing confidential information so that a spare key could be cut. What was taken was intangible information, not a tangible key. The court concluded that borrowing the lock for the purpose of obtaining this type of information violated the victim's property rights because the information was used to deprive the owner of the right of exclusive control of her property (her home). The court summed up the rationale for criminalizing this kind of theft in the following passage:[110]

> "'The ownership of a thing is the right of one or more persons to possess and use it to the exclusion of others. ... ownership is called property. Thus, property is something that one has the exclusive right to possess and use. A key to one's residence is clearly one's property. ...[t]he appellant's unauthorized possession of the [created] key would impair [the victim] right of ownership, *i.e.* her exclusive right of possession and use. This is so because a homeowner's ... property interest in his house key is not just the right to maintain possession of a tangible object—the key, but also the right to control the intangible benefit conferred by ownership of the key, *i.e.* the ability to control access to one's [property] residence. Courts

---

[106] See section 6 of the *Theft Act 1968* as discussed below.
[107] Cf. *R. v. Hamilton* [2008] Q.B. 224, where D took information that he was not entitled to take when he filmed up a woman's skirt in a supermarket. He was charged with outraging public decency, as there was no other specific offence available.
[108] 825 P.2d 758 (1992) at 761.
[109] 63 Cal. App. (4th) 1236 (1998) at 1251.
[110] *People v. Kwok*, 63 Cal. App. (4th) 1236 (1998) at 1251.

have said that the word 'property' is 'all-embracing so as to include every intangible benefit and prerogative susceptible of possession or disposition'. ... Making an unauthorized copy of a 'borrowed key', which is analogous to making an unauthorized copy of a trade secret[111] or an unauthorized copy of computer data,[112] destroys the 'intangible benefit and prerogative of being able to control access to one's residence' just as thoroughly as outright theft of the key itself."

When the defendant copies a key, door lock, or photographs without the owner's consent, his actions involve an assumption of the owners' rights. If the concept of appropriation involves an act expressly or impliedly authorized by the owner,[113] then it *a fortiori* involves an act that is not expressly or impliedly authorized by the owner.[114]

The information may be valuable in that its release could cause the owner humiliation and distress, or because it secures other tangible property. In the latter situation the information is akin to a "valuable security." The concept of valuable security normally refers to commercial documents[115] such as cheque forms,[116] which secure more tangible property; but it could also cover door keys, PIN codes and so on.[117] The American courts have held that PIN codes for bank accounts are property for the purposes of theft, because they are intangible forms of property. A PIN code or a cheque is intrinsically connected with the tangible property (hard cash) which it is used to control and protect. When a person steals a cheque or a PIN code he effectively denies the owner of the funds in the related bank account the exclusive right to use and control those funds.

29–039   As one U.S. court put it: "it may reasonably be said that a PIN code is property because it implies the right to use that access code—and to access the funds in the related bank account by means of that code."[118] As form of property one can own it and lose it and when it is lost because of another's appropriation it constitutes theft. The intangible property taken (PIN codes) or tangible property (cheques forms, door keys), are valuable because they can be used to secure other forms of property such as the victim's bank funds or private home.[119] It is hoped that when

---

[111] Trade secrets are regarded as property in the U.S. See *Williams v. Superior Court* 81 Cal. App. 3d 330 (1978); *People v. Gopal*, 171 Cal. App. 3d 524 (1985) and the cases cited therein.

[112] Stealing information from computers might be caught by sections 1 and 2 of the *Computer Misuse Act 1990* (U.K.).

[113] As for consent, see the erroneous decision in *D.P.P. v. Gomez* [1993] A.C. 442.

[114] *R. v. Morris* [1984] A.C. 320 at 331 *per* Lord Roskill in *obiter dictum*, as consent was not at issue as far as the label switching was concerned because it was clearly not authorized.

[115] See *R. v. Kassim* [1992] 1 A.C. 9; section 20 of the *Theft Act 1968*.

[116] *Parsons v. The Queen* (1999) 195 C.L.R. 619 at 633-634. *Aliter, R. v. Preddy* [1996] A.C. 815 at 836-837. Cf. the earlier cases which focused on the value of the paper that evidenced the intangible property: *R. v. Perry* (1845) 174 E.R. 1008.

[117] Something might have great value as "property" but no measurable value in the pecuniary sense. For instance, copying a person's PIN code is not information of any pecuniary value as the bank could issue a new number without any cost to the customer. But if the owner is not aware that it has been stolen, her account may be drained dry before she has a chance to inform the bank. In *People v. Kozlowski*, 96 Cal. App. (4th) 853 at 867 (2002) it was said: "We may take judicial notice of the common knowledge that a PIN code is more valuable if not disclosed to others—or, put another way, if it is exclusively possessed."

[118] *People v. Kozlowski*, 96 Cal. App. (4th) 853.

[119] Professor Smith argued: "The cheque remains a valuable security because it is an effective key to the drawer's bank account." See J.C. Smith, "Obtaining Cheques by Deception," [1997] *Crim. L.R.*

the Supreme Court revisits this issue it will follow the opinion of the High Court of Australia, which recognized that valuable securities such as cheque forms are property.[120]

In other cases, thieving a person's personal "information" will constitute identity theft. The theft of "identity" and stealing information by skimming a credit card[121] is not too different to copying another's house key or the PIN code (information) for his office building, because it results in the theft of a valuable security, which allows the owner to exclusively control his more tangible property. Generally, U.S. courts have held that information does constitute property for the purposes of the law of theft.[122] Such an interpretation would allow the reprehensible student who decides to steal an examination paper to be dealt with. After all, an identity thief might be caught by the *Fraud Act 2006*,[123] but those who copy examination papers would not necessarily come within its purview.

Section 6 of the *Fraud Act 2006* criminalizes the possession of "articles" that might be used in fraud. If D stands behind V as V enters the PIN code for his office and memorizes it and thereafter uses it to gain entry so that he can steal V's computer, he might be caught by section 6. It will depend on whether the information was used to commit *fraud* rather than theft. The courts are likely to focus on the burglary, since the deceiving of the machine is not directly aimed at making a gain or causing a loss. The theft seems to be a subsequent and independent act. (If D were to use the PIN code to get money from an ATM, the courts might hold that in entering a stolen but correct PIN code, D made a false representation to a machine with the aim of directly making a gain or causing a loss. After all, his direct aim is to have the machine dispense money, which he knows he has no right to receive.)

Confidential information such as a PIN Code could be interpreted as an "article"[124] that could be used to commit fraud (*i.e.* to trick a machine[125] into

29–040

---

396 at 400. Doctrinally this concept has not been discussed outside the context of commercial documents, but there is no logical reason for limiting it to documents. Cf. *R. v. Kasim* [1992] 1 A.C. 9; section 20 of the *Theft Act 1968*. But it has been extended to information used in electronic form, see *R. v. King* [1992] Q.B. 20; *Nolan v. Governor of Holloway Prison* [2003] EWHC 2709.

[120] *Parsons v. The Queen* (1999) 195 C.L.R. 619 at 633-634. As noted above, Lord Goff in *obiter* has suggested otherwise, see *R. v. Preddy* [1996] A.C. 815 at 836-837.

[121] See the Australian Model Criminal Code, *Credit Card Skimming Offences*, (Canberra: 2006) at Chap. 3.

[122] *United States v. Girard*, 601 F. 2d. 69 (1969); *United State v. Jones*, 677 F. Supp. 238 (1988); *People v. Gopal*, 171 Cal. App. 3d 524 (1985); *People v. Parker*, 217 Cal. App. 2d 422 (1963); *People v. Dolbeer*, 214 Cal. App. 2d 619 (1963); *Williams v. Superior Court*, 81 Cal. App. 3d 330 (1978).

[123] He might also be caught by more specific offences. See section 25 of the *Identity Cards Act 2006*. Some jurisdictions have introduced more specific identity theft offences. See Untited States 18 U.S.C.A. §1028(a) 7. The Supreme Court of the United States has held that the thief must steal an identity belonging to another and realize it did in fact belong to another, see *Flores-Figueroa v. U.S.*, 129 S.Ct. 1886 (2009). Wisconsin has a similar provision: Wis.Stat. Ann. §943.201(2) discussed in *State v. Baron*, 754 N.W. 2d. 175 (2008); *State v. Lis*, 751 N.W. 2d. 891 (2008) noting that it is a continuing offence, because it would normally involve recurring episodes of theft. See also South Australia: *Criminal Law Consolidation (Identity Theft) Amendment Act 2004* (S.A.).

[124] Section 8 of the *Fraud Act 2006* holds that "'article' includes any program or data held in electronic form."

[125] Section 2(5) of the *Fraud Act 2006*.

dispensing money (an ATM): the thief would also need to get his hands on the germane ATM card), but there remains the issue of whether memorizing it is sufficient. Is data stored in your memory an "article"? Does it need to be stored in a tangible way for it to constitute an article? There is no reason for requiring it to be written on paper or to be stored in a mobile telephone and so on; but there would have to be clear evidence demonstrating D possessed it (*i.e.* catching D using it would be sufficient for proving he possessed such information). Bank records and CCTV footage might also prove he used it on a given date, but if he went as far as using it he would be caught by the general provisions in the *Fraud Act 2006*. He would not, however, be caught by the *Fraud Act* if he misused the PIN Code for some purpose that did not involve fraud. Recognizing confidential information as property for the purposes of theft would fill this lacuna.

There is no rational basis for excluding theft of sensitive information from the law of theft. Those who steal million dollar trade secrets or examination papers are no less deserving of criminal censure than is the common shoplifter or the miser who downloads music illegally. The computer and information age has produced a range of new forms of property and also new ways of appropriating it; but the basic principles remain the same. There is nothing in the wording of section 4 of the *1968 Act* to prevent the law from being applied to these new forms of property.

29.8. STEALING CHEQUES AND INSTRUMENTS

29–041   When a cheque is stolen, three possible forms of theft may be committed: of the cheque a piece of paper,[126] of a thing in action, and of the proceeds of the cheque. If a person has a bank account he has a right to withdraw any money in it. The bank holds the funds but owes the account holder a debt for the balance in his account. The debt is a chose in action belonging to the account holder and is property for the purposes of section 4 of the *Theft Act*. When D steals a chose in action he steals V's right to take action to recover property from a third party such as the bank. An illustration of successful charges under the first two heads is *R. v. Kohn*.[127] Kohn was a company director who made out company cheques to third parties for his own benefit. He was convicted of theft of the cheques as pieces of paper, his theft occurring when he sent each cheque to the payee; it made no difference whether the bank account was in credit or not. He was also convicted of theft of a thing in action, namely the debt owed by the bank to the company in respect of the bank account.

---

[126] Several states in the U.S. have held that a cheque form *per se* is property which can be stolen: *People v. Carter*, 394 Ill. 403 (1946); *State v. Romero*, 146 Mont. 77 (1965); *Davenport v. State*, 127 Tex. Crim. 552 (1934).

[127] (1979) 69 Cr. App. R. 95. The account was overdrawn, so Kohn was unable to steal V's chose in action. Nowadays, he would be liable for an attempt. A forged cheque might be a "nullity" in law, but if it gets past the eye of the banks' staff, its being a nullity will not prevent D using it to thieve V's chose in action. But in such cases, the bank is the real victim! Cf. *Chan Man-sin v. The Queen* [1988] 1 W.L.R. 196; *R. v. Jack* [2002] 148 A.C.T.R. 1.

Conviction of the latter type of theft depended upon evidence that the account was in credit or that the cheque was within the agreed overdraft facility;[128] and that theft took place only when the bank honoured the cheque. The analysis on the second point appears to be that the bank owes a debt to its customer; this debt, the thing in action—the right to take action to recover the balance of the account from the bank, is *pro tanto* extinguished (or at least reduced by the value of the cheque) when the bank honours the cheque, and the extinguishment is regarded as an appropriation of the customer's chose in action (the debt the bank owes the customer). Alternatively, the defendant can be held to appropriate part of the account through the act of the payee in cashing or obtaining a credit in respect of the cheque, as he caused them to have the particular cheques.

When the drawer [victim] is deceived into writing a cheque "in favour of the payee [defendant], and delivers it to him. The cheque then constitutes a chose in action of the [defendant], which he can enforce against the [victim] drawer."[129] The defendant does not appropriate the victim's chose in action merely by receiving the cheque. The cheque creates a new chose in action which belongs to the defendant—it gives the defendant the right to sue for the sum stated on the cheque form. The victim's chose in action against the bank is what it always was: the balance of his bank account. The defendant must take further steps than merely receiving the cheque. The cheque is a new chose in action that is created by the drawer of the cheque (the deceived victim) writing out a cheque in favour of the defendant. The chose in action is created for the defendant (it names the defendant has having the right to sue for the sum of the cheque) and it belongs to the defendant. Nonetheless, when the defendant cashes/deposits the cheque (uses his ill-gotten chose in action) to cause a diminution in the balance of the drawer's bank account, he appropriates the victim's independent chose in action—*i.e.* the debt the bank owes to the victim. In *R. v. Duru*[130] the court erroneously held that merely inducing the drawer to write a cheque in your favour constitutes an appropriation of his chose in action regardless of whether you cash or deposit the cheque. In *R. v. Preddy*[131] the House of Lords overruled *R. v. Duru* in holding:

> "The point is simply that, when the cheque was obtained by the payee from the drawer, the chose in action represented by the cheque then came into existence and so had never belonged to the drawer. When it came into existence it belonged to the payee, and so there could be no question of his having obtained by deception property *belonging* to another."[132]

In *R. v. Williams*[133] the defendant dishonestly overcharged a number of elderly **29–042** and vulnerable customers for building work. When he cashed their cheques he stole a chose in action belonging to them (to the extent that the cheques were

---

[128] D does not assume "the rights of the bank to an *identifiable part of the bank's funds* which *corresponded* to the sum specified in" the *cheque*, when V's account is overdrawn. Consequently, D would "not appropriate the bank's property within the meaning of sections 1(1) and 3(1) of the *Theft Act* ..."either when the cheque was delivered to the payee or when the bank honoured the cheque." See *R. v. Navvabi* (1986) 83 Cr. App. R. 271. D might, however, be convicted of fraud under the *Fraud Act 2006*, because he defrauded the bank. Cf. *R. v. Christou* (1971) 115 S.J. 687.

[129] *R. v. Preddy* [1996] A.C. 815 at 835.

[130] [1974] 1 W.L.R. 2.

[131] [1996] A.C. 815.

[132] [1996] A.C. 815 at 818.

[133] (2001) 1 Cr. App. R. 23. See also *R. v. Hilton* (1997) 2 Cr. App. R. 445.

made out for more than they should have been),[134] because the defendant deposited the cheques in his own bank account thereby effecting a reduction of the credit balance in the victims' accounts, which was an appropriation under section 1 of the *Act*. If Williams' elderly customers had paid him by electronic transfer (debit cards and online electronic transfers are used to pay for most things these days—as cheques are being phased out of existence), or by directly depositing the cheques into his account for him, there would be no criminal liability for theft.

In *R. v. Preddy* V was deceived into electronically transferring its own funds to D's bank account, this caused the chose in action represented by the credit balance in V's account to be *pro tanto* extinguished or at least reduced by the value of the transfer and at the same time created a new chose in action in D's account. It was held that D did not obtain V's chose in action and, therefore, did not obtain property belonging to another. If the victim draws the cheque and also deposits it for the defendant, he would be depositing a cheque belonging to the defendant and also effecting a reduction of the credit balance of his own funds. V extinguishes his own chose in action by going to D's bank and depositing the cheque he has drawn in D's favour. At the same time, V creates a new chose in action for D, which never belonged to V. This in effect is no different to the electronic transfer in *R. v. Preddy*. Theft occurs when D appropriates V's chose in action, not *when V appropriates his own chose in action*. An appropriation would take place if D initiates the electronic transfer or takes V's cheque and deposits it himself thereby effecting a reduction in V's account.[135]

29–043   **What about theft of a cheque by a pickpocket or burglar?**   Once more the thief can be charged with stealing the cheque as a piece of paper (of the value of £x[136]) from the drawer (the person who has the bank account) or other person from whose possession the thing was taken. On conviction the thief can be punished according to the circumstances, and if he has cashed the cheque that is of course an important circumstance. Alternatively, if he has cashed the cheque (whether at a bank or by way of obtaining cash for it from someone else) he can be convicted either of stealing the cash or of fraud.

However, in a number of recent cases the courts have erroneously suggested that a cheque form is not property for the purposes of section 4 of the *Theft Act*. In *R. v. Preddy*[137] Lord Goff noted in an *obiter dictum* that a cheque form is not stolen when the defendant intends to cash/deposit it, because "[t]here can have been no intention on the part of the payee permanently to deprive the drawer of the cheque form, which would on presentation of the cheque for payment be

---

[134] It does not matter that the victim willingly wrote out the cheque for the overcharged sum. See *D.P.P. v. Gomez* [1993] A.C. 442.

[135] In *R. v. Hilton* [1997] 2 Cr. App. R. 445, D *instructed* the bank by faxes and cheques to *transfer* funds belonging to a charity to himself. In *R. v. Briggs* [2004] 1 Cr. App. R. 451 at 455 it was held: "where a victim causes a payment to be made in reliance on deceptive conduct by the defendant, there is no 'appropriation' by the defendant." In such a case D should be charged with fraud under the *Fraud Act 2006*.

[136] Though the cheque is a piece of paper, its value in law is that it is the obligation that it embodies. See Goode, *op. cit. infra note* 377, at 377 n. 69.

[137] [1996] A.C. 815.

returned to the drawer via his bank."[138] In *R. v. Graham*[139] the Court of Appeal adopted Lord Goff's *obiter* as law. The High Court of Australia has rejected Lord Goff's interpretation of the law.[140] It correctly observed that, in practice, banks almost never return cheque forms to the drawer. In addition, it held that the cheque form is a "valuable security" because "cheques drawn by a customer upon a bank contain a mandate by the drawer to its bank to reduce the credit of its account by payment in favour of a person answering the statutory description of a holder and thus have a value beyond that of their quality as pieces of paper."[141] It concluded that: "[t]he slip of paper that is returned to the drawer's bank has ceased to be a valuable security. Rather, it has become a record of what the valuable security was."[142] It is a piece of paper that empowers the holder (the defendant) to access the drawer's (victim) funds. This is so because a drawer's property interest in his cheque *form* is not just the right to maintain possession of a tangible object—the cheque form, but also the right to control the intangible benefit conferred by ownership of the cheque form *i.e.* the ability to control access to his funds.

29.9.   THE PROTECTION OF OWNERSHIP

Since theft can only be of property belonging to another, one cannot steal from a **29–044** person who according to the civil law is neither the owner nor the possessor of the property. Some examples:

V lends D money. Subsequently, D dishonestly decides not to repay the loan. Since the property in the money passed to D when it was lent to him, he is not guilty of theft (or any other offence) in respect of what is now his own money.

D consumes a meal in V's restaurant. The property in the food necessarily passes to him when he consumes it. Subsequently, he dishonestly decides not to pay the bill, and slips out when the waiter is not looking. He is not guilty of theft, but is guilty of the statutory offence of making off without having paid pursuant to section 3 of the *Theft Act 1978*.

A driver fills up with petrol. Nothing is said between the driver and the assistant as to the passing of property, but the intention must have been that the property in the petrol passed when the petrol entered the tank of the car. Petrol and food seem to be special cases in that the property by its nature is consumed in a way that makes it fairly clear that the owner intends title to pass when the customer is allowed to put it in his fuel tank or belly, as the case may be.[143] This is because the owner of the filling station does not contemplate the possibility of siphoning out the petrol if he is not paid. Similarly, it is impossible to retrieve the

---

[138] *R. v. Preddy* [1996] A.C. 815 at 836-837.

[139] (1997) 1 Cr. App. R. 302, followed by *R. v. Clark* [2002] 1 Cr. App. R. 14.

[140] *Parsons v. The Queen* (1999) 195 C.L.R. 619 at 633-634.

[141] *Parsons v. The Queen* (1999) 195 C.L.R. 619 at 633-634.

[142] *Parsons v. The Queen* (1999) 195 C.L.R. 619 at 634.

[143] Cf. *Hufsteler v. State*, 63 So. 2d 730 (1953) (U.S.), where it was held that driving off without paying for petrol was larceny by trick because the owner did not intend title to the petrol to pass until payment was made. In *Davies v. Leighton* (1979) 68 Cr. App. R. 4, it was held that property was not intended to pass until the time of payment. See also *Lucis v. Cashmarts* [1969] 2 Q.B. 400; *Pharmaceutical Society of Great Britain v. Boots Cash Chemists (Southern) Ltd.* [1952] 2 Q.B. 795.

restaurant meal intact from the dishonest customer's big belly! So if, when the assistant's back is turned, the driver suddenly conceives a dishonest intention and drives off without paying, he does not commit theft of the petrol—it is his petrol.[144] He is guilty of making off without having paid and might also be charged with fraud pursuant to the *Fraud Act 2006*.

29–045 **But suppose it was a self-service station and no assistant was looking on when D filled up. Would the property in the petrol still pass to D?** Yes. The installation of the self-service pump is an offer to drivers to help themselves. The driver accepts the offer, and thus creates a contract with the filling station proprietor. The property in the petrol passes to him under this contract.

29–046 **Suppose the diner and the driver intended not to pay when he consumed the meal or took the petrol.** Then he is guilty for falsely representing that he would pay for the meal or petrol and could be caught under section 2 of the *Fraud Act 2006*. Where they can, in the alternative, be convicted of theft in these circumstances is discussed below: 29.9. The above instances (summarizing the effect of decided cases) show that a person who agrees to buy goods cannot be guilty of theft by reason of anything he does with the goods after ownership and possession have passed to him. He can commit theft if either ownership or possession has not passed. (The problem presented by the passing of a voidable title is to be considered below (29.19.), as also is the fiction of ownership of another established by section 5(4) of the *Theft Act* (29.21.).

The possession of a thing is transferred in various ways, but chiefly by physical delivery. The ownership of a thing is also transferred in various ways, but chiefly by sale, or by delivery made with the intention of passing ownership. A gift, for example, is generally made by delivery (though it can be made in other ways, as by deed). The legal property (ownership) in goods can pass without the possession of the goods being transferred. As already mentioned it can pass by sale. Pursuant to section 17 of the *Sale of Goods Act 1979* the property in specific or ascertained goods passes under a contract of sale when it is intended to pass. Certain rules are set out in section 18 of that *Act* for establishing the intention of the parties unless a different intention appears. Rule 1 of section 18 of the *Sale of Goods Act 1979* is as follows:[145]

> "Where there is an unconditional contract for the sale of specific goods in a deliverable state the property in the goods passes to the buyer when the contract is made, and it is immaterial whether the time of payment or the time of delivery, be postponed."

---

[144] See as to the restaurant *Corcoran v. Whent* [1977] Crim. L.R. 52; and as to the petrol, see *Edwards v. Ddin* [1976] 1 W.L.R. 942. (In *R. v. McHugh* (1977) 64 Cr. App. R. 92 the Court of Appeal affirmed a conviction of theft under the proviso while conceding that the defendant was not guilty of it!).

[145] It is assumed that when a cheque is given in payment for goods that the owner intends to pass title on the basis the he takes the cheque as being valid—if he thought otherwise then he would not release the goods. The cheque itself is not much more than a promise to pay, but title to the property passes if there is an unconditional contract to that effect. See *R. (on the application of Valpak Ltd.) v. Environment Agency* [2002] EWHC 1510 (Admin.). For a deeper discussion see A. G. Guest, *Benjamin's Sale of Goods*, (London: Sweet & Maxwell, 7th edn. 2009) Chap. 5.

So if I choose a television set in a shop, and the seller promises to deliver it tomorrow and to bill me for it in due course, then if he dishonestly sells it to someone else (because supplies have run short and he can now get a better price) he commits theft from me. The set became my property under the contract, and it remains my property though it is still in his shop. The *Sale of Goods Act* provides a precise terminology for expressing these situations. Before the property passes in goods contracted to be sold, the contract of sale is called an "agreement to sell." The instant that the mystic property passes the agreement to sell becomes a "sale."[146] In the instance just given of the television set the contract of sale was a "sale" from the start; there was no point of time at which it was a mere "agreement to sell." If I rescind the contract because the television set is faulty, and send it back the seller will be free to repair it and sell it to someone else.[147]

Suppose I give a neighbour money to buy a certain used car for me, and he buys the car but immediately afterwards succumbs to the temptation of selling it again for his own dishonest purposes. Does he steal the car from me?   Yes. An agent is to be thought of as a kind of conduit pipe, transmitting property rights and obligations from his principal to a third party, and back from the third party to the principal. When he bought the car the property (ownership) passed directly from the seller to you as undisclosed principal in the transaction.[148] Conversely with an unauthorized *sale* by an agent: if the owner of a shop installs an assistant behind the counter, and a customer buys and pays for an article, the money becomes the employer's money as soon as it is handed over;[149] so if the assistant pockets it he steals from his employer.[150]

29–047

Suppose a customer in a shop chooses a camera and says he will take it away with him. The salesman has packed it up and written out the bill, and is expecting to be paid, when the customer runs out with the camera and disappears. Is that theft by the customer, or is it just another case of "making off without paying"?   In an ordinary shop transaction like this the court would have no difficulty in finding (under section 17 of the *Sale of Goods Act*) that the shopkeeper did not intend the property (ownership) to pass until payment had been made or credit expressly given.[151] The camera is still the property of the shopkeeper, and the customer has stolen it from him.

29–048

---

[146] Section 2 of the *Sale of Goods Act 1979*.

[147] *R. v. Walker* [1984] Crim. L.R. 112.

[148] Whether the ownership passes in law or only in equity is disputed, but even if it passes only in equity, that is enough to make the dishonest agent guilty of theft. See *Attorney-General of Hong Kong v. Reid* [1994] 1 A.C. 324.

[149] This might also include bribes intended for the employee, see *Attorney-General of Hong Kong v. Reid* [1994] 1 A.C. 324; *Tesco Stores Ltd. v. Pook* [2004] I.R.L.R. 618 (Ch.). Cf. *Powell v. MacRae* [1977] Crim. L.R. 571.

[150] Technically he could be charged, instead, with theft from the customer, though in practice this would not be done. The assistant (assuming that the customer knows he is an assistant, and does not suppose him to be the owner of the shop) impliedly represents to the customer that he is acting on behalf of his employer in receiving the money; if he then means to keep it for himself, he obtains it from the customer by fraudulent means, and therefore by theft.

[151] Verdicts to this effect have regularly been upheld in criminal cases. See *R. v. Slowly* (1873) 12 Cox C.C. 269; *R. v. Edmundson* (1912) 8 Cr. App. R. 107. In *Martin v. Puttick* [1968] 2 Q.B. 82 it was

29–049   **If an enterprising sales person sends me pornographic DVDs without my consent, in the hope that I will pay for them, can I put them on the fire?**   You would be an "involuntary bailee"—an odd name, since you would not be a bailee at all. A true bailee (a borrower, hirer, repairer, *etc.*) has agreed to receive temporary possession of the thing from the owner. You would technically be subject to the law of theft; but if you simply dispose of an embarrassing object, and are frank about it, you are unlikely to be thought dishonest.[152]

29–050   **I should like to ask a question about finders. The dishonesty section (section 2 of the *Theft Act*) says that a person is not generally dishonest if he believes that the owner cannot be found by taking reasonable steps. Suppose a finder says to himself: "I know how the owner can probably be found, but I think he must have abandoned this thing, so I will keep it."**   If he believes that he is not dishonest. But of course, the jury may refuse to credit that he really thought it.[153] Their opinion may be determined by the value of the article. An owner, when he loses an article of some value, does not abandon it merely by giving up the search and giving up hope of ever finding it again. It is still his, and nearly everyone would realize the fact. There are rules of civil law governing the rights or non-rights of finders of things on other people's land which can affect the law of theft, but the details may be left to the books on tort and property law. One rule may, however, be mentioned: a trespasser on property has no right to anything he finds there.[154] Failing any other claimant, the possessor of the land is entitled.[155] D is not a trespasser if D is an invited guest. In *Parker v. British Airways Board*[156] the plaintiff found an abandoned bracelet in the British Airways lounge and handed it in. When he handed it in he told the Board that if the owner failed to claim it that he would like it to be sent to him. It was held by the Court of Appeal

---

held to make no difference that the goods were wrapped and handed to the customer. In *R. v. Stephens* (1910) 4 Cr. App. R. 52 the rule was applied even where the shopkeeper allowed the defendant's confederate to go off with the goods, the defendant then refusing to pay for them. (In *Davies v. Leighton* (1979) 68 Cr. App. R. 4 the court suggested that the position might possibly be different if the salesman were a manager *sed quaere*.) Cf. *D.P.P. v. Gomez* [1993] A.C. 442, where the store manager passed a voidable title to the crooks.

[152] Under the *Unsolicited Goods and Services Act 1971* (as amended) it is an offence to demand payment for goods known to be unsolicited and the receiver who receives goods in such circumstances may retain them as an unconditional gift. In the case of goods received before 1 November 2000 recipients are required to give notice to the sender to collect them within 30 days, or otherwise to wait for six months, before being able to treat the goods as their own property. It is also an offence for a person to send pornographic publications to those who have not solicited them: see section 4 of the *Unsolicited Goods and Services Act 1971*.

[153] *R. v. Small* (1988) 86 Cr. App. R. 170.

[154] There is a difference between "mislaying" and "abandoning" property. In *R. v. Roston* [2003] EWCA Crim. 2206, D was charged with theft for going into a private golf green where he collected lost balls. The property in the balls remained with the golf club as they had only been misplaced on its own property. See also *R. v. Rowe* (1859) Bell C.C. 93. But if the property has been abandoned (*res derelicta*) there can be no theft because it belongs to no one (*res nullius*): *R. v. Thurborn* (1849) 1 Den. 387.

[155] *Hibbert v. McKiernan* [1948] 2 K.B. 142.

[156] [1982] Q.B. 100. See also *R. v. Woodman* [1974] Q.B. 754, where D was convicted of theft of scrap metal from a factory that had been closed for some years. In that case, the owner of closed the premises had fenced it in order to control access to it and therefore demonstrated that they continued to control the site.

that the plaintiff's rights "could only be displaced if D could show as occupiers, an obvious intention to exercise control over all articles in the lounge such that the bracelet was in their possession before the plaintiff found it." Thus, if D finds "uncontrolled" property in a public place and informs the occupier of his find his claim may have precedence. Exactly what the controller has to do to manifest its control is not clear. But if the item is buried in the land or otherwise attached to real property it is normally regarded as being in the landowner's possession and control.[157]

Obviously, I do not abandon a valuable bracelet simply by misplacing it in a public place. But surely I abandon my rubbish by disposing of it in a dustbin?   The refuse belongs to the householder until it is put out on the street for anyone to collect. In *Williams v. Phillips*[158] it was held that rubbish in a dustbin is not abandoned once title in it passes to the Corporation responsible for its disposal. The householder intends to give the refuse to the Corporation for proper disposal. In that case, the dustman was guilty of theft because he took refuse from his employer's dustcart. This is because title in it had passed to the Corporation. If the dustman was not on duty and found useful items abandoned on the street with other refuse, he would be entitled to take it as a finder.   **29–051**

Certain statutory offences are committed if a person who finds an article in a public conveyance or a taxi fails to hand it in. Also if a person finds a stray dog and keeps it without taking it to the police.[159] There are also statutory provisions covering abandoned treasure that is more than 300 years old and consists of more than 10 *per cent*. precious metal.[160] So if I were to find a valuable "lead" cross, I would be exempt from the treasure trove provisions? It appears you would be, because lead is not a precious metal.[161]

Suppose a "dip" is seen to steal something from a woman's handbag, but the woman was immediately lost in the crowd and cannot be traced. How is the indictment worded?   It lays the property in a person unknown.[162] The fact that the name or even the identity of the owner is unknown is never a bar to a charge of theft. However, the facts must make it clear that someone has been the victim of theft, even though we may not be certain who that someone is.[163] Although the   **29–052**

---

[157] *Elwes v. Briggs Gas Co.* (1886) 33 Ch. D. 562; *Moffatt v. Kazana* [1969] 2 W.L.R. 71.

[158] *Williams v. Phillips* (1957) 41 Cr. App. R. 5.

[159] By the *Dogs (Amendment) Act 1928* the finder must either return the dog to the owner or take it to the police station; if he does the latter he may remove it on condition that he keeps it for not less than a month. The police may destroy a stray dog under certain conditions: see sections 3 and 4 of the *Dogs Act 1906*, and also section 150(1) of the *Environmental Protection Act 1990*.

[160] See also section 4 of the *Treasure Act 1996*, which deals with ownership of treasure. Treasure is stealable if it meets the definition of treasure as set out in the *Act of 1996*: *Crown Estate Commissioners v. Roberts* [2008] 4 All E.R. 828. See also section 29 of the *Corners and Justice Act 2009*.

[161] *Enfield L.B.C. v. Mahoney* [1983] 2 All E.R. 901.

[162] Rule 8 of *the Indictment Rules 1971*. *Hibbert v. McKiernan* [1948] 2 K.B. 142; *Pike v. Morrison* [1981] Crim. L.R. 492.

[163] If the victim is dead, then his property will be held by the executor of his estate. If he is intestate and there are no heirs, then it becomes the property of the Crown as *bona vacantia*.

theft may be established by circumstantial evidence, circumstances of mere suspicion are not enough. The offence must, as always, be proved beyond reasonable doubt.

An example of suspicion being so strong as to amount to proof is the diverting tale of Noon at midnight.[164] A police constable saw Noon at 12:30 a.m. carrying a bundle which he suspiciously moved to the other arm when he observed the constable. When asked what he was carrying, Noon showed a cushion wrapped in a man's rain-coat, saying that they were his mother's. The constable pointed out that the raincoat was a man's, to which Noon replied: "So what, why can't my mother wear a man's rain-coat?" At that moment two tea towels fell from under Noon's coat. One of them bore a price tag. When asked where he got them he replied: "You've just found them on the floor." These evasive replies were held to constitute a case to answer, and a conviction of larceny from a person unknown was upheld. There was very considerable suspicion in that case, amounting to reasonable certainty of a theft. If it had not been so strong an inference the prosecution would have failed.

29–053   **Can one spouse (or civil partner) steal from the other?**   Formerly the law of theft did not apply between spouses, but section 30(1),(4)[165] of the *Theft Act* now makes no exception for husband and wife. However, it would obviously be unwise to use the criminal law for petty misappropriations of household articles by spouses. Spouses often contribute to a common fund, and it may not be clear what is whose; and a wife/husband who runs the home may feel morally entitled to things that legally belong to the other.[166] Often it would be hard to prove dishonesty. As a safeguard, therefore, the consent of the Director of Public Prosecutions is generally required in these cases.[167]

29.10. THE PROTECTION OF POSSESSION

29–054   The law protects not only owners but bare possessors. Even a person who has temporary control of a thing, like a clerk in respect of his office computer, is regarded for the purpose of an indictment as having "property" in it. It is the employer who in law has not only ownership but possession of the computer; the employee merely has "custody" or "control," but this custody is equivalent to ownership as against wrongdoers. On a charge of theft, the property may be laid in either the employer or the employee.

29–055   **Can someone possess a thing without knowing its existence?**   Yes, for the purpose of the law of theft.[168] The possessor of an old bureau possesses valuables in a secret drawer even though they are unknown to him. He has also the rights of

---

[164] *Noon v. Smith* [1964] 1 W.L.R. 1450. See also *Sturrock v. D.P.P.* [1996] R.T.R. 216; *R. v. Burton* (1854) Dears 282; *R. v. Joiner* (1910) 4 Cr. App. R. 64; *R. v. Fuschillo* [1940] 2 All E.R. 489; *R. v. Korniak* (1983) 76 Cr. App. R. 145.

[165] As amended by the *Civil Partnership Act 2004* c. 33 Sch. 27.

[166] Cf. *Roberts v. Western Australia* [2005] 189 F.L.R. 147.

[167] *R. v. Withers* [1975] Crim. L.R. 647.

[168] Cf. *R. v. Woodman* [1974] Q.B. 754. But a person cannot be charged with an offence of possession if he does not know the existence of the thing: 36.6.

an owner against third parties. So if an intruder or repairer finds the valuables, and dishonestly keeps them, he will be guilty of stealing from the owner of the bureau. If the owner of the bureau sells it, he is taken not to intend to sell the unknown contents so he is still entitled to these contents as against the buyer. Of course the seller would be subject to the same rule; he would be required to surrender the articles to the person who sold the bureau to him, if that person can be found, and so back to the person who originally hid the articles; but difficulties of proof would often prevent ownership being traced back so far. The buyer of the bureau who keeps an article he finds in it could not generally be convicted of theft, since he could so easily say that he thought he had a right to it. But if he had taken legal advice, for example, and been told that it was not his, he could probably be convicted.

If a person has a coin-operated gas meter, and dishonestly takes out of the meter coins he had himself put into it, he is guilty of theft of the coins or the gas? Of the coins. If the meter was provided by British Gas, he steals from it. As soon as a coin is inserted into the meter, it becomes the property of the supply company, because that was the intention of the parties to the agreement.[169] In much the same way, a person who takes coins from a parking meter steals from the owner of the meters, and those who use it know that in putting coins into the meter they are transferring the money to the local authority who has installed those meters.[170]

29–056

A similar rule (it may be called the container rule) applies where an employee who is not in a shop receives something from a stranger. It may sometimes be doubtful whether he has received it in his capacity of employee or privately, so if he acts dishonestly the question may arise whether he steals from the employer or the stranger. The question is readily answered if the employee put the thing into his employer's container before appropriating it; here it is well established that by putting it into the employer's container (which in law was in the employer's possession, the employee himself having only custody) he constructively put it into the possession of his employer, and at the same time it became the property of his employer.[171] When a dustman puts refuse in his employer's dustcart[172] and has agreed with his employer that the profits of gleaning from refuse ("totting" to use vernacular) should be shared between his employer (the Corporation) and its dustman, title in the refuse passes to the Corporation. If D dishonestly appropriates it from the cart he may be guilty of theft. The emergence of recycling means refuse is now big business. There might also be issues concerning privacy and identity theft, but that type of remote harm[173] should not be used to link the innocuous gleaner with the independent wrongdoing of a fraudster.

---

[169] *Martin v. Marsh* [1955] Crim. L.R. 781.

[170] Cf. *R. v. Krasniqi* [2008] EWCA Crim. 2257; *R. v. Rachis* [2009] EWCA Crim. 2809, where Ds were convicted of theft for stealing coins that others had put in the parking meter. Those cases also involved acts of criminal damage.

[171] *R. v. Mallison* (1902) 66 J.P. 503.

[172] *Williams v. Phillips* (1957) 41 Cr. App. R. 5.

[173] See Dennis J. Baker, "The Moral Limits of Criminalizing Remote Harms," (2007) 10(3) *New Criminal Law Review* 371.

29–057   **You told me before that I am statutorily barred from claiming ownership of treasure trove. What if I take my metal detector to the beach and find a new IWC watch in the sand?**   You may be liable of theft. This raises further issues of ownership and control. Finders are normally keepers, but an owner or lawful possessor of land owns all that is in or attached to it. In *Waverley BC v. Fletcher*[174] D took his metal detector to a public park and did some prospecting. He discovered a brooch. It was held that it was not treasure trove, so D thought he had ownership. The park belonged to Waverley Borough Council, so it too claimed ownership on the grounds that it owned the land where it was found. The Court of Appeal held that "where an object was found in or attached to land, the owner or lawful possessor of the land had a better title to the object than the finder, and where the object was unattached on land the owner or lawful possessor only had a better title than the finder where he had exercised such manifest control over the land as to indicate an intention to control it and anything found on it." It was irrelevant that the park was a public place as the act of digging was an act of trespass. One is not entitled to go around digging up parks. However, scratching through sand on a beach would hardly constitute an act of trespass. Otherwise, a child would be a trespasser every time he dug up sand to build a sandcastle. Unless the beach authorities indicate an intention to control any lost property found on it, you would have the right to take what you find.[175]

29.11.   TRUSTEES AND COMPANY DIRECTORS

29–058   As we have seen, even the trustee of property (who is its legal owner) can steal it if he dishonestly appropriates it with the intention of defeating the equitable interests of the beneficiaries. Although he is the legal owner of the property, he is not the beneficial owner—the owner in equity. In the ordinary case, therefore, the trustee will be guilty of theft on the general principle of section 5(1) of the *Theft Act*. Sometimes, as in the case of charitable trusts, there is no owner in equity, and a special provision is needed to bring the case within the net. Section 5(2) of the *Act* holds:

> "Where property is subject to a trust, the persons [to] whom it belongs shall be regarded as including any person having a right to enforce the trust, and an intention to defeat that trust shall be regarded accordingly as an intention to deprive of the property any person having that right."

If trust property is stolen by a third party, the indictment may lay the property either in the trustee (the legal owner) or in the beneficiary (the owner). If it is stolen by the trustee, the indictment will lay the property in the beneficiary or other person having right to enforce the trust (the Attorney-General in the case of charitable trusts).[176]

---

[174] [1996] Q.B. 334.

[175] It would be difficult to establish *mens rea*, if you did not know who the owner was, and genuinely believed he would never be found.

[176] A trust is normally created for the benefit of persons as *cestuis que trustent* and cannot have a purpose or object as a substitute to beneficiaries unless that purpose or object is charitable. A purpose

We have seen that failure to pay a debt or perform a contract—even a dishonest failure—is not in itself a theft. The victim must (in general) have some property right (*ius in rem*), that has been infringed, not just a right against a particular person (*ius in personam*). However, equity blurs the line between property and contract. A person whom the common law looks upon as a mere debtor may in equity be a constructive trustee of money, and the difference for the law of theft is vital. If D is the constructive trustee of a fund for V, then if D dishonestly appropriates the fund he is guilty of theft. We shall return to this in 29.14.

It will be remembered that section 5(1) excludes from proprietary interests "an equitable interest arising only from an agreement to transfer or grant an interest." These words do not apply the rule of civil law that when a person contracts to sell land, the purchaser is regarded as having an equitable interest in the land from the moment of the contract, even though the legal conveyance has not been made.[177] The owner (vendor) becomes a kind of trustee for him, but the subsection provides that this trust is to be ignored for the purpose of the law of theft. The reason is that if the owner wrongfully conveys the land to some other person, what he does is in substance a breach of his contract to sell the land to the first purchaser, and it was not thought right that the first purchaser should be protected by the law of theft.[178]

29–059

In *R. v. Sanders*[179] a debarred barrister was the executor of a deceased estate from which he took £100,000. The defendant had taken money belonging to the estate of his uncle. He argued that he had not stolen property belonging to another because a second will named him as a beneficiary. It is worth noting that the defendant only discovered the second will after he had taken the money. The defendant was convicted, because probate creates a trust empowering the executor to deal with the property belonging to the "deceased person in a particular way. The particular way is in accordance with the will that has been proved." When the defendant discovered the existence of the later will he was legally required to go back before the probate court to ask it to vary the terms of the trust so that the property would be held for the benefit of those named in the later will. "But unless and until that is done the trust is the one created by the probate court."[180]

---

or object cannot sue, but if it is charitable, the Attorney-General can sue to enforce it. *Morice v. Bishop of Durham* (1809) 34 E.R. 1046. See also *Charities Act 1993*. Cf. *R. v. Dyke* [2002] 1 Cr. App. R. 30. In *Parker v. The Queen* (1997) 186 C.L.R. 494, D took money from a mixed fund in a bank account that was set up to take donations for an election campaign. It was held that the donors were not co-owners of the funds in the account and that co-ownership would only be established if there was evidence of their intention to that effect, and there was no such evidence in that case. However, if a politician has been given funds for a particular purpose such as an entertainment allowance, and uses those funds to purchase a refrigerator for his private benefit then there is a clear case of theft. See *Adamson v. O'Brien* [2008] N.T.S.C. 8.

[177] The rule depends on the fact that the remedy of specific performance is available to enforce the contract, and it therefore applies also to contracts to sell shares, and even (it seems) to contracts to sell goods if they are of special value, not ordinary market commodities.

[178] Yet, as was mentioned before, a person who sells an ordinary chattel, passing title to it, and who then dishonestly sells it to someone else, does commit theft. He is unlikely to be prosecuted.

[179] [2003] EWCA Crim. 3079.

[180] *R. v. Sanders* [2003] EWCA Crim. 3079.

In *R. v. Clowes (No. 2)*[181] the defendants were convicted, *inter alia*, of theft. The defendants convinced many investors to invest millions of pounds in a company which they controlled called the BC Group. They provided brochures which stated that "investors' cheques were to be made payable to the BC group's international client account, that 'All moneys received are held in a designated client account and the clients are the beneficial owners of all securities purchased on their behalf' and that the BC group was authorised to buy and sell British government stock on investors' behalf on a fully discretionary basis...'" Not much of the investors' money was deposited in the designated client accounts and even less was used to purchase gilts. The defendants mingled the investors' money with their own and withdrew large sums for their personal use. The Court of Appeal held that the brochures and the terms of the portfolio investments, construed as a whole, demonstrated that the BC group had received funds from the investors on trust to invest them in stocks. The defendants had not been authorized to use the money for their own personal benefit:

> "The nature of the investment scheme stated in the brochures was investment in and the management of British government securities for the purpose of capital gain and the BC group's role was to act as a trustee of funds invested with it for that purpose and for that purpose only. No other form of investment was mentioned."[182]

29–060 **Can company directors steal from their own limited company?** Yes, unless the taking was for a legitimate company purpose and complied with the relevant company law and the company's memorandum or articles of association.[183] A sole director who *consents* to his company giving him its funds for his private use could hardly claim the company consented or that he acted honestly.[184] Directors must act in the interests of the company not their own interests.[185] In *Macleod v. The Queen*[186] the High Court of Australia held that it was irrelevant that the sole director (Macleod) of a limited private company (Trainex Pty. Ltd.[187]) consented on the company's behalf to him taking $2 million for his own personal use. Several thousand investors put money into Trainex Pty. Ltd. and the investor's deed required the company to hold the invested funds on trust for the purpose of producing films. The deed also obliged Trainex Pty. Ltd. to "deposit the invested

---

[181] [1994] 2 All E.R. 316.

[182] *R. v. Clowes (No. 2)* [1994] 2 All E.R. 316.

[183] The transaction would also have to comply with any duties imposed on the company where the company acts as a trustee of investment funds. *Macleod v. The Queen* [2003] 214 C.L.R. 230 at 264 *per* Callinan J. Justice Callinan held that the defendant's appropriation of the company's funds was unlawful in at least three ways: (1) it contravened his legal duties as a director; (2) it was a breach of trust; and (3) it was contrary to the memorandum and articles of association of Trainex, since it was "plain that the money used by the appellant was not used in pursuance of the objects of the company."

[184] *R. (on the application of A) v. Snaresbrook Crown Court* [2001] EWHC Admin. 456; *Re Attorney-General's Reference (No. 2 of 1982)* [1984] 2 W.L.R. 447.

[185] "Where a company is accused of a crime the act and intentions of those who are the directing minds and will of the company are attributed to the company. That is not the law where the charge is that those who are the directing minds and will have themselves committed a crime against the company." *D.P.P. v. Gomez* [1993] A.C. 442 at 496-97 *per* Lord Browne-Wilkinson.

[186] [2003] 214 C.L.R. 230. See also *R. v. Aylen* (1987) 49 S.A.S.R. 254.

[187] A "Pty. Ltd." company is the Australian equivalent of a British limited private company.

funds in a trust account and permitted the company to invest the funds in any interest bearing or discounted securities authorized by the *Trustee Act 1925* (N.S.W.)."

Of the funds raised, $718,000 was applied to film production, but more than $2 million was used by Macleod for his own personal use. This constituted approximately a third of all the funds that had been raised from investors. It was held that a sole beneficial shareholder's consent could not constitute the consent of the company so as to negate an allegation of fraud. Unlike *D.P.P. v. Gomez* where the defendant used fraud to obtain consent, Trainex Pty. Ltd. did not consent at all. The only consent Macleod received was from himself—not from the company. After all, there is a vital distinction between a director and the separate legal entity he represents. "The fact that the natural person so acting is in effective control of the company does not mean that he is the company, or that no distinction may be drawn between what he does and what the company should lawfully do."[188]

Notwithstanding the general duties of directors as set out in the relevant company law; in this case there was a deed which clearly spelt out the lawful obligations that the company had regarding its investors. A company being a fictitious legal entity cannot physically or mentally consent to anything, but a director consenting on its behalf can only consent to transactions that are *intra vires*. In this case, an *intra vires* transaction would have involved Macleod consenting to the company investing money in "any interest bearing or discounted securities authorized by the *Trustee Act 1925* (N.S.W.)" or in film production.[189] The money that was taken by Macleod "was not even beneficially owned by Trainex Pty. Ltd., but was for investment in accordance with a very explicit deed."[190] Trainex Pty. Ltd. was a trustee for investors who had invested funds, so Macleod could not consent on the company's behalf to the company violating its legal obligations as a trustee. The company had express fiduciary duties and it was absurd for the defendant to suggest that the company could authorize itself to steal from itself; and also breach its duties to its investors. In this country, Macleod's dishonest appropriation would also be caught by section 5 of the *Theft Act*, because the funds were not beneficially owned by Trainex.[191]

If I am the *only investor* in a private limited company and have not taken anyone else's funds either on trust or otherwise, then surely I should be allowed to dip into my company's till? You should not dip into the till without complying with the civil law governing company transactions. Companies pay

29–061

---

[188] In England and Wales such a transaction would be void and contrary to section 41 of the *Companies Act 2006*. In *Attorney-General Reference (No. 1 of 1985)* (1985) 41 S.A.S.R. 147 at 154 it was noted: "The company was not charged with stealing from itself, or anyone else. Nor was it charged with applying property for a purpose other than its own. The accused was not, and is not, the company. The fact that he is in dominant control of itself, does not make the company property his property." See also *R. v. Philippou* (1989) 89 Cr. App. R. 290.

[189] Company law imposes "affirmative duties of honesty, care and diligence on directors and officers…" *Macleod v. The Queen* [2003] 214 C.L.R. 230 at 263 *per* Callinan J. The position is no different in England and Wales. Of course, a discussion of those duties is beyond the scope of our present enquiry.

[190] *Macleod v. The Queen* [2003] 214 C.L.R. 230 at 262 *per* Callinan J.

[191] *R. v. Clowes (No. 2)* [1994] 2 All E.R. 316.

lower rates of tax and are able to borrow in their own right, so there may be tax implications or issues involving creditors. A person who registers a limited company creates a new legal person. A couple (perhaps a husband and wife) might turn themselves into a private company, transferring part of their assets to that company. The couple may both be directors, but if they dip into the till without proper authority given by the Board of Directors they may in suitable circumstances be convicted of theft from the company. If a business person merely goes into partnership with her husband, she and he together could not have stolen their own property,[192] even though what they did was meant to defraud their creditors. The possibility of stealing from a private limited[193] company arises only because the company itself is a legal person. If the company does not hold property on trust for other investors (and the director(s) is the only shareholder) the director(s) might claim that he was only taking what he was entitled to take (*i.e.* his own funds as invested by him) and therefore was not dishonest.[194] The case would be different if the appropriation was designed to defraud creditors[195] or the tax office. In most cases, a creditor will have an equitable or legal charge over identifiable property.

In summation, where the directors pass a resolution to sell off the company's assets below value to favoured relatives in order to defraud shareholders or creditors,[196] the directors might be guilty of theft or fraud as the property belongs to the company and they have acted dishonestly. The directors' would be acting *ultra vires* by consenting to such a transaction on the company's behalf and therefore the company could not be said to be consenting.[197] A company is not a person and cannot reason or change its mind, so there are legal limits as to what it can authorize. The legal limits are set out in the relevant company law,[198] the company's articles or memorandum of association, and sometimes in trust deeds. No company's memorandum or articles association would be drafted so as to authorize fraud against the company itself. It is legally impossible for a company to consent to such a transaction.[199] Any consent given by a director on a company's behalf, which allows the company's funds to be used in a way that is contrary to its lawful objects, is not true consent from the company. The courts would have no difficulty in convicting directors who fraudulently misappropriate company property. Depending on the facts, they could be charged with fraud

---

[192] Cf. section 9 of the *Fraud Act 2006*.

[193] Of course, a public company (plc) is axiomatically distinguishable as its assets belong to shareholders at large.

[194] See section 2(1)(b) of the *Theft Act 1968*.

[195] This conduct might also be caught by sections 206-211 of the *Insolvency Act 1986*.

[196] Cf. *D. M. Cannane v. J. Cannane Pty. Ltd. (In Liquidation)* (1998) 192 C.L.R. 557.

[197] As we have seen, a company might hold investments on trust: *R. v. Clowes (No. 2)* [1994] 2 All E.R. 316; *Macleod v. The Queen* [2003] 214 C.L.R. 230 at 263. The company is the trustee so the directors are limited to consenting to what the company is allowed to consent to.

[198] Directors have affirmative duties of honesty, care and diligence. See sections 171-177 of the *Companies Act 2006*.

[199] "A director or officer acting in breach of his obligations under statute law relating to companies, or in breach of its memorandum and articles of association, by using the money of the company for his own purpose is no more the voice or the amanuensis of the company, as between himself and the company, than a thief who gains access to its treasury and steals money from it, or a forger who forges a company cheque in his own favour." *Macleod v. The Queen* [2003] 214 C.L.R. 230 at 263 *per* Callinan J.

under the *Fraud Act 2006* or under section 993 of the *Companies Act 2006*. They might also be charged of a conspiracy to defraud the company. The fraud option would be preferable to charging theft.

The ruling of a circuit judge erroneously suggests that directors can consent on the company's behalf to fraud against the company.[200] In *R. v. Pearlberg* the directors of companies, acting (it seems) under the authority of resolutions that they themselves passed at meetings of the boards of directors, transferred part of the companies' bank accounts to their own private use. It was ruled that there was no case to answer on a charge of theft. The directors had authority from the companies (which owned the accounts) to do what they did, and so their acts could not be theft. The directors were the only shareholders, but the result should have been the same if there had been other shareholders, since it is the company, not the shareholders, that owns its property. A different legal result could be achieved by finding that the directors in not acting for the benefit of the company were acting beyond their powers (*i.e.* without the true consent of the company) and it is not easy to see why this conclusion was not reached by the judge.

Many unincorporated organizations have to do without legal personalities: most clubs, societies and associations, and even registered trade unions and friendly societies. The property of these organizations is put in the names of trustees, and if a trustee misappropriates the property he commits theft.

29.12. THEFT AND SUBSEQUENT POSSESSORS

When an article is stolen and passed from hand to hand, each fresh possessor is capable of stealing it—subject to certain principles of the law of property, and the overriding section 3(2) of the *Theft Act*:

29–062

> "Where property or a right or interest in property is or purports to be transferred for value to a person acting in good faith, no later assumption by him of rights which he believed himself to be acquiring shall, by reason of any defect in the transferor's title, amount to theft of the property."

The reason for this provision was that Parliament agreed with the C.L.R.C. in thinking that it would be too harsh to make an innocent purchaser guilty of theft merely because, after discovering the defect in his title, he could not bring himself to give up what he had bought.

For those who are interested, the main provisions of the law are as follows. They may be stated as a number of hypotheticals:

1. D1 makes off with V's thing, say his car from a car park, and disposes of it to D2. D1 is guilty of theft and gets no title to the thing; consequently, he passes no title to D2, even though D2 buys it from him in good faith, the maxim being *Nemo dat quod non habet*[201]—a person cannot give something that he has not got:

---

[200] *R. v. Pearlberg* [1982] Crim. L.R. 829.
[201] "*Nemo*" may be anglicized in pronunciation as "neemo."

(a)   If D2 knows the facts when he receives the car, he is guilty of theft by this act of appropriation,[202] as well as of handling stolen goods (Chap. 33).

(b)   If D2 does not know the facts when he receives the car, he can still become guilty of theft on account of what he does after coming to know the facts, unless he gave value for the car to D1. If he gave value for the car in good faith (that is, not knowing of the theft),[203] then section 3(2) protects him from a charge of theft in retaining it.[204]

2.   D1 obtains V's thing by fraud. This is an offence under the *Fraud Act 2006*, and it is also theft, at least sometimes (see the discussion *infra*). If V, by reason of the fraud, intends to pass the property in the car to D1, D1 will get the property, though his title will be voidable for fraud.[205] This means that he will become owner until V avoids (rescinds) the transaction according to certain rules:

(a)   If D1 then sells the thing to D2, who *knows* that the thing has been dishonestly come by, D2 gets only the title that D1 had—a voidable title. All the same, D2 is not dishonest in relation to D1. V no longer owns the thing; he has a right to avoid the transaction with D1, but the right to avoid is not ownership. D2's only offence is one of handling stolen goods (though this is in theory a more serious offence than theft itself).

(b)   If D1 *gives* the thing to D2, who takes it without knowing the facts, D2 commits no offence.[206]

In cases (a) and (b), even if V then avoids his transaction with D1, this will not make D2 a thief retrospectively. However, D2 must, on coming to know of V's rescission, return the thing to him; otherwise he will then commit an appropriation that is capable of being theftous:

(c)   If D1 *sells* the thing to D2, who takes it without knowing the facts, D2 obtains a completely valid title, as a *bona fide* purchaser. This is because the owner's rather fragile right to avoid his transfer to the cheat D1 comes to an end as soon as third party rights supervene. D2 will commit no offence even if he holds on to the thing after coming to know the facts, because the property no longer "belongs to another."

29–063   The last hypothetical, 2(c), is an exception to the *Nemo dat* rule. There are various other exceptions, two being specifically noteworthy:

---

[202] *Stapylton v. O'Callaghan* [1973] 2 All E.R. 782; *R. v. Devall* [1984] Crim. L.R. 428.

[203] *R. v. Wheeler* (1991) 92 Cr. App. R. 279, where it was emphasized that: "[A] purchaser in good faith and for value is in a more favourable position than other persons who come by property, whether innocently or not, without stealing."

[204] Neither is he guilty of handling. See 33.4.

[205] *D.P.P. v. Gomez* [1993] A.C. 442. There is an exception if D1 induced V to sell him the article by means of a fraud that created a fundamental mistake. This will make the contract of sale completely void (legally non-existent—void *ab initio*), and D1 will get no title to the thing, just as in case 1. This complexity is left for discussion in books on the law of contract.

[206] Even if D2 subsequently comes to know the facts, he will not become guilty of handling by reason of retaining the thing on his own behalf. See 33.4.

1.   If a trustee in breach of trust sells the trust property (thus committing theft, if he acts dishonestly) to a person who takes without notice of the breach of trust, the latter obtains good title.

2.   If money is stolen, the coins and notes initially continue to belong to the victim of the theft. But if the thief spends the money, the recipient taking in good faith, the recipient gets a good title to the money (because money is "negotiable").[207]

It follows that if the buyer from the trustee in the first case, or the person who received the money in good faith, giving value for it, in the second case, subsequently comes to know of the tainted origin of what he has got, he will still be safe from a charge of theft or of handling. His protection rests not upon section 3(2) but upon the fact that when he decides to hold the property after discovering the truth it is not property belonging to another. It is his property, and he is entitled to keep it.

29.13.   THEFT BY AN OWNER

An owner of goods can himself steal them. He may, for example, steal them from a co-owner—though in the case of co-ownership of chattels difficulty may arise in deciding what acts of use by one owner can be said to be dishonest against the other.[208]

29–064

It used to be held that larceny could be committed by an owner from a possessor who was not an owner but had an interest in the goods, such as a pawnbroker (pledgee);[209] and that same rule follows from section 5(1) of the *Theft Act*. The rule means that an owner can steal his own goods from an unpaid seller. Consider again the hypothetical where V sells D a television set. Even if the contract of sale in that case had expressly provided that the property should pass immediately, the seller would still have a seller's lien (right to retain the goods until the price is paid).[210] If the price is not paid, the seller can (after giving notice) resell the goods, deducting what is owed to him from the price obtained, and suing the buyer for any deficit.[211] It will be seen that the seller's lien is a substantial interest, and a dishonest taking by the buyer in order to evade the lien would be theft, notwithstanding that the buyer is technically the owner.

I must now ask you to consider one of the most extraordinary cases decided under the *Theft Act*, *R. v. Turner (No. 2)*.[212] To understand the case one must know that when an article is handed to a repairer for repair, the repairer has the

---

[207] Both these are known as the *bona fide* purchaser, colloquially (though not forensically) as the b.f.p. His full title is the *bona fide* purchaser for value without notice.

[208] *R. v. Bonner* [1970] 1 W.L.R. 838.

[209] *Rose v. Matt* [1951] 1 K.B. 810.

[210] Section 41 of the *Sale of Goods Act 1979*. A lien (pronounced "lee-en" or "leen") is a kind of charge upon goods somewhat similar to a mortgage. The goods are a security for a debt, the lienee being the creditor.

[211] Section 48 of the *Sale of Goods Act 1979*.

[212] [1971] 1 W.L.R. 901.

right to retain the article until he is paid his charges. This is the repairer's lien.[213] The owner cannot say: "Give me my property back, and I will pay your bill some other time." The rule applies, for example, to a motor mechanic who repairs a car.

29–065 **You don't mean to tell me that if I have my car repaired when I am on a journey, and cannot immediately pay the bill because it is a much larger repair than I expected, the repairer can refuse to give me back the car until I pay?** Probably the repairer would be reasonable and accept a cheque, but he would not be obliged to do so. (Your sensible course would have been to obtain an estimate in advance, not to be exceeded without your permission).

29–066 **What if the owner disputes the amount of the repair bill?** He must tender what he thinks he really owes. If he is right in his assessment of the sum properly due, and the tender is refused, he can safely go off with his car if he can get hold of it, or he can sue for damages for the illegal detention.

29–067 **And if he does not tender enough?** He is not supposed to go off with his article—though if he does not know about liens he would not commit theft in doing so, because he would believe that he has a legal right to deprive the repairer of the car.[214]

To go with *R. v. Turner (No. 2)*, the facts were as follows. Turner left his car at a garage for repair, and surreptitiously took it away when the repair was completed, without paying the bill.[215] The facts abundantly showed dishonest intent. He was convicted of stealing the car form the repairer, notwithstanding that the judge had directed the jury that they were not concerned with any question of lien. In fact the garage proprietor had a repairer's lien. It was because the repairer had a protected right to possession that Turner clearly acted wrongly in going off with the car, even though it was his own car. He owned the car, but there was a lien over the parts that had been put in it. If the judge had directed the jury in terms of the lien, therefore, Turner would certainly have been guilty of theft on the authorities, assuming that he knew of the lien. However, the judge told the jury that they need pay no attention to any question of lien.

29–068 **Why did the judge ignore the lien?** Judges are strongly inclined to exclude questions of civil law wherever they can from the law of theft. The effort cannot be wholly successful, since the *Act* requires the appropriation to be of "property belonging to another," which, as we have plentifully seen, imports civil law rules

---

[213] *Tappenden v. Artus* [1964] 2 Q.B. 185. Cf. *Xu v. Council of the Law Society of N.S.W.* (2009) 236 F.L.R. 480, where a solicitor held a client's passport because he had not paid his fees. It was held: "Although by statute the Commonwealth retains the general property in an Australian passport this does not prevent the recognition of a special property in a grantee as a bailee at will, or the creation of a subbailment in favour of a solicitor which entitles him to exercise a lien over a client's passport." At para 54 Handley A.J.A. said: "The solicitor having obtained possession of the passport for a legitimate forensic purpose, was entitled to retain possession against his client, and exercise a lien over it until his proper costs and disbursements were paid or payment thereof was secured. In my judgment he had a reasonable excuse for having and retaining possession of the passport for the purposes."

[214] See section 2(1)(a) of the *Theft Act*: discussed *infra*. Cf. *R. v. Kelly* [1998] 3 All E.R. 741 at 750.

[215] These days Turner might also be caught by section 11 of the *Fraud Act 2006*, which criminalizes those who dishonestly obtain a service.

of property (and their problems) into the criminal law. Where the judges have excluded the civil rules, the results have been to introduce confusion, uncertainty and anomalies into the criminal law.

The judge in effect directed the jury to assume that the owner of property could commit theft from his bailee at will. We must therefore suppose, against the fact, that the repairer of Turner's car had expressly agreed not to exercise a lien. In that case the repairer was a bailee at will. If the owner was entitled to repossess himself whenever he wished,[216] how could his act possibly be a crime? Yet not only was he convicted but the Court of Appeal affirmed the conviction. The court assumed that the only questions were: was the repairer in possession, and did the owner take the car from his possession with subjective dishonesty? If so, it is theft. Nothing else matters. This means that theft can be committed without an *actus reus* in the sense in which that term is generally used for consummated crimes. It is hard to believe that the decision represents the law.

The decision is open to the following objections:

- On the assumption that the repairer was a bailee at will, the bailment could be determined (ended) immediately, by the owner requesting the return of the car. The bailee, therefore, had no substantial interest in the property: no right to keep it, as against the owner, for any appreciable time. In these circumstances it is extraordinarily technical to say that Turner intended to deprive the bailee permanently of the thing. The bailee had no sufficient interest to make the statement substantially true. The bailee was not deprived because he had no interest of which he was deprived. It is perfectly lawful for the owner to demand the thing back from his bailee at will; and even if the owner neglects the formality of demand, still the bailee is not, except in the most technical sense, deprived of anything to which he has a right as against the owner.

- If the bailment was at will, Turner was hardly guilty of dishonesty in respect of the bailee's property-right in going off with his car. He would probably believe, within section 2(1) of the *Theft Act*, that he had a right to deprive the other of it. Technically he might be wrong, since he ought to have given notice to determine the bailment, the bailee then being bound to return the thing immediately. But a layman would be unlikely to know this, and even a lawyer might not. Turner's dishonesty in trying to get out of paying his bill ought not to make him guilty of theft, if he were not dishonest in respect of proprietary rights (including the right of the possessor, who has a charge upon the thing).

- If the bailment was at will, Turner did not intend to appropriate the car in any save the most technical sense. It was already his, and in substance he alone had the right to possession of it.

- Lastly, a person should not be held guilty of theft if he has the right to do what he does.

---

[216] Cf. *Carmichael v. Black* [1992] S.L.T. 897 at 900, where a wheelclamping firm was convicted of extortion under Scottish law for holding a motorcar. It was said, *obiter*, even if the firm had been owed money (and it was not because there was no contract), it had no right to detain the motorcar; or to use it to exhort money from its owner.

29–069   It seems possible that if the objections to the decision were argued in a later case, if the point arose again, *R. v. Turner (No. 2)* would not be followed.[217] Certainly that decision did not prevent a circuit judge from going the other way in *R. v. Meredith*.[218] Admittedly this is an authority lower in the judicial hierarchy than *R. v. Turner (No. 2)*, but much better bottomed in good sense. Meredith left his car in a road and it was towed away by the police under statutory powers. The statute then in force gave the police no right to retain the car when the owner came to collect it, though the owner was liable to pay a charge if his vehicle had caused obstruction, unless he preferred to face a prosecution for obstruction. Meredith went to the police station to collect his car, but the station was crowded so he simply drove his car away from the yard. A circuit judge ruled that he could not be convicted of stealing the car from the police, because the police had no right to retain the vehicle. Yet the police were undoubtedly in possession of it, and on a literal reading of *R. v. Turner (No. 2)* Meredith should have been convicted, at any rate if what he did was thought to be "dishonest." Even where there are statutory powers allowing the police to detain vehicles, the sensible approach is not to conflate theft with violating the legal obligation to pay a parking fine. If the police are granted powers to retain vehicles to force owners to pay parking fines and an owner decides to take his vehicle without paying then the latter should be labelled as an offence in its own right. Even if *R. v. Turner* is not likely to be followed, it may perhaps be held to be theft for an owner dishonestly to take his article back from a hirer. But the point is a difficult one, and has not been decided.

29.14.   PROPERTY TO BE DEALT WITH IN A PARTICULAR WAY

29–070   Section 5(3) states a rule that is often quite difficult to apply:

> "Where a person receives property from or on account of another, and is under an obligation to retain and deal with that property or its proceeds in a particular way, the property or proceeds shall be regarded (as against him) as belonging to the other."

29–071   **What does the subsection mean by an "obligation"? Is it a legal obligation or a moral obligation?**   Parliament is not in the habit of legislating about moral obligations as such; and that Parliament should do so without making its meaning plain is inconceivable. "Obligation," then, means a legal obligation, an obligation under the civil law; and there is ample authority for this view.[219] There must be a legal obligation even though it need not be enforceable.[220] It is for the judge to interpret the civil law and state to the jury, and for the jury to find any relevant facts.

---

[217] On an appeal against conviction by an unmeritorious defendant who can point to a substantial misdirection, the Court of Appeal prefers to hold that there has been no misdirection than to quash the conviction.

[218] [1973] Crim. L.R. 253.

[219] *R. v. Dubar* [1995] 1 Cr. App. R. 280. The decision to the contrary in *R. v. Hayes* (1977) 64 Cr. App. R. 82 was disapproved by the court in *R. v. Dubar*. See also *R. v. Mainwaring* (1982) 74 Cr. App. R. 99 at 107; *R. v. Cording* [1983] Crim. L.R. 175.

[220] *R. v. Meech* [1974] Q.B. 549.

The subsection is a compendious statement of a principle underlying a number of rules of the law of property.[221] Where a person receives property from or on account of another, and is under an obligation to the other to retain and deal with (it would have been better if the subsection had said "to retain or deal with") that property or its proceeds in a particular way, the property or proceeds generally *do* belong to that other, either at law or in equity.[222] If the recipient dishonestly appropriates the property he commits theft of property "belonging to another," the other having a "proprietary right or interest" within section 5(1). To this extent, section 5(3) is superfluous. Section 5(3)'s advantage over section 5(1) is simply that it does not require the court to determine whether V holds an equitable interest. The section also allows the prosecutor to circumvent the civil law barrier that arises when V creates a chose in action for D by electronic transfer. Section 5(3) was of no assistance in *R. v. Preddy*,[223] because the loan was used for the intended purpose, namely the purchase of a particular property.[224] As said before, that the notion of property is a key concept in the law of theft. It is a notion of the civil law, so the ambit of the law of theft depends directly upon the civil law. But there are exceptional cases where justice is served by allowing the criminal law to ride roughshod. The deeming provisions, most superlatively exemplified in sections 5(3) and 5(4), are an example of the criminal law riding roughshod.[225]

Section 5(3) does not require the "acquisition (the 'receiving') of the property" to involve an appropriation of another's property. It covers those who get property innocently and then appropriate it. A chose in action might be created for D, with instructions that it is ("received") created for D but is to be used for a

---

[221] For instance, a purpose trust hinges on a fiduciary duty to deal with property in a particular way. "The duty is fiduciary in character because a person who makes money available on terms that it is to be used for a particular purpose only and not for any other purpose thereby places his trust and confidence in the recipient to ensure that it is properly applied." *Cooper v. PRG Powerhouse Ltd.* [2008] EWHC 498 (Ch.) at para. 18.

[222] In *R. v. Arnold* [1997] 4 All E.R. 1 it was noted that: "section 5(3) of the *1968 Act* covered property received from another under an obligation short of actual trusteeship. Accordingly, provided that the obligation was one which clearly required the recipient to retain and deal with that property or its proceeds in a particular way, there was no good reason to introduce words of limitation in relation to the interest of the transferor, save that at the time of the handing over of the property he had lawful possession of it in circumstances which gave him a legal right *vis-à-vis* the recipient to require that it be retained or dealt with in a particular way for his benefit."

[223] [1996] A.C. 815 at 835.

[224] See *Klineberg v. Marsden* [1999] 1 Cr. App. R. 427 at 431. Cf. *Re Holmes* [2005] 1 Cr. App. R. 16.

[225] In *Klineberg v. Marsden* [1999] 1 Cr. App. R. 427 at 432-433, Kay J. (in the Court of Appeal, Rose L.J. and Baker J. concurring) said: "This clearly illustrates the significance of section 5(3). It is essentially a deeming provision by which property or its proceeds 'shall be regarded' as belonging to another, even though, on a strict civil law analysis, it does not. Moreover, it applies not only to property in its original form but also to 'its proceeds'. ... In our judgement the trial judge was right to conclude that section 5(3) could overcome the *Preddy* problem in the present case, provided that it was established that PCL and the appellants ... were under an obligation to the purchasers to retain and deal with 'the property or its proceeds' in a particular way and that what occurred was a breach of that obligation." *Per contra*, Ormerod and Williams suggest that section 5(3) does not apply when V has electronically paid D, because of the *R. v. Preddy* problem. They argue that: "5(3) does not apply and D can be guilty of theft only if the person whose bank account has been debited retains an equitable interest in the new property owned by D." See D. Ormerod & D. H. Williams, *Smith's Law of Theft*, (Oxford: O.U.P., 2007) at para. 2.226.

particular purpose. Similarly, a chose in action might be created for D by mistake. The appropriation for the purposes of theft only transpires when D dissipates the chose in action that was created for D on the basis that he would use it for a particular purpose, if he does not use it for that purpose.[226] The section only requires V (or his agent) to cause D to receive the property (*e.g.,* V causes D to receive property when he electronically creates a chose in action for D by reducing his own chose in action with his bank). The fact that the bank plays an intervening role is irrelevant. D's chose in action belongs to another within the meaning of section 1 in the *Theft Act 1968* from the moment D is made aware that it has been created for his use for a limited purpose.[227]

29–072 Such a reading of the deeming provisions found in section 5(3) and 5(4) is compatible with the idea of respect for property. Both sections use the words "the property or proceeds shall be regarded (as against him) as belonging to [V]." It makes no difference that section 5(4) uses the word "gets" whereas section 5(3) uses the word "receive," because in both cases D receives or gets a chose in action. When the *R. v. Preddy* problem arises, the newly created chose in action ("property") is regarded as belonging to V, because D has received it for a particular purpose. An electronic transfer in effect has the same implications for V as if he had drawn the cash and delivered it to D, and the deeming provisions adequately prevent D from relying on civil law technicalities to evade justice.

Unpicking the subsection, it will be seen to provide for two cases: where property is received from another, and where it is received on account of another. In the first case, where V transfers a chattel or money to D for a particular purpose, V will as a general principle be regarded as retaining either the legal or, at least, the equitable ownership; and both forms of ownership are protected by the law of theft.

An example would be where V gives D, a jobbing printer, £100 to buy paint for some work that V wants him to do. The jury (or magistrates) must decide whether the understanding was that the painter should spend that money (or money representing it: see later) on the paint, or whether the understanding was that the money was a general advance to D, which he could spend as he liked (as a contribution to a holiday on the Costa Brava if he wished), buying the paint perhaps later on with money not yet earned. If the jury find that the former was the understanding, and convict the painter of theft on the ground that he has dishonestly misappropriated the money, the conviction will be upheld on appeal.

29–073 That was an example of money received from another, the recipient being under an obligation to the payer to deal with the money in a particular way. Other examples of money received for a particular purpose might be where money is given on an agreement that it will be used for buying a car[228] or for paying a utility bill[229] and so on.

---

[226] *Klineberg v. Marsden* [1999] 1 Cr. App. R. 427 at 432. The chose in action might also be created for D by mistake, if so it is deemed as belonging to the person who caused the creation of the chose in action: see *Attorney-General's Reference (No. 1 of 1983)* [1985] Q.B. 182. *R. v. Gresham* [2003] EWCA Crim. 2070 at para. 14.

[227] *Klineberg v. Marsden* [1999] 1 Cr. App. R. 427 at 432.

[228] *R. v. Dubar* [1995] 1 Cr. App. R. 280.

[229] *Davidge v. Burnett* [1984] Crim. L.R. 297.

The second type of case envisaged in the subsection involves three parties, money or other property being received by D from X on account of V. The buyer of a house (X) pays a deposit to the estate agent, D who receives it in a fiduciary capacity on behalf of his principal, the seller (V). If D dishonestly misappropriates it the jury can convict him of theft from V. He has received money on account of V, and is under an obligation to V to deal with the money in a particular way, namely for the benefit of V. The legal position in the case of the estate agent is clarified by section 13 of the *Estate Agents Act 1979*, which declares that when an estate agent receives money he holds it on trust. A person may, of course, receive money on trust quite apart from any Act of Parliament, if such is the intention of the parties.

Compare the estate agent position with that of a travel agent who receives money from clients by way of payment in advance for tickets. The reasonable construction here may be that the travel agent is entitled to treat the money as an ordinary business receipt, being merely under a contractual obligation to buy the tickets for the client. In that case it cannot be said that the travel agent is under an obligation to retain and deal with that property in a particular way.[230] Nonetheless, if there is a clear agreement the travel agent may be liable. In *Germany v. Kumar (No. 1)*,[231] the travel agent appropriated the proceeds from ticket sales which he held on trust pursuant to an agreement that: "agreed a trustee relationship for the monies received from the sale of the tickets such that after deduction of commission the monies were duly to be accounted for by the 15th of the following month and transferred by direct debit...."[232] It was held that the "terms of the trust were sufficiently expressed to include an obligation on Kumar to pay the monies over by a given date and in not doing so, a charge of theft could be raised if the prosecution laid one against D."[233] Likewise, if D collects money for a charity he will be subject to an obligation in respect of the money or its proceeds in that he will be obliged to pass it on to the charity.[234]

Section 5(3) refers in one breath to "property or its proceeds," as though the two were virtually the same. This reflects certain rules of the civil law. Both the common law and equity allow property to be "followed" into its proceeds (the exchange product). Take again the hypothetical of the jobbing painter. If the understanding was that he was to spend the specific money on paint, and if he does so, the paint he buys will belong to his employer, being the "proceeds" of the money he was given. If he buys a coat for his wife instead of paint, the coat will belong to his employer: it does not matter that the exchange was wrongful. If painter does not need the paint immediately, there is nothing wrong in his paying the money into his bank account, provided that he keeps the account in credit to that amount, and that he eventually draws "the money" (*i.e.* a similar sum of money) out again to buy the paint.

29–074

---

[230] *R. v. Hall* [1973] Q.B. 126.

[231] [2000] Crim. L.R. 504.

[232] *Germany v. Kumar* (1999) Case No: CO/1786/98 (Queen's Bench Division Divisional Court). Cf. *D.P.P. v. Huskinson* (1988) 20 H.L.R. 562.

[233] [2000] Crim. L.R. 504. Kumar evaded justice, however, by claiming to be a single parent and thereby avoiding extradition to Germany.

[234] *R. v. Wain* [1995] 2 Cr. App. R. 660.

The rules of law and equity govern the "following" or "tracing" of funds[235] into an out of bank accounts, which need not be considered in this discussion of the law of theft. Nor will space allow for a discussion of the many legal and practical problems that are capable of arising.[236]

29.15. MAKING PROFITS WITH ANOTHER'S PROPERTY

29–075 A question of theft can arise where it is the law rather than the intention of the payer or other transferor that establishes the right of V to receive the money or other property. Section 5(3) does not state whether it is meant to apply to this case—whether property is received "on account of another" when the person handing over the property had no notion that the recipient would be required by law to hold it on account of another—it clearly does; and this was held before the *Act* under legislation similarly worded.[237]

A limitation upon the scope of the phrase "on account of another" established under the old law, should not operate as a restriction of the *Theft Act*. It was formerly held that if an employee improperly used his employer's property to make money (as, by letting out his tractor), and kept the proceeds, he did not commit embezzlement of the proceeds, because he did not receive the proceeds "on account of" his employer within the meaning of the embezzlement statute (now repealed). The proceeds were his, even though he was liable to his employer in damages in contract and tort. The employer's action for damages against his employee, for breach of contract or in tort, is an action *in personam*, not an action to recover property in the defendant's hands that belongs to the plaintiff. No doubt, the damages would be such as to wipe out the employee's profit; nevertheless the money he earned never was the employer's as a matter of law.[238]

Even if *Attorney-General's Reference (No. 1 of 1985)*[239] is determinative of the meaning of the words "on account of another" in section 5(3), that subsection plainly does not cover all contingencies. We must always remember section 5(1), which explains that it is theft to steal from a person having "any proprietary right or interest." Now although on the facts we are considering courts of law regarded the employee's illicit earning as his, courts of equity (that is to say, the courts in the exercise of their equitable jurisdiction, which all courts have) have developed a wide doctrine of constructive trust, meaning a trust not created expressly, but imposed by equity as a matter of justice. A person who occupies a fiduciary position (such as an employee) and who derives a profit from the unauthorized use of property belonging to another to whom he owes the fiduciary obligation becomes a constructive trustee for the proceeds.[240] The court would allow him fair remuneration for the work he has done (if outside his contract of employment

---

[235] See generally, Meagher *et al.*, *op. cit. supra*, note 10.

[236] For a fuller discussion see, in addition to the standard treatises, Glanville Williams, *Textbook of Criminal Law*, (London: Stevens & Sons, 1st edn., 1978) at 709-720.

[237] *R. v. Grubb* [1915] 2 K.B. 683.

[238] In *Attorney-General's Reference (No. 1 of 1985)* [1986] Q.B. 491, it was held that the employee received the secret profits on his own account. See also *R. v. Cullum* (1873) LR 2 C.C.R. 28. Cf. *R. v. Arnold* [1997] 4 All E.R. 1.

[239] [1986] Q.B. 491.

[240] *Zobory v. Federal Commissioner of Taxation* (1995) 129 A.L.R. 484.

with the owner) and for materials he has supplied in order to earn the profit, but the balance belongs in equity to the owner of the property.[241] The dishonest appropriation of this balance amounts to theft.[242]

In *Attorney-General's Reference (No. 1 of 1985)*[243] the defendant made a secret **29–076** profit by selling his own beer in a public house which he was managing for a brewer. The Court of Appeal held that the proceeds of the secret sales "was received by the manager not on account of the brewers but on his own account as a result of his private venture…"[244] The Court of Appeal was reluctant to import the constructive trust into the law of theft. Lord Lane C.J. basically asserted that a constructive trust should not be imposed, because the idea of telling a defendant that he holds money on trust when he uses another's property to make that money; and that he can be liable for stealing it, "is so abstruse and so far from ordinary people's understanding of what constitutes stealing that it should not amount to stealing."[245] Lord Lane C.J. said it was also too difficult to identify the illicit profits because the manager had not kept any records of his deceit.[246] Lord Lane C.J.'s reasoning is not convincing. It would not be necessary to identify all the profits for the purposes of theft.[247] If it could be shown that D had two empty beer barrels from a rival brewer on the premises at a given point in time and that he normally sells the contents of those barrels at £2 per pint, then he has stolen an identifiable sum. He may have sold many of his own barrels of beer, but it is not necessary to identify all his illicit profits, it is only necessary to prove he stole something.

Lord Lane C.J. relied in part on the decision of *Lister v. Stubbs*,[248] a decision that holds that those who make a secret profit need only account to their employer as a debtor. This cannot be reconciled with the modern law of equity and trusts.[249] Furthermore, the courts have imported the concept of constructive trust into the

---

[241] *Boardman v. Phipps* [1967] 2 A.C. 46.

[242] *R. v. Shadrokh-Cigari* [1988] Crim. L.R. 465. See also *Attorney-General of Hong Kong v. Reid* [1994] 1 A.C. 324; *Attorney-General v. Blake* [2001] 1 A.C. 268.

[243] [1986] Q.B. 491.

[244] This type of wrongdoing would now be caught by sections 1 and 4 of the *Fraud Act 2006*. Cf. *R. v. Cooke* [1986] A.C. 909.

[245] *Attorney-General's Reference (No. 1 of 1985)* [1986] Q.B. 491 at 507.

[246] Since the beer had been sold on the brewer's premises, it was the owner of any proceeds. But it could only successfully follow (or trace—in the case of proceeds) the property into the proceeds of sale if it were also able to identify them or the fund in which they were mixed. *Re Diplock, Diplock v. Wintle* [1948] Ch. 465 at 521; *Ministry of Health v. Simpson* [1951] A.C. 251; *Clark v. Cutland* [2004] 1 W.L.R. 783.

[247] As far as a constructive trust arises in equity: "It is for the defendant to establish that it is inequitable to order an account of the entire profits. If the defendant does not establish that that would be so, then the defendant must bear the consequences of mingling the profits attributable to the defendant's breach of fiduciary duty and the profits attributable to those earned by the defendant's efforts in investment, in the same way that a trustee of a mixed fund bears the onus of distinguishing what is his own." *Warman International Ltd. v. Dwyer* (1995) 182 C.L.R. 544 at 561-562.

[248] (1890) L.R. 45 Ch. D. 1.

[249] *Attorney-General of Hong Kong v. Reid* [1994] 1 A.C. 324 is to be preferred to *Lister v. Stubbs* (1890) L.R. 45 Ch. D. 1. See *Dyson Technology Ltd. v. Curtis* [2010] EWHC 3289; *Tesco Stores Ltd. v. Pook* [2004] I.R.L.R. 618; cf. *Sinclair Investments (UK) Ltd. v. Versailles Trade Finance Ltd.* [2010] EWHC 1614 (Ch).

law of theft.[250] For example, in *Zobory v. Federal Commissioner of Taxation*,[251] an employee (an accountant for Cannon) secretly borrowed $1,000,000 of his employer's funds and invested it for his own benefit. His investment made him a secret profit of $130,709 in interest income. The Federal Court of Australia accepted that the profits were held upon a constructive trust, of which Cannon was the beneficiary.[252]

It would be incongruous to send a shoplifter to jail for stealing £1,000 worth of goods, while at the same time leaving a person who has made a massive profit at his employer's expense to be dealt with by the civil courts. If Zobory had lost all the money gambling, and had been declared bankrupt, the civil courts would have been unable to provide a remedy. This type of grand fraud is clearly the business of the criminal law. It is clear that Parliament regards such conduct as criminal. The objective of section 4 of the *Fraud Act 2006* is to preclude a fiduciary, *inter alios*, from abusing his position of trust for his own personal advantage.

29-077   Another illustration of a constructive trust is where an agent is conducting a negotiation for his principal, and the other party gives the agent a bribe. The obvious course for the prosecutor is to charge the agent with corruption[253] or fraud, as charging theft presents difficulties. The better view of the civil law is that the agent becomes a constructive trustee of the bribe,[254] and therefore, given dishonesty, can steal it. The courts have accepted this argument. In *Attorney-General of Hong Kong v. Reid*,[255] the defendant was a prosecutor who had taken many bribes over a long period. It was held that he was in a fiduciary relationship and therefore had a fiduciary duty to his employer. By taking the bribes he breached that duty, so the property representing the bribes was held on constructive trust for his employer. Thus, those who make profits from their employer's property would now hold it on trust.

Yet another illustration relates to trade secrets. It was said above that a trade secret is not recognized as property for the law of theft. But a person who unlawfully uses a trade secret may sometimes be regarded as a constructive trustee of the profits, and in that case he may, other conditions being satisfied, be guilty of theft of the profits.

---

[250] See *Westdeutsche Landesbank Girozentrale v. Islington LBC* [1996] A.C. 669 at 717; *R. v. Shadrokh-Cigari* [1988] Crim. L.R. 465. See also *National Grid Electricity Transmission Plc. v. McKenzie* [2009] EWHC 1817 (Ch).

[251] (1995) 129 A.L.R. 484. See also *Agip (Africa) Ltd. v. Jackson* [1990] Ch. 265 at 289-291; *Black v. S Freedman & Co.* (1910) 12 C.L.R. 105 at 110.

[252] This meant that Cannon was entitled to the money, but had to pay tax on the profits which D made for it.

[253] Cf. the extraordinary decision in *Wheatley v. Commissioner of Police of the British Virgin Islands* [2006] 1 W.L.R. 1683, where a corrupt official was convicted of theft for awarding his own firm a construction contract. He failed to disclose his interest, but there was no evidence that he had overcharged for the building works or that the government lost any money on the contract. Notwithstanding this, instead of being charged with corruption, the Privy Council upheld his theft conviction for the sum paid for the work that his firm had contracted to undertake.

[254] *Reading v. Attorney-General* [1951] A.C. 507; *National Grid Electricity Transmission Plc. v. McKenzie* [2009] EWHC 1817 (Ch). Cf. *Powell v. MacRae* [1977] Crim. L.R. 571.

[255] [1994] 1 A.C. 324.

But the Brewer did not know that this profit had been earned. That does not **29–078** matter. A person can own property although he does not know it. The practical difficulty in these cases lies in establishing dishonesty. The employee is not to be expected to know the rules of equity, and he may well believe that the money he has earned with the employer's property is his own, especially if he has contributed his own property, labour or skill. The employee's knowledge that he has committed a civil wrong against the employer is not equivalent to knowledge that he is wrongfully appropriating the employer's property, or that he is under an obligation to deal with the earnings for the employer's benefit. Even if the employee betrays a feeling of guilt, as by lying about the matter, that can be attributed to his knowledge of having committed a civil wrong, not his knowledge that he has committed theft. So, unless the employee had legal advice before misappropriating the proceeds, he might succeed in a defence that he was not dishonest.[256] An intention to commit a breach of contract is not necessarily theftous dishonesty.

But is that position sound? The employee when prosecuted and cross- **29–079** **examined says: "I knew that what I did was not really honest and that I was not supposed to do it. I knew that if I was found out I would get into some kind of legal trouble. But I did the boss no harm, and I certainly had no notion that the money I made belonged to him." Surely he should be accounted dishonest. He made no effort to find out the legal position. He concealed what he had done because he knew that if the truth came out he would probably have to disgorge. Never mind that he did not know the difference between a debt and a trust. Very few laymen do. You make the law of theft unworkable, in its application to fiduciary relationships, if you make it depend on knowledge of the distinction.** There is something to be said for your view. The objection to it is that, as said before, theft must be of property belonging to another, and if the defendant did not realize that the proceeds belonged to another (or that he was under the obligation specified in subsection (3)) he lacked the *mens rea* for the crime. A breach of contract as such is not generally a crime. If the defendant believes that he is only committing a breach of contract, he lacks criminal intent. In practice, a charge of theft probably would not properly succeed unless the employer has warned the employee of the position, either before the misdemeanour or when the illicit proceeds are in the employee's bank.

Nevertheless, in many cases it will not be difficult to prove that D was dishonest. It is clearly dishonest to secretly invest your employer's funds for your own benefit. Likewise, the cost of purchasing a restaurant or public house and equipping it involves a substantial investment and most people would realize it would be dishonest to use another's substantial investment to make a profit at his expense.[257]

---

[256] It is worth noting that, the dishonesty standard under the *Fraud Act 2006* is no different from that used under the *Theft Act 1968*.

[257] Cf. *D.P.P. v. Gohill* [2007] EWHC 239 (Admin.)

29.16.   APPROPRIATION BY A NON-POSSESSOR

29–080   The thief must appropriate the property. The idea of theft at common law was that of taking a thing out of the possession of another without his consent. This was socially inadequate in two main ways:

- It was confined to theft of physical things; so if someone dishonestly effected a transfer from my bank account to his own, he did not commit theft. You could not steal an intangible like the bank's debt to its customer because you could not "take" it.
- The prohibition of taking did not affect people who were already in possession of the thing, borrowers, hirers, *etc.*; they could not "take" what they already possessed, so they could not steal it—even though they made off with it. Or so lawyers reasoned. The law of larceny was extended piecemeal to cover such situations, but it was a thing of fiction and patchwork.

When the C.L.R.C. embarked on its ambitious recasting of the law it needed a new word to express the basic *actus reus* of the new idea of theft. The law of tort had a concept called "converting property to one's own use," but the committee thought that the word "conversion" would not be readily intelligible to the jury (it might cause them to think that the property had to be changed into something else); so the committee chose instead the word "appropriation" to express the same idea.

An appropriation may come about either by a wrongful taking or in other ways. The essence of an appropriation in the ordinary sense is that it involves *taking control* of property in a way showing an intention to deprive the owner. The definition in the *Shorter Oxford English Dictionary*, approved by the Court of Appeal in *R. v. Morris*,[258] is "to take for one's own or to oneself." Putting this in another way, it is an act having the practical (though not necessarily legal) effect of giving someone else's property the character of being yours. We may call this the ordinary or dictionary meaning of the term. In this sense, it would obviously be an appropriation to eat another's food wrongfully, or ride off on his bicycle, or deliver his bicycle to another person, or spend his money, with intent in each case to deprive him of his property.

29–081   **You mean of course that these are all acts done without the consent of the owner.**   I wish I were allowed to mean that, but alas no. The *Theft Act 1968* does not specify that the owner must not consent (as the former *Larceny Act* did). If I ask to borrow your bike and ride off with it secretly intending to sell it, I appropriate it when I first take it even though I take it with your consent. It was held under the old law that although larceny was a taking without the owner's consent, this meant "without the owner's full and free consent." Some imperfect consent by the owner, marred by fraud or mistake, were not held to stand in the way of a conviction of larceny. In the last example, if a false pretence were used to get permission to borrow the bike; the borrower intending to steal it, he was

---

[258]   [1983] 2 W.L.R. 768.

guilty of theft from the moment he borrowed the bike; the law pretended that the owner had not consented to his having it at all. In order to avoid any fiction the C.L.R.C. decided to leave out the question of the owner's consent from the main definition of theft. This means consensual gifts might be caught by the *Theft Act*.[259]

You say that it is an appropriation to ride off on a person's bicycle with intent to deprive him of it. When exactly does the appropriation take place? When the thief begins to ride? At the latest then: perhaps when the thief merely lays hands on the bicycle. The C.L.R.C. was conscious that the concept of appropriation might cause problems in marginal cases like this, and therefore decided to give the expression more specific meaning in addition to its general dictionary meaning. We have already had part of section 3(1); it runs in full as follows:

29–082

> "Any assumption by a person of the rights of an owner amounts to an appropriation, and this includes, where he has come by the property (innocently or not) without stealing it, any later assumption of a right to it by keeping or dealing with it as owner."

We may call this the extended sense of appropriation. An assumption of rights in the subsection means a usurpation of rights; so the definition of appropriation includes doing anything in relation to the property that only the owner can lawfully do or authorize. It has been held that even the assumption of a single right is enough. In *R. v. Morris*[260] the defendant took articles from the shelves of a self-service store and attached to them price labels that he had removed from less expensive articles. At the check-out he was asked for and paid the lower prices. Then he was arrested.

Morris appropriated the articles in the dictionary sense, one might suppose, when he freed them from the owner's control by going off with them after passing the check-out point. But Lord Lane C.J., speaking for the Court of Appeal, expressed the opinion that there would be an appropriation in the extended sense at an earlier point in time: either when the customer dishonestly removed the articles from the shelves intending to steal them, or when he switched the price labels. The removal of an article from the shelf was an appropriation (moving the article being one of the rights of ownership), and the switching of the labels (whether it happened before or after the removal from the shelf) was evidence that the appropriation (the removal) was dishonest. If the jury were not satisfied that at the time of the removal from the shelf that Morris's intention was dishonest, the second part of section 3(1) came into operation: Morris had come by the property without stealing it, and the later switching of the labels was a dealing with the article as owner, and so there was an appropriation.

---

[259] See *R. v. Hinks* [2001] 2 A.C. 241, where a gullible man willingly gave away most of his money. The quality of consent in that case was questionable, as the victim arguably made the gifts because of the undue influence asserted by Hinks. See the discussion *infra*.

[260] [1983] 2 W.L.R. 768.

29–083   **But when Morris switched the labels he did not intend to deprive the owner starting from now. He was only preparing to deprive him later on, when he passed the check-out point.**   Your argument was apparently not presented to the court; but presumably a court faced with it would say that the intention may relate to the future. The thief need not intend his appropriation in the extended sense to be the act that deprives the owner; it is enough that the act is part of what he intends to do to deprive the owner. When Morris misbehaved at the supermarket shelves he intended to deprive the owner, even though he was not to get possession (and so actually deprive the owner) till later, when he had passed the check-out point. The supermarket consented to people taking things from the shelves, so surely that could not be an appropriation even in the extended sense. OK: we have to say that assuming the rights of an owner is an appropriation. But when Morris took down the articles from the shelves, he was acting with the implied consent of the owner, and so was not assuming the rights of an owner; he merely handled the thing in the way the owner allowed him to do. Lord Roskill took this view when the case went to the House of Lords:[261]

> "If one postulates an honest customer taking goods from a shelf to put in his trolley to take to the checkpoint there to pay the proper price, I am unable to see that any of these actions involves any assumption by the shopper of the rights of the supermarket. In the context of section 3(1), the concept of appropriation in my view involves not an act expressly or impliedly authorised by the owner but an act by way of adverse interference with or usurpation of those rights. When the honest shopper acts as I have just described, he is acting with the implied authority of the owner of the supermarket to take the goods from the shelf, put them in the trolley, take them to the checkpoint and there pay the correct price, at which moment the property in the goods will pass to the shopper for the first time. It is with the consent of the owners of the supermarket, be that consent express or implied, that the shopper does these acts and thus obtains at least control if not actual possession of the goods preparatory, at a later stage, to obtaining the property in them upon payment of the proper amount at the checkpoint."

The House of Lords held that changing the labels was an appropriation because it was an adverse interference with or usurpation of one of the rights of the owner.[262] An appropriation does not require an assumption of all of an owner's rights, rather any interference is sufficient. In *R. v. Morris* it was held that switching the labels was an appropriation because it was an unauthorized act which usurped the owner's rights. Only the owner has the right to decide whether or not to discount his own property. If the label-switcher had managed to leave the store without being detected, his removal of the goods without paying the full price would also constitute an appropriation as it too would involve an assumption by the shopper of the rights of the supermarket. But there would only be one act of theft, because only one item has been stolen. The course of conduct: the label switching, the presentation of the goods at the checkout and leaving the store with the goods for a lower price might be several appropriations, but they all relate to one theft. There may be several appropriations in the course of a

---

[261] *R. v. Morris* [1984] A.C. 320 at 331 *per* Lord Roskill in *obiter dictum*, as consent was not at issue as far as the label switching was concerned because it was clearly not authorized. *Aliter, D.P.P. v. Gomez* [1993] A.C. 442.

[262] *R. v. Morris* [1984] A.C. 320 at 331 *per* Lord Roskill.

single theft or several appropriations of different goods each constituting a separate theft,[263] but there cannot be successive thefts of the same property.

Are you telling me that if I merely switch labels on a pair shoes with the intention of getting them for less, I am guilty of theft even if I change my mind and put them back on the store's shelf? What if I hire a car with no intention of returning it, but change my mind two minutes later? As far as taking the goods from the store's shelf is concerned you have at least attempted theft as you usurped one of the rights of the owner, because you did not have any authority to switch the labels. Coupled with this, you switched the labels with the intention of permanently depriving the owner of the full price for those goods.

29–084

The hire car situation is more complex, since you had the owner's consent to take the car under a hire agreement and you did not go any further than authorized, as you returned the car. Nonetheless, you have committed theft. Any consent would be vitiated by your fraud, which was present when you took possession. The leading cases on this point have usually involved fraud and the fraud provided clear evidence of the bad intentions of the defendant when he initially took possession of the car. In these cases, the courts have held that the appropriation takes place as soon D takes possession of the car, because D has the intent to permanently deprive the owner of it.

There are some older cases that go the other way, but these cases have effectively been overruled by *D.D.P. v. Gomez*.[264] For example, in *R. v. Hircock*[265] the defendant gave a false name to obtain possession of a car under hire-purchase agreement as his real name was on a blacklist and therefore if he had told the truth he would not have obtained possession of the car. The defendant sold the car 14 days later. It was held that the initial act of taking possession of the car was an act of obtaining by deception and that the appropriation only took place when the defendant sold the car 14 days later. This case would now be caught by the *Fraud Act 2006,* but if an inept prosecutor were to charge it as theft the appropriation would be regarded as being complete from the moment the defendant took possession, since he had *mens rea* for theft from that moment onwards.[266]

In *R. v. Atakpu*[267] the defendants used fraud (fake passports and documents) to obtain possession of hire cars in Germany and Belgium. They were detained at the border into England by customs and their fraudulent documents gave them away. The issue for the court was to determine whether the theft of the motorcars took place in Germany/Belgium or England. Since the defendants used fraudulent documents to obtain possession of the cars (acted dishonestly), it could be

29–085

---

[263] *R. v. Atakpu* [1994] A.C. 69 at 79 citing Glanville Williams, "Appropriations: A Single or Continuous Act," [1978] Crim. L.R. 69, where Professor Williams wrote: "A man steals a watch, and two weeks later sells it. In common sense and ordinary language he is not guilty of a second theft when he sells it. Otherwise it would be possible, in theory, to convict a theft of a silver teapot every time he uses it to make the tea." See also *R. v. Skipp* [1975] Crim. L.R. 114.

[264] [1993] A.C. 442. The Court of Appeal applied *D.P.P. v. Gomez* in *R. v. Atakpu* [1993] 3 W.L.R. 812.

[265] (1978) 67 Cr. App. R. 278. Cf. *Kaur v. Chief Constable for Hampshire* [1981] 1 W.L.R. 578.

[266] *R. v. Atakpu* [1994] A.C. 69 applying *D.P.P. v. Gomez* [1993] A.C. 442.

[267] [1993] 3 W.L.R. 812.

inferred from the evidence that they intended to permanently deprive the owner of the vehicles from the moment they obtained possession. The Court of Appeal held that the cars were appropriated from the moment the defendants took possession in Germany and Belgium as they had the *mens rea* from that moment onwards. "The crime of theft occurs when the appropriation takes place. The appropriation may not be immediately apparent to the owner if a deception or fraud has been practised. Where property passes to a person as a result of a fraudulent representation an appropriation takes place, notwithstanding that the passing of property occurs with the owner's consent."[268]

In practice it would be impossible to prove when the driver formed *mens rea*. In *R. v. Atakpu* this obstacle was overcome because there was clear evidence of fraud (fraudulent documents and so forth), which demonstrated that the defendants had the *mens rea* for theft when they first took possession of the cars. In *R. v. Fritschy*[269] the defendant was asked to collect some Krugerands from bullion dealers in England and take them to Switzerland. He collected the coins but did not deliver them to the owner. It was held that there was no appropriation in England because there was no evidence that D acted outside the authority given by V until he was in Switzerland. It was suggested that it did not matter whether Fritschy had the *mens rea* for theft when he first took possession of the goods in England. The police will not be able to take action in such cases until the defendant acts outside the authority given by the owner, since it would be impossible to determine when he formed the *mens rea* for theft. (The point in time at which D formed the intent to permanently deprive V of his property will normally only be known by D.)

Unlike *R. v. Atakpu* and *R. v. Hircock* there was no evidence of fraud in *R. v. Fritschy*. We do not know what Fritschy was thinking when he took the coins. He may very well have intended to do the right thing when he left England. His bad intentions may have been formed after he arrived in Switzerland. In cases where there is no evidence of dishonesty when D took possession, it will be the later disposal that will provide evidence of D's dishonest intent—and the jury could infer that if D did not intend to appropriate the goods when he took possession he did when he disposed of them.

29–086   In *R. v. Morris* the House of Lords extended the definition of the *actus reus* for theft by holding *any* assumption of the owner's rights would be sufficient for satisfying the *actus reus* of theft. The *actus reus* (appropriation) for theft is complete once the shopper swaps the labels with an intent to permanently deprive the store of the full price for its property, regardless of whether the label-switcher changes his mind and decides to put the goods back on the shelf. The only limitation provided in *R. v. Morris* was that acts "expressly or impliedly authorised by the owner" do not adversely interfere with or usurp the owner's rights and therefore do not constitute an appropriation for the purposes of theft. However, the House of Lords in *D.P.P. v. Gomez* has since removed this qualification, which means even authorized acts such as removing goods from a shelf in a store constitute the *actus reus* of theft where the remover has the *mens rea* for theft.

---

[268] *R. v. Atakpu* [1993] 3 W.L.R. 812.
[269] [1985] Crim. L.R. 745.

Merely removing goods from a shelf would barely be an attempt let alone a consummated theft. Surely, applying the consent constraint is a sensible way of distinguishing mere thought crimes from attempts and completed acquisitions. The consent requirement would mean that the *actus reus* would require D to have done something more than merely touch the goods with the owner's consent. His thought crime should not be treated as consummated offending where he has taken hold of V's property with V's consent.

Suppose an undercover police officer overhears D in front of Berry Bros. & Rudd hatching a plan to go into the store to a steal a 1998 bottle of Penfolds Grange Hermitage. D goes in and picks up a bottle and looks at it but then changes his mind and puts it back. As he is heading for the exit he is arrested by the police officer.

D has not done much more than think about thieving the wine, he has not even attempted to act outside the owner's authority. The bottles are on the shelves for customers to view so that they can pick them up and read the comments on the labels. If D had put the bottle of wine in his overcoat pocket and then put it back there would have been an unauthorized dealing with the wine. In the latter situation D has at least attempted to appropriate the wine, and following Lord Roskill's analysis in *R. v. Morris* has also appropriated it.[270] But under *D.P.P. v. Gomez* the *actus reus* would have been complete from the moment D first picked up the bottle of wine.

In *D.P.P. v. Gomez* the House of Lords applied the law as set down in *Lawrence v. Commissioner of Police of the Metropolis*[271] by holding that an appropriation could occur even when the owner consented. *D.P.P. v. Gomez* and *Lawrence* were fraud cases that had been wrongly prosecuted as theft cases. A peculiarity of the English criminal appeal system is that the higher courts do not have the power to change an erroneous charge, so if the prosecution charges the wrong offence the options are to stretch the offence charged to cover the facts or acquit. The aforementioned cases involved the higher courts stretching doctrines to their limits to obtain convictions, because the defendants were clearly deserving of criminalization. There was no injustice in either case, as the defendants used fraud to "acquire" property belonging to another.[272]

29–087

---

[270] Subjectivists might not be too concerned about the distinction between attempted theft and consummated theft, but they would not criminalize D for merely thinking about thieving. See generally, Andrew Ashworth, "Taking the Consequences," at 107; R.A. Duff, "Acting, Trying, and Criminal Liability," and Richard H. S. Tur, "Subjectivism and Objectivism: Towards Synthesis," all in Shute *et al.* (eds) *Action and Value in Criminal Law*, (Oxford: Clarendon Press, 1993). See also Simon Gardner, "Appropriation in Theft: The Last Word," (1993) 109 *L.Q.R.* 194 noting that consent does not really make the defendant less culpable or less deserving of punishment as often the nature of his wrongdoing is no different than when consent is absence. Gardner seems to miss the middle ground, since the reality is that in most cases those who do unauthorized things with the property of another such as switching the price labels are getting closer to completing the crime than those who are too afraid to go past the stage of merely taking the goods from the shelf. The former wrongdoer poses a greater danger to society and his overt unauthorized act provides some guidance as to when the criminal law should be invoked.

[271] [1972] A.C. 626.

[272] See P. R. Glazebrook, "The Thief or Swindler: Who Cares?" (1991) 50 *Cambridge L.J.* 389. There has been some discussion of whether fraud is deserving of a greater sentence than theft, but in terms of harm and wrongness they are not too different. Cf. Stephen Shute and Jeremy Horder, "Thieving

In *D.D.P. v. Gomez*[273] the defendant, the assistant manager of a shop, was approached by a customer who wanted to purchase goods with two stolen cheques. The defendant knew the cheques were stolen and deceived the shop manager into authorizing the sale in exchange for the stolen cheques. He was charged with theft contrary to section 1(1) of the *Theft Act 1968*. The defendant argued that the goods had been sold under a contract between the customer and the shop and that there had been no appropriation of property belonging to another. The House of Lords held that "an act expressly or impliedly authorised by the owner of goods or consented to by him could amount to an appropriation of the goods."[274] In *D.P.P. v. Gomez* the Lords overruled a number of decisions that had been taking a more sensible line by holding that there was no appropriation under section 3(1) until the defendant began to act outside the owner's permission. The reason why the court decided the case as it did was that it thought that it was bound by the decision of the House of Lords in *Lawrence*;[275] but that case was distinguishable as a special case where "fraud" vitiated the title obtained by the takers. Fraud vitiated[276] the consent in *D.P.P. v. Gomez* and *Lawrence*, so it is arguable that the general requirement that an appropriation is ordinarily an adverse (non-consensual—unauthorized) usurpation of the rights of an owner, is compatible with the facts of those cases. If Lawrence has said to his victim, "Can I take £6 from your wallet for the taxi fare even though you owe me only 56 pence?" The answer would have been "No." Similarly, if Gomez had said to his manager "Will you accept these stolen cheques from my associate so that he can leave the store with valuable goods without really paying for them," the manager would have said, "No".

29–088   **What are the advantages of a consent requirement?**   In *R. v. Monaghan*[277] a cashier in a supermarket took money from a customer in payment for goods and put it in the till but did not ring it up (so there was no record of it). She dishonestly intended to take it out and keep it, but she was arrested before doing this. One would have thought that the forces of law pounced too soon; but the Court of Appeal upheld a conviction of theft on the ground that Monaghan was guilty of this offence when she put the money in the till. Assuming for the sake of argument that there was no other money in the till (an unlikely contingency), it is difficult to see how, on any view of the law, putting the money in was an appropriation. Monaghan did not appropriate the money in the dictionary meaning of the word; she did not, at that stage, keep it for herself. Nor was it an

---

and Deceiving: What is the Difference," (1993) 56 *Mod. L. Rev.* 548; C. M. V. Clarkson, "Theft and Fair Labelling," (1993) 56 *Mod. L. Rev.* 554. Glazebrook's argument is more convincing, as there is no discernable moral difference between the wrongness of fraud and theft—the difference is barely measurable in terms of harmfulness and culpableness. See Dennis J. Baker, "Constitutionalizing the Harm Principle," (2008) 27 *Crim. Just. Ethics* 3 at 17-22.

[273] [1993] A.C. 442.

[274] *D.P.P. v. Gomez* [1993] A.C. 442.

[275] [1970] 3 W.L.R. 1103. *R. v. Lawrence* involved a taxi driver asking an Italian student for a much higher fare for a taxi ride than was owed. The student did not speak English and did not understand the value of English pounds, so opened his wallet and indicated that the driver could take the owed fare, but the driver took nearly tenfold what he was owed.

[276] See 31:19(b) *infra*.

[277] [1979] Crim. L.R. 673.

appropriation within section 3(1), because Monaghan did not by putting the money into the firm's till assume the rights of an owner.

It may be said in reply that the decision can be supported on the ground that Monaghan was not authorized to put a customer's money into the till except on condition that she rang it up. But that would be a strange way to look at the employer's intention. He would surely rather have the money put in the till, even though with an irregularity, than not put in at all. Anyway the money belonged to the firm, and the till was the proper place for Monaghan to put it. The fact that she failed to ring it up would have grounded a charge of false accounting,[278] but ought not rationally have made her guilty of theft at that moment. The courts now say that a person can be guilty of theft in doing what he is entitled and even supposed to do; but it is a thoroughly dangerous and unprincipled rule. It makes theft depend not on anything wrongful that the defendant does but merely on what goes on in his mind. Monaghan supplied evidence of her dishonest intention, but evidence of criminal intent should not be sufficient for conviction of a consummated crime without proof of some objective illegality. Failing to ring up the till could not reasonably be regarded as an appropriation of money, and neither could the fact of putting the money into the till as her job required her to do.

The decision presents even greater difficulty if one makes the realistic supposition that there was other money in the till. Monaghan's intention in that case was not to remove the particular notes and coins received from the customer but any notes and coins amounting to that value. On that view, the prosecution had to face a second, and (one would have thought) equally insurmountable difficulty, relating to proof of intent. Monaghan was then not guilty of theft of the particular notes and coins she put into the till, because not only did she not take them but she did not necessarily intend to take them. They were merely part of a fund of money from which she intended to steal in future. Nor could the argument for the prosecution be helped by saying that Monaghan was guilty of theft of an unidentifiable part of the money in the till. There was no appropriation of an unidentifiable part.

Let me put to you another case, or more extreme case. This will often be found a good way to proceed. "'I took an extreme case,' was Alice's tearful reply. 'My excellent preceptress always used to say, When in doubt, take an extreme case. And I was in doubt.'" Suppose that the Duke of Omnium's[279] butler proposes to the first parlour-maid that they should seek a new and more rewarding life together in Australia. "I have found the key to his Grace's safe," he says; "so I will take off a tidy amount of cash and jewellery. You can take as much of his Grace's silver as you can get." Somebody has been listening, and the butler is arrested. Is he already guilty of stealing the Duke's silver? The butler has given his permission for the silver to be taken, and since only the Duke (acting personally or through his authorized agent) can lawfully permit the silver to be

29–089

---

[278] See section 17 of the *Theft Act 1968*.
[279] One of the characters in Anthony Trollope's, *The Pallisers: The Six Famous Parliamentary Novels*, (London: Coward, McCann & Geoghegan, 1974).

taken, the butler has assumed the rights of an owner. But of course a conclusion that he has already stolen the silver would be preposterous. *D.P.P. v. Gomez* does not even require an unauthorized act.[280]

The recent decisions from the House of Lords come close to dispensing altogether with the *actus reus* that is supposed to be required for a consummated crime. Merely picking up items from a store shelf with the owner's permission is too remote to constitute the *actus reus* of theft. This is the core disadvantage of dispensing with the consent requirement. In *Eddy v. Niman*[281] the defendant and a friend went to a large supermarket in an intoxicated state intending to steal goods. They placed a number of items in a trolley supplied by the store, but abandoned the goods before they reached the checkout. The court dismissed the charge of theft on the ground that there had been no appropriation by the defendant for the purposes of section 1(1). It was held the *actus reus* required some "overt act inconsistent with the true owner's rights" and that merely putting goods into receptacles provided by the store was not an overt act inconsistent with the rights of the owner. Alas, this is not the law. Coupled with this, the assumption of any single right of the owner constitutes an appropriation under *R. v. Morris*. Under the current law it is theoretically impossible to distinguish preparatory acts from actual attempts and actual attempts from consummated thefts. If we limit consummated theft to cases where the owner's rights have been assumed without the owner's genuine consent, it would be possible to gradate punishment and labelling with the defendant's actual level of wrongdoing. A consummated theft would surely have to involve an actual acquisition: of possession; of title (even if voidable); or a diminution of V's chose in action and so on.

29–090   **I suppose it would be theft if a postman wrongfully opens a letter, and then flushes it down the lavatory to conceal what he has done?**   Certainly. Section 1(2) provides:

> "It is immaterial whether the appropriation is made with a view to gain, or is made for the thief's own benefit."

Whether destroying a thing without taking possession of it is theft is doubtful. It is not an appropriation in the ordinary meaning of that word: a bomber does not appropriate the property he bombs. However, section 3(1) is peremptorily; any act falling within it is, we are told, an appropriation; and destroying property is certainly one of the rights of the owner of the property. In practice there would be

---

[280] Cf. *R. v. Pitham, Hehl* (1976) 65 Cr. App. R. 45, where M offered to sell V's goods to Pitham and Hehl. The only additional factor in that case was that both M, Pitham and Hehl entered V's house. However, the case is an anomaly as Pitham should have been charged with theft and M also as an accessory by instigating him. But the jury acquitted Pitham of theft and convicted him of handling stolen goods. Now, the rule is that a person cannot be convicted of handling if he merely dealt with the goods "in the course of the stealing." Therefore, in order to uphold Pitham's conviction of handling the Court of Appeal had to find that the theft was over and done before Pitham removed the goods. So this is what the court did. It held that the theftous appropriation took place when M made an offer of the goods (or invited Pitham to treat for them; it is not clear which M was regarded as having done). This act was an appropriation by M because it amounted to assuming the right of the owner.

[281] (1981) 73 Cr. App. R. 237.

no point in testing the scope of the law of theft; the sensible charge for destruction without taking is one of criminal damage.

Is it theft to set free someone's budgerigar?   It is probably an act of criminal   **29–091**
damage or destruction, but there is no reason why it should not, instead, be charged as theft. Here section 3(1) is valuable; setting the bird free is one of the rights of an owner. It should also be theft to let gas escape without authority and so on.

29.17.   APPROPRIATION BY A POSSESSOR

It seems that if a person receives possession of the property of another with intent   **29–092**
to steal, this is an appropriation. If he receives the property in good faith the theft is committed at the first subsequent dishonest and wrongful appropriation. It would be an appropriation if the hitherto innocent possessor wrongfully contracts to sell the article and delivers it, or gives it away, or destroys it. It would also be an appropriation to hide someone else's article with the object of keeping it; or for a possessor to tell the owner that it has been lost; or for the possessor to refuse to return it to the owner, or to deny his title to the property, which is only another way of informing him that he is not going to get it back. These are all modes of committing the old tort of conversion (now subsumed under wrongful interference with goods), and they are acts that can further an intention to steal. They can all be regarded as appropriations in the extended sense of section 3(1), which applies where a person who has come by the property without stealing it makes "any later assumption of a right to it by keeping or dealing with it as owner." Even *using* the thing should be enough if the bailee's right to keep is at an end.

Suppose the hire-purchaser of an article dishonestly sells it? Is this merely a   **29–093**
breach of contract to keep the article in his possession, or is it
theft?   Assuming *mens rea*, it is theft. A hire-purchaser is a hirer, a bailee; he does not become the owner till he makes all the payments that are due. In the usual contract of hire-purchase of a car, the car dealer sells the car to the hire-purchase company for cash, and the finance company lets the car to the hire-purchaser. This is done by documents signed by the hire-purchaser in the car dealer's office. So the answer is that if the hire-purchaser knows the law, and if he delivers the article to the person to whom he has wrongfully sold it, he is guilty of theft from the finance company, the owner of the car.

And if he does not deliver it?   If the bailee has contracted to sell the bailed   **29–094**
article and did not intend to deliver it, but was only defrauding the third party and intended to restore the article to its owner, he could not be guilty of theft because he would not intend to deprive the owner permanently.[282] But if he was to receive payment from the third party only upon delivering the article, it would be easy to

---

[282] The bailee cannot be said to intend to "treat the thing as his own to dispose of regardless of the [owner's] rights within the first limb of section 6 (1) of the *Theft Act*, because he does not actually dispose of the article (he does not pass either ownership or even possession of it), and he does not

prove the intent to deprive. In that case, he would be guilty of theft on the authority of *R. v. Pitham*[283] (if "authority" is not too strong a word to use for a case that is so unsatisfactory in its reasoning).[284] Even if *R. v. Pitham* is held to be wrong, the bailee in your hypothetical might perhaps be convicted of theft by reason of the second part of section 3(1); he has "come by" the article and has thereafter (it may be agreed) assumed the right to it by dealing with it as owner. However, one may still question whether a mere offer to sell, or even an actual sale[285] that is ineffective to pass title and is not accompanied by delivery, can properly be called "dealing" within the subsection. The bailee's act looks much more like an inchoate offence: an attempt to obtain money by fraudulent means, or (if the purchaser knows the facts) a conspiracy to defraud or to steal, or an attempt to steal. As was said before, a non-owner who offers the article for sale is not even guilty of a tort; he is not regarded as having converted the thing to his own use, because he has passed neither possession nor property.

29–095 **Can it be an appropriation for a possessor merely to retain an article intending not to return it?** Yes. The question can arise (1) in the case of a bailee, if he retains an article beyond the period of the bailment, or otherwise after his possession rights have come to an end, and (2) in the case of other persons who initially took possession in good faith, if they retain the article after coming to realize who the owner is.[286] The courts have taken the view that the intention of section 3(1) is to turn the wrongful "keeping as owner" into theft.[287] The statutory phrase does not settle the problem of duty. If a person consciously and by a positive act acquires possession of the property of another, and if his right to retain it comes to an end, it can be said that he is under a duty to return it, and that the *actus reus* of theft is committed when a reasonable time has elapsed for him to return it without his having done so. The question is more difficult if he did not acquire possession of the property of another consciously and by a positive act. For example, someone may send me through the post a valuable document to which I am not entitled and (when I open the package) know I am not entitled. If I put it on the mantelpiece and trouble myself no further, do I commit theft? Am I under a positive duty to bestir myself if I have done nothing to put myself under an obligation to do so? The authorities suggest that your keeping could constitute theft. What's more, it seems from *D.D.P. v. Gomez* that a

---

intend to dispose of it (*i.e.* sell, destroy or get rid of it); he intends only to pretend to dispose of it." If he maintains secure possession he does not even act recklessly: cf. *R. v. Fernandes* (1996) 1 Cr. App. R. 175 at 188 *per* Auld L.J.

[283] (1976) 65 Cr. App. R. 45.

[284] But there was a pre-*Act* case to the same effect for offers by bailees: *Rogers v. Arnott* [1960] 2 Q.B. 244.

[285] For a case involving an actual sale, see *Attorney-General of Hong Kong v. Nai-Keung* [1987] 1 W.L.R. 1339, where it was held that the defendant "had dishonestly sold his principal's property at an undervalue and exceeded his authority. He had thereby assumed the right of an owner in a way which amounted to an appropriation under the English and Hong Kong legislation."

[286] *D.D.P. v. Gomez* [1993] A.C. 442 at 475. Cf. *Walters v. Lunt* (1951) 35 Cr. App. R. 94.

[287] *Scholefield v. Greater Manchester Police* (2000) CO/2386/1999 (Q.B.D. (Divisional Court)). See also, *Broom v. Crowther*, (1984) 148 J.P. 592, where D was convicted because he kept the goods (which he already suspected were stolen) "[f]or a period of time after he had discovered that they were stolen." Goff L.J. held that D's actions made it clear that he was "keeping them as owner."

bailee commits theft simply by forming a dishonest intent, even when he has not begun to act outside the terms of the bailment.

One can exercise the right of an owner many times in succession with the same stolen object. Does one steal it every time? The general answer is no. The *Act* assumes that appropriation is one event—consider, for example, section 3(1), which makes keeping or dealing with a thing as owner a theftous appropriation only if the possessor has not already stolen the thing.[288] In common sense a thief does not steal the thing afresh every time he uses it; and the only firm rule, therefore, is that the first theftous appropriation is the last—for that particular thief. (Friends of his who borrow the thing can commit a new theft for themselves.) But a thief ought not to be able to use this rule purely as a technicality for his own advantage, arguing that he has been charged with the wrong act of appropriation—"no, I did not steal it on Tuesday I stole it on Monday." It would seem reasonable to say that the precise act of appropriation is an immaterial averment (like ownership), where nothing turns on it. Sometimes, for example, it is doubtful whether a person steals (1) by dishonesty coming into possession of property or (2) only later, by doing something wrong with the property;[289] on a charge of stealing by doing the wrong act in (2), it ought not generally to be a defence that the defendant had already stolen by obtaining the property.

29–096

When a purely technical point is raised on appropriation, the judge may think it wise to have the indictment amended; but this ought not to be essential except where the guilt of the defendant or someone else depends upon whether the theftous appropriation was one act or another. In the type of case last mentioned, where the time of appropriation is material to guilt, problems may arise. Readers will already have gathered the way in which appellate courts are likely to deal with them. They will define appropriation in the particular case in such a way as to affirm the conviction of a dishonest person. That is not a rule of law, but a proposition about how courts are likely to act in fact.

The precise time of a theft marks the dividing line between being an accessory to the theft and being a handler of stolen goods. To be an accessory to crime involves doing an act before the crime is completed; one cannot be an accessory to an act done afterwards. To be a handler of stolen goods, in contrast, one must handle them "otherwise than in the course of the stealing."[290] The object of this phrase is to prevent the actual thief and his helpers being convicted of handling by dealing with the goods that they have just stolen; so the phrase should rationally be read as meaning "after stealing." But what is likely to happen in practice may be illustrated by hypotheticals.

Case A. Suppose that burglars enter an unoccupied house and load its valuable contents into a van. They then call up an associate (who has not hitherto been in

29–097

---

[288] Even if successive acts closely related (a continuous act) in time can each be regarded as an appropriation, it is clear on principle that there should not be multiple convictions: see *R. v. Atakpu* [1994] Q.B. 69 at 79. An appropriation might also be achieved by using an innocent agent. See *R. v. Stringer* [1992] 94 Cr. App. R. 13.

[289] See *R. v. Fritschy* [1985] Crim. L.R. 745; *R. v. Hircock* (1978) 67 Cr. App. R. 278.

[290] Section 22(1) of the *Theft Act 1968*; see 33.1.

the plot) and ask him to drive the van to a hide-out and store the loot. This is done. If the associate is convicted of handling, an appellate court is likely to uphold the conviction, rightly, on the ground that the appropriation was completed before he arrived, so that his act was done otherwise than in the course of stealing—even though the act was commenced at the scene of the theft and shortly after the theft.[291]

Case B. The same facts as before, but the associate is convicted as an accessory to the theft. The appellate court is again likely to affirm the conviction, this time on the ground that the appropriation was not completed at the time of the defendant's intervention.[292]

Case A. In order to defend itself against a charge of inconsistency, the court may fudge the issue by saying that "the question of whether, when and by whom there has been an appropriation of property has always to be determined by the jury having regard to the circumstances of the case."[293]

The question of the time of appropriation is also important on a charge of robbery, which requires force or threats to be used "immediately before or at the time of" stealing.[294] These words in the statute were intended to exempt from a charge of robbery a thief who used force after the theft, even if he used it immediately afterwards. But if a thief uses force on his victim immediately after the theft, perhaps to prevent him from raising the alarm, and if he is convicted of robbery, the Court of Appeal will affirm the conviction on the ground that the time of stealing has certain spread: *R. v. Hale*.[295] This decision can then be cited in other cases[296] as a useful precedent for saying that theft continues after the act of appropriation had been completed; and the puzzlement of the commentators as to what is meant by an appropriation will be deepened.

29.18.   APPROPRIATION AND ILLEGALITY

29–098   The preceding discussion of the law of theft left to one side some of its grittiest complexities. These concern the common area covered by theft and obtaining by fraud, and the differences between fraudulent and non-fraudulent acquisitions. They also bear on the fundamental question whether the act of theft need be one that is illegal rather than merely criminal under the *Theft Act*.[297] In this section we shall be concerned with two main types of case. (1) Where D obtains ownership

---

[291] *R. v. Pitham, Hehl* (1976) 65 Cr. App. R. 45.
[292] Cf. the *dictum* in *R. v. Hale* (1979) 68 Cr. App. R. 415 quoted with approval in *R. v. Gregory* (1983) 77 Cr. App. R. 41.
[293] *R. v. Gregory* (1983) 77 Cr. App. R. 41 at 46 quoted with approval in *R. v. Atakpu* [1994] Q.B. 69 at 78.
[294] Section 8(1) of the *Theft Act 1968*.
[295] (1979) 68 Cr. App. R. 415.
[296] As it was in *R. v. Smartt* [2004] EWCA Crim. 2072 at para. 24; and in *R. v. Atakpu* [1994] Q.B. 69 at 78.
[297] For an earlier discussion see Glanville Williams, "Theft, Consent and Illegality," [1977] Crim. L.R. 127; Glanville Williams, "Theft, Consent and Illegality: Some Problems," [1977] Crim. L.R. 327.

in the goods before his dishonest act of appropriation. (2) Where D obtains ownership contemporaneously with the appropriation. In (1) D generally ought not be guilty of theft; in (2) he can be.

29.19.   WHERE D OBTAINS OWNERSHIP BEFORE THE APPROPRIATION

To state more exactly the rule already propounded above, there can be no act of theft under the general provision in section 1(1) of the *Theft Act 1968*[298] by a person who has obtained property (ownership) before the alleged act of appropriation. This follows from the rule that the theft must be of "property belonging to another." Suppose that V sells an antique piece to D, and immediately afterwards finds that he made a great mistake because it was worth vastly more than he thought. He goes at once to D and tells him of the mistake, but D refuses to give the thing back. D is not dishonest because he is entitled to keep his bargain; but in any case the jury are not allowed to convict him of theft merely because they think (rightly or wrongly) that a decent person would have given the thing back. It now belongs to D, so he cannot steal it.

29–099

It is the same when D obtains only a voidable title. A voidable title is one that can be avoided at the option of the other party, but still it is title (ownership, property) until the former owner's option to avoid is exercised. D buys a valuable piece of machinery from V, V allowing her credit on D's assurance that she has a Government contract under which she is about to receive a large advance, so that she will be able to settle the account within a month. D spoke in good faith, but it transpires that she was misinformed and the Government contract has not been completed. The contract between V and D for the sale of the machinery is voidable by V on account of D's innocent misrepresentation, but it is not void for mistake. Consequently, a voidable title passes to D under the contract, and D cannot steal the article under the general provision in section 1(1), in failing to restore it after she discovers the truth and before V has avoided the contract, even if she is regarded as acting dishonestly, because the machinery is hers. The civil law no longer regards it as belonging to V, even though V can get it back if he validly avoids the contract.

When a person has sold goods under a voidable contract and validly avoids the contract, the property revests in him. Thus, if the buyer thereafter dishonestly appropriates the goods (as by selling them knowing that the contract has been avoided, and that he ought to give the goods back), his act can be theft. Whereas a voidable title can pass under a voidable contract, no title at all passes under a void contract. The law of contract governs the question when there is only an apparent contract which is void, and when there is a true but voidable contract; this cannot be studied in detail here.

29.20.   OBTAINING OWNERSHIP BY FRAUD, THREATS OR UNDUE INFLUENCE

"They look upon fraud as a greater crime than theft, and therefore seldom fail to punish it with death: for, they allege, that care and vigilance, with a very common understanding, may preserve a man's goods from thieves; but honestly hath no fence against superior cunning; and

---

[298] That is to say, apart from sections 5(3) and 5(4) of the *Theft Act 1968*.

since it is necessary that there should be a perpetual intercourse of buying and selling, and dealing upon credit; where fraud is permitted and connived at, or hath no law to punish it, the honest dealer is always undone, and the knave gets the advantage."[299]

29–100   Swift conceived of theft as a crime of stealth or force. But the position in his day was that larceny was a graver crime than obtaining by false pretences; so the judges, always ready to tighten the law, created a certain overlap between the two crimes, with the result that a fraud case (obtaining by false pretences[300]) could sometimes be punished as larceny. This overlap is, perhaps unfortunately, continued and even extended by the *Theft Act 1968*. A person who acquires a thing by fraud steals it, provided that the other requirements of theft are satisfied, even though he obtains a voidable title to the thing. So much, at least, has been decided by the House of Lords in *Lawrence*[301] and *D.D.P. v. Gomez*.[302] In *R. v. Hinks*,[303] the Lords went even further by holding that it would be theft to accept a valid gift (indefeasible title), if the jury decide that D did something dishonest to influence V to make the gift.

In *Lawrence* an Italian student (Occhi by name) who had just arrived at Victoria station asked Lawrence, a taxi-driver, to take him to the Italian Centre. Lawrence said that the journey was very expensive. In fact the correct fare was about 10*s*. 6*d*. The student got into the taxi and proffered £1; Lawrence accepted this but then took from the student's open purse a further £6, the student making no protest. Lawrence was convicted of theft of "the approximate sum of £6," and this was affirmed on appeal by the Court of Appeal and House of Lords.

Two opinions are possible as to the overlap between theft and fraud offences and as to the effect of the decision in *Lawrence* in relation to that overlap. The opinion agrees that theft and obtaining by fraudulent[304] means are committed if a person dishonestly obtains possession (but not otherwise ownership) of money or some article by fraud, intending to keep it. Either offence can be charged,[305] or both offences can be charged and a conviction obtained of one of them.[306] It may be interjected here that even when the two offences overlap in this way, it is highly desirable as a matter of practice that prosecuting counsel should charge under the *Fraud Act 2006* rather than for theft. For one thing, the fraud charge gives the defendant better information of what is alleged against him, since the particulars will state the alleged fraudulent activity (which they will not do on a charge of theft). Moreover, charging fraud enables the judge to give a crisper direction to the jury as to the elements that they are to look for. The mysteries of appropriation are removed from the case.

---

[299] Jonathan Swift, *The Adventures of Captain Gulliver*, (London: Osborne & Griffin, 1785) at 50.
[300] The first false pretences offence was enacted in 1757. See 30 Geo. II, c. 24 §1 (1757).
[301] [1971] A.C. 626.
[302] *D.P.P. v. Gomez* [1993] A.C. 442.
[303] *R. v. Hinks* [2001] 2 A.C. 241.
[304] As seemed to be the case in *R. v. Hinks* [2001] 2 A.C. 241, but in that case the Lords thought that D's unconscionable acquisitive acts (arguably acts of undue influence), if relevant at all, would only establish dishonesty—*i.e.* would be relevant to *mens rea*, but not to establish the *actus reus*.
[305] That is, either an appropriate offence under the *Fraud Act 2006* or theft under the *Theft Act 1968*.
[306] If both theft and fraud are charged, the conviction should be of one only. Cf. the erroneous decision in *R. v. Hircock* (1978) 67 Cr. App. R. 278.

The difference of opinion arises if a cheat obtains ownership by fraud. If a cheat deceives another into (say) selling her an article, the victim intending to pass the ownership in the thing, the cheat gets title, even though the fraud means that it is only a voidable title. He can be charged with fraud, but according to one opinion (which may be called the restricted theft opinion) not theft. He is not guilty of theft because he has not got ownership. According to the other opinion (the unrestricted theft opinion) the prosecution once more have the option of charging him with theft, even though he has not got ownership. It will be seen that the unrestricted theory of theft makes theft completely cover the ground of fraud (except in certain minor respects, the chief being that theft does not apply to land).

29–101

Of the two opinions, the restricted theft opinion (which is advanced by Professor J. C. Smith)[307] is far preferable in as far as doctrinal clarity is concerned,[308] but the opinion is difficult (I think impossible) to derive from the words of the *Theft Act*. It was, therefore, rejected by the House of Lords in *Lawrence v. Commissioner of Police of the Metropolis* and again in *D.D.P. v. Gomez.*[309] The argument for the defence was that since Lawrence had obtained the ownership of the student's money (whether ownership unalloyed or voidable for fraud), the money did not "belong to another;" it belonged to Lawrence, so he could not steal it. Viscount Dilhorne, speaking for the Appellate Committee, produced a powerful reply:

> "The [former] offence of obtaining property by deception created by section 15 of the *Theft Act* also contained the words 'belonging to another'. 'A person who by any deception dishonestly obtains property belonging to another, with the intention of permanently depriving the other of it' commits that offence. 'Belonging to another' in section 1(1) and in section 15(1) in my view signifies no more than that, at the time of the appropriation or the obtaining, the property belonged to another … The short answer to this contention on behalf of the appellant is that the money in the wallet which he appropriated belonged to another, Mr. Occhi."

This is a convincing argument so far as it goes, but Smith sidesteps it by making a different point. He says that the question depends not on the words quoted by Viscount Dilhorne but upon the meaning of appropriation. In Smith's opinion, one does not appropriate another person's property if one gets the entire proprietary interest in the thing.

But there is no greater appropriation of property of another than getting the entire proprietary interest in it. If merely taking possession of another person's property is an appropriation (as you say everyone agrees), then getting both possession and ownership is *a fortiori* an appropriation. Similarly, when a person *obtains* a voidable title to another's property, he is only able to do so because the property belonged to another at the point in time when the fraudster obtained possession and (voidable) title. I think Smith would answer that the very meaning of appropriation is that one takes to oneself a thing that not only belongs to another at the moment of taking but

29–102

---

[307] See the debate between Professor Glanville Williams, "Theft and Voidable Title," [1981] Crim. L.R. 666 and J. C. Smith [1981] Crim. L.R. 679.

[308] See George P. Fletcher, *Rethinking Criminal Law*, (Boston: Little, Brown, 1978) at 29.

[309] Cf. the dissenting judgment of Lord Lowry in *D.P.P. v. Gomez* [1993] A.C. 442.

continues to belong to another. The moment that thing ceases to belong to another, and becomes the property of the taker, the taker can no longer appropriate it, because thereafter he holds it as owner. So Smith says. The old law of larceny made a distinction between cases where fraud was used to acquire control or possession and those cases where fraud was used to obtain both possession and title. The former offence of larceny by trick covered cases similar to *R. v. Atakpu*,[310] where the defendants used fraud (in that case fake passports and documents) to obtain possession (not title) of the hire cars, because the owner did not intend to transfer title. *D.P.P. v. Gomez* would have fallen into the former obtaining by false pretences category, on the basis that the owner intended to pass title and did in fact pass a voidable title.

Nonetheless, there was clearly an appropriation in *D.D.P. v. Gomez*—the defendant's unilateral acts allowed him and his confederates to gain possession, control and voidable title of the electrical goods. The appropriation was concurrent with the transfer of voidable title. The title was defective because it was granted on the false belief that valuable consideration was being provided in return for the goods. It is arguable that in such cases the seller does *not* intend title to pass until the cheque is cleared, but it would make no difference since the appropriation is concurrent with the passing of title in such cases.[311] When an owner has been tricked into handing over goods for a dodgy cheque, he might allow D to take those goods, but "[h]e had not in truth consented to D becoming owner without giving a valid draft drawn by the building society [or bank] for the price."[312] And this constitutes an appropriation pursuant to section 1(1) of the *Theft Act*.[313] Since the title is defective the victim can reclaim his property from D, but will not be able to reclaim the property if a third party has paid for it in good faith.[314]

29–103   **But in discussing appropriation you expressed the opinion that it is an appropriation to pass the victim's title to a third party without the victim's authority, and you cited the analogy of conversion in the law of tort. If so, it must be an appropriation to get the victim's title yourself. Smith's argument if it were valid, would mean that there is no appropriation in either case.** Yes. We have not yet finished this discussion, but must now return to examine the facts of *R. v. Lawrence* more closely. The transaction between Lawrence and the student needs legal analysis. Two interpretations are possible.

---

[310] [1993] 3 W.L.R. 812. See also *King v. Pear* (1779) 168 E.R. 208, where the rental agreement made it clear that title in the horse was not to pass with possession. See also *R. v. Thistle* (1849) 3 Cox C.C. 573; *Tunnard's Case* (1729) 2 East P.C. 687.

[311] Cf. *Hufsteler v. State*, 63 So. 2d 730 (1953), where it was held that driving off without paying for petrol was larceny by trick because the owner did not *intend title* to the petrol to pass until payment was made. See also *English v. State*, 80 Fla. 70 (1920). Cf. *People v. Norman*, 85 N.Y. 2d 609 (1995); *Braswell v. State*, 389 P. 2d 998 (1964).

[312] *Dobson v. General Accident Fire and Life Assurance Corporation Plc*. [1990] 1 Q.B. 274 at 289 *per* Bingham L.J.

[313] *Dobson v. General Accident Fire and Life Assurance Corporation Plc*. [1990] 1 Q.B. 274 at 289 *per* Bingham L.J. See also *D.P.P. v. Gomez* [1993] A.C. 442.

[314] *R. v. Wheeler* (1990) 92 Cr. App. R. 279; *R. v. Walker* [1984] Crim. L.R. 112; *R. v. Bloxham* [1983] 1 A.C. 109; *Shogun Finance v. Hudson* [2003] UKHL 62. Cf. section 24A of the *Theft Act 1968* with respect to a *bona fide* purchaser who dishonestly retains a wrongful credit.

The first is that it was a straight case of obtaining by deception (now an inchoate offence under the *Fraud Act 2006*), the courts holding that Lawrence could be convicted of theft instead of the former deception offence. The fraud was clear. Lawrence told a lie in saying that the journey was very far when he knew it was not. He also impliedly represented that the fare he was demanding and taking was the tariff fare for the journey. Throughout the Western world taxi fares in towns are governed by law, or otherwise by fixed scales of charges; they are not customarily matters of free bargaining on each occasion. (In London they are governed by law.) On the opinion now stated, the property in the notes passed to Lawrence when he took them, since the student was willing that it should pass (believing that this money represented the correct fare). Lawrence, however, got only voidable title to the money because of his fraud. He was convicted of theft, though he could have been convicted of obtaining by deception (and under the present law he would be convictable for fraud); and this implies acceptance of the unrestricted theft theory, according to which the two offences are concurrent in this respect. The interpretation is supported by the fact that Viscount Dilhorne thought it important to stress that the new definition of theft, unlike the old, does not require the act of theft to be committed without the owner's consent.

The alternative interpretation on the facts would deny that the actual decision in *R. v. Lawrence* supports the unrestricted theft theory. On this view, the student did not give any consent whatever to the taking of the excess fare, and therefore did not give Lawrence any title to the excess—not even a voidable one. It follows that there is nothing remarkable in the fact that Lawrence was convicted of theft. This interpretation is supported (1) by the statement in the Lords' opinion that it had not been established that the defrauded student consented to the taxi driver acquiring his money, and (2) by the doubt expressed in the opinion whether the property in the money had passed to Lawrence.

I cannot understand the doubt. The student allowed Lawrence to help   **29–104**
himself from his open purse, and then accepted the ride in the cab. So he
must have consented, and the property in his money must have
passed.   Smith thinks that a different conclusion can be reached, and he argues the point this way. The student impliedly authorized Lawrence to help himself from the purse to the extent of the proper fare, but no further. When Lawrence picked out (and appropriated) £6, he committed theft, because that was more than the proper fare (he had already more than received the proper fare when he was given the £1). It is true that the student then consented to Lawrence's retaining the money, but at that stage theft had already been committed. So the theft was a simple taking of money without consent.

I do not think Lawrence did appropriate the notes when he picked them out. He took them out provisionally, by way of demonstrating the amount he wanted. If the student had objected Lawrence would have given them back, and would have either gone off or done some haggling. Lawrence did not regard the matter as finalized, and did not appropriate the notes, until the student accepted the situation and allowed Lawrence to drive him. It was then that the theftous appropriation took place, and it took place with the student's implied consent, even though the consent was given under a mistake as to what the proper fare was. The ownership in the money passed to Lawrence, and it was at the same time theft.

Your analysis seems to me to be correct, but the important subject of enquiry is what the House of Lords held. For some reason their Lordships were not convinced that the student had consented to the £6 being taken, but they failed to explain the ground of their doubt. They cannot possibly have supposed that Lawrence took the money like a pickpocket or robber, so Smith's theory (legally defective though I think it is) seems to be the only possible explanation of what was in their minds. However, in *D.D.P. v. Gomez*[315] there was clearly consent. The victim knew exactly what he was handing over (valuable electrical) goods but was deceived into believing the cheques that were used for payment were valid. It is one thing to say: "I would not have consented to D taking the goods if I had known that the cheques were dodgy," and it is something rather different to say: "I did not consent to D taking the goods—he grabbed them and did a runner."

29–105   **Well, then, their Lordships in *Lawrence* were not convinced that property passed; but they held that even if it did pass Lawrence could be convicted of theft, because, since the property did not belong to him when he appropriated it, he appropriated the property of another. That is what they said, after all. So the decision still remains authority for the wider view of theft, and such a reading is supported by the majority opinion of the House of Lords in *D.P.P. v. Gomez*.**   I will now produce my own nostrum. The position would be saved if the courts could be induced to read into section 1(1) of the *Theft Act 1968* an implied requirement of unlawfulness. Appropriating a person's property without his consent is unlawful; so is appropriating it with consent obtained (and "vitiated") by fraud, duress[316] (or undue influence).[317] The actual design in *Gomez* and *Lawrence* is therefore correct. But I would suggest that some unlawfulness must be shown; and that is why there should be no conviction of theft in the hypothetical about nondisclosure. The money is not obtained unlawfully. This suggestion is not inconsistent with the decision in *Gomez* or *Lawrence*, because the Lords in those cases must have been convinced that the taking was either without V's consent or with consent induced by fraud, and either way it was unlawful.

By "unlawful" I mean unlawful by the civil law as a matter of property rights. The fact that the appropriation may amount to some minor criminal offence should not make it theft. Suppose that a London cab driver says to a prospective passenger: "Forget about fare tariffs. I am not going to take you unless you pay me £6." The passenger thereupon consents and pays up. Well, it is a dirty night, growing late, and no other cab is available. There is no deception, but the jury might hold it was dishonest of the cab driver to take advantage of the passenger's weak bargaining position; so the cabby might be convicted of theft on a wide

---

[315] [1991] 1 W.L.R. 1334.

[316] In *Louth v. Diprose* (1991) 175 C.L.R. 621, the wrongdoer threatened suicide in order to convince a solicitor who was besotted with her to convey a house to her.

[317] Borderline cases of undue influence should be left to the courts of equity to deal with. See *Allcard v. Skinner* (1887) L.R. 36; *Pesticcio v. Huet* [2004] W.T.L.R. 699.

view of the law. But it would be wrong to make a conviction of theft depend on such considerations; and the fact that the excessive fare is in breach of the cab fare tariff should not be regarded as turning the cabby's shabby conduct into the much more serious offence of theft.

Your suggestion may not be inconsistent with *Lawrence* and *D.D.P. v. Gomez*,   29–106
but it is with section 1(1), which does not require unlawfulness. There are certain ways in which I think that the requirement can be implied, even though section 1(1) does not express it. We shall return to this in due course. Consider the £1 note that the student handed to Lawrence at the start of the transaction. Presumably the student was not certain whether he might obtain change from it or not, but he intended to pass the ownership in the £1 to Lawrence, subject to the question of change.

Does it not follow that the £1 note became the property of Lawrence, so that   29–107
he could not steal it? The student intended to receive change if any was due, and change was due. It is not unreasonable to construe his intention to pass the property as subject to an implied condition, which condition was not fulfilled, so that the property did not pass. It is like the newsvendor who (in the old days when people could be trusted) left a pile of newspapers and a tin to receive the money. He impliedly consented to the taking of a newspaper if, but only if, the proper sum was placed in the tin. (Similarly, the manager in *D.P.P. v. Gomez* consented to the electrical goods being released into the custody of the customers, but only on the condition that they had been paid for.) The student consented to Lawrence keeping the note if, but only if, the proper change was given. There were several decisions under the old law of larceny holding that a fraudster who did not give the expected change was guilty of larceny of the note. So Lawrence could have been properly convicted of theft of the part of the value of the £1 note representing the change that he ought to have given.

Suppose property is obtained not by fraud but by threats? There is no doubt   29–108
that property obtained by duress is theft, and two reasons may be advanced, quite apart from the over-wide doctrine of *Gomez*. The first is that duress may totally nullify an apparent consent, and prevent property from passing, not merely make it voidable. Secondly, it is necessary to hold that an appropriation under duress is theft, in order to make sense of the offence of robbery.

I really like your unlawfulness requirement, because it allows *Lawrence* to be   29–109
reconciled with Lord Roskill's consent requirement as set out in *R. v. Morris*.
But in *R. v. Hinks*[318] a woman conned a vulnerable man for £60,000; and
according to the House of Lords did so without violating the civil law. She
was apparently sent to jail for obtaining a valid gift in civil law. And my
reading of the facts convinces me that she was a crook. Well, the facts of that case, I recall, were that Mrs. Hinks, a 38-year-old woman, befriended a fellow of low intelligence (who did not fully understand his finances) and convinced him to give her most of his savings. There was no apparent deception involved as the

---

[318] [2001] 2 A.C. 241.

victim consensually withdrew his cash and gave it to D, but the victim (Mr. Dolphin) was somewhat lacking in capacity and therefore did not understand that he was giving her *all* is money. Since D knew that V was not very bright and did not fully understand the nature of the gifts, it was dishonest of her to take them.

The House of Lords held that:[319] "'appropriation' ... was a neutral word which comprehended any assumption by a person of the owner's rights, and ... that the acquisition of an indefeasible title to property from a person who no longer retained any proprietary interest or any right to resume or recover any proprietary interest in the property was capable of amounting to 'appropriation' of that property." Undue influence would render such a gift voidable in equity, but it would not be theft to passively accept a gift from a fool knowing that he would not make such a gift if he had more information or was smarter! But if D actively pursues a gift and uses deceptive acquisitive techniques such as lies and false representations to cause the donor to make a gift in her favour, then her undue influence would involve fraud and V's consent may be vitiated. It is arguable that Hinks did not obtain an indefeasible title because she used undue influence to obtain the gift. Did her undue influence in fact vitiate V's consent? It would have to be shown that the gift was not given with true consent. This might be the case if it could be proved that V did not understand what he was doing, because he had no idea that he was giving away all is liquid assets.

29–110 **You told me before that the unlawfulness requirement specifies only a necessary, and not a sufficient condition, for establishing theft. Clearly, not every unlawful acquisition of another's property is theft.** Fraud[320] and duress clearly annuls V's consent, but so might undue influence when it involves pressure, influence and fraud. A lot would depend on the facts of the case. In *R. v. Hinks* the Lords apparently overlooked the obvious civil law unlawfulness of Hinks's acquisition. Hinks did not merely receive an overly generous gift; she took active steps to get V to make the gift. If Dolphin had decided that Hinks was a good friend and that he wanted to give her most of his assets, then the gift would be valid so long as he made the gift "only after free and fully informed thought about it." Dolphin gave away most of his money without understanding the nature of his financial situation and future needs and without receiving independent advice. The gift would have been invalid in civil law if that issue had been considered, as Hinks used a relationship of trust to influence Dolphin to make the gifts; and Dolphin was not free to consider the real implications of what he was doing. One cannot consent to what he does not understand! In most of these undue influence cases there will be dishonesty on the part of the donee.

29–111 **But is dishonesty enough?** No. It is not theft to dishonestly receive generous gifts if you have done nothing to influence the donor. If Hinks had done nothing to pressure Dolphin to give away his money, then her actions could not be said to have involved fraud or duress. One does not become a fraudster by passively

---

[319] *R. v. Hinks* [2001] 2 A.C. 241. Cf. *R. v. Cording* [1983] Crim. L.R. 175.

[320] It annuls but does not vitiate consent. In *Shogun Finance Ltd. v. Hudson* [2004] 1 A.C. 919 at 931 Lord Nicholls said, "[f]raud does not 'vitiate' consent. Professor Glanville Williams rightly said that the maxim 'fraud vitiates consent' is thoroughly misleading:" citing Glanville Williams, "Mistake As To Party in the Law of Contract" (1945) 23 *Canadian Bar Review* 271 at 291-292.

accepting a generous gift from a fool. Nor is it duress to passively accept such a gift. Nonetheless, passively accepting a gift from a vulnerable person of whom you have some influence might be the business of the civil courts.[321] In exceptional circumstances it might also be caught by section 5(4) of the *Theft Act*. An alternative might have been to say, "Mrs Hinks this money was given to you by mistake, you now have an obligation to return it or face a theft charge under section 5(4)." But Hinks took active steps—she did not sit back passively and accept a valid gift. Instead, the facts suggest that she went after Dolphin's money and actively influenced him to make the gifts. Dolphin's consent was defective and Hinks's did not get a valid title. Hinks committed theft in accordance with the unlawfulness requirement presented above. If the civil courts decided there was no civil law unlawfulness on the facts of *R. v. Hinks*, then it would be impossible to describe her conduct has theftous. One who does not engage in fraud, duress or undue influence and who obtains an indefeasible title to the gift cannot be a thief. The gift is valid as *ex post facto* no unlawfulness emerges to upset it. Lord Hobhouse in his dissenting opinion notes:[322]

> "It is unlikely that a charge of theft will be brought where there is not clear evidence of at least some conduct of the defendant which includes an element of fraud or overt dishonesty or some undue influence or knowledge of the deficient capacity of the alleged donor. This was the basis upon which the prosecution of the appellant was originally brought in the present case. On this basis there is no difficulty in explaining to the jury the relevant parts of section 5 and section 2(1) and the effect of the phrase 'assumption of the rights of an owner'. Where the basis is less specific and the possibility is that there may have been a valid gift of the relevant article or money to the defendant, the analysis of the prosecution case will break down under sections 2 and 5 as well as section 3 and it will not suffice simply to invite the jury to convict on the basis of their disapprobation of the defendant's conduct and their attribution to him of the knowledge that he must have known that they and other ordinary and decent persons would think it dishonest. Theft is a crime of dishonesty but dishonesty is not the only element in the commission of the crime."

If a 60-year-old partner in a law firm falls for a beautiful 21-year-old trainee lawyer and gives her gifts of an outrageously generous nature including a Chelsea apartment, would it be theft for her to accept the gifts? Unlike Dolphin, we could hardly claim the partner did not understand the nature of his finances or the magnitude of the gifts.[323] Let us imagine that the intern knows that the partner is

---

[321] The equitable doctrine of "undue influence" allows gifts to be invalidated in circumstances where there is a "relationship of trust and confidence" between donor and donee and the gift is made without "full, free and informed thought by the donor." See *Hammond v. Osborn* [2002] W.T.L.R. 1125, where the gift involved £297,005 which was more than 90 *per cent.* of V's liquid assets. Coupled with this, V was elderly and in poor health and had not received independent advice about the nature of the gift or the tax implications of giving way such a sum. See also *Goldsworthy v. Brickell* [1987] 1 All E.R. 853 where it was held that undue influence would be raised where "the gift or transaction was so large or the transaction *so improvident* that it could not be accounted for on the ground of friendship, relationship, charity, or other motives on which ordinary people acted, and if the person effecting it had reposed in the other such a degree of trust and confidence as to place the other in a position to influence him into effecting it."

[322] *R. v. Hinks* [2001] 2 A.C. 241 at 276.

[323] See the Australian case, *Louth v. Diprose* (1991) 175 C.L.R. 621, where a lawyer who was besotted with a woman he wanted to marry was able to establish undue influence to annul a transfer of real property. This case was somewhat borderline, because there comes a point in time when a fool has to bear the consequences of his actions.

totally besotted with her and that he wants to marry her, but decides not to disclose that she has no intention of ever marrying him. Instead, she is nice to him because she knows it might lead to more gifts. Surely this type of passive dishonestly does not make the trainee a thief? The trainee has not actively pursued the gifts nor even asked for them. Under the current law of theft the jury will have the discretion to decide whether this is theft.

29.21.　THE ARGUMENTS FOR A REQUIREMENT OF UNLAWFULNESS

29–112　**I do not understand why you are going to all this trouble to rationalize Hinks's conviction, she was clearly a rouge and the majority of the Lords have told you that you need only point to her dishonesty. The Lords have made it clear that Dolphin's consent and the supposed lawfulness of the gift in civil law were irrelevant.**　The advantage of the unlawfulness requirement is that it allows *Lawrence, D.D.P. v. Gomez* and *R. v. Hinks* to be reconciled with *R. v. Morris*.[324] These cases might be interpreted as unique cases (partly due to the fact that they were wrongly charged as theft cases) where the victims' consent was vitiated by fraud, duress and undue influence. From the *ex ante* perspective there was consent, but from the *ex post* perspective there was no consent. If so, the general proposition that appropriations are non-consensual usurpations of an owner's property rights could still apply.[325]

D.P.P. v. Gomez and *R. v. Hinks* have extended the law so that appropriation covers any dealing (whether lawful, consensual or otherwise) with property belonging to another. An alarming ramification of these decisions is that a person who interferes with another's property with an intent to permanently deprive him of it may be accounted guilty of theft without the necessity for proof of any other element. This could mean that a person who obtains a perfectly valid title to property can be guilty of theft of it by reason of some dishonesty in the transaction that gives him the title; so the rule would give the prospect of a chasm between the civil law (which would regard the contract and resulting title as valid and enforceable) and the criminal law (which would regard the transaction as tainted with criminality).

We have seen that this situation has already materialized when a person commits an appropriation in the extended sense of section 3(1) of the *Act*, "any assumption of the rights of an owner." A customer in a supermarket takes down an article from the shelf. The article remains the property of the supermarket, and the act done in relation to it is lawful (in the civil law) because the owner consents to it; moreover, the doer does not intend the act to deprive the owner immediately; yet it is regarded as a theftous appropriation. This is thoroughly anomalous, and the courts have gone the wrong way on this point. When the

---

[324]　See too *R. v. Baruday* [1984] V.R. 685.

[325]　In other areas of the criminal law, consent is negated when it is given by mistake or because D deceived V into consenting to something different from what V thought he was consenting to. If V consents to a medical procedure but in fact is used for the doctor's sexual gratification there is no consent for the latter. Likewise, if V consents to having sexual intercourse with her boyfriend but is raped by a stranger posing as her boyfriend her consent is negated by the rapist's deceptive act. See *R. v. Cort* [2004] Q.B. 388; *R. v. Green* [2002] EWCA Crim. 1501; *R. v. Devonald* [2008] EWCA Crim. 527; *R. v. Jheeta* (2008) 1 W.L.R. 2582; *R. v. Elbekkay* [2004] Crim. L.R. 163.

C.L.R.C. very unwisely voted to omit from section 1(1) of the *Act* both a requirement of unlawfulness and a requirement of absence of owner's consent, I do not think it contemplated that, as a result, the courts would use the flabby notion of dishonesty as a substitute for firm rules on the definition of theft.

The further distressing possibility now to be considered is that the courts may declare an act to be an appropriation although it not only is lawful but actually transfers title to the defendant—either a fully valid title or a voidable one. To make dishonesty almost the sole requirement for theft would put weight upon the notion of dishonesty that it was not meant to bear. The reference to dishonesty was intended as a restriction upon liability for what might *prima facie* look like theft. The C.L.R.C. proposed it as better conveying the meaning of the previous phrase "without a claim of right." Dishonesty was not thought of as the sole element saving people from conviction of theft in ordinary transactions like buying a bunch of bananas. To create an offence in which the *actus reus* is virtually nothing more than a dishonest act would offend against the principle of due notice of criminal prohibition (fair warning); it is too vague to be an adequate guide to conduct. As a restriction on liability for an act that is *ex facie* wrong the notion of dishonesty may be acceptable (though even there we have perceived trouble with it); but it is inadequate as a means of describing the forbidden act. **29–113**

Problems are unlikely to arise on a sale of bananas, but they might on the sale of an *objet d'art*.

Suppose that D buys an old sketch in an antique shop, for which he pays £5. He has made a special study of Leonardo, and knows that the sketch is his work; he also knows that it is worth tens of thousands of pounds. The dealer, of course, doesn't. D goes off proudly with the sketch.

It is inconceivable that on a charge of theft the jury would be left to decide whether they thought D was honest or not. No doubt they would find him honest, but they should not be left to make the decision. D is, in law, entitled to make a profit from his special knowledge. That is part of the fun of rummaging in antique shops and second-hand bookshops. D's contract to buy the sketch was valid, and D obtained a fully valid title. If the dealer refused to deliver the sketch, D could sue him in order to get it. It would be preposterous if on receipt of it D could be convicted of theft. And it would be almost as preposterous if the civil courts, taking notice of the *Theft Act*, decided that the law of contract is now to be modified by importing into it a vague injunction against dishonesty. Similarly, if Dolphin had unexpectedly surprised Hinks by giving her £60,000 out of the blue as a gift to thank her for watering his pot plants, without any encouragement or influence from her (but, with her thinking, "What an old fool, I cannot believe my luck, he is giving me most of his liquid assets"); it might be immoral or even a bit dishonest for her to accept the gift in such circumstances, but it would not be theft. It would be wrong to allow the jury to use its discretion to evaluate the dishonesty of her acceptance of the gift; and to ultimately decide whether it should be labelled as theft. **29–114**

Although section 1(1) does not make the absence of the owner's consent an element of theft, it cannot be imagined that an act done with the owner's full authority is theft. Suppose that V asks D to sell a horse for him. D sells the horse in accordance with his instructions, secretly intending to pocket the proceeds. Is

D guilty of theft of the horse by selling it? (Assume that he is arrested before he even gets possession of the sale price.) Literally he assumes the rights of an owner (he assumes them because he has been allowed to exercise them), and he has a dishonest mind; but he cannot, surely, be guilty of theft when what he does is lawful.

There are several ways of amending the *Theft Act* to make the legal position clearer, but the best hope for judicial correction of the law would be that already suggested: to imply a requirement of civil unlawfulness for theft. One way in which this could be achieved would be for the courts to hold that dishonesty implies unlawfulness.[326] Something like this appears to have been in the mind of the Court of Appeal in *Lawrence*:

> "Of course, where there is true consent by the owner of property to the appropriation of it by another, a charge of theft under section 1(1) must fail. This is not, however, because the words 'without consent' have to be implied in the new definition of theft. It is simply because, if there is such true consent, the essential element of dishonesty is not established. If, however, the apparent consent is brought about by dishonesty, there is nothing in the words of section 1(1) ... to make such apparent consent relevant as providing a defence."[327]

This passage is not very helpful as worded, but it would become helpful if the word "dishonesty" in the last sentence were changed to "deception" or "fraud." Consent brought about by an act of fraud or duress is defective. The question for the jury in the Leonardo hypothetical should be not whether the buyer was guilty of dishonesty but whether he was guilty of fraud; and on the facts stated there would be no evidence of fraud for the jury. If there was no fraud, and if therefore there was "true consent" on the part of the seller, then it would follow, as the court said, that "the essential element of dishonesty is not established." The Court of Appeal's *dictum* creates a concept of what may be called objective honesty, depending not upon the defendant's state of mind but upon the legal position. If the defendant acquired property from a person who gave "true consent," this presumably means that he gets a valid title to the property. Acting lawfully under the civil law, and getting a valid title, he is objectively honest (*i.e.* no unlawfulness vitiates V's consent from the *ex post* perspective); and it makes no difference that he may not have realized that he got a valid title and may have been subjectively dishonest.

29–115   In *R. v. Hinks*, Lord Steyn said: "Given the jury's conclusions, one is entitled to observe that the appellant's conduct should constitute theft, the only available charge. The tension between the civil and the criminal law is therefore not in my view a factor which justifies a departure from the law as stated in *Lawrence* and *Gomez*." But a proper analysis shows that there was no tension between the civil and criminal law in any of these cases. All these cases involved defective consent and therefore were voidable transactions in civil law. Hence, all three cases can be reconciled with the unlawfulness requirement. If there is a conflict between the civil law and the criminal law then the criminal law should ride roughshod.

---

[326] "Whether unlawfulness is or is not necessarily to be equated with fraud or dishonesty, it is relevant to the question whether fraud or dishonesty is present." *The Queen v. Macleod* [2003] 214 C.L.R. 230 at 264 *per* Callinan J.

[327] *Lawrence v. Commissioner of Police of the Metropolis* [1970] 3 W.L.R. 1103 at 1107.

For example, section 5(3) and 5(4) are designed to deal with a particular injustice that would arise if the civil law were to be applied literally to certain problems, but other conflicts are likely to be rare.

29.22.   PROPERTY OBTAINED BY TRANSFEROR'S MISTAKE

We saw that since *D.P.P. v. Gomez* it must be accepted that the acquisition of a **29–116** voidable title to property by fraud can be theft; and the same rule must apply to acquisitions by duress and undue influence involving obvious fraud, assuming that this makes the title voidable (*a fortiori* if no title passes). So far as the authority of *D.P.P. v. Gomez* goes, there is no need to extend the law any further. A person who obtains a title that is voidable on other grounds should not on so doing be liable to be convicted of theft, since these other grounds are for the most part too divorced from the idea of dishonesty, and the civil law is too fluid, to make a rule of this kind desirable. For example, contracts and titles are voidable for innocent misrepresentation by the transferor. These vitiating factors sometimes make the contract void, in which case no title to property passes and the transferee can commit theft; but sometimes they only make the contract voidable. The desirable rule is that in the latter cases theft can only be committed (fraud, duress and undue influence aside) by the operation of section 5(4) of the *Act* (to be considered presently), or where an appropriation is made dishonestly after the contract has been avoided. Once the courts were prepared to take this position; but the indications are now the other way. The following discussion will concentrate on voidability for mistake.

Whether a mistake on the part of the transferor of property affects the passing of the property depends on the circumstances. First, it may have no effect on the contract or on the passing of property, as in the hypothetical of the Leonardo sketch above. Secondly, it may make the contract void and prevent any property passing, as where V despatches goods to D by way of sale, believing that D is E. This mistake as to the identity of the parties, if known to D, will generally prevent D from obtaining title to the property, and if he dishonestly appropriates the property he commits theft. Thirdly, intermediate cases are possible in which V's mistake is not so fundamental as to make the contract void, but still is sufficiently substantial to make it voidable. We need not enquire what these cases are, since that is a matter for contract; but a single illustration may be given. A customer in a shop buys and pays for goods, knowing that the price charged, through mistake, is less than the seller had planned. The buyer probably obtains title to the goods, but only a voidable title.[328] Is he guilty of theft in taking them off? The question arose in *Kaur v. Chief Constable of Hampshire*.[329]

---

[328] A distinction must be drawn between two cases. One is where the seller, by a slip of the tongue asks less than he is meant to ask; if the buyer knows of the mistake there is no contract, because of the absence of consensus. The other case is where the seller knows the price that he is asking but was led to ask it through mistake; there is a consensus on the terms of the contract, but if the buyer knew of the mistake the contract is voidable by the seller. *Per contra*, J. C. Smith thinks (against the opinion of the court in *Kaur v. Chief Constable of Hampshire*) that there is no contract in either case. See [1981] Crim. L.R. 674-676.

[329] [1981] 1 W.L.R. 578.

Kaur selected a pair of shoes from the £6.99 rack in a shop. One shoe had a price label for £4.99 and the other for £6.99. She took them to the cashier without concealing either price label, and when asked for the lower price duly paid for it. Then she was arrested on leaving the shop. The Divisional Court held that she was not guilty of theft, notwithstanding a finding of fact by the justices that Kaur knew that £4.99 was not the correct price.

29–117   **How did she know it wasn't?**   Presumably because all the other shoes of the same kind were marked £6.99.

29–118   **All the same, it was a pretty trivial matter, I do not understand how Kaur came to be prosecuted. She was not dishonest. When there is some muddle or doubt about a price at a supermarket, the cashier or supervisor will normally give the customer the benefit of it. Kaur did not do anything dishonest to cause the double labelling.** Apparently Kaur was arrested because she was suspected of having switched the labels. The argument on appeal assumed that Kaur was dishonest, and turned on the question of law only. Everyone who is at all dishonest is adept at rationalizing or condoning dishonesty, Kaur was 75 *per cent*. honest, because she did not tamper with the price labels or endeavour to conceal them. A perfectly honest person like you, or anyway me, would have pointed out the discrepancy of labels to the cashier and said that the shoes came from the £6.99 rack. It is true, however, that vast multitudes of shoppers fall short of such a standard of honesty. They are quite willing to profit from a mistake by a large corporation if it does not involve telling a lie. Moreover, there is no great social need to extend the law of theft to these cases of marginal honesty. As Lord Lane C.J. said, in delivering judgment, "the court should be astute not to find theft where it would be straining the language and where an ordinary person would not regard the act to be theft."

Nevertheless the magistrates, who convicted Kaur, must have found her to be dishonest, perhaps because the issue of honesty was not contested before them. Nor was it contested on appeal. Honesty is a question of fact, and if the defendant had desired to appeal on that issue she should have taken the case to the Crown Court, which can consider points of both fact and law. This appeal was to the Divisional Court, which means that it was on a question of law only. It turned on the ownership of the shoes.

In the opinion of the court, the contract of sale was not void for the cashier's mistake, which was not fundamental; so property passed to Kaur under the contract. Her obtaining of ownership in this way was not theft. "She certainly assumed rights of an owner when, having paid, she took the shoes from the cashier in order to go home," but this gain was not theft, presumably because it was not an appropriation of property belonging to another. The contract was not voidable for fraud, since there was none; if it was voidable for the seller's mistake, "it had certainly not been avoided when the time came for the defendant to pick up the shoes and go."[330] Kaur obtained ownership by her purchase at the

---

[330] *Kaur v. Chief Constable of Hampshire* [1981] 1 W.L.R. 578 at 583G. If it had been so avoided, Kaur would have been deprived of the ownership, and could then have committed theft by walking out with the shoes.

cash desk before she took possession of the goods; when she did so take possession of them (thereby appropriating them), they were her goods so she could not be guilty of theft.

Why wasn't it an appropriation for Kaur to obtain ownership of the goods by paying for them at the cash desk, even though she did not immediately get possession of them? At that moment the goods belonged to the supermarket, and Kaur surely appropriated them by getting ownership of them. The court did not explain why not. Kaur obtained either a completely valid title[331] or a title that was voidable on account of the cashier's mistake (the court left open which); but even a voidable title is title, and a person who gets it "assumes the rights of an owner," even though he does not get possession until later. This line of reasoning, based on the literal words of sections 1 and 3 (and assuming that a requirement of unlawfulness is not read into section 1) would suggest that Kaur committed theft.

29–119

Kaur can be explained and distinguished from *Gomez* in one way. Gomez's obtaining of the electrical goods was unlawful because he was guilty of fraud (or, on an alternative interpretation of the facts, it was unlawful because the manager would not have consented to Gomez's acquisition of the store's property had he been told the cheques that were to be used to pay for the goods were dodgy), whereas Kaur had the cashier's consent and (as the Divisional Court expressly held) used no deception and committed no illegality in receiving the shoes. Even if her title to the shoes was voidable by reason of the cashier's mistake, it has already been suggested that a person who dishonestly obtains a voidable title to property should not necessarily be regarded as committing theft. If the defect in title does not arise from the use of unlawful means (and the unlawful means should be limited to fraud, duress—and perhaps the more extreme cases of undue influence, which involve fraud or duress), then obtaining title is a lawful act and so (on the thesis here presented) cannot, on a rational view, be theft. The actual decision in *Kaur* accords with this principle, and it is to be welcomed.

An act done with consent is not an appropriation if the defendant's act is an appropriation only by reason of section 3(1) or if the consent is not vitiated by some factor involving illegality as narrowly defined above, as was the case in *Kaur*. Kaur, therefore, was rightly held not guilty of theft, because her appropriation of the property was not unlawful. Alas, we are precluded by the decisions in *Gomez* and *R. v. Hinks* from saying this is now the law. It seems that the courts are now committed to saying that anything that can conceivably be called an appropriation within the terms of the *Act* is an appropriation, owner's genuine consent or not, even if the alleged appropriation is the obtaining of a completely valid title to the property in question.

29.23. WHERE THERE IS AN OBLIGATION TO MAKE RESTORATION

Some of the general propositions in this chapter are modified by section 5(4) of the *Theft Act*:

29–120

---

[331] You will recall that, *R. v. Hinks* criminalizes dishonest acquisitions regardless of whether D has obtained a valid title.

"Where a person gets property by another's mistake, and is under an obligation to make restoration (in whole or in part) of the property or its proceeds or of the value thereof, then to the extent of that obligation the property or proceeds shall be regarded (as against him) as belonging to the person entitled to restoration, and an intention not to make restoration shall be regarded accordingly as an intention to deprive that person of the property or proceeds."

29–121 **When is a person who gets property by mistake "under an obligation to make restoration of the property or its proceeds or the value thereof"?** The obligation may be to pay money as a matter of quasi-contract or by reason of an equitable obligation, or it may, presumably, be a liability in tort, such as liability for the tort of deceit. All these are matters of civil law into which we need not enter in depth.

The most important type of quasi-contractual liability is the liability to repay money received under a mistake of fact on the part of the payer. A "mistake of fact" for this purpose includes a mistake as to whether the money is legally due.[332] The payee is, in terms of the subsection, under a legal obligation to make restoration (by repaying an equivalent sum), and if he dishonestly decides not to do so he can be guilty of theft. Although section 5(4) is useful in avoiding questions of civil law that might otherwise cause difficulty, it is somewhat anomalous because it can operate to make a person guilty of stealing his own property, or rather the value of his own property. In *Moynes v. Cooper*[333] a wages clerk mistakenly overpaid an employee. The employee only discovered the overpayment later when he opened his pay packet. The employee avoided a conviction for larceny, because it was held that he did not have *animus furandi* when he took the property and that ownership in the excess funds had already passed to him when he discovered the overpayment.

So if a wages clerk makes a mistake when preparing the pay packets; and an employee in consequence finds too much money in his packet and dishonestly decides to say nothing about it, the employee would now be guilty of theft of the excess payment pursuant to section 5(4). It makes no difference whether the clerk's mistake was in putting the wrong name on the pay packet (mistake of identity of recipient),[334] or in putting a £50 note into the packet in mistake for a £20 note (mistake of identity of thing), or in putting ten £50 notes into the packet for nine (mistake as to quantity of the thing).[335] Indeed, the rule applies even though the clerk knew exactly what he was putting into the pay packet and mistook the number of hours that the employee had worked that week (mistake as to a motivating fact). Again, the rule applies whether the employee realized the mistake as soon as he received the pay packet, or whether he discovered it only after he had got home.

---

[332] However, in *Kleinwort Benson Ltd. (Appellant) v. Lincoln City Council* [1999] 2 A.C. 349, the House of Lords took the view that: "the rule precluding recovery of money paid under a mistake of law could no longer be maintained and recognition should be given to a general right to recover money paid under a mistake." See also *Deutsche Morgan Grenfell Group Plc. v. Inland Revenue Commissioners* [2007] 1 A.C. 558; *Fender v. National Westminster Bank Plc.* [2008] EWHC 2242 (Ch.).

[333] [1956] 1 Q.B. 439.

[334] Cf. *The Queen v. Middleton* (1872-75) L.R. 2 C.C.R. 38.

[335] *Attorney-General's Reference (No. 1 of 1983)* [1985] Q.B. 182.

But that raises the old problem of dishonesty. Many an employee who finds **29–122** his pay packet unexpectedly stuffed with notes merely regards it as a windfall. Nor might the same employee think of saying anything if he found himself undercharged at a supermarket. "They" have had their whack on sundry other occasions, and have doubtless made mistakes to our detriment. Now it's "their" turn to suffer. I haven't done anything to cause the mistake have I? The employee can readily be found to have known that he was or might be under a legal obligation to restore the excess sum to his employer, and the question for the jury will be whether he knew that his decision not to honour the obligation was out of accord with "current standards of ordinary decent people."[336]

So the conviction of Alan Lawrence could have been justified under section **29–123** 5(4)? Yes, and it is surprising that the subsection was not referred to in the opinions in the House of Lords. Lawrence was under an obligation to restore money received from the student because of the student's mistake as to the customary fare.

If an excessive sum is transferred by mistake, the transferee being entitled to **29–124** part of the sum, can he not be convicted of stealing the part he was entitled to? Of course not; and it does not matter that he was given, say, a £50 note when he was entitled to £20. If he dishonestly keeps the note he is guilty of theft of £30, the notional sum to which he is not entitled. In Lawrence, it will be remembered, the taxi-driver was convicted of stealing "the approximate sum of £6," although he had received £7—he was given credit for the proper fare that he could have charged.

Is a moral obligation to make restoration an "obligation" within section **29–125** 5(4)? No. That was decided in *R. v. Gilks*.[337] Gilks was convicted on a literal reading of section 1(1), not by applying section 5(4). The court expressly held that section 5(4) did not assist the prosecution, notwithstanding that Gilks was under a moral obligation to make repayment. This was a case in which a bookmaker made a payment by mistake. Gilks received a payment as though he had backed "Fighting Taffy," when in fact, as he knew, he had won a much smaller sum on "Fighting Scot." Gilks realized the mistake just before receiving the payment or at the moment when he was paid, but pocketed the money. When he was charged with theft, one submission made on his behalf was that the property in money passed to him notwithstanding the bookmaker's mistake. This was rejected by the Court of Appeal, which held that no property passed. But there remained a further point. Even if the property did pass to Gilks, he was (it was contended) under no legal obligation to return it. By statute, wagering agreements are void, the attitude of the law being that they are too frivolous to take up the time of the courts. It had already been held that in consequence of this statute a bookmaker cannot sue in quasi-contract to recover back a payment that

---

[336] *R. v. Ghosh* [1982] Q.B. 1053.
[337] [1972] 1 W.L.R. 1341 at 1345D.

he mistakenly made.[338] The Court of Appeal agreed that Gilks was under no legal obligation to return the money, but held nevertheless that he was rightly convicted of theft, on the literal reading of section 1(1).

It appears that Gilks was convicted on the grounds that title in the overpayment of money did not pass to him, because at the moment of payment he knew that he was not entitled to the money.[339] He did not discover the mistake *ex post facto*.

29–126 **You told me above that section 5(4) applies when V mistakenly passes both the legal and equitable title of his property to D, because D cannot steal property that he now owns; and that the subsection is needed to override the standard ownership rules. But you also told me that a "fundamental mistake" prevents title passing: so why not charge under section 1 of the *Theft Act*?** When there is a "fundamental mistake" ownership in the property does not normally pass. So if D retains property received because of a fundamental mistake with the intention of permanently depriving the owner of it, all the elements of theft as laid down by section (1) of the *Theft Act* would be satisfied.[340] This type of conduct would also be caught by section 5(4).

A mistake will only be "fundamental" when it is sufficient to completely negate the transferor's consent. Such a mistake shows that the transferor never "intended to deliver the thing transferred and so never gave consent to the transfer."[341] A fundamental mistake might arise because the transferor is mistaken as to the "identity" of the transferee[342] or as to the "identity" of the "thing" delivered[343] or as to the "quantity" of the thing delivered.[344] If no title passed to the defendant before or at the time of the dishonest appropriation, he is guilty of theft. The owner may not have intended to pass title, or he may have intended it to do so but his intention may have wholly failed of effect by reason of some fundamental mistake, whether the mistake results from the defendant's fraud or not. If on the other hand the mistake was not fundamental it will not prevent title from passing (whether a voidable title or even a completely valid title), and in this case the transferee would, apart from section 5(4), be protected from a charge of theft, if only because the rule that theft must be of property belonging to another.

The initial question, then, is what is meant by a fundamental mistake; and to explain this, a brief account must be given of the civil law, particularly the law of contract. In general, a mistake is fundamental when it relates to:

- The identity of the thing transferred;
- The quantity of the money or fungible goods transferred;

---

[338] *Ashcroft v. Morgan* [1938] 1 K.B. 49.

[339] The Australian High Court has held that *R. v. Gilks* was wrongly decided as far as this point is concerned. See *Ilich v. The Queen* (1987) 162 C.L.R. 110 at 127.

[340] *R. v. Davies* (1982) 74 Cr. App. R. 94.

[341] *Ilich v. The Queen* (1987) 162 C.L.R. 110 at 126-128. See also, Glanville Williams, "Mistake in the Law of Theft," (1977) 36 *Cambridge L.J.* 62.

[342] *R. v. Middleton* (1873) L.R. 2 C.C.R. 38.

[343] *R. v. Ashwell* (1885) 16 Q.B.D. 190.

[344] *Russell v. Smith* [1958] 1 Q.B. 27.

- The identity of the transferee;
- The terms of the transaction.

Most frauds do not result in fundamental mistake: they do not wholly nullify the   **29–127**
owner's intention to pass ownership, but merely make the defendant's title
voidable. A mistake is fundamental if its existence makes it plausible to say that
there is in fact no consent (intention, agreement) on the part of the transferor to
transfer *this* property to *this* person. Even in the cases of fundamental mistake
there is an element of consent. The transferor intends to send goods to a person of
a particular name at a particular address, but the person of that name at that
address is not the person he thinks he is dealing with (mistake of identity of
transferee). The transferor intends to transfer a currency note, but the note he
gives is a £50 when he thinks it is £20 (mistake of identify of thing transferred).
Here the element of mistake bulks so large that it is reasonable to deny the
transferor's consent to the transfer, notwithstanding that there is a small element
of consent.

A qualification arises when the fundamental mistake relates to the quantity of
the thing delivered, and that thing is money! Ordinarily, if you order 12 bottles of
Château Latour and the supplier mistakenly delivers 20 bottles, title would not
pass in the eight additional bottles. If you were to appropriate those additional
bottles you would be liable for theft,[345] as the supplier did not intend to give you
ownership of the additional bottles of wine.[346] The title to the eight bottles is void
ab initio. When a voidable title has passed in respect of goods, they are not due
back until the contract is avoided. When it is properly avoided the property
revests automatically, and any dishonest appropriation then made will be theft
without the need for section 5(4).

This type of case could be prosecuted literally under section 1(1) of the *Theft
Act* simply upon the basis that the fundamental mistake prevented ownership
passing, but if D is overpaid money a literal application of section 1(1) will not
ground a conviction. Why not? In the case of money title passes regardless of
whether there was a mistake as to the quantity. Therefore, you would be stealing
your own property and section 1(1) only protects property belonging to another.
When the oversupply relates to specific chattels (goods) a fundamental mistake as
to the quantity delivered prevents ownership from passing.[347] In *R. v. Webster* the
court held that the Crown retained an equitable proprietary interest in a medal
that was mistakenly sent to an army captain, because the captain had already
received his medal.[348] It was held that the mistake (belief that the captain was still
owed a medal) was causative of the sending of the second medal and therefore
the "Crown retained a proprietary interest in the second medal, within the

---

[345] *Russell v. Smith* [1958] 1 Q.B. 27.

[346] "With goods other than currency, property does not pass with possession unless it is the owner's
intention that it should and it has been held (not without some difficulty) that it is possible to conclude
in cases of over-delivery that appropriation of the whole of the goods involves the theft of the excess
goods without any need to identify them." *Ilich v. The Queen* (1987) 162 C.L.R. 110 at 129 citing *R.
v. Tideswell* [1905] 2 K.B. 273; *Pilgram v. Rice-Smith* [1977] 1 W.L.R. 671. Cf. *Lacis v. Cashmarts*
[1969] 2 Q.B. 400 at 411.

[347] *Ilich v. The Queen* (1987) 162 C.L.R. 110 at 127-128.

[348] *R. v. Webster* [2006] EWCA Crim. 2894.

meaning of section 5(1)."[349] (Nevertheless, the criminal courts would do well to steer clear of the law of contract when section 5(4) is available, as it provides a much clearer solution.) Coupled with this, when the mistake relates to the "money" that was overpaid, section 5(4) provides the only solution because title passes with money.

29–128   **Are you telling me that if I intend to give D money as a part of a *bona fide* transaction, but mistakenly overpay him that he will get off on a technicality?**   No. Section 5(4) will catch his conduct, as might section 5(1). In cases involving money the legal title will pass when the funds are mixed in D's account or when D is handed the notes. The core difference with money is that it becomes currency as soon as it is negotiated[350] by the recipient. So when the transferor intends to give the transferee money as a part of a *bona fide* transaction for value title passes in both the intended payment and the overpayment:

> "Apart from the insuperable difficulty of identifying the notes or coins which constituted the overpayment, it is the transaction itself which characterizes the payment. The transaction between the applicant and D was *bona fide* and for value. The payment, which was part of that transaction, was also of that character. It is not possible, in our view, to apportion the consideration to some of the chattels comprising the notes or coins transferred and not to others."[351]

A mistaken overpayment of money does not prevent property in the whole amount passing to the creditor. Nevertheless, V might "acquire" an equitable interest in the overpayment by way of constructive trust. If D is made aware of the fact that he has only received the money as a result of a "mistake," then he would breach his duty as a constructive trustee were he to dissipate those funds.[352] This type of non-expressed trust is created by operation of law and is referred to as a "constructive trust." In *Chase Manhattan Bank NA v. Israel-British Bank (London) Ltd.*,[353] Goulding J. was of the view that V retains an equitable interest in money that is transferred by mistake. In *Westdeutsche Landesbank Girozentrale v. Islington L.B.C.*,[354] Lord Browne-Wilkinson (correctly in my view) rejected such an argument. In *Westdeutsche Landesbank* the bank lent money to a local authority; the issue was whether the recipient of moneys paid under a contract that was void for mistake (or was *ultra vires*), held those moneys on a trust. Lord Browne-Wilkinson said:

---

[349]   *R. v. Webster* [2006] EWCA Crim. 2894 at para. 34.

[350]   When D obtains money as a part of a good faith for value transaction and spends that money (*i.e.* puts into circulation), D destroys the title of the former owner and creates new title.

[351]   *Ilich v. The Queen* (1987) 162 C.L.R. 110 at 129.

[352]   In *Muschinski v. Dodds* (1984-5) 160 C.L.R. 583, Deane J. said: "Once [a constructive trust's] predominantly remedial character is accepted, there is no reason to deny the availability of the constructive trust in any case where some principle of the law of equity calls for the imposition upon the legal owner of property, regardless of actual or presumed agreement or intention, of the obligation to hold or apply the property for the benefit of another." Cf. *Shields v. Westpac Banking Corporation* [2008] N.S.W.C.A. 268, where D had full knowledge of the mistake when he took control of the bank's funds. On this basis, it was held the trust arose immediately.

[353]   [1981] Ch. 105 at 120.

[354]   [1996] A.C. 669 at 706. This seems correct, after all, the local authority did not receive the money on behalf of another, because it received the money for itself. The mere relationship of debtor and creditor does not involve an entrustment.

"It is said that, since the bank only intended to part with its beneficial ownership of the moneys in performance of a valid contract, neither the legal nor the equitable title passed to the local authority at the date of payment. The legal title vested in the local authority by operation of law when the moneys became mixed in the bank account but, it is said, the bank '*retained* its equitable title'. ... I think this argument is fallacious. A person solely entitled to the full beneficial ownership of money or property, both at law and in equity, does not enjoy an equitable interest in that property. The legal title carries with it all rights. Unless and until there is a separation of the legal and equitable estates, there is no separate equitable title. Therefore to talk about the bank 'retaining its equitable interest' is meaningless. The only question is whether the circumstances under which the money was paid were such as, in equity, to impose a trust on the local authority. If so, an equitable interest arose for the first time under that trust."

It is a *non sequitur* to argue that the transferor retains an equitable interest in such circumstances. Whether the recipient holds the overpayment as constructive trustee is a separate question. The breach of trust would arise only once the recipient's conscience is affected by the knowledge of the mistake. "The ultimate question to be addressed in relation to the imposition of a constructive trust is whether the holder of the legal title to the property in question 'may not in good conscience retain the beneficial interest.'"[355] The mere receipt of the moneys without knowledge of V's mistake would not give rise to a breach of trust.[356]

If we accept that V acquires an equitable interest in a mistaken overpayment, then section 5(1) could apply. The courts have accepted such a proposition, even though they are yet to recognize the correct grounds that give rise to such an equitable interest. The Court of Appeal in *R. v. Shadrokh-Cigari*[357] and of the Court Martial Appeal Court in *R. v. Webster*[358] held that where property has been received as the result of a "basic" mistake, V retains an equitable proprietary interest in that property. As far as money is concerned, V does not retain an interest. Rather, the equitable interest arises because a constructive trust arises. In such circumstances, D has legal control of the funds but holds them on trust for V.

Where D has inadvertently dissipated an unnoticeable overpayment (for example, where his account has been credited with £100,100 instead of £100,000); his conscience might not be affected so he will not breach his obligations as a constructive trustee. Therefore, if D is aware of the overpayment and deliberately dissipates it, he could be liable for theft pursuant to section 5(1) of the *Theft Act 1968*.

So are you telling me that section 5(4) is superfluous? No. Section 5(4) is a catchall. It covers mistakes of both the fundamental[359] and non-fundamental kind.

29–129

29–130

---

[355] *Beatty v. Guggenheim Exploration Co.*, 122 N.E. 378 at 380 (1919) *per* Cardozo C.J. cited with approval in *White City Tennis Club Ltd. v. John Alexander's Clubs Pty Ltd.* [2009] N.S.W.C.A. 114. See also *Hospital Products Ltd. v. United States Surgical Corporation* (1984) 156 C.L.R. 41 at 108; *Baumgartner v. Baumgartner* (1987) 164 C.L.R. 137.

[356] *Westdeutsche Landesbank Girozentrale v. Islington LBC* [1996] A.C. 669 at 714-714 *per* Lord Browne-Wilkinson.

[357] [1988] Crim. L.R. 465 at 466. In this case, the Court of Appeal said that the conduct in question would also be caught by section 5(4), but held that a second ground for a conviction was that the bank retained a proprietary interest in the moneys paid by mistake.

[358] [2006] EWCA Crim. 2894 at paras. 32-33.

[359] In *R. v. Webster* and *R. v. Shadrokh-Cigari* [1988] Crim. L.R. 465 it was said that any mistake would have to be fundamental. (Fundamental mistakes mean that title never passes—the transaction is

Given the uncertainty of when a constructive trust will apply, the criminal courts would do well to avoid invoking section 5(1) when section 5(4) is clearly available. If a customer is given more change than she should have been given: would she hold that extra change on trust for the shopkeeper after discovering the mistake some time later? Would this type of trivial matter be an issue for the civil courts? I would think not! If such cases are to be prosecuted at all, they should be brought within the purview of section 5(4).

The real advantage of section 5(4) is that it does not require the criminal courts to decide complex issues of equity and trusts. Section 5(4) is a deeming provision which treats a mistaken transfer of money as a nullity. It effectively makes a mistaken but legitimate transfer in civil law void *ab initio*. For example, in *Attorney-General's Reference (No. 1 of 1983)*[360] D's employer mistakenly paid her £74 more than the amount to which she was owed. It was assumed she had done overtime which she had not. The payment was made by direct debit from the employer's bank account to D's bank account. D only learned of the excess credit in her account some time after it had appeared. D was tried on a count charging that she stole £74 belonging to her employer, contrary to section 1(1) of the *Act* and was acquitted. On a reference by the Attorney-General for the court's opinion on a point of law, Lord Lane C.J. said:[361]

> "• [F]irst of all: 'Did D get property?' The word 'get' is about as wide a word as could possibly have been adopted by the draftsman of the *Act*. The answer is 'Yes, D did get her chose in action'.
> • 'Did she get it by another's mistake?' The answer to that is plainly 'Yes'.
> • There were no proceeds of the chose in action to restore. 'Was she under an obligation to make restoration of the value thereof?'—the value of the chose in action. The answer to that seems to us to be 'Yes'.
> • Therefore the prosecution, up to this point, have succeeded in proving—remarkable though it may seem—that the 'property' in this case belonged to another within the meaning of section 1 in the *Theft Act 1968* from the moment when D became aware that this mistake had been made and that her account had been credited with the £74.74 and she consequently became obliged to restore the value."

What D obtained was her own chose in action. When the money left the employer's account its chose in action *quoad* that sum was extinguished. And when the equivalent sum was transferred to D's account it created in D a new chose in action being the right to demand payment of that sum from her bank.[362]

---

void *ab initio*; non-fundamental mistakes only make the transaction voidable). See also *Norwich Union Fire Insurance Society v. Wm. H. Price* [1934] A.C. 455 at 463. In the latter case, Lord Wright said: "But proof of mistake affirmatively excludes intention. It is, however, essential that the mistake relied on should be of such a nature that it can be properly described as a mistake in respect of the underlying assumption of the contract or transaction or as being fundamental or basic." In *R. v. Webster* [2006] EWCA Crim. 2894 at paras. 32-33, it was said: "To apply the approach taken by the court in *Shadrokh-Cigari*, it is necessary to ask whether the error was fundamental or basic, an error in respect of the underlying assumption of the transaction, so as to have the consequence that the Crown (represented by the Secretary of State for Defence) retained an equitable proprietary interest in the medal. ... In our judgement, the error in this case was plainly an error of that kind. We are satisfied that the Crown did retain a proprietary interest in the medal and was entitled to call for the return of the medal."

[360] [1985] Q.B. 182.

[361] *Attorney-General's Reference (No. 1 of 1983)* [1985] Q.B. 182 at 188-189 *per* Lane L.J.

[362] *R. v. Preddy* [1996] A.C. 815.

This only came into existence when the debt so created was owed to D by her bank, and so never belonged to her employer. However, section 5(4) treats the chose in action as though it was still the same chose in action that was in the employer's bank. It deems that the newly created chose in action belongs to the person whose mistake led to its creation. Furthermore, the section applies regardless of whether D did something to induce the mistake.[363]

It follows that the word "property" in the subsection was a mistake on the part of the draftspersons. It should have been "money," because that is the only form of property in respect of which the subsection has any practical operation.

29.24. LIMITATION OF AN AGENT'S AUTHORITY

Analogous to cases of fundamental mistake are those where property fails to pass because an agent has acted outside his authority. A cashier in a supermarket dishonestly charges a friend less than the proper price for goods. The friend, if he knows of the fraud, will be guilty of stealing goods.[364] There are other instances of a limitation of the agent's authority preventing property from passing, but they will not be considered here.[365]

29–131

29.25. ENTRAPMENT AND CONSENT

Before the *Theft Act*, when larceny was defined as being done without consent of the owner, the courts developed a sensible distinction between consent and facilitation.

29–132

If the owner, V, in order to catch a thief, puts out some marked money, or leaves a door or drawer unlocked, and lies in wait, he facilitates the theft but does not consent to it: his attitude is merely one of trying to find who the thief is, or to get evidence that a particular suspect is the thief. The same, if the owner tells his employee E to put out marked money. In such cases if the thief takes the bait he is guilty of theft.

But suppose that D incites E to join with him in stealing from V; E tells V of the approach that has been made to him, and V instructs him to pretend to co-operate with D; E then hands over the owner's property to D, pretending that he has stolen it from V. In these circumstances V was formerly taken to consent to the taking, which therefore was not larceny.[366]

Various writers assume that the *Act of 1968* has changed this by omitting the requirement of lack of owner's consent, and some of them welcome the conclusion that the thief can now be convicted of theft and not merely of an inchoate crime. For my part I think that such a conviction would be against principle, because D's act in receiving the money thrust into his hand on the owner's instructions is lawful, even though he imagines it to be unlawful. Unlawfulness does not follow merely from belief in unlawfulness, except in the

29–133

---

[363] *R. v. Gresham* [2003] EWCA Crim. 2070.
[364] *Pilgram v. Rice-Smith* [1977] 1 W.L.R. 671.
[365] *Attorney-General of Hong Kong v. Nai-Keung* [1987] 1 W.L.R. 1339.
[366] *R. v. Turvey* (1946) 31 Cr. App. R. 154.

case of inchoate crimes. Here D's crime was in encouraging E to steal, or of attempting to corrupt E; he is not guilty of a consummated theft.

If the *Theft Act* has changed the law, it would be not only contrary to principle but, in some circumstances, unjust. This is so if it was V who engineered the whole affair. Either from malice or because he wished to put the honesty of D to an extreme test, V got his employee E to thrust money into D's hands, pretending that he had stolen it from V. D succumbs to temptation and accepts the money. If this makes D guilty of theft, although he in fact had V's consent to do what he did, the law would be harsh, particularly because it does not recognize a defence of entrapment.[367] The right result can be reached under the *Act* by the means already suggested. It can be held that D's appropriation of the money is lawful, and therefore is not theft, though if he made any efforts to get the money they can still be charged as inchoate crimes.

29.26. THEFT: THE MENTAL ELEMENT

29–134   We may extract from the aforementioned definition of theft, amplified further by explanations in other sections and by judicial interpretation, a series of rules. The first two relate to the mental element:

1.   At the time of appropriation the thief must intend to deprive another person permanently of his property.
2.   The appropriation must be dishonest.

The phrase formerly used to describe the mental element in stealing was *animus furandi*. For the sake of speaking English (even though rather peculiar English) we shall speak of it as theftous intent. Its two elements are the intent to deprive the owner permanently, and dishonesty. The two elements are independent. One may dishonestly appropriate property intending to deprive the owner temporarily ("borrowing" another's lawn-mower when the taker knows that the owner does not wish the taker to do so). This is not theft. Or one may honestly appropriate goods intending to deprive the owner permanently of them. That is not theft either. (A diner at a restaurant intends to deprive the owner permanently of the food consumed, but he is not guilty of theft if he intends to pay for it, because he is honest. If, after consuming the meal, he declares that it was a culinary disaster and that he is not going to pay, he is still not guilty of theft, whatever his civil obligation may be. He will be guilty of the offence of "making off without paying" if his complaint was only a dishonest excuse for not paying: see 34.12).[368]

---

[367] *R. v. Latif* [1996] 2 Cr. App. R. 92; *R. v. Hooper* [2002] EWCA Crim. 621; *R. v. Byrne* [2003] EWCA Crim. 1073.
[368] Section 3 of *Theft Act 1978*. See also *R. v. Aziz* [1993] Crim. L.R. 708.

29.27. THE INTENT TO DEPRIVE

Theft requires an intention to deprive the owner; it is not concerned with any intention the thief may have to benefit himself.

29–135

But surely the thief doesn't want to deprive the owner for the hell of it, so to speak. He wants to get the property himself. Depriving the owner is incidental. So why doesn't the *Theft Act* say that the thief must intend to get the property himself? Exceptionally, the thief may simply want to deprive the owner—as where a postman, who has been too lazy to deliver letters, destroys them.[369] He wants to destroy the evidence against himself, and for that purpose wants to deprive the owner of them.[370] Even when the thief wants to acquire the property, this involves depriving the owner—and he intends this deprivation, because he knows it is an inseparable part of what he wants.

29–136

Could it be theft to deprive a person recklessly? It is not theft at common law, and would not be theft under the *Theft Act* except to the extent that section 6 applies.[371] The hole in the law is plugged to some extent by conspiracy to defraud,[372] which is committed by a conspiracy to subject another person to a financial risk that he would not have wished to run if he had known the facts. A remarkable example concerns company directors. They are in a peculiar position, since they are in charge of property of the company yet are not, technically, trustees for the shareholders. Although they may commit specific offences of dishonesty in relation to the company property, no statute declares that they commit a criminal offence in making use of the property in a rash way. Yet in *R. v. Sinclair*,[373] where directors took a risk by handing over the whole of the company's assets without security, they were held in the circumstances to be guilty of a conspiracy to defraud the company, its shareholders and creditors. The Court of Appeal said:

29–137

> "To cheat and defraud is to act with deliberate dishonesty to the prejudice of another person's proprietary right. In the context of this case the alleged conspiracy to cheat and defraud is an agreement by a director of the company and others dishonestly to take a risk with the assets of the company by using them in a manner which was known not to be in the best interests of the company and to be prejudicial to the minority of shareholders."[374]

---

[369] See *R. v. Lavender* [2007] EWCA Crim. 2679, where the defendant was found in possession of thousands of letters of which he failed to deliver. He was charged with theft and with "intentionally delaying postal packages" contrary to section 83 of the *Postal Services Act* (2000).

[370] *R. v. Sweeney* [2009] EWCA Crim. 1733, where a postman took "secure mail" packages in order to remove foreign currency worth £53,682 from them for his own benefit.

[371] "[S]ection 6 [would] apply to a person in possession or control of another's property who, dishonestly and for his own purpose, deals with that property in such a manner that he knows he is risking its loss." In *R. v. Fernandes* (1996) 1 Cr. App. R. 175 at 188 *per* Auld L.J.

[372] See also the offences in the *Fraud Act 2006*.

[373] [1968] 1 W.L.R. 1246.

[374] *R. v. Sinclair* [1968] 1 W.L.R. 1246 at 1250. See also *R. v. Rowland* [2007] EWCA Crim. 479. Similarly, the High Court of Australia citing *R. v. Sinclair* (a conspiracy defraud case) said: "It is sufficient that the conspirators intended to obtain some advantage for themselves by putting another person's property at risk." *Peters v. The Queen* (1998) 192 C.L.R. 493 at 525. The Supreme Court of Canada has held that the *mens rea* for "fraudulent deprivations" would be satisfied where the

The case shows that an intention to take a risk with someone else's property, or to cause him by fraud to take such a risk, for purposes of one's own, is capable of founding a charge of conspiracy to defraud. The essence of the offence is not causing a loss (because it does not matter whether loss is caused or not); it lies in subjecting another person to an unwanted pecuniary risk. The conspirators knowingly take this risk on the victim's behalf.

29.28. PERMANENT DEPRIVATION

29–138 The traditional notion of theft involves an intent to deprive the owner permanently, not just to make a temporary use of his property. A person is not guilty of theft in "borrowing" a neighbour's lawn-mower for the day while the neighbour is out, even if that is reckoned as dishonest. Is the law the same if a shop assistant "borrows" money from his employer's till, intending to replace it when his ship comes in? Unlike the taker of the mower he intends to deprive his employer of those particular coins or notes permanently, even if he has every prospect of replacing them in a short time. So he can be guilty of theft.[375]

29–139 **But is not this view a very technical view? One pound coin is as good as another. Nobody feels deprived if the pound in his pocket is changed into two 50p pieces.** Lawyers express the point by describing money as "fungible." A fungible is any property that is regarded as equivalent to other property of the same kind (corn, cement, petrol, postage stamps and so on).[376] In ordinary life, and for nearly all legal purposes, money is treated as a fund rather than as a number of pieces of small metal or paper. But in the present context there is a valid social reason for insisting that the actual money borrowed is not intended to be returned. The opposite view would let off any filcher of money who hoped one day to be able to restore it. True, a woman who takes another woman's pearl necklace to wear at a party is not guilty of theft if she intends to restore it, notwithstanding that she may lose it and so not be able to restore it. That is bad enough, but it would be worse if the same rule were extended to the high-handed "borrowing" of money with intent to spend it.

However, there are circumstances where a person who takes money intending to return an equivalent sum will not be guilty of theft, not because he does not intend to deprive the owner permanently (he does) but because he is not dishonest.[377] When an appropriation is and is not dishonest will be considered a little bit later.

---

defendant intended the deprivation or was reckless as to whether it would occur—and thus put the victim's pecuniary interests at risk. *R. v. Zlatic* (1993) 79 C.C.C. (3d) 466. See also American Law Institute: *Model Penal Code* (1985), §223.0(1).

[375] *Halstead v. Patel* [1972] 2 All E.R. 147; *R. v. Velumyl* [1989] Crim. L.R. 299.

[376] Although it is customary to instance these goods as fungibles, there is in reality no legal list. As Professor Goode says: "whether assets are fungibles depends not on their physical characteristics but upon the nature of the obligation owed with respect to them." Royston Miles Goode, "The Right to Trace and its Impact on Commercial Transactions," (1976) 92 *L.Q.R.* 360 at 383.

[377] See *R. v. O'Connell* [1992] 94 Cr. App. R. 39.

Is there not a danger of thieves getting off by saying that they intended to give the thing back? Sometimes yes. If a person makes off with a book from a library, or a picture from an art gallery, his defence that he intended to return it might have sufficient credibility to save him or her from conviction of theft, even though grave suspicion remains. But a more serious difficulty is presented by people who take up an article to see if it is worth stealing. The crook may, for example, take a lady's handbag, peer inside and finger the contents, returning the handbag when he finds only lipstick, *etc.* in it. It was held in *R. v. Easom*[378] that such a person cannot be convicted of theft (even though his general criminal intent is obvious), because his conduct shows that, as things turned out, he did not intend to steal what was actually in the bag.

29–140

Can such a person be guilty of attempted theft? Yes since the enactment of the *Criminal Attempts Act 1981*. Before the enactment of the *Attempts Act 1981*, *R. v. Easom* decided that the taker could not be convicted of an attempt since he lacked a present intent to steal. The Court of Appeal restated this opinion in a later case where Lord Scarman made a remark of which he must have repented afterwards (because it led to what came to be known as the "thieves charter"), that "it cannot be said that one who has a mind to steal only if what he finds is worth stealing has a present intent to steal."[379] The decision in *R. v. Eason* was right at the time, not because the defendant did not intend to steal but because the law then was that one could not attempt the impossible. One could not attempt to steal something that was not there. Easom did not intend to steal the things that were in the handbag (notebook, tissues, cosmetics and a pen, if you are curious to know), as was proved by the fact that he put them all back. But he did intend to steal anything of value that might be there. Following widespread criticism of the absurdity of the law, the Court of Appeal silently determined to repudiate its own decision, and even decisions of the House of Lords. Their Lordships said that in similar circumstances to those in *R. v. Easom* the crook could be convicted of attempting to steal "some or all of the contents of a handbag." This was laid down even before the *Criminal Attempts Act*, in two burglary cases before the Court of Appeal in which Lord Scarman's *dictum* was in effect acknowledged to be wrong. The court said:

29–141

> "If the jury ... are satisfied that at the moment of stealing he intended to steal anything in the building ... the fact that there was nothing in the building worth his while to steal seems to us to be immaterial. He nevertheless had an intent to steal.[380] Similarly, the court said that on a charge of attempting to steal from a receptacle where nothing of value was there, the thief can be convicted of attempting to steal 'some or all of the contents of the pocket/bureau' (or whatever it might be)."[381]

These *obiter dicta* were irreconcilable with the authorities on the impossibility rule when they were uttered, but have become undoubted since the *Attempts Act*

---

[378] [1971] 2 Q.B. 315. See *Carven v. Quilty* [1998] 148 F.L.R. 273 for a recent application of the rule.
[379] *R. v. Husseyn* (1977) 67 Cr. App. R. 131 at 132.
[380] *R. v. Walkington* [1979] 1 W.L.R. 1169 at 1179.
[381] *Attorney-General's Reference (No. 1 and 2 of 1979)* [1980] Q.B. 180.

1981.[382] If D raids V's taxi cab hoping to find V's proceeds, D would be guilty of theft if he manages to find the cash and appropriates it. However, if unbeknown to D the cash has been banked earlier that day and therefore is not in the taxi, he should be charged with attempted theft.[383] The indictment might read: "D intended to steal (cash) from the taxi." Or it might be even more general: "D intended to steal from the taxi."

If it is known what the thief hoped to find, he should be convictable of attempting to steal that.[384] If he thought the handbag contained the Kohinoor diamond, or a revolver, or a microchip of secret defence information (which MI6 had cleverly led him to believe was there), he is, on principle, guilty of attempting to steal it. It is right that his criminal record should show that he attempted to steal a priceless diamond or secret defence information, *etc.*, not that he attempted to steal lipstick. No importance attaches to the fact that the article in question was not there, or even that no such article existed, since we have now got rid of the "impossibility" rule in attempt.

29–142   On the last proposition, a possible snag that may occur to you relates to the wording of the indictment. If the indictment said: "attempted to steal a diamond known as the Kohinoor, the property of Mabel Bloggs" (the owner of the handbag), the answer might be made that, as everyone knows, the Kohinoor is one of the Crown jewels held in the Tower of London, and not the property of Mabel Bloggs or anyone other than the Queen. Although an argument of this type is clearly bad on principle. For one thing, averments of ownership in an indictment are immaterial. A more substantial and important answer to the objection is that by the *Criminal Attempts Act* a person is deemed to intend, and therefore to attempt, what it would be[385] his intention to do if the facts had been as he believed them to be (thus ponderously enacting the ordinary meaning of the English language).[386] If the crook thought that Mabel Bloggs had the diamond in her bag, he committed an attempt to steal that diamond from her. The rules of pleading must subordinate themselves to this legislative declaration, so that a charge of attempting to do something must always be read as a charge of attempting to do what it was in the defendant's mind to do, never mind the actual facts.

---

[382] However, one of the points decided in *R. v. Easom* is still law. If in a case like *Easom* the defendant is charged with stealing the contents of the handbag (which on inspection he found he did not want), he cannot even today be convicted of attempting to steal such contents (under a statute allowing conviction of an attempt on a charge of the substantive crime). If he did not steal the unwanted contents, he did not attempt to steal them either. So held in *Easom*, which is still good law on this point. Easom could nowadays be convicted of an attempt to steal, but there must be an express count for the attempt, and it must be so worded that it can be read as relating not to the objects actually in the container but the objects that the defendant hoped to find.

[383] Cf. *Garlett v. The Queen* (1987) A. Crim. R. 75.

[384] Glanville Williams, "Convictions and Fair Labelling," (1983) 42 *Cambridge L.J.* 85 at 94-95.

[385] *R. v. Tulloch* (1986) 83 Cr. App. R. 1; *R. v. Shivpuri* [1985] Q.B. 1029.

[386] See section 1(3) of the *Attempts Act 1981*.

29.29. CONSTRUCTIVE INTENT TO DEPRIVE PERMANENTLY

In order to widen the scope of theft, section 6 of the *Theft Act 1968* adopts the device deeming certain intents to be an intent to deprive the owner permanently. If you enjoy verbal puzzles, subsection (1) of this section may amuse you. If, on the other hand, you believe that the object of penal legislation is to give clear guidance to the citizen, judges and magistrates' clerks, advocates and their legal advisors, its wilful opacity will lower your spirits. Section 6(1) provides:

29–143

> "A person appropriating property belonging to another without meaning the other permanently to lose the thing itself is nevertheless to be regarded as having the intention of permanently depriving the other of it if his intention is to treat the thing as his own to dispose of regardless of the other's rights; and a borrowing or lending of it may amount to so treating it if, but only if, the borrowing or lending is for a period and in circumstances making it equivalent to an outright taking or disposal."

Unriddle me that. It is gobbledygook, but careful thought will extract some sense from it. The subsection has two limbs, divided by a semicolon, the second limb providing a partial definition of the word "treat" in the first limb. The second limb, within its limits, is overriding (because of the words "if and only if"). We may therefore restate the subsection (beginning with the second limb) as follows.

29–144

An appropriator is to be regarded as intending to deprive the owner permanently of the thing if his intention is:

1.   to borrow the thing from the owner, provided that the borrowing will be for a period and in circumstances making it equivalent to an outright taking;[387]
2.   to lend the thing to a third person, provided that the lending will be for a period and in circumstances making it equivalent to an outright disposal; or
3.   to treat the thing as his to dispose of (otherwise than by borrowing or lending as above) regardless of the owner's rights,[388]—even though in each of these cases the thief did not mean the owner to lose the thing itself.

But what is meant by borrowing in circumstances making it equivalent to an outright taking? Does it mean a real borrowing or a dishonest "swiping"? In this context, "borrowing" must signify an unauthorized "borrowing"—a temporary taking for use. Further, in the context of the whole subsection "borrowing" must be understood to mean a taking for temporary use, or for some other purpose involving temporary retention, not amounting to a disposal. If the taking is with a view to disposing of the thing it comes within proposition 3 above, not within proposition 1.

29–145

The most straightforward application of the principle is found in the "ransom" cases, because even a very restrictive interpretation of the provision catches such cases. In interpreting the law of larceny the courts applied what may be called a ransom principle.

---

[387] The *Act* says "is to be regarded" in the first limb and "may amount to so treating it" in the second limb. The reason for using "may" instead of "will" does not appear.
[388] See *D.P.P. v. Lavender* [1993] Crim. L.R. 279.

Suppose that D, noticing V's briefcase standing in a hotel lobby, took it off and then wrote to tell V that he could have it back if he paid a ransom. That was held to be theft. But if D took the suitcase as before and then returned it to V saying that he had found it, and hoping for a reward, this was not theft, because D intended V to have the article back in any event.

29–146 In *R. v. Raphael*[389] D took V's car and told V that the car would not be returned unless V paid D £500. The Court of Appeal held: "The express language of section 6 specifies that the subjective element necessary to establish the *mens rea* for theft includes an intention on the part of the taker 'to treat the thing as his own to dispose of regardless of the other's rights.'"[390] The court concluded that there is no better example of a violation of section 6 than an offer not to return another's property unless they pay for its return, because such a condition is inconsistent with the owner's "right to possession of his own property."[391]

There is no reason why these propositions should not apply also under the *Theft Act*, as a matter of interpretation of the words "with the intention of permanently depriving the other of it." In *R. v. Raphael* the owner was deprived permanently unless he paid up, and that can be regarded as an intent to deprive permanently without the assistance of section 6(1). It would also be caught by the subsection because D took the car with an intent to "temporarily deprive the owner" within the meaning of the subsection (under proposition 1 above). This would constitute theft within the subsection only if D intended to borrow the car for a period and in circumstances making it equivalent to an outright taking. These words are apt for a case where D takes the article intending to keep it for a long time, or for an appreciable part of its useful life: but in the case we are supposing the taking and holding to ransom may have been a brief affair. If the car were only taken temporarily and was not damaged in anyway, it would still be caught by the general principle: D intended to treat the car as his own to dispose of regardless of the proprietary rights of V, which effectively provides the circumstances that make it equivalent to an outright taking. The period of retention would not have to be long given the overall circumstances.

Another example is where a person appropriates a railway ticket dishonestly from the Railways Board, even though the Board will get it back on completion of the journey.[392] One cannot steal a railway journey, or a right to make it, but one can steal a document evidencing the right.[393] If the case is regarded as coming under proposition 1, it can well be held that the taking was equivalent to an outright taking because the taker got the full use of the ticket. After all when he had finished with it, it had no remaining value. In *R. v. Lloyd*[394] Ds clandestinely removed feature films due to be shown in the cinema so that they could make (pirate) copies of the films.[395] The films were returned by Ds before anyone

---

[389] [2008] EWCA Crim. 1014.

[390] *R. v. Raphael* [2008] EWCA Crim. 1014 at para. 47. See also *R. v. Coffey* [1987] Crim. L.R. 498; *R. v. Hall* (1848) 1 Den. C.C. 381.

[391] *R. v. Raphael* [2008] EWCA Crim.1014 at para. 47.

[392] For authority before the *Theft Act*, see *R. v. Beecham* (1851) Cox C.C. 181. Cf. *R. v. Boulton* (1849) 1 Den. C.C. 508; *R. v. Kilham* (1870) L.R. 1; *R. v. Chapman* (1910) 4 Cr. App. R. 276.

[393] Cf. *R. v. Marshall* (1998) 2 Cr. App. R. 282.

[394] [1985] Q.B. 829.

[395] There are also copyright piracy offences, but they are not our concern here.

missed them. Many pirated copies of the films were made and sold, but the success of the defendants' criminal enterprise depended on them successfully returning the films that had been borrowed for copying as soon as possible. The films were borrowed only for a few hours in most cases. The Court of Appeal held that section 6(1) "required an intention to return the thing in such a changed state that it has lost all its goodness or virtue; the borrowing had not been for such a period or in such circumstances as amounted to the equivalent of an outright taking or disposal and there was no theft."[396]

Are you telling me that if I thieve your £5,000 season rail ticket and only use   29–147
it for half of the season and return it so that you can use it for the remaining
half of the season, that I could invoke the _R. v. Lloyd_ doctrine to avoid
criminal liability?   I hope not. Recent authority suggests you might end up in
hot water if you substantially reduce the value of the item you have borrowed.
And rightly so, it would be absurd to allow you to evade justice where you have
used up £2,500 of my £5,000 season rail ticket. There is no need for the value to
be completely exhausted before one could argue that you have disposed of the
article pursuant to section 6(1).[397] A season ticket that has been half used,
changes completely in substance and value.[398] The subsection should be
interpreted in terms as referring to a "substantial" or "measurable loss of value,"
because any other interpretation would be nonsensical. Substantial should not
mean a 50 _per cent._ plus loss in value, it should refer to a measurable loss. There
is no reason why a person should not be punished for using up 10 _per cent._ of
another's expensive season ticket. Similarly, if you snatch another's expensive
watch and slam it into a rock face you exercise a right that belongs to the owner,
that is to decide what to do with the watch, whether to use it or dispose of it. It
should not matter that the watch is reparable and maintains half its value.[399] In
most cases, the portion used might be sufficiently identifiable and separable to
catch the user through a literal application of section 1(1) of the _Theft Act_, as the
user has an intention to permanently deprive the owner of the portion used.

A strict virtue analysis ("has lost _all_ its goodness or virtue"), would allow me   29–148
to borrow your antique desk for five years so long as it appreciates in value
(as it is likely to do because of its antiquity), without being liable for theft,
would it not?   It would, if we were to follow such a narrow reading of the
subsection. The subsection is not so limited as only to apply to a loss of value or
goodness. Therefore, you would be liable because you have treated the desk as
your own to dispose of by holding it for a _period_ and _in_ circumstances that make
your taking equivalent to an outright taking. You might argue that you meant only
to borrow it and would have given it back anytime if I had forced you to do so,
but such factors are irrelevant. If you keep V's property for a very unreasonable

---

[396] _R. v. Lloyd_ [1985] Q.B. 829.
[397] _D.P.P. v. SJ_ (A Juvenile) [2002] EWHC 291 (Admin.).
[398] Cf. _R. v. Bagshaw_ [1988] Crim. L.R. 321.
[399] In _D.P.P. v. SJ (A Juvenile)_ [2002] EWHC 291 (Admin.), the headphones might have been
reparable but they were badly damaged and by snapping and throwing them as hard as possible onto
the ground the defendant exercised a right of disposal—an ownership right which was not his to
exercise.

length of time this would satisfy the requirements of the subsection. Denying the owner of the enjoyment[400] and use of his property for an unreasonable period[401] of time is analogous to holding his property for ransom or temporarily taking a conveyance for a joyride.[402] Using up the value or goodness of the property is one situation where the subsection applies,[403] but it also covers unreasonable use or detention of another's property.

29–149   **Suppose I take your door lock to a locksmith and have a key cut for it so that I can access your house and read your private diary. Am I guilty of theft, if I borrow the lock only for a few hours and return it in pristine condition?**   You will be liable for theft, because you treat the door lock as your own to dispose of regardless of the rights of the owner. Furthermore, since you have had a key made for the lock it has lost all its goodness and value as a lock (that is, as a device for securing the owner's property).[404] The lock is no longer useful as a lock if it allows you to enter as you please.[405] It does not matter that you did not intend to permanently deprive the victim of his door lock.

Similarly, if you copy an examination paper you might not steal the actual paper that it is written on, but you would destroy all its goodness as an exam paper. It can no longer be used as an examination as its contents have leaked, and professors have to be paid to write a new paper. The printers would also have to be paid to reprint the new paper and so on.

29–150   **Suppose I am a professor who has noticed that the faculty has purchased comfy chairs for the administrative staff, but has failed to provide me with a nice chair. Could I not swap my old wooden chair for one of the comfy chairs from the administrative office in the faculty?**   You could but you would be risking a theft conviction.

---

[400] A similar provision in the Texas Penal Code catches "use" and "enjoyment" as well as diminution of value. See Tex. Pen. Code Ann. §31.03(a). "Deprivation of property occurs when property is withheld from the owner permanently or for so extended a period of time that a major portion of the value 'or' enjoyment of the property is lost to the owner, or when property is restored only upon payment of a reward or compensation, or when property is disposed of in a manner that makes recovery of the property to the owner unlikely." In *Winkley v. State*, 123 S.W.3d 707 (2003), it was held that the defendant's use of a hay dolly for a day constituted theft, "We conclude that this reading of the statute … comports with the societal desire to protect property rights. Further, we conclude that it was the legislature's intent to protect all property from theft, for it may have value to its owner even if it is completely void of any monetary value."

[401] Cf. *State v. Bautista*, 948 P 2d 1084 (1997), where D took a car to use for a weekend and was caught by a provision similar to section 6 of the *Theft Act 1968*.

[402] This type of conduct has its own offence. See sections 12 and 12A of the *Theft Act 1968*.

[403] Cf. *Clinton v. Cahill* [1998] N.I. 200.

[404] See *People v. Kwok*, 63 Cal. App. (4th) 1236 (1998); *Dreiman v. State*, 825 P.2d 758 (1992).

[405] The same applies to valuable securities such as cheque forms and bills of exchange. In *R. v. Arnold* [1997] 4 All E.R. 1 at 15 is was said: "where D has appropriated a valuable security handed over on the basis of an obligation that he will retain or deal with it for the benefit or to the account of the transferor, there is good reason for the application of section 6(1) if the intention of the transferee at the time of the appropriation is that the document should find its way back to the transferor only after all benefit to the transferor has been lost or removed as a result of its use in breach of such obligation." As for cheque forms, see *Parsons v. The Queen* (1999) 195 C.L.R. 619 at 633-634.

But surely I am not a thief, I have merely moved the chair to another part of   **29–151**
the faculty—my office. The chair might remain in the faculty's possession in the most technical sense, and you might not dare take it out of the faculty building, but making use of it without permission could result in a theft charge since you intend to treat the faculty's chair as your own. You would be exercising the faculty's ownership rights over the chair, its right to choose how to *use* its property (the property owner has the power to use, enjoy and dispose of his property as he pleases (*jus utendi et fruendi*)).[406] If there were not such a rule, faculty members could also take down the grand paintings in the public areas of the university and move them to their private faculty offices. It would be a free-for-all!

In *D.D.P. v. Lavender*[407] the defendant lived in a council house with his *de facto* partner. The defendant and his *de facto* partner (or their associates) damaged the doors on the council house in which they lived and requested new doors from the council. The council told the tenants that it could only replace doors that were damaged from normal wear and tear. Because the tenants destroyed the doors they were asked to pay for new doors. The defendant did not want to pay to replace the doors that he had damaged, so he walked 12 doors up the road and took doors from another house owned by the same council and used them to replace the damaged doors. The defendant was convicted of theft on the grounds that he "intended to treat the doors as his own in dealing with the council regardless of [its] rights."[408]

Converting, permanently or temporarily, the property of another for your use could constitute theft. Lavender's use of the council's doors extinguished the council's right to exclusive use. He deprived the council of its right[409] to have exclusive control over its property and *use* of that property. If a professor loses the key for her faculty office and decides to axe the door into bits to gain access to her office, she surely is not entitled to replace her door by permanently removing the door from the adjacent faculty office. This may seem a harsh interpretation. Some of you might be of the view that the council should have sued for the cost of the doors rather than use the criminal law. However, in many of these cases the tenants will be penniless and will be living on welfare. It might be infeasible to garnishee their income. The professor might be easier to deal with

---

[406] Planning laws might qualify how one can use one's real property (*jus abutendi*), but that is not our concern.

[407] [1994] Crim. L.R. 297.

[408] The court focused on the concept of "dealing". The doors had not lost their value, but they could no longer be used by the council for the legitimate purpose for which they were originally purchased. The council had no obligation to replace the defendants' doors free of charge because the council had not damaged them. The council suffered a permanent loss which could only have been rectified by removing the doors from the defendant's house, but the defendants would have been left in a door-less house—which no doubt would violate their human rights. Section 6's *raison d'être* was to prevent such dealings. Notably, the South Australia theft offence focuses on *dealing* with another's property without *consent*, and avoids the traditional physical *appropriation* problem. See section 134 of the *Criminal Law Consolidation Act 1935* (S.A.).

[409] Property rights at the most basic level involve an ownership claim which allows the owner to use or control (and possess) his property to the exclusion of others. Others cannot tell the exclusive owner how to use his property and if they permanently relocate or use (even if the property is still on the owner's premises) the property in a way that excludes the owner from using it for its intended purpose, then the owner has been in effect deprived of his property (right).

in a non-criminal way as he has something to lose if he does not return the chair to the administrative office—his job. All should be equal before the criminal law, but prosecution should be used as a last resort in cases where the property remains on the owner's premises.

29–152   There are cases where people borrow property belonging to another without permission and abandon it nearby hoping the owner will find it. These cases will usually be caught by section 6. Section 6 may apply, for example, where a person dishonestly takes a bicycle to travel for a distance and then abandons it. An appropriation with intent to abandon can be held to come within proposition 3; the taker, by abandoning the thing, "treats it as his own to dispose of." At common law, if there was a possibility of the owner getting the thing back the taker did not commit larceny (because he did not intend to deprive the owner permanently, but was only reckless as to permanent deprivation),[410] but it apparently becomes theft under section 6(1). It should be noted that theft is committed when the thing is abandoned, irrespective of whether the owner afterwards recovers it. The same applies if the bailee of the vehicle (a borrower or hirer) wrongfully abandons it. Although he may have "borrowed" within the second limb, the charge against him is based not on the borrowing but on the subsequent abandonment—the disposal, and so it is judged according to the first limb.

The proposition is doubtful where a person wrongfully takes an article and leaves it with someone, making sure that the owner is informed where his article is so that he can get it back. If the owner is given the information and is able to recover his property without having to pay for it, then the defendant seems to be considering the rights of the owner. He is not acting totally in disregard of the rights of the owner. If the defendant only intends a temporary deprivation and makes a genuine effort to ensure the owner will be able to recover the property without being unduly burdened, then it might be difficult for the prosecution to prove that he treated the property as his to dispose of. Suppose a Ph.D. student is vacating her college room to fly back to France but has forgotten to return five books belonging to the university library. It is 4.00 a.m. and she has a 5.00 a.m. flight, so is unable to return the books in person. She decides the best solution is to leave the books in the room that she is vacating with a note in the front of the books. But the note does not instruct the finder to return the books, but instead says, "A room without books is like a man without a soul." Suppose also that she knows the Ph.D. student that will be taking over her room and assumes that he will find the note amusing and also return the books to the university library.

29–153   She might also have assumed that the bedders would hand the books into the porters. Is she a thief? (Has she been dishonest? A conviction for theft also requires that the defendant was aware that her conduct would be considered dishonest by ordinary people.)[411] She has abandoned the books in a secure room within the university, so the books remain on university property.[412] Notwithstanding the idealistic note, she arguably took reasonable steps to ensure that the

---

[410] Glanville L. Williams, "Temporary Appropriation Should Be Theft," [1981] *Crim. L.R.* 129 at 134-135.

[411] We will examine the dishonesty requirement at length *infra*. See *R. v. Ghosh* [1982] Q.B. 1053.

[412] Cf. *DDP v. Lavender* [1994] Crim. L.R. 297.

books would be returned (or would be recoverable). After all, the books were taken out in her name and the university's computerized records would have prevented her from graduating until the books were returned. All the relevant circumstances suggest that our Ph.D. student has not committed theft, even though she abandoned property of which she had on loan.

It might seem reasonable at first sight to say that a case like *R. v. Easom*[413] furnishes another example of dishonest "borrowing" that should be regarded as equivalent to an outright taking. D takes up an article belonging to another, intending to steal it if he decides upon examination it is worth stealing. Then he satisfies himself that it is not, and relinquishes it. Since D has possessed himself of the article and it will be only by his own good grace that he gives it back, it is very near to being an outright taking. But it is hard to say that the taker intended to "borrow" the article for a period and in circumstances making it equivalent to an outright taking (merely taking up the article to look at it does not fall well within these words), or yet that he intended to treat the thing as his own to dispose of (he has not yet reached a final intention in the matter). Anyway, the court in *R. v. Easom* refused to apply section 6(1) to the case, and we must now regard it as beyond argument that theft is not committed.

Subsection 6(2) covers situations where D "parts with the property under a condition as to its return which he may not be able to perform ... this amounts to treating the property as his own to dispose of regardless of the other's rights." What does this proviso add? You told me that although I might not intend to thieve your property, that I can be liable for theft if I borrow it in circumstances where I know I might not be able to return it. Does this mean subjective recklessness is sufficient *mens rea* for theft? Yes.

29–154

Suppose X borrows his employer's laptop for the purpose of pawning/ pledging it, because he needs to raise some money to cover a gambling debt. X believes that he will have great difficulty in saving enough (because he has a serious gambling addiction) to get it back from the pawn shop within the set timeframe for paying. Let us assume that when the time comes for paying, he is unable to raise the funds to recover the property. Is he liable for theft? It appears so.[414] Constructive intent is used to treat X as though he actually intended to permanently deprive his employer of the laptop. This expanded definition of intention covers those who are subjectively reckless with property belonging to another. In such cases, D must not only intend to borrow or deal with the property regardless of the rights of the owner, but must also be "aware"[415] that his particular borrowing (or dealing) of that property creates a substantial risk[416] that the owner will not get the property back or will get it back only after its value has been substantially diminished.[417] A person would not, however, be criminally liable for theft for accidentally losing a library book, but

29–155

[413] [1971] 2 Q.B. 315.

[414] Section 6(2) of the *Theft Act 1968* makes specific reference to this type of situation.

[415] Since the decision of *R. v. G.* [2003] 3 W.L.R. 1060, the standard ought to be subjective recklessness.

[416] *R. v. Fernandes* (1996) 1 Cr. App. R. 175 at 188.

[417] *D.P.P. v. SJ (A Juvenile)* [2002] EWHC 291 (Admin.).

he may be required to compensate the library for its loss.[418] *Per contra*, if in a fit of rage a person throws a library book into a campfire (or snaps and destroys another's headphones), he would be treated as a thief, since he treats the book as though it were his own "to dispose of." The book has also lost all its value.

29–156 **If I honestly believe that I will be in a strong position to recover the property that I have borrowed and thereafter lent to a third party, would I still be liable if I am unable to recover the property?** That will depend on the circumstances. You might rebut a section 6(1) charge if you could demonstrate that you had an intent to return the property within the set timeframe and that you were in a position where you had a realistic and substantial ability of doing so.

Take the example of the banker who earns £600,000 *per annum*, but is strapped for cash as he has just purchased a house in Kensington. Suppose the banker needs to raise £20,000 cash urgently to pay for his grandfather's hip replacement. In order to raise the money, the banker decides to borrow (without permission) a Pro Hart painting which belongs to his wife's aunt, because the aunt is overseas and will not miss it for the time being. He pawns (pledges) it in order to raise the needed funds.[419] For the banker in our hypothetical, £20,000 is only two weeks' salary, so he genuinely believes that he will be able to return the painting within two weeks before the aunt returns. Alas, for the banker, he is fired the next day because of a credit crunch and the bank is unable to pay him his final salary as it has gone bankrupt.

The banker is now unable to recover the Pro Hart from the lendee (pawnbroker). The words "parts with the property under a condition as to its return which he may not be able to perform" seem to require the borrower to foresee that he was taking the risk of losing the property which he has borrowed. As the banker did not foresee the risk he was taking with the painting (he had no idea that he would lose his lucrative banking post) he was only negligent and therefore his dishonest borrowing should not be caught by section 6(2).[420]

29–157 In *R. v. Fernandes*[421] the defendant (an unscrupulous solicitor) had accumulated significant personal debts. Fenandes was in sole practice and had access to funds that he was holding on trust for his clients. In an attempt to overcome his financial difficulties, he borrowed money which belonged to two of his clients and invested the money in a risky backstreet investment scheme. Fenandes was hoping for a higher than normal return and also for a quick profit. No doubt he

---

[418] That would be a civil law matter, however.

[419] Outright taking arguably refers to borrowing and outright disposal to lending. See also A.T.H. Smith, *Property Offences: The Protection of Property Through the Criminal Law*, (London: Sweet & Maxwell, 1994) at 213.

[420] See *R. v. Fernandes* (1996) 1 Cr. App. R. 175 at 188, where it was held intention is imputable to D where he deals with property knowing that his dealing is risking its loss. There is nothing new about criminalizing reckless use that results in loss. See *R. v. Holloway* (1848) 169 E.R. 285, where it was held: if D "took [another's property] with a view only to a temporary user, intending, however, to keep them for a very unreasonable time, or to use them in a reckless, wanton, or injurious manner, and then to leave it to mere chance whether the owner ever recovered them or not, and if he recovered them at all, would probably recover them in a damaged or altered condition, such a taking would seem, in common sense, to be ample evidence of an intent wholly to deprive the owner of his property." See also *R. v. Medland* (1851) 5 Cox. C.C. 292.

[421] (1996) 1 Cr. App. R. 175 at 177-181.

expected that he would be able to return the money without being discovered. He might not have intended to permanently deprive his clients of their funds, but his actions resulted in their money being lost. Fenandes was convicted of theft pursuant to section 6(1) and (2).

The unauthorized[422] borrowing/dealing occurred after his firm acted for a client in matrimonial proceedings. Pursuant to a court order the client's home was sold, and since her husband was overseas at the time, the court ordered the defendant's firm to invest her husband's share of the proceeds of the sale in a high interest deposit account until he returned. The defendant initially invested the money in a high interest deposit account but thereafter closed it and transferred the funds to the firm's general client account. Shortly afterwards, the defendant transferred this money as part of a payment of £20,000 to his firm's book-keeper, Geoffrey Reynolds, for investment in "T & M Credit", a firm of licensed backstreet money-lenders of which Reynolds was a partner. All the money was lost—or at least disappeared and could not be recovered. Reynolds claimed that he returned the funds to Fenandes, but Fenandes denied this. Reynolds was found to be a totally unreliable witness, but the fact remained that it was Fenandes who borrowed the money and then invested it with a third party without his clients' authorization.

Fernandes appealed against his theft convictions. Counsel for the defence, referring to the examples provided by Lord Lane C.J. in *R. v. Lloyd*,[423] argued that the first limb of section 6(1) applied only to the ticket cases where a rail ticket, *etc.* had been returned to its owner as a valueless piece of paper and to the ransom cases where someone had taken another's property and offered to sell it back to the owner. Coupled with this, it was argued that the second limb is "restricted to a borrower's or lender's treatment of property in such a way as to render it valueless on return." It was also contended that any wider interpretation of section 6 would allow a jury to equate "what later turned out to have been an unwise and risky investment of the money with an intention, at the time of making it, permanently to deprive."[424] Auld L.J. said:

> "In our view, section 6(1), which is expressed in general terms, is not limited in its application to the illustrations given by Lord Lane C.J. in *Lloyd*.[425] Nor, in saying that in most cases it would be unnecessary to refer to the provision, did Lord Lane suggest that it should be so limited. The critical notion, stated expressly in the first limb and incorporated by reference in the second, is whether a defendant intended 'to treat the thing as his own to dispose of regardless of the other's rights'. The second limb of subsection (1), and also subsection (2), are merely specific illustrations of the application of that notion. We consider that section 6 may

---

[422] There was also a second *borrowing* involving a deceased estate.

[423] *R. v. Lloyd* [1985] Q.B. 829 at 836.

[424] *R. v. Fernandes* (1996) 1 Cr. App. R. 175 at 187.

[425] Lord Lane C.J. provided the following examples: "[T]he first part of section 6(1) seems to us to be aimed at the sort of case where a defendant takes things and then offers them back to the owner for the owner to buy if he wishes. If the taker intends to return them to the owner only upon such payment, then, on the wording of section 6(1), that is deemed to amount to the necessary intention permanently to deprive ..." Under the second limb: "Borrowing is *ex hypothesi* not something which is done with an intention permanently to deprive. This half of the subsection, we believe, is intended to make it clear that a mere borrowing is never enough to constitute the necessary guilty mind unless the intention is to return the 'thing' in such a changed state that it can truly be said that all its goodness or virtue has gone ...": *R. v. Lloyd* [1985] Q.B. 829 at 836.

apply to a person in possession or control of another's property who, dishonestly and for his own purpose, deals with that property in such a manner that he knows he is risking its loss."

This analysis of the scope of section 6 is welcome. The defendant did not invest the money for his client's benefit but for his own, and did so without any authorization. Furthermore, the investment was highly speculative. Even if D could show that he had intended to return the property within a reasonable time, his reckless use of the money demonstrated that it was very likely that he would not be in a position to do so.

29–158 **Would Fernandes had been guilty of theft had he invested his clients' funds in Lehman Brothers Holdings Inc. just before it crashed,[426] if he genuinely believed there was no risk involved in such an investment?** Lehman Brothers was a global giant, had a 158-year history and $US639 billion in assets when it filed for bankruptcy. Even prudent investors failed to anticipate its bankruptcy. Section 6(2) does not cover those who genuinely believe they are making a good investment or that the conditions are such that they should easily be able to regain possession of the property that they have put into the hands of third parties. Therefore, the "knows he is risking its loss" issue is not likely to arise in such a case. But whether or not the investment was speculative is not an issue under section 6(1). Even if Fernandes had invested his clients' funds wisely he would not have avoided liability under section 6(1), as section 6(2) operates "without prejudice to the generality of subsection (1)." The defendant did not invest the money he borrowed for his client's benefit but for his own *benefit*, and did so without any authorization. Section 6(1) catches this type of conduct. Section 6(2) is only a supplementary provision that applies when D "parts with the property under a condition as to its return which he may not be able to perform."

29.30. DISHONESTY

29–159 Even if the defendant appropriated property belonging to another with the intention of keeping it, he will still not be guilty of theft if he did not appropriate it dishonestly. (As we will see, the offences of fraud found in the *Fraud Act 2006*[427] also require dishonesty.)

The notion of dishonesty in theft fulfils a double function:

1. It expresses the ordinary *mens rea* principle applied to theft. The defendant must know that he is appropriating "property belonging to another," or (perhaps) be reckless in this regard. Not only a mistake of fact but a mistake as to the civil law can negative dishonesty. If you take someone else's umbrella believing it is yours you are not guilty of theft for two reasons: you were not dishonest, and even if the requirement of dishonesty

---

[426] When Lehman Brothers crashed it had assets worth $US639 billion. See "Lehman folds with record $613 billion debt," (New York: *Wall Street Journal*, Sept. 15, 2008).

[427] Although no provision has been made for a claim of right. Cf. *R. v. Wood* [1999] Crim. L.R. 564.

had not been inserted in the subsection the courts would undoubtedly hold that you lacked the mental element for theft.

2. The requirement of dishonesty also provides a special defence of morality. A historical note: It may seem strange that a moral concept should be introduced into the law of theft. The explanation goes back to the *Larceny Act 1916*, which put the common law into statutory form and incorporated into the definition of larceny the requirement that it should be done "fraudulently and without claim of right made in good faith."

A claim of right was a belief by the defendant that he owned the article or otherwise had the legal right to take it. Such a belief would negative *mens rea*, and so was a defence on ordinary principles. There was, therefore, no objection to the concept of claim of right, but the name was slightly misleading for a jury, who had to be made to understand that the question was not whether the defendant had an actual right to the property but whether he believed he had a right.

The second requirement, that the act be done fraudulently, was open to more serious objection, as being both vague and inapt. Inapt, because one would not ordinarily speak of a robber who makes a brusque demand as acting fraudulently. Vague, because no one knew what "fraudulently" meant in the context of larceny. In general it was not held to add anything to the meaning of "without claim of right." **29–160**

The C.L.R.C. thought the single word "dishonesty" (copied from the United States Model Penal Code) made a clearer substitute for both parts of the old phrase. Obviously a pickpocket acts dishonestly, while one who takes property believing it to be his own does not.

The notion of dishonesty is partly (but only partly) defined in section 2. Section 2(1):

"(1)   A person's appropriation of property belonging to another is not to be regarded as dishonest—
(a)   if he appropriates the property in the belief that he has in law the right to deprive the other of it, on behalf of himself or of a third person; or
(b)   if he appropriates the property in the belief that he would have the other's consent if the other knew of the appropriation and the circumstances of it; or
(c)   (except where the property came to him as trustee or personal representative) if he appropriates the property in the belief that the person to whom the property belongs cannot be discovered by taking reasonable steps."

In each of these cases the judge must instruct the jury that the defendant is to be acquitted if he satisfies or may satisfy the specified condition. Paragraph (a) means that a mistake as to the civil law can negative dishonesty.[428] (Not, of course, a mistake as to the criminal law: it is no excuse for a defendant that he did not know the existence of the basic law of theft,[429] but there is no hardship in that: one can hardly imagine anyone—apart from the most pitiable cases in

---

[428] It may be noted that, independently of the question of honesty, magistrates' courts have no jurisdiction to try a case where a question of title to land is involved. But it would seem that if the question is the defendant's belief in his title to land, they may try it: see the note to *Eagling v. Wheatley* [1977] Crim. L.R. 165.

[429] Cf. *R. v. Candy* (1990) *The Times*, 10 July (C.A.: Crim. Div.).

psychiatric hospitals—who does not know that theft is regarded as wrong.) The paragraph covers not only a mistaken belief that one owns the property but also a mistaken belief that one is otherwise entitled to it—*e.g.*, that one has contracted to buy it and is entitled to take it under the contract. Even a belief that one owns the property is no defence if one also knows that one is not entitled to posses it—as in the case where the owner surreptitiously takes the article back from an unpaid repairer who has a right to retain it until he is paid.

The burden of proving dishonesty rests on the prosecution.[430] If the defendant used a subterfuge, that is very strong evidence of dishonesty, but it is not conclusive. Honesty is not easily found when the act was done openly. The unreasonableness of a belief is not fatal to a defence of honesty,[431] but is of course some evidence that it was not genuinely held.[432]

29–161 **Suppose a man is owed money. Since the debtor refuses to pay, the creditor takes his wallet from him at knife-point, extracts the amount owing and returns the rest. Would that be theft?** No, because the taking is not dishonest. The rule has long been settled (and has been reaffirmed since the *Theft Act*) that such behaviour is not theft, the defendant having a claim of right. And because it is not theft it is not robbery either, since robbery presupposes a theft.[433] The judge must not ask the jury whether the defendant believed he had a right to use a knife to get the property, because that is not the question. The question of honesty relates to the defendant's belief in his right to the property, not to his belief in his right to use the particular means to get it.[434] One can be an honest ruffian.

If D admits he took the property and knew he had no right to do so then it is an open and shut case. In *R. v. Forrester*,[435] D took property in substitution for a debt he was owned, but believed that he had no right to take this type of action to recover the value of the debt. He was not mistaken as to whether he had a claim of right, since he knew he did not have a right to claim the substitute property. If D knows he has no claim of right over the given property, he cannot believe he does. Consequently, the subsection does not apply. If he mistakenly believes that he has such a right, the case would be different.

---

[430] See generally, *R. v. Flynn* [1970] Crim. L.R. 118.

[431] "A man may be ever so much mistaken in his reasoning processes and yet be honest, though you would not accept his mere statement of opinion unless there was some colour in the circumstances for his entertaining the opinion he claims to have had." *R. v. Nundah* (1916) 16 S.R. (N.S.W.) 482 at 489; *R. v. Hemmings* (1864) 176 E.R. 462; *R. v. Wade* (1869) 11 Cox C.C. 549. D might also raise evidence of his good character in support of his claim that he genuinely believed he had a claim of right: see *R. v. Bailey* [2004] EWCA Crim. 2530.

[432] *R. v. Holden* [1991] Crim. L.R. 478.

[433] *R. v. Hall* [2008] EWCA Crim. 2086; *R. v. Robinson* [1977] Crim. L.R. 173.

[434] Similarly, it is not burglary for a person to break into premises to take a thing to which he believes himself to be entitled. *R v. Knight* (1781) 2 East. PC 510. In *R. v. Lopatta* (1983) 10 A. Crim. R. 447 the "appellant admitted breaking into his former employer's warehouse at Dry Creek in the northern suburbs of Adelaide and taking therefrom 20 large drums of oil worth about $5,000, his estimated value of holiday and other pay and expenses which, he said, his former employer owed him but was neglecting or refusing to pay." It was held that the defence is available in such circumstances. See also *Barker v. The Queen* (1983) 153 C.L.R. 338, where the High Court of Australia dismissed the appeal but affirmed the availability of the "claim of right" for cases involving facts similar to those in *R. v. Lopatta*.

[435] [1992] Crim. L.R. 792.

But the creditor has no right to the specific notes and coins that happen to be in the debtor's pocket. He merely has a right to be paid. That is true. Lawyers distinguish between an obligation and a proprietary right, between a *ius in personam* and a *ius in rem*. The layman may not realize this; if he is kept out of his money by a debtor who has a stuffed wallet, he may see nothing illegal in helping himself. If so, he acts honestly. Paragraph (*a*) restates this position because it is not limited to a belief as to ownership. What matters is the defendant's belief in his right to appropriate the property.

29–162

Suppose the defendant is a lawyer, who knew the difference between obligation and property, and who nevertheless used high-handed methods to exact due payment. He does not come within the words of paragraph (*a*), because he lacked the required belief that what he did was legal. Nevertheless he may be found to have been honest if he believed that he acted morally.[436] That is a question for the jury.

29–163

Reverting to the honest ruffian: a forcible taker, though not guilty of theft or robbery, is guilty of assault,[437] and may be guilty of blackmail.

What if I believe the owner would consent to me making off with his property under the circumstances? Subsection 2(1)(b) allows for a defence in these circumstances. If you give your employer's goods to one of his debtors because you in fact believe (or believed that it was virtually certain that he would consent) that your employer would consent, then you might be able to demonstrate that you acted honestly. In *R. v. Close*,[438] D worked for a firm which owed Close's business £400. Close required some oil and D supplied Close with his employer's oil. D's defence was that he had not acted dishonestly. It was accepted by the jury that on these facts D did not act dishonestly. Similarly, if a person takes goods from a self-service stand and leaves the correct payment because he in fact believes that the owner would consent to him doing so, he should be able to demonstrate that he acted honestly.

29–164

Is the fact that I am willing to pay for the property sufficient for refuting dishonesty? Section 2(2) provides:

29–165

---

[436] Cf. the pre-*Act* position. *Harris v. Harrison* [1963] Crim. L.R. 497. In most cases, if one believes he has no legal claim the jury is not likely to accept he honestly believed he had a (moral) right to take the law into his own hands. Nevertheless, if D were to steal a loaf of bread to prevent his child from starving to death, or a car to rush his pregnant wife to an emergency ward, the jury might hold that such motives demonstrate an absence of dishonesty. D might avoid a conviction for theft if he could show that he took property in an emergency situation and intended to return an equal amount—this might negate *dishonesty* but the criminal law does not recognize a defence of "good motive." Cf. *State v. Savage*, 37 Del. 509 (1936). For a discussion of motives and honesty, see Martin Wasik, "*Mens Rea*, Motive, and the Problem of 'Dishonesty' in the Law of Theft," [1979] Crim. L.R. 543 at 549.

[437] *R. v. Skivington* [1968] 1 Q.B. 166; *R. v. Robinson* [1977] Crim. L.R. 173. Cf. *R. v. Boden* (1844) 174 E.R. 863. These cases show that ignorance of the civil law is not a defence in respect of offences against the person. Cf. *R. v. Bentley* (1850) 4 Cox C.C. 406; *Agnew v. Jobson* (1877) 13 Cox C.C. 625; *R. v. Tolson* (1889) 23 Q.B.D. 168 *per* Stephen J.; *Gelberg v. Miller* [1961] 1 W.L.R. 153.

[438] [1977] Crim. L.R. 107. See also, *R. v. Werchon* (1896) 3 A.L.R. (C.N.) 3, where a conviction for cutting bark with intent to steal was set aside as the accused had been informed that they were entitled to cut the bark.

"A person's appropriation of property belonging to another may be dishonest notwithstanding that he is willing to pay for the property."

This wholly useless provision does not say that the appropriation will be dishonest, only that it may be, which means that it may or may not be, the subsection leaves us no wiser. An offer to pay might manifest honesty, but it would depend on all the circumstances. If you are only offering to pay because you have been caught in the act, then it would be difficult for you to demonstrate that you were acting honestly.[439] Similarly, borrowing money from your employer's till with an intention to repay it would be dishonest.[440] In the case of self-service, it would depend on the objective facts. If the norm is for one to take milk, newspapers and so on from a self-service stand on the condition that one leaves the correct money, then it would not be dishonest for one to pay and take in such circumstances. A more borderline case would be where the defendant helps himself to beer (with a full intention of paying the next day) on the basis that he is a known and regular patron of the establishment from where he takes the beer.[441]

In general, it would be hard for the prosecution to convince a jury that a defendant who has paid full value in advance was acting dishonestly, if the defendant took goods that were for sale.[442] The case might be different if the goods were not on sale or were of a special nature. It would be no defence to argue that you paid market value for your friend's rare Ming vase, if it was not for sale. So an intention to pay is just another factor to be considered in all the circumstances.

29–166   **You told me earlier that if I forcibly take what I believe I am owed I will not be guilty of robbery. What about if I am refused service, so forcefully take what I want to buy? If I pay for it I should be able to claim a right to take it should I not?** No. You should be guilty of robbery. When D takes beer at gunpoint from a licensed seller who has refused to sell him beer because it is against the law to serve intoxicated patrons, he commits robbery. In *Jupiter v.*

---

[439] But even here there may be a genuine explanation of honesty. See for example, *Barnes v. State*, 31 Md. App. 25 (1976), where "[D] had a box of sugar worth about $2.00 which she placed in her pocketbook, which remained open at all times, to hold it. While she was waiting to pay she was accosted and arrested before she had a chance to get to the cashier to pay for the merchandise. D did not [fully] conceal the sugar. [And argued that] she did not have any intention to conceal it. She was merely holding it waiting to pay and had approximately $20.00 on her when she was arrested and had every intention of paying for it." See also *Hugo v. City of Fairbanks*, 658 P.2d 155 (1983); *People v. Jaso*, 84 Cal. Rptr. 567 (1970).

[440] *R. v. Williams* [1953] 1 Q.B. 660. See also *State v. Wilcox*, 17 Utah 2d 71 (1972). Cf. *State v. Labbitt*, 156 P 2d. 163 (1945); *Commonwealth v. Irvine*, 190 A. 171 (1937) on non-consensual debt collection.

[441] In *Mason v. State*, 32 Ark. 238 (1877) Ds served themselves 30 cents' worth of beer because the manager refused to get out of bed to serve them. They were regulars at the pub and intended to pay when the establishment reopened. They were acquitted of larceny. In that case, however, the publican tried to take advantage of the situation by demanding 10 times the value of the beer and this no doubt had some influence on the court.

[442] Some of the older U.S. larceny cases are illustrative of this point: see *Gettinger v. State*, 13 Neb. 308 (1882). Cf. *Pylee v. State*, 62 Tex. Crim, 49 (1911), where the oats that were taken were not for sale.

State[443] following a day's duck hunting, the defendant went to a public house and asked to purchase a six-pack of beer. The owner refused to sell the beer because Jupiter was intoxicated. Jupiter then asked the owner to sell him a single beer, but the owner refused because Jupiter was intoxicated. Jupiter went to his vehicle and then re-entered carrying a shotgun. The owner was forced to sell D a six-pack of beer. The defendant was ignorant of a criminal law, which prohibited the owner from selling liquor to intoxicated patrons. The defendant tried to rely on ancient English authorities to ground a claim of right.[444] The court held a "Claim of right defence is not applicable to robbery when the *transaction* that the robbery *effects* would be [criminal] even if it were consensual."[445] The victim does not consent to his property being taken and the payment does not make the non-consensual transaction consensual.

What if I mistakenly believe that the property has been abandoned? Sub-section 2(1)(c) above is intended chiefly to cover finding, particularly finding on the highway[446] (an expression that includes streets and public squares). There is no need for us to revisit the rules regarding abandoned property. You will recall that property that has been abandoned cannot be stolen, unless it is axiomatically the property of another because it is attached to his land or has been abandoned in a quasi-public area where he has "exercised such manifest control over the land as to indicate an intention to control it and anything found on it."[447] A person who finds an old brooch buried in a public park might not realize that the owner of the land has a better claim to the brooch than he does, but a mistake as to the civil law can negative dishonesty. D would not be dishonest if he believed that the property had been abandoned and that it would not be possible to find the owner by taking reasonable steps. If D finds a wallet bloated with cash on a public highway (and there is nothing in the wallet to suggest who owned it), he might believe it would be impossible to find the true owner.

29–167

However, if the wallet had the owner's driver's licence and other details in it, D would find it difficult to convince a jury that he truly believed it would be impossible to find the owner by taking reasonable steps such as handing it in at the local police station. But it would still be a question for the jury to consider. In

---

[443] 616 A.2d 412 (1992).

[444] The general principle as expressed in *The Fisherman's Case* (1584), cited in Michael Dalton, *The Country Justice*, (London: printed by William Rawlins *et al.*, 1705) at 364 is not likely to provide a defence in modern England and Wales. In that case, the only illegality was the robbery itself (or if you prefer sale by force), and it was held that the fact D paid meant he had not committed robbery. There might not have been any *incidental* illegality (such as V illegally selling intoxicated D alcohol), but surely no one in the 21st century could argue that he believed he had a clam of right to rob another merely because he paid. (For an earlier account (in French) of the *Fisherman's Case*, see Richard Crompton's 1606 edition of Sir Anthony Fitzherbert's, *L'office et Auctoritie de Iustices de Peace*, (London: Companie of Stationers, 1617) at 35.

[445] *Jupiter v. State*, 616 A.2d 412 (1992). Similarly, if D were to rob V for the value of *illegal* drugs he sold to V, because V is refusing to pay for the drugs, the illegality of the drug deal would prevent D from raising a claim of right defence. See *Martin v. State*, 174 Md. App. 510 (2007). However, this does not mean that illegal drugs are not property: *R. v. Smith* [2011] 1 Cr. App. R. 30. A discussion of whether property can pass on an illegal contact is beyond the scope of this treatise, but generally it can be said that it does not.

[446] *R. v. Glyde* (1868) L.R. 1 C.C.R. 139; *Thompson v. Nixon* [1966] 1 Q.B. 103.

[447] *Waverley BC v. Fletcher* [1996] Q.B. 334.

R. v. Small[448] the defendant took what appeared to be an abandoned car in circumstances where it seemed utterly unreasonable for him to claim he believed the vehicle had been abandoned. The Court of Appeal held that it did not matter that D's belief was unreasonable; the reasonableness of his belief might influence the assessment of whether he really held such a belief, but that is all.

29–168   **Does the judge exercise any control over the jury in deciding whether the appropriation was dishonest?** It might be thought, as a deduction from general principles of law, that the defendant would bear an evidential burden in respect of a defence of honesty[449] (just as he does in respect of private defence), and that the judge would be able to withdraw the issue from the jury if there is no "evidence that can properly be passed to the jury for their consideration."[450] When the C.L.R.C. proposed the use of the term "dishonesty" in defining theft it certainly did not contemplate that the jury would be left in complete freedom to uphold a defence that the defendant was carrying out a "Robin Hood" policy of robbing the rich to provide for the poor; or a policy of stealing from his employer on the ground that his services were so valuable that he was morally entitled to higher wages; or a policy of stealing from persons of some selected class (capitalists, bookmakers, and so on) who in his opinion should be made to pay money. Although a judge can never force a jury to convict, it was to be expected that he would strictly enjoin them that no possibility of honesty fell to be considered on such facts. However, things have developed in a way that seems to deprive the judge of almost all control, even the verbal control of giving a firm instruction to the jury on matters like those just listed.

The rot commenced with the decision of the Court of Appeal in *R. v. Feely*,[451] where it was held, applying the general rule in *Cozens v. Brutus*,[452] that "dishonesty" is an ordinary word which must be left to the jury to interpret, the court assuming that the jury will apply it according to "the standards of ordinary decent people."

R. v. Feely concerned the manager of a betting shop who took £30 from the till for his own purposes. This was contrary to his instructions, but he had a right of set-off for this amount in respect of money owed to him by his employer, so he did not put his employer financially at risk. His conviction of theft was quashed because the trial judge had removed the issue of dishonesty from the jury. The judge was wrong not to allow the jury to acquit on the dishonesty issue. Indeed, if the jury after a proper direction had convicted on such facts, the conviction should have been assailable on appeal as being unsafe. But the judgment of the Court of Appeal gave rise to foreboding, not because of the actual decision for the particular defendant but because of the rule stated by the court that honesty is entirely a question for the jury, applying their own assessment of decent current standards.

---

[448] (1988) 86 Cr. App. R. 170.

[449] The prosecution should lead evidence to demonstrate that the owner would not have consented. See generally, *R. v. Flynn* [1970] Crim. L.R. 118.

[450] The phrase used by Lord Morris: see *Bratty v. Attorney-General of Northern Ireland* [1963] A.C. 386 at 416-417.

[451] [1973] Q.B. 530.

[452] [1973] A.C. 854.

The practice of leaving the whole matter to the jury might be workable if our society were culturally homogeneous, with known and shared values, as it once very largely was. But the object of the law of theft is to protect property rights; and disrespect for these rights is now widespread. Since the jury are chosen at random, we have no reason to suppose that they will be any more honest and "decent" in their standards than the average person; indeed, it is not impossible that they will fail to achieve unanimity or near-unanimity except upon a standard lower than the average.

Evidence of the poor level of self-discipline now prevailing abounds—and this without taking any account of tax defaults. Those running corner stores, *inter alios*,[453] take as much cash as they can under the counter to avoid tax and see nothing wrong in doing so. Observers agree upon a very large scale of theft: not merely shoplifting and fare bilking but stealing from employers by employees and an assortment of frauds perpetuated upon customers by employees. Great numbers of employed people of all classes believe that systematic dishonesty of various kinds is a "perk." It is tolerated by many employers, provided that it does not exceed some ill-defined limit; and some employers even encourage fiddlers when they are at the expense of customers, since this is a way of increasing employees' remuneration without cost to the employers. For the employee, illicit remuneration has the advantage of being untaxed. Fiddling also brings non-material rewards: it is a pleasant departure from routine, a game of chance against the risk of detection, all the better since the consequences of detection are now rarely serious. Even the members of Parliament have been committing theft on a grand scale.[454] The members of the Commons and even those unelected members in the Lords stole millions and dressed it up as legitimate expenses. Some of the so-call legitimate expenses included private mortgages and home renovations: including having one's bell tower restored, and one's moat cleaned. If ordinary people in steady employment develop these lax notions about the right of property, it seems from the judgment in *R. v. Feely* that the law of theft is to be automatically adjusted to suit. So the law ceases to provide Holmes's "standard of reference by which conduct can be judged."[455]

The danger presented by *R. v. Feely* of encouraging a decline in standards is partly offset by the fact that minor charges of pilfering are likely to come before magistrates rather than juries, and magistrates may be better able to resist the decline than jurors. Also, whereas there is no appeal from acquittal by a jury, magistrates are kept on a rein by the Divisional Court; this gives the opportunity for the development of rules of law on the subject of honesty, binding on magistrates.[456]

---

[453] Tradesmen often demand cash too. (Taxicab operators a paid in full in cash, as unlike New York cabs, *inter alios*, one cannot use a debit or credit card in London cabs. No doubt taxicab operators have ways of fiddling their gauges so as to avoid paying the correct tax.)

[454] See Robert Winnett and Gordon Rayner, *No Expenses Spared*, (London: Bantam Press, 2009).

[455] What's more, giving the jury *carte blanche* to invoke conventional morality to determine whether to invoke the criminal law contravenes Sir Leo Cussen's great guiding rule: "Sir Leo Cussen insisted always most strongly that it was of little use to explain the law to the jury in general terms and then leave it to them to apply the law to the case before them. He held that the law should be given to the jury not merely with reference to the facts of the particular case but with an explanation of how it applied to the facts of the particular case." *Alford v. Magee* (1952) 85 C.L.R. 437 at 466.

[456] *Halstead v. Patel* [1972] 1 W.L.R. 661.

29–170   But in addition to the sociological objections to *R. v. Feely* there is the philosophical objection that it mistakes the meaning of honesty. Honesty, as the concept was used in the *Theft Act*, was not intended to refer to current standards of behaviour, in such a way that a dishonest society becomes honest by definition. Honesty means at least three things, all of them largely independent of prevailing mores:

1.   Respect for property rights.
2.   Refraining from fraud, at any rate where this would cause loss to another.
3.   Keeping a promise, at any rate where the promisee has supplied consideration for the promise or will suffer loss if it is not kept.[457]

The most important of these meanings for the law of theft is the first. Respect for property rights is not inconsistent with the invasion of property rights in specific cases for good reason (as in situations of necessity), but it is inconsistent with the appropriation of other people's property for personal advantage. The judge should therefore be able to rule that evidence of depredations approved by the opinions of the depredators is not evidence to support a defence of honesty.

Relying entirely on jury standards, without firm direction by the judge, was bad enough; but some decisions after *R. v. Freely* made matters worse by asking the jury to apply not even their own standard but that of the defendant himself whose behaviour was under scrutiny: did the defendant believe what he did was honest? In *Boggeln v. Williams*,[458] Boggeln was charged with dishonestly using electricity, an offence (akin to theft) provided for in section 13 of the *Theft Act 1968*. He had failed to pay his electricity bill, and was disconnected. He then told the Electricity Board employee that he intended to reconnect the supply, which he did. Convicted by magistrates, Boggeln successfully appealed to the Crown Court, which found as a fact that he was not dishonest, even though he knew that the Board did not consent to his use of the electricity, since he intended to pay for it and genuinely believed that he would be able to do so. On further appeal by case stated to the Divisional Court the acquittal was upheld, two members of the court attaching great importance to Boggeln's belief in his own honesty.

29–171   If one asks whether Boggeln respected property rights, the answer is clear-cut. He did not respect them, because he knew for a fact that the Board did not consent to his use of its property, and there were no circumstances entitling him to disregard that fact. But he did, in a sense, respect them, because he intended to pay and thought that the Board would not in fact be disadvantaged. The objection to the decision is not in respect of the outcome (though it certainly attaches an indulgent meaning to the notion of honesty) but to the judges' supposition that the defendant was entitled as a matter of law to set his own standards.

The danger of this attitude was shown in *R. v. Gilks*,[459] where a book-maker paid money by mistake to a punter, and the latter accepted the money although he knew he was not entitled to it. The punter, charged with theft, said in the witness box that in his view book-makers were fair game. The deputy chairman gravely

---

[457]   Williams, *op. cit. supra*, note 254 at 670-671.
[458]   [1978] 1 W.L.R. 873.
[459]   [1972] 1 W.L.R. 1341.

left this defence to the jury, asking them whether in their opinion the defendant thought he was acting honestly. The jury very sensibly rejected the defence, and that conviction was upheld on appeal; but the Court of Appeal did not question the propriety of leaving the defence to the jury, or the terms in which the judge had done so.

Subjectivism of this degree gives subjectivism a bad name. The subjective approach to criminal liability, properly understood, looks to the defendant's intention and to the facts as he believed them to be, not to his system of values. Gilks merely profited by the book-maker's mistake; but what if a person charged with robbing or burgling a book-maker says that in his opinion book-makers are fair game for robbers and burglars? Again, can the defendant go quit by avowing a belief that it is all right to "rip off" banks, insurance companies, multinationals, the taxman, and anyone else who is regarded as "undeserving"?

The extreme extension of the honesty defence to pure subjectivism has now been slightly, but only slightly, curtailed by a case that one can only with difficulty refrain from turning into an expletive: *R. v. Ghosh*.[460] Here the Court of Appeal failed to renounce the doctrine in *R. v. Feely*, and did not wholly reject (but only modified) the notion in *R. v. Gilks* that the defendant's views on honesty are important. The rule established by the court incorporates a double test of dishonesty, stated by Lord Lane C.J. in the following words:

29–172

> "• A jury must first of all decide whether according to the ordinary standards of decent and honest people what was done was dishonest. If it was not dishonest by those standards, that is the end of the matter and the prosecution fails.
>
> • If it was dishonest by those standards, then the jury must consider whether the defendant himself must have realised that what he was doing was by those standards dishonest."[461]

If the answer to the second question is no, the prosecution again fails, otherwise it succeeds on that issue.

The decision has one other importance: Lord Lane took the opportunity of affirming that the test of dishonesty is the same for conspiracy to defraud as for theft—a matter that had previously fallen into doubt.[462]

Lord Lane may have considered his judgment as a rescue operation, but if so, it is a rescue that still leaves this heroine in considerable peril. The second question stated in the decision presents an even greater threat to the standard of honesty than the first. If the defendant stoutly maintains that he considered his act

---

[460] [1982] Q.B. 1053.

[461] The Canadian Courts have rejected the subjective prong. See *R. v. Skalbania* [1996] 109 C.C.C. (3d) 515. See also *R. v. Théroux* [1993] 2 S.C.R. 5 at paras. 33 (a fraud case), where the Supreme Court of Canada said that the second prong of *Ghosh* "cannot be reconciled with the basic principles of criminal law relating to *mens rea*. ... A person who deprives another person of what the latter has should not escape criminal responsibility merely because, according to his moral or her personal code, he or she was doing nothing wrong or because of a sanguine belief that all will come out right in the end. Many frauds are perpetrated by people who think there is nothing wrong in what they are doing or who sincerely believe that their act of placing other people's property at risk will not ultimately result in actual loss to those persons. If the offence of fraud is to catch those who actually practise fraud, its *mens rea* cannot be cast so narrowly as this." See also Kenneth Campbell, "The Test of Dishonesty in *R. v. Ghosh*," (1984) 43 *Cambridge L.J.* 349.

[462] See *R. v. McIvor* [1982] 1 W.L.R. 409.

was honest, and that to his certain knowledge his friends (all of whom are decent and reasonable people) would agree with him ("Everyone I know regards book-makers as fair game;" "We all think it's OK to pad the expense account, to make up for the working time for which the boss doesn't pay us;" "Everyone whips paint and so on in this job; it's regarded as a fair perk"), the jury may be unable to agree upon a finding that in fact the defendant knew the opposite. This difficulty may beset even magistrates, who may be quite clear in their own minds what dishonesty is, but gravely hampered in applying the right standard when they are directed by the Court of Appeal to make enquiry into the defendant's idiosyncratic opinions.

29–173 **Is it a moral assessment of the "act" or the "actor"? In a way both, the actor is assessed on what he knew, believed, and intended. The *act* is assessed as dishonest by drawing on normative understandings of property rights.** The problem with assessing the objective dishonestness of a given type of "action," "act," or a "course of conduct" is that it is like asking whether it was "bad,", "good," "right," or "wrong." This is a philosophical question and opinion will differ as to what is dishonest. There will be disagreement about what is honest regardless of whether the judges provide instructions to the juries or not. But most people could understand the basic idea of respect of another's property. So, unless D can demonstrate that he had a justification or excuse for violating another's property right, he surely should be judged as having acted dishonestly. Focusing on the objectivity of the dishonestness of the act only takes us so far, because the appropriation is merely the means used to achieve either a dishonest or honest end. If D tells a lie to trick a thief into giving his property back, he acts dishonestly to achieve an honest end. If he intends to thieve property which he knows he has no claim of right over, then he acts with a dishonest end in mind—the end of unjustifiably and inexcusably disrespecting another's property rights. He is dishonest because he uses dishonest means (a surreptitious appropriation) to achieve the dishonest end of depriving the owner of his property. (His dishonesty hinges on the fact that he knows he has no right to the property, it is not a gift, he has not paid for it, and cannot point to social conventions to justify his appropriation).

Perhaps the only comfort to be derived from *R. v. Ghosh* is that the rule making honesty depend on what the defendant thinks about honesty must surely involve the placing of an evidential burden on the defendant. Otherwise the prosecution's position becomes impossible. So it should be acknowledged that the trial judge has the power to withdraw the issue of honesty from the jury if on no possible view of the evidence can it be taken to raise a doubt as to dishonesty. He might, for example, rule that the defendant's evidence of a widespread fiddle among his workmates is not evidence of the honesty of the practice fit for the consideration of the jury; nor is it evidence of the defendant's belief in honesty, because it is simply directed to the wrong question. Honesty, even in the sense of customary morality, refers to opinions of ordinary decent people, not just to the opinions of those who are subjected to the same temptations as the defendant and who succumb to them. Moreover, even if the judge has withheld the issue of dishonesty from the jury with technical impropriety, this should not be fatal if the evidence of dishonesty is overwhelming.[463]

The Divisional Court might be called on to correct a magistrates' court's assessment of dishonesty, when it is perverse. In *D.P.P. v. Gohill*[464] the magistrates thought it was not dishonest for D to cheat his employer for his own gain. D worked for a tool and plant hire company that hired equipment to members of the public. The company's policy was that if the equipment was returned to the store within two hours of being hired, because it was faulty, or because incorrect equipment had been chosen, no fee was charged. D allowed working and correctly chosen equipment to be returned within two hours on a number of occasions and was paid approximately £10 in tips whenever he turned a blind eye. D then altered the computer records to give the impression that the equipment had simply been reserved or was faulty in order to conceal the missing revenue. The magistrates' court held that reasonable and honest people would do the same thing and acquitted D. The Divisional Court held: "A magistrates' court's decision to acquit individuals, who allowed customers of a tool hire company to hire equipment without making a payment, of theft and false accounting on the grounds that the individuals' actions were not dishonest by the standards of reasonable and honest people was perverse."[465]

A majority of the Supreme Court of Victoria in *R. v. Salvo*[466] resoundingly **29–174** rejected the rule in *R. v. Feely*. In a forthright judgment, Fullagar J. (construing the similar provisions of the Victorian statute) shot down the English Court of Appeal's notion that the uninstructed juror would know the meaning of dishonesty as it appeared in the *Act* (and particularly as it appeared in the section corresponding to the former section 15). He rejected the "moral obloquy" test for the reason that it bases criminal liability upon shifting sands; and he held that the word "dishonesty" is to be understood to express an absence of a belief in legal (as opposed to moral) right to deprive the other of the property. In other words, he construed dishonesty as bearing the meaning formerly carried by the phrase "without claim of right." In his opinion, it is the duty of the judge in each case to indicate to the jury by reference to the facts what is required to constitute dishonesty in this sense.

Alas, Fullagar J.'s fusillade, splendid though it is, is not logically so effective as it may appear on first reading. In particular, a technical objection to his interpretation of "dishonesty" is that in effect the interpretation accepts section 2(1)(a) of the English *Act* (which is taken over into the Victorian *Act*) as expressing the full meaning of the word for the purpose of the *Act*. Thus, subject to the extension of that meaning made by paragraphs (*b*) and (*c*), the interpretation makes section 2 exhaustive of the meaning of the word, whereas the section shows that it is not meant to be exhaustive. This objection does not,

---

[463] See *R. v. Lewis* (1976) 62 Cr. App. R. 206. *R. v. Potger* (1971) 55 Cr. App. R. 42.

[464] [2007] EWHC 239 (Admin.).

[465] *D.P.P. v. Gohill* [2007] EWHC 239 (Admin.)

[466] [1980] V.R. 401. See also *R. v. Bonollo* [1981] V.R. 633; *R. v. Lawrence* [1997] 1 V.R. 45. See also *R. v. Todo* [2004] V.S.C.A.177 at para. 25 where it was noted that the decisions in *Peters v. The Queen* (1998) 192 C.L.R. 493 and *McLeod v. The Queen* (2003) 214 C.L.R. 230 did not interfere with the ruling in *R. v. Salvo*.

however, destroy the force of Fullagar J.'s criticism of the English practice of leaving the issue of dishonesty at large to an uninstructed jury.

The best solution, it may be suggested, would be legislation that in effect restores the former concept of conduct without a claim of right, in place of the concept of dishonesty, a claim of right being defined in section 2(1) (with some amendments). This would be a legislative acceptance of what Fullagar J. thinks the law should be. Professor Elliott suggests an addition in order to alleviate the law: it should be provided that to amount to theft an appropriation must be "detrimental to the interests of the other in a significant practical way."[467] However, such a provision would presumably leave it open to the defendant to say that he believed that his appropriation was not of this kind, and this may cause trouble—an employee can always believe that his said defalcations do not affect his employer in a significant and practical way. In the case of our MP, it could hardly be said that having his moat cleaned had any measurable impact on the treasury. It seems, therefore, to be better to go back to the unqualified rule of the common law. Moreover, section 2(2) should be rewritten to establish that dishonesty is never negatived merely by an intention to pay or repay for the property or money taken. The defendant would, however, have a defence where paragraph (*b*) or subsection (1) applies.

29–175 One always has a sense of hopelessness in proposing legislation in Britain, so the possibility of judicial reform is to be considered. The meaning of dishonesty has not yet come before the Supreme Court of the United Kingdom. When it does, there is some possibility that a bombardment of the Court based on *Salvo* will have an effect. What must be found is a definition of dishonesty (outside the specific situations mentioned in section 2)[468] that will not depend exclusively on general opinion, and one that will nevertheless go beyond the rules in section 2. I would suggest the definition should be that dishonesty involves disregard for rights of property without justification or excuse. If the defendant is not raising a claim of right under section 2, then he should raise evidence to demonstrate why it was excusable or justifiable for him to take V's property. Whether the claim of right falls within section 2 or under the general dishonesty standard, the jury should not accept the defendant's belief that what he did was honest unless there is something in the objective evidence that makes it plausible to hold that D did in fact hold such belief. There is a distinction between a belief that reasonable people would consider one's actions to be honest and a belief that one's actions do not violate the property rights of others. Section 2 allows D to put a totally unreasonable belief in a claim of right to the jury, but the unreasonableness of the belief could suggest that it was not in fact held. The assessment of D's subjective fault under the general standard of honesty should only focus on whether D believed he had a justification or excuse for violating V's property rights, and not on his subjective views of the honesty of the particular kind of acting.

---

[467] D. W. Elliott, "Dishonesty in Theft: A Dispensible Concept," [1982] Crim. L.R. 395.
[468] Cf. Peter Glazebrook, "Revisting the Theft Acts," (1993) 52 *Cambridge L.J.* 191.

CHAPTER 30

ROBBERY AND SIMILAR OFFENCES

"There be land rats and water rats, land thieves and water thieves,—I mean, pirates."

The Merchant of Venice I iii[1]

30.1.   ROBBERY

The non-lawyer speaks of "robbing a bank" by driving a tunnel into the strong-room; but this is not legal usage. In law, robbery implies force or the threat of it. It is a form of aggravated theft, not triable summarily.[2] Section 8 of the *Theft Act* provides:

30–001

> "(1)   A person is guilty of robbery if he steals, and immediately before or at the time of doing so, and in order to do so, he uses force on any person or puts or seeks to put any person in fear of being then and there subjected to force.
>
> (2)   A person guilty of robbery, or of an assault with intent to rob, shall on conviction on indictment be liable to imprisonment for life."

Its legal meaning is to be gathered chiefly from careful study of its terms and recent precedent; though a knowledge of some of the problems raised by the old case-law (when the definition of the offence was somewhat different) is of help.

Is robbery an offence against the person or against property?   The offence of robbery incorporates a combination of ingredients from the standard offences against the person (assault, *etc.*) and all the ingredients of the offence of theft. In times gone by, robbery was regarded as less serious than larceny because the robber's thieving was not surreptitious.[3] Eventually, robbery was labelled as more serious than larceny, because it is both an attack on property rights and on the person. Theft provides the robber with a fairly powerful incentive for using force, and force facilitates his taking, so robbery is regarded as very dangerous. It is the risk of bodily injury that underlies the labelling of robbery as a serious crime. The maximum sentence is imprisonment for life. There is, however, a remarkable difference between tugging a handbag from a lady's shoulder and robbing a bank with a machine gun, but the single offence of robbery covers both. The label of

30–002

---

[1]   William Shakespeare, *The Merchant of Venice*, (Leipzig: Bernard Tauchnitz, 1868) at 11.

[2]   Section 17 of the *Magistrates' Courts Act 1980* (Sch 1 para 28(a)).

[3]   Frederick Pollock and Frederick William Maitland, *The History of English Law Before the Time of Edward I*, (Cambridge: Cambridge University Press, Vol. I, 1923), 493-494.

robbery does not factor in the different levels of dangerousness posed by different offenders. The life sentence has also been applied in cases where the defendant was not armed with a dangerous weapon—at least not in an objective sense when assessed from the *ex post* perspective.[4]

In *Weeks v. United Kingdom*,[5] a 17-year old man was given a life sentence for robbing a store with a starter pistol. The robbery involved a sum of 35 pence, which was eventually found on the shop floor. The defendant went to a pet shop with a starter pistol loaded with blank cartridges, pointed it at the owner and demanded the contents of the till. After committing the robbery he confessed and gave himself up. It emerged that he carried out the robbery because he wanted to pay back £3 which he owed his mother, who had threatened him with eviction earlier that day. Nevertheless, the European Court held that the life sentence was not contrary to Article 3 of the *European Convention for the Protection of Human Rights and Fundamental Freedoms*. In a line of other cases, the European Commission of Human Rights has made it clear that the convention does not contain a "general right to call into question the length of a sentence imposed by a competent court".[6]

The sentencing judge has the discretion to give lighter sentences in cases where the offender has not been violent, has not used a dangerous weapon, has taken a trivial sum and so on.[7] Nonetheless, robbery should be labelled in proportion with its seriousness. The sensible approach would be to distinguish *simple* robbery from *aggravated* robbery. In the U.S. very few states bowl robbery into a single category. In the U.S. simple robbery is normally distinguished from aggravated robbery by factors such as whether the robber was "[a]rmed with a 'dangerous' (or 'deadly') ... weapon; used a dangerous instrumentality; inflicted serious bodily injury; and had an accomplice."[8] Thrashing out all the variables is beyond the scope of our present discussion, but core factors such as the dangerousness of the weapon and the level of violence used, seem to provide a clear starting point. Fair labeling means that it is important to distinguish seriously dangerous criminals such as *armed* robbers[9] from *unarmed* bag snatchers.

Since robbery is theft with the additional ingredient of the use or threat of force, a "person convicted of robbery must, by statutory definition, also be guilty

---

[4] If D intended the weapon to appear as a real weapon and it in fact had the effect of appearing as such, then he at least intends to cause V to apprehend that force might be used. Cf. *R. v. Bentham* [2005] 1 W.L.R. 1057; *R. v. Morris* (1985) 149 J.P. 60.

[5] (1988) 10 E.H.R.R. 293.

[6] See Michael Tonry and Richard S. Frase, *Sentencing and Sanctions in Western Countries*, (Oxford: Oxford University Press, 2001), 363. For a critique, see Dennis J. Baker, "Constitutionalizing the Harm Principle," (2008) 27 *Criminal Justice Ethics* 3; Dennis J. Baker, *The Right Not to be Criminalized: Demarcating Criminal Law's Authority*, (Farnham: Ashgate, 2011) at Chap. 2.

[7] *R. v. Roe* [2010] All E.R. 228; *R. v. Considine* [2008] EWCA Crim. 1407; *R. v. Allen* [2005] EWCA Crim. 667. For a good discussion of the issues, see Andrew Ashworth, "Robbery Re-assessed," [2002] Crim. L.R. 851.

[8] Wayne R. LaFave, *Substantive Criminal Law*, (Thompson/West Publishing, Vol. 3, 2003) at 193-194.

[9] It appears that the standard sentence for robberies involving aggravating factors is approximately 15 years. See *R. v. Turner* (1975) 61 Cr. App. R. 67 at 89 *et seq.*

of theft."[10] So the starting point is to establish all the elements of theft. D must appropriate property belonging to another. The wide reach of the concept of appropriation means that the theft element will not be too difficult to establish in most cases. Trying to tug a handbag from a person would constitute an appropriation for the purposes of the *Theft Act*, even if it was not successfully removed from the victim.[11] All the normal limitations apply. Therefore, it would not be robbery to use force to obtain confidential information.[12] Nor, it appears,[13] is it robbery to use force to take V's chequebook. There is a major *lacuna* here, which warrants the Supreme Court's attention.

If I frighten V into dropping his wallet with the intention of taking it, but do not touch the wallet, am I guilty of robbery?   You have not completed your robbery. If you stood by the wallet with an intent to prevent V from retrieving it so that you could take it, you would consummate the offence of robbery, because an appropriation under the very wide definition found in the current law of theft would be satisfied, since you (technically) have taken control of it. You will recall that the current law of theft does not make any real distinction between attempted theft and consummated theft. Alternatively, you might be guilty of assault with intent to rob contrary to section 8(2) of the *Theft Act 1968*.   **30–003**

What if I rob V to retrieve something that I believe belongs to me?   You will recall that the offence of *theft* requires dishonesty. If you have a genuine belief that you have a claim of right, you might convince the jury that you did not commit theft and therefore could not have committed robbery.[14] But your belief must actually be held.[15] Notwithstanding ancient authority to the contrary,[16] it is doubtful that a defendant would be able to rob a store and use the fact that he paid for the goods to ground a claim of right. Generally, a person would not believe he has a right to take goods that are for sale, if the seller has refused to sell him those goods. A person would have an even weaker claim when the goods are not for sale. D could not go to the National Gallery with his gun and chequebook to take all the paintings he desires, because the paintings are not for sale. Furthermore, a drug-dealer should not have a right to *rob* a client who has not paid him for illegal drugs, because he is trying to enforce an independent criminal transaction. Nor   **30–004**

---

[10] *R. v. Guy* (1990) 93 Cr. App. R. 108. However, the offence of assault is not an essential element of robbery. *R. v. Tennant* [1976] Crim. L.R. 133.

[11] *Corcoran v. Anderton* (1980) 71 Cr. App. R. 104. *DPP v. Gomez* [1993] A.C. 442.

[12] *Oxford v. Moss* (1979) 68 Cr. App. R. 183.

[13] *R. v. Preddy* [1996] A.C. 815 at 836-837. *Aliter, Parsons v. The Queen* (1999) 195 C.L.R. 619 at 633-634.

[14] See section 2 of the *Theft Act 1968*; *R. v. Hall* [2008] EWCA Crim. 2086; *R. v. Robinson* [1977] Crim. L.R. 173; *R. v. Skivington* [1968] 1 Q.B. 166.

[15] *R. v. Forrester* [1992] Crim. L.R. 792.

[16] In *The Fisherman's case,* cited in Michael Dalton, *The Country Justice,* (London: printed by William Rawlins *et al.*, 1705) at 364, it was held that: "whereupon the other took away some of the Fisherman's Fishes against his will, and gave him more Money for them than they were worth..." the other had a defence. See also William Hawkins, *A Treatise of the Pleas of the Crown*, (London: printed by E. Richardson *et al.*, 4th edn. 1762) at 98; William Blackstone, *Commentaries on the Laws of England*, (Dublin: printed for John Exshaw *et al.*, Vol. IV, 1769) at 242.

should D have the right to *force* other innocent people to sell him goods when it is a criminal offence to sell those goods to D.[17]

30–005 **Is actual force necessary?** There is no need for actual force. It is enough that D *intends* to make V fear that force will be applied then and there. It is not even necessary for V to feel threatened or to apprehend that force might be used, since it "is the intention of the perpetrator, rather than the fortitude of the victim, which is the touchstone of whether the offence was robbery or theft."[18] Criminalization and inculpation focuses on the unilateral intentions and actions of the defendant, not on how those actions affected a particular victim. If no force is applied and V does not in fact fear that any force will be used, D could still be guilty of robbery if it was his intention "to put any person in fear of being then and there subjected to force." So if D holds up V with a toy pistol (and unbeknown to D, V is a gun expert who recognizes the gun as a fake and thus does not fear that force will be used), D is guilty of robbery simply on the basis that he intended to put V "in fear of being then and there subjected to force." (And, of course, he would also have to appropriate the relevant property).

30–006 **How much force is necessary?** In effect, subsection (1) means that the theft must be accompanied by force or threat of force. The force may be minimal. In *R. v. Dawson*[19] the defendant, with two others, surrounded V; one of them "nudged" him so that he lost his balance, and while he was thus unbalanced another stole his wallet. A conviction of robbery was sustained on appeal. The judge had left it to the jury to decide whether "force" had been used within section 8(1), and this was held to be a proper course, since "force" is a word in ordinary use which juries understand. The judge had told the jury that the force had to be substantial, but the Court of Appeal left it open whether he was right to apply an adjective to the word of the *Act*. The outcome of the case is clearly right; force used in order to cause the victim to lose his balance is evidently within the *Act*; and the use of the word "substantial" would be an unwarranted gloss. At the same time, it is regrettable that the Court of Appeal did not give further guidance on the meaning of the word. The proper approach, it may be suggested, is to say that force of any degree is, with one exception, sufficient for robbery. So it should be sufficient if the force used was:

1. to prevent or overcome conscious resistance (a tug-of-war with the owner,[20] or applying a chloroform pad to the owner's nose), or
2. to sever an article attached to the owner (breaking a watch-chain),[21] or

---

[17] In *Jupiter v. State*, 616 A.2d 412 (1992) an intoxicated patron forced a publican to sell him beer and it was a criminal offence to sell beer to intoxicated patrons. In *Martin v. State*, 174 Md.App. 510 (2007), D used robbery to enforce an illegal drug deal.

[18] *R. v. D.P.P.* (2007) 171 J.P. 404.

[19] (1976) 64 Cr. App. R. 170; *R. v. Codsi* [2009] EWCA Crim. 1618. Cf. *R. v. Hale* 68 Cr. App. R. 415.

[20] *Corcoran v. Anderton* (1980) 71 Cr. App. R. 104.

[21] *R. v. Mason* (1820) 168 E.R. 876.

3.   in such a way as to cause injury (tearing an earring from the lobe of the ear).[22]

In each of these instances the force can reasonably be held to be within the section. But—and this is the exception—the force must be something more than slight exertion of strength used by a "dip" to lift the victim's wallet by stealth from his pocket.[23] Similarly, *gentle force* used to snatch an article by stealth or surprise should not be enough; otherwise robbery would include all theft from the person, which was obviously not the intention of the *Act*. Twitching a handbag from a woman caught unawares should not be robbery, but tugging it away when she offers resistance should be.[24]

But there is a very fine line here. If D sneaks up behind V and tugs her diamond necklace with the intent of using whatever force is necessary to get it off her neck, but by sheer chance her necklace has a faulty clip and falls from her neck without her even noticing, D's culpability and accompanying actions are no different than if he had used maximum force to remove the necklace. D should be convicted of robbery rather than of theft. After all, it was D's intention to use force and he attempted to use force by going through the motions of ripping the necklace from the lady's neck; it was only by pure chance that the intended force did not physically impact the particular victim's neck as severely as he had intended. (The appropriation was completed and the force attempted, but it is not attempted robbery since we can assume that he intended or sought to put V in fear of being subjected to force *not* immediately before the taking but "at the time of" the taking—as he was intending to use maximum force to rip the necklace from her neck. Actual fear is not necessary.) The case would be different if D had managed to complete the appropriation without any intention of putting V in fear of being then and there subjected to force, but it is difficult to imagine such a case.

If D slips a benzodiazepine drug such as rohipnol into V's drink so that he can get her purse while she is unconscious, he does not seem to commit robbery since he has not used any external force to administer the drug—nor does he intend V to fear that external force will be used then and there. *Per contra*, the fact that no external force was used to administer the drug seems to be irrelevant, because D indirectly inflicts force which has the same effect as if he had hit his victim over the head with a batten. The victim does not have to be aware of the fact that she has been subjected to force. If D sneaks up behind V and delivers a knockout blow, it is no defence to argue V did not see it coming. The question then, is this: does it make a difference if the (clandestine) administration of force is designed

30–007

---

[22] *R. v. Lapier* (1784) 168 E.R. 263.

[23] In the U.S. it has been held that: "[s]natching a purse from the fingertips of its unsuspecting possessor in itself did not constitute sufficient use of force" for robbery. See *People v. Patton*, 389 N.E. 2d 1174 (1979). See also *People v. Taylor*, 129 Ill.2d 80 at 84 (1989); *People v. Davis*, 935 P.2d 79 (1996); *State v. Harris*, 186 N.C.App. 437 (2007). Cf. *People v. Thomas*, 119 Ill.App.3d 464 (1983), where D removed V's purse which was tucked under her arm by giving it a quick jab with his fist, without actually touching V, but the purse left a red mark on her arm.

[24] In *R. v. Batchelor* [1977] Crim. L.R. 111 a man who snatched a bag from a woman pleaded guilty to robbery. It is surprising that the plea was offered and accepted on such facts. Cf. *R. v. Davis* (1980) 144 J.N.P. 707.

to *impact* V internally? In *People v. Dreast*[25] it was held: "A showing of 'force or fear' is not (and cannot be) limited to external forces such as bludgeoning the victim or displaying a lethal weapon to overcome his will and resistance. A poison or intoxicant, although internally applied, may also serve as a potent means to achieve the same goal and may also render the felonious taking of personal property a taking against the will of the victim, thereby constituting robbery."

This seems perfectly plausible. If D delivers a blow to knockout V, the actual cause of V's unconsciousness stems from the blow's impact on her internal physiological processes, as is the case when a person is poisoned by drugs. Our hypothetical was not a case of D finding an unconscious victim, but a case of him causing the victim's unconsciousness so that he could take her purse. There is no need for the force to be administered directly. The force might be applied indirectly by ripping at property which is attached to the victim[26] or by slipping drugs in his drink. It not possible to imagine all the likely physical consequences of drugging someone: Did it cause V to fall and make physical contact with the floor? Did it have violent physical side-effects such as causing pain? In the end, it should be for the jury to determine whether the indirect application of force was in fact force on a person.[27] The case would be different if D managed to hypnotize V into handing over his property, since this would not involve an application of force to V's inner workings. Its impact is psychological not physical. Given the penalty under section 22 of the *Offences Against the Person Act (1861)* for administering stupefying drugs is life, we need not delve any further.

The threat of force may be implied from conduct; so where several people surround the victim in such a way as to make resistance hazardous, if not vain, and steal from him, this amounts to robbery. Similarly, if D goes to a restaurant late at night dressed in a disguise to demand that the contents of the till be given to him, he would implicitly signal that force may be used. It would be reasonable to infer that the demands for cash are likely to be backed up with force. It is also worth noting that force used to overcome V's resistance is sufficient for the purposes of section 8(1) of the *Theft Act 1968*. So, if D attempts to remove V's wallet from his pocket and V fights back to thwart the appropriation, D's conviction could be elevated from (attempted) theft to robbery.

30–008 **Is a threat of using force on V's child sufficient?** The force threatened must be "on any person;" a threat to damage property[28] is insufficient for this crime (though sufficient for blackmail). And the threat must be of force to be applied to the recipient of the threat; so, oddly, it is not robbery to steal from a person by threatening to injure his baby if he resists, where the baby is not put in fear[29]; but such conduct is again punishable as blackmail.[30] However, the force need not be used on the person stolen from; it is robbery to use force on a signalman in order

---

[25] 153 Cal. App. 3d 623 at 625-629 (1984).

[26] *R. v. Clouden* [1987] Crim. L.R. 56.

[27] *R. v. Clouden* [1987] Crim. L.R. 56.

[28] Cf. the pre-*Act* position with respect to dwellings: *R. v. Simons* (1773) 2 East P.C. 712.

[29] *R. v. Taylor* [1996] C.L.Y. 1518. Cf. *Reane's Case* (1794) 168 E.R. 410.

[30] See section 21 of the *Theft Act 1968*.

to steal from a train. The force does not have to be used against a person who has a proprietary right or interest in the appropriated property. If D is trying to break into V's car to take his laptop computer and passer-by V2 tries to prevent him and is attacked, D is guilty of robbery. He has used force to appropriate property. Similarly, if D uses or threatens to use force against a security guard in order to get the goods from a warehouse, he will be guilty of robbery. There is no need to show that the guard has custody or control of the property.[31] The guard is no different to a passer-by stepping in.

Subsection (1) says: "puts or seeks to put any person in fear." Suppose that the defendant put the victim in fear without meaning to do so, and then took advantage of the fear to steal from him?   The subsection requires that the putting in fear must be "in order to steal." If the defendant did not intend to steal when he accidentally put the victim in fear, he is not guilty of robbery.[32] So, if D uses force in an attempt to rape V and she pays him money to avert the attack, he would not be guilty of robbery under the *Theft Act 1968*.[33] If a shoplifter dashes from a store in a panic and accidentally knocks over the doorman, he does not commit robbery. Our shoplifter is not guilty of robbery because he does not intend to use force to facilitate his appropriation. Likewise, if D gets into a fistfight with V and accidentally knocks him out, and thereafter decides (forms the intent) to take V's wallet, he does not commit robbery because he did not knockout V in order to steal his wallet. He could, however, be charged with an offence against the person and theft.

30–009

The subsection says that the force or threat must be "immediately before or at the time of" stealing. When is the time of the stealing?   The force or threat of it must be virtually contemporaneous with the appropriation. But the taking itself can span over a period of time. Theoretically, the stealing is complete upon the appropriation being made—whenever that is.[34] Using force to escape with the loot after committing a theft is not sufficient for robbery, (*a*) because this is used after the theft (*b*) because it is used in order to escape and not "in order to" steal. The previous legislation included force or threat made immediately after the theft; these words were purposely omitted from the *Theft Act 1968*. However, in *R. v. Hale*[35] the jury were allowed to find that an appropriation continued for some undefined time after the taking. This interpretation takes away the force of the limiting words, demonstrating that there are some changes in the law that Parliament is helpless to make.

30–010

In *R. v. Lockley*,[36] D and two others took cans of beer from an off-licence. When they were approached by the shopkeeper they used force in order to keep their stash. The defendant argued that he had not committed robbery, because the theft was complete before he used force. The court held that the appropriation

---

[31] Cf. *Smith v. Desmond* [1965] A.C. 960.

[32] Cf. *R. v. Bruce* [1975] 1 W.L.R. 1252.

[33] Cf. the pre-*Act* position: *R. v. Blackham* (1787) 2 East P.C. 711.

[34] See *R. v. Atakpu* [1994] Q.B. 69 at 79 citing Glanville Williams, "Appropriation: A Single or Continuous Act?" [1978] *Crim.L.R.* 69.

[35] (1979) 68 Cr. App. R. 415; *R. v. Smartt* [2004] EWCA Crim. 2072 at para. 24.

[36] [1995] Crim. L.R. 656.

was still in progress when D threatened to use force. Since the appropriation was still in progress and the force was designed to facilitate its completion, the force was contemporaneous with the taking. The appropriation would not be in progress if it is fully consummated (the wide definition of appropriation makes no distinction between consummated and non-consummated appropriations—since it merely requires D to assume a single right of the owner), but if D had left the store and had run a mile down the road the appropriation would no longer be in progress. Any force used at this stage would not be in order to steal as the defendant has already escaped with the goods. Thus, if D has made a fairly clear escape but V manages to catch up with him and is assaulted by D, it seems, unfortunately, that this cannot be robbery. Although, it might be argued that if V has chased D from the store and has stayed on his tail, that the appropriation was still continuing and thus was not consummated, but this would only apply if V had stayed in continuous pursuit.[37]

The threat must be to use force on the present occasion, not a threat to use it in the future by way of reprisal for failing now to submit to the proposed threat. It is not enough that a defendant persuades the victim to hand over property by threatening to use force in the future or on some unrelated occasion.[38] Future threats are blackmail and nothing more. It is not enough that a defendant persuades V to send him cash by courier, by phoning V and threatening to kill him at some future time if he does not send it, because even though the victim might be frightened he is not put in fear of "being then and there subjected to the force." If the force that V fears is "[s]eparated in *time* or *place* from the threat, the offence cannot be one of robbery."[39]

30–011   If D uses force to prevent V from retrieving his mobile phone from D's lawful possession, he could be guilty of robbery.[40] The theft element is satisfied because D's appropriation is concurrent with the physical force that he used to prevent V from regaining possession of his article. D did not appropriate the mobile phone when he took lawful possession, rather he appropriated it when he refused to return it and at the same time put V "in fear of being then and there subjected to force." This is to be distinguished from the case where D is in possession of V's gold ring because he appropriated it some time ago. If D appropriated V's gold ring weeks ago and V finds out and confronts him to regain possession of his ring—and D gives V a thorough hiding to prevent him from getting his ring back—D does not commit robbery. Since D appropriated the ring some weeks ago he cannot appropriate it again by refusing to hand it over to D. The appropriation and the hiding are separate acts taking place on different occasions. The force used by D to prevent V from regaining possession of the ring is not contemporaneous with D's appropriation of the ring. The appropriate charges in this situation are theft for the appropriation of the ring and assault for the subsequent hiding.

---

[37] Cf. *R. v. Jodie* (2000] 1 Cr. App. R. 17.

[38] *R. v. Kahn* [2001] EWCA Crim. 923.

[39] *R. v. Kahn* [2001] EWCA Crim. 923.

[40] See *R. v. Smartt* [2004] EWCA Crim. 2072 at para. 24 where V let D borrow his mobile phone and was threatened when he asked for its return.

Can the threat of fear also be a continuous event? A continuing threat of **30–012**
force may be sufficient.   The threat of present force will readily be held to
continue to operate on the victim's mind although the threat is not committed
until sometime afterwards. In *R. v. Donaghy*[41] the defendants (Donaghy and
Marshall) jumped in a cab and demanded to be driven to London. The cabdriver
took them because they had threatened his life. When they reached London,
Marshall stole £22 from the cabdriver. The Crown Court held that a conviction
for robbery could be sustained if the jury were satisfied that the "effect of the
threats was continuing, to the defendants' knowledge, and that they deliberately
used the effect of the threats in order to obtain the money and that by their
manner they gave the impression they were continuing the threats at the time of
the theft."

30.2.   ASSAULT WITH INTENT TO ROB

On a rational view of the law of attempt, every assault with intent to rob is an **30–013**
attempted robbery, and there is no need for a special provision. But before the
Criminal Attempts Act 1981 it was feared that on some facts an assault might be
held merely preparatory to a robbery; so the *Theft Act* provides this special form
of aggravated assault. Upon a charge of robbery there may be a conviction of
theft (since robbery is aggravated theft), or of attempted theft; but there cannot be
a conviction of assault with intent to rob, which needs a special count. Situations
are conceivable in which there is a robbery without assault, as where the thief
pulls an article from its owner who tries to prevent him from doing so. The
pulling should be sufficient force for robbery,[42] but it is not an assault, unless of
course there is an implied threat of physical assault.

Two offences similar to robbery that are outside the *Theft Act 1968* may be
briefly considered.

30.3.   HIJACKING

Hijacking does not normally fall within the definition of piracy, but its emergence **30–014**
as an offence of international dimensions has caused it to be governed by
international treaty. Legislation now in the *Aviation Act 1982* gives effect to this
treaty by creating an offence called "hijacking" in the marginal note. (If we are to
suffer a neologism it might as well have been called "skyjacking," since it is
confined to the hijacking of aircraft in flight.) In general, the offence is triable by
our courts regardless of where it was committed. The same *Act* creates various
offences of damaging or endangering aircraft, again triable by our courts
wherever the act is committed. Nonetheless, hijacking in the skies is more likely
to be related to terrorism (threats to the safety and wellbeing of the hostages)
rather than property rights. It might involve political blackmail, but it is not
usually done in order to steal.

---

[41] [1981] Crim. L.R. 644.
[42] *R. v. Sherriff* [1969] Crim. L.R. 260.

"Carjacking," however, does involve property rights. If D forcibly takes V's motorcar he may be guilty of robbery. The motorcar might also have valuable items inside it such as cash, a satellite navigation system, and mobile phones.[43] But if D takes the car with the intention of using it temporarily for a joyride, he would not commit robbery.[44] If theft is not made out because D did not intend to permanently deprive V of the vehicle, then robbery will not be available.[45]

30.4. PIRACY

30–015 Piracy has been described as robbery at sea.[46] English law recognizes two forms of piracy, which may be distinguished as piracy *jure gentium* and municipal piracy respectively. The first is recognized both by English law and by international law (*jus gentium* as it used to be called).[47] The offence found in the *United Nations Convention on the Law of the Sea 1982* is an offence that is justiciable (triable) by the courts in England and Wales.[48] Piracy is defined as follows:[49]

> "Piracy consists of any of the following acts:
> (a)   any illegal acts of violence or detention, or any act of depredation, committed for private ends by the crew or the passengers of a private ship or a private aircraft, and directed—
>   (i)   on the high seas, against another ship or aircraft, or against persons or property on board such ship or aircraft;
>   (ii) against a ship, aircraft, persons or property in a place outside the jurisdiction of any State;
> (b)   any act of voluntary participation in the operation of a ship or of an aircraft with knowledge of facts making it a pirate ship or aircraft;
> (c)   any act of inciting or of intentionally facilitating an act described in subparagraph (a) or (b)."

There is no case-law on this offence, so we need not take our investigation any further.

---

[43] *R. v. Meadley* [2009] EWCA Crim. 770; *R. v. Gbedje* [2007] 2 Cr.App.R.89. *R. v. Khan* [2007] 2 Cr.App.R. 95.

[44] *R. v. Mitchell* [2008] All E.R.109.

[45] In many cases the carjacker only intends to temporarily deprive the owner of the vehicle and has to be charged under section 12(1) of the *Theft Act 1968*. If it can be demonstrated that D intended to permanently deprive V of the car, then theft would be made out under section 1 of the *Theft Act 1968*. If the vehicle is held for ransom or is destroyed, then D might be guilty of theft under section 6 of the *Theft Act 1968*. See *R. v. Raphael* [2008] EWCA Crim. 1014.

[46] *A-G for Colony of Hong Kong v. Kwok-a-Sing* (1873) L.R. 5 P.C. 179 at 199.

[47] *Re Piracy Jure Gentium* [1934] A.C. 586.

[48] See section 26(1) of the *Merchant Shipping and Maritime Security Act 1997*; section 5(1) of the *Aviation Security Act 1982*.

[49] See schedule 5 of the *Merchant Shipping and Maritime Security Act 1997*.

CHAPTER 31

BLACKMAIL

"I can't believe *that*!" said Alice. "Can't you?" the Queen said in a pitying tone. "Try again: draw a long breath, and shut your eyes." Alice laughed. "There's no use trying," she said: "one *can't* believe impossible things." "I dare say you haven't had much practice," said the Queen. "When I was your age, I always did it for half an hour a day. Why, sometimes I've believed as many as six impossible things before breakfast."

Lewis Carroll, *Alice Through the Looking-Glass*

31.1.   THE DEFINITION OF BLACKMAIL

Blackmail has long been recognized as a crime,[1] but there is widespread disagreement about its criminalizability. Professor Feinberg once remarked, "Every *bona fide* philosopher of law tries his hand at least once at the ancient problem of punishing failed attempts."[2] The same might be said of the problem of criminalizing blackmail.[3] The literature on the ethics of criminalizing blackmail is too vast to footnote. The common arguments against criminalization are: (1) in many cases it would not normally be criminal for D to do what he threatens to do (*i.e.* spread a rumour after learning of some private scandal); and (2) D is offering V a *benefit* by offering to stay silent rather than reveal his secret (this is assuming, that the bargaining chip is "a promise of secrecy"). It is lawful for D to receive payment for his silence if V makes an unsolicited offer to pay for it. Of course, D

31–001

---

[1] Glanville Williams, "Blackmail," [1954] Crim. L.R. 7; W. H. D. Winder, "Development of Blackmail," (1941) 5 *Mod. L. Rev.* 21 at 24 *et seq.*; James Lindgren, "The Theory, History, and Practice of the Bribery-Extortion Distinction," (1993) 141 *U. Pa. L. Rev.* 1695; A. L., Goodhart, "Blackmail and Consideration in Contracts," (1928) 44 *L. Q. Rev.* 436. Offences under section 21 cannot be tried summarily: see section 17 of the *Magistrates' Courts Act 1980*.

[2] Joel Feinberg, *Problems at the Roots of Law*, (New York: Oxford University Press, 2003) at 77.

[3] See, *inter alia*, Leo Katz, *Ill-Gotten Gains: Evasion, Blackmail, Fraud and Kindred Puzzles of the Law*, (Chicago: Chicago University Press, 1998); Russell L. Christopher, "Trilemma of Meta-Blackmail: Is Conditionally Threatening Blackmail Worse, the Same, or Better than Blackmail Itself," (2006) 94 *Geo. L.J.* 813; Ken Levy, "Solution to the Real Blackmail Paradox: The Common Link between Blackmail and Other Criminal Threats," (2007) 39 *Conn. L. Rev.* 1051; Walter Block, "Crime of Blackmail: A Libertarian Critique," (1999) 18 *Crim. Just. Ethics* 3; George P. Fletcher, "Blackmail: the Paradigmatic Crime," (1993) 141 *U. Pa. L. Rev.* 1617; Richard A. Posner, "Blackmail, Privacy, and Freedom of Contract," (1993) 141 *U. Pa. L. Rev.* 1817; Henry E. Smith, "Harm in Blackmail," (1998) 92 *Nw. U. L. Rev.* 861; Jeffrie G. Murphy, "Blackmail: A Preliminary Inquiry," (1980) 62(2) *The Monist* 156; Joel Feinberg, "The Paradox of Blackmail," (1988) 1 *Ratio Juris* 83; these papers are also cornucopias of further references.

might also threaten to report V to the police for some crime V has committed unless V pays up, but this type of "promise of secrecy" could be criminalized independently of blackmail.[4] It is also worth noting, that in some cases the blackmail option will not be as economically fruitful as other legal alternatives, such as selling a celebrity's scandal to the tabloids. But not all victims of blackmail are celebrities, so often the secret will only be valuable to the victim.

31–002   **Suppose D (an undergraduate) is in the faculty late one evening to practice for the Jessup Moot when he notices an office door slightly ajar and decides to investigate. Upon investigation he discovers a married professor in a most compromising position with an undergraduate. D says to the professor: "I will not tell your husband, colleagues and undergraduates about your toy-boy, but it will cost you." Why should he be criminalized for offering to sell the professor a benefit?**   Does it make a difference if V offers to pay D without any encouragement from D? Would this make the bargain legitimate? Clearly, if the professor offers to pay D to hush things up, and D has not asked to be paid or made any threats, his actions fall outside the scope of blackmail. There is no basis for criminalizing the transaction if the professor's offer is unsolicited. What about if D is not interested in money, but is a great gossip who thoroughly enjoys telling everyone what he saw? We cannot criminalize everyday gossiping! It is tough luck for the professor. D would have a right to talk about what he saw. Similarly, if D has a secret about a celebrity he does not break the criminal law by selling it to the tabloids. Free speech is a cardinal value. Nor is it criminal for D to remain silent just out of respect for his professor.

31–003   **So, why is it criminal for him to remain silent for a small fee?**   The rationale seems fairly clear: he is using menacing demands to try and sell V her own information. V should not have to pay for her own privacy: and certainly should not be menaced for money for maintaining what she is entitled to maintain— basic privacy. Of course, in the real world privacy can only be protected in a limited sense. Free speech means that people can talk about what they like, tell stories and so forth. If a person discovers another's personal information by pure chance, without breaking into his home and so on, he can pass it on in conversation or in other forms. D may have a right to gossip about V, but he has no right to bully, coerce or otherwise intimidate V for his own economic gain. D has no entitlement to V's money as he is trying to sell what he does not own. He can use this information as gossip, but he cannot use coercive means to try and sell it to V. V has no right to stop D spreading the information as gossip, if the information is true and has been discovered legitimately, but she has the right not to be blackmailed. It is the fact that D tries to coerce V into paying (handing over her property) for something that D does not own to sell, that makes menacing threats for gain the business of the criminal law. D has earned no proprietary interest in V's information and therefore has no right to take V's cash for it. He can use it as gossip so far as it has ended up in the "commons," but that is it. A

---

[4] D has no right to cover up crime and certainly cannot sell silence in such a situation. See for example, section 5(1) of the *Criminal Law Act 1967*. The subsection does allow D to accept compensation if D is the victim of the crime that he is offering not to report.

more profound discussion of the theoretical foundations of the offence cannot be carried out here, but it is clear that this type of conduct can be brought within the purview of the harm principle.[5]

The crime of blackmail was formerly of great complexity. A revised and simplified form appears in section 21 of the *Theft Act*:

> "(1)   A person is guilty of blackmail if, with a view to gain for himself or another or with intent to cause loss to another, he makes any unwarranted demand with menaces; and for this purpose a demand with menaces is unwarranted unless the person making it does so in the belief—
>
> (a)   that he has reasonable grounds for making the demand; and
>
> (b)   that the use of the menaces is a proper means of reinforcing the demand.
>
> (2)   The nature of the act or omission demanded is immaterial, and it is also immaterial whether the menaces relate to action to be taken by the person making the demand.
>
> (3)   A person guilty of blackmail shall on conviction on indictment be liable to imprisonment for a term not exceeding fourteen years."

How does this crime differ from robbery?

1. The treat in robbery is made to get property, whereas a blackmailing demand under the section has the wider purpose of making any gain or causing a loss. The purpose may be, for example, to get a job.   **31–004**

2. The full offence of blackmail is committed as soon as the demand is made; nothing need have been handed over (whereas theftous appropriation is essential for the crime of robbery).

3. Blackmail requires menaces; robbery requires the threat of force (or actual force); in practice the threat of force will almost always be a menace.

Getting property from someone by threatening immediate force against him is both robbery and blackmail, though it would invariably be charged as robbery. Getting property by actual use of force without threats (striking the victim without giving him a chance of surrendering) is robbing but not blackmail, which needs a menace.

Menaces other than threats of immediate force against a person who is put in fear can be blackmail but cannot ripen into robbery. Examples are:

- a threat by a " protection racketeer" to blow up a building;
- a threat to kill a third party who does not know of the threat;
- a threat to get the victim dismissed from his job; and
- a threat to make known discreditable facts about the victim.

Taking a hostage and extorting a ransom would generally be prosecuted as blackmail, kidnapping or false imprisonment, but if the hostage knows what is happening and so is put in fear it would also be robbery. Blackmail is often severely punished by courts (sometimes with unnecessary severity), because of the distress that it causes[6] and the ease with which a victim by the use of such threats may be made to part with large sums of money. Where the blackmailing

---

[5] Dennis J. Baker, *The Right not to be Criminalized: Demarcating Criminal Law's Authority*, (Farnham: Ashgate, 2011).

[6] See *e.g.*, *R. v. Cossington* [1973] Crim. L.R. 319 where a blackmailer who obtained £20 from homosexuals was sentenced to 7 years.

threat is to reveal discreditable facts about the victim, judges generally allow the victim to give evidence in court under the name of "X."

31.2. THE *ACTUS REUS*: DEMAND WITH MENACES

31–005   Section 21 requires a demand[7] with menaces. If the demand is communicated by e-mail or post the demand will be complete regardless of whether the e-mail or letter reaches the intended recipient.[8] Arguably, the menacing demand is the legislation's *raison d'être*, as it is criminalized regardless of whether the demand results in D making a gain or causing a loss.

Normally the making of the demand will be clear (*i.e.* "give me money or else"), but it may be difficult to establish if dressed up as a reciprocal contract. In particular, an announced intention to write one's memoirs may violate the spirit but not the letter of the section. The most notorious instance of such moral blackmail was that by Harriette Wilson, a courtesan of the early 1800s. Finding that her charms alone could no longer sustain her style of life, she conceived the idea of writing an account of her many lovers, charging an honorarium for each name left out.[9] If adroitly executed, such a plan might well escape the law of blackmail. A man who, having heard of the projected book, took the initiative of offering money to have his own contribution to the author's life passed by, could hardly claim that he had received a demand. However, there would be a strong likelihood of a court finding an implied demand if this is at all possible on the facts. Harriette went so far as to publish her memoirs by instalments, which increased the pressure on her victims.

It is hard to see any difference in meaning between a blackmailing "menace" and an ordinary "threat,"[10] except that the more intensive word "menace" enables the court to ignore very trivial threats. (By a curiosity of language menaces are commonly spoken of in the plural, but of course one menace is enough.) So menaces are fairly serious threats such as threats to reveal sensitive information,[11] to use violence, to destroy property,[12] and so on.

31–006   **Is it blackmail to threaten evil to someone other than the person threatened?** The threat is still "menaces" within the section.

31–007   **Need the menace frighten the victim?**   The menace will still be such although, owing to facts unknown to the blackmailer, it makes no impression on the person to whom it is addressed.[13] The fact that the blackmailer thinks he has or may have produced an effective menace is enough. The advantage of this rule

---

[7] The demand is made where a blackmailing letter is posted: *Treacy v. D.P.P.* [1971] A.C. 537.

[8] *Teacy v. D.P.P.* [1971] A.C. 537; *R. v. Moran* (1952) 36 Cr. App. R. 10; *Austin v. The Queen* (1989) 166 C.L.R. 669.

[9] Kenneth Bourne, *The Blackmailing of the Chancellor*, (London: Lemon Tree Press, 1975).

[10] Cf. Lord Wright's comments in *Thorne v. Motor Trade Association* [1937] A.C. 797 at 817.

[11] *R. v. Cox* (1979) 1 Cr. App. R. 190; *R. v. Boyle* [1914] 3 K.B. 339; *R. v. Tomlinson* [1895] 1 Q.B. 706; *R. v. Chalmers* (1867) 10 Cox C.C. 450; *R. v. Miard* (1844) 1 Cox C.C. 22.

[12] *R. v. Taylor* (1859) 175 E.R. 831; *R. v. Smith* (1850) 2 Car. & Kir. 882.

[13] *R. v. Clear* [1968] 1 Q.B. 670. In that case, the threat had no impact on V because unbeknown to D, V's insurer was covering any loss.

to the defendant is illustrated by the cautionary tale of the student who, organizing a University Rag, sent letters to local shopkeepers telling them that they could avoid "inconvenience" on rag day if they paid up to £5 each into the rag fund. He found himself in the dock, charged with blackmail, no less. Luckily he was acquitted on the direction of the judge, who took the view that the threat was not a menace because it was not likely to affect "the mind of an ordinary person of normal stability."[14]

Although the ordinary person test may have a certain utility, it also raises problems: (1) Whether an ordinary person would accede unwillingly to the demand depends not only on the tenor of the threat but on the enormity of the demand. A millionaire, threatened with exposure of some youthful indiscretion, might prefer to pay up on a demand of £500, but the ordinary millionaire of normal stability and courage would probably balk at paying a million pounds. It can hardly be the law that what would otherwise be a blackmailing demand ceases to be so because of its enormity. So the rule must be that a threat that would intimidate an ordinary person to accede to a small demand is a menace, even if on a sliding scale V would eventually put up resistance because the price asked for is so great it outweighs the potential harm of the threat. (2) A blackmailer who pays upon the fears of a person whom he *knows*[15] to be particularly sensitive or timorous can hardly defend himself on the score of such sensitivity or timidity.[16]

On the whole, it may be thought that the ordinary person test creates more difficulties than it solves. The question should be left in the simple words of the *Act*: have menaces been used? The acquittal of the student can be explained on the ground that he was not apparently threatening anything more than good-natured horse-play, and this is how it was perceived by most of the shopkeepers.

Can a threat not to do something that it is one's duty to do be a blackmailing menace?   Obviously it can be. A threat not to feed someone whom the blackmailer has kidnapped would undoubtedly be sufficient, the blackmailer being under the usual duty to feed helpless persons in his charge.   **31–008**

Then would it be blackmail for a debtor to shake his creditor down for a 50 per cent. discount by saying that otherwise he will not pay any part of the debt?   The debtor may believe that he ought not reasonably be asked to pay the full debt, in which case he could argue at his trial that he lacked the unscrupulous mental element. Difficulty arises if the debtor acknowledges that the debt was   **31–009**

---

[14] *R. v. Harry* [1974] L.R. 32; see the valuable commentary on this case. But a blackmailer cannot get off merely by using the language of request: *R. v. Robinson* (1796) 168 E.R. 475 at 483.

[15] If D is aware that the likely effect of his actions will be to intimidate the particular victim, then this will be sufficient. *R. v. Garwood* [1987] 1 W.L.R. 319. The focus is on D's *mens rea*: Did D intend to make a menacing demand of a kind that would be sufficient to intimidate this particular V?

[16] It was held in *R. v. Lawrence* [1971] Crim. L.R. 645 that a conviction is not open to attack merely because the judge has not defined the word "menaces" for the jury; but the evidence made it clear that there was a threat of physical attack. The court added that in exceptional cases where because of special knowledge in special circumstances what would be a menace to an ordinary person was not a menace to the person to whom it was addressed, or *vice versa*, it was no doubt necessary to spell out the meaning of the word. See also *R. v. Garwood* [1987] 1 W.L.R. 319.

justly owing, and that he was acting unscrupulously. It seems obvious that some means of excluding the situation from the section must be found. The solution would be to say that the particular threat is not a "menace." It has always been common enough for debtors who are in difficulties to attempt to obtain an agreed reduction in their debts, and a threat not to pay a debt could not be called a "menace" in the ordinary meaning of that word.

31–010 **Who decides whether the threat is a menace?** The jury; but judges exercise the usual control.[17] In the case just put, if the judge left the case to the jury and the jury found that the threat to withhold payment of the debt was a menace, the Court of Appeal might perhaps quash a conviction, but the point is by no means clear.

31–011 **Can the threat to bring a civil action be a menace?** The question is of practical importance only if there is evidence that the threatener did not believe that he had a just cause of action. If he believed he had a just claim, he lacked the unscrupulous mental element. If he did not believe it, and therefore was unscrupulous (because of paragraph (a) of section 21(1) of the *Theft Act*), then a threat of civil action might well be found by the jury to be a menace, at any rate if the proceedings threatened would involve allegations against the defendant of discreditable conduct—for example, if it were a threatened action for sexual assault. Not only the claimant but his solicitor who lent himself to the false claim could be charged with blackmail.

31.3. THE ECONOMIC MENTAL ELEMENT

31–012 It will be noticed that there are two mental elements. The first, which we may call the economic mental element, is that the menacer must intend to make a gain or cause a loss. The second is expressed in the *Act* by saying that the demand must be unwarranted; but the *Act* immediately makes it clear that what is warranted or unwarranted is subjective to the defendant. The question relates not to the objective nature of the demand but to the defendant's state of mind about his demand. For want of a better name I propose to call it the unscrupulous mental element, a scrupulous defendant being required to believe both (a) and (b) of subsection (1). It is considered in 31.4.

The intent must be to obtain a gain or cause a loss—expressions that are defined in section 34(1) to extend only to "gain or loss in money or other property." It is irrelevant that D is owed the actual sum demanded or otherwise has a legitimate claim of right. One is not able to raise a claim or right as such. Blackmail is made out if D uses menacing demands to try to *gain* what he is legitimately owed, so long as D believes his menaces are not a "proper means of reinforcing the demand."[18] It is about D "getting what D has not,"[19] which

---

[17] See *R. v. Harry* [1974] Crim. L.R. 32.
[18] See also the discussion in Bernard Brown, "Claims of Right: Blackmail and Beyond," (1996) *N.Z. L. Rev.* 517. Roman law required D to demonstrate a public interest in disclosing secret information, *etc.* See the interesting discussion in R. H., Helmholz, "The Roman Law of Blackmail," (2001) 30 *J. Legal Stud.* 33.

includes property that is owed to him. Property also includes goods such as medicine. In *R. v. Bevans*[20] the defendant was in severe pain as he suffered from osteo-arthritis, so he called a doctor. When the medical doctor arrived at D's home to treat him, D pointed a gun at him and demanded a morphine injection. He threatened to shoot the medic if he did not give it to him. The Court of Appeal held that pursuant to the meaning of the words in section 34(2)(a) of the *Theft Act*, the defendant had obtained "what he had not," *i.e.* he got "something which consisted of money or other property." The injection into his body was property, "just as it would have been had the substance been contained in an ampoule which was handed over to him."

The object of the formula in section 21 of the *Act* is to exclude demands for things that are not regarded as property, such as sexual intercourse.[21] Such a demand does not fall within the notion of an offence in respect of property (with which alone the *Theft Act* is concerned). The requirement of an economic mental element means that many kinds of discreditable pressures are not an offence under the *Theft Act* or at all.[22] Examples of threats where there is or may be no economic motive are threats to accuse of discreditable conduct made:

- to get the victim to give a higher grade on a university essay; or
- to compel the victim to use his influence to procure an honorific but unremunerated appointment; or
- to compel the victim to procure a knighthood; or
- to get custody of the blackmailer's child when he is not entitled to the custody; or
- to dissuade the victim from prosecuting the blackmailer for some offence, or from reporting the offence to the police;[23] or

---

[19] This may be owned to D. D might also use *menacing threats* to cause V to part with what V has. *Attorney-General's Reference (No. 1 of 2001)* [2003] 1 Cr. App. R.131. See also section 34 of the *Theft Act 1968*.

[20] (1988) 87 Cr. App. R. 64.

[21] See section 4 of the *Sexual Offences Act 2003*. Cf. the former section 2 of the *Sexual Offences Act 1956*, which specifically targeted this type of blackmail. Cf. the general offence of "extortion" discussed by the Newfoundland Court of Appeal in *R. v. Davis* [1998] N.J. No. 16.

[22] Many states in the U.S. have general coercion offences. For example, Florida Penal Code, F.S.A. §836.05 provides: "Whoever, either verbally or by a written or printed communication, maliciously threatens to accuse another of any crime or offense, or by such communication maliciously threatens an injury to the person, property or reputation of another, or maliciously threatens to expose another to disgrace, or to expose any secret affecting another, or to impute any deformity or lack of chastity to another, with intent thereby to extort money or any pecuniary advantage whatsoever, or with intent to compel the person so threatened, or any other person, to do any act or refrain from doing any act against his or her will, shall be guilty of a felony of the second degree." See also §9A.36.070 of the Revised Code of Washington which provides: "(1) A person is guilty of coercion if by use of a threat he compels or induces a person to engage in conduct which the latter has a legal right to abstain from, or to abstain from conduct which he has a legal right to engage in. (2) 'Threat' as used in this section means: (a) To communicate, directly or indirectly, the intent immediately to use force against any person who is present at the time; or (b) Threats as defined in RCW 9A.04.110(25)(a), (b), or (c)." RCW 9A.56.110 (Washington Code) makes specific reference to sexual favours: "'Extortion' means knowingly to obtain or attempt to obtain by threat property or services of the owner, and specifically includes sexual favours."

[23] But this would be an attempt to obstruct justice.

- to induce the victim not to reveal past discreditable conduct by the blackmailer; or
- to induce the victim to introduce the blackmailer to high society, or to nominate him for membership of an exclusive club.

Even an attempt to make a married civil servant disclose military or political secrets by threatening to reveal that she used to be a porn star would not be blackmail, though it might be an offence under section 44 of the *Serious Crime Act 2007*, since D encourages V to commit an offence under section 2 of the *Official Secrets Act 1989*.

31–013   **But in some of these cases the threatener may have hoped to make a gain eventually. Being introduced to high society, or getting appointed to the House of Lords, might be turned to advantage.**   The courts have not had to consider whether a hope of indirect economic advantage, not directly derived from the advantage that is immediately sought, is sufficient for the crime of blackmail. It may be held that a general hope of advantage as a result of an improvement in the threatener's social, business or professional position is insufficient because it is too unquantifiable. But the more likely attitude of the judges would be to leave the jury to decide whether in all the circumstances a substantial part of the threatener's intention was to make a monetary gain.

31–014   **If V is suing D for a debt or damages, could it be blackmail for D to use menaces to V to make V discontinue the action?**   By section 34(2)(a), "'gain' includes a gain by keeping what one has." So the case is covered.[24]

31–015   **If a person demands payment of money that is due to him, is his intent to obtain a gain?**   Again yes.[25] A bird in the hand, *etc*. But the creditor who makes such a demand will not be guilty of blackmail unless he has the unscrupulous mental element. We are leaving this matter over at present. (In practice the charge against the creditor who uses high-handed methods of debt collection is likely to be the special offence of harassment of debtors,[26] and there may be other offences of more limited ambit, as well as licensing controls over debt-colleting agencies which might be sufficient.) In the unusual case where a person is convicted of a blackmailing threat to compel payment of money actually due, the courts sometimes take a very lenient line.[27]

---

[24] *Attorney-General's Reference (No. 1 of 2001)* [2003] 1 W.L.R. 395.

[25] *R. v. Parkes* [1973] Crim. L.R. 358.

[26] Section 40 of the *Administration of Justice Act 1970*.

[27] *R. v. Helal* (1980) 2 Cr. App. R. 383; *R. v. Kewell* [2000] 2 Cr. App. R.(S.) 38; *R. v. Mason* (1995) 16 Cr. App. R. 968; *R. v. Shah* (1993) 14 Cr. App. R. 503. This will not be the case if heavy handed tactics are used. Cf. *R. v. Simmons* (1991) 13 Cr. App. R. 242; *R. v. Killgallon* [1998] 1 Cr. App. R. 279.

31.4. THE UNSCRUPULOUS MENTAL ELEMENT

We now pass to the more difficult of the two mental elements specified in the section. The Crown must disprove one or other of the two beliefs mentioned in the section, satisfying the jury either:

31–016

(a)   that the defendant did not believe that he had reasonable grounds for making the demand, or

(b)   that the defendant did not believe that the use of the menaces was a proper means of reinforcing the demand.[28]

Suppose that the threatener knew he had no legal right to the property demanded; could he still be found to have believed that he had reasonable grounds for making the demand, thus lacking the unscrupulous element under (a)?   Certainly. He may have won money on a wager, which is void by statute but generally regarded as binding in honour. So if a bookmaker has not paid out winnings, the aggrieved punters may well threaten to have him posted at Tattersalls,[29] because this is a recognized sanction against defaulting bookmakers. A man's mistress may claim against him money he has promised her, though she has taken legal advice and knows she cannot in law recover money promised on what the law regards as an immoral consideration. In cases of this kind it is fully understandable that the threatener believed he (or she) had reasonable grounds for making the demand, and therefore he lacked the unscrupulous mental element under (a), even though he (or she) knew that it was not a legally enforceable demand.

31–017

Could the mistress threaten to expose the man to his wife if he does not pay money?   The question is for the jury. They may quite well find, at least in some circumstances, that the lady has skirted the law of blackmail. In the debate on the Theft Bill when it was before the House of Lords, Lord Stow Hill criticized the blackmail section as follows:

31–018

> "I instance the case of a lady who supposes that she is in an interesting condition as the result of her association with a gentleman who is married. She has asked him to make provision for the expected arrival in this world of a new child, and he has refused. He is well off and she thinks, no doubt rightly, that his conduct is indescribably evil and selfish. She passionately thinks it, and goes to him and says, 'Look here, if you dont make an adequate settlement on this child I will tell your wife, I will tell your employers; I will write letters to the Press; I will do everything I can to make you make settlement on the child.' Does she, in these circumstances, commit the crime of blackmail?
> In order to test the matter a little further, and possibly to make the example a little more difficult, may I assume this: that she is a lady who feels that this unfortunate infant is going to be born into the world, through no fault of his, labouring under the stigma of being an illegitimate child. What would be a reasonable settlement in the case of an infant born in lawful wedlock into a family is not sufficient in this case; it must be a much more generous settlement. The amount she has in mind might be such that ordinary people would think it a wholly unreasonable request. But if the jury are to ask themselves, what does she think about

---

[28] An evidential burden doubtless rests on the defendant. *R. v. Harvey* (1980) 72 Cr. App. R. 139 at 142; see also [1974] Crim. L.R. 33.

[29] Cf. *Burden v. Harris* [1937] 4 All E.R. 559. A horse owner may be reported to the Jockey Club: *Bubb v. Yelverton* (1870) L.R. 9 Eq. 471.

it, what is her belief, however unreasonable it may be, however it might beggar the family of the married man, ought they not to come to the conclusion that she is not guilty; that she has the belief that she has (a) reasonable grounds for making the demand, and (b) that her use of menaces is a proper means of reinforcing the demand? ...

May I put yet one more ingredient? Supposing it be the case that, contrary to her suspicions, she is not in the condition that I have described. She is in exactly the same condition, without knowing it, as she was before she met this man who is married. What then? A lady who has no anxieties of the sort that I have described, nevertheless believes that she has, and insists upon £1 million being settled. Where are we? Is that blackmail or is it not?"[30]

31–019   These questions receive no reply. Twenty-first century family law would mean that she would have a legal right to demand appropriate child support payments. Thus, the lady would have a fair chance of being acquitted. Indeed, it was the intention of the *Act* to remove this type of claim, in general, from the scope of blackmail. In one case before 1968, a poorly educated girl who wrote to a man of position that if he did not pay her money for an alleged indecent assault she would "summons" him and "let the town knowed [sic] about your going on" was convicted of blackmail,[31] but this occasioned some adverse comment. The girl could lawfully have instructed a solicitor to write the man a letter saying that unless he paid appropriate damages for the assault an action for damages would be brought for the assault; and the man would well understand the real point of the threat to sue in such circumstances would be the threat of publicity. So the girl was really punished for not making her claim through the usual professional channel. Since the *Theft Act* she could not be convicted if she believed that she had been assaulted and that her threat was a proper one. Of course, if it could be shown that she had not been assaulted, her claim to believe that she had been would almost certainly be discredited. Similarly, a lawyer could easily demand child support for a single mother who has had a child. The solicitor would not, however, be able to demand a million pounds to compensate the child for any stigma that might flow from being born out of wedlock. (In the 21st century many couples prefer not to get married and it is no longer stigmatizing for people to be born out of wedlock.)

There are further arguments in favour of keeping the law of blackmail to a narrow compass. We are accustomed to a considerable measure of anarchy in the harsh economic world. Under present arrangements, concurred in by all, trade unions are entitled to hold not only employers but the general public to ransom. Perhaps a powerful trade organization or trade union threatens a small retailer or industrialist to put him on a "stop list" unless he pays a so-called "fine" or agrees to conform to rules designed to benefit the organization. The leader of a trade union of public employees threatens to call a strike which will deprive the public of its ability to travel, water supply, fire service, electricity, sewage disposal, hospitals or schools unless his members have their pay substantially increased. For example, British Airways was losing £100s of millions of pounds in 2010 because of the recession, but its staff went on strike to demand even higher wages from the crippled company. A trade union sets up a "kangaroo court" to fine its members who have refused to take part in a strike, with the threat that if they do not pay the fines the union will procure their dismissal from their jobs. Thanks to

---

[30] *Parliamentary Debates*, House of Lords, vol. 289 cols. 248-249 (15 February 1968).
[31] *R. v. Dymond* [1920] 2 K.B. 260.

Baroness Thatcher, many militant unions lost most of their ransoming powers. In the U.S. some blackmail statutes target labour unions, but it seems, following the Thatcher reforms, that it would hardly be wise to extend the law of blackmail to economic pressures, except perhaps in extreme circumstances.

Take worse cases than those. The threatener says at his trial that he believed **31–020** **he had reasonable grounds because he was a poor man while the person threatened was a property tycoon who had made money in unconscionable ways. Or because the person threatened was a Jew and the funds were needed to re-establish Palestinians in their homeland. Or because funds were needed to finance an insurrection against "imperialism." Some people have warped minds and appear genuinely to believe complete absurdities. Since the *Act* words the unscrupulous mental element in purely subjective terms, doesn't it mean that every blackmailer who acquires the White Queen's ability must be let off?** There is force in your criticism of the *Act*. If section 21 were now being enacted I think that some restriction would be imposed on the subjective test. At least, the statute would create a class of menaces that are absolutely forbidden, such as a threat to injure.[32] However, the section need not be read as stating a rule of pure subjectivism. The question under (*b*) is whether the defendant believed his menaces were "proper", and "proper" was intended by the C.L.R.C. to mean, and can be read as meaning, "proper in the minds of people generally." On this view the question is whether the defendant believed people generally would approve (or not disapprove) of his conduct. The test accords with the model direction on dishonesty stated by the Court of Appeal in *R. v. Ghosh*.[33] In *R. v. Harvey*,[34] the Court of Appeal not only appeared to accept this interpretation of section 21 but in one respect went further.

The defendants had made threats to kill, maim and rape; and the judge had directed the jury as a matter of law that threats to commit such serious criminal offences could not be a proper means of reinforcing a demand—even though the demand was for payment of money that was thought to be morally due. On appeal against conviction the court said that the question whether the defendants believed that the injuries they threatened to inflict would be lawful should technically have been left to the jury; but since the threats were to do acts that any sane man knew were against the law of every civilized country, the court applied the proviso and affirmed the conviction. The decision is clearly correct, and seems in effect to extend to blackmail the rule in *R. v. Ghosh*, even though the court does not say so in certain terms. But the court went beyond the facts of the case before it, and (it may be strongly argued) went too far, when it said that if the defendant knows that the act he threatens is "unlawful," this is enough to show that the defendant knows that his menace is not "proper" within the meaning of paragraph (*b*):

---

[32] A threat to murder is an independent offence. See section 16 of the *Offences Against the Person Act 1861*. D might get a few years in jail if he makes such a threat. See *R. v. Donovan* [2009] EWCA Crim. 1258; *R. v. Robinson* [2009] EWCA Crim. 375.

[33] [1982] Q.B. 1053.

[34] (1981) 72 Cr. App. R. 139.

"'Proper' is plainly a word of wide meaning, certainly wider than (for example) 'lawful'. But the greater includes the lessor and no act which was not believed to be lawful could be believed to be proper within the meaning of the subsection."

The logic is defective. What the court evidently meant is that "proper" is a word of narrower denotation than "lawful" (though it says the opposite). But when the argument is rewritten to make it logical, it remains unconvincing because the major premise is unconvincing. Even a judge would probably find himself forced to admit in some circumstances that an act is proper although unlawful, and public opinion would concede the point more readily than a judge. It is one thing to say that people generally would certainly frown on a threat to kill and rape, another to say that they would certainly frown on a threat by a trade union leader to procure breaches of contract, or to organize a trespass upon factory premises; and it would be going even further to say that public opinion on such matters is so clear that the defendant, whoever he is, must have known of it. The *Act* makes the defendant's belief a jury question, not a matter to be settled by a misplaced reliance on logic.

31–021   Suppose, to take another example, that the defendant has threatened to continue to make harassing telephone calls to the debtor (a minor criminal offence) if the debt is not paid. A defence of belief in propriety must be left to the jury. As a rule the trial judge should always leave the question of the defendant's belief in the propriety to the jury.

Although modification of subjectivism in terms of what the defendant believed society would think proper solves some problems, it does not get over the difficulty of determining who constitutes the "society" whose opinions (as judged by the defendant) are decisive. A political gangster may realize that people generally would disapprove of him but might rest secure in the knowledge that he receives the approval of members of his own subculture. Whatever other people may think, he and his friends hold it to be perfectly right to wring money out of rich companies by holding their executives to ransom, or out of airline companies to secure safe return of their aircraft, and so on. To counter theses claims by asserting the supremacy of the general culture over the subculture would be to write into the *Act* a test that is not there, thought the courts will probably feel a drive to do so if the question arises.[35]

A factor of prime importance in a blackmail case will frequently be the secrecy or the openness of the transaction. A man who thinks he is acting properly in making a threat will not try to conceal his identity, and demand that money should be left in used pound notes at a telephone kiosk. Again, it is in practice impossible for a defendant both to argue that he did not utter the menaces and that if he did they were justified. So, if he chooses merely to deny the menaces, and the jury find against him and the menaces were *prima facie* improper, the judge need not direct the jury on the unscrupulous mental element.

---

[35] In 1967, during a strike by lorry drivers, some pickets exacted "contributions to strike funds" from firms not parties to the dispute as a condition of letting their lorries through. Their action was repudiated by their trade union, and presumably the pickets knew their behaviour would not be approved by general opinion; but no prosecutions were brought.

31.5. EXTORTION

It was an offence at common law for a public officer to take, by colour of his **31–022** office, any money or thing that is not due to him.[36] The common law offence of "obtaining property by threats, extortion by colour or office or franchise" was abolished by the *Theft Act 1968*.[37] However, the Scots still have such an offence called extortion, but it is conceptually akin to the English offence of blackmail. In *Black v. Carmichael*,[38] it was said: "Wheel clamping [motor vehicles] amounted to a demand for payment accompanied by the threat that until payment the vehicle would not be released. The placing of the notice on the windscreen stating the terms for release was a clear threat that the vehicle would remain immobilised until the levy was paid. This was attempted extortion, and if the levy was paid, extortion."

---

[36] J. W. C. Turner, *Russell on Crime*, (London: Stevens & Sons, 1958) at 370.
[37] See section 32(1)(a) and (b), of the *Theft Act 1968*, which also abrogated statutory offences of extortion by coroners and sheriffs.
[38] [1992] S.L.T. 897.

CHAPTER 32

BURGLARY

"With increasing well being, all people become aware, sooner or later, that they have something to protect."[1]

32.1. THE DEFINITION OF BURGLARY

Certain statutory offences of a preparatory kind are contained in the *Theft Act 1968* and other legislation. We shall include burglary in this list, because part of the definition of burglary makes it a preparatory offence, even though most burglars go beyond preparation and actually commit an offence in the building.

32–001

The common law crime of burglary was extremely technical, and the *Theft Act* makes a fresh start. Section 9 runs as follows:

"(1)   A person is guilty of burglary if—
  (a)   he enters any building or part of a building as a trespasser and with intent to commit any such offence as is mentioned in subsection (2) below; or
  (b)   having entered any building or part of a building as a trespasser he steals or attempts to steal anything in the building or that part of it or inflicts or attempts to inflict on any person therein any grievous bodily harm.

(2)   The offences referred to in subsection (1) (a) above are offences of stealing[2] anything in the building or part of a building in question, of inflicting on any person therein any grievous bodily harm therein, and of doing unlawful damage to the building or anything therein.

(3)   A person guilty of burglary shall on conviction on indictment be liable to imprisonment for a term not exceeding—
  (a)   where the offence was committed in respect of a building or part of a building which is a dwelling, fourteen years;
  (b)   in any other case, ten years.

(4)   References in subsections (1) and (2) above to a building, and the reference in subsection (3) above to a building which is a dwelling, shall apply also to an inhabited vehicle or vessel, and shall apply to any such vehicle or vessel *at times* when the person having a habitation in it is not there as well as at times when he is."

Section 10 creates an offence of aggravated burglary, punishable with imprisonment for life, if the burglar has with him at the time of the burglary[3] any firearm, any weapon of offence, or any explosive. Furthermore, burglary of a dwelling house is also treated as an aggravated form of burglary. Burglary of a

---

[1] J. K. Galbraith, *The Affluent Society*, (London: Hamish Hamilton, 1958), 89.
[2] This does not cover the offence of dishonestly using electricity: *Low v. Blease* [1975] Crim. L.R. 513. Nor the offence of taking a conveyance.
[3] *R. v. Francis* [1982] Crim. L.R. 363.

dwelling-house (whether anyone is there at the time or not) is rightly regarded as much more serious than simple theft from other buildings.[4]

Whereas most offences under the *Theft Act 1968* are triable either way, the more serious ones are purely indictable: robbery, assault with intent to rob, blackmail, and some forms of burglary.[5] The precise rule for burglary is somewhat complicated, and it is enough to say that ordinary burglary simply for the purpose of theft is triable either way, whereas burglary involving an intention to commit an offence which can only be tried on indictment or burglary in a dwelling involving violence is triable only on indictment.

32.2. ENTRY TO A BUILDING

32–002 Burglary requires an entry as a trespasser. It is not burglary to remain in a building as a trespasser with a burglarious intent.[6] Even an actual theft in the building by a person who has become a trespasser will not constitute burglary if the thief was not a trespasser when he entered.

32–003 **Is it an entry to get only part of your torso across the threshold?** Yes. Even putting a finger through a window with intent to steal was sufficient at common law.[7] The post-*Act* cases have suggested that the entry would have to be more "substantial," but not necessarily "effective." In *R. v. Collins*,[8] the Court of Appeal required a "substantial entry." How much of the body must be over the threshold to constitute a "substantial entry"? It is not against common sense to say that an entry with a small part of the body can constitute burglary. In *R. v. Brown*[9] it was held that D's insertion of the top half of his body inside a shop window was a "substantial" and "effective" entry. Does this mean less substantial entries such as putting one's hands on the inside of the window sill to pull oneself in to the premises would not be sufficient?[10] It is doubtful that the latter could be described as substantial, but D has effectively entered.

But does an effective entry mean that the entry also has to effectively facilitate D's ability to commit one of the ulterior offences? It appears not, because burglary is an inchoate offence. In *R. v. Ryan*[11] the defendant was found by an elderly resident with his head and one arm stuck through the window of the house. The defendant argued that since he was stuck and had to be removed by the fire brigade, his conduct did not constitute an entry in law as required by section 9(1) of the *Theft Act*. The Court of Appeal held that partial presence is all that is required and that it did not matter that the defendant was not physically able to steal from the premises.

---

[4] Section 26(2) of the *Criminal Justice Act 1991* amended section 9 of the *Theft Act 1968* to allow for a fourteen year sentence for those who burglarize dwellings.
[5] Section 17 of the *Magistrates' Courts Act 1980*.
[6] But if found in the building the unwelcome entrant may be guilty of an offence under the *Vagrancy Act 1824*. See the discussion *infra*.
[7] *R. v. Davis* (1823) 168 E.R. 917.
[8] [1973] Q.B. 100.
[9] [1985] Crim. L.R. 212.
[10] Cf. *R. v. Davis* (1823) 168 E.R. 917.
[11] (1996) 160 J.P. 610.

But surely Ryan only attempted to burgle the residence. Are you telling me 32–004
that double inchoate liability can be the basis of a burglary conviction?
Burglary is an inchoate version of itself, so the offence is made out whether D's
attempt is successful or not. The conviction will be for either attempted burglary
or burglary, depending on the facts. In some cases, the attempt will not overlap
with the inchoate elements of burglary (*i.e.* where D unsuccessfully attempts to
break into the building). Burglary is inchoate; it does not require an actual result
and this inchoate offence can also be attempted. (You might recall that attempts
are a form of inchoate criminality). Ryan entered the building as a trespasser with
an intent to steal and therefore was guilty of burglary, even though no harm
resulted (well, at least not in the sense of property being taken, or of g.b.h. or
unlawful damage being inflicted). He was not convicted of attempted burglary,
because his entry was sufficient to fulfil the elements of the inchoate offence of
burglary. If Ryan had got caught up on an outside fence (with his burglar tools in
hand), his actions would have been nothing more than attempted burglary, if
that.[12]

Can I avoid criminal liability for burglary if I use a prosthetic limb to hook 32–005
goods from a building?   No. But a distinction has to be made between
instruments that are used to directly extend D's person and the use of projectiles.
If one person standing at his bedroom window shoots at another person in a room
across the street, this is a trespass (because of the entry of the bullet) but it would
be absurd to call it burglary. In common sense, the marksman does not enter as a
trespasser. It is true that there was an entry in the old law of burglary, but it would
seem reasonable to require an entry by at least a part of the body or by an
instrument that directly extends the body. The instrument would have to remain
connected to the body, otherwise it would be impossible to draw a clear line.
Clearly, if D uses a hook or some other instrument to pull goods through a
house's letterbox, he in effect enters the building.[13] If a person has a hook on the
end of a pole which he uses to hook goods through a window, this is no different
than if he had reached in with his hand to take the goods. The pole is used to
extend his person and is inserted directly through the window and thus constitutes
an entry. The defendant's propinquity with the interior of the building means that
he is no less dangerous than a defendant who puts his torso or arm through a
window to grab goods. However, if D fires a bullet from a distance this does not
constitute an entry, as the bullet is in no way a *direct* extension of his person.
Entry as envisaged by the *Theft Act 1968*, does not cover the entry of inanimate
objects that are not a direct extension of the perpetrator's person (*i.e.* the use of
projectiles, because it is the projectile that enters, not D, or any (extended) part of
D either in the artificial or organic sense).

---

[12] Cf. *R. v. Campbell* [1991] 93 Cr. App. R. 350; *Mason v. D.P.P.* [2010] R.T.R. 11.

[13] See for example, *R. v. Sang* [2003] EWCA Crim. 2411, where D had a fishing rod bound with
sellotape and a magnet to hook goods from houses. See also the facts in the sentencing decisions, *R. v.
Horncastle* [2003] 1 Cr. App. R. (S.) 39; *R. v. Delaney* [2010] EWCA Crim. 988.

32–006   **Does the doctrine of innocent agency apply to burglary under the *Theft Act*?**
At common law one could enter through an innocent agent, *e.g.* through a small
child (under the age of responsibility) who was put into the premises to steal.[14]
There is little social need for this construction of the offence, since few people
would feel alarmed by the entry of a small child: the case of an entry by a child
could be adjudged as simply theft or attempted theft by the adult. The same
would also apply if someone trained a (non-savage) dog to steal.[15] But the courts
will probably continue the old rule if the question arises. If a person sends his
adult accomplice into a building, then obviously, both are burglars.

32–007   **Could an entry into an uninhabited building be burglary?**   Yes. Buildings
need not be habitations, so shops, offices, warehouses and churches are included.
At common law burglary could only be in a dwelling-house, but this probably
includes also small fixed structures like summerhouses and outhouses. A partially
constructed building is probably best defined as a construction site. If D steals
tools from a building site, the appropriate charge seems to be theft. Nonetheless,
if the building is near completion, it could be defined as a building.[16] The concept
of a "building" seems to operate on a continuum. Clearly, an open paddock is not
a building, but there is no need to go right to the other end of the continuum to
identify a building. Whether or not a structure is a building for the purpose of
section 9 will depend on the context.[17] In most cases it will be fairly obvious
whether or not the structure should be treated as a building. There was no desire
to extend the law to thefts from movables like a car or railway carriage. On the
other hand, mobile homes needed to be included, and they are therefore expressly
included provided that they are inhabited.

---

[14]   See Matthew Hale, *Historia Placitorum Coronae: The History of the Pleas of the Crown*, (London:
printed for F. Gyles, T. Woodward, and C. Davis, Vol. I, 1736) at 555-556.

[15]   It has been held that a dog cannot be substituted for a human for the purposes of trespassing. See
Pratt v. Martin [1911] 2 K.B. 90.

[16]   In *The Queen v. Manning* (1871) L.R. 1 C.C.R. 338, it was held that: "An unfinished house, of
which the walls were built and finished, the roof on and finished, a considerable part of the flooring
laid, and the internal walls and ceilings prepared ready for plastering [is] a building within the
meaning of the section." In *R. v. Ealing LBC Ex p. Zainuddain* [1994] E.G. 130 it was held that: "The
structure constituted a building even though it had not been completely roofed."

[17]   A "prefab" without foundations can be a building: *R. v. Leathley* [1979] Crim. L.R. 314. A heavy
goods vehicle is not a building: *Norfolk Constabulary v. Seekings* [1986] Crim. L.R. 167, but a
shipping container or cold-room might be. "The meaning of the word 'building', or, to put the point
another way, determining whether a particular structure is a 'building', must depend on the context in
which the word is used. ...There are many wooden or structures not made of 'brick or stonework',
such as chalets, stables, or industrial sheds, and there are many structures which are not 'inclosures',
such as wood-drying stores, bandstands, or Dutch barns, all of which, on the basis of the normal use
of the word, are 'buildings'. Other structures come easily to mind, such as the Pyramids or the
Colosseum, which are buildings in normal parlance, but do not fall within Lord Esher's [see Lord
Esher M.R.'s comment in *Moir v. Williams* [1892] 1 Q.B. 264 at 270) 'ordinar[y]' meaning. So, too, at
least some prefabricated structures, particularly if attached to a concrete, or similar, base, are naturally
described as buildings": *R. (on the application of Ghai) v. Newcastle City Council* [2010] EWCA Civ.
59 at pars. 20-25. A barbeque is a building, but in the context of burglary it would be ludicrous to call
it a building. For a context where it might be a building, see *Windsor Hotel (Newquay) Ltd. v. Allan*
(*The Times*, 2 July 1980).

Is a cabin cruiser within the law of burglary when it is moored and unoccupied during the winter?   The courts will probably say that if it is inhabited for part of the year by a person who, when he leaves, intends to resume habitation, it is within the law of burglary for the whole year. See subsection 3. The law is designed to protect trespasses into private habitations therefore it is not necessary to ask how often V visits or uses the residence. The question is simply, is it used as a residence? It would be no defence for D to argue that V only uses her London apartment for two weeks each year, so why should it be for him to argue that she only visited her houseboat for a month each year? After all, D might just happen to strike just as V arrives for her summer break.

32–008

So a person who steals from a motor caravan in a car park is a burglar even though the owner is not on holiday and is using the van for shopping?   It seems so, odd though that may be. The courts have to draw a line somewhere. Thus, the criminal takes the risk of being convicted of the more serious offence of burglary when he steals from vehicles that double as habitats and are being used off and on for that purpose.

32–009

32.3.   THE INTENT

The intent required for burglary is clearly set out in section 9 of the *Act*. A curiosity of the wording may be noticed. Whereas a person who trespassorily enters a building with an intent to do unlawful damage is a burglar, one who enters without burglarious intent but who actually does some unlawful damage after entry is not. On the other hand a trespasser in a building who actually steals or inflicts grievous bodily harm or attempts to do so is a burglar *even though he did not enter with that intent*. So just to ram the point home, we may sort out five types of burglary, which fall into two offence categories. In the first category (section 9(1)(a)) there is:

32–010

- Entry as a trespasser with intent to steal.[18]
- Entry as a trespasser with intent to inflict g.b.h.
- Entry as a trespasser with intent to do unlawful damage. (It must be shown that D intended to commit the ulterior offence, recklessness as to whether he would get in a fight and cause g.b.h[19] or unlawful damage is not sufficient).[20]

---

[18] And in the case of an attempt, it is sufficient that the intruder was prospecting for something that he might think worth stealing: *R. v. Walkington* [1979] 1 W.L.R. 1169.

[19] Cf. *R. v. Watson* [1989] 1 W.L.R. 684, where the defendants entered a house with the specific intention of stealing property and continued the act of burglary knowing that they were risking the safety of the occupant. It was held, "The unlawful act of burglary does not end with the offender crossing the threshold of the premises, so that if in the course of the burglary he becomes aware of the presence of a person of particular vulnerability, and the fact of his presence causes that person's death, he may be guilty of *manslaughter*." The latter of course, being a crime of recklessness. Cf. *R. v. Jenkins* (1983) 76 Cr. App. R. 313 at 318, where the Court of Appeal erroneously suggested that *causing* g.b.h. without even knowing that it had been *caused* would be sufficient. The court also suggested that the infliction of g.b.h. would not have to necessarily constitute an independent offence under the *Offences Against the Person Act 1861*. However, it is difficult to envisage a factual scenario

In the second category (section 9(1)(b)) there is:

- Stealing or attempting to steal after entry as a trespasser.
- Inflicting or attempting to inflict g.b.h. after entry as a trespasser.

32–011 **Is it possible to raise a claim of right, if D enters to retrieve goods which he believes he owns?** It is not burglary for a person to break into premises to take a thing to which he believes himself to be entitled. In *R. v. Lopatta*[21] the defendant admitted breaking into his former employer's warehouse from where he took 20 large drums of oil worth about $5,000AUD, "his estimated value of holiday and other pay and expenses which, he said, his former employer owed him but was neglecting or refusing to pay." It was held that a claim of right defence is available in such circumstances.

32–012 **Most people think of burglars as a specialized class of thieves. Isn't it strange to bring in other intents?** These other intents rarely arise, but the law of burglary has never been confined to cases where the intent is to steal. The historical justification for the special offence is the alarm that a criminal invasion of a dwelling-house causes. The alarm of the inhabitants would not be diminished by knowing that the intruders have come to steal rather than maim.

32–013 **Can you take it for granted that the intruder has entered with one of the specified intents?** Certainly not. But of course the jury may infer criminal intent if it is the only reasonable explanation of suspicious behaviour, but the alleged intent must be proved.[22]

32–014 **I can see that this gives burglary the edge over attempt from the prosecutor's point of view. But on the whole I don't see that there was sufficient reason to preserve burglary in the *Theft Act*.** It is true that if the crime of burglary were abolished, this need not make any appreciable difference to the enforcement of the criminal law. But trespassory entry into premises is such a distinctive feature of aggravation of crime that it is beneficial to have it recorded in that type of conviction. The Court of Appeal has emphasized that burglary of dwelling-houses is so serious an offence that even adolescents engaging in it should expect to lose their liberty,[23] which they might not do for theft without this aggravating feature.[24] There was an additional reason for the crime of burglary before the *Criminal Attempts Act 1981* was enacted, because the law of attempt was

---

where D has intentionally or recklessly *inflicted* g.b.h. (without justification or excuse) that would not constitute an offence. Clearly, the intentional or reckless infliction of g.b.h. is distinguishable from cases where D has entered as a trespasser and has accidentally or inadvertently *caused* g.b.h. In the case of criminal damage, section 9 makes it clear that it must be "unlawful" damage.

[20] *A v. D.P.P.* [2003] EWHC 1676 (Q.B.). The offence is one of specific intent. See *R. v. Durante* [1972] 1 W.L.R. 1612.

[21] (1983) 10 A. Crim. R. 447; *R v. Knight* (1781) 2 East. P.C. 510. See section 2(1)(a) of the *Theft Act 1968*.

[22] *Jones v. Brooks* (1968) 52 Cr. App. R. 614; *A v. D.P.P.* [2003] EWHC 1676 (Q.B.).

[23] *R. v. Smith and Woollard* (1978) 67 Cr. App. R. 211.

[24] This is reflected by the higher sentence for burglarizing dwellings. See section 26(2) of the *Criminal Justice Act 1991*.

traditionally so circumscribed that one could not be sure that the courts would hold every burglarious entry to be a sufficient act of attempt to commit the crime in view, as going beyond "mere preparation." There is also the point made just now, that the burglary charge saves the prosecution from having to prove the precise intent. And it means that one can apply the law of attempt to burglary itself: attempting to enter the premises can be attempted burglary.

32.4. THE TRESPASS

Trespass in the law of tort includes any presence on property without legal **32–015** right—that is to say, otherwise than with the consent of the possessor (occupier) or by authority of law. This is also its meaning in the present context.

On a prosecution for burglary, must the occupier of the building produce his **32–016** **title deeds?** Trespass is a wrong to possession, not to ownership. It is enough for evidence to be given that someone other than the defendant was in possession and that the defendant was wrongfully in the building.

Need the defendant know that he is trespassing? The *Act* seems to impose **32–017** objective liability in respect of the fact of trespass. But the courts imply a requirement of *mens rea*. The defendant must know he is a trespasser or be reckless as to this.[25] So a man who enters a caravan with intent to steal would commit burglary unless he believes that the caravan is not inhabited within the meaning of the *Act*. Such a belief is unlikely, because if the intruder knows that it may be a private caravan, he must realize that there is a possibility of the family having lived in it and coming to live in it again if they are not living in it at the moment.

When must the mental element exist? At the time of the *actus reus*. We must **32–018** therefore draw a distinction:

- If a man is charged with entering a building with intent to steal, *etc.*, he must have the full mental element at the time of entry, and therefore must know when he enters that he has or may have no right to enter.
- If he is charged with stealing in a building having entered as a trespasser (see section 9(1)(b)), it is enough that he knows he has no right to be there when he steals. If, therefore, a man enters the wrong house by mistake for one that he has a right to enter, discovers his mistake and steals in the house, he is guilty of burglary, notwithstanding that he did not know that he was trespassing when he entered. But he must have entered as a trespasser!

Suppose a customer in a shop slips into the cashier's office and helps himself **32–019** **from the till?** He is guilty of burglary in entering a part of the building as a trespasser and stealing therein. He knows that he has no right to be in the office.

---

[25] *R. v. Collins* [1973] Q.B. 100.

In this type of case, it is enough that the intruder has the burglarious intent when he enters the "part" of the building; he need not have had it when he first entered the building.[26]

32–020 **What if the owner assists the thief's entry in order to trap him?** If it is merely a question of leaving the street door unlocked, this is not consent to an entry, even though it is done to catch a thief. But the owner may do more. If D tries to bribe V's employee to let him in, and the employee, having informed V, on V's instructions lets D in, the authorities at common law were conflicting on whether burglary was committed.[27] On principle, it is not. An occupier who with full knowledge of the facts lets another into his premises can hardly be heard to say that the other is a trespasser against him. A person cannot simultaneously be a trespasser and a non-trespasser in the same premises.[28] Besides, the alarm caused by a criminal intruder in a building (which is the main concern of the law of burglary) hardly arises if the intruder has been let in knowing his criminal intention. D is, however, guilty of theft if he appropriates something inside.

32–021 **Suppose a man knocks at the door of a house occupied by an old lady living alone; she lets him enter, and he then asks her for money, which she gives to him. Could this be burglary?** Yes if the jury find that she was intimidated and the man knew it. The intimidation would vitiate her apparent consent to his entry and he would be a trespasser. He need not know the law of trespass; it is enough that he knows that the person who lets him is only doing so (or may be doing so) because of the intimidation. After all, D enters the private dwelling of a stranger.

32–022 **Then does the grisly doctrine of vitiation of consent by fraud rear itself again?** In burglary D might use fraud not only to gain entry, but also to obtain property from the invitee. If D cons V (by pretending to be a charity collector for Oxfam) not only to gain entry to V's house, but also to obtain V's property, he uses fraud to gain both entry and to acquire the goods. This could technically be brought within the purview of burglary, because D knows that V is not really

---

[26] It seems that a "part of a building" must be in some way physically marked off. Part of a shop marked off by counters on three sides, to which area the public are not admitted, comes within the notion: *R. v. Walkington* [1979] 1 W.L.R. 1169. The court said the if there were a single table in the middle of the shop to which the public were not intended to have access (and that is where most modern tills are located), it would be difficult for any jury to find properly that it was "part of a building" for this technical purpose. (Would they be allowed to find it improperly?) There must be some restriction on the notion of "part of a building," otherwise the rule requiring intent at the time of entry would lose its force. It would seem, however, that a notice excluding the public from say one end of a room would make that end "part of a building."

[27] *R. v. Egginton* (1801) 126 E.R. 1410 (not burglary where the employee opened the door on V's orders); *R. v. Johnson* (1841) 174 E.R. 479 (employee opened door on instructions of police; not burglary); *R. v. Chandler* [1913] 1 K.B. 125 (burglary where employee supplied D with a key). See more generally, Glanville Williams, *Criminal Law: The General Part*, (London: Stevens & Sons, 1961) at §§ 254, 255.

[28] *Healing (Sales) Pty Ltd. v. Inglis Elextrix Pty Ltd.* (1968) 121 C.L.R. 584 at 606.

consenting to his entry.[29] He enters as a trespasser, because he knows that V intends only to invite a genuine Oxfam representative to enter. Furthermore, he knows that he is using fraud to take property that he has no right to take.

Can a member of the family be a trespasser, or is he one of the occupiers? 32–023
In civil law, occupation (possession) is a technical concept. The parents of the family are the occupiers if they are the owners or tenants of the house. But other people may be there by the occupier's implied licence: the children, of course (who may be there even by authority of law so long as the occupier is bound to maintain them and they have no other home), guests, lodgers, and domestic employees. Some or all of these people have the occupier's implied authority to invite (licence) others to enter.

A thief sees a little boy of five playing at the open door of a house. He says: 32–024
"Can I come in, sonny?" The little boy assents, so the thief goes in and steals something. Is this burglary? Presumably the jury would be encouraged to find that a child of that age had no authority to invite a man to enter, and that the thief could not have believed that he had.

Suppose the son of the family came home one day intending to steal from his 32–025
father? Or brought in a boon companion who did so? There are two decided cases bearing on these questions, and since they appear to be partly in opposition they cannot both state the right rule. In the first case, *R. v. Collins*,[30] the defendant climbed a ladder and looked into an open window of a house and saw V asleep and naked in a bed close to the window. So he descended the ladder and stripped off all his clothes and went back up the ladder to the open window. Collins removed his clothes with the intention of raping the young woman he had just seen lying naked near the open window.[31] The victim awoke, and became aware that the form poised at the window was that of a blond naked male in a state of visible lust. Immediately coming to the conclusion that he was her regular boyfriend, she opened her arms to him. Collins, though doubtless surprised at this friendly reception, took advantage of it. Later, putting on the light and discovering her error, the girl slapped him on the face, bit him, and retired to the bathroom.

The next day Collins was charged not with rape or attempted rape, as he might have expected, but with burglary, of which offence he was in due course convicted. It was held on appeal that he was not guilty unless he knew at the time of entering that he was not invited by the girl to enter, or was reckless as to the fact. Since the jury had not been directed on this issue, a conviction of burglary was quashed. The victim was the adult daughter of the family and as such was not the legal occupier of the premises, and the young woman's mother, who appears

---

[29] The great overlap between fraud and theft (see *D.P.P. v. Gomez* [1993] A.C. 442) would allow this acquisition to be treated as either theft or fraud, but as he possibly entered as a trespasser (without V's real consent) the prosecution might try for burglary. This conduct would also come within the purview of section 2 of the *Fraud Act 2006*.

[30] [1973] 1 Q.B. 100.

[31] Section 140 and Sched. 7 of the *Sexual Offences Act 2003* have since removed trespasses with the intent to rape from section 9 of the *Theft Act 1968*.

to have been the occupier, would doubtless have objected to the stranger entering to have his way with her 18-year old daughter. But the court said:[32]

> "The point was raised that, the complainant [the girl] not being the tenant or occupier of the dwelling house and her mother being apparently in occupation, this girl herself could not in any sense have extended an effective invitation to enter. ... Whatever be the position in the law of tort, to regard such a proposition as acceptable in the criminal law would be unthinkable."

This seems to mean, and it is surely right, that an adult (or even younger) member of the family has a general implied authority to invite friends to the house, so as to prevent those friends being trespassers as a matter of criminal law, unless the parent (legal occupier) withdraws that authority in respect of a particular person. If the authority is not withdrawn, it does not matter that the parent would be highly displeased by the presence of the friend. The practical result of this view is supported by the *mens rea* doctrine. People are hazy about the law. When a member of the family invites his friend to the house, the friend naturally believes that he enters lawfully.

32–026 **Surely the daughter of the family cannot licence her boyfriend to come in to steal?** It is a reasonable restriction of the general principle to say that a person who is a member of the occupier's family or who has a licence from the occupier cannot sub-licence the entry of another person for a known burglarious purpose. In *R. v. Collins*, however, the young woman did not know of Collins's initial intention to rape (as she thought he was her boyfriend). Furthermore, Collins did not use deceptions, so he did not have a firm reason for believing he was not really being invited to enter. Whether or not he was reckless is another question.

32–027 **Where was Collins when he received the girl's invitation?** Collins was perched on the window sill, but whether on the outside sill or on the interior sill was not clear. The court first expressed the opinion that "that seemingly narrow point was of crucial importance," but later in the judgment said that:[33]

> "[U]nless the jury were entirely satisfied that the defendant made an effective and substantial entry into the bedroom without the complainant doing or saying anything to cause him to believe that she was consenting to his entering it, he ought not be convicted."

As far as the requirement that the entry should be substantial is concerned, it is not clear what force the adjective "effective" is intended to have beyond that of the word "substantial."

32–028 **Assume that (as the court held) the daughter was empowered to licence the young man's entry. Assume, too, that she purported to give him this licence before he entered the house. What effect did her mistake as to his identity have? Did Collins know that the girl believed him to be her boyfriend?** The court said:[34]

---

[32] *R. v. Collins* [1973] 1 Q.B. 100 at 107.
[33] *R. v. Collins* [1973] 1 Q.B. 100 at 106.
[34] *R. v. Collins* [1973] 1 Q.B. 100 at 106.

> "If she in fact appeared to be welcoming him, the Crown do not suggest that he should have realised or even suspected that she was so behaving because, despite the moonlight, she thought he was someone else."

This may be thought to imply that the girl's mistake as to Collins's identity vitiated her consent to his entry, so that he was a trespasser, and that if he had known of the mistake he would have had *mens rea* as to the trespass. But the court did not decide the point. Since Collins did not know of the girl's mistake, and was not reckless as to it, the question of the legal effect of her mistake of identity did not arise.[35]

An important point must now be made. In addition to mistaking Collins's identity, the girl mistook his intention. There is no reason to suppose that when Collins found that the girl was inviting him into her bedroom that he had given up his intention to use force if necessary to have her sexually. The attitude of mind of every rapist is that he will use force if necessary, and that was Collins's intention. Collins therefore entered as a would-be rapist, but this fact did not mean that he was a trespasser when he entered the room. A person who has a licence in fact to enter does not become a trespasser by reason of his criminal intent. Nor does a person who believes himself to have a licence to enter have the *mens rea* for trespass by reason of his independent criminal intent. This point was not expressly made by the court, but it is implicit in the decision.

The second case of the two cases concerned two defendants memorably named **32–029** *Jones and Smith*.[36] Smith's father had had two television sets stolen, and reported this to the police. The sets were then found in the joint possession of Smith Jnr. (who apparently lived on his own) and in his friend Jones. The precious pair had entered Smith Senior's house in the small hours and stole the sets. On the police ascertaining the facts they were prosecuted for burglary. At the trial Smith's father gave evidence to the effect that he had given his son unrestricted permission to enter the house, and that his son would "not be a trespasser in the house at any time." Nevertheless, the conviction of both defendants of burglary was affirmed.

There is no difficulty in this decision in relation to Jones's entry. For the reason already given, it could well be held that Smith Jnr. had no authority to admit Jones for the purpose of thievery. The problem arises from the view taken by the court that Smith Jnr. also was a trespasser. In common sense, a son cannot be a trespasser in his father's house unless the father expressly limits his right to enter. Even if the father had not given the evidence he did, there would surely be a strong presumption that a son, whatever his intention, is a licensee in the house. The father's evidence should have put the point beyond doubt.

There is, however, one ground on which Smith's conviction could properly have been affirmed. Granted that Jones was a trespasser, and therefore a burglar, Smith was guilty as accessory in letting him in. Unfortunately, the Court of Appeal did not consider this simple way of upholding the conviction. Instead, the

---

[35] In the law of contact mistake of identity generally does not vitiate consent if the imposter is present. The person under mistake is taken to intend to deal with the person actually present before him.

[36] [1976] 1 W.L.R. 672.

decision was rested on the fact, or assumed fact, that both defendants were trespasses in the civil law. The court said:[37]

> "The decision in *R. v. Collins* added to the concept of trespass as a civil wrong only the mental element of *mens rea*, which is essential to the criminal offence."

It may be doubted whether this attaches sufficient weight to the dictum in *R. v. Collins*, already quoted, relating to the consent given by the daughter of the family, which appears to regard the question of trespass as being possibly different in civil and criminal law. If the plain man were asked whether on the facts of *R. v. Jones and Smith* the son was a trespasser, he would surely have replied that although the son acted wrongfully in respect of the television sets, he was not a trespasser in the house.

32–030 The Court of Appeal decision laid down the following principle as the foundation of its decision:

> "[A] person is a trespasser for the purpose of section 9 (1) (b) of the *Theft Act 1968* if he enters premises of another knowing that he is entering in excess of the permission that has been given to him, or being reckless as to whether he is entering in excess of the permission that has been given to him to enter. Provided the facts are known to the accused which enable him to realise that he is acting in excess of the permission given or that he is acting recklessly as to whether he exceeds that permission, then that is sufficient for the jury to decide that he is in fact a trespasser."[38]

The trouble with judge-made law is that courts sometimes lay down a wide rule which serves their immediate purpose, without noticing the undesirable consequences that the rule may have in other applications. Entering "in excess of the permission that has been given to him" is a somewhat vague phrase, but what it evidently means is entering for a purpose not covered by the permission. In effect the decision implies (in contradiction of *R. v. Collins*) that a person who enters another's building with burglarious intent is always a trespasser at the moment of entry. If such a wide proposition is accepted, the consequence is that burglary is committed by various persons who may appear on the surface to be licensees; a customer in a shop, a house guest, and a butler, who steal in the building having entered for that purpose, notwithstanding that apart from their intention they would be lawfully there. It may even be burglary for a person to enter a telephone kiosk (which he is normally permitted to enter) to steal the contents of the coin box. A great extension is thus given to the crime.

There are strong reasons for saying this is not the correct view of the law. It makes the crime of burglary unnecessarily wide; it is founded on a misunderstanding of the pervious authorities; and it is inconsistent with the rationale of section 9.

32–031 The following are detailed arguments against the *dictum*:

- The rationale of burglary as a special offence is, to repeat, the danger and alarm caused by the presence of a criminally-minded intruder in a building.

---

[37] *R. v. Jones and Smith* [1976] 1 W.L.R. 672 at 675.
[38] *R. v. Jones and Smith* [1976] 1 W.L.R. 672 at 675.

This is unlikely to arise when the intruder has been permitted to enter—which is why the *Act* does not make it burglary for one who has been *permitted to enter* to commit one of the specified crimes after outstaying his welcome. The notion of consent or permission to enter should therefore be understood in its purely factual sense. Of course the commission of a crime may cause alarm, but the alarm is not increased by the fact that the judges describe the offender as a trespasser, when he has been permitted to enter in fact.

- The *Act* follows the recommendations of the C.L.R.C., and there is no hint in the committee's Report that it contemplated this extension of the offence.[39] The committee's purpose was to simplify the law of burglary but not to deprive it entirely of an element of objective illegality. For this reason the offence was to require a trespassory entry. What reception would the committee's Report have had if it had proposed that an ordinary shoplifter would be guilty of burglary if he was found to have intended to steal when he entered the shop? The dictum in *R. v. Jones and Smith* removes the objective requirement, because it makes the burglarious intent determinative of the legality of the entry. In the great majority of cases where *de facto* licensees steal, it fuses the two requirements of burglarious intent and trespassory entry into a single requirement, namely the burglarious intent. It is thus contrary to the clear intention of section 9.

- The construction of the *Act* offered in *R. v. Jones and Smith* is inconsistent not only with the separate requirement of trespass but with the separate requirement of entry as a trespasser. As we have seen, a person who, having entered a building lawfully, remains in it unlawfully and in order to steal *is not* for that reason a burglar. This implies that the object of the section is to strike at intruding strangers. If a person is lawfully on the spot, he does not become a burglar by remaining unlawfully. If *R. v. Jones and Smith* is right, the section covers many people who are known to the occupier, who are known to him to be present, and who have to all appearances his permission to enter. This seems to deprive the statute's insistence that the defendant must *enter* as a trespasser of most of its practical effect.

- The decision runs counter to *R. v. Collins*, where it was held, as we have seen, that the defendant was not a trespasser. Even if Collins intended to commit rape if necessary, this would not have made him a trespasser. Before rape was removed from section 9 of the *Theft Act*, entering a building as a trespasser with an intent to rape constituted an act of burglary, but if someone had been invited in as a genuine guest and then raped the invitee, the charge would normally have been for rape not for burglary. Thus, if the young lady in *R. v. Collins* had invited her *actual* boyfriend in for a chat and with him thereafter raping her, he would be a rapist not a burglar. The intent to rape would have to coincide with the trespassory entry for burglary to be satisfied. It is arguable that Collins's intention to rape did not cease to exist until after he had gained entry, but would have ceased when V mistakenly consented to sexual intercourse. Then again,

---

[39] See *Eighth Report on Theft and Related Offences by the Criminal Law Revision Committee in the United Kingdom*, Cmnd. 2977 (1966), paras. 35, 70 and 75.

Collins might not have had an intent to rape when he entered: he might have genuinely believed that the young woman was inviting him in for sex even though he was a stranger (after all they were both naked and he was in a state of visible lust, but she still invited him in). Therefore, his intention to rape might have ceased to exist before he entered the building. But there is no doubt what his intention was when he climbed back up the ladder in a state of visible lust. But Collins was not a trespasser, because he had permission to enter and the facts were not sufficient to prove that it was reckless of him to enter.

Mens rea cannot be established by pointing to what Collins discovered in retrospection (*i.e.* that V was not really consenting as she mistook him for her boyfriend), because Collins did not have this information when he entered. There is no such thing as retrospective intention or recklessness. D is not subjectively reckless merely because he learns from the *ex post* perspective that the victim would *not* have consented to him entering if she had known his intentions or who he really was. If he did not intend to enter as a trespasser then subjective recklessness must be established based on what D knew at the time of entry.

If D uses deception or duress to get V to consent to him entering the building, he enters as a trespasser because D knows that V is not really giving him permission to enter. If the young woman had said, "come in Billy, I have missed you" (assuming Billy was the name of her boyfriend), Collins would have realized that she was making a mistake as to his identity and that he was not really being invited in. Similarly, if Collins had known that the girl was in terror and was only agreeing to his entry out of fear, he would surely have had sufficient information to realize the consent was not real. The same could not be said of the shopper who enters a shop without money and without mentioning that he intends to do a bit of shoplifting—his silence as to his intentions does not make him a trespasser since he would believe that he has a right to enter as a member of the public. His silence is not used to gain entry (he gains entry by relying on the general offer that "shops" make for the world at large to enter), but rather it merely prevents the store from preventing him from using its general offer to enter.

- The authorities in the law of tort do not establish a secret intent can turn a licensee into a trespasser. They show that in the civil law, acting outside the implied condition of the licence can do so. A person who is *prima facie* licensed to enter is not a trespasser when he enters, even though he intends to act outside the terms of the licence. When he does so act, he becomes a trespasser in the civil law, but he did not enter as a trespasser. Therefore he cannot be guilty of burglary either under paragraph (*a*) or under paragraph (*b*), both of which require entry as a trespasser.

- The tort cases were motivated largely by a desire to prevent licensees from recovering damages for injury received when they were acting unlawfully on the premises. This has no bearing on the criminal law. In the criminal law, the notion of trespass should be given a broad, common sense interpretation in the defendant's favour.

- It was held in an immigration case that fraud in procuring leave to enter the country makes the leave voidable but not void,[40] and the same principle should apply in respect of burglary. Moreover, fraud presupposes (1) a fraudulent act (not a mere nondisclosure of criminal intent) and (2) an effect of the fraud on the mind of the person who consents. To "imply" a representation by the defendant that he has no illegal intention would be pure fiction—though one to which the courts are now, sadly, disposed.

  The court incorporated the mental element into its proposition of law (see the quotation above). But it may be questioned whether the jury acted reasonably in finding that Smith Jnr. knew that he might be entering in excess of the permission given to him. If Smith Jnr. were asked such a question, he might readily agree that he was stealing the television sets, but not that he was a trespasser in his father's house or had entered in excess of the permission given to him. His father did not mind his entry to house as such. No doubt he would have objected to the television sets being taken, but the ordinary person would probably regard a question framed in terms of trespass to the house as an extraordinary legalism and an irrelevance.

- The rule in *R. v. Jones and Smith* occasions particular difficulty if part of what the defendant does is clearly within the licence. A shoplifter enters a shop to make a purchase in the liquor department (which has tight security) and to steal anything else in the rest of the shop that he can. The butler enters the house in order to butle, and also later in the day to go off with the spoons. Is he a trespasser or not?

The main conclusions to be drawn from the two cases are as follows:　　　　**32–032**

1. It seems from *R. v. Jones and Smith* that a person who is normally licensed to enter premises is not licensed to enter them to steal from the occupier. Conceivably this rule, which has wide implications and is open to various legal objections, may not be followed, since that actual decision can be explained on the narrower ground next following.
2. Even if a person is licensed by the occupier to be on the premises himself, he cannot authorize another person to enter for a burglarious purpose of which he knows—or, very possibly, for the purpose of committing any crime against the occupier of which he knows. The thief who enters and steals will be a burglar, and the licensee who lets him in for the purpose of theft will be an accessory to the burglary.
3. Subject to rule 2 above, some person licensed by the occupier can sub-licence others to enter, and this is particularly so for members of the occupier's family, who can in general licence friends to enter, however, unwelcome their presence may be to the occupier, unless the occupier expressly withdraws the authority. This is the result of *R. v. Collins*. The point is important only in very exceptional circumstances.

---

[40] *R. v. Home Secretary, Ex p. Khawaja* [1984] A.C. 74.

In *Barker v. The Queen*,[41] the High Court of Australia tried to limit the scope *R. v. Jones and Smith* by holding: "If [the permission to enter] was subject to an actual express or implied limitation which excluded the actual entry, the entry was as a trespasser." In that case, V asked D to keep an eye on his house while he was on holiday. D had access to the house key and used it to steal from the house. The court took the view that the key had been given for the particular purpose of protecting the house and that there was no permission for D to enter for any other purpose, therefore D entered as a trespasser. But this distinction is very thin. Justice Murphy[42] thought that it was too thin to offer much in substance. In the following passage Justices Brennan and Deane (in the majority) tried identify a substantive distinction:[43]

> "As has been said, a permission to enter land need not be confined by reference to the purpose of the entry and, except in the case where it is so confined, a purpose of subsequently doing an unlawful act will not, under the common law, convert entry which was otherwise within the permission into entry as a trespasser. In particular, to take the example on which most reliance was placed, the implied invitation to enter which a shopkeeper extends to the public may ordinarily be limited to public areas of the shop and to hours in which the shop is open for business: it is not, however, ordinarily limited or confined by reference to purpose. Indeed, in the context of the importance of 'impulse buying', the mere presence of the prospective customer upon the premises is itself likely to be an object of the invitation and a person will be within the invitation if he enters for no particular purpose at all. The fact that a person enters with the purpose or some thought of possibly stealing an item of merchandise or of otherwise behaving in a manner which is beyond what he is authorized to do while on the premises does not, in the ordinary case where the invitation to enter is not confined by reference to purpose, result in the actual entry being outside the scope of the invitation and being trespassory."

32–033 This doctrine could be interpreted in two ways. Firstly, it might mean that the shoplifter enters as a trespasser if his sole purpose for entering the store is to steal. But it would be almost impossible in most cases to determine whether the shoplifter entered for the sole purpose of stealing, or whether he had mixed intentions,[44] such as an intention to browse, to purchase chewing gum and to steal.[45] If we have to establish that D entered the store for no other reason than to steal, then in many cases it will be almost impossible to establish that D entered as a trespasser. His intention to steal may have arisen after[46] he entered the store. Alternatively, D's intention to steal might have coexisted with a legitimate

---

[41] (1983) 153 C.L.R. 338 at 365.

[42] *Barker v. The Queen* (1983) 153 C.L.R. 338 at 349 *et seq.* dissenting.

[43] *Barker v. The Queen* (1983) 153 C.L.R. 338 at 361-362.

[44] If D, a luggage handler at the airport, enters the terminal building with the intention not only of doing his job, but also of stealing from suitcases, he does not enter as a trespasser. His legitimate intention of entering the building to do his job of unloading and loading suitcases means that he does not enter the airport terminal building as a trespasser, even though his ulterior intent is to steal. Furthermore, his separate entry into V's private suitcase does not make his theft burglary, since a suitcase is not a building. See *R. v. Dhunay* (1986) 8 Cr. App. R. 107, where D was charged with theft.

[45] In *Barker v. The Queen* (1983) 153 C.L.R. 338 at 348 Mason J. said: "If a person enters premises for a purpose which is within the scope of his authority his entry is authorized; it is not made unlawful because he enters with another and alien purpose in mind."

[46] D can become a trespasser if he misbehaves on another's premises after entering with V's consent, but as D only becomes a trespasser after he has lawfully gained entry he does not enter as a trespasser. See *Hillen v. I.C.I (Alkali) Ltd.* [1936] A.C. 65.

intention to buy goods, which he is generally permitted to enter the store to do. The shopkeeper's general invitation would protect him so long as he enters with more than theft on his mind.

Does this interpretation of the doctrine mean that if D enters a shop with nothing but theft on his avaricious mind he is a burglar? Yes. And it is for this reason that it has to be rejected. The *Barker v. The Queen* doctrine is only tenable, if it is accepted that the general right to enter shops (and the like) is not negated simply because D intends to enter only to steal. Of course, the invitee would object to such a shopper entering his store if he could read his mind, but in the real world it is not possible to read the minds of others. *Per contra*, D would be a trespasser, if the shopkeeper believed that D was entering his store for the sole purpose of stealing, so long as V had given D advanced[47] warning that he was barred from entering the shop. Thus, if a shopper knows that he is barred from a particular store because of his past shoplifting, he should realize that the general offer for the world at large to enter the store no longer applies to him. This type of case differs to the standard shoplifting case where the thief has not been told that he cannot enter. Generally, a shopper who enters a store for no other purpose other than to shoplift is not guilty of burglary, unless he has been given notice that he is barred from entering the particular store. It would be absurd to label this type of shoplifter as a burglar, if his fellow shoplifter is labelled as nothing more than a shoplifter simply because he not only intended to steal from the store, but also to "browse" or buy goods from the store. Likewise, the owner of a hotel or lodging-house who enters the room of a guest with an intent to steal is a thief rather than a burglar, because he does not enter as a trespasser. He would only enter as a trespasser if the guest's contract gave him a "right to immediate and exclusive possession."[48]

32–034

This also means that the butler who is off duty and drops by his employer's manor house for the sole purpose of stealing the silver candle holders is not guilty of burglary. The butler relies on the general permission he has been given to enter the house to access the goods he intends to steal. The dishonest butler would not be brave enough to enter the houses of strangers to steal. There is a big difference between those who thieve from places where they have been given a permission to enter and burglars who brazenly go into the homes of others without any permission. The defendant has to know that he had no right to enter or was reckless about this. This proviso seems to offer further protection to our butler and shoppers, because they would believe they have a right to enter.

The Australia *Model Criminal Code* has recommended that the law of burglary be limited to catching those who have not been given any permission to enter. It

---

[47] "If it is a general permission to enter in the sense that it is not limited, either expressly or by necessary implication, by reference to the purpose for which entry may be effected, it is not legitimate to cut back the generality of the permission to enter merely because it is probable that the grantor would, *if the matter had been raised*, have qualified it by excluding from its scope any entry for the purpose of committing an unauthorized act." *Barker v. The Queen* (1983) 153 C.L.R. 338 at 358 *per* Brennan and Deane J.J.

[48] *Barker v. The Queen* (1983) 153 C.L.R. 338 at 347.

expressly states that it is irrelevant that a person enters for some criminal purpose, if that person has been given permission to enter. Section 16.3(2) of the *Code* states:

> "A person is not a trespasser merely because the person is permitted to enter or remain in the building for a purpose that is not the person's intended purpose, or as a result of fraud, misrepresentation or another's mistake."[49]

32–035   The *Model Criminal Code*, however, goes too far. Clearly, in cases where there is no general permission for D to enter, fraud, mistake and misrepresentation should be considered when determining whether D knew that he had no right to enter or was reckless about this.[50] Of course, if D has a general permission to enter such issues do not arise because D would not need to use fraud to gain entry. Why would a shopper use fraud to enter a store if she has a general right to enter? If the shopper remains silent as to his sole intention to steal from a store, he does not gain entry on this basis. He merely avoids being barred on that occasion, which would be likely if he were to say to the store guard, "I am only here to steal."

Barker v. The Queen seems to apply only to cases where D did not have a general right to enter his neighbour's house. Barker was told that he could enter his neighbour's house in an emergency to protect the owner's property. He was not an employee or a family member who might have had a general right to enter. *Barker v. The Queen* also means that Smith Jnr. was not a trespasser, because he had a general right to enter his father's house. But because Smith did not act alone, and it was clear that his accomplice (Jones) knew he had no right to enter a private residence in the small hours for the sole purpose of stealing television sets, he should have been liable as an accessory.

32–036   **Suppose a man enters a museum as a member of the public. He hides in the lavatory until after closing time, then emerges and steals a gold statuette.** On the view of the law here put forward, the man's entry to the museum should not be accounted burglary, though this would involve the court in preferring *R. v. Collins* to *R. v. Jones and Smith*. For the same reason his entry to the lavatory is not burglary; he is licensed to enter the lavatory. Equally, when he emerges from it and enters the public rooms, it would be excessively technical to discover a burglary. In penal matters the judges should, in Bacon's words, "beware of hard constructions and strained inferences."[51] Substantially, the thief has simply remained in the building, which is not sufficient. If the defendant remains in the building after lawfully entering it, he has not entered it as a trespasser.[52] The law

---

[49] Australian Model Criminal Code, *Theft, Fraud and Bribery Related Offences*, (Canberra: 1995), chap. 3.

[50] See section 168(3) of the South Australian *Criminal Law Consolidation Act 1935*, which holds: "A person who enters or remains in a place with the consent of the occupier is not to be regarded as a trespasser unless that consent was obtained by— (a) force; or (b) a threat; or (c) an act of deception." Cf. *R. v. Boyle* [1954] 3 W.L.R. 364.

[51] Francis Bacon, *Bacon's Essays with annotations by Richard Whately*, (Boston: Lee & Shepard, 1868) at 550.

[52] *R. v. Laing* [1995] Crim. L.R. 395.

should be amended to catch those who enter a building lawfully and thereafter remain for the purpose of stealing. But such an amendment would be a matter for the legislature, not the courts.[53]

Suppose he hid in the broom cupboard?　He would be a trespasser in that "part of the building," namely the broom cupboard, but it is not burglary because he does not intend to steal in "that part of it" (see section 9(2)).

32–037

Suppose he has gone down to the nether regions to steal, where the public never had access?　That would be burglary, just as much as if the man had stolen in the private basement during opening hours.

32–038

Suppose D breaks into the Westfield Shopping Centre out of business hours (let us say, at 1 a.m.) for the sole purpose of stealing diamonds from the De Beers store. Is he guilty of burglary as soon as he enters the Westfield Centre as a trespasser, or does he have to enter the De Beers store as a trespasser?　The centre in London has 265 stores, which technically are 265 separate buildings connected in an overarching building. D has at least attempted burglary by entering the overarching area that connects all the stores, because his entry as a trespasser into the closed centre is an act that is more than merely preparatory. But it is likely that the courts would define the centre and its stores as one building, which means D's initial entry is an act of burglary regardless of whether he goes on to break into the De Beers store. Under the old law he would have been guilty of burglary only if he had entered the particular store (De Beers) as a trespasser with an intent to steal.[54] This is a critical issue in the context of burglary from a dwelling house, as it carries a much higher sentence. If D enters into the stairwell or lobby area of a large block of flats is he guilty of burglary from a dwelling even if he does not go on to break into a particular dwelling? It appears as though he could be guilty, because it need only be shown that D broke into the building with the intent to carry out the ulterior offence. Under the *Theft Act*, it is not necessary to demonstrate that D intended to target a particular part of the building or sub-building[55] within the overarching building. But a stairwell could hardly be described as a dwelling! Nor is a block of flats a particular dwelling. It is submitted that D's entry into the stairwell should be treated as an attempt. D should only be liable for burglarizing a dwelling house if he enters a particular dwelling such as a habitable flat within the block of flats.

32–039

---

[53] See, for example, section 168(1) of the South Australian *Criminal Law Consolidation Act 1935*, which holds: "For the purposes of this *Act*, a person commits a 'serious criminal trespass' if the person enters *or remains* in a place (other than a place that is open to the public) as a trespasser with the *intention of committing an offence* to which this section applies."

[54] Cf. *R. v. Wrigley* [1957] Crim. L.R. 57.

[55] *Pattrick v. Marley Estates Management* [2007] EWCA Civ. 1176; *Customs and Excise Commissioners v. Royal Exchange Theatre Trust* [1978] V.A.T.T.R. 139.

32.5. BEING FOUND ON PREMISES

32–040   Supplementing the law of theft and burglary is an offence in section 4 of the *Vagrancy Act 1824* which is worded as a breach of the "Eleventh Command-ment": thou shalt not be found out—or, rather, thou shalt not be found out at the time. The offence is committed only when a person is "found" on certain private premises "for any unlawful purpose." This and other offences in section 4 are triable only summarily.[56] The minutiae of the offence are as follows.

The place. The defendant must be found "in or upon any dwelling-house, warehouse coach-house, or in any inclosed yard, garden, or area." There are many decisions on the meaning of these words, not all of which need here be considered; it will be sufficient to summarize some of the main points.

The words "in or upon" include persons found on the roof of one of the specified buildings. A "dwelling house" probably means a house or flat[57] in which somebody habitually sleeps as his home, though he may be sleeping elsewhere at the time in question.

A "warehouse" probably includes a part of a shop used for the storage of goods and not open to the public,[58] but not part of the shop that is open to the public.[59] It does not include a building where goods are kept temporarily while something is done to them (*e.g.*, mail being sorted).[60]

Whether a "coach-house" now includes a garage is undecided. An "outhouse" must be closely connected with a house (and, it seems, it must be physically connected with it, as by a wall); a building in a field is not an outhouse.[61]

32–041   Then as to the words "inclosed yard, garden or area," they do not include a very large area, even though enclosed, but do cover an area of the size usually described as a yard, within the precincts of a building like a house or an inn, and enclosed to a substantial degree (even though some permanent openings are left for access).[62] The open space at the centre of Somerset House's quadrangle might be enclosed by the four grand wings of Somerset House (one of which houses the Faculty of Law, King's College London), but since King's College has not excluded the public from entering this area it does not constitute an enclosed yard for the purposes of section 4 of the *Vagrancy Act 1824*.[63] If the Law Faculty (and the other tenants) closed off the quadrangle and insisted on all visitors signing in at a security desk, then the space would constitute an enclosed yard for the

---

[56] Punishment is limited to three months. Before section 6 of the *Vagrancy Act 1824* was repealed anyone could arrest those found on or in premises for an unlawful purpose. Cf. *Gapper v. Chief Constable of Avon and Somerset* [2000] Q.B. 29.

[57] *Hollyhomes v. Hind* [1944] K.B. 571.

[58] *R. v. Hill* (1843) 174 L.R. 348.

[59] This was a "place of public resort" within the "suspected person" provision formerly contained in the *Vagrancy Act 1824* but now repealed.

[60] *Holloran v. Haughton* [1976] Crim. L.R. 270.

[61] *R. v. Borley* (1844) 8 J.P. 263.

[62] *Goodhew v. Morton* [1962] 1 W.L.R. 210.

[63] Cf. *Akhurst v. D.P.P.* (2009) 173 J.P. 499, where two men were found on the campus of a university. See also *Knott v. Blackburn* [1944] K.B. 77.

purposes of the *Act*. The words do not cover a tract of ground merely because it is called a "yard," as in "railway yard," "shipyard" and "vineyard."[64]

The meaning of "found." A suspect is "found" when he is perceived by the senses. A police officer who (being outside a house) hears the offender inside finds him there, even though the offender then makes an escape and is arrested outside. It seems that a person is found in a building if he is merely seen emerging (through a door or otherwise).[65] It seems, too, that the offence is not committed unless the suspect is trespassing in the place.

The purpose. The suspect must be found on the premises for an "unlawful purpose," which means any criminal purpose. The police can arrest and charge the offender even though it is not clear what precise mischief he was up to. If they get evidence of a particular unlawful purpose they may subsequently charge him with a more specific offence, such as burglary or attempt to steal. The unlawful purpose must relate to a planned crime, not a past crime. Therefore, if D is hiding in a garden to facilitate his escape from a burglary that is over and done, it could not be said that he was still intending to commit an offence for the purposes of satisfying section 4 of the *Vagrancy Act 1824*.[66] The intent may be to commit crime in the future.[67] But "unlawful purpose" does not include a purpose that is merely immoral or a matter of civil wrong; therefore it does not include the voyeur (Peeping Tom).[68]

The distinctions from attempt. (1) Entering premises, though an offence under section 4, may be held to be "mere preparation" and so not an attempt. This is particularly likely if the entry is into a yard and the intent is to steal in the building. (2) It may not be clear what crime the defendant intended; this would preclude a charge of attempt.

32.6. TRESPASS WITH INTENT TO COMMIT A SEXUAL OFFENCE

Section 63(1) of the *Sexual Offences Act 2003* holds: **32–042**

"(1)   A person commits an offence if–
   (a)   he is a trespasser on any premises,
   (b)   he intends to commit a relevant sexual offence on the premises, and
   (c)   he knows that, or is reckless as to whether, he is a trespasser.
(2)   In this section– "premises includes a structure or part of a structure;
   "relevant sexual offence has the same meaning as in section 62; "structure includes a tent, vehicle or vessel or other temporary or movable structure.
(3)   A person guilty of an offence under this section is liable–
   (a)   on summary conviction, to imprisonment for a term not exceeding 6 months or a fine not exceeding the statutory maximum or both;
   (b)   on conviction on indictment, to imprisonment for a term not exceeding 10 years."

---

[64] *Quatromini v. Peck* [1972] 3 All E.R. 521.

[65] *L v. Crown Prosecution Service* [2008] 1 Cr. App. R. 8.

[66] *L v. Crown Prosecution Service* [2008] 1 Cr. App. R. 8; *Smith v. Chief Superintendent, Woking Police Station* (1983) 76 Cr. App. R. 234.

[67] *Re Joy* (1853) 22 L.T. Jo. 80.

[68] *Hayes v. Stevenson* (1860) 3 L.T. 296. Cf. section 67 of the *Sexual Offences Act 2003*.

32.7. VEHICLE INTERFERENCE AND TAMPERING

32–043	Suppose that a person without authority tries the handle of a parked car. If, upon being arrested, he confesses that he intended to steal a car, or to steal the contents, or to take a conveyance for use, he can be convicted of attempting to commit the relevant offence.[69] To provide for these circumstances section 9 of the *Criminal Attempts Act 1981* creates a summary offence of vehicle interference.[70] Because it is only a summary offence it gives no right of trial and cannot be the subject of an attempt. But the offence is imprisonable, and a constable may arrest without warrant anyone who is or whom he with reasonable cause suspects to be guilty of it.

It must be proved that the defendant intended to commit one of the three offences mentioned above, but the prosecution need not prove which. If the defendant says that he only wanted to go to sleep in the car, or to look at the controls because he is interested in cars, and if this raises a reasonable doubt in the minds of the magistrates, he must be acquitted even though he clearly interfered with the vehicle.

32–044	**Could the police give evidence, to prove intent, that the defendant had previously been convicted of offences of dishonesty?**	The answer is no. The *Act* does not define the concept of "interfering with a motor vehicle or trailer." In *Reynolds v. Metropolitan Police* it was held that the conduct of two persons moving from one parked car to another, putting a hand on the door handle and looking inside, did not constitute interference, in the absence of evidence that they had opened the car doors or applied pressure to the door handles.[71] However, holding the handlebars of a motor-cycle so that another can attempt to use a crowbar to attempt to force the chain and padlock which secures it would be an interference.[72]

32.8. GOING EQUIPPED FOR STEALING *ETC.*

32–045	Section 25(1) of the *Theft Act* creates an important preparatory offence, triable either way,[73] which is given the above title in the marginal note:

> "(1)	A person shall be guilty of an offence if, when not at his place of abode, he has with him any article for use in the course of or in connection with any burglary or theft."

---

[69] *Jones v. Brooks* (1968) 52 Cr. App. R. 614.

[70] *Reynolds v. Metropolitan Police* [1982] Crim. L.R. 831; *M (Neil) (Juvenile) v. D.P.P.* [2000] Crim. L.R. 316.

[71] [1982] Crim. L.R. 831.

[72] *C. (A Minor) v. Director of Public Prosecutions* [1994] 3 W.L.R. 888.

[73] Section 17 of the *Magistrates' Courts Act 1980*.

The offence is punishable on indictment with 3 years imprisonment (subsection (2)),[74] which is less severe than the 4 years allowable for the offence of having offensive weapons.[75]

So the possession of a bunch of car keys can be an offence although the prosecution cannot prove whether the defendant's intention was to steal a car or only to make off with it temporarily. On the other hand, the subsection does not cover the possession of explosives for the purpose of salmon fishing, since poaching is not theft. The prosecution need not establish the particular burglary or theft that was intended.[76] Since the last three nouns in subsection (1) refer to the defendant's intention, it seems that an offence can be charged with all three words in the alternative, so the prosecution would not even have to prove whether the particular offence intended was a burglary or a theft, if it was clearly one of the two. In *R. v. Ellames*[77] it was held:

> "[I]n our view, to establish an offence under s.25(1) the prosecution must prove that the defendant was in possession the article, and intended the article to be used in the course of or in connection with some future burglary, theft. But it is not necessary to prove that he intended it to be used in the course of or in connection with any specific burglary or theft; it is enough to prove a general intention to use it for some burglary or theft....Nor, in our view, is it necessary to prove that the defendant intended to use it himself; it will be enough to prove that he had it with him with the intention that it should be used by someone else."

It will be seen that the offence is very widely defined. Although primarily aimed against the carrying of burglarious tools, it applies to the possession of a variety of other objects with the requisite intent, such as a car intended for use in a robbery, a pair of gloves to avoid leaving finger prints, and so on. The offence is valuable because it makes professional burglars wary of carrying articles like jemmies and duplicate keys; they try to work with non-incriminating articles, which are generally less effective for their purposes.

This last point does not wholly justify the statutory provision, because it covers articles that are not incriminating in themselves as well as those that are. For example, a shoplifter who has with him a bag in which he intends to put his loot would be covered. It has been suggested that the test should be whether the article is one that the defendant would not have had with him but for the contemplated offence; but it may be doubted whether even this restriction is inherent in the subsection. If a shopper carries a bag partly to carry articles that he is going to buy (because it is not practicable to steal them) and partly to conceal articles that he is going to steal, the bag would still seem to fall within the offence. (The trousers that the shopper is wearing would not fall within the offence, not because he would be wearing them anyway but because he does not intend to use them for the offence. If he intends to secrete stolen articles in his trousers pockets, the trousers would literally fall within it! In this respect the name given to the offence

32–046

---

[74] If the defendant intended to make off with a motor vehicle, the offence under section 25(1) carries endorsement of the defendant's driving licence and possible disqualification: sections 34 and 97 of the *Road Traffic Offenders Act 1988*.

[75] See section 1(1) of the *Prevention of Crime Act 1953* as amended by section 2(1) of the *Offensive Weapons Act 1996*.

[76] *R. v. Ellames* [1974] 1 W.L.R. 1391; *R. v. Mansfield* [1975] Crim. L.R. 101.

[77] [1974] 1 W.L.R. 1391 at 1397 *per* Browne J.

by the marginal note—"Going equipped for stealing, *etc.*"—is misleading. Marginal notes have no direct legislative effect, and it is doubtful how far they may be used as aids to construction.[78] But perhaps trousers could be excluded on the ground of avoiding absurdity.)

Like section 6 of the *Fraud Act 2006*, section 25 of the *Theft Act 1968* goes very far in making conviction depend upon little more than proof of intent. There are obvious risks of miscarriages of justice; so the court should be careful to scrutinize the evidence. A criminal who carries an article that is not incriminating in itself is likely to "get away with it" if, upon being questioned by the police, he can offer some plausible reason for carrying it.[79]

32–047 **Can a person who commits theft with an instrument be charged with both the theft and, under the subsection, with having the instrument?** Yes, if there is the appropriate evidence. But there would be little point in it. And the mere fact that the defendant is found to have committed the theft with the instrument is not enough for a conviction under section 25(1), because that subsection (it has been held) looks to an intended future use, not to possession of an article that has been used.[80]

32–048 **But if a person is found in possession of an article that he has just used to commit theft, he must previously have had it with him for the purpose of committing theft.** The Court of Appeal did not consider that point in the case just cited, presumably because it had not been argued. But presumably the prosecution would have to establish something more than momentary possession. If a person picks up a brick intending to use it to smash a shop widow in order to steal the things inside, this would hardly be enough to establish an offence under the subsection. Nor would an offence be committed if an article, carried innocently, is used on the spur of the moment for an offence.[81] "Has with him" would be construed to require something more continuous in the way of possession. The opinion is supported by the judicial interpretation of the similar phrase in the legislation against offensive weapons.[82]

---

[78] *D.P.P. v. Schildkamp* [1971] A.C. 1.

[79] The *Act* provides in subsection (3), that the article is "made or adapted" for criminal use, this is evidence that the defendant had it with him for the forbidden purpose. The provision simply places the evidential burden on the defendant and does not affect the prosecution's persuasive burden. A trial judge would be ill advised to rely on it unless the defendant submits that there is no case for him to answer; and even then the judge should use it only for the purpose of rejecting the submission and not for the purpose of directing the jury in terms of a presumption. *R. v. Harrison* [1970] Crim. L.R. 415.

[80] *R. v. Ellames* [1974] 1 W.L.R. 1391. Cf. *Minor v. Director of Public Prosecutions* (1988) 86 Cr. App. R. 378.

[81] *Per contra,* see the *obiter* in *R. v. Kelly* [1993] 97 Cr. App. R. 245, where D appealed against a conviction for aggravated burglary contrary to section 10 of the *Theft Act 1968* on the ground that "for aggravated burglary it was necessary to prove that he had the weapon with him with intent to cause injury before the occasion for the use of the weapon had arisen." It was held "that since the relevant time for consideration of the appellant's intent to use the weapon for causing injury was the time he actually stole the goods, the use of the screwdriver at the time of the theft with the requisite intent, namely, the intent to injure if the need arose, had been established."

[82] *R. v. Dayle* [1974] 1 W.L.R. 181; *Ohlson v. Hylton* [1975] 1 W.L.R. 724; *R. v. Giles* [1976] Crim. L.R. 253; *R. v. Ellis* [2010] EWCA Crim. 163.

Presumably "in connection with" is wider than "in the course of"?   Yes; so   **32–049**
much so that the latter phrase seems unnecessary. The Court of Appeal said on
one occasion:[83]

> "It is easy to think of cases where an article could be intended for use "in connection with
> though not 'in the course of a burglary, *etc.*, *e.g.*, articles intended to be used while doing
> preparatory acts or while escaping after a crime."

Wide as the subsection is, the courts do not apply it to what may be called
remote preparation for an offence. So it was held that where a defendant was in
possession of a driving licence belonging to another person, intending to use it to
obtain a job as a driver and subsequently to steal from his employer, his
possession was too remote from the intended theft to come within the
subsection.[84] However, this type of conduct would be caught by section 6 of the
Fraud Act 2006.[85]

If a person is walking along the street when the police arrest him for having   **32–050**
a burglarious implement with him, would it be a defence for him to show
that he did not intend to use the implement that day, but only the next day or
next week?   No. If he intended to use it, it does not matter when.[86]

Then if he takes it home with him, intending to have a good night's sleep   **32–051**
before committing the burglary, why can't he be guilty of the offence of
possessing the implement in his house?   The offence was not applied to the
"place of abode" because it was thought that this would be an undue invasion of
privacy. For example, such a provision might cause an over-zealous police force
to "turn-over" the houses of known criminals on a regular basis, which would
look like persecution.[87] Only the home is exempted, not the place of work. The
offence under section 6 of the *Fraud Act 2006* of possessing articles for use in
fraud is not limited in this way, and may be committed by those who keep such
articles in their private homes. The offence under section 4 of the *Explosive
Substances Act 1883* of possessing explosives for an unlawful object is not
limited in this way either, and may be committed by possessing explosives in the
home. But the latter *Act* is used only for the prosecution of those who intend to
commit large explosions, as for political objects. It is not the practice to make a
charge in respect of small amounts of explosive held for the purpose of blowing
safes.

---

[83] *R. v. Ellames* [1974] 1 W.L.R. 1391 at 1397.

[84] *R. v. Mansfield* [1975] Crim. L.R. 101.

[85] *R. v. Virciglo* [2010] EWCA Crim. 650.

[86] But it must be proved that the defendant had a firm intention to use the thing for a burglary or theft.
R. v. Hargreaves [1985] Crim. L.R. 243.

[87] It was held in *R. v. Bundy* [1977] 1 W.L.R. 914, that "place of abode" means a fixed place, so
although a car can be a place of abode if it is in one spot and the defendant sleeps there, it is not his
place of abode while he has it out on the road.

32–052 **Dart and Dash plan a robbery. They are to meet in Dart's house. Dash duly appears, equipped with his stocking-mask. Dart pockets his own mask, and they are about to leave the house when the police appear and they are arrested. Does the subsection mean that Dash is guilty of the offence but not Dart?** Dart is not guilty as perpetrator, since he is at his place of abode; but he is guilty as accessory to Dash's offence if (1) he knew that Dash had the mask with him for the forbidden purpose, and (2) he intended to assist him in the execution of the purpose; both these requisites are satisfied on the facts supposed.

CHAPTER 33

HANDLING STOLEN GOODS

"Cui prodest scelus,
Is fecit."[1]

33.1.   THE FORMS OF HANDLING

The rationale for criminalizing "handling" and "receiving" is that handlers and receivers of stolen goods create a market for theft. But do not innocent purchasers of stolen goods also contribute to that market? Yes, but their lack of culpability means that they will not come within the purview of the criminal law. The handler/receiver is only convicted of an offence when he knowingly (culpably) receives or handles the fruits of another's theft. By receiving or dealing with a good that can be produced only through wrongful harm, the possessor chooses to underwrite the thief's wrongful harm. The core justification for extending criminal liability to handlers and receivers is that they culpably choose to share the fruits (or, at least try to help others to do so) of the criminal harm of theft, burglary and robbery. The handler or receiver is only criminalized when he knows or believes the goods are stolen. The gravamen of the offence is the handling of the goods with knowledge that they were stolen. It is wrong for D2 to culpably possess, receive or to assist others to handle stolen goods, because D2 (handler) knows the goods have become available only because D1 (thief) has perpetrated a wrongful harm.[2]

33–001

In the war against theft the police can call certain ancillary provisions to their aid, such as the *Scrap Metal Dealers Act 1964* which requires such dealers to be registered and regulates the manner in which they may carry on their trade. Formerly, the offence of handling was called "receiving" stolen goods. The *Theft Act 1968* widened it and gave it a wider name, so that now the offence covers not

---

[1] This famous locution was used by Lucius Annaeus Seneca in his *Medea* where the protagonist stated: "the person who takes advantage of a crime, is the one who committed it."

[2] Dennis J. Baker, "Collective Criminalization and the Constitutional Right to Endanger Others," (2009) 28 *Crim. Just. Ethics* 168 at 190; Dennis J. Baker, *The Right Not to be Criminalized: Demarcating Criminal Law's Authority*, (Farnham: Ashgate, 2011) at Chap 4. See also Mike Sutton, "Supply by Theft: Does the Market for Second-hand Goods Play a Role in Keeping Crime Figures High?" (1995) 35(3) *Brit. J. Criminology* 400; Carl B. Klockars, *The Professional Fence* (New York: Free Press, 1974); Ted Roselius and Douglas Benton, "Marketing Theory and the Fencing of Stolen Goods," (1973-1974) 50 *Denv. L.J.* 177; Jerome Hall, *Theft, Law and Society*, (Bloomington IN: Bobbs-Merrill, 1952) at 164-189.

only the traditional receiver but the person who may be called a dealer in stolen goods (in a very wide sense of the expression). The definition in section 22(1) is a draftsman's omelette:

> "A person handles stolen goods if (otherwise than in the course of the stealing) knowing or believing them to be stolen goods he dishonestly receives the goods, or dishonestly undertakes or assists in their retention, removal, disposal or realisation by or for the benefit of another person, or if he arranges to do so."

The offence is punishable with 14 years' imprisonment, in other words more severely than theft.

33–002 **So handling is a graver offence than theft?**   Yes and no. Minor handlings are treated as lesser offences than theft. The reason why handling can be punished more severely than theft is because there have been notorious cases in the past where a professional receiver (like Jonathan Wild)[3] has been the centre of a great web of crime. (At the present day the most active professional "fences" are those who deal in laptops, mobile telephones, clothing, DVD players, household appliances, bikes and tools.)[4] But all is not as it seems. In the first place, sentences on handlers rarely exceed 7 years.[5] It does not look as though the increased punishment allowable for handling is needed. And if it is said that the extra dose is required for very large-scale handling, what about large-scale theft? This cannot be punished with more than 7 years' imprisonment unless burglary or robbery is involved. Why should there be any difference from handling?

In the second place, a conviction of handling is generally regarded as a lesser conviction than one of theft, and attracts a lighter sentence. The usual handler is a person of easy morals who succumbs to the temptation of buying something cheap, knowing it has been dishonestly acquired; he did not bring about the theft and is not, in the words of one commentator, "a facility whose existence is a reassuring part of the background against which thievery operates."[6] For these reasons he can expect to be sentenced more leniently than the thief himself. So a defendant who is charged with both theft and handling strives to get a conviction of handling (if he must be convicted) rather than one of theft.[7] He often offers a

---

[3] See Charles Hitchin, *A True Discovery of the Conduct of Receivers and Thief-takers in and about the City of London*, (London: printed for the author, 1718); Alexander Smith, *Memoirs of the Life and Times, of the Famous Jonathan Wild Together with the History and Lives of Modern Rogues*, (London: printed for Sam Briscoe, 1726). In Elizabethan times it was not an offence to receive or handle stolen goods. See *Dawson* (1601) Yel. 5, where it was said: "Thou art an arrant knave, for thou has bought stolen swine, and a stolen cow, knowing them to be stolen. And adjudg'd against the plaintiff, for the receipt or sale of goods stolen is not felony, nor makes any accessory, unless it is joined with a receipt or abetment of the felon himself."

[4] Jacqueline L. Schneider, "Stolen Goods Markets: Methods of Disposal," (2005) 45 *Brit. J. Criminology* 129 at 133.

[5] See *R. v. Webbe* [2002] 1 Cr. App. R. 22.

[6] D. W. Elliott, "Dialogues on the Theft Act," in P.R. Glazebrook (ed.), *Reshaping the Criminal Law: Essays in Honour of Glanville Williams*, (London: Stevens, 1978) at 294.

[7] This is particularly so if there has been, for example, a post office "snatch" totalling thousands of pounds, and D is found in possession of a mere £20 worth of the stolen postal orders. He will be anxious to say that he only handled this amount and was not a party to the theft as a whole. Handling is triable either way (section 17 of *the Magistrates' Courts Act 1980*), and most handlers are relatively happy to be dealt with summarily if given the chance.

plea of guilty to handling on condition that the theft charge is dropped; and the jury, if given the choice between the two charges, often choose to convict of handling if they view the offence indulgently. Logically, however, it should almost never be possible for a dishonest handler to avoid a conviction of theft of what he handles, because the handler is, by reason of the handling, a thief as well.

Let us unpick section 22(1). Begin by reading it carefully two or three times. It will be seen that the prosecution must prove three things: **33–003**

1. That the defendant handled the goods.
2. That they were stolen.
3. That at the time when the defendant handled the goods, (a) he was acting dishonestly and (b) knew or believed they were stolen.

As regards the first element, there are two main forms of the handling:

(a) receiving (where the defendant comes into possession of the goods), and
(b) a group of nouns referring to various forms of dealing with the goods (where the defendant need not come into possession).

Arranging to receive or deal with the goods is also the full offence, not simply an inchoate offence.

But doesn't the handler have to touch the goods? No. The person known in the underworld as a "placer" may simply talk on the telephone. He is guilty of handling if he "undertakes the realization" of the goods, as by finding a buyer for them. The subsection was drafted with the clear intention that it should create only one offence, capable of being committed in numerous different ways. But the courts, regarding this as undesirable, wish it to be treated as creating what are for most purposes two offences: **33–004**

> "The first is ... receiving .... The second is a new offence ... and can be committed in any of the various ways indicated by the words from 'undertakes to the end of the subsection. If follows that the new offence may and should be charged in a single count embodying in the particulars as much of the relevant language of the subsection including alternatives, as may be appropriate."[8]

In this statement Lord Bridge was summarizing, while slightly misunderstanding,[9] a rule previously developed in the Court of Appeal. We will give the first

---

[8] *R. v. Bloxham* [1983] A.C. 109 at 113.

[9] Lord Bridge said there are two offences. Previously, the Court of Appeal said simply the single offence in subs. (1) should be charged in two counts (an unorthodox procedure); but the rule was only advisory, and an information charging "handling" simpliciter was not bad for duplicity. Now Lord Bridge, obiter, says it is two offences. Notwithstanding that his Lordship was speaking on behalf of the House of Lords, he must be regarded as being wrong. There is only one offence on the wording of the statute; the Court of Appeal has decided that there is only one offence; and Lord Bridge did not refer to the precedents or purport to overrule them. Of course, prosecutors would be well advised to treat the subsection as creating two offences. But if an indictment or information charges Lord Bridge's two "offences" as a single offence, the charge should assuredly be regarded as valid. It is a pity that the courts have not gone further in splitting up the subsection de facto. The statement that

offence (or variety of the offence) the name of handling by receiving. The second is conveniently called, for short, handling by dealing. The reason offered by the Court of Appeal for having two counts was that they give the defendant better information than a single count, but it is difficult to see how. A more convincing reason would be that breaking the numerous alternatives into two major questions clarifies the task of the jury and the jury's findings. Also, since the traditional receiver is likely to get a heavier sentence than one who gives minor assistance, it is helpful for the verdict of the jury to distinguish between them. However, the legal distinction between receiving and dealing imperfectly reflects the amount of help that may be given. A placer, who simply acts as an agent for sale, may be a big-time professional criminal, while a receiver may be someone who buys a watch cheaply in a pub, or even a girl who is given a stolen watch by her thieving boyfriend. The judge in sentencing must take account of all the facts of the case, including his knowledge of the defendant's previous convictions.

33.2. HANDLING BY RECEIVING

33–005   Handling by receiving is committed by taking possession or control of the stolen goods.[10] The typical case is where the thief sells the goods to a professional receiver.[11] Sometimes the receiver's possession or control[12] is jointly with the thief or another person. Authorities establish that a person may receive by authorizing his agent to receive, or by having goods delivered to his premises.[13] The thief's wife is not guilty of handling merely because she is willing for goods to be kept and used in the matrimonial home and thinks it is nice to have these things.[14] But if she receives large sums of stolen money from the thief she can be

---

handling by dealing should be charged in a single count is an inconvenient rule when the prosecution desire to charge both handling by undertaking and handling by assisting. These two forms of handling would be much better put in separate counts.

[10] The offence apparently does not continue over separate receivings, so each receiving must generally go into a separate count. However, suppose the police have found an "Aladdin's Cave" of stolen property in the possession of the defendant, received over a considerable period of time, and they cannot identify the various receivings. In that case, it seems, all the receivings can go into one count. See *R. v. Smythe* (1981) 72 Cr. App. R. 8 at 13. Furthermore, "a continuous series of closely linked offences may be charged in one count where no particulars of the individual dates or amounts could be given." See *R. v. Cain* [1983] Crim. L.R. 802.

[11] In *R. v. Deakin* [1972] 1 W.L.R. 1618, the buyer, instead of being charged with receiving, was charged with undertaking the realization of the goods, under the later part of the subsection; and his conviction on this charge was upheld on appeal. The decision is obviously wrong, because it is the seller, not the buyer, who undertakes the realization of the goods. (The seller was not guilty of undertaking the realization because he did not sell for the benefit of another, so the buyer could not be brought in as an accessory to his sale.) The decision manifests the usual tendency of the Court of Appeal to uphold convictions of the wrong offence rather than let the fish out of the net. Cf. *R. v. Coleman* (1986) 150 J.P. 175.

[12] See *R. v. Forsyth* [1997] 2 Cr. App. R. 299; *Attorney-General's Reference (No.1 of 1974)* [1974] Q.B. 744.

[13] *R. v. Lloyd* [1992] Crim. L.R. 361; *R. v. Brook* [1993] Crim. L.R. 455; *R. v. Flynn* [2005] EWCA Crim. 452. See also the pre-*Act* authorities: *R. v. Frost* (1964) 48 Cr. App. R. 284; *R. v. Cavendish* [1961] 1 W.L.R. 1083; *R. v. Payne* (1910) 3 Cr. App. R. 259; *R. v. Seiga* (1961) 45 Cr. App. R. 26; *R. v. Wiley* (1850) 4 Cox C.C. 412; *R. v. Gleed* (1917) 12 Cr. App. R. 32.

[14] *R. v. Kanwar* [1982] 1 W.L.R. 845. Although this was decided on retaining, the same rule doubtless applies to receiving.

convicted of handling by receiving,[15] and she can sometimes be convicted of assisting her husband to retain the goods. The concluding words of the subsection, "or if he arranges to do so," appear to apply to all the preceding words, not merely to the words after "undertakes." If this is the correct reading, a person who arranges to receive stolen goods is guilty of handling as soon as he makes the arrangement.

You said that the receiver is also a thief. Doesn't that make an awful mix up? 33–006
The handler by receiving is almost always a thief.[16] (And so is the handler by dealing.) The handling is a fresh theft, distinct from the original theft that made the goods "stolen goods." The handler is guilty of handling, because his act is "otherwise than in the course of stealing" that made the goods stolen goods; and he is guilty of theft, by reason of his own dishonest appropriation.[17] But it is not customary to charge a clear handler with theft, because the charge of handling better represents what he has done.

Take the converse question. Isn't the thief a receiver in getting the goods? 33–007
Generally not, since he gets the goods "in the course of stealing." The goods must be stolen before the handling.[18]

Suppose two crooks break into a factory and fill a sack with assorted items. 33–008
After leaving they divide up the contents. Are they guilty of receiving from each other when they divide it up? No, because the sack and its contents are already in their joint possession. The goods are stolen, and they know it—because they were the thieves; but there is no receiving at that stage. However, this answer is largely theoretical. For reasons already given, your two crooks are unlikely to protest that they are thieves if they are being tried for handling; they prefer to be convicted of the handling, if anything. What may happen is that if they are convicted of handling they may appeal on the ground that there is no evidence that the goods were stolen when they received the goods. We shall return to this problem in a moment.

Can a thief be a handler of the same goods? Yes, by an act done after the 33–009
theft. If a master criminal who has got other people to carry out the actual theft subsequently handles the goods (as by receiving them), he may well be charged with the handling, even though he is an accessory to the theft, for here the handling is the more serious offence. His handling is not "in the course of the stealing" but distinctly subsequent to it.[19]

---

[15] *R. v. Dadd* [1974] Crim. L.R. 439.

[16] *Stapylton v. O'Callaghan* [1973] 2 All E.R. 782; *R. v. Dolan* (1976) 62 Cr. App. R. 36; *R. v. Sainthouse* [1980] Crim. L.R. 506.

[17] This point appears to have been thoroughly misunderstood in *R. v. Gregory* (1983) 77 Cr. App. R. 41.

[18] *R. v. Park* (1988) 87 Cr. App. R. 164.

[19] "A defendant may be convicted both of theft and of handling the same goods, if the evidence warrants such a conclusion. If the handling of the goods occurred only in the course of the theft, he cannot be found guilty of handling, by reason of section 22 (1) of the *Theft Act 1968*, but if he handles the goods later than the occasion of the theft, he may be convicted both of theft and handling." *R. v. Dolan* (1976) 62 Cr. App. R. 36. See also *R. v. Shelton* (1986) 83 Cr. App. R. 379 at 385.

33–010 **How long does "the course of the stealing" last? It seems a vague phrase.** In practice it means "after the theft,"[20] and it would have been better if the *Act* had said that. This is shown by *R. v Pitham*,[21] where the Court of Appeal rightly reduced "the course of stealing" to something approaching a Euclidean point. It will be remembered that in that case the court held that a non-owner who dishonestly offers another's goods for sale thereby appropriates them, so that they become stolen goods; when the offeree accepts the offer and receives the goods he is guilty of handling stolen goods, his act not being "in the course of stealing." *If* the court was right in *Pitham* in saying that X committed theft when he offered the goods to Pitham (a big "if"), then it was perfectly right in saying that Pitham's acceptance and removal of the goods was receiving. (The report does not make it clear whether Pitham removed the goods immediately on being made the offer or only on a return visit some time after, but there is no reason why the point should make any difference.) Of course, if Pitham had been an abettor in the actual commission of the theft by X, it could not possibly have been held that he was guilty of handling.

"Theft is a finite act—it has a beginning and it has an end; at what point the transaction is complete is a matter for the jury to decide upon the facts of each case."[22] But if Ds are still "on the job," the theft must continue at least for the purposes of the saving clause. For example, if D breaks into a house and takes up a gold cup, the theft is complete the moment he does so (perhaps the moment he touches it). Suppose that he then tosses it out of the window to a confederate. In common sense, the confederate receives it "in the course of stealing." Otherwise, the saving clause would hardly have any operation. "The course of stealing" must last for some time after the technical appropriation, even if only for a short time.[23]

33–011 **Suppose a person is found in possession of stolen articles. Is he charged with theft or with handling?** A clear thief should be charged as such; so should a clear handler, because these are generally the most straightforward charges. If there is no evidence how the man came by the stuff the usual practice is to charge him with both offences,[24] leaving the jury (or magistrates) to convict of whichever they think more likely.[25] The judge is not over-tender to the defendant

---

[20] Nothing turns on the distinction between "stealing" and "theft," because they mean the same.

[21] (1977) 65 Cr. App. R. 45.

[22] *R. v. Atakpu* [1994] Q.B. 69 at 78 *per* Ward J. See also Glanville Williams, "Appropriation: A Single or Continuous Act?" [1978] Crim. L. R. 69.

[23] *R. v. Atakpu* [1994] Q.B. 69 supports this view.

[24] "Mutually exclusive counts on a single indictment may be left to the jury where there is a *prima facie* case on both." *R. v. Bellman* [1989] A.C. 836; *R. v. Suter* [1997] C.L.Y. 1339. If there are alternative counts, the jury should be instructed to consider the more serious offence first. After the jury has returned their verdict on the theft, robbery or burglary count, then, the handling count should be considered. *R. v. Fernandez* [1997] 1 Cr.App.R. 123; *R. v. McEvilly* [2008] Crim. L.R. 968.

[25] Even charging both offences can lead to trouble, if the jury are divided between them. The best course would be for the judge to direct the jury that if in doubt between the two offences they convict of theft. In some jurisdictions, namely Australia and New Zealand, the courts have suggested that jury should be directed to convict D of the less serious offence. See *Gilson v. The Queen* (1991) 172 C.L.R. 353; *Police v. Waata* [2006] D.C.R. 738. But the seriousness of theses offences is circumstantially contingent. A professional handler would get a greater sentence than a petty thief, would he not? In *R. v. Torney* [2003] 141 A. Crim. R. 20, it was held: "The directions to the jury

in this situation, and will generally skate over the question of the burden of proving whether it is the one or the other. But in case of doubt, the prosecution should charge both offences, or else should charge theft only.

But how can he? The jury cannot convict the man of theft unless they are sure he stole, and they cannot convict him of handling unless they are sure that he obtained the goods "otherwise than in the course of stealing." Unless they can decide between these two offences beyond reasonable doubt, they ought not to convict either. The courts have not pointed at all clearly to the solution of this problem, but a solution is available. The judge should direct the jury that they can convict if they are satisfied that the defendant has dishonestly appropriated the property of another, whether he was the original thief or has since stolen it when he dishonestly came into possession of property previously stolen by another. The indictment should be worded so as to give sufficient latitude to the jury as to the time of the theft. 33–012

On one occasion when the defendant was charged only with handling and not with theft (a piece of folly on the part of the prosecutor, since the evidence left it uncertain which offence the defendant had committed) the Court of Appeal came to the prosecutor's assistance by holding that if there is no evidence that the defendant stole the property, the question of theft need not be left to the jury, who may then happily be allowed to convict of handling.[26] In effect the court put an evidential burden on the unfortunate defendant to raise the issue of his own guilt of theft, which obviously he would not want to do.[27] If in fact the defendant was a thief, he ought not be convicted of handling; yet obviously he is not going to raise that defence, because although he may be acquitted on the charge of handling he will inevitably be convicted as a thief.

If the handlers can be charged as thieves, what is the point of the handling offence? There are four answers to your question, none of them utterly conclusive. First, perhaps the best answer is that when a person has handled stolen goods a charge of handling is easier for the jury to understand than a charge of stealing. Second, handling in theory is punishable more severely; but, as we have seen, it is in practice generally treated more leniently. It therefore offers opportunities for plea-bargaining. Third, not all handlers are thieves. The 33–013

---

including that if they were satisfied by reason of the accused's possession, without satisfactory explanation, of recently stolen property, that the accused was either the thief or a handler of it, but were unable to be satisfied beyond reasonable doubt which, then they should convict on the lesser of the charges, that is, handling, and later correcting himself and directing that theft was the lesser offence, in all the circumstances, may well have created confusion in the minds of the jury and denied the applicants a real chance of acquittal."

[26] *R. v. Griffiths* (1974) 60 Cr. App. R. 14.

[27] *Per contra*, "Where counts of theft and handling are laid in the alternative and the accused pleads not guilty to both counts, it cannot be the intention of the section to produce the result that the Crown must attempt to prove theft beyond reasonable doubt on the first count and to disprove it beyond reasonable doubt on the second." *R. v. Koene* [1982] V.R. 916 (citing the first edition of this book at 827). Therefore, a direction on the: "otherwise than in the course of the stealing" element is not required unless the evidence of the case makes it an issue. See *R. v. Wells* [2004] EWCA Crim 792; *R. v. Cash* [1985] Q.B. 801. See also *R. v. Henderson* [2009] V.S.C.A. 136; *R. v. Torney* [2003] 141 A. Crim. R. 20 at 29.

law of handling is extended to goods obtained by fraud or blackmail, even when they would not for other purposes be regarded as being stolen (section 24(4) of the *Theft Act 1968*). Here the handler is not necessarily guilty of theft. If (as will usually be the case) the blackmailer or fraudster obtains a voidable title to the goods, a person who subsequently handles them will not be guilty of stealing them from the original owner, because the original owner is no longer the owner at the time of the act in question. Such a person can, however, be convicted of handling. A person who arranges to handle is a handler, though he is not guilty of theft but for a conspiracy to steal or a conspiracy to defraud. The point also applies to handlers by dealing.[28] Although some of these commit theft, it is not certain that all do. Fourth, if a person is charged with handling and not with theft, the prosecution may be assisted in proving the mental element by giving evidence of the defendant's previous convictions or similar conduct on other occasions, subject to certain conditions.[29]

This is not generally allowed on a charge of theft, or on a charge of both handling and theft. In order to get the benefit of the provision the prosecution may be tempted to charge handling when they really should charge theft; and the court should be astute to prevent this (instead of being astute to help the prosecutor, as it was in the case of the candlesticks). Normally, thieves, accessories and handlers[30] are tried together, and technically different charges are regarded as being alternative.

33.3. HANDLING BY DEALING: RETENTION

33–014 What we are calling handling by dealing turns on the four forbidden acts of retention, removal, disposal and realization of the goods. Like the other elements of handling by dealing (undertaking or assisting; arranging) these acts can be charged in the alternative. So a person can be charged with undertaking to retain, assisting to retain, arranging to undertake or arranging to assist the retention; and with removing, disposing of and realizing, through all the permutations.

33–015 **Why isn't the person who furthers the thief's plans in these respects punishable as an accessory to the theft?** Because theft is not a continuing offence; the appropriation is over by the time the handler comes on the scene. (I assume that the defendant did not help the thief by dealing with the goods "in the course of the stealing;" if he did, he is not a handler but an accessory to the theft. Also, if he agreed with the thief beforehand that he would handle the goods, he is both an accessory to the theft by encouraging it and, when he later deals with the stolen goods, a handler.)

---

[28] *R. v. Slater* [1996] Crim. L.R. 494.

[29] Section 27(3) of the *Theft Act 1968* provides: "(a) evidence that he has had in his possession, or has undertaken or assisted in the retention, removal, disposal or realisation of, stolen goods from any theft taking place not earlier than twelve months before the offence charged; and (b) (provided that seven days' notice in writing has been given to him of the intention to prove the conviction) evidence that he has within the five years preceding the date of the offence charged been convicted of theft or of handling stolen goods." See also *R. v. Duffus* (1994) 158 J.P. 224.

[30] For the joint trial of handlers and thieves, see section 27(1) and (2) of the *Theft Act 1968*.

Is there any common idea underlying the four prohibitions? What is the   **33–016**
subsection really aiming at?   The forms of handling by dealing are evidently
intended to cover acts enabling the thief (or some other person implicated in his
dishonesty) to retain (remain in possession of) his ill-gotten gains or to dispose of
them. For the moment we will assume that "removal" and "disposal" are roughly
comprised under the word "disposal." It may be convenient to say at once what
handling by dealing is intended to leave out. It is not intended to punish the thief
for using the loot: he can be dealt with for that as a thief, and need not be made a
handler as well. Nor does the subsection make his friends or employees guilty of
handling if they share in the use.[31]

As an example, one does not handle stolen goods merely by allowing oneself
to be driven in a stolen car, or by driving it on the general business of the thief.[32]
Although handling includes the "removal" of goods, this does not mean that
driving a stolen car, which is merely using it in the manner for which it is
designed, is to be regarded as removing it. It should not be so regarded unless the
driving is for the purpose of disposing of the stolen car, or of other stolen goods,
or more safely retaining them. In any case, the act of driving could not be a
handling if the driver was acting for his own purposes and not in order to benefit
or assist another.[33]

The two forbidden acts, then, are the retention and/or disposal of stolen goods.
These can each be committed in either of the two modes: by undertaking and by
assisting in their doing. "Undertaking" the act in question here means doing it.
The point may be briefly expanded. We saw in discussing manslaughter by
omission that this word is ambiguous in some contexts. In ordinary speech,
undertaking to do something is a promise to do it, while undertaking something
generally means doing it. ("He undertook to journey to Rome" = he went.) In
section 22(1) the undertaking is naturally read as the act of retention, *etc.* What
the statute evidently means by the word "undertakes" is that handling can be
committed by a person who retains, removes, disposes of or realizes goods for the
benefit of another.

In support of this opinion, it may be said that there would be little point in
reading "undertakes" as though it meant "promise," because an agreement for the
retention, *etc.* would be more naturally and explicitly charged as an arrangement
to retain, *etc.* under the concluding limb of the subsection. The word
"undertakes" is evidently put in not to carry the meaning of a promise but simply
to tie up grammatically with "assists." The draftsperson would have done better
to have avoided the ambiguity by rewriting the subsection.[34]

---

[31] *R. v. Sanders* (1982) 75 Cr. App. R. 84.
[32] *R. v. Kanwar* [1982] 1 W.L.R. 845.
[33] *R. v. Sloggett* [1972] 1 Q.B. 430. But driving or being driven in a stolen car could be charged under
section 12 of the *Theft Act 1968*. Probably it is not theft, since the person who drives the car for a
temporary purpose does not intend for his own part to deprive the owner permanently.
[34] Cf. C.L.R.C., *Eighth Report: Theft and Related Offences*, (London: Cmnd. 2977, 1966) at para.
128.

33–017 **What is the statute getting at when it says "by or for the benefit of another person"?** Fortunately we now have the authority of Lord Bridge telling us what it means. The word "undertakes" goes with "for the benefit of another person" and the word "assists" goes with "by... another person." Lord Bridge:[35]

> "The offence can be committed in relation to any one of these activities in one or other of two ways. First, the offender may himself undertake the activity for the benefit of another person. Secondly, the activity may be undertaken by another person and the offender may assist him."

Spelling this out again in the words of the subsection, the handler may (1) *undertake* the retention or disposal of the goods (two words that we are using to cover all four activities)—*i.e.* he may retain or dispose of the goods—for the benefit of another, or he may (2) assist another in retaining or disposing of the goods. With all these preliminaries over, we narrow our attention to the question of retaining stolen goods or assisting in their retention. The C.L.R.C. which proposed the offence in its present form, explained its rationale as follows (italics supplied):

> "We are in favour of extending the scope of the offence [from the receiving of stolen property] to certain other kinds of meddling with stolen property. *This is because the object should be to combat theft by making it more difficult and less profitable to dispose of stolen property.* Since thieves may be helped not only by buying the property but in other ways such as facilitating its disposal, it seems right that the offence should extend to these kinds of assistance."

The House of Lords quoted this passage in *R. v. Bloxham*[36] as a means of resolving any ambiguity that might be found in the subsection. Their Lordships held that they were entitled to look at the committee's Report on which the *Act* was based in order to ascertain what was the mischief that the subsection intended to cure, and they discovered from the Report that there was no mischief calling for legislative intervention on the particular point with which they were concerned. The Report was, therefore, a useful aid to the interpretation of the *Act*.

33–018 **The committee talks about the thief's disposal of goods. I don't see what "retention" of the goods has to do with disposal. It's the opposite.** The word "retention" does not appear in the committee's statement of policy; but it may be said that what section 22(1) does is to pick out certain particularly important activities by the thief after committing the theft, or by other persons in relation to the stolen goods, in which it is an offence to assist. The retention of goods is one of them.

33–019 **Who is the "another" that the subsection talks about?** Anyone other than the person(s) charged with handling.[37]

---

[35] *R. v. Bloxham* [1983] 1 A.C. 109 at 113. This interpretation of the subsection had previously been carefully worked out by the commentators. The draftsperson obscured his meaning by rolling the various alternatives into a complex sentence, and worse still, by getting the two halves of his variations mixed up: he should have said "for the benefit of or by another person as the case may be."
[36] [1983] 1 A.C. 109 at 115.
[37] See *R. v. Tokeley-Parry* [1999] Crim. L. R. 578, where D assisted the removal by another person by smuggling antiquities from Egypt including the door from the Tomb of Hetepka. See also *R. v. Roberts* (unreported 1993); *R. v. Gingell* [2000] 1 Cr. App. R. 88.

**But if the defendant can retain the stolen goods for his own benefit, why
can't he retain them for the benefit of his friend?**   Although the subsection
does not say so, what it is really aimed against is retaining (or disposing of) the
goods for the benefit of the thief (or of another handler), or helping the thief (or
handler) to retain (or dispose of) them. The draftsperson did not want to make the
thief himself guilty of handling by reason of his retention of the goods. If a
person knowingly retains stolen goods for his own benefit, he can be charged
with theft. The subsection states this limitation rather obscurely, by requiring that
the defendant was not acting for himself. If, for example, he agreed to warehouse
stolen goods, or if he let a garage to the thief, or to the thief's father (or his own
aunt, if you like), knowing that the garage was intended to house stolen goods, he
is a handler.[38]

33–020

**Underworld characters aren't generally altruistic. The chap who garages the
goods for the thief is being rewarded for it, so he is acting for his own benefit.**
Nevertheless, he is also acting for the benefit of the thief. We shall return to this
point below. A more unexpected illustration of the offence than those just given is
R. v. Kanwar.[39] A woman whose house contained (as she knew) goods stolen by
her husband lied to the police in the hope of protecting her husband and retaining
the goods. The Court of Appeal said that she committed no offence by having the
stolen goods in the house (presumably it was her husband who was the owner or
tenant of the house),[40] or in failing to disclose their presence to the police;[41] but
her lies led to her conviction of handling by assisting her husband to retain the
goods. This although the police knew she was lying and were not put off, since
the court read the word "assist," with doubtful propriety, to include a person who
did not assist but made an ineffectual effort to assist. This is not the only instance
of the courts construing a word in an extended sense to include an attempt.

33–021

It looks unrealistic to say that Mrs. Kanwar handled the stolen goods in talking
to the police, though perhaps that is the result of giving a conglomeration of
offences a conglomerate name. A more apt charge would have been under section
4(1) of the *Criminal Law Act 1967*; but that charge would have required the
consent of the Director of Public Prosecutions, and he would probably not have
consented to the prosecution of a wife for attempting to shield her husband.
Whether it was proper to use the *Theft Act* offence for the purpose of evading the
restriction on prosecution in the *Criminal Law Act* is a matter that the court did
not consider, since our judges do not regard it as part of their duty to control the
exercise by prosecutors of their discretion in prosecuting. It almost never occurs
to them to strike out a charge as being an abuse of process of the court, as this one
surely was.

---

[38] A difficult question may arise where a bailee dishonestly decides to keep the bailed article which is
being warehoused for him. The point of time at which the bailee steals may be hard to fix, and the
point of time at which the warehouse person acts "otherwise then in the course of the stealing" will be
similarly vague.

[39] [1982] 1 W.L.R. 845.

[40] Had the house been in her name her conviction would very likely have been upheld. In *R. v. Brown*
[1970] 1 Q.B. 105 it was held that an occupier who expressly or impliedly allows another to place
stolen goods on his property assists in their retention.

[41] *R. v. Brown* [1970] 1 Q.B. 105.

33–022 **Need there be *mens rea* at the beginning of the retaining? Suppose D agrees to warehouse goods for T, a thief, and after receiving them finds that they were stolen. He continues to keep them for T. Is he guilty of handling?** The subsection distinguishes between "receiving" (which may be for the defendant's own benefit) and "retaining for the benefit of another." The distinction relates to the time when the mental element is required. "Receiving" is once-for-all, but "retention" is a continuous affair:[42]

1. Handling by receiving (for oneself or another) requires that the defendant had the mental element at the time of receiving.[43] A person who receives goods innocently for his own benefit and dishonestly decides to keep them when he discovers they are stolen goods is not guilty of handling, because the *mens rea* comes after the *actus reus* is completed. (However, he can be convicted of theft, subject to the protection given to the buyer of goods by section 3(2) of the *Theft Act 1968*.)

2. Handling by retention for the benefit of another is committed as soon as the mental element arises, even though it arises after the commencement of the retention. This is because retaining is a continuing act (and similarly assisting another person to retain the goods can be a continuing act). Guilty knowledge acquired while the act is continuing, *i.e.* during the retention, can incriminate. Therefore, D in your hypothetical would not be charged with handling by receiving; he would be charged with handling by retention of the goods for the benefit of T, and could be convicted of that offence.[44] D's only safe course, when he comes to know that the goods are stolen, is to inform the police, or at least to wash his hands of the affair by dumping them somewhere and informing the police of their whereabouts.

33.4. HANDLING BY DEALING: DISPOSAL

33–023 Putting aside retention, we may say that the second part of the subsection is aimed against disposal of the goods, together with removal for the purpose of disposal.[45] (The word "realization" was unnecessary, since every realization of

---

[42] It has been objected to this that the offence is one of *undertaking* to retain, and that an undertaking is not a continuous transaction. The objection interprets an undertaking as a promise to retain, which I think is incorrect. For reasons given before, undertaking must be understood to refer to the act of retaining; and this act is performed continuously during the retention.

[43] *R. v. Alt* (1972) 56 Cr. App. R. 45; *R. v. Grainge* [1974] 1 W.L.R. 619; *R. v. Smythe* (1981) 72 Cr. App. R. 8. See also *R. v. Figures* [1976] Crim. L.R. 744, a ruling by a recorder which indicates that handling by receiving does not continue while the goods continue to be retained.

[44] *R. v. Brown* [1970] 1 Q.B. 105; *R. v. Pitchley* (1973) 57 Cr. App. R. 30 (where the conviction was of assisting to retain but should have been undertaking to retain; the actual decision is in any case open to question for a reason to be stated later). Applied by the Court of Appeal in *R. v. Burroughes* (2000) West Law 1791607.

[45] Griew (see Edward Griew, *The Theft Acts*, (London: Sweet & Maxwell, 7th edn., (1995) at 247)) takes disposal to include destruction. Doubtless the courts will so construe it, since they construe any conceivable ambiguity in a criminal statute against the immoral defendant. But the legal argument to the contrary in the present instance is strong. In legal usage, a disposal of property practically always refers to an alienation of it. In the context of section 22(1) of the *Theft Act*, where it is associated with the words "receives" and "realization," this is evidently what was intended. If Parliament meant to

goods is a disposal of them.) The subsection therefore operates against "placers," those who help the thief to find a buyer for the goods, and also against those who help to transport the goods for sale, as by unloading them from (or, presumably, loading them on) a lorry. One who agrees to supply oxygen cutting-equipment to open a stolen safe, to enable the contents to be spent or otherwise disposed of, becomes guilty of handling, because he arranges to assist in the realization of the loot. But if the object was only to enable the thief to get at and use the contents such as important documents that he wanted to keep, it should not be held to be handling, because then the person supplying the equipment is not assisting a disposal or retention but only an enjoyment.[46]

As we have seen, handling by dealing (whether the dealing is by way of retention or of disposal) may take either of two forms: undertaking (do-it-yourself) or assisting. The undertaking or assisting must be "by or for the benefit of another person or for the benefit of another person." This is a condensed way of saying that it must be by another person or for the benefit of another person. The limitation placed upon the offence by these words may be illustrated.

Suppose, to take the example of the safe already given, the thief had cut into the safe himself, to get at the money inside. In that case the opening of the safe would not be an offence under the subsection: the thief would not be doing the act for the benefit of another, and would not be assisting the doing of the act by another.

The idea underlying the subsection, though far from clearly expressed, is that there should be a distinction between handling by receiving (the first part of the subsection) and handling by dealing (the second part):

33–024

- The thief himself should be convictable of receiving if (for example) he were the master-mind behind the theft. He falls within the words of the subsection, because it covers the person who receives for his own benefit, provided that the receiving was after the theft, but received the goods from one of the other thieves afterwards.
- But the thief is not intended to be convictable of handling by dealing, because that would virtually efface the distinction between theft and handling. Every thief "handles" the goods (in a sense), unless he is arrested the moment after the theft. Accordingly, the intention of the subsection is that handling by dealing can only be undertaken for the benefit of another. In short, you receive for yourself (or for another), but can deal only for another.

This is the key to understanding the subsection. The handler may help a thief by undertaking the retention or disposal of the goods on his behalf. This is "undertaking for the benefit of another person." (Or the "other person" may be a receiver or other handler.) Alternatively, the handler may help the thief (or receiver) not by undertaking the job himself but by assisting the thief (or receiver or other handler) in doing the job. This is "assisting their retention, disposal *etc.*

---

turn criminal damage into an offence of handling it could and should have said so in plain terms and unambiguously, not relied upon an unusual meaning of the word "disposal."

[46] *R. v. Sanders* (1982) 75 Cr. App. R. 84.

by another person." Unfortunately, the draftsperson made two mistakes. First, he talked vaguely about "another person," when he should have said "the thief or (where the charge is not against the thief) another handler of the stolen goods." And instead of saying "for the benefit of" he should have used the more precise expression "on behalf of." One can only hope that the courts will perceive the sensible intention behind the lax drafting.

33–025   **Suppose the thief sells the stolen goods to a buyer who knows they are stolen. Is the thief guilty of handling by undertaking the disposal for the benefit of another, namely the buyer?**   No. The point was established in *R. v. Bloxham*.[47] Bloxham bought a stolen car, not knowing that it was stolen. When he discovered the truth he resold it at a low price to a man who was prepared to take it without documents. Bloxham could not be prosecuted for theft, because he was protected by section 3(2) of the *Theft Act 1968*,[48] so the prosecutor cunningly charged him instead with handling by undertaking the disposal of stolen goods for the benefit of another. His conviction of this offence was upheld by the Court of Appeal, which refused leave to appeal to the House of Lords; but the House itself gave leave, and quashed the conviction.

There were strong reasons of policy for this decision. The effect of section 3(2) is clearly to protect the person who initially came into possession of stolen goods in good faith from a charge of theft in selling them, and it would destroy the practical effect of this exemption if the same act were held to amount to handling. Besides, the decision of the Court of Appeal would have created a rule applicable equally to sales by thieves, even sales by thieves to innocent buyers, where as the C.L.R.C.'s policy statement (which the House of Lords quoted) referred only to those who help thieves in the disposal. Since thieves who steal goods generally do so with the intention of selling them, the decision would have made all such thieves guilty of handling when they sold—which was certainly not the intention of section 22(1).

But in addition to these reasons of policy there were arguments against the conviction based on the wording of the subsection. A person who sells an article does not assist the buyer to dispose of it, since the buyer does not dispose of it.[49] Further, such a seller in the ordinary way does not dispose of it for the benefit of another; he sells it for his own benefit, not for the benefit of the buyer.

33–026   **But there is a benefit to the buyer in the transaction. Otherwise he wouldn't have bought the article would he?**   Yes: the sale benefits the seller, and the purchase benefits the buyer, but they are different benefits. The seller gets the benefit of the buyer's money and the buyer gets the benefit of the article bought. The point remains that one party does not act for the benefit of the other within the meaning of the subsection.

---

[47] [1983] 1 A.C. 109.

[48] Section 3(2) provides: "Where property or a right or interest in property is or purports to be transferred for value to a person acting in good faith, no later assumption by him of rights which he believed himself to be acquiring shall, by reason of any defect in the transferor's title, amount to theft of the property."

[49] [1983] 1 A.C. 109 at 114 *per* Lord Bridge.

What about oblique intention?   This is a situation where one cannot apply   **33–027**
that concept, and it is because of cases of this kind that I suggested in 4.3. that
intention should not be taken to include oblique intention if this does not serve
the purposes of the law. The difficulty would have been avoided in the present
instance if the subsection had said "on behalf of" another person. Bloxham
obviously did not sell on behalf of the buyer. Nevertheless, the doctrine of
oblique intent must apply to some extent to charges of handling. Suppose that a
person assists a thief to dispose of the goods because he wants to earn a reward
from the thief. Obviously he will be held to have intended to assist. The intention
is either a direct intention (the person wants to help, in order to earn his reward)
or, at least an oblique intention (he wants to earn his reward, but believes for
certain that in doing so he is assisting). Either way he is guilty of the offence.

Could I put a problem for the sake of having a brief recap? Suppose a   **33–028**
student buys a book from a fellow student. He pays for it in good faith, but
later discovers that the seller is a thief who habitually steals from the local
booksellers. What is his position?   He is not guilty of handling, even if he
keeps the book, because he did not know it was stolen when he received it, and he
does not retain it for the benefit of another. Nor is he guilty of theft in retaining
the book: section 3(2).

Would the student be guilty of handling if he had sold the book or gave it   **33–029**
away?   *R. v. Bloxham* shows that he would not perpetrate handling by selling
the book, and section 3(2) protects him from a charge of theft. The student's
position if he gives the book away is more parlous. He would be in danger of
conviction of handling, absurd as that may sound, because it might be argued that
the gift is entirely for the benefit of another. The same could be said if he also lent
the book, or sold it and asked the buyer to pay the price to a charity or other
gratuitous recipient. In each of these hypotheticals the student would literally
have disposed of the book for the benefit of another. However, a court might be
persuaded to find that such cases are outside the intendment of the *Act*. They fall
outside the C.L.R.C.'s policy statement, since they are not cases of helping the
thief to dispose of the goods. They are not cases of helping a thief at all.

These problems again indicate defects in the drafting of the subsection. One
therapy would be to read "for the benefit of another" in a restrictive sense as
meaning "on behalf of another," as already suggested. Alternatively or
additionally, drastic surgery might be performed upon the meaning of the phrase
"another person." We may hope, though perhaps without much confidence, that
the courts would find that such cases as those just instanced fall outside any
rational understanding of the intention of the subsection. The words "any person"
should be taken as confined to the thief and (where the defendant is someone
other than the thief) any person guilty of handling the stolen goods. It would be
particularly absurd if a person who is not otherwise guilty of handling when he
retains another's property becomes guilty of that offence merely because he

allows a completely innocent person (his grandmother, perhaps) to use it, or uses it for the benefit of such person (driving his grandmother to church in a stolen car).[50]

The House of Lords could have settled these problems in *R. v. Bloxham* (they had all been ventilated in the literature), but it chose to confine its decision to the narrow facts of the case before it.

There are other perils of your unlucky student. Suppose he sells the book not to an innocent buyer[51] but to a buyer who knew the book was stolen. The buyer would be guilty of handling by receiving, and the student would, it seems, technically be guilty as accessory.[52] (He may even be accessory to theft by the buyer.) Fortunately, such charges appear to be unknown in present practice, and would look like an attempt to strain the law. Even a thief should not be convicted of being an accessory to handling if he sells stolen goods. The thief does not commit handling by the act of stealing, and it would be anomalous if the fact that he agrees to sell the goods were treated as making him a handler. (The problem would be solved if, as was before suggested, the law were changed to avoid implicating a party in a bilateral transaction which is forbidden only for the other party: 14.17).

33.5.   STOLEN GOODS

33–030   The *Act* speaks of "stolen goods," but the definition section makes goods include money, and also other property like things in action[53] (section 34(2)(*b*)). So a person who changes the thief's "hot" money for safe money can be guilty of handling by receiving.

The goods must be stolen. One consequence of this is that if a small child (under 10) brings home a bicycle that he has illegitimately "found," his parents who keep it are not guilty of receiving stolen goods, because the child is too young to be capable of stealing.[54] However, the parents may of course become guilty of theft (as perpetrators). The goods must already be "stolen" when the defendant handles them. He must "know or believe them to be stolen goods," not

---

[50] See J. R. Spencer, "The Mishandling of Handling," [1981] Crim. L.R. 682 at 685. The decision in *R. v. Bloxham* [1983] 1 A.C. 109 may also be cited as giving some encouragement to the argument against a wide interpretation of the offence, though the particular point was not there considered. The argument is also reinforced by the policy implications of section 3(2) of the *Act*, to which the House attached importance in *R. v. Bloxham*. According to the literal words of the handling section the friend of a b.f.p. who subsequently helps him to sell the goods, knowing the facts, would be guilty of handling, but this was obviously not in the mind of Parliament.

[51] In which case the student would be guilty of obtaining money from the buyer by an implied false representation (contrary to sections 1(a) and 2 *Fraud Act 2006*) as to his own title to sell, unless he believed that he had obtained a good title by buying in good faith.

[52] *Carter Patersons & Pickfords Carriers Limited v. Wessel* [1947] K.B. 849. In *R. v. Bloxham* [1983] 1 A.C. 109 at 115, Lord Bridge introduced a little healthy doubt into the position by saying that it was "conceivably" so.

[53] *R. v. Forsyth* [1997] 2 Cr. App. R. 299.

[54] *Walters v. Lunt* (1951) 35 Cr. App. R. 94; *D.P.P. v. K* [1997] 1 Cr. App. R. 36. While a person with a "legal immunity" cannot be "prosecuted for theft, the receiver should be subject to prosecution." See *R. v. Clark* [1977] 35 C.C.C. (2d) 319 citing Glanville Williams, *Criminal Law: The General Part* (London: Stevens & Sons, 2nd edn. 1961) at 391-2. See also *R. v. A. B.* [1941] 1 K.B. 454.

goods that are intended to be stolen. This point is easily overlooked in the case of handling by making an arrangement. A person who arranges to receive or deal with goods that are to be stolen subsequently is not guilty of handling stolen goods, though he is guilty of conspiring to handle. The fact that the goods were stolen may, of course, be found on the basis of circumstantial evidence, including the very low price at which they were sold to the defendant.[55] Nevertheless, several rules of law have the practical effect of hampering the prosecution in proving this issue. For example, a statement made by the thief (otherwise than on oath at the trial of the handler) is not admissible evidence against the handler, on account of the hearsay rule.[56] Also, the fact that the defendant thought the goods were stolen does not generally prove that they were.

Goods constructively stolen   The notion of "stolen goods" is extended by the **33–031** *Act* in three ways. First, as already said, the notion is made to cover property obtained by blackmail, or by fraud within the meaning of the *Fraud Act 2006*;[57] and also money "dishonestly withdrawn from an account to which a wrongful credit has been made."[58] Second, the offence is extended to cover handling in England of property criminally acquired abroad.[59] The third and most important extension is that "stolen goods" are defined to include (in general) the proceeds of the originally-stolen goods. In other words, the doctrine of following, which applies in connection with theft (29.14.), applies also to handling to a certain extent. There is a complicated provision in the *Act* (section 24(2)) the main aim of which is to prevent the thief effectively "laundering" stolen property by exchanging it for other property. The subsection provides that a disposal of stolen goods by a thief or (guilty) handler causes the proceeds also (when in the hands of the thief or guilty handler) to be "stolen." Instead of eliminating the stolen property the disposal generally doubles it, much as the Hydra of Greek legend responded to have its head cut off by immediately sprouting two more.

There is, however, an important difference between the goods originally stolen and goods received in exchange which are regarded as constructively stolen by the *Act* (let us call them the derivatively stolen goods). So long as the original owner has a right to recover the goods originally stolen, those goods remain stolen goods; so do goods received in exchange for them by a guilty possessor (thief or handler). But goods received in exchange for any of the foregoing goods

---

[55] *R. v. Overington* [1978] Crim. L.R. 692; *R. v. Hulbert* (1979) 69 Cr. App. R. 243; *R. v. MacDonald* (1980) 70 Cr. App. R. 288.

[56] *R. v. Korniak* (1983) 76 Cr. App. R. 145 at 150. The conditions for admitting hearsay evidence are set out in section 114 of the *Criminal Justice Act 2003*.

[57] See section 24(4) of the *Theft Act 1968*. Services obtained by fraud contrary to section 11 of the *Fraud Act 2006* are not declared to be "stolen" as the subsection covers "goods" only. If, say, D obtains the hire of a car by making a false representation, he can be convicted of obtaining services by fraud, but the car will not be stolen for the purpose of the offence of handling. Nor does the offence of handling cover goods obtained for the purpose of this offence by a conspiracy to defraud, unless of course the facts are such as to come within the definition of theft or under sections 1-4 of the *Fraud Act 2006*.

[58] Section 24A(8) of the *Theft Act 1968*.

[59] See section 24(1) of the *Theft Act 1968*. *R. v. Ofori* (1994) 99 Cr. App. R. 223. The prosecution must prove that D's conduct "amounted to an offence" under the relevant law in the foreign jurisdiction and the court cannot "take judicial notice that conduct which was unequivocally criminal in England was necessarily criminal elsewhere."

by an innocent possessor are not "stolen." In other words, the Hydra effect does not occur where the proceeds of the originally stolen goods or of derivatively stolen goods are received by a person who does not know the facts.

Some examples may clarify this. The Hydra effect (the doubling of the quantity of stolen goods) is seen if the thief of a wad of notes trades them with his underworld associate for other notes. The original notes remain "stolen," and the notes received in exchange become tainted in the same way.

33–032   The Hydra effect does not occur if the thief spends the notes (whether the originally-stolen or the substituted notes) with a seller who receives them in good faith. The latter, being a *bona fide* purchaser of the notes, obtains a good title to them (this being a special rule of the law of property for currency and negotiable instruments), so they cease to be stolen; but what the thief receives from him in return has that quality impressed on it.

The Hydra effect is seen at its most terrifying when the theft is of goods in the usual sense of the term (not money). If the thief of a dozen iPhones sells them, the proceeds in his hands are "stolen goods;" so if the thief hands these proceeds to his wife (who knows the facts), his wife can be convicted of handling the proceeds.[60] If Mrs. Thief spends the money on a MacBook, anybody who knowingly helps her to buy it is guilty of handling in helping her to dispose of the "stolen" money; and the MacBook will also be "stolen goods." The iPhones are still stolen goods; consequently, if the person who bought the iPhones from the thief knew they were stolen when he bought them, he is guilty of handling and receiving. And so the chain of guilt can go on, all of it depending on the original theft.

When "stolen goods" come into the hands of a person who does not know they are stolen, then if such a person changes the stolen goods for something else while still in that state of ignorance, the property he receives in exchange is not "stolen," but the goods he first received and now gives in exchange continue in the state of being stolen. So stolen "goods" in the narrow sense, unlike stolen money, can almost never be sanitized by being disposed of. (This is because the *Nemo date* rule applies to goods in the narrow sense but not to money). If, for example, a Constable painting is stolen from an art gallery, and passes through the hands of several buyers, it nevertheless remains the property of the art gallery and remains "stolen goods;" so if a dealer recognizes it and yet dishonestly buys it, he will be guilty of handling stolen property by receiving. The fact that the dealer buys from an innocent buyer makes no difference.

In suitable circumstances a fund may be traced into and through a bank account.[61] Suppose that X obtains a cheque by fraud. The cheque is as a piece of paper "stolen goods." X pays it into his bank account, thus converting it into a thing in action (X's right against his bank). X then draws on the account in favour of D, who takes X's cheque, knowing that it represents the "stolen" asset, in

---

[60] *R. v. Dadd* [1974] Crim. L.R. 439.

[61] *Serious Fraud Office v. Lexi Holdings Plc. (In Administration)* [2009] Q.B. 376; *Barclays Bank Plc. v. Kalamohan* [2010] EWHC 1383 (Ch.) (holding that in civil law "K was liable for knowing receipt and B was entitled to trace the proceeds of the banker's draft into the residential properties which were purchased using those moneys.") See also *Foskett v. McKeown* [2001] 1 A.C. 102. As for tracing into mixed funds, cf. *Parker v. The Queen* (1997) 186 C.L.R. 494.

whole or in part. D pays the cheque into his own bank account. If the fund received by D (by way of credit to his account) can be proved to represent the "stolen" fund, he can be convicted of receiving the relevant part of the fund as "stolen goods." But if that cannot be proved, D could be charged with dishonestly retaining a wrongful credit.[62] Section 24A of the *Theft Act 1968* deals with the *R. v. Preddy*[63] problem (see the discussion *infra*), but difficulties remain where the drawer of the cheque has both stolen and legitimate funds in her cheque account. If the payee is to be convicted under section 24A, then the prosecution will have to demonstrate that the wrongful credit came from funds that were stolen. This might only be possible in cases where the legitimate part of the drawer's mixed fund is not sufficient to cover the sum of the wrongful credit. If the drawer of the cheque has a £100,000 in her cheque account and only £5,000 of that balance represents stolen money, and she writes D (the payee) a cheque for less than £95,000, D does not obtain an identifiable wrongful credit when she deposits the cheque in her own account.[64]

So if the drawer had written a cheque for £95,001, D would have received an   33–033
identifiable wrongful credit of £1? Yes. £95,000 of the credit the payee received by depositing the cheque is legitimate and £1 is wrongful, because the drawer had to use at least £1 of the stolen funds in her cheque account to honour the cheque.

Suppose D dishonestly obtained for himself a credit balance (a thing in   33–034
action: the debt owing by the bank to him) by fraudulently arranging an
electronic money transfer. Does his fraud mean the thing in action (the
additional credit balance in his account) is stolen goods? When a person
obtains a money transfer by making a false representation he obtains property which never belonged to the victim. When V is deceived into electronically transferring his own funds to D's bank account the chose in action represented by the credit balance in V's account is *pro tanto* extinguished or at least reduced by the value of the transfer and at the same time a new chose in action is created in D's account. D does not obtain V's chose in action. Consequently, he does not steal property belonging to another.[65]

But D does obtain a chose in action at the expense of V. Surely this chose in   33–035
action is stolen goods? Section 24(4) provides that goods "obtained by ...
fraud (within the meaning of the *Fraud Act 2006*) shall be regarded as stolen."
For example, if D obtains V's car by making a false representation, the car will be deemed to be stolen for the purposes of section 22. Similarly, if D makes a false representation to secure an electronic transfer of money, then the thing in action

---

[62] See section 24A of the *Theft Act 1968*.

[63] [1996] A.C. 815.

[64] See *Attorney-General's Reference (No. 4 of 1979)* [1981] 1 W.L.R. 667.

[65] *R. v. Preddy* [1996] A.C. 815. However, this type of fraudulent transfer would come within the purview of the *Fraud Act 2006*. See *R. v. Kausar* [2009] EWCA Crim. 2242; *R. v. Briggs* [2004] 1 Cr. App. R. 34. Furthermore, under section 76(4) of the *Proceeds of Crime Act 2002* "all that is necessary is that a person obtains property as a result of or in connection with criminal conduct." See *R. v. Waya* [2010] EWCA Crim. 412. Cf. *R. v. Dabek* [1973] Crim. L.R. 527.

(the new balance in his bank account) is stolen goods in his hands. In *R. v. Forsyth*,[66] a fraudster, Nadir, fraudulently ordered an electronic transfer of £400,000 from PPI's company account with Midland Bank in London to an account controlled by him in Switzerland. Forsyth, Nadir's agent, collected the money from the bank in Switzerland and transferred it into an account in Switzerland.[67] Thereafter, Forsyth instructed the Swiss bank to transfer £307,000 to a bank in England and brought back the balance of £88,050 in cash to England. Forsyth was charged with handling a stolen thing in action by assisting in the retention, *etc.*, of the goods for the benefit of Nadir. Forsyth argued that "[a]ccording to *Preddy* the funds obtained by the transferee had never been in the hands of the thief at all; and the transferee in whose hands they are cannot be regarded as a handler until it has first been determined that he has handled the stolen goods."[68]

The Court of Appeal said:

> "It seems to us that the words 'in the hands of mean in the possession or under the control of the thief and there is no doubt [that Nadir] was exercising control over property representing PPI's right to the money when he gave instructions that it should be made available in the form of cash to be collected by [Forsyth]. ... [Therefore,] the balance in the sundry account with Warburg Soditic was in that sense in the hands of Nadir, it represented directly or indirectly PPI's chose in action against the Midland Bank."

The decision might also be explained as one where Nadir stole the thing in action.[69] Section 24(2) and (4) meant that the bank balance that Nadir acquired by fraud was stolen goods in his hands. Since section 24(4) deems that he actual thing in action was stolen goods, there was no need for the Court of Appeal to make reference to the deeming clause "directly or indirectly represent or have at any time represented the stolen goods in the hands of the thief." Furthermore, there was no need to consider whether the second thing in action created by Forsyth when she transferred £307,000 back to a bank represented property in the hands of the thief because by extinguishing the credit balance created by Nadir's original fraud, she was already guilty of handling stolen goods. By transferring £307,000 of Nadir's stolen thing in action back to England, and by withdrawing the rest in cash (£88,050 excluding bank fees), Forsyth disposed of the property Nadir had obtained by fraud which was stolen property notwithstanding the *R. v. Preddy* rule.[70]

33–036   **But what if Nadir had extinguished his stolen thing in action by transferring the funds to his bookmaker?**   Well, *R. v. Preddy* seems to rear its ugly head again.[71] Let us assume the money was transferred to settle a legitimate gambling

---

[66] [1997] 2 Cr. App. R. 299.

[67] D2 also took some of it in cash.

[68] *R. v. Forsyth* [1997] 2 Cr.App.R. 299 at 314.

[69] Since D1 initiated the transfer he arguably stole the chose in action. Cf. *R. v. Williams* [2001] 1 Cr. App. R. 23.

[70] The offences in the *Fraud Act 2006* are not constrained by the *Preddy* rule, and section 24(4) of the *Theft Act 1968* deems property obtained by fraud to be stolen property for the purposes of section 22 of the *Act*.

[71] Nadir would also be caught by section 24A of the *Theft Act 1968*, because the money ultimately ended up back in accounts controlled by him as a wrongful credit.

debt and that the bookmaker only learned after the transfer had been made that the money came from an illegitimate source. (This saves us considering issues of complicity). In doing this Nadir extinguishes his stolen thing in action and creates a new thing in action for the bookmaker. If the bookmaker knows that the credit balance was created by Nadir using stolen funds, is his retention of the credit balance an act of handling stolen goods? Following *R. v. Preddy*, the courts are likely to hold that the credit balance obtained by the bookmaker is goods which were never in the hands of Nadir.[72] If so, the bookmaker could not be convicted of handling stolen goods under sections 22 and 24. Section 24A of the *Theft Act 1968* tackles this problem and would be invoked instead. Section 24A provides:

> "(1)   A person is guilty of an offence if— (a) a wrongful credit has been made to an account kept by him or in respect of which he has any right or interest; (b) he knows or believes that the credit is wrongful; and (c) he dishonestly fails to take such steps as are reasonable in the circumstances to secure that the credit is cancelled.
>
> (2A) A credit to an account is wrongful to the extent that it derives from–
>
>   (a)   theft;
>   (b)   blackmail;
>   (c)   fraud (contrary to section 1 of the *Fraud Act 2006*); or
>   (d)   stolen goods.
>
> (5)   In determining whether a credit to an account is wrongful, it is immaterial (in particular) whether the account is overdrawn before or after the credit is made.
>
> (8)   References to stolen goods include money which is dishonestly withdrawn from an account to which a wrongful credit has been made, but only to the extent that the money derives from the credit."

The advantage of section 24A is that it catches the innocent receiver of a wrongful credit if he decides to dishonestly retain it. The section would catch the bookmaker, because he knows that the credit in his account "derives from Nadir's fraud." What does the bookmaker need to do to cancel the credit? Would a simple reversal be sufficient? It ought to be, but it might not be. If the bookmaker instructed his bank to transfer the money back the credit would be cancelled and reversed, but the money would be back in the hands of the fraudster, Nadir. Does section 24A require the bookmaker to return the money to the original victim? One would think not. It is doubtful that the bookmaker would have sufficient details of the underlying fraud to be able to return the money to its lawful owner. Nor would he have a duty to do so. All he needs to do is cancel the credit, and reversing it, even if that means returning it to the fraudster, should be sufficient for that purpose.

Section 24A would also catch the likes of Pitchley. Remember that if an innocent recipient of stolen goods sells them, the proceeds in his hands are not stolen in the eye of the criminal law. This point was overlooked in *R. v. Pitchley*.[73]   **33–037**

Pitchley's son stole some money and gave it to Pitchley for safe keeping; according to Pitchley he did not know that the money was stolen. He put it in his bank account, and the next day came to know that it was stolen. He then did

---

[72] They might also hold that section 24(2) is a deeming provision analogous to section 5(3) and 5(4) of the *Theft Act 1968* and, therefore, *R. v. Preddy* is no bar to conviction. See *Attorney-General's Reference (No. 4 of 1979)* [1981] 1 W.L.R. 667. This seems perfectly plausible given the aim of the subsection.

[73] (1973) 57 Cr. App. R. 30.

nothing because he did not wish to report his son to the police and did not think of returning the money to its owner. Pitchley's conviction of handling money by assisting to retain it was upheld by the Court of Appeal.

It will be observed that the money originally stolen was converted by Pitchley into a thing in action (the debt owing by the bank to him). This thing in action was property, and therefore goods within the meaning of the section. Nevertheless, the case was wrongly decided because, by paying the money into his bank account, Pitchley innocently turned currency into a thing in action, which was not the same property as that stolen. Section 24(2) states that the proceeds of stolen goods are stolen goods in the hands of a thief or guilty receiver, but Pitchley was neither; it follows that he could not be guilty of handling the thing in action as stolen goods. The point was missed by counsel and the court. However, the deposit created a wrongful credit in his account which he failed to cancel. Pitchley would now be caught by section 24A. (The same would apply if Pitchley's son had obtained the cash from blackmail, fraud or another thief.) D need not make the deposit himself, but he must not dishonestly retain it after he becomes aware of its existence.

Let us consider this section in light of *R. v. Forsyth*. In that case, Forsyth did not have any right or interest in the account kept by Nadir. She was merely acting as his agent. Nadir clearly committed an offence by obtaining a wrongful credit and by failing to cancel it. To cancel it he would had to have arranged to have it reversed. Forsyth seems to be caught by section 24A(8), because she withdrew cash on Nadir's behalf and as soon as she did, she received stolen property which she disposed for the benefit of Nadir.

33–038   **When goods cease to be stolen**   Goods cease to be "stolen" if they return to the possession of the owner or the police. If a police officer discovers goods which he suspects are stolen and decides to keep them under surveillance, this alone does not mean he has taken possession of the goods. He does not take them into "lawful custody" if he only intends to keep them under surveillance in order to catch the potential handlers:[74]

> "If the police officer seeing these goods in the back of the car had made up his mind that he would take them into custody, that he would reduce them into his possession or control, take charge of them so that they could not be removed and so that he would have the disposal of them, then it would be a perfectly proper conclusion to say that he had taken possession of the goods. On the other hand, if the truth of the matter is that he was of an entirely open mind at that stage as to whether the goods were to be seized or not and was of an entirely open mind as to whether he should take possession of them or not, but merely stood by so that when the driver of the car appeared he could ask certain questions of that driver as to the nature of the goods and why they were there, then there is no reason whatever to suggest that he had taken the goods into his possession or control."[75]

The rule stated in section 24(3):

---

[74] "In order to have possession of goods there must be an intention to possess, the *animus possidendi* of the old writers. Thus the policeman's mental attitude towards the goods … is very material." See *Attorney-General's Reference (No. 1 of 1974)* [1974] Q.B. 744. See also *R. v. Dolan* (1855) 6 Cox C.C. 44; *R. v. Schmidt* (1866) L.R. 1 C.C.R. 15; *R. v. Villensky* [1892] 2 Q.B. 597.
[75] *Attorney-General's Reference (No. 1 of 1974)* [1974] Q.B. 744 at 753.

"But no goods shall be regarded as having continued to be stolen goods after they have been restored to the person from whom they were stolen or to other lawful possession or custody."[76]

The rule is important if the owner of stolen goods or a police officer arrests the thief, takes the stolen goods from him, and then, hearing that a "fence" is about to arrive to collect the goods, sets a trap by concealing from the fence that things have taken an unexpected turn. The fence may take the goods, but if the court holds that the goods had then lost their character of stolen goods he will not be guilty of handling.[77] Exceptionally, since an arrangement to handle is handling, he can be convicted of handling stolen goods if it can be proved that his arrangement to receive them was made after they were stolen. In any case he can be convicted of attempting to handle, and this would be a perfectly proper case for using the law of attempt.[78] (If the goods had never been stolen it might look over sharp to charge an attempt, even though such a charge would be legally possible.)

Although the general rule stated in section 24(3) is undoubted, a police officer who comes across stolen goods and who thinks that a receiver is about to appear may evade the operation of the subsection by refraining from taking the goods and simply standing by to await developments. If he does not take the goods into his custody, a receiver who comes to carry off the goods can be convicted of handling them. It is for the jury to decide whether the officer intended to take charge of the goods or whether he intended merely to interrogate the suspect when he appeared and to seize the goods (and the suspect) only if his answers were unsatisfactory.[79] Obviously, this is a nebulous question, but the judge may encourage the jury in any doubtful situation to find that the goods are still "stolen."

33.6. THE MENTAL ELEMENT

The offence of receiving stolen goods requires knowledge or a belief that the goods are stolen. Negligence, or even recklessness, is insufficient.   **33–039**

But why isn't mere recklessness enough?   Because that would be an undue restraint upon commerce.[80] The offence of handling applies to all conceivable articles, which cannot be identified as being stolen merely by examining the   **33–040**

---

[76] The subsection "or after that person and any other person claiming through him have otherwise ceased as regards to those goods to have any right to restitution in respect of the theft." An example relating to money was given in the text. As another example, suppose that X induces V to sell him goods by making a false representation, X thus obtaining a voidable title. V, after discovering the fraud, decides nevertheless to affirm the contract, which he does. The goods now cease to be stolen, and D may safely buy them from X, even though he knows the facts.

[77] *Commissioner of Police of the Metropolis v. Streeter* (1980) 71 Cr. App. R. 113.

[78] *Haughton v. Smith* [1975] A.C. 476. Cf. *R. v. English* (1993) 68 A. Crim. R. 96; *Rich v. State* — So.3d —- (2009); *The Queen v. Donnelly* [1970] N.Z.L.R. 980; *R. v. Barbouttis* (1995) 82 A. Crim. R. 432.

[79] See Glanville Williams, *Textbook of Criminal Law*, (London: Stevens & Sons, 1st edn. 1978); *Commissioner of Police of the Metropolis v. Streeter* (1980) 71 Cr. App. R. 113.

[80] Glanville Williams, "Handling, Theft and the Purchaser Who Takes a Chance," [1985] Crim. L. R. 432. Cf. John Spencer, "Handling, Theft and the Mala Fides Purchaser," [1985] Crim. L. R. 92.

articles themselves. It is important not to incriminate honest dealers who make no enquiry whether the goods they are buying are stolen because they have no sufficient reason to think that they are. People must be free to buy unless they know or positively believe that the goods are stolen. The public interest in free trade is greater than the public interest in attempting to close every possibility of stolen goods being sold.

Section 22(1) allows what appears to be an alternative to knowledge; the defendant must have known or believed the goods to be stolen.[81] The C.L.R.C. proposed this alternative to cover a case where a person buys goods at a ridiculously low price from an unknown seller and deliberately asks no questions.[82] The aim was evidently to cover "wilful blindness," which in law is supposed to come within the notion of "knowledge"; but there is much doubt about what precisely wilful blindness means. Blindness can be "wilful" (subjective) or inadvertent (objective); if D is aware of the fact that the goods might be stolen he is subjectively aware of the risk he is taking by handling or receiving them. He chooses not to make inquiries to confirm whether or not the goods are stolen and therefore consciously runs the risk of receiving or handling stolen goods. If he did not believe or even consider that they might be stolen, then his blindness is inadvertent. If his inadvertent blindness was totally unreasonable, it might be said that he was objectively reckless in handling the goods since a reasonable person would have been aware of the risk of them being stolen, but negligence liability has no role to play in this area of the law.

The mere fact that the defendant ought to have known, *i.e.* that he was negligent or objectively reckless in not finding out, is insufficient. But although the jury may swallow an incredible tale, on account of the defendant's frank blue eyes, they are not bound to do so. In the first place, if any ordinary person would have believed that the goods were virtually certain to be stolen, the jury may infer that the defendant knew or believed they were stolen, simply because they cannot believe that he did not, in the circumstances, know or believe it. For example, if D purchases a Pro Hart painting for £100 from a person he believes to be a thief and of whom he knew was living on the dole, then the jury might hold that this evidence demonstrates that D in fact believed the goods were stolen. Similarly, if the defendant were to purchase an I.W.C. watch for £100 from a watch seller in Kowloon[83] to give to D2 in England, D2 would be liable if he really believed that the watch was a stolen one.

---

[81] He need not know the contents of the package, if he knows they are stolen. *R. v. McCullum* ((1973) 57 Cr. App. R. 645. Even a mistake as to the type of articles in the package would be no defence, being immaterial. It would be equally immaterial if the defendant thought that the goods had been "snatched" when actually they had been obtained by fraud.

[82] C.L.R.C., *Eighth Report: Theft and Related Offences*, (London: Cmnd. 2977, 1966) at para.128.

[83] The Hong Kong law of theft more or less mirrors the English law. See section 24(1) of the *Theft Act 1968*. See also *R. v. Ofori* (1994) 99 Cr. App. R. 223. The prosecution must prove that D's conduct "amounted to an offence" under the relevant law in the foreign jurisdiction and the court can "take judicial notice that conduct which was unequivocally criminal in England was necessarily criminal elsewhere."

But this is nothing more than D recklessly failing to obtain the relevant knowledge. I agree. However, there is a difference between recklessly failing to obtain knowledge and in having it! There is also a difference between intending to possess stolen goods, and in recklessly possessing them. If you know the goods are stolen, then you can intend to possess stolen goods. Similarly, if you believe that it is virtually certain that the goods are stolen, then, you obviously intend to possess what you believe to be stolen goods. But if you believe they might be stolen, you only risk handling stolen goods.

33–041

Can a person also recklessly fail to obtain a "belief"? No, his belief was whatever it was. If he did not form a belief that the goods were stolen, then he could not have in fact believed they were stolen. If he formed a belief that the goods were stolen then he believed they were stolen. More problematically, there are all those beliefs in between. D might have believed that there was a 90 *per cent.*, or 80 *per cent.* or 70 *per cent.* or 60 *per cent.* chance that the goods were stolen and so on. If D believed that the goods were virtually certain to be stolen he will come within the purview of the subsection. However, anything less will not do. If he only believed that it was probable that the goods were stolen he will not be caught by section 22.

33–042

The courts have made it clear that mere suspicion will not suffice.[84] If the suspicions of an incoming handler are aroused, and he deliberately refrains from making any inquiries for fear that he may learn the truth, his wilful blindness cannot be treated as equivalent to knowledge—he must actually *know* or believe that the goods are stolen.[85] If he is virtually certain that the goods are stolen but is wrong, then he attempts to handle or receive stolen goods. But if his belief is correct because the goods are in fact stolen, he will come within the purview of section 22.

So are you telling me "extreme subjective recklessness" applies? Yes, but only to the extent that it involves the defendant believing as a matter of virtual certainty that the goods are stolen. The preferable view is that the subsection extends the notion of "belief" to the case where the defendant, while lacking explicit information, is "certain" in his own mind that the goods are stolen. This is covered by the word "believes," otherwise it would follow that the reference to belief was an unnecessary (and therefore misleading) addition to the section. In other words, if the actor believed that the required circumstances, the definitional facts, were not present, then his act was neither intentional nor reckless as to them.

33–043

For a prosecution to succeed on a charge of receiving stolen property, it must establish that the property which the defendant received or handled was stolen

---

[84] *R. v. Adinga* [2003] EWCA Crim. 3201; *R. v. Toor* (1987) 85 Cr. App. R. 116; *R. v. Smith* (1977) 64 Cr. App. R. 217; *R. v. Ismail* [1977] Crim. L.R. 557; *R. v. Moys* (1984) 79 Cr. App. R. 72; *R. v. Reader* (1978) 66 Cr. App. R. 33; *Atwal v. Massey* (1972) 56 Cr. App. R. 6; *R. v. Grainge* [1974] 1 W.L.R. 619. See also *R. v. Havard* (1916) 11 Cr. App. R. 2; *R. v. Dykyj* (1993) 66 A. Crim. R. 567; *R. v. Fallon* (1981) 28 S.A.S.R. 394. One third of the states in the United States have also adopted the English "knowing" requirement. See Wayne R. LaFave, *Substantive Criminal Law*, (St Paul, Minn.: Thomson West Publishing, 2003) Vol. III at 162.

[85] *R. v. Forsyth* [1997] 2 Cr. App. R. 299.

and that he knew or believed it was stolen as a matter of certainty. The defendant would know the property was stolen as a matter of fact if he witnessed it being appropriated, but in most cases the defendant will not be present when the property is appropriated. But it is not necessary to demonstrate that the defendant knew as a matter of fact that the property was stolen. It is only necessary to demonstrate that the defendant believed as a matter of virtual certainty that they were stolen.

33–044 **Suppose a person acquires goods knowing that they are stolen but intending to return them to the owner?** Then he does not act "dishonestly." Apart from this point, it seems that the word has no useful function in relation to handling, but it may have other practical effects all the same.[86] If a handler argues that he was not dishonest in knowingly buying a stolen article in a pub, because everybody does it, his defence would presumably have to be left to the jury, who might sympathize.

It is even possible for an intermediary to arrange with the owner to get his goods back for him for reward, by paying the thief for them, without committing the offence of handling.[87] But it is a statutory offence for the owner or anyone else to advertize a reward for the return of stolen goods with no questions asked, or stating that money paid for the purchase of the stolen goods will be repaid.[88] The offence is not committed by making a private arrangement to the same effect.

---

[86] In some U.S. jurisdictions claim of right has been raised: see *Foskey v. State*, 188 S.E.2d 825 (1972).

[87] *R. v. Higgins* [1972] Crim. L.R. 213.

[88] Section 23 of the *Theft Act 1968*.

CHAPTER 34

FRAUD

"I will speak of one man more excelling in that craft[1] than others, that went about in King James his time, and long since, who called himself, The Kings Majesties most excellent *Hocus Pocus*, and so was called, because that at the playing of every Trick, he used to say, *Hocus pocus, tontus talontus, vade celeriter jubeo*, a dark composure of words, to blinde the eyes of the beholders, to make his Trick pass the more currantly without discovery."[2]

34.1.   THE FRAUD ACT 2006

The core offences in the *Fraud Act 2006* strike at certain fraud, whether it **34–001** produces the desired result. Under such legislation, an offence (apart from an inchoate offence like attempt) is committed even if the rogue does not succeed in acquiring the property, getting the goods out of the store and so on. The *Fraud Act 2006* recast the law, largely as a result of recommendations made by the Law Commission.[3] (All references hereinafter are to this *Act*, unless the contrary is expressed or clearly implied.) The core substantive offence is found in section 1 of the *Act*. It can be committed in three ways: 1) by making a false representation; 2) by failing to disclose certain information; and 3) by abusing a position. The offence is made out if the defendant engages in one of these three forms of conduct with an *intent* to make a gain or cause a loss or risk of loss to another. There is no need for the conduct to "result" in an actual gain for the perpetrator; or loss for the potential victim, because the offence is a "conduct" crime.

There are also a number of more specific offences in the *Act*. Section 6 makes it an offence to possess articles for use in frauds; section 7 makes it an offence to make or supply "articles for use in frauds"; section 9 makes it an offence for a sole trader to participate in a fraudulent business; and section 11 makes it an offence to dishonestly obtain services. Coupled with this, there are a number of fraud offences found in other statutes. Some of these offences cover the same territory as the new offences found in the *Fraud Act 2006*. For example:

---

[1] "Juggling" was the craft.

[2] Thomas Ady, *A Candle in the Dark: or, A Treatise Concerning the Nature of Witches & Witchcraft: Being advice to Judges, Sheriffes, Justices of the Peace and Grand-Jury-men, what to do, before they passe Sentence on such as are Arraigned for their Lives, as Witches*, (London: printed for R.I., 1656) at 29. Ady, of course, was referring to Hocus Pocus (William Vincent), the author of *Hocus Pocus Junior, The Anatomy of Legerdemain*, (London: printed by I. Dawson, 1638).

[3] The Law Commission Report 276, *Fraud*, (London, H.M.S.O., 2002). The Law Commission's report provides an extensive discussion of the problems in the old law.

- fraudulent trading by companies;[4]
- the making of false statements by company directors;[5]
- the making of misleading statements concerning financial markets;[6] and
- the making of dishonest representations to obtain welfare benefits.[7]

Other fraud type offences include:

- the dishonest suppression of certain documents;[8]
- false accounting;[9]
- forgery and counterfeiting;[10]
- tax evasion;[11] and
- insider trading.[12]

34–002   Some of these other offences will be dealt with in the next chapter. The focus of this chapter is on the new offences found in the *Fraud Act 2006*. The *Fraud Act* replaced a number of deception offences[13] with a number of new "conduct" offences. The core exception is section 11 of the *Act*, which criminalizes the obtaining of services by fraud. Section 11 is only satisfied if the offender actually obtains the services—an attempt to obtain them is not sufficient. (Thus, section 11 requires the fraudulent conduct, false representation, *etc.* to result in the defendant obtaining a service). If a man tries to obtain a free game of pool by inserting a washer instead of the correct coinage into a pool table, he is only guilty if he actually succeeds in obtaining the service. If the washer is not suitable for tricking the machine into releasing the balls, he will not be liable.

The most notable changes implemented by the new *Act* are twofold:

1.   The new offences do not require a deception.
2.   The new offences (barring the one just mentioned) are conduct crimes and thus are satisfied regardless of whether they result in a gain for the defendant; or whether a loss or risk of loss is caused to another. D need only engage in the conduct (make a "false representation," *etc.*) with an intent to bring about the criminal result (loss or gain).

---

[4] Companies are caught by section 993 of the *Companies Act 2006*. Sole traders are caught by section 9(1) of the *Fraud Act 2006*.

[5] Section 19 of the *Theft Act 1968*.

[6] Section 397 of the *Financial Services and Markets Act 2000*.

[7] Section 111A of the *Social Security Administration Act 1992*.

[8] Section 20 of the *Theft Act 1968*.

[9] Section 17 of the *Theft Act 1968*.

[10] See sections 1-5 and 14-19 of *Forgery and Counterfeiting Act 1981*.

[11] It is an offence at common law to cheat the public revenue: *R. v. Redford* (1989) 89 Cr. App. R. 1; *R. v. Stannard* [2005] B.T.C. 558. There are also statutory offences which need not concern us here.

[12] See section 52 of the *Criminal Justice Act 1993*.

[13] The offences that were repealed were "deception" offences, obtaining property by deception contrary to section 15 of the *Theft Act 1968*; obtaining electronic money transfers contrary to section 15A of the *Theft Act 1968*; obtaining pecuniary advantage by deception contrary to section 16 of the *Theft Act 1968*; procuring the execution of a valuable security contrary to section 20(2) of the *Theft Act 1968*; obtaining services by deception contrary to section 1 of the *Theft Act 1978*; evading liability by deception contrary to section 2 of the *Theft Act 1978*.

The deception requirement found in the old offences was problematic because a machine could not be deceived;[14] nor could a person, except by a stroke of legal fiction, be deceived by a false representation that was made to an uninterested third party.[15] In addition, a culpable defendant could evade conviction by demonstrating that his false representation did not in fact cause the victim to part with his property.[16] The deception had to be operative on the victim's mind. Even if there had been a deception, and property had been obtained, the defendant was not guilty under the former law unless there was a causal nexus between the deception and the obtaining. The rule meant that the deception had to have affected the victim's behaviour. Lord Roskill said in *R. v. Lambie*:[17] "the Crown must always prove its case and one element which will always be required to be proved is the effect of the dishonest representation upon the mind of the person to whom it is made." This problem is illustrated by the old case of *R. v. Mills*,[18] where it was held that if the victim of an attempted deception sees through the deception but nevertheless parts with his money, the fraudster cannot be convicted of obtaining by deception (though he can be convicted of an attempt to obtain). The *Act* has abolished the causal nexus requirement, but treats attempted fraud and consummated fraud as though they were one in the same.

The new fraud offences are almost unlimited as to the dishonest conduct they criminalize. A particular problem with the new offences is that everyone is labelled the same. Those who attempt fraud are labelled as though they consummated their act of fraud. Nonetheless, following *R. v. Morris*[19] and *D.P.P. v. Gomez*[20] many attempted thefts now have the potential to be labelled as consummated thefts. Furthermore, no distinction is made between petty frauds and those of the more serious kind. Some of the offences carry maximum penalties of 10 years imprisonment and it appears the categorization of the various degrees of wrongdoing involved will be left to the discretion of the sentencing judges. Again, the same can be said of theft. A further common feature is the "dishonesty" requirement. Since both theft and fraud offences rely on the jury to decide whether a given act was dishonest; and the jurors decide this by considering their own view of what is honest according to their understanding of conventional standards of honesty, it is arguable that there is a risk that people will not be given fair warning that they may be engaging in criminal conduct. But even the dishonesty defence would not have saved Mrs. Hinks,[21] since she must

34–003

---

[14] See *Holmes v. Governor of Brixton Prison* [2005] 1 W.L.R. 1857 at 1862.

[15] Fallaciously, the judges have held otherwise. See the discussion *infra* vis-à-vis the decisions in *Commissioner of Police of the Metropolis v. Charles* [1977] A.C. 177 and *R. v. Lambie* [1982] A.C. 449.

[16] See the discussion in Glanville Williams, *Textbook of Criminal Law*, (London: Stevens & Sons, 2nd edn., 1983) at 789-794.

[17] [1982] A.C. 449 at 461.

[18] (1857) 7 Cox. C.C. 263.

[19] [1984] A.C. 320.

[20] [1993] A.C. 442.

[21] If Mrs. Hinks were to be tried under the *Fraud Act 2006*, she would most likely be saved by the *actus reus* requirement. There is nothing in the facts of *Hinks* (at least in the judgments from the higher courts) to suggest that she made any false representations, or failed to disclose information or abused a position of trust. It appears from the facts she merely asked for the money knowing that Mr. Dolphin was not too intelligent and knowing that if he was smarter he might not give it. It appears that

have realized she was being dishonest, even if she did not realize that her given act of dishonesty could result in criminal liability.[22]

34.2. Fraud by False Representation

34–004   Section 1 of the *Fraud Act 2006* outlines the three core fraud offences:

"(1)   A person is guilty of fraud if he is in breach of any of the sections listed in subsection (2) (which provide for different ways of committing the offence).

(2)   The sections are–
(a)   section 2 (fraud by false representation),
(b)   section 3 (fraud by failing to disclose information), and
(c)   section 4 (fraud by abuse of position).

(3)   A person who is guilty of fraud is liable–
(a)   on summary conviction, to imprisonment for a term not exceeding 12 months or to a fine not exceeding the statutory maximum (or to both);
(b)   on conviction on indictment, to imprisonment for a term not exceeding 10 years or to a fine (or to both)."

The detail of these offences is set out in sections 2, 3 and 4. These offences therefore would be charged by making reference to section 1. Procedurally fraud by false representation would be charged as fraud contrary to sections 1(2)(a) and 2 of the *Fraud Act 2006*. Our study of the substantive law focuses on the wording of section 2, where the detail of the offence is set out.

Most acts of fraud, if not all, result from false representations. Therefore, it is of no surprise that the lead offence in the *Fraud Act 2006* is fraud by false representation. Section 2 provides:

"(1)   A person is in breach of this section if he–
(a)   dishonestly makes a false representation, and
(b)   intends, by making the representation– (i) to make a gain for himself or another, or (ii) to cause loss to another or to expose another to a risk of loss.

(2)   A representation is false if–
(a)   it is untrue or misleading, and
(b)   the person making it knows that it is, or might be, untrue or misleading.

(3)   "Representation means any representation as to fact or law, including a representation as to the state of mind of–
(a)   the person making the representation, or
(b)   any other person.

(4)   A representation may be express or implied.

(5)   For the purposes of this section a representation may be regarded as made if it (or anything implying it) is submitted in any form to any system or device designed to receive, convey or respond to communications (with or without human intervention)."

34–005   **What is the conduct element for the section 2 offence?**   The *actus reus* of this offence is the making of a false representation, express or implied. The most straightforward example of fraud by false representation is where D expressly

---

there was no act of fraud in *R. v. Hinks* [2001] 2 A.C. 241. Dolphin would have been better off recovering the money through civil action, as sending Mrs. Hinks to jail did not get him his money back.

[22] This begs the question of whether these offences are compatible with Article 7 of the *European Convention for the Protection of Human Rights and Fundamental Freedoms*, 4 November 1950, 213 U.N.T.S. 222, (entered into force generally on 3 September 1953).

makes a false representation about an existing fact. If D, a dishonest jeweller, tells his customer that the stone he is about to purchase is a pink diamond from the Argyle mine, when in fact D knows it is a cubic zirconia, he clearly makes a false representation about a present fact. If the same jeweller states that the watch he is selling is an I.W.C. when in fact it is a fake, it is easy to establish that he made a false representation about an existing fact. Regardless of the defendant's *mens rea*, the representation is in fact false if the watch is a fake. Similarly, if D states he is Honest John[23] when his real name is François Villon, he makes a false representation about his identity, which is an existing fact.[24] The false representation might also be about the existing state of the law. If D falsely claims that a zoning law has changed to encourage V to pay much more for his land than it is currently worth, he falsely represents the existing law.

Can there be a false representation of a future fact? A hotel proprietor accepts my cash for reserving a room in his new wing for August, saying that he fully expects the wing to be completed by then. In fact he knows that the prospects are slim, and the wing is not completed.   Section 2 of the *Fraud Act* expressly refers to false representations "as to fact and law" and also "as to states of minds," including a belief (as the civil law has long done). "The state of a person's mind," said Bowen L.J. in a civil case "is as much a fact as a state of his digestion."[25] So the proper way to word the charge against the hotel proprietor would be to make it fraud as to his belief that the future fact (the completion of the wing) will come about. Still, there is no profit in pedantry, and a charge worded in terms of a false representation as to the future should usually be read as relating to the defendant's present state of mind.[26] He presently believes that it is highly unlikely that the wing will be completed. Alternatively, a false representation that in terms refers to the future may be understood to mean that the existing facts are such that the future facts will occur.[27]   **34–006**

Could a person be punished under section 2 for falsely "promising" that he will do something?   If D represents that he will or intends to do X in return for a payment from V, but has no intention of keeping his promise he falsely represents his present intention. His present intention is not to do what he promises to do in the future.[28] Take the jobbing painter who gets money to buy paint. He says to one of his employers: "I'll paint your railings tomorrow; will you let me have £500 towards the paint?" The employer gives him the money. If   **34–007**

---

[23] The media's nickname for the former Prime Minster of Australia, John Winston Howard, A.C.

[24] This might be done with an intent to gain, *etc.* and thus would be caught by section 2 of the *Fraud Act 2006*. Cf. *Balcombe v. De Simoni* (1972) 126 C.L.R. 576; *R. v. Bryan* (1861) 2 F. & F. 567; *Shogun Finance Ltd. v. Hudson* [2004] 1 A.C. 919.

[25] *Edgington v. Fitzmaurice* (1885) 29 Ch. D. 459.

[26] See *British Airways Board v. Taylor* [1976] 1 W.L.R. 13. On the philosophical question see Alan R. White, "Trade Descriptions About the Future," (1974) 90 *L.Q.R.* 15.

[27] *Commissioner of Police of the Metropolis v. Charles* [1977] A.C. 177 at 191; *Lewin v. Barratt Homes Ltd.* (2000) 164 J.P. 182; *R. v. Sunair Holidays Ltd.* [1973] 1 W.L.R. 1105.

[28] See *Young v. The King* (1789) 100 E.R. 475. Some jurisdictions specifically target false promising. Cf. *People v. Abeel*, 888 N.Y.S.2d 696 (2009); *People v. Houghtaling*, 787 N.Y.S.2d 733 (2005). See also *R. v. Kanaris* [2005] Q.C.A. 473, where D obtained a loan from a friend by representing that the sale of his land was imminent.

the painter did not intend to do the work and obtained (or attempted to obtain) the money by this falsity he is guilty of fraud under section 2 of the *Act*. He has falsely represented his own state of mind. This being so, it seems obvious that the same result must follow if instead of the statement of intention there is what is in terms a promise. Suppose the conversation between the employer and the jobbing painter runs like this:

> "Employer: 'I want my railings painted. Can you promise to do them for me tomorrow?'
> Painter: 'Yes, but I shall need £500 to get the paint.'"

Clearly, the effect is the same as before. In other words, every promise is an implied representation that the promisor intends to keep his promise, because a promise makes no sense unless the promisor intends to perform it. This rule makes a certain breach in the traditional principle that the criminal law should not be used to enforce contracts. Furthermore, it applies whether or not the defendant manages to obtain the property (*e.g.*, the advance payment).

34–008　　**It is the same where there is no *express* promise? Micawber orders a meal in a restaurant, or buys petrol at a filling station, and departs without paying.**　　These are immediate payment transactions, and the customer impliedly represents that he is in a position to pay and intends to do so.[29] Lord Reid said:

> "Where a ... customer orders a meal in a restaurant, he must be held to make an implied representation that he can and will pay for it before he leaves."[30]

This applies to all transactions in which immediate payment is customarily expected. When a driver fills his petrol tank up with fuel at a self-service station he impliedly represents that he intends to pay for it before he drives off. It is on this basis that he is allowed to serve himself. Likewise, if a diner consumes food in a restaurant, he impliedly represents that he intends to pay for it. If a diner in a restaurant, having consumed a meal, confesses that he has no cash with which to pay, and does not offer a plausible explanation of mistake or forgetfulness, this will be strong evidence that when he consumed the meal he did not intend to pay for it. Similarly, dishonest intent may be evidenced by the immediately following conduct. If a diner leaves the restaurant hurriedly without paying, his subsequent conduct is evidence of his prior dishonest intention when he entered into the transaction.[31] (But if he had the money to pay, the police might not prosecute, because they might take the view that the defendant would probably be acquitted

---

[29] Nowadays, payment by cheque backed by a cheque card would be sufficient, or payment by credit or debit card if there is a sign accepting the kind of credit/debit card.

[30] *D.P.P. v. Ray* [1974] A.C. 370 at 379. Cf. *R. v. Nordeng* (1975) 62 Cr. App. R. 123 at 126, where the Court of Appeal said: "That the bill be paid at (or before) the end of his stay is a representation made by the conduct of the traveller who books in at a hotel." (Strictly speaking, the court should have said: "That he intends to pay the bill" *etc.*). See *Maple Leaf Macro Volatility Master Fund v. Rouvroy* [2009] 2 All E.R. 287 at 366.

[31] Cf. *R. v. Aston* [1970] 1 W.L.R. 1584.

on giving evidence of forgetfulness.) These hypotheticals exemplify acts of fraud, but in particular instances the charge would be for making off without having paid.[32]

Could a person be punished under section 2 for falsely promising that he will run a get-rich-quick scheme involving illegality, when in fact he had no intention of operating the scheme? Certainly. The "illegality" of what the fraudster promises is no defence to a charge of fraud. An example under the old law was where a woman obtained advance payments for promised prostitution, having no intention of supplying the expected service.[33]

34–009

False representations implied from conduct. Whether a representation is made by conduct is a question of fact for the jury, but whether a representation can be inferred from the defendant's conduct is a question of law for the judge.[34] Cases on the law of contract and tort as well as on the criminal law illustrate how a false representation may be implied from conduct. A person who dons a uniform (like an Oxbridge gown in the days when that was enough to gain credit from a local store) impliedly represents that he belongs to the organization that gives him the social right to wear it.[35] If he wears the gown to *try* to obtain credit, regardless of whether he succeeds or not, he may be guilty of fraud under section 2 of the *Fraud Act 2006*.

34–010

Similarly, a person who sells wine at a restaurant where he is employed as a waiter implies that he is selling the restaurant's wine (not his own),[36] a diner who orders and consumes a three course dinner in a cafe implies he will pay for it,[37] a hotel guest implies he will pay for the room at the end of his stay,[38] a bookmaker implies that he will pay out on winning wagers,[39] a driving instructor implies that he is a qualified and registered driving instructor[40] and so on. It has been held in the civil courts that a farmer who sends a cow to market impliedly represents that it is not diseased, and is fit to rub shoulders with other cows,[41] but whether such a representation should be implied in criminal matters is debatable.

Is there an implied representation of title to sell? An art dealer finds, after he has acquired a valuable painting, that it is stolen property. He sells it to an innocent purchaser without telling him that it is stolen, and later the purchaser has to give it back to the true owner. Has the art dealer committed fraud by failing to disclose that the painting was stolen? Yes. The criminal courts hold that it is open to the jury to imply a representation by the seller that he

34–011

---

[32] See section 3 of the *Theft Act 1978*.

[33] *R. v. Caslin* [1961] 1 W.L.R. 59; *R. v. B* (1953) 27 A.L.J. 745.

[34] *Commissioner of Police of the Metropolis v. Charles* [1977] A.C. 177 at 186-187.

[35] See *R. v. Barnard* (1837) 173 E.R. 342; *R. v. Robinson* (1884) 10 V.L.R. 131.

[36] *R. v. Doukas* [1978] 1 W.L.R. 372.

[37] *D.P.P. v. Ray* [1974] A.C. 370.

[38] *R. v. Nordeng* (1975) 62 Cr. App. R. 123 at 126; *R. v. Harris* (1976) 62 Cr. App. R. 28.

[39] *The Queen v. Buckmaster* (1887) 20 Q.B.D. 182.

[40] *R. v. Benli* [1998] 2 [1998] 2 V.R. 157; *R. v. Miller* (1992) 95 Cr. App. R. 421.

[41] *Bodger v. Nicholls* (1873) 28 L.T. 441. *Ward v. Hobbs* (1874) 2 A.C. 13 seems to depend entirely on the exclusion clause. Cf. *Roberts v. Leonard* (1995) 159 J.P. 711.

is able to pass the title that as a matter of law he purports to pass.[42] Therefore, fraud by false representation could be made out. If the section 2 offence is established, there would be no need to consider whether the art dealer committed fraud by failing to disclose the defect in title to the buyer.

34–012   **But when the ordinary person buys a picture in a shop, what is in his mind is that he is going to take it home with him. He doesn't think of some unknown person coming on the scene and claiming it. So what did D intend to achieve by remaining silent?**   I surmise that the answer the courts would give is that D remained silent for the purpose of falsely representing he was the legitimate owner of the painting, and did so with an intent to make a gain. He intended to falsely represent that the painting belonged to him and that he was in a position to pass good title. Even if V is not a lawyer and does not think in terms of ownership, he believes he is going to have the right to enjoy the picture "forever," which means that there is no other claimant who can lawfully dispossess him. This is his false belief. It is not necessary, however, to show that V formed a false belief (or was deceived) under the *2006 Act*. It is enough that D intended to make a false representation by remaining silent with an intent to gain or cause a loss or risk of loss to another.

The implied representation as to title is exceptional. A seller is not taken to make implied representations as to the quality or fitness of the article he sells. The civil law implies terms in the contract on these matters, but does not make breach of them fraud, any more than the criminal law makes them fraud. If a prosecution were brought under section 2 of the *Fraud Act* merely on the ground the article sold was unfit, to the knowledge of the seller,[43] the judge should, on principle, withdraw the case from the jury. A false representation is not to be implied merely because the buyer will be unpleasantly surprised when he discovers the truth. There may, however, be special circumstances in the case indicating that the seller did represent the article to be of a certain type or condition or to have a particular suitability. (An extreme example might be where D gives a car a new coat of paint to cover up serious corrosion with the aim of representing that it is in good condition).

Although it is common sense that a false representation can be implied from conduct (as in the case of the townsman wearing an Oxbridge academic gown),

---

[42] Section 12 of the *Sale of Goods Act 1979*; *Re Pinter* (1891) 17 Cox C.C. 497; *Eichholz v. Bannister* (1864) 144 E.R. 284; *R. v. Timperon [No. 2]* (1976) 15 S.A.S.R. 1. In *R. v. Edwards* [1978] Crim. L.R. 49, the application of the rule seems wrong; it was held that when a squatter in a house (who paid the rates) let some rooms to V, she could, on principle, be convicted of obtaining rent from V by deception under the former section 15 of the *Theft Act 1968*. The valid argument for the defence (rejected by the Court of Appeal) was that a squatter as a possessor can create a tenancy of the premises which is valid as between him and the lessee. Moreover, the facts made the inference almost irresistible that V knew he was dealing with a squatter, in which case there was in any case no false representation or information to disclose.

[43] This type of conduct could be caught by the offences found in the *Consumer Protection from Unfair Trading Regulations 2008*. See for example, regulations 5 and 6 and the corresponding offences in regulations 9 and 10. However, the penalties for violating these regulations are much lighter than those found in the *Fraud Act*, with the maxim sentence for a conviction on indictment being 2 years. Turning back the odometer on a motorcar could be caught by the consumer regulations. This type of offence used to be charged under the former section 1(1) of the *Trade Descriptions Act 1968*. See *R. (on the application of Donnachie) v. Cardiff Magistrates' Court* [2009] All E.R. 158.

the permission given to juries and magistrates to imply a representation puts them on a slide that can easily end in the punishment of mere nondisclosure where there is no duty to disclose, in the absence of tight control by judges; and unhappily that control is sometimes lacking. To find a representation truly implied by words or conduct is one thing; to "find" a fictitious representation, purely because the defendant is a scoundrel, is quite another. Two decisions of the House of Lords provide striking examples: *Commissioner of Police of the Metropolis v. Charles*[44] and *R. v. Lambie*.[45] The rules they establish are simple: that a person who uses a cheque card or credit card impliedly represents to the person who gives credit that he, the card-holder, is acting within the terms of his contract with the bank, notwithstanding that the person who gives the credit is not interested in this question. That the rule is politic cannot be denied, since it enables fraudulent persons to be convicted; but whether they should be convicted by this interpretation of the law is another matter, since it involves stretching the notion of implied representation beyond breaking point.

Charles concerned cheque cards. All the world knows (or at any rate all the world who reads the back of bank cheque cards), the bank promises the recipient of a cheque that the bank will honour the cheque provided that it complies with certain conditions expressed on the cheque card. The recipient of a cheque written in accordance with the conditions is not concerned with the state of the drawer's bank account, which is a matter solely between the drawer and the bank. It might be thought, therefore, that the drawer of the cheque that is valid under the terms of the cheque card cannot in so doing be guilty of making a false representation to the person who gives credit. It is because businesses do not trust customers they ask for a guarantee from the banks.

34–013

In *Charles*, the defendant wrote a series of cheques on the strength of his cheque card, knowing that the total greatly exceeded the overdraft he was allowed. The manager of a club to whom the cheques were given in payment for gaming chips was ignorant of this excess, and made no enquiry since he did not regard that matter as concerning the club (as, financially, it did not). Charles was convicted of obtaining an overdraft (resulting from the bank's honouring his cheques) by the deception impliedly addressed to the gambling club.[46] It was a case of obtaining a benefit (the overdraft) from A (his bank) by means of a deception addressed to B (the club manager). Charles was not charged with an offence under the former section 15(1) of the *Theft Act 1968* for obtaining the gaming chips from the club by the same deception, but on the court's reasoning he would clearly have been guilty of that as well.

In *Charles*, the fraud found by the House of Lords was based on an implied representation supposed to have been made by Charles that he was acting within his credit limit. Lord Diplock said that the card-holder:[47]

---

[44] [1977] A.C. 177.

[45] [1982] A.C. 449.

[46] Charles was convicted of obtaining a pecuniary advantage by deception contrary to the former section 16 of the *Theft Act 1968*.

[47] *Commissioner of Police of the Metropolis v. Charles* [1977] A.C. 177 at 182.

> "by exhibiting to the payee a cheque card … represents to the payee that he has actual authority from the bank to make a contract with the payee on the bank's behalf that it will honour the cheque on the presentment for payment."

If an implication of this kind were only to give commercial efficacy to the transaction, of course it should be made; but it is not the only way. The cheque card with its terms on the back is a general offer made directly by the bank to people who accept cheques on the strength of the card. The card-holder is a bearer of the offer, but need no more be regarded as the bank's agent to contract than was the newspaper that carried the celebrated advertisement by Carlisle and Cumberland Banking Co., or the newsagent who sold a copy of the newspaper to Mrs. Bragg, an agent for the Banking Co.[48] The position in *Charles* would have been the same if Charles' bank had written directly to the payee of each cheque in terms of its offer on the cheque card. And even if the card-holder was the bank's agent to contract on its behalf, his agency (his power to bind the bank towards the payee) did not incorporate the limitations expressed in the contract between him and the bank. The bank bound itself to the payee irrespective of the card-holder's observance of its rules.

34–014   *R. v. Lambie* concerned not a cheque card but a credit card, and the decision is open to much the same criticism as *Charles*. The main difference between the two types of card is that with the credit card the bank makes its own standing contracts in advance with the particular suppliers who are willing to accept its credit card. The question whether the abuse of credit card facilities involved any criminal offence had long been discussed in Whitehall, but no one had done anything about it. When, therefore, Miss Lambie went on a little shopping spree in a Mothercare shop, using a Barclaycard beyond her credit limit, someone selected her as a sacrificial lamb to get the law clarified by the soothsayers. Notwithstanding Lambie's transgression of the bank's rules, no harm could befall Mothercare, who could still claim from the bank under their contract with the bank. The department manager of Mothercare who dealt with the matter acted properly under the credit card contract and had no notice that Lambie was not entitled to use her card. In the result, Lambie was convicted of the former offence of dishonestly obtaining a pecuniary advantage by deception.

On appeal the Court of Appeal held that Lambie gave no implied representation to the shop as to her right to use the card. The shop was not interested in this question, being protected by its contract with the bank. The Oxford shop assistant who sold goods on credit to the townsman wearing the university gown certainly thought that he was an undergraduate; but the Mothercare manager did not suppose that Lambie was within Lambie's credit limit, because she was not concerned with the question. Indeed, she confirmed this in evidence. "I would not worry about what went on between the customer and Barclaycard." Alas, the decision of the Court of Appeal was reversed by the House of Lords, which restored the conviction.

The reason given by their Lordships followed the lines laid down in *Charles*. In the opinion of the House Lambie impliedly represented that she had authority from the bank to make a contract (as agent for the bank) with the shop, the

---

[48] See *Carlisle & Cumberland Banking Co. v. Bragg* [1911] 1 K.B. 489.

contact in question being not Lambie's purchase of goods but a collateral contract involving a promise by the bank to the shop to honour the Barclaycard.

This way of looking at the matter involved even greater difficulty than in *Charles*. In the credit card transaction there was already in existence a contract between the bank and Mothercare, a contract in the conclusion of which Lambie had played no part. (The bank represented that Mothercare would be paid regardless of whether one of its customers was dishonest). The fact that the contract operated only when a card-holder made a purchase did not make the card-holder an agent of the bank for its liability. The supposition of an agency on Lambie's part was, therefore, superfluous and unwarranted. Credit card agreements are drawn up with meticulous care by commercial lawyers, and nowhere do these agreements suggest that the card-holder acts as an agent in any capacity for the bank when he uses the card. From the point of view of the law of contract full efficacy can be given to the credit card arrangement without implying any such agency. The *only* purpose, it appears, of this implied agency asserted by the House of Lords is to convict the dishonest card-holder of fraud. In no other respect is the card-holder an agent of the bank. No agency need be implied in order to create a relationship between the bank and the shop, because that relationship is already established in the contract between the bank and the shop. The reason why the bank is liable to the shop is not because the card-holder has contracted on its behalf, but because the bank has directly contracted with the shop. **34–015**

If it must be taken that Lambie represented to the shop that the bank would under existing arrangements pay the shop, her representation was true. The bank would and did pay the shop. The criticism of Lambie was not that she defrauded the shop but that she defrauded the bank; but it is a strong thing to say that a person who deals with A impliedly represents to A that he is not defrauding B, A having no pecuniary interest in the question whether this fraud is committed or not. Section 2 of the *Fraud Act 2006* does not require an actual deception; nor does it matter whether the defendant makes the false representation to the victim as opposed to an uninterested third party. All the defendant has to do is make a false representation with an intent to gain or cause a loss, *etc*. This overcomes some of the issues raised in *Lambie*, but it raises the further question of whether Lambie would satisfy the *mens rea* requirement found in the fraud by false representation offence. After all, it is doubtful she "intended" to imply anything to the uninterested shopkeeper. (I will return to that issue shortly).

Are you telling me that if Lambie had stolen cash from her mother's purse, that her act of spending that money would have falsely represented that she had not stolen the money and thus have made her liable for fraud? The appropriate charge would be for theft, not theft and subsequently fraud for thereafter using the money. Clearly, if a person steals cash she does not commit fraud every time she spends some of it. The so-called implied representation in this case would not be sufficient to ground a fraud conviction, since section 2 of the *Act* requires the false representation be *made* for the purpose of making a gain or to cause loss to another or to expose another to a risk of loss. If Lambie had stolen cash the later implied representation that it was not stolen (or failure to **34–016**

disclose otherwise) could not be said to have been implied with an intent to make a gain or to cause a loss to another. The gain was made when the money was initially stolen—the later transaction of exchanging the money for goods does not allow her to gain a second time from the original victim.[49] Nor does it result in a further loss.

In all previous cases where representations had been implied, they concerned matters of importance to the alleged representee. The false representation must be made with an intent to gain or cause a loss to another. There must be some culpability link between D's gain and his false representation. The defendant must intend to create a false impression and must intend to do so for the purpose of making a gain or causing a loss or risk of loss to another.

34–017   **Are you telling me that Lambie did not in fact *intend* to make a false representation for the purpose of facilitating her purchase?** It is highly probable that she did not *intend* to imply that she was not defrauding her bank, because there was no need for her to do so.

If D makes a conscious choice to put on a uniform to falsely represent his identity for the purpose of making a gain he could not otherwise make, section 2 is satisfied because he not only intends to make a false representation by implication, but also intends to make a gain from that representation. It appears that Lambie did not think it was necessary for her to make an implied false representation to make the gain she made. She most likely would not have thought it was necessary to make such a representation in order to run up an overdraft, as it was the bank not the shopkeeper which had the power to stop her from running up an overdraft. What if she had presented her card to the shopkeeper and said: "I am running up an unauthorized overdraft to pay for this, it will take me months to pay it off?" Might not the shopkeeper have served her anyway?

There is no reason why the courts cannot imply a representation by a cardholder that she was not acting without the authority of her bank (regardless of whether it was immaterial to the alleged representee whether she was so acting or not), so long as it can be shown that the cardholder intended to make such a representation with an *intent* to make a gain or cause a loss *etc*. If such a representation was not causally needed or even thought about by the defendant, then it will be difficult to demonstrate that the defendant *made it* (either expressly or impliedly) with an *intent* to make a gain for herself, or to cause a loss to another. It is illogical to hold that Lambie falsely represented that she was not defrauding her bank in order to make the particular gain. She was more likely to have been thinking about how much interest she was going to have to pay on the overdraft she was running up. She might have genuinely believed (as many bankrupts have) that she was merely borrowing from the bank without its upfront approval. It is doubtful an *intentional* false representation even existed. It was not necessary for Lambie to implicitly represent, "I am not using stolen money," for her to make the gain she had in mind.

---

[49] Cf. *R. v. Hamilton* (1991) 92 Cr. App. R. 54, where D falsely represented that the money in his bank account was not stolen and that he had a right to withdraw it.

Per contra, it might be held that by allowing a shopkeeper (an innocent agent) to ring up the goods on the machine that transacts the credit/debit payment, and by inserting a PIN code into card reader to effect the payment, D falsely represents to the machine that she is entitled to the sum of money that is displayed as owed on the magnetic card reader's monitor. It would be necessary for her to make this claim to effect the transaction. She can see the value of the goods on the card reader's screen and enters her PIN code knowing she does not have sufficient funds to pay for the goods and thus might be caught by sections 1(2)(a) and 2(5).

34–018

An "intentional" (implied) false representation is easier to identify in the case of cheques, because the receiver of the cheque has an interest in establishing whether (from all appearances) it is likely to be honoured. Therefore, it is *necessary* for D to impliedly represent that the cheque will be honoured. It was settled in the old case of *R. v. Hazelton*[50] that when a person draws a cheque he can be taken as impliedly presenting that the cheque is a valid order for the payment of the amount stated. When *R. v. Hazelton* was decided there could be no representation as to intention, so the implied representation had to be worded in this way to make it look like a representation of external fact. But this poses no problem under the *Fraud Act*, since it is permissible to imply a general representation that the drawer *intends* and *expects* the cheque to be paid, and this is now a rational way to direct the jury.

34–019

In *D.P.P. v. Gomez*[51] the assistant manager of an electrical goods store was asked by an acquaintance to supply goods in exchange for two stolen building society cheques. The cheques were for £7,950 and £9,250 respectively and were undated and bore no payee's name. Gomez agreed and prepared a list of goods to the value of the stolen cheques which he submitted to the store's manager, Mr. Gilberd. He told Mr. Gilberd that the cheques represented a genuine order by one Johal and asked the sale to be authorized in return for the stolen cheques. Mr. Gilberd instructed the defendant to check with the bank to confirm the validity of the cheques, which of course Gomez did not do. Gomez falsely represented that the bank had told him that the cheques were "as good as cash." Gomez deposited the cheques in the firm's account, but soon after both cheques were returned by the bank stamped: "Orders not to pay. Stolen cheque."

In this case, Gomez expressly represented that the cheques would be honoured. He represented that he had confirmed with the bank that the cheques were valid and that there were no irregularities. Meanwhile, his confederates impliedly represented that they had an account on which the cheques were drawn, had the authority to draw the amount stated on the cheque forms, and that the cheques were valid orders for the sum stated on them. These cheques were stolen and were not valid orders so were not payable.

If a cheque is a valid order, will it be paid? Not necessarily. The drawer may secretly intend to stop payment or to empty his bank account after giving the cheque. The cheque is a valid order when drawn, but the drawer does not intend it to operate. Or he may give a cheque that he purposely omits to sign, hoping that

34–020

[50] (1872-75) L.R. 2 C.C.R. 134.
[51] [1993] A.C. 442 at 453.

the recipient will not notice; here the supposed cheque is not one at all, and so perhaps does not raise the *R. v. Hazelton* implication. In each of these cases the drawer will be guilty of fraud under the general representation stated above.

In the respects just stated the *R. v. Hazelton* representation is too narrow; but sometimes it is too wide, or at any rate misleading. The cheque as presented may be a valid order (no funds in the account and no overdraft arrangement), so that the giving of it may seem to be a breach of the *R. v. Hazelton* representation. But suppose that the drawer believes from his previous dealings with his bank that the bank will in fact allow him sufficient overdraft to honour the cheque; or suppose that he intends to pay in before the cheque is presented, or believes that a third party (his employer) will pay in, so that it will be met.[52] In these circumstances the implied representation that he intends and expects the cheque to be met is true; and anyway the drawer cannot be guilty of fraud, because he is not dishonest.

In short, as Lord Reid put it, the law now is that:

> "If nothing is said to the contrary, the law implies that the giver of a cheque represents that it will be honoured."[53]

—meaning, that he represents his intention and expectation to be that it will be honoured.

34–021   These arguments suggest that the *R. v. Hazelton* representation is a misleading statement of the law and should be modified. The persistence of former ideas is shown by the case[54] where the question arose whether the former deception offence could be committed where the defendant drew a post-dated cheque on his bank. It was held that it could, but the reason offered was that the giving of the cheque implied a representation that the state of facts at the date of its giving were such that it would be met on or after the date written on it. This reason is unconvincing and misses the mark. A person who gives a post-dated cheque promises to meet the cheque on it being presented after the stated date, but he does not warrant that he has already made arrangements for it to be met by the bank. The true reason why the fraudster can be guilty under section 2 of the *Fraud Act* notwithstanding that the cheque is post-dated is that same as the reason why fraudsters in general are liable on invalid cheques, post-dated or not, namely that he does not intend to meet the cheque.

34–022   **Does the section 2 provide a solution to the *Preddy* problem?**   False representations that are designed to induce another to electronically transfer funds

---

[52] That this intention prevents there being any false representation was recognized in *Commissioner of Police of the Metropolis v. Charles* [1977] A.C. 177 at 185, and in the court below *Commissioner of Police of the Metropolis v. Charles* [1976] 1 W.L.R. 248 at 254, quoting Phillimore L.J.

[53] *D.P.P. v. Turner* [1974] A.C. 357 at 367. See also *Commissioner of Police of the Metropolis v. Charles* [1977] A.C. 177 at 182, 186, 191.

[54] *R. v. Gilmartin* [1983] 2 W.L.R. 547. Cf. *R. v. Greenstein* [1975] 1 W.L.R. 1353. In addition, it is worth noting that D does not make a false representation if he provides V (a loan-shark) with post-dated cheques to evidence a loan, if D has made it clear that he is paying 40 *per cent.* interest because he is a high risk borrower who may not be able to repay the loan, because V has all the information—D is not concealing his high risk credit rating or that he might not be able to pay on the due date. See *R. v. Cabalza* [2002] 172 C.C.C. (3d) 436.

are clearly caught by section 2. Under section 2, D need not make a false representation with an intent to obtain property which "belongs to another." He need only intend to expose V to a risk of loss. If D secures a large mortgage by falsely representing that he is earning £100,000 *per annum* when in fact he is only earning £15,000 *per annum*, it is irrelevant that the mortgage funds are transferred electronically into his bank account thereby creating a new chose in action for D, which never belonged to the mortgagor, because the mortgagor suffers a loss or is at least exposed the risk of loss.[55]

How can a machine be misled?   The whole law of deception under the *Theft*   **34–023**
Acts was geared to the deception of humans.[56] Section 2(5) of the *Fraud Act* radically altered this by introducing a deeming provision. It deems that it is fraud to provide false information to a machine for the purpose of making a gain and so on. The new offence means the old problem of proving that a machine is "deceivable" no longer arises. A spate of technological advances meant that the fraudster could operate without needing to deceive a human being (as opposed to a machine) such as Internet banking facilities, A.T.M.s, and so on. If D puts a washer in the cigarette machine[57] with an intent to gain a free packet of cigarettes, he may be charged with fraud under sections 1(2)(a) and 2(5). If D closes his bank account and uses an expired debit card to continue to draw money from an A.T.M., because the A.T.M. is unable to tell whether he has a current account or whether the account is in credit, he would be caught by section 2(5) of the *Act*.[58] In addition, if D feeds false information into a machine to obtain a *service*, he may be liable for fraud. If D went to his local pub and put a washer into the coin slot of the pool table to obtain a free game of pool, he would obtain a service and may be liable for fraud under section 11 of the *Act*.

Suppose D is employed by H.M. Revenue & Customs. Suppose also that he has the capacity to access the office's computer by entering his user ID and password, and has *authority* to enter a "relief code" into the computer to exempt certain taxpayers from paying tax, but only "when relief has been granted to a taxpayer by an appropriate person with authority to do so."[59] "Relief" meaning that the taxpayer would be exempt from paying tax. Is D guilty of fraud if he exempts taxpayers without permission?

In a rather unusual Australian case, *Gilmour v. Director of Public Prosecutions (Cth.)*,[60] a tax office employee had on nineteen occasions inserted data into a computer (relief code "43," for those who are interested) to indicate that certain taxpayers had been granted relief from paying tax, even though he knew this was not the case. The "Relief Section" of the Australian Tax Office considers

---

[55] *R. v. PS* [2007] EWCA Crim. 2058; *R. v. Preddy* [1996] A.C. 815.

[56] See *Davies v. Flackett* [1973] R.T.R. 8; *R. v. Cooper* [1979] Crim. L.R. 42; *Holmes v. Governor of Brixton Prison* [2005] 1 W.L.R. 1857 at 1862.

[57] This would also be theft. See *R. v. Hands* (1887) 52 J.P. 24; *R. v. Mark* (1922) 18 Tas. L.R. 36.

[58] Cf. *Kennison v. Daire* (1986) 160 C.L.R. 129; *R. v. Baxter* (1988) 27 A. Crim. R. 18; *Shields v. New South Wales Crime Commission* (2007) 177 A. Crim. R. 130.

[59] *Gilmour v. Director of Public Prosecutions (Cth.)* (1995) 125 F.L.R. 114 at 116.

[60] (1995) 125 F.L.R. 114. As he did not intend to make a gain or cause a loss, he was convicted of a computer misuse type offence under section 76C of the *Crimes Act 1914 (Cth.)*: for "intentionally and without authority or lawful excuse inserting data into a Commonwealth computer."

applications by taxpayers for relief from payment of income tax. However, exemptions can only be granted by specialist employees in that section of the department (presumably, trained accountants). Once the appropriately qualified person grants relief, the taxpayer's application is then sent to a data-entry person so that he can enter the "relief code" to effectuate the tax relief.

34–024 The defendant had entered the relief code on nineteen occasions even though he had no "authority to grant relief." D had a user ID and password, which allowed him to access the tax office computer, but access was only authorized for data entry purposes. He was only permitted to enter relief code "43" when he had been authorized to exempt the particular taxpayer. Notably, the defendant did not intend to make a gain for himself. Rather, he exempted the taxpayers because of a "desire to expedite the process, a heavy workload and concern about suggested inconsistencies in determinations of applications for relief."[61]

34–025 **Would he be caught by the section 2(5) of the *Fraud Act 2006*?** He would be if he had entered the false information with an intent to make a gain for himself or for the taxpayers or to cause a loss or risk of loss to the tax office. It must be shown that he intended to either cause a loss or expose his employer to a risk of loss.

34–026 **What about cases where the false information is not received by the machine that is cable of effectuating the gain or loss, *etc.*?** Take the example of D who takes his roommate's debit card to purchase a flight to Australia so that he can attend his cousin's wedding. Suppose he goes to the Qantas Airlines webpage, brings up the relevant electronic form for purchasing the ticket, enters all his details and his roommate's debit card details, but does not hit the "make payment" option because he has forgotten the date of the wedding. Instead, he saves the form on his personal computer while he phones his cousin to get the date of the wedding. He simply saves the information so that he will not have to re-enter all the data. Suppose also that after he obtains the date of the wedding, he takes fright and decides not to proceed with the purchase. He has entered the information into a machine, but it is not the machine that can produce a gain or to cause a loss.

34–027 **Is entering false information into a personal computer sufficient to ground a conviction under section 2(5) of the *Fraud Act*?** No, it is not even an attempt. It appears to be an act that is no more than preparatory.[62] He would have to try to effectuate the transaction by clicking the "payment option" in the Qantas Airlines electronic form. His personal computer is not the machine that has to receive the false information for the transaction to be effectuated; rather it is the victim's bank's computer (and possibly the Qantas Airlines computer) that has the power to effectuate the transaction, and it can only do this if it receives the false information. It is the bank's machine that D has to *try* to feed the information. If D had clicked the payment option without the information being electronically transferred from his computer to the bank's computer, because he forgot to input

---

[61] *Gilmour v. Director of Public Prosecutions (Cth.)* (1995) 125 F.L.R. 114 at 116.
[62] See *Comer v. Bloomfield* (1971) 55 Cr. App. R. 305; *R. v. Ilyas* (1984) 78 Cr. App. R. 17.

mandatory information such as the type of debit card being use, then that would most likely be an attempt. It might not be difficult to prove an attempted fraud by false representation when the rogue is caught in the act of trying to post a false representation by *snail mail*, but it would be when he has attempted to send it electronically and it has bounced back as so to speak, because it has not left his personal computer.

There is a distinction between D storing another's debit card details on his computer and his using that information to make a false representation electronically. The former is no different than if the defendant had recorded the victim's debit card details by writing them down on a piece of paper. The representation has to be made even though it need not be communicated to the victim.[63] If it is not made there ought to be at least an attempt to make it. Unfortunately, "attempted" representations in an electronic form (*i.e.* bounced electronic messages) will very rarely be recorded in a way that would make it possible to prove that D attempted to make a false representation.

Storing information is not an attempt to make a representation. Similarly, writing down lies in a private notebook with an intent to use them in some later fraud does not constitute the making of a false representation, as the lies have not been *re*presented to anyone, nor does writing them down for future use amount to an attempt to present them to another. The false information must be represented to someone or something. If there is no false representation then the *actus reus* requirement will not be satisfied. When a defendant posts or e-mails his lies he represents them and thus makes a false representation. It is the conduct of representing the information that changes it from a mere act of storing information to the making of a false representation. Nonetheless, storing another's bank details could be caught by section 6 of the *Act of 2006*, as the information would constitute an article that could be used to commit fraud.

Continuing and consecutive representations

Suppose that D made a representation to V which he mistakenly believed to   **34–028**
be true when he made it. Afterwards he came to know of its untruth before
obtaining property from V on the strength of it, and did nothing to reveal the
true position to V.   The defendant's *mens rea* must coincide with the making of the false representation. On the authorities as they stand the courts are quite likely to hold him liable under section 2 of the *Fraud Act*. The legal question is whether the defendant's representation can be regarded as continuing until it is acted upon.[64] To put the point in general terms, the acceptance of the doctrine of continuing representation would meet the situation where there is a material change in circumstances between the making of the representation and its being acted upon. The question may arise in either of two ways:

---

[63] Section 2(3)(b) of the *Fraud Act* means that the representation can be made to either the victim or "any other person."

[64] A loose use of the phrase "continuing representation" may be noticed, but it has no bearing on the present discussion. The courts sometimes say that a fraudulent representation "continues" until it is acted upon, when all they mean is that the victim may act upon the representation after a lapse of time.

1. One, which you envisage is where the representor mistakenly believed that his representation was true at the time when he made it, but subsequently learnt of its untruth, before accepting the property offered to him on the strength of the representation.
2. The other type of case is where the representation was in fact true when made, but subsequently the representor discovered that it had become untrue, before he received the property.

In the first of these cases the criminal act precedes (or appears to precede) the criminal state of mind. In the second case, in addition, one of the external elements of the offence (the falsity of the representation) is missing at the time when the representation is (first) made.

The difficulty of convicting under section 2 may be overcome in both cases by finding that the defendant impliedly made a representation by "continuing" or "renewed" conduct of some sort. For the purpose of deciding whether such an implication can be made it is convenient to distinguish two types of case: where D co-opted in receiving the property (or attempting to receive it) after coming to know the truth (we may call this, for short, bilateral obtaining), and where he was merely sent it by V and passively received it (unilateral obtaining).

34–029   In bilateral obtaining D (for example) goes to V to receive the property at his hands. Here the probability is strong that the jury would be encouraged to find an implied representation by D at the time of the obtaining, reaffirming his previous representation. Since at the time he knew the truth, he would be guilty of fraud by false representation. The leading case is *Ray v. Sempers*,[65] which turned on evading a debt by deception, a statutory offence that has been superseded by section 2 of the *Fraud Act*. In that case, a student, Ray, entered a restaurant and ordered a meal with honest intent. After consuming it he decided to "bilk" the restaurant. He remained at the table for ten minutes till the waiter disappeared, then fled. The House of Lords held by majority that he had evaded the debt by deception; the deception consisting in sitting at the table until the waiter turned his back. While Ray was sitting at the table the waiter assumed he was honest and did not press for payment or call the police; this assumption was false, was deliberately caused by Ray, and was a false representation as to his intention. He was representing that he was about to pay, when in fact his real intention was to evade paying the debt which was due.

This case is limited to its special facts, because Ray's false representation was not implied from his act of consuming the meal, but from his subsequent act of remaining at the table for ten minutes. It was this subsequent act that implied that he was intending to pay. If there had been no subsequent act, he could not be said to have committed fraud by false representation, because he intended to pay when he consumed the meal. It was his subsequent conduct and his newly formed intention not to pay for their meal that falsified his earlier implied representation that he would pay.

---

[65] [1974] A.C. 370.

Suppose D fills up his diesel tank at his local filling station and subsequently learns that he is unable to pay because he has forgotten to bring his wallet. Suppose also that he decides the only solution is to speed off without paying and does so before the attendant notices him. (Let us assume the attendant only discovers D's crime when he is reviewing the store's CCTV footage later that day after being tipped off by another customer). Does D commit fraud by false representation?   No. You will recall title in petrol passes as soon as it is put into D's tank, and if D was honest when he filled up he became the lawful owner of the fuel. Most significantly, he acquired ownership without making a false representation, because he intended to pay for the fuel when he put it in his tank. He was implicitly telling the truth and acquired ownership before he formed his dishonest intent. Section 2 of the *Fraud Act* requires D to make his false representation with an intent to make a gain or to cause a loss or risk of loss to another. The defendant had made his gain with an honest intent, so could not be said to have made a false representation for the purpose of making a gain—the gain was over and done.

Furthermore, unlike Ray, he did not make a subsequent representation in order to evade a debt—he merely absconded without being noticed. If he had made a subsequent false representation such as promising to return to pay for the diesel and had no intention of doing so he would commit fraud. In *Ray v. Sempers* the second representation that the debt would be paid was implied from the continuing conduct of Ray and the other students sitting at the table so as to give the impression that they intended to pay the debt that was due. This representation was fully independent from Ray's earlier representation that he would pay for the meal, which was implied from him consuming the meal. Ray's *mens rea* coincided with the second continuing false representation that he intended to pay the bill, which was then due.

In the second type of case, unilateral obtaining (or attempted unilateral obtaining), D makes a representation to obtain property, discovers its falsity afterwards, does nothing, and intends to accept the property from the postman or other carrier if it is delivered to him. Here a representation cannot be implied when D orders the goods, since he lacked *mens rea*. However, upon learning of the falsity of his representation he "adopts" it by failing to disclose the truth because his deliberate silence implies that the representation continues to be true. It is because he has already claimed X to be true that his silence implies it continues to be true. He remains silent to imply that his representation is true; and does so with an intent to make a gain or cause a loss, *etc*. For example, in *R. v. Rai*[66] D applied to have the local authority pay for the installation of a £9,500 bathroom for his aged mother. The local authority approved his application and organized for a contractor to do the work. However, Rai's mother passed away before the work commenced. Rai did not tell the council that she had died. Instead, Rai stayed silent while the contractors built a new bathroom in his house at the council's expense.

Rai did not deny that he had not told the council of his mother's death until after the building works were completed. But it was argued on his behalf "that he had

34–030

34–031

---

[66] (2000) 1 Cr. App. R. 242 at 244-245.

no legal or contractual duty to inform the council and that mere silence or inactivity could not constitute such conduct."[67] The Court of Appeal rejected this argument. By remaining silent Rai made a straightforward false representation, "because, as he was aware, the local authority were still of the mind that the mother would occupy the premises. … [O]n a common-sense and purposive construction of the word 'conduct,' it does, in our judgment, cover positive acquiescence in knowingly letting this work proceed as D did in the present case." By remaining silent Rai falsified his earlier true representation that the bathroom was needed for his elderly mother.

The main advantage of this approach is that it applies to cases where there is no legal duty to disclose, as long as the defendant has made some kind of initial representation which was true. Supposing that the idea of the defendant falsifying his initial true representation by remaining silent to imply that it remains true is not recognized for the purposes of section 2, it may still be held that the representor who tries to accept the property after coming to know of the falsity of his representation is guilty of theft.

34–032   **If D makes several false representations, will he face several fraud convictions?**   Not necessarily. It will depend whether the false representations relates to a single event. Suppose D claims that his vintage Rolls Royce has only done 30,000 miles, once belonged to King George VI, is in immaculate condition, and that he has had an offer of £100,000 for it. Suppose the truth is that it has done 350,000 miles, never belonged to King George, has structural problems, a worn out engine, and he has had no offers for it. Despite the successive false representations there is only one act of fraud. D only attempts to sell the car to a single victim. If he had made the same claim to several customers, then he might be liable for further acts of fraud. As far as a particular victim is concerned, the jury would have to reach a unanimous agreement about whether a "single" representation was false.[68] It is not enough for *half* the jurors to agree that the representation about the mileage was false while the *other half* agree that the representation that it belonged to King George was false: there would have to be unanimous agreement that at least "one" of those "representations" was false.

34–033   **If D makes several false representations with an intent to make a new gain each time, does he commit a new act of fraud each time?**   Technically yes. Take the example of the unqualified driving instructor who has a hundred students because he has falsely represented to each of them that he is a qualified instructor. There is no doubt that his false representations to each customer is made with an intent to gain; and to cause a loss, *etc.* to that customer. As for each individual student, he only makes one continuous false representation. He falsely claims to be qualified to obtain the individual student's custom, and then continues that false representation every time he provides a driving lesson and

---

[67] *R. v. Rai* (2000) 1 Cr. App. R. 242 at 245.
[68] See *R. v. Brown* (1983) 79 Cr. App. Rep. 115. "[A] *Brown* direction will be necessary only in comparatively rare cases where there is a risk that the jury will not realise that they need to agree upon the particular ingredient [*i.e.* false representation, which is the *actus reus* of the section 2 offence] which they rely upon to find the defendant guilty of the offence charged." See *The Queen v. Lewis* [2010] EWCA Crim. 496 at para. 52.

takes further payment.[69] As for the independent representations made to the independent customers, they are distinct (continuing)[70] false representations and each forms the *actus reus* of the offence of fraud by false representation. The prosecution might be generous and charge him with a single offence under section 9(2)(b) of the *Fraud Act 2006* for carrying on a business for a "fraudulent purpose."[71]

Does one have to keep to the absolutely rigid truth? All sorts of petty humbugs are used in business matters. Assuming a false name, for instance. Do they fall foul of section 2 of the *Fraud Act*? You may be thinking of "puffery." As to names the English law is free and easy. "Lord" George Sanger ran a circus under a title of nobility that he simply assumed. Andreas Cornelis van Kuijk, Elvis Presley's manager, changed his name to Colonel Tom Parker, but his rank of "Colonel" was genuine. A person can give herself a new name or go under a business or professional name if she wishes, and many women still change their names when they get married. But if it can be shown that a name was assumed in order to try to get a fraudulent benefit, then fraud can be made out. An example is where a person of bad character assumes another name in order to get credit.

34–034

The representation must be false. Obviously, if D tells V a chain is 15-carat gold when he knows it is only 6-carat gold his statement is clearly untrue.[72] This is not mere puffery but a false representation about an existing fact. If it happens by accident to be true, the fraudster might be charged with attempted fraud but he could not be convicted of fraud.[73] He is guilty of an attempted fraud by false representation, and, strangely, may be guilty of theft.

What about ambiguous statements? If the utterer, like the witches of Macbeth, "palters in a double sense," intending his words to be understood in their untrue signification, it is a false representation.

34–035

Suppose V enters a "private" car park at his local shopping centre where there is no charge for the first hour of parking. Suppose also that unbeknown to V there is a massive penalty for those who stay longer than an hour.[74] Let us assume he has stayed 1 hour and 10 minutes and his breach of contract is detected by a camera. Within days he receives a demand in the post for £100 on a letter which is entitled: "*Parking* Charge Notice," (Penalty notices sent out by local authorities

---

[69] See *R. v. Benli* [1998] 2 V.R. 157.

[70] Assuming he has given them more than one lesson. Similarly, if D makes a false representation about his right to work in Britain, his dishonest representation as to his entitlement to work would continue while he remains employed on that basis. See *R. v. Nelson* [2010] 2 W.L.R. 788 at 803.

[71] *Morphitis v. Bernasconi* [2003] 2 WLR 1521; *In Re Gerald Cooper Chemicals Ltd. (In Liquidation)* [1978] Ch. 262 at 267.

[72] *The Queen v. Ardley* (1865-72) L.R. 1 C.C.R. 301.

[73] *R. v. Deller* (1952) 36 Cr. App. R. 184.

[74] In the law of contract, if a customer enters a car park subject to conditions, he is only bound by them if reasonably sufficient steps have been taken to bring them to his notice. *Thornton v. Shoe Lane Parking* [1971] 2 Q.B. 163; *Interfoto Picture Library Ltd. v Stiletto Visual Programmes Ltd.* [1989] Q.B. 433.

are almost identical, except they are called, "*Penalty* Charge Notices.") Let us assume the notice also states that if the sum of £100 is not paid within 14 days, a further penalty of £40 will be added.

Clearly this type of invoice (invoice, because in law that is what it is) would be misleading, because even though it does not expressly claim to be a "Penalty Charge Notice" from a local authority, it gives the impression that it is. Not only by using the identical words "Charge Notice," but also by claiming disproportionate punitive damages. The claim that punitive damages are owed is also a false representation, because a private firm cannot demand such excessive (punitive) damages for a standard breach of contract.[75] (Excessive overcharging is theft).[76] Such a notice is misleading in that if it gives the impression that failure to pay could result in criminal proceedings, and that the parking company is "authorised in some official capacity"[77] to collect and enforce punitive fines. Many would assume that the threatened proceedings are criminal rather than civil. The invoice is clearly misleading when it is designed to give the impression that the private firm is acting in some official character.

34–036   The notice is merely an invoice, but gives the impression that it is a state endorsed penal fine. The cost of overstaying for 10 minutes would be about 50 pence and it might cost the parking firm £2 at the most to send out a standard invoice. (Some people (lawyers) realize these Parking Charge Notices are mere invoices, so ask the parking company why it is charging £100 for a 10-minute overstay. In response, the firm normally claims it costs £100 to process the invoice). This too is a false representation. We get invoices for books and other items all the time and we know that a store could not provide an invoice for a £30 book, if it was going to cost it £100 to process the invoice.

This is a contractual matter therefore the firm's notice is merely an invoice to claim the cost of the over-parking. These types of invoices have misled thousands of motorists who pay them without question. The firm is only entitled to reasonable compensation for the over-parking which would normally be a few pounds at the most. The invoice should clearly state that it is an invoice and should only claim reasonable compensation for the over-parking. These firms normally know they are committing fraud as they have been exposed in the courts,[78] but still continue their practices. Even when their errors are pointed out to them, they continue to send very threatening letters. The parking company could be prosecuted for harassment, when it repeatedly threatens legal action and

---

[75] *Dunlop Pneumatic Tyre Co Ltd. v. New Garage & Motor Co Ltd.* [1915] A.C. 79. The best solution would be to bring this conduct to the attention of the Office of Fair Trading so that it could prosecute the offending corporation for committing offences under the *Consumer Protection from Unfair Trading Regulations 2008*. Alas, it would be difficult to get the police to bring a charge for the CPS to act on, because they are trained to look for street crime, not for corporate fraud.

[76] *R. v. Williams* (2001) 1 Cr. App. R. 23.

[77] See also section 40 of the *Administration of Justice Act 1970*.

[78] See, for example, Martin Delgado, "Judge quashes £300 Parking Fine … because it set out to frighten and intimidate the driver," (London: *The Daily Mail*, 22 March 2008).

repeatedly demands punitive sums that it is not owed.[79] It is hoped the some of these firms will be prosecuted under the *Fraud Act 2006*, as this practices is still widespread.

Can a person tell a lie if it is only a little one? A person may, to oil the wheels of a hire-purchase deal, exaggerate his weekly wage by half, or say he owns a house when he is only the tenant. Is that a crime?   Yes. In theory the law requires the absolute truth and full honesty; but the police are unlikely to prosecute trivial false representations. The examples you give are not trivial. How does your friend differ from a person who makes out he is earning double what he is to obtain a £500,000 mortgage?[80] The falsity is equivalent, the dishonesty is equivalent—the only difference is the value of the property he aims to acquire. At least as far as potential harm is concerned, the latter is a much more serious breach. 34–037

But surely it's all right to use a touch of blarney?   There have been indulgent decisions of both the criminal and civil courts to the effect that mere "puffery" (nebulous commendation) does not amount to a false representation.[81] Advertisers constantly suggest that a particular product will make a person look 10 years younger; they know that people don't believe this, but some may. The law cannot take a strict view of statements that any ordinary person[82] would realize are fanciful. Even the *Trade Descriptions Act 1968*, which quite generally prohibits false trade descriptions, has been held not to be offended against by a statement that particular goods were "extra value."[83] 34–038

Although such misrepresentations of opinion are not noticed by the law, this is so only when the statement is too frothy or too obviously fanciful to be nailed down as fraudulent. The courts are now more ready than they formerly were to hold:

- that a statement can be one of fact even though couched in extravagant and emotive language; and
- that a person who expresses an opinion on a particular matter impliedly states that he does hold that opinion, so that if it is clear that he could not have held it, it will be fraud by false representation.

---

[79] See *Ferguson v. British Gas Trading Ltd.* [2010] 1 W.L.R. 785 at 799 *per* Sedley L.J. discussing the *Protection from Harassment Act 1997*.

[80] See *R. v. Preddy* [1996] A.C. 815.

[81] *Wolkind v. Pura Foods* (1987) 151 J.P. 492; *R. v. Bryan* (1857) 21 J.P. 372. See generally, K.R. Handley *et al.*, *Actionable Misrepresentation*, (London: Butterworths, 2000).

[82] Regulation 5(2) of the *Consumer Protection from Unfair Trading Regulations 2008* refers to the "average" person, and criminalizes "truthful" representations, if the "[o]verall presentation in any way deceives or is likely to deceive the average consumer in relation to any of the matters in paragraph (4), even if the information is *factually correct*."

[83] *Cadbury Ltd. v. Halliday* [1975] 1 W.L.R. 649. See, however, *R. v. Bassett* (1966) 51 Cr. App. R. 28, where it was held that a representation that roof repairs had been done and that £35 was *a reasonable charge* was wholly a statement of fact, apparently because the sum indicated the extent of the repairs claimed to have been done. *Sed quaere*.

An example of "poetic" language being read as a statement of fact: where an unroadworthy car of pleasing appearance was described as a "beautiful car," this was held to be a false trade description because it was likely to be taken as intended to refer to the running of the car and not only its appearance.[84]

34–039 **What if D argues in defence to a fraud by false representation charge, "I did not say it is a diamond, I merely said in my opinion it is a diamond"?** In most cases, the victim will not take the defendant too seriously if he says, "I am not sure if it is a diamond, but I think it might be." If it is a diamond at stake, the victim will most likely demand proof or an expert opinion. Nonetheless, if D falsely represents his *opinion* by claiming that a stone is a diamond when he knows as a matter of fact that it is not, he makes a false representation about a present fact.[85] But not all false opinions incur liability. If D, an art expert, says, "I have examined this painting and have formed the opinion that it is definitely a Caravaggio," but thereafter discovers he was mistaken, he does not commit fraud. He may be negligent,[86] but if he genuinely believed it was a Caravaggio when he made his assessment he made his false representation without being dishonest. His opinion was based on what he really believed.

34–040 **Can D overcharge for a job if, in his opinion, he is worth more than other tradesman?** He can overcharge, but he might be charged with theft or fraud. If he were honest and said: "I am charging you three times what any other tradesman would charge, as I believe I am exceptionally good at what I do," he would not be liable for fraud or theft because he acts "honestly." Nonetheless, he would not have too many customers. In *R. v. Silverman*[87] two elderly spinsters were charged excessive amounts by an electrician. The electrician had been doing jobs for them for 15 years so they believed his excessive fees reflected the market value of the work he did. In fact, he was charging more than three times the market rate for the work. It was held that he made a false representation that the sum charged was a fair and proper charge for the work; and that he did so dishonestly. He knew that the rate he was charging was not close to the market value of such services as a matter of fact, so he could not have formed a genuine opinion that his quotation was fair and reasonable.

34–041 **What if D charges his customers 10 *per cent.* more than the going market rate? Does he have a duty to inform his potential customers that he is charging more than his competitors?** Common sense would suggest not. The *caveat emptor* doctrine has to take precedence in less extreme cases. If the

---

[84] *Robertson v. Dicicco* [1972] R.T.R. 431.

[85] Cf. *The Queen v. Francis* (1872-75) L.R. 2 C.C.R. 128.

[86] V may be able to claim civil damages, however. "[I]n so far as the court is concerned with negligent misrepresentation, the first question is whether [D] exercised due care to see that the opinion which he expressed was reliable. In relation to the more serious allegation of fraud [in civil law], the test is whether [D] in expressing his opinion acted dishonestly, because (i) he knew the representations were untrue, (ii) he had no belief in their truth, or (iii) he made the representations recklessly, careless whether they were true or false." *Cramaso LLP v. Viscount Reidhaven's Trustees* [2010] CSOH 62 at para. 90. See also *Food Co. U.K. LLP (t/a Muffin Break) v. Henry Boot Developments Ltd.* [2010] EWHC 358 (Ch).

[87] (1988) 86 Cr. App. R. 213.

overcharging is excessive, then clearly it would not be harsh to invoke the criminal law. Despite the talk of a relationship of trust in *R. v. Silverman*, under section 2 all that is required is a false representation. In *Lawrence*[88] there weren't any former dealings between Lawrence and the Italian student (Occhi by name), but Lawrence's false representation that the taxi fare was a fair and proper charge for the ride was no less reprehensible than Silverman's representation about the value of his work. If a person charges 10 *per cent.* more than his competitors, or even 20 *per cent.* more, this will not necessarily mean that he is falsely representing that his fees are a fair and proper charge for the work or goods, because such a difference in pricing would surely be within the range of what is reasonable and fair in an open market. If it is a regulated market (*e.g.*, taxi fares are regulated) then it may not be. But in the open market prices do vary between 10 and 20 *per cent.* and much more. This is probably why people shop around.

A tin of shortbread with Harrods stamped on it is going to be much more expensive than one with Marks & Spencer stamped on it: is this marketing or overcharging? When a lady purchases a Hermès Birkin bag for £40,000 plus she probably realizes that it does not cost anywhere near that much to produce. Clearly, there is no false representation made in such cases. It is the norm to charge outrageous sums for designer items and it is the overcharging that provides much of the demand for such products. Nor is the false celebrity hype that is used to market such items misleading, as ordinary people realize it is nonsense. In cases such as *Lawrence*, it would not be difficult to prove that the defendant made a false representation as to the fair and proper fare, because taxi fares are regulated. The overcharging cases are only likely to arise when it is clear that the defendant's overcharging is grossly excessive given the market average, as was the case in *R. v. Silverman*. The real danger will be in borderline cases, because the jury will be left to decide if a particular sharp but dishonest practice is also a dishonest practice that is caught by the *Fraud Act*.[89]

Gain and Loss

The *Fraud Act 2006* criminalizes those who use fraud to make a gain or to cause **34–042** a loss to another or a risk of a loss to another. It has a very wide reach, since it treats attempted fraud no differently from consummated fraud. Hence, a person will be liable for a fraud offence regardless of whether he *succeeds* in making a gain or causing a loss, *etc*. Furthermore, there is no need for the defendant's gain to correspond with the victim's loss. Nor does the defendant have to make a gain or attempt to make a gain. It is enough that he uses fraud to cause a loss to another or expose another to the risk of a loss. For example, if D knows he has a dodgy leg and falsely states on his health insurance application that he has perfect legs, he exposes the insurance firm to a risk of loss. He also gains, because he would be offered a cheaper premium on the basis that he is less likely to require a payout.

---

[88] *Lawrence v. Commissioner of Police of the Metropolis* [1971] A.C. 626.
[89] The defence team could produce evidence of the market to demonstrate that D's representation was reasonable within the given market. See *R. v. Mandry* [1973] 1 W.L.R. 1232.

But there might be cases where a person does not intend to make a gain, but merely intends to cause a loss or risk of loss to another.

Suppose D is upset with V because V had an affair with his girlfriend. V owns a winery and D seeks revenge by spreading a false rumour that V's wines are contaminated with a dangerous pesticide. Let us also assume that D does this with an intent to encourage people to stop purchasing V's wines.[90]

Since D makes his false representation intending to cause V a loss or expose V to a risk of loss,[91] he may be liable for fraud.

34–043   **What if D's rumour has no effect because D has a reputation for lying, and because V wins a prestigious wine award the next day?**   The offence does not require a loss. D would be liable as he *intended* to cause V a loss.

The gain or loss must be of money or other property. If D uses fraud to trick V into having sexual relations with him, he does not make a gain or cause a loss of property. Similarly, if a doctor makes a false representation to induce a person "to accept free medical services"[92] he does not commit fraud because the *Act* only protects property interests. If a person uses fraud to obtain confidential information that does not have any monetary value such as his housemate's nude photos, he does not commit fraud under the *Fraud Act 2006*. Not because confidential information is not property for the purposes of theft,[93] but because he does not take the photographs for the purpose of making a monetary gain or causing a monetary loss.

It does not matter that confidential information is not recognized as property under section 4(1) of the *Theft Act*, because it will be protected by the fraud provisions so long as it has a monetary value. It would be necessary to demonstrate that the defendant obtained the confidential information with an intent to make a financial gain or to cause a financial loss,[94] or risk of loss to another. If D uses fraud to obtain confidential information in order to make a financial gain or to cause a financial loss, he commits fraud. In *D.P.P. v. Withers*[95] the defendants used fraud to obtain confidential information about third parties. In that case, the defendants clearly made a financial gain as they were in the business of collecting such information and made a profit from doing so. This type of conduct would now be caught by section 2.

---

[90] See for example, *The King v. De Berenger* (1814) 3 M. and S. 67; *The King v. Parsons* (1762) 1 Wm. Bl. 392. Professor Turner cites section 4 of 7 & 8 Vict. C. 24, which specifically targeted "spreading false rumours to affect prices." See J. W. Cecil Turner, *Russell on Crime*, (London: Steven & Sons, Vol. II, 1958) at 1689 and the cases cited therein.

[91] For further examples of conduct that exposed others to a risk of loss, see *Mo Yuk Ping v. HKSAR* [2007] 3 H.K.L.R.D. 750; *Wai Yu-Tsang v. The Queen* [1992] 1 A.C. 269; *R. v. Allsop* (1977) 64 Cr. App. R. 29.

[92] Cf. *Bolitho v. Western Australia* (2007) 171 A. Crim. R. 108, where an elderly lady was conned into having medical treatment which she did not want or need. The court held that a similar provision in the Western Australian *Criminal Code* did not cover non-economic interests.

[93] Under section 4(1) of the *Theft Act 1968* the courts have not recognized confidential information, land, wild animals and so on as property, but this limitation does not apply to the *Fraud Act* offences. These items may be protected by the fraud provisions if they have some kind of economic value.

[94] Section 5(2)(a) of the *Fraud Act 2006* provides: "gain and loss ... extend only to gain or loss in money or other property."

[95] [1974] 2 W.L.R. 26.

Nonetheless, there should be some limits. If a person pretends she has been raped or robbed and thereby wastes[96] police time and resources, she causes a loss to the police department. But the indirect loss to taxpayers seems too remote[97] to justify treating her conduct as fraud. The gravamen of such wrongdoing is best dealt with by charging a more specific offence such as perverting the course of justice. In many of these types of cases, the defendants will not have acted with an intent to make a gain or to cause loss to the police department and thus will lack *mens rea*.

If D provides full consideration for the benefit that he *gains* (or loss he has caused), surely he is not guilty of fraud.   The fact that the defendant pays full consideration suggests that the victim has not suffered a pecuniary loss or been exposed to the risk of loss. It also suggests that the defendant has made no pecuniary gain. In some cases, the defendant's fraud will allow him to purchase property that he is legally prohibited from purchasing. D might lie about his age to purchase alcohol or make a false representation by forging a prescription to obtain medicines.[98] Despite the inchoate form of the offences, the *Fraud Act* aims to protect property interests. This raises the issue of whether a "sale" that has been induced by fraud is caught when D gives full consideration for the property he tries to obtain. In pecuniary terms D does not make a net gain when he pays market value for the goods taken. Likewise, in pecuniary terms D does not cause a net loss to another when he pays market value for the goods.

34–044

Suppose D fraudulently adds repeats to his prescription to obtain medication he is not entitled to.[99] Let us assume that he presents the prescription and pays the full price and even leaves a gargantuan tip for the pharmacist.

Does he intend to make a property gain or cause a property loss or risk of property loss to the pharmacist? It appears so. The pharmacist is deceived into handing over property (medicines) for "substitute" property (money), which he would not have done but for D's fraud. The defendant made the false representation with an intent to gain the substitute property—the medicines.[100]

Under the *Fraud Act* there is no need for an actual gain or loss to transpire. All that is required is that D made the false representation with an intent to make a gain or to cause a loss (or to expose another to the risk of loss). Is this what D intends when he forges his repeat prescriptions? Clearly, his false representation

34–045

---

[96] *The King v. Manley* [1933] 1 K.B. 529; *R. v. Cotter* [2003] Q.B. 951.

[97] This type of loss is barely measurable because it is borne collectively by taxpayers. See Dennis J. Baker, "Collective Criminalization and the Constitutional Right to Endanger Others," (2009) 28(2) *Criminal Justice Ethics* 3.

[98] This is an offence *per se*. See the *Forgery and Counterfeiting Act 1981*.

[99] Cf. *Brown v. Deveroux* (2008) 192 A. Crim. R. 190 at 202-203, where D forged her prescriptions to obtain medicines that she was not entitled. It was held under the Western Australian *Criminal Code* that "it is immaterial that the [defrauder] intended to give value for the property obtained or delivered, or the benefit gained, or the detriment caused." See also *Welham v. D.P.P.* [1961] A.C. 103 at 131, where Lord Denning said: "I cannot agree with them on this. If a drug addict forges a doctor's prescription so as to enable him to get drugs from a chemist, he has, I should have thought, an intent to defraud, even though he intends to pay the chemist the full price and no one is a penny the worse off." Cf. *R. v. A* [2010] EWCA Crim. 1949 where D made a false representation in an attempt to trick his wife into having an abortion—there was no financial loss or gain at stake here.

[100] He gets what he did not have: see section 5(3) of the *Fraud Act 2006*.

as to his entitlement to the medicines is made with an intent to gain property which he does not have: the medicines. He might intend to compensate the pharmacist for his loss of property by providing full consideration, but this does alter the fact that the pharmacist no longer has the medicines. Let us tease this out with a further example.

Suppose D, a loyal aficionado of Picasso paintings, attempts to purchase a Picasso from an elderly person, but his offer is rejected because the painting is a family heirloom and V wants to pass it down to a family member.

Would it be fraud for D to pay £3,000,000 for the painting which is worth £2,000,000, if his offer was accepted only because he falsely represented himself as a long lost member of the family? The courts are likely to hold that D intended to make a gain by obtaining the Picasso, because the painting is something he did not already have. The generous payment does not alter this fact. Clearly, D makes a false representation in order to obtain the Picasso. Money is handed over so V is not out of pocket as far as the value of the painting is concerned, but he has lost his rare painting. D's acquisition has resulted in him gaining a rare painting which he did not have before.

34–046   In *R. v. Parkes*[101] D was owed money and used blackmail to force his debtor to pay up. It was held even though he was owed the money he made a gain by acquiring it, because he got cash which was more than he already had. Gain means acquisition whether at a profit or not,[102] and regardless of whether more than adequate pecuniary compensation is provided.

A person might make the false representation to recover what he believes to be a genuine debt or to prevent another from defending what he believes is an unfounded claim. Making a false representation to persuade a debtor not to defend a civil action for the recovery of a debt could constitute a gain for the purposes of the fraud offences. Furthermore, D might have trouble showing he acted honesty, if he was dishonestly trying to prevent V from having the matter determined by an independent adjudicator. The court would have to be satisfied not only that D thought he had a right to use dishonest means to obtain the debt, but also that he believed it was appropriate to use such means to prevent V taking civil action to dispute the debt.[103]

34–047   **What if D only causes V to suffer a temporary property loss?** Section 5(2)(b) of the *Act* covers "any such gain or loss whether temporary or permanent." It means that a person who obtains a hire car by presenting an

---

[101] [1973] Crim. L.R. 358.

[102] *Attorney-General's Reference (No. 1 of 2001)* [2002] 3 All E.R. 840 at 849. A line of older cases make it clear that property was obtained by deception even when consideration of some kind was provided to obtain the property. *R. v. Bennett* (1914) 9 Cr. App. R. 146; *R. v. Potger* (1971) 55 Cr. App. R. 42; *R. v. King* [1987] Q.B. 547. See also *Balcombe v. De Simoni* (1972) 126 C.L.R. 576.

[103] In an Australian case King C.J. expounds: "I think that the intent to deprive a person of the opportunity of having a genuine dispute or a reasonably available defence properly adjudicated upon would be an intent to defraud for the purpose of the offences based upon obtaining money or property by dishonest or forbidden means. An intent by dishonest means to convince the supposed debtor that a defence which the accused believes the debtor to consider to be reasonably available to him, is without merit, and thereby to procure the payment of the claim would be an intent to defraud notwithstanding that the accused might genuinely believe that the defence should not be sustained and that his claim is just." *R. v. Kastratovic* (1985) 42 S.A.S.R. 59 at 65.

invalid driver's licence, intending to return the car at the end of the hiring, can be convicted under sections 1(2)(a) and 2 of the *Act*. He temporarily gains property that he would not otherwise have been able to gain but for his false representation. Similarly, if D abuses a position of trust by borrowing trust money to invest in a backstreet scheme for his own benefit, he would be liable for fraud even if he manages to return the money.[104]

Mens rea

What mental element is required under section 2?   Absent an *intent* to make   **34–048**
a gain or to cause a loss, or risk of loss to another, a false representation *per se* will not be enough to ground a conviction for fraud. In addition, the defendant must make the representation knowing "it is" false or knowing it "might be" false. If a person makes a false representation with an intent to gain or cause a loss, it is necessary to show that he knew as a matter of fact that his representation was false or might be false.

Does this mean that if D's knowledge of the attendant circumstances makes   **34–049**
him "aware" that his representation "might be" false he will come within the
purview of sections 1(2)(a) and 2 of the *Act*?   Yes. The subsection requires
actual knowledge. The subsection provides: "*knows* that it is, or might be, untrue or misleading." How can you "know" something might be untrue? The words "might be" are preceded by the word "know;" therefore, it is not a matter of "might know," but of "must know" that it "might be" false. In other words, the present facts must be sufficient to allow the defendant to know that his representation *is false*, or *might be* false.[105] Anything less would not constitute actual knowledge[106] of that probability—and the section requires actual knowledge of the "is" and/or the "might be."

But it is not possible to know anything for certain is it?   The word "know"   **34–050**
suggests certainty. If D, a man, falsely claims he is a woman, he would know for certain that his representation is false. Similarly, if a motor mechanic tells V that he changed the oil and all the filters when he serviced V's car, from the *ex post* perspective he knows as a matter of fact whether he really did. But it is not always possible to know whether a representation is false for certain. If a person asks an expert jeweller, "Is this really a silver teapot?" The jeweller might form a strong belief that it is by drawing on his expertise in metals and hallmarks, but unless he takes it to his laboratory to test it he would not know for sure. If he tests it he would be able to then say, "I know it is silver," as opposed to, "I believe it might be silver."

---

[104] Cf. *R. v. Fernandes* [1996] 1 Cr. App. R. 175, where the loss was permanent.

[105] This is what "actual knowledge" requires. See the discussion in Chapter 6.

[106] The Lords have held that "knowledge" requires true knowledge of the existing facts. *R. v. Saik* [2007] 1 A.C. 18.

34–051   **But a person cannot "know" whether something is a "probability" or a "might be" can he?**   Well, what about this, if you do not know for sure that something is true, then, you must know that it might be false. D will be caught by the subsection if the present facts are such that D does not know (or believe) that his representation is in fact true, because this means he knows that it could be false. In many cases, D will believe as a matter of certainty that his representation is false and it will turn out that he was right. In some cases he might believe it is false, but it turns out to be true. In the latter situation, he would only be liable for attempted fraud.

34–052   **Are you telling me that subjective recklessness as to the falsity of the representation is sufficient to ground liability?**   The defendant is not held liable for recklessly failing to check the facts, rather he is held liable for making a representation which he knows or believes might be false. It is submitted that "might be" means he would have to know that his representation was "probably" false, as opposed to "possibly" false. A person should not be criminalized for making a representation, merely because he believed there was a remote chance of it being false. Holding a defendant liable for merely being aware of the possibility that his statement is false would extend the tentacles of the subsection too far. If the defendant believes that his statement is probably untrue, then he should not pretend that it is absolutely true. He should provide an appropriate caveat.

34–053   **If a person is asked to evaluate the manuscript "Vortigern and Rowena"[107] to determine whether it is a genuine work of Shakespeare, does he make a false representation by stating his genuine but mistaken belief that it is authentic?**   If unbeknown to the appraiser the manuscript is in fact a fake he has made a false representation without believing it was false, but without knowing for sure that it was true. He could not be said to have *known* his false representation was true merely because he absolutely believed it was true, because all he knew about the truth about was his state of mind (hence, he knew he was telling the truth as he believed it to be, if anyone did). If the assessor mistakenly believes his representation is absolutely true, then he would lack an "awareness" of the fact that it "might be false." Consequently, he could not be said to have known that it might be false; and it does not matter whether a reasonable person would have been aware of its potential falseness. The subsection requires actual knowledge of the probability of falseness. If the assessor is blinded by professional arrogance, then he could not be said to be knowingly making a representation that might be false. All the evidence would allow the jury to infer that the defendant was not aware of the potential falseness of his representation. In any event, D's lack of dishonesty would provide an adequate defence.

If the assessor has a substantial doubt about the absolute truthfulness of his representation, then he would be aware of its probable falseness. He would only make a true representation if he included his doubts in that representation. It is

---

[107] For an interesting account of this great hoax, see W. H. Ireland, *The Confessions of William Henry Ireland*, (London: Printed by Ellerton and Byworth, for T. Goddard, 1805).

difficult to imagine a credible appraiser not making his doubts clear. If he does his representation is true, because he would be stating the truth about his state of mind, "I think it is genuine, but I cannot be absolutely sure." Even if he his guess is wrong, he acted honestly in stating his true belief. Palaeographers, antique dealers, art appraisers and other experts can only make reasonable estimates, such experts know better than anyone that it is almost impossible to have absolute knowledge of the authenticity of antique works.[108]

Can one intend a risk?   Yes, one can intend to take a risk. If D puts a wager on   **34–054**
a horse where the odds are 100 to 1, he intends to risk losing his money. If he gambles with money that he holds on trust, then he must intend to expose another to a risk of loss.[109] Similarly, if D starts a rumour for the sole purpose of causing a rival businessperson to lose some of his customers, *a fortiori* he intends to at least expose V to a risk of loss.

Under section 2, D need only intend to risk V's property interests. It is not necessary to show that he in fact endangered (endangerment is a state of affairs, but might also be labelled as a consequence after V's property interests have in fact been endangered) V's interests—he need only try. You will recall the tax office employee who exposed his employer to a risk of loss by randomly entering a relief code, which had the effect of randomly exempting taxpayers from paying income tax.[110] He may not have intended the consequence of causing an actual loss, but he intended to expose his employer to the risk of loss. Might D argue that he did not intend to risk V's property, but was merely reckless?[111] He might, but since he knew he was entering information that was probably false and that this could cause a loss, the jury are likely to infer that he intended to expose his employer to a risk of loss.

Does that mean that the "oblique intention" doctrine applies? Technically, that doctrine should not be invoked as a substitute for actual intention, unless the statute expressly recognizes oblique intention as a substitute.[112] But if it is not invoked, many fraudsters may be let off the hook. There may be cases where D

---

[108] It was once expounded: "Absolute knowledge can be had of very few things." *Story v. Buffum*, 90 Mass. 35 (1864) at 38 cited in *Attorney Grievance Com'n of Maryland v. Childress*, 364 Md. 48 (2001) at 61. Cited also in Rollin M. Perkins and Ronald N. Boyce, *Criminal Law*, (Mineola, N.Y.: The Foundation Press, 3rd ed., 1982) at 865.

[109]   *R. v. Fernandes* [1996] 1 Cr. App. R. 175.

[110]   *Gilmour v. Director of Public Prosecutions (Cth.)* (1995) 125 F.L.R. 114 at 116.

[111] If D had wrongly entered the relief code for taxpayers who were not entitled to an exemption because he was careless or reckless with his paperwork (for example, if he had a tendency to get all his files mixed up), then we might say, depending on whether his sloppiness was reckless or negligent, that he recklessly or negligently risked his employer's property. But when the risk taking is deliberate and informed, it is intentional risk taking.

[112] The "oblique intention" doctrine was developed by the courts towards the end of the 20th century: see *R. v. Woollin* [1999] 1 A.C. 82 at 96-97. If Parliament had intended such a doctrine to be applied in 21st century offences, then it would have expressly said so. See for example, section 44(2) of the *Serious Crime Act 2007*. When the relevant Bill was introduced, the Parliamentary Under-Secretary of State for Justice said: "The notion of intention is given a particular meaning by subsection (2) ... I hope that it assists the hon. Member for Hornchurch if I say that what we are trying to get at is that intention should be interpreted in a narrow way, and should exclude the concept of *virtual certainty*. It is equivalent to meaning that D's purpose must be to assist or encourage the offence." (Hansard, HC Public Bill Committee, 6th Sitting, 3 July 2007, col.211.)

can only be said to have obliquely intended to expose V to a risk of loss.[113] For example, where D does not intend to expose V to a risk of loss, but foresees the exposure to the risk of loss as an inevitable and inseparable consequence of him investing V's money in a backstreet scheme and so on. As soon as he invests the money he must foresee it is immediately put at risk and therefore D immediately exposes V to a risk of loss. If D foresees that the virtually certain effect of him doing X is that V will be exposed to a risk of loss, he should be liable as he intends to take a risk with V's property. Of course, this means that if he merely foresees the state of affairs (the risk of loss) as a possibility he may lack *mens rea*, even though he has done the conduct. He may foresee the risk as so remote that it cannot really be said that he intended to take it; but this too is intentional risk taking—he intends to take a very low risk. The risk of loss element seems to have been included merely to make the offence a conduct crime.

34–055 **Misleading representations** In most fraud cases such as the *D.P.P. v. Gomez*[114] type case, it will be fairly obvious that a false representation was dishonestly made. Gomez knew as a matter of fact that his representations were false. The first prong of the "knowledge of falsity" test clearly targets such cases. The second prong seems to be aimed at cases where the defendant knows his representation is probably false or misleading, and intentionally subjects an innocent party to the risk of loss for his own gain. But it is not enough to argue that the defendant *ought* to have known his representation was false; or *ought* to have known that it *might* have been false. The defendant "must know" that his representation is false or that it might be false.

To add a further layer of complexity, the subsection also catches knowledge of "misleading" statements. If D deliberately makes a misleading statement by telling a half-truth, it should not be too difficult to determine whether he knew it was misleading. It will be more difficult in complex cases to prove that D knew that his *true* representation might be "misleading."

34–056 **Suppose I am buying a used car and ask the seller whether all the gadgets are working. He replies: "The reserve tank is not operating," craftily failing to mention that the door locks, the automatic windows and the windscreen wipers are not working either.** Where there is no false representation and one cannot be implied, D cannot be guilty of fraud under section 2 unless his true representation is misleading. The jury or magistrates may find fraud if, as here, the defendant uttered a misleading half-truth. Blackburn J. once said, in a civil case:

> "I think it must in every case depend upon the nature of the transaction, whether the fact not disclosed is such that it is impliedly represented not to exist; and that must generally be a question of fact proper for a jury."[115]

---

[113] In some cases the money may be so well invested that there is no risk of loss, but an intention to gain is enough to satisfy sections 1-4 of the *Fraud Act 2006*. See the facts in *Zobory v. Federal Commissioner of Taxation* (1995) 129 A.L.R. 484.

[114] [1993] A.C. 442.

[115] *Lee v. Jones* (1864) 144 E.R. 194 at 244.

Or as Lord Hoffman recently put it: "A 'half truth' which, without disclosure of the other half, is, 'no better than a downright falsehood'"[116] A person's silence may be a tacit acceptance of a proposition put to him during negotiation. For example, V might say to the salesperson, "I am looking for the fastest computer available and have heard that X computer is it." Let us assume that the salesperson nods in agreeance despite the fact that he *knows* that X computer is to be superseded within a week by a much faster model. Let us also assume the salesperson acts as he does because he wants to get rid of old stock. Clearly the salesperson knows that his presently true representation is misleading or at least "might be" misleading. But the criminal law should not be used to target this type of sharp practice. It surely is up to the customer to do some research and shop around. Nonetheless, in less borderline cases a defendant could be caught by section 3 for dishonestly failing to disclose information that he had a legal duty to disclose. As we will see below, many acts will be caught by both section 2 and 3 of the *Fraud Act 2006*.

The case may be somewhat more complex where D has given V very technical information such as a mechanical inspection report on a second-hand Cessna 172 aircraft. In such a case the customer may be mislead as to the exact condition of the aircraft and the potential costs involved in repairing it, even though the engineer did not intend to provide misleading information. If the engineer knew his report might be misleading to the untrained eye, he would not be acting "dishonestly" by presenting the facts in the normal technical manner in which they would be presented by any engineer.

Can the defendant raise a claim of right defence?   The *Fraud Act 2006* does   **34–057** not expressly incorporate a "claim of right" defence. Therefore, claims of right will have to be raised as a part of a general claim of honesty. The general notion of "dishonestly" can be used to negate the *mens rea* element of the given fraud offence. The doctrine of dishonesty as expounded in *R. v. Ghosh*[117] applies in all fraud offences. A person who believes he has a *bona fide* claim of right to make a false representation in order to make a gain or cause a loss to another, *etc.* will be able to argue that he was not dishonest. The rule established by *R. v. Ghosh* incorporates a double test of dishonesty, stated by Lord Lane C.J. in the following words:

- "● A jury must first of all decide whether according to the ordinary standards of decent and honest people what was done was dishonest. If it was not dishonest by those standards, that is the end of the matter and the prosecution fails.
- ● If it was dishonest by those standards, then the jury must consider whether the defendant himself must have realized that what he was doing was by those standards dishonest."[118]

---

[116] *HIH Casualty and General Insurance Ltd. & Ors. v. Chase Manhattan Bank & Ors.* [2003] 1 C.L.C. 358 at 384 *per* Lord Hoffman citing Lord Macnaghten in *Gluckstein v. Barnes* [1900] A.C. 240 at 251. Cf. the facts in *Park's of Hamilton (Holdings) Ltd. v. Campbell* (2009) G.W.D. 1, where D fraudulently and negligently withheld vital information.

[117] [1982] Q.B. 1053.

[118] For a penetrating discussion of *Ghosh* see Kenneth Campbell, "The Test of Dishonesty in *R. v. Ghosh*," (1984) 43 *Cambridge L.J.* 349.

If the answer to the second question is no, the prosecution again fails, otherwise it succeeds on that issue. The decision has one other importance: Lord Lane took the opportunity of affirming that the test of dishonesty is the same for conspiracy to defraud as for theft—a matter that had previously fallen into doubt.[119] It was made clear in the Parliamentary Debates on the *Fraud Bill*[120] that the *Ghosh* test applies to the new fraud offences.

A judge is not always required to give a full *Ghosh* direction, but where a claim of honesty is raised the judge will have to make it clear to the jury that they must acquit if they conclude that the defendant actions were honest.[121] Given that the *Fraud Act* has not incorporated a claim of right provision,[122] judges will have to take care to provide crisp directions to ensure that valid claims of right are properly considered under the *Ghosh* test.[123] Section 2 of the *Theft Act 1968*, giving a partial definition of dishonesty in relation to theft, is not applied to the offence under section 2 of the *Fraud Act*, though a jury would be most unlikely to construe the latter offence more rigorously because they lack the assistance of a claim of right provision. Nonetheless, it would have been preferable to incorporate such a provision in the new legislation, because it would provide firmer guidance in cases involving a clear claim of right.

34–058 **One thing bothers me. I can see that there can be an honest obtaining of property even when dishonest "means" (a false representation) is used to effect the obtaining. How can there be an honest liar?** In fraud cases dishonesty arises at two different levels. Fraud by false representation provides a superlative exemplification of this, because the making of a false representation[124] is by its very nature dishonest. It is an act that is objectively dishonest in

---

[119] See *R. v. McIvor* [1982] 1 W.L.R. 409.

[120] See the Explanatory Notes to the *Fraud Bill* [H.L.] as introduced in the House of Lords on 25 May 2005.

[121] *R. v. McAleer* [2002] EWCA Crim. 1776; *R. v. Woolven* (1983) 77 Cr. App. R. 231.

[122] Cf. section 2 of the *Theft Act 1968*. The Law Commission provided a wholly unconvincing argument for not including a "claim of right" defence in the new *Fraud Act*. Firstly, it argued that as a matter of policy that the law of fraud which protects property rights should not be tied to civil law doctrines outlining property ownership, *etc*. Secondly, it argued that "[a] 'Robin Hood' defendant could seek to exploit legal 'loopholes' in order to redistribute property in a way, not amounting to theft, which she believes to be morally right, but knows most people would consider dishonest. She may argue that she genuinely believed that she had a legal right to act as she did, despite knowing that most reasonable, honest people would categorise her actions as dishonest. If there were a complete 'belief in a claim of right' defence, such a defendant would have to be acquitted. Under the *Ghosh* test, however, it would be for the jury to decide whether her exploitation of legal loopholes [use of the civil law] was in fact dishonest…": Law Commission, Report 276, *Fraud*, (London, H.M.S.O., 2002), at para. 7.69. What did the Law Commission mean by "exploitation of legal loopholes"? Presumably it was referring to D's belief that he had a right to exploit civil law doctrines *vis-à-vis* the rules of property ownership.

[123] In other jurisdictions, the lack of an express provision incorporating a "claim of right" in fraud provisions has not deterred judges from asserting that it exists. See *R. v. Sanders* (1991) 57 S.A.S.R. 102; *R. v. Timperon (No. 2)* (1976) 15 S.A.S.R. 1; *Roberts v. Western Australia* [2005]189 F.L.R. 147 at 155.

[124] The act of taking property is not inherently dishonest. The shoplifter does not tell a lie. He takes property but so does the person who pays. The only dishonesty in such cases relates to D's intention not to pay (that is, to violate another's property rights without justification or excuse), not the means used—the physical carrying away of property.

both the philosophical[125] and legal sense. The false representation is the dishonest *means* that are used to try to acquire another's property. In the second sense, dishonesty refers to the intent which the defendant had for using such dishonest means. In effect, dishonesty works as a defence, because the courts will consider whether the defendant used the dishonest means (false representation) with some further dishonest goal or purpose in mind. This is what the legislation requires, because it provides that the false representation (the dishonest means) must be "dishonestly *made.*"

Therefore the two levels of dishonesty in fraud are:

1.   D made a false representation (*i.e.* used dishonest means to try to obtain property or cause a loss or risk of loss of property to another).
2.   D made the false representation with a dishonest end in mind (*i.e.* the end of making a gain, or causing a loss or risk of loss to another). This end cannot be dishonest if D acted on the belief that he had a right to bring such an end about.

The defendant's dishonest intention must relate to the potential consequences of the prohibited *actus reus*. This means that his intention to gain or cause a loss or risk of loss to another must be dishonest. The consequences need not transpire as it is a conduct crime, but they must be intended. It is not simply a question of whether the defendant intentionally committed the prohibited conduct (made a false representation), but whether he did so with an intent to bring about the consequences proscribed by sections 1(2)(a) and 2 of the *Act* believing he had no right to do so.

Are you telling me that if D makes a false representation (uses dishonest   **34–059**
means) with the honest intent of obtaining stolen property from a thief so
that he can return it to its true owner[126] he does not act dishonestly?   Yes,[127]
D makes the false representation intending to achieve an honest end rather than the dishonest end of defrauding a rightful owner. In other words, the dishonest representation was honestly made, because it was not made with an intent to dishonestly make a gain or cause a loss or risk of loss to another.

Dishonestly relates to D's motive. For example, "a 'sting' operation involving an agreement by two or more persons to use dishonest means to obtain property which they believe they are legally entitled to take is not a conspiracy to defraud."[128] Put another way, a defendant will have the *mens rea* for fraud by false representation if his representation was made to allow him to make a gain

---

[125] See generally, Samuel W. Buell, "Novel Criminal Fraud" (2006) 81 *N.Y.U. L. Rev.* 1971; Stuart P. Green, "Lying, Misleading, and Falsely Denying: How Moral Concepts Inform The Law of Perjury, Fraud, and False Statements," (2001) 53 *Hastings L.J.* 157.

[126] The example might be better if D was using fraud to get his own property back, but there is authority to suggest that D can rely on D2's claim of right to negative dishonesty. See *R. v. Williams (No. 3)* [1962] Crim. L.R. 111; *R. v. Sanders* (1991) 57 S.A.S.R. 102. However, D would probably find it difficult to prove that he believed he had a claim of right to property belonging to V2 on the basis that V2 owed money to V1, and V1 owed money to D money. Cf. *R. v. Williams* (1836) 173 E.R. 158.

[127] *Peters v. The Queen* (1998) 192 C.L.R. 493 at 504.

[128] *Peters v. The Queen* (1998) 192 C.L.R. 493 at 508-509.

that he believed[129] he was not entitled to make or to cause a loss that he believed he was not entitled to cause, *etc.*, and he was conscious[130] of the fact that in so acting he was acting dishonestly according to the standards of ordinary people.

This approach enables a jury to find that although the defendant was dishonest in the sense that he made a false representation, he was not dishonest in obtaining (or attempting to obtain) the property, because he either was entitled to the property or thought he was. This means that it would be a misdirection for a judge to tell the jury to consider whether the defendant believed he had a right to obtain the property by fraud. The words "by fraud" must be omitted.[131] Even a lawyer who knows the general law should not be guilty under section 2 of the *Act* if he obtains or attempts to obtain property to which he believes he is entitled. However in conspiracy to defraud cases, the "dishonest means" (such as false representation) are not set out as the *actus reus* of the offence; therefore, any means that are used, even if not objectively dishonest, might be sufficient to ground a conviction if the jury decide the end aimed for was dishonest.

34–060   **Does a person act dishonestly if he intends to repay the money obtained by fraud?**   Yes. The defendant's intention to pay for the property he gains by making a false representation, and indeed his actual payment for it, does not necessarily negative dishonesty.[132] Where for example, a person obtains goods on an invalid cheque, intending to pay for them later knowing that he will be able to do so, it would be quite wrong if he were regarded as honest. Since *R. v. Ghosh*, the question would have to be left to the jury, but it would be far better if the courts held that on such facts there is no evidence on which a reasonable jury can find honesty.

Again, a person who by false representation obtains an advance of money to which he knows he is not entitled can be convicted under section 2 of the *Fraud Act* even thought he intends to repay. In the pre-Act case, *Halstead v. Patel*,[133] the holder of a Post Office Giro account (Patel) drew a cheque on it in return for cash received at the Post Office counter, knowing that the account was not in funds and that he was not allowed to draw on it. It was held that if Patel had intended to put funds into the account before the cheque was presented, this intention might negative dishonesty; but since his intention was to get the money and only later repay by paying into the account, he was guilty of obtaining by deception, notwithstanding that he would have had no difficulty later on in putting the account into credit.

The case illustrates the fact that an intention to make a delayed recompense may not negative dishonesty, where immediate recompense (in this case, by

---

[129] *R. v. McAleer* [2002] EWCA Crim. 1776; *R. v. Falconer-Atlee* (1974) 58 Cr. App. R. 348.

[130] In Canada the subjective prong is not applied in fraud cases. Therefore, it is irrelevant whether or not the defendant appreciated that his conduct was dishonest according to the standards of reasonable people. See *R. v. Théroux* [1993] 2 S.C.R. 5.

[131] See *R. v. Salvo* [1980] V.R. 401.

[132] See *R. v. Kritz* [1950] 1 K.B. 82 at 87.

[133] [1972] 1 W.L.R. 661. The court required the defendant's belief that he could meet the cheque to be "based on reasonable grounds," but this was corrected in *R. v. Lewis* (1976) 62 Cr. App. R. 206. Reasonableness has nothing to do with dishonesty, except to the usual extent that absence of reasonable grounds is evidence of non-belief.

putting a credit into the account) is required. Section 5(2)(b) of the *Fraud Act* provides: "gain or loss ... include any such gain or loss whether temporary or permanent." The evidential burden of honestly is on the defendant, and in some cases the defendant might raise evidence to support a claim that he genuinely believed he had a right to borrow the property or money. If the claim is supported with strong evidence the prosecution might have difficulty in rebutting it.

But you said that the dishonesty of the representation does not matter if the obtaining was honest. Patel was honest in respect of the obtaining, because he intended to repay. Patel had no claim of right. He knew he was breaking the rules. Clearly, a person cannot help himself to an overdraft or to a temporary line of credit, when he has no right to do so.   34–061

It isn't a question of claim of right. It is a question of honesty. Yes: the C.L.R.C. did not expect the new word to be interpreted more laxly than the old phrase. *Halstead v. Patel* came before magistrates, who do as they are told by a Divisional Court; and that court was clear that Patel had acted dishonestly. A Divisional Court would doubtless take the same view at the present day. If on the other hand the case had come before a jury, the jury would presumably have been given free rein. Before the *Theft Act 1968* the law was clear that an intention to repay money improperly taken did not generally give a claim of right. Persons were convicted of obtaining property by false pretences when they had obtained advances by deliberately overstating the value of their business, notwithstanding that they genuinely believed that the investors would not lose their money;[134] and this is socially right. A person who uses a false representation to expose another to a risk of loss would need to do more than claim he acted honestly because of a sanguine belief he would be able to return the money. The latter would not be sufficient evidence of honesty. His conduct would most likely be held to be dishonest when viewed against the "ordinary standards of honest and decent people."[135] Many frauds are perpetrated by people who put other people's property at risk.   34–062

34.3. FRAUD BY FAILING TO DISCLOSE INFORMATION

Section 3 of the *Fraud Act 2006* provides: 34–063
  A person is in breach of this section if he–

"(a) dishonestly fails to disclose to another person information which he is under a legal duty to disclose, and
(b) intends, by failing to disclose the information–
    (i) to make a gain for himself or another, or
    (ii) to cause loss to another or to expose another to a risk of loss."

What conduct element is required under section 3? The *actus reus* is satisfied if D fails to disclose information and he has a legal duty to do so. Where   34–064

---

[134] *R. v. Hamilton* (1845) 1 Cox C.C. 244; *R. v. Carpenter* (1911) 22 Cox. C.C. 618.
[135] Cf. *R. v. Fernandes* [1996] 1 Cr. App. R. 175, where the defendant "abused his position" as a solicitor to expose another to a risk of loss. Unfortunately for the victim, the loss eventuated.

there is no false representation and one cannot be implied, the general rule is that mere silence cannot amount to fraud. This is a historic principle not only of the criminal law but of the civil law.[136] Fraud involves something more than D simply failing to reveal the truth. Various civil remedies are available independently of fraud, but silence does constitute an act of fraud unless there is a legal duty to disclose. The line between silence and active fraud is more difficult to draw than may at first appear, particularly because the silence rule does not apply if a false representation can be genuinely implied, as in the instances given above. But the question arises whether there can be fraud without any false representation express or implied; and without any legal duty to disclose.

Consider a case where a customer in a shop sees an article bearing a price-tag so low that he believes there has been a mistake. He asks for the article and buys it at the marked price. Obviously, by buying it he does not impliedly represent that no mistake has been made as to the price, nor even that he knows of no mistake as to the price. Nor has he done anything positive to induce the seller's mistake. He merely presents the shop's own false representation to it. So he is not guilty of fraud under section 2 of the *Act*. (The case would be different if the shopper himself had been responsible for changing the price-tag, because he would then be making the false representation.)[137]

34–065   **Might your shopper be caught by section 1(2)(b) and 3 for failing to disclose the shopkeeper's mistake to the shopkeeper?**   No. The distinction between mere silence and actively making a misleading or false representation as to the value of the goods is the foundation of this part of the law, and the courts ought to maintain it strictly, even when they are tempted to depart from it to convict a rogue. If there are to be any "constructive false representations," or any moral duties of candour imposed by the criminal law, this should be done expressly by legislation stating when disclosure is required. Parliament chose to criminalize only those who fail to disclose when they have a legal duty to disclose. Shoppers might have a moral duty to disclose an obvious mistake, but they do not have a legal duty to report pricing errors to shopkeepers. Consequently, section 3 would not apply here. Nor do sections 1(2)(a) and 2 catch the shopper, because he did not change the price-tags. The tendering of the article to the cashier bearing the mistaken price marking is not a false representation made by the customer.[138] In

---

[136] *Smith v. Hughes* (1871) 19 W.R. 1059; *Statoil ASA v. Louis Dreyfus Energy Services LP* [2009] 1 All E.R. 1035. However, in some jurisdictions, a "legal duty" to disclose has long been recognized as sufficient for grounding a fraud conviction. Cf. *People v. Jory*, 443 Mich. 403 (1993); *People v. Johnson*, 150 N.Y.S. 331 (1914).

[137] The same would apply if his accomplice changed the price-tag. If D deliberately presents the false representation made on the price-tag by his accomplice to the cashier, he would be caught by section 2. However, it should not be enough that he makes use of an opportunity provided by the misdeed of another. If a customer in a supermarket sees a small boy changing price labels, and he then takes advantage of this by himself buying the article that he knows is less than its proper price, he should not be convicted of fraud by false representation, because he has not made the representation, either himself or through an accomplice. It would be very forced to find an implied representation by the customer that he knew that no one had altered the label.

[138] *Per curiam* in *Kaur v. Chief Constable of Hampshire* [1981] 1 W.L.R. 578 at 583D.

essence it is merely a failure by the customer to disclose his knowledge of the seller's own false representation, which the seller makes to the world at large.

Despite the wide reach of the implied representation doctrine, some cases will not be caught by it or by the duty of disclosure provision. It was noted before, that in some situations a person will have a duty to speak up if something takes place which makes his initial true representation false. In the case of *R. v. Rai*,[139] D made a true representation to his local council that he had an elderly mother who was entitled to a taxpayer funded bathroom. The council approved his application for a free bathroom but his mother passed away in the meantime. The council provided D with the bathroom because it continued to believe that his mother was alive and in need of the bathroom. This was not a case of pure omission, because D had actively made the initial true representation. Therefore, his silence implied that his initial true representation continued to be true. Since the shopper did not make an initial representation, he could not falsify a representation he never made by remaining silent.

34–066

A card-sharper keeps an ace up his sleeve, or a gambler throws with a loaded dice. Does he get winnings by fraud? One would think so; yet it is artificial to say that a player impliedly represents that he does not keep aces up his sleeve or has not got a loaded dice. But his very act of playing with others surely implies that he will not cheat? If not, no one would bother to play with him. What about bookmakers who "fix" a race by bribing the jockey riding the favourite not to win, or by doping his horse? With more subtle guile, a racehorse owner may enter an inferior runner, bet heavily on him, and then secretly switch for a much faster horse. Or he may dope the favourite to improve the chances of his own animal. It would impose an impossible strain upon the theory of representation to find implied representations in cases of this kind. Nor do these types have a general legal duty to disclose their dishonesty. These particular malpractices could be dealt with as offences under section 42 of the *Gaming Act 2005*, which is a comprehensive provision covering all cheating practices in relation to gambling. Where two or more persons are involved they are charged as conspiracies to defraud.

But the general question is capable of arising outside the limits of these offences. In more straightforward cases, the silence will be combined with positive acts which are clearly intended to present a false picture, as in the hilarious Irish case of *Gill v. McDowell*,[140] where the defendant sent to market a bullock, a heifer, and a hermaphrodite, dextrously revolving them so that the buyer thought they were all one-sexed (though he was unable to say in court whether he thought he was buying two bullocks and a heifer or two heifers and a bullock, so great was his confusion at the time). This type of case would be caught by section 3 (as there is a duty to disclose). V may be able to sue in damages if the cattle were to be sold to him as three bollocks, because D would most likely be under a contractual duty to disclose the sex of the animals. Given that D has by his conduct made a false representation about the sex of the animals, it would be better for the prosecution to charge him with fraud under

---

[139] (2000) 1 Cr. App. R. 242.
[140] [1903] 2 I.R. 463.

sections 1(2)(a) and 2, because this section does not require the courts to identify the source of the "legal duty" to disclose.

34–067 A historical note may help to elucidate this point. Formerly, the law of obtaining by false pretences[141] presupposed a representation, at least in theory. There was also an offence of being a common cheat (not necessarily involving a representation), which was almost entirely abolished by section 15(1) of the *Theft Act 1968*. Section 15(1) of the *Theft Act* has since been repealed by the *Fraud Act 2006*. The former offence merely required a deception. It did not say that the deception had to take the form of a representation, express or implied. It is clear that the intention of the *Theft Act* offence was that deception should implant a false belief in the victim's mind; and if this was achieved it made no difference whether it was produced by means of false representation or by what may generically be called a trick—provided in either case, that the defendant committed a positive act of deception and was not merely guilty of a failure to inform. In the above cases, deception is the trick the seller, player or gambler uses. It is not a mere omission, but a positive act to defraud. But unless these types of positive acts of trickery can also be properly conceptualized as false representations, they will not come within the purview of section 2 of the *Fraud Act*. Furthermore, if a legal duty of disclosure cannot be identified such cases will also fall outside the purview of section 3.

34–068 **When does a legal duty to disclose arise?** As we have seen, the courts have sometimes construed the law of theft so widely that a person who acquires money or other property by dishonestly failing to disclose something may possibly be guilty of theft even though the nondisclosure does not affect the validity of the transaction and he obtains a perfectly valid title[142] to the money or other property. In this respect, the courts have failed to introduce any limits into the law of theft. Properly considered, sections 1(2)(b) and 3 of the *Fraud Act* do not give a large extension to liability for fraud, because it only applies where there is a legal duty to disclose the relevant information. However, many civil law wrongs may now be brought within the purview of the criminal law. Most of the "legal duties" to disclose will be found in the civil law. Some cases will involve a criminal law duty to disclose, but breaching this type of duty would normally be an offence in

---

[141] *Rogers v. People*, 161 Colo. 317 (1966); *Stumpff v. People*, 51 Colo. 202 (1911); *Griffith v. State*, 3 Ga. App. 476 (1908). Cf. *People v. Jory*, 443 Mich. 403, 416 (1993), where D was convicted by a jury of obtaining money by false pretences, in part on the basis of his "failure to disclose the existence of a mortgage" on property he sold on a land contract. The court noted: "The concealment of a fact which one is bound to disclose is an indirect representation that such fact does not exist, and constitutes fraud:" citing *Groening v. Opsata*, 323 Mich. 73, 84 (1948). See also *United States Fidelity & Guaranty Co. v. Black*, 412 Mich. 99, 124-128 (1981); *McMullen v. Joldersma*, 174 Mich. App. 207 (1988). *State v. West*, 252 N.W.2d 457 (Iowa, 1977).

[142] The House of Lords thought Mrs. Hinks had obtained an indefeasible title to Dolphin's money. *R. v. Hinks* [2001] 2 A.C. 241. (As noted above, it is more likely she obtained a voidable title as she arguably engaged in undue influence).

itself.[143] It would not be necessary or appropriate to invoke section 3 where the non-disclosure is dealt with in more specific offences.

A legal duty of disclosure might be grounded on the following doctrines:[144]

- The fiduciary duty (*e.g.*, trustee and beneficiary; agent and principal; solicitor and client; employer and employee, *etc.*).[145]
- The duty of utmost good faith, *uberrima fides*, (*i.e.* the duty to make appropriate disclosures in insurance contracts, *etc.*).[146]
- Duties found in the express or implied terms of a contract.
- Statutory duties such as those imposed on companies with respect to prospectuses.[147]
- Failures to disclose that are legally actionable.[148] (That is, where the failure to disclose would give V a right to sue for damages or have the transaction rescinded, *etc.*).[149]

The courts have been reluctant to consider civil law concepts in the law of theft, but it appears they will have no choice as far as the fraud offences are concerned. The starting point will be for the courts to identify the source of the legal duty. Whether or not a legal duty has been breached is a question of fact for the jury. Some of the legal duties will be found in tort law, but the bulk of them

---

[143] For example, dishonestly failing to give a prompt notification of a change in one's circumstances for the purpose of obtaining benefits is an offence in itself which can result in a maximum sentence of seven years. See section 111A of the *Social Security Administration Act 1992*. See also *R. v. Lancaster* [2010] EWCA Crim. 370.

[144] See generally, Law Commission, Report 276, *Fraud*, (London, H.M.S.O., 2002) at 64.

[145] See *Imageview Management Ltd. v. Jack* [2009] Bus. L.R. 1034, where D breached a fiduciary duty by failing to "disclose" a secret commission.

[146] See *HIH Casualty & General Insurance Ltd. v. Chase Manhattan Bank* [2003] 1 C.L.C. 358, where it was held that an insurance contract of utmost good faith requires D to disclose any circumstance found as a fact to be material pursuant to section 18(4) of the *Marine Insurance Act 1906*. "If the non-disclosure or misrepresentation were other than innocent, the insurer might have rights additional to that of avoidance: the right to damages given by section 2(1) of the *Misrepresentation Act 1967* to the victim of a negligent misrepresentation; and the right to recover damages for deceit given by the common law to the victim of a fraudulent misrepresentation."

[147] The prospectus might state the risk involved in investing in the business and so on. See generally, the *Financial Services and Markets Act 2000*. There may also be more general duties on the directors to disclose whether they have a pending personal bankruptcy proceeding, *etc.* See also section 119 of the *Companies Act 2006*, which deals with offences in connection with request for or disclosure of information.

[148] A discussion of all the possibilities is not possible here. For those seeking a more detailed overview of the civil law in this area, see John Cartwright, *Misrepresentation, Mistake and Non-Disclosure*, (London: Sweet & Maxwell, 2nd edn. 2006).

[149] "Fraud in [civil law] enables the victim of the fraud to decline to proceed with a contract into which, by reason of the fraudulent misrepresentation, he was induced to enter, and he has a claim for damages for any loss he may suffer." *Shogun Finance Ltd. v. Hudson* [2004] 1 A.C. 919 at 931 *per* Lord Nicholls. If the contract is a nullity because D has lied about his real identity, then D would be caught by section 2 of the *Fraud Act 2006*. But his failure to disclose his real identity would also bring him within section 3 if he had a legal obligation to disclose his identity, or if his failure to disclose allows V to sue for damages. Cf. *Ainscough v. O'Shaughnessey*, 346 Mich. 307, 316 (1956), where it was held that where the "circumstances surrounding a particular transaction are such as to require the giving of information, a deliberate and intentional failure to do so may properly be regarded as fraudulent in character."

will be grounded on the "fiduciary" doctrine and contact law doctrines. For instance, in *R. v. Firth*[150] a consultant gynaecologist evaded a liability by avoiding being billed for N.H.S. hospital services by failing to inform the hospital of the private status of patients. Since the surgeon had a specific contractual obligation to disclose the status of his patients and he failed to do so, his mere silence would be caught by section 3. Furthermore, the continuing representations of the kind made in *R. v. Rai*,[151] would also be caught by section 3, if they are made as a part of contractual negotiations:

> "It is well settled that a representation made in the course of [contractual] negotiations may be treated as a continuing representation. The authoritative source of the principle in modern times is *With v. O'Flanagan* [1936] Ch. 575. In that case negotiations were entered into for the sale of a medical practice, and the vendor then represented to the purchasers that the takings of the practice were at the rate of £2000 *per annum*. The contract was signed some months later but by that date the circumstances had changed, as the practice had fallen off owing to the illness of the vendor. The change of circumstances was not disclosed to the purchasers, and when they took possession on that date they found that the practice was almost non-existent. The Court of Appeal held that the representation about the takings of the practice was a continuing representation. Since the purchaser had not been told of the change in takings before the contract was entered into, he was not bound by the contract. Lord Wright MR expressed his conclusion thus: 'I think that the change in circumstances ought to have been communicated to the plaintiffs before they were allowed to close the transaction.'"[152]

34–069   This may seem to be a massive extension of the criminal law, but it is clearly appropriate to bring some of these types within the scope of the criminal law. If we jail the hungry shoplifter for stealing bread, then we should also jail those who fleece others by dishonestly concealing facts to profit at another's expense. Take the rogue real estate agent who sells a house to a young couple without disclosing that the house is about to fall down as it is infested by termites.[153] Is this business or pure fraud? Suppose an employee who is on sick leave and is receiving workers compensation from his employer is found to be no longer disabled and working at a new job. Is it not fraud for him to receive payments from his former employer for what is now a non-existent disability, given that he has recovered and is earning a living elsewhere? There is nothing unfair about imposing criminal liability on these types.

Nonetheless, it will be difficult to reconcile borderline cases with the cardinal requirement of fair warning. People need to know in advance what is or is not criminal. Many rogues will not only be liable for civil law damages, but will now also risk being convicted of a serious criminal offence. What seems little more than sharp practice, may now constitute a serious criminal offence. For example in *Fitzroy Robinson Ltd. v. Mentmore Towers Ltd.*,[154]a firm of architects was found guilty of fraudulent misrepresentation because they failed to inform a client that, shortly before entering a contract, the project leader for that contract had

---

[150] (1990) 91 Cr. App. R. 217.

[151] (2000) 1 Cr. App. R. 242.

[152] *Food Co. U.K. LLP (t/a Muffin Break) v. Henry Boot Developments Ltd.* [2010] EWHC 358 (Ch) at para. 208.

[153] See *Sullivan v. Ulrich*, 40 N.W.2d 126 (1949).

[154] [2009] B.L.R. 505.

resigned. Since the partners of the firm intended to make a gain by failing to disclose material information, their actions would now be caught by sections 1(2)(b) and 3 of the *Fraud Act*.

What mental element is required under section 3? Like section 2, section 3 **34–070** merely requires D to intend, by failing to disclose the information, to make a gain for himself or another or cause loss to another or to expose another to a risk of loss. It is a conduct crime: no result (gain or loss) need transpire. D must, however, dishonestly intend to bring the result about. Therefore, D will have a defence if he is able to satisfy the evidential burden of honesty, and if the prosecution is unable to satisfy the persuasive burden to the contrary.

Suppose D is selling a filling station that is on a busy road and is turning over **34–071** **£2,000,000 *per annum*. Suppose also that D does not disclose to purchasers a pending plan to construct a highway bypass which would substantially divert all traffic away from filling station. Is he liable under section 3?** In the standard case, D would surely have a duty to disclose and thus would most likely come within the purview of section 3. However, the civil courts might hold that the vender is not guilty of an actionable fraud for failing to disclose the bypass plan if the Government's bypass plan was on the public record, and the purchasers employed a certified solicitor to investigate those facts, and at the time of purchase, the bypass was little more than a possibility contingent upon the Government approving funding.[155] (Furthermore, if the sale price had been reduced to reflect such a potentiality, this would be further evidence of honesty). In these circumstances, a jury in a criminal hearing might take the view that D was not dishonest.

34.4. FRAUD BY ABUSE OF POSITION

Section 4 of the *Fraud Act 2006* holds: **34–072**

"(1) A person is in breach of this section if he–
    (a) occupies a position in which he is expected to safeguard, or not to act against, the financial interests of another person,
    (b) dishonestly abuses that position, and
    (c) intends, by means of the abuse of that position– (i) to make a gain for himself or another, or (ii) to cause loss to another or to expose another to a risk of loss.
(2) A person may be regarded as having abused his position even though his conduct consisted of an omission rather than an act."

What is the conduct element for section 4? This offence can be committed **34–073** only by those who are deemed to be in a position where they are expected to safeguard the financial interests of the victim; and where their position empowers them to take "more than normal" advantage of the potential victim. When one examines the wording of the new offence, the old embezzlement type offences spring to mind. A person does not have to make a false representation to

---

[155] On almost identical facts in a U.S. case, *McMullen v. Joldersma*, 435 N.W.2d 428 (1988), the court held there was no legal duty to disclose.

embezzle his employer's funds. Nonetheless, he might commit fraud contrary to sections 1 and 4 of the *Act* if he takes advantage of a position which gives him an edge over the average fraudster. The essence of wrong is that the defendant takes advantage of a person who has put him in a "privileged position, by virtue of which he is expected to safeguard [that person's] financial interests."[156] The position need not be a formal legal position, such as fiduciary. If a family member or close friend has been trusted with an infirm person's debit card and PIN code, then he has been put in a "privileged position" and is expected not to abuse his position of trust.

To determine exactly which "positions" are covered, one has to carefully consider whether or not the defendant was entrusted to safeguard the victim's financial interests. Certain types of defendants will axiomatically come within the purview of the section because of their special relationship with the victim (for example, those who are in a fiduciary relationship with the victim such as solicitors, trustees, principals, accountants, company directors, and so on).

It is not clear how far this offence will reach. Did Mrs. Hinks[157] abuse a position of trust? Does it matter that Mr. Dolphin withdrew his own money and gave it to her? He knew the money was disappearing as he was giving it away, but the evidence suggested that he did not understand the nature of his gifts. Notwithstanding this, it is not clear that Mrs. Hinks occupied a special position of trust. Was she different to any other acquaintance? She was never put in a position where she was required to safeguard Mr. Dolphin's financial interests. In addition, her duty "not to act against" his financial interests was no different than the general duty that members of society owe each other? We all have a duty not to unjustifiably or inexcusably act against the financial interests of others. Would not a stranger also be expected not to act against the financial interests of a vulnerable person whom he has just met? It might be argued she abused a position of trust, because she was his friend, knew he was of low intelligence and knew that he did not understand that he was giving away most of his liquid assets. It might be said he was a mindless instrument and that she good as withdrew the money herself, but the evidence showed otherwise.

34–074   **But the subsection does not expressly limit itself to such cases.** The defendant must be in a "position" which requires him either to "safeguard" the victim's financial interests *or* "not to act against" them. The *not to act against* requirement is all-encompassing to say the least, because all thieves and fraudsters are expected not to unjustifiably and inexcusably act against the financial interests of others. Similarly, all employees are expected not to act against the financial interests of their employers', but do not necessarily engage in fraud by thieving. A shop assistant who takes goods from his place of employment acts against his employer's financial interests, because his position requires him to safeguard the storeowner's interests. A shoplifter might have a general duty not to act against the interests of the storeowner, but he does not have a duty to safeguard the storeowner's financial interests.

---

[156] *Cavell USA Inc & Anor v. Seaton Insurance Co. & Anor* [2009] 2 C.L.C. 991 at 1002-1003.

[157] *R. v. Hinks* [2001] 2 A.C. 241.

In these types of cases it would normally be possible to charge D with theft under the *Theft Act 1968*[158] or with fraud under section 2 of the *Act*. Similarly, when a nurse, a family member, a friend or a carer takes a mentally incapacitated person's debit card and PIN code and uses it for his own benefit, he would make a false representation to a machine or bank teller by claiming he has authority to use the card and is entitled to the funds that he withdraws. Beyond situations involving the *R. v. Preddy*[159] problem, or the secret profit problem,[160] and possibly certain situations where a non-fiduciary takes a bribe,[161] section 4 of the *Fraud Act* has little scope.

Are you telling me that the subsection only criminalizes those who abuse a special position of trust?   The shopkeeper allows people to enter his store because he trusts that they will not steal his goods, but he does not trust customers in the same way that he trusts his cashier, bookkeeper, or his accountant and solicitor. The Law Commission proposed this offence with a particular relationship of trust in mind. Its report provides:

34–075

> "The essence of the kind of relationship which in our view should be a prerequisite of this form of the offence is that the victim voluntarily put the defendant in a privileged position, by virtue of which the defendant is expected to safeguard the victim's financial interests or given power to damage those interests. ...[This] might arise, for example, because the defendant is given authority to exercise a discretion on the victim's behalf, or is given access to the victim's assets, premises, equipment or customers. ... In nearly all cases where it arises, it will be recognised by civil law as importing fiduciary duties."[162]

The most straightforward cases will be those where the defendant has breached a recognized fiduciary duty with an intent to make a gain or cause a loss. In *R. v. Fernandes*,[163] the defendant clearly abused his position as a solicitor by taking funds from his clients' account so that he could invest in a risky investment scheme for his own benefit. Fernandes had invested his clients' money in high risk schemes and had made a secret profit from doing so on many occasions. However, on this occasion he lost all the money. Even though he only intended to borrow the money temporarily he would be caught by sections 1(2)(c) and 4 of the *Act of 2006*, because he abused his position as a solicitor with an intent to gain. He might not have made a false representation, but he clearly committed fraud by taking advantage of a position of trust. Similarly, if a senior employee uses his position within a bank to transfer money from genuine

---

[158] See *R. v. Molcher* [2007] 1 Cr. App. R. 48, where D, a postman, stole letters containing pin codes and credit cards.

[159] [1996] A.C. 815. It is difficult to imagine the *Preddy* problem arising in the absence of D making a false representation.

[160] It was argued in the chapter on theft that those who make a "secret profit" by abusing a position of trust probably commit theft contrary to section 5(1),(3) of the *Theft Act 1968*. If such an argument is not accepted, as was the case in *Attorney-General's Reference (No.1 of 1985)* [1986] Q.B. 491, then, section 4 of the *Fraud Act 2006* could apply.

[161] See *R. v. Gayle* [2008] EWCA Crim. 1344. If the bribe is held on trust, then it will be caught by section 5(1) of the *Theft Act 1968*. See *Attorney-General of Hong Kong v. Reid Privy Council* [1994] 1 A.C. 324.

[162] Law Commission Report 276, *Fraud*, (London, H.M.S.O., 2002) at paragraphs 7.37-7.38.

[163] [1996] 1 Cr. App. R. 175. See also *R. v. Miles* [2007] 2 Cr. App. R. 5; *Zobory v. Federal Commissioner of Taxation* (1995) 129 A.L.R. 484.

customer accounts into accounts held by him he would commit fraud contrary to section 4.[164] He is expected to act in the bank's financial interests, because he has been hired by the bank to do so.

In *R. v. Butt*,[165] D abused a position of "trust" as the compliance officer of an investment bank, because he engaged in insider dealing contrary to section 52(1) the *Criminal Justice Act 1993*. D worked for an investment bank in a position which gave him privileged access to highly confidential inside information about the status and performance of companies which the bank was advising. He abused this position for his own personal gain and made a profit of £237,000. The bank clearly has a direct duty to those who entrust it with confidential information, trade secrets and so on. D as its employee had been put in a position where he was expected to safeguard the financial interests of the bank's clients. Section 4 merely requires D to abuse his position of trust to make a gain or cause a loss or risk of loss to another person. There would be no need to show either the bank or its client lost money, since D clearly intended to make a gain. (Of course, it would be best to rely on the insider trading provision, where possible, rather than section 4).

34–076　In other cases, the fraud will affect the financial interests of a company such as where a company director uses his position on the board of the company to make a personal gain. In *Spies v. The Queen*[166] D abused his position as a company director of Sterling Nicholas Pty. Ltd. "to gain directly an advantage for himself by causing it to purchase his shares in Holdings Pty. Ltd. for $500,000 which he caused to be credited to his account." He used his position with the company to get a resolution of the directors made which resolved that it should acquire all the issued shares in Holdings for $500,000. The latter company of course was bankrupt and its shares were worthless.

If a person memorizes a trade list or important aspects of a trade secret and uses it a year later whilst working in a new position, he would not be caught by section 4 unless he used his original position to obtain the information and did so with an intent to use it in some later fraud.

34–077　**There must be an abuse of trust.**　Suppose a cleaner in a nursing home finds mentally incapacitated V's debit card and PIN code (the latter is written on a bit of paper) under V's pillow.

If the cleaner takes the card and memorizes the PIN code and misuses them so that she might steal V's chose in action, she should be liable for theft. She does not commit an offence under section 4 of the *Fraud Act 2006*, because she has not been entrusted with the card or PIN code. Likewise, if D is visiting her elderly aunt in the nursing home and finds a debit card and PIN code belonging to V (another patient in the home), and misuses it, she could not be said to have taken advantage of a privileged position. V is a stranger to D and D's discovery of the card and PIN code was merely coincidental to her visiting the nursing home.

---

[164] Cf. *Attorney-General's Reference (No.86 of 2003)* [2004] 2 Cr. App. R. 79.

[165] [2006] 2 Cr. App. R. 44.

[166] *Spies v. The Queen* (2000) 201 C.L.R. 603. For further examples, see *Durovic v. The Queen* (1994) 71 A. Crim. R. 33; *Macleod v. The Queen* (2003) 214 C.L.R. 230; *Tarling v. Singapore* (1980) 70 Cr. App. R. 77.

Does section 4 catch only fiduciaries? No. Both the Law Commission and **34–078** Parliament took the view that it should apply to positions analogous to that of a fiduciary. The Explanatory Notes for the *Fraud Bill* make it clear that section 4 is intended to cover people who are in a similar position of trust to that of a fiduciary, whether or not they can be formally categorized as a fiduciary in the law of equity. The word "safeguard" as used in the subsection means that section 4 generally targets those who are in a special position of trust such as those who have access to the bank accounts of vulnerable people and so on.

The concept of fiduciary is instructive, however. "The essence of a fiduciary relationship ... is that one party pledges itself to act in the best interest of the other. The fiduciary relationship has trust, not self-interest, at its core, and when breach occurs, the balance favours the person wronged."[167] In *Hospital Products Ltd. v. United States Surgical Corporation*, Mason J. observed:[168]

> "The relationship between the parties is therefore one which gives the fiduciary a special opportunity to exercise the power or discretion to the detriment of that other person who is accordingly vulnerable to abuse by the fiduciary of his position ...
> It is partly because the fiduciary's exercise of the power or discretion can adversely affect the interests of the person to whom the duty is owed and because the latter is at the mercy of the former that the fiduciary comes under a duty to exercise his power or discretion in the interests of the person to whom it is owed."

As a matter of consistency, it would be unreasonable to criminalize those who have abused a fiduciary position, while at the same time exempting others from criminalization where they have taken advantage of an identical position of trust. Not all employees owe a fiduciary duty to their employer.[169] A hotel receptionist,[170] a cashier, a cleaner or carer might be in a position of great trust even though they may not be in a fiduciary relationship with their victims.[171] In *National Grid Electricity Transmission Plc v. McKenzie*,[172] the defendant's employment afforded him an opportunity to make a secret profit. It was held that Mr. McKenzie's rank meant that he owed a "duty to act honestly and faithfully ('in good faith') ... and ... not to make any secret profit by virtue of his position." However, the court said, "[t]he correct description of Mr. McKenzie is that he was an employee who (in certain limited respects) owed fiduciary duties: it is a mis-description to call him 'a fiduciary' and an error to treat him as a trustee." It is unlikely that the equity courts would hold that a junior employee such as a waiter is in a fiduciary relationship with his employer, but if the waiter were to

---

[167] *Canson Enterprises Ltd. v. Boughton & Co.* [1991] 3 S.C.R. 534 at 543 *per* McLachlin J. See also *Bristol and West Building Society v. Mothew* [1998] Ch 1 at 18 *per* Millett L.J.

[168] (1984) 156 C.L.R. 41 at 97, cited in *Pilmer v. Duke Group Ltd. (In Liq.)* (2001) 207 C.L.R. 165 at 196.

[169] Cf. *National Grid Electricity Transmission Plc. v. McKenzie* [2009] EWHC 1817 (Ch.); *Nottingham University v. Fischel* [2000] I.C.R. 1461; *Reading v. A-G* [1951] A.C. 507 at 516.

[170] *R. v. Cleall* [2009] EWCA Crim. 1807.

[171] A senior manager might owe a fiduciary duty even if he is not a "fiduciary" as such, see *National Grid Electricity Transmission Plc. v. McKenzie* [2009] EWHC 1817 (Ch). (For some examples of senior managers abusing positions of trust, see *Attorney-General's Reference (Nos. 29 and 30 of 2003)* [2003] EWCA Crim. 3065; *R. v. Barrick* (1985) 81 Cr. App. R. 78).

[172] [2009] EWHC 1817 (Ch) at para. 26. Cf. *Attorney-General of Hong Kong v. Reid Privy Council* [1994] 1 A.C. 324. (Obviously, in some cases involving government officials it would be easier and more sensible to charge them with a corruption offence).

make a secret profit by selling his own wine while on duty he should be treated no different to a senior manager who makes a secret profit.[173] Section 4 would apply regardless of whether there is a fiduciary relationship.[174]

34–079   In *R. v. Hardwick*[175] a social worker managed to acquire property worth £64,000 from an elderly lady who was suffering from dementia. The defendant not only committed theft, but also abused the trust that had been put in her by obtaining an enduring power of attorney. She used the power of attorney to sell victim's bungalow. The defendant deposited the money into the victim's account and thereafter made withdrawals in excess of £47,000 from that account. On similar facts in *R. v. Marshall*,[176] the defendant was convicted of fraud contrary sections 1 and 4 of the *Fraud Act 2006*. Marshall was the joint manager of a residential care home. One of the residents of the home had a mental age of a young child and therefore was not able to exercise control over her own bank account. The victim relied on her carers to do her banking on her behalf. Marshall was entrusted to handle the victim's banking and took advantage of the situation by withdrawing large sums for her own purposes. Even if Marshall was not a fiduciary, the relationship between her and the victim was one which gave her a special opportunity to exercise a power or discretion to the detriment of victim. A social worker and a manager of a residential home might be held to be in a fiduciary relationship, but a cleaner or carer working in the residential home might not be—even though the latter might also be afforded an opportunity to take advantage of a vulnerable resident. (There is a difference between being entrusted with property and in being afforded a general opportunity to thieve it.)

34–080   **The fact that an omission is sufficient for grounding a conviction adds to the uncertainty.**   Most people would realize that deliberately omitting to seek an opportunity which one is expected to seek is dishonest, but might not realize that criminal liability attaches. Section 4 is particularly wide in this sense. It is the only section which targets both positive acts and omissions. The example provided in the *Fraud Bill* Explanatory Notes is of an "employee who fails to take up the chance of a crucial contract in order that an associate or rival company can take it up instead at the expense of [his] employer." Apart from the difficulties in defining this type of wrongdoing with certainty, and in providing fair warning that what was once business is now fraud, there is nothing unjust about criminalizing these types of dishonest practices. This type of wrongdoer culpably harms another in a serious way. (Obviously, it will be necessary to show that D intentionally failed (recklessness or negligence will not do) to secure the opportunity with an intent to make a gain, or cause a loss or expose another to a risk of loss, and did so dishonestly).

34–081   **Who decides whether D was in position of trust?**   It is likely that the courts will hold that the question of whether D was in a relationship of trust with V is a

---

[173]   *R. v. Doukas* [1978] 1 W.L.R. 372. See also *R. v. Sutcliffe* [1986] A.C. 909.

[174]   In some cases, the fiduciary will also be caught by section 3 of the *Act* for failing to disclose certain information. See *Adams v. The Queen* [1995] 1 W.L.R. 52.

[175]   [2007] 1 Cr. App. R. 11.

[176]   [2009] EWCA Crim. 2076. See also *R. v. Seepersad* [2007] 2 Cr. App. R. 8.

question of law for the judge. The question of whether D dishonestly took advantage of the position will most likely be a question of fact for the jury. The Law Commission said: "The question whether the particular facts alleged can properly be described as giving rise to that relationship will be an issue capable of being ruled upon by the judge and, if the case goes to the jury, of being the subject of directions."[177]

Is it possible to vicariously abuse a position of trust?　No. But an employer might have to provide compensation for wrongs committed by their employees in certain situations.[178] As a general rule criminal liability is personal.

34–082

Does section 4 catch the police officer who abuses his position by offering not to book traffic offenders if they provide him with sexual favours?[179]　The officer is not guilty of blackmail because he did not act to make a gain of money or other property. As far as fraud for abuse of position is concerned, he might come within the reach of the *Fraud Act*. He might be caught for the gain he made for another (he arguably made a gain for his victims by sparing them the expense of paying their traffic fines) or for the loss he caused to his employer. He was paid to enforce the law and to issue the relevant enforcement notices so that the offenders would pay their fines. He clearly abused his position by exempting offenders from paying the relevant fines to the government. But the courts will most likely hold that the subsection does not cover remote or indirect loses or gains.[180]

34–083

Even if the courts hold otherwise, it will be difficult to prove that D intended to make a gain or cause a loss or expose his employer to a risk of loss in such cases. (The corrupt police officer probably did not even consider the financial and property implications of his seeking a sexual bribe). It would be better to charge the officer with "misconduct in a public office," because this offence directly targets the specific wrong involved.[181]

---

[177] Report 276, *Fraud*, (London, H.M.S.O., 2002) at paragraph 7.38.

[178] See *Ffrench v. Sestili* (2007) 98 S.A.S.R. 28, where Sestili (D2) was in the business of providing casual carers for disabled people living in their own homes. One of her clients, Ms Ffrench (V), was severely disabled and was physically dependent on her carers. Ms Sestili (the care provider) advertised for a qualified carer. She engaged Ms Brown (D1) to act as the carer for V. V, being a quadriplegic, was not able to operate an A.T.M., so required D1 to do her shopping as a part of her duties as her carer. V gave her credit card and PIN code to D1 for this purpose, but D1 stole $32,000. The issue for the purposes of civil law was whether the care provider and her insurer were vicariously liable for the loss. The Supreme Court of South Australia held: "(a) the employee's conduct in using the card to misappropriate money for her own purposes was so closely connected to her duties that the misappropriations must be regarded as occurring in the course of the employee's employment, and (b) the withdrawals were made in the ostensible pursuit of the employer's business."

[179] "Traffic PC Jailed for Having Sex With Women in Exchange for Letting Them off Driving Offences," (London, *Daily Mail*, Wednesday, Jun 16 2010).

[180] On remote harms, see Dennis J. Baker, "The Moral Limits of Criminalizing Remote Harms," (2007) 10 *New Crim. L. Rev.* 370; Dennis J. Baker, "Collective Criminalization and the Constitutional Right to Endanger Others," (2009) 28 *Crim. Just. Ethics* 168 at 189-190.

[181] Cf. *R. v. W(M)* (2010) 1 Cr. App. R. 28. It would not be a conspiracy to prevent the police officer from doing his public duty as more than one person does not conspire to prevent the police officer from doing is duty. (What's more, the office is the instigator). Cf. *Board of Trade v. Owen* [1957] A.C. 602 at 622; *R. v. Terry* [1984] A.C. 374.

34–084 **What mental element is required under section 4?** The core requirements are the same as for section 2 and 3, as outlined in detail above. It was noted above that ignorance of a duty to disclose is no defence under section 3. Likewise, D's ignorance of the fact that he occupies a position of trust is no defence under section 4. In many cases, D will be fully aware of the fact that he is stealing or attempting to steal property, or is otherwise committing fraud. However, there would be no great injustice in convicting a waiter who makes a secret profit by selling his own wines in his employer's cafe, simply because he was not aware that he was abusing a position of trust.

34.5. POSSESSION OF ARTICLES FOR USE IN FRAUD

34–085 Section 6 of the *Fraud Act 2006* holds:

> "(1)   A person is guilty of an offence if he has in his possession or under his control any article for use in the course of or in connection with any fraud.
> (2)   A person guilty of an offence under this section is liable–
>   (a)   on summary conviction, to imprisonment for a term not exceeding 12 months or to a fine not exceeding the statutory maximum (or to both);
>   (b)   on conviction on indictment, to imprisonment for a term not exceeding 5 years or to a fine (or to both)."

The focus of section 6 is not on outlawing inherently dangerous articles, but on fraud and the need to provide for intervention at an early opportunity. It will be seen that the offence is very widely defined. Although primarily aimed against the possession of articles that are inherently useful for use in fraud such as A.T.M card readers, fake passports, identity documents belonging to others and so on, it applies also to the possession of a large variety of other objects with the requisite intent, such as a laptop intended for use in fraud or an Old Wykehamist tie worn by a fraudster. The offence is valuable because it makes professional fraudsters wary of possessing articles such as A.T.M. card readers, fake passports and so on. If the defendant possesses non-incriminating articles such as a laptop with the requisite intent, he seems to be guilty of a thought crime. D may have purchased a computer and printer for a legitimate purpose, but now thinks to himself, "I could use my computer to make fake university degrees." The computer was originally possessed for a legitimate purpose, but since he now intends to possess it "for use" in fraud he probably commits an offence contrary to section 6.

34–086 **What conduct element is required under section 6?** The *actus reus* requires D to possess or control the articles. The articles need not be specifically designed to facilitate fraud. The offence only requires that the article be possessed "for use in the course of or in connection with any fraud." If D intends to possess a laptop computer "for use" in fraud, then he is in fact in possession of an article "for use" in fraud. He might use that laptop for some legitimate purpose, but that is irrelevant if it can be shown that it was also possessed for use in fraud.[182] In some

---

[182] Even innocuous articles such as a £50 pound note and washing up liquid could be possessed for use in fraud. See *R. v. Omgbwa* [2009] EWCA Crim. 1215. That "case involved a 'black money' scam or a 'wash wash' fraud which involves the use of a genuine bank note being coated with glue and

cases, the article will be specifically designed for use in fraud and the jury will most likely infer it was possessed for such a purpose (*e.g.*, an A.T.M. card reader, a false passport, *etc.*).[183] If there is nothing incriminating about the article, then liability will hinge almost entirely on D's intent.

What if the article is not suitable for use in fraud? It does not matter whether   **34–087**
the article turns out to be useful for committing a particular act of fraud. If D possesses paper which he intends to use to make bogus university degree certificates,[184] but gives up after discovering that the paper is not suitable he would be liable under section 6. He intended to possess it "for use" in fraud and that is all the subsection requires. This is not an attempt: he did not attempt to possess the paper because he actually possessed it. He only attempted to make the degrees, but that is attempted fraud[185] not attempted possession! If he had ordered the paper with his supplier failing to deliver it, he would have only attempted to possess an article for use in fraud. It is worth noting that if he intended to possess the same paper merely to write letters to his grandmother, he would not have committed any crime.

It will be seen that the offence is very widely defined. It applies to the possession of a large variety of objects and documents. Articles might include A.T.M. card reading devices, false passports, credit cards, utility bills, documents containing other people's bank account details, wage slips and any other documents which might be used in fraud.[186] As far as identity documents are concerned, section 25(1) and (2) of the *Identity Cards Act 2006* makes it an offence to possess false identity documents. (The latter, however, is not a property offence). An article also includes data held in electronic form.[187]

The articles might be held to be within D's control if they are on his premises, are stored on his personal computer, or are kept in an e-mail that he has not deleted.[188] Even if he has deleted the e-mail he may be liable if it can be proved that he intended to possess the information for use in fraud at the time when it existed in his possession. If the e-mail has been copied to someone else, the copied e-mail might provide sufficient proof of D's possession. The articles would also be in D's culpable control if he has arranged to have them stored at a friend's place or in a commercial depot and so on.[189]

---

iodine. This made the note black. A victim would then be shown the notes being treated with a 'special' chemical which washed the note and made it acceptable tender. The victim would then be persuaded to buy a pile of similar bank notes at a cut price and a quantity of the 'special' chemical. However, in reality the black notes would be merely pieces of blank paper cut to the size of the requisite currency note and the chemical would be nothing other than washing-up liquid."

[183] See the facts in *R. v. Ciorba* [2009] EWCA Crim. 1800; *R. v. Virciglo* [2010] EWCA Crim. 650.
[184] Producing fake degrees is a rather lucrative form of fraud. See *R. v. Huang* [2010] EWCA Crim. 375.
[185] If his conduct was aimed at making a gain or causing a loss, *etc.*
[186] See the facts in *R. v. Amusan* [2009] EWCA Crim. 690.
[187] See section 8 of the *Fraud Act 2006*.
[188] If he has deleted the e-mail, then he would no longer be in possession of the article. Cf. *R. v. Porter* [2007] 2 All E.R. 625.
[189] In *R. v. Kousar* [2009] 2 Cr. App. R. 5 the Court of Appeal held: "Knowledge or acquiescence was not enough to establish possession: actual control of the goods was needed. ... Nothing in the authorities supported the contention that 'ability to control' was enough." D would have to have

34–088   **Does it include data held in my memory such as the PIN code to V's bank account?**   The *Act* makes it clear that information or data constitutes an "article." It also expressly states that it does not matter if the information is stored in electronic form.[190] Parliament did not expressly mention the storage of data in the human mind, but this form of storage does not alter the fact that the memorized "information" is an "article." If a PIN code stored in electronic form or in a note book[191] is an article, then a PIN code stored in a person's memory should be treated as an article. It is the PIN code (confidential information) which is the article and the form in which it is stored does not alter its usefulness for committing fraud. Of course, issues of proof would mean that not many people would be caught if they were merely to memorize the information. But cases may arise; for example, where D1 is caught on C.C.T.V. telling D2 the PIN code for V's bank account. The video footage might be used to prove that D1 was in possession and control of an article—the PIN Code. If D2 uses it to commit fraud, he would commit a consummated act of fraud. D1 would be an accessory. D1 might also be charged with an offence under section 6, since he was in possession of the article with an intent that it would be used in fraud. It is not necessary to show that the defendant intended the article to be used in a particular fraud.

34–089   **What mental element is required under section 6?**   Generally, the *mens rea* element for a "possession" offence is satisfied if the defendant *knew* he was in possession of the offending article; *and* if he knew that the article was of a kind which he should not have possessed.[192] More importantly, the defendant must possess the article with an intent that it will be used "in the course of or in connection with *any* fraud." The offence does not criminalize D for knowingly being in possession of any article which "could be" used in fraud. The section expressly states that it must be possessed (*for the particular purpose*) "for use in the course of or in connection with any fraud." If D does not intend to possess the article for use in fraud, then he does not come within the purview of section 6.[193] Given that the offence does not include a dishonesty defence or any other kind of

---

control of the articles for use in fraud, as required by the *Act*. It would not be enough to show that her husband kept the articles in the matrimonial home, if she was not involved in his scam.

[190] Documents and information might be kept on a laptop, see *R. v. Mafe* [2009] EWCA Crim. 2752.

[191] Cf. *R. v. Rowe* [2007] Q.B. 975, where D had a "notebook containing his handwritten notes on the assembly and operation of a mortar and a coded list of explosive materials and potential targets." In *R. v. G* [2010] 1 A.C. 43 at 47 the House of Lords said that: "A document or record containing *information* is capable of being an 'article' for the purposes of the section 57" of the *Terrorism Act 2000*.

[192] Some offences do not contain a statutory defence, so the mental element is very limited, indeed. In *R. v. Deyemi* [2008] 1 Cr. App. R. 25 the Court of Appeal said: "On the question of whether the approach adopted by certain of their Lordships in *Warner* applies to a 'container' case under section 5 of the *Firearms Act 1968*, and presumably section 1 too of the *1968 Act*, so as to enable an accused to raise a defence that he did not know what was in the container, we are of the view that it does not."

[193] The courts have interpreted section 25 of the *Theft Act 1968* as requiring that: "the defendant was in possession of the article, and intended the article to be used in the course of or in connection with some future burglary, theft or cheat. ... Nor, in our view, is it necessary to prove that the defendant intended to use it himself; it will be enough to prove that he had it with him with the intention that it should be used by someone else." See *R. v. Ellames* [1974] 3 All E. R. 130 at 136 *per* Brown J; *Re. McAngus* [1994] Crim. L.R. 602.

statutory defence; and seems to cover non-incriminating items such as laptops and printers, it *must* require D to possess the article *with an intent* that it will be used in fraud.[194]

Many possession offences provide a reasonableness defence, but the section 6 offence does not. For example, section 58 of the *Terrorism Act 2000* makes it an offence to possess material which might be used in terrorism. That section does not require D to possess the offending material for terrorism purposes. Instead, the prosecution need only prove that "the defendant (i) had control of a record which contained information that was likely to provide practical assistance to a person committing or preparing an act of terrorism, (ii) knew that he had the record, and (iii) *knew* the kind of information which it contained. If the Crown establishes all three elements, then it has proved its case against the defendant and he falls to be convicted—unless he establishes a defence under subsection 58(3) of the *Terrorism Act 2000*."[195]

Under section 58(3) a defendant may demonstrate that his possession was not connected with a terrorist purpose, if he is able to provide a reasonable explanation for his possession. For example, he may be able to show he is a journalist who has merely gathered the offending information to expose a terrorist cell and so on. The defence allows the defendant to demonstrate that incriminating material was not possessed for the purpose of facilitating terrorism, but for some other reasonable purpose. If the prosecution is unable to demonstrate that the defendant knew he was in possession of material which he also knew could be used for terrorism, then there is no need for the defendant to raise the defence. The prosecution must prove that the defendant was in possession of the material and knew the nature of the material before the defendant need raise the defence of reasonable excuse. A reasonable excuse effectively is a way of arguing that the document or record was possessed for a purpose other than to assist in the commission or preparation of an act of terrorism.[196] If D is found in possession of a chemistry or physics textbook which contains information on building bombs, then he might raise the statutory defence by arguing that he possessed the books because he is reading for a Ph.D. in physics and has no connection with any terrorist organization and so on.

In *R. v. G*,[197] the House of Lords made it very clear that serious possession offences are "subject to the general presumption that criminal liability requires proof of *mens rea*." This seems particularly important for the offence found in section 6 of the *Fraud Act*, because it covers incriminating articles[198] such as fake passports as well as non-incriminating articles such as laptops and printers.

Does D have to be *aware* that he is "in possession" of an article which could be "used" to commit fraud?   If the section requires the defendant to possess the particular article with an intent that it be used in fraud, this question is superfluous. D cannot intend to possess something for use in fraud if he does not

34–090

---

[194] *B (A Child) v. D.P.P.* [2000] 2 A.C. 428; *R. v. G* [2010] 1 A.C. 43.

[195] *R. v. G* [2010] 1 A.C. 43.

[196] *R. v. G* [2010] 1 A.C. 43 at 84.

[197] [2010] 1 A.C. 43 at 55.

[198] Some *Acts* criminalize possession of articles that are inherently incriminating such as firearms and drugs, see *Firearms Act 1968*; *Misuse of Drugs Act 1971*.

know it is capable of being used in fraud. Nor can he intend to possess it if he does not know he is in possession of it.[199]

34–091 **The defendant might know that an article is in his possession and that it is something which "could be" used in fraud. Does that mean he is liable for possessing an article that could be used in fraud?** No. He knows he is in possession of articles which "could be" used in fraud, but he does not "intend to possess" those articles so that they might actually be used by him or someone else in fraud.

Suppose D has purchased a large Georgian house which used to be rented out to a dozen students. Suppose also that for some months after D moves in he is inundated with snail mail for the former tenants. Let us assume that it is obvious that many of the letters contain bank cards and statements. D is too busy to return the unwanted mail to the post office so keeps them in his possession for a couple of weeks before he takes them to his local post office. Let us assume he is a prosecutor and knows that bank statements, debit cards and PIN codes can be used to commit fraud.

Parliament cannot prohibit mere possession of innocuous articles such as mail and computers on the grounds that some people might use them to commit fraud. It must be shown that the particular defendant possessed the articles so that he or someone else could use them to carry out fraud. There is no other way to keep the offence within the bounds of justice.

34–092 **Is an "intention to possess" an article for use in fraud sufficient for grounding a conviction, or is actual "possession" required?** Suppose D has ordered software which he intends to use in fraud, but moves to Scotland before it is ever delivered. Let us also assume that the software is returned to the sender when it arrives at his old address. He should only be liable if his intent to possess the article for use in fraud coincided with his actual control and possession of that article. Merely "*intending* to possess" something for use in fraud is different to "possessing it with an intent" that it be used in fraud. The articles would have to at least be in his control.

Section 6 of the *Fraud Act 2006* goes very far in making conviction depend upon little more than proof of intent. There are obvious risks of miscarriages of justice; so the court should be careful to scrutinize the evidence. A person who is in possession of an article that is not incriminating in itself is likely to "get away with it" if, upon being questioned by the police, he can offer some plausible reason for possessing it. If the article or articles (*e.g.*, fake passports, masses of identity documents belonging to others, *etc.*) are incriminating, D will most likely be offering his plausible explanation to a jury rather than the police.

34.6. MAKING OR SUPPLYING ARTICLES FOR USE IN FRAUDS

34–093 Section 7 of the *Fraud Act 2006* holds:

---

[199] There is the odd aberrant decision to the contrary. Cf. *R. v. Lewis* (1988) 87 Cr. App. R. 270.

"(1) A person is guilty of an offence if he makes, adapts, supplies or offers to supply any article–
    (a) knowing that it is designed or adapted for use in the course of or in connection with fraud, or
    (b) intending it to be used to commit, or assist in the commission of, fraud.

(2) A person guilty of an offence under this section is liable–
    (a) on summary conviction, to imprisonment for a term not exceeding 12 months or to a fine not exceeding the statutory maximum (or to both);
    (b) on conviction on indictment, to imprisonment for a term not exceeding 10 years or to a fine (or to both)."

Again, this offence is aimed at those who facilitate fraud. The *actus reus* can be committed in five ways:

1. By *making* an article for use in the course or in connection with fraud.
2. By *adapting* an article for use in the course or in connection with fraud.
3. By *supplying* an article for use in the course or in connection with fraud.
4. By *offering* to supply any article for use in the course or in connection with fraud.
5. By *supplying* an article that has not been made or adapted for use in fraud. If the article is a normal item such as a computer or standard software that has not been adapted or made for use in fraud, then D will have to be charged under section 7(1)(b). This section applies only if D (offers) supplies the innocuous article "intending" it be used in fraud.

The mental element is satisfied under 7(1)(a) if:

1. D knows that the article which he adapts or makes is designed for use in property or financial fraud. (If he makes it or adapts it for use in fraud then he must know that it is made or adapted for such a purpose).

Or under section 7(1)(b):

1. D supplies or offers to supply an article that *has* been adapted or made for use in fraud; intending that it be "used to commit, or assist in the commission of, fraud."
2. D supplies or offers to supply an article, which is *not* specifically designed for use in fraud, intending that it be "used to commit, or assist in the commission of, fraud."

The section targets those who produce or supply articles which they know are **34–094** designed to facilitate fraud; or which they intend to be used to facilitate fraud.[200] The *actus reus* is narrower in section 7(1)(a) in that it must be shown that the article was made or adapted specifically for use in fraud. But the *mens rea* is wider in section 7(1)(a), since D need only supply or produce the article knowing that it is designed for use in fraud. If D makes and/or supplies A.T.M card readers or devices for reversing electricity meters, it does not matter that he does not intend his customer to use them to commit fraud. The mental element is satisfied

---

[200] Some of this conduct could be charged under sections 44-46 of the *Serious Crime Act 2007*.

because he knows that the article is "designed" for use in fraud. He need not make or adapt the article, but must at least supply or offer to supply it. If he knows that it has been made or adapted for use in fraud then it is a crime for him to supply it to another or even to *offer*[201] to supply it.

In the second formulation of the offence the *actus reus* is wider in that it covers the supply of any article, regardless of whether it has been made or adapted for use in fraud. However, the *mens rea* is narrower since it requires actual intention as to use. D must "supply"[202] the article intending that it be used "to commit, or assist in the commission of fraud." The mental element is tighter than that found in complicity offences, because an accessory would only have to foresee that there is a real possibility that the article would be used in the fraud.[203] The words "intending" and in the "commission of" suggest D would have to have a particular act of fraud in mind.

34–095   Suppose a shopkeeper supplies a laptop and printer to D believing that there is a real possibility that D will use these articles to commit fraud. Suppose also that the shopkeeper supplies the articles anyway, but hopes the customer will not use them in fraud.

If your shopkeeper sells the article "intending" merely to make a sale without a care as to what the customer does, he is not caught by the subsection.

Depending on all the evidence, the shopkeeper might be charged as an accessory under section 8 of the *Accessories and Abettors Act 1861*.[204] He could not, however, be convicted under section 7(1)(b) of the *Fraud Act 2006*, because he does not supply the articles intending that they be used in fraud. And since the laptop and printer are standard everyday items which have not been made or adapted for use in fraud, section 7(1)(a) does not apply.

34–096   **Does copying information for use in fraud constitute adapting or making it?**   If the information is specifically copied for use in fraud copying it might be a way to adapt it for use in fraud. The issue does not arise under section 7(1)(b), as it merely requires D to supply the article intending it be used in fraud.

34–097   **What if D makes a false divorce certificate to get a damsel to marry him?**   D commits bigamy, but the "article" is not used to commit property or financial fraud. Section 7 is a property offence, and as such, ought to be read in light of the enactment in which it sits. It is not designed to criminalize those who make articles that are not designed or intended for use in property or financial fraud. Thus, D would have to know that the particular article is suitable for

---

[201]   Cf. *R. v. Hollinshead* [1985] A.C. 975; *R. v. Levitz* (1990) 90 Cr. App. R. 33; *R. v. James* (1986) 82 Cr. App. R. 226.

[202]   "The word 'supply,' in its ordinary natural meaning, conveys the idea of furnishing or providing to another something which is wanted or required in order to meet the wants or requirements of that other. It connotes more than the mere transfer of physical control of some chattel or object from one person to another. No one would ordinarily say that to hand over something to a mere customer was to supply him with it. The additional concept is that of enabling the recipient to apply the thing handed over to purposes for which he desires or has a duty to apply it." *R. v. Maginnis* [1987] A.C. 303 at 309 *per* Lord Kinkel.

[203]   *R. v. Bryce* [2004] 2 Cr. App. R. 35.

[204]   See also, sections 44-46 of the *Serious Crime Act 2007*.

property or financial fraud. Of course, under subsection 7(1)(b) any type of article is caught, but D must intend that it be used in a property or financial fraud. If D supplies another with a forged a medical prescription so that person can acquire prescription drugs, he is caught by the subsection because he knows that the adapted article is of a kind that can be used to commit property fraud. Without the article D2 would not be able to get the property (medicines).

In *R. v. Huang*[205] the defendant did not make the offending articles, but merely "supplied" them. Huang supplied fake university degrees, which were made by a third party. He supplied documents to Chinese students attesting that the recipients had successfully graduated from English universities. "The documents purported to have been certified as authentic by the Chinese Embassy." The recipients of the degrees no doubt intended to pass "them off to their families in China, and to future employers in China." Huang, as the supplier, only took instructions from his potential customers and then had a third party make the documents. His customers usually provided him with a template of what they wanted. The police found hundreds of forged documents in both electronic and hardcopy in Huang's house; some of the electronic copies were stored on computers and memory sticks.

Huang received £130,000 in cash payments for the documents he supplied. The evidence showed that he knew full well that the articles were designed for use in fraud. What kind of fraud? Under section 7 there is no need to show that D1 (the supplier of the articles) in fact made a gain or caused a loss, or that his articles helped D2 (the receiver of the articles) make a gain or cause a loss; but it must be shown that he *knew* that the manufactured/adapted articles would be suitable for D2 to commit fraud within the meaning of the *Fraud Act 2006*. In this case, the students wanted the degrees to con their parents and future employers. Were the students able to use the articles to commit fraud within the meaning of the *Act*? If the degrees were purely designed to please the parents of the students, then this type of fraud would not come within the purview of the subsection. The *Fraud Act* deals with property crimes, not lying and dishonestly in general. It also appears that the parents would have already paid all the fees and maintenance if the students had got to the graduation stage. It is doubtful that it could be said that the fake degrees were suitable for committing financial fraud against the parents.

What about the financial gain that the student could make by gaining a job   34–098
with the fake degree?   The only judicial authority in point is *R. v. Lewis*.[206] This is a case of low authority (it was only a trial at assizes), but it has had significant results. The facts were that a woman obtained a post as a schoolmistress through a forged teacher's certificate. It was ruled that she had not obtained her salary by false pretences; the salary was paid in return for her services. Yet Lewis would not have got the job, and consequently her salary, if it had not been for the false representation. Her object in making the false representation was to get the salary. Assuming, as is likely, that the employer

---

[205] [2010] EWCA Crim. 375 (Unfortunately, this is only a sentencing decision, so other than providing useful facts, it tells us little about the compass of section 7).
[206] (1922) Somerset Assizes, cited in J.W.C. Turner, *Russell on Crime*, (London: Stevens & Sons, Vol. II, 1964) at 1186.

would not have made her any payment of salary if the lie had not been operating on his mind, there was certainly a factual causal connection between the lie and the obtaining of salary.

Why should it not have been a causal connection in law? Whatever the answer may be, the point has become largely theoretical because, in the unlikely event of a charge being made, it would now constitute an offence contrary to sections 1(a) and 2 of the *Fraud Act 2006*. That latter offence only requires the dishonest defendant to make the false representation with an intent to gain or cause a loss, *etc.* (But this does not catch the supplier of the fake degrees.)

If Huang *knew* that the fake degrees could be used in financial or property fraud he commits an offence contrary to section 7(1)(a). He clearly knew the articles were made and adapted specifically for use in fraud and most likely knew that degrees would be presented to future employers. Consequently, he knew the articles were of kind which could be used in "the course of or in connection with" property fraud. Using fake degrees to obtain a position that one is not qualified to hold would cause a financial loss to the employer. Not only in terms of productivity, but also in having to re-advertise the position and so on after discovering the fraud. Jurisdictionally, it could also be assumed that some of the students would use the fake degrees to obtain positions in the United Kingdom. At a stretch we could argue that he knew that the articles were of a kind which could be used in property fraud and culpably chose to "supply" them.

34–099   **Does it cover "making articles" for use in frauds involving services?**   Yes. The courts are likely to hold that it does. The maker only has to know that the article is of a kind that has been specifically adapted for use in financial or property fraud. This includes obtaining a service for free or at a reduced rate. If D is in the business of making fake railcards, then he must know that his customers will use these to obtain discounted rail fares. Similarly, if D adapts a washer to obtain a free game of pool (a service) by inserting it in a pool table, then section 7 would apply.

34–100   **What is the difference between "for use in the course of, or in connection with, fraud" and "to commit, or assist in the commission of, fraud"?**   Some preparatory acts might be caught. Furthermore, it might extend to acts done after the event, but the line needs to be drawn somewhere. Suppose D1 supplies D2 with a fake passport so that D2 can flee the country because he is on the run after committing a major property fraud. Does section 7(1)(a) apply? The act of leaving the country could hardly be said to be connected with the earlier property fraud.[207] Meanwhile, the words "in the commission of" appear to require that article be used in the commission of a particular property fraud.

---

[207] Of course, if a fake passport is an article which generally could be used in property fraud, and if D1 knew it, then he would be caught by the subsection regardless of what D2 did. D2's conduct is irrelevant in this sense, the focus is on the article's potentiality as an instrument for committing fraud, not on any given act of fraud, or after the fact evasion of justice.

34.7.   OBTAINING SERVICES DISHONESTLY

Section 11 of the *Fraud Act 2006* provides: **34–101**

"(1)   A person is guilty of an offence under this section if he obtains services for himself or
another–
(a)   by a dishonest act, and
(b)   in breach of subsection (2).
(2)   A person obtains services in breach of this subsection if–
(a)   they are made available on the basis that payment has been, is being or will be
made for or in respect of them,
(b)   he obtains them without any payment having been made for or in respect of
them or without payment having been made in full, and
(c)   when he obtains them, he knows–
(i)   that they are being made available on the basis described in paragraph
(a), or
(ii)   that they might be, but intends that payment will not be made, or will
not be made in full.
(3)   A person guilty of an offence under this section is liable–
(a)   on summary conviction, to imprisonment for a term not exceeding 12 months
or to a fine not exceeding the statutory maximum (or to both);
(b)   on conviction on indictment, to imprisonment for a term not exceeding 5 years
or to a fine (or to both)."

Two particular deficiencies in the former section 15 of the *Theft Act 1968*
(obtaining property by deception) were that it did not cover obtaining the hiring
of property, or the supply of services, by deception. Therefore, it failed to
provide, or to provide adequately, for various instances of what is popularly
called "bilking", a restaurant, a hotel, the railway, a taxi-driver, a car-hire firm
and so on. (In the first two cases, the restaurant and the hotel, there is an
obtaining of food, but prosecutors naturally felt that this did not express the real
offence.) Section 1 of the *Theft Act 1978* was introduced to fill the lacuna,[208] but
as a "deception" offence it did not catch those who dishonestly obtained services
from a machine. After some legislative vicissitudes, dishonestly obtaining a
service from a machine or otherwise is now covered by section 11 of the *Fraud
Act*.

Unlike the former offence, section 11 does not require an actual deception.
The requirement of deception under the former offence meant that if a person
snuck into a cinema through the exit door, in order to view a film without paying,
he committed no offence. However, such a defendant would be liable under
section 11 because he has in fact *obtained* the service. The wide definition of
"services" means that the offence covers the obtaining of an article or premises
for temporary use by way of hiring or tenancy. The offence does not require an
intent to deprive the owner permanently of anything, which adds little as a service
cannot be used up twice!

What is the conduct element for section 11?   Section 11 is a result crime.   **34–102**
Therefore the defendant must actually succeed in obtaining the service. The
services must be made available on the basis that payment would be received for

---

[208] See *R. v. Sofroniou* [2004] Q.B. 1218.

them. In addition, the defendant must either not pay or not pay in full for them. If he has paid in full for the service he will not come within the purview of section 11.

34–103 **Suppose a man hires a car. He pays the full hiring charge, but, having no driving licence, shows a licence belonging to someone else. Any offence?** What you are asking is whether the fraud must relate to the payment or promise of payment. The hirer of the car has paid full consideration for using the car and has no intention of avoiding paying for using it.[209] Consequently, D in your question does not offend against the section.

The following are further illustrations showing that the defendant need act for the purpose of avoiding paying for the service:

> D hires a hall saying that it is for a Church of England group; actually he intends it for a meeting of a terrorist organization.
> D signs into a hotel during an epidemic, falsely denying that he has been in contact with the disease.
> D jumps the queue for a council house by lying about his needs.
> D, a newspaper reporter, poses as a visitor in order to gain entrance to a hospital to interview a nurse.
> Underage D uses a fake ID to gain entry into a night club, but pays the full cover charge to enter.

In all these cases the offence is not committed, because D acted dishonestly but without an intent to avoid paying for the services. In all these cases the defendant has paid the full fee where required. If no question of payment enters into the transaction, it cannot constitute an offence under section 11. Section 11, unlike the former offence, does not embrace cases where the victim rightly knows that he has been paid, if the fraud relates to some matter other than payment. If the service is provided on the understanding that it has been or will be paid for, the fact that it has been paid for in full is material.

34–104 **Are you telling me that the fraud has to relate to obtaining a service for free, rather than obtaining the service *per se*?** It appears so. The defendant may be dishonest in getting the service by making a false representation, but section 11 is confined to cases relating to the other's prospect of being paid for the service. The *mens rea* requirement also makes this clear, as D must intend to avoid paying for the service. The offence is more restricted than the former offence, which was not limited to "payment" frauds.

34–105 **Is it a "service" to let a room without service? Does a theatre or museum provide services?** Yes, for the purpose of the *Act*. Service has a narrower meaning than the usual meaning of "services" because it does not cover gratuitous services. There is no reason why the payment should be specifically for the particular service, if it is for matters included in the service. So the provision would cover the case where a fraudster obtains entry to premises, or the

---

[209] *R. v. Waterfall* [1970] 1 Q.B. 148.

services of the Oxford & Cambridge Club or R.A.C., by falsely pretending to be a paid-up member. (There is no significance in the fact that the section speaks of services in plural; a single act is clearly covered).

Are aspects of the service which are not normally paid for covered by section 11?　When a guest books into a hotel his name is entered by the clerk into the hotel's computer, but this benefit alone would not constitute a service for the purposes of section 11. Unlike section 1 of the *Theft Act 1978*, section 11 of the new *Act* does not refer to "benefits." Section 11 should be read as covering only aspects of the service which are provided on the basis that they have been paid for or will be paid for.[210] Normally, one is not charged a separate fee for checking into a hotel. Nor is one normally charged a fee for opening a bank account, but one might be if he applies for a business loan. Similarly, if a person seeks a quotation from a builder intending not to pay him if he goes ahead and does the job, he could hardly be said to have obtained a service with an intent of not paying, if all he has received is the quotation, unless the builder normally charges for quotations. Under section 11 this would be no more than an attempt to obtain a service. In these types of cases, if the customer changes his mind and does not hire the builder or decides not to stay in the hotel, he is not normally charged for the quotation or for having his name logged into the hotel's computer. The defendant would have to obtain the builder's services (have him build something) or actually obtain the use of the hotel room to fall foul of section 11.

34–106

Another example would be the hiring of a car. The important "service" here is the use of the car; but giving the fraudster the keys of the car, or even entering his name in the computer as the hirer (thus creating a contract of hiring), is technically a part of the service. But unless there is a separate fee for these preliminary aspects of the service they should not be brought within the purview of section 11. When a person goes to a car hire centre he is not charged a fee if the clerk fills in all the paperwork and then he decides not to hire the car after all. (If the other elements can be proved, then this type of conduct should be treated as no more than an attempt). Similarly, if D tries to secure medical services for her pregnancy at a military hospital by lying about her ex-husband's status as an active duty military serviceman and by registering with the hospital, she does not obtain any of the medical services by merely registering for those services. She would need to obtain the ultrasound, consultation, and so on to come within the purview of section 11.[211]

What if the service is incidental to D's job?　In *United States v. May*[212] an air force officer used military aircraft to travel from his base to visit a female friend. He argued that "the military aircraft had to be used for training flights anyway and that any benefit he gained was incidental to any training use." This would certainly be the case if he had not chosen the destination for the training flight. For instance, if a British Airways pilot is scheduled to fly a passenger jet from

34–107

---

[210] *R. v. Dekson* [2005] 1 Cr. App. R. 114; *R. v. Sofroniou* [2004] Q.B. 1218.
[211] Registering for the medical service seems to be nothing more than "mere preparation" for obtaining the service. See *U.S. v. Lewis*, 938 F. Supp. 683 at 685-686 (1996).
[212] 625 F. 2d 186 (8th Cir.1980).

London to New York as a part of his job, he could hardly be said to be obtaining a service, if he is doing his job. Nor would it matter if he benefited because he has family in New York whom he visits each time he goes there as a part of his work. But the defendant in *United States v. May* had not been ordered to fly to the particular city where his girlfriend lived. Notwithstanding this, it is doubtful that the likes of May would satisfy the *mens rea* requirements of section 11. We would need more information: Did he use up more flight hours than he would have if he had flown to another city? Was it the norm for trainer pilots to have some discretion over where they would fly to so long as they kept within the set flying hours?

There is also the question of whether it was a service that was provided on the basis that it had been paid for or would be paid for. A normal flight on a commercial airline carrier is a service that is provided on the basis that it has been paid for or would be paid for. If a person is paid to take the training flights as a part of his employment, he is not likely to think he ought to be paying for them. Given that May thought the flight to his girlfriend's hometown was incidental to his training work, it might be difficult to prove that he knew it was or knew it might have been a service that was provided on the basis that it would be paid for.

34–108   **Is it possible to obtain a service without paying for it by omitting to do something?**   The defendant must do some dishonest act. The Act expressly states that a positive act is required. It is difficult to fathom omission which may properly be conceptualized as positive acts for this purpose. Nonetheless, certain omissions might constitute an offence under sections 1-4 of the *Act*.

34–109   **The services need not be of an ordinary commercial or transferrable kind.**   A person who obtains the services of a prostitute by promising to pay[213] might be caught by section 11.

34–110   **But it would not apply, if D obtains the consent of a non-prostitute by making a false representation as to his identity?**   Quite. As noted above, the *Act* limits itself to paid services because the legislation is designed primarily for the protection of property and transactions that do not cover offences against the person *per se*. Furthermore, the payment need not be due under an enforceable contract.[214]

34–111   **What if the service is illegal?**   Most of you will jump up in defence of the prostitute, because she has not been paid for sacrificially providing a service. Furthermore, you are likely to argue, "her wrongdoing was trivial to say the least." You will support bringing the dishonest punter within the purview of section 11.

---

[213] Cf. the facts in *R. v. Linekar* [1995] 2 Cr. App. R. 49.

[214] Cf. section 3(3) of the *Theft Act 1978* which expressly provides: "(3) Subsection (1) above shall not apply where the supply of the goods or the doing of the service is contrary to law, or where the service done is such that payment is not legally enforceable." So if D makes off with illegal drugs without paying for them, section 3 will not apply. As far as section 11 of the *Fraud Act 2006* is concerned, the courts might exclude the honesty defence in cases involving criminal transactions. Cf. *Martin v. State*, 174 Md.App. 510 (2007).

But does that not mean that we also have to criminalize those who have not paid a hit-man for his service of carrying out an assassination? After all, D obtains an illegal service when he has a rival assassinated by a hit-man. It would be utterly intolerable to use the criminal law to encourage people to pay hit-men. Similarly, V might pay the hit-man money because he falsely promises to carry out the assassination. If the assassin is not a real killer and does not intend to kill, but merely intends to make the false representation to make some money, as a matter of policy he should not be liable for fraud, since such a prosecution would effectively punish the potential assassin for not committing the more serious harm—that is, the assassination. Furthermore, a person who encourages another to commit an assassination is involved in very serious criminality and should not be able to use the criminal law to protect himself from the harmful side-effects[215] of his own criminal wrongdoing.

If the law is to be used to criminalize those who have not paid for illegal services, it should only be invoked when the criminality involved is extremely trivial, as is the case with prostitution.

The *Act* speaks of services that are provided on the basis that they have been or will be paid for. Does this mean with cash? It is not limited to cash payments. "Paid for" implies a payment in money or its legal equivalent (*e.g.*, payment by cheque, debit card, credit card and so on). A promise to transfer property or other services other than money (so-called "payment in kind") is not a promise for legal purposes. Nonetheless, the payment need not be due under an enforceable contract. Again, the section does not require that the payment should be made, or expected to be made, by the defendant. If a fraudster books a hotel saying that his company will pay, this can come within the *Act* if his company does not pay.   34–112

What if D pays in full for the service by using a stolen credit card or an unauthorized overdraft? In this case the defendant will not come within the purview of section 11, because he has paid in full for the service. It does not matter that D has stolen money to pay for the service. This might seem odd, but it is sensible given that his theft of the credit card or his unauthorized use of his own credit card would be caught by other offences. He has not obtained the service without paying for it. There is no need to stretch the meaning of the section to cover conduct that is caught elsewhere. The gravamen of stealing a credit card and using it to purchase services and the rest is that its owner, or at least his banker, will be out of pocket. (The same applies when D runs up an unauthorized overdraft—the bank is the victim not the person who is paid with the stolen money). The effect of stealing cash from V1 to purchase a service from X is that V1 is a victim and X benefits. (The same applies if funds are transferred electronically to X's account, as is the case when a credit or debit card is used.) Since the service provider has not been victimized, it is not necessary to bring those who use stolen money or unauthorized credit to purchase services within the purview of section 11. There is already more than enough duplication and overlap in sections 1-4 to cover such conduct. Furthermore, given the very   34–113

---

[215] So long as the harm only relates to property interests.

expansive reach of the law of theft, it is difficult to imagine such an offender being able to evade appropriate conviction elsewhere.

If the electronic payment does not go through for some reason, and D has already obtained the service, D might be caught by section 11. But it would be necessary to demonstrate that he did not intend to pay for the services in full, not that he intended to pay for them with someone else's money.

34–114 **What mental element is required under section 11?** Section 11 provides two alternatives for inculpating a defendant. The first alternative is the most straightforward as it is based on whether the defendant knew as a matter of fact that the services were being provided on the basis that they would be paid for. The defendant will be culpable if:

1. he obtains services "knowing" that they are services that "are" being made available on the basis that payment has been, is being or will be made for or in respect of them; and
2. he intends that payment will not be made, or will not be made in full; and
3. he acted dishonestly.

The alternative *mens rea* is looser. It is based on whether the defendant knew as a matter of fact that the services "might be" provided on the basis that they would be paid for:

1. The defendant "knows" that the services "might be" being made available on the basis that payment has been, is being or will be made for or in respect of them; and
2. he intends that payment will not be made, or will not be made in full; and
3. he acted dishonestly.

The first alternative will not raise too many difficulties. It will cover standard cases where it was fairly clear that the defendant knew that the service was being provided on the basis that it would be paid for and where he intentionally avoided paying for it. If D knows that he has already paid for a service and uses fraud to obtain it on the "belief" that it is owed to him, he might raise a lack of dishonestly as a defence.

34–115 Suppose D has paid in full for a rail ticket from London to Cambridge. Suppose also that when he enters the ticket into the ticket barrier machine, it swallows it and he loses his ticket. But luckily he has a receipt, which evidences his purchase. Let us assume when he tries to explain the situation to the train's conductor, the conductor tells him that there is nothing he can do and that D will have to purchase a new ticket. D has no money left so decides to sneak onto the train, believing that he has paid and, therefore, is owed the ride. (He also believes it is the railway's fault as its machine swallowed his ticket when he was entering the ticket barrier in the normal way).

Is he dishonest? That would be a question for the jury. If he has sufficient evidence of his purchase and of the railway's ineptitude he might satisfy the evidential burden of honesty. The jury might hold that he was not acting dishonestly according to the standards ordinary decent and honest people.

What about the person who is a genuine railcard holder, but has forgotten to take it with him on the train? Suppose he is given the option of either purchasing a new ticket at the full rate or getting off at the next stop. Suppose also that he takes the latter option, but sneaks back onto the same train by running down the platform and entering another carriage. He does this because he believes he has paid the right amount for the ride, is a genuine railcard holder, and thus should not have to pay the full fare. Again, he might be able to satisfy the evidential burden of honesty by raising evidence to show that he had a valid railcard at the time. Although he was acting dishonestly by sneaking back onto the train and did so to avoid paying the "full fare," the jury might accept that he did in fact *believe* that he had a right to use the discounted ticket that he had paid for, and thus was not acting dishonestly according to the standards ordinary decent and honest people.

34–116

A person who is not a railcard holder, but purchases a discounted rail ticket from a machine by selecting the student railcard option, would falsely represent that he is entitled to pay less than the *full amount* for the ticket. If he does so to avoid paying the full price of the ticket he could be caught by section 11. (In practice, he will merely be asked to purchase a new ticket.)

How will one "know" if the service is one where payment "might be" required? In most cases, it will be fairly obvious that the service is one which payment is normally due. Everyone knows that hairdressers, gardeners, lawyers, accountants, dentists, shoe repairers, taxi drivers and so on provide their services on the basis that they will be paid for. Whether a service is one that might be provided on the basis that payment will be provided will be determined by examining the context in which the defendant obtained the service. It will be important to ascertain whether the defendant "knew" that the service was one where payment "might be" required.

34–117

In *People v. Weg*[216] the defendant was charged with theft of services allegedly committed by using his employer's computer for his own personal benefit. It was held that the defendant was not guilty of obtaining a service when he used the Education Board's computer for his own use, because the Board was not in the business of supplying such a (computer) service. Under section 11 of the *Fraud Act 2006*, D could argue that he did not *know* that payment "might be" required for using his employer's computer. He could also raise the defence of dishonesty.

If D works for an Internet café and decides to sit on Facebook all day, he would know that he is using a service that his employer normally requires payment for, but would he know that it "is" or "might be" provided to him on that basis? Given the context in which he obtains the service, he probably does not see himself as a customer and would most likely not realize that payment "might be" required in this context. Similarly, the Army Captain who orders three junior officers to paint his house whilst they are on duty for the army, could not be said to "know" that the service he is ordering for himself is being provided on the

---

[216] 450 N.Y.S. (2d) 957 (1982).

basis that it is to be paid for.[217] The army is not in the business of painting houses. Nonetheless, he might be caught by section 4 of the *Act*, as he intends to cause a loss to another by abusing his position as Captain.

Thorny issues also arise in cases where scoundrels make false representations about their health to obtain disabled parking permits. The parking permit allows them to obtain a service for which payment is normally required. Each time they use the parking permit to avoid paying for "metered" parking they obtain a service that they would have paid for if they had not made a false representation. The dishonest use of the permit most likely would be caught by section 11. Otherwise, their false representations might be caught by section 1(2)(a) and 2 of the *Act*. (They make a false representation to get the permit; and every time they use it to get free parking they make a gain). They also imply that they are entitled to use the permit each time they use it.

34.8. PARTICIPATING IN FRAUDULENT BUSINESS

34–118   Section 9 of the *Fraud Act 2006* holds:

> "(1)   A person is guilty of an offence if he is knowingly a party to the carrying on of a business to which this section applies.
> (2)   This section applies to a business which is carried on–
>   (a)   by a person who is outside the reach of [section 993 of the *Companies Act 2006*] (offence of fraudulent trading), and
>   (b)   with *intent* to defraud creditors of any person or for any other fraudulent purpose.
> (3)   The following are within the reach of [that section] –
>   (a)   a company [(as defined in section 1(1) of the *Companies Act 2006*)];
>   (b)   a person to whom that section applies (with or without adaptations or modifications) as if the person were a company;
>   (c)   a person exempted from the application of that section."

34–119   **What conduct element is required under section 9(1)?**   The *actus reus* merely requires the defendant to carry on a business that is not registered as a corporation.

34–120   **What about a credit transaction? Two racketeers set up in business and at first pay the bills they incur to wholesalers. Then they run up a lot of large bills all at once, auction their stock and fade away. Will the police be on their tracks?**   Lawyers call this a "long firm fraud," for some arcane reason.[218] The ordinary person knows the phenomenon as the fly-by-night firm. The practice was to charge a single conspiracy to defraud. However, this would now be charged under section 9 of the *Fraud Act*, or, where a company is involved, the offence of fraudulent trading,[219] giving particulars of A, B, C, *etc.* who have been defrauded. You put each victim into the witness box and ask him: "Why did you

---

[217] See *Chappell v. United States*, 270 F. 2d. 274 (9th Cir. 1959). Cf. *U.S. v. Delano*, 55 F. 3d 720 (1995).

[218] Michael Levi, *The Phantom Capitalists: The Organisation and Control of Long-firm Fraud*, (London: Heinemann, 1981).

[219] See section 993 of the *Companies Act 2006*.

supply these goods to these men on credit?" Answer: "Because I thought they were an honest firm." Their mere ordering of the goods is an implied representation of honesty.

Does every firm guarantee its own solvency? Take the bank or travel agency **34–121** **that is financially ailing. A travel agent has lost a lot of money this season, and his debts exceed his assets. It is possible that if he continues to trade things may improve and all will be well. But it is also possible that they will get worse, in which case, when he takes a customer's advance payment on a holiday tour, he may not be able to provide the tour nor refund the cash. Faced with this dilemma, perhaps the very scrupulous agent would put up the shutters. But then his customers will certainly lose some of their money, whereas if he says nothing and goes on trading there is a chance that everyone will be happy.** You have put your finger on a difficult problem. In one case a judge ruled that the directors of a bank that failed could be charged with conspiracy to defraud when they took cash from customers knowing that they were insolvent.[220] The judge confined his opinion to bankers, who trade with other people's money, and said that the rule did not extend to ordinary traders. But on another occasion, when it was proved that the defendant traded through a company knowing that he was hopelessly insolvent, he was convicted of fraudulent trading.[221] Generally, the section is not confined to any particular type of trader or transaction, so long as the trader runs the business for the purpose of defrauding others.[222]

The difficulty relates to marginal cases, as in your question. If a firm is only marginally insolvent and there is hope of business picking up it would be harsh to say that fraud is established merely because the doors are not at once closed. Nonetheless, the subsection makes it clear that recklessness will not do: the defendant must carry on the business with an "intent to defraud."

Unlike the offences found in sections 2-4, the section 9 offence does not refer to "gain or loss." Instead, the defendant must carry on the business with an *intent* to "defraud." The concept of "defraud" does encapsulate "gain and loss,"[223] however. "[To] defraud ordinarily means ... to deprive a person dishonestly of something which is his or of something to which he is or would or might but for the perpetration of the fraud be entitled."[224] In *Kensington International Ltd. v. Congo*[225] Moore-Bick L.J. said:

> "The *Fraud Act 2006* does not contain a simple definition of fraud or fraudulent conduct; rather, it defines the statutory offence of fraud by reference to a breach of sections 2, 3 and 4, each of which contains a description of conduct which amounts to a breach of that section. In addition, section 9 makes it an offence knowingly to be a party to the carrying on of a business with intent to defraud creditors or for any other fraudulent purpose. Against that background I

---

[220] *R. v. Parker* (1916) 25 Cox C.C. 145. See also *R. v. Smith* [1996] 2 Cr. App. R. 1.

[221] *R. v. Inman* [1967] 1 Q.B. 140.

[222] In most cases, however, the victim is likely to be a creditor: see *R. v. Kemp* [1988] Q.B. 645.

[223] The concept "defraud" is even wider, since it is not limited to cases where there is an intention to cause the victim economic loss. See *Wai Yu-Tsang Appellant v. The Queen* [1992] 1 A.C. 269, at 270 and 279; *Welham v. D.P.P.* [1961] A.C. 103 at 123–124.

[224] *R. v. Scott* [1975] A.C. 819 at 839 *per* Viscount Dilhorne.

[225] [2008] 1 W.L.R. 1144 at 1163.

think that the expression "any form of fraudulent conduct or purpose in section 13 must be intended to refer to conduct, or to a purpose, that is fraudulent in the sense that it partakes of the essential characteristics of fraud as described in sections 2, 3 and 4. ... For my own part I think that the essence of fraud is deception of one kind or another coupled with injury or an intention to expose another to a risk of injury by means of that deception."

34–122 For example, selling someone a worthless college certificate would expose that person to a loss. It does not matter that the provider intends to provide some kind of service in return.[226] Suppose D sets up a driving school business knowing that he is not legally qualified to provide driving lessons, but provides them anyway.[227] He would be convictable under section 9 despite the fact he provided the lessons. He has defrauded his customers by failing to inform them of the fact that he is not a qualified driving instructor. If he had, they would probably have shopped around to find a qualified instructor to give their custom. Similarly, in *R. v. Smallman*[228] the defendant was charged with carrying on the business for a fraudulent purpose, namely with intent to defraud students by dishonestly "(i) pretending to the said students that the courses offered by the [business] were accredited by a recognized educational body; (ii) pretending to the said students that they would receive a recognized qualification upon completion of the course; and (iii) diverting funds from the company which had been paid to the company by, or on behalf of, the students, for the purposes of completion of their course training."

D must not only intend to defraud V, but must carry on the business for such a purpose. The subsection does not target legitimate businesses that engage in isolated acts of fraud. It is not sufficient that the some customers of the business have been defrauded in the course of doing business with D; the business must have been carried on with intent to achieve such a goal.[229]

In *Re Gerald Cooper Chemicals Ltd. (In Liquidation)*[230] it was said that this type of provision:

"is aimed at the carrying on of a business... and not at the execution of individual [fraudulent] transactions in the course of carrying on that business. I do not think that the words 'carried on' can be treated as synonymous with 'carried out', nor can I read the words 'any business' as synonymous with 'any transaction or dealing'. The director of a company dealing in second-hand motor cars who wilfully misrepresents the age and capabilities of a vehicle is, no doubt, a fraudulent rascal, but I do not think that he can be said to be carrying on the company's business for a fraudulent purpose, although no doubt he carries out a particular business transaction."

---

[226] A further example is where a person forges a prescription to obtain drugs: he defrauds the chemist "even though he intends to pay the chemist the full price and no one is a penny the worse off." *Welham v. D.P.P.* [1961] A.C. 103 at 131 *per* Lord Denning.

[227] *R. v. Benli* [1998] 2 [1998] 2 V.R. 157.

[228] [2010] EWCA Crim. 548. This case involved a company, but section 9 would apply in cases where the business is not registered as a corporation.

[229] *Morphitis v. Bernasconi* [2003] 2 W.L.R. 1521.

[230] [1978] Ch. 262 at 267.

34.9. CONSPIRACY TO DEFRAUD

Conspiracy to defraud is one of the open-ended forms of conspiracy that has **34–123** survived all attack. It even survived the reforms introduced by the *Fraud Act 2006*, notwithstanding the incredible reach of that enactment. A charge of conspiracy to defraud has been an attractive charge to the prosecution in serious cases not only because of its width but because the punishment is at large. The snag for ordinary cases is that it is not triable summarily. Moreover, conspiracy charges lend themselves to righteous indignation by defendants. It is a general stop-gap offence, but there are few, if any, gaps that remain unplugged. So, in practice, a charge of conspiracy to defraud should only be used as an absolute last resort. If there is any conduct that does not fall within any of the substantive offences of dishonesty, the prosecutor could consider whether it may not still be caught in the net of conspiracy to defraud.

The offence is doubly remarkable. First, in the width given to the notion of fraud. In ordinary speech this word generally demotes a deception—a false representation or trick working on the victim's mind, or sometimes a misappropriation of trust property by a trustee. But the judges, intent on catching crooks, and mindless of the niceties of language, held that the surreptitious or forcible taking of property without deception was also a defrauding at common law; so a robber, a burglar, and a pickpocket defrauded their victims.[231] Even where the conspirators have a state of mind that would in ordinary language be called fraudulent, there may be no false representation, failure to disclose or abuse of position as envisaged by the *Fraud Act* offences, and yet they may be guilty of conspiracy to defraud.

Secondly, the ends that the conspirators have in view may be of the most varied character. The object need not be to commit a crime, but may be to commit one of certain torts. It need not be to make a profit, but may merely be to inflict a loss.[232] It need not involve dishonesty in respect of property, but may be a dishonest endeavour to obtain certain acts or forbearances, such as to obtain a Government licence or permission.[233]

The major limiting factor in all forms of conspiracy to defraud is the necessity to prove dishonesty. A summing up is defective if it tells the jury that an intent to act to the prejudice of another's right *is* an intent to defraud. Such intent suffices for the offence only if it is dishonest, and this must be emphasized to the jury.[234]

---

[231] *Scott v. Commissioner of Police of the Metropolis* [1975] A.C. 819 at 837-838 *per* Viscount Dilhorne.

[232] *Scott v. Commissioner of Police of the Metropolis* [1975] A.C. 819 at 837-839.

[233] See *Board of Trade v. Owen* [1957] A.C. 602 at 622; *R. v. Terry* [1984] A.C. 374.

[234] *R. v. Landy* [1981] 1 W.L.R. 355 at 365-366. The court said that conduct such as acting to the prejudice of another's right is only possible evidence of defrauding. But if all the kinds of defrauding are only evidence of defrauding, what is defrauding? The answer, it seems, is that defrauding means dishonest conduct, and acting to the prejudice of another's right is one of the forms of conduct that juries may regard as dishonest. See also *R. v. Rowland* [2007] EWCA Crim. 479.

34–124 **I remember that a conspiracy to defraud remains a crime at common law, and cannot be charged as a statutory conspiracy. Is the difference between the two kinds of conspiracy important?** The rules do not differ markedly, apart from the fact that a statutory conspiracy must be to commit an offence, not just some wrong in general. Otherwise, the chief difference is that a conspiracy at common law (and therefore a conspiracy to defraud) is not an arrestable offence[235] while a statutory conspiracy can be.[236] And there is the procedural point that a statutory conspiracy should be charged under the *Criminal Law Act 1977*, while a conspiracy to defraud is charged as being contrary to the common law.

Then take, say, a conspiracy to obtain property by making a false representation. Is that a statutory conspiracy to violate section 2 of the *Fraud Act 2006*, or is it a common law conspiracy to defraud? Or both? This point has caused trouble, owing to the defective drafting of the *Criminal Law Act*. The answer, as settled by the courts with respect to the former section 15 of the *Theft Act*, is that the conspiracy *can* and (at least generally) *should* be charged as a statutory conspiracy to commit the specific offence (or offences).[237] In a clear case, where there is no doubt that the conspiracy, if it existed, was to commit a statutory offence, it should be charged as a statutory conspiracy.[238] Charges of conspiracy to defraud should be reserved for cases where at least part of the objects of the conspiracy were fraudulent objects that did not amount to any specific crimes.[239]

34.10. MAIN HEADS OF CONSPIRACY TO DEFRAUD

34–125 These generalizations, being somewhat negative, are perhaps un-illuminating. More positively, most conspiracies to defraud can be classified under the following heads:

1. *Conspiracies to obtain property dishonestly.* There are some ways in which conspiracy to defraud is wider than a charge of conspiracy to steal. A straightforward conspiracy to steal would be best charged as that, not as a conspiracy to defraud.[240]

2. *Conspiracies dishonestly to obtain a pecuniary advantage other than property.* While a conspiracy to obtain the pecuniary advantage should now be caught by sections 1-4 of the *Fraud Act 2006*, conspiracies to obtain such advantages are indictable as conspiracies to defraud. An example (where two or more wrongdoers are involved) is where a dishonest profit is made (or attempted to be made) from the property of another. This will not constitute theft of the property used, if there is in law no appropriation of

---

[235] *R. v. Spicer* (1970) 114 S.J. 824.

[236] That is to say, will be arrestable if the offence aimed at will be arrestable (as theft, for example, is).

[237] *R. v. Duncalf* [1979] 1 W.L.R. 918; *R. v. K.* [2007] 1 W.L.R. 3190 at 3205.

[238] *R. v. Levitz* (1990) 90 Cr. App. R. 33; *R. v. Pickford* [1995] Q.B. 203.

[239] *R. v. Levitz* (1990) 90 Cr. App. R. 33. The offences are not mutually exclusive. See section 12 of the *Criminal Justice Act 1987*.

[240] *R. v. Ascroft* [2003] Crim. L.R. 894.

that property with intent to deprive the owner permanently. An illustration is *Scott v. Commissioner of Police of the Metropolis*.[241]

This turned on a large-scale conspiracy to bribe cinema employees to hand over films that were being shown; the films were copied and distributed commercially. This amounted to a breach of copyright and the offence of corruption of employees, but, it was not theft of the copyright, and no deception was involved. It was held by the House of Lords that a charge of conspiracy to defraud the owners of the copyrights would lie.

Their Lordships assumed that what the defendants did not only made a profit for themselves, but inflicted a loss on the owners of the copyrights, which was no doubt true on the facts of the case; but circumstances can be imagined in which it would not be true. For example, the pirated films might be exhibited in China or Bora Bora, where perhaps the lawful owners of the copyrights were unable to distribute them. The scheme was fraudulent because its object was to make a profit from the unauthorized use of the property, when the exploitation of this use was part of the property right.[242]

3. *Conspiracies to cause a loss merely in malice.* Almost unknown: a conspiracy to cause criminal damage to property would be charged as such, not as conspiracy to defraud. Sometimes the courts emphasize an intent to cause a loss as indicative of a conspiracy to defraud, but swindlers are not actuated by old-fashioned malice. The loss they cause is incidental to the profit they make for themselves.

4. *Conspiracy to cause a person to act contrary to his duty.* (Including conspiracies to deceive a person into acting otherwise than as his duty would have obliged if it had not been for the deception practised upon him.) Although this type of charge has not been much used by prosecutors, it has enormous potential. There are innumerable statutes imposing "duties" on public officers and bodies, say to collect statistical information or to provide schooling or medical care, and any concerted action to prevent such duties from being punctiliously preformed would in theory be indictable.

The law is still somewhat uncertain on the last head. It certainly applies to conspiracies to use deception to obtain a government licence or permission to bring about other activity or inactivity by a public officer in breach of duty, but the doubt is whether it applies to the deception of private persons in respect of merely private duties. There have been some difficulties because of obscure and conflicting pronouncements from the Law Lords. All that emerges is that some Law Lords have said that the conspiracy may be to cause private persons to act contrary to their duty, while others have denied it. You may rest content with that knowledge, but the following summaries note the discordant views for those who are interested.

---

[241] [1975] A.C. 819.

[242] The defendants might have been charged with theft for taking the proceeds made from the infringement of copyright, but the point was not argued. Cf. *R. v. Shadrokh-Cigari* [1988] Crim. L.R. 465.

34–126   In *Board of Trade v. Owen*[243] Lord Tucker (speaking for the Judicial Committee of the Privy Council) said that a conspiracy to procure an export licence by fraud from a government department was an offence, primarily as a conspiracy to defraud the government; he followed this with a tentative remark indicating that he was prepared to consider that a conspiracy to defraud any person (even a private person) into acting to his detriment would constitute the offence. Lord Radcliffe cited this with approval in *Welham v. D.P.P.*,[244] a case on forgery where it was assumed that the mental element was the same as for conspiracy to defraud. On the whole the speeches in *Welham v. D.P.P.* agreed with Lord Denning who made no distinction between a public and a private duty.

Lord Radcliffe's enigmatic language may have misled some members of the House of Lords in *D.P.P. v. Withers*,[245] which is more directly relevant to our present subject. This was a decision that put an end to the doctrine of "public mischief" in our law. Enquiry agents obtained confidential information by fraud. They obtained the information from bank employees by pretending to be bank employees, and from government officers by pretending to be government officers. The House of Lords quashed convictions for conspiracy to defraud, but, apart from Viscount Dilhorne (with who Lord Reid concurred), none expressed the opinion that the conspiracy to deceive the banks might have been so charged. Lord Kilbrandon said expressly that bankers could not be accounted public officers within what he regarded as the rule in *Welham v. D.P.P.*

In *Scott v. Commissioner of Police of the Metropolis* (the facts of which were given earlier), Lord Diplock, alone among the Lords, said that on a charge of conspiracy to defraud an individual, the purpose of the conspirators must be to cause him economic loss by depriving him of some property right. Only where the victim is a public officer does the charge lie in respect of causing an act in breach of duty. This was *obiter*, and was probably influenced by the same misunderstanding of *Welham v. D.P.P.* as had occurred in *D.P.P. v. Withers*. Lord Dilhorne, who spoke for the rest of the House, did not express himself so dogmatically, though there is a passage in his speech, referring to *Welham v. D.P.P.*, that perhaps indicates the same misapprehension.

34–127   **Would the offence of conspiracy to defraud be committed by entering into an agreement to deceive a private person into committing an offence?**   An offence is an act contrary to duty, so the question is precisely that just discussed, whether a conspiracy to defraud a private person into acting contrary to his duty is punishable. As we have seen,[246] the courts seem now to be ready to hold that a person who causes the commission of an offence, or the *actus reus* of an offence, becomes implicated in it merely because of the element of causation. But that line of argument involves serious difficulties.

---

[243] [1957] A.C. 602 at 622. See also *R. v. Terry* [1984] A.C. 374.
[244] [1961] A.C. 103 at 129.
[245] [1975] A.C. 842.
[246] *Attorney-General's Reference (No. 1 of 1975)* [1975] Q.B. 773; *R. v. Millward* (1994) 158 J.P. 1091.

You said in the Chapter on conspiracy that the general offence of conspiracy   **34–128**
requires intention in relation to consequences. Is it a conspiracy to defraud
to subject another person to a financial risk that he would not have wished to
run if he had known the facts? Conspiracy to defraud does not require
anything more than conspiracy to take an unlawful risk.[247] A remarkable example
concerns company directors. They are in a peculiar position, since they are in
charge of the property of the company and yet are not, technically, trustees for the
shareholders. Although they may commit specific offences of dishonesty in
relation to the company property, no statute declares that they commit a criminal
offence in making use of it in a rash way. Yet in *R. v. Sinclair*,[248] where directors
took a risk by handing over the whole of the company's assets without security,
they were held in the circumstances to be guilty of a conspiracy to defraud the
company, its shareholders and creditors. The Court of Appeal said:[249]

> "To cheat and defraud is to act with deliberate dishonesty to the prejudice of another person's
> proprietary right. In the context of this case the alleged conspiracy to cheat and defraud is an
> agreement by a director of a company and others dishonestly to take a risk with the assets of
> the company by using them in a manner which was known to be not in the best interests of the
> company and to be prejudicial to the minority shareholders."

The case shows how intention to take a risk with someone else's property, or
to cause him by fraud to take such a risk, for purposes of one's own, is capable of
founding a charge of conspiracy to defraud. The essence of the offence is not
causing loss (because it does not matter whether loss is caused or not); it lies in
subjecting another person to an unwanted pecuniary risk.[250] The conspirators
knowingly take this risk on the victim's behalf.

The agreement to defraud might involve an agreement:

1.   To "deprive a person of something which is his or to which he would be or
   might be entitled or to injure some proprietary right of a person." The
   defendant need not intend to cause an actual loss, but he must be shown to
   have foreseen that such loss or prejudice would or might result.
2.   But conspiracies to defraud are not restricted to cases of intention to cause
   the victim an economic loss; if a person agrees with one or more other
   persons that they should deceive a public official to prevent him from
   performing his public duties, then, they too might be guilty of conspiracy to
   defraud.

---

[247] *Wai Yu-Tsang v. The Queen* [1992] 1 A.C. 269; *Adams v. The Queen* [1995] 1 W.L.R. 52.
[248] [1968] 1 W.L.R. 1246.
[249] *R. v. Sinclair* [1968] 1 W.L.R. 1246 at 1250.
[250] See *Wai Yu-Tsang v. The Queen* [1992] 1 A.C. 269; *Adams v. The Queen* [1995] 1 W.L.R. 52; *R. v. Allsop* (1976) 64 Cr. App. R. 29.

34.11.   DISHONESTY AND CONSPIRACY TO DEFRAUD

34–129   **Does a charge of conspiracy to defraud give proper notice to the defendant of what is alleged against him?**   The indictment should contain particulars of the fraud alleged, sufficient to identify it with reasonable precision;[251] and if particulars are lacking they may be ordered. Although the law has attained a certain degree of precision, it is open to objection on two grounds:

1. There is no reason for making liability depend upon the act being done by two people. If it is objectionable for two, it is objectionable for one. If it is unobjectionable for one, it should be unobjectionable for two.
2. The notion of defrauding is inherently vague. In itself it is merely a label for what the courts regard as dishonest. The law should be more certain than this. It should specify more exactly what is and is not allowed.[252]

34–130   **But the definitions of both theft and fraud include a requirement of dishonesty.[253] If you object to the requirement in conspiracy to defraud, you must object to it in other crimes also.**   Your first statement is correct, but your conclusion does not follow. In theft and fraud dishonesty is merely a limit on liability. As a philosopher would say, it is a necessary but not a sufficient condition. For theft you must appropriate property belonging to another, *etc.*, the requirement of dishonesty is an extra. For fraud you must make a false representation, fail to disclose information or abuse a position of trust. In the case of conspiracy to defraud there appears to be no other requirement, apart from the agreement. Anything that the jury labels (and is allowed to label) as dishonest becomes punishable as the object of a conspiracy to defraud. This is too vague a test to serve as the foundation of criminal liability.

You will recall that dishonesty can arise in two senses in fraud cases. Take the example of fraud by false representation, the false representation is the dishonest *means* used to achieve the dishonest *end* of obtaining another's property. (The end may be honest, if D used dishonest means to obtain what he believed was his own property). In *Peters v. The Queen*,[254] Justice McHugh said:

> "In most cases of conspiracy to defraud, to prove dishonest means the Crown will have to establish that the defendants intended to prejudice another person's right or interest or performance of public duty by:
> - making or taking advantage of representations or promises which they knew were false or would not be carried out;
> - concealing facts which they had a duty to disclose; or
> - engaging in conduct which they had no right to engage in."

---

[251] *R. v. Landy* [1981] 1 W.L.R. 355.

[252] See the discussion on the constitutional limits of the criminal law in Chapter 3.

[253] The *R. v. Ghosh* [1982] QB 1053 standard also applies in conspiracy to defraud cases.

[254] (1998) 192 C.L.R. 493 at 529.

We can add abuse of position of trust to that list.[255] But dishonesty is not determined by considering whether D used dishonest means. The focus should be on whether the conspirators had an honest "intent." The conspirators do not have a dishonest intent (unlawful motive) if they merely plan to carry out a "sting" operation to "obtain property which they believe they are legally entitled to take."[256] In case of conspiracy to defraud, agreement *per se* is not the means that are used to bring about the dishonest end. The conspirators' intent is dishonest, only if they aim for a dishonest end. The conspirators would act dishonestly if they intend to obtain property belonging to another believing they have no right to obtain it. (But so would a fraudster who intends the same, but does not "agree" with another to bring about such an end.) If the conspirators agree to obtain another's property believing they have no right to obtain it, they would be agreeing to bring about a dishonest end. If they agree to obtain the property because it was stolen from them, they agree to act honestly. (Put another way, their intent is honest because they aim to bring about a consequence which they are entitled to bring about).

The dishonest "means" are important in the law of fraud to the extent they provide a clear *actus reus* in fraud offences such as fraud by false representation, fraud by failing to disclose and fraud by abuse of position: these offences mean that the sole criterion for a fraud conviction is not mere dishonesty. But as I noted above, dishonest means can be used to achieve an honest end, as is the case where D uses a false representation to get his own property back from a thief. Hence, dishonesty will always be determined by considering the intent or lawful justification (or putatively lawful justifications in the case of mistakes) D had for bringing about the particular result: did he honestly intend to obtain his own property or did he dishonestly intend to obtain property belonging to another? The dishonest means form the *actus reus* of the fraud offences found in sections 1-4 and do not need to be analysed when considering the dishonesty defence.

34–131

Are there any "dishonest" means beyond false representation, failure to disclose and abuse of position that might be used to defraud another? If not, what role does the common law offence of conspiracy of defraud play? Would not all these statutory conspiracies since they are crimes in themselves? The inchoate form of criminalization provided for by the law of conspiracy would apply where D2 and D1 agree to make a false representation to make a gain or cause a loss, regardless of whether they make the representation.[257] But if two people agree to try to get money by making a representation, which may or may not be true, and at that time are reckless about whether it will be true or false, then, if the representation is untrue when they make it and get money, they will be guilty of fraud by false representation, but they are not guilty of conspiracy. It will be the same if one of the two knows that the representation

34–132

---

[255] An abuse of trust might involve a conspiracy to defraud (see *R. v. Darwin* [2009] EWCA Crim. 860), but using this type of dishonest means to achieve a dishonest end is caught by section 4 of the *Fraud Act 2006*.

[256] *Peters v. The Queen* (1998) 192 C.L.R. 493 at 508-509.

[257] This is basically a form of double inchoate liability to the extent that even if the representation is made, there is no need to show that it resulted in a gain/loss under the *Fraud Act 2006*.

is false; both must know that it is or will be false before there can be any criminal conspiracy. If the parties are found to have been "wilfully blind" to the possibility of falsity, they may be held to have known that the representation was false, but that doctrine of wilful blindness cannot be used to extend a requirement of knowledge to cases of mere recklessness.[258] In other words, where the offence can be committed without the perpetrator knowing of a required circumstance (*e.g.*, where he is liable for recklessness as to the circumstance), there can be no conspiracy except between those who intend that the circumstance shall exist at the time of the offence or know it will.

Similarly, if D2 and D1 agree to abuse a position of trust by using their employer's property to make a gain, they would be liable for making the agreement. There would be no need to show that they actually abused the position of trust, which would be required under section 4 of the *Fraud Act 2006*.[259] A conspiracy catches the agreement to do the conduct element. There is no need to show the conduct was done, only that there was an agreement to do it. Liability hinges on D2 and D1 agreeing to make the false representation, or to abuse the position of trust, or to fail to disclose information, regardless of whether they do that conduct.[260]

34.12.   MAKING OFF WITHOUT HAVING PAID

34–133   With the enactment of section 3 of the *Theft Act 1978* a new technical term entered the law—"making off." The section creates an either way offence to deal with debtors who do their tent-folding at a filling station or restaurant or other place where they are expected to pay on the spot. As usual, I set out the section with the omission of distracting words:

> "(1)   A person who, knowing that payment on the spot for any goods supplied or service done is required or expected from him, dishonestly makes off without having paid as required or expected and with intent to avoid payment of the amount due shall be guilty of an offence.
>
> (2)   Payment on the spot includes payment at the time of collecting goods on which work has been done or in respect of which service has been provided.
>
> (3)   Subsection (1) above shall not apply where the supply of the goods or the doing of the service is contrary to law, or where the service done is such that payment is not legally enforceable."

The advantage of the provision is that it enables a conviction to be obtained even when no proof is available that the defendant had a dishonest intent when he ordered the article or service, or when he obtained it.

So a motorist who "makes off" with a tank full of petrol, and the diner who slips out of the restaurant and melts in the crowd after the meal, can be convicted, even though some credence is given to his story that he did not form the

---

[258] *R. v. Saik* [2007] 1 A.C. 18.

[259] Again, under section 4 it is necessary to show the conduct element was committed, but not that it resulted in a gain or loss.

[260] For a discussion of the limits of double inchoate criminalization see Douglas N. Husak, "The Nature and Justifiability of Non-consummate Offences," (1995) 37 *Ariz. L. Rev.* 151; Ira P. Robbins, "Double Inchoate Crimes," (1989) 26 *Harv. J. on Legis.* 1.

fraudulent intent until the petrol was in his tank or the meal in his stomach. The provision also covers hotel and taxi cheats, and freeloaders on public transport.

But can you say that goods are "supplied" at a self-service filling station?   An acute question. The answer is yes, because the customer presses a button which alerts the supervising clerk before the customer fills up. On the other hand the surreptitious thief in a supermarket is probably not "supplied." He just takes.

34–134

What if a restaurant customer, having been served, creeps off but intends to pay later?   There seems to be a theoretical loophole in the offence as drafted, created by the words "and with intent to avoid payment of the amount due." They provide that even if the debtor does dishonestly make off without having paid as required or expected, he is not guilty if he can say with some plausibility that he intended to pay later.[261] However, the words may possibly be read as meaning "with intent to avoid payment as required or expected regardless of the particular spot where payment might normally be made."[262]

34–135

What if the diner is caught just outside the restaurant, trying to make his getaway?   The jury must be asked to consider what was the ambit of the "spot" where the payment was supposed to be made. Presumably the offence is committed as soon as the defendant has quitted the restaurant, filling station, *etc.* If he is only making for the restaurant door, that should on principle be only an attempt.[263]

34–136

Suppose the diner explains to the desk that he is going to his car to get his wallet, or gives a cheque; he never comes back, and the cheque is not honoured.   In both your hypotheticals the debtor obtains his creditor's consent to have, but the consent is procured by fraud. Thus, he could be charged with fraud by false representation.

34–137

In *R. v. Vincent*[264] the defendant stayed in two hotels and left without paying his bills in full. He was charged with two counts of making off without payment contrary to section 3(1) of the *Theft Act 1978*. Normally, the bill has to be paid before the customer leaves the premises. But on this occasion, the defendant told the proprietors of the hotels that he was waiting for money due to him for work which he had done, and would not be able to pay the bill until he received his wages. The trial judge directed the jury that, if the defendant was dishonest in getting the proprietors to agree to postponing payment, he should be taken as having made off without paying on the spot. The defendant was convicted on both counts.

---

[261] In *R. v. Allen* [1985] A.C. 1029 at 1034 it was held that it must be shown that the defendant intended to make off without paying altogether. In other words, he must be shown to have intended "to do more than delay or defer the payment." He must have intended to "evade payment altogether."

[262] *R. v. Aziz* [1993] Crim. L.R. 708.

[263] *R. v. Brooks* (1983) 76 Cr. App. R. 66.

[264] [2001] 1 W.L.R. 1172.

On appeal, the Court of Appeal said:[265]

> "The issue is whether, when the defendant left the premises, payment was at that time 'required or expected' from him. .... (There was no 'making off', giving that expression its ordinary meaning which may suggest a surreptitious departure). In circumstances such as these, the section does not in our view require or permit an analysis of whether the agreement actually made was obtained by deception. The wording and purpose of the section do not contemplate what could be a complex investigation of alleged fraud underlying the agreement. If the expectation is defeated by an agreement, it cannot be said to exist. The fact that the agreement was obtained dishonestly does not reinstate the expectation. While the customer would be liable to be charged with obtaining services by deception, if he continued to stay at the hotel with that dishonest intention, he would not infringe section 3."

34–138   **Would a tenant who flits without paying his rent be guilty under section 3?**   No. Service in section 3 is evidently intended to bear its ordinary meaning, whatever that is. The tenant of an unfurnished flat or house who bilks his landlord of the rent has not obtained a service, and anyway there is no requirement in an ordinary lease that the rent be paid on the spot.

---

[265] *R. v. Vincent* [2001] 1 W.L.R. 1172 at 1174-1176. *Contra*, the Court of Appeal said: "In taxi or restaurant cases, it would be more difficult for a customer to establish an agreement which defeated the expectation. The expectation may still exist if a customer leaves a restaurant on the pretext that he is going to get his wallet. The restaurateur's acquiescence in that departure, by not exercising a power of arrest, would not necessarily remove his expectation and the jury could be directed accordingly. The present circumstances were however different, if the defendant was believed, and the usual expectation of payment on the spot was removed by agreement."

CHAPTER 35

DAMAGE AND TRESPASS

"A ridiculously oversimplified misreading of history manages to present all human progress in terms of a battle between freedom, which is assumed to be good, and prohibition, which is assumed to be bad. In fact, of course, civilisation owes quite as much to those who limit freedom as to those who expand it. Stopping people doing things, that was the first necessity, with freedom only coming as a secondary luxury."

Peregrine Worsthorne

35.1. CRIMINAL DAMAGE

The offence of criminal damage (formerly called "malicious damage") now rests on the *Criminal Damage Act 1971*, and section references in the first part of this chapter will be to this *Act* unless otherwise stated. There are three main offences and two ancillary offences. The three main offences may be called, for short, (1) simple damage, (2) dangerous damage, and (3) arson. The two subsidiary offences are (1) threats and (2) custody with intent.   **35–001**

All are punishable with a maximum of imprisonment for 10 years, except arson and dangerous damage, which are punishable on indictment with imprisonment for life. All are triable either way, apart for the offences in sections 1(2) and 3. If a person is charged with the section 1(1) offence (apart from an offence charged as arson) and the value is less than £5,000 he has to be tried summarily.[1] "The court is required to 'proceed as if the offence were triable only summarily' if, but only if, 'it appears to the court clear that' it is considering a low value offence. If that remains unclear, then the justices have to proceed as if the offence was not scheduled and the value of the offence never falls to be considered again."[2] Other cases of dangerous damage (and arson when it complies with the definition of dangerous damage) are triable only on indictment. In fact the vast majority of cases of vandalism are disposed of summarily.

Simple damage is defined in section 1(1):

---

[1] Section 22 of the *Magistrates' Courts Act 1980*; section 22(11) provides: "where (a) the accused is charged on the same occasion with two or more scheduled offences and it appears to the court that they constitute or form part of a series of two or more offences of the same or a similar character; or (b) the offence charged consists in incitement to commit two or more scheduled offences, this section shall have effect as if any reference in it to the value involved were a reference to the aggregate of the values involved."

[2] *R. v. Bristol Magistrates Court Ex p. E* [1999] 1 W.L.R. 390 at 39; see also *R. v. Fennell* [2000] 1 W.L.R. 2011 at 2017; *R. v. Alden* [2002] 2 Cr. App. R. (S.) 74.

> "(1) A person who without lawful excuse destroys or damages any property belonging to another intending to destroy or damage any such property or being reckless as to whether any such property would be destroyed or damaged shall be guilty of an offence."

35.2. THE DAMAGE

35–002 Although the *Act* carefully says "destroys or damages," every case of destroying must be one of damaging.[3] Actual damage is required, and the court may refuse to find damage where minimal damage has been caused without direct intent—as where a few men play football in a grass field used for grazing.[4] But quite small provable damage is sufficient.[5]

35–003 **Could that ubiquitous, Bill Stickers,[6] be prosecuted under the *Act*?** For acts done without authority he is usually charged under the local *Acts* or bylaws;[7] but on principle he could be charged with criminal damage.[8] Dirt has been jocularly defined as a matter in place, and affixing matter in an unwanted place is capable of being regarded as damage.[9] Other examples would be: spreading jam on someone's car seat, putting sugar in his petrol, and defacing his walls with aerosol paint.[10] In *R. v. Fiak*[11] the defendant flooded a police cell by placing a blanket down the lavatory. Judge P. (as he then was) said:[12]

> "it is true that the effect of the appellant's actions in relation to the blanket and the cell were both remediable, the simple reality is that the blanket could not be used as a blanket by any other prisoner until it had been dried out (and, we believe, also cleaned) and the flooded cells remained out of action until the water was cleared. In our judgment it is clear that both sustained damage for the purposes of the *1971 Act*."

The law on the subject of minor damage was cast into some doubt by the decision of a Crown Court on appeal from magistrates in *"A" (a Juvenile)*.[13] The defendant had been convicted of criminal damage for spitting on the back of a police sergeant's uniform which he was wearing. The conviction was set aside on the ground that the spittle could readily have been wiped off with a damp cloth,

---

[3] But the distinction can be important in respect of jurisdiction and compensation.

[4] Cf. *Eley v. Lytle* (1885) 50 J.P. 308, decided under the previous legislation. See also *Gardner v. Mansbridge* [1887] 19 Q.B.D. 217; cf. *Gayford v. Chouler* [1898] 1 Q.B. 316; *Laws v. Eltringham* (1881-82) 8 Q.B.D. 283.

[5] For the old law, see *e.g.*, *R. v. Foster* (1852) 6 Cox C.C. 25.

[6] That is, the person who pastes up posters on walls or billboards.

[7] Marking or billposting on a wall, *etc.* in London is an offence under section 54(10) of the *Metropolitan Police Act 1839*.

[8] Cf. *R. v. Austin* [2009] 2 Cr. App. R. (S.) 74, Ds was jailed for 20 months for spraying graffiti in the carriages of trains. See also *Roe v. Kingerlee* [1986] Crim. L.R. 735, where D smeared mud graffiti on a police cell wall.

[9] *Henderson & Battley* (November 29, 1984) quoted in *Cox v. Riley* (1986) 83 Cr. App. R. 54 at 56-57.

[10] Cf. *Roper v. Knott* [1898] 1 Q.B. 868 (damaging milk by adding water); *King v. Lees* (1949) 65 T.L.R. 21 (urinating in a taxi-cab). But it appears that daubing a wall would not be damage if it is regarded as amelioration: *R. v. Fancy* [1980] Crim. L.R. 171.

[11] [2005] Po. L.R. 211.

[12] *R. v. Fiak* [2005] Po. L.R. 211.

[13] [1978] Crim. L.R. 689.

and the raincoat was not rendered "inoperative." Spitting upon a silk dress, on the other hand, could be damage if removing the spittle left a mark.

The case is not of high authority, and seems to be a lenient application of the law. On the occasion in question the officer's raincoat was already covered with similar spittle, and if the one youth before the court who spat upon it was not guilty of damage, neither were any of the others; yet collectively they had made it necessary to wash the coat (and during the period of washing it would be what would be called "inoperative"). Displacing the parts of a machine in order to render it temporarily unless amounts to damaging it even though the parts are not damaged.[14] Similarly, it should be damage to separate a fixture from a building.[15]

Enabling someone's pet animal to escape would doubtless be a constructive destruction of it! Releasing breeding mink from their cages, whereby their value was reduced although they were recovered and were not physically damaged, was held to cause damage by the Supreme Court of the Republic of Ireland.[16] Letting the air out of someone's tyres would best be dealt with as an offence of tampering with a vehicle,[17] but it should also be accounted damage and, theoretically, theft of the air.

What if I wheel-clamp a person's car so that he cannot use it? Would it make   35–004
any difference if I were to offer to unclamp it in return for pecuniary
payment?   You should be liable for criminal damage, but there is an aberrant decision which holds otherwise.[18] It is true that detention *per se* would not damage the car or diminish its value, but the car cannot be used as a car until it is released. This type of interference with "use" has been held to constitute criminal damage.[19] "What the *Act* requires to be proved is that tangible property has been damaged, not necessarily that the damage itself should be tangible. … If the appellant was proved to have intentionally and without lawful excuse [interfered] in such a way as to cause an impairment of the value or usefulness of the [property] to the owner, there would be damage within the meaning of section 1."[20] The value of property will be impaired where the owner has to pay to have it repaired or cleaned. If a person has to have her dress dried cleaned because someone has poured red wine on it, the value of the dress is reduced. Similarly, if

---

[14] The damage need not be permanent. *Cox v. Riley* (1986) 83 Cr. App. R. 54. This was also held under the *Malicious Damage Act 1861*. See *R. v. Fisher* (1865-72) L.R. 1 C.C.R. 7; *R. v. Tacey* (1821) Russ. & R. 452.

[15] Where a metal sheet is removed from a house without damaging the sheet, the charge should be of damage to the house (the aggregate entity), not to the sheet. See *R. v. Woolstock* [1977] Crim. L.R. 104. Magistrates have held that squatters who take off a Yale lock and replace it with one of their own do not commit criminal damage (*The Times*, 22 August 1975). Cf. *Johnson v. D.P.P.* [1994] Crim. L.R. 673.

[16] *Rexi Irish Mink Ltd. v. Dublin County Council* [1972] I.R. 123.

[17] Section 25 of the *Road Traffic Act 1988*.

[18] See *Drake v. D.P.P.* [1994] R.T.R. 411 at 418, where it was held that wheel-clamping a vehicle did not damage it because it did not cause any physical damage to it. If the vehicle had been marked or scratched by the clamp that would have constituted criminal damage. But if the scratch had been of a kind that would have resulted from normal use, that would not be criminal damage. See *Morphitis v. Salmon* (1990) 154 J.P. 365.

[19] *R. v. Fiak* [2005] Po. L.R. 211; *Morphitis v. Salmon* [1990] Crim. L.R. 48; *R. v. Fisher* (1865-72) L.R. 1 C.C.R. 7.

[20] *R. v. Whiteley* [1991] 93 Cr. App. R. 25 at 28 *per* Lord Lane C.J.

D dumps five tonnes of scrap steel on V's front lawn, he damages V's land because V will have to expend his own labour to remove it or pay others to do so.[21] Property's usefulness might be impaired where it is detained or temporarily put out of use. If a wheel-clamper takes a part from a car to prevent the owner from using it, he would be liable for criminal damage. If the wheel-clamper were to jack up the car to take one of its wheels to prevent the owner from using it, he would be liable for criminal damage even though he does not physically damage the car or its wheel.[22] His detention of the wheel impairs the usefulness of the car. It should make no difference whether he clamps the wheel or removes it!

The wheel-clamper might also be liable for theft[23] or blackmail. In *Black v. Carmichael*,[24] it was held that it is criminal extortion for car park operators to hold a person's vehicle for ransom. This was a Scottish decision, but the offence of blackmail should apply in England and Wales. Car park operators include "penalty" clauses in small print on signs in their car parks, but these "penalty" clauses are unlawful in civil law.[25] Private organizations are not empowered to punish citizens; they are entitled only to reasonable compensation for the loss of use of their car park space. A claim of £100 for £1 worth of unpaid parking would be an unlawful claim for a penalty sum and the use of a wheel-clamp to force a person to pay it would, theoretically, be blackmail. The criminal law should be used wherever possible to punish those who engage in these types of dodgy consumer practices;[26] unfortunately it isn't, because prosecutors are trained to focus on street crime.[27]

35–005   **Would it be damage if a dissatisfied employee sabotaged the business by instructing its computer to wipe clean the company's computer programmes and files?**   Your example shows that the notion of damage must include any deleterious change in the condition of property.[28] Section 10(5) of the *Act of 1971* provides: "For the purposes of this *Act* a modification of the contents of a computer shall not be regarded as damaging any computer or computer storage medium unless its effect on that computer or computer storage medium impairs its physical condition."[29]

---

[21] *Henderson & Battley* (November 29, 1984) quoted in *Cox v. Riley* (1986) 83 Cr. App. R. 54 at 56-57.

[22] This is assuming he put the car on appropriate blocks after jacking it up and thus did not cause any physical damage to it.

[23] See section 6 of the *Theft Act 1968* as discussed in *R. v. Raphael* [2008] EWCA Crim. 1014. See also sections 12 and 12A of the *Theft Act 1968*.

[24] [1992] S.L.T. 897.

[25] *Dunlop Pneumatic Tyre Co Ltd. v. New Garage & Motor Co Ltd.* [1915] A.C. 79.

[26] Parliament has now licensed wheel-clamping, which means the clamper can obtain an illegal penalty as long as he is licensed. See sections 3 and 4A of the *Private Security Industry Act 2001*.

[27] See the comments of Sedley L.J. in *Ferguson v. British Gas Trading Ltd.* [2010] 1 W.L.R. 785 at 799. See also Jeffrey H. Reiman and Paul Leighton, *The Rich Get Richer and the Poor Get Prison: Ideology, Class, and Criminal Justice*, (Boston: Allyn & Bacon, 9th edn. 2010).

[28] See *Cox v. Riley* (1986) 83 Cr. App. R. 54; *R. v. Whiteley* (1991) 93 Cr. App. R. 25 (damage to a computer disk by removing the "information" from them).

[29] But see the offence in section 3 of the *Computer Misuse Act 1990*.

35.3.   PROPERTY

The definition of property for the propose of criminal damage in section 10 **35–006**
broadly follows that in the *Theft Act 1968*, but there are two main divergences:

1.   There can generally be no theft of land or a building as such, but criminal
     damage can be committed to land or a building.[30]
2.   Taking wild mushrooms and flowers, fruit or foliage of "a plant growing
     wild" can be theft if the taking is for a commercial purpose. But wilfully
     squashing the mushrooms, or damaging the foliage, *etc.* of such a plant, is
     not criminal damage whatever the purpose. The test of commercial purpose
     is not incorporated into the *Criminal Damage Act*, because it is hardly
     apposite.

Felling someone else's tree can be criminal damage,[31] because a tree is
presumably not just a plant, and anyway the felling is not merely damage to
foliage, *etc.* Burning the gorse is regarded as an amelioration.[32] The exclusion of
"foliage" presumably allows one to take a small branch of foliage from a shrub
without being guilty of criminal damage (query if from a tree); but it would not
extend to damaging the whole of a shrub. Taking the whole plant would be
criminal damage to the land, and it would also be theft of the plant, even though
not for a commercial purpose. Questions may arise on what is meant by "growing
wild." A shrub is not "growing wild" if it has been planted; but what if, though
self-sown, it has been fertilized or pruned? On principle the prosecution would
have to show that the defendant knew the plant was cultivated or was reckless as
to this. (For a discussion of when wild animals become property, see Chapter 29).

35.4.   BELONGING TO ANOTHER

Subsection (1) is confined to "property belonging to another;"[33] so it does not **35–007**
penalize the anti-social destruction of one's own property.[34] However, this can
sometimes be an offence under subsection (2), to be dealt with presently.

---

[30] See the decision of Court of Appeal in the unreported case of *Henderson & Battley* (November 29,
1984) quoted in *Cox v. Riley* (1986) 83 Cr. App. R. 54 at 56-57. That case involved D dumping
rubbish on a development site thereby forcing the owner to pay to have it removed.

[31] *Unsworth v. D.P.P.* [2010] EWHC 3037 (Admin).

[32] Cf. *R. v. Fancy* [1980] Crim. L.R. 171.

[33] Nevertheless, an allegation that a particular person owns the property is, as in theft, an immaterial
averment. See *Pike v. Morrison* [1981] 1 All E.R. 65, where the rule was applied though the burning
was carried out by an employee on the employer's directions. The court overlooked the fact that the
property was vested in a company.

[34] There may be certain laws covering listed property and antiquities of national importance, but
beyond that you may burn your Caravaggio if you wish! For an interesting account of damage to art
see Thomas Wurtenberger, "Criminal Damage to Art –A Criminological Study," (1965) 14 *DePaul L.
Rev.* 83.

Formerly, setting fire to one's own house as a step towards defrauding the insurance company was arson; this is not so under the *Act of 1971*,[35] though it can be an offence under subsection (2), or alternatively fraud, in appropriate circumstances.

Section 10(2) provides:

"(1)   In this *Act* 'property' means of a tangible nature, whether real or personal, including money and—

(a)   including wild creatures which have been tamed or are ordinarily kept in captivity, and any other wild creatures or their carcasses if, but only if, they have been reduced into possession which has not been lost or abandoned or are in the course of being reduced into possession; but

(b)   not including mushrooms growing wild on any land or flowers, fruit or foliage of a plant growing wild on any land.

For the purposes of this subsection 'mushroom' includes any fungus and 'plant' includes any shrub or tree.

(2)   Property shall be treated for the purposes of this *Act* as belonging to any person—

(a)   having the custody or control of it;

(b)   having in it any proprietary right or interest (not being an equitable interest arising only from an agreement to transfer or grant an interest); or

(c)   having a charge on it.

(3)   Where property is subject to a trust, the persons to whom it belongs shall be so treated as including any person having a right to enforce the trust.

(4)   Property of a corporation sole shall be so treated as belonging to the corporation notwithstanding a vacancy in the corporation."

This provision is fairly self-explanatory. It is clear that even if D owns the property he may be liable for damaging it if there are other co-owners, or if another person has a proprietary interest in the property. If a bank has a "charge" on D's chattels (paintings, *etc.*)[36] or a "mortgage" on his house, then it has an interest in his property. Although a husband can be guilty of damaging his wife's property, and *vice versa*, a charge requires the consent of the Director of Prosecutions, as for theft.[37] If no one has a proprietary interest in the defendant's property, he will be the absolute owner. In such circumstances, his property will not belong to another.

35–008   **Can a person be guilty of criminal damage to property in his own possession?**   Yes, if he does not own it. A tenant who sets fire to the house would be guilty; so would a person who first drives off in someone else's car and then deliberately damages it.

---

[35] *R. v. Denton* [1981] 1 W.L.R. 1446, where the rule was applied although the burning was carried out by an employee on the employee's directions. The court overlooked the fact that the property was vested in a company.

[36] On legal charges see *Scottish & Newcastle Plc. v. Lancashire Mortgage Corp Ltd.* [2007] N.P.C. 84. On fixed and floating charges, see *Re ASRS Establishment Ltd.* [2002] B.C.C. 64 at 70; *In Re Bond Worth Ltd.* [1980] Ch. 228 at 249.

[37] Section 30(4) of the *Theft Act 1968*. The same applies apropos civil partners.

Will a landlord commit an offence if he sets fire to his tenant's house?   The   **35–009**
Act provides that custody by another person is equivalent to ownership,[38] so that
the landlord would be guilty of criminal damage.

There are certain statutory offences of damaging or destroying property even
though it may be one's own and in one's own possession—cutting down a tree
that is the subject of a Tree Preservation Order, demolishing a listed building,[39]
and catching and killing a protected wild animal. These offences are trivial in
comparison with the spectacular wastes in our society that have in the past gone
uncontrolled and unpunished. Minerals are used when replaceable resources
would do as well; they are used and then cast away as garbage so thinly that they
will be impossible to recover. If a gas strike at sea goes wrong, although it can be
capped, it is sometimes left to bubble away, so that gas that has lain in the ground
for millions of years runs to waste. The law has now caught up with these
activities, but a discussion of the relevant provisions is beyond the scope of this
book.

Injuring animals can be an offence under the *Animal Welfare Act 2006* or one
of the statutes protecting animals, whether or not they belong to the defendant;
but the *raison d'être* of this legislation of course, is the prevention not of waste
but of cruelty.

35.5.   THE MENTAL ELEMENT

The mental element is intention or recklessness. We have seen that the   **35–010**
requirement of recklessness is interpreted in a subjective sense.[40] There is no
negligent damage to property, but this is embraced in the offences of negligent
driving, and there are a few statutory provisions.[41]

Can the doctrine of transferred intention be applied under the *Act*?   **35–011**
Almost certainly yes. At common law, the doctrine of transferred intention
applies whenever the statute permits it by its wording, provided that one can find
both the *mens rea* and the *actus reus* for the offence charged, though in respect of
different property.

The question relates to the meaning of "any such property" in section 1(1).

Probably this means "any property belonging to another" (the word "such"
referring back to the earlier phrase "belonging to another").[42] If so, the word

---

[38] Section 10(2). However, if a bailor at will determines the bailment and retakes the article, even
though only momentarily, he cannot thereafter commit criminal damage to it; and similarly if he has
agreed to sell the article with payment by instalment and has validly retaken the article for
non-payment. See *R. v. Judge* (1974) 138 J.P.N. 649.

[39] The law is too feeble to prevent listed buildings from being reduced to rubble by unscrupulous
developers, when the development value of the land is greater than that of the building. The only way
to make the law effective would be to provide for compulsory sale of the land in such cases, even
when the demolition is supposed to have been a mistake, the owner being allowed the value of the
listed building and the rest of the proceeds being forfeited.

[40] *R. v. G* [2004] 1 A.C. 1034.

[41] Section 3 of the *Submarine Telegraph Act 1885* as amended (negligent injury to submarine cables);
section 1 of the *Dogs (Protection of Livestock) Act 1953* (sheep-worrying by dogs).

[42] Cf. the wording of section 1(2), where "such" is omitted because under that subsection the property
need not belong to another.

"any" brings in the doctrine of transferred intention. If the *Act* had said merely "such property," it would have been pretty clear that the doctrine was excluded.

35–012 An alternative interpretation is that "any such property" means "any property of the same kind." This would involve the courts in inventing numberless classifications of property. What is a thing of the same kind as a watch, apart from another watch? Is a watch the same kind of thing as a car? Is a horse the same as a dog? Not only would such an enquiry result is uncertainty and complexity, but it might mean that intention could be transferred from the defendant's own property to the property of another person—which would be anomalous. So pretty clearly (1) is the preferable interpretation. "Such property" means not "property of the same kind" but "property belonging to another."[43]

However, the legal transference of intention should not be a reason for increasing punishment. If D tries to break what he knows to be a cheap vase but accidentally (*i.e.* without intention or recklessness) knocks over a very valuable one, he may be convicted of criminal damage to the expensive vase, but should obviously be sentenced on the basis of his actual intention.[44]

35.6. WITHOUT LAWFUL EXCUSE

35–013 Several excuses for damaging property of another are recognized by the general law. For example, a landowner (or occupier, or probably licensee) may eject trespassing property, notwithstanding that this may inevitably involve some damage to property (as where he demolishes a shed that has been placed on his land by way of trespass). A person may abate a nuisance by removing any unlawful obstruction to a public or private right of way.[45] Property may be damaged, it is suggested in a situation of necessity, and of course it may be damaged with the consent of the owner.[46] In addition, a non-exhaustive definition

---

[43] This was clearly the intention of the Law Commission, which said: "The intention or recklessness need not be related to the particular property damaged, provided that it is related to another's property. If, for example, a person throws a stone at a passing motorcar intending to damage it, but misses and breaks a shop window, he will have the necessary intention in respect of the damage to the window as he intended to damage the property of another": Law Commission, *Report on Offences of Damage to Property*, (Law Com. No. 29 of 1970) at para. 45.

[44] Ashworth uses this type of case as part of his argument that the law of transferred intention should be abolished. See Andrew Ashworth, "Transferred Malice and Punishment for Unforeseen Consequences," in Peter Glazebrook (ed.), *Reshaping the Criminal Law: Essays in Honour of Glanville Williams*, (London: Steven & Sons, 1978) at 77 *et seq*. This is plausible in respect of criminal damage. See the discussion in Glanville Williams, "Convictions and Fair Labelling," (1983) 42 *Cambridge L.J.* 85 at 86-87. Practical instances are in any case rare. There is not the same difficulty for offences against the person, because here the legal distinction between a.b.h. and g.b.h. or death should generally prevent great anomaly arising.

[45] *Chamberlain v. Lindon* [1998] 1 W.L.R. 1252. See also *Unsworth v. D.P.P.* [2010] EWHC 3037 (Admin).

[46] Section 5 (a provision about to be discussed) allows a defence of belief in the owner's consent, but the drafters of the *Act* did not think it necessary to say that the owner's actual consent is a defence, evidently because this falls under the general defence of "lawful excuse" in section 1(1). The Court of Appeal in *R. v. Denton* [1981] 1 W.L.R. 1446 said that this is "probably" so; but why "probably"? Where the owner consents to the act there is no *actus reus*; and this is true even though the defendant did not know that the owner consented.

of "lawful excuse" is provided by section 5. Subsection 5(2) specifies two particular types of lawful excuse for the purpose of the *Act*; belief in consent and belief in defence. Belief in consent:

> "(a)   if at the time of the act or acts alleged to constitute the offence he believed that the person or persons whom he believed to be entitled to consent to the destruction of or damage to the property in question had so consented, or would have so consented to it if he or they had known of the destruction or damage and its circumstances."

Belief in defence:

> "...
>
> (b)   if he destroyed or damaged or threatened to destroy or damage the property in question or, in the case of a charge of an offence under section 3 above, intended to use or cause or permit the use of something to destroy or damage it, in order to protect property belonging to himself or another or a right or interest in property which was or which he believed to be vested in himself or another, and at the time of the act or acts alleged to constitute the offence he believed—
>
>   (i)   that the property, right or interest was in immediate need of protection; and
>
>   (ii)   that the means of protection adopted or proposed to be adopted were or would be reasonable having regard to all the circumstances.
>
> (3)   For the purposes of this section it is immaterial whether a belief is justified or not if it is honestly held.
>
> (4)   For the purposes of subsection (2) above a right or interest in property includes any right or privilege in or over land, whether created by grant, licence or otherwise.
>
> (5)   This section shall not be construed as casting doubt on any defence recognised by law as a defence to criminal charges."

These two paragraphs apply to cases where there is to the defendant's knowledge an actual consent of the owner,[47] or an actual necessity for protecting property, as well as to cases where the defendant makes a mistake as to these matters. It is clear on principle that the burden of negativing the defence rests on the prosecution.

Paragraph (*b*) means, for example, that a sheep farmer who has shot a marauding dog is not guilty of criminal damage if he believed that this was immediately necessary and reasonable in the protection of his sheep.[48] The qualification that the property must be believed to be in "immediate need of protection" is regrettable. Action in defence of property may be necessary and reasonable even though the threat is not immediate. A hill farmer does not live among his sheep, and it may be reasonable for him to kill a marauding dog even though his sheep are safe so long as he is with them. Notwithstanding this restriction in paragraph (*b*), the defendant should have the defence of necessity in such circumstances. It must be said, however, that the decided cases do not give much encouragement to the argument that necessity can supplement the right of private defence.[49]

35–014

---

[47] *R. v. Denton* [1981] 1 W.L.R. 1446.

[48] By section 3 of *Dogs Act 1906* and section 2(2) of the *Dogs (Protection of Livestock) Act 1953*, a police officer may "seize" stray dogs in certain circumstances, and after a certain time have them destroyed.

[49] See particularly *Workman v. Cowper* [1961] 2 Q.B. 143. See also *Monsanto Plc. v. Tilly* [2000] Env. L.R. 313.

It is not clear how far anticipatory action is justified when it takes the form of creating static deterrents. A farmer surrounds his field with barbed wire, on which a trespasser tears his clothes. Has the farmer intentionally or recklessly damaged the clothes? On the causation principles studied in Chapter 8 it may be held that it is not the farmer who has done this, but the trespasser in trying to climb over an obvious danger. Assuming, however, that the courts find a *prima facie* case of criminal damage caused by recklessness, the question is whether the defence under paragraph (*b*) applies. This turns on whether the requirement of immediate danger rules out anticipatory measures by way of static defence. The prosecution may advance the argument that when the anti-trespasser device operates it is immediately necessary. But the difficulty is the question of timing. If "the time of the act or acts alleged to constitute the offence" is when the wire is put up, the farmer does not then believe that immediate protection is required. If the time is when the damage is caused to the trespasser, the farmer may then be asleep, and have no belief that his property is in "immediate need of protection." So, in addition to relying on paragraph (*b*), the farmer would do well to seek to establish the defence of "lawful excuse" as a matter of private defence. The barbed wire is a customary and reasonable form of static defence against trespassers (see 21.8.).

35–015   **Doesn't the ultra-subjectivism of paragraph (b) raise the same problem as in blackmail?**   It is true that the paragraph is widely drawn in that it makes the issue depend on whether the defendant himself thought the act was reasonable. This means that he must have thought that right-thinking people would regard what he did as reasonable. Of course, the more unreasonable the defendant's conduct was in an objective sense, the less the tribunal is likely to credit his claim that he believed his conduct was reasonable. Some of the decisions before the *Act of 1971* took an extremely costive attitude towards the defence of claim of right. The intention of the *Act of 1971* is to remove from the criminal law any damage done under a supposition of right, since such conduct is adequately provided for by civil law. So the message to police is: do not prosecute in these circumstances.

Another liberality in the drafting in paragraph (*b*) applies not only in respect of acts done to protect property but also in respect of those done for the protection of what the defendant believed was "a right or interest in property."[50] It therefore covers not only what is usually called private defence but such matters as abatement of nuisance.

If a person, mistakenly believing that he is entitled to a right of way over another's land, moves what he regards as an obstruction, he is not protecting physical property against attack but regards himself as protecting his right or way. The paragraph therefore applies. Similarly, the paragraph applies if a person, having or believing that he has an incorporeal interest, does something that he believes to be reasonably necessary to protect the interest even though the law does not authorize the interest to be protected in that way. A person who has sporting rights over the land of another is not entitled to shoot a strange dog that is disturbing the game and spoiling his sport;[51] but if he does so, believing that this is reasonable, he has a defence under section 5.

---

[50] Cf. subsection (4), reproduced above, which makes doubly sure by repeating the point.

[51] *Gott v. Measures* [1948] 1 K.B. 234.

It should follow that if a person has had a parking space allotted to him, and if he **35–016** damages a trespassing car in endeavouring to remove it from the space, the defence provided by paragraph (*b*) should apply.[52] It may be that the law gives him the right to take reasonable steps to eject the car (certainly it does if he is a lessee of it);[53] but even if it does not, he has a defence if he believed his parking right gave him a right or interest in property and that what he did was reasonable.[54] Note that subsection (4) expressly extends protection to licensees. Indeed, even if the defendant did not believe that he was entitled to act on his own account, the paragraph gives him a defence if he believed he was acting to protect property rights of the owner of the ground. The intention of the paragraph to rest the defence on a subjective basis is clear; all that creates a doubt is the constant tendency of the courts to distrust subjectively worded defences, and indeed to construe defences narrowly whenever possible.[55]

One restriction has already been imposed by the judges on the defence under paragraph (*b*). The statutory defence is held not to apply where the act (starting a small fire to demonstrate that fire alarms do not work) was done merely to call the attention of the authorities to present a dangerous situation, even though the object of the defendant was to reduce this danger. The defensive act is apparently regarded as not being related significantly closely to the avoidance of danger. In *R. v. Hunt*, D believed that the council was doing nothing about repairing the faulty fire alarms in a block of old people's flats, so he got the residents out of the flats and set fire to a bed in a fairly isolated part of the block. Thereafter, he summoned the fire brigade and broke the alarm to show it was not working. The Court of Appeal held that the question of whether D acted "'in order to protect property belonging to another' within section 5(2) was objective and that the defence was not made out because D's 'act was not one which did or could in itself protect property.'"

In *R. v. Hill*,[56] the defendants intended to use hacksaw blades to cut a strand of a chain link fence surrounding a U.S. naval base at Brawdy. Their defence to charges of possession of the blades with intent to damage property was that their aim was to protect property belonging to themselves or another and that such property was in immediate need of protection. They asserted that if the naval base was not closed down that there was a risk of devastation of property by a sudden Soviet nuclear attack. Lord Lane C.J. said:[57]

> "There are two aspects to this type of question. The first aspect is to decide what it was that D in her own mind thought. The learned judge assumed, and so do we, for the purposes of this decision, that everything she said about her reasoning was true. I have already perhaps given a sufficient outline of what it was she believed to demonstrate what is meant by that. Up to that point the test was subjective. In other words one is examining what is going on in the applicant's mind. ... Having done that, the judges in the present cases—turned to the second aspect of the case, and that is this. He had to decide as a matter of law which means objectively, whether it could be said that on those facts as believed by the applicant, snipping

---

[52] Cf. *Chamberlain v. Lindon* [1998] 1 W.L.R. 1252.
[53] *Hall v. Davis* (1825) 172 E.R. 16; cf. *R. v. Tao* [1977] Q.B. 141.
[54] *Chamberlain v. Lindon* [1998] 1 W.L.R. 1252.
[55] *R. v. Hunt* (1978) 66 Cr. App. R. 105; *R. v. Hill* (1989) 89 Cr. App. R. 74; *Unsworth v. D.P.P.* [2010] EWHC 3037 (Admin).
[56] (1989) 89 Cr. App. R. 74.
[57] *R. v. Hill* (1989) 89 Cr. App. R. 74 at 79.

the strand of the wire, which she intended to do, could amount to something done to protect either the applicant's own home or the homes of her adjacent friends in Pembrokeshire."

35–017 According to the above authorities, it does not matter whether the defendant intended to damage the property in order to protect her own property, if objectively judged the criminal damage was not capable of protecting her property. But a person's purpose for acting does not depend on whether the means adopted were capable of achieving the end aimed for. On the other hand, a Divisional Court in *Jaggard v. Dickinson*[58] gave a thoroughly subjectivist interpretation to paragraph (*a*).

The real issue in *R. v. Hunt* and *R. v. Hill* was whether the defendants acted to protect the property in question, not whether their conduct was capable of protecting the property. Hunt on his own admission said his primary aim was to get the council to do something about the faulty fire alarms. In other words, he admitted that he was not acting to protect the given property from an immediate threat. If the defence is put to the jury when the evidence supporting it is thin, they are likely to reject it. The more unreasonable the defendant's claim that he was acting to protect his property or the property of another was in an objective sense, the less the tribunal is likely to credit his claim that he acted to protect his property or property belonging to another. It is one thing to infer from the evidence that the defendant is not telling the truth, it is another to hold that he was telling the truth and then deny him the defence merely because his act was not capable of protecting the property in question. However, where there is no evidence to support his claim, the defence need not be put to the jury.[59]

35–018 **Does "the immediate need of protection" element incorporate an objective test?** The subsection makes it clear that if the defendant in fact believed that the property was in need of immediate protection, the defence should be available. "It is immaterial whether a belief is justified or not if it is honestly held." The defence applies where there was an actual necessity for protecting property, as well as to cases where the defendant makes a *mistake* as to this matter. Consequently, if there is some evidence to support the defendant's mistaken belief, the defence should be considered by the tribunal of fact. If the objective evidence shows that it was totally unreasonable for the defendant to believe that the property was under immediate threat, the jury may infer that the defendant did not in fact believe it was. If tribunal of fact find that the defendant did in fact believe the property was in need of immediate protection, it cannot ignore this finding merely because his belief was unreasonable.

Alternatively, if there is no evidence to support the claim that the property was in need of immediate protection, the defence need not be put to the jury. In *R. v. Hunt* there was little evidence to support the defendant's claim that he believed the flats where in need of immediate protection. The flats were not on fire and there was nothing to suggest that they would catch fire in the imminent future. Rather, the evidence made it clear that the defendant believed that precautions needed to be taken by the council, not himself, to ensure that the flats would not

---

[58] [1981] Q.B. 527. See 19.6. See also Glanville Williams, "Two Nocturnal Blunders," (1990) 140 *N.L.J.* 1564.
[59] *R. v. Hunt* (1989) 89 Cr. App. R. 74 at 79; see also *Ayliffe v. D.P.P.* [2006] Q.B. 227.

be vulnerable to the threat of fire at some stage in the future. Arguably this is what Lord Lane C.J. had in mind in *R. v. Hill*, when he said: "[T]here must be evidence that the defendant *believed* that immediate action had to be taken to do something which would otherwise be a crime in order to prevent the immediate risk of something worse happening."[60] (Lord Lane C.J. was not suggesting that the question under section 5(2)(b)(i) is partly objective, he was merely stating that where there is no evidence to support a claim under that subsection, the defence need not be put to the jury).

Need the defendant's act of criminal damage be a proportionate or   **35–019**
reasonable way of avoiding the threat to his property? No. It is enough that the defendant believed that the means used to protect his property were reasonable.[61] As noted above, the paragraph is widely drawn on that it makes the issue depend not on whether the defendant's conduct was in fact reasonable (reasonable in the estimate of the jury or magistrates) but on whether the defendant himself thought it was reasonable. (The issue is whether the defendant thought that right-thinking people would regard what he did as reasonable.) Of course, the more unreasonable the defendant's conduct was in an objective sense, the less the tribunal is likely to credit his claim that he believed his conduct was reasonable. So the notion of subjective unreasonableness, though abstruse, is not unworkable.

The two paragraphs leave out something. A person may destroy property in   **35–020**
the honest but mistaken belief that it is his own. Clearly he would be acquitted on the general issue of *mens rea*. The two paragraphs exemplify cases where *mens rea* is absent but do not preclude a defence for other cases. Under section 1(1) the defendant must have the required mental element in relation to the property of another. The point was decided, it may be remembered, in *R. v. Smith*.[62] The court proceeded not on the wording of the *Act*, which was silent on the point, but on "the ordinary principles of *mens rea*."

What if the defendant's belief that he owned the property was the result of a   **35–021**
mistake not of fact but of the civil law? These were the circumstances in *R. v. Smith*, above. The reason why Smith thought the property was his own was that he was the tenant of a flat and had made certain improvements in the flat; but the improvements became the property of the landlord by virtue of the rule of law that things attached to the land become the property of the landowner. (There are exceptions to the principle, but none was relevant.) When quitting the flat, Smith damaged the fixtures in removing some of them (which he was not in law entitled to do). On a charge of criminal damage, his defence that he thought the fixtures were his own succeeded; yet his mistake was as to the general law of property in fixtures, not as to a matter of observable fact.

---

[60] *R. v. Hill* (1989) 89 Cr. App. R. 74.
[61] *Chamberlain v. Lindon* [1998] 1 W.L.R. 1252 at 1262.
[62] [1974] Q.B. 354.

35–022 **What if the defendant mistakenly believes something that is not recognized as property is property belonging to another?** To the extent that the mistake is one of civil law it will provide a defence. Similarly, if the defendant mistakenly believes that abandoned property belongs to another. If the mistake is one of criminal law, then it will not count. For instance, section 10 of the *Act of 1971* provides:

> "(1)   In this *Act* 'property' means of a tangible nature, whether real or personal, including money and—
>
> (a)   including wild creatures which have been tamed or are ordinarily kept in captivity, and any other wild creatures or their carcasses if, but only if, they have been reduced into possession which has not been lost or abandoned or are in the course of being reduced into possession."

The *Act* does not make it a criminal offence to damage wild creatures that "have not been reduced into possession." The logical corollary is that the defence of lawful excuse found in section 5(2)(b) is available only when the defendant acts to protect property as recognised by the *Act*. The wider question of what is or is not property is one of civil law, but section 10 expressly states that wild animals that have not been reduced into possession are not property for the purposes of the *Act*. Ignorance of this provision cannot provide a defence.

If wild animals that have not been reduced into possession are not property, then people cannot destroy other property (traps belonging to a government department) in an attempt to protect wild animals in this context. In *Cresswell v. D.P.P.*,[63] the defendants mistakenly believed that wild badgers were property belonging to the Department for Environment, Food and Rural Affairs ("DEFRA"). DEFRA set a number of traps to catch badgers at a particular location because it was believed that the badgers were the source of bovine tuberculosis in that area. The appellants were animal activists who sincerely and passionately believed that badgers were not causing the local cattle to contract bovine tuberculosis, and that the culling of badgers was unnecessary as a step towards dealing with the problem. The appellants went onto farmland armed with bolt croppers, which they used to destroy four badger traps that had been set by officers of DEFRA. It was not disputed that they had destroyed property belonging to another (the traps) and that they intended to do so. The appellants attempted to raise the section 5(2)(b) defence, but failed because the wild badgers were not property.

35–023 If their mistake had merely been one of civil law, the defence would have been available because the appellants genuinely believed that the badgers were property belonging to another. The *Act* makes it clear that the defence is not available where a person destroys non-property, and section 10 expressly states that wild animals are not property unless they have been reduced into possession.

35–024 **Paragraph *(b)* provides for damaging property in defence of property, but what about damaging property in defence of the person?** Acts done in defence of the person are generally those causing injury to the person, but you are right: it is perfectly possible to damage property when defending the person, as

---

[63] [2006] EWHC 3379 (Admin).

when one kills an attacking dog.[64] The *Act*, evidently by oversight, leaves this to fall under the general category of lawful excuse.

This may have two consequences, peculiar in principle but unlikely to cause difficulty in practice:

1. Paragraph (*b*) allows a person to protect property of someone who is a stranger to him. But this applies only if he damages property. If he injures the person of an attacker, he cannot justify at common law the ground that he was protecting property of a stranger,[65] unless the doctrine of necessity helps him.

2. The Law Commission, who originated the *Criminal Damage Act 1971*, took a strongly subjective position, and in paragraph (*b*) made the defendant's belief in right a defence. As we saw in Chapter 21, the general view of the common law is that the belief for self-defence may be unreasonable but must be genuine; and this applies to damaging property in defence of a person, which the *Act of 1971* leaves to the common law. In this respect, the two defences are now compatible.[66] If a man strikes at and injures a snarling dog, and is prosecuted for damaging the dog, his belief that it was about to tear his clothes is a defence although the belief was unreasonable. Similarly, his unreasonable belief that the dog was about to bite his leg is a defence at common law, if it was in fact held.

It may be mentioned here that there is a rule of common law ousting the jurisdiction of magistrates in certain cases involving title to land. The reason for the rule is that title to land may involve complicated questions which are thought not to be suitable for magistrates to determine. All the same, the rule has caused much difficulty, and the section 7(2) of the *Criminal Damage Act 1971* solves the problem by excluding it in charges of damage.

35.7. DANGEROUS CRIMINAL DAMAGE

This phrase is used here merely as a convenient, though unofficial, abbreviation. **35–025** The offence is defined in section 1(2):

> "A person who without lawful excuse destroys or damages any property, whether belonging to himself or another—
>
> (a)   intending to destroy or damage any property or being reckless as to whether any property would be destroyed or damaged; and
>
> (b)   intending by the destruction or damage to endanger the life of another or being reckless as to whether the life of another would be thereby endangered; shall be guilty of an offence."

---

[64] *Morris v. Nugent* (1836) 173 E.R. 252.

[65] But, as said above, a licensee can probably defend the property at common law against wrongdoers. *Hall v. Davis* (1825) 172 E.R. 16; cf. *R. v. Tao* [1977] Q.B. 141.

[66] Prior to the decision in *R. v. Williams* (1984) 78 Cr. App. R. 276 at 281-282 *per* Lord Lane C.J., the belief that it was necessary to act in self-defence had to be reasonable. The subjective approach now governs the whole law of private defence. See also section 76(4) of the *Criminal Justice and Immigration Act 2008*.

The offence is similar to what I have called the offence of simple damage, except as follows:

1.   It applies where a person damages his own property,[67] as well as where he damages the property of another.
2.   It is confined to cases where life is intentionally or recklessly endangered.[68] This element is thought to justify the increase in the maximum punishment to imprisonment for life. It should be noticed that the offence can be committed although no one was in fact endangered (as where no one was in fact in the building).[69]
3.   Although "lawful excuse" is a defence, the partial definition of "lawful excuse" in section 5 is not applied. Presumably the "lawful excuse" under this subsection must be something that excuses not only the damage to the property but the peril to life. The excuses of private defence, and (perhaps) necessity can sometimes operate to justify imperilling life.

While the measure was under discussion, the inclusion of this offence was criticized (without avail) as being illogical, because the offence is really an offence against the person and not one against property. If D tampers with the brakes of his own car, which he knows his father is going to use, hoping that his father will be killed or injured, it is strange to treat the case as one of criminal damage. (If D had built a car with bad brakes for the same purpose he could not be said to have damaged the car, and therefore could not be punished under section 1(1); yet his purpose and the danger would be the same.)

35–026   **Need the criminal damage be the source of danger?**   The defendant must intend "by the destruction or damage to endanger the life;" or at least foresee that the "damage" will endanger the life of another. In *R. v. Steer*,[70] D went to the home of his former business partner, against whom he bore a grudge. After ringing the door bell he fired a rifle at the windows of the bedroom and lounge and at the front door. No injuries were caused to the occupants of the house. The defendant was charged, *inter alia*, with damaging property with intent, being reckless as to whether the life of another would be thereby endangered, contrary to section 1(2) of the *Criminal Damage Act 1971*. Counsel for the defendant submitted that there was no case to answer because the danger had not been caused by the damage done to the house, but rather was caused by the stray bullets that were fired from the rifle. Lord Bridge said:[71]

> "Of course, it is obvious that any danger to life in this case was caused by the shot from the rifle itself, not by any trifling damage done to the bedroom window or to any property in the bedroom. ... To be guilty under subsection (1) the defendant must have intended or been reckless as to the damage to property which he caused. To be guilty under subsection (2) he must additionally have intended to endanger life or been reckless as to whether life would be

---

[67]   *R. v. Harding* [2000] 1 Cr. App. R. (S.) 327; *Attorney-General's Reference (No.98 of 2001)* [2002] 2 Cr. App. R. (S.) 25; *R. v. Brewis* [2004] EWCA Crim. 1919.
[68]   See *R. v. Steer* [1988] A.C. 111; *R. v. Webster* [1995] 2 All E.R. 168.
[69]   *R. v. Steer* [1988] A.C. 111 at 116; *R. v. Parker* [1993] Crim. L.R. 856.
[70]   [1988] A.C. 111.
[71]   *R. v. Steer* [1988] A.C. 111 at 116–117.

endangered 'by the damage to property which he caused. This is the context in which the words must be construed and it seems to me impossible to read the words 'by the damage as meaning 'by the damage or by the act which caused the damage."

The defendant was not liable for criminal damage because he did not intend the damage to the house (the bullet holes through the doors and windows) for the purpose of endangering the life of its occupants; rather he intended to endanger the occupants by shooting them. The bullet holes *per se* could not endanger anyone. A person could stand near a door or a window with a bullet hole in it all day without being endangered. A bullet hole in a door is no more dangerous than a keyhole. The source of the danger was the mobile bullets that were coming from the barrel of the rifle. Nor could it be said that D foresaw that this damage would endanger the occupants, because clearly the damage was not capable of endangering the life of the occupants. D intended to endanger the occupants of the house, but he did not intend to use criminal damage as the means of achieving that end. He intended to use a rifle as the means for achieving that end.

In *R. v. Wenton*,[72] D threw a brick through a window of a house to knock its glass windowpane out. Thereafter, he tossed a petrol bomb through the opening. The petrol spilled on the floor but did not ignite so there was no fire. D submitted that there were two distinct and separate acts involved: (1) the breaking of the window with the brick; and (2) and the projection of the petrol canister into the house. D also asserted that the act that caused the criminal damage (the breaking of the windowpane) did not endanger of the lives of the occupants, and since the second act (the tossing of the canister) did not cause any damage, it could not be used to ground a conviction for aggravated criminal damage.

Leveson L.J. said:[73]

> "By no stretch of argument could it be said that the damage to the window threatened the occupants. Indeed, this case is one removed from that in *R. v. Steer* because in that case it was in fact the same act that caused the damage that also created the risk, namely the discharge of the rifle into the house. Here, the act which caused the damage was the projection of the brick through the window. The act which caused the threat and endangerment was the projection of a petrol bomb into the house which was subsequent to and followed the breaking of the window."

The case would be different were D to fire a bullet at a large glass wall in V's beach house foreseeing that massive slabs of glass would fall on V and cut him to bits.[74] In this case, D foresees that the damage itself will endanger V's life.

35.8. ARSON

Section 1 of the *Act of 1971*, after creating the offence of simple damage in subsection (1) and the offence of dangerous damage in subsection (2), provides in subsection (3) as follows. Arson under subsection 1(2) and (3) is triable only on indictment. Arson charged under subsections 1(1) and (3) is triable either way: **35–027**

---

[72] (2010) 174 J.P. 577.
[73] (2010) 174 J.P. 577 at para. 10.
[74] Cf. *R. v. Webster* [1995] 1 Cr. App. R. 492.

"An offence committed under this section by destroying or damaging property by fire shall be charged as arson."

It follows that there are two forms of arson; one under subsection (2), combined in each case with subsection (3).[75] The difference of substance between what may be called simple arson and dangerous arson (apart from the difference of definition) is that dangerous arson may be committed in respect of one's own property.

35–028 **Is arson a separate offence or just a way of charging criminal damage?** It seems to be a separate offence. Consequently, an intent to cause damage otherwise than by fire cannot be transferred to make the offender guilty of arson of something else if fire is accidentally caused.[76]

There was an offence of arson at common law, and in the discussion leading to the enactment of the *Act* some disagreement emerged as to whether a special offence of damaging by fire was worth preserving. The Law Commission stated the arguments for the view that prevailed (though it was not their own view) as follows:

"There are two main arguments for treating damage by fire differently from other ways of damaging property. The first is that damage by fire, particularly to buildings and stacks, is an offence which has always been regarded with abhorrence. It is argued that this is of itself a reason for allowing a higher maximum penalty. The second argument, which we find much more persuasive, is that many people who resort to damage by fire are mentally unbalanced and in need of treatment, and yet frequently do not qualify for committal to hospital. If damage by burning is punishable by a maximum sentence of life imprisonment, a person so convicted may be kept in detention for psychiatric treatment for as long as proves necessary.[77]"

35–029 **Surely it would not be arson if D lit up someone else's cigar without his permission?** Technically it would be. The cases on the former offence of arson established that it was committed if the thing were caused to smoulder at red heat, though there were no actual flame;[78] and doubtless the same construction still applies. Doubtless, too, your imaginary case will never come to court.

The availability of charges of serious damage and serious arson means that if the conviction (by verdict or on plea) is only of simple damage or simple arson, the judge in sentencing must assume that the defendant neither intended to endanger life nor was even reckless as to this—however obvious the risk may appear to the sentencer.[79]

In charging dangerous damage or dangerous arson the courts regard it as important for the prosecutor to charge intention and recklessness in separate

---

[75] The offence should be charged under both subsection (1) and subsection (3), or both subsection (2) and subsection (3): *R. v. Aylesbury Crown Court Ex p. Simons* (1972) 56 Cr. App. R. 818.

[76] Glanville Williams, "Convictions and Fair Labelling," (1983) 42 *Cambridge L.J.* 85. *Contra*, Andrew Ashworth, "Transferred Malice and Punishment for Unforeseen Consequences," in Peter Glazebrook (ed.), *Reshaping the Criminal Law: Essays in Honour of Glanville Williams*, (London: Steven & Sons, 1978) at 92.

[77] Law Commission, *Report on Offences of Damage to Property*, (London: H.M.S.O., Law Com. No. 29, 1970) at para. 29.

[78] *R. v. Parker* (1839) 173 E.R. 733; cf. *R. v. Russell* (1842) 174 E.R. 626.

[79] *R. v. Booker* [1982] Crim. L.R. 378.

counts, not in the alternative in the same count. The chief reason that, if the two kinds of fault are charged in the alternative in the same count, a conviction on plea will give the judge no guidance on whether the defendant intended to endanger life or acted recklessly. The judge can hear evidence to establish the degree of the defendant's fault, but if he neglects to do this he must sentence on the basis of the smallest degree of fault implied by the plea, *i.e.* recklessness.

Notice the parallel offence to dangerous arson created by the section 2 of the *Explosive Substances Act 1883* (causing an explosion likely to endanger life or cause serious injury to property).

35.9.   THREATS

Section 2 provides:

35–030

> "A person who without lawful excuse makes to another a threat, intending that that other would fear it would be carried out,—
> (a)   to destroy or damage any property belonging to that other or a third person; or
> (b)   to destroy or damage his own property in a way which he knows is likely to endanger the life of that other or third person; shall be guilty of an offence."

It will be noticed that the threat may be made in any way—*e.g.*, over the telephone. The threat need not be made directly to the victim of the threatened attack, and it need not be a threat of immediate damage. The threat might be implied from D's conduct, if a reasonable person in the same position as the victim would have believed that D was threatening to damage V's (or his own in the case of endangerment) property.[80] Nevertheless, it must be shown that the defendant intended the other party to fear that the implied threat would be carried out. Recklessness will not do.[81] The partial definition of "lawful excuse" in section 5 applies to an offence under this section (with appropriate modifications) unless the threat is to damage property in a way that the threatener knows is likely to endanger the life of another.

35.10.   CUSTODY WITH INTENT

Section 3 provides:

35–031

> "A person who has anything in his custody or under his control intending without lawful excuse to use it or cause or permit another to use it—
> (a)   to destroy or damage any property belonging to some other person; or
> (b)   to destroy or damage his own or the user's property in a way which he knows is likely to endanger the life of some other person; shall be guilty of an offence."

The effect of this is to create a kind of statutory attempt; it has a wide ambit, because the "thing" may be something quite ordinary, like a tin of aerosol paint, a

---

[80] Cf. *R. v. Cakmak* [2002] 2 Cr. App. R. 158, where Ds threatened to burn themselves whilst on the London Eye. The direct threat was to burn themselves, but this also implied that they were threatening to set the London Eye on fire.

[81] *R. v. Cakmak* [2002] 2 Cr. App. R. 158.

hacksaw blade[82] or even a box of matches, and there is no requirement of an intent to use it immediately.[83] The partial definition of "lawful excuse" again applies (with appropriate modifications), unless the defendant intended to damage property in a way that he knew was likely to endanger the life of another.

It may be noticed that there are also offences of possessing explosives in sections 3 and 4 of the *Explosive Substances Act 1883*.[84]

35.11. TRESPASS

35–032   Traditionally, and exceptions apart, trespass upon land is a wrong noticed only by the civil law. The reason is not easy to state. Of course, trespassing on a man's land is not a grave matter in comparison with trespassing on his head, or among his insides; but there are plenty of minor offences, and it is slightly surprising that this does not feature among them.

Not only does the criminal law turn a blind eye to the rambler through farms and woods, but it is not generally an offence to disport oneself in someone else's garden, to "gate-crash" a party by slipping in among the guests (except that the consumption of food or drink by the gate-crasher would be theft or fraud); to enter a house surreptitiously in order to "bug" it, or to sleep in the best bed; even to intrude into Buckingham Palace, sit on the Queen's bed, and engage her in unwelcome conversation;[85] to creep into a cinema or climb the fence to a football match without paying;[86] to organize a "pop festival" without the landowner's permission; to park one's car in someone else's parking space; for a newspaper reporter to gain admission to a private house or conference by a "ruse" (*i.e.* by deception) or by stealth; for a person to wander round a hospital making a nuisance of himself; for hunt and shooting saboteurs to trespass in order to disturb the sportsmen's quarry; or for demonstrators to invade a football or cricket pitch during a match in order to make a political protest. At one time the anaemic state of the law might have been justified on the ground that these events were too rare to be a serious social evil, but that argument cannot stand examination at the present day, when such forms of lawfulness are commonplace.

The most serious consequence is that the police are without legal reasons for interfering if they feel so disposed. At the least, they often arrest or at least detain a trespasser for an apprehended breach of the peace,[87] and have him bound over to keep the peace. In many cases a charge under one of the offences found in sections 1-5 of the *Public Order Act 1986* would be justified. In serious cases involving a number of people, the police may consider charging a trespassory

---

[82] *R. v. Hill* (1989) 89 Cr. App. R. 74.

[83] *R. v. Buckingham* (1976) 63 Cr. App. R. 159.

[84] Other inchoate offences are contained in unrepealed sections of the *Malicious Damage Act 1861*; sections 35 and 36, relating to the obstruction or endangering of railway engines.

[85] In July 1982 one Fagan did this, and no charge was brought. However, he may now be caught by section 128 of the *Serious Organised Crime and Police Act 2005*; there is a defence in subsection 128(4).

[86] However, see section 11(1) of the *Fraud Act 2006*.

[87] The limits of this option were discussed in Chapter 9. See *R. (on the application of Laporte) v. Chief Constable of Gloucestershire* [2007] 2 A.C. 105.

assembly under section 14A(2) of the *Public Order Act 1986*.[88] In other cases, the police can stand by while the occupier ejects the trespasser, and if the trespasser makes forcible resistance they can charge him with assault. It would be more sensible, however, if the police saw him out on the occupier's behalf.

Miscellaneous statutes provide special offences of trespass. For example, section 128 of the *Serious Organised Crime and Police Act 2005* provides: **35–033**

> "(1)   A person commits an offence if he enters, or is on, any protected site in England and Wales or Northern Ireland as a trespasser.
>
> (1A)   In this section 'protected site' means–
> (a)   a nuclear site; or
> (b)   a designated site.
>
> (1B)   In this section 'nuclear site' means–
> (a)   so much of any premises in respect of which a nuclear site licence (within the meaning of the *Nuclear Installations Act 1965*) is for the time being in force as lies within the outer perimeter of the protection provided for those premises; and
> (b)   so much of any other premises of which premises falling within paragraph (a) form a part as lies within that outer perimeter.
>
> (1C)   For this purpose–
> (a)   the outer perimeter of the protection provided for any premises is the line of the outermost fences, walls or other obstacles provided or relied on for protecting those premises from intruders; and
> (b)   that line shall be determined on the assumption that every gate, door or other barrier across a way through a fence, wall or other obstacle is closed.
>
> 2(2)   A 'designated site' means a site—
> (a)   specified or described (in any way) in an order made by the Secretary of State, and
> (b)   designated for the purposes of this section by the order.
>
> (3)   The Secretary of State may only designate a site for the purposes of this section if—
> (a)   it is comprised in Crown land; or
> (b)   it is comprised in land belonging to Her Majesty in Her private capacity or to the immediate heir to the Throne in his private capacity; or
> (c)   it appears to the Secretary of State that it is appropriate to designate the site in the interests of national security.
>
> (4)   It is a defence for a person charged with an offence under this section to prove that he did not know, and had no reasonable cause to suspect, that the site in relation to which the offence is alleged to have been committed was a [protected]1 site.
>
> (5)   A person guilty of an offence under this section is liable on summary conviction—
> (a)   to imprisonment for a term not exceeding 51 weeks, or
> (b)   to a fine not exceeding level 5 on the standard scale, or to both."

Furthermore, it is an offence to trespass on military lands,[89] a military camp,[90] the premises of a foreign mission,[91] or a public garden.[92] It is an offence for a trespasser on educational premises to cause (or permit!) nuisance or disturbance[93]

---

[88]   *D.P.P. v. Jones* [1999] 2 A.C. 240. Cf. *Mayor of London v. Hall* [2011] 1 W.L.R. 504, where the court "remitted for reconsideration the question of whether it was proportionate to grant applications for an order for possession and an injunction against a protestor in respect of his protest and camping on an area of Parliament Square Gardens."

[89]   See sections 14, 17(2) of the *Military Lands Act 1892*.

[90]   Section 8 of the *Manoeuvres Act 1958*.

[91]   Section 9 of the *Criminal Law Act 1977*.

[92]   Section 5 of the *Town Gardens Protection Act 1863*.

[93]   Section 547 of the *Education Act 1996* (as amended).

(student demonstrators beware!); to interfere with a designated wreck;[94] or to abandon litter (including derelict vehicles dumped on land);[95] or to drive a motor vehicle without lawful authority off a road "upon any common land, moor land or other land of whatsoever description"; there is an exception for driving within 15 yards of a road for the purpose of parking.[96] At one time an unauthorized climber of Nelson's column could be convicted of an offence;[97] but this is no longer the case. Similarly, the climber on the dome of St. Paul's or the statue of Eros in Piccadilly Circus appears to commit no specific offence; he is likely, however, to be charged with criminal damage if this can be found, or failing that to be bound over. (Magistrates are given remarkable *carte blanche* in exercising this last power,[98] and from time to time bind over trespassers on the ground of an apprehended breach of the peace which is a mere figment of their imagination.)

Occasionally a trespass becomes criminal by reason of the intent, as in the case of trespass in pursuit of game (which can be committed by shooting on a country road),[99] burglarious entry to a building,[100] and trespasses forbidden by section 1 of the *Official Secrets Act 1911*.[101] It is also forbidden for a trespasser in a building (or on land ancillary to a building) to have with him a weapon of offence,[102] or for a trespasser to have with him a firearm,[103] or (as we shall presently see) for certain people to seek to enter premises by violence.[104]

35.12. TRESPASSORY ENTRY TO A BUILDING

35–034 The most serious form of trespass is trespassory entry to a building, and particularly a dwelling, and even more particularly a cuckoo-like trespass, involving the ouster of the lawful owner or other occupier. Even so, the peaceable invasion of buildings is not an offence.[105]

Here again the police have generally adopted an attitude of studied indifference to the problems of the unfortunate owner.[106] Failing all else the

---

[94] Section 1 of the *Protection of Wrecks Act 1973*.

[95] Section 3 of the *Refuse Disposal (Amenity) Act 1978*; cf. Part IV *et passim* of the *Environmental Protection Act 1990*. See also section 3 of the *Control of Pollution Act 1974*.

[96] Section 34 of the *Road Traffic Act 1988*. The penalty is low, and in any case the police do not seem to enforce the section. Section 193(4) of the *Property Law Act 1925* (as amended) has a similar provision for certain commons without the parking exemption. See also *Phillips v. D.P.P.* [2003] L.L.R. 98; *Bakewell Management Ltd. v. Brandwood* [2004] 2 A.C. 519.

[97] See the revoked *Trafalgar Square Regulations 1952 (SI 1952/776)*. See also *Allmond & "Negotiate Now" v. United Kingdom* (1995) 19 E.H.R.R. CD93.

[98] Cf. *R. (on the application of Laporte) v. Chief Constable of Gloucestershire* [2007] 2 A.C. 105.

[99] *R. v. Pratt* (1855) 119 E.R. 319.

[100] Section 9 of the *Theft Act 1968*.

[101] As extensively interpreted in *Chandler v. D.P.P.* [1964] A.C. 763.

[102] Section 8 of the *Criminal Law Act 1977*.

[103] Section 20 of the *Firearms Act 1968*.

[104] Section 6 of the *Criminal Law Act 1977*.

[105] Although the law may change very soon. See Tom Whitehead, "Squatting to be made illegal, vows Clarke," (London: *The Telegraph*, 18 March 2011), noting the Lord Chancellor intends to criminalize squatting.

[106] But even before the passage of the *Criminal Law Act 1977* the *Metropolitan Police Commissioner Act* undertook to assist the displaced occupier of a furnished residence. On the old law of forcible entry, see Michael Dalton, *The Country Justice*, (London: William Rawlins et al, 1697) at 297-818.

owner must face the costs of a court action—costs that he is unlikely to be able to recover from the indulgent trespassers. He may sue for an injunction to prevent a threatened occupancy if he can identify the threateners.[107] After the illegal occupancy has taken place he can sue for damages (but this remedy is not likely to be enforceable); more importantly, he may ask for a court order for recovery of his property. An expeditious summary procedure has been devised, under which an order can be made in a matter of days—even as little as a day.[108] The order will be enforced by the sheriff and his officers (in the case of the High Court) or by the bailiff and his officers (in the case of the county court). The sheriff can call upon the police to assist him under section 8 of the *Sheriffs Act 1887*. The bailiff is too low in rank to be given this right; but under section 10 of the *Criminal Law Act 1977* it is an offence to obstruct any court officer enforcing an order for recovery of premises, and the police, if they can be persuaded to stand by, can arrest offenders and so in effect assist their eviction.

The criminal law does, however, concern itself with violent entry into buildings (and associated with buildings). Before the *Criminal Law Act 1977* the prohibition of violence in trespassing depended upon ancient Statutes of Forcible Entry. The Law Commission decided to modernize this antiquated legislation, and as a result the *Act of 1977* superseded it by a new summary offence set out in section 6. The offence consists in using violence or the threat of violence to secure entry to a building where there is someone present who is opposed. (It does not matter that entrance is not gained).

Section 6(1) provides:
35–035

"(1)   Subject to the following provisions of this section, any person who, without lawful authority, uses or threatens violence for the purpose of securing entry into any premises for himself or for any other person is guilty of an offence, provided that—
    (a)   there is someone present on those premises at the time who is opposed to the entry which the violence is intended to secure; and
    (b)   the person using or threatening the violence knows that that is the case.
(1A)   Subsection (1) above does not apply to a person who is a displaced residential occupier or a protected intending occupier of the premises in question or who is acting on behalf of such an occupier; and if the accused adduces sufficient evidence that he was, or was acting on behalf of, such an occupier he shall be presumed to be, or to be acting on behalf of, such an occupier unless the contrary is proved by the prosecution.[109]
(2)   Subject to subsection (1A) above,[110] the fact that a person has any interest in or right to possession or occupation of any premises shall not for the purposes of subsection (1) above constitute lawful authority for the use or threat of violence by him or anyone else for the purpose of securing his entry into those premises."

---

[107] For practical limitations see A. M. Prichard, *Squatting*, (London: Sweet & Maxwell, 1981) at 42-45.
[108] For further details as to the procedure *vis-à-vis* interim possession orders against squatters see *Civil Procedure Rules (1998/*3132), rules 55.20–55.28. See also *Rules of the Supreme Court*, Or. 113; *County Court Rules*, Ord. 24, rules 1-7. See *Secretary of State for the Environment, Food and Rural Affairs v. Meier* [2009] 1 W.L.R. 2780 at 2785, 2791, 2797-2799.
[109] Added by *Criminal Justice and Public Order Act 1994*, Pt V section 72(2).
[110] Words inserted by *Criminal Justice and Public Order Act 1994*, Pt V section 72(3).

35–036   **But why does the offence require violence? Isn't it just as much of an outrage for squatters to move into another person's house during his temporary absence without violence?**   For the framers of the *Act of 1977*, political considerations were paramount. Some squatters receive a measure of public sympathy. Besides, the intruders may not be squatters; they may be workpeople (championed by their trade unions) engaged in a "sit in" or "work in" by way of protest against closure of the factory or against an announcement of redundancies; or they may be students peaceably occupying the administrative block on the university premises for political reasons in order to impede the work of the University. So, to reduce opposition, it was felt that the offence had to be confined to cases of violence. However, the "displaced residential occupier"[111] and the "protected intending occupier"[112] are exempt from section 6.

35–037   **By "violence" does the subsection mean violence against the occupier or violence to the building—smashing windows and suchlike?**   Both. Subsection 4:

> "It is immaterial for the purposes of this section—(a) whether the violence in question is directed against the person or against property."

35–038   **I can't see why the lawful occupiers need protection from this law. If the invaders use violence to an occupier, they are guilty of assault, *etc.*; and if they smash their way into the building they are guilty of criminal damage.**   Yes. Section 6 is of very little use to lawful occupiers. Sometimes it may clarify the position if there has only doubtfully been an assault, and it has the advantage that the prosecution can charge a summary offence which carries no right of trial. But anyway, the unlawful invaders who are likely to be encountered will probably not offend against section 6. Squatters and demonstrators sneak into premises when no one is there, or unlawfully stay after lawful entry, or fiddle the locks; and in none of these cases will section 6 apply.

35–039   **Then the section is not much use?**   Its chief "use", if that is the right word, is in restraining the owner from forcibly re-entering his building after he has been illegally ousted from it. The Law Commission decided that the owner was (with certain exceptions to be discussed in a moment) liable to be charged with the offence just as much as if he were a trespasser. Subsection (2) provides that "the fact that a person has any interest in ... premises shall not ... constitute lawful authority..." It follows that a university employee can commit the offence when faced with a sit-in; so can the local authority when it finds its empty building overrun with squatters. Unless they employ tactics about to be mentioned, such owners must go to court if they want to get the intruders out. We see, therefore, that subsection (1) is not an enactment primarily motivated by concern for the owner of the property invaded. In its practical effect it is a legislative provision for the aid and security of lawbreakers, though of course its purpose is to preserve the peace.

---

[111] This means a person who was already living in a property before being excluded by squatters. See section 12(3) of the *Criminal Act 1977*.

[112] See section 12A of the *Criminal Law Act 1977*.

Whether the decision of policy was right may be doubted. There was no evidence of serious disorder arising from evicted owners using reasonable force to give effect to their right to enter. Normally, the evicted owner will go to the courts, whether he is given the option of self-help or not. Although the offence in section 6(1) was meant to be generally neutral between owners and aggressors, in practice, as we shall see, it works lopsidedly—not lopsidedly against the aggressor, but against the owner.

But the *Act* makes an important exception for the "displaced residential occupier" or "protected intending occupier." If you are wrongfully dispossessed of the dwelling or flat you have been occupying, by someone who entered as a trespasser or are an intending occupier, you are given the privileged position of displaced residential occupier or protected intending occupier and can smash and fight your way in to evict the usurper; this right you have at common law, and it is limited only by the requirement that the force you use against the trespassers must be necessary and reasonable.

We commence with persons other than the aforementioned. Taking subsection (2) **35–040** at its face value (and putting aside certain arguments, to be noticed hereafter, that may be used to deflect it, but not have come before the courts), it means that the owner is allowed to do little more than fight on (using reasonable force) until he is ejected; once he is run out, he must generally accept defeat until the forces of law put him back in. If the owner defies the section and fights his way back in, he very likely commits assault as well as offending against the section, at any rate up to the time when he gets back over the threshold.

The section covers all buildings and land ancillary thereto. But it does not apply to other land;[113] so a farmer who has been evicted from any part of his acres (say by gypsies making an encampment) can use force to get back in and evict his evictors as at common law.

"Uses or threatens violence." It seems that a threat of violence can be an offence even though it is made some time before the projected entry. The threat may be implied, and if an invading mob seeks to enter premises illegally, its mere numbers may be an implied threat of violence to the occupier in case of resistance. But if a particular invader were prosecuted it would have to be shown, first, that he intended to obtain entry, and secondly, that he intended to threaten violence or was reckless as to such a threat being so understood.

Although the main object of the *Acts* is to preserve the peace, it does not pursue **35–041** that aim consistently. It does not prohibit the owner entering peaceably and then using force to turn the squatters out again. The displaced owner may get in by stealth, persuasion of fraud; once in, he can admit his friends, and together they may (so far as subsection (1) is concerned) set upon the intruders. (There may be argument on when the owner can be regarded as having got back in; if he or his friend simply gets a foot inside the door without the use of violence, can he then use violence to expel the usurpers? It appears not.)

You may suppose from the foregoing that a good plan for the displaced owner would be to collect his friends and at dead of night break a window, get in and join battle. Not so: the prohibition of using "violence" against property in order to

---

[113] Section 12 of the *Act of 1977*.

get in applies against the ousted owner as much as against trespassers. This is remarkable, since the window is the owner's. The explanation of the anomaly lies in the section's duality of purpose. If the section had created two distinct offences, one of unlawful entry by trespassers and one of the use of force by owners to re-enter, each offence could have been drafted in terms appropriate to it. Instead, those who drafted the legislation decided to get it all in to one offence. They wished to prevent trespassers getting in by breaking windows, and since they had (foolishly) decided to treat owners generally with the same medicine as trespassers, they applied the same rule to owners. No sensible reason can be given for saying that the owner can get back in with his own key but not by breaking his own window.

Another oddity is in speaking of violence against property. One would not call it "violence" if a blacksmith at his anvil hammers a horse shoe. Presumably the word in this context means destructive violence. A distinction may be drawn between the technical force used in unscrewing a lock (which is not violence) and smashing a door or windowpane (which is). Difficult intermediate cases may arise; gently levering a door off its hinges, for instance. But what is the reason for distinguishing? We may offer our answer: none. Even if one is thinking only of invasion by trespassers, the lawful inhabitant may be just as frightened when invaders are seen unscrewing his door locks as if they are smashing his windows; in either case their object is clearly to get in. Or the inhabitant may not, at first, be frightened at all, because he does not know his window is being broken or his door lock unscrewed; he is frightened only when he finds that the trespassers have entered. If they get into the building unlawfully, does it greatly matter how they got there? Legally, it does; but that only shows how easily the law becomes nonsensical.

35–042 Suppose the owner has been pushed or locked out by invaders; but he has an ally left on the premises (for example, his son or a watchman). Can the owner use violence to get back in? The general answer is no. The section is evidently intended to enact a precise rule. It does not use vague words like "possession," but says distinctly that no one must use violence to secure entry. So anyone once pushed out cannot legally fight his way back in, merely on the ground that he is the owner and has been ejected.

But the full answer to the question depends upon what his happening inside. If the ally has accepted defeat and is sitting philosophically in a chair, the owner, as has just been said, will commit the offence if he uses violence to re-enter. He can steal in by the back door, because it is still his property. He must not break in. (Except in the unlikely event of the invaders leaving the place unoccupied for a short time; if they make this mistake, the owner can smash his way in—he does not commit the offence of using violence to enter, because no one is inside who is opposing his entry; and he does not commit criminal damage, because it is his own property).

If on the other hand the ally is fighting on, as he is entitled to, or even if he is continuing to demand that the invaders retreat, then if they use force against him they are guilty of assaulting him, and the owner who perceives this happening may use reasonable force to re-enter in order to protect his ally from attack. The section denies that the owner has lawful authority to enter as owner, but does not deny that he or anyone else has lawful authority to enter to prevent an offence being committed inside. It is true that section 6(4)(b) says that: "it is immaterial … whether the entry which the violence is intended to secure is for the purpose of acquiring possession of the premises or for any other purpose"; this provision affects the forcible gate-crasher who has no lawful authority to enter, but it should not affect the owner or police officer who is entering in pursuance of a power given to him otherwise than in virtue of ownership of the building, namely, for the purpose of defending another person and of preventing the continuation of offences. He therefore has "lawful authority" to enter. Having got back in, he may himself renew the struggle against the intruders.

The same argument applies if the owner enters in order to prevent any other crime (*e.g.*, the abstraction of electricity, if the trespassers are burning the lights at night). **35–043**

Another possible gap may be seen in the protection apparently given by section 6 to illegal entrants. At common law the owner of chattels may *recapt* (retake) them from one who is in unlawful possession of them (21.11.). It has accordingly been suggested[114] that the displaced owner can use reasonable force to enter his own building to recapt his private papers or any other article that are being unlawfully detained from him; and this right to enter (it may be argued) is not excluded by subsection (2). If the owner enters to recapt, having got his article he may again turn round to expel the intruders. Only invaders in an empty building are safe from an argument along these lines. The argument, if accepted, may reduce subsection (2) to a virtual nullity, but if so it will be a well deserved fate.

Where are the police all this time? Can't they, if they are willing to help, join in on the side of the owner? The answer is yes if (but only if) the intruders have committed an offence for which they can be arrested, or are committing an offence that the police are entitled to put a stop to, or if the police are acting at the request of the owner to assist him in recapting a chattel (perhaps his iPad, which may contain a valuable trade secret) under the argument set out above. The police are most likely to act if the intruders used violence to gain entry and so offended against the section; the police can arrest them for the offence, and can use force to enter in order to do this.[115] When the intruders are arrested the place is naturally cleared.

If the intruders got in without violence, and are simply keeping the owner out, then they commit no offence merely by seizing and retaining possession. The owner cannot authorize the police to use violence on his behalf (except as his agent to recapt a chattel, if the owner himself has that right); nor have the police, in general, any other "lawful authority" to act. The owner can bring a civil action, but meanwhile the intruders may be vandalizing his property, spreading filth and germs upon it, or prying into the confidential papers in his office. It is true that, as already said, if the police reasonably suspect the commission of an arrestable offence like criminal damage, or abstracting electricity, they may use force to enter in order to make an arrest for that. But, in the case of damage, if there are **35–044**

---

[114] Prichard, *op. cit. supra*, note 108 at 63 *et seq.*
[115] Section 2(6) of the *Criminal Law Act 1967*.

many trespassers it may not be possible to establish that the damage was caused by any particular one of them, in which case no arrest can lawfully be made unless it can be inferred from the circumstances that all the trespassers had a common purpose to cause such damage.

We now come to the exceptions for the displaced "residential" occupier and protected intending occupier. First of all, no offence is committed if the person who re-enters was living in the dwelling, from which he has been excluded by someone who has entered as a trespasser. Such a "displaced residential occupier" is allowed to exercise self-help. Take the example of a person who keeps a flat in London because he works there but spends his weekends in his country house; if he arrives one Monday morning to find squatters, as a current resident, he would be taken to be in occupation. Even if he left the flat for the entire summer, he would still be in occupation if it is one of his primary residences where he lives. He will be a displaced residential occupier, so if it is taken over by trespassers he will be able to use reasonable force to oust them.

The prohibition of violent entry by the owner applies even where squatters occupy a house or flat, if the place was uninhabited because it was for sale or to let, or because it was a holiday home not occupied at the time. So if you find your seaside bungalow (which you have left uninhabited since its last letting) occupied by squatters, you must leave them respectfully there until you have taken the right steps. For dwellings of this type, the *Act* is a "squatters charter," enabling them to live in the house with little fear of being evicted for a period of time dependent on the state of congestion of the local county court and the financial ability of the owner to undertake litigation.

35–045 Section 12A of the *Act of 1977* is slightly wider:

> "(1) For the purposes of this Part of this *Act* an individual is a protected intending occupier of any premises at any time if at that time he falls within subsection (2), (4) or (6) below.
>
> (2) An individual is a protected intending occupier of any premises if—
>
> (a) he has in those premises a freehold interest or a leasehold interest with not less than two years still to run;
>
> (b) he requires the premises for his own occupation as a residence;
>
> (c) he is excluded from occupation of the premises by a person who entered them, or any access to them, as a trespasser."

This is wider because intending occupiers will normally have more than two years to run on the lease. Section 7 of the *Act* gives further protection in respect of residential premises. It applies, within certain limits, whenever such premises have been invaded, whether the invasion was accompanied by violence or not. Subsection (1) provides:

> "(1) Subject to the following provisions of this section and to section 12A(9) below, any person who is on any premises as a trespasser after having entered as such is guilty of an offence if he fails to leave those premises on being required to do so by or on behalf of—
>
> (a) a displaced residential occupier of the premises; or
>
> (b) an individual who is a protected intending occupier of the premises.
>
> (d) he or a person acting on his behalf holds a written statement—
>
> (i) which specifies his interest in the premises;

(ii)   which states that he requires the premises for occupation as a residence for himself; and

(iii)   with respect to which the requirements in subsection (3) below are fulfilled."

The latter expression ("protected intending occupier") is elaborately defined in the *Act*; roughly, it means a purchaser or a person let in by the local authority, the Housing Corporation or a housing association, bearing written evidence of his claim.

With extraordinary pusillanimity, the section is confined to residential premises. **35–046** Subsection 7(3) provides:

"(3)   In any proceedings for an offence under this section it shall be a defence for the accused to prove—

(a)   that the premises in question are or form part of premises used mainly for non-residential purposes; and

(b)   that he was not on any part of the premises used wholly or mainly for residential purposes."

This definition suited the trade unions and ensured that there would be no political opposition to the measure. It means that workpeople who bar factory gates against their employer cannot be peremptorily required to leave under section 7, whereas the employer, if he tries to evict them, is liable to be charged under section 6. Similarly, a firm that finds its offices occupied by demonstrators who are busy examining its files is given no protection under section 7, while the demonstrators are again protected by section 6. Even if the premises are residential and the owner is excluded from them, the offence under section 7 is not committed if the owner was not in residence at the time of the invasion. He may, for example, have vacated the house because he was going to let or sell it; here the offence is not committed unless (in the case of private owner) he has actually sold it,[116] in which case the buyer is a "protected intending occupier." If a prospective buyer is put off by the fact that the house is now in the hands of squatters, and so refuses to buy it, or if the owner has granted a periodic tenancy of it instead of selling it, the trespassers will be immune from the criminal law however long they remain, unless they commit some other offence.

Again, section 7 does not apply to the ordinary trespasser (even one on residential premises) if the owner is not excluded, since such an owner is not a displaced residential occupier or a protected intending occupier.[117] Nor does the section apply to a trespasser if, although the owner is excluded, the trespasser did not enter as a trespasser but only became one after entry. So if a person's guest (or son, or mistress) locks him out of his own house, the *Act* provides him with no remedy. He is not a displaced residential occupier (because he has not been

---

[116] Or granted a long-term lease of it.

[117] See the definition in sections 12 and 12A of the *Act of 1977*.

excluded by someone who entered as a trespasser), and he cannot make a notification under section 7 (because, again, the trespasser did not enter as such).[118]

35–047 The advantage of section 7, where it operates, is that, by creating an offence it increases the likelihood of the police bestirring themselves. If they do, the owner is likely to get his property back without court action. Where the section does not apply, the police may quite possibly take no interest in the affair, even to help a bailiff to execute a court order for possession.

Such is the attempt made by the legislature to reconcile the owner's claim with the preservation of the peace. All in all it is of more interest as a social document evidencing the nervelessness of government in the fact of social unrest, and political sympathy for illegal action, than as a rational piece of legislation. The law still does not concede any rights to squatters, but it leaves them largely free from penal control. Squatters are sometimes in a miserable plight, rendered homeless by a combination of personal misfortune and ineptitude. But it is the wrong answer to allow either squatters or demonstrators to take over other people's property with freedom from criminal sanctions. The law enables the owner to get them out in a few days (if he is lucky) by court order, but this will cost him money and time, and it is hard to see why the police should not be given a general permission to assist the owner in the first place.

---

[118] So if a wife locks her husband out he cannot use violence to get back in, even though the dispute is essentially a domestic matter; and a charge against him under section 6 does not require the consent of the Director of Public Prosecutions.

CHAPTER 36

STRICT LIABILITY

"It must needs be that offences come; but woe to that many by whom the offence cometh!"

St Matthew 18: xviii. 7.

36.1. *MENS REA* AND STRICT LIABILITY

The *mens rea* doctrine is excluded in cases of strict liability, even though a   **36–001**
question of pure fact is involved. Here it is sufficient for the prosecution to prove
the doing of the prohibited act, the existence of the circumstance or happening of
the consequence as the case may be.[1] In other words, any defence of ignorance,
mistake or reasonable care is excluded unless the law allows it to some limited
extent. The reason offered by some judges for construing an offence as one of
strict liability is that the statute is silent on the question of *mens rea*; yet if there is
in law an implied requirement of *mens rea* (as the Lords have held to be the case),
the fact that the *Act* does not express the requirement should not affect the
matter.[2]

Strict liability is sometimes called "absolute liability," but this, although
accepted usage, is a misnomer, because all the usual defences are available except
the defence of lack of intention, recklessness or negligence. For example, the
defendant can set up a defence of duress,[3] necessity,[4] insanity,[5] automatism,[6] and

---

[1] It is preferable not to say that an offence requiring the prosecution to prove negligence is one of
strict liability. Lord Diplock on one occasion said that careless driving is an offence of strict liability:
Commissioner of Police of the Metropolis Appellant v. Caldwell [1982] A.C. 341, but this would be
inconvenient usage. For other aberrational uses of the term, which sometimes result in faulty
conclusions, see Glanville Williams "'Absolute liability,' in Traffic Offences," [1967] Crim. L.R. 142
at 143-145.
[2] *Sweet v. Parsley* [1970] A.C. 132; *B (A Child) v. D.P.P.* [2000] 2 A.C. 428; *Crown Prosecution
Service v. M* [2010] 2 Cr. App. R. 33. For an overview of the older authorities see G. L., Peiris, "Strict
Liability in Commonwealth Criminal Law," (1983) 3 *Legal Stud.* 117.
[3] *O'Sullivan v. Fisher* [1954] S.A.S.R. 33 at 37.
[4] See for example, *U.S. v. Panter*, 688 F.2d 268 (1982); *U.S. v. Unser*, 165 F.3d 755 (1999).
[5] See (27.4); *Tollefson v. State*, 525 So. 2d 957 at 961 (1988); *Clucas v. State*, 815 P. 2d 384 (1991).
See also the authorities cited in Vera Bergelson, "Fair Punishment for Humbert Humbert: Strict
Liability and Affirmative Defences," (2011) 14 *New Crim. L. Rev.* 55 at 67 n. 48; Ellen Byers,
"Mentally Ill Criminal Offenders and the Strict Liability Effect: Is There Hope for a Just
Jurisprudence in an Era of Responsibility/Consequences Talk," (2005) 57 *Ark. L. Rev.* 447. Cf. *D.P.P.
v. Harper* [1997] 1 W.L.R. 1406.
[6] See *R. v. Metro News Ltd.* (1986) 56 O.R. (2d) 321 (Can.) and *R.v. Stokes* (2009) O.N.C.J 8 at
paragraph 10 citing Glanville Williams, *Textbook of Criminal Law*, (London: Stevens & Sons, 1978).

perhaps impossibility in some circumstances. An offence may be of strict liability in one respect but require a fault element in another. Driving while disqualified is an offence of strict liability in respect of the disqualification (the driver is guilty although he firmly, but mistakenly, believed that he was not then disqualified), but it requires an intentional act of driving. We can call it an offence of strict liability because that is the predominant feature.

When it is held that an element of a serious crime is a matter of strict liability, this is probably because the courts fear that the prosecution would find it too difficult to establish *mens rea* in respect of that element. It is also economically impractical to try people for minor violations such as illegal parking, speeding and so on.

36.2. THE NOTION OF STRICT LIABILITY

36–002 In legal speech an offence of absolute or strict liability means one in which some element does not require proof of fault. As we have seen, an offence may carry strict liability in one respect but not in all. An unsophisticated lawgiver tends to word offences in absolute terms, but this does not necessarily mean that he wishes them to be construed absolutely. Take the commandment "Thou shall not kill." Whatever this meant three thousand years ago, the meaning it now conveys to us is that we must not kill intentionally or recklessly, or negligently. An accidental killing is not a breach of it, because no one can help pure accidents.

Unfortunately, there is no fixed rule of interpretation in respect of edicts absolute in their terms. Generally the courts read them straight, so that people who are without fault are convicted. Occasionally, however, the crime (particularly if it is of a grave kind) will be taken to require *mens rea*. In the absence of a rule, the legislative policy question is decided as it arises, uncertainly and expensively, not by our elected legislators but by a few lawyers arguing on supposedly legal grounds before a few judges.

A far better solution of the problem would be to lay down the kind of fault generally required for penal liability, this requirement being implied by law where the particular offence does not specify that a particular kind of fault is required nor yet that no fault is required. The solution could give effect to generally accepted principles of justice. It would give certainty to the law, and would often save the legislature (whether Parliament or Government departments) the complications of drafting involved in specifying required fault elements.

In *R. v. Charlson* (1955) 1 W.L.R. 317 at 319, it was held that the prosecution did not have to prove intent in relation to the third charge relating to the infliction of grievous bodily harm, but that it had to prove that the harm was caused by "a conscious act of the accused". See also *State v. Kremer*, 262 Minn. 190 (1962); *Cordwell v. Carley* (1985) 31 A. Crim. R. 291. Strict liability for robotic-acting—that is, for an *actus reus* that is robotic because the volitional element incorporated in that notion is missing, would be contrary to the requirements of proportionate punishment. *State v. Campbell*, 117 Ohio App. 3d 762 (1997); *R. v. Hudson* [1971] 2 Q.B. 202. See also R. S. Clark, "Automatism and Strict Liability," (1970) 5 *Victoria U. Wellington L. Rev.* 12.

There should be a fixed rule, granted, but is there any need to have a requirement of fault for minor offences? If it helps to repress offences to punish people although they are not thought to have been at fault, why not do so? Too high a price may be paid for full "efficiency"[7] in the criminal process. Strict liability is apt to create a burning sense of grievance and a loss of confidence in the administration of law.[8]

36–003

Aren't you overstating the position? It would take up too much time if magistrates' courts had to go into the question of fault on minor charges. Besides, one may shrewdly suspect the defendant has been negligent even though this cannot be proved. Magistrates must go into the question of fault, even on a charge involving strict liability, if the defendant wants to show that he was not at fault in order to mitigate punishment.

36–004

There are, it is true, some types of case, though they are few, where proof of negligence would in practice be impossible, even though negligence is very likely. When driving at night one sees quite a number of vehicles running on only one sidelight, or with tail lamps extinguished; many of these drivers may have been negligent in maintaining their vehicles, but the possibility cannot be excluded that some of the lamps will have only just burnt out. A fixed penalty of a minor amount can be justified on the ground that separating the sheep from the goats would be impossible; but even in this type of case liability is best imposed merely by way of a "ticket" fine.

It isn't only a question of magistrates' time. Where offences are very numerous, a requirement that the prosecutor should prove fault would impose a burden upon the resources of law-enforcement out of proportion to the end achieved. It might mean that the police, or inspectors of health and safety at work, or traffic examiners, or trading standards officers, would have to possess a larger investigative staff than they do now. This is an argument used by the enforcing officers; but it needs to be viewed with suspicion, particularly since every professional class tends to aggrandize itself. It is always pleasanter to be uncontrolled. But the law enforcers cannot charge every minor offence. They have to be selective, and naturally charge offences when they believe the offender has been at fault. If the prosecutor must consider evidence of negligence before instituting proceedings, why should he not produce the evidence for the consideration of the court?

36–005

There is an important distinction between civil and criminal law in relation to strict liability. The law of tort is concerned with cases where a loss or damage has occurred and the question is who should bear it. Occasionally it is thought right that the burden should be placed on the shoulders of a person, usually an entrepreneur of some kind, who is made to act as a sort of compulsory insurer of

---

[7] Cf. Stephen Shavell, "Strict Liability Versus Negligence," (1980) 9 *J. Legal Stud.* 1.

[8] For a penetrating overview of the academic debate, see Douglas N. Husak, "Varieties of Strict Liability," (1995) 8 *Can. J. L. & Jurisprudence* 189; Kenneth W. Simons, "When is Strict Criminal Liability Just," (1997) 87 *J. Crim. L. & Criminology* 1075; John Stanton-Ife, "Strict Liability: Stigma and Regret," (2007) 27 *Oxford J. Legal Stud.* 151; see also the essays collected in A. P. Simester (ed.), *Appraising Strict Liability*, (Oxford: Oxford University Press, 2005); Andrew Ashworth, "Should Strict Liability be Removed from all Imprisonable Offences," (2010) 45 *Irish Jurist* 1.

the public against risk—*e.g.*, someone who brings a collection of dangerous things on his land. The object of the criminal law, on the other hand, is to secure compliance with rules of behaviour, primarily through the threat of punishment if they are broken; and it seems logically to follow that punishment should not be imposed upon a person who has no criminal mind, at any rate if he is not even negligent, unless there are compelling administrative reasons for excluding the trial of fault in very trivial cases. Criminal punishment is not a transfer of a loss that has already occurred: it is an evil deliberately created by the law for imposition upon offenders, and normally has no rational foundation (it may be argued) if the offence could not have been avoided. Murphy and Coleman try to answer this type of objection to strict liability:[9]

> "Widespread strict liability would destroy meaningful lives because it would force us to be overly cautious in areas (*e.g.*, travel, pursuing ordinary activities, *etc.*) where we should not be overly cautious. But this is not true for all areas of social activity. Thus in order to prevent great harm, what is ultimately the matter with society saying this: 'Certain areas of activity (food processing, banking, sexual experimentation with children) have great potential for harm. Since individuals do not have fundamental rights to do those things and since there is no social value in having people casually experiment in these areas (indeed much potential for harm), then what is wrong with making the price for entry into these selected areas a willingness to risk strict liability prosecution. …Even if one function of the criminal law is to express society's moral condemnation for certain acts and thereby stigmatise the criminal, a person who lacks the wisdom to heed the warning that he stay out of a dangerous area of conduct for which he is unsuited may not be an unfitting object for such ostracism.'"

Early law, which was briefly discussed in 4.1, recognized something very near to absolute criminal responsibility. Its disappearance or submergence was due to the influence of the Church and the increasing awareness of moral ideas. By the first half of the 19th century, one could say that crime required not merely fault in general, but some kind of *mens rea*.[10] (There were exceptions which still, very largely, survive: a few crimes, such as manslaughter, can be committed by negligence without a positive wrongful mental state, and a few other crimes carry strict liability in some respects.)[11] Even when Parliament created a new offence without inserting an express requirement of *mens rea*, the courts usually hold that

---

[9] Jeffrie G. Murphy and Jules L. Coleman, *Philosophy of Law*, (Westview Press, 1990) at 128. See also *Sweet v. Parsley* [1970] A.C. 132 at 163.

[10] For a survey of the older English law, see Richard G. Singer, "Resurgence of Mens Rea: III—The Rise and Fall of Strict Criminal Liability," (1989) 30 *B.C. L. Rev.* 337 at 340-356.

[11] These crimes, not treated at large in this book, have been said to be exceptions to the general requirement of *mens rea* at common law; but how far this is true has never been altogether clear. *Blasphemy* and *obscenity* are of strict liability in respect of the judgment of what is blasphemous or obscene, but the judgment is very close to being a value-judgment rather than a question of fact. See 6.10. It is arguable that *criminal libel* requires *mens rea*, except in respect of the judgment of what is defamatory, and except also that the employer is attributively liable for a publication by his employee. Libel has been turned by statute into a crime of negligence in some cases. Contempt of court was perhaps a crime of strict liability in certain respects at common law; this rule is affirmed, with modifications in sections 1-7 of the *Contempt of Court Act 1981*. Public nuisance can apparently be committed by negligence; and is a crime of strict liability to the extent that it carries attributive liability, committed by negligence, and is a crime of strict liability to the extent that it carries attributive liability, which it does in at least some cases; but it has lost much of its importance because indictments are now uncommon. The common law crime has been replaced with statutory offences, which continue strict liability.

the offence could be committed only by one who knew the relevant facts, since the requirement of *mens rea* was, in the words of Cockburn C.J. "the foundation of all criminal justice."[12] "Acts of Parliament" said Coke C.J., "are to be so construed as no man that is innocent, or free from injury or wrong, be by a literal construction punished or endamaged."[13]

The beautiful sentiment, reaffirmed in *R. v. Tolson*,[14] was already in doubt towards the close of the 19th century, when the courts began to edge away from the *mens rea* doctrine. Parliament had commenced a trickle of social legislation, which has since become a flood. This protects consumers from sharp practices, safeguards public health and safety, gives special protection to workpeople, tenants, and others deemed to be in need of it, and regulates economic activities in a myriad of ways. The regular practice in such legislation is to state the prohibited act without bothering to specify a fault element. In these circumstances, the mind of Parliament might be read in either of two ways. It might be assumed that Parliament intended to create strict liability; and this assumption is confirmed by the fact that when the courts interpret the legislation in this way, Parliament (which in effect means the Government) frequently leaves the *Act* unamended. Or it might be assumed that Parliament meant the court to interpret the statute in the light of general principles of law, including the requirement of *mens rea*, and this assumption is in turn confirmed by the fact that on the rare occasions when the courts do this Parliament never makes the legislation more severe, while when the courts fail to do it Parliament frequently amends the legislation to allow a defence of absence of knowledge or absence of no-negligence. The second assumption would have the advantage of leaving the point for Parliament to clarify, thus clearing the judges of the reproach that they have themselves abandoned a principle of justice. Moreover, if the courts insisted upon a requirement of fault this would almost certainly influence Parliament in the same direction, while the ready concession of liability without fault by the judges naturally has the effect of devaluing the principle of justice.

36–006

For decades, it was fairly regular practice, on the part of both the legislature and judges, to exclude or qualify the requirement of *mens rea*. Sometimes it abandoned it entirely, as in *R. v. Larsonneur*.[15] But fortunately, in recent times, (at least as far as *mala in se* crimes are concerned), the courts have moved in a different direction.[16] In *R. v. K*[17] Lord Steyn said: "It is well established that there is a constitutional principle of general application that 'whenever a section is silent as to *mens rea* there is a presumption that, in order to give effect to the will of Parliament, we must read in words appropriate to require *mens rea*.'" Surely, if it is a constitutional principle, it would apply regardless of whether the section

---

[12] *R. v. Sleep* [1861] 8 Cox C.C. 472 at 477.
[13] Sir Edward Coke, *Institutes of the laws of England: Third Part*, (London: Printed by William Rawlins *et al.*, Part 1. 1684) at 360. Quoted with approval in *Margate Pier Co. v. Hannam* (1819) 106 E.R. 661 at 664.
[14] (1889) 23 Q.B.D. 168.
[15] (1934) 24 Cr. App. R. 74.
[16] *B (A Child) v. D.P.P.* [2000] 2 A.C. 428; *Crown Prosecution Service v. M* [2010] 2 Cr. App. R. 33. See Kenneth Campbell, "New Directions in Strict Liability," (2000) 11 *K.C.L.J.* 261.
[17] [2002] 1 A.C. 462 at 477.

expressly states strict liability is sufficient. The principle would be: every serious crime carrying a jail sentence requires fault.[18] However, the courts are yet to recognize this as a constitutional right.

Many of the offences found in the *Sexual Offences Act 2003* have elements of strict liability and also carry hefty jail terms, but the courts have not been willing to hold that these provisions are incompatible with the *Human Rights Act 1998*.[19] Some of the offences that have strict liability elements in the *Sexual Offences Act 2003* do not expressly state that strict liability is sufficient. But it is clear that is what Parliament intended, because the majority of the offences found in the *Act of 2003* expressly state that fault is required. Other provisions expressly provide for strict liability. For example, section 53A of the *Sexual Offences Act 2003* creates a strict liability offence. That offence is committed if a person pays or promises payment for the sexual services of a prostitute who has been subject to exploitative conduct (has been forced into prostitution). D is liable "whether D is, or ought to be, aware that [the third party] has engaged in exploitative conduct." (It is a summary offence punishable by fine only, but can still involve court proceedings and a conviction.) This type of criminalization holds an innocent person liable for the criminality of others and thus violates his constitutional right not be unfairly criminalized.[20]

36–007   Usually a mental element is partly retained in the statutory offence, but it may be abandoned in respect of some element where *mens rea* would be difficult to prove.[21] When the legislature, in creating a minor offence of a regulatory character, has not made express reference to a mental element (as by using the word "wilfully" or "knowingly"), the courts generally take the view that the statute is to be read literally in some respect, thus creating strict liability. Even when the statutes create serious crimes and explicitly require a mental element, the courts may attach the mental element to something less than the full crime, even where the statutory words seem strong enough to prevent this: in other words they may create crimes of half *mens rea*.[22]

---

[18] To the extent that an offence can result in jail time, the presumption is underwritten by the constitutional right not be unfairly punished. See generally, Dennis J. Baker, *The Right Not to be Criminalized: Demarcating Criminal Law's Authority*, (Ashgate: Farnham, 2011) at Chap. 2.

[19] *R. v. G* [2009] 1 A.C. 92. However, the issue of whether it is just to "jail" a non-culpable offender was not considered in *R. v. G*. That case only considered whether strict liability conflicted with the Convention right to a fair trial and presumption of innocence; and the right to respect for private life.

[20] See Dennis J. Baker, "Collective Criminalization and the Constitutional Right to Endanger Others," (2009) 28 *Crim. Just. Ethics* 168 at 190 *et seq.*; Dennis J. Baker, "The Moral Limits of Criminalizing Remote Harms," (2007) 10 *New Crim. L. Rev.* 370.

[21] For example, in *R. v. G* [2009] 1 A.C. 92 at 96H, Lord Hoffman said: "The mental element of the offence under section 5 of the *Sexual Offences Act 2003*, as the language and structure of the section makes clear, is that penetration must be intentional but there is no requirement that the accused must have known that the other person was under 13."

[22] *R. v. Savage* [1992] 1 A.C. 699 (the Lords decision in *R. v. Savage* cannot be reconciled with its decision in *B (A Child) v. D.P.P.* [2000] 2 A.C. 428, since the latter rejects *elements of strict liability* being imposed in serious crimes where the statute does not provide for such—so part *mens rea* and part strict liability will not do unless the statute provides for such.) *R. v. Mowatt* [1968] 1 Q.B. 421; *R. v. Phekoo* [1981] 1 W.L.R. 1117; and *R. v. Prince* (1875) 2 C.C.R. 154 (though the statute in the last case did not explicitly require a mental element.) Compare, *State v. Brown*, 140 Wash.2d 456 at 473-474 (2000).

Perhaps it was this development that was in Gilbert's mind when he wrote a celebrated parody of judicial reasoning. To a defence that the accused persons had no idea and knew nothing about it and were not there, the Mikado replies:[23]

> "That's the pathetic part of it. Unfortunately, the fool of the *Act* says 'Compassing the death of the heir apparent. There's not a word about a mistake, or not knowing, or having no notion, or not being there. There should be, of course, but there isnt. That's the slovenly way in which these *Acts* are always drawn."

Gilbert had been called to the Bar, and the Mikado was first performed in 1885, 10 years after the severe decision in *R. v. Prince*,[24] which was discussed earlier.

Granted that a mental element should be required for grave crimes, aren't the courts justified in regarding it as inappropriate to require it for minor offences? Offences like selling impure milk are offences of negligence, not of knowledge.   You are right in saying that there should be a larger place for negligence in relation to minor offences than the courts allow as a matter of common law. In practice they assume that there is nothing between the requirement of *mens rea* and strict liability: every offence must fall into one class or the other unless legislation has expressly introduced a question of negligence. The judges reason thus: the statute does not expressly require a mental element; to find the requirement by implication would narrow the offence too much; therefore it is an absolute offence (an offence of strict liability); therefore no fault is required. But the reasoning is fallacious. One does not establish that negligence is not required by establishing that *mens rea* is not required.

36–008

Anyway, one can surely say that in practice a defendant who is held to be strictly liable will have at least been negligent.   Often, but not necessarily so. Consider (to take a single illustration) the case of *Parker v. Alder*.[25] A farmer (Alder) despatched milk by rail to a purchaser. Some unknown person meddled with the churns,[26] and added water, presumably after abstracting some milk. Alder was convicted of selling an article of food not of the nature, substance and quality demanded, since it was held that the property in the milk did not pass until it reached its destination, and so the milk was adulterated at the point of sale.

36–009

This case shows the great difference between an absolute offence and an offence of negligence. To make a person responsible for negligence the prosecution must point to some feature of his conduct that was negligent; they must suggest some step that he could reasonably have taken which would have avoided the evil result. If the defendant is convicted he will know that in similar circumstances in future he can avoid legal proceedings by taking the step thus pointed out to him. But the only certain way for the suppliers of milk to avoid the fine imposed upon Alder would be to give up supplying milk. They might be able

---

[23] W.S. Gilbert and Arthur Sullivan, *The Mikado, or, The town of Titipu*, (London: Chappell, 1911).

[24] (1875) 2 C.C.R. 154.

[25] [1899] 1 Q.B. 20; cf. *Watson v. Coupland* [1945] 1 All E.R. 217.

[26] Sections 20 of the *Food Safety Act 1990* provides a defences where another person has committed the offence. Meanwhile, section 21 of the same *Act* provides a defence of "due diligence." See also section 22 of the *Act of 1990*.

to minimize the risk if they could put tamper-proof locks on milk churns. However, a suggestion like this would invite consideration of the question whether such an expenditure was worthwhile, having regard to the smallness of the risk, and the very small social harm resulting from the watering down of a single churn of milk.[27] In commercial matters the taking of precautions costs money, and if perfection were really insisted upon the cost of the product would rise substantially, without compensating advantage to the consumer.

It is, in a way, only a minor evil that a farmer should be made to pay a fine of a few pounds, which he can well afford, for the adulteration of milk, even though he could not help it.[28] However, if this is an evil it has the characteristic of being an unnecessary one, since there is generally no compelling need to have strict liability crime. Careless breaches of regulatory offences abound, and prosecutions for these are usually sufficient to be a standing warning to people to obey the law. Little purpose is served by adding to the large numbers of truly guilty defendants the small number of persons who are morally innocent. The social argument is all the other way. For whereas natural evils can often be accepted as part of the price of living, a man-made evil may be strongly and even bitterly resented because it is felt to be unjust.

36–010 A fine imposed upon a business concern irrespective of fault is not so much an affront as is a fine imposed upon an individual. But even if the defendant is a trading concern, the result of a rule disregarding fault may be that business people come to regard fines as part of their overhead costs. The attitude of indifference thus engendered towards the criminal process through inflation of the law may well spread to other offences, where an element of fault is present. Often it is cheaper to run the risk of an occasional small fine than to make the alterations in business arrangements necessary to avoid it.[29] If the trader becomes habituated to the atmosphere of the criminal court, and is taught to regard the criminal process as something that has no connection with responsibility and fault, he may adopt a

---

[27] This may not always be the case, if more than water is added. In a recent scandal in China a number of suppliers added melamine to diluted milk to conceal the fact that they had diluted the milk. This resulted in six infants being fatally poisoned and tens of thousands more being poisoned. See Dennis J. Baker & Lucy X. Zhao, "Responsibility Links, Fair Labelling and Proportionality in China: A Comparative Analysis," (2009) 14(2) *UCLA J. Int'l L. & Foreign Aff.* 274.

[28] The injustice may sometimes be alleviated if the faultless defendant is allowed a civil action to recover his fine and costs from a person who was at fault. Whether this is permissible is doubtful. Martin Wasik, "Shifting the Burden of Strict Liability," [1982] Crim. L.R. 567. But such an action, even if allowable and practicable, would not solve the grievance of being unjustly convicted. This is now a moot point as far as supplying food is concerned, since the defences found in sections 21-22 of the *Food Safety Act 1990* provide an appropriate solution.

[29] See Raymond W. Mushal, "Reflections upon American Environmental Enforcement Experience as it may Relate to Post-Hampton Developments in England and Wales," (2007) 19(2) *J. Environmental Law* 201; Melanie Newman, "Bitter Pills for Drug Companies," (2010) *B.M.J.* 341: c5095; Jeffrey H. Reiman, *The Rich Get Richer and the Poor Get Prison*, (Boston: Allyn & Bacon, 4th edn. 1995); Cf. Nelson, G. Smith, "No Longer Just a Cost of Doing Business: Criminal Liability of Corporate Officials for Violations of the *Clean Water Act* and the *Resource Conservation and Recovery Act*," (1993) 53 *La. L. Rev.* 119.

cynical and self-interested attitude on many of the questions to which legal regulations are directed. The ultimate result may actually be a decrease in the preventive effect of the law.[30]

But come back to the milk churns. How do you know that Alder was telling the truth when he said that he put the milk on the rail in a pure state? Perhaps he had adulterated it himself. Strict liability prevents people getting away with dishonest defences.

- It was found by the magistrate as a fact that the milk was pure when put on the rail.

36–011

- If dishonest defences are thought to be a problem, this could be eased by shifting the burden on the defendant.
- Strict liability exempts the prosecution from having to prove fault, but not from having to prove the act done in breach of statute. Suppose that in *Parker v. Alder* the buyer had transferred the milk from Alder's churns to his own, and had only later discovered water in it. Alder asserts that the milk in his churns was pure, and that the adulteration must have occurred after transfer. The buyer says that the adulteration did not occur after transfer, so it must have been Alder's fault. In these circumstances the burden would be on the prosecution to show that Alder had violated the statute by supplying diluted milk, and he would be entitled to the benefit of the doubt. So the law does not say that, on a charge of an offence of strict liability, the defendant's word is always to be disregarded.
- It seems improbable that the deterrent effect of the law would be weakened greatly or at all if the occasional defendant escaped with a dishonest defence. He would be very unlikely to get away with it often.

We must now say something on the history of the subject. The way in which strict liability has evolved may be illustrated by the construction of the *Food and Drugs Acts* which first came on to the statute book in the 19th century and are now represented by the *Food Safety Act 1990*. Section 14(1) of the *1990 Act* makes it an offence to sell to the prejudice of the purchaser any food that is not of the nature, substance or quality demanded.[31] (It was under the predecessor of the predecessor of this section that Alder was convicted.)[32] The purchaser is deemed to demand an article as it is expressly or impliedly represented by the seller to be,[33] and sellers are taken to represent impliedly that their wares are pure. So the offence is committed if, for example, a nail is found in a bun, a mouse in a meat roll, or water in milk, or if a sausage is deficient in meat content. As we have

---

[30] Sanford H. Kadish, "Some Observations on the Use of Criminal Sanctions in Enforcing Economic Regulations," (1963) 30 *U. Chi. L. Rev.* 423 at 440-444.

[31] Section 14(2) of the *Food Safety Act 1990* provides, "(2) In subsection (1) above the reference to sale shall be construed as a reference to sale for human consumption; and in proceedings under that subsection it shall not be a defence that the purchaser was not prejudiced because he bought for analysis or examination." Cf. sections 8 and 15 of the *Act of 1990*.

[32] See section 2 of the now repealed *Food and Drugs Act 1955*. Drugs are now dealt with in a separate enactment. See *Nottingham City Council v. Wolverhampton & Dudley Breweries Plc.* [2004] Q.B. 1274.

[33] *Per* Lord Diplock in *Smedleys Ltd. v. Breed* [1974] A.C. 839 at 857-858.

seen, the offence is held not to require *mens rea* (subject to statutory defences which we are leaving aside for the moment).[34] The earlier decisions were rested upon a critical examination of the words of the statute and a comparison of one section with another, leading to the conclusion that Parliament must have intended to dispense with *mens rea* for the particular offence although there were no express words in the statute to that effect. Later judges became bolder, and placed their decisions not on the language of the statute but on broad social grounds, saying that the purpose of the legislation would be defeated if it were held necessary for the prosecution to prove *mens rea*. (No one has suggested the question is whether the prosecution should not at least have to prove negligence. This point is now moot, because the *Food Safety Act 1990* provides a due diligence defence.)

36–012   Section 21 provides:

> "(1)   It shall, subject to subsection (5) below, be a defence for the person charged to prove that he took all reasonable precautions and exercised all due diligence to avoid the commission of the offence by himself or by a person under his control.
>
> (2)   Without prejudice to the generality of subsection (1) above, a person charged with an offence under section 14 or 15 above who neither—
>
> > (a)   prepared the food in respect of which the offence is alleged to have been committed; nor (b) imported it into Great Britain, shall be taken to have established the defence provided by that subsection if he satisfies the requirements of subsection (3) or (4) below.
>
> (3)   A person satisfies the requirements of this subsection if he proves—
>
> > (a)   that the commission of the offence was due to an act or default of another person who was not under his control, or to reliance on information supplied by such a person;
> >
> > (b)   that he carried out all such checks of the food in question as were reasonable in all the circumstances, or that it was reasonable in all the circumstances for him to rely on checks carried out by the person who supplied the food to him; and
> >
> > (c)   that he did not know and had no reason to suspect at the time of the commission of the alleged offence that his act or omission would amount to an offence under the relevant provision.
>
> (4)   A person satisfies the requirements of this subsection if he proves—(a) that the commission of the offence was due to an act or default of another person who was not under his control, or to reliance on information supplied by such a person; (b) that the sale or intended sale of which the alleged offence consisted was not a sale or intended sale under his name or mark; and (c) that he did not know, and could not reasonably have been expected to know, at the time of the commission of the alleged offence that his act or omission would amount to an offence under the relevant provision."

36.3.   EXTENSIONS OF THE DOCTRINE

36–013   Once the notion of justice had been jettisoned in favour of *raison d'État* strict liability could readily be extended to penal legislation in general, at any rate when the offence was not of a particularly serious character. So it was read into *Acts* relating to the sale of intoxicants, *Acts* governing weights and measures,[35] *Acts* regulating the relation of employer and employee (such as hours of work and

---

[34] See sections 20-22 of the *Food Safety Act 1990*.

[35] Many of these offences now provide a due diligence defence. See for example, section 34 of *Weights and Measures Act 1985*.

rates of pay), various provisions of the *Road Traffic Act 1988*, and other legislation too diverse to be enumerated.[36]

The theory that strict liability results from the will of Parliament rather than the predilection of judges rings particularly hollow when one discovers instances of strict liability being construed even where the legislature has used words indicating a requirement of dishonesty or other fault.

Suppose that you and I were arguing, and I told you that your conclusion was false. This might not be impolite, because the word "false" in that context would simply mean "not true." But if I told you that you were making false statements, you would understandably regard my words as offensive, because in that context the word "false" would generally carry a charge of lying. To avoid misunderstanding one must say that one's opponent is "mistaken," not that he is uttering falsities. Therefore, it might be thought that an *Act* of Parliament penalize the making of a "false" statement would be construed in favour of the defendant as impliedly requiring *mens rea*—knowledge that the statement is false, or recklessness as to whether it is true or false. But it has been held that a number of offences worded in this way carry strict liability.[37]

A regulation requiring the brakes of the vehicle to be "maintained" in good condition efficient working order might be thought to be satisfied if there has in fact been proper maintenance. Not a bit of it: however good your maintenance is, if your brakes fail, even quite unforeseeably, you will be liable under the regulation.[38] This construction makes the regulation equivalent to one requiring the brakes at all times to be in a non-dangerous state.[39] **36–014**

A statute requires a bankrupt to give a satisfactory explanation of the manner in which a loss occurred. It is held that he commits an offence even if he uses all due diligence to give an explanation, if the explanation is not satisfactory.[40] In other words the bankrupt is legally obliged to do more than can reasonably be expected of him.

---

[36] See also Meredith Blake and Andrew Ashworth, "The Presumption of Innocence in English Criminal Law," (1996) Crim. L.R. 306 at 313, where it is noted that: "244 offences [with more than one element of strict liability [are] triable in the Crown Court [and] carry maximum prison sentences of over six months."

[37] *Laird v. Dobell* [1906] 1 K.B. 131; *R. v. Cummerson* [1968] 2 Q.B. 534. But as regards the second decision, Parliament intervened and has since included the words "knowingly" and "wilfully" in the subsections of the "false statements" offence found in section 174 of the *Road Traffic Act 1988*. Whatever view may be taken of these cases in general, the interpretation is reasonable where (as in the case of the *Trade Descriptions Act 1968*) a prohibition of making a false statement is accompanied by a defence of no negligence; here the word "false" obviously carries an objective meaning, and applies to false statements: see *e.g.*, *Taylor v. Smith* [1974] R.T.R. 190. Most of the provisions in the *Trade Descriptions Act* have been replaced with consumer regulations: see *Consumer Protection from Unfair Trading Regulations 2008*. Regulation 17 contains a "due diligence" defence which provides: "17(1) In any proceedings against a person for an offence under regulation 9, 10, 11 or 12 it is a defence for that person to prove—(a) that the commission of the offence was due to— (i) a mistake; (ii) reliance on information supplied to him by another person; (iii) the act or default of another person; (iv) an accident; or (v) another *cause beyond his control*; and (b) that he took all reasonable precautions and exercised all due diligence to avoid the commission of such an offence by himself or any person under his control."

[38] *Hawkins v. Holmes* [1974] R.T.R. 436.

[39] See section 40A of the *Road Traffic Act 1988*.

[40] *R. v. Salter* [1968] 2 Q.B. 793.

36.4. PRINCIPLES OF CONSTRUCTION

36–015   In general, the authorities on strict liability are so conflicting that it is impossible to abstract any coherent principle on when this form of liability arises and when it does not. A particular position affirming strict liability can almost always be matched by its contradictory position affirming fault liability. The result is that in the absence of express words in the statute judges can generally attach any fault element to it that they please, or refuse to attach any fault element; and they can always find some apparent authority or argument for what they propose to do.

Take *Reynolds v. GH Austin & Sons Ltd.*[41] The defendant company operated motor coaches, but were allowed to carry private parties only, not members of the public in general. A woman's guild organized an outing, and the company agreed to provide a coach. The organizer of the outing, without the knowledge of the company, advertised the outing to the public, and some members of the public were therefore included in it. The result was that this particular use of the coach was not covered by the company's licence. The company was charged with the statutory offence of using a vehicle without a road service licence. In view of the many authorities on strict liability the prosecution doubtless thought they had an open and shut case, but the Divisional Court directed an acquittal. Lord Goddard C.J. said: "This is not to throw any doubt on the well established principle that if there is an absolute prohibition and the prohibited act is done a penalty is incurred, but hitherto that doctrine has never been applied to a case where the prohibited act was not that of the defendant, but of some person over whom he had no control and for whom he had no responsibility."

36–016   **I think that was an untenable reason. The prohibited act was not advertise the outing to the public; it was using a vehicle without a road service licence, which the company did.**   Yes, it was a Homeric nod on Lord Goddard's part, I fear. There was indeed an act by another person, but, as you say, the act charged was that of the defendant company.

Another criticism is that Lord Goddard overlooked *Parker v. Alder*,[42] and the two decisions stand in opposition to each other. Austin & Sons had committed the act forbidden by statute; they had used a vehicle without having the proper license covering the use. In the same way, Adler had committed the forbidden act; he had sold food not of the nature, substance or quality demanded. In both cases, no breach would have taken place but for the unauthorized act of another person who was not the defendant's employee. If this was an excuse for Austin & Sons it should have been an excuse for Alder. A distinction between the two cases is that the actual offender in *Parker v. Alder* was unknown and presumably unascertainable, whereas the actual offender in *Reynolds v. GH Austin & Sons Ltd.* was known or traceable. But this fact should have made no difference to the liability of the defendant.

---

[41] [1951] 2 K.B. 135.
[42] [1899] 1 Q.B. 20.

Recent legislation has tended to include a no negligence defence; so the likes of Alder will not always be held liable for the independent wrongdoing of third parties. Alder would now have a defence. Section 20 of the *Food Safety Act 1990* provides:

"Where the commission by any person of an offence under any of the preceding provisions of this Part is due to an act or default of some other person, that other person shall be guilty of the offence; and a person may be charged with and convicted of the offence by virtue of this section whether or not proceedings are taken against the first-mentioned person.[43]"

There are other cases in which the court has intimated that although the defendant was in general strictly liable, he might perhaps escape liability by showing that the default occurred by the act of a third party.[44] Half a loaf is provisionally better than no bread, but all the same the restriction of the no-fault defence to cases where there has been an act of a third party is illogical. As J.C. Smith has commented:[45]

36–017

"If the event is unforeseeable, the defendant is no more responsible for its occurrence when it is brought about by some natural phenomenon than when it is brought about by the intervention of a third party. The only explanation would seem to be that there is an assumption [by the courts] that someone must be responsible—the intervening third party if there is one, the defendant if there is not."

The judges frequently claim that the absence of the word "knowingly" in a statute is evidence that Parliament meant the offence to carry strict liability, but this is obviously a *non sequitur*. Parliament may have left out "knowingly" because it was not bothering itself about the fault element (and sometimes this is held to be the case);[46] or Parliament may have meant that the offence can be committed knowingly or recklessly; or it may have meant that the offence can be committed negligently. To say: "this offence does not require knowledge; therefore it is of absolute liability; therefore it does not require negligence" exhibits the fallacy of ambiguous middle.

Another example of contradiction: in *Harding v. Price*[47] it was held that a driver could not be convicted under a statute for failing to stop after an accident if he was not aware of the accident. This might suggest the proposition that offences of omission depend on the defendant having knowledge of the facts that create a duty to act. Until one knows the facts one is not galvanized into action. But, like *Reynolds v. Austin*, *Harding v. Price* represents only a brief lucid internal and an irrational part of the law. Other offences of omission have been interpreted to involve no consideration of justice. For example, the parents of a girl who played

---

[43] A similar defence can be found in reg. 16 of the *Consumer Protection from Unfair Trading Regulations 2008.*

[44] *Alphacell Ltd. v. Woodward* [1972] A.C. 824; *Strowger v. John*[1974] R.T.R. 124; *James & Son v. Smee* [1955] 1 Q.B. 78 at 91 *per* Parker J.

[45] [1974] Crim. L.R. 124.

[46] See Devlin J's celebrated statement (or rather, alas, over-statement) that "all that the word 'knowingly' does is to expressly state what is normally implied." *Roper v. Taylor's Central Garage* [1951] 2 T.L.R. 284 at 288.

[47] [1948] 1 K.B. 695; principle applied in *Hampson v. Powell* [1970] R.T.R. 293; *Bentley v. Dickinson* [1983] R.T.R. 356. Cf. *D.P.P. v. Pidhajeckyi* [1991] R.T.R. 136.

truant from school were held to be guilty of an offence[48] under the former *Education Act 1944* although they had no knowledge of the absences.[49]

36–018   **Can one say that strict liability applies to purely technical offences?**   This idea was advanced by Lord Reid in *Sweet v. Parsley*.[50] Strict liability is said to be imposed where the offence is the result of modern legislative policy and not of traditional morality, or in other words where it is a matter of *malum prohibitum* rather than *malum in se*. *Mala prohibita* crimes are sometimes called "quasi-criminal offences"—offences that are regarded as "not criminal in any real sense, but acts which in the public interest are prohibited under penalty."[51] They are also called "public welfare offences" or "regulatory offences."

The difficulty with trying to establish a category of this kind is to say exactly what it means. All offences are, in a sense, public welfare offences, and all result from legal regulation. The so-called quasi-criminal offences are followed by the same procedure for prosecution as other offences. One might have thought it impossible for any judge to hold that an offence carrying a possible prison sentence is "not criminal in any real sense," but three Lords felt no incongruity in saying so. People have in fact languished in jail for offending without proof of fault. But as a matter of constitutional justice, offences carrying jail terms provide a very clear line.[52] As a matter of principle, no one should be sent to jail when he is blameless. Everyone has a fundamental and constitutional right not be "jailed" for blameless harm-doing.[53]

If the violation cannot result in a jail term, then perhaps the argument is that a person's reputation is not lowered because he is found guilty of committing a technical offence, and in such a case people are not interested to know whether he committed the offence knowingly or not. One can indeed make a broad distinction between technical offences and particularly disgraced acts, but it is a

---

[48] This is a strict liability offence contrary to section 444 of the *Education Act 1996*. It does not matter whether the parent's actions were reasonable. See *Bath and North East Somerset DC v. Warman* [1999] Ed. C.R. 517. The offence has been held to be compatible with the *Human Rights Act 1998*: *Barnfather v. Islington Education Authority* [2003] 1 W.L.R. 2318.

[49] *Crump v. Gilmore* (1969) 113 S.J. 998. See also, *Atkinson v. Sir Alfred McAlphine & Sons Ltd.* [1974] Crim. L.R. 668, where a company employed men to remove lagging from steel beams. The lagging contained asbestos, but the company did not know and had no reason to know this. It was held liable for failing to adopt the precautions enjoined in the *Asbestos Regulations*. These regulations were intended to apply to firms working with asbestos. In the ordinary use of language the defendant company did not work with asbestos, and it did not know that asbestos was involved even in a minor degree.

[50] [1970] A.C. 132 at 149, affirmed by the House of Lords in *B (A Child) v. D.P.P.* [2000] 2 A.C. 428; *R. v. K* [2002] 1 A.C. 462 at 477. Applied by the Court of Appeal in *Crown Prosecution Service v. M* [2010] 2 Cr. App. R. 33; *R. v. Matudi* [2003] E.H.L.R. 13.

[51] *Sherras v. De Rutzen* [1895] 1 Q.B. 918 at 922 *per* Wright J.

[52] Dennis J. Baker, "Constitutionalizing the Harm Principle," (2008) 27 *Crim. Just. Ethics* 3.

[53] This means intention or recklessness is required, if a person is to be sent to prison. In extreme cases gross negligence is acceptable (gross negligence manslaughter, causing death by dangerous driving, *etc.*, but strict liability is never enough to justify sending a person to jail). Even one day in prison would be a cruel and unusual punishment for blameless harm-doing. *Robinson v. California*, 360 U.S. 660, 667 (1962). See also Dennis J. Baker, *The Right Not to be Criminalized: Demarcating Criminal Law's Authority*, (Ashgate: Farnham, 2011). Cf. *R. v. Muhamad* [2003] Q.B. 1031, where the court suggests that the type sentence should be influenced by the level of culpability required for a conviction.

matter of degree. If the principle is that strict liability applies only to technical offences, the courts have an idiosyncratic idea of what constitutes such an offence. But strict liability has been read by the courts into various offences involving long jail sentences, including:

- A serious offence under the *Firearms Act 1968*.[54]
- Sexual offences (in respect of the age of a young person).[55]
- Statutory rape.[56]

The truth is that judges have an open-ended list of reasons for imposing strict liability, and the fact that the offence is technical is only one of them. If the offence is technical, that will be a reason for dispensing with proof of fault;[57] if it is a serious offence involving odium, it must threaten "danger to the community," which will be another reason for reaching the same conclusion. The former pattern of judicial thinking was biased in one direction: in favour of the prosecution,[58] but the trend is now to require *mens rea* unless the statute expressly states otherwise.[59]   **36–019**

If the doctrine of quasi-criminal offences is taken seriously, it should mean that these offences should be punishable only as "contraventions" by a small or moderate fine, enforced not by the police or (primarily) the courts but by enforcement agencies, with recourse to the courts only on appeal.[60] But, this would need wide-ranging legislation, for which Parliament has no time. The best that can be hoped for is that, if a change of attitude can be brought about,[61] gradual progress may be made towards this goal as new offences are created.

Can a secondary party be held liable for a strict liability offence?   It has been pointed out before that strict liability does not apply to inchoate offences or complicity. To be guilty as attempter or accessory, the defendant must know the relevant facts.   **36–020**

---

[54] *R. v. Deyemi* [2008] 1 Cr. App. R. 2; *R. v. Zahid* [2010] EWCA Crim. 2158; *R. v. Waller* [1991] Crim. L.R. 381; *R. v. Bradish* (1990) 90 Cr. App. R. 271.

[55] *R. v. Prince* (1875) 2 C.C.R. 154; cf. *B (A Child) v. D.P.P.* [2000] 2 A.C. 428 where the Lords disapproved *R. v. Prince*.

[56] *R. v. G.* [2009] 1 A.C. 92.

[57] As in *Strowger v. John* [1974] R.T.R. 124.

[58] However, isolated instances of benevolent interpretation did occur. For example, *Cain v. Campbell* [1978] Crim. L.R. 292 ("taking"); *Pharmaceutical Society v. Harwood* [1981] Crim. L.R. 255.

[59] *B (A Child) v. D.P.P.* [2000] 2 A.C. 428; *R. v. K* [2002] 1 A.C. 462; *Crown Prosecution Service v. M* [2010] 2 Cr. App. R. 33; *R. v. Matudi* [2003] E.H.L.R. 13.

[60] See "Justice," *Breaking the Rules*, (London: Justice, 1980).

[61] Especially, if the higher courts were to declare that offences of strict liability involving jail terms are unconstitutional. They have not gone this far, but have held that such offences will be unconstitutional if the wording of the statute does not expressly provide for strict liability: see *B (A Child) v. D.P.P.* [2000] 2 A.C. 428; *R. v. K* [2002] 1 A.C. 462.

36.5. USING AND CAUSING

36–021 The verbs occurring in a subsection of the road traffic legislation have been subject of much judicial labour. By a provision now in section 40A of the *Road Traffic Act 1988*, an offence is created in respect of motor vehicles in the following words:

> "A person is guilty of an offence if he uses, or causes or permits another to use, a motor vehicle or trailer on a road when—(a) the condition of the motor vehicle or trailer, or of its accessories or equipment, or (b) the purpose for which it is used, or (c) the number of passengers carried by it, or the manner in which they are carried, or (d) the weight, position or distribution of its load, or the manner."

Each of the three verbs "uses," "causes," and "permits" has been held to create a separate offence. "Uses" is understood to create strict liability, in the sense that one need not know the quality of the thing one uses.[62] So if the vehicle is used by an employee on his employer's business, and the vehicle does not comply with the regulations (though without fault on anybody's part), the prosecutor's clear course if he decides to bring a charge is to frame it against the employer (and also the employee, if he wishes) in terms of using the vehicle in breach of the section.[63]

A prosecutor who charges the employer with having "permitted" the use will face a solid body of authority to the effect that an offence of "permitting," "suffering" or "allowing"[64] anything can be committed only by one who knows the facts (or, perhaps, the possibility of the facts) that he is supposed to have permitted, suffered or allowed.[65] This verb, therefore, imports a requirement of *mens rea*.[66]

36–022 The courts have placed a curiously restrictive interpretation upon the "word" causes. It was held that the verb in this context implies the giving of an order or direction to use the vehicle. When, therefore, a motor mechanic negligently carried out work on a van so that it contravened the former regulations, his employer was held not liable when the owner subsequently drove the van on a road;[67] and it follows that the mechanic would not have been liable either.

Here the criminal liability is placed solely on the unfortunate van owner, who takes his van on the road believing that it has been put in order by the repairer. The courts thus achieve a double failure of justice. On causal principles it is the negligent repairer who has caused the violation, since he caused the owner to

---

[62] *R. (on the application of Vehicle & Operator Services Agency) v. Henderson* [2004] EWHC 3118; *Hatton v. Hall* [1997] R.T.R. 212. See also *James & Son v. Smee* [1955] 1 Q.B. 78 (defective brakes); *Gifford v. Whittaker* [1942] 1 K.B. 501 (insecure load).

[63] Cf. *Richardson v. Baker* [1976] R.T.R. 56. Note that in some contexts the verb "use" does not bring in a subordinate employee. *Jenks v. Turpin* (1883-84) 13 Q.B.D. 505.

[64] One must, however, have a legal duty not to permit, allow, cause. We are not expected to police the world at large. *R. v. Tilley* [2010] 1 W.L.R. 605.

[65] See 6.4. *Vehicle Inspectorate v. Nuttall* [1999] 1 W.L.R. 629 *per* Lord Steyn; cf. the judgment of Lord Hobhouse. See also *Cambridgeshire CC v. Associated Lead Mills Ltd.* [2006] R.T.R. 8.

[66] See the exception mentioned in 6.4.

[67] *Shave v. Rosner* [1954] 2 Q.B. 113. Cf. *Thompson v. Lodwick*[1983] R.T.R. 76.

believe that the work had been properly done; and on a rational view of the law the owner should be regarded as free from blame.

Suppose D tells his son to go to the railway station in D's car to pick up a parcel. Unknown to D the car has defective brakes. Does D cause the use of the car? It has been held that a person does not cause the use of a vehicle by another person in breach of the law unless he knows the facts, and it does not matter whether the person he directs to drive the vehicle is his employee or not. "Causes" is interpreted to carry the same *mens rea* requirement as the word "permits."[68]

36–023

Strictly speaking, if the autonomy principle of *novus actus*[69] were applied it should be held that a person does not commit an offence of "causing" a result if the causing is immediately by another free agent. The responsibility, if any, of the remote causer should be either as perpetrator when he comes within the statutory verb (as when he is held to "use" something) or as accessory to the immediate causer, and liability should carry the usual requirement of knowledge. But it is understandable that courts should overlook this technicality and convict the employer of an offence of causing where he too knows the facts.

A person who causes an event other than an act may be held to be strictly liable. So in *Alphacell v. Woodward*[70] the House of Lords upheld the conviction of a company of "causing" polluted matter to enter a river without the need for either *mens rea* or negligence. Their Lordships reserved the question whether the company would have been liable if the result had been brought about by the act of a stranger or of God.[71] But the House has since held that a company would be liable on such facts.[72] Where an event other than an act (and event such as injury, or danger of injury) is factually caused by two persons acting independently, the courts are likely to find that the person who was negligent was the cause of the event in law, not the person who took due care.[73] This may be regarded as an application of the reasonable foresight principle in causation.[74]

36.6.   OFFENCES OF POSSESSION

Some offences are worded in terms of "possessing" a forbidden object (such objects being here called contraband). Examples are the offences of unlawfully possessing explosives, firearms and controlled drugs (which in general are drugs capable of affecting consciousness and behaviour). Other statutes use different

36–024

---

[68] So held in *Ross Hillman Ltd. v. Bond* [1974] Q.B. 435, see also *Cambridgeshire CC v. Associated Lead Mills Ltd.* [2006] R.T.R. 8.

[69] See generally, Glanville Williams, "Finis for *Novus Actus*," (1989) 48 *Cambridge L.J.* 391.

[70] [1972] A.C. 824.

[71] This is an unusual incursion of the notion of an act of God into the criminal law. For its use in the law of tort, see, *e.g.*, Anthony Dugdale and Michael Jones, *Clerk & Lindsell on Torts*, (London: Sweet & Maxwell, 20th edn. 2010).

[72] *Environmental Agency v. Empress Car Co. (Abertillery) Ltd.* [1998] 1 All E.R. 481, cf. *Impress (Worcester) Ltd. v. Rees* [1971] 2 All E.R. 357. See the discussion at 8.9.

[73] See *Sever v. Duffy* [1977] R.T.R. 429, which is especially noteworthy because the person at fault was not in breach of the regulation.

[74] 8.8.

language having much the same effect, for instance "keeping" a dangerous wild animal without a license,[75] "receiving" stolen goods (one form of handling), and the offence where a person "has with him" an offensive weapon. (But "has with him" refers to immediate personal possession,[76] whereas a person can be guilty of an ordinary possession offence if he entrusts the contraband to another person for safe keeping on his behalf.[77]

According to the theory of possession, this concept involves both a physical and a mental component: the corpus to control the thing in question. We need not go into the theory of this in detail, beyond observing that it can have importance in contraband offences. Some possession offences specifically require knowledge, the most prominent example being receiving stolen goods.[78] Where the statute creating an offence of possession does not specifically require knowledge, the present tendency is to say that it imposes strict liability, and this even though the offence is a serious one with a potentially severe penalty. The point will be developed in connection with drug and firearms offences.

36.7. THE POSSESSION OF CONTROLLED DRUGS

36–025   The law relating to drug offences is now largely settled by section 28(3) of the *Misuse of Drugs Act 1971*. This makes liability depend, for the most part, on knowledge by the defendant that he has the thing, or negligence in not ascertaining what he has. The subsection, omitting non-essentials, runs as follows:

> "Where it is necessary for the prosecution to prove that some substance or product was [a] controlled drug, and it is proved that the substance or product in question was that controlled drug, the accused shall be acquitted thereof—
> (i)   if he proves that he neither believed nor suspected nor had reasons to suspect that the substance or product in question was a controlled drug; or
> (ii)   if he proves that he believed the substance or product in question to be a controlled drug, or a controlled drug of a description, such that, if it had in fact been that controlled drug or a controlled drug of that description, he would not at the material time have been committing any offence to which this section applies."

Paragraph (i) provides a defence of no negligence when the defendant did not know he had a controlled drug. Paragraph (ii) allows a very limited defence if the defendant thought he had a different controlled drug: the facts must be such that if it had been that drug he would have committed no offence. He must show, for example, that he had a prescription for the drug he believed it to be. Otherwise he can be punished for possessing the drug he in fact has. So he can be punished for possessing a packet of heroin when he reasonably believed that he was committing the much less serious offence of possessing cannabis resin.[79]

---

[75] *Dangerous Wild Animals Act 1976.*

[76] It can, however, extend to possession of articles in a parked vehicle. *R. v. Doukas* [1978] 1 W.L.R. 372; *R. v. Jones* [1987] 1 W.L.R. 692; *R. v. Pawlicki* [1992] 1 W.L.R. 827.

[77] *R. v. Kelt* [1977] 1 W.L.R. 1365.

[78] We have seen that the alternative of belief merely refers to wilful blindness, which would be the equivalent to knowledge in any case.

[79] *R. v. Leeson* [2000] 1 Cr. App. R. 233.

However, the *Act* is spatchcocked on to the existing case-law, which draws complicated distinctions in relation to the doctrine of possession. These would now be of small practical importance were it not for the fact that they can still affect the technical correctness of a summing-up, and can therefore lead to acquittals, merited or otherwise. This means that the common law must be set out if the law is to be fully stated.

Under the legislation before 1971, unauthorized possession of a controlled drug **36–026** was declared to be an offence in unqualified terms, and the courts held that the offence carried strict liability. This was finally settled by the decision of the House of Lords in *Warner v. Metropolitan Police Commissioner*.[80] Warner was found with a box containing 20,000 amphetamine tablets; he first said that the box contained rubbish, and then said that he thought it contained scent. His story as to his belief was evidently highly suspect; but the trial judge told the jury that his belief was irrelevant to guilt, so that the appellate courts were faced with the alternative of either agreeing that the offence was of strict liability or upsetting the conviction. In these circumstances their Lordships had every temptation to agree with the trial judge, which they did. Lord Reid vigorously dissented, holding, in accordance with *R. v. Tolson*,[81] that although the legislation then in force was silent on the mental element, *mens rea* was impliedly required. The offence carried stiff penalties and could be said to belong to the realm of traditional morality since they would incur moral disapproval from many people; they could not be dismissed as relating to mere matters of convenience.[82] The majority of the Lords, however, were moved by what they regarded as the social importance of closing loopholes in the anti-drug legislation. Their speculation of what Parliament probably intended was perhaps partly falsified by the *Act of 1971*, which provides the no-negligence defence already mentioned, the burden of establishing which is placed on the defendant.[83]

A person who read section 28(3) by itself would understand that if he is charged with unlawfully possessing, say, cannabis, and he did not know he had a controlled drug, he must prove that he was not at fault. But the position is more complicated. Such proof would indeed be a defence; but the need for the no-negligence defence arises only if the defendant is proved to have been in possession of the drug, and the doctrine of possession at common law contains ingredients that can work to his advantage.

To explain: it might be supposed that in an offence of possession the *actus reus* consists in the physical control of the contraband; and if the *Misuse of Drugs Act*

---

[80] [1969] 2 A.C. 256.

[81] (1889) 23 Q.B.D. 168.

[82] Lord Reid swung his colleagues round to his general approach the next year in: *Sweet v. Parsley* [1970] A.C. 132.

[83] However, in *R. v. Lambert* [2002] 2 A.C. 545 at 563, Lord Slynn said, *obiter*: "If read in isolation there is obviously much force in the contention that section 28(2) imposes the legal burden of proof on the accused, in which case serious arguments arise as to whether this is justified or so disproportionate that there is a violation of article 6(2) of the *European Convention of Human Rights*. . . . Even if the most obvious way to read section 28(2) is that it imposes a legal burden of proof I have no doubt that it is 'possible', without doing violence to the language or to the objective of that section, to read the words as imposing only the evidential burden of proof. Such a reading would in my view be compatible with Convention rights..."

1971 had enacted that proposition we should have been saved much agonizing. But it did not; it left the law of possession as it was settled in *Warner v. Metropolitan Police Commissioner*. In that case the House of Lords, having thrown the notion of fault out of the offence, with mistaken ingenuity put a bit of it back in again via the doctrine of possession. They were able to do this because it has always been accepted that possession involves a mental element, known as *animus possidendi*, the intention to possess.[84]

36–027 In relation to the law of theft, we have seen that *animus possidendi* on the part of the victim is readily found. Since possession is ownership as against wrongdoers, theft and criminal damage may be committed against possessors. And, for this purpose, a person can be credited with possession of a thing although he does not know of its identity, or even of its existence, as in the container cases.[85] Being in possession of a house, conveyance, bureau or other container, he is deemed to intend to possess all its contents, unless they are in the immediate possession of someone else. Everybody, except perhaps thieves, would agree that this is a reasonable doctrine. The mental element required of a victim for the purpose of protecting him in his possession is therefore minimal.

It is otherwise with the possession of contraband. Where the alleged possessor is not the complainant in the witness box but the defendant in the dock, he cannot, in general, be convicted of possessing a forbidden object, according to the House of Lords, unless he is in some tenuous way aware of it.[86] However, the concession so made is extremely limited. It is held that a person can be held to possess contraband in three cases, even when he is unaware of what precisely he has. Three rules may be stated.

First, where a person invites contraband to be delivered to him, he is guilty of unlawfully possessing it the moment it arrives on his premises, even though at that moment he does not know it has come. So the tenant of a house in multiple occupation is guilty of possessing cannabis he has ordered as soon as it drops through the letter-box addressed to him.[87] This was decided by the Court of Appeal after the decision in *Warner*, showing that that case has not exhausted the ingenuity of the courts in creating new rules on this subject.

36–028 *Secondly*, the fair inference from the opinions expressed in *Warner* is that a person who is morally irreproachable when he comes into possession of a contraband object has a reasonable, though short, time to examine the thing to find whether it is contraband, and, if it is, to purge himself of its pollution.[88] This view is supported by their Lordships acceptance of the proposition that substantial possession must be established, not momentary control.

---

[84] For details, reference may be made to the specialized literature, particularly Sir Frederick Pollock and R. S. Wright, *An Essay on Possession in the Common Law*, (Oxford: Clarendon Press, 1888).

[85] 29.10.

[86] For an aberrant decision to the contrary, see *R. v. Lewis* (1988) 87 Cr. App. R. 270.

[87] *R. v. Peaston* (1979) 69 Cr. App. R. 203. Cf. *Adams v. D.P.P.* [2002] EWHC 438 (Admin).

[88] *R. v. Wright* (1976) 62 Cr. App. R. 169 endorses the view that the defendant has a reasonable time to examine a container, but states that this is so only when he does not suspect and has no reason to suspect that it contains drugs. It would seem harsh if a person who accepts a box doubtfully, suspecting that it may contain contraband and intending to examine it immediately, with a view to turning it over to the police if it is contraband, is guilty of possessing contraband.

While Warner appears to give the defendant a short period of grace to examine what he has, it does not allow him to make a mistake. If he thinks he has sweets and so does not bother to examine the contents of the box, he possesses the contents whatever they are. If, realizing that he does not know what he has, he conscientiously examines the contents and erroneously comes to the conclusion that they are sweets, he is again deemed to be in possession of the contents.

The *Misuse of Drugs Act 1971*[89] explains when a person may lawfully acquire what he knows is (or suspects may be) a controlled drug. The defendant may prove:

> "(a)   that, knowing or suspecting it to be a controlled drug, he took possession of it for the purpose of preventing another from committing or continuing to commit an offence in connection with that drug and that as soon as possible after taking possession of it he took all such steps as were reasonably open to him to destroy the drug or to deliver it into the custody of a person lawfully entitled to take custody of it; or
>
> (b)   that, knowing or suspecting it to be a controlled drug, he took possession of it for the purpose of delivering it into the custody of a person lawfully entitled to take custody of it and that as soon as possible after taking possession of it he took all such steps as were reasonably open to him to deliver it into the custody of such a person."

It will be observed that the subsection does not give the defendant a defence merely because on ascertaining the illegal nature of the drug he threw it away or gave it back to the transferor. But either of these facts may perhaps induce the court to hold that the defendant did not have a sufficiently substantial relation to the thing to be accounted as possession.[90]   **36–029**

Thirdly, a person is held to be in possession of uninvited objects (even though he neither knows nor suspects them to be contraband) according to certain rules which we are to study, the minimum requirement being that he must know that he possesses *something*. Everyone who knows he has something must immediately examine what it is, on pain of otherwise being held to be in possession of contraband if it is in fact contraband.

This rule, that the defendant must know he has something, may sound an extraordinarily anaemic requirement, as indeed it is, but at least it has the effect that if the article has been delivered into the hands of the defendant's employee, or into his building, or put into his backpack or car, he does not acquire possession of contraband if he does not know that anything has been so delivered or put.[91] The House of Lords, by affirming this rule in *Warner*, gave tepid support to the idea that contraband offences should require some mental state; but instead of expressing the rule in terms of a basic fault element (which would have been open to the objection that it would have let Warner off), their Lordships concealed the mental requirement under a refinement of the doctrine of possession, applicable only to contraband offences.

---

[89] Section 5(4).
[90] *R. v. Wright* (1976) 62 Cr. App. R. 169; *R. v. McNamara* (1988) 87 Cr. App. R. 246.
[91] Cf. *R. v. Lewis* (1988) 87 Cr. App. R. 270.

36–030   Although Warner was decided before the *Act of 1971*, and although the technicalities thus introduced into the doctrine of possession became unnecessary after the *Act* allowed a no-fault defence, the decision has been followed since.[92]

Suppose the defendant charged with possession of a controlled drug knew that a box had been delivered to his house, and believed it to be empty, but in fact it contained cannabis. Assuming that the defendant has not ordered cannabis, he cannot be convicted (even apart from section 28(3)) of unlawfully possessing cannabis. The trial judge must direct the jury (or the clerk must advise magistrates) that the burden is on the prosecution to prove that the defendant was in possession of cannabis, which means that it must be proved that he knew there was X in the box. The judge must not tell the jury that the defendant can be convicted if he "had reason to suspect that X was in the box." This "objective" formula, under the *Misuse of Drugs Act*, applies only when the defendant is in possession of the contraband, and at present we are considering whether he *is* in possession of it.

What (you will want to know) is this mysterious algebraical quantity that has suddenly entered the discussion? The defendant is charged with possessing cannabis; must it not be shown that he knew he possessed cannabis? No. What must be proved we do not precisely know; and that is why I inserted the symbol in the previous paragraph. As a partial definition, it means "something additional to the contents that the defendant does not dispute he knew were there." Consequently, he is not liable in what may be called the "planting" cases.

36–031   He may know that there are many small items in his car, but he is not guilty of an offence if a cannabis cigarette has been put there by someone else without his knowledge.[93] He may know that he has a bottle of stomach pills, but is not guilty of an offence if an amphetamine tablet (a controlled drug) has been introduced among those pills without his knowledge.[94] He may know that he has a knife, but is not guilty of an offence if traces of cannabis resin are found on it, and he did not put them there and did not know they were there.[95]

It will be seen that the law is, to use the kindest possible adjective, extremely subtle. It supposes that a person can possess the six sides of a box without possessing what is inside. The defendant possesses the container or other article, and also any known contents or adherents, but not (for the purpose of a contraband offence) the unknown contents or adherents. In general, he can be guilty of a contraband offence only in respect of the contents or adherents that he knows are there.

This brings me to the question that I am sure is trembling on your lips. When we speak of "the contents that the defendant knows are there," do we postulate that he knows the nature of those contents? Suppose he knows that he has a packet of cigarettes; he thinks they are tobacco, but in fact they are cannabis. He knows he has a bottle of pills; he thinks they are all his wife's stomach pills, but in fact they are his son's amphetamine tablets—the whole lot of them. He knows

---

[92] See *R. v. Leeson* [2000] 1 Cr. App. R. 233; see also *R. v. McNamara* (1988) 87 Cr. App. R. 246, where the decision was explained.
[93] *R. v. Ashton-Rickhardt* [1978] 1 W.L.R. 37.
[94] *R. v. Irving* [1970] Crim. L.R. 642.
[95] *R. v. Marriott* [1971] 1 W.L.R. 187.

there is something brown on his knife; he thinks it is toffee, but in fact it is cannabis. Does he know that the thing in question is there?

This was the problem considered by the House of Lords in *Warner*. The majority (having an eye to Warner and his unconvincing defence) regarded a person's mistake as to the "qualities" of the thing as not preventing him from being in possession of it. In all the instances just given the defendant would be held to be in possession of contraband. If he knows he has the substance, he possesses it, even though he mistakes its nature.[96] It has been held, for example, that if the defendant knows he has a cigarette he possesses it, even though it contains cannabis and not, as he thinks, tobacco.[97]

36–032

But the line drawn by the law is so fine that sometimes common sense disappears:

1. A person knows that he has a packet of 20 cigarettes. He thinks they are all tobacco, but they are all cannabis. Conclusion; he possesses the cannabis.
2. The same, except that only one of the 20 is cannabis. The law seems to be that this is essentially the same as in case (1), so that the person is in unlawful possession of the one reefer. He knows that he has 20 cigarettes, and this is one of them. But:
3. if he only knew that he had an indeterminate number of cigarettes, and this one had got among them without his knowledge, he would not be in possession of it.[98]

It seems strange that so much should depend on whether the defendant knows the total number. And is it not crazy that a person's criminality should depend on whether he thinks he has a clean knife or whether he thinks he has a knife with a little toffee on the blade?

It will be seen that the rule in *Warner* is an abstruse and irrational compromise between liability for fault and strict liability. As the cases on theft show, it is not

36–033

---

[96] In *Warner v. Commissioner of Police of the Metropolis* [1969] 2 A.C. 256 the defendant thought he had scent (or so he said); in fact the box contained cannabis, and the House of Lords held that the defendant was in possession of cannabis. Lord Pearce, whose speech appears in effect to state the *ratio decidendi* of the majority, said (at 305): "I think that the term 'possession' is satisfied by a knowledge only of the existence of the thing itself and not its qualities, and that ignorance or mistake as to its qualities is not an excuse. This would comply with the general understanding of the word 'possess.' Though I reasonably believe the tablets which I possess to be aspirin, yet if they turn out to be heroin I am in possession of heroin tablets. This would be so I think even if I believed them to be sweets. It would be otherwise if I believed them to be something of a wholly different nature. At this point a question of degree arises as to when a difference in qualities amounts to a difference in kind. That is a matter for a jury who would probably decide it sensibly in favour of the genuinely innocent but against the guilty." His Lordship is struggling valiantly to state a rule that may seem to make sense and yet will save Warner's conviction, but there is a conflict between the first part of this statement and the last, for if a mistake as to the kind of object is a defence, then surely aspirin or sweets and heroin are different in kind; and similarly scent and cannabis are different in kind, so that Warner should have been acquitted. It seems that in practice the courts do not apply the latter part of Lord Pearce's *dictum*, and that a mistake as to the kind of object does not negative possession of it. See *R. v. Leeson* [2000] 1 Cr. App. R. 233; *R. v. McNamara* (1988) 87 Cr. App. R. 246.

[97] *Searle v. Randolph* [1972] Crim. L.R. 779.

[98] *R. v. Irving* [1970] Crim. L.R. 642.

an essential part of the notion of possession that a person should know of the existence of the thing that is under his control. The only reasons for insisting on knowledge when the question of possession arises in contraband cases is the feeling that it is unfair to the defendant to convict him if he does not know that he possesses a thing. This was made plain by Lord Pearce, who became the architect of the law by the accidental fact that he held the balance between two Lords who would have supported a more stringent liability and two who were more lenient. Lord Pearce avowedly used the notion of *animus possidendi* as a substitute, though an imperfect substitute, for *mens rea*.[99] But if fairness is the issue, it is surely unfair to convict the defendant of possessing a controlled drug when he believes that what he has is something totally different, such as a bottle of scent. To distinguish between the defendant who believes he has an empty box and the defendant who believes he has a box containing scent, when in fact in both instances the box contains cannabis, is to reduce the law to complete artificiality. The beauty of the distinction in *Warner* (as it appeared to their Lordships) was that it ensured that Warner stayed convicted; but that was an ephemeral advantage, and now we are lumbered with absurd law for the indefinite future.

However, the rule in *Warner* is important only on the issue of possession. The *Misuse of Drugs Act 1971* leaves untouched the conceptual mess of *Warner* but sits on top of it the new statutory defence of section 28(3). So, even if the defendant is found to be in possession of the drug, he now gets off (by virtue of the subsection) if he did not know or suspect and had no reason to suspect that it was a controlled drug that he was supposed to have. The upshot is that, under the *Act*, a person is not guilty of illegally possessing the drug if there was nothing to put him on enquiry as to its being a controlled drug.

The awkward consequence may be illustrated. The defendant is found to have a cigarette containing cannabis in his car, and his defence is that he did not know it was there and that it must have been placed there by someone else. The judge must direct the jury, first, that the burden rests on the prosecution to satisfy them so that they feel sure that the defendant knew he had the cigarette. (Goodness knows if the jury will understand it.) If they find in the affirmative, then the burden rests on the defendant under section 28(3) to establish on the balance of probability[100] that he did not know or suspect or have reason to suspect that the something was or included cannabis.

36–034   This is an entirely artificial separation of the issues. The substantial question is not whether the defendant knew he had a tobacco cigarette, that is to say he knew he had something, and that something was the cigarette (the possession of which is no offence) but whether he knew (or, since the *Act* says so, had reason to suspect) he had a reefer; and in common sense the issue should be confined to that, and should be a single issue carrying a single burden of proof.

Having spoken of things in boxes (and the same remarks apply to things that are wrapped up so that the contents of the wrapping are invisible), we must now consider the case where the possessor of the box or parcel has no right to open it. Suppose a person is given a box for safe keeping, or to give to someone else. He

---

[99] See his remark on "planting" [1969] 2 A.C. 256 at 360G.
[100] Cf. *R. v. Lambert* [2002] 2 A.C. 545.

knows there is something inside it, but he believes this to be innocent, such as sweets. Actually it is a controlled drug. It seems unfair to make him guilty, if he had no right to open the box.

The House of Lords invented a special rule for this situation in *Warner*. The majority view appears to have been that the defendant possesses the thing if he:

- knows that he possesses something, and
- has an opportunity to ascertain what it is, and
- either has a right to ascertain what it is (*e.g.*, by opening the container) or came by the thing in suspicious circumstances.

The above was specifically the view of Lord Pearce, who, as said before, expressed the highest common factor of opinion in favour of liability.

It need not be observed that this complex rule cannot be deduced from any theory of possession. It is judicial legislation pure and simple, the object being to give a defence to apparently honest people but not to those who evoke suspicion (an object that it achieves only very imperfectly). The fact that the defendant is an employee or bailee who has no right to open the box entrusted to him is no defence, either under the rule in *Warner* or under the *Act*, if he came by the box in suspicious circumstances—which presumably means, if he ought to have suspected the truth. **36–035**

The rule does not operate against the defendant if he did not know that he had anything (as if he thought he was being entrusted with an empty box, when in fact it was full of controlled drugs). However stupid he was, and however suspicious the circumstances, he cannot be convicted of possessing the drugs. But if he knew there was something in the box, such as aspirins, he can be convicted if the box contained controlled drugs and if he came into possession in objectively suspicious circumstances.

The rule in *Warner* means, further, that if the defendant comes into possession of a box for a safe custody otherwise than in suspicious circumstances, believing the box to contain scent, then he is not guilty although it actually contains cannabis, because he has no right to open the box.

What if drugs have been dumped in my shed without my knowledge? In the Irish case, *The People v. Boyle*,[101] Boyle was convicted of unlawful possession of a controlled drug. The offence related to the possession of cocaine in a shed and container. When the police searched the shed they found three men, cocaine and drug processing equipment. The two men who were with Boyle had rubber gloves on and quantities of cannabis resin on their persons. Boyle did not have rubber gloves on and had no controlled substances on his person, but he had been in the shed with the other men and had opened the doors to let them in. Denham J. said:[102] **36–036**

---

[101] [2010] 1 I.R. 787.
[102] [2010] 1 I.R. 787 at 798.

"In the instant case there was no evidence directly connecting the accused with actual possession or control of the items on the bench in the shed or in the filing cabinet. However, there was evidence that the accused was a lawful and also a *de facto* occupier of this shed. There was evidence that he was there every day. From this it was open to a jury properly to conclude that the drugs and drug handling equipment, not least the adapted compressor, could not have come and remained there without his knowledge and at least tacit, in the sense of passive, consent. This was not a shared space, as in *R. v. Bland* [1988] Crim. L.R. 41, over which the accused had no control and to which others were free to come and go and do as they pleased. While this might not be sufficient to establish actual physical possession or control over these items it was evidence sufficient to go to a jury of offering assistance and encouragement to the two other men in using the shed for the unlawful purpose."

In *R. v. Lewis*,[103] D was the sole tenant of a house where drugs had been found. His defence was that he did not know or suspect that someone might have put drugs in his house. The evidence was that many people frequented the house, but that Lewis only visited it on rare occasions. Unlike Boyle, there was little evidence to support the claim that "drugs could not have come and remained there without [Lewis's] knowledge and at least tacit, in the sense of passive, consent." Lewis did not even suspect that the drugs (or suspicious package or container and so on) were in his house. It is true that Lewis had an opportunity to search his own premises to ascertain whether or not there were any drugs there, but a person is not likely to go looking for drugs that he does not even suspect exist. Lewis had no knowledge of the extras in his house.

36–037   **What if a fellow resident brings drugs into a shared home?**   In *R. v. Bland*,[104] a couple lived together in a house that was frequented by many visitors. Some of the visitors were found leaving the premises in possession of drugs. Traces of the drugs were also found on the premises. The prosecution case against Bland was that she was living with a man who was dealing in drugs and thus was in joint possession. Bland's conviction of possession of a controlled drug with intent to supply was quashed, because there was no evidence of active or passive assistance. She asserted that she had no idea that her boyfriend was a drug-dealer. It was held that the fact that she lived with the dealer in "the same room was insufficient evidence from which an inference of assistance could be drawn. Assistance required more than mere knowledge that [the boyfriend] was drug-dealing."

In *R. v. Kousar*,[105] trading standards officers found a large quantity of counterfeit items in the matrimonial home of the defendant and her husband. They were charged with offences under section 92(1)(c) of the *Trade Marks Act 1994*. The Crown's case was that the husband sold counterfeit goods at the local markets and that since they were kept in the matrimonial home the defendant was also in possession of them. It was argued on the defendant's behalf that she had no involvement in her husband's business and that she had no idea that the goods were counterfeit. It was asserted that the goods were therefore not within her possession for the purposes of section 92(1)(c).

Clarke J. said:

---

[103] (1988) 87 Cr. App. R. 270.
[104] (1987) 151 J.P. 857; *R. v. Arshad* [2002] EWCA Crim. 1549; *R. v. Conway* [1994] Crim. L.R. 826.
[105] [2009] 2 Cr. App. R. 88 at 93.

"In the course of argument some discussion was engendered about the normal domestic situation: is a husband or wife to be regarded as in joint possession of items in that house which are in fact the property of the other spouse? Is a husband to be regarded as in possession of clothing and cosmetics, for example, of which his wife is both the owner and the possessor? We venture to suggest that that concept is quite inappropriate. One is not in possession of one's spouse's personal property in that sense. The term 'permission has been used, that she permitted this property to be in the house. Permission may be something more than an acquiescence but even then is not in our judgment sufficient to render the permittor a person in possession of the goods. In the field of drugs offences, there is a specific offence of permitting premises to be used for certain activities but there is no equivalent in the legislation with which we are concerned. A finding of being able to exercise a measure of control, which is the basis upon which this issue was in due course left to the jury, is not the same as a finding that she did exercise control. ... [H]er so-called ability or right to control the goods was [insufficient] to render her in possession of them."

A final question relating to the possession of drugs is the liability of the occupier of premises where drugs are consumed. Is it, for example, an offence to allow your guest to use drugs at a party? Section 8 of the *Act of 1971* provides the answer: **36–038**

"A person commits an offence if, being the occupier or concerned in the management of any premises, he knowingly permits or suffers any of the following activities to take place on those premises, that is to say—
(a) producing or attempting to produce a controlled drug in contravention of section 4(1) of this Act;
(b) supplying or attempting to supply a controlled drug to another in contravention of section 4(1) of this Act, or offering to supply a controlled drug to another in contravention of section 4(1);
(c) preparing opium for smoking;
(d) smoking cannabis, cannabis resin or prepared opium."

This section requires *mens rea*. It applies not only to occupiers but to landladies of lodging houses, and presumably, to universities and colleges in respect of the activities of students. (A student who lives in a college hostel is himself an "occupier" of his room within the meaning of the section,[106] even though the college would seem to be an occupier as well. A similar remark applies to the lodger.)

36.8. THE POSSESSION OF FIREARMS

The unauthorized possession of firearms is an offence under the *Firearms Act 1968*. Problems arise particularly with regard to antique and toy guns, some of which are firearms within the *Act* while others are not. If a prosecution is brought, it will be for the jury, under the direction of the judge, to decide whether the particular gun comes within the definition in the *Act*. Suppose, then, that a person possesses a gun which he believes to be an antique or toy falling outside the *Act*, but the jury (or magistrates on summary trial) find that it is a prohibited firearm. Has an offence been committed? **36–039**

The sensible (though not the law's)[107] answer to this question would be that although the police can seize and forfeit the prohibited weapon, the defendant is

---

[106] *R. v. Tao* [1977] Q.B. 141.
[107] *R. v. Deyemi* [2008] 1 Cr. App. R. 345.

not guilty of an offence in possessing it. His mistake may be either one of fact or one of law. He may mistakenly believe that the gun has a particular attribute (that there is some fact relating to the gun); and this attribute may be one that if true would take the gun out of the class of prohibited firearms. Or the defendant may not make a mistake of fact but simply be ignorant of the statutory definition of a firearm, or apply it wrongly (*i.e.* in a way that the jury or magistrates do not apply it). Here his mistake may be said to be one of law.[108] On *mens rea* principles, the mistake of fact should be a defence, but not the mistake of law.

The courts apparently do not distinguish between the two situations: they hold that the defendant is liable either way. In two earlier decisions on the subject, on a supposed antique and a supposed toy respectively,[109] the court said that the offence of possessing firearms is "absolute," and quoted *Warner v. Commissioner of Police of the Metropolis*. The distinction from *R. v. Tolson*,[110] (and other similar decisions) was stated to be, principally, "the danger to the community resulting from possession of lethal weapons." It is to be observed, however, that in both cases the defendant knew he had a gun of some sort. What if he did not know that he had a gun at all? Suppose, for example, that he thought that what he had in a particular box (inherited from his grandmother) was a power drill. Again, the courts have held such a person would be liable.[111]

36–040   Two hypotheticals will illustrate the current law.

D was found with a gun in his car; he had no gun licence, and his defence is that the gun (rapped in brown paper) was planted on him: he did not know that the parcel or any gun was there. The gun was something additional to the objects that he knew were in the car. On the doctrine of *Warner*, if this defence cannot be disproved, D was not in possession of the gun. This must be the law where D does not know that something exists; it is one thing to hold a person liable when he accepts a container without checking its contents or sees a parcel in his car an omits to check it, but something entirely different to hold him liable where there is no voluntary "act" or "omission" of any kind.

As before, but D admits that he saw a brown paper parcel in his car, which he says he assumed to contain a constructional toy belonging to his small son. According to a line of cases D is strictly liable for possessing the gun.[112]

In *R. v. Bradish*,[113] it was held that if the offence is one of strict liability it does not matter whether the defendant knows what is in the container (bag, backpack, and so on) or whether he thinks the ammunition he has is fake. It is a strict liability offence, and it would be no defence for the defendant to maintain that he did not know or could not reasonably have been expected to know what type of weapon was in the container. However, it has been held without qualification that a person cannot be convicted of "having with him an offensive weapon" if he did

---

[108] Although this distinction may seem clear in theory, it can raise subtle problems. As an example from a different context, see *R. v. Champ* (1981) 73 Cr. App. R. 367.

[109] *R. v. Howells* (1977) 65 Cr. App. R. 86; *R. v. Hussain* (1981) 72 Cr. App. R. 143; *R. v. Deyemi* [2008] 1 Cr. App. R. 345. See also *R. v. Bradish* (1990) 90 Cr. App. R. 271.

[110] (1889) 23 Q.B.D. 168.

[111] *R. v. Zahid* [2010] EWCA Crim. 2158; *R. v. Deyemi* [2008] 1 Cr. App. R. 345.

[112] *R. v. Zahid* [2010] EWCA Crim. 2158; *R. v. Waller* [1991] Crim. L.R. 381; *R. v. Bradish* (1990) 90 Cr. App. R. 271.

[113] *R. v. Bradish* (1990) 90 Cr. App. R. 271; *R. v. Waller* [1991] Crim. L.R. 381.

not know he had it,[114] and the same rule should be applied to firearms. It is regrettable, but must now be accepted, that if a person knows that he has a gun of any kind he takes the risk of its coming within the *Act*, even though he reasonably believes that the gun falls outside it.

---

[114] *R. v. Cugullere* [1961] 1 W.L.R. 858; *R. v. Russell* (1985) 81 Cr. App. R. 315.

CHAPTER 37

ATTRIBUTED ACTS: VICARIOUS LIABILITY

"*Qui peccat per alium peccat per se* is not a maximum of criminal law."

Lord Diplock[1]

37.1. STRICT LIABILITY WITHOUT AN ACT BY THE DEFENDANT

Some cases of strict liability require at least a physical act by the defendant in violation of law. Nevertheless, as was observed in Chapter 7, there are also situational and status offences carrying strict liability. To take a case that has been mentioned above, the parents of a girl who truanted were held guilty of an offence under a statute providing that in such circumstances "the parent of the child shall be guilty of an offence," although they did not know, and quite possibly had no reason to know, of their daughter's misbehaviour.[2]

37–001

The most prominent instances of situational and strict liability are the offences of unlawful possession already studied. Nowadays, legislation that *prima facie* creates situational liability (though by no means always) allows a defence.[3] In typical situational offences the external element is defined simply in terms of the event occurring, it being immaterial whether the event results from the defendant's act. The event may be defined without reference as the conduct of a human being (one's child is absent from school).

It may be tempting to categorize some cases of the last type, where the conduct of another person is involved, as "vicarious liability," an expression properly belonging to the law of tort, which does not sit well in the criminal law. The civil courts hold that if an employee commits a tort in the course of his employment the employer, as well as the employee, is liable for it.[4] Thus vicarious liability is difficult (I do not say impossible) to support if considered in terms of justice; but one of the objects of the law of tort is to compensate the victim of the wrong, and it is thought that the object is best effected by giving

---

[1] *Tesco Supermarkets Ltd. v. Nattrass* [1972] A.C. 153 at 199.

[2] *Crump v. Gilmore* (1969) 113 S.J. 998. The offence is now found in section 444 of the *Education Act 1996*. See *Bath and North East Somerset DC v. Warman* [1999] Ed. C.R. 517; *R. v. Leeds Magistrates Court* [2005] E.L.R. 589. It has been held to be compatible with the *European Convention on Human Rights 1950*; see *Barnfather v. Islington LBC* [2003] 1 W.L.R. 2318.

[3] Section 28 of the *Misuse of Drugs Act 1971*. Many *Acts* also incorporate no-negligence defences. See sections 3(1)(b) and (3) of the *Prevention of Oil Pollution Act 1971* as discussed in *Amoco (UK) Exploration Co. v. Frame* [2009] Env. L.R. 653.

[4] See, for example, *Maga v. Archbishop of Birmingham* [2010] 1 W.L.R. 1441; *Lister v. Hesley Hall Ltd.* [2002] 1 A.C. 215; *Majrowski v. Guy's and St Thomas's NHS Trust* [2007] 1 A.C. 224. Cf. *Safeway Stores Ltd. v. Twigger* [2011] 1 Lloyd's Rep. 462.

him a remedy against the employer, who is more likely to satisfy the judgment than the employee, and who can, after all, insure against his liability.

37–002
The reasoning does not apply in criminal law,[5] the chief object of which is deterrence and retribution. Here it would seem to be an elementary principle both of justice and of utility that one person should not be held accountable for the wrong of another. For the utilitarian, punishment can be justified only by its useful effect for the future. In general, utility[6] and retribution[7] cannot be achieved by imposing punishment on a person who did not do the act and could not have prevented it by any reasonable precaution.

The notion of justice seems so instinctive that it is hard to imagine any society so callous to punish people severely for the crimes of others; yet examples abound.[8] In the earliest extant code of law, Code of Hammurabi (dating from the second millennium BC), one section provided that if a builder built a house so poorly that it fell upon the owner's son and killed him, the builder's son should be put to death.[9] In the Old Testament, too, group responsibility was accepted, though the prophets Jeremiah and Ezekiel protested against it. By the time of the New Testament, the personal, atomistic conception of duty had become fully established in religious thought.[10] Even then it did not completely permeate against it. In medieval England, men of the hundred were fined for murders and robberies committed in the locality, and not so long ago the collective punishment of towns and villages was used as a means of colonial rule. Through the legal mechanism of a bill of attainder, the legislature could also declare a person or group of persons guilty of some serious crime without a trial.[11]

Notwithstanding that the criminal courts do not apply a wide general principle on this subject, something like vicarious liability is still recognized for certain minor criminal offences, the object being to induce the defendant to exercise control over others. One instance occurs in relation to juveniles. The court may order that fines, compensation and costs awarded against a young person shall be paid by his parent or guardian unless, in the circumstances, the court thinks it

---

[5] *R. v. Huggins* (1730) 92 E.R. 518; *Lee v. Dangar Grant & Co.* [1892] 2 Q.B. 337 at 348; *Bagge v. Whitehead* [1892] 2 Q.B. 355; *R. (on the application of Chief Constable of Northumbria) v. Newcastle upon Tyne Magistrates' Court* [2010] EWHC 935.

[6] Paul H. Robinson, *Distributive Principles of Criminal Law: Who Should be Punished How Much?*, (New York: Oxford University Press, 2008) at Chap. 8; David Beetham, *The Legitimation of Power*, (Basingstoke, Macmillian, 1991).

[7] See Andrew von Hirsch, *Censure and Sanctions*, (Oxford: Clarendon Press, 1993).

[8] See Dennis J. Baker, *The Right Not to be Criminalized: Demarcating Criminal Law's Authority*, (Ashgate: Farnham, 2011) at 101 *et seq.*; L.H. Leigh, *Strict and Vicarious Liability: A Study in Administrative Criminal Law*, (London: Sweet & Maxwell, 1982).

[9] See Albert Kocourek and John H. Wigmore, *Sources of Ancient and Primitive Law*, (Boston: Little, Brown, 1915) at 433. The ancient Chinese Codes also relied heavily on the notion of collective responsibility. See Dennis J Baker & Lucy X. Zhao, "Responsibility Links, Fair Labelling and Proportionality in China: Comparing China's Criminal Law Theory and Doctrine," (2009) 14(2) *UCLA J. Int'l L. Foreign Aff.* 274; Daryl J. Levinson, "Collective Sanctions," (2004) 56 *Stan. L. Rev.* 345.

[10] Mary Sturt and Margaret Hobling, *Practical Ethics: A Sketch of the Moral Structure of Society*, (London: Routledge & K. Paul, 1949) at 56.

[11] Michael P. Lehmann, "The Bill of Attainder Doctrine: A Survey of the Decisional Law," (1978) 5 *Hastings Const. L.Q.* 767.

would be unreasonable to make them pay.[12] Again, the registered owner of a vehicle is liable by statute in respect of certain and excess parking charges, even though the fault was that of some other person (not being a person in possession of the vehicle without the owner's consent).[13] This provision was found to be necessary because it was too burdensome for the police to trace the actual offender, when offences were numerous and so trivial.

There are various other examples of criminal liability for the act of another (particularly of employees) which we are now to study. It is sometimes argued, in favour of this liability, that if an employer is fined for his underlying contraventions he is likely to discipline his staff better in the future. But much the same result could be achieved if the employer were allowed a no-negligence defence. He would still be under considerable pressure to supervise those under his control, because otherwise he would fail in his defence.

37.2.   THE ATTRIBUTION OF ACTS

Some statutes that on their face seem to refer to the defendant's conduct are interpreted to attribute liability to a non-doer. This arises because the courts interpreting these particular statutes deem the act of some person other than the defendant (generally his employee,[14] or a person closely similar to an employee) to be the act of the defendant. **37–003**

An example of a statute encouraging such interpretation is section 163 of the *Licensing Act 1964* (now repealed), which provided that "a person shall not, either himself or by his servant or agent," do certain things. The section shrank from saying anything so barbarous as that A shall be liable for the offence of B. The wording might perhaps have been understood by the MPs who passed it to apply only when the employer ordered the commission of the offence; but in fact it was doubtless intended to make the employer punishable also for the unauthorized act of his employee in the course of the employment; and this is how the courts interpreted it. So here we have a situational offence masquerading as an ordinary offence of personal act.[15]

The reason for legislation of this kind rests largely on difficulties of proof. The employer will frequently have been guilty of negligence in failing to prevent the offence, even though negligence cannot be proved by the prosecution from its own hand, so to speak—particularly when no one is obliged to answer questions. Attributive responsibility enables a conviction to be registered and the employing firm to be mulcted in a monetary penalty. This penalty may persuade the firm to discipline its employees, even to the extent of dismissing them when this seems the only way of preventing a repetition.

---

[12] See *R. v. JJB* [2004] 2 Cr. App. R. (S.) 41; sections 136-138 of the *Powers of Criminal Courts (Sentencing) Act 2000*.

[13] Section 107 of the *Road Traffic Regulation Act 1984*; see also section 64 of the *Road Traffic Offenders Act 1988*.

[14] *Harrow London Borough Council v. Shah* [2000] 1 W.L.R. 83; *Coppen v. Moore (No.2)* [1898] 2 Q.B. 306; *R. v. Bleasdale* (1848) 175 E.R. 321. The traditional expressions are "master" and "servant"; these have largely gone out of use because they belong to an antiquated social order (though the second survives honourably for "civil servants").

[15] For an even more remarkable example, see *Lindsay v. Vickers* [1978] Crim. L.R. 55.

37–004   To a large extent, of course, the purpose of the law could be satisfied by making the employer liable for negligence, the burden of establishing the absence of fault being placed on him.[16] But the argument in favour of a severe rule is the same as that for strict liability. It is said that penalties for these offences are light, and that the prosecutor ought not to be put to the trouble of investigating too closely what the employer has done. Whether this is a convincing answer must be a matter of opinion. As was pointed out before, the issue of fault may arise on the question of penalty, so that the prosecutor cannot avoid the issue if the defendant wishes to raise it.

This type of penal liability differs from vicarious liability in tort in the fact that the provisions creating it are only fragmentary, depending upon particular statutes or their interpretation.[17] Vicarious liability in tort, on the other hand, is a general principle of law. Further, the theory is different. The theory of the criminal law in these cases of pseudo-personal liability is not that the employee commits a crime for which the employer is made liable but that in certain cases the employer is debited with the act of the employee (or certain other persons) more or less as though it were his own act. These practical and conceptual differences from the law of tort make it desirable to give the criminal doctrine a distinctive name, for which reason it will here be called "the doctrine of attributed acts." It may also be called for convenience, "attributive liability," but only on the understanding in legal theory what is attributed to the defendant is not the offence of another (since that other person need not have perpetrated an offence) but the other's act or default.[18]

37.3.   IMPLIED ATTRIBUTION: THE LICENSEE CASES

37–005   The courts frequently hold that acts may be attributed to another person without express words in the legislation to suggest it; but many doubts exist. As said before, there is no general principle whereby a person is held criminally liable merely because a criminal act is committed by his employee in the course of his employment. These courts often seem to be pressing towards such a principle, but have not yet reached it. The basic stance of the criminal law is therefore the opposite of the law of tort, and to that extent the *dictum* of Lord Diplock quoted at the head of this chapter is clearly correct. A defendant to a criminal charge is liable only if he falls within the words of the statute, as interpreted by the courts—except that in the licensee cases, to be noticed in a moment, the courts

---

[16] Cf. section 40 of the *Health and Safety at Work etc. Act 1974* as examined in *R. v. Chargot Ltd. (t/a Contract Services)* [2009] 1 W.L.R. 1.

[17] There were three crimes at common law in which something like vicarious liability is or was recognized: criminal libel (see *R. v. Walter* (1799) 170 E.R. 524; but see section 7 of the *Libel Act 1843* which provides a defence for the employer who did not know of the libel or authorize it: *R. v. Holbrook* (1877) 13 Cox C.C. 650), nuisance (*R. v. Medley* (1834) 6 C. & P. 292; cf. *Chisholm v. Doulton* (1889) L.R. 22 Q.B.D. 736), and contempt of court (cf. the civil case, *Director General of Fair Trading v. Pioneer Concrete (UK) Ltd.* [1995] 1 A.C. 456). The instances of attributed acts discussed in this chapter rest on the judicial interpretation of certain statutes.

[18] See Glazebrook's criticism of the term "vicarious liability" in P. R. Glazebook, "Situational Liability," in P. R. Glazebrook, *Reshaping the Criminal Law: Essays in Honour of Glanville Williams*, (London: Stevens & Sons, 1978) at 108 *et seq.*

have interpreted the statutory words so strangely that they have in reality created an exception to the principle. The point to be understood is that the courts often find that the defendant does fall within the words of the statute because of what has been physically done by his employee or agent. This will become clearer as we proceed.

The cases come from different dates, and there has been a notable shift in judicial interpretation; even the modern authorities do not state a completely coherent doctrine. However, we may perhaps perceive two main principles which explain most of them. One concerns public licenses; the other concerns construction of statutory verbs.

The defendant may have a licence from a public authority to do something that would otherwise be forbidden, and the statute providing for the licence may contain special offences capable of being committed by the licensee.[19] This is certainly the case with the licence to sell intoxicating liquor. In interpreting the offences, the courts hold that the keeper or licensee of certain premises is responsible for the acts of his manager or other delegate.[20]

For example, section 44 of the *Metropolitan Police Act 1839* provides: **37–006**

> "Every person who shall have or keep any house, shop, room, or place of public resort within the metropolitan police district, wherein provisions, liquors, or refreshments of any kind shall be sold or consumed, (whether the same shall be kept or retailed therein or procured elsewhere,) and who shall wilfully or knowingly permit drunkenness or other disorderly conduct in such house, shop, room, or place or knowingly permit or suffer prostitutes or persons of notoriously bad character to meet together and remain therein, shall for every such offence."

The word "permit" is generally read as a *mens rea* word, *i.e.* as presupposing the defendant's knowledge of what is happening. Suppose that the owner or the keeper of the house, *etc.* has installed a manager who knowingly permits drunkenness on the premises. Paradoxically, under the *Act of 1844* it is impossible to convict as perpetrator the manager who is the real offender[21] because the *Act* strikes only at the keeper. If the keeper could not be convicted as perpetrator then the manager could not be convicted as accessory, so the legislation would wholly fail of effect in these circumstances.

The legislation has been held to mean that when a keeper "delegates" the management of the premises he can be convicted of the act of this manager.[22] Even when a statute expressly requires *mens rea*, as when it punishes a keeper who "knowingly allows" prostitutes to resort to the premises, the keeper is liable

---

[19] Such offences have existed for centuries. See William Oldnall Russell, *A Treatise on Crimes and Indictable Misdemeanours*, (Boston: Lilly & Wait, 1831) at 301.

[20] Including a partner or co-licensee: *Linnett v. MPC* [1946] K.B. 290.

[21] Cf. section 140 of the *Licensing Act 2003*. The section provides: "(1) A person to whom subsection (2) applies commits an offence if he knowingly allows disorderly conduct on relevant premises. (2) This subsection applies—(a) to *any person who works at the premises in a capacity*, whether paid or unpaid, which authorises him to prevent the conduct, (b) in the case of licensed premises, to—(i) the holder of a premises licence in respect of the premises, and (ii) the designated premises supervisor (if any) under such a licence."

[22] *Allen v. Whitehead* [1930] 1 K.B. 211.

on account of his manager's knowledge, though he himself has none.[23] Thus the doctrine of delegation allows a person to be convicted of violating the statute when he quite clearly does not come within its terms. Since the keeper can be convicted as perpetrator, the manager can be convicted as accessory.

37–007　The delegation doctrine has been applied frequently in the licensing cases. Cave J. explained the rationale for invoking the delegation doctrine in the early licensing cases in *Massey v. Morriss*.[24] In that case the owner of a ship was charged with an offence because the master of one of his ships had overloaded it, even though he had not authorized the overloading and had no knowledge of it. Cave J. said:

> "Did the appellant allow the ship to be so loaded? There is no evidence whatever that he did so unless the mere fact that he appointed the master who allowed it to be done amounted to an 'allowing' of it by himself. But I do not think that that could possibly have been the intention of the legislature. Of course, there may in some cases be circumstances from which you may fairly draw the conclusion that the owner appointed a particular master knowing that he would overload the ship, and intending that he should do so; but there is no evidence of any such circumstances here. There is nothing beyond the bare fact that the appellant appointed the master, and that is not enough. Reference was made to the alehouse cases. But the explanation of those cases is this: licences to keep alehouses are only granted to persons of good personal character, and it is obvious that the object of so restricting the grant of licences would be defeated if the licensed person could, by delegating the control and management of the house to another person who was altogether unfit to keep it, free himself from responsibility for the manner in which the house was conducted. The cases are not analogous."[25]

It is not clear why the cases are not analogous. Might not a shipping operator also benefit by using a manager to break the rules? If Cave J.'s judgment does anything, it highlights that the delegation doctrine allows licensees to be convicted on a fictitious basis.

37–008　**But if you forget academic purism, isn't the delegation doctrine really a good wheeze?**　In a way, but one may ask whether it is proper for the courts to convict people in contradiction of the words of a statute. When the draftsperson of an *Act* has confined an offence to one who knowingly allows, the draftsperson must have considered and rejected (or been instructed to reject) the possibility of extending the scope of the offence to include one who negligently fails to prevent. No self-respecting Parliamentary counsel would use the phrase "knowingly allows" if he meant to include negligence in failing to prevent an occurrence that is not known; yet that is how the courts read the phrase in the licence cases. Indeed, the interpretation favoured by the courts not only takes in negligence but enables the publican who could not have discovered the facts to be punished, if his manager knew. The publican may end up with an array of convictions for what purport to be *mens rea* offences, and when he applies to the justices for the renewal of his licence these convictions may count against him. No one will know from the record that he was not at fault. Is it right to convict people on a fictitious basis?

---

[23] *Allen v. Whitehead* [1930] 1 K.B. 211. See also *Southwark LBC v. Allied Domecq Leisure Ltd.* [1999] E.H.L.R. 231. Cf. *Hall & Woodhouse Ltd. v. Poole Borough Council* [2010] P.T.S.R. 741.

[24] [1894] 2 Q.B. 412.

[25] [1894] 2 Q.B. 412 at 413–414.

To add to the anomaly of the present law, the courts hold that if the publican has not delegated the management of the premises but is personally present, he is not responsible for the act of his barman or other employee when the offence requires personal knowledge. If, for example, the licensee is charged with "permitting" drunkenness, and the permitting was by his employee without his knowledge, but he himself was personally present, he will not be liable, because permitting requires knowledge.[26] The effect of the rule is that the licensee's responsibility depends on the delegation means that his responsibility varies inversely with the possibility of control. Take two contrasting situations:

1. A barperson allows prostitutes to resort almost under the publican's nose, but without the publican's knowledge. The publican genuinely does not know what is going on, because he is busy with something else at the time, though he has not delegated control of the premises. Here he cannot be convicted of the statutory offence under section 44 of the *Metropolitan Police Act 1839* for knowingly permitting prostitutes to meet together and remain on his premises.
2. The barperson tolerates prostitutes as before, but the publican is on holiday in Australia, and has installed the barperson as a responsible manager whom he has chosen with care. Here the rule is that the publican can be convicted, because he has delegated authority.

Yet it is obvious in case (2) that the publican is, if anything, less able to control the situation than he is in case (1). So the result of this judge-made rule is that the less control the publican has in fact, the more likely he is to be penalized. The anomaly is the result of illegitimately introducing into the criminal law a concept of general agency developed in the civil law, where it admits of an altogether different justification.

But if the publican were present it would almost always be possible to find   **37–009** **that he knew of the prostitutes or drunks on his premises, or was wilfully blind to their presence, so there would be no difficulty in convicting him.** Even if this assumption is invariably true for offences of permitting prostitutes and drunks to be on the premises (which may be doubted), there may be other offences where the publican's awareness is by no means a necessary inference. Take the facts of *Vane v. Yiannopoullos*.[27] By a provision of the now repealed *Licensing Act 1964*, "if the holder of a justices" on-licence knowingly sells or supplies intoxicating liquor to persons to whom he is not permitted by the conditions of the licence to sell or supply it he shall be guilty of an offence." The licensee of the restaurant was allowed by the conditions of his licence to serve drinks only with meals. His waitress, contrary to his instructions, served drinks without a meal, while he was in another part of the restaurant. The House of Lords held that the licensee could not be convicted of the offence. Lord Donovan

---

[26] *Somerset v. Wade* [1894] 1 Q.B. 574. Even if the employee commits an offence of strict liability the licensee will not be liable as accessory in the absence of knowledge. This is because of the rule in *Callow v. Tillstone* (1900) 64 J.P. 823; *Robinson v. D.P.P.* [1991] R.T.R. 315; *Vehicle Inspectorate v. Nuttall* [1999] 1 W.L.R. 629 *per* Lord Steyn; cf. *Ferguson v. Weaving* [1951] 1 K.B. 814.
[27] [1965] A.C. 486.

expressed the position succinctly when he said: "If a decision that 'knowingly' means 'knowingly' will make the provision difficult to enforce, the remedy lies with the legislature."[28]

The speeches in the House of Lords left undecided the question whether their Lordships would be prepared to overrule the decisions making the publican liable for the *mens rea* of his manager in the case of delegation. However, the Divisional Courts have not shared these doubts,[29] and have continued to apply the traditional rule that a licensee is liable when he delegates—a matter that depends almost exclusively on the question whether he is present or absent.[30]

37–010 **How far away must the publican be to be "absent"?** At one time it was thought that the absence meant complete absence from the premises; but the Divisional Court has now stretched the law still further by holding that a licensee who himself happens to be in a different room can be found to have delegated the management of the room in which the offence takes place.[31] A waitress can therefore become a "manager" for the purpose of the rule as soon as the licensee goes into the next room. This is impossible to reconcile with *Vane v. Yiannopoullos*, where the licensee who was on a different floor from that on which the offence was committed was held not to have delegated his authority. The licensee who is on a different floor is likely to be more remote than one who is merely in a different room. Why should the law distinguish between a different floor and a different room in the same building; and if it does distinguish, should it not be the other way round? The truth seems to be that the intermediate appellate courts find the decision in the House of Lords unpalatable, and will not apply it if they can by any means distinguish it.

If only the licensee can commit the offence as perpetrator,[32] and if on the facts he has not delegated but his employee commits the forbidden act, then, on principle, no one can be convicted. For instance, in *Vane v. Yiannopoullos* the waitress knew all the facts that made what she did a *de facto* breach of the conditions of the employer's licence. Although the waitress was morally an offender, it has never been suggested that she could be convicted as accessory to a non-existent offence of the licensee. It is only when the delegation doctrine applies, and the licensee can be convicted, that the employee who does the actual selling can be convicted as accessory. If it were always possible to convict the employee who commits the offence in fact, so to speak, it is unlikely that the courts would have felt obliged to convict the licensee, in defence of the statute requiring the licensee to have *mens rea*. This is a strong argument against the validity of the *dictum* in *R. v. Cogan*.[33]

It seems that where the offence requires knowledge the licensee's delegate must know the facts. If he does not, the licensee is not liable. Also, the doctrine

---

[28] *Vane v. Yiannopoullos* [1965] A.C. 486 at 511.

[29] *Howker v. Robinson* [1973] Q.B. 178.

[30] *Howker v. Robinson* [1973] Q.B. 178.

[31] *Howker v. Robinson* [1973] Q.B. 178.

[32] Since the enactment of the *Licensing Act 2003* such cases are likely to be rare, because that *Act* targets both the perpetrator and the licensee.

[33] [1976] Q.B. 217.

applies only to acts of the delegate manager, not to those of his assistant;[34] but there is at least one difficult decision on this.[35]

The doctrine of delegation is not necessarily confined to the liquor cases, but may be applied to other statutes with licensing provisions.[36] One may hope that the courts will call a halt at this point and not extend it outside offences by licensees, though from time to time there are threatening signs that this may be done.[37] **37–011**

The provisions of the repealed *Licensing Act 1964*[38] were limited in that they only struck at the licensee who was generally the employer, and was silent as to the employee's liability. However, the provisions of the *Licensing Act 2003* plug this gap, because they target both the perpetrator and the allower. Many of its provisions criminalize the perpetrator for his actions and also any person who "allows" the perpetrator to perpetrate. For instance, compare section 146 with section 147. Section 146 catches those who actually sell alcohol to minors. (If the statute by its terms imposes liability on the barman/manager alone, the licensee will not normally be vicariously liable for him. The licensee can be liable as accessory, but only if he knows the facts). Nevertheless, section 147 of the *Act of 2003* catches those who "knowingly allow" alcohol to be sold to children, as long as that person is in a position to prevent the sale. (The "knowingly allow" provisions in the *Act of 2003* do not merely target the licensee, but also managers and supervisors as defined in the *Act*.) It is yet to be seen whether the courts will deem that a licensee who is on holiday in Australia has the knowledge of the manager who he has installed to run his London pub in his absence. It would be wrong to convict the licensee of the section 147 offence if he has no knowledge of his manager's offending. It ought to be enough to convict the manager. The manager is the perpetrator and should be liable if the Crown can prove that he perpetrated the offence by knowingly allowing alcohol to be sold to a child. (If the delegation doctrine is applied, the licensee would be deemed to be a joint-perpetrator even though he had no knowledge of the sale and was not personally in a position to prevent it.)

Section 140 of *Licensing Act 2003* makes special reference to the licensee and the designated premises supervisor, but again requires all the potential offenders to have actual knowledge of the fact that disorderly conduct is taking place on the given premises. That section provides:

---

[34] Cf. *Rowlands v. Gee* [1977] Crim. L.R. 481. See also *Southwark LBC v. Allied Domecq Leisure Ltd.* [1999] E.H.L.R. 231.

[35] In *R. v. Winson* [1969] 1 Q.B. 371 an absent licensee was held guilty of an offence requiring knowledge when it was committed by his assistant manager without his knowledge, although the full manager was on the premises. Section 147 of the *Licensing Act 2003*, among others, treats any employee (or other person) who has the power to prevent a criminal sale of alcohol from taking place as a perpetrator of the section 147 offence, so long has he has been given the authority to prevent such a sale from taking place.

[36] *United Dairies (London) v. Beckenham Corp.* [1963] 1 Q.B. 434.

[37] In *Allen v. Whitehead* [1930] 1 K.B. 211 the doctrine was applied where the offence was confined to persons "who shall have or keep a house," even though not licensed; but there are authorities the other way. See Glanville Williams, *Criminal Law: The General Part*, (London: Stevens & Sons, 2nd edn. 1961) at 272-273.

[38] Cf. *Licensing Act 2003*.

"(1)   A person to whom subsection (2) applies commits an offence if he knowingly allows disorderly conduct on relevant premises.

(2)   This subsection applies—

    (a)   to any person who works at the premises in a capacity, whether paid or unpaid, which authorises him to prevent the conduct,

    (b)   in the case of licensed premises, to—

        (i)   the holder of a premises licence in respect of the premises, and

        (ii)   the designated premises supervisor (if any) under such a licence."

One cannot fail to prevent what one does not know is taking place. Thus, if the licensee is in Australia, only the manager and other bar staff who have knowledge of the disorderly conduct, and who knowingly allow it to continue, should be convicted of the offence. There is no case for invoking the delegation doctrine in such cases, because the modern statute provides the manager and other relevant staff with ample incentive for complying with the law; it criminalizes such parties for their own personal choice to break the law.

37.4.   THE CONSTRUCTION OF STATUTORY VERBS: SALE

37–012   As I just noted, a peculiarity of the provisions of the repealed *Licensing Act 1964*[39] was that it only struck at the licensee who was generally the employer, and was silent as to the employee, who was left to be brought in, if at all, only under the doctrine of accessoryship. Many other enactments do the opposite; they strike at the actual doer, who in matters of trade and industry will often be the employee, and appear to be silent as far as the responsibility of the employer is concerned. However, the courts have for many years groped for some principle that would bring in the employer.

This represents another effort to get away from *mens rea*. The courts had held, in an indulgent moment, that a person cannot be convicted as accessory without *mens rea*; but it was thought that it should be possible, all the same, to convict an employer where his employee committed an offence of strict liability, without casting on the prosecution the necessity for proving the employer's *mens rea*. To effect this end, the courts had to find that the employer himself perpetrated the offence.[40]

A few cases apply to other statutes the distinction drawn in the older licensee cases; has the employer delegated his authority generally? (in which case he is responsible for his delegate) or has he merely appointed the employee to do some specific task? (in which case he is not liable).[41] But this distinction has generally been dropped, except in the licence cases. It is irrational in the context of the criminal law, because it does not succeed in picking out either those employers who are most likely to have had effective control or those who are most likely to have been at fault. Also, it involves an unwarranted exercise of legislative power by the courts.

---

[39] Cf. *Licensing Act 2003.*

[40] E.g., *Harrow London Borough Council v. Shah* [2000] 1 W.L.R. 83; *St Helens BC v. Hill* (1992) 156 J.P. 602; *Coppen v. Moore (No.2)* [1898] 2 Q.B. 306; cf. *R. v. Bleasdale* (1848) 175 E.R. 321.

[41] *E.g., Barker v. Levinson* [1951] 1 K.B. 342.

A certain break-through occurred when the courts discovered (as they thought) that the verbs used in penal statutes can sometimes be interpreted to include the conduct of persons other than the immediate doer. Take again section 14 of the *Food Safety Act 1990* (re-enacting earlier legislation). This penalizes a person who "sells" "food which is not of the nature or substance or quality demanded by the purchaser." In its legal meaning the word "sells" refers to a legal transaction, a sale under a contract of sale. When a person makes a purchase in (say) a department store, the sale in law is by the store company,[42] which owns the goods that are sold, not by the assistant who deals with the customer. Therefore, the store company can be convicted of the offence of improper selling under section 14 of the *Food Safety Act 1990*.[43] The employer, who himself performs no physical act at the time of the sale, is made liable as perpetrator although the sale is physically arranged by his employee, because the employer is regarded in law as making the sale.[44] Contractual verbs, then, are almost inevitably read to apply to the employer who is the contracting party. The argument for this interpretation is not so strong when applied to factual verbs, which on traditional principles should be read as applying to the actual doer; otherwise vicarious penal liability would be let in by the back door.

37–013

Suppose that the employee disregards instructions by the employer when he sells goods, and therefore violates the statute?   The contract of sale is still binding on the employer (if the employee had a general authority to sell and if the limitation of his authority was not known to the buyer), so the employer still commits an offence if the sale is wrongful.[45] But a sale by an employee (like an errand boy) who is not authorized to sell at all does not involve the employer.[46]

37–014

What if the sale is not by an employee?   The same principle applies. In the civil law, a person may authorize any other person to make a contract as his agent. The agent need not be his employee. An agent is anyone who is authorized to make a contract on the principal's behalf; he may, for example, be an auctioneer.

37–015

---

[42] Cf. *Nottingham City Council v. Wolverhampton and Dudley Breweries Plc.* [2004] Q.B. 1274.

[43] "Section 14 applies to all foods, and it is obviously desirable for the achievement of the legislative purpose that it should be possible to hold to account the owner of the goods prior to the sale. Furthermore it is not an unreasonable burden because he has available the defence of due diligence." *Nottingham City Council v. Wolverhampton and Dudley Breweries Plc.* [2004] Q.B. 1274 at 1286 *per* Kennedy L.J.

[44] See also *Harrow London Borough Council v. Shah* [2000] 1 W.L.R. 83, where an employee in a newsagent sold a lottery ticket to a minor. *St Helens BC v. Hill* (1992) 156 J.P. 602, where an employee sold tobacco to a minor. Hence, there is no need to consider whether authority was delegated when the offence is one of strict liability: *R. v. Winson* [1969] 1 Q.B. 371 at 382.

[45] *Per cur.* in *Anderton v. Rodgers* (1981) 145 J.P. 181.

[46] *Adams v. Camfoni* [1929] 1 K.B. 95. The same rule applies in respect of other contractual verbs, e.g., "employ": *Portsea Island Mutual Cooperative Society Ltd. v. Leyland* [1978] I.C.R. 1195.

37–016 **I suppose the employee or other agent who does the actual selling is liable as accessory?**   More than this; he is held to be liable as co-perpetrator, so that he is (in the absence of an express statutory defence) strictly responsible (which he could not be if his liability were only as accessory).[47]

The decisions on this point, though settled, are open to challenge on grounds of logic. As we have just seen, the courts have held that the word "sell" in a penal statute refers to a legal relationship. A shop assistant is not a party to that relationship, so his liability should be only as accessory. To say that he is a perpetrator of an improper sale involves reading the statutory word "sells" in two different ways at once: as applying to the creation of a legal relationship (legally sells) and the making of a factual arrangement (physically sells). It is highly unlikely that a Parliamentary draftsperson would have intended such a double meaning; if he had wished to bring in both the employer and employee as perpetrators he would have done so by appropriate language. Nor is the interpretation necessary in order to place a legal duty on the employee; if he were held liable as accessory he could still be convicted, but only on proof of *mens rea*. The unpersuasive reading of the word "sells" in a double meaning is due simply to the desire of the judges to bring in as many people as possible within the net of strict liability.

An even more extensive notion of "selling" has been adopted. To understand this, the scheme of the *Sale of Goods Act 1979* must be known. The *Act of 1979*, which is the general code regulating the contract of sale of goods in the civil law, provides (in section 2(4)) that an "agreement to sell" turns into a "sale" when the property (ownership) in the goods passes to the buyer. Property may pass at the time of the contract; but sometimes its passes at a later time. When the contract is for the sale of "unascertained goods" no property can pass until the goods are ascertained (section 16), and they become ascertained when they are "appropriated" to the contract (designated as being the goods agreed to be sold). Suppose I telephone my coal merchant and order ten sacks of coal. My order is taken, so that the contact of sale is between myself and the coal merchant. The next morning the coalmen employed by the merchant (who took no part in forming the contract) set out with a full load of sacks. None bears my name, and there is at that time no appropriation. Unknown to the coalmen, the sacks contain short weight. The coalman takes ten sacks off the lorry and delivers them to me with a ticket showing a false weight. This is the point of the appropriation, the time when the agreement to sell turns into a "sale" (section 18 r. 5). The courts held, under legislation preceeding the *Trade Descriptions Act 1968*, that a coalman, by delivering goods with the false ticket and passing the ownership in the goods under the contract of sale, "sold" them and so could be convicted of selling them with a false trade description.[48] The same result might not be reached under the *Consumer Protection from Unfair Trading Regulations 2008/1277*, since those

---

[47] See, for example, *Caldwell v. Bethell* [1913] 1 K.B. 119; *Knapp v. Bedwell* (1916) 80 J.P. 336. In *Sandford Motor Sales v. Habgood* [1962] Crim. L.R. 487 liability was extended to an auctioneer. (The decision in *Lester v. Balfour Williamson Merchant Shippers* [1953] 2 Q.B. 168 is irreconcilable with these cases, though perfectly correct in point of general legal principle.) See also *Merton LBC v. Sinclair Collis Ltd.* (2010) 175 J.P. 11, where cigarettes were sold to a minor via a cigarette vending machine.

[48] *Preston v. Albuery* [1964] 2 Q.B. 796.

regulations focus on the "trader who engages in a *commercial practice*." It would be stretching it to hold that the coalmen are traders, or that they are engaging in a commercial practice.

The reasoning is even less convincing than before, because a person whose act happens to pass the ownership in goods cannot reasonably be described as selling. Nor could such a person be a trader: he is not a trader and does not engage in a commercial practice. All he does is assist his employer (a trader) to engage in a commercial practice. Suppose I sell you a horse on condition that a third person, X, signifies approval of him. When X signifies that the horse is sound, the contract becomes unconditional and the ownership passes; but it would be strange to say that X's approval meant that X "sold" the horse. X's approval is simply an event on the happening of which the contract becomes fully effective. I might sell you the horse on condition that it rained tomorrow, but that rain would not sell the horse. In the same way, the delivery man who appropriates goods to the contract does not sell them in any sensible meaning of the words. What he may do is assist the sale, but then his liability should depend on *mens rea*.

37–017

37.5. "USING" UNDER THE CONSTRUCTION AND USE REGULATIONS

When the statutory verb refers not to a legal but to a purely factual situation the task of bringing the employer within it is not so easy. The traditional principle, exemplified by 19th century cases, is that the employer of the doer is not affected. If a statute makes it a crime (for example) to "make" a forgery or to "enter" a building, an employee who "makes" or "enters" does not automatically inculpate his employer, for it is the employee who violates the statutory prohibition, not the employer. It is only the employee who can be convicted of forgery or burglary or of some other serious crime, unless of course the employer has encouraged or assisted the crime. These cases are still law, because in crimes requiring *mens rea* the employee's intention cannot usually be attributed to the employer. But in regulatory offences, not requiring *mens rea*, the courts have succeeded in interpreting certain statutory verbs in such an extensive sense as to include the employer, even when such verbs do not refer to contracts.

37–018

One example is the verb "cause." It was shown in the last chapter that an employer may be held to "cause" a result by employing someone who causes it, though in this case he is not liable if he has no knowledge of the facts.[49]

Much more prominent in the case-law is the verb "use." Section 40A of the *Road Traffic Act 1988* provides:

"A person is guilty of an offence if he uses, or causes or permits *another*[50] to use, a motor vehicle or trailer on a road when—

---

[49] *Cornish v. Ferry Masters Ltd.* [1975] R.T.R. 292; *Dent v. Coleman* [1978] R.T.R. 1. Cf. *National Rivers Authority (Southern Region) v. Alfred McAlpine Homes East Ltd.* [1994] Env. L.R. 198.

[50] The reference to "another" in section 40A of the *Road Traffic Act 1988* technically means that it should only catch those who permit or cause "another" to "use." If the employee user uses without being caused or permitted to use, then the employer should not be liable. *Per contra*, in *James & Son Ltd. v. Smee* [1955] 1 Q.B. 78, the now repealed regulation 101 of the *Motor Vehicles (Construction*

(a)   the condition of the motor vehicle or trailer, or of its accessories or equipment, or

(b)   the purpose for which it is used, or

(c)   the number of passengers carried by it, or the manner in which they are carried, or

(d)   the weight, position or distribution of its load, or the manner in which it is secured, is such that the use of the motor vehicle or trailer involves a danger of injury to any person."

37–019   Suppose that A drives a vehicle, B loads goods on it and C rides in it. Common speech allows us to say that all three "use" the vehicle (at least in some circumstances), and so does their employer D if they are acting in the course of the employment. How far should the legal interpretation follow common speech? The question arose under the old law in *James & Son Ltd. v. Smee*.[51] James & Son Ltd.'s employee used a motor vehicle in the course of his employment. Unknown to the company's management the brakes were out of order, which was a breach of the now repealed *Construction and Use Regulations 1973*.[52] It was held that the company should not be convicted of permitting the offence, since the defect in the brakes was not known; but the company could have been convicted of "using" the vehicle through its employee, if it had been charged with that, this being an offence of absolute prohibition. Parker J. (later Lord Parker C.J.) said: "In common parlance a master is using his vehicle if it is being used by his servant on his business."

The reasoning is plausible, and has been accepted even since;[53] but it is legally fallacious. The orthodox principle is that it is the actual physical doer of the act who is the perpetrator of an offence (apart from the law of innocent agency). Therefore, in an offence of using a thing it should be the person who handles the thing who perpetuates the offence. The employer should not be regarded as perpetrating the offence even if he has expressly ordered it; his liability should be as accessory, and accessorial liability requires *mens rea*. The fact that the employer can be said to use the thing via his employee is nothing to purpose; Lady Macbeth could be said to have killed Duncan by the hand of her husband, but she was an accessory, not a perpetrator of murder. Nor is it *à propos* that the accessory can be charged as a principal; this procedural rule does not affect the substantive law. Moreover, Lord Parker's interpretation is basically inconsistent with the legislation. This distinguishes between using and permitting a use, which suggests that the legislature intended the notion of using to be confined to personal use.[54]

The courts had no sooner established the new rule than they repented of the width of the attributive liability they had created. They realized that in interpreting the notion of using so extensively they were in danger of making nonsense of the statute depriving the alternative of permitting use of any practical

---

and Use) Regulations, 1951 was in issue. That regulation provided: "If any person uses or causes or permits to be used on any road a motor vehicle..." Cf. section 143 of the *Road Traffic Act 1988*.

[51] [1955] 1 Q.B. 78.

[52] The latest regulations are the *Road Vehicles (Construction and Use) Regulations 1986/1078* (as amended). See also *Pedal Cycles (Construction and Use) Regulations 1983/1176*. However, many of the "use," "permitting" and "causing" offences are found in other road traffic enactments.

[53] *Drysdale v. Harrison* [1973] R.T.R. 45; *Jones v. D.P.P.* [1999] R.T.R. 1; *O'Mahony v. Joliffe* [1999] R.T.R. 245.

[54] Cf. *R. (on the application of Vehicle & Operator Services Agency) v. Henderson* [2004] EWHC 3118.

effect. So they took the commendable course of qualifying the "common parlance" approach and cutting down the doctrine of attribution in this context by holding that the only person who "uses" a vehicle without driving it is the driver's employer.[55] Anyone else is liable only if he can be said to cause or permit the use (or, of course, to abet it). Therefore, the owner of a vehicle who asks a friend to drive it on such an owner's business does not use the vehicle;[56] and a person who lets a vehicle on hire does not use it either.

But it might be the owner's fault, not the hirer's, that the van was maintained badly.　That is the trouble with the wording of an offence, which **37–020** does not provide for negligence. The owner is liable only for permitting (or causing) the use by the hirer, and permitting requires knowledge of the defence (or possibly recklessness).[57] As for causing, it was noted in the last chapter that the verb in this context implies the giving of an order or direction to use the vehicle. Therefore, when a motor mechanic negligently carried out work on a van so that it contravened the former regulations, his employer was held not liable when the owner subsequently drove the van on a road;[58] and it follows that the mechanic would not have been liable either.

There is no attribution even in respect of the acts of a partner. In civil law a partner is liable for the acts of his co-partners on the partnership business, and in the criminal law a partner is liable for an offence in connection with the sale or supply by his co-partners, as if they were his employees.[59] The sale or supply by any partner is a sale and supply by each of them. But the same rule does not apply in respect of partnership "use." A partner in a firm is held not to "use" the vehicle when it is being driven by his co-partner, even when it is being used on the partnership business and even when he is a travelling passenger.[60] His co-partner is not his employee. The justification for this decision is that it sets relatively

---

[55] *Bennett v. Richardson* [1980] R.T.R. 358. On "use" the owner of course can be charged with causing or permitting the use if he knows of the condition of the vehicle. See *Vehicle Inspectorate v. Nuttall* [1999] 1 W.L.R. 629 *per* Lord Steyn; *Yorkshire Traction Co Ltd. v. Vehicle Inspectorate* [2001] R.T.R. 34.

[56] *Crawford v. Haughton* [1972] 1 W.L.R. 572. In the law of tort, a voluntary assister can be an employee, or sufficiently in the position of an employee to inculpate the person assisted, at any rate where use is made of the latter's property; but it is right that the criminal law should eschew this nebulous extension of liability. The position of a wife who gives her husband a hand now and again in his business is doubtful. In *Brandish v. Poole* [1968] 1 W.L.R. 544, a wife who helped her husband in his business on one occasion was held not to be his "servant" within the meaning of the given statute. This is difficult to reconcile with some criminal cases such as *R. v. Foulkes* (1875) L.R. 2 C.C.R. 150; and *Boucher v. D.P.P.* (1996) 160 J.P. 650, as well as with civil cases. However, since a partner is not liable for a use by his co-partner, it is reasonable that the same exemption should apply to use by a wife.

[57] *Robinson v. D.P.P.* [1991] R.T.R. 315; *Lloyd-Wolper v. Moore* [2004] R.T.R. 30; *D.P.P. v. Fisher* [1992] R.T.R. 93.

[58] *Shave v. Rosner* [1954] 2 Q.B. 113. Cf. *Thompson v. Lodwick* [1983] R.T.R. 76. Cf. section 5 of the *Domestic Violence, Crime and Victims Act 2004* which deems that one can negligently allow or cause. Conceptually, it is illogical to suggest that one negligently causes autonomous others to do deliberate acts.

[59] *Clode v. Barnes* [1974] 1 W.L.R. 544; cf. *Parsons v. Barnes* [1973] Crim. L.R. 537; *Linnett v. MPC* [1946] K.B. 290.

[60] *Bennett v. Richardson* [1980] R.T.R. 358.

clear bounds to the notion of "use." However, a partner "uses" the vehicle when it is being driven by the firm's employee.[61]

Unfortunately, the courts have qualified their concession and impaired the clarity of their rule by holding that a person can "use" a vehicle in some circumstances when it is being driven by someone other than his employee. This is when the defendant was being driven in a vehicle "directly for his own purposes." In a case where D was being driven in his own car by a friend in order to get him home, he was held to be using the car.[62] In *Hatton v. Hall*[63] this approach was qualified. Henry L.J. said:[64] "We have no quarrel with the proposition that where the passenger does procure the making of the journey, he may be exercising sufficient control or management to be a 'user.'... The question: 'Was he then exercising a sufficient degree of control or management over the car ... to be jointly using it?'"[65] So, if the passenger of a vehicle exercises a sufficient degree of control or management over the vehicle, she will be deemed to be a user, even though she was not operating it.[66] The exception not only smudges what was thought to be a clear rule but creates anomalies. It is strange that a partner who is being driven on partnership business is not regarded as having sufficient degree of control or management over the vehicle to be deemed a user.

37–021 Even when an employer can be convicted of an offence of using, the employee who drives the vehicle can also be convicted, and can be held strictly liable,[67] notwithstanding that the defect in the vehicle of which complaint is made was not his fault but that of the firm's maintenance department. The law has nothing to do with justice.

The driver might not be charged, because the prosecutor will be gunning for the employer. But an unwary prosecutor may perhaps charge the driver with using in order to charge the employer with abetting, depending on the wording of the statute. In that event, the prosecution while succeeding against the unfortunate driver, will collapse against the employer unless it can be shown that the employer knew all the facts of the offence.[68] To get home against the employer

---

[61] *Passmooe v. Gibbons* [1979] R.T.R. 53. But the director of a limited company does not use the company's vehicles when driven by employees, because the company, not he, is the employer.

[62] *Cobb v. Williams* [1973] R.T.R. 113. The owner was convicted of using a car without insurance (which at the time was an offence under section 201 of the *Road Traffic Act 1960*), which also referred to using or causing or permitting another to use); no enquiry was made whether he knew or should have known of the driver's lack of insurance. See also *Leathley v. Tatton* [1980] R.T.R. 21.

[63] [1997] R.T.R. 212.

[64] *Hatton v. Hall* [1997] R.T.R. 212.

[65] It was also said, a joint enterprise, such as "a trip to a public house by motorcycle on a summer's evening, [would] not involve a sufficient vesting of control or management of the motorcycle in the pillion passenger to make him a user of that vehicle on that trip." *Hatton v. Hall* [1997] R.T.R. 212 at 224.

[66] *O'Mahony v. Joliffe* [1999] R.T.R. 245.

[67] Cf. *R. (on the application of Vehicle & Operator Services Agency) v. Henderson* [2004] EWHC 3118.

[68] *Robinson v. D.P.P.* [1991] R.T.R. 315. In *Vehicle Inspectorate v. Nuttall* [1999] 1 W.L.R. 629 at 635 Lord Steyn said: "It is not an offence of strict or absolute liability. Nothing less than wilfulness or recklessness will be sufficient. In practice recklessness will be the relevant *mens rea*. There was some controversy about where the line between recklessness and negligence in respect of an offence under section 96(11A) *Transport Act 1968* should be drawn. ... I am satisfied that if the defendant's state of

where the given offence allows for "strict liability" you must charge him not with "permitting" or "causing"[69] nor with abetting the offence, but with "using."[70]

Problems may arise where an employee is pursuing his own purposes. The employer's liability will depend on the precise facts:

- Suppose the employee takes out the firm's van in the evening on some private frolic. In that case, obviously, the employer does not "use" the van, since he has not authorized the use in any way.[71]
- The position is not necessarily the same if the employee starts out on an authorized journey but deviates from his round of toil to call on his girlfriend. Cases on vicarious liability in tort show that the test then is the degree of deviation. If the employee merely takes a roundabout route (on the outward or return journey) he is still within the general course of his employment and the employer is therefore still "using" the vehicle. If the employee goes off in an entirely wrong direction, that is a frolic of his own. But no precise angle of deviation can be laid down as a way of deciding these cases. One has to make an impressionistic judgment.[72]

The employer cannot escape liability by giving the employee a list of "Don'ts" **37–022** unless he puts the whole category of conduct in question outside the employee's authority. If a bus *conductor* is told not to drive the bus, he will be acting outside the course of his employment if he drives it.[73] But if the *driver* is told not to drive the bus without first checking the brakes, he will still be acting within the course of his employment if he disregards the order, so that his employer will still in law be "using" the bus. If the law were otherwise, employers would merely instruct their employees not to break the law, and the employers would escape liability even though they made no serious effort to see that the law was obeyed.[74]

---

mind is one of not caring whether a contravention of the provisions of the Regulation took place that would generally be sufficient to establish recklessness and that that is the necessary mental element in a charge under section 96(11A) of the *Act of 1968*. If recklessness in at least this sense is not established no offence is committed." Lord Nicholls (at 631) said: "So does the driver's employer if he 'caused or permitted' the contravention. 'Permitted' is a word commonly found in statutes creating criminal offences. Its meaning depends upon the context. Its meaning, for instance, may be confined to 'allowed' or 'authorised.' Or it may be wider and embrace 'failed to take reasonable steps to prevent.' In the present case, in agreement with all your Lordships, I consider that 'permitted' in section 96(11A) of the *Transport Act 1968* bears the latter, wider meaning." Clearly, the Lords require the employer to *know* that they are failing to take reasonable steps to prevent a criminal use of their vehicles. Cf. *Henshall (Quarries) v. Harvey* [1965] 2 Q.B. 233.

[69] *Cornish v. Ferry Masters Ltd.* [1975] R.T.R. 292; *Dent v. Coleman* [1978] R.T.R. 1. In *Vehicle Inspectorate v. Nuttall* [1999] 1 W.L.R. 629 at 640 Lord Hobhouse said: "Where the employer is charged with having caused the employee's breach, the need for the prosecutor to prove such a causal relationship is obvious." Cf. *National Rivers Authority (Southern Region) v. Alfred McAlpine Homes East Ltd.* [1994] Env. L.R. 198.

[70] *Jones v. D.P.P.* [1999] R.T.R. 1.

[71] *McKnight v. Davies* [1974] R.T.R. 4; see also *Singh v. Rathour* [1988] 1 W.L.R. 422; cf. *R. v. Phipps* (1970) 54 Cr. App. R. 300.

[72] For a criminal case in which the question arose see *Jack Motors Ltd. v. Fazackerley* [1962] Crim. L.R. 486. See also *Jones v. D.P.P.* [1999] R.T.R. 1.

[73] For a civil case to this effect see *Iqbal v. London Transport Executive* (1973) 16 K.I.R. 329.

[74] See, for example, *Vehicle Inspectorate v. Nuttall* [1999] 1 W.L.R. 629; cf. *Surrey CC v. Burton Retail Ltd.* (1998) 162 J.P. 545; *R. v. Lowe* (1850) 175 E.R. 489.

An intermediate case is where the driver is instructed to make a certain journey, and he uses not his ordinary vehicle but another vehicle that he is not authorized to drive. Here again it is held that the employer "uses" the unauthorized vehicle. The fact that the vehicle is being used on his business by the employee who is authorized to drive on that journey is decisive.[75] The interpretation of the law is distinctly hard on the employer if the authorized vehicle was well maintained (or insured) and the unauthorized vehicle was not supposed to be driven at all.[76]

37–023   **If I "use" the vehicles driven by my employees, do I "use" those driven by a builder whom I employ to build a house?**   No. The builder is an independent contractor, not an employee. The general rule of civil law is that vicarious liability does not extend to independent contractors, and the rule is followed by the criminal courts in cases of the type here being considered. The law would be reduced to absurdity if the employer of a building contractor, or the passenger in a taxi, were deemed to "use" the vehicle in such a way as to make him responsible for its defective brakes.[77]

37.6.   "USING" BY ITSELF

37–024   The previous discussion was concerned primarily with legislation in relation to "using or causing or permitting to be used." Where the legislation penalizes "using" only, the principles appear to be identical except in one respect. The simple "using" offence has been held to be wider than the "using or permitting" offence because it includes use by independent contractors. However, the authorities are in conflict. In *Charman (F.E.) v. Clow*[78] the defendant company, Charman Ltd., contracted to supply a quantity of ash to V. To fulfil their contract, they ordered the ash from a supplier and engaged the owner-driver of a lorry to deliver it. The lorry did not comply with the *Weights and Measures Act 1963*[79] as a cubic measure, so that a short measure of ash was delivered. The *Act* made it an offence to "use" an article for trade as a cubic measure unless it has been passed by an inspector. It was held by a Divisional Court that Charman Ltd. was guilty of the offence, since it "used" the lorry through the contractor. Cases on the *Construction and Use Regulation* were distinguished, since here the statute did not refer in the alternative to "permitting" to use.

The *ratio decidendi* was that the word "use" was in itself wide enough to cover use through an independent contractor, and that the narrower meaning adopted in relation to the "using or permitting" sections was due entirely to a desire to leave an ambit of operation to the alternative of "permitting." The court

---

[75] *Richardson v. Baker* [1976] R.T.R. 56; *Jones v. D.P.P.* [1999] R.T.R. 1.

[76] Clearly, the employer has not "permitted" or "caused" the unauthorized use where it has instructed its drivers not to use a vehicle that is not insured and so on; so such an employer can only be held liable as a user.

[77] On the distinction between employees and independent contractors, and the problems that arise when a vehicle is hired along with a driver (or a driver is hired from an agency), see Glanville Williams, *Textbook of Criminal Law*, (London: Stevens and Sons, 1978) at 937-940.

[78] [1974] 1 W.L.R. 1384.

[79] This *Act* was repealed by the *Weights and Measures Act 1985*.

thought itself constrained by authority[80] to reach this conclusion, but expressed regret that the law should thus be made so complicated (and, it might have added, so flagrantly unjust). The attention of the court was not called to a contrary decision, later in date than the authority on which it relied. This was the decision of *United Dairies (London) v. Beckenham Corp.*[81] United Dairies, a milk distributing company, supplied bottles to a farmer from whom it bought milk. The farmer filled the bottles with milk and returned them, so filled, to United Dairies. The bottles proved to be dirty. Regulations (in force at the time) provided that milk bottles be thoroughly cleaned before "use." It was held that "use" referred to filling the bottle; only the farmer filled the bottle, and only he was liable under the regulations.

Certainly the farmer used the bottles by filling them. No doubt it was the practice that he, rather than the milk distributor, should wash the bottles; so it was the farmer who was at fault if the bottles were dirty. These would have been excellent reasons for convicting the farmer. But the food inspector, for some obscure bureaucratic reason, chose to charge the distributor; and the decision in its favour was a matter of common sense. Yet if the view expressed in *Charman (F.E.) v. Clow* is accepted, did not the distributor "use" its bottles by having them filled by the farmer as an independent contractor? Filling was simply part of the general use of the bottles for conveying milk to the public, and that use was, on the principle of *Charman (F.E.) v. Clow*, a use by the distributor (employer) as well as by the farmer (contractor). Consequently, there seems to be an antinomy between the two decisions, and the result reached in *United Dairies (London) v. Beckenham Corp.* case is greatly preferable. To interpret the word "use" to include use through contractors gives it a vast extension; it could mean, for example, that a passenger in a taxi is liable for breach of regulations governing the use of the taxi, when in common sense they are none of his business.

Apart from the question mark hanging over independent contractors, it appears that (as already said) the word "use" is construed in the same way whether or not it appears as an alternative to permitting or causing use. Perhaps the commonest situation in which the question arises is where a vehicle is taken without authority and a passenger is charged with using the vehicle without insurance.[82] If he was a party to the unlawful taking he is clearly guilty as accessory to the unlawful taking of the conveyance, and as an accessory to the uninsured use,[83] and he can therefore be convicted of the unlawful taking and uninsured use.[84] If he was not party to the unlawful taking but knew at the beginning of the ride that the vehicle had been unlawfully taken, he is guilty of allowing himself to be carried in the vehicle,[85] but not (at least generally) of using the vehicle without insurance (even as an accessory).[86] This seems to be an application of the principle discussed above: he is not the driver or the driver's employer, and has not commissioned

37–025

---

[80] *Quality Dairies (York) v. Pedley* [1952] 1 K.B. 275.

[81] [1963] 1 Q.B. 434.

[82] Section 143 of the *Road Traffic Act 1988.*

[83] *Ross v. Rivenall* [1959] 1 W.L.R. 713; *per cur. Boldizsar v. Knight* [1980] Crim. L.R. 653.

[84] *Ross v. Rivenall* [1959] 1 W.L.R. 713.

[85] Section 12 of the *Theft Act 1968.*

[86] *Hatton v. Hall* [1997] R.T.R. 212.

the use.[87] Perhaps if he commissioned the use of the vehicle (though after it had been unlawfully taken) he would be guilty of using it on the "direct purposes"[88] rule, or "exercising sufficient control or management" rule.[89]

In *Hall v. Hatton*,[90] Henry L.J. said:

> "[I]t is apparent from that summary that while every passenger, in ordinary language, uses the vehicle he is driven in, 'use' must be given a restricted meaning, for if it were not, very many passengers in cars, cabs, and buses, have unwittingly but potentially been committing criminal offences in accepting lifts in ignorance of the precise insurance position (or indeed, of the mechanical condition) of the vehicle. .... (It is also useful to notice that the passenger claiming against the [insurance company] is not defeated simply by the finding that he knew that there was no sufficient third-party cover in force, but only if additionally he was liable as an owner or user for failure to provide that cover). The leading authority is *Brown v. Roberts* [1965] 1 Q.B. 1, in that case Megaw J. imposed a restricted construction on the statutory phrase 'use a motor vehicle on the road. The *ratio* for the decision was that merely being a passenger did not make you a user: 'unless there is present, in the person alleged to be the user, an element of controlling, managing or operating the vehicle at the particular time.'"

37.7. "PERSONAL" VERBS

37–026 In the instances studied in this chapter offences of strict liability have been extended to include employers by construing a verb attributively, to cover someone other than the immediate doer. How far the courts will go with this practice of attribution remains in doubt, but certainly there are some verbs that cannot be construed attributively but only "personally."

An important instance is the verb "drives." The owner of a lorry might say that he "used" it for a journey to Sheffield even though he was not in it; but he would never say that he "drove" it to Sheffield unless he were at the wheel. As was pointed out before,[91] the notion of driving strongly connotes the physical act of controlling the vehicle in motion. Besides, to hold that an employer drives through his employee would have absurd results. It would mean the multi-millionaire who has never learnt to drive, lounging in the back of his limousine, could be convicted of driving without a licence; although the actual driving was done by his chauffeur who had a licence. If the multi-millionaire were being driven back from a good dinner he might be convicted of driving under the influence of drink. No one deserves to be treated so unjustly. Statutes referring to driving can sensibly only be understood as referring to the actual driving; and that is how they are construed.

---

[87] Cf. *O'Mahony v. Joliffe* [1999] R.T.R. 245.

[88] *D. v. Parsons* [1960] 1 W.L.R. 797. *A fortiori* if he only came to know of the unlawfulness during the ride: *Boldizsar v. Knight* [1980] Crim. L.R. 653.

[89] *Hatton v. Hall* [1997] R.T.R. 212; *O'Mahony v. Joliffe* [1999] R.T.R. 245.

[90] [1997] R.T.R. 212 at 218. At 225 Henry L.J. goes on to say: "If a passenger employs a driver to drive against the clock to catch an aeroplane he clearly has a greater power to control and/or manage the vehicle than would be the case if a father agreed to drive his 18-year-old son and 80-year-old mother-in-law, neither able to drive, to visit his wife in hospital. Similarly, if a bank-robber is a pillion passenger on a get-away motorcycle, it may be inferred that he has a greater degree of management and control over the driver than the pillion passenger in the instant case. It is a question of fact and degree in each case, but in all cases the user must be given the restricted meaning found by Megaw J." However, it would be better to rely on accessorial liability in such cases.

[91] 14.18.

What if the millionaire tells his chauffeur to drive at 60 m.p.h. in a built-up   **37–027**
area?   Then, of course, the millionaire would be an accessory to the offence (of
dangerous driving, or of exceeding the speed limit) committed by the chauffeur.

It may be suggested that another instance of a personal verb is "knowingly."
An employer does not make a demand if it is made by his employee without his
authority.[92] In one case,[93] an employer was held to have been rightly convicted of
wilfully obstructing the highway by reason of an act of his employee which he
had not authorized; but this is clearly wrong. In the first place the offence in
question was once of wilfulness,[94] which (this not being a licensee case) should
not have carried attributive liability. In the second place, it is not law that an
employer is to be regarded as doing everything that his employee does. *Tesco
Supermarkets Ltd. v. Nattrass*,[95] which is to be dealt with in the next chapter, was
full of remarks by the Lords to the effect that the concept of vicarious liability has
no general application in the criminal law.[96] If employers are to be made
vicariously responsible for offences of this kind it should be done by specific
legislation.

37.8.   *MENS REA*

On principle and on the clear balance of authority, legislation requiring *mens rea*   **37–028**
does not saddle the employer with the mental state of his employee. The
construction of some statutory verbs in an attributive sense settles the question of
the employer's liability if the only fault is that of an employee. This is expressed
or implied in various of the licensee cases and cases on corporate liability, which
recognize that *mens rea* cannot be attributed to the employer outside the special
liability attached by those cases.[97] Similarly, with negligence.[98] One or two
decisions go the other way,[99] but they are out of line the current authority.

The following well-established rules may be listed in support of this view; all
of them show that the *mens rea* of the employee is not automatically transferred
to the employer:

- Even a licensee is not liable for a *mens rea* offence committed by an
  employee if he does not delegate to that employee: *Vane v. Yiannopoullos*.[100]

---

[92] *Barker v. Levinson* [1951] 1 K.B. 342.

[93] *C. Gabriel Ltd. v. Enfield L.B.C.* [1971] R.T.R. 265.

[94] *Contra*, if the offence is one of absolute liability: *R. v. British Steel Plc.* [1995] 1 W.L.R. 1356.

[95] [1972] A.C. 153.

[96] This was affirmed in *R. (on the application of Chief Constable of Northumbria) v. Newcastle upon Tyne Magistrates' Court* [2010] EWHC 935 *per* Munby L.J.

[97] This principle was reaffirmed in *Coupe v. Guyett* [1973] 1 W.L.R. 669; *Essendon Engineering Co. v. Maile* [1982] R.T.R. 260. It may be suggested that even if the offence in the latter case had not required a mental element, the employer should still not have been regarded as "issuing" a test certificate by the hand of its employee, except as accessory.

[98] *Tesco Supermarkets Ltd. v. Nattrass* [1972] A.C. 153.

[99] *C. Gabriel Ltd. v. Enfield L.B.C.* [1971] R.T.R. 265; *Mousell Bros Ltd. v. London & North Western Railway Co.* [1917] 2 K.B. 836.

[100] [1965] A.C. 486.

- Since "permitting" or "causing" a person to do something requires *mens rea*, an employer is not liable for permitting or causing an employee to do something if he has no *mens rea*.[101]
- Even where an employer is attributively liable for an offence of strict liability directly committed by his employee, he is not liable for the employee's attempt to commit it, because an attempt requires *mens rea* in the defendant, and the *mens rea* of his employee is not sufficient.[102]
- Even where an employer is attributively liable for an offence of strict liability committed by his employee, he cannot be convicted without proof of *mens rea* if he is charged with abetting the offence.[103]

---

[101] *Ross Hillman Ltd. v. Bond* [1974] Q.B. 435; *John v. Matthews* [1970] 2 Q.B. 443.

[102] 15.4.

[103] *Somerset v. Wade* [1894] 1 Q.B. 574; *Callow v. Tillstone* (1900) 64 J.P. 823; *McKnight v. Davies* [1974] R.T.R. 4.

CHAPTER 38

CORPORATIONS; EXCEPTIONS TO STRICT LIABILITY

"I'm Lingley of Lingley Ltd. Not one of you can touch me. I turned myself into a company years ago."

Sutton Vane[1]

"And it is great reason that an hospital, in expectancy or intendment, or nomination, should be sufficient to support the name of an incorporation when the corporation itself is only in abstracto, and rests only in intendment and consideration of the law; for a corporation aggregate of many is invisible, immortal, and rests only in intendment and consideration of the law. ... They cannot commit treason, nor be outlawed, nor excommunicate, for they have no souls, neither can they appear in person, but by attorney."[2]

38.1. CORPORATIONS

Sutton Vane's unpleasant business person has grasped a certain truth in regard to the civil law of corporations, but directors of companies are by no means immune in the criminal courts.　　**38–001**

What is the difference between a company and a corporation? The strict technical term at common law was "corporation." A "company" may be an unincorporated firm (partnership). But when we speak of a company we usually mean an incorporated company, a corporation, and that is what "company" will mean in this chapter. A group of people may have been incorporated:　　**38–002**

- by royal charter (*e.g.*, a University such as King's College London, or an Oxford[3] or Cambridge college),

---

[1] *Outward Bound*, (New York: Liveright, 1930) at 96.

[2] *The Case of Sutton's Hospital* (1612) 10 Coke Reports 23a at 32b. An earlier reference to a fictitious manmade *alter ego* appears in an anonymous case reported in (1608) 7 Coke Reports 2a at 10b, where Sir Edward Coke wrote: "First, every subject (as it hath been affirmed by those that argued against the plaintiff) is presumed by law to be sworn to the King, which is to his natural person, and likewise the King is sworn to his subjects, ... which oath he taketh in his natural person: for the politic capacity is invisible and immortal; nay, the politic body hath no soul, for it is framed by the policy of man." But the corporation appears in the reports long before this: see (1327) 77 E.R. 17 at 21, where it is said: "Where the Abbot of Westminster had a prior and convent who were regular and mort (dead) in law, yet the King by his charter did divide that corporation, and made the prior and convent a distinct and capable body, to sue and be sued by themselves."

[3] Some of the oldest corporation cases involve Oxbridge colleges: see *Merton College in Oxford* (1347) Jenkins 21.

- by special statute (*e.g.*, a public corporation), or
- by registration under the *Companies Act 2006* or its predecessors (by far the commonest way).[4]

38–003   **What is the difference between a company registered under the *Companies Act 2006* and a company that is a partnership?** A partnership ("Binjour & Co.") is rarely recognized in the criminal law,[5] and only receives limited recognition in the civil law. The same applies to other unincorporated associations such as a club.[6] When a member of a members club "buys" a drink in the bar, there is no "sale" or "supply" to him for the purpose of (say) the *Trade Descriptions Act 1968*, because in law he is already the beneficial owner of all the property of the club, in common with the other members.[7] If the club were registered as a company, then the company would own the property and there would be a sale. The point about a registered company ("Binjour & Co. Ltd.") is that it is a corporation, *i.e.* a notional entity, a ghostly person—what lawyers call a "legal person." It is based upon but is distinct from a number of human beings who sign the memorandum of association and so bring the company into existence; these human beings may afterwards die without affecting the existence of a company. What needs to be understood is that when Mr. Burke and Mr. Wills "turn themselves" into a limited company, they have between them given birth to a new person in law, which may hold property and make contracts on its own account, and that these are not the contracts and property of Mr. Burke and Mr. Wills.

38–004   **What is the point of saying that a company is a person in law?** The independent legal existence of the company is useful because individual shareholders may come and go; and it has the great advantage of creating limited liability. Only the company is liable for its debts.[8] If the company is insolvent, creditors cannot go against the private property of the shareholders. The shareholders are responsible only to the extent of their shares, and when their

---

[4] See also "limited liability" partnerships as provided for in the *Limited Liability Partnerships Act 2000*.

[5] Cf. *R. v. W Stevenson & Sons (A Partnership)* [2008] Bus. L.R. 1200, where a partnership was convicted of committing a strict liability offence. Some provisions expressly provide that a partnership may commit certain serious offences. See section 1 of the *Corporate Manslaughter and Corporate Homicide Act 2007* provides: "(2) The organisations to which this section applies are–(a) a corporation; (b) a department or other body listed in Schedule 1; (c) a police force; (d) a partnership, or a trade union or employers' association, that is an employer."

[6] See *Attorney-General v. Able* [1984] Q.B. 795 at 810 where Woolf J. held that an unincorporated association was incapable of committing the particular offence. Cf. *R. v. L* [2009] 1 Cr. App. R. 230, where it was held that it is possible to prosecute unincorporated associations for certain statutory offences. The court said: "However, it was a necessary consequence of the nature of an unincorporated association that all its members were jointly and severally liable for its actions done within their authority. The members of the golf club were all maintainers of the storage tank and all liable for the strict liability offence of causing the leakage. It followed that on the facts a prosecution under section 85 of the *Water Resources Act 1991* [a strict liability pollution offence] could be brought either against either the club in its own name, or against its individual members."

[7] *John v. Matthews* [1970] 2 Q.B. 443.

[8] Compare limited partnerships.

shares are fully paid up they are not liable at all. Few people would invest in a large company if they were liable without limit for the debts of the company if things went wrong.

Do you mean that a person can commit crimes under the disguise of a company? The law recognizes corporate liability, but the device of incorporation is not a bolt-hole for people who commit offences. A company can act only through human beings, and a human being who commits an offence on account of the benefit of a company will be responsible for that offence himself, just as any employee committing an offence for a human employer is liable. The importance of incorporation is that it makes the company itself liable in certain circumstances for offences, as well as human beings.

38–005

38.2. IDENTIFICATION

Corporate liability was slowly developed by the judges, with some help from statute on the procedural points.[9] Companies are liable in three ways; either (1) directly; (2) attributively; or (3) by virtue of a special kind of legal attribution know as the identification doctrine:

38–006

1. There are certain statutory offences that target companies directly.[10] If a statute creates an offence of omission—say, requiring the corporation to make a return of information—there may be no "person" to convict of failure to do the act other than the company itself. For the duty is imposed only on the company. (Parliament may impose it also on the officers, but generally it does not do so.) Similarly, if a statute imposes a duty upon the occupier of property, there would be difficulty in convicting anyone but a company as perpetrator of the offence where it is the company that owns or occupies the property in question. And unless the company can be convicted as perpetrator the directors cannot be convicted as accessories.[11]

2. They are liable for the misdeeds of their employees to the same extent as a human employer would be. We have seen that attributive liability does not (except in the licensee cases) apply to offences requiring mens rea, and the same limitation applies to companies, in so far as their liability is based upon ordinary rules of attribution for rank-and-file employees.[12]

3. However, the identification doctrine goes a step beyond this. A company is identified with its controlling officers. The doctrine owes its origin to a civil law case, where it was held that, for the purpose of a statute referring

---

[9] See Glanville Williams, *Criminal Law: The General Part*, (London: Stevens & Sons, 2nd edn. 1961) at §278.

[10] See for example, sections 386-389 of the *Companies Act 2006*.

[11] This is subject, however, to the possible effect of *R. v. Cogan* [1976] Q.B. 217.

[12] *Ross Hillman v. Bond* [1974] 2 All E.R. 287; see also *Tesco Stores Ltd. v. Brent L.B.C.* [1993] 1 W.L.R. 1037 at 1043 where it was said: "The language here draws no distinction between the defendant and those under his control.... It is, as I have already suggested, absurd to suppose that those who manage a vast company would have any knowledge or any information as to the age of a casual purchaser of a video film." See also the discussion in *Ferguson v. British Gas Trading Ltd.* [2010] 1 W.L.R. 785 at 795.

to "actual fault or privity," the privity of the manager was that of the company. Viscount Haldane L.C. said:

> "My Lords, a corporation is an abstraction. It has no mind of its own any more than it has a body of its own; its active and directing will must consequently be sought in the person of somebody who for some purposes may be called an agent, but who is really the directing mind and will of the corporation, the very *ego* and centre of the personality of the corporation."[13]

In other words, those who control or manage the affairs of the company are regarded in a sense as the company itself. Whenever they are acting in their capacity of controlling officers, the company is identified with both:

- their acts, even in respect of verbs that would not be read attributively for a human employer, and also
- their states of mind.

38–007 In this way, the company can become liable for an offence requiring *mens rea*, even in circumstances where a human employer would not be liable. In *R. v. ICR Haulage Ltd.*,[14] a company, its managing director, and others were indicted for conspiracy to defraud. The Court of Criminal Appeal upheld the indictment. Although the crime charged required a state of mind, and although a corporation has no mind of its own, yet the state of mind of its managing director is imputed to it, so that his fraud is its fraud.

Notice that other persons besides the company and the one director were involved in the conspiracy; if there had not been, there could have been no conviction. A company, through its director, may conspire with another person. But a director who does something illegal on behalf of the company cannot be convicted on that account of conspiring with the company, because then there is only one mind at work, whereas conspiracy needs two.[15]

Where a company is liable under the identification doctrine, the director or other controlling officer will almost always be a co-perpetrator of or accessory in the offence, or commit one of the special statutory offences for company officers.[16]

The doctrine of identification applies not only to private companies but to public corporations like local authorities and public utilities. But a corporation that is an "emanation of the Crown" can be protected by the Crown's general immunity from statutes.[17]

---

[13] *Lennard's Carrying Co Ltd. v. Asiatic Petroleum Co. Ltd.* [1915] A.C. 705 at 713.
[14] [1944] K.B. 551.
[15] *R. v. McDonnell* [1966] 1 Q.B. 233.
[16] See section 1255 of the *Companies Act 2006*.
[17] 27.1.

You speak of the controlling officers, but isn't it impossible to draw a sharp line between the top brass and the lower ranks in a large company? Even a workman who is sent out with his mate to do a routine maintenance job is invested with a certain discretion. The law provides no clear principle for deciding who is a controller.[18] According to Lord Reid in *Tesco Supermarkets Ltd. v. Nattrass*:[19]

38–008

> "It must be a question of law whether, once the facts have been ascertained, a person in doing particular things is to be regarded as the company or merely as the company's servant or agent. … the judge must direct the jury that if they find certain facts proved then as a matter of law they must find that the criminal act of the officer, servant or agent including his state of mind, intention, knowledge or belief is the act of the company."

Unfortunately, the decision does not make it clear what are these facts to which the judge must direct the jury's attention.[20] It can certainly be said that the directors are controllers, but the company manager or even secretary[21] will join the select circle if he has an important say. Denning L.J. in a civil case described the distinction as being between the "brain" of the company and its "hands,"[22] but that is no more than a metaphor.

In the *Tesco* case, the question arose whether the branch manager of a supermarket firm was sufficiently in control of the company's affairs to have his negligence attributed to the company as the personal fault of the company. The House of Lords held not. Lord Reid restated the general principle as follows:[23]

> "Normally the board of directors, the managing director and perhaps other superior officers of a company carry out the functions of management and speak and act as the company. Their subordinates do not. They carry out orders from above and it can make no difference that they are given some measure of discretion. But the board of directors may delegate some part of their functions of management giving to their delegate full discretion to act independently of instructions from them. I see no difficulty in holding that they have thereby put such a delegate in their place so that within the scope of the delegation he can act as the company. It may not always be easy to draw the line but there are cases in which the line must be drawn."

Lord Reid made it plain that the liability of a company for its controllers is equivalent to the personal liability of a human being. "There is no question of the company being vicariously liable." Although it is not clear that a branch manager is not necessarily to be regarded as a member of the top echelon with which the company is identified, the actual decision was helped by the fact that Tesco branch managers were tightly controlled by visiting branch inspectors and above them by area managers. But it seems that even without this fact the branch manager would not have had sufficient administrative powers to be identified with the corporation. Lord Pearson said:

38–009

---

[18] See *Meridian Global Funds Management Asia Ltd. v. Securities Commission* [1995] 2 A.C. 500.

[19] [1972] A.C. 153 at 170, 173.

[20] For the resulting difficulty, see *R. v. Andrews Weatherfoil Ltd.* [1972] 1 W.L.R. 118.

[21] *Moore v. I Bresler Ltd.* [1944] 2 All E.R. 515. In *D.P.P. v. Kent and Sussex Contractors Co.* [1944] K.B. 146 the company's transport manager was included, but that decision may perhaps be reconsidered since *Tesco*.

[22] *HL Bolton Engineering Co Ltd. v. TJ Graham & Sons Ltd.* [1957] 1 Q.B. 159.

[23] *Tesco Supermarkets Ltd. v. Nattrass* [1972] A.C. 153 at 171.

"In the present case the company has some hundreds of retail shops, and it would be far from reasonable to say that every one of its shop managers is the same person as the company. ... supervision of the details of operations is not normally a function of higher management: it is normally carried out by employees at the level of foremen, charge hands, over lookers, floor managers and 'shop' managers (in the factory sense of 'shop')."[24]

38–010   **I find it strange if the number of retail shops is a factor. Is it the law that a company with two retail shops is identified with branch managers, while a giant company with hundreds of shops has its brain located entirely at HQ? Why should such a line be drawn?**   Lord Pearson's remark was probably no more than rhetoric. We have no reason to suppose that the matter depends upon the number of branches.

More generally, it can only be said that the identification doctrine is a compromise on the difficult question of policy. On the one hand, it would be possible to say that every company employee is identified with the company, in which case the company would be liable for a *mens rea* offence committed by the lowliest workman. This makes a remarkable contrast with the rule for human employers. At the other extreme it would be possible to say that the company is never liable except for an offence of strict liability. But then it could not be liable for an inchoate offence (even one committed for the purpose of committing an offence of strict liability), nor could it be liable as accessory, even to an offence of strict liability. Both inchoate offences and accessoryship require *mens rea*. A company could not even be liable for an offence of negligence; and since the present legislative tendency is to turn strict liability into negligence liability, this might eventually exclude corporate liability altogether.

If it is to be accepted that a compromise is necessary, the view may still be taken that the "voices of infallibility" drew the line too tightly in the *Tesco* case.[25] There is no absolute right or wrong about this, but the practical effect of *Tesco* appears to be to confine the identification doctrine to the behaviour of a few people meeting, say, in London, when the activities of the corporation are country-wide or even world-wide. It would seem on the whole to have been more sensible to have extended the identification doctrine to cover the person or persons in control of local branches.

38–011   In crimes requiring *mens rea* it does not matter if the range of persons inculpating the company is restricted, since the purposes of deterrence are generally best served by prosecuting those who are responsible. It is offences of negligence that the limitation of liability imposed in *Tesco* is most injurious.[26] That a company should not be liable for an offence of negligence committed by its branch manager, who after all represents the company in the particular locality, is a

---

[24] *Tesco Supermarkets Ltd. v. Nattrass* [1972] A.C. 153 at 191, 193. Cf. Lord Diplock at 199-200, attaching importance to the person empowered by the articles of association of the company.

[25] Compare the proposals in Brent Fisse and John Braithwaite, *Corporations, Crime and Accountability*, (Cambridge: Cambridge University Press, 1993) (where a reactive fault theory is proposed); Celia Wells, *Corporations and Criminal Responsibility*, (Oxford: Oxford University Press, 2nd edn. 2001) (where an aggregate fault theory is proposed). See also the useful comparative study by Sara Sun Beale and Adam G. Safwat, "What Developments in Western Europe Tell Us about American Critiques of Corporate Criminal Liability," (2004) 8 *Buff. Crim. L. Rev.* 89.

[26] See *Attorney-General's Reference (No. 2 of 1999)* [2000] Q.B. 796; *R. v. P & O European Ferries (Dover) Ltd.* (1991) 93 Cr. App. R. 72.

considerable defect in the law. (The importance of negligence in these offences will appear presently.) What is evidently needed is a statutory redefinition of the officers whose acts and mental states implicate the company.[27]

For example, §18-1-606 of the *Colorado Revised Statutes (2003)* provides:

"(1)   A business entity is guilty of an offense if:

  (a)   The conduct constituting the offense consists of an omission to discharge a specific duty of affirmative performance imposed on the business entity by law; or

  (b)   The conduct constituting the offense is engaged in, authorized, solicited, requested, commanded, or knowingly tolerated by the governing body or individual authorized to manage the affairs of the business entity or by a high managerial agent acting within the scope of his or her employment or in behalf of the business entity.

(2)   As used in this section:

  (a)   'Agent' means any director, officer, or employee of a business entity, or any other person who is authorized to act in behalf of the business entity, and 'high managerial agent' means an officer of a business entity or any other agent in a position of comparable authority with respect to the formulation of the business entity's policy or the supervision in a managerial capacity of subordinate employees.

  (b)   'Business entity' means a corporation ..."

The analogous Arizona[28] provision was recently invoked to ground a manslaughter and aggravated assault convictions against a corporation. In *Meridian Global Funds Management Asia Ltd. v. Securities Commission*,[29] Lord Hoffman invoked the concepts of "agency" and "authorization" to attribute the acts and mental state of a chief investment manager to the corporation that employed him. Meridian was a Hong Kong based investment management corporation. Its chief investment manager and another senior investment manager purchased a large stake in a New Zealand based company with a view of gaining control of it.[30] Because of the size of the investment, Meridian was required by statute to notify the New Zealand stock exchange of its investment. The members of the corporation who were part of its "directing mind and will" (the directors) failed to inform the stock exchange of the investment, because the chief investment manager had failed to inform them of the investment. The investment manager was not held to be a part of the "directing mind and will" of the company himself, but was held to be acting in that capacity to the extent that he had been "authorized"[31] to act for the company at a corresponding level.

---

[27] See, for example, Haw. Rev. Stat. §702-227 (1993); Ark. Code Ann. §5-2-502 (1997); see also §2.07(1),(3) of the ALI Model Penal Code.

[28] See Ariz. Rev. Stat. Ann. §13-305 (2001), which was applied to manslaughter and assault charges in *State v. Far West Water & Sewer Inc.*, 224 Ariz. 173 (2010).

[29] [1995] 2 A.C. 500.

[30] The aim was to take it over and strip it of its valuable assets.

[31] This can be reconciled with *Tesco Supermarkets Ltd. v. Nattrass* [1972] A.C. 153 at 193, where Lord Pearson said: "A company may have an *alter ego*, if those persons who are or have its *ego* delegate to some other person the control and management, with full discretionary powers, of some section of the company's business." Meanwhile (at 199) Lord Diplock said those who are the "directing mind and will" of a corporation are to be "found by identifying those natural persons who by the memorandum and articles of association or as a result of action taken by the directors, or by the company in general meeting pursuant to the articles, are entrusted with the exercise of the powers of the company."

38–012   The Privy Council had to decide whether the knowledge of the chief investment manager could be attributed to Meridian. Lord Hoffman said:

> "So far as anyone in the hierarchy had *functions corresponding* to those to be expected of an individual owner, his failure to discharge them was attributable to the company. So far as there was no such person, the superior management was at fault in failing to ensure that there was. In either case, the fault was attributable to the company."[32]

The court may find that a given "statute" makes a human agent a part of the "directing mind and will" of the company in a given context. For example, a chief investment manager might be regarded as acting as a part of the "directing mind and will" of a company, to the extent that he is making large authorized investments for the company. However, he would not generally be regarded as a part of the "directing mind and will" of the company, so if his wrongful act did not relate to a large-scale investment decision, he would not be regarded as acting as a part of the "directing mind and will" of the company. In the non-investment context, he is just another employee of the company:

> "This is always a matter of interpretation: given that it was intended to apply to a company, how was it intended to apply? Whose act (or knowledge, or state of mind) was for this purpose intended to count as the act *etc.* of the company? One finds the answer to this question by applying the usual canons of interpretation, taking into account the language of the rule (if it is a statute) and its content and policy."[33]

Later in the judgment, Lord Hoffman said:

> "In the case of a corporate security holder, what rule should be implied as to the person whose knowledge for this purpose is to count as the knowledge of the company? Surely the person who, with the authority of the company, acquired the relevant interest. Otherwise the policy of the *Act* would be defeated. Companies would be able to allow employees to acquire interests on their behalf which made them substantial security holders but would not have to report them until the board or someone else in senior management got to know about it. This would put a premium on the board paying as little attention as possible to what its investment managers were doing. Their Lordships would therefore hold that upon the true construction of section 20(4)(e), the company knows that it has become a substantial security holder when that is known to the person who had authority to do the deal. It is then obliged to give notice under section 20(3). The fact that Koo did the deal for a corrupt purpose and did not give such notice because he did not want his employers to find out cannot in their Lordships view affect the attribution of knowledge and the consequent duty to notify."[34]

The approach adopted in *Meridian Global Funds Management Asia Ltd. v. Securities Commission* is not as inventive as some commentators think. The Privy Council merely held that the statute meant that in the given context, the large-scale investment context, the chief investment officer was acting in the capacity of someone who was part of the "directing mind and will" of the company. Therefore, when he failed to notify the New Zealand stock exchange of the investment, the company also failed. Lord Hoffman's human agent, therefore, need not be part of the "directing mind and will" of the company, he need only be

---

[32] *Meridian Global Funds Management Asia Ltd. v. Securities Commission* [1995] 2 A.C. 500 at 510.
[33] *Meridian Global Funds Management Asia Ltd. v. Securities Commission* [1995] 2 A.C. 500 at 507.
[34] *Meridian Global Funds Management Asia Ltd. v. Securities Commission* [1995] 2 A.C. 500 at 511.
See also *Ferguson v. British Gas Trading Ltd.* [2010] 1 W.L.R. 785 at 794-795.

acting in that capacity. This may resemble the agency approach that is adopted in the more expansive penal codes in the United States, but it is clear that it is much more limited. Unlike the U.S. statutes,[35] the *Meridian* doctrine does not rope in lower level managers and supervisors, it merely catches the high level manager who has been authorized to act at the "directly mind and will" level. Hence, the decision in *Meridian* has not extended the identification doctrine.

What if a controller of a company commits an offence for his own fell   **38–013**
purposes? It has been held that the acts of a controller are attributed to the company even when the controller is acting in fraud of the company.[36] This is the sort of reasoning that has been characterized as "mechanical jurisprudence." There is little sense in punishing the company by a fine when the act was directed against the company and therefore against the shareholders.

The identification doctrine can be important not only when a company is the defendant but when it is the victim of an offence. The knowledge of a controller, and the consent of a controller if given within his powers,[37] is a defence to the same extent as that of a human victim. But, of course, it is no answer to a charge based on fraud committed against an honest director to say that a dishonest director knew the truth.[38]

It can be argued that identification applies only in respect of acts done on company business, not in the manager's private concerns, and that it applies only in respect of acts done in a managerial or directorial capacity.[39] For example, suppose that the managing director of a London based company drives to Cambridge to see a branch manager, and in the course of driving is guilty of gross negligence causing the death of a pedestrian. A corporation can in an appropriate case be held guilty of manslaughter; but it is not guilty here, since the act of the director, though within the course of his employment for the purpose of the law of tort, is not what may be called a managerial act. It is not an exercise of the corporate powers, or a decision relating to the corporate activities.

Might the director come within the purview of section 1 of the *Corporate*   **38–014**
***Manslaughter and Corporate Homicide Act 2007*?** The identification doctrine is not invoked in corporate manslaughter cases, because the *Act of 2007* creates

---

[35] See *U.S. v. Ionia Management*, 526 F. Supp.2d 319 (2007).

[36] *Moore v. I Bresler Ltd.* [1944] 2 All E.R. 515. *Per contra, Attorney-General's Reference (No.2 of 1982)* [1984] Q.B. 624; see also *Greener Solutions Ltd. v. Revenue and Customs Commissioners* [2010] UKFTT 412; and *Belmont Finance Corp. Ltd. v. Williams Furniture Ltd.* [1978] 3 W.L.R. 712.

[37] *Attorney-General's Reference (No. 2 of 1982)* [1984] Q.B. 624; *R. v. Philippou* (1989) 89 Cr. App. R. 290; cf. *R. v. Pearlberg* [1982] Crim. L.R. 829. See also *Attorney-General's Reference (No. 1 of 1985)* (1985) 41 S.A.S.R. 147 at 154; *Macleod v. The Queen* [2003] 214 C.L.R. 230 at 263.

[38] *R. v. Buono* [1970] Crim. L.R. 154.

[39] The all-embracing U.S. provisions also include such a constraint. In *Grace v. Thomason Nissan*, 76 F.Supp.2d 1083 (1999) V was sexually assaulted by a fellow employee of the company where she was employed and attempted to have the company held liable for the assault. The court held that: "the proper standard of corporate liability under §13981(c) requires a showing that (1) the person who committed the gender-motivated crime of violence has final policymaking authority; (2) a final policymaker 'ratified' a subordinate's unlawful conduct; or (3) a final policymaker acted with deliberate indifference to the subordinate's unlawful conduct." No one of high managerial authority ratified the sexual assault, so it could not be attributed to the corporation.

its own rules of attribution for such cases. Nevertheless, the director's negligent driving is too remote to come within the purview of section 1.

Section 1 provides:

"(1)   An organisation to which this section applies is guilty of an offence if the way in which its activities are managed or organised–
    (a)   causes a person's death, and
    (b)   amounts to a gross breach of a relevant duty of care owed by the organisation to the deceased.

(2)   The organisations to which this section applies are–(a) a corporation; (b) a department or other body listed in Schedule 1; (c) a police force; (d) a partnership, or a trade union or employers association; that is an employer.

(3)   An organisation is guilty of an offence under this section only if the way in which its activities are managed or organised by its senior management is a substantial element in the breach referred to in subsection (1).

(4)   For the purposes of this *Act*–
    (a)   'relevant duty of care' has the meaning given by section 2, read with sections 3 to 7;
    (b)   a breach of a duty of care by an organisation is a 'gross breach' if the conduct alleged to amount to a breach of that duty falls far below what can reasonably be expected of the organisation in the circumstances;
    (c)   'senior management', in relation to an organisation, means the persons who play significant roles in–(i) the making of decisions about how the whole or a substantial part of its activities are to be managed or organised, or (ii) the actual managing or organising of the whole or a substantial part of those activities."

This provision does not require the act of negligent driving to be imputed to those who form a part of the directing will and mind of the company, but it clearly does not catch personal wrongdoing that has nothing to do with the corporation's operations. The way the corporation organized and managed its activities did not facilitate or cause the director to drive negligently. *Per contra*, if a transport company organizes and manages its activities so that its drivers are regularly sent out in trucks that are not roadworthy and a driver's brakes fail thereby causing him to kill a pedestrian, the company will most likely be liable for corporate manslaughter. Similarly, if a corporation organizes its activities so that its manual workers are continuously asked to work in dangerous conditions without proper safety equipment, and this results in the death of one of the workmen, the corporation will be liable for corporate manslaughter.[40]

Obviously, the factual inquiry into gross negligence will become more complex where several layers of negligence culminate in a fatal accident, but if the various acts of negligence can be linked to the way the company has managed or organized its activities, then it should be liable. Only acts of negligence that can be linked to the way that a company managed or organized its activities will be aggregated to ground a corporate manslaughter conviction. Remote acts of negligence will not count.

38–015   **Is there any kind of legal trouble that a company cannot get into?** Virtually none, but it would be almost impossible for a company to commit bigamy, rape[41] and so on. Since a company cannot be put behind bars, the only possible penalty is a fine, apart from any forfeiture of property or cancellation of licence that may

---

[40] *State v. Far West Water & Sewer Inc.*, 224 Ariz. 173 (2010).
[41] *Grace v. Thomason Nissan*, 76 F.Supp.2d 1083 (1999).

be allowable by law on conviction of the offence in question. But all offences except murder, treason and some forms of piracy are now finable.[42]

A company cannot perpetrate perjury and similar false statements on oath, because no one has tried to put a corporation on oath; but there is no reason why a company should not be convicted as accessory to perjury.[43]

38.3.   THE POLICY OF CORPORATE LIABILITY

The liability of corporations, like strict liability, exemplifies utilitarian theory in criminal law. It is based not on the theory of retributive justice but upon the need for deterrence. The law is designed to encourage corporations to ensure that their employees comply with standards that may ensure that others will not be harmed.[44] It is because no individual is sufficiently culpable, that the law has to go after the corporation. The law uses a combination of direct liability, strict liability and vicarious liability to try to influence the behaviour of the collective of individuals who control the physical actions of a corporation at any given time. **38–016**

I can see that slapping a large fine on a company may cause it to pull up its corporate socks. But surely criminal responsibility should be human, because in the last resort only human beings can be punished. Why not simply convict the directors or other persons responsible for the offence within the corporation? That is an important question. The main answer is that companies generally fight quite hard to avoid conviction, even when only a modest fine[45] is involved—and sometimes the fine is far from modest.[46] Those responsible for the affairs of the company dislike the possibility of adverse publicity involved in a conviction, because they may have been trying to build up the fair name of the company in the minds of the public.[47] If there is social justification for bringing the name of the company before the public when it is involved in an offence of strict liability, then with much stronger reason it should be possible to bring in the company when there has been negligence or wilful misbehaviour by its controlling officers. Given the sheer size and international structure of many modern corporations, bad publicity is not likely to have the **38–017**

---

[42] For an idea of the types of fines that might be imposed in serious cases see *R. v. Balfour* [2007] Bus. L.R. 77.

[43] Cf. *Re Odyssey (London) Ltd. v. OIC Run Off Ltd.* (2000) 150 *N.L.J.* 430.

[44] Corporations may struggle to find the right mechanisms to ensure that their employees comply with the relevant standards. For a discussion of this issue see Donald C. Langevoort, "Monitoring: The Behavioural Economics of Corporate Compliance with Law," (2002) 2002 *Colum. Bus. L. Rev.* 71; Carlos Gomez-Jara Diez, "Corporate Culpability as a Limit to the Overcriminalization of Corporate Criminal Liability: The Interplay between Self-Regulation, Corporate Compliance, and Corporate Citizenship," (2011) 14 *New Crim. L. Rev.* 78.

[45] *HM Advocate v. Munro & Sons (Highland) Ltd.* (2009) S.L.T. 233.

[46] For example, Greenhouse notes that: "The oil giant BP said on Friday that it would challenge a record $87.4 million fine imposed for what regulators said was the company's failure to correct problems after a 2005 explosion killed 15 workers at a refinery in Texas City, Tex." Steven Greenhouse, "BP to Challenge Fine for Refinery Blast," (New York: *New York Times*, 30 October 2009).

[47] David A. Skeel, "Shaming in Corporate Law," (2001) 149 *U. Pa. L. Rev.* 1811 at 1823 *et seq.*

same deterrent impact as punitive fines.[48] If the bad publicity concerns product safety, then it may have a significant impact, but if it merely involves exposing a one-off disaster, or an isolated case of corporate manslaughter,[49] the public might not pay too much attention.

However, massive fines for oil spills and corporate manslaughter could encourage corporations to take extra care. Such fines could impact the share price of a company in a dramatic fashion and companies are in business to make money, not to lose it. Consequently, fines that are tailored to proportionately impact the given corporation's wealth,[50] may achieve greater social utility in promoting obedience to the law.[51]

38–018   **You said that besmirching the company's image might not be as effective as imposing an appropriate fine. But, the reality of a fine imposed on a company is that it is imposed upon the shareholders (or the taxpayers in the case of a government entity), whose assets are depleted by that amount. Or, if the company is insolvent, the fine falls upon the creditors. Perhaps the employees may be affected, because if the company is impoverished their jobs may be in peril. But the shareholders, the creditors and the employees are probably, for the most part, innocent of the offence. Where is the justice in punishing them?**   I think we must leave the creditors out of it. Whenever anyone is fined, his creditors may be affected.

As to the others, one answer is that the fine has not the same effect upon the shareholders and employees as if it were imposed on them directly. A shareholder does not feel the punishment in his body or reputation. He suffers it only in his bank account—and perhaps imperceptibly at that. (Shareholders risk their funds by choosing to invest; they benefit when a corporation cuts corners, but also pay, indirectly, for the company's shoddy practices when those practices result in harm.) Employees are unlikely to be affected unless the fine has a crippling effect upon the company.[52]

---

[48] Mary K. Ramirez, "The Science Fiction of Corporate Criminal Liability: Containing the Machine through the Corporate Death Penalty," (2005) 47 *Ariz. L. Rev.* 933 at 938 *et seq.*

[49] Notably, section 10(1) of the *Corporate Manslaughter and Corporate Homicide Act 2007* provides: "A court before which an organisation is convicted of corporate manslaughter or corporate homicide may make an order (a 'publicity order') requiring the organisation to publicise in a specified manner–(a) the fact that it has been convicted of the offence; (b) specified particulars of the offence; (c) the amount of any fine imposed; (d) the terms of any remedial order made."

[50] It would be pointless impose a £1m fine on a multibillion pound corporation for corporate manslaughter, while at the same time imposing the same size fine on a small company that is not worth much more than £1m, because the former is likely to treat such a fine as the cost of doing business.

[51] Cf. Darryl K. Brown, "Street Crime, Corporate Crime, and the Contingency of Criminal Liability," (2001) 149 *U. Pa. L. Rev.* 1295;. Jennifer Arlen, "Potentially Perverse Effects of Corporate Criminal Liability," (1994) 23 *J. Legal Stud.* 833; Einer Elhauge, "Sacrificing Corporate Profits in the Public Interest," (2005) 80 *N.Y.U. L. Rev.* 733; Samuel W. Buell, "The Blaming Function of Entity Criminal Liability," (2006) 81 *Ind. L.J.* 473.

[52] In some cases, where a major disaster occurs, such as a major oil spill, the share price might fall dramatically. Nonetheless, an isolated case of corporate manslaughter or moderate level of environmental vandalism is not likely to have such a dramatic effect on the share price. In a case concerning one of Lord Kagan's companies, the judge fined the company £375,000 and intimated that it would have been higher but for the risk of causing unemployment. (*The Times*, 13 December 1983).

The company itself is a legal figment. Its physical embodiment is only a piece of paper—in the case of a registered company, the memorandum of association. It has no feelings. It can hardly be said to be convicted "justly" or "unjustly." Upon being convicted it never becomes neurotic, or spends the rest of its life writing letters to the Lord Chancellor complaining of having been unjustly dealt with. So any analogy with a human being is inapt. Whether a company should be liable to conviction depends entirely on whether this subserves the general good of society.

To say that a company can commit virtually any crime does not mean that it **38–019** always makes sense to prosecute the company. Where the directors commit a *mens rea* offence, it may be better policy to concentrate upon them, and some prosecuting counsel take this view.[53] Success in the prosecution depends, generally, upon proving that the directors (1) perpetrated the offence or (2) were accessories to it, knowing the facts,[54] or (3) were guilty of what we may call a "company officer's offence."[55] We have seen that it is now common form in statutes creating new offences relating to trade and numerous other activities to provide that when an offence under the statute is committed by a company, any director, manager or other officer with whose consent or connivance[56] (or even by whose negligence)[57] the offence is committed becomes implicated in it.[58]

For example, section 1255 of the *Companies Act 2006*, which provides:

---

[53] The danger that corporate liability can shield guilty individuals is again illustrated by the *Kagan* case, where the directors of the company, under Kagan's influence, wished to cause the company to plead guilty to a charge of fraud arising out of Kagan's machinations, in order to shift to the shareholders part of the fine that would otherwise fall upon Kagan. A High Court Injunction was issued on behalf of minority shareholders to forbid the plea.

[54] *R. v. Love* (1955) 39 Cr. App. R. 30.

[55] There is also a litany of offences that regulate the way a company is managed, formed, listed on the stock exchange, audited and so on. See *Companies Act 2006*.

[56] Consent and connivance mean that it must be shown that director had "knowledge" of the offending and "agreed" to it. See *Attorney-General's Reference (No. 1 of 1995)* [1996] 1 W.L.R. 970.

[57] Cf. *R. v. Chargot Ltd. (trading as Contract Services)* [2009] 1 W.L.R. 1 at 16.

[58] See, for example, section 50(2) of the *Children and Families (Wales) Measure 2010*; section 61 of the *Data Protection Act 1998*; section 65 of the *Charities Act 2006*; section 87 of the *Childcare Act 2006*; section 143 of the *Adoption and Children Act 2002*; section 39 of the *Bank of England Act 1998*; section 7 of the *City of Westminster Act 1996*; section 4(6) of the *Children and Young Persons (Protection from Tobacco) Act 1991*; section 52 of the *Clean Air Act 1993*; section 50 of the *Aviation and Maritime Security Act 1990*; section 195 of the *Broadcasting Act 1990*; section 78 of the *Airports Act 1986*; section 11(9) of the *Anatomy Act 1984*; section 11 of the *Animal Health and Welfare Act 1984*; section 14 of the *Atomic Energy Act 1946*; section 99 of the *Civil Aviation Act 1982*; section 2 of the *Agricultural Land (Removal of Surface Soil) Act 1953*; section 110 of the *Agriculture Act 1970*; section 19 of the *Agriculture and Horticulture Act 1964*; section 9(5) of the *Building Control Act 1964*; section 55 of the *Cable and Broadcasting Act 1984*; section 64 of the *Coal Industry Act 1994*; section 10 of the *Coinage Act 1971*; section 40(2) of the *Consumer Protection Act 1987*; section 87 of the *Control of Pollution Act 1974*; section 14 of the *Deer Act 1991*; section 108 of the *Electricity Act 1989*; section 45 of the *Gas Act 1986*; section 314 of the *Highways Act 1980*; section 432(2) of the *Insolvency Act 1986*; section 48 of the *London Local Authorities Act 1995*; sections 10(4) and 41(3) of the *Petroleum Act 1998*; section 36 of the *Plant Varieties Act 1997*; section 36 of the *Radioactive Substances Act 1993*; section 147 of the *Railways Act 1993*; section 177 of the *Water Act 1989*; section 210 of the *Water Industry Act 1991*; section 82 of the *Weights and Measures Act 1985*; reg. 23 of the *Merchant Shipping and Fishing Vessels (Health and Safety at Work) (Biological Agents) Regulations 2010*; reg. 15 of the *Wine Regulations 2009*; section 14 of the *Bribery Act 2010*, among others.

"(1)   Where an offence under this Part committed by a body corporate is proved to have been committed with the consent or connivance of, or to be attributable to any neglect on the part of, an officer of the body, or a person purporting to act in any such capacity, he as well as the body corporate is guilty of the offence and liable to be proceeded against and punished accordingly.

(2)   Where an offence under this Part committed by a partnership is proved to have been committed with the consent or connivance of, or to be attributable to any neglect on the part of, a partner, he as well as the partnership is guilty of the offence and liable to be proceeded against and punished accordingly.

(3)   Where an offence under this Part committed by an unincorporated association (other than a partnership) is proved to have been committed with the consent or connivance of, or to be attributable to any neglect on the part of, any officer of the association or any member of its governing body, he as well as the association is guilty of the offence and liable to be proceeded against and punished accordingly."

One difficulty in confining liability to the human perpetrator is that it may not always be possible to identify the individual within the company who was at fault. Even when he is found, he may have been blatantly "leaned on" or subtly influenced by the pressures from his superiors, which makes it unjust to treat him as solely responsible. William Whyte's book *The Organisation Man*[59] showed how the vast business corporation tends to produce a subculture, an environment in which individuality becomes submerged, exacting complete conformity to the organization's norms as the price of financial security. Coupled with this, many corporate disasters are the result of layer upon layer of managerial sloppiness and also from sloppiness at the ground level.[60] In these circumstances it may be necessary to punish not only the offending individuals where possible, but also the organization as a whole, in order to compel a change of behaviour in the group. The fine may help to call down upon the offender the displeasure of his equals or superiors, or it may cause the officers of the company to change their policies.

38–020   Instead of talking about punishment, wouldn't it be more sensible to justify fines upon a company as a way of compensating the community for the breach of law?   Sometimes that may be so, as when a shipping company is fined for illegally discharging oil at sea. Or the fine may make the company disgorge ill-gotten gains, as when it trades without obtaining a licence that is legally required. But the company can generally be fined a really large sum only if the offence is indictable and is tried on indictment (magistrates are limited in their power to fine, and cannot commit a company to the Crown Court for sentence). Moreover, in so far as the penal law pays attention to the question of fault it is inappropriate for cases where a large illegal profit has been made without fault. This difficulty has become particularly acute since *Tesco Supermarkets Ltd. v. Nattrass*;[61] if a Tesco-type branch manager commits a *mens rea* offence to make a big profit for the company, the company, since it cannot be convicted, cannot be fined in order to claw back the gain. What is obviously needed, apart from reforms, is a civil proceeding for compensation on behalf of

---

[59] (New York: Simon & Schuster, 1956). See also the more recent literature discussed in James Gobert and Maurice Punch, *Rethinking Corporate Crime*, (London: Butterworths, 2003).

[60] See Wells, *op. cit. supra*, note 25.

[61] [1972] A.C. 153.

the public where illegal profits have been made with or without fault. It may be mentioned in conclusion that an effective civil sanction for use against a company that is given to fraudulent trading is to have it wound up.

38.4. HUMAN EMPLOYERS AND THE IDENTIFICATION DOCTRINE

The notion of identification is not applied to human employers, or at any rate it never has been. In *Tesco Supermarkets Ltd. v. Nattrass*,[62] Lord Reid disapproved a *dictum* of Lord Parker C.J. that a human employer would be liable if his manager was "a person whom delegation in the true sense of the delegation of management has passed." On the other hand Lord Pearson, speaking specifically with regard to the defence of "no negligence" under section 24 of the *Trade Descriptions Act*, said:

38–021

> "Section 24 requires a dividing line to be drawn between the master and any other person. The defendant cannot disclaim liability for an act or omission of his *ego* or his *alter ego*.[63] In the case of an individual defendant, his *ego* is simply himself, but he may have an *alter ego*. For instance, if he has only one shop and he appoints a manager of that shop with full discretion to manage it as he thinks fit, the manager is doing what the employer would normally do and may be held to be the employer's *alter ego*. But if the defendant has hundreds of shops, he could not be expected personally to manage each one of them and the manager of one of his shops cannot in the absence of exceptional circumstances be considered his *alter ego*."[64]

This opinion, that the identification doctrine applies to human employers, was not voiced by the other Lords, and was evidently a minority view of Lord Pearson's.

But why shouldn't the identification doctrine be extended to non-corporate employers? If the big shots in a company are identified with the company, why shouldn't a manager employed by a partnership be identified with the partners? The delegation rule for companies is a response to the difficulty that otherwise no company could be convicted of an offence requiring *mens rea*. This difficulty does not arise in the case of a sole trader or a partnership, because here the human beings who are carrying on the business can have *mens rea*.

38–022

If Snoopy Hudson trades as the Superfood Co. (even an individual may call himself "Co." if he wishes), and through his negligence unfit food is exposed for sale, a prosecution will not name the Superfood Co. as a defendant. Nor will it do so if Snoopy is trading in partnership. Neither an individual business name nor a partnership name is regarded by the criminal law. Snoopy (and any partner of his) will be charged personally, though the public may of course gather from the report that the fault was associated with the Superfood stores.

Perhaps the law should be altered to allow a business to be charged under its trading name, and to make the owner liable for his manager to the same extent as

---

[62] [1972] A.C. 153 at 173.
[63] "Other self."
[64] *Tesco Supermarkets Ltd. v. Nattrass* [1972] A.C. 153 at 192-193.

a limited company would be.[65] But the point is important chiefly for chain stores, and few chain store businesses are unincorporated; moreover, as we have seen, corporate liability is rather ineffective for branch activities. For human defendants the question of justice is paramount. Even if the business in the hypothetical above could be charged under its name, a conviction would still, in law, be a conviction of Snoopy Hudson (and any partner of his) personally; and it would be wrong to convict them of an offence requiring fault if they have not been at fault.

38–023   **Can a trade union be prosecuted?**   If members of the union's executive council authorize the commission of a crime they can be charged as individuals, and the trade union can also be charged.[66]

38.5.   THE DEFENCE OF NO NEGLIGENCE

38–024   We must now return to the general problem of strict liability. The English courts (unlike the High Court of Australia and the Supreme Court of Canada) having failed to develop a no-negligence defence to charges involving strict liability; the Government, through Parliament, has to some extent stepped in. What precisely has moved them to reactivate the issue of fault is not clear. The majority of the offences under the *Road Traffic Act 1988* (for example) still retain full strict liability.[67] The common characteristic of this statute, which the modern changes have passed by, is that it is administered not by special inspectors but by the police; but there is no obvious reason why this fact should deny the defendant a no-negligence defence.

When a no-negligence defence is allowed, the language varies. Sometimes the defence is expressed broadly, as in the following examples.

Section 67 of the *Offices, Shops and Railway Premises Act 1963* provides: "It shall be a defence for a person charged with a contravention of a provision of this *Act* or of regulations thereunder to prove that he used all due diligence to secure compliance with that provision."[68]

Meanwhile section 21 of the *Food Safety Act 1990*: "In any proceedings for an offence under any of the preceding provisions of this Part … it shall … be a

---

[65] Cf. section 1(2) of the *Corporate Manslaughter and Corporate Homicide Act 2007*, which provides: "The organisations to which this section applies are–(a) a corporation; (b) a department or other body listed in Schedule 1; (c) a police force; (d) a partnership, or a trade union or employers' association, that is an employer."

[66] Section 10 of the *Trade Union and Labour Relations (Consolidation) Act 1992*. See also the preceding footnote.

[67] However, Schedule 1, para. 1(2)(b) of the *Road Traffic Act 1988* provides: "if the original accused further proves that he has used all due diligence to secure that section 15A, 17 or, as the case may be, 18(4) was complied with, he shall be acquitted of the offence."

[68] Similarly worded provisions appear in many statutes such as section 22(8)(b) of the *Petroleum Act 1998*; reg. 9 of the *Children (Protection at Work) Regulations 1998*; reg. 5 of the *Offshore Installations (Emergency Pollution Control) Regulations 2002*; section 12(5) of the *Outer Space Act 1986*; section 156 of the *Mines and Quarries Act 1954*; section 3(5) of the *Farm and Garden Chemicals Act 1967*; section 63(2)(b) of the *Building Act 1984*; section 16 of the *Agriculture (Safety, Health and Welfare Provisions) Act 1956*, among others.

defence for the person charged to prove that he took all reasonable precautions and exercised all due diligence to avoid the commission of the offence by himself or by a person under his control."[69]

These are defences of no negligence, since "diligence" in law is the opposite of negligence and the equivalent of care.[70]   **38–025**

Even when a defence is given in these wide terms, the Divisional Court will not allow magistrates to dismiss a charge by lightly assuming that the defendant has taken care.[71] It is insufficient, for instance, for the seller of dangerous goods to say that he imported them and that he relied on the certificate of the foreign seller that the goods complied with English law.[72] The questions, as always on an issue of negligence, are: What precautions could the defendant have taken to comply with the law? Was it reasonable to expect him to take those precautions? If so, did he take them? Where the fault is that of the defendant's employee, the defendant, to disprove his own negligence, must show what steps he took to train, instruct, and control his employee.

In *Croydon L.B.C. v. Pinch a Pound (UK) Ltd.*,[73] trading standards officers sent two 15-year-old youths (as test purchasers) into a store to purchase knives. The youths selected two knives and made their way to the till, which was operated by an employee of the defendant company. The employee completed the sale without challenging either youth. (The managing director of the defendant company was not present at the shop when the sale was made by his employee.) The defendant company was charged under section 141A of the *Criminal Justice Act 1988*, which provides:

> "(1)   Any person who sells to a person under the age of eighteen years an article to which this section applies shall be guilty of an offence.
>
> (2)   Subject to subsection (3) below, this section applies to— (a) any knife, knife blade or razor blade, (b) any axe, and (c) any other article which has a blade or which is sharply pointed and which is made or adapted for use for causing injury to the person.
>
> (4)   It shall be a defence for a person charged with an offence under subsection (1) above to prove that he took all reasonable precautions and exercised all due diligence to avoid the commission of the offence."

---

[69] Similarly worded provisions appear in many statutes such as reg. 17(1)(b) of the *Consumer Protection from Unfair Trading Regulations 2008*; section 11(3) of the *Anatomy Act 1984*; section 60(8) of the *Charities Act 1992*; section 1250 of the *Companies Act 2006*; section 2(6),(7) of the *Ancient Monuments and Archaeological Areas Act 1979*; section 112 of the *Building Societies Act 1986*; section 1(3) of the *Children and Young Persons (Protection from Tobacco) Act 1991*; section 12C of the *Children and Young Persons Act 1933* (as amended by section 143 of the *Criminal Justice and Immigration Act 2008*); section 33(7)(a) of the *Environmental Protection Act 1990*; section 23(3) of the *Financial Services and Markets Act 2000*, sections 139, 156(3)(b), of the *Licensing Act 2003*; section 109 of the *Marine and Coastal Access Act 2009*; section 16(4) of the *Legal Services Act 2007*; section 4(3) of the *Knives Act 1997*; section 109 of the *Friendly Societies Act 1992*, among others.

[70] *Tesco Supermarkets Ltd. v. Nattrass* 1972] A.C. 153 at 199 *per* Lord Diplock.

[71] *Merton LBC v. Sinclair Collis Ltd.* (2010) 175 J.P. 11; *R. (on the application of Tesco Stores Ltd.) v. City of London Corp.* [2010] EWHC 2920; *Kilhey Court Hotels Ltd. v. Wigan MBC* (2005) 169 J.P. 1.

[72] *Taylor v. Lawrence Fraser (Bristol) Ltd.* [1978] Crim. L.R. 43.

[73] [2010] EWHC 3283.

38–026   The burden of proving the statutory defence, on the balance of probabilities, falls upon the defendant. The defendant succeeded in the Crown Court. On appeal to the Divisional Court, it was held that the defence had not been made out. Roderick Evans J. said:

> "[T]he statutory defence requires proof of two elements: (1) the taking of all reasonable precautions and (2) the exercise of all due diligence. These are cumulative requirements although circumstances no doubt arise where they overlap. For example, all due diligence must be exercised in instituting a preventative regime whereby an employer takes all reasonable precautions to avoid the commission of the offence created by the act by his employees. However, the employer must go further and exercise all due diligence to ensure that the measures he put in place are maintained, adhered to by his employees and continue to be adequate in the context of the risk at which the statute is directed and of the nature of his own business."[74]

Roderick Evans J. accepted the factual findings of the magistrates and concluded that the defendant had not exercised due diligence. Similarly, Pill L.J. observed that the justices had found that the defendant had not implemented an effective system to prevent such sales. It only registered refused sales on an *ad hoc* basis; it had not installed adequate signage, and had failed to provide adequate training for its staff.[75]

---

[74] *Croydon L.B.C. v. Pinch a Pound (UK) Ltd.* [2010] EWHC 3283 at para. 19.
[75] *Croydon L.B.C. v. Pinch a Pound (UK) Ltd.* [2010] EWHC 3283 at para. 49.

INDEX

All references are to paragraph number

INDEX

INDEX